Literature of the
Western World

LITERATURE OF THE WESTERN WORLD

VOLUME I

*The Ancient World Through
the Renaissance*

SECOND EDITION

BRIAN WILKIE ❧ JAMES HURT

University of Arkansas   *University of Illinois*

MACMILLAN PUBLISHING COMPANY
NEW YORK

Macmillan Publishing Company
866 Third Avenue, New York, New York 10022

Collier Macmillan Canada, Inc.

Library of Congress Cataloging-in-Publication Data
(Revised for vol. 1)

Literature of the Western world.

  Includes index.
  Contents: v. 1. The ancient world through the
Renaissance—v. 2. Neoclassicism through the modern period.
  1. Literature—Collections. I. Wilkie, Brian,
     II. Hurt, James,
PN6014.L615 1988   808.8   86-27656
ISBN 0-02-427800-9 (v. 1)
ISBN 0-02-427810-6 (v. 2)

   PRINTING   8 9 YEAR   1 2 3 4 5

ISBN 0-02-427800-9 (v.1)

ISBN 0-02-427810-6 (v.2)

ISBN 0-02-427670-7 (v.1) (pbk)

ISBN 0-02-427680-4 (v.2) (pbk)

Acknowledgments

WALTER J. BLACK, INC.: Selections from Aristotle, *Poetics,* translated by Samuel Henry Butcher and revised by Louise Ropes Loomis, from Aristotle, *On Man in the Universe,* the Classics Club Edition published by Walter J. Black, Inc., 1943. Reprinted by verbal permission of Walter J. Black, Inc.

THE BOBBS-MERRILL COMPANY, INC.: Selections from *Song of Roland,* translated by Patricia Terry. Copyright © 1965 by The Bobbs-Merrill Company, Inc., Indianapolis, Indiana. Reprinted by permission of The Bobbs-Merrill Company, Inc.

ALISON M. BOND: Poems numbers 1, 3, 5, 8, 11, 39, 51, 62, 76, 85, 101, 109 from *The Poems of Catullus,* translated by Horace Gregory. Copyright © 1956 by Horace Gregory. Reprinted by permission of the Estate of Horace Gregory from *The Poems of Catullus,* W. W. Norton, New York, 1972.

CBS COLLEGE PUBLISHING: The complete "Inferno" and selections from "Purgatory" and from "Paradise" from *The Divine Comedy* by Dante Alighieri, translated by H. R. Huse, Holt, Rinehart and Winston, New York, 1954. Copyright © 1954 by Holt, Rinehart and Winston. Reprinted by permission of Holt, Rinehart and Winston, CBS College Publishing.

ROSICA COLIN LIMITED: Selections from *The Decameron* by Boccaccio, translated by Richard Aldington. Copyright © by Catherine Guillaume, 1983. Reprinted by permission of Rosica Colin Limited, authors' representatives, London, England.

DOUBLEDAY & COMPANY, INC.: Excerpts from Homer, *The Iliad,* translated by Robert Fitzgerald. Copyright © 1974 by Robert Fitzgerald. Reprinted by permission of Doubleday & Company, Inc. *The Odyssey* by Homer, translated by Robert Fitzgerald. Translation copyright © 1961 by Robert Fitzgerald. Reprinted by permission of Doubleday & Company, Inc.

FARRAR, STRAUS & GIROUX, INC.: *Beowulf,* translated by Kevin Crossley-Holland. Copyright © 1968 by Kevin Crossley-Holland. Reprinted by permission of Farrar, Straus & Giroux, Inc.

ANGEL FLORES: Garcilaso de la Vega: translated by Edwin Morgan, "Your Face Is Written in My Soul" and "While There Is Still the Color of a Rose"; Fray Luis de León: translated by Edwin Morgan, "Ode to Francisco Salinas"; translated by James Edward Tobin, "At the Ascension"; San Juan de la Cruz: translated by Kate Flores, "One Dismal Night"; translated by Stephen Stepanchev, "O Living Flame of Love"; translated by Willis Barnstone, "I Entered Where I Did Not Know"; translated by James Edward Tobin, "A Shepherd, Young and Mournful, Grieves Alone" and "I Know Full Well the Water's Flowing Power"; Luis de Góngora: translated by Roy Campbell, "Allegory of the Brevity of Things Human"; Lope de Vega: translated by W. S. Merwin, "At Dawn the Virgin Is Born," "Ice and Fires Contend with My Child," and "Where Are You Going, Maiden?"; translated by Denise Levertov, "A Little Carol of the Virgin"; translated by Doreen Bell, "A Sonnet All of a Sudden." Selections from Angel Flores, ed., *An Anthology of Spanish Poetry from Garcilaso to García Lorca in English Translation* (Garden City: Doubleday Anchor Books, 1961).

HARCOURT BRACE JOVANOVICH, INC.: *Lysistrata,* by Aristophanes. An English Version by Dudley Fitts, copyright 1954 by Harcourt Brace Jovanovich, Inc.; renewed 1982 by Cornelia Fitts, Daniel H. Fitts and Deborah W. Fitts. Reprinted by permission of the publisher.

INDIANA UNIVERSITY PRESS: Selections from *Metamorphoses* by Ovid, translated by Rolfe Humphries. Reprinted by permission of Indiana University Press. All rights reserved.

THE LABYRINTH PRESS: "Bisclavret" and "Yonec" from *The Lais of Marie de France,* trans. Robert Hanning and Joan Ferrante. New York: Dutton, 1978, pp. 92–100 and 137–152. Reprinted: Labyrinth Press.

MACMILLAN LTD., LONDON: Selections from *Don Quixote* by Cervantes, translated by Walter Starkie. Reprinted by permission of Macmillan Ltd., London and Basingstoke.

MACMILLAN PUBLISHING CO., INC., NEW YORK: *King Lear* by William Shakespeare, from *The Living Shakespeare,* edited by Oscar James Campbell. Copyright © 1949 by Macmillan Publishing Company, Inc., renewed 1977 by Robert F. Campbell, Eunice C. Goodale and Emily F. C. Meyer. Reprinted by permission of Macmillan Publishing Co., Inc., New York.

MBI Books Division/The Heritage Press: Selections from *The Five Books of Gargantua and Pantagruel* by Rabelais, translated by Jacques LeClercq. Used by the permission of The Heritage Press, Norwalk, Connecticut.

Oxford University Press, Inc., U.S.A.: *Antigone* by Sophocles, from *Three Theban Plays*, translated by Theodore Howard Banks. Copyright © 1956 by Theodore Howard Banks. Reprinted by permission of Oxford University Press, Inc. *Oedipus the King* by Sophocles, translated by Stephen Berg and Diskin Clay. Copyright © 1978 by Stephen Berg and Diskin Clay. Reprinted by permission of Oxford University Press, Inc.

Penguin Books Ltd.: *Medea* by Euripides, from *MEDEA and Other Plays*, translated by Philip Vellacott (Penguin Classics, 1963). Copyright © 1963 by Philip Vellacott. Reprinted by permission of Penguin Books Ltd., Harmondsworth, Middlesex, England. Stories 8, 15, 18, 19, 36, and 55 from Marguerite de Navarre: *The Heptameron* translated by P. A. Chilton (Penguin Classics, 1984), copyright © P. A. Chilton, 1984.

Persea Books, Inc.: Selections from Christine de Pizan, *The Book of the City of Ladies*, translated by Earl Jeffrey Richards. Copyright © 1982 by Persea Books. Reprinted by permission of Persea Books, Inc., 225 Lafayette Street, New York, N.Y. 10012.

David Sanders: Translations by David Sanders of Pierre de Ronsard, "To Cassandre," "On the Death of Marie," "To Hélène," "Sonnet to an Unnamed Person"; of Joachim Du Bellay, "Regrets, XXXI" and "From a Winnower of Wheat to the Winds."

Scott, Foresman and Company: Selections from *Paradise Lost* by John Milton, from *The Poems of John Milton*, 2nd edition, edited by James Holly Hanford. Copyright © 1953 by Scott, Foresman and Company. Reprinted by permission.

Charles Scribner's Sons: Selections from *The Aeneid* by Virgil, translated by Rolfe Humphries. Copyright © 1951 by Charles Scribner's Sons. Reprinted by permission of Charles Scribner's Sons.

Simon & Schuster: Books I and II of *Utopia* by Thomas More, translated by Peter K. Marshall. Copyright © 1965 by Washington Square Press, Inc. Reprinted by permission of Simon & Schuster.

University of Alabama Press: Selected poems from *Selected Poems* by Petrarch, translated by Anthony Mortimer. Copyright © 1977 by Anthony Mortimer. Reprinted by permission of the University of Alabama Press.

University of California Press: Poems numbered 30, 34, 37, 38, 39, 40, 41, 42, 43, 97 by Sappho, from *Sappho: A New Translation*, translated by Mary Barnard. Copyright © 1958 by the Regents of the University of California. Reprinted by permission of the University of California Press.

University of Chicago Press: Euripides, *The Bacchae*, translated by William Arrowsmith, from *The Complete Greek Tragedies*, Volume IV, Euripides, 1958.

Viking Penguin Inc.: *The Oresteia* by Aeschylus, translated by Robert Fagles. Copyright © 1966, 1967, 1975 by Robert Fagles. Reprinted by permission of Viking Penguin Inc. All rights reserved. Selections from *The Canterbury Tales* by Geoffrey Chaucer, from *The Portable Chaucer*, translated by Theodore Morrison. Copyright 1949, © 1975, © renewed 1977 by Theodore Morrison. Reprinted by permission of Viking Penguin Inc.

Preface

❧❧❧❧❧❧❧❧❧❧

The first edition of *Literature of the Western World* was intended to fill a need for an anthology suitable to world-literature surveys as they are taught today. The editors were committed to several principles. First, no author was to be represented by a mere snippet. Works were to be presented in their entirety; with those few works, such as *Don Quixote*, where complete reprinting was impossible, full, readable selections that accurately suggested the shape of the entire work were to be presented. Second, the anthology was to offer a wide range of choices. The book was designed to be capacious enough to include far more in each volume than would be read in any one version of the course, so that teachers could tailor assignments to their individual needs and tastes. Whenever possible, more than one selection by an author was to be included, to offer either a choice or an opportunity to compare and trace common themes through two or three works. Third, the book was to use the best translations available, the ones that best combined accuracy and sensitivity to the style of the original. This did not always mean selecting the most recent or the best-known translations (though it frequently did); it did mean choosing the translations that best revealed why the original was a great work of art. Fourth, the anthology was to be thoroughly contemporary, serving the needs of students today rather than those of a quarter-century ago. The selections, as well as the introductions, bibliographies, and notes, were to reflect the rereadings of the traditional canon of Western literature that are going on in the best classrooms today, while also recognizing that many long-established masterpieces have retained their central place. Fifth, and finally, the book was designed to be as useful as possible to teachers and students. Period and author introductions were to be detailed and accessible, in content, style, and format; notes were to be very full; and such aids as diagrams, chronologies, and suggestions for further reading were to be provided wherever possible. The book, in other words, was to supply everything needed up to the point where instruction begins but was not to usurp the instructor's responsibility for—and delight in—exploration and interpretation.

The enthusiastic reception of the first edition encouraged the editors to believe that they had been correct in identifying a need for such a collection. One of the most pleasant benefits of their work has been the opportunity to meet and correspond with a great many users of the book across the country. Every aspect of the book has been thoroughly examined from the perspectives of both teachers and students—resulting in tough, realistic correctives to armchair speculations. After several years of such ex tion, the time came for a revision that would incorporate the sugg the editors had received.

The response to the collection did not suggest that any basic changes in the conception of the book were needed. Therefore, the goals of the second edition remain the same as those of the first: complete works, a range of choice, the best translations, a contemporary point of view, and ample support material. Within these boundaries, however, a great many changes, both large and small, have been made.

While preserving our policy of using complete works by retaining the complete *Odyssey,* we have responded to the good suggestions of many readers by including a generous, coherently readable selection from *The Iliad.* We have added Euripides' *The Bacchae,* the resonant masterpiece that rang the curtain down on the great age of Greek tragedy. Virgil's *Aeneid* is more fully represented, notably by the inclusion of the poem's great climax and all of Book VI, often regarded as the summit of Latin literature. The medieval section has been expanded and strengthened by the inclusion of the complete *Beowulf,* two fascinating *lais* by Marie de France, an expanded representation of Chaucer, and a selection from Christine de Pizan's *Book of the City of Ladies.* Lyric poetry is difficult to present satisfactorily in translation, but we have addressed the need to represent it by including a substantial selection—a mini-anthology, really—of English and continental Renaissance lyrics. The Renaissance section is further enriched by the inclusion of Marguerite de Navarre's *Heptameron,* an intriguing companion piece to Boccaccio's *Decameron.* Our Enlightenment section is considerably expanded by a selection of the brilliant letters of Mme de Sévigné, the complete *Princesse de Clèves* by Mme de La Fayette, and Pope's "Epistle to Dr. Arbuthnot." Again in line with our preference for complete works, we have replaced excerpted versions of several long Romantic works with a more generous selection of lyrics and the complete text of Jane Austen's *Persuasion.* In our revisions of our nineteenth- and twentieth-century sections, we sought a better representation of non-English-language authors, adding such writers as Pushkin, Machado de Assis, and Isaac Babel, as well as a generous selection of French symbolist and modernist poetry parallel to the Renaissance lyrics earlier in the book. Virginia Woolf is represented not only by a short story but also by a powerful selection from *A Room of One's Own,* T. S. Eliot not only by the early "Love Song of J. Alfred Prufrock" and *The Waste Land* but by "Burnt Norton" as well. The treatment of contemporary literature has been thoroughly revised and updated, with an expanded introduction and a balanced range of authors that include Doris Lessing, Gabriel García Márquez, Adrienne Rich, Milan Kundera, Athol Fugard, and Joyce Carol Oates, as well as, from the first edition, Jorge Luis Borges, Samuel Beckett, Ralph Ellison, James Baldwin, and Peter Handke.

For the new material, we have been fortunate to obtain translations well up to the high standard set in the first edition. *The Iliad* appears in Robert Fitzgerald's brilliant translation and *The Bacchae* in that of William Arrowsmith. We have been reluctant to represent narrative poetry in prose paraphrases and so have happily selected Kevin Crossley-Holland's wonderful verse translation of *Beowulf,* an almost uncanny recreation of the effects of Anglo-Saxon verse in modern English, and the charming verse renderings of Marie de France by Robert Hanning and Joan Ferrante. Christine de Pizan appears in the vigorous recent version by Earl Jeffrey Richards. We have been especially attentive to translations of the Renaissance lyrics and of nineteenth- and twentieth-century French lyrics, many of which have been rendered by distinguished poets. Mme de Sévigné's letters, ordinarily badly represented in English, appear in the translation by Leonard Tancock, the only one based on the recent authoritative French edition. *The Princesse de Clèves* is presented in a witty, stylish translation by Nancy Mitford.

In addition to major changes in selections, there have been innumerable small changes in presentation. Introductions have been revised, in some cases heavily, and many annotations have been rewritten for thoroughness and clarity. We have revised and updated the suggestions for further reading, though we remain deeply indebted to Nancy K. Barry, Frances Stickney Newman, and Willard J. Rusch for the bibliographies they compiled for the first edition and have continued to signal this debt by using their respective initials where appropriate. As in the first edition, our aim has been to list works that are reliable and authoritative but also appropriate for non-expert readers; many works indispensable to advanced scholarly study have been consciously omitted.

To attempt to represent almost three thousand years of literature within a single book, even a large one, is of course a quixotic undertaking. But we believe that our second-edition changes have moved the book closer to our goals. In any anthology, the part must stand for the whole, of course. But we have tried to represent the great national literatures—French, German, Russian, Spanish, English, American—in a balanced if necessarily noncomprehensive way. In the nineteenth and twentieth centuries, especially, we have also at least suggested the riches of literature outside Western Europe and the United States with such writers as Machado de Assis, Babel, Borges, García Márquez, Kundera, and Fugard. We have also been concerned to represent literature by women with an approach to adequacy. But more important than numbers is the fullness with which issues of gender are represented, from Christine de Pizan's *Book of the City of Ladies* and Marguerite de Navarre's *Heptameron* through Mme de La Fayette's *Princesse de Clèves*, Austen's *Persuasion*, Ibsen's *A Doll House*, and Chopin's *The Awakening* to Woolf's *A Room of One's Own* and the poetry of Adrienne Rich. Care has also been taken to present a balanced range of genres, from the sweep of epic to the miniature world of the lyric poem. Nineteen plays are included: a sizable drama anthology within the larger one. We are especially proud of our representation of longer fiction. Our decision, taken in the first edition, not to represent the novel by one massive text but rather to enlarge the area of choice has been vindicated by the users of the book. Our five novels—*The Princesse de Clèves, The Sorrows of Young Werther, Persuasion, A Hero of Our Time,* and *The Awakening*—represent five national literatures, and they are supplemented by such substantial novellas and other prose narratives as the Gospel of Matthew, *Candide, Notes from Underground, The Death of Ivan Ilyitch, Heart of Darkness, The Metamorphosis,* and *A Sorrow Beyond Dreams,* all complete. We hope that *Literature of the Western World,* second edition, will please its many old friends and win many new ones.

Among old friends are a great many who took an active role in planning and advising on the first edition, the second edition, or both. Among these we would like to thank especially Roberta Rubenstein of American University, our Senior Consultant. Professor Rubenstein participated in every stage of the planning and production of the second edition, advising on the evolution of the table of contents, suggesting texts and translations to consider, and reading and editing our introductions. The book—and our prose styles—are much improved because of her wisdom, her tactful criticism, and her sharp blue pencil.

Other valued advisors include:

Professor Anthony W. Annunziata, State University of New York at Oswego; Professor Kenneth Baughman, University of Northern Iowa; Professor Paula Berggren, Baruch College; Professor Ronald Bogue, The University of Georgia; Professor Gary Brodsky, Northeastern Illinois University; Professor Robert Burlingame, The University of Texas at El Paso; Professor Sondra M. Cooney, Kent State University; Professor Raymond E. Fitch, Ohio University; Professor Earl E. Fitz, The Pennsylvania State University; Professor Alan Friedman, University of Texas; Professor Phyllis Goodman, Millersville University; Professor Ervene Gulley, Bloomsburg University; Professor Joseph C. Harrison, Jackson State Community College; Professor Dabney Hart, Georgia State University; Professor Jeffrey D. Hoeper, Arkansas State University; Professor Alfred Kloeckner, Norwich University; Professor Susan M. Levin, Stevens Institute of Technology; Professor Nancy F. Lewis, North Shore Community College; Professor Dean McWilliams, Ohio University; Professor Charles Piltch, John Jay College of Criminal Justice; Professor J. E. Rivers, University of Colorado at Boulder; Professor Evan Seymour, Community College of Philadelphia; Professor Robert L. Stringer, Delaware State University; Professor James Vanden Bosch, Calvin College; Professor William A. Vincent, Michigan State University.

Advisors for the first edition, whose good influence on the book remains great, include:

Professor Jesse T. Airaudi, Baylor University; Professor Beatrice Batson, Wheaton College; Professor J. A. Bryant, University of Kentucky; Professor Leslie Chard, University of Cincinnati; Professor Keith Cohen, University of Wisconsin, Madison; Professor Charles L. Crow, Bowling Green State University; Professor Prescott Evarts, Jr., Monmouth College; Professor Robert Fagles, Princeton University; Professor Betty S. Flowers, The University of Texas at Austin; Professor Barbara L. Gerber; Professor John F. Hennedy, Providence College; Professor Thomas G. Jones, Jr., Western Kentucky University; Professor Beuford W. Keene, University of Tennessee, Martin; Professor James King, Hillsdale College; Professor Alfred Kloeckner, Norwich University; Professor Stanley J. Kozikowski, Bryant College; Professor Lawrence F. Laban, Virginia Commonwealth University; Professor Frederick Z. Lesher, University of Wisconsin, La Crosse; Professor Irving Lord, South Oregon State College; Professor Christiaan T. Lievestro, University of Santa Clara; Professor John M. Long, Eastern Kentucky University; Professor Littleton Long, University of Vermont; Professor Joan McCarthy, Southern Connecticut State University; Professor H. Thomas McCracken; Professor Ronald E. MacFarland, University of Idaho; Professor Ronald E. McReynolds, Central Missouri State University; Professor Charles Miller, Western State College; Professor Zenobia Mistri, Purdue University, Calumet Campus; Professor Martin Mueller, Northwestern University; Professor Helen H. Naugle, Georgia Institute of Technology; Professor R. W. Parker, Wittenberg University; Professor Erling W. Peterson, Indiana Central University; Professor Willard Potts, Oregon State University; Professor Carroll Y. Rich, North Texas State University; Professor William Patrick Riley, Mississippi Valley State University; Professor J. E. Rivers, University of Colorado, Boulder; Professor Allen Robb, Florida State University; Professor Thomas G. Rosenmeyer, University of California, Berkeley; Professor Silvia Ruffo-Fiore, University of South Florida; Professor Susan Rusinko, Bloomsburg University; Professor Richard Savage, Bloomsburg University; Professor Gerald H. Strauss, Bloomsburg University; Professor Woodruff C. Thomson, Brigham Young University; Professor Willa F. Valencia, Valdosta State College; Professor Robert A. Wiggins, University of California, Davis; Professor Heinz D. Woehlk, Northeast Missouri State University; Professor Edith Williams, Eastern Kentucky University.

For advice on particular authors and periods we warmly thank Lynn Altenbernd, John Bateman, Barbara Bowen, Vincent Bowen, Edward Brandabur, David Bright, Jackson Campbell, Howard Cole, John Dussinger, Karen Ford, Chester Fontenot, Eva Frayne, John Frayne, John Friedman, Stanley Gray, Achsah Guibbory, Jan Hinely, Bernard Hirsch, Frank Hodgins, Allan Holaday, Anthony Kaufman, David Kay, Keneth Kinnamon, Joan Klein, Dale Kramer, James Marchand, Donald Masterson, Linda Mazer, Michael Mullin, Cary Nelson, John K. Newman, Michael Palencia-Roth, Vernon Robbins, Michael Shapiro, Charles Shattuck, Janet Levarie Smarr, Arnold Stein, Jack Stillinger, Zohreh Sullivan, Benjamin Uroff, Leon Waldoff, Emily Watts, and Richard Wheeler.

For conceiving the idea of this anthology and expert guidance throughout the project, we thank D. Anthony English. Our production editor, Patricia Cabeza, performed intelligently and heroically the immense task of guiding the book through the press. Berta Lewis provided excellent assistance with design. The alertness, sensitivity to style, and literary expertise of our copy editor, Joyce Rappaport, have been of great value. For further help with copy editing and proofreading, we are deeply indebted to Suzanne McCray, Kevin McLaughlin, and Ann Wilkie.

Contents

The Ancient World   ₁

VIRGIL 983
(*70–19 B.C.*)

OVID 1094
(*43 B.C.–17 A.D.*)

Renaissance Lyric Poetry 2279
(C. 1500–C. 1660)

The Ancient World

THE "ancient world," as it is here represented, consists of three civilizations that flourished in the millennium before Christ in a comparatively small area around the Mediterranean Sea: those of the ancient Hebrews, the Greeks, and the Romans. To the far-sighted anthropologist taking a long view of time, such a sampling of the ancient world would be too limited both chronologically and geographically. By the tenth century B.C., man was already old upon the earth and had created many other civilizations, some of them highly developed. Some of them, too, flourished in areas far from the Mediterranean—in the Orient, in Africa, and in the Americas. Nevertheless, it is to the Hebrews, the Greeks, and the Romans that we look for the main literary traditions of Western culture that concern this anthology. These traditions are the riverhead of Western literature, although we can discern other contributions near the source and continuing tributary streams from Africa and the East.

The core of Hebrew culture has always been religion, and it is through religion that it has most strongly influenced the Western world. It would be neither possible nor very useful to review here the course of the development of the Hebrews' culture and conception of God. But much of their view of the world is summed up in the prophet Micah's deceptively simple words: "He has showed you, O man, what is good; and what does the Lord require of you but to do justice, and to love kindness, and to walk humbly with your God?" No Greek or Roman could have written, or even have understood, these words. They imply a cluster of ideas wholly alien to the Greek and Roman world views but at the very heart of Hebraism: the existence of a single God, from whom the idea of "the good" derives, and a moral role for man in which he, along with everything else, is subordinated to God. (Micah's terms for ethical behavior in this world—"justice" and "kindness"—would not have puzzled either a Greek or a Roman, but both would have defined these words differently.) The Hebrew "Yahveh" came to be the God of all mankind and, at the same time, the God of each individual. The result of this personal relationship was a stress upon individual experience, an emphasis upon conscience (including a social conscience), and a concentration upon introspection and the spiritual life. The Hebrews were continually involved in negotiations, individual and collective, with a father-God.

The course of Greek thought was significantly different. When the people we now know as Greeks began to filter into the Greek peninsula in about 2000 B.C., they brought with them a primitive polytheism based on personifications of natural forces, which they humanized and attempted to propitiate by means of prayers, libations, and sacrifices. Greek religion

1

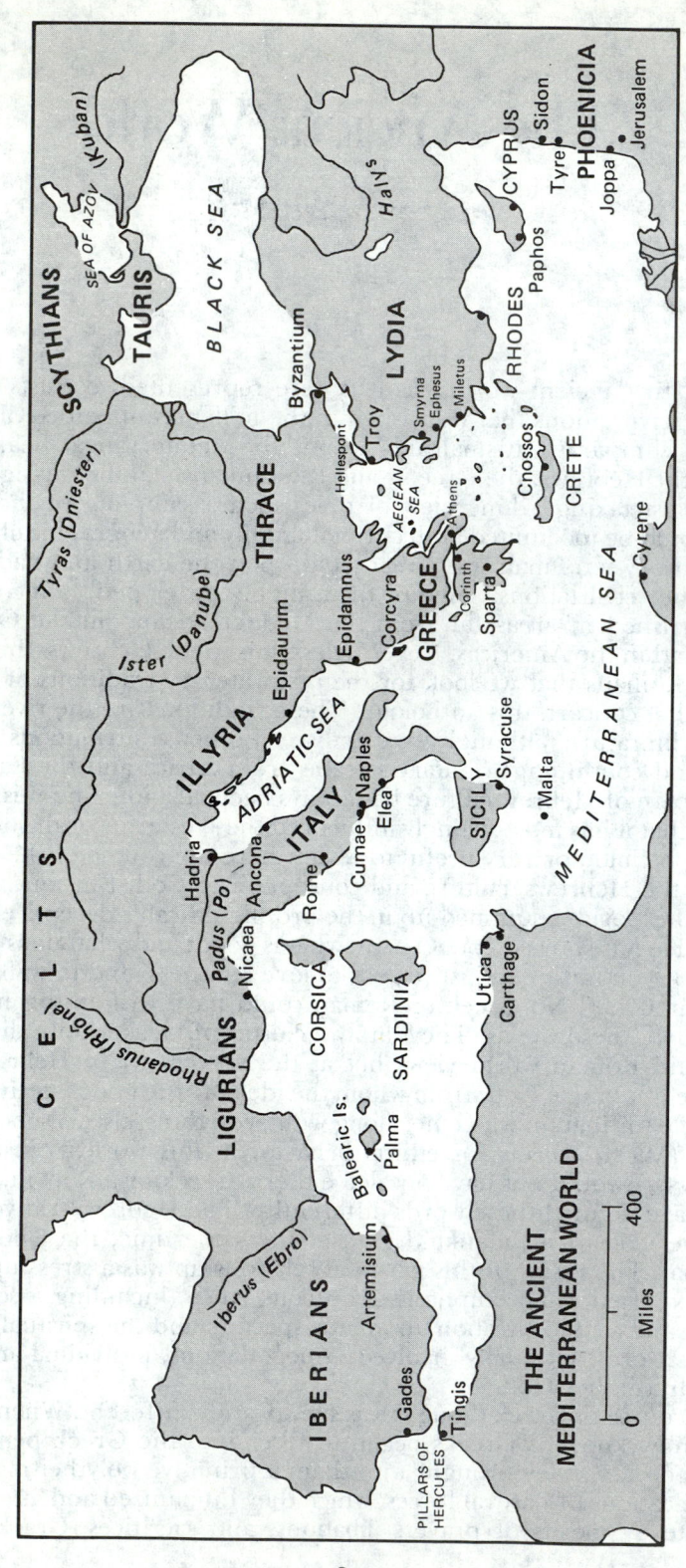

THE ANCIENT MEDITERRANEAN WORLD

2

changed and developed, of course, over its long history, but even in its most fully developed form it carried few if any implications for morality or conscience in the Hebrew sense. The Greek gods were superior to men, in power, beauty, and immortality, but they were not ethically superior, and, unlike Yahveh, they did not demand that men follow an exacting code of morality. The Greeks looked not to their gods for an ethical code, but to their own reason and innate sense of the good. The result was a culture that seems, even to a modern "post-Christian" reader, remarkably serene and guiltfree. The Greeks, it has been said, had a strong sense of crime, but none at all of sin.

The Greeks found the main significance of life not in the relation of man with God, but in man's relations with himself and with his fellows. If, for the sake of focus, we simplify the Greek view of the world as we did the Hebrew, we may find it stated best in the mottoes the Greeks inscribed over the gates of the temple to Apollo at Delphi: "Know thyself" and "Nothing too much." An ancient Hebrew would have misunderstood these phrases as badly as an ancient Greek would have misunderstood Micah's words. "Knowing" himself implied to a Greek none of the spiritual struggles or the wrestling with angels with which the Hebrew was preoccupied. A person came to know himself in Greece through experience, through involvement in the world. The crucial tableau in Hebrew history is one man alone on a mountaintop, learning directly from God "what is good." The Greeks had their mountaintops, too, but the messages they received there from the gods were characteristically riddling and enigmatic; the responsibility for knowledge was thrown squarely back upon the questioner. The Greek tableau corresponding to the man on the mountaintop is a group of men in lively, earnest conversation, exercising the privilege Socrates said was characteristic of free citizens: "They can have their talk out in peace, wandering at will from one subject to another, their only aim to attain the truth."

Or the emblematic tableau might be a group of men at the great Olympic Games, competing in athletics or in horseracing, drama, music, or poetry; or it could be the audience at a production of an Aeschylean tragedy at the City Dionysia in the theater of Dionysus in Athens. For to the Greeks there were no sharp divisions between the intellectual, physical, and spiritual sides of human nature. To "know oneself" was to know one's mind, body, and spirit as a harmonious balanced system. The Greek view of human nature as a seamless unity was so deep and so thoroughgoing that it provides a stumbling block to our understanding of their institutions and their literature. We attend class, or watch the Rose Bowl on television, or go to a play or to church, and all of these are separate activities, each carried on by specialists and directed at different aspects of our personalities. It is hard for us to understand the very different Greek attitude toward, for example, the Great Games, in which the same contestants might compete in the five athletic events of the *pentathlon* and in music and poetry. The Games were a religious festival as well, dedicated to the worship of Zeus or Apollo or Poseidon. And were the great dramatic festivals artistic events or religious ceremonies? No Greek would have understood such a question, any more than he would have understood our attempts to distinguish between "sin" and "error" in such dramatic characters as King Oedipus. In institu-

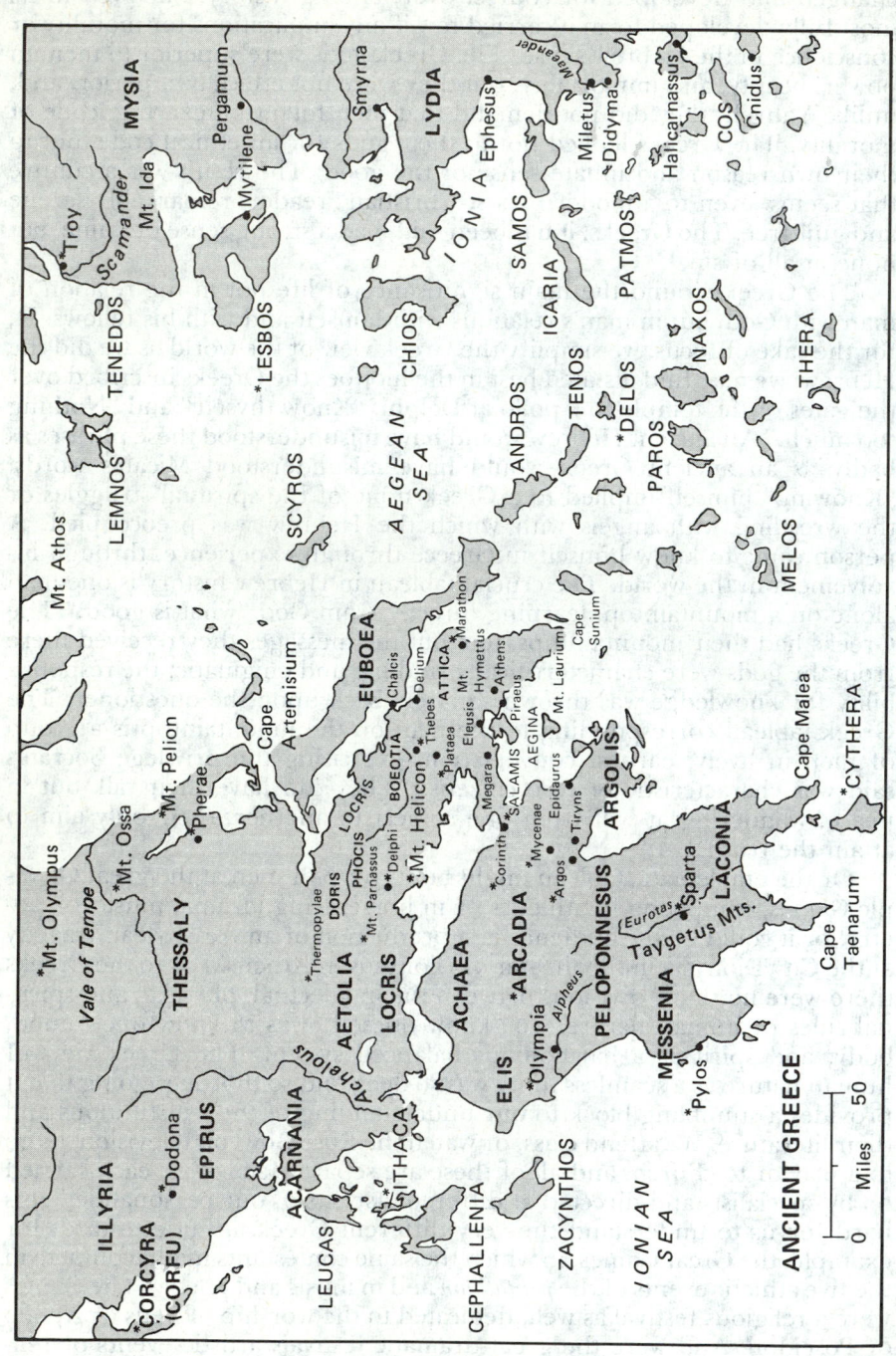

ANCIENT GREECE

MYSIA
Pergamum
Mt. Ida
Scamander
Troy
TENEDOS
LESBOS
Mytilene
Smyrna
LYDIA
Ephesus
Maeander
IONIA
Miletus
Didyma
Halicarnassus
Cnidus
COS
SAMOS
ICARIA
PATMOS
CHIOS
NAXOS
THERA
Mt. Athos
LEMNOS
SCYROS
AEGEAN SEA
TENOS
ANDROS
DELOS
PAROS
MELOS
Cape Artemisium
Mt. Pelion
Mt. Ossa
*Mt. Olympus
Vale of Tempe
Pherae
THESSALY
EUBOEA
Chalcis
Delium
Marathon
Thebes
Mt. Hymettus
ATTICA
Plataea
Athens
BOEOTIA
Eleusis
Piraeus
*Delphi
LOCRIS
Megara
SALAMIS
Cape Sunium
Mt. Parnassus
*Mt. Helicon
AEGINA
Mt. Laurium
PHOCIS
Corinth
Epidaurus
DORIS
*Thermopylae
Mycenae
Tiryns
ARGOLIS
Argos
Cape Malea
AETOLIA
LOCRIS
ARCADIA
PELOPONNESUS
*CYTHERA
ACHAEA
Eurotas
Achelous
ELIS
*Olympia
Sparta
LACONIA
Alpheus
Taygetus Mts.
EPIRUS
Dodona
ACARNANIA
MESSENIA
Cape Taenarum
*Mt. Olympus
ILLYRIA
CORCYRA (CORFU)
LEUCAS
ITHACA
Pylos
CEPHALLENIA
ZACYNTHOS
IONIAN SEA
0   Miles   50

4

Ancient Greece. NOTE: Some of the names below are spelled in various ways by translators. Asterisks (*) indicate the places described in the list.

ARCADIA. Setting of much ancient pastoral poetry.

ARGOS. In Aeschylus, the city of Agamemnon, Clytemnestra, Orestes, and Electra.

CORCYRA (Corfu). Conjectural home island of the Phaeacians in Homer's *Odyssey*.

CORINTH. Center of wealth, commerce, and shipbuilding; setting of Euripides' *Medea*.

CYTHERA. Island where Aphrodite came to land after being born of the sea foam.

DELOS. Birthplace of Apollo and Artemis.

DELPHI. Site of the great oracle of Apollo; the center of Greek prophetic utterance. The Omphalos (Navelstone), believed to be the center of the Earth, was located there.

DODONA. Site of the great oracle of Zeus.

HELICON. Mountain sacred to the Muses; location of the Hippocrene, the fountain of poetic inspiration.

ITHACA. Home island of Odysseus.

LESBOS. Home island of Sappho.

MARATHON. Plain (26 miles from Athens) where the Greeks defeated the Persians in 490 B.C.

MYCENAE. Center of a great ancient culture; in Homer, the city of Agamemnon.

OLYMPIA. With Delphi, one of the two greatest religious centers of Greece; site of the ancient Olympic Games.

OLYMPUS. Mountain home of the gods.

OSSA, PELION. Mountains piled atop one another in an attempt by the Titans to take the gods by storm.

PARNASSUS. Mountain associated with Apollo and the Muses and hence with learning and the arts.

PELION. See Ossa.

PLATAEA. Site of victory by the Greeks, under Pausanias, over the Persians in 479 B.C.

PYLOS. Home of Nestor; visited by Telemachus in Homer's *Odyssey*.

SALAMIS. Site of defeat of Xerxes and the Persian navy by the Greeks in 480 B.C.

SPARTA. Principal enemy of Athens in the Peloponnesian War (431–404 B.C.); home of Menelaus and Helen of Troy in Homer's *Odyssey*.

THEBES. City of Pentheus, Oedipus, and Antigone.

THERMOPYLAE. A mountain pass heroically defended in 480 B.C. by the Spartans, under Leonidas, against the Persian invaders.

TROY. Site of the Trojan War, fought by the Greeks to reclaim Helen.

tions, as in human personalities, the Greeks did not differentiate the spirit, the mind, and the flesh.

The other Delphic inscription, "Nothing too much," is also a deceptively simple statement. The concept does not suggest a timid moderation, "playing it safe," but something almost the opposite. It insists that men confront reality unflinchingly, refusing the temptation to retreat into defensive and self-deluding inflations and exaggerations. This principle is consistent with "knowing oneself," since self-knowledge ends in accepting what it is to be human and avoiding the temptation to be either less or more than human. Morally, exaggeration and excess manifest themselves in *hubris,* which is not just pride but also a self-deluding rejection of human limitations. To the fifth-century Greeks, the luxurious and despotic Persian emperor Xerxes represented the sort of overweening man who closed his eyes to human boundaries and whom the gods delighted in cutting down. Greek tragedy is full of parallel examples of men who fall through attempting to be something other than human. Artistically, the principle of "nothing too much" was also expressed in a deep dislike of any elaboration or ornamentation that shielded the viewer from a direct view of "the thing itself." Greek art, whether it be the epics of Homer, the architecture of the Parthenon, or a sculpted Apollo, is characterized by a direct, unblinking view of reality and a combination of passion and restraint that is the essence of classicism. This is not to say that Greek art was "realistic" in the modern sense. Idealization—the attempt to capture the essence of a thing—was also fundamental to Greek art. But the ideal originated in the recognizable.

The leisure which made possible the Greeks' passionate but clear-eyed exploration of themselves and the world around them had a price: slavery and the subjugation of women. The Greek male was freed from demanding physical labor by the existence of a sizable slave class, made up mostly of "barbarians" (non-Greeks) captured in war. The institution of slavery was rarely questioned by the Greeks; one of the ironies of history is that its most freedom-loving culture accepted slavery, for the most part, as a matter of course. Nor did women share in the free exploration of the world men enjoyed. Greek women had few rights and were confined to the home. They managed domestic matters, and they bore and raised the children (at least in Athens; customs differed among the city-states). Greek children were almost exclusively in the company of women until the age of seven and then were rigidly segregated by sex; the result, predictably, was a perpetuation of traditional attitudes on the part of Greek women and a deep-seated distrust and even fear of women on the part of Greek men. This fear expressed itself in widespread homosexuality ("Greek love"), a rigid compartmentalization of sexual qualities, a glorification of "male" at the expense of "female" qualities, and a mythology full of female fright-figures, from the shrewish Hera to the Medusa, whose gaze turned men to stone, to the fearsome Furies, goddesses of blood vengeance, to the fierce Medea, who killed her children to avenge herself upon her faithless husband. (They were, of course, idealized women in myth, too: Athena, the patroness of Athens, was the goddess of wisdom.) The tragedian Euripides, in many ways an ironic commentator upon the ways of his contemporaries, questioned his culture's attitudes toward both slaves and women, but his was a rare voice in an intensely male-oriented society.

Greek culture reached its peak in the fifth century B.C. and was centered in Athens, which dominated the city-states of the peninsula and its islands for most of the century. But the power of Athens and Greece alike was severely eroded during a series of bitter internecine wars which ended in 338 B.C. when the kingdom of Macedonia conquered Greece. Greek art and learning had a brief Indian summer, the third-century "Hellenistic" (as opposed to the earlier "Hellenic") period, in the city of Alexandria in northern Egypt. Greek culture maintained some of its integrity through the days of the Roman Empire, and it passed on part of its legacy to Christianity. But the deathblow to even nominal Greek political independence came in 146 B.C., when the armies of the rising Republic of Rome marched into Greece and turned it into a mere province for the growing Roman Empire.

If the Hebrews looked to God for the meaning of life and the Greeks looked for it in the world around them, the Romans looked to earthly, human authority. It was a Roman, Horace, who wrote that it is "sweet and seemly to die for one's country," a phrase which encapsulates a number of Roman attitudes, including the subordination of the individual to the state, an obsession with death, and the cultivation of a stoic denial of personal feeling. Many Greeks suffered or risked death for their country, but it is hard to imagine their idealizing their sacrifice in this way. The Roman tableau to match the Hebrew on his mountaintop and the Greek talking with his friends might be the uniformed centurion marching in a column behind his commander to triumph or death. The Roman empire took shape over centuries of constant war; in our first glimpse of Rome at the end of the sixth century B.C., it is at war, attacking neighbor after neighbor until by 133 B.C. the nation was the undisputed ruler of the whole Mediterranean. The Roman virtues were those of the soldier: discipline, control, and obedience to authority.

Authority hedged the Roman around from his earliest childhood. The Roman family was a miniature of the state, headed by a stern father whose power was almost absolute. He owned all the property and could, by writing a letter, divorce his wife or even condemn her to death. The Greek family, male-oriented as it was, was never paternalistic in the Roman sense; the Greek grew up thinking of himself as an individual, but the Roman was above all else a member of a family and, later, of a clan and a nation. Roman religion reinforced these feelings of subordination to authority. The earliest Roman religion, which continued to be the domestic religion throughout the years of the Empire, rested on a belief in spirits that inhabited particular localities; each household had its own *lares, penates,* and *manes* which, respectively, watched over its lands and buildings, guarded the family's other possessions, and embodied the spirits of its male ancestors. The Roman must have grown up feeling that he was constantly observed by such spirits. When the more generalized gods of the Romans—Jupiter, Juno, Venus, and Mars—were merged, under Greek influence, with the Greek pantheon of Zeus, Hera, Aphrodite, and Ares, the result was a state religion the outward observances of which were enforced with a rigidity totally alien to the Greek mentality. In the late Empire, Stoic philosophy deeply influenced thoughtful Romans; it has been called the true Roman religion. Although Stoicism originated with a Greek—Zeno of Citium—its emphasis upon endurance and the repression of feeling made

7

a strong appeal to the Romans' instinct for authority. The version of Stoicism developed in Rome taught the individual to subordinate his own will to the family, to the state, and to God. He was to do his duty without question, cultivating self-denial and impassive reserve. Altogether, the Stoic view of the world was ideally suited to the Roman temperament.

The great Roman contribution to civilization was the instrument of social organization—law. The Romans were able to extend their sway over so much of the world and maintain it so long because wherever they went they brought with them the concept of authority. In their system, no one was wholly exempt from the rule of an impersonal force. Forbidding as such impersonality may seem, it also left a cherished legacy to posterity. We owe to the Romans the principles that a person must be assumed innocent until proven guilty, that the law must be applied judiciously, with due regard to the particular situation, and that all individuals are equal before the law.

Roman art was largely derivative from the Greeks. After 272 B.C., when the Romans captured the Greek city of Tarentum, Greek artists and scholars poured into Rome, and as Horace expressed it, "Conquered Greece took captive her fierce conqueror." Roman architecture, sculpture, drama, poetry, and painting were all copied from Greek models, often with a considerable distortion through inflation, as in the gigantic Roman temples copied from small Greek originals, or through refinement, as in Seneca's polished imitations of Greek tragedy.

In a survey of ancient literature (limited even to the works of the Hebrews, the Greeks, and the Romans), variety is more apparent than unity. But we can follow a few threads related to the development of the major literary genres: narrative, drama, poetry, and expository literary prose.

The characteristic narrative forms of the ancient world are the folk tale, the epic, and the history. We may pass over the folk tale fairly quickly, since our knowledge of it in the ancient world is indirect and inferential. We know that a large body of folk narrative must have been in oral circulation since earliest times among the Hebrews, the Greeks, and the Romans. But these tales have reached us only as they were incorporated into written narratives. We can detect signs of them in, for example, the Hebrew Bible, Homer, and Virgil.

In narrative, the greatest achievement of the ancient world was the epic. Long heroic poems seem to be a natural form in most early literatures. There are the Exodus epic in the Bible and the *Iliad* and the *Odyssey* at the dawn of Greek literature. But we can also point to, among others, the Babylonian *Gilgamesh* (C. 2000 B.C.), the Indian *Mahabharata* (A.D. 350–500), the Old English *Beowulf* (eighth century A.D.), and the German *Nibelungenlied* (C. A.D. 1200). These are all "folk epics"—that is, although they may have been put into final form by single authors, they were developed by folk poets, over extended periods of time, from traditional materials that dealt with the legendary histories of their peoples. The folk epics have a wide variety of forms, but they are linked by certain recurring characteristics. Though not all regarded as, like the Bible, "sacred books," all hold special places in their cultures as major statements of national or cultural identity. They purport to tell the stories of the formation or the early history of an entire people; thus they are never regarded as mere fictional entertainment but are held in some degree of reverence. All of them, too,

8

center on heroes, drawn from history or legend, who are regarded not merely as individuals but as embodiments of the special values of their cultures. The settings are vast, ranging across nations or the entire world. Even when the action is confined to a limited place, as in Homer's *Iliad,* that place is the scene of great events determining the fate of nations. The action is similarly grand, involving deeds that exemplify extraordinary qualities treasured by the culture, especially military prowess, physical strength, and spiritual force. Often the action takes the hero on a journey which consists of a series of trials testing his heroism. The gods of the culture often involve themselves in the action, as the Lord does in the Exodus story, or as, in a very different way, the Olympian gods enter the plots of the Homeric epics. The style is at once exalted and simple, grand but not highly embellished. And the point of view is objective; the action is seen from an impersonal angle, without authorial intrusion and with the emphasis upon external action rather than upon inner motivations.

The epic form captured the imaginations of a great many poets who attempted to incorporate its qualities in original works, or art epics. In addition to employing the features of folk epics, these poets developed a number of epic conventions, which refine and develop the features inherent in the folk epic, especially the epics of Homer. The art epic opens with a statement of a grand governing theme and an invocation to an appropriate muse to inspire and instruct the poet. The poet plunges *in medias res,* or "into the middle of things," with earlier action recounted at a later point in the epic. There are, characteristically, catalogues of warriors, ships, armies; extended formal speeches by the main characters; and epic similes, extended set-pieces which develop comparisons at length. The greatest ancient art epic is Virgil's *Aeneid;* Ovid's *Metamorphoses* is another, in some ways, though he introduces the epic conventions in a playful and deliberately trivializing way.

The other major narrative form of the ancient world is the history. The dividing line between epic and history is not always precise; the epic finds its roots in legendary history, and history is often seen through epic lenses. About half of the Old Testament is presented as a history of the Hebrews, though a good part of it—the Exodus saga—blends history with folk epic. But we cannot reconstruct from the Old Testament a factual account of early Israel such as a modern historian would write. Hebrew history is history seen through faith; and the purpose of the Hebrew Bible is not to record precise dates and circumstances, but rather to trace out the underlying design of history as a revelation of religious truth.

History in the modern sense begins in the fifth century B.C. with Herodotus and his Greek history of the Persian Wars. Here too fact and fancy are often mingled; Herodotus begins with a lively travelogue of the Persian Empire, reporting everything he has seen and heard, though he is careful to say he does not necessarily believe all of it. The modern critical and scientific treatment of history begins with Herodotus' younger contemporary Thucydides, whose history of the Peloponnesian War makes a quite modern attempt not only at factual accuracy but also at historical interpretation. The Romans carried on the tradition of historical writing. The romantic and patriotic Livy's *History of Rome* is the historical counterpart to Virgil's epic *Aeneid,* while Tacitus' *Histories* and *Annals* chronicle Rome's later degeneracy, in a savage parallel to the contemporary verse satires of Juvenal. The beginning of modern notions of how to organize and develop a sustained narrative lies as much in the work of these historians as in that of the more frankly "literary" writers.

Of the major literary kinds, drama has had the most sporadic history. Perhaps because a fairly complex set of social and intellectual circumstances are necessary to make theatrical production possible, drama has flourished in only three fairly brief periods in Western history, and the first of these is in the Greece of the fifth century B.C. (the other two ages are the late Renaissance and early neoclassical period, between about 1580 and 1700, and the modern period, since about 1860).

There is some evidence that a dramatic tradition existed in Egypt as early as 3000 B.C., but practically nothing is known of it. The Hebrews had no theater, although the Book of Job shows some evidence of the influence of Greek tragedy, and the Song of Solomon may have some relation to a quasi-dramatic wedding performance. It is to Greece that we look for the beginnings of Western drama.

Greek drama originated in the sixth century B.C., in the worship of Dionysus. Four annual festivals were consecrated to him: the Rural Dionysia (in December), the Lenaia (in January), the Anthesteria (in February), and the City or Great Dionysia (in March). The god was worshiped at these festivals through the performances of dithyrambs, which were hymns of ecstasy narrating an incident in the life of the god and performed by choruses of singers and dancers. The step from narration to drama presumably was taken when a chorus leader moved from telling about the god to impersonating him and acting out his story. The Greeks believed that this revolutionary innovator was a man named Thespis, who is therefore traditionally regarded as the first actor in history. It was Thespis, too, who won the prize for tragedy in 534 B.C., when the City Dionysia was reorganized and a contest for tragedy was established. Dithyrambic performances took place on the circular stone platforms which were used as threshing floors in the center of Greek villages; these platforms seem to have provided the model for the *orchestra,* or circular dancing place, which served as the central acting area of the fully developed Greek theater.

It is in the fifth century that we emerge from theatrical legend into theatrical history. By the time Aeschylus, the oldest of the Greek dramatists whose works survive, began competing in the tragedy contests in 499 B.C., the contests had been held for about thirty-five years and the methods of production had assumed essentially the form they kept throughout the great age of the Greek theater. The festivals were civic and religious rituals, occasions for exploring the fundamental ideas and values that made Athens a unified community. The annual dramatic festivals were organized, and the plays produced, by a cooperative effort of the civic leaders of the city, eminent private sponsors, and the artists themselves, in accordance with rules that by the fifth century and become standard. The audience consisted, in effect, of the whole citizenry, brought together not in a spirit of playgoing whim but of communal solidarity. (Women attended the tragedies but not the comedies.) During the fifth century, the Great Dionysia, the most important of the annual festivals, included four days devoted to plays. On the first day, five comedies, by different authors, were presented.

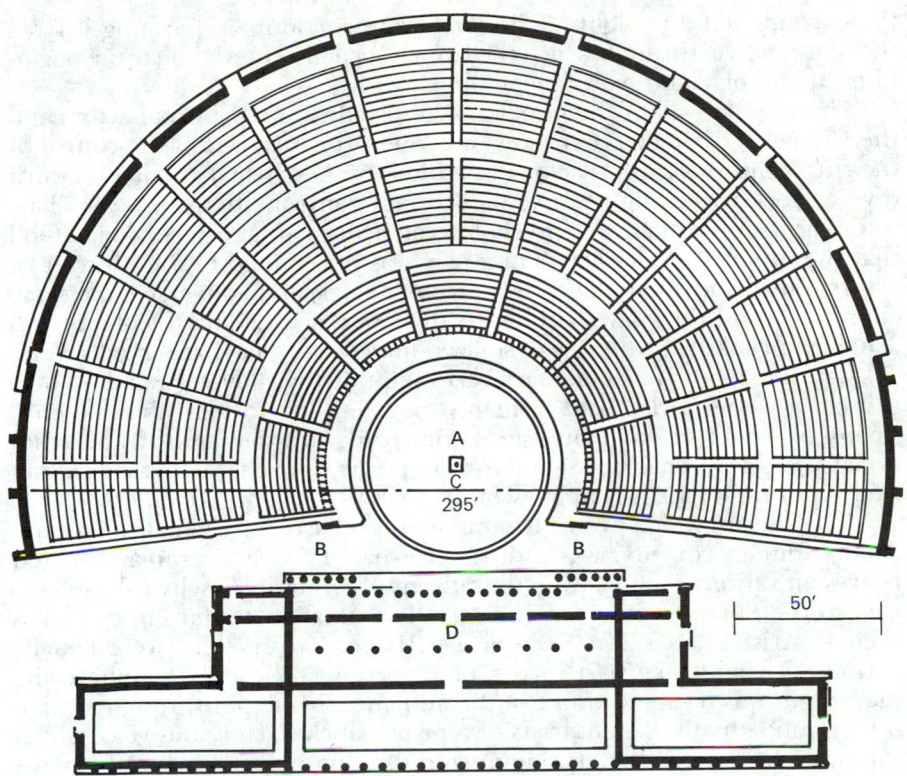

Plan of the theater of Dionysus at Athens. A. Orchestra B. Chorus Entrance C. Altar to Dionysus D. Skene.

On each of the next three days, plays by a single author were acted: three tragedies, followed by a broadly comic "satyr play" designed to relieve the intensity of the tragedies. Prizes were awarded to the best actor and to the best combination of playwright and producer.

At Athens, plays were acted in the Theater of Dionysus, a vast outdoor arena located on sloping ground near the Acropolis. Between the sixth and fourth centuries, the most important era of Greek drama, the theater evolved considerably. At first it was little more than a circular acting space, or *orchestra,* at the foot of a concave hillside where the audience sat on the ground. By the fifth century, permanent seats for the audience had been built and a long building called the *skene* had been constructed behind the *orchestra.* The *skene,* which became increasingly elaborate architecturally as time passed, provided dressing rooms, a backdrop for the action (scenery was apparently minimal), and a place through which the principal actors could make their entrances and exits. The *skene* often represented an edifice, integral to the story, where indoor actions could be imagined to happen, offstage—in Agamemnon's palace, for example. (The direct presentation of indoor scenes is unusual in Greek plays, as are killings and other violent episodes.) It is possible, though not certain, that a raised platform directly in front of the *skene* formed a stage slightly elevated above the *orchestra.* At

11

the extreme left and right of the *skene* were corridors, separating it from the seating area, through which the Chorus usually entered near the beginning of the play and exited near the end.

The players—all of them males—consisted of the principal actors and the Chorus. Originally, there was only one principal, but in the course of the fifth century a second actor was added (by Aeschylus) and later a third (by Sophocles), making possible face-to-face confrontations between characters and thus enhancing psychological realism. It must be understood that the number of characters in a play was not limited to the number of actors; one actor often played two or more roles, and conversely the same character could be played by more than one actor. This flexibility was achieved primarily by the use of stylized masks, a device that served several purposes: to maintain elementary verisimilitude (by allowing an adult male to play a young girl or old woman, for example); to help the audience (many of whom sat far from the action) recognize the identity and emotional state of the characters; and to help portray the characters as generalized types rather than simply as individuals.

The Chorus, which probably numbered twelve or fifteen in tragedy and twenty-four in comedy, was a distinctive part of Greek drama. It could represent various groups, from the citizens of Argos in Aeschylus' *Agamemnon,* to the Furies in his *Eumenides,* to the animal grotesques in comedies such as Aristophanes' *The Frogs* or *The Wasps.* Its functions were equally various: it could take part in the play's action, reflect the response the playwright was trying to evoke in the audience, bring out through sympathy or antipathy the salient traits of a principal character, and voice philosophical ideals. Not least, its singing and dancing helped sustain the play's mood and enhance it as spectacle.

Music and dance were important in both tragedy and comedy, helping to create elevated, festive, or ceremonial effects. The choral poems were sung, in a variety of lyric verse forms, to the accompaniment of dance and of musical instruments including the flute. Ordinary dialogue was probably delivered as a quasi-musical chant or in some other way that distinguished it from the tone of ordinary speech. A number of people have pointed out that, in its stylized manner, its spectacle, and its integration of different art media, Greek drama has its closest modern analogue in grand opera. (And indeed, opera originated in a seventeenth-century attempt to reconstruct the staging of Greek drama.)

Only forty-five Greek plays have survived: seven tragedies by Aeschylus, seven tragedies by Sophocles, seventeen tragedies and one satyr play by Euripides, eleven comedies by Aristophanes, and two comedies by Menander (only one of which is intact). Even this small sampling, hardly likely to encompass the full range of Greek drama, is highly varied. Tragedy ranges from the titanic culture-histories of Aeschylus, through the marvelously crafted humanistic dramas of Sophocles, to Euripides' ironic dramas of inner division and self-deception (some of which are more like comedies of manners than like tragedies). Aristophanes' Old Comedy is the Greek dramatic form most remote from modern drama. He strings upon a sketchy, fantastic, often perfunctory plot, scenes of farce, parody, and topical satire, punctuated with choruses of beautiful lyric poetry. It was not Old Comedy but the New Comedy—surviving only in the works of the fourth-century Menander—that was to establish the pattern of later comedy. New Comedy turned from fantasy and satire to deal with contemporary middle-class private life. The choruses were subordinated to intrigue-plots which usually dealt with a young man's attempt to marry against his father's opposition.

The Roman theater, like many aspects of Roman culture, was modeled on that of the Greeks. In Rome, where Greek-inspired plays began to be performed in the third century B.C., plays were performed at festivals honoring the gods, or for special occasions such as a state funeral or a military victory. The theaters were constructed along Greek lines, although by the first century A.D. they had come to be much larger and more elaborate than the Greek theaters, reflecting the Roman love of excess. Thirty-seven Roman plays survive: twenty-one comedies by Plautus (c. 254–184 B.C.); six comedies by Terence (195–159 B.C.); nine tragedies by Seneca (4 B.C.–65 A.D.), the Stoic philosopher and adviser to the Emperor Nero; and one tragedy formerly attributed to Seneca but now agreed to be the work of a later, anonymous author. Roman comedy, like Greek New Comedy, dealt with intrigues arising from middle-class life, while Seneca's stiff, melodramatic dramas, not meant for production, are reworkings of Greek tragedies. (Five of his nine extant plays are adapted from Euripides.)

Greek tragedy expressed the Greek spirit both in its unflinching treatment of basic issues in human life ("Know thyself") and in its strict economy of means ("Nothing too much"). Greek comedy embodied the Greeks' freedom of thought and expression, as well as their involvement in public life. Roman drama carried on the Greek achievement and was to be the version of classical drama that initially influenced the theater when it was reborn during the Renaissance.

Of all the genres, lyric poetry travels least well. Narrative and drama lose a great deal with the passage of time and loss of cultural associations. Subtleties disappear with translation into other languages. But the broad outlines of a story and the power of the stage are rugged—thus epic and drama can survive the passing of time and changes in language better than lyric poetry, which depends so much on nuance and the precise word.

"Lyric" originally meant "sung to the lyre," and perhaps the central fact about lyric poetry in the ancient world is its close connection with music. The lyric poet was literally a "lyricist" in Hebrew and Greek culture, as we are reminded by stories by David as a harpist and of Sappho's skill upon the lyre.

The Hebrew Bible is full of song, and the lyric portions of it should be read with imaginary, if not real, music in the background. The role of music and poetry in Hebrew worship is suggested by many passages in the Old Testament, among them the description of David's bringing of the ark to Jerusalem (I Chron. 16:7–36) and the descriptions of worship in the Psalms. In Psalm 42, the speaker tells of leading the throng to the House of God "with glad shouts and songs of thanksgiving," while in Psalm 68 another procession is described, "the singers in front, the minstrels last, between them maidens playing timbrels."

Hebrew poetry, like most ancient Near Eastern poetry, did not depend upon rhyme or a fixed line length, but rather upon a loose rhythm and parallelism. A unit of Hebrew verse characteristically consists of two lines,

13

each with three or four heavily stressed syllables, the second line parallel to the first in that it either paraphrases, develops, or completes it:

> What is man, that thou art mindful of him?
>   and the son of man, that thou visitest him? [PSALMS 8:4]

The simple, exalted power of this form is perceptible even in English translation.

The early Greeks described poetry as either "lyric" or "choric." Lyric poetry was the expression of a single singer accompanied by the lyre, while choric poetry was a group expression, sung by a chorus, usually also with instrumental accompaniment. The greatest school of lyric poets in Greece was centered among the Aeolians, on the eastern coast of the Aegean Sea and on the island of Lesbos, in the sixth century B.C. The great Aeolian lyricists, Sappho and Alcaeus, also inspired an Ionian school of lyricists on the mainland of Greece. The major successor to Sappho and Alcaeus was Anacreon, who was born in Teos in Asia Minor but spent much of his life in Athens. The leader of the "Dorian school" of the fifth century was the "choric" poet Pindar. Late Greek poetry of the Hellenistic period is best represented by Theocritus, whose *Idylls* established the pattern for centuries to come of pastoral poetry, in which the subject matter, whatever it may be, is cast in terms of rural scenes and characters.

In lyric poetry, as in much else, the Greeks set out on paths we still follow. The very conception of a "lyric" voice, intensely individual and personal, uncovering the subtle movements of thought and emotion and linking them to musicality, was Greek. Perhaps the most direct heir to Greek lyricism among the Romans was the first-century B.C. Catullus, whose most famous poems, those about his mistress "Lesbia," seem to explore all the convolutions of a self in the grip of an ambivalent passion. The other great Latin lyricists seem tame by comparison—they are polished and even elegant but they lack the naked self-revelation of the Greeks and of Catullus. Virgil is almost as well known for his *Eclogues* as for the *Aeneid;* in these poems he follows Theocritus in urbanely surveying many subjects under the cloak of the pastoral idiom. The other great Augustan lyricist was Horace, whose polished style, charm, and tone of detached common sense made him the most imitated classical poet of the European Enlightenment. Ovid was primarily a storyteller rather than a lyricist, but in his *Art of Love, Amores,* and *Metamorphoses,* we see again the Greek lyric inspiration, translated into Roman smartness and a cynical, amusing detachment.

Finally, a narrow definition of literary genres should not rule out such masterpieces of discursive prose as we find in much of the Old Testament and in Plato and Aristotle. Such works have had an incalculable impact upon later literature. The voices of the Hebrew prophets, of Plato's genial and humane Socrates, and of Aristotle, the indefatigable analyst of the nature and meaning of almost everything, must be included among the voices of the ancient world.

FURTHER READING *(prepared by J. H.): The Oxford History of the Classical World,* ed. by John Boardman, Jasper Griffin, and Oswyn Murray, 1986, is a very fine comprehensive treatment of the ancient Greek and Roman world, lavishly illustrated, combining history and sociology with good essays on ancient literature, art, and philosophy. An excellent overview of ancient history is provided by Chester G. Starr, *A History of the Ancient World*, 1965. A standard brief introduction to Hebrew history is John Bright, *A History of Israel*, 2nd ed., 1972. Even briefer and very useful are B. K. Rattey, *A Short History of the Hebrews*, 2nd ed., 1964, and Harry Orlinsky, *Ancient Israel*, 2nd ed., 1960. J. B. Bury's *History of Greece*, revised by R. Meiggs, 1951, and Michael Grant's *History of Rome*, 1978, are recommended for what their titles promise. Classical Greece is well treated in S. Hornblower, *The Greek World, 479–323*, 1983, and J. K. Davies, *Democracy and Classical Greece*, 1978. T. Cornell and J. Matthews, *Atlas of the Roman World*, 1982, includes, besides good maps and illustrations, a general history of Rome. Also useful are studies of the history of ideas in the ancient world. For the Hebrews, see James Muilenburg, *The Way of Israel*, 1961, and Norman Snaith, *Distinctive Ideas of the Old Testament*, 1947. Important special topics are treated in Frank M. Cross, *Canaanite Myth and Hebrew Epic*, 1973; Dennis J. McCarthy, *Old Testament Covenant: A Survey of Current Opinions*, 1972; and John H. Otwell, *And Sarah Laughed*, 1977, which examines the role of women in the Old Testament. Of special importance in understanding the literary practice of the Hebrews, as well as individual books of the Bible, is Northrop Frye's *The Great Code: The Bible and Literature*, 1982. H. D. F. Kitto's *The Greeks*, 1951, C. M. Bowra's *The Greek Experience*, 1957, A. Andrewes' *The Greeks*, 1967, and K. J. Dover's lavishly illustrated *The Greeks*, 1981, are all clear, accurate introductions to Greek ideas and culture. An important literary history of Greece is Albin Lesky, *A History of Greek Literature*, 1963, trans. James Willis and Cornelis de Heer, 1966. Briefer, but still valuable, overviews are provided by C. M. Bowra, *Ancient Greek Literature*, 1933, and K. J. Dover, ed., *Ancient Greek Literature*, 1980. On Greek drama and the Greek theater, T. B. L. Webster's *Greek Theatre Production*, 1962, Peter Arnott's *Greek Scenic Conventions*, 1962, and Margarete Bieber's *The History of the Greek and Roman Theater*, 2nd ed., 1961, are authoritative. Albin Lesky's *Greek Tragic Poetry*, 1983, is a comprehensive account. H. D. F. Kitto's *Greek Tragedy*, 3rd ed., 1961, is a standard critical survey; Jan Kott's *The Eating of the Gods*, 1973, surveys the plays from a more recent perspective. Hugh Lloyd-Jones, *The Justice of Zeus*, 2nd ed., 1984, puts Greek tragic drama in a broad perspective. M. I. Finley, ed., *The Legacy of Greece*, 1981, collects major essays reappraising the Greek heritage. R. H. Barrow's *The Romans*, 1949, is a useful brief introduction to Roman thought and culture. J. Wight Duff's two-volume history of Roman literature has not been superseded: *A Literary History of Rome from the Origins to the Close of the Golden Age*, 3rd ed., 1953; and *A Literary History of Rome in the Silver Age*, 3rd ed., 1964. Michael Grant's *Roman Literature*, 1954, is also accurate and readable, as is Moses Hadas' *History of Latin Literature*, 1952. Hadas' *Ancilla to Classical Reading*, 1954, is a thoughtful and lively handbook for the student of both Greek and Roman literature. R. M. Ogilvie's *Roman Literature and Society*, 1980, is a good author-by-author introduction and survey. On the forging of the ancient epic tradition and its modern heritage, see John Kevin Newman, *The Classical Epic Tradition*, 1986.

The Old Testament

(Tenth Century B.C. to Second Century B.C.)

The Old Testament develops a single central theme: the history of the ancient Hebrews' evolving perceptions of God. The setting is the tiny land of Palestine, the characters are the members of a small group of nomadic, Semitic tribes, and the time is a span of about fourteen centuries, from about 1800 B.C. to about 400 B.C. The story is above all a history, for the Hebrews—the ancient people whose culture has been transmitted by the Jews—were unusual, though not unique, among early peoples in conceiving of their religion not as the product of a single magnificent revelation, but as the result of a long series of experiences with their God. To the Hebrews, history was the story of a series of transactions with a stern but loving deity.

Although the Book of Genesis deals with the earliest events in the history of mankind, it was, in its final form, one of the last written books of the Old Testament. A group of Priestly revisers constructed the book, in about the middle of the fourth century B.C. Their sources were a much earlier version (the "J document") and an undetermined number of intermediate accounts.

The book as we have it divides into two parts. The first section is an account of prehistorical racial beginnings, and the second is a history of the origin of the Hebrews, descendants of the three patriarchs Abraham, Isaac, and Jacob. The account of the Creation that opens the book is a poetic treatment that in concrete narrative embodies certain basic Hebrew beliefs. Some of the matters "explained" in this account are fairly trivial: why snakes crawl on the ground, for example, and why women are afraid of them. But most of the questions raised are of the grandest magnitude: Who rules the world? What is man's relationship to God? How can we account for the presence of suffering in the world? Why do people wage war against each other? Genesis provides no final answers to these questions; the rest of the Old Testament, and the New Testament as well, is devoted to exploring the questions more fully, and people today are still engaged in debating some of the issues raised by the Creation story: Should women be subordinate to men, and must there be mistrust between men and women? Is work to be conceived of as a punishment? Are human beings by nature sinful, and is their natural relation to God that of suppliants seeking to atone for their sins?

Such questions do not obscure the major assumptions about the world that the first part of Genesis establishes. The Hebrews maintained that there is a Supreme Being, that He makes certain ethical demands upon human beings, and that man's chief duty is to serve God and to carry out His will.

With the eleventh chapter of Genesis, the focus abruptly narrows from the prehistory of mankind as a whole to the Hebrew people in particular and to their origins in the family of Abraham. The stories of Abraham, Isaac, Jacob, Esau, and Joseph, which follow, bear, like the earlier part of Genesis, the marks of primitive, folktale origins and later, more sophisticated revision. The key episodes, as in the earlier portion, are those in which God reveals Himself to man and establishes a series of "covenants" or agreements. These covenants represent a series of unfolding or developing perceptions of God, from the first (broken) covenant in the Garden, through the covenant of the rainbow, to the great covenant made with Abraham, and subsequently repeatedly renewed, that He would "make of thee a great nation."

The books of Exodus, Leviticus, Numbers, Deuteronomy, and Joshua are largely devoted to the Hebrew national epic. These books tell the story of the escape from Egyptian bondage under the leadership of Moses, the forty-years wandering in the Wilderness, and the final triumphant entry into the Promised Land. The books contain much else as well, notably large bodies of legislation, but the selections presented here form the narrative basis of the books. In its grand scope and its nationalistic fervor, the Exodus saga suggests comparisons with the Greek Iliad *and* Odyssey *and the Roman* Aeneid. *Like these other works, it recounts heroic actions from the early history of a people, centered around strong, dominating heroes. Like the* Odyssey *and the* Aeneid, *it is built upon the strong but simple basis of a journey through heroic challenges and perils, a journey that ends in a triumphant "homecoming." And, as in the classical epics, its action moves between the human and divine levels.*

The chief difference is in the nature of the divine element in the Hebrew and the Graeco-Roman epics. The Olympian gods, in the classical epics, remain above the action, observing and occasionally intervening either to help or to hinder the hero, but leaving the central action to unfold on the human plane. In the Exodus saga, by contrast, the entire story turns around the complex relationship between the Lord and the Hebrew people, as He both chastises and encourages them in their slow progress not only toward Canaan but toward an understanding of the Lord as God and of themselves as a nation.

Moses emerges almost immediately as the hero of the story, with the romantic tale of his discovery in the bulrushes by the Pharaoh's daughter. We read of his rearing at court, where he is nursed by his own mother in the role of foster mother. He kills an Egyptian oppressor and flees into the land of Midian. And then occurs the mysterious event that sets the epic action in motion: God appears to Moses in a burning bush and tells him to "bring forth the children of Israel out of Egypt." This event thus takes its place in the series of "theophanies," or direct experiences of God, that form the spine of the Pentateuch (the first five books of the Bible). The event is mysterious because no reason is ever given for the Lord's choosing Moses for this great work. Moses must grow into the role God has assigned him. At first he is reluctant and protests that he is not capable of the task God has laid on him. But as the epic progresses, Moses increases in moral stature to true epic proportions: he becomes fearless, commanding, and resourceful—the kind of man the Lord speaks with "face to face, as a man speaketh unto his friend." As the German poet Heinrich Heine wrote, "How tiny the mountain seems when Moses stands upon it!"

The dramatic interest in the Exodus epic is provided not only by the heroic growth of Moses, but also by his struggles with the Hebrew people. It is paradoxical that, in this nationalistic epic, the Hebrews represent themselves as deeply flawed. They are hardly out of Egypt before they are complaining and wishing they were back there, "when we sat by the flesh pots, and when we did eat bread to the full." When Moses obtains the gift of manna for them and conveys the Lord's command that they not store it overnight, they immediately disobey him and "it bred worms and stank." Even when Moses is on Mount Sinai, receiving the law, written upon tablets of stone by the finger of God, the people quickly become discouraged and build a "molten calf" to worship, Egyptian-fashion. No wonder the Lord's recurrent cry is "Behold, it is a stiffnecked people!"

The Exodus saga thus becomes not just a militaristic tale of battles against external enemies, but also the story of an education and a maturation for a whole people. God, through Moses, leads them into the Wilderness for forty years, on the most circuitous route possible to the Promised Land, not arbitrarily but in order to give them time to transform themselves from a slave people to a nation, with a government, a body of civil and religious law, and a sense of national identity.

The action of the Exodus saga, though sometimes repetitive and anecdotal, in a folk-like way, is highly unified as a whole. It sweeps toward four great climaxes: the Hebrews' crossing of the Red Sea and their defeat of the forces of the Pharaoh, the receiving of the Law of God atop Mount Sinai, the death of Moses, and the triumphant entry into the Promised Land under Joshua. This last part of the saga, which takes up the entire book of Joshua and which is represented here only by the history of the initial campaign against Jericho, presents the story as a swift and almost wholly triumphant military action under the leadership of a brilliant general. We are later told in Judges and First Samuel that the conquest was a slow and laborious process. The character of Joshua in the earlier books seems to be the result of a deliberate attempt to create an epic hero in a mold more familiar than that of Moses. Joshua is the hero as warrior rather than as spiritual leader. But he never comes fully to life, and Moses remains the memorable figure of the epic.

It is generally agreed that the Book of Job is the literary masterpiece of the Old Testament and one of the great works of all literature. It contains some of the most magnificent poetry in the Bible, and its seemingly simple structure, on rereading, reveals itself as endlessly resonant in its implications. And yet it is somewhat surprising that this book should be in the Bible at all, so sharp is its questioning of traditional Hebrew thought. Its subject is an eternal one—why do the good suffer?—and although of course it arrives at no answer to the unanswerable question, its reasoning is so keen and its emotional power so deep that the careful reader of Job can never again accept easy and shallow answers to the question.

Nothing is known of the author of Job, and its precise date is uncertain, but scholars now generally date it in the fifth century B.C. *Such dating would make it roughly contemporary with Aeschylus'* Prometheus Bound *and Sophocles'* Oedipus Rex, *both of which also deal profoundly with the question of human suffering. This common theme and the book's dramatic form have tempted critics to speculate that the author was directly influenced by Greek tragedy, though there is no external evidence of such influence.*

Job's debate with his conventional friends Eliphaz, Bildad, and Zophar sharply challenges the traditional Deuteronomic view of human suffering. Job and his "Comforters" agree that his suffering comes from God, but they differ radically on its meaning. The Comforters reconcile God's absolute power and absolute goodness by insisting that Job's suffering is a just punishment for sin. Job insists with equal vehemence that he has not deserved his fate and that no simple equation can be made between sin and suffering. But his lament is directed as much to God Himself as to the Comforters, as he calls into question not only their facile explanations but also the fundamental idea of any sort of justice or "covenant" between limited man and limitless God. "How should man be just with God?" he cries, "If he will contend with Him, he cannot answer Him one of a thousand."

The resolution of the book comes when God speaks "out of the whirlwind" in a theophany which recalls God's other appearances to man throughout the Old Testament. God's reply is simultaneously a rebuke to Job and a vindication of his position that God's power is too great to be reckoned in human terms. Ultimately, God approves the tormented questioner more than the complacent moralizers: "My wrath is kindled against thee, and against thy two friends," He tells Eliphaz, "for ye have not spoken of me the thing that is right, as my servant Job hath." The wager won, God

*restores to Job all that he has lost, and the book ends. The central question is still
unanswered, but the issue has been dramatized more vividly than ever before or since.*

*The Psalms (a word that literally means "Songs") are thoroughly and obviously
an expression of Hebrew ideas, expressed in some of the most beautiful lyric poetry in
world literature. Martin Luther called these 150 songs "a Bible in miniature," and
indeed they do encapsulate much of Hebrew history, psychology, and theology. Written over almost the entire time-span of the Old Testament, they were used in ancient
times for liturgical purposes (the exact nature of which is a subject of controversy)
and continue to be so used in modern Jewish and Christian worship. They include
hymns, meditations, exhortations, songs of praise, and commentaries on the significance of historical events for the Hebrew people. In tone they range widely, from
quietude to rage, from exultation to deep grief. They are deeply Hebraic in their
celebration of nature, not for its own sake but as God's handiwork, in their portrayal
of God as transcendently great and powerful but in intimate touch with His people,
and in their expression of communal ideals through an intensely personal tone.*

*The Book of Jonah is generally grouped with the Prophetic books, because its
protagonist is a prophet (although a surprisingly reluctant and inept one). It is not,
however, a prophecy itself, but rather a delightful short story, or perhaps a parable,
full of comic irony which makes an essentially serious point, a point about the universality of God's rule and the dangers of narrowness and xenophobia.*

*The story is full of delicate ironies. Jonah, to whom, as to Moses, God has ap-
peared, tries to escape the task God has demanded of him. The heathen sailors, by
contrast, are quite willing to believe in the Lord and to serve Him, once they understand the situation. God saves Jonah from the sea, with a loving charity Jonah
himself lacks. (His prayer in the belly of the fish is a later interpolation that suggests a
piety he does not have at this point in the story.) The Ninevites, like the sailors, are
quite willing to be converted, even by so surly a message as Jonah's: "Yet forty days,
and Nineveh shall be overthrown." But Jonah is petty enough to sulk and pout when
God does not make good his prophecy that He will kill "sixscore thousand persons" in
Nineveh. God teaches Jonah a lesson through the gourd which first flourishes and
then dies. We are not told whether or not Jonah profits from the lesson, but the
message is clear to us: God does not hate "foreigners," as some of his self-satisfied
followers do.*

NOTE ON THE TEXT

*These selections from the Old Testament are from the King James Version of 1611.
There are a number of more accurate, modern translations, but none has had comparable influence upon English speech and literature. The first six books have
been condensed for the sake of narrative continuity. Omissions of large sections
(such as the Joseph story in Genesis) are marked in footnotes.*

FURTHER READING *(prepared by F. S. N.):* George A. Buttrick, ed., *The Interpreter's
Bible,* 12 vols., 1952, gives, in addition to background material on the Old Testament
(vol. 7), introductions, exegesis and exposition on individual books. John E.
Steinmueller and Kathryn Sullivan, eds., *Catholic Biblical Encyclopedia: Old Testament,*
1956, have compiled a valuable work of reference. Dealing with the books as literary types is Georg Fohrer's *Introduction to the Old Testament,* 1965, trans. by David E.
Green, 1968. The relationship between literary art and biblical strategy and mean-

ing is explored incisively in Meir Sternberg's *The Poetics of Biblical Narrative: Ideological Literature and the Drama of Reading*, 1985, and in two books by Robert Alter: *The Art of Biblical Narrative*, 1981, and *The Art of Biblical Poetry*, 1985. John B. Gabel and Charles B. Wheeler, *The Bible as Literature: An Introduction*, 1986, is especially useful for basic background. Kenneth R. R. Gros Louis, ed., *Literary Interpretations of Biblical Narratives*, 1982, is accurately described by its title. General studies, including information on background, canon, literary merits and individual books, are offered by Otto Eissfeldt, *The Old Testament*, 1934, trans. by Peter R. Ackroyd, 1965, repr. 1974; and by Aage Bentzen, *Introduction to the Old Testament*, 1948, 7th ed. 1967.

THE OLD TESTAMENT

King James Version (1611)

from GENESIS

THE CREATION OF THE WORLD

(Genesis 1:1–2:3)

In the beginning God created the heaven and the earth. And the earth was without form, and void; and darkness was upon the face of the deep. And the Spirit of God moved upon the face of the waters. And God said, "Let there be light": and there was light. And God saw the light, that it was good: and God divided the light from the darkness. And God called the light Day, and the darkness he called Night. And the evening and the morning were the first day.

And God said, "Let there be a firmament in the midst of the waters, and let it divide the waters from the waters." And God made the firmament, and divided the waters which were under the firmament from the waters which were above the firmament: and it was so.[1] And God called the firmament Heaven. And the evening and the morning were the second day.

And God said, "Let the waters under the heaven be gathered together unto one place, and let the dry land appear": and it was so. And God called the dry land Earth; and the gathering together of the waters called he Seas: and God saw that it was good. And God said, "Let the earth bring forth grass, the herb yielding seed, and the fruit tree yielding fruit after his kind, whose seed is in itself, upon the earth": and it was so. And the earth brought forth grass, and herb yielding seed after his kind, and the tree yielding fruit, whose seed was in itself, after his kind: and God saw that it was good. And the evening and the morning were the third day.

And God said: "Let there be lights in the firmament of the heaven to divide the day from the night; and let them be for signs, and for seasons, and for days, and years; and let them be for lights in the firmament of the heaven to give light upon the earth." And it was so. And God made two great lights; the greater light to rule the day, and the lesser light to rule the night: he made the stars also. And God set them in the firmament of the

---

[1] These lines rest upon a belief that the world was created out of a watery chaos. The "firmament" was thought of as a solid dome which divided the "waters above" from the "waters below."

heaven to give light upon the earth. And to rule over the day and over the night, and to divide the light from the darkness: and God saw that it was good. And the evening and the morning were the fourth day.

And God said, "Let the waters bring forth abundantly the moving creature that hath life, and fowl that may fly above the earth in the open firmament of heaven." And God created great whales, and every living creature that moveth, which the waters brought forth abundantly, after their kind, and every winged fowl after his kind: and God saw that it was good. And God blessed them, saying, "Be fruitful, and multiply, and fill the waters in the seas, and let fowl multiply in the earth." And the evening and the morning were the fifth day.

And God said, "Let the earth bring forth the living creature after his kind, cattle,[2] and creeping thing, and beast of the earth after his kind": and it was so. And God made the beast of the earth after his kind, and cattle after their kind, and every thing that creepeth upon the earth after his kind: and God saw that it was good.

And God said, "Let us make man in our image, after our likeness: and let them have dominion over the fish of the sea, and over the fowl of the air, and over the cattle, and over all the earth, and over every creeping thing that creepeth upon the earth." So God created man in his own image, in the image of God created he him; male and female created he them. And God blessed them, and God said unto them, "Be fruitful, and multiply, and replenish the earth, and subdue it: and have dominion over the fish of the sea, and over the fowl of the air, and over every living thing that moveth upon the earth." And God said, "Behold, I have given you every herb bearing seed, which is upon the face of all the earth, and every tree, in the which is the fruit of a tree yielding seed; to you it shall be for meat. And to every beast of the earth, and to every fowl of the air, and to every thing that creepeth upon the earth, wherein there is life, I have given every green herb for meat." And it was so. And God saw every thing that he had made, and, behold, it was very good. And the evening and the morning were the sixth day.

Thus the heavens and the earth were finished, and all the host of them. And on the seventh day God ended his work which he had made; and he rested on the seventh day from all his work which he had made. And God blessed the seventh day, and sanctified it: because that in it he had rested from all his work which God created and made. . . .

THE FALL OF MAN

(*Genesis 2:4–3:24*)
In the day that the Lord God made the earth and the heavens, and every plant of the field before it was in the earth, and every herb of the field before it grew (for the Lord God had not caused it to rain upon the earth, and there was not a man to till the ground) there went up a mist from the earth, and watered the whole face of the ground. And the Lord God formed man of the dust of the ground, and breathed into his nostrils the

---

[2] All domestic animals.

breath of life; and man became a living soul. And the Lord God planted a garden eastward in Eden; and there he put the man whom he had formed. And out of the ground made the Lord God to grow every tree that is pleasant to the sight, and good for food; the tree of life also in the midst of the garden, and the tree of knowledge of good and evil. And a river went out of Eden to water the garden; and from thence it was parted, and became into four heads. The name of the first is Pison: that is it which compasseth the whole land of Havilah, where there is gold; and the gold of that land is good: there is bdellium[3] and the onyx stone. And the name of the second river is Gihon: the same is it that compasseth the whole land of Ethiopia. And the name of the third river is Hiddekel: that is it which goeth toward the east of Assyria. And the fourth river is Euphrates.

And the Lord God took the man, and put him into the garden of Eden to dress[4] it and to keep it. And the Lord God commanded the man, saying, "Of every tree of the garden thou mayest freely eat: but of the tree of the knowledge of good and evil, thou shalt not eat of it: for in the day that thou eatest thereof thou shalt surely die."

And the Lord God said, "It is not good that the man should be alone; I will make him a help meet for him." And out of the ground the Lord God formed every beast of the field, and every fowl of the air; and brought them unto Adam[5] to see what he would call them: and whatsoever Adam called every living creature, that was the name thereof. And Adam gave names to all cattle, and to the fowl of the air, and to every beast of the field; but for Adam there was not found a help meet for him. And the Lord God caused a deep sleep to fall upon Adam, and he slept: and he took one of his ribs, and closed up the flesh instead thereof; and the rib, which the Lord God had taken from man, made he a woman, and brought her unto the man.

And Adam said,

> "This is now bone of my bones,
>   and flesh of my flesh:
> She shall be called Woman,
>   because she was taken out of Man."

Therefore shall a man leave his father and his mother, and shall cleave unto his wife: and they shall be one flesh. And they were both naked, the man and his wife, and were not ashamed.

Now the serpent was more subtil than any beast of the field which the Lord God had made. And he said unto the woman, "Yea, hath God said, 'Ye shall not eat of every tree of the garden'?" And the woman said unto the serpent, "We may eat of the fruit of the trees of the garden: but of the fruit of the tree which is in the midst of the garden, God hath said, 'Ye shall not eat of it, neither shall ye touch it, lest ye die.'" And the serpent said unto the woman, "Ye shall not surely die: for God doth know that in the day ye

---

[3] The meaning of this word is obscure. It may be either a fragrant gum resin or a precious stone such as carbuncle, crystal, or pearl.
[4] Tend or cultivate.   [5] "Adam" means "man."

eat thereof, then your eyes shall be opened, and ye shall be as gods, knowing good and evil."[6]

And when the woman saw that the tree was good for food, and that it was pleasant to the eyes, and a tree to be desired to make one wise, she took of the fruit thereof, and did eat, and gave also unto her husband with her; and he did eat. And the eyes of them both were opened, and they knew that they were naked; and they sewed fig leaves together, and made themselves aprons.

And they heard the voice of the Lord God walking in the garden in the cool of the day: and Adam and his wife hid themselves from the presence of the Lord God amongst the trees of the garden. And the Lord God called unto Adam, and said unto him, "Where art thou?" And he said, "I heard thy voice in the garden, and I was afraid, because I was naked; and I hid myself." And he said, "Who told thee that thou wast naked? Hast thou eaten of the tree, whereof I commanded thee that thou shouldest not eat?" And the man said, "The woman whom thou gavest to be with me, she gave me of the tree, and I did eat." And the Lord God said unto the woman, "What is this that thou hast done?" And the woman said, "The serpent beguiled me, and I did eat." And the Lord God said unto the serpent,

> "Because thou hast done this,
>   thou are cursed above all cattle,
>   and above every beast of the field.
> Upon thy belly shalt thou go,
>   and dust shall thou eat
>   all the days of thy life:
> And I will put enmity between thee and the woman,
>   and between thy seed[7] and her seed;
> It shall bruise thy head,
>   and thou shalt bruise his heel."

Unto the woman he said,

> "I will greatly multiply thy sorrow and thy conception;
> In sorrow thou shalt bring forth children;
> And thy desire shall be to thy husband,
> And he shall rule over thee."

And unto Adam he said, "Because thou hast hearkened unto the voice of thy wife, and hast eaten of the tree, of which I commanded thee, saying, 'Thou shalt not eat of it':

> "Cursed is the ground for thy sake;
>   in sorrow shalt thou eat of it all the days of thy life.
> Thorns also and thistles shall it bring forth to thee;
>   and thou shalt eat the herb of the field;

---

[6] Only the tree of "the knowledge of good and evil" is mentioned in the temptation story. The previously mentioned "tree of life" does not appear.

[7] Descendants.

> In the sweat of thy face
>> shalt thou eat bread,
> Till thou return unto the ground;
>> for out of it wast thou taken:
> For dust thou art,
>> and unto dust shalt thou return."

And Adam called his wife's name Eve; because she was the mother of all living.[8] Unto Adam also and to his wife did the Lord God make coats of skins, and clothed them.

And the Lord God said, "Behold, the man is become as one of us, to know good and evil: and now, lest he put forth his hand, and take also of the tree of life, and eat, and live for ever—" therefore the Lord God sent him forth from the garden of Eden, to till the ground from whence he was taken. So he drove out the man; and he placed at the east of the garden of Eden Cherubims,[9] and a flaming sword which turned every way, to keep the way of the tree of life.

CAIN AND ABEL

(Genesis 4:1–5:5)

And Adam knew[10] Eve his wife; and she conceived, and bore Cain, and said, "I have gotten a man from the Lord." And she again bore his brother Abel. And Abel was a keeper of sheep, but Cain was a tiller of the ground. And in process of time it came to pass that Cain brought of the fruit of the ground an offering unto the Lord. And Abel, he also brought of the firstlings of his flock and of the fat thereof. And the Lord had respect unto Abel and to his offering: but unto Cain and to his offering he had not respect.[11] And Cain was very wroth, and his countenance fell. And the Lord said unto Cain, "Why are thou wroth? and why is thy countenance fallen? If thou doest well, shalt thou not be accepted? and if thou doest not well, sin lieth at the door. And unto thee shall be his desire, and thou shalt rule over him."

And Cain talked with Abel his brother: and it came to pass, when they were in the field, that Cain rose up against Abel his brother, and slew him. And the Lord said unto Cain, "Where is Abel thy brother?" And he said, "I know not: am I my brother's keeper?" And he said, "What hast thou done? the voice of thy brother's blood crieth unto me from the ground. And now art thou cursed from the earth, which hath opened her mouth to receive thy brother's blood from thy hand. When thou tillest the ground, it shall not henceforth yield unto thee her strength; a fugitive and a vagabond shalt thou be in the earth." And Cain said unto the Lord, "My punishment

---

[8] "Eve" in Hebrew resembles the word for "living."

[9] Guardians of sacred areas, depicted as winged creatures, half human and half lion.

[10] Had sexual intercourse with.

[11] The Cain and Abel story reflects the tensions between nomadic shepherds and farmers. (Compare the tension between hunter and shepherd in the story of Jacob and Esau.) No reason is given for God's refusal of Cain's offering.

is greater than I can bear. Behold, thou hast driven me out this day from the face of the earth; and from thy face shall I be hid; and I shall be a fugitive and a vagabond in the earth; and it shall come to pass that every one that findeth me shall slay me." And the Lord said unto him, "Therefore whosoever slayeth Cain, vengeance shall be taken on him sevenfold." And the Lord set a mark upon Cain, lest any finding him should kill him. And Cain went out from the presence of the Lord, and dwelt in the land of Nod, on the east of Eden. . . .

And Adam knew his wife again; and she bore a son, and called his name Seth: "For God," said she, "hath appointed me another seed instead of Abel, whom Cain slew." And to Seth, to him also there was born a son; and he called his name Enos; then began men to call upon the name of the Lord. . . .

And the days of Adam after he had begotten Seth were eight hundred years: and he begot sons and daughters. And all the days that Adam lived were nine hundred and thirty years: and he died. . . .[12]

THE FLOOD

(Genesis 6:1–9:29)

And it came to pass, when men began to multiply on the face of the earth, and daughters were born unto them, that the sons of God saw the daughters of men that they were fair; and they took them wives of all which they chose.[13] And the Lord said, "My spirit shall not always strive with man, for that he also is flesh: yet his days shall be a hundred and twenty years." There were giants in the earth in those days; and also after that, when the sons of God came in unto the daughters of men, and they bore children to them, the same became mighty men which were of old, men of renown. And God saw that the wickedness of man was great in the earth, and that every imagination of the thoughts of his heart was only evil continually. And it repented the Lord that he had made man on the earth, and it grieved him at his heart. And the Lord said, "I will destroy man whom I have created from the face of the earth; both man, and beast, and the creeping thing, and the fowls of the air; for it repenteth me that I have made them." But Noah found grace in the eyes of the Lord. . . .

Noah was a just man and perfect in his generations, and Noah walked with God. And Noah begot three sons, Shem, Ham, and Japheth. . . .

And God said unto Noah, "The end of all flesh is come before me; for the earth is filled with violence through them; and, behold, I will de-

[12] Various explanations have been offered to account for the extraordinary life spans attributed to figures of the Old Testament. The simplest is that they are exaggerations—such as appear in other national legends—intended to glorify the beginnings of the race.

[13] This account of the mating of "the sons of God" and "the daughters of men" is a good example of the primitive conceptions of divinity which still survive in the Old Testament. The story was perhaps originally intended to account for the existence of the Nephilim, a tribe of men of gigantic size and strength; this narrative may be compared to the stories of the matings of gods and mortal women in Greek mythology.

stroy them with the earth.[14] Make thee an ark of gopher wood;[15] rooms shalt thou make in the ark, and shalt pitch it within and without with pitch. And this is the fashion which thou shalt make it of: the length of the ark shall be three hundred cubits,[16] the breadth of it fifty cubits, and the height of it thirty cubits. A window shalt thou make to the ark, and in a cubit shalt thou finish it above; and the door of the ark shalt thou set in the side thereof; with lower, second, and third stories shalt thou make it. And, behold, I, even I, do bring a flood of waters upon the earth, to destroy all flesh, wherein is the breath of life, from under heaven; and everything that is in the earth shall die. But with thee will I establish my covenant;[17] and thou shalt come into the ark, thou, and thy sons, and thy wife, and thy sons' wives with thee. And of every living thing of all flesh, two of every sort shalt thou bring into the ark, to keep them alive with thee; they shall be male and female. Of fowls after their kind, and of cattle after their kind, of every creeping thing of the earth after his kind, two of every sort shall come unto thee, to keep them alive. And take thou unto thee of all food that is eaten, and thou shalt gather it to thee; and it shall be for food for thee, and for them." Thus did Noah; according to all that God commanded him, so did he. And the Lord said unto Noah, "Come thou and all thy house into the ark; for thee have I seen righteous before me in this generation. Of every clean beast thou shalt take to thee by sevens, the male and his female; and of beasts that are not clean by two, the male and his female.[18] Of fowls also of the air by sevens, the male and the female; to keep seed alive upon the face of all the earth. For yet seven days, and I will cause it to rain upon the earth forty days and forty nights; and every living substance that I have made will I destroy from off the face of the earth."

And Noah did according unto all that the Lord commanded him. And Noah went in, and his sons, and his wife, and his sons' wives with him, into the ark, because of the waters of the flood. Of clean beasts, and of beasts that are not clean, and of fowls, and of every thing that creepeth upon the earth, there went in two and two unto Noah into the ark, the male and the female, as God had commanded Noah. And it came to pass after seven days

[14] The Biblical account of the Flood has much in common with other accounts of great floods, especially in the Babylonian Gilgamesh Epic. In this other work, the hero also builds an ark, it comes to rest on a mountain, birds are sent out to see if the flood is subsiding, and the hero makes burnt offerings for his deliverance. The Genesis version differs, however, in that the Flood is not sent capriciously but as a punishment for man's wickedness.

[15] An ark is a large ship. The kind of wood used is unidentified; "gopher" simply means "tree" in Hebrew.

[16] A cubit is an ancient unit of measurement based on the length of the forearm, usually about twenty inches.

[17] This "covenant," or agreement, between God and Noah, which is expanded after the Flood and marked with the sign of the rainbow, is the first of several such covenants in the Old Testament. The agreements culminate in the repeated covenant with Abraham and his descendants, which has become the central idea in Judaism. The conditions under which God allowed Adam and Eve to live in the Garden are an implicit covenant that anticipates these later covenants.

[18] "Clean beasts" include those which have cloven hooves and chew a cud. See Leviticus, Chapter 11. The distinction between clean and unclean here is apparently a later addition, not harmonized with the rest of the text, since Noah takes in two of each animal, regardless of status.

that the waters of the flood were upon the earth. In the six hundredth year of Noah's life in the second month, the seventeenth day of the month, the same day were all the fountains of the great deep broken up, and the windows of heaven were opened.[19] And the waters prevailed, and were increased greatly upon the earth; and the ark went upon the face of the waters. And the waters prevailed exceedingly upon the earth; and all the high hills, that were under the whole heaven, were covered. Fifteen cubits upward did the waters prevail; and the mountains were covered. And all flesh died that moved upon the earth, both of fowl, and of cattle, and of beast, and of every creeping thing that creepeth upon the earth, and every man. All in whose nostrils was the breath of life, of all that was in the dry land, died. And every living substance was destroyed which was upon the face of the ground, both man, and cattle, and the creeping things, and the fowl of the heaven; and they were destroyed from the earth: and Noah only remained alive, and they that were with him in the ark. And the waters prevailed upon the earth a hundred and fifty days.

And God remembered Noah, and every living thing, and all the cattle that was with him in the ark: and God made a wind to pass over the earth, and the waters assuaged. The fountains also of the deep and the windows of heaven were stopped, and the rain from heaven was restrained; and the waters returned from off the earth continually: and after the end of the hundred and fifty days the waters were abated. And the ark rested in the seventh month, on the seventeenth day of the month, upon the mountains of Ararat. And the waters decreased continually until the tenth month: in the tenth month, on the first day of the month, were the tops of the mountains seen.

And it came to pass at the end of forty days that Noah opened the window of the ark which he had made: and he sent forth a raven, which went forth to and fro, until the waters were dried up from off the earth. Also he sent forth a dove from him, to see if the waters were abated from off the face of the ground; but the dove found no rest for the sole of her foot, and she returned unto him into the ark, for the waters were on the face of the whole earth: then he put forth his hand, and took her, and pulled her in unto him into the ark. And he stayed yet other seven days; and again he sent forth the dove out of the ark; and the dove came in to him in the evening; and, lo, in her mouth was an olive leaf plucked off: so Noah knew that the waters were abated from off the earth. And he stayed yet other seven days; and sent forth the dove; which returned not again unto him any more.

And it came to pass in the six hundredth and first year, in the first month, the first day of the month, the waters were dried up from off the earth: and Noah removed the covering of the ark, and looked, and, behold the face of the ground was dry. And in the second month, on the seven and twentieth day of the month, was the earth dried. And God spoke unto Noah, saying, "Go forth of the ark, thou, and thy wife, and thy sons, and

---

[19] As a result of the blending of different accounts, two explanations are given for the Flood. The first is that it rained for forty days and forty nights, while here it is said that "all the fountains of the great deep [were] broken up, and the windows of heaven were opened." In other words, chaos returned through the opening up of subterranean seas and the opening of the dome-like firmament that restrained "the waters above." See the beginning of Genesis.

thy sons' wives with thee. Bring forth with thee every living thing that is
with thee, of all flesh, both of fowl, and of cattle, and of every creeping
thing that creepeth upon the earth; that they may breed abundantly in the
earth, and be fruitful, and multiply upon the earth." And Noah went forth,
and his sons, and his wife, and his sons' wives with him. Every beast, every
creeping thing, and every fowl, and whatsoever creepeth upon the earth,
after their kinds, went forth out of the ark.

And Noah builded an altar unto the Lord; and took of every clean
beast, and of every clean fowl, and offered burnt offerings on the altar.
And the Lord smelled a sweet savor; and the Lord said in his heart, "I will not
again curse the ground any more for man's sake; for the imagination of man's
heart is evil from his youth; neither will I again smite any more every thing
living, as I have done. While the earth remaineth, seedtime and harvest, and
cold and heat, and summer and winter, and day and night shall not cease."

And God blessed Noah and his sons, and said unto them, "Be fruitful,
and multiply, and replenish the earth. And the fear of you and the dread
of you shall be upon every beast of the earth, and upon every fowl of the
air, upon all that moveth upon the earth, and upon all the fishes of the sea;
into your hand are they delivered. Every moving thing that liveth shall be
meat for you; even as the green herb have I given you all things. But flesh
with the life thereof, which is the blood thereof, shall ye not eat. And surely
your blood of your lives will I require; at the hand of every beast will I
require it, and at the hand of man; at the hand of every man's brother will I
require the life of man. Whoso sheddeth man's blood, by man shall his
blood be shed: for in the image of God made he man." . . . And God spoke
unto Noah, and to his sons with him, saying, "And I, behold, I establish my
covenant with you, and with your seed after you; and with every living
creature that is with you, of the fowl, of the cattle, and of every beast of the
earth with you; from all that go out of the ark, to every beast of the earth.
And I will establish my covenant with you; neither shall all flesh be cut off
any more by the waters of a flood; neither shall there any more be a flood
to destroy the earth."

And God said, "This is the token of the covenant which I make between
me and you and every living creature that is with you, for perpetual generations: I do set my bow in the cloud, and it shall be for a token of a covenant
between me and the earth. And it shall come to pass, when I bring a cloud
over the earth, that the bow shall be seen in the cloud: and I will remember
my covenant, which is between me and you and every living creature of all
flesh; and the waters shall no more become a flood to destroy all flesh. And
the bow shall be in the cloud; and I will look upon it, that I may remember
the everlasting covenant between God and every living creature of all flesh
that is upon the earth."[20] And God said unto Noah, "This is the token of
the covenant, which I have established between me and all flesh that is
upon the earth." . . .

And Noah began to be a husbandman, and he planted a vineyard: and
he drank of the wine, and was drunken; and he was uncovered within his

---

[20] The rainbow was often regarded by primitive peoples as God's bow from which he shot
arrows of lightning. Here it becomes rather a sign in the heavens that God's anger has abated.

tent. And Ham, the father of Canaan, saw the nakedness of his father, and told his two brethren without. And Shem and Japheth took a garment, and laid it upon both their shoulders, and went backward, and covered the nakedness of their father; and their faces were backward, and they saw not their father's nakedness.[21] And Noah awoke from his wine, and knew what his younger son had done unto him. And he said, "Cursed be Canaan; a servant of servants shall he be unto his brethren." And he said, "Blessed be the Lord God of Shem; and Canaan shall be his servant. God shall enlarge Japheth, and he shall dwell in the tents of Shem; and Canaan shall be his servant."

And Noah lived after the flood three hundred and fifty years. And all the days of Noah were nine hundred and fifty years: and he died. . . .

THE TOWER OF BABEL

(*Genesis 11:1–11:9*)
And the whole earth was of one language, and of one speech. And it came to pass, as they journeyed from the east, that they found a plain in the land of Shinar; and they dwelt there. And they said one to another, "Go to, let us make brick, and burn them thoroughly." And they had brick for stone, and slime had they for mortar. And they said, "Go to, let us build us a city and a tower, whose top may reach unto heaven; and let us make us a name, lest we be scattered abroad upon the face of the whole earth."[22] And the Lord came down to see the city and the tower, which the children of men builded. And the Lord said, "Behold, the people is one, and they have all one language; and this they begin to do: and now nothing will be restrained from them, which they have imagined to do. Go to, let us go down, and there confound their language, that they may not understand one another's speech." So the Lord scattered them abroad from thence upon the face of all the earth: and they left off to build the city. Therefore is the name of it called Babel; because the Lord did there confound the language of all the earth: and from thence did the Lord scatter them abroad upon the face of all the earth. . . .

THE STORY OF ABRAHAM AND ISAAC

(*Genesis 11:27–25:28*)
Now these are the generations of Terah: Terah begot Abram, Nahor and Haran; and Haran begot Lot. And Haran died before his father Terah in the land of his nativity, in Ur of the Chaldees. And Abram and Nahor took them wives: the name of Abram's wife was Sarai; and the name of Nahor's

---

[21] There is some confusion here in names. God places the curse on Canaan rather than on Ham, who is said to have committed the offense. The incident implies that Israel's later subjugation of Canaan was the consequence of the Canaanites' sexual perversions.

[22] Mesopotamian cities were marked by *ziggurats*, pyramid-like towers regarded as the gateways to heaven. The story of the Tower of Babel not only alludes to such structures, but also is an etiological story accounting for the origin of languages and cultural magnificence of Babylon. The episode also emphasizes man's continuing pride and sinfulness even after the Flood.

wife, Milcah, the daughter of Haran, the father of Milcah, and the father of Iscah. But Sarai was barren; she had no child.

And Terah took Abram his son, and Lot the son of Haran his son's son, and Sarai his daughter-in-law, his son Abram's wife; and they went forth with them from Ur of the Chaldees, to go into the land of Canaan; and they came unto Haran, and dwelt there. And the days of Terah were two hundred and five years: and Terah died in Haran.

Now the Lord had said unto Abram, "Get thee out of thy country, and from thy kindred, and from thy father's house, unto a land that I will show thee: and I will make of thee a great nation, and I will bless thee, and make thy name great; and thou shalt be a blessing. And I will bless them that bless thee, and curse him that curseth thee: and in thee shall all families of the earth be blessed."[23]

So Abram departed, as the Lord had spoken unto him; and Lot went with him: and Abram was seventy and five years old when he departed out of Haran. And Abram took Sarai his wife, and Lot his brother's son, and all their substance that they had gathered, and the souls that they had gotten in Haran; and they went forth to go into the land of Canaan; and into the land of Canaan they came. And Abram passed through the land unto the place of Sichem, unto the plain of Moreh. And the Canaanite was then in the land. And the Lord appeared unto Abram, and said, "Unto thy seed will I give this land." And there builded he an altar unto the Lord, who appeared unto him. And he removed from thence unto a mountain on the east of Beth-el, and pitched his tent, having Beth-el on the west, and Hai on the east: and there he builded an altar unto the Lord, and called upon the name of the Lord. And Abram journeyed, going on still toward the south. . . .[24]

And it came to pass after these things that God did tempt Abraham, and said unto him, "Abraham": and he said, "Behold, here I am." And he said, "Take now thy son, thine only son Isaac, whom thou lovest, and get thee into the land of Moriah; and offer him there for a burnt offering upon one of the mountains which I will tell thee of." And Abraham rose up early in the morning, and saddled his ass, and took two of his young men with him, and Isaac his son, and cleft the wood for the burnt offering, and rose up, and went unto the place of which God had told him. Then on the third day Abraham lifted up his eyes, and saw the place afar off. And Abraham said unto his young men, "Abide ye here with the ass; and I and the lad will go yonder and worship, and come again to you." And Abraham took the wood of the burnt offering, and laid it upon Isaac his son; and he took the fire in his hand, and a knife; and they went both of them together.

And Isaac spoke unto Abraham his father, and said, "My father": and he said, "Here am I, my son." And he said, "Behold the fire and the wood:

---

[23] This is the first statement of the often-repeated "covenant" with Israel around which much of Old Testament history revolves.

[24] Abram and his family migrate to Egypt and then return to Canaan. His nephew Lot settles in the cities of the fertile plain of Jordan. To mark His covenant with the Hebrews, God changes Abram's name to Abraham and Sarai's to Sarah, requires that all males of Abraham's line shall be circumcised, and miraculously causes Sarah to bear a son, Isaac, in her very old age. Angered by the practice of sodomy, God sends down fire and brimstone to destroy the cities of the plain, Sodom and Gomorrah, sparing only Lot and some of his kin.

but where is the lamb for a burnt offering?" And Abraham said, "My son, God will provide himself a lamb for a burnt offering": so they went both of them together. And they came to the place which God had told him of; and Abraham built an altar there, and laid the wood in order, and bound Isaac his son, and laid him on the altar upon the wood. And Abraham stretched forth his hand, and took the knife to slay his son. And the angel of the Lord called unto him out of heaven, and said, "Abraham, Abraham": and he said, "Here am I." And he said, "Lay not thine hand upon the lad, neither do thou any thing unto him: for now I know that thou fearest God, seeing thou hast not withheld thy son, thine only son from me." And Abraham lifted up his eyes, and looked, and beheld behind him a ram caught in a thicket by his horns: and Abraham went and took the ram, and offered him up for a burnt offering in the stead of his son. And Abraham called the name of that place Jehovah-jireh: as it is said to this day, "In the mount of the Lord it shall be seen. . . . [25] So Abraham returned unto his young men, and they rose up and went together to Beer-sheba; and Abraham dwelt at Beer-sheba. . . . [26]

And Isaac was forty years old when he took Rebekah to wife, the daughter of Bethuel the Syrian of Padan-aram, the sister to Laban the Syrian. And Isaac intreated the Lord for his wife, because she was barren: and the Lord was intreated of him, and Rebekah his wife conceived. And the children struggled together within her; and she said, "If it be so, why am I thus?" And she went to enquire of the Lord. And the Lord said unto her,

> "Two nations are in thy womb,
>   and two manner of people shall be separated from thy bowels;
> And the one people shall be stronger than the other people;
>   and the elder shall serve the younger."

And when her days to be delivered were fulfilled, behold, there were twins in her womb. And the first came out red, all over like a hairy garment; and they called his name Esau. And after that came his brother out, and his hand took hold on Esau's heel; and his name was called Jacob:[27] and Isaac was threescore years old when she bore them. And the boys grew: and Esau was a cunning hunter, a man of the field; and Jacob was a plain man, dwelling in tents. And Isaac loved Esau, because he did eat of his venison: but Rebekah loved Jacob.

---

[25] The story of the near-sacrifice of Isaac has many analogues in other religions and literatures, including the story of Agamemnon's sacrifice of his daughter Iphigenia, referred to in the *Iliad* and in Aeschylus' *Agamemnon*. The form the story takes here seems to celebrate perfect faith and to condemn human sacrifice.

[26] After Sarah dies, Abraham seeks a bride for Isaac. Resolved that his son shall marry a woman of his own Mesopotamian people rather than any of the local Canaanite women, Abraham sends his steward to his former homeland. While stopping by a well, the steward providentially encounters Rebekah, Isaac's first cousin. She travels to her new homeland in Canaan and is married to Isaac. Abraham dies and is buried beside Sarah.

[27] The name Jacob can mean either "he takes by the heel" or "he supplants." The second meaning is particularly relevant in the light of Jacob's later history. The character of Jacob is a version of the "trickster hero," and his often rather crudely comic exploits in the sections which follow still betray their origins in folk tales.

THE STORY OF JACOB

(Genesis 25:29–35:29)

And Jacob sod pottage:[28] and Esau came from the field, and he was faint: and Esau said to Jacob, "Feed me, I pray thee, with that same red pottage; for I am faint" (therefore was his name called Edom). And Jacob said, "Sell me this day thy birthright." And Esau said, "Behold, I am at the point to die: and what profit shall this birthright do to me?" And Jacob said, "Swear to me this day!" And he swore unto him: and he sold his birthright unto Jacob. Then Jacob gave Esau bread and pottage of lentils; and he did eat and drink, and rose up, and went his way: thus Esau despised his birthright. . . .

And Esau was forty years old when he took to wife Judith the daughter of Beeri the Hittite, and Bashemath the daughter of Elon the Hittite: which were a grief of mind unto Isaac and to Rebekah.

And it came to pass that when Isaac was old, and his eyes were dim, so that he could not see, he called Esau his eldest son, and said unto him, "My son": and he said unto him, "Behold, here am I." And he said, "Behold now, I am old, I know not the day of my death. Now therefore take, I pray thee, thy weapons, thy quiver and thy bow, and go out to the field, and take me some venison; and make me savory meat, such as I love, and bring it to me, that I may eat; that my soul may bless thee before I die."

And Rebekah heard when Isaac spoke to Esau his son. And Esau went to the field to hunt for venison, and to bring it. And Rebekah spoke unto Jacob her son, saying, "Behold, I heard thy father speak unto Esau thy brother, saying, 'Bring me venison, and make me savory meat, that I may eat, and bless thee before the Lord before my death.' Now therefore, my son, obey my voice according to that which I command thee. Go now to the flock, and fetch me from thence two good kids of the goats; and I will make them savory meat for thy father, such as he loveth: and thou shalt bring it to thy father, that he may eat, and that he may bless thee before his death." And Jacob said to Rebekah his mother, "Behold, Esau my brother is a hairy man, and I am a smooth man. My father peradventure will feel me, and I shall seem to him as a deceiver; and I shall bring a curse upon me, and not a blessing." And his mother said unto him, "Upon me be thy curse, my son; only obey my voice, and go fetch me them." And he went, and fetched, and brought them to his mother; and his mother made savory meat, such as his father loved. And Rebekah took goodly raiment of her eldest son Esau, which were with her in the house, and put them upon Jacob her younger son; and she put the skins of the kids of the goats upon his hands, and upon the smooth of his neck; and she gave the savory meat and the bread, which she had prepared, into the hand of her son Jacob.

And he came unto his father, and said, "My father": and he said, "Here am I; who art thou, my son?" And Jacob said unto his father, "I am Esau thy firstborn; I have done according as thou badest me: arise, I pray thee, sit and eat of my venison, that thy soul may bless me." And Isaac said unto his son, "How is it that thou hast found it so quickly, my son?" And he said, "Because the Lord thy God brought it to me." And Isaac said unto Jacob,

[28] Cooked food.

"Come near, I pray thee, that I may feel thee, my son, whether thou be my very son Esau or not." And Jacob went near unto Isaac his father; and he felt him, and said, "The voice is Jacob's voice, but the hands are the hands of Esau." And he discerned him not, because his hands were hairy, as his brother Esau's hands; so he blessed him. And he said, "Art thou my very son Esau?" And he said, "I am." And he said, "Bring it near to me, and I will eat of my son's venison, that my soul may bless thee." And he brought it near to him, and he did eat: and he brought the wine, and he drank. And his father Isaac said unto him, "Come near now, and kiss me, my son." And he came near, and kissed him: and he smelled the smell of his raiment, and blessed him, and said,

> "See, the smell of my son
>> is as the smell of a field which the Lord hath blessed:
> Therefore God give thee of the dew of heaven,
>> and the fatness of the earth,
>> and plenty of corn and wine:
> Let people serve thee,
>> and nations bow down to thee:
> Be lord over thy brethren,
>> and let thy mother's sons bow down to thee:
> Cursed be every one that curseth thee,
>> and blessed be he that blesseth thee."

And it came to pass, as soon as Isaac had made an end of blessing Jacob, and Jacob was yet scarce gone out from the presence of Isaac his father, that Esau his brother came in from his hunting. And he also had made savory meat, and brought it unto his father, and said unto his father, "Let my father arise, and eat of his son's venison, that thy soul may bless me." And Isaac his father said unto him, "Who art thou?" And he said, "I am thy son, thy firstborn Esau." And Isaac trembled very exceedingly, and said, "Who? where is he that hath taken venison, and brought it me, and I have eaten of all before thou camest, and have blessed him? yea, and he shall be blessed." And when Esau heard the words of his father, he cried with a great and exceeding bitter cry, and said unto his father, "Bless me, even me also, O my father." And he said, "Thy brother came with subtilty, and hath taken away thy blessing." And he said, "Is not he rightly named Jacob? for he hath supplanted me these two times: he took away my birthright; and, behold, now he hath taken away my blessing." And he said, "Hast thou not reserved a blessing for me?" And Isaac answered and said unto Esau, "Behold, I have made him thy lord, and all his brethren have I given to him for servants; and with corn and wine have I sustained him: and what shall I do now unto thee, my son?" And Esau said unto his father, "Hast thou but one blessing, my father? bless me, even me also, O my father." And Esau lifted up his voice, and wept. And Isaac his father answered and said unto him,

> "Behold, thy dwelling shall be the fatness of the earth,
>> and of the dew of heaven from above;
> And by thy sword shalt thou live,
>> and shalt serve thy brother;

And it shall come to pass when thou shalt have the dominion,
  that thou shalt break his yoke from off thy neck."

And Esau hated Jacob because of the blessing wherewith his father
blessed him: and Esau said in his heart, "The days of mourning for my
father are at hand; then will I slay my brother Jacob."[29] And these words of
Esau her elder son were told to Rebekah: and she sent and called Jacob her
younger son, and said unto him, "Behold, thy brother Esau, as touching
thee, doth comfort himself, purposing to kill thee. Now therefore, my son,
obey my voice; and arise, flee thou to Laban my brother to Haran. And
tarry with him a few days, until thy brother's fury turn away; until thy
brother's anger turn away from thee, and he forget that which thou hast
done to him. Then I will send, and fetch thee from thence: why should I
be deprived also of you both in one day?"

And Rebekah said to Isaac, "I am weary of my life because of the
daughters of Heth: if Jacob take a wife of the daughters of Heth, such as
these which are of the daughters of the land, what good shall my life do
me?" And Isaac called Jacob, and blessed him, and charged him, and said
unto him, "Thou shalt not take a wife of the daughters of Canaan. Arise, go
to Padan-aram, to the house of Bethuel thy mother's father; and take thee
a wife from thence of the daughters of Laban thy mother's brother. And
God Almighty bless thee, and make thee fruitful, and multiply thee, that
thou mayest be a multitude of people; and give thee the blessing of Abraham, to thee, and to thy seed with thee; that thou mayest inherit the land
wherein thou art a stranger, which God gave unto Abraham." . . .

And Jacob went out from Beer-sheba, and went toward Haran. And he
lighted upon a certain place, and tarried there all night, because the sun
was set; and he took of the stones of that place, and put them for his
pillows, and lay down in that place to sleep. And he dreamed, and, behold,
a ladder set up on the earth, and the top of it reached to heaven: and,
behold, the angels of God ascending and descending on it. And, behold,
the Lord stood above it, and said, "I am the Lord God of Abraham thy
father, and the God of Isaac: the land whereon thou liest, to thee will I give
it, and to thy seed; and thy seed shall be as the dust of the earth, and thou
shalt spread abroad to the west, and to the east, and to the north, and to the
south: and in thee and in thy seed shall all the families of the earth be
blessed. And, behold, I am with thee, and will keep thee in all places
whither thou goest, and will bring thee again into this land; for I will not
leave thee until I have done that which I have spoken to thee of." And
Jacob awaked out of his sleep, and he said, "Surely the Lord is in this place;
and I knew it not." And he was afraid, and said, "How dreadful is this
place! this is none other but the house of God, and this is the gate of
heaven."

And Jacob rose up early in the morning, and took the stone that he had
put for his pillows, and set it up for a pillar, and poured oil upon the top of

---

[29] Jacob's hoodwinking of Isaac reflects the ancient belief in the magical nature of formal
blessings and curses; once a blessing had been pronounced, even in error, it could not be
withdrawn.

it. And he called the name of that place Beth-el:[30] but the name of that city was called Luz at the first. And Jacob vowed a vow, saying, "If God will be with me, and will keep me in this way that I go, and will give me bread to eat, and raiment to put on, so that I come again to my father's house in peace; then shall the Lord be my God: and this stone, which I have set for a pillar, shall be God's house: and of all that thou shalt give me I will surely give the tenth unto thee."

Then Jacob went on his journey, and came into the land of the people of the east. And he looked, and beheld a well in the field, and, lo, there were three flocks of sheep lying by it; for out of that well they watered the flocks: and a great stone was upon the well's mouth. And thither were all the flocks gathered: and they rolled the stone from the well's mouth, and watered the sheep, and put the stone again upon the well's mouth in his place. And Jacob said unto them, "My brethren, whence be ye?" And they said, "Of Haran are we." And he said unto them, "Know ye Laban the son of Nahor?" And they said, "We know him." And he said unto them, "Is he well?" And they said, "He is well: and, behold, Rachel his daughter cometh with the sheep." And he said, "Lo, it is yet high day, neither is it time that the cattle should be gathered together: water ye the sheep, and go and feed them." And they said, "We cannot, until all the flocks be gathered together, and till they roll the stone from the well's mouth; then we water the sheep." And while he yet spoke with them, Rachel came with her father's sheep: for she kept them. And it came to pass, when Jacob saw Rachel the daughter of Laban his mother's brother, and the sheep of Laban his mother's brother, that Jacob went near, and rolled the stone from the well's mouth, and watered the flock of Laban his mother's brother. And Jacob kissed Rachel, and lifted up his voice, and wept. And Jacob told Rachel that he was her father's brother, and that he was Rebekah's son: and she ran and told her father.

And it came to pass, when Laban heard the tidings of Jacob his sister's son, that he ran to meet him, and embraced him, and kissed him, and brought him to his house. And he told Laban all these things. And Laban said to him, "Surely thou art my bone and my flesh." And he abode with him the space of a month. And Laban said unto Jacob, "Because thou art my brother, shouldest thou therefore serve me for nought? tell me, what shall thy wages be?" And Laban had two daughters: the name of the elder was Leah, and the name of the younger was Rachel. Leah was tender-eyed;[31] but Rachel was beautiful and well favored. And Jacob loved Rachel; and said, "I will serve thee seven years for Rachel thy younger daughter." And Laban said, "It is better that I give her to thee than that I should give her to another man. Abide with me."

And Jacob served seven years for Rachel; and they seemed unto him but a few days, for the love he had to her. And Jacob said unto Laban, "Give me my wife, for my days are fulfilled, that I may go in unto her." And Laban gathered together all the men of the place, and made a feast. And it came to pass in the evening that he took Leah his daughter, and

---

[30] "The House of God."
[31] The word here translated "tender-eyed" apparently means, more precisely, "dull-eyed."

brought her to him; and he went in unto her. And Laban gave unto his daughter Leah Zilpah his maid for a handmaid. And it came to pass that in the morning, behold, it was Leah: and he said to Laban, "What is this thou hast done unto me? did not I serve with thee for Rachel? wherefore then hast thou beguiled me?" And Laban said, "It must not be so done in our country, to give the younger before the firstborn. Fulfil her week, and we will give thee this also for the service which thou shalt serve with me yet seven other years."[32] And Jacob did so, and fulfilled her week: and he gave him Rachel his daughter to wife also. And Laban gave to Rachel his daughter Bilhah his handmaid to be her maid. And he went in also unto Rachel, and he loved also Rachel more than Leah, and served with him yet seven other years.

And when the Lord saw that Leah was hated, he opened her womb: but Rachel was barren. And Leah conceived, and bore a son, and she called his name Reuben: for she said, "Surely the Lord hath looked upon my affliction; now therefore my husband will love me."[33] And she conceived again, and bore a son; and said, "Because the Lord hath heard that I was hated, he hath therefore given me this son also": and she called his name Simeon. And she conceived again, and bore a son; and said, "Now this time will my husband be joined unto me, because I have borne him three sons": therefore was his name called Levi. And she conceived again, and bore a son: and she said, "Now will I praise the Lord": therefore she called his name Judah; and left bearing.

And when Rachel saw that she bore Jacob no children, Rachel envied her sister; and said unto Jacob, "Give me children, or else I die." And Jacob's anger was kindled against Rachel: and he said "Am I in God's stead, who hath withheld from thee the fruit of the womb?" And she said, "Behold my maid Bilhah, go in unto her; and she shall bear upon my knees, that I may also have children by her." And she gave him Bilhah her handmaid to wife: and Jacob went in unto her. And Bilhah conceived, and bore Jacob a son. And Rachel said, "God hath judged me, and hath also heard my voice, and hath given me a son": therefore called she his name Dan.[34] And Bilhah Rachel's maid conceived again, and bore Jacob a second son. And Rachel said, "With great wrestlings have I wrestled with my sister, and I have prevailed": and she called his name Naphtali.

When Leah saw that she had left bearing, she took Zilpah her maid, and gave her Jacob to wife. And Zilpah Leah's maid bore Jacob a son. And Leah said, "A troop cometh": and she called his name Gad.[35] And Zilpah Leah's maid bore Jacob a second son. And Leah said, "Happy am I, for the daughters will call me blessed": and she called his name Asher.[36]

And Reuben went in the days of wheat harvest, and found mandrakes in the field, and brought them unto his mother Leah. Then Rachel said to Leah, "Give me, I pray thee, of thy son's mandrakes."[37] And she said unto

[32] Laban's cheating of Jacob, an example of "the trickster out-tricked," succeeds because of the custom of leading the bride to the bridal tent in darkness.

[33] "Reuben" means "See, a son!"   [34] "Dan" means "He judged."

[35] "Gad" means "Fortune."   [36] "Asher" means "Happy."

[37] Mandrakes are the roots of a potato-like plant which were thought to have aphrodisiac qualities and to stimulate conception.

her, "Is it a small matter that thou hast taken my husband? and wouldest thou take away my son's mandrakes also?" And Rachel said, "Therefore he shall lie with thee to-night for thy son's mandrakes." And Jacob came out of the field in the evening, and Leah went out to meet him, and said, "Thou must come in unto me; for surely I have hired thee with my son's mandrakes." And he lay with her that night. And God hearkened unto Leah, and she conceived, and bore Jacob the fifth son. And Leah said, "God hath given me my hire, because I have given my maiden to my husband": and she called his name Issachar. And Leah conceived again, and bore Jacob the sixth son. And Leah said, "God hath endued me with a good dowry; now will my husband dwell with me, because I have borne him six sons": and she called his name Zebulun. And afterwards she bore a daughter, and called her name Dinah. And God remembered Rachel, and God hearkened to her, and opened her womb. And she conceived, and bore a son; and said, "God hath taken away my reproach": and she called his name Joseph; and said, "The Lord shall add to me another son."[38]

And it came to pass, when Rachel had borne Joseph, that Jacob said unto Laban, "Send me away, that I may go unto mine own place, and to my country. Give me my wives and my children, for whom I have served thee, and let me go: for thou knowest my service which I have done thee." And Laban said unto him, "I pray thee, if I have found favor in thine eyes, tarry: for I have learned by experience that the Lord hath blessed me for thy sake." And he said, "Appoint me thy wages, and I will give it." And he said unto him, "Thou knowest how I have served thee, and how thy cattle was with me. For it was little which thou hadst before I came, and it is now increased unto a multitude; and the Lord hath blessed thee since my coming: and now when shall I provide for mine own house also?" And he said, "What shall I give thee?" And Jacob said, "Thou shalt not give me any thing: if thou wilt do this thing for me, I will again feed and keep thy flock. I will pass through all thy flock to-day, removing from thence all the speckled and spotted cattle, and all the brown cattle among the sheep, and the spotted and speckled among the goats: and of such shall be my hire. So shall my righteousness answer for me in time to come, when it shall come for my hire before thy face: everyone that is not speckled and spotted among the goats, and brown among the sheep, that shall be counted stolen with me." And Laban said, "Behold, I would it might be according to thy word." And he removed that day the he-goats that were ringstreaked and spotted, and all the she-goats that were speckled and spotted, and every one that had some white in it, and all the brown among the sheep, and gave them into the hand of his sons. And he set three days' journey betwixt himself and Jacob: and Jacob fed the rest of Laban's flocks.

And Jacob took him rods of green poplar, and of the hazel and chestnut tree; and peeled white strakes in them, and made the white appear which was in the rods. And he set the rods which he had peeled before the flocks in the gutters in the watering troughs when the flocks came to drink, that they should conceive when they came to drink. And the flocks conceived

[38] "Joseph" means "He adds."

before the rods, and brought forth cattle ringstreaked, speckled, and spotted.[39] And Jacob did separate the lambs, and set the faces of the flocks toward the ringstreaked, and all the brown in the flock of Laban; and he put his own flocks by themselves, and put them not unto Laban's cattle. And it came to pass, whensoever the stronger cattle did conceive, that Jacob laid the rods before the eyes of the cattle in the gutters, that they might conceive among the rods. But when the cattle were feeble, he put them not in: so the feebler were Laban's, and the stronger Jacob's. And the man increased exceedingly, and had much cattle, and maidservants, and menservants, and camels, and asses.

And he heard the words of Laban's sons, saying, "Jacob hath taken away all that was our father's; and of that which was our father's hath he gotten all this glory." And Jacob beheld the countenance of Laban and, behold, it was not toward him as before. And the Lord said unto Jacob, "Return unto the land of thy fathers, and to thy kindred; and I will be with thee." And Jacob sent and called Rachel and Leah to the field unto his flock and said unto them, "I see your father's countenance, that it is not toward me as before; but the God of my father hath been with me. And ye know that with all my power I have served your father. And your father hath deceived me, and changed my wages ten times; but God suffered him not to hurt me. If he said thus, 'The speckled shall be thy wages'; then all the cattle bore speckled: and if he said thus, 'The ringstreaked shall be thy hire'; then bore all the cattle ringstreaked. Thus God hath taken away the cattle of your father, and given them to me. And it came to pass at the time that the cattle conceived, that I lifted up mine eyes, and saw in a dream, and, behold, the rams which leaped upon the cattle were ringstreaked, speckled, and grisled. And the angel of God spoke unto me in a dream, saying, 'Jacob.' And I said, 'Here am I.' And he said, 'Lift up now thine eyes, and see, all the rams which leap upon the cattle are ringstreaked, speckled, and grisled: for I have seen all that Laban doeth unto thee. I am the God of Beth-el, where thou anointedst the pillar, and where thou vowedst a vow unto me: now arise, get thee out from this land, and return unto the land of thy kindred.' " And Rachel and Leah answered and said unto him, "Is there yet any portion or inheritance for us in our father's house? Are we not counted of him strangers? for he hath sold us, and hath quite devoured also our money. For all the riches which God hath taken from our father, that is ours, and our children's: now then, whatsoever God hath said unto thee, do."

Then Jacob rose up, and set his sons and his wives upon camels; and he carried away all his cattle, and all his goods which he had gotten, the cattle of his getting, which he had gotten in Padan-aram, for to go to Isaac his father in the land of Canaan. And Laban went to shear his sheep: and Rachel had stolen the images that were her father's.[40] And Jacob stole away unawares to Laban the Syrian, in that he told him not that he fled. So he

---

[39] Jacob's trick depends upon the notion of prenatal influence, the belief that a pregnant animal's experiences influence her offspring. The cows and ewes see spotted rods and give birth to spotted offspring.

[40] These "images," later called "gods," are either small statues of household deities (like the Roman Lares and Penates) or images of ancestors.

fled with all that he had; and he rose up, and passed over the river, and set his face toward the mount Gilead.

And it was told Laban on the third day that Jacob was fled. And he took his brethren with him, and pursued after him seven days' journey; and they overtook him in the mount Gilead. And God came to Laban the Syrian in a dream by night, and said unto him, "Take heed that thou speak not to Jacob either good or bad."

Then Laban overtook Jacob. Now Jacob had pitched his tent in the mount: and Laban with his brethren pitched in the Mount of Gilead. And Laban said to Jacob, "What hast thou done, that thou hast stolen away unawares to me, and carried away my daughters, as captives taken with the sword? Wherefore didst thou flee away secretly, and steal away from me; and didst not tell me, that I might have sent thee away with mirth, and with songs, with tabret, and with harp? And hast not suffered me to kiss my sons and my daughters? thou has now done foolishly in so doing. It is in the power of my hand to do you hurt: but the God of your father spoke unto me yesternight, saying, 'Take thou heed that thou speak not to Jacob either good or bad.' And now, though thou wouldest needs be gone, because thou sore longedst after thy father's house, yet wherefore hast thou stolen my gods?" And Jacob answered and said to Laban, "Because I was afraid: for I said, 'Peradventure thou wouldest take by force thy daughters from me.' With whomsoever thou findest thy gods, let him not live: before our brethren discern thou what is thine with me, and take it to thee." For Jacob knew not that Rachel had stolen them.

And Laban went into Jacob's tent, and into Leah's tent, and into the two maidservants' tents; but he found them not. Then went he out of Leah's tent, and entered into Rachel's tent. Now Rachel had taken the images, and put them in the camel's furniture, and sat upon them. And Laban searched all the tent, but found them not. And she said to her father, "Let it not displease my lord that I cannot rise up before thee; for the custom of women is upon me."[41] And he searched, but found not the images.

And Jacob was wroth, and chid with Laban: and Jacob answered and said to Laban, "What is my trespass? what is my sin, that thou hast so hotly pursued after me? Whereas thou hast searched all my stuff, what hast thou found of all thy household stuff? set it here before my brethren and thy brethren, that they may judge betwixt us both. This twenty years have I been with thee; thy ewes and thy she-goats have not cast their young, and the rams of thy flock have I not eaten. That which was torn of beasts I brought not unto thee;[42] I bore the loss of it; of my hand didst thou require it, whether stolen by day, or stolen by night. Thus I was; in the day the drought consumed me, and the frost by night; and my sleep departed from mine eyes. Thus have I been twenty years in thy house; I served thee fourteen years for thy two daughters, and six years for thy cattle: and thou hast changed my wages ten times. Except the God of my father, the God of

---

[41] I.e., she is menstruating.

[42] According to the Code of Hammurabi, then the law in Mesopotamia, a shepherd was not responsible to his employer for animals "torn by beasts." Despite his trickery and sharp dealing, Jacob represents himself as one who goes even beyond the law in his honesty and hard work.

Abraham, and the fear of Isaac, had been with me, surely thou hadst sent
me away now empty. God hath seen mine affliction and the labor of my
hands, and rebuked thee yesternight."

And Laban answered and said unto Jacob, "These daughters are my
daughters, and these children are my children, and these cattle are my
cattle, and all that thou seest is mine: and what can I do this day unto these
my daughters, or unto their children which they have borne? Now therefore come thou, let us make a covenant, I and thou; and let it be for a
witness between me and thee." And Jacob took a stone, and set it up for a
pillar. And Jacob said unto his brethren, "Gather stones"; and they took
stones, and made a heap: and they did eat there upon the heap. And Laban
called it Jegar-sahadutha: but Jacob called it Galeed.[43] And Laban said,
"This heap is a witness between me and thee this day." Therefore was the
name of it called Galeed and Mizpah,[44] for he said, "The Lord watch between me and thee, when we are absent one from another. If thou shalt
afflict my daughters, or if thou shalt take other wives beside my daughters,
no man is with us; see, God is witness betwixt me and thee."

And Laban said to Jacob, "Behold this heap, and behold this pillar,
which I have cast betwixt me and thee! This heap be witness, and this pillar
be witness, that I will not pass over this heap to thee, and that thou shalt not
pass over this heap and this pillar unto me, for harm. The God of Abraham, and the God of Nahor, the God of their father, judge betwixt us."
Then Jacob offered sacrifice upon the mount, and called his brethren to
eat bread: and they did eat bread, and tarried all night in the mount. And
early in the morning Laban rose up, and kissed his sons and his daughters,
and blessed them: and Laban departed, and returned unto his place.

And Jacob went on his way, and the angels of God met him. And when
Jacob saw them, he said, "This is God's host": and he called the name of
that place Mahanaim.[45] And Jacob sent messengers before him to Esau his
brother unto the land of Seir, the country of Edom. And he commanded
them, saying, "Thus shall ye speak unto my lord Esau: 'Thy servant Jacob
saith thus, "I have sojourned with Laban, and stayed there until now; and I
have oxen, and asses, flocks, and menservants, and womenservants; and I
have sent to tell my lord, that I may find grace in thy sight." ' "

And the messengers returned to Jacob, saying, "We came to thy brother
Esau, and also he cometh to meet thee, and four hundred men with him."
Then Jacob was greatly afraid and distressed; and he divided the people
that was with him, and the flocks, and herds, and the camels, into two
bands; and said, "If Esau come to the one company, and smite it, then the
other company which is left shall escape."

And Jacob said, "O God of my father Abraham, and God of my father
Isaac, the Lord which saidst unto me, 'Return unto thy country, and to thy
kindred, and I will deal well with thee!' I am not worthy of the least of all
the mercies, and of all the truth, which thou hast showed unto thy servant;
for with my staff I passed over this Jordan; and now I am become two
bands. Deliver me, I pray thee, from the hand of my brother, from the

---

[43] Both these names mean "the heap of witness," in Laban's Aramaic and Jacob's Hebrew.
[44] "Mizpah" means "Watchpost."   [45] "Two armies."

hand of Esau: for I fear him, lest he will come and smite me, and the mother with the children. And thou saidst, 'I will surely do thee good, and make thy seed as the sand of the sea, which cannot be numbered for multitude.' "

And he lodged there that same night; and took of that which came to his hand a present for Esau his brother: two hundred she-goats, and twenty he-goats, two hundred ewes, and twenty rams, thirty milch camels with their colts, forty kine, and ten bulls, twenty she-asses, and ten foals. And he delivered them into the hand of his servants, every drove by themselves; and said unto his servants, "Pass over before me, and put a space betwixt drove and drove." And he commanded the foremost, saying, "When Esau my brother meeteth thee, and asketh thee, saying, 'Whose art thou? and whither goest thou? and whose are these before thee?' then thou shalt say, 'They be thy servant Jacob's; it is a present sent unto my lord Esau: and, behold, also he is behind us.' " And so commanded he the second, and the third, and all that followed the droves, saying, "On this manner shall ye speak unto Esau, when ye find him. And say ye moreover, 'Behold, thy servant Jacob is behind us.' " For he said, "I will appease him with the present that goeth before me, and afterward I will see his face; peradventure he will accept of me." So went the present over before him: and himself lodged that night in the company.

And he rose up that night, and took his two wives, and his two womenservants, and his eleven sons, and passed over the ford Jabbok. And he took them, and sent them over the brook, and sent over that he had. And Jacob was left alone; and there wrestled a man with him until the breaking of the day. And when he saw that he prevailed not against him, he touched the hollow of his thigh; and the hollow of Jacob's thigh was out of joint, as he wrestled with him. And he said, "Let me go, for the day breaketh." And he said, "I will not let thee go, except thou bless me." And he said unto him, "What is thy name?" And he said "Jacob." And he said, "Thy name shall be called no more Jacob, but Israel: for as a prince hast thou power with God and with men, and hast prevailed." And Jacob asked him, and said, "Tell me, I pray thee, thy name." And he said, "Wherefore is it that thou dost ask after my name?" And he blessed him there. And Jacob called the name of the place Peniel: "For I have seen God face to face, and my life is preserved." And as he passed over Penuel the sun rose upon him, and he halted upon his thigh. Therefore the children of Israel eat not of the sinew which shrank, which is upon the hollow of the thigh, unto this day: because he touched the hollow of Jacob's thigh in the sinew that shrank.[46]

And Jacob lifted up his eyes, and looked, and, behold, Esau came, and with him four hundred men. And he divided the children unto Leah, and unto Rachel, and unto the two handmaids. And he put the handmaids and their children foremost, and Leah and her children after, and Rachel

---

[46]The meaning of this strange wrestling episode is rather obscure. Jacob's wrestling with God may be intended to represent symbolically his own inner struggle to throw off his rather defective past character and become a worthier man. The reference to the "sinew which shrank" in "the hollow of the thigh" seems to be an attempt to account for the Jewish ritual of removing the sciatic nerves, with the arteries and tendons of the thigh, in meat intended to be eaten.

and Joseph hindermost. And he passed over before them, and bowed himself to the ground seven times, until he came near to his brother.

And Esau ran to meet him, and embraced him, and fell on his neck, and kissed him: and they wept. And he lifted up his eyes, and saw the women and the children; and said, "Who are those with thee?" And he said, "The children which God hath graciously given thy servant." Then the hand-maidens came near, they and their children and they bowed themselves. And Leah also with her children came near, and bowed themselves: and after came Joseph near and Rachel, and they bowed themselves. And he said, "What meanest thou by all this drove which I met?" And he said, "These are to find grace in the sight of my lord."

And Esau said, "I have enough, my brother; keep that thou hast unto thyself." And Jacob said, "Nay, I pray thee, if now I have found grace in thy sight, then receive my present at my hand: for therefore I have seen thy face, as though I had seen the face of God, and thou wast pleased with me. Take, I pray thee, my blessing that is brought to thee; because God hath dealt graciously with me, and because I have enough."

And he said, "Let us take our journey, and let us go, and I will go before thee." And he said unto him, "My lord knoweth that the children are tender, and the flocks and herds with young are with me: and if men should overdrive them one day, all the flock will die. Let my lord, I pray thee, pass over before his servant: and I will lead on softly, according as the cattle that goeth before me and the children be able to endure, until I come unto my lord unto Seir."

And Esau said, "Let me now leave with thee some of the folk that are with me." And he said, "What needeth it? let me find grace in the sight of my lord." So Esau returned that day on his way unto Seir. And Jacob journeyed to Succoth, and built him a house, and made booths for his cattle: therefore the name of the place is called Succoth.[47] And Jacob came to Shalem, a city of Shechem, which is in the land of Canaan, when he came from Padan-aram; and pitched his tent before the city. And he bought a parcel of a field, where he had spread his tent, at the hand of the children of Hamor, Shechem's father, for a hundred pieces of money. And he erected there an altar, and called it El-elohe-Israel. . . .[48]

And God said unto Jacob, "Arise, go up to Beth-el, and dwell there: and make there an altar unto God, that appeared unto thee when thou fleddest from the face of Esau thy brother." Then Jacob said unto his household, and to all that were with him, "Put away the strange gods that are among you, and be clean, and change your garments: and let us arise, and go up to Beth-el; and I will make there an altar unto God, who answered me in the day of my distress, and was with me in the way which I went." And they gave unto Jacob all the strange gods which were in their hand, and all their earrings which were in their ears; and Jacob hid them under the oak which was by Shechem.[49] And they journeyed: and the terror of God[50] was upon

---

[47] "Booths."   [48] "God, the God of Israel."

[49] The worshipers had to undergo ceremonial purification (washing and changing clothes), and they were required to renounce strange (or foreign) gods. The earrings which they surrendered were magical amulets used in pagan worship.

[50] The "Terror of God" was a mysterious panic said to seize and paralyze the enemy in early accounts of holy wars.

the cities that were round about them, and they did not pursue after the sons of Jacob.

So Jacob came to Luz, which is in the land of Canaan, that is, Beth-el, he and all the people that were with him. And he built there an altar, and called the place El-beth-el: because there God appeared unto him, when he fled from the face of his brother. But Deborah Rebekah's nurse died, and she was buried beneath Beth-el under an oak: and the name of it was called Allon-bachuth.

And God appeared unto Jacob again, when he came out of Padan-aram, and blessed him. And God said unto him, "Thy name is Jacob: thy name shall not be called any more Jacob, but Israel shall be thy name": and he called his name Israel. And God said unto him, "I am God Almighty: be fruitful and multiply; a nation and a company of nations shall be of thee, and kings shall come out of thy loins; and the land which I gave Abraham and Isaac, to thee I will give it, and to thy seed after thee will I give the land." And God went up from him in the place where he talked with him. And Jacob set up a pillar in the place where he talked with him, even a pillar of stone: and he poured a drink offering thereon, and he poured oil thereon. And Jacob called the name of the place where God spoke with him, Beth-el.

And they journeyed from Beth-el; and there was but a little way to come to Ephrath: and Rachel travailed, and she had hard labor. And it came to pass, when she was in hard labor, that the midwife said unto her, "Fear not; thou shalt have this son also." And it came to pass, as her soul was in departing (for she died), that she called his name Ben-oni: but his father called him Benjamin.[51] And Rachel died, and was buried in the way to Ephrath, which is Beth-lehem. And Jacob set a pillar upon her grave: that is the pillar of Rachel's grave unto this day. And Israel journeyed, and spread his tent beyond the tower of Edar.

And it came to pass, when Israel dwelt in that land, that Reuben went and lay with Bilhah his father's concubine: and Israel heard it. . . .[52]

And Jacob came unto Isaac his father unto Mamre, unto the city of Arbah, which is Hebron, where Abraham and Isaac sojourned. And the days of Isaac were a hundred and fourscore years. And Isaac gave up the ghost, and died, and was gathered unto his people, being old and full of days: and his sons Esau and Jacob buried him. . . .[53]

---

[51] "Ben-oni" means "son of my sorrow," but "Benjamin" means "son of my right hand" or "son of the South."

[52] This mysterious episode apparently accounts for Reuben's loss of prestige as the first-born son.

[53] The last fourteen chapters of Genesis, here omitted, tell the story of Jacob's son Joseph and his rise to power in the land of Egypt.

THE EXODUS SAGA

THE ESCAPE FROM EGYPT

(Exodus 1:8–14:31)

Now there arose up a new king over Egypt, which knew not Joseph.[1] And he said unto his people, "Behold, the people of the children of Israel are more and mightier than we. Come on, let us deal wisely with them; lest they multiply, and it come to pass that, when there falleth out any war, they join also unto our enemies, and fight against us, and so get them up out of the land." Therefore they did set over them taskmasters to afflict them with their burdens. And they built for Pharaoh treasure cities, Pithom and Rameses. But the more they afflicted them, the more they multiplied and grew. And they were grieved because of the children of Israel. And the Egyptians made the children of Israel to serve with rigor: and they made their lives bitter with hard bondage, in mortar, and in brick, and in all manner of service in the field: all their service, wherein they made them serve, was with rigor. And the king of Egypt spoke to the Hebrew midwives, of which the name of the one was Shiphrah, and the name of the other Puah: and he said, "When ye do the office of a midwife to the Hebrew women, and see them upon the stools;[2] if it be a son, then ye shall kill him: but if it be a daughter, then she shall live." But the midwives feared God, and did not as the king of Egypt commanded them, but saved the men children alive. And the king of Egypt called for the midwives, and said unto them, "Why have ye done this thing, and have saved the men children alive?" And the midwives said unto Pharaoh, "Because the Hebrew women are not as the Egyptian women; for they are lively, and are delivered ere the midwives come in unto them." Therefore God dealt well with the midwives: and the people multiplied, and waxed very mighty. And it came to pass, because the midwives feared God, that he made them houses. And Pharaoh charged all his people, saying, "Every son that is born ye shall cast into the river, and every daughter ye shall save alive."

And there went a man of the house of Levi, and took to wife a daughter of Levi. And the woman conceived, and bore a son; and when she saw him that he was a goodly child, she hid him three months. And when she could not longer hide him, she took for him an ark of bulrushes,[3] and daubed it with slime and with pitch, and put the child therein; and she laid it in the flags by the river's brink. And his sister stood afar off, to wit[4] what would be done to him.[5] And the daughter of Pharaoh came down to wash herself at the river; and her maidens walked along by the river's side; and when she

---

[1] Genesis ends with the long story of Jacob's son Joseph, of how he was sold into slavery in Egypt, and of how he rose to a position of power there, winning favor for his fellow Hebrews. Exodus opens four centuries later, and the Hebrews in Egypt have sunk to the status of slaves, brutally employed in building the Pharaoh's monuments and public works. The "new king" is now thought to belong to a native Egyptian dynasty which drove out the foreign Hyksos kings, who had been friendly to the Hebrews, in the sixteenth century B.C.

[2] Birth-stools.   [3] Sedge plants which grow in marshy areas.   [4] To know or find out.

[5] The story of an infant hero being saved by being put in a basket in the water appears in other ancient hero-tales, including that of Sargon of Agade, from about 2600 B.C.

saw the ark among the flags, she sent her maid to fetch it. And when she had opened it, she saw the child: and, behold, the babe wept. And she had compassion on him, and said, "This is one of the Hebrews' children." Then said his sister to Pharaoh's daughter, "Shall I go and call to thee a nurse of the Hebrew women, that she may nurse the child for thee?" And Pharaoh's daughter said to her, "Go!" And the maid went and called the child's mother.

And Pharaoh's daughter said unto her, "Take this child away, and nurse it for me, and I will give thee thy wages." And the woman took the child, and nursed it. And the child grew, and she brought him unto Pharaoh's daughter, and he became her son. And she called his name Moses; and she said, "Because I drew him out of the water."

And it came to pass in those days, when Moses was grown, that he went out unto his brethren, and looked on their burdens; and he spied an Egyptian smiting an Hebrew, one of his brethren. And he looked this way and that way, and when he saw that there was no man, he slew the Egyptian, and hid him in the sand. And when he went out the second day, behold, two men of the Hebrews strove together: and he said to him that did the wrong, "Wherefore smitest thou thy fellow?" And he said, "Who made thee a prince and a judge over us? intendest thou to kill me, as thou killedst the Egyptian?" And Moses feared, and said, "Surely this thing is known."

Now when Pharaoh heard this thing, he sought to slay Moses. But Moses fled from the face of Pharaoh, and dwelt in the land of Midian:[6] and he sat down by a well. Now the priest of Midian had seven daughters: and they came and drew water, and filled the troughs to water their father's flock. And the shepherds came and drove them away: but Moses stood up and helped them, and watered their flock. And when they came to Reuel their father, he said, "How is it that ye are come so soon to-day?" And they said, "An Egyptian delivered us out of the hand of the shepherds, and also drew water enough for us, and watered the flock." And he said unto his daughters, "And where is he? why is it that ye have left the man? call him, that he may eat bread." And Moses was content to dwell with the man: and he gave Moses Zipporah his daughter. And she bore him a son, and he called his name Gershom: for he said, "I have been a stranger in a strange land."[7]

And it came to pass in process of time that the king of Egypt[8] died: and the children of Israel sighed by reason of the bondage, and they cried, and their cry came up unto God by reason of the bondage. And God heard their groaning, and God remembered his covenant with Abraham, with Isaac, and with Jacob. And God looked upon the children of Israel, and God had respect unto them.

Now Moses kept the flock of Jethro his father-in-law, the priest of

---

[6] The location of the land of Midian is not known, but it has been suggested that it was from the Midianites and from his father-in-law that Moses acquired his concept of God, especially since his faith before his flight into Midian is not mentioned. Moses' father-in-law, called Reuel here, is later called Jethro (Exodus 3:1) and Raguel (Numbers 10:29). This variation is due to the existence of different compositional strands in the book.

[7] "Gershom," as indicated, means "stranger in a strange land."

[8] The king was probably Seit I; the oppressive new king was Rameses II.

Midian: and he led the flock to the backside of the desert, and came to the mountain of God, even to Horeb. And the angel of the Lord appeared unto him in a flame of fire out of the midst of a bush: and he looked, and, behold, the bush burned with fire, and the bush was not consumed. And Moses said, "I will now turn aside, and see this great sight, why the bush is not burnt." And when the Lord saw that he turned aside to see, God called unto him out of the midst of the bush, and said, "Moses, Moses." And he said, "Here am I." And he said, "Draw not nigh hither: put off thy shoes from off thy feet, for the place whereon thou standest is holy ground." Moreover he said, "I am the God of thy father, the God of Abraham, the God of Isaac, and the God of Jacob." And Moses hid his face; for he was afraid to look upon God.

And the Lord said, "I have surely seen the affliction of my people which are in Egypt, and have heard their cry by reason of their taskmasters; for I know their sorrows. And I am come down to deliver them out of the hand of the Egyptians, and to bring them up out of that land unto a good land and a large, unto a land flowing with milk and honey; unto the place of the Canaanites, and the Hittites, and the Amorites, and the Perizzites, and the Hivites, and the Jebusites. Now therefore, behold, the cry of the children of Israel is come unto me: and I have also seen the oppression wherewith the Egyptians oppress them. Come now therefore, and I will send thee unto Pharaoh, that thou mayest bring forth my people the children of Israel out of Egypt." And Moses said unto God, "Who am I, that I should go unto Pharaoh, and that I should bring forth the children of Israel out of Egypt?" And he said, "Certainly I will be with thee; and this shall be a token unto thee, that I have sent thee. When thou hast brought forth the people out of Egypt, ye shall serve God upon this mountain."

And Moses said unto God, "Behold, when I come unto the children of Israel, and shall say unto them, 'The God of your fathers hath sent me unto you'; and they shall say to me, 'What is his name?' what shall I say unto them?" And God said unto Moses, "I AM THAT I AM":[9] and he said, "Thus shalt thou say unto the children of Israel, I AM hath sent me unto you." And God said moreover unto Moses, "Thus shalt thou say unto the children of Israel, 'The Lord God of your fathers, the God of Abraham, the God of Isaac, and the God of Jacob, hath sent me unto you.' And they shall hearken to thy voice: and thou shalt come, thou and the elders of Israel, unto the king of Egypt, and ye shall say unto him, 'The Lord God of the Hebrews hath met with us: and now let us go, we beseech thee, three days' journey into the wilderness, that we may sacrifice to the Lord our God.' And I am sure that the king of Egypt will not let you go, no, not by a mighty hand. And I will stretch out my hand, and smite Egypt with all my wonders which I will do in the midst thereof: and after that he will let you go. And I will give this people favor in the sight of the Egyptians: and it shall come to

---

[9] "I am that I am" is a play on the four Hebrew consonants represented in English as Y-H-V-H. The English version of the name of the Hebrew God, originally written only in consonants, has been a source of some confusion. The correct version is apparently "Yahweh," but the King James Version regularly uses merely "The Lord." The name "Jehovah," used only four times in the King James Version, results from a misunderstanding on the part of early English translators, who inserted the vowels of the Hebrew "Adonai" (Lord) into the consonants Y (or J)-H-V-H.

pass that, when ye go, ye shall not go empty: but every woman shall borrow of her neighbor, and of her that sojourneth in her house, jewels of silver, and jewels of gold, and raiment: and ye shall put them upon your sons, and upon your daughters; and ye shall spoil the Egyptians."

And Moses answered and said, "But, behold, they will not believe me, nor hearken unto my voice: for they will say, 'The Lord hath not appeared unto thee.'" And the Lord said unto him, "What is that in thine hand?" And he said, "A rod." And he said, "Cast it on the ground." And he cast it on the ground, and it became a serpent; and Moses fled from before it. And the Lord said unto Moses, "Put forth thine hand, and take it by the tail." And he put forth his hand, and caught it, and it became a rod in his hand. And the Lord said furthermore unto him, "Put now thine hand into thy bosom." And he put his hand into his bosom: and when he took it out, behold, his hand was leprous as snow. And he said, "Put thine hand into thy bosom again." And he put his hand into his bosom again; and plucked it out of his bosom, and, behold, it was turned again as his other flesh. "And it shall come to pass, if they will not believe thee, neither hearken to the voice of the first sign, that they will believe the voice of the latter sign. And it shall come to pass, if they will not believe also these two signs, neither hearken unto thy voice, that thou shalt take of the water of the river, and pour it upon the dry land: and the water which thou takest out of the river shall become blood upon the dry land."

And Moses said unto the Lord, "O my Lord, I am not eloquent, neither heretofore, nor since thou hast spoken unto thy servant: but I am slow of speech, and of a slow tongue." [10] And the Lord said unto him, "Who hath made man's mouth? or who maketh the dumb, or deaf, or the seeing, or the blind? have not I the Lord? Now therefore go, and I will be with thy mouth, and teach thee what thou shalt say." And he said, "O my Lord, send, I pray thee, by the hand of him whom thou wilt send." And the anger of the Lord was kindled against Moses, and he said, "Is not Aaron the Levite thy brother? I know that he can speak well. And also, behold, he cometh forth to meet thee: and when he seeth thee, he will be glad in his heart. And thou shalt speak unto him, and put words in his mouth: and I will be with thy mouth, and with his mouth, and will teach you what ye shall do. And he shall be thy spokesman unto the people: and he shall be, even he shall be to thee instead of a mouth, and thou shalt be to him instead of God. And thou shalt take this rod in thine hand, wherewith thou shalt do signs."

And Moses went and returned to Jethro his father-in-law, and said unto him, "Let me go, I pray thee, and return unto my brethren which are in Egypt, and see whether they be yet alive." And Jethro said to Moses, "Go in peace." And the Lord said unto Moses in Midian, "Go, return into Egypt: for all the men are dead which sought thy life." And Moses took his wife and his sons, and set them upon an ass, and he returned to the land of Egypt: and Moses took the rod of God in his hand. . . .

And Moses and Aaron went and gathered together all the elders of the

[10] The tradition that Moses had a speech impediment stems from this passage and from a later passage which says that his brother Aaron spoke for Moses when he reported what the Lord had said to the elders of Israel.

children of Israel; and Aaron spoke all the words which the Lord had spoken unto Moses, and did the signs in the sight of the people. And the people believed; and when they heard that the Lord had visited the children of Israel, and that he had looked upon their affliction, then they bowed their heads and worshipped.

And afterward Moses and Aaron went in, and told Pharaoh, "Thus saith the Lord God of Israel, 'Let my people go, that they may hold a feast unto me in the wilderness.'" And Pharaoh said, "Who is the Lord, that I should obey his voice to let Israel go? I know not the Lord, neither will I let Israel go." And they said, "The God of the Hebrews hath met with us: let us go, we pray thee, three days' journey into the desert, and sacrifice unto the Lord our God; lest he fall upon us with pestilence, or with the sword." And the king of Egypt said unto them, "Wherefore do ye, Moses and Aaron, let the people from their works? get you unto your burdens." And Pharaoh commanded the same day the taskmasters of the people, and their officers, saying, "Ye shall no more give the people straw to make brick, as heretofore: let them go and gather straw for themselves.[11] And the tale[12] of the bricks, which they did make heretofore, ye shall lay upon them; ye shall not diminish ought thereof: for they be idle; therefore they cry, saying, 'Let us go and sacrifice to our God.' Let there more work be laid upon the men, that they may labor therein; and let them not regard vain words."

And the taskmasters of the people went out, and their officers, and they spoke to the people, saying, "Thus saith Pharaoh, 'I will not give you straw. Go ye, get you straw where ye can find it: yet not ought of your work shall be diminished.'" So the people were scattered abroad throughout all the land of Egypt to gather stubble instead of straw. And the taskmasters hastened them, saying, "Fulfil your works, your daily tasks, as when there was straw." And the officers of the children of Israel, which Pharaoh's taskmasters had set over them, were beaten, and demanded, "Wherefore have ye not fulfilled your task in making brick both yesterday and to-day, as heretofore?"

Then the officers of the children of Israel came and cried unto Pharaoh, saying, "Wherefore dealest thou thus with thy servants? There is no straw given unto thy servants, and they say to us, 'Make brick': and, behold, thy servants are beaten; but the fault is in thine own people." But he said, "Ye are idle, ye are idle: therefore ye say, 'Let us go and do sacrifice to the Lord.' Go therefore now, and work; for there shall no straw be given you, yet shall ye deliver the tale of bricks." And the officers of the children of Israel did see that they were in evil case, after it was said, "Ye shall not minish[13] ought from your bricks of your daily task." And they met Moses and Aaron, who stood in the way, as they came forth from Pharaoh; and they said unto them, "The Lord look upon you, and judge; because ye have made our savor to be abhorred in the eyes of Pharaoh, and in the eyes of his servants, to put a sword in their hand to slay us."

And Moses returned unto the Lord, and said, "Lord, wherefore hast

[11] Bricks were made with clay and then dried in the sun (rather than fired). They would be brittle unless the clay was mixed with sand or with chopped straw.
[12] Number or quota.   [13] Archaic form of "diminish."

thou so evil entreated this people? why is it that thou hast sent me? For since I came to Pharaoh to speak in thy name, he hath done evil to this people; neither hast thou delivered thy people at all." . . . And God spoke unto Moses, and said unto him, "I am the Lord; and I appeared unto Abraham, unto Isaac, and unto Jacob, by the name of God Almighty, but by my name JEHOVAH was I not known to them. And I have also established my covenant with them, to give them the land of Canaan, the land of their pilgrimage, wherein they were strangers. And I have also heard the groaning of the children of Israel, whom the Egyptians keep in bondage; and I have remembered my covenant. Wherefore say unto the children of Israel, 'I am the Lord, and I will bring you out from under the burdens of the Egyptians, and I will rid you out of their bondage, and I will redeem you with a stretched out arm, and with great judgments; and I will take you to me for a people, and I will be to you a God; and ye shall know that I am the Lord your God, which bringeth you out from under the burdens of the Egyptians. And I will bring you in unto the land, concerning the which I did swear to give it to Abraham, to Isaac, and to Jacob; and I will give it you for an heritage: I am the Lord.'" And Moses spoke so unto the children of Israel: but they hearkened not unto Moses for anguish of spirit, and for cruel bondage.

And the Lord said unto Moses, "See, I have made thee a god to Pharaoh: and Aaron thy brother shall be thy prophet. Thou shalt speak all that I command thee: and Aaron thy brother shall speak unto Pharaoh, that he send the children of Israel out of his land. And I will harden Pharaoh's heart, and multiply my signs and my wonders in the land of Egypt. But Pharaoh shall not hearken unto you, that I may lay my hand upon Egypt, and bring forth mine armies, and my people the children of Israel, out of the land of Egypt by great judgments. And the Egyptians shall know that I am the Lord, when I stretch forth mine hand upon Egypt, and bring out the children of Israel from among them." . . .

And the Lord spoke unto Moses and unto Aaron, saying, "When Pharaoh shall speak unto you, saying, 'Show a miracle for you'; then thou shalt say unto Aaron, 'Take thy rod, and cast it before Pharaoh,' and it shall become a serpent." And Moses and Aaron went in unto Pharaoh, and they did so as the Lord had commanded: and Aaron cast down his rod before Pharaoh, and before his servants, and it became a serpent. Then Pharaoh also called the wise men and the sorcerers: now the magicians of Egypt, they also did in like manner with their enchantments. For they cast down every man his rod, and they became serpents: but Aaron's rod swallowed up their rods. And he hardened Pharaoh's heart, that he hearkened not unto them; as the Lord had said. . . .

And the Lord spoke unto Moses, "Say unto Aaron, 'Take thy rod, and stretch out thine hand upon the waters of Egypt, upon their streams, upon their rivers, and upon their ponds, and upon all their pools of water, that they may become blood; and that there may be blood throughout all the land of Egypt, both in vessels of wood, and in vessels of stone.'" And Moses and Aaron did so, as the Lord commanded; and he lifted up the rod, and smote the waters that were in the river, in the sight of Pharaoh, and in the sight of his servants; and all the waters that were in the river were turned to blood.[14] And the fish that was in the river died; and the river stank, and the Egyptians could not drink of the water of the river; and there was blood throughout all the land of Egypt. And the magicians of Egypt did so with their enchantments: and Pharaoh's heart was hardened, neither did he hearken unto them; as the Lord had said. And Pharaoh turned and went into his house, neither did he set his heart to this also. And all the Egyptians digged round about the river for water to drink; for they could not drink of the water of the river. And seven days were fulfilled, after that the Lord had smitten the river.[15]

And the Lord said unto Moses, "Yet will I bring one plague more upon Pharaoh, and upon Egypt; afterwards he will let you go hence: when he shall let you go, he shall surely thrust you out hence altogether. Speak now in the ears of the people, and let every man borrow of his neighbor, and every woman of her neighbor, jewels of silver, and jewels of gold." And the Lord gave the people favor in the sight of the Egyptians. Moreover the man Moses was very great in the land of Egypt, in the sight of Pharaoh's servants, and in the sight of the people.

And Moses said, "Thus saith the Lord, 'About midnight will I go out into the midst of Egypt. And all the firstborn in the land of Egypt shall die, from the firstborn of Pharaoh that sitteth upon his throne, even unto the firstborn of the maidservant that is behind the mill; and all the firstborn of beasts. And there shall be a great cry throughout all the land of Egypt, such as there was none like it, nor shall be like it any more.' But against any of the children of Israel shall not a dog move his tongue, against man or beast: that ye may know how the Lord doth put a difference between the Egyptians and Israel. And all these thy servants shall come down unto me, and bow down themselves unto me, saying, 'Get thee out, and all the people that follow thee': and after that I will go out." And he went out from Pharaoh in great anger.

And the Lord said unto Moses, "Pharaoh shall not hearken unto you; that my wonders may be multiplied in the land of Egypt." And Moses and Aaron did all these wonders before Pharaoh: and the Lord hardened Pharaoh's heart, so that he would not let the children of Israel go out of his land. . . .

Then Moses called for all the elders of Israel, and said unto them, "Draw out and take you a lamb according to your families, and kill the passover. And ye shall take a bunch of hyssop,[16] and dip it in the blood that is in the basin, and strike the lintel and the two side posts with the blood that is in the basin; and none of you shall go out at the door of his house until the morning. For the Lord will pass through to smite the Egyptians; and when he seeth the blood upon the lintel, and on the two side posts, the Lord will pass over the door, and will not suffer the destroyer to come in

---

[14] This plague, like the subsequent ones, appears to be a heightening of natural phenomena. The Nile, in the middle of the summer, often turns a reddish color because of small organisms in the water.

[15] Eight of the ten plagues visited by God on the Egyptians are omitted here: the plagues of frogs, lice, flies, murrain (a disease of animals), boils, hail, locusts, and darkness. Several times Pharaoh agrees to let the Israelites go, but when the plagues are remitted he hardens his heart again.

[16] An aromatic plant, possibly a form of mint.

unto your houses to smite you. And ye shall observe this thing for an ordinance to thee and to thy sons for ever. And it shall come to pass, when ye be come to the land which the Lord will give you, according as he hath promised, that ye shall keep this service. And it shall come to pass, when your children shall say unto you, 'What mean ye by this service?' that ye shall say, 'It is the sacrifice of the Lord's passover, who passed over the houses of the children of Israel in Egypt, when he smote the Egyptians, and delivered our houses.'" And the people bowed the head and worshipped. And the children of Israel went away, and did as the Lord had commanded Moses and Aaron, so did they.

And it came to pass that at midnight the Lord smote all the firstborn in the land of Egypt, from the firstborn of Pharaoh that sat on his throne unto the firstborn of the captive that was in the dungeon; and all the firstborn of cattle. And Pharaoh rose up in the night, he, and all his servants, and all the Egyptians; and there was a great cry in Egypt; for there was not a house where there was not one dead.[17] And he called for Moses and Aaron by night, and said, "Rise up, and get you forth from among my people, both ye and the children of Israel; and go, serve the Lord, as ye have said. Also take your flocks and your herds, as ye have said, and be gone; and bless me also."

And the Egyptians were urgent upon the people, that they might send them out of the land in haste; for they said, "We be all dead men."

And the people took their dough before it was leavened, their kneading troughs being bound up in their clothes upon their shoulders. And the children of Israel did according to the word of Moses; and they borrowed of the Egyptians jewels of silver, and jewels of gold, and raiment: and the Lord gave the people favor in the sight of the Egyptians, so that they lent unto them such things as they required. And they spoiled the Egyptians.

And the children of Israel journeyed from Rameses to Succoth, about six hundred thousand on foot that were men, beside children. And a mixed multitude went up also with them; and flocks and herds, even very much cattle. And they baked unleavened cakes of the dough which they brought forth out of Egypt, for it was not leavened; because they were thrust out of Egypt, and could not tarry, neither had they prepared for themselves any victual.

(Now the sojourning of the children of Israel, who dwelt in Egypt, was four hundred and thirty years. And it came to pass at the end of the four hundred and thirty years, even the selfsame day it came to pass, that all the hosts of the Lord went out from the land of Egypt. It is a night to be much observed unto the Lord for bringing them out from the land of Egypt: this is that night of the Lord to be observed of all the children of Israel in their generations.) . . .

And it came to pass, when Pharaoh had let the people go, that God led them not through the way of the land of the Philistines, although that was near; for God said, "Lest peradventure the people repent when they see

---

[17] This story is the basis for the Jewish festival of Passover, one of the oldest religious festivals in the world. It is observed in March or April and lasts for seven or eight days. Work is prohibited on the first and last days; other features of the festival include the eating of unleavened bread ("matzot") and of bitter herbs with the evening meal.

war, and they return to Egypt": but God led the people about, through the
way of the wilderness of the Red Sea.[18] And the children of Israel went up
harnessed out of the land of Egypt. And Moses took the bones of Joseph
with him: for he had straitly[19] sworn the children of Israel, saying, "God
will surely visit you; and ye shall carry up my bones away hence with
you." . . . And the Lord went before them by day in a pillar of a cloud, to
lead them the way; and by night in a pillar of fire, to give them light; to go
by day and night: he took not away the pillar of the cloud by day, nor the
pillar of fire by night, from before the people. . . .

And it was told the king of Egypt that the people fled: and the heart of
Pharaoh and of his servants was turned against the people, and they said,
"Why have we done this, that we have let Israel go from serving us?" And
he made ready his chariot, and took his people with him: and he took six
hundred chosen chariots, and all the chariots of Egypt, and captains over
every one of them. And the Lord hardened the heart of Pharaoh king
of Egypt, and he pursued after the children of Israel: and the children
of Israel went out with a high hand. But the Egyptians pursued after them,
all the horses and chariots of Pharaoh, and his horsemen, and his army,
and overtook them encamping by the sea, beside Pi-hahiroth, before Baal-
zephon.

And when Pharaoh drew nigh, the children of Israel lifted up their
eyes, and, behold, the Egyptians marched after them; and they were sore
afraid: and the children of Israel cried out unto the Lord. And they said
unto Moses, "Because there were no graves in Egypt, hast thou taken us
away to die in the wilderness? wherefore hast thou dealt thus with us, to
carry us forth out of Egypt? Is not this the word that we did tell thee in
Egypt, saying, 'Let us alone, that we may serve the Egyptians'? For it had
been better for us to serve the Egyptians, than that we should die in the
wilderness." And Moses said unto the people, "Fear ye not, stand still, and
see the salvation of the Lord, which he will show to you to-day: for the
Egyptians whom ye have seen to-day, ye shall see them again no more for
ever. The Lord shall fight for you, and ye shall hold your peace." . . .

And the angel of God, which went before the camp of Israel, removed
and went behind them; and the pillar of the cloud went from before their
face, and stood behind them: and it came between the camp of the Egyptians and the camp of Israel; and it was a cloud and darkness to them, but it
gave light by night to these: so that the one came not near the other all
night. And Moses stretched out his hand over the sea; and the Lord caused
the sea to go back by a strong east wind all that night, and made the sea dry
land, and the waters were divided. And the children of Israel went into the
midst of the sea upon the dry ground: and the waters were a wall unto

---

[18] It is possible to reconstruct Moses' route out of Egypt, taking not the direct route to
Canaan, about two hundred miles along the coast, but an indirect route southeast to the Sea of
Reeds (not the Red Sea). The reason given here is anachronistic, since the Philistines did not
settle in Palestine until after the Hebrew invasion. Possibly Moses took the indirect, "wandering" route to allow the Hebrews time to become a disciplined, united people before they
invaded Canaan, or perhaps he wanted to lead them toward the mountain where they would
receive the Law.

[19] Strictly.

them on their right hand, and on their left. And the Egyptians pursued, and went in after them to the midst of the sea, even all Pharaoh's horses, his chariots, and his horsemen. And it came to pass that in the morning watch the Lord looked unto the host of the Egyptians through the pillar of fire and of the cloud, and troubled the host of the Egyptians, and took off their chariot wheels, that they drove them heavily: so that the Egyptians said, "Let us flee from the face of Israel; for the Lord fighteth for them against the Egyptians."

And the Lord said unto Moses, "Stretch out thine hand over the sea, that the waters may come again upon the Egyptians, upon their chariots, and upon their horsemen." And Moses stretched forth his hand over the sea, and the sea returned to his strength when the morning appeared; and the Egyptians fled against it; and the Lord overthrew the Egyptians in the midst of the sea. And the waters returned, and covered the chariots, and the horsemen, and all the host of Pharaoh that came into the sea after them; there remained not so much as one of them. But the children of Israel walked upon dry land in the midst of the sea; and the waters were a wall unto them on their right hand, and on their left.

Thus the Lord saved Israel that day out of the hand of the Egyptians; and Israel saw the Egyptians dead upon the sea shore. And Israel saw that great work which the Lord did upon the Egyptians: and the people feared the Lord, and believed the Lord and his servant Moses.

THE JOURNEY TO SINAI

(Exodus 15:22–18:27)
So Moses brought Israel from the Red Sea, and they went out into the wilderness of Shur; and they went three days in the wilderness, and found no water. And when they came to Marah, they could not drink of the waters of Marah, for they were bitter: therefore the name of it was called Marah. And the people murmured against Moses, saying, "What shall we drink?"

And he cried unto the Lord; and the Lord showed him a tree, which when he had cast into the waters, the waters were made sweet: there he made for them a statute and an ordinance, and there he proved them, and said, "If thou wilt diligently hearken to the voice of the Lord thy God, and wilt do that which is right in his sight, and wilt give ear to his commandments, and keep all his statutes, I will put none of these diseases upon thee, which I have brought upon the Egyptians: for I am the Lord that healeth thee."

And they came to Elim, where were twelve wells of water, and threescore and ten palm trees: and they encamped there by the waters.

And they took their journey from Elim, and all the congregation of the children of Israel came unto the wilderness of Sin, which is between Elim and Sinai, on the fifteenth day of the second month after their departing out of the land of Egypt. And the whole congregation of the children of Israel murmured against Moses and Aaron in the wilderness; and the children of Israel said unto them, "Would to God we had died by the hand of the Lord in the land of Egypt, when we sat by the flesh pots, and when we did eat bread to the full; for ye have brought us forth into this wilderness, to kill this whole assembly with hunger."

Then said the Lord unto Moses, "Behold, I will rain bread from heaven for you; and the people shall go out and gather a certain rate every day, that I may prove them, whether they will walk in my law, or no. And it shall come to pass that on the sixth day they shall prepare that which they bring in; and it shall be twice as much as they gather daily." And Moses and Aaron said unto all the children of Israel, "At even, then ye shall know that the Lord hath brought you out from the land of Egypt; and in the morning, then ye shall see the glory of the Lord; for that he heareth your murmurings against the Lord: and what are we, that ye murmur against us?" . . .

And it came to pass, that at even the quails came up, and covered the camp: and in the morning the dew lay round about the host. And when the dew that lay was gone up, behold, upon the face of the wilderness there lay a small round thing, as small as the hoar frost on the ground. And when the children of Israel saw it, they said one to another, "It is manna": for they wist not what it was.[20] And Moses said unto them, "This is the bread which the Lord hath given you to eat. This is the thing which the Lord hath commanded, 'Gather of it every man according to his eating, an omer for every man, according to the number of your persons; take ye every man for them which are in his tents.'" And the children of Israel did so, and gathered, some more, some less. And when they did mete it with an omer,[21] he that gathered much had nothing over, and he that gathered little had no lack; they gathered every man according to his eating. And Moses said, "Let no man leave of it till the morning." Notwithstanding they hearkened not unto Moses; but some of them left of it until the morning, and it bred worms, and stank: and Moses was wroth with them. And they gathered it every morning, every man according to his eating: and when the sun waxed hot, it melted.

And it came to pass that on the sixth day they gathered twice as much bread, two omers for one man: and all the rulers of the congregation came and told Moses. And he said unto them, "This is that which the Lord hath said, 'To-morrow is the rest of the holy sabbath unto the Lord: bake that which ye will bake to-day, and seethe[22] that ye will seethe; and that which remaineth over lay up for you to be kept until the morning.'" And they laid it up till the morning, as Moses bade: and it did not stink, neither was there any worm therein. And Moses said, "Eat that to-day; for to-day is a sabbath unto the Lord: to-day ye shall not find it in the field. Six days ye shall gather it; but on the seventh day, which is the sabbath, in it there shall be none." And it came to pass that there went out some of the people on the seventh day for to gather, and they found none. . . . And the house of Israel called the name thereof Manna: and it was like coriander seed, white; and the taste of it was like wafers made with honey. And Moses said, "This is the thing which the Lord commandeth, 'Fill an omer of it to be

[20] "Manna" means "What is it?"
[21] "Mete" means "measure." An "omer" is an ancient Hebrew unit of dry capacity equal to about a tenth of a bushel.
[22] Boil or stew.

kept for your generations; that they may see the bread wherewith I have fed you in the wilderness, when I brought you forth from the land of Egypt.'" And Moses said unto Aaron, "Take a pot, and put an omer full of manna therein, and lay it up before the Lord, to be kept for your generations."

As the Lord commanded Moses, so Aaron laid it up before the Testimony,[23] to be kept. And the children of Israel did eat manna forty years, until they came to a land inhabited; they did eat manna until they came unto the borders of the land of Canaan. . . .

And all the congregation of the children of Israel journeyed from the wilderness of Sin, after their journeys, according to the commandment of the Lord, and pitched in Rephidim: and there was no water for the people to drink. Wherefore the people did chide with Moses, and said, "Give us water that we may drink." And Moses said unto them, "Why chide ye with me? wherefore do ye tempt the Lord?" And the people thirsted there for water; and the people murmured against Moses, and said, "Wherefore is this that thou hast brought us up out of Egypt, to kill us and our children and our cattle with thirst?" And Moses cried unto the Lord, saying, "What shall I do unto this people? they be almost ready to stone me." And the Lord said unto Moses, "Go on before the people, and take with thee of the elders of Israel; and thy rod, wherewith thou smotest the river, take in thine hand, and go. Behold, I will stand before thee there upon the rock in Horeb; and thou shalt smite the rock, and there shall come water out of it, that the people may drink." And Moses did so in the sight of the elders of Israel. And he called the name of the place Massah, and Meribah, because of the chiding of the children of Israel, and because they tempted the Lord, saying, "Is the Lord among us, or not?"[24]

Then came Amalek, and fought with Israel in Rephidim. And Moses said unto Joshua,[25] "Choose us out men, and go out, fight with Amalek: tomorrow I will stand on the top of the hill with the rod of God in mine hand." So Joshua did as Moses had said to him, and fought with Amalek: and Moses, Aaron, and Hur went up to the top of the hill. And it came to pass, when Moses held up his hand, that Israel prevailed: and when he let down his hand, Amalek prevailed. But Moses' hands were heavy; and they took a stone, and put it under him, and he sat thereon; and Aaron and Hur stayed up his hands, the one on the one side, and the other on the other side; and his hands were steady until the going down of the sun. And Joshua discomfited Amalek and his people with the edge of the sword. . . .

Jethro, the priest of Midian, Moses' father-in-law, heard of all that God had done for Moses, and for Israel his people, and that the Lord had brought Israel out of Egypt. Then Jethro, Moses' father-in-law, took Zipporah, Moses' wife, after he had sent her back, and her two sons; of which the name of the one was Gershom: for he said, "I have been an alien in a strange land," and the name of the other was Eliezer: "For the God of

[23] The tablets inscribed with the Mosaic law. The passage anticipates the giving of the Law later in Exodus.

[24] "Massah" means "proof" and "Meribah" means "contention."

[25] This is the first reference to Joshua, the young warrior who was to lead the Israelite armies into Canaan after the death of Moses.

my father," said he, "was mine help, and delivered me from the sword of Pharaoh."[26]

And Jethro, Moses' father-in-law, came with his sons and his wife unto Moses into the wilderness, where he encamped at the mount of God: and he said unto Moses, "I thy father-in-law Jethro am come unto thee, and thy wife, and her two sons with her." And Moses went out to meet his father-in-law, and did obeisance, and kissed him; and they asked each other of their welfare; and they came into the tent. And Moses told his father-in-law all that the Lord had done unto Pharaoh and to the Egyptians for Israel's sake, and all the travail that had come upon them by the way, and how the Lord delivered them. And Jethro rejoiced for all the goodness which the Lord had done to Israel, whom he had delivered out of the hand of the Egyptians. And Jethro said, "Blessed be the Lord, who hath delivered you out of the hand of the Egyptians, and out of the hand of Pharaoh, who hath delivered the people from under the hand of the Egyptians. Now I know that the Lord is greater than all gods: for in the thing wherein they dealt proudly he was above them."

And Jethro, Moses' father-in-law, took a burnt offering and sacrifices for God: and Aaron came, and all the elders of Israel, to eat bread with Moses' father-in-law before God. And it came to pass on the morrow that Moses sat to judge the people: and the people stood by Moses from the morning unto the evening. And when Moses' father-in-law saw all that he did to the people, he said, "What is this thing that thou doest to the people? why sittest thou thyself alone, and all the people stand by thee from morning unto even?" And Moses said unto his father-in-law, "Because the people come unto me to enquire of God. When they have a matter, they come unto me; and I judge between one and another, and I do make them know the statutes of God, and his laws." And Moses' father-in-law said unto him, "The thing that thou doest is not good. Thou wilt surely wear away, both thou, and this people that is with thee: for this thing is too heavy for thee; thou art not able to perform it thyself alone. Hearken now unto my voice, I will give thee counsel, and God shall be with thee: Be thou for the people to God-ward, that thou mayest bring the causes unto God: and thou shalt teach them ordinances and laws, and shalt show them the way wherein they must walk, and the work that they must do. Moreover thou shalt provide out of all the people able men, such as fear God, men of truth, hating covetousness; and place such over them, to be rulers of thousands, and rulers of hundreds, rulers of fifties, and rulers of tens: and let them judge the people at all seasons: and it shall be that every great matter they shall bring unto thee, but every small matter they shall judge: so shall it be easier for thyself, and they shall bear the burden with thee. If thou shalt do this thing, and God command thee so, then thou shalt be able to endure, and all this people shall also go to their place in peace."

So Moses hearkened to the voice of his father-in-law, and did all that he had said. And Moses chose able men out of all Israel, and made them heads over the people, rulers of thousands, rulers of hundreds, rulers of fifties, and rulers of tens. And they judged the people at all seasons: the hard

[26] "Eliezer" means "God is my help."

causes they brought unto Moses, but every small matter they judged themselves. And Moses let his father-in-law depart; and he went his way into his own land.

THE GIVING OF THE LAW

(Exodus 19:1–31:18)
In the third month, when the children of Israel were gone forth out of the land of Egypt, the same day came they into the wilderness of Sinai. For they were departed from Rephidim, and were come to the desert of Sinai, and had pitched in the wilderness; and there Israel camped before the mount. And Moses went up unto God, and the Lord called unto him out of the mountain, saying, "Thus shalt thou say to the house of Jacob, and tell the children of Israel: 'Ye have seen what I did unto the Egyptians, and how I bore you on eagles' wings, and brought you unto myself. Now therefore, if ye will obey my voice indeed, and keep my covenant, then ye shall be a peculiar treasure unto me above all people: for all the earth is mine.'"[27] . . . And the Lord said unto Moses, "Go unto the people, and sanctify them to-day and to-morrow, and let them wash their clothes, and be ready against the third day: for the third day the Lord will come down in the sight of all the people upon Mount Sinai. And thou shalt set bounds unto the people round about, saying, 'Take heed to yourselves, that ye go not up into the mount, or touch the border of it: whosoever toucheth the mount shall be surely put to death.' There shall not a hand touch it, but he shall surely be stoned, or shot through; whether it be beast or man, it shall not live: when the trumpet soundeth long, they shall come up to the mount."

And Moses went down from the mount unto the people, and sanctified the people; and they washed their clothes. And he said unto the people, "Be ready against the third day: come not at your wives." And it came to pass on the third day in the morning, that there were thunders and lightnings, and a thick cloud upon the mount, and the voice of the trumpet exceeding loud; so that all the people that was in the camp trembled. And Moses brought forth the people out of the camp to meet with God; and they stood at the nether part of the mount. And Mount Sinai was altogether on a smoke, because the Lord descended upon it in fire; and the smoke thereof ascended as the smoke of a furnace, and the whole mount quaked greatly. And when the voice of the trumpet sounded long, and waxed louder and louder, Moses spoke, and God answered him by a voice. And the Lord came down upon Mount Sinai, on the top of the mount: and the Lord called Moses up to the top of the mount; and Moses went up. . . .

And God spoke all these words, saying, "I am the Lord thy God, which have brought thee out of the land of Egypt, out of the house of bondage.

---

[27] The first part of this sentence identifies the Hebrews as God's Chosen People or "peculiar treasure," while the last part emphasizes that their God is the God of the entire universe. The sufferings the Hebrews later undergo suggest that they are not "chosen" in the sense of being uniquely favored but rather in the sense of being the medium for God's ethical and spiritual teachings to mankind.

"Thou shalt have no other gods before me.

"Thou shalt not make unto thee any graven image, or any likeness of any thing that is in heaven above, or that is in the earth beneath, or that is in the water under the earth: thou shalt not bow down thyself to them, nor serve them: for I the Lord thy God am a jealous God, visiting the iniquity of the fathers upon the children unto the third and fourth generation of them that hate me; and showing mercy unto thousands of them that love me, and keep my commandments.[28]

"Thou shalt not take the name of the Lord thy God in vain; for the Lord will not hold him guiltless that taketh his name in vain.

"Remember the sabbath day, to keep it holy. Six days shalt thou labor, and do all thy work: but the seventh day is the sabbath of the Lord thy God: in it thou shalt not do any work, thou, nor thy son, nor thy daughter, thy manservant, nor thy maidservant, nor thy cattle, nor thy stranger that is within thy gates: for in six days the Lord made heaven and earth, the sea, and all that in them is, and rested the seventh day: wherefore the Lord blessed the sabbath day, and hallowed it.

"Honor thy father and thy mother: that thy days may be long upon the land which the Lord thy God giveth thee.

"Thou shalt not kill.

"Thou shalt not commit adultery.

"Thou shalt not steal.

"Thou shalt not bear false witness against thy neighbor.

"Thou shalt not covet thy neighbor's house, thou shalt not covet thy neighbor's wife, nor his manservant, nor his maidservant, nor his ox, nor his ass, nor any thing that is thy neighbor's. . . .[29]

And he gave unto Moses, when he had made an end of communing with him upon Mount Sinai, two tables of testimony, tables of stone, written with the finger of God.

THE GOLDEN CALF

(Exodus 32:1–34:32)

And when the people saw that Moses delayed to come down out of the mount, the people gathered themselves together unto Aaron, and said unto him, "Up, make us gods, which shall go before us; for as for this Moses, the man that brought us up out of the land of Egypt, we wot not what is become of him." And Aaron said unto them, "Break off the golden earrings, which are in the ears of your wives, of your sons, and of your daughters, and bring them unto me." And all the people broke off the golden earrings which were in their ears, and brought them unto Aaron. And he received them at their hand, and fashioned it with a graving tool,

[28] This ban upon "graven images" to be set up for worship is one of the distinctive features of the Hebrew religion. It should be noted that the ban is only against images to be worshiped, not against images of any kind, as in Islam.

[29] A long section is omitted here (Exodus 20:18–31:17), which contains detailed provisions of the Covenant Code, much of it of little contemporary interest. The most important omission is the instructions for the building of the Tabernacle and for public worship.

after he had made it a molten calf:[30] and they said, "These be thy gods, O Israel, which brought thee up out of the land of Egypt." And when Aaron saw it, he built an altar before it; and Aaron made proclamation, and said, "To-morrow is a feast to the Lord." And they rose up early on the morrow, and offered burnt offerings, and brought peace offerings; and the people sat down to eat and to drink, and rose up to play.

And the Lord said unto Moses, "Go, get thee down; for thy people, which thou broughtest out of the land of Egypt, have corrupted themselves. They have turned aside quickly out of the way which I commanded them: they have made them a molten calf, and have worshipped it, and have sacrificed thereunto, and said, 'These be thy gods, O Israel, which have brought thee up out of the land of Egypt.'" And the Lord said unto Moses, "I have seen this people, and, behold, it is a stiffnecked people. Now therefore let me alone, that my wrath may wax hot against them, and that I may consume them: and I will make of thee a great nation." And Moses besought the Lord his God, and said, "Lord, why doth thy wrath wax hot against thy people, which thou hast brought forth out of the land of Egypt with great power, and with a mighty hand? Wherefore should the Egyptians speak, and say, 'For mischief did he bring them out, to slay them in the mountains, and to consume them from the face of the earth'? Turn from thy fierce wrath, and repent of this evil against thy people. Remember Abraham, Isaac, and Israel, thy servants, to whom thou sworest by thine own self, and saidst unto them, 'I will multiply your seed as the stars of heaven, and all this land that I have spoken of will I give unto your seed, and they shall inherit it for ever.'"

And the Lord repented of the evil which he thought to do unto his people. And Moses turned, and went down from the mount, and the two tables of the testimony were in his hand: the tables were written on both their sides; on the one side and on the other were they written. And the tables were the work of God, and the writing was the writing of God, graven upon the tables. And when Joshua heard the noise of the people as they shouted, he said unto Moses, "There is a noise of war in the camp." And he said, "It is not the voice of them that shout for mastery, neither is it the voice of them that cry for being overcome: but the noise of them that sing do I hear." And it came to pass, as soon as he came nigh unto the camp, that he saw the calf, and the dancing: and Moses' anger waxed hot, and he cast the tables out of his hands, and broke them beneath the mount. And he took the calf which they had made, and burnt it in the fire, and ground it to powder, and strewed it upon the water, and made the children of Israel drink of it.[31]

And Moses said unto Aaron, "What did this people unto thee, that thou hast brought so great a sin upon them?" And Aaron said, "Let not the anger of my lord wax hot: thou knowest the people, that they are set on mischief. For they said unto me, 'Make us gods, which shall go before us: for as for this Moses, the man that brought us up out of the land of Egypt,

---

[30] The fashioning of the "molten calf," which directly violates the second commandment, probably refers to a small bull. The ritual echoes practices of the fertility religions of Egypt and of the rest of the ancient Near East.

[31] The drinking of water mixed with pulverized gold from the golden calf constitutes a "trial by ordeal." Those who suffered ill effects were regarded as proven guilty.

we wot not what is become of him.' And I said unto them, 'Whosoever hath any gold, let them break it off.' So they gave it me: then I cast it into the fire, and there came out this calf."

And when Moses saw that the people were naked (for Aaron had made them naked unto their shame among their enemies), then Moses stood in the gate of the camp, and said, "Who is on the Lord's side? let him come unto me." And all the sons of Levi gathered themselves together unto him. And he said unto them, "Thus saith the Lord God of Israel, 'Put every man his sword by his side, and go in and out from gate to gate throughout the camp, and slay every man his brother, and every man his companion, and every man his neighbor.'" And the children of Levi did according to the word of Moses: and there fell of the people that day about three thousand men. . . .[32]

And it came to pass on the morrow that Moses said unto the people, "Ye have sinned a great sin: and now I will go up unto the Lord; peradventure I shall make an atonement for your sin." And Moses returned unto the Lord, and said, "Oh, this people have sinned a great sin, and have made them gods of gold. Yet now, if thou wilt forgive their sin—; and if not, blot me, I pray thee, out of thy book which thou hast written." And the Lord said unto Moses, "Whosoever hath sinned against me, him will I blot out of my book. Therefore now go, lead the people unto the place of which I have spoken unto thee: behold, mine Angel shall go before thee: nevertheless in the day when I visit I will visit their sin upon them."

And the Lord plagued the people, because they made the calf, which Aaron made.

And the Lord said unto Moses, "Depart, and go up hence, thou and the people which thou hast brought up out of the land of Egypt, unto the land which I swore unto Abraham, to Isaac, and to Jacob, saying, 'Unto thy seed will I give it': . . . unto a land flowing with milk and honey: for I will not go up in the midst of thee; for thou art a stiffnecked people: lest I consume thee in the way."

And when the people heard these evil tidings, they mourned: and no man did put on him his ornaments. . . . And the children of Israel stripped themselves of their ornaments by the mount Horeb. And Moses took the tabernacle, and pitched it without the camp, afar off from the camp, and called it the tabernacle of the congregation. And it came to pass that every one which sought the Lord went out unto the tabernacle of the congregation, which was without the camp. And it came to pass, when Moses went out unto the tabernacle, that all the people rose up, and stood every man at his tent door, and looked after Moses, until he was gone into the tabernacle. And it came to pass, as Moses entered into the tabernacle, the cloudy pillar descended, and stood at the door of the tabernacle, and the Lord talked with Moses. And all the people saw the cloudy pillar stand at the tabernacle door: and all the people rose up and worshipped, every man in his tent door. And the Lord spoke unto Moses face to face, as a man speaketh unto his friend. . . .

---

[32]This shocking story seems to suggest that the priests of Levi were consecrated to the priesthood by demonstrating that they could place loyalty to the Lord above ties of friendship or kinship.

And Moses said unto the Lord, "See, thou sayest unto me, 'Bring up this people': and thou hast not let me know whom thou wilt send with me. Yet thou hast said, 'I know thee by name, and thou hast also found grace in my sight.' Now therefore, I pray thee, if I have found grace in thy sight, show me now thy way, that I may know thee, that I may find grace in thy sight: and consider that this nation is thy people." And he said, "My presence shall go with thee, and I will give thee rest." And he said unto him, "If thy presence go not with me, carry us not up hence. For wherein shall it be known here that I and thy people have found grace in thy sight? is it not in that thou goest with us? so shall we be separated, I and thy people, from all the people that are upon the face of the earth."

And the Lord said unto Moses, "I will do this thing also that thou hast spoken: for thou hast found grace in my sight, and I know thee by name." And he said, "I beseech thee, show me thy glory." And he said, "I will make all my goodness pass before thee, and I will proclaim the name of the Lord before thee; and will be gracious to whom I will be gracious, and will show mercy on whom I will show mercy." And he said, "Thou canst not see my face: for there shall no man see me, and live." And the Lord said, "Behold, there is a place by me, and thou shalt stand upon a rock: and it shall come to pass, while my glory passeth by, that I will put thee in a cleft of the rock, and will cover thee with my hand while I pass by: and I will take away mine hand, and thou shalt see my back parts: but my face shall not be seen."

And the Lord said unto Moses, "Hew thee two tables of stone like unto the first: and I will write upon these tables the words that were in the first tables, which thou brokest. And be ready in the morning, and come up in the morning unto Mount Sinai, and present thyself there to me in the top of the mount. And no man shall come up with thee, neither let any man be seen throughout all the mount; neither let the flocks nor herds feed before that mount." . . . And he hewed two tables of stone like unto the first; and Moses rose up early in the morning, and went up unto Mount Sinai, as the Lord had commanded him, and took in his hand the two tables of stone. And it came to pass, when Moses came down from Mount Sinai with the two tables of testimony in Moses' hand, when he came down from the mount, that Moses wist not that the skin of his face shone while he talked with him. And when Aaron and all the children of Israel saw Moses, behold, the skin of his face shone; and they were afraid to come nigh him. And Moses called unto them; and Aaron and all the rulers of the congregation returned unto him: and Moses talked with them. And afterward all the children of Israel came nigh: and he gave them in commandment all that the Lord had spoken with him in Mount Sinai. . . .[33]

THE HOLINESS CODE

(*Leviticus 19:1–19:36*)
And the Lord spoke unto Moses, saying, "Speak unto all the congregation

[33] The last six chapters of Exodus, omitted here, contain a further set of cultic laws and describe the building of the Tabernacle.

of the children of Israel, and say unto them, 'Ye shall be holy: for I the Lord your God am holy.[34]

"'Ye shall fear every man his mother, and his father, and keep my sabbaths: I am the Lord your God.

"'Turn ye not unto idols, nor make to yourselves molten gods: I am the Lord your God.

"'And if ye offer a sacrifice of peace offerings unto the Lord, ye shall offer it at your own will. It shall be eaten the same day ye offer it, and on the morrow: and if ought remain until the third day, it shall be burnt in the fire. And if it be eaten at all on the third day, it is abominable; it shall not be accepted. Therefore every one that eateth it shall bear his iniquity, because he hath profaned the hallowed thing of the Lord: and that soul shall be cut off from among his people.

"'And when ye reap the harvest of your land, thou shalt not wholly reap the corners of thy field, neither shalt thou gather the gleanings of thy harvest. And thou shalt not glean thy vineyard, neither shalt thou gather every grape of thy vineyard; thou shalt leave them for the poor and stranger: I am the Lord your God.

"'Ye shall not steal, neither deal falsely, neither lie one to another.

"'And ye shall not swear by my name falsely, neither shalt thou profane the name of thy God: I am the Lord.

"'Thou shalt not defraud thy neighbor, neither rob him: the wages of him that is hired shall not abide with thee all night until the morning.

"'Thou shalt not curse the deaf, nor put a stumblingblock before the blind, but shalt fear thy God: I am the Lord.

"'Ye shall do no unrighteousness in judgment: thou shalt not respect the person of the poor, nor honor the person of the mighty: but in righteousness shalt thou judge thy neighbor.

"'Thou shalt not go up and down as a talebearer among thy people: neither shalt thou stand against the blood of thy neighbor: I am the Lord.

"'Thou shalt not hate thy brother in thine heart: thou shalt in any wise rebuke thy neighbor, and not suffer sin upon him. Thou shalt not avenge, nor bear any grudge against the children of thy people, but thou shalt love thy neighbor as thyself: I am the Lord.

"'Ye shall keep my statutes. Thou shalt not let thy cattle gender with a diverse kind: thou shalt not sow thy field with mingled seed: neither shall a garment mingled of linen and woollen come upon thee.[35]

"'And whosoever lieth carnally with a woman, that is a bondmaid, betrothed to a husband, and not at all redeemed, nor freedom given her; she shall be scourged; they shall not be put to death, because she was not free. And he shall bring his trespass offering unto the Lord, unto the door of the

---

[34] The Old Testament contains four major "codes" or bodies of laws: the Covenant Code in Exodus, the Deuteronomic Code in Deuteronomy, the Holiness Code in Leviticus, and the Priestly Code, which is scattered through Exodus, Leviticus, and Numbers. Leviticus is largely devoted to Hebrew laws, including laws of the sacrifice and consecration to the priesthood and laws of the "clean" and the "unclean," regulating sex and childbirth, diet, disease, and care of the dead. The passage given here constitutes the Holiness Code, devoted more to ethical than to practical matters.

[35] This odd law against the "mixing of kinds" is repeated in Deuteronomy; it apparently is directed against erasing distinctions which God has ordained.

tabernacle of the congregation, even a ram for a trespass offering. And the priest shall make an atonement for him with the ram of the trespass offering before the Lord for his sin which he hath done: and the sin which he hath done shall be forgiven him.

"'And when ye shall come into the land, and shall have planted all manner of trees for food, then ye shall count the fruit thereof as uncircumcised: three years shall it be as uncircumcised unto you: it shall not be eaten of. But in the fourth year all the fruit thereof shall be holy to praise the Lord withal. And in the fifth year shall ye eat of the fruit thereof, that it may yield unto you the increase thereof: I am the Lord your God.

"'Ye shall not eat any thing with the blood: neither shall ye use enchantment, nor observe times.[36]

"'Ye shall not round the corners of your heads, neither shalt thou mar the corners of thy beard.

"'Ye shall not make any cuttings in your flesh for the dead, nor print any marks upon you: I am the Lord.

"'Do not prostitute thy daughter, to cause her to be a whore; lest the land fall to whoredom, and the land become full of wickedness.

"'Ye shall keep my sabbaths, and reverence my sanctuary: I am the Lord.

"'Regard not them that have familiar spirits, neither seek after wizards, to be defiled by them: I am the Lord your God.

"'Thou shalt rise up before the hoary head, and honor the face of the old man, and fear thy God: I am the Lord.

"'And if a stranger sojourn with thee in your land, ye shall not vex him. But the stranger that dwelleth with you shall be unto you as one born among you, and thou shalt love him as thyself; for ye were strangers in the land of Egypt: I am the Lord your God.

"'Ye shall do no unrighteousness in judgment, in meteyard, in weight, or in measure. Just balances, just weights, a just ephah, and a just hin, shall ye have:[37] I am the Lord your God, which brought you out of the land of Egypt.'" . . .

THE WANDERINGS IN THE WILDERNESS

(Numbers 9:15–21:35)
And on the day that the tabernacle was reared up the cloud covered the tabernacle, namely, the tent of the testimony: and at even there was upon the tabernacle as it were the appearance of fire, until the morning. So it was always: the cloud covered it by day, and the appearance of fire by night. And when the cloud was taken up from the tabernacle, then after that the children of Israel journeyed: and in the place where the cloud abode, there the children of Israel pitched their tents. . . .

And they departed from the mount of the Lord three days' journey:

[36] This and the five following laws are directed against the practices of other religions: witchcraft, heathen mourning customs, sacred prostitution, and necromancy, or the conjuring of spirits to predict the future.

[37] "Meteyard": balances of scales. "Ephah": unit of dry measure, a little over a bushel. "Hin": unit of liquid measure, about one and a half gallons.

and the ark of the covenant[38] of the Lord went before them in the three days' journey, to search out a resting place for them. And the cloud of the Lord was upon them by day, when they went out of the camp. And it came to pass, when the ark set forward, that Moses said, "Rise up, Lord, And let thine enemies be scattered; And let them that hate thee flee before thee." And when it rested, he said, "Return, O Lord, Unto the many thousands of Israel." . . .

And the Lord spoke unto Moses, saying, "Send thou men, that they may search the land of Canaan, which I give unto the children of Israel: of every tribe of their fathers shall ye send a man, every one a ruler among them." And Moses by the commandment of the Lord sent them from the wilderness of Paran: all those men were heads of the children of Israel. . . . And Moses sent them to spy out the land of Canaan, and said unto them, "Get you up this way southward, and go out into the mountain: and see the land, what it is; and the people that dwelleth therein, whether they be strong or weak, few or many; and what the land is that they dwell in, whether it be good or bad; and what cities they be that they dwell in, whether in tents, or in strong holds; and what the land is, whether it be fat or lean, whether there be wood therein, or not. And be ye of good courage, and bring of the fruit of the land." . . .

And they returned from searching of the land after forty days. And they went and came to Moses, and to Aaron, and to all the congregation of the children of Israel, unto the wilderness of Paran, to Kadesh; and brought back word unto them, and unto all the congregation, and showed them the fruit of the land. And they told him, and said, "We came unto the land whither thou sentest us, and surely it floweth with milk and honey; and this is the fruit of it. Nevertheless the people be strong that dwell in the land, and the cities are walled, and very great: and moreover we saw the children of Anak there. The Amalekites dwell in the land of the south: and the Hittites, and the Jebusites, and the Amorites, dwell in the mountains: and the Canaanites dwell by the sea, and by the coast of Jordan."

And Caleb stilled the people before Moses, and said, "Let us go up at once, and possess it; for we are well able to overcome it." But the men that went up with him said, "We be not able to go up against the people; for they are stronger than we." And they brought up an evil report of the land which they had searched unto the children of Israel, saying, "The land, through which we have gone to search it, is a land that eateth up the inhabitants thereof; and all the people that we saw in it are men of a great stature. And there we saw the giants, the sons of Anak, which come of the giants: and we were in our own sight as grasshoppers, and so we were in their sight."

And all the congregation lifted up their voice, and cried; and the people wept that night. And all the children of Israel murmured against Moses and against Aaron: and the whole congregation said unto them, "Would God that we had died in the land of Egypt! or would God we had died in

---

[38] The Ark of the Covenant, built according to the instructions given Moses in Exodus, was the physical symbol of the presence of God among the Hebrews. Its contents are unclear; it may have held the stone tablets of the Law or perhaps the brazen serpent made by Moses. The "arks" in modern synagogues hold the scrolls of the Torah.

this wilderness! And wherefore hath the Lord brought us unto this land, to fall by the sword, that our wives and our children should be a prey? were it not better for us to return into Egypt?"

And they said one to another, "Let us make a captain, and let us return into Egypt." Then Moses and Aaron fell on their faces before all the assembly of the congregation of the children of Israel. And Joshua the son of Nun, and Caleb the son of Jephunneh, which were of them that searched the land, rent their clothes: and they spoke unto all the company of the children of Israel, saying, "The land, which we passed through to search it, is an exceeding good land. If the Lord delight in us, then he will bring us into this land, and give it us; a land which floweth with milk and honey. Only rebel not ye against the Lord, neither fear ye the people of the land; for they are bread for us: their defense is departed from them, and the Lord is with us: fear them not." But all the congregation bade stone them with stones.

And the glory of the Lord appeared in the tabernacle of the congregation before all the children of Israel. And the Lord said unto Moses, "How long will this people provoke me? and how long will it be ere they believe me, for all the signs which I have showed among them? I will smite them with the pestilence, and disinherit them, and will make of thee a greater nation and mightier than they."

And Moses said unto the Lord, "Then the Egyptians shall hear it (for thou broughtest up this people in thy might from among them); and they will tell it to the inhabitants of this land: for they have heard that thou Lord art among this people, that thou Lord art seen face to face, and that thy cloud standeth over them, and that thou goest before them, by day time in a pillar of a cloud, and in a pillar of fire by night. Now if thou shalt kill all this people as one man, then the nations which have heard the fame of thee will speak, saying, 'Because the Lord was not able to bring this people into the land which he swore unto them, therefore he hath slain them in the wilderness.' And now, I beseech thee, let the power of my Lord be great, according as thou hast spoken, saying, 'The Lord is longsuffering, and of great mercy, forgiving iniquity and transgression, and by no means clearing the guilty, visiting the iniquity of the fathers upon the children unto the third and fourth generation.' Pardon, I beseech thee, the iniquity of this people according unto the greatness of thy mercy; and as thou hast forgiven this people, from Egypt even until now."

And the Lord said, "I have pardoned according to thy word: but as truly as I live, all the earth shall be filled with the glory of the Lord. Because all those men which have seen my glory, and my miracles, which I did in Egypt and in the wilderness, and have tempted me now these ten times, and have not hearkened to my voice; surely they shall not see the land which I swore unto their fathers, neither shall any of them that provoked me see it. . . . How long shall I bear with this evil congregation, which murmur against me? I have heard the murmurings of the children of Israel, which they murmur against me. Say unto them, 'As truly as I live,' saith the Lord, 'as ye have spoken in mine ears, so will I do to you: your carcases shall fall in this wilderness; and all that were numbered of you, according to your whole number, from twenty years old and upward, which have murmured against me, doubtless ye shall not come into the land, concerning which I swore to make you dwell therein, save Caleb the son of Jephunneh, and Joshua the son of Nun. But your little ones, which ye said should be a prey, them will I bring in, and they shall know the land which ye have despised. But as for you, your carcases, they shall fall in this wilderness. And your children shall wander in the wilderness forty years, and bear your whoredoms, until your carcases be wasted in the wilderness. After the number of the days in which ye searched the land, even forty days, each day for a year, shall ye bear your iniquities, even forty years, and ye shall know my breach of promise. I the Lord have said, "I will surely do it unto all this evil congregation, that are gathered together against me: in this wilderness they shall be consumed, and there they shall die."'"

And the men, which Moses sent to search the land, who returned, and made all the congregation to murmur against him, by bringing up a slander upon the land, even those men that did bring up the evil report upon the land, died by the plague before the Lord. But Joshua the son of Nun, and Caleb the son of Jephunneh, which were of the men that went to search the land, lived still.

And Moses told these sayings unto all the children of Israel: and the people mourned greatly. And they rose up early in the morning, and got them up into the top of the mountain, saying, "Lo, we be here, and will go up unto the place which the Lord hath promised: for we have sinned." And Moses said, "Wherefore now do ye transgress the commandment of the Lord? but it shall not prosper. Go not up, for the Lord is not among you; that ye be not smitten before your enemies. For the Amalekites and the Canaanites are there before you, and ye shall fall by the sword: because ye are turned away from the Lord, therefore the Lord will not be with you." But they presumed to go up unto the hill top: nevertheless the ark of the covenant of the Lord, and Moses, departed not out of the camp. Then the Amalekites came down, and the Canaanites which dwelt in that hill, and smote them, and discomfited them, even unto Hormah. . . .

Then came the children of Israel, even the whole congregation, into the desert of Zin in the first month: and the people abode in Kadesh; and Miriam died there, and was buried there. And there was no water for the congregation: and they gathered themselves together against Moses and against Aaron. And the people chid with Moses, and spoke, saying, "Would God that we had died when our brethren died before the Lord! And why have ye brought up the congregation of the Lord into this wilderness, that we and our cattle should die there? And wherefore have ye made us to come up out of Egypt, to bring us in unto this evil place? it is no place of seed, or of figs, or of vines, or of pomegranates; neither is there any water to drink."

And Moses and Aaron went from the presence of the assembly unto the door of the tabernacle of the congregation, and they fell upon their faces: and the glory of the Lord appeared unto them. And the Lord spoke unto Moses, saying, "Take the rod, and gather thou the assembly together, thou, and Aaron thy brother, and speak ye unto the rock before their eyes; and it shall give forth his water, and thou shalt bring forth to them water out of the rock: so thou shalt give the congregation and their beasts drink."

And Moses took the rod from before the Lord, as he commanded him. And Moses and Aaron gathered the congregation together before the rock, and he said unto them, "Hear now, ye rebels; must we fetch you water out of this rock?" And Moses lifted up his hand, and with his rod he smote the rock twice: and the water came out abundantly, and the congregation drank, and their beasts also.

And the Lord spoke unto Moses and Aaron, "Because ye believed me not, to sanctify me in the eyes of the children of Israel, therefore ye shall not bring this congregation into the land which I have given them. This is the water of Meribah; because the children of Israel strove with the Lord, and he was sanctified in them."[39] . . .

And the children of Israel, even the whole congregation, journeyed from Kadesh, and came unto Mount Hor. And the Lord spoke unto Moses and Aaron in Mount Hor, by the coast of the land of Edom, saying, "Aaron shall be gathered unto his people: for he shall not enter into the land which I have given unto the children of Israel, because ye rebelled against my word at the water of Meribah. Take Aaron and Eleazar his son, and bring them up unto Mount Hor: and strip Aaron of his garments, and put them upon Eleazar his son: and Aaron shall be gathered unto his people, and shall die there."

And Moses did as the Lord commanded: and they went up into Mount Hor in the sight of all the congregation. And Moses stripped Aaron of his garments, and put them upon Eleazar his son; and Aaron died there in the top of the mount: and Moses and Eleazar came down from the mount. And when all the congregation saw that Aaron was dead, they mourned for Aaron thirty days, even all the house of Israel. . . .

THE DEATH OF MOSES

(Deuteronomy 31:14–34:12)[40]
And the Lord said unto Moses, "Behold, thy days approach that thou must die: call Joshua, and present yourselves in the tabernacle of the congregation, that I may give him a charge." And Moses and Joshua went, and presented themselves in the tabernacle of the congregation. And the Lord appeared in the tabernacle in a pillar of a cloud: and the pillar of the cloud stood over the door of the tabernacle.

And the Lord said unto Moses, "Behold, thou shalt sleep with thy fathers; and this people will rise up, and go a-whoring after the gods of the strangers of the land, whither they go to be among them, and will forsake me, and break my covenant which I have made with them. Then my anger shall be kindled against them in that day, and I will forsake them, and I will hide my face from them, and they shall be devoured, and many evils and troubles shall befall them; so that they will say in that day, 'Are not these evils come upon us, because our God is not among us?' " . . .

[39] It is not clear what happened in the incident of the water to justify the Lord's refusal to let Aaron and Moses enter the land of Canaan. Later, the accusation is repeated: "Ye rebelled against my commandment" (Numbers 27:14). "Meribah" means "contention" or "strife."

[40] The end of Numbers is devoted to the story of Balaam and to the appointment of Joshua as the successor to Moses. Most of Deuteronomy is devoted to a recasting of the Covenant Code. ("Deuteronomy" is Greek for "second law.") These important sections are omitted here in order to preserve the narrative emphasis.

And Moses went up from the plains of Moab unto the mountain of Nebo, to the top of Pisgah, that is over against Jericho. And the Lord showed him all the land of Gilead, unto Dan, and all Naphtali, and the land of Ephraim, and Manasseh, and all the land of Judah, unto the utmost sea, and the south, and the plain of the valley of Jericho, the city of palm trees, unto Zoar. And the Lord said unto him, "This is the land which I swore unto Abraham, unto Isaac, and unto Jacob, saying, 'I will give it unto thy seed': I have caused thee to see it with thine eyes, but thou shalt not go over thither." So Moses the servant of the Lord died there in the land of Moab, according to the word of the Lord. And he buried him in a valley in the land of Moab, over against Beth-peor: but no man knoweth of his sepulchre unto this day. And Moses was a hundred and twenty years old when he died: his eye was not dim, nor his natural force abated. And the children of Israel wept for Moses in the plains of Moab thirty days: so the days of weeping and mourning for Moses were ended. And Joshua the son of Nun was full of the spirit of wisdom; for Moses had laid his hands upon him: and the children of Israel hearkened unto him, and did as the Lord commanded Moses. And there arose not a prophet since in Israel like unto Moses, whom the Lord knew face to face, in all the signs and the wonders, which the Lord sent him to do in the land of Egypt to Pharaoh, and to all his servants, and to all his land, and in all that mighty hand, and in all the great terror which Moses showed in the sight of all Israel.

THE DESTRUCTION OF JERICHO

(Joshua 1:1–6:27)
Now after the death of Moses the servant of the Lord it came to pass that the Lord spoke unto Joshua the son of Nun, Moses' minister, saying, "Moses my servant is dead; now therefore arise, go over this Jordan, thou, and all this people, unto the land which I do give to them, even to the children of Israel. Every place that the sole of your foot shall tread upon, that have I given unto you, as I said unto Moses. From the wilderness and this Lebanon even unto the great river, the river Euphrates, all the land of the Hittites, and unto the great sea toward the going down of the sun, shall be your coast. There shall not any man be able to stand before thee all the days of thy life: as I was with Moses, so I will be with thee: I will not fail thee, nor forsake thee. Be strong and of a good courage: for unto this people shalt thou divide for an inheritance the land, which I swore unto their fathers to give them. Only be thou strong and very courageous, that thou mayest observe to do according to all the law, which Moses my servant commanded thee: turn not from it to the right hand or to the left, that thou mayest prosper whithersoever thou goest. This book of the law[41] shall not depart out of thy mouth; but thou shalt meditate therein day and night, that thou mayest observe to do according to all that is written therein: for then thou shalt make thy way prosperous, and then thou shalt have good success. Have not I commanded thee? Be strong and of a good courage; be

[41] The legal provisions of the Book of Deuteronomy.

not afraid, neither be thou dismayed: for the Lord thy God is with thee whithersoever thou goest."

Then Joshua commanded the officers of the people, saying, "Pass through the host, and command the people, saying, 'Prepare you victuals; for within three days ye shall pass over this Jordan, to go in to possess the land, which the Lord your God giveth you to possess it.'" . . .

And Joshua the son of Nun sent out of Shittim two men to spy secretly, saying, "Go view the land, even Jericho." And they went, and came into a harlot's house, named Rahab, and lodged there. And it was told the king of Jericho, saying, "Behold, there came men in hither to-night of the children of Israel to search out the country." And the king of Jericho sent unto Rahab, saying, "Bring forth the men that are come to thee, which are entered into thine house: for they be come to search out all the country." And the woman took the two men and hid them, and said thus, "There came men unto me, but I wist not whence they were: and it came to pass about the time of shutting of the gate, when it was dark, that the men went out: whither the men went I wot not: pursue after them quickly; for ye shall overtake them." But she had brought them up to the roof of the house, and hid them with the stalks of flax, which she had laid in order upon the roof. And the men pursued after them the way to Jordan unto the fords: and as soon as they which pursued after them were gone out, they shut the gate.

And before they were laid down, she came up unto them upon the roof; and she said unto the men, "I know that the Lord hath given you the land, and that your terror is fallen upon us, and that all the inhabitants of the land faint because of you. For we have heard how the Lord dried up the water of the Red Sea for you, when ye came out of Egypt; and what ye did unto the two kings of the Amorites, that were on the other side Jordan, Sihon and Og, whom ye utterly destroyed.[42] And as soon as we had heard these things, our hearts did melt, neither did there remain any more courage in any man, because of you: for the Lord your God, he is God in heaven above, and in earth beneath. Now therefore, I pray you, swear unto me by the Lord, since I have showed you kindness, that ye will also show kindness unto my father's house, and give me a true token: and that ye will save alive my father, and my mother, and my brethren, and my sisters, and all that they have, and deliver our lives from death." And the men answered her, "Our life for yours, if ye utter not this our business. And it shall be, when the Lord hath given us the land, that we will deal kindly and truly with thee."

Then she let them down by a cord through the window: for her house was upon the town wall, and she dwelt upon the wall. And she said unto them, "Get you to the mountain, lest the pursuers meet you; and hide yourselves there three days, until the pursuers be returned: and afterward may ye go your way." And the men said unto her, "We will be blameless of this thine oath which thou hast made us swear. Behold, when we come into the land, thou shalt bind this line of scarlet thread in the window which thou didst let us down by: and thou shalt bring thy father, and thy mother,

---

[42] A clearer translation would be: "what you did to the two kings of the Amorites that were beyond the Jordan, to Sihon and Og, whom you utterly destroyed."

and thy brethren, and all thy father's household, home unto thee. And it shall be, that whosoever shall go out of the doors of thy house into the street, his blood shall be upon his head, and we will be guiltless: and whosoever shall be with thee in the house, his blood shall be on our head, if any hand be upon him. And if thou utter this our business, then we will be quit of thine oath which thou hast made us to swear." And she said, "According unto your words, so be it." And she sent them away, and they departed: and she bound the scarlet line in the window.

And they went, and came unto the mountain, and abode there three days, until the pursuers were returned: and the pursuers sought them throughout all the way, but found them not. So the two men returned, and descended from the mountain, and passed over, and came to Joshua the son of Nun, and told him all things that befell them: and they said unto Joshua, "Truly the Lord hath delivered into our hands all the land; for even all the inhabitants of the country do faint because of us."

And Joshua rose early in the morning; and they removed from Shittim, and came to Jordan, he and all the children of Israel, and lodged there before they passed over. And it came to pass after three days that the officers went through the host; and they commanded the people, saying, "When ye see the ark of the covenant of the Lord your God, and the priests the Levites bearing it, then ye shall remove from your place, and go after it. Yet there shall be a space between you and it, about two thousand cubits by measure: come not near unto it, that ye may know the way by which ye must go: for ye have not passed this way heretofore." And Joshua said unto the people, "Sanctify yourselves: for to-morrow the Lord will do wonders among you." And Joshua spoke unto the priests, saying, "Take up the ark of the covenant, and pass over before the people." And they took up the ark of the covenant, and went before the people.

And the Lord said unto Joshua, "This day will I begin to magnify thee in the sight of all Israel, that they may know that, as I was with Moses, so I will be with thee. And thou shalt command the priests that bear the ark of the covenant, saying, 'When ye are come to the brink of the water of Jordan, ye shall stand still in Jordan.'" And Joshua said unto the children of Israel, "Come hither, and hear the words of the Lord your God." And Joshua said, "Hereby ye shall know that the living God is among you, and that he will without fail drive out from before you the Canaanites, and the Hittites, and the Hivites, and the Perizzites, and the Girgashites, and the Amorites, and the Jebusites. Behold, the ark of the covenant of the Lord of all the earth passeth over before you into Jordan. Now therefore take you twelve men out of the tribes of Israel, out of every tribe a man. And it shall come to pass, as soon as the soles of the feet of the priests that bear the ark of the Lord, the Lord of all the earth, shall rest in the waters of Jordan, that the waters of Jordan shall be cut off from the waters that come down from above; and they shall stand upon a heap." . . .

And it came to pass, as they that bore the ark were come unto Jordan, and the feet of the priests that bore the ark were dipped in the brim of the water (for Jordan overfloweth all his banks all the time of harvest), that the waters which came down from above stood and rose up upon a heap very far from the city Adam, that is beside Zaretan: and those that came down toward the sea of the plain, even the Salt Sea, failed, and were cut off: and the people passed over right against Jericho. And the priests that bore the ark of the covenant of the Lord stood firm on dry ground in the midst of Jordan, and all the Israelites passed over on dry ground, until all the people were passed clean over Jordan. . . .

Now Jericho was straitly shut up because of the children of Israel: none went out, and none came in. And the Lord said unto Joshua, "See, I have given into thine hand Jericho, and the king thereof, and the mighty men of valor. And ye shall compass the city, all ye men of war, and go round about the city once. Thus shalt thou do six days. And seven priests shall bear before the ark seven trumpets of rams' horns: and the seventh day ye shall compass the city seven times, and the priests shall blow with the trumpets.[43] And it shall come to pass, that when they make a long blast with the ram's horn, and when ye hear the sound of the trumpet, all the people shall shout with a great shout; and the wall of the city shall fall down flat, and the people shall ascend up every man straight before him." . . .

And Joshua rose early in the morning, and the priests took up the ark of the Lord. And seven priests bearing seven trumpets of rams' horns before the ark of the Lord went on continually, and blew with the trumpets: and the armed men went before them; but the rearward came after the ark of the Lord, the priests going on, and blowing with the trumpets. And the second day they compassed the city once, and returned into the camp: so they did six days. And it came to pass on the seventh day that they rose early about the dawning of the day, and compassed the city after the same manner seven times: only on that day they compassed the city seven times. And it came to pass at the seventh time, when the priests blew with the trumpets, Joshua said unto the people, "Shout; for the Lord hath given you the city. And the city shall be accursed, even it, and all that are therein, to the Lord: only Rahab the harlot shall live, she and all that are with her in the house, because she hid the messengers that we sent. And ye, in any wise keep yourselves from the accursed thing, lest ye make yourselves accursed, when ye take of the accursed thing, and make the camp of Israel a curse, and trouble it. But all the silver, and gold, and vessels of brass and iron, are consecrated unto the Lord: they shall come into the treasury of the Lord." So the people shouted when the priests blew with the trumpets: and it came to pass, when the people heard the sound of the trumpet, and the people shouted with a great shout, that the wall fell down flat, so that the people went up into the city, every man straight before him, and they took the city. And they utterly destroyed all that was in the city, both man and woman, young and old, and ox, and sheep, and ass, with the edge of the sword.[44]

But Joshua had said unto the two men that had spied out the country, "Go into the harlot's house, and bring out thence the woman, and all that she hath, as ye swore unto her." And the young men that were spies went in, and brought out Rahab, and her father, and her mother, and her brethren, and all that she had; and they brought out all her kindred, and left them without the camp of Israel. And they burnt the city with fire, and all

[43] The sacred number seven occurs repeatedly in this chapter.
[44] This grim annihilation of an entire city, even of the animals, because it was "accursed," is repugnant to modern readers; there are, however, many parallels in the early history of the Semites.

that was therein: only the silver, and the gold, and the vessels of brass and of iron, they put into the treasury of the house of the Lord. And Joshua saved Rahab the harlot alive, and her father's household, and all that she had; and she dwelleth in Israel even unto this day; because she hid the messengers, which Joshua sent to spy out Jericho. And Joshua adjured them at that time, saying, "Cursed be the man before the Lord, that riseth up and buildeth this city Jericho: he shall lay the foundation thereof in his firstborn, and in his youngest son shall he set up the gates of it."

So the Lord was with Joshua; and his fame was noised throughout all the country. . . .[45]

from JOB

CHAPTER 1

There was a man in the land of Uz, whose name was Job; and that man was perfect and upright, and one that feared God, and eschewed evil. And there were born unto him seven sons and three daughters. His substance also was seven thousand sheep, and three thousand camels, and five hundred yoke of oxen, and five hundred she asses, and a very great household; so that this man was the greatest of all the men of the east.

And his sons went and feasted in their houses, every one his day; and sent and called for their three sisters to eat and to drink with them. And it was so, when the days of their feasting were gone about, that Job sent and sanctified them, and rose up early in the morning, and offered burnt offerings according to the number of them all: for Job said, "It may be that my sons have sinned, and cursed God in their hearts." Thus did Job continually.

Now there was a day when the sons of God came to present themselves before the Lord, and Satan[1] came also among them. And the Lord said unto Satan, "Whence comest thou?" Then Satan answered the Lord, and said, "From going to and fro in the earth, and from walking up and down in it." And the Lord said unto Satan, "Hast thou considered my servant Job, that there is none like him in the earth, a perfect and an upright man, one that feareth God, and escheweth evil?" Then Satan answered the Lord, and said, "Doth Job fear God for nought? Hast not thou made an hedge about him, and about his house, and about all that he hath on every side? thou hast blessed the work of his hands, and his substance is increased in the land. But put forth thine hand now, and touch all that he hath, and he will curse thee to thy face." And the Lord said unto Satan, "Behold, all that

[45] The rest of the Book of Joshua, eighteen more chapters, continues the story of Israel's conquest of Palestine in a series of triumphant sieges and battles under Joshua. The book ends with an account of Joshua's death.

[1] As the ruler of a band of evil spirits opposed to God, Satan appears by name only three times in the King James Version of the Old Testament, though he appears frequently in the New Testament. In Job, he appears in the Prologue but is never mentioned in the debate with the Comforters.

he hath is in thy power; only upon himself put not forth thine hand." So Satan went forth from the presence of the Lord.

And there was a day when his sons and his daughters were eating and drinking wine in their eldest brother's house: and there came a messenger unto Job, and said, "The oxen were plowing, and the asses feeding beside them: and the Sabeans fell upon them, and took them away; yea, they have slain the servants with the edge of the sword; and I only am escaped alone to tell thee." While he was yet speaking, there came also another, and said, "The fire of God is fallen from heaven, and hath burned up the sheep, and the servants, and consumed them; and I only am escaped alone to tell thee." While he was yet speaking, there came also another, and said, "The Chaldeans made out three bands, and fell upon the camels, and have carried them away, yea, and slain the servants with the edge of the sword; and I only am escaped alone to tell thee." While he was yet speaking, there came also another, and said, "Thy sons and thy daughters were eating and drinking wine in their eldest brother's house: and, behold, there came a great wind from the wilderness, and smote the four corners of the house, and it fell upon the young men, and they are dead; and I only am escaped alone to tell thee."

Then Job arose, and rent his mantle, and shaved his head, and fell down upon the ground, and worshipped, and said,

> "Naked came I out of my mother's womb,
> And naked shall I return thither:
> The Lord gave, and the Lord hath taken away;
> Blessed be the name of the Lord."

In all this Job sinned not, nor charged God foolishly.

CHAPTER 2

Again there was a day when the sons of God came to present themselves before the Lord, and Satan came also among them to present himself before the Lord. And the Lord said unto Satan, "From whence comest thou?" And Satan answered the Lord, and said, "From going to and fro in the earth, and from walking up and down in it." And the Lord said unto Satan, "Hast thou considered my servant Job, that there is none like him in the earth, a perfect and an upright man, one that feareth God, and escheweth evil? and still he holdeth fast his integrity, although thou movedst me against him, to destroy him without cause." And Satan answered the Lord, and said, "Skin for skin,[2] yea, all that a man hath will he give for his life. But put forth thine hand now, and touch his bone and his flesh, and he will curse thee to thy face." And the Lord said unto Satan, "Behold, he is in thine hand; but save his life."

So went Satan forth from the presence of the Lord, and smote Job with sore boils from the sole of his foot unto his crown. And he took him a

---

[2]"A hide for a hide"—a proverbial expression used by tradesmen.

potsherd[3] to scrape himself withal; and he sat down among the ashes. Then said his wife unto him, "Dost thou still retain thine integrity? curse God, and die." But he said unto her, "Thou speakest as one of the foolish women speaketh. What? shall we receive good at the hand of God, and shall we not receive evil?" In all this did not Job sin with his lips.

Now when Job's three friends heard of all this evil that was come upon him, they came every one from his own place; Eliphaz the Temanite, and Bildad the Shuhite, and Zophar the Naamathite: for they had made an appointment together to come to mourn with him and to comfort him. And when they lifted up their eyes afar off, and knew him not, they lifted up their voice, and wept; and they rent every one his mantle, and sprinkled dust upon their heads toward heaven. So they sat down with him upon the ground seven days and seven nights, and none spake a word unto him: for they saw that his grief was very great.

CHAPTER 3

After this opened Job his mouth, and cursed his day. And Job spake, and said,

"Let the day perish wherein I was born,
    and the night in which it was said, There is a man child conceived.
Let that day be darkness;
    let not God regard it from above,
    neither let the light shine upon it.
Let darkness and the shadow of death stain it;
    let a cloud dwell upon it;
    let the blackness of the day terrify it.
As for that night, let darkness seize upon it;
    let it not be joined unto the days of the year,
    let it not come into the number of the months.
Lo, let that night be solitary,
    let no joyful voice come therein.
Let them curse it that curse the day,
    who are ready to raise up their mourning.
Let the stars of the twilight thereof be dark;
    let it look for light, but have none;
    neither let it see the dawning of the day:
Because it shut not up the doors of my mother's womb,
    nor hid sorrow from mine eyes.

"Why died I not from the womb?
    why did I not give up the ghost when I came out of the belly?
Why did the knees prevent me?
    or why the breasts that I should suck?
For now should I have lain still and been quiet,
    I should have slept: then had I been at rest,

[3] A piece of broken pottery.

With kings and counsellors of the earth,
    which built desolate places for themselves;
Or with princes that had gold,
    who filled their houses with silver:
Or as an hidden untimely birth I had not been;
    as infants which never saw light.
There the wicked cease from troubling;
    and there the weary be at rest.
There the prisoners rest together;
    they hear not the voice of the oppressor.
The small and great are there;
    And the servant is free from his master.

"Wherefore is light given to him that is in misery,
    and life unto the bitter in soul;
Which long for death, but it cometh not;
    and dig for it more than for hid treasures;
Which rejoice exceedingly,
    and are glad, when they can find the grave?
Why is light given to a man whose way is hid,
    and whom God hath hedged in?
For my sighing cometh before I eat,
    and my roarings are poured out like the waters.
For the thing which I greatly feared is come upon me,
    and that which I was afraid of is come unto me.
I was not in safety, neither had I rest,
    neither was I quiet; yet trouble came."

CHAPTER 4

Then Eliphaz the Temanite answered and said,

"If we assay to commune with thee, wilt thou be grieved?
    but who can withhold himself from speaking?
Behold, thou hast instructed many,
    and thou hast strengthened the weak hands.
Thy words have upholden him that was falling,
    and thou hast strengthened the feeble knees.
But now it is come upon thee, and thou faintest;
    it toucheth thee, and thou art troubled.
Is not this thy fear, thy confidence, thy hope,
    and the uprightness of thy ways?
Remember, I pray thee, who ever perished, being innocent?
    or where were the righteous cut off?[4]
Even as I have seen, they that plow iniquity,
    and sow wickedness, reap the same.

---

[4] Here, as throughout, Eliphaz upholds the doctrine that the good prosper and the wicked are punished in this world. Suffering is thus a proof of sin.

By the blast of God they perish,
    and by the breath of his nostrils are they consumed.
The roaring of the lion, and the voice of the fierce lion,
    and the teeth of the young lions, are broken.
The old lion perisheth for lack of prey,
    and the stout lion's whelps are scattered abroad.

"Now a thing was secretly brought to me,
    and mine ear received a little thereof.
In thoughts from the visions of the night,
    when deep sleep falleth on men,
Fear came upon me, and trembling,
    which made all my bones to shake.
Then a spirit passed before my face;
    the hair of my flesh stood up:
It stood still,
    but I could not discern the form thereof:
An image was before mine eyes,
    there was silence, and I heard a voice, saying,
Shall mortal man be more just than God?
    shall a man be more pure than his maker?
Behold, he put no trust in his servants;
    and his angels he charged with folly:
How much less in them that dwell in houses of clay,
    whose foundation is in the dust,
    which are crushed before the moth?
They are destroyed from morning to evening:
    they perish for ever without any regarding it.
Doth not their excellency which is in them go away?
    they die, even without wisdom."

CHAPTER 5

"Call now, if there be any that will answer thee;
    and to which of the saints wilt thou turn?
For wrath killeth the foolish man,
    and envy slayeth the silly one.
I have seen the foolish taking root:
    but suddenly I cursed his habitation.
His children are far from safety,
    and they are crushed in the gate,
    neither is there any to deliver them.
Whose harvest the hungry eateth up,
    and taketh it even out of the thorns,
    and the robber swalloweth up their substance.
Although affliction cometh not forth of the dust,
    neither doth trouble spring out of the ground;
Yet man is born unto trouble,
    as the sparks fly upward.

"I would seek unto God,
    and unto God would I commit my cause:
Which doeth great things and unsearchable;
    marvellous things without number:
Who giveth rain upon the earth,
    and sendeth waters upon the fields:
To set up on high those that be low;
    that those which mourn may be exalted to safety.
He disappointeth the devices of the crafty,
    so that their hands cannot perform their enterprise.
He taketh the wise in their own craftiness:
    and the counsel of the froward is carried headlong.
They meet with darkness in the daytime,
    and grope in the noonday as in the night.
But he saveth the poor from the sword,
    from their mouth, and from the hand of the mighty.
So the poor hath hope,
    And iniquity stoppeth her mouth.

"Behold, happy is the man whom God correcteth:
    therefore despise not thou the chastening of the Almighty:[5]
For he maketh sore, and bindeth up:
    he woundeth, and his hands make whole.
He shall deliver thee in six troubles:
    yea, in seven there shall no evil touch thee.
In famine he shall redeem thee from death:
    and in war from the power of the sword.
Thou shalt be hid from the scourge of the tongue:
    neither shalt thou be afraid of destruction when it cometh.
At destruction and famine thou shalt laugh:
    neither shalt thou be afraid of the beasts of the earth.
For thou shalt be in league with the stones of the field:
    and the beasts of the field shall be at peace with thee.
And thou shalt know that thy tabernacle shall be in peace;
    and thou shalt visit thy habitation, and shalt not sin.
Thou shalt know also that thy seed shall be great,
    and thine offspring as the grass of the earth.
Thou shalt come to thy grave in a full age,
    like as a shock of corn cometh in in his season.
Lo this, we have searched it, so it is;
    hear it, and know thou it for thy good."

CHAPTER 6

But Job answered and said,

"Oh that my grief were thoroughly weighed,
    and my calamity laid in the balances together!

---

[5] This is the orthodox Jewish doctrine of *musar;* God imposes suffering to chasten or correct.

For now it would be heavier than the sand of the sea:
    therefore my words are swallowed up.[6]
For the arrows of the Almighty are within me,
    the poison whereof drinketh up my spirit:
    the terrors of God do set themselves in array against me.
Doth the wild ass bray when he hath grass?
    or loweth the ox over his fodder?
Can that which is unsavory be eaten without salt?
    or is there any taste in the white of an egg?
The things that my soul refused to touch
    are as my sorrowful meat.
Oh that I might have my request;
    and that God would grant me the thing that I long for!
Even that it would please God to destroy me;
    that he would let loose his hand, and cut me off!
Then should I yet have comfort;
    yea, I would harden myself in sorrow: let him not spare;
    for I have not concealed the words of the Holy One.
What is my strength, that I should hope?
    and what is mine end, that I should prolong my life?
Is my strength the strength of stones?
    or is my flesh of brass?
Is not my help in me?
    and is wisdom driven quite from me?

"To him that is afflicted pity should be showed from his friend;
    but he forsaketh the fear of the Almighty.
My brethren have dealt deceitfully as a brook,
    and as the stream of brooks they pass away;
Which are blackish by reason of the ice,
    and wherein the snow is hid:
What time they wax warm, they vanish:
    when it is hot, they are consumed out of their place.
The paths of their way are turned aside;
    they go to nothing, and perish.
The troops of Tema looked,
    the companies of Sheba waited for them.
They were confounded because they had hoped;
    they came thither, and were ashamed.
For now ye are nothing;
    ye see my casting down, and are afraid.
Did I say, 'Bring unto me'?
    or, 'Give a reward for me of your substance'?
Or, 'Deliver me from the enemy's hand'?
    or, 'Redeem me from the hand of the mighty'?

"Teach me, and I will hold my tongue:
    and cause me to understand wherein I have erred.

---

[6] Job replies to Eliphaz by saying that the orthodox explanation cannot be valid in his case, since his suffering exceeds any possible cause.

How forcible are right words!
　　but what doth your arguing reprove?
Do ye imagine to reprove words,
　　and the speeches of one that is desperate, which are as wind?
Yea, ye overwhelm the fatherless,
　　and ye dig a pit for your friend.

"Now therefore be content, look upon me;
　　for it is evident unto you if I lie.
Return, I pray you, let it not be iniquity;
　　yea, return again, my righteousness is in it.[7]
Is there iniquity in my tongue?
　　cannot my taste discern perverse things?"

CHAPTER 7

"Is there not an appointed time to man upon earth?
　　are not his days also like the days of an hireling?
As a servant earnestly desireth the shadow,
　　and as an hireling looketh for the reward of his work:
So am I made to possess months of vanity,
　　and wearisome nights are appointed to me.
When I lie down, I say, 'When shall I arise, and the night be gone?'
　　and I am full of tossings to and fro unto the dawning of the day.
My flesh is clothed with worms and clods of dust;
　　my skin is broken, and become loathsome.
My days are swifter than a weaver's shuttle,
　　and are spent without hope.

"O remember that my life is wind:
　　mine eye shall no more see good.
The eye of him that hath seen me shall see me no more:
　　thine eyes are upon me, and I am not.
As the cloud is consumed and vanisheth away:
　　so he that goeth down to the grave shall come up no more.
He shall return no more to his house,
　　neither shall his place know him any more.

"Therefore I will not refrain my mouth;
　　I will speak in the anguish of my spirit;
　　I will complain in the bitterness of my soul.
Am I a sea, or a whale,
　　that thou settest a watch over me?
When I say, 'My bed shall comfort me,
　　my couch shall ease my complaint';
Then thou scarest me with dreams,
　　and terrifiest me through visions:
So that my soul chooseth strangling,
　　and death rather than my life.

[7] This line would be clearer if translated "Let no injustice be done; my cause is righteous."

I loathe it; I would not live alway:
    let me alone; for my days are vanity.
What is man, that thou shouldest magnify him?
    and that thou shouldest set thine heart upon him?
And that thou shouldest visit him every morning,
    and try him every moment?
How long wilt thou not depart from me,
    nor let me alone till I swallow down my spittle?
I have sinned; what shall I do unto thee, O thou preserver of men?
    why hast thou set me as a mark against thee,
    so that I am a burden to myself?
And why dost thou not pardon my transgression,
    and take away mine iniquity?
For now shall I sleep in the dust;
    and thou shalt seek me in the morning, but I shall not be."

CHAPTER 8

Then answered Bildad the Shuhite, and said,

"How long wilt thou speak these things?
    and how long shall the words of thy mouth be like a strong wind?
Doth God pervert judgment?
    or doth the Almighty pervert justice?
If thy children have sinned against him,
    and he have cast them away for their transgression;
If thou wouldest seek unto God betimes,
    and make thy supplication to the Almighty;
If thou wert pure and upright;
    surely now he would awake for thee,
    and make the habitation of thy righteousness prosperous.
Though thy beginning was small,
    yet thy latter end should greatly increase.

"For enquire, I pray thee, of the former age,
    and prepare thyself to the search of their fathers:[8]
(For we are but of yesterday, and know nothing,
    because our days upon earth are a shadow:)
Shall not they teach thee, and tell thee,
    and utter words out of their heart?
Can the rush grow up without mire?
    can the flag grow without water?
Whilst it is yet in his greenness, and not cut down,
    It withereth before any other herb.
So are the paths of all that forget God;
    and the hypocrite's hope shall perish:

---

[8] In his eagerness to uphold orthodoxy, Bildad suggests that the cause of Job's suffering may be not in his own sins but in those of his family.

Whose hope shall be cut off,
    and whose trust shall be a spider's web.
He shall lean upon his house, but it shall not stand:
    he shall hold it fast, but it shall not endure.
He is green before the sun,
    and his branch shooteth forth in his garden.
His roots are wrapped about the heap,
    and seeth the place of stones.
If he destroy him from his place,
    then it shall deny him, saying, 'I have not seen thee.'
Behold, this is the joy of his way,
    and out of the earth shall others grow.

"Behold, God will not cast away a perfect man,
    neither will he help the evil doers:
Till he fill thy mouth with laughing,
    and thy lips with rejoicing.
They that hate thee shall be clothed with shame;
    and the dwelling place of the wicked shall come to nought."

CHAPTER 9

Then Job answered and said,

"I know it is so of a truth:
    but how should man be just with God?
If he will contend with him,
    he cannot answer him one of a thousand.
He is wise in heart, and mighty in strength:
    who hath hardened himself against him, and hath prospered?
Which removeth the mountains, and they know not:
    which overturneth them in his anger.
Which shaketh the earth out of her place,
    and the pillars thereof tremble.
Which commandeth the sun, and it riseth not;
    and sealeth up the stars.
Which alone spreadeth out the heavens,
    and treadeth upon the waves of the sea.
Which maketh Arcturus, Orion, and Pleiades,
    and the chambers of the south.
Which doeth great things past finding out;
    yea, and wonders without number.
Lo, he goeth by me, and I see him not:
    he passeth on also, but I perceive him not.
Behold, he taketh away, who can hinder him?
    Who will say unto him, 'What doest thou?'

"If God will not withdraw his anger,
    the proud helpers do stoop under him.
How much less shall I answer him,
    and choose out my words to reason with him?

Whom, though I were righteous, yet would I not answer,
  but I would make supplication to my judge.
If I had called, and he had answered me;
  yet would I not believe that he had hearkened unto my voice.
For he breaketh me with a tempest,
  and multiplieth my wounds without cause.
He will not suffer me to take my breath,
  but filleth me with bitterness.
If I speak of strength, lo, he is strong:
  and if of judgment, who shall set me a time to plead?
If I justify myself, mine own mouth shall condemn me:
  if I say, I am perfect, it shall also prove me perverse.
Though I were perfect, yet would I not know my soul:
  I would despise my life.
This is one thing, therefore I said it,
  he destroyeth the perfect and the wicked.
If the scourge slay suddenly,
  he will laugh at the trial of the innocent.
The earth is given into the hand of the wicked:
  he covereth the faces of the judges thereof;
  if not, where, and who is he?

"Now my days are swifter than a post:[9]
  they flee away, they see no good.
They are passed away as the swift ships:
  as the eagle that hasteth to the prey.
If I say, 'I will forget my complaint,
  I will leave off my heaviness, and comfort myself':
I am afraid of all my sorrows,
  I know that thou wilt not hold me innocent.
If I be wicked, why then labor I in vain?
If I wash myself with snow water,
  and make my hands never so clean;
Yet shalt thou plunge me in the ditch,
  and mine own clothes shall abhor me.
For he is not a man, as I am, that I should answer him,
  and we should come together in judgment.
Neither is there any daysman[10] betwixt us,
  that might lay his hand upon us both.
Let him take his rod away from me,
  and let not his fear terrify me:
Then would I speak, and not fear him;
  but it is not so with me.

CHAPTER 10

"My soul is weary of my life; I will leave my complaint upon myself;
  I will speak in the bitterness of my soul.

[9]Runner.   [10]Umpire.

I will say unto God, 'Do not condemn me;
 show me wherefore thou contendest with me.
Is it good unto thee that thou shouldest oppress,
 that thou shouldest despise the work of thine hands,
 and shine upon the counsel of the wicked?
Hast thou eyes of flesh?
 or seest thou as man seeth?
Are thy days as the days of man?
 are thy years as man's days,
That thou enquirest after mine iniquity,
 and searchest after my sin?
Thou knowest that I am not wicked;
 and there is none that can deliver out of thine hand.
Thine hands have made me and fashioned me together round about;
 yet thou dost destroy me.
Remember, I beseech thee, that thou hast made me as the clay;
 And wilt thou bring me into dust again?
Hast thou not poured me out as milk,
 and curdled me like cheese?
Thou hast clothed me with skin and flesh,
 and hast fenced me with bones and sinews:
Thou hast granted me life and favor,
 and thy visitation hath preserved my spirit.
And these things hast thou hid in thine heart:
 I know that this is with thee.
If I sin, then thou markest me,
 and thou wilt not acquit me from mine iniquity.
If I be wicked, woe unto me;
 and if I be righteous, yet will I not lift up my head.
I am full of confusion;
 therefore see thou mine affliction;
For it increaseth. Thou huntest me as a fierce lion:
 and again thou showest thyself marvellous upon me.
Thou renewest thy witnesses against me,
 and increasest thine indignation upon me;
 changes and war are against me.

"Wherefore then hast thou brought me forth out of the womb?
 Oh that I had given up the ghost, and no eye had seen me!
I should have been as though I had not been;
 I should have been carried from the womb to the grave.
Are not my days few? cease then,
 and let me alone, that I may take comfort a little,
Before I go whence I shall not return,
 even to the land of darkness[11] and the shadow of death;

---

[11] The concept of hell, like the figure of Satan, is late in developing in the Old Testament period. The "land of darkness" mentioned here is the Hebrew *sheol*, a shadowy place where the dead go, similar to the Greek "Hades." It does not imply reward or punishment for one's life on earth.

A land of darkness, as darkness itself;
    and of the shadow of death, without any order,
    and where the light is as darkness."

CHAPTER 11

Then answered Zophar the Naamathite, and said,

"Should not the multitude of words be answered?
    and should a man full of talk be justified?
Should thy lies make men hold their peace?
    and when thou mockest, shall no man make thee ashamed?
For thou hast said, 'My doctrine is pure,
    and I am clean in thine eyes.'
But oh that God would speak,
    and open his lips against thee;
And that he would show thee the secrets of wisdom,
    that they are double to that which is!
Know therefore that God exacteth of thee less than thine iniquity
        deserveth.[12]

"Canst thou by searching find out God?
    canst thou find out the Almighty unto perfection?
It is as high as heaven; what canst thou do?
    deeper than hell; what canst thou know?
The measure thereof is longer than the earth,
    and broader than the sea.
If he cut off, and shut up,
    or gather together, then who can hinder him?
For he knoweth vain men:
    he seeth wickedness also; will he not then consider it?
For vain man would be wise,
    though man be born like a wild ass's colt.

"If thou prepare thine heart,
    and stretch out thine hands toward him;
If iniquity be in thine hand, put it far away,
    and let not wickedness dwell in thy tabernacles.
For then shalt thou lift up thy face without spot;
    yea, thou shalt be steadfast, and shalt not fear:
Because thou shalt forget thy misery,
    and remember it as waters that pass away:
And thine age shall be clearer than the noonday;
    thou shalt shine forth, thou shalt be as the morning.
And thou shalt be secure, because there is hope;
    yea thou shalt dig about thee, and thou shalt take thy rest in safety.
Also thou shalt lie down, and none shall make thee afraid;
    yea, many shall make suit unto thee.

[12] Zophar, too, insists that Job has deserved his suffering and that God dispenses justice on earth.

But the eyes of the wicked shall fail, and they shall not escape,
 and their hope shall be as the giving up of the ghost."

CHAPTER 12

And Job answered and said,

"No doubt but ye are the people,
 and wisdom shall die with you.
But I have understanding as well as you;
 I am not inferior to you:
 yea, who knoweth not such things as these?
I am as one mocked of his neighbor,
 who calleth upon God, and he answereth him:
 the just upright man is laughed to scorn.
He that is ready to slip with his feet
 is as a lamp despised in the thought of him that is at ease.
The tabernacles of robbers prosper,
 and they that provoke God are secure;
 into whose hand God bringeth abundantly.

"But ask now the beasts, and they shall teach thee;
 and the fowls of the air, and they shall tell thee:
Or speak to the earth, and it shall teach thee:
 and the fishes of the sea shall declare unto thee.
Who knoweth not in all these
 that the hand of the Lord hath wrought this?
In whose hand is the soul of every living thing,
 and the breath of all mankind.
Doth not the ear try words?
 and the mouth taste his meat?
With the ancient is wisdom;
 and in length of days understanding.

"With him is wisdom and strength,
 he hath counsel and understanding.
Behold, he breaketh down, and it cannot be built again:
 he shutteth up a man, and there can be no opening.
Behold, he withholdeth the waters, and they dry up:
 also he sendeth them out, and they overturn the earth.
With him is strength and wisdom:
 the deceived and the deceiver are his.
He leadeth counsellors away spoiled,
 and maketh the judges fools.
He looseth the bond of kings,
 and girdeth their loins with a girdle.
He leadeth princes away spoiled,
 and overthroweth the mighty.
He removeth away the speech of the trusty,
 and taketh away the understanding of the aged.

He poureth contempt upon princes,
  and weakeneth the strength of the mighty.
He discovereth deep things out of darkness,
  and bringeth out to light the shadow of death.
He increaseth the nations, and destroyeth them:
  he enlargeth the nations, and straiteneth them again.
He taketh away the heart of the chief of the people of the earth,
  and causeth them to wander in a wilderness where there is no way.
They grope in the dark without light,
  and he maketh them to stagger like a drunken man."

CHAPTER 13

"Lo, mine eye hath seen all this,
  mine ear hath heard and understood it.
What ye know, the same do I know also:
  I am not inferior unto you.
Surely I would speak to the Almighty,
  and I desire to reason with God.
But ye are forgers of lies,
  ye are all physicians of no value.
O that ye would altogether hold your peace!
  and it should be your wisdom.
Hear now my reasoning,
  and hearken to the pleadings of my lips.
Will ye speak wickedly for God?
  and talk deceitfully for him?
Will ye accept his person?
  will ye contend for God?
Is it good that he should search you out?
  or as one man mocketh another, do ye so mock him?
He will surely reprove you,
  if ye do secretly accept persons.
Shall not his excellency make you afraid?
  and his dread fall upon you?
Your remembrances are like unto ashes,
  your bodies to bodies of clay.
Hold your peace, let me alone, that I may speak,
  and let come on me what will.
Wherefore do I take my flesh in my teeth,
  and put my life in mine hand?
Though he slay me, yet will I trust in him:[13]
  but I will maintain mine own ways before him.
He also shall be my salvation:
  for an hypocrite shall not come before him.[14]

---

[13] The latter part of this line should read "I have no hope," a more defiant and despairing statement.

[14] Job argues that his eagerness to confront God is a proof of his blamelessness, for a guilty man would not dare to come before Him.

Hear diligently my speech,
    and my declaration with your ears.
Behold now, I have ordered my cause;
    I know that I shall be justified.
Who is he that will plead with me?
    for now, if I hold my tongue, I shall give up the ghost.
Only do not two things unto me:
    then will I not hide myself from thee.
Withdraw thine hand far from me:
    and let not thy dread make me afraid.
Then call thou, and I will answer:
    or let me speak, and answer thou me.
How many are mine iniquities and sins?
    make me to know my transgression and my sin.
Wherefore hidest thou thy face,
    and holdest me for thine enemy?
Wilt thou break a leaf driven to and fro?
    and wilt thou pursue the dry stubble?
For thou writest bitter things against me,
    and makest me to possess the iniquities of my youth.
Thou puttest my feet also in the stocks,
    and lookest narrowly unto all my paths;
    thou settest a print upon the heels of my feet.
And he, as a rotten thing, consumeth,
    as a garment that is moth eaten."

CHAPTER 14

"Man that is born of a woman
    is of few days, and full of trouble.
He cometh forth like a flower, and is cut down:
    he fleeth also as a shadow, and continueth not.
And dost thou open thine eyes upon such an one,
    and bringest me into judgment with thee?
Who can bring a clean thing out of an unclean?
    not one.
Seeing his days are determined,
    the number of his months are with thee,
    thou hast appointed his bounds that he cannot pass;
Turn from him, that he may rest,
    till he shall accomplish, as an hireling, his day.

"For there is hope of a tree, if it be cut down, that it will sprout again,
    and that the tender branch thereof will not cease.
Though the root thereof wax old in the earth,
    and the stock thereof die in the ground;
Yet through the scent of water it will bud,
    and bring forth boughs like a plant.
But man dieth, and wasteth away:
    yea, man giveth up the ghost, and where is he?

As the waters fail from the sea,
    and the flood decayeth and drieth up:
So man lieth down, and riseth not:
    till the heavens be no more, they shall not awake,
    nor be raised out of their sleep.
O that thou wouldest hide me in the grave,
    that thou wouldest keep me secret, until thy wrath be past,
    that thou wouldest appoint me a set time, and remember me!
If a man die, shall he live again?
    all the days of my appointed time will I wait,
    till my change come.
Thou shalt call, and I will answer thee:
    thou wilt have a desire to the work of thine hands.
For now thou numberest my steps:
    dost thou not watch over my sin?
My transgression is sealed up in a bag,
    and thou sewest up mine iniquity.

"And surely the mountain falling cometh to nought,
    and the rock is removed out of his place.
The waters wear the stones:
    thou washest away the things which grow out of the dust of the earth;
    and thou destroyest the hope of man.
Thou prevailest for ever against him, and he passeth:
    thou changest his countenance, and sendest him away.
His sons come to honor, and he knoweth it not;
    and they are brought low, but he perceiveth it not of them.
But his flesh upon him shall have pain,
    and his soul within him shall mourn."

CHAPTER 19

Then Job answered [the Comforters] and said,

"How long will ye vex my soul,
    and break me in pieces with words?
These ten times have ye reproached me:
    ye are not ashamed that ye make yourselves strange to me.
And be it indeed that I have erred,
    mine error remaineth with myself.
If indeed ye will magnify yourselves against me,
    and plead against me my reproach:
Know now that God hath overthrown me,
    and hath compassed me with his net.
Behold, I cry out of wrong, but I am not heard:
    I cry aloud, but there is no judgment.
He hath fenced up my way that I cannot pass,
    and he hath set darkness in my paths.

He hath stripped me of my glory,
and taken the crown from my head.
He hath destroyed me on every side, and I am gone:
and mine hope hath he removed like a tree.
He hath also kindled his wrath against me,
and he counteth me unto him as one of his enemies.
His troops come together,
and raise up their way against me,
and encamp round about my tabernacle.

"He hath put my brethren far from me,
and mine acquaintance are verily estranged from me.
My kinsfolk have failed,
and my familiar friends have forgotten me.
They that dwell in mine house, and my maids, count me for a stranger:
I am an alien in their sight.
I called my servant, and he gave me no answer;
I intreated him with my mouth.
My breath is strange to my wife,
though I intreated for the children's sake of mine own body.
Yea, young children despised me;
I arose, and they spake against me.
All my inward friends abhorred me:
and they whom I loved are turned against me.
My bone cleaveth to my skin and to my flesh,
and I am escaped with the skin of my teeth.
Have pity upon me, have pity upon me, O ye my friends;
for the hand of God hath touched me.
Why do ye persecute me as God,
and are not satisfied with my flesh?

"Oh that my words were now written!
Oh that they were printed in a book!
That they were graven with an iron pen
and lead in the rock for ever!
For I know that my redeemer liveth,
and that he shall stand at the latter day upon the earth:
And though after my skin worms destroy this body,
yet in my flesh shall I see God:
Whom I shall see for myself,
and mine eyes shall behold, and not another;[15]
though my reins be consumed within me.
But ye should say, 'Why persecute we him,
seeing the root of the matter is found in me?'
Be ye afraid of the sword:
for wrath bringeth the punishments of the sword,
that ye may know there is a judgment."

[15] The Hebrew text is unclear at this point. The word translated "Redeemer" here was a legal term meaning "avenger" or "vindicator." Job probably is saying that after his death he will see God, in the role of "avenger," vindicate him posthumously in the eyes of the world.

CHAPTER 29

Moreover Job continued his parable, and said,

"Oh that I were as in months past,
        as in the days when God preserved me;
When his candle shined upon my head,
        and when by his light I walked through darkness;
As I was in the days of my youth,
        when the secret of God was upon my tabernacle;
When the Almighty was yet with me,
        when my children were about me;
When I washed my steps with butter,
        and the rock poured me out rivers of oil;
When I went out to the gate through the city,
        when I prepared my seat in the street!
The young men saw me, and hid themselves:
        and the aged arose, and stood up.
The princes refrained talking,
        and laid their hand on their mouth.
The nobles held their peace,
        and their tongue cleaved to the roof of their mouth.
When the ear heard me, then it blessed me;
        and when the eye saw me, it gave witness to me:
Because I delivered the poor that cried,
        and the fatherless, and him that had none to help him.
The blessing of him that was ready to perish came upon me:
        and I caused the widow's heart to sing for joy.
I put on righteousness, and it clothed me:
        my judgment was as a robe and a diadem.
I was eyes to the blind,
        and feet was I to the lame.
I was a father to the poor:
        and the cause which I knew not I searched out.
And I brake the jaws of the wicked,
        and plucked the spoil out of his teeth.
Then I said, 'I shall die in my nest,
        and I shall multiply my days as the sand.'
My root was spread out by the waters,
        and the dew lay all night upon my branch.
My glory was fresh in me,
        and my bow was renewed in my hand.

"Unto me men gave ear,
        and waited, and kept silence at my counsel.
After my words they spake not again;
        and my speech dropped upon them.
And they waited for me as for the rain;
        and they opened their mouth wide as for the latter rain.
If I laughed on them, they believed it not;
        and the light of my countenance they cast not down.

I chose out their way, and sat chief,
    and dwelt as a king in the army,
    as one that comforteth the mourners."

CHAPTER 30

"But now they that are younger than I
    have me in derision,
Whose fathers I would have disdained
    to have set with the dogs of my flock.
Yea, whereto might the strength of their hands profit me,
    in whom old age was perished?
For want and famine they were solitary;
    fleeing into the wilderness in former time desolate and waste.
Who cut up mallows by the bushes,
    and juniper roots for their meat.
They were driven forth from among men,
    (they cried after them as after a thief;)
To dwell in the cliffs of the valleys,
    in caves of the earth, and in the rocks.
Among the bushes they brayed;
    under the nettles they were gathered together.
They were children of fools, yea, children of base men:
    they were viler than the earth.

"And now am I their song,
    yea, I am their byword.
They abhor me, they flee far from me,
    and spare not to spit in my face.
Because he hath loosed my cord, and afflicted me,
    they have also let loose the bridle before me.
Upon my right hand rise the youth;
    they push away my feet,
And they raise up against me
    the ways of their destruction.
They mar my path,
    they set forward my calamity, they have no helper.
They came upon me as a wide breaking in of waters:
    in the desolation they rolled themselves upon me.
Terrors are turned upon me:
    they pursue my soul as the wind:
    and my welfare passeth away as a cloud.

"And now my soul is poured out upon me;
    the days of affliction have taken hold upon me.
My bones are pierced in me in the night season:
    and my sinews take no rest.
By the great force of my disease is my garment changed:
    it bindeth me about as the collar of my coat.

He hath cast me into the mire,
    and I am become like dust and ashes.
I cry unto thee, and thou dost not hear me:
    I stand up, and thou regardest me not.
Thou art become cruel to me:
    with thy strong hand thou opposest thyself against me.
Thou liftest me up to the wind;
    thou causest me to ride upon it,
    and dissolvest my substance.
For I know that thou wilt bring me to death,
    and to the house appointed for all living.

"Howbeit he will not stretch out his hand to the grave,
    though they cry in his destruction.
Did not I weep for him that was in trouble?
    was not my soul grieved for the poor?
When I looked for good, then evil came unto me:
    and when I waited for light, there came darkness.
My bowels boiled, and rested not:
    the days of affliction prevented me.
I went mourning without the sun:
    I stood up, and I cried in the congregation.
I am a brother to dragons,
    and a companion to owls.
My skin is black upon me,
    and my bones are burned with heat.
My harp also is turned to mourning,
    and my organ into the voice of them that weep."

CHAPTER 31

"I made a covenant with mine eyes;
    why then should I think upon a maid?
For what portion of God is there from above?
    and what inheritance of the Almighty from on high?
Is not destruction to the wicked?
    and a strange punishment to the workers of iniquity?
Doth not he see my ways,
    and count all my steps?

If I have walked with vanity,
    or if my foot hath hasted to deceit;
Let me be weighed in an even balance,
    that God may know mine integrity.
If my step hath turned out of the way,
    and mine heart walked after mine eyes,
    and if any blot hath cleaved to mine hands;
Then let me sow, and let another eat;
    yea, let my offspring be rooted out.

"If mine heart have been deceived by a woman,
    or if I have laid wait at my neighbor's door;
Then let my wife grind unto another,[16]
    and let others bow down upon her.
For this is an heinous crime;
    yea, it is an iniquity to be punished by the judges.
For it is a fire that consumeth to destruction,
    and would root out all mine increase.

"If I did despise the cause of my manservant or of my maidservant,
    when they contended with me;
What then shall I do when God riseth up?
    and when he visiteth, what shall I answer him?
Did not he that made me in the womb make him?
    and did not one fashion us in the womb?

"If I have withheld the poor from their desire,
    or have caused the eyes of the widow to fail;
Or have eaten my morsel myself alone,
    and the fatherless hath not eaten thereof;
(For from my youth he was brought up with me, as with a father,
    and I have guided her from my mother's womb;)
If I have seen any perish for want of clothing,
    or any poor without covering;
If his loins have not blessed me,
    and if he were not warmed with the fleece of my sheep;
If I have lifted up my hand against the fatherless,
    when I saw my help in the gate:
Then let mine arm fall from my shoulder blade,
    and mine arm be broken from the bone.
For destruction from God was a terror to me,
    and by reason of his highness I could not endure.

"If I have made gold my hope,
    or have said to the fine gold, 'Thou art my confidence';
If I rejoiced because my wealth was great,
    and because mine hand had gotten much;
If I beheld the sun when it shined,
    or the moon walking in brightness;
And my heart hath been secretly enticed,
    or my mouth hath kissed my hand:
This also were an iniquity to be punished by the judge:
    for I should have denied the God that is above.

"If I rejoiced at the destruction of him that hated me,
    or lifted up myself when evil found him:
Neither have I suffered my mouth to sin
    by wishing a curse to his soul.

[16] That is, grind grain as a servant for someone else.

If the men of my tabernacle said not,
    'Oh that we had of his flesh! we cannot be satisfied.'
The stranger did not lodge in the street:
    but I opened my doors to the traveller.
If I covered my transgressions as Adam,
    by hiding mine iniquity in my bosom:
Did I fear a great multitude,
    or did the contempt of families terrify me,
    that I kept silence, and went not out of the door?
Oh that one would hear me!
    behold, my desire is, that the Almighty would answer me,
    and that mine adversary had written a book.
Surely I would take it upon my shoulder,
    and bind it as a crown to me.
I would declare unto him the number of my steps;
    as a prince would I go near unto him.

"If my land cry against me,
    or that the furrows likewise thereof complain;
If I have eaten the fruits thereof without money,
    or have caused the owners thereof to lose their life:
Let thistles grow instead of wheat,
    and cockle instead of barley."

The words of Job are ended.

CHAPTER 38

Then the Lord answered Job out of the whirlwind,[17] and said,

"Who is this that darkeneth counsel
    by words without knowledge?
Gird up now thy loins like a man;
    for I will demand of thee, and answer thou me.

"Where wast thou when I laid the foundations of the earth?
    declare, if thou hast understanding.
Who hath laid the measures thereof, if thou knowest?
    or who hath stretched the line upon it?
Whereupon are the foundations thereof fastened?
    or who laid the corner stone thereof;
When the morning stars sang together,
    and all the sons of God shouted for joy?

"Or who shut up the sea with doors,
    when it brake forth, as if it had issued out of the womb?
When I made the cloud the garment thereof,
    and thick darkness a swaddlingband for it,

---

[17] God appears in a whirlwind elsewhere in the Old Testament as well, notably in Nahum
1:3 and Psalms 18:7–15.

And brake up for it my decreed place,
    and set bars and doors,
And said, 'Hitherto shalt thou come, but no further:
    and here shall thy proud waves be stayed'?
Hast thou commanded the morning since thy days;
    and caused the dayspring[18] to know his place;
That it might take hold of the ends of the earth,
    that the wicked might be shaken out of it?
It is turned as clay to the seal;
    and they stand as a garment.
And from the wicked their light is withholden,
    and the high arm shall be broken.

"Hast thou entered into the springs of the sea?
    or hast thou walked in the search of the depth?
Have the gates of death been opened unto thee?
    or hast thou seen the doors of the shadow of death?
Hast thou perceived the breadth of the earth?
    declare if thou knowest it all.

"Where is the way where light dwelleth?
    and as for darkness, where is the place thereof,
That thou shouldest take it to the bound thereof,
    and that thou shouldest know the paths to the house thereof?
Knowest thou it, because thou wast then born?
    or because the number of thy days is great?

"Hast thou entered into the treasures of the snow?
    or hast thou seen the treasures of the hail,
Which I have reserved against the time of trouble,
    against the day of battle and war?
By what way is the light parted,
    which scattereth the east wind upon the earth?
Who hath divided a watercourse for the overflowing of waters,
    or a way for the lightning of thunder;
To cause it to rain on the earth, where no man is;
    on the wilderness, wherein there is no man;
To satisfy the desolate and waste ground;
    and to cause the bud of the tender herb to spring forth?

"Hath the rain a father?
    or who hath begotten the drops of dew?
Out of whose womb came the ice?
    and the hoary frost of heaven, who hath gendered it?
The waters are hid as with a stone,
    and the face of the deep is frozen.

"Canst thou bind the sweet influences of Pleiades,
    or loose the bands of Orion?
Canst thou bring forth Mazzaroth in his season?
    or canst thou guide Arcturus with his sons?[19]

[18] Dawn.   [19] These are all stars or constellations.

Knowest thou the ordinances of heaven?
    canst thou set the dominion thereof in the earth?

"Canst thou lift up thy voice to the clouds,
    that abundance of waters may cover thee?
Canst thou send lightnings, that they may go,
    and say unto thee, 'Here we are'?
Who hath put wisdom in the inward parts?
    or who hath given understanding to the heart?
Who can number the clouds in wisdom?
    or who can stay the bottles of heaven,
When the dust groweth into hardness,
    and the clods cleave fast together?

"Wilt thou hunt the prey for the lion?
    or fill the appetite of the young lions,
When they couch in their dens,
    and abide in the covert to lie in wait?
Who provideth for the raven his food?
    when his young ones cry unto God,
    they wander for lack of meat."

CHAPTER 39

"Knowest thou the time when the wild goats of the rock bring forth?
    or canst thou mark when the hinds do calve?
Canst thou number the months that they fulfil?
    or knowest thou the time when they bring forth?
They bow themselves, they bring forth their young ones,
    they cast out their sorrows.
Their young ones are in good liking, they grow up with corn;
    they go forth, and return not unto them.

"Who hath sent out the wild ass free?
    or who hath loosed the bands of the wild ass?
Whose house I have made the wilderness,
    and the barren land his dwellings.
He scorneth the multitude of the city,
    neither regardeth he the crying of the driver.
The range of the mountains is his pasture,
    and he searcheth after every green thing.

"Will the unicorn[20] be willing to serve thee,
    or abide by thy crib?
Canst thou bind the unicorn with his band in the furrow?
    or will he harrow the valleys after thee?
Wilt thou trust him, because his strength is great?
    or wilt thou leave thy labor to him?

[20] Or wild ox.

Wilt thou believe him, that he will bring home thy seed,
    and gather it into thy barn?

"Gavest thou the goodly wings unto the peacocks?
    or wings and feathers unto the ostrich?
Which leaveth her eggs in the earth,
    and warmeth them in dust,
And forgetteth that the foot may crush them,
    or that the wild beast may break them.
She is hardened against her young ones, as though they were not hers:
    her labor is in vain without fear;
Because God hath deprived her of wisdom,
    neither hath he imparted to her understanding.
What time she lifteth up herself on high,
    she scorneth the horse and his rider.

"Hast thou given the horse strength?
    hast thou clothed his neck with thunder?
Canst thou make him afraid as a grasshopper?
    the glory of his nostrils is terrible.
He paweth in the valley, and rejoiceth in his strength:
    he goeth on to meet the armed men.
He mocketh at fear, and is not affrighted;
    neither turneth he back from the sword.
The quiver rattleth against him,
    the glittering spear and the shield.
He swalloweth the ground with fierceness and rage:
    neither believeth he that it is the sound of the trumpet.
He saith among the trumpets, 'Ha, ha';
    and he smelleth the battle afar off,
    the thunder of the captains, and the shouting.

"Doth the hawk fly by thy wisdom,
    and stretch her wings toward the south?
Doth the eagle mount up at thy command,
    and make her nest on high?
She dwelleth and abideth on the rock,
    upon the crag of the rock, and the strong place.
From thence she seeketh the prey,
    and her eyes behold afar off.
Her young ones also suck up blood:
    and where the slain are, there is she."

CHAPTER 40

Moreover the Lord answered Job, and said,

"Shall he that contendeth with the Almighty instruct him?
He that reproveth God, let him answer it."

Then Job answered the Lord, and said,

"Behold, I am vile; what shall I answer thee?
  I will lay mine hand upon my mouth.
Once have I spoken; but I will not answer:
  yea, twice; but I will proceed no further."

Then answered the Lord unto Job out of the whirlwind, and said,

"Gird up thy loins now like a man:
  I will demand of thee, and declare thou unto me.
Wilt thou also disannul my judgment?
  wilt thou condemn me, that thou mayest be righteous?
Hast thou an arm like God?
  or canst thou thunder with a voice like him?

"Deck thyself now with majesty and excellency;
  and array thyself with glory and beauty.
Cast abroad the rage of thy wrath:
  and behold every one that is proud, and abase him.
Look on every one that is proud, and bring him low;
  and tread down the wicked in their place.
Hide them in the dust together;
  and bind their faces in secret.
Then will I also confess unto thee
  that thine own right hand can save thee.

"Behold now behemoth,[21] which I made with thee;
  he eateth grass as an ox.
Lo now, his strength is in his loins,
  and his force is in the navel of his belly.
He moveth his tail like a cedar:
  the sinews of his stones are wrapped together.
His bones are as strong pieces of brass;
  his bones are like bars of iron.

"He is the chief of the ways of God:
  he that made him can make his sword to approach unto him.
Surely the mountains bring him forth food,
  where all the beasts of the field play.
He lieth under the shady trees,
  in the covert of the reed, and fens.
The shady trees cover him with their shadow;
  the willows of the brook compass him about.
Behold, he drinketh up a river, and hasteth not:
  he trusteth that he can draw up Jordan into his mouth.
He taketh it with his eyes:
  his nose pierceth through snares."

---

[21] Probably the hippopotamus, here presented as a primeval monster.

CHAPTER 41

"Canst thou draw out leviathan[22] with an hook?
　　or his tongue with a cord which thou lettest down?
Canst thou put an hook into his nose?
　　or bore his jaw through with a thorn?
Will he make many supplications unto thee?
　　will he speak soft words unto thee?
Will he make a covenant with thee?
　　wilt thou take him for a servant for ever?
Wilt thou play with him as with a bird?
　　or wilt thou bind him for thy maidens?
Shall the companions make a banquet of him?
　　shall they part him among the merchants?
Canst thou fill his skin with barbed irons?
　　or his head with fish spears?
Lay thine hand upon him,
　　remember the battle, do no more.
Behold, the hope of him is in vain:
　　shall not one be cast down even at the sight of him?
None is so fierce that dare stir him up:
　　who then is able to stand before me?
Who hath prevented me, that I should repay him?
　　whatsoever is under the whole heaven is mine.

"I will not conceal his parts,
　　nor his power, nor his comely proportion.
Who can discover the face of his garment?
　　or who can come to him with his double bridle?
Who can open the doors of his face?
　　his teeth are terrible round about.
His scales are his pride,
　　shut up together as with a close seal.
One is so near to another,
　　that no air can come between them.
They are joined one to another,
　　they stick together, that they cannot be sundered.
By his neesings[23] a light doth shine,
　　and his eyes are like the eyelids of the morning.
Out of his mouth go burning lamps,
　　and sparks of fire leap out.
Out of his nostrils goeth smoke,
　　as out of a seething pot or caldron.
His breath kindleth coals,
　　and a flame goeth out of his mouth.

[22] A mythological version of the crocodile, here presented as a sea monster emblematic of primeval chaos.
[23] Sneezes (which send out drops of water reflecting the sun).

In his neck remaineth strength,
    and sorrow is turned into joy before him.
The flakes of his flesh are joined together:
    they are firm in themselves; they cannot be moved.
His heart is as firm as a stone;
    yea, as hard as a piece of the nether millstone.
When he raiseth up himself, the mighty are afraid:
    by reason of breakings they purify themselves.
The sword of him that layeth at him cannot hold:
    the spear, the dart, nor the habergeon.
He esteemeth iron as straw,
    and brass as rotten wood.
The arrow cannot make him flee:
    slingstones are turned with him into stubble.
Darts are counted as stubble:
    he laugheth at the shaking of a spear.
Sharp stones are under him:
    he spreadeth sharp pointed things upon the mire.
He maketh the deep to boil like a pot:
    he maketh the sea like a pot of ointment.
He maketh a path to shine after him;
    one would think the deep to be hoary.
Upon earth there is not his like,
    who is made without fear.
He beholdeth all high things:
    he is a king over all the children of pride."

CHAPTER 42

Then Job answered the Lord, and said,

"I know that thou canst do every thing,
    and that no thought can be withholden from thee.
'Who is he that hideth counsel without knowledge?'
Therefore have I uttered that I understood not;
    things too wonderful for me, which I knew not.
'Hear, I beseech thee, and I will speak:
    I will demand of thee, and declare thou unto me.'
I have heard of thee by the hearing of the ear:
    but now mine eye seeth thee.
Wherefore I abhor myself, and repent
    in dust and ashes."

And it was so, that after the Lord had spoken these words unto Job, the Lord said to Eliphaz the Temanite, "My wrath is kindled against thee, and against thy two friends: for ye have not spoken of me the thing that is right, as my servant Job hath. Therefore take unto you now seven bullocks and seven rams, and go to my servant Job, and offer up for yourselves a burnt offering; and my servant Job shall pray for you: for him will I accept: lest I deal with you after your folly, in that ye have not spoken of me the thing which is right, like my servant Job." So Eliphaz the Temanite and Bildad the Shuhite and Zophar the Naamathite went, and did according as the Lord commanded them: the Lord also accepted Job. And the Lord turned the captivity of Job, when he prayed for his friends: also the Lord gave Job twice as much as he had before. Then came there unto him all his brethren, and all his sisters, and all they that had been of his acquaintance before, and did eat bread with him in his house: and they bemoaned him, and comforted him over all the evil that the Lord had brought upon him: every man also gave him a piece of money, and every one an earring of gold. So the Lord blessed the latter end of Job more than his beginning: for he had fourteen thousand sheep, and six thousand camels, and a thousand yoke of oxen, and a thousand she asses. He had also seven sons and three daughters. And he called the name of the first, Jemima; and the name of the second, Kezia; and the name of the third, Keren-happuch. And in all the land were no women found so fair as the daughters of Job: and their father gave them inheritance among their brethren. After this lived Job an hundred and forty years, and saw his sons, and his sons' sons, even four generations. So Job died, being old and full of days.

from PSALMS

PSALM 8

1   O Lord our Lord,[1]
      how excellent is thy name in all the earth!
      who has set thy glory above the heavens.
2   Out of the mouth of babes and sucklings[2] hast thou ordained
      strength
      because of thine enemies,
      that thou mightest still the enemy and the avenger.

3   When I consider thy heavens, the work of thy fingers,
      the moon and the stars, which thou hast ordained;
4   What is man, that thou art mindful of him?
      and the son of man,[3] that thou visitest him?

5   For thou hast made him a little lower than the angels,
      and hast crowned him with glory and honor.
6   Thou madest him to have dominion over the works of thy hands;
      thou hast put all things under his feet:
7   All sheep and oxen,
      yea, and the beasts of the field;
8   The fowl of the air, and the fish of the sea,
      and whatsoever passeth through the paths of the sea.

---

[1] Numbers in left margin are biblical verse numbers.   [2] Infants at the breast.
[3] "Son of man" means any individual person.

9   O Lord our Lord,
            how excellent is thy name in all the earth!

PSALM 23

1   The Lord is my shepherd;
            I shall not want.
2   He maketh me to lie down in green pastures:
            he leadeth me beside the still waters.
3   He restoreth my soul:
            he leadeth me in the paths of righteousness for his name's sake.

4   Yea, though I walk through the valley of the shadow of death,
            I will fear no evil: for thou art with me;
            thy rod and thy staff[4] they comfort me.

5   Thou preparest a table before me in the presence of mine enemies:
            thou anointest my head with oil;
            my cup runneth over.[5]
6   Surely goodness and mercy shall follow me all the days of my life:
            and I will dwell in the house of the Lord for ever.[6]

PSALM 91

1   He that dwelleth in the secret place of the Most High[7]
            shall abide under the shadow of the Almighty.
2   I will say of the Lord, He is my refuge and my fortress:
            my God; in him will I trust.
3   Surely he shall deliver thee from the snare of the fowler,[8]
            and from the noisome[9] pestilence.
4   He shall cover thee with his feathers,
            and under his wings shalt thou trust:
            his truth shall be thy shield and buckler.[10]
5   Thou shalt not be afraid for the terror by night;
            nor for the arrow that flieth by day;
6   Nor for the pestilence that walketh in darkness;
            nor for the destruction that wasteth at noonday.

7   A thousand shall fall[11] at thy side,
            and ten thousand at thy right hand;
            but it shall not come nigh thee.
8   Only with thine eyes shalt thou behold
            and see the reward of the wicked.

---

[4] The rod keeps off enemies; the staff is an emblem of protection.
[5] In verse 5, the metaphor shifts; God is a host lavishing attentions on a dinner guest.
[6] One possible meaning is "I will spend my life worshiping in God's temple."
[7] Dwells in God's presence, or perhaps, more specifically, in the Temple.
[8] Hunter of game birds.   [9] Harmful.   [10] Shield; defense.
[11] Shall be stricken by the plague.

9   Because thou hast made the Lord, which is my refuge,
  even the Most High, thy habitation;
10   There shall no evil befall thee,
  neither shall any plague come nigh thy dwelling.

11   For he shall give his angels charge over thee,
  to keep thee in all thy ways.
12   They shall bear thee up in their hands,
  lest thou dash thy foot against a stone.
13   Thou shalt tread upon the lion and adder:
  the young lion and the dragon shalt thou trample under feet.

14   Because he hath set his love upon me,[12]
  therefore will I deliver him:
  I will set him on high, because he hath known my name.
15   He shall call upon me, and I will answer him:
  I will be with him in trouble;
  I will deliver him, and honor him.
16   With long life will I satisfy him,
  and show him my salvation.

PSALM 103

1   Bless the Lord, O my soul:
  and all that is within me, bless his holy name.
2   Bless the Lord, O my soul,
  and forget not all his benefits:
3   Who forgiveth all thine iniquities;
  Who healeth all thy diseases;
4   Who redeemeth thy life from destruction;
  who crowneth thee with loving-kindness and tender mercies;
5   Who satisfieth thy mouth with good things;
  so that thy youth is renewed like the eagle's.

6   The Lord executeth righteousness
  and judgment for all that are oppressed.
7   He made known his ways unto Moses,
  his acts unto the children of Israel.
8   The Lord is merciful and gracious,
  slow to anger, and plenteous in mercy.
9   He will not always chide:
  neither will he keep his anger for ever.
10   He hath not dealt with us after[13] our sins;
  nor rewarded us according to our iniquities.

11   For as the heaven is high above the earth,
  so great is his mercy toward them that fear him.
12   As far as the east is from the west,
  so far hath he removed our transgressions from us.

---

[12] Verses 14–16 are thought of as spoken by God. [13] In proportion to.

13   Like as a father pitieth his children,
          so the Lord pitieth them that fear him.
14   For he knoweth our frame;
          he remembereth that we are dust.

15   As for man, his days are as grass:
          as a flower of the field, so he flourisheth.
16   For the wind passeth over it, and it is gone;
          and the place thereof shall know it no more.
17   But the mercy of the Lord is from everlasting to everlasting
          upon them that fear him,
          and his righteousness unto children's children;
18   To such as keep his covenant,
          and to those that remember his commandments to do them.

19   The Lord hath prepared his throne[14] in the heavens;
          and his kingdom ruleth over all.
20   Bless the Lord, ye his angels, that excel in strength,
          that do his commandments, hearkening unto the voice of his
              word.
21   Bless ye the Lord, all ye his hosts;
          ye ministers of his, that do his pleasure.
22   Bless the Lord, all his works in all places of his dominion:
          bless the Lord, O my soul.

PSALM 114

1   When Israel went out of Egypt,
          the house of Jacob from a people of strange language;
2   Judah was his sanctuary,
          and Israel[15] his dominion.

3   The sea saw it,[16] and fled:
          Jordan was driven back.
4   The mountains skipped like rams,
          and the little hills like lambs.

5   What ailed thee, O thou sea, that thou fleddest?
          thou Jordan, that thou wast driven back?
6   Ye mountains, that ye skipped like rams;
          and ye little hills, like lambs?

7   Tremble, thou earth, at the presence of the Lord,
          at the presence of the God of Jacob;

[14] Established His (God's own) throne.

[15] Judah was the southern kingdom of Palestine, settled by the tribes of Judah and Benjamin; Israel was the northern kingdom, settled by the tribes descended from Jacob's ten other sons.

[16] Saw God's presence. The reference is to the miraculous dividing of the waters when the Hebrews escaped from Egypt (Exodus 14); Jordan, in the following line, is the river crossed by the Hebrews forty years later, when they entered the Promised Land (Joshua 3). The Jordan too was miraculously dried up to allow a crossing.

8   Which turned the rock into a standing water,[17]
        the flint into a fountain of waters.

PSALM 130

1   Out of the depths have I cried unto thee, O Lord.
2   Lord, hear my voice:
        let thine ears be attentive to the voice of my supplications.

3   If thou, Lord, shouldest mark iniquities,
        O Lord, who shall stand?
4   But there is forgiveness with thee,
        that thou mayest be feared.

5   I wait for the Lord,
        my soul doth wait, and in his word do I hope.
6   My soul waiteth for the Lord more than they that watch for the
          morning:
        I say, more than they that watch for the morning.

7   Let Israel hope in the Lord:
        for with the Lord there is mercy,
        and with him is plenteous redemption.
8   And he shall redeem Israel from all his iniquities.

PSALM 137

1   By the rivers of Babylon,[18] there we sat down,
        yea, we wept, when we remembered Zion.
2   We hanged our harps upon the willows in the midst thereof.
3   For there they that carried us away captive required of us a song;
        and they that wasted[19] us required of us mirth, saying,
        Sing us one of the songs of Zion.
4   How shall we sing the Lord's song in a strange land?

5   If I forget thee, O Jerusalem,
        let my right hand forget her cunning.
6   If I do not remember thee,
        let my tongue cleave to the roof of my mouth;
        if I prefer not Jerusalem above my chief joy.

7   Remember, O Lord, the children of Edom[20]
        in the day of Jerusalem;

[17] A pool. During the Hebrews' forty years of wandering, God empowered Moses to draw water from a rock by striking it with his staff (Exodus 17).

[18] The irrigation canals of the Tigris and Euphrates rivers, in Babylonia. The Babylonians conquered the Hebrews' homeland (Zion) in 597 B.C., inaugurating sixty years of exile and captivity.

[19] Laid waste.

[20] A land south of the Dead Sea; an ally of the Babylonians in the sack of Jerusalem.

who said, Rase[21] it, rase it,
    even to the foundation thereof.

8   O daughter of Babylon, who are to be destroyed;
      happy shall he be, that rewardeth thee as thou hast served us.

9   Happy shall he be, that taketh and dasheth
      thy little ones against the stones.

PSALM 139

1   O Lord, thou hast searched me, and known me.

2   Thou knowest my downsitting and mine uprising;
      thou understandest my thought afar off.

3   Thou compassest my path and my lying down,
      and art acquainted with all my ways.

4   For there is not a word in my tongue,
      but, lo, O Lord, thou knowest it altogether.

5   Thou hast beset me behind and before,
      and laid thine hand upon me.

6   Such knowledge is too wonderful for me;
      it is high, I cannot attain unto it.

7   Whither shall I go from thy Spirit?
      or whither shall I flee from thy presence?

8   If I ascend up into heaven, thou art there:
      if I make my bed in hell,[22] behold, thou art there.

9   If I take the wings of the morning,[23]
      and dwell in the uttermost parts of the sea;

10   Even there shall thy hand lead me,
      and thy right hand shall hold me.

11   If I say, Surely the darkness shall cover me;
      even the night shall be light about me.

12   Yea, the darkness hideth not from thee;
      but the night shineth as the day:
      the darkness and the light are both alike to thee.

13   For thou hast possessed my reins:[24]
      thou has covered me in my mother's womb.

14   I will praise thee; for I am fearfully and wonderfully made:
      marvelous are thy works; and that my soul knoweth right well.

15   My substance was not hid from thee
      when I was made in secret,
      and curiously wrought in the lowest parts of the earth.[25]

16   Thine eyes did see my substance, yet being unperfect;
      and in thy book all my members were written,
      which in continuance were fashioned,
      when as yet there was none of them.

---

[21] Raze; demolish.
[22] Sheol, the place of the dead (roughly equivalent to the Greek Hades).
[23] Travel as fast as the dawn spreads.
[24] "Didst form my inward parts" (Revised Standard Version).
[25] A metaphor for the womb.

17 How precious also are thy thoughts unto me, O God!
How great is the sum of them!
18 If I should count them, they are more in number than the sand:
when I awake, I am still with thee.

19 Surely thou wilt slay the wicked, O God:
depart from me therefore, ye bloody men.
20 For they speak against thee wickedly,
and thine enemies take thy name in vain.
21 Do not I hate them, O Lord, that hate thee?
And am not I grieved with those that rise up against thee?
22 I hate them with perfect hatred:
I count them mine enemies.
23 Search me, O God, and know my heart:
try me, and know my thoughts:
24 And see if there be any wicked way in me,
and lead me in the way everlasting.

JONAH

Now the word of the Lord came unto Jonah[1] the son of Amittai, saying, "Arise, go to Nineveh, that great city, and cry against it; for their wickedness is come up before me." But Jonah rose up to flee unto Tarshish from the presence of the Lord, and went down to Joppa; and he found a ship going to Tarshish: so he paid the fare thereof, and went down into it, to go with them unto Tarshish from the presence of the Lord.

But the Lord sent out a great wind into the sea, and there was a mighty tempest in the sea, so that the ship was like to be broken. Then the mariners were afraid, and cried every man unto his god, and cast forth the wares that were in the ship into the sea, to lighten it of them. But Jonah was gone down into the sides of the ship; and he lay, and was fast asleep. So the shipmaster came to him, and said unto him, "What meanest thou, O sleeper? arise, call upon thy God, if so be that God will think upon us, that we perish not."

And they said every one to his fellow, "Come, and let us cast lots, that we may know for whose cause this evil is upon us." So they cast lots, and the lot fell upon Jonah. Then said they unto him, "Tell us, we pray thee, for whose cause this evil is upon us; what is thine occupation? and whence comest thou? what is thy country; and of what people art thou?" And he said unto them, "I am a Hebrew; and I fear the Lord, the God of heaven, which hath made the sea and the dry land." Then were the men exceedingly afraid, and said unto him, "Why hast thou done this?" For the men knew that he fled from the presence of the Lord, because he had told them.

Then said they unto him, "What shall we do unto thee, that the sea may be calm unto us?" for the sea wrought, and was tempestuous. And he said unto them, "Take me up, and cast me forth into the sea; so shall the sea be

[1] The name Jonah means "dove," the symbol of Israel.

calm unto you: for I know that for my sake this great tempest is upon you."
Nevertheless the men rowed hard to bring it to the land; but they could
not: for the sea wrought, and was tempestuous against them. Wherefore
they cried unto the Lord, and said, "We beseech thee, O Lord, we beseech
thee, let us not perish for this man's life, and lay not upon us innocent
blood: for thou, O Lord, hast done as it pleased thee." So they took up
Jonah, and cast him forth into the sea: and the sea ceased from her raging.
Then the men feared the Lord exceedingly, and offered a sacrifice unto
the Lord, and made vows.

Now the Lord had prepared a great fish to swallow up Jonah. And
Jonah was in the belly of the fish three days and three nights. Then Jonah
prayed unto the Lord his God out of the fish's belly and said,

> "I cried by reason of mine affliction unto the Lord,
>   and he heard me;
> Out of the belly of hell cried I,
>   and thou heardest my voice.
> For thou hadst cast me into the deep,
>   in the midst of the seas;
>   and the floods compassed me about:
>   all thy billows and thy waves passed over me.
> Then I said, 'I am cast out of thy sight;
>   yet I will look again toward thy holy temple.'
> The waters compassed me about, even to the soul:
>   the depth closed me round about,
> The weeds were wrapped about my head.
>   I went down to the bottoms of the mountains;
>   the earth with her bars was about me for ever:
> Yet hast thou brought up my life from corruption,
>   O Lord my God.
> When my soul fainted within me
>   I remembered the Lord:
> And my prayer came in unto thee,
>   into thine holy temple.
> They that observe lying vanities
>   forsake their own mercy.
> But I will sacrifice unto thee
>   with the voice of thanksgiving;
> I will pay that that I have vowed;
>   salvation is of the Lord."

And the Lord spoke unto the fish, and it vomited out Jonah upon the
dry land.

And the word of the Lord came unto Jonah the second time, saying,
"Arise, go unto Nineveh, that great city, and preach unto it the preaching
that I bid thee." So Jonah arose, and went unto Nineveh, according to the
word of the Lord. Now Nineveh was an exceedingly great city of three
days' journey. And Jonah began to enter into the city a day's journey, and
he cried, and said, "Yet forty days, and Nineveh shall be overthrown." So

the people of Nineveh believed God, and proclaimed a fast, and put on sackcloth,[2] from the greatest of them even to the least of them.

For word came unto the king of Nineveh, and he arose from his throne, and he laid his robe from him, and covered him with sackcloth, and sat in ashes. And he caused it to be proclaimed and published through Nineveh by the decree of the king and his nobles, saying, "Let neither man nor beast, herd nor flock, taste any thing: let them not feed, nor drink water: but let man and beast be covered with sackcloth, and cry mightily unto God: yea, let them turn every one from his evil way, and from the violence that is in their hands. Who can tell if God will turn and repent, and turn away from his fierce anger, that we perish not?"

And God saw their works, that they turned from their evil way; and God repented of the evil that he had said that he would do unto them; and he did it not.

But it displeased Jonah exceedingly, and he was very angry. And he prayed unto the Lord, and said, "I pray thee, O Lord, was not this my saying, when I was yet in my country? Therefore I fled before unto Tarshish: for I knew that thou art a gracious God, and merciful, slow to anger, and of great kindness, and repentest thee of the evil. Therefore now, O Lord, take, I beseech thee, my life from me; for it is better for me to die than to live." Then said the Lord, "Doest thou well to be angry?" So Jonah went out of the city, and sat on the east side of the city, and there made him a booth, and sat under it in the shadow, till he might see what would become of the city.

And the Lord God prepared a gourd, and made it to come up over Jonah, that it might be a shadow over his head, to deliver him from his grief. So Jonah was exceeding glad of the gourd. But God prepared a worm when the morning rose the next day, and it smote the gourd that it withered. And it came to pass, when the sun did arise, that God prepared a vehement east wind; and the sun beat upon the head of Jonah, that he fainted, and wished in himself to die, and said, "It is better for me to die than to live." And God said to Jonah, "Doest thou well to be angry for the gourd?" And he said, "I do well to be angry, even unto death." Then said the Lord, "Thou hast had pity on the gourd, for the which thou hast not labored, neither madest it grow; which came up in a night, and perished in a night. And should not I spare Nineveh, that great city, wherein are more than sixscore thousand persons, that cannot discern between their right hand and their left hand; and also much cattle?"

---

[2] A garment made of coarse goat or camel's hair, worn as a sign of mourning or penitence.

Homer
(*Eighth Century* B.C.)

Like the Bible, Homer's Iliad *and* Odyssey *are fundamental sources of the culture and literature of the Western world. These epics have been revered not only as masterpieces of language and narrative but also as expressions of central truths about human beings and their place in the scheme of things. They grow out of a story the elements of which are as follows: While a guest at the palace of Meneláos* (Menelaus *in the more familiar English spelling), who was king of Sparta in southern Greece, the Trojan prince Paris fell in love with Helen, his host's supremely beautiful wife, and carried her off to Troy, apparently with her consent. Under the command of Meneláos' brother Agamémnon, the Greeks organized an army and sailed to Troy in order to recapture Helen, to avenge the dishonor of her husband, and to punish Paris for his violation of the sacred code of hospitality. But, despite outnumbering the Trojans, the Greeks were long frustrated in their attempt to take the city, which was to fall only after ten years of siege. The* Iliad *focuses on one important episode in the war, a quarrel between Agamémnon and Akhilleus* (Achilles) *over ownership of a prisoner slave-girl. The epic then records the tragic consequences of the quarrel: it describes the death of Akhilleus' beloved companion Patróklos* (Patroclus) *while Akhilleus was sulking on the sidelines and the subsequent revenge taken by Akhilleus on the Trojan hero Hektor* (Hector), *who had killed his friend. The action of the* Odyssey *takes place after the war is over. The poem concentrates on one of the foremost Greek warriors against Troy, the resourceful Odysseus, who must overcome many obstacles and tribulations in order to return to his wife and homeland. The actual fall of Troy is not described in either of the two Homeric poems. (One ancient account of the city's fall was written many centuries later by the Roman poet Virgil in his* Aeneid, *Book II.)*

Again like the Bible, the two Homeric epics have for centuries caused controversy. Debates continue today as strongly as ever. To say that the Iliad *and* Odyssey *were written by Homer is in fact almost a nonstatement, since the meaning of its very terms is ambiguous. What exactly* are *the two poems? Are some parts more authentic than others? Were they composed as wholes or did they evolve? Was Homer a real person or is his name merely a convenient label for a legendary figure or group? Are both poems the work of the same author? If he was an individual, when and where did he live? At what stage of their history were the poems (originally meant to be sung or recited) put into the written form we know? To what extent does the written version preserve the oral version? Were Troy and the Trojan war as described in the* Iliad *historical? Many of these questions, some of which date to early antiquity, still cannot be answered with complete certainty.*

Some probabilities have emerged, however. In the later nineteenth century, the great amateur archaeologist Heinrich Schliemann proved by his excavations that Troy did indeed once exist. A war similar to the one Homer describes probably did occur, around the early twelfth century B.C. Most authorities now believe also that Homer was a single person, who lived around the eighth century B.C. and was a professional bard or minstrel like Demódokos and Phêmios in the Odyssey. *His homeland was probably Ionia, a region south of Troy in Asia Minor (modern Turkey) that faces Greece across the Aegean Sea. Tradition says that he was blind.*

His role in composing the Iliad *and* Odyssey *is harder to define. Undoubtedly he inherited a large store of traditional material that included many prominent*

*incidents and characters of the tale of Troy. He regarded this material as history, and
many poems on the subject would have been familiar to him and to his audience. But
he probably deserves the main credit at least for shaping and refining this material
into the monumental works we know, giving to them the unity, power, and artistry
that Aristotle later praised so highly in his* Poetics. *These qualities have caused
Homer to be honored as one of the supreme poets of the world. Whether the* Iliad *and*
Odyssey *were actually put in written form by him (he lived in an age and place
barely emerging from several centuries of illiteracy), were recorded by a scribe to
whom he dictated, or were written down only after a considerable period of oral
transmission, is still much debated.*

That the Iliad *and* Odyssey *were originally intended to be heard rather than
read is the first thing new readers need to know about the poems. The fact explains,
for example, the frequent repetitions—of single phrases, of whole lines, and sometimes of long passages. Such repetition is characteristic of all forms of oral communication, since—as lecturers, auctioneers, playwrights, and orators know—repetition
enhances clarity and helps achieve the desired emphasis. The repetition may even be,
as some scholars now believe, a key to the poems' origins, in the oral-formulaic
method, a process by which singers improvised by combining traditional phrases with
original ones to flesh out a memorized narrative outline. If we ignore the poems' oral
manner we put an unnecessary distance between ourselves and their original audience. Moreover, we can misinterpret many of their strategies, especially the "Homeric
epithets," the recurrent brief phrases used to describe things or persons. The reader
may wonder why Hera, the queen of the gods, is called "white-armed" in some passages and "Goddess of the Golden Chair" in others, where either label (or neither)
would seem appropriate, or why Akhilleus is "the great runner" even when he is not
running, or why the striking phrase "tamer of horses" should be applied to two
different men. The answer is that Homer inserted such phrases in places where they
fit the poetic rhythm, even where they are not especially relevant to the narrative
context. (The Greek meter, dactyllic hexameter, combines long [—] and short [˘]
syllables in the pattern —˘˘—˘˘—˘˘—˘˘—˘˘——, with certain substitutions
permitted.) It is a mistake, then, to read too much into such phrases or to use them to
interpret particular passages, even when the phrases do sound appropriate.*

*An even more serious error is to look down on Homer as a simple, primitive poet,
one whose accomplishments, like those of a precocious child, are impressive mainly
because of his early age. In fact, there have been few if any greater artists than
Homer. The stories he tells are vivid and powerful in their sweep, but they are also
subtle and skillfully shaded. For example, all the principal men in the* Iliad, *Greeks
and Trojans, are brave in battle, but their styles of bravery are distinctive: Agamémnon is savage, Akhilleus is proud and supremely confident, Hektor is patriotic, Odysseus is pragmatic (as in the* Odyssey *as well). Seemingly fleeting details can be quite
significant. When, in Book IV of the* Odyssey, *Telémakhos approaches the palace of
Meneláos, one of the king's men hesitates to admit the young man as the code of
hospitality would dictate. Meneláos is furious, but we can guess why his man is
nervous: years before, another guest named Paris had been welcomed by Meneláos
but had gone on to abduct his beautiful wife Helen and thus had set off the entire
Trojan war. We must be alert to such subtleties, since Homer's objective manner
usually leaves connections unstated. Characterizations are fully individualized. Penélopê in the* Odyssey *is not merely the object of the suitors' lust and greed but also a
fully imagined, resourceful wife and woman, a fit mate for the crafty Odysseus. The
green young man Telémakhos and the inexperienced but enterprising Phaiákian*

princess Nausikaa (Nausicaä) are richly realized characters in themselves and also effective foils for Odysseus, the seasoned veteran of life and experience. One of the major achievements of the Homeric poems is that they combine richness of detail and nuance with a masterful control of the poems' general movement and pattern.

Homer's control results partly, as Aristotle later pointed out, from his careful limiting of his material; the Iliad treats a single episode in the ten-year Trojan war and the Odyssey centers on the troubled homecoming of a single warrior. But the poems have also a far more ambitious aim: to describe as fully as possible the heroic world. Heroism is the theme of both poems. Since the Iliad is a tragedy and a war poem, it celebrates the heroism that faces and suffers death. The Odyssey is a kind of comedy, and the heroism it celebrates is that of survival, the triumph over death. The Iliad derives much of its intensity from its almost claustrophobic atmosphere, its setting confined to a few square miles in and around the besieged city of Troy where thousands of men are cramped together. The closeness of atmosphere is relieved only occasionally by scenes involving the Olympian gods and through similes reminding the audience of the world of nature and peacetime. The Odyssey is wholly different. Its geographical vistas are almost endless, taking in the far, romantic reaches of the known and fabled Mediterranean world and even the realm of the dead. In intriguing contrast is the second half of the poem, where the setting narrows to that of a domestic drama on Odysseus' home island. Here the arena of heroism is neither the defeat of an army nor the perils of distant travel but a struggle to reassert private rights to home and property. The suspense of Odysseus' plot against the suitors emerges from a context not of the cosmic but of familiar human detail—a world of good and bad servants, favorite beds, kitchen logistics. In different ways, then, the Odyssey is both more panoramic and more intimate than the Iliad.

The Homeric divinities, similarly, seem both remote and familiar. Their role and relationship to human beings are very difficult to define. In some ways they seem like projections (often in a comic vein) of human activities and the human environment: Poseidon of the sea, Hephaistos of fire and metalworking, Apollo of medicine and archery, Athena of resourcefulness, Aphroditê of love and sex, and so forth. They are thoroughly humanized, and in their rivalries, loyalties, plots, and bickerings they sometimes seem to parody the human beings, on a scale actually smaller than life. On the other hand, they are utterly superior to human beings, in power and above all in their exemption from death. (Paradoxically, the strictest limitation of their power is their inability to share their immortality with their human protégés.) They continually intervene, especially at key moments, to shape the course of events on earth. In doing so they would seem to limit human freedom. Yet the poems also make it clear that men are responsible for their deeds and that they do have choices. The immortals' actions frequently seem to be confirmations rather than causes of what happens; we can say that Odysseus is resourceful because the goddess Athena aids him or that she aids him because, like her, he is resourceful. In any event, the presence of the divinities in the world of the poems emphasizes both the brevity and the urgency of human life and thus enhances our sense of the mystery in the world.

The Iliad and Odyssey are the oldest epics in the Western tradition. Seven centuries after Homer, Virgil creatively imitated and synthesized the two Homeric epics in the Aeneid, a story of the Trojan survivors who, under Ainéias, or Aeneas, journeyed like Odysseus through hardships to lay in Italy the foundations of Roman greatness after a battle resembling that in the Iliad. Virgil sophisticated the epic, making it a more strictly literary form and using it for doctrinal purposes, as a vehicle for fostering Roman political and religious values. Seventeen hundred years after Virgil, Milton wrote the definitive English epic, Paradise Lost, *in an attempt to "justify the ways of God to men" and to preach an essentially Christian heroism. Both Milton and Virgil depict a universe governed by an ultimately just providential force, and each either implies or states that his form of heroism has superseded earlier epic values. Each found a model in Homer, despite the vast differences between their metaphysics and Homer's apparent unconcern with it. That indebtedness testifies that Homer was not only a great poet but also one whose vision has universal application.*

FURTHER READING (*prepared by F.S.N.*): Oliver Taplin provides an introductory essay on Homer, with a useful bibliography, in *The Oxford History of the Classical World*, ed. by John Boardman, Jasper Griffin, and Oswyn Murray, 1986. A description of the life and culture of pre-Homeric civilization is given by John Chadwick, *The Decipherment of Linear B*, 1960. Howard Clarke's *Homer's Readers*, 1981, surveys clearly what is known of the circumstances under which the Homeric epics were composed. Two introductory works on Homer are W. A. Camps, *An Introduction to Homer*, 1980; and Jasper Griffin, *Homer* (in the Past Masters series), 1980. On the Homeric problem, G. S. Kirk, *Homer and the Oral Tradition*, 1976, is useful. A stimulating sampling of essays by artists such as Tolstoy, Pound, and Cavafy has been edited by George Steiner and Robert Fagles, *Homer: A Collection of Critical Essays*, 1962; while learned studies by classical scholars such as Bowra, Lord, and Blegen have been assembled by Alan J. B. Wace and Frank H. Stubbings, *A Companion to Homer*, 1962. An informative and readable critical commentary on the *Iliad*, based specifically on the Robert Fitzgerald translation and including a foreword by him, is James C. Hogan's *A Guide to the Iliad*, 1979. On the *Iliad* as tragedy, see C. W. Macleod's introduction to his edition of and commentary on the *Iliad*, Book XXIV, 1982. For a treatment of human mortality in the poem, along with discussion of the Homeric deities, see J. Griffin's *Homer on Life and Death*, 1980. Analysis of individual scenes in the *Odyssey* as they contribute to the poem's effect appears in B. Fenik, *Studies in the Odyssey*, 1974. The poem's effect is also well captured in N. Austin, *Archery at the Dark of the Moon*, 1975. M. I. Finley, *The World of Odysseus*, 1964, discusses the sociology of the *Odyssey*. Charles Taylor, ed., *Essays on the Odyssey: Selected Modern Criticism*, 1963, provides twentieth-century interpretations of the work.

THE ILIAD

Translated by Robert Fitzgerald

For the events leading up to the Trojan war, see the first paragraph of the Introduction to Homer. As *The Iliad* opens, Troy is undergoing its tenth year of siege by the Greek coalition (called at different times Akhaians, Danáäns, and Argives). Although they outnumber the Trojans, the Greeks have not been able to take Troy and win back Helen—this despite the presence on the Greek side of the great warrior Akhilleus (Achilles) and the Myrmidons, his tough and disciplined army.

The gods take a strong interest in the war and are divided in their allegiances, some supporting the Greeks and some the Trojans. The division is explained in part by a mythological episode that occurred before Paris and Helen eloped. Paris had judged a dispute among Hêra (queen of the gods), the warlike goddess Athêna, and Aphrodítê (goddess of love and beauty) over which of the three was most beautiful. He decided for Aphrodítê, who had promised him as a reward the most beautiful woman in the world and then kept her promise by giving him Helen. As a result, Aphrodítê sides with Paris and his people while Hêra and Athêna oppose them bitterly.

Many persons and places in the *Iliad* are best known to readers by their Latinized names, such as *Achilles* and *Ajax*. The present translator has used forms (*Akhilleus, Aías*) closer to the Greek spelling and pronunciation. An acute accent (´) indicates stress; thus *Aías* is accented on the first syllable, *Agamémnon* on the third one. A circumflex accent (^) indicates that the vowel sound is long; thus *Lêto* is pronounced Laytoe. A dieresis (¨) indicates pronunciation as a separate syllable; thus *Danáäns* has three syllables rather than two. [*Editors' headnote.*]

BOOK ONE: QUARREL, OATH, AND PROMISE

Anger be now your song, immortal one,[1]
Akhilleus' anger, doomed and ruinous,
that caused the Akhaians[2] loss on bitter loss
and crowded brave souls into the undergloom,[3]
leaving so many dead men—carrion
for dogs and birds; and the will of Zeus was done.[4]
Begin it when the two men first contending
broke with one another—

the Lord Marshal

Agamémnon, Atreus' son, and Prince Akhilleus.

Among the gods, who brought this quarrel on?   10
The son of Zeus by Lêto.[5] Agamémnon
angered him, so he made a burning wind
of plague rise in the army: rank and file
sickened and died for the ill their chief had done
in despising a man of prayer.
This priest, Khrysês, had come down to the ships[6]
with gifts, no end of ransom for his daughter;
on a golden staff he carried the god's white bands[7]
and sued for grace from the men of all Akhaia,
the two Atreidai[8] most of all:

"O captains   20

Meneláos and Agamémnon, and you other

---

[1] The first lines are the model for the "opening formula" used by epic poets after Homer: the invocation of the Muse, or spirit of inspiration; the request that she "sing" the poem; the statement of the main theme, along with a hint at its consequences; the abrupt leap into the story itself. Compare the opening lines of Homer's *Odyssey*, Virgil's *Aeneid*, and Milton's *Paradise Lost*.

[2] The Greek forces.   [3] Aïdês (Hades), the shadowy realm of the dead.

[4] Zeus was the king of the gods. Homer considers all events in the poem and life in general as manifestations of Zeus' will, although human beings do have a limited but significant freedom to choose and are responsible for their actions; the interrelationship of human and divine will is complex and ambiguous. Even Zeus is to some extent limited by fate; in later Greek literature fate is regarded as an even more mysterious and impersonal force.

[5] *son . . . Lêto.* Apollo, god of archery, prophecy, and healing (as well as its opposite, disease).

[6] The Greek fleet is drawn up on the beach bordering the plain of Troy.

[7] The staff and ribbons are symbolic of Apollo, who as god of prophecy is patron of the prophet-priest Khrysês.

[8] Sons of Atreus. For the history of the house of Atreus, see Aeschylus' *Oresteia.*

Akhaians under arms!
The gods who hold Olympos,[9] may they grant you
plunder of Priam's[10] town and a fair wind home,
but let me have my daughter back for ransom
as you revere Apollo, son of Zeus!"

Then all the soldiers murmured their assent:

"Behave well to the priest. And take the ransom!"

But Agamémnon would not. It went against his desire,
and brutally he ordered the man away: 30

"Let me not find you here by the long ships
loitering this time or returning later,
old man; if I do,
the staff and ribbons of the god will fail you.
Give up the girl? I swear she will grow old
at home in Argos,[11] far from her own country,
working my loom and visiting my bed.
Leave me in peace and go, while you can, in safety."

So harsh he was, the old man feared and obeyed him,
in silence trailing away   40
by the shore of the tumbling clamorous whispering sea,
and he prayed and prayed again, as he withdrew,
to the god whom silken-braided Lêto bore:

"O hear me, master of the silver bow,
protector of Ténedos and the holy towns,
Apollo, Sminthian,[12] if to your liking
ever in any grove I roofed a shrine
or burnt thighbones in fat upon your altar—
bullock or goat flesh—let my wish come true:
your arrows on the Danááns[13] for my tears!"   50

Now when he heard this prayer, Phoibos Apollo
walked with storm in his heart from Olympos' crest,
quiver and bow at his back, and the bundled arrows
clanged on the sky behind as he rocked in his anger,
descending like night itself. Apart from the ships
he halted and let fly, and the bowstring slammed
as the silver bow sprang, rolling in thunder away.
Pack animals were his target first, and dogs,
but soldiers, too, soon felt transfixing pain
from his hard shots, and pyres[14] burned night and day.   60
Nine days the arrows of the god came down

[9] The mountain where the gods live.   [10] The king of Troy.
[11] A region of southern Greece, ruled by Agamémnon.
[12] *Ténedos.* An island nearby. *Sminthian.* A name of Apollo meaning "mouse god," perhaps a reference to the god's ability to bring on plague, rodents being carriers.
[13] Another name for the Greek forces.   [14] Bonfires for cremating the dead.

broadside upon the army. On the tenth,
Akhilleus called all ranks to assembly. Hêra,[15]
whose arms are white as ivory, moved him to it,
as she took pity on Danáäns dying.
All being mustered, all in place and quiet,
Akhilleus, fast in battle as a lion,
rose and said:

                             "Agamémnon, now, I take it,
the siege is broken, we are going to sail,
and even so may not leave death behind: 70
if war spares anyone, disease will take him . . .
We might, though, ask some priest or some diviner,
even some fellow good at dreams—for dreams
come down from Zeus as well—
why all this anger of the god Apollo?

Has he some quarrel with us for a failure
in vows or hekatombs?[16] Would mutton burned
or smoking goat flesh make him lift the plague?"

Putting the question, down he sat. And Kalkhas,
Kalkhas Thestórides,[17] came forward, wisest   80
by far of all who scanned the flight of birds.[18]
He knew what was, what had been, what would be,
Kalkhas, who brought Akhaia's ships to Ilion[19]
by the diviner's gift Apollo gave him.
Now for their benefit he said:

                                 "Akhilleus,
dear to Zeus, it is on me you call
to tell you why the Archer God is angry.
Well, I can tell you. Are you listening? Swear
by heaven that you will back me and defend me,
because I fear my answer will enrage   90
a man with power in Argos, one whose word
Akhaian troops obey.

                    A great man in his rage is formidable
for underlings: though he may keep it down,
he cherishes the burning in his belly
until a reckoning day. Think well
if you will save me."

---

[15] Queen of the gods who strongly supports the Greeks. See headnote to the *Iliad*. The phrase "whose arms are white as ivory" is one of many repeated verbal formulas; some of them can have a particular, appropriate effect, but most of them are used more automatically, in accordance with the needs of poetic meter in oral poetry.

[16] Lavish sacrifices to the gods.   [17] The suffix *-ides* means "son of."

[18] Prophets, or diviners, discovered the gods' will by observing omens such as the direction of birds in flight.

[19] Troy.

Said Akhilleus:

"Courage.

Tell what you know, what you have light to know.
I swear by Apollo, the lord god to whom
you pray when you uncover truth,   100
never while I draw breath, while I have eyes to see,
shall any man upon this beachhead dare
lay hands on you—not one of all the army,
not Agamémnon, if it is he you mean,
though he is first in rank of all Akhaians."

The diviner then took heart and said:

"No failure

in hekatombs or vows is held against us.
It is the man of prayer whom Agamémnon
treated with contempt: he kept his daughter,
spurned his gifts: for that man's sake the Archer   110
visited grief upon us and will again.
Relieve the Danääns of this plague he will not
until the girl who turns the eyes of men
shall be restored to her own father—freely,
with no demand for ransom—and until
we offer up a hekatomb at Khrysê.[20]
Then only can we calm him and persuade him."

He finished and sat down. The son of Atreus,
ruler of the great plain, Agamémnon,
rose, furious. Round his heart resentment   120
welled, and his eyes shone out like licking fire.
Then, with a long and boding look at Kalkhas,
he growled at him:

"You visionary of hell,

never have I had fair play in your forecasts.
Calamity is all you care about, or see,
no happy portents; and you bring to pass
nothing agreeable. Here you stand again
before the army, giving it out as oracle
the Archer made them suffer because of me,
because I would not take the gifts   130
and let the girl Khrysêis go; I'd have her
mine, at home. Yes, if you like, I rate her
higher than Klytaimnestra, my own wife!
She loses nothing by comparison
in beauty or womanhood, in mind or skill.

---

[20] Khrysês' town; the names of priest, town, and daughter (Khrysêis) are virtually the same word.

For all of that, I am willing now to yield her
if it is best; I want the army saved
and not destroyed. You must prepare, however,
a prize of honor for me, and at once,
that I may not be left without my portion—   140
I, of all Argives. It is not fitting so.
While every man of you looks on, my girl
goes elsewhere."

Prince Akhilleus answered him:

"Lord Marshall, most insatiate of men,
how can the army make you a new gift?
Where is our store of booty? Can you see it?
Everything plundered from the towns has been
distributed; should troops turn all that in?[21]
Just let the girl go, in the god's name, now;   150
we'll make it up to you, twice over, three
times over, on that day Zeus gives us leave
to plunder Troy behind her rings of stone."

Agamémnon answered:

                                                              "Not that way

will I be gulled, brave as you are, Akhilleus.
Take me in, would you? Try to get around me?
What do you really ask? That you may keep
your own winnings, I am to give up mine
and sit here wanting her? Oh, no:
the army will award a prize to me   160
and make sure that it measures up, or if
they do not, I will take a girl myself,
your own, or Aías', or Odysseus' prize![22]
Take her, yes, to keep. The man I visit
may choke with rage; well, let him.
But this, I say, we can decide on later.

Look to it now, we launch on the great sea
a well-found ship, and get her manned with oarsmen,
load her with sacrificial beasts and put aboard
Khrysêis in her loveliness. My deputy,   170
Aías, Idómeneus,[23] or Prince Odysseus,
or you, Akhilleus, fearsome as you are,
will make the hekatomb and quiet the Archer."

---

[21] The Greeks have made several side-raids on towns near Troy.

[22] *Aías, Odysseus.* Two of the principal Greek warriors and leaders. There are two Aíases; the one referred to here is the "greater" Aías, son of Télamôn. Odysseus, noted for his resourcefulness, is the hero of Homer's other epic, the *Odyssey.*

[23] Ruler of Krete (Crete); another prominent leader among the Greeks.

Akhilleus frowned and looked at him, then said:

"You thick-skinned, shameless, greedy fool!
Can any Akhaian care for you, or obey you,
after this on marches or in battle?
As for myself, when I came here to fight,
I had no quarrel with Troy or Trojan spearmen:
they never stole my cattle or my horses,   180
never in the black farmland of Phthía[24]
ravaged my crops. How many miles there are
of shadowy hills between, and foaming seas!
No, no, we joined for you, you insolent boor,
to please you, fighting for your brother's sake
and yours, to get revenge upon the Trojans.
You overlook this, dogface, or don't care,
and now in the end you threaten to take my girl,
a prize I sweated for, and soldiers gave me!

Never have I had plunder like your own   190
from any Trojan stronghold battered down
by the Akhaians. I have seen more action
hand to hand in those assaults than you have,
but when the time for sharing comes, the greater
share is always yours. Worn out with battle
I carry off some trifle to my ships.
Well, this time I make sail for home.
Better to take now to my ships. Why linger,
cheated of winnings, to make wealth for you?"

To this the high commander made reply: 200

"Desért, if that's the way the wind blows. Will I
beg you to stay on my account? I will not.
Others will honor me, and Zeus who views
the wide world most of all.

                              No officer

is hateful to my sight as you are, none
given like you to faction,[25] as to battle—
rugged you are, I grant, by some god's favor.
Sail, then, in your ships, and lord it over
your own battalion of Myrmidons.[26] I do not
give a curse for you, or for your anger.   210
But here is warning for you:

                              Khrysêis

being required of me by Phoibos Apollo,
she will be sent back in a ship of mine,
manned by my people. That done, I myself

[24] Akhilleus' homeland, in northern Greece.   [25] Insubordination; subversive dissent.
[26] Akhilleus' troops.

will call for Brisêis at your hut, and take her,
flower of young girls that she is, your prize,
to show you here and now who is the stronger
and make the next man sick at heart—if any
think of claiming equal place with me."

A pain like grief weighed on the son of Pêleus,[27]   220
and in his shaggy chest this way and that
the passion of his heart ran: should he draw
longsword from hip, stand off the rest, and kill
in single combat the great son of Atreus,
or hold his rage in check and give it time?
And as this tumult swayed him, as he slid
the big blade slowly from the sheath, Athêna
came to him from the sky.[28] The white-armed goddess,
Hêra, sent her, being fond of both,
concerned for both men. And Athêna, stepping   230
up behind him, visible to no one
except Akhilleus, gripped his red-gold hair.

Startled, he made a half turn, and he knew her
upon the instant for Athêna: terribly
her grey eyes blazed at him. And speaking softly
but rapidly aside to her he said:

"What now, O daughter of the god of heaven
who bears the stormcloud, why are you here? To see
the wolfishness of Agamémnon?
Well, I give you my word: this time, and soon,   240
he pays for his behavior with his blood."

The grey-eyed goddess Athêna said to him:

"It was to check this killing rage I came
from heaven, if you will listen. Hêra sent me,
being fond of both of you, concerned for both.
Enough: break off this combat, stay your hand
upon the sword hilt. Let him have a lashing
with words, instead: tell him how things will be.
Here is my promise, and it will be kept:
winnings three times as rich, in due season,   250
you shall have in requital for his arrogance.
But hold your hand. Obey."

                                            The great runner,
Akhilleus, answered:

---

[27] Akhilleus' father.

[28] Associated with crafts, resourcefulness, and skill in general, Athêna is a powerful agent of divine assistance to the Greeks in the *Iliad* and the faithful patron of Odysseus in the *Odyssey*. For her opposition to Troy and allegiance to the Greeks, see the headnote to the *Iliad*.

                              "Nothing for it, goddess,
but when you two immortals speak, a man
complies, though his heart burst. Just as well.
Honor the gods' will, they may honor ours."

On this he stayed his massive hand
upon the silver pommel, and the blade
of his great weapon slid back in the scabbard.
The man had done her bidding. Off to Olympos,   260
gaining the air, she went to join the rest,
the powers of heaven in the home of Zeus.

But now the son of Pêleus turned on Agamémnon
and lashed out at him, letting his anger ride
in execration:

                                     "Sack of wine,
you with your cur's eyes and your antelope heart!
You've never had the kidney to buckle on
armor among the troops, or make a sortie
with picked men—oh, no; that way death might lie.
Safer, by god, in the middle of the army—   270
is it not?—to commandeer the prize
of any man who stands up to you! Leech!
Commander of trash! If not, I swear,
you never could abuse one soldier more!

But here is what I say: my oath upon it
by this great staff: look: leaf or shoot
it cannot sprout again, once lopped away
from the log it left behind in the timbered hills;
it cannot flower, peeled of bark and leaves;
instead, Akhaian officers in council   280
take it in hand by turns, when they observe
by the will of Zeus due order in debate:[29]
let this be what I swear by then: I swear
a day will come when every Akhaian soldier
will groan to have Akhilleus back. That day
you shall no more prevail on me than this
dry wood shall flourish—driven though you are,
and though a thousand men perish before
the killer, Hektor.[30] You will eat your heart out,
raging with remorse for this dishonor   290
done by you to the bravest of Akhaians."

He hurled the staff, studded with golden nails,
before him on the ground. Then down he sat,
and fury filled Agamémnon, looking across at him.

---

[29] To hold the staff signifies that one has the floor in the discussion.
[30] Son of Priam and chief warrior on the Trojan side; a central character in the *Iliad*.

But for the sake of both men Nestor arose,
the Pylians' orator, eloquent and clear;
argument sweeter than honey rolled from his tongue.
By now he had outlived two generations
of mortal men, his own and the one after,
in Pylos land, and still ruled in the third.   300
In kind reproof he said:

                                                            "A black day, this.

Bitter distress comes this way to Akhaia.
How happy Priam and Priam's sons would be,
and all the Trojans—wild with joy—if they
got wind of all these fighting words between you,
foremost in council as you are, foremost
in battle. Give me your attention. Both
are younger men than I, and in my time
men who were even greater have I known
and none of them disdained me. Men like those   310
I have not seen again, nor shall: Peiríthoös,
the Lord Marshal Dryas, Kaineus, Exádios,
Polyphêmos, Theseus—Aigeus' son,
a man like the immortal gods. I speak
of champions among men of earth, who fought
with champions, with wild things of the mountains,
great centaurs[31] whom they broke and overpowered.
Among these men I say I had my place
when I sailed out of Pylos, my far country,
because they called for me. I fought   320
for my own hand among them. Not one man
alive now upon earth could stand against them.
And I repeat: they listened to my reasoning,
took my advice. Well, then, you take it too.
It is far better so.

                                                      Lord Agamémnon,
do not deprive him of the girl, renounce her.
The army had allotted her to him.
Akhilleus, for your part, do not defy
your King and Captain. No one vies in honor
with him who holds authority from Zeus.   330
You have more prowess, for a goddess bore you;[32]
his power over men surpasses yours.

But, Agamémnon, let your anger cool.
I beg you to relent, knowing Akhilleus
a sea wall for Akhaians in the black waves of war."

---

[31] Mythological beings, shaped like horses but having human torsos and heads.
[32] Thetis, a sea-nymph, had been the mate of Akhilleus' father Pêleus.

Lord Agamémnon answered:

"All you say

is fairly said, sir, but this man's ambition,
remember, is to lead, to lord it over
everyone, hold power over everyone,
give orders to the rest of us! Well, one   340
will never take his orders! If the gods
who live forever made a spearman of him,
have they put insults on his lips as well?"

Akhilleus interrupted:

"What a poltroon,[33]

how lily-livered I should be called, if I
knuckled under to all you do or say!
Give your commands to someone else, not me!
And one more thing I have to tell you: think it
over: this time, for the girl, I will not
wrangle in arms with you or anyone,   350
though I am robbed of what was given me;
but as for any other thing I have
alongside my black ship, you shall not take it
against my will. Try it. Hear this, everyone:
that instant your hot blood blackens my spear!"

They quarreled in this way, face to face, and then
broke off the assembly by the ships. Akhilleus
made his way to his squadron and his quarters,
Patróklos[34] by his side, with his companions.

Agamémnon proceeded to launch a ship,   360
assigned her twenty oarsmen, loaded beasts
for sacrifice to the god, then set aboard
Khryseîs in her loveliness. The versatile
Odysseus took the deck, and, all oars manned,
they pulled out on the drenching ways of sea.
The troops meanwhile were ordered to police camp
and did so, throwing refuse in the water;
then to Apollo by the barren surf
they carried out full-tally hekatombs,
and the savor curled in crooked smoke toward heaven.   370

That was the day's work in the army.

Agamémnon
had kept his threat in mind, and now he acted,

---

[33] Coward.
[34] Akhilleus' chariot-driver and dearest friend; a central character in the *Iliad*.

called Eurýbatês and Talthýbios,
his aides and criers:[35]

                         "Go along," he said,
"both of you, to the quarters of Akhilleus
and take his charming Brisêis by the hand
to bring to me. And if he balks at giving her
I shall be there myself with men-at-arms
in force to take her—all the more gall for him."

So, ominously, he sent them on their way,   380
and they who had no stomach for it went
along the waste sea shingle toward the ships
and shelters of the Myrmidons. Not far
from his black ship and hut they found the prince
in the open, seated. And seeing these two come
was cheerless to Akhilleus. Shamefast, pale
with fear of him, they stood without a word;
but he knew what they felt and called out:

                         "Peace to you,
criers and couriers of Zeus and men!
Come forward. Not one thing have I against you: 390
Agamémnon is the man who sent you
for Brisêis. Here then, my lord Patróklos,
bring out the girl and give her to these men.
And let them both bear witness before the gods
who live in bliss, as before men who die,
including this harsh king, if ever hereafter
a need for me arises to keep the rest
from black defeat and ruin.

                      Lost in folly,
the man cannot think back or think ahead
how to come through a battle by the ships."   400

Patróklos did the bidding of his friend,
led from the hut Brisêis in her beauty
and gave her to them. Back along the ships
they took their way, and the girl went, loath to go.

Leaving his friends in haste, Akhilleus wept,
and sat apart by the grey wave, scanning the endless sea.
Often he spread his hands in prayer to his mother:

"As my life came from you, though it is brief,
honor at least from Zeus who storms in heaven
I call my due. He gives me precious little.   410
See how the lord of the great plains, Agamémnon,

---

[35] Heralds.

humiliated me! He has my prize,
by his own whim, for himself."

                                    Eyes wet with tears,
he spoke, and her ladyship his mother heard him
in green deeps where she lolled near her old father.[36]
Gliding she rose and broke like mist from the inshore
grey sea face, to sit down softly before him,
her son in tears; and fondling him she said:

"Child, why do you weep? What grief is this?
Out with it, tell me, both of us should know."   420
Akhilleus, fast in battle as a lion,
groaned and said:

                        "Why tell you what you know?
We sailed out raiding, and we took by storm
that ancient town of Eëtíôn called Thêbê,
plundered the place, brought slaves and spoils away.[37]
At the division, later,
they chose a young girl, Khrysêis, for the king.
Then Khrysês, priest of the Archer God, Apollo,
came to the beachhead we Akhaians hold,
bringing no end of ransom for his daughter;   430
he had the god's white bands on a golden staff
and sued for grace from the army of Akhaia,
mostly the two Atreidai, corps commanders.
All of our soldiers murmured in assent:
'Behave well to the priest. And take the ransom!'
But Agamémnon would not. It went against his desire,
and brutally he ordered the man away.
So the old man withdrew in grief and anger.
Apollo cared for him: he heard his prayer
and let black bolts of plague fly on the Argives.   440

One by one our men came down with it
and died hard as the god's shots raked the army
broadside. But our priest divined the cause
and told us what the god meant by the plague.

I said, 'Appease the god!' but Agamémnon
could not contain his rage; he threatened me,
and what he threatened is now done—
one girl the Akhaians are embarking now
for Khrysê beach with gifts for Lord Apollo;
the other, just now, from my hut—the criers   450

---

[36] Nêreus, father of the Nereids (sea-nymphs).
[37] Elaborate, sometimes verbatim, repetitions of earlier material are frequent in Homer.
Eëtíôn is the father of Andrómakhê, wife of the Trojan hero Hektor.

came and took her, Briseus' girl, my prize,
given by the army.
                                        If you can, stand by me:
go to Olympos, pray to Zeus, if ever
by word or deed you served him—
and so you did, I often heard you tell it
in Father's house: that time when you alone
of all the gods shielded the son of Krónos[38]
from peril and disgrace—when other gods,
Pallas Athêna, Hêra, and Poseidon,[39]
wished him in irons, wished to keep him bound,   460
you had the will to free him of that bondage,
and called up to Olympos in all haste
Aigaion, whom the gods call Briareus,
the giant with a hundred arms, more powerful
than the sea-god, his father. Down he sat
by the son of Krónos, glorying in that place.
For fear of him the blissful gods forbore
to manacle Zeus.
                                Remind him of these things,
cling to his knees and tell him your good pleasure
if he will take the Trojan side   470
and roll the Akhaians back to the water's edge,
back on the ships with slaughter! All the troops
may savor what their king has won for them,
and he may know his madness, what he lost
when he dishonored me, peerless among Akhaians."

Her eyes filled, and a tear fell as she answered:

"Alas, my child, why did I rear you, doomed
the day I bore you?[40] Ah, could you only be
serene upon this beachhead through the siege,
your life runs out so soon.   480
Oh early death! Oh broken heart! No destiny
so cruel! And I bore you to this evil!

But what you wish I will propose
To Zeus, lord of the lightning, going up
myself into the snow-glare of Olympos
with hope for his consent.
                                        Be quiet now
beside the long ships, keep your anger bright
against the army, quit the war.
                                        Last night

---

[38] Krónos was father of Zeus and ruler of the gods in the divine generation overthrown by Zeus and the Olympians.
[39] God of the ocean, brother of Zeus, and a supporter of the Greeks in the war.
[40] Akhilleus is fated to die young and will in fact be killed in the Trojan war, though his death is not described in the *Iliad*. See also Akhilleus' somewhat different account in Book IX of his "two possible destinies."

Zeus made a journey to the shore of Ocean
to feast among the Sunburned,[41] and the gods   490
accompanied him. In twelve days he will come
back to Olympos. Then I shall be there
to cross his bronze doorsill and take his knees.
I trust I'll move him."

                                        Thetis left her son
still burning for the softly belted girl
whom they had wrested from him.

                                        Meanwhile Odysseus
with his shipload of offerings came to Khrysê.
Entering the deep harbor there
they furled the sails and stowed them, and unbent
forestays to ease the mast down quickly aft   500
into its rest; then rowed her to a mooring.
Bow-stones were dropped, and they tied up astern,
and all stepped out into the wash and ebb,
then disembarked their cattle for the Archer,
and Khrysêis, from the deepsea ship. Odysseus,
the great tactician, led her to the altar,
putting her in her father's hands, and said:

"Khrysês, as Agamémnon's emissary
I bring your child to you, and for Apollo
a hekatomb in the Danáäns' name.   510
We trust in this way to appease your lord,
who sent down pain and sorrow on the Argives."

So he delivered her, and the priest received her,
the child so dear to him, in joy. Then hastening
to give the god his hekatomb, they led
bullocks to crowd around the compact altar,
rinsed their hands and delved in barley baskets,
as open-armed to heaven Khrysês prayed:

"Oh hear me, master of the silver bow,
protector of Ténedos and the holy towns,   520
if while I prayed you listened once before
and honored me, and punished the Akhaians,
now let my wish come true again. But turn
your plague away this time from the Danáäns."

And this petition, too, Apollo heard.
When prayers were said and grains of barley strewn,
they held the bullocks for the knife, and flayed them,
cutting out joints and wrapping these in fat,

---

[41] The Ethiopians, a people believed to live at the edge of the world, which was envisaged
as flat and surrounded by a body of water called Ocean.

two layers, folded, with raw strips of flesh,
for the old man to burn on cloven faggots,   530
wetting it all with wine.

                                             Around him stood
young men with five-tined forks in hand, and when
the vitals had been tasted, joints consumed,
they sliced the chines and quarters for the spits,
roasted them evenly and drew them off.
Their meal being now prepared and all work done,
they feasted to their hearts' content and made
desire for meat and drink recede again,
then young men filled their winebowls to the brim,
ladling drops for the god in every cup.   540
Propitiatory songs rose clear and strong
until day's end, to praise the god, Apollo,
as One Who Keeps the Plague Afar; and listening
the god took joy.

                                             After the sun went down
and darkness came, at last Odysseus' men
lay down to rest under the stern hawsers.

When Dawn spread out her finger tips of rose
they put to sea for the main camp of Akhaians,
and the Archer God sent them a following wind.
Stepping the mast they shook their canvas out,   550
and wind caught, bellying the sail. A foaming
dark blue wave sang backward from the bow
as the running ship made way against the sea,
until they came offshore of the encampment.
Here they put in and hauled the black ship high,
far up the sand, braced her with shoring timbers,
and then disbanded, each to his own hut.

Meanwhile unstirring and with smoldering heart,
the godlike athlete, son of Pêleus, Prince
Akhilleus waited by his racing ships.   560
He would not enter the assembly
of emulous men, nor ever go to war,
but felt his valor staling in his breast
with idleness, and missed the cries of battle.

Now when in fact twelve days had passed, the gods
who live forever turned back to Olympos,
with Zeus in power supreme among them.

                                             Thetis
had kept in mind her mission for her son,
and rising like a dawn mist from the sea
into a cloud she soared aloft in heaven   570
to high Olympos. Zeus with massive brows
she found apart, on the chief crest enthroned,

and slipping down before him, her left hand
placed on his knees and her right hand held up
to cup his chin, she made her plea to him:[42]

"O Father Zeus, if ever amid immortals
by word or deed I served you, grant my wish
and see to my son's honor! Doom for him
of all men comes on quickest.

                            Now Lord Marshal

Agamémnon has been highhanded with him,   580
has commandeered and holds his prize of war.
But you can make him pay for this, profound
mind of Olympos!

                        Lend the Trojans power,

until the Akhaians recompense my son
and heap new honor upon him!"

                           When she finished,

the gatherer of cloud said never a word
but sat unmoving for a long time, silent.
Thetis clung to his knees then spoke again:

"Give your infallible word, and bow your head,
or else reject me. Can you be afraid   590
to let me see how low in your esteem
I am of all the gods?"

                         Greatly perturbed,

Lord Zeus who masses cloud said:

                          "Here is trouble.

You drive me into open war with Hêra
sooner or later:
she will be at me, scolding all day long.
Even as matters stand she never rests
from badgering me before the gods: I take
the Trojan side in battle, so she says.

Go home before you are seen. But you can trust me   600
to put my mind on this; I shall arrange it.
Here let me bow my head, then be content
to see me bound by that most solemn act
before the gods. My word is not revocable
nor ineffectual, once I nod upon it."

He bent his ponderous black brows down, and locks
ambrosial[43] of his immortal head
swung over them, as all Olympos trembled.

---

[42] This posture—one hand on the knees, the other on the chin—was conventional for
seekers of help from the powerful.

[43] Celestial; literally, ambrosia is the food of the gods. Their drink is nectar, which is later
served to them.

After this pact they parted: misty Thetis
from glittering Olympos leapt away   610
into the deep sea; Zeus to his hall retired.
There all the gods rose from their seats in deference
before their father; not one dared
face him unmoved, but all stood up before him,
and thus he took his throne.

                                        But Hêra knew
he had new interests; she had seen
the goddess Thetis, silvery-footed daughter
of the Old One of the sea, conferring with him,
and, nagging, she inquired of Zeus Kroníon:

"Who is it this time, schemer? Who has your ear?   620
How fond you are of secret plans, of taking
decisions privately! You could not bring yourself,
could you, to favor me with any word
of your new plot?"

                        The father of gods and men
said in reply:

                        "Hêra, all my provisions
you must not itch to know.
You'll find them rigorous, consort though you are.
In all appropriate matters no one else,
no god or man, shall be advised before you.
But when I choose to think alone,   630
don't harry me about it with your questions."

The Lady Hêra answered with wide eyes:

"Majesty, what a thing to say. I have not
'harried' you before with questions, surely;
you are quite free to tell what you will tell.
This time I dreadfully fear—I have a feeling—
Thetis, the silvery-footed daughter
of the Old One of the sea, led you astray.
Just now at daybreak, anyway, she came
to sit with you and take your knees; my guess is   640
you bowed your head for her in solemn pact
that you will see to the honor of Akhilleus—
that is, to Akhaian carnage near the ships."

Now Zeus the gatherer of cloud said:

                                        "Marvelous,
you and your guesses; you are near it, too.
But there is not one thing that you can do about it,
only estrange yourself still more from me—
all the more gall for you. If what you say
is true, you may be sure it pleases me.

And now you just sit down, be still, obey me,   650
or else not all the gods upon Olympos
can help in the least when I approach your chair
to lay my inexorable hands upon you."

At this the wide-eyed Lady Hêra feared him,
and sat quite still, and bent her will to his.
Up through the hall of Zeus now all the lords
of heaven were sullen and looked askance. Hêphaistos,[44]
master artificer, broke the silence,
doing a kindness to the snowy-armed
lady, his mother Hêra.

                                                    He began: 660

"Ah, what a miserable day, if you two
raise your voices over mortal creatures!
More than enough already! Must you bring
your noisy bickering among the gods?
What pleasure can we take in a fine dinner
when baser matters gain the upper hand?
To Mother my advice is—what she knows—
better make up to Father, or he'll start
his thundering and shake our feast to bits.
You know how he can shock us if he cares to—   670
out of our seats with lightning bolts!
Supreme power is his. Oh, soothe him, please,
take a soft tone, get back in his good graces.
Then he'll be benign to us again."
He lurched up as he spoke, and held a winecup
out to her, a double-handed one,
and said:

                    "Dear Mother, patience, hold your tongue,
no matter how upset you are. I would not
see you battered, dearest.

                                        It would hurt me,
and yet I could not help you, not a bit.   680
The Olympian is difficult to oppose.
One other time I took your part he caught me
around one foot and flung me
into the sky from our tremendous terrace.
I soared all day! Just as the sun dropped down
I dropped down, too, on Lemnos—nearly dead.
The island people nursed a fallen god."

He made her smile—and the goddess, white-armed Hêra,
smiling took the winecup from his hand.

[44] The lame god of fire and of metal-crafts. He had once before been thrown from Olympos for taking Hêra's side against Zeus, landing on the Aegean island of Lemnos.

Then, dipping from the winebowl, round he went   ₆₉₀
from left to right, serving the other gods
nectar of sweet delight.

                  And quenchless laughter
broke out among the blissful gods
to see Hêphaistos wheezing down the hall.
So all day long until the sun went down
they spent in feasting, and the measured feast
matched well their hearts' desire.
So did the flawless harp held by Apollo
and heavenly songs in choiring antiphon
that all the Muses sang.

                 And when the shining   ₇₀₀
sun of day sank in the west, they turned
homeward each one to rest, each to that home
the bandy-legged wondrous artisan
Hêphaistos fashioned for them with his craft.
The lord of storm and lightning, Zeus, retired
and shut his eyes where sweet sleep ever came to him,
and at his side lay Hêra, Goddess of the Golden Chair.

BOOK II. *Persuaded by Thetis to side with Akhilleus, Zeus sends a deceiving dream to Agamémnon which leads him to believe that the fall of Troy is at hand. As a test of his army's determination, Agamémnon calls the troops together and tells them that they must abandon the siege of Troy and admit defeat despite their superior numbers. The soldiers, all too happy to go home, rush toward the ships; but Odysseus, under the influence of Hêra and Athêna, rallies them. Thersîtês, a repulsive common soldier, reviles Agamémnon for his greed, lust, and ill-treatment of Akhilleus. Nestor proposes that, to foster loyalty and discipline, the army should be mustered by nation and clan. A long catalogue follows, listing the Greek commanders, giving information about their geographical and family backgrounds, and specifying the number of ships each leader commands. (The total number of ships is over 1,200.) A briefer catalogue of the Trojans and of their allies from other regions concludes the Book.*

BOOK III. *As the armies approach each other, Paris offers single combat; he is soon recognized by Meneláos, the husband whom Paris has cuckolded. At first Paris is cowed, but after Hektor expresses contempt for his softness he agrees to face Meneláos. (We learn in this Book that Paris is hated or despised by both armies and even by Helen.) A treaty is proposed by which the victor in the duel is to have Helen and the armies are to end the war, without further fighting. Next we see Helen herself in Troy; the aged counsellors of Priam, the Trojan king, are awed by Helen's beauty but desire that she should go back to her husband so that the war can end. Priam himself, however, is fond of Helen. From atop the city walls he points out to him, at his request, the chief leaders of the Greeks. Priam goes out onto the plain to ratify the treaty but returns before the duel, which he considers too painful to watch. The single combat begins; Meneláos is about to triumph when Aphrodítê, goddess of love and protector of Paris, rescues Paris and returns him to the safety of his bedchamber in Troy. The goddess then sends to him the reluctant Helen, who goes to bed with Paris but only after taunting him. Since the mysteriously vanished Paris cannot be found, the Greeks claim victory and demand that Helen and other agreed-upon compensation be delivered up to them.*

BOOK IV. *The gods are feasting on Mount Olympos. Zeus deliberately provokes his wife Hêra by suggesting that, since Meneláos has won the duel, he should be awarded Helen and the war should end now, with Troy spared. Predictably, the fiercely vindictive goddess is angered; she wins from Zeus permission for Athêna to incite some Trojan to break the pledged truce-agreement and thus rekindle the hostilities. Athêna, in disguise, tempts the archer Pán-daros, who is fighting for the Trojans, to launch an arrow at Meneláos; he is slightly wounded by the shot. The truce broken, Agamémnon rouses the Greeks to battle through a combination of flattery and taunts. Fierce fighting breaks out between the two armies.*

BOOK V. *The war continues to rage—man against man, man against god, god against god. Athêna and Hêra aid the Greeks; Apollo, Aphrodítê, and Arês aid the Trojans. The central human figure is the great Greek warrior Diomêdês; he kills the truce-breaker Pándaros after being wounded by an arrow from him and puts the Trojan hero Aineías in grave danger before Aineías is assisted by Apollo and his mother Aphrodítê. Aphrodítê and Arês are both wounded by Diomêdês and retire to Olympos; the beautiful goddess is told by Zeus, affection-ately, that she is too soft for battle, but Zeus expresses loathing for the universally hated war-god. The battle itself is indecisive.*

from BOOK SIX: INTERLUDES IN FIELD AND CITY

The immortals having retired from the field, battle continues; the Trojans begin to retreat. Agamémnon vows to kill the whole Trojan people, including children. Hek-tor's brother Hélenos, a prophet, urges him to return to Troy and have the women offer propitiatory offerings to Athêna so that the goddess may restrain her protégé Diomêdês. Diomêdês is about to fight a stranger (Glaukos) when they discover that their grandfathers were sworn friends; the two agree not to fight each other. Hektor arrives at Troy. Book VI continues:

Now, when Hektor reached the Skaian Gates[1]
daughters and wives of Trojans rushed to greet him
with questions about friends, sons, husbands, brothers.
"Pray to the gods!" he said to each in turn,
as grief awaited many. He walked on
and into Priam's palace, fair and still,
made all of ashlar,[2] with bright colonnades.
Inside were fifty rooms of polished stone
one by another, where the sons of Priam
slept beside their wives;[3] apart from these   290
across an inner court were twelve rooms more
all in one line, of polished stone, where slept
the sons-in-law of Priam and their wives.
Approaching these, he met his gentle mother
going in with Laódikê, most beautiful
of all her daughters. Both hands clasping his,
she looked at him and said:

                                        "Why have you come
from battle, child? Those fiends, the Akhaians, fighting
around the town, have worn you out; you come
to climb our Rock[4] and lift your palms to Zeus!   300

---

[1] The main portal of the city.   [2] Rectangular building-blocks.
[3] Priam had fifty sons, by his queen Hékabê and by other women.
[4] The hill on which the city stands.

Wait, and I'll serve you honeyed wine.
First you may offer up a drop to Zeus,
to the immortal gods, then slake your thirst.
Wine will restore a man when he is weary
as you are, fighting to defend your own."

Hektor answered her, his helmet flashing:

"No, my dear mother, ladle me no wine;
You'd make my nerve go slack: I'd lose my edge.
May I tip wine to Zeus with hands unwashed?
I fear to—a bespattered man, and bloody,   310
may not address the lord of gloomy cloud.
No, it is you I wish would bring together
our older women, with offerings, and go visit
the temple of Athêna, Hope of Soldiers.
Pick out a robe, most lovely and luxurious,
most to your liking in the women's hall;
place it upon Athêna's knees;[5] assure her
a sacrifice of heifers, twelve young ones
ungoaded ever in their lives, if in her mercy
relenting toward our town, our wives and children,   320
she keeps Diomêdês out of holy Troy.
He is a wild beast now in combat and pursuit.
Make your way to her shrine, visit Athêna,
Hope of Soldiers.

                                        As for me, I go
for Paris, to arouse him, if he listens.
If only earth would swallow him here and now!
What an affliction the Olympian
brought up for us in him—a curse for Priam
and Priam's children![6] Could I see that man
dwindle into Death's night, I'd feel my soul   330
relieved of its distress!"

So Hektor spoke, and she walked slowly on
into the mégaron.[7] She called her maids,
who then assembled women from the city.
But Hékabê went down to the low chamber
fragrant with cedar, where her robes were kept,
embroidered work by women of Sidonia
Aléxandros[8] had brought, that time he sailed
and ravished Helen, princess, pearl of kings.
Hékabê lifted out her loveliest robe,   340

[5] The knees of her statue.
[6] It is worth remembering that Paris as well as Hektor is a son of Hékabê, the addressee here.
[7] The great hall of the house.
[8] Another name for Paris. He and Helen had stopped in Sidonia (Phoenicia) on their way to Troy.

most ample, most luxurious in brocade,
and glittering like starlight under all.
This offering she carried to Athêna
with a long line of women in her train.
On the Akrópolis,[9] Athêna's shrine
was opened for them by Theanô, stately
daughter of Kisseus, wife to Antênor,[10]
and chosen priestess of Athêna. Now
all crying loud stretched out their arms in prayer,
while Theanô with grace took up the robe   350
to place it on fair-haired Athêna's knees.
She made petition then to Zeus's daughter:

                                                            "Lady,

excellent goddess, towering friend of Troy,
smash Diomêdês' lance-haft! Throw him hard
below the Skaian Gates, before our eyes!
Upon this altar we'll make offering
of twelve young heifers never scarred!
Only show mercy to our town,
mercy to Trojan men, their wives and children."

These were Theanó's prayers, her vain prayers.   360
Pallas Athêna turned away her head.

During the supplication at the shrine,
Hektor approached the beautiful house Aléxandros
himself had made, with men who in that time
were master-builders in the land of Troy.
Bedchamber, hall, and court, in the upper town,
they built for him near Priam's hall and Hektor's.
Now Hektor dear to Zeus went in, his hand
gripping a spear eleven forearms long,
whose bronze head shone before him in the air   370
as shone, around the neck, a golden ring.
He found his brother in the bedchamber
handling a magnificent cuirass[11] and shield
and pulling at his bent-horn bow, while Helen
among her household women sat nearby,
directing needlecraft and splendid weaving.
At sight of him, to shame him, Hektor said:

"Unquiet soul, why be aggrieved in private?
Our troops are dying out there where they fight
around our city, under our high walls.   380
The hue and cry of war, because of you,
comes in like surf upon this town.
You'd be at odds with any other man

---

[9] The most elevated part of the city.   [10] A Trojan lord and counsellor.
[11] A piece of armor designed to cover the chest and back.

you might see quitting your accursèd war.
Up; into action, before torches thrown
make the town flare!"

                                        And shining like a god

Aléxandros replied:

                                                "Ah, Hektor,

this call to order is no more than just.
So let me tell you something: hear me out.
No pettishness, resentment toward the Trojans,   390
kept me in this bedchamber so long,
but rather my desire, on being routed,
to taste grief to the full.

                                        In her sweet way

my lady rouses me to fight again—
and I myself consider it better so.
Victory falls to one man, then another.
Wait, while I put on the wargod's gear,
or else go back; I'll follow, sure to find you."

For answer, Hektor in his shining helm
said not a word, but in low tones   400
enticing Helen murmured:

                                        "Brother dear—

dear to a whore, a nightmare of a woman!
That day my mother gave me to the world
I wish a hurricane blast had torn me away
to wild mountains, or into tumbling sea
to be washed under by a breaking wave,
before these evil days could come!—or, granted
terrible years were in the gods' design,
I wish I had had a good man for a lover
who knew the sharp tongues and just rage of men.   410
This one—his heart's unsound, and always will be,
and he will win what he deserves. Come here
and rest upon this couch with me, dear brother.
You are the one afflicted most
by harlotry in me and by his madness,
our portion, all of misery, given by Zeus
that we may live in song for men to come."

Great Hektor shook his head, his helmet flashing,
and said:

                                        "No, Helen, offer me no rest;
I know you are fond of me. I cannot rest.   420
Time presses, and I grow impatient now
to lend a hand to Trojans in the field

who feel a gap when I am gone. Your part
can be to urge him—let him feel the urgency
to join me in the city. He has time:
I must go home to visit my own people,
my own dear wife and my small son. Who knows
if I shall be reprieved again to see them,
or beaten down under Akhaian blows
as the immortals will."

He turned away   430

and quickly entered his own hall, but found
Princess Andrómakhê was not at home.
With one nursemaid and her small child, she stood
upon the tower of Ilion, in tears,
bemoaning what she saw.

Now Hektor halted

upon his threshold, calling to his maids:

"Tell me at once, and clearly, please,
my lady Andrómakhê, where has she gone?
To see my sisters, or my brothers' wives?
Or to Athêna's temple? Ladies of Troy   440
are there to make petition to the goddess."

The busy mistress of the larder answered:

"Hektor, to put it clearly as you ask,
she did not go to see your sisters, nor
your brothers' wives, nor to Athêna's shrine
where others are petitioning the goddess.
Up to the great square tower of Ilion
she took her way, because she heard our men
were spent in battle by Akhaian power.
In haste, like a madwoman, to the wall   450
she went, and Nurse went too, carrying the child."

At this word Hektor whirled and left his hall,
taking the same path he had come by,
along byways, walled lanes, all through the town
until he reached the Skaian Gates, whereby
before long he would issue on the field.
There his warmhearted lady
came to meet him, running: Andrómakhê,
whose father, Eëtíôn, once had ruled
the land under Mount Plakos, dark with forest,   460
at Thêbê under Plakos—lord and king
of the Kilikians. Hektor was her lord now,
head to foot in bronze; and now she joined him.
Behind her came the maid, who held the child
against her breast, a rosy baby still,

Hektoridês, the world's delight, as fresh
as a pure shining star. Skamándrios[12]
his father named him; other men would say
Astýanax, "Lord of the Lower Town,"
as Hektor singlehandedly guarded Troy.   470
How brilliantly the warrior smiled, in silence,
his eyes upon the child! Andrómakhê
rested against him, shook away a tear,
and pressed his hand in both her own, to say:

"Oh, my wild one, your bravery will be
your own undoing! No pity for our child,
poor little one, or me in my sad lot—
soon to be deprived of you! soon, soon
Akhaians as one man will set upon you
and cut you down! Better for me, without you,   480
to take cold earth for mantle. No more comfort,
no other warmth, after you meet your doom,
but heartbreak only. Father is dead, and Mother.[13]
My father great Akhilleus killed when he
besieged and plundered Thêbê, our high town,
citadel of Kilikians. He killed him,
but, reverent at least in this, did not
despoil him. Body, gear, and weapons forged
so handsomely, he burned, and heaped a barrow
over the ashes. Elms were planted round   490
by mountain-nymphs of him who bears the stormcloud.[14]
Then seven brothers that I had at home
in one day entered Death's dark place. Akhilleus,
prince and powerful runner, killed all seven
amid their shambling cattle and silvery sheep.
Mother, who had been queen of wooded Plakos,
he brought with other winnings home, and freed her,
taking no end of ransom. Artemis
the Huntress shot her in her father's house.[15]
Father and mother—I have none but you,   500
nor brother, Hektor; lover none but you!
Be merciful! Stay here upon the tower!
Do not bereave your child and widow me!
Draw up your troops by the wild figtree; that way
the city lies most open, men most easily
could swarm the wall where it is low:
three times, at least, their best men tried it there
in company of the two called Aías, with

[12] Hektor's son is named for Skamánder, a river on the Trojan plain.
[13] Khrysêis, the woman awarded to Agamémnon, was also taken during the raid on Thêbê that Andrómakhê describes in the following lines; the same expedition included a raid on another city where Akhilleus captured Brisêis, whom he has given up to Agamémnon.
[14] Nymphs associated with Zeus.
[15] The arrows of Artemis, goddess of the hunt, were a symbol of death for women.

Idómeneus, the Atreidai, Diomêdes—
whether someone who had it from oracles   510
had told them, or their own hearts urged them on."

Great Hektor in his shimmering helmet answered:

"Lady, these many things beset my mind
no less than yours. But I should die of shame
before our Trojan men and noblewomen
if like a coward I avoided battle,
nor am I moved to. Long ago I learned
how to be brave, how to go forward always
and to contend for honor, Father's and mine.
Honor—for in my heart and soul I know   520
a day will come when ancient Ilion falls,
when Priam and the folk of Priam perish.
not by the Trojans' anguish on that day
am I so overborne in mind—the pain
of Hékabê herself, or Priam king,
or of my brothers, many and valorous,
who will have fallen in dust before our enemies—
as by your own grief, when some armed Akhaian
takes you in tears, your free life stripped away.
Before another woman's loom in Argos   530
it may be you will pass, or at Messêis
or Hypereiê fountain, carrying water,
against your will—iron constraint upon you.
And seeing you in tears, a man may say:
'There is the wife of Hektor, who fought best
of Trojan horsemen when they fought at Troy.'
So he may say—and you will ache again
for one man who could keep you out of bondage.
Let me be hidden dark down in my grave
before I hear you cry or know you captive!"   540

As he said this, Hektor held out his arms
to take his baby. But the child squirmed round
on the nurse's bosom and began to wail,
terrified by his father's great war helm—
the flashing bronze, the crest with horsehair plume
tossed like a living thing at every nod.
His father began laughing, and his mother
laughed as well. Then from his handsome head
Hektor lifted off his helm and bent
to place it, bright with sunlight, on the ground.   550
When he had kissed his child and swung him high
to dandle him, he said this prayer:

                                                    "O Zeus

and all immortals, may this child, my son,

become like me a prince among the Trojans.[16]
Let him be strong and brave and rule in power
at Ilion; then someday men will say
'This fellow is far better than his father!'
seeing him home from war, and his arms
the bloodstained gear of some tall warrior slain—
making his mother proud."

After this prayer,   560
into his dear wife's arms he gave his baby,
whom on her fragrant breast
she held and cherished, laughing through her tears.
Hektor pitied her now. Caressing her,
he said:

"Unquiet soul, do not be too distressed
by thoughts of me. You know no man dispatches me
into the undergloom against my fate;
no mortal, either, can escape his fate,
coward or brave man, once he comes to be.
Go home, attend to your own handiwork   570
at loom and spindle, and command the maids
to busy themselves, too. As for the war,
that is for men, all who were born at Ilion,
to put their minds on—most of all for me."

He stooped now to recover his plumed helm
as she, his dear wife, drew away, her head
turned and her eyes upon him, brimming tears.
She made her way in haste then to the ordered
house of Hektor and rejoined her maids,
moving them all to weep at sight of her.   580
In Hektor's home they mourned him, living still
but not, they feared, again to leave the war
or be delivered from Akhaian fury.

Paris in the meantime had not lingered:
after he buckled his bright war-gear on
he ran through Troy, sure-footed with long strides.
Think how a stallion fed on clover and barley,
mettlesome, thundering in a stall, may snap
his picket rope and canter down a field
to bathe as he would daily in the river—   590
glorying in freedom! Head held high
with mane over his shoulders flying,
his dazzling work of finely jointed knees

---

[16] Hektor's prayer for his son would seem to contradict what he has just said about the inevitable destruction of the Trojans. His mood changes during this episode.

takes him around the pasture haunts of horses.[17]
That was the way the son of Priam, Paris,
ran from the height of Pergamos,[18] his gear
ablaze like the great sun,
and laughed aloud. He sprinted on, and quickly
met his brother, who was slow to leave
the place where he had discoursed with his lady.   600
Aléxandros was first to speak:

                                                        "Dear fellow,"

he said, "have I delayed you, kept you waiting?
Have I not come at the right time, as you asked?"

And Hektor in his shimmering helm replied:

"My strange brother! No man with justice in him
would underrate your handiwork in battle;
you have a powerful arm. But you give way
too easily, and lose interest, lose your will.
My heart aches in me when I hear our men,
who have such toil of battle on your account,   610
talk of you with contempt. Well, come along.
Someday we'll make amends for that, if ever
we drive the Akhaians from the land of Troy—
if ever Zeus permit us, in our hall,
to set before the gods of heaven, undying
and ever young, our winebowl of deliverance."[19]

BOOK VII. *Athêna and Apollo collaborate to arrange a temporary halt in the fighting, by instigating another single combat, this time between Hektor and a Greek opponent. Hektor utters the challenge, stipulating that the corpse of the man defeated is to be given proper rites. After the Greeks hesitate, Meneláos comes forward, but he is then dissuaded and the foremost Greek warriors volunteer. The greater Aías is chosen by lot to face Hektor. Their duel ends indecisively, and the two men exchange gifts. A truce is arranged during which both armies are to recover their dead and give them proper funerals. The Greeks intend also to build a wall around their encampment near the ships. During a council of the Trojans it is proposed that Helen be surrendered; Paris insists that he will keep her, though he is willing to give up the treasure he had brought to Troy with her. When that offer is made to the Greeks, they refuse it and indicate that even the restoration of Helen will not satisfy them. The dead are cremated and the Greeks build their ramparts.*

BOOK VIII. *Asserting his supreme power over the other deities, Zeus commands them not to intervene in the fighting. Led by the exultant Hektor, the Trojans drive the Greeks back to their seaside encampment behind the walls. When Hêra and Athêna prepare to enter the battle on*

---

[17] This extended comparison is an example of the "Homeric simile," which typically illustrates an action or state of mind but is also, to some extent, a small, self-contained picture or story. Most of Homer's similes are drawn from nature (storms, the sea, etc.) or from the familiar activities of shepherd, farmer, or hunter.

[18] The citadel of Troy.

[19] Hektor hopes that some day they may celebrate a ritual thanksgiving to the gods for the city's survival.

the Greek side, Zeus again asserts his will, forcing them to return reluctantly to Olympos. Zeus decrees that Hektor shall give the Greeks no respite until the time when Akhilleus, roused by the death of his good friend Patróklos, shall return to action. At nightfall the Trojans do not return to the city as usual but encamp on the field, preparing what they hope will be a decisive attack the next day.

BOOK NINE: A VISIT OF EMISSARIES

So Trojans kept their watch that night.

                              To seaward

Panic that attends blood-chilling Rout
now ruled the Akhaians. All their finest men
were shaken by this fear, in bitter throes,
as when a shifting gale
blows up over the cold fish-breeding sea,
north wind and west wind wailing out of Thrace
in squall on squall, and dark waves crest, and shoreward
masses of weed are cast up by the surf:
so were Akhaian hearts torn in their breasts.   10

By that great gloom hard hit, the son of Atreus[1]
made his way amid his criers and told them
to bid each man in person to assembly
but not raise a general cry. He led them,
making the rounds himself, and soon the soldiers
grimly took their places. Then he rose,
with slow tears trickling, as from a hidden spring
dark water runs down, staining a rock wall;
and groaning heavily he addressed the Argives:

"Friends, leaders of Argives, all my captains,   20
Zeus Kronidês entangled me in folly
to my undoing. Wayward god, he promised
solemnly that I should not sail away
before I stormed the inner town of Troy.
Crookedness and duplicity, I see now!
He calls me to return to Argos beaten
after these many losses. That must be
his will and his good pleasure, who knows why?
Many a great town's height has he destroyed
and will destroy, being supreme in power.   30
Enough. Now let us act on what I say:
Board ship for our own fatherland! Retreat!
We cannot hope any longer to take Troy!"

At this a stillness overcame them all,
the Akhaian soldiers. Long they sat in silence,

---

[1] Agamémnon (the higher-ranking son), not Meneláos.

hearing their own hearts beat. Then Diomêdês
rose at last to speak. He said:

"My lord,

I must contend with you for letting go,
for losing balance. I may do so here
in assembly lawfully. Spare me your anger.   40
Before this you have held me up to scorn
for lack of fighting spirit;[2] old and young,
everyone knows the truth of that. In your case,
the son of crooked-minded Krónos gave you
one gift and not both: a staff of kingship
honored by all men, but no staying power—
the greatest gift of all.
What has come over you, to make you think
the Akhaians weak and craven as you say?
If you are in a passion to sail home,   50
sail on: the way is clear, the many ships
that made the voyage from Mykênê[3] with you
stand near the sea's edge. Others here will stay
until we plunder Troy! Or if they, too,
would like to, let them sail for their own country!
Sthênelos[4] and I will fight alone
until we see the destined end of Ilion.
We came here under god."

When Diomêdês

finished, a cry went up from all Akhaians
in wonder at his words. Then Nestor stood   60
and spoke among them:

"Son of Tydeus, formidable

above the rest in war, in council, too,
you have more weight than others of your age.
No one will cry down what you say, no true
Akhaian will, or contradict you. Still,
you did not push on to the end.
I know you are young; in years you might well be
my last-born son, and yet for all of that
you kept your head and said what needed saying
before the Argive captains. My own part,   70
as I am older, is to drive it home.
No one will show contempt for what I say,
surely not Agamémnon, our commander.
Alien to clan and custom and hearth fire

---

[2] Agamémnon made this charge in Book IV; in fact, Diomêdês is one of the bravest warriors among the Greeks.
[3] Agamémnon's chief city (also spelled *Mycenae*).
[4] Diomêdês' comrade and charioteer.

is he who longs for war—heartbreaking war—
with his own people.

                                    Let us yield to darkness
and make our evening meal. But let the sentries
take their rest on watch outside the rampart
near the moat;[5] those are my orders for them.
Afterward, you direct us, Agamémnon,   80
by right of royal power. Provide a feast
for older men, your counselors. That is duty
and no difficulty: your huts are full of wine
brought over daily in our ships from Thrace
across the wide sea, and all provender
for guests is yours, as you are high commander.
Your counselors being met, pay heed to him
who counsels best. The army of Akhaia
bitterly needs a well-found plan of action.
The enemy is upon us, near the ships,   90
burning his thousand fires. What Akhaian
could be highhearted in that glare? This night
will see the army saved or brought to ruin."

They heeded him and did his will. Well-armed,
the sentries left to take their posts, one company
formed around Thrasymêdês, Nestor's son,
another mustered by Askálaphos
and Iálmenos, others commanded by
Meríonês, Aphareus, Dêípyros,
and Kreion's son, the princely Lykomêdês.   100
Seven lieutenants, each with a hundred men,
carrying long spears, issued from the camp
for outposts chosen between ditch and rampart.
Campfires were kindled, and they took their meal.

The son of Atreus led the elder men
together to his hut, where he served dinner,
and each man's hand went out upon the meal.
When they had driven hunger and thirst away,
Old Nestor opened their deliberations—
Nestor, whose counsel had seemed best before,   110
point by point weaving his argument:

"Lord Marshal of the army, Agamémnon,
as I shall end with you, so I begin,
since you hold power over a great army
and are responsible for it: the Lord Zeus
put in your keeping staff and precedent
that you might gather counsel for your men.
You should be first in discourse, but attentive

[5] The defensive ditch outside the walls.

to what another may propose, to act on it
if he speak out for the good of all. Whatever   120
he may initiate, action is yours.
On this rule, let me speak as I think best.
A better view than mine no man can have,
the same view that I've held these many days
since that occasion when, my lord, for all
Akhilleus' rage, you took the girl Brisêis
out of his lodge—but not with our consent.
Far from it; I for one had begged you not to.
Just the same, you gave way to your pride,
and you dishonored a great prince,   130
a hero to whom the gods themselves do honor.
Taking his prize, you kept her and still do.
But even so, and even now, we may
contrive some way of making peace with him
by friendly gifts, and by affectionate words."

Then Agamémnon, the Lord Marshal, answered:

"Sir, there is nothing false in your account
of my blind errors. I committed them;
I will not now deny it. Troops of soldiers
are worth no more than one man cherished by Zeus   140
as he has cherished this man and avenged him,
overpowering the army of Akhaians.
I lost my head, I yielded to black anger,
but now I would retract it and appease him
with all munificence. Here before everyone
I may enumerate the gifts I'll give.
Seven new tripods and ten bars of gold,
then twenty shining caldrons, and twelve horses,
thoroughbreds, who by their wind and legs
have won me prizes: any man who owned   150
what these have brought me could not lack resources,
could not be pinched for precious gold—so many
prizes have these horses carried home.
Then I shall give him seven women, deft
in household handicraft—women of Lesbos
I chose when he himself took Lesbos town,
as they outshone all womankind in beauty.
These I shall give him, and one more, whom I
took away from him then: Briseus' daughter.
Concerning her, I add my solemn oath   160
I never went to bed or coupled with her,
as custom is with men and women.
These will be his at once. If the immortals
grant us the plundering of Priam's town,
let him come forward when the spoils are shared
and load his ship with bars of gold and bronze.

Then he may choose among the Trojan women
twenty that are most lovely, after Helen.
If we return to Argos of Akhaia,
flowing with good things of the earth, he'll be   170
my own adopted son, dear as Orestês,
born long ago and reared in bounteous peace.[6]
I have three daughters now at home, Khrysóthemis,
Laódikê, and Iphiánassa.
He may take whom he will to be his bride
and pay no bridal gift, leading her home
to Pêleus' hall. But I shall add a dowry
such as no man has given to his daughter.
Seven flourishing strongholds I'll give him:
Kardamylê and Ênopê and Hirê   180
in the wild grassland; holy Phêrai too,
and the deep meadowland of Ántheia,
Aipeia and the vineyard slope of Pêdasos,
all lying near the sea in the far west
of sandy Pylos. In these lands are men
who own great flocks and herds; now as his liegemen,
they will pay tithes[7] and sumptuous honor to him,
prospering as they carry out his plans.
These are the gifts I shall arrange if he
desists from anger. Let him be subdued!   190
Lord Death indeed is deaf to appeal, implacable;
of all gods therefore he is most abhorrent
to mortal men. So let Akhilleus bow to me,
considering that I hold higher rank
and claim the precedence of age."

                                                                To this

Lord Nestor of Gerênia replied:

"Lord Marshal of the army, Agamémnon,
this time the gifts you offer Lord Akhilleus
are not to be despised. Come, we'll dispatch
our chosen emissaries to his quarters   200
as quickly as possible. Those men whom I
may designate, let them perform the mission.
Phoinix,[8] dear to Zeus, may lead the way.
Let Aías follow him, and Prince Odysseus.
The criers, Hódios and Eurýbatês,
may go as escorts. Bowls for their hands here!

---

[6] The murder of Agamémnon by his wife, and his son Orestês' later murder of her in revenge, are mentioned in Homer's *Odyssey* and are the central incidents of Aeschylus' *Oresteia*. The following lines fail to mention Agamémnon's best-known daughters, Iphigeneia and Electra. The sacrifice of Iphigeneia by Agamémnon in order to gain favorable winds for the voyage to Troy and Electra's support of her brother in the murder of their mother are important in Aeschylus' plays.

[7] Shares of crops, animals, and so on.   [8] Akhilleus' tutor.

Tell them to keep silence, while we pray
that Zeus the son of Krónos will be merciful."

Nestor's proposal fell on willing ears,
and criers came at once to tip out water   210
over their hands, while young men filled the winebowls
and dipped a measure into every cup.
They spilt their offerings[9] and drank their fill,
then briskly left the hut of Agamémnon.
Nestor accompanied them with final words
and sage looks, especially for Odysseus,
as to the effort they should make to bring
the son of Pêleus round.

                                   Following Phoinix,

Aías and Odysseus walked together
beside the tumbling clamorous whispering sea,   220
praying hard to the girdler of the islands[10]
that they might easily sway their great friend's heart.
Amid the ships and huts of the Myrmidons
they found him, taking joy in a sweet harp
of rich and delicate make—the crossbar set
to hold the strings being silver. He had won it
when he destroyed the city of Eëtíôn,
and plucking it he took his joy: he sang
old tales of heroes, while across the room
alone and silent sat Patróklos, waiting   230
until Akhilleus should be done with song.
Phoinix had come in unremarked,[11] but when
the two new visitors, Odysseus leading,
entered and stood before him, then Akhilleus
rose in wonderment, and left his chair,
his harp still in his hand. So did Patróklos
rise at sight of the two men. Akhilleus
made both welcome with a gesture, saying:

"Peace! My two great friends, I greet your coming.
How I have needed it! Even in my anger,   240
of all Akhaians, you are closest to me."

And Prince Akhilleus led them in. He seated them
on easy chairs with purple coverlets,
and to Patróklos who stood near he said:

"Put out an ampler winebowl, use more wine
for stronger drink,[12] and place a cup for each.
Here are my dearest friends beneath my roof."

---

[9] That is, as tribute to the gods. [10] Poseidon, god of the ocean.
[11] *Phoinix . . . unremarked.* Like "Following Phoinix" a few lines earlier, these words are inserted by the translator as a way of coping with a major problem in the Greek text, which does not mention Phoinix as walking from Agamémnon's hut to that of Akhilleus.
[12] Wine was usually served mixed, often with water.

Patróklos did as his companion bade him.
Meanwhile the host set down a carving block
within the fire's rays; a chine of mutton   250
and a fat chine of goat he placed upon it,
as well as savory pork chine. Automédôn[13]
steadied the meat for him, Akhilleus carved,
then sliced it well and forked it on the spits.
Meanwhile Patróklos, like a god in firelight,
made the hearth blaze up. When the leaping flame
had ebbed and died away, he raked the coals
and in the glow extended spits of meat,
lifting these at times from the firestones
to season with pure salt. When all was done   260
and the roast meat apportioned into platters,
loaves of bread were passed round by Patróklos
in fine baskets. Akhilleus served the meat.
He took his place then opposite Odysseus,
back to the other wall, and told
Patróklos to make offering to the gods.
This he did with meat tossed in the fire,
then each man's hand went out upon the meal.
When they had put their hunger and thirst away,
Aías nodded silently to Phoinix,   270
but Prince Odysseus caught the nod. He filled
a cup of wine and lifted it to Akhilleus,
saying:

                        "Health, Akhilleus. We've no lack
of generous feasts this evening—in the lodge
of Agamémnon first, and now with you,
good fare and plentiful each time.
It is not feasting that concerns us now,
however, but a ruinous defeat.
Before our very eyes we see it coming
and are afraid. By a blade's turn, our good ships   280
are saved or lost, unless you arm your valor.
Trojans and allies are encamped tonight
in pride before our ramparts, at our sterns,
and through their army burn a thousand fires.
These men are sure they cannot now be stopped
but will get through to our good ships. Lord Zeus
flashes and thunders for them on the right,[14]
and Hektor in his ecstasy of power
is mad for battle, confident in Zeus,
deferring to neither men nor gods. Pure frenzy   290
fills him, and he prays for the bright dawn
when he will shear our stern-post beaks away
and fire all our ships, while in the shipways

---

[13] Third-ranking man among the Myrmidons, after Akhilleus and Patróklos.
[14] Favorable omens appeared on the observer's right.

amid that holocaust he carries death
among our men, driven out by smoke. All this
I gravely fear; I fear the gods will make
good his threatenings, and our fate will be
to die here, far from the pastureland of Argos.
Rouse yourself, if even at this hour
you'll pitch in for the Akhaians and deliver them   300
from Trojan havoc. In the years to come
this day will be remembered pain for you
if you do not. No remedy, no remedy
will come to hand, once the great ill is done.
While there is time, think how to keep this evil
day from the Danäans!

                           My dear lad,

how rightly in your case your father, Pêleus,
put it in his farewell, sending you out
from Phthía to take ship with Agamémnon!
'Now as to fighting power, child,' he said,   310
'if Hêra and Athêna wish, they'll give it.
Control your passion, though, and your proud heart,
for gentle courtesy is a better thing.
Break off insidious quarrels, and young and old,
the Argives will respect you for it more.'
That was your old father's admonition:
you have forgotten. Still, even now, abandon
heart-wounding anger. If you will relent,
Agamémnon will match this change of heart
with gifts. Now listen and let me list for you   320
what just now in his quarters he proposed:
seven new tripods, and ten bars of gold,
then twenty shining caldrons, and twelve horses,
thoroughbreds, that by their wind and legs
have won him prizes: any man who owned
what these have brought him would not lack resources,
could not be pinched for precious gold—so many
prizes have these horses carried home.
Then he will give you seven women, deft
in household handicraft: women of Lesbos   330
chosen when you yourself took Lesbos town,
as they outshone all womankind in beauty.
These he will give you, and one more, whom he
took away from you then: Briseus' daughter,
concerning whom he adds a solemn oath
never to have gone to bed or coupled with her,
as custom is, my lord, with men and women.
These are all yours at once. If the immortals
grant us the pillaging of Priam's town,
you may come forward when the spoils are shared   340
and load your ship with bars of gold and bronze.
Then you may choose among the Trojan women

twenty that are most lovely, after Helen.
And then, if we reach Argos of Akhaia,
flowing with good things of the earth, you'll be
his own adopted son, dear as Orestês,
born long ago and reared in bounteous peace.
He has three daughters now at home, Khrysóthemis,
Laódikê, and Iphiánassa.
You may take whom you will to be your bride   350
and pay no gift when you conduct her home
to your ancestral hall. He'll add a dowry
such as no man has given to his daughter.
Seven flourishing strongholds he'll give to you:
Kardamylê and Enopê and Hirê
in the wild grassland; holy Phêrai too,
and the deep meadowland of Ántheia,
Aipeia and the vineyard slope of Pêdasos,
all lying near the sea in the far west
of sandy Pylos. In these lands are men   360
who own great flocks and herds; now as your liegemen,
they will pay tithes and sumptuous honor to you,
prospering as they carry out your plans.
These are the gifts he will arrange if you
desist from anger.

                                        Even if you abhor
the son of Atreus all the more bitterly,
with all his gifts, take pity on the rest,
all the old army, worn to rags in battle.
These will honor you as gods are honored!
And ah, for these, what glory you may win!   370
Think: Hektor is your man this time: being crazed
with ruinous pride, believing there's no fighter
equal to him among those that our ships
brought here by sea, he'll put himself in range!"

Akhilleus the great runner answered him:

"Son of Laërtês and the gods of old,
Odysseus, master soldier and mariner,
I owe you a straight answer, as to how
I see this thing, and how it is to end.
No need to sit with me like mourning doves   380
making your gentle noise by turns. I hate
as I hate Hell's own gate that man who hides
one thought within him while he speaks another.
What I shall say is what I see and think.
Give in to Agamémnon? I think not,
neither to him nor to the rest. I had
small thanks for fighting, fighting without truce
against hard enemies here. The portion's equal
whether a man hangs back or fights his best;

the same respect, or lack of it, is given   390
brave man and coward. One who's active dies
like the do-nothing. What least thing have I
to show for it, for harsh days undergone
and my life gambled, all these years of war?
A bird will give her fledglings every scrap
she comes by, and go hungry, foraging.
That is the case with me.
Many a sleepless night I've spent afield
and many a day in bloodshed, hand to hand
in battle for the wives of other men.   400
In sea raids I plundered a dozen towns,
eleven in expeditions overland
through Trojan country, and the treasure taken
out of them all, great heaps of handsome things,
I carried back each time to Agamémnon.
He sat tight on the beachhead, and shared out
a little treasure; most of it he kept.
He gave prizes of war to his officers;
the rest have theirs, not I; from me alone
of all Akhaians, he pre-empted her.   410
He holds my bride,[15] dear to my heart. Aye, let him
sleep with her and enjoy her!

                                                    Why must Argives
fight the Trojans? Why did he raise an army
and lead it here? For Helen, was it not?
Are the Atreidai of all mortal men
the only ones who love their wives? I think not.
Every sane decent fellow loves his own
and cares for her, as in my heart I loved
Brisêis, though I won her by the spear.
Now, as he took my prize out of my hands,   420
tricked and defrauded me, he need not tempt me;
I know him, and he cannot change my mind.
Let him take thought, Odysseus, with you
and others how the ships may be defended
against incendiary attack. By god,
he has achieved imposing work without me,
a rampart piled up overnight, a ditch
running beyond it, broad and deep,
with stakes implanted in it! All no use!
He cannot hold against the killer's charge.   430
As long as I was in the battle, Hektor
never cared for a fight far from the walls;
his limit was the oak tree by the gate.
When I was alone one day he waited there,
but barely got away when I went after him.
Now it is I who do not care to fight.

---

[15] Brisêis; she is not literally his wife, however.

Tomorrow at dawn when I have made offering
to Zeus and all the gods, and hauled my ships
for loading in the shallows, if you like
and if it interests you, look out and see   440
my ships on Hellê's waters in the offing,[16]
oarsmen in line making the sea-foam scud!
And if the great Earthshaker[17] gives a breeze,
the third day out I'll make it home to Phthía.
Rich possessions are there I left behind
when I was mad enough to come here; now
I take home gold and ruddy bronze, and women
belted luxuriously, and hoary iron,
all that came to me here. As for my prize,
he who gave her took her outrageously back.   450
Well, you can tell him all this to his face,
and let the other Akhaians burn
if he in his thick hide of shamelessness
picks out another man to cheat. He would not
look me in the eye, dog that he is!
I will not share one word of counsel with him,
nor will I act with him; he robbed me blind,
broke faith with me: he gets no second chance
to play me for a fool. Once is enough.
To hell with him, Zeus took his brains away!   460
His gifts I abominate, and I would give
not one dry shuck for him. I would not change,
not if he multiplied his gifts by ten,
by twenty times what he has now, and more,
no matter where they came from: if he gave
what enters through Orkhómenos' town gate
or Thebes of Egypt, where the treasures lie—
that city where through each of a hundred gates
two hundred men drive out in chariots.[18]
Not if his gifts outnumbered the sea sands   470
or all the dust grains in the world could Agamémnon
ever appease me—not till he pays me back
full measure, pain for pain, dishonor for dishonor.
The daughter of Agamémnon, son of Atreus,
I will not take in marriage. Let her be
as beautiful as pale-gold Aphrodítê,
skilled as Athêna of the sea-grey eyes,
I will not have her, at any price. No, let him
find someone else, an eligible Akhaian,
kinglier than I.

                                                   Now if the gods   480

---

[16] *Hellê's waters:* The Hellespont (the modern Dardanelles). *offing:* horizon.
[17] Poseidon.
[18] *Orkhómenos:* an important city northwest of Athens. *Thebes:* an ancient, royal city of
Egypt.

preserve me and I make it home, my father
Pêleus will select a bride for me.
In Hellas[19] and in Phthîa there are many
daughters of strong men who defend the towns.
I'll take the one I wish to be my wife.
There in my manhood I have longed, indeed,
to marry someone of congenial mind
and take my ease, enjoying the great estate
my father had acquired.

                                Now I think

no riches can compare with being alive,   490
not even those they say this well-built Ilion
stored up in peace before the Akhaians came.
Neither could all the Archer's shrine contains
at rocky Pytho,[20] in the crypt of stone.
A man may come by cattle and sheep in raids;
tripods he buys, and tawny-headed horses;
but his life's breath cannot be hunted back
or be recaptured once it pass his lips.
My mother, Thetis of the silvery feet,
tells me of two possible destinies   500
carrying me toward death: two ways:
if on the one hand I remain to fight
around Troy town, I lose all hope of home
but gain unfading glory; on the other,
if I sail back to my own land my glory
fails—but a long life lies ahead for me.
To all the rest of you I say: 'Sail home:
you will not now see Ilion's last hour,'
for Zeus who views the wide world held his sheltering
hand over that city, and her troops   510
have taken heart.

                         Return, then, emissaries,
deliver my answer to the Akhaian peers—
it is the senior officer's privilege—
and let them plan some other way, and better,
to save their ships and save the Akhaian army.
This one cannot be put into effect—
their scheme this evening—while my anger holds.
Phoinix may stay and lodge the night with us,
then take ship and sail homeward at my side
tomorrow, if he wills. I'll not constrain him."   520

After Akhilleus finished, all were silent,
awed, for he spoke with power.
Then the old master-charioteer, Lord Phoinix,

---

[19] This word later came to mean all of Greece; here it refers to a region in northern Greece.
[20] Temple of Apollo at Delphi in Greece; visitors seeking the god's oracular guidance made rich offerings.

answered at last, and let his tears come shining,
fearing for the Akhaian ships:

                                                                    "Akhilleus,

if it is true you set your heart on home
and will not stir a finger to save the ships
from being engulfed by fire—all for this rage
that has swept over you—how, child, could I
be sundered from you, left behind alone?
For your sake the old master-charioteer,   530
Pêleus, made provision that I should come,
that day he gave you godspeed out of Phthía
to go with Agamémnon. Still a boy,
you knew nothing of war that levels men
to the same testing, nothing of assembly
where men become illustrious. That is why
he sent me, to instruct you in these matters,
to be a man of eloquence and action.
After all that, dear child, I should not wish   540
to be left here apart from you—not even
if god himself should undertake to smooth
my wrinkled age and make me fresh and young,
as when for the first time I left the land
of lovely women, Hellas. I went north
to avoid a feud with Father, Amyntor
Orménidês. His anger against me rose
over a fair-haired slave girl whom he fancied,
without respect for his own wife, my mother.
Mother embraced my knees and begged that I   550
make love to this girl, so that afterward
she might be cold to the aging man. I did it.
My father guessed the truth at once, and cursed me,
praying the ghostly Furies[21] that no son
of mine should ever rest upon his knees:
a curse fulfilled by the immortals—Lord
Zeus of undergloom and cold Perséphonê.[22]
I planned to put a sword in him, and would have,
had not some god unstrung my rage, reminding me
of country gossip and the frowns of men;   560
I shrank from being called a parricide
among the Akhaians. But from that time on
I felt no tie with home, no love for lingering
under the rooftree of a raging father.
Our household and our neighbors, it is true,
urged me to stay. They made a handsome feast
of shambling cattle butchered, and fat sheep;
young porkers by the litter, crisp with fat,
were singed and spitted in Hêphaistos' fire,

---

[21] Spirits who avenge sins, especially against blood kindred.
[22] *Zeus of undergloom:* Aïdês (Hades), ruler of the dead. *Perséphonê:* his queen.

rivers of wine drunk from the old man's store.   570
Nine times they spent the night and slept beside me,
taking the watch by turns, leaving a fire
to flicker under the entrance colonnade,
and one more in the court outside my room.
But when the tenth night came, starless and black,
I cracked the tight bolt on my chamber door,
pushed out, and scaled the courtyard wall, unseen
by household men on watch or women slaves.
Then I escaped from that place, made my way
through Hellas where the dancing floors are wide,   580
until I came to Phthía's fertile plain,
mother of flocks, and Pêleus the king.
He gave me welcome, treated me with love,
as a father would an only son, his heir
to rich possessions. And he made me rich,
appointing me great numbers of retainers
on the frontier of Phthía, where I lived
as lord of Dolopês. Now, it was I
who formed your manhood, handsome as a god's,
Akhilleus: I who loved you from the heart;   590
for never in another's company
would you attend a feast or dine in hall—
never, unless I took you on my knees
and cut your meat, and held your cup of wine.
Many a time you wet my shirt, hiccuping
wine-bubbles in distress, when you were small.
Patient and laborious as a nurse
I had to be for you, bearing in mind
that never would the gods bring into being
any son of mine. Godlike Akhilleus,   600
you were the manchild that I made my own
to save me someday, so I thought, from misery.
Quell your anger, Akhilleus! You must not
be pitiless! The gods themselves relent,
and are they not still greater in bravery,
in honor and in strength? Burnt offerings,
courteous prayer, libation, smoke of sacrifice,
with all of these, men can placate the gods
when someone oversteps and errs. The truth is,
prayers[23] are daughters of almighty Zeus—   610
one may imagine them lame, wrinkled things
with eyes cast down, that toil to follow after
passionate Folly. Folly is strong and swift,
outrunning all the prayers, and everywhere

[23]*prayers:* pleas for forgiveness, uttered by a man who, after harming another while possessed by a kind of madness (Folly), repents of his misdeed. If the injured man accepts the plea or prayer he is rewarded, but if he rejects it he may himself be visited by a fit of Folly that drives him to a ruinous act. The allegory is prophetic of what will happen to Akhilleus.

arriving first to injure mortal men;
still they come healing after. If a man
reveres the daughters of Zeus when they come near,
he is rewarded, and his prayers are heard;
but if he spurns them and dismisses them,
they make their way to Zeus again and ask   620
that Folly dog that man till suffering
has taken arrogance out of him.

                                                                      Relent,

be courteous to the daughters of Zeus, you too,
as courtesy sways others, and the best.
If Agamémnon had no gifts for you,
named none to follow, but inveighed against you
still in fury, then I could never say,
'Discard your anger and defend the Argives—'
never, no matter how they craved your help.
But this is not so: he will give many things   630
at once; he promised others; he has sent
his noblest men to intercede with you,
the flower of the army, and your friends,
dearest among the Argives. Will you turn
their words, their coming, into humiliation?
Until this moment, no one took it ill
that you should suffer anger; we learned this
from the old stories of how towering wrath
could overcome great men; but they were still
amenable to gifts and to persuasion.   640
Here is an instance I myself remember
not from our own time but in ancient days:
I'll tell it to you all, for all are friends.
The Kourêtês were fighting a warlike race,[24]
Aitolians, around the walls of Kálydôn,
with slaughter on both sides: Aitolians
defending their beloved Kálydôn
while the Kourêtês longed to sack the town.
The truth is, Artemis of the Golden Chair
had brought the scourge of war on the Aitolians;   650
she had been angered because Oineus made
no harvest offering from his vineyard slope.

---

[24] The story Phoinix proceeds to tell is a parable, drawn from mythology and adapted here to make it fit Akhilleus' situation. Reordered chronologically, the story is as follows: Artemis, goddess of the hunt and of wild life ("Mistress of Long Arrows"), was offended by the failure of Oineus, king of the Aitolians, to honor her. In revenge, she sent a great boar to ravage his land. The king's son, Meléagros, organized a band of men to kill the boar. After it was killed, the Aitolians quarreled with the Kourêtês, a neighboring people, over the animal's head and hide; in the ensuing war the Kourêtês threatened Kálydôn, Oineus' city. In the fighting Meléagros killed his mother Althaié's brother, who was fighting on the Kourêtês' side. She cursed her son, who therefore retired from battle, putting his city in peril. His people and family implored him to defend it and offered him gifts, but he resisted their pleas until his wife Kleopátrê persuaded him. He them saved the city, but only after it was too late for him to receive the gifts.

While other gods enjoyed his hekatombs
he made her none, either forgetful of it
or careless—a great error, either way.
In her anger, the Mistress of Long Arrows
roused against him a boar with gleaming tusks
out of his wild grass bed, a monstrous thing
that ravaged the man's vineyard many times
and felled entire orchards, roots, 660
blooms, apples and all. Now this great boar
Meléagros, the son of Oineus, killed
by gathering men and hounds from far and near.
So huge the boar was, no small band could master him,
and he brought many to the dolorous pyre.[25]
Around the dead beast Artemis set on
a clash with battlecries between Kourêtês
and proud Aitolians over the boar's head
and shaggy hide. As long, then, as Meléagros,
backed by the wargod, fought, the Kourêtês 670
had the worst of it for all their numbers
and could not hold a line outside the walls.
But then a day came when Meléagros
was stung by venomous anger that infects
the coolest thinker's heart: swollen with rage
at his own mother, Althaiê, he languished
in idleness at home beside his lady,
Kleopátrê.

                                This lovely girl was born

to Marpessê of ravishing pale ankles,[26]
Euênos' child, and Idês, who had been 680
most powerful of men on earth. He drew
the bow against the Lord Phoibos Apollo
over his love, Marpessê, whom her father
and gentle mother called Alkýonê,
since for her sake her mother gave that seabird's
forlorn cry when Apollo ravished her.
With Kleopátrê lay Meléagros,
nursing the bitterness his mother stirred,
when in her anguish over a brother slain
she cursed her son. She called upon the gods, 690
beating the grassy earth with both her hands
as she pitched forward on her knees, with cries
to the Lord of Undergloom and cold Perséphonê,
while tears wetted her veils—in her entreaty
that death come to her son. Inexorable

---

[25] The fire in which the dead were cremated.
[26] The poem digresses for a few lines to describe the parents of Meléagros' wife, Kleopátrê. Her father Idês and the god Apollo had been rivals for the love of her mother Marpessê (who chose her human lover), also called Alkýonê, a name denoting a sea-bird with a mournful cry.

in Érebos[27] a vampire Fury listened.
Soon, then, about the gates of the Aitolians
tumult and din of war grew loud; their towers
rang with blows. And now the elder men
implored Meléagros to leave his room,   700
and sent the high priests of the gods, imploring him
to help defend the town. They promised him
a large reward: in the green countryside
of Kálydôn, wherever it was richest,
there he might choose a beautiful garden plot
of fifty acres, half in vineyard, half
in virgin prairie for the plow to cut.
Oineus, master of horsemen, came with prayers
upon the doorsill of the chamber, often
rattling the locked doors, pleading with his son.   710
His sisters, too, and then his gentle mother
pleaded with him. Only the more fiercely
he turned away. His oldest friends, his dearest,
not even they could move him—not until
his room was shaken by a hail of stones
as Kourêtês began to scale the walls
and fire the city.

                      Then at last his lady
in her soft-belted gown besought him weeping,
speaking of all the ills that come to men
whose town is taken: soldiers put to the sword;   720
the city razed by fire; alien hands
carrying off the children and the women.
Hearing these fearful things, his heart was stirred
to action: he put on his shining gear
and fought off ruin from the Aitolians.
Mercy prevailed in him. His folk no longer
cared to award him gifts and luxuries,
yet even so he saved that terrible day.
Oh, do not let your mind go so astray!
Let no malignant spirit   730
turn you that way, dear son! It will be worse
to fight for ships already set afire!
Value the gifts; rejoin the war; Akhaians
afterward will give you a god's honor.
If you reject the gifts and then, later,
enter the deadly fight, you will not be
accorded the same honor, even though
you turn the tide of war!"

                      But the great runner
Akhilleus answered:

---

[27] Part of the realm of the dead.

"Old uncle Phoinix, bless you,

that is an honor I can live without. 740
Honored I think I am by Zeus's justice,
justice that will sustain me by the ships
as long as breath is in me and I can stand.
Here is another point: ponder it well:
best not confuse my heart with lamentation
for Agamémnon, whom you must not honor;
you would be hateful to me, dear as you are.
Loyalty should array you at my side
in giving pain to him who gives me pain.
Rule with me equally, share half my honor,[28] 750
but do not ask my help for Agamémnon.
My answer will be reported by these two.
Lodge here in a soft bed, and at first light
we can decide whether to sail or stay."

He knit his brows and nodded to Patróklos
to pile up rugs for Phoinix' bed—a sign
for the others to be quick about departing.
Aías, however, noble son of Télamôn
made the last appeal. He said:

"Odysseus,

master soldier and mariner, let us go. 760
I do not see the end of this affair
achieved by this night's visit. Nothing for it
but to report our talk for what it's worth
to the Danáäns, who sit waiting there.
Akhilleus hardened his great heart against us,
wayward and savage as he is, unmoved
by the affections of his friends who made him
honored above all others on the beachhead.
There is no pity in him. A normal man
will take the penalty for a brother slain 770
or a dead son. By paying much, the one
who did the deed may stay unharmed at home.
Fury and pride in the bereaved are curbed
when he accepts the penalty. Not you.
Cruel and unappeasable rage the gods
put in you for one girl alone. We offer
seven beauties, and much more besides!
Be gentler, and respect your own rooftree
whereunder we are guests who speak for all
Danáäns as a body. Our desire 780
is to be closest to you of them all."

---

[28] This is not meant literally; Akhilleus is saying, in effect, "Ask any favor except that I help Agamémnon."

Akhilleus the great runner answered him:

"Scion[29] of Télamôn and gods of old,
Aías, lord of fighting men, you seemed
to echo my own mind in what you said!
And yet my heart grows large and hot with fury
remembering that affair: as though I were
some riffraff or camp follower, he taunted me
before them all!

                                        Go back, report the news:
I will not think of carnage or of war   790
until Prince Hektor, son of Priam, reaches
Myrmidon huts and ships in his attack,
slashing through Argives, burning down their ships.
Around my hut, my black ship, I foresee
for all his fury, Hektor will break off combat."[30]

That was his answer. Each of the emissaries
took up a double-handed cup and poured
libation by the shipways. Then Odysseus
led the way on their return. Patróklos
commanded his retainers and the maids   800
to make at once a deep-piled bed for Phoinix.
Obediently they did so, spreading out
fleeces and coverlet and a linen sheet,
and down the old man lay, awaiting Dawn.
Akhilleus slept in the well-built hut's recess,
and with him lay a woman he had brought
from Lesbos, Phorbas' daughter, Diomêdê.
Patróklos went to bed at the other end,
and with him, too, a woman lay—soft-belted
Iphis, who had been given to him by Akhilleus   810
when he took Skyros, ringed by cliff, the mountain
fastness of Enyéus.

                                        Now the emissaries
arrived at Agamémnon's lodge. With cups
of gold held up, and rising to their feet
on every side, the Akhaians greeted them,
curious for the news. Lord Agamémnon
put the question first:

                                        "Come, tell me, sir,
Odysseus, glory of Akhaia—will Akhilleus
fight off ravenous fire from the ships
or does he still refuse, does anger still   820
hold sway in his great heart?"

---

[29] Offspring.
[30] Akhilleus is apparently modifying his earlier resolve to sail away the next morning.

That patient man,
the Prince Odysseus, made reply:

"Excellency,

Lord Marshal of the army, son of Atreus,
the man has no desire to quench his rage.
On the contrary, he is more than ever
full of anger, spurns you and your gifts,
calls on you to work out your own defense
to save the ships and the Akhaian army.
As for himself, he threatens at daybreak
to drag his well-found ships into the surf,   830
and says he would advise the rest as well
to sail for home. 'You shall not see,' he says,
'the last hour that awaits tall Ilion,
for Zeus who views the wide world held his sheltering
hand over the city, and her troops
have taken heart.' That was Akhilleus' answer.
Those who were with me can confirm all this,
Aías can, and the two clearheaded criers.
As to old Phoinix, he is sleeping there
by invitation, so that he may sail   840
to his own country, homeward with Akhilleus,
tomorrow, if he wills, without constraint."

When he had finished everyone was still,
sitting in silence and in perturbation
for a long time. At last brave Diomêdês,
lord of the warcry, said:

"Excellency,

Lord Marshal of the army, Agamémnon,
you never should have pled with him, or given
so many gifts to him. At the best of times
he is a proud man; now you have pushed him far   850
deeper into his vanity and pride.
By god, let us have done with him—
whether he goes or stays! He'll fight again
when the time comes, whenever his blood is up
or the god rouses him. As for ourselves,
let everyone now do as I advise
and go to rest. Your hearts have been refreshed
with bread and wine, the pith and nerve of men.
When the fair Dawn with finger tips of rose
makes heaven bright, deploy your men and horses   860
before the ships at once, and cheer them on,
and take your place, yourself, in the front line
to join the battle."

All gave their assent

in admiration of Diomêdês,
breaker of horses. When they had spilt their wine
they all dispersed, each man to his own hut,
and lying down they took the gift of sleep.

BOOK X. *The troubled Agamémnon and his brother Meneláos, unable to sleep, assemble
the Greek chieftains in the night. After they inspect the sentries, Nestor proposes that a recon-
naissance patrol try to discover the Trojan plans. Diomêdês volunteers for the dangerous
mission, choosing the wily Odysseus as his partner. Meanwhile the Trojans too decide to send
out a scout, a man named Dolôn. Diomêdês and Odysseus capture him, lead him to believe he
will be taken prisoner alive, get information from him, and then kill him. The two Greeks,
acting on what they have learned, raid the camp of King Rhêsos of Thrace, a newcomer to the
war, kill him and several of his men, steal his wondrous horses, and then return triumphantly
to the ships.*

BOOK XI. *The next day brings fierce general fighting, gods and goddesses remaining out
of action. At first Agamémnon inflicts severe damage on the Trojans, who retreat before him.
Zeus sends his messenger-goddess Iris to tell Hektor that he should not engage the enemy
himself until Agamémnon shall be wounded. Soon thereafter the Greek commander is in fact
wounded and forced to return to the camp. Hektor leads a counterattack. Diomêdês is
wounded, by an arrow from Paris, and then Odysseus is wounded too. Meneláos and the
greater Aías come to Odysseus' aid. Nestor takes the wounded Greek physician Makháôn back
to the camp as Aías slowly retreats before a swarm of Trojans. At this point almost all the
important Greek leaders have been put out of action. Akhilleus, aboard his ship, exults over the
Greeks' plight but sends his friend Patróklos to Nestor for information about the wounded man
he is attending. Nestor reminds Patróklos that the latter's proper mission is to counsel Akhilleus
and goes on to suggest that Akhilleus authorize Patróklos to lead the Myrmidons, Akhilleus'
rested troops, against the Trojans. Patróklos feels sympathy for the desperate Greeks.*

from BOOK TWELVE: THE RAMPART BREACHED

The immortals still inactive, Hektor leads an assault on the palisaded fort that protects the Greek camp and ships. (The main defenders are now the two Aíases and
the archer Teukros.) Poulýdamas, a Trojan, suggests to Hektor that the Trojan
forces should breach the moat on foot rather than with chariots; Hektor accepts the
advice. But a later suggestion by Poulýdamas, that the army should retreat in accordance with an apparent ill omen, is scornfully rejected by Hektor. Sarpêdôn—
king of Lykia, son of Zeus, and ally of the Trojans—prepares to attack the wall.

But even so, and even now, the Trojans
led by great Hektor could not yet have breached
the wall and gate with massive bar, had not
Lord Zeus impelled Sarpêdôn, his own son,   330
against the Argives like a lion on cattle.
Circular was the shield he held before him,
hammered out of pure bronze: aye, the smith
had hammered it, and riveted the plates
to thick bull's hide on golden rods rigged out
to the full circumference. Now gripping this,

hefting a pair of spears, he joined the battle,
formidable as some hill-bred lion, ravenous
for meat after long abstinence. His valor
summons him to attempt homesteads and flocks— 340
and though he find herdsmen on hand with dogs
and spears to guard the sheep, he will not turn
without a fling at the stockade. One thing
or the other: a mighty leap and a fresh kill,
or he will fall at the spearmen's feet, brought down
by a javelin thrown hard.

                                   So valor drove

Sarpêdôn to the wall to make a breakthrough.
Turning to Glaukos, Hippólokhos' son, he said:

"What is the point of being honored so
with precedence at table, choice of meat, 350
and brimming cups, at home in Lykia,
like gods at ease in everyone's regard?
And why have lands been granted you and me
on Xánthos bank: to each his own demesne,
with vines and fields of grain?

                                So that we two

at times like this in the Lykian front line
may face the blaze of battle and fight well,
that Lykian men-at-arms may say:
'They are no common men, our lords who rule
in Lykia. They eat fat lamb at feasts 360
and drink rare vintages, but the main thing is
their fighting power, when they lead in combat!'

Ah, cousin, could we but survive this war
to live forever deathless, without age,
I would not ever go again to battle,
nor would I send you there for honor's sake!
But now a thousand shapes of death surround us,
and no man can escape them, or be safe.
Let us attack—whether to give some fellow
glory or to win it from him." 370

BOOK XII (continued). *After this speech to Glaukos, Sarpêdôn assaults the wall and is partially successful. It is Hektor, however, who finally breaks down one of the gates. His troops swarm into the fort after him, the Greeks fleeing toward the ships.*

BOOK XIII. *Confident that his earlier prohibition will keep the other gods from interfering in the war, Zeus relaxes his vigilance. The sea-god Poseidon, however, takes advantage of the opportunity and comes covertly to the Greeks' aid, inciting them to stiff resistance. Fierce battle continues, reflected in many scattered engagements. Zeus' plan, we learn, is to give the Trojans a limited victory in answer to Thetis' plea in Book I that Akhilleus be vindicated, but the god will not let the Greeks be utterly defeated. Idómeneus the king of Krete (Crete) performs valiant deeds on the Greek side. The Trojans falter, but Hektor rallies them. The Book ends as the Greeks prepare to resist still another Trojan offensive.*

BOOK XIV. *With Agamémnon, Diomêdês, and Odysseus all wounded, the Greeks are on the point of being routed. Agamémnon proposes to launch the ships, but Odysseus scorns the idea as cowardice and bad strategy. Diomêdês urges that the three return to the fight, at least to encourage their comrades. Poseidon continues to help the Greeks; to support him, Hêra decides to hoodwink Zeus by seducing him and then making him fall asleep—a project in which she wins the help of Aphroditê by deception and of the god Sleep by bribes. With Zeus asleep, Poseidon is able to help the Greeks even more than before, and the tide of battle is turned. The greater Aías wounds Hektor with a large stone so that he has to be carried out of battle. The Trojans withdraw in panic.*

BOOK XV. *Zeus awakens, sees the Trojans being routed by the Greeks and Poseidon, and is enraged at the trick Hêra has played on him. He predicts the future course of the war: the Greeks will be driven back to the ships again, Akhilleus will send Patróklos into the fight, Hektor will kill Patróklos and then be killed by Akhilleus, the Greeks will take Troy. But for the time being Zeus will continue to humiliate the Greeks as part of his plan to vindicate Akhilleus. He sends Hêra back to Olympos with instructions to summon Iris and Apollo. When they come to him, he sends Iris to order Poseidon out of the action and Apollo to reinvigorate the wounded Hektor. Poseidon angrily and reluctantly obeys, and Apollo leads Hektor and the Trojans back to the ships, leveling the protective walls and making a causeway across the moat. The dismayed Patróklos, who since the end of Book XI has been attending one of the wounded in the Greeks' camp, hurries away to persuade Akhilleus to come to the rescue. Zeus' will is that the Trojans shall set fire to part of the Grecian fleet.*

BOOK SIXTEEN: A SHIP FIRED, A TIDE TURNED

That was the way the fighting went
for one seagoing ship. Meanwhile Patróklos
approached Akhilleus his commander, streaming
warm tears—like a shaded mountain spring
that makes a rockledge run with dusky water.
Akhilleus watched him come, and felt a pang for him.
Then the great prince and runner said:

                                        "Patróklos,

why all the weeping? Like a small girlchild
who runs beside her mother and cries and cries
to be taken up, and catches at her gown,   10
and will not let her go, looking up in tears
until she has her wish: that's how you seem,
Patróklos, winking out your glimmering tears.
Have you something to tell the Myrmidons
or me? Some message you alone have heard
from Phthía? But they say that Aktor's son,
Menoitios, is living still, and Pêleus,
the son of Aíakos, lives on
amid his Myrmidons.[1] If one of these
were dead, we should be grieved.

                                   Or is this weeping   20

---

[1] *Menoitios, Pêleus.* The fathers of, respectively, Patróklos and Akhilleus.

over the Argives, seeing how they perish
at the long ships by their own bloody fault!
Speak out now, don't conceal it, let us share it."

And groaning, Patróklos, you replied:

"Akhilleus, prince and greatest of Akhaians,
be forbearing. They are badly hurt.
All who were the best fighters are now lying
among the ships with spear or arrow wounds.
Diomêdês, Tydeus' rugged son, was shot;
Odysseus and Agamémnon, the great spearman,   30
have spear wounds; Eurýpylos[2]
took an arrow shot deep in his thigh.
Surgeons with medicines are attending them
to ease their wounds.

                            But you are a hard case,
Akhilleus! God forbid this rage you nurse
should master me. You and your fearsome pride!
What good will come of it to anyone, later,
unless you keep disaster from the Argives?
Have you no pity?
Pêleus, master of horse, was not your father,   40
Thetis was not your mother! Cold grey sea
and sea-cliffs bore you, making a mind so harsh.
If in your heart you fear some oracle,
some word of Zeus, told by your gentle mother,
then send me out at least, and send me quickly,[3]
give me a company of Myrmidons,
and I may be a beacon to Danááns!
Lend me your gear to strap over my shoulders;
Trojans then may take me for yourself
and break off battle, giving our worn-out men   50
a chance to breathe. Respites are brief in war.
We fresh troops with one battlecry might easily
push their tired men back on the town,
away from ships and huts."

                                 So he petitioned,

witless as a child that what he begged for
was his own death, hard death and doom.

                                    Akhilleus

out of his deep anger made reply:

"Hard words, dear prince. There is no oracle
I know of that I must respect, no word

---

[2] A wounded Greek warrior whom Patróklos has been tending since the action of Book XI.
[3] This suggestion, like certain other points in Patróklos' speech, was made first by Nestor in Book XI.

from Zeus reported by my gentle mother.[4]   60
Only this bitterness eats at my heart
when one man would deprive and shame his equal,
taking back his prize by abuse of power.
The girl whom the Akhaians chose for me
I won by my own spear. A town with walls
I stormed and sacked for her. Then Agamémnon
stole her back, out of my hands, as though
I were some vagabond held cheap.

                                                  All that

we can let pass as being over and done with;
I could not rage forever. And yet, by heaven, I swore   70
I would not rest from anger till the cries
and clangor of battle reached my very ships!
But you, now, you can strap my famous gear
on your own shoulders, and then take command
of Myrmidons on edge and ripe for combat,
now that like a dark stormcloud the Trojans
have poured round the first ships, and Argive troops
have almost no room for maneuver left,
with nothing to their rear but sea. The whole
townful of Trojans joins in, sure of winning,   80
because they cannot see my helmet's brow
aflash in range of them. They'd fill the gullies
with dead men soon, in flight up through the plain,
if Agamémnon were on good terms with me.
As things are, they've outflanked the camp. A mercy
for them that in the hands of Diomêdês
no great spear goes berserk, warding death
from the Danääns! Not yet have I heard
the voice of Agamémnon, either, shouting
out of his hateful skull. The shout of Hektor,   90
the killer, calling Trojans, makes a roar
like breaking surf, and with long answering cries
they hold the whole plain where they drove the Akhaians.
Even so, defend the ships, Patróklos.
Attack the enemy in force, or they
will set the ships ablaze with whirling fire
and rob Akhaians of their dear return.
Now carry out the purpose I confide,
so that you'll win great honor for me, and glory
among Danääns; then they'll send me back   100
my lovely girl, with bright new gifts as well.
Once you expel the enemy from the ships,
rejoin me here. If Hêra's lord,
the lord of thunder, grants you the day's honor,

---

[4] These words seem to contradict what Akhilleus has said in Book IX about his "two possible destinies"; possibly the excited Akhilleus means something like "That is not the point right now."

covet no further combat far from me
with Trojan soldiers. That way you'd deny me
recompense of honor. You must not,
for joy of battle, joy of killing Trojans,
carry the fight to Ilion![5] Some power
out of Olympos, one of the immortal gods,   110
might intervene for them. The Lord Apollo
loves the Trojans. Turn back, then, as soon
as you restore the safety of the ships,
and let the rest contend, out on the plain.
Ah, Father Zeus, Athêna, and Apollo!
If not one Trojan of them all
should get away from death, and not one Argive
save ourselves were spared, we two alone
could pull down Troy's old coronet of towers!"

These were the speeches they exchanged. Now Aías   120
could no longer hold:[6] he was dislodged
by spear-throws, beaten by the mind of Zeus
and Trojan shots. His shining helm rang out
around his temples dangerously with hits
as his helmplates were struck and struck again;
he felt his shoulder galled on the left side
hugging the glittering shield—and yet they could not
shake it, putting all their weight in throws.
In painful gasps his breath came, sweat ran down
in rivers off his body everywhere;   130
no rest for him, but trouble upon trouble.

Now tell me, Muses, dwellers on Olympos,
how fire first fell on the Akhaian ships!
Hektor moved in to slash with his long blade
at Aías' ashwood shaft, and near the spearhead
lopped it off. Then Telamônian Aías
wielded a pointless shaft, while far away
the flying bronze head rang upon the ground,
and Aías shivered knowing in his heart
the work of gods: how Zeus, the lord of thunder,   140
cut off his war-craft in that fight, and willed
victory to the Trojans. He gave way
before their missiles as they rushed in throwing
untiring fire into the ship. It caught
at once, a-gush with flame, and fire lapped
about the stern.

Akhilleus smote his thighs

and said to Patróklos:

"Now go into action,

---

[5] To the city of Troy itself.
[6] Aías is aboard one of the beached ships, using a long spear to ward off attackers.

prince and horseman! I see roaring fire
burst at the ships. Action, or they'll destroy them,
leaving no means of getting home. Be quick,   150
strap on my gear, while I alert the troops!"

Patróklos now put on the flashing bronze.
Greaves were the first thing, beautifully fitted
to calf and shin with silver ankle chains;
and next he buckled round his ribs the cuirass,
blazoned with stars, of swift Aiákidês;[7]
then slung the silver-studded blade of bronze
about his shoulders, and the vast solid shield;
then on his noble head he placed the helm,
its plume of terror nodding high above,   160
and took two burly spears with his own handgrip.
He did not take the great spear of Akhilleus,
weighty, long, and tough. No other Akhaian
had the strength to wield it, only Akhilleus.
It was a Pêlian ash, cut on the crest
of Pêlion, given to Akhilleus' father
by Kheirôn[8] to deal death to soldiery.
He then ordered his war-team put in harness
by Automédôn,[9] whom he most admired
after Prince Akhilleus, breaker of men,   170
for waiting steadfast at his call in battle.
Automédôn yoked the fast horses for him—
Xánthos and Balíos, racers in wind.
The stormgust Podargê, who once had grazed
green meadowland by the Ocean stream, conceived
and bore them to the west wind, Zephyros.
In the side-traces Pêdasos, a thoroughbred,
was added to the team; Akhilleus took him
when he destroyed the city of Eëtíôn.
Mortal, he ran beside immortal horses.   180
Akhilleus put the Myrmidons in arms,
the whole detachment near the huts. Like wolves,
carnivorous and fierce and tireless,
who rend a great stag on a mountainside
and feed on him, their jaws reddened with blood,
loping in a pack to drink springwater,
lapping the dark rim up with slender tongues,
their chops a-drip with fresh blood, their hearts
unshaken ever, and their bellies glutted:
such were the Myrmidons and their officers,   190
running to form up round Akhilleus' brave

[7] Akhilleus' father Pêleus (son of Aíakos).
[8] A centaur who had tutored Akhilleus; also spelled *Chiron*.
[9] When Patróklos assumes command, his normal post as charioteer is assumed by
Automédôn, the third-ranking among Akhilleus' Myrmidons.

companion-in-arms.
And like the god of war

among them was Akhilleus: he stood tall
and sped the chariots and shieldmen onward.

Fifty ships there were that Lord Akhilleus,
favored of heaven, led to Troy. In each
were fifty soldiers, shipmates at the rowlocks.
Five he entrusted with command and made
lieutenants, while he ruled them all as king.
One company was headed by Menésthios   200
in his glittering breastplate, son of Spérkheios,
a river fed by heaven. Pêleus' daughter,
beautiful Polydôrê, had conceived him
lying with Spérkheios, untiring stream,
a woman with a god; but the world thought
she bore her child to Periêrês' son,
Bôros, who married her in the eyes of men
and offered countless bridal gifts. A second
company was commanded by Eudôros,
whose mother was unmarried: Polymêlê,   210
Phylas' daughter, a beautiful dancer
with whom the strong god Hermês fell in love,
seeing her among singing girls who moved
in measure for the lady of belling hounds,
Artemis of the golden shaft. And Hermês,
pure Deliverer, ascending soon
to an upper room, lay secretly with her
who was to bear his brilliant son, Eudôros,
a first-rate man at running and in war.
When Eileithyía,[10] sending pangs of labor,   220
brought him forth to see the sun-rays, then
strong-minded Ekheklêos, Aktor's son,
led the girl home with countless bridal gifts;
but Phylas in his age brought up the boy
with all kind care, as though he were a son.
Company three was led by Peísandros
Maimálidês, the best man with a spear,
of all Myrmidons after Patróklos.
Company four the old man, master of horse,
Phoinix, commanded. Alkimédôn, son   230
of Laérkês, commanded company five.
When all were mustered under their officers,
Akhilleus had strict orders to impart:

"Myrmidons, let not one man forget
how menacing you were against the Trojans
during my anger and seclusion: how

---

[10] Goddess of childbirth.

each one reproached me, saying, 'Ironhearted
son of Pêleus, now we see: your mother
brought you up on rage, merciless man,
the way you keep your men confined to camp   240
against their will! We might as well sail home
in our seagoing ships, now this infernal
anger has come over you!' That way
you often talked, in groups around our fires.
Now the great task of battle is at hand
that you were longing for! Now every soldier
keep a fighting heart and face the Trojans!"

He stirred and braced their spirit; every rank
fell in more sharply when it heard its king.
As when a builder fitting stone on stone   250
lays well a high house wall to buffet back
the might of winds, just so
they fitted helms and studded shields together:
shield-rim on shield-rim, helmet on helmet, men
all pressed on one another, horsehair plumes
brushed on the bright crests as the soldiers nodded,
densely packed as they were.

                                   Before them all
two captains stood in gear of war: Patróklos
and Automédôn, of one mind, resolved
to open combat in the lead.

                                      Akhilleus   260
went to his hut. He lifted up the lid
of a seachest, all intricately wrought,
that Thetis of the silver feet had stowed
aboard his ship for him to take to Ilion,
filled to the brim with shirts, wind-breaking cloaks,
and fleecy rugs. His hammered cup was there,
from which no other man drank the bright wine,
and he made offering to no god but Zeus.
Lifting it from the chest, he purified it
first with brimstone,[11] washed it with clear water,   270
and washed his hands, then dipped it full of wine.
Now standing in the forecourt, looking up
toward heaven, he prayed and poured his offering out,
and Zeus who plays in thunder heard his prayer:

"Zeus of Dôdôna,[12] god of Pelasgians,
O god whose home lies far! Ruler of wintry
harsh Dôdôna! Your interpreters,
the Selloi, live with feet like roots, unwashed,

[11] Sulphur.
[12] A shrine of Zeus near Akhilleus' homeland, supervised by the Selloi, primitive people
who interpreted the god's oracles.

and sleep on the hard ground. My lord, you heard me
praying before this, and honored me 280
by punishing the Akhaian army. Now,
again, accomplish what I most desire.
I shall stay on the beach, behind the ships,
but send my dear friend with a mass of soldiers,
Myrmidons, into combat. Let your glory,
Zeus who view the wide world, go beside him.
Sir, exalt his heart,
so Hektor too may see whether my friend
can only fight when I am in the field,
or whether singlehanded he can scatter them 290
before his fury! When he has thrown back
their shouting onslaught from the ships, then let him
return unhurt to the shipways and to me,
his gear intact, with all his fighting men."

That was his prayer, and Zeus who views the wide world
heard him. Part he granted, part denied:
he let Patróklos push the heavy fighting
back from the ships, but would not let him come
unscathed from battle.
                              Now, after Akhilleus
had made his prayer and offering to Zeus, 300
he entered his hut again, restored the cup
to his seachest, and took his place outside—
desiring still to watch the savage combat
of Trojans and Akhaians. Brave Patróklos'
men moved forward with high hearts until
they charged the Trojans—Myrmidons in waves,
like hornets that small boys, as boys will do,
the idiots, poke up with constant teasing
in their daub chambers on the road,
to give everyone trouble. If some traveler 310
who passes unaware should then excite them,
all the swarm comes raging out
to defend their young. So hot, so angrily
the Myrmidons came pouring from the ships
in a quenchless din of shouting. And Patróklos
cried above them all:
                              "O Myrmidons,
brothers-in-arms of Pêleus' son, Akhilleus,
fight like men, dear friends, remember courage,
let us win honor for the son of Pêleus!
He is the greatest captain on the beach, 320
his officers and soldiers are the bravest!
Let King Agamémnon learn his folly
in holding cheap the best of the Akhaians!"

Shouting so, he stirred their hearts. They fell
as one man on the Trojans, and the ships
around them echoed the onrush and the cries.
On seeing Menoitios' powerful son, and with him
Automédôn, aflash with brazen gear,
the Trojan ranks broke, and they caught their breath,
imagining that Akhilleus the swift fighter   330
had put aside his wrath for friendship's sake.
Now each man kept an eye out for retreat
from sudden death. Patróklos drove ahead
against their center with his shining spear,
into the huddling mass, around the stern
of Prôtesílaos' burning ship. He hit
Pyraikhmês, who had led the Paiônês
from Amydôn, from Áxios' wide river—
hit him in the right shoulder. Backward in dust
he tumbled groaning, and his men at-arms,   340
the Paiônês, fell back around him. Dealing
death to a chief and champion, Patróklos
drove them in confusion from the ship,
and doused the tigerish fire. The hull half-burnt
lay smoking on the shipway. Now the Trojans
with a great outcry streamed away; Danáäns
poured along the curved ships, and the din
of war kept on. As when the lightning master,
Zeus, removes a dense cloud from the peak
of some great mountain, and the lookout points   350
and spurs and clearings are distinctly seen
as though pure space had broken through from heaven:
so when the dangerous fire had been repelled
Danáäns took breath for a space. The battle
had not ended, though; not yet were Trojans
put to rout by the Akhaian charge
or out of range of the black ships. They withdrew
but by regrouping tried to make a stand.

                                                   In broken

ranks the captains sought and killed each other,
Menoitios' son making the first kill.   360
As Arêilykos wheeled around to fight,
he caught him with his spearhead in the hip,
and drove the bronze through, shattering the bone.
He sprawled face downward on the ground.

                                                   Now veteran

Meneláos thrusting past the shield
of Thoas to the bare chest brought him down.[13]
Rushed by Ámphiklos, the alert Mégês
got his thrust in first, hitting his thigh
where a man's muscles bunch. Around the spearhead

---

[13] The victors in lines 365–409 are all Greeks.

tendons were split, and darkness veiled his eyes.   370
Nestor's sons were in action: Antílokhos
with his good spear brought down Atýmnios,
laying open his flank; he fell headfirst.
Now Maris moved in, raging for his brother,
lunging over the dead man with his spear,
but Thrasymêdês had already lunged
and did not miss, but smashed his shoulder squarely,
tearing his upper arm out of the socket,
severing muscles, breaking through the bone.
He thudded down and darkness veiled his eyes.   380
So these two, overcome by the two brothers,[14]
dropped to the underworld of Érebos.
They were Sarpêdôn's true brothers-in-arms
and sons of Amisôdaros, who reared
the fierce Khimaira,[15] nightmare to many men.
Aías,[16] Oïleus' son, drove at Kleóboulos
and took him alive, encumbered in the press,
but killed him on the spot with a sword stroke
across the nape—the whole blade running hot
with blood, as welling death and his harsh destiny   390
possessed him. Now Pênéleos
and Lykôn clashed; as both had cast and missed
and lunged and missed with spears,
they fought again with swords. The stroke of Lykôn
came down on the other's helmet ridge
but his blade broke at the hilt. Pênéleos
thrust at his neck below the ear and drove
the blade clear in and through; his head toppled,
held only by skin, and his knees gave way.
Meríonês on the run overtook Akámas   400
mounting behind his horses and hit his shoulder,
knocking him from the car. Mist swathed his eyes.
Idómeneus thrust hard at Erýmas' mouth
with his hard bronze. The spearhead passed on through
beneath his brain and split the white brain-pan.
His teeth were dashed out, blood filled both his eyes,
and from his mouth and nostrils as he gaped
he spurted blood. Death's cloud enveloped him.
There each Danáän captain killed his man.
As ravenous wolves come down on lambs and kids   410
astray from some flock that in hilly country
splits in two by a shepherd's negligence,
and quickly wolves bear off the defenseless things,
so when Danáäns fell on Trojans, shrieking

[14] Antílokhos and Thrasymêdês, the sons of Nestor.
[15] In fable, the Khimaira (or Chimera) was a monster having a lion's head, a goat's body, and a dragon's tail.
[16] This is the "lesser" Aías.

flight was all they thought of, not of combat.
Aías the Tall[17] kept after bronze-helmed Hektor,
casting his lance, but Hektor, skilled in war,
would fit his shoulders under the bull's-hide shield,
and watch for whizzing arrows, thudding spears.
Aye, though he knew the tide of battle turned,   420
he kept his discipline and saved his friends.
As when Lord Zeus would hang the sky with storm,
a cloud may enter heaven from Olympos
out of crystalline space, so terror and cries
increased about the shipways. In disorder
men withdrew. Then Hektor's chariot team
cantering bore him off with all his gear,
leaving the Trojans whom the moat confined;
and many chariot horses in that ditch,
breaking their poles off at the tip, abandoned   430
war-cars and masters. Hard on their heels
Patróklos kept on calling all Danáäns
onward with slaughter in his heart. The Trojans,
yelling and clattering, filled all the ways,
their companies in pieces. High in air
a blast of wind swept on, under the clouds,
as chariot horses raced back toward the town
away from the encampment. And Patróklos
rode shouting where he saw the enemy mass
in uproar: men fell from their chariots   440
under the wheels and cars jounced over them,
and running horses leapt over the ditch—
immortal horses, whom the gods gave Pêleus,
galloping as their mettle called them onward
after Hektor, target of Patróklos.
But Hektor's battle-team bore him away.

As under a great storm black earth is drenched
on an autumn day, when Zeus pours down the rain
in scudding gusts to punish men, annoyed
because they will enforce their crooked judgments   450
and banish justice from the market place,
thoughtless of the gods' vengeance; all their streams
run high and full, and torrents cut their way
down dry declivities into the swollen sea
with a hoarse clamor, headlong out of hills,
while cultivated fields erode away—
such was the gasping flight of the Trojan horses.

When he had cut their first wave off, Patróklos
forced it back again upon the ships
as the men fought toward the city. In between   460

[17] The "greater" Aías.

the ships and river and the parapet[18]
he swept among them killing, taking toll
for many dead Akhaians. First,
thrusting past Prónoös' shield, he hit him
on the bare chest; and made him crumple: down
he tumbled with a crash. Then he rushed Thestôr,
Enop's son, who sat all doubled up
in a polished war-car, shocked out of his wits,
the reins flown from his hands—and the Akhaian   470
got home his thrust on the right jawbone, driving
through his teeth. He hooked him by the spearhead
over the chariot rail, as a fisherman
on a point of rock will hook a splendid fish
with line and dazzling bronze out of the ocean:
so from his chariot on the shining spear
he hooked him gaping and face downward threw him,
life going out of him as he fell.

                                               Patróklos

now met Erýlaos' rush and hit him square
mid-skull with a big stone. Within his helm
the skull was cleft asunder, and down he went   480
headfirst to earth; heartbreaking death engulfed him.
Next Erýmas, Amphóteros, Epaltês,
Tlêpolemos Damastoridês, Ekhíos,
Pyris, Ipheus, Euíppos, Polymêlos,
all in quick succession he brought down
to the once peaceful pastureland.

                                           Sarpêdôn,

seeing his brothers-in-arms in their unbelted
battle jackets downed at Patróklos' hands,
called in bitterness to the Lykians:[19]

"Shame, O Lykians, where are you running?   490
Now you show your speed!

                           I'll take on this one,

and learn what man he is that has the power
to do such havoc as he has done among us,
cutting down so many, and such good men."

He vaulted from his car with all his gear,
and on his side Patróklos, when he saw him,
leapt from his car. Like two great birds of prey
with hooked talons and angled beaks, who screech
and clash on a high ridge of rock, these two
rushed one another with hoarse cries. But Zeus,   500
the son of crooked-minded Krónos, watched,
and pitied them. He said to Hêra:

---

[18] The wall of Troy. The river Skamánder, also called Xánthos, flows by the plain.
[19] Lykia, of which Sarpêdôn is king, is a region about two hundred miles southeast of Troy.

                                                              "Ai!
Sorrow for me, that in the scheme of things
the dearest of men to me must lie in dust
before the son of Menoitios, Patróklos.
My heart goes two ways as I ponder this:
shall I catch up Sarpêdôn
out of the mortal fight with all its woe
and put him down alive in Lykia,
in that rich land? Or shall I make him fall   510
beneath Patróklos' hard-thrown spear?"

                                         Then Hêra
of the wide eyes answered him:

                                         "O fearsome power,
my Lord Zeus, what a curious thing to say.
A man who is born to die, long destined for it,
would you set free from that unspeakable end?
Do so; but not all of us will praise you.
And this, too, I may tell you: ponder this:
should you dispatch Sarpêdôn home alive,
anticipate some other god's desire
to pluck a man he loves out of the battle.   520
Many who fight around the town of Priam
sprang from immortals; you'll infuriate these.
No, dear to you though he is, and though you mourn him,
let him fall, even so, in the rough battle,
killed by the son of Menoitios, Patróklos.
Afterward, when his soul is gone, his lifetime
ended, Death and sweetest Sleep can bear him
homeward to the broad domain of Lykia.
There friends and kin may give him funeral
with tomb and stone, the trophies of the dead."   530

To this the father of gods and men agreed,
but showered bloody drops upon the earth
for the dear son Patróklos would destroy
in fertile Ilion, far from his home.
When the two men had come in range, Patróklos
turned like lightning against Thrasydêmos,
a tough man ever at Sarpêdôn's side,
and gave him a death-wound in the underbelly.
Sarpêdôn's counterthrust went wide, but hit
the trace horse, Pêdasos, in the right shoulder.[20]   540
Screaming harshly, panting his life away,
he crashed and whinnied in the dust; the spirit
left him with a wingbeat. The team shied
and strained apart with a great creak of the yoke

---

[20] Pêdasos is the third, auxiliary horse harnessed with Akhilleus' two immortal horses.

as reins were tangled over the dead weight
of their outrider fallen. Automédôn,
the good soldier, found a way to end it:
pulling his long blade from his hip
he jumped in fast and cut the trace horse free.
The team then ranged themselves beside the pole,   550
drawing the reins taut, and once more,
devoured by fighting madness, the two men clashed.
Sarpêdôn missed again. He drove his spearhead
over the left shoulder of Patróklos,
not even grazing him. Patróklos then
made his last throw, and the weapon left his hand
with flawless aim. He hit his enemy
just where the muscles of the diaphragm
encased his throbbing heart. Sarpêdôn fell
the way an oak or poplar or tall pine   560
goes down, when shipwrights in the wooded hills
with whetted axes chop it down for timber.
So, full length, before his war-car lay
Sarpêdôn raging, clutching the bloody dust.
Imagine a greathearted sultry bull
a lion kills amid a shambling herd:
with choking groans he dies under the claws.
So, mortally wounded by Patróklos
the chief of Lykian shieldsmen lay in agony
and called his friend by name:

                       "Glaukos, old man,   570
old war-dog, now's the time to be a spearman!
Put your heart in combat! Let grim war
be all your longing! Quickly, if you can,
arouse the Lykian captains, round them up
to fight over Sarpêdôn. You, too, fight
to keep my body, else in later days
this day will be your shame.[21] You'll hang your head
all your life long, if these Akhaians take
my armor here, where I have gone down fighting
before the ships. Hold hard; cheer on the troops!"   580

The end of life came on him as he spoke,
closing his eyes and nostrils. And Patróklos
with one foot on his chest drew from his belly
spearhead and spear; the diaphragm came out,
so he extracted life and blade together.
Myrmidons clung to the panting Lykian horses,
rearing to turn the car left by their lords.

---

[21] Proper funeral rites were essential for the honor of the dead man and for his well-being
after death—an important theme in the poem.

But bitter anguish at Sarpêdôn's voice
had come to Glaukos, and his heart despaired
because he had not helped his friend. He gripped   590
his own right arm and squeezed it, being numb
where Teukros with a bowshot from the rampart
had hit him while he fought for his own men,[22]
and he spoke out in prayer to Lord Apollo:

"Hear me, O lord, somewhere in Lykian farmland
or else in Troy: for you have power to listen
the whole world round to a man hard pressed as I!
I have my sore wound, all my length of arm
a-throb with lancing pain; the flow of blood
cannot be stanched; my shoulder's heavy with it.   600
I cannot hold my spear right or do battle,
cannot attack them. Here's a great man destroyed,
Sarpêdôn, son of Zeus. Zeus let his own son
die undefended. O my lord, heal this wound,
lull me my pains, put vigor in me! Let me
shout to my Lykians, move them into combat!
Let me give battle for the dead man here!"

This way he prayed, and Phoibos Apollo heard him,
cutting his pain and making the dark blood dry
on his deep wound, then filled his heart with valor.   610
Glaukos felt the change, and knew with joy
how swiftly the great god had heard his prayer.
First he appealed to the Lykian captains, going
right and left, to defend Sarpêdôn's body,
then on the run he followed other Trojans,
Poulýdamas, Pánthoös' son, Agênor,
and caught up with Aineías and with Hektor,
shoulder to shoulder, urgently appealing:

"Hektor, you've put your allies out of mind,
those men who give their lives here for your sake   620
so distant from their friends and lands: you will not
come to their aid! Sarpêdôn lies there dead,
commander of the Lykians, who kept
his country safe by his firm hand, in justice!
Arês in bronze has brought him down: the spear
belonged to Patróklos. Come, stand with me, friends,
and count it shame if they strip off his gear
or bring dishonor on his body—these
fresh Myrmidons enraged for the Danääns
cut down at the shipways by our spears!"   630

At this, grief and remorse possessed the Trojans,
grief not to be borne, because Sarpêdôn

---

[22] Teukros had wounded Glaukos in Book XII.

had been a bastion of the town of Troy,
foreigner though he was. A host came with him,
but he had fought most gallantly of all.
They made straight for the Danáäns, and Hektor
led them, hot with anger for Sarpêdôn.
Patróklos in his savagery cheered on
the Akhaians, first the two named Aías, both
already aflame for war:

"Aías and Aías,   640
let it be sweet to you to stand and fight!
You always do; be lionhearted, now.
The man who crossed the rampart of Akhaians
first of all lies dead: Sarpêdôn.[23] May we
take him, dishonor him, and strip his arms,
and hurl any friend who would defend him
into the dust with our hard bronze!"

At this they burned to throw the Trojans back.
And both sides reinforced their battle lines,
Trojans and Lykians, Myrmidons and Akhaians,   650
moving up to fight around the dead
with fierce cries and clanging of men's armor.
Zeus unfurled a deathly gloom of night
over the combat, making battle toil
about his dear son's body a fearsome thing.
At first, the Trojans drove back the Akhaians,
fiery-eyed as they were; one Myrmidon,
and not the least, was killed: noble Epeigeus,
a son of Agaklês. In Boudeion,
a flourishing town, he ruled before the war,   660
but slew a kinsman. So he came as suppliant
to Pêleus and to Thetis, who enlisted him
along with Lord Akhilleus, breaker of men,
to make war in the wild-horse country of Ilion
against the Trojans. Even as he touched the dead man,
Hektor hit him square upon the crest
with a great stone: his skull split in the helmet,
and he fell prone upon the corpse. Death's cloud
poured round him, heart-corroding. Grief and pain
for this friend dying came to Lord Patróklos,   670
who pounced through spear-play like a diving hawk
that puts jackdaws and starlings wildly to flight:
straight through Lykians, through Trojans, too,
you drove, Patróklos, master of horse,
in fury for your friend. Sthenélaos
the son of Ithaiménês was the victim:
Patróklos with a great stone broke his nape-cord.

[23] The reference is to Book XII; it was actually Hektor who first broke through the defensive wall around the ships, though Sarpêdôn had threatened and damaged it.

Backward the line bent, Hektor too gave way,
as far as a hunting spear may hurtle, thrown
by a man in practice or in competition   680
or matched with deadly foes in war. So far
the Trojans ebbed, as the Akhaians drove them.
Glaukos, commander of Lykians, turned first,
to bring down valorous Báthyklês, the son
of Khalkôn, one who had his home in Hellas,
fortunate and rich among the Myrmidons.
Whirling as this man caught him, Glaukos hit him
full in the breastbone with his spear, and down
he thudded on his face. The Akhaians grieved
to see their champion fallen, but great joy   690
came to the Trojans, and they thronged about him.
Not that Akhaians now forgot their courage,
no, for their momentum carried them on.
Meríonês brought down a Trojan soldier,
Laógonos, Onêtor's rugged son,
a priest of Zeus on Ida, honored there
as gods are. Gashed now under jaw and ear
his life ran out, and hateful darkness took him.
Then at Meríonês Aineías cast
his bronze-shod spear, thinking to reach his body   700
under the shield as he came on. But he
looked out for it and swerved, slipping the spear-throw,
bowing forward, so the long shaft stuck
in earth behind him and the butt quivered;
the god Arês deprived it of its power.
Aineías raged and sneered:

                                                    "Meríonês,
fast dodger that you are, if I had hit you
my spearhead would have stopped your dance for good!"

Meríonês, good spearman, answered him:

"For all your power, Aineías, you could hardly   710
quench the fighting spirit of every man
defending himself against you. You are made
of mortal stuff like me. I, too, can say,
if I could hit you square, then tough and sure
as you may be, you would concede the game
and give your soul to the lord of nightmare, Death."

Patróklos said to him sharply:

                                                    "Meríonês,
you have your skill, why make a speech about it?
No, old friend, rough words will make no Trojans
back away from the body. Many a one   720
will be embraced by earth before they do.

War is the use of arms, words are for council.
More talk's pointless now; we need more fighting!"

He pushed on, and godlike Meríonês
fought at his side. Think of the sound of strokes
woodcutters make in mountain glens, the echoes
ringing for listeners far away: just so
the battering din of these in combat rose
from earth where the living go their ways—the clang
of bronze, hard blows on leather, on bull's hide,   730
as longsword blades and spearheads met their marks.
And an observer could not by now have seen
the Prince Sarpêdôn, since from head to foot
he lay enwrapped in weapons, dust, and blood.
Men kept crowding around the corpse. Like flies
that swarm and drone in farmyards round the milkpails
on spring days, when the pails are splashed with milk:
just so they thronged around the corpse. And Zeus
would never turn his shining eyes away
from this mêlée, but watched them all and pondered   740
long over the slaughter of Patróklos—
whether in that place, on Sarpêdôn's body,
Hektor should kill the man and take his gear,
or whether he, Zeus, should augment the moil[24]
of battle for still other men. He weighed it
and thought this best: that for a while Akhilleus'
shining brother-in-arms should drive his foes
and Hektor in the bronze helm toward the city,
taking the lives of many. First of all
he weakened Hektor, made him mount his car   750
and turn away, retreating, crying out
to others to retreat: for he perceived
the dipping scales of Zeus.[25] At this the Lykians
themselves could not stand fast, but all turned back,
once they had seen their king struck to the heart,
lying amid swales of dead—for many
fell to earth beside him when Lord Zeus
had drawn the savage battle line. So now
Akhaians lifted from Sarpêdôn's shoulders
gleaming arms of bronze, and these Patróklos   760
gave to his soldiers to be carried back
to the decked ships. At this point, to Apollo
Zeus who gathers cloud said:

                                   "Come, dear Phoibos,
wipe away the blood mantling Sarpêdôn;
take him up, out of the play of spears,

[24]Turmoil.
[25]Zeus uses a balance scale to weigh alternative results of a conflict. The loser's side of the scale tips down, the winner's up.

a long way off, and wash him in the river,
anoint him with ambrosia, put ambrosial
clothing on him. Then have him conveyed
by those escorting spirits quick as wind,
sweet Sleep and Death, who are twin brothers. These   770
will set him down in the rich broad land of Lykia,
and there his kin and friends may bury him
with tomb and stone, the trophies of the dead."

Attentive to his father, Lord Apollo
went down the foothills of Ida[26] to the field
and lifted Prince Sarpêdôn clear of it.
He bore him far and bathed him in the river,
scented him with ambrosia, put ambrosial
clothing on him, then had him conveyed
by those escorting spirits quick as wind,   780
sweet Sleep and Death, who are twin brothers. These
returned him to the rich broad land of Lykia.

Patróklos, calling to his team, commanding
Automédôn, rode on after the Trojans
and Lykians—all this to his undoing,
the blunderer. By keeping Akhilleus' mandate,
he might have fled black fate and cruel death.
But overpowering is the mind of Zeus
forever, matched with man's. He turns in fright
the powerful man and robs him of his victory   790
easily, though he drove him on himself.
So now he stirred Patróklos' heart to fury.

Whom first, whom later did you kill in battle,
Patróklos, when the gods were calling deathward?
First it was Adrêstos, Autônoös,
and Ekheklos; then Périmos Megadês,
Eristôr, Melánippos; afterward,
Elasos, Moulios, Pylartês. These
he cut down, while the rest looked to their flight.
Troy of the towering gates was on the verge   800
of being taken by the Akhaians, under
Patróklos' drive: he raced with blooded spear
ahead and around it. On the massive tower
Phoibos Apollo stood as Troy's defender,
deadly toward him. Now three times Patróklos
assaulted the high wall at the tower joint,
and three times Lord Apollo threw him back
with counterblows of his immortal hands
against the resplendent shield. The Akhaian then
a fourth time flung himself against the wall,   810

[26] A mountain near Troy from which Zeus often observes the war.

more than human in fury. But Apollo
thundered:

                    "Back, Patróklos, lordly man!
Destiny will not let this fortress town
of Trojans fall to you! Not to Akhilleus,
either, greater far though he is in war!"[27]

Patróklos now retired, a long way off
and out of range of Lord Apollo's anger.
Hektor had held his team at the Skaian Gates,
being of two minds: should he re-engage,
or call his troops to shelter behind the wall?   820
While he debated this, Phoibos Apollo
stood at his shoulder in a strong man's guise:
Ásïos, his maternal uncle, brother
of Hékabê and son of Dymas, dweller
in Phrygia on Sangaríos river.
Taking his semblance now, Apollo said:

"Why break off battle, Hektor? You need not.
Were I superior to you in the measure
that I am now inferior, you'd suffer
from turning back so wretchedly from battle.   830
Action! Lash your team against Patróklos,
and see if you can take him. May Apollo
grant you the glory!"

                    And at this, once more
he joined the mêlée, entering it as a god.
Hektor in splendor called Kebríonês
to whip the horses toward the fight. Apollo,
disappearing into the ranks, aroused
confusion in the Argives, but on Hektor
and on the Trojans he conferred his glory.
Letting the rest go, Hektor drove his team   840
straight at Patróklos; and Patróklos faced him
vaulting from his war-car, with his spear
gripped in his left hand; in his right
he held enfolded a sparkling jagged stone.
Not for long in awe of the other man,
he aimed and braced himself and threw the stone
and scored a direct hit on Hektor's driver,
Kebríonês, a bastard son of Priam,
smashing his forehead with the jagged stone.
Both brows were hit at once, the frontal bone   850
gave way, and both his eyes burst from their sockets
dropping into the dust before his feet,
as like a diver from the handsome car

---

[27] Akhilleus will be slain before the city is finally taken.

he plummeted, and life ebbed from his bones.
You jeered at him then, master of horse, Patróklos:

"God, what a nimble fellow, somersaulting!
If he were out at sea in the fishing grounds
this man could feed a crew, diving for oysters,
going overboard even in rough water,
the way he took that earth-dive from his car.   860
The Trojans have their acrobats, I see."

With this, he went for the dead man with a spring
like a lion, one that has taken a chest wound
while ravaging a cattle pen—his valor
his undoing. So you sprang, Patróklos,
on Kebríonês. Then Hektor, too, leapt down
out of his chariot, and the two men fought
over the body like two mountain lions
over the carcass of a buck, both famished,
both in pride of combat. So these two   870
fought now for Kebríonês, two champions,
Patróklos son of Menoitios, and Hektor,
hurling their bronze to tear each other's flesh.
Hektor caught hold of the dead man's head and held,
while his antagonist clung to a single foot,
as Trojans and Danáäns pressed the fight.
As south wind and the southeast wind, contending
in mountain groves, make all the forest thrash,
beech trees and ash trees and the slender cornel
swaying their pointed boughs toward one another   880
in roaring wind, and snapping branches crack:
so Trojans and Akhaians made a din
as lunging they destroyed each other. Neither
considered ruinous flight. Many sharp spears
and arrows trued by feathers from the strings
were fixed in flesh around Kebríonês,
and boulders crashed on shields, as they fought on
around him. And a dustcloud wrought
by a whirlwind hid the greatness of him slain,
minding no more the mastery of horses.   890
Until the sun stood at high noon in heaven
spears bit on both sides, and the soldiers fell;
but when the sun passed toward unyoking time,
the Akhaians outfought destiny to prevail.
Now they dragged off gallant Kebríonês
out of range, away from the shouting Trojans,
to strip his shoulders of his gear. And fierce
Patróklos hurled himself upon the Trojans
in onslaughts fast as Arês, three times, wild
yells in his throat. Each time he killed nine men.   900
But on the fourth demonic foray, then

the end of life loomed up for you, Patróklos.
Into the combat dangerous Phoibos came
against him, but Patróklos could not see
the god, enwrapped in cloud as he came near.
He stood behind and struck with open hand
the man's back and broad shoulders, and the eyes
of the fighting man were dizzied by the blow.
Then Phoibos sent the captain's helmet rolling
under the horses' hooves, making the ridge   910
ring out, and dirtying all the horsehair plume
with blood and dust. Never in time before
had this plumed helmet been befouled with dust,
the helmet that had kept a hero's brow
unmarred, shielding Akhilleus' head. Now Zeus
bestowed it upon Hektor, let him wear it,
though his destruction waited. For Patróklos
felt his great spearshaft shattered in his hands,
long, tough, well-shod, and seasoned though it was;
his shield and strap fell to the ground; the Lord   920
Apollo, son of Zeus, broke off his cuirass.
Shock ran through him, and his good legs failed,
so that he stood agape. Then from behind
at close quarters, between the shoulder blades,
a Dardan fighter speared him: Pánthoös' son,
Euphórbos, the best Trojan of his age
at handling spears, in horsemanship and running:
he had brought twenty chariot fighters down
since entering combat in his chariot,
already skilled in the craft of war. This man   930
was first to wound you with a spear, Patróklos,
but did not bring you down. Instead, he ran back
into the mêlée, pulling from the flesh
his ashen spear, and would not face his enemy,
even disarmed, in battle. Then Patróklos,
disabled by the god's blow and the spear wound,
moved back to save himself amid his men.
But Hektor, seeing that his brave adversary
tried to retire, hurt by the spear wound, charged
straight at him through the ranks and lunged for him   940
low in the flank, driving the spearhead through.
He crashed, and all Akhaian troops turned pale.
Think how a lion in his pride brings down
a tireless boar; magnificently they fight
on a mountain crest for a small gushing spring—
both in desire to drink—and by sheer power
the lion conquers the great panting boar:
that was the way the son of Priam, Hektor,
closed with Patróklos, son of Menoitios,
killer of many, and took his life away.   950
Then glorying above him he addressed him:

"Easy to guess, Patróklos, how you swore
to ravage Troy, to take the sweet daylight
of liberty from our women, and to drag them
off in ships to your own land—you fool!
Between you and those women there is Hektor's
war-team, thundering out to fight! My spear
has pride of place among the Trojan warriors,
keeping their evil hour at bay.
The kites[28] will feed on you, here on this field.   960
Poor devil, what has that great prince, Akhilleus,
done for you? He must have told you often
as you were leaving and he stayed behind,
'Never come back to me, to the deepsea ships,
Patróklos, till you cut to rags
the bloody tunic on the chest of Hektor!'
That must have been the way he talked, and won
your mind to mindlessness."

                                               In a low faint voice,
Patróklos, master of horse, you answered him:

"This is your hour to glory over me,   970
Hektor. The Lord Zeus and Apollo gave you
the upper hand and put me down with ease.
They stripped me of my arms. No one else did.
Say twenty men like you had come against me,
all would have died before my spear.
No, Lêto's son and fatal destiny
have killed me; if we speak of men, Euphórbos.
You were in third place, only in at the death.
I'll tell you one thing more; take it to heart.
No long life is ahead for you. This day   980
your death stands near, and your immutable end,
at Prince Akhilleus' hands."

                                                            His own death
came on him as he spoke, and soul from body,
bemoaning severance from youth and manhood,
slipped to be wafted to the underworld.
Even in death Prince Hektor still addressed him:

"Why prophesy my sudden death, Patróklos?
Who knows, Akhilleus, son of bright-haired Thetis,
might be hit first; he might be killed by me."

At this he pulled his spearhead from the wound,   990
setting his heel upon him; then he pushed him
over on his back, clear of the spear,
and lifting it at once sought Automédôn,
companion of the great runner, Akhilleus,
longing to strike him. But the immortal horses,
gift of the gods to Pêleus, bore him away.

---

[28] Birds of prey.

from BOOK SEVENTEEN: CONTENDING FOR A SOLDIER FALLEN

Hektor has seized the armor of Akhilleus that the dead Patróklos had worn. A long and bitter struggle ensues for possession of his body. The Greeks want to return it to Akhilleus, the Trojans to desecrate it; moreover, Glaukos, mistakenly believing that the Greeks now have the corpse of his dead comrade Sarpêdôn, hopes they may trade it for the corpse of Patróklos. Meneláos defends Patróklos' body with the help of the greater Aías and other warriors. Glaukos charges Hektor with cowardice; Hektor, aroused, puts on the armor of Akhilleus/Patróklos (as Zeus predicts Hektor's death) and leads his followers into the fight for the body. Aineías joins in. This part of the battlefield has been shrouded in near-darkness by Zeus, though in other places the sky is clear. Akhilleus is still unaware of his friend's death.

At the end of Book XVI Automédôn, charioteer for Patróklos, withdrew from the battle along with Akhilleus' immortal horses. We see them again:

                                                            Out of range,
the horses of Akhilleus, from the time
they sensed their charioteer[1] downed in the dust   480
at the hands of deadly Hektor, had been weeping.
Automédôn, the son of Diorês,
laid often on their backs his flickering whip,
pled often in a low tone—or he swore at them—
but neither toward the shipways and the beach
by Hellê's waters would they budge, nor follow
Akhaians into battle. No: stock-still
as a gravestone, fixed above the tomb
of a dead man or woman, they stood fast,
holding the beautiful war-car still: their heads   490
curved over to the ground, and warm tears flowed
from under eyelids earthward as they mourned
their longed-for driver. Manes along the yoke
were soiled as they hung forward under yokepads.
Seeing their tears flow, pitying them, Lord Zeus
bent his head and murmured in his heart:

"Poor things, why did I give you to King Pêleus,
a mortal, you who never age nor die,
to let you ache with men in their hard lot?
For of all creatures that breathe and move on earth   500
none is more to be pitied than a man.
Never at least shall Hektor, son of Priam,
ride behind you in your painted car.
That I will not allow. Is it not enough
that he both has the gear and brags about it?
I shall put fire in your knees and hearts
to rescue Automédôn, bear him away
from battle to the decked ships. Glory of killing,

---

[1] Patróklos, who normally serves as charioteer (i.e., when Akhilleus is in action).

even so, I reserve to his enemies
until they reach the ships, until sundown,   510
until the dusk comes, full of stars."

    BOOK XVII *(continued). Hektor and Aineías try to capture Akhilleus' horses but are
driven back by the two Aíases. Zeus allows Athêna to encourage Meneláos; Apollo encourages
Hektor once more. Zeus now gives victory to the Trojans. The greater Aías and Meneláos send
a runner to Akhilleus with the news of Patróklos' death. With immense difficulty, and sustained by the two Aíases, the Greeks carry Patróklos' body to the rear as the triumphant Trojans
advance again, led by Hektor and Aineías.*

BOOK EIGHTEEN: THE IMMORTAL SHIELD

While they were still in combat, fighting seaward
raggedly as fire, Antílokhos[1]
ran far ahead with tidings for Akhilleus.
In shelter of the curled, high prows he found him
envisioning what had come to pass,
in gloom and anger saying to himself:

"Ai! why are they turning tail once more,
unmanned, outfought, and driven from the field
back on the beach and ships? I pray the gods
this may not be the last twist of the knife!   10
My mother warned me once that, while I lived,
the most admirable of Myrmidons
would quit the sunlight under Trojan blows.
It could indeed be so. He has gone down,
my dear and wayward friend!
Push their deadly fire away, I told him,
then return! You must not fight with Hektor!"

And while he called it all to mind,
the son of gallant Nestor came up weeping
to give his cruel news:

                                "Here's desolation,   20
son of Pêleus, the worst news for you—
would god it had not happened!—Lord Patróklos
fell, and they are fighting over his body,
stripped of armor. Hektor has your gear."

A black stormcloud of pain shrouded Akhilleus.
On his bowed head he scattered dust and ash
in handfuls and befouled his beautiful face,
letting black ash sift on his fragrant khiton.[2]
Then in the dust he stretched his giant length

[1] Son of Nestor, sent in Book XVII to inform Akhilleus of Patróklos' death.
[2] A loose, knee-length garment.

and tore his hair with both hands.

the women who had been spoils of war to him
and to Patróklos flocked in haste around him,
crying loud in grief. All beat their breasts,
and trembling came upon their knees.

wept where he stood, bending to hold the hero's
hands when groaning shook his heart: he feared
the man might use sharp iron to slash his throat.
And now Akhilleus gave a dreadful cry.

his mother heard him, in the depths offshore
lolling near her ancient father.[3] Nymphs   40
were gathered round her: all Nêrëïdês
who haunted the green chambers of the sea.
Glaukê, Thaleia, and Kymodokê,
Nesaiê, Speiô, Thoê, Haliê
with her wide eyes; Kymothoê, Aktaiê,
Limnôreia, Melitê, and Iaira,   .
Amphitoê, Agauê, Dôtô, Prôtô,
Pherousa, Dynaménê, Dexaménê,
Amphinomê, Kallianeira, Dôris,
Panopê, and storied Galateia,   50
Nêmertês and Apseudês, Kallianassa,
Klyméne, Ianeira, Ianassa,
Maira, Oreithyia, Amathyia,
and other Nêrëïdês of the deep sea,
filling her glimmering silvery cave. All these
now beat their breasts as Thetis cried in sorrow:

"Sisters, daughters of Nêreus, hear and know
how sore my heart is! Now my life is pain
for my great son's dark destiny! I bore
a child flawless and strong beyond all men.   60
He flourished like a green shoot, and I brought him
to manhood like a blossoming orchard tree,
only to send him in the ships to Ilion
to war with Trojans. Now I shall never see him
entering Pêleus' hall, his home, again.
But even while he lives, beholding sunlight,
suffering is his lot. I have no power
to help him, though I go to him. Even so,
I'll visit my dear child and learn what sorrow
came to him while he held aloof from war."   70

On this she left the cave, and all in tears
her company swam aloft with her. Around them

---

[3] Nêreus, a sea-god.

a billow broke and foamed on the open sea.
As they made land at the fertile plain of Troy,
they went up one by one in line to where,
in close order, Myrmidon ships were beached
to right and left of Akhilleus. Bending near
her groaning son, the gentle goddess wailed
and took his head between her hands in pity,
saying softly:

                        "Child, why are you weeping?   80
What great sorrow came to you? Speak out,
do not conceal it. Zeus
did all you asked: Akhaian troops,
for want of you, were all forced back again
upon the ship sterns, taking heavy losses
none of them could wish."

                                The great runner
groaned and answered:

                         "Mother, yes, the master
of high Olympos brought it all about,
but how have I benefited? My greatest friend
is gone: Patróklos, comrade in arms, whom I   90
held dear above all others—dear as myself—
now gone, lost; Hektor cut him down, despoiled him
of my own arms, massive and fine, a wonder
in all men's eyes. The gods gave them to Pêleus
that day they put you in a mortal's bed—
how I wish the immortals of the sea
had been your only consorts! How I wish
Pêleus had taken a mortal queen! Sorrow
immeasurable is in store for you as well,
when your own child is lost: never again   100
on his homecoming day will you embrace him!
I must reject this life, my heart tells me,
reject the world of men,
if Hektor does not feel my battering spear
tear the life out of him, making him pay
in his own blood for the slaughter of Patróklos!"

Letting a tear fall, Thetis said:

                                "You'll be
swift to meet your end, child, as you say:
your doom comes close on the heels of Hektor's own."

Akhilleus the great runner ground his teeth   110
and said:

                      "May it come quickly. As things were,
I could not help my friend in his extremity.
Far from his home he died; he needed me

to shield him or to parry the death stroke.
For me there's no return to my own country.
Not the slightest gleam of hope did I
afford Patróklos or the other men
whom Hektor overpowered. Here I sat,
my weight a useless burden to the earth,
and I am one who has no peer in war   120
among Akhaian captains—

                                though in council

there are wiser. Ai! let strife and rancor
perish from the lives of gods and men,
with anger that envenoms even the wise
and is far sweeter than slow-dripping honey,
clouding the hearts of men like smoke: just so
the marshal of the army, Agamémnon,
moved me to anger. But we'll let that go,
though I'm still sore at heart; it is all past,
and I have quelled my passion as I must.   130

Now I must go to look for the destroyer
of my great friend. I shall confront the dark
drear spirit of death at any hour Zeus
and the other gods may wish to make an end.
Not even Hêraklês[4] escaped that terror
though cherished by the Lord Zeus. Destiny
and Hêra's bitter anger mastered him.
Likewise with me, if destiny like his
awaits me, I shall rest when I have fallen!
Now, though, may I win my perfect glory   140
and make some wife of Troy break down,
or some deep-breasted Dardan[5] woman sob
and wipe tears from her soft cheeks. They'll know then
how long they had been spared the deaths of men,
while I abstained from war!
Do not attempt to keep me from the fight,
though you love me; you cannot make me listen."

Thetis, goddess of the silvery feet,
answered:

                         "Yes, of course, child: very true.
You do no wrong to fight for tired soldiers   150
and keep them from defeat. But still, your gear,
all shining bronze, remains in Trojan hands.
Hektor himself is armed with it in pride!—
Not that he'll glory in it long, I know,
for violent death is near him.

---

[4] In myth, Hêraklês (Hercules) was a great Greek hero, a kind of superman. In some versions he was deified at the end of his life.
[5] From the vicinity of Troy.

Patience, then.
Better not plunge into the moil of Arês
until you see me here once more. At dawn,
at sunrise, I shall come
with splendid arms for you from Lord Hêphaistos."

She rose at this and, turning from her son,   160
told her sister Nêrêïdês:

"Go down

into the cool broad body of the sea
to the sea's Ancient; visit Father's hall,
and make all known to him. Meanwhile, I'll visit
Olympos' great height and the lord of crafts,
Hêphaistos, hoping he will give me
new and shining armor for my son."

At this they vanished in the offshore swell,
and to Olympos Thetis the silvery-footed
went once more, to fetch for her dear son   170
new-forged and finer arms.

Meanwhile, Akhaians,
wildly crying, pressed by deadly Hektor,
reached the ships, beached above Hellê's water.
None had been able to pull Patróklos clear
of spear- and swordplay: troops and chariots
and Hektor, son of Priam, strong as fire,
once more gained upon the body. Hektor
three times had the feet within his grasp
and strove to wrest Patróklos backward, shouting
to all the Trojans—but three times the pair   180
named Aías in their valor shook him off.
Still he pushed on, sure of his own power,
sometimes lunging through the battle-din,
or holding fast with a great shout: not one step
would he give way. As from a fresh carcass
herdsmen in the wilds cannot dislodge
a tawny lion, famished: so those two
with fearsome crests could not affright the son
of Priam or repel him from the body.
He might have won it, might have won unending   190
glory, but Iris running on the wind
came from Olympos to the son of Pêleus,
bidding him gird for battle. All unknown
to Zeus and the other gods she came, for Hêra
sent her down. And at his side she said:

"Up with you, Pêleidês, who strike cold fear
into men's blood! Protect your friend Patróklos,
for whom, beyond the ships, desperate combat
rages now. They are killing one another

on both sides: the Akhaians to defend him,   200
Trojans fighting for that prize
to drag to windy Ilion. And Hektor
burns to take it more than anyone—
to sever and impale Patróklos' head
on Trojan battlements. Lie here no longer.
It would be shameful if wild dogs of Troy
made him their plaything! If that body suffers
mutilation, you will be infamous!"

Prince Akhilleus answered:

                                   "Iris of heaven,
what immortal sent you to tell me this?"   210

And she who runs upon the wind replied:

"Hêra, illustrious wife of Zeus,
but he on his high throne knows nothing of it.
Neither does any one of the gods undying
who haunt Olympos of eternal snows."

Akhilleus asked:

                              "And now how shall I go
into the fighting? Those men have my gear.
My dear mother allows me no rearming
until I see her again here.
She promises fine arms from Lord Hêphaistos.   220
I don't know whose armor I can wear,
unless I take Aías' big shield.
But I feel sure he's in the thick of it,
contending with his spear over Patróklos."

Then she who runs upon the wind replied:

"We know they have your arms, and know it well.
Just as you are, then, stand at the moat; let Trojans
take that in; they will be so dismayed
they may break off the battle, and Akhaians
in their fatigue may win a breathing spell,   230
however brief, a respite from the war."

                                        At this,
Iris left him, running downwind. Akhilleus,
whom Zeus loved, now rose. Around his shoulders
Athêna hung her shield,[6] like a thunderhead
with trailing fringe. Goddess of goddesses,
she bound his head with golden cloud, and made

---

[6] The aegis, a terror-inspiring shield given by Hêphaistos to Zeus and often used by
Athêna.

his very body blaze with fiery light.
Imagine how the pyre of a burning town
will tower to heaven and be seen for miles
from the island under attack, while all day long   240
outside their town, in brutal combat, pikemen
suffer the wargod's winnowing; at sundown
flare on flare is lit, the signal fires
shoot up for other islanders to see,
that some relieving force in ships may come:
just so the baleful radiance from Akhilleus
lit the sky. Moving from parapet
to moat, without a nod for the Akhaians,
keeping clear, in deference to his mother,
he halted and gave tongue. Not far from him   250
Athêna shrieked. The great sound shocked the Trojans
into tumult, as a trumpet blown
by a savage foe shocks an encircled town,
so harsh and clarion was Akhilleus' cry.
The hearts of men quailed, hearing that brazen voice.
Teams, foreknowing danger, turned their cars
and charioteers blanched, seeing unearthly fire,
kindled by the grey-eyed goddess Athêna,
brilliant over Akhilleus. Three great cries
he gave above the moat. Three times they shuddered,   260
whirling backward, Trojans and allies,
and twelve good men took mortal hurt
from cars and weapons in the rank behind.
Now the Akhaians leapt at the chance
to bear Patrôklos' body out of range.
They placed it on his bed,
and old companions there with brimming eyes
surrounded him. Into their midst Akhilleus
came then, and he wept hot tears to see
his faithful friend, torn by the sharp spearhead,   270
lying cold upon his cot. Alas,
the man he sent to war with team and chariot
he could not welcome back alive.

                                                                       Her majesty,
wide-eyed Hêra, made the reluctant sun,
unwearied still, sink in the streams of Ocean.
Down he dropped, and the Akhaian soldiers
broke off combat, resting from the war.[7]
The Trojans, too, retired. Unharnessing
teams from war-cars, before making supper,
they came together on the assembly ground,   280
every man on his feet; not one could sit,
each being still in a tremor—for Akhilleus,

---

[7] This day's fighting had begun in Book XI.

absent so long, had once again appeared.
Clearheaded Poulýdamas, son of Pánthoös,
spoke up first, as he alone could see
what lay ahead and all that lay behind.
He and Hektor were companions-in-arms,
born, as it happened, on the same night; but one
excelled in handling weapons, one with words.
Now for the good of all he spoke among them: 290

"Think well of our alternatives, my friends.
What I say is, retire upon the town,
instead of camping on the field till dawn
here by the ships. We are a long way
from our stone wall. As long as that man raged
at royal Agamémnon, we could fight
the Akhaians with advantage. I was happy
to spend last night so near the beach and think
of capturing ships today. Now, though, I fear
the son of Pêleus to my very marrow!   300
There are no bounds to the passion of that man.
He will not be contained by the flat ground
where Trojans and Akhaians share between them
raging war: he will strive on to fight
to win our town, our women. Back to Troy!
Believe me, this is what we face!
Now, starry night has made Akhilleus pause,
but when day comes, when he sorties in arms
to find us lingering here, there will be men
who learn too well what he is made of. Aye,   310
I daresay those who get away will reach
walled Ilion thankfully, but dogs and kites
of Troy will feed on many. May that story
never reach my ears! If we can follow
my battle plan, though galled by it, tonight
we'll husband strength, at rest in the market place.
Towers, high gates, great doors of fitted planking,
bolted tight, will keep the town secure.
Early tomorrow we shall arm ourselves
and man the walls. Worse luck then for Akhilleus,   320
if he comes looking for a head-on fight
on the field around the wall! He can do nothing
but trot back, after all, to the encampment,
his proud team in a lather from their run,
from scouring every quarter below the town.
Rage as he will, he cannot force an entrance,
cannot take all Troy by storm. Wild dogs
will eat him first!"

                        Under his shimmering helmet
Hektor glared at the speaker. Then he said:

"Poulýdamas, what you propose no longer   330
serves my turn. To go on the defensive
inside the town again? Is anyone
not sick of being huddled in those towers?
In past days men told tales of Priam's city,
rich in gold and rich in bronze, but now
those beautiful treasures of our home are lost.[8]
Many have gone for sale to Phrygia
and fair Mêïoniê, since Lord Zeus
grew hostile toward us.

                   Now when the son of Krónos
Crooked Wit has given me a chance   340
of winning glory, pinning the Akhaians
back on the sea—now is no time to publish
notions like these to troops, you fool! No Trojan
goes along with you, I will not have it!
Come, let each man act as I propose.
Take your evening meal by companies;
remember sentries; keep good watch; and any
Trojan tired of his wealth, who wants
to lose everything, let him turn it over
to the army stores to be consumed in common!   350
Better our men enjoy it than Akhaians.
At first light we shall buckle armor on
and bring the ships under attack. Suppose
the man who stood astern there was indeed
Akhilleus, then worse luck for him,
if he will have it so. Shall I retreat
from him, from clash of combat? No, I will not.
Here I'll stand, though he should win; I might
just win, myself: the battle-god's impartial,
dealing death to the death-dealing man."   360

This was Hektor's speech. The Trojans roared
approval of it—fools, for Pallas Athêna
took away their wits. They all applauded
Hektor's poor tactics, but Poulýdamas
with his good judgment got not one assent.
They took their evening meal now, through the army,
while all night long Akhaians mourned Patróklos.

Akhilleus led them in their lamentation,
laying those hands deadly to enemies
upon the breast of his old friend, with groans   370
at every breath, bereft as a lioness
whose whelps a hunter seized out of a thicket;
late in returning, she will grieve, and roam

---

[8]*treasures . . . are lost.* That is, sold to pay the expenses of the war.

through many meandering valleys on his track
in hope of finding him; heart-stinging anger
carries her away. Now with a groan
he cried out to the Myrmidons:

                                      "Ah, god,

what empty prophecy I made that day
to cheer Menoitios in his mégaron!
I promised him his honored son, brought back   380
to Opoeis,[9] as pillager of Ilion
bearing his share of spoils,
But Zeus will not fulfill what men design,
not all of it. Both he and I were destined
to stain the same earth dark red here at Troy.
No going home for me; no welcome there
from Pêleus, master of horse, or from my mother,
Thetis. Here the earth will hold me under.
Therefore, as I must follow you into the grave,
I will not give you burial, Patróklos,   390
until I carry back the gear and head
of him who killed you, noble friend.
Before your funeral pyre I'll cut the throats
of twelve resplendent children of the Trojans—
that is my murdering fury at your death.
But while you lie here by the swanlike ships,
night and day, close by, deep-breasted women
of Troy, and Dardan women, must lament
and weep hot tears, all those whom we acquired
by labor in assault, by the long spear,   400
pillaging the fat market towns of men."

With this Akhilleus called the company
to place over the campfire a big tripod
and bathe Patróklos of his clotted blood.
Setting tripod and caldron on the blaze
they poured it full, and fed the fire beneath,
and flames licked round the belly of the vessel
until the water warmed and bubbled up
in the bright bronze. They bathed him then, and took
sweet oil for his anointing, laying nard[10]   410
in the open wounds; and on his bed they placed him,
covering him with fine linen, head to foot,
and a white shroud over it.

                                    So all that night

beside Akhilleus the great runner,
the Myrmidons held mourning for Patróklos.
Now Zeus observed to Hêra, wife and sister:

---

[9] The home of Menoitios, Patróklos' father.
[10] Balm made from the aromatic spikenard plant.

"You had your way, my lady, after all,
my wide-eyed one! You brought him to his feet,
the great runner! One would say the Akhaian
gentlemen were progeny of yours."   420

And Hêra with wide eyes replied:

                                         "Dread majesty,

Lord Zeus, why do you take this tone? May not
an ordinary mortal have his way,
though death awaits him, and his mind is dim?
Would anyone suppose that I, who rank
in two respects highest of goddesses—
by birth[11] and by my station, queen to thee,
lord of all gods—that I should not devise
ill fortune for the Trojans whom I loathe?"

So ran their brief exchange. Meanwhile   430
the silvery-footed Thetis reached Hêphaistos'
lodging, indestructible and starry,
framed in bronze by the bandy-legged god.
She found him sweating, as from side to side
he plied his bellows; on his forge were twenty
tripods to be finished, then to stand
around his mégaron. And he wrought wheels
of gold for the base of each, that each might roll
as of itself into the gods' assembly,
then roll home, a marvel to the eyes.   440
The caldrons were all shaped but had no handles.
These he applied now, hammering rivets in;
and as he toiled surehandedly at this,
Thetis arrived.

                              Grace in her shining veil
just going out encountered her—that Grace
the bowlegged god had taken to wife.[12] She greeted
Thetis with a warm handclasp and said:

"My lady Thetis, gracious goddess, what
has brought you here? You almost never honor us!
Please come in, and let me give you welcome."   450

Loveliest of goddesses, she led the way,
to seat her guest on a silver-studded chair,
elaborately fashioned, with a footrest.
Then she called to Hêphaistos:

                                   "Come and see!
Thetis is here, in need of something from you!"

---

[11] Hêra and Zeus are both children of the former supreme deity, Krónos.

[12] Hêphaistos' wife is generally identified as Aphrodîtê. Here she is identified as Grace, perhaps to indicate that metal-working entails not just strength but also elegant beauty.

To this the Great Gamelegs replied:

"Ah, then we have a visitor I honor.
She was my savior, after the long fall
and fractures that I had to bear, when Mother,[13]
bitch that she is, wanted to hide her cripple.   460
That would have been a dangerous time, had not
Thetis and Eurýnomê[14] taken me in—
Eurýnomê, daughter of the tidal Ocean.
Nine years I stayed, and fashioned works of art,
brooches and spiral bracelets, necklaces,
in their smooth cave, round which the stream of Ocean
flows with a foaming roar: and no one else
knew of it, gods or mortals. Only Thetis
knew, and Eurýnomê, the two who saved me.
Now she has come to us. Well, what I owe   470
for life to her ladyship in her soft braids
I must repay. Serve her our choicest fare
while I put up my bellows and my tools."

At this he left the anvil block, and hobbled
with monstrous bulk on skinny legs to take
his bellows from the fire. Then all the tools
he had been toiling with he stowed
in a silver chest.
                          That done, he sponged himself,
his face, both arms, bull-neck and hairy chest,
put on a tunic, took a weighty staff,   480
and limped out of his workshop. Round their lord
came fluttering maids of gold, like living girls:
intelligences, voices, power of motion
these maids have, and skills learnt from immortals.
Now they came rustling to support their lord,
and he moved on toward Thetis, where she sat
upon the silvery chair. He took her hand
and warmly said:
                          "My Lady Thetis, gracious
goddess, why have you come? You almost never honor us.
Tell me the favor that you have in mind,   490
for I desire to do it if I can,
and if it is a thing that one may do."

Thetis answered, tear on cheek:
                                        "Hêphaistos,

who among all Olympian goddesses
endured anxiety and pain like mine?
Zeus chose me, from all of them, for this!

---

[13] Hêra.   [14] Thetis' aunt.

Of sea-nymphs I alone was given in thrall
to a mortal warrior, Pêleus Aiákidês,
and I endured a mortal warrior's bed
many a time, without desire. Now Pêleus   500
lies far gone in age in his great hall,
and I have other pain. Our son, bestowed
on me and nursed by me, became a hero
unsurpassed. He grew like a green shoot;
I cherished him like a flowering orchard tree,
only to send him in the ships to Ilion
to war with Trojans. Now I shall never see him
entering Pêleus' hall, his home, again.
But even while he lives, beholding sunlight,
suffering is his lot. I have no power   510
to help him, though I go to him. A girl,
his prize from the Akhaians, Agamémnon
took out of his hands to make his own,
and ah, he pined with burning heart! The Trojans
rolled the Akhaians back on the ship sterns,
and left them no escape. Then Argive officers
begged my son's help, offering every gift,
but he would not defend them from disaster.
Arming Patróklos in his own war-gear,
he sent him with his people into battle.   520
All day long, around the Skaian Gates,
they fought, and would have won the city, too,
had not Apollo, seeing the brave son
of Menoitios wreaking havoc on the Trojans,
killed him in action, and then given Hektor
the honor of that deed.

                                        On this account
I am here to beg you: if you will, provide
for my doomed son a shield and crested helm,
good legging-greaves, fitted with ankle clasps,
a cuirass, too. His own armor was lost   530
when his great friend went down before the Trojans.
Now my son lies prone on the hard ground in grief."

The illustrious lame god replied:

                                        "Take heart.
No trouble about the arms. I only wish
that I could hide him from the power of death
in his black hour—wish I were sure of that
as of the splendid gear he'll get, a wonder
to any one of the many men there are!"

He left her there, returning to his bellows,
training them on the fire, crying, "To work!"   540
In crucibles the twenty bellows breathed

every degree of fiery air: to serve him
a great blast when he labored might and main,
or a faint puff, according to his wish
and what the work demanded.

                                        Durable

fine bronze and tin he threw into the blaze
with silver and with honorable gold,
then mounted a big anvil in his block
and in his right hand took a powerful hammer,
managing with his tongs in his left hand.   550

His first job was a shield, a broad one, thick,
well-fashioned everywhere.[15] A shining rim
he gave it, triple-ply, and hung from this
a silver shoulder strap. Five welded layers
composed the body of the shield. The maker
used all his art adorning this expanse.
He pictured on it earth, heaven, and sea,
unwearied sun, moon waxing, all the stars
that heaven bears for garland: Plêïadês,
Hyadês, Oríôn in his might,   560
the Great Bear, too, that some have called the Wain,
pivoting there, attentive to Oríôn,
and unbathed ever in the Ocean stream.[16]

He pictured, then, two cities, noble scenes:
weddings in one, and wedding feasts, and brides
led out through town by torchlight from their chambers
amid chorales, amid the young men turning
round and round in dances: flutes and harps
among them, keeping up a tune, and women
coming outdoors to stare as they went by.   570
A crowd, then, in a market place, and there
two men at odds over satisfaction owed
for a murder done:[17] one claimed that all was paid,
and publicly declared it; his opponent
turned the reparation down, and both
demanded a verdict from an arbiter,
as people clamored in support of each,
and criers restrained the crowd. The town elders

[15] The pictures on the shield are an attempt to describe comprehensively life in Homer's time and the cosmos as then conceived. Though in its physical structure the shield is modeled on man-made shields as described elsewhere in the *Iliad*, both the craftsmanship and the content clearly go beyond what a human artisan could achieve.

[16] The Great Bear (Ursa Major), also called the Wain and the Big Dipper, is close to the North Star, or Polaris, and therefore seems to rotate around it; for people in the northern latitudes, then, the constellation is always above the northern horizon, regardless of season or time of day.

[17] The penalty for a killing could be paid by a gift of money to the dead man's kin. Here, the elders and arbiter argue and judge the case, two measures of gold being awarded for the best argument or solution.

sat in a ring, on chairs of polished stone,
the staves of clarion criers in their hands,   580
with which they sprang up, each to speak in turn,
and in the middle were two golden measures
to be awarded him whose argument
would be the most straightforward.

                                                   Wartime then;
around the other city were emplaced
two columns of besiegers, bright in arms,
as yet divided on which plan they liked:
whether to sack the town, or treat for half
of all the treasure stored in the citadel.
The townsmen would not bow to either: secretly   590
they armed to break the siege-line. Women and children
stationed on the walls kept watch, with men
whom age disabled. All the rest filed out,
as Arês led the way, and Pallas Athêna,
figured in gold, with golden trappings, both
magnificent in arms, as the gods are,
in high relief, while men were small beside them.
When these had come to a likely place for ambush,
a river with a watering place for flocks,
they there disposed themselves, compact in bronze.   600
Two lookouts at a distance from the troops
took their posts, awaiting sight of sheep
and shambling cattle. Both now came in view,
trailed by two herdsmen playing pipes, no hidden
danger in their minds. The ambush party
took them by surprise in a sudden rush;
swiftly they cut off herds and beautiful flocks
of silvery grey sheep, then killed the herdsmen.
When the besiegers from their parleying ground
heard sounds of cattle in stampede, they mounted   610
behind mettlesome teams, following the sound,
and came up quickly. Battle lines were drawn,
and on the riverbanks the fight began
as each side rifled javelins at the other.
Here then Strife and Uproar joined the fray,
and ghastly Fate, that kept a man with wounds
alive, and one unwounded, and another
dragged by the heels through battle-din in death.
This figure wore a mantle dyed with blood,
and all the figures clashed and fought   620
like living men, and pulled their dead away.

Upon the shield, soft terrain, freshly plowed,
he pictured: a broad field, and many plowmen
here and there upon it. Some were turning
ox teams at the plowland's edge, and there
as one arrived and turned, a man came forward

putting a cup of sweet wine in his hands.
They made their turns-around, then up the furrows
drove again, eager to reach the deep field's
limit; and the earth looked black behind them,   630
as though turned up by plows. But it was gold,
all gold—a wonder of the artist's craft.

He put there, too, a king's field. Harvest hands
were swinging whetted scythes to mow the grain,
and stalks were falling along the swath
while binders girded others up in sheaves
with bands of straw—three binders, and behind them
children came as gleaners, proffering
their eager armfuls. And amid them all
the king stood quietly with staff in hand,   640
happy at heart, upon a new-mown swath.
To one side, under an oak tree his attendants
worked at a harvest banquet. They had killed
a great ox, and were dressing it; their wives
made supper for the hands, with barley strewn.

A vineyard then he pictured, weighted down
with grapes: this all in gold; and yet the clusters
hung dark purple, while the spreading vines
were propped on silver vine-poles. Blue enamel
he made the enclosing ditch, and tin the fence,   650
and one path only led into the vineyard
on which the loaded vintagers took their way
at vintage time. Lighthearted boys and girls
were harvesting the grapes in woven baskets,
while on a resonant harp a boy among them
played a tune of longing, singing low
with delicate voice a summer dirge. The others,
breaking out in song for the joy of it,
kept time together as they skipped along.

The artisan made next a herd of longhorns,   660
fashioned in gold and tin: away they shambled,
lowing, from byre[18] to pasture by a stream
that sang and rippled in a reedy bed.
Four cowherds all of gold were plodding after
with nine lithe dogs beside them.

                                              On the assault,

in two tremendous bounds, a pair of lions
caught in the van a bellowing bull, and off
they dragged him, followed by the dogs and men.
Rending the belly of the bull, the two
gulped down his blood and guts, even as the herdsmen   670

[18] Barn.

tried to set on their hunting dogs, but failed:
no trading bites with lions for those dogs,
who halted close up, barking, then ran back.

And on the shield the great bowlegged god
designed a pasture in a lovely valley,
wide, with silvery sheep, and huts and sheds
and sheepfolds there.

                             A dancing floor as well
he fashioned, like that one in royal Knossos[19]
Daidalos made for the Princess Ariadnê.
Here young men and the most desired young girls   680
were dancing, linked, touching each other's wrists,
the girls in linen, in soft gowns, the men
in well-knit khitons given a gloss with oil;
the girls wore garlands, and the men had daggers
golden-hilted, hung on silver lanyards.
Trained and adept, they circled there with ease
the way a potter sitting at his wheel
will give it a practice twirl between his palms
to see it run; or else, again, in lines
as though in ranks, they moved on one another: 690
magical dancing! All around, a crowd
stood spellbound as two tumblers led the beat
with spins and handsprings through the company.

Then, running round the shield-rim, triple-ply,
he pictured all the might of the Ocean stream.

Besides the densely plated shield, he made
a cuirass, brighter far than fire light,
a massive helmet, measured for his temples,
handsomely figured, with a crest of gold;
then greaves[20] of pliant tin.

                          Now when the crippled god   700
had done his work, he picked up all the arms
and laid them down before Akhilleus' mother,
and swift as a hawk from snowy Olympos' height
she bore the brilliant gear made by Hêphaistos.

---

[19] A city in Krete, ruled by the legendary king Minos and renowned for, among other things, dancing. Daidalos (Daedalus) was a master craftsman best known for constructing a labyrinth to contain the Minotaur, a monster half man and half bull.
[20] Armor for the lower legs.

BOOK NINETEEN: THE AVENGER FASTS AND ARMS

Dawn in her yellow robe rose in the east
out of the flowing Ocean, bearing light
for deathless gods and mortal men. And Thetis
brought to the beach her gifts from the god of fire.
She found her dear son lying beside Patróklos,
wailing, while his men stood by
in tears around him. Now amid that throng
the lovely goddess bent to touch his shoulder
and said to him:

> "Ah, child, let him lie dead,
for all our grief and pain, we must allow it;   10
he fell by the gods' will.
But you, now—take the war-gear from Hêphaistos.
No man ever bore upon his shoulders
gear so magnificent."

> And she laid the armor
down before Akhilleus, clanging loud
in all its various glory. Myrmidons
began to tremble at the sound, and dared not
look straight at the armor; their knees shook.
But anger entered Akhilleus as he gazed,
his eyes grown wide and bright as blazing fire,   20
with fierce joy as he handled the god's gifts.
After appraising them in his delight
he spoke out to his mother swiftly:

> "Mother,
these the god gave are miraculous arms,
handiwork of immortals, plainly—far
beyond the craft of men. By heaven, I'll wear them!
Only, I feel the dread that while I fight
black carrion flies may settle on Patróklos'
wounds, where the spearheads marked him, and I fear
they may breed maggots to defile the corpse,   30
now life is torn from it. His flesh may rot."

But silvery-footed Thetis answered:

> "Child,
you must not let that prey on you. I'll find
a way to shield him from the black fly hordes
that eat the bodies of men killed in battle.
Though he should lie unburied a long year,
his flesh will be intact and firm. Now, though,
for your part, call the Akhaians to assembly.
Tell them your anger against Agamémnon

is over and done with!
After that, at once   40
put on your gear, prepare your heart, for war!"

Her promise gave her son wholehearted valor.
Then, turning to Patróklos, she instilled
red nectar and ambrosia[1] in his nostrils
to keep his body whole.

                                       And Prince Akhilleus

passed along the surf-line with a shout
that split the air and roused men of Akhaia,
even those who, up to now, had stayed
amid the massed ships—navigators, helmsmen,   50
men in charge of rations and ship stores.
Aye, even these now headed for assembly,
since he who for so long had shunned the battle,
Akhilleus, now appeared upon the field.
Resolute Diomêdês and Odysseus,
familiars[2] of the wargod, limped along,
leaning on spears, for both had painful wounds.
They made their way to the forefront and sat down,
and last behind them entered the Lord Marshal
Agamémnon, favoring his wound: he too   60
had taken a slash, from Antênor's son, Koôn.
When everyone had crowded in, Akhilleus,
the great battlefield runner, rose and said:

"Agamémnon, was it better for us
in any way, when we were sore at heart,
to waste ourselves in strife over a girl?
If only Artemis had shot her down[3]
among the ships on the day I made her mine,
after I took Lyrnessos!
Fewer Akhaians would have died hard   70
at enemy hands, while I abstained in anger—
Hektor's gain, the Trojans' gain. Akhaians
years hence will remember our high words,
mine and yours. But now we can forget them,
and, as we must, forego our passion. Aye,
by heaven, I drop my anger now!
No need to smolder in my heart forever! Come,
send your long-haired Akhaians into combat,
and let me see how Trojans will hold out,
if camping near the beachhead's their desire!   80
I rather think some will be glad to rest,
provided they get home, away from danger,
out of my spear's range!"

---

[1] Literally, the drink and food of the gods.   [2] Attendants.
[3] Had brought death to her.

These were his words,
and all the Akhaians gave a roar of joy
to hear the prince abjure his rage.
Lord Marshal Agamémnon then addressed them,
standing up, not in the midst of them,
but where he had been sitting:

"Friends, fighters,

Danáäns, companions of Arês: it is fair
to listen to a man when he has risen   90
and not to interrupt him. That's vexation
to any speaker, able though he may be.
In a great hubbub how can any man
attend or speak? A fine voice will be muffled.
While I open my mind to the son of Pêleus,
Argives, attention! Each man weigh my words!
The Akhaians often brought this up against me,
and chided me. But I am not to blame.[4]
Zeus and Fate and a nightmare Fury are,
for putting savage Folly in my mind   100
in the assembly that day, when I wrested
Akhilleus' prize of war from him. In truth,
what could I do? Divine will shapes these things.
Ruinous Folly, eldest daughter of Zeus,
beguiles us all. Her feet are soft, from walking
not on earth but over the heads of men
to do them hurt. She traps one man or another.
Once indeed she deluded Zeus, most noble
of gods and men, they say. But feminine
Hêra with her underhanded ways   110
tricked him, the day Alkmênê, in high Thebes,
was to have given birth to Hêraklês.[5]
Then glorying Zeus remarked to all the gods:
'Hear me, all gods and goddesses, I'll tell you
of something my heart dwells upon. This day
the childbirth goddess, Eileithyía, brings
into the light a man who will command
all those around him, being of the race of men
who come of my own blood!' But in her guile
the Lady Hêra said: 'You may be wrong,   120
unable to seal your word with truth hereafter.
Come, Olympian, swear me a great oath

---

[4] *I am not to blame.* Despite these words and his accusation of Folly, Agamémnon does to
some extent admit his fault. His account is roughly analogous to modern expressions like
"What possessed me to do that?"

[5] Alkmênê was a mortal woman who, after being seduced by Zeus in the guise of her
husband, gave birth to the hero Hêraklês, whom Hêra hated out of jealousy of his mother.
During one period of his life he was required to serve Eurýstheus (grandson of Perseus,
another son of Zeus) by performing twelve superhumanly difficult labors.

he will indeed be lord of all his neighbors,
the child of your own stock in the race of men
who drops between a woman's legs today!'

Zeus failed to see her crookedness: he swore
a mighty oath, and mightily went astray,
for flashing downward from Olympos crest
Hêra visited Argos of Akhaia,
aware that the strong wife of Perseus' son,   130
Sthénelos, was big with child,
just entering her seventh month. But Hêra
brought this child into the world's daylight
beforehand by two months, and checked Alkmênê's
labor, to delay the birth of hers.
To Zeus the son of Krónos then she said:
'Zeus of the bright bolt, father, let me add
a new event to your deliberations.
Even now a superior man is born
to be a lord of Argives: Eurýstheus,   140
a son of Sthénelos, the son of Perseus,
of your own stock. And it is not unfitting
for him to rule the Argives.' This report
sharply wounded the deep heart of Zeus.
He picked up Folly by her shining braids
in sudden anger—swearing a great oath
that never to starred heaven or Olympos
Folly, who tricks us all, should come again.
With this he whirled her with one hand and flung her
out of the sky. So to men's earth she came,   150
but ever thereafter made Zeus groan to see
his dear son toil at labors for Eurýstheus.

So, too, with me: when in his shimmering helm
great Hektor slaughtered Argives near the ships,
could I ignore my folly, my delusion?
Zeus had stolen my wits, my act was blind.
But now I wish to make amends, to give
all possible satisfaction. Rouse for war,
send in your troops! I here repeat my offer
of all that Odysseus promised yesterday![6]   160
Stay if you will, though the wargod presses you.
Men in my service will unload the gifts
from my own ship, that you may see how richly
I reward you!"

                             Akhilleus answered:
                                     "Excellency,

Lord Marshal Agamémnon, make the gifts
if you are keen to—gifts are due; or keep them.

[6]Agamémnon refers to the offer he made in Book IX.

It is for you to say. Let us recover
joy of battle soon, that's all!
No need to dither here and lose our time,
our great work still undone. When each man sees   170
Akhilleus in a charge, crumpling the ranks
of Trojans with his bronze-shod spear, let each
remember that is the way to fight his man!"

Replied Odysseus, the shrewd field commander:

"Brave as you are, and like a god in looks,
Akhilleus, do not send Akhaian soldiers
into the fight unfed! Today's mêlée
will not be brief, when rank meets rank, and heaven
breathes fighting spirit into both contenders.
No, tell all troops who are near the ships to take   180
roast meat and wine, for heart and staying power.
No soldier can fight hand to hand, in hunger,
all day long until the sun goes down!
Though in his heart he yearns for war, his legs
go slack before he knows it: thirst and famine
search him out, and his knees fail as he moves.
But that man stayed with victualing and wine
can fight his enemies all day: his heart
is bold and happy in his chest, his legs
hold out until both sides break off the battle!   190
Come, then, dismiss the ranks to make their breakfast.
Let the Lord Marshal Agamémnon
bring his gifts to the assembly ground
where all may see them; may your heart be warmed.
Then let him swear to you, before the Argives,
never to have made love to her, my lord,
as men and women by their nature do.
So may your heart be peaceable toward him!
And let him sate your hunger with rich fare
in his own shelter, that you may lack nothing   200
due you in justice. Afterward, Agamémnon,
you'll be more just to others, too. There is
no fault in a king's wish to conciliate
a man with whom he has been quick to anger!"

And the Lord Marshal Agamémnon answered:

"Glad I am to hear you, son of Laërtês,
finding the right word at the right time
for all these matters. And the oath you speak of
I'll take willingly, with all my heart,
and will not, before heaven, be forsworn.   210
Now let Akhilleus wait here, though the wargod
tug his arm; and all the rest of you
wait here assembled till the gifts have come

down from our quarters, and our peace is made.
For you, Odysseus, here is my command:
choose the finest young peers of all Akhaia
to fetch out of my ship those gifts we pledged
Akhilleus yesterday; and bring the women.
Let Talthýbios[7] prepare for sacrifice,
in the army's name, a boar to Zeus and Hêlios."[8]   220

Replied Akhilleus:

                              "Excellency, Lord Marshal,
another time were better for these ceremonies,
some interval in the war, and when I feel
less passion in me. Look, those men lie dead
whom Hektor killed when Zeus allowed him glory,
and yet you two propose a meal! By god,
I'd send our soldiers into action now
unfed and hungry. Have a feast, I'd say,
at sundown, when our shame has been avenged!
Before that, for my part, I will not swallow   230
food or drink—my dear friend being dead,
lying before my eyes, bled white by spear-cuts,
feet turned to his hut's door, his friends in mourning
around him. Your concerns are none of mine.
Slaughter and blood are what I crave, and groans
of anguished men!"

                              But the shrewd field commander
Odysseus answered:

                              "Akhilleus, flower and pride
of the Akhaians, you are more powerful
than I am—and a better spearman, too—
only in sizing matters up I'd say   240
I'm just as far beyond you, being older,
knowing more of the world. So bear with me.
Men quickly reach satiety with battle
in which the reaping bronze will bring to earth
big harvests, but a scanty yield, when Zeus,
war's overseer for mankind, tips the scales.
How can a fasting belly mourn our dead?
So many die, so often, every day,
when would soldiers come to an end of fasting?
No, we must dispose of him who dies   250
and keep hard hearts, and weep that day alone.
And those whom the foul war has left unhurt
will do well to remember food and drink,
so that we may again close with our enemies,
our dangerous enemies, and be tough soldiers,

---

[7] Agamémnon's crier, or herald.   [8] The sun or sun-god.

hardened in mail of bronze. Let no one, now,
be held back waiting for another summons:
here is your summons! Woe to the man who lingers
beside the Argive ships! No, all together,
let us take up the fight against the Trojans!"   260

He took as escort sons of illustrious Nestor:
Phyleus' son Mégês, Thoas, and Meríonês,
and the son of Kreion, Lykomêdês, and
Melánippos, to Agamémnon's quarters.
No sooner was the work assigned than done:
they brought the seven tripods Agamémnon
promised Akhilleus, and the twenty caldrons
shining, and the horses, a full dozen;
then they conducted seven women, skilled
in housecraft, with Brisêis in her beauty.   270
Odysseus weighed ten bars of purest gold
and turned back, followed by his young Akhaians,
bearing the gifts to place in mid-assembly.

Now Agamémnon rose. Talthýbios
the crier, with his wondrous voice, stood near him,
holding the boar. The son of Atreus drew
the sheath knife that he carried, hung
beside the big sheath of his sword, and cut
first bristles from the boar. Arms wide to heaven
he prayed to Zeus, as all the troops kept still,   280
all sitting in due order in their places,
hearing their king. In prayer he raised his eyes
to the broad sky and said:

                              "May Zeus, all-highest
and first of gods, be witness first, then Earth
and Hêlios and the Furies underground
who punish men for having broken oaths,
I never laid a hand on your Brisêis,
proposing bed or any other pleasure;
in my quarters the girl has been untouched.
If one word that I swear is false,   290
may the gods plague me for a perjured liar!"

He slit the boar's throat with his blade of bronze.
Then Talthýbios, wheeling, flung the victim
into the offshore water, bait for fish.
Akhilleus rose amid the Argive warriors,
saying:

                              "Father Zeus, you send mankind
prodigious follies. Never otherwise
had Agamémnon stung me through and through;
never would he have been so empty-headed

as to defy my will and take the girl!   300
No, for some reason Zeus had death at heart
for the Akhaians, and for many.

                                               Well:

go to your meat, then we'll resume the fighting."

Thus he dismissed the assembly. All the men
were quick to scatter, each to his own ship.
As for the gifts, the Myrmidons took over
and bore them all to Akhilleus' ship, to stow
within his shelter. There they left the women
and drove the horses to the herd.

                                            The girl   310
Brisêis, in her grace like Aphrodítê,
on entering saw Patróklos lying dead
of spear wounds, and she sank down to embrace him
with a sharp sobbing cry, lifting her hands
to tear her breast, soft throat, and lovely face,
this girl, shaped like the goddesses of heaven.
Weeping, she said:

                                    "Patróklos, very dear,
most dear to me, cursed as I am, you were
alive still when I left you, left this place!
Now I come back to find you dead, my captain!
Evil follows evil so, for me.   320
The husband to whom father and mother gave me
I saw brought down by spears before our town,
with my three brothers, whom my mother bore.
Dear brothers, all three met their day of wrath.
But when Akhilleus killed my lord, and sacked
the city of royal Mynês, not a tear
would you permit me: no, you undertook
to see me married to the Prince Akhilleus,[9]
conveyed by ship to Phthía, given a wedding
among the Myrmidons. Now must I mourn   330
your death forever, who were ever gentle."

She wailed again, and women sobbed about her,
first for Patróklos, then for each one's grief.
Meanwhile Akhaian counselors were gathered
begging Akhilleus to take food. He spurned it,
groaning:

                              "No, I pray you, my dear friends,
if anyone will listen!—do not nag me
to glut and dull my heart with food and drink!

---

[9] Patróklos was presumably trying to console Brisêis; for Akhilleus to marry a woman taken
captive would be unlikely.

A burning pain is in me. I'll hold out
till sundown without food. I say I'll bear it." 340

With this he sent the peers away, except
the two Atreidai[10] and the great Odysseus,
Nestor, Idómeneus, and old Lord Phoinix.
These would have comforted him, but none
could quiet or comfort him until he entered
the bloody jaws of war. Now pierced by memory,
he sighed and sighed again, and said:

                "Ah, once

you, too, poor fated friend, and best of friends,
would set a savory meal deftly before us
in our field shelter, when the Akhaians wished 350
no time lost between onsets against Trojans.
Now there you lie, broken in battle. Ah,
lacking you, my heart will fast this day
from meat and drink as well. No greater ill
could come to me, not news of Father's death—
my father, weeping soft tears now in Phthía
for want of that son in a distant land
who wars on Troy for Helen's sake—that woman
who makes the blood run cold. No greater ill,
even should my son die, who is being reared 360
on Skyros, Neoptólemos, if indeed
he's living still.[11] My heart's desire had been
that I alone should perish far from Argos
here at Troy; that you should sail to Phthía,
taking my son aboard your swift black ship
at Skyros, to introduce him to his heritage,
my wide lands, my servants, my great hall.
In this late year Pêleus may well be dead
and buried, or have few days yet to live,
beset by racking age, always awaiting 370
dire news of me, of my own death."

As he said this he wept. The counselors groaned,
remembering each what he had left at home;
and seeing them sorrow, Zeus took pity on them,
saying quickly to Athêna:

                "Daughter,

you seem to have left your fighting man alone.

---

[10] Sons of Atreus—i.e., Agamémnon and Meneláos.
[11] Skyros was an island east of Greece, in the Aegean Sea. According to some versions of the legend, the mother of Neoptólemos was a princess of Skyros whom Akhilleus had loved while hiding out there to avoid the Trojan War. Neoptólemos (also called Pyrrhus) joined the Greek forces after his father's death and killed Priam when Troy was finally taken (compare the account in Virgil's *Aeneid*, Book II).

Should one suppose you care no more for Akhilleus?
There he sits, before the curving prows,
and grieves for his dear friend. The other soldiers
flock to meat; he thirsts and hungers. Come,   380
infuse in him sweet nectar and ambrosia,
that an empty belly may not weaken him."

He urged Athêna to her own desire,
and like a gliding sea hawk, shrilling high,
she soared from heaven through the upper air,
while the Akhaians armed throughout the ranks.
Nectar and ambrosia she instilled
within Akhilleus, that his knees be not
assailed by hollow famine; then she withdrew
to her mighty father's house. Meanwhile the troops   390
were pouring from the shipways to the field.
As when cold snowflakes fly from Zeus in heaven,
thick and fast under the blowing north wind,
just so, that multitude of gleaming helms
and bossed shields issued from the ships, with plated
cuirasses and ashwood spears. Reflected
glintings flashed to heaven, as the plain
in all directions shone with glare of bronze
and shook with trampling feet of men. Among them
Prince Akhilleus armed. One heard his teeth   400
grind hard together, and his eyes blazed out
like licking fire, for unbearable pain
had fixed upon his heart. Raging at Trojans,
he buckled on the arms Hêphaistos forged.
The beautiful greaves, fitted with silver anklets,
first he put upon his legs, and next
the cuirass on his ribs; then over his shoulder
he slung the sword of bronze with silver scabbard;
finally he took up the massive shield
whence came a radiance like the round full moon.   410
As when at sea to men on shipboard comes
the shining of a campfire on a mountain
in a lone sheepfold, while the gusts of nightwind
take them, loath to go, far from their friends
over the teeming sea: just so
Akhilleus' finely modeled shield sent light
into the heavens: Lifting his great helm
he placed it on his brows, and like a star
the helm shone with its horsetail blowing free,
all golden, that Hêphaistos had set in   420
upon the crest. Akhilleus tried his armor,
shrugging and flexing, making sure it fitted,
sure that his gleaming legs had play. Indeed
the gear sat on him light as wings: it buoyed him!

Now from a spear-case he withdrew a spear—
his father's—weighty, long, and tough. No other
Akhaian had the strength to handle it,
this great Pêlian shaft
of ashwood, given his father by the centaur
Kheirôn from the crest of Pêlion   430
to be the death of heroes.

                                                   Automédôn

and Álkimos with swift hands yoked his team,
making firm the collars on the horses,
placing the bits between their teeth, and pulling
reins to the war-car. Automédôn then
took in hand the shining whip and mounted
the chariot, and at his back Akhilleus
mounted in full armor, shining bright
as the blinding Lord of Noon.[12] In a clarion voice
he shouted to the horses of his father: 440

"Xánthos and Balíos! Known to the world
as foals of great Podargê! In this charge
care for your driver in another way!
Pull him back, I mean, to the Danáäns,
back to the main body of the army,
once we are through with battle; this time,
no leaving him there dead, like Lord Patróklos!"

To this, from under the yoke, the nimble Xánthos
answered, and hung his head, so that his mane
dropped forward from the yokepad to the ground—   450
Hêra whose arms are white as ivory
gave him a voice to say:

                                    "Yes, we shall save you,
this time, too, Akhilleus in your strength!
And yet the day of your destruction comes,
and it is nearer. We are not the cause,
but rather a great god is, and mighty Fate.
Nor was it by our sloth or sluggishness
the Trojans stripped Patróklos of his armor.
No, the magnificent god[13] that Lêto bore
killed him in action and gave Hektor glory.   460
We might run swiftly as the west wind blows,
most rapid of all winds, they say; but still
it is your destiny to be brought low
by force, a god's force and a man's!"[14]

---

[12] The sun.   [13] Apollo.
[14] Akhilleus will one day be slain by the bow of Paris with the help of Apollo, god of archers.

On this,
the Furies put a stop to Xánthos' voice.[15]
In anger and gloom Akhilleus said to him:

"Xánthos, why prophesy my death? No need.
What is in store for me I know, know well:
to die here, far away from my dear father,
my mother, too. No matter. All that matters   470
is that I shall not call a halt today
till I have made the Trojans sick of war!"

And with a shout he drove his team
of trim-hooved horses into the front line.

BOOK XX. *Zeus assembles the gods and tells them that they now have a free hand to intervene in the war. A brief catalogue of the gods follows: on the Greek side Hêra, Athêna, Poseidon, Hermês, and Hêphaistos; on the Trojan side Arês, Apollo, Artemis (Apollo's sister and goddess of the hunt), Lêto (mother of Apollo and Artemis), the river-god Xánthos, and Aphrodítê. (For the time being, however, most of the gods stay out of action.) Aineías, incited by Apollo, engages Akhilleus; Poseidon (though he favors the Greeks) saves the Trojan hero by spiriting him away, since Aineías is fated to live and rule over the Trojan survivors of the war. Akhilleus and Hektor exhort their respective armies to fight. At Apollo's suggestion, Hektor stays out of Akhilleus' range, but when one of Hektor's brothers is slain he attacks Akhilleus. Hektor is saved when Apollo hides him in a cloud. Cheated of his prey a second time, Akhilleus rages, killing many Trojans.*

BOOK XXI. *Akhilleus divides the Trojan forces, driving half of them toward the city, half into the river Xánthos (also called Skamánder), which flows by the plain. In the river he kills many men and takes twelve alive who are to pay later for the death of Patróklos. Xánthos, the god and personification of the river, angered by the pollution of his waters and by Akhilleus' slaughter of Trojans, attacks him and puts him in sore danger of drowning. Poseidon, Athêna, and Hêra come to Akhilleus' aid, and the fire god Hêphaistos uses his flames to overcome the raging river, which bubbles with the heat. Now the gods begin a general battle with one another: Athêna against Arês, Athêna against Aphrodítê, Hêra against Artemis. Challenged half-heartedly by Poseidon, Apollo declines to fight, remarking that it is foolish for gods to fight one another for the sake of mere mortals. The deities who favor the Greeks having emerged as victors, all the gods return to Olympos except Apollo, who helps the fleeing Trojans to withdraw safely within the city walls, by impersonating a Trojan and leading Akhilleus on a wild-goose chase. But Hektor remains outside the walls, stranded.*

BOOK TWENTY-TWO: DESOLATION BEFORE TROY

Once in the town, those who had fled like deer
wiped off their sweat and drank their thirst away,
leaning against the cool stone of the ramparts.
Meanwhile Akhaians with bright shields aslant
came up the plain and nearer. As for Hektor,

---

[15] That a horse should speak violates natural law, of which the Furies are guardians. (Xánthos is also the name of a river-god who appears in Books XX and XXI.)

fatal destiny pinned him where he stood
before the Skaian Gates, outside the city.

Now Akhilleus heard Apollo calling
back to him:

                                        "Why run so hard, Akhilleus,
mortal as you are, after a god?   10
Can you not comprehend it? I am immortal.
You are so hot to catch me, you no longer
think of finishing off the men you routed.
They are all in the town by now, packed in
while you were being diverted here. And yet
you cannot kill me; I am no man's quarry."

Akhilleus bit his lip and said:
"Archer of heaven, deadliest
of immortal gods, you put me off the track,
turning me from the wall this way. A hundred   20
might have sunk their teeth into the dust
before one man took cover in Ilion!
You saved my enemies with ease and stole
my glory, having no punishment to fear.
I'd take it out of you, if I had the power."

Then toward the town with might and main he ran,
magnificent, like a racing chariot horse
that holds its form at full stretch on the plain.
So light-footed Akhilleus held the pace.
And aging Priam was the first to see him   30
sparkling on the plain, bright as that star
in autumn rising, whose unclouded rays
shine out amid a throng of stars at dusk—
the one they call Oríôn's dog, most brilliant,
yes, but baleful as a sign: it brings
great fever to frail men.[1] So pure and bright
the bronze gear blazed upon him as he ran.
The old man gave a cry. With both his hands
thrown up on high he struck his head, then shouted,
groaning, appealing to his dear son. Unmoved,   40
Lord Hektor stood in the gateway, resolute
to fight Akhilleus.
                            Stretching out his hands,
old Priam said, imploring him:

                                        "No, Hektor!
Cut off as you are, alone, dear son,
don't try to hold your ground against this man,

---

[1] Sirius, the brightest of the stars, reappears in the eastern skies in the "dog days" of
August, a time associated with disease.

or soon you'll meet the shock of doom, borne down
by the son of Pêleus. He is more powerful
by far than you, and pitiless. Ah, were he
but dear to the gods as he is dear to me!
Wild dogs and kites would eat him where he lay   50
within the hour, and ease me of my torment.
Many tall sons he killed, bereaving me,
or sold them to far islands. Even now
I cannot see two sons of mine, Lykáôn
and Polydôros,[2] among the Trojans massed
inside the town. A queen, Laóthoê,
conceived and bore them. If they are alive
amid the Akhaian host, I'll ransom them
with bronze and gold: both I have, piled at home,
rich treasures that old Altês, the renowned,   60
gave for his daughter's dowry. If they died,
if they went under to the homes of Death,
sorrow has come to me and to their mother.
But to our townsmen all this pain is brief,
unless you too go down before Akhilleus.
Come inside the wall, child; here you may
fight on to save our Trojan men and women.
Do not resign the glory to Akhilleus,
losing your own dear life! Take pity, too,
on me and my hard fate, while I live still.   70
Upon the threshold of my age, in misery,
the son[3] of Krónos will destroy my life
after the evil days I shall have seen—
my sons brought down, my daughters dragged away,
bedchambers ravaged, and small children hurled
to earth in the atrocity of war,
as my sons' wives are taken by Akhaians'
ruinous hands. And at the end, I too—
when someone with a sword-cut or a spear
has had my life—I shall be torn apart   80
on my own doorstep by the hounds
I trained as watchdogs, fed from my own table.
These will lap my blood with ravenous hearts
and lie in the entranceway.

                                  Everything done
to a young man killed in war becomes his glory,
once he is riven by the whetted bronze:
dead though he be, it is all fair, whatever
happens then. But when an old man falls,
and dogs disfigure his grey head and cheek

---

[2] They were slain by Akhilleus in, respectively, Books XXI and XX. Laóthoê, daughter of Altês, is one of Priam's concubines. (Hektor's mother, Hékabê, is Priam's principal wife and queen of Troy.)
[3] Zeus.

and genitals, that is most harrowing   90
of all that men in their hard lives endure."

The old man wrenched at his grey hair and pulled out
hanks of it in both hands, but moved
Lord Hektor not at all. The young man's mother
wailed from the tower across, above the portal,
streaming tears, and loosening her robe
with one hand, held her breast out in the other,
saying:

                "Hektor, my child, be moved by this,
and pity me, if ever I unbound
a quieting breast for you. Think of these things,   100
dear child; defend yourself against the killer
this side of the wall, not hand to hand.
He has no pity. If he brings you down,
I shall no longer be allowed to mourn you
laid out on your bed, dear branch in flower,
born of me! And neither will your lady,
so endowed with gifts. Far from us both,
dogs will devour you by the Argive ships."

With tears and cries the two implored their son,
and made their prayers again, but could not shake him.   110
Hektor stood firm, as huge Akhilleus neared.
The way a serpent, fed on poisonous herbs,
coiled at his lair upon a mountainside,
with all his length of hate awaits a man
and eyes him evilly: so Hektor, grim
and narrow-eyed, refused to yield. He leaned
his brilliant shield against a spur of wall
and in his brave heart bitterly reflected:
"Here I am badly caught. If I take cover,
slipping inside the gate and wall, the first   120
to accuse me for it will be Poulýdamas,
he who told me I should lead the Trojans
back to the city on that cursed night
Akhilleus joined the battle. No, I would not,
would not, wiser though it would have been.
Now troops have perished for my foolish pride,
I am ashamed to face townsmen and women.
Someone inferior to me may say:
'He kept his pride and lost his men, this Hektor!'
So it will go. Better, when that time comes,   130
that I appear as he who killed Akhilleus
man to man, or else that I went down
fighting him to the end before the city.
Suppose, though, that I lay my shield and helm
aside, and prop my spear against the wall,

and go meet the noble Prince Akhilleus,
promising Helen, promising with her
all treasures that Aléxandros[4] brought home
by ship to Troy—the first cause of our quarrel—
that he may give these things to the Atreidai?   140
Then I might add, apart from these, a portion
of all the secret wealth the city owns.
Yes, later I might take our counselors' oath
to hide no stores, but share and share alike
to halve all wealth our lovely city holds,
all that is here within the walls. Ah, no,
why even put the question to myself?
I must not go before him and receive
no quarter, no respect! Aye, then and there
he'll kill me, unprotected as I am,   150
my gear laid by, defenseless as a woman.
No chance, now, for charms[5] from oak or stone
in parley with him—charms a girl and boy
might use when they enchant each other talking!
Better we duel, now at once, and see
to whom the Olympian awards the glory."

These were his shifts of mood. Now close at hand
Akhilleus like the implacable god of war
came on with blowing crest, hefting the dreaded
beam of Pêlian ash on his right shoulder.   160
Bronze light played around him, like the glare
of a great fire or the great sun rising,
and Hektor, as he watched, began to tremble.
Then he could hold his ground no more. He ran,
leaving the gate behind him, with Akhilleus
hard on his heels, sure of his own speed.
When that most lightning-like of birds, a hawk
bred on a mountain, swoops upon a dove,
the quarry dips in terror, but the hunter,
screaming, dips behind and gains upon it,   170
passionate for prey. Just so, Akhilleus
murderously cleft the air, as Hektor
ran with flashing knees along the wall.
They passed the lookout point, the wild figtree
with wind in all its leaves, then veered away
along the curving wagon road, and came
to where the double fountains well, the source
of eddying Skamánder. One hot spring
flows out, and from the water fumes arise
as though from fire burning; but the other   180
even in summer gushes chill as hail

---

[4] Paris.
[5] Pleasing words. The meaning of the phrase "from oak or stone" is uncertain.

or snow or crystal ice frozen on water.
Near these fountains are wide washing pools
of smooth-laid stone, where Trojan wives and daughters
laundered their smooth linen in the days
of peace before the Akhaians came. Past these
the two men ran, pursuer and pursued,
and he who fled was noble, he behind
a greater man by far. They ran full speed,
and not for bull's hide or a ritual beast   190
or any prize that men compete for: no,
but for the life of Hektor, tamer of horses.
Just as when chariot-teams around a course
go wheeling swiftly, for the prize is great,
a tripod or a woman,[6] in the games
held for a dead man, so three times these two
at full speed made their course round Priam's town,
as all the gods looked on. And now the father
of gods and men turned to the rest and said:

"How sad that this beloved man is hunted   200
around the wall before my eyes! My heart
is touched for Hektor; he has burned thigh flesh
of oxen for me often, high on Ida,
at other times on the high point of Troy.
Now Prince Akhilleus with devouring stride
is pressing him around the town of Priam.
Come, gods, put your minds on it, consider
whether we may deliver him from death
or see him, noble as he is, brought down
by Pêleus' son, Akhilleus."

Grey-eyed Athêna   210

said to him:

"Father of the blinding bolt,
the dark stormcloud, what words are these? The man
is mortal, and his doom fixed, long ago.
Would you release him from his painful death?
Then do so, but not all of us will praise you."

Zeus who gathers cloud replied:

"Take heart,

my dear and honored child. I am not bent
on my suggestion, and I would indulge you.
Act as your thought inclines, refrain no longer."

So he encouraged her in her desire,   220
and down she swept from ridges of Olympos.

---

[6] In Book XXIII these prizes are offered to the winner of the chariot race in the ceremonial funeral games honoring Patróklos.

Great Akhilleus, hard on Hektor's heels,
kept after him, the way a hound will harry
a deer's fawn he has startled from its bed
to chase through gorge and open glade, and when
the quarry goes to earth under a bush
he holds the scent and quarters till he finds it;
so with Hektor: he could not shake off
the great runner, Akhilleus. Every time
he tried to spring hard for the Dardan gates   230
under the towers, hoping men could help him,
sending missiles down, Akhilleus loomed
to cut him off and turn him toward the plain,
as he himself ran always near the city.
As in a dream a man chasing another
cannot catch him, nor can he in flight
escape from his pursuer, so Akhilleus
could not by his swiftness overtake him,
nor could Hektor pull away. How could he
run so long from death, had not Apollo   240
for the last time, the very last, come near
to give him stamina and speed?

                                     Akhilleus

shook his head at the rest of the Akhaians,
allowing none to shoot or cast at Hektor—
none to forestall him, and to win the honor.
But when, for the fourth time, they reached the springs,
the Father poised his golden scales.

                                    He placed

two shapes of death, death prone and cold, upon them,
one of Akhilleus, one of the horseman, Hektor,
and held the midpoint, pulling upward. Down   250
sank Hektor's fatal day, the pan went down
toward undergloom, and Phoibos Apollo left him.
Then came Athêna, grey-eyed, to the son
of Pêleus, falling in with him, and near him,
saying swiftly:

                                "Now at last I think

the two of us, Akhilleus loved by Zeus,
shall bring Akhaians triumph at the ships
by killing Hektor—unappeased
though he was ever in his thirst for war.
There is no way he may escape us now,   260
not though Apollo, lord of distances,
should suffer all indignity for him
before his father Zeus who bears the stormcloud,
rolling back and forth and begging for him.
Now you can halt and take your breath, while I
persuade him into combat face to face."

These were Athêna's orders. He complied,
relieved, and leaning hard upon the spearshaft
armed with its head of bronze. She left him there
and overtook Lord Hektor—but she seemed   270
Dêíphobos in form and resonant voice,
appearing at his shoulder, saying swiftly:

"Ai! Dear brother, how he runs, Akhilleus,
harrying you around the town of Priam!
Come, we'll stand and take him on."

To this,

great Hektor in his shimmering helm replied:

"Dêíphobos, you were the closest to me
in the old days, of all my brothers, sons
of Hékabê and Priam. Now I can say
I honor you still more   280
because you dared this foray for my sake,
seeing me run. The rest stay under cover."

Again the grey-eyed goddess spoke:

"Dear brother, how your father and gentle mother
begged and begged me to remain! So did
the soldiers round me, all undone by fear.
But in my heart I ached for you.
Now let us fight him, and fight hard.
No holding back. We'll see if this Akhilleus
conquers both, to take our armor seaward,   290
or if he can be brought down by your spear."

This way, by guile, Athêna led him on.
And when at last the two men faced each other,
Hektor was the first to speak. He said:

"I will no longer fear you as before,
son of Pêleus, though I ran from you
round Priam's town three times and could not face you.
Now my soul would have me stand and fight,
whether I kill you or am killed. So come,
we'll summon gods here as our witnesses,   300
none higher, arbiters of a pact: I swear
that, terrible as you are,
I'll not insult your corpse should Zeus allow me
victory in the end, your life as prize.
Once I have your gear, I'll give your body
back to Akhaians. Grant me, too, this grace."

But swift Akhilleus frowned at him and said:

"Hektor, I'll have no talk of pacts with you,
forever unforgiven as you are.
As between men and lions there are none,   310
no concord between wolves and sheep, but all
hold one another hateful through and through,
so there can be no courtesy between us,
no sworn truce, till one of us is down
and glutting with his blood the wargod Arês.
Summon up what skills you have. By god,
you'd better be a spearman and a fighter!
Now there is no way out. Pallas Athêna
will have the upper hand of you. The weapon
belongs to me. You'll pay the reckoning   320
in full for all the pain my men have borne,
who met death by your spear."

                                                   He twirled and cast
his shaft with its long shadow. Splendid Hektor,
keeping his eye upon the point, eluded it
by ducking at the instant of the cast,
so shaft and bronze shank passed him overhead
and punched into the earth. But unperceived
by Hektor, Pallas Athêna plucked it out
and gave it back to Akhilleus. Hektor said:

"A clean miss. Godlike as you are,   330
you have not yet known doom for me from Zeus.
You thought you had, by heaven. Then you turned
into a word-thrower, hoping to make me lose
my fighting heart and head in fear of you.
You cannot plant your spear between my shoulders
while I am running. If you have the gift,
just put it through my chest as I come forward.
Now it's for you to dodge my own. Would god
you'd give the whole shaft lodging in your body!
War for the Trojans would be eased   340
if you were blotted out, bane that you are."

With this he twirled his long spearshaft and cast it,
hitting his enemy mid-shield, but off
and away the spear rebounded. Furious
that he had lost it, made his throw for nothing,
Hektor stood bemused. He had no other.
Then he gave a great shout to Dêíphobos
to ask for a long spear. But there was no one
near him, not a soul. Now in his heart
the Trojan realized the truth and said: 350

"This is the end. The gods are calling deathward.
I had thought
a good soldier, Dêíphobos, was with me.

He is inside the walls. Athêna tricked me.
Death is near, and black, not at a distance,
not to be evaded. Long ago
this hour must have been to Zeus's liking
and to the liking of his archer son.
They have been well disposed before, but now
the appointed time's upon me. Still, I would not   360
die without delivering a stroke,
or die ingloriously, but in some action
memorable to men in days to come."

With this he drew the whetted blade that hung
upon his left flank, ponderous and long,
collecting all his might the way an eagle
narrows himself to dive through shady cloud
and strike a lamb or cowering hare: so Hektor
lanced ahead and swung his whetted blade.
Akhilleus with wild fury in his heart   370
pulled in upon his chest his beautiful shield—
his helmet with four burnished metal ridges
nodding above it, and the golden crest
Hêphaistos locked there tossing in the wind.
Conspicuous as the evening star that comes,
amid the first in heaven, at fall of night,
and stands most lovely in the west, so shone
in sunlight the fine-pointed spear
Akhilleus poised in his right hand, with deadly
aim at Hektor, at the skin where most   380
it lay exposed. But nearly all was covered
by the bronze gear he took from slain Patróklos,
showing only, where his collarbones
divided neck and shoulders, the bare throat
where the destruction of a life is quickest.
Here, then, as the Trojan charged, Akhilleus
drove his point straight through the tender neck,
but did not cut the windpipe, leaving Hektor
able to speak and to respond. He fell
aside into the dust. And Prince Akhilleus   390
now exulted:

                                        "Hektor, had you thought
that you could kill Patróklos and be safe?
Nothing to dread from me; I was not there.
All childishness. Though distant then, Patróklos'
comrade in arms was greater far than he—
and it is I who had been left behind
that day beside the deepsea ships who now
have made your knees give way. The dogs and kites
will rip your body. His will lie in honor
when the Akhaians give him funeral."   400

Hektor, barely whispering, replied:

"I beg you by your soul and by your parents,
do not let the dogs feed on me
in your encampment by the ships. Accept
the bronze and gold my father will provide
as gifts, my father and her ladyship
my mother. Let them have my body back,
so that our men and women may accord me
decency of fire when I am dead."

Akhilleus the great runner scowled and said: 410

"Beg me no beggary by soul or parents,
whining dog! Would god my passion drove me
to slaughter you and eat you raw, you've caused
such agony to me! No man exists
who could defend you from the carrion pack—
not if they spread for me ten times your ransom,
twenty times, and promise more as well;
aye, not if Priam, son of Dárdanos,
tells them to buy you for your weight in gold!
You'll have no bed of death, nor will you be   420
laid out and mourned by her who gave you birth.
Dogs and birds will have you, every scrap."

Then at the point of death Lord Hektor said:

"I see you now for what you are. No chance
to win you over. Iron in your breast
your heart is. Think a bit, though: this may be
a thing the gods in anger hold against you
on that day when Paris and Apollo
destroy you at the Gates,[7] great as you are."

Even as he spoke, the end came, and death hid him;   430
spirit from body fluttered to undergloom,
bewailing fate that made him leave his youth
and manhood in the world. And as he died
Akhilleus spoke again. He said:

"Die, make an end. I shall accept my own
whenever Zeus and the other gods desire."

At this he pulled his spearhead from the body,
laying it aside, and stripped
the bloodstained shield and cuirass from his shoulders.
Other Akhaians hastened round to see   440
Hektor's fine body and his comely face,

---

[7] The gates of Troy.

and no one came who did not stab the body.
Glancing at one another they would say:

"Now Hektor has turned vulnerable, softer
than when he put the torches to the ships!"

And he who said this would inflict a wound.
When the great master of pursuit, Akhilleus,
had the body stripped, he stood among them,
saying swiftly:

"Friends, my lords and captains
of Argives, now that the gods at last have let me   450
bring to earth this man who wrought
havoc among us—more than all the rest—
come, we'll offer battle around the city,
to learn the intentions of the Trojans now.
Will they give up their strongpoint at this loss?
Can they fight on, though Hektor's dead?

But wait:
why do I ponder, why take up these questions?
Down by the ships Patróklos' body lies
unwept, unburied. I shall not forget him
while I can keep my feet among the living.   460
If in the dead world they forget the dead,
I say there, too, I shall remember him,
my friend. Men of Akhaia, lift a song!
Down to the ships we go, and take this body,
our glory. We have beaten Hektor down,
to whom as to a god the Trojans prayed."

Indeed, he had in mind for Hektor's body
outrage and shame. Behind both feet he pierced
the tendons, heel to ankle. Rawhide cords
he drew through both and lashed them to his chariot,   470
letting the man's head trail. Stepping aboard,
bearing the great trophy of the arms,
he shook the reins, and whipped the team ahead
into a willing run. A dustcloud rose
above the furrowing body; the dark tresses
flowed behind, and the head so princely once
lay back in dust. Zeus gave him to his enemies
to be defiled in his own fatherland.
So his whole head was blackened. Looking down,
his mother tore her braids, threw off her veil,   480
and wailed, heartbroken to behold her son.
Piteously his father groaned, and round him
lamentation spread throughout the town,

most like the clamor to be heard if Ilion's
towers, top to bottom, seethed in flames.
They barely stayed the old man, mad with grief,
from passing through the gates. Then in the mire
he rolled, and begged them all, each man by name:

"Relent, friends. It is hard; but let me go
out of the city to the Akhaian ships.   490
I'll make my plea to that demonic heart.
He may feel shame before his peers, or pity
my old age. His father, too, is old,
Pêleus, who brought him up to be a scourge
to Trojans, cruel to all, but most to me,
so many of my sons in flower of youth
he cut away. And, though I grieve, I cannot
mourn them all as much as I do one,
for whom my grief will take me to the grave—
and that is Hektor. Why could he not have died   500
where I might hold him? In our weeping, then,
his mother, now so destitute, and I
might have had surfeit and relief of tears."

These were the words of Priam as he wept,
and all his people groaned. Then in her turn
Hékabê led the women in lamentation:

"Child, I am lost now. Can I bear my life
after the death of suffering your death?
You were my pride in all my nights and days,
pride of the city, pillar to the Trojans   510
and Trojan women. Everyone looked to you
as though you were a god, and rightly so.
You were their greatest glory while you lived.
Now your doom and death have come upon you."

These were her mournful words. But Hektor's lady
still knew nothing; no one came to tell her
of Hektor's stand outside the gates. She wove
upon her loom, deep in the lofty house,
a double purple web with rose design.
Calling her maids in waiting,   520
she ordered a big caldron on a tripod
set on the hearthfire, to provide a bath
for Hektor when he came home from the fight.
Poor wife, how far removed from baths he was
she could not know, as at Akhilleus' hands
Athêna brought him down.

                                        Then from the tower
she heard a wailing and a distant moan.
Her knees shook, and she let her shuttle fall,
and called out to her maids again:

"Come here.   530
Two must follow me, to see this action.
I heard my husband's queenly mother cry.
I feel my heart rise, throbbing in my throat.
My knees are like stone under me. Some blow
is coming home to Priam's sons and daughters.
Ah, could it never reach my ears! I die
of dread that Akhilleus may have cut off Hektor,
blocked my bold husband from the city wall,
to drive him down the plain alone! By now
he may have ended Hektor's deathly pride.
He never kept his place amid the chariots   540
but drove ahead. He would not be outdone
by anyone in courage."

                              Saying this, she ran
like a madwoman through the mégaron,
her heart convulsed. Her maids kept at her side.
On reaching the great tower and the soldiers,
Andrómakhê stood gazing from the wall
and saw him being dragged before the city.
Chariot horses at a brutal gallop
pulled the torn body toward the decked ships.
Blackness of night covered her eyes; she fell   550
backward swooning, sighing out her life,
and let her shining headdress fall, her hood
and diadem, her plaited band and veil
that Aphrodítê once had given her,
on that day when, from Eëtíôn's house,
for a thousand bridal gifts, Lord Hektor led her.
Now, at her side, kinswomen of her lord
supported her among them, dazed and faint
to the point of death. But when she breathed again
and her stunned heart recovered, in a burst   560
of sobbing she called out among the women:

"Hektor! Here is my desolation. Both
had this in store from birth—from yours in Troy
in Priam's palace, mine by wooded Plakos
at Thêbê in the home of Eëtíôn,
my father, who took care of me in childhood,
a man cursed by fate, a fated daughter.
How I could wish I never had been born!
Now under earth's roof to the house of Death
you go your way and leave me here, bereft,   570
lonely, in anguish without end. The child
we wretches had is still in infancy;
you cannot be a pillar to him, Hektor,
now you are dead, nor he to you. And should
this boy escape the misery of the war,

there will be toil and sorrow for him later,
as when strangers move his boundary stones.[8]
The day that orphans him will leave him lonely,
downcast in everything, cheeks wet with tears,
in hunger going to his father's friends   580
to tug at one man's cloak, another's khiton.
Some will be kindly: one may lift a cup
to wet his lips at least, though not his throat;
but from the board some child with living parents
gives him a push, a slap, with biting words:
'Outside, you there! Your father is not with us
here at our feast!' And the boy Astýanax
will run to his forlorn mother. Once he fed
on marrow only and the fat of lamb,
high on his father's knees. And when sleep came   590
to end his play, he slept in a nurse's arms,
brimful of happiness, in a soft bed.
But now he'll know sad days and many of them,
missing his father. 'Lord of the lower town'[9]
the Trojans call him. They know, you alone,
Lord Hektor, kept their gates and their long walls.
Beside the beaked ships now, far from your kin,
the blowflies' maggots in a swarm will eat you
naked, after the dogs have had their fill.
Ah, there are folded garments in your chambers,   600
delicate and fine, of women's weaving.
These, by heaven, I'll burn to the last thread
in blazing fire! They are no good to you,
they cannot cover you in death. So let them
go, let them be burnt as an offering
from Trojans and their women in your honor."

Thus she mourned, and the women wailed in answer.

BOOK XXIII. *Led by Akhilleus and his Myrmidons, the Greeks mourn Patróklos. Akhilleus continues to dishonor Hektor's corpse. Patróklos' ghost appears to Akhilleus, asks for speedy burial so that he may be accepted among the dead, and reminds Akhilleus of his own approaching death in the Trojan war. The Greeks conduct Patróklos' funeral rites, which include the slaying by Akhilleus of the twelve Trojans he earlier captured for that purpose. (Hektor's body, meanwhile, is being preserved by Aphrodîtê and Apollo from defacement and corruption.) Akhilleus presides over ceremonial athletic contests (the gods still intervening on occasion): chariot-racing, boxing, wrestling, foot-racing, armed combat, weight-throwing, archery, javelin-throwing. But the last of these contests is not actually held; Akhilleus awards the victory to Agamémnon in advance.*

[8]Encroach on his land.   [9]The meaning of the child's nickname, Astýanax.

BOOK TWENTY-FOUR: A GRACE GIVEN IN SORROW

The funeral games were over. Men dispersed
and turned their thoughts to supper in their quarters,
then to the boon of slumber. But Akhilleus
thought of his friend, and sleep that quiets all things
would not take hold of him. He tossed and turned
remembering with pain Patróklos' courage,
his buoyant heart; how in his company
he fought out many a rough day full of danger,
cutting through ranks in war and the bitter sea.
With memory his eyes grew wet. He lay   10
on his right side, then on his back, and then
face downward—but at last he rose, to wander
distractedly along the line of surf.
This for eleven nights. The first dawn, brightening
sea and shore, became familiar to him,
as at that hour he yoked his team, with Hektor
tied behind, to drag him out, three times
around Patróklos' tomb. By day he rested
in his own hut, abandoning Hektor's body
to lie full-length in dust—though Lord Apollo,   20
pitying the man, even in death,
kept his flesh free of disfigurement.
He wrapped him in his great shield's[1] flap of gold
to save him from laceration. But Akhilleus
in rage visited indignity on Hektor
day after day, and, looking on,
the blessed gods were moved. Day after day
they urged the Wayfinder[2] to steal the body—
a thought agreeable to all but Hêra,
Poseidon, and the grey-eyed one, Athêna.   30
These opposed it, and held out, since Ilion
and Priam and his people had incurred
their hatred first, the day Aléxandros
made his mad choice and piqued two goddesses,
visitors in his sheepfold: he praised
a third, who offered ruinous lust.[3]
Now when Dawn grew bright for the twelfth day,
Phoibos Apollo spoke among the gods:

"How heartless and how malevolent you are!
Did Hektor never make burnt offering   40

---

[1] The aegis, or shield of Zeus, sometimes lent by him to other immortals.
[2] Hermês, messenger of the gods and also the patron of tricksters and thieves.
[3] For the decision by Paris (Aléxandros) that had offended Hêra and Athêna, see the
headnote to the *Iliad*. Paris had been a shepherd at the time of the incident. Poseidon's hatred
of the Trojans originated when he was forced to serve as a laborer under Priam's father
Laomédôn, who added insult to injury by withholding the god's wages.

of bulls' thighbones to you, and unflawed goats?
Even in death you would not stir to save him
for his dear wife to see, and for his mother,
his child, his father, Priam, and his men:
they'd burn the corpse at once and give him burial.
Murderous Akhilleus has your willing help—
a man who shows no decency, implacable,
barbarous in his ways as a wild lion
whose power and intrepid heart
sway him to raid the flocks of men for meat.   50
The man has lost all mercy;
he has no shame—that gift that hinders mortals
but helps them, too. A sane one may endure
an even dearer loss: a blood brother,
a son; and yet, by heaven, having grieved
and passed through mourning, he will let it go.
The Fates have given patient hearts to men.
Not this one: first he took Prince Hektor's life
and now he drags the body, lashed to his car,
around the barrow[4] of his friend, performing   60
something neither nobler in report
nor better in itself. Let him take care,
or, brave as he is, we gods will turn against him,
seeing him outrage the insensate earth!"

Hêra whose arms are white as ivory
grew angry at Apollo. She retorted:

"Lord of the silver bow, your words would be
acceptable if one had a mind to honor
Hektor and Akhilleus equally.
But Hektor suckled at a woman's breast,   70
Akhilleus is the first-born of a goddess—
one I nursed myself. I reared her, gave her
to Pêleus, a strong man whom the gods loved.
All of you were present at their wedding—
you too—friend of the base, forever slippery!—
came with your harp and dined there!"

                                         Zeus the stormking
answered her:

                                "Hêra, don't lose your temper
altogether. Clearly the same high honor
cannot be due both men. And yet Lord Hektor,
of all the mortal men in Ilion,   80
was dearest to the gods, or was to me.
He never failed in the right gift; my altar
never lacked a feast

---

[4] A large mound covering a grave.

of wine poured out and smoke of sacrifice—
the share assigned as ours. We shall renounce
the theft of Hektor's body; there is no way;
there would be no eluding Akhilleus' eye,
as night and day his mother comes to him.
Will one of you now call her to my presence?
I have a solemn message to impart: 90
Akhilleus is to take fine gifts from Priam,
and in return give back Prince Hektor's body."

At this, Iris who runs on the rainy wind
with word from Zeus departed. Midway between
Samos and rocky Imbros,[5] down she plunged
into the dark grey sea, and the brimming tide
roared over her as she sank into the depth—
as rapidly as a leaden sinker, fixed
on a lure of wild bull's horn, that glimmers down
with a fatal hook among the ravening fish.   100
Soon Iris came on Thetis in a cave,
surrounded by a company of Nereïds
lolling there, while she bewailed the fate
of her magnificent son, now soon to perish
on Troy's rich earth, far from his fatherland.
Halting before her, Iris said:

                                                   "Come, Thetis,
Zeus of eternal forethought summons you."

Silvery-footed Thetis answered:

                                                   "Why?

Why does the great one call me to him now,
when I am shy of mingling with immortals,   110
being so heavyhearted? But I'll go.
Whatever he may say will have its weight."

That loveliest of goddesses now put on
a veil so black no garment could be blacker,
and swam where windswift Iris led. Before them
on either hand the ground swell fell away.
They rose to a beach, then soared into the sky
and found the viewer of the wide world, Zeus,
with all the blissful gods who live forever
around him seated. Athêna yielded place,   120
and Thetis sat down by her father, Zeus,
while Hêra handed her a cup of gold
and spoke a comforting word. When she had drunk,
Thetis held out the cup again to Hêra.
The father of gods and men began:

[5] Islands in the Aegean Sea, northwest of Troy.

"You've come
to Olympos, Thetis, though your mind is troubled
and insatiable pain preys on your heart.
I know, I too. But let me, even so,
explain why I have called you here. Nine days   130
of quarreling we've had among the gods
concerning Hektor's body and Akhilleus.
They wish the Wayfinder to make off with it.
I, however, accord Akhilleus honor
as I now tell you—in respect for you
whose love I hope to keep hereafter. Go, now,
down to the army, tell this to your son:
the gods are sullen toward him, and I, too,
more than the rest, am angered at his madness,
holding the body by the beaked ships
and not releasing it. In fear of me   140
let him relent and give back Hektor's body!
At the same time I'll send Iris to Priam,
directing him to go down to the beachhead
and ransom his dear son. He must bring gifts
to melt Akhilleus' rage."

                                                        Thetis obeyed,

leaving Olympos' ridge and flashing down
to her son's hut. She found him groaning there,
inconsolable, while men-at-arms
went to and fro, making their breakfast ready—
having just put to the knife a fleecy sheep.   150
His gentle mother sat down at his side,
caressed him, and said tenderly:

                                                        "My child,

will you forever feed on your own heart
in grief and pain, and take no thought of sleep
or sustenance? It would be comforting
to make love with a woman. No long time
will you live on for me: Death even now
stands near you, appointed and all-powerful.
But be alert and listen: I am a messenger
from Zeus, who tells me the gods are sullen toward you   160
and he himself most angered at your madness,
holding the body by the beaked ships
and not releasing it. Give Hektor back.
Take ransom for the body."

                                                        Said Akhilleus:

"Let it be so. Let someone bring the ransom
and take the dead away, if the Olympian
commands this in his wisdom."

So, that morning,

in camp, amid the ships, mother and son
conversed together, and their talk was long.
Lord Zeus meanwhile sent Iris to Ilion.   170

"Off with you, lightfoot, leave Olympos, take
my message to the majesty of Priam
at Ilion. He is to journey down
and ransom his dear son upon the beachhead.
He shall take gifts to melt Akhilleus' rage,
and let him go alone, no soldier with him,
only some crier, some old man, to drive
his wagon team and guide the nimble wagon,
and afterward to carry home the body
of him that Prince Akhilleus overcame.   180
Let him not think of death, or suffer dread,
as I'll provide him with a wondrous guide,
the Wayfinder, to bring him across the lines
into the very presence of Akhilleus.
And he, when he sees Priam within his hut,
will neither take his life nor let another
enemy come near. He is no madman,
no blind brute, nor one to flout the gods,
but dutiful toward men who beg his mercy."

Then Iris at his bidding ran   190
on the rainy winds to bear the word of Zeus,
until she came to Priam's house and heard
voices in lamentation. In the court
she found the princes huddled around their father,
faces and clothing wet with tears. The old man,
fiercely wrapped and hooded in his mantle,
sat like a figure graven—caked in filth
his own hands had swept over head and neck
when he lay rolling on the ground. Indoors
his daughters and his sons' wives were weeping,   200
remembering how many and how brave
the young men were who had gone down to death
before the Argive spearmen.

Zeus's courier,

appearing now to Priam's eyes alone,
alighted whispering, so the old man trembled:

"Priam, heir of Dárdanos,[6] take heart,
and have no fear of me; I bode no evil,
but bring you friendly word from Zeus,
who is distressed for you and pities you
though distant far upon Olympos. He   210

---

[6] A son of Zeus and ancestor of Priam (five generations earlier).

commands that you shall ransom the Prince Hektor,
taking fine gifts to melt Akhilleus' rage.
And go alone: no soldier may go with you,
only some crier, some old man, to drive
your wagon team and guide the nimble wagon,
and afterward to carry home the body
of him that Prince Akhilleus overcame.
Put away thoughts of death, shake off your dread,
for you shall have a wondrous guide,
the Wayfinder, to bring you across the lines   220
into the very presence of Akhilleus.
He, for his part, seeing you in his quarters,
will neither take your life nor let another
enemy come near. He is no madman,
no blind brute, nor one to flout the gods,
but dutiful toward men who beg his mercy."

Iris left him, swift as a veering wind.
Then Priam spoke, telling the men to rig
a four-wheeled wagon with a wicker box,
while he withdrew to his chamber roofed in cedar,   230
high and fragrant, rich in precious things.
He called to Hékabê, his lady:

                                                        "Princess,

word from Olympian Zeus has come to me
to go down to the ships of the Akhaians
and ransom our dead son. I am to take
gifts that will melt Akhilleus' anger. Tell me
how this appears to you, tell me your mind,
for I am torn with longing, now, to pass
inside the great encampment by the ships."

The woman's voice broke as she answered:

                                                        "Sorrow,   240

sorrow. Where is the wisdom now that made you
famous in the old days, near and far?
How can you ever face the Akhaian ships
or wish to go alone before those eyes,
the eyes of one who stripped your sons in battle,
how many, and how brave? Iron[7] must be
the heart within you. If he sees you, takes you,
savage and wayward as the man is,
he'll have no mercy and no shame. Better
that we should mourn together in our hall.   250
Almighty fate spun this thing for our son
the day I bore him: destined him to feed
the wild dogs after death, being far from us

---

[7] Courageous.

when he went down before the stronger man.
I could devour the vitals of that man,
leeching into his living flesh! He'd know
pain then—pain like mine for my dead son.
It was no coward the Akhaian killed;
he stood and fought for the sweet wives of Troy,
with no more thought of flight or taking cover."   260

In majesty old Priam said:

                                                              "My heart

is fixed on going. Do not hold me back,
and do not make yourself a raven[8] crying
calamity at home. You will not move me.
If any man on earth had urged this on me—
reader of altar smoke,[9] prophet or priest—
we'd say it was a lie, and hold aloof.
But no: with my own ears I heard the voice,
I saw the god before me. Go I shall,
and no more words. If I must die alongside   270
the ships of the Akhaians in their bronze,
I die gladly. May I but hold my son
and spend my grief; then let Akhilleus kill me."

Throwing open the lids of treasure boxes
he picked out twelve great robes of state, and twelve
light cloaks for men, and rugs, an equal number,
and just as many capes of snowy linen,
adding a dozen khitons to the lot;
then set in order ten pure bars of gold,
a pair of shining tripods, four great caldrons,   280
and finally one splendid cup, a gift
Thracians had made him on an embassy.
He would not keep this, either—as he cared
for nothing now but ransoming his son.

And now, from the colonnade,
he made his Trojan people keep their distance,
berating and abusing them:

                                                              "Away,

you craven fools and rubbish! In your own homes
have you no one to mourn, that you crowd here,
to make more trouble for me? Is this a show,   290
that Zeus has crushed me, that he took the life
of my most noble son? You'll soon know what it means,
as you become child's play for the Akhaians
to kill in battle, now that Hektor's gone.
As for myself, before I see my city

---

[8] Traditionally, the bird forebodes evil.   [9] Interpreter of omens.

taken and ravaged, let me go down blind
to Death's cold kingdom!"

                                                              Staff in hand,
he herded them, until they turned away
and left the furious old man. He lashed out
now at his sons, at Hélenos and Paris,   300
Agathôn, Pammôn, Antíphonos,
Polítês, Dêíphobos, Hippóthoös,
and Dios—to these nine the old man cried:

"Bestir yourselves, you misbegotten whelps,
shame of my house! Would god you had been killed
instead of Hektor at the line of ships.
How curst I am in everything! I fathered
first-rate men, in our great Troy; but now
I swear not one is left: Mêstôr, Trôílos,
laughing amid the war-cars; and then Hektor—   310
a god to soldiers, and a god among them,
seeming not a man's child, but a god's.
Arês[10] killed them. These poltroons are left,
hollow men, dancers, heroes of the dance,
light-fingered pillagers of lambs and kids
from the town pens!
                                            Now will you get a wagon
ready for me, and quickly? Load these gifts
aboard it, so that we can take the road."

Dreading the rough edge of their father's tongue,
they lifted out a cart, a cargo wagon,   320
neat and maneuverable, and newly made,
and fixed upon it a wicker box; then took
a mule yoke from a peg, a yoke of boxwood
knobbed in front, with rings to hold the reins.
They brought out, too, the band nine forearms long
called the yoke-fastener, and placed the yoke
forward at the shank of the polished pole,
shoving the yoke-pin firmly in. They looped
three turns of the yoke-fastener round the knob
and wound it over and over down the pole,   330
tucking the tab end under. Next, the ransom:
bearing the weight of gifts for Hektor's person
out of the inner room, they piled them up
on the polished wagon. It was time to yoke
the mule-team, strong in harness, with hard hooves,
a team the Mysians had given Priam.
Then for the king's own chariot they harnessed

[10] Here, as often, the word is not so much the name of a god as a synonym for war itself.

a team of horses of the line of Trôs,[11]
reared by the old king in his royal stable.
So the impatient king and his sage crier   340
had their animals yoked in the palace yard
when Hékabê in her agitation joined them,
carrying in her right hand a golden cup
of honeyed wine, with which, before they left,
they might make offering. At the horses' heads
she stood to tell them:

                                        "Here, tip wine to Zeus,
the father of gods. Pray for a safe return
from the enemy army, seeing your heart is set
on venturing to the camp against my will.
Pray in the second place to Zeus the stormking,   350
gloomy over Ida, who looks down
on all Troy country. Beg for an omen-bird,
the courier dearest of all birds to Zeus
and sovereign in power of flight,[12]
that he appear upon our right in heaven.
When you have seen him with your own eyes, then,
under that sign, you may approach the ships.
If Zeus who views the wide world will not give you
vision of his bird, then I at least
cannot bid godspeed to your journey,   360
bent on it though you are."

                                                    In majesty
Priam replied:

                                        "My lady, in this matter
I am disposed to trust you and agree.
It is an excellent thing and salutary
to lift our hands to Zeus, invoking mercy."

The old king motioned to his housekeeper,
who stood nearby with a basin and a jug,
to pour clear water on his hands. He washed them,
took the cup his lady held, and prayed
while standing there, midway in the walled court.   370
Then he tipped out the wine, looking toward heaven,
saying:

                                "Zeus, our Father, reigning from Ida,
god of glory and power, grant I come
to Akhilleus' door as one to be received
with kindliness and mercy. And dispatch

---

[11] Great-grandfather of Priam. The horses of Trôs, which he received from Zeus, were the best in the world.
[12] The eagle. Good omens appeared on the right side.

your courier bird, the nearest to your heart
of all birds, and the first in power of flight.
Let him appear upon our right in heaven
that I may see him with my own eyes
and under that sign journey to the ships."   380

Zeus all-foreseeing listened to this prayer
and put an eagle, king
of winged creatures, instantly in flight:
a swamp eagle, a hunter, one they call
the duskwing. Wide as a doorway in a chamber
spacious and high, built for a man of wealth,
a door with long bars fitted well, so wide
spread out each pinion. The great bird appeared
winging through the town on their right hand,
and all their hearts lifted with joy to see him.   390
In haste the old king boarded his bright car
and clattered out of the echoing colonnade.
Ahead, the mule-team drew the four-wheeled wagon,
driven by Idaíos,[13] and behind
the chariot rolled, with horses that the old man
whipped into a fast trot through the town.
Family and friends all followed weeping
as though for Priam's last and deathward ride.
Into the lower town they passed, and reached
the plain of Troy. Here those who followed after   400
turned back, sons and sons-in-law. And Zeus
who views the wide world saw the car and wagon
brave the plain. He felt a pang for Priam
and quickly said to Hermês, his own son:

"Hermês, as you go most happily
of all the gods with mortals,[14] and give heed
to whom you will, be on your way this time
as guide for Priam to the deepsea ships.
Guide him so that not one of the Danáäns
may know or see him till he reach Akhilleus."   410

Argeiphontês[15] the Wayfinder obeyed.
He bent to tie his beautiful sandals on,
ambrosial, golden, that carry him over water
and over endless land on a puff of wind,
and took the wand with which he charms asleep—
or, when he wills, awake—the eyes of men.
So, wand in hand, the strong god glittering
paced into the air. Quick as a thought

---

[13] Priam's crier, or herald.
[14] Hermês often acts as a guide, and one of his functions is to conduct the spirits of the
dead to the underworld.
[15] A name for Hermês; see Homer's *Odyssey*, I.53 and note.

he came to Hellê's waters and to Troy,
appearing as a boy whose lip was downy   420
in the first bloom of manhood, a young prince,
all graciousness.

                           After the travelers
drove past the mound of Ilos,[16] at the ford
they let the mules and horses pause to drink
the running stream. Now darkness had come on
when, looking round, the crier
saw Hermês near at hand. He said to Priam:

"You must think hard and fast, your grace;
there is new danger; we need care and prudence.
I see a man-at-arms there—ready, I think,   430
to prey on us. Come, shall we whip the team
and make a run for it? Or take his knees
and beg for mercy?"

                           Now the old man's mind
gave way to confusion and to terror.
On his gnarled arms and legs the hair stood up,
and he stared, breathless. But the affable god
came over and took his hand and asked:

                                "Old father,
where do you journey, with your cart and car,
while others rest, below the evening star?
Do you not fear the Akhaians where they lie   440
encamped, hard, hostile outlanders, nearby?
Should someone see you, bearing stores like these
by night, how would you deal with enemies?
You are not young, your escort's ancient, too.
Could you beat off an attacker, either of you?
I'll do no hurt to you but defend you here.
You remind me of my father, whom I hold dear."

Old Priam answered him:

                                "Indeed, dear boy,
the case is as you say. And yet some god
stretched out his hand above me, he who sent   450
before me here—and just at the right time—
a traveler like yourself, well-made, well-spoken,
clearheaded, too. You come of some good family."

The Wayfinder rejoined:

                            "You speak with courtesy,
dear sir. But on this point enlighten me:

---

[16] Ilos' burial mound. He was grandfather of Priam and founder of Troy (which is therefore sometimes called Ilion).

are you removing treasure here amassed
for safety abroad, until the war is past?
Or can you be abandoning Ilion
in fear, after he perished, that great one
who never shirked a battle, your own princely son?"   460

Old Priam replied:

                     "My brave young friend, who are you?
Born of whom? How nobly you acknowledge
the dreadful end of my unfortunate son."

To this the Wayfinder replied:

                               "Dear sir,

you question me about him? Never surmise
I have not seen him with my very eyes,
and often, on the field. I saw him chase
Argives with carnage to their own shipways,
while we stood wondering, forbidden war
by the great anger that Akhilleus bore   470
Lord Agamémnon. I am of that company
Akhilleus led. His own ship carried me
as one of the Myrmidons. My father is old,
as you are, and his name's Polyktôr;[17] gold
and other wealth he owns;
and I am seventh and last of all his sons.
When I cast lots among them, my lot fell
to join the siege against Troy citadel.
Tonight I've left the camp to scout this way
where, circling Troy, we'll fight at break of day;   480
our men are tired of waiting and will not stand
for any postponement by the high command."

Responded royal Priam:

                             "If you belong
to the company of Akhilleus, son of Pêleus,
tell me this, and tell me the whole truth:
is my son even now beside the ships?
Or has Akhilleus by this time dismembered him
and thrown him to the wild dogs?"

                               The Wayfinder
made reply again:

                               "Dear sir,
no dogs or birds have yet devoured your son.   490
Beside Akhilleus' ship, out of the sun,
he lies in a place of shelter. Now twelve days

---

[17] The name means "having wealth."

the man has lain there, yet no part decays,
nor have the blowfly's maggots, that devour
dead men in war, fed on him to this hour.
True that around his dear friend's barrow tomb
Akhilleus drags him when dawn-shadows come,
driving pitilessly; but he mars him not.
You might yourself be witness, on the spot,
how fresh with dew he lies, washed of his gore,   500
unstained, for the deep gashes that he bore
have all closed up—and many thrust their bronze
into his body. The blest immortal ones
favor your prince, and care for every limb
even in death, as they so cherished him."

The old king's heart exulted, and he said:

"Child, it was well to honor the immortals.
He never forgot, at home in Ilion—
ah, did my son exist? was he a dream?—
the gods who own Olympos. They in turn   510
were mindful of him when he met his end.
Here is a goblet as a gift from me.
Protect me, give me escort, if the gods
attend us, till I reach Akhilleus' hut."

And in response Hermês the Wayfinder
said:

                    "You are putting a young man to the test,
dear sir, but I may not, as you request,
accept a gift behind Akhilleus' back.
Fearing, honoring him, I could not lack
discretion to that point. The consequence, too,   520
could be unwelcome. As for escorting you,
even to Argos' famous land I'd ride
a deck with you, or journey at your side.
No cutthroat ever will disdain your guide."

With this, Hermês who lights the way for mortals
leapt into the driver's place. He caught up
reins and whip, and breathed a second wind
into the mule-team and the team of horses.
Onward they ran toward parapet and ships,
and pulled up to the moat.
                                        Now night had fallen,   530
bringing the sentries to their supper fire,
but the glimmering god Hermês, the Wayfinder,
showered a mist of slumber on them all.
As quick as thought, he had the gates unbarred
and open to let the wagon enter, bearing
the old king and the ransom.

                                                    Going seaward
they came to the lofty quarters of Akhilleus,
a lodge the Myrmidons built for their lord
of pine trees cut and trimmed, and shaggy thatch
from mowings in deep meadows. Posts were driven   540
round the wide courtyard in a palisade,
whose gate one crossbar held, one beam of pine.
It took three men to slam this home, and three
to draw the bolt again—but great Akhilleus
worked his entryway alone with ease.
And now Hermês, who lights the way for mortals,
opened for Priam, took him safely in
with all his rich gifts for the son of Pêleus.
Then the god dropped the reins, and stepping down
he said:

                                        "I am no mortal wagoner,   550
but Hermês, sir. My father sent me here
to be your guide amid the Akhaian men.
Now that is done, I'm off to heaven again
and will not visit Akhilleus. That would be
to compromise an immortal's dignity—
to be received with guests of mortal station.
Go take his knees, and make your supplication:
invoke his father, his mother, and his child;
pray that his heart be touched, that he be reconciled."

Now Hermês turned, departing for Olympos,   560
and Priam vaulted down. He left Idaíos
to hold the teams in check, while he went forward
into the lodge. He found Akhilleus, dear
to Zeus, there in his chair, with officers
at ease across the room. Only Automédôn
and Álkimos were busy near Akhilleus,
for he had just now made an end of dinner,
eating and drinking, and the laden boards
lay near him still upon the trestles.

                                                        Priam,
the great king of Troy, passed by the others,   570
knelt down, took in his arms Akhilleus' knees,
and kissed the hands of wrath that killed his sons.

When, taken with mad Folly in his own land,
a man does murder and in exile finds
refuge in some rich house, then all who see him
stand in awe.
So these men stood.

                                                    Akhilleus
gazed in wonder at the splendid king,
and his companions marveled too, all silent,

with glances to and fro. Now Priam prayed   580
to the man before him:

                          "Remember your own father,
Akhilleus, in your godlike youth: his years
like mine are many, and he stands upon
the fearful doorstep of old age.[18] He, too,
is hard pressed, it may be, by those around him,
there being no one able to defend him
from bane of war and ruin. Ah, but he
may nonetheless hear news of you alive,
and so with glad heart hope through all his days
for sight of his dear son, come back from Troy,   590
while I have deathly fortune.

                                 Noble sons
I fathered here, but scarce one man is left me.
Fifty I had when the Akhaians came,
nineteen out of a single belly, others
born of attendant women. Most are gone.
Raging Arês cut their knees from under them.
And he who stood alone among them all,
their champion, and Troy's, ten days ago
you killed him, fighting for his land, my prince,
Hektor.

                  It is for him that I have come   600
among these ships, to beg him back from you,
and I bring ransom without stint.

                           Akhilleus,
be reverent toward the great gods! And take
pity on me, remember your own father.
Think me more pitiful by far, since I
have brought myself to do what no man else
has done before—to lift to my lips the hand
of one who killed my son."

                         Now in Akhilleus
the evocation of his father stirred
new longing, and an ache of grief. He lifted   610
the old man's hand and gently put him by.
Then both were overborne as they remembered:
the old king huddled at Akhilleus' feet
wept, and wept for Hektor, killer of men,
while great Akhilleus wept for his own father
as for Patróklos once again; and sobbing
filled the room.

                     But when Akhilleus' heart
had known the luxury of tears, and pain
within his breast and bones had passed away,

[18] Upon the threshold of death.

he stood then, raised the old king up, in pity   620
for his grey head and greybeard cheek, and spoke
in a warm rush of words:

                                            "Ah, sad and old!
Trouble and pain you've borne, and bear, aplenty.
Only a great will could have brought you here
among the Akhaian ships, and here alone
before the eyes of one who stripped your sons,
your many sons, in battle. Iron must be
the heart within you. Come, then, and sit down.
We'll probe our wounds no more but let them rest,
though grief lies heavy on us. Tears heal nothing,   630
drying so stiff and cold. This is the way
the gods ordained the destiny of men,
to bear such burdens in our lives, while they
feel no affliction. At the door of Zeus
are those two urns of good and evil gifts
that he may choose for us; and one for whom
the lightning's joyous king dips in both urns
will have by turns bad luck and good. But one
to whom he sends all evil[19]—that man goes
contemptible by the will of Zeus; ravenous   640
hunger drives him over the wondrous earth,
unresting, without honor from gods or men.
Mixed fortune came to Pêleus. Shining gifts
at the gods' hands he had from birth: felicity,
wealth overflowing, rule of the Myrmidons,
a bride immortal at his mortal side.
But then Zeus gave afflictions too—no family
of powerful sons grew up for him at home,
but one child, of all seasons and of none.
Can I stand by him in his age? Far from my country   650
I sit at Troy to grieve you and your children.
You, too, sir, in time past were fortunate,
we hear men say. From Makar's isle of Lesbos
northward, and south of Phrygia and the Straits,
no one had wealth like yours, or sons like yours.[20]
Then gods out of the sky sent you this bitterness:
the years of siege, the battles and the losses.
Endure it, then. And do not mourn forever
for your dead son. There is no remedy.
You will not make him stand again. Rather   660
await some new misfortune to be suffered."

---

[19] Misfortune.
[20] Lesbos (of which Makar was a legendary king) is an island off the coastline, south of
Troy; Phrygia lies inland, to the east; the Straits (the Hellespont, or modern Dardanelles) lie to
the north.

The old king in his majesty replied:

"Never give me a chair, my lord, while Hektor
lies in your camp uncared for. Yield him to me
now. Allow me sight of him. Accept
the many gifts I bring. May they reward you,
and may you see your home again.
You spared my life at once and let me live."

Akhilleus, the great runner, frowned and eyed him
under his brows:

                "Do not vex me, sir," he said.   670
"I have intended, in my own good time,
to yield up Hektor to you. She who bore me,
the daughter of the Ancient of the sea,
has come with word to me from Zeus. I know
in your case, too—though you say nothing, Priam—
that some god guided you to the shipways here.
No strong man in his best days could make entry
into this camp. How could he pass the guard,
or force our gateway?

                  Therefore, *let me be.*
Sting my sore heart again, and even here,   680
under my own roof, suppliant though you are,
I may not spare you, sir, but trample on
the express command of Zeus!"

                   When he heard this,
the old man feared him and obeyed with silence.
Now like a lion at one bound Akhilleus
left the room. Close at his back the officers
Automédôn and Álkimos went out—
comrades in arms whom he esteemed the most
after the dead Patróklos. They unharnessed
mules and horses, led the old king's crier   690
to a low bench and sat him down.
Then from the polished wagon
they took the piled-up price of Hektor's body.
One khiton and two capes they left aside
as dress and shrouding for the homeward journey.
Then, calling to the women slaves, Akhilleus
ordered the body bathed and rubbed with oil—
but lifted, too, and placed apart, where Priam
could not see his son—for seeing Hektor
he might in his great pain give way to rage,   700
and fury then might rise up in Akhilleus
to slay the old king, flouting Zeus's word.
So after bathing and anointing Hektor
they drew the shirt and beautiful shrouding over him.

Then with his own hands lifting him, Akhilleus
laid him upon a couch, and with his two
companions aiding, placed him in the wagon.
Now a bitter groan burst from Akhilleus,
who stood and prayed to his own dead friend:

"Patróklos,
710

do not be angry with me, if somehow
even in the world of Death you learn of this—
that I released Prince Hektor to his father.[21]
The gifts he gave were not unworthy. Aye,
and you shall have your share, this time as well."[22]

The Prince Akhilleus turned back to his quarters.
He took again the splendid chair that stood
against the farther wall, then looked at Priam
and made his declaration:

"As you wished, sir,

the body of your son is now set free.
He lies in state. At the first sight of Dawn   720
you shall take charge of him yourself and see him.
Now let us think of supper. We are told
that even Niobê in her extremity
took thought for bread—though all her brood had perished,
her six young girls and six tall sons.[23] Apollo,
making his silver longbow whip and sing,
shot the lads down, and Artemis with raining
arrows killed the daughters—all this after
Niobê had compared herself with Lêto,
the smooth-cheeked goddess.

She has borne two children, 730

Niobê said, How many have I borne!
But soon those two destroyed the twelve.

Besides,

nine days the dead lay stark, no one could bury them,
for Zeus had turned all folk of theirs to stone.
The gods made graves for them on the tenth day,
and then at last, being weak and spent with weeping,
Niobê thought of food. Among the rocks
of Sipylos' lonely mountainside, where nymphs
who race Akhelôïos river go to rest,

---

[21] When Patróklos' funeral was held, in Book XXIII, Akhilleus had promised his dead friend that he would not return Hektor's body to Priam or allow it to be burned or buried.

[22] The gifts are more than a bribe given to Akhilleus; they are valued not only in themselves but also—as in many primitive heroic cultures—as an outward symbol of the recipient's honor. Moreover, Akhilleus promises to give Patróklos his share—by burning it as he had burned other treasures at the funeral.

[23] Niobê's presumptuous boast of superiority to Lêto (mother of Artemis and Apollo) and the transformation of the grieving mother to stone are traditional elements of the myth, but much of the story as given here was invented by Homer in order to create a parallel with Priam and Hektor. The poet does something similar with the Meléagros story in Book IX.

she, too, long turned to stone, somewhere broods on   740
the gall immortal gods gave her to drink.

Like her we'll think of supper, noble sir.
Weep for your son again when you have borne him
back to Troy; there he'll be mourned indeed."

In one swift movement now Akhilleus caught
and slaughtered a white lamb. His officers
flayed it, skillful in their butchering
to dress the flesh; they cut bits for the skewers,
roasted, and drew them off, done to a turn.
Automédôn dealt loaves into the baskets   750
on the great board; Akhilleus served the meat.
Then all their hands went out upon the supper.
When thirst and appetite were turned away,
Priam, the heir of Dárdanos, gazed long
in wonder at Akhilleus' form and scale—
so like the gods in aspect. And Akhilleus
in his turn gazed in wonder upon Priam,
royal in visage as in speech. Both men
in contemplation found rest for their eyes,
till the old hero, Priam, broke the silence: 760

"Make a bed ready for me, son of Thetis,
and let us know the luxury of sleep.
From that hour when my son died at your hands
till now, my eyelids have not closed in slumber
over my eyes, but groaning where I sat
I tasted pain and grief a thousandfold,
or lay down rolling in my courtyard mire.
Here for the first time I have swallowed bread
and made myself drink wine.

                                        Before, I could not."

Akhilleus ordered men and serving women   770
to make a bed outside, in the covered forecourt,
with purple rugs piled up and sheets outspread
and coverings of fleeces laid on top.
The girls went out with torches in their hands
and soon deftly made up a double bed.
Then Akhilleus, defiant of Agamémnon,
told his guest:

                                        "Dear venerable sir,
you'll sleep outside tonight, in case an Akhaian
officer turns up, one of those men
who are forever taking counsel with me—   780
as well they may. If one should see you here
as the dark night runs on, he would report it
to the Lord Marshal Agamémnon. Then

return of the body would only be delayed.
Now tell me this, and give me a straight answer:
How many days do you require
for the funeral of Prince Hektor?—I should know
how long to wait, and hold the Akhaian army."

Old Priam in his majesty replied:

"If you would have me carry out the burial,   790
Akhilleus, here is the way to do me grace.
As we are penned in the town, but must bring wood
from the distant hills, the Trojans are afraid.
We should have mourning for nine days in hall,
then on the tenth conduct his funeral
and feast the troops and commons;
on the eleventh we should make his tomb,
and on the twelfth give battle, if we must."

Akhilleus said:

                                "As you command, old Priam,
the thing is done. I shall suspend the war   800
for those eleven days that you require."

He took the old man's right hand by the wrist
and held it, to allay his fear.

                                                        Now crier
and king with hearts brimful retired to rest
in the sheltered forecourt, while Akhilleus slept
deep in his palisaded lodge. Beside him,
lovely in her youth, Brisêis lay.
And other gods and soldiers all night long,
by slumber quieted, slept on. But slumber
would not come to Hermês the Good Companion,   810
as he considered how to ease the way
for Priam from the camp, to send him through
unseen by the formidable gatekeepers.
Then Hermês came to Priam's pillow, saying:

"Sir, no thought of danger shakes your rest,
as you sleep on, being great Akhilleus' guest,
amid men fierce as hunters in a ring.
You triumphed in a costly ransoming,
but three times costlier your own would be
to your surviving sons—a monarch's fee—   820
if this should come to Agamémnon's ear
and all the Akhaian host should learn that you are here."

The old king started up in fright, and woke
his herald. Hermês yoked the mules and horses,

took the reins, then inland like the wind
he drove through all the encampment, seen by no one.
When they reached Xánthos, eddying and running
god-begotten river, at the ford,
Hermês departed for Olympos. Dawn
spread out her yellow robe on all the earth,   830
as they drove on toward Troy, with groans and sighs,
and the mule-team pulled the wagon and the body.
And no one saw them, not a man or woman,
before Kassandra.[24] Tall as the pale-gold
goddess Aphrodítê, she had climbed
the citadel of Pergamos at dawn.
Now looking down she saw her father come
in his war-car, and saw the crier there,
and saw Lord Hektor on his bed of death
upon the mulecart. The girl wailed and cried   840
to all the city:

                                        "Oh, look down, look down,
go to your windows, men of Troy, and women,
see Lord Hektor now! Remember joy
at seeing him return alive from battle,
exalting all our city and our land!"

Now, at the sight of Hektor, all gave way
to loss and longing, and all crowded down
to meet the escort and body near the gates,
till no one in the town was left at home.
There Hektor's lady and his gentle mother   850
tore their hair for him, flinging themselves
upon the wagon to embrace his person
while the crowd groaned. All that long day
until the sun went down they might have mourned
in tears before the gateway. But old Priam
spoke to them from his chariot:

                                                        "Make way,
let the mules pass. You'll have your fill of weeping
later, when I've brought the body home."

They parted then, and made way for the wagon,
allowing Priam to reach the famous hall.   860
They laid the body of Hektor in his bed,
and brought in minstrels, men to lead the dirge.
While these wailed out, the women answered, moaning.
Andrómakhê of the ivory-white arms
held in her lap between her hands

---

[24] A daughter of Priam and Hékabê. She is prominent in later Greek literature as a prophetess doomed to have her prophecies disbelieved. See, for example, Aeschylus' *Agamemnon*,
which shows her as a captive taken from Troy by Agamémnon.

the head of Hektor who had killed so many.
Now she lamented:

          "You've been torn from life,
my husband, in young manhood, and you leave me
empty in our hall. The boy's a child
whom you and I, poor souls, conceived; I doubt   870
he'll come to manhood. Long before, great Troy
will go down plundered, citadel and all,
now that you are lost, who guarded it
and kept it, and preserved its wives and children.
They will be shipped off in the murmuring hulls
one day, and I along with all the rest.
You, my little one, either you come with me
to do some grinding labor, some base toil
for a harsh master, or an Akhaian soldier
will grip you by the arm and hurl you down   880
from a tower here to a miserable death—
out of his anger for a brother, a father,
or even a son that Hektor killed. Akhaians
in hundreds mouthed black dust under his blows.
He was no moderate man in war, your father,
and that is why they mourn him through the city.
Hektor, you gave your parents grief and pain
but left me loneliest, and heartbroken.
You could not open your strong arms to me
from your deathbed, or say a thoughtful word,   890
for me to cherish all my life long
as I weep for you night and day."

               Her voice broke,
and a wail came from the women. Hékabê
lifted her lamenting voice among them:

"Hektor, dearest of sons to me, in life
you had the favor of the immortal gods,
and they have cared for you in death as well.
Akhilleus captured other sons of mine
in other years, and sold them overseas
to Samos, Imbros, and the smoky island,   900
Lemnos. That was not his way with you.
After he took your life, cutting you down
with his sharp-bladed spear, he trussed and dragged you
many times round the barrow of his friend,
Patróklos, whom you killed—though not by this
could that friend live again. But now I find you
fresh as pale dew, seeming newly dead,
like one to whom Apollo of the silver bow
had given easy death with his mild arrows."[25]

[25] The arrows of Apollo bring death to men as those of his sister Artemis do to women.

Hékabê sobbed again, and the wails redoubled.   910
Then it was Helen's turn to make lament:

"Dear Hektor, dearest brother to me by far!
My husband is Aléxandros,
who brought me here to Troy—God, that I might
have died sooner! This is the twentieth year
since I left home, and left my fatherland.[26]
But never did I have an evil word
or gesture from you. No—and when some other
brother-in-law or sister would revile me,
or if my mother-in-law spoke to me bitterly—   920
but Priam never did, being as mild
as my own father—you would bring her round
with your kind heart and gentle speech. Therefore
I weep for you and for myself as well,
given this fate, this grief. In all wide Troy
no one is left who will befriend me, none;
they all shudder at me."

                                        Helen wept,
and a moan came from the people, hearing her.
Then Priam, the old king, commanded them:

"Trojans, bring firewood to the edge of town.   930
No need to fear an ambush of the Argives.
When he dismissed me from the camp, Akhilleus
told me clearly they will not harass us,
not until dawn comes for the twelfth day."

Then yoking mules and oxen to their wagons
the people thronged before the city gates.
Nine days they labored, bringing countless loads
of firewood to the town. When Dawn that lights
the world of mortals came for the tenth day,
they carried greathearted Hektor out at last,   940
and all in tears placed his dead body high
upon its pyre, then cast a torch below.
When the young Dawn with finger tips of rose
made heaven bright, the Trojan people massed
about Prince Hektor's ritual fire.
All being gathered and assembled, first
they quenched the smoking pyre with tawny wine
wherever flames had licked their way, then friends
and brothers picked his white bones from the char
in sorrow, while the tears rolled down their cheeks.   950
In a golden urn they put the bones,

---

[26] This statement is puzzling, since the war lasted only ten years. Perhaps we are to understand that the Greeks spent ten years in preparation or that the expedition was delayed ten years en route.

shrouding the urn with veiling of soft purple.
Then in a grave dug deep they placed it
and heaped it with great stones. The men were quick
to raise the death-mound, while in every quarter
lookouts were posted to ensure against
an Akhaian surprise attack. When they had finished
raising the barrow, they returned to Ilion,
where all sat down to banquet in his honor
in the hall of Priam king. So they performed   960
the funeral rites of Hektor, tamer of horses.

THE ODYSSEY

Translated by Robert Fitzgerald

The ten-year war waged by the Greeks against Troy, culminating in the overthrow of the city, is now itself ten years in the past. Helen, whose flight to Troy with the Trojan prince Paris had prompted the Greek expedition to seek revenge and reclaim her, is now home in Sparta, living harmoniously once more with her husband Meneláos (Menelaus). His brother Agamémnon, commander-in-chief of the Greek forces, was murdered on his return from the war by his wife and her paramour. Of the Greek chieftains who have survived both the war and the perilous homeward voyage, all have returned except Odysseus, the crafty and astute ruler of Ithaka (Ithaca), an island in the Ionian Sea off western Greece. Since he is presumed dead, suitors from Ithaka and other regions have overrun his house, paying court to his attractive wife Penélopê, endangering the position of his son Telémakhos (Telemachus), corrupting many of the servants, and literally eating up Odysseus' estate. Penélopê has stalled for time but is finding it increasingly difficult to deny the suitors' demands that she marry one of them; Telémakhos, who is just approaching young manhood, is becoming actively resentful of the indignities suffered by his household.

Many persons and places in the *Odyssey* are best known to readers by their Latinized names, such as *Telemachus*. The present translator has used forms (*Telémakhos*) closer to the Greek spelling and pronunciation. A slanted accent-mark (´) indicates stress; thus *Agamémnon* is accented on the third syllable. A circumflex accent (ˆ) indicates that the vowel sound is long; thus *Kêrês* is pronounced "Care-ace." A dieresis (¨) indicates pronunciation as a separate syllable; thus, *Thoösa* has three syllables rather than two. [*Editors' headnote.*]

BOOK ONE: A GODDESS INTERVENES

Sing in me, Muse, and through me tell the story
of that man skilled in all ways of contending,
the wanderer, harried for years on end,
after he plundered the stronghold
on the proud height of Troy.[1]

---

[1] These lines contain the traditional epic "opening formula" that includes the invocation of the inspiring Muse, the statement of the theme, the identification of the hero (in this case Odysseus), and a glance at the significance of the story.

He saw the townlands
and learned the minds of many distant men,
and weathered many bitter nights and days
in his deep heart at sea, while he fought only
to save his life, to bring his shipmates home.
But not by will nor valor could he save them,   10
for their own recklessness destroyed them all—
children and fools, they killed and feasted on
the cattle of Lord Hêlios,[2] the Sun,
and he who moves all day through heaven
took from their eyes the dawn of their return.

Of these adventures, Muse, daughter of Zeus,
tell us in our time, lift the great song again.
Begin when all the rest who left behind them
headlong death in battle or at sea
had long ago returned, while he alone still hungered   20
for home and wife. Her ladyship Kalypso
clung to him in her sea-hollowed caves—
a nymph, immortal and most beautiful,
who craved him for her own.

                              And when long years and seasons
wheeling brought around that point of time
ordained for him to make his passage homeward,
trials and dangers, even so, attended him
even in Ithaka,[3] near those he loved.
Yet all the gods had pitied Lord Odysseus,
all but Poseidon,[4] raging cold and rough   30
against the brave king till he came ashore
at last on his own land.

                              But now that god
had gone far off among the sunburnt races,
most remote of men, at earth's two verges,
in sunset lands and lands of the rising sun,
to be regaled by smoke of thighbones burning,
haunches of rams and bulls, a hundred fold.
He lingered delighted at the banquet side.

In the bright hall of Zeus upon Olympos
the other gods were all at home, and Zeus,   40
the father of gods and men, made conversation.
For he had meditated on Aigísthos,[5] dead

[2] The offense against Hêlios is described in Book XII.
[3] Odysseus' island homeland, in the Ionian sea off western Greece (sometimes the spelling is *Ithaca*).
[4] God of the ocean and brother of the chief of the gods who dwelled on Mount Olympos (Olympus), Zeus.
[5] While the Greek commander Agamémnon was away fighting against Troy, Aigísthos (Aegisthus) entered into an adulterous union with Klytaimnéstra (Clytaemnestra), Agamémnon's wife; they murdered Agamémnon upon his return. The murder was later avenged by Orestês, son of Agamémnon and Klytaimnéstra, as is related in Aeschylus' trilogy of plays known as *The Oresteia*.

by the hand of Agamémnon's son, Orestês,
and spoke his thought aloud before them all:

"My word, how mortals take the gods to task!
All their afflictions come from us, we hear.
And what of their own failings? Greed and folly
double the suffering in the lot of man.
See how Aigísthos, for his double portion,
stole Agamémnon's wife and killed the soldier   50
on his homecoming day. And yet Aigísthos
knew that his own doom lay in this. We gods
had warned him, sent down Hermês Argeiphontês,[6]
our most observant courier, to say:
'Don't kill the man, don't touch his wife,
or face a reckoning with Orestês
the day he comes of age and wants his patrimony.'
Friendly advice—but would Aigísthos take it?
Now he has paid the reckoning in full."

The grey-eyed goddess Athena replied to Zeus: 60

"O Majesty, O Father of us all,
that man is in the dust indeed, and justly.
So perish all who do what he had done.
But my own heart is broken for Odysseus,
the master mind of war, so long a castaway
upon an island in the running sea;
a wooded island, in the sea's middle,
and there's a goddess in the place, the daughter
of one whose baleful mind knows all the deeps
of the blue sea—Atlas,[7] who holds the columns   70
that bear from land the great thrust of the sky.
His daughter will not let Odysseus go,
poor mournful man; she keeps on coaxing him
with her beguiling talk, to turn his mind
from Ithaka. But such desire is in him
merely to see the hearthsmoke leaping upward
from his own island, that he longs to die.
Are you not moved by this, Lord of Olympos?
Had you no pleasure from Odysseus' offerings
beside the Argive[8] ships, on Troy's wide seaboard?   80
O Zeus, what do you hold against him now?"

To this the summoner of cloud replied:

"My child, what strange remarks you let escape you.

---

[6] God of messengers and messenger of the gods; he was also associated sometimes with the wind. "Argeiphontês" connotes brightness or the ability to clear the sky of clouds.
[7] In myth, Atlas is the titanic being who supports the sky. Here he is described as father of the nymph Kalypso, who is holding Odysseus prisoner on her island, Ogýgia.
[8] The collective name for the Greek forces who fought under Agamémnon against Troy.

Could I forget that kingly man, Odysseus?
There is no mortal half so wise; no mortal
gave so much to the lords of open sky.
Only the god who laps the land in water,
Poseidon, bears the fighter an old grudge
since he poked out the eye of Polyphêmos,
brawniest of the Kyklopês.[9] Who bore   90
that giant lout? Thoösa, daughter of Phorkys,
an offshore sea lord: for this nymph had lain
with Lord Poseidon in her hollow caves.
Naturally, the god, after the blinding—
mind you, he does not kill the man;
he only buffets him away from home.
But come now, we are all at leisure here,
let us take up this matter of his return,
that he may sail. Poseidon must relent
for being quarrelsome will get him nowhere,   100
one god, flouting the will of all the gods."

The grey-eyed goddess Athena answered him:

"O Majesty, O Father of us all,
if it now please the blissful gods
that wise Odysseus reach his home again,
let the Wayfinder, Hermês, cross the sea
to the island of Ogýgia; let him tell
our fixed intent to the nymph with pretty braids,
and let the steadfast man depart for home.
For my part, I shall visit Ithaka   110
to put more courage in the son, and rouse him
to call an assembly of the islanders,
Akhaian[10] gentlemen with flowing hair.
He must warn off that wolf pack of the suitors
who prey upon his flocks and dusky cattle.
I'll send him to the mainland then, to Sparta
by the sand beach of Pylos;[11] let him find
news of his dear father where he may
and win his own renown about the world."

She bent to tie her beautiful sandals on,   120
ambrosial, golden, that carry her over water
or over endless land on the wings of the wind,
and took the great haft of her spear in hand—
that bronzeshod spear this child of Power can use
to break in wrath long battle lines of fighters.

---

[9] The encounter with these one-eyed giants (also spelled *Polyphemus* and *Cyclops*) is described in Book IX.

[10] In a general sense, "Greek"; more especially, descriptive of men living in a region not far from Ithaka.

[11] A city and region of southern Greece ruled by Nestor, an aged king and counsellor.

Flashing down from Olympos' height she went
to stand in Ithaka, before the Manor,
just at the doorsill of the court. She seemed
a family friend, the Taphian captain, Mentês,
waiting, with a light hand on her spear.   130
Before her eyes she found the lusty suitors
casting dice inside the gate, at ease
on hides of oxen—oxen they had killed.
Their own retainers made a busy sight
with houseboys, mixing bowls of water and wine,
or sopping water up in sponges, wiping
tables to be placed about in hall,
or butchering whole carcasses for roasting.

Long before anyone else, the prince Telémakhos
now caught sight of Athena—for he, too,   140
was sitting there, unhappy among the suitors,
a boy, daydreaming. What if his great father
came from the unknown world and drove these men
like dead leaves through the place, recovering
honor and lordship in his own domains?
Then he who dreamed in the crowd gazed out at Athena.

Straight to the door he came, irked with himself
to think a visitor had been kept there waiting,
and took her right hand, grasping with his left
her tall bronze-bladed spear. Then he said warmly: 150

"Greetings, stranger! Welcome to our feast.
There will be time to tell your errand later."

He led the way, and Pallas Athena followed
into the lofty hall. The boy reached up
and thrust her spear high in a polished rack
against a pillar, where tough spear on spear
of the old soldier, his father, stood in order.
Then, shaking out a splendid coverlet,
he seated her on a throne with footrest—all
finely carved—and drew his painted armchair   160
near her, at a distance from the rest.
To be amid the din, the suitors' riot,
would ruin his guest's appetite, he thought,
and he wished privacy to ask for news
about his father, gone for years.

                                                             A maid

brought them a silver finger bowl and filled it
out of a beautiful spouting golden jug,
then drew a polished table to their side.
The larder mistress with her tray came by
and served them generously. A carver lifted   170

cuts of each roast meat to put on trenchers[12]
before the two. He gave them cups of gold,
and these the steward as he went his rounds
filled and filled again.

                  Now came the suitors,
young bloods trooping in to their own seats
on thrones or easy chairs. Attendants poured
water over their fingers, while the maids
piled baskets full of brown loaves near at hand,
and houseboys brimmed the bowls with wine.
Now they laid hands upon the ready feast   180
and thought of nothing more. Not till desire
for food and drink had left them were they mindful
of dance and song, that are the grace of feasting.
A herald gave a shapely cithern harp
to Phêmios,[13] whom they compelled to sing—
and what a storm he plucked upon the strings
for prelude! High and clear the song arose.

Telémakhos now spoke to grey-eyed Athena,
his head bent close, so no one else might hear:

"Dear guest, will this offend you, if I speak?   190
It is easy for these men to like these things,
harping and song; they have an easy life,
scot free, eating the livestock of another—
a man whose bones are rotting somewhere now,
white in the rain on dark earth where they lie,
or tumbling in the groundswell of the sea.
If he returned, if these men ever saw him,
faster legs they'd pray for, to a man,
and not more wealth in handsome robes or gold.
But he is lost; he came to grief and perished,   200
and there's no help for us in someone's hoping
he still may come; that sun has long gone down.
But tell me now, and put it for me clearly—
who are you? Where do you come from? Where's your home
and family? What kind of ship is yours,
and what course brought you here? Who are your sailors?
I don't suppose you walked here on the sea.
Another thing—this too I ought to know—
is Ithaka new to you, or were you ever
a guest here in the old days? Far and near   210
friends knew this house; for he whose home it was
had much acquaintance in the world."

                          To this
the grey-eyed goddess answered:

---

[12] Plates.   [13] The house bard, or minstrel.

                                                                    "As you ask,
I can account most clearly for myself.
Mentês I'm called, son of the veteran
Ankhíalos; I rule seafaring Taphos.
I came by ship, with a ship's company,
sailing the winedark[14] sea for ports of call
on alien shores—to Témesê, for copper,
bringing bright bars of iron in exchange.   220
My ship is moored on a wild strip of coast
in Reithron Bight, under the wooded mountain.
Years back, my family and yours were friends,
as Lord Laërtês[15] knows; ask when you see him.
I hear the old man comes to town no longer,
stays up country, ailing, with only one
old woman to prepare his meat and drink
when pain and stiffness take him in the legs
from working on his terraced plot, his vineyard.
As for my sailing here—   230
the tale was that your father had come home,
therefore I came. I see the gods delay him.
But never in this world is Odysseus dead—
only detained somewhere on the wide sea,
upon some island, with wild islanders;
savages, they must be, to hold him captive.
Well, I will forecast for you, as the gods
put the strong feeling in me—I see it all,
and I'm no prophet, no adept in bird-signs.
He will not, now, be long away from Ithaka,   240
his father's dear land; though he be in chains
he'll scheme a way to come; he can do anything.

But tell me this now, make it clear to me:
You must be, by your looks, Odysseus' boy?
The way your head is shaped, the fine eyes—yes,
how like him! We took meals like this together
many a time, before he sailed for Troy
with all the lords of Argos in the ships.
I have not seen him since, nor has he seen me."

And thoughtfully Telémakhos replied: 250

"Friend, let me put it in the plainest way.
My mother says I am his son; I know not
surely. Who has known his own engendering?
I wish at least I had some happy man
as father, growing old in his own house—

---

[14] This adjective is repeatedly used by Homer to describe the sea. Such "Homeric epithets"
are taken as one sign that the *Iliad* and *Odyssey* were designed for oral delivery.
[15] Father of Odysseus. At this point Laërtês is living in retirement on a farm.

but unknown death and silence are the fate
of him that, since you ask, they call my father."

Then grey-eyed Athena said:

                               "The gods decreed
no lack of honor in this generation:
such is the son Penélopê bore in you.   260
But tell me now, and make this clear to me:
what gathering, what feast is this? Why here?
A wedding? Revel? At the expense of all?
Not that, I think. How arrogant they seem,
these gluttons, making free here in your house!
A sensible man would blush to be among them."

To this Telémakhos answered:

"Friend, now that you ask about these matters,
our house was always princely, a great house,
as long as he of whom we speak remained here.   270
But evil days the gods have brought upon it,
making him vanish, as they have, so strangely.
Were his death known, I could not feel such pain—
if he had died of wounds in Trojan country
or in the arms of friends, after the war.
They would have made a tomb for him, the Akhaians,
and I should have all honor as his son.
Instead, the whirlwinds got him, and no glory.
He's gone, no sign, no word of him; and I inherit
trouble and tears—and not for him alone,   280
the gods have laid such other burdens on me.
For now the lords of the islands,
Doulíkhion and Samê, wooded Zakynthos,
and rocky Ithaka's young lords as well,
are here courting my mother; and they use
our house as if it were a house to plunder.
Spurn them she dare not, though she hates that marriage,
nor can she bring herself to choose among them.
Meanwhile they eat their way through all we have,
and when they will, they can demolish me."   290

Pallas Athena was disturbed, and said:

"Ah, bitterly you need Odysseus, then!
High time he came back to engage these upstarts.
I wish we saw him standing helmeted
there in the doorway, holding shield and spear,
looking the way he did when I first knew him.
That was at our house, where he drank and feasted
after he left Ephyra, homeward bound
from a visit to the son of Mérmeris, Ilos.

He took his fast ship down the gulf that time   300
for a fatal drug to dip his arrows in
and poison the bronze points; but young Ilos
turned him away, fearing the gods' wrath.
My father gave it, for he loved him well.
I wish these men could meet the man of those days!
They'd know their fortune quickly: a cold bed.
Aye! but it lies upon the gods' great knees
whether he can return and force a reckoning
in his own house, or not.

                                                 If I were you,

I should take steps to make these men disperse.   310
Listen, now, and attend to what I say:
at daybreak call the islanders to assembly,
and speak your will, and call the gods to witness:
the suitors must go scattering to their homes.
Then here's a course for you, if you agree:
get a sound craft afloat with twenty oars
and go abroad for news of your lost father—
perhaps a traveller's tale, or rumored fame
issued from Zeus abroad in the world of men.
Talk to that noble sage at Pylos, Nestor,   320
then go to Meneláos,[16] the red-haired king
at Sparta, last man home of all the Akhaians.
If you should learn your father is alive
and coming home, you could hold out a year.
Or if you learn that he is dead and gone,
then you can come back to your own dear country
and raise a mound for him, and burn his gear,
with all the funeral honors due the man,
and give your mother to another husband.

When you have done all this, or seen it done,   330
it will be time to ponder
concerning these contenders[17] in your house—
how you should kill them, outright or by guile.
You need not bear this insolence of theirs,
you are a child no longer. Have you heard
what glory young Orestês won
when he cut down that two-faced man, Aigísthos,
for killing his illustrious father?
Dear friend, you are tall and well set up, I see;
be brave—you, too—and men in times to come   340
will speak of you respectfully.

[16] Brother of Agamémnon and husband of Helen of Troy. Also spelled *Menelaus*. Helen's elopement with their Trojan guest Paris precipitated the Trojan war.

[17] Suitors for the hand in marriage of the presumably widowed Penélopê, wife of Odysseus.

Now I must join my ship;
my crew will grumble if I keep them waiting.
Look to yourself; remember what I told you."

Telémakhos replied:

"Friend, you have done me
kindness, like a father to his son,
and I shall not forget your counsel ever.
You must get back to sea, I know, but come
take a hot bath, and rest; accept a gift
to make your heart lift up when you embark—
some precious thing, and beautiful, from me,   350
a keepsake, such as dear friends give their friends."

But the grey-eyed goddess Athena answered him:

"Do not delay me, for I love the sea ways.
As for the gift your heart is set on giving,
let me accept it on my passage home,
and you shall have a choice gift in exchange."

With this Athena left him
as a bird rustles upward, off and gone.
But as she went she put new spirit in him,
a new dream of his father, clearer now,   360
so that he marvelled to himself
divining that a god had been his guest.
Then godlike in his turn he joined the suitors.

The famous minstrel still sang on before them,
and they sat still and listened, while he sang
that bitter song, the Homecoming of Akhaians—
how by Athena's will they fared from Troy;
and in her high room careful Penélopê,
Ikários' daughter, heeded the holy song.
She came, then, down the long stairs of her house,   370
this beautiful lady, with two maids in train
attending her as she approached the suitors;
and near a pillar of the roof she paused,
her shining veil drawn over across her cheeks,
the two girls close to her and still,
and through her tears spoke to the noble minstrel:

"Phêmios, other spells you know, high deeds
of gods and heroes, as the poets tell them;
let these men hear some other; let them sit
silent and drink their wine. But sing no more   380
this bitter tale that wears my heart away.
It opens in me again the wound of longing

for one incomparable, ever in my mind—
his fame all Hellas[18] knows, and midland Argos."

But Telémakhos intervened and said to her:

"Mother, why do you grudge our own dear minstrel
joy of song, wherever his thought may lead?
Poets are not to blame, but Zeus who gives
what fate he pleases to adventurous men.
Here is no reason for reproof: to sing   390
the news of the Danaans![19] Men like best
a song that rings like morning on the ear.
But you must nerve yourself and try to listen.
Odysseus was not the only one at Troy
never to know the day of his homecoming.
Others, how many others, lost their lives!"

The lady gazed in wonder and withdrew,
her son's clear wisdom echoing in her mind.
But when she had mounted to her rooms again
with her two handmaids, then she fell to weeping   400
for Odysseus, her husband. Grey-eyed Athena
presently cast a sweet sleep on her eyes.

Meanwhile the din grew loud in the shadowy hall
as every suitor swore to lie beside her,
but Telémakhos turned now and spoke to them:

"You suitors of my mother! Insolent men,
now we have dined, let us have entertainment
and no more shouting. There can be no pleasure
so fair as giving heed to a great minstrel
like ours, whose voice itself is pure delight.   410
At daybreak we shall sit down in assembly
and I shall tell you—take it as you will—
you are to leave this hall. Go feasting elsewhere,
consume your own stores. Turn and turn about,
use one another's houses. If you choose
to slaughter one man's livestock and pay nothing,
this is rapine; and by the eternal gods
I beg Zeus you shall get what you deserve:
a slaughter here, and nothing paid for it!"

By now their teeth seemed fixed in their under-lips,   420
Telémakhos' bold speaking stunned them so.
Antínoös, Eupeithês' son, made answer:

"Telémakhos, no doubt the gods themselves
are teaching you this high and mighty manner.

[18]Greece.   [19]The Greeks who fought against the Trojans.

Zeus forbid you should be king in Ithaka,[20]
though you are eligible as your father's son."

Telémakhos kept his head and answered him:

"Antínoös, you may not like my answer,
but I would happily be king, if Zeus
conferred the prize. Or do you think it wretched?   430
I shouldn't call it bad at all. A king
will be respected, and his house will flourish.
But there are eligible men enough,
heaven knows, on the island, young and old,
and one of them perhaps may come to power
after the death of King Odysseus.
All I insist on is that I rule our house
and rule the slaves my father won for me."

Eurýmakhos, Pólybos' son, replied:

"Telémakhos, it is on the gods' great knees   440
who will be king in sea-girt Ithaka.
But keep your property, and rule your house,
and let no man, against your will, make havoc
of your possessions, while there's life on Ithaka.
But now, my brave young friend,
a question or two about the stranger.
Where did your guest come from? Of what country?
Where does he say his home is, and his family?
Has he some message of your father's coming,
or business of his own, asking a favor?   450
He left so quickly that one hadn't time
to meet him, but he seemed a gentleman."

Telémakhos made answer, cool enough:

"Eurýmakhos, there's no hope for my father.
I would not trust a message, if one came,
nor any forecaster my mother invites
to tell by divination of time to come.
My guest, however, was a family friend,
Mentês, son of Ankhíalos.
He rules the Taphian people of the sea."   460

So said Telémakhos, though in his heart
he knew his visitor had been immortal.
But now the suitors turned to play again
with dance and haunting song. They stayed till nightfall,
indeed black night came on them at their pleasure,
and half asleep they left, each for his home.

[20] At the time of the poem's action, the rulership of most Greek city-states was not automatically passed from father to son.

Telémakhos' bedroom was above the court,
a kind of tower, with a view all round;
here he retired to ponder in the silence,
while carrying brands of pine alight beside him   470
Eurýkleia went padding, sage and old.
Her father had been Ops, Peisênor's son,
and she had been a purchase of Laërtês
when she was still a blossoming girl. He gave
the price of twenty oxen[21] for her, kept her
as kindly in his house as his own wife,
though, for the sake of peace, he never touched her.
No servant loved Telémakhos as she did,
she who had nursed him in his infancy.
So now she held the light, as he swung open   480
the door of his neat freshly painted chamber.
There he sat down, pulling his tunic off,
and tossed it into the wise old woman's hands.
She folded it and smoothed it, and then hung it
beside the inlaid bed upon a bar;
then, drawing the door shut by its silver handle
she slid the catch in place and went away.
And all night long, wrapped in the finest fleece,
he took in thought the course Athena gave him.

BOOK TWO: A HERO'S SON AWAKENS

When primal Dawn spread on the eastern sky
her fingers of pink light, Odysseus' true son
stood up, drew on his tunic and his mantle,
slung on a sword-belt and a new-edged sword,
tied his smooth feet into good rawhide sandals,
and left his room, a god's brilliance upon him.
He found the criers with clarion voices and told them
to muster the unshorn[1] Akhaians in full assembly.
The call sang out, and the men came streaming in;
and when they filled the assembly ground, he entered,   10
spear in hand, with two quick hounds at heel;
Athena lavished on him a sunlit grace
that held the eye of the multitude. Old men
made way for him as he took his father's chair.

Now Lord Aigýptios, bent down and sage with years,
opened the assembly. This man's son

---

[21] In the Greek civilization of Homeric times, the ox was a common standard of value. Articles of clothing, weapons, women taken as war prizes, and servants were evaluated in terms of how many oxen they were worth.
[1] Having long or flowing hair.

had served under the great Odysseus, gone
in the decked ships with him to the wild horse country
of Troy—a spearman, Ántiphos by name.
The ravenous Kyklops in the cave destroyed him[2]   20
last in his feast of men. Three other sons
the old man had, and one, Eurýnomos,
went with the suitors; two farmed for their father;
but even so the old man pined, remembering
the absent one, and a tear welled up as he spoke:

"Hear me, Ithakans! Hear what I have to say.
No meeting has been held here since our king,
Odysseus, left port in the decked ships.
Who finds occasion for assembly, now?
one of the young men? one of the older lot?   30
Has he had word our fighters are returning[3]—
news to report if he got wind of it—
or is it something else, touching the realm?
The man has vigor, I should say; more power to him.
Whatever he desires, may Zeus fulfill it."

The old man's words delighted the son of Odysseus,
who kept his chair no longer but stood up,
eager to speak, in the midst of all the men.
The crier, Peisênor, master of debate,
brought him the staff[4] and placed it in his hand;   40
then the boy touched the old man's shoulder, and said:

"No need to wonder any more, Sir,
who called this session. The distress is mine.
As to our troops returning, I have no news—
news to report if I got wind of it—
nor have I public business to propose;
only my need, and the trouble of my house—
the troubles.

                     My distinguished father is lost,
who ruled among you once, mild as a father,
and there is now this greater evil still: 50
my home and all I have are being ruined.
Mother wanted no suitors, but like a pack
they came—sons of the best men here among them—
lads with no stomach for an introduction
to Ikários, her father across the sea;
he would require a wedding gift, and give her
to someone who found favor in her eyes.

[2] This incident is described in Book IX.
[3] Except for Odysseus and his Ithakans, all the Greek warriors against Troy had by this time returned home or were known to be dead.
[4] The emblem which, placed by the herald in the speaker's hand, gave him the right to speak as a public official.

No; these men spend their days around our house
killing our beeves and sheep and fatted goats,
carousing, soaking up our good dark wine,   60
not caring what they do. They squander everything.
We have no strong Odysseus to defend us,
and as to putting up a fight ourselves—
we'd only show our incompetence in arms.
Expel them, yes, if I only had the power;
the whole thing's out of hand, insufferable.
My house is being plundered: is this courtesy?
Where is your indignation? Where is your shame?
Think of the talk in the islands all around us,
and fear the wrath of the gods,   70
or they may turn, and send you some devilry.
Friends, by Olympian Zeus and holy Justice
that holds men in assembly and sets them free,
make an end of this! Let me lament in peace
my private loss. Or did my father, Odysseus,
ever do injury to the armed Akhaians?
Is this your way of taking it out on me,
giving free rein to these young men?
I might as well—might better—see my treasure
and livestock taken over by you all;   80
then, if you fed on them, I'd have some remedy,
and when we met, in public, in the town,
I'd press my claim; you might make restitution.
This way you hurt me when my hands are tied."

And in hot anger now he threw the staff to the ground,
his eyes grown bright with tears. A wave of sympathy
ran through the crowd, all hushed; and no one there
had the audacity to answer harshly
except Antínoös, who said:

                                   "What high and mighty
talk, Telémakhos! No holding you!   90
You want to shame us, and humiliate us,
but you should know the suitors are not to blame—
it is your own dear, incomparably cunning mother.
For three years now—and it will soon be four—
she has been breaking the hearts of the Akhaians,
holding out hope to all, and sending promises
to each man privately—but thinking otherwise.

Here is an instance of her trickery:
she had her great loom standing in the hall
and the fine warp of some vast fabric on it;   100
we were attending her, and she said to us:
'Young men, my suitors, now my lord is dead,
let me finish my weaving before I marry,

or else my thread will have been spun in vain.
It is a shroud I weave for Lord Laërtês,
when cold death comes to lay him on his bier.
The country wives would hold me in dishonor
if he, with all his fortune, lay unshrouded.'
We have men's hearts; she touched them; we agreed.
So every day she wove on the great loom—   110
but every night by torchlight she unwove it;
and so for three years she deceived the Akhaians.
But when the seasons brought the fourth around,
one of her maids, who knew the secret, told us;
we found her unraveling the splendid shroud.
She had to finish then, although she hated it.

Now here is the suitors' answer—
you and all the Akhaians, mark it well:
dismiss your mother from the house, or make her marry
the man her father names and she prefers.   120
Does she intend to keep us dangling forever?
She may rely too long on Athena's gifts—
talent in handicraft and a clever mind;
so cunning—history cannot show the like
among the ringleted ladies of Akhaia,
Mykênê with her coronet, Alkmênê, Tyro.
Wits like Penélopê's never were before,
but this time—well, she made poor use of them.
For here are suitors eating up your property
as long as she holds out—a plan some god   130
put in her mind. She makes a name for herself,
but you can feel the loss it means for you.
Our own affairs can wait; we'll never go anywhere else,
until she takes an Akhaian to her liking."

But clear-headed Telémakhos replied:

"Antínoös, can I banish against her will
the mother who bore me and took care of me?
My father is either dead or far away,
but dearly I should pay for this
at Ikários' hands, if ever I sent her back.   140
The powers of darkness would requite it, too,
my mother's parting curse would call hell's furies[5]
to punish me, along with the scorn of men.
No: I can never give the word for this.
But if your hearts are capable of shame,
leave my great hall, and take your dinner elsewhere,
consume your own stores. Turn and turn about,

---

[5] In mythology, the primitive female agents of retribution for evil, especially for evil committed against blood-kindred.

use one another's houses. If you choose
to slaughter one man's livestock and pay nothing,
this is rapine; and by the eternal gods   150
I beg Zeus you shall get what you deserve:
a slaughter here, and nothing paid for it!"

Now Zeus who views the wide world sent a sign to him,
launching a pair of eagles from a mountain crest
in gliding flight down the soft blowing wind,
wing-tip to wing-tip quivering taut, companions,
till high above the assembly of many voices
they wheeled, their dense wings beating, and in havoc
dropped on the heads of the crowd—a deathly omen—
wielding their talons, tearing cheeks and throats;   160
then veered away on the right hand through the city.
Astonished, gaping after the birds, the men
felt their hearts flood, foreboding things to come.
And now they heard the old lord Halithersês,
son of Mastor, keenest among the old
at reading birdflight into accurate speech;
in his anxiety for them, he rose and said:

"Hear me, Ithakans! Hear what I have to say,
and may I hope to open the suitors' eyes
to the black wave towering over them. Odysseus   170
will not be absent from his family long:
he is already near, carrying in him
a bloody doom for all these men, and sorrow
for many more on our high seamark, Ithaka.
Let us think how to stop it; let the suitors
drop their suit; they had better, without delay.
I am old enough to know a sign when I see one,
and I say all has come to pass for Odysseus
as I foretold when the Argives massed on Troy,
and he, the great tactician, joined the rest.   180
My forecast was that after nineteen years,[6]
many blows weathered, all his shipmates lost,
himself unrecognized by anyone,
he would come home. I see this all fulfilled."

But Pólybos' son, Eurýmakhos, retorted:

"Old man, go tell the omens for your children
at home, and try to keep them out of trouble.
I am more fit to interpret this than you are.
Bird life aplenty is found in the sunny air,
not all of it significant. As for Odysseus,   190
he perished far from home. You should have perished with him—
then we'd be spared this nonsense in assembly,

---

[6] These include the ten years of war against Troy.

as good as telling Telémakhos to rage on;
do you think you can gamble on a gift from him?
Here is what I foretell, and it's quite certain:
if you, with what you know of ancient lore,
encourage bitterness in this young man,
it means, for him, only the more frustration—
he can do nothing whatever with two eagles—
and as for you, old man, we'll fix a penalty   200
that you will groan to pay.
Before the whole assembly I advise Telémakhos
to send his mother to her father's house;
let them arrange her wedding there, and fix
a portion suitable for a valued daughter.
Until he does this, courtship is our business,
vexing though it may be; we fear no one,
certainly not Telémakhos, with his talk;
and we care nothing for your divining, uncle,
useless talk; you win more hatred by it.   210
We'll share his meat, no thanks or fee to him,
as long as she delays and maddens us.
It is a long, long time we have been waiting
in rivalry for this beauty. We could have gone
elsewhere and found ourselves very decent wives."

Clear-headed Telémakhos replied to this:

"Eurýmakhos, and noble suitors all,
I am finished with appeals and argument.
The gods know, and the Akhaians know, these things.
But give me a fast ship and a crew of twenty   220
who will see me through a voyage, out and back.
I'll go to sandy Pylos, then to Sparta,
for news of Father since he sailed from Troy—
some traveller's tale, perhaps, or rumored fame
issued from Zeus himself into the world.
If he's alive, and beating his way home,
I might hold out for another weary year;
but if they tell me that he's dead and gone,
then I can come back to my own dear country
and raise a mound for him, and burn his gear,   230
with all the funeral honors that befit him,
and give my mother to another husband."

The boy sat down in silence. Next to stand
was Mentor, comrade in arms of the prince Odysseus,
an old man now. Odysseus left him authority
over his house and slaves, to guard them well.
In his concern, he spoke to the assembly:

"Hear me, Ithakans! Hear what I have to say.
Let no man holding scepter as a king

be thoughtful, mild, kindly, or virtuous;   240
let him be cruel, and practice evil ways;
it is so clear that no one here remembers
how like a gentle father Odysseus ruled you.
I find it less revolting that the suitors
carry their malice into violent acts;
at least they stake their lives
when they go pillaging the house of Odysseus—
their lives upon it, he will not come again.
What sickens me is to see the whole community
sitting still, and never a voice or a hand raised   250
against them—a mere handful compared with you."

Leókritos, Euênor's son, replied to him:

"Mentor, what mischief are you raking up?
Will this crowd risk the sword's edge over a dinner?
Suppose Odysseus himself indeed
came in and found the suitors at his table:
he might be hot to drive them out. What then?
Never would he enjoy his wife again—
the wife who loves him well; he'd only bring down
abject death on himself against those odds.   260
Madness, to talk of fighting in either case.
Now let all present go about their business!
Halithersês and Mentor will speed the traveller;
they can help him: they were his father's friends.
I rather think he will be sitting here
a long time yet, waiting for news on Ithaka;
that seafaring he spoke of is beyond him."

On this note they were quick to end their parley.
The assembly broke up; everyone went home—
the suitors home to Odysseus' house again.   270
But Telémakhos walked down along the shore
and washed his hands in the foam of the grey sea,
then said this prayer:

                                        "O god of yesterday,
guest in our house, who told me to take ship
on the hazy sea for news of my lost father,
listen to me, be near me:
The Akhaians only wait, or hope to hinder me,
the damned insolent suitors most of all."

Athena was nearby and came to him,
putting on Mentor's figure and his tone,   280
the warm voice in a lucid flight of words:

"You'll never be fainthearted or a fool,
Telémakhos, if you have your father's spirit;

he finished what he cared to say,
and what he took in hand he brought to pass.
The sea routes will yield their distances
to his true son, Penélopê's true son,—
I doubt another's luck would hold so far.
The son is rare who measures with his father,
and one in a thousand is a better man,   290
but you will have the sap and wit
and prudence—for you get that from Odysseus—
to give you a fair chance of winning through.
So never mind the suitors and their ways,
there is no judgment in them, neither do they
know anything of death and the black terror
close upon them—doom's day on them all.
You need not linger over going to sea.
I sailed beside your father in the old days,
I'll find a ship for you, and help you sail her.   300
So go on home, as if to join the suitors,
but get provisions ready in containers—
wine in two-handled jugs and barley meal,
the staying power of oarsmen,
in skin bags, watertight. I'll go the rounds
and call a crew of volunteers together.
Hundreds of ships are beached on sea-girt Ithaka;
let me but choose the soundest, old or new,
we'll rig her and take her out on the broad sea."

This was the divine speech Telémakhos heard   310
from Athena, Zeus's daughter. He stayed no longer,
but took his heartache home,
and found the robust suitors there at work,
skinning goats and roasting pigs in the courtyard.
Antínoös came straight over, laughing at him,
and took him by the hand with a bold greeting:

"High-handed Telémakhos, control your temper!
Come on, get over it, no more grim thoughts,
but feast and drink with me, the way you used to.
The Akhaians will attend to all you ask for—   320
ship, crew, and crossing to the holy land
of Pylos, for the news about your father."

Telémakhos replied with no confusion:

"Antínoös, I cannot see myself again
taking a quiet dinner in this company.
Isn't it enough that you could strip my house
under my very nose when I was young?
Now that I know, being grown, what others say,
I understand it all, and my heart is full.
I'll bring black doom upon you if I can—   330

either in Pylos, if I go, or in this country.
And I will go, go all the way, if only
as someone's passenger. I have no ship,
no oarsmen: and it suits you that I have none."

Calmly he drew his hand from Antínoös' hand.
At this the suitors, while they dressed their meat,
began to exchange loud mocking talk about him.
One young toplofty gallant set the tone:

                        "Well, think of that!

Telémakhos has a mind to murder us.
He's going to lead avengers out of Pylos,   340
or Sparta, maybe; oh, he's wild to do it.
Or else he'll try the fat land of Ephyra—
he can get poison there, and bring it home,
doctor the wine jar and dispatch us all."

Another took the cue:

                        "Well now, who knows?

He might be lost at sea, just like Odysseus,
knocking around in a ship, far from his friends.
And what a lot of trouble that would give us,
making the right division of his things!
We'd keep his house as dowry for his mother—   350
his mother and the man who marries her."

That was the drift of it. Telémakhos
went on through to the storeroom of his father,
a great vault where gold and bronze lay piled
along with chests of clothes, and fragrant oil.
And there were jars of earthenware in rows
holding an old wine,
mellow, unmixed, and rare; cool stood the jars
against the wall, kept for whatever day
Odysseus, worn by hardships, might come home.   360
The double folding doors were tightly locked
and guarded, night and day, by the serving woman,
Eurýkleia, grand-daughter of Peisênor,
in all her duty vigilant and shrewd.
Telémakhos called her to the storeroom, saying:

"Nurse, get a few two-handled travelling jugs
filled up with wine—the second best, not that
you keep for your unlucky lord and king,
hoping he may have slipped away from death
and may yet come again—royal Odysseus.   370
Twelve amphorai[7] will do; seal them up tight.

---

[7] Plural form of "amphora," a jar with two handles and a thin neck.

And pour out barley into leather bags—
twenty bushels of barley meal ground fine.
Now keep this to yourself! Collect these things,
and after dark, when mother has retired
and gone upstairs to bed, I'll come for them.
I sail to sandy Pylos, then to Sparta,
to see what news there is of Father's voyage."

His loving nurse Euríkleia gave a cry,
and tears sprang to her eyes as she wailed softly: 380

"Dear child, whatever put this in your head?
Why do you want to go so far in the world—
and you our only darling? Lord Odysseus
died in some strange place, far from his homeland.
Think how, when you have turned your back, these men
will plot to kill you and share all your things!
Stay with your own, dear, do. Why should you suffer
hardship and homelessness on the wild sea?"

But seeing all clear, Telémakhos replied:

"Take heart, Nurse, there's a god behind this plan.   390
And you must swear to keep it from my mother,
until the eleventh day, or twelfth, or till
she misses me, or hears that I am gone.
She must not tear her lovely skin lamenting."

So the old woman vowed by all the gods,
and vowed again, to carry out his wishes;
then she filled up the amphorai with wine
and sifted barley meal into leather bags.
Telémakhos rejoined the suitors.

                                               Meanwhile
the goddess with grey eyes had other business: 400
disguised as Telémakhos, she roamed the town
taking each likely man aside and telling him:
"Meet us at nightfall at the ship!" Indeed,
she asked Noêmon, Phronios' wealthy son,
to lend her a fast ship, and he complied.
Now when at sundown shadows crossed the lanes
she dragged the cutter to the sea and launched it,
fitted out with tough seagoing gear,
and tied it up, away at the harbor's edge.
The crewmen gathered, sent there by the goddess.   410
Then it occurred to the grey-eyed goddess Athena
to pass inside the house of the hero Odysseus,
showering a sweet drowsiness on the suitors,
whom she had presently wandering in their wine;
and soon, as they could hold their cups no longer,
they straggled off to find their beds in town,

eyes heavy-lidded, laden down with sleep.
Then to Telémakhos the grey-eyed goddess
appeared again with Mentor's form and voice,
calling him out of the lofty emptied hall: 420

"Telémakhos, your crew of fighting men
is ready at the oars, and waiting for you;
come on, no point in holding up the sailing."

And Pallas Athena turned like the wind, running
ahead of him. He followed in her footsteps
down to the seaside, where they found the ship,
and oarsmen with flowing hair at the water's edge.
Telémakhos, now strong in the magic, cried:

"Come with me, friends, and get our rations down!
They are all packed at home, and my own mother   430
knows nothing!—only one maid was told."

He turned and led the way, and they came after,
carried and stowed all in the well-trimmed ship
as the dear son of Odysseus commanded.
Telémakhos then stepped aboard; Athena
took her position aft, and he sat by her.
The two stroke oars cast off the stern hawsers
and vaulted over the gunnels to their benches.
Grey-eyed Athena stirred them a following wind,
soughing from the north-west on the winedark sea,   440
and as he felt the wind, Telémakhos
called to all hands to break out mast and sail.
They pushed the fir mast high and stepped it firm
amidships in the box, made fast the forestays,
then hoisted up the white sail on its halyards
until the wind caught, booming in the sail;
and a flushing wave sang backward from the bow
on either side, as the ship got way upon her,
holding her steady course.
Now they made all secure in the fast black ship,   450
and, setting out the winebowls all a-brim,
they made libation to the gods,
                                        the undying, the ever-new,
most of all to the grey-eyed daughter of Zeus.
And the prow sheared through the night into the dawn.

BOOK THREE: THE LORD OF THE
WESTERN APPROACHES

The sun rose on the flawless brimming sea
into a sky all brazen—all one brightening

for gods immortal and for mortal men
on plowlands kind with grain.

        And facing sunrise

the voyagers now lay off Pylos town,
compact stronghold of Neleus.[1] On the shore
black bulls were being offered by the people
to the blue-maned god who makes the islands tremble:
nine congregations, each five hundred strong,
led out nine bulls apiece to sacrifice,   10
taking the tripes to eat, while on their altars
thighbones in fat lay burning for the god.
Here they put in, furled sail, and beached the ship;
but Telémakhos hung back in disembarking,
so that Athena turned and said:

"Not the least shyness, now, Telémakhos.
You came across the open sea for this—
to find out where the great earth hides your father
and what the doom was that he came upon.
Go to old Nestor, master charioteer,   20
so we may broach the storehouse of his mind.
Ask him with courtesy, and in his wisdom
he will tell you history and no lies."

But clear-headed Telémakhos replied:

"Mentor, how can I do it, how approach him?
I have no practice in elaborate speeches, and
for a young man to interrogate an old man
seems disrespectful—"

       But the grey-eyed goddess said:

"Reason and heart will give you words, Telémakhos;
and a spirit will counsel others. I should say   30
the gods were never indifferent to your life."

She went on quickly, and he followed her
to where the men of Pylos had their altars.
Nestor appeared enthroned among his sons,
while friends around them skewered the red beef
or held it scorching. When they saw the strangers
a hail went up, and all that crowd came forward
calling out invitations to the feast.
Peisístratos in the lead, the young prince,
caught up their hands in his and gave them places   40
on curly lambskins flat on the sea sand
near Thrasymêdês, his brother, and his father;

---

[1] Son of the sea-god Poseidon (the "blue-maned god"), he was the founder of Pylos and the father of Nestor.

he passed them bits of the food of sacrifice,
and, pouring wine in a golden cup,
he said to Pallas Athena, daughter of Zeus:

"Friend, I must ask you to invoke Poseidon:
you find us at this feast, kept in his honor.
Make the appointed offering then, and pray,
and give the honeyed winecup to your friend
so he may do the same. He, too,   50
must pray to the gods on whom all men depend,
but he is just my age, you are the senior,
so here, I give the goblet first to you."

And he put the cup of sweet wine in her hand.
Athena liked his manners, and the equity
that gave her precedence with the cup of gold,
so she besought Poseidon at some length:

"Earthshaker, listen and be well disposed.
Grant your petitioners everything they ask:
above all, honor to Nestor and his sons;   60
second, to every man of Pylos town
a fair gift in exchange for this hekatomb;[2]
third, may Telémakhos and I perform
the errand on which last night we put to sea."

This was the prayer of Athena—
granted in every particular by herself.
She passed the beautiful wine cup to Telémakhos,
who tipped the wine and prayed as she had done.
Meanwhile the spits were taken off the fire,
portions of crisp meat for all. They feasted,   70
and when they had eaten and drunk their fill, at last
they heard from Nestor, prince of charioteers:

"Now is the time,"[3] he said, "for a few questions,
now that our young guests have enjoyed their dinner.
Who are you, strangers? Where are you sailing from,
and where to, down the highways of sea water?
Have you some business here? or are you, now,
reckless wanderers of the sea, like those corsairs
who risk their lives to prey on other men?"

Clear-headed Telémakhos responded cheerfully,   80
for Athena gave him heart. By her design
his quest for news about his father's wandering
would bring him fame in the world's eyes. So he said:

[2] A grand public sacrifice and offering to the gods.
[3] Hospitality required that no such questions be asked of guests until they had been welcomed and fed.

"Nestor, pride of Akhaians, Neleus' son,
you ask where we are from, and I can tell you:
our home port is under Mount Neion, Ithaka.
We are not here on Ithakan business, though,
but on my own. I want news of my father,
Odysseus, known for his great heart, and I
will comb the wide world for it. People say   90
he fought along with you when Troy was taken.
As to the other men who fought that war,
we know where each one died, and how he died;
but Zeus allotted my father death and mystery.
No one can say for sure where he was killed,
whether some hostile landsmen or the sea,
the stormwaves on the deep sea, got the best of him.
And this is why I come to you for help.
Tell me of his death, sir, if perhaps
you witnessed it, or have heard some wanderer   100
tell the tale. The man was born for trouble.
Spare me no part of it for kindness' sake,
but put the scene before me as you saw it.
If ever Odysseus my noble father
served you by promise kept or work accomplished
in the land of Troy, where you Akhaians suffered,
recall those things for me the way they were."

Then Nestor, prince of charioteers, made answer:

"Dear friend, you take me back to all the trouble
we went through in that country, we Akhaians: 110
rough days aboard ship on the cloudy sea
cruising away for pillage after Akhilleus;[4]
rough days of battle around Priam's[5] town.
Our losses, then—so many good men gone:
Arês' great Aias[6] lies there, Akhilleus lies there,
Patróklos,[7] too, the wondrous counselor,
and my own strong and princely son, Antílokhos—
fastest man of them all, and a born fighter.
Other miseries, and many, we endured there.
Could any mortal man tell the whole story?   120
Not if you stayed five years or six to hear
how hard it was for the flower of the Akhaians;
you'd go home weary, and the tale untold.
Think: we were there nine years, and we tried everything,
all stratagems against them,

---

[4] The foremost Greek warrior, central figure of the *Iliad*.   [5] King of Troy.
[6] Another great Greek warrior (also spelled *Ajax*), associated here with Arês, the god of war.
[7] The closest friend of Akhilleus; it was to avenge his death at the hand of the Trojan leader Hektor that Akhilleus—as is narrated in the *Iliad*—re-entered the battle and killed Hektor.

up to the bitter end that Zeus begrudged us.
And as to stratagems, no man would claim
Odysseus' gift for those. He had no rivals,
your father, at the tricks of war.

                                                        Your father?   130

Well, I must say I marvel at the sight of you:
your manner of speech couldn't be more like his;
one would say No; no boy could speak so well.
And all that time at Ilion,[8] he and I
were never at odds in council or assembly—
saw things the same way, had one mind between us
in all the good advice we gave the Argives.
But when we plundered Priam's town and tower
and took to the ships, God scattered the Akhaians.
He had a mind to make homecoming hard for them,
seeing they would not think straight nor behave,   140
or some would not. So evil days came on them,
and she who had been angered,
Zeus's dangerous grey-eyed daughter, did it,
starting a fight between the sons of Atreus.[9]
First they were fools enough to call assembly
at sundown, unheard of hour;
the Akhaian soldiers turned out, soaked with wine,
to hear talk, talk about it from their commanders:
Meneláos harangued them to get organized—
time to ride home on the sea's broad back, he said;   150
but Agamémnon wouldn't hear of it. He wanted
to hold the troops, make sacrifice, a hekatomb,
something to pacify Athena's rage.
Folly again, to think that he could move her.
Will you change the will of the everlasting gods
in a night or a day's time?
The two men stood there hammering at each other
until the army got to its feet with a roar,
and no decision, wanting it both ways.
That night no one slept well, everyone cursing   160
someone else. Here was the bane[10] from Zeus.
At dawn we dragged our ships to the lordly water,
stowed aboard all our plunder
and the slave women in their low hip girdles.
But half the army elected to stay behind
with Agamémnon as their corps commander;
the other half embarked and pulled away.
We made good time, the huge sea smoothed before us,

---

[8] Troy.

[9] Atreus was father of Agamémnon and Meneláos, the brothers who commanded the Greek forces. Athena's hostility to the Greeks (whom she generally favored and aided) was occasioned by outrages committed against the Trojan princess and prophetess Kassandra, who during the sack of Troy had tried to take refuge at Athena's shrine.

[10] Ruin; poison.

and held our rites when we reached Ténedos,[11]
being wild for home. But Zeus, not willing yet,   170
now cruelly set us at odds a second time,
and one lot turned, put back in the rolling ships,
under command of the subtle captain, Odysseus;
their notion was to please Lord Agamémnon.
Not I. I fled, with every ship I had;
I knew fate had some devilment brewing there.
Diomêdês roused his company and fled, too,
and later Meneláos, the red-haired captain,
caught up with us at Lesbos,
while we mulled over the long sea route, unsure   180
whether to lay our course northward of Khios,
keeping the Isle of Psyria off to port,
or inside Khios, coasting by windy Mimas.
We asked for a sign from heaven, and the sign came
to cut across the open sea to Euboia,
and lose no time putting our ills behind us.
The wind freshened astern, and the ships ran
before the wind on paths of the deep sea fish,
making Geraistos before dawn. We thanked Poseidon
with many a charred thighbone for that crossing.   190
On the fourth day, Diomêdês' company
under full sail put in at Argos port,
and I held on for Pylos. The fair wind,
once heaven set it blowing, never failed.

So this, dear child, was how I came from Troy,
and saw no more of the others, lost or saved.
But you are welcome to all I've heard since then
at home; I have no reason to keep it from you.
The Myrmidon spearfighters returned, they say,
under the son of lionhearted Akhilleus;   200
and so did Poias' great son, Philoktêtês.
Idómeneus brought his company back to Krete;[12]
the sea took not a man from him, of all
who lived through the long war.
And even as far away as Ithaka
you've heard of Agamémnon—how he came
home, how Aigísthos waited to destroy him
but paid a bitter price for it in the end.
That is a good thing, now, for a man to leave

---

[11] The problem described by Nestor in the following lines is whether the part of the Greek fleet that decided to sail immediately should follow a circuitous course homeward among the islands of the Aegean Sea or head straight across it, by a course that was shorter but farther removed from ports.

[12] The Myrmidons were Akhilleus' troops; his son was Pyrrhus, also called Neoptólemus. Philoktêtês was a Greek warrior who, after having been abandoned on the way to Troy because of a malodorous wound, later rejoined the Greek forces and was crucial to their success in the war. Idómeneus, an ally of the Greeks against the Trojans, was king of Krete (Crete).

a son behind him, like the son who punished   210
Aigísthos for the murder of his great father.
You, too, are tall and well set-up, I see;
be brave, you too, so men in times to come
will speak well of you."

                                        Then Telémakhos said:

"Nestor, pride of Akhaians, Neleus' son,
that was revenge, and far and wide the Akhaians
will tell the tale in song for generations.
I wish the gods would buckle his arms on me!
I'd be revenged for outrage
on my insidious and brazen enemies.   220
But no such happy lot was given to me
or to my father. Still, I must hold fast."

To this Lord Nestor of Gerênia said:

"My dear young friend, now that you speak of it,
I hear a crowd of suitors for your mother
lives with you, uninvited, making trouble.
Now tell me how you take this. Do the people
side against you, hearkening to some oracle?
Who knows, your father might come home someday
alone or backed by troops, and have it out with them.   230
If grey-eyed Athena loved you
the way she did Odysseus in the old days,
in Troy country, where we all went through so much—
never have I seen the gods help any man
as openly as Athena did your father—
well, as I say, if she cared for you that way,
there would be those to quit this marriage game."

But prudently Telémakhos replied:

"I can't think what you say will ever happen, sir.
It is a dazzling hope. But not for me.   240
It could not be—even if the gods willed it."

At this grey-eyed Athena broke in, saying:

"What strange talk you permit yourself, Telémakhos.
A god could save the man by simply wishing it—
from the farthest shore in the world.
If I were he, I should prefer to suffer
years at sea, and then be safe at home;
better that than a knife at my hearthside
where Agamémnon found it—killed by adulterers.
Though as for death, of course all men must suffer it: 250

the gods may love a man, but they can't help him
when cold death comes to lay him on his bier."[13]

Telémakhos replied:

"Mentor, grievously though we miss my father, why
go on as if that homecoming could happen?
You know the gods had settled it already,
years ago, when dark death came for him.
But there is something else I imagine Nestor
can tell us, knowing as he does the ways of men.
They say his rule goes back over three generations,   260
so long, so old, it seems death cannot touch him.
Nestor, Neleus' son, true sage, say how
did the Lord of the Great Plains, Agamémnon, die?
What was the trick Aigísthos used
to kill the better man? And Meneláos,
where was he? Not at Argos[14] in Akhaia,
but blown off course, held up in some far country,
is that what gave the killer nerve to strike?"

Lord Nestor of Gerênia made answer:

"Well, now, my son, I'll tell you the whole story.   270
You know, yourself, what would have come to pass
if red-haired Meneláos, back from Troy,
had caught Aigísthos in that house alive.
There would have been no burial mound for him,
but dogs and carrion birds to huddle on him
in the fields beyond the wall, and not a soul
bewailing him, for the great wrong he committed.
While we were hard-pressed in the war at Troy
he stayed safe inland in the grazing country,
making light talk to win Agamémnon's queen.   280
But the Lady Klytaimnéstra, in the first days,
rebuffed him, being faithful still;
then, too, she had at hand as her companion
a minstrel Agamémnon left attending her,
charged with her care, when he took ship for Troy.

---

[13] This final sentence is a definitive expression of the ancient Greek understanding of the difference between human beings and deities. Though gods may be champions and even comrades of mortals, the latter are doomed to die and the gods are not. The distinction has little to do with morality or metaphysics. The gods belong to a different order of beings, though not necessarily to a superior order.

[14] The region ruled by Agamémnon, brother to Meneláos, whose wife Helen had run off with the Trojan prince Paris. Homer's account of the slaying of Agamémnon at his homecoming is at this point a fairly simple justification of Agamémnon and his avenging son Orestês; Aeschylus' account in the *Oresteia* is more psychologically complex. For other accounts of the story, by the Ancient of the Salt Sea and by Agamémnon himself, see Books IV and XI of the *Odyssey*.

Then came the fated hour when she gave in.[15]
Her lover tricked the poet and marooned him
on a bare island for the seabirds' picking,
and took her home, as he and she desired.
Many thighbones he burned on the gods' altars   290
and many a woven and golden ornament
hung to bedeck them, in his satisfaction;
he had not thought life held such glory for him.

Now Meneláos and I sailed home together
on friendly terms, from Troy,
but when we came off Sunion Point[16] in Attika,
the ships still running free, Onêtor's son
Phrontis, the steersman of Meneláos' ship,
fell over with a death grip on the tiller:
some unseen arrow from Apollo hit him.   300
No man handled a ship better than he did
in a high wind and sea, so Meneláos
put down his longing to get on, and landed
to give this man full honor in funeral.
His own luck turned then. Out on the winedark sea
in the murmuring hulls again, he made Cape Malea,[17]
but Zeus who views the wide world sent a gloom
over the ocean, and a howling gale
came on with seas increasing, mountainous,
parting the ships and driving half toward Krete   310
where the Kydonians live by Iardanos river.
Off Gortyn's coastline in the misty sea there
a reef, a razorback, cuts through the water,
and every westerly piles up a pounding
surf along the left side, going toward Phaistos—
big seas buffeted back by the narrow stone.
They were blown here, and fought in vain for sea room;
the ships kept going in to their destruction,
slammed on the reef. The crews were saved. But now
those five that weathered it got off to southward,   320
taken by wind and current on to Egypt;
and there Meneláos stayed. He made a fortune
in sea traffic among those distant races,
but while he did so, the foul crime was planned
and carried out in Argos by Aigísthos,

---

[15] This passage presents both Klytaimnéstra and her paramour Aigísthos as frivolous and irresponsible dalliers; in other versions of the story, notably in Aeschylus' *Oresteia*, both these adulterers are given an understandable, if not necessarily justifiable, motive for revenge against Agamémnon.

[16] The tip of a promontory, near Athens, in southeastern Greece. The fleet is trying to sail westward around the southern coast.

[17] Located at the extreme southern point of the Grecian mainland, directly north of the western end of the island of Krete.

who ruled over golden Mykênai[18] seven years.
Seven long years, with Agamémnon dead,
he held the people down, before the vengeance.
But in the eighth year, back from exile in Attika,
Orestês killed the snake who killed his father. 330
He gave his hateful mother and her soft man
a tomb together, and proclaimed the funeral day
a festal day for all the Argive people.
That day Lord Meneláos of the great war cry
made port with all the gold his ships could carry.
And this should give you pause, my son:
don't stay too long away from home, leaving
your treasure there, and brazen suitors near;
they'll squander all you have or take it from you,
and then how will your journey serve? 340
I urge you, though, to call on Meneláos,
he being but lately home from distant parts
in the wide world. A man could well despair
of getting home at all, if the winds blew him
over the Great South Sea—that weary waste,
even the wintering birds delay
one winter more before the northward crossing.
Well, take your ship and crew and go by water,
or if you'd rather go by land, here are
horses, a car, and my own sons for company 350
as far as the ancient land of Lakedaimon[19]
and Meneláos, the red-haired captain there.
Ask him with courtesy, and in his wisdom
he will tell you history and no lies."

While Nestor talked, the sun went down the sky
and gloom came on the land,
and now the grey-eyed goddess Athena said:

"Sir, this is all most welcome and to the point,
but why not slice the bulls' tongues now, and mix
libations for Poseidon and the gods? 360
Then we can all retire; high time we did;
the light is going under the dark world's rim,
better not linger at the sacred feast."

When Zeus's daughter spoke, they turned to listen
and soon the squires brought water for their hands,
while stewards filled the winebowls and poured out
a fresh cup full for every man. The company
stood up to fling the tongues and a shower of wine

---

[18] The capital city of the plain of Argos, ruled over by Agamémnon. Also spelled "Mycenae."

[19] Sparta; in the far south of Greece. Also spelled "Lacedaemon."

over the flames, then drank their thirst away.
Now finally Telémakhos and Athena   370
bestirred themselves, turning away to the ship,
but Nestor put a hand on each, and said:

"Now Zeus forbid, and the other gods as well,
that you should spend the night on board, and leave me
as though I were some pauper without a stitch,
no blankets in his house, no piles of rugs,
no sleeping soft for host or guest! Far from it!
I have all these, blankets and deep-piled rugs,
and while I live the only son of Odysseus
will never make his bed on a ship's deck—   380
no, not while sons of mine are left at home
to welcome any guest who comes to us."

The grey-eyed goddess Athena answered him:

"You are very kind, sir, and Telémakhos
should do as you ask. That is the best thing.
He will go with you, and will spend the night
under your roof. But I must join our ship
and talk to the crew, to keep their spirits up,
since I'm the only senior in the company.
The rest are boys who shipped for friendship's sake,   390
no older than Telémakhos, any of them.
Let me sleep out, then, by the black hull's side,
this night at least. At daybreak I'll be off
to see the Kaukonians[20] about a debt they owe me,
an old one and no trifle. As for your guest,
send him off in a car, with one of your sons,
and give him thoroughbreds, a racing team."

Even as she spoke, Athena left them—seeming
a seahawk, in a clap of wings,—and all
the Akhaians of Pylos town looked up astounded.   400
Awed then by what his eyes had seen, the old man
took Telémakhos' hand and said warmly:

"My dear child, I can have no fears for you,
no doubt about your conduct or your heart,
if, at your age, the gods are your companions.
Here we had someone from Olympos—clearly
the glorious daughter of Zeus, his third child,
who held your father dear among the Argives.
O, Lady, hear me! Grant an illustrious name
to me and to my children and my dear wife!   410
A noble heifer shall be yours in sacrifice,
one that no man has ever yoked or driven;
my gift to you—her horns all sheathed in gold."

[20] A people who lived near Pylos.

So he ended, praying; and Athena heard him.
Then Nestor of Gerênia led them all,
his sons and sons-in-law, to his great house;
and in they went to the famous hall of Nestor,
taking their seats on thrones and easy chairs,
while the old man mixed water in a wine bowl
with sweet red wine, mellowed eleven years   420
before his housekeeper uncapped the jar.
He mixed and poured his offering, repeating
prayers to Athena, daughter of royal Zeus.
The others made libation, and drank deep,
then all the company went to their quarters,
and Nestor of Gerênia showed Telémakhos
under the echoing eastern entrance hall
to a fine bed near the bed of Peisístratos,
captain of spearmen, his unmarried son.
Then he lay down in his own inner chamber   430
where his dear faithful wife had smoothed his bed.

When Dawn spread out her finger tips of rose,
Lord Nestor of Gerênia, charioteer,
left his room for a throne of polished stone,
white and gleaming as though with oil, that stood
before the main gate of the palace; Neleus here
had sat before him—masterful in kingship,
Neleus, long ago a prey to death, gone down
to the night of the underworld.
So Nestor held his throne and scepter now,   440
lord of the western approaches to Akhaia.
And presently his sons came out to join him,
leaving the palace: Ekhéphron and Stratíos,
Perseus and Arêtós and Thrasymêdês,
and after them the prince Peisístratos,
bringing Telémakhos along with him.
Seeing all present, the old lord Nestor said:

"Dear sons, here is my wish, and do it briskly
to please the gods, Athena first of all,
my guest in daylight at our holy feast.   450
One of you must go for a young heifer
and have the cowherd lead her from the pasture.
Another call on Lord Telémakhos' ship
to invite his crewmen, leaving two behind;
and someone else again send for the goldsmith,
Laerkês, to gild the horns.
The rest stay here together. Tell the servants
a ritual feast will be prepared in hall.
Tell them to bring seats, firewood and fresh water."

Before he finished, they were about these errands.   460
The heifer came from pasture,

the crewmen of Telémakhos from the ship,
the smith arrived, bearing the tools of his trade—
hammer and anvil, and the precision tongs
he handled fiery gold with,—and Athena
came as a god comes, numinous, to the rites.

The smith now gloved each horn in a pure foil
beaten out of the gold that Nestor gave him—
a glory and delight for the goddess' eyes—
while Ekhéphron and Stratíos held the horns.   470
Arêtós brought clear lustral water
in a bowl quivering with fresh-cut flowers,
a basket of barley in his other hand.
Thrasymêdês, who could stand his ground in war,
stood ready, with a sharp two-bladed axe,
for the stroke of sacrifice, and Perseus
held a bowl for the blood. And now Nestor,
strewing the barley grains, and water drops,
pronounced his invocation to Athena
and burned a pinch of bristles from the victim.   480
When prayers were said and all the grain was scattered
great-hearted Thrasymêdês in a flash
swung the axe, at one blow cutting through
the neck tendons. The heifer's spirit failed.
Then all the women gave a wail of joy—
daughters, daughters-in-law, and the Lady Eurydíkê,
Klyménos' eldest daughter. But the men
still held the heifer, shored her up
from the wide earth where the living go their ways,
until Peisístratos cut her throat across,   490
the black blood ran, and life ebbed from her marrow.
The carcass now sank down, and they disjointed
shoulder and thigh bone, wrapping them in fat,
two layers, folded, with raw strips of flesh.
These offerings Nestor burned on the split-wood fire
and moistened with red wine. His sons took up
five-tined forks in their hands, while the altar flame
ate through the bones, and bits of tripe went round.
Then came the carving of the quarters, and they spitted
morsels of lean meat on the long sharp tines   500
and broiled them at arm's length upon the fire.

Polykástê, a fair girl, Nestor's youngest,
had meanwhile given a bath to Telémakhos—
bathing him first, then rubbing him with oil.
She held fine clothes and a cloak to put around him
when he came godlike from the bathing place;
then out he went to take his place with Nestor.
When the best cuts were broiled and off the spits,
they all sat down to banquet. Gentle squires

kept every golden wine cup brimming full. 510
And so they feasted to their heart's content,
until the prince of charioteers commanded:

"Sons, harness the blood mares for Telémakhos;
hitch up the car, and let him take the road."

They swung out smartly to do the work, and hooked
the handsome horses to a chariot shaft.
The mistress of the stores brought up provisions
of bread and wine, with victuals fit for kings,
and Telémakhos stepped up on the painted car.
Just at his elbow stood Peisístratos, 520
captain of spearmen, reins in hand. He gave
a flick to the horses, and with streaming manes
they ran for the open country. The tall town
of Pylos sank behind them in the distance,
as all day long they kept the harness shaking.

The sun was low and shadows crossed the lanes
when they arrived at Phêrai.[21] There Dióklês,
son of Ortílokhos whom Alpheios fathered,
welcomed the young men, and they slept the night.
But up when the young Dawn's finger tips of rose 530
opened in the east, they hitched the team
once more to the painted car,
and steered out eastward through the echoing gate,
whipping their fresh horses into a run.
That day they made the grainlands of Lakedaimon,
where, as the horses held to a fast clip,
they kept on to their journey's end. Behind them
the sun went down and all the roads grew dark.

BOOK FOUR: THE RED-HAIRED
KING AND HIS LADY

By vales and sharp ravines in Lakedaimon
the travellers drove to Meneláos' mansion,
and found him at a double wedding feast
for son and daughter.

Long ago at Troy

he pledged her to the heir of great Akhilleus,
breaker of men—a match the gods had ripened;
so he must send her with a chariot train
to the town and glory of the Myrmidons.
And that day, too, he brought Alektor's daughter

[21] A stopping-place on the eastward route from Pylos to Lakedaimon.

to marry his tall scion,[1] Megapénthês,   10
born of a slave girl during the long war—
for the gods had never after granted Helen
a child to bring into the sunlit world
after the first, rose-lipped Hermionê,
a girl like the pale-gold goddess Aphroditê.[2]

Down the great hall in happiness they feasted,
neighbors of Meneláos, and his kin,
for whom a holy minstrel harped and sang;
and two lithe tumblers moved out on the song
with spins and handsprings through the company.   20
Now when Telémakhos and Nestor's son
pulled up their horses at the main gate,
one of the king's companions in arms, Eteóneus,
going outside, caught sight of them. He turned
and passed through court and hall to tell the master,
stepping up close to get his ear. Said he:

"Two men are here—two strangers,[3] Meneláos,
but nobly born Akhaians, they appear.
What do you say, shall we unhitch their team,
or send them on to someone free to receive them?"   30

The red-haired captain answered him in anger:

"You were no idiot before, Eteóneus,
but here you are talking like a child of ten.
Could we have made it home again—and Zeus
give us no more hard roving!—if other men
had never fed us, given us lodging?

                                                        Bring
these men to be our guests: unhitch their team!"

Eteóneus left the long room like an arrow,
calling equerries[4] after him, on the run.
Outside, they freed the sweating team from harness,   40
stabled the horses, tied them up, and showered
bushels of wheat and barley in the feed box;
then leaned the chariot pole
against the gleaming entry wall of stone
and took the guests in. What a brilliant place
that mansion of the great prince seemed to them!
A-glitter everywhere, as though with fiery
points of sunlight, lusters of the moon.
The young men gazed in joy before they entered

---

[1] Descendant; son.   [2] Goddess of love and beauty.
[3] The near-breach of hospitality by Eteóneus, which angers Meneláos, is probably explained by wariness; another guest, Paris, had once abducted Helen and thus set off the war.
[4] Men who tended to the horses.

into a room of polished tubs to bathe.   50
Maidservants gave them baths, anointed them,
held out fresh tunics, cloaked them warm; and soon
they took tall thrones beside the son of Atreus.
Here a maid tipped out water for their hands
from a golden pitcher into a silver bowl,
and set a polished table near at hand;
the larder mistress with her tray of loaves
and savories came, dispensing all her best,
and then a carver heaped their platters high
with various meats, and put down cups of gold.   60
Now said the red-haired captain, Meneláos,
gesturing:

                              "Welcome; and fall to; in time,
when you have supped, we hope to hear your names,
forbears and families—in your case, it seems,
no anonymities, but lordly men.
Lads like yourselves are not base born."

                                                              At this,
he lifted in his own hands the king's portion,
a chine of beef, and set it down before them.
Seeing all ready then, they took their dinner;
but when they had feasted well,   70
Telémakhos could not keep still, but whispered,
his head bent close, so the others might not hear:

"My dear friend, can you believe your eyes?—
the murmuring hall, how luminous it is
with bronze, gold, amber, silver, and ivory!
This is the way the court of Zeus must be,
inside, upon Olympos. What a wonder!"

But splendid Meneláos had overheard him
and spoke out on the instant to them both:

"Young friends, no mortal man can vie with Zeus.   80
His home and all his treasures are for ever.
But as for men, it may well be that few
have more than I. How painfully I wandered
before I brought it home! Seven years at sea,
Kypros, Phoinikia, Egypt, and still farther
among the sun-burnt races.
I saw the men of Sidon[5] and Arabia
and Libya, too, where lambs are horned at birth.
In every year they have three lambing seasons,
so no man, chief or shepherd, ever goes   90
hungry for want of mutton, cheese, or milk—

[5] An important city in Phoinikia (Phoenicia), an area along the Syrian coast noted for
commerce and craftsmanship.

all year at milking time there are fresh ewes.
But while I made my fortune on those travels
a stranger killed my brother, in cold blood,—
tricked blind, caught in the web of his deadly queen.
What pleasure can I take, then, being lord
over these costly things?
You must have heard your fathers tell my story,
whoever your fathers are; you must know of my life,
the anguish I once had, and the great house   100
full of my treasure, left in desolation.
How gladly I should live one third as rich
to have my friends back safe at home!—my friends
who died on Troy's wide seaboard, far
from the grazing lands of Argos.
But as things are, nothing but grief is left me
for those companions. While I sit at home
sometimes hot tears come, and I revel in them,
or stop before the surfeit makes me shiver.
And there is one I miss more than the other   110
dead I mourn for; sleep and food alike
grow hateful when I think of him. No soldier
took on so much, went through so much, as Odysseus.
That seems to have been his destiny, and this mine—
to feel each day the emptiness of his absence,
ignorant, even, whether he lived or died.
How his old father and his quiet wife,
Penélopê, must miss him still!
And Telémakhos, whom he left as a new-born child."

Now hearing these things said, the boy's heart rose   120
in a long pang for his father, and he wept,
holding his purple mantle with both hands
before his eyes. Meneláos knew him now,
and so fell silent with uncertainty
whether to let him speak and name his father
in his own time, or to inquire, and prompt him.
And while he pondered, Helen came
out of her scented chamber, a moving grace
like Artemis,[6] straight as a shaft of gold.
Beside her came Adrastê, to place her armchair,   130
Alkippê, with a rug of downy wool,
and Phylo, bringing a silver basket, once
given by Alkandrê, the wife of Pólybos,
in the treasure city, Thebes of distant Egypt.
He gave two silver bathtubs to Meneláos
and a pair of tripods, with ten pure gold bars,
and she, then, made these beautiful gifts to Helen:
a golden distaff,[7] and the silver basket

---

[6]Goddess of the hunt.   [7]A staff used in spinning thread.

rimmed in hammered gold, with wheels to run on.
So Phylo rolled it in to stand beside her,   140
heaped with fine spun stuff, and cradled on it
the distaff swathed in dusky violet wool.
Reclining in her light chair with its footrest,
Helen gazed at her husband and demanded:

"Meneláos, my lord, have we yet heard
our new guests introduce themselves? Shall I
dissemble what I feel? No, I must say it.
Never, anywhere, have I seen so great a likeness
in man or woman—but it is truly strange!
This boy must be the son of Odysseus,   150
Telémakhos, the child he left at home
that year the Akhaian host made war on Troy—
daring all for the wanton that I was."

And the red-haired captain, Meneláos, answered:

"My dear, I see the likeness as well as you do.
Odysseus' hands and feet were like this boy's;
his head, and hair, and the glinting of his eyes.
Not only that, but when I spoke, just now,
of Odysseus' years of toil on my behalf
and all he had to endure—the boy broke down   160
and wept into his cloak."

                                                      Now Nestor's son,
Peisístratos, spoke up in answer to him:

"My lord marshal, Meneláos, son of Atreus,
this is that hero's son as you surmise,
but he is gentle, and would be ashamed
to clamor for attention before your grace
whose words have been so moving to us both.
Nestor, Lord of Gerênia, sent me with him
as guide and escort; he had wished to see you,
to be advised by you or assisted somehow.   170
A father far from home means difficulty
for an only son, with no one else to help him;
so with Telémakhos:
his father left the house without defenders."

The king with flaming hair now spoke again:

"His son, in my house! How I loved the man,
And how he fought through hardship for my sake!
I swore I'd cherish him above all others
if Zeus, who views the wide world, gave us passage
homeward across the sea in the fast ships.   180
I would have settled him in Argos, brought him
over with herds and household out of Ithaka,

his child and all his people. I could have cleaned out
one of my towns to be his new domain.
And so we might have been together often
in feasts and entertainments, never parted
till the dark mist of death lapped over one of us.
But God himself must have been envious,
to batter the bruised man so that he alone
should fail in his return."   190

A twinging ache of grief rose up in everyone,
and Helen of Argos wept, the daughter of Zeus,[8]
Telémakhos and Meneláos wept,
and tears came to the eyes of Nestor's son—
remembering, for his part, Antílokhos,
whom the son of shining Dawn[9] had killed in battle.
But thinking of that brother, he broke out:

"O son of Atreus, when we spoke of you
at home, and asked about you, my old father
would say you have the clearest mind of all.   200
If it is not too much to ask, then, let us not
weep away these hours after supper;
I feel we should not: Dawn will soon be here!
You understand, I would not grudge a man
right mourning when he comes to death and doom:
what else can one bestow on the poor dead?—
a lock of hair sheared,[10] and a tear let fall.
For that matter, I, too,
lost someone in the war at Troy—my brother,
and no mean soldier, whom you must have known,   210
although I never did,—Antílokhos.
He ranked high as a runner and fighting man."

The red-haired captain Meneláos answered:

"My lad, what you have said is only sensible,
and you did well to speak. Yes, that was worthy
a wise man and an older man than you are:
you speak for all the world like Nestor's son.
How easily one can tell the man whose father
had true felicity, marrying and begetting!
And that was true of Nestor, all his days,   220
down to his sleek old age in peace at home,
with clever sons, good spearmen into the bargain.
Come, we'll shake off this mourning mood of ours
and think of supper. Let the men at arms

---

[8] Helen was daughter of Zeus by the mortal woman Lêda. (Lêda was ravished by the god, who took the form of a swan.)
[9] Memnon, an Ethiopian king, was the son of Eos, the goddess of the dawn.
[10] To strew a lock of one's hair on the dead was a customary part of funeral ritual.

rinse our hands again! There will be time
for a long talk with Telémakhos in the morning."

The hero Meneláos' companion in arms,
Asphalion, poured water for their hands,
and once again they touched the food before them.
But now it entered Helen's mind   230
to drop into the wine that they were drinking
an anodyne, mild magic of forgetfulness.
Whoever drank this mixture in the wine bowl
would be incapable of tears that day—
though he should lose mother and father both,
or see, with his own eyes, a son or brother
mauled by weapons of bronze at his own gate.
The opiate of Zeus's daughter bore
this canny power. It had been supplied her
by Polydamna, mistress of Lord Thôn,   240
in Egypt, where the rich plantations grow
herbs of all kinds, maleficent and healthful;
and no one else knows medicine as they do,
Egyptian heirs of Paian,[11] the healing god.
She drugged the wine, then, had it served, and said—
taking again her part in the conversation—

"O Meneláos, Atreus' royal son,
and you that are great heroes' sons, you know
how Zeus gives all of us in turn
good luck and bad luck, being all powerful.   250
So take refreshment, take your ease in hall,
and cheer the time with stories. I'll begin.
Not that I think of naming, far less telling,
every feat of that rugged man, Odysseus,
but here is something that he dared to do
at Troy, where you Akhaians endured the war.
He had, first, given himself an outrageous beating
and thrown some rags on—like a household slave—
then slipped into that city of wide lanes
among his enemies. So changed, he looked   260
as never before upon the Akhaian beachhead,
but like a beggar, merged in the townspeople;
and no one there remarked him. But I knew him—
even as he was, I knew him,
and questioned him. How shrewdly he put me off!
But in the end I bathed him and anointed him,
put a fresh cloak around him, and swore an oath
not to give him away as Odysseus to the Trojans,
till he got back to camp where the long ships lay.
He spoke up then, and told me   270

---

[11] An epithet for Apollo in his role as god of physicians.

all about the Akhaians, and their plans—
then sworded many Trojans through the body
on his way out with what he learned of theirs.
The Trojan women raised a cry—but my heart
sang—for I had come round, long before,
to dreams of sailing home, and I repented
the mad day Aphroditê
drew me away from my dear fatherland,
forsaking all—child, bridal bed, and husband—
a man without defect in form or mind."   280

Replied the red-haired captain, Meneláos:

"An excellent tale, my dear, and most becoming.
In my life I have met, in many countries,
foresight and wit in many first rate men,
but never have I seen one like Odysseus
for steadiness and a stout heart. Here, for instance,
is what he did—had the cold nerve to do—
inside the hollow horse,[12] where we were waiting,
picked men all of us, for the Trojan slaughter,
when all of a sudden, you came by—I dare say   290
drawn by some superhuman
power that planned an exploit for the Trojans;
and Deïphobos,[13] that handsome man, came with you.
Three times you walked around it, patting it everywhere,
and called by name the flower of our fighters,
making your voice sound like their wives, calling.
Diomêdês and I crouched in the center
along with Odysseus; we could hear you plainly;
and listening, we two were swept
by waves of longing—to reply, or go.   300
Odysseus fought us down, despite our craving,
and all the Akhaians kept their lips shut tight,
all but Antiklos. Desire moved his throat
to hail you, but Odysseus' great hands clamped
over his jaws, and held. So he saved us all,
till Pallas Athena led you away at last."

Then clear-headed Telémakhos addressed him:

"My lord marshal, Meneláos, son of Atreus,
all the more pity, since these valors
could not defend him from annihilation—   310
not if his heart were iron in his breast.

---

[12] The Greeks had hidden some of their best warriors inside a huge wooden horse, which
the Trojans hauled into their city, thus precipitating its overthrow. For a detailed version of
the incident, see Virgil's *Aeneid*, Book II.
[13] By the time of the fall of Troy, Helen had been married to this Trojan prince.

But will you not dismiss us for the night now?
Sweet sleep will be a pleasure, drifting over us."

He said no more, but Helen called the maids
and sent them to make beds, with purple rugs
piled up, and sheets outspread, and fleecy
coverlets, in the porch inside the gate.
The girls went out with torches in their hands,
and presently a squire led the guests—
Telémakhos and Nestor's radiant son—   320
under the entrance colonnade, to bed.
Then deep in the great mansion, in his chamber,
Meneláos went to rest, and Helen,
queenly in her long gown, lay beside him.

When the young Dawn with finger tips of rose
made heaven bright, the deep-lunged man of battle
stood up, pulled on his tunic and his mantle,
slung on a swordbelt and a new edged sword,
tied his smooth feet into fine rawhide sandals
and left his room, a god's brilliance upon him.   330
He sat down by Telémakhos, asking gently:

"Telémakhos, why did you come, sir, riding
the sea's broad back to reach old Lakedaimon?
A public errand or private? Why, precisely?"

Telémakhos replied:

"My lord marshal Meneláos, son of Atreus,
I came to hear what news you had of Father.
My house, my good estates are being ruined.
Each day my mother's bullying suitors come
to slaughter flocks of mine and my black cattle;   340
enemies crowd our home. And this is why
I come to you for news of him who owned it.
Tell me of his death, sir, if perhaps
you witnessed it, or have heard some wanderer
tell the tale. The man was born for trouble.
Spare me no part for kindness' sake; be harsh;
but put the scene before me as you saw it.
If ever Odysseus my noble father
served you by promise kept or work accomplished
in the land of Troy, where you Akhaians suffered,   350
recall those things for me the way they were."

Stirred now to anger, Meneláos said:

"Intolerable—that soft men, as those are,
should think to lie in that great captain's bed.

Fawns in a lion's lair! As if a doe
put down her litter of sucklings there, while she
quested a glen or cropped some grassy hollow.
Ha! Then the lord returns to his own bed
and deals out wretched doom on both alike.
So will Odysseus deal out doom on these.   360
O Father Zeus, Athena, and Apollo!
I pray he comes as once he was, in Lesbos,
when he stood up to wrestle Philomeleidês—
champion and Island King—
and smashed him down. How the Akhaians cheered!
If only that Odysseus met the suitors,
they'd have their consummation, a cold bed!
Now for your questions, let me come to the point.
I would not misreport it for you; let me
tell you what the Ancient of the Sea,[14]   370
who is infallible, said to me—every word.

During my first try at a passage homeward
the gods detained me, tied me down to Egypt—
for I had been too scant in hekatombs,
and gods will have the rules each time remembered.
There is an island washed by the open sea
lying off Nile mouth—seamen call it Pharos—
distant a day's sail in a clean hull
with a brisk land breeze behind. It has a harbor,
a sheltered bay, where shipmasters   380
take on dark water for the outward voyage.
Here the gods held me twenty days becalmed.
No winds came up, seaward escorting winds
for ships that ride the sea's broad back, and so
my stores and men were used up; we were failing
had not one goddess intervened in pity—
Eidothea, daughter of Proteus,
the Ancient of the Sea. How I distressed her!
I had been walking out alone that day—
my sailors, thin-bellied from the long fast,   390
were off with fish hooks, angling on the shore—
then she appeared to me, and her voice sang:

'What fool is here, what drooping dunce of dreams?
Or can it be, friend, that you love to suffer?
How can you linger on this island, aimless
and shiftless, while your people waste away?'

To this I quickly answered:

                                              'Let me tell you,
goddess, whatever goddess you may be,

---

[14] Proteus, who is described in the following passage.

these doldrums are no will of mine. I take it
the gods who own broad heaven are offended.   400
Why don't you tell me—since the gods know everything—
who has me pinned down here?
How am I going to make my voyage home?'

Now she replied in her immortal beauty:

'I'll put it for you clearly as may be, friend.
The Ancient of the Salt Sea haunts this place,
immortal Proteus of Egypt; all the deeps
are known to him; he serves under Poseidon,
and is, they say, my father.
If you could take him by surprise and hold him,   410
he'd give you course and distance for your sailing
homeward across the cold fish-breeding sea.
And should you wish it, noble friend, he'd tell you
all that occurred at home, both good and evil,
while you were gone so long and hard a journey.'

To this I said:

                              'But you, now—you must tell me
how I can trap this venerable sea-god.
He will elude me if he takes alarm;
no man—god knows—can quell a god with ease.'

That fairest of unearthly nymphs replied: 420

'I'll tell you this, too, clearly as may be.
When the sun hangs at high noon in heaven,
the Ancient glides ashore under the Westwind,
hidden by shivering glooms on the clear water,
and rests in caverns hollowed by the sea.
There flippered seals, brine children, shining come
from silvery foam in crowds to lie around him,
exhaling rankness from the deep sea floor.
Tomorrow dawn I'll take you to those caves
and bed you down there. Choose three officers   430
for company—brave men they had better be—
the old one has strange powers, I must tell you.
He goes amid the seals to check their number,
and when he sees them all, and counts them all,
he lies down like a shepherd with his flock.
Here is your opportunity: at this point
gather yourselves, with all your heart and strength,
and tackle him before he bursts away.
He'll make you fight—for he can take the forms
of all the beasts, and water, and blinding fire;   440
but you must hold on, even so, and crush him
until he breaks the silence. When he does,

he will be in that shape you saw asleep.
Relax your grip, then, set the Ancient free,
and put your questions, hero:
Who is the god so hostile to you,
and how will you go home on the fish-cold sea.'

At this she dove under a swell and left me.
Back to the ships in the sandy cove I went,
my heart within me like a high surf running;   450
but there I joined my men once more
at supper, as the sacred Night came on,
and slept at last beside the lapping water.
When Dawn spread out her finger tips of rose
I started, by the sea's wide level ways,
praying the gods for help, and took along
three lads I counted on in any fight.
Meanwhile the nereid[15] swam from the lap of Ocean
laden with four sealskins, new flayed
for the hoax she thought of playing on her father.   460
In the sand she scooped out hollows for our bodies
and sat down, waiting. We came close to touch her,
and, bedding us, she threw the sealskins over us—
a strong disguise; oh, yes, terribly strong
as I recall the stench of those damned seals.
Would any man lie snug with a sea monster?
But here the nymph, again, came to our rescue,
dabbing ambrosia under each man's nose—
a perfume drowning out the bestial odor.
So there we lay with beating hearts all morning   470
while seals came shoreward out of ripples, jostling
to take their places, flopping on the sand.
At noon the Ancient issued from the sea
and held inspection, counting off the sea-beasts.
We were the first he numbered; he went by,
detecting nothing. When at last he slept
we gave a battlecry and plunged for him,
locking our hands behind him. But the old one's
tricks were not knocked out of him; far from it.
First he took on a whiskered lion's shape,   480
a serpent then; a leopard; a great boar;
then sousing water; then a tall green tree.
Still we hung on, by hook or crook, through everything,
until the Ancient saw defeat, and grimly
opened his lips to ask me:

                                             'Son of Atreus,

who counselled you to this? A god: what god?
Set a trap for me, overpower me—why?'

[15] A sea-nymph.

He bit it off, then, and I answered:

                                      'Old one,
you know the reason—why feign not to know?
High and dry so long upon this island   490
I'm at my wits' end, and my heart is sore.
You gods know everything; now you can tell me:
which of the immortals chained me here?
And how will I get home on the fish-cold sea?'

He made reply at once:

                            'You should have paid
honor to Zeus and the other gods, performing
a proper sacrifice before embarking:
that was your short way home on the winedark sea.
You may not see your friends, your own fine house,
or enter your own land again,   500
unless you first remount the Nile in flood
and pay your hekatomb to the gods of heaven.
Then, and then only,
the gods will grant the passage you desire.'

Ah, how my heart sank, hearing this—
hearing him send me back on the cloudy sea
in my own track, the long hard way of Egypt.
Nevertheless, I answered him and said:

'Ancient, I shall do all as you command.
But tell me, now, the others—   510
had they a safe return, all those Akhaians
who stayed behind when Nestor and I left Troy?
Or were there any lost at sea—what bitterness!—
any who died in camp, after the war?'

To this he said:

                        'For you to know these things
goes beyond all necessity, Meneláos.
Why must you ask?—you should not know my mind,
and you will grieve to learn it, I can tell you.
Many there were who died, many remain,
but two high officers alone were lost—   520
on the passage home, I mean; you saw the war.
One is alive, a castaway at sea;
the other, Aîas, perished with all hands—
though first Poseidon landed him on Gyrai[16]
promontory, and saved him from the ocean.

---

[16] An island in the Aegean. Aîas, who in the following lines is described as punished for his insolent and sacrilegious boasting, is the "lesser," "Locrian" Aîas (Ajax), the son of Oileus; he is not the "greater" Aîas who was the son of Télamon.

Despite Athena's hate, he had lived on,
but the great sinner in his insolence
yelled that the gods' will and the sea were beaten,
and this loud brag came to Poseidon's ears.
He swung the trident[17] in his massive hands   530
and in one shock from top to bottom split
that promontory, toppling into the sea
the fragment where the great fool sat.
So the vast ocean had its will with Aîas,
drunk in the end on salt spume as he drowned.
Meanwhile your brother left that doom astern
in his decked ships—the Lady Hera[18] saved him;
but as he came round Malea
a fresh squall caught him, bearing him away
over the cold sea, groaning in disgust,   540
to the Land's End of Argos, where Thyestês[19]
lived in the days of old, and then his son,
Aigísthos. Now, again, return seemed easy:
the high gods wound the wind into the east,
and back he sailed, this time to his own coast.
He went ashore and kissed the earth in joy,
hot tears blinding his eyes at sight of home.
But there were eyes that watched him from a height—
a lookout, paid two bars of gold to keep
vigil the year round for Aigísthos' sake,   550
that he should be forewarned, and Agamémnon's
furious valor sleep unroused.
Now this man with his news ran to the tyrant,
who made his crooked arrangements in a flash,
stationed picked men at arms, a score of men
in hiding; set a feast in the next room;
then he went out with chariots and horses
to hail the king and welcome him to evil.
He led him in to banquet, all serene,
and killed him, like an ox felled at the trough;   560
and not a man of either company
survived that ambush in Aigísthos' house.'

Before the end my heart was broken down.
I slumped on the trampled sand and cried aloud,
caring no more for life or the light of day,
and rolled there weeping, till my tears were spent.
Then the unerring Ancient said at last:

[17] The three-pronged spear wielded by the sea-god Poseidon.
[18] Consort of Zeus; queen of the gods. She consistently sided with the Greeks against the
Trojans.
[19] Brother of Atreus (the father of Agamémnon and Meneláos). See the headnote to
Aeschylus' *Oresteia*. Homer's account here of the murder of Agamémnon differs considerably
from the version in Aeschylus; in the *Oresteia*, Agamémnon's wife Klytaimnéstra plays a more
significant role than does Aigísthos in the murder.

'No more, no more; how long must you persist?
Nothing is gained by grieving so. How soon
can you return to Argos? You may take him   570
alive there still—or else meanwhile Orestês
will have despatched him. You'll attend the feast.'

At this my heart revived, and I recovered
the self command to question him once more:

'Of two companions now I know. The third?
Tell me his name, the one marooned at sea;
living, you say, or dead? Even in pain
I wish to hear.'

                               And this is all he answered:

'Laërtês' son, whose home is Ithaka.
I saw him weeping, weeping on an island.   580
The nymph Kalypso has him, in her hall.
No means of faring home are left him now;
no ship with oars, and no ship's company
to pull him on the broad back of the sea.
As to your own destiny, prince Meneláos,
you shall not die in the bluegrass land of Argos;
rather the gods intend you for Elysion[20]
with golden Rhadamanthos[21] at the world's end,
where all existence is a dream of ease.
Snowfall is never known there, neither long   590
frost of winter, nor torrential rain,
but only mild and lulling airs from Ocean
bearing refreshment for the souls of men—
the West Wind always blowing.

                               For the gods

hold you, as Helen's lord, a son of Zeus.'

At this he dove under a swell and left me,
and I went back to the ship with my companions,
feeling my heart's blood in me running high;
but in the long hull's shadow, near the sea,
we supped again as sacred Night came on   600
and slept at last beside the lapping water.

When Dawn spread out her finger tips of rose,
in first light we launched on the courtly breakers,
setting up masts and yards in the well-found ships;
went all on board, and braced on planks athwart

[20] As presented here in Homer, this realm (also called *Elysium*) is not part of the underground Hades which Odysseus visits later in the *Odyssey*. It is, rather, a happy land on the extreme western surface of the earth.
[21] Ruler of Elysion (sometimes portrayed in ancient literature as a judge of the dead in Hades).

oarsmen in line dipped oars in the grey sea.
Soon I drew in to the great stream[22] fed by heaven
and, laying by, slew bulls in the proper number,
until the immortal gods were thus appeased;
then heaped a death mound on that shore against   610
all-quenching time for Agamémnon's honor,
and put to sea once more. The gods sent down
a sternwind for a racing passage homeward.

So ends the story. Now you must stay with me
and be my guest eleven or twelve days more.
I'll send you on your way with gifts, and fine ones:
three chariot horses, and a polished car;
a hammered cup, too, so that all your days,
tipping the red wine for the deathless gods,
you will remember me."

                                    Telémakhos answered: 620

"Lord, son of Atreus, no, you must not keep me.
Not that a year with you would be too long:
I never could be homesick here—I find
your tales and all you say so marvellous.
But time hangs heavy on my shipmates' hands
at holy Pylos, if you make me stay.
As for your gift, now, let it be some keepsake.
Horses I cannot take to Ithaka;
let me bestow them back on you, to serve
your glory here. My lord, you rule wide country,   630
rolling and rich with clover, galingale
and all the grains: red wheat and hoary barley.
At home we have no level runs or meadows,
but highland, goat land—prettier than plains, though.
Grasses, and pasture land, are hard to come by
upon the islands tilted in the sea,
and Ithaka is the island of them all."

At this the deep-lunged man of battle smiled.
Then he said kindly, patting the boy's hand:

"You come of good stock, lad. That was well spoken.   640
I'll change the gift, then—as indeed I can.
Let me see what is costliest and most beautiful
of all the precious things my house contains:
a wine bowl, mixing bowl, all wrought of silver,
but rimmed with hammered gold. Let this be yours.
It is Hephaistos'[23] work, given me by Phaidimos,

---

[22] The Nile, believed to have a divine source in the sky.
[23] The god of fire and of metal-working. Also spelled *Hephaestus*.

captain and king of Sidon. He received me
during my travels. Let it be yours, I say."

This was their discourse on that morning. Meanwhile
guests were arriving at the great lord's house,   650
bringing their sheep, and wine, the ease of men,
with loaves their comely kerchiefed women sent,
to make a feast in hall.

                                      At that same hour,
before the distant manor of Odysseus,
the suitors were competing at the discus throw
and javelin, on a measured field they used,
arrogant lords at play. The two best men,
Antínoös and Eurýmakhos, presided.
Now Phronios' son, Noêmon, came to see them
with a question for Antínoös. He said: 660

"Do any of us know, or not, Antínoös,
what day Telémakhos will be home from Pylos?
He took my ship, but now I need it back
to make a cruise to Elis, where the plains are.
I have a dozen mares at pasture there
with mule colts yet unweaned. My notion is
to bring one home and break him in for labor."

His first words made them stare—for they knew well
Telémakhos could not have gone to Pylos,
but inland with his flocks, or to the swineherd.   670
Eupeithês' son, Antínoös, quickly answered:

"Tell the story straight. He sailed? Who joined him—
a crew he picked up here in Ithaka,
or his own slaves? He might have done it that way.
And will you make it clear
whether he took the ship against your will?
Did he ask for it, did you lend it to him?"

Now said the son of Phronios in reply:

"Lent it to him, and freely. Who would not,
when a prince of that house asked for it, in trouble?   680
Hard to refuse the favor, it seems to me.
As for his crew, the best men on the island,
after ourselves, went with him. Mentor I noted
going aboard—or a god who looked like Mentor.
The strange thing is, I saw Lord Mentor here
in the first light yesterday—although he sailed
five days ago for Pylos."

                                           Turning away,
Noêmon took the path to his father's house,

leaving the two men there, baffled and hostile.
They called the rest in from the playing field   690
and made them all sit down, so that Antínoös
could speak out from the stormcloud of his heart,
swollen with anger; and his eyes blazed:

"A bad business. Telémakhos had the gall
to make that crossing, though we said he could not.
So the young cub rounds up a first rate crew
in spite of all our crowd, and puts to sea.
What devilment will he be up to next time?—
Zeus blast the life out of him before he's grown!
Just give me a fast ship and twenty men;   700
I'll intercept him, board him in the strait
between the crags of Samê[24] and this island.
He'll find his sea adventure after his father
swamping work in the end!"

                                        They all cried "Aye!"
and "After him!" and trailed back to the manor.

Now not much time went by before Penélopê
learned what was afoot among the suitors.
Medôn the crier told her. He had been
outside the wall, and heard them in the court
conspiring. Into the house and up the stairs   710
he ran to her with his news upon his tongue—
but at the door Penélopê met him, crying:

"Why have they sent you up here now? To tell
the maids of King Odysseus—'Leave your spinning:
Time to go down and slave to feed those men?'
I wish this were the last time they came feasting,
courting me or consorting here! The last!
Each day you crowd this house like wolves
to eat away my brave son's patrimony.
When you were boys, did your own fathers tell you   720
nothing of what Odysseus was for them?
In word and act impeccable, disinterested
toward all the realm—though it is king's justice
to hold one man abhorred and love another;
no man alive could say Odysseus wronged him.
But your own hearts—how different!—and your deeds!
How soon are benefactions all forgotten!"

Now Medôn, the alert and cool man, answered:

"I wish that were the worst of it, my Lady,
but they intend something more terrible—   730

---

[24] An island, modern Cephalonia, south and west of Ithaka; also called Kephallênia in this
poem.

may Zeus forfend and spare us!
They plan to drive the keen bronze through Telémakhos
when he comes home. He sailed away, you know,
to hallowed Pylos and old Lakedaimon
for news about his father."

                                         Her knees failed,
and her heart failed as she listened to the words,
and all her power of speech went out of her.
Tears came; but the rich voice could not come.
Only after a long while she made answer:

"Why has my child left me? He had no need   740
of those long ships on which men shake out sail
to tug like horses, breasting miles of sea.
Why did he go? Must he, too, be forgotten?"

Then Medôn, the perceptive man, replied:

"A god moved him—who knows?—or his own heart
sent him to learn, at Pylos, if his father
roams the wide world still, or what befell him."

He left her then, and went down through the house.
And now the pain around her heart benumbed her;
chairs were a step away, but far beyond her;   750
she sank down on the door sill of the chamber,
wailing, and all her women young and old
made a low murmur of lament around her,
until at last she broke out through her tears:

"Dearest companions, what has Zeus given me?
Pain—more pain than any living woman.
My lord, my lion heart, gone, long ago—
the bravest man, and best, of the Danaans,
famous through Hellas and the Argive midlands—
and now the squalls have blown my son, my dear one,   760
an unknown boy, southward. No one told me.
O brute creatures, not one soul would dare
to wake me from my sleep; you knew
the hour he took the black ship out to sea!
If I had seen that sailing in his eyes
he should have stayed with me, for all his longing,
stayed—or left me dead in the great hall.
Go, someone, now, and call old Dólios,
the slave my father gave me before I came,
my orchard keeper—tell him to make haste   770
and put these things before Laërtês; he
may plan some kind of action; let him come
to cry shame on these ruffians who would murder
Odysseus' son and heir, and end his line!"

The dear old nurse, Eurýkleia, answered her:

"Sweet mistress, have my throat cut without mercy
or what you will; it's true, I won't conceal it,
I knew the whole thing; gave him his provisions;
grain and sweet wine I gave, and a great oath
to tell you nothing till twelve days went by,   780
or till you heard of it yourself, or missed him;
he hoped you would not tear your skin lamenting.
Come, bathe and dress your loveliness afresh,
and go to the upper rooms with all your maids
to ask help from Athena, Zeus's daughter.
She it will be who saves this boy from death.
Spare the old man this further suffering;
the blissful gods cannot so hate his line,
heirs of Arkêsios; one will yet again
be lord of the tall house and the far fields."   790

She hushed her weeping in this way, and soothed her.
The Lady Penélopê arose and bathed,
dressing her body in her freshest linen,
filled a basket with barley, and led her maids
to the upper rooms, where she besought Athena:

"Tireless child of Zeus, graciously hear me!
If ever Odysseus burned at our altar fire
thighbones of beef or mutton in sacrifice,
remember it for my sake! Save my son!
Shield him, and make the killers go astray!"   800

She ended with a cry, and the goddess heard her.
Now voices rose from the shadowy hall below
where the suitors were assuring one another:

"Our so-long-courted Queen is even now
of a mind to marry one of us, and knows
nothing of what is destined for her son."

Of what was destined they in fact knew nothing,
But Antínoös addressed them in a whisper:

"No boasting—are you mad?—and no loud talk:
someone might hear it and alarm the house.   810
Come along now, be quiet, this way; come,
we'll carry out the plan our hearts are set on."

Picking out twenty of the strongest seamen,
he led them to a ship at the sea's edge,
and down they dragged her into deeper water,
stepping a mast in her, with furled sails,
and oars a-trail from thongs looped over thole pins,

ready all; then tried the white sail, hoisting,
while men at arms carried their gear aboard.
They moored the ship some way off shore, and left her
to take their evening meal there, waiting for night to come.

Penélopê at that hour in her high chamber
lay silent, tasting neither food nor drink,
and thought of nothing but her princely son—
could he escape, or would they find and kill him?—
her mind turning at bay, like a cornered lion
in whom fear comes as hunters close the ring.
But in her sick thought sweet sleep overtook her,
and she dozed off, her body slack and still.

Now it occurred to the grey-eyed goddess Athena
to make a figure of dream in a woman's form—
Iphthimê, great Ikários' other daughter,
whom Eumêlos of Phêrai took as bride.
The goddess sent this dream to Odysseus' house
to quiet Penélopê and end her grieving.
So, passing by the strap-slit[25] through the door,
the image came a-gliding down the room
to stand at her bedside and murmur to her:

"Sleepest thou, sorrowing Penélopê?
The gods whose life is ease no longer suffer thee
to pine and weep, then; he returns unharmed,
thy little one; no way hath he offended."

Then pensive Penélopê made this reply,
slumbering sweetly in the gates of dream:

"Sister, hast thou come hither? Why? Aforetime
never wouldst come, so far away thy dwelling.
And am I bid be done with all my grieving?
But see what anguish hath my heart and soul!
My lord, my lion heart, gone, long ago—
the bravest man, and best, of the Danaans,
famous through Hellas and the Argive midlands—
and now my son, my dear one, gone seafaring,
a child, untrained in hardship or in council.
Aye, 'tis for him I weep, more than his father!
Aye, how I tremble for him, lest some blow
befall him at men's hands or on the sea!
Cruel are they and many who plot against him,
to take his life before he can return."

Now the dim phantom spoke to her once more:

---

[25] A hole in a door through which a strap was passed. It allowed a person outside to bolt the door on the inside.

"Lift up thy heart, and fear not overmuch.   860
For by his side one goes whom all men else
invoke as their defender, one so powerful—
Pallas Athena; in thy tears she pitied thee
and now hath sent me that I so assure thee."

Then said Penélopê the wise:

                                                        "If thou art
numinous[26] and hast ears for divine speech,
O tell me, what of Odysseus, man of woe?
Is he alive still somewhere, seeth he day light still?
Or gone in death to the sunless underworld?"

The dim phantom said only this in answer: 870

"Of him I may not tell thee in this discourse,
alive or dead. And empty words are evil."

The wavering form withdrew along the doorbolt
into a draft of wind, and out of sleep
Penélopê awoke, in better heart
for that clear dream in the twilight of the night.

Meanwhile the suitors had got under way,
planning the death plunge for Telémakhos.
Between the Isles of Ithaka and Samê
the sea is broken by an islet, Asteris,   880
with access to both channels from a cove.
In ambush here that night the Akhaians lay.

BOOK FIVE: SWEET NYMPH AND OPEN SEA

Dawn came up from the couch of her reclining,
leaving her lord Tithonos'[1] brilliant side
with fresh light in her arms for gods and men.
And the master of heaven and high thunder, Zeus,
went to his place among the gods assembled
hearing Athena tell Odysseus' woe.
For she, being vexed that he was still sojourning
in the sea chambers of Kalypso,[2] said:

"O Father Zeus and gods in bliss forever,
let no man holding scepter as a king   10

    [26] Gifted with uncanny spiritual powers.
    [1] The lover of Eos, goddess of the dawn. No mention is made here of the most famous
version of his myth, in which Eos wins for him the gift of immortality but forgets, fatefully, to
ensure that Tithonus will never grow older. See Tennyson's poem "Tithonus."
    [2] The nymph's island, Ogýgia, is located in a western region of the Mediterranean. The
geography of Odysseus' wanderings west of Greece is uncertain.

think to be mild, or kind, or virtuous;
let him be cruel, and practice evil ways,
for those Odysseus ruled cannot remember
the fatherhood and mercy of his reign.
Meanwhile he lives and grieves upon that island
in thralldom to the nymph; he cannot stir,
cannot fare homeward, for no ship is left him,
fitted with oars—no crewmen or companions
to pull him on the broad back of the sea.
And now murder is hatched on the high sea   20
against his son, who sought news of his father
in the holy lands of Pylos and Lakedaimon."

To this the summoner of cloud replied:

"My child, what odd complaints you let escape you.
Have you not, you yourself, arranged this matter—
as we all know—so that Odysseus
will bring these men to book, on his return?
And are you not the one to give Telémakhos
a safe route for sailing? Let his enemies
encounter no one and row home again."   30

He turned then to his favorite son and said:

"Hermês, you have much practice on our missions,
go make it known to the softly-braided nymph
that we, whose will is not subject to error,
order Odysseus home; let him depart.
But let him have no company, gods or men,
only a raft that he must lash together,
and after twenty days, worn out at sea,
he shall make land upon the garden isle,
Skhería,[3] of our kinsmen, the Phaiákians.   40
Let these men take him to their hearts in honor
and berth him in a ship, and send him home,
with gifts of garments, gold, and bronze—
so much he had not counted on from Troy
could he have carried home his share of plunder.
His destiny is to see his friends again
under his own roof, in his father's country."

No words were lost on Hermês the Wayfinder,
who bent to tie his beautiful sandals on,
ambrosial, golden, that carry him over water   50
or over endless land in a swish of the wind,
and took the wand with which he charms asleep—

---

[3] The land (also spelled Scheria) of the Phaiákians (Phaeacians), possibly located on the southern shore of the Mediterranean, opposite Ithaka, possibly in Corfu, an island northwest of Ithaka off the west coast of Greece.

or when he wills, awake—the eyes of men.
So wand in hand he paced into the air,
shot from Pieria[4] down, down to sea level,
and veered to skim the swell. A gull patrolling
between the wave crests of the desolate sea
will dip to catch a fish, and douse his wings;
no higher above the whitecaps Hermês flew
until the distant island lay ahead,   60
then rising shoreward from the violet ocean
he stepped up to the cave. Divine Kalypso,
the mistress of the isle, was now at home.
Upon her hearthstone a great fire blazing
scented the farthest shores with cedar smoke
and smoke of thyme, and singing high and low
in her sweet voice, before her loom a-weaving,
she passed her golden shuttle to and fro.
A deep wood grew outside, with summer leaves
of alder and black poplar, pungent cypress.   70
Ornate birds here rested their stretched wings—
horned owls, falcons, cormorants—long-tongued
beachcombing birds, and followers of the sea.
Around the smoothwalled cave a crooking vine
held purple clusters under ply of green;
and four springs, bubbling up near one another
shallow and clear, took channels here and there
through beds of violets and tender parsley.
Even a god who found this place
would gaze, and feel his heart beat with delight: 80
so Hermês did; but when he had gazed his fill
he entered the wide cave. Now face to face
the magical Kalypso recognized him,
as all immortal gods know one another
on sight—though seeming strangers, far from home.
But he saw nothing of the great Odysseus,
who sat apart, as a thousand times before,
and racked his own heart groaning, with eyes wet
scanning the bare horizon of the sea.
Kalypso, lovely nymph, seated her guest   90
in a bright chair all shimmering, and asked:

"O Hermês, ever with your golden wand,
what brings you to my island?
Your awesome visits in the past were few.
Now tell me what request you have in mind;
for I desire to do it, if I can,
and if it is a proper thing to do.
But wait a while, and let me serve my friend."

---

[4] An area on the slopes of Mount Olympos.

She drew a table of ambrosia near him
and stirred a cup of ruby-colored nectar[5]— 100
food and drink for the luminous Wayfinder,
who took both at his leisure, and replied:

"Goddess to god, you greet me, questioning me?
Well, here is truth for you in courtesy.
Zeus made me come, and not my inclination;
who cares to cross that tract of desolation,
the bitter sea, all mortal towns behind
where gods have beef and honors from mankind?
But it is not to be thought of—and no use—
for any god to elude the will of Zeus. 110

He notes your friend, most ill-starred by renown
of all the peers who fought for Priam's town—
nine years of war they had, before great Troy was down.
Homing, they wronged the goddess[6] with grey eyes,
who made a black wind blow and the seas rise,
in which his troops were lost, and all his gear,
while easterlies and current washed him here.
Now the command is: send him back in haste.
His life may not in exile go to waste.
His destiny, his homecoming, is at hand, 120
when he shall see his dearest, and walk on his own land."

That goddess most divinely made
shuddered before him, and her warm voice rose:

"Oh you vile gods, in jealousy supernal!
You hate it when we choose to lie with men—
immortal flesh by some dear mortal side.
So radiant Dawn once took to bed Orion[7]
until you easeful gods grew peevish at it,
and holy Artemis, Artemis throned in gold,
hunted him down in Delos with her arrows. 130
Then Dêmêtêr of the tasseled tresses yielded
to Iasion,[8] mingling and making love
in a furrow three times plowed; but Zeus found out
and killed him with a white-hot thunderbolt.
So now you grudge me, too, my mortal friend.
But it was I who saved him—saw him straddle
his own keel board, the one man left afloat
when Zeus rent wide his ship with chain lightning
and overturned him in the winedark sea.

[5] Ambrosia and nectar were the food and drink of the gods.
[6] Compare the passage in Book IV alluding to the insolence of the lesser Aîas, or Ajax.
[7] A gigantic hunter, loved by Eos.
[8] Probably symbolic of harvest-wealth, since the offspring of his union with Dêmêtêr, goddess of the fields, was Plutus, who symbolized wealth.

Then all his troops were lost, his good companions,   140
but wind and current washed him here to me.
I fed him, loved him, sang that he should not die
nor grow old, ever, in all the days to come.
But now there's no eluding Zeus's will.
If this thing be ordained by him, I say
so be it, let the man strike out alone
on the vast water. Surely I cannot 'send' him.
I have no long-oared ships, no company
to pull him on the broad back of the sea.
My counsel he shall have, and nothing hidden,   150
to help him homeward without harm."

To this the Wayfinder made answer briefly:

"Thus you shall send him, then. And show more grace
in your obedience, or be chastised by Zeus."

The strong god glittering left her as he spoke,
and now her ladyship, having given heed
to Zeus's mandate, went to find Odysseus
in his stone seat to seaward—tear on tear
brimming his eyes. The sweet days of his life time
were running out in anguish over his exile,   160
for long ago the nymph had ceased to please.
Though he fought shy of her and her desire,
he lay with her each night, for she compelled him.
But when day came he sat on the rocky shore
and broke his own heart groaning, with eyes wet
scanning the bare horizon of the sea.
Now she stood near him in her beauty, saying:

"O forlorn man, be still.
Here you need grieve no more; you need not feel
your life consumed here; I have pondered it,   170
and I shall help you go.
Come and cut down high timber for a raft
or flatboat; make her broad-beamed, and decked over,
so you can ride her on the misty sea.
Stores I shall put aboard for you—bread, water,
and ruby-colored wine, to stay your hunger—
give you a seacloak and a following wind
to help you homeward without harm—provided
the gods who rule wide heaven wish it so.
Stronger than I they are, in mind and power."   180

For all he had endured, Odysseus shuddered.
But when he spoke, his words went to the mark:

"After these years, a helping hand? O goddess,
what guile is hidden here?

A raft, you say, to cross the Western Ocean,[9]
rough water, and unknown? Seaworthy ships
that glory in god's wind will never cross it.
I take no raft you grudge me out to sea.
Or yield me first a great oath, if I do,
to work no more enchantment to my harm."   190

At this the beautiful nymph Kalypso smiled
and answered sweetly, laying her hand upon him:

"What a dog you are! And not for nothing learned,
having the wit to ask this thing of me!
My witness then be earth and sky
and dripping Styx[10] that I swear by—
the gay gods cannot swear more seriously—
I have no further spells to work against you.
But what I shall devise, and what I tell you,
will be the same as if your need were mine.   200
Fairness is all I think of. There are hearts
made of cold iron—but my heart is kind."

Swiftly she turned and led him to her cave,
and they went in, the mortal and immortal.
He took the chair left empty now by Hermês,
where the divine Kalypso placed before him
victuals and drink of men; then she sat down
facing Odysseus, while her serving maids
brought nectar and ambrosia to her side.
Then each one's hands went out on each one's feast   210
until they had had their pleasure; and she said:

"Son of Laërtês, versatile Odysseus,
after these years with me, you still desire
your old home? Even so, I wish you well.
If you could see it all, before you go—
all the adversity you face at sea—
you would stay here, and guard this house, and be
immortal—though you wanted her forever,
that bride for whom you pine each day.
Can I be less desirable than she is?   220
Less interesting? Less beautiful? Can mortals
compare with goddesses in grace and form?"

To this the strategist Odysseus answered:

"My lady goddess, here is no cause for anger.
My quiet Penélopê—how well I know—
would seem a shade before your majesty,

---

[9] The western Mediterranean.
[10] A river in Hades, the realm of the dead. To swear by Styx was the most solemn oath a deity could utter.

death and old age being unknown to you,
while she must die. Yet, it is true, each day
I long for home, long for the sight of home.
If any god has marked me out again   230
for shipwreck, my tough heart can undergo it.
What hardship have I not long since endured
at sea, in battle! Let the trial come."

Now as he spoke the sun set, dusk drew on,
and they retired, this pair, to the inner cave
to revel and rest softly, side by side.

When Dawn spread out her finger tips of rose
Odysseus pulled his tunic and his cloak on,
while the sea nymph dressed in a silvery gown
of subtle tissue, drew about her waist   240
a golden belt, and veiled her head, and then
took thought for the great-hearted hero's voyage.
A brazen axehead first she had to give him,
two-bladed, and agreeable to the palm
with a smooth-fitting haft of olive wood;
next a well-polished adze; and then she led him
to the island's tip where bigger timber grew—
besides the alder and poplar, tall pine trees,
long dead and seasoned, that would float him high.
Showing him in that place her stand of timber   250
the loveliest of nymphs took her way home.
Now the man fell to chopping; when he paused
twenty tall trees were down. He lopped the branches,
split the trunks, and trimmed his puncheons true.
Meanwhile Kalypso brought him an auger tool
with which he drilled through all his planks, then drove
stout pins to bolt them, fitted side by side.
A master shipwright, building a cargo vessel,
lays down a broad and shallow hull; just so
Odysseus shaped the bottom of his craft.   260
He made his decking fast to close-set ribs
before he closed the side with longer planking,
then cut a mast pole, and proper yard,
and shaped a steering oar to hold her steady.
He drove long strands of willow in all the seams
to keep out waves, and ballasted with logs.
As for a sail, the lovely nymph Kalypso
brought him a cloth so he could make that, too.
Then he ran up his rigging—halyards, braces—
and hauled the boat on rollers to the water.   270

This was the fourth day, when he had all ready;
on the fifth day, she sent him out to sea.
But first she bathed him, gave him a scented cloak,

and put on board a skin of dusky wine
with water in a bigger skin, and stores—
boiled meats and other victuals—in a bag.
Then she conjured a warm landbreeze to blowing—
joy for Odysseus when he shook out sail!
Now the great seaman, leaning on his oar,
steered all the night unsleeping, and his eyes   280
picked out the Pleiadês, the laggard Ploughman,
and the Great Bear, that some have called the Wain,
pivoting in the sky before Orion;
of all the night's pure figures, she alone
would never bathe or dip in the Ocean stream.[11]
These stars the beautiful Kalypso bade him
hold on his left hand as he crossed the main.
Seventeen nights and days in the open water
he sailed, before a dark shoreline appeared;
Skhería then came slowly into view   290
like a rough shield of bull's hide on the sea.

But now the god of earthquake, storming home
over the mountains of Asia from the Sunburned land,
sighted him far away. The god grew sullen
and tossed his great head, muttering to himself:

"Here is a pretty cruise! While I was gone
the gods have changed their minds about Odysseus.
Look at him now, just offshore of that island
that frees him from the bondage of his exile!
Still I can give him a rough ride in, and will."   300

Brewing high thunderheads, he churned the deep
with both hands on his trident—called up wind
from every quarter, and sent a wall of rain
to blot out land and sea in torrential night.
Hurricane winds now struck from the South and East
shifting North West in a great spume of seas,
on which Odysseus' knees grew slack, his heart
sickened, and he said within himself:

"Rag of man that I am, is this the end of me?
I fear the goddess told it all too well—   310
predicting great adversity at sea
and far from home. Now all things bear her out:
the whole rondure[12] of heaven hooded so
by Zeus in woeful cloud, and the sea raging
under such winds. I am going down, that's sure.

---

[11] In northern latitudes, the Big Dipper (the Great Bear, or Wain) never sets but rather
circles around Polaris, the North Star. For Odysseus to keep the constellation on his left would
require him to sail eastward.
[12] Circle or sphere.

How lucky those Danaans were who perished
on Troy's wide seaboard, serving the Atreidai![13]
Would God I, too, had died there—met my end
that time the Trojans made so many casts at me
when I stood by Akhilleus after death.   320
I should have had a soldier's burial
and praise from the Akhaians—not this choking
waiting for me at sea, unmarked and lonely."

A great wave drove at him with toppling crest
spinning him round, in one tremendous blow,
and he went plunging overboard, the oar-haft
wrenched from his grip. A gust that came on howling
at the same instant broke his mast in two,
hurling his yard and sail far out to leeward.
Now the big wave a long time kept him under,   330
helpless to surface, held by tons of water,
tangled, too, by the seacloak of Kalypso.
Long, long, until he came up spouting brine,
with streamlets gushing from his head and beard;
but still bethought him, half-drowned as he was,
to flounder for the boat and get a handhold
into the bilge—to crouch there, foiling death.
Across the foaming water, to and fro,
the boat careered like a ball of tumbleweed
blown on the autumn plains, but intact still.   340
So the winds drove this wreck over the deep,
East Wind and North Wind, then South Wind and West,
coursing each in turn to the brutal harry.

But Ino[14] saw him—Ino, Kadmos' daughter,
slim-legged, lovely, once an earthling girl,
now in the seas a nereid, Leukothea.
Touched by Odysseus' painful buffeting
she broke the surface, like a diving bird,
to rest upon the tossing raft and say:

"O forlorn man, I wonder   350
why the Earthshaker, Lord Poseidon, holds
this fearful grudge—father of all your woes.
He will not drown you, though, despite his rage.
You seem clear-headed still; do what I tell you.
Shed that cloak, let the gale take your craft,
and swim for it—swim hard to get ashore
upon Skhería, yonder,
where it is fated that you find a shelter.
Here: make my veil your sash; it is not mortal;

[13] Sons of Atreus—Agamémnon and Meneláos.
[14] Maddened by Hera, who was jealous of her for helping to rear the young god Dionysos,
Ino leaped into the sea and was transformed into a nereid, or sea-nymph.

you cannot, now, be drowned or suffer harm.   360
Only, the instant you lay hold of earth,
discard it, cast it far, far out from shore
in the winedark sea again, and turn away."

After she had bestowed her veil, the nereid
dove like a gull to windward
where a dark waveside closed over her whiteness.
But in perplexity Odysseus
said to himself, his great heart laboring:

"O damned confusion! Can this be a ruse
to trick me from the boat for some god's pleasure?   370
No I'll not swim; with my own eyes I saw
how far the land lies that she called my shelter.
Better to do the wise thing, as I see it.
While this poor planking holds, I stay aboard;
I may ride out the pounding of the storm,
or if she cracks up, take to the water then;
I cannot think it through a better way."

But even while he pondered and decided,
the god of earthquake heaved a wave against him
high as a rooftree and of awful gloom.   380
A gust of wind, hitting a pile of chaff,
will scatter all the parched stuff far and wide;
just so, when this gigantic billow struck
the boat's big timbers flew apart. Odysseus
clung to a single beam, like a jockey riding,
meanwhile stripping Kalypso's cloak away;
then he slung round his chest the veil of Ino
and plunged headfirst into the sea. His hands
went out to stroke, and he gave a swimmer's kick.
But the strong Earthshaker had him under his eye,   390
and nodded as he said:

                             "Go on, go on;
wander the high seas this way, take your blows,
before you join that race the gods have nurtured.[15]
Nor will you grumble, even then, I think,
for want of trouble."

                             Whipping his glossy team
he rode off to his glorious home at Aigai.[16]
But Zeus's daughter Athena countered him:
she checked the course of all the winds but one,
commanding them, "Be quiet and go to sleep."
Then sent a long swell running under a norther   400

---

[15] The Phaiákians, or Phaeacians.   [16] An Akhaian city.

to bear the prince Odysseus, back from danger,
to join the Phaiákians, people of the sea.

Two nights, two days, in the solid deep-sea swell
he drifted, many times awaiting death,
until with shining ringlets in the East
the dawn confirmed a third day, breaking clear
over a high and windless sea; and mounting
a rolling wave he caught a glimpse of land.
What a dear welcome thing life seems to children
whose father, in the extremity, recovers   410
after some weakening and malignant illness:
his pangs are gone, the gods have delivered him.
So dear and welcome to Odysseus
the sight of land, of woodland, on that morning.
It made him swim again, to get a foothold
on solid ground. But when he came in earshot
he heard the trampling roar of sea on rock,
where combers, rising shoreward, thudded down
on the sucking ebb—all sheeted with salt foam.
Here were no coves or harborage or shelter,   420
only steep headlands, rockfallen reefs and crags.
Odysseus' knees grew slack, his heart faint,
a heaviness came over him, and he said:

"A cruel turn, this. Never had I thought
to see this land, but Zeus has let me see it—
and let me, too, traverse the Western Ocean—
only to find no exit from these breakers.
Here are sharp rocks off shore, and the sea a smother
rushing around them; rock face rising sheer
from deep water; nowhere could I stand up   430
on my two feet and fight free of the welter.
No matter how I try it, the surf may throw me
against the cliffside; no good fighting there.
If I swim down the coast, outside the breakers,
I may find shelving shore and quiet water—
but what if another gale comes on to blow?
Then I go cursing out to sea once more.
Or then again, some shark of Amphitritê's[17]
may hunt me, sent by the genius of the deep.
I know how he who makes earth tremble hates me."   440

During this meditation a heavy surge
was taking him, in fact, straight on the rocks.
He had been flayed there, and his bones broken,
had not grey-eyed Athena instructed him:
he gripped a rock-ledge with both hands in passing

---

[17] A sea-nymph, consort of Poseidon and thus queen of the ocean.

and held on, groaning, as the surge went by,
to keep clear of its breaking. Then the backwash
hit him, ripping him under and far out.
An octopus, when you drag one from his chamber,
comes up with suckers full of tiny stones: 450
Odysseus left the skin of his great hands
torn on that rock-ledge as the wave submerged him.
And now at last Odysseus would have perished,
battered inhumanly, but he had the gift
of self-possession from grey-eyed Athena.
So, when the backwash spewed him up again,
he swam out and along, and scanned the coast
for some landspit that made a breakwater.
Lo and behold, the mouth of a calm river
at length came into view, with level shores 460
unbroken, free from rock, shielded from wind—
by far the best place he had found.
But as he felt the current flowing seaward
he prayed in his heart:

                 "O hear me, lord of the stream:
how sorely I depend upon your mercy!
derelict as I am by the sea's anger.
Is he not sacred, even to the gods,
the wandering man who comes, as I have come,
in weariness before your knees, your waters?
Here is your servant; lord, have mercy on me." 470

Now even as he prayed the tide at ebb
had turned, and the river god made quiet water,
drawing him in to safety in the shallows.
His knees buckled, his arms gave way beneath him,
all vital force now conquered by the sea.
Swollen from head to foot he was, and seawater
gushed from his mouth and nostrils. There he lay,
scarce drawing breath, unstirring, deathly spent.
In time, as air came back into his lungs
and warmth around his heart, he loosed the veil, 480
letting it drift away on the estuary
downstream to where a white wave took it under
and Ino's hands received it. Then the man
crawled to the river bank among the reeds
where, face down, he could kiss the soil of earth,
in his exhaustion murmuring to himself:

"What more can this hulk suffer? What comes now?
In vigil through the night here by the river
how can I not succumb, being weak and sick,
to the night's damp and hoarfrost of the morning? 490
The air comes cold from rivers before dawn.
But if I climb the slope and fall asleep

in the dark forest's undergrowth—supposing
cold and fatigue will go, and sweet sleep come—
I fear I make the wild beasts easy prey."

But this seemed best to him, as he thought it over.
He made his way to a grove above the water
on open ground, and crept under twin bushes
grown from the same spot—olive and wild olive—
a thicket proof against the stinging wind   500
or Sun's blaze, fine soever the needling sunlight;
nor could a downpour wet it through, so dense
those plants were interwoven. Here Odysseus
tunnelled, and raked together with his hands
a wide bed—for a fall of leaves was there,
enough to save two men or maybe three
on a winter night, a night of bitter cold.
Odysseus' heart laughed when he saw his leaf-bed,
and down he lay, heaping more leaves above him.

A man in a distant field, no hearthfires near,   510
will hide a fresh brand in his bed of embers
to keep a spark alive for the next day;
so in the leaves Odysseus hid himself,
while over him Athena showered sleep
that his distress should end, and soon, soon.
In quiet sleep she sealed his cherished eyes.

BOOK SIX: THE PRINCESS AT THE RIVER

Far gone in weariness, in oblivion,
the noble and enduring man slept on;
but Athena in the night went down the land
of the Phaiákians, entering their city.
In days gone by, these men held Hypereia,
a country of wide dancing grounds, but near them
were overbearing Kyklopês,[1] whose power
could not be turned from pillage. So the Phaiákians
migrated thence under Nausíthoös
to settle a New World across the sea,   10
Skhería Island. That first captain walled
their promontory, built their homes and shrines,
and parcelled out the black land for the plow.
But he had gone down long ago to Death.
Alkínoös ruled, and Heaven gave him wisdom,
so on this night the goddess, grey-eyed Athena,

[1] These monstrous giants of Sicily are described in Book IX. *Hypereia* means "highlands"; their location is uncertain.

entered the palace of Alkínoös
to make sure of Odysseus' voyage home.
She took her way to a painted bedchamber
where a young girl lay fast asleep—so fine   20
in mould and feature that she seemed a goddess—
the daughter of Alkínoös, Nausikaa.
On either side, as Graces[2] might have slept,
her maids were sleeping. The bright doors were shut,
but like a sudden stir of wind, Athena
moved to the bedside of the girl, and grew
visible as the shipman Dymas' daughter,
a girl the princess' age, and her dear friend.
In this form grey-eyed Athena said to her:

"How so remiss, and yet thy mother's daughter?   30
leaving thy clothes uncared for, Nausikaa,
when soon thou must have store of marriage linen,
and put thy minstrelsy in wedding dress!
Beauty, in these, will make folk admire,
and bring thy father and gentle mother joy.
Let us go washing in the shine of morning!
Beside thee will I drub, so wedding chests
will brim by evening. Maidenhood must end!
Have not the noblest born Phaiákians
paid court to thee, whose birth none can excel?   40
Go beg thy sovereign father, even at dawn,
to have the mule cart and the mules brought round
to take thy body-linen, gowns and mantles.
Thou shouldst ride, for it becomes thee more,
the washing pools are found so far from home."

On this word she departed, grey-eyed Athena,
to where the gods have their eternal dwelling—
as men say—in the fastness of Olympos.
Never a tremor of wind, or a splash of rain,
no errant snowflake comes to stain that heaven,   50
so calm, so vaporless, the world of light.
Here, where the gay gods live their days of pleasure,
the grey-eyed one withdrew, leaving the princess.

And now Dawn took her own fair throne, awaking
the girl in the sweet gown, still charmed by dream.
Down through the rooms she went to tell her parents,
whom she found still at home: her mother seated
near the great hearth among her maids—and twirling
out of her distaff yarn dyed like the sea—;
her father at the door, bound for a council   60

_____

[2] Three goddesses who personify grace and beauty.

of princes on petition of the gentry.
She went up close to him and softly said:

"My dear Papà, could you not send the mule cart
around for me—the gig with pretty wheels?
I must take all our things and get them washed
at the river pools; our linen is all soiled.
And you should wear fresh clothing, going to council
with counselors and first men of the realm.
Remember your five sons at home: though two
are married, we have still three bachelor sprigs;   70
they will have none but laundered clothes each time
they go to the dancing. See what I must think of!"

She had no word to say of her own wedding,
though her keen father saw her blush. Said he:

"No mules would I deny you, child, nor anything.
Go along, now; the grooms will bring your gig
with pretty wheels and the cargo box upon it."

He spoke to the stableman, who soon brought round
the cart, low-wheeled and nimble;
harnessed the mules, and backed them in their traces.   80
Meanwhile the girl fetched all her soiled apparel
to bundle in the polished wagon box.
Her mother, for their luncheon, packed a hamper
with picnic fare, and filled a skin of wine,
and, when the princess had been handed up,
gave her a golden bottle of olive oil
for softening girls' bodies, after bathing.
Nausikaa took the reins and raised her whip,
lashing the mules. What jingling! What a clatter!
But off they went in a ground-covering trot,   90
with princess, maids, and laundry drawn behind.
By the lower river where the wagon came
were washing pools, with water all year flowing
in limpid spillways that no grime withstood.
The girls unhitched the mules, and sent them down
along the eddying stream to crop sweet grass.
Then sliding out the cart's tail board, they took
armloads of clothing to the dusky water,
and trod them in the pits, making a race of it.
All being drubbed, all blemish rinsed away,   100
they spread them, piece by piece, along the beach
whose pebbles had been laundered by the sea;
then took a dip themselves, and, all anointed
with golden oil, ate lunch beside the river
while the bright burning sun dried out their linen.
Princess and maids delighted in that feast;
then, putting off their veils,

they ran and passed a ball to a rhythmic beat,
Nausikaa flashing first with her white arms.

So Artemis goes flying after her arrows flown   110
down some tremendous valley-side—
                              Taÿgetos, Erymanthos—
chasing the mountain goats or ghosting deer,
with nymphs of the wild places flanking her;
and Lêto's[3] heart delights to see them running,
for, taller by a head than nymphs can be,
the goddess shows more stately, all being beautiful.
So one could tell the princess from the maids.

Soon it was time, she knew, for riding homeward—
mules to be harnessed, linen folded smooth—
but the grey-eyed goddess Athena made her tarry,   120
so that Odysseus might behold her beauty
and win her guidance to the town.

                                                 It happened

when the king's daughter threw her ball off line
and missed, and put it in the whirling stream,—
at which they all gave such a shout, Odysseus
awoke and sat up, saying to himself:

"Now, by my life, mankind again! But who?
Savages, are they, strangers to courtesy?
Or gentle folk, who know and fear the gods?
That was a lust cry of tall young girls—   130
most like the cry of nymphs, who haunt the peaks,
and springs of brooks, and inland grassy places.
Or am I amid people of human speech?
Up again, man; and let me see for myself."

He pushed aside the bushes, breaking off
with his great hand a single branch of olive,
whose leaves might shield him in his nakedness;
so came out rustling, like a mountain lion,
rain-drenched, wind-buffeted, but in his might at ease,
with burning eyes—who prowls among the herds   140
or flocks, or after game, his hungry belly
taking him near stout homesteads for his prey.
Odysseus had this look, in his rough skin
advancing on the girls with pretty braids;
and he was driven on by hunger, too.
Streaked with brine, and swollen, he terrified them,
so that they fled, this way and that. Only
Alkínoös' daughter stood her ground, being given
a bold heart by Athena, and steady knees.

---

[3] Mother of Artemis, goddess of the hunt. Taÿgetos and Erymanthos are mountainous
places in Greece.

She faced him, waiting. And Odysseus came,   150
debating inwardly what he should do:
embrace this beauty's knees in supplication?
or stand apart, and, using honeyed speech,
inquire the way to town, and beg some clothing?
In his swift reckoning, he thought it best
to trust in words to please her—and keep away;
he might anger the girl, touching her knees.
So he began, and let the soft words fall:

"Mistress: please: are you divine, or mortal?
If one of those who dwell in the wide heaven,   160
you are most near to Artemis, I should say—
great Zeus's daughter—in your grace and presence.
If you are one of earth's inhabitants,
how blest your father, and your gentle mother,
blest all your kin. I know what happiness
must send the warm tears to their eyes, each time
they see their wondrous child go to the dancing!
But one man's destiny is more than blest—
he who prevails, and takes you as his bride.
Never have I laid eyes on equal beauty   170
in man or woman. I am hushed indeed.
So fair, one time, I thought a young palm tree
at Delos[4] near the altar of Apollo—
I had troops under me when I was there
on the sea route that later brought me grief—
but that slim palm tree filled my heart with wonder:
never came shoot from earth so beautiful.
So now, my lady, I stand in awe so great
I cannot take your knees. And yet my case is desperate:
twenty days, yesterday, in the winedark sea,   180
on the ever-lunging swell, under gale winds,
getting away from the Island of Ogýgia.
And now the terror of Storm has left me stranded
upon this shore—with more blows yet to suffer,
I must believe, before the gods relent.
Mistress, do me a kindness!
After much weary toil, I come to you,
and you are the first soul I have seen—I know
no others here. Direct me to the town,
give me a rag that I can throw around me,   190
some cloth or wrapping that you brought along.
And may the gods accomplish your desire:
a home, a husband, and harmonious
converse with him—the best thing in the world
being a strong house held in serenity

---

[4] An island in the Aegean Sea, birthplace of Apollo and sacred to him.

where man and wife agree. Woe to their enemies,
joy to their friends! But all this they know best."

Then she of the white arms, Nausikaa, replied:

"Stranger, there is no quirk or evil in you   200
that I can see. You know Zeus metes out fortune
to good and bad men as it pleases him.
Hardship he sent to you, and you must bear it.
But now that you have taken refuge here
you shall not lack for clothing, or any other
comfort due to a poor man in distress.
The town lies this way, and the men are called
Phaiákians, who own the land and city.
I am daughter to the Prince Alkínoös,
by whom the power of our people stands."
Turning, she called out to her maids-in-waiting: 210

"Stay with me! Does the sight of a man scare you?
Or do you take this one for an enemy?
Why, there's no fool so brash, and never will be,
as to bring war or pillage to this coast,
for we are dear to the immortal gods,
living here, in the sea that rolls forever,
distant from other lands and other men.
No: this man is a castaway, poor fellow;
we must take care of him. Strangers and beggars
come from Zeus: a small gift, then, is friendly.   220
Give our new guest some food and drink, and take him
into the river, out of the wind, to bathe."

They stood up now, and called to one another
to go on back. Quite soon they led Odysseus
under the river bank, as they were bidden;
and there laid out a tunic, and a cloak,
and gave him olive oil in the golden flask.
"Here," they said, "go bathe in the flowing water."
But heard now from that kingly man, Odysseus:

"Maids," he said, "keep away a little; let me   230
wash the brine from my own back, and rub on
plenty of oil. It is long since my anointing.
I take no bath, however, where you can see me—
naked before young girls with pretty braids."

They left him, then, and went to tell the princess.
And now Odysseus, dousing in the river,
scrubbed the coat of brine from back and shoulders
and rinsed the clot of sea-spume from his hair;
got himself all rubbed down, from head to foot,
then he put on the clothes the princess gave him.   240

Athena lent a hand, making him seem
taller, and massive too, with crisping hair
in curls like petals of wild hyacinth,
but all red-golden. Think of gold infused
on silver by a craftsman, whose fine art
Hephaistos taught him, or Athena: one
whose work moves to delight: just so she lavished
beauty over Odysseus' head and shoulders.
Then he went down to sit on the sea beach
in his new splendor. There the girl regarded him,   250
and after a time she said to the maids beside her:

"My gentlewomen, I have a thing to tell you.
The Olympian gods cannot be all averse
to this man's coming here among our islanders.
Uncouth he seemed, I thought so, too, before;
but now he looks like one of heaven's people.
I wish my husband could be fine as he
and glad to stay forever on Skhería!
But have you given refreshment to our guest?"

At this the maids, all gravely listening, hastened   260
to set out bread and wine before Odysseus,
and ah! how ravenously that patient man
took food and drink, his long fast at an end.

The princess Nausikaa now turned aside
to fold her linens; in the pretty cart
she stowed them, put the mule team under harness,
mounted the driver's seat, and then looked down
to say with cheerful prompting to Odysseus:

"Up with you now, friend; back to town we go;
and I shall send you in before my father   270
who is wondrous wise; there in our house with him
you'll meet the noblest of the Phaiákians.
You have good sense, I think; here's how to do it:
while we go through the countryside and farmland
stay with my maids, behind the wagon, walking
briskly enough to follow where I lead.
But near the town—well, there's a wall with towers
around the Isle, and beautiful ship basins
right and left of the causeway of approach;
seagoing craft are beached beside the road   280
each on its launching ways. The agora,[5]
with fieldstone benches bedded in the earth,
lies either side Poseidon's shrine—for there
men are at work on pitch-black hulls and rigging,
cables and sails, and tapering of oars.

[5] Public meeting-place.

The archer's craft is not for the Phaiákians,
but ship designing, modes of oaring cutters
in which they love to cross the foaming sea.
From these fellows I will have no salty talk,
no gossip later. Plenty are insolent.   290
And some seadog might say, after we passed:
'Who is this handsome stranger trailing Nausikaa?
Where did she find him? Will he be her husband?
Or is she being hospitable to some rover
come off his ship from lands across the sea—
there being no lands nearer. A god, maybe?
a god from heaven, the answer to her prayer,
descending now—to make her his forever?
Better, if she's roamed and found a husband
somewhere else: none of our own will suit her,   300
though many come to court her, and those the best.'
This is the way they might make light of me.
And I myself should hold it shame
for any girl to flout her own dear parents,
taking up with a man, before her marriage.

Note well, now, what I say, friend, and your chances
are excellent for safe conduct from my father.
You'll find black poplars in a roadside park
around a meadow and fountain—all Athena's—
but Father has a garden in the place—   310
this within earshot of the city wall.
Go in there and sit down, giving us time
to pass through town and reach my father's house.
And when you can imagine we're at home,
then take the road into the city, asking
directions to the palace of Alkínoös.
You'll find it easily: any small boy
can take you there; no family has a mansion
half so grand as he does, being king.
As soon as you are safe inside, cross over   320
and go straight through into the mégaron[6]
to find my mother. She'll be there in firelight
before a column, with her maids in shadow,
spinning a wool dyed richly as the sea.
My father's great chair faces the fire, too;
there like a god he sits and takes his wine.
Go past him; cast yourself before my mother,
embrace her knees—and you may wake up soon
at home rejoicing, though your home be far.
On Mother's feeling much depends; if she   330
looks on you kindly, you shall see your friends
under your own roof in your father's country."

---

[6] The great hall of the house.

At this she raised her glistening whip, lashing
the team into a run; they left the river
cantering beautifully, then trotted smartly.
But then she reined them in, and spared the whip,
so that her maids could follow with Odysseus.
The sun was going down when they went by
Athena's grove. Here, then, Odysseus rested,
and lifted up his prayer to Zeus's daughter: 340

"Hear me, unwearied child of royal Zeus!
O listen to me now—thou so aloof
while the Earthshaker wrecked and battered me.
May I find love and mercy among these people."

He prayed for that, and Pallas Athena heard him—
although in deference to her father's brother[7]
she would not show her true form to Odysseus,
at whom Poseidon smoldered on
until the kingly man came home to his own shore.

BOOK SEVEN: GARDENS AND FIRELIGHT

As Lord Odysseus prayed there in the grove
the girl rode on, behind her strapping team,
and came late to the mansion of her father,
where she reined in at the courtyard gate. Her brothers
awaited her like tall gods in the court,
circling to lead the mules away and carry
the laundered things inside. But she withdrew
to her own bedroom, where a fire soon shone,
kindled by her old nurse, Eurymedousa.
Years ago, from a raid on the continent,   10
the rolling ships had brought this woman over
to be Alkínoös' share—fit spoil for him
whose realm hung on his word as on a god's.
And she had schooled the princess, Nausikaa,
whose fire she tended now, making her supper.

Odysseus, when the time had passed, arose
and turned into the city. But Athena
poured a sea fog around him as he went—
her love's expedient, that no jeering sailor
should halt the man or challenge him for luck.   20
Instead, as he set foot in the pleasant city,
the grey-eyed goddess came to him, in figure
a small girl child, hugging a water jug.

---

[7] Poseidon, brother of Athena's father, Zeus.

Confronted by her, Lord Odysseus asked:

"Little one, could you take me to the house
of that Alkínoös, king among these people?
You see, I am a poor old stranger here;
my home is far away; here there is no one
known to me, in countryside or city."

The grey-eyed goddess Athena replied to him: 30

"Oh, yes, good grandfer, sir, I know, I'll show you
the house you mean; it is quite near my father's.
But come now, hush, like this, and follow me.
You must not stare at people, or be inquisitive.
They do not care for strangers in this neighborhood;
a foreign man will get no welcome here.
The only things they trust are the racing ships
Poseidon gave, to sail the deep blue sea
like white wings in the sky, or a flashing thought."

Pallas Athena turned like the wind, running   40
ahead of him, and he followed in her footsteps.
And no seafaring men of Phaiákia
perceived Odysseus passing through their town:
the awesome one in pigtails barred their sight
with folds of sacred mist. And yet Odysseus
gazed out marvelling at the ships and harbors,
public squares, and ramparts towering up
with pointed palisades along the top.
When they were near the mansion of the king,
grey-eyed Athena in the child cried out: 50

"Here it is, grandfer, sir—that mansion house
you asked to see. You'll find our king and queen
at supper, but you must not be dismayed;
go in to them. A cheerful man does best
in every enterprise—even a stranger.
You'll see our lady just inside the hall—
her name is Arêtê; her grandfather
was our good king Alkínoös's father—
Nausithoös by name, son of Poseidon
and Periboia. That was a great beauty,   60
the daughter of Eurymedon, commander
of the Gigantês[1] in the olden days,
who led those wild things to their doom and his.
Poseidon then made love to Periboia,
and she bore Nausíthoös, Phaiákia's lord,
whose sons in turn were Rhêxênor and Alkínoös.
Rhêxênor had no sons; even as a bridegroom

---

[1] The Giants, enormous semihuman beings, offspring of Ge, an ancient earth-goddess.

he fell before the silver bow of Apollo,
his only child a daughter, Arêtê.
When she grew up, Alkínoös married her   70
and holds her dear. No lady in the world,
no other mistress of a man's household,
is honored as our mistress is, and loved,
by her own children, by Alkínoös,
and by the people. When she walks the town
they murmur and gaze, as though she were a goddess.
No grace or wisdom fails in her; indeed
just men in quarrels come to her for equity.
Supposing, then, she looks upon you kindly,
the chances are that you shall see your friends   80
under your own roof, in your father's country."

At this the grey-eyed goddess Athena left him
and left that comely land, going over sea
to Marathon, to the wide roadways of Athens
and her retreat in the stronghold of Erekhtheus.[2]
Odysseus, now alone before the palace,
meditated a long time before crossing
the brazen threshold of the great courtyard.
High rooms he saw ahead, airy and luminous
as though with lusters of the sun and moon,   90
bronze-paneled walls, at several distances,
making a vista, with an azure molding
of lapis lazuli.[3] The doors were golden
guardians of the great room. Shining bronze
plated the wide door sill; the posts and lintel
were silver upon silver; golden handles
curved on the doors, and golden, too, and silver
were sculptured hounds, flanking the entrance way,
cast by the skill and ardor of Hephaistos
to guard the prince Alkínoös's house—   100
undying dogs that never could grow old.
Through all the rooms, as far as he could see,
tall chairs were placed around the walls, and strewn
with fine embroidered stuff made by the women.
Here were enthroned the leaders of Phaiákia
drinking and dining, with abundant fare.
Here, too, were boys of gold on pedestals
holding aloft bright torches of pitch pine
to light the great rooms, and the night-time feasting.
And fifty maids-in-waiting of the household   110
sat by the round mill, grinding yellow corn,

---

[2] Legendary ruler of Athens, Athena's city. Marathon (several centuries after Homer's time
the site of a great Greek victory over the Persians) was a plain near Athens, cherished by
Athena.
[3] Fine blue stone.

or wove upon their looms, or twirled their distaffs,
flickering like the leaves of a poplar tree;
while drops of oil glistened on linen weft.
Skillful as were the men of Phaiákia
in ship handling at sea, so were these women
skilled at the loom, having this lovely craft
and artistry as talents from Athena.

To left and right, outside, he saw an orchard
closed by a pale—four spacious acres planted   120
with trees in bloom or weighted down for picking:
pear trees, pomegranates, brilliant apples,
luscious figs, and olives ripe and dark.
Fruit never failed upon these trees: winter
and summer time they bore, for through the year
the breathing Westwind ripened all in turn—
so one pear came to prime, and then another,
and so with apples, figs, and the vine's fruit
empurpled in the royal vineyard there.
Currants were dried at one end, on a platform   130
bare to the sun, beyond the vintage arbors
and vats the vintners trod; while near at hand
were new grapes barely formed as the green bloom fell,
or half-ripe clusters, faintly coloring.
After the vines came rows of vegetables
of all the kinds that flourish in every season,
and through the garden plots and orchard ran
channels from one clear fountain, while another
gushed through a pipe under the courtyard entrance
to serve the house and all who came for water.   140
These were the gifts of heaven to Alkínoös.

Odysseus, who had borne the barren sea,
stood in the gateway and surveyed this bounty.
He gazed his fill, then swiftly he went in.
The lords and nobles of Phaiákia
were tipping wine to the wakeful god, to Hermês—
a last libation before going to bed—
but down the hall Odysseus went unseen,
still in the cloud Athena cloaked him in,
until he reached Arêtê, and the king.   150
He threw his great hands round Arêtê's knees,
whereon the sacred mist curled back;
they saw him; and the diners hushed amazed
to see an unknown man inside the palace.
Under their eyes Odysseus made his plea:

"Arêtê, admirable Rhêxênor's daughter,
here is a man bruised by adversity, thrown
upon your mercy and the king your husband's,

begging indulgence of this company—
may the gods' blessing rest on them! May life   160
be kind to all! Let each one leave his children
every good thing this realm confers upon him!
But grant me passage to my father land.
My home and friends lie far. My life is pain."

He moved, then, toward the fire, and sat him down
amid the ashes. No one stirred or spoke
until Ekhenêos broke the spell—an old man,
eldest of the Phaiákians, an oracle,
versed in the laws and manners of old time.
He rose among them now and spoke out kindly: 170

"Alkínoös, this will not pass for courtesy:
a guest abased in ashes at our hearth?
Everyone here awaits your word; so come, then,
lift the man up; give him a seat of honor,
a silver-studded chair. Then tell the stewards
we'll have another wine bowl for libation
to Zeus, lord of the lightning—advocate
of honorable petitioners. And supper
may be supplied our friend by the larder mistress."

Alkínoös, calm in power, heard him out,   180
then took the great adventurer by the hand
and led him from the fire. Nearest his throne
the son whom he loved best, Laódamas,
had long held place; now the king bade him rise
and gave his shining chair to Lord Odysseus.
A serving maid poured water for his hands
from a gold pitcher into a silver bowl,
and spead a polished table at his side;
the mistress of provisions came with bread
and other victuals, generous with her store.   190
So Lord Odysseus drank, and tasted supper.
Seeing this done, the king in majesty
said to his squire:

                                        "A fresh bowl, Pontónoös;
we make libation to the lord of lightning,
who seconds honorable petitioners."

Mixing the honey-hearted wine, Pontónoös
went on his rounds and poured fresh cups for all,
whereof when all had spilt they drank their fill.
Alkínoös then spoke to the company:

"My lords and leaders of Phaiákia: 200
hear now, all that my heart would have me say.
Our banquet's ended, so you may retire;

but let our seniors gather in the morning
to give this guest a festal day, and make
fair offerings to the gods. In due course we
shall put our minds upon the means at hand
to take him safely, comfortably, well
and happily, with speed, to his own country,
distant though it may lie. And may no trouble
come to him here or on the way; his fate   210
he shall pay out at home, even as the Spinners[4]
spun for him on the day his mother bore him.
If, as may be, he is some god, come down
from heaven's height, the gods are working strangely:
until now, they have shown themselves in glory
only after great hekatombs—those figures
banqueting at our side, throned like ourselves.
Or if some traveller met them when alone
they bore no least disguise; we are their kin; Gigantês,
Kyklopês, rank no nearer gods than we."   220

Odysseus' wits were ready, and he replied:

"Alkínoös, you may set your mind at rest.
Body and birth, a most unlikely god
am I, being all of earth and mortal nature.
I should say, rather, I am like those men
who suffer the worst trials that you know,
and miseries greater yet, as I might tell you—
hundreds; indeed the gods could send no more.
You will indulge me if I finish dinner—?
grieved though I am to say it. There's no part   230
of man more like a dog than brazen Belly,
crying to be remembered—and it must be—
when we are mortal weary and sick at heart;
and that is my condition. Yet my hunger
drives me to take this food, and think no more
of my afflictions. Belly must be filled.
Be equally impelled, my lords, tomorrow
to berth me in a ship and send me home!
Rough years I've had; now may I see once more
my hall, my lands, my people before I die!"   240

Now all who heard cried out assent to this:
the guest had spoken well; he must have passage.
Then tipping wine they drank their thirst away,
and one by one went homeward for the night.
So Lord Odysseus kept his place alone
with Arêtê and the king Alkínoös
beside him, while the maids went to and fro

---

[4] The fates, mythological women who determined the span of a human life by spinning,
measuring, and cutting the thread symbolic of it.

clearing away the wine cups and the tables.
Presently the ivory-skinned lady
turned to him—for she knew his cloak and tunic   250
to be her own fine work, done with her maids—
and arrowy came her words upon the air:

"Friend, I, for one, have certain questions for you.
Who are you, and who has given you this clothing?
Did you not say you wandered here by sea?"

The great tactician carefully replied:

"Ah, majesty, what labor it would be
to go through the whole story! All my years
of misadventures, given by those on high!
But this you ask about is quickly told: 260
in mid-ocean lies Ogýgia, the island
haunt of Kalypso, Atlas' guileful daughter,
a lovely goddess and a dangerous one.
No one, no god or man, consorts with her;
but supernatural power brought me there
to be her solitary guest: for Zeus
let fly with his bright bolt and split my ship,
rolling me over in the winedark sea.
There all my shipmates, friends were drowned, while I
hung on the keelboard of the wreck and drifted   270
nine full days. Then in the dead of night
the gods brought me ashore upon Ogýgia
into her hands. The enchantress in her beauty
fed and caressed me, promised me I should be
immortal, youthful, all the days to come;
but in my heart I never gave consent
though seven years detained. Immortal clothing
I had from her, and kept it wet with tears.
Then came the eighth year on the wheel of heaven
and word to her from Zeus, or a change of heart,   280
so that she now commanded me to sail,
sending me out to sea on a craft I made
with timber and tools of hers. She gave me stores,
victuals and wine, a cloak divinely woven,
and made a warm land breeze come up astern.
Seventeen days I sailed in the open water
before I saw your country's shore, a shadow
upon the sea rim. Then my heart rejoiced—
pitiable as I am! For blows aplenty
awaited me from the god who shakes the earth.   290
Cross gales he blew, making me lose my bearings,
and heaved up seas beyond imagination—
huge and foundering seas. All I could do
was hold hard, groaning under every shock,
until my craft broke up in the hurricane.

I kept afloat and swam your sea, or drifted,
taken by wind and current to this coast
where I went in on big swells running landward.
But cliffs and rock shoals made that place forbidding,
so I turned back, swimming off shore, and came   300
in the end to a river, to auspicious water,
with smooth beach and a rise that broke the wind.
I lay there where I fell till strength returned.
Then sacred night came on, and I went inland
to high ground and a leaf bed in a thicket.
Heaven sent slumber in an endless tide
submerging my sad heart among the leaves.
That night and next day's dawn and noon I slept;
the sun went west; and then sweet sleep unbound me,
when I became aware of maids—your daughter's—   310
playing along the beach; the princess, too,
most beautiful. I prayed her to assist me,
and her good sense was perfect; one could hope
for no behavior like it from the young,
thoughtless as they most often are. But she
gave me good provender and good red wine,
a river bath, and finally this clothing.
There is the bitter tale. These are the facts."

But in reply Alkínoös observed:

"Friend, my child's good judgment failed in this—   320
not to have brought you in her company home.
Once you approached her, you became her charge."

To this Odysseus tactfully replied:

"Sir, as to that, you should not blame the princess.
She did tell me to follow with her maids,
but I would not. I felt abashed, and feared
the sight would somehow ruffle or offend you.
All of us on this earth are plagued by jealousy."

Alkínoös' answer was a declaration:

"Friend, I am not a man for trivial anger: 330
better a sense of measure in everything.
No anger here. I say that if it should please
our father Zeus, Athena, and Apollo—
seeing the man you are, seeing your thoughts
are my own thoughts—my daughter should be yours
and you my son-in-law, if you remained.
A home, lands, riches you should have from me
if you could be contented here. If not,
by Father Zeus, let none of our men hold you!
On the contrary, I can assure you now   340

of passage late tomorrow: while you sleep
my men will row you through the tranquil night
to your own land and home or where you please.
It may be, even, far beyond Euboia—
called most remote by seamen of our isle
who landed there, conveying Rhadamanthos
when he sought Títyos, the son of Gaia.[5]
They put about, with neither pause nor rest,
and entered their home port the selfsame day.
But this you, too, will see: what ships I have,   350
how my young oarsmen send the foam a-scudding!"

Now joy welled up in the patient Lord Odysseus
who said devoutly in the warmest tones:

"O Father Zeus, let all this be fulfilled
as spoken by Alkínoös! Earth of harvests
remember him! Return me to my homeland!"

In this manner they conversed with one another;
but the great lady called her maids, and sent them
to make a kingly bed, with purple rugs
piled up, and sheets outspread, and fleecy   360
coverlets, in an eastern colonnade.
The girls went out with torches in their hands,
swift at their work of bedmaking; returning
they whispered at the lord Odysseus' shoulder:

"Sir, you may come; your bed has been prepared."

How welcome the word "bed" came to his ears!
Now, then, Odysseus laid him down and slept
in luxury under the Porch of Morning,
while in his inner chamber Alkínoös
retired to rest where his dear consort lay.   370

BOOK EIGHT: THE SONGS OF THE HARPER

Under the opening fingers of the dawn
Alkínoös, the sacred prince, arose,
and then arose Odysseus, raider of cities.
As the king willed, they went down by the shipways
to the assembly ground of the Phaiákians.
Side by side the two men took their ease there

---

[5] The lines "It may be . . . Gaia" are somewhat obscure, since Rhadamanthos is pictured in Book IV as dwelling in Elysion, and Títyos, in Book XI, is punished in Hades. The main point is clear, though: Alkínoös is boasting of the nautical range and speed of his seafaring people. Euboia is an island east of Greece. Gaia is another name for Ge, the earth-deity.

on smooth stone benches. Meanwhile Pallas Athena
roamed through the byways of the town, contriving
Odysseus' voyage home—in voice and feature
the crier of the king Alkínoös   10
who stopped and passed the word to every man:

"Phaiákian lords and counselors, this way!
Come to assembly: learn about the stranger,
the new guest at the palace of Alkínoös—
a man the sea drove, but a comely man;
the gods' own light is on him."

                                        She aroused them,
and soon the assembly ground and seats were filled
with curious men, a throng who peered and saw
the master mind of war, Laërtês' son.
Athena now poured out her grace upon him,   20
head and shoulders, height and mass—a splendor
awesome to the eyes of the Phaiákians;
she put him in a fettle to win the day,
mastering every trial they set to test him.
When all the crowd sat marshalled, quieted,
Alkínoös addressed the full assembly:

"Hear me, lords and captains of the Phaiákians!
Hear what my heart would have me say!
Our guest and new friend—nameless to me still—
comes to my house after long wandering   30
in Dawn lands, or among the Sunset races.
Now he appeals to me for conveyance home.
As in the past, therefore, let us provide
passage, and quickly, for no guest of mine
languishes here for lack of it. Look to it:
get a black ship afloat on the noble sea,
and pick our fastest sailer; draft a crew
of two and fifty from our younger townsmen—
men who have made their names at sea. Loop oars
well to your tholepins,[1] lads, then leave the ship,   40
come to our house, fall to, and take your supper:
we'll furnish out a feast for every crewman.
These are your orders. As for my older peers
and princes of the realm, let them foregather
in festival for our friend in my great hall;
and let no man refuse. Call in our minstrel,
Demódokos, whom God made lord of song,
heart-easing, sing upon what theme he will."

He turned, led the procession, and those princes
followed, while his herald sought the minstrel.   50

---

[1] Pegs on the side of a boat, used as oarlocks.

Young oarsmen from the assembly chose a crew
of two and fifty, as the king commanded,
and these filed off along the waterside
to where the ship lay, poised above open water.
They hauled the black hull down to ride the sea,
rigging a mast and spar in the black ship,
with oars at trail from corded rawhide, all
seamanly; then tried the white sail, hoisting,
and moored her off the beach. Then going ashore
the crew went up to the great house of Alkínoös.   60

Here the enclosures, entrance ways, and rooms
were filled with men, young men and old, for whom
Alkínoös had put twelve sheep to sacrifice,
eight tuskers[2] and a pair of shambling oxen.
These, now, they flayed and dressed to make their banquet.

The crier soon came, leading that man of song
whom the Muse cherished; by her gift he knew
the good of life, and evil—
for she who lent him sweetness made him blind.[3]
Pontónoös fixed a studded chair for him   70
hard by a pillar amid the banqueters,
hanging the taut harp from a peg above him,
and guided up his hands upon the strings;
placed a bread basket at his side, and poured
wine in a cup, that he might drink his fill.
Now each man's hand went out upon the banquet.

In time, when hunger and thirst were turned away,
the Muse brought to the minstrel's mind a song
of heroes whose great fame rang under heaven:
the clash between Odysseus and Akhilleus,   80
how one time they contended[4] at the godfeast
raging, and the marshal, Agamémnon,
felt inward joy over his captains' quarrel;
for such had been foretold him by Apollo
at Pytho[5]—hallowed height—when the Akhaian
crossed that portal of rock to ask a sign—
in the old days when grim war lay ahead
for Trojans and Danaans, by God's will.
So ran the tale the minstrel sang. Odysseus
with massive hand drew his rich mantle down   90
over his brow, cloaking his face with it,
to make the Phaiákians miss the secret tears

[2] Animals with tusks, such as boars.
[3] According to tradition, Homer himself was blind.
[4] This incident probably took place before the action of the *Iliad*.
[5] The shrine of Apollo at Delphi, on Mount Parnassos (Parnassus); the god uttered oracular pronouncements there.

that started to his eyes. How skillfully
he dried them when the song came to a pause!
threw back his mantle, spilt his gout of wine!
But soon the minstrel plucked his note once more
to please the Phaiákian lords, who loved the song;
then in his cloak Odysseus wept again.
His tears flowed in the mantle unperceived:
only Alkínoös, at his elbow, saw them,   100
and caught the low groan in the man's breathing.
At once he spoke to all the seafolk round him:

"Hear me, lords and captains of the Phaiákians.
Our meat is shared, our hearts are full of pleasure
from the clear harp tone that accords with feasting;
now for the field and track; we shall have trials
in the pentathlon.[6] Let our guest go home
and tell his friends what champions we are
at boxing, wrestling, broadjump and foot racing."

On this he led the way and all went after.   110
The crier unslung and pegged the shining harp
and, taking Demódokos's hand,
led him along with all the rest—Phaiákian
peers, gay amateurs of the great games.
They gained the common, where a crowd was forming,
and many a young athlete now came forward
with seaside names like Tipmast, Tiderace, Sparwood,
Hullman, Sternman, Beacher and Pullerman,
Bluewater, Shearwater, Runningwake, Boardalee,
Seabelt, son of Grandfleet Shipwrightson;   120
Seareach stepped up, son of the Launching Master,
rugged as Arês,[7] bane of men; his build
excelled all but the Prince Laódamas;
and Laódamas made entry with his brothers,
Halios and Klytóneus, sons of the king.
The runners, first, must have their quarter mile.
All lined up tense; then Go! and down the track
they raised the dust in a flying bunch, strung out
longer and longer behind Prince Klytóneus.
By just so far as a mule team, breaking ground,   130
will distance oxen, he left all behind
and came up to the crowd, an easy winner.
Then they made room for wrestling—grinding bouts
that Seareach won, pinning the strongest men;
then the broadjump; first place went to Seabelt;
Sparwood gave the discus the mightiest fling,
and Prince Laódamas outboxed them all.

---

[6] An athletic contest consisting of five events.   [7] God of war.

Now it was he, the son of Alkínoös,
who said when they had run through these diversions:

"Look here, friends, we ought to ask the stranger   140
if he competes in something. He's no cripple;
look at his leg muscles and his forearms.
Neck like a bollard;[8] strong as a bull, he seems;
and not old, though he may have gone stale under
the rough times he had. Nothing like the sea
for wearing out the toughest man alive."

Then Seareach took him up at once, and said:

"Laódamas, you're right, by all the powers.
Go up to him, yourself, and put the question."

At this, Alkínoös' tall son advanced   150
to the center ground, and there addressed Odysseus:

"Friend, Excellency, come join our competition,
if you are practiced, as you seem to be.
While a man lives he wins no greater honor
than footwork and the skill of hands can bring him.
Enter our games, then; ease your heart of trouble.
Your journey home is not far off, remember;
the ship is launched, the crew all primed for sea."

Odysseus, canniest of men, replied:

"Laódamas, why do you young chaps challenge me?   160
I have more on my mind than track and field—
hard days, and many, have I seen, and suffered.
I sit here at your field meet, yes; but only
as one who begs your king to send him home."

Now Seareach put his word in, and contentiously:

The reason being, as I see it, friend,
you never learned a sport, and have no skill
in any of the contests of fighting men.
You must have been the skipper of some tramp
that crawled from one port to the next, jam full   170
of chaffering hands: a tallier of cargoes,
itching for gold—not, by your looks, an athlete."

Odysseus frowned, and eyed him coldly, saying:

"That was uncalled for, friend, you talk like a fool.
The gods deal out no gift, this one or any—
birth, brains, or speech—to every man alike.
In looks a man may be a shade, a specter,

---

[8] A sturdy post to which a ship's ropes were tied.

and yet be master of speech so crowned with beauty
that people gaze at him with pleasure. Courteous,
sure of himself, he can command assemblies,   180
and when he comes to town, the crowds gather.
A handsome man, contrariwise, may lack
grace and good sense in everything he says.
You now, for instance, with your fine physique—
a god's, indeed—you have an empty noddle.[9]
I find my heart inside my ribs aroused
by your impertinence. I am no stranger
to contests, as you fancy. I rated well
when I could count on youth and my two hands.
Now pain has cramped me, and my years of combat   190
hacking through ranks in war, and the bitter sea.
Aye. Even so I'll give your games a trial.
You spoke heart-wounding words. You shall be answered."

He leapt out, cloaked as he was, and picked a discus,
a rounded stone, more ponderous than those
already used by the Phaiákian throwers,
and, whirling, let it fly from his great hand
with a low hum. The crowd went flat on the ground—
all those oar-pulling, seafaring Phaiákians—
under the rushing noise. The spinning disk   200
soared out, light as a bird, beyond all others.
Disguised now as a Phaiákian, Athena
staked it and called out:

                                        "Even a blind man,
friend, could judge this, finding with his fingers
one discus, quite alone, beyond the cluster.
Congratulations; this event is yours;
not a man here can beat you or come near you."

That was a cheering hail, Odysseus thought,
seeing one friend there on the emulous field,
so, in relief, he turned among the Phaiákians   210
and said:

                                 "Now come alongside that one, lads.
The next I'll send as far, I think, or farther.
Anyone else on edge for competition
try me now. By heaven, you angered me.
Racing, wrestling, boxing—I bar nothing
with any man except Laódamas,
for he's my host. Who quarrels with his host?
Only a madman—or no man at all—
would challenge his protector among strangers,

[9] Head.

cutting the ground away under his feet.   220
Here are no others I will not engage,
none but I hope to know what he is made of.
Inept at combat, am I? Not entirely.
Give me a smooth bow; I can handle it,
and I might well be first to hit my man
amid a swarm of enemies, though archers
in company around me drew together.
Philoktêtês[10] alone, at Troy, when we
Akhaians took the bow, used to outshoot me.
Of men who now eat bread upon the earth   230
I hold myself the best hand with a bow—
conceding mastery to the men of old,
Heraklês, or Eurýtos[11] of Oikhalía,
heroes who vied with gods in bowmanship.
Eurýtos came to grief, it's true; old age
never crept over him in his long hall;
Apollo took his challenge ill, and killed him.
What then, the spear? I'll plant it like an arrow.
Only in sprinting, I'm afraid, I may
be passed by someone. Roll of the sea waves   240
wearied me, and the victuals in my ship
ran low; my legs are flabby."

                                              When he finished,
the rest were silent, but Alkínoös answered:

"Friend, we take your challenge in good part,
for this man angered and affronted you
here at our peaceful games. You'd have us note
the prowess that is in you, and so clearly,
no man of sense would ever cry it down!
Come, turn your mind, now, on a thing to tell
among your peers when you are home again,   250
dining in hall, beside your wife and children:
I mean our prowess, as you may remember it,
for we, too, have our skills, given by Zeus,
and practiced from our father's time to this—
not in the boxing ring nor the palestra[12]
conspicuous, but in racing, land or sea;
and all our days we set great store by feasting,
harpers, and the grace of dancing choirs,
changes of dress, warm baths, and downy beds.
O master dancers of the Phaiákians!   260
Perform now: let our guest on his return

---

[10] Philoktêtês had inherited the magical bow of the fabled hero Heraklês (Hercules); a version of his story is dramatized in Sophocles' *Philoctetes*.

[11] Grandson of Apollo, and Heraklês' instructor in bowmanship. He was killed in a competition with Apollo, god of archery. Eurýtos' bow descended to Odysseus.

[12] A public athletics-ground.

tell his companions we excel the world
in dance and song, as in our ships and running.
Someone go find the gittern harp in hall
and bring it quickly to Demódokos!"

At the serene king's word, a squire ran
to bring the polished harp out of the palace,
and place was given to nine referees—
peers of the realm, masters of ceremony—
who cleared a space and smoothed a dancing floor.   270
The squire brought down, and gave Demódokos,
the clear-toned harp; and centering on the minstrel
magical young dancers formed a circle
with a light beat, and stamp of feet. Beholding,
Odysseus marvelled at the flashing ring.

Now to his harp the blinded minstrel sang
of Arês' dalliance with Aphroditê:
how hidden in Hephaistos'[13] house they played
at love together, and the gifts of Arês,
dishonoring Hephaistos' bed—and how   280
the word that wounds the heart came to the master
from Hêlios,[14] who had seen the two embrace;
and when he learned it, Lord Hephaistos went
with baleful calculation to his forge.
There mightily he armed his anvil block
and hammered out a chain, whose tempered links
could not be sprung or bent; he meant that they should hold.
Those shackles fashioned, hot in wrath Hephaistos
climbed to the bower and the bed of love,
pooled all his net of chain around the bed posts   290
and swung it from the rafters overhead—
light as a cobweb even gods in bliss
could not perceive, so wonderful his cunning.
Seeing his bed now made a snare, he feigned
a journey to the trim stronghold of Lemnos,[15]
the dearest of earth's towns to him. And Arês?
Ah, golden Arês' watch had its reward
when he beheld the great smith leaving home.
How promptly to the famous door he came,
intent on pleasure with sweet Kythereia![16]   300
She, who had left her father's side but now,
sat in her chamber when her lover entered;
and tenderly he pressed her hand and said:

---

[13] The lame god of fire and metalworking, husband of Aphroditê.   [14] The sun-god.
[15] An island in the Aegean, center of the worship of Hephaistos; it was there that he fell after Zeus, during a fit of anger, threw him out of heaven.
[16] Aphroditê. Also spelled *Cytherea*.

"Come and lie down, my darling, and be happy!
Hephaistos is no longer here, but gone
to see his grunting Sintian[17] friends on Lemnos."

As she, too, thought repose would be most welcome,
the pair went in to bed—into a shower
of clever chains, the netting of Hephaistos.
So trussed, they could not move apart, nor rise,   310
at last they knew there could be no escape,
they were to see the glorious cripple now—
for Hêlios had spied for him, and told him;
so he turned back, this side of Lemnos Isle,
sick at heart, making his way homeward.
Now in the doorway of the room he stood
while deadly rage took hold of him; his voice,
hoarse and terrible, reached all the gods:

"O Father Zeus, O gods in bliss forever,
here is indecorous entertainment for you,   320
Aphroditê, Zeus's daughter,
caught in the act, cheating me, her cripple,
with Arês—devastating Arês.
Cleanlimbed beauty is her joy, not these
bandylegs I came into the world with:
no one to blame but the two gods[18] who bred me!
Come see this pair entwining here
in my own bed! How hot it makes me burn!
I think they may not care to lie much longer,
pressing on one another, passionate lovers;   330
they'll have enough of bed together soon.
And yet the chain that bagged them holds them down
till Father sends me back my wedding gifts—
all that I poured out for his damned pigeon,
so lovely, and so wanton."

                                              All the others
were crowding in, now, to the brazen house—
Poseidon who embraces earth, and Hermês
the runner, and Apollo, lord of Distance.
The goddesses stayed home for shame; but these
munificences ranged there in the doorway,   340
and irrepressible among them all
arose the laughter of the happy gods.
Gazing hard at Hephaistos' handiwork
the gods in turn remarked among themselves:

"No dash in adultery now."

---

[17] The Sintians, of Lemnos, had a reputation for crudity.   [18] Zeus and Hera.

"The tortoise tags the hare—
Hephaistos catches Arês—and Arês outran the wind."

"The lame god's craft has pinned him. Now shall he
pay what is due from gods taken in cuckoldry."

They made these improving remarks to one another,
but Apollo leaned aside to say to Hermês: 350

"Son of Zeus, beneficent Wayfinder,
would you accept a coverlet of chain, if only
you lay by Aphroditê's golden side?"

To this the Wayfinder replied, shining:

"Would I not, though, Apollo of distances!
Wrap me in chains three times the weight of these,
come goddesses and gods to see the fun;
only let me lie beside the pale-golden one!"

The gods gave way again to peals of laughter,
all but Poseidon, and he never smiled,   360
but urged Hephaistos to unpinion Arês,
saying emphatically, in a loud voice:

                                                      "Free him:
you will be paid, I swear; ask what you will;
he pays up every jot the gods decree."

To this the Great Gamelegs replied:

                                                      "Poseidon,
lord of the earth-surrounding sea, I should not
swear to a scoundrel's honor. What have I
as surety from you, if Arês leaves me
empty-handed, with my empty chain?"

The Earth-shaker for answer urged again: 370

"Hephaistos, let us grant he goes, and leaves
the fine unpaid; I swear, then, I shall pay it."

Then said the Great Gamelegs at last:

                                                      "No more:
you offer terms I cannot well refuse."

And down the strong god bent to set them free,
till disencumbered of their bond, the chain,
the lovers leapt away—he into Thrace,
while Aphroditê, laughter's darling, fled
to Kypros Isle and Paphos,[19] to her meadow

---

[19] A city in ancient Cyprus (Kypros), an island south of Turkey where Aphroditê had a cult.

and altar dim with incense. There the Graces   380
bathed and anointed her with golden oil—
a bloom that clings upon immortal flesh alone—
and let her folds of mantle fall in glory.

So ran the song the minstrel sang.

                                                                      Odysseus

listening, found sweet pleasure in the tale,
among the Phaiákian mariners and oarsmen.
And next Alkínoös called upon his sons,
Halios and Laódamas, to show
the dance no one could do as well as they—
handling a purple ball carven by Pólybos.   390
One made it shoot up under the shadowing clouds
as he leaned backward; bounding high in air
the other cut its flight far off the ground—
and neither missed a step as the ball soared.

The next turn was to keep it low, and shuttling
hard between them, while the ring of boys
gave them a steady stamping beat.
Odysseus now addressed Alkínoös:

"O majesty, model of all your folk,
your promise was to show me peerless dancers;   400
here is the promise kept. I am all wonder."

At this Alkínoös in his might rejoicing
said to the seafarers of Phaiákia:

"Attend me now, Phaiákian lords and captains:
our guest appears a clear-eyed man and wise.
Come, let him feel our bounty as he should.
Here are twelve princes of the kingdom—lords
paramount, and I who make thirteen;
let each one bring a laundered cloak and tunic,
and add one bar of honorable gold.   410
Heap all our gifts together; load his arms;
let him go joyous to our evening feast!
As for Seareach—why, man to man
he'll make amends, and handsomely; he blundered."

Now all as one acclaimed the king's good pleasure,
and each one sent a squire to bring his gifts.
Meanwhile Seareach found speech again, saying:

"My lord and model of us all, Alkínoös,
as you require of me, in satisfaction,
this broadsword of clear bronze goes to our guest.   420

Its hilt is silver, and the ringed sheath
of new-sawn ivory—a costly weapon."

He turned to give the broadsword to Odysseus,
facing him, saying blithely:

                                                    "Sir, my best

wishes, my respects; if I offended,
I hope the seawinds blow it out of mind.
God send you see your lady and your homeland
soon again, after the pain of exile."

Odysseus, the great tactician, answered:

"My hand, friend; may the gods award you fortune.   430
I hope no pressing need comes on you ever
for this fine blade you give me in amends."

He slung it, glinting silver, from his shoulder,
as the light shone from sundown. Messengers
were bearing gifts and treasure to the palace,
where the king's sons received them all, and made
a glittering pile at their grave mother's side;
then, as Alkínoös took his throne of power,
each went to his own high-backed chair in turn,
and said Alkínoös to Arêtê: 440

"Lady, bring here a chest, the finest one;
a clean cloak and tunic; stow these things;
and warm a cauldron for him. Let him bathe,
when he has seen the gifts of the Phaiákians,
and so dine happily to a running song.
My own wine-cup of gold intaglio[20]
I'll give him, too; through all the days to come,
tipping his wine to Zeus or other gods
in his great hall, he shall remember me."

Then said Arêtê to her maids:

                                                    "The tripod: 450

stand the great tripod legs about the fire."

They swung the cauldron on the fire's heart,
poured water in, and fed the blaze beneath
until the basin simmered, cupped in flame.
The queen set out a rich chest from her chamber
and folded in the gifts—clothing and gold
given Odysseus by the Phaiákians;

[20] A design cut into the surface.

then she put in the royal cloak and tunic,
briskly saying to her guest:

                                                    "Now here, sir,

look to the lid yourself, and tie it down   460
against light fingers, if there be any,
on the black ship tonight while you are sleeping."

Noble Odysseus, expert in adversity,
battened the lid down with a lightning knot
learned, once, long ago, from the Lady Kirkê.[21]
And soon a call came from the Bathing Mistress
who led him to a hip-bath, warm and clear—
a happy sight, and rare in his immersions
after he left Kalypso's home—where, surely,
the luxuries of a god were ever his.   470
When the bath maids had washed him, rubbed him down,
put a fresh tunic and a cloak around him,
he left the bathing place to join the men
at wine in hall.

                                        The princess Nausikaa,

exquisite figure, as of heaven's shaping,
waited beside a pillar as he passed
and said swiftly, with wonder in her look:

"Fare well, stranger; in your land remember me
who met and saved you. It is worth your thought."

The man of all occasions now met this: 480

"Daughter of great Alkínoös, Nausikaa,
may Zeus the lord of thunder, Hera's consort,
grant me daybreak again in my own country!
But there and all my days until I die
may I invoke you as I would a goddess,
princess, to whom I owe my life."

                                                            He left her

and went to take his place beside the king.

Now when the roasts were cut, the winebowls full,
a herald led the minstrel down the room
amid the deference of the crowd, and paused   490
to seat him near a pillar in the center—
whereupon that resourceful man, Odysseus,
carved out a quarter from his chine of pork,
crisp with fat, and called the blind man's guide:

"Herald! here, take this to Demódokos:
let him feast and be merry, with my compliments.
All men owe honor to the poets—honor

---

[21] A sorceress; Odysseus' encounter with her is described in Book X. Also spelled *Circe*.

and awe, for they are dearest to the Muse
who puts upon their lips the ways of life."

Gentle Demódokos took the proffered gift   500
and inwardly rejoiced. When all were served,
every man's hand went out upon the banquet,
repelling hunger and thirst, until at length
Odysseus spoke again to the blind minstrel:

"Demódokos, accept my utmost praise.
The Muse, daughter of Zeus in radiance,
or else Apollo[22] gave you skill to shape
with such great style your songs of the Akhaians—
their hard lot, how they fought and suffered war.
You shared it, one would say, or heard it all.   510
Now shift your theme, and sing that wooden horse
Epeios built, inspired by Athena—
the ambuscade Odysseus filled with fighters
and sent to take the inner town of Troy.
Sing only this for me, sing me this well,
and I shall say at once before the world
the grace of heaven has given us a song."

The minstrel stirred, murmuring to the god, and soon
clear words and notes came one by one, a vision
of the Akhaians in their graceful ships   520
drawing away from shore: the torches flung
and shelters flaring: Argive soldiers crouched
in the close dark around Odysseus: and
the horse, tall on the assembly ground of Troy.
For when the Trojans pulled it in, themselves,
up to the citadel, they sat nearby
with long-drawn-out and hapless argument—
favoring, in the end, one course of three:
either to stave the vault with brazen axes,
or haul it to a cliff and pitch it down,   530
or else to save it for the gods, a votive glory—
the plan that could not but prevail.
For Troy must perish, as ordained, that day
she harbored the great horse of timber; hidden
the flower of Akhaia lay, and bore
slaughter and death upon the men of Troy.
He sang, then, of the town sacked by Akhaians
pouring down from the horse's hollow cave,
this way and that way raping the steep city,
and how Odysseus came like Arês to   540
the door of Deïphobos,[23] with Meneláos,

---

[22] God of music and prophecy. He would naturally have an affinity with bards.
[23] Meneláos' wife, Helen, had in Troy been given in marriage to Deïphobos.

and braved the desperate fight there—
conquering once more by Athena's power.

The splendid minstrel sang it.

                                                          And Odysseus

let the bright molten tears run down his cheeks,
weeping the way a wife mourns for her lord
on the lost field where he has gone down fighting
the day of wrath that came upon his children.
At sight of the man panting and dying there,
she slips down to enfold him, crying out;   550
then feels the spears, prodding her back and shoulders,
and goes bound into slavery and grief.
Piteous weeping wears away her cheeks:
but no more piteous than Odysseus' tears,
cloaked as they were, now, from the company.
Only Alkínoös, at his elbow, knew—
hearing the low sob in the man's breathing—
and when he knew, he spoke:

"Hear me, lords and captains of Phaiákia!
And let Demódokos touch his harp no more.   560
His theme has not been pleasing to all here.
During the feast, since our fine poet sang,
our guest has never left off weeping. Grief
seems fixed upon his heart. Break off the song!
Let everyone be easy, host and guest;
there's more decorum in a smiling banquet!
We had prepared here, on our friend's behalf,
safe conduct in a ship, and gifts to cheer him,
holding that any man with a grain of wit
will treat a decent suppliant like a brother.   570
Now by the same rule, friend, you must not be
secretive any longer! Come, in fairness,
tell me the name you bore in that far country;
how were you known to family, and neighbors?
No man is nameless—no man, good or bad,
but gets a name in his first infancy,
none being born, unless a mother bears him!
Tell me your native land, your coast and city—
sailing directions for the ships, you know—
for those Phaiákian ships of ours   580
that have no steersman, and no steering oar,
divining the crew's wishes, as they do,
and knowing, as they do, the ports of call
about the world. Hidden in mist or cloud
they scud the open sea, with never a thought
of being in distress or going down.
There is, however, something I once heard
Nausíthoös, my father, say: Poseidon

holds it against us that our deep sea ships
are sure conveyance for all passengers.   590
My father said, some day one of our cutters
homeward bound over the cloudy sea
would be wrecked by the god, and a range of hills
thrown round our city. So, in his age, he said,
and let it be, or not, as the god please.
But come, now, put it for me clearly, tell me
the sea ways that you wandered, and the shores
you touched; the cities, and the men therein,
uncivilized, if such there were, and hostile,
and those godfearing who had kindly manners.   600
Tell me why you should grieve so terribly
over the Argives and the fall of Troy.
That was all gods' work, weaving ruin there
so it should make a song for men to come!
Some kin of yours, then, died at Ilion,
some first rate man, by marriage near to you,
next your own blood most dear?
Or some companion of congenial mind
and valor? True it is, a wise friend
can take a brother's place in our affection."   610

BOOK NINE: NEW COASTS AND POSEIDON'S SON

Now this was the reply Odysseus made:

"Alkínoös, king and admiration of men,
how beautiful this is, to hear a minstrel
gifted as yours: a god he might be, singing!
There is no boon in life more sweet, I say,
than when a summer joy holds all the realm,
and banqueters sit listening to a harper
in a great hall, by rows of tables heaped
with bread and roast meat, while a steward goes
to dip up wine and brim your cups again.   10
Here is the flower of life, it seems to me!
But now you wish to know my cause for sorrow—
and thereby give me cause for more.

                                        What shall I
say first? What shall I keep until the end?
The gods have tried me in a thousand ways.
But first my name: let that be known to you,
and if I pull away from pitiless death,
friendship will bind us, though my land lies far.

I am Laërtês' son, Odysseus.

                                        Men hold me
formidable for guile in peace and war: 20

this fame has gone abroad to the sky's rim.
My home is on the peaked sea-mark of Ithaka
under Mount Neion's wind-blown robe of leaves,
in sight of other islands—Doulíkhion,
Samê, wooded Zakynthos—Ithaka
being most lofty in that coastal sea,
and northwest, while the rest lie east and south.
A rocky isle, but good for a boy's training;
I shall not see on earth a place more dear,
though I have been detained long by Kalypso,   30
loveliest among goddesses, who held me
in her smooth caves, to be her heart's delight,
as Kirkê of Aiaia, the enchantress,
desired me, and detained me in her hall.
But in my heart I never gave consent.
Where shall a man find sweetness to surpass
his own home and his parents? In far lands
he shall not, though he find a house of gold.

What of my sailing, then, from Troy?

                              What of those years
of rough adventure, weathered under Zeus?   40
The wind that carried west from Ilion
brought me to Ísmaros,[1] on the far shore,
a strongpoint on the coast of the Kikonês.
I stormed that place and killed the men who fought.
Plunder we took, and we enslaved the women,
to make division, equal shares to all—
but on the spot I told them: 'Back, and quickly!
Out to sea again!' My men were mutinous,
fools, on stores of wine. Sheep after sheep
they butchered by the surf, and shambling cattle,   50
feasting,—while fugitives went inland, running
to call to arms the main force of Kikonês.
This was an army, trained to fight on horseback
or, where the ground required, on foot. They came
with dawn over that terrain like the leaves
and blades of spring. So doom appeared to us,
dark word of Zeus for us, our evil days.
My men stood up and made a fight of it—
backed on the ships, with lances kept in play,
from bright morning through the blaze of noon   60
holding our beach, although so far outnumbered;
but when the sun passed toward unyoking time,
then the Akhaians, one by one, gave way.
Six benches were left empty in every ship
that evening when we pulled away from death.

---

[1] The land of the Kikonês, in Thrace (on the northern coast of the Aegean Sea).

And this new grief we bore with us to sea:
our precious lives we had, but not our friends.
No ship made sail next day until some shipmate
had raised a cry, three times, for each poor ghost
unfleshed by the Kikonês on that field.   70

Now Zeus the lord of cloud roused in the north
a storm against the ships, and driving veils
of squall moved down like night on land and sea.
The bows went plunging at the gust; sails
cracked and lashed out strips in the big wind.
We saw death in that fury, dropped the yards,
unshipped the oars, and pulled for the nearest lee:
then two long days and nights we lay offshore
worn out and sick at heart, tasting our grief,
until a third Dawn came with ringlets shining.   80
Then we put up our masts, hauled sail, and rested,
letting the steersmen and the breeze take over.

I might have made it safely home, that time,
but as I came round Malea[2] the current
took me out to sea, and from the north
a fresh gale drove me on, past Kythera.
Nine days I drifted on the teeming sea
before dangerous high winds. Upon the tenth
we came to the coastline of the Lotos Eaters,
who live upon that flower. We landed there   90
to take on water. All ships' companies
mustered alongside for the mid-day meal.
Then I sent out two picked men and a runner
to learn what race of men that land sustained.
They fell in, soon enough, with Lotos Eaters,
who showed no will to do us harm, only
offering the sweet Lotos to our friends—
but those who ate this honeyed plant, the Lotos,
never cared to report, nor to return:
they longed to stay forever, browsing on   100
the native bloom, forgetful of their homeland.
I drove them, all three wailing, to the ships,
tied them down under their rowing benches,
and called the rest: 'All hands aboard;
come, clear the beach and no one taste
the Lotos, or you lose your hope of home.'
Filing in to their places by the rowlocks
my oarsmen dipped their long oars in the surf,
and we moved out again on our sea faring.

[2] The cape at the southernmost end of Greece; Kythera, mentioned two lines below, is a
sizable island just southwest of Malea.

In the next land we found were Kyklopês,[3]   110
giants, louts, without a law to bless them.
In ignorance leaving the fruitage of the earth in mystery
to the immortal gods, they neither plow
nor sow by hand, nor till the ground, though grain—
wild wheat and barley—grows untended, and
wine-grapes, in clusters, ripen in heaven's rain.
Kyklopês have no muster and no meeting,
no consultation or old tribal ways,
but each one dwells in his own mountain cave
dealing out rough justice to wife and child,   120
indifferent to what the others do.

                                                              Well, then:

across the wide bay from the mainland
there lies a desert island, not far out,
but still not close inshore. Wild goats in hundreds
breed there; and no human being comes
upon the isle to startle them—no hunter
of all who ever tracked with hounds through forests
or had rough going over mountain trails.
The isle, unplanted and untilled, a wilderness,
pastures goats alone. And this is why: 130
good ships like ours with cheekpaint at the bows
are far beyond the Kyklopês. No shipwright
toils among them, shaping and building up
symmetrical trim hulls to cross the sea
and visit all the seaboard towns, as men do
who go and come in commerce over water.
This isle—seagoing folk would have annexed it
and built their homesteads on it: all good land,
fertile for every crop in season: lush
well-watered meads along the shore, vines in profusion,   140
prairie, clear for the plow, where grain would grow
chin high by harvest time, and rich sub-soil.
The island cove is landlocked, so you need
no hawsers out astern, bow-stones or mooring:
run in and ride there till the day your crews
chafe to be under sail, and a fair wind blows.
You'll find good water flowing from a cavern
through dusky poplars into the upper bay.
Here we made harbor. Some god guided us
that night, for we could barely see our bows   150
in the dense fog around us, and no moonlight
filtered through the overcast. No look-out,
nobody saw the island dead ahead,
nor even the great landward rolling billow
that took us in: we found ourselves in shallows,
keels grazing shore: so furled our sails

---

[3] One-eyed giants, inhabitants of Sicily. Also spelled *Cyclops*.

and disembarked where the low ripples broke.
There on the beach we lay, and slept till morning.

When Dawn spread out her finger tips of rose
we turned out marvelling, to tour the isle,   160
while Zeus's shy nymph daughters flushed wild goats
down from the heights—a breakfast for my men.
We ran to fetch our hunting bows and long-shanked
lances from the ships, and in three companies
we took our shots. Heaven gave us game a-plenty:
for every one of twelve ships in my squadron
nine goats fell to be shared; my lot was ten.
So there all day, until the sun went down,
we made our feast on meat galore, and wine—
wine from the ship, for our supply held out,   170
so many jars were filled at Ísmaros
from stores of the Kikonês that we plundered.
We gazed, too, at Kyklopês Land, so near,
we saw their smoke, heard bleating from their flocks.
But after sundown, in the gathering dusk,
we slept again above the wash of ripples.

When the young Dawn with finger tips of rose
came in the east, I called my men together
and made a speech to them:

                                        'Old shipmates, friends,
the rest of you stand by; I'll make the crossing   180
in my own ship, with my own company,
and find out what the mainland natives are—
for they may be wild savages, and lawless,
or hospitable and god fearing men.'

At this I went aboard, and gave the word
to cast off by the stern. My oarsmen followed,
filing in to their benches by the rowlocks,
and all in line dipped oars in the grey sea.

As we rowed on, and nearer to the mainland,
at one end of the bay, we saw a cavern   190
yawning above the water, screened with laurel,
and many rams and goats about the place
inside a sheepfold—made from slabs of stone
earthfast between tall trunks of pine and rugged
towering oak trees.

                                        A prodigious man
slept in this cave alone, and took his flocks
to graze afield—remote from all companions,
knowing none but savage ways, a brute
so huge, he seemed no man at all of those

who eat good wheaten bread; but he seemed rather   200
a shaggy mountain reared in solitude.
We beached there, and I told the crew
to stand by and keep watch over the ship;
as for myself I took my twelve best fighters
and went ahead. I had a goatskin full
of that sweet liquor that Euanthês' son,
Maron, had given me. He kept Apollo's
holy grove at Ísmaros; for kindness
we showed him there, and showed his wife and child,
he gave me seven shining golden talents   210
perfectly formed, a solid silver winebowl,
and then this liquor—twelve two-handled jars
of brandy, pure and fiery. Not a slave
in Maron's household knew this drink; only
he, his wife and the storeroom mistress knew;
and they would put one cupful—ruby-colored,
honey-smooth—in twenty more of water,
but still the sweet scent hovered like a fume
over the winebowl. No man turned away
when cups of this came round.

                                   A wineskin full   220

I brought along, and victuals in a bag,
for in my bones I knew some towering brute
would be upon us soon—all outward power,
a wild man, ignorant of civility.

We climbed, then, briskly to the cave. But Kyklops
had gone afield, to pasture his fat sheep,
so we looked round at everything inside:
a drying rack that sagged with cheeses, pens
crowded with lambs and kids, each in its class:
firstlings apart from middlings, and the 'dewdrops,'   230
or newborn lambkins, penned apart from both.
And vessels full of whey were brimming there—
bowls of earthenware and pails for milking.
My men came pressing round me, pleading:

                                                       'Why not

take these cheeses, get them stowed, come back,
throw open all the pens, and make a run for it?
We'll drive the kids and lambs aboard. We say
put out again on good salt water!'

                                                       Ah,

how sound that was! Yet I refused. I wished
to see the caveman, what he had to offer—   240
no pretty sight, it turned out, for my friends.
We lit a fire, burnt an offering,
and took some cheese to eat; then sat in silence

around the embers, waiting. When he came
he had a load of dry boughs on his shoulder
to stoke his fire at suppertime. He dumped it
with a great crash into that hollow cave,
and we all scattered fast to the far wall.
Then over the broad cavern floor he ushered
the ewes he meant to milk. He left his rams
and he-goats in the yard outside, and swung
high overhead a slab of solid rock
to close the cave. Two dozen four-wheeled wagons,
with heaving wagon teams, could not have stirred
the tonnage of that rock from where he wedged it
over the doorsill. Next he took his seat
and milked his bleating ewes. A practiced job
he made of it, giving each ewe her suckling;
thickened his milk, then, into curds and whey,[4]
sieved out the curds to drip in withy baskets,
and poured the whey to stand in bowls
cooling until he drank it for his supper.
When all these chores were done, he poked the fire,
heaping on brushwood. In the glare he saw us.

'Strangers,' he said, 'who are you? And where from?
What brings you here by sea ways—a fair traffic?
Or are you wandering rogues, who cast your lives
like dice, and ravage other folk by sea?'

We felt a pressure on our hearts, in dread
of that deep rumble and that mighty man.
But all the same I spoke up in reply:

'We are from Troy, Akhaians, blown off course
by shifting gales on the Great South Sea;
homeward bound, but taking routes and ways
uncommon; so the will of Zeus would have it.
We served under Agamémnon, son of Atreus—
the whole world knows what city
he laid waste, what armies he destroyed.
It was our luck to come here; here we stand,
beholden for your help, or any gifts
you give—as custom is to honor strangers.
We would entreat you, great Sir, have a care
for the gods' courtesy; Zeus will avenge
the unoffending guest.'[5]

He answered this
from his brute chest, unmoved:

'You are a ninny,

---

[4] The liquid part of separated milk, as distinguished from the lumpy curds.
[5] Zeus was the protector and guarantor of the laws of hospitality.

or else you come from the other end of nowhere,
telling me, mind the gods! We Kyklopês
care not a whistle for your thundering Zeus
or all the gods in bliss; we have more force by far.
I would not let you go for fear of Zeus—   290
you or your friends—unless I had a whim to.
Tell me, where was it, now, you left your ship—
around the point, or down the shore, I wonder?'

He thought he'd find out, but I saw through this,
and answered with a ready lie:

                                                                        'My ship?

Poseidon Lord, who sets the earth a-tremble,
broke it up on the rocks at your land's end.
A wind from seaward served him, drove us there.
We are survivors, these good men and I.'

Neither reply nor pity came from him,   300
but in one stride he clutched at my companions
and caught two in his hands like squirming puppies
to beat their brains out, spattering the floor.
Then he dismembered them and made his meal,
gaping and crunching like a mountain lion—
everything: innards, flesh, and marrow bones.
We cried aloud, lifting our hands to Zeus,
powerless, looking on at this, appalled;
but Kyklops[6] went on filling up his belly
with manflesh and great gulps of whey,   310
then lay down like a mast among his sheep.
My heart beat high now at the chance of action,
and drawing the sharp sword from my hip I went
along his flank to stab him where the midriff
holds the liver. I had touched the spot
when sudden fear stayed me: if I killed him
we perished there as well, for we could never
move his ponderous doorway slab aside.
So we were left to groan and wait for morning.

When the young Dawn with finger tips of rose   320
lit up the world, the Kyklops built a fire
and milked his handsome ewes, all in due order,
putting the sucklings to the mothers. Then,
his chores being all dispatched, he caught
another brace of men to make his breakfast,
and whisked away his great door slab
to let his sheep go through—but he, behind,
reset the stone as one would cap a quiver.

---

[6] Here used as a singular; his name, we learn later, is Polyphêmos.

There was a din of whistling as the Kyklops
rounded his flock to higher ground, then stillness.   330
And now I pondered how to hurt him worst,
if but Athena granted what I prayed for.
Here are the means I thought would serve my turn:

a club, or staff, lay there along the fold—
an olive tree, felled green and left to season
for Kyklops' hand. And it was like a mast
a lugger of twenty oars, broad in the beam—
a deep-sea-going craft—might carry:
so long, so big around, it seemed. Now I
chopped out a six foot section of this pole   340
and set it down before my men, who scraped it;
and when they had it smooth, I hewed again
to make a stake with pointed end. I held this
in the fire's heart and turned it, toughening it,
then hid it, well back in the cavern, under
one of the dung piles in profusion there.
Now came the time to toss for it: who ventured
along with me? whose hand could bear to thrust
and grind that spike in Kyklops' eye, when mild
sleep had mastered him? As luck would have it,   350
the men I would have chosen won the toss—
four strong men, and I made five as captain.

At evening came the shepherd with his flock,
his woolly flock. The rams as well, this time,
entered the cave: by some sheep-herding whim—
or a god's bidding—none were left outside.
He hefted his great boulder into place
and sat him down to milk the bleating ewes
in proper order, put the lambs to suck,
and swiftly ran through all his evening chores.   360
Then he caught two more men and feasted on them.
My moment was at hand, and I went forward
holding an ivy bowl of my dark drink,
looking up, saying:

                              'Kyklops, try some wine.
Here's liquor to wash down your scraps of men.
Taste it, and see the kind of drink we carried
under our planks. I meant it for an offering
if you would help us home. But you are mad,
unbearable, a bloody monster! After this,
will any other traveller come to see you?'   370

He seized and drained the bowl, and it went down
so fiery and smooth he called for more:

'Give me another, thank you kindly. Tell me,
how are you called? I'll make a gift will please you.

Even Kyklopês know the wine-grapes grow
out of grassland and loam in heaven's rain,
but here's a bit of nectar and ambrosia!'

Three bowls I brought him, and he poured them down.
I saw the fuddle and flush come over him,
then I sang out in cordial tones:

                                              'Kyklops,   380
you ask my honorable name? Remember
the gift you promised me, and I shall tell you.
My name is Nohbdy: mother, father, and friends,
everyone calls me Nohbdy.'

                                    And he said:

'Nohbdy's my meat, then, after I eat his friends.
Others come first. There's a noble gift, now.'

Even as he spoke, he reeled and tumbled backward,
his great head lolling to one side; and sleep
took him like any creature. Drunk, hiccuping,
he dribbled streams of liquor and bits of men.   390

Now, by the gods, I drove my big hand spike
deep in the embers, charring it again,
and cheered my men along with battle talk
to keep their courage up: no quitting now.
The pike of olive, green though it had been,
reddened and glowed as if about to catch.
I drew it from the coals and my four fellows
gave me a hand, lugging it near the Kyklops
as more than natural force nerved them; straight
forward they sprinted, lifted it, and rammed it   400
deep in his crater eye, and I leaned on it
turning it as a shipwright turns a drill
in planking, having men below to swing
the two-handled strap that spins it in the groove.
So with our brand we bored that great eye socket
while blood ran out around the red hot bar.
Eyelid and lash were seared; the pierced ball
hissed broiling, and the roots popped.

                                    In a smithy
one sees a white-hot axehead or an adze
plunged and wrung in a cold tub, screeching steam—   410
the way they make soft iron hale and hard—:
just so that eyeball hissed around the spike.
The Kyklops bellowed and the rock roared round him,
and we fell back in fear. Clawing his face

he tugged the bloody spike out of his eye,
threw it away, and his wild hands went groping;
then he set up a howl for Kyklopês
who lived in caves on windy peaks nearby.
Some heard him; and they came by divers ways
to clump around outside and call:

'What ails you,   420

Polyphêmos? Why do you cry so sore
in the starry night? You will not let us sleep.
Sure no man's driving off your flock? No man
has tricked you, ruined you?'

Out of the cave

the mammoth Polyphêmos roared in answer:

'Nohbdy, Nohbdy's tricked me, Nohbdy's ruined me!'

To this rough shout they made a sage reply:

'Ah well, if nobody has played you foul
there in your lonely bed, we are no use in pain
given by great Zeus. Let it be your father,   430
Poseidon Lord, to whom you pray.'

So saying

they trailed away. And I was filled with laughter
to see how like a charm the name deceived them.
Now Kyklops, wheezing as the pain came on him,
fumbled to wrench away the great doorstone
and squatted in the breach with arms thrown wide
for any silly beast or man who bolted—
hoping somehow I might be such a fool.
But I kept thinking how to win the game:
death sat there huge; how could we slip away?   440
I drew on all my wits, and ran through tactics,
reasoning as a man will for dear life,
until a trick came—and it pleased me well.
The Kyklops' rams were handsome, fat, with heavy
fleeces, a dark violet.

Three abreast

I tied them silently together, twining
cords of willow from the ogre's bed;
then slung a man under each middle one
to ride there safely, shielded left and right.
So three sheep could convey each man. I took   450
the woolliest ram, the choicest of the flock,
and hung myself under his kinky belly,
pulled up tight, with fingers twisted deep
in sheepskin ringlets for an iron grip.
So, breathing hard, we waited until morning.

When Dawn spread out her finger tips of rose
the rams began to stir, moving for pasture,
and peals of bleating echoed round the pens
where dams with udders full called for a milking.
Blinded, and sick with pain from his head wound,   460
the master stroked each ram, then let it pass,
but my men riding on the pectoral fleece
the giant's blind hands blundering never found.
Last of them all my ram, the leader, came,
weighted by wool and me with my meditations.
The Kyklops patted him, and then he said:

'Sweet cousin ram, why lag behind the rest
in the night cave? You never linger so,
but graze before them all, and go afar
to crop sweet grass, and take your stately way   470
leading along the streams, until at evening
you run to be the first one in the fold.
Why, now, so far behind? Can you be grieving
over your Master's eye? That carrion rogue
and his accurst companions burnt it out
when he had conquered all my wits with wine.
Nohbdy will not get out alive, I swear.
Oh, had you brain and voice to tell
where he may be now, dodging all my fury!
Bashed by this hand and bashed on this rock wall   480
his brains would strew the floor, and I should have
rest from the outrage Nohbdy worked upon me.'

He sent us into the open, then. Close by,
I dropped and rolled clear of the ram's belly,
going this way and that to untie the men.
With many glances back, we rounded up
his fat, stiff-legged sheep to take aboard,
and drove them down to where the good ship lay.
We saw, as we came near, our fellows' faces
shining; then we saw them turn to grief   490
tallying those who had not fled from death.
I hushed them, jerking head and eyebrows up,
and in a low voice told them: 'Load this herd;
move fast, and put the ship's head toward the breakers.'
They all pitched in at loading, then embarked
and struck their oars into the sea. Far out,
as far off shore as shouted words would carry,
I sent a few back to the adversary:

'O Kyklops! Would you feast on my companions?
Puny, am I, in a Caveman's hands?   500
How do you like the beating that we gave you,
you damned cannibal? Eater of guests
under your roof! Zeus and the gods have paid you!'

The blind thing in his doubled fury broke
a hilltop in his hands and heaved it after us.
Ahead of our black prow it struck and sank
whelmed in a spuming geyser, a giant wave
that washed the ship stern foremost back to shore.
I got the longest boathook out and stood
fending us off, with furious nods to all   510
to put their backs into a racing stroke—
row, row, or perish. So the long oars bent
kicking the foam sternward, making head
until we drew away, and twice as far.
Now when I cupped my hands I heard the crew
in low voices protesting:

                                   'Godsake, Captain!
Why bait the beast again? Let him alone!'

'That tidal wave he made on the first throw
all but beached us.'

                              'All but stove us in!'

'Give him our bearing with your trumpeting,   520
he'll get the range and lob a boulder.'

                                    'Aye
He'll smash our timbers and our heads together!'

I would not heed them in my glorying spirit,
but let my anger flare and yelled:

                                 'Kyklops,
if ever mortal man inquire
how you were put to shame and blinded, tell him
Odysseus, raider of cities, took your eye:
Laërtês' son, whose home's on Ithaka!'

At this he gave a mighty sob and rumbled:

'Now comes the weird[7] upon me, spoken of old.   530
A wizard, grand and wondrous, lived here—Télemos,
a son of Eurymos; great length of days
he had in wizardry among the Kyklopês,
and these things he foretold for time to come:
my great eye lost, and at Odysseus' hands.
Always I had in mind some giant, armed
in giant force, would come against me here.
But this, but you—small, pitiful and twiggy—
you put me down with wine, you blinded me.
Come back, Odysseus, and I'll treat you well,   540
praying the god of earthquake to befriend you—

---

[7] Inescapable destiny.

his son I am, for he by his avowal
fathered me, and, if he will, he may
heal me of this black wound—he and no other
of all the happy gods or mortal men.'

Few words I shouted in reply to him:

'If I could take your life I would and take
your time away, and hurl you down to hell!
The god of earthquake could not heal you there!'

At this he stretched his hands out in his darkness   550
toward the sky of stars, and prayed Poseidon:

'O hear me, lord, blue girdler of the islands,
if I am thine indeed, and thou art father:
grant that Odysseus, raider of cities, never
see his home: Laërtês' son, I mean,
who kept his hall on Ithaka. Should destiny
intend that he shall see his roof again
among his family in his father land,
far be that day, and dark the years between.
Let him lose all companions, and return   560
under strange sail to bitter days at home.'

In these words he prayed, and the god heard him.
Now he laid hands upon a bigger stone
and wheeled around, titanic for the cast,
to let it fly in the black-prowed vessel's track.
But it fell short, just aft the steering oar,
and whelming seas rose giant above the stone
to bear us onward toward the island.
                                            There

as we ran in we saw the squadron waiting,
the trim ships drawn up side by side, and all   570
our troubled friends who waited, looking seaward.
We beached her, grinding keel in the soft sand,
and waded in, ourselves, on the sandy beach.
Then we unloaded all the Kyklops' flock
to make division, share and share alike,
only my fighters voted that my ram,
the prize of all, should go to me. I slew him
by the sea side and burnt his long thighbones
to Zeus beyond the stormcloud, Kronos'[8] son,
who rules the world. But Zeus disdained my offering;   580
destruction for my ships he had in store
and death for those who sailed them, my companions.
Now all day long until the sun went down

---

[8] Equivalent of the Roman Saturn. Chief of the gods in the divine generation preceding
Zeus and the Olympian dynasty; dethroned by his son Zeus.

we made our feast on mutton and sweet wine,
till after sunset in the gathering dark
we went to sleep above the wash of ripples.

When the young Dawn with finger tips of rose
touched the world, I roused the men, gave orders
to man the ships, cast off the mooring lines;
and filing in to sit beside the rowlocks   590
oarsmen in line dipped oars in the grey sea.
So we moved out, sad in the vast offing,
having our precious lives, but not our friends.

BOOK TEN: THE GRACE OF THE WITCH

We made our landfall on Aiolia Island,
domain of Aiolos[1] Hippotadês,
the wind king, dear to the gods who never die—
an isle adrift upon the sea, ringed round
with brazen ramparts on a sheer cliffside.
Twelve children had old Aiolos at home—
six daughters and six lusty sons—and he
gave girls to boys to be their gentle brides;
now those lords, in their parents' company,
sup every day in hall—a royal feast   10
with fumes of sacrifice and winds that pipe
'round hollow courts; and all the night they sleep
on beds of filigree beside their ladies.
Here we put in, lodged in the town and palace,
while Aiolos played host to me. He kept me
one full month to hear the tale of Troy,
the ships and the return of the Akhaians,
all which I told him point by point in order.
When in return I asked his leave to sail
and asked provisioning, he stinted nothing,   20
adding a bull's hide sewn from neck to tail
into a mighty bag, bottling storm winds;
for Zeus had long ago made Aiolos
warden of winds, to rouse or calm at will.
He wedged this bag under my afterdeck,
lashing the neck with shining silver wire
so not a breath go through; only the west wind
he lofted for me in a quartering breeze
to take my squadron spanking home.

                                                No luck:
the fair wind failed us when our prudence failed.   30

[1] God of the winds, son of Hippotês. Commonly spelled *Aeolus*. A tradition locates his island off the north coast of Sicily.

Nine days and nights we sailed without event,
till on the tenth we raised our land. We neared it,
and saw men building fires along the shore;
but now, being weary to the bone, I fell
into deep slumber; I had worked the sheet
nine days alone, and given it to no one,
wishing to spill no wind on the homeward run.
But while I slept, the crew began to parley:
silver and gold, they guessed, were in that bag
bestowed on me by Aiolos' great heart;   40
and one would glance at his benchmate and say:
'It never fails. He's welcome everywhere:
hail to the captain when he goes ashore!
He brought along so many presents, plunder
out of Troy, that's it. How about ourselves—
his shipmates all the way? Nigh home we are
with empty hands. And who has gifts from Aiolos?
He has. I say we ought to crack that bag,
there's gold and silver, plenty, in that bag!'

Temptation had its way with my companions,   50
and they untied the bag.

                Then every wind

roared into hurricane; the ships went pitching
west with many cries; our land was lost.
Roused up, despairing in that gloom, I thought:
'Should I go overside for a quick finish
or clench my teeth and stay among the living?'
Down in the bilge I lay, pulling my sea cloak
over my head, while the rough gale blew the ships
and rueful crews clear back to Aiolia.

We put ashore for water; then all hands   60
gathered alongside for a mid-day meal.
When we had taken bread and drink, I picked
one soldier, and one herald, to go with me
and called again on Aiolos. I found him
at meat with his young princes and his lady,
but there beside the pillars, in his portico,
we sat down silent at the open door.
The sight amazed them, and they all exclaimed:

'Why back again, Odysseus?'

                          'What sea fiend

rose in your path?'

                    'Did we not launch you well   70
for home, or for whatever land you chose?'

Out of my melancholy I replied:

'Mischief aboard and nodding at the tiller—
a damned drowse—did for me. Make good my loss,
dear friends! You have the power!'

                           Gently I pleaded,
but they turned cold and still. Said Father Aiolos:

'Take yourself out of this island, creeping thing—
no law, no wisdom, lays it on me now
to help a man the blessed gods detest—
out! Your voyage here was cursed by heaven!'   80

He drove me from the place, groan as I would,
and comfortless we went again to sea,
days of it, till the men flagged at the oars—
no breeze, no help in sight, by our own folly—
six indistinguishable nights and days
before we raised the Laistrygonian height
and far stronghold of Lamos.[2] In that land
the daybreak follows dusk, and so the shepherd
homing calls to the cowherd setting out;
and he who never slept could earn two wages,   90
tending oxen, pasturing silvery flocks,
where the low night path of the sun is near
the sun's path by day. Here, then, we found
a curious bay with mountain walls of stone
to left and right, and reaching far inland,—
a narrow entrance opening from the sea
where cliffs converged as though to touch and close.
All of my squadron sheltered here, inside
the cavern of this bay.

                       Black prow by prow
those hulls were made fast in a limpid calm   100
without a ripple, stillness all around them.
My own black ship I chose to moor alone
on the sea side, using a rock for bollard;
and climbed a rocky point to get my bearings.
No farms, no cultivated land appeared,
but puffs of smoke rose in the wilderness;
so I sent out two picked men and a herald
to learn what race of men this land sustained.

My party found a track—a wagon road
for bringing wood down from the heights to town;   110
and near the settlement they met a daughter

---

[2] Son of Poseidon and king of the Laistrygonians. Traditions place their land in southwest
Italy or in Sicily. The following lines describe the almost continuous daylight of summer in the
far north, but it would have been impossible for Odysseus and his men to reach such latitudes.
Traditionally, the shepherd grazes his flock during the night.

of Antiphatês the Laistrygon—a stalwart
young girl taking her pail to Artakía,
the fountain where these people go for water.
My fellows hailed her, put their questions to her:
who might the king be? ruling over whom?
She waved her hand, showing her father's lodge,
so they approached it. In its gloom they saw
a woman like a mountain crag, the queen—
and loathed the sight of her. But she, for greeting,   120
called from the meeting ground her lord and master,
Antiphatês, who came to drink their blood.
He seized one man and tore him on the spot,
making a meal of him; the other two
leaped out of doors and ran to join the ships.
Behind, he raised the whole tribe howling, countless
Laistrygonês—and more than men they seemed,
gigantic when they gathered on the sky line
to shoot great boulders down from slings; and hell's own
crashing rose, and crying from the ships,   130
as planks and men were smashed to bits—poor gobbets[3]
the wildmen speared like fish and bore away.
But long before it ended in the anchorage—
havoc and slaughter—I had drawn my sword
and cut my own ship's cable. 'Men,' I shouted,
'man the oars and pull till your hearts break
if you would put this butchery behind!'
The oarsmen rent the sea in mortal fear
and my ship spurted out of range, far out
from that deep canyon where the rest were lost.   140
So we fared onward, and death fell behind,
and we took breath to grieve for our companions.

Our next landfall was on Aiaia,[4] island
of Kirkê, dire beauty and divine,
sister of baleful Aiêtês, like him
fathered by Hêlios the light of mortals
on Persê, child of the Ocean stream.

                                                        We came

washed in our silent ship upon her shore,
and found a cove, a haven for the ship—
some god, invisible, conned us in. We landed,   150
to lie down in that place two days and nights,
worn out and sick at heart, tasting our grief.
But when Dawn set another day a-shining
I took my spear and broadsword, and I climbed

---

[3] Lumps of raw meat.

[4] Later legend placed this island, home of Kirkê (Circe), near the west coast of Italy, near
Rome. Aiêtês was the king of Colchis who lost the magical Golden Fleece to Iêson (Jason) and
the Argonauts; see the headnote to Euripides' *Medea*. Medea, Aiêtês' daughter, was also a
sorceress; witchcraft ran in the family.

a rocky point above the ship, for sight
or sound of human labor. Gazing out
from that high place over a land of thicket,
oaks and wide watercourses, I could see
a smoke wisp from the woodland hall of Kirkê.
So I took counsel with myself: should I   160
go inland scouting out that reddish smoke?
No: better not, I thought, but first return
to waterside and ship, and give the men
breakfast before I sent them to explore.
Now as I went down quite alone, and came
a bowshot from the ship, some god's compassion
set a big buck in motion to cross my path—
a stag with noble antlers, pacing down
from pasture in the woods to the riverside,
as long thirst and the power of sun constrained him.   170
He started from the bush and wheeled: I hit him
square in the spine midway along his back
and the bronze point broke through it. In the dust
he fell and whinnied as life bled away.
I set one foot against him, pulling hard
to wrench my weapon from the wound, then left it,
butt-end on the ground. I plucked some withies
and twined a double strand into a rope—
enough to tie the hocks of my huge trophy;
then pickaback I lugged him to the ship,   180
leaning on my long spearshaft; I could not
haul that mighty carcass on one shoulder.
Beside the ship I let him drop, and spoke
gently and low to each man standing near:

'Come, friends, though hard beset, we'll not go down
into the House of Death before our time.
As long as food and drink remain aboard
let us rely on it, not die of hunger.'

At this those faces, cloaked in desolation
upon the waste sea beach, were bared;   190
their eyes turned toward me and the mighty trophy,
lighting, foreseeing pleasure, one by one.
So hands were washed to take what heaven sent us.
And all that day until the sun went down
we had our fill of venison and wine,
till after sunset in the gathering dusk
we slept at last above the line of breakers.
When the young Dawn with finger tips of rose
made heaven bright, I called them round and said:

'Shipmates, companions in disastrous time,   200
O my dear friends, where Dawn lies, and the West,

and where the great Sun, light of men, may go
under the earth by night, and where he rises—
of these things we know nothing. Do we know
any least thing to serve us now? I wonder.
All that I saw when I went up the rock
was one more island in the boundless main,
a low landscape, covered with woods and scrub,
and puffs of smoke ascending in mid-forest.'

They were all silent, but their hearts contracted,   210
remembering Antiphatês the Laistrygon
and that prodigious cannibal, the Kyklops.
They cried out, and the salt tears wet their eyes.
But seeing our time for action lost in weeping,
I mustered those Akhaians under arms,
counting them off in two platoons, myself
and my godlike Eurýlokhos commanding.
We shook lots in a soldier's dogskin cap
and his came bounding out—valiant Eurýlokhos!—
So off he went, with twenty-two companions   220
weeping, as mine wept, too, who stayed behind.

In the wild wood they found an open glade,
around a smooth stone house—the hall of Kirkê—
and wolves and mountain lions lay there, mild
in her soft spell, fed on her drug of evil.
None would attack—oh, it was strange, I tell you—
but switching their long tails they faced our men
like hounds, who look up when their master comes
with tidbits for them—as he will—from table.
Humbly those wolves and lions with mighty paws   230
fawned on our men—who met their yellow eyes
and feared them.
                              In the entrance way they stayed
to listen there: inside her quiet house
they heard the goddess Kirkê.

                                            Low she sang
in her beguiling voice, while on her loom
she wove ambrosial fabric sheer and bright,
by that craft known to the goddesses of heaven.
No one would speak, until Politês—most
faithful and likable of my officers, said:

'Dear friends, no need for stealth: here's a young weaver   240
singing a pretty song to set the air
a-tingle on these lawns and paven courts.
Goddess she is, or lady. Shall we greet her?'

So reassured, they all cried out together,
and she came swiftly to the shining doors

to call them in. All but Eurýlokhos—
who feared a snare—the innocents went after her.
On thrones she seated them, and lounging chairs,
while she prepared a meal of cheese and barley
and amber honey mixed with Pramnian wine,   250
adding her own vile pinch, to make them lose
desire or thought of our dear father land.
Scarce had they drunk when she flew after them
with her long stick and shut them in a pigsty—
bodies, voices, heads, and bristles, all
swinish now, though minds were still unchanged.
So, squealing, in they went. And Kirkê tossed them
acorns, mast, and cornel berries—fodder
for hogs who rut and slumber on the earth.

Down to the ship Eurýlokhos came running   260
to cry alarm, foul magic doomed his men!
But working with dry lips to speak a word
he could not, being so shaken; blinding tears
welled in his eyes; foreboding filled his heart.
When we were frantic questioning him, at last
we heard the tale: our friends were gone. Said he:

'We went up through the oak scrub where you sent us,
Odysseus, glory of commanders,
until we found a palace in a glade,
a marble house on open ground, and someone   270
singing before her loom a chill, sweet song—
goddess or girl, we could not tell. They hailed her,
and then she stepped through shining doors and said,
"Come, come in!" Like sheep they followed her,
but I saw cruel deceit, and stayed behind.
Then all our fellows vanished. Not a sound,
and nothing stirred, although I watched for hours.'

When I heard this I slung my silver-hilted
broadsword on, and shouldered my long bow,
and said, "Come, take me back the way you came.'   280
But he put both his hands around my knees
in desperate woe, and said in supplication:

'Not back there, O my lord! Oh, leave me here!
You, even you, cannot return, I know it,
I know you cannot bring away our shipmates;
better make sail with these men, quickly too,
and save ourselves from horror while we may.'

But I replied:

                                        'By heaven, Eurýlokhos,
rest here then; take food and wine;

stay in the black hull's shelter. Let me go,   290
as I see nothing for it but to go.'

I turned and left him, left the shore and ship,
and went up through the woodland hushed and shady
to find the subtle witch in her long hall.
But Hermês met me, with his golden wand,
barring the way—a boy whose lip was downy
in the first bloom of manhood, so he seemed.
He took my hand and spoke as though he knew me:

> 'Why take the inland path alone,
> poor seafarer, by hill and dale   300
> upon this island all unknown?
> Your friends are locked in Kirkê's pale;[5]
> all are become like swine to see;
> and if you go to set them free
> you go to stay, and never more make sail
> for your old home upon Thaki.[6]

> But I can tell you what to do
> to come unchanged from Kirkê's power
> and disenthrall your fighting crew:
> take with you to her bower   310
> as amulet, this plant I know—
> it will defeat her horrid show,
> so pure and potent is the flower;
> no mortal herb was ever so.

> Your cup with numbing drops of night
> and evil, stilled of all remorse,
> she will infuse to charm your sight;
> but this great herb with holy force
> will keep your mind and senses clear:
> when she turns cruel, coming near   320
> with her long stick to whip you out of doors,
> then let your cutting blade appear,

> Let instant death upon it shine,
> and she will cower and yield her bed—
> a pleasure you must not decline,
> so may her lust and fear bestead
> you and your friends, and break her spell;
> but make her swear by heaven and hell
> no witches' tricks, or else, your harness shed,
> you'll be unmanned by her as well.'   330

He bent down glittering for the magic plant
and pulled it up, black root and milky flower—

[5] An enclosed area.   [6] Ithaka.

a *molü*[7] in the language of the gods—
fatigue and pain for mortals to uproot;
but gods do this, and everything, with ease.

Then toward Olympos through the island trees
Hermês departed, and I sought out Kirkê,
my heart high with excitement, beating hard.
Before her mansion in the porch I stood
to call her, all being still. Quick as a cat   340
she opened her bright doors and sighed a welcome;
then I strode after her with heavy heart
down the long hall, and took the chair she gave me,
silver-studded, intricately carved,
made with a low footrest. The lady Kirkê
mixed me a golden cup of honeyed wine,
adding in mischief her unholy drug.
I drank, and the drink failed. But she came forward
aiming a stroke with her long stick, and whispered:

'Down in the sty and snore among the rest!'   350

Without a word, I drew my sharpened sword
and in one bound held it against her throat.
She cried out, then slid under to take my knees,
catching her breath to say, in her distress:

'What champion, of what country, can you be?
Where are your kinsmen and your city?
Are you not sluggish with my wine? Ah, wonder!
Never a mortal man that drank this cup
but when it passed his lips he had succumbed.
Hale must your heart be and your tempered will.   360
Odysseus then you are, O great contender,
of whom the glittering god with golden wand
spoke to me ever, and foretold
the black swift ship would carry you from Troy.
Put up your weapon in the sheath. We two
shall mingle and make love upon our bed.
So mutual trust may come of play and love.'

To this I said:

       'Kirkê, am I a boy,
that you should make me soft and doting now?
Here in this house you turned my men to swine;   370
now it is I myself you hold, enticing
into your chamber, to your dangerous bed,
to take my manhood when you have me stripped.
I mount no bed of love with you upon it.

[7] Usually spelled *moly.*

Or swear me first a great oath, if I do,
you'll work no more enchantment to my harm.'

She swore at once, outright, as I demanded,
and after she had sworn, and bound herself,
I entered Kirkê's flawless bed of love.

Presently in the hall her maids were busy,   380
the nymphs who waited upon Kirkê: four,
whose cradles were in fountains, under boughs,
or in the glassy seaward-gliding streams.
One came with richly colored rugs to throw
on seat and chairback, over linen covers;
a second pulled the tables out, all silver,
and loaded them with baskets all of gold;
a third mixed wine as tawny-mild as honey
in a bright bowl, and set out golden cups.
The fourth came bearing water, and lit a blaze   390
under a cauldron. By and by it bubbled,
and when the dazzling brazen vessel seethed
she filled a bathtub to my waist, and bathed me,
pouring a soothing blend on head and shoulders,
warming the soreness of my joints away.
When she had done, and smoothed me with sweet oil,
she put a tunic and a cloak around me
and took me to a silver-studded chair
with footrest, all elaborately carven.
Now came a maid to tip a golden jug   400
of water into a silver finger bowl,
and draw a polished table to my side.
The larder mistress brought her tray of loaves
with many savory slices, and she gave
the best, to tempt me. But no pleasure came;
I huddled with my mind elsewhere, oppressed.

Kirkê regarded me, as there I sat
disconsolate, and never touched a crust.
Then she stood over me and chided me:

'Why sit at table mute, Odysseus?   410
Are you mistrustful of my bread and drink?
Can it be treachery that you fear again,
after the gods' great oath I swore for you?'

I turned to her at once, and said:

                                                        'Kirkê,

where is the captain who could bear to touch
this banquet, in my place? A decent man
would see his company before him first.

Put heart in me to eat and drink—you may,
by freeing my companions. I must see them.'

But Kirkê had already turned away.   420
Her long staff in her hand, she left the hall
and opened up the sty. I saw her enter,
driving those men turned swine to stand before me.
She stroked them, each in turn, with some new chrism;[8]
and then, behold! their bristles fell away,
the course pelt grown upon them by her drug
melted away, and they were men again,
younger, more handsome, taller than before.
Their eyes upon me, each one took my hands,
and wild regret and longing pierced them through,   430
so the room rang with sobs, and even Kirkê
pitied that transformation. Exquisite
the goddess looked as she stood near me, saying:

'Son of Laërtês and the gods of old,
Odysseus, master mariner and soldier,
go to the sea beach and sea-breasting ship;
drag it ashore, full length upon the land;
stow gear and stores in rock-holes under cover;
return; be quick; bring all your dear companions.'

Now, being a man, I could not help consenting.   440
So I went down to the sea beach and the ship,
where I found all my other men on board,
weeping, in despair along the benches.
Sometimes in farmyards when the cows return
well fed from pasture to the barn, one sees
the pens give way before the calves in tumult,
breaking through to cluster about their mothers,
bumping together, bawling. Just that way
my crew poured round me when they saw me come—
their faces wet with tears as if they saw   450
their homeland, and the crags of Ithaka,
even the very town where they were born.
And weeping still they all cried out in greeting:

'Prince, what joy this is, your safe return!
Now Ithaka seems here, and we in Ithaka!
But tell us now, what death befell our friends?'

And, speaking gently, I replied:

'First we must get the ship high on the shingle,
and stow our gear and stores in clefts of rock

---

[8] An oil, usually having sacred or supernatural properties.

for cover. Then come follow me, to see   460
your shipmates in the magic house of Kirkê
eating and drinking, endlessly regaled.'

They turned back, as commanded, to this work;
only one lagged, and tried to hold the others:
Eurýlokhos it was, who blurted out:

'Where now, poor remnants? is it devil's work
you long for? Will you go to Kirkê's hall?
Swine, wolves, and lions she will make us all,
beasts of her courtyard, bound by her enchantment.
Remember those the Kyklops held, remember   470
shipmates who made that visit with Odysseus!
The daring man! They died for his foolishness!'

When I heard this I had a mind to draw
the blade that swung against my side and chop him,
bowling his head upon the ground—kinsman
or no kinsman, close to me though he was.
But others came between, saying, to stop me,

'Prince, we can leave him, if you say the word;
let him stay here on guard. As for ourselves,
show us the way to Kirkê's magic hall.'   480

So all turned inland, leaving shore and ship,
and Eurýlokhos—he, too, came on behind,
fearing the rough edge of my tongue. Meanwhile
at Kirkê's hands the rest were gently bathed,
anointed with sweet oil, and dressed afresh
in tunics and new cloaks with fleecy linings.
We found them all at supper when we came.
But greeting their old friends once more, the crew
could not hold back their tears; and now again
the rooms rang with sobs. Then Kirkê, loveliest   490
of all immortals, came to counsel me:

'Son of Laërtês and the gods of old,
Odysseus, master mariner and soldier,
enough of weeping fits. I know—I, too—
what you endured upon the inhuman sea,
what odds you met on land from hostile men.
Remain with me, and share my meat and wine;
restore behind your ribs those gallant hearts
that served you in the old days, when you sailed
from stony Ithaka. Now parched and spent,   500
your cruel wandering is all you think of,
never of joy, after so many blows.'

As we were men we could not help consenting.
So day by day we lingered, feasting long

on roasts and wine, until a year grew fat.
But when the passing months and wheeling seasons
brought the long summery days, the pause of summer,
my shipmates one day summoned me and said:

'Captain, shake off this trance, and think of home—
if home indeed awaits us,

if we shall ever see   510
your own well-timbered hall on Ithaka.'

They made me feel a pang, and I agreed.
That day, and all day long, from dawn to sundown,
we feasted on roast meat and ruddy wine,
and after sunset when the dusk came on
my men slept in the shadowy hall, but I
went through the dark to Kirkê's flawless bed
and took the goddess' knees in supplication,
urging, as she bent to hear:

'O Kirkê,

now you must keep your promise; it is time.   520
Help me make sail for home. Day after day
my longing quickens, and my company
give me no peace, but wear my heart away
pleading when you are not at hand to hear.'

The loveliest of goddesses replied:

'Son of Laërtês and the gods of old,
Odysseus, master mariner and soldier,
you shall not stay here longer against your will;
but home you may not go
unless you take a strange way round and come   530
to the cold homes of Death and pale Perséphonê.[9]
You shall hear prophecy from the rapt shade
of blind Teirêsias[10] of Thebes, forever
charged with reason even among the dead;
to him alone, of all the flitting ghosts,
Perséphonê has given a mind undarkened.'

At this I felt a weight like stone within me,
and, moaning, pressed my length against the bed,
with no desire to see the daylight more.
But when I had wept and tossed and had my fill   540
of this despair, at last I answered her:

'Kirkê, who pilots me upon this journey?
No man has ever sailed to the land of Death.'

---

[9] *Death* refers to Hades, ruler of the land of the dead. *Perséphonê* was his consort.
[10] A famous soothsayer who figures in many Greek myths and legends; see, for example,
Sophocles' *Oedipus the King.*

That loveliest of goddesses replied:

'Son of Laërtês and the gods of old,
Odysseus, master of land ways and sea ways,
feel no dismay because you lack a pilot;
only set up your mast and haul your canvas
to the fresh blowing North; sit down and steer,
and hold that wind, even to the bourne of Ocean,   550
Perséphonê's deserted strand and grove,
dusky with poplars and the drooping willow.
Run through the tide-rip, bring your ship to shore,
land there, and find the crumbling homes of Death.
Here, toward the Sorrowing Water, run the streams
of Wailing, out of Styx, and quenchless Burning—
torrents[11] that join in thunder at the Rock.
Here then, great soldier, setting foot obey me:
dig a well shaft a forearm square; pour out
libations round it to the unnumbered dead: 560
sweet milk and honey, then sweet wine, and last
clear water, scattering handfulls of white barley.
Pray now, with all your heart, to the faint dead;
swear you will sacrifice your finest heifer,
at home in Ithaka, and burn for them
her tenderest parts in sacrifice; and vow
to the lord Teirêsias, apart from all,
a black lamb, handsomest of all your flock—
thus to appease the nations of the dead.
Then slash a black ewe's throat, and a black ram,   570
facing the gloom of Erebos;[12] but turn
your head away toward Ocean. You shall see, now
souls of the buried dead in shadowy hosts,
and now you must call out to your companions
to flay those sheep the bronze knife has cut down,
for offerings, burnt flesh to those below,
to sovereign Death and pale Perséphonê.
Meanwhile draw sword from hip, crouch down, ward off
the surging phantoms from the bloody pit
until you know the presence of Teirêsias.   580
He will come soon, great captain; be it he
who gives you course and distance for your sailing
homeward across the cold fish-breeding sea.'

As the goddess ended, Dawn came stitched in gold.
Now Kirkê dressed me in my shirt and cloak,
put on a gown of subtle tissue, silvery,
then wound a golden belt about her waist
and veiled her head in linen,

---

[11] The rivers of Hades. The Sorrowing Water is Acheron; the river of wailing is Cocytus;
the burning river is Phlegethon.
[12] Part of the realm of Hades; the equivalent of primitive darkness. Also spelled *Erebus*.

while I went through the hall to rouse my crew.
I bent above each one, and gently said: 590

'Wake from your sleep: no more sweet slumber. Come,
we sail: the Lady Kirkê so ordains it.'

They were soon up, and ready at that word;
but I was not to take my men unharmed
from this place, even from this. Among them all
the youngest was Elpênor—
no mainstay in a fight nor very clever—
and this one, having climbed on Kirkê's roof
to taste the cool night, fell asleep with wine.
Waked by our morning voices, and the tramp   600
of men below, he started up, but missed
his footing on the long steep backward ladder
and fell that height headlong. The blow smashed
the nape cord, and his ghost fled to the dark.
But I was outside, walking with the rest,
saying:

                'Homeward you think we must be sailing
to our own land; no, elsewhere is the voyage
Kirkê has laid upon me. We must go
to the cold homes of Death and pale Perséphonê
to hear Teirêsias tell of time to come.'   610

They felt so stricken, upon hearing this,
they sat down wailing loud, and tore their hair.
But nothing came of giving way to grief.
Down to the shore and ship at last we went,
bowed with anguish, cheeks all wet with tears,
to find that Kirkê had been there before us
and tied nearby a black ewe and a ram:
she had gone by like air.
For who could see the passage of a goddess
unless she wished his mortal eyes aware?   620

BOOK ELEVEN: A GATHERING OF SHADES

We bore down on the ship at the sea's edge
and launched her on the salt immortal sea,
stepping our mast and spar in the black ship;
embarked the ram and ewe and went aboard
in tears, with bitter and sore dread upon us.
But now a breeze came up for us astern—
a canvas-bellying landbreeze, hale shipmate
sent by the singing nymph with sun-bright hair;
so we made fast the braces, took our thwarts,

and let the wind and steersman work the ship   10
with full sail spread all day above our coursing,
till the sun dipped, and all the ways grew dark
upon the fathomless unresting sea.

                                                                   By night

our ship ran onward toward the Ocean's[1] bourne,
the realm and region of the Men of Winter,
hidden in mist and cloud. Never the flaming
eye of Hêlios lights on those men
at morning, when he climbs the sky of stars,
nor in descending earthward out of heaven;
ruinous night being rove[2] over those wretches.   20
We made the land, put ram and ewe ashore,
and took our way along the Ocean stream
to find the place foretold for us by Kirkê.
There Perimêdês and Eurýlokhos
pinioned the sacred beasts. With my drawn blade
I spaded up the votive pit, and poured
libations round it to the unnumbered dead:
sweet milk and honey, then sweet wine, and last
clear water; and I scattered barley down.
Then I addressed the blurred and breathless dead,   30
vowing to slaughter my best heifer for them
before she calved, at home in Ithaka,
and burn the choice bits on the altar fire;
as for Teirêsias, I swore to sacrifice
a black lamb, handsomest of all our flock.
Thus to assuage the nations of the dead
I pledged these rites, then slashed the lamb and ewe,
letting their black blood stream into the wellpit.
Now the souls gathered, stirring out of Erebos,
brides and young men, and men grown old in pain,   40
and tender girls whose hearts were new to grief;
many were there, too, torn by brazen lanceheads,
battle-slain, bearing still their bloody gear.
From every side they came and sought the pit
with rustling cries; and I grew sick with fear.
But presently I gave command to my officers
to flay those sheep the bronze cut down, and make
burnt offerings of flesh to the gods below—
to sovereign Death, to pale Perséphonê.
Meanwhile I crouched with my drawn sword to keep   50
the surging phantoms from the bloody pit
till I should know the presence of Teirêsias.

---

[1] The great river believed to encompass the entire (flat) world. In the present passage,
Homer locates Hades in the north and not, as is more usual, beneath the surface of the earth.
  [2] Fastened; a nautical term. Hêlios is the sun god.

One shade came first—Elpênor, of our company,
who lay unburied still on the wide earth
as we had left him—dead in Kirkê's hall,
untouched, unmourned, when other cares compelled us.
Now when I saw him there.I wept for pity
and called out to him:

                        'How is this, Elpênor,
how could you journey to the western gloom
swifter afoot than I in the black lugger?'   60

He sighed, and answered:

                        'Son of great Laërtês,
Odysseus, master mariner and soldier,
bad luck shadowed me, and no kindly power;
ignoble death I drank with so much wine.
I slept on Kirkê's roof, then could not see
the long steep backward ladder, coming down,
and fell that height. My neck bone, buckled under,
snapped, and my spirit found this well of dark.
Now hear the grace I pray for, in the name
of those back in the world, not here—your wife   70
and father, he who gave you bread in childhood,
and your own child, your only son, Telémakhos,
long ago left at home.

                    When you make sail
and put these lodgings of dim Death behind,
you will moor ship, I know, upon Aiaia Island;
there, O my lord, remember me, I pray,
do not abandon me unwept, unburied,
to tempt the gods' wrath,[3] while you sail for home;
but fire my corpse, and all the gear I had,
and build a cairn for me above the breakers—   80
an unknown sailor's mark for men to come.
Heap up the mound there, and implant upon it
the oar I pulled in life with my companions.'

He ceased, and I replied:

                        'Unhappy spirit,
I promise you the barrow and the burial.'

So we conversed, and grimly, at a distance,
with my long sword between, guarding the blood,
while the faint image of the lad spoke on.
Now came the soul of Antikleía, dead,
my mother, daughter of Autólykos,   90

[3] The wrath of the gods would be provoked if a body on earth was left unburied and
visible.

dead now, though living still when I took ship
for holy Troy. Seeing this ghost I grieved,
but held her off, through pang on pang of tears,
till I should know the presence of Teirêsias.
Soon from the dark that prince of Thebes came forward
bearing a golden staff; and he addressed me:

'Son of Laërtês and the gods of old,
Odysseus, master of land ways and sea ways,
why leave the blazing sun, O man of woe,
to see the cold dead and the joyless region?   100
Stand clear, put up your sword;
let me but taste of blood, I shall speak true.'

At this I stepped aside, and in the scabbard
let my long sword ring home to the pommel silver,
as he bent down to the sombre blood. Then spoke
the prince of those with gift of speech:

                                                        'Great captain,
a fair wind and the honey lights of home
are all you seek. But anguish lies ahead;
the god who thunders on the land prepares it,
not to be shaken from your track, implacable,   110
in rancor for the son whose eye you blinded.
One narrow strait may take you through his blows:
denial of yourself, restraint of shipmates.
When you make landfall on Thrinákia[4] first
and quit the violet sea, dark on the land
you'll find the grazing herds of Hêlios
by whom all things are seen, all speech is known.
Avoid those kine, hold fast to your intent,
and hard seafaring brings you all to Ithaka.
But if you raid the beeves, I see destruction   120
for ship and crew. Though you survive alone,
bereft of all companions, lost for years,
under strange sail shall you come home, to find
your own house filled with trouble: insolent men
eating your livestock as they court your lady.
Aye, you shall make those men atone in blood!
But after you have dealt out death—in open
combat or by stealth—to all the suitors,
go overland on foot, and take an oar,
until one day you come where men have lived   130
with meat unsalted, never known the sea,
nor seen seagoing ships, with crimson bows
and oars that fledge light hulls for dipping flight.
The spot will soon be plain to you, and I

---

[4] Sicily. For the outcome of this prophetic warning about molesting the sun-god's cattle, see
Book XII.

can tell you how: some passerby will say,
"What winnowing fan[5] is that upon your shoulder?"
Halt, and implant your smooth oar in the turf
and make fair sacrifice to Lord Poseidon:
a ram, a bull, a great buck boar; turn back,
and carry out pure hekatombs at home   140
to all wide heaven's lords, the undying gods,
to each in order. Then a seaborne death
soft as this hand of mist will come upon you
when you are wearied out with rich old age,
your country folk in blessed peace around you.
And all this shall be just as I foretell.'

When he had done, I said at once,

                                                        'Teirêsias,
my life runs on then as the gods have spun it.
But come, now, tell me this; make this thing clear:
I see my mother's ghost among the dead   150
sitting in silence near the blood. Not once
has she glanced this way toward her son, nor spoken.
Tell me, my lord,
may she in some way come to know my presence?'

To this he answered:

                                                'I shall make it clear
in a few words and simply. Any dead man
whom you allow to enter where the blood is
will speak to you, and speak the truth; but those
deprived will grow remote again and fade.'

When he had prophesied, Teirêsias' shade   160
retired lordly to the halls of Death;
but I stood fast until my mother stirred,
moving to sip the black blood; then she knew me
and called out sorrowfully to me:

                                                        'Child,
how could you cross alive into this gloom
at the world's end?—No sight for living eyes;
great currents run between, desolate waters,
the Ocean first, where no man goes a journey
without ship's timber under him.

                                                        Say, now,
is it from Troy, still wandering, after years,   170
that you come here with ship and company?
Have you not gone at all to Ithaka?
Have you not seen your lady in your hall?'

---

[5] A tool used to separate grain from chaff.

She put these questions, and I answered her:

'Mother, I came here, driven to the land of death
in want of prophecy from Teirêsias' shade;
nor have I yet coasted Akhaia's hills
nor touched my own land, but have had hard roving
since first I joined Lord Agamémnon's host
by sea for Ilion, the wild horse country,   180
to fight the men of Troy.
But come now, tell me this, and tell me clearly,
what was the bane that pinned you down in Death?
Some ravaging long illness, or mild arrows
a-flying down one day from Artemis?[6]
Tell me of Father, tell me of the son
I left behind me; have they still my place,
my honors, or have other men assumed them?
Do they not say that I shall come no more?
And tell me of my wife: how runs her thought,   190
still with her child, still keeping our domains,
or bride again to the best of the Akhaians?'

To this my noble mother quickly answered:

'Still with her child indeed she is, poor heart,
still in your palace hall. Forlorn her nights
and days go by, her life used up in weeping.
But no man takes your honored place. Telémakhos
has care of all your garden plots and fields,
and holds the public honor of a magistrate,
feasting and being feasted. But your father   200
is country bound and comes to town no more.
He owns no bedding, rugs, or fleecy mantles,
but lies down, winter nights, among the slaves,
rolled in old cloaks for cover, near the embers.
Or when the heat comes at the end of summer,
the fallen leaves, all round his vineyard plot,
heaped into windrows,[7] make his lowly bed.
He lies now even so, with aching heart,
and longs for your return, while age comes on him.
So I, too, pined away, so doom befell me,   210
not that the keen-eyed huntress with her shafts
had marked me down and shot to kill me; not
that illness overtook me—no true illness
wasting the body to undo the spirit;
only my loneliness for you, Odysseus,
for your kind heart and counsel, gentle Odysseus,
took my own life away.'

---

[6] As archer-goddess, Artemis provided the gift of painless death. Among other things, she was protectress of the weak.
[7] Drifted heaps, as of leaves or snow.

                                                    I bit my lip,

rising perplexed, with longing to embrace her,
and tried three times, putting my arms around her,
but she went sifting through my hands, impalpable   220
as shadows are, and wavering like a dream.
Now this embittered all the pain I bore,
and I cried in the darkness:

                                                    'O my mother,

will you not stay, be still, here in my arms,
may we not, in this place of Death, as well,
hold one another, touch with love, and taste
salt tears' relief, the twinge of welling tears?
Or is this all hallucination, sent
against me by the iron queen, Perséphonê,
to make me groan again?'

                                          My noble mother   230

answered quickly:

                                          'O my child—alas,

most sorely tried of men—great Zeus's daughter,
Perséphonê, knits no illusion for you.
All mortals meet this judgment when they die.
No flesh and bone are here, none bound by sinew,
since the bright-hearted pyre consumed them down—
the white bones long exanimate[8]—to ash;
dreamlike the soul flies, insubstantial.

You must crave sunlight soon.

                                    Note all things strange

seen here, to tell your lady in after days.'   240

So went our talk; then other shadows came,
ladies in company, sent by Perséphonê—
consorts or daughters of illustrious men—
crowding about the black blood.

                                          I took thought

how best to separate and question them,
and saw no help for it, but drew once more
the long bright edge of broadsword from my hip,
that none should sip the blood in company
but one by one, in order; so it fell
that each declared her lineage and name.   250

Here was great loveliness of ghosts! I saw
before them all, that princess of great ladies,

---

[8] Separated from the vital spirit, or "soul."

Tyro,[9] Salmoneus' daughter, as she told me,
and queen to Krêtheus, a son of Aiolos.
She had gone daft for the river Enipeus,
most graceful of all running streams, and ranged
all day by Enipeus' limpid side,
whose form the foaming girdler of the islands,
the god who makes earth tremble, took and so
lay down with her where he went flooding seaward,   260
their bower a purple billow, arching round
to hide them in a sea-vale, god and lady.
Now when his pleasure was complete, the god
spoke to her softly, holding fast her hand:

'Dear mortal, go in joy! At the turn of seasons,
winter to summer, you shall bear me sons;
no lovemaking of gods can be in vain.
Nurse our sweet children tenderly, and rear them.
Home with you now, and hold your tongue, and tell
no one your lover's name—though I am yours,   270
Poseidon, lord of surf that makes earth tremble.'

He plunged away into the deep sea swell,
and she grew big with Pelias and Neleus,
powerful vassals, in their time, of Zeus.
Pelias lived on broad Iolkos seaboard
rich in flocks, and Neleus at Pylos.
As for the sons borne by that queen of women
to Krêtheus, their names were Aison, Pherês,
and Amytháon, expert charioteer.

Next after her I saw Antiopê,   280
daughter of Ásopos. She too could boast
a god for lover, having lain with Zeus
and borne two sons to him: Amphion and
Zêthos, who founded Thebes, the upper city,
and built the ancient citadel. They sheltered
no life upon that plain, for all their power,
without a fortress wall.

                                And next I saw
Amphitrion's true wife, Alkmênê,[10] mother,
as all men know, of lionish Heraklês,
conceived when she lay close in Zeus's arms;   290
and Megarê, high-hearted Kreon's daughter,
wife of Amphitrion's unwearying son.

---

[9] A queen of Thessaly, enamored of the river-god Enipeus, in whose guise Poseidon made love to her. She bore him two sons: Pelias, the usurper-king of Iolkos (see headnote to Euripides' *Medea*), and Neleus (the father of Nestor, who appears earlier in the *Odyssey*).

[10] She is a "true wife" because Zeus had adopted the disguise of her husband Amphitrion in order to lie with her; the offspring of this union was Heraklês (Hercules).

I saw the mother of Oidipous, Epikastê,[11]
whose great unwitting deed it was
to marry her own son. He took that prize
from a slain father; presently the gods
brought all to light that made the famous story.
But by their fearsome wills he kept his throne
in dearest Thebes, all through his evil days,
while she descended to the place of Death,   300
god of the locked and iron door. Steep down
from a high rafter, throttled in her noose,
she swung, carried away by pain, and left him
endless agony from a mother's Furies.

And I saw Khloris, that most lovely lady,
whom for her beauty in the olden time
Neleus wooed with countless gifts, and married.
She was the youngest daughter of Amphion,
son of Iasos. In those days he held
power at Orkhómenos, over the Minyai.   310
At Pylos then as queen she bore her children—
Nestor, Khromios, Periklýmenos,
and Pêro, too, who turned the heads of men
with her magnificence. A host of princes
from nearby lands came courting her; but Neleus
would hear of no one, not unless the suitor
could drive the steers of giant Íphiklos
from Phylakê—longhorns, broad in the brow,
so fierce that one man only, a diviner,[12]
offered to round them up. But bitter fate   320
saw him bound hand and foot by savage herdsmen.
Then days and months grew full and waned, the year
went wheeling round, the seasons came again,
before at last the power of Íphiklos,
relenting, freed the prisoner, who foretold
all things to him. So Zeus's will was done.

And I saw Lêda,[13] wife of Tyndareus,
upon whom Tyndareus had sired twins
indomitable: Kastor, tamer of horses,

[11] More commonly known as *Jocasta*. She was mother and wife of the Theban ruler Oidipous (Oedipus). The story, in which he unwittingly kills his father and marries his mother, is best known through Sophocles' drama *Oedipus the King*. Jocasta committed suicide after learning that she had been guilty of incest.

[12] Melampous, who was gifted with prophetic power; the giant released him in return for his services as a prophet. In some versions of the myth, Melampous performs the described feats as a service to his brother Bias, who courts and eventually marries Pêro.

[13] Mother, by Zeus, of Helen of Troy. By her mortal husband, Tyndareus, she is also mother of Agamémnon's wife Klytaimnéstra and of the twins named Kastor and Polydeukês (better known in later myth and in astronomy as the "Gemini," Castor and Pollux). The twins are granted life after death but can never be both alive at the same time. In some versions of the myth the twins' father is Zeus.

and Polydeukês, best in the boxing ring.   330
Those two live still, though life-creating earth
embraces them: even in the underworld
honored as gods by Zeus, each day in turn
one comes alive, the other dies again.

Then after Lêda to my vision came
the wife of Aloeus, Iphimedeia,
proud that she once had held the flowing sea
and borne him sons, thunderers for a day,
the world-renowned Otos and Ephialtês.
Never were men on such a scale   340
bred on the plowlands and the grainlands, never
so magnificent any, after Orion.
At nine years old they towered nine fathoms tall,
nine cubits in the shoulders, and they promised
furor upon Olympos, heaven broken by battle cries,
the day they met the gods in arms.

                                            With Ossa's
mountain peak they meant to crown Olympos
and over Ossa Pelion's[14] forest pile
for footholds up the sky. As giants grown
they might have done it, but the bright son[15] of Zeus   350
by Lêto of the smooth braid shot them down
while they were boys unbearded; no dark curls
clustered yet from temples to the chin.

Then I saw Phaidra, Prokris; and Ariadnê,
daughter of Minos,[16] the grim king. Theseus took her
aboard with him from Krete for the terraced land
of ancient Athens; but he had no joy of her.
Artemis killed her on the Isle of Dia
at a word from Dionysos.

                                    Maira, then,
and Klymênê, and that detested queen,   360
Eríphylê,[17] who betrayed her lord for gold . . .
but how name all the women I beheld there,

[14] The mountains Ossa and Pelion are near Olympos, where Zeus and his generation of deities dwell.

[15] Apollo.

[16] King of Krete (Crete), in some myths regarded as a just man who posthumously became a judge of the dead. In other myths he is a savage ruler who demanded that Athens provide victims for human sacrifice to the monstrous bull called the Minotaur. The Athenian ruler Theseus, husband of Phaidra (Phaedra), killed the Minotaur with the aid of Ariadnê, her sister. After eloping with Ariadnê, Theseus abandoned her on the island of Dia (Naxos). Ariadnê then incurred the anger of the god Dionysos, though in most versions of the myth she wedded him.

[17] Corrupted by Polyneices (son of Oidipous of Thebes) with the gift of a gold necklace, Eríphylê treacherously persuaded her husband Amphiaraos to take part in an ill-fated assault on Thebes in which he was killed.

daughters and wives of kings? The starry night
wanes long before I close.

                                        Here, or aboard ship,

amid the crew, the hour for sleep has come.
Our sailing is the gods' affair and yours."

Then he fell silent. Down the shadowy hall
the enchanted banqueters were still. Only
the queen with ivory pale arms, Arêtê, spoke,
saying to all the silent men:

                                        "Phaiákians,   370

how does he stand, now, in your eyes, this captain,
the look and bulk of him, the inward poise?
He is my guest, but each one shares that honor.
Be in no haste to send him on his way
or scant your bounty in his need. Remember
how rich, by heaven's will, your possessions are."

Then Ekhenêos, the old soldier, eldest
of all Phaiákians, added his word:

"Friends, here was nothing but our own thought spoken,
the mark hit square. Our duties to her majesty.   380
For what is to be said and done,
we wait upon Alkínoös' command."

At this the king's voice rang:

                                        "I so command—

as sure as it is I who, while I live,
rule the sea rovers of Phaiákia. Our friend
longs to put out for home, but let him be
content to rest here one more day, until
I see all gifts bestowed. And every man
will take thought for his launching and his voyage,
I most of all, for I am master here."   390

Odysseus, the great tactician, answered:

"Alkínoös, king and admiration of men,
even a year's delay, if you should urge it,
in loading gifts and furnishing for sea—
I too could wish it; better far that I
return with some largesse of wealth about me—
I shall be thought more worthy of love and courtesy
by every man who greets me home in Ithaka."

The king said:

                                        "As to that, one word, Odysseus:
from all we see, we take you for no swindler—   400

though the dark earth be patient of so many,
scattered everywhere, baiting their traps with lies
of old times and of places no one knows.
You speak with art, but your intent is honest.
The Argive troubles, and your own troubles,
you told as a poet would, a man who knows the world.
But now come tell me this: among the dead
did you meet any of your peers, companions
who sailed with you and met their doom at Troy?
Here's a long night—an endless night—before us,   410
and no time yet for sleep, not in this hall.
Recall the past deeds and the strange adventures.
I could stay up until the sacred Dawn
as long as you might wish to tell your story."

Odysseus the great tactician answered:

"Alkínoös, king and admiration of men,
there is a time for story telling; there is
also a time for sleep. But even so,
if, indeed, listening be still your pleasure,
I must not grudge my part. Other and sadder   420
tales there are to tell, of my companions,
of some who came through all the Trojan spears,
clangor and groan of war,
only to find a brutal death at home—
and a bad wife behind it.

                                                        After Perséphonê,
icy and pale, dispersed the shades of women,
the soul of Agamémnon, son of Atreus,
came before me, sombre in the gloom,
and others gathered round, all who were with him
when death and doom struck in Aegísthos' hall.   430
Sipping the black blood, the tall shade perceived me,
and cried out sharply, breaking into tears;
then tried to stretch his hands toward me, but could not,
being bereft of all the reach and power
he once felt in the great torque of his arms.
Gazing at him, and stirred, I wept for pity,
and spoke across to him:

                                                        'O son of Atreus,
illustrious Lord Marshal, Agamémnon,
what was the doom that brought you low in death?
Were you at sea, aboard ship, and Poseidon   440
blew up a wicked squall to send you under,
or were you cattle-raiding on the mainland
or in a fight for some strongpoint, or women,
when the foe hit you to your mortal hurt?'

But he replied at once:

'Son of Laërtês,
Odysseus, master of land ways and sea ways,
neither did I go down with some good ship
in any gale Poseidon blew, nor die
upon the mainland, hurt by foes in battle.
It was Aigísthos who designed my death,   450
he and my heartless wife,[18] and killed me, after
feeding me, like an ox felled at the trough.
That was my miserable end—and with me
my fellows butchered, like so many swine
killed for some troop, or feast, or wedding banquet
in a great landholder's household. In your day
you have seen men, and hundreds, die in war,
in the bloody press, or downed in single combat,
but these were murders you would catch your breath at:
think of us fallen, all our throats cut, winebowl   460
brimming, tables laden on every side,
while blood ran smoking over the whole floor.
In my extremity I heard Kassandra,[19]
Priam's daughter, piteously crying
as the traitress Klytaimnéstra made to kill her
along with me. I heaved up from the ground
and got my hands around the blade, but she
eluded me, that whore. Nor would she close
my two eyes[20] as my soul swam to the underworld
or shut my lips. There is no being more fell,   470
more bestial than a wife in such an action,
and what an action that one planned!
The murder of her husband and her lord.
Great god, I thought my children and my slaves
at least would give me welcome. But that woman,
plotting a thing so low, defiled herself
and all her sex, all women yet to come,
even those few who may be virtuous.'

He paused then, and I answered:

'Foul and dreadful.
That was the way that Zeus who views the wide world   480
vented his hatred on the sons of Atreus—
intrigues of women, even from the start.

Myriads
died by Helen's fault, and Klytaimnéstra
plotted against you half the world away.'

---

[18] In Agamémnon's version here, his wife (as in Aeschylus' *Oresteia*) bears a greater responsibility for the murder than in the version outlined in Book IV.

[19] A Trojan princess and prophetess. Agamémnon brought her home from Troy as a slave. Also spelled *Cassandra*.

[20] That is, she would not perform the customary funeral rites.

And he at once said:

'Let it be a warning

even to you. Indulge a woman never,
and never tell her all you know. Some things
a man may tell, some he should cover up.
Not that I see a risk for you, Odysseus,
of death at your wife's hands. She is too wise,   490
too clear-eyed, sees alternatives too well,
Penélopê, Ikários' daughter—
that young bride whom we left behind—think of it!—
when we sailed off to war. The baby boy
still cradled at her breast—now he must be
a grown man, and a lucky one. By heaven,
you'll see him yet, and he'll embrace his father
with old fashioned respect, and rightly.

My own

lady never let me glut my eyes
on my own son, but bled me to death first.   500
One thing I will advise, on second thought;
stow it away and ponder it.

Land your ship

in secret on your island; give no warning.
The day of faithful wives is gone forever.

But tell me, have you any word at all
about my son's[21] life? Gone to Orkhómenos
or sandy Pylos, can he be? Or waiting
with Meneláos in the plain of Sparta?
Death on earth has not yet taken Orestês.'

But I could only answer:

'Son of Atreus,   510

why do you ask these questions of me? Neither
news of home have I, nor news of him,
alive or dead. And empty words are evil.'

So we exchanged our speech, in bitterness,
weighed down by grief, and tears welled in our eyes,
when there appeared the spirit of Akhilleus,
son of Peleus; then Patróklos' shade,
and then Antílokhos, and then Aias,
first among all the Danaans in strength
and bodily beauty, next to prince Akhilleus.   520
Now that great runner, grandson of Aíakhos,
recognized me and called across to me:

[21] Agamémnon asks about Orestês, who avenged his father's murder.

'Son of Laërtês and the gods of old,
Odysseus, master mariner and soldier,
old knife, what next? What greater feat remains
for you to put your mind on, after this?
How did you find your way down to the dark
where these dimwitted dead are camped forever,
the after images of used-up men?'

                                        I answered:

'Akhilleus, Peleus' son, strongest of all   530
among the Akhaians, I had need of foresight
such as Teirêsias alone could give
to help me, homeward bound for the crags of Ithaka.
I have not yet coasted Akhaia, not yet
touched my land; my life is all adversity.
But was there ever a man more blest by fortune
than you, Akhilleus? Can there ever be?
We ranked you with immortals in your lifetime,
we Argives did, and here your power is royal
among the dead men's shades. Think, then, Akhilleus: 540
you need not be so pained by death.'

                                        To this
he answered swiftly:

                        'Let me hear no smooth talk
of death from you, Odysseus, light of councils.
Better, I say, to break sod as a farm hand
for some poor country man, on iron rations,
than lord it over all the exhausted dead.
Tell me, what news of the prince my son:[22] did he
come after me to make a name in battle
or could it be he did not? Do you know
if rank and honor still belong to Peleus[23]   550
in the towns of the Myrmidons? Or now, may be,
Hellas and Phthia[24] spurn him, seeing old age
fetters him, hand and foot. I cannot help him
under the sun's rays, cannot be that man
I was on Troy's wide seaboard, in those days
when I made bastion for the Argives
and put an army's best men in the dust.
Were I but whole again, could I go now
to my father's house, one hour would do to make
my passion and my hands no man could hold   560
hateful to any who shoulder him aside.'

---

[22] Neoptólemos, or Pyrrhus, who was brought to the Trojan war after his father's death and killed Priam, the Trojan king.
[23] Akhilleus' father.   [24] Greece and Peleus' kingdom.

Now when he paused I answered:

                                            'Of all that—

of Peleus' life, that is—I know nothing;
but happily I can tell you the whole story
of Neoptólemos, as you require.
In my own ship I brought him out from Skyros
to join the Akhaians under arms.

                                  And I can tell you,

in every council before Troy thereafter
your son spoke first and always to the point;
no one but Nestor and I could out-debate him.   570
And when we formed against the Trojan line
he never hung back in the mass, but ranged
far forward of his troops—no man could touch him
for gallantry. Aye, scores went down before him
in hard fights man to man. I shall not tell
all about each, or name them all—the long
roster of enemies he put out of action,
taking the shock of charges on the Argives.
But what a champion his lance ran through
in Eurýpulos[25] the son of Télephos! Keteians   580
in throngs around that captain also died—
all because Priam's gifts had won his mother
to send the lad to battle; and I thought
Memnon alone in splendor ever outshone him.

But one fact more: while our picked Argive crew
still rode that hollow horse Epeios built,
and when the whole thing lay with me, to open
the trapdoor of the ambuscade or not,
at that point our Danaan lords and soldiers
wiped their eyes, and their knees began to quake,   590
all but Neoptólemos. I never saw
his tanned cheek change color or his hand
brush one tear away. Rather he prayed me,
hand on hilt, to sortie, and he gripped
his tough spear, bent on havoc for the Trojans.
And when we had pierced and sacked Priam's tall city
he loaded his choice plunder and embarked
with no scar on him; not a spear had grazed him
nor the sword's edge in close work—common wounds
one gets in war. Arês in his mad fits   600
knows no favorites.'

                                  But I said no more,
for he had gone off striding the field of asphodel,[26]

---

[25] Leader of a force persuaded to join the war in support of the Trojans.
[26] A flower, possibly a variety of narcissus.

the ghost of our great runner, Akhilleus Aiákidês,
glorying in what I told him of his son.

Now other souls of mournful dead stood by,
each with his troubled questioning, but one
remained alone, apart: the son of Télamon,
Aîas, it was—the great shade burning still[27]
because I had won favor on the beachhead
in rivalry over Akhilleus' arms. 610
The Lady Thetis, mother of Akhilleus,
laid out for us the dead man's battle gear,
and Trojan children, with Athena,
named the Danaan fittest to own them. Would
god I had not borne the palm that day!
For earth took Aîas then to hold forever,
the handsomest and, in all feats of war,
noblest of the Danaans after Akhilleus.
Gently therefore I called across to him:

'Aîas, dear son of royal Télamon, 620
you would not then forget, even in death,
your fury with me over those accurst
calamitous arms?—and so they were, a bane
sent by the gods upon the Argive host.
For when you died by your own hand we lost
a tower, formidable in war. All we Akhaians
mourn you forever, as we do Akhilleus;
and no one bears the blame but Zeus.
He fixed that doom for you because he frowned
on the whole expedition of our spearmen. 630
My lord, come nearer, listen to our story!
Conquer your indignation and your pride.'

But he gave no reply, and turned away,
following other ghosts toward Erebos.
Who knows if in that darkness he might still
have spoken, and I answered?

But my heart

longed, after this, to see the dead elsewhere.

And now there came before my eyes Minos,
the son of Zeus, enthroned, holding a golden staff,
dealing out justice among ghostly pleaders 640
arrayed about the broad doorways of Death.

And then I glimpsed Orion, the huge hunter,
gripping his club, studded with bronze, unbreakable,

---

[27] After the death of Akhilleus, the "greater" Aîas (Ajax) and Odysseus had been rival claimants for Akhilleus' weapons; when the arms were awarded to Odysseus, Aîas killed himself.

with wild beasts he had overpowered in life
on lonely mountainsides, now brought to bay
on fields of asphodel.

                                        And I saw Títyos,

the son of Gaia, lying
abandoned over nine square rods of plain.
Vultures, hunched above him, left and right,
rifling his belly, stabbed into the liver,   650
and he could never push them off.

                                        This hulk

had once committed rape of Zeus's mistress,
Lêto, in her glory, when she crossed
the open grass of Panopeus toward Pytho.

Then I saw Tántalos[28] put to the torture:
in a cool pond he stood, lapped round by water
clear to the chin, and being athirst he burned
to slake his dry weasand[29] with drink, though drink
he would not ever again. For when the old man
put his lips down to the sheet of water   660
it vanished round his feet, gulped underground,
and black mud baked there in a wind from hell.
Boughs, too, drooped low above him, big with fruit,
pear trees, pomegranates, brilliant apples,
luscious figs, and olives ripe and dark;
but if he stretched his hand for one, the wind
under the dark sky tossed the bough beyond him.

Then Sísyphos[30] in torment I beheld
being roustabout to a tremendous boulder.
Leaning with both arms braced and legs driving,   670
he heaved it toward a height, and almost over,
but then a Power spun him round and sent
the cruel boulder bounding again to the plain.
Whereon the man bent down again to toil,
dripping sweat, and the dust rose overhead.
Next I saw manifest the power of Heraklês—
a phantom,[31] this, for he himself has gone
feasting amid the gods, reclining soft
with Hêbê of the ravishing pale ankles,
daughter of Zeus and Hêra, shod in gold.   680
But, in my vision, all the dead around him

[28] The sin for which Tántalos (Tantalus) is being punished here is uncertain—possibly it is for revealing the gods' secrets, possibly for his serving his son's flesh to the gods (see the headnote to Aeschylus' *Oresteia*).

[29] Throat.

[30] A Corinthian ruler, noted during his lifetime for cunning treachery. More commonly spelled *Sisyphus*.

[31] Heraklês, or Hercules, was taken to heaven after his death. He was thereafter wedded to the goddess Hêbê.

cried like affrighted birds; like Night itself
he loomed with naked bow and nocked arrow
and glances terrible as continual archery.
My hackles rose at the gold swordbelt he wore
sweeping across him: gorgeous intaglio
of savage bears, boars, lions with wildfire eyes,
swordfights, battle, slaughter, and sudden death—
the smith who had that belt in him, I hope
he never made, and never will make, another.   690
The eyes of the vast figure rested on me,
and of a sudden he said in kindly tones:

'Son of Laërtês and the gods of old,
Odysseus, master mariner and soldier,
under a cloud, you too? Destined to grinding
labors like my own in the sunny world?
Son of Kroníon Zeus or not, how many
days I sweated out, being bound in servitude
to a man far worse than I, a rough master![32]
He made me hunt this place one time   700
to get the watchdog of the dead: no more
perilous task, he thought, could be; but I
brought back that beast, up from the underworld;
Hermês and grey-eyed Athena showed the way.'

And Heraklês, down the vistas of the dead,
faded from sight; but I stood fast, awaiting
other great souls who perished in times past.
I should have met, then, god-begotten Theseus
and Peirithoös,[33] whom both I longed to see,
but first came shades in thousands, rustling   710
in a pandemonium of whispers, blown together,
and the horror took me that Perséphonê
had brought from darker hell some saurian death's head.[34]
I whirled then, made for the ship, shouted to crewmen
to get aboard and cast off the stern hawsers,
an order soon obeyed. They took their thwarts,
and the ship went leaping toward the stream of Ocean
first under oars, then with a following wind.

BOOK TWELVE: SEA PERILS AND DEFEAT

The ship sailed on, out of the Ocean Stream,
riding a long swell on the open sea
for the Island of Aiaia.

[32] Eurystheus, in whose service Heraklês was forced to perform many superhumanly difficult feats, including the capture of Cerberus, the dog who guarded the realm of the dead.
[33] A friend of Theseus.   [34] Reptilian specter.

                                        Summering Dawn
has dancing grounds there, and the Sun his rising;[1]
but still by night we beached on a sand shelf
and waded in beyond the line of breakers
to fall asleep, awaiting the Day Star.

When the young Dawn with finger tips of rose
made heaven bright, I sent shipmates to bring
Elpênor's body from the house of Kirkê.   10
We others cut down timber on the foreland,
on a high point, and built his pyre of logs,
then stood by weeping while the flame burnt through
corse and equipment.

                                    Then we heaped his barrow,
lifting a gravestone on the mound, and fixed
his light but unwarped oar against the sky.
These were our rites in memory of him. Soon, then,
knowing us back from the Dark Land, Kirkê came
freshly adorned for us, with handmaids bearing
loaves, roast meats, and ruby-colored wine.   20

She stood among us in immortal beauty
jesting:

                              'Hearts of oak, did you go down
alive into the homes of Death? One visit
finishes all men but yourselves, twice mortal!
Come, here is meat and wine, enjoy your feasting
for one whole day; and in the dawn tomorrow
you shall put out to sea. Sailing directions,
landmarks, perils, I shall sketch for you, to keep you
from being caught by land or water
in some black sack of trouble.'

                                        In high humor   30
and ready for carousal, we agreed;
so all that day until the sun went down
we feasted on roast meat and good red wine,
till after sunset, at the fall of night,
the men dropped off to sleep by the stern hawsers.
She took my hand then, silent in the hush,
drew me apart, made me sit down, and lay
beside me, softly questioning, as I told
all I had seen, from first to last.

                                    Then said the Lady Kirkê:
'So: all those trials are over.

                                    Listen with care   40
to this, now, and a god will arm your mind.

---

[1] Aiaia is distinguished from the sunless land of the dead which they have just left behind.

Square in your ship's path are Seirênês,[2] crying
beauty to bewitch men coasting by;
woe to the innocent who hears that sound!
He will not see his lady nor his children
in joy, crowding about him, home from sea;
the Seirênês will sing his mind away
on their sweet meadow lolling. There are bones
of dead men rotting in a pile beside them
and flayed skins shrivel around the spot.

Steer wide; 50

keep well to seaward; plug your oarsmen's ears
with beeswax kneaded soft; none of the rest
should hear that song.

But if you wish to listen,

let the men tie you in the lugger,[3] hand
and foot, back to the mast, lashed to the mast,
so you may hear those harpies'[4] thrilling voices;
shout as you will, begging to be untied,
your crew must only twist more line around you
and keep their stroke up, till the singers fade.
What then? One of two courses you may take,   60
and you yourself must weigh them. I shall not
plan the whole action for you now, but only
tell you of both.

Ahead are beetling rocks

and dark blue glancing Amphitritê,[5] surging,
roars around them. Prowling Rocks,[6] or Drifters,
the gods in bliss have named them—named them well.
Not even birds can pass them by, not even
the timorous doves that bear ambrosia
to Father Zeus; caught by downdrafts, they die
on rockwall smooth as ice.

Each time, the Father 70

wafts a new courier to make up his crew.

Still less can ships get searoom of these Drifters,
whose boiling surf, under high fiery winds,
carries tossing wreckage of ships and men.
Only one ocean-going craft, the far-famed
Argo,[7] made it, sailing from Aiêta;
but she, too, would have crashed on the big rocks

---

[2] In Grecian fable, women who could lure men to their destruction through their entrancing song. Also spelled *Sirens.*

[3] A small boat.

[4] In this passage, the word "harpies" means "temptresses." They are not the obscene and filthy females who appear in Virgil's *Aeneid,* Book III.

[5] Sea-nymph; consort of Poseidon. She is the female personification of the ocean.

[6] Possibly the Planctae, islands at the north end of what is now called the Strait of Messina, which divides Sicily from the Italian mainland.

[7] The fabled ship, manned by great heroes and captained by Iêson (Jason), that sailed to capture the Golden Fleece.

if Hêra had not pulled her through, for love
of Iêson, her captain.

A second course[8]

lies between headlands. One is a sharp mountain   80
piercing the sky, with stormcloud round the peak
dissolving never, not in the brightest summer,
to show heaven's azure there, nor in the fall.
No mortal man could scale it, nor so much
as land there, not with twenty hands and feet,
so sheer the cliffs are—as of polished stone.
Midway that height, a cavern full of mist
opens toward Erebos and evening. Skirting
this in the lugger, great Odysseus,
your master bowman, shooting from the deck,   90
would come short of the cavemouth with his shaft;
but that is the den of Skylla, where she yaps
abominably, a newborn whelp's cry,
though she is huge and monstrous. God or man,
no one could look on her in joy. Her legs—
and there are twelve—are like great tentacles,
unjointed, and upon her serpent necks
are borne six heads like nightmares of ferocity,
with triple serried rows of fangs and deep
gullets of black death. Half her length, she sways   100
her heads in air, outside her horrid cleft,
hunting the sea around that promontory
for dolphins, dogfish, or what bigger game
thundering Amphitritê feeds in thousands.
And no ship's company can claim
to have passed her without loss and grief; she takes,
from every ship, one man for every gullet.

The opposite point seems more a tongue of land
you'd touch with a good bowshot, at the narrows.
A great wild fig, a shaggy mass of leaves,   110
grows on it, and Kharybdis lurks below
to swallow down the dark sea tide. Three times
from dawn to dusk she spews it up
and sucks it down again three times, a whirling
maelstrom; if you come upon her then
the god who makes earth tremble could not save you.
No, hug the cliff of Skylla, take your ship
through on a racing stroke. Better to mourn
six men than lose them all, and the ship, too.'

[8] The following lines describe the two fabled monsters Skylla (Scylla) and Kharybdis (Charybdis), who presumably personify the dangers of the Strait of Messina. Skylla is a treacherous reef, Kharybdis a whirlpool. The proverbial phrase "between Scylla and Charybdis" has come to mean a situation in which one has to choose between equally dreadful alternatives.

So her advice ran; but I faced her, saying: 120

'Only instruct me, goddess, if you will,
how, if possible, can I pass Kharybdis,
or fight off Skylla when she raids my crew?'

Swiftly that loveliest goddess answered me:

'Must you have battle in your heart forever?
The bloody toil of combat? Old contender,
will you not yield to the immortal gods?
That nightmare cannot die, being eternal
evil itself—horror, and pain, and chaos;
there is no fighting her, no power can fight her,   130
all that avails is flight.

                       Lose headway there
along that rockface while you break out arms,
and she'll swoop over you, I fear, once more,
taking one man again for every gullet.
No, no, put all your backs into it, row on;
invoke Blind Force, that bore this scourge of men,
to keep her from a second strike against you.

Then you will coast Thrinákia,[9] the island
where Hêlios' cattle graze, fine herds, and flocks
of goodly sheep. The herds and flocks are seven,   140
with fifty beasts in each.

                        No lambs are dropped,
or calves, and these fat cattle never die.
Immortal, too, their cowherds are—their shepherds—
Phaëthousa and Lampetía, sweetly braided
nymphs that divine Neaira bore
to the overlord of high noon, Hêlios.
These nymphs their gentle mother bred and placed
upon Thrinákia, the distant land,
in care of flocks and cattle for their father.

Now give those kine a wide berth, keep your thoughts   150
intent upon your course for home,
and hard seafaring brings you all to Ithaka.
But if you raid the beeves, I see destruction
for ship and crew.

                     Rough years then lie between
you and your homecoming, alone and old,
the one survivor, all companions lost.'

As Kirkê spoke, Dawn mounted her golden throne,
and on the first rays Kirkê left me, taking

---

[9] Sicily.

her way like a great goddess up the island.
I made straight for the ship, roused up the men   160
to get aboard and cast off at the stern.
They scrambled to their places by the rowlocks
and all in line dipped oars in the grey sea.
But soon an off-shore breeze blew to our liking—
a canvas-bellying breeze, a lusty shipmate
sent by the singing nymph with sunbright hair.
So we made fast the braces, and we rested,
letting the wind and steersman work the ship.
The crew being now silent before me, I
addressed them, sore at heart:

                                  'Dear friends,   170
more than one man, or two, should know those things
Kirkê foresaw for us and shared with me,
so let me tell her forecast: then we die
with our eyes open, if we are going to die,
or know what death we baffle if we can. Seirênês
weaving a haunting song over the sea
we are to shun, she said, and their green shore
all sweet with clover; yet she urged that I
alone should listen to their song. Therefore
you are to tie me up, tight as a splint,   180
erect along the mast, lashed to the mast,
and if I shout and beg to be untied,
take more turns of the rope to muffle me.'

I rather dwelt on this part of the forecast,[10]
while our good ship made time, bound outward down
the wind for the strange island of Seirênês.
Then all at once the wind fell, and a calm
came over all the sea, as though some power
lulled the swell.

                      The crew were on their feet
briskly, to furl the sail, and stow it; then,   190
each in place, they poised the smooth oar blades
and sent the white foam scudding by. I carved
a massive cake of beeswax into bits
and rolled them in my hands until they softened—
no long task, for a burning heat came down
from Hêlios, lord of high noon. Going forward
I carried wax along the line, and laid it
thick on their ears. They tied me up, then, plumb
amidships, back to the mast, lashed to the mast,
and took themselves again to rowing. Soon,   200
as we came smartly within hailing distance,

---

[10]Odysseus shrewdly failed to mention the inevitable devouring of some of his men by
Skylla.

the two Seirênês, noting our fast ship
off their point, made ready, and they sang:

> *This way, oh turn your bows,*
>   *Akhaia's glory,*
> *As all the world allows—*
>   *Moor and be merry.*
>
> *Sweet coupled airs we sing.*
>   *No lonely seafarer*
> *Holds clear of entering*   210
>   *Our green mirror.*
>
> *Pleased by each purling note*
>   *Like honey twining*
> *From her throat and my throat,*
>   *Who lies a-pining?*
>
> *Sea rovers here take joy*
>   *Voyaging onward,*
> *As from our song of Troy*
> *Greybeard and rower-boy*
>   *Goeth more learnèd.*   220
>
> *All feats on that great field*
>   *In the long warfare,*
> *Dark days the bright gods willed,*
>   *Wounds you bore there,*
>
> *Argos' old soldiery*
>   *On Troy beach teeming,*
> *Charmed out of time we see.*
> *No life on earth can be*
>   *Hid from our dreaming.*

The lovely voices in ardor appealing over the water   230
made me crave to listen, and I tried to say
'Untie me!' to the crew, jerking my brows;
but they bent steady to the oars. Then Perimêdês
got to his feet, he and Eurýlokhos,
and passed more line about, to hold me still.
So all rowed on, until the Seirênês
dropped under the sea rim, and their singing
dwindled away.
                                My faithful company
rested on their oars now, peeling off
the wax that I had laid thick on their ears;   240
then set me free.
                                But scarcely had that island

faded in blue air than I saw smoke
and white water, with sound of waves in tumult—
a sound the men heard, and it terrified them.
Oars flew from their hands; the blades went knocking
wild alongside till the ship lost way,
with no oarblades to drive her through the water.

Well, I walked up and down from bow to stern,
trying to put heart into them, standing over
every oarsman, saying gently,

                                     'Friends,   250
have we never been in danger before this?
More fearsome, is it now, than when the Kyklops
penned us in his cave? What power he had!
Did I not keep my nerve, and use my wits
to find a way out for us?

                                Now I say
by hook or crook this peril too shall be
something that we remember.

                              Heads up, lads!
We must obey the orders as I give them.
Get the oarshafts in your hands, and lay back
hard on your benches; hit these breaking seas.   260
Zeus help us pull away before we founder.
You at the tiller, listen, and take in
all that I say—the rudders are your duty;
keep her out of the combers and the smoke;
steer for that headland; watch the drift, or we
fetch up in the smother, and you drown us.'

That was all, and it brought them round to action.
But as I sent them on toward Skylla, I
told them nothing, as they could do nothing.
They would have dropped their oars again, in panic,   270
to roll for cover under the decking. Kirkê's
bidding against arms had slipped my mind,
so I tied on my cuirass and took up
two heavy spears, then made my way along
to the foredeck—thinking to see her first from there,
the monster of the grey rock, harboring
torment for my friends. I strained my eyes
upon that cliffside veiled in cloud, but nowhere
could I catch sight of her.

                           And all this time,
in travail, sobbing, gaining on the current,   280
we rowed into the strait—Skylla to port
and on our starboard beam Kharybdis, dire
gorge of the salt sea tide. By heaven! when she
vomited, all the sea was like a cauldron

seething over intense fire, when the mixture
suddenly heaves and rises.

The shot spume

soared to the landside heights, and fell like rain.

But when she swallowed the sea water down
we saw the funnel of the maelstrom, heard
the rock bellowing all around, and dark   290
sand raged on the bottom far below.
My men all blanched against the gloom, our eyes
were fixed upon that yawning mouth in fear
of being devoured.

Then Skylla made her strike,

whisking six of my best men from the ship.
I happened to glance aft at ship and oarsmen
and caught sight of their arms and legs, dangling
high overhead. Voices came down to me
in anguish, calling my name for the last time.

A man surfcasting on a point of rock   300
for bass or mackerel, whipping his long rod
to drop the sinker and the bait far out,
will hook a fish and rip it from the surface
to dangle wriggling through the air:

so these

were borne aloft in spasms toward the cliff.

She ate them as they shrieked there, in her den,
in the dire grapple, reaching still for me—
and deathly pity ran me through
at that sight—far the worst I ever suffered,
questing the passes of the strange sea.

We rowed on.   310

The Rocks were now behind; Kharybdis, too,
and Skylla dropped astern.

Then we were coasting

the noble island of the god, where grazed
those cattle with wide brows, and bounteous flocks
of Hêlios, lord of noon, who rides high heaven.

From the black ship, far still at sea, I heard
the lowing of the cattle winding home
and sheep bleating; and heard, too, in my heart
the words of blind Teirêsias of Thebes
and Kirkê of Aiaia: both forbade me   320
the island of the world's delight, the Sun.
So I spoke out in gloom to my companions:

'Shipmates, grieving and weary though you are,
listen: I had forewarning from Teirêsias

and Kirkê, too; both told me I must shun
this island of the Sun, the world's delight.
Nothing but fatal trouble shall we find here.
Pull away, then, and put the land astern.'

That strained them to the breaking point, and, cursing,
Eurýlokhos cried out in bitterness: 330

'Are you flesh and blood, Odysseus, to endure
more than a man can? Do you never tire?
God, look at you, iron is what you're made of.
Here we all are, half dead with weariness,
falling asleep over the oars, and you
say "No landing"—no firm island earth
where we could make a quiet supper. No:
pull out to sea, you say, with night upon us—
just as before, but wandering now, and lost.
Sudden storms can rise at night and swamp   340
ships without a trace.

                   Where is your shelter
if some stiff gale blows up from south or west—
the winds that break up shipping every time
when seamen flout the lord gods' will? I say
do as the hour demands and go ashore
before black night comes down.

                         We'll make our supper
alongside, and at dawn put out to sea.'

Now when the rest said 'Aye' to this, I saw
the power of destiny devising ill.
Sharply I answered, without hesitation: 350

'Eurýlokhos, they are with you to a man.
I am alone, outmatched.

                   Let this whole company
swear me a great oath: Any herd of cattle
or flock of sheep here found shall go unharmed;
no one shall slaughter out of wantonness
ram or heifer; all shall be content
with what the goddess Kirkê put aboard.'

They fell at once to swearing as I ordered,
and when the round of oaths had ceased, we found
a halfmoon bay to beach and moor the ship in,   360
with a fresh spring nearby. All hands ashore
went about skillfully getting up a meal.
Then, after thirst and hunger, those besiegers,
were turned away, they mourned for their companions
plucked from the ship by Skylla and devoured,
and sleep came soft upon them as they mourned.

In the small hours of the third watch, when stars
that shone out in the first dusk of evening
had gone down to their setting, a giant wind
blew from heaven, and clouds driven by Zeus   370
shrouded land and sea in a night of storm;
so, just as Dawn with finger tips of rose
touched the windy world, we dragged our ship
to cover in a grotto, a sea cave
where nymphs had chairs of rock and sanded floors.
I mustered all the crew and said:

                       'Old shipmates,
our stores are in the ship's hold, food and drink;
the cattle here are not for our provision,
or we pay dearly for it.

                  Fierce the god is
who cherishes these heifers and these sheep: 380
Hêlios; and no man avoids his eye.'

To this my fighters nodded. Yes. But now
we had a month of onshore gales, blowing
day in, day out—south winds, or south by east.
As long as bread and good red wine remained
to keep the men up, and appease their craving,
they would not touch the cattle. But in the end,
when all the barley in the ship was gone,
hunger drove them to scour the wild shore
with angling hooks, for fishes and sea fowl,   390
whatever fell into their hands; and lean days
wore their bellies thin.

                The storms continued.
So one day I withdrew to the interior
to pray the gods in solitude, for hope
that one might show me some way of salvation.
Slipping away, I struck across the island
to a sheltered spot, out of the driving gale.
I washed my hands there, and made supplication
to the gods who own Olympos, all the gods—
but they, for answer, only closed my eyes   400
under slow drops of sleep.

              Now on the shore Eurýlokhos
made his insidious plea:

                  'Comrades,' he said,
'You've gone through everything; listen to what I say.
All deaths are hateful to us, mortal wretches,
but famine is the most pitiful, the worst
end that a man can come to.

Will you fight it?
Come, we'll cut out the noblest of these cattle
for sacrifice to the gods who own the sky;
and once at home, in the old country of Ithaka,
if ever that day comes—   410
we'll build a costly temple and adorn it
with every beauty for the Lord of Noon.
But if he flares up over his heifers lost,
wishing our ship destroyed, and if the gods
make cause with him, why, then I say: Better
open your lungs to a big sea once for all
than waste to skin and bones on a lonely island!'

Thus Eurýlokhos; and they murmured 'Aye!'
trooping away at once to round up heifers.
Now, that day tranquil cattle with broad brows   420
were grazing near, and soon the men drew up
around their chosen beasts in ceremony.
They plucked the leaves that shone on a tall oak—
having no barley meal—to strew the victims,
performed the prayers and ritual, knifed the kine
and flayed each carcass, cutting thighbones free
to wrap in double folds of fat. These offerings,
with strips of meat, were laid upon the fire.
Then, as they had no wine, they made libation
with clear spring water, broiling the entrails first;   430
and when the bones were burnt and tripes shared,
they spitted the carved meat.
                              Just then my slumber
left me in a rush, my eyes opened,
and I went down the seaward path. No sooner
had I caught sight of our black hull, than savory
odors of burnt fat eddied around me;
grief took hold of me, and I cried aloud:

'O Father Zeus and gods in bliss forever,
you made me sleep away this day of mischief!
O cruel drowsing, in the evil hour!   440
Here they sat, and a great work they contrived.'

Lampetía[11] in her long gown meanwhile
had borne swift word to the Overlord of Noon:

'They have killed your kine.'

                              And the Lord Hêlios
burst into angry speech amid the immortals:

[11] One of the nymphs who tended her father Hêlios' cattle.

'O Father Zeus and gods in bliss forever,
punish Odysseus' men! So overweening,
now they have killed my peaceful kine, my joy
at morning when I climbed the sky of stars,
and evening, when I bore westward from heaven.   450
Restitution or penalty they shall pay—
and pay in full—or I go down forever
to light the dead men in the underworld.'

Then Zeus who drives the stormcloud made reply:

'Peace, Hêlios: shine on among the gods,
shine over mortals in the fields of grain.
Let me throw down one white-hot bolt, and make
splinters of their ship in the winedark sea.'

—Kalypso later told me of this exchange,
as she declared that Hermês had told her.   460
Well, when I reached the sea cave and the ship,
I faced each man, and had it out; but where
could any remedy be found? There was none.
The silken beeves of Hêlios were dead.
The gods, moreover, made queer signs appear:
cowhides began to crawl, and beef, both raw
and roasted, lowed like kine upon the spits.

Now six full days my gallant crew could feast
upon the prime beef they had marked for slaughter
from Hêlios' herd; and Zeus, the son of Kronos,   470
added one fine morning.

                       All the gales
had ceased, blown out, and with an offshore breeze
we launched again, stepping the mast and sail,
to make for the open sea. Astern of us
the island coastline faded, and no land
showed anywhere, but only sea and heaven,
when Zeus Kroníon piled a thunderhead
above the ship, while gloom spread on the ocean.
We held our course, but briefly. Then the squall
struck whining from the west, with gale force, breaking   480
both forestays, and the mast came toppling aft
along the ship's length, so the running rigging
showered into the bilge.

                       On the after deck
the mast had hit the steersman a slant blow
bashing the skull in, knocking him overside,
as the brave soul fled the body, like a diver.
With crack on crack of thunder, Zeus let fly
a bolt against the ship, a direct hit,

so that she bucked, in reeking fumes of sulphur,
and all the men were flung into the sea.   490
They came up 'round the wreck, bobbing a while
like petrels[12] on the waves.

                                 No more seafaring

homeward for these, no sweet day of return;
the god had turned his face from them.

                                    I clambered

fore and aft my hulk until a comber
split her, keel from ribs, and the big timber
floated free; the mast, too, broke away.
A backstay floated dangling from it, stout
rawhide rope, and I used this for lashing
mast and keel together. These I straddled,   500
riding the frightful storm.

                               Nor had I yet

seen the worst of it: for now the west wind
dropped, and a southeast gale came on—one more
twist of the knife—taking me north again,
straight for Kharybdis. All that night I drifted,
and in the sunrise, sure enough, I lay
off Skylla mountain and Kharybdis deep.
There, as the whirlpool drank the tide, a billow
tossed me, and I sprang for the great fig tree,
catching on like a bat under a bough.   510
Nowhere had I to stand, no way of climbing,
the root and bole being far below, and far
above my head the branches and their leaves,
massed, overshadowing Kharybdis pool.
But I clung grimly, thinking my mast and keel
would come back to the surface when she spouted.
And ah! how long, with what desire, I waited!
till, at the twilight hour, when one who hears
and judges pleas in the marketplace all day
between contentious men, goes home to supper,   520
the long poles at last reared from the sea.

Now I let go with hands and feet, plunging
straight into the foam beside the timbers,
pulled astride, and rowed hard with my hands
to pass by Skylla. Never could I have passed her
had not the Father of gods and men, this time,
kept me from her eyes. Once through the strait,
nine days I drifted in the open sea
before I made shore, buoyed up by the gods,
upon Ogýgia Isle. The dangerous nymph   530

[12] Sea-birds.

Kalypso lives and sings there, in her beauty,
and she received me, loved me.

But why tell

the same tale that I told last night in hall
to you and to your lady? Those adventures
made a long evening, and I do not hold
with tiresome repetition of a story."

BOOK THIRTEEN: ONE MORE STRANGE ISLAND

He ended it, and no one stirred or sighed
in the shadowy hall, spellbound as they all were,
until Alkínoös answered:

"When you came

here to my strong home, Odysseus, under
my tall roof, headwinds were left behind you.
Clear sailing shall you have now, homeward now,
however painful all the past.

My lords,

ever my company, sharing the wine of Council,
the songs of the blind harper, hear me further:
garments are folded for our guest and friend   10
in the smooth chest, and gold
in various shaping of adornment lies
with other gifts, and many, brought by our peers;
let each man add his tripod and deep-bellied
cauldron: we'll make levy upon the realm
to pay us for the loss each bears in this."

Alkínoös had voiced their own hearts' wish.
All gave assent, then home they went to rest;
but young Dawn's finger tips of rose, touching
the world, roused them to make haste to the ship,   20
each with his gift of noble bronze. Alkínoös,
their ardent king, stepping aboard himself,
directed the stowing under the cross planks,
not to cramp the long pull of the oarsmen.
Going then to the great hall, lords and crew
prepared for feasting.

As the gods' anointed,

Alkínoös made offering on their behalf—an ox
to Zeus beyond the stormcloud, Kronos' son,
who rules the world. They burnt the great thighbones
and feasted at their ease on fresh roast meat,   30
as in their midst the godlike harper sang—
Demódokos, honored by all that realm.

Only Odysseus

time and again turned craning toward the sun,
impatient for day's end, for the open sea.
Just as a farmer's hunger grows, behind
the bolted plow and share, all day afield,
drawn by his team of winedark oxen: sundown
is benison for him, sending him homeward
stiff in the knees from weariness, to dine;
just so, the light on the sea rim gladdened Odysseus,   40
and as it dipped he stood among the Phaiákians,
turned to Alkínoös, and said:

"O king and admiration of your people,
give me fare well, and stain the ground with wine;
my blessings on you all! This hour brings
fulfillment to the longing of my heart:
a ship for home, and gifts the gods of heaven
make so precious and so bountiful.

After this voyage

god grant I find my own wife in my hall
with everyone I love best, safe and sound!   50
And may you, settled in your land, give joy
to wives and children; may the gods reward you
every way, and your realm be free of woe."

Then all the voices rang out, "Be it so!"
and "Well spoken!" and "Let our friend make sail!"

Whereon Alkínoös gave command to his crier:

"Fill the winebowl, Pontónoös: mix and serve:
go the whole round, so may this company
invoke our Father Zeus, and bless our friend,
seaborne tonight and bound for his own country."   60

Pontónoös mixed the honey-hearted wine
and went from chair to chair, filling the cups;
then each man where he sat poured out his offering
to the gods in bliss who own the sweep of heaven.
With gentle bearing Odysseus rose, and placed
his double goblet in Arêtê's hands,
saying:

"Great Queen, farewell;

be blest through all your days till age comes on you,
and death, last end for mortals, after age.
Now I must go my way. Live in felicity,   70
and make this palace lovely for your children,
your countrymen, and your king, Alkínoös."

Royal Odysseus turned and crossed the door sill,
a herald at his right hand, sent by Alkínoös

to lead him to the sea beach and the ship.
Arêtê, too, sent maids in waiting after him,
one with a laundered great cloak and a tunic,
a second balancing the crammed sea chest,
a third one bearing loaves and good red wine.
As soon as they arrived alongside, crewmen   80
took these things for stowage under the planks,
their victualling and drink; then spread a rug
and linen cover on the after deck,
where Lord Odysseus might sleep in peace.
Now he himself embarked, lay down, lay still,
while oarsmen took their places at the rowlocks
all in order. They untied their hawser,
passing it through a drilled stone ring; then bent
forward at the oars and caught the sea
as one man, stroking.

                                   Slumber, soft and deep   90
like the still sleep of death, weighed on his eyes
as the ship hove seaward.

                                   How a four horse team
whipped into a run on a straightaway
consumes the road, surging and surging over it!
So ran that craft and showed her heels to the swell,
her bow wave riding after, and her wake
on the purple night-sea foaming.

                                   Hour by hour
she held her pace; not even a falcon wheeling
downwind, swiftest bird, could stay abreast of her
in that most arrowy flight through open water,   100
with her great passenger—godlike in counsel,
he that in twenty years had borne such blows
in his deep heart, breaking through ranks in war
and waves on the bitter sea.

                                   This night at last
he slept serene, his long-tried mind at rest.

When on the East the sheer bright star arose
that tells of coming Dawn, the ship made landfall
and came up islandward in the dim of night.
Phorkys, the old sea baron, has a cove
here in the realm of Ithaka; two points   110
of high rock, breaking sharply, hunch around it,
making a haven from the plunging surf
that gales at sea roll shoreward. Deep inside,
at mooring range, good ships can ride unmoored.
There, on the inmost shore, an olive tree
throws wide its boughs over the bay; nearby
a cave of dusky light is hidden
for those immortal girls, the Naiadês.[1]

---

[1] Sea-nymphs.

Within are winebowls hollowed in the rock
and amphorai; bees bring their honey here;   120
and there are looms of stone, great looms, whereon
the weaving nymphs make tissues, richly dyed
as the deep sea is; and clear springs in the cavern
flow forever. Of two entrances,
one on the north allows descent of mortals,
but beings out of light alone, the undying,
can pass by the south slit; no men come there.

This cove the sailors knew. Here they drew in,
and the ship ran half her keel's length up the shore,
she had such way on her from those great oarsmen.   130
Then from their benches forward on dry ground
they disembarked. They hoisted up Odysseus
unruffled on his bed, under his cover,
handing him overside still fast asleep,
to lay him on the sand; and they unloaded
all those gifts the princes of Phaiákia
gave him, when by Athena's heart and will
he won his passage home. They bore this treasure
off the beach, and piled it close around
the roots of the olive tree, that no one passing   140
should steal Odysseus' gear before he woke.
That done, they pulled away on the homeward track.

But now the god that shakes the islands, brooding
over old threats of his against Odysseus,
approached Lord Zeus to learn his will. Said he:

"Father of gods, will the bright immortals ever
pay me respect again, if mortals do not?—
Phaiákians, too, my own blood kin?

                                                    I thought

Odysseus should in time regain his homeland;
I had no mind to rob him of that day—   150
no, no; you promised it, being so inclined;
only I thought he should be made to suffer
all the way.

                                    But now these islanders
have shipped him homeward, sleeping soft, and put him
On Ithaka, with gifts untold
of bronze and gold, and fine cloth to his shoulder.
Never from Troy had he borne off such booty
if he had got home safe with all his share."

Then Zeus who drives the stormcloud answered, sighing:

"God of horizons, making earth's underbeam   160
tremble, why do you grumble so?
The immortal gods show you no less esteem,

and the rough consequence would make them slow
to let barbs fly at their eldest and most noble.
But if some mortal captain, overcome
by his own pride of strength, cuts or defies you,
are you not always free to take reprisal?
Act as your wrath requires and as you will."

Now said Poseidon, god of earthquake:

                                               "Aye,
god of the stormy sky, I should have taken   170
vengeance, as you say, and on my own;
but I respect, and would avoid, your anger.
The sleek Phaiákian cutter, even now,
has carried out her mission and glides home
over the misty sea. Let me impale her,
end her voyage, and end all ocean-crossing
with passengers, then heave a mass of mountain
in a ring around the city."

Now Zeus who drives the stormcloud said benignly:

"Here is how I should do it, little brother: 180
when all who watch upon the wall have caught
sight of the ship, let her be turned to stone—
an island like a ship, just off the bay.
Mortals may gape at that for generations!
But throw no mountain round the sea port city."

When he heard this, Poseidon, god of earthquake,
departed for Skhería, where the Phaiákians
are born and dwell. Their ocean-going ship
he saw already near, heading for harbor;
so up behind her swam the island-shaker   190
and struck her into stone, rooted in stone, at one
blow of his palm,

                          then took to the open sea.
Those famous ship handlers, the Phaiákians,
gazed at each other, murmuring in wonder;
you could have heard one say:

                       "Now who in thunder
has anchored, moored that ship in the seaway,
when everyone could see her making harbor?"

The god had wrought a charm beyond their thought.
But soon Alkínoös made them hush, and told them:

"This present doom upon the ship—on me—   200
my father prophesied in the olden time.
If we gave safe conveyance to all passengers
we should incur Poseidon's wrath, he said,

whereby one day a fair ship, manned by Phaiákians,
would come to grief at the god's hands; and great
mountains would hide our city from the sea.
So my old father forecast.

                                        Use your eyes:
these things are even now being brought to pass.
Let all here abide by my decree:

                                    We make
an end henceforth of taking, in our ships,   210
castaways who may land upon Skhería;
and twelve choice bulls we dedicate at once
to Lord Poseidon, praying him of his mercy
not to heave up a mountain round our city."

In fearful awe they led the bulls to sacrifice
and stood about the altar stone, those captains,
peers of Phaiákia, led by their king in prayer
to Lord Poseidon.

                               Meanwhile, on his island,
his father's shore, that kingly man, Odysseus,
awoke, but could not tell what land it was   220
after so many years away; moreover,
Pallas Athena, Zeus's daughter, poured
a grey mist all around him, hiding him
from common sight—for she had things to tell him
and wished no one to know him, wife or townsmen,
before the suitors paid up for their crimes.

The landscape then looked strange, unearthly strange
to the Lord Odysseus: paths by hill and shore,
glimpses of harbors, cliffs, and summer trees.
He stood up, rubbed his eyes, gazed at his homeland,   230
and swore, slapping his thighs with both his palms,
then cried aloud:

                               "What am I in for now?
Whose country have I come to this time? Rough
savages and outlaws, are they, or
godfearing people, friendly to castaways?
Where shall I take these things? Where take myself,
with no guide, no directions? These should be
still in Phaiákian hands, and I uncumbered,
free to find some other openhearted
prince who might be kind and give me passage.   240
I have no notion where to store this treasure;
first-comer's trove it is, if I leave it here.

My lords and captains of Phaiákia
were not those decent men they seemed, not honorable,

landing me in this unknown country—no,
by god, they swore to take me home to Ithaka
and did not! Zeus attend to their reward,
Zeus, patron of petitioners, who holds
all other mortals under his eye; he takes
payment from betrayers!

I'll be busy.   250

I can look through my gear. I shouldn't wonder
if they pulled out with part of it on board."

He made a tally of his shining pile—
tripods, cauldrons, cloaks, and gold—and found
he lacked nothing at all.

And then he wept,

despairing, for his own land, trudging down
beside the endless wash of the wide, wide sea,
weary and desolate as the sea. But soon
Athena came to him from the nearby air,
putting a young man's figure on—a shepherd,   260
like a king's son, all delicately made.
She wore a cloak, in two folds off her shoulders,
and sandals bound upon her shining feet.
A hunting lance lay in her hands.

At sight of her

Odysseus took heart, and he went forward
to greet the lad, speaking out fair and clear:

"Friend, you are the first man I've laid eyes on
here in this cove. Greetings. Do not feel
alarmed or hostile, coming across me; only
receive me into safety with my stores.   270
Touching your knees I ask it, as I might
ask grace of a god.

O sir, advise me,

what is this land and realm, who are the people?
Is it an island all distinct, or part
of the fertile mainland, sloping to the sea?"

To this grey-eyed Athena answered:

"Stranger,

you must come from the other end of nowhere,
else you are a great booby, having to ask
what place this is. It is no nameless country.
Why, everyone has heard of it, the nations   280
over on the dawn side, toward the sun,
and westerners in cloudy lands of evening.
No one would use this ground for training horses,
it is too broken, has no breadth of meadow;
but there is nothing meager about the soil,

the yield of grain is wondrous, and wine, too,
with drenching rains and dewfall.

                              There's good pasture

for oxen and for goats, all kinds of timber,
and water all year long in the cattle ponds.
For these blessings, friend, the name of Ithaka   290
has made its way even as far as Troy—
and they say Troy lies far beyond Akhaia."

Now Lord Odysseus, the long-enduring,
laughed in his heart, hearing his land described
by Pallas Athena, daughter of Zeus who rules
the veering stormwind; and he answered her
with ready speech—not that he told the truth,
but, just as she did, held back what he knew,
weighing within himself at every step
what he made up to serve his turn.

                                    Said he: 300

"Far away in Krete I learned of Ithaka—
in that broad island over the great ocean.
And here I am now, come myself to Ithaka!
Here is my fortune with me. I left my sons
an equal part, when I shipped out. I killed
Orsílokhos, the courier, son of Idómeneus.[2]
This man could beat the best cross country runners
in Krete, but he desired to take away
my Trojan plunder, all I had fought and bled for,
cutting through ranks in war and the cruel sea.   310
Confiscation is what he planned; he knew
I had not cared to win his father's favor
as a staff officer in the field at Troy,
but led my own command.

                                    I acted: I

hit him with a spearcast from a roadside
as he came down from the open country. Murky
night shrouded all heaven and the stars.
I made that ambush with one man at arms.
We were unseen. I took his life in secret,
finished him off with my sharp sword. That night   320
I found asylum on a ship off shore
skippered by gentlemen of Phoinikia;[3] I gave
all they could wish, out of my store of plunder,
for passage, and for landing me at Pylos
or Elis Town, where the Epeioi are in power.
Contrary winds carried them willy-nilly

---

[2] The king of Krete (Crete).
  [3] Phoenicia; an area of the Syrian coast noted for commerce. Sidon was one of its principal
cities.

past that coast; they had no wish to cheat me,
but we were blown off course.

Here, then, by night

we came, and made this haven by hard rowing.
All famished, but too tired to think of food,   330
each man dropped in his tracks after the landing,
and I slept hard, being wearied out. Before
I woke today, they put my things ashore
on the sand here beside me where I lay,
then reimbarked for Sidon, that great city.
Now they are far at sea, while I am left
forsaken here."

At this the grey-eyed goddess

Athena smiled, and gave him a caress,
her looks being changed now, so she seemed a woman,
tall and beautiful and no doubt skilled   340
at weaving splendid things. She answered briskly:

"Whoever gets around you must be sharp
and guileful as a snake; even a god
might bow to you in ways of dissimulation.
You! You chameleon!
Bottomless bag of tricks! Here in your own country
would you not give your stratagems a rest
or stop spellbinding for an instant?
You play a part as if it were your own tough skin.

No more of this, though. Two of a kind, we are,   350
contrivers, both. Of all men now alive
you are the best in plots and story telling.
My own fame is for wisdom among the gods—
deceptions, too.

Would even you have guessed

that I am Pallas Athena, daughter of Zeus,
I that am always with you in times of trial,
a shield to you in battle, I who made
the Phaiákians befriend you, to a man?
Now I am here again to counsel with you—
but first to put away those gifts the Phaiákians   360
gave you at departure—I planned it so.
Then I can tell you of the gall and wormwood
it is your lot to drink in your own hall.
Patience, iron patience, you must show;
so give it out to neither man nor woman
that you are back from wandering. Be silent
under all injuries, even blows from men."

His mind ranging far, Odysseus answered:

"Can mortal man be sure of you on sight,
even a sage, O mistress of disguises?   370

Once you were fond of me—I am sure of that—
years ago, when we Akhaians made
war, in our generation, upon Troy.
But after we had sacked the shrines of Priam
and put to sea, God scattered the Akhaians;
I never saw you after that, never
knew you aboard with me, to act as shield
in grievous times—not till you gave me comfort
in the rich hinterland of the Phaiákians
and were yourself my guide into that city.   380

Hear me now in your father's name, for I
cannot believe that I have come to Ithaka.
It is some other land. You made that speech
only to mock me, and to take me in.
Have I come back in truth to my home island?"

To this the grey-eyed goddess Athena answered:

"Always the same detachment! That is why
I cannot fail you, in your evil fortune,
coolheaded, quick, well-spoken as you are!
Would not another wandering man, in joy,   390
make haste home to his wife and children? Not
you, not yet. Before you hear their story
you will have proof about your wife.

                                            I tell you,

she still sits where you left her, and her days
and nights go by forlorn, in lonely weeping.
For my part, never had I despaired; I felt
sure of your coming home, though all your men
should perish; but I never cared to fight
Poseidon, Father's brother, in his baleful
rage with you for taking his son's eye.   400

Now I shall make you see the shape of Ithaka.
Here is the cove the sea lord Phorkys owns,
there is the olive spreading out her leaves
over the inner bay, and there the cavern
dusky and lovely, hallowed by the feet
of those immortal girls, the Naiadês—
the same wide cave under whose vault you came
to honor them with hekatombs—and there
Mount Neion, with his forest on his back!"

She had dispelled the mist, so all the island
stood out clearly. Then indeed Odysseus'   410
heart stirred with joy. He kissed the earth,
and lifting up his hands prayed to the nymphs:

"O slim shy Naiadês, young maids of Zeus,
I had not thought to see you ever again!

O listen smiling

to my gentle prayers, and we'll make offering
plentiful as in the old time, granted I
live, granted my son grows tall, by favor
of great Athena, Zeus's daughter,
who gives the winning fighter his reward!"   420

The grey-eyed goddess said directly:

"Courage;

and let the future trouble you no more.
We go to make a cache now, in the cave,
to keep your treasure hid. Then we'll consider
how best the present action may unfold."

The goddess turned and entered the dim cave,
exploring it for crannies, while Odysseus
carried up all the gold, the fire-hard bronze,
and well-made clothing the Phaiákians gave him.
Pallas Athena, daughter of Zeus the storm king,   430
placed them, and shut the cave mouth with a stone,
and under the old grey olive tree those two
sat down to work the suitors death and woe.
Grey-eyed Athena was the first to speak, saying:

"Son of Laërtês and the gods of old,
Odysseus, master of land ways and sea ways,
put your mind on a way to reach and strike
a crowd of brazen upstarts.

Three long years

they have played master in your house: three years
trying to win your lovely lady, making   440
gifts as though betrothed. And she? Forever
grieving for you, missing your return,
she has allowed them all to hope, and sent
messengers with promises to each—
though her true thoughts are fixed elsewhere."

At this

the man of ranging mind, Odysseus, cried:

"So hard beset! An end like Agamémnon's
might very likely have been mine, a bad end,
bleeding to death in my own hall. You forestalled it,
goddess, by telling me how the land lies.   450
Weave me a way to pay them back! And you, too,
take your place with me, breathe valor in me
the way you did that night when we Akhaians

unbound the bright veil from the brow of Troy!
O grey-eyed one, fire my heart and brace me!
I'll take on fighting men three hundred strong
if you fight at my back, immortal lady!"

The grey-eyed goddess Athena answered him:

"No fear but I shall be there; you'll go forward
under my arm when the crux comes at last.   460
And I foresee your vast floor stained with blood,
spattered with brains of this or that tall suitor
who fed upon your cattle.

                                        Now, for a while,

I shall transform you; not a soul will know you,
the clear skin of your arms and legs shriveled,
your chestnut hair all gone, your body dressed
in sacking that a man would gag to see,
and the two eyes, that were so brilliant, dirtied—
contemptible, you shall seem to your enemies,
as to the wife and son you left behind.   470

But join the swineherd first—the overseer
of all your swine, a good soul now as ever,
devoted to Penélopê and your son.
He will be found near Raven's Rock and the well
of Arethousa,[4] where the swine are pastured,
rooting for acorns to their hearts' content,
drinking the dark still water. Boarflesh grows
pink and fat on that fresh diet. There
stay with him, and question him, while I
am off to the great beauty's land of Sparta,   480
to call your son Telémakhos home again—
for you should know, he went to the wide land
of Lakedaimon, Meneláos' country,
to learn if there were news of you abroad."

Odysseus answered:

                                        "Why not tell him, knowing
my whole history, as you do? Must he
traverse the barren sea, he too, and live
in pain, while others feed on what is his?"

At this the grey-eyed goddess Athena said:

"No need for anguish on that lad's account.   490
I sent him off myself, to make his name
in foreign parts—no hardship in the bargain,

[4]The fountain identified with the water-nymph Arethousa (Arethusa) is more often located in Sicily.

taking his ease in Meneláos' mansion,
lapped in gold.

The young bucks here, I know,

lie in wait for him in a cutter, bent
on murdering him before he reaches home.
I rather doubt they will. Cold earth instead
will take in her embrace a man or two
of those who fed so long on what is his."

Speaking no more, she touched him with her wand,   500
shriveled the clear skin of his arms and legs,
made all his hair fall out, cast over him
the wrinkled hide of an old man, and bleared
both his eyes, that were so bright. Then she
clapped an old tunic, a foul cloak, upon him,
tattered, filthy, stained by greasy smoke,
and over that a mangy big buck skin.
A staff she gave him, and a leaky knapsack
with no strap but a loop of string.

Now then,

their colloquy at an end, they went their ways—   510
Athena toward illustrious Lakedaimon
Far over sea, to join Odysseus' son.

BOOK FOURTEEN: HOSPITALITY IN THE FOREST

He went up from the cove through wooded ground,
taking a stony trail into the high hills, where
the swineherd lived, according to Athena.
Of all Odysseus' field hands in the old days
this forester cared most for the estate;
and now Odysseus found him
in a remote clearing, sitting inside the gate
of a stockade he built to keep the swine
while his great lord was gone.

Working alone,

far from Penélopê and old Laërtês,   10
he had put up a fieldstone hut and timbered it
with wild pear wood. Dark hearts of oak he split
and trimmed for a high palisade around it,
and built twelve sties adjoining in this yard
to hold the livestock. Fifty sows with farrows
were penned in each, bedded upon the earth,
while the boars lay outside—fewer by far,
as those well-fatted were for the suitors' table,
fine pork, sent by the swineherd every day.
Three hundred sixty now lay there at night,   20

guarded by dogs—four dogs like wolves, one each
for the four lads the swineherd reared and kept
as under-herdsmen.

                                        When Odysseus came,
the good servant sat shaping to his feet
oxhide for sandals, cutting the well-cured leather.
Three of his young men were afield, pasturing
herds in other woods; one he had sent
with a fat boar for tribute into town,
the boy to serve while the suitors got their fill.

The watch dogs, when they caught sight of Odysseus,   30
faced him, a snarling troop, and pelted out
viciously after him. Like a tricky beggar
he sat down plump, and dropped his stick. No use.
They would have rolled him in the dust and torn him
there by his own steading[1] if the swineherd
had not sprung up and flung his leather down,
making a beeline for the open. Shouting,
throwing stone after stone,
he made them scatter; then turned to his lord
and said:

                                        "You might have got a ripping, man!   40
Two shakes more and a pretty mess for me
you could have called it, if you had the breath.
As though I had not trouble enough already,
given me by the gods, my master gone,
true king that he was. I hang on here,
still mourning for him, raising pigs of his
to feed foreigners, and who knows where the man is,
in some far country among strangers! Aye—
if he is living still, if he still sees the light of day.

Come to the cabin. You're a wanderer too.   50
You must eat something, drink some wine, and tell me
where you are from and the hard times you've seen."

The forester now led him to his hut
and made a couch for him, with tips of fir
piled for a mattress under a wild goat skin,
shaggy and thick, his own bed covering.

                                                                Odysseus,

in pleasure at this courtesy, gently said:

"May Zeus and all the gods give you your heart's desire
for taking me in so kindly, friend."

---

[1] Farmhouse or farm.

Eumaios—

O my swineherd![2]—answered him:

"Tush, friend,   60

rudeness to a stranger is not decency,
poor though he may be, poorer than you.

All wanderers

and beggars come from Zeus. What we can give
is slight but well-meant—all we dare. You know
that is the way of slaves,[3] who live in dread
of masters—new ones like our own.

I told you

the gods, long ago, hindered our lord's return.
He had a fondness for me, would have pensioned me
with acres of my own, a house, a wife
that other men admired and courted; all   70
gifts good-hearted kings bestow for service,
for a life work the bounty of god has prospered—
for it does prosper here, this work I do.
Had he grown old in his own house, my master
would have rewarded me. But the man's gone.
God curse the race of Helen and cut it down,
that wrung the strength out of the knees of many!
And he went, too—for the honor of Agamémnon
he took ship overseas for the wild horse country
of Troy, to fight the Trojans."

This being told,   80

he tucked his long shirt up inside his belt
and strode into the pens for two young porkers.
He slaughtered them and singed them at the fire,
flayed and quartered them, and skewered the meat
to broil it all; then gave it to Odysseus
hot on the spits. He shook out barley meal,
took a winebowl of ivy wood and filled it,
and sat down facing him, with a gesture, saying:

"There is your dinner, friend, the pork of slaves.
Our fat shoats are all eaten by the suitors,   90
cold-hearted men, who never spare a thought
for how they stand in the sight of Zeus. The gods
living in bliss are fond of no wrongdoing,
but honor discipline and right behavior.
Even the outcasts of the earth, who bring
piracy from the sea, and bear off plunder

---

[2] This kind of direct address by the poet, expressing affection, is used in the *Odyssey* only for Eumaios.

[3] Though owned by masters as in modern forms of slavery, and often obtained by forced capture, "slaves" in the aristocratic Homeric times were often more like trusted and responsible servants than like maltreated property. Eumaios and Telémakhos' old nurse Eurýkleia, described elsewhere in the *Odyssey*, are representative examples.

given by Zeus in shiploads—even those men
deep in their hearts tremble for heaven's eye.
But the suitors, now, have heard some word, some oracle
of my lord's death, being so unconcerned   100
to pay court properly or to go about their business.
All they want is to prey on his estate,
proud dogs; they stop at nothing. Not a day
goes by, and not a night comes under Zeus,
but they make butchery of our beeves and swine—
not one or two beasts at a time, either.
As for swilling down wine, they drink us dry.
Only a great domain like his could stand it—
greater than any on the dusky mainland
or here in Ithaka. Not twenty heroes   110
in the whole world were as rich as he. I know:
I could count it all up; twelve herds in Elis,
as many flocks, as many herds of swine,
and twelve wide-ranging herds of goats, as well,
attended by his own men or by others—
out at the end of the island, eleven herds
are scattered now, with good men looking after them,
and every herdsman, every day, picks out
a prize ram to hand over to those fellows.
I too as overseer, keeper of swine,   120
must go through all my boars and send the best."

While he ran on, Odysseus with zeal
applied himself to the meat and wine, but inwardly
his thought shaped woe and ruin for the suitors.
When he had eaten all that he desired
and the cup he drank from had been filled again
with wine—a welcome sight—,
he spoke, and the words came light upon the air:

"Who is this lord who once acquired you,
so rich, so powerful, as you describe him?   130
You think he died for Agamémnon's honor.
Tell me his name: I may have met someone
of that description in my time. Who knows?
Perhaps only the immortal gods could say
if I should claim to have seen him: I have roamed
about the world so long."

                                    The swineherd answered
as one who held a place of trust:

                                                      "Well, man,
his lady and his son will put no stock
in any news of him brought by a rover.
Wandering men tell lies for a night's lodging,   140
for fresh clothing; truth doesn't interest them.

Every time some traveller comes ashore
he has to tell my mistress his pretty tale,
and she receives him kindly, questions him,
remembering her prince, while the tears run
down her cheeks—and that is as it should be
when a woman's husband has been lost abroad.
I suppose you, too, can work your story up
at a moment's notice, given a shirt or cloak.
No: long ago wild dogs and carrion   150
birds, most like, laid bare his ribs on land
where life had left him. Or it may be, quick fishes
picked him clean in the deep sea, and his bones
lie mounded over in sand upon some shore.
One way or another, far from home he died,
a bitter loss, and pain, for everyone,
certainly for me. Never again shall I
have for my lot a master mild as he was
anywhere—not even with my parents
at home, where I was born and bred. I miss them   160
less than I do him—though a longing comes
to set my eyes on them in the old country.
No, it is the lost man I ache to think of—
Odysseus. And I speak the name respectfully,
even if he is not here. He loved me, cared for me.
I call him dear my lord, far though he be."

Now royal Odysseus, who had borne the long war,
spoke again:

                    "Friend, as you are so dead sure
he will not come—and so mistrustful, too—
let me not merely talk, as others talk,   170
but swear to it: your lord is now at hand.
And I expect a gift for this good news
when he enters his own hall. Till then I would not
take a rag, no matter what my need.
I hate as I hate Hell's own gate that weakness
that makes a poor man into a flatterer.
Zeus be my witness, and the table garnished
for true friends, and Odysseus' own hearth—
by heaven, all I say will come to pass!
He will return, and he will be avenged   180
on any who dishonor his wife and son."

Eumaios—O my swineherd!—answered him:

"I take you at your word, then: you shall have
no good news gift from me. Nor will Odysseus
enter his hall. But peace! drink up your wine.
Let us talk now of other things. No more
imaginings. It makes me heavy-hearted

when someone brings my master back to mind—
my own true master.

                                                        No, by heaven,   190
let us have no oaths! But if Odysseus
can come again god send he may! My wish
is that of Penélopê and old Laërtês
and Prince Telémakhos.

                                                        Ah, he's another
to be distressed about—Odysseus' child,
Telémakhos! By the gods' grace he grew
like a tough sapling, and I thought he'd be
no less a man than his great father—strong
and admirably made; but then someone,
god or man, upset him, made him rash,
so that he sailed away to sandy Pylos   200
to hear news of his father. Now the suitors
lie in ambush on his homeward track,
ready to cut away the last shoot of Arkêsios'[4]
line, the royal stock of Ithaka.

                                                        No good
dwelling on it. Either he'll be caught
or else Kroníon's[5] hand will take him through.

Tell me, now, of your own trials and troubles.
And tell me truly first, for I should know,
who are you, where do you hail from, where's your home
and family? What kind of ship was yours,   210
and what course brought you here? Who are your sailors?
I don't suppose you walked here on the sea."

To this the master of improvisation answered:

"I'll tell you all that, clearly as I may.
If we could sit here long enough, with meat
and good sweet wine, warm here, in peace and quiet
within doors, while the work of the world goes on—
I might take all this year to tell my story
and never end the tale of misadventures
that wore my heart out, by the gods' will.   220

My native land is the wide seaboard of Krete
where I grew up. I had a wealthy father,
and many other sons were born to him
of his true lady. My mother was a slave,
his concubine; but Kastor Hylákidês,
my father, treated me as a true born son.
High honor came to him in that part of Krete
for wealth and ease, and sons born for renown,

---

[4] Odysseus' paternal grandfather.   [5] Zeus, son of Kronos.

before the death-bearing Kêrês[6] drew him down
to the underworld. His avid sons thereafter   230
dividing up the property by lot
gave me a wretched portion, a poor house.
But my ability won me a wife
of rich family. Fool I was never called,
nor turn-tail in a fight.

                       My strength's all gone,
but from the husk you may divine the ear
that stood tall in the old days. Misery owns me
now, but then great Arês and Athena
gave me valor and man-breaking power,
whenever I made choice of men-at-arms   240
to set a trap with me for my enemies.
Never, as I am a man, did I fear Death
ahead, but went in foremost in the charge,
putting a spear through any man whose legs
were not as fast as mine. That was my element,
war and battle. Farming I never cared for,
nor life at home, nor fathering fair children.
I reveled in long ships with oars; I loved
polished lances, arrows in the skirmish,
the shapes of doom that others shake to see.   250
Carnage suited me; heaven put those things
in me somehow. Each to his own pleasure!
Before we young Akhaians shipped for Troy
I led men on nine cruises in corsairs
to raid strange coasts, and had great luck, taking
rich spoils on the spot, and even more
in the division. So my house grew prosperous,
my standing therefore high among the Kretans.
Then came the day when Zeus who views the wide world
drew men's eyes upon that way accurst   260
that wrung the manhood from the knees of many!
Everyone pressed me, pressed King Idómeneus
to take command of ships for Ilion.
No way out; the country rang with talk of it.
So we Akhaians had nine years of war.
In the tenth year we sacked the inner city,
Priam's town, and sailed for home; but heaven
dispersed the Akhaians. Evil days for me
were stored up in the hidden mind of Zeus.
One month, no more, I stayed at home in joy   270
with children, wife, and treasure. Lust for action
drove me to go to sea then, in command
of ships and gallant seamen bound for Egypt.
Nine ships I fitted out; my men signed on
and came to feast with me, as good shipmates,

---

[6] That is, the forces of death.

for six full days. Many a beast I slaughtered
in the gods' honor, for my friends to eat.
Embarking on the seventh, we hauled sail
and filled away from Krete on a fresh north wind
effortlessly, as boats will glide down stream.   280
All rigging whole and all hands well, we rested,
letting the wind and steersmen work the ships,
for five days; on the fifth we made the delta.[7]
I brought my squadron in to the river bank
with one turn of the sweeps. There, heaven knows,
I told the men to wait and guard the ships
while I sent out patrols to rising ground.
But reckless greed carried them all away
to plunder the rich bottomlands; they bore off
wives and children, killed what men they found.   290

When this news reached the city, all who heard it
came at dawn. On foot they came, and horsemen,
filling the river plain with dazzle of bronze;
and Zeus lord of lightning
threw my men into blind panic: no one dared
stand against that host closing around us.
Their scything weapons left our dead in piles,
but some they took alive, into forced labor.
And I—ah, how I wish that I had died
in Egypt, on that field! So many blows   300
awaited me!—Well, Zeus himself inspired me;
I wrenched my dogskin helmet off my head,
dropped my spear, dodged out of my long shield,
ran for the king's chariot and swung on
to embrace and kiss his knees. He pulled me up,
took pity on me, placed me on the footboards,
and drove home with me crouching there in tears.
Aye—for the troops, in battle fury still,
made one pass at me after another, pricking me
with spears, hoping to kill me. But he saved me,   310
for fear of the great wrath of Zeus that comes
when men who ask asylum are given death.

Seven years, then, my sojourn lasted there,
and I amassed a fortune, going about
among the openhanded Egyptians.
But when the eighth came round, a certain
Phoinikian adventurer came too,
a plausible rat, who had already done
plenty of devilry in the world.

---

[7] The estuary of the Nile river. Though the entire present account by Odysseus of his past
life is meant to deceive, many of his invented stories correspond to what in fact did happen to
him.

This fellow

took me in completely with his schemes, 320
and led me with him to Phoinikia,
where he had land and houses. One full year
I stayed there with him, to the month and day,
and when fair weather came around again
he took me in a deepsea ship for Libya,
pretending I could help in the cargo trade;
he meant, in fact, to trade me off, and get
a high price for me. I could guess the game
but had to follow him aboard. One day
on course due west, off central Krete, the ship 330
caught a fresh norther, and we ran southward
before the wind while Zeus piled ruin ahead.
When Krete was out of sight astern, no land
anywhere to be seen, but sky and ocean,
Kroníon put a dark cloud in the zenith
over the ship, and gloom spread on the sea.
With crack on crack of thunder, he let fly
a bolt against the ship, a direct hit,
so that she bucked, in sacred fumes of sulphur,
and all the men were flung into the water. 340
They came up round the wreck, bobbing a while
like petrels on the waves. No homecoming
for these, from whom the god had turned his face!
Stunned in the smother as I was, yet Zeus
put into my hands the great mast of the ship—
a way to keep from drowning. So I twined
my arms and legs around it in the gale
and stayed afloat nine days. On the tenth night,
a big surf cast me up in Thesprotia.[8]
Pheidon the king there gave me refuge, nobly, 350
with no talk of reward. His son discovered me
exhausted and half dead with cold, and gave me
a hand to bear me up till he reached home
where he could clothe me in a shirt and cloak.
In that king's house I heard news of Odysseus,
who lately was a guest there, passing by
on his way home, the king said; and he showed me
the treasure that Odysseus had brought:
bronze, gold, and iron wrought with heavy labor—
in that great room I saw enough to last 360
Odysseus' heirs for ten long generations.
The man himself had gone up to Dodona[9]
to ask the spelling leaves of the old oak

---

[8] In Epirus, on the northwest shore of Greece, somewhat north of Ithaka along the mainland coast.

[9] Site of the oldest oracle of Zeus, where the god's utterances were interpreted from the rustling of oak-leaves.

the will of God: how to return, that is,
to the rich realm of Ithaka, after so long
an absence—openly, or on the quiet.
And, tipping wine out, Pheidon swore to me
the ship was launched, the seamen standing by
to take Odysseus to his land at last.
But he had passage first for me: Thesprotians   370
were sailing, as luck had it, for Doulíkhion,[10]
the grain-growing island; there, he said,
they were to bring me to the king, Akastos.
Instead, that company saw fit to plot
foul play against me; in my wretched life
there was to be more suffering.

                                                    At sea, then,

when land lay far astern, they sprang their trap.
They'd make a slave of me that day, stripping
cloak and tunic off me, throwing around me
the dirty rags you see before you now.   380
At evening, off the fields of Ithaka,
they bound me, lashed me down under the decking
with stout ship's rope, while they all went ashore
in haste to make their supper on the beach.
The gods helped me to pry the lashing loose
until it fell away. I wound my rags
in a bundle round my head and eased myself
down the smooth lading plank into the water,
up to the chin, then swam an easy breast stroke
out and around, putting that crew behind,   390
and went ashore in underbrush, a thicket,
where I lay still, making myself small.
They raised a bitter yelling, and passed by
several times. When further groping seemed
useless to them, back to the ship they went
and out to sea again. The gods were with me,
keeping me hid; and with me when they brought me
here to the door of one who knows the world.
My destiny is yet to live awhile."

The swineherd bowed and said:

                                        "Ah well, poor drifter,   400
you've made me sad for you, going back over it,
all your hard life and wandering. That tale
about Odysseus, though, you might have spared me;
you will not make me believe that.
Why must you lie, being the man you are,
and all for nothing?

                                        I can see so well

---

[10] An island near Ithaka.

what happened to my master, sailing home!
Surely the gods turned on him, to refuse him
death in the field, or in his friends' arms
after he wound up the great war at Troy.   410
They would have made a tomb for him, the Akhaians,
and paid all honor to his son thereafter. No,
stormwinds made off with him. No glory came to him.

I moved here to the mountain with my swine.
Never, now, do I go down to town
unless I am sent for by Penélopê
when news of some sort comes. But those who sit
around her go on asking the old questions—
a few who miss their master still,
and those who eat his house up, and go free.   420
For my part, I have had no heart for inquiry
since one year an Aitolian[11] made a fool of me.
Exiled from land to land after some killing,
he turned up at my door; I took him in.
My master he had seen in Krete, he said,
lodged with Idómeneus, while the long ships,
leaky from gales, were laid up for repairs.
But they were all to sail, he said, that summer,
or the first days of fall—hulls laden deep
with treasure, manned by crews of heroes.

                                      This time   430
you are the derelict the Powers bring.
Well, give up trying to win me with false news
or flattery. If I receive and shelter you,
it is not for your tales but for your trouble,
and with an eye to Zeus, who guards a guest."

Then said that sly and guileful man, Odysseus:

"A black suspicious heart beats in you surely;
the man you are, not even an oath could change you.
Come then, we'll make a compact; let the gods
witness it from Olympos, where they dwell.   440
Upon your lord's homecoming, if he comes
here to this very hut, and soon—
then give me a new outfit, shirt and cloak,
and ship me to Doulíkhion—I thought it
a pleasant island. But if Odysseus
fails to appear as I predict, then Swish!
let the slaves pitch me down from some high rock,
so the next poor man who comes will watch his tongue."

The forester gave a snort and answered:

---

[11] Aitolia (or Aetolia) was part of the western Greek mainland, east of Ithaka.

"Friend,   450
if I agreed to that, a great name
I should acquire in the world for goodness—
at one stroke and forever: your kind host
who gave you shelter and the hand of friendship,
only to take your life next day!
How confidently, after that, should I
address my prayers to Zeus, the son of Kronos!

It is time now for supper. My young herdsmen
should be arriving soon to set about it.
We'll make a quiet feast here at our hearth."

At this point in their talk the swine had come   460
up to the clearing, and the drovers followed
to pen them for the night—the porkers squealing
to high heaven, milling around the yard.
The swineherd then gave orders to his men:

"Bring in our best pig for a stranger's dinner.
A feast will do our hearts good, too; we know
grief and pain, hard scrabbling with our swine,
while the outsiders live on our labor."

                                                  Bronze
axe in hand, he turned to split up kindling,
while they drove in a tall boar, prime and fat,   470
planting him square before the fire. The gods,
as ever, had their due in the swineherd's thought,
for he it was who tossed the forehead bristles
as a first offering on the flames, calling
upon the immortal gods to let Odysseus
reach his home once more.

                                 Then he stood up
and brained the boar with split oak from the woodpile.
Life ebbed from the beast; they slaughtered him,
singed the carcass, and cut out the joints.
Eumaios, taking flesh from every quarter,   480
put lean strips on the fat of sacrifice,
floured each one with barley meal, and cast it
into the blaze. The rest they sliced and skewered,
roasted with care, then took it off the fire
and heaped it up on platters. Now their chief,
who knew best the amenities, rose to serve,
dividing all that meat in seven portions—
one to be set aside, with proper prayers,
for the wood nymphs and Hermês, Maia's son;
the others for the company. Odysseus   490
he honored with long slices from the chine—

warming the master's heart. Odysseus looked at him
and said:

> "May you be dear to Zeus

as you are dear to me for this, Eumaios,
favoring with choice cuts a man like me."

And—O my swineherd!—you replied, Eumaios:

"Bless you, stranger, fall to and enjoy it
for what it is. Zeus grants us this or that,
or else refrains from granting, as he wills;
all things are in his power."

> He cut and burnt   500

a morsel for the gods who are young forever,
tipped out some wine, then put it in the hands
of Odysseus, the old soldier, raider of cities,
who sat at ease now with his meat before him.
As for the loaves, Mesaúlios dealt them out,
a yard boy, bought by the swineherd on his own,
unaided by his mistress or Laërtês,
from Taphians,[12] while Odysseus was away.
Now all hands reached for that array of supper,
until, when hunger and thirst were turned away   510
Mesaúlios removed the bread and, heavy
with food and drink, they settled back to rest.

Now night had come on, rough, with no moon,
but a nightlong downpour setting in, the rainwind
blowing hard from the west. Odysseus
began to talk, to test the swineherd, trying
to put it in his head to take his cloak off
and lend it, or else urge the others to.
He knew the man's compassion.

> "Listen," he said,   520

"Eumaios, and you others, here's a wishful
tale that I shall tell. The wine's behind it,
vaporing wine, that makes a serious man
break down and sing, kick up his heels and clown,
or tell some story that were best untold.
But now I'm launched, I can't stop now.

> Would god I felt

the hot blood in me that I had at Troy!
Laying an ambush near the walls one time,
Odysseus and Meneláos were commanders
and I ranked third. I went at their request.

[12] Inhabitants of western Greece. That Eumaios the slave himself acquired a servant is another sign that in Homeric times slavery was not always degrading serfdom.

We worked in toward the bluffs and battlements   530
and, circling the town, got into canebrakes,[13]
thick and high, a marsh where we took cover,
hunched under arms.

                The northwind dropped, and night
came black and wintry. A fine sleet descending
whitened the cane like hoarfrost, and clear ice
grew dense upon our shields. The other men,
all wrapt in blanket cloaks as well as tunics,
rested well, in shields up to their shoulders,
but I had left my cloak with friends in camp,
foolhardy as I was. No chance of freezing hard,   540
I thought, so I wore kilts and a shield only.
But in the small hours of the third watch, when stars
that rise at evening go down to their setting,
I nudged Odysseus, who lay close beside me;
he was alert then, listening, and I said:

'Son of Laërtês and the gods of old,
Odysseus, master mariner and soldier,
I cannot hold on long among the living.
The cold is making a corpse of me. Some god
inveigled me to come without a cloak.   550
No help for it now; too late.'

                    Next thing I knew
he had a scheme all ready in his mind—
and what a man he was for schemes and battles!
Speaking under his breath to me, he murmured:

'Quiet; none of the rest should hear you.'

                          Then,
propping his head on his forearm, he said:

'Listen, lads, I had an ominous dream,
the point being how far forward from our ships
and lines we've come. Someone should volunteer
to tell the corps commander, Agamémnon;   560
he may reinforce us from the base.'

                          At this,
Thoas jumped up, the young son of Andraimon,
put down his crimson cloak and headed off,
running shoreward.

                Wrapped in that man's cloak
how gratefully I lay in the bitter dark
until the dawn came stitched in gold! I wish
I had that sap and fiber in me now!"

---

[13] Thick growths of cane.

Then—O my swineherd!—you replied, Eumaios:

"That was a fine story, and well told,
not a word out of place, not a pointless word.   570
No, you'll not sleep cold for lack of cover,
or any other comfort one should give
to a needy guest. However, in the morning,
you must go flapping in the same old clothes.
Shirts and cloaks are few here; every man
has one change only. When our prince arrives,
the son of Odysseus, he will make you gifts—
cloak, tunic, everything—and grant you passage
wherever you care to go."

On this he rose
and placed the bed of balsam near the fire,   580
strewing sheepskins on top, and skins of goats.
Odysseus lay down. His host threw over him
a heavy blanket cloak, his own reserve
against the winter wind when it came wild.
So there Odysseus dropped off to sleep,
while herdsmen slept nearby. But not the swineherd:
not in the hut could he lie down in peace,
but now equipped himself for the night outside;
and this rejoiced Odysseus' heart, to see him
care for the herd so, while his lord was gone.   590
He hung a sharp sword from his shoulder, gathered
a great cloak round him, close, to break the wind,
and pulled a shaggy goatskin on his head.
Then, to keep at a distance dogs or men,
he took a sharpened lance, and went to rest
under a hollow rock where swine were sleeping
out of the wind and rain.

BOOK FIFTEEN: HOW THEY CAME TO ITHAKA

South into Lakedaimon[1]
into the land where greens are wide for dancing
Athena went, to put in mind of home
her great-hearted hero's honored son,
rousing him to return.

And there she found him
with Nestor's lad in the late night at rest
under the portico of Meneláos,
the famous king. Stilled by the power of slumber
the son of Nestor lay, but honeyed sleep

---

[1] The story of Telémakhos, broken off after Book IV, is here resumed.

had not yet taken in her arms Telémakhos.   10
All through the starlit night, with open eyes,
he pondered what he had heard about his father,
until at his bedside grey-eyed Athena
towered and said:

                "The brave thing now, Telémakhos,
would be to end this journey far from home.
All that you own you left behind
with men so lost to honor in your house
they may devour it all, shared out among them.
How will your journey save you then?

                             Go quickly
to the lord of the great war cry, Meneláos;   20
press him to send you back. You may yet find
the queen your mother in her rooms alone.
It seems her father and her kinsmen say
Eurýmakhos is the man for her to marry.
He has outdone the suitors, all the rest,
in gifts to her, and made her pledges double.
Check him, or he will have your lands and chattels
in spite of you.

                    You know a woman's pride
at bringing riches to the man she marries.
As to her girlhood husband, her first children,   30
he is forgotten, being dead—and they
no longer worry her.[2]

                        So act alone.
Go back; entrust your riches to the servant
worthiest in your eyes, until the gods
make known what beauty you yourself shall marry.

This too I have to tell you: now take heed:
the suitors' ringleaders are hot for murder,
waiting in the channel between Ithaka
and Samê's rocky side; they mean to kill you
before you can set foot ashore. I doubt   40
they'll bring it off. Dark earth instead
may take to her cold bed a few brave suitors
who preyed upon your cattle.

                      Bear well out
in your good ship, to eastward of the islands,
and sail again by night. Someone immortal
who cares for you will make a fair wind blow.
Touch at the first beach, go ashore, and send
your ship and crew around to port by sea,
while you go inland to the forester,

---

[2] These last three lines are a comment on widows in general, not on Penélopê in particular.
Athena assumes this cynical view in order to hasten Telémakhos' return.

your old friend, loyal keeper of the swine.   50
Remain that night with him; send him to town
to tell your watchful mother Penélopê
that you are back from Pylos safe and sound."

With this Athena left him for Olympos.
He swung his foot across and gave a kick
and said to the son of Nestor:

                                        "Open your eyes,
Peisístratos. Get our team into harness.
We have a long day's journey."

                                        Nestor's son
turned over and answered him:

                                        "It is still night,
and no moon. Can we drive now? We can not,   60
itch as we may for the road home. Dawn is near.
Allow the captain of spearmen, Meneláos,
time to pack our car with gifts and time
to speak a gracious word, sending us off.
A guest remembers all his days
that host who makes provision for him kindly."

The Dawn soon took her throne of gold, and Lord
Meneláos, clarion in battle,
rose from where he lay beside the beauty   70
of Helen with her shining hair. He strode
into the hall nearby.

                                        Hearing him come,
Odysseus' son pulled on his snowy tunic
over the skin, gathered his long cape
about his breadth of shoulder like a captain,
the heir of King Odysseus. At the door
he stood and said:

                                        "Lord Marshal, Meneláos,
send me home now to my own dear country:
longing has come upon me to go home."

The lord of the great war cry said at once: 80
"If you are longing to go home, Telémakhos,
I would not keep you for the world, not I.
I'd think myself or any other host
as ill-mannered for over-friendliness
as for hostility.

                                        Measure is best in everything.
To send a guest packing, or cling to him
when he's in haste—one sin equals the other.

'Good entertaining ends with no detaining.'
Only let me load your car with gifts
and fine ones, you shall see.

I'll bid the women   90

set out breakfast from the larder stores;
honor and appetite—we'll attend to both
before a long day's journey overland.
Or would you care to try the Argive midlands
and Hellas, in my company? I'll harness
my own team, and take you through the towns.
Guests like ourselves no lord will turn away;
each one will make one gift, at least,
to carry home with us: tripod or cauldron
wrought in bronze, mule team, or golden cup."   100

Clearheaded Telémakhos replied:

"Lord Marshal

Meneláos, royal son of Atreus,
I must return to my own hearth. I left
no one behind as guardian of my property.
This going abroad for news of a great father—
heaven forbid it be my own undoing,
or any precious thing be lost at home."

At this the tall king, clarion in battle,
called to his lady and her waiting women
to give them breakfast from the larder stores.   110
Eteóneus, the son of Boethoös, came
straight from bed, from where he lodged nearby,
and Meneláos ordered a fire lit
for broiling mutton. The king's man obeyed.
Then down to the cedar chamber Meneláos
walked with Helen and Prince Megapénthês.
Amid the gold he had in that place lying
the son of Atreus picked a wine cup, wrought
with handles left and right, and told his son
to take a silver winebowl.

Helen lingered   120

near the deep coffers filled with gowns, her own
handiwork.

Tall goddess among women,

she lifted out one robe of state so royal,
adorned and brilliant with embroidery,
deep in the chest it shimmered like a star.
Now all three turned back to the door to greet
Telémakhos. And red-haired Meneláos
cried out to him:

"O prince Telémakhos,

may Hêra's Lord of Thunder see you home

and bring you to the welcome you desire!   130
Here are your gifts—perfect and precious things
I wish to make your own, out of my treasure."

And gently the great captain, son of Atreus,
handed him the goblet. Megapénthês
carried the winebowl glinting silvery
to set before him, and the Lady Helen
drew near, so that he saw her cheek's pure line.
She held the gown and murmured:

"I, too,
bring you a gift, dear child, and here it is;   140
remember Helen's hands by this; keep it
for your own bride, your joyful wedding day;
let your dear mother guard it in her chamber.
My blessing: may you come soon to your island,
home to your timbered hall."

       So she bestowed it,
and happily he took it. These fine things
Peisístratos packed well in the wicker carrier,
admiring every one. Then Meneláos
led the two guests in to take their seats
on thrones and easy chairs in the great hall.   150
Now came a maid to tip a golden jug
of water over a silver finger bowl,
and draw the polished tables up beside them;
the larder mistress brought her tray of loaves,
with many savories to lavish on them;
viands were served by Eteóneus, and wine
by Meneláos' son. Then every hand
reached out upon good meat and drink to take them,
driving away hunger and thirst. At last,
Telémakhos and Nestor's son led out   160
their team to harness, mounted their bright car,
and drove down under the echoing entrance way,
while red-haired Meneláos, Atreus' son,
walked alongside with a golden cup—
wine for the wayfarers to spill at parting.
Then by the tugging team he stood, and spoke
over the horses' heads:

       "Farewell, my lads.

Homage to Nestor, the benevolent king;
in my time he was fatherly to me,
when the flower of Akhaia warred on Troy."   170

Telémakhos made this reply:

"No fear
but we shall bear at least as far as Nestor

your messages, great king. How I could wish
to bring them home to Ithaka! If only
Odysseus were there, if he could hear me tell
of all the courtesy I have had from you,
returning with your finery and your treasure."

Even as he spoke, a beat of wings went skyward
off to the right—a mountain eagle, grappling   180
a white goose in his talons, heavy prey
hooked from a farmyard. Women and men-at-arms
made hubbub, running up, as he flew over,
but then he wheeled hard right before the horses—
a sight that made the whole crowd cheer, with hearts
lifting in joy. Peisístratos called out:

"Read us the sign, O Meneláos, Lord
Marshal of armies! Was the god revealing
something thus to you, or to ourselves?"

At this the old friend of the god of battle   190
groped in his mind for the right thing to say,
but regal Helen put in quickly:

"Listen:
I can tell you—tell what the omen means,
as light is given me, and as I see it
point by point fulfilled. The beaked eagle
flew from the wild mountain of his fathers
to take for prey the tame house bird. Just so,
Odysseus, back from his hard trials and wandering,
will soon come down in fury on his house.   200
He may be there today, and a black hour
he brings upon the suitors."

                                                Telémakhos
gazed and said:

                                "May Zeus, the lord of Hêra,
make it so! In far-off Ithaka, all my life,
I shall invoke you as a goddess, lady."

He let the whip fall, and the restive mares
broke forward at a canter through the town
into the open country.

                                                All that day

they kept their harness shaking, side by side,
until at sundown when the roads grew dim   210
they made a halt at Pherai. There Dióklês
son of Ortílokhos whom Alpheios fathered,
welcomed the young men, and they slept the night.

Up when the young Dawn's finger tips of rose
opened in the east, they hitched the team
once more to the painted car
and steered out westward through the echoing gate,
whipping their fresh horses into a run.
Approaching Pylos Height at the day's end,
Telémakhos appealed to the son of Nestor: 220

"Could you, I wonder, do a thing I'll tell you,
supposing you agree?
We take ourselves to be true friends—in age
alike, and bound by ties between our fathers,
and now by partnership in this adventure.
Prince, do not take me roundabout,
but leave me at the ship, else the old king
your father will detain me overnight
for love of guests, when I should be at sea."

The son of Nestor nodded, thinking swiftly   230
how best he could oblige his friend.
Here was his choice: to pull the team hard over
along the beach till he could rein them in
beside the ship. Unloading Meneláos'
royal keepsakes into the stern sheets,
he sang out:

                                        "Now for action! Get aboard,
and call your men, before I break the news
at home in hall to father. Who knows better
the old man's heart than I? If you delay,
he will not let you go, but he'll descend on you   240
in person and imperious; no turning
back with empty hands for him, believe me,
once his blood is up."

                                        He shook the reins
to the lovely mares with long manes in the wind,
guiding them full tilt toward his father's hall.
Telémakhos called in the crew, and told them:

"Get everything shipshape aboard this craft;
we pull out now, and put sea miles behind us."

The listening men obeyed him, climbing in
to settle on their benches by the rowlocks,   250
while he stood watchful by the stern. He poured out
offerings there, and prayers to Athena.

Now a strange man came up to him, an easterner
fresh from spilling blood in distant Argos,

a hunted man. Gifted in prophecy,
he had as forebear that Melampous,[3] wizard
who lived of old in Pylos, mother city
of western flocks.
                                    Melampous, a rich lord,
had owned a house unmatched among the Pylians,
until the day came when king Neleus, noblest   260
in that age, drove him from his native land.
And Neleus for a year's term sequestered
Melampous' fields and flocks, while he lay bound
hand and foot in the keep of Phylakos.
Beauty of Neleus' daughter put him there
and sombre folly the inbreaking Fury
thrust upon him. But he gave the slip
to death, and drove the bellowing herd of Iphiklos
from Phylakê to Pylos, there to claim
the bride that ordeal won him from the king.   270
He led her to his brother's house, and went on
eastward into another land, the bluegrass
plain of Argos. Destiny held for him
rule over many Argives. Here he married,
built a great manor house, fathered Antíphatês
and Mantios, commanders both, of whom
Antíphatês begot Oikleiês
and Oikleiês the firebrand Amphiaraos.
This champion the lord of stormcloud, Zeus,
and strong Apollo loved; nor had he ever   280
to cross the doorsill into dim old age.
A woman, bought by trinkets, gave him over
to be cut down in the assault on Thebes.
His sons were Alkmáon and Amphílokhos.
In the meantime Lord Mantios begot
Polypheidês, the prophet, and
Kleitos—famous name! For Dawn[4] in silks
of gold carried off Kleitos for his beauty
to live among the gods. But Polypheidês,
high-hearted and exalted by Apollo   290
above all men for prophecy, withdrew
to Hyperesia[5] when his father angered him.
He lived on there, foretelling to the world
the shape of things to come.
                                    His son it was,

Theoklýmenos, who came upon Telémakhos
as he poured out the red wine in the sand
near his trim ship, with prayer to Athena;
and he called out, approaching:

---

[3] For the stories of Melampous and Amphiaraos, see Book XI and the notes to it.
[4] Eos, goddess of the dawn.
[5] A town on the Corinthian bay; part of Agamémnon's kingdom.

"Friend, well met
here at libation before going to sea.
I pray you by the wine you spend, and by   300
your god, your own life, and your company;
enlighten me, and let the truth be known.
Who are you? Of what city and what parents?"

Telémakhos turned to him and replied:

"Stranger, as truly as may be, I'll tell you.
I am from Ithaka, where I was born;
my father is, or he once was, Odysseus.
But he's a long time gone, and dead, may be;
and that is what I took ship with my friends
to find out—for he left long years ago."   310

Said Theoklýmenos in reply:

"I too
have had to leave my home. I killed a cousin.
In the wide grazing lands of Argos live
many kinsmen of his and friends in power,
great among the Akhaians. These I fled.
Death and vengeance at my back, as Fate
has turned now, I came wandering overland.
Give me a plank aboard your ship, I beg,
or they will kill me. They are on my track."   320

Telémakhos made answer:

"No two ways

about it. Will I pry you from our gunnel[6]
when you are desperate to get to sea?
Come aboard; share what we have, and welcome."

He took the bronze-shod lance from the man's hand
and laid it down full-length on deck; then swung
his own weight after it aboard the cutter,
taking position aft, making a place
for Theoklýmenos near him. The stern lines
were slacked off, and Telémakhos commanded: 330

"Rig the mast; make sail!" Nimbly they ran
to push the fir pole high and step it firm
amidships in the box, make fast the forestays,
and hoist aloft the white sail on its halyards.
A following wind came down from grey-eyed Athena,
blowing brisk through heaven, and so steady
the cutter lapped up miles of salt blue sea,

---

[6]Gunwale; the top edge of the ship's side.

passing Krounoi[7] abeam and Khalkis estuary
at sundown when the sea ways all grew dark.
Then, by Athena's wind borne on, the ship   340
rounded Pheai by night and coasted Elis,
the green domain of the Epeioi; thence
he put her head north toward the running pack
of islets, wondering if by sailing wide
he sheered off Death, or would be caught.

                                              That night

Odysseus and the swineherd supped again
with herdsmen in their mountain hut. At ease
when appetite and thirst were turned away,
Odysseus, while he talked, observed the swineherd
to see if he were hospitable still—   350
if yet again the man would make him stay
under his roof, or send him off to town.

"Listen," he said, "Eumaios; listen, lads.
At daybreak I must go and try my luck
around the port. I burden you too long.
Direct me, put me on the road with someone.
Nothing else for it but to play the beggar
in populous parts. I'll get a cup or loaf,
maybe, from some householder. If I go
as far as the great hall of King Odysseus   360
I might tell Queen Penélopê my news.
Or I can drift inside among the suitors
to see what alms they give, rich as they are.
If they have whims, I'm deft in ways of service—
that I can say, and you may know for sure.
By grace of Hermês the Wayfinder, patron
of mortal tasks, the god who honors toil,
no man can do a chore better than I can.
Set me to build a fire, or chop wood,
cook or carve, mix wine and serve—or anything   370
inferior men attend to for the gentry."

Now you were furious at this, Eumaios,
and answered—O my swineherd!—

                                              "Friend, friend,
how could this fantasy take hold of you?
You dally with your life, and nothing less,
if you feel drawn to mingle in that company—
reckless, violent, and famous for it
out to the rim of heaven. Slaves
they have, but not like you. No—theirs are boys

[7] The following lines describe the ship's northwest course along the southwest coast of Greece.

in fresh cloaks and tunics, with pomade 380
ever on their sleek heads, and pretty faces.
These are their minions, while their tables gleam
and groan under big roasts, with loaves and wine.
Stay with us here. No one is burdened by you,
neither myself nor any of my hands.
Wait here until Odysseus' son returns.
You shall have clothing from him, cloak and tunic,
and passage where your heart desires to go."

The noble and enduring man replied:

"May you be dear to Zeus for this, Eumaios, 390
even as you are to me. Respite from pain
you give me—and from homelessness. In life
there's nothing worse than knocking about the world,
no bitterness we vagabonds are spared
when the curst belly rages! Well, you master it
and me, making me wait for the king's son.
But now, come, tell me:
what of Odysseus' mother, and his father
whom he took leave of on the sill of age?
Are they under the sun's rays, living still, 400
or gone down long ago to lodge with Death?"

To this the rugged herdsman answered:

"Aye,
that I can tell you; it is briefly told.
Laërtês lives, but daily in his hall
prays for the end of life and soul's delivery,
heartbroken as he is for a son long gone
and for his lady. Sorrow, when she died,
aged and enfeebled him like a green tree stricken;
but pining for her son, her brilliant son, 410
wore out her life.

                Would god no death so sad
might come to benefactors dear as she!
I loved always to ask and hear about her
while she lived, although she lived in sorrow.
For she had brought me up with her own daughter,
Princess Ktimenê, her youngest child.
We were alike in age and nursed as equals
nearly, till in the flower of our years
they gave her, married her, to a Samian prince,
taking his many gifts. For my own portion 420
her mother gave new clothing, cloak and sandals,
and sent me to the woodland. Well she loved me.
Ah, how I miss that family! It is true
the blissful gods prosper my work; I have
meat and drink to spare for those I prize;

but so removed I am, I have no speech
with my sweet mistress, now that evil days
and overbearing men darken her house.
Tenants all hanker for good talk and gossip
around their lady, and a snack in hall,   430
a cup or two before they take the road
to their home acres, each one bearing home
some gift to cheer his heart."

                                            The great tactician
answered:

                             "You were still a child, I see,
when exiled somehow from your parents' land.
Tell me, had it been sacked in war, the city
of spacious ways in which they made their home,
your father and your gentle mother? Or
were you kidnapped alone, brought here by sea
huddled with sheep in some foul pirate squadron,   440
to this landowner's hall? He paid your ransom?"

The master of the woodland answered:

                                                   "Friend,

now that you show an interest in that matter,
attend me quietly, be at your ease,
and drink your wine. These autumn nights are long,
ample for story-telling and for sleep.
You need not go to bed before the hour;
sleeping from dusk to dawn's a dull affair.
Let any other here who wishes, though,
retire to rest. At daybreak let him breakfast   450
and take the king's own swine into the wilderness.
Here's a tight roof; we'll drink on, you and I,
and ease our hearts of hardships we remember,
sharing old times. In later days a man
can find a charm in old adversity,
exile and pain. As to your question, now:

A certain island, Syriê by name—
you may have heard the name—lies off Ortýgia[8]
due west, and holds the sunsets of the year.
Not very populous, but good for grazing   460
sheep and kine; rich too in wine and grain.
No dearth is ever known there, no disease
wars on the folk, of ills that plague mankind;
but when the townsmen reach old age, Apollo

---

[8] Though there were actual places bearing the names of Syriê and Ortýgia, in the present
context they refer vaguely to unidentifiable localities, probably in northwestern Greece, and
possibly invented by the poet.

with his longbow of silver comes, and Artemis,
showering arrows of mild death.

Two towns

divide the farmlands of that whole domain,
and both were ruled by Ktêsios, my father,
Orménos' heir, and a great godlike man.

Now one day some of those renowned seafaring   470
men, sea-dogs, Phoinikians, came ashore
with bags of gauds for trading. Father had
in our household a woman of Phoinikia,
a handsome one, and highly skilled. Well, she
gave in to the seductions of those rovers.
One of them found her washing near the mooring
and lay with her, making such love to her
as women in their frailty are confused by,
even the best of them.

In due course, then,

he asked her who she was and where she hailed from: 480
and nodding toward my father's roof, she said:

'I am of Sidon town, smithy of bronze
for all the East. Arubas Pasha's daughter.
Taphian pirates caught me in a byway
and sold me into slavery overseas
in this man's home. He could afford my ransom.'

The sailor who had lain with her replied:

'Why not ship out with us on the run homeward,
and see your father's high-roofed hall again,
your father and your mother? Still in Sidon   490
and still rich, they are said to be.'

She answered:

'It could be done, that, if you sailors take
oath I'll be given passage home unharmed.'

Well, soon she had them swearing it all pat
as she desired, repeating every syllable,
whereupon she warned them:

'Not a word

about our meeting here! Never call out to me
when any of you see me in the lane
or at the well. Some visitor might bear
tales to the old man. If he guessed the truth,   500
I'd be chained up, your lives would be in peril.
No: keep it secret. Hurry with your peddling,
and when your hold is filled with livestock, send
a message to me at the manor hall.

Gold I'll bring, whatever comes to hand,
and something else, too, as my passage fee—
the master's child, my charge: a boy so high,
bright for his age; he runs with me on errands.
I'd take him with me happily; his price
would be I know not what in sale abroad.'   510

Her bargain made, she went back to the manor.
But they were on the island all that year,
getting by trade a cargo of our cattle;
until, the ship at length being laden full,
ready for sea, they sent a messenger
to the Phoinikian woman. Shrewd he was,
this fellow who came round my father's hall,
showing a golden chain all strung with amber,
a necklace. Maids in waiting and my mother
passed it from hand to hand, admiring it,   520
engaging they would buy it. But that dodger,
as soon as he had caught the woman's eye
and nodded, slipped away to join the ship.
She took my hand and led me through the court
into the portico. There by luck she found
winecups and tables still in place—for Father's
attendant counselors had dined just now
before they went to the assembly. Quickly
she hid three goblets in her bellying dress
to carry with her, while I tagged along   530
in my bewilderment. The sun went down
and all the lanes grew dark as we descended,
skirting the harbor in our haste to where
those traders of Phoinikia held their ship.
All went aboard at once and put to sea,
taking the two of us. A favoring wind
blew from the power of heaven. We sailed on
six nights and days without event. Then Zeus
the son of Kronos added one more noon—and sudden
arrows from Artemis pierced the woman's heart.   540
Stone-dead she dropped
into the sloshing bilge the way a tern
plummets; and the sailors heaved her over
as tender pickings for the seals and fish.
Now I was left in dread, alone, while wind
and current bore them on to Ithaka.
Laërtês purchased me. That was the way
I first laid eyes upon this land."

                                                    Odysseus,
the kingly man, replied:

                                                "You rouse my pity,
telling what you endured when you were young.   550

But surely Zeus put good alongside ill:
torn from your own far home, you had the luck
to come into a kind man's service, generous
with food and drink. And a good life you lead,
unlike my own, all spent in barren roaming
from one country to the next, till now."

So the two men talked on, into the night,
leaving few hours for sleep before the Dawn
stepped up to her bright chair.

The ship now drifting

under the island lee, Telémakhos'   560
companions took in sail and mast, unshipped
the oars and rowed ashore. They moored her stern
by the stout hawser lines, tossed out the bow stones,
and waded in beyond the wash of ripples
to mix their wine and cook their morning meal.
When they had turned back hunger and thirst, Telémakhos
arose to give the order of the day.

"Pull for the town," he said, "and berth our ship,
while I go inland across country. Later,
this evening, after looking at my farms,   570
I'll join you in the city. When day comes
I hope to celebrate our crossing, feasting
everyone on good red meat and wine."

His noble passenger, Theoklýmenos,
now asked:

"What as to me, my dear young fellow,

where shall I go? Will I find lodging here
with some one of the lords of stony Ithaka?
Or go straight to your mother's hall and yours?"

Telémakhos turned round to him and said:

"I should myself invite you to our hall   580
if things were otherwise; there'd be no lack
of entertainment for you. As it stands,
no place could be more wretched for a guest
while I'm away. Mother will never see you;
she almost never shows herself at home
to the suitors there, but stays in her high chamber
weaving upon her loom. No, let me name
another man for you to go to visit:
Eurýmakhos,[9] the honored son of Pólybos.

---

[9] *Eurýmakhos.* Since he is one of Penélopê's principal suitors, it is odd that Eurýmakhos should be recommended by Telémakhos as a host for his passenger. Indeed, Telémakhos soon changes his mind and asks the trusted crewman Peiraios to house Theoklýmenos. Possibly Telémakhos, with something of his father's wariness, hesitates until he has some evidence of Theoklýmenos' good will.

In Ithaka they are dazzled by him now—   590
the strongest of their princes, bent on making
mother and all Odysseus' wealth his own.
Zeus on Olympos only knows
if some dark hour for them will intervene."

The words were barely spoken, when a hawk,
Apollo's courier, flew up on the right,
clutching a dove and plucking her—so feathers
floated down to the ground between Telémakhos
and the moored cutter. Theoklýmenos
called him apart and gripped his hand, whispering: 600

"A god spoke in this bird-sign on the right.
I knew it when I saw the hawk fly over us.
There is no kinglier house than yours, Telémakhos,
here in the realm of Ithaka. Your family
will be in power forever."

                                                    The young prince,
clear in spirit, answered:

                                                       "Be it so,
friend, as you say. And may you know as well
the friendship of my house, and many gifts
from me, so everyone may call you fortunate."

He called a trusted crewman named Peiraios,   610
and said to him:

                                    "Peiraios, son of Klýtios,
can I rely on you again as ever, most
of all the friends who sailed with me to Pylos?
Take this man home with you, take care of him,
treat him with honor, till I come."

                                                         To this
Peiraios the good spearman answered:

"Aye,
stay in the wild country while you will,
I shall be looking after him, Telémakhos.
He will not lack good lodging."

                                          Down to the ship   620
he turned, and boarded her, and called the others
to cast off the stern lines and come aboard.
So men climbed in to sit beside the rowlocks.
Telémakhos now tied his sandals on
and lifted his tough spear from the ship's deck;
hawsers were taken in, and they shoved off

to reach the town by way of the open sea
as he commanded them—royal Odysseus'
own dear son, Telémakhos.

On foot 630

and swiftly he went up toward the stockade
where swine were penned in hundreds, and at night
the guardian of the swine, the forester,
slept under arms on duty for his masters.

BOOK SIXTEEN: FATHER AND SON

But there were two men in the mountain hut—
Odysseus and the swineherd. At first light
blowing their fire up, they cooked their breakfast
and sent their lads out, driving herds to root
in the tall timber.

When Telémakhos came,

the wolvish troop of watchdogs only fawned on him
as he advanced. Odysseus heard them go
and heard the light crunch of a man's footfall—
at which he turned quickly to say:

"Eumaios,

10

here is one of your crew come back, or maybe
another friend: the dogs are out there snuffling
belly down; not one has even growled.
I can hear footsteps—"

But before he finished

his tall son stood at the door.

The swineherd

rose in surprise, letting a bowl and jug
tumble from his fingers. Going forward,
he kissed the young man's head, his shining eyes
and both hands, while his own tears brimmed and fell.
Think of a man whose dear and only son,
born to him in exile, reared with labor,
has lived ten years abroad and now returns:
how would that man embrace his son! Just so
the herdsman clapped his arms around Telémakhos
and covered him with kisses—for he knew
the lad had got away from death. He said:

20

"Light of my days, Telémakhos,
you made it back! When you took ship for Pylos
I never thought to see you here again.
Come in, dear child, and let me feast my eyes;
here you are, home from the distant places!

30

How rarely, anyway, you visit us,
your own men, and your own woods and pastures!
Always in the town, a man would think
you loved the suitors' company, those dogs!"

Telémakhos with his clear candor said:

"I am with you, Uncle. See now, I have come
because I wanted to see you first, to hear from you
if Mother stayed at home—or is she married
off to someone, and Odysseus' bed
left empty for some gloomy spider's weaving?"   40

Gently the forester replied to this:

"At home indeed your mother is, poor lady,
still in the women's hall. Her nights and days
are wearied out with grieving."

                                              Stepping back
he took the bronze-shod lance, and the young prince
entered the cabin over the worn door stone.
Odysseus moved aside, yielding his couch,
but from across the room Telémakhos checked him:

"Friend, sit down; we'll find another chair
in our own hut. Here is the man to make one!"   50

The swineherd, when the quiet man sank down,
built a new pile of evergreens and fleeces—
a couch for the dear son of great Odysseus—
then gave them trenchers of good meat, left over
from the roast pork of yesterday, and heaped up
willow baskets full of bread, and mixed
an ivy bowl of honey-hearted wine.
Then he in turn sat down, facing Odysseus,
their hands went out upon the meat and drink
as they fell to, ridding themselves of hunger,   60
until Telémakhos paused and said:

                                                      "Oh, Uncle,
what's your friend's home port? How did he come?
Who were the sailors brought him here to Ithaka?
I doubt if he came walking on the sea."

And you replied, Eumaios—O my swineherd—

"Son, the truth about him is soon told.
His home land, and a broad land, too, is Krete,
but he has knocked about the world, he says,
for years, as the Powers wove his life. Just now
he broke away from a shipload of Thesprotians   70

to reach my hut. I place him in your hands.
Act as you will. He wishes your protection."

The young man said:

                            "Eumaios, my protection!
The notion cuts me to the heart. How can I
receive your friend at home? I am not old enough
or trained in arms. Could I defend myself
if someone picked a fight with me?

                                       Besides,

mother is in a quandary, whether to stay with me
as mistress of our household, honoring
her lord's bed, and opinion in the town,   80
or take the best Akhaian who comes her way—
the one who offers most.

                              I'll undertake,

at all events, to clothe your friend for winter,
now he is with you. Tunic and cloak of wool,
a good broadsword, and sandals—these are his.
I can arrange to send him where he likes
or you may keep him in your cabin here.
I shall have bread and wine sent up; you need not
feel any pinch on his behalf.

                                 Impossible

to let him stay in hall, among the suitors.   90
They are drunk, drunk on impudence, they might
injure my guest—and how could I bear that?
How could a single man take on those odds?
Not even a hero could.

                        The suitors are too strong."

At this the noble and enduring man, Odysseus,
addressed his son:

                        "Kind prince, it may be fitting
for me to speak a word. All that you say
gives me an inward wound as I sit listening.
I mean this wanton game they play, these fellows,
riding roughshod over you in your own house,   100
admirable as you are. But tell me,
are you resigned to being bled? The townsmen,
stirred up against you, are they, by some oracle?
Your brothers—can you say your brothers fail you?
A man should feel his kin, at least, behind him
in any clash, when a real fight is coming.
If my heart were as young as yours, if I were
son to Odysseus, or the man himself,
I'd rather have my head cut from my shoulders
by some slashing adversary, if I   110
brought no hurt upon that crew! Suppose

I went down, being alone, before the lot,
better, I say, to die at home in battle
than see these insupportable things, day after
day the stranger cuffed, the women slaves
dragged here and there, shame in the lovely rooms,
the wine drunk up in rivers, sheer waste
of pointless feasting, never at an end!"

Telémakhos replied:

        "Friend, I'll explain to you.
There is no rancor in the town against me,   120
no fault of brothers, whom a man should feel
behind him when a fight is in the making;
no, no—in our family the First Born
of Heaven, Zeus, made single sons the rule.
Arkeísios had but one, Laërtês; he
in turn fathered only one, Odysseus,
who left me in his hall alone, too young
to be of any use to him.
And so you see why enemies fill our house
in these days: all the princes of the islands,   130
Doulíkhion, Samê, wooded Zakýnthos,
Ithaka, too—lords of our island rock—
eating our house up as they court my mother.
She cannot put an end to it; she dare not
bar the marriage that she hates; and they
devour all my substance and my cattle,
and who knows when they'll slaughter me as well?
It rests upon the gods' great knees.

            Uncle,
go down at once and tell the Lady Penélopê
that I am back from Pylos, safe and sound.   140
I stay here meanwhile. You will give your message
and then return. Let none of the Akhaians
hear it; they have a mind to do me harm."

To this, Eumaios, you replied:

            "I know.
But make this clear, now—should I not likewise
call on Laërtês with your news? Hard hit
by sorrow though he was, mourning Odysseus,
he used to keep an eye upon his farm.
He had what meals he pleased, with his own folk.
But now no more, not since you sailed for Pylos; 150
he has not taken food or drink, I hear,
sitting all day, blind to the work of harvest,
groaning, while the skin shrinks on his bones."

Telémakhos answered:

                              "One more misery,
but we had better leave it so.
If men choose, and have their choice, in everything,
we'd have my father home.

                                   Turn back
when you have done your errand, as you must,
not to be caught alone in the countryside.
But wait—you may tell Mother   160
to send our old housekeeper on the quiet
and quickly; she can tell the news to Grandfather."

The swineherd, roused, reached out to get his sandals,
tied them on, and took the road.

                                   Who else
beheld this but Athena? From the air
she walked, taking the form of a tall woman,
handsome and clever at her craft, and stood
beyond the gate in plain sight of Odysseus,
unseen, though, by Telémakhos, unguessed,
for not to everyone will gods appear.   170
Odysseus noticed her; so did the dogs,
who cowered whimpering away from her. She only
nodded, signing to him with her brows,
a sign he recognized. Crossing the yard,
he passed out through the gate in the stockade
to face the goddess. There she said to him:

"Son of Laërtês and the gods of old,
Odysseus, master of land ways and sea ways,
dissemble to your son no longer now.
The time has come: tell him how you together   180
will bring doom on the suitors in the town.
I shall not be far distant then, for I
myself desire battle."

                            Saying no more,
she tipped her golden wand upon the man,
making his cloak pure white, and the knit tunic
fresh around him. Lithe and young she made him,
ruddy with sun, his jawline clean, the beard
no longer grey upon his chin. And she
withdrew when she had done.
                         Then Lord Odysseus
reappeared—and his son was thunderstruck.   190
Fear in his eyes, he looked down and away
as though it were a god, and whispered:

                                              "Stranger,

you are no longer what you were just now!
Your cloak is new; even your skin! You are
one of the gods who rule the sweep of heaven!
Be kind to us, we'll make you fair oblation
and gifts of hammered gold. Have mercy on us!"

The noble and enduring man replied:

"No god. Why take me for a god? No, no.
I am that father whom your boyhood lacked   200
and suffered pain for lack of. I am he."

Held back too long, the tears ran down his cheeks
as he embraced his son.

                                Only Telémakhos,

uncomprehending, wild
with incredulity, cried out:

                                              "You cannot

be my father Odysseus! Meddling spirits
conceived this trick to twist the knife in me!
No man of woman born could work these wonders
by his own craft, unless a god came into it
with ease to turn him young or old at will.   210
I swear you were in rags and old,
and here you stand like one of the immortals!"

Odysseus brought his ranging mind to bear
and said:

                      "This is not princely, to be swept
away by wonder at your father's presence.
No other Odysseus will ever come,
for he and I are one, the same; his bitter
fortune and his wanderings are mine.
Twenty years gone, and I am back again
on my own island.

                                As for my change of skin,   220
that is a charm Athena, Hope of Soldiers,
uses as she will; she has the knack
to make me seem a beggar man sometimes
and sometimes young, with finer clothes about me.
It is no hard thing for the gods of heaven
to glorify a man or bring him low."

When he had spoken, down he sat.

                                Then, throwing

his arms around this marvel of a father
Telémakhos began to weep. Salt tears
rose from the wells of longing in both men,   230

and cries burst from both as keen and fluttering
as those of the great taloned hawk,
whose nestlings farmers take before they fly.
So helplessly they cried, pouring out tears,
and might have gone on weeping so till sundown,
had not Telémakhos said:

                              "Dear father! Tell me
what kind of vessel put you here ashore
on Ithaka? Your sailors, who were they?
I doubt you made it, walking on the sea!"

Then said Odysseus, who had borne the barren sea: 240

"Only plain truth shall I tell you, child.
Great seafarers, the Phaiákians, gave me passage
as they give other wanderers. By night
over the open ocean, while I slept,
they brought me in their cutter, set me down
on Ithaka, with gifts of bronze and gold
and stores of woven things. By the gods' will
these lie all hidden in a cave. I came
to this wild place, directed by Athena,
so that we might lay plans to kill our enemies.   250
Count up the suitors for me, let me know
what men at arms are there, how many men.
I must put all my mind to it, to see
if we two by ourselves can take them on
or if we should look round for help."

                                        Telémakhos
replied:

                    "O Father, all my life your fame
as a fighting man has echoed in my ears—
your skills with weapons and the tricks of war—
but what you speak of is a staggering thing,
beyond imagining, for me. How can two men   260
do battle with a houseful in their prime?
For I must tell you this is no affair
of ten or even twice ten men, but scores,
throngs of them. You shall see, here and now.
The number from Doulíkhion alone
is fifty-two, picked men, with armorers,
a half dozen; twenty-four came from Samê,
twenty from Zakýnthos; our own island
accounts for twelve, high-ranked, and their retainers,
Medôn the crier, and the Master Harper   270
besides a pair of handymen at feasts.
If we go in against all these
I fear we pay in salt blood for your vengeance.

You must think hard if you would conjure up
the fighting strength to take us through."

                                                          Odysseus

who had endured the long war and the sea
answered:

                                                    "I'll tell you now.

Suppose Athena's arm is over us, and Zeus
her father's, must I rack my brains for more?"

Clearheaded Telémakhos looked hard and said: 280

"Those two are great defenders, no one doubts it,
but throned in the serene clouds overhead;
other affairs of men and gods they have
to rule over."

                                          And the hero answered:

"Before long they will stand to right and left of us
in combat, in the shouting, when the test comes—
our nerve against the suitors' in my hall.
Here is your part: at break of day tomorrow
home with you, go mingle with our princes.
The swineherd later on will take me down   290
the port-side trail—a beggar, by my looks,
hangdog and old. If they make fun of me
in my own courtyard, let your ribs cage up
your springing heart, no matter what I suffer,
no matter if they pull me by the heels
or practice shots at me, to drive me out.
Look on, hold down your anger. You may even
plead with them, by heaven! in gentle terms
to quit their horseplay—not that they will heed you,
rash as they are, facing their day of wrath.   300
Now fix the next step in your mind.

                                                          Athena,

counseling me, will give me word, and I
shall signal to you, nodding: at that point
round up all armor, lances, gear of war
left in our hall, and stow the lot away
back in the vaulted store room. When the suitors
miss those arms and question you, be soft
in what you say: answer:

                                          'I thought I'd move them
out of the smoke. They seemed no longer those
bright arms Odysseus left us years ago   310
when he went off to Troy. Here where the fire's
hot breath came, they had grown black and drear.

One better reason, too, I had from Zeus:
suppose a brawl starts up when you are drunk,
you might be crazed and bloody one another,
and that would stain your feast, your courtship. Tempered
iron can magnetize a man.'

                                        Say that.

But put aside two broadswords and two spears
for our own use, two oxhide shields nearby
when we go into action. Pallas Athena   320
and Zeus All Provident will see you through,
bemusing our young friends.

                              Now one thing more.

If son of mine you are and blood of mine,
let no one hear Odysseus is about.
Neither Laërtês, nor the swineherd here,
nor any slave, nor even Penélopê.
But you and I alone must learn how far
the women are corrupted; we should know
how to locate good men among our hands,
the loyal and respectful, and the shirkers   330
who take you lightly, as alone and young."

His admirable son replied:

                                        "Ah, Father,

even when danger comes I think you'll find
courage in me. I am not scatterbrained.
But as to checking on the field hands now,
I see no gain for us in that. Reflect,
you make a long toil, that way, if you care
to look men in the eye at every farm,
while these gay devils in our hall at ease
eat up our flocks and herds, leaving us nothing.   340

As for the maids I say, Yes: make distinction
between good girls and those who shame your house;
all that I shy away from is a scrutiny
of cottagers just now. The time for that
comes later—if in truth you have a sign
from Zeus the Stormking."

                              So their talk ran on,
while down the coast, and round toward Ithaka,
hove the good ship that had gone out to Pylos
bearing Telémakhos and his companions.
Into the wide bay waters, on to the dark land,   350
they drove her, hauled her up, took out the oars
and the canvas for light-hearted squires to carry
homeward—as they carried, too, the gifts

of Meneláos round to Klýtios'[1] house.
But first they sped a runner to Penélopê.
They knew that quiet lady must be told
the prince her son had come ashore, and sent
his good ship round to port; not one soft tear
should their sweet queen let fall.

                                        Both messengers,

crewman and swineherd—reached the outer gate   360
in the same instant, bearing the same news,
and went in side by side to the king's hall.
He of the ship burst out among the maids:

"Your son's ashore this morning, O my Queen!"

But the swineherd calmly stood near Penélopê
whispering what her son had bade him tell
and what he had enjoined on her. No more.
When he had done, he left the place and turned
back to his steading in the hills.

                                        By now,

sullen confusion weighed upon the suitors.   370
Out of the house, out of the court they went,
beyond the wall and gate, to sit in council.
Eurýmakhos, the son of Pólybos,
opened discussion:

                        "Friends, face up to it;
that young pup, Telémakhos, has done it;
he made the round trip, though we said he could not.
Well—now to get the best craft we can find
afloat, with oarsmen who can drench her bows,
and tell those on the island to come home."

He was yet speaking when Amphínomos,   380
craning seaward, spotted the picket ship
already in the roadstead under oars
with canvas brailed up; and this fresh arrival
made him chuckle. Then he told his friends:

"Too late for messages. Look, here they come
along the bay. Some god has brought them news,
or else they saw the cutter pass—and could not
overtake her."

                                On their feet at once,
the suitors took the road to the sea beach,
where, meeting the black ship, they hauled her in.   390
Oars and gear they left for their light-hearted

[1] Father of the trusty Peiraios; see the end of Book XV.

squires to carry, and all in company
made off for the assembly ground. All others,
young and old alike, they barred from sitting.
Eupeithês' son, Antínoös, made the speech:

"How the gods let our man escape a boarding,
that is the wonder.

We had lookouts posted
up on the heights all day in the sea wind,
and every hour a fresh pair of eyes;
at night we never slept ashore   400
but after sundown cruised the open water
to the southeast, patrolling until Dawn.
We were prepared to cut him off and catch him,
squelch him for good and all. The power of heaven
steered him the long way home.

Well, let this company plan his destruction,
and leave him no way out, this time. I see
our business here unfinished while he lives.
He knows, now, and he's no fool. Besides,
his people are all tired of playing up to us.   410
I say, act now, before he brings the whole
body of Akhaians to assembly—
and he would leave no word unsaid, in righteous
anger speaking out before them all
of how we plotted murder, and then missed him.
Will they commend us for that pretty work?
Take action now, or we are in for trouble;
we might be exiled, driven off our lands.
Let the first blow be ours.
If we move first, and get our hands on him   420
far from the city's eye, on path or field,
then stores and livestock will be ours to share;
the house we may confer upon his mother—
and on the man who marries her. Decide
otherwise you may—but if, my friends,
you want that boy to live and have his patrimony,
then we should eat no more of his good mutton,
come to this place no more.

Let each from his own hall
court her with dower gifts. And let her marry
the destined one, the one who offers most."   430

He ended, and no sound was heard among them,
sitting all hushed, until at last the son
of Nísos Aretíadês arose—
Amphínomos.

He led the group of suitors
who came from grainlands on Doulíkhion,

and he had lightness in his talk that pleased
Penélopê, for he meant no ill.
Now, in concern for them, he spoke:

"O Friends

I should not like to kill Telémakhos.
It is a shivery thing to kill a prince   440
of royal blood.

We should consult the gods.

If Zeus hands down a ruling for that act,
then I shall say, 'Come one, come all,' and go
cut him down with my own hand—
but I say Halt, if gods are contrary."

Now this proposal won them, and it carried.
Breaking their session up, away they went
to take their smooth chairs in Odysseus' house.
Meanwhile Penélopê the Wise,
decided, for her part, to make appearance   450
before the valiant young men.

She knew now

they plotted her child's death in her own hall,
for once more Medôn, who had heard them, told her.
Into the hall that lovely lady came,
with maids attending, and approached the suitors,
till near a pillar of the well-wrought roof
she paused, her shining veil across her cheeks,
and spoke directly to Antínoös:

"Infatuate,

steeped in evil! Yet in Ithaka they say
you were the best one of your generation   460
in mind and speech. Not so, you never were.
Madman, why do you keep forever knitting
death for Telémakhos? Have you no piety
toward men dependent on another's mercy?
Before Lord Zeus, no sanction can be found
for one such man to plot against another!
Or are you not aware that your own father
fled to us when the realm was up in arms
against him? He had joined the Taphian pirates
in ravaging Thesprotian folk, our friends.   470
Our people would have raided *him,* then—breached
his heart, butchered his herds to feast upon—
only Odysseus took him in, and held
the furious townsmen off. It is Odysseus'
house you now consume, his wife you court,
his son you kill, or try to kill. And me
you ravage now, and grieve. I call upon you
to make an end of it!—and your friends too!"

The son of Pólybos it was, Eurýmakhos,
who answered her with ready speech:

                                        "My lady   480

Penélopê, wise daughter of Ikários,
you must shake off these ugly thoughts. I say
that man does not exist, nor will, who dares
lay hands upon your son Telémakhos,
while I live, walk the earth, and use my eyes.
The man's life blood, I swear,
will spurt and run out black around my lancehead!
For it is true of me, too, that Odysseus,
raiders of cities, took me on his knees
and fed me often—tidbits and red wine.   490
Should not Telémakhos, therefore, be dear to me
above the rest of men? I tell the lad
he must not tremble for his life, at least
alone in the suitors' company. Heaven
deals death no man avoids."

                                    Blasphemous lies

in earnest tones he told—the one who planned
the lad's destruction!

                                    Silently the lady

made her way to her glowing upper chamber,
there to weep for her dear lord, Odysseus,
until grey-eyed Athena   500
cast sweet sleep upon her eyes.

                                    At fall of dusk

Odysseus and his son heard the approach
of the good forester. They had been standing
over the fire with a spitted pig,
a yearling. And Athena coming near
with one rap of her wand made of Odysseus
an old old man again, with rags about him—
for if the swineherd knew his lord were there
he could not hold the news; Penélopê
would hear it from him.

                                    Now Telémakhos   510

greeted him first:

                            "Eumaios, back again!

What was the talk in town? Are the tall suitors
home again, by this time, from their ambush,
or are they still on watch for my return?"

And you replied, Eumaios—O my swineherd:

"There was no time to ask or talk of that;
I hurried through the town. Even while I spoke

my message, I felt driven to return.
A runner from your friends turned up, a crier,
who gave the news first to your mother. Ah!   520
One thing I do know; with my own two eyes
I saw it. As I climbed above the town
to where the sky is cut by Hermês' ridge,
I saw a ship bound in for our own bay
with many oarsmen in it, laden down
with sea provisioning and two-edged spears,
and I surmised those were the men.

                                                    Who knows?"

Telémakhos, now strong with magic, smiled
across at his own father—but avoided
the swineherd's eye.

                                    So when the pig was done,   530
the spit no longer to be turned, the table
garnished, everyone sat down to feast
on all the savory flesh he craved. And when
they had put off desire for meat and drink,
they turned to bed and took the gift of sleep.

BOOK SEVENTEEN: THE BEGGAR AT THE MANOR

When the young Dawn came bright into the East
spreading her finger tips of rose, Telémakhos
the king's son, tied on his rawhide sandals
and took the lance that bore his handgrip. Burning
to be away, and on the path to town,
he told the swineherd:

                                    "Uncle, the truth is
I must go down myself into the city.
Mother must see me there, with her own eyes,
or she will weep and feel forsaken still,
and will not set her mind at rest. Your job   10
will be to lead this poor man down to beg.
Some householder may want to dole him out
a loaf and pint. I have my own troubles.
Am I to care for every last man who comes?
And if he takes it badly—well, so much
the worse for him. Plain truth is what I favor."

At once Odysseus the great tactician
spoke up briskly:

                                    "Neither would I myself
care to be kept here, lad. A beggar man
fares better in the town. Let it be said   20

I am not yet so old I must lay up
indoors and mumble, 'Aye, Aye' to a master.[1]
Go on, then. As you say, my friend can lead me
as soon as I have had a bit of fire
and when the sun grows warmer. These old rags
could be my death, outside on a frosty morning,
and the town is distant, so they say."

                                        Telémakhos

with no more words went out, and through the fence,
and down hill, going fast on the steep footing,
nursing woe for the suitors in his heart.   30

Before the manor hall, he leaned his lance
against a great porch pillar and stepped in
across the door stone.

                              Old Eурýkleia

saw him first, for that day she was covering
handsome chairs nearby with clean fleeces.
She ran to him at once, tears in her eyes;
and other maidservants of the old soldier
Odysseus gathered round to greet their prince,
kissing his head and shoulders.

                                    Quickly, then,

Penélopê the Wise, tall in her beauty   40
as Artemis or pale-gold Aphroditê,
appeared from her high chamber and came down
to throw her arms around her son. In tears
she kissed his head, kissed both his shining eyes,
then cried out, and her words flew:

                                        "Back with me!

Telémakhos, more sweet to me than sunlight!
I thought I should not see you again, ever,
after you took the ship that night to Pylos—
against my will, with not a word! you went
for news of your dear father. Tell me now   50
of everything you saw!"

                              But he made answer:

"Mother, not now. You make me weep. My heart
already aches—I came near death at sea.
You must bathe, first of all, and change your dress,
and take your maids to the highest room to pray.
Pray, and burn offerings to the gods of heaven,
that Zeus may put his hand to our revenge.

---

[1] Odysseus means that he is not yet so old that he must remain in one place, subject to a
single master.

I am off now to bring home from the square
a guest, a passenger I had. I sent him
yesterday with all my crew to town.   60
Peiraios was to care for him, I said,
and keep him well, with honor, till I came."

She caught back the swift words upon her tongue.
Then softly she withdrew
to bathe and dress her body in fresh linen,
and make her offerings to the gods of heaven,
praying Almighty Zeus
to put his hand to their revenge.

                                              Telémakhos
had left the hall, taken his lance, and gone
with two quick hounds at heel into the town,   70
Athena's grace in his long stride
making the people gaze as he came near.
And suitors gathered, primed with friendly words,
despite the deadly plotting in their hearts—
but these, and all their crowd, he kept away from.
Next he saw sitting some way off, apart,
Mentor, with Antiphos and Halithersês,
friends of his father's house in years gone by.
Near these men he sat down, and told his tale
under their questioning.

                            His crewman, young Peiraios,   80
guided through town, meanwhile, into the Square,
the Argive exile, Theoklýmenos.
Telémakhos lost no time in moving toward him;
but first Peiraios had his say:

                                 "Telémakhos,
you must send maids to me, at once, and let me
turn over to you those gifts from Meneláos!"

The prince had pondered it, and said:

                                   "Peiraios,
none of us knows how this affair will end.
Say one day our fine suitors, without warning,
draw upon me, kill me in our hall,   90
and parcel out my patrimony—I wish
you, and no one of them, to have those things.
But if my hour comes, if I can bring down
bloody death on all that crew,
you will rejoice to send my gifts to me—
and so will I rejoice!"

                              Then he departed,
leading his guest, the lonely stranger, home.

Over chair-backs in hall they dropped their mantles
and passed in to the polished tubs, where maids
poured out warm baths for them, anointed them,   100
and pulled fresh tunics, fleecy cloaks around them.
Soon they were seated at their ease in hall.
A maid came by to tip a golden jug
over their fingers into a silver bowl
and draw a gleaming table up beside them.
The larder mistress brought her tray of loaves
and savories, dispensing each.

                                In silence

across the hall, beside a pillar, propped
in a long chair, Telémakhos' mother
spun a fine wool yarn.

                         The young men's hands   110
went out upon the good things placed before them,
and only when their hunger and thirst were gone
did she look up and say:

                            "Telémakhos,

what am I to do now? Return alone
and lie again on my forsaken bed—
sodden how often with my weeping
since that day when Odysseus put to sea
to join the Atreidai[2] before Troy?

                            Could you not

tell me, before the suitors fill our house,
what news you have of his return?"

                             He answered: 120

"Now that you ask a second time, dear Mother,
here is the truth.

                      We went ashore at Pylos
to Nestor, lord and guardian of the West,
who gave me welcome in his towering hall.
So kind he was, he might have been my father
and I his long-lost son—so truly kind,
taking me in with his own honored sons.
But as to Odysseus' bitter fate,
living or dead, he had no news at all
from anyone on earth, he said. He sent me   130
overland in a strong chariot
to Atreus' son, the captain, Meneláos.
And I saw Helen there, for whom the Argives
fought, and the Trojans fought, as the gods willed.
Then Meneláos of the great war cry
asked me my errand in that ancient land

---

[2] Sons of Atreus—Agamémnon and Meneláos.

of Lakedaimon. So I told our story,
and in reply he burst out:[3]

'Intolerable!

That feeble men, unfit as those men are,
should think to lie in that great captain's bed,   140
fawns in the lion's lair! As if a doe
put down her litter of sucklings there, while she
sniffed at the glen or grazed a grassy hollow.
Ha! Then the lord returns to his own bed
and deals out wretched doom on both alike.

So will Odysseus deal out doom on these.
O Father Zeus, Athena, and Apollo!
I pray he comes as once he was, in Lesbos,
when he stood up to wrestle Philomeleidês—
champion and Island King—   150
and smashed him down. How the Akhaians cheered!
If that Odysseus could meet the suitors,
they'd have a quick reply, a stunning dowry!
Now for your questions, let me come to the point.
I would not misreport it for you; let me
tell you what the Ancient of the Sea,
that infallible seer, told me.

On an island

your father lies and grieves. The Ancient saw him
held by a nymph, Kalypso, in her hall;
no means of sailing home remained to him,   160
no ship with oars, and no ship's company
to pull him on the broad back of the sea.'

I had this from the lord marshal, Meneláos,
and when my errand in that place was done
I left for home. A fair breeze from the gods
brought me swiftly back to our dear island."

The boy's tale made her heart stir in her breast,
but this was not all. Mother and son now heard
Theoklýmenos, the diviner, say:

"He does not see it clear—

O gentle lady,   170

wife of Odysseus Laërtiadês,
listen to me, I can reveal this thing.
Zeus be my witness, and the table set
for strangers and the hearth to which I've come—
the lord Odysseus, I tell you,
is present now, already, on this island!

---

[3] The following quotation of Meneláos' words summarizes his narrative in Book IV.

Quartered somewhere, or going about, he knows
what evil is afoot. He has it in him
to bring a black hour on the suitors. Yesterday,
still at the ship, I saw this in a portent.   180
I read the sign aloud, I told Telémakhos!"

The prudent queen, for her part, said:

                                              "Stranger,

if only this came true—
our love would go to you, with many gifts;
aye, every man who passed would call you happy!"

So ran the talk between these three.

                                         Meanwhile,

swaggering before Odysseus' hall,
the suitors were competing at the discus throw
and javelin, on the level measured field.
But when the dinner hour drew on, and beasts   190
were being driven from the fields to slaughter—
as beasts were, every day—Medôn spoke out:
Medôn, the crier, whom the suitors liked;
he took his meat beside them.

                                 "Men," he said,

"each one has had his work-out and his pleasure,
come in to Hall now; time to make our feast.
Are discus throws more admirable than a roast
when the proper hour comes?"

                              At this reminder
they all broke up their games, and trailed away
into the gracious, timbered hall. There, first,   200
they dropped their cloaks on chairs; then came their ritual:
putting great rams and fat goats to the knife—
pigs and a cow, too.

                         So they made their feast.

During these hours, Odysseus and the swineherd
were on their way out of the hills to town.
The forester had got them started, saying:

"Friend, you have hopes, I know, of your adventure
into the heart of town today. My lord
wishes it so, not I. No, I should rather
you stood by here as guardian of our steading.   210
But I owe reverence to my prince, and fear
he'll make my ears burn later if I fail.
A master's tongue has a rough edge. Off we go.
Part of the day is past; nightfall will be
early, and colder, too."

Odysseus,
who had it all timed in his head, replied:

"I know, as well as you do. Let's move on.
You lead the way—the whole way. Have you got
a staff, a lopped stick, you could let me use
to put my weight on when I slip? This path   220
is hard going, they said."

Over his shoulders
he slung his patched-up knapsack, an old bundle
tied with twine. Eumaios found a stick for him,
the kind he wanted, and the two set out,
leaving the boys and dogs to guard the place.
In this way good Eumaios led his lord
down to the city.

And it seemed to him
he led an old outcast, a beggar man,
leaning most painfully upon a stick,
his poor cloak, all in tatters, looped about him.   230

Down by the stony trail they made their way
as far as Clearwater, not far from town—
a spring house where the people filled their jars.
Ithakos, Nêritos, and Polýktor[4] built it,
and round it on the humid ground a grove,
a circular wood of poplars grew. Ice cold
in runnels from a high rock ran the spring,
and over it there stood an altar stone
to the cool nymphs, where all men going by
laid offerings.

Well, here the son of Dólios   240
crossed their path—Melánthios.[5]

He was driving
a string of choice goats for the evening meal,
with two goatherds beside him; and no sooner
had he laid eyes upon the wayfarers
than he began to growl and taunt them both
so grossly that Odysseus' heart grew hot:

"Here comes one scurvy type leading another!
God pairs them off together, every time.
Swineherd, where are you taking your new pig,
that stinking beggar there, licker of pots?   250
How many doorposts has he rubbed his back on

---

[4] These three were the founding fathers of the island; Ithakos' name represents the island itself, Nêritos' name an important mountain on the island.

[5] Dólios was a trusty steward of Odysseus' father, Laërtes. As we learn later, Melánthios' sister Melántho, maid to Penélopê, is a mistress of the suitor Eurýmakhos, a fact that probably accounts for the intimacy of her goatherd brother with the suitors.

whining for garbage, where a noble guest
would rate a cauldron or a sword?

                                                    Hand him

over to me, I'll make a farmhand of him,
a stall scraper, a fodder carrier! Whey
for drink will put good muscle on his shank!
No chance: he learned his dodges long ago—
no honest sweat. He'd rather tramp the country
begging, to keep his hoggish belly full.
Well, I can tell you this for sure: 260
in King Odysseus' hall, if he goes there,
footstools will fly around his head—good shots
from strong hands. Back and side, his ribs will catch it
on the way out!"

                                  And like a drunken fool
he kicked at Odysseus' hip as he passed by.
Not even jogged off stride, or off the trail,
the Lord Odysseus walked along, debating
inwardly whether to whirl and beat
the life out of this fellow with his stick,
or toss him, brain him on the stony ground.   270
Then he controlled himself, and bore it quietly.
Not so the swineherd.

                             Seeing the man before him,
he raised his arms and cried:

                            "Nymphs of the spring,
daughters of Zeus, if ever Odysseus
burnt you a thighbone in rich fat—a ram's
or kid's thighbone, hear me, grant my prayer:
let our true lord come back, let heaven bring him
to rid the earth of these fine courtly ways
Melánthios picks up around the town—
all wine and wind! Bad shepherds ruin flocks!"   280

Melánthios the goatherd answered:

                                  "Bless me!
The dog can snap: how he goes on! Some day
I'll take him in a slave ship overseas
and trade him for a herd!

                             Old Silverbow
Apollo, if he shot clean through Telémakhos[6]
in hall today, what luck! Or let the suitors
cut him down!

                          Odysseus died at sea;
no coming home for him."

---

[6] That is, if Telémakhos should drop dead.

                                                    He flung this out
and left the two behind to come on slowly,
while he went hurrying to the king's hall.   290
There he slipped in, and sat among the suitors,
beside the one he doted on—Eurýmakhos.
Then working servants helped him to his meat
and the mistress of the larder gave him bread.

Reaching the gate, Odysseus and the forester
halted and stood outside, for harp notes came
around them rippling on the air
as Phêmios picked out a song. Odysseus
caught his companion's arm and said:

                                                    "My friend,
here is the beautiful place—who could mistake it?   300
Here is Odysseus' hall: no hall like this!
See how one chamber grows out of another;
see how the court is tight with wall and coping;
no man at arms could break this gateway down!
Your banqueting young lords are here in force,
I gather, from the fumes of mutton roasting
and strum of harping—harping, which the gods
appoint sweet friend of feasts!"

                                        And—O my swineherd!
you replied:

                                        "That was quick recognition;
but you are no numbskull—in this or anything.   310
Now we must plan this action. Will you take
leave of me here, and go ahead alone
to make your entrance now among the suitors?
Or do you choose to wait?—Let me go forward
and go in first.

                                        Do not delay too long;
someone might find you skulking here outside
and take a club to you, or heave a lance.
Bear this in mind, I say."

                                                    The patient hero
Odysseus answered:

                                        "Just what I was thinking.
You go in first, and leave me here a little.   320
But as for blows and missiles,
I am no tyro[7] at these things. I learned
to keep my head in hardship—years of war

---

[7] Inexperienced beginner.

and years at sea. Let this new trial come.
The cruel belly, can you hide its ache?
How many bitter days it brings! Long ships
with good stout planks athwart—would fighters rig them
to ride the barren sea, except for hunger?
Seawolves—woe to their enemies!"

                                        While he spoke   330
an old hound, lying near, pricked up his ears
and lifted up his muzzle. This was Argos,
trained as a puppy by Odysseus,
but never taken on a hunt before
his master sailed for Troy. The young men, afterward,
hunted wild goats with him, and hare, and deer,
but he had grown old in his master's absence.
Treated as rubbish now, he lay at last
upon a mass of dung before the gates—
manure of mules and cows, piled there until
fieldhands could spread it on the king's estate.   340
Abandoned there, and half destroyed with flies,
old Argos lay.

                      But when he knew he heard
Odysseus' voice nearby, he did his best
to wag his tail, nose down, with flattened ears,
having no strength to move nearer his master.
And the man looked away,
wiping a salt tear from his cheek; but he
hid this from Eumaios. Then he said:

"I marvel that they leave this hound to lie
here on the dung pile;   350
he would have been a fine dog, from the look of him,
though I can't say as to his power and speed
when he was young. You find the same good build
in house dogs, table dogs landowners keep
all for style."

                          And you replied, Eumaios:

"A hunter owned him—but the man is dead
in some far place. If this old hound could show
the form he had when Lord Odysseus left him,
going to Troy, you'd see him swift and strong.
He never shrank from any savage thing   360
he'd brought to bay in the deep woods; on the scent
no other dog kept up with him. Now misery
has him in leash. His owner died abroad,
and here the women slaves will take no care of him.
You know how servants are: without a master
they have no will to labor, or excel.

For Zeus who views the wide world takes away
half the manhood of a man, that day
he goes into captivity and slavery."

Eumaios crossed the court and went straight forward   370
into the mégaron[8] among the suitors;
but death and darkness in that instant closed
the eyes of Argos, who had seen his master,
Odysseus, after twenty years.

                                   Long before anyone else
Telémakhos caught sight of the grey woodsman
coming from the door, and called him over
with a quick jerk of his head. Eumaios'
narrowed eyes made out an empty bench
beside the one the carver used—that servant
who had no respite, carving for the suitors.   380
This bench he took possession of, and placed it
across the table from Telémakhos
for his own use. Then the two men were served
cuts from a roast and bread from a bread basket.

At no long interval, Odysseus came
through his own doorway as a mendicant,
humped like a bundle of rags over his stick.
He settled on the inner ash wood sill,
leaning against the door jamb—cypress timber
the skilled carpenter planed years ago   390
and set up with a plumbline.

                              Now Telémakhos
took an entire loaf and a double handful
of roast meat; then he said to the forester:

"Give these to the stranger there. But tell him
to go among the suitors, on his own;
he may beg all he wants. This hanging back
is no asset to a hungry man."

The swineherd rose at once, crossed to the door,
and halted by Odysseus.

                                "Friend," he said,
"Telémakhos is pleased to give you these,   400
but he commands you to approach the suitors;
you may ask all you want from them. He adds,
your shyness is no asset to a beggar."

[8] The great hall of the house.

The great tactician, lifting up his eyes,
cried:

> "Zeus aloft! A blessing on Telémakhos!
Let all things come to pass as he desires!"

Palms held out, in the beggar's gesture, he
received the bread and meat and put it down
before him on his knapsack—lowly table!—
then he fell to, devouring it. Meanwhile   410
the harper in the great room sang a song.
Not till the man was fed did the sweet harper
end his singing—whereupon the company
made the walls ring again with talk.

> Unseen,
Athena took her place beside Odysseus
whispering in his ear:

> "Yes, try the suitors.
You may collect a few more loaves, and learn
who are the decent lads, and who are vicious—
although not one can be excused from death!"

So he appealed to them, one after another,   420
going from left to right, with open palm,
as though his life time had been spent in beggary.
And they gave bread, for pity—wondering, though,
at the strange man. Who could this beggar be,
where did he come from? each would ask his neighbor;
till in their midst the goatherd, Melánthios,
raised his voice:

> "Hear just a word from me,
my lords who court our illustrious queen!

> This man,
this foreigner, I saw him on the road;
the swineherd here was leading him this way;   430
who, what, or whence he claims to be, I could not
say for sure."

> At this, Antínoös
turned on the swineherd brutally, saying:

> "You famous
breeder of pigs, why bring this fellow here?
Are we not plagued enough with beggars,
foragers and such rats?

> You find the company
too slow at eating up your lord's estate—
is that it? So you call this scarecrow in?"

The forester replied:

"Antínoös, 440

well born you are, but that was not well said.
Who would call in a foreigner?—unless
an artisan with skill to serve the realm,
a healer, or a prophet, or a builder,
or one whose harp and song might give us joy.
All these are sought for on the endless earth,
but when have beggars come by invitation?
Who puts a field mouse in his granary? My lord,
you are a hard man, and you always were,
more so than others of this company—hard
on all Odysseus' people and on me. 450
But this I can forget
as long as Penélopê lives on, the wise and tender
mistress of this hall; as long
as Prince Telémakhos—"

But he broke off
at a look from Telémakhos, who said:

"Be still.

Spare me a long-drawn answer to this gentleman.
With his unpleasantness, he will forever make
strife where he can—and goad the others on."

He turned and spoke out clearly to Antínoös:

"What fatherly concern you show me! Frighten 460
this unknown fellow, would you, from my hall
with words that promise blows—may God forbid it!
Give him a loaf. Am I a niggard? No,
I call on you to give. And spare your qualms
as to my mother's loss, or anyone's—
not that in truth you have such care at heart:
your heart is all in feeding, not in giving."

Antínoös replied:

"What high and mighty
talk, Telémakhos! No holding you!
If every suitor gave what I may give him,
he could be kept for months—kept out of sight!" 470

He reached under the table for the footstool
his shining feet had rested on—and this
he held up so that all could see his gift.

But all the rest gave alms,
enough to fill the beggar's pack with bread
and roast meat.

So it looked as though Odysseus
had had his taste of what these men were like
and could return scot free to his own doorway—
but halting now before Antínoös   480
he made a little speech to him. Said he:

"Give a mite, friend. I would not say, myself,
you are the worst man of the young Akhaians.
The noblest, rather; kingly, by your look;
therefore you'll give more bread than others do.
Let me speak well of you as I pass on
over the boundless earth!

I, too, you know,
had fortune once, lived well, stood well with men,
and gave alms, often, to poor wanderers
like this one that you see—aye, to all sorts,   490
no matter in what dire want. I owned
servants—many, god knows—and all the rest
that goes with being prosperous, as they say.
But Zeus the son of Kronos brought me down.

No telling
why he would have it, but he made me go
to Egypt with a company of rovers—
a long sail to the south—for my undoing.
Up the broad Nile and in to the river bank
I brought my dipping squadron. There, indeed,   500
I told the men to stand guard at the ships;
I sent patrols out—out to rising ground;
but reckless greed carried my crews away
to plunder the Egyptian farms; they bore off
wives and children, killed what men they found.
The news ran on the wind to the city, a night cry,
and sunrise brought both infantry and horsemen,
filling the river plain with dazzle of bronze;
then Zeus lord of lightning
threw my men into a blind panic; no one dared   510
stand against that host closing around us.
Their scything weapons left our dead in piles,
but some they took alive, into forced labor,
myself among them. And they gave me, then,
to one Dmêtor, a traveller, son of Iasos,
who ruled at Kypros.[9] He conveyed me there.
From that place, working northward, miserably—"

But here Antínoös broke in, shouting:

"God!

What evil wind blew in this pest?

[9] Cyprus, a large island off the Syrian coast.

                                        Get over,   520
stand in the passage! Nudge my table, will you?
Egyptian whips are sweet
to what you'll come to here, you nosing rat,
making your pitch to everyone!
These men have bread to throw away on you
because it is not theirs. Who cares? Who spares
another's food, when he has more than plenty?"

With guile Odysseus drew away, then said:

"A pity that you have more looks than heart.
You'd grudge a pinch of salt from your own larder
to your own handy man. You sit here, fat   530
on others' meat, and cannot bring yourself
to rummage out a crust of bread for me!"

Then anger made Antínoös' heart beat hard,
and, glowering under his brows, he answered:

                                        "Now!

You think you'll shuffle off and get away
after that impudence? Oh, no you don't!"

The stool he let fly hit the man's right shoulder
on the packed muscle under the shoulder blade—
like solid rock, for all the effect one saw.
Odysseus only shook his head, containing   540
thoughts of bloody work, as he walked on,
then sat, and dropped his loaded bag again
upon the door sill. Facing the whole crowd
he said, and eyed them all:

                                "One word only,
my lords, and suitors of the famous queen.
One thing I have to say.
There is no pain, no burden for the heart
when blows come to a man, and he defending
his own cattle—his own cows and lambs.
Here it was otherwise. Antínoös   550
hit me for being driven on by hunger—
how many bitter seas men cross for hunger!
If beggars interest the gods, if there are Furies
pent in the dark to avenge a poor man's wrong, then may
Antínoös meet his death before his wedding day!"

Then said Eupeithês' son, Antínoös:

                                        "Enough.

Eat and be quiet where you are, or shamble elsewhere,
unless you want these lads to stop your mouth

pulling you by the heels, or hands and feet,
over the whole floor, till your back is peeled!"   560

But now the rest were mortified, and someone
spoke from the crowd of young bucks to rebuke him:

"A poor show, that—hitting this famished tramp—
bad business, if he happened to be a god.
You know they go in foreign guise, the gods do,
looking like strangers, turning up
in towns and settlements to keep an eye
on manners, good or bad."

                                 But at this notion
Antínoös only shrugged.

                                 Telémakhos,
after the blow his father bore, sat still   570
without a tear, though his heart felt the blow.
Slowly he shook his head from side to side,
containing murderous thoughts.

                               Penélopê
on the higher level of her room had heard
the blow, and knew who gave it. Now she murmured:

"Would god you could be hit yourself, Antínoös—
hit by Apollo's bowshot!"

                               And Eurýnomê
her housekeeper, put in:

                               "He and no other?
If all we pray for came to pass, not one
would live till dawn!"

                             Her gentle mistress said: 580
"Oh, Nan,[10] they are a bad lot; they intend
ruin for all of us; but Antínoös
appears a blacker-hearted hound than any.
Here is a poor man come, a wanderer,
driven by want to beg his bread, and everyone
in hall gave bits, to cram his bag—only
Antínoös threw a stool, and banged his shoulder!"

So she described it, sitting in her chamber
among her maids—while her true lord was eating.
Then she called in the forester and said: 590

---

[10] Affectionate diminutive for an old woman.

"Go to that man on my behalf, Eumaios,
and send him here, so I can greet and question him.
Abroad in the great world, he may have heard
rumors about Odysseus—may have known him!"

Then you replied—O swineherd!

                       "Ah, my queen,

if these Akhaian sprigs would hush their babble
the man could tell you tales to charm your heart.
Three days and nights I kept him in my hut;
he came straight off a ship, you know, to me.
There was no end to what he made me hear   600
of his hard roving; and I listened, eyes
upon him, as a man drinks in a tale
a minstrel sings—a minstrel taught by heaven
to touch the hearts of men. At such a song
the listener becomes rapt and still. Just so
I found myself enchanted by this man.
He claims an old tie with Odysseus, too—
in his home country, the Minoan[11] land
of Krete. From Krete he came, a rolling stone
washed by the gales of life this way and that   610
to our own beach.

                  If he can be believed

he has news of Odysseus near at hand
alive, in the rich country of Thesprotia,
bringing a mass of treasure home."

Then wise Penélopê said again:

"Go call him, let him come here, let him tell
that tale again for my own ears.

                         Our friends

can drink their cups outside or stay in hall,
being so carefree. And why not? Their stores
lie intact in their homes, both food and drink,   620
with only servants left to take a little.
But these men spend their days around our house
killing our beeves, our fat goats and our sheep,
carousing, drinking up our good dark wine;
sparing nothing, squandering everything.
No champion like Odysseus takes our part.
Ah, if he comes again, no falcon ever
struck more suddenly than he will, with his son,
to avenge this outrage!"

                     The great hall below
at this point rang with a tremendous sneeze[12]—   630

---

[11] Minos, to whom the adjective *Minoan* refers, had been king of Krete (Crete).
[12] A sneeze was regarded as a sign of good luck.

"kchaou!" from Telêmakhos—like an acclamation.
And laughter seized Penélopê.

Then quickly,

lucidly she went on:

"Go call the stranger

straight to me. Did you hear that, Eumaios?
My son's thundering sneeze at what I said!
May death come of a sudden so; may death
relieve us, clean as that, of all the suitors!
Let me add one thing—do not overlook it—
if I can see this man has told the truth,
I promise him a warm new cloak and tunic."   640

With all this in his head, the forester
went down the hall, and halted near the beggar,
saying aloud:

"Good father, you are called

by the wise mother of Telémakhos,
Penélopê. The queen, despite her troubles,
is moved by a desire to hear your tales
about her lord—and if she finds them true,
she'll see you clothed in what you need, a cloak
and a fresh tunic.

You may have your belly

full each day you go about this realm   650
begging. For all may give, and all they wish."

Now said Odysseus, the old soldier:

"Friend,
I wish this instant I could tell my facts
to the wise daughter of Ikários, Penélopê—
and I have much to tell about her husband;
we went through much together.

But just now

this hard crowd worries me. They are, you said
infamous to the very rim of heaven
for violent acts: and here, just now, this fellow   660
gave me a bruise. What had I done to him?
But who would lift a hand for me? Telémakhos?
Anyone else?

No; bid the queen be patient,

Let her remain till sundown in her room,
and then—if she will seat me near the fire—
inquire tonight about her lord's return.
My rags are sorry cover; you know that;
I showed my sad condition first to you."

The woodsman heard him out, and then returned;
but the queen met him on her threshold, crying: 670

"Have you not brought him? Why? What is he thinking?
Has he some fear of overstepping? Shy
about these inner rooms? A hangdog beggar?"

To this you answered, friend Eumaios:

"No:
he reasons as another might, and well,
not to tempt any swordplay from these drunkards.
Be patient, wait—he says—till darkness falls.
And, O my queen, for you too that is better:
better to be alone with him, and question him,   680
and hear him out."

                                        Penélopê replied:

"He is no fool; he sees how it could be.
Never were mortal men like these
for bullying and brainless arrogance!"

Thus she accepted what had been proposed,
so he went back into the crowd. He joined
Telémakhos, and said at once in whispers—
his head bent, so that no one else might hear:

"Dear prince, I must go home to keep good watch
on hut and swine, and look to my own affairs.   690
Everything here is in your hands. Consider
your own safety before the rest; take care
not to get hurt. Many are dangerous here.
May Zeus destroy them first, before we suffer!"

Telémakhos said:

                              "Your wish is mine, Uncle.
Go when your meal is finished. Then come back
at dawn, and bring good victims for a slaughter.
Everything here is in my hands indeed—
and in the disposition of the gods."

Taking his seat on the smooth bench again,   700
Eumaios ate and drank his fill, then rose
to climb the mountain trail back to his swine,
leaving the mégaron and court behind him
crowded with banqueters.
                                        These had their joy
of dance and song, as day waned into evening.

BOOK EIGHTEEN: BLOWS AND A QUEEN'S BEAUTY

Now a true scavenger came in—a public tramp
who begged around the town of Ithaka,
a by-word for his insatiable swag-belly,
feeding and drinking, dawn to dark. No pith
was in him, and no nerve, huge as he looked.
Arnaios, as his gentle mother called him,
he had been nicknamed "Iros"[1] by the young
for being ready to take messages.

This fellow

thought he would rout Odysseus from his doorway,
growling at him:

"Clear out, grandfather,   10

or else be hauled out by the ankle bone.
See them all giving me the wink? That means,
'Go on and drag him out!' I hate to do it.
Up with you! Or would you like a fist fight?"

Odysseus only frowned and looked him over,
taking account of everything, then said:

"Master, I am no trouble to you here.
I offer no remarks. I grudge you nothing.
Take all you get, and welcome. Here is room
for two on this doorslab—or do you own it?   20
You are a tramp, I think, like me. Patience:
a windfall from the gods will come. But drop
that talk of using fists; it could annoy me.
Old as I am, I might just crack a rib
or split a lip for you. My life would go
even more peacefully, after tomorrow,
looking for no more visits here from you."

Iros the tramp grew red and hooted:

"Ho,
listen to him! The swine can talk your arm off,   30
like an old oven woman! With two punches
I'd knock him snoring, if I had a mind to—
and not a tooth left in his head, the same
as an old sow caught in the corn! Belt up!
And let this company see the way I do it
when we square off. Can you fight a fresher man?"

Under the lofty doorway, on the door sill
of wide smooth ash, they held this rough exchange.

[1] A pun on Iris, goddess of the rainbow and a messenger of the gods.

And the tall full-blooded suitor, Antínoös,
overhearing, broke into happy laughter.   40
Then he said to the others:

                                                        "Oh, my friends,
no luck like this ever turned up before!
What a farce heaven has brought this house!

                                                        The stranger
and Iros have had words, they brag of boxing!
Into the ring they go, and no more talk!"

All the young men got on their feet now, laughing,
to crowd around the ragged pair. Antínoös
called out:

                                "Gentlemen, quiet! One more thing:
here are goat stomachs ready on the fire
to stuff with blood and fat, good supper pudding.   50
The man who wins this gallant bout
may step up here and take the one he likes.
And let him feast with us from this day on:
no other beggar will be admitted here
when we are at our wine."

                                                This pleased them all.
But now that wily man, Odysseus, muttered:

"An old man, an old hulk, has no business
fighting a young man, but my belly nags me;
nothing will do but I must take a beating.
Well, then, let every man here swear an oath   60
not to step in for Iros. No one throw
a punch for luck. I could be whipped that way."

So much the suitors were content to swear,
but after they reeled off their oaths, Telémakhos
put in a word to clinch it, saying:

                                                        "Friend,
if you will stand and fight, as pride requires,
don't worry about a foul blow from behind.
Whoever hits you will take on the crowd.
You have my word as host; you have the word
of these two kings, Antínoös and Eurýmakhos—   70
a pair of thinking men."

                                                All shouted, "Aye!"

So now Odysseus made his shirt a belt
and roped his rags around his loins, baring
his hurdler's thighs and boxer's breadth of shoulder,
the dense rib-sheath and upper arms. Athena
stood nearby to give him bulk and power,

while the young suitors watched with narrowed eyes—
and comments went around:

"By god, old Iros now retiros."

                                                    "Aye,
he asked for it, he'll get it—bloody, too."

"The build this fellow had, under his rags!"

Panic made Iros' heart jump, but the yard-boys
hustled and got him belted by main force,
though all his blubber quivered now with dread.
Antínoös' angry voice rang in his ears:

"You sack of guts, you might as well be dead,
might as well never have seen the light of day,
if this man makes you tremble! Chicken-heart,
afraid of an old wreck, far gone in misery!
Well, here is what I say—and what I'll do.
If this ragpicker can outfight you, whip you,
I'll ship you out to that king in Epeíros,
Ékhetos²—he skins everyone alive.
Let him just cut your nose off and your ears
and pull your privy parts out by the roots
to feed raw to his hunting dogs!"

                                        Poor Iros
felt a new fit of shaking take his knees.
But the yard-boys pushed him out. Now both contenders
put their hands up. Royal Odysseus
pondered if he should hit him with all he had
and drop the man dead on the spot, or only
spar, with force enough to knock him down.
Better that way, he thought—a gentle blow,
else he might give himself away.

                                        The two
were at close quarters now, and Iros lunged
hitting the shoulder. Then Odysseus hooked him
under the ear and shattered his jaw bone,
so bright red blood came bubbling from his mouth,
as down he pitched into the dust, bleating,
kicking against the ground, his teeth stove in.
The suitors whooped and swung their arms, half dead
with pangs of laughter.

                            Then, by the ankle bone,
Odysseus hauled the fallen one outside,
crossing the courtyard to the gate, and piled him

²Probably a nonhistorical tyrannical ruler whose name was a byword for cruelty. Epeíros
(Epirus), in the preceding line, is the Grecian mainland north of Ithaka.

against the wall. In his right hand he stuck
his begging staff, and said:

                                        "Here, take your post.
Sit here to keep the dogs and pigs away.
You can give up your habit of command
over poor waifs and beggarmen—you swab.
Another time you may not know what hit you."   120

When he had slung his rucksack by the string
over his shoulder, like a wad of rags,
he sat down on the broad door sill again,
as laughing suitors came to flock inside;
and each young buck in passing gave him greeting,
saying, maybe,

                                "Zeus fill your pouch for this!
May the gods grant your heart's desire!"

                                                "Well done
to put that walking famine out of business."

"We'll ship him out to that king in Epeíros,
Ékhetos—he skins everyone alive."   130

Odysseus found grim cheer in their good wishes—
his work had started well.

                                Now from the fire
his fat blood pudding came, deposited
before him by Antínoös—then, to boot,
two brown loaves from the basket, and some wine
in a fine cup of gold. These gifts Amphínomos
gave him. Then he said:

                                "Here's luck, grandfather;
a new day; may the worst be over now."

Odysseus answered, and his mind ranged far:

"Amphínomos, your head is clear, I'd say;   140
so was your father's—or at least I've heard
good things of Nísos the Doulíkhion,
whose son you are, they tell me—an easy man.
And you seem gently bred.

                                In view of that,
I have a word to say to you, so listen.

Of mortal creatures, all that breathe and move,
earth bears none frailer than mankind. What man
believes in woe to come, so long as valor
and tough knees are supplied him by the gods?
But when the gods in bliss bring miseries on,   150

then willy-nilly, blindly, he endures.
Our minds are as the days are, dark or bright,
blown over by the father of gods and men.

So I, too, in my time thought to be happy;
but far and rash I ventured, counting on
my own right arm, my father, and my kin;
behold me now.

                               No man should flout the law,
but keep in peace what gifts the gods may give.

I see you young blades living dangerously,
a household eaten up, a wife dishonored—   160
and yet the master will return, I tell you,
to his own place, and soon; for he is near.
So may some power take you out of this,
homeward, and softly, not to face that man
the hour he sets foot on his native ground.
Between him and the suitors I foretell
no quittance,[3] no way out, unless by blood,
once he shall stand beneath his own roof-beam."

Gravely, when he had done, he made libation
and took a sip of honey-hearted wine,   170
giving the cup, then, back into the hands
of the young nobleman. Amphínomos, for his part,
shaking his head, with chill and burdened breast,
turned in the great hall.

                             Now his heart foreknew
the wrath to come, but he could not take flight,
being by Athena bound there.

                           Death would have him
broken by a spear thrown by Telémakhos.
So he sat down where he had sat before.

And now heart-prompting from the grey-eyed goddess
came to the quiet queen, Penélopê: 180
a wish to show herself before the suitors;
for thus by fanning their desire again
Athena meant to set her beauty high
before her husband's eyes, before her son.
Knowing no reason, laughing confusedly,
she said:

                           "Eurýnomê, I have a craving
I never had at all—I would be seen
among those ruffians, hateful as they are.

[3] Repayment.

I might well say a word, then, to my son,
for his own good—tell him to shun that crowd;   190
for all their gay talk, they are bent on evil."

Mistress Eurýnomê replied:

"Well said, child,

now is the time. Go down, and make it clear,
hold nothing back from him.

But you must bathe

and put a shine upon your cheeks—not this way,
streaked under your eyes and stained with tears.
You make it worse, being forever sad,
and now your boy's a bearded man! Remember
you prayed the gods to let you see him so."

Penélopê replied:

"Eurýnomê,   200

it is a kind thought, but I will not hear it—
to bathe and sleek with perfumed oil. No, no,
the gods forever took my sheen away
when my lord sailed for Troy in the decked ships.
Only tell my Autonoë to come,
and Hippodameía; they should be attending me
in hall, if I appear there. I could not
enter alone into that crowd of men."

At this the good old woman left the chamber
to tell the maids her bidding. But now too   210
the grey-eyed goddess had her own designs.
Upon the quiet daughter of Ikários
she let clear drops of slumber fall, until
the queen lay back asleep, her limbs unstrung,
in her long chair. And while she slept the goddess
endowed her with immortal grace to hold
the eyes of the Akhaians. With ambrosia
she bathed her cheeks and throat and smoothed her brow—
ambrosia, used by flower-crowned Kythereia[4]
when she would join the rose-lipped Graces dancing.   220
Grandeur she gave her, too, in height and form,
and made her whiter than carved ivory.
Touching her so, the perfect one was gone.
Now came the maids, bare-armed and lovely, voices
breaking into the room. The queen awoke
and as she rubbed her cheek she sighed:

"Ah, soft

that drowse I lay embraced in, pain forgot!
If only Artemis the Pure would give me

----

[4]Aphroditê, goddess of love.

death as mild, and soon! No heart-ache more,
no wearing out my lifetime with desire   230
and sorrow, mindful of my lord, good man
in all ways that he was, best of the Akhaians!"

She rose and left her glowing upper room,
and down the stairs, with her two maids in train,
this beautiful lady went before the suitors.
Then by a pillar of the solid roof
she paused, her shining veil across her cheek,
the two girls close to her and still;
and in that instant weakness took those men
in the knee joints, their hearts grew faint with lust;   240
not one but swore to god to lie beside her.

But speaking for her dear son's ears alone
she said:

                  "Telémakhos, what has come over you?
Lightminded you were not, in all your boyhood.
Now you are full grown, come of age; a man
from foreign parts might take you for the son
of royalty, to go by your good looks;
and have you no more thoughtfulness or manners?
How could it happen in our hall that you
permit the stranger to be so abused?   250
Here, in our house, a guest, can any man
suffer indignity, come by such injury?
What can this be for you but public shame?"

Telémakhos looked in her eyes and answered,
with his clear head and his discretion:

"Mother,
I cannot take it ill that you are angry.
I know the meaning of these actions now,
both good and bad. I had been young and blind.
How can I always keep to what is fair   260
while these sit here to put fear in me?—princes
from near and far whose interest is my ruin;
are any on my side?

                          But you should know
the suitors did not have their way, matching
the stranger here and Iros—for the stranger
beat him to the ground.

                             O Father Zeus!

Athena and Apollo! could I see
the suitors whipped like that! Courtyard and hall
strewn with our friends, too weak-kneed to get up,
chapfallen to their collarbones, the way   270
old Iros rolls his head there by the gate

as though he were pig-drunk! No energy
to stagger on his homeward path; no fight
left in his numb legs!"

                                        Thus Penélopê
reproached her son, and he replied. Now, interrupting,
Eurýmakhos called out to her:

                                              "Penélopê,

deep-minded queen, daughter of Ikários,
if all Akhaians in the land of Argos
only saw you now! What hundreds more
would join your suitors here to feast tomorrow!   280
Beauty like yours no woman had before,
or majesty, or mastery."

                                        She answered:

"Eurýmakhos, my qualities—I know—
my face, my figure, all were lost or blighted
when the Akhaians crossed the sea to Troy,
Odysseus my lord among the rest.
If he returned, if he were here to care for me,
I might be happily renowned!
But grief instead heaven sent me—years of pain.
Can I forget?—the day he left this island,   290
enfolding my right hand and wrist in his,
he said:

                          'My lady, the Akhaian troops
will not easily make it home again
full strength, unhurt, from Troy. They say the Trojans
are fighters too; good lances and good bowmen,
horsemen, charioteers—and those can be
decisive when a battle hangs in doubt.
So whether God will send me back, or whether
I'll be a captive there, I cannot tell.
Here, then, you must attend to everything.   300
My parents in our house will be a care for you
as they are now, or more, while I am gone.
Wait for the beard to darken our boy's cheek;
then marry whom you will, and move away.'

The years he spoke of are now past; the night
comes when a bitter marriage overtakes me,
desolate as I am, deprived by Zeus
of all the sweets of life.

                                        How galling, too,
to see newfangled manners in my suitors!
Others who go to court a gentlewoman,   310
daughter of a rich house, if they are rivals,

bring their own beeves and sheep along; her friends
ought to be feasted, gifts are due to her;
would any dare to live at her expense?"

Odysseus' heart laughed when he heard all this—
her sweet tones charming gifts out of the suitors
with talk of marriage, though she intended none.
Eupeithês' son, Antínoös, now addressed her:

"Ikários' daughter, O deep-minded queen!
If someone cares to make you gifts, accept them!   320
It is no courtesy to turn gifts away.
But we go neither to our homes nor elsewhere
until of all Akhaians here you take
the best man for your lord."

                                     Pleased at this answer,
every man sent a squire to fetch a gift—
Antínoös, a wide resplendent robe,
embroidered fine, and fastened with twelve brooches,
pins pressed into sheathing tubes of gold;
Eurýmakhos, a necklace, wrought in gold,
with sunray pieces of clear glinting amber.   330
Eurýdamas's men came back with pendants,
ear-drops in triple clusters of warm lights;
and from the hoard of Lord Polýktor's son,
Peisándros, came a band for her white throat,
jewelled adornment. Other wondrous things
were brought as gifts from the Akhaian princes.
Penélopê then mounted the stair again,
her maids behind, with treasure in their arms.

And now the suitors gave themselves to dancing,
to harp and haunting song, as night drew on;   340
black night indeed came on them at their pleasure.
But three torch fires were placed in the long hall
to give them light. On hand were stores of fuel,
dry seasoned chips of resinous wood, split up
by the bronze hatchet blade—these were mixed in
among the flames to keep them flaring bright;
each housemaid of Odysseus took her turn.

Now he himself, the shrewd and kingly man,
approached and told them:

                               "Housemaids of Odysseus,
your master so long absent in the world,   350
go to the women's chambers, to your queen.
Attend her, make the distaff whirl, divert her,
stay in her room, comb wool for her.

                                      I stand here

ready to tend these flares and offer light
to everyone. They cannot tire me out,
even if they wish to drink till Dawn.
I am a patient man."

                                        But the women giggled,
glancing back and forth—laughed in his face;
and one smooth girl, Melántho, spoke to him
most impudently. She was Dólios' daughter,   360
taken as ward in childhood by Penélopê
who gave her playthings to her heart's content
and raised her as her own. Yet the girl felt
nothing for her mistress, no compunction,
but slept and made love with Eurýmakhos.
Her bold voice rang now in Odysseus' ears:

"You must be crazy, punch drunk, you old goat.
Instead of going out to find a smithy
to sleep warm in—or a tavern bench—you stay
putting your oar in, amid all our men.   370
Numbskull, not to be scared! The wine you drank
has clogged your brain, or are you always this way,
boasting like a fool? Or have you lost
your mind because you beat that tramp, that Iros?
Look out, or someone better may get up
and give you a good knocking about the ears
to send you out all bloody."

                                                    But Odysseus
glared at her under his brows and said:

                                            "One minute:

let me tell Telémakhos how you talk
in hall, you slut; he'll cut your arms and legs off!"   380

This hard shot took the women's breath away
and drove them quaking to their rooms, as though
knives were behind: they felt he spoke the truth.
So there he stood and kept the firelight high
and looked the suitors over, while his mind
roamed far ahead to what must be accomplished.

They, for their part, could not now be still
or drop their mockery—for Athena wished
Odysseus mortified still more.

                                            Eurýmakhos,
the son of Pólybos, took up the baiting,   390
angling for a laugh among his friends.

"Suitors of our distinguished queen," he said,
"hear what my heart would have me say.

This man

comes with a certain aura of divinity
into Odysseus' hall. He shines.

He shines

around the noggin, like a flashing light,
having no hair at all to dim his lustre."

Then turning to Odysseus, raider of cities,
he went on:

"Friend, you have a mind to work,
do you? Could I hire you to clear stones   400
from wasteland for me—you'll be paid enough—
collecting boundary walls and planting trees?
I'd give you a bread ration every day,
a cloak to wrap in, sandals for your feet.
Oh no: you learned your dodges long ago—
no honest sweat. You'd rather tramp the country
begging, to keep your hoggish belly full."

The master of many crafts replied:

"Eurýmakhos,

we two might try our hands against each other
in early summer when the days are long,   410
in meadow grass, with one good scythe for me
and one as good for you: we'd cut our way
down a deep hayfield, fasting to late evening.
Or we could try our hands behind a plow,
driving the best of oxen—fat, well-fed,
well-matched for age and pulling power, and say
four strips apiece of loam the share could break:
you'd see then if I cleft you a straight furrow.
Competition in arms? If Zeus Kroníon
roused up a scuffle now, give me a shield,   420
two spears, a dogskin cap with plates of bronze
to fit my temples, and you'd see me go
where the first rank of fighters lock in battle.
There would be no more jeers about my belly.
You thick-skinned menace to all courtesy!
You think you are a great man and a champion,
but up against few men, poor stuff, at that.
Just let Odysseus return, those doors
wide open as they are, you'd find too narrow
to suit you on your sudden journey out."   430

Now fury mounted in Eurýmakhos,
who scowled and shot back:

"Bundle of rags and lice!

By god, I'll make you suffer for your gall,
your insolent gabble before all our men."

He had his foot-stool out: but now Odysseus
took to his haunches by Amphínomos' knees,
fearing Eurýmakhos' missile, as it flew.
It clipped a wine steward on the serving hand,
so that his pitcher dropped with a loud clang
while he fell backward, cursing, in the dust.   440
In the shadowy hall a low sound rose—of suitors
murmuring to one another.

                                      "Ai!" they said,

"This vagabond would have done well to perish
somewhere else, and make us no such rumpus.
Here we are, quarreling over tramps; good meat
and wine forgotten; good sense gone by the board."

Telémakhos, his young heart high, put in:

"Bright souls, alight with wine, you can no longer
hide the cups you've taken.[5] Aye, some god
is goading you. Why not go home to bed?—   450
I mean when you are moved to. No one jumps
at my command."

                            Struck by his blithe manner,
the young men's teeth grew fixed in their under lips,
but now the son of Nísos, Lord Amphínomos
of Aretíadês, addressed them all:

"O friends, no ruffling replies are called for;
that was fair counsel.
                      Hands off the stranger, now,
and hands off any other servant here
in the great house of King Odysseus. Come,
let my own herald wet our cups once more,   460
we'll make an offering, and then to bed.
The stranger can be left behind in hall;
Telémakhos may care for him; he came
to Telémakhos' door, not ours."

                             This won them over.
The soldier Moulios, Doulíkhion herald,
comrade in arms of Lord Amphínomos,
mixed the wine and served them all. They tipped out
drops for the blissful gods, and drank the rest,
and when they had drunk their thirst away
they trailed off homeward drowsily to bed.   470

---

[5] That is, they cannot hide the fact that they have drunk so much.

BOOK NINETEEN: RECOGNITIONS AND A DREAM

Now by Athena's side in the quiet hall
studying the ground for slaughter, Lord Odysseus
turned to Telémakhos.

          "The arms," he said.
"Harness and weapons must be out of sight
in the inner room. And if the suitors miss them,
be mild; just say 'I had a mind to move them
out of the smoke. They seemed no longer
the bright arms that Odysseus left at home
when he went off to Troy. Here where the fire's
hot breath came, they had grown black and drear.   10
One better reason struck me, too:
suppose a brawl starts up when you've been drinking—
you might in madness let each other's blood,
and that would stain your feast, your courtship.

            Iron

itself can draw men's hands.'"

         Then he fell silent,
and Telémakhos obeyed his father's word.
He called Eurýkleia, the nurse, and told her:

"Nurse, go shut the women in their quarters
while I shift Father's armor back
to the inner rooms—these beautiful arms unburnished,   20
caked with black soot in his years abroad.
I was a child then. Well, I am not now.
I want them shielded from the draught and smoke."

And the old woman answered:

         "It is time, child,
you took an interest in such things. I wish
you'd put your mind on all your house and chattels.[1]
But who will go along to hold a light?[2]
You said no maids, no torch-bearers."

           Telémakhos

looked at her and replied:

         "Our friend here.
A man who shares my meat can bear a hand,   30
no matter how far he is from home."

---

[1] Possessions other than house and lands.
[2] Maids would normally have been the torch-bearers.

He spoke so soldierly
her own speech halted on her tongue. Straight back
she went to lock the doors of the women's hall.
And now the two men sprang to work—father
and princely son, loaded with round helms
and studded bucklers, lifting the long spears,
while in their path Pallas Athena
held up a golden lamp of purest light.
Telémakhos at last burst out:

                            "Oh, Father,
here is a marvel! All around I see   40
the walls and roof beams, pedestals and pillars,
lighted as though by white fire blazing near.
One of the gods of heaven is in this place!"

Then said Odysseus, the great tactician,

"Be still: keep still about it: just remember it.
The gods who rule Olympos make this light.
You may go off to bed now. Here I stay
to test your mother and her maids again.
Out of her long grief she will question me."

Telémakhos went across the hall and out   50
under the light of torches—crossed the court
to the tower chamber where he had always slept.
Here now again he lay, waiting for dawn,
while in the great hall by Athena's side
Odysseus waited with his mind on slaughter.

Presently Penélopê from her chamber
stepped in her thoughtful beauty.

                         So might Artemis
or golden Aphroditê have descended;
and maids drew to the hearth her own smooth chair
inlaid with silver whorls and ivory. The artisan   60
Ikmálios had made it, long before,
with a footrest in a single piece, and soft
upon the seat a heavy fleece was thrown.
Here by the fire the queen sat down. Her maids,
leaving their quarters, came with white arms bare
to clear the wine cups and the bread, and move
the trestle boards where men had lingered drinking.
Fiery ashes out of the pine-chip flares
they tossed, and piled on fuel for light and heat.
And now a second time Melántho's voice   70
rang brazen in Odysseus' ears:

                            "Ah, stranger,
are you still here, so creepy, late at night
hanging about, looking the women over?

You old goat, go outside, cuddle your supper;
get out, or a torch may kindle you behind!"

At this Odysseus glared under his brows
and said:

                      "Little devil, why pitch into me again?
Because I go unwashed and wear these rags,
and make the rounds? But so I must, being needy;
that is the way a vagabond must live.   80
And do not overlook this: in my time
I too had luck, lived well, stood well with men,
and gave alms, often, to poor wanderers
like him you see before you—aye, to all sorts,
no matter in what dire want. I owned
servants—many, I say—and all the rest
that goes with what men call prosperity.
But Zeus the son of Kronos brought me down.
Mistress, mend your ways, or you may lose
all this vivacity of yours. What if her ladyship   90
were stirred to anger? What if Odysseus came?—
and I can tell you, there is hope of that—
or if the man is done for, still his son
lives to be reckoned with, by Apollo's will.
None of you can go wantoning on the sly
and fool him now. He is too old for that."

Penélopê, being near enough to hear him,
spoke out sharply to her maid:

                           "Oh, shameless,
through and through! And do you think me blind,
blind to your conquest?[3] It will cost your life.   100
You knew I waited—for you heard me say it—
waited to see this man in hall and question him
about my lord; I am so hard beset."

She turned away and said to the housekeeper:

"Eurýnomê, a bench, a spread of sheepskin,
to put my guest at ease. Now he shall talk
and listen, and be questioned."

                               Willing hands
brought a smooth bench, and dropped a fleece upon it.
Here the adventurer and king sat down;
then carefully Penélopê began: 110

---

[3] The reference is to Melántho's sexual dalliance with Eurýmakhos. The following words are probably less a threat than a warning that Melántho will have brought on her own punishment.

"Friend, let me ask you first of all:
who are you, where do you come from, of what nation
and parents were you born?"

                                                    And he replied:

"My lady, never a man in the wide world
should have a fault to find with you. Your name
has gone out under heaven like the sweet
honor of some god-fearing king, who rules
in equity over the strong: his black lands bear
both wheat and barley, fruit trees laden bright,
new lambs at lambing time—and the deep sea   120
gives great hauls of fish by his good strategy,
so that his folk fare well.

                                        O my dear lady,
this being so, let it suffice to ask me
of other matters—not my blood, my homeland.
Do not enforce me to recall my pain.
My heart is sore; but I must not be found
sitting in tears here, in another's house:
it is not well forever to be grieving.
One of the maids might say—or you might think—
I had got maudlin over cups of wine."   130

And Penélopê replied:

                                        "Stranger, my looks,
my face, my carriage, were soon lost or faded
when the Akhaians crossed the sea to Troy,
Odysseus my lord among the rest.
If he returned, if he were here to care for me,
I might be happily renowned!
But grief instead heaven sent me—years of pain.
Sons of the noblest families on the islands,
Doulíkhion, Samê, wooded Zakýnthos,
with native Ithakans, are here to court me,   140
against my wish; and they consume this house.
Can I give proper heed to guest or suppliant
or herald on the realm's affairs?

                                        How could I?
wasted with longing for Odysseus, while here
they press for marriage.

                                        Ruses served my turn
to draw the time out—first a close-grained web
I had the happy thought to set up weaving
on my big loom in hall. I said, that day:
'Young men—my suitors, now my lord is dead,
let me finish my weaving before I marry,   150
or else my thread will have been spun in vain.
It is a shroud I weave for Lord Laërtês

when cold Death comes to lay him on his bier.
The country wives would hold me in dishonor
if he, with all his fortune, lay unshrouded.'
I reached their hearts that way, and they agreed.
So every day I wove on the great loom,
but every night by torchlight I unwove it;
and so for three years I deceived the Akhaians.
But when the seasons brought a fourth year on,   160
as long months waned, and the long days were spent,
through impudent folly in the slinking maids
they caught me—clamored up to me at night;
I had no choice then but to finish it.
And now, as matters stand at last,
I have no strength left to evade a marriage,
cannot find any further way; my parents
urge it upon me, and my son
will not stand by while they eat up his property.
He comprehends it, being a man full grown,   170
able to oversee the kind of house
Zeus would endow with honor.

                                        But you too

confide in me, tell me your ancestry.
You were not born of mythic oak or stone."

And the great master of invention answered:

"O honorable wife of Lord Odysseus,
must you go on asking about my family?
Then I will tell you, though my pain
be doubled by it: and whose pain would not
if he had been away as long as I have   180
and had hard roving in the world of men?
But I will tell you even so, my lady.

One of the great islands of the world
in midsea, in the winedark sea, is Krete:
spacious and rich and populous, with ninety
cities and a mingling of tongues.
Akhaians there are found, along with Kretan
hillmen of the old stock, and Kydonians,
Dorians in three blood-lines, Pelasgians[4]—
and one among their ninety towns is Knossos.   190
Here lived King Minos[5] whom great Zeus received
every ninth year in private council—Minos,

---

[4] Kydonians, Dorians, Pelasgians were various ethnic groups, natives of Krete or immigrants.

[5] Minos, sometimes represented as a cruel king (as in Book XI), is here represented as supremely honored. Knossos is on the north shore of Krete. In this version of his autobiography, Odysseus obviously departs from what he had told Eumaios (Book XIV) and Antínoös (Book XVII).

the father of my father, Deukálion.
Two sons Deukálion had: Idómeneus,
who went to join the Atreidai before Troy
in the beaked ships of war; and then myself,
Aithôn by name—a stripling next my brother.
But I saw with my own eyes at Knossos once
Odysseus.

                    Gales had caught him off Cape Malea,
driven him southward on the coast of Krete,   200
when he was bound for Troy. At Ámnisos,
hard by the holy cave of Eileithuía,[6]
he lay to, and dropped anchor, in that open
and rough roadstead riding out the blow.
Meanwhile he came ashore, came inland, asking
after Idómeneus: dear friends he said they were;
but now ten mornings had already passed,
ten or eleven, since my brother sailed.
So I played host and took Odysseus home,
saw him well lodged and fed, for we had plenty;   210
then I made requisitions—barley, wine,
and beeves for sacrifice—to give his company
abundant fare along with him.

                               Twelve days

they stayed with us, the Akhaians, while that wind
out of the north shut everyone inside—
even on land you could not keep your feet,
such fury was abroad. On the thirteenth,
when the gale dropped, they put to sea."

Now all these lies he made appear so truthful
she wept as she sat listening. The skin   220
of her pale face grew moist the way pure snow
softens and glistens on the mountains, thawed
by Southwind after powdering from the West,
and, as the snow melts, mountain streams run full:
so her white cheeks were wetted by these tears
shed for her lord—and he close by her side.
Imagine how his heart ached for his lady,
his wife in tears; and yet he never blinked;
his eyes might have been made of horn or iron
for all that she could see. He had this trick—   230
wept, if he willed to, inwardly.

                                Well, then,

as soon as her relieving tears were shed
she spoke once more:

                    "I think that I shall say, friend,
give me some proof, if it is really true

---

[6]Ámnisos is an anchorage off Krete. Eileithuía was a goddess, daughter of Hera, who controlled maternal labor and childbirth.

that you were host in that place to my husband
with his brave men, as you declare. Come, tell me
the quality of his clothing, how he looked,
and some particular of his company."

Odysseus answered, and his mind ranged far:

"Lady, so long a time now lies between,   240
it is hard to speak of it. Here is the twentieth year
since that man left the island of my father.
But I shall tell what memory calls to mind.
A purple cloak, and fleecy, he had on—
a double thick one. Then, he wore a brooch
made of pure gold with twin tubes for the prongs,
and on the face a work of art: a hunting dog
pinning a spotted fawn in agony
between his forepaws—wonderful to see
how being gold, and nothing more, he bit   250
the golden deer convulsed, with wild hooves flying.
Odysseus' shirt I noticed, too—a fine
closefitting tunic like dry onion skin,
so soft it was, and shiny.

                                        Women there,

many of them, would cast their eyes on it.
But I might add, for your consideration,
whether he brought these things from home, or whether
a shipmate gave them to him, coming aboard,
I have no notion: some regardful host
in another port perhaps it was. Affection   260
followed him—there were few Akhaians like him.
And I too made him gifts: a good bronze blade,
a cloak with lining and a broidered shirt,
and sent him off in his trim ship with honor.
A herald, somewhat older than himself,
he kept beside him; I'll describe this man:
round-shouldered, dusky, woolly-headed;
Eurýbatês, his name was—and Odysseus
gave him preferment over the officers.
He had a shrewd head, like the captain's own."   270

Now hearing these details—minutely true—
she felt more strangely moved, and tears flowed
until she had tasted her salt grief again.
Then she found words to answer:

                                        "Before this

you won my sympathy, but now indeed
you shall be our respected guest and friend.
With my own hands I put that cloak and tunic
upon him—took them folded from their place—
and the bright brooch for ornament.

Gone now,   280
I will not meet the man again
returning to his own home fields. Unkind
the fate that sent him young in the long ship
to see that misery at Ilion, unspeakable!"

And the master improviser answered:

"Honorable
wife of Odysseus Laërtiadês,
you need not stain your beauty with these tears,
nor wear yourself out grieving for your husband.
Not that I can blame you. Any wife
grieves for the man she married in her girlhood,
lay with in love, bore children to—though he   290
may be no prince like this Odysseus,
whom they compare even to the gods. But listen:
weep no more, and listen:
I have a thing to tell you, something true.
I heard but lately of your lord's return,
heard that he is alive, not far away,
among Thesprótians in their green land
amassing fortune to bring home. His company
went down in shipwreck in the winedark sea
off the coast of Thrinákia. Zeus and Hêlios   300
held it against him that his men had killed
the kine of Hêlios. The crew drowned for this.
He rode the ship's keel. Big seas cast him up
on the island of Phaiákians, godlike men
who took him to their hearts. They honored him
with many gifts and a safe passage home,
or so they wished. Long since he should have been here,
but he thought better to restore his fortune
playing the vagabond about the world;
and no adventurer could beat Odysseus   310
at living by his wits—no man alive.
I had this from King Phaidôn of Thesprótia;
and, tipping wine out, Phaidôn swore to me
the ship was launched, the seamen standing by
to bring Odysseus to his land at last,
but I got out to sea ahead of him
by the king's order—as it chanced a freighter
left port for the grain bins of Doulíkhion.
Phaidôn, however, showed me Odysseus' treasure.
Ten generations of his heirs or more   320
could live on what lay piled in that great room.
The man himself had gone up to Dodona
to ask the spelling leaves of the old oak
what Zeus would have him do—how to return to Ithaka
after so many years—by stealth or openly.

You see, then, he is alive and well, and headed
homeward now, no more to be abroad
far from his island, his dear wife and son.
Here is my sworn word for it. Witness this,
god of the zenith, noblest of the gods,   330
and Lord Odysseus' hearthfire, now before me:
I swear these things shall turn out as I say.
Between this present dark and one day's ebb,
after the wane, before the crescent moon,[7]
Odysseus will come."

                                      Penélopê,
the attentive queen, replied to him:

                                       "Ah, stranger,
if what you say could ever happen!
You would soon know our love! Our bounty, too:
men would turn after you to call you blessed.
But my heart tells me what must be.   340
Odysseus will not come to me; no ship
will be prepared for you. We have no master
quick to receive and furnish out a guest
as Lord Odysseus was.

                             Or did I dream him?

Maids, maids: come wash him, make a bed for him,
bedstead and colored rugs and coverlets
to let him lie warm into the gold of Dawn.
In morning light you'll bathe him and anoint him
so that he'll take his place beside Telémakhos
feasting in hall. If there be one man there   350
to bully or annoy him, that man wins
no further triumph here, burn though he may.
How will you understand me, friend, how find in me,
more than in common women, any courage
or gentleness, if you are kept in rags
and filthy at our feast? Men's lives are short.
The hard man and his cruelties will be
cursed behind his back, and mocked in death.
But one whose heart and ways are kind—of him
strangers will bear report to the wide world,   360
and distant men will praise him."

                                       Warily
Odysseus answered:

---

[7] Between now and the time of the new moon. As it happens, the day specified will be the morrow.

"Honorable lady,
wife of Odysseus Laërtiadês,
a weight of rugs and cover? Not for me.
I've had none since the day I saw the mountains
of Krete, white with snow, low on the sea line
fading behind me as the long oars drove me north.
Let me lie down tonight as I've lain often,
many a night unsleeping, many a time
afield on hard ground waiting for pure Dawn.   370
No: and I have no longing for a footbath
either; none of these maids will touch my feet,
unless there is an old one, old and wise,
one who has lived through suffering as I have:
I would not mind letting my feet be touched
by that old servant."

                                              And Penélopê said:

"Dear guest, no foreign man so sympathetic
ever came to my house, no guest more likeable,
so wry and humble are the things you say.
I have an old maidservant ripe with years,   380
one who in her time nursed my lord. She took him
into her arms the hour his mother bore him.
Let her, then, wash your feet, though she is frail.
Come here, stand by me, faithful Eurýkleia,
and bathe—bathe your master, I almost said,
for they are of an age, and now Odysseus'
feet and hands would be enseamed like his.
Men grow old soon in hardship."

                                              Hearing this,
the old nurse hid her face between her hands
and wept hot tears, and murmured:

                                              "Oh, my child!   390
I can do nothing for you! How Zeus hated you,
no other man so much! No use, great heart,
O faithful heart, the rich thighbones you burnt
to Zeus who plays in lightning—and no man
ever gave more to Zeus—with all your prayers
for a green age, a tall son reared to manhood.
There is no day of homecoming for you.
Stranger, some women in some far off place
perhaps have mocked my lord when he'd be home
as now these strumpets[8] mock you here. No wonder   400
you would keep clear of all their whorishness
and have no bath. But here am I. The queen
Penélopê, Ikários' daughter, bids me;

_____
[8] Whores.

so let me bathe your feet to serve my lady—
to serve you, too.

My heart within me stirs,

mindful of something. Listen to what I say:
strangers have come here, many through the years,
but no one ever came, I swear, who seemed
so like Odysseus—body, voice and limbs—
as you do."

Ready for this, Odysseus answered: 410

"Old woman, that is what they say. All who have seen
the two of us remark how like we are,
as you yourself have said, and rightly, too."

Then he kept still, while the old nurse filled up
her basin glittering in firelight; she poured
cold water in, then hot.

But Lord Odysseus

whirled suddenly from the fire to face the dark.
The scar: he had forgotten that. She must not
handle his scarred thigh, or the game was up.
But when she bared her lord's leg, bending near, 420
she knew the groove at once.

An old wound

a boar's white tusk inflicted, on Parnassos[9]
years ago. He had gone hunting there
in company with his uncles and Autólykos,
his mother's father—a great thief and swindler
by Hermês'[10] favor, for Autólykos pleased him
with burnt offerings of sheep and kids. The god
acted as his accomplice. Well, Autólykos
on a trip to Ithaka
arrived just after his daughter's boy was born. 430
In fact, he had no sooner finished supper
than Nurse Eurýkleia put the baby down
in his own lap and said:

"It is for you, now,

to choose a name for him, your child's dear baby;
the answer to her prayers."

Autólykos replied:

"My son-in-law, my daughter, call the boy
by the name I tell you. Well you know, my hand
has been against the world of men and women;
odium and distrust I've won. Odysseus

---

[9] The famous mountain near Delphi. Also spelled *Parnassus*.
[10] Noted for cleverness, Hermês was the patron god of thieves, though he is not usually presented in that role by Homer.

should be his given name.[11] When he grows up,   440
when he comes visiting his mother's home
under Parnassos, where my treasures are,
I'll make him gifts and send him back rejoicing."

Odysseus in due course went for the gifts,
and old Autólykos and his sons embraced him
with welcoming sweet words; and Amphithéa,
his mother's mother, held him tight and kissed him,
kissed his head and his fine eyes.

                                             The father

called on his noble sons to make a feast,
and going about it briskly they led in   450
an ox of five years, whom they killed and flayed
and cut in bits for roasting on the skewers
with skilled hands, with care; then shared it out.
So all the day until the sun went down
they feasted to their hearts' content. At evening,
after the sun was down and dusk had come,
they turned to bed and took the gift of sleep.

When the young Dawn spread in the eastern sky
her finger tips of rose, the men and dogs
went hunting, taking Odysseus. They climbed   460
Parnassos' rugged flank mantled in forest,
entering amid high windy folds at noon
when Hêlios beat upon the valley floor
and on the winding Ocean whence he came.
With hounds questing ahead, in open order,
the sons of Autólykos went down a glen,
Odysseus in the lead, behind the dogs,
pointing his long-shadowing spear.

                                             Before them

a great boar lay hid in undergrowth,
in a green thicket proof against the wind   470
or sun's blaze, fine soever the needling sunlight,
impervious too to any rain, so dense
that cover was, heaped up with fallen leaves.
Patter of hounds' feet, men's feet, woke the boar
as they came up—and from his woody ambush
with razor back bristling and raging eyes
he trotted and stood at bay. Odysseus,
being on top of him, had the first shot,
lunging to stick him; but the boar
had already charged under the long spear.   480
He hooked aslant with one white tusk and ripped out
flesh above the knee, but missed the bone.

---

[11] *Odysseus* means something like "wrathful."

Odysseus' second thrust went home by luck,
his bright spear passing through the shoulder joint;
and the beast fell, moaning as life pulsed away.
Autólykos' tall sons took up the wounded,
working skillfully over the Prince Odysseus
to bind his gash, and with a rune[12] they stanched
the dark flow of blood. Then downhill swiftly
they all repaired to the father's house, and there   490
tended him well—so well they soon could send him,
with Grandfather Autólykos' magnificent gifts,
rejoicing, over sea to Ithaka.
His father and the Lady Antikleía
welcomed him, and wanted all the news
of how he got his wound; so he spun out
his tale, recalling how the boar's white tusk
caught him when he was hunting on Parnassos.

This was the scar the old nurse recognized;
she traced it under her spread hands, then let go,   500
and into the basin fell the lower leg
making the bronze clang, sloshing the water out.
Then joy and anguish seized her heart; her eyes
filled up with tears; her throat closed, and she whispered,
with hand held out to touch his chin:

                                               "Oh yes!

You are Odysseus! Ah, dear child! I could not
see you until now—not till I knew
my master's very body with my hands!"

Her eyes turned to Penélopê with desire
to make her lord, her husband, known—in vain,   510
because Athena had bemused the queen,
so that she took no notice, paid no heed.
At the same time Odysseus' right hand
gripped the old throat; his left hand pulled her near,
and in her ear he said:

                                        "Will you destroy me,
nurse, who gave me milk at your own breast?
Now with a hard lifetime behind I've come
in the twentieth year home to my father's island.
You found me out, as the chance was given you.
Be quiet; keep it from the others, else   520
I warn you, and I mean it, too,
if by my hand god brings the suitors down
I'll kill you, nurse or not, when the time comes—
when the time comes to kill the other women."

[12] Magic spell or charm.

Eurýkleia kept her wits and answered him:

"Oh, what mad words are these you let escape you!
Child, you know my blood, my bones are yours;
no one could whip this out of me. I'll be
a woman turned to stone, iron I'll be.
And let me tell you too—mind now—if god   530
cuts down the arrogant suitors by your hand,
I can report to you on all the maids,
those who dishonor you, and the innocent."

But in response the great tactician said:

"Nurse, no need to tell me tales of these.
I will have seen them, each one, for myself.
Trust in the gods, be quiet, hold your peace."

Silent, the old nurse went to fetch more water,
her basin being all spilt.

                                        When she had washed
and rubbed his feet with golden oil, he turned,   540
dragging his bench again to the fire side
for warmth, and hid the scar under his rags.
Penélopê broke the silence, saying:

                                                        "Friend,

allow me one brief question more. You know,
the time for bed, sweet rest, is coming soon,
if only that warm luxury of slumber
would come to enfold us, in our trouble. But for me
my fate at night is anguish and no rest.
By day being busy, seeing to my work,
I find relief sometimes from loss and sorrow;   550
but when night comes and all the world's abed
I lie in mine alone, my heart thudding,
while bitter thoughts and fears crowd on my grief.
Think, how Pandáreos'[13] daughter, pale forever,
sings as the nightingale in the new leaves
through those long quiet hours of night,
on some thick-flowering orchard bough in spring;
how she rills out and tilts her note, high now, now low,
mourning for Itylos whom she killed in madness—
her child, and her lord Zêthos' only child.   560
My forlorn thought flows variable as her song,
wondering: shall I stay beside my son
and guard my own things here, my maids, my hall,
to honor my lord's bed and the common talk?

[13] In this version of the nightingale-myth, Aedon (daughter of Pandáreos and wife of
Zêthos) was metamorphosed into a nightingale, through the compassion of Zeus, after she had
killed her only son, Itylos, by mistake. She had intended to kill the eldest son of Niobe, her
sister-in-law, who had aroused her jealousy by having so many children.

Or had I best join fortunes with a suitor,
the noblest one, most lavish in his gifts?
Is it now time for that?
My son being still a callow boy forbade
marriage, or absence from my lord's domain;
but now the child is grown, grown up, a man,   570
he, too, begins to pray for my departure,
aghast at all the suitors gorge on.

                                                  Listen:

interpret me this dream: From a water's edge
twenty fat geese have come to feed on grain
beside my house. And I delight to see them.
But now a mountain eagle with great wings
and crooked beak storms in to break their necks
and strew their bodies here. Away he soars
into the bright sky; and I cry aloud—
all this in dream—I wail and round me gather   580
softly braided Akhaian women mourning
because the eagle killed my geese.

                                             Then down

out of the sky he drops to a cornice beam
with mortal voice telling me not to weep.
'Be glad,' says he, 'renowned Ikários' daughter:
here is no dream but something real as day,
something about to happen. All those geese
were suitors, and the bird was I. See now,
I am no eagle but your lord come back
to bring inglorious death upon them all!'   590
As he said this, my honeyed slumber left me.
Peering through half-shut eyes, I saw the geese
in hall, still feeding at the self-same trough."

The master of subtle ways and straight replied:

"My dear, how can you choose to read the dream
differently? Has not Odysseus himself
shown you what is to come? Death to the suitors,
sure death, too. Not one escapes his doom."

Penélopê shook her head and answered:

                                           "Friend,

many and many a dream is mere confusion,   600
a cobweb of no consequence at all.
Two gates for ghostly dreams there are: one gateway
of honest horn, and one of ivory.
Issuing by the ivory gate are dreams
of glimmering illusion, fantasies,
but those that come through solid polished horn
may be borne out, if mortals only know them.

I doubt it came by horn, my fearful dream—
too good to be true, that, for my son and me.
But one thing more I wish to tell you: listen   610
carefully. It is a black day, this that comes.
Odysseus' house and I are to be parted.
I shall decree a contest for the day.
We have twelve axe heads. In his time, my lord
could line them up, all twelve, at intervals
like a ship's ribbing; then he'd back away
a long way off and whip an arrow through.
Now I'll impose this trial on the suitors.
The one who easily handles and strings the bow
and shoots through all twelve axes I shall marry,   620
whoever he may be—then look my last
on this my first love's beautiful brimming house.
But I'll remember, though I dream it only."

Odysseus said:

                                        "Dear honorable lady,
wife of Odysseus Laërtiadês,
let there be no postponement of the trial.
Odysseus, who knows the shifts of combat,
will be here: aye, he'll be here long before
one of these lads can stretch or string that bow
or shoot to thread the iron!"

                                        Grave and wise,   630
Penélopê replied:

                                        "If you were willing
to sit with me and comfort me, my friend,
no tide of sleep would ever close my eyes.
But mortals cannot go forever sleepless.
This the undying gods decree for all
who live and die on earth, kind furrowed earth.
Upstairs I go, then, to my single bed,
my sighing bed, wet with so many tears
after my Lord Odysseus took ship
to see that misery at Ilion, unspeakable.   640
Let me rest there, you here. You can stretch out
on the bare floor, or else command a bed."

So she went up to her chamber softly lit,
accompanied by her maids. Once there, she wept
for Odysseus, her husband, till Athena
cast sweet sleep upon her eyes.

BOOK TWENTY: SIGNS AND A VISION

Outside in the entry way he made his bed—
raw oxhide spread on level ground, and heaped up
fleeces, left from sheep the Akhaians killed.
And when he had lain down, Eurýnomê
flung out a robe to cover him. Unsleeping
the Lord Odysseus lay, and roved in thought
to the undoing of his enemies.

                                  Now came a covey of women
laughing as they slipped out, arm in arm,
as many a night before, to the suitors' beds;
and anger took him like a wave to leap   10
into their midst and kill them, every one—
or should he let them all go hot to bed
one final night? His heart cried out within him
the way a brach[1] with whelps between her legs
would howl and bristle at a stranger—so
the hackles of his heart rose at that laughter.
Knocking his breast he muttered to himself:

"Down; be steady. You've seen worse, that time
the Kyklops like a rockslide ate your men
while you looked on. Nobody, only guile,   20
got you out of that cave alive."

                                      His rage
held hard in leash, submitted to his mind,
while he himself rocked, rolling from side to side,
as a cook turns a sausage, big with blood
and fat, at a scorching blaze, without a pause,
to broil it quick: so he rolled left and right,
casting about to see how he, alone,
against the false outrageous crowd of suitors
could press the fight.

                        And out of the night sky
Athena came to him; out of the nearby dark   30
in body like a woman; came and stood
over his head to chide him:

                        "Why so wakeful,
most forlorn of men? Here is your home,
there lies your lady; and your son is here,
as fine as one could wish a son to be."

Odysseus looked up and answered:

"Aye,
goddess, that much is true; but still

---

[1] Female dog; bitch.

I have some cause to fret in this affair.
I am one man; how can I whip those dogs?   40
They are always here in force. Neither
is that the end of it, there's more to come.
If by the will of Zeus and by your will
I killed them all, where could I go for safety?
Tell me that!"

                             And the grey-eyed goddess said:

"Your touching faith! Another man would trust
some villainous mortal, with no brains—and what
am I? Your goddess-guardian to the end
in all your trials. Let it be plain as day:
if fifty bands of men surrounded us   50
and every sword sang for your blood,
you could make off still with their cows and sheep.
Now you, too, go to sleep. This all night vigil
wearies the flesh. You'll come out soon enough
on the other side of trouble."

                                  Raining soft

sleep on his eyes, the beautiful one was gone
back to Olympos. Now at peace, the man
slumbered and lay still, but not his lady.
Wakeful again with all her cares, reclining
in the soft bed, she wept and cried aloud
until she had had her fill of tears, then spoke   60
in prayer first to Artemis:

                                   "O gracious

divine lady Artemis, daughter of Zeus,
if you could only make an end now quickly,
let the arrow fly, stop my heart,
or if some wind could take me by the hair
up into running cloud, to plunge in tides of Ocean,
as hurricane winds took Pandáreos' daughters[2]
when they were left at home alone. The gods
had sapped their parents' lives. But Aphroditê   70
fed those children honey, cheese, and wine,
and Hêra gave them looks and wit, and Artemis,
pure Artemis, gave lovely height, and wise
Athena made them practised in her arts—
till Aphroditê in glory walked on Olympos,
begging for each a happy wedding day
from Zeus, the lightning's joyous king, who knows

---

[2] Pandáreos stole a statue from a temple of Zeus; after the death of Pandáreos, his three daughters (Aedon and two of her sisters), though pitied by the greatest of the goddesses, were carried away by the Furies, the avengers of the father's wickedness. This story differs from the one in Book XIX, in which Aedon was changed into a nightingale.

all fate of mortals, fair and foul—
but even at that hour the cyclone winds
had ravished them away   80
to serve the loathsome Furies.

                                        Let me be

blown out by the Olympians! Shot by Artemis,
I still might go and see amid the shades
Odysseus in the rot of underworld.
No coward's eye should light by my consenting!
Evil may be endured when our days pass
in mourning, heavy-hearted, hard beset,
if only sleep reign over nighttime, blanketing
the world's good and evil from our eyes.
But not for me: dreams too my demon sends me.   90
Tonight the image of my lord came by
as I remember him with troops. O strange
exultation! I thought him real, and not a dream."

Now as the Dawn appeared all stitched in gold,
the queen's cry reached Odysseus at his waking,
so that he wondered, half asleep: it seemed
she knew him, and stood near him! Then he woke
and picked his bedding up to stow away
on a chair in the mégaron. The oxhide pad
he took outdoors. There, spreading wide his arms,   100
he prayed:

                    "O Father Zeus, if over land and water,
after adversity, you willed to bring me home,
let someone in the waking house give me good augury,
and a sign be shown, too, in the outer world."

He prayed thus, and the mind of Zeus in heaven
heard him. He thundered out of bright Olympos
down from above the cloudlands, in reply—
a rousing peal for Odysseus. Then a token
came to him from a woman grinding flour
in the court nearby. His own handmills were there,   110
and twelve maids had the job of grinding out
whole grain and barley meal, the pith of men.
Now all the rest, their bushels ground, were sleeping;
one only, frail and slow, kept at it still.
She stopped, stayed her hand, and her lord heard
the omen from her lips:

                              "Ah, Father Zeus

almighty over gods and men!
A great bang of thunder that was, surely,
out of the starry sky, and not a cloud in sight.
It is your nod to someone. Hear me, then,   120
make what I say come true:

let this day be the last the suitors feed
so dainty in Odysseus' hall!
They've made me work my heart out till I drop,
grinding barley. May they feast no more!"

The servant's prayer, after the cloudless thunder
of Zeus, Odysseus heard with lifting heart,
sure in his bones that vengeance was at hand.
Then other servants, wakening, came down
to build and light a fresh fire at the hearth.   130
Telémakhos, clear-eyed as a god, awoke,
put on his shirt and belted on his sword,
bound rawhide sandals under his smooth feet,
and took his bronze-shod lance. He came and stood
on the broad sill of the doorway, calling Eurýkleia:

"Nurse, dear Nurse, how did you treat our guest?
Had he a supper and a good bed? Has he lain
uncared for still? My mother is like that,
perverse for all her cleverness:
she'd entertain some riff-raff, and turn out   140
a solid man."

                          The old nurse answered him:
"I would not be so quick to accuse her, child.
He sat and drank here while he had a mind to;
food he no longer hungered for, he said—
for she did ask him. When he thought of sleeping,
she ordered them to make a bed. Poor soul!
Poor gentleman! So humble and so miserable,
he would accept no bed with rugs to lie on,
but slept on sheepskins and a raw oxhide
in the entry way. We covered him ourselves."   150

Telémakhos left the hall, hefting his lance,
with two swift flickering hounds for company,
to face the island Akhaians in the square;
and gently born Eurýkleia, the daughter
of Ops Peisenóridês, called to the maids:

"Bestir yourselves! you have your brooms, go sprinkle
the rooms and sweep them, robe the chairs in red,
sponge off the tables till they shine.
Wash out the winebowls and two-handled cups.
You others go fetch water from the spring;   160
no loitering; come straight back. Our company
will be here soon; morning is sure to bring them;
everyone has a holiday today."[3]

---

[3] The day is a special festival.

The women ran to obey her—twenty girls
off to the spring with jars for dusky water,
the rest at work inside. Then tall woodcutters
entered to split up logs for the hearth fire,
the water carriers returned; and on their heels
arrived the swineherd, driving three fat pigs,
chosen among his pens. In the wide court   170
he let them feed, and said to Odysseus kindly:

"Friend, are they more respectful of you now,
or still insulting you?"

                                                        Replied Odysseus:

"The young men, yes. And may the gods requite
those insolent puppies for the game they play
in a home not their own. They have no decency."

During this talk, Melánthios the goatherd
came in, driving goats for the suitors' feast,
with his two herdsmen. Under the portico
they tied the animals, and Melánthios   180
looked at Odysseus with a sneer. Said he:

                                                        "Stranger,
I see you mean to stay and turn our stomachs
begging in this hall. Clear out, why don't you?
Or will you have to taste a bloody beating
before you see the point? Your begging ways
nauseate everyone. There are feasts elsewhere."

Odysseus answered not a word, but grimly
shook his head over his murderous heart.
A third man came up now: Philoítios
the cattle foreman, with an ox behind him   190
and fat goats for the suitors. Ferrymen
had brought these from the mainland, as they bring
travellers, too—whoever comes along.
Philoítios tied the beasts under the portico
and joined the swineherd.

                                                "Who is this," he said,
"Who is the new arrival at the manor?
Akhaian? or what else does he claim to be?
Where are his family and fields of home?
Down on his luck, all right: carries himself like a captain.
How the immortal gods can change and drag us down   200
once they begin to spin dark days for us!—
Kings and commanders, too."

                                                Then he stepped over
and took Odysseus by the right hand, saying:

"Welcome, Sir. May good luck lie ahead
at the next turn. Hard times you're having, surely.
O Zeus! no god is more berserk in heaven
if gentle folk, whom you yourself begot,[4]
you plunge in grief and hardship without mercy!
Sir, I began to sweat when I first saw you,
and tears came to my eyes, remembering   210
Odysseus: rags like these he may be wearing
somewhere on his wanderings now—
I mean, if he's alive still under the sun.
But if he's dead and in the house of Death,
I mourn Odysseus. He entrusted cows to me
in Kephallênia,[5] when I was knee high,
and now his herds are numberless, no man else
ever had cattle multiply like grain.
But new men tell me I must bring my beeves
to feed them, who care nothing for our prince,   220
fear nothing from the watchful gods. They crave
partition of our lost king's land and wealth.
My own feelings keep going round and round
upon this tether: can I desert the boy
by moving, herds and all, to another country,
a new life among strangers? Yet it's worse
to stay here, in my old post, herding cattle
for upstarts.
                            I'd have gone long since,
gone, taken service with another king; this shame
is no more to be borne; but I keep thinking   230
my own lord, poor devil, still might come
and make a rout of suitors in his hall."

Odysseus, with his mind on action, answered:

"Herdsman, I make you out to be no coward
and no fool: I can see that for myself.
So let me tell you this. I swear by Zeus
all highest, by the table set for friends,
and by your king's hearthstone to which I've come,
Odysseus will return. You'll be on hand
to see, if you care to see it,   240
how those who lord it here will be cut down."

The cowman said:

                                "Would god it all came true!
You'd see the fight that's in me!"

---

[4]To say that Zeus was their father was a way of describing great leaders.
[5]A large island near Ithaka; modern Cephalonia.

Then Eumaios

echoed him, and invoked the gods, and prayed
that his great-minded master should return.
While these three talked, the suitors in the field
had come together plotting—what but death
for Telémakhos?—when from the left an eagle
crossed high with a rockdove in his claws.

Amphínomos got up. Said he, cutting them short: 250

"Friends, no luck lies in that plan for us,
no luck,[6] knifing the lad. Let's think of feasting."

A grateful thought, they felt, and walking on
entered the great hall of the hero Odysseus,
where they all dropped their cloaks on chairs or couches
and made a ritual slaughter, knifing sheep,
fat goats and pigs, knifing the grass-fed steer.
Then tripes were broiled and eaten. Mixing bowls
were filled with wine. The swineherd passed out cups,
Philoítios, chief cowherd, dealt the loaves   260
into the panniers, Melánthios poured wine,
and all their hands went out upon the feast.

Telémakhos placed his father to advantage
just at the door sill of the pillared hall,
setting a stool there and a sawed-off table,
gave him a share of tripes, poured out his wine
in a golden cup, and said:

"Stay here, sit down

to drink with our young friends. I stand between you
and any cutting word or cuffing hand
from any suitor. Here is no public house   270
but the old home of Odysseus, my inheritance.
Hold your tongues then, gentlemen, and your blows,
and let no wrangling start, no scuffle either."

The others, disconcerted, bit their lips
at the ring in the young man's voice. Antínoös,
Eupeithês' son, turned round to them and said:

"It goes against the grain, my lords, but still
I say we take this hectoring by Telémakhos.
You know Zeus balked at it, or else
we might have shut his mouth a long time past,   280
the silvery speaker."

---

[6] The bird's appearance on the left is an ill omen.

                                                          But Telémakhos
paid no heed to what Antínoös said.

Now public heralds wound through Ithaka
leading a file of beasts for sacrifice, and islanders
gathered under the shade trees of Apollo,
in the precinct of the Archer—while in hall
the suitors roasted mutton and fat beef
on skewers, pulling off the fragrant cuts;
and those who did the roasting served Odysseus
a portion equal to their own, for so   290
Telémakhos commanded.

                                                          But Athena
had no desire now to let the suitors
restrain themselves from wounding words and acts.
Laërtês' son again must be offended.
There was a scapegrace[7] fellow in the crowd
named Ktésippos, a Samian, rich beyond
all measure, arrogant with riches, early
and late a bidder for Odysseus' queen.
Now this one called attention to himself:

"Hear me, my lords, I have a thing to say.   300
Our friend has had his fair share from the start
and that's polite; it would be most improper
if we were cold to guests of Telémakhos—
no matter what tramp turns up. Well then, look here,
let me throw in my own small contribution.
He must have prizes to confer, himself,
on some brave bathman or another slave
here in Odysseus' house."

                                        His hand went backward
and, fishing out a cow's foot from the basket,
he let it fly.

                                        Odysseus rolled his head   310
to one side softly, ducking the blow, and smiled
a crooked smile with teeth clenched. On the wall
the cow's foot struck and fell. Telémakhos
blazed up:

                        "Ktésippos, lucky for you, by heaven,
not to have hit him! He took care of himself,
else you'd have had my lance-head in your belly;
no marriage, but a grave instead on Ithaka
for your father's pains.

                                You others, let me see
no more contemptible conduct in my house!
I've been awake to it for a long time—by now   320

[7] Unprincipled.

I know what is honorable and what is not.
Before, I was a child. I can endure it
while sheep are slaughtered, wine drunk up, and bread—
can one man check the greed of a hundred men?—
but I will suffer no more viciousness.
Granted you mean at last to cut me down:
I welcome that—better to die than have
humiliation always before my eyes,
the stranger buffeted, and the serving women
dragged about, abused in a noble house."   330

They quieted, grew still, under his lashing,
and after a long silence, Ageláos,
Damástor's son, spoke to them all:

                                 "Friends, friends,
I hope no one will answer like a fishwife.
What has been said is true. Hands off this stranger,
he is no target, neither is any servant
here in the hall of King Odysseus.
Let me say a word, though, to Telémakhos
and to his mother, if it please them both:
as long as hope remained in you to see   340
Odysseus, that great gifted man, again,
you could not be reproached for obstinacy,
tying the suitors down here; better so,
if still your father fared the great sea homeward.
How plain it is, though, now, he'll come no more!
Go sit then by your mother, reason with her,
tell her to take the best man, highest bidder,
and you can have and hold your patrimony,
feed on it, drink it all, while she
adorns another's house."

                                 Keeping his head,   350

Telémakhos replied:

                              "By Zeus Almighty,
Ageláos, and by my father's sufferings,
far from Ithaka, whether he's dead or lost,
I make no impediment to Mother's marriage.
'Take whom you wish,' I say, 'I'll add my dowry.'
But can I pack her off against her will
from her own home? Heaven forbid!"

                                    At this,

Pallas Athena touched off in the suitors
a fit of laughter, uncontrollable.[8]
She drove them into nightmare, till they wheezed   360

---

[8] The laughter is a sign that the suitors are out of their right minds.

and neighed as though with jaws no longer theirs,
while blood defiled their meat,[9] and blurring tears
flooded their eyes, heart-sore with woe to come.
Then said the visionary, Theoklýmenos:

"O lost sad men, what terror is this you suffer?
Night shrouds you to the knees, your heads, your faces;
dry retch of death runs round like fire in sticks;
your cheeks are streaming; these fair walls and pedestals
are dripping crimson blood. And thick with shades
is the entry way, the courtyard thick with shades   370
passing athirst toward Érebos, into the dark,
the sun is quenched in heaven, foul mist hems us in . . . ."

The young men greeted this with shouts of laughter,
and Eurýmakhos, the son of Pólybos, crowed:

"The mind of our new guest has gone astray.
Hustle him out of doors, lads, into the sunlight;
he finds it dark as night inside!"

The man of vision looked at him and said:

"When I need help, I'll ask for it, Eurýmakhos.
I have my eyes and ears, a pair of legs,   380
and a straight mind, still with me. These will do
to take me out. Damnation and black night
I see arriving for yourselves: no shelter,
no defence for any in this crowd—
fools and vipers in the king's own hall."

With this he left that handsome room and went
home to Peiraios, who received him kindly.
The suitors made wide eyes at one another
and set to work provoking Telémakhos
with jokes about his friends. One said, for instance: 390

"Telémakhos, no man is a luckier host
when it comes to what the cat dragged in. What burning
eyes your beggar had for bread and wine!
But not for labor, not for a single heave—
he'd be a deadweight on a field. Then comes
this other, with his mumbo-jumbo. Boy,
for your own good, I tell you, toss them both
into a slave ship for the Sikels.[10] That would pay you."

Telémakhos ignored the suitors' talk.
He kept his eyes in silence on his father,   400
awaiting the first blow. Meanwhile

[9] That is, in the eyes of Odysseus, Telémakhos, and Theoklýmenos.   [10] Sicilians.

the daughter of Ikários, Penélopê,
had placed her chair to look across and down
on father and son at bay; she heard the crowd,
and how they laughed as they resumed their dinner,
a fragrant feast, for many beasts were slain—
but as for supper, men supped never colder
than these, on what the goddess and the warrior
were even then preparing for the suitors,
whose treachery had filled that house with pain.   410

BOOK TWENTY-ONE: THE TEST OF THE BOW

Upon Penélopê, most worn in love and thought,
Athena cast a glance like a grey sea
lifting her. Now to bring the tough bow out and bring
the iron blades. Now try those dogs at archery
to usher bloody slaughter in.

                         So moving stairward
the queen took up a fine doorhook of bronze,
ivory-hafted, smooth in her clenched hand,
and led her maids down to a distant room,
a storeroom where the master's treasure lay:
bronze, bar gold, black iron forged and wrought.   10
In this place hung the double-torsion bow
and arrows in a quiver, a great sheaf—
quills of groaning.

                     In the old time in Lakedaimon[1]
her lord had got these arms from Íphitos,
Eurýtos'[2] son. The two met in Messenia[3]
at Ortílokhos' table, on the day
Odysseus claimed a debt owed by that realm—
sheep stolen by Messenians out of Ithaka
in their long ships, three hundred head, and herdsmen.
Seniors of Ithaka and his father sent him   20
on that far embassy when he was young.
But Íphitos had come there tracking strays,
twelve shy mares, with mule colts yet unweaned.
And a fatal chase they led him over prairies
into the hands of Heraklês. That massive
son of toil and mortal son of Zeus
murdered his guest at wine[4] in his own house—
inhuman, shameless in the sight of heaven—

[1] The region of Sparta, in southern Greece.   [2] A famous archer.
[3] A region down the coast from Ithaka, in southwestern Greece.
[4] Íphitos' pursuit of his lost mares brought him to Tiryns, the city of the great hero-adventurer Heraklês, who, according to certain versions of the story, had something to do with the mares' disappearance. By some accounts, Heraklês killed Íphitos by throwing him down from the city walls.

to keep the mares and colts in his own grange.
Now Íphitos, when he knew Odysseus, gave him   30
the master bowman's arm; for old Eurýtos
had left it on his deathbed to his son.
In fellowship Odysseus gave a lance
and a sharp sword. But Heraklês killed Íphitos
before one friend could play host to the other.
And Lord Odysseus would not take the bow
in the black ships to the great war at Troy.
As a keepsake he put it by:
it served him well at home in Ithaka.

Now the queen reached the storeroom door and halted.   40
Here was an oaken sill, cut long ago
and sanded clean and bedded true. Foursquare
the doorjambs and the shining doors were set
by the careful builder. Penélopê untied the strap
around the curving handle, pushed her hook
into the slit, aimed at the bolts inside
and shot them back. Then came a rasping sound
as those bright doors the key had sprung gave way—
a bellow like a bull's vaunt in a meadow—
followed by her light footfall entering   50
over the plank floor. Herb-scented robes
lay there in chests, but the lady's milkwhite arms
went up to lift the bow down from a peg
in its own polished bowcase.

                                        Now Penélopê
sank down, holding the weapon on her knees,
and drew her husband's great bow out, and sobbed
and bit her lip and let the salt tears flow.
Then back she went to face the crowded hall
tremendous bow in hand, and on her shoulder hung
the quiver spiked with coughing death. Behind her   60
maids bore a basket full of axeheads, bronze
and iron implements for the master's game.
Thus in her beauty she approached the suitors,
and near a pillar of the solid roof
she paused, her shining veil across her cheeks,
her maids on either hand and still,
then spoke to the banqueters:

                                        "My lords, hear me:
suitors indeed, you commandeered this house
to feast and drink in, day and night, my husband
being long gone, long out of mind. You found   70
no justification for yourselves—none
except your lust to marry me. Stand up, then:
we now declare a contest for that prize.
Here is my lord Odysseus' hunting bow.
Bend and string it if you can. Who sends an arrow

through iron axe-helve sockets,[5] twelve in line?
I join my life with his, and leave this place, my home,
my rich and beautiful bridal house, forever
to be remembered, though I dream it only."

Then to Eumaios:

                              "Carry the bow forward.   80

Carry the blades."

                    Tears came to the swineherd's eyes
as he reached out for the big bow. He laid it
down at the suitors' feet. Across the room
the cowherd sobbed, knowing the master's weapon.
Antínoös growled, with a glance at both:

                                        "Clods.

They go to pieces over nothing.

                              You two, there,

why are you sniveling? To upset the woman
even more? Has she not pain enough
over her lost husband? *Sit down.*
Get on with dinner quietly, or cry about it   90
outside, if you must. Leave us the bow.
A clean-cut game, it looks to me.
Nobody bends that bowstave easily
in this company. Is there a man here
made like Odysseus? I remember him
from childhood: I can see him even now."

That was the way he played it, hoping inwardly
to span the great horn bow with corded gut
and drill the iron with his shot—he, Antínoös,
destined to be the first of all to savor   100
blood from a biting arrow at his throat,
a shaft drawn by the fingers of Odysseus
whom he had mocked and plundered, leading on
the rest, his boon companions. Now they heard
a gay snort of laughter from Telémakhos,
who said then brilliantly:

                              "A queer thing, that!

Has Zeus almighty made me a half-wit?
For all her spirit, Mother has given in,
promised to go off with someone—and
is that amusing? What am I cackling for?   110
Step up, my lords, contend now for your prize.
There is no woman like her in Akhaia,

---

[5] The details of the feat to be performed have been much discussed and are not entirely
clear; in any case, the archer had to send an arrow through twelve openings—notches, holes,
or other apertures—in the handles or blades of the axes.

not in old Argos, Pylos, or Mykênê,
neither in Ithaka nor on the mainland,
and you all know it without praise of mine.
Come on, no hanging back, no more delay
in getting the bow bent. Who's the winner?
I myself should like to try that bow.
Suppose I bend it and bring off the shot,
my heart will be less heavy, seeing the queen my mother   120
go for the last time from this house and hall,
if I who stay can do my father's feat."

He moved out quickly, dropping his crimson cloak,
and lifted sword and sword belt from his shoulders.
His preparation was to dig a trench,
heaping the earth in a long ridge beside it
to hold the blades half-bedded. A taut cord
aligned the socket rings. And no one there
but looked on wondering at his workmanship,
for the boy had never seen it done.

                               He took his stand then   130
on the broad door sill to attempt the bow.
Three times he put his back into it and sprang it,
three times he had to slack off. Still he meant
to string that bow and pull for the needle shot.
A fourth try, and he had it all but strung—
when a stiffening in Odysseus made him check.
Abruptly then he stopped and turned and said:

"Blast and damn it, must I be a milksop
all my life? Half-grown, all thumbs,
no strength or knack at arms, to defend myself   140
if someone picks a fight with me.

                                         Take over,

O my elders and betters, try the bow,
run off the contest."

                                  And he stood the weapon
upright against the massy-timbered door
with one arrow across the horn aslant,
then went back to his chair. Antínoös
gave the word:

                              "Now one man at a time
rise and go forward. Round the room in order;
left to right from where they dip the wine."

As this seemed fair enough, up stood Leódês   150
the son of Oinops. This man used to find
vision for them in the smoke of sacrifice.
He kept his chair well back, retired by the winebowl,
for he alone could not abide their manners

but sat in shame for all the rest. Now it was he
who had first to confront the bow,
standing up on the broad door sill. He failed.
The bow unbending made his thin hands yield,
no muscle in them. He gave up and said:

"Friends, I cannot. Let the next man handle it.   160
Here is a bow to break the heart and spirit
of many strong men. Aye. And death is less
bitter than to live on and never have
the beauty that we came here laying siege to
so many days. Resolute, are you still,
to win Odysseus' lady Penélopê?
Pit yourselves against the bow, and look
among Akhaians for another's daughter.
Gifts will be enough to court and take her.
Let the best offer win."

                              With this Leódês   170
thrust the bow away from him, and left it
upright against the massy-timbered door,
with one arrow aslant across the horn.
As he went down to his chair he heard Antínoös'
voice rising:

                          "What is that you say?
It makes me burn. You cannot string the weapon,
so 'Here is a bow to break the heart and spirit
of many strong men.' Crushing thought!
You were not born—you never had it in you—
to pull that bow or let an arrow fly.   180
But here are men who can and will."

He called out to the goatherd, Melánthios:

"Kindle a fire there, be quick about it,
draw up a big bench with a sheepskin on it,
and bring a cake of lard out of the stores.
Contenders from now on will heat and grease the bow.
We'll try it limber, and bring off the shot."

Melánthios darted out to light a blaze,
drew up a bench, threw a big sheepskin over it,
and brought a cake of lard. So one by one   190
the young men warmed and greased the bow for bending,
but not a man could string it. They were whipped.
Antínoös held off; so did Eurýmakhos,
suitors in chief, by far the ablest there.

Two men had meanwhile left the hall:
swineherd and cowherd, in companionship,

one downcast as the other. But Odysseus
followed them outdoors, outside the court,
and coming up said gently:

                                                 "You, herdsman
and you, too, swineherd, I could say a thing to you,   200
or should I keep it dark?

                                       No, no; speak,

my heart tells me. Would you be men enough
to stand by Odysseus if he came back?
Suppose he dropped out of a clear sky, as I did?
Suppose some god should bring him?
Would you bear arms for him, or for the suitors?"

The cowherd said:

                                       "Ah, let the master come!
Father Zeus, grant our old wish! Some courier
guide him back! Then judge what stuff is in me
and how I manage arms!"

                                       Likewise Eumaios   210

fell to praying all heaven for his return,
so that Odysseus, sure at least of these,
told them:

                                       "I am at home, for I am he.
I bore adversities, but in the twentieth year
I am ashore in my own land. I find
the two of you, alone among my people,
longed for my coming. Prayers I never heard
except your own that I might come again.
So now what is in store for you I'll tell you:
If Zeus brings down the suitors by my hand   220
I promise marriages to both, and cattle,
and houses built near mine. And you shall be
brothers-in-arms of my Telémakhos.
Here, let me show you something else, a sign
that I am he, that you can trust me, look:
this old scar from the tusk wound that I got
boar hunting on Parnassos—
Autólykos' sons and I."

                                       Shifting his rags
he bared the long gash. Both men looked, and knew,
and threw their arms around the old soldier, weeping,   230
kissing his head and shoulders. He as well
took each man's head and hands to kiss, then said—
to cut it short, else they might weep till dark—

"Break off, no more of this.
Anyone at the door could see and tell them.

Drift back in, but separately at intervals
after me.
                              Now listen to your orders:
when the time comes, those gentlemen, to a man,
will be dead against giving me bow or quiver.
Defy them. Eumaios, bring the bow   240
and put it in my hands there at the door.
Tell the women to lock their own door tight.
Tell them if someone hears the shock of arms
or groans of men, in hall or court, not one
must show her face, but keep still at her weaving.
Philoítios, run to the outer gate and lock it.
Throw the cross bar and lash it."

                                        He turned back
into the courtyard and the beautiful house
and took the stool he had before. They followed
one by one, the two hands loyal to him.   250

Eurýmakhos had now picked up the bow.
He turned it round, and turned it round
before the licking flame to warm it up,
but could not, even so, put stress upon it
to jam the loop over the tip
                              though his heart groaned to bursting.
Then he said grimly:

                                        "Curse this day.

What gloom I feel, not for myself alone,
and not only because we lose that bride.
Women are not lacking in Akhaia,
in other towns, or on Ithaka. No, the worst   260
is humiliation—to be shown up for children
measured against Odysseus—we who cannot
even hitch the string over his bow.
What shame to be repeated of us, after us!"

Antínoös said:

                                        "Come to yourself. You know
that is not the way this business ends.
Today the islanders held holiday, a holy day,[6]
no day to sweat over a bowstring.
                              Keep your head.

Postpone the bow. I say we leave the axes
planted where they are. No one will take them.   270
No one comes to Odysseus' hall tonight.
Break out good wine and brim our cups again,

---

[6] With ironic appropriateness, a feast day of Apollo, god of archery. Antínoös makes this
an excuse for putting off the present challenge.

we'll keep the crooked bow safe overnight,
order the fattest goats Melánthios has
brought down tomorrow noon, and offer thighbones burning
to Apollo, god of archers,
while we try out the bow and make the shot."

As this appealed to everyone, heralds came
pouring fresh water for their hands, and boys
filled up the winebowls. Joints of meat went round,   280
fresh cuts for all, while each man made his offering,
tilting the red wine to the gods, and drank his fill.
Then spoke Odysseus, all craft and gall:

"My lords, contenders for the queen, permit me:
a passion in me moves me to speak out.
I put it to Eurýmakhos above all
and to that brilliant prince, Antínoös. Just now
how wise his counsel was, to leave the trial
and turn your thoughts to the immortal gods! Apollo
will give power tomorrow to whom he wills.   290
But let me try my hand at the smooth bow!
Let me test my fingers and my pull
to see if any of the oldtime kick is there,
or if thin fare and roving took it out of me."

Now irritation beyond reason swept them all,
since they were nagged by fear that he could string it.
Antínoös answered, coldly and at length:

"You bleary vagabond, no rag of sense is left you.
Are you not coddled here enough, at table
taking meat with gentlemen, your betters,   300
denied nothing, and listening to our talk?
When have we let a tramp hear all our talk?
The sweet goad of wine has made you rave!
Here is the evil wine can do
to those who swig it down. Even the centaur
Eurýtion,[7] in Peiríthoös' hall
among the Lapíthai, came to a bloody end
because of wine; wine ruined him: it crazed him,
drove him wild for rape in that great house.
The princes cornered him in fury, leaping on him   310
to drag him out and crop his ears and nose.
Drink had destroyed his mind, and so he ended
in that mutilation—fool that he was.

---

[7]The centaurs were an uncivilized tribe (often represented in myth as having horses'
trunks and legs and human torsos and heads), inhabitants of Thessaly, in northeastern
Greece. They were invited to the wedding of Peiríthoös, king of the Lapíthai, a neighboring
people, and at the wedding tried to carry off the bride; the present version tells the story in the
singular, of Eurýtion. In the ensuing battle the centaurs were defeated.

Centaurs and men made war for this,
but the drunkard first brought hurt upon himself.

The tale applies to you: I promise you
great trouble if you touch that bow. You'll come by
no indulgence in our house; kicked down
into a ship's bilge, out to sea you go,
and nothing saves you. Drink, but hold your tongue.   320
Make no contention here with younger men."

At this the watchful queen Penélopê
interposed:

                                        "Antínoös, discourtesy
to a guest of Telémakhos—whatever guest—
that is not handsome. What are you afraid of?
Suppose this exile put his back into it
and drew the great bow of Odysseus—
could he then take me home to be his bride?
You know he does not imagine that! No one
need let that prospect weigh upon his dinner!   330
How very, very improbable it seems."

It was Eurýmakhos who answered her:

"Penélopê, O daughter of Ikários,
most subtle queen, we are not given to fantasy.
No, but our ears burn at what men might say
and women, too. We hear some jackal whispering:
'How far inferior to the great husband
her suitors are! Can't even budge his bow!
Think of it; and a beggar, out of nowhere,
strung it quick and made the needle shot!'   340
That kind of disrepute we would not care for."

Penélopê replied, steadfast and wary:

"Eurýmakhos, you have no good repute
in this realm, nor the faintest hope of it—
men who abused a prince's house for years,
consumed his wine and cattle. Shame enough.
Why hang your heads over a trifle now?
The stranger is a big man, well-compacted,
and claims to be of noble blood.
Ai!   350
Give him the bow, and let us have it out!
What I can promise him I will:
if by the kindness of Apollo he prevails
he shall be clothed well and equipped.
A fine shirt and a cloak I promise him;
a lance for keeping dogs at bay, or men;

a broadsword; sandals to protect his feet;
escort, and freedom to go where he will."

Telémakhos now faced her and said sharply:

"Mother, as to the bow and who may handle it   360
or not handle it, no man here
has more authority than I do—not one lord
of our own stony Ithaka nor the islands lying
east toward Elis: no one stops me if I choose
to give these weapons outright to my guest.
Return to your own hall. Tend your spindle.
Tend your loom. Direct your maids at work.
This question of the bow will be for men to settle,
most of all for me. I am master here."

She gazed in wonder, turned, and so withdrew,   370
her son's clearheaded bravery in her heart.
But when she had mounted to her rooms again
with all her women, then she fell to weeping
for Odysseus, her husband. Grey-eyed Athena
presently cast a sweet sleep on her eyes.

The swineherd had the horned bow in his hands
moving toward Odysseus, when the crowd
in the banquet hall broke into an ugly din,
shouts rising from the flushed young men:

                                          "Ho! Where
do you think you are taking that, you smutty slave?"   380

"What is this dithering?"

                              "We'll toss you back alone
among the pigs, for your own dogs to eat,
if bright Apollo nods and the gods are kind!"

He faltered, all at once put down the bow, and stood
in panic, buffeted by waves of cries,
hearing Telémakhos from another quarter
shout:

"Go on, take him the bow!

                              Do you obey this pack?
You will be stoned back to your hills! Young as I am
my power is over you! I wish to God   390
I had as much the upper hand of these!
There would be suitors pitched like dead rats
through our gate, for the evil plotted here!"

Telémakhos' frenzy struck someone as funny,
and soon the whole room roared with laughter at him,

so that all tension passed. Eumaios picked up
bow and quiver, making for the door,
and there he placed them in Odysseus' hands.
Calling Eurýkleia to his side he said:

"Telémakhos

trusts you to take care of the women's doorway.   400
Lock it tight. If anyone inside
should hear the shock of arms or groans of men
in hall or court, not one must show her face,
but go on with her weaving."

The old woman

nodded and kept still. She disappeared
into the women's hall, bolting the door behind her.
Philoítios left the house now at one bound,
catlike, running to bolt the courtyard gate.
A coil of deck-rope of papyrus fiber
lay in the gateway; this he used for lashing,   410
and ran back to the same stool as before,
fastening his eyes upon Odysseus.

And Odysseus took his time,

turning the bow, tapping it, every inch,
for borings that termites might have made
while the master of the weapon was abroad.
The suitors were now watching him, and some
jested among themselves:

"A bow lover!"

"Dealer in old bows!"

"Maybe he has one like it

at home!"

"Or has an itch to make one for himself."

"See how he handles it, the sly old buzzard!"   420

And one disdainful suitor added this:

"May his fortune grow an inch for every inch he bends it!"

But the man skilled in all ways of contending,
satisfied by the great bow's look and heft,
like a musician, like a harper, when
with quiet hand upon his instrument
he draws between his thumb and forefinger
a sweet new string upon a peg: so effortlessly
Odysseus in one motion strung the bow.
Then slid his right hand down the cord and plucked it,   430
so the taut gut vibrating hummed and sang
a swallow's note.

       In the hushed hall it smote the suitors
and all their faces changed. Then Zeus thundered
overhead, one loud crack for a sign.
And Odysseus laughed within him that the son
of crooked-minded Kronos had flung that omen down.
He picked one ready arrow from his table
where it lay bare: the rest were waiting still
in the quiver for the young men's turn to come.
He nocked it, let it rest across the handgrip,   440
and drew the string and grooved butt of the arrow,
aiming from where he sat upon the stool.

                        Now flashed

arrow from twanging bow clean as a whistle
through every socket ring, and grazed not one,
to thud with heavy brazen head beyond.

                      Then quietly

Odysseus said:

                "Telémakhos, the stranger
you welcomed in your hall has not disgraced you.
I did not miss, neither did I take all day
stringing the bow. My hand and eye are sound,
not so contemptible as the young men say.   450
The hour has come to cook their lordships' mutton—
supper by daylight. Other amusements later,
with song and harping that adorn a feast."

He dropped his eyes and nodded, and the prince
Telémakhos, true son of King Odysseus,
belted his sword on, clapped hand to his spear,
and with a clink and glitter of keen bronze
stood by his chair, in the forefront near his father.

BOOK TWENTY-TWO: DEATH IN THE GREAT HALL

Now shrugging off his rags the wiliest fighter of the islands
leapt and stood on the broad door sill, his own bow in his hand.
He poured out at his feet a rain of arrows from the quiver
and spoke to the crowd:

            "So much for that. Your clean-cut game is over.
Now watch me hit a target that no man has hit before,
if I can make this shot. Help me, Apollo."

He drew to his fist the cruel head of an arrow for Antínoös
just as the young man leaned to lift his beautiful drinking cup,
embossed, two-handled, golden: the cup was in his fingers:
the wine was even at his lips: and did he dream of death?   10
How could he? In that revelry amid his throng of friends

who would imagine a single foe—though a strong foe indeed—
could dare to bring death's pain on him and darkness on his eyes?
Odysseus' arrow hit him under the chin
and punched up to the feathers through his throat.

Backward and down he went, letting the winecup fall
from his shocked hand. Like pipes his nostrils jetted
crimson runnels, a river of mortal red,
and one last kick upset his table
knocking the bread and meat to soak in dusty blood.   20
Now as they craned to see their champion where he lay
the suitors jostled in uproar down the hall,
everyone on his feet. Wildly they turned and scanned
the walls in the long room for arms; but not a shield,
not a good ashen spear was there for a man to take and throw.
All they could do was yell in outrage at Odysseus:

"Foul! to shoot at a man! That was your last shot!"

"Your own throat will be slit for this!"

                          "Our finest lad is down!
You killed the best on Ithaka."

                    "Buzzards will tear your eyes out!"

For they imagined as they wished—that it was a wild shot,   30
an unintended killing—fools, not to comprehend
they were already in the grip of death.
But glaring under his brows Odysseus answered:

"You yellow dogs, you thought I'd never make it
home from the land of Troy. You took my house to plunder,
twisted my maids to serve your beds. You dared
bid for my wife while I was still alive.
Contempt was all you had for the gods who rule wide heaven,
contempt for what men say of you hereafter.
Your last hour has come. You die in blood."   40

As they all took this in, sickly green fear
pulled at their entrails, and their eyes flickered
looking for some hatch or hideaway from death.
Eurýmakhos alone could speak. He said:

"If you are Odysseus of Ithaka come back,
all that you say these men have done is true.
Rash actions, many here, more in the countryside.
But here he lies, the man who caused them all.
Antínoös was the ringleader, he whipped us on
to do these things. He cared less for a marriage   50
than for the power Kroníon has denied him
as king of Ithaka. For that
he tried to trap your son and would have killed him.

He is dead now and has his portion. Spare
your own people. As for ourselves, we'll make
restitution of wine and meat consumed,
and add, each one, a tithe of twenty oxen
with gifts of bronze and gold to warm your heart.
Meanwhile we cannot blame you for your anger."

Odysseus glowered under his black brows   60
and said:

                              "Not for the whole treasure of your fathers,
all you enjoy, lands, flocks, or any gold
put up by others, would I hold my hand.
There will be killing till the score is paid.
You forced yourselves upon this house. Fight your way out,
or run for it, if you think you'll escape death.
I doubt one man of you skins by."

They felt their knees fail, and their hearts—but heard
Eurýmakhos for the last time rallying them.

"Friends," he said, "the man is implacable.   70
Now that he's got his hands on bow and quiver
he'll shoot from the big door stone there
until he kills us to the last man.

                              Fight, I say,
let's remember the joy of it. Swords out!
Hold up your tables to deflect his arrows.
After me, everyone: rush him where he stands.
If we can budge him from the door, if we can pass
into the town, we'll call out men to chase him.
This fellow with his bow will shoot no more."

He drew his own sword as he spoke, a broadsword of fine bronze,   80
honed like a razor on either edge. Then crying hoarse and loud
he hurled himself at Odysseus. But the kingly man let fly
an arrow at that instant, and the quivering feathered butt
sprang to the nipple of his breast as the barb stuck in his liver.
The bright broadsword clanged down. He lurched and fell aside,
pitching across his table. His cup, his bread and meat,
were spilt and scattered far and wide, and his head slammed on the
        ground.
Revulsion, anguish in his heart, with both feet kicking out,
he downed his chair, while the shrouding wave of mist closed on his
        eyes.

Amphínomos now came running at Odysseus,   90
broadsword naked in his hand. He thought to make
the great soldier give way at the door.
But with a spear throw from behind Telémakhos hit him

between the shoulders, and the lancehead drove
clear through his chest. He left his feet and fell
forward, thudding, forehead against the ground.
Telémakhos swerved around him, leaving the long dark spear
planted in Amphínomos. If he paused to yank it out
someone might jump him from behind or cut him down with a sword
at the moment he bent over. So he ran—ran from the tables   100
to his father's side and halted, panting, saying:

"Father let me bring you a shield and spear,
a pair of spears, a helmet.
I can arm on the run myself; I'll give
outfits to Eumaios and this cowherd.
Better to have equipment."

                                          Said Odysseus:

"Run then, while I hold them off with arrows
as long as the arrows last. When all are gone
if I'm alone they can dislodge me."

                                                Quick
upon his father's word Telémakhos   110
ran to the room where spears and armor lay.
He caught up four light shields, four pairs of spears,
four helms of war high-plumed with flowing manes,
and ran back, loaded down, to his father's side.
He was the first to pull a helmet on
and slide his bare arm in a buckler strap.
The servants armed themselves, and all three took their stand
beside the master of battle.

                                    While he had arrows
he aimed and shot, and every shot brought down
one of his huddling enemies.   120
But when all barbs had flown from the bowman's fist,
he leaned his bow in the bright entry way
beside the door, and armed: a four-ply shield
hard on his shoulder, and a crested helm,
horsetailed, nodding stormy upon his head,
then took his tough and bronze-shod spears.

                                    The suitors
who held their feet, no longer under bowshot,
could see a window high in a recess of the wall,
a vent, lighting the passage to the storeroom.
This passage had one entry, with a door,   130
at the edge of the great hall's threshold, just outside.[1]

---

[1] The window in the *mégaron,* or great hall, connects with an external corridor that runs to
the rear of the house, past the women's chambers, to the storeroom; the only exit from the
corridor to the outdoor courtyard is close to where Odysseus and his three allies have posted
themselves. It is therefore, as Mélanthios soon points out, not a safe escape route.

Odysseus told the swineherd to stand over
and guard this door and passage. As he did so,
a suitor named Ageláos asked the others:

"Who will get a leg up on that window
and run to alarm the town? One sharp attack
and this fellow will never shoot again."

His answer
came from the goatherd, Melánthios:

"No chance, my lord.
The exit into the courtyard is too near them,
too narrow. One good man could hold that portal   140
against a crowd. No: let me scale the wall
and bring you arms out of the storage chamber.
Odysseus and his son put them indoors,
I'm sure of it; not outside."

The goatish goatherd
clambered up the wall, toes in the chinks,
and slipped through to the storeroom. Twelve light shields,
twelve spears he took, and twelve thick-crested helms,
and handed all down quickly to the suitors.
Odysseus, when he saw his adversaries
girded and capped and long spears in their hands   150
shaken at him, felt his knees go slack,
his heart sink, for the fight was turning grim.
He spoke rapidly to his son:

"Telémakhos, one of the serving women
is tipping the scales against us in this fight,
or maybe Melánthios."

But sharp and clear
Telémakhos said:

"It is my own fault, Father,
mine alone. The storeroom door—I left it
wide open. They were more alert than I.
Eumaios, go and lock that door,   160
and bring back word if a woman is doing this
or Melánthios, Dólios' son. More likely he."

Even as they conferred, Melánthios
entered the storeroom for a second load,
and the swineherd at the passage entry saw him.
He cried out to his lord:

"Son of Laërtês,
Odysseus, master mariner and soldier,
there he goes, the monkey, as we thought,

there he goes into the storeroom.

Let me hear your will:
put a spear through him—I hope I am the stronger—   170
or drag him here to pay for his foul tricks
against your house?"

Odysseus said:

"Telémakhos and I
will keep these gentlemen in hall, for all their urge to leave.
You two go throw him into the storeroom, wrench his arms
and legs behind him, lash his hands and feet
to a plank, and hoist him up to the roof beams.
Let him live on there suffering at his leisure."

The two men heard him with appreciation
and ducked into the passage. Melánthios,
rummaging in the chamber, could not hear them   180
as they came up; nor could he see them freeze
like posts on either side the door.
He turned back with a handsome crested helmet
in one hand, in the other an old shield
coated with dust—a shield Laërtês bore
soldiering in his youth. It had lain there for years,
and the seams on strap and grip had rotted away.
As Melánthios came out the two men sprang,
jerked him backward by the hair, and threw him.
Hands and feet they tied with a cutting cord   190
behind him, so his bones ground in their sockets,
just as Laërtês' royal son commanded.
Then with a whip of rope they hoisted him
in agony up a pillar to the beams,
and—O my swineherd—you were the one to say:

"Watch through the night up there, Melánthios.
An airy bed is what you need.
You'll be awake to see the primrose Dawn
when she goes glowing from the streams of Ocean
to mount her golden throne.

No oversleeping   200
the hour for driving goats to feed the suitors."

They stooped for helm and shield and left him there
contorted, in his brutal sling,
and shut the doors, and went to join Odysseus,
whose mind moved through the combat now to come.
Breathing deep, and snorting hard, they stood
four at the entry, facing two score men.
But now into the gracious doorway stepped
Zeus's daughter Athena. She wore the guise of Mentor,
and Odysseus appealed to her in joy: 210

"O Mentor, join me in this fight! Remember
how all my life I've been devoted to you,
friend of my youth!"

                    For he guessed it was Athena,
Hope of Soldiers. Cries came from the suitors,
and Ageláos, Damástor's son, called out:

"Mentor, don't let Odysseus lead you astray
to fight against us on his side.
Think twice: we are resolved—and we will do it—
after we kill them, father and son,
you too will have your throat slit for your pains   220
if you make trouble for us here. It means your life.
Your life—and cutting throats will not be all.
Whatever wealth you have, at home, or elsewhere,
we'll mingle with Odysseus' wealth. Your sons
will be turned out, your wife and daughters
banished from the town of Ithaka."

Athena's anger grew like a storm wind as he spoke
until she flashed out at Odysseus:

                    "Ah, what a falling off!
Where is your valor, where is the iron hand
that fought at Troy for Helen, pearl of kings,   230
no respite and nine years of war? How many foes
your hand brought down in bloody play of spears?
What stratagem but yours took Priam's town?
How is it now that on your own door sill,
before the harriers[2] of your wife, you curse your luck
not to be stronger?
                  Come here, cousin, stand by me,
and you'll see action! In the enemies' teeth
learn how Mentor, son of Álkimos,
repays fair dealing!"

                    For all her fighting words
she gave no overpowering aid—not yet;   240
father and son must prove their mettle still.
Into the smoky air under the roof
the goddess merely darted to perch on a blackened beam—
no figure to be seen now but a swallow.

Command of the suitors had fallen to Ageláos.
With him were Eurýnomos, Amphímedon,
Demoptólemos, Peisándros, Pólybos,
the best of the lot who stood to fight for their lives

---

[2] Predatory dogs or hawks.

after the streaking arrows downed the rest.
Ageláos rallied them with his plan of battle: 250

"Friends, our killer has come to the end of his rope,
and much good Mentor did him, that blowhard, dropping in.
Look, only four are left to fight, in the light there at the door.
No scattering of shots, men, no throwing away good spears;
we six will aim a volley at Odysseus alone,
and may Zeus grant us the glory of a hit.
If he goes down, the others are no problem."

At his command, then, "Ho!" they all let fly
as one man. But Athena spoiled their shots.
One hit the doorpost of the hall, another   260
stuck in the door's thick timbering, still others
rang on the stone wall, shivering hafts[3] of ash.
Seeing his men unscathed, royal Odysseus
gave the word for action.

                                                    "Now I say, friends,
the time is overdue to let them have it.
Battlespoil they want from our dead bodies
to add to all they plundered here before."

Taking aim over the steadied lanceheads
they all let fly together. Odysseus killed
Demoptólemos; Telémakhos   270
killed Euryádês; the swineherd, Élatos;
and Peisándros went down before the cowherd.
As these lay dying, biting the central floor,
their friends gave way and broke for the inner wall.
The four attackers followed up with a rush
to take spears from the fallen men.

                                                    Re-forming,
the suitors threw again with all their strength,
but Athena turned their shots, or all but two.
One hit a doorpost in the hall, another
stuck in the door's thick timbering, still others   280
rang on the stone wall, shivering hafts of ash.
Amphímedon's point bloodied Telémakhos'
wrist, a superficial wound, and Ktésippos'
long spear passing over Eumaios' shield
grazed his shoulder, hurtled on and fell.
No matter: with Odysseus the great soldier
the wounded threw again. And Odysseus raider of cities
struck Eurýdamas down. Telémakhos
hit Amphímedon, and the swineherd's shot

[3] Shafts.

killed Pólybos. But Ktésippos, who had last evening thrown   290
a cow's hoof at Odysseus, got the cowherd's heavy cast
full in the chest—and dying heard him say:

"You arrogant joking bastard!
Clown, will you, like a fool, and parade your wit?
Leave jesting to the gods who do it better.
This will repay your cow's-foot courtesy
to a great wanderer come home."

                                                        The master
of the black herds had answered Ktésippos.
Odysseus, lunging at close quarters, put a spear
through Ageláos, Damástor's son. Telémakhos   300
hit Leókritos from behind and pierced him,
kidney to diaphragm. Speared off his feet,
he fell face downward on the ground.

At this moment that unmanning thunder cloud,
the aegis,[4] Athena's shield,
took form aloft in the great hall.

                                    And the suitors mad with fear
at her great sign stampeded like stung cattle by a river
when the dread shimmering gadfly strikes in summer,
in the flowering season, in the long-drawn days.
After them the attackers wheeled, as terrible as falcons   310
from eyries in the mountains veering over and diving down
with talons wide unsheathed on flights of birds,
who cower down the sky in chutes and bursts along the valley—
but the pouncing falcons grip their prey, no frantic wing avails,
and farmers love to watch those beakèd hunters.
So these now fell upon the suitors in that hall,
turning, turning to strike and strike again,
while torn men moaned at death, and blood ran smoking
over the whole floor.

                                          Now there was one
who turned and threw himself at Odysseus' knees—   320
Leódês, begging for his life:

                                                        "Mercy,
mercy on a suppliant, Odysseus!
Never by word or act of mine, I swear,
was any woman troubled here. I told the rest
to put an end to it. They would not listen,
would not keep their hands from brutishness,
and now they are all dying like dogs for it.
I had no part in what they did: my part
was visionary—reading the smoke of sacrifice.
Scruples go unrewarded if I die."   330

---

[4] The shield of Zeus, lent by him to Athena.

The shrewd fighter frowned over him and said:

"You were diviner to this crowd? How often
you must have prayed my sweet day of return
would never come, or not for years!—and prayed
to have my dear wife, and beget children on her.
No plea like yours could save you
from this hard bed of death. Death it shall be!"

He picked up Ageláos' broadsword
from where it lay, flung by the slain man,
and gave Leódês' neck a lopping blow   340
so that his head went down to mouth in dust.

One more who had avoided furious death
was the son of Terpis, Phêmios, the minstrel,
singer by compulsion to the suitors.
He stood now with his harp, holy and clear,
in the wall's recess, under the window, wondering
if he should flee that way to the courtyard altar,
sanctuary of Zeus, the Enclosure God.
Thighbones in hundreds had been offered there
by Laërtês and Odysseus. No, he thought;   350
the more direct way would be best—to go
humbly to his lord. But first to save
his murmuring instrument he laid it down
carefully between the winebowl and a chair,
then he betook himself to Lord Odysseus,
clung hard to his knees, and said:

                                                    "Mercy,
mercy on a suppliant, Odysseus!
My gift is song for men and for the gods undying.
My death will be remorse for you hereafter.
No one taught me: deep in my mind a god   360
shaped all the various ways of life in song.
And I am fit to make verse in your company
as in the god's. Put aside lust for blood.
Your own dear son Telémakhos can tell you,
never by my own will or for love
did I feast here or sing amid the suitors.
They were too strong, too many; they compelled me."

Telémakhos in the elation of battle
heard him. He at once called to his father:

"Wait: that one is innocent: don't hurt him.   370
And we should let our herald live—Medôn;
he cared for me from boyhood. Where is *he?*
Has he been killed already by Philoítios
or by the swineherd? Else he got an arrow
in that first gale of bowshots down the room."

Now this came to the ears of prudent Medôn
under the chair where he had gone to earth,
pulling a new-flayed bull's hide over him.
Quiet he lay while blinding death passed by.
Now heaving out from under   380
he scrambled for Telémakhos' knees and said:

"Here I am, dear prince; but rest your spear!
Tell your great father not to see in me
a suitor for the sword's edge—one of those
who laughed at you and ruined his property!"

The lord of all the tricks of war surveyed
this fugitive and smiled. He said:

"Courage: my son has dug you out and saved you.
Take it to heart, and pass the word along:
fair dealing brings more profit in the end.   390
Now leave this room. Go and sit down outdoors
where there's no carnage, in the court,
you and the poet with his many voices,
while I attend to certain chores inside."

At this the two men stirred and picked their way
to the door and out, and sat down at the altar,
looking around with wincing eyes
as though the sword's edge hovered still.
And Odysseus looked around him, narrow-eyed,
for any others who had lain hidden   400
while death's black fury passed.

                                       In blood and dust
he saw that crowd all fallen, many and many slain.

Think of a catch that fishermen haul in to a halfmoon bay
in a fine-meshed net from the white-caps of the sea:
how all are poured out on the sand, in throes for the salt sea,
twitching their cold lives away in Hêlios' fiery air:
so lay the suitors heaped on one another.

Odysseus at length said to his son:

"Go tell old Nurse I'll have a word with her.
What's to be done now weighs on my mind."   410

Telémakhos knocked at the women's door and called:

"Eurýkleia, come out here! Move, old woman.
You kept your eye on all our servant girls.
Jump, my father is here and wants to see you."

His call brought no reply, only the doors
were opened, and she came. Telémakhos

led her forward. In the shadowy hall
full of dead men she found his father
spattered and caked with blood like a mountain lion
when he has gorged upon an ox, his kill—   420
with hot blood glistening over his whole chest,
smeared on his jaws, baleful and terrifying—
even so encrimsoned was Odysseus
up to his thighs and armpits. As she gazed
from all the corpses to the bloody man
she raised her head to cry over his triumph,
but felt his grip upon her, checking her.
Said the great soldier then:

                                                    "Rejoice

inwardly. No crowing aloud, old woman.
To glory over slain men is no piety.   430
Destiny and the gods' will vanquished these,
and their own hardness. They respected no one,
good or bad, who came their way.
For this, and folly, a bad end befell them.
Your part is now to tell me of the women,
those who dishonored me, and the innocent."

His own old nurse Eurýkleia said:

                                            "I will, then.

Child, you know you'll have the truth from me.
Fifty all told they are, your female slaves,
trained by your lady and myself in service,   440
wool carding and the rest of it, and taught
to be submissive. Twelve went bad,
flouting me, flouting Penélopê, too.
Telémakhos being barely grown, his mother
would never let him rule the serving women—
but you must let me go to her lighted rooms
and tell her. Some god sent her a drift of sleep."

But in reply the great tactician said:

"Not yet. Do not awake her. Tell those women
who were the suitors' harlots to come here."   450

She went back on this mission through his hall.
Then he called Telémakhos to his side
and the two herdsmen. Sharply Odysseus said:

"These dead must be disposed of first of all.
Direct the women. Tables and chairs will be
scrubbed with sponges, rinsed and rinsed again.
When our great room is fresh and put in order,
take them outside, these women,

between the roundhouse[5] and the palisade,
and hack them with your swordblades till you cut   460
the life out of them, and every thought of sweet
Aphroditê under the rutting suitors,
when they lay down in secret."

                                                              As he spoke

here came the women in a bunch, all wailing,
soft tears on their cheeks. They fell to work
to lug the corpses out into the courtyard
under the gateway, propping one
against another as Odysseus ordered,
for he himself stood over them. In fear
these women bore the cold weight of the dead.   470
The next thing was to scrub off chairs and tables
and rinse them down. Telémakhos and the herdsman
scraped the packed earth floor with hoes, but made
the women carry out all blood and mire.
When the great room was cleaned up once again,
at swordpoint they forced them out, between
the roundhouse and the palisade, pell-mell
to huddle in that dead end without exit.
Telémakhos, who knew his mind,[6] said curtly:

"I would not give the clean death of a beast   480
to trulls[7] who made a mockery of my mother
and of me too—you sluts, who lay with suitors."

He tied one end of a hawser to a pillar
and passed the other about the roundhouse top,
taking the slack up, so that no one's toes
could touch the ground. They would be hung like doves
or larks in springès[8] triggered in a thicket,
where the birds think to rest—a cruel nesting.
So now in turn each woman thrust her head
into a noose and swung, yanked high in air,   490
to perish there most piteously.
Their feet danced for a little, but not long.

From storeroom to the court they brought Melánthios,
chopped with swords to cut his nose and ears off,
pulled off his genitals to feed the dogs
and raging hacked his hands and feet away.

---

[5] A building, with a cone-shaped roof, near the wall surrounding the courtyard; probably a place for storing implements.
[6] Telémakhos departs from Odysseus' instructions; he gives the offending women a dishonorable death by hanging rather than death by the knife or sword, as in the ritual sacrifice of an innocent animal.
[7] Harlots.
[8] Nooses, attached to tied branches, used to trap birds and other small animals.

As their own hands and feet called for a washing,
they went indoors to Odysseus again.
Their work was done. He told Eurýkleia:

           "Bring me

brimstone[9] and a brazier—medicinal   500
fumes to purify my hall. Then tell
Penélopê to come, and bring her maids.
All servants round the house must be called in."

His own old nurse Eurýkleia replied:

"Aye, surely that is well said, child. But let me
find you a good clean shirt and cloak and dress you.
You must not wrap your shoulders' breadth again
in rags in your own hall. That would be shameful."

Odysseus answered:

         "Let me have the fire.
The first thing is to purify this place."   510

With no more chat Eurýkleia obeyed
and fetched out fire and brimstone. Cleansing fumes
he sent through court and hall and storage chamber.
Then the old woman hurried off again
to the women's quarters to announce her news,
and all the servants came now, bearing torches
in twilight, crowding to embrace Odysseus,
taking his hands to kiss, his head and shoulders,
while he stood there, nodding to every one,
and overcome by longing and by tears.   520

BOOK TWENTY-THREE: THE TRUNK OF
THE OLIVE TREE

The old nurse went upstairs exulting,
with knees toiling, and patter of slapping feet,
to tell the mistress of her lord's return,
and cried out by the lady's pillow:

             "Wake,

wake up, dear child! Penélopê, come down,
see with your own eyes what all these years you longed for!
Odysseus is here! Oh, in the end, he came!
And he has killed your suitors, killed them all
who made his house a bordel[1] and ate his cattle
and raised their hands against his son!"

 [9] Sulfur.   [1] Bordello; brothel.

Penélopê said: 10

"Dear nurse . . . the gods have touched you.
They can put chaos into the clearest head
or bring a lunatic down to earth. Good sense
you always had. They've touched you. What is this
mockery you wake me up to tell me,
breaking in on my sweet spell of sleep?
I had not dozed away so tranquilly
since my lord went to war, on that ill wind
to Ilion.

                                Oh, leave me! Back down stairs!
If any other of my women came in babbling   20
things like these to startle me, I'd see her
flogged out of the house! Your old age spares you that."

Eurýkleia said:

"Would I play such a trick on you, dear child?
It is true, true, as I tell you, he has come!
That stranger they were baiting was Odysseus.
Telémakhos knew it days ago—
cool head, never to give his father away,
till he paid off those swollen dogs!"

The lady in her heart's joy now sprang up   30
with sudden dazzling tears, and hugged the old one,
crying out:

                            "But try to make it clear!
If he came home in secret, as you say,
could he engage them singlehanded? How?
They were all down there, still in the same crowd."

To this Eurýkleia said:

                                        "I did not see it,
I knew nothing; only I heard the groans
of men dying. We sat still in the inner rooms
holding our breath, and marvelling, shut in,
until Telémakhos came to the door and called me—   40
your own dear son, sent this time by his father!
So I went out, and found Odysseus
erect, with dead men littering the floor
this way and that. If you had only seen him!
It would have made your heart glow hot!—a lion
splashed with mire and blood.

                                        But now the cold
corpses are all gathered at the gate,
and he has cleansed his hall with fire and brimstone,
a great blaze. Then he sent me here to you.
Come with me: you may both embark this time   50

for happiness together, after pain,
after long years. Here is your prayer, your passion,
granted: your own lord lives, he is at home,
he found you safe, he found his son. The suitors
abused his house, but he has brought them down."

The attentive lady said:

"Do not lose yourself
in this rejoicing: wait: you know
how splendid that return would be for us,
how dear to me, dear to his son and mine;
but no, it is not possible, your notion   60
must be wrong.

Some god has killed the suitors,
a god, sick of their arrogance and brutal
malice—for they honored no one living,
good or bad, who ever came their way.
Blind young fools, they've tasted death for it.
But the true person of Odysseus?
He lost his home, he died far from Akhaia."

The old nurse sighed:

"How queer, the way you talk!
Here he is, large as life, by his own fire,
and you deny he ever will get home!   70
Child, you always were mistrustful!
But there is one sure mark that I can tell you:
that scar left by the boar's tusk long ago.
I recognized it when I bathed his feet
and would have told you, but he stopped my mouth,
forbade me, in his craftiness.

Come down,
I stake my life on it, he's here!
Let me die in agony if I lie!"

Penélopê said:

"Nurse dear, though you have your wits about you,
still it is hard not to be taken in   80
by the immortals. Let us join my son, though,
and see the dead and that strange one who killed them."

She turned then to descend the stair, her heart
in tumult. Had she better keep her distance
and question him, her husband? Should she run
up to him, take his hands, kiss him now?
Crossing the door sill she sat down at once
in firelight, against the nearest wall,
across the room from the lord Odysseus.

                                                          There   90
leaning against a pillar, sat the man
and never lifted up his eyes, but only waited
for what his wife would say when she had seen him.
And she, for a long time, sat deathly still
in wonderment—for sometimes as she gazed
she found him—yes, clearly—like her husband,
but sometimes blood and rags were all she saw.
Telémakhos' voice came to her ears:

                                              "Mother,
cruel mother, do you feel nothing,
drawing yourself apart this way from Father?
Will you not sit with him and talk and question him?   100
What other woman could remain so cold?
Who shuns her lord, and he come back to her
from wars and wandering, after twenty years?
Your heart is hard as flint and never changes!"

Penélopê answered:

                                  "I am stunned, child.
I cannot speak to him. I cannot question him.
I cannot keep my eyes upon his face.
If really he is Odysseus, truly home,
beyond all doubt we two shall know each other
better than you or anyone. There are   110
secret signs we know, we two."

                                          A smile
came now to the lips of the patient hero, Odysseus,
who turned to Telémakhos and said:

"Peace: let your mother test me at her leisure.
Before long she will see and know me best.
These tatters, dirt—all that I'm caked with now—
make her look hard at me and doubt me still.
As to this massacre, we must see the end.
Whoever kills one citizen, you know,
and has no force of armed men at his back,   120
had better take himself abroad by night
and leave his kin. Well, we cut down the flower of Ithaka,
the mainstay of the town. Consider that."

Telémakhos replied respectfully:

                                              "Dear Father,
enough that you yourself study the danger,
foresighted in combat as you are,
they say you have no rival.

                                  We three stand

ready to follow you and fight. I say
for what our strength avails, we have the courage."

And the great tactician, Odysseus, answered:

"Good.   130

Here is our best maneuver, as I see it:
bathe, you three, and put fresh clothing on,
order the women to adorn themselves,
and let our admirable harper choose a tune
for dancing, some lighthearted air, and strum it.
Anyone going by, or any neighbor,
will think it is a wedding feast he hears.
These deaths must not be cried about the town
till we can slip away to our own woods. We'll see
what weapon, then, Zeus puts into our hands."   140

They listened attentively, and did his bidding,
bathed and dressed afresh; and all the maids
adorned themselves. Then Phêmios the harper
took his polished shell and plucked the strings,
moving the company to desire
for singing, for the sway and beat of dancing,
until they made the manor hall resound
with gaiety of men and grace of women.
Anyone passing on the road would say:

"Married at last, I see—the queen so many courted.   150
Sly, cattish wife! She would not keep—not she!—
the lord's estate until he came."

So travellers'
thoughts might run—but no one guessed the truth.
Greathearted Odysseus, home at last,
was being bathed now by Eurýnomê
and rubbed with golden oil, and clothed again
in a fresh tunic and a cloak. Athena
lent him beauty, head to foot. She made him
taller, and massive, too, with crisping hair
in curls like petals of wild hyacinth   160
but all red-golden. Think of gold infused
on silver by a craftsman, whose fine art
Hephaistos taught him, or Athena: one
whose work moves to delight: just so she lavished
beauty over Odysseus' head and shoulders.
He sat then in the same chair by the pillar,
facing his silent wife, and said:

"Strange woman,
the immortals of Olympos made you hard,
harder than any. Who else in the world

would keep aloof as you do from her husband   170
if he returned to her from years of trouble,
cast on his own land in the twentieth year?

Nurse, make up a bed for me to sleep on.
Her heart is iron in her breast."

                                              Penélopê

spoke to Odysseus now. She said:

                                        "Strange man,

if man you are . . . This is no pride on my part
nor scorn for you—not even wonder, merely.
I know so well how you—how he—appeared
boarding the ship for Troy. But all the same . . .

Make up his bed for him, Eurýkleia.   180
Place it outside the bedchamber my lord
built with his own hands. Pile the big bed
with fleeces, rugs, and sheets of purest linen."

With this she tried him to the breaking point,
and he turned on her in a flash raging:

"Woman, by heaven you've stung me now!
Who dared to move my bed?
No builder had the skill for that—unless
a god came down to turn the trick. No mortal
in his best days could budge it with a crowbar.   190
There is our pact and pledge, our secret sign,
built into that bed—my handiwork
and no one else's!

                              An old trunk of olive

grew like a pillar on the building plot,
and I laid out our bedroom round that tree,
lined up the stone walls, built the walls and roof,
gave it a doorway and smooth-fitting doors.
Then I lopped off the silvery leaves and branches,
hewed and shaped that stump from the roots up
into a bedpost, drilled it, let it serve   200
as model for the rest. I planed them all,[2]
inlaid them all with silver, gold and ivory,
and stretched a bed between—a pliant web
of oxhide thongs dyed crimson.

                              There's our sign!

I know no more. Could someone else's hand
have sawn that trunk and dragged the frame away?"

---

[2] That is, planed all the bedposts, of which one was the shaped tree trunk.

Their secret! as she heard it told, her knees
grew tremulous and weak, her heart failed her.
With eyes brimming tears she ran to him,
throwing her arms around his neck, and kissed him,   210
murmuring:

                        "Do not rage at me, Odysseus!
No one ever matched your caution! Think
what difficulty the gods gave: they denied us
life together in our prime and flowering years,
kept us from crossing into age together.
Forgive me, don't be angry. I could not
welcome you with love on sight! I armed myself
long ago against the frauds of men,
impostors who might come—and all those many
whose underhanded ways bring evil on!   220
Helen of Argos, daughter of Zeus and Leda,
would she have joined the stranger,[3] lain with him,
if she had known her destiny? known the Akhaians
in arms would bring her back to her own country?
Surely a goddess moved her to adultery,
her blood unchilled by war and evil coming,
the years, the desolation; ours, too.
But here and now, what sign could be so clear
as this of our own bed?
No other man has ever laid eyes on it—   230
only my own slave, Aktoris, that my father
sent with me as a gift—she kept our door.
You make my stiff heart know that I am yours."

Now from his breast into his eyes the ache
of longing mounted, and he wept at last,
his dear wife, clear and faithful, in his arms,
longed for
                as the sunwarmed earth is longed for by a swimmer
spent in rough water where his ship went down
under Poseidon's blows, gale winds and tons of sea.
Few men can keep alive through a big surf   240
to crawl, clotted with brine, on kindly beaches
in joy, in joy, knowing the abyss behind:
and so she too rejoiced, her gaze upon her husband,
her white arms round him pressed as though forever.

The rose Dawn might have found them weeping still
had not grey-eyed Athena slowed the night
when night was most profound, and held the Dawn

---

[3] Paris, the Trojan guest of Meneláos and Helen, with whom she ran away.

under the Ocean of the East. That glossy team,
Firebright and Daybright, the Dawn's horses
that draw her heavenward for men—Athena   250
stayed their harnessing.

                                  Then said Odysseus:

"My dear, we have not won through to the end.
One trial—I do not know how long—is left for me
to see fulfilled. Teirêsias' ghost forewarned me[4]
the night I stood upon the shore of Death, asking
about my friends' homecoming and my own.
But now the hour grows late, it is bed time,
rest will be sweet for us; let us lie down."

To this Penélopê replied:

                                      "That bed,
that rest is yours whenever desire moves you,   260
now the kind powers have brought you home at last.
But as your thought has dwelt upon it, tell me:
what is the trial you face? I must know soon;
what does it matter if I learn tonight?"

The teller of many stories said:

                                  "My strange one,
must you again, and even now,
urge me to talk? Here is a plodding tale;
no charm in it, no relish in the telling.
Teirêsias told me I must take an oar
and trudge the mainland, going from town to town,   270
until I discover men who have never known
the salt blue sea, nor flavor of salt meat—
strangers to painted prows, to watercraft
and oars like wings, dipping across the water.
The moment of revelation he foretold
was this, for you may share the prophecy:
some traveller falling in with me will say:
'A winnowing fan, that on your shoulder, sir?'
There I must plant my oar,[5] on the very spot,
with burnt offerings to Poseidon of the Waters: 280
a ram, a bull, a great buck boar. Thereafter
when I come home again, I am to slay
full hekatombs to the gods who own broad heaven,
one by one.

                            Then death will drift upon me
from seaward, mild as air, mild as your hand,
in my well-tended weariness of age,

---

[4] See Book XI.
[5] The point of this gesture would be to appease the sea-god by spreading his fame even into places where the sea is unknown. This excursion does not, in fact, take place in the *Odyssey*.

contented folk around me on our island.
He said all this must come."

Penélopê said:

"If by the gods' grace age at least is kind,
we have that promise—trials will end in peace."   290

So he confided in her, and she answered.
Meanwhile Eurýnomê and the nurse together
laid soft coverlets on the master's bed,
working in haste by torchlight. Eurýkleia
retired to her quarters for the night,
and then Eurýnomê, as maid-in-waiting,
lighted her lord and lady to their chamber
with bright brands.

She vanished.

So they came

into that bed so steadfast, loved of old,
opening glad arms to one another.   300
Telémakhos by now had hushed the dancing,
hushed the women. In the darkened hall
he and the cowherd and the swineherd slept.

The royal pair mingled in love again
and afterward lay revelling in stories:
hers of the siege her beauty stood at home
from arrogant suitors, crowding on her sight,
and how they fed their courtship on his cattle,
oxen and fat sheep, and drank up rivers
of wine out of the vats.

Odysseus told   310

of what hard blows he had dealt out to others
and of what blows he had taken—all that story.
She could not close her eyes till all was told.

His raid on the Kikonês, first of all,
then how he visited the Lotos Eaters,
and what the Kyklops did, and how those shipmates,
pitilessly devoured, were avenged.
Then of his touching Aiolos's isle
and how that king refitted him for sailing
to Ithaka; all vain: gales blew him back   320
groaning over the fishcold sea. Then how
he reached the Laistrygonians' distant bay
and how they smashed his ships and his companions.
Kirkê, then: of her deceits and magic,
then of his voyage to the wide underworld
of dark, the house of Death, and questioning
Teirêsias, Theban spirit.

Dead companions,
many, he saw there, and his mother, too.
Of this he told his wife, and told how later
he heard the choir of maddening Seirênês,   330
coasted the Wandering Rocks, Kharybdis' pool
and the fiend Skylla who takes toll of men.
Then how his shipmates killed Lord Hêlios' cattle
and how Zeus thundering in towering heaven
split their fast ship with his fuming bolt,
so all hands perished.

                                        He alone survived,
cast away on Kalypso's isle, Ogýgia.
He told, then, how that nymph detained him there
in her smooth caves, craving him for her husband,
and how in her devoted lust she swore   340
he should not die nor grow old, all his days,
but he held out against her.

                                                Last of all

what sea-toil brought him to the Phaiákians;
their welcome; how they took him to their hearts
and gave him passage to his own dear island
with gifts of garments, gold and bronze . . .

                                        Remembering,

he drowsed over the story's end. Sweet sleep
relaxed his limbs and his care-burdened breast.

Other affairs were in Athena's keeping.
Waiting until Odysseus had his pleasure   350
of love and sleep, the grey-eyed one bestirred
the fresh Dawn from her bed of paling Ocean
to bring up daylight to her golden chair,
and from his fleecy bed Odysseus
arose. He said to Penélopê:

                                                "My lady,

what ordeals have we not endured! Here, waiting
you had your grief, while my return dragged out—
my hard adventures, pitting myself against
the gods' will, and Zeus, who pinned me down
far from home. But now our life resumes: 360
we've come together to our longed-for bed.
Take care of what is left me in our house;
as to the flocks that pack of wolves laid waste
they'll be replenished: scores I'll get on raids
and other scores our island friends will give me
till all the folds are full again.

                                                This day

I'm off up country to the orchards. I must see
my noble father, for he missed me sorely.
And here is my command for you—a strict one,

though you may need none, clever as you are.   370
Word will get about as the sun goes higher
of how I killed those lads. Go to your rooms
on the upper floor, and take your women. Stay there
with never a glance outside or a word to anyone."

Fitting cuirass and swordbelt to his shoulders,
he woke his herdsmen, woke Telémakhos,
ordering all in arms. They dressed quickly,
and all in war gear sallied from the gate,
led by Odysseus.

                                Now it was broad day
but these three men Athena hid in darkness,   380
going before them swiftly from the town.

BOOK TWENTY-FOUR: WARRIORS, FAREWELL

Meanwhile the suitors' ghosts were called away
by Hermês of Kyllênê,[1] bearing the golden wand
with which he charms the eyes of men or wakens
whom he wills.

                  He waved them on, all squeaking
as bats will in a cavern's underworld,
all flitting, flitting criss-cross in the dark
if one falls and the rock-hung chain is broken.
So with faint cries the shades trailed after Hermês,
pure Deliverer.

                  He led them down dank ways,
over grey Ocean tides, the Snowy Rock,   10
past shores of Dream and narrows of the sunset,
in swift flight to where the Dead inhabit
wastes of asphodel at the world's end.

Crossing the plain they met Akhilleus'[2] ghost,
Patróklos and Antílokhos, then Aîas,
noblest of Danaans after Akhilleus
in strength and beauty. Here the newly dead
drifted together, whispering. Then came
the soul of Agamémnon, son of Atreus,
in black pain forever, surrounded by men-at-arms   20
who perished with him in Aigísthos' hall.
Akhilleus greeted him:

                        "My lord Atreidês,
we held that Zeus who loves the play of lightning

---

[1] Birthplace and home of Hermês, in Arcadia.
[2] The following passage mentions several heroes of the Trojan war. Patróklos and Antílokhos were especially close friends of Akhilleus.

would give you length of glory, you were king
over so great a host of soldiery
before Troy, where we suffered, we Akhaians.
But in the morning of your life
you met that doom that no man born avoids.
It should have found you in your day of victory,
marshal of the army, in Troy country;   30
then all Akhaia would have heaped your tomb
and saved your honor for your son. Instead
piteous death awaited you at home."

And Atreus' son replied:

                                              "Fortunate hero,
son of Pêleus, godlike and glorious,
at Troy you died, across the sea from Argos,
and round you Trojan and Akhaian peers
fought for your corpse and died. A dustcloud wrought
by a whirlwind hid the greatness of you slain,
minding no more the mastery of horses.   40
All that day we might have toiled in battle
had not a storm from Zeus broken it off.
We carried you out of the field of war
down to the ships and bathed your comely body
with warm water and scented oil. We laid you
upon your long bed, and our officers
wept hot tears like rain and cropped their hair.
Then hearing of it in the sea, your mother, Thetis,[3]
came with nereids of the grey wave crying
unearthly lamentation over the water,   50
and trembling gripped the Akhaians to the bone.
They would have boarded ship that night and fled
except for one man's wisdom—venerable
Nestor, proven counselor in the past.
He stood and spoke to allay their fear: 'Hold fast,
sons of the Akhaians, lads of Argos.
His mother it must be, with nymphs her sisters,
come from the sea to mourn her son in death.'

Veteran hearts at this contained their dread
while at your side the daughters of the ancient   60
seagod wailed and wrapped ambrosial shrouding
around you.

                              Then we heard the Muses sing
a threnody[4] in nine immortal voices.

---

[3] A nereid (sea-nymph), mother of Akhilleus.
[4] Dirge; lament. The Muses are goddesses of song, literature, and the arts. Homer does not describe them elsewhere as being nine in number; this is one of several anomalies about the present scene in Hades that have caused certain commentators to reject it as unauthentic.

No Argive there but wept, such keening[5] rose
from that one Muse who led the song.

                                        Now seven

days and ten, seven nights and ten, we mourned you,
we mortal men, with nymphs who know no death,
before we gave you to the flame, slaughtering
longhorned steers and fat sheep on your pyre.

Dressed by the nereids and embalmed with honey,   70
honey and unguent in the seething blaze,
you turned to ash. And past the pyre Akhaia's
captains paraded in review, in arms,
clattering chariot teams and infantry.
Like a forest fire the flame roared on, and burned
your flesh away. Next day at dawn, Akhilleus,
we picked your pale bones from the char to keep
in wine and oil. A golden amphora[6]
your mother gave for this—Hephaistos' work,
a gift from Dionysos.[7] In that vase,   80
Akhilleus, hero, lie your pale bones mixed
with mild Patróklos' bones, who died before you,
and nearby lie the bones of Antílokhos,
the one you cared for most of all companions
after Patróklos.

                           We of the Old Army,
we who were spearmen, heaped a tomb for these
upon a foreland over Hellê's waters,[8]
to be a mark against the sky for voyagers
in this generation and those to come.
Your mother sought from the gods magnificent trophies   90
and set them down midfield for our champions. Often
at funeral games after the death of kings
when you yourself contended, you've seen athletes
cinch their belts when trophies went on view.
But these things would have made you stare—the treasures
Thetis on her silver-slippered feet
brought to your games—for the gods held you dear.
You perished, but your name will never die.
It lives to keep all men in mind of honor
forever, Akhilleus.

                       As for myself, what joy   100
is this, to have brought off the war? Foul death
Zeus held in store for me at my coming home;
Aigísthos and my vixen cut me down.''

---

[5] Loud, shrill lamenting for the dead.   [6] A type of jar.   [7] God of wine and revelry.
[8] The Hellespont; the modern Dardanelles, the strait connecting the Aegean Sea with the
Sea of Marmara; located just north of Troy.

While they conversed, the Wayfinder[9] came near,
leading the shades of suitors overthrown
by Lord Odysseus. The two souls of heroes
advanced together, scrutinizing these.
Then Agamémnon recognized Amphímedon,
son of Meláneus—friends of his on Ithaka—
and called out to him:

                                                        "Amphímedon,   110

what ruin brought you into this undergloom?
All in a body, picked men, and so young?
One could not better choose the kingdom's pride.
Were you at sea, aboard ship, and Poseidon
blew up a dire wind and foundering waves,
or cattle-raiding, were you, on the mainland,
or in a fight for some stronghold, or women,
when the foe hit you to your mortal hurt?
Tell me, answer my question. Guest and friend
I say I am of yours—or do you not remember   120
I visited your family there? I came
with Prince Meneláos, urging Odysseus
to join us in the great sea raid on Troy.
One solid month we beat our way, breasting
south sea and west, resolved to bring him round,
the wily raider of cities."

                                                 The new shade said:

"O glory of commanders, Agamémnon,
all that you bring to mind I remember well.
As for the sudden manner of our death
I'll tell you of it clearly, first to last.   130
After Odysseus had been gone for years
we were all suitors of his queen. She never
quite refused, nor went through with a marriage,
hating it, ever bent on our defeat.
Here is one of her tricks: she placed her loom,
her big loom, out for weaving in her hall,
and the fine warp of some vast fabric on it.
We were attending her, and she said to us:
'Young men, my suitors, now my lord is dead,
let me finish my weaving before I marry,   140
or else my thread will have been spun in vain.
This is a shroud I weave for Lord Laërtês
when cold Death comes to lay him on his bier.
The country wives would hold me in dishonor
if he, with all his fortune, lay unshrouded.'
We had men's hearts; she touched them; we agreed.
So every day she wove on the great loom—

   [9]Hermês.

but every night by torchlight she unwove it,
and so for three years she deceived the Akhaians.
But when the seasons brought the fourth around,   150
as long months waned, and the slow days were spent,
one of her maids, who knew the secret, told us.
We found her unraveling the splendid shroud,
and then she had to finish, willy nilly—
finish, and show the big loom woven tight
from beam to beam with cloth. She washed the shrouding
clean as sun or moonlight.

                              Then, heaven knows
from what quarter of the world, fatality
brought in Odysseus to the swineherd's wood
far up the island. There his son went too   160
when the black ship put him ashore from Pylos.
The two together planned our death-trap. Down
they came to the famous town—Telémakhos
long in advance: we had to wait for Odysseus.
The swineherd led him to the manor later
in rags like a foul beggar, old and broken,
propped on a stick. These tatters that he wore
hid him so well that none of us could know him
when he turned up, not even the older men.
We jeered at him, took potshots at him, cursed him.   170
Daylight and evening in his own great hall
he bore it, patient as a stone. That night
the mind of Zeus beyond the stormcloud stirred him
with Telémakhos at hand to shift his arms
from mégaron to storage room and lock it.
Then he assigned his wife her part: next day
she brought his bow and iron axeheads out
to make a contest. Contest there was none;
that move doomed us to slaughter. Not a man
could bend the stiff bow to his will or string it,   180
until it reached Odysseus. We shouted,
'Keep the royal bow from the beggar's hands
no matter how he begs!' Only Telémakhos
would not be denied.

                       So the great soldier
took his bow and bent it for the bowstring
effortlessly. He drilled the axeheads clean,
sprang, and decanted arrows on the door sill,
glared, and drew again. This time he killed
Antínoös.

                      There facing us he crouched
and shot his bolts of groaning at us, brought us   190
down like sheep. Then some god, his familiar,[10]
went into action with him round the hall,

---

[10] A friendly attendant spirit.

after us in a massacre. Men lay groaning,
mortally wounded, and the floor smoked with blood.

That was the way our death came, Agamémnon.
Now in Odysseus' hall untended still
our bodies lie,[11] unknown to friends or kinsmen
who should have laid us out and washed our wounds
free of the clotted blood, and mourned our passing.
So much is due the dead."

                                         But Agamémnon's   200
tall shade when he heard this cried aloud:

"O fortunate Odysseus, master mariner
and soldier, blessed son of old Laërtês!
The girl you brought home made a valiant wife!
True to her husband's honor and her own,
Penélopê, Ikários' faithful daughter!
The very gods themselves will sing her story
for men on earth—mistress of her own heart,
Penélopê!
Tyndáreus' daughter waited, too—how differently!   210
Klytaimnéstra, the adulteress,
waited to stab her lord and king. That song
will be forever hateful. A bad name
she gave to womankind, even the best."

These were the things they said to one another
under the rim of earth where Death is lord.

Leaving the town, Odysseus and his men
that morning reached Laërtês' garden lands,
long since won by his toil from wilderness—
his homestead, and the row of huts around it   220
where fieldhands rested, ate and slept. Indoors
he had an old slave woman, a Sikel,[12] keeping
house for him in his secluded age.

Odysseus here took leave of his companions.

"Go make yourselves at home inside," he said.
"Roast the best porker and prepare a meal.
I'll go to try my father. Will he know me?
Can he imagine it, after twenty years?"

He handed spear and shield to the two herdsmen,
and in they went, Telémakhos too. Alone   230
Odysseus walked the orchard rows and vines.

---

[11] It is unusual in Homer that the souls of unburied men should be admitted to Hades.
[12] Sicilian.

He found no trace of Dólios and his sons
nor the other slaves—all being gone that day
to clear a distant field, and drag the stones
for a boundary wall.

But on a well-banked plot
Odysseus found his father in solitude
spading the earth around a young fruit tree.

He wore a tunic, patched and soiled, and leggings—
oxhide patches, bound below his knees
against the brambles; gauntlets[13] on his hands   240
and on his head a goatskin cowl of sorrow.[14]
This was the figure Prince Odysseus found—
wasted by years, racked, bowed under grief.
The son paused by a tall pear tree and wept,
then inwardly debated: should he run
forward and kiss his father, and pour out
his tale of war, adventure, and return,
or should he first interrogate him, test him?
Better that way, he thought—
first draw him out with sharp words, trouble him.   250
His mind made up, he walked ahead. Laërtês
went on digging, head down, by the sapling,
stamping the spade in. At his elbow then
his son spoke out:

"Old man, the orchard keeper
you work for is no townsman. A good eye
for growing things he has; there's not a nurseling,
fig tree, vine stock, olive tree or pear tree
or garden bed uncared for on this farm.
But I might add—don't take offense—your own
appearance could be tidier. Old age   260
yes—but why the squalor, and rags to boot?
It would not be for sloth, now, that your master
leaves you in this condition; neither at all
because there's any baseness in your self.
No, by your features, by the frame you have,
a man might call you kingly,
one who should bathe warm, sup well, and rest easy
in age's privilege. But tell me:
who are your masters? whose fruit trees are these
you tend here? Tell me if it's true this island   270
is Ithaka, as that fellow I fell in with
told me on the road just now? He had
a peg loose, that one: couldn't say a word
or listen when I asked about my friend,
my Ithakan friend. I asked if he were alive

---

[13] Gloves with protective cuffs.
[14] The goatskin cap is an expression of his mourning.

or gone long since into the underworld.
I can describe him if you care to hear it:
I entertained the man in my own land
when he turned up there on a journey; never
had I a guest more welcome in my house.   280
He claimed his stock was Ithakan: Laërtês
Arkeísiadês, he said his father was.
I took him home, treated him well, grew fond of him—
though we had many guests—and gave him
gifts in keeping with his quality: seven
bars of measured gold, a silver winebowl
filigreed with flowers, twelve light cloaks,
twelve rugs, robes and tunics—not to mention
his own choice of women trained in service,
the four well-favored ones he wished to take."   290

His father's eyes had filled with tears. He said:

"You've come to that man's island, right enough,
but dangerous men and fools hold power now.
You gave your gifts in vain. If you could find him
here in Ithaka alive, he'd make
return of gifts and hospitality,
as custom is, when someone has been generous.
But tell me accurately—how many years
have now gone by since that man was your guest?
your guest, my son—if he indeed existed—   300
born to ill fortune as he was. Ah, far
from those who loved him, far from his native land,
in some sea-dingle[15] fish have picked his bones,
or else he made the vultures and wild beasts
a trove[16] ashore! His mother at his bier
never bewailed him, nor did I, his father,
nor did his admirable wife, Penélopê,
who should have closed her husband's eyes in death
and cried aloud upon him as he lay.
So much is due the dead.

                                But speak out, tell me further: 310
who are you, of what city and family?
where have you moored the ship that brought you here,
where is your admirable crew? Are you a peddler
put ashore by the foreign ship you came on?"

Again Odysseus had a fable ready.

"Yes," he said, "I can tell you all those things.
I come from Rover's Passage where my home is,

[15] Dell; valley.   [16] A valuable find.

and I'm King Allwoes' only son. My name
is Quarrelman.[17]

                          Heaven's power in the westwind
drove me this way from Sikania,[18]   320
off my course. My ship lies in a barren
cove beyond the town there. As for Odysseus,
now is the fifth year since he put to sea
and left my homeland—bound for death, you say.
Yet landbirds flying from starboard crossed his bow—
a lucky augury. So we parted joyously,
in hope of friendly days and gifts to come."

A cloud of pain had fallen on Laërtês.
Scooping up handfuls of the sunburnt dust
he sifted it over his grey head, and groaned,   330
and the groan went to the son's heart. A twinge
prickling up through his nostrils warned Odysseus
he could not watch this any longer.
He leaped and threw his arms around his father,
kissed him, and said:

                             "Oh, Father, I am he!
Twenty years gone, and here I've come again
to my own land!

                      Hold back your tears! No grieving!
I bring good news—though still we cannot rest.
I killed the suitors to the last man!
Outrage and injury have been avenged!"   340

Laërtês turned and found his voice to murmur:

"If you are Odysseus, my son, come back,
give me some proof, a sign to make me sure."

His son replied:

                          "The scar then, first of all.
Look, here the wild boar's flashing tusk
wounded me on Parnassos; do you see it?
You and my mother made me go, that time,
to visit Lord Autólykos, her father,
for gifts he promised years before on Ithaka.
Again—more proof—let's say the trees you gave me   350
on this revetted[19] plot of orchard once.
I was a small boy at your heels, wheedling
amid the young trees, while you named each one.
You gave me thirteen pear, ten apple trees,

[17] Rover's Passage, Allwoes, and Quarrelman are imaginary assumed (though appropriate) names.
[18] Sicily, perhaps.   [19] Buttressed by stones.

and forty fig trees. Fifty rows of vines
were promised too, each one to bear in turn.
Bunches of every hue would hang there ripening,
weighed down by the god of summer days."

The old man's knees failed him, his heart grew faint,
recalling all that Odysseus calmly told.   360
He clutched his son. Odysseus held him swooning
until he got his breath back and his spirit
and spoke again:

       "Zeus, Father! Gods above!—
you still hold pure Olympos, if the suitors
paid for their crimes indeed, and paid in blood!
But now the fear is in me that all Ithaka
will be upon us. They'll send messengers
to stir up every city of the islands."

Odysseus the great tactician answered:

"Courage, and leave the worrying to me.   370
We'll turn back to your homestead by the orchard.
I sent the cowherd, swineherd, and Telémakhos
ahead to make our noonday meal."

            Conversing

in this vein they went home, the two together,
into the stone farmhouse. There Telémakhos
and the two herdsmen were already carving
roast young pork, and mixing amber wine.
During these preparations the Sikel woman
bathed Laërtês and anointed him,
and dressed him in a new cloak. Then Athena,   380
standing by, filled out his limbs again,
gave girth and stature to the old field captain
fresh from the bathing place. His son looked on
in wonder at the godlike bloom upon him,
and called out happily:

          "Oh, Father,

surely one of the gods who are young forever
has made you magnificent before my eyes!"

Clearheaded Laërtês faced him, saying:

"By Father Zeus, Athena and Apollo,
I wish I could be now as once I was,   390
commander of Kephallenians,[20] when I took
the walled town, Nérikos, on the promontory!

[20] Inhabitants of the large island (modern Cephalonia) near Ithaka. Nérikos is on a nearby
island.

Would god I had been young again last night
with armor on me, standing in our hall
to fight the suitors at your side! How many
knees I could have crumpled, to your joy!"

While son and father spoke, cowherd and swineherd
attended, waiting, for the meal was ready.
Soon they were all seated, and their hands
picked up the meat and bread.

                                    But now old Dólios   400
appeared in the bright doorway with his sons,
work-stained from the field. Laërtês' housekeeper,
who reared the boys and tended Dólios
in his bent age, had gone to fetch them in.
When it came over them who the stranger was
they halted in astonishment. Odysseus
hit an easy tone with them. Said he:

"Sit down and help yourselves. Shake off your wonder.
Here we've been waiting for you all this time,
and our mouths watering for good roast pig!"   410

But Dólios came forward, arms outstretched,
and kissed Odysseus' hand at the wrist bone,
crying out:

                              "Dear master, you returned!
You came to us again! How we had missed you!
We thought you lost. The gods themselves have brought you!
Welcome, welcome; health and blessings on you!
And tell me, now, just one thing more: Penélopê,
does she know yet that you are on the island?
or should we send a messenger?"

Odysseus gruffly said,

                                    "Old man, she knows.   420
Is it for you to think of her?"

                                          So Dólios
quietly took a smooth bench at the table
and in their turn his sons welcomed Odysseus,
kissing his hands; then each went to his chair
beside his father. Thus our friends
were occupied in Laërtês' house at noon.

Meanwhile to the four quarters of the town
the news ran: bloody death had caught the suitors;
and men and women in a murmuring crowd
gathered before Odysseus' hall. They gave   430

burial to the piteous dead, or bore
the bodies of young men from other islands
down to the port, thence to be ferried home.
Then all the men went grieving to assembly
and being seated, rank by rank, grew still,
as old Eupeithês rose to address them. Pain
lay in him like a brand for Antínoös,
the first man that Odysseus brought down,
and tears flowed for his son as he began:

"Heroic feats that fellow did for us   440
Akhaians, friends! Good spearmen by the shipload
he led to war and lost—lost ships and men,
and once ashore again killed these, who were
the islands' pride.

                           Up with you! After him!—
before he can take flight to Pylos town
or hide at Elis, under Epeian law!
We'd be disgraced forever! Mocked for generations
if we cannot avenge our sons' blood, and our brothers!
Life would turn to ashes—at least for me;
rather be dead and join the dead!

                                   I say   450
we ought to follow now, or they'll gain time
and make the crossing."

                            His appeal, his tears,
moved all the gentry listening there;
but now they saw the crier and the minstrel
come from Odysseus' hall, where they had slept.
The two men stood before the curious crowd,
and Medôn said:

                        "Now hear me, men of Ithaka.
When these hard deeds were done by Lord Odysseus
the immortal gods were not far off. I saw
with my own eyes someone divine who fought   460
beside him, in the shape and dress of Mentor;
it was a god who shone before Odysseus,
a god who swept the suitors down the hall
dying in droves."

                       At this pale fear assailed them,
and next they heard again the old forecaster,
Halithérsês Mastóridês. Alone
he saw the field of time, past and to come.
In his anxiety for them he said:

"Ithakans, now listen to what I say.
Friends, by your own fault these deaths came to pass.   470
You would not heed me nor the captain, Mentor;

would not put down the riot of your sons.
Heroic feats they did!—all wantonly
raiding a great man's flocks, dishonoring
his queen, because they thought he'd come no more.
Let matters rest; do as I urge; no chase,
or he who wants a bloody end will find it."

The greater number stood up shouting "Aye!"
But many held fast, sitting all together
in no mind to agree with him. Eupeithês   480
had won them to his side. They ran for arms,
clapped on their bronze, and mustered
under Eupeithês at the town gate
for his mad foray.

          Vengeance would be his,
he thought, for his son's murder; but that day
held bloody death for him and no return.

At this point, querying Zeus, Athena said:

"O Father of us all and king of kings,
enlighten me. What is your secret will?
War and battle, worse and more of it,   490
or can you not impose a pact on both?"

The summoner of cloud replied:

           "My child,
why this formality of inquiry?
Did you not plan that action by yourself—
see to it that Odysseus, on his homecoming,
should have their blood?

         Conclude it as you will.
There is one proper way, if I may say so:
Odysseus' honor being satisfied,
let him be king by a sworn pact forever,
and we, for our part, will blot out the memory   500
of sons and brothers slain. As in the old time
let men of Ithaka henceforth be friends;
prosperity enough, and peace attend them."

Athena needed no command, but down
in one spring she descended from Olympos
just as the company of Odysseus finished
wheat crust and honeyed wine, and heard him say:

"Go out, someone, and see if they are coming."

One of the boys went to the door as ordered
and saw the townsmen in the lane. He turned   510
swiftly to Odysseus.

                                                        "Here they come,"
he said, "best arm ourselves, and quickly."

All up at once, the men took helm and shield—
four fighting men, counting Odysseus,
with Dólios' half dozen sons. Laërtês
armed as well, and so did Dólios—
greybeards, they could be fighters in a pinch.
Fitting their plated helmets on their heads
they sallied out, Odysseus in the lead.

Now from the air Athena, Zeus's daughter,   520
appeared in Mentor's guise, with Mentor's voice,
making Odysseus' heart grow light. He said
to put cheer in his son:

                                                        "Telémakhos,
you are going into battle against pikemen
where hearts of men are tried. I count on you
to bring no shame upon your forefathers.
In fighting power we have excelled this lot
in every generation."

                                                        Said his son:
"If you are curious, Father, watch and see
the stuff that's in me. No more talk of shame."   530

And old Laërtês cried aloud:
"Ah, what a day for me, dear gods!
to see my son and grandson vie in courage!"

Athena halted near him, and her eyes
shone like the sea. She said:

                                                        "Arkeísiadês,
dearest of all my old brothers-in-arms,
invoke the grey-eyed one and Zeus her father,
heft your spear and make your throw."

Power flowed into him from Pallas Athena,
whom he invoked as Zeus's virgin child,   540
and he let fly his heavy spear.

                                                        It struck
Eupeithês on the cheek plate of his helmet,
and undeflected the bronze head punched through.
He toppled, and his armor clanged upon him.
Odysseus and his son now furiously
closed, laying on with broadswords, hand to hand,
and pikes: they would have cut the enemy down
to the last man, leaving not one survivor,

had not Athena raised a shout
that stopped all fighters in their tracks.

"Now hold!" 550

she cried, "Break off this bitter skirmish;
end your bloodshed, Ithakans, and make peace."

Their faces paled with dread before Athena,
and swords dropped from their hands unnerved, to lie
strewing the ground, at the great voice of the goddess.
Those from the town turned fleeing for their lives.
But with a cry to freeze their hearts
and ruffling like an eagle on the pounce,
the lord Odysseus reared himself to follow—
at which the son of Kronos dropped a thunderbolt 560
smoking at his daughter's feet.

Athena

cast a grey glance at her friend and said:

"Son of Laërtês and the gods of old,
Odysseus, master of land ways and sea ways,
command yourself. Call off this battle now,
or Zeus who views the wide world may be angry."

He yielded to her, and his heart was glad.
Both parties later swore to terms of peace
set by their arbiter, Athena, daughter
of Zeus who bears the stormcloud as a shield— 570
though still she kept the form and voice of Mentor.

Sappho
(Seventh Century B.C. to Sixth Century B.C.)

What we know about Sappho can be briefly stated: She lived in the late seventh and early sixth centuries B.C.; she was born and spent most of her life on the island of Lesbos in the Aegean Sea; her mother's name was Cleis; she had a daughter also named Cleis; her husband's name was Cercolas (probably); she had two brothers named Charaxos and Larichos and possibly a third named Eurygyos; she had a number of young female companions, perhaps her students; and she wrote magnificent poetry. The voice of this earliest woman poet is intensely personal and intensely musical even in the muffled and distorted form in which it has reached us.

Sappho was well known in classical times. She seems to have been rather prolific, writing perhaps five hundred poems, and she was widely quoted by critics, commentators, and grammarians down through late Roman times. She was one of the poets most parodied on the late Greek comic stage; at least six Greek comedies dealt with her (all are now lost). From these plays sprang a number of legends about Sappho—that she was short, dark, and ugly ("a nightingale with misshapen wings"), that she was a prostitute, and that she died by throwing herself off the Leucadian cliffs when her love for a ferryman named Phaon was not reciprocated. All these legends are now thoroughly discredited.

The earliest surviving manuscript of Sappho's poems dates from the third century B.C., hundreds of years after her death, and its link with what she actually composed is indirect, depending on a long chain of singers who, over that time, transmitted the lyrics orally, at some undetermined point putting them into writing. Sappho was literally a lyric poet, singing or chanting the poems to her own accompaniment on the lyre, and she may never have put them into writing herself at all. The method of transmission, then, was one obstacle to the accurate preservation of her texts.

But Sappho's reputation as a lesbian (in a sexual as well as a geographical sense) was also a major reason why so little of her work survives. Even in classical times, her homosexuality was the source of some disapproval; Ovid wrote that she "taught how to love girls." But this mild disapproval hardened into hatred in the early Middle Ages. About 380 A.D., St. Gregory of Nazianzos, Bishop of Constantinople, ordered all copies of Sappho's works burned wherever they were found, and again in the eleventh century Pope Gregory VII ordered her poems publicly burned in Rome and Constantinople. As a result of such attacks and of the general loss of classical manuscripts during the Middle Ages, not a single collection of Sappho's poems survived the medieval period.

Interest in Sappho reawakened in the Renaissance, however, and scholars attempted to reconstruct her work by assembling all the lines quoted by other Greek and Latin writers. Longinus' Essay on the Sublime, for example, contained the complete text of Sappho's "He is more than a hero" (number 39 in this text), and Dionysios of Halikarnassos' Treatise on Style contained all of "Prayer to Aphrodite" (number 38). Even so, the results were pitifully small.

And then, incredibly, in 1879, new poems by Sappho were discovered in an ancient rubbish heap in Egypt; further manuscripts came to light during a series of archeological expeditions in the 1890's. Papyrus scrolls upon which the poems had been copied had been torn, lengthwise, into strips and used as mummy wrappings. Others had been used to stuff mummified crocodiles. As a result of this shredding, the new texts of Sappho, while valuable, include many partial lines; reconstructing what Sappho wrote involves a great deal of guesswork. We now have about seven hundred intelligible lines of Sappho's voluminous verse.

The poet that emerges from this sadly mutilated work is nevertheless powerful and distinctive. Sappho wrote a number of epithalamia (wedding songs), to be chanted by a chorus before the bridal chamber. But her favorite poetic form was the short, intensely personal lyric, written to be chanted to the lyre by a solo singer. Most of her poems in this form deal with the passions and relationships within her circle of female companions, and especially with her own feelings about these women. Who these companions were is a matter of some speculation. Earlier critics believed that Sappho was a priestess and the leader of a thiasos, an organized group of women devoted to the worship of Aphrodite. More recent scholars have vigorously opposed this view and held that the circle of girls, if it had any formal standing at all, was at most a group of students or apprentices who studied poetry and the lyre with Sappho.

Fortunately, this question does not have to be resolved before we can understand the poems. Whatever her official relationship to the circle of girls, Sappho's emphasis in her poems is almost exclusively personal and passionate. Even the prayers to Aphrodite are full of an aching, human passion, and the pain of longing has seldom been better described than in Number 39, where the glimpse of her loved one sitting by a man eclipses the world of perception, leaving only a feeling like death. If Sappho's world has a "hothouse atmosphere," as one critic has said, within its limits it is a psychologically realistic and extraordinarily moving one.

The passion and the intensity in Sappho's poetry are expressed with a limpid simplicity. The English critic C. M. Bowra describes her poetry as "ordinary speech raised to the highest level of expressiveness." The translator of this selection, Mary Barnard, states that her ambition is to capture in English Sappho's "fresh colloquial directness of speech," the quality that, along with her passion and her lyricism, led an anonymous Roman critic to write that "Sappho was not ninth among men but rather tenth among the lovely Muses."

NOTE ON THE TEXT

Because of complex problems of textual reconstruction, the first lines of the poems included here are sometimes to be read as titles, sometimes as integral parts of the poems. Their numbering corresponds to that in the Barnard translation.

FURTHER READING (*prepared by F.S.N.*): Discussion of Sappho's life and work is found in Bruno Snell, *The Discovery of the Mind*, 1948, trans. T. G. Rosenmeyer, 1953, pp. 43–70; Albin Lesky, *A History of Greek Literature*, 1957, 2nd ed. 1963, trans. J. Willis and C. de Heer, 1966, pp. 138–148; and Willis Barnstone, *Sappho: Lyrics in the Original Greek with Translations*, 1965. Denys L. Page, in his *Sappho and Alcaeus: An Introduction to the Study of Ancient Lesbian Poetry*, 1955, presents twelve of the longer poems, with translation, commentary and interpretative material; these analyses are followed by useful general remarks on Sappho's writings. On the form of Sappho's poetry, see Anne Pippin Burnett's lucidly written critical and historical study *Three Archaic Poets: Archilochus, Alcaeus, Sappho*, 1983. Discussions of Sappho in a feminist context are included in *Reflections of Women in Antiquity*, ed. Helene P. Foley, 1981. Guidance to writings on Sappho can be found in the apparatus of Richard Jenkyns' *Three Classical Poets: Sappho, Catullus, and Juvenal*, 1982.

POEMS

Translated by Mary Barnard

30

We drink your health

Lucky bridegroom!
Now the wedding you
asked for is over

and your wife is the   5
girl you asked for;
she's a bride who is

charming to look at,
with eyes as soft as
honey, and a face   10

that Love has lighted
with his own beauty.
Aphrodite[1] has surely

outdone herself in
doing honor to you!   15

34

Lament for a maidenhead

FIRST   Like a quince-apple
VOICE   ripening on a top
             branch in a tree top

             not once noticed by   5
             harvesters or if
             not unnoticed, not reached

SECOND   Like a hyacinth in
VOICE   the mountains, trampled
             by shepherds until   10
             only a purple stain
             remains on the ground

37

You[1] know the place: then

Leave Crete and come to us
waiting where the grove is
pleasantest, by precincts

sacred to you; incense   5
smokes on the altar, cold
streams murmur through the

[1] Goddess of love, as well as of the sea and of beauty, flowers, and seasons.
[1] The poem is addressed to Aphrodite (the "Cyprian" of line 14).

    apple branches, a young
    rose thicket shades the ground
    and quivering leaves pour   10

    down deep sleep; in meadows
    where horses have grown sleek
    among spring flowers, dill

    scents the air. Queen! Cyprian!
    Fill our gold cups with love   15
    stirred into clear nectar

38

Prayer to my lady of Paphos[1]

Dapple-throned Aphrodite,
eternal daughter of God,
snare-knitter! Don't, I beg you,

cow my heart with grief! Come,   5
as once when you heard my far-
off cry and, listening, stepped

from your father's house to your
gold car, to yoke the pair whose
beautiful thick-feathered wings[2]   10

oaring down mid-air from heaven
carried you to light swiftly
on dark earth; then, blissful one,

smiling your immortal smile
you asked, What ailed me now that   15
made me call you again? What

was it that my distracted
heart most wanted? "Whom has
Persuasion to bring round now

to your love? Who, Sappho, is   20
unfair to you? For, let her
run, she will soon run after;

[1] Aphrodite, who was born of the sea foam and washed ashore at Paphos.
[2] The sparrows that drew Aphrodite's chariot.

if she won't accept gifts, she
will one day give them; and if
she won't love you—she soon will   25

love, although unwillingly. . . ."
If ever—come now! Relieve
this intolerable pain!

What my heart most hopes will
happen, make happen; you your-   30
self join forces on my side!

39

He is more than a hero

He is a god in my eyes—
the man who is allowed
to sit beside you—he

who listens intimately   5
to the sweet murmur of
your voice, the enticing

laughter that makes my own
heart beat fast. If I meet
you suddenly, I can't   10

speak—my tongue is broken;
a thin flame runs under
my skin; seeing nothing,

hearing only my own ears
drumming, I drip with sweat;   15
trembling shakes my body

and I turn paler than
dry grass. At such times
death isn't far from me

40

Yes, Atthis,[1] you may be sure

                                                  Even in Sardis
Anactoria will think often of us

[1] Atthis and Anactoria were two of the girls in Sappho's circle.

of the life we shared here, when you seemed
the Goddess incarnate
to her and your singing pleased her best

Now among Lydian women she in her
turn stands first as the red-
fingered moon rising at sunset takes

precedence over stars around her;
her light spreads equally
on the salt sea and fields thick with bloom

Delicious dew pours down to freshen
roses, delicate thyme
and blossoming sweet clover; she wanders

aimlessly, thinking of gentle
Atthis, her heart hanging
heavy with longing in her little breast

She shouts aloud, Come! we know it;
thousand-eared night repeats that cry
across the sea shining between us

41

To an army wife, in Sardis:

Some say a cavalry corps,
some infantry, some, again,
will maintain that the swift oars

of our fleet are the finest
sight on dark earth; but I say
that whatever one loves, is.

This is easily proved: did
not Helen[1]—she who had scanned
the flower of the world's manhood—

choose as first among men one
who laid Troy's honor in ruin?
warped to his will, forgetting

love due her own blood, her own
child, she wandered far with him.
So Anactoria, although you

---

[1] Helen of Troy, whose choice of Paris as a lover and subsequent flight with him to Troy began the Trojan War.

being far away forget us,
the dear sound of your footstep
and light glancing in your eyes

would move me more than glitter   20
of Lydian horse or armored
tread of mainland infantry

42

I have had not one word from her

Frankly I wish I were dead.
When she left, she wept

a great deal; she said to
me, "This parting must be   5
endured, Sappho. I go unwillingly."

I said, "Go, and be happy
but remember (you know
well) whom you leave shackled by love   ✓

"If you forget me, think   10
of our gifts to Aphrodite
and all the loveliness that we shared

"all the violet tiaras,
braided rosebuds, dill and
crocus twined around your young neck   15

"myrrh poured on your head
and on soft mats girls with
all that they most wished for beside them

"while no voices chanted
choruses without ours,
no woodlot bloomed in spring without song . . ."   20

43

It was you, Atthis, who said

"Sappho, if you will not get
up and let us look at you
I shall never love you again!

"Get up, unleash your suppleness,   5
lift off your Chian nightdress[1]
and, like a lily leaning into

"a spring, bathe in the water.
Cleis[2] is bringing your best
purple frock and the yellow   10

"tunic down from the clothes chest;
you will have a cloak thrown over
you and flowers crowning your hair . . .

"Praxinoa, my child, will you please
roast nuts for our breakfast? One   15
of the gods is being good to us:

"today we are going at last
into Mitylene, our favorite
city, with Sappho, loveliest

"of its women; she will walk   20
among us like a mother with
all her daughters around her

"when she comes home from exile . . ."

But you forget everything

97

I have often asked you
not to come now
Hermes,[1] Lord, you
who lead the ghosts
home: 5
     But this time
I am not happy; I
want to die, to see
the moist lotus open
along Acheron[2]   10

---

[1] From the island of Chios, off the coast of Asia Minor.   [2] Sappho's daughter.
[1] The god who guided the dead to the underworld.   [2] The river of Death.

Aeschylus

(C. 525–456 B.C.)

The oldest of the three great Greek tragedians, Aeschylus was born around 525 B.C. in Eleusis, a town near Athens, and died in Sicily in 456. He fought in the Persian wars, taking part in the great Athenian victory at Marathon in 490 and later in other climactic victories over the invading Persians, including the naval battle of Salamis in 480. Earlier that year, the Persians had partially destroyed Athens. Aeschylus' sense of pride in his city's accomplishments and triumphant survival is expressed most directly in his play The Persians *(472), the only surviving Greek tragedy based on history, but also in the Orestes trilogy, or* Oresteia. *Aeschylus is a definitive spokesman for central Athenian values during the noblest age of ancient Greece. It is probable, in fact, that the eminent political and civic leader Pericles was the "choregus" (roughly equivalent of "producer") for one of Aeschylus' plays.*

Today, as was true in antiquity, Aeschylus is called the "Father of Tragedy." He earned the title not only by his achievements as an artist, as typified by the power and loftiness of his stories, themes, and style, but also by his technical innovations. He is said to have introduced the "second actor" (earlier there had been only one and a Chorus), thus making possible more complex plots and interactions. (The addition of an actor multiplied the number of possible characters, since parts were regularly doubled and men played female as well as male roles.) At the same time, he preserved the major lyrical and dramatic role of the Chorus, which both participates in and comments on the action—this in addition to its musical and choreographic function. His output was impressive: some eighty or ninety plays. Of these, seven have survived: The Persians, Seven Against Thebes, The Suppliant Maidens, Prometheus Bound, *and the three plays that make up the* Oresteia.

Greek tragedies were regularly written and performed as cycles of three, each cycle followed by a raucous "satyr play" designed to contrast with the emotional loftiness and intensity of the tragedies. Aeschylus' Oresteia, *performed in 458 just two years before his death, is the only such cycle of tragedies to have survived in its entirety.*

Much of the power of this awesome work lies in the universality of its theme. Like the Book of Job, Virgil's Aeneid, *and Milton's* Paradise Lost, *the* Oresteia *explores the perennially urgent question of whether suffering and evil can be reconciled with cosmic justice—and, if it can be, how. The literal story, however, focuses on a concrete and practical form of the question: What is the relationship between strict justice and human welfare, individual and communal? Social order, even more obviously than cosmic justice, would seem to demand that evil acts be punished—especially when, as in Aeschylus' trilogy, these acts violate the most fundamental relationships, husband-wife and parent-child. Yet the act of punishment itself frequently seems an obscenity, at odds with our sense of what is noble in humanity and worth loving or emulating in the divine order, however we define it. In our own time the question, independent of theology, underlies the debate about the function of punishment, mercy, rehabilitation, and deterrence in the judicial and penal systems. It is not at all coincidental that the* Oresteia *ends with the establishment of a law court.*

Aeschylus explores the question by dramatizing the events growing out of the curse on the lineage of Atreus. The family has been guilty of unspeakable atrocities for generations before the plays' action begins, culminating in Agamemnon's sacrifice of his daughter Iphigeneia and the excesses committed against the innocents of Troy. (See the Headnote to the Oresteia.) *Within the plays themselves, the chain of violence is extended by two further acts: the murder of Agamemnon by his wife Clytaemnestra, and the successful conspiracy of their children, Orestes and Electra, to kill their mother in the cause of justice. The main agency and symbol of retaliation are the Furies, repellent primitive beings who in their very unsophistication embody an uncompromising honesty in dealing with elemental evil, especially violations of blood-kinship.*

"Tragedy" seems hardly the right term for this superdrama, either for the whole or for its separate plays. In Aeschylus' early plays, such as the surviving Persians *and* Seven Against Thebes, *he placed human affairs in the foreground, with the gods relegated to the background. But in the* Oresteia, *as apparently also in the late* Prometheus *and Danaid trilogies (now represented only in the surviving* Prometheus Bound *and* The Suppliant Maidens), *he brought the cosmos itself on stage as he dramatized the divisions within the universe and their ultimate reconciliation. The* Oresteia *is not so much a tragedy, in the Aristotelian sense, as it is a Divine Comedy, tracing the emergence of civilization out of darkness into light. This process is presented in terms of sexual conflict and its resolution, conflict which penetrates all levels of existence, from the psychological through the domestic and political to the cosmic.* Agamemnon *presents a world trapped in a net (a crucial image throughout the trilogy) of blood-vengeance, a primitive code presided over by the conservative, irrational, female Furies. The nightmare world of* Agamemnon *is shot through with sexual conflict and confusion. The unwifely Clytaemnestra "maneuvers like a man," while Aegisthus is a womanly man, and the heart of Cassandra's premonitory vision (which no one understands) is, "What outrage—the woman kills the man!" Confusion of personal sexual identity is echoed on the domestic level in the marital hatred of Agamemnon and his queen and on the political level in the Trojan War, fought "all for another's woman." The Greek victory has been a rape—"for their mad outrage of a queen we raped their city"—and Agamemnon, who killed his own daughter, has been "the darling of all the golden girls who spread the gates of Troy."*

The Libation Bearers *introduces the title character of the trilogy, Orestes, who is to become the pivotal figure in the revolution of values the* Oresteia *traces. The law of blood-vengeance still reigns, but the vengeance of Orestes and Electra, so reluctant and self-doubting, is very different from the self-confident exultation of Clytaemnestra's bloodletting. Sexual conflict and confusion here are translated into the agonized ambivalence of a son and daughter forced to choose between love for a mother and honor for a father. And by the end of the play, sexual conflicts on the familial and political levels have broadened to a cosmic level in the conflict of the embodied Furies with the male Olympian Apollo, who authorized Orestes' vengeance. This conflict is brought directly on stage as we move from the nightmarish mode of* Agamemnon *and the comparatively realistic and Sophoclean manner of* The Libation Bearers *to the allegorical theomachy of* The Eumenides. *The curiously bisexual Athena, female but motherless, since she sprang straight from the head of Zeus, becomes the instrument for the resolution of sexual conflict, personally for Orestes, politically for Athens, and cosmically, in the reconciliation of the gods. The male Olympians triumph, but the female Furies are honored too, as they are transformed into the Eumenides, the "Kindly Ones," watchers over the rain, sunshine, and fertility of nature. This "Divine Comedy" ends with a distinctly nontragic hymn of triumph to the Athenian balance between the claims of earth and sky, female and male, fertility and control, with an optimism unclouded by the darker visions of Sophocles and Euripides.*

Aeschylus' poetic and dramatic style matches the grandeur of his theme. The language, with its daring metaphors and bold dislocations of syntax, mirrors an emotional and intellectual unrest perfectly in keeping with the dramatic excitement and the profundity of theme. Image patterns are used with dazzling skill to heighten effects and to convey nuances of theme and meaning. The patterns are many and omnipresent: of fire, light and darkness, nets, wealth, wind, storm, yokes, animals, hunting, lawsuits, wrestling and other sports, "threeness," and so on. These images are not a code, each image having a static meaning; their significance is always shaped by the immediate context. For example, a yoke can suggest enslavement but also the intimacy of a harmonious bond such as happy marriage. (The word "bond" itself has the same ambiguous meaning.) Moreover, the images evolve in parallel with the evolution of action and values; an example is the ominous torch flame that at the beginning of the Agamemnon *signals the fall of Troy and the imminent fall of the returning general but at the end of* The Eumenides *symbolizes fertility and deep joy.*

As a stage craftsman, Aeschylus is the most daring and flamboyant of the three Greek tragedians. His contemporaries called him the poet of "shock," and a persistent story insisted that he wrote his plays while drunk. He served both as composer and choreographer for his own plays, and the dances he arranged for his choruses were famous for their violence and extravagance: the Persian Lords, for example, in The Persians, *howl and scrape at the earth to conjure up the ghost of Darius. Shock follows shock in the* Oresteia. *The entrance of Agamemnon and his army is an impressive spectacle, and the dark red carpet running out from the palace door like a stream of blood is one of the most brilliant uses of a stage property in Greek drama. A contemporary testified that the first appearance of the Furies in* The Eumenides, *moaning and dripping blood from their eye sockets, caused children in the audience to faint and women to miscarry. The comment is possibly an exercise of critical license, but it nevertheless captures the shock the scene must have created. And the final great procession of the entire cast out of the theater and up to the hill of the Areopagus, in full view of the audience, is an extraordinary dramatic effect that suddenly moves the timeless, legendary action of the plays into the here and now.*

The Oresteia *is an allusive work that, like Virgil's* Aeneid, *brings together the two wellsprings of Greek literature, the* Iliad *and the* Odyssey, *while also transforming them. The Trojan War is the immediate occasion of the acts that bring on Agamemnon's murder and the ensuing events of the three plays. But the Odyssean themes of the warrior's return to his wife and of the loyal son determined to preserve his father and his house from harm are also reworked by Aeschylus with penetrating irony and insight.*

The trilogy makes a political and religious statement, through the medium of great art. But it is more than ideology or theology, and more than art in a narrow sense of the word. It is an emblem of the full range of human nature, one of those rare works—like Dante's Comedy, *Shakespeare's last plays, Beethoven's last music— that can explore vastness and mystery without losing touch with the human, including the earthy and even the homely. Dante included jokes and personal reminiscences in his account of the cosmos; Beethoven in his last symphony inserted a grunting German-band episode into an Olympian, ecstatic hymn to joy. Aeschylus, in* The Libation Bearers, *reminds us through Orestes' old nurse that the agent and victim of large tragic and providential forces was once a baby who needed to have his diapers changed. The magnificence of the Oresteia is ultimately a product of its range, its clear understanding and respect for man as a many-layered being. "Beneath" us lie elemental forces like the Furies; "above" us beckon the Olympian forces of the sky; "around" us lie the familiar facts of our condition in the actual world. All three of these levels, though, are within us, needing to be humanized and synthesized if we are to realize our full potential, individually and communally.*

FURTHER READING (*prepared by F.S.N.*): John Herington, *Aeschylus*, 1986, is a clearly-written introductory overview of the author's work, especially valuable for its attention to patterns of diction and theatrical effect. Helen Bacon's essay on Aeschylus in Volume I of *Ancient Writers: Greece and Rome*, ed. T. James Luce, 1982, and Oliver Taplin's *The Stagecraft of Aeschylus*, 1977, are also recommended. Gilbert Murray in his classic *Aeschylus: The Creator of Tragedy*, 1940, deals not only with the extant works, but also with Aeschylus' contribution to tragedy. Anthony J. Podlecki, *The Political Background of Aeschylean Tragedy*, 1966, comments on all seven plays. H. D. F. Kitto in *Form and Meaning in Drama*, 1956, is concerned mainly with the writings of Aeschylus and Sophocles; while Albin Lesky in *Greek Tragedy*, 1938, trans. H. A. Frankfort, 1965, presents material on all three tragedians. Stimulating essays on many aspects of Aeschylean drama are offered by Marsh H. McCall, ed., *Aeschylus: A Collection of Critical Essays*, 1972. The Greek text of the three plays, a translation, and general remarks are given by W. Headlam and George Thomson, ed., *The Oresteia of Aeschylus*, 1938, 2nd ed. 1966. Anne Lebeck in *The Oresteia: A Study in Language and Structure*, 1971, shows how the imagery in the three dramas is interconnected. Hugh Lloyd-Jones' introductions in his translation of the *Oresteia*, 1979, are first-rate.

THE ORESTEIA

Translated by Robert Fagles

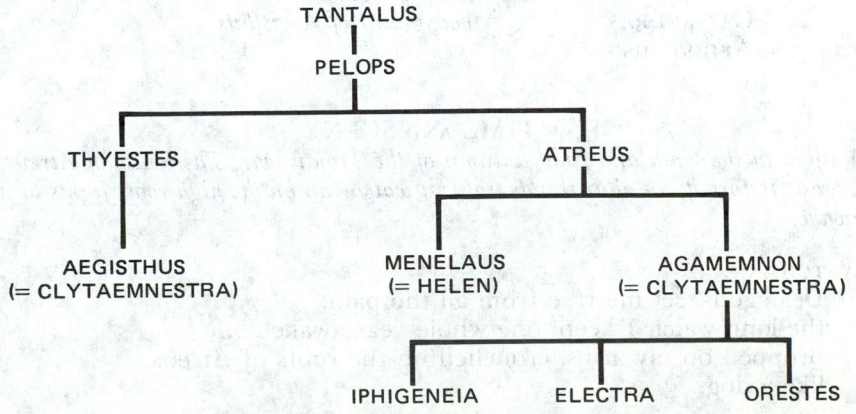

The genealogy of Orestes, according to Aeschylus.

Before the action of the first play *(Agamemnon)* begins, a line of evil acts, each inciting an act of terrible retaliation, already extends back several generations. Tantalus, the mythical great-grandfather of Agamemnon, murdered his son Pelops and tried to deceive the gods by serving them his son's flesh at a banquet. The gods saw through his deception, however, restoring Pelops to life and punishing Tantalus in Hades in a manner expressed by the word "tantalize." (The sinner was immersed in water up to his neck, with fruit trees over his head, both the water and the fruit receding when he tried to drink or eat.) Pelops in his turn double-crossed and then murdered Myrtilus, a conspirator with him in a plot to win a bride for Pelops.

Pelops had two sons, Atreus and Thyestes. Thyestes seduced his brother's wife; in revenge, Atreus first banished Thyestes and then, after luring him home again, served the flesh of Thyestes' children to him at a banquet. Thyestes cursed the house of Atreus and fled. Aegisthus, a surviving son of Thyestes, inherited his father's hatred of the line of Atreus.

Agamemnon and Menelaus are sons of Atreus. Menelaus married the beautiful Helen. She later eloped with Paris (son of King Priam of Troy), whom Menelaus had been entertaining as a guest. Agamemnon and Menelaus then organized a Greek coalition to recapture Helen from Troy and to take revenge on the Trojans. But the Greek fleet was threatened and detained at the port of Aulis by adverse winds and weather. In order to propitiate the gods, especially Artemis, and secure favorable winds, Agamemnon sacrificed the life of his daughter Iphigeneia, thereby extending the line of sacrilegious killings and incurring the hatred of his wife Clytaemnestra (half-sister to Helen). During Agamemnon's absence at Troy, Clytaemnestra has entered into an adulterous union with Aegisthus, both of whom have a motive for killing Agamemnon. [*Editors' headnote.*]

AGAMEMNON

CHARACTERS

WATCHMAN	CHORUS, THE OLD MEN OF ARGOS
CLYTAEMNESTRA	AND THEIR LEADER
HERALD	*Attendants of Clytaemnestra*
AGAMEMNON	*and of Agamemnon,*
CASSANDRA	*bodyguard of Aegisthus*
AEGISTHUS	

TIME AND SCENE

A night in the tenth and final autumn of the Trojan war. The house of Atreus in Argos.[1] Before it, an altar stands unlit; a watchman on the high roofs fights to stay awake.

WATCHMAN.
  Dear gods, set me free from all the pain,
  the long watch I keep, one whole year awake . . .
  propped on my arms, crouched on the roofs of Atreus
  like a dog.

[1] According to Homer, Agamemnon lived in Mycenae; Aeschylus changes the scene of the tragedy to Argos. Both cities were located in the plain of Argolis, in south-central Greece.

I know the stars by heart,
the armies of the night, and there in the lead
the ones that bring us snow or the crops of summer,
bring us all we have—
our great blazing kings of the sky,
I know them, when they rise and when they fall . . .
and now I watch for the light, the signal-fire
breaking out of Troy, shouting Troy is taken.
So she commands,[2] full of her high hopes.
That woman—she maneuvers like a man.

And when I keep to my bed, soaked in dew,
and the thoughts go groping through the night
and the good dreams that used to guard my sleep . . .
not here, it's the old comrade, terror at my neck.
I mustn't sleep, no—

                    [*Shaking himself awake.*]
                    Look alive, sentry.
And I try to pick out tunes, I hum a little,
a good cure for sleep, and the tears start,
I cry for the hard times come to the house,
no longer run like the great place of old.

Oh for a blessed end to all our pain,
some godsend burning through the dark—

                    [*Light appears slowly in the east; he
                    struggles to his feet and scans it.*]
                    I salute you!
You dawn of the darkness, you turn night to day—
I see the light at last.
They'll be dancing in the streets of Argos
thanks to you, thanks to this new stroke of—
                    Aieeeeee!
There's your signal clear and true, my queen!
Rise up from bed—hurry, lift a cry of triumph
through the house, praise the gods for the beacon,
if they've taken Troy . . .
                    But there it burns,
fire all the way. I'm for the morning dances.
Master's luck is mine. A throw of the torch
has brought us triple-sixes[3]—we have won!
My move now—

---

[2] Clytaemnestra, Agamemnon's queen, has established a chain of fire-beacons that will relay quickly the news that Troy has fallen.
[3] A winning throw of the dice in a game related to backgammon.

[*Beginning to dance, then breaking
off, lost in thought.*]

       Just bring him home. My king,
I'll take your loving hand in mine and then . . .
the rest is silence. The ox is on my tongue.[4]
Aye, but the house and these old stones,
give them a voice and what a tale they'd tell.   40
And so would I, gladly . . .
I speak to those who know; to those who don't
my mind's a blank. I never say a word.

[*He climbs down from the roof and
disappears into the palace through a
side entrance. A* CHORUS, *the old
men of Argos who have not learned
the news, enters and marches around
the altar.*]

CHORUS.
Ten years gone, ten to the day
  our great avenger[5] went for Priam—   45
    Menelaus and lord Agamemnon,
two kings with the power of Zeus,
the twin throne, twin scepter,
Atreus' sturdy yoke of sons
launched Greece in a thousand ships,   50
armadas cutting loose from the land,
armies massed for the cause, the rescue—

[*From within the palace* CLYTAEM-
NESTRA *raises a cry of triumph.*]

the heart within them screamed for all-out war!
Like vultures robbed of their young,
  the agony sends them frenzied,   55
soaring high from the nest, round and
round they wheel, they row their wings,
stroke upon churning thrashing stroke,
but all the labor, the bed of pain,
  the young are lost forever.   60
Yet someone hears on high—Apollo,
Pan or Zeus[6]—the piercing wail
these guests of heaven raise,

---

[4] A proverbial phrase, the equivalent of "my lips are sealed." The watchman is probably thinking ominously of the guilty affair between Clytaemnestra and Aegisthus.

[5] Agamemnon and his brother Menelaus (whose wife Helen had run away with Paris, thus occasioning the war against Troy). Priam was the Trojan King.

[6] Apollo, Pan, and Zeus are, respectively, the god of prophecy, the god of nature, and the king of the gods.

and drives at the outlaws, late
but true to revenge, a stabbing Fury![7]   65

> [CLYTAEMNESTRA *appears at the*
> *doors and pauses with her entourage.*]

So towering Zeus the god of guests[8]
drives Atreus' sons at Paris,
all for a woman manned by many[9]
the generations wrestle, knees
grinding the dust, the manhood drains,   70
the spear snaps in the first blood rites
   that marry Greece and Troy.
And now it goes as it goes
and where it ends is Fate.
And neither by singeing flesh   75
nor tipping cups of wine[10]
nor shedding burning tears can you
enchant away the rigid Fury.

> [CLYTAEMNESTRA *lights the altar-*
> *fires.*]

We are the old, dishonored ones,
the broken husks of men.   80
Even then they cast us off,
the rescue mission[11] left us here
to prop a child's strength upon a stick.
What if the new sap rises in his chest?
He has no soldiery in him,   85
   no more than we,
and we are aged past aging,
gloss of the leaf shriveled,
three legs at a time we falter on.
Old men are children once again,   90
   a dream that sways and wavers
into the hard light of day.

But you,
daughter of Leda, queen Clytaemnestra,

[7] The Furies are female personifications and agents of vengeance for crime, especially crime against blood-kin. In the last play of the trilogy they are redefined as "the Eumenides," or "kindly ones."

[8] One of the roles of Zeus. Paris had violated the laws of hospitality by stealing Helen away from the house of his host, Menelaus.

[9] Helen had been courted by innumerable suitors in addition to the man she married (Menelaus) and the man she ran away with (Paris).

[10] Ritual offerings to the gods included sacrificed animals and poured-out wine. The imagery here and the two following lines could refer to any of several persons in the play. Such ambiguity is recurrent in the trilogy.

[11] The naval and military expedition to bring Helen back from Troy.

what now, what news, what message
drives you through the citadel   95
    burning victims? Look,
the city gods, the gods of Olympus,
gods of the earth and public markets—
all the altars blazing with your gifts!
    Argos blazes! Torches   100
race the sunrise up her skies—
drugged by the lulling holy oils,
    unadulterated,
run from the dark vaults of kings.
    Tell us the news!   105
What you can, what is right—
Heal us, soothe our fears!
Now the darkness comes to the fore,
now the hope glows through your victims,
beating back this raw, relentless anguish   110
    gnawing at the heart.

> [CLYTAEMNESTRA *ignores them and
> pursues her rituals; they assemble
> for the opening chorus.*]

O but I still have power to sound the gods' command at the roads[12]
that launched the kings. The gods breathe power through my
        song,
    my fighting strength, Persuasion grows with the years—
I sing how the flight of fury hurled the twin command,   115
            one will that hurled young Greece
and winged the spear of vengeance straight for Troy!
The kings of birds to kings of the beaking prows,[13] one black,
    one with a blaze of silver
        skimmed the palace spearhand right   120
            and swooping lower, all could see,
                plunged their claws in a hare, a mother
        bursting with unborn young—the babies spilling,
quick spurts of blood—cut off the race just dashing into life!
Cry, cry for death, but good win out in glory in the end.   125

But the loyal seer[14] of the armies studied Atreus' sons,
two sons with warring hearts—he saw two eagle-kings

[12] In lines 112–258 the chorus recalls fearfully the ominous beginning of the expedition
against Troy. The eagles' devouring of the hare was understood by Calchas, the Greek
soothsayer, to foreshadow the destruction of Troy. But Artemis, goddess of the hunt (and
thus protector of pregnant animals) and of childbirth (thus offended by the anticipated
slaughter of innocents at Troy) was angered. Unfavorable winds threatened the Greek fleet
anchored at Aulis. Ironically, Artemis had to be appeased by the sacrificial killing at Aulis of
Agamemnon's daughter Iphigeneia—an example of strict retribution in kind, a central theme
in the Orestes trilogy.

[13] The kings of birds are eagles; the kings of the beaking prows are Agamemnon and
Menelaus.

[14] Calchas.

    devour the hare and spoke the things to come,
"Years pass, and the long hunt nets the city of Priam,
                 the flocks beyond the walls, 130
a kingdom's life and soul—Fate stamps them out.
Just let no curse of the gods lour on us first,
        shatter our giant armor
            forged to strangle Troy. I see
                pure Artemis bristle in pity— 135
                   yes, the flying hounds of the Father
      slaughter for armies . . . their own victim . . . a woman
trembling young, all born to die—She loathes the eagles' feast!"[15]
Cry, cry for death, but good win out in glory in the end.

    "Artemis, lovely Artemis, so kind 140
to the ravening lion's tender, helpless cubs,
the suckling young of beasts that stalk the wilds—
      bring this sign for all its fortune,
          all its brutal torment home to birth!
I beg you, Healing Apollo,[16] soothe her before 145
her crosswinds hold us down and moor the ships too long,
pressing us on to another victim . . .
        nothing sacred, no
          no feast to be eaten
            the architect of vengeance 150

                 [Turning to the palace.]
        growing strong in the house
      with no fear of the husband
here she waits
the terror raging back and back in the future
      the stealth, the law of the hearth, the mother— 155
         Memory womb of Fury child-avenging Fury!"
    So as the eagles wheeled at the crossroads,
Calchas clashed out the great good blessings mixed with doom
    for the halls of kings and singing with our fate
we cry, cry for death, but good win out in glory in the end. 160

        Zeus, great nameless all in all,
        if that name will gain his favor,
         I will call him Zeus.
      I have no words to do him justice,
         weighing all in the balance, 165
        all I have is Zeus, Zeus—
Lift this weight, this torment from my spirit,
        cast it once for all.

---

[15] We are meant to recall also the abominable meal at which Thyestes was served his children's flesh by Atreus.
[16] Apollo, god of healing, is brother to Artemis.

He who was so mighty once,[17]
   storming for the wars of heaven,   170
     he has had his day.
And then his son who came to power
met his match in the third fall
and he is gone. Zeus, Zeus—
   raise your cries and sing him Zeus the Victor!   175
     You will reach the truth:

     Zeus has led us on to know,
   the Helmsman lays it down as law
   that we must suffer, suffer into truth.
We cannot sleep, and drop by drop at the heart   180
   the pain of pain remembered comes again,
   and we resist, but ripeness comes as well.
From the gods enthroned on the awesome rowing-bench
     there comes a violent love.

     So it was that day the king,   185
   the steersman at the helm of Greece,
would never blame a word the prophet said—
swept away by the wrenching winds of fortune
he conspired! Weatherbound we could not sail,
   our stores exhausted, fighting strength hard-pressed,   190
   and the squadrons rode in the shallows off Chalkis[18]
     where the riptide crashes, drags,

and winds from the north pinned down our hulls at Aulis,
port of anguish . . . head winds starving,
sheets and the cables snapped   195
   and the men's minds strayed,
   the pride, the bloom of Greece
   was raked as time ground on,
ground down, and then the cure for the storm
and it was harsher—Calchas cried,   200
"My captains, Artemis must have blood!"—
   as harsh the sons of Atreus
     dashed their scepters on the rocks,
   could not hold back the tears,

and I still can hear the older warlord saying,   205
"Obey, obey, or a heavy doom will crush me—
Oh but doom *will* crush me
   once I rend my child,
     the glory of my house—
   a father's hands are stained,   210

---

[17] The following lines describe the overthrow of Ouranos (Uranus) by his son Kronos (Saturn) and of the latter by his son Zeus, who now reigns as supreme god.
[18] Chalkis, on the island Euboea, faced the port of Aulis on the mainland.

blood of a young girl streaks the altar.
Pain both ways and what is worse?
Desert the fleets, fail the alliance?
    No, but stop the winds with a virgin's blood,
        feed their lust, their fury?—feed their fury!—   215
Law is law!—
      Let all go well."

And once he slipped his neck in the strap of Fate,
his spirit veering black, impure, unholy,
once he turned he stopped at nothing,
      seized with the frenzy   220
            blinding driving to outrage—
wretched frenzy, cause of all our grief!
Yes, he had the heart
    to sacrifice his daughter!—
    to bless the war that avenged a woman's loss,   225
        a bridal rite that sped the men-of-war.

"My father, father!"—she might pray to the winds;
no innocence moves her judges mad for war.
Her father called his henchmen on,
    on with a prayer,   230
        "Hoist her over the altar
like a yearling, give it all your strength!
She's fainting—lift her,
    sweep her robes around her,
    but slip this strap in her gentle curving lips . . .   235
        here, gag her hard, a sound will curse the house"—
and the bridle chokes her voice . . . her saffron[19] robes
pouring over the sand
            her glance like arrows showering
wounding every murderer through with pity
      clear as a picture, live,   240
she strains to call their names . . .
I remember often the days with father's guests
when over the feast her voice unbroken,
    pure as the hymn her loving father
bearing third libations, sang to Saving Zeus—   245
transfixed with joy, Atreus' offspring
    throbbing out their love.

What comes next? I cannot see it, cannot say.
The strong techniques of Calchas do their work.
But Justice turns the balance scales,   250
    sees that we suffer
and we suffer and we learn.
And we will know the future when it comes.

[19]Orange-yellow, the traditional color of the bridal garment.

Greet it too early, weep too soon.
    It all comes clear in the light of day.   255
Let all go well today, well as she could want,

                        [*Turning to* CLYTAEMNESTRA.]

our midnight watch, our lone defender,
        single-minded queen.
LEADER.[20]
                                We've come,
Clytaemnestra. We respect your power.
Right it is to honor the warlord's woman   260
once he leaves the throne.
                                But why these fires?
Good news, or more good hopes? We're loyal,
we want to hear, but never blame your silence.
CLYTAEMNESTRA.
Let the new day shine, as the proverb says,
glorious from the womb of Mother Night.[21]   265

                        [*Lost in prayer, then turning to the*
                        CHORUS.]

You will hear a joy beyond your hopes.
Priam's citadel—the Greeks have taken Troy!
LEADER.
No, what do you mean? I can't believe it.
CLYTAEMNESTRA.
Troy is ours. Is that clear enough?
LEADER.
                                The joy of it,
stealing over me, calling up my tears—   270
CLYTAEMNESTRA.
Yes, your eyes expose your loyal hearts.
LEADER.
And you have proof?
CLYTAEMNESTRA.
                                I do,
I must. Unless the god is lying.
LEADER.
                                That,
or a phantom spirit sends you into raptures.
CLYTAEMNESTRA.
No one takes me in with visions—senseless dreams.   275
LEADER.
Or giddy rumor, you haven't indulged yourself—

[20] The principal spokesman for the Chorus.
[21] Ironically, the avenging Furies are also offspring of the primeval Night.

CLYTAEMNESTRA.
    You treat me like a child, you mock me?
LEADER.
    Then when did they storm the city?
CLYTAEMNESTRA.
    Last night, I say, the mother of this morning.
LEADER.
    And who on earth could run the news so fast?   280
CLYTAEMNESTRA.
    The god of fire—rushing fire from Ida![22]
    And beacon to beacon rushed it on to me,
    my couriers riding home the torch.
                                      From Troy
    to the bare rock of Lemnos, Hermes' Spur,
    and the Escort winged the great light west   285
    to the Saving Father's face, Mount Athos hurled it
    third in the chain and leaping Ocean's back
    the blaze went dancing on to ecstasy—pitch-pine
    streaming gold like a newborn sun—and brought
    the word in flame to Mount Makistos' brow.   290
    No time to waste, straining, fighting sleep,
    that lookout heaved a torch glowing over
    the murderous straits of Euripos to reach
    Messapion's watchmen craning for the signal.
    Fire for word of fire! tense with the heather   295
    withered gray, they stack it, set it ablaze—
    the hot force of the beacon never flags,
    it springs the Plain of Asôpos, rears
    like a harvest moon to hit Kithairon's crest
    and drives new men to drive the fire on.   300
    That relay pants for the farflung torch,
    they swell its strength outstripping my commands
    and the light inflames the marsh, the Gorgon's Eye,
    it strikes the peak where the wild goats range—
    my law, my fire whips that camp!   305
    They spare nothing, eager to build its heat,
    and a huge beard of flame overcomes the headland
    beetling down the Saronic Gulf, and flaring south
    it brings the dawn to the Black Widow's face—
    the watch that looms above your heads—and now   310

---

[22] A mountain range near Troy. Clytaemnestra's description of the progress of the flame-signal from Troy to Argos is filled with ironic overtones. Mount Athos, here associated with Zeus as "Saving Father," recalls by contrast Agamemnon's slaying of his daughter Iphigeneia; the "murderous" straits of Euripos are the location of her death; the "Black Widow" (Mount Arachnaion, or "Spider Mountain") suggests both Clytaemnestra herself and a web, one of the variants of the net-imagery ubiquitous in the play; the "true son" of Ida suggests the causal link between Agamemnon's Trojan adventure and his fate at his homecoming as well as foreshadowing the avenging role of his son Orestes.

the true son of the burning flanks of Ida
crashes on the roofs of Atreus' sons!

And I ordained it all.
Torch to torch, running for their lives,
one long succession racing home my fire.
                                                                One,   315
first in the laps and last,[23] wins out in triumph.
There you have my proof, *my* burning sign, I tell you—
the power my lord passed on from Troy to me.

LEADER.
We'll thank the gods, my lady—first this story,
let me lose myself in the wonder of it all!   320
Tell it start to finish, tell us all.

CLYTAEMNESTRA.
The city's ours—in our hands this very day!
I can hear the cries in crossfire rock the walls.
Pour oil and wine in the same bowl,
what have you, friendship? A struggle to the end.   325
So with the victors and the victims—outcries,
you can hear them clashing like their fates.

They are kneeling by the bodies of the dead,
embracing men and brothers, infants over
the aged loins that gave them life, and sobbing,   330
as the yoke constricts their last free breath,
for every dear one lost.
                              And the others,
there, plunging breakneck through the night—
the labor of battle sets them down, ravenous,
to breakfast on the last remains of Troy.   335
Not by rank but the lots of chance they draw,
they lodge in the houses captured by the spear,
settling in so soon, released from the open sky,
the frost and dew. Lucky men, off guard at last,
they sleep away their first good night in years.   340

If only they are revering the city's gods,
the shrines of the gods who love the conquered land,
no plunderer will be plundered in return.
Just let no lust, no mad desire seize the armies
to ravish what they must not touch—   345
overwhelmed by all they've won!
                              The run for home
and safety waits, the swerve at the post,[24]
the final lap of the grueling two-lap race.

---

[23] A winning relay team ("first in the laps") achieves the victory when the runner of the
anchor leg (the "last") crosses the finish line.

[24] The turning-post in a race, where the racers turn and head back for where they started.

And even if the men come back with no offense
to the gods, the avenging dead[25] may never rest—   350
Oh let no new disaster strike! And here
you have it, what a woman has to say.
Let the best win out, clear to see.
A small desire but all that I could want.

LEADER.

Spoken like a man, my lady, loyal,   355
full of self-command. I've heard your sign
and now your vision.

                             [Reaching toward her as she turns
                             and re-enters the palace.]

                 Now to praise the gods.
The joy is worth the labor.

CHORUS.

O Zeus my king and Night, dear Night,[26]
queen of the house who covers us with glories,   360
you slung your net on the towers of Troy,
neither young nor strong could leap
the giant dredge net of slavery,
    all-embracing ruin.
I adore you, iron Zeus of the guests   365
and your revenge—you drew your longbow
year by year to a taut full draw
till one bolt, not falling short
or arching over the stars,
    could split the mark of Paris!   370
The sky stroke of god!—it is all Troy's to tell,
but even I can trace it to its cause:
god does as god decrees.
    And still some say
that heaven would never stoop to punish men   375
who trample the lovely grace of things
untouchable. How wrong they are!
    A curse burns bright on crime—
      full-blown, the father's crimes will blossom,
      burst into the son's.   380
Let there be less suffering . . .
give us the sense to live on what we need.

             Bastions of wealth
             are no defense for the man
             who treads the grand altar of Justice   385
                down and out of sight.

[25] The Chorus is meant to apply the phrase to the Trojan dead; Clytaemnestra also alludes cryptically to her dead daughter.

[26] The Chorus in this passage concentrates on Paris as the evil man whom the gods punish, but much of what they say applies also to Agamemnon and the whole line of Atreus. In the latter part of the song (lines 426 ff.), the Chorus begins to sense dimly this more general guilt.

Persuasion, maddening child of Ruin
overpowers him—Ruin plans it all.
And the wound will smolder on,
    there is no cure,   390
a terrible brilliance kindles on the night.
He is bad bronze scraped on a touchstone:[27]
put to the test, the man goes black.
    Like the boy who chases
       a bird on the wing,[28] brands his city,   395
        brings it down and prays,
but the gods are deaf
to the one who turns to crime, they tear him down.

           So Paris learned:
           he came to Atreus' house   400
           and shamed the tables spread for guests,
              he stole away the queen.

And she left her land *chaos*, clanging shields,
companions tramping, bronze prows, men in bronze,
    and she came to Troy with a dowry, death,   405
strode through the gates
        defiant in every stride,
as prophets of the house looked on and wept,
"Oh the halls and the lords of war,
    the bed and the fresh prints of love.   410
I *see* him,[29] unavenging, unavenged,
the stun of his desolation is so clear—
   he longs for the one who lies across the sea
until her phantom seems to sway the house.

           Her curving images,   415
           her beauty hurts her lord,
           the eyes starve and the touch
             of love is gone,

"and radiant dreams are passing in the night,
the memories throb with sorrow, joy with pain . . .   420
   it is pain to dream and see desires
slip through the arms,
        a vision lost forever
winging down the moving drifts of sleep."
So he grieves at the royal hearth   425
   yet others' grief is worse, far worse.
All through Greece for those who flocked to war
they are holding back the anguish now,

[27] A stone that, rubbed against a metal, shows whether the metal is true or counterfeit.
[28] To chase a bird on the wing is foolishly to attempt the impossible.
[29] The primary reference is to Menelaus left alone without Helen.

you can feel it rising now in every house;
I tell you there is much to tear the heart.   430

> They knew the men they sent,
> but now in place of men
> ashes and urns come back
> to every hearth.

War, War, the great gold-broker of corpses   435
holds the balance of the battle on his spear!
Home from the pyres he sends them,
   home from Troy to the loved ones,
weighted with tears, the urns brimmed full,
   the heroes return in gold-dust,   440
dear, light ash for men; and they weep,
they praise them, "He had skill in the swordplay,"
   "He went down so tall in the onslaught,"
"All for another's woman." So they mutter
in secret and the rancor steals   445
toward our staunch defenders, Atreus' sons.

> And there they ring the walls, the young,
> the lithe, the handsome hold the graves
> they won in Troy; the enemy earth
>   rides over those who conquered.   450

The people's voice is heavy with hatred,
now the curses of the people must be paid,
and now I wait, I listen . . .
   there—there is something breathing
under the night's shroud. God takes aim   455
   at the ones who murder many;
the swarthy Furies stalk the man
gone rich beyond all rights—with a twist
   of fortune grind him down, dissolve him
into the blurring dead—there is no help.   460
The reach for power can recoil,
the bolt of god can strike you at a glance.

> Make me rich with no man's envy,
> neither a raider of cities, no,
> nor slave come face to face with life   465
>   overpowered by another.

[Speaking singly.]

—Fire comes and the news is good,
   it races through the streets
   but is it true? Who knows?
   Or just another lie from heaven?   470

—Show us the man so childish, wonderstruck,
   he's fired up with the first torch,
    then when the message shifts
    he's sick at heart.

              —Just like a woman
    to fill with thanks before the truth is clear.   475

    —So gullible. Their stories spread like wildfire,
       they fly fast and die faster;
     rumors voiced by women come to nothing.

LEADER.
    Soon we'll know her fires for what they are,
    her relay race of torches hand-to-hand—   480
    know if they're real or just a dream,
    the hope of a morning here to take our senses.
    I see a herald running from the beach
    and a victor's spray of olive shades his eyes
    and the dust he kicks, twin to the mud of Troy,   485
    shows he has a voice—no kindling timber
    on the cliffs, no signal-fires for him.
    He can shout the news and give us joy,
    or else . . . please, not that.
                 Bring it on,
    good fuel to build the first good fires.   490
    And if anyone calls down the worst on Argos
    let him reap the rotten harvest of his mind.

                [*The* HERALD *rushes in and kneels
                 on the ground.*]

HERALD.
    Good Greek earth, the soil of my fathers!
    Ten years out, and a morning brings me back.
    All hopes snapped but one—I'm home at last.   495
    Never dreamed I'd die in Greece, assigned
    the narrow plot I love the best.
                     And now
    I salute the land, the light of the sun,
    our high lord Zeus and the king of Pytho[30]—
    no more arrows, master, raining on our heads!   500
    At Scamander's banks we took our share,
    your longbow brought us down like plague.
    Now come, deliver us, heal us—lord Apollo!
    Gods of the market, here, take my salute.
    And you, my Hermes, Escort,   505
    loving Herald, the herald's shield and prayer!—

---

[30] The archer-god Apollo, who had sided with the Trojans and launched the arrows of plague against the Greeks.

And the shining dead of the land who launched the armies,
warm us home . . . we're all the spear has left.

You halls of the kings, you roofs I cherish,
sacred seats—you gods that catch the sun,   510
if your glances ever shone on him in the old days,
greet him well—so many years are lost.
He comes, he brings us light in the darkness,
free for every comrade, Agamemnon lord of men.

Give him the royal welcome he deserves!   515
He hoisted the pickax of Zeus who brings revenge,
he dug Troy down, he worked her soil down,
the shrines of her gods and the high altars, gone!—
and the seed of her wide earth he ground to bits.
That's the yoke he claps on Troy. The king,   520
the son of Atreus comes. The man is blest,
the one man alive to merit such rewards.

Neither Paris nor Troy, partners to the end,
can say their work outweighs their wages now.
Convicted of rapine, stripped of all his spoils,   525
and his father's house and the land that gave it life—
he's scythed them to the roots. The sons of Priam
pay the price twice over.

LEADER.
                              Welcome home
from the wars, herald, long live your joy.

HERALD.
                                        Our joy—
now I could die gladly. Say the word, dear gods.   530

LEADER.
Longing for your country left you raw?

HERALD.
The tears fill my eyes, for joy.

LEADER.
                              You too,
down the sweet disease that kills a man
with kindness . . .

HERALD.
                    Go on, I don't see what you—

LEADER.
                                              Love
for the ones who love you—that's what took you.

HERALD.
                                              You mean   535
the land and the armies hungered for each other?

LEADER.
There were times I thought I'd faint with longing.

HERALD.
So anxious for the armies, why?
LEADER.
                                        For years now,
only my silence kept me free from harm.
HERALD.
                                        What,
with the kings gone did someone threaten you?
LEADER.
                                        So much . . .   540
now as you say, it would be good to die.
HERALD.
True, we *have* done well.
Think back in the years and what have you?
A few runs of luck, a lot that's bad.
Who but a god can go through life unmarked?   545

A long, hard pull we had, if I would tell it all.
The iron rations, penned in the gangways
hock by jowl like sheep. Whatever miseries
break a man, our quota, every sunstarved day.

Then on the beaches it was worse. Dug in   550
under the enemy ramparts—deadly going.
Out of the sky, out of the marshy flats
the dews soaked us, turned the ruts we fought from
into gullies, made our gear, our scalps
crawl with lice.
                                And talk of the cold,   555
the sleet to freeze the gulls, and the big snows
come avalanching down from Ida. Oh but the heat,
the sea and the windless noons, the swells asleep,
dropped to a dead calm . . .

But why weep now?   560
It's over for us, over for them.
The dead can rest and never rise again;
no need to call their muster. We're alive,
do we have to go on raking up old wounds?
Good-by to all that. Glad I am to say it.   565

For us, the remains of the Greek contingents,
the good wins out, no pain can tip the scales,
not now. So shout this boast to the bright sun—
fitting it is—wing it over the seas and rolling earth:
"Once when an Argive expedition captured Troy   570
they hauled these spoils back to the gods of Greece,
they bolted them high across the temple doors,
the glory of the past!"
                                And hearing that,

men will applaud our city and our chiefs,
and Zeus will have the hero's share of fame—   575
he did the work.

              That's all I have to say.

LEADER.

I'm convinced, glad that I was wrong.
Never too old to learn; it keeps me young.

                        [CLYTAEMNESTRA *enters with her*
                        women.]

First the house and the queen, it's their affair,
but I can taste the riches.

CLYTAEMNESTRA.

                  I cried out long ago!—   580
for joy, when the first herald came burning
through the night and told the city's fall.
And there were some who smiled and said,
"A few fires persuade you Troy's in ashes.
Women, women, elated over nothing."   585

You made me seem deranged.
For all that I sacrificed—a woman's way,
you'll say—station to station on the walls
we lifted cries of triumph that resounded
in the temples of the gods. We lulled and blessed   590
the fires with myrrh and they consumed our victims.

                 [*Turning to the* HERALD.]

But enough. Why prolong the story?
From the king himself I'll gather all I need.
Now for the best way to welcome home
my lord, my good lord . . .

                No time to lose!   595
What dawn can feast a woman's eyes like this?
I can see the light, the husband plucked from war
by the Saving God and open wide the gates.

Tell him that, and have him come with speed,
the people's darling—how they long for him.   600
And for his wife,
may he return and find her true at hall,
just as the day he left her, faithful to the last.
A watchdog gentle to him alone,

               [*Glancing toward the palace.*]

            savage
to those who cross his path. I have not changed.   605
The strains of time can never break our seal.

In love with a new lord, in ill repute I am
as practiced as I am in dyeing bronze.

That is my boast, teeming with the truth.
I am proud, a woman of my nobility—   610
I'd hurl it from the roofs!

                                [*She turns sharply, enters the palace.*]

LEADER.
She speaks well, but it takes no seer to know
she only says what's right.

                              [*The* HERALD *attempts to leave; the
                              leader takes him by the arm.*]

                      Wait, one thing.
Menelaus, is he home too, safe with the men?
The power of the land—dear king.   615
HERALD.
I doubt that lies will help my friends,
in the lean months to come.
LEADER.
Help us somehow, tell the truth as well.
But when the two conflict it's hard to hide—
out with it.
HERALD.
               He's lost, gone from the fleets!   620
He and his ship, it's true.
LEADER.
                  After you watched him
pull away from Troy? Or did some storm
attack you all and tear him off the line?
HERALD.
                        There,
like a marksman, the whole disaster cut to a word.
LEADER.
How do the escorts give him out—dead or alive?   625
HERALD.
No clear report. No one knows . . .
only the wheeling sun that heats the earth to life.
LEADER.
But then the storm—how did it reach the ships?
How did it end? Were the angry gods on hand?
HERALD.
This blessed day, ruin it with *them*?   630
Better to keep their trophies far apart.

When a runner comes, his face in tears,
saddled with what his city dreaded most,
the armies routed, two wounds in one,

one to the city, one to hearth and home. . .   635
our best men, droves of them, victims
herded from every house by the two-barb whip
that Ares[31] likes to crack,
                            that charioteer
who packs destruction shaft by shaft,
careening on with his brace of bloody mares—   640
When he comes in, I tell you, dragging that much pain,
wail your battle-hymn to the Furies, and high time!

But when he brings salvation home to a city
singing out her heart—
how can I mix the good with so much bad   645
and blurt out this?—
                    "Storms swept the Greeks,
and not without the anger of the gods!"

Those enemies for ages, fire and water,
sealed a pact and showed it to the world—
they crushed our wretched squadrons.
                                    Night looming,   650
breakers lunging in for the kill
and the black gales come brawling out of the north—
ships ramming, prow into hooking prow, gored
by the rush-and-buck of hurricane pounding rain
by the cloudburst—
                    ships stampeding into the darkness,   655
lashed and spun by the savage shepherd's hand!

But when the sun comes up to light the skies
I see the Aegean heaving into a great bloom
of corpses . . . Greeks, the pick of a generation
scattered through the wrecks and broken spars.   660

But not us, not our ship, our hull untouched.
Someone stole us away or begged us off.
No mortal—a god, death grip on the tiller,
or lady luck herself, perched on the helm,
she pulled us through, she saved us. Aye,   665
we'll never battle the heavy surf at anchor,
never shipwreck up some rocky coast.

But once we cleared that sea-hell, not even
trusting luck in the cold light of day,
we battened on our troubles, they were fresh—   670
the armada punished, bludgeoned into nothing.

And now if one of them still has the breath
he's saying *we* are lost. Why not?

---

[31] God of war.

We say the same of him. Well,
here's to the best.
               And Menelaus?   675
Look to it, he's come back, and yet . . .
if a shaft of the sun can track him down,
alive, and his eyes full of the old fire—
thanks to the strategies of Zeus, Zeus
would never tear the house out by the roots—   680
then there's hope our man will make it home.

You've heard it all. Now you have the truth.

                     [*Rushing out.*]

CHORUS.
Who—what power named the name that drove your fate?—[32]
what hidden brain could divine your future,
steer that word to the mark,   685
to the bride of spears,
      the whirlpool churning armies,
              Oh for all the world a Helen!
Hell at the prows, hell at the gates
hell on the men-of-war,   690
from her lair's sheer veils she drifted
     launched by the giant western wind,
        and the long tall waves of men in armor,
huntsmen trailing the oarblades' dying spoor[33]
slipped into her moorings,   695
     Simois'[34] mouth that chokes with foliage,
                  bayed for bloody strife,

for Troy's Blood Wedding Day—she drives her word,
her burning will to the birth, the Fury
late but true to the cause,   700
to the tables shamed
     and Zeus who guards the hearth—
            the Fury makes the Trojans pay!
Shouting their hymns, hymns for the bride
hymns for the kinsmen doomed   705
to the wedding march of Fate,
     Troy changed her tune in her late age,
        and I think I hear the dirges mourning
"Paris, born and groomed for the bed of Fate!"

[32] The foregoing inquiries about Menelaus lead naturally to the theme of this choral passage: the significance of Helen, whom Menelaus was bringing home. The Chorus, punning on the root meaning of Helen's name in Greek ("destruction," rendered here as "hell"), see her as an agent of ruin inflicted as just punishment for Paris and the Trojans. She is also, however, a scourge to Greece and to the house of Atreus.

[33] The track of a wild animal. Having sailed from her home to Troy, Helen is pursued by the Greek fleet ("huntsmen") sailing to recover her.

[34] A river near Troy.

They mourn with their life breath, 710
    they sing their last, the sons of Priam
          born for bloody slaughter.

    So a man[35] once reared
a lion cub at hall, snatched
from the breast, still craving milk 715
    in the first flush of life.
A captivating pet for the young,
and the old men adored it, pampered it
    in their arms, day in, day out,
like an infant just born. 720
Its eyes on fire, little beggar,
fawning for its belly, slave to food.

    But it came of age
and the parent strain broke out
and it paid its breeders back. 725
    Grateful it was,[36] it went
through the flock to prepare a feast,
an illicit orgy—the house swam with blood,
    none could resist that agony—
          massacre vast and raw! 730
From god there came a priest of ruin,
adopted by the house to lend it warmth.

And the first sensation Helen brought to Troy . . .
call it a spirit
    shimmer of winds dying 735
        glory light as gold
    shaft of the eyes dissolving, open bloom
    that wounds the heart with love.
But veering wild in mid-flight
she whirled her wedding on to a stabbing end, 740
slashed at the sons of Priam—hearthmate, friend to the death,
    sped by Zeus who speeds the guest,
a bride of tears, a Fury.

There's an ancient saying,[37] old as man himself:
men's prosperity 745
    never will die childless,
        once full-grown it breeds.

---

[35] Helen is compared to a lion cub reared as a household pet until, having grown, its latent nature asserts itself in bloodshed. The house can be the Trojans' or that of Agamemnon and Menelaus.

[36] Grim humor; the grown lion is like someone thankfully repaying parents for rearing him.

[37] In the following lines the Chorus echoes the traditional belief that excess of prosperity in itself brings on punishment by the gods, but the old men go on to insist that the more important cause is evil deeds. Wealth acquired through evil combines both incitements to divine retribution.

    Sprung from the great good fortune in the race
      comes bloom on bloom of pain—
insatiable wealth. But not I,   750
I alone say this. Only the reckless act
can breed impiety, multiplying crime on crime,
      while the house kept straight and just
is blessed with radiant children.

        But ancient Violence longs to breed,   755
            new Violence comes
    when its fatal hour comes, the demon comes
    to take her toll—no war, no force, no prayer
      can hinder the midnight Fury stamped
    with parent Fury moving through the house.   760

        But Justice shines in sooty hovels,
            loves the decent life.
    From proud halls crusted with gilt by filthy hands
      she turns her eyes to find the pure in spirit—
spurning the wealth stamped counterfeit with praise,   765
    she steers all things toward their destined end.

                     [AGAMEMNON *enters in his chariot,*
                     his plunder borne before him by his
                     entourage; behind him, half hidden,
                     stands CASSANDRA.[38] *The old men*
                     press toward him.]

Come, my king, the scourge of Troy,
    the true son of Atreus—
How to salute you, how to praise you
neither too high nor low, but hit   770
the note of praise that suits the hour?
So many prize some brave display,
they prefer some flaunt of honor
    once they break the bounds.
When a man fails they share his grief,   775
but the pain can never cut them to the quick.
When a man succeeds they share his glory,
torturing their faces into smiles.
But the good shepherd[39] knows his flock.
When the eyes seem to brim with love   780
    and it is only unction,
he will know, better than we can know.
That day you marshaled the armies
all for Helen—no hiding it now—
I drew you in my mind in black;   785
you seemed a menace at the helm,

---

[38] A prophetess, daughter of King Priam of Troy, taken captive by Agamemnon.
[39] Agamemnon, regarded as protector of his subjects.

        sending men to the grave
to bring her home, that hell on earth.
But now from the depths of trust and love
I say Well fought, well won—   790
      the end is worth the labor!
Search, my king, and learn at last
who stayed at home and kept their faith
      and who betrayed the city.

AGAMEMNON.
                           First,
with justice I salute my Argos and my gods,   795
my accomplices who brought me home and won
my rights from Priam's Troy—the just gods.
No need to hear our pleas. Once for all
they consigned their lots to the urn[40] of blood,
they pitched on death for men, annihilation   800
for the city. Hope's hand, hovering
over the urn of mercy, left it empty.
Look for the smoke—it is the city's seamark,
building even now.
                The storms of ruin live!
Her last dying breath, rising up from the ashes   805
send us gales of incense rich in gold.

For that we must thank the gods with a sacrifice
our sons will long remember. For their mad outrage
of a queen we raped their city—we were right.
The beast of Argos, foals of the wild mare,[41]   810
thousands massed in armor rose on the night
the Pleiades[42] went down, and crashing through
their walls our bloody lion lapped its fill,
gorging on the blood of kings.
                     Our thanks to the gods,
long drawn out, but it is just the prelude.   815

                        [CLYTAEMNESTRA *approaches with*
                        her women; they are carrying dark
                        red tapestries. AGAMEMNON *turns*
                        to the leader.]

And your concern, old man, is on my mind.
I hear you and agree, I will support you.
How rare, men with the character to praise
a friend's success without a trace of envy,

---

[40] In deciding law cases, an Athenian juror cast his vote by dropping a pebble into one of two urns signifying conviction and acquittal.

[41] Agamemnon refers to the Greek soldiers who, hidden inside the wooden horse, brought about the fall of Troy. The story is told in Virgil's *Aeneid,* Book II.

[42] The setting of this constellation is associated in the present context with the approach of winter and storms.

poison to the heart—it deals a double blow.   820
Your own losses weigh you down but then,
look at your neighbor's fortune and you weep.
Well I know. I understand society,
the fawning mirror of the proud.
                                   My comrades . . .
they're shadows, I tell you, ghosts of men   825
who swore they'd die for me. Only Odysseus:
I dragged that man to the wars but once in harness
he was a trace-horse, he gave his all for me.
Dead or alive, no matter, I can praise him.

And now this cause involving men and gods.   830
We must summon the city for a trial,
found a national tribunal. Whatever's healthy,
shore it up with law and help it flourish.
Wherever something calls for drastic cures
we make our noblest effort: amputate or wield   835
the healing iron, burn the cancer at the roots.

Now I go to my father's house—
I give the gods my right hand, my first salute.
The ones who sent me forth have brought me home.

                              [*He starts down from the chariot,
                              looks at* CLYTAEMNESTRA, *stops,
                              and offers up a prayer.*]

Victory, you have sped my way before,   840
now speed me to the last.

                              [CLYTAEMNESTRA *turns from the
                              king to the* CHORUS.]

CLYTAEMNESTRA.
                              Old nobility of Argos
gathered here, I am not ashamed to tell you
how I love the man. I am older,
and the fear dies away . . . I am human.
Nothing I say was learned from others.   845
This is my life, my ordeal, long as the siege
he laid at Troy and more demanding.
                                   First,
when a woman sits at home and the man is gone,
the loneliness is terrible,
unconscionable . . .   850
and the rumors spread and fester,
a runner comes with something dreadful,
close on his heels the next and his news worse,
and they shout it out and the whole house can hear;
and wounds—if he took one wound for each report   855

to penetrate these walls, he's gashed like a dragnet,
more, if he had only died . . .
for each death that swelled his record, he could boast
like a triple-bodied Geryon[43] risen from the grave,
"Three shrouds I dug from the earth, one for every body   860
that went down!"

                     The rumors broke like fever,
broke and then rose higher. There were times
they cut me down and eased my throat from the noose.
I wavered between the living and the dead.

                 [*Turning to* AGAMEMNON.]

                       And so
our child is gone, not standing by our side,   865
the bond of our dearest pledges, mine and yours;
by all rights our child should be here . . .
Orestes.[44] You seem startled.
You needn't be. Our loyal brother-in-arms
will take good care of him, Strophios the Phocian.   870
He warned from the start we court two griefs in one.
You risk all on the wars—and what if the people
rise up howling for the king, and anarchy
should dash our plans?

                Men, it is their nature,
trampling on the fighter once he's down.   875
Our child is gone. That is my self-defense
and it is true.

             For me, the tears that welled
like springs are dry. I have no tears to spare.
I'd watch till late at night, my eyes still burn,
I sobbed by the torch I lit for you alone.   880

              [*Glancing toward the palace.*]

I never let it die . . . but in my dreams
the high thin wail of a gnat would rouse me,
piercing like a trumpet—I could see you
suffer more than all
the hours that slept with me could ever bear.   885

I endured it all. And now, free of grief,
I would salute that man the watchdog of the fold,
the mainroyal, saving stay[45] of the vessel,
rooted oak that thrusts the roof sky-high,

---

[43] A three-headed giant.

[44] One of the many ironies in Clytaemnestra's speech; the preceding lines suggest Orestes' dead sister Iphigeneia. Clytaemnestra has sent Orestes away to the city of Phocis, to clear the way for Aegisthus and herself, or to protect Orestes against civil mutiny while his father was away, or perhaps for both reasons.

[45] A cable that supports the mainroyal mast of a ship.

the father's one true heir.   890
Land at dawn to the shipwrecked past all hope,
light of the morning burning off the night of storm,
the cold clear spring to the parched horseman—
O the ecstasy, to flee the yoke of Fate!

It is right to use the titles he deserves.   895
Let envy keep her distance. We have suffered
long enough.

> [*Reaching toward* AGAMEMNON.]

      Come to me now, my dearest,
down from the car of war, but never set the foot
that stamped out Troy on earth again, my great one.

Women, why delay? You have your orders.   900
Pave his way with tapestries.

> [*They begin to spread the crimson
> tapestries between the king and the
> palace doors.*]

      Quickly.
Let the red stream flow and bear him home
to the home he never hoped to see[46]—Justice,
lead him in!
      Leave all the rest to me.
The spirit within me never yields to sleep.   905
We will set things right, with the gods' help.
We will do whatever Fate requires.
AGAMEMNON.
      There
is Leda's daughter,[47] the keeper of my house.
And the speech to suit my absence, much too long.
But the praise that does us justice,   910
let it come from others, then we prize it.
      This—
You treat me like a woman, groveling, gaping up at me!
What am I, some barbarian peacocking out of Asia?
Never cross my path with robes and draw the lightning.
Never—only the gods deserve the pomps of honor   915
and the stiff brocades of fame. To walk on them . . .
I am human, and it makes my pulses stir
with dread.[48]
      Give me the tributes of a man

---

[46] A grim pun: both "the home in Argos he had lost hope of seeing again" and "the home (death) he hoped never to see."

[47] Clytaemnestra; she and Helen are half sisters, Leda being mother to both.

[48] Agamemnon feels (or perhaps feigns) reluctance to commit an act of *hubris*, the overweening pride of a man which will bring on angry retribution by the gods.

and not a god, a little earth to walk on,
not this gorgeous work.   920
There is no need to sound my reputation.
I have a sense of right and wrong, what's more—
heaven's proudest gift. Call no man blest
until he ends his life in peace, fulfilled.
If I can live by what I say, I have no fear.   925
CLYTAEMNESTRA.
One thing more. Be true to your ideals and tell me—
AGAMEMNON.
True to my ideals? Once I violate them I am lost.
CLYTAEMNESTRA.
Would you have sworn this act[49] to god in a time of terror?
AGAMEMNON.
Yes, if a prophet called for a last, drastic rite.
CLYTAEMNESTRA.
But Priam—can you see him if he had your success?   930
AGAMEMNON.
Striding on the tapestries of god, I see him now.
CLYTAEMNESTRA.
And *you* fear the reproach of common men?
AGAMEMNON.
The voice of the people—aye, they have enormous power.
CLYTAEMNESTRA.
Perhaps, but where's the glory without a little gall?[50]
AGAMEMNON.
And where's the woman in all this lust for glory?   935
CLYTAEMNESTRA.
But the great victor—it becomes him to give away.
AGAMEMNON.
Victory in this . . . war of ours, it means so much to you?
CLYTAEMNESTRA.
O give way! The power is yours[51] if you surrender
all of your own free will to me.
AGAMEMNON.
                                   Enough.
If you are so determined—   940

                         [*Turning to the women, pointing to
                         his boots.*]

Let someone help me off with these at least.
Old slaves, they've stood me well.

---

[49] Clytaemnestra refers to the act of walking on the splendid "red carpet." She also has in mind Agamemnon's willingness in the past to commit an outrage like the killing of his daughter when such an outrage served his purpose.

[50] Clytaemnestra implies that great men must be prepared to endure the "gall" of inferior men's envy.

[51] That is, "If you yield freely and magnanimously to my whim, it is you who will have overcome me" (in their little dispute, what Agamemnon calls "this . . . war of ours").

Hurry,
and while I tread his splendors dyed red in the sea,[52]
may no god watch and strike me down with envy
from on high. I feel such shame—   945
to tread the life of the house, a kingdom's worth
of silver in the weaving.

> [*He steps down from the chariot to
> the tapestries and reveals* CASSAN-
> DRA, *dressed in the sacred regalia,
> the fillets,*[53] *robes, and scepter of*
> APOLLO.]

Done is done.
Escort this stranger in, be gentle.
Conquer with compassion. Then the gods
shine down upon you, gently. No one chooses   950
the yoke of slavery, not of one's free will—
and she least of all. The gift of the armies,
flower and pride of all the wealth we won,
she follows me from Troy.
                                                            And now,
since you have brought me down with your insistence,   955
just this once I enter my father's house,
trampling royal crimson as I go.

> [*He takes his first steps and pauses.*]

CLYTAEMNESTRA.
                                                            There is the sea
and who will drain it dry? Precious as silver,[54]
inexhaustible, ever-new, it breeds the more we reap it—
tides on tides of crimson dye our robes blood-red.   960
Our lives are based on wealth, my king,
the gods have seen to that.
Destitution, our house has never heard the word.
I would have sworn to tread on legacies of robes,
at one command from an oracle, deplete the house—   965
suffer the worst to bring that dear life back!

> [*Encouraged,* AGAMEMNON *strides
> to the entrance.*]

When the root lives on, the new leaves come back,
spreading a dense shroud of shade across the house

---

[52] The red dye of the tapestry-carpet was derived from a kind of sea snail.

[53] Ribbons. Cassandra had been wooed by Apollo, the god of prophecy, but because she resisted him, she had been cursed with the gift of prophesying to hearers who would always refuse to believe her.

[54] The red fabric had silver woven into it.

to thwart the Dog Star's[55] fury. So you return
to the father's hearth, you bring us warmth in winter   970
like the sun—

And you are Zeus when Zeus
tramples the bitter virgin grape for new wine[56]
and the welcome chill steals through the halls, at last
the master moves among the shadows of his house, fulfilled.

[AGAMEMNON *goes over the threshold; the women gather up the tapestries while* CLYTAEMNESTRA *prays.*]

Zeus, Zeus, master of all fulfillment, now fulfill our prayers—   975
speed our rites to their fulfillment once for all!

[*She enters the palace, the doors
close, the old men huddle in terror.*]

CHORUS.
Why, why does it rock me,[57] never stops,
this terror beating down my heart,
            this seer that sees it all—
it beats its wings, uncalled unpaid   980
thrust on the lungs
the mercenary song beats on and on
singing a prophet's strain—
            and I can't throw it off
like dreams that make no sense,   985
and the strength drains
that filled the mind with trust,
and the years drift by and the driven sand
            has buried the mooring lines
that churned when the armored squadrons cut for Troy . . .   990
and now I believe it, I can prove he's home,
            my own clear eyes for witness—

Agamemnon!

Still it's chanting, beating deep so deep in the heart
this dirge of the Furies, oh dear god,
not fit for the lyre,[58] its own master   995
        it kills our spirit
kills our hopes
and it's real, true, no fantasy—
        stark terror whirls the brain

[55] The star Sirius, considered as a harbinger of killing heat, disease, and madness.
[56] An allusion to the shedding of the young Iphigeneia's blood.
[57] The anguished choral song that follows expresses two levels of awareness by the Chorus:
1) its consciousness of the old hereditary curse on the lineage of Atreus and 2) the more
immediate suspicion of Clytaemnestra based on the knowledge of her adulterous relationship
with Aegisthus.
[58] Not fit for joyous song.

and the end is coming
                    Justice comes to birth—   1000
I pray my fears prove false and fall
and die and never come to birth!
Even exultant health, well we know,
          exceeds its limits,[59] comes so near disease   1005
it can breach the wall between them.

Even a man's fate, held true on course,
          in a blinding flash rams some hidden reef;
but if caution only casts the pick of the cargo[60]—
one well-balanced cast—   1010
the house will not go down, not outright;
laboring under its wealth of grief
the ship of state rides on.

Yes, and the great green bounty of god,
sown in the furrows year by year and reaped each fall   1015
can end the plague of famine.

But a man's lifeblood
          is dark and mortal.
Once it wets the earth
what song can sing it back?   1020
Not even the master-healer[61]
          who brought the dead to life—
Zeus stopped the man before he did more harm.

Oh, if only the gods had never forged
the chain that curbs our excess,   1025
          one man's fate curbing the next man's fate,
my heart would outrace my song, I'd pour out all I feel—
                    but no, I choke with anguish,
          mutter through the nights.
Never to ravel out a hope in time   1030
and the brain is swarming, burning—

                              [CLYTAEMNESTRA *emerges from*
                              the palace and goes to CASSANDRA,
                              impassive in the chariot.]

CLYTAEMNESTRA.
     Won't you come inside? I mean you, Cassandra.
     Zeus in all his mercy wants you to share

---

[59] The principle of the golden mean, of steering between too little and too much, applies even to health, according to the Chorus.

[60] A ship in peril can be saved by jettisoning cargo so as to lighten it; similarly, a man may salvage his happiness and his "house" by forsaking his most prized wealth.

[61] Asclepios, a physician so gifted that he brought a dead man back to life. As punishment for thus violating the natural order, Zeus killed him with a thunderbolt.

some victory libations[62] with the house.
The slaves are flocking. Come, lead them   1035
up to the altar of the god who guards
our dearest treasures.
            Down from the chariot,
no time for pride. Why even Heracles,[63]
they say, was sold into bondage long ago,
he had to endure the bitter bread of slaves.   1040
But if the yoke descends on you, be grateful
for a master born and reared in ancient wealth.
Those who reap a harvest past their hopes[64]
are merciless to their slaves.
                From us
you will receive what custom says is right.   1045

            [CASSANDRA *remains impassive.*]

LEADER.
It's *you* she is speaking to, it's all too clear.
You're caught in the nets of doom—obey
if you can obey, unless you cannot bear to.
CLYTAEMNESTRA.
Unless she's like a swallow, possessed
of her own barbaric song, strange, dark.   1050
I speak directly as I can—she must obey.
LEADER.
Go with her. Make the best of it, she's right.
Step down from the seat, obey her.
CLYTAEMNESTRA.
               Do it *now*—
I have no time to spend outside. Already
the victims crowd the hearth, the Navelstone,[65]   1055
to bless this day of joy I never hoped to see!—
our victims[66] waiting for the fire and the knife,
and you,
if you want to taste our mystic rites, come now.
If my words can't reach you—

           [*Turning to the leader.*]

           Give her a sign,   1060
one of her exotic handsigns.

[62] Ritual pourings of liquids.
[63] The heroic Heracles (Hercules) had served as a slave to Omphale, queen of Lydia in Asia
Minor.
[64] Men whose wealth ("harvest") is not "ancient" but recent.
[65] Also the name of a stone at Apollo's shrine in Delphi; Orestes goes to that Navelstone, to
be purged of his blood-guilt, at the beginning of *The Eumenides.*
[66] The animals to be sacrificed in the ritual; but Clytaemnestra's statement has also a more
sinister private meaning.

LEADER.
                                   I think
the stranger needs an interpreter, someone clear.
She's like a wild creature, fresh caught.
CLYTAEMNESTRA.
                                              She's mad,
her evil genius murmuring in her ears.
She comes from a *city* fresh caught.   1065
She must learn to take the cutting bridle
before she foams her spirit off in blood—
and that's the last I waste on her contempt!

> [*Wheeling, re-entering the palace.
> The leader turns to* CASSANDRA,
> *who remains transfixed.*]

LEADER.
    Not I, I pity her. I will be gentle.
    Come, poor thing. Leave the empty chariot—   1070
    Of your own free will try on the yoke of Fate.

CASSANDRA.
    Aieeeeee! Earth—Mother—
                        Curse of the Earth—Apollo Apollo!
LEADER.
    Why cry to Apollo?
    He's not the god to call with sounds of mourning.
CASSANDRA.
    Aieeeeee! Earth—Mother—   1075
                        Rape of the Earth—Apollo Apollo!
LEADER.
    Again, it's a bad omen.
    She cries for the god who wants no part of grief.[67]

> [CASSANDRA *steps from the chariot,
> looks slowly toward the rooftops of
> the palace.*]

CASSANDRA.
    God of the long road,
                Apollo *Apollo* my destroyer—
    you destroy me once, destroy me twice—   1080
LEADER.
    She's about to sense her own ordeal, I think.
    Slave that she is, the god lives on inside her.
CASSANDRA.
    God of the iron marches,
                Apollo *Apollo* my destroyer—
    where, where have you led me now? what house—   1085

---

[67] Apollo is more typically associated with joy.

LEADER.
    The house of Atreus and his sons. Really—
    don't you know? It's true, see for yourself.
CASSANDRA.
    No . . . the house that hates god,
            an echoing womb of guilt, kinsmen
                  torturing kinsmen, severed heads,   1090
    slaughterhouse of heroes, soil streaming blood—
LEADER.
    A keen hound, this stranger.
    Trailing murder, and murder she will find.
CASSANDRA.
    See, my witnesses—
            I trust to them, to the babies   1095
                  wailing, skewered on the sword,
    their flesh charred, the father gorging on their parts—
LEADER.
    We'd heard your fame as a seer,
    but no one looks for seers in Argos.
CASSANDRA.
    Oh no, what horror, what new plot,   1100
    new agony this?—
    it's growing, massing, deep in the house,
                a plot, a monstrous—*thing*
                    to crush the loved ones, no,
        there is no cure, and rescue's far away and—   1105
LEADER.
    I can't read these signs; I knew the first,[68]
    the city rings with them.
CASSANDRA.
    You, you godforsaken—you'd do *this*?
    The lord of your bed,
    you bathe him . . . his body glistens, then—   1110
                  how to tell the climax?—
                    comes so quickly, see,
    hand over hand shoots out, hauling ropes—
                         then lunge!
LEADER.
    Still lost. Her riddles, her dark words of god—
    I'm groping, helpless.
CASSANDRA.
                  No no, look *there*!—   1115
    what's that? some net flung out of hell—
        No, *she* is the snare,
    the bedmate, deathmate, murder's strong right arm!
             Let the insatiate discord in the race
    rear up and shriek "Avenge the victim—stone them dead!"   1120

---

[68]The Leader had understood Cassandra's earlier reference to the familiar story of
Thyestes' feast but does not understand her allusion to the imminent murder of Agamemnon.

LEADER.
   What Fury is this? Why rouse it, lift its wailing
   through the house? I hear you and lose hope.
CHORUS.
   Drop by drop at the heart, the gold of life ebbs out.
       We are the old soldiers . . . wounds will come
   with the crushing sunset of our lives.   1125
   Death is close, and quick.
CASSANDRA.
                             Look out! *look out!*—
   Ai, drag the great bull from the mate!—
       a thrash of robes, she traps him—
   writhing—
              black horn glints, twists—
                                 she gores him through!
           And now he buckles, look, the bath swirls red—   1130
   There's stealth and murder in that caldron, do you hear?
LEADER.
   I'm no judge, I've little skill with the oracles,
   but even I know danger when I hear it.
CHORUS.
   What good are the oracles to men? Words, more words,
       and the hurt comes on us, endless words   1135
   and a seer's techniques have brought us
   terror and the truth.
CASSANDRA.
   The agony—O I am breaking!—Fate's so hard,
       and the pain that floods my voice is mine alone.
   Why have you brought me here, tormented as I am?   1140
   Why, unless to die with him, why else?
LEADER AND CHORUS.
   Mad with the rapture—god speeds you on
       to the song, the deathsong,
   like the nightingale[69] that broods on sorrow,
       mourns her son, her son,   1145
   her life inspired with grief for him,
   she lilts and shrills, dark bird that lives for night.
CASSANDRA.
   The nightingale—O for a song, a fate like hers!
       The gods gave her a life of ease, swathed her in wings,
   no tears, no wailing. The knife waits for me.   1150
   They'll splay me on the iron's double edge.
LEADER AND CHORUS.
   Why?—what god hurls you on, stroke on stroke
       to the long dying fall?

[69] Tereus, husband of Procne, raped his wife's sister Philomela. In revenge, after being
informed of the rape by her sister, Procne killed Itys, her son by Tereus, and served the son's
flesh as a meal for the father. In some versions of the myth Procne was later metamorphosed
into a nightingale, Philomela into a swallow. (In other versions the metamorphoses are reversed, Procne becoming the swallow and Philomela the nightingale.)

Why the horror clashing through your music,
    terror struck to song?—   1155
why the anguish, the wild dance?
Where do your words of god and grief begin?

CASSANDRA.
Ai, the wedding, wedding of Paris,
death to the loved ones. Oh Scamander,[70]
you nursed my father . . . once at your banks   1160
    I nursed and grew, and now at the banks
of Acheron,[71] the stream that carries sorrow,
it seems I'll chant my prophecies too soon.

LEADER AND CHORUS.
    What are you saying? Wait, it's clear,
a child could see the truth, it wounds within,   1165
                      like a bloody fang it tears—
      I hear your destiny—breaking sobs,
                  cries that stab the ears.

CASSANDRA.
Oh the grief, the grief of the city
ripped to oblivion. Oh the victims,   1170
the flocks my father burned at the wall,
    rich herds in flames . . . no cure for the doom
that took the city after all, and I,
her last ember, I go down with her.

LEADER AND CHORUS.
    You cannot stop, your song goes on—   1175
some spirit drops from the heights and treads you down
                 and the brutal strain grows—
      your death-throes come and come and
               I cannot see the end!

CASSANDRA.
Then off with the veils that hid the fresh young bride—   1180
we will see the truth.
Flare up once more, my oracle! Clear and sharp
as the wind that blows toward the rising sun,
I can feel a deeper swell now, gathering head
to break at last and bring the dawn of grief.   1185

No more riddles. I will teach you.
Come, bear witness, run and hunt with me.
We trail the old barbaric works of slaughter.

These roofs—look up—there is a dancing troupe
that never leaves. And they have their harmony   1190
but it is harsh, their words are harsh, they drink
beyond the limit. Flushed on the blood of men
their spirit grows and none can turn away
their revel breeding in the veins—the Furies!

[70] A river at Troy.   [71] A river in Hades, the underground world of the dead.

They cling to the house for life. They sing,   1195
sing of the frenzy that began it all,
strain rising on strain, showering curses
on the man who tramples on his brother's bed.[72]

There. Have I hit the mark or not? Am I a fraud,
a fortune-teller babbling lies from door to door?   1200
Swear how well I know the ancient crimes
that live within this house.
LEADER.
                              And if I did?
Would an oath bind the wounds and heal us?
But you amaze me. Bred across the sea,
your language strange and still you sense the truth   1205
as if you had been here.
CASSANDRA.
                         Apollo the Prophet
introduced me to his gift.
LEADER.
    A *god*—and moved with love?
CASSANDRA.
    I was ashamed to tell this once,
    but now . . .
LEADER.
                   We spoil ourselves with scruples,   1210
    long as things go well.
CASSANDRA.
                          He came like a wrestler,
magnificent, took me down and breathed his fire
    through me and—
LEADER.
                      You bore him a child?
CASSANDRA.
                                        I yielded,
then at the climax I recoiled—I deceived Apollo!
LEADER.
    But the god's skills—they seized you even then?   1215
CASSANDRA.
    Even then I told my people all the grief to come.
LEADER.
    And Apollo's anger never touched you?—is it possible?
CASSANDRA.
    Once I betrayed him I could never be believed.
LEADER.
    We believe you. Your visions seem so true.
CASSANDRA.
                                        Aieeee!—

---

[72]Thyestes had provoked Atreus' anger by seducing his wife, thus bringing on Atreus'
revenge and the lineal curse.

the pain, the terror! the birth-pang of the seer   1220
who tells the truth—
                              it whirls me, oh,
the storm comes again, the crashing chords!

Look, you see them nestling at the threshold?
Young, young in the darkness like a dream,
like children really, yes, and their loved ones   1225
brought them down . . .
                              their hands, they fill their hands
with their own flesh, they are serving it like food,
holding out their entrails . . . now it's clear,
I can see the armfuls of compassion, see the father
reach to taste and—
                              For so much suffering,   1230
I tell you, someone plots revenge.
A lion[73] who lacks a lion's heart,
he sprawled at home in the royal lair
and set a trap for the lord on his return.
My lord . . . I must wear his yoke, I am his slave.   1235
The lord of the men-of-war, he obliterated Troy—
he is so blind, so lost to that detestable hellhound[74]
who pricks her ears and fawns and her tongue draws out
her glittering words of welcome—
                              No, he cannot see
the stroke that Fury's hiding, stealth, murder.   1240
What outrage—the woman kills the man!
                              What to call
that . . . monster of Greece, and bring my quarry down?
Viper coiling back and forth?
                              Some sea-witch?—
Scylla[75] crouched in her rocky nest—nightmare of sailors?
Raging mother of death, storming deathless war against   1245
the ones she loves!
                              And how she howled in triumph,
boundless outrage. Just as the tide of battle
broke her way, she seems to rejoice that he
is safe at home from war, saved for her.

Believe me if you will. What will it matter   1250
if you won't? It comes when it comes,
and soon you'll see it face to face
and say the seer was all too true.
You will be moved with pity.
LEADER.
                              Thyestes' feast,

[73] The "lion" is Aegisthus.   [74] Clytaemnestra.

[75] A female monster, imagined as dwelling in a cave, personifying the dangerous rocks on one side of the strait of Messina, which separates Italy from Sicily. She is described in both Homer's *Odyssey* and Virgil's *Aeneid*.

the children's flesh—that I know,   1255
and the fear shudders through me. It's true,
real, no dark signs about it. I hear the rest
but it throws me off the scent.
CASSANDRA.

                                    Agamemnon.
You will see him dead.
LEADER.

                            Peace, poor girl!
Put those words to sleep.
CASSANDRA.

                                    No use,   1260
the Healer[76] has no hand in this affair.
LEADER.
Not if it's true—but god forbid it is!
CASSANDRA.
You pray, and they close in to kill!
LEADER.
What man prepares this, this dreadful—
CASSANDRA.

                                            Man?
You *are* lost, to every word I've said.[77]
LEADER.

                            Yes—   1265
I don't see who can bring the evil off.
CASSANDRA.
And yet I know my Greek, too well.
LEADER.
So does the Delphic oracle,
but he's hard to understand.
CASSANDRA.

                            His *fire*!—
sears me, sweeps me again—the torture!   1270
Apollo Lord of the Light, you burn,
you blind me—
                    Agony!
                                    She is the lioness,
she rears on her hind legs, she beds with the wolf
when her lion king goes ranging—
                                            she will kill me—
Ai, the torture!
                            She is mixing her drugs,   1275
adding a measure more of hate for me.
She gloats as she whets the sword for him.
He brought me home and we will pay in carnage.

---

[76] Apollo.   [77] Cassandra means that she has been referring to a woman, not a man.

Why mock yourself with these—trappings, the rod,
the god's wreath, his yoke around my throat?   1280
Before I die I'll tread you—

> [*Ripping off her regalia, stamping it into the ground.*]

                    Down, out,
die die die!
Now you're down. I've paid you back.
Look for another victim—I am free at last—
make her rich in all your curse and doom.

> [*Staggering backward as if wrestling with a spirit tearing at her robes.*]

                              See,   1285
Apollo himself, his fiery hands—I feel him again,
he's stripping off my robes, the Seer's robes!
And after he looked down and saw me mocked,
even in these, his glories, mortified by friends[78]
I loved, and they hated me, they were so blind   1290
to their own demise—

                    I went from door to door,
I was wild with the god, I heard them call me
"Beggar! Wretch! Starve for bread in hell!"

And I endured it all, and now he will
extort me as his due. A seer for the Seer.   1295
He brings me here to die like this,
not to serve at my father's altar. No,
the block is waiting. The cleaver steams
with my life blood, the first blood drawn
for the king's last rites.

> [*Regaining her composure and moving to the altar.*]

                    We will die,   1300
but not without some honor from the gods.
There will come another[79] to avenge us,
born to kill his mother, born
his father's champion. A wanderer, a fugitive
driven off his native land, he will come home   1305
to cope the stones of hate that menace all he loves.
The gods have sworn a monumental oath: as his father lies
upon the ground he draws him home with power like a prayer.

[78] The Trojans; Cassandra's own people did not heed her.
[79] Orestes, son of Agamemnon and Clytaemnestra.

Then why so pitiful, why so many tears?
I have seen my city faring as she fared,   1310
and those who took her, judged by the gods,
faring as they fare. I must be brave.
It is my turn to die.

                                    [*Approaching the doors.*]

I address you as the Gates of Death.
I pray it comes with one clean stroke,   1315
no convulsions, the pulses ebbing out
in gentle death. I'll close my eyes and sleep.
LEADER.
    So much pain, poor girl, and so much truth,
    you've told so much. But if you *see* it coming,
    clearly—how can you go to your own death,   1320
    like a beast to the altar driven on by god,
    and hold your head so high?
CASSANDRA.
                            No escape, my friends,
    not now.
LEADER.
        But the last hour should be savored.
CASSANDRA.
    My time has come. Little to gain from flight.
LEADER.
    You're brave, believe me, full of gallant heart.   1325
CASSANDRA.
    Only the wretched go with praise like that.
LEADER.
    But to go nobly lends a man some grace.
CASSANDRA.
    My noble father—you and your noble children.

                                    [*She nears the threshold and recoils,
                                    groaning in revulsion.*]

LEADER.
    What now? what terror flings you back?
    Why? Unless some horror in the brain—
CASSANDRA.
                                    Murder.   1330
    The house breathes with murder—bloody shambles![80]
LEADER.
    No, no, only the victims at the hearth.
CASSANDRA.
    I know that odor. I smell the open grave.

---

[80] A place of bloodshed; a slaughterhouse.

LEADER.
But the Syrian myrrh, it fills the halls with splendor,
can't you sense it?
CASSANDRA.
                              Well, I must go in now,   1335
mourning Agamemnon's death and mine.
Enough of life!

                    [*Approaching the doors again and
                    crying out.*]
              Friends—I cried out,
not from fear like a bird fresh caught,
but that you will testify to *how* I died.
When the queen, woman for woman, dies for me,   1340
and a man falls for the man who married grief.
That's all I ask, my friends. A stranger's gift
for one about to die.
LEADER.
                    Poor creature, you
and the end you see so clearly. I pity you.
CASSANDRA.
I'd like a few words more, a kind of dirge,   1345
it is my own. I pray to the sun,
the last light I'll see,
that when the avengers cut the assassins down
they will avenge me too, a slave who died,
an easy conquest.
                    Oh men, your destiny.   1350
When all is well a shadow can overturn it.
When trouble comes a stroke of the wet sponge,
and the picture's blotted out. And that,
I think that breaks the heart.

                    [*She goes through the doors.*]
CHORUS.
But the lust for power never dies—   1355
     men cannot have enough.
No one will lift a hand to send it
from his door, to give it warning,
"Power, never come again!"
Take this man: the gods in glory   1360
gave him Priam's city to plunder,
brought him home in splendor like a god.
But now if he must pay for the blood
his fathers shed, and die for the deaths
he brought to pass, and bring more death   1365
to avenge his dying, show us one
     who boasts himself born free
of the raging angel, once he hears—

[*Cries break out within the palace.*]

AGAMEMNON.

                                              Aagh!
Struck deep—the death-blow, deep—
LEADER.

                                    Quiet. Cries,
but who? Someone's stabbed—
AGAMEMNON.

                              Aaagh, again . . .   1370
second blow—struck home.
LEADER.

                        The work is done,
you can feel it. The king, and the great cries—
Close ranks now, find the right way out.

                              [*But the old men scatter, each speaks
                              singly.*]

CHORUS.
 —I say send out heralds, muster the guard,
    they'll save the house.

                              —And I say rush in now,   1375
  catch them red-handed—butchery running on their blades.

 —Right with you, do something—now or never!

 —Look at them, beating the drum for insurrection.

                                              —Yes,
  we're wasting time. They rape the name of caution,
    their hands will never sleep.

                              —Not a plan in sight.   1380
  Let men of action do the planning too.

 —I'm helpless. Who can raise the dead with words?

 —What, drag out our lives? bow down to the tyrants,
    the ruin of the house?

                    —Never, better to die
  on your feet than live on your knees.

                              —Wait,   1385
  do we take the cries for signs, prophesy like seers
    and give him up for dead?

                    —No more suspicions,
  not another word till we have proof.

—Confusion
on all sides—one thing to do. See how it stands
with Agamemnon, once and for all we'll see—   1390

> [*He rushes at the doors. They open
> and reveal a silver caldron that
> holds the body of* Agamemnon
> *shrouded in bloody robes, with the
> body of* Cassandra *to his left and*
> Clytaemnestra *standing to his
> right, sword in hand. She strides
> toward the chorus.*]

Clytaemnestra.
Words, endless words I've said to serve the moment!
Now it makes me proud to tell the truth.
How else to prepare a death for deadly men
who seem to love you? How to rig the nets
of pain so high no man can overleap them?   1395

I brooded on this trial, this ancient blood feud
year by year. At last my hour came.
Here I stand and here I struck
and here my work is done.
I did it all. I don't deny it, no.   1400
He had no way to flee or fight his destiny—

> [*Unwinding the robes from* Aga-
> memnon's *body, spreading them be-
> fore the altar where the old men
> cluster around them, unified as a
> chorus once again.*]

our never-ending, all-embracing net, I cast it
wide for the royal haul, I coil him round and round
in the wealth, the robes of doom, and then I strike him
once, twice, and at each stroke he cries in agony—   1405
he buckles at the knees and crashes here!
And when he's down I add the third, last blow,
to the Zeus who saves the dead beneath the ground
I send that third blow home in homage like a prayer.

So he goes down, and the life is bursting out of him—   1410
great sprays of blood, and the murderous shower
wounds me, dyes me black and I, I revel
like the Earth when the spring rains come down,
the blessed gifts of god, and the new green spear
splits the sheath and rips to birth in glory!   1415

So it stands, elders of Argos gathered here.
Rejoice if you can rejoice—I glory.

And if I'd pour upon his body the libation
it deserves, what wine could match my words?
It is right and more than right. He flooded   1420
the vessel of our proud house with misery,
with the vintage of the curse and now
he drains the dregs. My lord is home at last.

LEADER.
You appall me, you, your brazen words—
exulting over your fallen king.

CLYTAEMNESTRA.
                                                And you,   1425
you try me like some desperate woman.
My heart is steel, well you know. Praise me,
blame me as you choose. It's all one.
Here is Agamemnon, my husband made a corpse
by this right hand—a masterpiece of Justice.   1430
Done is done.

CHORUS.
                    Woman!—what poison cropped from the soil
or strained from the heaving sea, what nursed you,
drove you insane? You brave the curse of Greece.
        You have cut away and flung away and now
the people cast you off to exile,   1435
broken with our hate.

CLYTAEMNESTRA.
                            And now you sentence me?—
you banish *me* from the city, curses breathing
down my neck? But *he*—
name one charge you brought against him then.
He thought no more of it than killing a beast,   1440
and his flocks were rich, teeming in their fleece,
but he sacrificed his own child, our daughter,
the agony I labored into love
to charm away the savage winds of Thrace.

Didn't the law demand you banish him?—   1445
hunt him from the land for all his guilt?
But now you witness what I've done
and you are ruthless judges.
                                    Threaten away!
I'll meet you blow for blow. And if I fall
the throne is yours. If god decrees the reverse,   1450
late as it is, old men, you'll learn your place.

CHORUS.
    Mad with ambition,
                    shrilling pride!—some Fury
crazed with the carnage rages through your brain—
                    I can see the flecks of blood inflame your eyes!   1455
But vengeance comes—you'll lose your loved ones,
stroke for painful stroke.

CLYTAEMNESTRA.
  Then learn this too, the power of my oaths.
  By the child's Rights I brought to birth,
  by Ruin, by Fury—the three gods to whom   1460
  I sacrificed this man—I swear my hopes
  will never walk the halls of fear so long
  as Aegisthus lights the fire on my hearth.
  Loyal to me as always, no small shield
  to buttress my defiance.
                              Here he lies.   1465
  He brutalized me. The darling of all
  the golden girls who spread the gates of Troy.
  And here his spearprize . . . what wonders she beheld!—
  the seer of Apollo shared my husband's bed,
  his faithful mate who knelt at the rowing-benches,   1470
  worked by every hand.
                              They have their rewards.
  He as you know. And she, the swan[81] of the gods
  who lived to sing her latest, dying song—
  his lover lies beside him.
  She brings a fresh, voluptuous relish to my bed!   1475
CHORUS.
  Oh quickly, let me die—
  no bed of labor, no, no wasting illness . . .
  bear me off in the sleep that never ends,
              now that he has fallen,
  now that our dearest shield lies battered—   1480
      Woman made him suffer,
                  woman struck him down.

  Helen the wild, maddening Helen,
  one for the many, the thousand lives
  you murdered under Troy. Now you are crowned   1485
  with this consummate wreath, the blood
  that lives in memory, glistens age to age.
  Once in the halls she walked and she was war,
  angel of war, angel of agony, lighting men to death.
CLYTAEMNESTRA.
  Pray no more for death, broken   1490
  as you are. And never turn
      your wrath on her, call her
  the scourge of men, the one alone
  who destroyed a myriad Greek lives—
  Helen the grief that never heals.   1495
CHORUS.
  The *spirit!*—you who tread
  the house and the twinborn sons[82] of Tantalus—

[81] In folklore, the swan sings for the first and last time just before its death.
[82] "Sons" can refer either to Tantalus' grandsons, Thyestes and Atreus, or to his great-grandsons, Agamemnon and Menelaus, who married the sisters Clytaemnestra and Helen.

you empower the sisters, Fury's twins
        whose power tears the heart!
Perched on the corpse your carrion raven   1500
      glories in her hymn,
               her screaming hymn of pride.

CLYTAEMNESTRA.
    Now you set your judgment straight,
    you summon *him!* Three generations
        feed the spirit in the race.   1505
    Deep in the veins he feeds our bloodlust—
    aye, before the old wound dies
    it ripens in another flow of blood.
CHORUS.
    The great curse of the house, the spirit,
        dead weight wrath—and you can praise it!   1510
    Praise the insatiate doom that feeds
    relentless on our future and our sons.
    Oh all through the will of Zeus,
    the cause of all, the one who works it all.
        What comes to birth that is not Zeus?   1515
    Our lives are pain, what part not come from god?

    Oh my king, my captain,
    how to salute you, how to mourn you?
    What can I say with all my warmth and love?
    Here in the black widow's web you lie,   1520
    gasping out your life
    in a sacrilegious death, dear god,
    reduced to a slave's bed,
    my king of men, yoked by stealth and Fate,
    by the wife's hand that thrust the two-edged sword.   1525
CLYTAEMNESTRA.
    You claim the work is mine, call me
    Agamemnon's wife—you are so wrong.
    Fleshed in the wife of this dead man,
        the spirit lives within me,
    our savage ancient spirit of revenge.   1530
    In return for Atreus' brutal feast
    he kills his perfect son—for every
    murdered child, a crowning sacrifice.
CHORUS.
    And *you,* innocent of his murder?
        And who could swear to that? and how? . . .   1535
    and still an avenger could arise,
    bred by the fathers' crimes, and lend a hand.
    He wades in the blood of brothers,
    stream on mounting stream—black war erupts
        and where he strides revenge will stride,   1540
    clots will mass for the young who were devoured.

Oh my king, my captain,
how to salute you, how to mourn you?
What can I say with all my warmth and love?
Here in the black widow's web you lie,   1545
gasping out your life
in a sacrilegious death, dear god,
reduced to a slave's bed,
my king of men, yoked by stealth and Fate,
by the wife's hand that thrust the two-edged sword.   1550

CLYTAEMNESTRA.

No slave's death, I think—
no stealthier than the death he dealt
our house and the offspring of our loins,
          Iphigeneia, girl of tears.
Act for act, wound for wound!   1555
Never exult in Hades, swordsman,
here you are repaid. By the sword
you did your work and by the sword you die.

CHORUS.

          The mind reels—where to turn?
     All plans dashed, all hope! I cannot think . . .   1560
the roofs are toppling, I dread the drumbeat thunder
the heavy rains of blood will crush the house
          the first light rains are over—
     Justice brings new acts of agony, yes,
on new grindstones Fate is grinding sharp the sword of Justice.   1565

Earth, dear Earth,
if only you'd drawn me under
long before I saw him huddled
in the beaten silver bath.
Who will bury him, lift his dirge?   1570

          [*Turning to* CLYTAEMNESTRA.]

You, can you dare *this*?
To kill your lord with your own hand
then mourn his soul with tributes, terrible tributes—
do his enormous works a great dishonor.
This godlike man, this hero. Who at the grave   1575
will sing his praises, pour the wine of tears?
Who will labor there with truth of heart?

CLYTAEMNESTRA.

This is no concern of yours.
The hand that bore and cut him down
will hand him down to Mother Earth.
This house will never mourn for him.   1580
          Only our daughter Iphigeneia,
by all rights, will rush to meet him
first at the churning straits,

the ferry[83] over tears—   1585
she'll fling her arms around her father,
pierce him with her love.

CHORUS.
     Each charge meets countercharge.
    None can judge between them. Justice.
   The plunderer plundered, the killer pays the price.   1590
The truth still holds while Zeus still holds the throne:
    the one who acts must suffer—
  that is law. Who, who can tear from the veins
the bad seed, the curse? The race is welded to its ruin.

CLYTAEMNESTRA.
  At last you see the future and the truth!   1595
But I will swear a pact with the spirit
born within us. I embrace his works,
cruel as they are but done at last,
   if he will leave our house[84]
in the future, bleed another line   1600
with kinsmen murdering kinsmen.
Whatever he may ask. A few things
are all I need, once I have purged
our fury to destroy each other—
   purged it from our halls.

         [AEGISTHUS *has emerged from the*
         palace with his bodyguard and
         stands triumphant over the body of
         AGAMEMNON.]

AEGISTHUS.
        O what a brilliant day   1605
it is for vengeance! Now I can say once more
there are gods in heaven avenging men,
blazing down on all the crimes of earth.
Now at last I see this man brought down
in the Furies' tangling robes. It feasts my eyes—   1610
he pays for the plot his father's hand contrived.

Atreus, this man's father, was king of Argos.
My father, Thyestes—let me make this clear—
Atreus' brother challenged him for the crown,
and Atreus drove him out of house and home   1615
then lured him back, and home Thyestes came,
poor man, a suppliant to his own hearth,
to pray that Fate might save him.
        So it did.
There was no dying, no staining our native ground

---

[83] The boat in which Charon ferried the dead across the river Styx to Hades.
[84] As the later plays of the trilogy show, there is sad irony in Clytaemnestra's hope that her
deed of revenge will have ended the chain of retributive acts.

with *his* blood. Thyestes was the guest, 1620
and this man's godless father—

[*Pointing to* AGAMEMNON.]

the zeal of the host outstripping a brother's love,
made my father a feast that seemed a feast for gods,
a love feast of his children's flesh.
He cuts
the extremities, feet and delicate hands 1625
into small pieces, scatters them over the dish
and serves it to Thyestes throned on high.
He picks at the flesh he cannot recognize,
the soul of innocence eating the food of ruin—
look,

[*Pointing to the bodies at his feet.*]

that feeds upon the house! And then, 1630
when he sees the monstrous thing he's done, he shrieks,
he reels back head first and vomits up that butchery,
tramples the feast—brings down the curse of Justice:
"Crash to ruin, all the race of Pleisthenes,[85] crash down!"

So you see him, down. And I, the weaver of Justice, 1635
plotted out the kill. Atreus drove us into exile,
my struggling father and I, a babe-in-arms,
his last son, but I became a man
and Justice brought me home. I was abroad
but I reached out and seized my man, 1640
link by link I clamped the fatal scheme
together. Now I could die gladly, even I—
now I see this monster in the nets of Justice.

LEADER.
Aegisthus, you revel in pain—you sicken me.
You say you killed the king in cold blood, 1645
singlehanded planned his pitiful death?
I say there's no escape. In the hour of judgment,
trust to this, your head will meet the people's
rocks and curses.

AEGISTHUS.
You say! you slaves at the oars—
while the master on the benches cracks the whip? 1650
You'll learn, in your late age, how much it hurts
to teach old bones their place. We have techniques—
chains and the pangs of hunger,
two effective teachers, excellent healers.
They can even cure old men of pride and gall. 1655

---

[85] Apparently an ancestor of Agamemnon, his exact identity is vague.

Look—can't you see? The more you kick
against the pricks, the more you suffer.
LEADER.
   You, pathetic—
the king had just returned from battle.
You waited out the war and fouled his lair,   1660
you planned my great commander's fall.
AEGISTHUS.

                         Talk on—
you'll scream for every word, my little Orpheus.[86]
We'll see if the world comes dancing to your song,
your absurd barking—snarl your breath away!
I'll make you dance, I'll bring you all to heel.   1665
LEADER.
   You rule Argos? You who schemed his death
but cringed to cut him down with your own hand?
AEGISTHUS.
   The treachery was the woman's work, clearly.
I was a marked man, his enemy for ages.
But I will use his riches, stop at nothing   1670
to civilize his people. All but the rebel:
him I'll yoke and break—
no cornfed colt, running free in the traces.
Hunger, ruthless mate of the dark torture-chamber,
trains her eyes upon him till he drops!   1675
LEADER.
   Coward, why not kill the man yourself?
Why did the woman, the corruption of Greece
and the gods of Greece, have to bring him down?
Orestes—
          If he still sees the light of day,
bring him home, good Fates, home to kill   1680
this pair at last. Our champion in slaughter!
AEGISTHUS.
   Bent on insolence? Well, you'll learn, quickly.
At them, men—you have your work at hand!

                 [*His men draw swords; the old men
                    take up their sticks.*]

LEADER.
   At them, fist at the hilt, to the last man—
AEGISTHUS.
   Fist at the hilt, I'm not afraid to die.   1685
LEADER.
   It's death you want and death you'll have—
we'll make that word your last.

---

[86] The archetypal poet-musician whose song compelled even nature to listen. See Ovid's
Metamorphoses, Book X.

[CLYTAEMNESTRA *moves between
them, restraining* AEGISTHUS.]

CLYTAEMNESTRA.

No more, my dearest,
no more grief. We have too much to reap
right here, our mighty harvest of despair.
Our lives are based on pain. No bloodshed now.   1690

Fathers of Argos, turn for home before you act
and suffer for it. What we did was destiny.
If we could end the suffering, how we would rejoice.
The spirit's brutal hoof has struck our heart.
And that is what a woman has to say.   1695
Can you accept the truth?

[CLYTAEMNESTRA *turns to leave.*]

AEGISTHUS.

But these . . . mouths
that bloom in filth—spitting insults in my teeth.
You tempt your fates, you insubordinate dogs—
to hurl abuse at me, your master!

LEADER.

No Greek
worth his salt would grovel at your feet.   1700

AEGISTHUS.

I—I'll stalk you all your days!

LEADER.

Not if the spirit brings Orestes home.

AEGISTHUS.

Exiles feed on hope—well I know.

LEADER.

More,
gorge yourself to bursting—soil justice, while you can.

AEGISTHUS.

I promise you, you'll pay, old fools—in good time too!   1705

LEADER.

Strut on your own dunghill, you cock beside your mate.

CLYTAEMNESTRA.

Let them howl—they're impotent. You and I have power now.
We will set the house in order once for all.

[*They enter the palace; the great
doors close behind them; the old men
disband and wander off.*]

THE LIBATION BEARERS

CHARACTERS

ORESTES, *son of Agamemnon*   CLYTAEMNESTRA
   and Clytaemnestra   CILISSA, *Orestes' old nurse*
PYLADES, *his companion*   AEGISTHUS
ELECTRA, *his sister*   *A servant of Aegisthus*
CHORUS OF SLAVEWOMEN   *Attendants of Orestes,*
   AND THEIR LEADER   *bodyguard of Aegisthus*

TIME AND SCENE
*Several years have passed since Agamemnon's death. At Argos, before the tomb of
the king and his fathers, stands an altar; behind it looms the house of Atreus.*
ORESTES *and* PYLADES *enter, dressed as travelers.* ORESTES *kneels and prays.*

ORESTES.
   Hermes,[1] lord of the dead, look down and guard
   the fathers' power. Be my savior, I beg you,
   be my comrade now.
               I have come home
   to my own soil, an exile home at last.
   Here at the mounded grave I call my father,   5
   Hear me—I am crying out to you . . .

                           [*He cuts two locks of hair*[2] *and lays
                           them on the grave.*]

   There is a lock for Inachos[3] who nursed me
   into manhood, there is one for death.

   I was not here to mourn you when you died,
   my father, never gave the last salute   10
   when they bore your corpse away.

                           [ELECTRA *and a chorus of slave-
                           women enter in procession. They are
                           dressed in black and bear libations,
                           moving toward* ORESTES *at the
                           grave.*]

---

[1] The messenger of the gods, patron of human messengers and heralds. He also guided
the dead to Hades.
[2] The locks were customary ritual tributes to the dead.
[3] River at Argos; Orestes pays tribute to his original fatherland as well as to his dead father,
Agamemnon.

What's this?
Look, a company moving toward us. Women,
robed in black . . . so clear in the early light.

I wonder what they mean, what turn of fate?—
some new wound to the house? 15
Or perhaps they come to honor you, my father,
bearing cups to soothe and still the dead.
That's right, it must be . . .
Electra, I think I see *her* coming, there,
my own sister, worn, radiant in her grief— 20
Dear god, let me avenge my father's murder—
fight beside me now with all your might!

Out of their way, Pylades.[4] I must know
what they mean, these women turning toward us,
what their prayers call forth. 25

[*They withdraw behind the tomb.*]
CHORUS.[5]
Rushed from the house we come
  escorting cups for the dead,
in step with the hands' hard beat,
          our cheeks glistening,
flushed where the nails have raked new furrows running blood; 30
and life beats on, and through it all
we nurse our lives with tears,
to the sound of ripping linen beat our robes in sorrow,
      close to the breast the beats throb
and laughter's gone and fortune throbs and throbs. 35

Aie!—bristling Terror[6] struck—
  Terror the seer of the house,
the nightmare ringing clear
          breathed its wrath in sleep,
in the midnight watch a cry!—the voice of Terror 40
deep in the house, bursting down
on the women's darkened chambers, yes,
and the old ones, skilled at dreams, swore oaths to god and called,
      "The proud dead stir under earth,
they rage against the ones who took their lives." 45

---

[4] Son of Strophios, with whom the exiled Orestes had lived in Phokis after Clytaemnestra
sent him away (see the *Agamemnon*).
[5] The Chorus consists of women brought back from Troy as slaves. In the lament that
follows they express grief for both the house of Atreus and that of Troy.
[6] Clytaemnestra has been frightened by a nightmare; she has therefore sent the women to
Agamemnon's tomb with propitiatory libations (mixtures of honey and wine).

But the gifts, the empty gifts
          she hopes will ward them off—
good Mother Earth!—that godless woman sends me here . . .
          I dread to say her prayer.
What can redeem the blood that wets the soil?   50
Oh for the hearthfire banked with grief,
   the ramparts down, a fine house down—
dark, dark, and the sun, the life is curst,
     and mist enshrouds the halls
          where the lords of war went down.   55

And the ancient pride no war,
               no storm, no force could tame,
ringing in all men's ears, in all men's hearts is gone.
          They are afraid. Success,
they bow to success, more god than god himself.   60
But Justice waits and turns the scales:
     a sudden blow for some at dawn,
for some in the no man's land of dusk
     her torments grow with time,
          and the lethal night takes others.   65

And the blood that Mother Earth consumes
clots hard, it won't seep through, it breeds revenge
                         and frenzy goes through the guilty,
seething like infection, swarming through the brain.

For the one who treads a virgin's bed   70
there is no cure. All the streams of the world,
     all channels run into one
to cleanse a man's red hands will swell the bloody tide.

And I . . . Fate and the gods brought down their yoke,
they ringed our city, out of our fathers' halls   75
          they led us here as slaves.
And the will breaks, we kneel at their command—
               our masters right or wrong!
     And we beat the tearing hatred down,
          behind our veils we weep for her,   80

                    [*Turning to* ELECTRA.]

her senseless fate.
Sorrow turns the secret heart to ice.
ELECTRA.
                         Dear women,
you keep the house in order, best you can;
and now you've come to the grave to say a prayer
with me, my escorts. I'll need your help with this.   85
What to say when I pour the cup of sorrow?

[*Lifting her libation cup.*]

What kindness, what prayer can touch my father?
Shall I say I bring him love for love, a woman's
love for husband? My mother, love from her?
I've no taste for that, no words to say   90
as I run the honeyed oil on father's tomb.

Or try the salute we often use at graves?
"A wreath for a wreath. Now bring the givers
gifts to match" . . . no, give them pain for pain.[7]

Or silent, dishonored, just as father died,   95
empty it out for the soil to drink and then
retrace my steps, like a slave sent out with scourings
left from the purging of the halls, and throw
the cup behind me, looking straight ahead.

Help me decide, my friends. Join me here.   100
We nurse a common hatred in the house.
Don't hide your feelings—no, fear no one.
Destiny waits us all,

[*Looking toward the tomb.*]

        born free,
or slaves who labor under another's hand.
Speak to me, please. Perhaps you've had   105
a glimpse of something better.
LEADER.
               I revere
your father's death-mound like an altar.
I'll say a word, now that you ask,
that comes from deep within me.
ELECTRA.
              Speak on,
with everything you feel for father's grave.   110
LEADER.
Say a blessing as you pour, for those who love you.
ELECTRA.
And of the loved ones, whom to call my friends?
LEADER.
First yourself, then all who hate Aegisthus.
ELECTRA.
I and you. I can say a prayer for us
and then for—
LEADER.
        You know, try to say it.   115

---

[7] Electra possibly means "pain for the murderers to match the pain they gave my father."

ELECTRA.
There is someone else to rally to our side?
LEADER.
Remember Orestes, even abroad and gone.
ELECTRA.
Well said, the best advice I've had.
LEADER.
Now for the murderers. Remember them and—
ELECTRA.
                                             What?

I'm so unseasoned, teach me what to say.   120
LEADER.
Let some god or man come down upon them.
ELECTRA.
Judge or avenger, which?
LEADER.
Just say "the one who murders in return!"
ELECTRA.
How can I ask the gods for that
and keep my conscience clear?
LEADER.
                         How not,   125
and pay the enemy back in kind?

                          [ELECTRA *kneels at the grave in
                          prayer.*]

ELECTRA.
                       —Herald king
of the world above and the quiet world below,
lord of the dead, my Hermes, help me now.
Tell the spirits underground to hear my prayers,
and the high watch hovering over father's roofs,   130
and have her listen too, the Earth herself
who brings all things to life and makes them strong,
then gathers in the rising tide once more.

And I will tip libations to the dead.
I call out to my father, Pity me,   135
dear Orestes too.
Rekindle the light that saves our house!
We're auctioned off, drift like vagrants now.
Mother has pawned us for a husband, Aegisthus,
her partner in her murdering.
                       I go like a slave,   140
Orestes driven from his estates while they,
they roll in the fruits of all your labors,
magnificent and sleek. O bring Orestes home,
with a happy twist of fate, my father. Hear me,

make me far more self-possessed than mother,   145
make this hand more pure.

These prayers for us. For our enemies I say,
Raise up your avenger, into the light, my father—
kill the killers in return, with justice!
So in the midst of prayers for good I place   150
this curse for them.
               Bring up your blessings,
up into the air, led by the gods and Earth
and all the rights that bring us triumph.

                        [*Pouring libations on the tomb and
                        turning to the women.*]

These are my prayers. Over them I pour libations.
Yours to adorn them with laments, to make them bloom,   155
so custom says—sing out and praise the dead.
CHORUS.
Let the tears fall, ring out and die,
           die with the warlord at this bank,
this bulwark of the good, defense against the bad,
the guilt, the curse we ward away   160
with prayer and all we pour. Hear me, majesty, hear me,
    lord of glory, from the darkness of your heart.
                       Ohhhhhh!—
       Dear god, let him come! Some man
with a strong spear, born to free the house,
    with the torsion bow of Scythia[8] bent for slaughter,   165
splattering shafts like a god of war—sword in fist
       for the slash-and-hack of battle!

                    [ELECTRA *remains at the grave,
                  staring at the ground.*]
ELECTRA.
                       Father,
you have it now, the earth has drunk your wine.
Wait, friends, here's news. Come share it.
LEADER.
                     Speak on,
my heart's a dance of fear.
ELECTRA.
                 A lock of hair,   170
here on the grave . . .
LEADER.
             Whose? A man's?
A growing girl's?

—————

[8] A region in southwest Asia, noted for its archers and their powerful bows.

ELECTRA.
               And it has the marks,
and anyone would think—
LEADER.
                     What?
We're old. You're young, now you teach us.
ELECTRA.
No one could have cut this lock but I and—   175
LEADER.
Callous they are, the ones who ought to shear
the hair and mourn.
ELECTRA.
            Look at the texture, just like—
LEADER.
Whose? I want to know.
ELECTRA.
              Like mine, identical,
can't you see?
LEADER.
         Orestes . . . he brought a gift
in secret?
ELECTRA.
      It's *his*—I can see his curls.   180
LEADER.
And how could he risk the journey here?
ELECTRA.
He sent it, true, a lock to honor father.
LEADER.
All the more cause for tears. You mean
he'll never set foot on native ground again.
ELECTRA.
                        Yes!

It's sweeping over me too—anguish   185
like a breaker—a sword ripping through my heart!
Tears come like the winter rains that flood the gates—
can't hold them back, when I see this strand of hair.

How could I think another Greek could play
the prince with this?
            She'd never cut it,   190
the murderess, my mother. She insults the name,
she and her godless spirit preying on her children.

But how, how can I come right out and say it *is*
the glory of the dearest man I know, Orestes?
Stop, I'm fawning on hope.
               Oh, if only   195
it had a herald's voice, kind and human—
I'm so shaken, torn—and told me clearly
to throw it away, they severed it from a head

that I detest. Or it could sorrow with me
like a brother, aye,   200
this splendor come to honor father's grave.

We call on the gods, and the gods well know
what storms torment us, sailors whirled to nothing.
But if we are to live and reach the haven,
one small seed could grow a mighty tree—   205
Look, tracks.
     A new sign to tell us more.
Footmarks . . . pairs of them, like mine.
Two outlines, two prints, his own, and there,
a fellow traveler's.

       [*Putting her foot into* ORESTES'
       print.]

    The heel, the curve of the arch
like twins.

       [*While* ORESTES *emerges from be-
       hind the grave, she follows cau-
       tiously in his steps until they come
       together.*]

   Step by step, my step in his . . .
         we meet—   210
Oh the pain, like pangs of labor—this is madness!
ORESTES.
Pray for the future. Tell the gods they've brought
your prayers to birth, and pray that we succeed.

       [ELECTRA *draws back, struggling
       for composure.*]

ELECTRA.
The gods—why now? What have I ever won from them?
ORESTES.
The sight you prayed to see for many years.   215
ELECTRA.
And you know the one I call?
ORESTES.
       I know Orestes,
know he moves you deeply.
ELECTRA.
      Yes,
but now what's come to fill my prayers?
ORESTES.
Here I am. Look no further.
No one loves you more than I.

ELECTRA.
                                        No,   220
    it's a trap, stranger . . . a net you tie around me?
ORESTES.
    Then I tie myself as well.
ELECTRA.
                            But the pain,
    you're laughing at all—
ORESTES.
                                        Your pain is mine.
    If I laugh at yours, I only laugh at mine.
ELECTRA.
    Orestes—   225
    can I call you?—are you really—
ORESTES.
                                        I am!
    Open your eyes. So slow to learn.
    You saw the lock of hair I cut in mourning.
    You scanned my tracks, you could see my marks,
    your breath leapt, you all but saw me in the flesh—   230
    Look—

                                        [*Holding the lock to his temple, then
                                        to* ELECTRA'S]

                put it where I cut it.
    It's your brother's. Try, it matches yours.

                                        [*Removing a strip of weaving from
                                        his clothing.*]

    Work of your own hand, you tamped the loom,
    look, there are wild creatures in the weaving.

                                        [*She kneels beside him, weeping; he
                                        lifts her to her feet and they em-
                                        brace.*]

    No, no, control yourself—don't lose yourself in joy!   235
    Our loved ones, well I know, would slit our throats.
LEADER.
    Dearest, the darling of your father's house,
    hope of the seed we nursed with tears—you save us.
    Trust to your power, win your father's house once more!
ELECTRA.
    You light to my eyes, four loves in one!   240
    I have to call you father, it is fate;
    and I turn to you the love I gave my mother—
    I despise her, she deserves it, yes,
    and the love I gave my sister,[9] sacrificed

---

[9] Iphigeneia, sacrificed at Aulis. See headnote to the *Oresteia*.

on the cruel sword, I turn to you.   245
You were my faith, my brother—
you alone restore my self-respect.

[*Praying.*]

Power and Justice, Saving Zeus, Third Zeus,[10]
almighty all in all, be with us now.
Orestes.
Zeus, Zeus, watch over all we do,   250
fledglings reft of the noble eagle father.
He died in the coils, the viper's dark embrace.
We are his orphans worn down with hunger,
weak, too young to haul the father's quarry
home to shelter.
                    Look down on us!   255
I and Electra too, I tell you, children
robbed of our father, both of us bound
in exile from our house.
                    And what a father—
a priest at sacrifice, he showered you
with honors. Put an end to his nestlings now   260
and who will serve you banquets rich as his?
Destroy the eagle's brood, you can never
send a sign that wins all men's belief.
Rot the stock of a proud dynastic tree—
it can never shore your altar steaming   265
with the oxen in the mornings.
                    Tend us—
we seem in ruins now, I know. Up from nothing
rear a house to greatness.
Leader.
                    Softly, children,
white hopes of your father's hearth. Someone
might hear you, children, charmed with his own voice   270
blurt all this out to the masters. Oh, just once
to see them—live bones crackling in the fire
spitting pitch!
Orestes.
                    Apollo will never fail me, no,
his tremendous power, his oracle charges me
to see this trial through.
                    I can still hear the god—   275
a high voice ringing with winters of disaster,
piercing the heart within me, warm and strong,
unless I hunt my father's murderers, cut them down
in their own style—they destroyed my birthright.

---

[10]Zeus in his role as savior. Compare the more material and pragmatic emphasis in the following prayer to Zeus by Orestes.

"Gore them like a bull!" he called, "or pay their debt   280
with your own life, one long career of grief."

He revealed[11] so much about us,
told how the dead take root beneath the soil,
they grow with hate and plague the lives of men.
He told of the leprous boils that ride the flesh,   285
their wild teeth gnawing the mother tissue, aye,
and a white scurf spreads like cancer over these,
and worse, he told how assaults of Furies spring
to life on the father's blood . . .
                                   You can *see* them—
the eyes burning, grim brows working over you in the dark—   290
the dark sword of the dead—your murdered kinsmen
pleading for revenge. And the madness haunts
the midnight watch, the empty terror shakes you,
harries, drives you on—an exile from your city—
a brazen whip will mutilate your back.   295

For such as us, no share in the winebowl,
no libations poured in love. You never see
your father's wrath but it pulls you from the altars.
There is no refuge, none to take you in.
A pariah, reviled, at long last you die,   300
withered in the grip of all this dying.

Such oracles are persuasive,
don't you think? And even if I am not convinced,
the rough work of the world is still to do.
So many yearnings meet and urge me on.   305
The god's commands. Mounting sorrow for father.
Besides, the lack of patrimony[12] presses hard;
and my compatriots, the glory of men
who toppled Troy with nerves of singing steel,
go at the beck and call of a brace of women.   310
Womanhearted he is[13]—if not, we'll soon see.

> [*The leader lights the altar fires.*
> ORESTES, ELECTRA *and the chorus*
> *gather for the invocation at the*
> *grave.*]

CHORUS.
          Powers of destiny, mighty queens of Fate!—
          by the will of Zeus your will be done,

---

[11] In the following lines Orestes describes the physical, psychological, and social ills that, according to Apollo's oracle, Orestes will have to endure if he does not avenge his father's murder.
[12] What Orestes ought rightfully to inherit.
[13] That is, Aegisthus, who now rules Argos with Clytaemnestra.

press on to the end now,
    Justice turns the wheel.   315
"Word for word, curse for curse
be born now," Justice thunders,
    hungry for retribution,
"stroke for bloody stroke be paid.
    The one who acts must suffer."   320
Three generations strong the word resounds.

ORESTES.
    Dear father, father of dread,
what can I do or say to reach you now?
    What breath can reach from here
to the bank where you lie moored at anchor?[14]   325
What light can match your darkness? None,
    but there is a kind of grace that comes
        when the tears revive a proud old house
and Atreus' sons, the warlords lost and gone.

LEADER.
    The ruthless jaws of the fire,[15]   330
    my child, can never tame the dead,
              his rage inflames his sons.
Men die and the voices rise, they light the guilty, true—
cries raised for the fathers, clear and just,
    will hunt their killers harried to the end.   335

ELECTRA.
    Then hear me now, my father,
it is my turn, my tears are welling now,
    as child by child we come
to the tomb and raise the dirge, my father.
Your grave receives a girl in prayer   340
and a man in flight, and we are one,
    and the pain is equal, whose is worse?
And who outwrestles death—what third last fall?[16]

CHORUS.
    But still some god, if he desires,
    may work our strains to a song of joy,   345
    from the dirges chanted over the grave
        may lift a hymn in the kings' halls
and warm the loving cup you stir this morning.

ORESTES.
    If only at Troy
a Lycian[17] cut you down, my father—   350
gone, with an aura left at home behind you,
    children to go their ways

[14] In the world of the dead; but the phrase calls up also the memory of the Greek fleet at Aulis, where Agamemnon had committed the outrage on Iphigeneia that ultimately brought on his murder.
[15] The fire in which the dead are cremated.
[16] The deciding round in a wrestling match.
[17] The Lycians fought in aid of the Trojans.

and the eyes look on them bright with awe,
and the tomb you win on headlands seas away
    would buoy up the house . . .   355
LEADER.
    And loved by the men you loved
      who died in glory, there you'd rule
                      beneath the earth—lord, prince,
    stern aide to the giant kings who judge the shadows there.[18]
    You were a king of kings when you drew breath;   360
      the mace you held could make men kneel or die.
ELECTRA.
      No, not under Troy!—
    not dead and gone with them, my father,
    hordes pierced by the spear Scamander[19] washes down.
      Sooner the killers die   365
    as they killed you—at the hands of friends,
    and the news of death would come from far away,
      we'd never know this grief.[20]
CHORUS.
      You are dreaming, children,
      dreams dearer than gold, more blest   370
      than the Blest beyond the Northwind's raging.[21]
        Dreams are easy, oh,
      but the double lash is striking home.
      Now our comrades group underground.
      Our masters' reeking hands are doomed—   375
        the children take the day!
ORESTES.
    That thrills his ear,
            that arrow lands!
                    Zeus, Zeus, force up from the earth
    destruction, late but true to the mark,   380
    to the reckless heart, the killing hand—
      for parents of revenge revenge be done.
LEADER.
    And the ripping cries of triumph mine
    to sing when the man is stabbed,
                    the woman[22] dies—   385
      why, why hide what's deep inside me,
      black wings beating, storming the spirit's prow—
                    hurricane, slashing hatred!

---

[18] The giant kings are Minos, Rhadamanthus, and Aeacus, who were rewarded for their just lives by being made judges of the dead in Hades.
[19] The river Scamander, near Troy.
[20] Electra wishes that Clytaemnestra and Aegisthus had died before they killed Agamemnon.
[21] The Chorus refers to the Hyperboreans, a mythical people supposed to live happily in the far north, beyond Boreas (the north wind). They had a special devotion to Apollo.
[22] Aegisthus is "the man"; Clytaemnestra is "the woman."

ELECTRA.
>   Both fists at once
>   come down, come down—
>   Zeus, *crush* their skulls! Kill! Kill!   390
>   Now give the land some faith, I beg you,
>   from these ancient wrongs bring forth our rights.
>   Hear me, Earth, and all you lords of death.

CHORUS.
>   It is the law: when the blood of slaughter
>   wets the ground it wants more blood.   395
>   Slaughter cries for the Fury
>   of those long dead to bring destruction
>   on destruction churning in its wake!

ORESTES.
>   Sweet Earth, how long?—great lords of death, look on,
>   you mighty curses of the dead. Look on   400
>   the last of Atreus' children, here, the remnant
>   helpless, cast from home . . . god, where to turn?

LEADER.
>   And again my pulses race and leap,
>   I can feel your sobs, and hope
>   becomes despair   405
>   and the heart goes dark to hear you—
>   then the anguish ebbs, I see you stronger,
>   hope and the light come on me.

ELECTRA.
>   *What* hope?—what force to summon, what can help?
>   What but the pain we suffer, bred by her?   410
>   So let her fawn. She can never soothe her young wolves—
>   Mother dear, you bred our wolves' raw fury.

LEADER AND CHORUS.
>   I beat and beat the dirge like a Persian mourner,[23]
>   hands clenched tight and the blows are coming thick and fast,
>   you can see the hands shoot out,   415
>   now hand over hand and down—the head pulsates,
>   blood at the temples pounding to explode!

ELECTRA.
>   Reckless, brutal mother—oh dear god!—
>   The brutal, cruel cortege,[24]
>   the warlord stripped of his honor guard   420
>   and stripped of mourning rites—
>   you dared entomb your lord unwept, unsung.

ORESTES.
>   Shamed for all the world, you mean—
>   dear god, my father degraded so!

---

[23] Noted for violent demonstrations of grief.

[24] Followers of or ceremony at a funeral. Agamemnon's mutilated body had received no funeral rites.

Oh she'll pay,   425
she'll pay, by the gods and these bare hands—
    just let me take her life and *die*!
LEADER AND CHORUS.
    Shamed? *Butchered,* I tell you—hands lopped,
strung to shackle his neck and arms!
So she worked,   430
she buried him, made your life a hell.
      Your father mutilated—do you hear?
ELECTRA.
    You tell him of father's death, but I was an outcast,
worthless, leashed like a vicious dog in a dark cell.
    I wept—laughter died that day . . .   435
    I wept, pouring out the tears behind my veils.
        Hear *that,* my brother, carve it on your heart!
LEADER AND CHORUS.
    Let it ring in your ears
      but let your heart stand firm.
    The outrage stands as it stands,   440
      you burn to know the end,
but first be strong, be steel, then down and fight.
ORESTES.
    I am calling you, my father—be with all you love!
ELECTRA.
    I am with you, calling through my tears.
LEADER AND CHORUS.
    We band together now, the call resounds—   445
      hear us now, come back into the light.
    Be with us, battle all you hate.
ORESTES.
    Now force *clash* with force, right with right!
ELECTRA.
    Dear gods, be just—win back our rights.
LEADER AND CHORUS.
    The flesh crawls to hear them pray.   450
      The hour of doom has waited long . . .
pray for it once, and oh my god, it comes.
CHORUS.
    Oh, the torment bred in the race,
        the grinding scream of death
          and the stroke that hits the vein,   455
   the hemorrhage none can stanch, the grief,
   the curse no man can bear.

    But there is a cure in the house
      and not outside it, no,
        not from others but from *them,*   460
    their bloody strife. We sing to you,
dark gods beneath the earth.

Now hear, you blissful powers underground—
    answer the call, send help.
Bless the children, give them triumph now.   465

> [*They withdraw, while* ELECTRA
> *and* ORESTES *come to the altar.*]

ORESTES.
    Father, king, no royal death you died—
    give me the power now to rule our house.
ELECTRA.
    I need you too, my father.
    Help me kill her lover, then go free.
ORESTES.
    Then men will extend the sacred feast to you.   470
    Or else, when the steam and the rich savor burn
    for Mother Earth, you will starve for honor.
ELECTRA.
    And I will pour my birthright out to you—
    the wine of the fathers' house, my bridal wine,[25]
    and first of all the shrines revere your tomb.   475
ORESTES.
    O Earth, bring father up to watch me fight.
ELECTRA.
    O Persephone,[26] give us power—lovely, gorgeous power!
ORESTES.
    Remember the bath—they stripped away your life, my father.
ELECTRA.
    Remember the all-embracing net—they made it first for you.
ORESTES.
    Chained like a beast—chains of hate, not bronze, my father!   480
ELECTRA.
    Shamed in the schemes, the hoods they slung around you!
ORESTES.
    Does our taunting wake you, oh my father?
ELECTRA.
    Do you lift your beloved head?
ORESTES.
    Send us justice, fight for all you love,
    or help us pin them grip for grip. They threw you—   485
    don't you long to throw them down in turn?
ELECTRA.
    One last cry, father. Look at your nestlings
    stationed at your tomb—pity
    your son and daughter. We are all you have.

---

[25] Electra has been barred from marrying while Clytaemnestra and Aegisthus are alive, lest she bear a son to avenge Agamemnon.
[26] Queen of the land of the dead.

ORESTES.
    Never blot out the seed of Pelops here.   490
    Then in the face of death you cannot die.

                       [The leader comes forward again.]

LEADER.
    The voices of children—salvation to the dead!
    Corks[27] to the net, they rescue the linen meshes
    from the depths. This line will never drown!
ELECTRA.
    Hear us—the long wail we raise is all for you.   495
    Honor our call and you will save yourself.
LEADER.
    And a fine thing it is to lengthen out the dirge;
    you adore a grave and fate they never mourned.
    But now for action—now you're set on action,
    put your stars to proof.
ORESTES.
                   So we will.   500
    One thing first, I think it's on the track.
    Why did she send libations? What possessed her,
    so late, to salve a wound past healing?
    To the unforgiving dead she sends this sop,
    this . . . who am I to appreciate her gifts?   505
    They fall so short of all her failings. True,
    "pour out your all to atone an act of blood,
    you work for nothing." So the saying goes.
    I'm ready. Tell me what you know.
LEADER.
                 I know, my boy,
    I was there. She had bad dreams. Some terror   510
    came groping through the night—it shook her,
    and she sent these cups, unholy woman.
ORESTES.
    And you know the dream, you can tell it clearly?
LEADER.
    She dreamed she bore a snake, said so herself and . . .
ORESTES.
    Come to the point—where does the story end?   515
LEADER.
    . . . she swaddled it like a baby, laid it to rest.
ORESTES.
    And food, what did the little monster want?
LEADER.
    She gave it her breast to suck—she was dreaming.
ORESTES.
    And didn't it tear her nipple, the brute inhuman—

---

[27] Floats to keep the net from sinking.

LEADER.
Blood curdled the milk with each sharp tug . . .   520
ORESTES.
No empty dream. The vision of a man.
LEADER.
. . . and she woke with a scream, appalled,
and rows of torches, burning out of the blind dark,
flared across the halls to soothe the queen,
and then she sent the libations for the dead,   525
an easy cure she hopes will cut the pain.
ORESTES.
                                                  No,
I pray to the Earth and father's grave to bring
that dream to life in me. I'll play the seer—
it all fits together, watch!
If the serpent came from the same place as I,   530
and slept in the bands that swaddled me, and its jaws
spread wide for the breast that nursed me into life
and clots stained the milk, mother's milk,
and she cried in fear and agony—so be it.
As she bred this sign, this violent prodigy,   535
so she dies by violence. I turn serpent,
I kill her. So the vision says.
LEADER.
You are the seer for me, I like your reading.
Let it come! But now rehearse your friends.
Say do this, or don't do that—   540
ORESTES.
The plan is simple. My sister goes inside.
And I'd have her keep the bond with me a secret.
They killed an honored man by cunning, so
they die by cunning, caught in the same noose.
So he commands,   545
Apollo the Seer who's never lied before.

And I like a stranger, equipped for all events,
go to the outer gates with this man here,
Pylades, a friend, the house's friend-in-arms.
And we both will speak Parnassian, both try   550
for the native tones of Delphi.[28]
                                    Now, say none
at the doors will give us a royal welcome
(after all the house is ridden by a curse),[29]
well then we wait . . . till a passer-by will stop

---

[28] Delphi and Mount Parnassus, both associated with the god Apollo, are in the region (Phokis) where Orestes has lived in exile. He may mean that he will adopt the regional dialect of Delphi or that his words will be delphic (obscure but faithful to the commission given him by Apollo).

[29] The curse would cause the house's inhabitants to sin against the laws of hospitality and also to fear visitors.

and puzzle and make insinuations at the house,   555
"Aegisthus shuts his door on the man who needs him.
Why, I wonder—does he know? Is he home?"

But once through the gates, across the threshold,
once I find that man on *my* father's throne,
or returning late to meet me face to face,   560
and his eyes shift and fall—
                              I promise you,
before he can ask me, "Stranger, who are you?"—
I drop him dead, a thrust of the sword, and twist!
Our Fury never wants for blood. *His* she drinks unmixed,
our third libation poured to Saving Zeus.   565

                    [*Turning to* ELECTRA.]

Keep a close watch inside, dear, be careful.
We must work together step by step.

                    [*To the chorus.*]

                              And you,
better hold your tongues, religiously.
Silence, friends, or speak when it will help.

                    [*Looking toward* PYLADES *and the
                    death-mound and beyond.*]

For the rest, watch over me, I need you—   570
guide my sword through struggle, guide me home!

                    [*As* ORESTES, PYLADES *and* ELEC-
                    TRA *leave, the women reassemble for
                    the chorus.*]

CHORUS.
    Marvels, the Earth breeds many marvels,
            terrible marvels overwhelm us.
    The heaving arms of the sea embrace and swarm
with savage life. And high in the no man's land of night   575
        torches[30] hang like swords. The hawk on the wing,
            the beast astride the fields
    can tell of the whirlwind's fury roaring strong.

    Oh but a man's high daring spirit,
            who can account for that? Or woman's   580
    desperate passion daring past all bounds?
    She couples with every form of ruin known to mortals.

---

[30] Strange celestial bodies, such as comets.

Woman, frenzied, driven wild with lust,
           twists the dark warm harness
of wedded love—tortures man and beast.   585

Well you know, you with a sense of truth
          recall Althaia,[31]
the heartless mother
who killed her son,
ai! what a scheme she had—   590
        she rushed his destiny,
            lit the bloody torch
preserved from the day he left her loins with a cry—
           the life of the torch paced his,
burning on till Fate burned out his life.   595

There is one more in the tales of hate:
        remember Scylla,[32]
the girl of slaughter
seduced by foes
to take her father's life.   600
        The gift of Minos,
          a choker forged in gold
turned her head and Nisos' immortal lock she cut
          as he slept away his breath . . .
ruthless bitch, now Hermes takes her down.   605

Now that I call to mind old wounds that never heal—
  Stop, it's time for the wedded love-in-hate,
for the curse of the halls,
        the woman's brazen cunning
          bent on her lord in arms,   610
  her warlord's power—
             Do you respect such things?
I prize the hearthstone warmed by faith,
a woman's temper nothing bends to outrage.

First at the head of legendary crime stands Lemnos.[33]
  People shudder and moan, and can't forget—   615

[31] The Chorus in the following passage cites three examples of perverted parental, filial, or conjugal love, all of which in the present context are ironic or double-edged, like the matricide Orestes and Electra are planning. Althaia, in mythology, had been warned at the birth of her son Meleager that his life would end when a certain torch, or brand from the fire, was burnt out. She hid it away, but later her anger with her son, who had killed her brothers, impelled her to burn the torch, bringing on his death.

[32] This Scylla (not to be confused with the monster of the same name who threatened navigators of the straits of Messina) was in myth the daughter of Nisos, king of Megara, whose city was besieged by King Minos of Crete. In Aeschylus' version of her story she succumbed to bribery (in other versions her motive is love for Minos) and cut off a lock of her father's hair on which his life depended.

[33] An island in the Aegean. It is associated in mythology and legend with atrocities, the most notorious being the attempted slaughter of all husbands and other males by the women of the island, who were jealous of their mistresses.

each new horror that comes
        we call the hells of Lemnos.
                Loathed by the gods for guilt,
    cast off by men, disgraced, their line dies out.
Who could respect what god detests?   620
What of these tales have I not picked with justice?

        The sword's at the lungs!—it stabs deep,
            the edge cuts through and through
        and Justice drives it—Outrage still lives on,
        not trodden to pieces underfoot, not yet,   625
         though the laws lie trampled down,
              the majesty of Zeus.

        The anvil of Justice stands fast
        and Fate beats out her sword.
        Tempered for glory, a child will wipe clean   630
        the inveterate stain of blood shed long ago—
         Fury brings him home at last,
            the brooding mother Fury!

                 [*The women leave.* ORESTES *and*
                 PYLADES *approach the house of*
                 ATREUS.]

ORESTES.

                              Slave, the slave!—
where is he? Hear me pounding the gates?
Is there a man inside the house?   635
For the third time, come out of the halls!
If Aegisthus has them welcome friendly guests.

                [*A voice from inside.*]

PORTER.

   All right, I hear you. . . .
   Where do you come from, stranger? Who are you?

ORESTES.

   Announce me to the masters of the house.   640
I've come for them, I bring them news.
                            Hurry,
the chariot of the night is rushing on the dark!
The hour falls, the traveler casts his anchor
in an inn where every stranger feels at home.
                          Come out!
Whoever rules the house. The woman in charge.   645
No, the man, better that way.
No scruples then. Say what you mean,
man to man launch in and prove your point,
make it clear, strong.

[Clytaemnestra *emerges*[34] *from
the palace, attended by* Electra.]

Clytaemnestra.

Strangers, please,
tell me what you would like and it is yours.   650
We've all you might expect in a house like ours.
We have warm baths and beds to charm away your pains
and the eyes of Justice[35] look on all we do.
But if you come for higher things, affairs
that touch the state, that is the men's concern   655
and I will stir them on.

Orestes.

I am a stranger,
from Daulis, close to Delphi. I'd just set out,
packing my own burden bound for Argos
(here I'd put my burden down and rest),
when I met a perfect stranger, out of the blue,   660
who asks about my way and tells me his.

Strophios,
a Phocian, so I gathered in conversation.
"Well, my friend," he says, "out for Argos
in any case? Remember to tell the parents
he is dead, Orestes . . .

promise me please   665
(it's only right), it will not slip your mind.
Then whatever his people want, to bring him home
or bury him here, an alien, all outcast here
forever, won't you ferry back their wishes?
As it is, a bronze urn is armor to his embers.   670
The man's been mourned so well . . ."

I only tell you
what I heard. And am I speaking now
with guardians, kinsmen who will care?
It's hard to say. But a parent ought to know.[36]

---

[34] Orestes had hoped that Aegisthus, about whom he feels "no scruples," would encounter
him first, but (by dramatic logic and the logic of the curse) he is brought immediately face-
to-face with his mother, who is simultaneously his fundamental antagonist, a person whose
intimate relationship to him causes the ambivalent human feelings in both of them, and the
most recent carrier of the self-propagating retaliatory curse that lies on the lineage of Atreus.

[35] A typical specimen of the irony omnipresent in the trilogy. In extending the expected
hospitable welcome to the guest, Clytaemnestra evokes her murder of her husband Agamemnon in his bath; the "eyes of Justice" are those that enforce the rites of hospitality and (for the
audience) are the forces that punish an adulterous wife for murdering her husband. The
dialogue here between Clytaemnestra and Orestes epitomizes the tragedy of the entire story:
Clytaemnestra had killed her husband because he had murdered their daughter Iphigeneia at
Aulis; now she is engaged in a life-or-death struggle with another of her own children.

[36] This poignant line has at least three meanings: a) "Shouldn't a mother know her own
son?"; b) "It is only right that this tragic message be delivered to a parent, not a more distant
kinsman or guardian"; c) "Any mother who killed her son's father should be told what has
happened to the son she exiled so that she could commit her crimes." Clytaemnestra's reply, in
her lines that follow, shows her mixed feelings as mother of the man she has most to fear.

CLYTAEMNESTRA.

                                                   I, I—
your words, you storm us, raze us to the roots,   675
you curse of the house so hard to wrestle down!
How you range—targets at peace, miles away,
and a shaft from your lookout brings them down.
You strip me bare of all I love, destroy me,
now—Orestes.   680

And he was trained so well, we'd been so careful,
kept his footsteps clear of the quicksand of death.
Just now, the hope of the halls, the surgeon to cure
our Furies' lovely revel—he seemed so close,
he's written off the rolls.

ORESTES.

                         If only I were . . .   685
my friends, with hosts as fortunate as you
if only I *could* be known for better news[37]
and welcomed like a brother. The tie between
the host and stranger, what is kinder?
But what an impiety, so it seemed to me,   690
not to bring this to a head for loved ones.
I was bound by honor, bound by the rights
of hospitality.

CLYTAEMNESTRA.

              Nothing has changed.
For all that you receive what you deserve,
as welcome in these halls as one of us.
Wouldn't another bear the message just as well?   695
But you must be worn from the long day's journey—
time for your rewards.

                         [*To* ELECTRA.]

                    Escort him in,
where the men who come are made to feel at home.
He and his retinue, and fellow travelers.   700
Let them taste the bounty of our house.
Do it, as if you depended on his welfare.

And we will rouse the powers in the house
and share the news. We never lack for loved ones,
we will probe this turn of fortune every way.   705

[37] Messengers were frequently (if illogically) rewarded for bringing good news and were hated or punished for bringing bad news. Clytaemnestra's reply, that the messenger will "receive what you deserve," is another ambiguity; does she mean that he will be rewarded for bringing to Aegisthus (and perhaps to her) the good news that a potentially avenging son is dead, or that the news of this son's death, welcome or not, is a service to the dead son's family, or both? And does Clytaemnestra's reassurance that the messenger will be "as welcome in these halls as one of us" mean that he will be treated kindly or that he will be given the same kind of unnatural treatment that all the house of Atreus has given to its kindred?

> [ELECTRA *leads* ORESTES, PYLA-
> DES *and their retinue into the
> halls;* CLYTAEMNESTRA *follows,
> while the chorus reassembles.*]

LEADER.

 Oh dear friends who serve the house,
  when can we speak out, when
 can the vigor of our voices serve Orestes?

CHORUS.

 Queen of the Earth, rich mounded Earth,
 breasting over the lord of ships,   710
 the king's corpse at rest,
 hear us now, now help us,
  now the time is ripe—
 Down to the pit Persuasion goes
 with all her cunning. Hermes of Death,   715
 the great shade patrols the ring
 to guide the struggles, drive the tearing sword.

LEADER.

 And I think our new friend is at his mischief.
 Look, Orestes' nurse in tears.

      [*Enter* CILISSA.]

 Where now, old-timer, padding along the gates?   720
 With pain a volunteer to go your way.

NURSE.

        "Aegisthus,"[38]
 your mistress calling, "hurry and meet your guests.
 There's news. It's clearer man to man, you'll see."

 And she looks at the maids and pulls that long face
 and down deep her eyes are laughing over the work   725
 that's done. Well and good for her. For the house
 it's the curse all over—the strangers make that plain.
 But let *him* hear, he'll revel once he knows.
         Oh god,
 the life is hard. The old griefs, the memories
 mixing, cups of pain, so much pain in the halls,   730
 the house of Atreus . . . I suffered, the heart within me
 always breaking, oh, but I never shouldered
 misery like this. So many blows, good slave,
 I took my blows.
     Now dear Orestes—
 the sweetest, dearest plague of all our lives!   735

[38] In addition to revealing the nurse Cilissa's hatred for Aegisthus, her words introduce a poignantly human note. Like his mother Clytaemnestra, Orestes is more, and less, than an instrument in a cosmic system of right and wrong; he was also a human baby who needed feeding and diaper-changing. The nurse's comparison of herself to a "prophet" (line 745) in her dealings with a baby join together the most cosmic, theological implications and the most homely, personal ones.

Red from your mother's womb I took you, reared you . . .
nights, the endless nights I paced, your wailing
kept me moving—led me a life of labor,
all for what?
                        And such care I gave it . . .
baby can't think for itself, poor creature.   740
You have to nurse it, don't you? Read its mind,
little devil's got no words, it's still swaddled.
Maybe it wants a bite or a sip of something,
or its bladder pinches—a baby's soft insides
have a will of their own. I had to be a prophet.   745
Oh I tried, and missed, believe you me, I missed,
and I'd scrub its pretty things until they sparkled.
Washerwoman and wetnurse shared the shop.
A jack of two trades, that's me,
and an old hand at both . . .
                              and so I nursed Orestes,   750
yes, from his father's arms I took him once,
and now they say he's dead,
I've suffered it all, and now I'll fetch that man,
the ruination of the house—give him the news,
he'll relish every word.
LEADER.
                        She tells him to come,   755
but how, prepared?
NURSE.
                        Prepared, how else?
I don't see . . .
LEADER.
                        With his men, I mean, or all alone?
NURSE.
Oh, she says to bring his bodyguard, his cutthroats.
LEADER.
No, not now, not if you hate our master—
tell him to come alone.   760
Nothing for him to fear then, when he hears.
Have him come quickly too, rejoicing all the way!
The teller sets the crooked message straight.
NURSE.
                                        What,
you're *glad* for the news that's come?
LEADER.
                                        Why not,
if Zeus will turn the evil wind to good?   765
NURSE.
But how? Orestes, the hope of the house is gone.
LEADER.
Not yet. It's a poor seer who'd say so.
NURSE.
What are you saying—something I don't know?

LEADER.
  Go in with your message. Do as you're told.
  May the gods take care of cares that come from them.   770
NURSE.
  Well, I'm off. Do as I'm told.
  And here's to the best . . .
  some help, dear gods, some help.

[*Exit.*]

CHORUS.
  O now bend to my prayer, Father Zeus,
      lord of the gods astride the sky—   775
  grant them all good fortune,
  the lords of the house who strain to see
              strict discipline return.
  Our cry is the cry of Justice,
              Zeus, safeguard it well.

                                  Zeus,   780
  set him against his enemies in the halls!
      Do it, rear him to greatness—two, threefold
      he will repay you freely, gladly.

  Look now—watch the colt of a man you loved,
      yoked to the chariot of pain.   785
  Now the orphan needs you—
  harness his racing, rein him in,
              preserve his stride so we
  can watch him surge in the homestretch,
              storming for the goal.   790

      And you who haunt the vaults
  where the gold glows in the darkness,
  hear us now, good spirits of the house,
      conspire with us—come,
      and wash old works of blood   795
  in the fresh-drawn blood of Justice.
  Let the gray retainer, murder, breed no more.

  And you, Apollo, lord of the glorious masoned cavern,[39]
      grant that this man's house lift up its head,
          that we may see with loving eyes   800
      the light of freedom burst from its dark veil!

      And lend a hand and scheme
  for the rights, my Hermes, help us,
  sail the action on with all your breath.

---

[39] Apollo's temple at Delphi and the cleft in the earth over which it was built.

Reveal what's hidden, please,   805
  or say a baffling word
in the night and blind men's eyes—
when the morning comes your word is just as dark.

Soon, at last, in the dawn that frees the house,
  we sea-widows wed to the winds   810
      will beat our mourning looms of song
           and sing, "Our ship's come in!
     Mine, mine is the wealth that swells her holds—
those I love are home and free of death."

But you, when your turn in the action comes, be strong.   815
    When she cries "Son!" cry out "My *father's* son!"
        Go through with the murder—innocent at last.

Raise up the heart of Perseus[40] in your breast!
  And for all you love under earth
and all above its rim, now scarf your eyes   820
       against the Gorgon's fury—
  In, go in for the slaughter now!

             [*Enter* AEGISTHUS, *alone.*]

The butcher comes. Wipe out death with death.
AEGISTHUS.
  Coming, coming. Yes, I have my summons.
There's news, I gather, travelers here to tell it.   825
No joy in the telling though—Orestes dead.
Saddle the house with a bloody thing like that
and it might just collapse. It's still raw
from the last murders, galled and raw.

But how to take the story, for living truth?   830
Or work of a woman's panic, gossip starting up
in the night to flicker out and die?[41]

           [*Turning to the leader.*]

          Do you know?
Tell me, clear my mind.
LEADER.
             We've heard a little.
But get it from the strangers, go inside.
Messengers have no power. Nothing like   835
a face-to-face encounter with the source.

---

[40] The mythical hero Perseus, with the help of Pluto, Hermes, and Athena, killed Medusa, one of the three female monsters (the Gorgons) with snakes in their hair; anyone who looked at her was turned to stone. Athena gave Perseus a mirror so that he would not have to look directly at Medusa.

[41] Compare the Chorus's skepticism about Clytaemnestra's report of the fall of Troy, in *Agamemnon.*

AEGISTHUS.
　—Must see him, test the messenger. Where was he
when the boy died, standing on the spot?
Or is he dazed with rumor, mouthing hearsay?
No, he'll never trap me open-eyed! 840

　　　　　　　　　　　[*Striding through the doors.*]

CHORUS.
　Zeus, Zeus, what can I say?—
how to begin this prayer, call down
　　the gods for help? what words
can reach the depth of all I feel?
Now they swing to the work, 845
the red edge of the cleaver
hacks at flesh and men go down.
Agamemnon's house goes down—
　　all-out disaster now,
or a son ignites the torch of freedom, 850
wins the throne, the citadel,
　　the fathers' realms of gold.
The last man on the bench,[42] a challenger
must come to grips with two. Up,
like a young god, Orestes, wrestle— 855
　　let it be to win.

　　　　　　　　　[*A scream inside the palace.*]

　—Listen!
　　　　　—What's happening?
　　　　　　　　　　—The house,
　what have they done to the house?
LEADER.
　　　　　　　　　　　　Back,
till the work is over! Stand back—
they'll count us clean of the dreadful business. 860

　　　　　　　　　　[*The women scatter; a wounded
　　　　　　　　　　servant of* AEGISTHUS *enters.*]

　Look, the die is cast, the battle's done.
SERVANT.
　　　　　　　　　　　　Ai,
Ai, all over, master's dead—Aie,
a third, last salute. Aegisthus is no more.

　　　　　　　　　　[*Rushing at a side door, struggling
　　　　　　　　　　to work it open.*]

　Open up, wrench the bolts on the women's doors.
Faster! A strong young arm it takes, 865

---

[42] The wrestler who must meet the winner of the earlier match or matches.

but not to save him now, he's finished.
What's the use?
                              Look—wake up!
                                                    No good,
I call to the deaf, to sleepers . . . a waste of breath.
Where are you, Clytaemnestra? What are you doing?
LEADER.
Her head is ripe for lopping on the block.   870
She's next, and justice wields the ax.

                              [*The door opens, and* CLYTAEM-
                              NESTRA *comes forth.*]

CLYTAEMNESTRA.

                                                    What now?
Why this shouting up and down the halls?
SERVANT.
The dead are killing the living,[43] I tell you!
CLYTAEMNESTRA.
Ah, a riddle. I do well at riddles.
By cunning we die, precisely as we killed.   875
Hand me the man-ax, someone, hurry!

                              [*The servant dashes out.*]

Now we will see. Win all or lose all,
we have come to this—the crisis of our lives.

                              [*The main doors open;* ORESTES,
                              *sword in hand, is standing over the
                              body of* AEGISTHUS, *with* PYLADES
                              close behind him.]

ORESTES.
It's you I want. This one's had enough.
CLYTAEMNESTRA.
Gone, my violent one—Aegisthus, very dear.   880
ORESTES.
You love your man? Then lie in the same grave.
You can never be unfaithful to the dead.

                              [*Pulling her toward* AEGISTHUS'
                              body.]

CLYTAEMNESTRA.
Wait, son—no feeling for this, my child?
The breast[44] you held, drowsing away the hours,
soft gums tugging the milk that made you grow?   885

---

[43] The line means a) the supposedly dead Orestes is killing Aegisthus, and b) all the dead victims of the curse on the house are taking revenge.
[44] Either Clytaemnestra has exposed her breast or Orestes has done so in his violence.

[ORESTES *turns to* PYLADES.]

ORESTES.
What will I do, Pylades—I dread to kill my mother!
PYLADES.
What of the future? What of the Prophet God Apollo,
the Delphic voice, the faith and oaths we swear?
Make all mankind your enemy, not the gods.
ORESTES.
O you win me over—good advice.

[*Wheeling on* CLYTAEMNESTRA,
thrusting her toward AEGISTHUS.]

      This way—   890
I want to butcher you—right across his body!
In life you thought he dwarfed my father—*Die!*—
go down with him forever!
        You love this man,
the man you should have loved you hated.
CLYTAEMNESTRA.
I gave you life. Let me grow old with you.   895
ORESTES.
What—kill my father, then you'd live with me?
CLYTAEMNESTRA.
Destiny had a hand in that, my child.
ORESTES.
This too: destiny is handing you your death.
CLYTAEMNESTRA.
You have no fear of a mother's curse, my son?
ORESTES.
Mother? You flung me to a life of pain.   900
CLYTAEMNESTRA.
Never flung you, placed you in a comrade's house.
ORESTES.
—Disgraced me, sold me, a freeborn father's son.
CLYTAEMNESTRA.
Oh? then name the price I took for you.
ORESTES.
I am ashamed to mention it[45] in public.
CLYTAEMNESTRA.
Please, and tell your father's failings too.   905
ORESTES.
Never judge him—he suffered, you sat here at home.
CLYTAEMNESTRA.
It hurts women, being kept from men, my son.
ORESTES.
Perhaps . . . but the man slaves to keep them safe at home.

[45] Orestes probably means both the killing of Agamemnon in the son's absence and his
mother's adultery. Her reply in the next line balances these crimes against Agamemnon's
killing of Iphigeneia and his adulteries with Trojan women such as his captive, Cassandra.

CLYTAEMNESTRA.

—I see murder in your eyes, my child—mother's murder!

ORESTES.

You are the murderer, not I—and you will kill yourself.[46]   910

CLYTAEMNESTRA.

Watch out—the hounds of a mother's curse will hunt you down.

ORESTES.

But how to escape a father's if I fail?

CLYTAEMNESTRA.

I must be spilling live tears on a tomb of stone.

ORESTES.

Yes, my father's destiny—it decrees your death.

CLYTAEMNESTRA.

Ai—you are the snake I bore—I gave you life!

ORESTES.

                                          Yes!   915

That was the great seer, that terror in your dreams.
You killed and it was outrage—suffer outrage now.

> [*He draws her over the threshold;
> the doors close behind them, and the
> chorus gathers at the altar.*]

LEADER.

I even mourn the victims' double fates.
But Orestes fought, he reached the summit
of bloodshed here—we'd rather have it so.   920
The bright eye of the halls must never die.

CHORUS.

Justice came at last to the sons of Priam,
late but crushing vengeance, yes,
but to Agamemnon's house returned
    the double lion,[47]   925
            the double onslaught
    drove to the hilt—the exile sped by god,
by Delphi's just command that drove him home.

Lift the cry of triumph O! the master's house
wins free of grief, free of the ones   930
who bled its wealth, the couple stained with murder,
            free of Fate's rough path.

He came back with a lust for secret combat,
stealthy, cunning vengeance, yes,
but his hand was steered in open fight   935
    by god's true daughter,

---

[46]That is, she will have brought on her own death through her evil acts.

[47]Orestes and Pylades. The optimism expressed throughout this choral passage, the belief that the curse has finally been put to rest and that the chain of acts of revenge has been broken, is shortsighted and premature. Later, the Chorus will become aware of this fact.

Right, Right we call her,
we and our mortal voices aiming well—
she breathes her fury, shatters all she hates.

Lift the cry of triumph O! the master's house   940
wins free of grief, free of the ones
who bled its wealth, the couple stained with murder,
free of Fate's rough path.

Apollo wills it so!—
Apollo, clear from the Earth's deep cleft   945
his voice came shrill, "Now stealth will master stealth!"
And the pure god came down and healed our ancient wounds,
the heavens come, somehow, to lift our yoke of grief—
Now to praise the heavens' just command.

Look, the light is breaking!   950
The huge chain that curbed the halls gives way.
Rise up, proud house, long, too long
your walls lay fallen, strewn along the earth.

Time brings all to birth—
soon Time will stride through the gates with blessings,   955
once the hearth burns off corruption, once
the house drives off the Furies. Look, the dice of Fate
fall well for all to see. We sing how fortune smiles—
the aliens in the house are routed out at last!

Look, the light is breaking!   960
The huge chain that curbed the halls gives way.
Rise up, proud house, long, too long
your walls lay fallen, strewn along the earth.

[*The doors open. Torches light*
PYLADES *and* ORESTES, *sword in*
hand, standing over the bodies of
CLYTAEMNESTRA *and* AEGISTHUS,
as CLYTAEMNESTRA *stood over the*
bodies of AGAMEMNON *and* CAS-
SANDRA.]

ORESTES.
Behold the double tyranny of our land!
They killed my father, stormed my fathers' house.   965
They had their power when they held the throne.
Great lovers still, as you may read their fate.
True to their oath, hand in hand they swore
to kill my father, hand in hand to die.
Now they keep their word.

*[Unwinding from the bodies on the
bier the robes that entangled* AGA-
MEMNON, *he displays them, as* CLY-
TAEMNESTRA *had displayed them,
to the chorus at the altar.]*

Look once more on this,   970
you who gather here to attend our crimes—
the master-plot that bound my wretched father,
shackled his ankles, manacled his hands.
Spread it out! Stand in a ring around it,
a grand shroud for a man.

Here, unfurl it   975
so the Father—no, not mine but the One
who watches over all, the Sun can behold
my mother's godless work. So he may come,
my witness when the day of judgment comes,
that I pursued this bloody death with justice,   980
mother's death.

Aegisthus, why mention him?
The adulterer dies. An old custom, justice.

But she who plotted this horror against her husband,
she carried his children, growing in her womb
and she—I loved her once   985
and now I loathe, I have to loathe—

what is she?

[Kneeling by the body of his mother.]

Some moray eel, some viper born to rot her mate
with a single touch, no fang to strike him,
just the wrong, the reckless fury in her heart!

*[Glancing back and forth from
* CLYTAEMNESTRA *to the robes.]*

This—how can I dignify this . . . snare for a beast?—   990
sheath for a corpse's feet?

This winding-sheet,
this tent for the bath of death!

No, a hunting net,
a coiling—what to call—?

Foot-trap—
woven of robes . . .
why, this is perfect gear for the highwayman   995
who entices guests and robs them blind and plies
the trade of thieves. With a sweet lure like this
he'd hoist a hundred lives and warm his heart,

Live with such a woman, marry *her*? Sooner
the gods destroy me—die without an heir!   1000
CHORUS.
    Oh the dreadful work . . .
    Death calls and she is gone.
      But oh, for you, the survivor,
    suffering is just about to bloom.
ORESTES.
    Did she do the work or not?—Here, come close—   1005
This shroud's my witness, dyed with Aegisthus' blade[48]—
Look, the blood ran here, conspired with time to blot
the swirling dyes, the handsome old brocade.

                      [*Clutching* AGAMEMNON'S *robes,*
                      *burying his face in them and
                      weeping.*]

Now I can praise you, now I am here to mourn.
You were my father's death, great robe, I hail you!   1010
Even if I must suffer the work and the agony
and all the race of man—
                        I embrace you . . . you,
my victory, are my guilt, my curse, and still—
CHORUS.
    No man can go through life
    and reach the end unharmed.   1015
      Aye, trouble is now,
    and trouble still to come.
ORESTES.
                  But *still*,
that you may know—
                  I see no end in sight,
I am a charioteer—the reins are flying, look,
the mares plunge off the track—
                     my bolting heart,   1020
it beats me down and terror beats the drum,
my dance-and-singing master pitched to fury—

And still, while I still have some self-control,
I say to my friends in public: I killed my mother,
not with a little justice. She was stained   1025
with father's murder, she was cursed by god.
And the magic spells that fired up my daring?
One comes first. The Seer of Delphi who declared,
"Go through with this and you go free of guilt.
Fail and—"

---

[48] Presumably the blade used by Clytaemnestra to kill Agamemnon.

I can't repeat the punishment.   1030
What bow could hit the crest of so much pain?

> [PYLADES *gives* ORESTES *a branch
> of olive and invests him in the robes
> of Apollo, the wreath and insignia
> of suppliants to Delphi.*][49]

Now look on me, armed with the branch and wreath,
a suppliant bound for the Navelstone of Earth,
Apollo's sacred heights
where they say the fire of heaven can never die.   1035

> [*Looking at his hand that still re-
> tains the sword.*]

I must escape this blood . . . it is my own.
—Must turn toward his hearth,
none but his, the Prophet God decreed.

I ask you, Argos and all my generations,
remember how these brutal things were done.   1040
Be my witness to Menelaus[50] when he comes.
And now I go, an outcast driven off the land,
in life, in death, I leave behind a name for—
LEADER.
But you've done well. Don't burden yourself
with bad omens, lash yourself with guilt.   1045
You've set us free, the whole city of Argos,
lopped the heads of these two serpents once for all.

> [*Staring at the women and beyond,*
> ORESTES *screams in terror.*]

ORESTES.
No, no! Women[51]—look—like Gorgons,
shrouded in black, their heads wreathed,
swarming serpents!
                    —Cannot stay, I must move on.   1050
LEADER.
What dreams can whirl you so? You of all men,
you have your father's love. Steady,
nothing to fear with all you've won.
ORESTES.
                              No dreams,
these torments, not to me, they're clear, real—the hounds
of mother's hate.

[49] Apollo has promised to purge Orestes from blood-guilt after Orestes returns to the god's temple.
[50] Brother of Agamemnon and husband of Helen; he has not yet returned to Argos.
[51] The women are the Furies, avengers of blood-guilt. In the final play of the trilogy they will confront Orestes; eventually they will be renamed "the Eumenides" ("kindly ones").

LEADER.

                     The blood's still wet on your hands.   1055
It puts a kind of frenzy in you . . .

ORESTES.

                           God Apollo!
Here they come, thick and fast,
their eyes dripping hate—

LEADER.

                      One thing
will purge you. Apollo's touch will set you free
from all your . . . torments.

ORESTES.

                    You can't see them—   1060
I can, they drive me on! I must move on—

            [*He rushes out;* PYLADES *follows
            close behind.*]

LEADER.

Farewell then. God look down on you with kindness,
guard you, grant you fortune.

CHORUS.

    Here once more, for the third time,
the tempest in the race has struck   1065
the house of kings and run its course.
  First the children eaten,
the cause of all our pain, the curse.
And next the kingly man's ordeal,
the bath where the proud commander,   1070
lord of Achaea's armies lost his life.
And now a third has come, but who?
  A third like Saving Zeus?
Or should we call him death?
Where will it end?—   1075
where will it sink to sleep and rest,
  this murderous hate, this Fury?

THE EUMENIDES

CHARACTERS

THE PYTHIA, *the priestess of Apollo*
APOLLO
ORESTES
HERMES
THE GHOST OF CLYTAEMNESTRA

CHORUS OF FURIES AND THEIR LEADER
ATHENA
Escorting Chorus of Athenian women
Men of the jury, herald, citizens

TIME AND SCENE

The FURIES *have pursued* ORESTES *to the temple of* APOLLO *at Delphi. It is morning. The priestess of the god appears at the great doors and offers up her prayer.*

PYTHIA.[1]

First of the gods I honor in my prayer is Mother Earth,
the first of the gods to prophesy, and next I praise
Tradition, second to hold her Mother's mantic seat,
so legend says, and third by the lots of destiny,
by Tradition's free will—no force to bear her down—   5
another Titan, child of the Earth, took her seat
and Phoebe passed it on as a birthday gift to Phoebus,
Phoebus a name for clear pure light derived from hers.
Leaving the marsh and razorback of Delos,[2] landing
at Pallas' headlands flocked by ships, here he came   10
to make his home Parnassus[3] and the heights.
And an escort filled with reverence brought him on,
the highway-builders, sons of the god of fire who tamed
the savage country, civilized the wilds—on he marched
and the people lined his way to cover him with praise,   15
led by Delphos,[4] lord, helm of the land, and Zeus
inspired his mind with the prophet's skill, with godhead,
made him fourth in the dynasty of seers to mount this throne,
but it is Zeus that Apollo speaks for, Father Zeus.
These I honor in the prelude of my prayers—these gods.   20
But Athena at the Forefront of the Temple[5] crowns our legends.
I revere the nymphs who keep the Corycian rock's[6] deep hollows,
loving haunt of birds where the spirits drift and hover.
And Great Dionysos rules the land. I never forget that day
he marshaled his wild women in arms—he was all god,   25
he ripped Pentheus[7] down like a hare in the nets of doom.
And the rushing springs of Pleistos, Poseidon's[8] force I call,
and the king of the sky, the king of all fulfillment, Zeus.

---

[1] The name of the priestess derives from the Python, a dragon killed by Apollo when the god assumed power at Delphi. Omitting this incident, the priestess traces the history of the Delphic oracle (the "mantic," or prophetic, center of Greece) in terms of the successive powers or deities who prophesied there. The first was Earth, a primitive maternal being or principle, followed by Themis ("Tradition," associated with justice and custom), followed by Phoebe, a Titaness associated with the moon, followed by her grandson Phoebus, or Apollo, whom the priestess associates in her speech with highway-building, the taming of savagery, and generally the advent of the civilized. But in fact, despite the Pythia's natural inclination toward the "Apollonian" values of reason and moderation, the play will be much more evenhanded in its treatment of the conflicting claims of the primitive forces represented by the Furies, Mother Night, and Mother Earth, and on the other hand the more "civilized" forces Apollo represents.

[2] The island where Apollo was born.

[3] The mountain at Delphi; generally associated with Apollo, it actually had two peaks, one sacred to him and one to Dionysos, the god of wine who embodies the libidinal energies antithetical to Apollo's moderation. Dionysos rules the temple at Delphi during the winter, when Apollo is absent.

[4] The original king from whom Delphi was supposed to derive its name.

[5] Athena had a shrine near the temple's entrance.

[6] An area of Mount Parnassus; it contained a cave sacred to Pan, god of nature.

[7] The rationalistic Pentheus, opposed to the orgiastic worship of Dionysos, was torn apart by his mother and other frenzied female worshipers of the god.

[8] God of the ocean.

Now the prophet goes to take her seat.[9] God speed me—
grant me a vision greater than all my embarkations past! 30

[*Turning to the audience.*]

Where are the Greeks among you? Draw your lots and enter.
It is the custom here. I will tell the future
only as the god will lead the way.

[*She goes through the doors and
reappears in a moment, shaken,
thrown to her knees by some terrific
force.*]

Terrors—
terrors to tell, terrors all can see!—
they send me reeling back from Apollo's house. 35
The strength drains, it's very hard to stand,
crawling on all fours, no spring in the legs . . .
an old woman,[10] gripped by fear, is nothing,
a child, nothing more.

[*Struggling to her feet, trying to
compose herself.*]

I'm on my way to the vault, 40
it's green with wreaths, and there at the Navelstone[11]
I see a man—an abomination to god—
he holds the seat where suppliants sit for purging;[12]
his hands dripping blood, and his sword just drawn,
and he holds a branch (it must have topped an olive) 45
wreathed with a fine tuft of wool, all piety,
fleece gleaming white. So far it's clear, I tell you.
But there in a ring around the man, an amazing company—
women,[13] sleeping, nestling against the benches . . .
women? No, 50
Gorgons I'd call them; but then with Gorgons
you'd see the grim, inhuman . . .

---

[9] The seat is a tripod situated over the underground cleft beneath the temple. The Pythia's role was to relay the utterances of Apollo.

[10] The Pythia was always an elderly woman.

[11] The Omphalos, a cone-shaped rock near or in the temple. It was believed to be the center of the earth.

[12] Because he has taken his mother Clytaemnestra's life, Orestes must be ritually "purged" of the pollution of blood before he can be tried at law. Here he carries the emblems customary for those seeking purgation.

[13] The Furies, who pursue Orestes in revenge for his act of matricide. Appropriately, the priestess of Apollo does not recognize these primitive beings; she guesses that they may be the Gorgons (female monsters the sight of whom turned gazers to stone) or Harpies (hideous bird-women sent by Helios the sun-god to punish the king Phineus by defiling his food; compare the description of the Harpies in Virgil's *Aeneid*, Book III).

                                                 I saw a picture
years ago, the creatures tearing the feast
away from Phineus—
                             These have no wings,
I looked. But black they are, and so repulsive.   55
Their heavy, rasping breathing makes me cringe.
And their eyes ooze a discharge, sickening,
and what they wear—to flaunt *that* at the gods,
the idols, sacrilege! even in the homes of men.
The tribe that produced that brood I never saw,   60
or a plot of ground to boast it nursed their kind
without some tears, some pain for all its labor.

Now for the outcome. This is his concern,
Apollo the master of this house, the mighty power.
Healer, prophet, diviner of signs, he purges   65
the halls of others—He must purge his own.

                             [*She leaves. The doors of the temple
                             open and reveal* APOLLO *rising
                             over* ORESTES; *he kneels in prayer
                             at the Navelstone, surrounded by the
                             FURIES who are sleeping.* HERMES
                             waits in the background.]

APOLLO.
No, I will never fail you, through to the end
your guardian standing by your side or worlds away!
I will show no mercy to your enemies! Now
look at these—

                             [*Pointing to the* FURIES]

                             these obscenities!—I've caught them,   70
beaten them down with sleep.
                             They disgust me.
These gray, ancient children never touched
by god, man or beast—the eternal virgins.
Born for destruction only, the dark pit,
they range the bowels of Earth, the world of death,   75
loathed by men and the gods who hold Olympus.[14]

Nevertheless keep racing on and never yield.
Deep in the endless heartland they will drive you,
striding horizons, feet pounding the earth forever,
on, on over seas and cities swept by tides!   80
Never surrender, never brood on the labor.

---

[14] There is a natural antipathy between the elemental and ancient force represented by the
Furies and the modern, supposedly more advanced Olympian gods, especially Apollo.

And once you reach the citadel of Pallas,[15] kneel
and embrace her ancient idol in your arms and there,
with judges of your case, with a magic spell—
with words—we will devise the master-stroke   85
that sets you free from torment once for all.
I persuaded you to take your mother's life.

ORESTES.
    Lord Apollo, you know the rules of justice,
    know them well. Now learn compassion too.
    No one doubts your power to do great things.   90

APOLLO.
    Remember that. No fear will overcome you.

                                    [*Summoning* HERMES *from the
                                    shadows.*]

You, my brother, blood of our common Father,
Hermes, guard him well. Live up to your name,
good Escort. Shepherd him well, he is my suppliant,
and outlaws have their rights that Zeus reveres.   95
Lead him back to the world of men with all good speed.

                                    [APOLLO *withdraws to his inner
                                    sanctuary;* ORESTES *leaves with
                                    HERMES in the lead. The* GHOST
                                    OF CLYTAEMNESTRA *appears at the
                                    Navelstone, hovering over the* FUR-
                                    IES *as they sleep.*]

THE GHOST OF CLYTAEMNESTRA.
    You—how can you *sleep?*
    Awake, awake—what use are sleepers now?
    I go stripped of honor, thanks to you,
    alone among the dead. And for those I killed   100
    the charges of the dead will never cease, never—
    I wander in disgrace, I feel the guilt, I tell you,
    withering guilt from all the outraged dead!

    But I suffered too, terribly, from dear ones,
    and none of my spirits rages to avenge me.   105
    I was slaughtered by his matricidal hand.
    See these gashes—

                                    [*Seizing one of the* FURIES *weak
                                    with sleep.*]

    Carve them in your heart!

---

[15] Athena; Apollo directs Orestes to her city, Athens. The "ancient idol" was a wooden
statue of the goddess located there.

The sleeping brain has eyes that give us light;
we can never see our destiny by day.

And after all my libations . . . how you lapped   110
the honey, the sober offerings poured to soothe you,
awesome midnight feasts I burned at the hearthfire,
your dread hour never shared with gods.
All those rites, I see them trampled down.
And he springs free like a fawn, one light leap   115
at that—he's through the thick of your nets,
he breaks away!
Mocking laughter twists across his face.
Hear me, I am pleading for my life.
Awake, my Furies, goddesses of the Earth!   120
A dream is calling—Clytaemnestra calls you now.

                    [*The* Furies *mutter in their sleep.*]

Mutter on. Your man is gone, fled far away.
My son has friends to defend him, not like mine.

                    [*They mutter again.*]

You sleep too much, no pity for my ordeal.
Orestes murdered his mother—he is gone.   125

                    [*They begin to moan.*]

Moaning, sleeping—onto your feet, quickly.
What is your work? What but causing pain?
Sleep and toil, the two strong conspirators,
they sap the mother dragon's deadly fury—

                    [*The* Furies *utter a sharp moan
                    and moan again, but they are still
                    asleep.*]

Furies.
   Get him, get him, get him, get him—   130
   there he goes.
The Ghost of Clytaemnestra.
                    The prey you hunt is just a dream—
like hounds mad for the sport you bay him on,
you never leave the kill.
                    But what are you *doing*?
Up! don't yield to the labor, limp with sleep.
Never forget my anguish.   135
Let my charges hurt you, they are just;
deep in the righteous heart they prod like spurs.
You, blast him on with your gory breath,
the fire of your vitals—wither him, after him,
one last foray—waste him, burn him out!

[She vanishes. The lead FURY *urges on the pack.]*

LEADER.

                                    Wake up!   140
I rouse you, you rouse her. Still asleep?
Onto your feet, kick off your stupor.
See if this prelude has some grain of truth.

[The FURIES *circle, pursuing the scent with hunting calls, and cry out singly when they find* ORESTES *gone.]*

FURIES.
—Aieeeeee—no, no, *no,* they do us wrong, dear sisters.

  —The miles of pain, the pain I suffer . . .   145
and all for nothing, all for pain, more pain,
        the anguish, oh, the grief too much to bear.

—The quarry's slipped from the nets, our quarry lost and gone.

      —Sleep defeats me . . . I have lost the prey.

—You—child of Zeus[16]—*you,* a common thief!   150

  —Young god, you have ridden down the powers
proud with age. You worship the suppliant,
        the godless man who tears his parent's heart—

—The matricide, you steal him away, and you a god!

      —Guilt both ways, and who can call it justice?   155

—Not I: her charges stalk my dreams,
  yes, the charioteer rides hard,
        her spurs digging the vitals,
    under the heart, under the heaving breast—

—I can feel the executioner's lash, it's searing   160
        deeper, sharper, the knives of burning ice—

—Such is your triumph, you young gods,
  world dominion past all rights.
        Your throne is streaming blood,
    blood at the foot, blood at the crowning head—   165

—I can see the Navelstone of the Earth, it's bleeding,
        bristling corruption, oh, the guilt it has to bear—

[16] Apollo.

Stains on the hearth! The Prophet stains the vault,
  he cries it on, drives on the crime himself.
      Breaking the god's first law, he rates men first,   170
          destroys the old dominions of the Fates.

He wounds me too, yet *him* he'll never free,
  plunging under the earth, no freedom then:
      curst as he comes for purging, at his neck
          he feels new murder springing from his blood.   175

> [APOLLO *strides from his sanctuary
> in full armor, brandishing his bow
> and driving back the* FURIES.]

APOLLO.
  Out, I tell you, out of these halls—fast!—
  set the Prophet's chamber free!

> [*Seizing one of the* FURIES, *shaking
> an arrow across her face.*]

                    Or take
  the flash and stab of this, this flying viper
  whipped from the golden cord that strings my bow!

Heave in torment, black froth erupting from your lungs,   180
  vomit the clots of all the murders you have drained.
  But never touch my halls, you have no right.

Go where heads are severed, eyes gouged out,
  where Justice and bloody slaughter are the same . . .
  castrations, wasted seed, young men's glories butchered,   185
  extremities maimed, and huge stones at the chest,
  and the victims wail for pity—
  spikes inching up the spine, torsos stuck on spikes.

> [*The* FURIES *close in on him.*]

So, you hear your love feast, yearn to have it all?
  You revolt the gods. Your look,   190
  your whole regalia gives you away—your kind
  should infest a lion's cavern reeking blood.
  But never rub your filth on the Prophet's shrine.
  Out, you flock without a herdsman—out!
  No god will ever shepherd you with love.   195
LEADER.
  Lord Apollo, now it is your turn to listen.
  You are no mere accomplice in this crime.
  You did it all, and all the guilt is yours.
APOLLO.
  No, how? Enlarge on that, and only that.

LEADER.
You commanded the guest to kill his mother.   200
APOLLO.
—Commanded him to avenge his father, what of it?
LEADER.
And then you dared embrace him, fresh from bloodshed.
APOLLO.
Yes, I ordered him on, to my house, for purging.
LEADER.
And we sped him on, and you revile us?
APOLLO.
Indeed, you are not fit to approach this house.   205
LEADER.
And yet we have our mission and our—
APOLLO.
Authority—you? Sound out your splendid power.
LEADER.
Matricides: we drive them from their houses.
APOLLO.
And what of the wife who strikes her husband down?
LEADER.
That murder would not destroy one's flesh and blood.   210
APOLLO.
Why, you'd disgrace—obliterate the bonds of Zeus
and Hera queen of brides! And the queen of love
you'd throw to the winds at a word, disgrace love,
the source of mankind's nearest, dearest ties.
Marriage of man and wife is Fate itself,   215
stronger than oaths, and Justice guards its life.
But if one destroys the other and you relent—
no revenge, not a glance in anger—then
I say your manhunt of Orestes is unjust.
Some things stir your rage, I see. Others,   220
atrocious crimes, lull your will to act.
                                        Pallas
will oversee this trial. She is one of us.[17]
LEADER.
I will never let that man go free, never.
APOLLO.
Hound him then, and multiply your pains.
LEADER.
Never try to cut my power with your logic.   225
APOLLO.
I'd never touch it, not as a gift—your power.
LEADER.
                                        Of course,
great as you are, they say, throned on high with Zeus.

---

[17] One of the modern Olympian gods, whom the primitive Furies oppose.

But blood of the mother draws me on—must hunt
the man for Justice. Now I'm on his trail!

> [*Rushing out, with the* FURIES *in
> full cry.*]

APOLLO.
And I will defend my suppliant and save him.   230
A terror to gods and men, the outcast's anger,
once I fail him, all of my own free will.

> [APOLLO *leaves. The scene changes
> to the Acropolis in Athens. Escorted
> by* HERMES, ORESTES *enters and
> kneels, exhausted, before the ancient
> shrine and idol of* ATHENA.]

ORESTES.
                                                    Queen Athena,
under Apollo's orders I have come.
Receive me kindly. Curst and an outcast,
no suppliant for purging . . . my hands are clean.   235
My murderous edge is blunted now, worn down at last
on the outland homesteads, beaten paths of men.

On and out over seas and dry frontiers,
I kept alive the Prophet's strong commands.
Struggling toward your house, your idol—

> [*Taking the knees of* ATHENA'S *idol
> in his arms.*]

                                                    Goddess,   240
here I keep my watch,
I await the consummation of my trial.

> [*The* FURIES *enter in pursuit but
> cannot find* ORESTES *who is en-
> twined around* ATHENA'S *idol. The
> leader sees the footprints.*]

LEADER.
                                          At last!
The clear trail of the man. After it, silent
but it tracks his guilt to light. He's wounded—
go for the fawn, my hounds, the splash of blood,   245
hunt him, rake him down.

                                Oh, the labor,
the man-killing labor. My lungs are bursting . . .
over the wide rolling earth we've ranged in flock,
hurdling the waves in wingless flight and now we come,
all hot pursuit, outracing ships astern—and now   250

he's here, somewhere, cowering like a hare . . .
the reek of human blood—it's laughter to my heart!

[*Inciting a pair of* FURIES.]

Look, look again, you two,
scour the ground before he escapes—one dodge
and the matricide slips free.

[*Seeing* ORESTES, *one by one they
press around him and* ATHENA'S
idol.]

FURIES.

     —There he is!   255
 Clutching the knees of power once again,
  twined in the deathless goddess' idol, look,
 he wants to go on trial for his crimes.

       —Never . . .
  the mother's blood that wets the ground,
 you can never bring it back, dear god,   260
 the Earth drinks, and the running life is gone.

       —No,
you'll give me blood for blood, you must!
  Out of your living marrow I will drain
 my red libation, out of your veins I suck my food,
  my raw, brutal cups—

      —Wither you alive,   265
  drag you down and there you pay, agony
for mother-killing agony!

     —And there you will see them all.
Every mortal who outraged god or guest or loving parent:
each receives the pain his pains exact.

—A mighty god is Hades. There   270
 at the last reckoning underneath the earth
  he scans all, he squares all men's accounts
 and graves them on the tablets of his mind.

[ORESTES *remains impassive.*]

ORESTES.
I have suffered into truth. Well I know
the countless arts of purging, where to speak,   275
where silence is the rule.[18] In this ordeal
a compelling master urges me to speak.

---

[18] A person who had not been ritually purged might spread pollution merely by speaking.

[*Looking at his hands.*]

The blood sleeps, it is fading on my hands,
the stain of mother's murder washing clean.
It was still fresh at the god's hearth. Apollo   280
killed the swine[19] and the purges drove it off.
Mine is a long story
if I'd start with the many hosts I met,
I lived with, and I left them all unharmed.[20]
Time refines all things that age with time.   285

And now with pure, reverent lips I call
the queen of the land. Athena, help me!
Come without your spear—without a battle
you will win myself, my land, the Argive people[21]
true and just, your friends-in-arms forever.   290
Where are you now? The scorching wilds of Libya,
bathed by the Triton pool[22] where you were born?
Robes shrouding your feet
or shod and on the march to aid allies?
Or striding the Giants' Plain,[23] marshal of armies,   295
hero scanning, flashing through the ranks?
                                                        Come—
you can hear me from afar, you are a god.
Set me free from this!
LEADER.
                              Never—neither
Apollo's nor Athena's strength can save you.
Down you go, abandoned,   300
searching your soul for joy but joy is gone.
Bled white, gnawed by demons, a husk, a wraith—

                          [*She breaks off, waiting for reply,*
                          but ORESTES *prays in silence.*]

No reply? you spit my challenge back?
You'll feast me alive, my fatted calf,
not cut on the altar first. Now hear my spell,   305
the chains of song I sing to bind you tight.
FURIES.
                              Come, Furies, dance!—
link arms for the dancing hand-to-hand,

---

[19] The animals normally sacrificed in rites of purgation.
[20] That he has not brought misfortune to his hosts indicates that Orestes has been successfully purged.
[21] Athens had contracted an alliance with Argos (the city where the action of the two earlier
plays occurs) a few years before the *Oresteia* was performed.
[22] This lake in Libya, according to one version of the myth, was Athena's birthplace.
[23] The place where the Giants (offspring of Ouranos and Ge, the personification of Earth)
unsuccessfully challenged the gods of Olympus. The present passage emphasizes Athena's
role as warrior and guardian of her city, Athens.

now we long to reveal our art,
our terror, now to declare our right
   to steer the lives of men,   310
we all conspire, we dance! we are
the just and upright, we maintain.
Hold out your hands, if they are clean
   no fury of ours will stalk you,
you will go through life unscathed.   315
But show us the guilty—one like this
   who hides his reeking hands,
and up from the outraged dead we rise,
witness bound to avenge their blood
we rise in flames against him to the end!   320

Mother who bore me,
  O dear Mother Night,
to avenge the blinded dead
and those who see by day,
  now hear me! The whelp Apollo   325
spurns my rights, he tears this trembling victim
          from my grasp—the one to bleed,
   to atone away the mother-blood at last.

   Over the victim's burning head
this chant this frenzy striking frenzy   330
      lightning crazing the mind
          this hymn of Fury
chaining the senses, ripping cross the lyre,[24]
       withering lives of men!

This, this is our right,
  spun for us by the Fates,[25]   335
the ones who bind the world,
and none can shake our hold.
  Show us the mortals overcome,
insane to murder kin—we track them down
      till they go beneath the earth,   340
and the dead find little freedom in the end.

   Over the victim's burning head
this chant this frenzy striking frenzy
      lightning crazing the mind
          this hymn of Fury   345
chaining the senses, ripping cross the lyre,
      withering lives of men!

[24] The lyre was associated with Apollo in his role as god of song and of joyful poetry.
[25] In mythology, the three sisters who control the "thread" of a human life. The first spins the thread, the second measures its length, and the third cuts it off at its destined end, the time of death.

Even at birth, I say, our rights were so ordained.
   The deathless gods must keep their hands far off—
no god may share our cups, our solemn feasts.   350
We want no part of their pious white robes—
   the Fates who gave us power made us free.

   Mine is the overthrow of houses, yes,
when warlust reared like a tame beast
      seizes near and dear—   355
         down on the man we swoop, aie!
            for all his power black him out!—
for the blood still fresh from slaughter on his hands.

So now, striving to wrench our mandate from the gods,
   we make ourselves exempt from their control,   360
we brook no trial—no god can be our judge.[26]

[Reaching toward ORESTES.]

His breed, worthy of loathing, streaked with blood,
   Zeus slights, unworthy his contempt.

   Mine is the overthrow of houses, yes,
when warlust reared like a tame beast   365
      seizes near and dear—
         down on the man we swoop, aie!
            for all his power black him out!—
for the blood still fresh from slaughter on his hands.

And all men's dreams of grandeur,   370
         tempting the heavens,
all melt down, under earth their pride goes down—
      lost in our onslaught, black robes swarming,
        Furies throbbing, dancing out our rage.

Yes! leaping down from the heights,   375
   dead weight in the crashing footfall
         down we hurl on the runner
           breakneck for the finish—
cut him down, our fury stamps him down!

Down he goes, sensing nothing,   380
         blind with defilement . . .

---

[26] What the Furies are fighting for is not merely the punishment of Orestes as an individual. They also question the basic grounds of justice. How, they protest, can an Olympian—Athena, for example—be legally competent to decide the question of whether the Olympians or the more primeval powers should be the final court of appeal? And, even more fundamentally, should the primitive law of retaliation for crimes against kindred be subordinated to *any* court or technical legal system?

darkness hovers over the man, dark guilt,
  and a dense pall overhangs his house,
   legend tells the story through her tears.

Yes! leaping down from the heights,   385
 dead weight in the crashing footfall
    down we hurl on the runner
     breakneck for the finish—
cut him down, our fury stamps him down!

   So the center holds.   390
  We are the skilled, the masterful,
   we the great fulfillers,
  memories of grief, we awesome spirits
   stern, unappeasable to man,
 disgraced, degraded, drive our powers through;   395
 banished far from god to a sunless, torchlit dusk,[27]
  we drive men through their rugged passage,
  blinded dead and those who see by day.

   Then where is the man
  not stirred with awe, not gripped by fear   400
   to hear us tell the law that
  Fate ordains, the gods concede the Furies,
   absolute till the end of time?
 And so it holds, our ancient power still holds.
We are not without our pride, though beneath the earth   405
  our strict battalions form their lines,
 groping through the mist and sunstarved night.

      [*Enter* ATHENA, *armed for combat
     with her aegis*[28] *and her spear.*]

ATHENA.
 From another world I heard a call for help.
 I was on the Scamander's banks, just claiming Troy.[29]

---

[27] These two lines, applicable to either the Furies or their victims, are a good gloss on the Furies. Both they and the punished sinners dwell in a dark underground world that is the polar opposite of the heaven and light where the newer gods dwell on Mount Olympus (above, not below, humanity). Since the Furies and the sinners inhabit the same dark place, the Furies can be understood not just as an external force of punishment but also as the internal force of guilty conscience; the sinner is ultimately his or her own avenger. The concept is akin to what Dante intimates in his *Inferno*, that the outer and internal forces that punish sin are not clearly separable. Intriguingly, then, the Furies can be interpreted as either a primitive force superseded by an advance in ethical understanding or—as a modern depth-psychologist might argue—the personification of a timeless fact about human psychology that has been obscured by the illusory progress of "civilization."

[28] Here, a cape worn by Athena.

[29] In Aeschylus' time the Athenians had a colony near Troy that they claimed had been given them by right after the Trojan war. "Theseus' sons" (line 413) are the Athenians; he was the legendary hero of their city.

The Achaean warlords chose the hero's share   410
of what their spear had won—they decreed that land,
root and branch all mine, for all time to be,
for Theseus' sons a rare, matchless gift.

Home from the wars I come, my pace unflagging,
wingless, flown on the whirring, breasting cape   415
that yokes my racing spirit in her prime.

> [*Unfurling the aegis, seeing* ORES-
> TES *and the* FURIES *at her shrine.*]

And I see some new companions on the land.
Not fear, a sense of wonder fills my eyes.

Who are you? I address you all as one:
you, the stranger seated at my idol,   420
and you, like no one born of the sown seed,
no goddess watched by the gods, no mortal either,
not to judge by your look at least, your features . . .
Wait, I call my neighbors into question.
They've done nothing wrong. It offends the rights,   425
it violates tradition.
LEADER.
                        You will learn it all,
young daughter of Zeus, cut to a few words.
We are the everlasting children of the Night.
Deep in the halls of Earth they call us Curses.
ATHENA.
Now I know your birth, your rightful name—   430
LEADER.
But not our powers, and you will learn them quickly.
ATHENA.
I can accept the facts, just tell them clearly.
LEADER.
Destroyers of life: we drive them from their houses.
ATHENA.
And the murderer's flight, where does it all end?
LEADER.
Where there is no joy, the word is never used.   435
ATHENA.
Such flight for him? You shriek him on to that?
LEADER.
                                                    Yes,
he murdered his mother—called that murder just.
ATHENA.
And nothing forced him on, no fear of someone's anger?
LEADER.
What spur could force a man to kill his mother?

ATHENA.
Two sides are here, and only half is heard.   440

LEADER.
But the oath[30]—he will neither take the oath nor give it,
no, his will is set.

ATHENA.
               And you are set
on the name of justice rather than the act.

LEADER.
How? Teach us. You have a genius for refinements.

ATHENA.
Injustice, I mean, should never triumph thanks to oaths.   445

LEADER.
Then examine him yourself, judge him fairly.

ATHENA.
You would turn over responsibility to me,
to reach the final verdict?

LEADER.
              Certainly.[31]
We respect you. You show us respect.

[ATHENA turns to ORESTES.]

ATHENA.
Your turn, stranger. What do you say to this?   450
Tell us your land, your birth, your fortunes.
Then defend yourself against their charge,
if trust in your rights has brought you here to guard
my hearth and idol, a suppliant for purging
like Ixion,[32] sacred. Speak to all this clearly,   455
speak to me.

ORESTES.
          Queen Athena, first,
the misgiving in your final words is strong.
Let me remove it. I haven't come for purging.
Look, not a stain on the hands that touch your idol.
I have proof for all I say, and it is strong.   460

The law condemns the man of the violent hand
to silence, till a master trained at purging
slits the throat of a young suckling victim,
blood absolves his blood. Long ago
at the halls of others I was fully cleansed   465

---

[30] The ritual oath of innocence. Orestes refuses it because the fact itself of matricide is for him not the main issue. A few lines later Athena argues that such rituals should not govern in legal contests.

[31] The Furies now agree to be bound by Athena's verdict.

[32] After murdering his father-in-law, Ixion was absolved by Zeus. (Later, after trying to seduce Zeus's consort, Hera, Ixion was punished by being tied in the underworld to an ever-revolving wheel.)

in the cleansing springs, the blood of many victims.
Threat of pollution, sweep it from your mind.

Now for my birth. You will know at once.
I am from Argos. My father, well you ask,
was Agamemnon, sea-lord of the men-of-war,   470
your partisan when you made the city Troy
a city of the dead.
                      What an ignoble death he died
when he came home—Ai! my blackhearted mother
cut him down, enveloped him in her handsome net—
it still attests his murder in the bath.   475
But I came back, my years of exile weathered—
killed the one who bore me, I won't deny it,
killed her in revenge. I loved my father,
fiercely.
            And Apollo shares the guilt—
he spurred me on, he warned of the pains I'd feel   480
unless I acted, brought the guilty down.
But were we just or not? Judge us now.
My fate is in your hands. Stand or fall
I shall accept your verdict.
ATHENA.
                      Too large a matter,
some may think, for mortal men to judge.   485
But by all rights not even I should decide
a case of murder—murder whets the passions.
Above all, the rites have tamed your wildness.
A suppliant, cleansed, you bring my house no harm.
If you are innocent, I'd adopt you for my city.   490

[*Turning to the* FURIES.]

But they have their destiny too, hard to dismiss,
and if they fail to win their day in court—
how it will spread, the venom of their pride,
plague everlasting blights our land, our future . . .

So it stands. A crisis either way.   495

[*Looking back and forth from*
ORESTES *to the* FURIES.]

Embrace the one? expel the other? It defeats me.

But since the matter comes to rest on us,
I will appoint the judges of manslaughter,
swear them in, and found a tribunal here
for all time to come.[33]

---

[33] The court of the Areopagus, the main forum of the Athenian judicial system.

[*To* ORESTES *and the* FURIES.]

My contestants, 500
summon your trusted witnesses and proofs,
your defenders under oath to help your cause.
And I will pick the finest men of Athens,
return and decide the issue fairly, truly—
bound to our oaths, our spirits bent on justice. 505

[ATHENA *leaves. The* FURIES *form
their chorus.*]

FURIES.
Here, now,[34] is the overthrow
of every binding law—once his appeal,
his outrage wins the day,
his matricide! One act links all mankind,
hand to desperate hand in bloody license. 510
Over and over deathstrokes
dealt by children wait their parents,
mortal generations still unborn.

We are the Furies still, yes,
but now our rage that patrolled the crimes of men, 515
that stalked their rage dissolves—
we loose a lethal tide to sweep the world!
Man to man foresees his neighbor's torments,
groping to cure his own—
poor wretch, there is no cure, no use, 520
the drugs that ease him speed the next attack.

Now when the sudden blows come down,
let no one sound the call that once brought help,
"Justice, hear me—Furies throned in power!"
Oh I can hear the father now 525
or the mother sob with pain
at the pain's onset . . . hopeless now,
the house of Justice falls.

There is a time when terror helps,
the watchman must stand guard upon the heart. 530
It helps, at times, to suffer into truth.
Is there a man who knows no fear
in the brightness of his heart,
or a man's city, both are one,
that still reveres the rights? 535

---

[34] In the following chorus, the Furies argue that the force they represent, of vengeance and fear of punishment, is the very foundation of social order; if Orestes is acquitted, the whole community will be engulfed by general chaos, since the distinction between good and evil will no longer govern human behavior.

Neither the life of anarchy
nor the life enslaved by tyrants, no,
worship neither.
Strike the balance all in all and god will give you power;
the laws of god may veer from north to south—   540
we Furies plead for Measure.
Violence is Impiety's child, true to its roots,
but the spirit's great good health breeds all we love
and all our prayers call down,
prosperity and peace.   545

All in all I tell you people,
bow before the altar of the rights,
revere it well.
Never trample it underfoot, your eyes set on spoils;
revenge will hunt the godless day and night—   550
the destined end awaits.
So honor your parents first with reverence, I say,
and the stranger guest you welcome to your house,
turn to attend his needs,
respect his sacred rights.   555

All of your own free will, all uncompelled,
be just and you will never want for joy,
you and your kin can never be uprooted from the earth.
The reckless one—I warn the marauder
dragging plunder, chaotic, rich beyond all rights: 560
he'll strike his sails,
harried at long last,
stunned when the squalls of torment break his spars to bits.

He cries to the deaf, he wrestles walls of sea
sheer whirlpools down, down, with the gods' laughter   565
breaking over the man's hot heart—they see him flailing, crushed.
The one who boasted never to shipwreck
now will never clear the cape and steer for home;
he lived for wealth,
golden his life long—   570
he rams on the reef of law and drowns unwept, unseen.

[*The scene has shifted to the Areopa-*
gus, the tribunal on the Crag of
Ares.[35] ATHENA *enters in proces-*
sion with a herald and ten citizens
she has chosen to be judges.]

---

[35] Ares, the god of war, had according to legend once been tried on the Areopagus (the "Crag of Ares" in Athens), for murder.

ATHENA.

    Call for order, herald, marshal our good people.
    Lift the Etruscan battle-trumpet,[36]
    strain it to full pitch with human breath,
    crash out a stabbing blast along the ranks.   575

> [*The trumpet sounds. The judges
> take up positions between the audi-
> ence and the actors.* ATHENA *sepa-
> rates the* FURIES *and* ORESTES, *di-
> recting him to the Stone of Outrage
> and the leader to the Stone of
> Unmercifulness, where the* FURIES
> *form their chorus. Then* ATHENA
> *takes her stand between two urns
> that will receive the ballots.*]

    And while this court of judgment fills, my city,
    silence will be best. So that you can learn
    my everlasting laws. And you too,

> [*To* ORESTES *and the* FURIES.]

    that our verdict may be well observed by all.

> [APOLLO *enters suddenly and looms
> behind* ORESTES.]

    Lord Apollo—rule it over your own sphere!   580
    What part have you in this? Tell us.

APOLLO.

                          I come
    as a witness. This man, according to custom,
    this suppliant sought out my house and hearth.
    I am the one who purged his bloody hands.
    His champion too, I share responsibility   585
    for his mother's execution.
                       Bring on the trial.
    You know the rules, now turn them into justice.

> [ATHENA *turns to the* FURIES.]

ATHENA.

    The trial begins! Yours is the first word—
    the prosecution opens. Start to finish,
    set the facts before us, make them clear.   590

LEADER.

    Numerous as we are, we will be brief.

---

[36] Athena's battle-trumpet, supposedly made in a region of northern Italy.

[*To* ORESTES.]

Answer count for count, charge for charge.
First, tell us, did you kill your mother?
ORESTES.
I killed her. There's no denying that.
LEADER.
Three falls in the match. One is ours[37] already.   595
ORESTES.
You exult before your man is on his back.
LEADER.
But *how* did you kill her? You must tell us that.
ORESTES.
I will. I drew my sword—more, I cut her throat.
LEADER.
And who persuaded you? who led you on?
ORESTES.
This god and his command.

[*Indicating* APOLLO.]

He bears me witness.   600
LEADER.
The Seer? He drove you on to matricide?
ORESTES.
                                        Yes,
and to this hour I have no regrets.
LEADER.
                                        If the verdict
brings you down, you'll change your story quickly.
ORESTES.
I have my trust; my father will help me from the grave.
LEADER.
Trust to corpses now! You made your mother one.   605
ORESTES.
I do. She had two counts against her, deadly crimes.
LEADER.
How? Explain that to your judges.
ORESTES.
She killed her husband—killed my father too.
LEADER.
But murder set her free, and you live on for trial.
ORESTES.
She lived on. You never drove *her* into exile—why?   610
LEADER.
The blood of the man she killed was not her own.
ORESTES.
And I? Does mother's blood run in my veins?

---

[37] Three overthrows of the opponent were required to win a wrestling match; the Leader claims to have won the first.

LEADER.
> How could she breed you in her body, murderer?
> Disclaim your mother's blood? She gave you life.

> [ORESTES *turns to* APOLLO.]

ORESTES.
> Bear me witness—show me the way, Apollo!   615
> Did I strike her down with justice?
> Strike I did, I don't deny it, no.
> But how does our bloody work impress you now?—
> Just or not? Decide.
> I must make my case to them.

> [*Looking to the judges.*]

APOLLO.
>   *Just,*   620
> I say, to you and your high court, Athena.
> Seer that I am, I never lie. Not once
> from the Prophet's thrones have I declared
> a word that bears on man, woman or city
> that Zeus did not command, the Olympian Father.   625
> This is *his* justice—omnipotent, I warn you.
> Bend to the will of Zeus. No oath can match
> the power of the Father.
LEADER.
>   Zeus, you say,
> gave that command to your oracle? He charged
> Orestes here to avenge his father's death   630
> and spurn his mother's rights?
APOLLO.
>   —Not the same
> for a noble man to die, covered with praise,
> his scepter the gift of god—murdered, at that,
> by a woman's hand, no arrows whipping in
> from a distance as an Amazon[38] would fight.   635
> But as you will hear, Athena, and your people
> poised to cast their lots and judge the case.
> Home from the long campaign he came, more won
> than lost on balance, home to her loyal, waiting arms,
> the welcome bath . . .
>   he was just emerging at the edge,   640
> and there she pitched her tent, her circling shroud—
> she shackled her man in robes,
> in her gorgeous never-ending web she chopped him down!

> Such was the outrage of his death, I tell you,
> the lord of the squadrons, that magnificent man.   645

---

[38] The Amazons were women warriors, noted especially as archers.

Her I draw to the life to lash your people,
marshaled to reach a verdict.
LEADER.

                                        Zeus, you say,
sets more store by a father's death? He shackled
his own father, Kronos[39] proud with age.
Doesn't that contradict you?   650

                    [*To the judges.*]

Mark it well. I call you all to witness.
APOLLO.
You grotesque, loathsome—the gods detest you!
Zeus can break chains, we've cures for that,
countless ingenious ways to set us free.
But once the dust drinks down a man's blood,   655
he is gone, once for all. No rising back,
no spell sung over the grave can sing him back—
not even Father can. Though all things else
he can overturn and never strain for breath.
LEADER.

                                            So
you'd force this man's acquittal? Behold, Justice!   660

            [*Exhibiting* APOLLO *and* ORESTES.]

Can a son spill his mother's blood on the ground,
then settle into his father's halls in Argos?
Where are the public altars he can use?
Can the kinsmen's holy water touch his hands?
APOLLO.
Here is the truth, I tell you—see how right I am.   665
The woman you call the mother of the child
is not the parent,[40] just a nurse to the seed,
the new-sown seed that grows and swells inside her.
The *man* is the source of life—the one who mounts.
She, like a stranger for a stranger, keeps   670
the shoot alive unless god hurts the roots.

I give you proof that all I say is true.
The father can father forth without a mother.
Here she stands, our living witness. Look—

                [*Exhibiting* ATHENA.]

[39] Zeus had overcome his father Kronos (the Roman Saturn) and imprisoned him in the underworld; Apollo will reply to this charge by arguing that imprisonment is not the same as irrevocable death.
[40] This genetic theory is proved, Apollo goes on to argue, by Athena herself, who was born from Zeus's head.

Child sprung full-blown from Olympian Zeus,   675
never bred in the darkness of the womb
but such a stock no goddess could conceive!

And I, Pallas, with all my strong techniques
will rear your host and battlements to glory.
So I dispatched this suppliant to your hearth   680
that he might be your trusted friend forever,
that you might win a new ally,[41] dear goddess.
He and his generations arm-in-arm with yours,
your bonds stand firm for all posterity—

ATHENA.

                                    Now

have we heard enough? May I have them cast   685
their honest lots as conscience may decide?

LEADER.

For us, we have shot our arrows, every one.
I wait to hear how this ordeal will end.

ATHENA.

                              Of course.

And what can I do to merit your respect?

APOLLO.

You have heard what you have heard.   690

[To the judges.]

Cast your lots, my friends,
strict to the oath that you have sworn.

ATHENA.

                             And now

if you would hear my law, you men of Greece,
you who will judge the first trial of bloodshed.
Now and forever more, for Aegeus' people[42]   695
this will be the court where judges reign.
This is the Crag of Ares, where the Amazons
pitched their tents when they came marching down
on Theseus, full tilt in their fury, erecting
a new city to overarch his city, towers thrust   700
against his towers—they sacrificed to Ares,
named this rock from that day onward Ares' Crag.

Here from the heights, terror and reverence,
my people's kindred powers
will hold them from injustice through the day   705
and through the mild night. Never pollute
our law with innovations. No, my citizens,

[41] The people of Argos; at the time of the *Oresteia*, Athens had recently concluded an alliance with them.

[42] The Athenians; Aegeus was a legendary ruler of the city and father of Theseus.

foul a clear well and you will suffer thirst.
Neither anarchy nor tyranny, my people.
Worship the Mean, I urge you,   710
shore it up with reverence and never
banish terror from the gates, not outright.[43]
Where is the righteous man who knows no fear?
The stronger your fear, your reverence for the just,
the stronger your country's wall and city's safety,   715
stronger by far than all men else possess
in Scythia's rugged steppes or Pelops' level plain.[44]
Untouched by lust for spoil, this court of law
majestic, swift to fury, rising above you
as you sleep, our night watch always wakeful,   720
guardian of our land—I found it here and now.

So I urge you, Athens. I have drawn this out
to rouse you to your future. You must rise,
each man must cast his lot and judge the case,
reverent to his oath. Now I have finished.   725

> [*The judges come forward, pass be-
> tween the urns and cast their lots.*]

LEADER.
  Beware. Our united force can break your land.
  Never wound our pride, I tell you, never.
APOLLO.
  The oracles, not mine alone but Zeus's too—
  dread them, I warn you, never spoil their fruit.

> [*The leader turns to* APOLLO.]

LEADER.
  You dabble in works of blood beyond your depth.   730
  Oracles, your oracles will be stained forever.
APOLLO.
  Oh, so the Father's judgment faltered when Ixion,
  the first man-slayer came to him for purging?
LEADER.
  Talk on, talk on. But if I lose this trial
  I will return in force to crush the land.   735
APOLLO.
  Never—among the gods, young and old,
  you go disgraced. I will triumph over you!

---

[43] The phrase probably means two things: a) maintain as part of your conscience a wholesome fear of committing evil, and b) do not summarily turn away from your city a frightened
stranger seeking asylum.
[44] That is, in the wild land of faraway Scythia or in the Grecian land of Pelops that included
Argos.

LEADER.
> Just as you triumphed in the house of Pheres,[45]
> luring the Fates to set men free from death.

APOLLO.
> What?—is it a crime to help the pious man,   740
> above all, when his hour of need has come?

LEADER.
> You brought them down, the oldest realms of order,
> seduced the ancient goddesses with wine.

APOLLO.
> *You* will fail this trial—in just a moment
> spew your venom and never harm your enemies.   745

LEADER.
> You'd ride me down, young god, for all my years?
> Well here I stand, waiting to learn the verdict.
> Torn with doubt . . . to rage against the city or—

ATHENA.
> My work is here, to render the final judgment.
> Orestes,

> [*Raising her arm, her hand
> clenched as if holding a ballot-stone.*]

> I will cast my lot for you.   750
> No mother gave me birth.
> I honor the male, in all things but marriage.
> Yes, with all my heart I am my Father's child.
> I cannot set more store by the woman's death—
> she killed her husband, guardian of their house.   755
> Even if the vote is equal, Orestes wins.[46]

> Shake the lots from the urns. Quickly,
> you of the jury charged to make the count.

> [*Judges come forward, empty the
> urns, and count the ballot-stones.*]

ORESTES.
> O God of the Light, Apollo, how will the verdict go?

LEADER.
> O Night, dark mother, are you watching now?   760

---

[45] Father of Admetus, a favorite of Apollo, who preserved Admetus from destined death by overcoming "the ancient goddesses"—that is, the Fates—"with wine" (line 743) so that they agreed to accept an alternative victim. Admetus' wife Alcestis offered her own life instead of his. The story is told in Euripides' *Alcestis*.

[46] In interpreting Athena's decision here, we can accept her own explanation, that she is her father Zeus's child (an Olympian who is biased toward males). But these reasons seem incompatible with her evenhandedness elsewhere in the play. That she has not simply ignored the Furies' side of the case is proved by her later actions and words.

ORESTES.
  Now for the goal—the noose, or the new day!
LEADER.
  Now we go down, or forge ahead in power.
APOLLO.
  Shake out the lots and count them fairly, friends.
  Honor Justice. An error in judgment now
  can mean disaster. The cast of a single lot   765
  restores a house to greatness.

                                  [*Receiving the judges' count,* ATHENA
                                  lifts her arm once more.]

ATHENA.

                                  The man goes free,
  cleared of the charge of blood. The lots are equal.
ORESTES.
  O Pallas Athena—you, you save my house!
  I was shorn of the fatherland but you
  reclaim it for me. Now any Greek will say,   770
  "He lives again, the man of Argos lives
  on his fathers' great estates. Thanks to Pallas,
  Apollo and Zeus, the lord of all fulfillment,
  Third, Saving Zeus." He respected father's death,
  looked down on mother's advocates—

                                  [*Indicating the* FURIES.]

                                  he saved me.   775

  And now I journey home. But first I swear
  to you, your land and assembled host, I swear
  by the future years that bring their growing yield
  that no man, no helmsman of Argos wars on Athens,
  spears in the vanguard moving out for conquest.   780
  We ourselves, even if we must rise up from the grave,
  will deal with those who break the oath I take—
  baffle them with disasters, curse their marches,
  send them hawks aloft on the left[47] at every crossing—
  make their pains recoil upon their heads.   785
  But all who keep our oath, who uphold your rights
  and citadel forever, comrade spear to spear,
  we bless with all the kindness of our heart.

  Now farewell, you and the people of your city.
  Good wrestling—a grip no foe can break.   790
  A saving hope, a spear to bring you triumph!

---

[47] The left was the side on which ill omens supposedly appeared. Compare the eagles
(mentioned in *Agamemnon,* lines 118 ff.) who appeared on the right before the sacrifice of
Iphigeneia at Aulis.

> [*Exit* ORESTES, *followed by*
> APOLLO. *The* FURIES *reel in wild*
> *confusion around* ATHENA.]

FURIES.
    You, you younger gods!—you have ridden down
        the ancient laws, wrenched them from my grasp—
    and I, robbed of my birthright, suffering, great with wrath,
        I loose my poison over the soil, aieee!—   795
    poison to match my grief comes pouring out my heart,
            cursing the land to burn it sterile and now
    rising up from its roots a cancer blasting leaf and child,
            now for Justice, Justice!—cross the face of the earth
    the bloody tide comes hurling, all mankind destroyed.   800
    . . . Moaning, only moaning? What will I do?
        The mockery of it, Oh unbearable,
    mortified by Athens,
    we the daughters of Night,
    our power stripped, cast down.
ATHENA.
                            Yield to me.   805
    No more heavy spirits. You were not defeated—
    the vote was tied, a verdict fairly reached
    with no disgrace to you, no, Zeus brought
    luminous proof before us. He who spoke
    god's oracle, he bore witness that Orestes   810
    did the work but should not suffer harm.

    And now you'd vent your anger, hurt the land?
    Consider a moment. Calm yourself. Never
    render us barren, raining your potent showers
    down like spears, consuming every seed.   815
    By all my rights I promise you your seat
    in the depths of earth,[48] yours by all rights—
    stationed at hearths equipped with glistening thrones,
    covered with praise! My people will revere you.
FURIES.
    You, you younger gods!—you have ridden down   820
        the ancient laws, wrenched them from my grasp—
    and I, robbed of my birthright, suffering, great with wrath,
        I loose my poison over the soil, aieee!—
    poison to match my grief comes pouring out my heart,
            cursing the land to burn it sterile and now   825
    rising up from its roots a cancer blasting leaf and child,
            now for Justice, Justice!—cross the face of the earth
    the bloody tide comes hurling, all mankind destroyed.

---

[48] Appropriately, the Furies, who have been all along portrayed as forces of earth and night, will be given cave-shrines at the Athenian Acropolis, where they will combine their old role as ministers of avenging justice with a new role as agents of fertility and the blessings symbolized by it.

. . . Moaning, only moaning? What will I do?
    The mockery of it, Oh unbearable,   830
mortified by Athens,
we the daughters of Night,
our power stripped, cast down.
ATHENA.
                           You have your power,
you are goddesses—but not to turn
on the world of men and ravage it past cure.   835
I put my trust in Zeus and . . . must I add this?
I am the only god who knows the keys
to the armory where his lightning-bolt is sealed.
No need of that, not here.
                     Let me persuade you.
The lethal spell of your voice, never cast it   840
down on the land and blight its harvest home.
Lull asleep that salt black wave of anger—
awesome, proud with reverence, live with me.
The land is rich, and more, when its first fruits,
offered for heirs and the marriage rites, are yours   845
to hold forever, you will praise my words.
FURIES.
    But for me to suffer such disgrace . . . I,
the proud heart of the past, driven under the earth,
condemned, like so much filth,
    and the fury in me breathing hatred—   850
O good Earth,
       what is this stealing under the breast,
what agony racks the spirit? . . . Night, dear Mother Night!
All's lost, our ancient powers torn away by their cunning,
ruthless hands, the gods so hard to wrestle down   855
obliterate us all.
ATHENA.
                I will bear with your anger.
You are older. The years have taught you more,
much more than I can know. But Zeus, I think,
gave me some insight too, that has its merits.
If you leave for an alien land and alien people,   860
you will come to love this land, I promise you.
As time flows on, the honors flow through all
my citizens, and you, throned in honor
before the house of Erechtheus,[49] will harvest
more from men and women moving in solemn file   865
than you can win throughout the mortal world.

Here in our homeland never cast the stones
that whet our bloodlust. Never waste our youth,

---

[49] A legendary ruler of Athens; a temple named for him (the Erechtheum) stood on the
Acropolis.

inflaming them with the burning wine of strife.
Never pluck the heart of the battle cock   870
and plant it in our people—intestine war
seething against themselves. Let our wars
rage on abroad, with all their force, to satisfy
our powerful lust for fame. But as for the bird
that fights at home—my curse on civil war.   875

This is the life I offer, it is yours to take.
Do great things, feel greatness, greatly honored.
Share this country cherished by the gods.

FURIES.
    But for me to suffer such disgrace . . . I,
the proud heart of the past, driven under the earth,   880
condemned, like so much filth,
    and the fury in me breathing hatred—
O good Earth,
        what is this stealing under the breast,
what agony racks the spirit? . . . Night, dear Mother Night!   885
All's lost, our ancient powers torn away by their cunning,
ruthless hands, the gods so hard to wrestle down
obliterate us all.

ATHENA.
                        No, I will never tire
of telling you your gifts. So that you,
the older gods, can never say that I,   890
a young god and the mortals of my city
drove you outcast, outlawed from the land.

But if you have any reverence for Persuasion,
the majesty of Persuasion,
the spell of my voice that would appease your fury—   895
Oh please stay . . .
                    and if you refuse to stay,
it would be wrong, unjust to afflict this city
with wrath, hatred, populations routed. Look,
it is all yours, a royal share of our land—
justly entitled, glorified forever.

LEADER.
                                Queen Athena,   900
where is the home you say is mine to hold?

ATHENA.
Where all the pain and anguish end. Accept it.

LEADER.
And if I do, what honor waits for me?

ATHENA.
No house can thrive without you.

LEADER.
                            You would do that—
grant me that much power?

ATHENA.
                              Whoever reveres us—   905
we will raise the fortunes of their lives.
LEADER.
     And you will pledge me that, for all time to come?
ATHENA.
     Yes—I must never promise things I cannot do.
LEADER.
     Your magic is working . . . I can feel the hate,
the fury slip away.
ATHENA.
                              At last! And now take root   910
in the land and win yourself new friends.
LEADER.
                                        A spell—
what spell to sing? to bind the land forever? Tell us.
ATHENA.
     Nothing that strikes a note of brutal conquest. Only peace—
blessings, rising up from the earth and the heaving sea,
and down the vaulting sky let the wind-gods breathe   915
a wash of sunlight streaming through the land,
and the yield of soil and grazing cattle flood
our city's life with power and never flag
with time. Make the seed of men live on,
the more they worship you the more they thrive.   920
I love them as a gardener loves his plants,
these upright men, this breed fought free of grief.
All that is yours to give.
                         And I,
in the trials of war where fighters burn for fame,
will never endure the overthrow of Athens—   925
all will praise her, victor city, pride of man.

                              [*The* FURIES *assemble, dancing
                              around* ATHENA, *who becomes their
                              leader.*]

FURIES.
                    I will embrace
          one home with you, Athena,
                    never fail the city
          you and Zeus almighty, you and Ares   930
     hold as the fortress of the gods, the shield
of the high Greek altars, glory of the powers.
     Spirit of Athens, hear my words, my prayer
          like a prophet's warm and kind,
               that the rare good things of life   935
               come rising crest on crest,
          sprung from the rich black earth and
     gleaming with the bursting flash of sun.

ATHENA.

    These blessings I bestow on you, my people, gladly.
    I enthrone these strong, implacable spirits here   940
    and root them in our soil.
                          Theirs,
    theirs to rule the lives of men,
       it is their fated power.
    But he who has never felt their weight,
    or known the blows of life and how they fall,   945
    the crimes of his fathers hale him toward their bar,
    and there for all his boasts—destruction,
       silent, majestic in anger,
    crushes him to dust.

FURIES.

               Yes and I ban
       the winds that rock the olive—   950
       hear my love, my blessing—
    thwart their scorching heat that blinds the buds,
     hold from our shores the killing icy gales,
    and I ban the blight that creeps on fruit and withers—
      God of creation, Pan, make flocks increase   955
       and the ewes drop fine twin lambs
         when the hour of labor falls.
         And silver, child of Earth,
        secret treasure of Hermes,
     come to light and praise the gifts of god.   960

ATHENA.

    Blessings—now do you hear, you guards of Athens,
     all that she will do?
    Fury the mighty queen, the dread
    of the deathless gods and those beneath the earth,
    deals with mortals clearly, once for all.   965
    She delivers songs to some, to others
     a blinding life of tears—
    Fury works her will.

FURIES.

          And the lightning stroke
      that cuts men down before their prime, I curse,
       but the lovely girl who finds a mate's embrace,   970
    the deep joy of wedded life—O grant that gift, that prize,
    you gods of wedlock, grant it, goddesses of Fate!
      Sisters born of the Night our mother,
        spirits steering law,
       sharing at all our hearths,   975
       at all times bearing down
        to make our lives more just,
      all realms exalt you highest of the gods.

ATHENA.

    Behold, my land, what blessings Fury kindly,
     gladly brings to pass—   980

I am in my glory! Yes, I love Persuasion;
she watched my words, she met their wild refusals.
Thanks to Zeus of the Councils who can turn
dispute to peace—he won the day.

[*To the* FURIES.]

    Thanks to our duel for blessings;   985
we win through it all.
FURIES.
                  And the brutal strife,
        the civil war devouring men, I pray
    that it never rages through our city, no,
that the good Greek soil never drinks the blood of Greeks,
      shed in an orgy of reprisal life for life—   990
        that Fury like a beast will never
          rampage through the land.
        Give joy in return for joy,
         one common will for love,
        and hate with one strong heart: 995
    such union heals a thousand ills of man.
ATHENA.
Do you *hear* how Fury sounds her blessings forth,
   how Fury finds the way?
Shining out of the terror of their faces
I can see great gains for you, my people.   1000
Hold them kindly, kind as they are to you.
Exalt them always, you exalt your land,
   your city straight and just—
its light goes through the world.
FURIES.
                  Rejoice,
        rejoice in destined wealth,   1005
        rejoice, Athena's people—
      poised by the side of Zeus,
   loved by the loving virgin girl,[50]
      achieve humanity at last,
        nestling under Pallas' wings   1010
      and blessed with Father's love.
ATHENA.
You too rejoice! and I must lead the way
to your chambers by the holy light of these,
   your escorts bearing fire.

                    [*Enter* ATHENA'S *entourage of*
                    women, bearing offerings and vic-
                    tims and torches still unlit.]

---

[50]The "virgin goddess" Athena; her kinship with the Furies, who are now also kindly
Eumenides, ironically recalls Apollo's sneer at the Furies earlier as "the eternal virgins" (line
73).

Come, and sped beneath the earth 1015
  by our awesome sacrifices,
keep destruction from the country,
bring prosperity home to Athens,
triumph sailing in its wake.
                                        And you,
my people born of the Rock King,[51] 1020
lead on our guests for life, my city—
May they treat you with compassion,
compassionate as you will be to them.

FURIES.

                              Rejoice!—
            rejoice—the joy resounds—
        all those who dwell in Athens, 1025
            spirits and mortals, come,
            govern Athena's city well,
        revere us well, we are your guests;
        you will learn to praise your Furies,
            you will praise the fortunes of your lives. 1030

ATHENA.

My thanks! and I will speed your prayers, your blessings—
lit by the torches breaking into flame
I send you home, home to the core of Earth,
escorted by these friends who guard my idol
duty-bound.

                    [ATHENA's *entourage comes for-
                    ward, bearing crimson robes.*[52]]

            Bright eye of the land of Theseus, 1035
come forth, my splendid troupe. Girls and mothers,
trains of aged women grave in movement,
dress our Furies now in blood-red robes.
Praise them—let the torch move on!
So the love this family bears toward our land 1040
will bloom in human strength from age to age.

                    [*The women invest the* FURIES *and
                    sing the final chorus. Torches blaze;
                    a procession forms, including the
                    actors and the judges and the audi-
                    ence.* ATHENA *leads them from the
                    theater and escorts them through the
                    city.*]

THE WOMEN OF THE CITY.

    On, on, good spirits born for glory,
Daughters of Night, her children always young,

---

[51] The primitive king of the Acropolis.
[52] The red robes and torches recall and reverse the ominous symbolism of robes, blood,
and torches in the *Agamemnon*.

now under loyal escort—
Blessings, people of Athens, sing your blessings out.   1045

Deep, deep in the first dark vaults of Earth,
sped by the praise and victims we will bring,
                reverence will attend you—
Blessings now, all people, sing your blessings out.

You great good Furies, bless the land with kindly hearts,   1050
you Awesome Spirits, come—exult in the blazing torch,
                exultant in our fires, journey on.
Cry, cry in triumph, carry on the dancing on and on!

This peace between Athena's people and their guests
must never end. All-seeing Zeus and Fate embrace,   1055
                down they come to urge our union on—
Cry, cry in triumph, carry on the dancing on and on!

Sophocles
(496–406 B.C.)

*In more than one sense, Sophocles is the central figure among the three great Greek
tragedians. He was born in 496 B.C. in Colonus, the suburb of Athens celebrated in
his last play,* Oedipus at Colonus; *he died in 406. Much of his life-span thus overlapped that of his predecessor, Aeschylus, who died when Sophocles was forty. The
third of the great triumvirate, Euripides, was sixteen years younger than Sophocles
but died slightly before him. As a dramatist, Sophocles was a consummate artist who
combined the high ethical and religious concerns of Aeschylus with the intense interest
in individual human psychology characteristic of Euripides. Sophocles' ninety years
of life therefore coincided with the entire history—the rise and fall—of the golden
age of Greek tragedy. His years also coincided with the rise and fall of the uniquely
splendid—and historically tragic—Athenian culture of the fifth century. In 480,
when Sophocles was sixteen years old, he took part in a public celebration of the naval
victory over the Persians at Salamis, a victory that—coincidentally or not—raised
the curtain on the awesome cultural and social achievements of the ensuing age.
Sophocles' death occurred only two years before the definitive collapse of Athenian
supremacy, when in 404 the city succumbed to Sparta and its allies.*

*By most accounts, Sophocles was a man comfortably at home in his world and at
the center of its public life. He was enormously successful and popular as a man of
the theater. His temperament was urbane, gregarious, balanced. He held several
important public positions during the years of Athens' primacy—as treasurer, as a
diplomatic and military policy-maker, as an ambassador, even as a priest. In short, he
was what we have come to call a member of the establishment. And yet, intriguingly,*

he wrote dramas that call into question—though they do not necessarily under-mine—the values generally associated with that role. Oedipus, in Oedipus the King, *is the model of a good ruler, a humanely intelligent and vigorously active leader, a man who earlier saved his adopted city Thebes from disaster. Yet Oedipus is finally driven to self-mutilation and self-imposed exile because he has committed, though unwittingly, the most horrendous crimes against the divine order, the natural order, and the polity: patricide, incest, and the pollution of his city. In* Antigone, *Oedipus' brave, lovable, headstrong daughter confronts her uncle Kreon, the new ruler of Thebes, over an issue—the conflicting demands of civic, familial, and religious principles—that few establishmentarians would press urgently. Probings of these themes, stories, or issues are not what one would expect of a religious pietist or of a politically complacent conservative.*

That paradox, along with others, makes Sophocles an especially challenging artist and personality. Scholars disagree on how to interpret him, as man or playwright. He wrote more than 120 plays, of which only seven have survived intact (two are included in this volume; the others are Ajax, The Women of Trachis, Electra, Philoctetes, *and* Oedipus at Colonus). *His artistic control of plot and other elements of the drama have helped identify Sophocles as the perfect "classicist," and the extravagant praise given him by Aristotle in his* Poetics *has reinforced that image. Yet "classicist" is an inadequate term, and a seriously misleading one if we make the simple-minded but familiar identification of the classical with calm, serene detachment. Sophocles tends to represent in his characters general human types, an approach generally considered classical. Antigone is the archetype of the martyr to principle, Oedipus of the intelligent man brought low by the very intellectual gifts and compulsion to understand that make him admirable (not to mention the universality found in him by Sigmund Freud, who discerned in the "Oedipus complex" a fundamental law of filial and psychic experience). Yet at no time do we lose sight of these characters as individuals, and indeed as individuals racked by conflict, pain, or both. Antigone is indeed a type, but (like Cordelia in Shakespeare's* King Lear, *who has a similar blend of gentleness and toughness) she embodies that type in a distinct individual personality. For example, Antigone's awareness of the sanctity of the family bond makes her compassionate toward her dead brother Polyneices but incongruously, brutally contemptuous of her sister Ismene.*

One of the pervading themes in Sophocles is the justice of the universe. We are to understand that, in some sense, cosmic justice ultimately prevails, but any cosmic order that demands the blinding and exile of the essentially just Oedipus and the death of the heroic Antigone would seem ambiguous and indeed frightening. Few authors of any age have rendered the experience of raw pain—psychological and physical—so compellingly. Significantly, the nineteenth-century poet Matthew Arnold described Sophocles as a man who "saw life steadily and saw it whole" but also as one who heard "the eternal note of sadness" and was preeminently sensitive to "the turbid ebb and flow of human misery."

Sophocles does not treat issues in a vacuum; he is above all a dramatist. The innovations he made in dramatic method and staging have the effect of making conflict more humanly immediate—if not necessarily more powerful—than in Aeschylus. By increasing the number of speaking actors from two to three, Sophocles made possible even more intricate interpersonal relationships than Aeschylus had portrayed; by reducing the lyrical role of the Chorus (though he increased its size) Sophocles was able to focus more directly, and in a less stylized way, on complexities of character as conveyed in dialogue. He also expanded the use of stage machinery. The total effect is to intensify our awareness of conflict, both external and within individual characters.

Oedipus the King *has a special place in literature; it may well be the most important and influential drama ever written. Aristotle seems to have considered it the definitive tragedy, just as he considered Homer's* Iliad *and* Odyssey *the definitive epics. The play is the best known and most frequently cited example of "dramatic irony," where the audience possesses information of which the main characters in the play are ignorant. The gradual revelation to Oedipus of his past history, an already familiar story the audience would have known from the very beginning of the play, makes for powerful suspense, especially since it is Oedipus himself who relentlessly investigates and puts together the case that—for all the elaborate precautions he has taken not to commit unspeakable crimes—will in the end damn him in his own eyes and in those of other people. The gigantic metaphor of eyes, of seeing, and blindness, is worked with virtuoso skill. But the metaphor is not a mere "literary" device; it typifies Sophocles' view of man's place in the totality of things. Humanity in his plays is an integral part of a world-order that can be only partially understood at best. The cosmic system includes, besides human beings and nature, those darkly inscrutable forces identified—inadequately—as the gods and fate.*

Yet Sophocles is not a fatalist either. Despite the sense of inevitability his plays convey, human beings are considered responsible for their acts. But this belief in responsibility raises an even deeper question about necessity and human freedom, for if the lives of men and women are governed by themselves and not by their stars, are not these human beings themselves determined in their behavior by what they "are"? Character may be destiny, but to what extent is character itself an unchangeable given? Even more than such difficult but relatively concrete issues as the conflict between the person and polity, this mind-bending question makes Sophocles' plays touchstones for an appreciation of the human dilemma.

FURTHER READING *(prepared by F.S.N.):* An excellent general introduction to Sophocles and to each of his plays is Ruth Scodel, *Sophocles,* 1984. Now available in English is the classic by Karl Reinhardt, *Sophocles,* 1947, trans. Hazel and David Harvey, 1979, which discusses all the extant plays. Other works dealing with all or some of the Sophoclean dramas are S. M. Adams, *Sophocles the Playwright,* 1957; William Nickerson Bates, *Sophocles: Poet and Dramatist,* 1940, repr. 1961; Bernard M. W. Knox, *The Heroic Temper: Studies in Sophoclean Tragedy,* 1964. Further critical works on the life and thought of Sophocles are T. B. L. Webster, *An Introduction to Sophocles,* 1936, repr. 1969; and H. D. F. Kitto, *Sophocles: Dramatist and Philosopher,* 1958, repr. 1981. A number of modern interpretations of Sophocles are edited by Thomas Marion Woodard, *Sophocles: A Collection of Critical Essays,* 1966. The theatrical production of Sophocles' plays is the subject of David Seale, *Vision and Stagecraft in Sophocles,* 1982; see also the discussion of Sophocles' theater in J. Michael Walton, *The Greek Sense of Theatre: Tragedy Reviewed,* 1985. A close analysis of the word patterns in *Antigone* is given by R. F. Goheen, *The Imagery of Sophocles' Antigone,* 1951. The staging of *Antigone* is discussed in Leo Aylen, *The Greek Theater,* 1985. Luci Berkowitz and Theodore F. Brunner, ed., *Sophocles: Oedipus Tyrannus,* 1970, includes both a translation and a number of essays by various scholars on themes such as religion and psychology. See further M. J. O'Brien, ed., *Twentieth Century Interpretations of Oedipus Rex: A Collection of Critical Essays,* 1968.

OEDIPUS THE KING

Translated by Stephen Berg and Diskin Clay

CHARACTERS

OEDIPUS, *king of Thebes*
PRIEST *of Zeus*
KREON, *Oedipus' brother-in-law*
CHORUS OF THEBAN ELDERS
LEADER OF THE CHORUS
TEIRESIAS, *prophet, servant to*
   Apollo
JOCASTA, *wife of Oedipus*
MESSENGER *from Corinth*
SHEPHERD, *member of Laios'*
   household

SERVANT, *household slave of*
   Oedipus
Delegation of Thebans, servants
   to lead Teiresias and
   Oedipus; attendants to
   Oedipus, Kreon, Jocasta;
   and Antigone and Ismene,
   the daughters of Oedipus.

TIME AND SCENE

Dawn. Silence. The royal palace of Thebes. The altar of Apollo[1] to the left of the central palace. A delegation of Thebans—old men, boys, young children—enters the orchestra[2] by the steps below the altar, assembles, and waits. They carry suppliant boughs—olive branches tied with strips of wool. Some climb the steps between the orchestra and the altar, place their branches on the altar, and return to the orchestra. A PRIEST stands apart from the suppliants at the foot of one of the two stairs. Silence. Waiting. The central doors open. From inside the palace, limping,[3] OEDIPUS comes through the palace doors and stands at the top of the steps leading down into the orchestra. He is dressed in gold and wears a golden crown.

OEDIPUS. Why children,
   why are you here, why
   are you holding those branches tied with wool,
   begging me for help? Children,
   the whole city smolders with incense.[4]
   Wherever I go I hear sobbing, praying. Groans fill the air.
   Rumors, news from messengers, they are not enough for me.
   Others cannot tell me what you need.
   I am king, I had to come. As king,
   I had to know. Know for myself, know for me.   10

---

[1] The utterances of Apollo, god of prophecy, are central to the play's action. He was also god of healing and, conversely, of plague.

[2] In a Greek theater, the open space in front of the stage.

[3] In Greek, the name Oedipus means "swell-foot." The cause of his lameness is revealed later in the play.

[4] The city has been making religious offerings to appease the angry gods who have visited plague on Thebes.

Everybody everywhere knows who I am: Oedipus. King.
Priest of Zeus, we respect your age, your high office.
Speak.
Why are you kneeling? Are you afraid, old man?
What can I give you?
How can I help? Ask.
Ask me anything. Anything at all.
My heart would be a stone
if I felt no pity for these poor shattered people of mine
kneeling here, at my feet.   20
PRIEST. Oedipus, lord of Thebes, you see us, the people of Thebes,
     your people,
crowding in prayer around your altar,
these small children here, old men bent with age, priests, and I,
     the priest of Zeus,
and our noblest young men, the pride and strength of Thebes.
And there are more of us, lord Oedipus, more—gathered in the
     city, stunned,
kneeling, offering their branches, praying before the two great
     temples of Athena[5]
or staring into the ashes of burnt offerings,[6] staring,
waiting, waiting for the god to speak.
Look,
look at it,   30
lord Oedipus—right there,
in front of your eyes—this city—
it reels under a wild storm of blood, wave after wave battering
     Thebes.
We cannot breathe or stand.
We hunger, our world shivers with hunger. A disease hungers,
nothing grows, wheat, fruit, nothing grows bigger than a seed.
Our women bear
dead things,
all they can do is grieve,
our cattle wither, stumble, drop to the ground,   40
flies simmer on their bloated tongues,
the plague spreads everywhere, a stain seeping through our
     streets, our fields, our houses,
look—god's fire eating everyone, everything,
stroke after stroke of lightning, the god stabbing it alive—
it can't be put out, it can't be stopped,
its heat thickens the air, it glows like smoking metal,
this god of plague guts our city and fills the black world under us
     where the dead go
with the shrieks of women,

---

[5] Goddess of wisdom and knowledge; also, the patron of Athens and of Greek cities in general.
[6] Sacrifices to the gods; the inspection of the ashes, it was hoped, would reveal the gods' will.

living women, wailing.
You are a man, not a god—I know.   50
We all know this, the young kneeling here before you know it, too,
but we know how great you are, Oedipus, greater than any man.
When crisis struck, you saved us[7] here in Thebes,
you faced the mysterious, strange disasters hammered against us
    by the gods.
This is our history—
we paid our own flesh to the Sphinx until you set us free.
You knew no more than anyone, but you knew.
There was a god in it, a god in you.

[*The* PRIEST *kneels.*]

Help us. Oedipus, we beg you, we all turn to you, kneeling to your
    greatness.
Advice from the gods or advice from human beings—you will
    know which is needed.   60
But help us. Power and experience are yours, all yours.
Between thought and action, between
our plans and their results a distance opens.
Only a man like you, Oedipus, tested by experience,
can make them one. That much I know.
Oedipus, more like a god than any man alive,
deliver us, raise us to our feet. Remember who you are.
Remember your love for Thebes. Your skill was our salvation once
    before.
For this Thebes calls you savior.
Don't let us remember you as the king—godlike in power—   70
who gave us back our life, then let us die.
Steady us forever. You broke the riddle for us then.
It was a sign. A god was in it. Be the man you were—
rule now as you ruled before.
Oh Oedipus,
how much better to rule a city of men than be king of empty earth.
A city is nothing, a ship is nothing
where no men live together, where no men work together.
OEDIPUS. Children, poor helpless children.
I know what brings you here, I know.   80
You suffer, this plague is agony for each of you,
but none of you, not one suffers as I do.
Each of you suffers for himself, only himself.
My whole being wails and breaks
for this city, for myself, for all of you,

---

[7] Thebes had earlier been ravaged by the Sphinx, a monster with a lion's body and a
woman's head, who proposed a famous riddle, a wrong solution to which was punished by
death. The question was, "What animal moves first on four legs, then on two, then on three,
and is weakest when moving on four legs?" Oedipus correctly solved the riddle: Man, who
first crawls, then walks, then goes with a walking stick. The solution of the riddle destroyed the
Sphinx and established Oedipus in power as savior of Thebes.

old man, all of you.
Everything ends here, with me. I am the man.
You have not wakened me from some kind of sleep.
I have wept, struggled, wandered in this maze of thought,
tried every road, searched hard—   90
finally I found one cure, only one:
I sent my wife's brother, Kreon, to great Apollo's shrine at
    Delphi;[8]
I sent him to learn what I must say or do to save Thebes.
But his long absence troubles me. Why isn't he here? Where is he?
When he returns, what kind of man would I be
if I failed to do everything the god reveals?

> [*Some of the suppliants by the steps
> to the orchestra stand to announce
> *KREON'S* arrival to the* PRIEST.
> KREON *comes in by the entrance to
> the audience's left with a garland on
> his head.*]

PRIEST. You speak of Kreon, and Kreon is here.
OEDIPUS. [*turning to the altar of Apollo, then to* KREON]
    Lord Apollo, look at him—his head is crowned with laurel, his
        eyes glitter.
    Let his words blaze, blaze like his eyes, and save us.
PRIEST. He looks calm, radiant, like a god. If he brought bad news,   100
    would he be wearing that crown of sparkling leaves?
OEDIPUS. At last we will know.
    Lord Kreon, what did the god Apollo say?
KREON. His words are hopeful.
    Once everything is clear, exposed to the light,
    we will see our suffering is blessing. All we need is luck.
OEDIPUS. What do you mean? What did Apollo say? What should we
        do?
    Speak.
KREON. Here? Now? In front of all these people?
    Or inside, privately?   110

[KREON *moves toward the palace.*]

OEDIPUS. Stop. Say it. Say it to the whole city.
    I grieve for them, for their sorrow and loss, far more than I grieve
        for myself.
KREON. This is what I heard—there was no mistaking the god's mean-
        ing—
    Apollo commands us:
    Cleanse the city of Thebes, cleanse the plague from that city,
    destroy the black stain spreading everywhere, spreading,

---

[8] The most important center of prophecy in Greece; see the description at the beginning of
Aeschylus' *The Eumenides.*

poisoning the earth, touching each house, each citizen,
sickening the hearts of the people of Thebes!
Cure this disease that wastes all of you, spreading, spreading,
before it grows so vast nothing can cure it.   120

OEDIPUS. What is this plague?
How can we purify the city?

KREON. A man must be banished. Banished or killed.
Blood for blood. The plague is blood,
blood, breaking over Thebes.

OEDIPUS. *Who* is the man? *Who* is Apollo's victim?

KREON. My lord, before you came to Thebes, before you came to
        power,
Laios was our king.

OEDIPUS. I know. But I never saw Laios.

KREON. Laios was murdered. Apollo's command was very clear: 130
Avenge the murderers of Laios. Whoever they are.

OEDIPUS. But where *are* his murderers?
The crime is old. How will we find their tracks?
The killers could be anywhere.

KREON. Apollo said the killers are still here, here in Thebes.
Pursue a thing, and you may catch it;
ignored, it slips away.

OEDIPUS. And Laios—where was he murdered?
At home? Or was he away from Thebes?

KREON. He told us before he left—he was on a mission to Delphi, 140
his last trip away from Thebes. He never returned.

OEDIPUS. Wasn't there a witness, someone with Laios who saw what
        happened?

KREON. They were all killed, except for one man. He escaped.
But he was so terrified he remembered only one thing.

OEDIPUS. What was it? One small clue might lead to others.

KREON. This is what he said: bandits ambushed Laios, not one man.
They attacked him like hail crushing a stalk of wheat.

OEDIPUS. How could a single bandit dare attack a king
unless he had supporters, people with money, here,
here in Thebes?   150

KREON. There were suspicions. But after Laios died we had no leader,
        no king.
Our life was turmoil, uncertainty.

OEDIPUS. But once the throne was empty,
what threw you off the track, what kept you from searching
until you uncovered everything, knew every detail?

KREON. The intricate, hard song of the Sphinx
persuaded us the crime was not important, not then.
It seemed to say we should focus on what lay at our feet, in front of
        us,
ignore what we could not see.

OEDIPUS. Now *I* am here.   160
I will begin the search again, I
will reveal the truth, expose everything, let it all be seen.

Apollo and you were right to make us wonder about the dead
    man.
Like Apollo, I am your ally.
Justice and vengeance are what I want,
for Thebes, for the god.
Family, friends—I won't rid myself of this stain, this disease, for
    them—
they're far from here.[9] I'll do it for myself, for me.
The man who killed Laios might take revenge on me
just as violently.   170
So by avenging Laios' death, I protect myself.
[*turning to the suppliants*] Rise, children,
pick up your branches,
let someone announce my decision to the whole city of Thebes.
[*to the* PRIEST] I will do everything. Everything.
And, with the god's help, we will be saved.
Bright Apollo, let your light help us see.
Our happiness is yours to give, our failure and ruin yours.
PRIEST. Rise. We have the help we came for, children.
The king himself has promised.   180
May Apollo, who gave these oracles, come as our savior now.
Apollo, heal us, save us from this plague!

> [OEDIPUS *enters the palace. Its
> doors close.* KREON *leaves by a door
> to the right on the wing of the stage.
> The* PRIEST *and suppliants go
> down into the orchestra and leave by
> the entrance to the left as a chorus of
> fifteen Theban elders files into the
> orchestra by the entrance on the
> right, preceded by a flute player.*]

CHORUS. voice   voice   voice
    voice who knows everything o god
    glorious voice of Zeus[10]
    how have you come from Delphi bathed in gold
    what are you telling our bright city Thebes
    what are you bringing me
    health death fear
    I know nothing   190
    so frightened rooted here
    awed by you
    healer what have you sent
    is it the sudden doom of grief

---

[9] Oedipus means that his wife's first husband, Laios, is now far removed by time and death;
in addition, at this point Oedipus wrongly believes that he is the son of parents who reside in
another city (Corinth).

[10] The message or communication from Zeus, king of the gods. More concretely, the
"voice" is Apollo, the prophetic spokesman of the supreme god's will and knowledge.

or the old curse the darkness
looming in the turning season

o holy immortal voice
hope golden seed of the future
listen be with me speak
these cries of mine rise   200
tell me
I call to you reach out to you first
holy Athena god's daughter who lives forever
and your sister Artemis[11]
who cradles the earth our earth
who sits on her great throne at the hub of the market place
and I call to Apollo who hurls light
from deep in the sky
o gods be with us now
shine on us your three shields[12]   210
blazing against the darkness
come in our suffering as you came once before
to Thebes o bright divinities
and threw your saving light against the god of grief
o gods
be with us now

pain pain my sorrows have no sound
no name no word no pain like this
plague sears my people everywhere
everyone army citizens no one escapes   220
no spear of strong anxious thought protects us
great Thebes grows nothing
seeds rot in the ground
our women when they labor
cry Apollo Apollo but their children die
and lives one after another split the air
birds taking off
wingrush hungrier than fire
souls leaping away they fly
to the shore   230
of the cold god of evening[13]
west

the death stain spreads
so many corpses lie in the streets everywhere
nobody grieves for them
the city dies and young wives

[11] Athena was the daughter of Zeus, born directly without a mother from his head; Artemis, born of Zeus and Leto, is her half sister and also Apollo's full sister.
[12] The protective power of the three deities invoked (Athena, Artemis, Apollo).
[13] Hades, god of the underworld and of the dead.

and mothers gray-haired mothers wail
sob on the altar steps
they come from the city everywhere mourning their bitter days
prayers blaze to the Healer   240
grief cries a flute mingling
daughter of Zeus[14] o shining daughter show us
the warm bright face of peace of help
of our salvation

                    [*The doors of the palace open.* OE-
                    DIPUS *enters.*]

and turn back the huge raging jaws of the death god Ares[15]
drive him back drive him away
his flames lash at me
this is his war these are his shields
shouts pierce us on all sides
turn him back lift him on a strong wind   250
rush him away
to the two seas[16] at the world's edge
the sea where the waters boil
the sea where no traveler can land
because if night leaves anything alive
day destroys it
o Zeus
god beyond all other gods
handler of the fire
father   260
make the god of our sickness
ashes

Apollo
great bowman of light draw back your bow
fire arrow after arrow
make them a wall circling us
shoot into our enemy's eyes
draw the string twined with gold
come goddess[17]
who dances on the mountains   270
sowing light where your feet brush the ground
blind our enemy come
god of golden hair
piled under your golden cap Bacchus
your face blazing like the sea when the sun falls on it
like sunlight on wine

---

[14] His daughter Athena.
[15] The god of war—often regarded as the personification of any kind of destruction.
[16] The Atlantic at the western edge of the world, the Black Sea at the eastern.
[17] Artemis, goddess of the hunt.

god whose name is our name Bacchus[18]
god of joy god of terror
be with us now your bright face
like a pine torch roaring   280
thrust into the face of the slaughtering war god
blind him
drive him down from Olympos
drive him away from Thebes
forever

OEDIPUS. Every word of your prayers has touched me.
    Listen. Follow me. Join me in fighting this sickness, this plague,
    and all your sufferings may end, like a dark sky,
    clear suddenly, blue, after a week of storms,
    soothing the torn face of the sea,   290
    soothing our fears.
    Your fate looms in my words—
    I heard nothing about Laios' death.
    I know nothing about the murder,
    I was alone, how could I have tracked the killer, without a clue,
    I came to Thebes after the crime was done,
    I was made a Theban after Laios' death. Listen carefully—
    these words come from an innocent man.

[*Addressing the* CHORUS.]

One of *you* knows who killed Laios.
Where is that man?   300
Speak.
I command it. Fear is no excuse.
He must clear himself of the dangerous charge.
Who did this thing?
Was it a stranger?
Speak.
I will not harm him. The worst he will suffer is exile.
I will pay him well. He will have a king's thanks.
But if he will not speak because he fears me,
if he fears what I will do to him or to those he loves,   310
if he will not obey me,
I say to him:
My power is absolute in Thebes, my rule reaches everywhere,
my words will drive the guilty man, the man who *knows*,
out of this city, away from Thebes, forever.

Nothing.
My word for him is nothing.
Let him *be* nothing.
Give him nothing.

---

[18] The god of wine, Bacchus or Dionysos, had special associations with Thebes.

Let him touch nothing of yours, he is nothing to you.   320
Lock your doors when he approaches.
Say nothing to him, do not speak.
No prayers with him, no offerings with him.
No purifying water.
Nothing.
Drive him from your homes. Let him have no home, nothing.
No words, no food, shelter, warmth of hand, shared worship.
Let him have nothing. Drive him out, let him die.
He is our disease.
                              I know.
                                        Apollo has made it clear.
Nothing can stop me, nothing can change my words.   330
I fight for Apollo, I fight for the dead man.
You see me, you hear me, moving against the killer.
My words are his doom.
Whether he did it alone, and escaped unseen,
whether others helped him kill, it makes no difference—
let my hatred burn out his life, hatred, always.
Make him an ember of suffering.
Make all his happiness
ashes.
If he eats at my side, sits at my sacred hearth, and I know these
     things,   340
let every curse I spit out against him find *me,*
come home to *me.*
Carry out my orders. You must,
for me, for Apollo, and for Thebes, Thebes,
this poor wasted city,
deserted by its gods.
I know—the gods have given us this disease.
That makes no difference. You should have acted,
you should have done something long ago to purge our guilt.
The victim was noble, a king—   350
you should have done everything to track his murderer down.
And so,
because I rule now where he ruled;
because I share his bed, his wife;
because the same woman who mothered my children might have
     mothered his;
because fate swooped out of nowhere and cut him down;
because of all these things
I will fight for him as I would fight for my own murdered
     father.
Nothing will stop me.
No man, no place, nothing will escape my gaze. I will not stop   360
until I know it all, all, until everything is clear.
For every king, every king's son and his sons,
for every royal generation of Thebes, *my* Thebes,
I will expose the killer, I will reveal him

to the light.
Oh gods, gods,
destroy all those who will not listen, will not obey.
Freeze the ground until they starve.
Make their wives barren as stone.
Let this disease that shakes Thebes to its roots—   370
or any worse disease, if there is any worse than this—waste them,
crush everything they have, everything they are.
But you men of Thebes—
you, who know my words are right, who obey me—
may justice and the gods defend you, bless you,
graciously, forever.
LEADER. Your curse forces me to speak, Master.
I cannot escape it.
I did not murder the king, I cannot show you the man who did.
Apollo told us to search for the killer.   380
Apollo must name him.
OEDIPUS. No man can force the gods to speak.
LEADER. Then I will say the next best thing.
OEDIPUS. If there's a third best thing, say that too.
LEADER. Teiresias sees what the god Apollo sees.
Truth, truth.
If you heard the god speaking, heard his voice,
you might see more, more, and more.
OEDIPUS. Teiresias? I have seen to that already.
Kreon spoke of Teiresias, and I sent for him. Twice.   390
I find it strange he still hasn't come.
LEADER. And there's an old story, almost forgotten,
a dark, faded rumor.
OEDIPUS. What rumor? I must sift each story,
see it, understand it.
LEADER. Laios was killed by bandits.
OEDIPUS. I have heard that story: but who can show me the man who
saw the murderer?
Has anyone seen him?
LEADER. If he knows the meaning of fear,
if he heard those curses you spoke against him,   400
those words still scorching the air,
you won't find him now, not in Thebes.
OEDIPUS. The man *murdered*. Why would words frighten him?

> [TEIRESIAS *has appeared from the
> stage entrance to the right of the
> audience. He walks with a staff and
> is helped by a slave boy and attend-
> ants. He stops at some distance from
> center stage.*]

LEADER. Here is the man who can catch the criminal
They're bringing him now—

the godlike prophet who speaks with the voice of god.
He, only he, knows truth.
The truth is rooted in his soul.

OEDIPUS. Teiresias, you understand all things,
    what can be taught, what is locked in silence,   410
    the distant things of heaven, and things that crawl the earth.
    You cannot see, yet you know the nature of this plague infesting
        our city.
    Only you, my lord, can save us, only you can defend us.
    Apollo told our messenger—did you hear?—
    that we could be saved only by tracking down Laios' killers,
    only by killing them, or sending them into exile.
    Help us, Teiresias.
    Study the cries of birds, study their wild paths,
    ponder the signs of fire, use all your skills of prophecy.
    Rescue us, preserve us.   420
    Rescue yourself, rescue Thebes, rescue me.
    Cleanse every trace of the growing stain left by the dead man's
        blood.
    We are in your hands, Teiresias.
    No work is more nobly human than helping others,
    helping with all the strength and skill we possess.

TEIRESIAS. Wisdom is a curse
    when wisdom does nothing for the man who has it.
    Once I knew this well, but I forgot.
    I never should have come.

OEDIPUS. Never should have come? Why this reluctance, prophet?   430

TEIRESIAS. Let me go home.
    That way is best, for you, for me.
    Let me live my life, and you live yours.

OEDIPUS. Strange words. Teiresias, cruel to the city that gave you life.
    Your holy knowledge could save Thebes. How can you keep
        silent?

TEIRESIAS. What have you said that helps Thebes? Your words are
        wasted.
    I would rather be silent than waste my words.

OEDIPUS. Look at us,   [OEDIPUS *stands, the* CHORUS *kneel.*]
    kneeling to you, Teiresias, imploring you.
    In the name of the gods, if you know—   440
    help us, tell us what you know.

TEIRESIAS. You kneel because you do not understand.
    But I will never let you see my grief. Never.
    My grief is yours.

OEDIPUS. What? You know and won't speak?
    You'd betray us all, you'd destroy the city of Thebes?

TEIRESIAS. I will do nothing to hurt myself, or you. Why insist?
    I will not speak.

OEDIPUS. Stubborn old fool, you'd make a rock angry!
    Tell me what you know! Say it!   450
    Where are your feelings? Won't you ever speak?

TEIRESIAS. You call me cold, stubborn, unfeeling, you insult me. But *you*,
    Oedipus, what do you know about yourself,
    about your real feelings?
    You don't see how much alike we are.
OEDIPUS. How can *I* restrain my anger when I see how little you care
    for Thebes.
TEIRESIAS. The truth will come, by itself,
    the truth will come
    no matter how I shroud it in silence.
OEDIPUS. All the more reason why you should speak.   460
TEIRESIAS. Not another word.
    Rage away. You will never make me speak.
OEDIPUS. I'll rage, prophet, I'll give you all my anger.
    I'll say it all—
    Listen: I think you were involved in the murder of Laios,
    you helped plan it, I think you
    did everything in your power to kill Laios,
    everything but strike him with your own hands,
    and if you weren't blind, if you still had eyes to see with,
    I'd say you, and *you* alone, did it all.   470
TEIRESIAS. Do you think so? Then obey your own words, obey
    the curse everyone heard break from your own lips:
    Never speak again to these men of Thebes,
    never speak again to me.
                    You, it's
  you.
  What plagues the city is *you*.
  The plague is *you*.
OEDIPUS. Do you know what you're saying?
  Do you think I'll let you get away with these vile accusations?
TEIRESIAS. I am safe.   480
    Truth lives in me, and the truth is strong.
OEDIPUS. Who taught you this truth of yours? Not your prophet's
    craft.
TEIRESIAS. You taught me. You forced me to speak.
OEDIPUS. Speak what? Explain. Teach me.
TEIRESIAS. Didn't you understand?
    Are you trying to make me say the word?
OEDIPUS. What word? Say it. Spit it out.
TEIRESIAS. Murderer.
    I say *you*,
    you are the killer you're searching for.   490
OEDIPUS. You won't say *that* again to me and get away with it.
TEIRESIAS. Do you want more? Shall I make you really angry?
OEDIPUS. Say anything you like. Your words are wasted.
TEIRESIAS. I say you live in shame, and you do not know it,
    do not know that you
    and those you love most
    wallow in shame,

you do not know
in what shame you live.
OEDIPUS. You'll pay for these insults, I swear it.   500
TEIRESIAS. Not if the truth is strong.
OEDIPUS. The truth *is* strong, but not your truth.
  You have no truth. You're blind.
  Blind in your eyes. Blind in your ears. Blind in your mind.
TEIRESIAS. And I pity you for mocking my blindness.
  Soon everyone in Thebes will mock you, Oedipus. They'll
    mock you
  as you have mocked me.
OEDIPUS. One endless night swaddles you in its unbroken black sky.
  You can't hurt me, you can't hurt anyone who sees the light of day.
TEIRESIAS. True. Nothing I do will harm you. You, you   510
  and your fate belong to Apollo.
  Apollo will see to *you.*
OEDIPUS. Are these your own lies, prophet—or Kreon's?
TEIRESIAS. Kreon? Your plague is *you,* not Kreon.
OEDIPUS. Money, power, one great skill surpassing another,
  if a man has these things, other men's envy grows and grows,
  their greed and hunger are insatiable.
  Most men would lust for a life like mine—but I did not demand
    my life,
  Thebes gave me my life, and from the beginning, my good friend
    Kreon,
  loyal, trusted Kreon,   520
  was reaching for my power, wanted to ambush me, get rid of me
    by hiring this cheap wizard,
  this crass, conniving priest, who sees nothing but profit,
  whose prophecy is simple profit. *You,*
  what did *you* ever do that proves you a real seer? What did you
    ever *see,* prophet?
  And when the Sphinx who sang mysteriously
  imprisoned us
  why didn't you speak and set us free?
  No ordinary man could have solved her riddle,
  it took prophecy, prophecy and skill you clearly never had.
  Even the paths of birds, even the gods' voices were useless.   530
  But I showed up, I, Oedipus,
  stupid, untutored Oedipus,
  I silenced her, I destroyed her, I used my wits, not omens,
  to sift the meaning of her song.
  And this is the man you want to kill so you can get close to King
    Kreon,
  weigh his affairs for him, advise him, influence him.
  No, I think you and your master, Kreon, who contrived this plot,
  will be whipped out of Thebes.
  Look at you.
  If you weren't so old, and weak, oh   540

I'd make you pay
for this conspiracy of yours.
LEADER. Oedipus, both of you spoke in anger.
　　Anger is not what we need.
　　We need all our wits, all our energy to interpret Apollo's words.
　　Then we will know what to do.
TEIRESIAS. Oedipus, you are king, but you must hear my reply.
　　My right to speak is just as valid as yours.
　　I am not your slave. Kreon is not my patron.
　　My master is Apollo. I can say what I please.　　　　　　　　　　550
　　You insulted me. You mocked me. You called me blind.
　　Now hear *me* speak, Oedipus.
　　You have eyes to see with,
　　but you do not see yourself, you do not see
　　the horror shadowing every step of your life,
　　the blind shame in which you live,
　　you do not see where you live and who lives with you,
　　lives always at your side.
　　Tell me, Oedipus, who are your parents?
　　Do you know?　　　　　　　　　　　　　　　　　　　　　　　　560
　　You do not even know
　　the shame and grief you have brought your family,
　　those still alive, those buried beneath the earth.
　　But the curse of your mother, the curse of your father
　　will whip you, whip you again and again, wherever you turn,
　　it will whip you out of Thebes forever,
　　your clear eyes flooded with darkness.
　　That day will come.
　　And then what scoured, homeless plain, what leafless tree,
　　what place on Kithairon,[19]　　　　　　　　　　　　　　　　　570
　　where no other humans are or ever will be,
　　where the wind is the only thing that moves,
　　what raw track of thorns and stones, what rock, gulley,
　　or blind hill won't echo your screams, your howls of anguish
　　when you find out that the marriage song,
　　sung when you came to Thebes, heard in your house,
　　guided you to *this* shore, this wilderness
　　you thought was home, *your* home?
　　And you do not see
　　all the other awful things　　　　　　　　　　　　　　　　　　580
　　that will show you who you really are, show you
　　to your children, face to face.
　　Go ahead! Call me quack, abuse Kreon, insult Apollo, the god
　　who speaks through me, whose words move on my lips.

---

[19] Also spelled *Cithaeron*. A mountain range near Thebes. Oedipus, as later events will
reveal, was abandoned there as a child; it will also be his destination when he goes into exile
later. Sophocles' audience knew this detail, and all the other significant elements of the story,
at the outset of the play.

No man will ever know worse suffering than you,
your life, your flesh, your happiness an ember of pain. Ashes.
Oedipus. [*to the* Chorus] Must I stand here and listen to these attacks?
Teiresias. [*beginning to move away*] I am here, Oedipus, because you
     sent for me.
Oedipus. You old fool,
    I'd have thought twice before asking you to come   590
    if I had known you'd spew out such idiocy.
Teiresias. Call me fool, if you like, but your parents,
    who gave you life, they respected my judgment.
Oedipus. Parents?
             What do you mean?
                Who are my mother and father?
Teiresias. This day is your mother and father—this day will give you
    your birth,
    it will destroy you too.
Oedipus. How you love mysterious, twisted words.
Teiresias. Aren't you the great solver of riddles?
    Aren't you Oedipus?
Oedipus. Taunt me for the gift of my brilliant mind.   600
    That gift is what makes me great.
Teiresias. That gift is your destiny. It made you everything you are,
    and it has ruined you.
Oedipus. But if this gift of mine saved Thebes, who cares what
    happens to me?
Teiresias. I'm leaving. Boy, take me home.
Oedipus. Good. Take him home. Here
    I keep stumbling over you, here you're in my way.
    Scuttle home, and leave us in peace!
Teiresias. I'm going. I said what I came to say,
    and that scowl, darkening your face, doesn't frighten me. How can
     you hurt me?   610
    I tell you again:
    the man you've been trying to expose—
    with all your threats, with your inquest into Laios' murder—
    that man is here, in Thebes.
    Now people think he comes from Corinth, but later
    they will see he was born in Thebes.
    When they know, he'll have no pleasure in that news.
    Now he has eyes to see with, but they will be slashed out;
    rich and powerful now, he will be a beggar,
    poking his way with a stick, feeling his way to a strange country.   620
    And his children—the children he lives with—
    will see him at last, see what he is, see who he really is:
    their brother and their father; his wife's son, his mother's
     husband;
    the lover who slept with his father's wife; the man who murdered
     his father—
    the man whose hands still drip with his father's blood.
    These truths will be revealed.

Go inside and ponder *that* riddle, and if you find I've lied,
then call me a prophet who cannot see.

> [OEDIPUS *turns and enters the pal-*
> *ace.* TEIRESIAS *is led out through*
> *the stage entrance on the right.*]

CHORUS. who did crimes unnameable things
    things words cringe at   630
    which man did the rock of prophecy at Delphi say
    did these things
    his hands dripping with blood
    he should run now flee
    his strong feet swallowing the air
    stronger than the horses of storm winds
    their hooves slicing the air
    now in his armor
    Apollo lunges at him
    his infinite branching fire reaches out   640
    and the steady dread death-hungry Fates follow and never stop
    their quick scissors[20] seeking the cloth of his life

    just now
    from high snowy Parnassus[21]
    the god's voice exploded its blazing message
    follow his track find the man
    no one knows
    a bull loose under wild bushes and trees
    among caves and gray rocks
    cut from the herd he runs and runs but runs nowhere   650
    zigzagging desperate to get away
    birds of prophecy birds of death circling his head
    forever
    voices forged at the white stone core of the earth[22]
    they go where he goes always

    terror's in me flooding me
    how can I judge
    what the god Apollo says
    trapped hoping confused
    I do not see what is here now   660
    when I look to the past I see nothing
    I know nothing about a feud
    wounding the families of Laios or Oedipus
    no clue to the truth then or now

---

[20] The three Fates were spinners of the thread of human life; the third, Atropos, cut the thread at a point that determined the moment of death.
[21] The mountain near Apollo's oracle at Delphi.
[22] The Omphalos, or Navelstone, at Delphi. It was believed to be the center of the earth.

nothing to blacken his golden fame in Thebes
and help Laios' family
solve the mystery of his death

Zeus and Apollo know
they understand
only they see   670
the dark threads crossing beneath our life
but no man can say a prophet sees more than I
one man surpasses another
wisdom against wisdom skill against skill
but I will not blame Oedipus
whatever anyone says
until words are as real as things

one thing is clear
years back the Sphinx tested him
his answer was true   680
he was wise and sweet to the city
so he can never be evil
not to me

> [KREON *enters through the stage
> entrance at right, and addresses the*
> CHORUS.]

KREON. Men of Thebes, I hear Oedipus, our king and master,
　　has brought terrible charges against me.
　　I have come to face those charges. I resent them bitterly.
　　If he imagines I have hurt him, spoken or acted against him
　　while our city dies, believe me—I have nothing left to live for.
　　His accusations pierce me, wound me mortally—
　　nothing they touch is trivial, private—   690
　　if you, my family and friends,
　　think I'm a traitor, if all Thebes believes it, says it.
LEADER. Perhaps he spoke in anger, without thinking,
　　perhaps his anger made him accuse you.
KREON. Did he really say I persuaded Teiresias to lie?
LEADER. I heard him say these things,
　　but I don't know what they mean.
KREON. Did he look you in the eyes when he accused me?
　　Was he in his right mind?
LEADER. I do not know or see what great men do.   700

> [*turning to* OEDIPUS, *who has
> emerged from the palace*]

But here he is—Oedipus.
OEDIPUS. What? *You* here? Murderer!
　　You dare come here, to my palace, when it's clear

you've been plotting to murder me and seize the throne of
    Thebes?
You're the bandit, *you're* the killer.

Answer me—

Did you think I was cowardly or stupid?
Is that why you betrayed me?
Did you really think I wouldn't see what you were plotting,
how you crept up on me like a cloud inching across the sun?
Did you think I wouldn't defend myself against you?   710
You thought I was a fool, but the fool was you, Kreon.
Thrones are won with money and men, you fool!

KREON. You have said enough, Oedipus. Now let me reply.
    Weigh my words against your charges, then judge for yourself.

OEDIPUS. Eloquent, Kreon. But you won't convince me now.
    Now that I know your hatred, your malice.

KREON. Let me explain.

OEDIPUS. Explain?
    What could explain your treachery?

KREON. If you think this stubborn anger of yours, this perversity,   720
    is something to be proud of, you're mad.

OEDIPUS. And if you think you can injure your sister's husband,
    and not pay for it, *you're* mad.

KREON. I would be mad to hurt you. How have I hurt you?

OEDIPUS. Was it you who advised me to send for that great holy
    prophet?

KREON. Yes, and I'd do it again.

OEDIPUS. How long has it been since Laios disappeared?

KREON. Disappeared?

OEDIPUS. Died. Was murdered . . .

KREON. Many, many years.   730

OEDIPUS. And this prophet of yours—was he practicing his trade at
    the time?

KREON. With as much skill, wisdom and honor as ever.

OEDIPUS. Did he ever mention my name?

KREON. Not in my presence.

OEDIPUS. Was there an inquest? A formal inquiry?

KREON. Of course. Nothing was ever discovered.

OEDIPUS. Then why didn't our wonderful prophet, our Theban
    wizard,
    denounce me as the murderer then?

KREON. I don't know. And when I don't know, I don't speak.

OEDIPUS. But you know this. You know it with perfect certainty.   740

KREON. What do you mean?

OEDIPUS. This: if you and Teiresias were not conspiring against me,
    Teiresias would never have charged *me* with Laios' murder.

KREON. If he said that, you should know.
    But now, Oedipus, it's my right, my turn to question you.

OEDIPUS. Ask anything. You'll never prove I killed Laios.

KREON. Did you marry my sister, Jocasta?

OEDIPUS. I married Jocasta.
KREON. And you gave her an equal share of the power in Thebes?
OEDIPUS. Whatever she wants is hers.   750
KREON. And I share that power equally with you and her?
OEDIPUS. Equally.
    And that's precisely why it's clear you're false, treacherous.
KREON. No, Oedipus.
    Consider it rationally, as I have. Reflect:
What man, what sane man, would prefer a king's power
with all its dangers and anxieties,
when he could enjoy that same power, without its cares,
and sleep in peace each night? Power?
I have no instinct for power, no hunger for it either.   760
It isn't royal power I want, but its advantages.
And any sensible man would want the same.
Look at the life I lead. Whatever I want, I get from you,
with your goodwill and blessing. I have nothing to fear.
If I were king, my life would be constant duty and constraint.
Why would I want your power or the throne of Thebes
more than what I enjoy now—the privilege of power
without its dangers? I would be a fool to want more
than what I have—the substance, not the show, of power.
As matters stand, no man envies me, I am courted   770
and admired by all. Men wear no smiling masks for Kreon.
And those who want something from you come to me
because the way to royal favor lies through me.
Tell me, Oedipus, why should I give these blessings up
to seize your throne and all the dangers it confers?
A man like me, who knows his mortal limits and accepts them,
cannot be vicious or treacherous by nature.
The love of power is not my nature, nor is treason
or the thoughts of treason that go with love of power.
I would never dare conspire against your life.   780

Do you want to test the truth of what I say?
Go to Delphi, put the question to the oracle,
ask if I have told you exactly what Apollo said.
Then if you find that Teiresias and I have plotted against you,
seize me and put me to death. Convict me
not by one vote alone, but two—yours *and* mine, Oedipus.
But don't convict me on the strength of your suspicions,
don't confuse friends with traitors, traitors with friends.
There's no justice in that.
To throw away a good and loyal friend   790
is to destroy what you love most—
your own life, and what makes life worth living.
Someday you will know the truth:
time, only time reveals the good man;
one day's light reveals the evil man.

LEADER. Good words
for someone careful, afraid he'll fall.
But a mind like lightning
stumbles.
OEDIPUS. When a clever man plots against me and moves swiftly   800
I must move just as swiftly, I must plan.
But if I wait, if I do nothing, he will win, win everything,
and I will lose.
KREON. What do you want? My exile?
OEDIPUS. No. Your death.
KREON. You won't change your mind? You won't believe me?
OEDIPUS. I'll believe you when you teach me the meaning of envy.
KREON. Envy? You talk about envy. You don't even know what
sense is.
Can't you listen to me?
OEDIPUS. I *am* listening. To my own good sense.   810
KREON. Listen to *me*. I have sense on my side too.
OEDIPUS. You? You were born devious.
KREON. And if you're wrong?
OEDIPUS. I still must govern.
KREON. Not if you govern badly.
OEDIPUS. Oh Thebes, Thebes . . .
KREON. Thebes is mine too.
LEADER. [*turning to* JOCASTA, *who has entered from the palace,*
accompanied by a woman attendant]
Stop. I see
Jocasta coming from the palace
just in time, my lords, to help you   820
settle this deep, bitter feud raging between you.
Listen to what she says.
JOCASTA. Oedipus! Kreon! Why this insane quarreling?
You should be ashamed, both of you. Forget yourselves.
This is no time for petty personal bickering.
Thebes is sick, dying.
—Come inside, Oedipus
—And you, Kreon, leave us.
Must you create all this misery over nothing, nothing?
KREON. Jocasta,
Oedipus has given me two impossible choices: 830
Either I must be banished from Thebes, my city, my home,
or be arrested and put to death.
OEDIPUS. That's right.
I caught him plotting against me, Jocasta.
Viciously, cunningly plotting against the king of Thebes.
KREON. Take every pleasure I have in life, curse me, let me die,
if I've done what you accuse me of, let the gods
destroy everything I have, let them do anything to me.
I stand here, exposed to their infinite power.
JOCASTA. Oedipus, in the name of the gods, believe him.   840

His prayer has made him holy, naked to the mysterious
whims of the gods, has taken him beyond what is human.
Respect his words, respect me, respect these men standing at your
     side.
CHORUS. [*beginning a dirge-like appeal to* OEDIPUS]
     listen to her
     think yield
     we implore you
OEDIPUS. What do you want?
CHORUS. be generous to Kreon give him respect
     he was never foolish before
     now his prayer to the gods has made him great   850
     great and frightening
OEDIPUS. Do you know what you're asking?
CHORUS. I know
OEDIPUS. Then say it.
CHORUS. don't ever cut him off
     without rights or honor
     blood binds you both
     his prayer has made him sacred
     don't accuse him
     because some blind suspicion hounds you   860
OEDIPUS. Understand me:
     when you ask for these things
     you ask for my death or exile.
CHORUS. no
     by the sun
     the god who bathes us in his light
     who sees all
     I will die godless no family no friends
     if what I ask means that
     it is Thebes   870
     Thebes dying wasting away life by life
     this is the misery
     that breaks my heart
     and now this quarrel raging between you and Kreon
     is more more than I can bear
OEDIPUS. Then let him go, if it means I must die
     or be forced out of Thebes forever, stripped of all my rights, all
          my honors.
     Your grief, *your* words touch me. Not his.
     I pity you. But him,
     my hatred will reach him wherever he goes.   880
KREON. It's clear you hate to yield, clear
     you yield only under pressure, only
     when you've worn out the fierceness of your anger.
     Then all you can do is sit, and brood.
     Natures like yours are a torment to themselves.
OEDIPUS. Leave. Go!
KREON. I'm going. Now I know

you do not know me.
But these men know I am the man I seem to be, a just man,
not devious, not a traitor.   890

[KREON *leaves.*]

CHORUS. woman why are you waiting
    lead him inside comfort him
JOCASTA. Not before I know what has happened here.
CHORUS. blind ignorant words suspicion without proof
    the injustice of it
    gnaws at us
JOCASTA. From both men?
CHORUS. yes
JOCASTA. What caused it?
CHORUS. enough enough   900
    no more words
    Thebes is so tormented now
    let it rest where it ended
OEDIPUS. Look where cooling my rage,
    where all your decent, practical thoughts have led you.
CHORUS. Oedipus I have said this many times
    I would be mad helpless to give advice
    if I turned against you now
    once
    you took our city in her storm of pain   910
    straightened her course found fair weather
    o lead her to safety now
    if you can
JOCASTA. If you love the gods, tell me, too, Oedipus—I implore you—
    why are you still so angry, why can't you let it go?
OEDIPUS. I will tell you, Jocasta.
    You mean more, far more to me than these men here.
    Jocasta, it is Kreon—Kreon and his plots against me.
JOCASTA. What started your quarrel?
OEDIPUS. He said I murdered Laios.   920
JOCASTA. Does he know something? Or is it pure hearsay?
OEDIPUS. He sent me a vicious, trouble-making prophet
    to avoid implicating himself. He did not say it to my face.
JOCASTA. Oedipus, forget all this. Listen to me:
    no mortal can practise the art of prophecy, no man can see the
        future.
    One experience of mine will show you why.
    Long ago an oracle came to Laios.
    It came not from Apollo himself but from his priests.
    It said Laios was doomed to be murdered by a son, his son and
        mine.
    But Laios, from what we heard, was murdered by bandits from a
        foreign country,   930
    cut down at a crossroads. My poor baby

was only three days old when Laios had his feet pierced together
    behind the ankles
and gave orders to abandon our child on a mountain, leave him
    alone to die
in a wilderness of rocks and bare gray trees
where there were no roads, no people.
So you see—Apollo didn't make that child his father's killer,
Laios wasn't murdered by his son. That dreadful act which so
    terrified Laios—
it never happened.

All those oracular voices meant was nothing, nothing.
Ignore them.   940
Apollo creates. Apollo reveals. He needs no help from men.
OEDIPUS. [*who has been very still*]
    While you were speaking, Jocasta, it flashed through my mind
    like wind suddenly ruffling a stretch of calm sea.
    It stuns me. I can almost see it—some memory, some image.
    My heart races and swells—
JOCASTA. Why are you so strangely excited, Oedipus?
OEDIPUS. You said Laios was cut down *near* a crossroads?
JOCASTA. That was the story. It hasn't changed.
OEDIPUS. Where did it happen? Tell me. Where?
JOCASTA. In Phokis. Where the roads from Delphi and Daulia meet.   950
OEDIPUS. When?
JOCASTA. Just before you came to Thebes and assumed power.
    Just before you were proclaimed King.
OEDIPUS. O Zeus, Zeus,
    what are you doing with my life?
JOCASTA. Why are you so disturbed, Oedipus?
OEDIPUS. Don't ask me. Not yet.
                       Tell me about Laios.
    How old was he? What did he look like?
JOCASTA. Streaks of gray were beginning to show in his black hair.
    He was tall, strong—built something like you.   960
OEDIPUS. No! O gods, o
    it seems each hard, arrogant curse
    I spit out
    was meant for me, and I
    didn't
    know it!
JOCASTA. Oedipus, what do you mean? Your face is so strange.
    You frighten me.
OEDIPUS. It *is* frightening—can the blind prophet see, can he
    really see?
    I would know if you told me . . .   970
JOCASTA. I'm afraid to ask, Oedipus.
    Told you what?
OEDIPUS. Was Laios traveling with a small escort
    or with many armed men, like a king?

Jocasta. There were five, including a herald.
    Laios was riding in his chariot.
Oedipus. Light, o light, light
    now everything, everything is clear. All of it.
    Who told you this? Who was it?
Jocasta. A household slave. The only survivor.   980
Oedipus. Is he here, in Thebes?
Jocasta. No. When he returned and saw that you were king
    and learned Laios was dead, he came to me and clutched my hand,
    begged me to send him to the mountains
    where shepherds graze their flocks, far from the city,
    so he could never see Thebes again.
    I sent him, of course. He deserved that much, for a slave, and
        more.
Oedipus. Can he be called back? Now?
Jocasta. Easily. But why?
Oedipus. I am afraid I may have said too much—   990
    I *must* see him.
    Now.
Jocasta. Then he will come.
    But surely I have a right to know what disturbs you, Oedipus.
Oedipus. Now that I've come this far, Jocasta,
    hope torturing me, each step of mine heavy with fear,
    I won't keep anything from you.
    Wandering through the mazes of a fate like this,
    how could I confide in anyone but you?

    My father was Polybos, of Corinth.   1000
    My mother, Merope, was Dorian.
    Everyone in Corinth saw me as its first citizen,
    but one day something happened,
    something strange, puzzling. Puzzling, but nothing more.
    Still, it worried me.
    One night, I was at a banquet,
    and a man—he was very drunk—said I wasn't my father's son,
    called me "bastard." That stung me, I was shocked.
    I could barely control my anger, I lay awake all night.
    The next day I went to my father and mother,   1010
    I questioned them about the man and what he said.
    They were furious with him, outraged by his insult,
    and I was reassured. But I kept hearing the word "bastard"
        "bastard"—
    I couldn't get it out of my head.
    Without my parents' knowledge, I went to Delphi: I wanted the
        truth,
    but Apollo refused to answer me.
    And yet he did reveal other things, he did show me
    a future dark with torment, evil, horror,
    he made me *see*—
    see myself, doomed to sleep with my own mother, doomed   1020

to bring children into this world where the sun pours down,
children no one could bear to see, doomed
to murder the man who gave me life, whose blood is *my* blood. My
    father.
And after I heard all this, I fled Corinth,
measuring my progress by the stars, searching for a place
where I would never see those words, those dreadful predictions
come true. And on my way
I came to the place where you say King Laios was murdered.

Jocasta, the story I'm about to tell you is the truth:
I was on the road, near the crossroads you mentioned,   1030
when I met a herald, with an old man, just as you described him.
The man was riding in a chariot
and his driver tried to push me off the road
and when he shoved me I hit him. I hit him.
The old man stood quiet in the chariot until I passed under him,
then he leaned out and caught me on the head with an ugly
    goad[23]—
its two teeth wounded me—and with this hand of mine,
this hand clenched around my staff,
I struck him back even harder—so hard, so quick he couldn't
    dodge it,
and he toppled out of the chariot and hit the ground, face up.   1040
I killed them. Every one of them. I still see them.

[*to the* CHORUS]

If this stranger and Laios
are somehow linked by blood,
tell me what man's torment equals mine?

Citizens, hear my curse again—
Give this man nothing. Let him touch nothing of yours.
Lock your doors when he approaches.
Say nothing to him when he approaches.
                              And these, these curses,
with my own mouth I
spoke these monstrous curses against myself.   1050

[OEDIPUS *turns back to* JOCASTA]

These hands, these bloodstained hands made love to you in your
    dead husband's bed,
these hands murdered him.

---

[23] A barbed stick used to prod animals.

If I must be exiled, never to see my family,
never to walk the soil of my country
so I will not sleep with my mother
and kill Polybos, my father, who raised me—his son!—
wasn't I born evil—answer me!—isn't every part of me
unclean? Oh
some unknown god, some savage venomous demon must have
    done this,
raging, swollen with hatred. Hatred   1060
for me.

Holiness, pure, radiant powers, o gods
don't let me see that day,
don't let it come, take me away
from men, men with their eyes, hide me
before I see
the filthy black stain reaching down over me, into me.

> [*The* Chorus *have moved away*
> *from the stage*]

Leader. Your words make us shudder, Oedipus,
    but hope, hope
    until you hear more from the man who witnessed the murder.   1070
Oedipus. That is the only hope I have. Waiting.
    Waiting for that man to come from the pastures.
Jocasta. And when he finally comes, what do you hope to learn?
Oedipus. If his story matches yours, I am saved.
Jocasta. What makes you say that?
Oedipus. Bandits—you said he told you bandits killed Laios.
    So if he still talks about bandits,
    more than one, I couldn't have killed Laios.
    One man is not the same as many men.
    But if he speaks of one man, traveling alone,   1080
    then all the evidence points to me.
Jocasta. Believe me, Oedipus, those were his words.
    And he can't take them back: the whole city heard him, not
        only me.
    And if he changes only the smallest detail of his story,
    that still won't prove Laios was murdered as the oracle foretold.
    Apollo was clear—it was Laios' fate to be killed by my son,
    but my poor child died before his father died.
    The future has no shape. The shapes of prophecy lie.
    I see nothing in them, they are all illusions.
Oedipus. Even so, I want that shepherd summoned here.   1090
    Now. Do it now.
Jocasta. I'll send for him immediately. But come inside.
    My only wish is to please you.

> [Jocasta *dispatches a servant.*]

CHORUS. fate[24]
   be here let what I say be pure
   let all my acts be pure
   laws forged in the huge clear fields of heaven
   rove the sky
   shaping my words limiting what I do
   Olympos[25] made those laws not men who live and die   1100
   nothing lulls those laws to sleep
   they cannot die
   and the infinite god in them never ages

   arrogance insatiable pride
   breed the tyrant
   feed him on thing after thing blindly
   at the wrong time uselessly
   and he grows reaches so high
   nothing can stop his fall
   his feet thrashing the air standing on nothing   1110
   and nowhere to stand he plunges down
   o god shatter the tyrant
   but let men compete let self-perfection grow
   let men sharpen their skills
   soldiers citizens building the good city
   Apollo
   protect me always
   always the god I will honor

   if a man walks through his life arrogant
   strutting proud   1120
   says anything does anything
   does not fear justice
   fear the gods bow to their shining presences
   let fate make him stumble in his tracks
   for all his lecheries and headlong greed
   if he takes whatever he wants right or wrong
   if he touches forbidden things
   what man who acts like this would boast
   he can escape the anger of the gods
   why should I join these sacred public dances   1130
   if such acts are honored

   no
   I will never go to the holy untouchable stone

---

[24] The choral passage that follows seems central to the play, but its application is problematical. The Chorus expresses a pious revulsion from the kind of evil acts that bring on divine punishment; it then proceeds to define *hubris*, the state of overweening pride that is especially dangerous in provoking divine wrath. The passage implies that if these ancient moral principles and the gods' oracles no longer can be depended on, all order has been lost. But no character in the play seems to have *deliberately* committed such acts of impiety as the Chorus describes.

[25] The mountain home of the gods.

navel of the earth at Delphi
never again
go to the temples at Olympia at Abai[26]
if all these things are not joined
if past present future are not made one
made clear to mortal eyes
o Zeus if that is your name   1140
power above all immortal king
see these things look
those great prophecies are fading
men say they're nothing
nobody prays to the god of light no one believes
nothing of the gods stays

> [JOCASTA *enters from the palace,
> carrying a branch tied with strands
> of wool, and a jar of incense. She is
> accompanied by a servant woman.
> She addresses the* CHORUS.]

JOCASTA. Lords of Thebes, I come to the temples of the god
with offerings—this incense and this branch.
So many thoughts torture Oedipus. He never rests.
He acts without reason. He is like a man   1150
who has lost everything he knows—the past
is useless to him; strange, new things baffle him.
And if someone talks disaster, it stuns him: he listens, he is afraid.
I have tried to reassure him, but nothing helps.
So I have come to you—
Apollo, close to my life, close to this house,
listen to my prayers: [*she kneels*]
                           help us purify ourselves of this disease,
help us survive the long night of our suffering,
protect us. We are afraid when we see Oedipus confused
and frightened—Oedipus, the only man who can pilot Thebes   1160
to safety.

> [*A* MESSENGER *from Corinth has
> arrived by the entrance to the orches-
> tra on the audience's left. He sees*
> JOCASTA *praying, then turns to
> address the* CHORUS.]

MESSENGER. Friends,
can you tell me where King Oedipus lives
or better still, where I can find him?
LEADER. Here, in this house.
This lady is his wife and mother
of his children.

---

[26] Sites of oracles, of Apollo and Zeus respectively.

MESSENGER. May you and your family prosper.
    May you be happy always under this great roof.
JOCASTA. Happiness and prosperity to you, too, for your kind words.   1170
    But why are you here? Do you bring news?
MESSENGER. Good news for your house, good news for King Oedipus.
JOCASTA. What is your news? Who sent you?
MESSENGER. I come from Corinth, and what I have to say I know will
    bring you joy.
    And pain perhaps. . . . I do not know.
JOCASTA. Both joy and pain? What news could do that?
MESSENGER. The people of Corinth want Oedipus as their king.
    That's what they're saying.
JOCASTA. But isn't old Polybos still king of Corinth?
MESSENGER. His kingdom is his grave.   1180
JOCASTA. Polybos is *dead?*
MESSENGER. If I'm lying, my lady, let me die for it.
JOCASTA. You. [*to a servant*] Go in and tell Oedipus.
    O oracles of the gods, where are you now!
    This man, the man Oedipus was afraid he would murder,
    the man he feared, the man he fled from has died a natural death.
    Oedipus didn't kill him, it was luck, luck.

                           [*She turns to greet* OEDIPUS *as he*
                           comes out of the palace.]

OEDIPUS. Jocasta, why did you send for me? [*taking her gently by the
    arm*]
JOCASTA. Oedipus,
    listen to this man, see what those ominous, holy predictions of
        Apollo mean now.   1190
OEDIPUS. Who is this man? What does he say?
JOCASTA. He comes from Corinth.
    Your father is dead. Polybos is dead!
OEDIPUS. What?
    Let me hear those words from your own mouth, stranger.
    Tell me yourself, in your own words.
MESSENGER. If that's what you want to hear first, then I'll say it:
    Polybos is dead.
OEDIPUS. How did he die? Assassination? Illness? How?
MESSENGER. An old man's life hangs by a fragile thread. Anything can
        snap it.   1200
OEDIPUS. That poor old man. It was illness then?
MESSENGER. Illness and old age.
OEDIPUS. Why, Jocasta,
    why should men look to the great hearth at Delphi
    or listen to birds shrieking and wheeling overhead—
    cries meaning I was doomed to kill my father?
    He is dead, gone, covered by the earth.
    And here I am—my hands never even touched a spear—
    I did not kill him,

unless he died from wanting me to come home.   1210
No. Polybos has bundled up all these oracles
and taken them with him to the world below.
They are only words now, lost in the air.
JOCASTA. Isn't that what I predicted?
OEDIPUS. You were right. My fears confused me.
JOCASTA. You have nothing to fear. Not now. Not ever.
OEDIPUS. But the oracle said I am doomed to sleep with my mother.
  How can I live with that and not be afraid?
JOCASTA. Why should men be afraid of anything? Fortune rules our
    lives.
  Luck is everything. Things happen. The future is darkness.   1220
  No human mind can know it.
  It's best to live in the moment, live for today, Oedipus.
  Why should the thought of marrying your mother make you so
    afraid?
  Many men have slept with their mothers in their dreams.
  Why worry? See your dreams for what they are—nothing, nothing
    at all.
  Be happy, Oedipus.
OEDIPUS. All that you say is right, Jocasta. I know it.
  I should be happy,
  but my mother is still living. As long as she's alive,
  I live in fear. This fear is necessary.   1230
  I have no choice.
JOCASTA. But Oedipus, your father's death is a sign, a great sign—
  the sky has cleared, the sun's gaze holds us in its warm, hopeful
    light.
OEDIPUS. A great sign, I agree. But so long as my mother is alive,
  my fear lives too.
MESSENGER. Who is this woman you fear so much?
OEDIPUS. Merope, King Polybos' wife.
MESSENGER. Why does Merope frighten you so much?
OEDIPUS. A harrowing oracle hurled down upon us by some
    great god.
MESSENGER. Can you tell me? Or did the god seal your lips?   1240
OEDIPUS. I can.
  Long ago, Apollo told me I was doomed to sleep with my mother
  and spill my father's blood, murder him
  with these two hands of mine.
  That's why I never returned to Corinth. Luckily, it would seem.
  Still, nothing on earth is sweeter to a man's eyes
  than the sight of his father and mother.
MESSENGER. And you left Corinth because of this prophecy?
OEDIPUS. Yes. And because of my father. To avoid killing my father.
MESSENGER. But didn't my news prove you have nothing to fear?   1250
  I brought good news.
OEDIPUS. And I will reward you for your kindness.
MESSENGER. That's why I came, my lord. I knew you'd remember me
    when you returned to Corinth.

OEDIPUS. I will never return, never live with my parents again.
MESSENGER. Son, it's clear you don't know what you're doing.
OEDIPUS. What do you mean? In the name of the gods, speak.
MESSENGER. If you're afraid to go home because of your parents.
OEDIPUS. I *am* afraid, afraid
    Apollo's prediction will come true, all of it,   1260
    as god's sunlight grows brighter on a man's face at dawn
    when he's in bed, still sleeping,
    and reaches into his eyes and wakes him.
MESSENGER. Afraid of murdering your father, of having his blood
    on your hands?
OEDIPUS. Yes. His blood. The stain of his blood. That terror never
    leaves me.
MESSENGER. But Oedipus, then you have no reason to be afraid.
OEDIPUS. I'm their son, they're my parents, aren't they?
MESSENGER. Polybos is nothing to you.
OEDIPUS. Polybos is not my father?   1270
MESSENGER. No more than I am.
OEDIPUS. But you are nothing to me. Nothing.
MESSENGER. And Polybos is nothing to you either.
OEDIPUS. Then why did he call me his son?
MESSENGER. Because I gave you to him. With these hands
    I gave you to him.
OEDIPUS. How could he have loved me like a father if I am not
    his son?
MESSENGER. He had no children. That opened his heart.
OEDIPUS. And what about you?
    Did you buy me from someone? Or did you find me?   1280
MESSENGER. I found you squawling, left alone to die in the thickets of
    Kithairon.
OEDIPUS. Kithairon? What were you doing on Kithairon?
MESSENGER. Herding sheep in the high summer pastures.
OEDIPUS. You were a shepherd, a drifter looking for work?
MESSENGER. A drifter, yes, but it was I who saved you.
OEDIPUS. Saved me? Was I hurt when you picked me up?
MESSENGER. Ask your feet.
OEDIPUS. Why,
    why did you bring up that childhood pain?
MESSENGER. I cut you free. Your feet were pierced, tied together at
    the ankles   1290
    with leather thongs strung between the tendons and the bone.
OEDIPUS. That mark of my shame—I've worn it from the cradle.
MESSENGER. That mark is the meaning of your name:
    Oedipus, Swollenfoot, Oedipus.
OEDIPUS. Oh gods
    who did this to me?
    My mother?
    My father?
MESSENGER. I don't know. The man I took you from—he would
    know.

OEDIPUS. So you didn't find me? Somebody else gave me to you?   1300
MESSENGER. I got you from another shepherd.
OEDIPUS. What shepherd? Who was he? Do you know?
MESSENGER. As I recall, he worked for Laios.
OEDIPUS. The same Laios who was king of Thebes?
MESSENGER. The same Laios. The man was one of Laios' shepherds.
OEDIPUS. Is he still alive? I want to see this man.
MESSENGER. [*pointing to the* CHORUS] These people would know that
    better than I do.
OEDIPUS. Do any of you know this shepherd he's talking about?
    Have you ever noticed him in the fields or in the city?
    Answer, if you have.   1310
    It is time everything came out, time everything was made clear.
    Everything.
LEADER. I think he's the shepherd you sent for.
    But Jocasta, she would know.
OEDIPUS. [*to* JOCASTA]
    Jocasta, do you know this man?
    Is he the man this shepherd here says worked for Laios?
JOCASTA. What man? Forget about him. Forget what was said.
    It's not worth talking about.
OEDIPUS. How can I forget
    with clues like these in my hands?   1320
    With the secret of my birth staring me in the face?
JOCASTA. No, Oedipus!
    No more questions.
    For god's sake, for the sake of your own life!
    Isn't my anguish enough—more than enough?
OEDIPUS. You have nothing to fear,[27] Jocasta.
    Even if my mother
    and her mother before her were both slaves,
    that doesn't make *you* the daughter of slaves.
JOCASTA. Oedipus, you *must* stop.
                        I beg you—stop!   1330
OEDIPUS. Nothing can stop me now. I must know everything.
    Everything!
JOCASTA. I implore you, Oedipus. For your own good.
OEDIPUS. Damn my own good!
JOCASTA. Oh, Oedipus, Oedipus,
    I pray to god you never see who you are!
OEDIPUS. [*to one of the attendants, who hurries off through the
    exit stage left*]
    You there, go find that shepherd, bring him here.
    Let that woman bask in the glory of her noble birth.
JOCASTA. God help you, Oedipus—
    you were born to suffer, born   1340
    to misery and grief.

---

[27] Oedipus believes Jocasta's anguish is caused by fears that he is of lowly birth and social station.

These are the last words I will ever speak, ever
Oedipus.

> [JOCASTA *rushes offstage into the*
> *palace. Long silence.*]

LEADER. Why did Jocasta rush away,
    Oedipus, fleeing in such pain?
    I fear disaster, or worse,
    will break from this silence of hers.
OEDIPUS. Let it break! Let everything break!
    I must discover who I am, know the secret of my birth,
    no matter how humble, how vile.   1350
    Perhaps Jocasta is ashamed of my low birth, ashamed to be my
        wife.
    Like all women she's proud.
    But Luck, goddess who gives men all that is good, made *me*,
    and I won't be cheated of what is mine, nothing can dishonor me,
        ever.
    I am like the months, my brothers the months—they shaped me
    when I was a baby in the cold hills of Kithairon,
    they guided me, carved out my times of greatness,
    and they still move their hands over my life.
    I am the man I am. I will not stop
    until I discover who my parents are.   1360
CHORUS. if I know if I see
    if the dark force of prophecy is mine
    Kithairon
    when the full moon
    rides over us tomorrow
    listen listen to us sing to you
    dance worship praise you
    mountain where Oedipus was found
    know Oedipus will praise you
    praise his nurse country and mother   1370
    who blessed our king
    I call on you Apollo
    let these visions please you
    god Apollo
    healer

    Oedipus son
    who was your mother
    which of the deathless mountain nymphs who lay
    with the great god Pan[28]
    on the high peaks he runs across   1380
    or with Apollo
    who loves the high green pastures above

---

[28] God of the forest, of mountains, and of wild nature.

which one bore you
did the god of the bare windy peaks Hermes[29]
or the wild, dervish Dionysos
living in the cool air of the hills
take you
a foundling
from one of the nymphs he plays with
joyously lift you hold you in his arms   1390
OEDIPUS. Old men, I think the man coming toward us now
  must be the shepherd we are looking for.
  I have never seen him, but the years, chalking his face and hair,
    tell me
  he's the man. And my men are with him. But you probably
    know him.
LEADER. I do know him. If Laios ever had a man he trusted,
  this was the man.
OEDIPUS. [*to the* MESSENGER]
  You—is this the man you told me about?
MESSENGER. That's him. You're looking at the man.
OEDIPUS. [*to the* SHEPHERD *who has been waiting, hanging back*]
  You there, come closer.
                                    Answer me, old man.
  Did you work for Laios?   1400
SHEPHERD. I was born his slave, and grew up in his household.
OEDIPUS. What was your work?
SHEPHERD. Herding sheep, all my life.
OEDIPUS. Where?
SHEPHERD. Kithairon, mostly. And the country around Kithairon.
OEDIPUS. Do you remember ever seeing this man?
MESSENGER. Which man?
OEDIPUS. [*pointing to the* MESSENGER]
  This man standing here. Have you ever seen him before?
SHEPHERD. Not that I remember.
MESSENGER. No wonder, master. But I'll make him remember.   1410
  He knows who I am. We used to graze our flocks together
  in the pastures around Kithairon.
  Every year, for six whole months, three years running.
  From March until September, when the Dipper rose, signaling the
    harvest.
  I had one flock, he had two.
  And when the frost came, I drove my sheep back to their winter
    pens
  and he drove his back to Laios' fold.
  Remember, old man? Isn't that how it was?
SHEPHERD. Yes. But it was all so long ago.
MESSENGER. And do you remember giving me a baby boy at the
    time—   1420
  to raise as my own son?

[29] Hermes was born on a mountain (Cyllene); he was also the god of shepherds.

SHEPHERD. What if I do? Why all these questions?
MESSENGER. That boy became King Oedipus, friend.
SHEPHERD. Damn you, can't you keep quiet.
OEDIPUS. Don't scold him, old man.
  It's you who deserve to be punished, not him.
SHEPHERD. What did I say, good master?
OEDIPUS. You haven't answered his question about the boy.
SHEPHERD. He's making trouble, master. He doesn't know a thing.

[OEDIPUS *takes the* SHEPHERD *by
the cloak*]

OEDIPUS. Tell me or you'll be sorry.   1430
SHEPHERD. For god's sake, don't hurt me, I'm an old man.
OEDIPUS. [*to one of his men*] You there, hold him. We'll make him talk.

[*The attendant pins the* SHEP-
HERD'S *arms behind his back*]

SHEPHERD. Oedipus, Oedipus,
  god knows I pity you.
  What more do you want to know?
OEDIPUS. Did you give the child to this man?
                                        Speak.   Yes or no?
SHEPHERD. Yes.
  And I wish to god I'd died that day.
OEDIPUS. You *will* be dead unless you tell me the whole truth.
SHEPHERD. And worse than dead if I do.   1440
OEDIPUS. It seems our man won't answer.
SHEPHERD. No. I told you already. I gave him the boy.
OEDIPUS. Where did you get him? From Laios' household? Or where?
SHEPHERD. He wasn't *my* child. He was given to me.
OEDIPUS. [*turning to the* CHORUS *and the audience*]
  By whom? Someone here in Thebes?
SHEPHERD. Master, please, in god's name, no more questions.
OEDIPUS. You're a dead man if I have to ask you once more.
SHEPHERD. He was one
  of the children
  from Laios'   1450
  household.
OEDIPUS. A slave child? Or Laios' own?
SHEPHERD. I can't say it . . . it's
  awful, the words
  are awful . . . awful.
OEDIPUS. And I,
  I am afraid to hear them . . .
  but I must.
SHEPHERD. He was Laios' own child.
  Your wife, inside the palace, she can explain it all.   1460
OEDIPUS. *She* gave you the child?
SHEPHERD. My lord . . . yes.

OEDIPUS. Why?

SHEPHERD. She wanted me to abandon the child on a mountain.

OEDIPUS. His own mother?

SHEPHERD. Yes. There were prophecies, horrible oracles. She was afraid.

OEDIPUS. What oracles?

SHEPHERD. Oracles predicting he would murder his own father.

OEDIPUS. But why did you give the boy to this old man?

SHEPHERD. Because I pitied him, master, because I   1470
 thought the man would take the child away, take him to another
  country.
 Instead he saved him. Saved him for—oh gods,
 a fate so horrible, so awful, words can't describe it.
 If you were the baby that man took from me, Oedipus,
 what misery, what grief is yours!

OEDIPUS. [*looking up at the sun*]
 LIGHT   LIGHT   LIGHT
 never again flood these eyes with your white radiance, oh gods, my
  eyes. All, all
 the oracles have proven true. I, Oedipus, I
 am the child
 of parents who should never have been mine—doomed, doomed!   1480
 Now everything is clear—I
 lived with a woman, she was my mother, I slept in my mother's
  bed, and I
 murdered, murdered my father,
 the man whose blood flows in these veins of mine,
 whose blood stains these two hands red.

        [OEDIPUS *raises his hands to the*
        sun, then turns and walks into the
        palace.]

CHORUS. man after man after man
 o mortal generations
 here once
 almost not here
 what are we   1490
 dust ghosts images a rustling of air
 nothing nothing
 we breathe on the abyss
 we are the abyss
 our happiness no more than traces of a dream
 the high noon sun sinking into the sea
 the red spume of its wake raining behind it
 we are you
 we are you Oedipus
 dragging your maimed foot   1500
 in agony
 and now that I see your life finally revealed

your life fused with the god
blazing out of the black nothingness of all we know
I say
no happiness lasts nothing human lasts

wherever you aimed you hit
no archer had your skill
you grew rich powerful great
everything came falling to your feet   1510
o Zeus
after he killed the Sphinx
whose claws curled under
whose weird song of the future[30] baffled and destroyed
he stood like a tower high above our country
warding off death
and from then on Oedipus we called you
king our king
draped you in gold
our highest honors were yours   1520
and you ruled this shining city
Thebes   Thebes

now
your story is pain pity no story is worse
than yours Oedipus
ruined savage blind
as you struggle with your life
as your life changes
and breaks and shows you who you are
Oedipus   Oedipus   1530
son father you harbored in the selfsame place[31]
the same place sheltered you both
bridegroom
how could the furrow your father plowed
not have cried out all this time
while you lay there unknowing
and saw the truth too late

time like the sun sees all things
and it sees you
you cannot hide from that light   1540
your own life opening itself to you
to all
married unmarried father son
for so long

[30] The Sphinx was a kind of oracle; specifically, her riddle about the three states of man
reflects this play's focus on Oedipus' infancy, prime of manhood, and final weakness when,
blinded, he must use a walking stick.
[31] Harbored sexually, with Jocasta; geographically, the place alluded to is the mountain
Kithairon, where Laios died and to which Oedipus will flee.

justice comes like the dawn
always
and it shows the world your marriage now

I wish
o child of Laios
I wish I had never seen you   1550
I grieve for you
wail after wail fills me and pours out
because of you my breath came flowing back
but now
the darkness of your life
floods my eyes

> [*The palace doors open. A* SERVANT
> *enters and approaches the* CHORUS
> *and audience.*]

SERVANT. Noble citizens, honored above all others in Thebes,
    if you still care for the house of Laios,
    if you still can feel the spirit of those who ruled before, now
    the horrors you will hear, the horrors you will see, will shake   1560
        your hearts and shatter you with grief beyond enduring.
    Not even the waters of those great rivers Ister and Phasis[32]
    could wash away the blood
    that now darkens every stone of this shining house,
    this house that will reveal, soon, soon
    the misery and evil two mortals,
    both masters of this house, have brought upon themselves.

    The griefs we cause ourselves cut deepest of all.[33]
LEADER. What we already know
    has hurt us enough,   1570
    has made us cry out in pain.
    What more can you say?
SERVANT. This:
    Jocasta is dead. The queen is dead.
LEADER. Ah, poor
    unhappy Jocasta,
    how did she die?
SERVANT. She killed herself. She did it.
    But you did not see what happened there,
    you were not there, in the palace. You did not see it.   1580
    I did.
    I will tell you how Queen Jocasta died,
    the whole story, all of it. All I can remember.

---

[32] Ister is the Danube River; Phasis is a river flowing into the Black Sea.
[33] The reference may be to the acts of Laios and Oedipus in the distant past or to the recent suicide and self-blinding of Jocasta and Oedipus. The words "cut deepest of all" can also apply to the Thebans and to the theatrical audience.

After her last words to Oedipus
she rushed past us through the entrance hall, screaming,
raking her hair with both hands, and flew into the bedroom, *their*
    bedroom,
and slammed the doors shut as she lunged at her bridal bed,
crying "Laios" "Laios"—dead all these years—
remembering Laios—how his own son years ago
grew up and then killed him, leaving her to   1590
sleep with her own son, to have his children, *their* children,
children—not sons, not daughters, something else, monsters. . . .
Then she collapsed, sobbing, cursing the bed where she held both
    men in her arms,
got husband from husband, children from her child.
We heard it all, but suddenly, I couldn't tell what was happening.
Oedipus came crashing in, he was howling,
stalking up and down—we couldn't take our eyes off him—
and we stopped listening to her pitiful cries.
We stood there, watching him move like a bull, lurching, charging,
shouting at each of us to give him a sword, demanding we tell him   1600
where his wife was, that woman whose womb carried him,
him and his children, that wife who gave him birth.
Some god, some demon, led him to her, and he knew—
none of us showed him—
suddenly a mad, inhuman cry burst from his mouth
as if the wind rushed through his tortured body,
and he heaved against those bedroom doors so the hinges whined
and bent from their sockets and the bolts snapped,
and he stood in the room.
There she was—   1610
we could see her—his wife
dangling by her neck from a noose of braided, silken cords
tied to a rafter, still swaying.
And when he saw her he bellowed and stretched up and loosened
    the rope,
cradling her in one arm,
and slowly laid her body on the ground.

That's when it happened—he
ripped off the gold
brooches she was wearing—one on each shoulder of her gown—
and raised them over his head—you could see them flashing—   1620
and tilted his face up and
brought them right down into his eyes
and the long pins sank deep, all the way back into the sockets,
and he shouted at his eyes:
"Now you won't see me, you won't see
my agonies or my crimes,
but in endless darkness, always, there you'll see
those I never should have seen.

And those I should have known were my parents, father and
    mother—
these eyes will never see their faces in the light.   1630
These eyes will never see the light again, never."
Cursing his two blind eyes over and over, he
lifted the brooches again and drove their pins through his
    eyeballs up
to the hilts until they were pulp, until the blood streamed out
soaking his beard and cheeks,
a black storm splashing its hail across his face.

Two mortals acted. Now grief tears their lives apart
as if that pain sprang from a single, sorrowing root
to curse each one, man and wife. For all those years
their happiness was truly happiness, but now, now   1640
wailing, madness, shame and death,
every evil men have given a name,
everything criminal and vile
that mankind suffers they suffer. Not one evil is missing.

LEADER. But now
    does this torn, anguished man
    have any rest from his pain?
SERVANT. No, no—
    then he shouted at us to open the doors and show everyone in
        Thebes
    his father's killer, his mother's—I cannot say it.   1650
    Once we have seen him as he is
    he will leave Thebes, lift the curse from his city—
    banish himself, cursed by his own curses.
    But his strength is gone, his whole life is pain,
    more pain than any man can bear.
    He needs help, someone to guide him.
    He is alone, and blind. Look,
    look—the palace doors are opening—now
    a thing
    so horrible will stand before you   1660
    you will shudder with disgust and try to turn away
    while your hearts will swell with pity for what you see.

                              [*The central doors open.* OEDIPUS
                              enters, led by his household servants.
                              His mask is covered with blood. The
                              CHORUS *begin a dirge to which*
                              OEDIPUS *responds antiphonally.*]

CHORUS. horror horror o what suffering
    men see
    but none is worse than this
    Oedipus o

how could you have slashed out your eyes
what god leaped on you
from beyond that last border of space
what madness entered you   1670
clawing even more misery into you
I cannot look at you

but there are questions
so much I would know
so much that I would see
no   no
the shape of your life makes me shudder
OEDIPUS. I   I
this voice of agony
I am   what place am I   1680
where? Not here, nowhere I know!
What force, what tide breaks over my life?
Pain, demon stabbing into me
leaving nothing, nothing, no man I know, not human,
fate howling out of nowhere   what am I
fire   a voice   where   where
is it being taken?
LEADER. Beyond everything to a place
so terrible nothing is seen there, nothing is heard.
OEDIPUS. [*reaching out, groping*]
Thing   thing   darkness   1690
spilling into me, my
black cloud smothering me forever,
nothing can stop you, nothing can escape,
I cannot push you away.

I am
nothing but my own cries breaking
again and again
the agony of those gold pins
the memory of what I did
stab me   1700
again
again.
LEADER. What can you feel but pain.
It all comes back, pain in remorse,
remorse in pain, to tear you apart with grief.
OEDIPUS. Dear, loyal friend
you, only you, are still here with me, still care
for this blind, tortured man.
Oh,
I know you are there, I know you, friend,   1710
even in this darkness, friend, touched by your voice.

Leader. What you did was horrible,
    but how could you quench the fire of your eyes,
    what demon lifted your hands?
Oedipus. Apollo   Apollo
    it was Apollo, always Apollo,
    who brought each of my agonies to birth,
    but I,
    nobody else, *I*,
    I raised these two hands of mine, held them above my head,   1720
    and plunged them down,
    I stabbed out these eyes.
    Why should I have eyes? Why,
    when nothing I saw was worth seeing?
    Nothing.
Leader. Nothing. Nothing.
Oedipus. Oh friends. Nothing.
    No one to see, no one to love,
    no one to speak to, no one to hear!
                Friends, friends, lead me away now.
    Lead me away from Thebes—Oedipus,   1730
    destroyer and destroyed,
    the man whose life is hell
    for others and for himself, the man
    more hated by the gods than any other man, ever.
Leader. Oh I pity you,
    I weep for your fate
    and for your mind,
    for what it is to be you, Oedipus.
    I wish you had never seen the man you are.
Oedipus. I hate   1740
    the man who found me, cut the thongs from my feet,
    snatched me from death, cared for me—
    I wish he were dead!
    I should have died up there on those wild, desolate slopes of
        Kithairon.
    Then my pain and the pain
    those I love suffer now
    never would have been.
Leader. These are my wishes too.
Oedipus. Then I never would have murdered my father,
    never heard men call me my mother's husband.   1750

    Now
    I am
    Oedipus!
    Oedipus, who lay in that loathsome bed, made love there in
        that bed,
    his father's and mother's bed, the bed
    where he was born.

No gods anywhere now, not for me,[34] now,
unholy, broken man.
What man ever suffered grief like this?
LEADER. How can I say that what you did was right?   1760
    Better to be dead than live blind.
OEDIPUS. I did what I had to do. No more advice.
    How could *my* eyes,
    when I went down into that black, sightless place beneath the
        earth,
    the place where the dead go down, how,
    how could I have looked at anything,
    with what human eyes could I have gazed
    on my father, on my mother—
    oh gods, my mother!
    What I did against those two   1770
    not even strangling could punish.

    And my children, how would the sight of them, born as they were
        born,
    be sweet? Not to these eyes of mine, never to these eyes.
    Nothing, nothing is left me now—no city with its high walls,
    no shining statues of the gods. I stripped all these things from
        myself—
    I, Oedipus, fallen lower than any man now, born nobler than the
        best,
    born the king of Thebes! Cursed with my own curses, I
    commanded Thebes to drive out the killer.
    I banished the royal son of Laios, the man the gods revealed
    is stained with the awful stain. The secret stain   1780
    that I myself revealed is *my* stain. And now, revealed at last,
    how could I ever look men in the eyes?
    Never. Never.

    If I could, I would have walled my ears so they heard nothing,
    I would have made this body of mine a wall.
    I would have heard nothing, tasted nothing, smelled nothing, seen
    nothing.
            No thought. No feeling. Nothing. Nothing.
    So pain would never reach me any more.

    O Kithairon,
    why did you shelter me and take me in?   1790
    Why did you let me live? Better to have died on that bare slope of
        yours
    where no man would ever have seen me or known the secret of my
        birth!

    Polybos, Corinth, that house I thought was my father's home,
    how beautiful I was when you sheltered me as a child

---

[34] Oedipus means that he has been forsaken by the gods.

and oh what disease festered beneath that beauty.
Now everyone knows the secret of my birth, knows
how vile I am.

O roads, secret valley, cluster of oaks,
O narrow place where two roads join a third,[35]
roads that drank my blood as it streamed from my hands,   1800
flowing from my dead father's body,
do you remember me now?
Do you remember what I did with my own two hands, there in
    your presence,
and what I did after that, when I came here to Thebes?
O marriage, marriage, you gave me my life, and then
from the same seed, *my* seed, spewed out
fathers, brothers, sisters, children, brides, wives—
nothing, no words can express the shame.
No more words. Men should not name what men should never do.

[*To the* Chorus]

Gods, oh gods, gods,   1810
hide me, hide me
now
far away from Thebes,
kill me,
cast me into the sea,
drive me where you will never see me—never again.

[*Reaching out to the* Chorus, *who
back away*]

Touch this poor man, touch me,
don't be afraid to touch me. Believe me, nobody,
nobody but me can bear
this fire of anguish.   1820
It is mine. Mine.

Leader. Kreon has come.
    Now he, not you, is the sole guardian of Thebes,
    and only he can grant you what you ask.
Oedipus. [*turning toward the palace*]
    What can I say to him, how can anything I say
    make him listen now?
    I wronged him. I accused him, and now everything I said
    proves I am vile.
Kreon. [*enters from the entrance to the right. He is accompanied by men who
        gather around* Oedipus]

---

[35] Not only the crossroads where Oedipus killed his father, but also the sexual "narrow place" where Oedipus, his father, and Jocasta conjoined.

I have not come to mock you, Oedipus; I have not come to blame
    you for the past.

[*To attendants*]

You men, standing there, if you have no respect for human dig-
    nity,   1830
at least revere the master of life,
the all-seeing sun whose light nourishes
every living thing on earth.
Come, cover this cursed, naked, holy thing,[36] hide him
from the earth and the sacred rain and the light,
you powers who cringe from his touch.
Take him. Do it now. Be reverent.
Only his family should see and hear his grief.
Their grief.

OEDIPUS. I beg you, Kreon, if you love the gods,   1840
grant me what I ask.
I have been vile to you, worse than vile.
I have hurt you, terribly, and yet
you have treated me with kindness, with nobility.
You have calmed my fear, you did not turn away from me.
Do what I ask. Do it for yourself, not for me.

KREON. What do you want from me, Oedipus?

OEDIPUS. Drive me out of Thebes, do it now, now—
drive me someplace where no man can speak to me,
where no man can see me anymore.   1850

KREON. Believe me, Oedipus, I would have done it long ago.
But I refuse to act until I know precisely what the god desires.

OEDIPUS. Apollo has revealed what he desires. Everything is clear.
I killed my father, I am polluted and unclean.
I must die.

KREON. That is what the god commanded, Oedipus.
But there are no precedents for what has happened.
We need to *know* before we act.

OEDIPUS. Do you care so much for me, enough to ask Apollo?
For *me*, Oedipus?   1860

KREON. Now even you will trust the god, I think.

OEDIPUS. I will. And I turn to you, I implore you, Kreon—
the woman lying dead inside, your sister,
give her whatever burial you think best.

                                  As for me,
never let this city of my fathers see me here in Thebes.
Let me go and live on the mountain, on Kithairon—the mountain
my parents intended for my grave.
Let me die the way they wanted me to die: slowly, alone—
die *their* way.

---

[36] Because he bears a burden of guilt that transforms ordinary human nature, Oedipus has
paradoxically become a kind of sacred being.

And yet this much I know—

no sickness,   1870
no ordinary, natural death[37] is mine.
I have been saved, preserved, kept alive
for some strange fate, for something far more awful still.
When that thing comes, let it take me
where it will.

[OEDIPUS *turns, looking for something, waiting*]

As for my sons,[38] Kreon,
they are grown men, they can look out for themselves.
But my daughters, those two poor girls of mine,
who have never left their home before, never left their father's
    side,
who ate at my side every day, who shared whatever was mine,   1880
I beg you, Kreon,
care for them, love them.
But more than anything, Kreon,
I want to touch them,

[*he begins to lift his hands*]

let me touch them with these hands of mine,
let them come to me so we can grieve together.
My noble lord, if only I could touch them with my hands,
they would still be mine just as they were
when I had eyes that could still see.

[*Oedipus' two small daughters are
brought out of the palace*]

O gods, gods, is it possible? Do I hear   1890
my two daughters crying? Has Kreon pitied me and brought me
what I love more than my life—
my daughters?
KREON. I brought them to you, knowing how much you love them,
    Oedipus,
knowing the joy you would feel if they were here.
OEDIPUS. May the gods who watch over the path of your life, Kreon,
prove kinder to you than they were to me.

---

[37] In his play *Oedipus at Colonus*, Sophocles continues the story of *Oedipus the King* (though
the plays, along with the further continuation, *Antigone*, were written at different periods of
Sophocles' life). Since Oedipus died at Colonus, a suburb of Athens that included a place
sacred to the Furies, the personified forces of atonement celebrated in the last play of
Aeschylus' *Orestes* trilogy, the present reference to Oedipus' mysterious and sacred death and
resting place would have been important to Sophocles' Athenian audience as a sign of the
redemptive value of Oedipus' wanderings and sufferings.
[38] Eteocles and Polyneices. Their enmity in a subsequent war for control of the city of
Thebes, and the related ordeals of Oedipus' daughters Antigone and Ismene, are central to
Sophocles' *Oedipus at Colonus* and *Antigone*.

Where are you, children?
Come, come to your brother's hands—

[*taking his daughters into his arms*]

his mother was your mother, too,   1900
come to these hands which made these eyes, bright clear eyes once,
sockets seeing nothing, the eyes
of the man who fathered you. Look . . . your father's eyes,
your father—
who knew nothing until now, saw nothing until now, and became
the husband of the woman who gave him birth.
                                                       I weep for you
when I think how men will treat you, how bitter your lives will be.
What festivals will you attend, whose homes will you visit
and not be assailed by whispers, and people's stares?
Where will you go and not leave in tears?   1910
And when the time comes for you to marry,
what men will take you as their brides, and risk the shame of mar-
     rying
the daughters of Oedipus?
What sorrow will not be yours?
Your father killed his father, made love
to the woman who gave birth to him. And he fathered you
in the same place where he was fathered.
That is what you will hear; that is what they will say.
Who will marry you then? You will never marry,
but grow hard and dry like wheat so far beyond harvest   1920
that the wind blows its white flakes into the winter sky.
Oh Kreon,
now you are the only father my daughters have.
Jocasta and I, their parents, are lost to them forever.
These poor girls are yours. Your blood.
Don't let them wander all their lives,
begging, alone, unmarried, helpless.
Don't let them suffer as their father has. Pity them, Kreon,
pity these girls, so young and helpless except for you.
Promise me this. Noble Kreon,   1930
touch me with your hand, give me a sign.

[KREON *takes his hands*]

                                                       Daughters,
daughters, if you were older, if you could understand,
there is so much more I would say to you.
But for now, I give you this prayer—
                                        Live,
live your lives, live each day as best you can,
  may your lives be happier than your father's was.
KREON. No more grief. Come in.
OEDIPUS. I must. But obedience comes hard.

KREON. Everything has its time.
OEDIPUS. First, promise me this. 1940
KREON. Name it.
OEDIPUS. Banish me from Thebes.
KREON. I cannot.   Ask the gods for that.
OEDIPUS. The gods hate me.
KREON. Then you will have your wish.
OEDIPUS. You promise?
KREON. I say only what I mean.
OEDIPUS. Then lead me in.

> [OEDIPUS *reaches out and touches his daughters, trying to take them with him*]

KREON. Oedipus, come with me. Let your daughters go. Come.
OEDIPUS. No. You will not take my daughters. I forbid it. 1950
KREON. You *forbid* me?
> You have no power any more.
> All the great power you once had is gone,
> gone forever.

> [*The* CHORUS *turn to face the audience.* KREON *leads* OEDIPUS *toward the palace. His daughters follow. He moves slowly, and disappears into the palace as the* CHORUS *ends.*]

CHORUS. O citizens of Thebes, this is Oedipus,
> who solved the famous riddle, who held more power than any
> > mortal.
> See what he is: all men gazed on his fortunate life,
> all men envied him, but look at him, look.
> All he had, all this man was,
> pulled down and swallowed by the storm of his own life, 1960
> and by the god.
> Keep your eyes on that last day, on your dying.
> Happiness and peace, they were not yours
> unless at death you can look back on your life and say
> I lived, I did not suffer.

ANTIGONE

Translated by Theodore Howard Banks

CHARACTERS IN THE PLAY

CREON,[1] *King of Thebes, brother
of Jocasta, the mother and wife
of Oedipus*
EURYDICE, *Queen of Thebes,
wife of Creon*
HAEMON, *son of Creon*
ANTIGONE } *daughters of Oedipus*
ISMENE   } *and Jocasta*

TIRESIAS, *a prophet*
BOY, *attendant of Tiresias*
GUARD
MESSENGER
CHORUS *of Theban Elders*
ATTENDANTS

SCENE
Courtyard of the royal palace at Thebes. Daybreak.

[*Enter* ANTIGONE *and* ISMENE]

ANTIGONE. Dear sister! Dear Ismene! How many evils
  Our father, Oedipus, bequeathed to us![2]
  And is there one of them—do you know of one
  That Zeus has not showered down upon our heads?
  I have seen pain, dishonor, shame, and ruin,
  I have seen them all, in what we have endured.
  And now comes this new edict by the King
  Proclaimed throughout the city. Have you heard?
  Do you not know, even yet, our friends are threatened?
  They are to meet the fate of enemies.   10
ISMENE. Our friends, Antigone? No, I have heard
  Nothing about them either good or bad.
  I have no news except that we two sisters
  Lost our two brothers when they killed each other.[3]
  I know the Argive army fled last night,
  But what that means, or whether it makes my life
  Harder or easier, I cannot tell.
ANTIGONE. This I was sure of. So I brought you here
  Beyond the palace gates to talk alone.

[1] The Kreon of *Oedipus the King*. The names in this translation sometimes are spelled differently.

[2] The two sisters had accompanied their self-blinded father Oedipus in his wanderings and sufferings after his banishment from Thebes. (The banishment is described at the end of *Oedipus the King*.) Possibly we are to regard Oedipus' lineage as afflicted by an inherited curse. Oedipus' crimes, committed unwittingly, had been to kill his father Laius, the king of Thebes, and to marry his mother.

[3] Oedipus' two sons, Eteocles and Polyneices, had been rivals for the rulership of the city. After being exiled by Eteocles, Polyneices had recruited a military force in Argos to attack Thebes. In the ensuing battle, the Thebans had defeated the Argives and the brothers Eteocles and Polyneices had killed each other, leaving Creon to rule Thebes.

ISMENE. What is the matter? I know you are deeply troubled. 20
ANTIGONE. Yes, for our brothers' fate.[4] Creon has given
  An honored burial to one, to the other
  Only unburied shame. Eteocles
  Is laid in the earth with all the rites observed
  That give him his due honor with the dead.
  But the decree concerning Polyneices
  Published through Thebes is that his wretched body
  Shall lie unmourned, unwept, unsepulchered.
  Sweet will he seem to the vultures when they find him,
  A welcome feast that they are eager for. 30
  This is the edict the good Creon uttered
  For your observance and for mine—yes, mine.
  He is coming here himself to make it plain
  To those who have not heard. Nor does he think it
  Of little consequence, because whoever
  Does not obey is doomed to death by stoning.
  Now you can show you are worthy of your birth,
  Or bring disgrace upon a noble house.
ISMENE. What can I do, Antigone? As things are,
  What can I do that would be of any help? 40
ANTIGONE. You can decide if you will share my task.
ISMENE. What do you mean? What are you planning to do?
ANTIGONE. I intend to give him burial. Will you help?
ISMENE. To give him burial! Against the law?
ANTIGONE. He is our brother. I will do my duty,
  Yours too, perhaps. I never will be false.
ISMENE. Creon forbids it! You are too rash, too headstrong.
ANTIGONE. He has no right to keep me from my own.
ISMENE. Antigone! Think! Think how our father perished[5]
  In scorn and hatred when his sins, that he 50
  Himself discovered, drove him to strike blind
  His eyes by his own hand. Think how his mother,
  His wife—both names were hers—ended her life
  Shamefully hanging in a twisted noose.
  Think of that dreadful day when our two brothers,
  Our wretched brothers, fought and fell together,
  Each slayer and each slain. And now we too,
  Left all alone, think how in turn we perish,
  If, in defiance of the law, we brave
  The power of the commandment of a king. 60
  O think Antigone! We who are women
  Should not contend with men; we who are weak
  Are ruled by the stronger, so that we must obey

---

[4] It was believed that the unburied were treated with contempt in the underground realm of the dead. Moreover, to mourn and to prepare bodies for proper burial was the special duty of the women.

[5] The version in *Oedipus at Colonus* is that Oedipus, after long suffering, died a holy and mysterious death. The events Ismene describes here (her mother Jocasta's suicide and Oedipus' self-blinding) take place in *Oedipus the King*.

In this and in matters that are yet more bitter.
And so I pray the dead to pardon me
If I obey our rulers, since I must.
To be too bold in what we do is madness.
ANTIGONE. I will not urge you. And I would not thank you
For any help that you might care to give me.
Do what you please, but I will bury him,   70
And if I die for that, I shall be happy.
Loved, I shall rest beside the one I loved.
My crime is innocence, for I owe the dead
Longer allegiance than I owe the living.
With the dead I lie forever. Live, if you choose,
Dishonoring the laws the gods have hallowed.
ISMENE. No, I dishonor nothing. But to challenge
Authority—I have not strength enough.
ANTIGONE. Then make that your excuse. I will go heap
The earth above the brother that I love.   80
ISMENE. O Sister, Sister! How I fear for you!
ANTIGONE. No, not for me. Set your own life in order.
ISMENE. Well then, at least, tell no one of your plan.
Keep it close hidden, as I too will keep it.
ANTIGONE. Oh! Publish it! Proclaim it to the world!
Then I will hate you less than for your silence.
ISMENE. Your heart is hot for deeds that chill the blood.
ANTIGONE. I know that I give pleasure where I should.
ISMENE. Yes, if you can, but you will try in vain.
ANTIGONE. When my strength fails, then I shall try no longer.   90
ISMENE. A hopeless task should never be attempted.
ANTIGONE. Your words have won their just reward: my hatred
And the long-lasting hatred of the dead.
But leave me and the folly that is mine
To undergo the worst that can befall me.
I shall not suffer an ignoble death.
ISMENE. Go then, Antigone, if you must go.
And yet remember, though your act is foolish,
That those who love you do so with all their hearts.

> [*Exeunt* ANTIGONE *and* ISMENE.
> *Enter* CHORUS]

CHORUS.
Sunbeam, eye of the golden day, on Thebes the seven-gated,   100
On Dircé's[6] streams you have dawned at last, O fairest of light.
Dawned on our foes, who had come enflamed by the quarrel of
Polyneices,
Shone on their glittering arms, made swifter their headlong
flight.
From Argos they came with their white shields flashing,

---

[6] A river near Thebes.

Their helmets, crested with horsehair, agleam:
An army that flew like a snow-white eagle
Across our borders with shrilling scream.

Above our roofs it soared, at our gates with greedy jaws it was
      gaping;
  But before their spears tasted our blood, and before our circle
    of towers
Felt the flame of their torches, they turned to flight. The foes of
    the Theban dragon[7]   110
Found the surge and clamor of battle too fierce for their feebler
    powers.
  For Zeus, who abhors a proud tongue's boasting,
    Seeing their river of armor flow
Clashing and golden, struck with his lightning
    To silence the shout of our foremost foe.[8]

He crashed to the earth with his torch, who had scaled the top of
    our ramparts,
  Raging in frenzy against us, breathing tempestuous hate,
Raging and threatening in vain. And mighty Ares,[9] our ally,
  Dealing havoc around him, apportioned to other foemen
    their fate.
  For at seven portals, their seven leaders,   120
    Down to the earth their bronze arms threw
  In tribute to Zeus, the lord of the battle;
    Save the fated brothers, the wretched two,
Who went to their common doom together,
    Each wielding a spear that the other slew.

Now glorious Victory smiles upon jubilant Thebes rich in chariots.
  Let us give free rein to our joy, forgetting our late-felt war;
Let us visit in night-long chorus the temples of all the immortals,
  With Bacchus,[10] who shakes the land in the dances, going be-
    fore.
  But behold! The son of Menoeceus approaches,   130
    Creon, the new-crowned King of the land,
  Made King by new fortunes the gods have allotted.
    What step has he pondered? What has he planned
To lay before us, his council of elders,
    Who have gathered together at his command?

[*Enter* CREON]

---

[7] According to myth, the Thebans were descendants of men metamorphosed from the teeth of a dragon killed by Cadmus, founder of the city.

[8] The foe is Capaneus. Having scaled the walls of Thebes, he boasted that not even Zeus, king of the gods, could stop him, but Zeus killed him with a thunderbolt.

[9] God of war and of destruction.

[10] God of wine; his mother Semele, who was ravished by Zeus in the form of lightning, was a Theban.

CREON. Elders of Thebes, our city has been tossed
    By a tempestuous ocean, but the gods
    Have steadied it once more and made it safe.
    You, out of all the citizens, I have summoned,
    Because I knew that you once reverenced   140
    The sovereignty of Laius, and that later,
    When Oedipus was King and when he perished,
    Your steadfast loyalty upheld his children.
    And now his sons have fallen, each one stained
    By his brother's blood, killed by his brother's hand,
    So that the sovereignty devolves on me,
    Since I by birth am nearest to the dead.[11]
    Certainly no man can be fully known,
    Known in his soul, his will, his intellect,
    Until he is tested and has proved himself   150
    In statesmanship. Because a city's ruler,
    Instead of following the wisest counsel,
    May through some fear keep silent. Such a man
    I think contemptible. And one whose friend
    Has stronger claims upon him than his country,
    Him I consider worthless.[12] As for me,
    I swear by Zeus, forever all-beholding,
    That I would not keep silence, if I saw
    Ruin instead of safety drawing near us;
    Nor would I think an enemy of the state   160
    Could be my friend. For I remember this:
    Our country bears us all securely onward,
    And only while it sails a steady course
    Is friendship possible. Such are the laws
    By which I guard the greatness of the city.
    And kindred to them is the proclamation
    That I have made to all the citizens
    Concerning the two sons of Oedipus:
    Eteocles, who has fallen in our defence,
    Bravest of warriors, shall be entombed   170
    With every honor, every offering given
    That may accompany the noble dead
    Down to their rest. But as for Polyneices,
    He came from exile eager to consume
    The city of his fathers with his fire
    And all the temples of his fathers' gods,
    Eager to drink deep of his kindred's blood,
    Eager to drag us off to slavery.
    To this man, therefore, nothing shall be given.
    None shall lament him, none shall do him honor.   180

---

[11] Creon is the brother of the dead rivals' mother, Jocasta; he is also a cousin of the former king Laius.

[12] Creon here states his side of the play's central moral and political issue. The word "friend" has also the meaning of "kindred."

He shall be left without a grave, his corpse
Devoured by birds and dogs, a loathsome sight.
Such is my will. For never shall the wicked
Be given more approval than the just,
If I have power to stop it. But whoever
Feels in his heart affection for his city
Shall be rewarded both in life and death.

CHORUS. Creon, son of Menoeceus, it has pleased you
So to pass judgment on our friend and foe.
And you may give commands to all of us,   190
The living and the dead. Your will is law.

CREON. Then see that this command is carried out.

CHORUS. Sir, lay that burden on some younger man.

CREON. Sentries have been assigned to guard the body.

CHORUS. Then what additional duty would you give us?

CREON. Never to countenance the disobedient.

CHORUS. Who is so stupid as to long for death?

CREON. Death is indeed the punishment. Yet men
Have often been destroyed by hope of gain.

[*Enter* GUARD]

GUARD. My Lord, I cannot say that I have hurried,   200
Or that my running has made me lose my breath.
I often stopped to think, and turned to go back.
I stood there talking to myself: 'You fool,'
I said, 'Why do you go to certain death?'
And then: 'You idiot, are you still delaying?
If someone else tells Creon, you will suffer.'
I changed my mind this way, getting here slowly,
Making a short road long. But still, at last,
I did decide to come. And though my story
Is nothing much to tell, yet I will tell it.   210
One thing I know. I must endure my fate,
But nothing more than that can happen to me.

CREON. What is the matter? What is troubling you?

GUARD. Please let me tell you first about myself.
I did not do it. I did not see who did.
It is not right for me to be punished for it.

CREON. You take good care not to expose yourself.
Your news must certainly be something strange.

GUARD. Yes, it is strange—dreadful. I cannot speak.

CREON. Oh, tell it, will you? Tell it and go away!   220

GUARD. Well, it is this. Someone has buried the body,
Just now, and gone—has sprinkled it with dust
And given it other honors it should have.

CREON. What are you saying? Who has dared to do it?

GUARD. I cannot tell. Nothing was to be seen:
No mark of pickaxe, no spot where a spade
Had turned the earth. The ground was hard and dry,

Unbroken—not a trace of any wheels—
No sign to show who did it. When the sentry
On the first watch discovered it and told us,   230
We were struck dumb with fright. For he was hidden
Not by a tomb but a light coat of dust,
As if a pious hand had scattered it.
There were no tracks of any animal,
A dog or wild beast that had come to tear him.
We all began to quarrel, and since no one
Was there to stop us, nearly came to blows.
Everyone was accused, and everyone
Denied his guilt. We could discover nothing.
We were quite willing to handle red-hot iron,   240
To walk through fire, to swear by all the gods
That we were innocent of the deed itself,
And innocent of taking any part
In planning it or doing it. At last
One of us spoke. We trembled and hung our heads,
For he was right; we could not argue with him,
Yet his advice was bound to cause us trouble.
He told us all this had to be reported,
Not kept a secret. We all agreed to that.
We drew lots for it, and I had no luck.   250
I won the prize and was condemned to come.
So here I stand, unwilling, because I know
The bringer of bad news is never welcome.
CHORUS. Sir, as he spoke, I have been wondering.
   Can this be, possibly, the work of gods?
CREON. Be silent![13] Before you madden me! You are old.
   Would you be senseless also? What you say
   Is unendurable. You say the gods
   Cared for this corpse. Then was it for reward,
   Mighty to match his mighty services,   260
   That the gods covered him? He who came to burn
   Their pillared temples and their votive offerings,
   Ravage their land, and trample down the state.
   Or is it your opinion that the gods
   Honor the wicked? Inconceivable!
   However, from the first, some citizens
   Who found it difficult to endure this edict,
   Muttered against me, shaking their heads in secret,
   Instead of bowing down beneath the yoke,
   Obedient and contented with my rule.   270
   These are the men who are responsible,
   For I am certain they have bribed the guards

---

[13] The Chorus's surmise about divine intervention in this first burial is conceivably true; the play is somewhat ambiguous on the matter. The possibility that the Chorus is right emphasizes Creon's departure from his earlier-stated principle that rulers should listen to counsel (line 152).

To bury him. Nothing is worse than money.
Money lays waste to cities, banishes
Men from their homes, indoctrinates the heart,
Perverting honesty to works of shame,
Showing men how to practice villainy,
Subduing them to every godless deed.
But all those men who got their pay for this
Need have no doubt their turn to pay will come. 280
[*to the* GUARD] Now, you. As I still honor Zeus the King,
I tell you, and I swear it solemnly,
Either you find the man who did this thing,
The very man, and bring him here to me,
Or you will not just die. Before you die,
You will be tortured until you have explained
This outrage; so that later when you steal
You will know better where to look for money
And not expect to find it everywhere.
Ill-gotten wealth brings ruin and not safety. 290
GUARD. Sir, may I speak? Or shall I merely go?
CREON. You can say nothing that is not offensive.
GUARD. Do I offend your hearing or your heart?
CREON. Is it your business to define the spot?
GUARD. The criminal hurts your heart, and I your ears.
CREON. Still talking? Why, you must have been born talking!
GUARD. Perhaps. But I am not the guilty man.
CREON. You are. And what is more you sold yourself.
GUARD. You have judged me, sir, and have misjudged me, too.
CREON. Be clever about judging if you care to. 300
But you will say that treachery leads to sorrow
Unless you find the man and show him to me.

[*Exit* CREON]

GUARD. Finding him is the best thing that could happen.
Fate will decide. But however that may be,
You never are going to see me here again.
I have escaped! I could not have hoped for that.
I owe the gods my thanks for guarding me.

[*Exit* GUARD]

CHORUS.
Many the marvelous things; but none that can be
More of a marvel than man! This being that braves
With the south wind of winter the whitened streaks of the sea, 310
Threading his way through the troughs of engulfing waves.
And the earth most ancient, the eldest of all the gods,
Earth, undecaying, unwearied, he wears away with his toil;
Forward and back with his plowshare, year after year, he plods,
With his horses turning the soil.

Man in devising excels. The birds of the air,
    That light-minded race, he entangles fast in his toils.
Wild creatures he catches, casting about them his snare,
    And the salt-sea brood he nets in his woven coils.
The tireless bull he has tamed, and the beast whose lair   320
    Is hidden deep in the wilds, who roams in the wooded hills.
He has fitted a yoke that the neck of the shaggy-maned horse
        will bear;
    He is master of all through his skills.

He has taught himself speech, and wind-like thought, and the
        lore
 Of ruling a town. He has fled the arrows of rain,
The searching arrows of frost he need fear no more,
    That under a starry sky are endured with pain.
Provision for all he has made—unprovided for naught,
    Save death itself, that in days to come will take shape.
From obscure and deep-seated disease he has subtly wrought   330
    A way of escape.

Resourceful and skilled, with an inconceivable art,
    He follows his course to a good or an evil end.
When he holds the canons of justice high in his heart
    And has sworn to the gods the laws of the land to defend,
Proud stands his city; without a city is he
    Who with ugliness, rashness, or evil dishonors the day.
Let me shun his thoughts. Let him share no hearthstone with me,
    Who acts in this way!

CHORUS. Look there! Look there! What portent can this be?   340
    Antigone! I know her, it is she!
    Daughter of Oedipus a prisoner brought?
    You defied Creon? You in folly caught?

               [*Enter* GUARD *with* ANTIGONE]

GUARD. She did it. Here she is. We caught this girl
    As she was burying him. Where is the King?
CHORUS. Leaving the palace there, just as we need him.

               [*Enter* CREON]

CREON. Why do you need my presence? What has happened?
GUARD. My Lord, no one should take a solemn oath
    Not to do something, for his second thoughts
    Make him a liar. I vowed not to hurry back.   350
    I had been battered by your storm of threats.
    But when a joy comes that exceeds our hopes,
    No other happiness can equal it.
    So I have broken my vow. I have returned,
    Bringing this girl along. She was discovered

Busy with all the rites of burial.
There was no casting lots, no, not this time!
Such luck as this was mine and no one else's.
Now sir, take her yourself, examine her,
Convict her, do what you like. But as for me,   360
I have the right to a complete acquittal.

CREON. This is the girl you caught? How? Where was she?

GUARD. Burying the dead man, just as I have told you.

CREON. Do you mean that? Or have you lost your mind?

GUARD. Your order was that he should not be buried.
    I saw her bury him. Is that all clear?

CREON. How was she seen? You caught her in the act?

GUARD. This was what happened. When we had gotten back,
    With your threats following us, we swept away
    The dust that covered him. We left him bare,   370
    A rotting corpse. And then we sat to windward,
    Up on the hillside, to avoid the stench.
    All of us were alert, and kept awake
    Threatening each other. No one could get careless.
    So the time passed, until the blazing sun
    Stood at the zenith, and the heat was burning.
    Then suddenly the wind came in a blast,
    Lifting a cloud of dust up from the earth,
    Troubling the sky and choking the whole plain,
    Stripping off all the foliage of the woods,   380
    Filling the breadth of heaven. We closed our eyes
    And bore the affliction that the gods had sent us.
    When it had finally stopped, we saw this girl.
    She wailed aloud with a sharp, bitter cry,
    The cry a bird gives seeing its empty nest
    Robbed of its brood. And she too, when she saw
    The naked body, was loud in her lament
    And cursed the men who had uncovered him.
    Quickly she sprinkled him with dust, and then
    Lifting a pitcher, poured out three libations[14]   390
    To do him honor. When we ran and caught her,
    She was unterrified. When we accused her
    Both of her earlier and her present act,
    She made no effort to deny the charges.
    I am part glad, part sorry. It is good
    To find that you yourself have gotten clear,
    But to bring trouble on your friends is hard.
    However, nothing counts except my safety.

CREON [*to* ANTIGONE]. You there. You, looking at the ground. Tell me.
    Do you admit this or deny it? Which?   400

ANTIGONE. Yes, I admit it. I do not deny it.

CREON [*to* GUARD]. Go. You are free. The charge is dropped.

[14] Ritual pourings of liquids.

[*Exit* GUARD]

Now you,

Answer this question. Make your answer brief.
You knew there was a law forbidding this?
ANTIGONE. Of course I knew it. Why not? It was public.
CREON. And you have dared to disobey the law?
ANTIGONE. Yes. For this law[15] was not proclaimed by Zeus,
  Or by the gods who rule the world below.
  I do not think your edicts have such power
  That they can override the laws of heaven,   410
  Unwritten and unfailing, laws whose life
  Belongs not to today or yesterday
  But to time everlasting; and no man
  Knows the first moment that they had their being.
  If I transgressed these laws because I feared
  The arrogance of man, how to the gods
  Could I make satisfaction? Well I know,
  Being a mortal, that I have to die,
  Even without your proclamations. Yet
  If I must die before my time is come,   420
  That is a blessing. Because to one who lives,
  As I live, in the midst of sorrows, death
  Is of necessity desirable.
  For me, to face death is a trifling pain
  That does not trouble me. But to have left
  The body of my brother, my own brother,
  Lying unburied would be bitter grief.
  And if these acts of mine seem foolish to you,
  Perhaps a fool accuses me of folly.
CHORUS. The violent daughter of a violent father,   430
  She cannot bend before a storm of evils.
CREON [*to* ANTIGONE]. Stubborn? Self-willed? People like that, I tell
      you,
  Are the first to come to grief. The hardest iron,
  Baked in the fire, most quickly flies to pieces.
  An unruly horse is taught obedience
  By a touch of the curb. How can you be so proud?
  You, a mere slave?[16] [*to* CHORUS] She was well schooled already
  In insolence, when she defied the law.
  And now look at her! Boasting, insolent,
  Exulting in what she did. And if she triumphs   440
  And goes unpunished, I am no man—she is.
  If she were more than niece, if she were closer
  Than anyone who worships at my altar,

---

[15] In the following lines Antigone states her creed; compare Creon's maxim in lines 154–156. Both antagonists can cite religious or political principles. A major question in the play is whether Antigone and Creon are actually governed by these large principles or by more personal motives (good or bad).

[16] This is arrogantly false; Antigone is not in fact a slave.

She would not even then escape her doom,
A dreadful death. Nor would her sister. Yes,
Her sister had a share in burying him.
[*to* ATTENDANT] Go bring her here. I have just seen her, raving,
Beside herself. Even before they act,
Traitors who plot their treason in the dark
Betray themselves like that. Detestable!   450
[*to* ANTIGONE] But hateful also is an evil-doer
Who, caught red-handed, glorifies the crime.

ANTIGONE. Now you have caught me, will you do more than kill me?
CREON. No, only that. With that I am satisfied.
ANTIGONE. Then why do you delay? You have said nothing
 I do not hate. I pray you never will.
 And you hate what I say. Yet how could I
 Have won more splendid honor than by giving
 Due burial to my brother? All men here
 Would grant me their approval, if their lips   460
 Were not sealed up in fear. But you, a king,
 Blessed by good fortune in much else besides,
 Can speak and act with perfect liberty.
CREON. All of these Thebans disagree with you.
ANTIGONE. No. They agree, but they control their tongues.
CREON. You feel no shame in acting without their help?
ANTIGONE. I feel no shame in honoring a brother.
CREON. Another brother died who fought against him.
ANTIGONE. Two brothers. The two sons of the same parents.
CREON. Honor to one is outrage to the other.   470
ANTIGONE. Eteocles will not feel himself dishonored.
CREON. What! When his rites are offered to a traitor?
ANTIGONE. It was his brother, not his slave, who died.
CREON. One who attacked the land that he defended.
ANTIGONE. The gods still wish those rites to be performed.
CREON. Are the just pleased with the unjust as their equals?
ANTIGONE. That may be virtuous in the world below.
CREON. No. Even there a foe is never a friend.
ANTIGONE. I am not made for hatred but for love.
CREON. Then go down to the dead. If you must love,   480
 Love them. While I yet live, no woman rules me.
CHORUS. Look there. Ismene, weeping as sisters weep.
 The shadow of a cloud of grief lies deep
 On her face, darkly flushed; and in her pain
 Her tears are falling like a flood of rain.

[*Enter* ISMENE *and* ATTENDANTS]

CREON. You viper! Lying hidden in my house,
 Sucking my blood in secret, while I reared,
 Unknowingly, two subverters of my throne.
 Do you confess that you have taken part
 In this man's burial, or deny it? Speak.   490

ISMENE. If she will recognize my right to say so,
  I shared the action and I share the blame.
ANTIGONE. No. That would not be just. I never let you
  Take any part in what you disapproved of.
ISMENE. In your calamity, I am not ashamed
  To stand beside you, beaten by this tempest.
ANTIGONE. The dead are witnesses of what I did,
  To love in words alone is not enough.
ISMENE. Do not reject me, Sister! Let me die
  Beside you, and do honor to the dead.   500
ANTIGONE. No. You will neither share my death nor claim
  What I have done. My death will be sufficient.
ISMENE. What happiness can I have when you are gone?
ANTIGONE. Ask Creon that. He is the one you value.
ISMENE. Do you gain anything by taunting me?
ANTIGONE. Ah, no! By taunting you, I hurt myself.
ISMENE. How can I help you? Tell me what I can do.
ANTIGONE. Protect yourself. I do not grudge your safety.
ISMENE. Antigone! Shall I not share your fate?
ANTIGONE. We both have made our choices: life, and death.   510
ISMENE. At least I tried to stop you. I protested.
ANTIGONE. Some have approved your way; and others, mine.
ISMENE. Yet now I share your guilt. I too am ruined.
ANTIGONE. Take courage. Live your life. But I long since
  Gave myself up to death to help the dead.
CREON. One of them has just lost her senses now.
  The other has been foolish all her life.
ISMENE. We cannot always use our reason clearly.
  Suffering confuses us and clouds our minds.
CREON. It clouds your mind. You join in her wrong-doing.   520
ISMENE. How is life possible without my sister?
CREON. Your sister? You have no sister. She is dead.
ISMENE. Then you will kill the wife your son has chosen?
CREON. Yes. There are other fields that he can plow.
ISMENE. He will not find such an enduring love.
CREON. A wicked woman for my son? No, never!
ANTIGONE. O Haemon, Haemon! How your father wrongs you![17]
CREON. You and your marriage! Let me hear no more!
CHORUS. You are unyielding? You will take her from him?
CREON. Death will act for me. Death will stop the marriage.   530
CHORUS. It seems, then, you have sentenced her to death.
CREON. Yes. And my sentence you yourselves accepted.
  Take them inside. From now on, they are women,
  And have no liberty. For even the bold
  Seek an escape when they see death approaching.

                              [*Exeunt* ANTIGONE, ISMENE, *and*
                              ATTENDANTS]

---

[17] In some versions, this line is given to Ismene.

CHORUS.
Blesséd the life that has no evil known,
For the gods, striking, strike down a whole race—
Doomed parent and doomed child both overthrown.
As when the fierce breath of the winds of Thrace
Across the darkness of the sea has blown 540
A rushing surge; black sand from deep below
Comes boiling up; wind-beaten headlands moan,
Fronting the full shock of the billow's blow.

The race of Oedipus, from days of old,
To long dead sorrows add new sorrows' weight.[18]
Some god has sent them sufferings manifold.
None may release another, for their fate
Through generations loosens not its hold.
Now is their last root cut, their last light fled,
Because of frenzy's curse, words overbold, 550
And dust, the gods' due, on the bloodstained dead.

O Zeus, what human sin restricts thy might?
Thou art unsnared by all-ensnaring sleep
Or tireless months. Unaging thou dost keep
Thy court in splendor of Olympian light.
And as this law was true when time began,
Tomorrow and forever it shall be:
Naught beyond measure in the life of man
From fate goes free.

For hope, wide-ranging, that brings good to some, 560
To many is a false lure of desire
Light-minded, giddy; and until the fire
Scorches their feet, they know not what will come.
Wise is the famous adage: that to one
Whom the gods madden, evil, soon or late,
Seems good; then can he but a moment shun
The stroke of fate.

But Haemon comes, of your two sons the last.[19]
Is his heart heavy for the sentence passed
Upon Antigone, his promised bride, 570
And for his hope of marriage now denied?

[*Enter* HAEMON]

---

[18] The sorrows of the family extend farther into the past than to Oedipus' acts of patricide and incest; for example, his father Laius had been cursed by Pelops (the ancestor of the cursed family treated in Aeschylus' Orestes trilogy) after Laius had wronged Pelops, his protector during a period of exile, by stealing his son.

[19] According to one version of the Thebes saga, Haemon's brother Megareus had committed suicide in order to propitiate the war-god Ares and thus save Thebes.

CREON. We soon shall know better than seers could tell us.
    My son, Antigone is condemned to death.
    Nothing can change my sentence. Have you learned
    Her fate and come here in a storm of anger,
    Or do you love me and support my acts?
HAEMON. Father, I am your son. Your greater knowledge
    Will trace the pathway that I mean to follow.
    My marriage cannot be of more importance
    Than to be guided always by your wisdom.   580
CREON. Yes, Haemon, this should be the law you live by!
    In all things to obey your father's will.
    Men pray for children round them in their homes
    Only to see them dutiful and quick
    With hatred to requite their father's foe,
    With honor to repay their father's friend.
    But what is there to say of one whose children
    Prove to be valueless? That he has fathered
    Grief for himself and laughter for his foes.
    Then, Haemon, do not, at the lure of pleasure,   590
    Unseat your reason for a woman's sake.
    This comfort soon grows cold in your embrace:
    A wicked wife to share your bed and home.
    Is there a deeper wound than to find worthless
    The one you love? Turn from this girl with loathing,
    As from an enemy, and let her go
    To get a husband in the world below.
    For I have found her openly rebellious,
    Her only out of all the city. Therefore,
    I will not break the oath that I have sworn.   600
    I will have her killed. Vainly she will invoke
    The bond of kindred blood the gods make sacred.
    If I permit disloyalty to breed
    In my own house, I nurture it in strangers.
    He who is righteous with his kin is righteous
    In the state also. Therefore, I cannot pardon
    One who does violence to the laws or thinks
    To dictate to his rulers; for whoever
    May be the man appointed by the city,
    That man must be obeyed in everything,   610
    Little or great, just or unjust. And surely
    He who was thus obedient would be found
    As good a ruler as he was a subject;
    And in a storm of spears he would stand fast
    With loyal courage at his comrade's side.
    But disobedience is the worst of evils.
    For it is this that ruins cities; this
    Makes our homes desolate; armies of allies
    Through this break up in rout. But most men find
    Their happiness and safety in obedience.   620
    Therefore we must support the law, and never

Be beaten by a woman. It is better
To fall by a man's hand, if we must fall,
Than to be known as weaker than a girl.
CHORUS. We may in our old age have lost our judgment,
And yet to us you seem to have spoken wisely.
HAEMON. The gods have given men the gift of reason,
Greatest of all things that we call our own.
I have no skill, nor do I wish to have it,
To show where you have spoken wrongly. Yet 630
Some other's thought, beside your own, might prove
To be of value. Therefore it is my duty,
My natural duty as your son, to notice,
On your behalf, all that men say, or do,
Or find to blame. For your frown frightens them,
So that the citizen dares not say a word
That would offend you. I can hear, however,
Murmurs in darkness and laments for her.
They say: 'No woman ever less deserved
Her doom, no woman ever was to die 640
So shamefully for deeds so glorious.
For when her brother fell in bloody battle,
She would not let his body lie unburied
To be devoured by carrion dogs or birds.
Does such a woman not deserve reward,
Reward of golden honor?' This I hear,
A rumor spread in secrecy and darkness.
Father, I prize nothing in life so highly
As your well-being. How can children have
A nobler honor than their father's fame 650
Or father than his son's? Then do not think
Your mood must never alter; do not feel
Your word, and yours alone, must be correct.
For if a man believes that he is right
And only he, that no one equals him
In what he says or thinks, he will be found
Empty when searched and tested. Because a man
Even if he be wise, feels no disgrace
In learning many things, in taking care
Not to be over-rigid. You have seen 660
Trees on the margin of a stream in winter:
Those yielding to the flood save every twig,
And those resisting perish root and branch.
So, too, the mariner who never slackens
His taut sheet overturns his craft and spends
Keel uppermost the last part of his voyage.
Let your resentment die. Let yourself change.
For I believe—if I, a younger man,
May have a sound opinion—it is best
That men by nature should be wise in all things. 670
But most men find they cannot reach that goal;

And when this happens, it is also good
To learn to listen to wise counselors.
CHORUS. Sir, when his words are timely, you should heed them.
And Haemon, you should profit by his words.
Each one of you has spoken reasonably.
CREON. Are men as old as I am to be taught
How to behave by men as young as he?
HAEMON. Not to do wrong. If I am young, ignore
My youth. Consider only what I do.   680
CREON. Have you done well in honoring the rebellious?
HAEMON. Those who do wrong should not command respect.
CREON. Then that disease has not infected her?
HAEMON. All of our city with one voice denies it.
CREON. Does Thebes give orders for the way I rule?
HAEMON. How young you are! How young in saying that!
CREON. Am I to govern by another's judgment?
HAEMON. A city that is one man's is no city.
CREON. A city is the king's. That much is sure.
HAEMON. You would rule well in a deserted country.   690
CREON. This boy defends a woman, it appears.
HAEMON. If you are one. I am concerned for you.
CREON. To quarrel with your father does not shame you?
HAEMON. Not when I see you failing to do justice.
CREON. Am I unjust when I respect my crown?
HAEMON. Respect it! When you trample down religion?
CREON. Infamous! Giving first place to a woman!
HAEMON. But never to anything that would disgrace me.
CREON. Each word you utter is a plea for her.
HAEMON. For you, too, and for me, and for the gods.   700
CREON. You shall not marry her this side of death.
HAEMON. Then if she dies, she does not die alone.
CREON. What! Has it come to this? You threaten me?
HAEMON. No. But I tell you your decree is useless.
CREON. You will repent this. You! Teaching me wisdom!
HAEMON. I will not call you mad. You are my father.
CREON. You woman's slave! Your talk will not persuade me.
HAEMON. Then what you want is to make all the speeches.
CREON. So. Now by all the gods in heaven above us,
One thing is certain: you are going to pay   710
For taunting and insulting me. [*to* ATTENDANTS] Bring out
That hated object. Let her die this moment,
Here, at her bridegroom's feet, before his eyes.
HAEMON. No, you are wrong. Not at my feet. And never
Will you set eyes upon my face again.
Rage, rave, with anyone who can bear to listen.

[*Exit* HAEMON]

CHORUS. Sir, he is gone; his anger gives him speed.
Young men are bitter in their agony.

CREON. Let him imagine more than man can do,
    Or let him do more. Never shall he save 720
    These two girls; they are going to their doom.
CHORUS. Do you intend to put them both to death?
CREON. That was well said. No, not the innocent.
CHORUS. And the other? In what way is she to die?
CREON. Along a desolate pathway I will lead her,
    And shut her, living, in a rocky vault
    With no more food than will appease the gods,[20]
    So that the city may not be defiled.
    Hades,[21] who is the only god she worships,
    May hear her prayers, and rescue her from death. 730
    Otherwise she will learn at last, though late,
    That to revere the dead is useless toil.

[Exit CREON]

CHORUS.
    None may withstand you, O love unconquered,
        Seizing the wealth of man as your prey,
    In the cheek of a maiden keeping your vigil,
        Till night has faded again to day.
    You roam the wilds to men's farthest dwellings,
        You haunt the boundless face of the sea.
    No god may escape you, no short-lived mortal
        From the madness that love inflicts may flee. 740

    You twist our minds until ruin follows.
        The just to unrighteous ways you turn.
    You have goaded kinsman to strive with kinsman
        Till the fires of bitter hatred burn.
    In the eyes of a bride you shine triumphant;
        Beside the eternal laws your throne
    Eternal stands, for great Aphrodite,[22]
        Resistless, works her will on her own.

    But now I too am moved. I cannot keep
        Within the bounds of loyalty. I weep 750
    When I behold Antigone, the bride,
        Nearing the room where all at last abide.

[Enter ANTIGONE, *guarded]*

ANTIGONE.
    See me, my countrymen! See with what pain

---

[20] This method of execution is inconsistent with the earlier passage that decrees death by stoning (lines 26–36). Creon apparently believes, legalistically, that he can avoid the crime of shedding kindred blood by merely shutting Antigone up alone and by providing her with food. Technically no act of execution will have been committed.

[21] King of the realm of the dead. The name can also mean the realm itself.

[22] Goddess of love.

I tread the path I shall not tread again,
Looking my last upon the light of day
 That shines for me no more.
Hades, who gives his sleep to all, me, living, leads away
 To Acheron's[23] dark shore.
Not mine the hymeneal chant, not mine the bridal song,
 For I, a bride, to Acheron belong.   760

CHORUS.
 Glorious, therefore, and with praise you tread
The pathway to the deep gulf of the dead.
You have not felt the force of fate's decrees,
Struck down by violence, wasted by disease;
But of your own free will you choose to go,
Alone of mortals, to the world below.

ANTIGONE.
I know how sad a death she suffered, she
Who was our guest here, Phrygian Niobe.[24]
Stone spread upon her, close as ivy grows,
 And locked her in its chains.   770
Now on her wasted form, men say, fall ceaselessly the snows,
 Fall ceaselessly the rains;
While from her grieving eyes drop tears, tears that her bosom
   steep.
 And like hers, my fate lulls me now to sleep.

CHORUS.
 She was a goddess[25] of the gods' great race;
Mortals are we and mortal lineage trace.
But for a woman the renown is great
In life and death to share a godlike fate.

ANTIGONE.
 By our fathers' gods, I am mocked! I am mocked![26] Ah! why, 780
 You men of wealth, do you taunt me before I die?
O sacred grove of the city! O waters that flow
 From the spring of Dircé! Be witness; to you I cry.
What manner of woman I am you know
And by what laws, unloved, unlamented, I go
 To my rocky prison, to my unnatural tomb.
  Alas, how ill-bestead!
 No fellowship have I; no others can share my doom,
Neither mortals nor corpses, neither the quick[27] nor the dead.

---

[23] A river in the land of the dead.

[24] Niobe, originally from Phrygia in Asia Minor, was the wife of Amphion, a former ruler of Thebes. Mother of fourteen children, she boasted of her superiority to the goddess Leto, who had only two, Apollo and Artemis. In revenge for her impiety, all Niobe's children were killed and she herself was turned into a stone from which flowed a perpetual stream of her tears. There is an irony: Niobe was punished for flouting the gods, while Antigone is being killed for her piety.

[25] Niobe was daughter of Tantalus, whose father was Zeus.

[26] Antigone's protest probably reflects her bitter reaction to the elders' implication that she is lucky (in sharing the fate of the famed Niobe).

[27] The living.

CHORUS.
    You have rushed forward with audacious feet   790
    And dashed yourself against the law's high seat.
    That was a grievous fall, my child, and yet
    In this ordeal you pay your father's debt.
ANTIGONE.
    You have touched on the heaviest grief that my heart can hold:
    Grief for my father, sorrow that never grows old
    For our famous house and its doom that the fates have spun.
        My mother's bed! Ah! How can its horrors be told?
    My mother who yielded her love to one
    Who was at once my father and her son.
        Born of such parents, with them henceforth I abide,   800
            Wretched, accursed, unwed.
        And you, Polyneices, you found an ill-fated bride,[28]
    And I, the living, am ruined by you, the dead.
CHORUS.
    A pious action may of praise be sure,
    But he who rules a land cannot endure
    An act of disobedience to his rule.
    Your own self-will you have not learned to school.
ANTIGONE.
    Unwept, unfriended, without marriage song,
    Forth on my road I miserable am led;
        I may not linger. Not for long   810
    Shall I, most wretched, see the holy sun.
    My fate no friend bewails, not one;
        For me no tear is shed.

                    [*Enter* CREON]

CREON. Do you not know that singing and lamentation
    Would rise incessantly as death approached,
    If they could be of service? Lead her away!
    Obey my orders. Shut her in her grave
    And leave her there, alone. Then she can take
    Her choice of living in that home, or dying.
    I am not stained by the guilt of this girl's blood,   820
    But she shall see the light of day no longer.
ANTIGONE. O tomb! O cavern! Everlasting prison!
    O bridal-chamber! To you I make my way
    To join my kindred, all those who have died
    And have been greeted by Persephone.[29]
    The last and far most miserable of all,
    I seek them now, before I have lived my life.
    Yet high are the hopes I cherish that my coming

---

[28] Polyneices, as part of his plan to enlist the aid of Argos in attacking Thebes, married a daughter of the Argive king. The war, and Polyneices' death, have brought death to Antigone too.

[29] Consort of Hades, king of the dead.

Will be most welcome to my father; welcome,
Mother, to you; and welcome to you, Brother.   830
For when you died I ministered to you all,
With my own hands washed you and dressed your bodies,
And poured libations at your graves. And now,
Because I have given to you, too, Polyneices,
Such honors as I could, I am brought to this.
And yet all wise men will approve my act.
Not for my children, had I been a mother,
Not for a husband, for his moldering body,
Would I have set myself against the city
As I have done. And the law sanctions me.   840
Losing a husband, I might find another.
I could have other children. But my parents
Are hidden from me in the underworld,
So that no brother's life can bud and bloom
Ever again.[30] And therefore, Polyneices,
I paid you special honor. And for this
Creon has held me guilty of evil-doing,
And leads me captive for my too great boldness.
No bridal bed is mine, no bridal song,
No share in the joys of marriage, and no share   850
In nursing children and in tending them.
But thus afflicted, destitute of friends,
Living, I go down to the vaults of death.
What is the law of heaven that I have broken?
Why should I any longer look to the gods,
Ill-fated as I am? Whose aid should I invoke,
When I for piety am called impious?
If this pleases the gods, then I shall learn
That sin brought death upon me. But if the sin
Lies in my judges, I could wish for them   860
No harsher fate than they have decreed for me.
CHORUS. Still the storm rages; still the same gusts blow,
    Troubling her spirit with their savage breath.
CREON. Yes. And her guards will pay for being slow.
ANTIGONE. Ah! With those words I have drawn close to death.
CREON. You cannot hope that you will now be freed
    From the fulfillment of the doom decreed.
ANTIGONE.
        O Thebes, O land of my fathers, O city!

[30] For various reasons, including the opinion that Antigone's fine distinctions and perhaps
insensitivity here are inconsistent with the rest of the play, some editors and translators reject
lines 836–844. The appropriateness of the passage has been defended, on grounds of dramatic psychology (for example, the marital and maternal roles must be merely imagined by
Antigone, while her role of sister is one she has experienced) and more technical grounds (for
example, the notion that the sibling-bond is closer than either the marital one which involves
no blood-kinship or the "half-interest" bond of blood-kinship that links a child with one of its
two parents).

O gods who begot and guarded my house from of old![31]
    They seize me, they snatch me away!   870
    Now, now! They show no pity.
    They give no second's delay.
You elders, you leaders of Thebes, behold me, behold!
    The last of the house of your kings, the last.
    See what I suffer. See the doom
    That is come upon me, and see from whom,
Because to the laws of heaven I held fast.

                     [*Exeunt* ANTIGONE *and* GUARDS]

CHORUS.
    This likewise Danaë[32] endured:
The light of heaven she changed for a home brass-bound,
    In a tomb-like chamber close immured.   880
And yet, O my child, her race was with honor crowned.
    And she guarded the seed of Zeus gold-showered.
But naught from the terrible power of fate is free:
    Neither war, nor city walls high-towered,
Nor wealth, nor black ships beaten by the sea.

    He too bowed down beneath his doom,
The son of Dryas,[33] swift-angered Edonian king,
    Shut fast in a rocky prison's gloom.
How he roused the god with his mad tongue's mocking sting,
    As his frenzy faded, he came to know;   890
For he sought to make the god-filled maenads mute,
    To quench the Bacchic torches' glow,
And angered the Muses, lovers of the flute.

    By the double sea[34] and the dark rocks steely blue
    The beach of Bosporus lies and the savage shore
Of Thracian Salmydessus. There the bride
    Of Phineus, whose fierce heart no mercy knew,
Dealt his two sons a blow that for vengeance cried;
    Ares beheld her hand, all stained with gore,
Grasping the pointed shuttle that pierced through   900
    Their eyes that saw no more.

---

[31] According to the myths, several of Antigone's forebears in the Theban dynasty were related to the gods, by blood or marriage.

[32] Danaë's father Acrisius, a king of Argos, had imprisoned her because of a prophecy that she would bear a son who would kill him. Zeus came to her in a shower of golden rain, begetting Perseus, who did later kill Acrisius.

[33] Lycurgus, a legendary Thracian king. He had been imprisoned after being driven to madness by the gods for opposing the worship of Bacchus (Dionysus). Maenads (line 891) were orgiastic female worshipers of the god.

[34] The following lines allude to a third story of imprisonment; most interpreters have found the story itself and its application to Antigone obscure. Phineus, a king of Thrace, divorced his wife Cleopatra (daughter of Boreas, the north wind), who had borne him two sons, and cast her into prison; his second wife blinded the two children and entombed them.

In misery pining, their lot they lamented aloud,
    Sons of a mother whose fortune in marriage was ill.
From the ancient line of Erechtheus[35] her blood she traced;
    Nurtured in caves far-distant and nursed in cloud,
Daughter of Boreas, daughter of gods, she raced
    Swift as a steed on the slope of the soaring hill.
And yet, O child, O child, she also bowed
    To the long-lived fates' harsh will.

              [*Enter* TIRESIAS *and* BOY]

TIRESIAS. Elders of Thebes, we have come to you with one   910
    Finding for both the pathway that we followed,
    For in this fashion must the blind be guided.
CREON. What tidings, old Tiresias, are you bringing?
TIRESIAS. I will inform you, I the seer. Give heed.
CREON. To ignore your counsel has not been my custom.
TIRESIAS. Therefore you kept Thebes on a steady course.
CREON. I can bear witness to the help you gave.
TIRESIAS. Mark this. You stand upon the brink of ruin.
CREON. What terrible words are those? What do you mean?
TIRESIAS. My meaning is made manifest by my art   920
    And my art's omens. As I took my station
    Upon my ancient seat of augury,
    Where round me birds of every sort come flocking,
    I could no longer understand their language.
    It was drowned out in a strange, savage clamor,
    Shrill, evil, frenzied, inarticulate.
    The whirr of wings told me their murderous talons
    Tore at each other. Filled with dread, I then
    Made trial of burnt sacrifice. The altar
    Was fully kindled, but no clear, bright flame   930
    Leaped from the offering; only fatty moisture
    Oozed from the flesh and trickled on the embers,
    Smoking and sputtering. The bladder burst,
    And scattered in the air. The folds of fat
    Wrapping the thigh-bones melted and left them bare.
    Such was the failure of the sacrifice,
    That did not yield the sign that I was seeking.
    I learned these things from this boy's observation;
    He is my guide as I am guide to others.
    Your edict brings this suffering to the city,   940
    For every hearth of ours has been defiled
    And every altar. There the birds and dogs
    Have brought their carrion, torn from the corpse
    Of ill-starred Polyneices. Hence, the gods
    Refuse our prayers, refuse our sacrifice,

---

[35] A legendary Athenian king, grandfather of Cleopatra.

Refuse the flame of our burnt-offerings.
No birds cry clearly and auspiciously,
For they are glutted with a slain man's blood.
Therefore, my son, consider what has happened.
All men are liable to grievous error;   950
But he who, having erred, does not remain
Inflexible, but rather makes amends
For ill, is not unwise or unrewarded.
Stubborn self-will incurs the charge of folly.
Give to the fallen the honors he deserves
And do not stab him. Are you being brave
When you inflict new death upon the dead?
Your good I think of; for your good I speak,
And a wise counselor is sweet to hear
When the advice he offers proves of value.   960

CREON. Old man, all of you shoot your arrows at me
Like archers at a target. You have used
Even the art of prophecy in your plotting.
Long have the tribe of prophets traded in me,[36]
Like a ship's cargo. Drive whatever bargain
May please you, buy, sell, heap up for yourself
Silver of Sardis, gold of India. Yet
I tell you this: that man shall not be buried,
Not though the eagles of Zeus himself should bear
The carrion morsels to their master's throne.   970
Not even from the dread of such pollution
Will I permit his burial, since I know
There is no mortal can defile the gods.
But even the wisest men disastrously
May fall, Tiresias, when for money's sake
They utter shameful words with specious wisdom.

TIRESIAS. Ah! Do men understand, or even consider—
CREON. Consider what? Doubtless some platitude!
TIRESIAS. How precious beyond any wealth is prudence.
CREON. How full of evil is the lack of prudence.   980
TIRESIAS. Yet you are sick, sick with that same disease.
CREON. I will not in reply revile a prophet.
TIRESIAS. You do. You say my prophecy is false.
CREON. Well, all the race of seers are mercenary.
TIRESIAS. And love of base wealth marks the breed of tyrants.
CREON. Are you aware that you address your King?
TIRESIAS. I made you King by helping you save Thebes.
CREON. Wise in your art and vicious in your acts.
TIRESIAS. Do not enrage me. I should keep my secret.
CREON. Reveal it. Speak. But do not look for profit.   990
TIRESIAS. You too will find no profit in my words.

---

[36] Ironically, Oedipus (in *Oedipus the King*) had accused Tiresias and Creon himself of a similar, and equally imaginary, mercenary plot.

CREON. How can you earn your pay? I will not change.
TIRESIAS. Then know this. Yes, be very sure of it.
    Only a few more times will you behold
    The swift course of the chariot of the sun
    Before you give as payment for the dead
    Your own dead flesh and blood. For you have thrust
    A living soul to darkness, in a tomb
    Imprisoned without pity. And a corpse,
    Belonging to the gods below you keep   1000
    Unpurified, unburied, unrevered.
    The dead are no concern either of yours
    Or of the gods above, yet you offend them.
    So the avengers, the destroyers, Furies[37]
    Of Hades and the gods, lurking in ambush,
    Wait to inflict your sins upon your head.
    Do you still think my tongue is lined with silver?
    A time will come, and will not linger coming,
    That will awaken in your house the wailing
    Of men and women. Hatred shakes the cities,[38]   1010
    Hatred of you. Their sons are mangled corpses,
    Hallowed with funeral rites by dogs or beasts
    Or birds who bear the all-polluting stench
    To every city having hearth or altar.
    You goaded me, and therefore like an archer
    I shoot my angry arrows at your heart,
    Sure arrows; you shall not escape their sting.
    Boy, lead me home. Let him expend his rage
    On younger men, and let him learn to speak
    With a more temperate tongue, and school his heart   1020
    To feelings finer than his present mood.

                       [*Exeunt* TIRESIAS *and* BOY]

CHORUS. Sir, he is gone, with fearful prophecies.
    And from the time that these dark hairs have whitened,
    I have known this: never has he foretold
    Anything that proved false concerning Thebes.
CREON. I also know it well, and it dismays me.
    To yield is bitter. But to resist, and bring
    A curse upon my pride is no less bitter.
CHORUS. Son of Menoeceus, listen. You must listen.
CREON. What should I do? Tell me, I will obey.   1030
CHORUS. Go. Free the girl. Release her from the cavern,
    And build a tomb for the man you would not bury.
CREON. So that is your advice—that I should yield?
CHORUS. Sir, you should not delay. The gods are swift
    In cutting short man's folly with their curse.
CREON. How hard it is to change! Yet I obey.

---

[37] Primitive personifications of vengeance, especially for crimes against kindred.
[38] The cities that organized the army to attack Thebes.

I will give up what I had set my heart on.
No one can stand against the blows of fate.
CHORUS. Go. Go yourself. These things are not for others.
CREON. I will go this moment. Guards there! All of you!   1040
Take up your axes. Quick! Quick! Over there.
I imprisoned her myself, and I myself
Will set her free. And yet my mind misgives me.
Never to break the ancient law is best.

[*Exit* CREON]

CHORUS.
     Thou[39] art known by many a name.
  O Bacchus! To thee we call.
  Cadmean Semele's glory and pride,
Begotten of Zeus, whose terrible lightnings flame,
    Whose thunders appall.
Bacchus, thou dost for us all in thy love provide.   1050
  Over Icaría thou dost reign,
  And where the worshippers journey slow
  To the rites of Eleusis,[40] where mountains shield
The multitudes crossing Demeter's welcoming plain.
Thou makest this mother-city of maenads thine own,
  A city beside the rippling flow
Of the gentle river, beside the murderous field
  Where the teeth of the dragon were sown.

    In the torches' wind-blown flare
  Thou art seen, in their flicker and smoke.   1060
  Where the two-fold peaks of Parnassus[41] gleam,
Corycian nymphs, as they move through the ruddy glare,
    Thee, Bacchus, invoke.
They move in their dance beside the Castalian stream.[42]
  O Bacchus, guardian divine!
  Down from the slopes of Nysa's[43] hills
  Where a mantle of ivy covers the ground,
From headlands rich with the purple grape and the vine,
Thou comest to us, thou comest. O be not long!
  Thy triumph the echoing city fills.   1070
The streets are loud with thy praises; the highways resound,
  Resound with immortal song.

[39] The Chorus invokes Bacchus as the patron deity of Thebes.
[40] Icaria is an island in the Aegean Sea; Eleusis, a town near Athens, was the center of the mysterious fertility rites of Demeter, goddess of the fields and harvest.
[41] A mountain near Apollo's shrine at Delphi; one of the peaks was sacred to Apollo, one to Bacchus (Dionysus). The Corycian cave, sacred to the god Pan and the Nymphs, was located on the mountain.
[42] A spring and pool on Mount Parnassus.
[43] A mountain where Bacchus had been reared by nymphs.

Thou honorest highly our Theban city,
   Thou, and thy mother by lightning slain.
Our people sicken. O Bacchus have pity!
   Across the strait with its moaning wave,
Down from Parnassus, come thou again!
   Come with thy healing feet, and save!

O thou who leadest the stars in chorus,
   Jubilant stars with their breath of fire,   1080
Offspring of Zeus, appear before us!
   Lord of the tumult of night, appear!
With the frenzied dance of thy maenad choir,
   Bacchus, thou giver of good, draw near!

[Enter MESSENGER]

MESSENGER. You of the house of Cadmus and Amphíon,[44]
   No man's estate can ever be established
   Firmly enough to warrant praise or blame.
   Fortune, from day to day, exalts the lucky
   And humbles the unlucky. No one knows
   Whether his present lot can long endure.   1090
   For Creon once was blest, as I count blessings;
   He had saved this land of Cadmus from its foes;
   He was the sovereign and ruled alone,
   The noble father of a royal house.
   And now, all has been lost. Because a man
   Who has forfeited his joy is not alive,
   He is a living corpse. Heap, if you will,
   Your house with riches; live in regal pomp.
   Yet if your life is unhappy, all these things
   Are worth not even the shadow of a vapor   1100
   Put in the balance against joy alone.
CHORUS. What new disaster has the King's house suffered?
MESSENGER. Death. And the guilt of death lies on the living.
CHORUS. The guilt of death! Who has been killed? Who killed him?
MESSENGER. Haemon is killed, and by no stranger's hand.
CHORUS. He killed himself? Or did his father kill him?
MESSENGER. He killed himself, enraged by his murderous father.
CHORUS. Tiresias! Now your prophecy is fulfilled.
MESSENGER. Consider, therefore, what remains to do.
CHORUS. There is the Queen, wretched Eurydice.   1110
   Perhaps mere chance has brought her from the palace;
   Perhaps she has learned the news about her son.

[Enter EURYDICE]

EURYDICE. Thebans, I heard you talking here together
   When I was on my way to greet the goddess,

---

[44] Amphíon was a former ruler of Thebes; he had helped build the city's walls by his harp-music, which was so powerful that even stones were moved by it.

Pallas Athene, and to pray to her.
Just as I loosed the fastening of the door,
The words that told of my calamity
Struck heavily upon my ear. In terror
I fell back fainting in my women's arms.
But now, repeat your story. I shall hear it   1120
As one who is not ignorant of grief.
MESSENGER. My Lady, I will bear witness to what I saw,
And will omit no syllable of the truth.
Why should I comfort you with words that later
Would prove deceitful? Truth is always best.—
Across the plain I guided my Lord Creon
To where unpitied Polyneices lay,
A corpse mangled by dogs. Then we besought
Hecate, goddess of the roads, and Pluto[45]
To moderate their wrath, and to show mercy.   1130
We washed the dead with ceremonial water.
Gathering the scattered fragments that remained,
With fresh-cut boughs we burned them. We heaped up
A mound of native earth above his ashes.
Then we approached the cavern of Death's bride,
The rock-floored marriage-chamber. While as yet
We were far distant, someone heard the sound
Of loud lament in that unhallowed place,
And came to tell our master. As the King
Drew near, there floated through the air a voice,   1140
Faint, indistinct, that uttered a bitter cry.
The King burst out in anguish: 'Can it be
That I, in my misery, have become a prophet?
Will this be the saddest road I ever trod?
My son's voice greets me. Quickly, slaves! Go quickly!
When you have reached the sepulcher, get through
The opening where the stones are wrenched away,
Get to the mouth of the burial chamber. Look,
See if I know his voice—Haemon's, my son's—
Or if I am deluded by the gods.'   1150
We followed our despairing master's bidding
And in the farthest recess of the tomb
We found Antigone, hanging, with her veil
Noosed round her neck. And with her we found Haemon,
His arms flung round her waist, grieving aloud
For his bride lost in death, his ruined marriage,
His father's deeds. But when his father saw him,
Creon cried piteously and going in,
Called to him brokenly: 'My son, my son,
What have you done? What are you thinking of?   1160
What dreadful thing has driven you out of your mind?

[45] Hecate, associated with crossroads, was a goddess of night, magic, and the underworld;
Pluto is another name for Hades, god of the dead.

Son, come away. I beg you. I beseech you.'
But Haemon glared at him with furious eyes
Instead of answering, spat in his face,
And drew his sword. His father turned to fly
So that he missed his aim. Immediately,
In bitter self-reproach, the wretched boy
Leaned hard against his sword, and drove it deep
Into his side. Then while his life yet lingered,
With failing strength he drew Antigone close;   1170
And as he lay there gasping heavily,
Over her white cheek his blood ebbed away.
The dead lie clasped together. He is wedded,
Not in this world but in the house of Death.
He has borne witness that of all the evils
Afflicting man, the worst is lack of wisdom.

                           [*Exit* EURYDICE]

CHORUS. What does that mean? Who can interpret it?
    The Queen has gone without a single word.
MESSENGER. It startles me. And yet I hope it means
    That hearing these dreadful things about her son,   1180
    She will not let herself show grief in public
    But will lament in private with her women.
    Schooled in discretion, she will do no wrong.
CHORUS. How can we tell? Surely too great a silence
    Is no less ominous than too loud lament.
MESSENGER. Then I will enter. Perhaps she is concealing
    Some secret purpose in her passionate heart.
    I will find out, for you are right in saying
    Too great a silence may be ominous.

                    [*Exit* MESSENGER. *Enter* CREON
                    with ATTENDANTS, *carrying the*
                    body of HAEMON *on a bier*]

CHORUS. Thebans, look there! The King himself draws near,   1190
    Bearing a load whose tale is all too clear.
    This is a work—if we dare speak our thought—
    That not another's but his own hands wrought.
CREON.
        O, how may my sin be told?
    The stubborn, death-fraught sin of a darkened brain!
        Behold us here, behold
    Father and son, the slayer and the slain!
        Pain, only pain
    Has come of my design.
        Fate struck too soon; too soon your spirit fled.   1200
        My son, my young son, you are lying dead
    Not for your folly, but for mine, for mine.

CHORUS. Sir, you have come to learn the right too late.
CREON.
    My lesson has been bitter and complete.
Some god has struck me down with crushing weight,
Filling my heart with cruelty and hate.
    Trampling my happiness beneath his feet.
      Grief, bitter grief, is man's fate.

[*Enter* MESSENGER]

MESSENGER [*indicating* HAEMON].
    Your load is heavy, Sir, but there is more.
    That is the burden you are bearing now.   1210
    Soon you must bear new woe within your house.
CREON. And what worse misery can follow this?
MESSENGER. Your wife is dead, a mother like her son.
    Poor woman, by her own hand she has died.
CREON.
    By her own hand she died.
Death, spare me! Can you never have your fill?
    Never be satisfied?
Herald of evil, messenger of ill,
    Your harsh words kill,
They smite me now anew.   1220
    My wife is dead—You tell me my wife is dead.
    Death after death is heaped upon my head.
Speak to me, boy. Is what you tell me true?
MESSENGER. It is no longer hidden. Sir, look there.

[*The body of* EURYDICE *is disclosed
through the palace doors*]

CREON.
    Another horror that makes blind mine eyes!
What further agony has fate in store?
My dead son's body in my arms I bore,
    And now beside him his dead mother lies.
      I can endure no more.
MESSENGER. There at the altar with a keen-edged knife   1230
    She stabbed herself; and as her eyes were darkened,
    She wailed the death of Megareus,[46] her son,
    Who earlier had met a noble fate;
    She wailed for Haemon; then, with her last breath,
    You, as the slayer of your sons, she cursed.
CREON.
    I am shaken with terror, with terror past belief.
    Is there none here to end my anguish? None?

---

[46] The other son of Creon and Eurydice; he had bravely committed suicide to save Thebes.

No sword to pierce me? Broken with my grief,
So steeped in agony that we are one.
MESSENGER. Sir, as she died, she burdened you with guilt,   1240
Charging you with the death of both your sons.
CREON. And by what act of violence did she die?
MESSENGER. Hearing the shrill lament for Haemon's fate,
Deep in her heart she drove the bright blade home.
CREON [*to* HAEMON].
I am your slayer, I alone.
I am guilty, only I.
I, and none other, must atone.
Lead me away. The truth I own.
Nothing is left, except to die.
CHORUS. If anything can be good, those words are good.   1250
For when calamity has come upon us,
The thing that is the briefest is the best.
CREON.
Draw near me, death! O longed for death, draw near!
Most welcome destiny, make no delay.
Tell me my last hour, my last breath, is here.
I have no wish to see another day.
CHORUS. Such things are yet to come. We are concerned
With doing what must needs be done today.
The future rests in other hands than ours.
CREON. That is my whole desire. That is my prayer.   1260
CHORUS. No. Do not pray. Men must accept their doom.
CREON.
My life's work there before me lies.
My folly slew my wife, my son.
I know not where to turn mine eyes.
All my misdeeds before me rise.
Lead me away, brought low, undone.

[*Exit* CREON]

CHORUS.
The crown of happiness is to be wise.
Honor the gods, and the gods' edicts prize.
They strike down boastful men and men grown bold.
Wisdom we learn at last, when we are old.   1270

Euripides

(C. 480–406 B.C.)

Aeschylus fought in the momentous Greek naval victory at Salamis in 480 B.C. The adolescent Sophocles helped to celebrate it publicly. Tradition has it that Euripides was born in Salamis on the very day of the battle. Even if, or especially if, the tradition is historically inaccurate (he may have been born a few years earlier), it symbolizes a desire by the ancients to link Euripides with his two mighty predecessors as the third definitive playwright of the greatest age of Greece.

Unlike Aeschylus and Sophocles, Euripides seems to have taken little active part in the official public life of Athens; he was not a social man by temperament. The size of his library indicates that he was extensively learned. From the year 455 on, he participated regularly in the dramatic contests held annually in Athens, but he won first prize less often than did Aeschylus or Sophocles, possibly because of the "irregularities" later alleged, by Aristotle and other critics, to exist in his work, or possibly because of his nonconformist attitude toward Greek religion and Athenian politics. His political dissidence intensified during the last two decades of his life as the tragic and misguided Peloponnesian war against Sparta and its allies moved inexorably toward a dismal conclusion. His play The Trojan Women, *for example (produced in 415), exposes the brutality of "heroic" conquerors and, indirectly, shows Euripides' distaste for Athenian imperialism. He spent the last two years of his life in Macedonia, where he died in 406, slightly earlier than Sophocles, who conducted a scene of public mourning for him in the theater. After his death, Euripides' plays were immensely popular; of the ninety he wrote, eighteen have survived, as compared with seven apiece by Aeschylus and Sophocles. Among these is* The Cyclops, *the only extant specimen of the grotesque "satyr play" that in Athenian dramatic practice regularly followed the set of three tragedies performed earlier in the same day.*

The two violent and disturbing plays included in this volume, Medea *(431) and* The Bacchae *(written just before the author's death), constitute a rough frame for Euripides' surviving work.* Medea *was one of the earlier of these extant plays, and* The Bacchae *was his last one (thus also the last of the great ancient Greek tragedies). One needs to keep in mind, however, that* Medea *was the work not of a novice but rather of a veteran playwright who, when he wrote the play, had had a quarter-century of experience in composing for the theater.* The Bacchae, *written when the aged and embittered Euripides had exiled himself in the north, was among the most daring and speculative of his plays; ironically, however, it comes untypically close in its organizational structure to the model generally employed by Euripides' predecessors.*

Euripides' work as a whole illustrates several new departures. The formal structure (The Bacchae *notwithstanding) is looser than in Aeschylus or Sophocles, though perhaps we ought rather to call it freer. He made extensive use of the Prologue and, at the end of his plays, was partial to the* deus ex machina *device, whereby a deity intervenes to impose an arbitrary resolution. The endings of his plays are frequently ambiguous or disturbing, as in Medea's escape to Athens and in the harsh, rather ambiguous judgments passed by Dionysus on the survivors of the house of Cadmus. In Euripides, the Chorus often sings magnificent lyrics, but they tend to be less integral to the dramatic action than in the plays of Aeschylus or Sophocles. Another recurrent device is the* agon, *a direct and usually hostile confrontation* *between two characters in which arguments or accusations are exchanged in rapid-fire fashion. Euripides also helped popularize the mode of drama we now call tragicomedy; his* Alcestis, *in which the dead heroine is reclaimed from the grave, is an example. To regard such innovations as regrettable departures from the kind of coherent unity Aristotle called for is unjust to Euripides, who created several powerful forms of drama that are best allowed to operate by their own organically functional rules, without being measured against arbitrary norms of what ancient drama, or tragedy, is supposed to be.*

Some of these formal, or antiformal, elements, but more especially the ideas conveyed or implied in his plays, have earned Euripides a reputation as the most "romantic" of the three great tragedians. The alleged untidiness of his dramatic construction often parallels and indeed emphasizes the central Euripidean theme of irrationality, in people and in the cosmos. Throughout Medea, *the heroine, like many other characters in Euripides, is overcome by passion (sometimes tender, more often violent in the extreme). As an exploration of human values, the play seems to many readers to present an almost maddening stalemate; it is equally impossible either to dismiss Medea's motives or to endorse them, not to mention her hair-raising acts. The same ambivalence informs* The Bacchae, *a play that addresses, not incidentally but head-on, the value of the irrational Dionysian drives. This tragedy, generally recognized as among the supreme achievements of ancient Greece, has been interpreted both as a return by Euripides to religious piety and as profound skepticism, both as an indictment of rationality and as an indictment of irrational fanaticism.*

According to the Chorus in Aeschylus' Oresteia, *humanity suffers into truth. In Sophocles much the same thing is true, though the theology is less explicit; for example, in* Oedipus at Colonus *the unspeakable suffering endured by the blinded and exiled king is redeemed at his death, when he is mysteriously transfigured. In the last analysis, both these dramatists are optimists—though by no means facile ones. Euripides is more pessimistic. For him, an intellectual and a skeptic, whatever force governs the world—whether we call that force Fate, the divine will, Necessity, or by any other name—is amoral and entirely indifferent to humanity. As* Medea *shows, human acts of good and evil are thrown into a moral void. Certainly suffering has meaning for Euripides. But, for him, education through suffering is something humanity has to undergo alone, without much theological comfort. The world, for him, is both utterly unpredictable and also utterly predictable, in the sense that its operation is affected by neither piety nor virtue. Granted that it is dangerous to translate the values of an ancient Athenian into modern terms, it still seems tempting, if not inevitable, to read Euripides as a quintessentially modern man, for better or worse. His view of the world, as in modern scientific determinism, posits a universe (in which laws cannot be changed by human moral acts) almost indistinguishable—from the human point of view—from one that is not governed at all. The universe most metaphysically determined is morally the most chaotic.*

Euripides' attitude toward the sexes is another crucial topic. Legend surrounds his birth; at the other end, legend has it that at his death he was torn apart, by dogs or women. Again, the legend may be quaint, but the fact remains that, beginning in his own time, Euripides has been charged with misogyny. Aristophanes, for one, gave weight to the charge, in Lysistrata *and in other comedies. It is easy to see how, superficially, the creator of a violent and male-threatening witch such as Medea could be regarded as defaming women. It is just as easy, however, and especially from the viewpoint of modern feminism, to see Euripides as a master psychologist and critic of the masculine and feminine mystiques that operate on a powerful thematic and symbolic level in Greek tragedy from Aeschylus' Oresteia on. As Aristophanes explored these mystiques in a comic vein, so Euripides explored them in a tragic vein, above all in* The Bacchae. *The athletic male rationalist Pentheus sees the women of Thebes as having been delivered over to lasciviousness, but from the women's point of view they have been freed for something else, whether from the literal prison in which Pentheus has ineffectually locked them or from the more symbolic prison of their domestic weaving-looms. The identification of this freedom with erotic sexuality and with violence exists largely in Pentheus' tortured and sex-ridden imagination; before being invaded by males intent on ambush or moral entrapment, the liberated life of the Bacchae is innocently pastoral, not especially aphrodisiac, and pacific, not violent. The phallic thyrsus carried by the initiates of Dionysus becomes most unambiguously a weapon of literal warfare when the literal spears of their male adversaries are turned against the women. Moreover, this kind of sociological tension is a correlative of an equally tortured tension in the psyche, again epitomized by Pentheus, who is both repelled by the "effeminate" Dionysian foreigner and titillated by the furtive adventure of wearing curls and a dress. It is entirely possible to see* The Bacchae *as a sermon to the effect that the libidinal forces embodied in women are dangerous when they get out of hand; it is equally possible, however, to see it as exploring the tragic insight that sexual hostility is born of repression and that the fantasies of sexual division and fear are inevitably self-fulfilling.*

FURTHER READING *(prepared by F.S.N.):* Gilbert Murray's popular work *Euripides and His Age*, 1913, 2nd ed. 1946, remains an excellent introduction to the historical and cultural context of Euripides' drama. For material on the life and writings of Euripides see D. J. Conacher, *Euripidean Drama: Myth, Theme and Structure*, 1967; and T. B. L. Webster, *The Tragedies of Euripides*, 1967, which also compares the works of Euripides with those of Aeschylus and Sophocles. A challenging modern selection of studies is given by E. Segal, ed., *Euripides: A Collection of Critical Essays*, 1968. Pietro Pucci in his full-scale discussion of *Medea, The Violence of Pity in Euripides' Medea*, 1980, tackles major problems in interpreting this work. Excellent chapters on *Medea* and *The Bacchae* appear (along with chapters on all the other ancient Greek tragedies) in John Ferguson, *A Companion to Greek Tragedy*, 1972. This book also contains good bibliographies of ancient Greek tragedy in general, of each of the great tragedians in general, and of each separate tragedy. Demanding but extremely rewarding is Charles Segal's comprehensive study *Dionysiac Poetics and Euripides' "Bacchae,"* 1982. For discussion of the theatrical production of Euripides' plays, see J. Michael Walton, *The Greek Sense of Theatre: Tragedy Reviewed*, 1985.

MEDEA

Translated by Philip Vellacott

The kingship of the city of Iolcus (in Thessaly, the northeastern region of Greece) had been usurped by Pelias. Jason's father, Aeson, was half brother of Pelias and rightful ruler of Iolcus. After a period of protective exile under the tutelage of Chiron the Centaur, Jason returned to Iolcus. His usurper-uncle Pelias then sent Jason off to Colchis (on the Black Sea) to capture the magically potent Golden Fleece of a ram. Jason made the adventurous voyage, in company with some of the most famous and fabled Greek heroes, called the Argonauts after the name of their ship the *Argo*. When Jason reached Colchis, its king Aeetes (Medea's father) agreed to give up the Golden Fleece if Jason performed certain superhumanly difficult tasks. He was able to perform them with the help of Medea, who had fallen in love with him and who possessed magical arts. The heroes then returned with the Golden Fleece to Iolcus, along with Medea, who assisted their return by killing her brother so that her father Aeetes would be delayed in his pursuit. In Iolcus, Medea continued to aid Jason by using her witchcraft to cause the death of Pelias at the hands of his daughters. But Jason was unable to claim his throne, and he and Medea were banished from Iolcus. They settled in Corinth, the setting of the play *Medea*. After some time there, Jason has decided to cast off Medea and to marry Glauce, daughter of Creon, the king of Corinth. This Creon should not be confused with the Creon who, in Sophocles' Oedipus plays, rules Thebes. [*Editors' headnote.*]

CHARACTERS

NURSE	JASON
TUTOR *to Medea's sons*	AEGEUS, *king of Athens*
MEDEA	MESSENGER
CHORUS *of Corinthian women*	MEDEA'S TWO CHILDREN
CREON, *king of Corinth*	

SCENE
Before Jason's house in Corinth

NURSE. If only they had never gone! If the Argo's hull
  Never had winged out through the grey-blue jaws of rock[1]
  And on towards Colchis! If that pine on Pelion's[2] slopes
  Had never felt the axe, and fallen, to put oars
  Into those heroes' hands, who went at Pelias' bidding
  To fetch the golden fleece! Then neither would Medea,
  My mistress, ever have set sail for the walled town
  Of Iolcus, mad with love for Jason; nor would she,
  When Pelias' daughters, at her instance, killed their father,
  Have come with Jason and her children to live here   10
  In Corinth; where, coming as an exile, she has earned
  The citizens' welcome; while to Jason she is all
  Obedience—and in marriage that's the saving thing,
  When a wife obediently accepts her husband's will.

  But now her world has turned to enmity, and wounds her
  Where her affection's deepest. Jason has betrayed
  His own sons, and my mistress, for a royal bed,
  For alliance with the king of Corinth. He has married
  Glauce, Creon's daughter. Poor Medea! Scorned and shamed,
  She raves, invoking every vow and solemn pledge   20

[1] The Symplegades, two mythical rocks at the north end of the strait of Bosporus, the entrance to the Black Sea. The rocks were supposed to crush ships that sailed between them.
[2] A mountain in Thessaly.

That Jason made her, and calls the gods as witnesses
What thanks she has received for her fidelity.
She will not eat; she lies collapsed in agony,
Dissolving the long hours in tears. Since first she heard
Of Jason's wickedness, she has not raised her eyes,
Or moved her cheek from the hard ground; and when her friends
Reason with her, she might be a rock or wave of the sea,
For all she hears—unless, maybe, she turns away
Her lovely head, speaks to herself alone, and wails
Aloud for her dear father, her own land and home,   30
Which she betrayed and left, to come here with this man
Who now spurns and insults her. Poor Medea! Now
She learns through pain what blessings they enjoy who are not
Uprooted from their native land. She hates her sons:
To see them is no pleasure to her. I am afraid
Some dreadful purpose is forming in her mind. She is
A frightening woman; no one who makes an enemy
Of her will carry off an easy victory.

Here come the boys, back from their running. They've no thought
Of this cruel blow that's fallen on their mother. Well,   40
They're young; young heads and painful thoughts don't go
    together.

> [*Enter the* TUTOR *with* MEDEA'S
> TWO SONS.]

TUTOR. Old nurse and servant of my mistress's house, tell me,
    What are you doing, standing out here by the door,
    All alone, talking to yourself, harping on trouble?
    Eh? What does Medea say to being left alone?
NURSE. Old friend, tutor of Jason's sons, an honest slave
    Suffers in her own heart the blow that strikes her mistress.
    It was too much, I couldn't bear it; I had to come
    Out here and tell my mistress's wrongs to earth and heaven.
TUTOR. Poor woman! Has she not stopped crying yet?   50
NURSE.   Stopped crying?
    I envy you. Her grief's just born—not yet half-grown.
TUTOR. Poor fool—though she's my mistress and I shouldn't say it—
    She had better save her tears. She has not heard the worst.
NURSE. The worst? What now? Don't keep it from me. What has hap-
    pened?
TUTOR. Why, nothing's happened. I'm sorry I said anything.
NURSE. Look—we're both slaves together: don't keep me in the dark.
    Is it so great a secret? I can hold my tongue.
TUTOR. I'd gone along to the benches where the old men play
    At dice, next to the holy fountain of Peirene;   60
    They thought I was not listening; and I heard one say
    That Creon king of Corinth means to send these boys
    Away from here—to banish them, and their mother too.
    Whether the story's true I don't know. I hope not.

NURSE. But surely Jason won't stand by and see his sons
    Banished, even if he has a quarrel with their mother?
TUTOR. Old love is ousted by new love. Jason's no friend
    To this house.
NURSE.   Then we're lost, if we must add new trouble
    To old, before we're rid of what we had already.
TUTOR. But listen: it's no time to tell Medea this.   70
    Keep quiet, say nothing about it.
NURSE.   Children, do you hear
    What sort of father Jason is to you? My curse
    On—No! No curse; he is my master. All the same,
    He is guilty: he has betrayed those near and dear to him.
TUTOR. What man's not guilty? It's taken you a long time to learn
    That everybody loves himself more than his neighbour.
    These boys are nothing to their father: he's in love.
NURSE. Run into the house, boys. Everything will be all right.

                 [*The children move away a little.*]

You do your best to keep them by themselves, as long
As she's in this dark mood; don't let them go to her.   80
I've watched her watching them, her eye like a wild bull's.
There's something that she means to do; and I know this:
She'll not relax her rage till it has found its victim.
God grant she strike her enemies and not her friends!

                 [MEDEA's *voice is heard from inside
                 the house.*]

MEDEA. Oh, oh! What misery, what wretchedness!
    What shall I do? If only I were dead!
NURSE. There! You can hear; it is your mother
    Racking her heart, racking her anger.
    Quick, now, children, hurry indoors;
    And don't go within sight of her,   90
    Or anywhere near her; keep a safe distance.
    Her mood is cruel, her nature dangerous,
    Her will fierce and intractable.
    Come on, now, in with you both at once.

                 [*The* CHILDREN *go in, and the*
                 TUTOR *follows.*]

The dark cloud of her lamentations
Is just beginning. Soon, I know,
It will burst aflame as her anger rises.
Deep in passion and unrelenting,
What will she do now, stung with insult?
MEDEA [*indoors*]. Do I not suffer? Am I not wronged? Should I not
    weep?   100
    Children, your mother is hated, and you are cursed:
    Death take you, with your father, and perish his whole house!

NURSE. Oh, the pity of it! Poor Medea!
    Your children—why, what have *they* to do
    With their father's wickedness? Why hate *them?*
    I am sick with fear for you, children, terror
    Of what may happen. The mind of a queen
    Is a thing to fear. A queen is used
    To giving commands, not obeying them;
    And her rage once roused is hard to appease.   110

    To have learnt to live on the common level
    Is better. No grand life for me,
    Just peace and quiet as I grow old.
    The middle way, neither great nor mean,
    Is best by far, in name and practice.
    To be rich and powerful brings no blessing;
    Only more utterly
    Is the prosperous house destroyed, when the gods are angry.

                        [*Enter the* CHORUS *of Corinthian*
                        women.]

CHORUS.
    I heard her voice, I heard
    That unhappy woman from Colchis   120
    Still crying, not calm yet.
    Old Nurse, tell us about her.
    As I stood by the door I heard her
    Crying inside the palace.
    And my own heart suffers too
    When Jason's house is suffering;
    For that is where my loyalty lies.
NURSE. Jason's house? It no longer exists; all that is finished.
    Jason is a prisoner in a princess's bed;
    And Medea is in her room   130
    Melting her life away in tears;
    No word from any friend can give her comfort.
MEDEA [*still from indoors*].
    Come, flame of the sky,
    Pierce through my head!
    What do I gain from living any longer?
    Oh, how I hate living! I want
    To end my life, leave it behind, and die.
CHORUS.
    O Zeus, and Earth, and Light,
    Do you hear the chanted prayer
    Of a wife in her anguish?   140

                        [*turning to the door and address-*
                        ing MEDEA]

What madness is this? The bed you long for—
Is it what others shrink from?

Is it death you demand?
Do not pray that prayer, Medea!
If your husband is won to a new love—
The thing is common; why let it anger you?
Zeus will plead your cause.
Check this passionate grief over your husband
Which wastes you away.

MEDEA. Mighty Themis! Dread Artemis![3]   150
Do you see how I am used—
In spite of those great oaths I bound him with—
By my accursed husband?
Oh, may I see Jason and his bride
Ground to pieces in their shattered palace
For the wrong they have dared to do to me, unprovoked!
O my father, my city, you I deserted;
My brother I shamefully murdered!

NURSE. Do you hear what my mistress is saying,
Clamouring to Themis, hearer of prayer,   160
And to Zeus, who is named guardian of men's oaths?
It is no trifling matter
That can end a rage like hers.

CHORUS. I wish she would come out here and let us see her
And talk to her; if she would listen
Perhaps she would drop this fierce resentful spirit,
This passionate indignation.
As a friend I am anxious to do whatever I can.
Go, nurse, persuade her to come out to us.
Tell her we are all on her side.   170
Hurry, before she does harm—to those in there;
This passion of hers is an irresistible flood.

NURSE. I will. I fear I shall not persuade her;
Still, I am glad to do my best.
Yet as soon as any of us servants
Goes near to her, or tries to speak,
She glares at us like a mad bull
Or a lioness guarding her cubs.

> [*The* NURSE *goes to the door, where
> she turns.*]

The men of old times had little sense;
If you called them fools you wouldn't be far wrong.   180
They invented songs, and all the sweetness of music,
To perform at feasts, banquets, and celebrations;
But no one thought of using
Songs and stringed instruments
To banish the bitterness and pain of life.
Sorrow is the real cause

---

[3] Themis is the personification of justice; Artemis is the virgin goddess of the hunt who
protects young creatures and women in childbirth.

Of deaths and disasters and families destroyed.
If music could cure sorrow it would be precious;
But after a good dinner why sing songs?
When people have fed full they're happy already.   190

> [*The* NURSE *goes in.*]

CHORUS.
    I heard her sobbing and wailing,
    Shouting shrill, pitiful accusations
    Against her husband who has betrayed her.
    She invokes Themis, daughter of Zeus,
    Who witnessed those promises which drew her
    Across from Asia to Hellas, setting sail at night,
    Threading the salt strait,
    Key and barrier to the Pontic Sea.[4]

> [MEDEA *comes out. She is not
> shaken with weeping, but cool and
> self-possessed.*]

MEDEA. Women of Corinth, I would not have you censure me,
    So I have come. Many, I know, are proud at heart,   200
    Indoors or out; but others are ill spoken of
    As supercilious, just because their ways are quiet.
    There is no justice in the world's censorious eyes.
    They will not wait to learn a man's true character;
    Though no wrong has been done them, one look—and they hate.
    Of course a stranger must conform; even a Greek
    Should not annoy his fellows by crass stubbornness.
    I accept my place; but this blow that has fallen on me
    Was not to be expected. It has crushed my heart.
    Life has no pleasure left, dear friends. I want to die.   210
    Jason was my whole life; he knows that well. Now he
    Has proved himself the most contemptible of men.

    Surely, of all creatures that have life and will, we women
    Are the most wretched. When, for an extravagant sum,
    We have bought a husband,[5] we must then accept him as
    Possessor of our body. This is to aggravate
    Wrong with worse wrong. Then the great question: will the man
    We get be bad or good? For women, divorce is not
    Respectable; to repel the man, not possible.

    Still more, a foreign woman, coming among new laws,   220
    New customs, needs the skill of magic, to find out
    What her home could not teach her, how to treat the man
    Whose bed she shares. And if in this exacting toil
    We are successful, and our husband does not struggle

---

[4] The Black Sea.   [5] The reference is to the dowry given with the bride in marriage.

Under the marriage yoke, our life is enviable.
Otherwise, death is better. If a man grows tired
Of the company at home, he can go out, and find
A cure for tediousness. We wives are forced to look
To one man only. And, they tell us, we at home
Live free from danger, they go out to battle: fools!   230
I'd rather stand three times in the front line than bear
One child.

        But the same arguments do not apply
To you and me. You have this city, your father's home,
The enjoyment of your life, and your friends' company.
I am alone; I have no city; now my husband
Insults me. I was taken as plunder from a land
At the earth's edge. I have no mother, brother, nor any
Of my own blood to turn to in this extremity.

So, I make one request. If I can find a way
To work revenge on Jason for his wrongs to me,   240
Say nothing. A woman's weak and timid in most matters;
The noise of war, the look of steel, makes her a coward.
But touch her right in marriage, and there's no bloodier spirit.
CHORUS. I'll do as you ask. To punish Jason will be just.
I do not wonder that you take such wrongs to heart.

[CREON *approaches.*]

But look, Medea; I see Creon, King of Corinth;
He must have come to tell you of some new decision.
CREON. You there, Medea, scowling rage against your husband!
I order you out of Corinth; take your sons and go
Into exile. Waste no time; I'm here to see this order   250
Enforced. And I'm not going back into my palace
Until I've put you safe outside my boundaries.
MEDEA. Oh! this is the cruel end of my accursed life!
My enemies have spread full sail; no welcoming shore
Waits to receive and save me. Ill-treated as I am,
Creon, I ask: for what offence do you banish me?
CREON. I fear you. Why wrap up the truth? I fear that you
May do my daughter some irreparable harm.
A number of things contribute to my anxiety.
You're a clever woman, skilled in many evil arts;   260
You're barred from Jason's bed, and that enrages you.
I learn too from reports, that you have uttered threats
Of revenge on Jason and his bride and his bride's father.
I'll act first, then, in self-defence. I'd rather make you
My enemy now, than weaken, and later pay with tears.
MEDEA. My reputation, yet again! Many times, Creon,
It has been my curse and ruin. A man of any shrewdness
Should never have his children taught to use their brains
More than their fellows. What do you gain by being clever?

You neglect your own affairs; and all your fellow citizens   270
Hate you. Those who are fools will call you ignorant
And useless, when you offer them unfamiliar knowledge.
As for those thought intelligent, if people rank
You above *them*, that is a thing they will not stand.
I know this from experience: because I am clever,
They are jealous; while the rest dislike me. After all,
I am not so clever as all that.
                                    So you, Creon,
Are afraid—of what? Some harm that I might do to you?
Don't let *me* alarm you, Creon. I'm in no position—
A woman—to wrong a king. You have done me no wrong.   280
You've given your daughter to the man you chose. I hate
My husband—true; but you had every right to do
As you have done. So now I bear no grudge against
Your happiness: marry your daughter to him, and good luck
To you both. But let me live in Corinth. I will bear
My wrongs in silence, yielding to superior strength.
CREON. Your words are gentle: but my blood runs cold to think
What plots you may be nursing deep within your heart.
In fact, I trust you so much less now than before.
A woman of hot temper—and a man the same—   290
Is a less dangerous enemy than one quiet and clever.
So out you go, and quickly; no more arguing.
I've made my mind up; you're my enemy. No craft
Of yours will find a way of staying in my city.
MEDEA. I kneel to you, I beseech you by the young bride, your child.
CREON. You're wasting words; you'll never make me change my mind.
MEDEA. I beg you! Will you cast off pity, and banish me?
CREON. I will: I have more love for my family than for you.
MEDEA. My home, my country! How my thoughts turn to you now!
CREON. I love my country too—next only to my daughter.   300
MEDEA. Oh, what an evil power love has in people's lives!
CREON. That would depend on circumstances, I imagine.
MEDEA. Great Zeus, remember who caused all this suffering!
CREON. Go, you poor wretch, take all my troubles with you! Go!
MEDEA. I know what trouble is; I have no need of more.
CREON. In a moment you'll be thrown out neck and crop. Here, men!
MEDEA. No, no, not that! But, Creon, I have one thing to ask.
CREON. You seem inclined, Medea, to give me trouble still.
MEDEA. I'll go. [*She still clings to him.*] It was not *that* I begged.
CREON.   Then why resist?
Why will you not get out?
MEDEA.   This one day let me stay,   310
To settle some plan for my exile, make provision
For my two sons, since their own father is not concerned
To help them. Show some pity: you are a father too,
You should feel kindly towards them. For myself, exile
Is nothing. I weep for them; their fate is very hard.
CREON. I'm no tyrant by nature. My soft heart has often

Betrayed me; and I know it's foolish of me now;
Yet none the less, Medea, you shall have what you ask.
But take this warning: if tomorrow's holy sun
Finds you or them inside my boundaries, you die.   320
That is my solemn word. Now stay here, if you must,
This one day. You can hardly in one day accomplish
What I am afraid of.

                         [*Exit* CREON.]

CHORUS.
        Medea, poor Medea!
        Your grief touches our hearts.
        A wanderer, where can you turn?
        To what welcoming house?
        To what protecting land?
        How wild with dread and danger
        Is the sea where the gods have set your course!   330
MEDEA. A bad predicament all round—yes, true enough;
        But don't imagine things will end as they are now.
        Trials are yet to come for this new-wedded pair;
        Nor shall those nearest to them get off easily.

        Do you think I would ever have fawned so on this man,
        Except to gain my purpose, carry out my schemes?
        Not one touch, not one word: yet he—oh, what a fool!
        By banishing me at once he could have thwarted me
        Utterly; instead, he allows me to remain one day.
        Today three of my enemies I shall strike dead: 340
        Father and daughter; and *my* husband.

        I have in mind so many paths of death for them,
        I don't know which to choose. Should I set fire to the house,
        And burn the bridal chamber? Or creep up to their bed
        And drive a sharp knife through their guts? There is one fear:
        If I am caught entering the house, or in the act,
        I die, and the last laugh goes to my enemies.
        The best is the direct way, which most suits my bent:
        To kill by poison.

        So—say they are dead: what city will receive me then?   350
        What friend will guarantee my safety, offer land
        And home as sanctuary? None. I'll wait a little.
        If some strong tower of help appears, I'll carry out
        This murder cunningly and quietly. But if Fate
        Banishes me without resource, I will myself
        Take sword in hand, harden my heart to the uttermost,
        And kill them both, even if I am to die for it.

For, by Queen Hecate,[6] whom above all divinities
I venerate, my chosen accomplice, to whose presence
My central hearth is dedicated, no one of them   360
Shall hurt me and not suffer for it! Let me work:
In bitterness and pain they shall repent this marriage,
Repent their houses joined, repent my banishment.

Come! Lay your plan, Medea; scheme with all your skill.
On to the deadly moment that shall test your nerve!
You see now where you stand. Your father was a king,
His father was the Sun-god:[7] you must not invite
Laughter from Jason and his new allies, the tribe
Of Sisyphus.[8] You know what you must do. Besides—

[*She turns to the* CHORUS.]

We were born women—useless for honest purposes,   370
But in all kinds of evil skilled practitioners.
CHORUS. Streams of the sacred rivers flow uphill;
    Tradition, order, all things are reversed:
        Deceit is *men*'s device now,
        Men's oaths are gods' dishonour.
    Legend will now reverse our reputation;
    A time comes when the female sex is honoured;
        That old discordant slander
        Shall no more hold us subject.
    Male poets of past ages, with their ballads   380
    Of faithless women, shall go out of fashion;
        For Phoebus,[9] Prince of Music,
    Never bestowed the lyric inspiration
        Through female understanding—
        Or we'd find themes for poems,
    We'd counter with our epics against man.
    Oh, Time is old; and in his store of tales
        Men figure no less famous
        Or infamous than women.

    So you, Medea, wild with love,   390
    Set sail from your father's house,
    Threading the Rocky Jaws of the eastern sea;
    And here, living in a strange country,
    Your marriage lost, your bed solitary,
    You are driven beyond the borders,
    An exile with no redress.
    The grace of sworn oaths is gone;

[6] Goddess of witchcraft, though also in some contexts a protective deity.
[7] Helios, father of Aeetes.
[8] An earlier, legendary king of Corinth, noted for deceitfulness.
[9] Apollo, god of music and poetry.

Honour remains no more
In the wide Greek world, but is flown to the sky.
Where can you turn for shelter?   400
Your father's door is closed against you;
Another is now mistress of your husband's bed;
A new queen rules in your house.

[*Enter* JASON.]

JASON. I have noticed—this is not the first occasion—
What fatal results follow from ungoverned rage.
You could have stayed in Corinth, still lived in this house,
If you had quietly accepted the decisions
Of those in power. Instead, you talked like a fool; and now
You are banished. Well, your angry words don't upset *me;*
Go on as long as you like reciting Jason's crimes.   410
But after your abuse of the King and the princess
Think yourself lucky to be let off with banishment.
I have tried all the time to calm them down; but you
Would not give up your ridiculous tirades against
The royal family. So, you're banished. However, I
Will not desert a friend. I have carefully considered
Your problem, and come now, in spite of everything,
To see that you and the children are not sent away
With an empty purse, or unprovided. Exile brings
With it a train of difficulties. You no doubt   420
Hate me: but I could never bear ill-will to you.
MEDEA. You filthy coward!—if I knew any worse name
For such unmanliness I'd use it—so, you've come!
You, my worst enemy, come to me! Oh, it's not courage,
This looking friends in the face after betraying them.
It is not even audacity; it's a disease,
The worst a man can have, pure shamelessness. However,
It is as well you came; to say what I have to say
Will ease my heart; to hear it said will make you wince.

I will begin at the beginning. When you were sent   430
To master the fire-breathing bulls, yoke them, and sow
The deadly furrow, then I saved your life; and that
Every Greek who sailed with you in the Argo knows.
The serpent that kept watch over the Golden Fleece,
Coiled round it fold on fold, unsleeping—it was I
Who killed it, and so lit the torch of your success.[10]
I willingly deceived my father; left my home;
With you I came to Iolcus by Mount Pelion,
Showing much love and little wisdom. There I put
King Pelias to the most horrible of deaths[11]   440

---

[10] Medea refers in the preceding six lines to the difficult tasks Jason had to accomplish in Colchis to win the Golden Fleece.

[11] Medea had deceitfully persuaded Pelias' daughters that they could magically restore their father's youth by boiling him in a cauldron.

By his own daughters' hands, and ruined his whole house.
And in return for this you have the wickedness
To turn me out, to get yourself another wife,
Even after I had borne you sons! If you had still
Been childless I could have pardoned you for hankering
After this new marriage. But respect for oaths has gone
To the wind. Do you, I wonder, think that the old gods
No longer rule? Or that new laws are now in force?
You must know you are guilty of perjury to me.

My poor right hand, which you so often clasped! My knees 450
Which you then clung to! How we are besmirched and mocked
By this man's broken vows, and all our hopes deceived!

Come, I'll ask your advice as if you were a friend.
Not that I hope for any help from you; but still,
I'll ask you, and expose your infamy. Where now
Can I turn? Back to my country and my father's house,
Which I betrayed to come with you? Or to Iolcus,
To Pelias's wretched daughters? What a welcome they
Would offer me, who killed their father! Thus it stands:
My friends at home now hate me; and in helping you 460
I have earned the enmity of those I had no right
To hurt. For my reward, you have made me the envy
Of Hellene women everywhere! A marvellous
Husband I have, and faithful too, in the name of pity;
When I'm banished, thrown out of the country without a friend,
Alone with my forlorn waifs. Yes, a shining shame
It will be to you, the new-made bridegroom, that your own sons,
And I who saved your life, are begging beside the road!

O Zeus! Why have you given us clear signs to tell
True gold from counterfeit; but when we need to know 470
Bad *men* from good, the flesh bears no revealing mark?
CHORUS. The fiercest anger of all, the most incurable,
 Is that which rages in the place of dearest love.
JASON. I have to show myself a clever speaker, it seems.
 This hurricane of recrimination and abuse
 Calls for good seamanship: I'll furl all but an inch
 Of sail, and ride it out. To begin with, since you build
 To such a height your services to me, I hold
 That credit for my successful voyage was solely due
 To Aphrodite,[12] no one else divine or human. 480
 I admit, you have intelligence; but, to recount
 How helpless passion drove you then to save my life
 Would be invidious; and I will not stress the point.
 Your services, so far as they went, were well enough;
 But in return for saving me you got far more

[12] Goddess of love.

Than you gave. Allow me, in the first place, to point out
That you left a barbarous land to become a resident
Of Hellas;[13] here you have known justice; you have lived
In a society where force yields place to law.
Moreover, here your gifts are widely recognized,   490
You are famous; if you still lived at the ends of the earth
Your name would never be spoken. Personally, unless
Life brings me fame, I long neither for hoards of gold,
Nor for a voice sweeter than Orpheus![14]—Well, *you* began
The argument about my voyage; and that's my answer.

As for your scurrilous taunts against my marriage with
The royal family, I shall show you that my action
Was wise, not swayed by passion, and directed towards
Your interests and my children's.—No, keep quiet! When I
Came here from Iolcus as a stateless exile, dogged   500
And thwarted by misfortunes—why, what luckier chance
Could I have met, than marriage with the King's daughter?
It was not, as you resentfully assume, that I
Found your attractions wearisome, and was smitten with
Desire for a new wife; nor did I specially want
To raise a numerous family—the sons we have
Are enough, I'm satisfied; but I wanted to ensure
First—and the most important—that we should live well
And not be poor; I know how a poor man is shunned
By all his friends. Next, that I could bring up my sons   510
In a manner worthy of my descent; have other sons,
Perhaps, as brothers to your children; give them all
An equal place, and so build up a closely-knit
And prosperous family. *You* need no more children, do you?
While *I* thought it worth while to ensure advantages
For those I have, by means of those I hope to have.

Was such a plan, then, wicked? Even you would approve
If you could govern your sex-jealousy. But you women
Have reached a state where, if all's well with your sex-life,
You've everything you wish for; but when *that* goes wrong,   520
At once all that is best and noblest turns to gall.
If only children could be got some other way,
Without the female sex! If women didn't exist,
Human life would be rid of all its miseries.
CHORUS. Jason, you have set your case forth very plausibly.
     But to my mind—though you may be surprised at this—
     You are acting wrongly in thus abandoning your wife.
MEDEA. No doubt I differ from many people in many ways.
     To me, a wicked man who is also eloquent

[13] Greece.
[14] A legendary poet, and one of the Argonauts; his music was so wonderful that he could
enchant nature itself. See the account in Ovid's *Metamorphoses*, Book X.

Seems the most guilty of them all. He'll cut your throat   530
As bold as brass, because he knows he can dress up murder
In handsome words. He's not so clever after all.
You dare outface me now with glib high-mindedness!
One word will throw you: if you were honest, you ought first
To have won me over, not got married behind my back.

JASON. No doubt, if I had mentioned it, you would have proved
Most helpful. Why, even now you will not bring yourself
To calm this raging temper.

MEDEA.   That was not the point;
But you're an ageing man, and an Asiatic wife
Was no longer respectable.

JASON.   Understand this: 540
It's not for the sake of any woman that I have made
This royal marriage, but, as I've already said,
To ensure your future, and to give my children brothers
Of royal blood, and build security for us all.

MEDEA. I loathe your prosperous future; I'll have none of it,
Nor none of your security—it galls my heart.

JASON. You know—you'll change your mind and be more sensible.
You'll soon stop thinking good is bad, and striking these
Pathetic poses when in fact you're fortunate.

MEDEA. Go on, insult me: you have a roof over your head.   550
I am alone, an exile.

JASON.   It was your own choice.
Blame no one but yourself.

MEDEA.   *My* choice? What did I do?
Did I make you my wife and then abandon you?

JASON. You called wicked curses on the King and his house.

MEDEA. I did. On your house too Fate sends me as a curse.

JASON. I'll not pursue this further. If there's anything else
I can provide to meet the children's needs or yours,
Tell me: I'll gladly give whatever you want, or send
Letters of introduction, if you like, to friends
Who will help you.—Listen: to refuse such help is mad.   560
You've everything to gain if you give up this rage.

MEDEA. Nothing would induce me to have dealings with your friends,
Nor to take any gift of yours; so offer none.
A lying traitor's gifts carry no luck.

JASON.   Very well.
I call the gods to witness that I have done my best
To help you and the children. You make no response
To kindness; friendly overtures you obstinately
Reject. So much the worse for you.

MEDEA.   Go! You have spent
Too long out here. You are consumed with craving for
Your newly-won bride. Go, enjoy her.

[*Exit* JASON.]

It may be—   570
And God uphold my words—that this your marriage-day
Will end with marriage lost, loathing and horror left.
CHORUS.
    Visitations of love that come
    Raging and violent on a man
    Bring him neither good repute nor goodness.
    But if Aphrodite descends in gentleness
    No other goddess brings such delight.
    Never, Queen Aphrodite,
    Loose against me from your golden bow,
    Dipped in sweetness of desire,   580
    Your inescapable arrow!

    Let Innocence, the gods' loveliest gift,
    Choose me for her own;
    Never may the dread Cyprian[15]
    Craze my heart to leave old love for new,
    Sending to assault me
    Angry disputes and feuds unending;
    But let her judge shrewdly the loves of women
    And respect the bed where no war rages.

    O my country, my home!   590
    May the gods save me from becoming
    A stateless refugee
    Dragging out an intolerable life
    In desperate helplessness!
    That is the most pitiful of all griefs;
    Death is better. Should such a day come to me
    I pray for death first.
    Of all pains and hardships none is worse
    Than to be deprived of your native land.

    This is no mere reflection derived from hearsay;   600
    It is something we have seen.
    You, Medea, have suffered the most shattering of blows;
    Yet neither the city of Corinth
    Nor any friend has taken pity on you.
    May dishonour and ruin fall on the man
    Who, having unlocked the secrets
    Of a friend's frank heart, can then disown him!
    He shall be no friend of mine.

[*Enter* AEGEUS.[16]]

---

[15] Aphrodite, goddess of love. Born of the foam of the sea, she made her first appearance in Cyprus.

[16] In myth, the father of Theseus, the great Athenian ruler.

AEGEUS. All happiness to you, Medea! Between old friends
  There is no better greeting.
MEDEA.   All happiness to you,   610
  Aegeus, son of Pandion the wise! Where have you come from?
AEGEUS. From Delphi, from the ancient oracle of Apollo.
MEDEA. The centre of the earth,[17] the home of prophecy:
  Why did you go?
AEGEUS.   To ask for children; that my seed
  May become fertile.
MEDEA.   Why, have you lived so many years
  Childless?
AEGEUS.   Childless I am; so some fate has ordained.
MEDEA. You have a wife, or not?
AEGEUS.   I am married.
MEDEA.   And what answer
  Did Phoebus give you about children?
AEGEUS.   His answer was
  Too subtle for me or any human interpreter.
MEDEA. Is it lawful for me to hear it?
AEGEUS.   Certainly; a brain   620
  Like yours is what is needed.
MEDEA.   Tell me, since you may.
AEGEUS. He commanded me 'not to unstop the wineskin's neck'—
MEDEA. Yes—until when?
AEGEUS.   Until I came safe home again.
MEDEA. I see. And for what purpose have you sailed to Corinth?
AEGEUS. You know the King of Troezen, Pittheus, son of Pelops?
MEDEA. Yes, a most pious man.
AEGEUS.   I want to ask his advice
  About this oracle.
MEDEA.   He is an expert in such matters.
AEGEUS. Yes, and my closest friend. We went to the wars together.
MEDEA. I hope you will get all you long for, and be happy.
AEGEUS. But you are looking pale and wasted: what is the matter?   630
MEDEA. Aegeus, my husband's the most evil man alive.
AEGEUS. Why, what's this? Tell me all about your unhappiness.
MEDEA. Jason has betrayed me, though I never did him wrong.
AEGEUS. What has he done? Explain exactly.
MEDEA.   He has taken
  Another wife, and made her mistress of *my* house.
AEGEUS. But such a thing is shameful! He has never dared–
MEDEA. It is so. Once he loved me; now I am disowned.
AEGEUS. Was he tired of you? Or did he fall in love elsewhere?
MEDEA. Oh, passionately. He's not a man his friends can trust.
AEGEUS. Well, if—as you say—he's a bad lot, let him go.   640

---

[17] The "Navelstone," believed to be the center of the earth, was located at Delphi. Compare the opening of Aeschylus' *The Eumenides*.

MEDEA. It's royalty and power he's fallen in love with.
AEGEUS.   What?
    Go on. Who's the girl's father?
MEDEA.   Creon, King of Corinth.
AEGEUS. I see. Then you have every reason to be upset.
MEDEA. It is the end of everything! What's more, I'm banished.
AEGEUS. Worse still—extraordinary! Why, who has banished you?
MEDEA. Creon has banished me from Corinth.
AEGEUS.   And does Jason
    Accept this? How disgraceful!
MEDEA.   Oh, no! He protests.
    But he's resolved to bear it bravely.—Aegeus, see,
    I touch your beard as a suppliant, embrace your knees,
    Imploring you to have pity on my wretchedness.   650
    Have pity! I am an exile; let me not be friendless.
    Receive me in Athens;[18] give me a welcome in your house.
    So may the gods grant you fertility, and bring
    Your life to a happy close. You have not realized
    What good luck chance has brought you. I know certain drugs
    Whose power will put an end to your sterility.
    I promise you shall beget children.
AEGEUS.   I am anxious,
    For many reasons, to help you in this way, Medea;
    First, for the gods' sake, then this hope you've given me
    Of children—for I've quite despaired of my own powers.   660
    This then is what I'll do: once you can get to Athens
    I'll keep my promise and protect you all I can.
    But I must make this clear first: I do not intend
    To take you with me away from Corinth. If you come
    Yourself to Athens, you shall have sanctuary there;
    I will not give you up to anyone. But first
    Get clear of Corinth without help; the Corinthians too
    Are friends of mine, and I don't wish to give offence.
MEDEA. So be it. Now confirm your promise with an oath,
    And all is well between us.
AEGEUS.   Why? Do you not trust me?   670
    What troubles you?
MEDEA.   I trust you; but I have enemies—
    Not only Creon, but the house of Pelias.
    Once you are bound by oaths you will not give me up
    If they should try to take me out of your territory.
    But if your promise is verbal, and not sworn to the gods,
    Perhaps you will make friends with them, and agree to do
    What they demand. I've no power on my side, while they
    Have wealth and all the resources of a royal house.
AEGEUS. Your forethought is remarkable; but since you wish it
    I've no objection. In fact, the taking of an oath   680
    Safeguards me; since I can confront your enemies

---

[18] Athens often boasted of its hospitality to aliens.

With a clear excuse; while *you* have full security.
So name your gods.
MEDEA.   Swear by the Earth under your feet,
By the Sun, my father's father, and the whole race of gods.
AEGEUS. Tell me what I shall swear to do or not to do.
MEDEA. Never yourself to expel me from your territory;
And, if my enemies want to take me away, never
Willingly, while you live, to give me up to them.
AEGEUS. I swear by Earth, and by the burning light of the Sun,
And all the gods, to keep the words you have just spoken.   690
MEDEA. I am satisfied. And if you break your oath, what then?
AEGEUS. Then may the gods do to me as to all guilty men.
MEDEA. Go now, and joy be with you. Everything is well.
I'll reach your city as quickly as I can, when I
Have carried out my purpose and achieved my wish.

> [AEGEUS *clasps her hand and hurries off.*]

CHORUS. May Hermes, protector of travellers, bring you
Safe to your home, Aegeus; may you accomplish
All that you so earnestly desire;
For your noble heart wins our goodwill.
MEDEA. O Zeus! O Justice, daughter of Zeus! O glorious Sun!   700
Now I am on the road to victory; now there's hope!
I shall see my enemies punished as they deserve.
Just where my plot was weakest, at that very point
Help has appeared in this man Aegeus; he is a haven
Where I shall find safe mooring, once I reach the walls
Of the city of Athens. Now I'll tell you all my plans:
They'll not make pleasant hearing.

> [*Medea's* NURSE *has entered; she listens in silence.*]

                              First I'll send a slave
To Jason, asking him to come to me; and then
I'll give him soft talk; tell him he has acted well,
Tell him I think this royal marriage which he has bought   710
With my betrayal is for the best and wisely planned.
But I shall beg that my children be allowed to stay.
Not that I would think of leaving sons of mine behind
On enemy soil for those who hate me to insult;
But in my plot to kill the princess they must help.
I'll send them to the palace bearing gifts, a dress
Of soft weave and a coronet of beaten gold.
If she takes and puts on this finery, both she
And all who touch her will expire in agony;
With such a deadly poison I'll anoint my gifts.   720

However, enough of that. What makes me cry with pain
Is the next thing I have to do. I will kill my sons.

No one shall take my children from me. When I have made
Jason's whole house a shambles,[19] I will leave Corinth
A murderess, flying from my darling children's blood.
Yes, I can endure guilt, however horrible;
The laughter of my enemies I will not endure.

Now let things take their course. What use is life to me?
I have no land, no home, no refuge from despair.
My folly was committed long ago, when I   730
Was ready to desert my father's house, won over
By eloquence from a Greek, whom with God's help I now
Will punish. He shall never see alive again
The sons he had from me. From his new bride he never
Shall breed a son; she by my poison, wretched girl,
Must die a hideous death. Let no one think of me
As humble or weak or passive; let them understand
I am of a different kind: dangerous to my enemies,
Loyal to my friends. To such a life glory belongs.
CHORUS. Since you have told us everything, and since I want   740
To be your friend, and also to uphold the laws
Of human life—I tell you, you must not do this!
MEDEA. No other thing is possible. You have excuse
For speaking so: you have not been treated as I have.
CHORUS. But—to kill your own children! Can you steel your heart?
MEDEA. This is the way to deal Jason the deepest wound.
CHORUS. This way will bring you too the deepest misery.
MEDEA. Let be. Until it is done words are unnecessary.
Nurse! You are the one I use for messages of trust.
Go and bring Jason here. As you're a loyal servant,   750
And a woman, breathe no word about my purposes.

[*Exit* NURSE.]

CHORUS. The people of Athens, sons of Erechtheus, have enjoyed
        their prosperity
Since ancient times. Children of blessed gods,
They grew from holy soil unscorched by invasion.[20]
Among the glories of knowledge their souls are pastured;
They walk always with grace under the sparkling sky.
There long ago, they say, was born golden-haired Harmony,
Created by the nine virgin Muses[21] of Pieria.

They say that Aphrodite dips her cup
In the clear stream of the lovely Cephisus;[22]   760

---

[19] A slaughterhouse.
[20] An irony and a significant phrase, for *Medea* was produced in 431, on the eve of the long Peloponnesian War between Athens and the confederacy headed by Sparta. The Athenians ultimately were conquered.
[21] The nine goddesses of the arts, worshiped at Pieria, on the slopes of Mount Olympus.
[22] The main river near Athens.

It is she who breathes over the land the breath
Of gentle honey-laden winds; her flowing locks
She crowns with a diadem of sweet-scented roses,
And sends the Loves to be enthroned beside Knowledge,
And with her to create excellence in every art.

Then how will such a city,
Watered by sacred rivers,
A country giving protection to its friends—
How will Athens welcome
You, the child-killer   770
Whose presence is pollution?
Contemplate the blow struck at a child,
Weigh the blood you take upon you.
Medea, by your knees,
By every pledge or appeal we beseech you,
Do not slaughter your children!

Where will you find hardness of purpose?
How will you build resolution in hand or heart
To face horror without flinching?
When the moment comes, and you look at them—   780
The moment for you to assume the role of murderess—
How will you do it?
When your sons kneel to you for pity,
Will you stain your fingers with their blood?
Your heart will melt; you will know you cannot.

> [*Enter* JASON *from the palace. Two
> maids come from the house to attend*
> MEDEA.]

JASON. You sent for me: I have come. Although you hate me, I
    Am ready to listen. You have some new request; what is it?
MEDEA. Jason, I ask you to forgive the things I said.
    You must bear with my violent temper; you and I
    Share many memories of love. I have been taking   790
    Myself to task. 'You are a fool,' I've told myself,
    'You're mad, when people try to plan things for the best,
    To be resentful, and pick quarrels with the King
    And with your husband; what he's doing will help us all.
    His wife is royal; her sons will be my sons' brothers.
    Why not throw off your anger? What is the matter, since
    The gods are making kind provision? After all
    I have two children still to care for; and I know
    We came as exiles, and our friends are few enough.'
    When I considered this, I saw my foolishness;   800
    I saw how useless anger was. So now I welcome
    What you have done; I think you are wise to gain for us
    This new alliance, and the folly was all mine.

I should have helped you in your plans, made it my pleasure
To get ready your marriage-bed, attend your bride.
But we women—I won't say we are bad by nature,
But we are what we are. You, Jason, should not copy
Our bad example, or match yourself with us, showing
Folly for folly. I give in; I was wrong just now,
I admit. But I have thought more wisely of it since.   810
Children, children! Are you indoors? Come out here.

[*The* CHILDREN *come out. Their* TU-
TOR *follows.*]

                                                  Children,
Greet your father, as I do, and put your arms round him.
Forget our quarrel, and love him as your mother does.
We have made friends; we are not angry any more.
There, children; take his hand.

[*She turns away in a sudden flood
of weeping.*]

                          Forgive me; I recalled
What pain the future hides from us.

[*After embracing* JASON *the* CHIL-
DREN *go back to* MEDEA.]

                                    Oh children! Will you
All your lives long, stretch out your hands to me like this?
Oh, my tormented heart is full of tears and terrors.
After so long, I have ended my quarrel with your father;
And now, see! I have drenched this young face with my tears.   820
CHORUS. I too feel fresh tears fill my eyes. May the course of evil
Be checked now, go no further!
JASON.   I am pleased, Medea,
That you have changed your mind; though indeed I do not blame
Your first resentment. Only naturally a woman
Is angry when her husband marries a second wife.
You have had wiser thoughts; and though it has taken time,
You have recognized the right decision. This is the act
Of a sensible woman. As for you, my boys, your father
Has taken careful thought, and, with the help of the gods,
Ensured a good life for you. Why, in time, I'm sure,   830
You with your brothers will be leading men in Corinth.
Only grow big and strong. Your father, and those gods
Who are his friends, have all the rest under control.
I want to see you, when you're strong, full-grown young men,
Tread down my enemies.

[*Again* MEDEA *breaks down and
weeps.*]

What's this? Why these floods of tears?
Why are you pale? Did you not like what I was saying?
Why do you turn away?
MEDEA.   It is nothing. I was thinking
About these children.
JASON.   I'll provide for them. Cheer up.
MEDEA. I will. It is not that I mean to doubt your word.
But women—are women; tears come naturally to us.   840
JASON. Why do you grieve so over the children?
MEDEA.   I'm their mother.
When you just now prayed for them to live long, I wondered
Whether it would be so; and grief came over me.
But I've said only part of what I had to say;
Here is the other thing. Since Creon has resolved
To send me out of Corinth, I fully recognize
That for me too this course is best. If I lived here
I should become a trouble both to you and him.
People believe I bear a grudge against you all.
So I must go. But the boys—I would like *them* to be   850
Brought up in your care. Beg Creon to let them stay.
JASON. I don't know if I can persuade him; but I'll try.
MEDEA. Then—get your wife to ask her father to let them stay.
JASON. Why, certainly; I'm pretty sure she'll win him over.
MEDEA. She will, if she's like other women. But I too
Can help in this. I'll send a present to your wife—
The loveliest things to be found anywhere on earth.
The boys shall take them.—One of you maids, go quickly, bring
The dress and golden coronet.—They will multiply
Her happiness many times, when she can call her own   860
A royal, noble husband, and these treasures, which
My father's father the Sun bequeathed to his descendants.

> [*A slave has brought a casket, which*
> MEDEA *now hands to her sons.*]

Boys, hold these gifts. Now carry them to the happy bride,
The princess royal; give them into her own hands.
Go! She will find them all that such a gift should be.
JASON. But why deprive yourself of such things, foolish woman?
Do you think a royal palace is in want of dresses?
Or gold, do you suppose? Keep them, don't give them away.
If my wife values me at all she will yield to *me*
More than to costly presents, I am sure of that.   870
MEDEA. Don't stop me. Gifts, they say, persuade even the gods;
With mortals, gold outweighs a thousand arguments.
The day is hers; from now on *her* prosperity
Will rise to new heights. She is royal and young. To buy
My sons from exile I would give life, not just gold.
Come, children, go both of you into this rich palace;
Kneel down and beg your father's new wife, and my mistress,

That you may not be banished. And above all, see
That she receives my present into her own hands.
Go quickly; be successful, and bring good news back,   880
That what your mother longs for has been granted you.

[*Exit* JASON *followed by the* CHIL-
DREN *and the* TUTOR.]

CHORUS.
    Now I have no more hope,
    No more hope that the children can live;
    They are walking to murder at this moment.
    The bride will receive the golden coronet,
    Receive her merciless destroyer;
    With her own hands she will carefully fit
    The adornment of death round her golden hair.

    She cannot resist such loveliness, such heavenly gleaming;
    She will enfold herself   890
    In the dress and the wreath of wrought gold,
    Preparing her bridal beauty
    To enter a new home—among the dead.
    So fatal is the snare she will fall into,
    So inevitable the death that awaits her;
    From its cruelty there is no escape.

    And you, unhappy Jason, ill-starred in marriage,
    You, son-in-law of kings:
    Little you know that the favour you ask
    Will seal your sons' destruction   900
    And fasten on your wife a hideous fate.
    O wretched Jason!
    So sure of destiny, and so ignorant!

    Your sorrow next I weep for, pitiable mother;
    You, for jealousy of your marriage-bed,
    Will slaughter your children;
    Since, disregarding right and loyalty,
    Your husband has abandoned you
    And lives with another wife.

[*The* TUTOR *returns from the palace with the two* CHILDREN.]

TUTOR. Mistress! These two boys are reprieved from banishment.   910
    The princess took your gifts from them with her own hand,
    And was delighted. They have no enemies in the palace.

[MEDEA *is silent.*]

Well, bless my soul!
Isn't that good news? Why do you stand there thunderstruck?
MEDEA [*to herself*]. How cruel, how cruel!
TUTOR.   That's out of tune with the news I brought.
MEDEA. How cruel life is!
TUTOR.   Have I, without knowing it,
Told something dreadful, then? I thought my news was good.
MEDEA. Your news is what it is. I am not blaming you.
TUTOR. Then why stand staring at the ground, with streaming eyes?   920
MEDEA. Strong reason forces me to weep, old friend. The gods,
And my own evil-hearted plots, have led to this.
TUTOR. Take heart, mistress; in time your sons will bring you home.
MEDEA. Before then, I have others to send home.—Oh, gods!

[*She weeps.*]

TUTOR. You're not the only mother parted from her sons.
We are all mortal; you must not bear grief so hard.
MEDEA. Yes, friend. I'll follow your advice. Now go indoors
And get things ready for them, as on other days.

[*Exit* TUTOR. *The* CHILDREN *come
to* MEDEA.]

O children, children! You have a city, and a home;
And when we have parted, there you both will stay for ever,   930
You motherless, I miserable. And I must go
To exile in another land, before I have had
My joy of you, before I have seen you growing up,
Becoming prosperous. I shall never see your brides,
Adorn your bridal beds, and hold the torches high.
My misery is my own heart, which will not relent.
All was for nothing, then—these years of rearing you,
My care, my aching weariness, and the wild pains
When you were born. Oh, yes, I once built many hopes
On you; imagined, pitifully, that you would care   940
For my old age, and would yourselves wrap my dead body
For burial. How people would envy me my sons!
That sweet, sad thought has faded now. Parted from you,
My life will be all pain and anguish. You will not
Look at your mother any more with these dear eyes.
You will have moved into a different sphere of life.

Dear sons, why are you staring at me so? You smile
At me—your last smile: why?

[*She weeps. The* CHILDREN *go from
her a little, and she turns to the*
CHORUS.]

                       Oh, what am I to do?
Women, my courage is all gone. Their young, bright faces—
I can't do it. I'll think no more of it. I'll take them   950
Away from Corinth. Why should I hurt *them,* to make
Their father suffer, when I shall suffer twice as much
Myself? I won't do it. I won't think of it again.

What is the matter with me? Are my enemies
To laugh at me? Am I to let them off scot free?
I must steel myself to it. What a coward I am,
Even tempting my own resolution with soft talk.
Boys, go indoors.

                      [The CHILDREN *go to the door, but
                      stay there watching her.]*

If there is any here who finds it
Not lawful to be present at my sacrifice,
Let him see to it. My hand shall not weaken.   960

Oh, my heart, don't, don't do it! Oh, miserable heart,
Let them be! Spare your children! We'll all live together
Safely in Athens; and they will make you happy. . . . No!
No! No! By all the fiends of hate in hell's depths, no!
I'll not leave sons of mine to be the victims of
My enemies' rage. In any case there is no escape,
The thing's done now. Yes, now—the golden coronet
Is on her head, the royal bride is in her dress,
Dying, I know it. So, since I have a sad road
To travel, and send these boys on a still sadder road,   970
I'll speak to them. Come, children; give me your hand, dear son;
Yours too. Now we must say goodbye. Oh, darling hand,
And darling mouth; your noble, childlike face and body!
Dear sons, my blessing on you both—but there, not here!
All blessing here your father has destroyed. How sweet
To hold you! And children's skin is soft, and their breath pure.
Go! Go away! I can't look at you any longer;
My pain is more than I can bear.

                      [The CHILDREN *go indoors.]*

                   I understand
The horror of what I am going to do; but anger,
The spring of all life's horror, masters my resolve.   980

                      *[*MEDEA *goes to stand looking to-
                      wards the palace.]*

CHORUS.
    I have often engaged in arguments,
    And become more subtle, and perhaps more heated,

Than is suitable for women;
Though in fact women too have intelligence,
Which forms part of our nature and instructs us—
Not all of us, I admit; but a certain few
You might perhaps find, in a large number of women—
A few not incapable of reflection;

And this is my opinion: those men or women
Who never had children of their own at all   990
Enjoy the advantage in good fortune
Over those who are parents. Childless people
Have no means of knowing whether children are
A blessing or a burden; but being without them
They live exempt from many troubles.

While those who have growing up in their homes
The sweet gift of children I see always
Burdened and worn with incessant worry,
First, how to rear them in health and safety,
And bequeath them, in time, enough to live on;   1000
And then this further anxiety:
They can never know whether all their toil
Is spent for worthy or worthless children.

And beyond the common ills that attend
All human life there is one still worse:
Suppose at last they are pretty well off,
Their children have grown up, and, what's more,
Are kind and honest: then what happens?
A throw of chance—and there goes Death
Bearing off your child into the unknown.   1010

Then why should mortals thank the gods,
Who add to their load, already grievous,
This one more grief, for their children's sake,
Most grievous of all?
MEDEA. Friends, I have long been waiting for a message from the
    palace.
  What is to happen next? I see a slave of Jason's
  Coming, gasping for breath. He must bring fearful news.

[*Enter a* MESSENGER.]

MESSENGER. Medea! Get away, escape! Oh, what a thing to do!
  What an unholy, horrible thing! Take ship, or chariot,
  Any means you can, but escape!
MEDEA.   Why should I escape?   1020
MESSENGER. She's dead—the princess, and her father Creon too,
  They're both dead, by your poisons.
MEDEA.   Your news is excellent.
  I count you from today my friend and benefactor.

MESSENGER. What? Are you sane, or raving mad? When you've com-
    mitted
  This hideous crime against the royal house, you're glad
  At hearing of it? Do you not tremble at such things?
MEDEA. I could make suitable reply to that, my friend.
  But take your time now; tell me, how did they die? You'll give
  Me double pleasure if their death was horrible.
MESSENGER. When your two little boys came hand in hand, and en-
    tered   1030
  The palace with their father, where the wedding was,
  We servants were delighted. We had all felt sorry
  To hear how you'd been treated; and now the word went round
  From one to another, that you and Jason had made it up.
  So we were glad to see the boys; one kissed their hand,
  Another their fair hair. Myself, I was so pleased,
  I followed with them to the princess's room. Our mistress—
  The one we now call mistress in your place—before
  She saw your pair of boys coming, had eyes only
  For Jason; but seeing them she dropped her eyes, and turned   1040
  Her lovely cheek away, upset that they should come
  Into her room. Your husband then began to soothe
  Her sulkiness, her girlish temper. 'You must not,'
  He said, 'be unfriendly to our friends. Turn your head round,
  And give up feeling angry. Those your husband loves
  You must love too. Now take these gifts,' he said, 'and ask
  Your father to revoke their exile for my sake.'
  So, when she saw those lovely things, she was won over,
  And agreed to all that Jason asked. At once, before
  He and your sons were well out of the house, she took   1050
  The embroidered gown and put it round her. Then she placed
  Over her curls the golden coronet, and began
  To arrange her hair in a bright mirror, smiling at
  Her lifeless form reflected there. Then she stood up,
  And to and fro stepped daintily about the room
  On white bare feet, and many times she would twist back
  To see how the dress fell in clear folds to the heel.

  Then suddenly we saw a frightening thing. She changed
  Colour; she staggered sideways, shook in every limb.
  She was just able to collapse on to a chair,   1060
  Or she would have fallen flat. Then one of her attendants,
  An old woman, thinking that perhaps the anger of Pan[23]
  Or some other god had struck her, chanted the cry of worship.
  But then she saw, oozing from the girl's lips, white froth;
  The pupils of her eyes were twisted out of sight;
  The blood was drained from all her skin. The old woman knew
  Her mistake, and changed her chant to a despairing howl.

---

[23] The old woman at first suspects some attack of unreasonable terror such as was associated with the nature-god Pan (from whose name the word "panic" derives).

One maid ran off quickly to fetch the King, another
To look for Jason and tell him what was happening
To his young bride; the whole palace was filled with a clatter
Of people running here and there. 1070
                     All this took place
In a few moments, perhaps while a fast runner might run
A hundred yards; and she lay speechless, with eyes closed.
Then she came to, poor girl, and gave a frightful scream,
As two torments made war on her together: first
The golden coronet round her head discharged a stream
Of unnatural devouring fire: while the fine dress
Your children gave her—poor miserable girl!—the stuff
Was eating her clear flesh. She leapt up from her chair,
On fire, and ran, shaking her head and her long hair 1080
This way and that, trying to shake off the coronet.
The ring of gold was fitted close and would not move;
The more she shook her head the fiercer the flame burned.
At last, exhausted by agony, she fell to the ground;
Save to her father, she was unrecognizable.
Her eyes, her face, were one grotesque disfigurement;
Down from her head dripped blood mingled with flame; her
    flesh,
Attacked by the invisible fangs of poison, melted
From the bare bone, like gum-drops from a pine-tree's bark—
A ghastly sight. Not one among us dared to touch 1090
Her body. What we'd seen was lesson enough for us.

But suddenly her father came into the room.
He did not understand, poor man, what kind of death
Had struck his child. He threw himself down at her side,
And sobbed aloud, and kissed her, and took her in his arms,
And cried, 'Poor darling child, what god destroyed your life
So cruelly? Who robs me of my only child,
Old as I am, and near my grave? Oh, let me die
With you, my daughter!' Soon he ceased his tears and cries,
And tried to lift his aged body upright; and then, 1100
As ivy sticks to laurel-branches, so he stuck
Fast to the dress. A ghastly wrestling then began;
He struggled to raise up his knee, she tugged him down.
If he used force, he tore the old flesh off his bones.
At length the King gave up his pitiful attempts;
Weakened with pain, he yielded, and gasped out his life.
Now, joined in death, daughter and father—such a sight
As tears were made for—they lie there.
                         To you, Medea,
I have no more to say. You will yourself know best
How to evade reprisal. As for human life, 1110
It is a shadow, as I have long believed. And this
I say without hesitation: those whom most would call
Intelligent, the propounders of wise theories—

Their folly is of all men's the most culpable.
Happiness is a thing no man possesses. Fortune
May come now to one man, now to another, as
Prosperity increases; happiness never.

[*Exit* MESSENGER.]

CHORUS. Today we see the will of Heaven, blow after blow,
    Bring down on Jason justice and calamity.
MEDEA. Friends, now my course is clear: as quickly as possible   1120
    To kill the children and then fly from Corinth; not
    Delay and so consign them to another hand
    To murder with a better will. For they must die,
    In any case; and since they must, then I who gave
    Them birth will kill them. Arm yourself, my heart: the thing
    That you must do is fearful, yet inevitable.
    Why wait, then? My accursed hand, come, take the sword;
    Take it, and forward to your frontier of despair.
    No cowardice, no tender memories; forget
    That you once loved them, that of your body they were born.   1130
    For one short day forget your children; afterwards
    Weep: though you kill them, they were your beloved sons.
    Life has been cruel to me.

[MEDEA *goes into the house.*]

CHORUS. Earth, awake! Bright arrows of the Sun,
    Look! Look down on the accursed woman
    Before she lifts up a murderous hand
    To pollute it with her children's blood!
    For they are of your own golden race;
    And for mortals to spill blood that grew
    In the veins of gods is a fearful thing.   1140
    Heaven-born brightness, hold her, stop her,
    Purge the palace of her, this pitiable
    Bloody-handed fiend of vengeance!

    All your care for them lost! Your love
    For the babes you bore, all wasted, wasted!
    Why did you come from the blue Symplegades
    That hold the gate of the barbarous sea?
    Why must this rage devour your heart
    To spend itself in slaughter of children?
    Where kindred blood pollutes the ground   1150
    A curse hangs over human lives;
    And murder measures the doom that falls
    By Heaven's law on the guilty house.

[*A child's scream is heard from inside the house.*]

CHORUS. Do you hear? The children are calling for help.
   O cursed, miserable woman!
CHILDREN'S VOICES. Help, help! Mother, let me go!
   Mother, don't kill us!
CHORUS. Shall we go in?
   I am sure we ought to save the children's lives.
CHILDREN'S VOICES. Help, help, for the gods' sake! She is killing us!   1160
   We can't escape from her sword!
CHORUS. O miserable mother, to destroy your own increase,
   Murder the babes of your body!
   Stone and iron you are, as you resolved to be.

   There was but one in time past,
   One woman that I have heard of,
   Raised hand against her own children.
   It was Ino,[24] sent out of her mind by a god,
   When Hera, the wife of Zeus,
   Drove her from her home to wander over the world.   1170
   In her misery she plunged into the sea
   Being defiled by the murder of her children;
   From the steep cliff's edge she stretched out her foot,
   And so ended,
   Joined in death with her two sons.

   What can be strange or terrible after this?
   O bed of women, full of passion and pain,
   What wickedness, what sorrow you have caused on the earth!

   [*Enter* JASON, *running and breathless.*]

JASON. You women standing round the door there! Is Medea
   Still in the house?—vile murderess!—or has she gone   1180
   And escaped? I swear she must either hide in the deep earth
   Or soar on wings into the sky's abyss, to escape
   My vengeance for the royal house.—She has killed the King
   And the princess! Does she expect to go unpunished?

   Well, I am less concerned with her than with the children.
   Those who have suffered at her hands will make her suffer;
   I've come to save my sons, before Creon's family
   Murder them in revenge for this unspeakable
   Crime of their mother's.
CHORUS.   Jason, you have yet to learn
   How great your trouble is; or you would not have spoken so.   1190
JASON. What trouble? Is Medea trying to kill me too?
CHORUS. Your sons are dead. Their mother has killed both your sons.

---

[24] Ino had helped to bring up the god Dionysus, who was born of Zeus and Semele. Hera,
Zeus' consort, drove Ino to madness in revenge for Zeus' begetting of Dionysus.

JASON. What? Killed my sons? That word kills me.
CHORUS.   They are both dead.
JASON. Where are they? Did she kill them out here, or indoors?
CHORUS. Open that door, and see them lying in their blood.
JASON. Slaves, there! Unbar the doors! Open, and let me see
    Two horrors: my dead sons, and the woman I will kill.

> [JASON *batters at the doors.* MEDEA
> *appears above the roof, sitting in
> a chariot drawn by dragons, with
> the bodies of the two children be-
> side her.*]

MEDEA. Jason! Why are you battering at these doors, seeking
    The dead children and me who killed them? Stop! Be quiet.
    If you have any business with me, say what you wish.   1200
    Touch us you cannot, in this chariot which the Sun
    Has sent to save us from the hands of enemies.
JASON. You abomination! Of all women most detested
    By every god, by me, by the whole human race!
    You could endure—a mother!—to lift sword against
    Your own little ones; to leave me childless, my life wrecked.
    After such murder do you outface both Sun and Earth—
    Guilty of gross pollution? May the gods blast your life!
    I am sane now; but I was mad before, when I
    Brought you from your palace in a land of savages   1210
    Into a Greek home—you, a living curse, already
    A traitor both to your father and your native land.
    The vengeance due for your sins the gods have cast on me.
    You had already murdered your brother at his own hearth
    When first you stepped on board my lovely Argo's hull.
    That was your beginning. Then you became my wife, and bore
    My children; now, out of mere sexual jealousy,
    You murder them! In all Hellas there is not one woman
    Who could have done it; yet in preference to them
    I married you, chose hatred and murder for my wife—   1220
    No woman, but a tiger; a Tuscan Scylla[25]—but more savage.
    Ah, what's the use? If I cursed you all day, no remorse
    Would touch you, for your heart's proof against feeling. Go!
    Out of my sight, polluted fiend, child-murderer!
    Leave me to mourn over my destiny: I have lost
    My young bride; I have lost the two sons I begot
    And brought up; I shall never see them alive again.
MEDEA. I would if necessary have answered at full length
    Everything you have said; but Zeus the father of all
    Knows well what service I once rendered you, and how   1230
    You have repaid me. You were mistaken if you thought
    You could dishonour my bed and live a pleasant life

---

[25] A monster who attacked mariners sailing between Italy and Sicily through what is now
called the strait of Messina.

And laugh at me. The princess was wrong too, and so
Was Creon, when he took you for his son-in-law
And thought he could exile me with impunity.
So now, am I a tiger, Scylla?—Hurl at me
What names you please! I've reached your heart; and that is right.
JASON. You suffer too; my loss is yours no less.
MEDEA.   It is true;
But my pain's a fair price, to take away your smile.
JASON. O children, what a wicked mother Fate gave you!   1240
MEDEA. O sons, your father's treachery cost you your lives.
JASON. It was not my hand that killed my sons.
MEDEA.   No, not your hand;
But your insult to me, and your new-wedded wife.
JASON. You thought *that* reason enough to murder them, that I
No longer slept with you?
MEDEA.   And is that injury
A slight one, do you imagine, to a woman?
JASON.   Yes,
To a modest woman; but to you—the whole world lost.
MEDEA. I can stab too: your sons are dead!
JASON.   Dead? No! They live
To haunt your life with vengeance.
MEDEA.   Who began this feud?
The gods know.
JASON.   Yes—they know the vileness of your heart.   1250
MEDEA. Loathe on! Your bitter voice—how I abhor the sound!
JASON. As I loathe yours. Let us make terms and part at once.
MEDEA. Most willingly. What terms? What do you bid me do?
JASON. Give me my sons for burial and mourning rites.
MEDEA. Oh, no! I will myself convey them to the temple
Of Hera[26] Acraea; there in the holy precinct I
Will bury them with my own hand, to ensure that none
Of my enemies shall violate or insult their graves.
And I will ordain an annual feast and sacrifice
To be solemnized for ever by the people of Corinth,   1260
To expiate this impious murder. I myself
Will go to Athens, city of Erechtheus,[27] to make my home
With Aegeus son of Pandion. You, as you deserve,
Shall die an unheroic death,[28] your head shattered
By a timber from the Argo's hull. Thus wretchedly
Your fate shall end the story of your love for me.
JASON. The curse of children's blood be on you!
Avenging Justice blast your being!
MEDEA. What god will hear your imprecation,
Oath-breaker, guest-deceiver, liar?   1270

[26] The goddess was regarded as defender of wives and marriage.
[27] Legendary Athenian king.
[28] One version of Jason's death is that he died in this way, at Corinth, struck by a falling
beam as he sat near his old ship, the *Argo*.

JASON. Unclean, abhorrent child-destroyer!
MEDEA. Go home: your wife waits to be buried.
JASON. I go—a father once; now childless.
MEDEA. You grieve too soon. Old age is coming.
JASON. Children, how dear you were!
MEDEA. To their mother; not to you.
JASON. Dear—and you murdered them?
MEDEA. Yes, Jason, to break your heart.
JASON. I long to fold them in my arms;
  To kiss their lips would comfort me.   1280
MEDEA. *Now* you have loving words, now kisses for them:
  Then you disowned them, sent them into exile.
JASON. For God's sake, let me touch their gentle flesh.
MEDEA. You shall not. It is waste of breath to ask.
JASON.
      Zeus, do you hear how I am mocked,
      Rejected, by this savage beast
      Polluted with her children's blood?

      But now, as time and strength permit,
      I will lament this grievous day,
      And call the gods to witness, how   1290
      You killed my sons, and now refuse
      To let me touch or bury them.
      Would God I had not bred them,
      Or ever lived to see
      Them dead, you their destroyer!

                                    [*During this speech the chariot has
                                    moved out of sight.*]

CHORUS. Many are the Fates which Zeus in Olympus dispenses;
  Many matters the gods bring to surprising ends.
  The things we thought would happen do not happen;
  The unexpected God makes possible;
  And such is the conclusion of this story.[29]   1300

─────────

[29] The last five lines are a formulaic ending, used also at the conclusion of several other plays by Euripides, including *Alcestis*, *Andromache*, *Helen*, and *The Bacchae*.

THE BACCHAE

Translated by William Arrowsmith

CHARACTERS

DIONYSUS, *also called Bromius, Evius,*
  and Bacchus
CHORUS OF ASIAN BACCHAE, *followers*
  of Dionysus
TEIRESIAS
CADMUS

PENTHEUS
ATTENDANT
FIRST MESSENGER
SECOND MESSENGER
AGAVE
CORYPHAEUS, *chorus leader*

SCENE

Before the royal palace at Thebes. On the left is the way to Cithaeron; on the right, to the city. In the center of the orchestra stands, still smoking, the vine-covered tomb of Semele, mother of DIONYSUS.[1]

Enter DIONYSUS. *He is of soft, even effeminate, appearance. His face is beardless; he is dressed in a fawn-skin and carries a thyrsus (i.e., a stalk of fennel tipped with ivy leaves).*[2] *On his head he wears a wreath of ivy, and his long blond curls ripple down over his shoulders. Throughout the play he wears a smiling mask.*

DIONYSUS.
  I am Dionysus, the son of Zeus,
come back to Thebes, this land where I was born.
My mother was Cadmus' daughter, Semele by name,
midwived by fire, delivered by the lightning's
blast.
          And here I stand, a god incognito,
disguised as man, beside the stream of Dirce
and the waters of Ismenus. There before the palace
I see my lightning-married mother's grave,
and there upon the ruins of her shattered house
the living fire of Zeus still smolders on   10
in deathless witness of Hera's violence and rage
against my mother. But Cadmus wins my praise:
he has made this tomb a shrine, sacred to my mother.

[1] Thebes, where the tragedies of Oedipus and Antigone are enacted in a time later than that of *The Bacchae*, was a city about forty miles northwest of Athens. Cithaeron was a mountain range nearby. Semele, the mortal mother of Dionysus by Zeus the king of the gods, was incited by Zeus' jealous queen, Hera, to wish that he would appear to Semele in all his divine glory; the ensuing lightning struck her dead. Zeus saved Dionysus, however, supposedly by placing the embryonic infant inside his thigh to conceal him from Hera. (The "orchestra" in the ancient Greek theater was the circular arena between the stage and the spectators.)

[2] The thyrsus (tipped by a pine cone surrounded by ivy) was a distinctive emblem of Dionysus' worshipers.

It was I who screened her grave with the green
of the clustering vine.
                              Far behind me lie
those golden-rivered lands, Lydia and Phrygia,
where my journeying began. Overland I went,
across the steppes of Persia where the sun strikes hotly
down, through Bactrian fastness[3] and the grim waste
of Media. Thence to rich Arabia I came;   20
and so, along all Asia's swarming littoral[4]
of towered cities where Greeks and foreign nations,
mingling, live, my progress made. There
I taught my dances to the feet of living men,
establishing my mysteries and rites
that I might be revealed on earth for what I am:
a god.
            And thence to Thebes.
                                    This city, first
in Hellas,[5] now shrills and echoes to my women's cries,
their ecstasy of joy. Here in Thebes
I bound the fawn-skin to the women's flesh and armed   30
their hands with shafts of ivy. For I have come
to refute that slander spoken by my mother's sisters—
those who least had right to slander her.
They said that Dionysus was no son of Zeus,
but Semele had slept beside a man in love
and fathered off her shame on Zeus—a fraud, they sneered,
contrived by Cadmus to protect his daughter's name.
They said she lied, and Zeus in anger at that lie
blasted her with lightning.
                              Because of that offense
I have stung them with frenzy, hounded them from home   40
up to the mountains where they wander, crazed of mind,
and compelled to wear my orgies' livery.
Every woman in Thebes—but the women only—
I drove from home, mad. There they sit,
rich and poor alike, even the daughters of Cadmus,
beneath the silver firs on the roofless rocks.
Like it or not, this city must learn its lesson:
it lacks initiation in my mysteries;
that I shall vindicate my mother Semele
and stand revealed to mortal eyes as the god   50
she bore to Zeus.
                      Cadmus the king has abdicated,
leaving his throne and power to his grandson Pentheus;
who now revolts against divinity, in *me;*

---

[3] Stronghold, in Bactria, an eastern province of the Persian empire. Dionysus had grown
up in Asia, from which he has just traveled to Greece. Lydia and Phrygia were regions of Asia
Minor (in modern Turkey) near the ancient site of Troy. Media was for the Greeks roughly
synonymous with Persia.
[4] Coastal area.   [5] Greece.

thrusts *me* from his offerings; forgets *my* name
in his prayers. Therefore I shall *prove* to him
and every man in Thebes that I am god
indeed. And when my worship is established here,
and all is well, then I shall go my way
and be revealed to other men in other lands.
But if the men of Thebes attempt to force 60
my Bacchae[6] from the mountainside by threat of arms,
I shall marshal my Maenads and take the field.
To these ends I have laid my deity aside
and go disguised as man.

                    [*He wheels and calls offstage.*]
               On, my women,
women who worship me, women whom I led
out of Asia where Tmolus[7] heaves its rampart
over Lydia!
          On, comrades of my progress here!
Come, and with your native Phrygian drum—
Rhea's[8] drum and mine—pound at the palace doors
of Pentheus! Let the city of Thebes behold you, 70
while I return among Cithaeron's forest glens
where my Bacchae wait and join their whirling dances.[9]

                   [*Exit* DIONYSUS *as the* CHORUS OF
                   ASIAN BACCHAE *comes dancing in
                   from the right. They are dressed in
                   fawn-skins, crowned with ivy, and
                   carry thyrsi, timbrels,[10] and flutes.*]

CHORUS.
Out of the land of Asia,
down from holy Tmolus,
speeding the service of god,
for Bromius[11] we come!
Hard are the labors of god;
hard, but his service is sweet.
Sweet to serve, sweet to cry:
          Bacchus!   *Evohé!*[12] 80
—You on the streets!
        —You on the roads!
               —Make way!

---

[6] The Bacchae, also called Bacchantes and Maenads, were frenzied female worshipers of Dionysus (for whom Bacchus is another name).

[7] A mountain range.

[8] Rhea, identified with the Asiatic earth-goddess Cybele, the Great Mother or "mother of the gods," was wife of Cronus and Zeus' mother.

[9] The rapidly spinning dance movement characteristic of Dionysus' worshipers was wholly unlike the choric dances generally performed in Greek dramas.

[10] Tambourines. Percussion instruments were also extremely unusual in Greek dramatic choruses.

[11] This alternative name for Dionysus means "thunderous."

[12] The cry acclaiming Evius, still another name for Dionysus.

—Let every mouth be hushed. Let no ill-omened words
   profane your tongues.
                                —Make way! Fall back!
                                              —Hush.
—For now I raise the old, old hymn to Dionysus.

—Blessèd, blessèd are those who know the mysteries of god.
—Blessèd is he who hallows his life in the worship of god,
      he whom the spirit of god possesseth, who is one
      with those who belong to the holy body of god.
—Blessèd are the dancers and those who are purified,
      who dance on the hill in the holy dance of god.   90
—Blessèd are they who keep the rite of Cybele the Mother.
—Blessèd are the thyrsus-bearers, those who wield in their hands
      the holy wand of god.
—Blessèd are those who wear the crown of the ivy of god.
—Blessèd, blessèd are they: Dionysus is their god!

—On, Bacchae, on, you Bacchae,
   bear your god in triumph home!
   Bear on the god, son of god,
   escort your Dionysus home!
   Bear him down from Phrygian hill,   100
   attend him through the streets of Hellas!

—So his mother bore him once
   in labor bitter; lightning-struck,
   forced by fire that flared from Zeus,
   consumed, she died, untimely torn,
   in childbed dead by blow of light!
   Of light the son was born!

—Zeus it was who saved his son;
   with speed outrunning mortal eye,
   bore him to a private place,   110
   bound the boy with clasps of gold;
   in his thigh as in a womb,
   concealed his son from Hera's eyes.

—And when the weaving Fates fulfilled the time,
   the bull-horned god was born of Zeus. In joy
   he crowned his son, set serpents on his head—
   wherefrom, in piety, descends to us
   the Maenad's writhing crown, her *chevelure*[13] of snakes.

—O Thebes, nurse of Semele,
   crown your hair with ivy!   120
   Grow green with bryony![14]

---

[13] Head of hair; tresses.   [14] Vines.

Redden with berries! O city,
with boughs of oak and fir,
come dance the dance of god!
Fringe your skins of dappled fawn
with tufts of twisted wool!
Handle with holy care
the violent wand of god!
And let the dance begin!
He is Bromius who runs   130
to the mountain!
        to the mountain!
where the throng of women waits,
driven from shuttle and loom,
possessed by Dionysus!

—And I praise the holies of Crete,
the caves of the dancing Curetes,[15]
there where Zeus was born,
where helmed in triple tier
around the primal drum
the Corybantes[16] danced. They,   140
they were the first of all
whose whirling feet kept time
to the strict beat of the taut hide
and the squeal of the wailing flute.
Then from them to Rhea's hands
the holy drum was handed down;
but, stolen by the raving Satyrs,[17]
fell at last to me and now
accompanies the dance
which every other year   150
celebrates your name:
   Dionysus!

—He is sweet upon the mountains. He drops to the earth
   from the running packs.
He wears the holy fawn-skin. He hunts the wild goat
   and kills it.
He delights in the raw flesh.
He runs to the mountains of Phrygia, to the mountains
   of Lydia he runs!
He is Bromius who leads us! *Evohé!*   160

—With milk the earth flows! It flows with wine!
   It runs with the nectar of bees!

[15] The people, inhabitants of Crete, whose loud singing and dancing drowned out the cries of the infant Zeus and thus concealed him from his cannibalistic father Cronus.

[16] Frenzied, armor-clad male worshipers and priests of Cybele; sometimes identified with the Curetes.

[17] Forest creatures, half man, half goat, in the service of Dionysus and the nature-god Pan.

—Like frankincense in its fragrance
  is the blaze of the torch he bears.
  Flames float out from his trailing wand
    as he runs, as he dances,
    kindling the stragglers,
    spurring with cries,
  and his long curls stream to the wind!

—And he cries, as they cry, *Evohé!*—   170
    On, Bacchae!
    On, Bacchae!
  Follow, glory of golden Tmolus,
    hymning god
    with a rumble of drums,
  with a cry, *Evohé!* to the Evian god,
  with a cry of Phrygian cries,
  when the holy flute like honey plays
  the sacred song of those who go
  to the mountain!
                    to the mountain!   180

—Then, in ecstasy, like a colt by its grazing mother,
  the Bacchante runs with flying feet, she leaps!
                         [*The* CHORUS *remains grouped in
                         two semicircles about the orchestra
                         as* TEIRESIAS[18] *makes his entrance.
                         He is incongruously dressed in the
                         bacchant's*[19] *fawn-skin and is
                         crowned with ivy. Old and blind, he
                         uses his thyrsus to tap his way.*]

TEIRESIAS.
  Ho there, who keeps the gates?
                         Summon Cadmus—
  Cadmus, Agenor's son, the stranger from Sidon
  who built the towers of our Thebes.[20]
                         Go, someone.
  Say Teiresias wants him. He will know what errand
  brings me, that agreement, age with age, we made
  to deck our wands, to dress in skins of fawn
  and crown our heads with ivy.
                         [*Enter* CADMUS *from the palace.
                         Dressed in Dionysiac costume and
                         bent almost double with age, he is an
                         incongruous and pathetic figure.*]

---

[18] A Theban prophet, in the service of the prophet-god Apollo; he appears also in *Oedipus the King* and *Antigone*. (Or his name may be a generic term for a prophet.)
[19] The male term equivalent to female *bacchante*.
[20] An emigrant from Sidon, in Phoenicia (the region north of Palestine at the far-eastern end of the Mediterranean Sea), Cadmus had founded Thebes and populated it with warriors who grew from the planted teeth of a dragon he had killed.

CADMUS.

My old friend,
I knew it must be you when I heard your summons.   190
For there's a wisdom in his voice that makes
the man of wisdom known.

But here I am,
dressed in the costume of the god, prepared to go.
Insofar as we are able, Teiresias, we must
do honor to this god, for he was born
my daughter's son, who has been revealed to men,
the god, Dionysus.

Where shall we go, where
shall we tread the dance, tossing our white heads
in the dances of god?

Expound to me, Teiresias.
For in such matters you are wise.

Surely   200
I could dance night and day, untiringly
beating the earth with my thyrsus! And how sweet it is
to forget my old age.

TEIRESIAS.

It is the same with me.
I too feel young, young enough to dance.

CADMUS.

Good. Shall we take our chariots to the mountain?

TEIRESIAS.

Walking would be better. It shows more honor
to the god.

CADMUS.

So be it. I shall lead, my old age
conducting yours.

TEIRESIAS.

The god will guide us there
with no effort on our part.

CADMUS.

Are we the only men
who will dance for Bacchus?

TEIRESIAS.

They are all blind.   210
Only we can see.

CADMUS.

But we delay too long.
Here, take my arm.

TEIRESIAS.

Link my hand in yours.

CADMUS.

I am a man, nothing more. I do not scoff
at heaven.

TEIRESIAS.

We do not trifle with divinity.

No, we are the heirs of customs and traditions
hallowed by age and handed down to us
by our fathers. No quibbling logic can topple *them*,
whatever subtleties this clever age invents.
People may say: "Aren't you ashamed? At your age,
going dancing, wreathing your head with ivy?"   220
Well, I am *not* ashamed. Did the god declare
that just the young or just the old should dance?
No, he desires his honor from all mankind.
He wants no one excluded from his worship.

CADMUS.

Because you cannot see, Teiresias, let me be
interpreter for you this once. Here comes
the man to whom I left my throne, Echion's son,
Pentheus, hastening toward the palace. He seems
excited and disturbed. Yes, listen to him.

> [*Enter* PENTHEUS *from the right.
> He is a young man of athletic build,
> dressed in traditional Greek dress;
> like* DIONYSUS, *he is beardless. He
> enters excitedly, talking to the at-
> tendants who accompany him.*]

PENTHEUS.

I happened to be away, out of the city,   230
but reports reached me of some strange mischief here,
stories of our women leaving home to frisk
in mock ecstasies among the thickets on the mountain,
dancing in honor of the latest divinity,
a certain Dionysus, whoever he may be!
In their midst stand bowls brimming with wine.
And then, one by one, the women wander off
to hidden nooks where they serve the lusts of men.
Priestesses of Bacchus they claim they are,
but it's really Aphrodite[21] they adore.   240
I have captured some of them; my jailers
have locked them away in the safety of our prison.
Those who run at large shall be hunted down
out of the mountains like the animals they are—
yes, my own mother Agave, and Ino
and Autonoë, the mother of Actaeon.
In no time at all I shall have them trapped
in iron nets and stop this obscene disorder.
    I am also told a foreigner has come to Thebes
from Lydia, one of those charlatan magicians,   250
with long yellow curls smelling of perfumes,
with flushed cheeks and the spells of Aphrodite
in his eyes. His days and nights he spends
with women and girls, dangling before them the joys

---

[21] Goddess of sex and love.

of initiation in his mysteries.
But let me bring him underneath that roof
and I'll stop his pounding with his wand and tossing
his head. By god, I'll have his head cut off!
And *this* is the man who claims that Dionysus
is a god and was sewn into the thigh of Zeus,   260
when, in point of fact, that same blast of lightning
consumed him and his mother both for her lie
that she had lain with Zeus in love. Whoever
this stranger is, aren't such impostures,
such unruliness, worthy of hanging?

> [*For the first time he sees* TEIRESIAS
> *and* CADMUS *in their Dionysiac cos-*
> *tumes.*]
>   *What!*

But this is incredible! Teiresias the seer
tricked out in a dappled fawn-skin!

>   And *you,*

you, my own grandfather, playing at the bacchant
with a wand!

>   Sir, I shrink to see your old age

so foolish. Shake that ivy off, grandfather!   270
Now drop that wand. Drop it, I say.

> [*He wheels on* TEIRESIAS.]
>   Aha,

I see: this is *your* doing, Teiresias.
Yes, you want still another god revealed to men
so you can pocket the profits from burnt offerings
and bird-watching.[22] By heaven, only your age
restrains me now from sending you to prison
with those Bacchic women for importing here to Thebes
these filthy mysteries. When once you see
the glint of wine shining at the feasts of women,
then you may be sure the festival is rotten.   280

CORYPHAEUS.[23]

What blasphemy! Stranger, have you no respect
for heaven? For Cadmus who sowed the dragon teeth?
Will the son of Echion disgrace his house?

TEIRESIAS.

Give a wise man an honest brief to plead
and his eloquence is no remarkable achievement.
But you are glib; your phrases come rolling out
smoothly on the tongue, as though your words were wise
instead of foolish. The man whose glibness flows
from his conceit of speech declares the thing he is:
a worthless and a stupid citizen.

>   I tell you,   290

---

[22] Observing the flight of birds was one way in which prophets foretold the future.
[23] Not a proper name but a noun meaning "Chorus Leader."

this god whom you ridicule shall someday have
enormous power and prestige throughout Hellas.
Mankind, young man, possesses two supreme blessings.
First of these is the goddess Demeter,[24] or Earth—
whichever name you choose to call her by.
It was she who gave to man his nourishment of grain.
But after her there came the son of Semele,
who matched her present by inventing liquid wine
as his gift to man. For filled with that good gift,
suffering mankind forgets its grief; from it   300
comes sleep; with it oblivion of the troubles
of the day. There is no other medicine
for misery. And when we pour libations[25]
to the gods, we pour the god of wine himself
that through his intercession man may win
the favor of heaven.
                              You sneer, do you, at that story
that Dionysus was sewed into the thigh of Zeus?
Let me teach you what that really means. When Zeus
rescued from the thunderbolt his infant son,
he brought him to Olympus.[26] Hera, however,   310
plotted at heart to hurl the child from heaven.
Like the god he is, Zeus countered her. Breaking off
a tiny fragment of that ether which surrounds the world,
he molded from it a dummy Dionysus.
This he *showed* to Hera, but with time men garbled
the word and said that Dionysus had been *sewed*
into the thigh of Zeus. This was their story,
whereas, in fact, Zeus *showed* the dummy to Hera
and gave it as a hostage for his son.
                                      Moreover,
this is a god of prophecy. His worshippers,   320
like madmen, are endowed with mantic[27] powers.
For when the god enters the body of a man
he fills him with the breath of prophecy.
                                      Besides,
he has usurped even the functions of warlike Ares.[28]
Thus, at times, you see an army mustered under arms
stricken with panic before it lifts a spear.
This panic comes from Dionysus.
                                      Someday
you shall even see him bounding with his torches
among the crags at Delphi,[29] leaping the pastures
that stretch between the peaks, whirling and waving   330

[24] The goddess of agriculture.   [25] Ritually spilled drink-offerings.
[26] The mountain home of the gods.   [27] Prophetic.   [28] The god of war.
[29] The site of the great temple of Apollo; a symbol of the older, established Greek religion.
Delphi had in fact come to have a shrine of the libidinal god Dionysus near that of the
rationalist god Apollo; one of the twin peaks of the nearby Mount Parnassus was sacred to
Dionysus.

his thyrsus: great throughout Hellas.
                              Mark my words,
Pentheus. Do not be so certain that power
is what matters in the life of man; do not mistake
for wisdom the fantasies of your sick mind.
Welcome the god to Thebes; crown your head;
pour him libations and join his revels.
   Dionysus does not, I admit, *compel* a woman
to be chaste. Always and in every case
it is her character and nature that keeps
a woman chaste. But even in the rites of Dionysus,   340
the chaste woman will not be corrupted.
                              Think:
you are pleased when men stand outside your doors
and the city glorifies the name of Pentheus.
And so the god: he too delights in glory.
But Cadmus and I, whom you ridicule, will crown
our heads with ivy and join the dances of the god—
an ancient foolish pair perhaps, but dance
we must. Nothing you have said would make me
change my mind or flout the will of heaven.
You are mad, grievously mad, beyond the power   350
of any drugs to cure, for you are drugged
with madness.
CORYPHAEUS.
                         Apollo would approve your words.
Wisely you honor Bromius: a great god.
CADMUS.
                              My boy,
Teiresias advises well. Your home is here
with us, with our customs and traditions, not
outside, alone. Your mind is distracted now,
and what you think is sheer delirium.
Even if this Dionysus is no god,
as you assert, persuade yourself that he is.
The fiction is a noble one, for Semele will seem   360
to be the mother of a god, and this confers
no small distinction on our family.
                         You saw
that dreadful death your cousin Actaeon died
when those man-eating hounds he had raised himself
savaged him and tore his body limb from limb
because he boasted that his prowess in the hunt surpassed
the skill of Artemis.[30]
                    Do not let his fate be yours.

---

[30] Sister of Apollo; the virgin goddess of the hunt. The more familiar version of the myth,
apt in the context of *The Bacchae*, relates that Actaeon, having seen the chaste goddess bathing,
was punished by being changed into a stag and dismembered by his own hunting dogs.

Here, let me wreathe your head with leaves of ivy.
Then come with us and glorify the god.
PENTHEUS.
    Take your hands off me! Go worship your Bacchus,   370
but do not wipe your madness off on me.
By god, I'll make him pay, the man who taught you
this folly of yours.

                [*He turns to his attendants.*]
            Go, someone, this instant,
to the place where this prophet prophesies.
Pry it up with crowbars, heave it over,
upside down; demolish everything you see.
Throw his fillets[31] out to wind and weather.
That will provoke him more than anything.
As for the rest of you, go and scour the city
for that effeminate stranger, the man who infects our women   380
with this strange disease and pollutes our beds.
And when you take him, clap him in chains
and march him here. He shall die as he deserves—
by being stoned to death. He shall come to rue
his merrymaking here in Thebes.
                [*Exeunt attendants.*]
TEIRESIAS.
                   Reckless fool,
you do not know the consequences of your words.
You talked madness before, but this is raving
lunacy!
        Cadmus, let us go and pray
for this raving fool and for this city too,
pray to the god that no awful vengeance strike   390
from heaven.
            Take your staff and follow me.
Support me with your hands, and I shall help you too
lest we stumble and fall, a sight of shame,
two old men together.
            But go we must,
acknowledging the service that we owe to god,
Bacchus, the son of Zeus.
            And yet take care
lest someday your house repent of Pentheus[32]
in its sufferings. I speak not prophecy
but fact. The words of fools finish in folly.
        [*Exeunt* TEIRESIAS *and* CADMUS.
        PENTHEUS *retires into the palace.*]
CHORUS.
    —Holiness, queen of heaven,   400
      Holiness on golden wing
      who hover over earth,

---

[31] Ceremonial headbands.   [32] The name means "grief."

do you hear what Pentheus says?
Do you hear his blasphemy
against the prince of the blessèd,
the god of garlands and banquets,
Bromius, Semele's son?
These blessings he gave:
laughter to the flute
and the loosing of cares   410
when the shining wine is spilled
at the feast of the gods,
and the wine-bowl casts its sleep
on feasters crowned with ivy.

—A tongue without reins,
defiance, unwisdom—
their end is disaster.
But the life of quiet good,
the wisdom that accepts—
these abide unshaken,   420
preserving, sustaining
the houses of men.
Far in the air of heaven,
the sons of heaven live.
But they watch the lives of men.
And what passes for wisdom is not;
unwise are those who aspire,
who outrange the limits of man.
Briefly, we live. Briefly,
then die. Wherefore, I say,   430
he who hunts a glory, he who tracks
some boundless, superhuman dream,
may lose his harvest here and now
and garner death. Such men are mad,
        their counsels evil.

—O let me come to Cyprus,
island of Aphrodite,
homes of the loves that cast
their spells on the hearts of men!
Or Paphos where the hundred-   440
mouthed barbarian river
brings ripeness without rain!33
To Pieria, haunt of the Muses,34
and the holy hill of Olympus!
O Bromius, leader, god of joy,

33 Cyprus is a large eastern-Mediterranean island, west of modern Syria and south of modern Turkey. Paphos, the principal center of the rites of Aphrodite, was a town in western Cyprus.

34 Pieria was a district in northern Greece. The nine Muses, minor goddesses, were sponsors of the arts, learning, and culture.

Bromius, take me there!
There the lovely Graces[35] go,
and there Desire, and there
the right is mine to worship
　　as I please.   450

—The deity, the son of Zeus,
in feast, in festival, delights.
He loves the goddess Peace,
generous of good,
preserver of the young.
To rich and poor he gives
the simple gift of wine,
the gladness of the grape.
But him who scoffs he hates,
and him who mocks his life,   460
the happiness of those
for whom the day is blessed
but doubly blessed the night;
whose simple wisdom shuns the thoughts
of proud, uncommon men and all
their god-encroaching dreams.
But what the common people do,
the things that simple men believe,
　　　I too believe and do.

> [*As* PENTHEUS *reappears from the*
> *palace, enter from the left several*
> *attendants leading* DIONYSUS *cap-*
> *tive.*]

ATTENDANT.
Pentheus, here we are; not empty-handed either.   470
We captured the quarry you sent us out to catch.
But our prey here was tame: refused to run
or hide, held out his hands as willing as you please,
completely unafraid. His ruddy cheeks were flushed
as though with wine, and he stood there smiling,
making no objection when we roped his hands
and marched him here. It made me feel ashamed.
"Listen, stranger," I said, "I am not to blame.
We act under orders from Pentheus. He ordered
your arrest."

　　　　　　　As for those women you clapped in chains   480
and sent to the dungeon, they're gone, clean away,
went skipping off to the fields crying on their god
Bromius. The chains on their legs snapped apart
by themselves. Untouched by any human hand,

---

[35] The three Graces, also minor goddesses, were attendants on Aphrodite who personified
charm, brilliance, and youthful freshness.

the doors swung wide, opening of their own accord.
Sir, this stranger who has come to Thebes is full
of many miracles. I know no more than that.
The rest is your affair.
PENTHEUS.

                Untie his hands.
We have him in our net. He may be quick,
but he cannot escape us now, I think.

                      [*While the servants untie* DIONYSUS'
                      hands, PENTHEUS *attentively scruti-*
                      nizes his prisoner. Then the servants
                      step back, leaving PENTHEUS *and*
                      DIONYSUS *face to face.*]
                      So,   490
you *are* attractive, stranger, at least to women—
which explains, I think, your presence here in Thebes.
Your curls are long. You do not wrestle, I take it.
And what fair skin you have—you must take care of it—
no daylight complexion; no, it comes from the night
when you hunt Aphrodite with your beauty.

                         Now then,
who are you and from where?
DIONYSUS.

                   It is nothing
to boast of and easily told. You have heard, I suppose,
of Mount Tmolus and her flowers?
PENTHEUS.

                    I know the place.
It rings the city of Sardis.[36]
DIONYSUS.

                   I come from there.   500
My country is Lydia.
PENTHEUS.

              Who is this god whose worship
you have imported into Hellas?
DIONYSUS.

               Dionysus, the son of Zeus.
He initiated me.
PENTHEUS.

            You have some local Zeus
who spawns new gods?
DIONYSUS.

            He is the same as yours—
the Zeus who married Semele.
PENTHEUS.

             How did you see him?
In a dream or face to face?

---

[36] A very wealthy city, capital of Lydia in Asia Minor.

DIONYSUS.
                              Face to face.
He gave me his rites.
PENTHEUS.
                         What form do they take,
these mysteries of yours?
DIONYSUS.
                         It is forbidden
to tell the uninitiate.
PENTHEUS.
                    Tell me the benefits
that those who know your mysteries enjoy.   510
DIONYSUS.
I am forbidden to say. But they are worth knowing.
PENTHEUS.
Your answers are designed to make me curious.
DIONYSUS.
                                             No:
our mysteries abhor an unbelieving man.
PENTHEUS.
You say you saw the god. What form did he assume?
DIONYSUS.
Whatever form he wished. The choice was his,
not mine.
PENTHEUS.
              You evade the question.
DIONYSUS.
                              Talk sense to a fool
and he calls you foolish.
PENTHEUS.
                         Have you introduced your rites
in other cities too? Or is Thebes the first?
DIONYSUS.
Foreigners everywhere now dance for Dionysus.
PENTHEUS.
They are more ignorant than Greeks.
DIONYSUS.
                              In this matter   520
they are not. Customs differ.
PENTHEUS.
                         Do you hold your rites
during the day or night?
DIONYSUS.
                         Mostly by night.
The darkness is well suited to devotion.
PENTHEUS.
Better suited to lechery and seducing women.
DIONYSUS.
You can find debauchery by daylight too.

PENTHEUS.
You shall regret these clever answers.
DIONYSUS.

                                          And you,
your stupid blasphemies.
PENTHEUS.

                              What a bold bacchant!
You wrestle well—when it comes to words.
DIONYSUS.

                                          Tell me,
what punishment do you propose?
PENTHEUS.

                              First of all,
I shall cut off your girlish curls.
DIONYSUS.

                              My hair is holy.   530
My curls belong to god.

                              [PENTHEUS *shears away the god's*
                              curls.]

PENTHEUS.

                          Second, you will surrender
your wand.
DIONYSUS.

          You take it. It belongs to Dionysus.
                              [PENTHEUS *takes the thyrsus.*]
PENTHEUS.
Last, I shall place you under guard and confine you
in the palace.
DIONYSUS.

              The god himself will set me free
whenever I wish.
PENTHEUS.

                  You will be with your women in prison
when you call on him for help.
DIONYSUS.

                              He is here now
and sees what I endure from you.
PENTHEUS.

                                  Where is he?
I cannot see him.
DIONYSUS.

                  With me. Your blasphemies
have made you blind.
PENTHEUS [*to attendants*].

                        Seize him. He is mocking me
and Thebes.
DIONYSUS.

              I give you sober warning, fools: 540
place no chains on *me*.

PENTHEUS.

                    But *I* say: chain him.
And I am the stronger here.

DIONYSUS.

                          You do not know
the limits of your strength. You do not know
what you do. You do not know who you are.

PENTHEUS.

I am Pentheus, the son of Echion and Agave.

DIONYSUS.

Pentheus: you shall repent that name.

PENTHEUS.

                              Off with him.
Chain his hands; lock him in the stables by the palace.
Since he desires the darkness, give him what he wants.
Let him dance down there in the dark.

                        [*As the attendants bind* DIONYSUS'
                        hands, the CHORUS *beats on its*
                        drums with increasing agitation as
                        though to emphasize the sacrilege.]
                        As for these women,
your accomplices in making trouble here,   550
I shall have them sold as slaves or put to work
at my looms. That will silence their drums.

                        [*Exit* PENTHEUS.]

DIONYSUS.

                                I go,
though not to suffer, since that cannot be.
But Dionysus whom you outrage by your acts,
who you deny is god, will call you to account.
When you set chains on me, you manacle the god.

                        [*Exeunt attendants with* DIONYSUS
                        captive.]

CHORUS.

    —O Dirce, holy river,
        child of Achelöus' water,[37]
        yours the springs that welcomed once
        divinity, the son of Zeus!
    For Zeus the father snatched his son   560
        from deathless flame, crying:
    Dithyrambus,[38] *come!*
    Enter my male womb.
    I name you Bacchus and to Thebes
    proclaim you by that name.
    But now, O blessèd Dirce,
    you banish me when to your banks I come,

---

[37] Dirce, a nymph identified with the spring at Thebes, was daughter of the god of the north-Grecian river Achelöus.

[38] An epithet for Dionysus; a dithyramb was a wildly ecstatic choric hymn to the god.

crowned with ivy, bringing revels.
O Dirce, why am I rejected? 570
By the clustered grapes I swear,
by Dionysus' wine,
someday you shall come to know
  the name of *Bromius!*

—With fury, with fury, he rages,
Pentheus, son of Echion,
born of the breed of Earth,
spawned by the dragon, whelped by Earth!
Inhuman, a rabid beast,
a giant in wildness raging, 580
storming, defying the children of heaven.
He has threatened me with bonds
though my body is bound to god.
He cages my comrades with chains;
he has cast them in prison darkness.
O lord, son of Zeus, do you see?
O Dionysus, do you see
how in shackles we are held
unbreakably, in the bonds of oppressors?
Descend from Olympus, lord! 590
Come, whirl your wand of gold
and quell with death this beast of blood
whose violence abuses man and god
  outrageously.

—O lord, where do you wave your wand
among the running companies of god?
There on Nysa,[39] mother of beasts?
There on the ridges of Corycia?[40]
Or there among the forests of Olympus
where Orpheus fingered his lyre 600
and mustered with music the trees,
mustered the wilderness beasts?[41]
O Pieria, you are blessed!
Evius honors you. He comes to dance,
bringing his Bacchae, fording the race
where Axios[42] runs, bringing his Maenads
whirling over Lydias,
generous father of rivers
and famed for his lovely waters
that fatten a land of good horses. 610

[39] The childhood home of Dionysus; its location is uncertain.
[40] A cave on Mount Parnassus.
[41] In myth, Orpheus was a supremely gifted poet-singer whose songs enchanted all nature, including the trees and animals.
[42] A river in Thrace, the region north of the Aegean Sea.

*[Thunder and lightning. The earth
trembles. The* CHORUS *is crazed with
fear.]*

DIONYSUS [*from within*].
  Ho!
  Hear me! Ho, Bacchae!
  Ho, Bacchae! Hear my cry!
CHORUS.
  Who cries?
  Who calls me with that cry
  of Evius? Where are you, lord?
DIONYSUS.
  Ho! Again I cry—
  the son of Zeus and Semele!
CHORUS.
  O lord, lord Bromius!
  Bromius, come to us now!   620
DIONYSUS.
Let the earthquake come! Shatter the floor of the world!
CHORUS.
  —Look there, how the palace of Pentheus totters.
  —Look, the palace is collapsing!
  —Dionysus is within. Adore him!
  —We adore him!
  —Look there!
              —Above the pillars, how the great stones
    gape and crack!
              —Listen. Bromius cries his victory!
DIONYSUS.
*Launch the blazing thunderbolt of god! O lightnings,
come! Consume with flame the palace of Pentheus!*
                          *[A burst of lightning flares across
                          the façade of the palace and tongues
                          of flame spurt up from the tomb of
                          Semele. Then a great crash of thun-
                          der.]*
CHORUS.
  Ah,   630
  look how the fire leaps up
  on the holy tomb of Semele,
  the flame of Zeus of Thunders,
  his lightnings, still alive,
  blazing where they fell!
  Down, Maenads,
  fall to the ground in awe! He walks
  among the ruins he has made!
  He has brought the high house low!
  He comes, our god, the son of Zeus!   640
                          [The CHORUS *falls to the ground in
                          oriental fashion, bowing their heads*

                                        in the direction of the palace. A
                                        hush; then DIONYSUS *appears,*
                                        lightly picking his way among the
                                        rubble. Calm and smiling still, he
                                        speaks to the CHORUS *with a solici-*
                                        tude approaching banter.]

DIONYSUS.
    What, women of Asia? Were you so overcome with fright
    you fell to the ground? I think then you must have seen
    how Bacchus jostled the palace of Pentheus. But come, rise.
    Do not be afraid.
CORYPHAEUS.
                    O greatest light of our holy revels,
    how glad I am to see your face! Without you I was lost.
DIONYSUS.
    Did you despair when they led me away to cast me down
    in the darkness of Pentheus' prison?
CORYPHAEUS.
                                    What else could I do?
    Where would I turn for help if something happened to you?
    But how did you escape that godless man?
DIONYSUS.
                                    With ease.
    No effort was required.
CORYPHAEUS.
                    But the manacles on your wrists?   650
DIONYSUS.
    There I, in turn, humiliated him, outrage for outrage.
    He seemed to think that he was chaining me but never once
    so much as touched my hands. He fed on his desires.
    Inside the stable he intended as my jail, instead of me,
    he found a bull and tried to rope its knees and hooves.
    He was panting desperately, biting his lips with his teeth,
    his whole body drenched with sweat, while I sat nearby,
    quietly watching. But at that moment Bacchus came,
    shook the palace and touched his mother's grave with tongues
    of fire. Imagining the palace was in flames,   660
    Pentheus went rushing here and there, shouting to his slaves
    to bring him water. Every hand was put to work: in vain.
    Then, afraid I might escape, he suddenly stopped short,
    drew his sword and rushed to the palace. There, it seems,
    Bromius had made a shape, a phantom which resembled me,
    within the court. Bursting in, Pentheus thrust and stabbed
    at that thing of gleaming air as though he thought it me.
    And then, once again, the god humiliated him.
    He razed the palace to the ground where it lies, shattered
    in utter ruin—his reward for my imprisonment.   670
    At that bitter sight, Pentheus dropped his sword, exhausted
    by the struggle. A man, a man, and nothing more,
    yet he presumed to wage a war with god.

For my part,
I left the palace quietly and made my way outside.
For Pentheus I care nothing.
                              But judging from the sound
of tramping feet inside the court, I think our man
will soon be here. What, I wonder, will he have to say?
But let him bluster. I shall not be touched to rage.
Wise men know constraint: our passions are controlled.

> [*Enter* PENTHEUS, *stamping heav-
> ily, from the ruined palace.*]

PENTHEUS.
But this is mortifying. That stranger, that man   680
I clapped in irons, has escaped.

> [*He catches sight of* DIONYSUS.]

                              What! *You?*
Well, what do you have to say for yourself?
How did you escape? Answer me.
DIONYSUS.
                              Your anger
walks too heavily. Tread lightly here.
PENTHEUS.
How did you escape?
DIONYSUS.
                      Don't you remember?
Someone, I said, would set me free.
PENTHEUS.
                                    Someone?
But who? Who is this mysterious someone?
DIONYSUS.
[He who makes the grape grow its clusters
for mankind.][43]
PENTHEUS.
            A splendid contribution, that.
DIONYSUS.
You disparage the gift that is his chiefest glory.   690
PENTHEUS.
[If I catch him here, he will not escape my anger.]
I shall order every gate in every tower
to be bolted tight.
DIONYSUS.
                    And so? Could not a god
hurdle your city walls?
PENTHEUS.
                        You are clever—very—
but not where it counts.

---

[43] The bracketed lines in this passage and later in the play are supplied by the translator to
replace lines missing from the manuscript.

DIONYSUS.

                                        Where it counts the most,
there I *am* clever.

                              [*Enter a messenger, a herdsman
                              from Mount Cithaeron.*]
                    But hear this messenger
who brings you news from the mountain of Cithaeron.
We shall remain where we are. Do not fear:
we will not run away.

MESSENGER.

                    Pentheus, king of Thebes,
I come from Cithaeron where the gleaming flakes of snow   700
fall on and on forever—

PENTHEUS.

                        Get to the point.
What is your message, man?

MESSENGER.

                              Sir, I have seen
the holy Maenads, the women who ran barefoot
and crazy from the city, and I wanted to report
to you and Thebes what weird fantastic things,
what miracles and more than miracles,
these women do. But may I speak freely
in my own way and words, or make it short?
I fear the harsh impatience of your nature, sire,
too kingly and too quick to anger.

PENTHEUS.

                                    Speak freely.   710
You have my promise: I shall not punish you.
Displeasure with a man who speaks the truth is wrong.
However, the more terrible this tale of yours,
that much more terrible will be the punishment
I impose upon that man who taught our womenfolk
this strange new magic.

MESSENGER.

                        About that hour
when the sun lets loose its light to warm the earth,
our grazing herds of cows had just begun to climb
the path along the mountain ridge. Suddenly
I saw three companies of dancing women,   720
one led by Autonoë, the second captained
by your mother Agave, while Ino led the third.
There they lay in the deep sleep of exhaustion,
some resting on boughs of fir, others sleeping
where they fell, here and there among the oak leaves—
but all modestly and soberly, not, as you think,
drunk with wine, nor wandering, led astray
by the music of the flute, to hunt their Aphrodite
through the woods.

                          But your mother heard the lowing
of our horned herds, and springing to her feet,   730
gave a great cry to waken them from sleep.
And they too, rubbing the bloom of soft sleep
from their eyes, rose up lightly and straight—
a lovely sight to see: all as one,
the old women and the young and the unmarried girls.
First they let their hair fall loose, down
over their shoulders, and those whose straps had slipped
fastened their skins of fawn with writhing snakes
that licked their cheeks. Breasts swollen with milk,
new mothers who had left their babies behind at home   740
nestled gazelles and young wolves in their arms,
suckling them. Then they crowned their hair with leaves,
ivy and oak and flowering bryony. One woman
struck her thyrsus against a rock and a fountain
of cool water came bubbling up. Another drove
her fennel in the ground, and where it struck the earth,
at the touch of god, a spring of wine poured out.
Those who wanted milk scratched at the soil
with bare fingers and the white milk came welling up.
Pure honey spurted, streaming, from their wands.   750
If you had been there and seen these wonders for yourself,
you would have gone down on your knees and prayed
to the god you now deny.
                          We cowherds and shepherds
gathered in small groups, wondering and arguing
among ourselves at these fantastic things,
the awful miracles those women did.
But then a city fellow with the knack of words
rose to his feet and said: "All you who live
upon the pastures of the mountain, what do you say?
Shall we earn a little favor with King Pentheus   760
by hunting his mother Agave out of the revels?"
Falling in with his suggestion, we withdrew
and set ourselves in ambush, hidden by the leaves
among the undergrowth. Then at a signal
all the Bacchae whirled their wands for the revels
to begin. With one voice they cried aloud:
"O Iacchus![44] Son of Zeus!" "O Bromius!" they cried
until the beasts and all the mountain seemed
wild with divinity. And when they ran,
everything ran with them.
                          It happened, however,   770
that Agave ran near the ambush where I lay
concealed. Leaping up, I tried to seize her,
but she gave a cry: "Hounds who run with me,

---

[44] Still another epithet for Dionysus.

men are hunting us down! Follow, follow me!
Use your wands for weapons."
At this we fled
and barely missed being torn to pieces by the women.
Unarmed, they swooped down upon the herds of cattle
grazing there on the green of the meadow. And then
you could have seen a single woman with bare hands
tear a fat calf, still bellowing with fright,   780
in two, while others clawed the heifers to pieces.
There were ribs and cloven hooves scattered everywhere,
and scraps smeared with blood hung from the fir trees.
And bulls, their raging fury gathered in their horns,
lowered their heads to charge, then fell, stumbling
to the earth, pulled down by hordes of women
and stripped of flesh and skin more quickly, sire,
than you could blink your royal eyes. Then,
carried up by their own speed, they flew like birds
across the spreading fields along Asopus'[45] stream   790
where most of all the ground is good for harvesting.
Like invaders they swooped on Hysiae
and on Erythrae in the foothills of Cithaeron.
Everything in sight they pillaged and destroyed.
They snatched the children from their homes. And when
they piled their plunder on their backs, it stayed in place,
untied. Nothing, neither bronze nor iron,
fell to the dark earth. Flames flickered
in their curls and did not burn them. Then the villagers,
furious at what the women did, took to arms.   800
And *there*, sire, was something terrible to see.
For the men's spears were pointed and sharp, and yet
drew no blood, whereas the wands the women threw
inflicted wounds. And then the men *ran*,
routed by women! Some god, I say, was with them.
The Bacchae then returned where they had started,
by the springs the god had made, and washed their hands
while the snakes licked away the drops of blood
that dabbled their cheeks.
Whoever this god may be,
sire, welcome him to Thebes. For he is great   810
in many other ways as well. It was he,
or so they say, who gave to mortal men
the gift of lovely wine by which our suffering
is stopped. And if there is no god of wine,
there is no love, no Aphrodite either,
nor other pleasure left to men.
[*Exit messenger.*]
CORYPHAEUS.
I tremble

---

[45] A river in Boeotia, the region surrounding Thebes.

to speak the words of freedom before the tyrant.
But let the truth be told: there is no god
greater than Dionysus.

PENTHEUS.
       Like a blazing fire
this Bacchic violence spreads. It comes too close.   820
We are disgraced, humiliated in the eyes
of Hellas. This is no time for hesitation.
         [*He turns to an attendant.*]
You there. Go down quickly to the Electran gates[46]
and order out all heavy-armored infantry;
call up the fastest troops among our cavalry,
the mobile squadrons and the archers. We march
against the Bacchae! Affairs are out of hand
when we tamely endure such conduct in our women.
         [*Exit attendant.*]

DIONYSUS.
Pentheus, you do not hear, or else you disregard
my words of warning. You have done me wrong,   830
and yet, in spite of that, I warn you once
again: do not take arms against a god.
Stay quiet here. Bromius will not let you
drive his women from their revels on the mountain.

PENTHEUS.
Don't you lecture me. You escaped from prison.
Or shall I punish you again?

DIONYSUS.
        If I were you,
I would offer him a sacrifice, not rage
and kick against necessity, a man defying
god.

PENTHEUS.
  I shall give your god the sacrifice
that he deserves. His victims will be his women.   840
I shall make a great slaughter in the woods of Cithaeron.

DIONYSUS.
You will all be routed, shamefully defeated,
when their wands of ivy turn back your shields
of bronze.

PENTHEUS.
    It is hopeless to wrestle with this man.
Nothing on earth will make him hold his tongue.

DIONYSUS.
            Friend,
you can still save the situation.

PENTHEUS.
        How?
By accepting orders from my own slaves?

---

[46] One of the gates of the city.

DIONYSUS.

> No.

I undertake to lead the women back to Thebes.
Without bloodshed.

PENTHEUS.

> This is some trap.

DIONYSUS.

> A trap?

How so, if I save you by my own devices?

PENTHEUS.

> I know.   850

You and they have conspired to establish your rites
forever.

DIONYSUS.

> True, I *have* conspired—with god.

PENTHEUS.

Bring my armor, someone. And *you* stop talking.

> [PENTHEUS *strides toward the left,
> but when he is almost offstage,* DIO-
> NYSUS *calls imperiously to him.*]

DIONYSUS.

Wait!
Would you like to *see* their revels on the mountain?

PENTHEUS.

I would pay a great sum to see that sight.

DIONYSUS.

Why are you so passionately curious?

PENTHEUS.

> Of course

I'd be sorry to see them drunk—

DIONYSUS.

> But for all your sorrow,

you'd like very much to see them?

PENTHEUS.

> Yes, very much.

I could crouch beneath the fir trees, out of sight.   860

DIONYSUS.

But if you try to hide, they may track you down.

PENTHEUS.

Your point is well taken. I will go openly.

DIONYSUS.

Shall I lead you there now? Are you ready to go?

PENTHEUS.

The sooner the better. The loss of even a moment
would be disappointing now.

DIONYSUS.

> First, however,

you must dress yourself in women's clothes.

PENTHEUS.

> *What?*

You want *me*, a man, to wear a woman's dress. But why?
DIONYSUS.
If they knew you were a man, they would kill you instantly.
PENTHEUS.
True. You are an old hand at cunning, I see.
DIONYSUS.
Dionysus taught me everything I know.   870
PENTHEUS.
Your advice is to the point. What I fail to see
is what we do.
DIONYSUS.
                        I shall go inside with you
and help you dress.
PENTHEUS.
                        Dress? In a *woman's* dress,
you mean? I would die of shame.
DIONYSUS.
                                    Very well.
Then you no longer hanker to see the Maenads?
PENTHEUS.
What is this costume I must wear?
DIONYSUS.
                        On your head
I shall set a wig with long curls.
PENTHEUS.
                        And then?
DIONYSUS.
Next, robes to your feet and a net for your hair.
PENTHEUS.
Yes? Go on.
DIONYSUS.
                Then a thyrsus for your hand
and a skin of dappled fawn.
PENTHEUS.
                                I could not bear it.   880
I *cannot* bring myself to dress in women's clothes.
DIONYSUS.
Then you must fight the Bacchae. That means bloodshed.
PENTHEUS.
Right. First we must go and reconnoiter.
DIONYSUS.
Surely a wiser course than that of hunting bad
with worse.
PENTHEUS.
                But how can we pass through the city
without being seen?
DIONYSUS.
                        We shall take deserted streets.
I will lead the way.

PENTHEUS.
>   Any way you like,
> provided those women of Bacchus don't jeer at me.
> First, however, I shall ponder your advice,
> whether to go or not.

DIONYSUS.
>   Do as you please.   890
> I am ready, whatever you decide.

PENTHEUS.
>   Yes.
> Either I shall march with my army to the mountain
> or act on your advice.

> [*Exit* PENTHEUS *into the palace.*]

DIONYSUS.
>   Women, our prey now thrashes
> in the net we threw. He shall see the Bacchae
> and pay the price with death.
>   O Dionysus,
> now action rests with you. And you are near.
> Punish this man. But first distract his wits;
> bewilder him with madness. For sane of mind
> this man would never wear a woman's dress;
> but obsess his soul and he will not refuse.   900
> After those threats with which he was so fierce,
> I want him made the laughingstock of Thebes,
> paraded through the streets, a woman.
>   Now
> I shall go and costume Pentheus in the clothes
> which he must wear to Hades[47] when he dies, butchered
> by the hands of his mother. He shall come to know
> Dionysus, son of Zeus, consummate god,
> most terrible, and yet most gentle, to mankind.

> [*Exit* DIONYSUS *into the palace.*]

CHORUS.
> —When shall I dance once more
>   with bare feet the all-night dances,   910
>   tossing my head for joy
>   in the damp air, in the dew,
>   as a running fawn might frisk
>   for the green joy of the wide fields,
>   free from fear of the hunt,
>   free from the circling beaters[48]
>   and the nets of woven mesh
>   and the hunters hallooing on
>   their yelping packs? And then, hard pressed,
>   she sprints with the quickness of wind,   920

---

[47] The underworld realm of the dead.
[48] Persons who flush game animals from cover.

bounding over the marsh, leaping
to frisk, leaping for joy,
gay with the green of the leaves,
to dance for joy in the forest,
to dance where the darkness is deepest,
    where no man is.

—What is wisdom? What gift of the gods
is held in honor like this:
to hold your hand victorious
over the heads of those you hate?   930
Honor is precious forever.

—Slow but unmistakable
the might of the gods moves on.
It punishes that man,
infatuate of soul
and hardened in his pride,
who disregards the gods.
The gods are crafty:
they lie in ambush
a long step of time   940
to hunt the unholy.
Beyond the old beliefs,
no thought, no act shall go.
Small, small is the cost
to believe in this:
whatever is god is strong;
whatever long time has sanctioned,
that is a law forever;
the law tradition makes
is the law of nature.   950

—What is wisdom? What gift of the gods
is held in honor like this:
to hold your hand victorious
over the heads of those you hate?
Honor is precious forever.

—Blessèd is he who escapes a storm at sea,
    who comes home to his harbor.
—Blessèd is he who emerges from under affliction.
—In various ways one man outraces another in the
    race for wealth and power.   960
—Ten thousand men possess ten thousand hopes.
—A few bear fruit in happiness; the others go awry.
—But he who garners day by day the good of life,
    he is happiest. Blessèd is he.

                        [*Re-enter* DIONYSUS *from the pal-
                        ace. At the threshold he turns and
                        calls back to* PENTHEUS.]

DIONYSUS.
    Pentheus if you are still so curious to see
    forbidden sights, so bent on evil still,
    come out. Let us see you in your woman's dress,
    disguised in Maenad clothes so you may go and spy
    upon your mother and her company.

> [*Enter* PENTHEUS *from the palace.*
> *He wears a long linen dress which*
> *partially conceals his fawn-skin. He*
> *carries a thyrsus in his hand; on his*
> *head he wears a wig with long blond*
> *curls bound by a snood. He is dazed*
> *and completely in the power of the*
> *god who has now possessed him.*]
>   Why,

    you look exactly like one of the daughters of Cadmus.   970
PENTHEUS.
    I seem to see two suns blazing in the heavens.
    And now two Thebes, two cities, and each
    with seven gates. And you—you are a bull
    who walks before me there. Horns have sprouted
    from your head. Have you always been a beast?
    But now I see a bull.
DIONYSUS.
                It is the god you see.
    Though hostile formerly, he now declares a truce
    and goes with us. You see what you could not
    when you were blind.
PENTHEUS [*coyly primping*].
             Do I look like anyone?
    Like Ino or my mother Agave?
DIONYSUS.
                So much alike   980
    I almost might be seeing one of them. But look:
    one of your curls has come loose from under the snood
    where I tucked it.
PENTHEUS.
            It must have worked loose
    when I was dancing for joy and shaking my head.
DIONYSUS.
    Then let me be your maid and tuck it back.
    Hold still.
PENTHEUS.
       Arrange it. I am in your hands
    completely.

> [DIONYSUS *tucks the curl back under*
> *the snood.*]

DIONYSUS.
         And now your strap has slipped. Yes,
    and your robe hangs askew at the ankles.

PENTHEUS [*bending backward to look*].

                                                              I think so.
At least on my right leg. But on the left the hem
lies straight.
DIONYSUS.

                                        You will think me the best of friends   990
when you see to your surprise how chaste the Bacchae are.
PENTHEUS.

But to be a real Bacchante, should I hold
the wand in my right hand? Or this way?
DIONYSUS.

                                                                        No.
In your right hand. And raise it as you raise
your right foot. I commend your change of heart.
PENTHEUS.

Could I lift Cithaeron up, do you think?
Shoulder the cliffs, Bacchae and all?
DIONYSUS.

                                                        If you wanted.
Your mind was once unsound, but now you think
as sane men do.
PENTHEUS.

                                Should we take crowbars with us?
Or should I put my shoulder to the cliffs   1000
and heave them up?
DIONYSUS.

                                        What? And destroy the haunts
of the nymphs, the holy groves where Pan plays
his woodland pipe?
PENTHEUS.

                                        You are right. In any case,
women should not be mastered by brute strength.
I will hide myself beneath the firs instead.
DIONYSUS.

You will find all the ambush you deserve,
creeping up to spy on the Maenads.
PENTHEUS.

                                                              Think.
I can see them already, there among the bushes,
mating like birds, caught in the toils of love.
DIONYSUS.

Exactly. This is your mission: you go to watch.   1010
You may surprise them—or they may surprise you.
PENTHEUS.

Then lead me through the very heart of Thebes,
since I, alone of all this city, dare to go.
DIONYSUS.

You and you alone will suffer for your city.
A great ordeal awaits you. But you are worthy

of your fate. I shall lead you safely there;
someone else shall bring you back.
PENTHEUS.

                                        Yes, my mother.
DIONYSUS.
An example to all men.
PENTHEUS.

                            It is for that I go.
DIONYSUS.
You will be carried home—
PENTHEUS.

                            O luxury!
DIONYSUS.
cradled in your mother's arms.
PENTHEUS.

                                You will be spoil me.   1020
DIONYSUS.
I *mean* to spoil you.
PENTHEUS.

                        I go to my reward.
DIONYSUS.
You are an extraordinary young man, and you go
to an extraordinary experience. You shall win
a glory towering to heaven and usurping
god's.

                                [*Exit* PENTHEUS.]
        Agave and you daughters of Cadmus,
reach out your hands! I bring this young man
to a great ordeal. The victor? Bromius.
Bromius—and I. The rest the event shall show.
                                [*Exit* DIONYSUS.]

CHORUS.
    —Run to the mountain, fleet hounds of madness!
    Run, run to the revels of Cadmus' daughters!   1030
    Sting them against the man in women's clothes,
    the madman who spies on the Maenads, who peers
    from behind the rocks, who spies from a vantage!
    His mother shall see him first. She will cry
    to the Maenads: "Who is this spy who has come
    to the mountains to peer at the mountain-revels
    of the women of Thebes? What bore him, Bacchae?
    This man was born of no woman. Some lioness
    give him birth, some one of the Libyan gorgons!"[49]

    —O Justice, principle of order, spirit of custom,   1040
    come! Be manifest; reveal yourself with a sword!

[49] A set of three female monsters, with snakes for hair, who turned to stone those who
gazed on them.

Stab through the throat that godless man,
the mocker who goes, flouting custom and outraging god!
O Justice, stab the evil earth-born spawn of Echion!

—Uncontrollable, the unbeliever goes,
in spitting rage, rebellious and amok,
madly assaulting the mysteries of god,
profaning the rites of the mother of god.
Against the unassailable he runs, with rage
obsessed. Headlong he runs to death.   1050
For death the gods exact, curbing by that bit
the mouths of men. They humble us with death
that we remember what we are who are not god,
but men. We run to death. Wherefore, I say,
accept, accept:
humility is wise; humility is blest.
But what the world calls wise I do not want.
Elsewhere the chase. I hunt another game,
those great, those manifest, those certain goals,
achieving which, our mortal lives are blest.   1060
Let these things be the quarry of my chase:
purity; humility; an unrebellious soul,
accepting all. Let me go the customary way,
the timeless, honored, beaten path of those who walk
with reverence and awe beneath the sons of heaven.

—O Justice, principle of order, spirit of custom,
come! Be manifest; reveal yourself with a sword!
Stab through the throat that godless man,
the mocker who goes, flouting custom and outraging god!
O Justice, destroy the evil earth-born spawn of Echion!   1070

—O Dionysus, reveal yourself a bull! Be manifest,
a snake with darting heads, a lion breathing fire!
O Bacchus, come! Come with your smile!
Cast your noose about this man who hunts
your Bacchae! Bring him down, trampled
underfoot by the murderous herd of your Maenads!
                                        [*Enter a messenger from Cithaeron.*]
MESSENGER.
How prosperous in Hellas these halls once were,
this house founded by Cadmus, the stranger from Sidon
who sowed the dragon seed in the land of the snake!
I am a slave and nothing more, yet even so   1080
I mourn the fortunes of this fallen house.
CORYPHAEUS.

                                                What is it?

Is there news of the Bacchae?
MESSENGER.

                                        This is my news:

Pentheus, the son of Echion, is dead.
CORYPHAEUS.
   All hail to Bromius! Our god is a great god!
MESSENGER.
   What is this you say, women? You dare to rejoice
   at these disasters which destroy this house?
CORYPHAEUS.
   I am no Greek. I hail my god
   in my own way. No longer need I
   shrink with fear of prison.
MESSENGER.
   If you suppose this city is so short of men—   1090
CORYPHAEUS.
   Dionysus, Dionysus, not Thebes,
   has power over me.
MESSENGER.
   Your feelings might be forgiven, then. But this,
   this exultation in disaster—it is not right.
CORYPHAEUS.
   Tell us how the mocker died.
   How was he killed?
MESSENGER.
   There were three of us in all: Pentheus and I,
   attending my master, and that stranger who volunteered
   his services as guide. Leaving behind us
   the last outlying farms of Thebes, we forded   1100
   the Asopus and struck into the barren scrubland
   of Cithaeron.
                  There in a grassy glen we halted,
   unmoving, silent, without a word,
   so we might see but not be seen. From that vantage,
   in a hollow cut from the sheer rock of the cliffs,
   a place where water ran and the pines grew dense
   with shade, we saw the Maenads sitting, their hands
   busily moving at their happy tasks. Some
   wound the stalks of their tattered wands with tendrils
   of fresh ivy; others, frisking like fillies   1110
   newly freed from the painted bridles, chanted
   in Bacchic songs, responsively.
                  But Pentheus—
   unhappy man—could not quite see the companies
   of women. "Stranger," he said, "from where I stand,
   I cannot see these counterfeited Maenads.
   But if I climbed that towering fir that overhangs
   the banks, then I could see their shameless orgies
   better."
                  And now the stranger worked a miracle.
   Reaching for the highest branch of a great fir,
   he bent it down, down, down to the dark earth,   1120
   till it was curved the way a taut bow bends

or like a rim of wood when forced about the circle
of a wheel. Like that he forced that mountain fir
down to the ground. No mortal could have done it.
Then he seated Pentheus at the highest tip
and with his hands let the trunk rise straightly up,
slowly and gently, lest it throw its rider.
And the tree rose, towering to heaven, with my master
huddled at the top. And now the Maenads saw him
more clearly than he saw them. But barely had they seen,   1130
when the stranger vanished and there came a great voice
out of heaven—Dionysus', it must have been—
crying: "Women, I bring you the man who has mocked
at you and me and at our holy mysteries.
Take vengeance upon him." And as he spoke
a flash of awful fire bound earth and heaven.
The high air hushed, and along the forest glen
the leaves hung still; you could hear no cry of beasts.
The Bacchae heard that voice but missed its words,
and leaping up, they stared, peering everywhere.   1140
Again that voice. And now they knew his cry,
the clear command of god. And breaking loose
like startled doves, through grove and torrent,
over jagged rocks, they flew, their feet maddened
by the breath of god. And when they saw my master
perching in his tree, they climbed a great stone
that towered opposite his perch and showered him
with stones and javelins of fir, while the others
hurled their wands. And yet they missed their target,
poor Pentheus in his perch, barely out of reach   1150
of their eager hands, treed, unable to escape.
Finally they splintered branches from the oaks
and with those bars of wood tried to lever up the tree
by prying at the roots. But every effort failed.
Then Agave cried out: "Maenads, make a circle
about the trunk and grip it with your hands.
Unless we take this climbing beast, he will reveal
the secrets of the god." With that, thousands of hands
tore the fir tree from the earth, and down, down
from his high perch fell Pentheus, tumbling   1160
to the ground, sobbing and screaming as he fell,
for he knew his end was near. His own mother,
like a priestess with her victim, fell upon him
first. But snatching off his wig and snood
so she would recognize his face, he touched her cheeks,
screaming, *"No, no, Mother! I am Pentheus,*
your own son, the child you bore to Echion!
Pity me, spare me, Mother! I have done a wrong,
but do not kill your own son for my offense."
But she was foaming at the mouth, and her crazed eyes   1170

rolling with frenzy. She was mad, stark mad,
possessed by Bacchus. Ignoring his cries of pity,
she seized his left arm at the wrist; then, planting
her foot upon his chest, she pulled, wrenching away
the arm at the shoulder—not by her own strength,
for the god had put inhuman power in her hands.
Ino, meanwhile, on the other side, was scratching off
his flesh. Then Autonoë and the whole horde
of Bacchae swarmed upon him. Shouts everywhere,
he screaming with what little breath was left,   1180
they shrieking in triumph. One tore off an arm,
another a foot still warm in its shoe. His ribs
were clawed clean of flesh and every hand
was smeared with blood as they played ball with scraps
of Pentheus' body.

        The pitiful remains lie scattered,
one piece among the sharp rocks, others
lying lost among the leaves in the depths
of the forest. His mother, picking up his head,
impaled it on her wand. She seems to think it is
some mountain lion's head which she carries in triumph   1190
through the thick of Cithaeron. Leaving her sisters
at the Maenad dances, she is coming here, gloating
over her grisly prize. She calls upon Bacchus:
he is her "fellow-huntsman," "comrade of the chase,
crowned with victory." But all the victory
she carries home is her own grief.

                    Now,
before Agave returns, let me leave
this scene of sorrow. Humility,
a sense of reverence before the sons of heaven—
of all the prizes that a mortal man might win,   1200
these, I say, are wisest; these are best.
                [*Exit* MESSENGER.]

CHORUS.
  —We dance to the glory of Bacchus!
    We dance to the death of Pentheus,
    the death of the spawn of the dragon!
      He dressed in woman's dress;
      he took the lovely thyrsus;
      it waved him down to death,
        led by a bull to Hades.
    Hail, Bacchae! Hail, women of Thebes!
    Your victory is fair, fair the prize,   1210
      this famous prize of grief!
    Glorious the game! To fold your child
    in your arms, streaming with his blood!
CORYPHAEUS.
  But look: there comes Pentheus' mother, Agave,

running wild-eyed toward the palace.

—Welcome,

welcome to the reveling band of the god of joy!

> [*Enter* AGAVE *with other* BAC-
> CHANTES. *She is covered with blood
> and carries the head of* PENTHEUS
> *impaled upon her thyrsus.*]

AGAVE.
Bacchae of Asia—
CHORUS.
Speak, speak.
AGAVE.
We bring this branch to the palace,
this fresh-cut spray from the mountains.
Happy was the hunting.
CHORUS.
I see.   1220
I welcome our fellow-reveler of god.
AGAVE.
The whelp of a wild mountain lion,
and snared by me without a noose.
Look, look at the prize I bring.
CHORUS.
Where was he caught?
AGAVE.
On Cithaeron—
CHORUS.
On Cithaeron?
AGAVE.
Our prize was killed.
CHORUS.
Who killed him?
AGAVE.
I struck him first.
The Maenads call me "Agave the blest."
CHORUS.
And then?
AGAVE.
Cadmus'—
CHORUS.
Cadmus'?
AGAVE.
Daughters.
After me, they reached the prey.   1230
After me. Happy was the hunting.
CHORUS.
Happy indeed.
AGAVE.
Then share my glory,
share the feast.

CHORUS.
                    Share, unhappy woman?
AGAVE.
  See, the whelp is young and tender.
  Beneath the soft mane of its hair,
  the down is blooming on the cheeks.
CHORUS.
  With that mane he *looks* a beast.
AGAVE.
  Our god is wise. Cunningly, cleverly,
  Bacchus the hunter lashed the Maenads
  against his prey.
CHORUS.
                    Our king is a hunter.   1240
AGAVE.
  You praise me now?
CHORUS.
                    I praise you.
AGAVE.
  The men of Thebes—
CHORUS.
                    And Pentheus, your son?
AGAVE.
  Will praise his mother. She caught
  a great quarry, this lion's cub.
CHORUS.
  Extraordinary catch.
AGAVE.
                    Extraordinary skill.
CHORUS.
  You are proud?
AGAVE.
                    Proud and happy.
  I have won the trophy of the chase,
  a great prize, manifest to all.
CORYPHAEUS.
  Then, poor woman, show the citizens of Thebes
  this great prize, this trophy you have won   1250
  in the hunt.

                              [AGAVE *proudly exhibits her thyrsus*
                              with the head of PENTHEUS *impaled*
                              upon the point.]

AGAVE.
                    You citizens of this towered city,
  men of Thebes, behold the trophy of your women's
  hunting! *This* is the quarry of our chase, taken
  not with nets nor spears of bronze but by the white
  and delicate hands of women. What are they worth,
  your boastings now and all that uselessness
  your armor is, since we, with our bare hands,

captured this quarry and tore its bleeding body
limb from limb?
      —But where is my father Cadmus?
He should come. And my son. Where is Pentheus?   1260
Fetch him. I will have him set his ladder up
against the wall and, there upon the beam,
nail the head of this wild lion I have killed
as a trophy of my hunt.

         [Enter CADMUS, *followed by attend-*
         ants who bear upon a bier the dis-
         membered body of PENTHEUS.]

CADMUS.
        Follow me, attendants.
Bear your dreadful burden in and set it down,
there before the palace.

        [The attendants set down the bier.]
      This was Pentheus
whose body, after long and weary searchings
I painfully assembled from Cithaeron's glens
where it lay, scattered in shreds, dismembered
throughout the forest, no two pieces   1270
in a single place.

      Old Teiresias and I
had returned to Thebes from the orgies on the mountain
before I learned of this atrocious crime
my daughters did. And so I hurried back
to the mountain to recover the body of this boy
murdered by the Maenads. There among the oaks
I found Aristaeus' wife, the mother of Actaeon,
Autonoë, and with her Ino, both
still stung with madness. But Agave, they said,
was on her way to Thebes, still possessed.   1280
And what they said was true, for there she is,
and not a happy sight.

AGAVE.
       Now, Father,
yours can be the proudest boast of living men.
For you are now the father of the bravest daughters
in the world. All of your daughters are brave,
but I above the rest. I have left my shuttle
at the loom; I raised my sight to higher things—
to hunting animals with my bare hands.

          You see?
Here in my hands I hold the quarry of my chase,
a trophy for our house. Take it, Father, take it.   1290
Glory in my kill and invite your friends to share
the feast of triumph. For you are blest, Father,
by this great deed I have done.

CADMUS.
        This is a grief

so great it knows no size. I cannot look.
This is the awful murder your hands have done.
This, this is the noble victim you have slaughtered
to the gods. And to share a feast like this
you now invite all Thebes and me?
O gods,
how terribly I pity you and then myself.
Justly—too, too justly—has lord Bromius,   1300
this god of our own blood, destroyed us all,
every one.

AGAVE.
How scowling and crabbed is old age
in men. I hope my son takes after his mother
and wins, as she has done, the laurels of the chase
when he goes hunting with the younger men of Thebes.
But all my son can do is quarrel with god.
He should be scolded, Father, and you are the one
who should scold him. Yes, someone call him out
so he can see his mother's triumph.

CADMUS.
Enough. No more.
When you realize the horror you have done,   1310
you shall suffer terribly. But if with luck
your present madness lasts until you die,
you will seem to have, not having, happiness.

AGAVE.
Why do you reproach me? Is there something wrong?

CADMUS.
First raise your eyes to the heavens.

AGAVE.
There.
But why?

CADMUS.
Does it look the same as it did before?
Or has it changed?

AGAVE.
It seems—somehow—clearer,
brighter than it was before.

CADMUS.
Do you still feel
the same flurry inside you?

AGAVE.
The same—flurry?
No, I feel—somehow—calmer. I feel as though—   1320
my mind were somehow—changing.

CADMUS.
Can you still hear me?
Can you answer clearly?

AGAVE.
No. I have forgotten

what we were saying, Father.
CADMUS.
                                        Who was your husband?
AGAVE.
Echion—a man, they said, born of the dragon seed.
CADMUS.
What was the name of the child you bore your husband?
AGAVE.
    Pentheus.
CADMUS.
                        And whose head do you hold in your hands?
AGAVE [*averting her eyes*].
A lion's head—or so the hunters told me.
CADMUS.
Look directly at it. Just a quick glance.
AGAVE.
What is it? What am I holding in my hands?
CADMUS.
Look more closely still. Study it carefully.   1330
AGAVE.
No! O gods, I see the greatest grief there is.
CADMUS.
Does it look like a lion now?
AGAVE.
                        No, no. It is—
Pentheus' head—I hold—
CADMUS.
                        And mourned by me
before you ever knew.
AGAVE.
                        But *who* killed him?
Why am *I* holding him?
CADMUS.
                        O savage truth,
what a time to come!
AGAVE.
                        For god's sake, speak.
My heart is beating with terror.
CADMUS.
                            You killed him.
You and your sisters.
AGAVE.
                        But where was he killed?
Here at home? Where?
CADMUS.
                        He was killed on Cithaeron,
there where the hounds tore Actaeon to pieces.   1340
AGAVE.
But why? Why had Pentheus gone to Cithaeron?

CADMUS.
He went to your revels to mock the god.
AGAVE.
                                    But *we*—
what were we doing on the mountain?
CADMUS.
                                You were mad.
The whole city was possessed.
AGAVE.
                        Now, now I see:
Dionysus has destroyed us all.
CADMUS.
                            You outraged him.
You denied that he was truly god.
AGAVE.
                            Father,
where is my poor boy's body now?
CADMUS.
                            There it is.
I gathered the pieces with great difficulty.
AGAVE.
Is his body entire? Has he been laid out well?
CADMUS.
[All but the head. The rest is mutilated   1350
horribly.]
AGAVE.
              But why should Pentheus suffer for my crime?
CADMUS.
He, like you, blasphemed the god. And so
the god has brought us all to ruin at one blow,
you, your sisters, and this boy. All our house
the god has utterly destroyed and, with it,
me. For I have no sons left, no male heir;
and I have lived only to see this boy,
this branch of your own body, most horribly
and foully killed.

                    [*He turns and addresses the corpse.*]
              —To you my house looked up.
Child, you were the stay of my house; you were   1360
my daughter's son. Of you this city stood in awe.
No one who once had seen your face dared outrage
the old man, or if he did, you punished him.
Now I must go, a banished and dishonored man—
I, Cadmus the great, who sowed the soldiery
of Thebes and harvested a great harvest. My son,
dearest to me of all men—for even dead,
I count you still the man I love the most—
never again will your hand touch my chin;
no more, child, will you hug me and call me   1370

"Grandfather" and say, "Who is wronging you?
Does anyone trouble you or vex your heart, old man?
Tell me, Grandfather, and I will punish him."
No, now there is grief for me; the mourning
for you; pity for your mother; and for her sisters,
sorrow.
        If there is still any mortal man
who despises or defies the gods, let him look
on this boy's death and believe in the gods.

CORYPHAEUS.
Cadmus, I pity you. Your daughter's son
has died as he deserved, and yet his death   1380
bears hard on you.[50]

AGAVE.
               O Father, now you can see
how everything has changed. I am in anguish now,
tormented, who walked in triumph minutes past,
exulting in my kill. And that prize I carried home
with such pride was my own curse. Upon these hands
I bear the curse of my son's blood. How then
with these accursed hands may I touch his body?
How can I, accursed with such a curse, hold him
to my breast? O gods, what dirge can I sing
[that there might be] a dirge [for every]   1390
broken limb?
.   .   .   .
        Where is a shroud to cover up his corpse?
O my child, what hands will give you proper care
unless with my own hands I lift my curse?
                   [*She lifts up one of* PENTHEUS'
                   limbs and asks the help of CADMUS
                   in piecing the body together. She
                   mourns each piece separately before
                   replacing it on the bier.]
Come, Father. We must restore his head
to this unhappy boy. As best we can, we shall make
him whole again.
            —O dearest, dearest face!
Pretty boyish mouth! Now with this veil
I shroud your head, gathering with loving care
these mangled bloody limbs, this flesh I brought
to birth   1400
.   .   .   .

---

[50]"At this point there is a break in the manuscript of nearly fifty lines. The following speeches of Agave and Coryphaeus and the first part of Dionysus' speech have been conjecturally reconstructed from fragments and later material which made use of the *Bacchae*. Lines which can plausibly be assigned to the lacuna [missing portion] are otherwise not indicated. My own inventions are designed, not to complete the speeches, but to effect a transition between the fragments, and are bracketed." (Translator's note.)

CORYPHAEUS.
　　Let this scene teach those [who see these things:
　　Dionysus is the son] of Zeus.

> [*Above the palace* DIONYSUS *appears in epiphany.*[51]]

DIONYSUS.
　　　　　　　　　　　　[I am Dionysus,
　　the son of Zeus, returned to Thebes, revealed,
　　a god to men.] But the men [of Thebes] blasphemed me.
　　They slandered me; they said I came of mortal man,
　　and not content with speaking blasphemies,
　　[they dared to threaten my person with violence.]
　　These crimes this people whom I cherished well
　　did from malice to their benefactor. Therefore,
　　I now disclose the sufferings in store for them.　　　　　　1410
　　Like [enemies], they shall be driven from this city
　　to other lands; there, submitting to the yoke
　　of slavery, they shall wear out wretched lives,
　　captives of war, enduring much indignity.

> [*He turns to the corpse of* PEN-THEUS.]

　　This man has found the death which he deserved,
　　torn to pieces among the jagged rocks.
　　You are my witnesses: he came with outrage;
　　he attempted to chain my hands, abusing me
　　[and doing what he should least of all have done.]
　　And therefore he has rightly perished by the hands　　　　1420
　　of those who should the least of all have murdered him.
　　What he suffers, he suffers justly.
　　　　　　　　　　　　　　　Upon you,
　　Agave, and on your sisters I pronounce this doom:
　　you shall leave this city in expiation
　　of the murder you have done. You are unclean,
　　and it would be a sacrilege that murderers
　　should remain at peace beside the graves [of those
　　whom they have killed].[52]

> [*He turns to* CADMUS.]

· · · · · · · · · · · · · · · · · · ·

　　　　　　　　Next I shall disclose the trials
　　which await this man. You, Cadmus, shall be changed
　　to a serpent, and your wife, the child of Ares,　　　　　　1430
　　immortal Harmonia, shall undergo your doom,
　　a serpent too. With her, it is your fate
　　to go a journey in a car drawn on by oxen,
　　leading behind you a great barbarian host.
　　For thus decrees the oracle of Zeus.

---

[51] The revelation, or manifestation, of a god.
[52] Here ends the break in the manuscript.

With a host so huge its numbers cannot be counted,
you shall ravage many cities; but when your army
plunders the shrine of Apollo, its homecoming
shall be perilous and hard.[53] Yet in the end
the god Ares shall save Harmonia and you   1440
and bring you both to live among the blest.[54]
   So say I, born of no mortal father,
Dionysus, true son of Zeus. If then,
when you would not, you had muzzled your madness,
you should have an ally now in the son of Zeus.

CADMUS.

We implore you, Dionysus. We have done wrong.[55]

DIONYSUS.

Too late. When there was time, you did not know me.

CADMUS.

We have learned. But your sentence is too harsh.

DIONYSUS.

I am a god. I was blasphemed by you.

CADMUS.

Gods should be exempt from human passions.   1450

DIONYSUS.

Long ago my father Zeus ordained these things.

AGAVE.

It is fated, Father. We must go.

DIONYSUS.

                          Why then delay?
For you must go.

CADMUS.

                   Child, to what a dreadful end
have we all come, you and your wretched sisters
and my unhappy self. An old man, I must go
to live a stranger among barbarian peoples, doomed
to lead against Hellas a motley foreign army.
Transformed to serpents, I and my wife,
Harmonia, the child of Ares, we must captain
spearsmen against the tombs and shrines of Hellas.   1460
Never shall my sufferings end; not even
over Acheron[56] shall I have peace.

AGAVE [*embracing* CADMUS].

                      O Father,
to be banished, to live without you!

---

[53] It will be a "homecoming" because the "barbarian host" (that is, army of non-Greeks) led by Cadmus and his wife will be invading their own country, Greece. The "shrine of Apollo" is Delphi.

[54] Among the spirits in Elysium, the realm of special happiness in the afterlife.

[55] Although Cadmus has been shown earlier in the play as eager to join in the rites of Dionysus, his faith was flawed; for example, he suggested to Pentheus that they should pretend Dionysus was divine even if he was not.

[56] A river in the realm of the dead.

CADMUS.

　　　　　　　　　　　　Poor child,
like a white swan warding its weak old father,
why do you clasp those white arms about my neck?

AGAVE.

But banished! Where shall I go?

CADMUS.

　　　　　　　　　　　I do not know,
my child. Your father can no longer help you.

AGAVE.

Farewell, my home! City, farewell.
O bridal bed, banished I go,
in misery, I leave you now.　　　　　　　　　　　　　1470

CADMUS.

Go, poor child, seek shelter in Aristaeus'[57] house.

AGAVE.

I pity you, Father.

CADMUS.

　　　　　　　　　And I pity you, my child,
and I grieve for your poor sisters. I pity them.

AGAVE.

Terribly has Dionysus brought
disaster down upon this house.

DIONYSUS.

I was terribly blasphemed,
my name dishonored in Thebes.

AGAVE.

Farewell, Father.

CADMUS.

　　　　　　　Farewell to you, unhappy child.
Fare well. But you shall find your faring hard.

　　　　　　　　　　　[*Exit* CADMUS.]

AGAVE.

Lead me, guides, where my sisters wait,　　　　　　1480
poor sisters of my exile. Let me go
where I shall never see Cithaeron more,
where that accursed hill may not see me,
where I shall find no trace of thyrsus!
　　　　That I leave to other Bacchae.

　　　　　　　　　[*Exit* AGAVE *with attendants.*]

CHORUS.

The gods have many shapes.
The gods bring many things
to their accomplishment.
And what was most expected
has not been accomplished.　　　　　　　　　　　　1490
But god has found his way
for what no man expected.
　　　　So ends the play.[58]

---

[57] Husband of Agave's sister Autonoë. Autonoë was the mother of Actaeon, who was destroyed by the goddess Artemis.

[58] These last eight lines are a formula used to conclude several other plays by Euripides, including *Medea, Alcestis, Andromache,* and *Helen.*

Aristophanes

(C. 450–C. 386 B.C.)

Aristophanes was born around 450 B.C., and his death some time during the 380's marks the end of the great century of ancient Greek drama. The chronological sequence of the four pre-eminent playwrights—the tragedians Aeschylus, Sophocles, and Euripides and the comedian Aristophanes—coincides with two important trends in the theater. In aesthetic form, drama moved from the loftily stylized to the more realistic (as typified in the "New Comedy" of the fourth century, which stressed the individual actors and took away from the Chorus its role in the action); in mood and attitude, there was a shift from idealistic optimism to disillusioned cynicism. These trends in the drama parallel trends in Athenian political, religious, and philosophical attitudes. In the epoch ending shortly before 400 B.C., Athens endured military, political, and cultural ordeals that culminated in the overthrow of Athenian democracy and independence. The period when Athens was the moral and political exemplar of what was best in ancient Greece was at an end.

Aristophanes is the only representative of the fifth-century "Old Comedy" whose works have survived. Since biographical information about him is scant, it is difficult to isolate what is distinctive in him from what is characteristic of the Old Comedy; the man and the movement are not clearly separable. If we are thinking about dramaturgy, neither can be called realistic, since the settings, costumes, and freewheeling plots of Aristophanes' plays are often fantastic to the point of surrealism. In The Wasps (a play about the Athenian judicial system; 422), in The Frogs (a literary satire pitting the deceased tragedians Aeschylus and Euripides against each other; 405), and in The Birds (a utopian fantasy-satire; 414), characters or Chorus or both are costumed and portrayed grotesquely in the guise of the animals after which the plays are named.

Yet Aristophanes is a realist in his own way—in subject and theme, if not in theatrical style. His plays (of the forty he wrote, eleven have survived) repeatedly present unflattering portraits of actual people—people who may well have been in his audience—disguised thinly or not at all (they include Socrates, Euripides, and the Athenian political leader Cleon, whom Aristophanes despised). His favorite subjects were literary satire, particularly lampoons of Euripides and what Aristophanes chose to see as the other dramatist's hatred of women; intellectual satire of newfangled trends in education, philosophy, and moral values; and above all, political satire, directed mainly against the Athenian effort in the Peloponnesian War. Aristophanes consistently regarded the war as cruelty toward the enemies and allies of Athens and as suicidal folly from the vantage-point of Athens itself. In fact, early in his career he was once prosecuted for disloyalty. He got off lightly and immediately resumed his role of political gadfly, which says something about Aristophanes and perhaps about Athenian political tolerance even in its days of militaristic jingoism. Spectators of Aristophanes' plays saw the world pictured not in the long vistas of myth and perennial archetypes about the human condition but in the context of what had happened yesterday and what was likely to happen tomorrow. For all his zany exuberance, Aristophanes was an intellectual, and one concerned intimately with current events.

Lysistrata (411) is one of his masterpieces. A witty specimen of antiwar propaganda, it includes also some of his typical wisecracks about tragedy, literature, and Euripides, though it does not demonstrate much if any of his concern with philosophi-

cal issues. The affection and respect Aristophanes felt for women as capable agents and as custodians of ultimate human sanity come across warmly and brilliantly. The same sympathy and admiration emerge in his plays Thesmophoriazusae, *or Ladies' Day (411), in which women plot to avenge themselves on Euripides, and in* Ecclesiazusae, *or* Women in Parliament *(392).*

Roman comedy, which established the model for subsequent comedy in Western theater, was modeled on the Greek New Comedy, a form that thrived after the accession of Alexander the Great, when Athens lost its political freedom. New Comedy abandoned the Aristophanic Old Comedy's freedom of structure and political comment in favor of comparatively realistic plots that usually turned around a young man's attempts to marry over his father's objections. But in many ways the spirit of comedy—laughter, irreverence, the celebration of sexuality, and a movement toward liberation from social and personal bonds—was already established in Old Comedy and was transmitted intact to New Comedy and thence to later dramatic history. In Aristophanes, as in comedy ever since, the action begins with a society constricted by authority, proceeds through a series of laughable irreverent events to dissolve that authority, and ends with a new, liberated society, reconstituted around the values of youth, vitality, and sexuality. Many of Aristophanes' plays end with a feast or a dance, forerunners of the boy-gets-girl celebrations of modern comedy. Sexuality triumphs, and as the modern critic Northrop Frye wittily puts it, "the plot usually moves toward an act which, like death in Greek tragedy, takes place offstage, and is symbolized by a closing embrace."

Lysistrata is not far removed from a fertility celebration, and its cheerful, innocent obscenity is basic to its meaning. Underlying its bawdy, topical jokes and its absurd, incredible plot is a serious confrontation of values. Aristophanes, like his epic and tragic predecessors, almost instinctively defines this confrontation along sexual lines. Lysistrata begins with a comic Athens in thrall to sterile, destructive "male" values, in pursuit of a war that Aristophanes regards as misguided and hopeless. "War's a man's affair," says Lysistrata; she is quoting Homer, but she gives the line an ironic twist very far from Homer's meaning. To the male thirst for glory and self-destructive competitiveness, Lysistrata opposes not only sexuality but also common sense and a respect for nonheroic ordinary life. In the most famous passage in the play, she compares the state to a ball of tangled yarn, which the housewife must untangle, wash, and weave together into a seamless unity. "It would take a woman," the Commissioner exclaims, "to reduce state questions to a matter of carding and weaving!"

Who "wins" in Lysistrata? Just as it is typically Greek to see the world as divided between "male" rationality and abstraction and "female" desire and vitality, so it is typically Greek to see the solution as a balance between the two forces. The women do stop the war (a bit of unhistorical wishful thinking on the part of Aristophanes), but the men's claims of honor are satisfied, too, in the peace negotiations. The real winner is "Reconciliation," a concept represented on stage by a statue under whose eyes the resolution is effected and given significance in the form of an enormous naked woman. We seem to be witnessing an earthy, comic echo of the sexual reconciliation and the hymn to Athens at the end of the Oresteia *when Lysistrata says, "Each man be kind to his woman, and you, women, be equally kind," and the play ends with a joyous hymn to "Athena of the House of Brass."*

FURTHER READING *(prepared by F.S.N.):* On the festivals, staging and production of ancient comedy, see F. H. Sandbach, *The Comic Theatre of Greece and Rome,* 1977;

Kenneth McLeish, *The Theatre of Aristophanes, 1980;* Leo Aylen, *The Greek Theater,*
1985 (with special attention to *The Frogs*); Katherine Lever, *The Art of Greek Comedy,*
1956; and C. W. Dearden, *The Stage of Aristophanes, 1976.* Useful general material
on Aristophanes' life and writings may be found in K. J. Dover, *Aristophanic Comedy,*
1972; and Lois Spatz, *Aristophanes, 1978.* Victor Ehrenberg, *The People of Aristophanes: A Sociology of Old Attic Comedy,* 1943, 3rd ed. 1962, introduces the reader to the
farmers, tradesmen, slaves and family members of the late fifth century B.C. *Yale
Classical Studies,* Vol. XXVI (1980), is devoted to essays on the interpretation of
Aristophanes. Gilbert Murray in *Aristophanes: A Study,* 1933, in addition to presenting background material on Aristophanes and on comedy in general, devotes a
chapter to *Lysistrata.*

LYSISTRATA

Translated by Dudley Fitts

The political and military background of the play is the Peloponnesian war, a series
of conflicts between confederacies led by Athens and Sparta. The Peloponnese, of
which Sparta was the capital, was a large peninsula that makes up southern Greece.
The period of the war, from 431 B.C. to 404, was a tragic era, especially for Athens,
whose defeat in the latter year marked the end of its greatest political and cultural
age. In 413, two years before *Lysistrata* was produced in Athens, the city's naval and
military forces had suffered a calamitous defeat in connection with the ill-fated
Sicilian expedition that Athenian patriots—or imperialists—had hoped would establish Athenian dominance of the Mediterranean. Through comedy that is sometimes caustic and sometimes good-humored, Aristophanes' play was intended to
show the folly of both political power-lust and civil war among Greeks. As art,
Lysistrata is a triumph; judged in the light of historical consequences, the play was a
failure, since the war went on to its disastrous end.

Some of the jokes can be understood only if one keeps in mind that the usual
costume in fifth-century Greek comedy included an exaggeratedly prominent
leather phallus.

The characters' names are in many instances significant puns: for example,
Lysistrata's name means "Dismisser of Armies" and "Myrrhine" puns on the word
meaning female genitals. [*Editors' headnote.*]

PERSONS REPRESENTED

LYSISTRATA	COMMISSIONER
KALONIKE	KINESIAS
MYRRHINE	SPARTAN HERALD
LAMPITO	SPARTAN AMBASSADOR
CHORUS	A SENTRY

SCENE: *Athens. First, a public square; later, beneath the walls of the
Akropolis; later, a courtyard within the Akropolis.*[1]

---

[1] The hill upon which the main civic and religious centers of Athens were located.

Until the *éxodos*, the CHORUS is divided into two hemichori: the first, of Old Men; the second, of Old Women. Each of these has its KORYPHAIOS. In the *éxodos*, the hemichori return as Athenians and Spartans.[2]

The supernumeraries include the BABY SON of Kinêsias; STRATYLLIS, a member of the hemichorus of Old Women; various individual speakers, both Spartan and Athenian.

PROLOGUE

Athens; a public square; early morning; LYSISTRATA *sola.*

LYSISTRATA.
    If someone had invited them to a festival—
    of Bacchos, say; or to Pan's shrine, or to Aphroditê's
    over at Kôlias[3]—, you couldn't get through the streets,
    what with the drums and the dancing. But now,
    not a woman in sight!
                       Except—oh, yes!

[*Enter* KALONIKE]

    Here's one of my neighbors, at last. Good
    morning, Kalonikê.
KALONIKE.
                Good morning, Lysistrata.
                                  Darling,
    don't frown so! You'll ruin your face!
LYSISTRATA.
                            Never mind my face.
    Kalonikê,
    the way we women behave! Really, I don't blame the men   10
    for what they say about us.
KALONIKE.
                   No; I imagine they're right.
LYSISTRATA.
    For example: I call a meeting
    to think out a most important matter—and what happens?
    The women all stay in bed!
KALONIKE.
                Oh, they'll be along.
    It's hard to get away, you know: a husband, a cook,
    a child . . . Home life can be *so* demanding!
LYSISTRATA.
    What I have in mind is even more demanding.

---

[2] The *éxodus* is the last choral song of the play. The *koryphaios* is the principal spokesman for the Chorus or, as here, for a division of it.
[3] An area of the Greek coast where Aphroditê, goddess of love, had a temple.

KALONIKE.
Tell me: what is it?
LYSISTRATA.
                                It's big.
KALONIKE.
                                        Goodness! *How* big?
LYSISTRATA.
Big enough for all of us.
KALONIKE.
                                But we're not all here!
LYSISTRATA.
We would be, if *that's* what was up!
                                        No, Kalonikê,   20
this is something I've been turning over for nights,
long sleepless nights.
KALONIKE.
                        It must be getting worn down, then,
if you've spent so much time on it.
LYSISTRATA.
                                Worn down or not,
it comes to this: Only we women can save Greece!
KALONIKE.
Only we women? Poor Greece!
LYSISTRATA.
                                Just the same,
it's up to us. First, we must liquidate
the Peloponnesians—
KALONIKE.
                        Fun, fun!
LYSISTRATA.
                                —and then the Boiotians.[4]
KALONIKE.
Oh! But not those heavenly eels!
LYSISTRATA.
                                You needn't worry.
I'm not talking about eels.—But here's the point:
If we can get the women from those places—   30
all those Boiotians and Peloponnesians—
to join us women here, why, we can save
all Greece!
KALONIKE.
                But dearest Lysistrata!
How can women do a thing so austere, so
political? We belong at home. Our only armor's
our perfumes, our saffron dresses and
our pretty little shoes!

---

[4] Inhabitants of a region opposed to Athens in the war. The area was noted for its succulent eels and other seafood. Athenian sophisticates regarded Boiotia as a crude and backward place.

LYSISTRATA.

Exactly. Those
transparent dresses, the saffron, the
perfume, those pretty shoes—
KALONIKE.

Oh?

LYSISTRATA.

Not a single man would lift
his spear—
KALONIKE.

I'll send my dress to the dyer's tomorrow! 40
LYSISTRATA.
—or grab a shield—
KALONIKE.

The sweetest little negligée—
LYSISTRATA.
—or haul out his sword.
KALONIKE.

I know where I can buy
the dreamiest sandals!
LYSISTRATA.

Well, so you see. Now, shouldn't
the women have come?
KALONIKE.

Come? They should have *flown!*

LYSISTRATA.
Athenians are always late.

But imagine!
There's no one here from the South Shore, or from Sálamis.[5]
KALONIKE.
Things are hard over in Sálamis, I swear.
They have to get going at dawn.
LYSISTRATA.

And nobody from Acharnai.[6]
I thought they'd be here hours ago.
KALONIKE.

Well, you'll get
that awful Theagenês woman;[7] she'll be 50
a sheet or so in the wind.

But look!
Someone at last! Can you see who they are?

[*Enter* MYRRHINE *and other women*]

---

[5] An island south of Greece, site of the memorable Greek naval victory over the Persians in
480. Lysistrata (whose name means "dismisser of armies") intends to gather women from
Greek cities, both allied with and opposed to Athens.
[6] A town near Athens.
[7] The wife of Theagenês, a notoriously superstitious man. The phrase "a sheet or so in the
wind" means drunk.

LYSISTRATA.
They're from Anagyros.[8]
KALONIKE.
                         They certainly are.
You'd know them anywhere, by the scent.
MYRRHINE.
Sorry to be late, Lysistrata.
                        Oh come,
don't scowl so. Say something!
LYSISTRATA.
                      My dear Myrrhinê,
what is there to say? After all,
you've been pretty casual about the whole thing.
MYRRHINE.
                              Couldn't find
my girdle in the dark, that's all.
                    But what *is*
'the whole thing'?
KALONIKE.
                 No, we've got to wait   60
for those Boiotians and Peloponnesians.
LYSISTRATA.
That's more like it.—But, look!
Here's Lampitô!

               [*Enter* LAMPITO *with women from
               Sparta*]

LYSISTRATA.
                 Darling Lampitô,
how pretty you are today! What a nice color!
Goodness, you look as though you could strangle a bull!
LAMPITO.
Ah think Ah could! It's the work-out
in the gym every day; and, of co'se that dance of ahs
where y' kick yo' own tail.[9]
KALONIKE.
                    What an adorable figure!
LAMPITO.
Lawdy, when y' touch me lahk that,
Ah feel lahk a heifer at the altar!
LYSISTRATA.
                   And this young lady?   70
Where is she from?

---

[8] A malodorous marshland.
[9] The Spartans were proverbially associated with discipline and the more austere virtues.
Lampito here refers to a strenuous dance performed as exercise by Spartan females. The
translator renders Spartan speech as backwoods American-Southern because the Athenians
condescendingly viewed Spartans as unsophisticated.

LAMPITO.
                        Boiotia. Social-Register type.
LYSISTRATA.
    Ah. 'Boiotia of the fertile plain.'
KALONIKE.
                            And if you look,
you'll find the fertile plain has just been mowed.
LYSISTRATA.
    And this lady?
LAMPITO.
                Hagh, wahd, handsome. She comes from Korinth.
KALONIKE.
    High and wide's the word for it.
LAMPITO.
                         Which one of you
called this heah meeting, and why?
LYSISTRATA.
                    I did.
LAMPITO.
                    Well, then, tell us:
What's up?
MYRRHINE.
            Yes, darling, what *is* on your mind, after all?
LYSISTRATA.
    I'll tell you.—But first, one little question.
MYRRHINE.
                           Well?
LYSISTRATA.
    It's your husbands. Fathers of your children. Doesn't it bother you
that they're always off with the Army? I'll stake my life,
not one of you has a man in the house this minute!
              80
KALONIKE.
    Mine's been in Thrace the last five months, keeping an eye
on that General.[10]
MYRRHINE.
               Mine's been in Pylos for seven.
LAMPITO.
                        And mahn,
whenever he gets a *dis*charge, he goes raht back
with that li'l ole shield of his, and enlists again!
LYSISTRATA.
    And not the ghost of a lover to be found!
From the very day the war began—
                      those Milesians![11]
I could skin them alive!
              —I've not seen so much, even,

---

[10] Eukrates, an Athenian commander of doubtful loyalty.

[11] Former allies of Athens who had defected shortly before *Lysistrata* was produced. The Milesians reputedly manufactured a kind of dildo, or phallic substitute.

as one of those leather consolation prizes.—
But there! What's important is: If I've found a way   90
to end the war, are you with me?
MYRRHINE.
                                        I should *say* so!
Even if I have to pawn my best dress and
drink up the proceeds.
KALONIKE.
                              Me, too! Even if they split me
right up the middle, like a flounder.
LAMPITO.
                                        Ah'm shorely with you.
Ah'd crawl up Taÿgetos[12] on mah knees
if that'd bring peace.
LYSISTRATA.
                            All right, then; here it is:
Women! Sisters!
If we really want our men to make peace,
we must be ready to give up—
MYRRHINE.
                                        Give up what!
Quick, tell us!
LYSISTRATA.
                  But *will* you?
MYRRHINE.
                                        We will, even if it kills us.   100
LYSISTRATA.
Then we must give up going to bed with our men.

                        [*Long silence*]

Oh? So now you're sorry? Won't look at me?
Doubtful? Pale? All teary-eyed?
                              But come: be frank with me.
Will you do it, or not? Well? Will you do it?
MYRRHINE.
                                        I couldn't. No.
Let the war go on.
KALONIKE.
                  Nor I. Let the war go on.
LYSISTRATA.
You, you little flounder,
ready to be split up the middle?
KALONIKE.
                              Lysistrata, no!
I'd walk through fire for you—you *know* I would!—but don't
ask us to give up *that!* Why, there's nothing like it!

---

[12] A mountain range near Sparta.

LYSISTRATA.
   And you?
BOIOTIAN.
         No. I must say *I'd* rather walk through fire.   110
LYSISTRATA.
   What an utterly perverted sex we women are!
   No wonder poets write tragedies about us.
   There's only one thing we can think of.
                       But you from Sparta:
   if you stand by me, we may win yet! Will you?
   It means so much!
LAMPITO.
            Ah sweah, it means *too* much!
   By the Two Goddesses,[13] it does! Asking a girl
   to sleep—Heaven knows how long!—in a great big bed
   with nobody there but herself! But Ah'll stay with you!
   Peace comes first!
LYSISTRATA.
           Spoken like a true Spartan!
KALONIKE.
   But if—
       oh dear!
            —if we give up what you tell us to,   120
   will there *be* any peace?
LYSISTRATA.
           Why, mercy, of course there will!
   We'll just sit snug in our very thinnest gowns,
   perfumed and powdered from top to bottom, and those men
   simply won't stand still! And when we say No,
   they'll go out of their minds! And there's your peace.
   You can take my word for it.
LAMPITO.
           Ah seem to remember
   that Colonel Menelaos threw his sword away
   when he saw Helen's breast[14] all bare.
KALONIKE.
           But, goodness me!
   What if they just get up and leave us?
LYSISTRATA.
           In that case
   we'll have to fall back on ourselves, I suppose.   130
   But they won't.
KALONIKE.
        I must say that's not much help. But
   what if they drag us into the bedroom?

[13] Demeter, goddess of the fields and fertility, and her daughter Persephone, who was associated with both death and fertility.

[14] The reference is to Euripides' play *Andromache;* Menelaos (Menelaus), the cuckolded husband of Helen of Troy, is so struck with Helen's beauty that he abandons his plan to kill her in revenge.

LYSISTRATA.

Hang on to the door.

KALONIKE.

What if they slap us?

LYSISTRATA.

If they do, you'd better give in.
But be sulky about it. Do I have to teach you how?
You know there's no fun for men when they have to force you.
There are millions of ways of getting them to see reason.
Don't you worry: a man
doesn't like it unless the girl co-operates.

KALONIKE.

I suppose so. Oh, all right. We'll go along.

LAMPITO.

Ah imagine us Spahtans can arrange a peace. But you   140
Athenians! Why, you're just war-mongerers!

LYSISTRATA.

Leave that to me.

I know how to make them listen.

LAMPITO.

Ah don't see how.

After all, they've got their boats; and there's lots of money[15]
piled up in the Akropolis.

LYSISTRATA.

The Akropolis? Darling,
we're taking over the Akropolis today!
That's the older women's job. All the rest of us
are going to the Citadel to sacrifice—you understand me?
And once there, we're in for good!

LAMPITO.

Whee! Up the rebels!

Ah can see you're a good strat*ee*gist.

LYSISTRATA.

Well, then, Lampitô,
what we have to do now is take a solemn oath.[16]   150

LAMPITO.

Say it. We'll sweah.

LYSISTRATA.

This is it.
—But where's our Inner Guard?
                    —Look, Guard: you see this shield?
Put it down here. Now bring me the victim's entrails.

KALONIKE.

But the oath?

LYSISTRATA.

You remember how in Aischylos' *Seven*
they killed a sheep and swore on a shield? Well, then?

---

[15] A fund stored on the Akropolis, designed to finance the war effort.
[16] What follows is a parody of a standard ritual sacrifice and oath of loyalty.

KALONIKE.
But I don't see how you can swear for peace on a shield.
LYSISTRATA.
What else do you suggest?
KALONIKE.
                              Why not a white horse?[17]
We could swear by that.
LYSISTRATA.
                     And where will you get a white horse?
KALONIKE.
I never thought of that. *What* can we do?
LYSISTRATA.
                              I have it!
Let's set this big black wine-bowl on the ground   160
and pour in a gallon or so of Thasian,[18] and swear
not to add one drop of water.
LAMPITO.
                    Ah lahk *that* oath!
LYSISTRATA.
Bring the bowl and the wine-jug.
KALONIKE.
                    Oh, what a simply *huge* one!
LYSISTRATA.
Set it down. Girls, place your hands on the gift-offering.

O Goddess of Persuasion! And thou, O Loving-cup
Look upon this our sacrifice, and
be gracious!
KALONIKE.
See the blood spill out. How red and pretty it is!
LAMPITO.
And Ah must say it smells good.
MYRRHINE.
                  Let me swear first!
KALONIKE.
No, by Aphroditê, we'll match for it!   170
LYSISTRATA.
Lampitô: all of you women: come, touch the bowl,
and repeat after me—remember, this is an oath—:
I WILL HAVE NOTHING TO DO WITH MY HUSBAND OR
    MY LOVER
KALONIKE.
I will have nothing to do with my husband or my lover
LYSISTRATA.
THOUGH HE COME TO ME IN PITIABLE CONDITION

---

[17] In Aeschylus' tragedy *Seven Against Thebes*, the seven leaders attacking the city take an oath on a shield. (This war provides the background of Sophocles' *Antigone*.) The reference to the white horse is possibly some kind of sexual joke, but commentators are puzzled by the phrase.

[18] A wine of high quality.

KALONIKE.
Though he come to me in pitiable condition
(Oh Lysistrata! This is killing me!)
LYSISTRATA.
IN MY HOUSE I WILL BE UNTOUCHABLE
KALONIKE.
In my house I will be untouchable
LYSISTRATA.
IN MY THINNEST SAFFRON SILK   180
KALONIKE.
In my thinnest saffron silk
LYSISTRATA.
AND MAKE HIM LONG FOR ME.
KALONIKE.
And make him long for me.
LYSISTRATA.
I WILL NOT GIVE MYSELF
KALONIKE.
I will not give myself
LYSISTRATA.
AND IF HE CONSTRAINS ME
KALONIKE.
And if he constrains me
LYSISTRATA.
I WILL BE COLD AS ICE AND NEVER MOVE
KALONIKE.
I will be cold as ice and never move
LYSISTRATA.
I WILL NOT LIFT MY SLIPPERS TOWARD THE CEILING   190
KALONIKE.
I will not lift my slippers toward the ceiling
LYSISTRATA.
OR CROUCH ON ALL FOURS LIKE THE LIONESS IN THE
    CARVING
KALONIKE.
Or crouch on all fours like the lioness in the carving
LYSISTRATA.
AND IF I KEEP THIS OATH LET ME DRINK FROM THIS
    BOWL
KALONIKE.
And if I keep this oath let me drink from this bowl
LYSISTRATA.
IF NOT, LET MY OWN BOWL BE FILLED WITH WATER
KALONIKE.
If not, let my own bowl be filled with water.
LYSISTRATA.
You have all sworn?
MYRRHINE.
                    We have.

Lysistrata.

                         Then thus
I sacrifice the victim.

                    [*Drinks largely*]

Kalonike.

                    Save some for us!
Here's to you, darling, and to you, and to you!   200

                    [*Loud cries off-stage*]

Lampito.
What's all *that* whoozy-goozy?

Lysistrata.

                         Just what I told you.
The older women have taken the Akropolis.
Now you, Lampitô,
rush back to Sparta. We'll take care of things here. Leave
these girls here for hostages.
                         The rest of you,
up to the Citadel: and mind you push in the bolts.

Kalonike.
But the men? Won't they be after us?

Lysistrata.

                              Just you leave
the men to me. There's not fire enough in the world,
or threats either, to make me open these doors
except on my own terms.

Kalonike.

              I hope not, by Aphroditê!   210
After all,
we've got a reputation for bitchiness to live up to.

                    [*Exeunt*]

PÁRODOS:[19] CHORAL EPISODE

The hillside just under the Akropolis. Enter Chorus of Old Men *with burning torches and braziers; much puffing and coughing.*

Koryphaios[m].
Forward march, Drakês, old friend: never you mind
that damn big log banging hell down on your back.

Chorus[m].
There's this to be said for longevity: [strophe 1]
You see things you thought that you'd never see.
Look, Strymodôros, who would have thought it?

---

[19] The song sung at the first entrance of the Chorus.

We've caught it—
                    the New Femininity!
The wives of our bosom, our board, our bed—
Now, by the gods, they've gone ahead   220
And taken the Citadel (Heaven knows why!),
Profanèd the sacred statuar-y,[20]
                                        And barred the doors,
                                        The subversive whores!

KORYPHAIOS[m].
  Shake a leg there, Philûrgos, man: the Akropolis or bust!
  Put the kindling around here. We'll build one almighty big
  bonfire for the whole bunch of bitches, every last one;
  and the first we fry will be old Lykôn's woman.[21]

CHORUS[m].

                                                  [ANTISTROPHE 1]
  They're not going to give me the old horse-laugh!
  No, by Deméter, they won't pull this off!   230
    Think of Kleómenés:[22] even he
    Didn't go free
                    till he brought me his stuff.
  A good man he was, all stinking and shaggy,
  Bare as an eel except for the bag he
  Covered his rear with. God, what a mess!
  Never a bath in six years, I'd guess.
                    Pure Sparta, man!
                    He also ran.

KORYPHAIOS[m].
  That was a siege, friends! Seventeen ranks strong
  we slept at the Gate. And shall we not do as much   240
  against these women, whom God and Euripides[23] hate?
  If we don't, I'll turn in my medals from Marathon.

CHORUS[m].

                                                      [STROPHE 2]
  Onward and upward! A little push,
    And we're there.
  Ouch, my shoulders! I could wish
    For a pair
  Of good strong oxen. Keep your eye
  On the fire there, it mustn't die.
                    Akh! Akh!
  The smoke would make a cadaver cough!   250

[20] An old and revered wooden statue of Athêna in her role as protectress of Athens.
  [21] A woman noted for lax morality; here, as often elsewhere, Aristophanes refers to actual people of his time.
  [22] A Spartan king who, in 508, had occupied the Akropolis in aid of the aristocratic party during a civil conflict in Athens. His occupation was brief, not the six years the senile Chorus remembers. The reference to this incident, like the following reminiscence of the great victory at Marathon (490), would make the members of the Chorus a hundred or more years old—probably a joke by Aristophanes, designed to emphasize the old men's decrepitude.
  [23] Often represented by Aristophanes, perhaps only half-seriously, as a misogynist.

Holy Heraklês, a hot spark   [ANTISTROPHE 2]
  Bit my eye!
Damn this hellfire, damn this work!
  So say I.
Onward and upward just the same.
(Lachês, remember the Goddess: for shame!)
    Akh! Akh!
    The smoke would make a cadaver cough!

KORYPHAIOS[m].

At last (and let us give suitable thanks to God
for his infinite mercies) I have managed to bring   260
my personal flame to the common goal. It breathes, it lives.
Now, gentlemen, let us consider. Shall we insert
the torch, say, into the brazier, and thus extract
a kindling brand? And shall we then, do you think,
push on to the gate like valiant sheep? On the whole, yes.
But I would have you consider this, too: if they—
I refer to the women—should refuse to open,
what then? Do we set the doors afire
and smoke them out? At ease, men. Meditate.
Akh, the smoke! Woof! What we really need   270
is the loan of a general or two from the Samos[24] Command.
At least we've got this lumber off our backs.
That's something. And now let's look to our fire.

O Pot, brave Brazier, touch my torch with flame!
Victory, Goddess, I invoke thy name!
Strike down these paradigms of female pride,
And we shall hang our trophies up inside.

           [*Enter* CHORUS OF OLD WOMEN
           on the walls of the Akropolis, carry-
           ing jars of water]

KORYPHAIOS[w].

Smoke, girls, smoke! There's smoke all over the place!
Probably fire, too. Hurry, girls! Fire! Fire!

CHORUS[w].

      Nikodikê, run!   [STROPHE 1]   280
      Or Kalyké's done
      To a turn, and poor Kritylla's
      Smoked like a ham.
             Damn
      These old men! Are we too late?
      I nearly died down at the place
      Where we fill our jars:
        Slaves pushing and jostling—
        Such a hustling
      I never saw in all my days.

---

[24] An island near Asia Minor. At the time of the play it was the headquarters of Athenian forces.

But here's water at last.   [ANTISTROPHE 1]   290
Haste, sisters, haste!
Slosh it on them, slosh it down,
The silly old wrecks!
                              Sex
Almighty! What they want's
A hot bath? Good. Send one down.
Athêna of Athens town,
    Trito-born![25] Helm of Gold!
    Cripple the old
Firemen! Help us help them drown!

> [*The* OLD MEN *capture a woman,*
> STRATYLLIS]

STRATYLLIS.
  Let me go! Let me go!
KORYPHAIOS[w].
                    You walking corpses,   300
  have you no shame?
KORYPHAIOS[m].
                    I wouldn't have believed it!
  An army of women in the Akropolis!
KORYPHAIOS[w].
  So we scare you, do we? Grandpa, you've seen
  only our pickets yet!
KORYPHAIOS[m].
                    Hey, Phaidrias!
  Help me with the necks of these jabbering hens!
KORYPHAIOS[w].
  Down with your pots, girls! We'll need both hands
  if these antiques attack us.
KORYPHAIOS[m].
                    Want your face kicked in?
KORYPHAIOS[w].
  Want your balls chewed off?
KORYPHAIOS[m].
                    Look out! I've got a stick!
KORYPHAIOS[w].
  You lay a half-inch of your stick on Stratyllis,
  and you'll never stick again!   310
KORYPHAIOS[m].
  Fall apart!
KORYPHAIOS[w].
                    I'll spit up your guts!
KORYPHAIOS[m].
                    Euripides! Master!
  How well you knew women!

---

[25] Athêna, by one account, was born near Tritonis, a lake in Libya.

KORYPHAIOS^w.
                              Listen to him! Rhodippê,
   up with the pots!
KORYPHAIOS^m.
                         Demolition of God,
   what good are your pots?
KORYPHAIOS^w.
                              You refugee from the tomb,
   what good is your fire?
KORYPHAIOS^m.
                              Good enough to make a pyre
   to barbecue you!
KORYPHAIOS^w.
                              We'll squizzle your kindling!
KORYPHAIOS^m.
   You think so?
KORYPHAIOS^w.
                    Yah! Just hang around a while!
KORYPHAIOS^m.
   Want a touch of my torch?
KORYPHAIOS^w.
                              It needs a good soaping.
KORYPHAIOS^m.
   How about you?
KORYPHAIOS^w.
                         Soap for a senile bridegroom!
KORYPHAIOS^m.
   Senile? Hold your trap!
KORYPHAIOS^w.
                              Just *you* try to hold it!   320
KORYPHAIOS^m.
   The yammer of women!
KORYPHAIOS^w.
                              Oh is that so?
   You're not in the jury room[26] now, you know.
KORYPHAIOS^m.
   Gentlemen, I beg you, burn off that woman's hair!
KORYPHAIOS^w.
   Let it come down!

                              [*They empty their pots on the men*]

KORYPHAIOS^m.
   What a way to drown!
KORYPHAIOS^w.
                         Hot, hey?
KORYPHAIOS^m.
                              Say,
   enough!

[26] Elderly Athenians frequently served as jurors in law cases.

KORYPHAIOS[w].
        Dandruff
needs watering. I'll make you
nice and fresh.
KORYPHAIOS[m].
                For God's sake, you,
hold off!

SCENE I

[*Enter a* COMMISSIONER[27] *accompanied by four constables*]

COMMISSIONER.
    These degenerate women! What a racket of little drums,   330
    what a yapping for Adonis on every house-top!
    It's like the time in the Assembly when I was listening
    to a speech—out of order, as usual—by that fool
    Demostratos,[28] all about troops for Sicily,
    that kind of nonsense—
                        and there was his wife
    trotting around in circles howling
    Alas for Adonis!—
                    and Demostratos insisting
    we must draft every last Zakynthian[29] that can walk—
    and his wife up there on the roof,
    drunk as an owl, yowling   340
    Oh weep for Adonis!—
                        and that damned ox Demostratos
    mooing away through the rumpus. That's what we get
    for putting up with this wretched woman-business!
KORYPHAIOS[m].
    Sir, you haven't heard the half of it. They laughed at us!
    Insulted us! They took pitchers of water
    and nearly drowned us! We're still wringing out our clothes,
    for all the world like unhousebroken brats.
COMMISSIONER.
    Serves you right, by Poseidon![30]
    Whose fault is it if these women-folk of ours
    get out of hand? We coddle them,   350
    we teach them to be wasteful and loose. You'll see a husband
    go into a jeweler's. 'Look,' he'll say,

---

[27] One of a group of men appointed to oversee the Athenian legislature after the defeat in Sicily.

[28] One of the most aggressive supporters of the recent disastrous campaign in Sicily. At the time the expedition set forth, the women were celebrating the rituals of Adonis, a god who represented the death-and-resurrection cycle in nature. The women's ritual laments for his death were interpreted as having put a hex on the military expedition.

[29] Dwellers on the island of Zakynthos; they were allies of Athens who, it had been hoped, would strengthen the Athenian forces in the Sicilian campaign.

[30] God of water and ocean.

'jeweler,' he'll say, 'you remember that gold choker
'you made for my wife? Well, she went to a dance last night
'and broke the clasp. Now, I've got to go to Sálamis,
'and can't be bothered. Run over to my house tonight,
'will you, and see if you can put it together for her.'
Or another one
goes to a cobbler—a good strong workman, too,
with an awl that was never meant for child's play. 'Here,'   360
he'll tell him, 'one of my wife's shoes is pinching
'her little toe. Could you come up about noon
'and stretch it out for her?'
                                        Well, what do you expect?
Look at me, for example. I'm a Public Officer,
and it's one of my duties to pay off the sailors.
And where's the money? Up there in the Akropolis!
And those blasted women slam the door in my face!
But what are we waiting for?
                                —Look here, constable,
stop sniffing around for a tavern, and get us
some crowbars. We'll force their gates! As a matter of fact,   370
I'll do a little forcing myself.

                          [*Enter* LYSISTRATA, *above, with*
                          MYRRHINE, KALONIKE, *and the*
                          BOIOTIAN]

LYSISTRATA.
                              No need of forcing.
Here I am, of my own accord. And all this talk
about locked doors—! We don't need locked doors,
but just the least bit of common sense.
COMMISSIONER.
    Is that so, ma'am!
                      —Where's my constable?
                                      —Constable,
arrest that woman, and tie her hands behind her.
LYSISTRATA.
    If he touches me, I swear by Artemis[31]
    there'll be one scamp dropped from the public pay-roll tomorrow!
COMMISSIONER.
    Well, constable? You're not afraid, I suppose? Grab her,
    two of you, around the middle!
KALONIKE.
                        No, by Pándrosos![32]   380
    Lay a hand on her, and I'll jump on you so hard
    your guts will come out the back door!

---

[31] The virgin goddess of the hunt, the moon, and childbirth. In the following lines, she is referred to as "the Moon-Goddess" and "the Taurian."
[32] Daughter of a legendary ruler of Athens.

COMMISSIONER.

                                        That's what *you* think!
Where's the sergeant?—Here, you: tie up that trollop first,
the one with the pretty talk!

MYRRHINE.

                                        By the Moon-Goddess,
just try! They'll have to scoop you up with a spoon!

COMMISSIONER.

        Another one!
                        Officer, seize that woman!
                                                        I swear
I'll put an end to this riot!

BOIOTIAN.

                                        By the Taurian,
one inch closer, you'll be one screaming bald-head!

COMMISSIONER.

        Lord, what a mess! And my constables seem ineffective.
But—women get the best of us? By God, no!
                                                —Skythians![33]   390

Close ranks and forward march!

LYSISTRATA.

                                        'Forward,' indeed!
By the Two Goddesses, what's the sense in *that*?
They're up against four companies of women
armed from top to bottom.

COMMISSIONER.

                                Forward, my Skythians!

LYSISTRATA.

        Forward, yourselves, dear comrades!
You grainlettucebeanseedmarket girls!
You garlicandonionbreadbakery girls!
Give it to 'em! Knock 'em down! Scratch 'em!
Tell 'em what you think of 'em!

                        [*General mêlée; the Skythians yield*]

                                        —Ah, that's enough!
Sound a retreat: good soldiers don't rob the dead.   400

COMMISSIONER.

        A nice day *this* has been for the police!

LYSISTRATA.

        Well, there you are.—Did you really think we women
would be driven like slaves? Maybe now you'll admit
that a woman knows something about spirit.

COMMISSIONER.

                                        Spirit enough,
especially spirits in bottles! Dear Lord Apollo!

[33] Archers from the north who made up much of the Athenian police force.

KORYPHAIOS[m].
　　Your Honor, there's no use talking to them. Words
　　mean nothing whatever to wild animals like these.
　　Think of the sousing they gave us! and the water
　　was not, I believe, of the purest.
KORYPHAIOS[w].
　　You shouldn't have come after us. And if you try it again,　　　410
　　you'll be one eye short!—Although, as a matter of fact,
　　what I like best is just to stay at home and read,
　　like a sweet little bride: never hurting a soul, no,
　　never going out. But if you *must* shake hornets' nests,
　　look out for the hornets.
CHORUS[m].
　　　　Of all the beasts that God hath wrought　　　[STROPHE 1]
　　　　　What monster's worse than woman?
　　　　Who shall encompass with his thought
　　　　　Their guile unending? No man.

　　　　They've seized the Heights, the Rock, the Shrine—　　　420
　　　　　But to what end? I wot not.
　　　　Sure there's some clue to their design!
　　　　　Have you the key? I thought not.
KORYPHAIOS[m].
　　We might question them, I suppose. But I warn you, sir,
　　don't believe anything you hear! It would be un-Athenian
　　not to get to the bottom of this plot.
COMMISSIONER.
　　　　　　　　　　　　　　Very well.
　　My first question is this: Why, so help you God,
　　did you bar the gates of the Akropolis?
LYSISTRATA.
　　　　　　　　　　　　　　Why?
　　To keep the money, of course. No money, no war.
COMMISSIONER.
　　You think that money's the cause of war?
LYSISTRATA.
　　　　　　　　　　　　　　I do.　　　430
　　Money brought about that Peisandros[34] business
　　and all the other attacks on the State. Well and good!
　　They'll not get another cent here!
COMMISSIONER.
　　　　　　　　　　　　And what will you do?
LYSISTRATA.
　　What a question! From now on, we intend
　　to control the Treasury.

---

[34] A corrupt and venal Athenian politician who plotted to overthrow the city's democratic
regime.

COMMISSIONER.
                                        Control the Treasury!
LYSISTRATA.
    Why not? Does that seem strange? After all,
    we control our household budgets.
COMMISSIONER.
                                        But that's different!
LYSISTRATA.
    'Different'? What do you mean?
COMMISSIONER.
                                        I mean simply this:
    it's the Treasury that pays for National Defense.
LYSISTRATA.
    Unnecessary. We propose to abolish war.   440
COMMISSIONER.
    Good God.—And National Security?
LYSISTRATA.
                                        Leave that to us.
COMMISSIONER.
    You?
LYSISTRATA.
            Us.
COMMISSIONER.
            We're done for, then!
LYSISTRATA.
                                        Never mind.
    We women will save you in spite of yourselves.
COMMISSIONER.
                                        What nonsense!
LYSISTRATA.
    If you like. But you must accept it, like it or not.
COMMISSIONER.
    Why, this is downright subversion!
LYSISTRATA.
                                        Maybe it is.
    But we're going to save you, Judge.
COMMISSIONER.
                                        I don't *want* to be saved.
LYSISTRATA.
    Tut. The death-wish. All the more reason.
COMMISSIONER.
                                        But the idea
    of women bothering themselves about peace and war!
LYSISTRATA.
    Will you listen to me?
COMMISSIONER.
                        Yes. But be brief, or I'll—
LYSISTRATA.
    This is no time for stupid threats.

COMMISSIONER.
                              By the gods,   450
    I can't stand any more!
AN OLD WOMAN.
                         Can't stand? Well, well.
COMMISSIONER.
    That's enough out of you, you old buzzard!
    Now, Lysistrata: tell me what you're thinking.
LYSISTRATA.
    Glad to.
            Ever since this war began
    We women have been watching you men, agreeing with you,
    keeping our thoughts to ourselves. That doesn't mean
    we were happy: we *weren't*, for we saw how things were going;
    but we'd listen to you at dinner
    arguing this way and that.
                         —Oh you, and your big
    Top Secrets!—
                And then we'd grin like little patriots   460
    (though goodness knows we didn't feel like grinning) and ask you:
    'Dear, did the Armistice come up in Assembly today?'
    And you'd say, 'None of your business! Pipe down!' you'd say.
    And so we would.
AN OLD WOMAN.
                    I wouldn't have by God!
COMMISSIONER.
    You'd have taken a beating, then!
                              —Go on.
LYSISTRATA.
    Well, we'd be quiet. But then, you know, all at once
    you men would think up something worse than ever.
    Even *I* could see it was fatal. And, 'Darling,' I'd say,
    'have you gone completely mad?' And my husband would look at
        me
    and say, 'Wife, you've got your weaving to attend to.   470
    'Mind your tongue, if you don't want a slap. "War's
    "a man's affair"!'[35]
COMMISSIONER.
                    Good words, and well pronounced.
LYSISTRATA.
    You're a fool if you think so.
                              It was hard enough
    to put up with all this banquet-hall strategy.
    But then we'd hear you out in the public square:
    'Nobody left for the draft-quota here in Athens?'
    you'd say; and, 'No,' someone else would say, 'not a man!'

---

[35] Hector addresses these last four words to his wife, Andromache, in Homer's *Iliad*,
Book VI.

And so we women decided to rescue Greece.
You might as well listen to us now: you'll have to, later.
COMMISSIONER.
You rescue Greece? Absurd.
LYSISTRATA.

                    You're the absurd one.   480
COMMISSIONER.
You expect me to take orders from a woman?

                             I'd die first!
LYSISTRATA.
Heavens, if that's what's bothering you, take my veil,
here, and wrap it around your poor head.
KALONIKE.

                           Yes,
and you can have my market-basket, too.
Go home, tighten your girdle, do the washing, mind
your beans! 'War's
a woman's affair'!
KORYPHAIOS[w].

               Ground pitchers! Close ranks!
CHORUS[w].

                                   [ANTISTROPHE]

    This is a dance that I know well.
      My knees shall never yield.
    Wobble and creak I may, but still   490
      I'll keep the well-fought field.

    Valor and grace march on before,
      Love prods us from behind.
    Our slogan is EXCELSIOR.[36]
      Our watchword SAVE MANKIND.
KORYPHAIOS[w].
Women, remember your grandmothers! Remember
that little old mother of yours, what a stinger she was!
On, on, never slacken. There's a strong wind astern!
LYSISTRATA.
O Erôs of delight! O Aphroditê! Kyprian![37]
If ever desire has drenched our breasts or dreamed   500
in our thighs, let it work so now on the men of Hellas
that they shall tail us through the land, slaves, slaves
to Woman, Breaker of Armies!
COMMISSIONER.

                    And if we do?
LYSISTRATA.
Well, for one thing, we shan't have to watch you
going to market, a spear in one hand, and heaven knows
what in the other.

---

[36] A Latin motto meaning, roughly, "On to nobler things," or, literally, "higher."
[37] Erôs, Aphroditê, and Kyprian are names for the god and goddess of love.

KALONIKE.
                            Nicely said, by Aphroditê!
LYSISTRATA.
   As things stand now, you're neither men nor women.
   Armor clanking with kitchen pans and pots—
   you sound like a pack of Korybantês![38]
COMMISSIONER.
   A man must do what a man must do.
LYSISTRATA.
                                      So I'm told.   510
   But to see a General, complete with Gorgon-shield,[39]
   jingling along the dock to buy a couple of herrings!
KALONIKE.
   I saw a Captain the other day—lovely fellow he was,
   nice curly hair—sitting on his horse; and—can you believe it?—
   he'd just bought some soup, and was pouring it into his helmet!
   And there was a soldier from Thrace
   swishing his lance like something out of Euripides,
   and the poor fruit-store woman got so scared
   that she ran away and let him have his figs free!
COMMISSIONER.
   All this is beside the point.
                                Will you be so kind   520
   as to tell me how you mean to save Greece?
LYSISTRATA.
                                      Of course.
   Nothing could be simpler.
COMMISSIONER.
                            I assure you, I'm all ears.
LYSISTRATA.
   Do you know anything about weaving?
   Say the yarn gets tangled: we thread it
   this way and that through the skein, up and down,
   until it's free. And it's like that with war.
   We'll send our envoys
   up and down, this way and that, all over Greece,
   until it's finished.
COMMISSIONER.
                   Yarn? Thread? Skein?
   Are you out of your mind? I tell you,   530
   war is a serious business.
LYSISTRATA.
                        So serious
   that I'd like to go on talking about weaving.
COMMISSIONER.
   All right. Go ahead.

---

[38] Devotees of the earth-goddess Cybele, whose rites included frenzied dancing and music.
[39] The Gorgon's head, in myth, turned gazers to stone; it was therefore a common design on warriors' shields.

LYSISTRATA.
                         The first thing we have to do
is to wash our yarn, get the dirt out of it.
You see? Isn't there too much dirt here in Athens?
You must wash those men away.
                          Then our spoiled wool—
that's like your job-hunters, out for a life
of no work and big pay. Back to the basket,
citizens or not, allies or not,
or friendly immigrants.
                       And your colonies?   540
Hanks of wool lost in various places. Pull them
together, weave them into one great whole,
and our voters are clothed for ever.
COMMISSIONER.
                           It would take a woman
to reduce state questions to a matter of carding and weaving.
LYSISTRATA.
You fool! Who were the mothers whose sons sailed off
to fight for Athens in Sicily?
COMMISSIONER.
                    Enough!
I beg you, do not call back those memories.
LYSISTRATA.
                         And then,
instead of the love that every woman needs,
we have only our single beds, where we can dream
of our husbands off with the Army.
                       Bad enough for wives!   550
But what about our girls, getting older every day,
and older, and no kisses?
COMMISSIONER.
                   Men get older, too.
LYSISTRATA.
Not in the same sense.
                 A soldier's discharged,
and he may be bald and toothless, yet he'll find
a pretty young thing to go to bed with.
                      But a woman!
Her beauty is gone with the first grey hair.
She can spend her time
consulting the oracles and the fortune-tellers,
but they'll never send her a husband.
COMMISSIONER.
Still, if a man can rise to the occasion—   560
LYSISTRATA.
Rise? Rise, yourself!

                     [*Furiously*]

Go invest in a coffin!
You've money enough.
I'll bake you
a cake[40] for the Underworld.
And here's your funeral
wreath!

[*She pours water upon him*]

MYRRHINE.
And here's another!

[*More water*]

KALONIKE.
And here's
my contribution!

[*More water*]

LYSISTRATA.
What are you waiting for?
All aboard Styx Ferry![41]
Charôn's calling for you!
It's sailing-time: don't disrupt the schedule!

COMMISSIONER.
The insolence of women! And to me!
No, by God, I'll go back to town and show   570
the rest of the Commission what might happen to them.

[*Exit* COMMISSIONER]

LYSISTRATA.
Really, I suppose we should have laid out his corpse
on the doorstep, in the usual way.
But never mind.
We'll give him the rites of the dead tomorrow morning.

[*Exit* LYSISTRATA *with* MYRRHINE
and KALONIKE]

PARÁBASIS:[42] CHORAL EPISODE

KORYPHAIOS^m.

[ODE 1]
Sons of Liberty, awake! The day of glory is at hand.

---

[40] Part of the customary funeral ritual; a honey cake was the offering with which the dead person was to propitiate Cerberus, the monster-dog who guarded the Underworld, or realm of the dead.

[41] The dead were ferried by the boatman Charôn across the river Styx to the Underworld.

[42] An address to the audience by the Chorus.

CHORUS[m].

I smell tyranny afoot, I smell it rising from the land.
I scent a trace of Hippias,[43] I sniff upon the breeze
A dismal Spartan hogo that suggests King Kleisthenês.[44]
  Strip, strip for action, brothers!
  Our wives, aunts, sisters, mothers   580
Have sold us out: the streets are full of godless female rages.
Shall we stand by and let our women confiscate our wages?[45]

KORYPHAIOS[m].

[EPIRRHEMA[46] 1]

Gentlemen, it's a disgrace to Athens, a disgrace
to all that Athens stands for, if we allow these grandmas
to jabber about spears and shields and making friends
with the Spartans. What's a Spartan? Give me a wild wolf
any day. No. They want the Tyranny back, I suppose.
Are we going to take that? No. Let us look like
the innocent serpent, but be the flower under it,
as the poet sings. And just to begin with,   590
I propose to poke a number of teeth
down the gullet of that harridan[47] over there.

KORYPHAIOS[w].

[ANTODE 1]

Oh, is that so? When you get home, your own mammá won't know
    you!

CHORUS[w].

Who do you think we are, you senile bravos? Well, I'll show you.
I bore the sacred vessels[48] in my eighth year, and at ten
I was pounding out the barley for Athêna Goddess; then
    They made me Little Bear
    At the Braunonian Fair;
I'd held the Holy Basket by the time I was of age,
The Blessed Dry Figs had adorned my plump décolletage.   600

KORYPHAIOS[w].

[ANTEPIRRHEMA 1]

A 'disgrace to Athens', am I, just at the moment
I'm giving Athens the best advice she ever had?
Don't I pay taxes to the State? Yes, I pay them
in baby boys. And what do you contribute,
you impotent horrors? Nothing but waste: all
our Treasury,[49] dating back to the Persian Wars,

---

[43] The last of the Athenian tyrants; he ruled about a century before the present action.
[44] A notoriously effeminate bisexual.
[45] The fund from which the elderly jurors' fees were paid was kept at the Akropolis.
[46] Along with the following "Antode" and "Antepirrhema," this section is a choral song that customarily made a satiric comment on current events.
[47] A sharp-tongued old woman.
[48] In the following lines, the women describe various roles in the rites of Athêna and Artemis. Selected preadolescent Athenian girls of good family were privileged to perform these roles.
[49] A fund originally established in the days of Greek unity to finance the war against Persia; the money had since been misappropriated by unscrupulous politicians.

gone! rifled! And not a penny out of your pockets!
Well, then? Can you cough up an answer to that?
Look out for your own gullet, or you'll get a crack
from this old brogan that'll make your teeth see stars!   610
Chorus[m].

          Oh insolence!   [ODE 2]
          Am I unmanned?
          Incontinence!
          Shall my scarred hand
          Strike never a blow
          To curb this flow-
          ing female curse?

          Leipsydrion![50]
          Shall I betray
          The laurels won   620
          On that great day?
          Come, shake a leg,
          Shed old age, beg
          The years reverse!

Koryphaios[m].

                                   [EPIRRHEMA 2]
Give them an inch, and we're done for! We'll have them
launching boats next and planning naval strategy,
sailing down on us like so many Artemisias.[51]
Or maybe they have ideas about the cavalry.
That's fair enough, women are certainly good
in the saddle. Just look at Mikôn's paintings,   630
all those Amazons[52] wrestling with all those men!
On the whole, a straitjacket's their best uniform.
Chorus[w].

          Tangle with me,   [ANTODE 2]
          And you'll get cramps.
          Ferocity
          's no use now, Gramps!
          By the Two,
          I'll get through
          To you wrecks yet!

          I'll scramble your eggs,   640
          I'll burn your beans,
          With my two legs.
          You'll see such scenes
          As never yet
          Your two eyes met.
          A curse? You bet!

[50] Another site of patriotic Athenian heroism from the great days (in this instance about a century earlier) of the city's fight against tyranny.
[51] A queen who had commanded a naval unit in the Persian war against Greece.
[52] Fabled women-warriors; Mikôn was a famous contemporary painter.

KORYPHAIOS^W.

    If Lampitô stands by me, and that delicious Theban girl,
    Ismênia—what good are *you?* You and your seven
    Resolutions! Resolutions? Rationing Boiotian eels
    and making our girls go without them at Hekatê's Feast!   650
    That was statesmanship! And we'll have to put up with it
    and all the rest of your decrepit legislation
    until some patriot—God give him strength!—
    grabs you by the neck and kicks you off the Rock.

SCENE II

[*Re-enter* LYSISTRATA *and her lieutenants*]

KORYPHAIOS^W [*Tragic tone*].
        Great Queen, fair Architect of our emprise,
        Why lookst thou on us with foreboding eyes?
LYSISTRATA.
    The behavior of these idiotic women!
    There's something about the female temperament
    that I can't bear!
KORYPHAIOS^W.
                What in the world do you mean?
LYSISTRATA.
    Exactly what I say.
KORYPHAIOS^W.
      What dreadful thing has happened?   660
    Come, tell us: we're all your friends.
LYSISTRATA.
                        It isn't easy
    to say it; yet, God knows, we can't hush it up.
KORYPHAIOS^W.
    Well, then? Out with it!
LYSISTRATA.
               To put it bluntly,
    we're dying to get laid.
KORYPHAIOS^W.
              Almighty God!
LYSISTRATA.
    Why bring God into it?—No, it's just as I say.
    I can't manage them any longer: they've gone man-crazy,
    they're all trying to get out.
                  Why, look:
    one of them was sneaking out the back door
    over there by Pan's cave; another
    was sliding down the walls with rope and tackle;   670
    another was climbing aboard a sparrow,⁵³ ready to take off

---

⁵³ The bird was associated with Aphroditê, goddess of love.

for the nearest brothel—I dragged *her* back by the hair!
They're all finding some reason to leave.

Look there!

There goes another one.

—Just a minute, you!

Where are you off to so fast?

FIRST WOMAN.

I've got to get home.

I've a lot of Milesian wool, and the worms are spoiling it.

LYSISTRATA.

Oh bother you and your worms! Get back inside!

FIRST WOMAN.

I'll be back right away, I swear I will.
I just want to get it stretched out on my bed.

LYSISTRATA.

You'll do no such thing. You'll stay right here.

FIRST WOMAN.

And my wool? 680

You want it ruined?

LYSISTRATA.

Yes, for all I care.

SECOND WOMAN.

Oh dear! My lovely new flax from Amorgos[54]—
I left it at home, all uncarded!

LYSISTRATA.

Another one!

And all she wants is someone to card her flax.
Get back in there!

SECOND WOMAN.

But I swear by the Moon-Goddess,

the minute I get it done, I'll be back!

LYSISTRATA.

I say No.

If you, why not all the other women as well?

THIRD WOMAN.

O Lady Eileithyia![55] Radiant goddess! Thou
intercessor for women in childbirth! Stay, I pray thee,
oh stay this parturition. Shall I pollute
a sacred spot?

690

LYSISTRATA.

And what's the matter with *you*?

THIRD WOMAN.

I'm having a baby—any minute now.

LYSISTRATA.

But you weren't pregnant yesterday.

---

[54] An Aegean island noted for the excellence of its flax.
[55] A goddess of childbirth. To give birth in the precincts of the Akropolis would be sacrilegious.

THIRD WOMAN.
                                        Well, I am today.
Let me go home for a midwife, Lysistrata:
there's not much time.
LYSISTRATA.
                              I never heard such nonsense.
What's that bulging under your cloak?
THIRD WOMAN.
                                        A little baby boy.

LYSISTRATA.
It certainly isn't. But it's something hollow,
like a basin or—Why, it's the helmet of Athêna!
And you said you were having a baby.
THIRD WOMAN.
                                  Well, I am! So there!

LYSISTRATA.
Then why the helmet?
THIRD WOMAN.
                              I was afraid that my pains   700
might begin here in the Akropolis; and I wanted
to drop my chick into it, just as the dear doves do.
LYSISTRATA.
Lies! Evasions!—But at least one thing's clear:
you can't leave the place before your purification.
THIRD WOMAN.
But I can't stay here in the Akropolis! Last night I dreamed
of the Snake.[56]
FIRST WOMAN.
                    And those horrible owls,[57] the noise they make!
I can't get a bit of sleep; I'm just about dead.
LYSISTRATA.
You useless girls, that's enough: Let's have no more lying.
Of course you want your men. But don't you imagine
that they want you just as much? I'll give you my word,   710
their nights must be pretty hard.
                                  Just stick it out!
A little patience, that's all, and our battle's won.
I have heard an Oracle. Should you like to hear it?
FIRST WOMAN.
An Oracle? Yes, tell us!
LYSISTRATA.
                        Here is what it says:
WHEN SWALLOWS SHALL THE HOOPOE[58] SHUN
    AND SPURN HIS HOT DESIRE,
ZEUS WILL PERFECT WHAT THEY'VE BEGUN
    AND SET THE LOWER HIGHER.

___

[56] Though never seen, this mythical snake was considered the guardian of Athêna's temple on the Akropolis.
[57] Birds sacred to Athêna.   [58] A bird, here identified with the male sex.

FIRST WOMAN.
   Does that mean we'll be on top?
LYSISTRATA.
   BUT IF THE SWALLOWS SHALL FALL OUT   720
      AND TAKE THE HOOPOE'S BAIT,
   A CURSE MUST MARK THEIR HOUR OF DOUBT,
      INFAMY SEAL THEIR FATE.
THIRD WOMAN.
   I swear, *that* Oracle's all too clear.
FIRST WOMAN.

                                        Oh the dear gods!
LYSISTRATA.
   Let's not be downhearted, girls. Back to our places!
   The god has spoken. How can we possibly fail him?

                              [*Exit* LYSISTRATA *with the dissi-
                              dent women*]

CHORAL EPISODE

CHORUS^m.

                                                    [STROPHE]
   I know a little story that I learned way back in school
   Goes like this:
   Once upon a time there was a young man—and no fool—
   Named Melanion;[59] and his   730
   One aversi-on was marriage. He loathed the very thought.
   So he ran off to the hills, and in a special grot
   Raised a dog, and spent his days
   Hunting rabbits. And it says
   That he never never never did come home.
   It might be called a refuge *from* the womb.
   All right,
            all right,
                     all right!
   We're as bright as young Melanion, and we hate the very sight
   Of you women!
A MAN.
   How about a kiss, old lady?   740
A WOMAN.
   Here's an onion for your eye!
A MAN.
   A kick in the guts, then?
A WOMAN.
   Try, old bristle-tail, just try!

[59] An obscure personage; in this context, he is a kind of male equivalent of Artemis, the
determinedly virgin goddess of the hunt.

A MAN.
>   Yet they say Myronidês[60]
>   On hands and knees
>   Looked just as shaggy fore and aft as I!

CHORUS[W].

[ANTISTROPHE]

>   Well, *I* know a little story, and it's just as good as yours.
>   Goes like this:
>   Once there was a man named Timon[61]—a rough diamond, of
>   course,
>   And that whiskery face of his   750
>   Looked like murder in the shrubbery. By God, he was a son
>   Of the Furies, let me tell you! And what did he do but run
>   From the world and all its ways,
>   Cursing mankind! And it says
>   That his choicest execrations as of then
>   Were leveled almost wholly at *old* men.
>   All right,
>   all right,
>   all right!
>   But there's one thing about Timon: he could always stand the
>   sight
>   Of us women.

A WOMAN.
>   How about a crack in the jaw, Pop?   760

A MAN.
>   I can take it, Ma—no fear!

A WOMAN.
>   How about a kick in the face?

A MAN.
>   You'd reveal your old caboose?

A WOMAN.
>   What I'd show
>   I'll have you know,
>   Is an instrument you're too far gone to use.

SCENE III

[*Re-enter* LYSISTRATA]

LYSISTRATA.
>   Oh, quick, girls, quick! Come here!

A WOMAN.
>   What is it?

LYSISTRATA.
>   A man.

---

[60] An Athenian general.

[61] A noted misanthrope (the titular character of one of Shakespeare's plays). The women choose here to present him as an enemy to males rather than to humankind.

A man simply bulging with love.

                    O Kyprian Queen,[62]

O Paphian, O Kythereian! Hear us and aid us!

A WOMAN.

Where is this enemy?

LYSISTRATA.

                    Over there, by Demêter's shrine.   770

A WOMAN.

Damned if he isn't. But who *is* he?

MYRRHINE.

                       My husband.

Kinêsias.

LYSISTRATA.

     Oh then, get busy! Tease him! Undermine him!

Wreck him! Give him everything—kissing, tickling, nudging,

whatever you generally torture him with—: give him everything

except what we swore on the wine we would not give.

MYRRHINE.

Trust me.

LYSISTRATA.

     I do. But I'll help you get him started.

The rest of you women, stay back.

                [Enter KINESIAS]

KINESIAS.

                 Oh God! Oh my God!

I'm stiff from lack of exercise. All I can do to stand up.

LYSISTRATA.

Halt! Who are you, approaching our lines?

KINESIAS.

                      Me? I.

LYSISTRATA.

A man?

KINESIAS.

     You have eyes, haven't you?

LYSISTRATA.

                  Go away.   780

KINESIAS.

Who says so?

LYSISTRATA.

          Officer of the Day.

KINESIAS.

               Officer, I beg you,

by all the gods at once, bring Myrrhinê out.

LYSISTRATA.

Myrrhinê? And who, my good sir, are you?

---

[62] *Kyprian* and the names in the following line are epithets for Aphroditê, goddess of love.

KINESIAS.
Kinêsias. Last name's Pennison. Her husband.
LYSISTRATA.
Oh, of course. I beg your pardon. We're glad to see you.
We've heard so much about you. Dearest Myrrhinê
is always talking about 'Kinêsias'—never nibbles an egg
or an apple without saying
'Here's to Kinêsias!'
KINESIAS.
Do you really mean it?
LYSISTRATA.
I do.
When we're discussing men, she always says   790
'Well, after all, there's nobody like Kinêsias!'
KINESIAS.
Good God.—Well, then, please send her down here.
LYSISTRATA.
And what do *I* get out of it?
KINESIAS.
A standing promise.
LYSISTRATA.
I'll take it up with her.

[*Exit* LYSISTRATA]

KINESIAS.
But be quick about it!
Lord, what's life without a wife? Can't eat. Can't sleep.
Every time I go home, the place is so empty, so
insufferably sad. Love's killing me. Oh,
hurry!

[*Enter* MANES, *a slave, with* KINES-
IAS' *baby; the voice of* MYRRHINE *is
heard off-stage.*]

MYRRHINE.
But of course I love him! Adore him!—But no,
he hates love. No. I won't go down.

[*Enter* MYRRHINE, *above*]

KINESIAS.
Myrrhinê!
Darlingest Myrrhinette! Come down quick!   800
MYRRHINE.
Certainly not.
KINESIAS.
Not? But why, Myrrhinê?

MYRRHINE.
  Why? You don't need me.
KINESIAS.
                    Need you? My God, *look* at me!
MYRRHINE.
  So long!

                    [*Turns to go*]

KINESIAS.
        Myrrhinê, Myrrhinê, Myrrhinê!
  If not for my sake, for our child!

                    [*Pinches* BABY]

        —All right, you: pipe up!
BABY.
  Mummie! Mummie! Mummie!
KINESIAS.
                    You hear that?
  Pitiful, I call it. Six days now
  with never a bath; no food; enough to break your heart!
MYRRHINE.
  My darlingest child! What a father *you* acquired!
KINESIAS.
  At least come down for his sake.
MYRRHINE.
                    I suppose I must.
  Oh, this mother business!

                    [*Exit*]

KINESIAS.
                    How pretty she is! And younger!   810
  The harder she treats me, the more bothered I get.

                    [MYRRHINE *enters, below*]

MYRRHINE.
                              Dearest child,
  you're as sweet as your father's horrid. Give me a kiss.
KINESIAS.
  Now don't you see how wrong it was to get involved
  in this scheming League of women? It's bad
  for us both.
MYRRHINE.
        Keep your hands to yourself!
KINESIAS.
                    But our house
  going to rack and ruin?

MYRRHINE.
                                    I don't care.
KINESIAS.
                                                And your knitting
all torn to pieces by the chickens? Don't you care?
MYRRHINE.
Not at all.
KINESIAS.
                        And our debt to Aphroditê?
Oh, *won't* you come back?
MYRRHINE.
                                    No.—At least, not until you men
make a treaty and stop this war.
KINESIAS.
                                                Why, I suppose   820

that might be arranged.
MYRRHINE.
                                    Oh? Well, I suppose
I might come down then. But meanwhile,
I've sworn not to.
KINESIAS.
                        Don't worry.—Now, let's have fun.
MYRRHINE.
No! Stop it! I said no!
                                    —Although, of course,
I *do* love you.
KINESIAS.
                        I know you do. Darling Myrrhinê:
come, shall we?
MYRRHINE.
                Are you out of your mind? In front of the child?
KINESIAS.
Take him home, Manês.

                                [*Exit* MANES *with* BABY]
                        There. He's gone.
                                                Come on!
There's nothing to stop us now.
MYRRHINE.
                                    You devil! But where?
KINESIAS.
In Pan's cave. What could be snugger than that?
MYRRHINE.
But my purification before I go back to the Citadel?   830
KINESIAS.
Wash in the Klepsydra.[63]

---

[63] A spring on the Akropolis.

MYRRHINE.

                     And my oath?

KINESIAS.

                              Leave the oath to me.

After all, I'm the man.

MYRRHINE.

                  Well . . . if you say so.

                          I'll go find a bed.

KINESIAS.

Oh, bother a bed! The ground's good enough for me.

MYRRHINE.

No. You're a bad man, but you deserve something better than dirt.

                     [*Exit* MYRRHINE]

KINESIAS.

What a love she is! and how thoughtful!

                  [*Re-enter* MYRRHINE]

MYRRHINE.

                      Here's your bed.

Now let me get my clothes off.

               But, good horrors!

We haven't a mattress.

KINESIAS.

            Oh, forget the mattress!

MYRRHINE.

                         No.

Just lying on blankets? Too sordid.

KINESIAS.

                Give me a kiss.

MYRRHINE.

Just a second.

                 [*Exit* MYRRHINE]

KINESIAS.

          I swear, I'll explode!

               [*Re-enter* MYRRHINE]

MYRRHINE.

              Here's your mattress.

I'll just take my dress off.

              But look—   840

where's our pillow?

KINESIAS.

         I don't *need* a pillow!

MYRRHINE.

                 Well, *I* do.

[*Exit* MYRRHINE]

KINESIAS.
I don't suppose even Heraklês[64]
would stand for this!

[*Re-enter* MYRRHINE]

MYRRHINE.
                              There we are. Ups-a-daisy!
KINESIAS.
So we are. Well, come to bed.
MYRRHINE.
                              But I wonder:
is everything ready now?
KINESIAS.
                              I can swear to that. Come, darling!
MYRRHINE.
Just getting out of my girdle.
                              But remember, now,
what you promised about the treaty.
KINESIAS.
                              Yes, yes, yes!
MYRRHINE.
But no coverlet!
KINESIAS.
              Damn it, I'll be
your coverlet!
MYRRHINE.
              Be right back.

[*Exit* MYRRHINE]

KINESIAS.
                              This girl and her coverlets
will be the death of me.

[*Re-enter* MYRRHINE]

MYRRHINE.
                              Here we are. Up you go!   850
KINESIAS.
Up? I've been up for ages.
MYRRHINE.
                          Some perfume?
KINESIAS.
No, by Apollo!
MYRRHINE.
              Yes, by Aphroditê!
I don't care whether you want it or not.

---

[64] A lustful womanizer, Heraklês (Hercules) could also be chivalrous and even self-abasing
in his relations with women.

[*Exit* Myrrhine]

Kinesias.
For love's sake, hurry!

[*Re-enter* Myrrhine]

Myrrhine.
Here, in your hand. Rub it right in.
Kinesias.
                              Never cared for perfume.
And this is particularly strong. Still, here goes.
Myrrhine.
What a nitwit I am! I brought you the Rhodian bottle.
Kinesias.
Forget it.
Myrrhine.
                No trouble at all. You just wait here.

[*Exit* Myrrhine]

Kinesias.
God damn the man who invented perfume!

[*Re-enter* Myrrhine]

Myrrhine.
At last! The right bottle!
Kinesias.
                              I've got the rightest   860
bottle of all, and it's right here waiting for you.
Darling, forget everything else. Do come to bed.
Myrrhine.
Just let me get my shoes off.
                              —And, by the way,
you'll vote for the treaty?
Kinesias.
                        I'll think about it.

[Myrrhine *runs away*]

There! That's done it! The damned woman,
she gets me all bothered, she half kills me,
and she runs! What'll I do? Where
can I get laid?
                —And you, little prodding pal,
who's going to take care of *you?* No, you and I
had better get down to old Foxdog's[65] Nursing Clinic.   870
Chorus[m].
        Alas for the woes of man, alas
        Specifically for you.

[65] A well known pimp.

She's brought you to a pretty pass:
    What are you going to do?
Split, heart! Sag, flesh! Proud spirit, crack!
Myrrhinê's got you on your back.

KINESIAS.
    The agony, the protraction!

KORYPHAIOS[m].
                       Friend,
    What woman's worth a damn?
    They bitch us all, world without end.

KINESIAS.
    Yet they're so damned sweet, man!   880

KORYPHAIOS[m].
    Calamitous, that's what I say.
    You should have learned that much today.

CHORUS[m].
    O blessed Zeus, roll womankind
        Up into one great ball;
    Blast them aloft on a high wind,
        And once there, let them fall.
    Down, down they'll come, the pretty dears,
    And split themselves on our thick spears.

                  [*Exit* KINESIAS]

SCENE IV

[*Enter a* SPARTAN HERALD]

HERALD.
    Gentlemen, Ah beg you will be so kind
    as to direct me to the Central Committee.   890
    Ah have a communication.

                  [*Re-enter* COMMISSIONER]

COMMISSIONER.
                    Are you a man,
    or a fertility symbol?

HERALD.
                 Ah refuse to answer that question!
    Ah'm a certified herald from Spahta, and Ah've come
    to talk about an ahmistice.

COMMISSIONER.
                   Then why
    that spear under your cloak?

HERALD.
                Ah have no speah!

COMMISSIONER.
    You don't walk naturally, with your tunic

poked out so. You have a tumor, maybe,
or a hernia?
HERALD.

                You lost yo' mahnd, man?
COMMISSIONER.

                            Well,
something's up, I can see that. And I don't like it.
HERALD.
Colonel, Ah resent this.
COMMISSIONER.

                        So I see. But what *is* it?
HERALD.

                                 A staff   900
with a message from Spahta.
COMMISSIONER.

                      Oh. I know about those staffs.[66]
Well, then, man, speak out: How are things in Sparta?
HERALD.
Hahd, Colonel, hahd! We're at a standstill.
Cain't seem to think of anything but women.
COMMISSIONER.
How curious! Tell me, do you Spartans think
that maybe Pan's[67] to blame?
HERALD.
Pan? No. Lampitô and her little naked friends.
They won't let a man come nigh them.
COMMISSIONER.
How are you handling it?
HERALD.

                      Losing our mahnds,
if y' want to know, and walking around hunched over   910
lahk men carrying candles in a gale.
The women have swohn they'll have nothing to do with us
until we get a treaty.
COMMISSIONER.

                Yes, I know.
It's a general uprising, sir, in all parts of Greece.
But as for the answer—

                Sir: go back to Sparta
and have them send us your Armistice Commission.
I'll arrange things in Athens.

                And I may say
that my standing is good enough to make them listen.

---

[66] The pun alludes to a Spartan method of cryptography: a message was written on fabric wound around a staff (like an overlapping bandage). It was then unwound, despatched by messenger, and rewound on a staff identical in shape with the sender's. Only then could the scrambled lines of writing be realigned to make sense.

[67] The nature-god Pan was held accountable for sudden and inexplicable fits of madness, or "panic." The god could also cause sexual excesses.

HERALD.
> A man after mah own haht! Seh, Ah thank you.

[*Exit* HERALD]

CHORAL EPISODE

CHORUS^m.

Oh these women! Where will you find	[STROPHE] 920

> Oh these women! Where will you find   [STROPHE] 920
> A slavering beast that's more unkind?
>   Where a hotter fire?
> Give me a panther, any day.
> He's not so merciless as they,
>   And panthers don't conspire.

CHORUS^w.

> We may be hard, you silly old ass,   [ANTISTROPHE]
> But who brought you to this stupid pass?
>   You're the ones to blame.
> Fighting with us, your oldest friends,
> Simply to serve your selfish ends—   930
>   Really, you have no shame!

KORYPHAIOS^m.

> No, I'm through with women for ever.

KORYPHAIOS^w.

>   If you say so.
> Still, you might put some clothes on. You look too absurd
> standing around naked. Come, get into this cloak.

KORYPHAIOS^m.

> Thank you; you're right. I merely took it off
> because I was in such a temper.

KORYPHAIOS^w.

>   That's much better.
> Now you resemble a man again.
>   Why have you been so horrid?
> And look: there's some sort of insect in your eye.
> Shall I take it out?

KORYPHAIOS^m.

>   An insect, is it? So that's
> what's been bothering me. Lord, yes: take it out!   940

KORYPHAIOS^w.

> You might be more polite.
>   —But, heavens!
> What an enormous mosquito!

KORYPHAIOS^m.

>   You've saved my life.
> That mosquito was drilling an artesian well
> in my left eye.

KORYPHAIOS^w.

>   Let me wipe
> those tears away.—And now: one little kiss?

KORYPHAIOS^m.
  No, no kisses.
KORYPHAIOS^w.
                You're so difficult.
KORYPHAIOS^m.
  You impossible women! How you do get around us!
  The poet was right: Can't live with you, or without you.
  But let's be friends.
  And to celebrate, you might join us in an Ode.   950
CHORUS^{m and w}.
                Let it never be said   [STROPHE 1]
                That my tongue is malicious:
                Both by word and by deed
  I would set an example that's noble and gracious.
                We've had sorrow and care
                Till we're sick of the tune.
                Is there anyone here
                Who would like a small loan?
                  My purse is crammed,
                  As you'll soon find;   960
  And you needn't pay me back if the Peace gets signed.

                I've invited to lunch   [STROPHE 2]
                Some Karystian rips[68]—
                An esurient bunch,
  But I've ordered a menu to water their lips.
                I can still make soup
                And slaughter a pig.
                You're all coming, I hope?
                But a bath first, I beg!
                  Walk right up   970
                  As though you owned the place,
  And you'll get the front door slammed to in your face.

                        SCENE V

[*Enter* SPARTAN AMBASSADOR, *with entourage*]

KORYPHAIOS^m.
  The Commission has arrived from Sparta.
                                          How oddly
  they're walking!
                Gentlemen, welcome to Athens!
  How is life in Lakonia?[69]
AMBASSADOR.
                        Need we discuss that?
  Simply use your eyes.

---

[68] People from Karystos, allied with Athens. They were considered uninhibited and morally loose.
[69] The southern area of Greece. Sparta was its most important city.

CHORUS[m].

The poor man's right:
What a sight!

AMBASSADOR.

Words fail me.
But come, gentlemen, call in your Commissioners,
and let's get down to a Peace.

CHORAGOS[m].

The state we're in! Can't bear
a stitch below the waist. It's a kind of pelvic   980
paralysis.

COMMISSIONER.

Won't somebody call Lysistrata?—Gentlemen,
we're no better off than you.

AMBASSADOR.

So I see.

A SPARTAN.

Seh, do y'all feel a certain strain
early in the morning?

AN ATHENIAN.

I do, sir. It's worse than a strain.
A few more days, and there's nothing for us but Kleisthenês,
that broken blossom.

CHORAGOS[m].

But you'd better get dressed again.
You know these people going around Athens with chisels,
looking for statues of Hermês.[70]

ATHENIAN.

Sir, you are right.

SPARTAN.

He certainly is! Ah'll put mah own clothes back on.

[*Enter* ATHENIAN COMMISSIONERS]

COMMISSIONER.

Gentlemen from Sparta, welcome. This is a sorry business.   990

SPARTAN.   [*To one of his own group*]:
Colonel, we got dressed just in time. Ah sweah,
if they'd seen us the way we were, there'd have been a new wah
between the states.

COMMISSIONER.

Shall we call the meeting to order?

Now, Lakonians,
what's your proposal?

AMBASSADOR.

We propose to consider peace.

---

[70]Opponents of the expedition to Sicily had mutilated these phallic statues (commonly
located in front of homes) just before the fleet set sail. Some Athenians believed that the
vandalism had jinxed the Sicilian campaign.

COMMISSIONER.
    Good. That's on our minds, too.
                    —Summon Lysistrata.
We'll never get anywhere without her.

AMBASSADOR.
                           Lysistrata?
Summon Lysis-*any*body! Only, summon!

KORYPHAIOS^m.
                    No need to summon:
here she is, herself.

                  [*Enter* LYSISTRATA]

COMMISSIONER.
             Lysistrata! Lion of women!
This is your hour to be   1000
hard and yielding, outspoken and shy, austere and
gentle. You see here
the best brains of Hellas (confused, I admit,
by your devious charming) met as one man
to turn the future over to you.

LYSISTRATA.
                  That's fair enough,
unless you men take it into your heads
to turn to each other instead of to us. But I'd know
soon enough if you did.
              —Where is Reconciliation?
Go, some of you: bring her here.

                [*Exeunt two women*]
                And now, women,
lead the Spartan delegates to me: not roughly   1010
or insultingly, as our men handle them, but gently,
politely, as ladies should. Take them by the hand,
or by anything else if they won't give you their hands.

           [*The* SPARTANS *are escorted over*]

There.—The Athenians next, by any convenient handle.

           [*The* ATHENIANS *are escorted*]

Stand there, please.—Now, all of you, listen to me.

           [*During the following speech the
           two women re-enter, carrying an
           enormous statue of a naked girl; this
           is* RECONCILIATION.]

I'm only a woman, I know; but I've a mind,
and, I think, not a bad one: I owe it to my father

and to listening to the local politicians.
So much for that.
                              Now, gentlemen,
since I have you here, I intend to give you a scolding.   1020
We are all Greeks. ·
Must I remind you of Thermopylai, of Olympia,
of Delphoi?[71] names deep in all our hearts?
Are they not a common heritage?
                              Yet you men
go raiding through the country from both sides,
Greek killing Greek, storming down Greek cities—
and all the time the Barbarian[72] across the sea
is waiting for his chance!
                              —That's my first point.

AN ATHENIAN.
Lord! I can hardly contain myself.

LYSISTRATA.
                              As for you Spartans:
Was it so long ago that Perikleidês[73]   1030
came here to beg our help? I can see him still,
his grey face, his sombre gown. And what did he want?
An army from Athens. All Messênê
was hot at your heels, and the sea-god splitting your land.
Well, Kimôn and his men,
four thousand strong, marched out and saved all Sparta.
And what thanks do we get? You come back to murder us.

AN ATHENIAN.
They're aggressors, Lysistrata!

A SPARTAN.
                              Ah Admit it.
When Ah look at those laigs, Ah sweah Ah'll aggress mahself!

LYSISTRATA.
And you, Athenians: do you think you're blameless?   1040
Remember that bad time when we were helpless,
and an army came from Sparta,
and that was the end of the Thessalian menace,
the end of Hippias[74] and his allies.
                              And that was Sparta,
and only Sparta; but for Sparta, we'd be
cringing slaves today, not free Athenians.

                              [*From this point, the male responses
                              are less to* LYSISTRATA *than to the
                              statue*]

---

[71] The place-names evoke the former days of Greek unity and glory before the tragic civil war.

[72] Foreign; non-Greek.

[73] An emissary sent from Sparta, earlier in the fifth century, to request help from Athens in putting down civil war in Sparta and rebellion by Spartan-controlled Messênê. Athens responded by sending a rescue-force led by Kimôn.

[74] The Spartans had helped Athens to overthrow and expel the tyrant Hippias.

A SPARTAN.
A well shaped speech.
AN ATHENIAN.
                         Certainly it has its points.
LYSISTRATA.
Why are we fighting each other? With all this history
of favors given and taken, what stands in the way
of making peace?
AMBASSADOR.
                         Spahta is ready, ma'am,   1050
so long as we get that place back.
LYSISTRATA.
                         What place, man?

AMBASSADOR.
Ah refer to Pylos.[75]
COMMISSIONER.
                         Not a chance, by God!
LYSISTRATA.
Give it to them, friend.
COMMISSIONER.
                         But—what shall we have to bargain with?
LYSISTRATA.
Demand something in exchange.
COMMISSIONER.
                         Good idea.—Well, then:
Cockeville first, and the Happy Hills, and the country
between the Legs of Mêgara.
AMBASSADOR.
                         Mah government objects.
LYSISTRATA.
Over-ruled. Why fuss about a pair of legs?

                    [*General assent. The statue is re-
                    moved.*]

AN ATHENIAN.
I want to get out of these clothes and start my plowing.
A SPARTAN.
Ah'll fertilize mahn first, by the Heavenly Twins!
LYSISTRATA.
And so you shall,   1060
once you've made peace. If you are serious,
go, both of you, and talk with your allies.
COMMISSIONER.
Too much talk already. No, we'll stand together.

---

[75] A town; the root meaning of its name is "flank." This and the following lines make a
series of puns referring both to control of geographical areas and to portions of the female
body as visible in the statue of the nude "Reconciliation." Conventional diplomatic bargaining
for territory is thus blended with the sexual diplomacy employed by the women in the play.

We've only one end in view. All that we want
is our women; and I speak for our allies.

AMBASSADOR.
Mah government concurs.

AN ATHENIAN.
                          So does Karystos.

LYSISTRATA.
Good.—But before you come inside
to join your wives at supper, you must perform
the usual lustration.[76] Then we'll open
our baskets for you, and all that we have is yours.   1070
But you must promise upright good behavior
from this day on. Then each man home with his woman!

AN ATHENIAN.
Let's get it over with.

A SPARTAN.
                          Lead on. Ah follow.

AN ATHENIAN.
Quick as a cat can wink!

                                      [*Exeunt all but the* CHORUSES]

CHORUS[W].
                    Embroideries ánd   [ANTISTROPHE 1]
                    Twinkling ornaments ánd
                    Pretty dresses—I hand
Them all over to you, and with never a qualm.
                    They'll be nice for your daughters
                    On festival days   1080
                    When the girls bring the Goddess
                    The ritual prize.
                          Come in, one and all:
                          Take what you will.
I've nothing here so tightly corked that you can't make it spill.

                    You may search my house,   [ANTISTROPHE 2]
                    But you'll not find
                    The least thing of use,
Unless your two eyes are keener than mine.
                    Your numberless brats
                    Are half starved? and your slaves?   1090
                    Courage, grandpa! I've lots
                    Of grain left, and big loaves.
                          I'll fill your guts
                          I'll go the whole hog;
But if you come too close to me, remember: 'ware the dog!

                                            [*Exeunt* CHORUSES]

_____
[76]Ceremonial purification.

ÉXODOS

[*A* DRUNKEN CITIZEN *enters, approaches the gate, and is halted by a* SENTRY]

CITIZEN.
　　Open. The. Door.
SENTRY.
　　　　　　　　　　Now, friend, just shove along!
　　—So you want to sit down. If it weren't such an old joke,
　　I'd tickle your tail with this torch. Just the sort of gag
　　this audience appreciates.
CITIZEN.
　　　　　　　　　　I. Stay. Right. Here.   1100
SENTRY.
　　Get away from there, or I'll scalp you! The gentlemen from Sparta
　　are just coming back from dinner.

> [*Exit* CITIZEN; *the general com-
> pany re-enters; the two* CHORUSES
> *now represent* SPARTANS *and*
> ATHENIANS.]

A SPARTAN.
　　　　　　　　　　Ah must say,
　　Ah never tasted better grub.
AN ATHENIAN.
　　　　　　　　　　And those Lakonians!
　　They're gentlemen, by the Lord! Just goes to show,
　　a drink to the wise is sufficient.
COMMISSIONER.
　　　　　　　　　　And why not?
　　A sober man's an ass.
　　Men of Athens, mark my words: the only efficient
　　Ambassador's a drunk Ambassador. Is that clear?
　　Look: we go to Sparta,
　　and when we get there we're dead sober. The result?   1110
　　Everyone cackling at everyone else. They make speeches;
　　and even if we understand, we get it all wrong
　　when we file our reports in Athens. But today—!
　　Everybody's happy. Couldn't tell the difference
　　between *Drink to Me Only* and
　　The Star-Spangled Athens.
　　　　　　　　　　What's a few lies,
　　washed down in good strong drink?

> [*Re-enter the* DRUNKEN CITIZEN]

SENTRY.
　　　　　　　　　　God almighty,
　　he's back again!

CITIZEN.

I. Resume. My. Place.

[*To an* ATHENIAN]

A SPARTAN.

Ah beg yo', seh,
take yo' instrument in yo' hand and play for us.   1120
Ah'm told
yo' understand the in*tric*acies of the floot?
Ah'd lahk to execute a song and dance
in honor of Athens,
                    and, of cohse, of Spahta.

CITIZEN.

Toot. On. Your. Flute.

> [*The following song is a solo—an
> aria—accompanied by the flute.
> The* CHORUS OF SPARTANS *begins
> a slow dance.*]

A SPARTAN.

O Memory,
Let the Muse speak once more
In my young voice. Sing glory.
Sing Artemision's shore,[77]
Where Athens fluttered the Persians. *Alalaí*,   1130
Sing glory, that great
Victory! Sing also
Our Leonidas and his men,
Those wild boars, sweat and blood
Down in a red drench. Then, then
The barbarians broke, though they had stood
Numberless as the sands before!

O Artemis,
Virgin Goddess, whose darts
Flash in our forests: approve   1140
This pact of peace and join our hearts,
From this day on, in love.
Huntress, descend!

LYSISTRATA.

All that will come in time.
                    But now, Lakonians,
take home your wives. Athenians, take yours.
Each man be kind to his woman; and you, women,
be equally kind. Never again, pray God,
shall we lose our way in such madness.

---

[77] In the former days of Grecian unity, the Athenian fleet had fought against the Persians near Artemision while the Spartans, led by the hero Leonidas, had bravely fought the Persians on land, at Thermopylae. *Alalaí* is a battle cry.

KORYPHAIOS[a].

And now

let's dance our joy.

[*From this point the dance becomes
general*]

CHORUS[a].
Dance, you Graces
Artemis, dance   1150
Dance, Phoibos, Lord of dancing
Dance,
In a scurry of Maenads, Lord Dionysos
Dance, Zeus Thunderer
Dance, Lady Hêra
Queen of the Sky
Dance, dance, all you gods
Dance witness everlasting of our pact
Evohí Evohé
Dance for the dearest
the Bringer of Peace
Deathless Aphroditê!
COMMISSIONER.
Now let us have another song from Sparta.   1160
CHORUS[s].
From Taÿgetos, from Taÿgetos,
Lakonian Muse, come down.
Sing to the Lord Apollo
Who rules Amyklai[78] Town.

Sing Athêna of the House of Brass![79]

Sing Lêda's Twins,[80] that chivalry
Respondent on the shore
Of our Eurôtas;[81] sing the girls
That dance along before:

Sparkling in dust their gleaming feet,   1170
Their hair a Bacchant[82] fire,
And Lêda's daughter,[83] thyrsos raised,
Leads their triumphant choir.

---

[78] A town, associated with Apollo, in the Spartan region.
[79] The temple of Athena in Sparta.
[80] The "Heavenly Twins," Castor and Pollux, protectors of their sister, Helen of Troy.
[81] The river of Sparta.
[82] Associated with the Bacchantes, female worshipers of Bacchus (Dionysus), the god of wine, sex, and revelry.
[83] Helen of Troy, symbol of woman as cause of war but here of woman as reconciler. The thyrsos is a staff carried by worshipers of Dionysus/Bacchus.

Choruses[s] and a[.]
> Evohé!
>> Evohaí!
>>> Evohé!
>>>> We pass
>>> Dancing
>>>> dancing
>>>>> to greet
>>> Athêna of the House of Brass.

Plato
(C.427–C.348 B.C.)

Except for certain great religious teachers, Plato has probably been the most influential thinker in the history of Western culture. Because he believed that dialectic, in the form of oral give-and-take, was a higher form of discourse and a more reliable avenue to wisdom than written treatises, his writings are not necessarily a complete or wholly reliable record of what he believed. But the high reverence in which Plato was held, in his own day and since, has caused his written work to survive more completely than that of virtually any other ancient Greek author. Moreover, the written work itself reflects Plato's dedication to the spoken word, since his most typical literary form is the "Dialogue." The thirty or more works by Plato that have come down to us concentrate mainly on ethical, political, and metaphysical issues, but they also treat in depth or at least touch on many other important matters that have pre-occupied philosophers, including issues in mathematics, logic, and physical science.

Plato was a pioneering thinker, but he was much more than a groundbreaker. Are words merely arbitrary symbols for things and human ideas, or do words have a more absolute relationship to what they signify? Are goodness and beauty realities in themselves—independent of the accidents of our observation and tastes—or are they merely attributes that the human mind generalizes from particular objects it considers good or beautiful? Do we know truth through reason or through some more mysterious or intuitive process? If love helps us become our best selves and induces ecstatic states of happiness and generosity, why does it also bring out what is most absurd, irrational, and malignant in us? In forming a just political community, should the first task be to perfect individual citizens, in the hope that they will add up to a just polity, or should individuals model their private virtues on a general conception of what the community needs? These questions raised by Plato, and many others like them, have obsessed countless people—practical men and women as well as abstract theoreticians. And—which is most remarkable—in trying to answer such questions, people have again and again gone directly to Plato's works themselves, not merely to later "sophistications" of his thought.

Plato was born around 427 B.C., in Athens, of an aristocratic lineage that claimed descent from preeminent legendary ancestors. He came under the influence of Socrates—the central figure in most of Plato's Dialogues—when Plato was about twenty, at which time Socrates was in his early sixties. During the eight or so years before Socrates was tried and condemned to death in 399, Plato was one of many bright and well-born young Athenians who listened and learned in the public places of Athens where Socrates held forth. Plato's family was active in Athenian politics, and he himself was drawn toward public life in the critical last decade of the fifth century (years which witnessed among other dramatic events the final defeat of Athens in its civil war against Sparta). But at this time Plato opted against a political career. Significantly, in the Apology, *his account of Socrates' trial, he reports Socrates' opinion that to be apolitical is the only way to retain integrity. In Plato's middle and old age, however (he died around 348), he made several journeys to Sicily, partly with the hope of helping the ruling family of Syracuse realize in practical terms the political principles Plato had come to believe in. The effort failed for several reasons, but the fact that Plato did make the attempt to reconcile theoretical principles with actual practice testifies that he was not simply the otherworldly mystic that many people associate with the term "Platonic."*

Apart from his own direct teaching, whether or not it was preserved in writing, Plato's most distinctive achievement was to found and lead the "Academy" (located in an olive grove near Athens, and named after the hero Academus). This assemblage of brilliant original thinkers, brought together under Plato's direction, was the prototype of modern universities and "think tanks."

The greatness of Plato, and his incalculable influence, are mainly attributable to the inherent profundity and originality of his thought. Even if it had come down to us in the severely colorless vehicle that in our time is considered normal or even essential for hard thinking in philosophy and science, Plato would occupy a central position among intellectuals. But his appeal has been much broader, and that fact is largely due to the literary forms he used, mainly the Dialogue. Plato has often, and rightly, been called a poet (despite the ambiguous view of poetry in works like the Ion), *because of the high eloquence and supernal beauty he often attains. But Plato is also a master of fiction and, almost literally, of drama. His credentials as a dramatist are revealed on two levels. On one level, ideas themselves are the dramatic "characters," and Plato's triumph is to make these competing ideas compelling in themselves, so that we are drawn to one or another of them, our sympathies evoked as if the ideas were our friends or enemies. In addition, though, the human persons who espouse or oppose various ideological positions are drawn with great subtlety and psychological realism. Most of these people were actual historical human beings, so that Plato portrayed from life and not merely from his imagination. But many authors whose explicit aim is biography have not succeeded nearly as well as did Plato in the vivid rendering of personalities.*

Chief among Plato's triumphs of characterization is, of course, Socrates. This multifaceted man—by turns earnest and playful, ironic and unguarded, elevated in mind but physically unprepossessing—emerges as one of the most memorable human beings in history or fiction. To treat him as a mere creature of Plato's art would be absurd, of course, just as it would be absurd to treat Jesus as an invention of the New Testament evangelists. Socrates was a distinct historical individual, in his own right an important personage and an eminent teacher-thinker. But to what extent Plato represented him and his ideas accurately is uncertain. That there was much distortion in Plato's portrait seems unlikely, since Socrates was the most publicly accessible of Athenians, and many of the readers in Plato's audience would have remembered him personally. A much more difficult and important problem is to what extent Plato's ideas coincide with those of his mentor. Plato could hardly have given Socrates so central a place in the Dialogues if the pupil had not embraced and retained many of Socrates' ideas. On the other hand, Socrates died a half-century before Plato did, and Plato's ideas must inevitably have developed during that period. Other complications include the fact that the Dialogues are not always consistent with one another; in some of them Plato may be dramatizing the clash of ideas for its own sake without trying to propose a solution to which either Socrates or Plato himself would have subscribed. And, on top of these difficulties, there is the question of how nearly "Neo-Platonism"—the occultist developments of his ideas during the two millennia after Plato—is consonant with Plato's thought.

Although such critical, biographical, and historical questions are important, in some ways they are distractions. In one sense Platonism is no more or less than what is contained in Plato's works: a set of ideas and a method for testing and exploring them. Whether or not either Plato or Socrates would have endorsed the ideas, and whether they and their adherents are treated ironically or not, are from the thinker's point of view less important than the truth or falsity of various positions. In the Symposium, *for example, a fable explaining sexual attraction as the result of a primordial splitting of people into halves is treated facetiously, but the notion of "soul mates" implied in the fable has survived the ironic context and has become one fundamental "model" of the nature of love. Part of the power of Plato's works is due to the fact that the concepts expressed in them have a reality that can transcend the human drama through which they are so vividly expressed.*

For many people, "Platonism" has come to suggest otherworldliness, ecstasy, and mysticism. And it is undeniable that the tone and content of the Dialogues is sometimes elevated and rhapsodic. The metaphysical doctrine of "Ideas" or "Forms" (introduced in the Republic *and other Dialogues) does indeed seem to suggest that the material world is flawed exactly because it is material. But to regard Plato as a mystic—if by that term we mean a devotee of mystery—is misleading, to say the least. Mind, the senses, the mundane, are central in Plato's works; the reasoning is razor-edged, and the frequent analogies are usually to such homely creatures as pack-asses and tanners, even when Socrates is leading the way to sublime insights. One of the challenges Plato poses for the modern reader is that of reconciling the mental states of rationalism and excitement. For most people today, those terms are irreconcilable; for example (the cliché goes), poets and other artists* feel, *while scientists* think. *Plato's works suggest that hard thinking can be a positively sensuous experience. To present it through a literary medium that uses comedy, characterization, local setting, and the like is to imply that thinking is not an alternative to living but one of the best parts of living.*

FURTHER READING *(prepared by F. S. N.):* The standard treatment of Plato as writer, philosopher, and influential thinker is Paul Friedländer's *Plato,* 1928–1930, 2nd ed. 1953–1957, 3 vols., trans. Hans Meyerhoff, 1958–1969. Other useful works on Plato's life and writings are by Paul Shorey, *What Plato Said,* 1933, repr. 1965; and by G. C. Field, *The Philosophy of Plato,* 1949, 2nd ed. 1969. On the development of Plato's thought see especially I. M. Crombie, *An Examination of Plato's Doctrines,* 2 vols., 1962–1963, and, by the same author, the shortened version *Plato: The Midwife's Apprentice,* 1964. On the role of poetic language and myth in Plato, see Julius A. Elias, *Plato's Defence of Poetry,* 1984. On the *Apology,* see the introductory materials in R. E. Allen's translation *The Dialogues of Plato,* Volume I, 1985. Plato's lasting influence is treated in A. H. Armstrong, ed., *The Cambridge History of Later Greek and Early Medieval Philosophy,* 1967.

from *THE REPUBLIC*

Translated by Benjamin Jowett

The Republic, the second-longest (after the *Laws*) of Plato's works, is an inquiry into the nature of justice. The inquiry leads, in turn, to an attempt to define the ideal state. The form is that of a dialogue between Socrates and six other speakers. Book VII begins with the famous Parable of the Cave (or Den), in which Socrates, addressing an older brother of Plato named Glaucon, illustrates the difference between unenlightened men and enlightened philosophers. The parable also suggests the difficulty philosophers will have in returning to the sphere of practical affairs after having envisioned the ideal, supra-earthly form of the good. (Nevertheless, in the just commonwealth such civic service will be the duty of philosopher-rulers.) [*Editors' headnote*.]

BOOK VII

THE PARABLE OF THE CAVE

And now, I said,[1] let me show in a figure how far our nature is enlightened or unenlightened:—Behold! human beings living in an underground den, which has a mouth open towards the light and reaching all along the den; here they have been from their childhood, and have their legs and necks chained so that they cannot move, and can only see before them, being prevented by the chains from turning round their heads. Above and behind them a fire is blazing at a distance, and between the fire and the prisoners there is a raised way; and you will see, if you look, a low wall built along the way, like the screen which marionette players have in front of them, over which they show the puppets.

I see.

And do you see, I said, men passing along the wall carrying all sorts of vessels, and statues and figures of animals made of wood and stone and various materials, which appear over the wall? Some of them are talking, others silent.

You have shown me a strange image, and they are strange prisoners.

Like ourselves, I replied; and they see only their own shadows, or the shadows of one another, which the fire throws on the opposite wall of the cave?

True, he said; how could they see anything but the shadows if they were never allowed to move their heads?

And of the objects which are being carried in like manner they would only see the shadows?

Yes, he said.

---

[1] The entire dialogue is related, by Socrates, on the day after it is supposed to have occurred.

And if they were able to converse with one another, would they not suppose that they were naming what was actually before them?

Very true.

And suppose further that the prison had an echo which came from the other side, would they not be sure to fancy when one of the passers-by spoke that the voice which they heard came from the passing shadow?

No question, he replied.

To them, I said, the truth would be literally nothing but the shadows of the images.

That is certain.

And now look again, and see what will naturally follow if the prisoners are released and disabused of their error. At first, when any of them is liberated and compelled suddenly to stand up and turn his neck round and walk and look towards the light, he will suffer sharp pains; the glare will distress him, and he will be unable to see the realities of which in his former state he had seen the shadows; and then conceive some one saying to him, that what he saw before was an illusion, but that now, when he is approaching nearer to being and his eye is turned towards more real existence, he has a clearer vision,—what will be his reply? And you may further imagine that his instructor is pointing to the objects as they pass and requiring him to name them,—will he not be perplexed? Will he not fancy that the shadows which he formerly saw are truer than the objects which are now shown to him?

Far truer.

And if he is compelled to look straight at the light, will he not have a pain in his eyes which will make him turn away to take refuge in the objects of vision which he can see, and which he will conceive to be in reality clearer than the things which are now being shown to him?

True, he said.

And suppose once more, that he is reluctantly dragged up a steep and rugged ascent, and held fast until he is forced into the presence of the sun himself, is he not likely to be pained and irritated? When he approaches the light his eyes will be dazzled, and he will not be able to see anything at all of what are now called realities.

Not all in a moment, he said.

He will require to grow accustomed to the sight of the upper world. And first he will see the shadows best, next the reflections of men and other objects in the water, and then the objects themselves; then he will gaze upon the light of the moon and the stars and the spangled heaven; and he will see the sky and the stars by night better than the sun or the light of the sun by day?

Certainly.

Last of all he will be able to see the sun, and not mere reflections of him in the water, but he will see him in his own proper place, and not in another; and he will contemplate him as he is.

Certainly.

He will then proceed to argue that this is he who gives the season and the years, and is the guardian of all that is in the visible world, and in a certain way the cause of all things which he and his fellows have been accustomed to behold?

Clearly, he said, he would first see the sun and then reason about him.

And when he remembered his old habitation, and the wisdom of the den and his fellow-prisoners, do you not suppose that he would felicitate himself on the change, and pity them?

Certainly, he would.

And if they were in the habit of conferring honors among themselves on those who were quickest to observe the passing shadows and to remark which of them went before, and which followed after, and which were together; and who were therefore best able to draw conclusions as to the future, do you think that he would care for such honors and glories, or envy the possessors of them? Would he not say with Homer,

"Better to be the poor servant of a poor master,"[2]

and to endure anything, rather than think as they do and live after their manner?

Yes, he said, I think that he would rather suffer anything than entertain these false notions and live in this miserable manner.

Imagine once more, I said, such an one coming suddenly out of the sun to be replaced in his old situation; would he not be certain to have his eyes full of darkness?

To be sure, he said.

And if there were a contest, and he had to compete in measuring the shadows with the prisoners who had never moved out of the den, while his sight was still weak, and before his eyes had become steady (and the time which would be needed to acquire this new habit of sight might be very considerable), would he not be ridiculous? Men would say of him that up he went and down he came without his eyes; and that it was better not even to think of ascending; and if any one tried to loose another and lead him up to the light, let them only catch the offender, and they would put him to death.

No question, he said.

This entire allegory, I said, you may now append, dear Glaucon, to the previous argument; the prison-house is the world of sight, the light of the fire is the sun, and you will not misapprehend me if you interpret the journey upwards to be the ascent of the soul into the intellectual world according to my poor belief, which, at your desire, I have expressed— whether rightly or wrongly God knows. But, whether true or false, my opinion is that in the world of knowledge the idea of good appears last of all, and is seen only with an effort; and, when seen, is also inferred to be the universal author of all things beautiful and right, parent of light and of the lord of light in this visible world, and the immediate source of reason and truth in the intellectual; and that this is the power upon which he who would act rationally either in public or private life must have his eye fixed.

I agree, he said, as far as I am able to understand you.

Moreover, I said, you must not wonder that those who attain to this

---

[2] In the dim underworld of Hades visited by Odysseus in the *Odyssey*, Book XI, the shade of the great warrior Achilles says that he would rather be alive as the lowliest servant than reign as king of the underworld.

beatific vision are unwilling to descend to human affairs; for their souls are ever hastening into the upper world where they desire to dwell; which desire of theirs is very natural, if our allegory may be trusted.

Yes, very natural.

And is there anything surprising in one who passes from divine contemplations to the evil state of man, misbehaving himself in a ridiculous manner; if, while his eyes are blinking and before he has become accustomed to the surrounding darkness, he is compelled to fight in courts of law, or in other places, about the images or the shadows of images of justice, and is endeavoring to meet the conceptions of those who have never yet seen absolute justice?

Anything but surprising, he replied.

Any one who has common sense will remember that the bewilderments of the eyes are of two kinds, and arise from two causes, either from coming out of the light or from going into the light, which is true of the mind's eye, quite as much as of the bodily eye; and he who remembers this when he sees any one whose vision is perplexed and weak, will not be too ready to laugh; he will first ask whether that soul of man has come out of the brighter life, and is unable to see because unaccustomed to the dark, or having turned from darkness to the day is dazzled by excess of light. And he will count the one happy in his condition and state of being, and he will pity the other; or, if he have a mind to laugh at the soul which comes from below into the light, there will be more reason in this than in the laugh which greets him who returns from above out of the light into the den.

That, he said, is a very just distinction.

But then, if I am right, certain professors of education must be wrong when they say that they can put a knowledge into the soul which was not there before, like sight into blind eyes.

They undoubtedly say this, he replied.

Whereas, our argument shows that the power and capacity of learning exists in the soul already; and that just as the eye was unable to turn from darkness to light without the whole body, so too the instrument of knowledge can only by the movement of the whole soul be turned from the world of becoming into that of being, and learn by degrees to endure the sight of being, and of the brightest and best of being, or in other words, of the good. . . .

THE APOLOGY

Translated by Benjamin Jowett

In 399 B.C. the seventy-year-old Socrates had made enemies of certain prominent Athenians to the extent that he was brought to trial, on two counts: for atheism and for the corruption of Athenian youth. The *Apology* is Socrates' defense of himself against the charges, both the immediate and specific ones on which he was arraigned and those brought against him during his entire life and career. If the word "apology" is mistakenly understood in its ordinary modern sense, the title of this work will be puzzling, for Socrates' speech is not a confession of guilt or error; it is quite the contrary. Socrates' words are an "apology" in the older sense of *apologia*, meaning an aggressive vindication of himself and of his principles. In keeping with his distinctive style of behavior, Socrates conducts his defense in an utterly personal way, with little regard for expediency or for legal forms and procedures.

Plato himself, then in his late twenties, is mentioned in the *Apology* as among the followers of Socrates present at the trial. If he was indeed present, Plato was in a position to record Socrates' words accurately. To what extent he actually did so, we cannot be sure; as with other Socratic dialogues, we must assume that the *Apology* is a combination of Socrates' ideas and his pupil Plato's own emphases and artistry. But the image of Socrates that emerges is so compelling that it conveys a strong impression of historical and even reportorial accuracy.

For many centuries readers have been irresistibly drawn to compare Socrates and Jesus. The accounts of their trials and executions are especially worthy of comparison—for both the similarities and the differences. See, for example, Matthew 26-27 and John 18-19. [*Editors' headnote.*]

How you, O Athenians, have been affected by my accusers, I cannot tell; but I know that they almost made me forget who I was—so persuasively did they speak; and yet they have hardly uttered a word of truth. But of the many falsehoods told by them, there was one which quite amazed me;—I mean when they said that you should be upon your guard and not allow yourselves to be deceived by the force of my eloquence. To say this, when they were certain to be detected as soon as I opened my lips and proved myself to be anything but a great speaker, did indeed appear to me most shameless—unless by the force of eloquence they mean the force of truth; for if such is their meaning, I admit that I am eloquent. But in how different a way from theirs! Well, as I was saying, they have scarcely spoken the truth at all; but from me you shall hear the whole truth: not, however, delivered after their manner in a set oration duly ornamented with words and phrases. No, by heaven! but I shall use the words and arguments which occur to me at the moment; for I am confident in the justice of my cause: at my time of life I ought not to be appearing before you, O men of Athens, in the character of a juvenile orator—let no one expect it of me. And I must beg of you to grant me a favor:—If I defend myself in my accustomed manner, and you hear me using the words which I have been in the habit of using in the agora,[1] at the tables of the money-changers, or anywhere else, I would ask you not to be surprised, and not to interrupt me on this account. For I am more than seventy years of age, and appearing now for the first time in a court of law, I am quite a stranger to the language of the place; and therefore I would have you regard me as if I were really a stranger,[2] whom you would excuse if he spoke in his native tongue, and after the fashion of his country:—Am I making an unfair request of you? Never mind the manner, which may or may not be good; but think only of the truth of my words, and give heed to that: let the speaker speak truly and the judge decide justly.

And first, I have to reply to the older charges and to my first accusers, and then I will go on to the later ones. For of old I have had many accusers, who have accused me falsely to you during many years; and I am more

---

[1] The public marketplace where citizens congregated.

[2] A noncitizen of Athens, whose dialect would have sounded uncouth to Athenians. Socrates' ironic point is that, though he is a genuine and lifelong Athenian, his manner of discourse will sound unconventional, like that of a "stranger" or foreigner.

afraid of them than of Anytus and his associates,[3] who are dangerous, too, in their own way. But far more dangerous are the others, who began when you were children, and took possession of your minds with their falsehoods, telling of one Socrates, a wise man, who speculated about the heaven above, and searched into the earth beneath, and made the worse appear the better cause.[4] The disseminators of this tale are the accusers whom I dread; for their hearers are apt to fancy that such enquirers do not believe in the existence of the gods. And they are many, and their charges against me are of ancient date, and they were made by them in the days when you were more impressible than you are now—in childhood, or it may have been in youth—and the cause when heard went by default, for there was none to answer. And hardest of all, I do not know and cannot tell the names of my accusers; unless in the chance case of a Comic poet.[5] All who from envy and malice have persuaded you—some of them having first convinced themselves—all this class of men are most difficult to deal with; for I cannot have them up here, and cross-examine them, and therefore I must simply fight with shadows in my own defense, and argue when there is no one who answers. I will ask you then to assume with me, as I was saying, that my opponents are of two kinds; one recent, the other ancient: and I hope that you will see the propriety of my answering the latter first, for these accusations you heard long before the others, and much oftener.

Well, then, I must make my defense, and endeavor to clear away in a short time, a slander which has lasted a long time. May I succeed, if to succeed be for my good and yours, or likely to avail me in my cause! The task is not an easy one; I quite understand the nature of it. And so leaving the event with God, in obedience to the law I will now make my defense.

I will begin at the beginning, and ask what is the accusation which has given rise to the slander of me, and in fact has encouraged Meletus to prefer this charge against me. Well, what do the slanderers say? They shall be my prosecutors, and I will sum up their words in an affidavit: 'Socrates is an evil-doer, and a curious person, who searches into things under the earth and in heaven, and he makes the worse appear the better cause; and he teaches the aforesaid doctrines to others.' Such is the nature of the accusation: it is just what you have yourselves seen in the comedy of Aristophanes, who has introduced a man whom he calls Socrates, going about and saying that he walks in air, and talking a deal of nonsense concerning matters of which I do not pretend to know either much or little—not that I mean to speak disparagingly of any one who is a student of natural philosophy. I should be very sorry if Meletus could bring so grave a charge against

---

[3] The three men who pressed charges against Socrates were Anytus, Meletus, and Lycon. Anytus was a wealthy leather merchant who disliked Socrates partly on political grounds and partly because Socrates had tried to persuade Anytus to let his son pursue a career different from his father's. Meletus (cross-examined by Socrates later in the *Apology*) may have been a poet (poets were both adulated and despised by Socrates/Plato). Of Lycon little is known; he may have been a professional orator.

[4] Socrates was almost entirely concerned with ethical human values, as distinguished from both natural science and the tricks of logic and language associated with the Sophists (professional teachers of rhetoric and logic or pseudo-logic). Nevertheless, his dexterity in discourse and his subtleties of argument caused some people to believe that he was a Sophist.

[5] Aristophanes, who in his play *The Clouds* represented Socrates unfavorably, as a pretender to miraculous powers.

me. But the simple truth is, O Athenians, that I have nothing to do with physical speculations. Very many of those here present are witnesses to the truth of this, and to them I appeal. Speak then, you who have heard me, and tell your neighbors whether any of you have ever known me hold forth in few words or in many upon such matters. . . . You hear their answer. And from what they say of this part of the charge you will be able to judge of the truth of the rest.

As little foundation is there for the report that I am a teacher, and take money; this accusation has no more truth in it than the other. Although, if a man were really able to instruct mankind, to receive money for giving instruction would, in my opinion, be an honor to him. There is Gorgias of Leontium, and Prodicus of Ceos, and Hippias of Elis,[6] who go the round of the cities, and are able to persuade the young men to leave their own citizens by whom they might be taught for nothing, and come to them whom they not only pay, but are thankful if they may be allowed to pay them. There is at this time a Parian philosopher residing in Athens, of whom I have heard; and I came to hear of him in this way:—I came across a man who has spent a world of money on the Sophists, Callias, the son of Hipponicus, and knowing that he had sons, I asked him: 'Callias,' I said, 'if your two sons were foals or calves, there would be no difficulty in finding some one to put over them; we should hire a trainer of horses, or a farmer probably, who would improve and perfect them in their own proper virtue and excellence; but as they are human beings, whom are you thinking of placing over them? Is there any one who understands human and political virtue? You must have thought about the matter, for you have sons; is there any one?' 'There is,' he said. 'Who is he?' said I; 'and of what country? and what does he charge?' 'Evenus[7] the Parian,' he replied; 'he is the man, and his charge is five minae.' Happy is Evenus, I said to myself, if he really has this wisdom, and teaches at such a moderate charge. Had I the same, I should have been very proud and conceited; but the truth is that I have no knowledge of the kind.

I dare say, Athenians, that some one among you will reply, 'Yes, Socrates, but what is the origin of these accusations which are brought against you; there must have been something strange which you have been doing? All these rumors and this talk about you would never have arisen if you had been like other men: tell us, then, what is the cause of them, for we should be sorry to judge hastily of you.' Now I regard this as a fair challenge, and I will endeavor to explain to you the reason why I am called wise and have such an evil fame. Please to attend then. And although some of you may think that I am joking, I declare that I will tell you the entire truth. Men of Athens, this reputation of mine has come of a certain sort of wisdom which I possess. If you ask me what kind of wisdom, I reply, wisdom such as may perhaps be attained by man, for to that extent I am inclined to believe that I am wise; whereas the persons of whom I was speaking have a superhuman wisdom, which I may fail to describe, because I have it not myself; and he who says that I have, speaks falsely, and is taking away my character.

---

[6] Noted Sophists and teachers, mainly of rhetoric and logic.

[7] A poet and teacher of oratory, from the island of Paros. The low sum he charged may indicate his low repute as a teacher. A mina was worth about forty dollars.

And here, O men of Athens, I must beg you not to interrupt me, even if I seem to say something extravagant. For the word which I will speak is not mine. I will refer you to a witness who is worthy of credit; that witness shall be the God of Delphi[8]—he will tell you about my wisdom, if I have any, and of what sort it is. You must have known Chaerephon; he was early a friend of mine, and also a friend of yours, for he shared in the recent exile of the people,[9] and returned with you. Well, Chaerephon, as you know, was very impetuous in all his doings, and he went to Delphi and boldly asked the oracle to tell him whether—as I was saying, I must beg you not to interrupt—he asked the oracle to tell him whether any one was wiser than I was, and the Pythian prophetess answered, that there was no man wiser. Chaerephon is dead himself; but his brother, who is in court, will confirm the truth of what I am saying.

Why do I mention this? Because I am going to explain to you why I have such an evil name. When I heard the answer, I said to myself, What can the god mean? and what is the interpretation of his riddle? for I know that I have no wisdom, small or great. What then can he mean when he says that I am the wisest of men? And yet he is a god, and cannot lie; that would be against his nature. After long consideration, I thought of a method of trying the question. I reflected that if I could only find a man wiser than myself, then I might go to the god with a refutation in my hand. I should say to him, 'Here is a man who is wiser than I am; but you said that I was the wisest.' Accordingly I went to one who had the reputation of wisdom, and observed him—his name I need not mention; he was a politician whom I selected for examination—and the result was as follows: When I began to talk with him, I could not help thinking that he was not really wise, although he was thought wise by many, and still wiser by himself; and thereupon I tried to explain to him that he thought himself wise, but was not really wise; and the consequence was that he hated me, and his enmity was shared by several who were present and heard me. So I left him, saying to myself, as I went away: Well, although I do not suppose that either of us knows anything really beautiful and good, I am better off than he is,—for he knows nothing, and thinks that he knows; I neither know nor think that I know. In this latter particular, then, I seem to have slightly the advantage of him. Then I went to another who had still higher pretensions to wisdom, and my conclusion was exactly the same. Whereupon I made another enemy of him, and of many others beside him.

Then I went to one man after another, being not unconscious of the enmity which I provoked, and I lamented and feared this: but necessity was laid upon me,—the word of God, I thought, ought to be considered first. And I said to myself, Go I must to all who appear to know, and find out the meaning of the oracle. And I swear to you, Athenians, by the dog I swear!—for I must tell you the truth—the result of my mission was just

---

[8] Site of the most famous temple of Apollo; the god's oracles were pronounced there by the Pythia, his priestess.

[9] Five years earlier, after the defeat of Athens by Sparta in 404, the "Thirty Tyrants" had temporarily ruled and terrorized Athens, driving the democratic leaders (who included Socrates' friend Chaerephon) into temporary exile. The democracy had been reestablished in 403.

this: I found that the men most in repute were all but the most foolish; and that others less esteemed were really wiser and better. I will tell you the tale of my wanderings and of the 'Herculean'[10] labors, as I may call them, which I endured only to find at last the oracle irrefutable. After the politicians, I went to the poets; tragic, dithyrambic, and all sorts. And there, I said to myself, you will be instantly detected; now you will find out that you are more ignorant than they are. Accordingly, I took them some of the most elaborate passages in their own writings, and asked what was the meaning of them—thinking that they would teach me something. Will you believe me? I am almost ashamed to confess the truth, but I must say that there is hardly a person present who would not have talked better about their poetry than they did themselves. Then I knew that not by wisdom do poets write poetry, but by a sort of genius and inspiration; they are like diviners or soothsayers who also say many fine things, but do not understand the meaning of them.[11] The poets appeared to me to be much in the same case; and I further observed that upon the strength of their poetry they believed themselves to be the wisest of men in other things in which they were not wise. So I departed, conceiving myself to be superior to them for the same reason that I was superior to the politicians.

At last I went to the artisans,[12] for I was conscious that I knew nothing at all, as I may say, and I was sure that they knew many fine things; and here I was not mistaken, for they did know many things of which I was ignorant, and in this they certainly were wiser than I was. But I observed that even the good artisans fell into the same error as the poets;—because they were good workmen they thought that they also knew all sorts of high matters, and this defect in them overshadowed their wisdom; and therefore I asked myself on behalf of the oracle, whether I would like to be as I was, neither having their knowledge nor their ignorance, or like them in both; and I made answer to myself and to the oracle that I was better off as I was.

This inquisition has led to my having many enemies of the worst and most dangerous kind, and has given occasion also to many calumnies. And I am called wise, for my hearers always imagine that I myself possess the wisdom which I find wanting in others: but the truth is, O men of Athens, that God only is wise; and by his answer he intends to show that the wisdom of men is worth little or nothing; he is not speaking of Socrates, he is only using my name by way of illustration, as if he said, He, O men, is the wisest, who, like Socrates, knows that his wisdom is in truth worth nothing. And so I go about the world, obedient to the god, and search and make enquiry into the wisdom of any one, whether citizen or stranger, who appears to be wise; and if he is not wise, then in vindication of the oracle I show him that he is not wise; and my occupation quite absorbs me, and I have no time to give either to any public matter of interest or to any concern of my own, but I am in utter poverty by reason of my devotion to the god.

[10] The legendary hero Hercules had been forced to undertake a series of superhumanly difficult tasks.

[11] This view of poets and of their interpreters is elaborated, half-playfully, by Socrates in Plato's *Ion.*

[12] Craftsmen.

There is another thing:—young men of the richer classes, who have not much to do, come about me of their own accord; they like to hear the pretenders examined, and they often imitate me, and proceed to examine others; there are plenty of persons, as they quickly discover, who think that they know something, but really know little or nothing; and then those who are examined by them instead of being angry with themselves are angry with me: This confounded Socrates, they say; this villainous misleader of youth!—and then if somebody asks them, Why, what evil does he practice or teach? they do not know, and cannot tell; but in order that they may not appear to be at a loss, they repeat the ready-made charges which are used against all philosophers about teaching things up in the clouds and under the earth, and having no gods, and making the worse appear the better cause; for they do not like to confess that their pretense of knowledge has been detected—which is the truth; and as they are numerous and ambitious and energetic, and are drawn up in battle array and have persuasive tongues, they have filled your ears with their loud and inveterate calumnies. And this is the reason why my three accusers, Meletus and Anytus and Lycon, have set upon me; Meletus, who has a quarrel with me on behalf of the poets; Anytus, on behalf of the craftsmen and politicians; Lycon, on behalf of the rhetoricians: and as I said at the beginning, I cannot expect to get rid of such a mass of calumny all in a moment. And this, O men of Athens, is the truth and the whole truth; I have concealed nothing, I have dissembled nothing. And yet, I know that my plainness of speech makes them hate me, and what is their hatred but a proof that I am speaking the truth?—Hence has arisen the prejudice against me; and this is the reason of it, as you will find out either in this or in any future enquiry.

I have said enough in my defense against the first class of my accusers; I turn to the second class. They are headed by Meletus, that good man and true lover of his country, as he calls himself. Against these, too, I must try to make a defense:—Let their affidavit be read: it contains something of this kind: It says that Socrates is a doer of evil, who corrupts the youth; and who does not believe in the gods of the state, but has other new divinities of his own. Such is the charge; and now let us examine the particular counts. He says that I am a doer of evil, and corrupt the youth; but I say, O men of Athens, that Meletus is a doer of evil, in that he pretends to be in earnest when he is only in jest, and is so eager to bring men to trial from a pretended zeal and interest about matters in which he really never had the smallest interest. And the truth of this I will endeavor to prove to you.

Come hither, Meletus, and let me ask a question of you. You think a great deal about the improvement of youth?

Yes, I do.

Tell the judges, then, who is their improver; for you must know, as you have taken the pains to discover their corrupter, and are citing and accusing me before them. Speak, then, and tell the judges who their improver is.—Observe, Meletus, that you are silent, and have nothing to say. But is not this rather disgraceful, and a very considerable proof of what I was saying, that you have no interest in the matter? Speak up, friend, and tell us who their improver is.

The laws.

But that, my good sir, is not my meaning. I want to know who the person is, who, in the first place, knows the laws.[13]

The judges, Socrates, who are present in court.

What, do you mean to say, Meletus, that they are able to instruct and improve youth?

Certainly they are.

What, all of them, or some only and not others?

All of them.

By the goddess Herè,[14] that is good news! There are plenty of improvers, then. And what do you say of the audience,—do they improve them?

Yes, they do.

And the senators?

Yes, the senators improve them.

But perhaps the members of the assembly corrupt them?—or do they too improve them?

They improve them.

Then every Athenian improves and elevates them; all with the exception of myself; and I alone am their corrupter? Is that what you affirm?

That is what I stoutly affirm.

I am very unfortunate if you are right. But suppose I ask you a question: How about horses? Does one man do them harm and all the world good? Is not the exact opposite the truth? One man is able to do them good, or at least not many;—the trainer of horses, that is to say, does them good, and others who have to do with them rather injure them? Is not that true, Meletus, of horses, or of any other animals? Most assuredly it is; whether you and Anytus say yes or no. Happy indeed would be the condition of youth if they had one corrupter only, and all the rest of the world were their improvers. But you, Meletus, have sufficiently shown that you never had a thought about the young: your carelessness is seen in your not caring about the very things which you bring against me.

And now, Meletus, I will ask you another question—by Zeus I will: Which is better, to live among bad citizens, or among good ones? Answer, friend, I say; the question is one which may be easily answered. Do not the good do their neighbors good, and the bad do them evil?

Certainly.

And is there any one who would rather be injured than benefited by those who live with him? Answer, my good friend, the law requires you to answer—does any one like to be injured?

Certainly not.

And when you accuse me of corrupting and deteriorating the youth, do you allege that I corrupt them intentionally or unintentionally?

Intentionally, I say.

[13] In the following lines, Socrates calls into play his notorious talent for reducing his opponent's view to foolishness. The half-defiant, half-squirming Meletus is forced to define the noncorrupters of youth first as the "judges" (that is, the men empowered to render the verdict), then the entire audience, then the "senators" (the five hundred select members of the assembly who constituted the Athenian civic council), then the whole "assembly" which in law included the entire adult citizenry of Athens.

[14] Hera, queen of the gods; this oath is often used by Socrates.

But you have just admitted that the good do their neighbors good, and the evil do them evil. Now, is that a truth which your superior wisdom has recognized thus early in life, and am I, at my age, in such darkness and ignorance as not to know that if a man with whom I have to live is corrupted by me, I am very likely to be harmed by him; and yet I corrupt him, and intentionally, too—so you say, although neither I nor any other human being is ever likely to be convinced by you. But either I do not corrupt them, or I corrupt them unintentionally; and on either view of the case you lie. If my offense is unintentional, the law has no cognizance of unintentional offenses: you ought to have taken me privately, and warned and admonished me; for if I had been better advised, I should have left off doing what I only did unintentionally—no doubt I should; but you would have nothing to say to me and refused to teach me. And now you bring me up in this court, which is a place not of instruction, but of punishment.

It will be very clear to you, Athenians, as I was saying, that Meletus has no care at all, great or small, about the matter. But still I should like to know, Meletus, in what I am affirmed to corrupt the young. I suppose you mean, as I infer from your indictment, that I teach them not to acknowledge the gods which the state acknowledges, but some other new divinities or spiritual agencies in their stead. These are the lessons by which I corrupt the youth, as you say.

Yes, that I say emphatically.

Then, by the gods, Meletus, of whom we are speaking, tell me and the court, in somewhat plainer terms, what you mean! for I do not as yet understand whether you affirm that I teach other men to acknowledge some gods, and therefore that I do believe in gods, and am not an entire atheist—this you do not lay to my charge,—but only you say that they are not the same gods which the city recognizes—the charge is that they are different gods. Or, do you mean that I am an atheist simply, and a teacher of atheism?

I mean the latter—that you are a complete atheist.

What an extraordinary statement! Why do you think so, Meletus? Do you mean that I do not believe in the godhead of the sun or moon,[15] like other men?

I assure you, judges, that he does not: for he says that the sun is stone, and the moon earth.

Friend Meletus, you think that you are accusing Anaxagoras:[16] and you have but a bad opinion of the judges, if you fancy them illiterate to such a degree as not to know that these doctrines are found in the books of Anaxagoras the Clazomenian, which are full of them. And so, forsooth,

---

[15] Apollo was the god of the sun, Artemis the goddess of the moon; but, whether the sun and moon were literally identified with these deities or not, reverence for the two great celestial bodies was a hallmark of religious piety for the Greeks. Socrates did, in fact, hold the sun and moon in awe, as is shown in Plato's *Symposium*.

[16] A philosopher-scientist, born around 500 B.C. Socrates, concerned almost entirely with ethics, would have resisted such materialist astrophysical theories. The reference to the theater a few lines later may mean that Anaxagoras' ideas were explored by the playwrights (particularly Euripides and Aristophanes) or that the philosopher's writings could be purchased there (or in some similar public place). In any event, Socrates' point is that such religiously heterodox ideas were freely available to the public apart from anything he might have taught.

the youth are said to be taught them by Socrates, when there are not unfrequently exhibitions of them at the theater (price of admission one drachma at the most); and they might pay their money, and laugh at Socrates if he pretends to father these extraordinary views. And so, Meletus, you really think that I do not believe in any god?

I swear by Zeus that you believe absolutely in none at all.

Nobody will believe you, Meletus, and I am pretty sure that you do not believe yourself. I cannot help thinking, men of Athens, that Meletus is reckless and impudent, and that he has written this indictment in a spirit of mere wantonness and youthful bravado. Has he not compounded a riddle, thinking to try me? He said to himself:—I shall see whether the wise Socrates will discover my facetious contradiction, or whether I shall be able to deceive him and the rest of them. For he certainly does appear to me to contradict himself in the indictment as much as if he said that Socrates is guilty of not believing in the gods, and yet of believing in them—but this is not like a person who is in earnest.

I should like you, O men of Athens, to join me in examining what I conceive to be his inconsistency; and do you, Meletus, answer. And I must remind the audience of my request that they would not make a disturbance if I speak in my accustomed manner:

Did ever man, Meletus, believe in the existence of human things, and not of human beings? . . . I wish, men of Athens, that he would answer, and not be always trying to get up an interruption. Did ever any man believe in horsemanship, and not in horses? or in flute-playing, and not in flute-players? No, my friend; I will answer to you and to the court, as you refuse to answer for yourself. There is no man who ever did. But now please to answer the next question: Can a man believe in spiritual and divine agencies, and not in spirits or in demigods?[17]

He cannot.

How lucky I am to have extracted that answer, by the assistance of the court! But then you swear in the indictment that I teach and believe in divine or spiritual agencies (new or old, no matter for that); at any rate, I believe in spiritual agencies,—so you say and swear in the affidavit; and yet if I believe in divine beings, how can I help believing in spirits or demigods;—must I not? To be sure I must; and therefore I may assume that your silence gives consent. Now what are spirits or demigods? are they not either gods or the sons of gods?

Certainly they are.

But this is what I call the facetious riddle invented by you: the demigods or spirits are gods, and you say first that I do not believe in gods, and then again that I do believe in gods; that is, if I believe in demigods. For if the demigods are the illegitimate sons of gods, whether by the nymphs or by any other mothers, of whom they are said to be the sons—what human being will ever believe that there are no gods if they are the sons of gods? You might as well affirm the existence of mules,[18] and deny that of horses

[17] The ensuing cross-examination of Meletus, logically sound or not, should probably be understood as an attempt by Socrates to prove contemptuously that he could easily defeat his opponents at their legalistic game if he did not have more substantial arguments to make (the ones that emerge in the following parts of his speech).

[18] A mule is a sterile animal produced by the union of a jackass with a mare.

and asses. Such nonsense, Meletus, could only have been intended by you to make trial of me. You have put this into the indictment because you had nothing real of which to accuse me. But no one who has a particle of understanding will ever be convinced by you that the same men can believe in divine and superhuman things, and yet not believe that there are gods and demigods and heroes.

I have said enough in answer to the charge of Meletus: any elaborate defense is unnecessary; but I know only too well how many are the enmities which I have incurred, and this is what will be my destruction if I am destroyed;—not Meletus, nor yet Anytus, but the envy and detraction of the world, which has been the death of many good men, and will probably be the death of many more; there is no danger of my being the last of them.

Some one will say: And are you not ashamed, Socrates, of a course of life which is likely to bring you to an untimely end? To him I may fairly answer: There you are mistaken: a man who is good for anything ought not to calculate the chance of living or dying; he ought only to consider whether in doing anything he is doing right or wrong—acting the part of a good man or of a bad. Whereas, upon your view, the heroes who fell at Troy were not good for much, and the son of Thetis[19] above all, who altogether despised danger in comparison with disgrace; and when he was so eager to slay Hector, his goddess mother said to him, that if he avenged his companion Patroclus, and slew Hector, he would die himself—'Fate,' she said, in these or the like words, 'waits for you next after Hector;' he, receiving this warning, utterly despised danger and death, and instead of fearing them, feared rather to live in dishonor, and not to avenge his friend. 'Let me die forthwith,' he replies, 'and be avenged of my enemy, rather than abide here by the beaked ships, a laughing-stock and a burden of the earth.' Had Achilles any thought of death and danger? For wherever a man's place is, whether the place which he has chosen or that in which he has been placed by a commander, there he ought to remain in the hour of danger; he should not think of death or of anything but of disgrace. And this, O men of Athens, is a true saying.

Strange, indeed, would be my conduct, O men of Athens, if I who, when I was ordered by the generals whom you chose to command me at Potidaea and Amphipolis and Delium,[20] remained where they placed me, like any other man, facing death—if now, when, as I conceive and imagine, God orders me to fulfil the philosopher's mission of searching into myself and other men, I were to desert my post through fear of death, or any other fear; that would indeed be strange, and I might justly be arraigned in court for denying the existence of the gods, if I disobeyed the oracle because I was afraid of death, fancying that I was wise when I was not wise. For the fear of death is indeed the pretense of wisdom, and not real

----

[19] A sea nymph, mother of Achilles, the hero of Homer's *Iliad*. The Trojan prince and hero Hector had killed Achilles' best friend, Patroclus, an event that brought Achilles back into the battle after a period of sulky neutrality occasioned by his quarrel with the Greek commander, Agamemnon. The dialogue cited here, between Achilles and Thetis, occurs in Book XVIII of the *Iliad*.

[20] Sites of battles (fought respectively in 432, 422, and 424) in which Socrates had served bravely as a soldier. At Potidaea Socrates had saved the life of the Athenian soldier-playboy Alcibiades; see Plato's *Symposium*.

wisdom, being a pretense of knowing the unknown; and no one knows whether death, which men in their fear apprehend to be the greatest evil, may not be the greatest good. Is not this ignorance of a disgraceful sort, the ignorance which is the conceit that a man knows what he does not know? And in this respect only I believe myself to differ from men in general, and may perhaps claim to be wiser than they are:—that whereas I know but little of the world below, I do not suppose that I know: but I do know that injustice and disobedience to a better, whether God or man, is evil and dishonorable, and I will never fear or avoid a possible good rather than a certain evil. And therefore if you let me go now, and are not convinced by Anytus, who said that since I had been prosecuted I must be put to death; (or if not that I ought never to have been prosecuted at all); and that if I escape now, your sons will all be utterly ruined by listening to my words—if you say to me, Socrates, this time we will not mind Anytus, and you shall be let off, but upon one condition, that you are not to enquire and speculate in this way any more, and that if you are caught doing so again you shall die;—if this was the condition on which you let me go, I should reply: Men of Athens, I honor and love you; but I shall obey God rather than you, and while I have life and strength I shall never cease from the practice and teaching of philosophy, exhorting any one whom I meet and saying to him after my manner: You, my friend,—a citizen of the great and mighty and wise city of Athens,—are you not ashamed of heaping up the greatest amount of money and honor and reputation, and caring so little about wisdom and truth and the greatest improvement of the soul, which you never regard or heed at all? And if the person with whom I am arguing, says: Yes, but I do care; then I do not leave him or let him go at once; but I proceed to interrogate and examine and cross-examine him, and if I think that he has no virtue in him, but only says that he has, I reproach him with undervaluing the greater, and overvaluing the less. And I shall repeat the same words to every one whom I meet, young and old, citizen and alien, but especially to the citizens, inasmuch as they are my brethren. For know that this is the command of God; and I believe that no greater good has ever happened in the state than my service to the God. For I do nothing but go about persuading you all, old and young alike, not to take thought for your persons or your properties, but first and chiefly to care about the greatest improvement of the soul. I tell you that virtue is not given by money, but that from virtue comes money and every other good of man, public as well as private. This is my teaching, and if this is the doctrine which corrupts the youth, I am a mischievous person. But if any one says that this is not my teaching, he is speaking an untruth. Wherefore, O men of Athens, I say to you, do as Anytus bids or not as Anytus bids, and either acquit me or not; but whichever you do, understand that I shall never alter my ways, not even if I have to die many times.

Men of Athens, do not interrupt, but hear me; there was an understanding between us that you should hear me to the end: I have something more to say, at which you may be inclined to cry out; but I believe that to hear me will be good for you, and therefore I beg that you will not cry out. I would have you know, that if you kill such an one as I am, you will injure yourselves more than you will injure me. Nothing will injure me, not Meletus nor yet Anytus—they cannot, for a bad man is not permitted to injure a better than himself. I do not deny that Anytus may, perhaps, kill him, or drive him into exile, or deprive him of civil rights; and he may imagine, and others may imagine, that he is inflicting a great injury upon him: but there I do not agree. For the evil of doing as he is doing—the evil of unjustly taking away the life of another—is greater far.

And now, Athenians, I am not going to argue for my own sake, as you may think, but for yours, that you may not sin against the God by condemning me, who am his gift to you. For if you kill me you will not easily find a successor to me, who, if I may use such a ludicrous figure of speech, am a sort of gadfly, given to the state by God; and the state is a great and noble steed who is tardy in his motions owing to his very size, and requires to be stirred into life. I am that gadfly which God has attached to the state, and all day long and in all places am always fastening upon you, arousing and persuading and reproaching you. You will not easily find another like me, and therefore I would advise you to spare me. I dare say that you may feel out of temper (like a person who is suddenly awakened from sleep), and you think that you might easily strike me dead as Anytus advises, and then you would sleep on for the remainder of your lives, unless God in his care of you sent you another gadfly. When I say that I am given to you by God, the proof of my mission is this:—if I had been like other men, I should not have neglected all my own concerns or patiently seen the neglect of them during all these years, and have been doing yours, coming to you individually like a father or elder brother, exhorting you to regard virtue; such conduct, I say, would be unlike human nature. If I had gained anything, or if my exhortations had been paid, there would have been some sense in my doing so; but now, as you will perceive, not even the impudence of my accusers dares to say that I have ever exacted or sought pay of any one; of that they have no witness. And I have a sufficient witness to the truth of what I say—my poverty.

Some one may wonder why I go about in private giving advice and busying myself with the concerns of others, but do not venture to come forward in public and advise the state. I will tell you why. You have heard me speak at sundry times and in divers places of an oracle or sign which comes to me, and is the divinity which Meletus ridicules in the indictment. This sign, which is a kind of voice, first began to come to me when I was a child; it always forbids but never commands me to do anything which I am going to do. This is what deters me from being a politician. And rightly, as I think. For I am certain, O men of Athens, that if I had engaged in politics, I should have perished long ago, and done no good either to you or to myself. And do not be offended at my telling you the truth: for the truth is, that no man who goes to war with you or any other multitude, honestly striving against the many lawless and unrighteous deeds which are done in a state, will save his life; he who will fight for the right, if he would live even for a brief space, must have a private station and not a public one.

I can give you convincing evidence of what I say, not words only, but what you value far more—actions. Let me relate to you a passage of my own life which will prove to you that I should never have yielded to injustice from any fear of death, and that 'as I should have refused to yield' I must have died at once. I will tell you a tale of the courts, not very interesting perhaps, but nevertheless true. The only office of state which I ever held, O men of Athens, was that of senator: the tribe Antiochis, which is my tribe, had the presidency at the trial of the generals who had not taken up the bodies of the slain after the battle of Arginusae; and you proposed to try them in a body, contrary to law, as you all thought afterwards; but at the time I was the only one of the Prytanes who was opposed to the illegality, and I gave my vote against you; and when the orators threatened to impeach and arrest me, and you called and shouted, I made up my mind that I would run the risk, having law and justice with me, rather than take part in your injustice because I feared imprisonment and death. This happened in the days of the democracy.[21] But when the oligarchy of the Thirty was in power, they sent for me and four others into the rotunda, and bade us bring Leon[22] the Salaminian from Salamis, as they wanted to put him to death. This was a specimen of the sort of commands which they were always giving with the view of implicating as many as possible in their crimes; and then I showed, not in word only but in deed, that, if I may be allowed to use such an expression, I cared not a straw for death, and that my great and only care was lest I should do an unrighteous or unholy thing. For the strong arm of that oppressive power did not frighten me into doing wrong; and when we came out of the rotunda the other four went to Salamis and fetched Leon, but I went quietly home. For which I might have lost my life, had not the power of the Thirty shortly afterwards come to an end. And many will witness to my words.

Now do you really imagine that I could have survived all these years, if I had led a public life, supposing that like a good man I had always maintained the right and had made justice, as I ought, the first thing? No indeed, men of Athens, neither I nor any other man. But I have been always the same in all my actions, public as well as private, and never have I yielded any base compliance to those who are slanderously termed my disciples, or to any other. Not that I have any regular disciples. But if anyone likes to come and hear me while I am pursuing my mission, whether he be young or old, he is not excluded. Nor do I converse only with those who pay; but any one, whether he be rich or poor, may ask and answer me and listen to my words; and whether he turns out to be a bad man or a good one, neither result can be justly imputed to me; for I never taught or professed to teach him anything. And if any one says that he has ever learned or heard anything from me in private which all the world has not heard, let me tell you that he is lying.

But I shall be asked, Why do people delight in continually conversing with you? I have told you already, Athenians, the whole truth about this matter: they like to hear the cross-examination of the pretenders to wisdom; there is amusement in it. Now this duty of cross-examining other

---

[21] The Athenian senate consisted of five hundred members, fifty from each of the ten phylae, or "tribes." Socrates belonged to a tribe named for the mythical figure Antiochus. Each tribe served for one-tenth of the year as the executive body of the senate; during that period they were called "Prytanes." While Socrates was serving in that capacity, certain Athenian commanders were indicted for allegedly neglecting the dead after the naval battle of Arginusae in 406. Socrates refused to participate in the trial, which violated due process of Athenian law in a number of ways.

[22] As he had defied the authority of the democratic state, Socrates also defied the tyrannical "Thirty" who ruled in 404, by refusing to extradite Leon from Salamis after he had fled there to escape the despotic regime.

men has been imposed upon me by God; and has been signified to me by oracles, visions, and in every way in which the will of divine power was ever intimated to any one. This is true, O Athenians; or, if not true, would be soon refuted. If I am or have been corrupting the youth, those of them who are now grown up and have become sensible that I gave them bad advice in the days of their youth should come forward as accusers, and take their revenge; or if they do not like to come themselves, some of their relatives, fathers, brothers, or other kinsmen, should say what evil their families have suffered at my hands. Now is their time. Many of them I see in the court. There is Crito, who is of the same age and of the same deme[23] with myself, and there is Critobulus his son, whom I also see. Then again there is Lysanias of Sphettus, who is the father of Aeschines—he is present; and also there is Antiphon of Cephisus, who is the father of Epigenes; and there are the brothers of several who have associated with me. There is Nicostratus the son of Theosdotides, and the brother of Theodotus (now Theodotus himself is dead, and therefore he, at any rate, will not seek to stop him); and there is Paralus the son of Demodocus, who had a brother Theages; and Adeimantus the son of Ariston, whose brother Plato[24] is present; and Aeantodorus, who is the brother of Apollodorus, whom I also see. I might mention a great many others, some of whom Meletus should have produced as witnesses in the course of his speech; and let him still produce them, if he has forgotten—I will make way for him. And let him say, if he has any testimony of the sort which he can produce. Nay, Athenians, the very opposite is the truth. For all these are ready to witness on behalf of the corrupter, of the injurer of their kindred, as Meletus and Anytus call me; not the corrupted youth only—there might have been a motive for that—but their uncorrupted elder relatives. Why should they too support me with their testimony? Why, indeed, except for the sake of truth and justice, and because they know that I am speaking the truth, and that Meletus is a liar.

Well, Athenians, this and the like of this is all the defense which I have to offer. Yet a word more. Perhaps there may be some one who is offended at me, when he calls to mind how he himself on a similar, or even a less serious occasion, prayed and entreated the judges with many tears, and how he produced children in court, which was a moving spectacle, together with a host of relations and friends; whereas I, who am probably in danger of my life, will do none of these things. The contrast may occur to his mind, and he may be set against me, and vote in anger because he is displeased at me on this account. Now if there be such a person among you,—mind, I do not say that there is,—to him I may fairly reply: My friend, I am a man, and like other men, a creature of flesh and blood, and not 'of wood or stone,' as Homer says;[25] and I have a family, yes, and sons, O Athenians, three in number, one almost a man, and two others who are still young; and yet I will not bring any of them hither in order to petition you for an

---

[23] District.

[24] The author of the present work. Several of the persons mentioned appear in other works by Plato.

[25] The words are addressed to the disguised Odysseus by his wife Penelope, in Book XIX of Homer's *Odyssey*.

acquittal. And why not? Not from any self-assertion or want of respect for you. Whether I am or am not afraid of death is another question, of which I will not now speak. But, having regard to public opinion, I feel that such conduct would be discreditable to myself, and to you, and to the whole state. One who has reached my years, and who has a name for wisdom, ought not to demean himself. Whether this opinion of me be deserved or not, at any rate the world has decided that Socrates is in some way superior to other men. And if those among you who are said to be superior in wisdom and courage, and any other virtue, demean themselves in this way, how shameful is their conduct! I have seen men of reputation, when they have been condemned, behaving in the strangest manner: they seemed to fancy that they were going to suffer something dreadful if they died, and that they could be immortal if you only allowed them to live; and I think that such are a dishonor to the state, and that any stranger coming in would have said of them that the most eminent men of Athens, to whom the Athenians themselves give honor and command, are no better than women. And I say that these things ought not to be done by those of us who have a reputation; and if they are done, you ought not to permit them; you ought rather to show that you are far more disposed to condemn the man who gets up a doleful scene and makes the city ridiculous, than him who holds his peace.

But, setting aside the question of public opinion, there seems to be something wrong in asking a favor of a judge, and thus procuring an acquittal, instead of informing and convincing him. For his duty is, not to make a present of justice, but to give judgment; and he has sworn that he will judge according to the laws, and not according to his own good pleasure; and we ought not to encourage you, nor should you allow yourselves to be encouraged, in this habit of perjury—there can be no piety in that. Do not then require me to do what I consider dishonorable and impious and wrong, especially now, when I am being tried for impiety on the indictment of Meletus. For if, O men of Athens, by force of persuasion and entreaty I could overpower your oaths, then I should be teaching you to believe that there are no gods, and in defending should simply convict myself of the charge of not believing in them. But that is not so—far otherwise. For I do believe that there are gods, and in a sense higher than that in which any of my accusers believe in them. And to you and to God I commit my cause, to be determined by you as is best for you and me.[26]

There are many reasons why I am not grieved, O men of Athens, at the vote of condemnation. I expected it, and am only surprised that the votes are so nearly equal; for I had thought that the majority against me would have been far larger; but now, had thirty votes gone over to the other side, I should have been acquitted. And I may say, I think, that I have escaped Meletus. I may say more; for without the assistance of Anytus and Lycon, any one may see that he would not have had a fifth part of the votes, as the

---

[26] At this point the jurors cast their votes; about 280 vote for conviction, 220 for acquittal. (Plato does not describe these deliberations; there has been no omission from the text.) The next decision is on the sentence.

law requires, in which case he would have incurred a fine of a thousand drachmae.[27]

And so he proposes death as the penalty. And what shall I propose on my part, O men of Athens? Clearly that which is my due. And what is my due? What return shall be made to the man who has never had the wit to be idle during his whole life; but has been careless of what the many care for—wealth, and family interests, and military offices, and speaking in the assembly, and magistracies, and plots, and parties. Reflecting that I was really too honest a man to be a politician and live, I did not go where I could do no good to you or to myself; but where I could do the greatest good privately to every one of you, thither I went, and sought to persuade every man among you that he must look to himself, and seek virtue and wisdom before he looks to his private interests, and look to the state before he looks to the interests of the state; and that this should be the order which he observes in all his actions. What shall be done to such an one? Doubtless some good thing, O men of Athens, if he has his reward; and the good should be of a kind suitable to him. What would be a reward suitable to a poor man who is your benefactor, and who desires leisure that he may instruct you? There can be no reward so fitting as maintenance in the Prytaneum,[28] O men of Athens, a reward which he deserves far more than the citizen who has won the prize at Olympia in the horse or chariot race, whether the chariots were drawn by two horses or by many. For I am in want, and he has enough; and he only gives you the appearance of happiness, and I give you the reality. And if I am to estimate the penalty fairly, I should say that maintenance in the Prytaneum is the just return.

Perhaps you think that I am braving you in what I am saying now, as in what I said before about the tears and prayers. But this is not so. I speak rather because I am convinced that I never intentionally wronged any one, although I cannot convince you—the time has been too short; if there were a law in Athens, as there is in other cities, that a capital cause should not be decided in one day, then I believe that I should have convinced you. But I cannot in a moment refute great slanders; and, as I am convinced that I never wronged another, I will assuredly not wrong myself. I will not say of myself that I deserve any evil, or propose any penalty. Why should I? Because I am afraid of the penalty of death which Meletus proposes? When I do not know whether death is a good or an evil, why should I propose a penalty which would certainly be an evil? Shall I say imprisonment? And why should I live in prison, and be the slave of the magistrates of the year—of the Eleven?[29] Or shall the penalty be a fine, and imprisonment until the fine is paid? There is the same objection. I should have to lie in prison, for money I have none, and cannot pay. And if I say exile (and this

[27] Socrates ironically intimates that each of his three accusers has captured a third of the vote cast against him—approximately ninety-three apiece, a number lower than the one-fifth (about one hundred) necessary for an accuser to avoid paying a fine. The fine was intended to discourage capricious prosecutions.

[28] A place on the Acropolis where benefactors of Athens were honored. Olympia, in southwestern Greece, was the site of a great festival, held every four years, featuring athletic contests. The modern Olympic games are named for this festival.

[29] A public committee that enforced and supervised criminal penalties, including executions. It was made up of a representative from each of the ten "tribes," plus a secretary.

may possibly be the penalty which you will affix), I must indeed be blinded by the love of life, if I am so irrational as to expect that when you, who are my own citizens, cannot endure my discourses and words, and have found them so grievous and odious that you will have no more of them, others are likely to endure me. No indeed, men of Athens, that is not very likely. And what a life should I lead, at my age, wandering from city to city, ever changing my place of exile, and always being driven out! For I am quite sure that wherever I go, there, as here, the young men will flock to me; and if I drive them away, their elders will drive me out at their request; and if I let them come, their fathers and friends will drive me out for their sakes.

Some one will say: Yes, Socrates, but cannot you hold your tongue, and then you may go into a foreign city, and no one will interfere with you? Now I have great difficulty in making you understand my answer to this. For if I tell you that to do as you say would be a disobedience to the God, and therefore that I cannot hold my tongue, you will not believe that I am serious; and if I say again that daily to discourse about virtue, and of those other things about which you hear me examining myself and others, is the greatest good of man, and that the unexamined life is not worth living,[30] you are still less likely to believe me. Yet I say what is true, although a thing of which it is hard for me to persuade you. Also, I have never been accustomed to think that I deserve to suffer any harm. Had I money I might have estimated the offense at what I was able to pay, and not have been much the worse. But I have none, and therefore I must ask you to proportion the fine to my means. Well, perhaps I could afford a mina, and therefore I propose that penalty:[31] Plato, Crito, Critobulus, and Apollodorus, my friends here, bid me say thirty minae, and they will be the sureties. Let thirty minae be the penalty; for which sum they will be ample security to you.[32]

Not much time will be gained, O Athenians, in return for the evil name which you will get from the detractors of the city, who will say that you killed Socrates, a wise man; for they will call me wise, even although I am not wise, when they want to reproach you. If you had waited a little while, your desire would have been fulfilled in the course of nature. For I am far advanced in years, as you may perceive, and not far from death. I am speaking now not to all of you, but only to those who have condemned me to death. And I have another thing to say to them: You think that I was convicted because I had no words of the sort which would have procured my acquittal—I mean, if I had thought fit to leave nothing undone or unsaid. Not so; the deficiency which led to my conviction was not of words—certainly not. But I had not the boldness or impudence or inclination to address you as you would have liked me to do, weeping and wailing and lamenting, and saying and doing many things which you have been accustomed to hear from others, and which, as I maintain, are unworthy of me. I thought at the time that I ought not to do anything common or mean when in danger: nor do I now repent of the style of my defense; I would

---

[30] One of Socrates' most memorable axioms.

[31] Socrates' decision to propose a monetary penalty is not mercenary but just the opposite: it is a dramatization of his contempt for money as a measure of life and values.

[32] At this point, the five hundred judges cast another split vote, for the death penalty. (Again, Plato does not describe these deliberations; the text given here is complete.)

rather die having spoken after my manner, than speak in your manner and live. For neither in war nor yet at law ought I or any man to use every way of escaping death. Often in battle there can be no doubt that if a man will throw away his arms, and fall on his knees before his pursuers, he may escape death; and in other dangers there are other ways of escaping death, if a man is willing to say and do anything. The difficulty, my friends, is not to avoid death, but to avoid unrighteousness; for that runs faster than death. I am old and move slowly, and the slower runner has overtaken me, and my accusers are keen and quick, and the faster runner, who is unrighteousness, has overtaken them. And now I depart hence condemned by you to suffer the penalty of death,—they too go their ways condemned by the truth to suffer the penalty of villainy and wrong; and I must abide by my award—let them abide by theirs. I suppose that these things may be regarded as fated,—and I think that they are well.

And now, O men who have condemned me, I would fain prophesy to you; for I am about to die, and in the hour of death men are gifted with prophetic power. And I prophesy to you who are my murderers, that immediately after my departure punishment far heavier than you have inflicted on me will surely await you. Me you have killed because you wanted to escape the accuser, and not to give an account of your lives. But that will not be as you suppose: far otherwise. For I say that there will be more accusers of you than there are now; accusers whom hitherto I have restrained: and as they are younger they will be more inconsiderate with you, and you will be more offended at them. If you think that by killing men you can prevent some one from censuring your evil lives, you are mistaken; that is not a way of escape which is either possible or honorable; the easiest and the noblest way is not to be disabling others, but to be improving yourselves. This is the prophecy which I utter before my departure to the judges who have condemned me.

Friends, who would have acquitted me, I would like also to talk with you about the thing which has come to pass, while the magistrates are busy, and before I go to the place at which I must die. Stay then a little, for we may as well talk with one another while there is time. You are my friends, and I should like to show you the meaning of this event which has happened to me. O my judges—for you I may truly call judges—I should like to tell you of a wonderful circumstance. Hitherto the divine faculty of which the internal oracle is the source has constantly been in the habit of opposing me even about trifles, if I was going to make a slip or error in any matter; and now as you see there has come upon me that which may be thought, and is generally believed to be, the last and worst evil. But the oracle made no sign of opposition, either when I was leaving my house in the morning, or when I was on my way to the court, or while I was speaking, at anything which I was going to say; and yet I have often been stopped in the middle of a speech, but now in nothing I either said or did touching the matter in hand has the oracle opposed me. What do I take to be the explanation of this silence? I will tell you. It is an intimation that what has happened to me is a good, and that those of us who think that death is an evil are in error. For the customary sign would surely have opposed me had I been going to evil and not to good.

Let us reflect in another way, and we shall see that there is great reason to hope that death is a good; for one of two things—either death is a state of nothingness and utter unconsciousness, or, as men say, there is a change and migration of the soul from this world to another. Now if you suppose that there is no consciousness, but a sleep like the sleep of him who is undisturbed even by dreams, death will be an unspeakable gain. For if a person were to select the night in which his sleep was undisturbed even by dreams, and were to compare with this the other days and nights of his life, and then were to tell us how many days and nights he had passed in the course of his life better and more pleasantly than this one, I think that any man, I will not say a private man, but even the great king will not find many such days or nights, when compared with the others. Now if death be of such a nature, I say that to die is gain; for eternity is then only a single night. But if death is the journey to another place, and there, as men say, all the dead abide, what good, O my friends and judges, can be greater than this? If indeed when the pilgrim arrives in the world below, he is delivered from the professors of justice in this world, and finds the true judges who are said to give judgment there, Minos and Rhadamanthus and Aeacus and Triptolemus,[33] and other sons of God who were righteous in their own life, that pilgrimage will be worth making. What would not a man give if he might converse with Orpheus and Musaeus and Hesiod and Homer?[34] Nay, if this be true, let me die again and again. I myself, too, shall have a wonderful interest in there meeting and conversing with Palamedes, and Ajax[35] the son of Telamon, and any other ancient hero who has suffered death through an unjust judgment; and there will be no small pleasure, as I think, in comparing my own sufferings with theirs. Above all, I shall then be able to continue my search into true and false knowledge; as in this world, so also in the next; and I shall find out who is wise, and who pretends to be wise, and is not. What would not a man give, O judges, to be able to examine the leader of the great Trojan expedition; or Odysseus or Sisyphus,[36] or numberless others, men and women too! What infinite delight would there be in conversing with them and asking them questions! In another world they do not put a man to death for asking questions: assuredly not. For besides being happier than we are, they will be immortal, if what is said is true.

Wherefore, O judges, be of good cheer about death, and know of a certainty, that no evil can happen to a good man, either in life or after death. He and his are not neglected by the gods; nor has my own approaching end happened by mere chance. But I see clearly that the time had arrived when it was better for me to die and be released from trouble; wherefore the oracle gave no sign. For which reason, also, I am not angry with my condemners, or with my accusers; they have done me no harm, although they did not mean to do me any good; and for this I may gently blame them.

---

[33] The four judges of the dead in the afterlife.   [34] Great poets, legendary and real.
[35] Two victims of unjust or dubious trials or verdicts.
[36] Both were noted for their cunning. In mentioning them here, Socrates is anticipating a meeting not merely with eminent men but with adversaries whose mental agility will put his powers to a real test.

Still I have a favor to ask of them. When my sons are grown up, I would ask you, O my friends, to punish them; and I would have you trouble them, as I have troubled you, if they seem to care about riches, or anything, more than about virtue; or if they pretend to be something when they are really nothing,—then reprove them, as I have reproved you, for not caring about that for which they ought to care, and thinking that they are something when they are really nothing. And if you do this, both I and my sons will have received justice at your hands.

The hour of departure has arrived, and we go our ways—I to die, and you to live. Which is better God only knows.[37]

---

[37] In two other dialogues, the *Crito* and the *Phaedo,* the story of Socrates' last days is concluded. In the former, his friend Crito pleads with Socrates to accept an opportunity to escape from Athens, to which Socrates replies (in his usual style of reasoned argument) that such a course would be wrong, since to defy the Athenian laws that have condemned him is the equivalent of rejecting parents who have nurtured him and whose authority he has implicitly accepted throughout his life. The *Phaedo* includes Socrates' argument for the immortality and inviolability of the soul and narrates his serene death, imposed by his drinking of the poison liquid called hemlock.

Aristotle
(384–322 B.C.)

Probably the most versatile and encyclopedic philosopher who ever lived, Aristotle inherited the Platonic tradition but pointed it in important new directions. He was born in 384 B.C. in Stagira (hence his epithet "the Stagirite"), a town in Macedonia on the far northern border of Greece. Since his father was court physician to the Macedonian king, Aristotle absorbed in his early years a good deal of information about the life sciences—a fact that permanently influenced the tendency of his thought. In 367, at the age of seventeen, he went to Athens and studied there in the Academy directed by Plato. Plato admired his pupil and had a strong influence on him; the young Aristotle seems to have believed even more strongly than Plato that the human soul suffered from the prison-house of the body, a view he later changed radically.

When Plato died (in 348 or 347), Aristotle left Athens for twelve years. At Assus, in Asia Minor, he undertook the education of the ruler and wrote part of his Politics, *arguing that the main purpose of the state was to promote the philosophic life among its best citizens. He also married the ruler's niece and had a daughter by her; after his wife's death he had a son, Nicomachus, by another woman. (It is this son who, because he was believed to have edited the work, gave his name to the* Nicomachean Ethics, *one of two treatises by Aristotle on the subject.) After spending three years at Assus, Aristotle moved to the island of Lesbos, where he resumed his investigation of the life sciences, especially marine biology. Here he*

*combined with his characteristic close observation of objective data an equally char-
acteristic conviction that the various creatures are designed to have distinctive
purposes.*

*Around 342 he returned to his homeland, Macedonia, where the great king
Philip now reigned. There he was entrusted with the education of Philip's teen-aged
son, Alexander. Aristotle's intention was to instill in the prince a combination of the
martial and philosophic virtues. When Philip was murdered in 336, Alexander
succeeded him, going on to complete the conquest of Greece that his father had begun
and thereafter subjugating the Greeks' inveterate Persian enemies and other empires
in a vast region stretching as far east as India. In the process, Alexander made
obsolete the traditional Greek city-state that Aristotle, anachronistically, continued
throughout his life to think of as the political norm.*

*By 335 Aristotle had returned to Athens (which was now controlled by Macedo-
nia), where he established the Lyceum, a rival institution to the Academy. At the
Lyceum, which had an unprecedented library and extensive facilities for scientific
work, Aristotle and his colleagues investigated virtually all areas of science, philosophy, and other branches of learning. In 323, at Alexander's death, the Athenians
rebelled against Macedonian domination, with which Aristotle (accurately or not)
was associated in the public mind. A charge of impiety was brought against him. His
life endangered, Aristotle left Athens, apparently in order to prevent the Athenians
from repeating the crime they had committed in executing Plato's mentor, Socrates.
One year later, in 322, Aristotle died in Chalcis, a town north of Athens.*

*Most people today find Plato's dialogues more readable than the works of Aris-
totle, but this difference is misleading. A great deal of Aristotle's writings, especially
his earlier ones, has been lost, including many works in a popular vein: letters,
poems, and dialogues that in form and content resembled Plato's. Except for fragments, the works of Aristotle known today were not intended by him for written
publication; they are, rather, notes for his teaching at the Lyceum. Moreover, ancient
editors transformed his work by grouping together under a single title different treatises on the same subject that he wrote at different times. Partly because of such
editing, and partly because Aristotle felt obliged to record positions different from his
own, he sometimes appears inconsistent or redundant. Ancient testimony indicates
that Aristotle's mind, personality, and literary style were warmer than is evident in
the matter-of-fact writings that have come down to us.*

*Aristotle at least touched on virtually all the fields of human knowledge, treating
many of them in depth: natural sciences including zoology, embryology, physics,
meteorology, astronomy, even chemistry in a rudimentary way; mathematics (most of
his work on this subject has been lost); psychology; politics and ethics (which for him
were closely related to each other); the language arts including rhetoric and poetics.
In many of these disciplines he pioneered and made striking discoveries. Nor was he
content to investigate the subjects in isolation; he tried to bring them together, partly
by applying consistent principles of systematic method, partly by subsuming them
under the axioms of "first philosophy" developed in his* Metaphysics. *This reli-
gious-philosophic work is logically prior to the more particular studies, because it
treats of the nature of being in itself and delineates the broad principles that govern
and differentiate more specific fields of investigation. But both metaphysics and its
subsidiary studies depend on a methodology of thinking in general. That methodology, largely developed by Aristotle, is outlined in his* Organon, *a group of tracts
dealing with logic and the precise use of language in discourse.*

The Organon *is probably the most permanently valuable of all Aristotle's works;*

it remains an indispensable sourcebook on how to think straight, both deductively and inductively. The works on natural science have inevitably been superseded by those of researchers who have been able to use modern instruments and modern mathematics, though some of Aristotle's ideas (on the classification of animals, for example) remain roughly valid. His shrewd observations on political science in the Politics *are still meaningful and provocative, though they are limited somewhat by Aristotle's preoccupation with the peculiar circumstances of the Greek city-state. Much of what he wrote about the humanities, especially ethics and literary theory, is as valuable today as ever; for example, a group of Aristotelian literary critics has been prominent in the twentieth century, and the doctrine of the "tragic flaw" enunciated in the* Poetics *has wide general currency.*

Even where Aristotle's ideas have been superseded, they often remain valuable because they constitute so large a part of our intellectual and cultural history. During the Middle Ages and until after the Renaissance, university education was thoroughly grounded in Aristotle, and indeed one of the most fascinating episodes in the emergence of modern science is its efforts, especially in the seventeenth century, to throw off the weight of what had become Aristotelian dogma. (That this struggle had to occur is ironic, since Aristotle himself believed firmly in the inductive method; he taught emphatically that mere theory must yield to observed facts.) Philosophers and theologians like Thomas Aquinas, and poets like Dante, are impossible to understand adequately without an awareness of Aristotle's contributions to their thought. The doctrine of the unmoved first mover of the universe; the idea of a continuous chain of being running up a scale from inanimate matter to God; the tripartite classification of souls into nutritive (animals, plants, man), sensitive (animals, man), and rational (man, God); the distinction between substance (what a thing really is) *and accident (nonessential properties); the condemnation of taking interest for money (which in works like Dante's* Inferno *is considered usury); the ethical doctrine of the golden mean between two extremes—these ideas, originated or definitively expressed by Aristotle, are fundamental to Western history, literature, and thought. Perhaps the most frequently recurring intellectual model in his works, and one of the most influential, is his fourfold treatment of causes: the material cause (what a thing is made of); the formal cause (its shape or governing principle); the efficient cause (the process by which it was made); and the final cause (its purpose). His concern with final causes pervades Aristotle's analysis of everything from the parts of animals, to man, to the cosmos as a whole.*

Plato and Aristotle are sometimes treated as polar opposites—Plato being an idealist and Aristotle a materialist. That is a serious mistake: both were staunchly opposed to any view of man or the universe as strictly material in their natures, and both considered the philosophic life the highest of human vocations. (Part of the apparent difference between them arises from the literary vehicles in which their work has survived.) There remains a significant distinction between them, however, in what they say and how they reach their conclusions. Though both are rationalist logicians, Aristotle depends more than Plato on data derived from the visible world; in short, his thought is more empirical. His political and ethical thought is more pragmatic, having less of the visionary emphasis than does Plato's. The two also differ in their views of the relationship between spirit and matter; Plato regards the soul as the true human identity, yoked with an essentially unreal, alien body, while Aristotle teaches that in man soul (or form) and body are intimately united and interdependent.

FURTHER READING *(prepared by F.S.N.):* Two excellent general introductions to Aristotle for undergraduates are Jonathan Barnes, *Aristotle*, 1983, and J. L. Ackrill, *Aristotle the Philosopher*, 1981; also valuable is Marjorie Grene, *Portrait of Aristotle*, 1963. Valuable material on the life, thought, and writings of Aristotle may be found in W. D. Ross, *Aristotle*, 1924, 5th ed. repr. 1960; D. J. Allan, *The Philosophy of Aristotle*, 1952; and J. H. Randall, Jr., *Aristotle*, 1960. Werner W. Jaeger, *Aristotle: Fundamentals of the History of His Development*, 1923, trans. Richard Robinson, 1934, 2nd ed. 1948, treats the works in chronological sequence, in order to show Aristotle's intellectual development. On Aristotle's main ethical doctrines, see W. F. R. Hardie, *Aristotle's Ethical Theory*, 1968. Humphry House, *Aristotle's Poetics*, 1956, repr. 1967; and John Jones, *On Aristotle and Greek Tragedy*, 1962, survey what Aristotle has to say about the three great tragedians, and about plot, character, action, catharsis, and imitation.

from *POETICS*

Translation by Samuel Henry Butcher
as revised by Louise Ropes Loomis
Footnotes by Louise Ropes Loomis

I

I propose to treat of Poetry in itself and of its various kinds, noting the essential quality of each; to inquire into the structure of the plot required for a good poem; into the number and nature of the parts of which a poem is composed; and similarly into whatever else falls within the same inquiry. Following, then, the order of nature, let us begin with the principles which come first.

Epic poetry and tragedy, comedy also and dithyrambic[1] poetry, and the music of the flute and of the lyre in most of their forms, are all in their general conception modes of imitation. They differ, however, from one another in three respects—their mediums, their objects, their manner or mode of imitation being in each case distinct.

For as there are persons who, by conscious art or mere habit, imitate and represent various objects through the medium of color and form, or, again, by the voice; so in the group of arts above mentioned, taken as a whole, the imitation is produced by rhythm, language, or harmony, either singly or combined.

Thus in the music of the flute and of the lyre, harmony and rhythm alone are employed; also in other arts, such as that of the shepherd's pipe, which are essentially similar to these. In dancing, rhythm alone is used without harmony; for even dancing imitates character, emotion, and action, by rhythmical movement. . . .

There are, again, some arts which employ all the means above mentioned—namely, rhythm, tune, and meter. Such are dithyrambic and

[1] For dithyrambic poetry the ordinary English reader may understand what we call lyric poetry. More strictly defined the dithyramb was a hymn or ode in rapturous style, such as were sung at the festivals of the god Dionysus.

nomic[2] poetry, and also tragedy and comedy; but between them the difference is that in the first two cases these means are all employed in combination, in the latter, now one means is employed, now another.

Such, then, are the differences of the arts with respect to the medium of imitation.

II

Since the objects of imitation are men in action, and these men must be either of a high or a low type (for moral character mainly answers to this division, goodness and badness being the distinguishing marks of moral differences), it follows that we must represent men either as better than in real life, or as worse, or as they are. It is the same in painting. Polygnotus depicted men as nobler than they are, Pauson as less noble, Dionysius drew them true to life.[3]

Now it is evident that each of the arts of imitation above mentioned will exhibit these differences, and itself become a distinct kind in imitating objects that are thus distinct. Such diversities may be found even in dancing, flute playing, and lyre playing. So again in language, whether prose or verse, unaccompanied by music. Homer, for example, makes men better than they are; Cleophon as they are; Hegemon of Thasos, the inventor of parodies, worse than they are.[4] The same distinction marks off tragedy from comedy; for comedy aims at representing men as worse, tragedy as better than in actual life.

III

There is still a third difference—the manner in which each of these objects may be imitated. For the medium being the same, the objects the same, the poet may imitate by narration—in which case he can either take another personality as Homer does, or speak in his own person, unchanged—or he may present all his characters as living and moving before us.

These, then, as we said at the beginning, are the three differences which distinguish artistic imitation—the medium, the objects, and the manner. So that from one point of view, Sophocles[5] is an imitator of the same kind as Homer—for both imitate higher types of character; from another point of view, he is of the same kind as Aristophanes[6]—for both imitate persons acting and doing. Hence, some say, the name of "drama" is given to such plays, as representing action. . . .

---

[2] Nomic poetry is instructive poetry, maxims or wise sayings in the form of verse.

[3] Unfortunately no work by any of these famous Greek painters has come down to us.

[4] The writings of Cleophon and Hegemon are also lost.

[5] Sophocles was one of the great trio of fifth-century Athenian tragedians, the other two being Aeschylus and Euripides. Seven of Sophocles' tragedies have been preserved.

[6] The famous satirical comedy writer of the end of the fifth century B.C.

IV

Poetry in general seems to have sprung from two sources, each of them lying deep in our nature. First, the instinct of imitation is implanted in man from childhood, one difference between him and other animals being that he is the most imitative of living creatures, and through imitation learns his earliest lessons. And no less universal is the pleasure he takes in seeing things imitated. We have evidence of this in the facts of experience. Objects which in themselves we view with pain, we delight to contemplate when reproduced with minute fidelity: such as the forms of the most ignoble animals and of dead bodies. The cause of this, again, is that to learn gives the liveliest pleasure, not only to philosophers but to men in general, although their capacity of learning is more limited. Thus the reason why men enjoy seeing a likeness is that in contemplating it they find themselves learning or inferring, and saying perhaps, "Ah, that is he." If they happen not to have seen the original, their pleasure will be due not to the imitation as such, but to the execution, the coloring, or some such other cause.

Imitation, then, is one instinct of our nature. Next there is the instinct for harmony and rhythm, meters being manifestly sections of rhythm. Persons, therefore, starting with this natural gift developed by degrees their special aptitudes, until their rude improvisations gave birth to poetry.

Poetry now diverged in two directions, according to the individual character of the writers. The graver spirits imitated noble actions and the actions of good men. The more trivial sort imitated the actions of meaner persons, at first composing satires, as the former did hymns to the gods and praises of famous men. A poem of the satirical kind cannot indeed be put down to any author earlier than Homer; though there were probably many such writers. But from Homer onward, instances can be cited—his own *Margites*,[7] for example, and other similar compositions. The appropriate meter was also here introduced; hence the measure is still called the iambic[8] or lampooning measure, being that in which people lampooned one another. Thus the older poets were distinguished as writers either of heroic or of lampooning verse.

As in the serious style Homer is pre-eminent among poets, for he alone combined dramatic form with excellence of imitation, so he too first laid down the main lines of comedy, by dramatizing the ludicrous instead of writing personal satire. His *Margites* bears the same relation to comedy that the *Iliad* and *Odyssey* do to tragedy. And when tragedy and comedy appeared, the two classes of poets still followed their natural bent: the lampooners became writers of comedy, and the epic poets were succeeded by tragedians, since the drama was a larger and higher form of art. . . .

---

[7] The mock battle epic that went by the name of *Margites* has long been lost. Whether it was really the work of the author of the *Iliad*, as Aristotle thought, we cannot judge.

[8] The pattern of the iambic meter was a line composed of a series of pairs of syllables, a short syllable, followed by a long one. We in English still use its equivalent, an unaccented syllable followed by an accented, both in comic verse, such as

"O oysters, come and walk with us,
The walrus did beseech,"

and also in grand and serious poetry, such as *Paradise Lost*.

Tragedy advanced by slow degrees; each new element that showed itself was in turn developed. Having passed through many changes, it found its natural form, and there it stopped.

Aeschylus first introduced a second actor;[9] he diminished the importance of the chorus, and assigned the leading part to the dialogue. Sophocles raised the number of actors to three, and added scene painting. It was not till late that the short plot was discarded for one of greater compass, and the grotesque diction of the earlier satiric form for the stately manner of tragedy.

V

Comedy is, as we have said, an imitation of characters of a lower type—not, however, in the full sense of the word bad, the ludicrous being merely a subdivision of the ugly. It consists of some defect or ugliness which is not painful or destructive. To take an obvious example, the comic mask is ugly and distorted, but does not imply pain.

The successive changes through which tragedy passed, and the authors of these changes, are well known, whereas comedy has had no history, because it was not at first treated seriously. . . .

Epic poetry agrees with tragedy in so far as it is an imitation in verse of characters of a higher type. They differ in that epic poetry admits but one kind of meter[10] and is narrative in form. They differ, again, in their length: for tragedy endeavors, as far as possible, to confine itself to a single circuit of the sun, or but slightly to exceed this limit; whereas the epic action has no limits of time. This, then, is a second point of difference; though at first the same freedom was admitted in tragedy as in epic poetry. . . .

VI

Tragedy, then, is an imitation of an action that is serious, complete, and of a certain magnitude; in language embellished with every kind of artistic ornament, the several kinds being found in separate parts of the play; in the form of dramatic action, not of narrative; through pity and fear effecting the proper purification of these emotions.[11] By "language embellished," I mean language into which rhythm, harmony, and song enter. By

[9] Before Aeschylus' time the embryonic Greek tragedy consisted of speeches by a single actor or narrator telling the chorus what had happened and a series of songs, dances, and responses by the chorus, expressing their wonder, joy, or grief at the news.

[10] To a Greek the only meter admissible in an epic poem was the meter of the *Iliad* and the *Odyssey*, or what was called hexameter verse. Virgil used the same meter for the *Aeneid*. In English a well known example of hexameter verse is Longfellow's *Evangeline:*
    "This is the forest primeval: the murmuring pines and the hemlocks"—

[11] Note that an unhappy or what we call a tragic ending was not one of the Greek requirements for a tragedy, though Aristotle thought it the perfect ending. See XIII. Many tragedies ended with a solemn reconciliation after a conflict or quiet after pain, to please the audience, Aristotle says.

"the several kinds in separate parts," I mean that some parts are rendered through the medium of verse alone, others again with the aid of song.

Now as tragic imitation implies persons acting, it necessarily follows, in the first place, that spectacular equipment will be a part of tragedy. Next, song and diction, for these are the medium of imitation. By diction, I mean the metrical arrangement of the words: as for song, it is a term whose sense everyone understands.

Again, tragedy is the imitation of an action, and an action implies personal actors, who necessarily possess certain distinctive qualities of character and thought; for it is by these that we form our estimate of their actions and these two—thought and character—are the natural causes from which their actions spring, and on their actions all success or failure depends. Now, the imitation of the action is the plot; by plot I here mean the arrangement of the incidents. By character I mean that because of which we ascribe certain qualities to the actors. Thought is needed whenever they speak to prove a statement or declare a general truth. Every tragedy, therefore, must have six parts, which parts determine its quality—namely, plot, character, diction, thought, spectacle, song. . . .

But most important of all is the structure of the incidents. For tragedy is an imitation, not of men, but of action and life, of happiness and misery. And life consists of action, and its end is a mode of activity,[12] not a quality. Now character determines men's qualities, but it is their actions that make them happy or wretched. The purpose of action in the tragedy, therefore, is not the representation of character: character comes in as contributing to the action. Hence the incidents and the plot are the end of the tragedy; and the end is the chief thing of all. So without action there cannot be a tragedy; there may be one without character. . . .

Again, you may string together a set of speeches expressive of character, and well finished in point of diction and thought, and not produce the essential tragic effect nearly so well as with a play which, however deficient in these respects, yet has a plot and artistically constructed incidents. Besides which, the most powerful elements of emotional interest in tragedy—reversal of the situation and recognition scenes[13]—are parts of the plot. A further proof is that novices in the art attain to finish of diction and precision of portraiture before they can construct the plot. It is the same with almost all the early poets.

The plot, then, is the first principle, and, as it were, the soul of a tragedy: character holds the second place. A similar statement is true of painting. The most beautiful colors, laid on confusedly, will not give as much pleasure as a simple chalk outline of a portrait. Thus tragedy is the imitation of an action, and of actors mainly with a view to the action. . . .

The spectacle is, indeed, an attraction in itself, but of all the parts it is the least artistic, and connected least with the art of poetry. For the power of tragedy is felt even apart from representation and actors. Besides, the production of scenic effects is more a matter for the property man than for the poet.

---

[12] See the *Ethics*, Book I, Chapter 6.
[13] These two admired features of many old dramatic plots Aristotle explains further on.

VII

These principles being established, let us now discuss the proper structure
of the plot, since this is the first and most important thing in tragedy.

Now, according to our definition, tragedy is an imitation of an action
that is complete and whole and of a certain magnitude; for there may be a
whole that is wanting in magnitude. A whole is that which has a beginning,
a middle, and an end. A beginning is that which does not have to follow
anything else, but after which something else naturally takes place. An end,
on the contrary, is that which itself naturally follows something else, either
by necessity or as a general rule, but has nothing coming after it. A middle
is that which follows something else as some other thing follows it. A well-
constructed plot must neither begin nor end at haphazard, but conform to
these principles.

Again, a beautiful object, whether it be a living organism or any whole
composed of parts, must not only have an orderly arrangement of parts,
but must also be of a certain magnitude; for beauty depends on magnitude
and order. Hence a very tiny creature cannot be beautiful; for the view of it
is confused, the object being seen in an almost imperceptible moment of
time. Nor, again, can one of vast size be beautiful; for as the eye cannot take
it all in at once, the unity and sense of the whole is lost for the spectator; as
it would be if there were a creature a thousand miles long. As, therefore, in
the case of living bodies and organisms, a certain magnitude is necessary,
and a magnitude which may be easily embraced in one view; so in the plot,
a certain length is necessary, and a length which can be easily embraced by
the memory. . . . And to state the matter roughly, we may say that the
proper length is such as to allow for a sequence of necessary or probable
events that will bring about a change from calamity to good fortune, or
from good fortune to calamity.

VIII

Unity of plot does not, as some persons think, consist of having a single
man as the hero. For infinitely various are the incidents in one man's life
which cannot be reduced to unity; and so, too, there are many actions of
one man out of which we cannot make one action. Hence the error, as it
appears, of all poets who have composed a Heracleid, a Theseid,[14] or other
poems of the kind. They imagine that as Heracles was one man, the story of
Heracles must also be a unity. But Homer, as in all else he is of surpassing
merit, here too—whether from art or natural genius—seems to have happily discerned the truth. In composing the *Odyssey* he did not include all the
adventures of Odysseus—such as his wound on Parnassus, or his feigned
madness at the mustering of the host[15]—incidents between which there
was no necessary or probable connection: but he made the *Odyssey* and
likewise the *Iliad* center around an action that in our sense of the word is
one. As therefore, in the other imitative arts, the imitation is one when the
object imitated is one, so the plot, being an imitation of an action, must

---

[14] That is, a long-drawn narrative of all the exploits of a Heracles or a Theseus.
[15] Incidents said to have occurred before the opening of the *Iliad*.

imitate one action and that a whole, the structural union of the parts being such that, if any one of them is displaced or removed, the whole will be disjointed and disturbed. For a thing whose presence or absence makes no visible difference is not an organic part of the whole.

IX

It is, moreover, evident from what has been said that it is not the function of the poet to relate what has happened but what may happen—what is possible according to the law of probability or necessity. The poet and the historian differ not by writing in verse or in prose. The work of Herodotus[16] might be put into verse, and it would still be a species of history, with meter no less than without it. The true difference is that one relates what has happened, the other what may happen. Poetry, therefore, is a more philosophical and a higher thing than history: for poetry tends to express the universal, history the particular. . . .

But even if a poet chances to take an historical subject, he is nonetheless a poet; for there is no reason why some events that have actually happened should not conform to the law of the probable and the possible, and in virtue of that aspect of them he is their poet or maker.

Of all plots and actions the episodic are the worst. I call a plot "episodic" in which the episodes or acts succeed one another without probable or necessary sequence. Bad poets compose such pieces by their own fault, good poets, to please the players; for, as they write show pieces for competition, they stretch the plot beyond its capacity, and are often forced to break the natural continuity.

But again, tragedy is an imitation not only of a complete action, but of events inspiring fear or pity. Such an effect is best produced when the events come on us by surprise and when, at the same time, they follow as cause and effect. The wonder will then be greater than if they happened of themselves or merely by accident; for coincidences too are most marvelous when they have a look of design. We may instance the statue of Mitys at Argos, which fell upon his murderer while he was watching a festival, and killed him. Such events seem the result of more than chance. Plots, therefore, constructed on these principles are necessarily the best.

X

Plots are either simple or complex, for the actions in real life, of which they are an imitation, are obviously either one or the other. An action which is one and continuous in the sense above defined, I call simple, when the change in the hero's fortune takes place without reversal of the situation and without recognition.

A complex action is one in which the change is accompanied by such a reversal, or by recognition, or by both. These all should arise from the internal structure of the plot, so that what follows should be the necessary

---

[16] The first of the great Greek historians, who wrote the story of the world, as he knew it, down through the Persian wars.

or probable result of what went before. It makes a great difference whether the event is caused by or simply happens after the previous action.

XI

Reversal of the situation is a change by which conditions in the play are transformed into their opposite, keeping always to our rule of probability or necessity. Thus in the Oedipus,[17] the messenger comes to cheer Oedipus and free him from his alarms about his mother, but by revealing who Oedipus really is produces the opposite effect. . . .

Recognition, as the name indicates, is a change from ignorance to knowledge, producing love or hate between the persons destined by the poet for good or bad fortune. The best form of recognition is coincident with a reversal of the situation, as in the Oedipus.[18]

Even inanimate things of the most trivial kind may in a sense be objects of recognition. Again, we may recognize or discover whether a person has done a thing or not. But the recognition which is most intimately connected with the plot and action is, as we have said, the recognition of persons. This recognition, combined with a reversal, will produce either pity or fear; and actions producing these effects are those which, by our definition, tragedy represents. Moreover, it is upon such situations that the issue of good or bad fortune will depend. Recognition, then, being between persons, it may happen that one person only is recognized by the other—when the latter is already known—or it may be necessary that the recognition should be on both sides. Thus Iphigenia is revealed to Orestes by the sending of the letter; but another act of recognition is required to make Orestes known to Iphigenia.[19]

---

[17] The *Oedipus Tyrannus [Oedipus the King]* of Sophocles is a tragedy which Aristotle much admired and which happily has come down to us. At its opening, Oedipus is the prosperous king of Thebes, with a wife, Jocasta, whom he dearly loves. In the course of the play he discovers that . . . he is the child of Jocasta and her former husband, the late King of Thebes, exposed to die in infancy because of an ominous prophecy and rescued by [a shepherd]. He learns also that an arrogant old man he killed in a roadside quarrel was the late king, his father. He is therefore the unwitting murderer of his own father and for years has lived in incest with his own mother. At the news, Jocasta hangs herself and Oedipus puts out his eyes and goes blinded and accursed into banishment.

[18] Shakespeare frequently uses these classical dramatic devices of reversal of situation and recognition. The tragedy of *King Lear* is an outstanding illustration of the first. The themes of disguise, mistaken identity, and revelation or recognition occur again and again; notably in *As You Like It, Twelfth Night, Winter's Tale* and *The Tempest*.

[19] The reference here is to Euripides' play of *Iphigenia in Tauris*. Aristotle summarizes briefly the story of Iphigenia in XVII. As the young daughter of King Agamemnon, she was brought from her home to the port of Aulis to be sacrificed, that her father and his fleet might have a favorable wind to sail to Troy. She was snatched from the altar by the goddess Artemis and disappeared. Years later she is a priestess serving in the savage country of Tauris. Her brother Orestes, whom she left at home, a little child, is now a maddened wanderer, seeking absolution for his crime of killing his mother, Clytemnestra, in revenge for her murder of his father, Agamemnon. When Iphigenia finds Orestes on the shore at Tauris, neither, of course, knows the other. In fact, he has no idea that his long lost sister is alive. Through a letter which she gives him he learns who she is, but meanwhile by a law of the country he is condemned to die as a sacrilegious intruder. Through some words of his at the last moment she discovers that he is Orestes and saves him.

Two parts, then, of the plot—reversal of the situation and recognition—turn upon surprises. A third part is the scene of suffering. The scene of suffering is a destructive or painful action, such as a death on the stage, bodily agony, wounds, and the like. . . .

XIII

As a sequel to what has already been said, we must proceed to consider what the poet should aim at, and what he should avoid in constructing his plots; and by what means the specific effect of tragedy will be produced.

A perfect tragedy should, as we have seen, be arranged not on the simple but on the complex plan. It should, moreover, imitate actions which excite pity and fear, this being the distinctive mark of tragic imitation. It follows plainly, in the first place, that the change of fortune presented must not be the spectacle of a virtuous man brought from prosperity to adversity: for this moves neither pity nor fear: it merely shocks us. Nor, again, that of a bad man passing from adversity to prosperity: for nothing can be more alien to the spirit of tragedy; it possesses no single tragic quality; it neither satisfies the moral sense nor calls forth pity or fear. Nor, again, should the downfall of an utter villain be exhibited. A plot of this kind would, doubtless, satisfy the moral sense, but it would inspire neither pity nor fear;[20] for pity is aroused by unmerited misfortune, fear by the misfortune of a man like ourselves. Such an event, therefore, will be neither pitiful nor terrible.

There remains, then, the character between these two extremes—that of a man extraordinarily good and just, who yet brings misfortune on himself not by vice or depravity, but by some error or frailty.[21] He must be one who is highly renowned and prosperous, a personage like Oedipus, Thyestes, or other illustrious men of great families.

The best constructed plot should, therefore, be single in its issue, rather than double, as some maintain. The change of fortune should be not from bad to good, but, reversely, from good to bad. It should come about as the result not of vice, but of some great error or frailty, in a character either such as we have described, or better rather than worse. . . . A tragedy, to be perfect according to the rules of art, should be of this construction. Hence they are in error who censure Euripides just because he follows this principle in his plays, many of which end unhappily. It is, as we have said, the right ending. The best proof is that on the stage and in dramatic competition, such plays, if well worked out, are the most tragic in effect; and Euripides, faulty though he may be in the general management of his subject, yet is felt to be the most tragic of the poets.

In the second rank comes the kind of tragedy which some place first. Like the Odyssey, it has a double thread of plot, and also an opposite ending for the good and for the bad actors. It is accounted the best only

---

[20] Shakespeare's tragedy of *Richard III* is sometimes cited in disproof of this statement. Richard is an "utter villain" but we take a keen interest in his bold struggle to master fate.

[21] Two notably brave and generous tragic heroes, whose downfall is due to one shortcoming in character or judgment, are, of course, Lear and Othello. Some readers would include Hamlet.

because of the weakness of the spectators; for the poet is guided in what he writes by the wishes of his audience. The pleasure, however, thence derived is not the true tragic pleasure. It is proper rather to comedy, where those who, in the piece, are the deadliest enemies—like Orestes and Aegisthus[22]—quit the stage as friends at the close, and no one slays or is slain.

XIV

Fear and pity may be aroused by spectacular means; but they may also result from the inner structure of the piece, which is the better way, and indicates a superior poet. For the plot ought to be so constructed that, even without the aid of the eye, he who hears the tale told will thrill with horror and melt to pity at what takes place. This is the impression we should receive from hearing the story of Oedipus. But to produce this effect by the mere spectacle is a less artistic method, and dependent on extraneous aids. Those who employ spectacular means to create a sense not of the terrible but of the merely monstrous are strangers to the purpose of tragedy; for we must not demand of tragedy any and every kind of pleasure, but only that which is proper to it. And since the pleasure the tragic poet should offer is that which comes from pity and fear through imitation, it is evident that this quality must be impressed on the incidents.

Let us then determine what circumstances strike us as terrible or pitiful.

Actions of this sort must happen between persons who are either friends or enemies or indifferent to one another. If an enemy kills an enemy, there is nothing to excite pity either in the act or the intention—except in so far as the suffering itself is pitiful. So too with indifferent persons. But when the tragic incident occurs between those who are near or dear to one another—if, for example, a brother kills, or intends to kill, a brother, a son his father, a mother her son, a son his mother, or any other deed of the kind is done—these are situations to be looked for by the poet. He may not indeed destroy the framework of the received legends—the fact, for instance, that Clytemnestra was slain by Orestes . . . but he ought to show invention of his own, and skillfully handle the traditional material. . . .

Enough has now been said concerning the structure of the incidents and the right kind of plot.

XV

With regard to the characters there are four things to be aimed at. First, and most important, they must be good. Now any speech or action that manifests some kind of moral purpose will be expressive of character: the

---

[22] In the tragic story of Agamemnon and his son Orestes, Aegisthus is the paramour of Agamemnon's wife, Clytemnestra, who influences her to murder her husband on his return from Troy. Orestes, her son, kills Aegisthus as well as his mother when he finally avenges his father. (See Aeschylus' *Oresteia*—Editors' note.)

character will be good if the purpose is good. The goodness is possible in every class of persons. Even a woman may be good, and also a slave, though the one is liable to be an inferior being, and the other quite worthless. The second thing to aim at is appropriateness. There is a type of manly valor, but manliness in a woman, or unscrupulous cleverness, is inappropriate. Thirdly, a character must be true to life: which is something different from goodness and appropriateness, as here described. The fourth point is consistency: for even though the person being imitated, who suggested the type, is inconsistent, still he must be consistently inconsistent.

As in the structure of the plot, so too in the portraiture of character, the poet should always aim at either the necessary or the probable. Thus a person of a given character should speak or act as it is necessary or probable that he would; just as this event should follow that as a necessary or probable consequence. It is therefore evident that the unraveling of the plot, no less than the complication, must arise out of the plot itself; it must not be brought about by supernatural interference—as in the *Medea*.[23] The supernatural should be employed only for events outside the drama—for past or future events, beyond the range of human knowledge, which need to be reported or foretold; for to the gods we ascribe the power of seeing all things. Within the action there must be nothing improbable. If the improbable cannot be excluded, it should be outside the field of the tragedy, as is the improbable element in the *Oedipus* of Sophocles.

Again, since tragedy is an imitation of persons above the common level, the example of good portrait painters should be followed. They, while reproducing the distinctive features of the original, make a likeness true to life and yet more beautiful. So too the poet, in representing men hot tempered or indolent or with other defects of character, should preserve the type and yet ennoble it. In this way Agathon and Homer have portrayed Achilles.[24]

These, then, are rules the poet should observe. Nor should he neglect those appeals to the eye, which, though not among the essentials, are the concomitants of poetry; for here too there is much room for error. But of this enough has been said in our published treatise. . . .[25]

XVII

In constructing the plot and working it out with the proper diction, the poet should put the scene, as far as possible, before his eyes. In this way, seeing everything with the utmost vividness, as if he were an actual eyewit-

---

[23] In Euripides' play of *Medea*, the heroine, who out of indignation at her wrongs has killed her two children and brought about the death of her husband's new bride, escapes from his fury into the sky in a magic chariot.

[24] We have nothing left of any work by Agathon. We know only that he was a playwright who promised to rival Euripides but who left Athens for some reason at the age of forty and died disappointed in a foreign land. At the banquet celebrated in Plato's dialogue of the *Symposium* he was the happy and admired host. For Homer's noble treatment of Achilles, see especially the *Iliad*, Books IX, XIX, XXIV.

[25] Aristotle wrote a dialogue *On Poets,* now lost.

ness, he will discover what is in keeping with it, and be most unlikely to overlook inconsistencies. . . .

Again, the poet should act out his own play to the best of his power, with the gestures that go with it; for those with a sympathetic nature, who themselves feel the emotion, are most convincing; and one who is grieved himself despairs, one who is angry rages with the most lifelike reality. Hence poetry implies either a special gift of nature or a strain of madness. In the one case a man can take the mold of any character; in the other, he is lifted out of his proper self.

As for the story, whether the poet takes it ready-made or constructs it for himself, he should first sketch its general outline and then fill in the episodes and amplify in detail. The general plan may be illustrated by the *Iphigenia*.[26] A young girl is sacrificed; she disappears mysteriously from the eyes of those who sacrificed her; she is transported to another country, where the custom is to offer up all strangers to the goddess. To this ministry she is appointed. Some time later her own brother chances to arrive. The fact that the oracle for some reason ordered him to go there is outside the general plan of the play. The purpose, again, of his coming is outside the action proper. However, he comes, he is seized, and, when on the point of being sacrificed, reveals who he is. The mode of recognition may be either that of Euripides or of Polyidus,[27] in whose play he exclaims very naturally: "So it was not my sister only, but I too who was doomed to be sacrificed"; and by that remark he is saved.

After this, the names being once given, it remains to fill in the episodes. We must see, however, that they are relevant to the action. In the case of Orestes, for example, there is the madness which led to his capture and his deliverance by means of the purificatory rite. In a play the episodes are short, but in epic poetry they lengthen out the tale. Thus the story of the *Odyssey* can be stated briefly. A certain man is absent from home for many years; he is jealously watched by Poseidon, and quite alone. Meanwhile his home is in a wretched plight—suitors are wasting his substance and plotting against his son. At length, tempest-tossed, he arrives and makes himself known; he attacks the suitors with his own hand, and is himself preserved while he destroys them. This is the essence of the plot; the rest is episode.

XVIII

Every tragedy falls into two parts—complication and unraveling or *dénouement*. Incidents before the play opens and often others within the play itself form the complication; the rest is the unraveling. By the complication I mean all that extends from the beginning of the action to the part which marks the turning point to good or bad fortune. The unraveling is that which extends from the beginning of the change to the end. . . .

Again, the poet should remember what has been often said, and not make an epic structure into a tragedy. By an epic structure I mean one with a multiplicity of plots—as if, for instance, you were to make a tragedy out

[26] On the story of Iphigenia see XI, note.   [27] We have no plays of Polyidus.

of the entire story of the *Iliad*. In the epic poem, owing to its length, each part can assume its proper magnitude. In the drama the result is far from answering to the poet's expectation. The proof is that the poets who have dramatized the whole story of the fall of Troy, instead of selecting portions, like Euripides; or who have taken the whole tale of Niobe, and not a part of her story, like Aeschylus, either fail utterly or meet with poor success on the stage. . . .

XXIII

As for that poetry which is narrative in form and imitates in meter, the plot manifestly ought, as in a tragedy, to be constructed on dramatic principles. It should have for its subject a single action, whole and complete, with a beginning, a middle, and an end. It will thus resemble a living organism in all its unity, and produce the pleasure proper to it. It will differ in structure from historical compositions, which of necessity present not a single action, but a single period, and all that happened within that period to one person or to many, however little connected together the events may be. For as the sea fight at Salamis and the battle with the Carthaginians in Sicily took place at the same time but did not tend to any one result, so in the ordinary course of events one thing sometimes follows another, and yet no single end is thereby produced. Such is the way, we may say, most poets write.

Here again, then, as has been already observed, the transcendent excellence of Homer is manifest. He never attempts to make the whole war of Troy the subject of his poem, though that war had a beginning and an end. It would have been too vast a theme, and not easily embraced in a single view. If not that, it would have been overcomplicated by the variety of the incidents in it. As it is, he detaches a single portion, though he admits as episodes many events from the general story of the war—such as the Catalogue of Ships[28] and others—thus diversifying the poem. . . . For this reason the *Iliad* and the *Odyssey* each furnish the subject of but one tragedy, or, at most, of two. . . .

XXIV

Again, epic poetry may have as many kinds as tragedy: it may be simple, or complex, a tale of character or of suffering. The parts also, with the exception of song and spectacle, are the same; for it requires reversals of the situation, recognitions, and scenes of suffering. Moreover, the thought and the diction must be artistic. In all these respects, Homer is our earliest and sufficient model. Indeed each of his poems has a twofold character. The *Iliad* is at once simple and a tale of suffering, and the *Odyssey* complex (for recognition scenes run through it), and at the same time a tale of character. Moreover, in diction and thought they are supreme.

---

[28] In the second half of Book II of the *Iliad*, Homer interrupts the course of his story to insert a catalogue of the ships that came to Troy and their leaders.

Epic poetry differs from tragedy in the scale on which it is constructed, and in its meter. As regards scale or length, we have already laid down an adequate limit: the beginning and the end must be capable of being brought within a single view. This condition will be satisfied by poems on a smaller scale than the old epics, and answering in length to the group of tragedies presented at a single sitting.[29]

Epic poetry has, however, a great—a special—capacity for enlarging its dimensions, and we can see the reason. In tragedy we cannot imitate several lines of action carried on at one and the same time; we must confine ourselves to the action on the stage and the part taken by the players. But in epic poetry, owing to the narrative form, many events simultaneously transacted can be presented; and these, if relevant to the subject, add mass and dignity to the poem. The epic has here an advantage, and one that conduces to grandeur of effect, to diverting the mind of the hearer, and relieving the story with varying episodes. For sameness of incident soon produces satiety, and makes tragedies fail on the stage. . . .

Homer, admirable in all respects, has the special merit of being the only poet who rightly appreciates the part he should take himself. The poet should speak as little as possible in his own person, for it is not this that makes him an imitator. Other poets appear themselves upon the scene throughout, and imitate but little and rarely. Homer, after a few prefatory words, at once brings in a man or woman or other personage, none of them wanting in characteristic qualities, but each with a character of his own.

The element of the wonderful is required in tragedy. But the improbable, on which the wonderful depends for its chief effects, has wider scope in epic poetry, because there the person acting is not seen. Thus, the pursuit of Hector would be ludicrous if placed upon the stage—the Greeks standing still and not joining in the pursuit, and Achilles waving them back.[30] But in the epic poem the absurdity passes unnoticed. Now the wonderful is pleasing, as may be inferred from the fact that everyone tells a story with some addition of his own, knowing that his hearers like it. . . .

But the poet should prefer probable impossibilities to improbable possibilities. The tragic plot must not be composed of improbable parts. Everything improbable should, if possible, be excluded; or, at all events, it should lie outside the action of the play itself. . . .

But once the improbable has been introduced and an air of likelihood imparted to it, we must accept it in spite of the absurdity. Take even the incidents in the *Odyssey* where Odysseus is left upon the shore of Ithaca.[31] How intolerable even these might have been would be apparent if an inferior poet were to treat the subject! As it is, the absurdity is veiled by the poetic charm with which the poet invests it.

The diction should be elaborated in the pauses of the action where there is no expression of character or thought. For, conversely, character and thought are merely obscured by a diction that is over brilliant.

---

[29] Greek dramatists of the great period used to produce their plays in groups of four, three more or less connected tragedies followed by a comic or satiric play, all seen by the audience in one sitting.

[30] Achilles' pursuit of Hector is described in the *Iliad*, Book XXII.

[31] *Odyssey*, Book XIII.

XXV

With respect to problems and their solutions, the number and nature of the sources from which they spring may be thus set forth.

The poet being an imitator, like a painter or any other artist, must of necessity imitate one of three objects: things as they were or are, things as they are said or thought to be, or things as they ought to be. This he does in language—using either current expressions or, it may be, rare words or metaphors. There are also many modifications of language, which we concede to the poets. Add to this, that the standard of correctness is not the same in poetry and in politics, any more than in poetry and in any other art. Within the art of poetry itself there are two kinds of faults—those which touch its essence, and those which are accidental. If the poet intended to describe something right, but described it incorrectly through lack of ability to express himself, his art is faulty. But if his failure was due to a wrong intention—if, for instance, he represented a horse as throwing out both his off legs at once, or introduced technical inaccuracies in medicine, or some other science—the error was not in the essentials of his art. These are the points of view from which we should consider and answer the questions raised in the problems.

First as to questions which concern the poet's own art. If he describes the impossible, he is guilty of an error; but the error may be justified, if the end of the art be thereby attained (the end being that already mentioned)—if, that is, the effect of this or any other part of the poem is thus rendered more striking. A case in point is the pursuit of Hector. If, however, the end might have been as well or better attained without violating the rules of poetic correctness, the error is not justified; for every kind of error should, if possible, be avoided.

Again, does the error touch the essentials of the poetic art or some accident of it? For example, not to know that a hind has no horns is a less serious matter than to paint it inartistically.

Further, if it be objected that a description is not true to fact, the poet may perhaps reply, "But the objects are as they ought to be"; just as Sophocles said that he drew men as they ought to be, Euripides as they are. In this way the objection may be met. If, however, the description is neither true nor of the thing as it should be, the poet may answer, "This is how men say the thing is." This dictum applies to the tales about the gods. It may well be that these stories are not loftier than the facts nor yet true to fact; they are, very possibly, what Xenophanes[32] says of them. But anyhow, "this is what is said."

XXVI

The question may be raised whether the epic or tragic form of imitation is the higher. If the more refined art is the higher, and the more refined in every case is that which appeals to the better sort of audience, the art which

[32] Xenophanes of Colophon, who lived almost two hundred years before Aristotle, seems to have been remembered largely for his attacks on and ridicule of the popular polytheism of Greece.

addresses itself to any and everyone is manifestly most unrefined. The audience then is supposed to be too dull to comprehend unless the performers throw in something of their own, who therefore indulge in perpetual movements.

So we are told that epic poetry is addressed to a cultivated audience, who do not need gestures, tragedy to an inferior public. Being then unrefined, it is evidently the lower of the two.

Now, in the first place, this censure attaches not to the poetic but to the actors' art; for gesticulation may be equally overdone in epic recitation. . . . Next, all action is not to be condemned—any more than all dancing—but only that of bad performers. . . . Again, tragedy, like epic poetry, produces its effect even without action; it reveals its power by mere reading. If, then, in all other respects it is superior, this fault, we say, is not inherent in it.

And superior it is, because it has all the epic elements—it may even use the epic meter, with music and spectacular effects as important accessories; and these produce the most lively of pleasures. Further, it creates a vivid impression when read as well as when acted. Moreover, the art in it attains its end within narrower limits; and the concentrated effect is more pleasurable than one which is spread over a long time and so diluted. What, for example, would be the effect of the *Oedipus* of Sophocles, if it were cast into a form as long as the *Iliad*? Once more, the epic imitation has less unity; as is shown by this, that any epic poem will furnish subjects for several tragedies. . . .

If, then, tragedy is superior to epic poetry in all these respects and, moreover, fulfills its specific function better as an art—for each art ought to produce, not any chance pleasure, but the pleasure proper to it, as already stated—it plainly follows that tragedy is the higher art, as attaining its end more perfectly.

Thus much may suffice concerning tragic and epic poetry in general; their several kinds and parts, with the number of each and their differences; the causes that make a poem good or bad; the objections of the critics and the answer to their objections.

Catullus
(C.84–C.54 B.C.)

Gaius Valerius Catullus, one of the world's great lyric poets and (with Horace) one of the two greatest in Latin literature, was born around 84 B.C. and died young, at about the age of thirty. His birthplace was Verona, in a northern Italian province ("Cisalpine Gaul") that was controlled by Rome in Catullus' lifetime but whose inhabitants did not acquire the rights of Roman citizenship until shortly after his death. His father was wealthy and prominent enough to entertain Julius Caesar as a guest. Although Catullus made one long journey in 57–56, to Asia Minor (where he visited the grave of his brother, as is recorded in Poem 101), most of his life was divided between his home province and Rome. He lived during the eventful last days of the Roman republic, but, although his acquaintances included leading political figures like Caesar, Pompey, and Cicero, Catullus apparently had little interest in politics as such. Although he lampooned Caesar and Pompey, for instance, he did so on personal rather than on political grounds. The social set in which he moved seems to have been smart, sophisticated, and for the most part modernist in its insouciantly easygoing morality.

The most intense of his attachments was with a woman whom in his poems Catullus calls Lesbia, in honor of the Greek poet Sappho of Lesbos, whose poetry was in some respects a model for Catullus. It seems virtually certain that Lesbia was in real life a woman named Clodia, seven to ten years older than Catullus, married but scarcely bound to a rather pompous husband. She was an aristocrat, probably, the center of a set of political adventurers, a woman of brilliance and beauty, probably a nymphomaniac, and, if the gossip of the time was accurate, the lover of her brother and the poisoner of her husband. Something is known of her from a hostile portrait in a speech by Cicero defending one of her former lovers against a charge of attempting to poison her. Her husband, Metellus Celer, was governor of Cisalpine Gaul in the year 62, and if Catullus met Clodia then (which is possible though not certain), he would have been twenty-two years old at the time the affair began. The twenty-five poems that depict it can be arranged to form a dramatic sequence (which does not necessarily reflect their order of composition), beginning in idealism and fire (see Poem 51, a close paraphrase of Sappho's "He is more than a hero") and progressing through disillusionment, reconciliation, jealousy, anger, self-pity, and brooding resolution to shake off his passion, to his final dismissal of Lesbia in the elaborately contemptuous Poem 11, where Catullus ironically returns to the verse form named for Sappho. Whether the obloquy heaped on Lesbia-Clodia is entirely just can be questioned; Cicero's attack on her is that of an adversary lawyer in the courtroom, and the resentment felt by rejected lovers is not always reasonable. But she seems to have been wicked enough.

Catullus' personal social set overlapped with a set of poets he was associated with, the "Neoterics" or "new poets." Catullus, and the others if they were like him (their work has not survived), broke from the main tradition of Roman poetry and its high-serious epic and tragic concern with public themes like history and war; he preferred more personal and occasional topics. The new poetry has a colloquialism drawn in part from Roman comedy overlaid with the influence of Alexandrianism, the school of the late (fourth and third centuries) Greek poet-scholars. The Alexandrian influence helps account for Catullus' concern with meticulous elegance of form, learned allusion, and taste. There is a good deal of art-for-art's-sake estheticism in Catullus. Yet, paradoxically, his art is above all one of intensely personal expression, treating subjects drawn from life, and his feelings are expressed with a directness and intimacy that are distinctly romantic. The sound, of Catullus' short lyrics at least, is that of a personal conversational voice easily recognizable as his. The viewpoint is unabashedly subjective. The range is astonishing. The playfully mock-solemn dirge for Lesbia's dead pet sparrow is delicately light of touch, but Catullus can also be grossly obscene (Poem 39 gives a hint, though only a hint, of this side of him). The rapturous first address to Lesbia (51) is in violent contrast with the blistering farewell (11). Each lyric seems a total indulgence of the poet's mood, at least as the poet's art defines it. The control of tones is masterful. Poem 11, for example, has three distinct tones: mock-heroic inflation, scathing hatred, and self-pity.

Catullus' influence on ancient literature was great, extending even to poets very

*dissimilar to him like Virgil and Horace. All the same, his poetry came precariously
close to disappearing as almost all of Sappho's has done. Poem 62 exists in a ninth-
century manuscript; Catullus would else be unknown (except for brief fragments)
without the discovery around 1300 of a manuscript of the other 115 or so poems of
his that we have. Even this manuscript was soon lost again, but fortunately not before
it had been copied. To these lucky accidents we owe the survival of a voice expressive
of the passion and the dissipation that coexisted with Roman austerity.*

FURTHER READING *(prepared by F. S. N.):* Three good comprehensive introductions to Catullus are Stuart G. P. Small, *Catullus: A Reader's Guide to the Poems*, 1983;
Kenneth Quinn, *Catullus: An Interpretation*, 1973; and the translation and apparatus
in G. P. Goold's *Catullus*, 1983. Also helpful are the pertinent sections of the volume
Latin Literature, ed. E. J. Kenney and W. V. Clausen, 1982, in *The Cambridge History
of Classical Literature;* and Michael Grant, *Greek and Latin Authors, 800 B.C.–A.D.
1000*, 1980. C. J. Fordyce, *Catullus: A Commentary*, 1961, offers an excellent commentary, with the Latin text, on most of the poems. T. P. Wiseman, *Catullus and His
World: A Reappraisal*, 1985, and Tenney Frank, *Catullus and Horace: Two Poets in
Their Environment*, 1928, attempt to place Catullus in his historical setting. Kenneth
Quinn, ed., in *Approaches to Catullus*, 1972, assembles a number of respected essays
on Catullus which had previously appeared in scholarly journals.

POEMS

Translated by Horace Gregory

1[1]

Who shall receive my new-born book,
my poems, elegant and shy,
neatly dressed and polished?[2]

You, Cornelius,
shall be my single patron,   5
for, long ago, you praised
my slender lines and stanzas;

You, the only man in Italy
whose genius had the vigour
to write the history of the world   10
in three sturdy volumes;

---

[1] This dedicatory poem was written to introduce a collection of Catullus' poems; his surviving work would take up more than one book (that is, scroll), and so it is uncertain which
poems the dedication applies to. The addressee is Cornelius Nepos, who had written a history
of the world in three scrolls and who, like Catullus, came from Cisalpine Gaul, south of the
Alps in northern Italy.

[2] Polished with pumice (volcanic rock), used to smooth the ends of the papyrus and give the
volume elegance.

These were books, by Jupiter,
that showed a learned mind and
the strength for heavy labour.

Then, take this little book   15
for what it is, my friend.

Patroness and Muse,
keep these poems green for
a day or so beyond a hundred years,
                                O Virgin!³   20

51¹

He is changed to a god he who looks on her,
godlike he shines when he's seated beside her,
immortal joy to gaze and hear the fall of
                        her sweet laughter.

All of my senses are lost and confounded;   5
Lesbia rises before me and trembling
I sink into earth and swift dissolution
                        seizes my body.

Limbs are pierced with fire and the heavy tongue fails,
ears resound with noise of distant storms shaking   10
this earth, eyes gaze on stars that fall forever
                        into deep midnight.

*   *   *

This languid madness destroys you Catullus,
long day and night shall be desolate, broken,
as long ago ancient kings and rich cities   15
                        fell into ruin.

*   *   *

---

³*Virgin.* The Muse.
¹This poem, the first in the "Lesbia" sequence, records the poet's feelings at or near the beginning of his relationship with the woman usually identified as Clodia, a fashionable and emancipated beauty. (The numbering of Catullus' poems does not correspond to the order of their composition or of the events recorded.) The first three stanzas are a near-translation from a poem by Sappho of Lesbos, part of which survives ("He is more than a hero"). Authorities do not agree on whether the last four lines of Catullus's poem are really part of it or represent instead an error in the manuscript. The Latin meter ("sapphics") is also derived from Sappho and, as far as we know, was used only twice by Catullus: once here and once in his bitter farewell to Lesbia (Poem 11). "He" in line one is presumably a rival, possibly Clodia's husband.

3

Dress now in sorrow, O all
you shades of Venus,
and your little cupids weep.

My girl has lost her darling sparrow;
he is dead, her precious toy   5
that she loved more than her two eyes,
O, honeyed sparrow following her
as a girl follows her mother,
never to leave her breast, but tripping
now here, now there, and always singing   10
his sweet falsetto
song to her alone.

Now he is gone; poor creature,
lost in darkness,
to a sad place   15
from which no one returns.

O ravenous hell!
My evil hatred rises against your power,
you that devour
all things beautiful;   20
and now this pitiful, broken sparrow,
who is the cause of my girl's grief,
making her eyes weary and red with sorrow.

5

Come, Lesbia, let us live and love,
nor give a damn what sour old men say.
The sun that sets may rise again
but when our light has sunk into the earth,
it is gone forever.   5
          Give me a thousand kisses,
then a hundred, another thousand,
another hundred
          and in one breath
still kiss another thousand,   10
another hundred.
          O then with lips and bodies joined
many deep thousands;
          confuse
their number,   15
          so that poor fools and cuckolds (envious

even now) shall never
learn our wealth and curse us
with their
evil eyes.   20

85

I hate and love.
    And if you ask me why,
I have no answer, but I discern,
can feel, my senses rooted in eternal torture.

109

My life, my love, you say our love will last forever;
O gods remember
her pledge, convert the words of her avowal into a prophecy.
Now let her blood speak, let sincerity govern each syllable fallen
from her lips, so that the long years of our lives shall be   5
a contract of true love inviolate
against time itself, a symbol of eternity.

39[1]

Egnatius has white teeth and therefore always pleasant, always smiling;
and if a lawyer is telling a sad tale for the defense[2] (a pitiful client),
Egnatius is there with his eternal smile.
If there's a funeral with the mother weeping
over the body of her only son,   5
Egnatius arrives gleaming with his happy smile:
no matter where he is or who he sees or what he does,
he is forever smiling.
        O what a foul disease,
this smile,   10
      not sweet nor gracious,
nor a sign of social charm.
              Listen to me, my dear,
good, fine Egnatius,
        if you were Roman, Sabine, Tibertine,   15
or a starved greedy pig from Umbria,

---

[1] Egnatius, a Spaniard, was one of Clodia/Lesbia's lovers.
[2] Egnatius is pictured as sitting among the defendant's supporters, where sadness and concern would be fitting.

or an Etruscan, short and round, or a dark Lanuvian
with glittering teeth or a man from my own province,[3]
or anybody at all who scrubs his teeth with good clean water daily—
your smile would still offend me; nothing is worse   20
than senseless laughter from a foolish face. But you're a Spaniard,
and we already know the Spanish custom:
                          how Spaniards clean their teeth
and scour their gums with the same water that issues
from their bladders.   25
              So if your teeth are clean, my friend, we know how
you have used your urine.

8

Poor damned Catullus, here's no time for nonsense,
open your eyes, O idiot, innocent boy, look at what has happened:
once there were sunlit days when you followed after
where ever a girl would go, she loved with greater
love than any woman knew.   5
Then you took your pleasure
and the girl was not unwilling. Those were the bright days, gone;
now she's no longer yielding; you must be, poor idiot,
more like a man! not running after
her your mind all tears; stand firm, insensitive.   10
Say with a smile, voice steady, "Good-bye, my girl," Catullus
strong and manly no longer follows you, nor comes when you are
    calling
him at night and you shall need him.
You whore! Where's your man to cling to, who will praise your
    beauty,
where's the man that you love and who will call you his,   15
and when you fall to kissing, whose lips will you devour?
But always, your Catullus will be as firm as rock is.

76

If man can find rich consolation, remembering his good deeds and all
    he has done,
if he remembers his loyalty to others, nor abuses his religion by heart-
    less betrayal
of friends to the anger of powerful gods,[1]

---

[3] Six non-Roman peoples who were nevertheless socially accepted. The people of Catullus'
own province, in northern Italy south of the Alps, had still not acquired full Roman citizenship in Catullus' lifetime.
[1] That is, does not make dishonest oaths.

then, my Catullus, the long years before you shall not sink in darkness
   with all hope gone,
wandering, dismayed, through the ruins of love.   5
All the devotion that man gives to man, you have given, Catullus,
your heart and your brain flowed into a love that was desolate,
   wasted, nor can it return.
But why, why do you crucify love and yourself through the years?
Take what the gods have to offer and standing serene, rise forth as a
   rock against darkening skies;
and yet you do nothing but grieve, sunken deep in your sorrow, Catullus,   10
for it is hard, hard to throw aside years lived in poisonous love that
   has tainted your brain
and must end.
If this seems impossible now, you must rise
to salvation. O gods of pity and mercy, descend and witness my sorrow, if ever
you have looked upon man in his hour of death, see me now in despair.   15
Tear this loathsome disease from my brain. Look, a subtle corruption
   has entered my bones,[2]
no longer shall happiness flow through my veins like a river. No
   longer I pray
that she love me again, that her body be chaste, mine forever.
Cleanse my soul of this sickness of love, give me power to rise, resur-
   rected, to thrust love aside,
I have given my heart to the gods, O hear me, omnipotent heaven,   20
and ease me of love and its pain.

11[1]

Furius, Aurelius, bound to Catullus
though he marches piercing farthest India
where echoing waves of the Eastern Oceans
      break upon the shores:

Under Caspian seas, to mild Arabia,   5
east of Parthia,[2] dark with savage bowmen,
or where the Nile, sevenfold and uprising,
      stains its leveled sands,—

[2] These words echo and contrast with the description of ardent love in Poem 51: "swift dissolution/seizes my body./Limbs are pierced with fire."

[1] This poem marks the final contemptuous farewell to Lesbia/Clodia. In the original Latin, Catullus uses for the second and last time the sapphic verse form used in Poem 51, the overture to the love affair. Furius and Aurelius have apparently been sent as envoys from Lesbia to seek a reconciliation; since they were not in fact friends of Catullus, his address to them as fellow comrades-in-arms is perhaps heavily sarcastic. Before getting to the point—his message to Lesbia—the poet surveys the entire known world, from India in the east to Britain in the west.

[2] A country in what is now northeastern Iran.

Even though he marches over Alps to gaze on
great Caesar's monuments:[3] the Gallic Rhine and   10
Britons who live beyond torn seas, remotest
    men of distant lands—

Friends who defy with me all things, whatever
gods may send us, go now, friends, deliver
these words to my lady, nor sweet—flattering,   15
    nor kind nor gentle:

Live[4] well and sleep with adulterous lovers,
three hundred men between your thighs, embracing
all love turned false, again, again, and breaking
    their strength, now sterile.   20

She will not find my love (once hers) returning;
she it was who caused love, this lonely flower,[5]
tossed aside, to fall by the plow dividing
    blossoming meadows.

62[1]

Boys

Twilight and star we hope to see arise, pouring bright rain from
    Mount Olympus[2] down
over the wedding feast, have now arrived, we sing our praise to the
    advancing bride,
rise now to greet her singing:
O Hymen, Hymenaee, come now, O Hymen.[3]

Girls

And is it true that Hesperus is here? Witness this company of boys
    now standing   5
facing us and the star of night flames with the fire of Mount Oeta,[4]

---

[3] Reminders of Julius Caesar's exploits. Caesar crossed the Rhine in the summer of 55 B.C., and later in that year he crossed the English Channel to Britain.

[4] The word recalls its use in the first line of the rapturous Poem 5.

[5] The image is another reminiscence of Sappho, who uses a similar image of a damaged flower in "Lament for a maidenhead."

[1] This epithalamium, or wedding song, was not written for any particular wedding. Influenced strongly by Greek poetry, it describes a mixture of Greek and Roman nuptial ceremonies. The setting is the end of an evening feast in the house of the bride's parents; the form is that of a choral competition between the young male and female guests, who are seated apart from each other. The bride makes her appearance in the course of the poem.

[2] That is, the sky; Mount Olympus was the dwelling place of the gods.

[3] A ritual refrain at weddings. (Later Hymen was personified as the god of marriage.) The refrain is probably an interjection by the poet, not by the singers.

[4] There may have been a cult of Hesperus, the evening star, on Oeta, a mountain in central Greece.

O hear them sing and see their ritual, wonder and joy for us to gaze
  upon
O Hymen, Hymenaee, come now, O Hymen.

BOYS

Hear how the girls have set their song in perfect measures, and each
  word recited
sounds from an infallible memory, surely their minds were rooted   10
deep in memorable music while we (our minds and ears distracted)
  wandered, and we shall be outdone;
O victory shall fall to those who sing in perfect rhythm, we must equal
  them and what they say must find
our words a perfect complement.
O Hymen, Hymenaee, come now, O Hymen.

GIRLS

What are these flames that roll against the skies, divorcing mother
  and child, more terrible   15
than earthly fires? These flames of Hesperus that seize a daughter
  from her mother's arms
delivering the girl into the quick embrace of a young husband—here
  is destruction greater
than a tall city given to its enemies.
O Hymen, Hymenaee, come now, O Hymen.

BOYS

What is more beautiful than this rich fire, the crown of heaven rising,   20
the fire that joins the marriage a true contract spoken by husband and
  parents of the bride,
and yet does not disclose its vital power until the marriage bed is
  made. What a gift from heaven
greater than this gift from gods to man in a superlative hour of happiness?
O Hymen, Hymenaee, come now, O Hymen.

*   *   *

GIRLS

O friends who love us, Hesperus has taken one of us, our sister,
  taken. . . .[5]   25

*   *   *

[5] Most of the young women's words here and the beginning of the men's reply have been
lost. The women apparently charge Hesperus, herald of night, with being the ally of thieves.
The men answer that, besides alerting the night police to be on guard, Hesperus as morning
star also brings daylight and thus catches thieves (Venus can be either a morning or an evening
star).

BOYS

O Hesperus when you rise, our guardian, eyes open the night long,
you come, disguised as dawn star now disclosing thieves hidden under
    night's vast shadow
but virgins cry against you, a false lamentation against him who is
    desire
coiled in their brains, a secret never spoken.
O Hymen, Hymenaee, come now, O Hymen.   30

GIRLS

We are as flowers[6] in a garden hidden from all men's eyes, no crea-
    ture of the field walks in this place,
no plow divides us; only the gentlest wind, rain from a soft warm
    cloud and the quickening sun to nourish us.
We are the treasure that many girls and boys desire; but once de-
    flowered (the flower stained and torn)
the virgin's body rancid, neither boys nor girls will turn to her again
nor can she wake their passion.   35

BOYS

You are as a vine in a barren field that cannot climb by its own
    strength
nor its fruit prosper (the vine driven downward with its own weight
    neither the ox nor plowman shall teach it how
to grow, but if its body twined round an elm, gives promise of fruit,
    then by this marriage
many a farmer and his beast will wait upon it). So is it with you O
    virgins.
The virgin, perfect, wastes until she ripens in the marriage bed and
    there receives   40
her father's blessing and her husband's love.
Never resist the power of this union made, O virgin; father and
    mother have given you to him, this man, your husband
your maidenhead by this division is not yours alone, you hold one
    third of that which is the treasure
of parents and your husband—this is the lawful contract given to him
    whose hands receive your dowry.
O Hymen, Hymenaee, come now, O Hymen.   45

101[1]

Dear brother, I have come these many miles, through strange lands to
    this Eastern Continent

---

    [6] The following flower-simile, like the one in Catullus's Poem 11, is probably a reminis-
cence of Sappho's "Lament for a maidenhead."
    [1] Catullus' brother had died young, in Asia Minor near the site of ancient Troy. In 57 B.C.,
during a term of service abroad, in nearby Bithynia, Catullus visited his brother's grave. He
offers ritual gifts to the dead.

to see your grave, a poor sad monument of what you were, O brother.
And I have come too late; you cannot hear me; alone now I must
   speak
to these few ashes that were once your body and expect no answer.
I shall perform an ancient ritual over your remains, weeping,   5
(this plate of lentils for dead men to feast upon, wet with my tears)
O brother, here's my greeting: here's my hand forever welcoming you
and I forever saying: good-bye, good-bye.

Virgil
(70 B.C. – 19 B.C.)

Because of the nobility of his conceptions and his poetic genius, Virgil has had a more continuous and profound impact on European culture, antique and Christian, than any other single classical author. Since his own day his works have been the fare of schoolchildren and of connoisseurs of poetry alike. He has been regarded not only as a prototype of the consummate artist but also as a sage, a religious prophet, and even a sorcerer. Perhaps his most distinctive achievement is to have defined heroism, and its costs, in a context not of primitive social conditions but of a sophisticated, intricately organized civilization and its values.

Like several other great Roman poets, notably Catullus, Horace, and Ovid, Virgil came from the provinces. He was born, like Catullus, in the part of northern Italy called Cisalpine Gaul, in 70 B.C. There he learned the deep love of rural nature that would later shine through his poetry. His father seems to have been a man of humble stock who acquired farm land near Mantua. Virgil nevertheless got a very good education—especially in language and literature, science, and philosophy—at Cremona, Milan, and finally at Rome, where he arrived at the age of seventeen. He is said to have contemplated a career in law but to have lacked the quickness and hardihood necessary for success in it. Although he was amiable and made influential friends in the political and cultural circles of Rome, he was a shy, studious person who never married and who took no direct part in public life. A professional poet, he devoted almost all his time to his art and the studies ancillary to it.

His three principal works were the Eclogues (written between 42 and 37), the Georgics (36–29), and the Aeneid (29–19). The Eclogues are pastoral poems, in the tradition of the Greek poet Theocritus, depicting the idyllic life of shepherds, but Virgil intriguingly combines with the escapist setting references to actual persons and current topics. Two of the Eclogues deal with dispossession from one's land—a poignant, typically Virgilian theme—and are believed to refer to the expropriation of Virgil's family farm for the benefit of soldiers in the army of Mark Antony and Octavian after they defeated the assassins of Julius Caesar at Philippi. (The property was apparently returned to Virgil at a later date.) The Fourth Eclogue, which prophesies the birth of a wondrous child who is to restore the Golden Age, was later interpreted by Christians as a prophecy of Jesus; hence its name the "Messianic eclogue." The Georgics too has a rural theme and setting; in fact, it is largely a practical handbook for farmers, though the work also has a broad patriotic theme in keeping with Virgil's desire to help restore Italian agriculture and the moral values associated with it. It counterpoints dream and reality, tragedy and comedy, pessimism and optimism. The Georgics, *composed slowly and carefully, at the rate of less than one line a day, is often praised as the most perfect of all Latin poems. After completing it, Virgil turned to his greatest work, the* Aeneid, *to which he devoted his remaining years. At the time of his death in* 19 B.C. *he had not quite perfected it and asked that it be burned. Octavian (the emperor Caesar Augustus) is said to have rescued it.*

Despite his retiring temperament, Virgil lived at a time when it was not easy for any Roman to avoid the impact of public events. The wars of Roman against Roman had begun decades before Virgil's birth. During his boyhood the republican form of Roman government was proving less and less capable of curbing the ambitions of powerful men. Pompey the Great, one of the two consuls (chief magistrates) in 70, the year Virgil was born, had a meteoric career as general and legislator. In 55, as Virgil reached the traditional age of manhood, Pompey was consul a second time, and in 52 the leader assumed the unprecedented office of sole consul to deal with the gang warfare and street disorders which were racking the life of the capital. Cicero, the eminent Roman thinker and statesman, dreamed that in some such central and autocratic figure as Pompey Rome might find salvation from the ills that were too widespread for its traditional government to control.

In fact, Rome's first autocracy in almost five centuries was to be established not by Pompey but by Julius Caesar, who, at first simply a popular politician from an impoverished noble family, gradually had begun to emerge as an unmatched leader and a strategist of ruthless brilliance. Caesar defeated Pompey in 48 at the Battle of Pharsalus, and during four breathless years he attempted to reshape Roman government as a centralized monarchy on the model of Alexander the Great. But Caesar's audacity went too far. In 44 a group of conspirators led by Brutus assassinated him in Pompey's Theater at Rome. The conspirators had no clear plan of action. It looked as if Rome would collapse under the sheer size of its own problems, when out of the welter of confusion and carnage emerged Caesar's ailing nineteen-year-old grandnephew Octavian. A skilled politician driven by an extraordinary genius, Octavian maneuvered his way through the labyrinth of Roman power politics over the next thirteen years, winning at length the general support of Rome. His most formidable rival, his brother-in-law Mark Antony, had become infatuated with Cleopatra, the queen of Egypt, and even planned to yield her part of the Roman domain. In the climactic naval battle of Actium in 31 (an event foreshadowed in Book III and described in Book VIII of the Aeneid), *Octavian defeated Antony and Cleopatra. Their subsequent suicide left Octavian supreme in authority, and in 23 he became known as Caesar Augustus. His regime aimed at several goals: the civic renewal of Rome, the revival of traditional religious devotion, and the fostering of a new patriotism. The arts were to be important vehicles for these ideals, all of which are reflected in the* Aeneid.

For Virgil, as for many other Romans, the restoration of peace was in itself a blessed achievement, an occasion and opportunity for Roman national glory. In Book I of the Aeneid *Jupiter prophesies a time when*

> *wars will cease, and a rough age grow gentler,*
> *White Faith and Vesta, Romulus and Remus,*
> *Give law to nations. War's grim gates will close,*

> Tight-shut with bars of iron, and inside them
> The wickedness of war sit bound and silent,
> The red mouth straining and the hands held tight
> In fastenings of bronze, a hundred hundred.

> (I. 305–311)

To "give law to nations"—this, and not mere narrow chauvinism, is the distinctive Roman mission. The shade of Anchises tells his son Aeneas in Book VI:

> Others, no doubt, will better mould the bronze
> To the semblance of soft breathing, draw, from marble,
> The living countenance; and others plead
> With greater eloquence, or learn to measure,
> Better than we, the pathways of the heaven,
> The risings of the stars: remember, Roman,
> To rule the people under law, to establish
> The way of peace, to battle down the haughty,
> To spare the meek. Our fine arts, these, forever.

> (VI. 888–896)

Although Anchises is historically right in conceding superiority in the fine arts to other nations, specifically Greece, and identifying government as the epitome of Roman greatness, it is somewhat ironic that his exhortation, at once modest and proud, should appear in a poem that is one of the world's aesthetic masterpieces.

The Aeneid is, then, a eulogy of Roman values. But it also puts those values in perspective by showing insistently the great cost at which they are achieved and sustained. The poem, particularly in the second half, treats political negotiation and war at length, but war is presented there as a moral tragedy, however necessary, and even admirable, martial prowess and courage may be. Aeneas is no Homeric hero, free to demonstrate valor and prowess for their own sake, with no social obligation beyond himself, his family, and the cohorts banded together under him. The distinctively Virgilian melancholy, combined inextricably with tones of triumph, arises largely from the poet's awareness that public duty requires again and again the sacrifice of personal fulfillment. Aeneas, the mirror of Augustus and of Roman potential, must be educated in suffering before he can perform his mission and become a worthy embodiment of the Roman ideal. His affair with Dido is a personal tragedy on both sides. Since Carthage, the city she rules, was to become an inveterate enemy of Rome in three major wars during the two centuries before Virgil, it would have been easy for him to present this African queen as merely ignoble, a focus for propaganda. That instead he portrays her sympathetically, indeed creating in her the most memorable character in Latin literature, both enhances her own tragic stature and underlines Aeneas' tragic dilemma in having to renounce her in the name of duty.

For the formal vehicle of his story and message, Virgil chose the epic, a literary genre he had aspired to since early in his life. His handling of epic owes something to the Greek Alexandrians, but his primary models are the two Homeric epics. Books I to VI are, like the Odyssey, a tale of wandering; Books VII to XII are a war story, like the Iliad. But those general correspondences are, in themselves, only the most superficial marks of Homeric influence, and there are ironic differences too. The journey of Homer's Odysseus is a true homecoming; Aeneas' odyssey, despite the *ancestral roots the Trojans have in Italy, is a leavetaking, a deracination. Virgil's echoing of Homer is intricate but also intricately varied, so that the echoing is less imitative than expressive. Virgil's synthesizing tour de force overlies a radical originality of the utmost importance in the history of epic. Aristotle, in his* Poetics, *had praised Homer for his objectivity, his effacement of himself, and had identified such self-effacement as the epic poet's proper role. In his own way, of course, Virgil too is objective; that is, he combines with his didacticism flexibility of sympathy with individual human beings, realistic insight into human psychology, and a sense that there is often right on both sides. Yet the* Aeneid *is, after all, a subjective poem—in the sense that the author's presence can be felt everywhere, in the ideas and in the characteristic Virgilian tone of pathos, introspectiveness, and poignancy.*

An even more important innovation is Virgil's imaginative redefinition of the role of history in epic. Rather than narrating and directly celebrating modern Roman history, which is ultimately his main concern, he chooses to return to the legendary roots of the Roman experience nearly a millennium earlier, in the wanderings and wars of the Trojans after the fall of their city. In treating the seeds of later Roman history, Roman religious ritual, Roman character traits as having been sown in that era of the dim past, the Aeneid, *unlike the Homeric models, envisions time and history as a meaningful linear movement toward goals ordained by a mysterious but purposeful providence. Understood in this way, the fall of Troy is ultimately a fortunate fall. In ancient literature the closest thing we have to this is not in pagan literature but in the Bible, especially in the Exodus saga. Both there and in the* Aeneid *we see a guiding providence operating through divinely appointed, half-reluctant heroes, Moses and Aeneas, both of whom must grow into their roles but then rest content not quite to reach the ultimate goal of their people. In both works the journey is out of a disastrous past toward a new promised land that is also an ancestral homeland. Both leaders must mediate between the exigencies of providence and the weariness and backslidings of their followers. It is no wonder that poets in the Judaeo-Christian tradition could retrospectively claim Virgil as one of their own.*

Except for the Bible, the Aeneid *may well be the most highly revered book in European literary history, especially before the reemergence of the Greek classics in Europe during the Renaissance. Like the Bible, Virgil's works were used by people seeking supernatural guidance; they opened a copy at random and found wisdom in the first passage their eyes struck. That practice (the* Sortes Vergilianae) *reflects the moral sententiousness of the* Aeneid, *but it also reflects the poem's style. To translate Virgil is especially challenging, for almost every line is dense with meaning, nuance, implication. That is partly owing to the nature of classical Latin, which can produce special effects because the word order is freer than in modern English, and partly to Virgil's painstaking method of composition, which is utterly different from the essentially oral manner of Homer's verse (though Virgil did sometimes read his poetry aloud). The meter is the standard epic meter, dactylic hexameter—each of the six feet made up of a long syllable and two short ones (dactyl) or of two long ones (spondee). But in addition to this quantitative meter, based on the actual time-duration of syllables, Virgil's verse recognizes the stress accents that words possessed in spoken Latin as they do in English, and this stress-accent pattern is played against the quantitative pattern in ways from which Virgil elicits enormously varied expressive effects. It should be noted too that, in the last two feet of Virgil's hexameter line, the stress-accent pattern and the quantitative pattern coincide, so that each line sustains rhythmic tensions that are resolved in the last two feet. The first seven lines of the*

*Aeneid, quoted below, are given as a sample; the slash marks indicate the divisions
into feet; the long and short syllables are indicated, respectively, by the marks — and
˘; and the normal spoken stress accents are indicated by italics:*

Ārmă vĭ/*rum* quĕ *ca*/no, Tro/iae quī / *pri* mŭs ăb / ōrĭs

Ītă lĭ/am, *fa*/to *pro* fu/gŭs, La/*vin* iăquĕ / vē nĭt

li tŏră, / *mul* tum *il*/le et *ter*/rĭs iac/tā tŭs ĕt / *al* to

vi su pē/rum, sae/vae *me* mŏ/rēm Iu/*no* nĭs ŏb / ī rām,

mul tă *quo*/quĕ ēt bel/lo *pas*/sŭs, dŭm / *con* dĕrĕt / ūr bĕm,

infer/*ret* quĕ *de*/os La tĭ/o, gĕ nŭs / ūn dĕ La/*ti* nŭm,

Ālbă/*ni* quĕ *pa*/trēs, āt/que al tae / *mœ* nĭă / *Ro* mae.

*In his poem "To Virgil," composed in 1882 for the 1,900th anniversary of Virgil's
death, Tennyson paid tribute to what he called Virgil's "ocean-roll of rhythm":*

I salute thee, Mantovano [Mantuan], I that loved thee since my day began,
Wielder of the stateliest measure ever molded by the lips of man.

FURTHER READING *(prepared by F. S. N.):* W. F. Jackson Knight, *Roman Vergil,*
1944, 2nd ed. 1966, is especially useful on Virgil's language and style. For a comprehensive treatment of Virgil's work and his debt to Homer and to the Alexandrians, see Brooks Otis, *Virgil: A Study in Civilized Poetry,* 1964. Also valuable on the
Alexandrian background to Augustan poetry is J. K. Newman, *Augustus and the New
Poetry,* 1967. Lively and stimulating twentieth-century interpretations are presented
by Steele Commager, ed., *Virgil: A Collection of Critical Essays,* 1966; by Donald R.
Dudley, ed., *Virgil,* 1969; and by John D. Bernard, ed., *Vergil at 2000: Commemora-
tive Essays on the Poet and His Influence,* 1986. Viktor Pöschl, *The Art of Vergil: Image
and Symbol in the Aeneid,* 1950, trans. Gerda Seligson, 1962, shows how the epic is
unified thematically, symbolically, and artistically. Kenneth Quinn, *Virgil's "Aeneid":
A Critical Description,* 1968, brings twentieth-century critical methods to bear on
traditional material. Also helpful and incisive are W. A. Camps, *An Introduction to
Virgil's Aeneid,* 1969, and the Introduction to R. D. Williams' commentary *The Aeneid
of Virgil,* 1973. Gordon Williams, *Technique and Ideas in the "Aeneid",* 1983, is excellent, though intellectually demanding. A more accessible recent work, Jasper Griffin's *Virgil,* 1986, can be strongly recommended.

from *THE AENEID*

Translated by Rolfe Humphries

BOOK I: THE LANDING NEAR CARTHAGE

Arms and the man I sing,[1] the first who came,
Compelled by fate, an exile out of Troy,
To Italy and the Lavinian coast,[2]

---

[1] Lines 1–16 use the standard epic "opening formula," including the identification of the
hero, the proclamation of the theme and of its significance, and the invocation of the inspiring
Muse.
[2] The west coast of Italy.

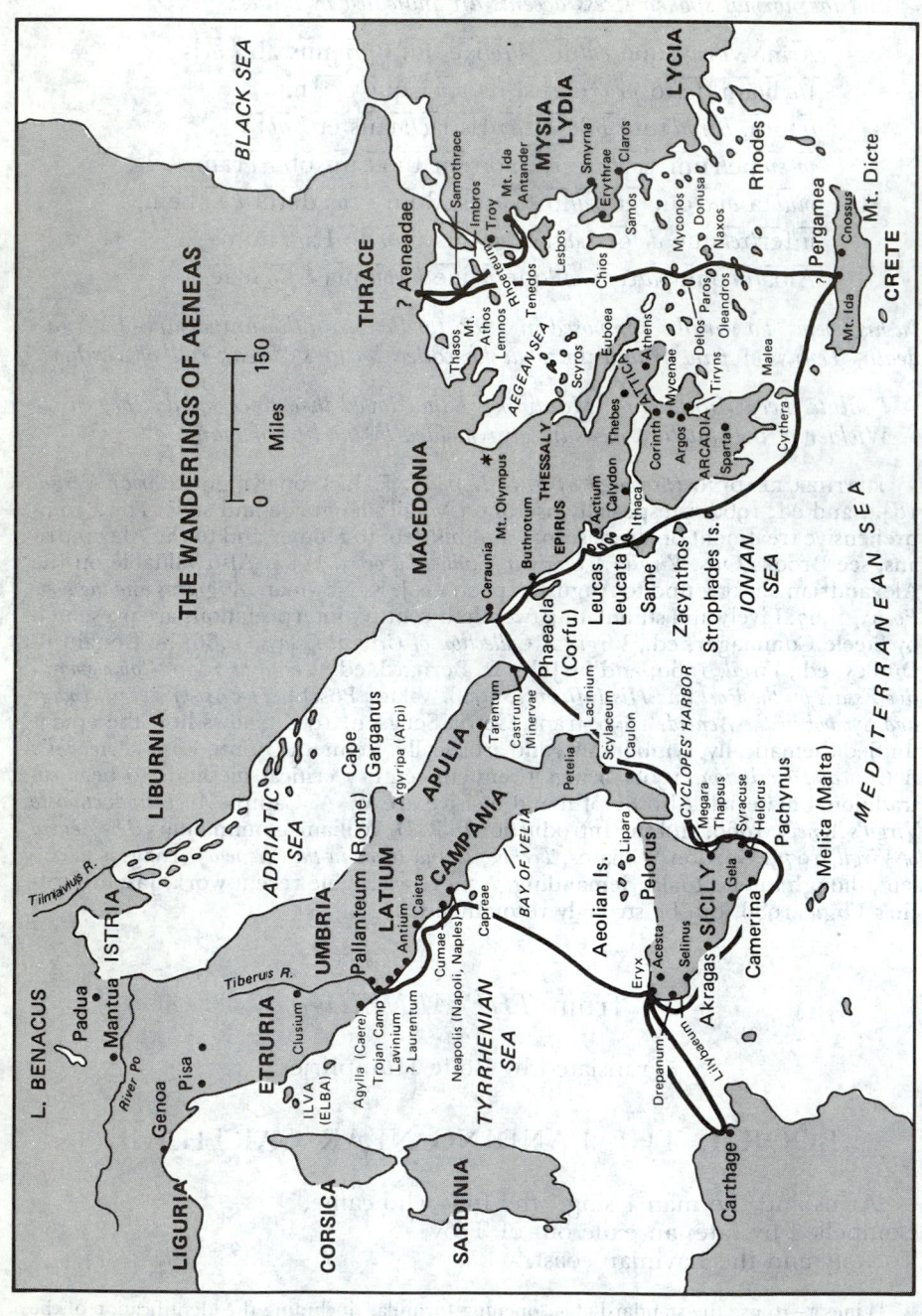

THE WANDERINGS OF AENEAS

0 _____ 150

Miles

Much buffeted on land and on the deep
By violence of the gods, through that long rage,
That lasting hate, of Juno's. And he suffered
Much, also, in war, till he should build his town
And bring his gods to Latium,[3] whence, in time,
The Latin race, the Alban[4] fathers, rose
And the great walls of everlasting Rome.   10

   Help me, O Muse, recall the reasons: why,
Why did the queen of heaven[5] drive a man
So known for goodness, for devotion, through
So many toils and perils? Was there slight,
Affront, or outrage? Is vindictiveness
An attribute of the celestial mind?

   There was an ancient city, Carthage, once
Founded by Tyrians,[6] facing Italy
And Tiber's[7] mouth, far-off, a wealthy town,
War-loving, and aggressive; and Juno held   20
Even her precious Samos[8] in less regard.
Here were her arms, her chariot, and here,
Should fate at all permit, the goddess burned
To found the empire of the world forever.
But, she had heard, a Trojan race would come,
Some day, to overthrow the Tyrian towers,
A race would come, imperious people,[9] proud
In war, with wide dominion, bringing doom
For Libya. Fate willed it so. And Juno
Feared, and remembered: there was the old war   30
She fought at Troy for her dear Greeks; her mind
Still fed on hurt and anger; deep in her heart
Paris' decision[10] rankled, and the wrong
Offered her slighted beauty; and the hatred
Of the whole race; and Ganymede's[11] honors—
All that was fuel to fire; she tossed and harried
All over the seas, wherever she could, those Trojans
Who had survived the Greeks and fierce Achilles,
And so they wandered over many an ocean,
Through many a year, fate-hounded. Such a struggle   40
It was to found the race of Rome!

---

[3] The area of Italy destined to be settled by the Trojans.

[4] The city Alba Longa was founded by Ascanius, Aeneas' son. It produced Romulus, who was according to legend the founder of Rome.

[5] Juno, queen of the gods and inveterate enemy of the Trojans.

[6] People from Tyre, a city on the Syrian coast, noted for commerce.

[7] The river of Rome. The epithet *War-loving* refers to the fact that Rome and Carthage fought three wars against each other during the third and second centuries B.C.

[8] An island in the Aegean Sea, site of the great temple of Juno.   [9] The Romans.

[10] Paris, one of the sons of King Priam of Troy, had been asked to judge which of the three goddesses Juno, Minerva, and Venus was most beautiful. He chose Venus, who rewarded him with Helen; Helen's abduction by Paris from her husband Menelaus then ignited the Trojan War.

[11] Promoted over Juno's daughter Hebe as cupbearer to the gods.

                                                    They were happy
Spreading the sail, rushing the foam with bronze,
And Sicily hardly out of sight, when Juno,
Still nourishing the everlasting wound,
Raged to herself: "I am beaten, I suppose;
It seems I cannot keep this Trojan king
From Italy. The fates, no doubt, forbid me.[12]
Pallas, of course, could burn the Argive ships,
Could drown the sailors, all for one man's guilt,
The crazy acts of Ajax.[13] Her own hand   50
Hurled from the cloud Jove's thunderbolt, and shattered
Their ships all over the sea; she raised up storm
And tempest; she spiked Ajax on the rocks,
Whirled him in wind, blasted his heart with fire.
And I, who walk my way as queen of the gods,
Sister of Jove, and wife of Jove, keep warring
With one tribe through the long, long years. Who cares
For Juno's godhead? Who brings sacrifice
Devoutly to her altars?"
                                            Brooding, burning,
She sought Aeolia, the storm-clouds' dwelling,   60
A land that sweeps and swarms with the winds' fury,
Whose monarch, Aeolus, in his deep cave rules
Imperious, weighing down with bolt and prison
Those boisterous struggling roarers, who go raging
Around their bars, under the moan of the mountain.
High over them their sceptered lord sits watching,
Soothing, restraining, their passionate proud spirit,
Lest, uncontrolled, they seize, in their wild keeping,
The land, the sea, the arch of sky, in ruin
Sweeping through space. This Jupiter feared; he hid them   70
Deep in dark caverns, with a mass of mountain
Piled over above them, and a king to give them
Most certain regulation, with a knowledge
When to hold in, when to let go. Him Juno
Approached in supplication:—"Aeolus,
Given by Jove the power to still the waters,
Or raise them with a gale, a tribe I hate
Is on its way to Italy, and they carry
Troy with them, and their household gods, once beaten.
Shake anger into those winds of yours, turn over   80
Their ships, and drown them; drive them in all directions,
Litter the sea with bodies! For such service
The loveliest nymph I have, Deiopea,
Shall be your bride forever, and you will father
Fair children on her fairness." Aeolus

---

[12] Even the gods were considered subject to the superior power of Fate.
[13] Pallas, or Athena (the Greek equivalent of Minerva, goddess of wisdom), had inflicted
the punishment described in revenge for the rape by Ajax of the prophetess Cassandra.

Made answer: "Yours, O Queen, the task of seeking
Whatever it is you will; and mine the duty
To follow with performance. All my empire,
My sceptre, Jove's indulgence, are beholden
To Juno's favor, by whose blessing I   90
Attend the feasts of the gods and rule this storm-land."
   His spear-butt struck the hollow mountain-side,
And the winds, wherever they could, came sweeping forth,
Whirled over the land, swooped down upon the ocean.
East, South, Southwest, they heave the billows, howl,
Storm, roll the giant combers toward the shore.
Men cry; the rigging creaks and strains; the clouds
Darken, and men see nothing; a weight of darkness
Broods over the deep; the heavy thunder rumbles
From pole to pole; the lightning rips and dazzles;   100
There is no way out but death. Aeneas shudders
In the chill shock, and lifts both hands to heaven:—
"O happy men, thrice happy, four times happy,
Who had the luck to die, with their fathers watching
Below the walls of Troy! Ah, Diomedes,
Bravest of Greeks, why could I not have fallen,
Bleeding my life away on plains of Ilium[14]
In our encounter there, where mighty Hector
Went down before Achilles'[15] spear, and huge
Sarpedon[16] lay in dust, and Simois river   110
Rolled to the sea so many noble heroes,
All drowned in all their armor?" And the gale
Howls from the north, striking the sail, head on;
The waves are lifted to the stars; the oars
Are broken, and the prow slews round; the ship
Lies broadside on; a wall of water, a mountain,
Looms up, comes pouring down; some ride the crest,
Some, in the trough, can see the boil of the sand.
The South wind hurls three ships on the hidden rocks,
That sea-reef which Italians call the Altars;   120
The West takes three, sweeping them from the deep
On shoal and quicksand; over the stern of one,
Before Aeneas' eyes, a great sea falls,
Washing the helmsman overboard; the ship
Whirls thrice in the suck of the water and goes down
In the devouring gulf; and here and there
A few survivors swim, the Lycian men
Whose captain was Orontes; now their arms,
Their Trojan treasures, float with the broken timbers
On the swing and slide of the waves. The storm, triumphant, 130

[14] Troy.
[15] Hector and Achilles were the chief warriors of the Trojans and Greeks, respectively. The slaying of Hector by Achilles is described in Homer's *Iliad*, Book XXII.
[16] King of Lycia, killed while fighting on the side of the Trojans. The Simois was a river at the battlefield of Troy.

Rides down more boats, and more; there goes Achates;
Abas, Aletes, Ilioneus,
Receive the hostile water; the walls are broken;
The enemy pours in.
                      But meanwhile Neptune[17]
Saw ocean in a welter of confusion,
The roar of storm, and deep and surface mingled.
Troublesome business, this; he rose, majestic,
From under the waves, and saw the Trojan vessels
Scattered all over the sea by the might of the waves
And the wreck of sky; he recognized the anger   140
And cunning of his sister, and he summoned
The winds by name:—"What arrogance is this,
What pride of birth, you winds, to meddle here
Without my sanction, raising all this trouble?
I'll—No, the waves come first: but listen to me,
You are going to pay for this! Get out of here!
Go tell your king the lordship of the ocean,
The trident, are not his, but mine. His realm
Reaches no further than the rocks and caverns
You brawlers dwell in; let him rule that palace,   150
Big as he pleases, shut you in, and stay there!"
    This said, he calmed the swollen sea and cloud,
Brought back the sun; Cymothoe and Triton,[18]
Heaving together, pulled the ships from the reef,
As Neptune used his trident for a lever,
Opened the quicksand, made the water smooth,
And the flying chariot skimmed the level surface.
Sometimes, in a great nation, there are riots
With the rabble out of hand, and firebrands fly
And cobblestones; whatever they lay their hands on   160
Is a weapon for their fury, but should they see
One man of noble presence, they fall silent,
Obedient dogs, with ears pricked up, and waiting,
Waiting his word, and he knows how to bring them
Back to good sense again. So ocean, roaring,
Subsided into stillness, as the sea-god
Looked forth upon the waters, and clear weather
Shone over him as he drove his flying horses.
    Aeneas' weary children make for harbor,
Whichever lies most near, and the prows are turned   170
To Libya's coast-line. In a bay's deep curve
They find a haven, where the water lies
With never a ripple. A little island keeps
The sea-swell off, and the waves break on its sides
And slide back harmless. The great cliffs come down
Steep to deep water, and the background shimmers,

[17] God of the ocean.
[18] Cymothoe and Triton were, respectively, a sea-nymph and a sea-god.

Darkens and shines, the tremulous aspen moving
And the dark fir pointing still. And there is a cave
Under the overhanging rocks, alive
With water running fresh, a home of the Nymphs,   180
With benches for them, cut from the living stone.
No anchor is needed here for weary ships,
No mooring-cable. Aeneas brings them in,
Seven weary vessels, and the men are glad
To be ashore again, to feel dry sand
Under the salt-stained limbs. Achates[19] strikes
The spark from the flint, catches the fire on leaves,
Adds chips and kindling, blows and fans the flame,
And they bring out the soaked and salty corn,
The hand-mills, stone and mortar, and make ready,   190
As best they can, for bread.
                Meanwhile Aeneas
Climbs to a look-out, for a view of the ocean,
Hoping for some good luck; the Phrygian galleys
Might meet his gaze, or Capys' boats, or a pennon
On a far-off mast-head flying. There is nothing,
Nothing to see out yonder, but near the water
Three stags are grazing, with a herd behind them,
A long line browsing through the peaceful valley.
He reaches for the bow and the swift arrows
Borne by Achates, and he shoots the leaders,   200
High-antlered, routs the common herd, and ceases
Only when seven are slain, a number equal
To the ships' tally, and then he seeks the harbor,
Divides the spoil, broaches the wine Acestes
Had stowed for them at Drepanum on their leaving,
A kingly present, and he calms their trouble,
Saying: "O comrades, we have been through evil
Together before this; we have been through worse,
Scylla, Charybdis, and the Cyclops' dwelling,[20]
The sounding rocks. This, too, the god will end.   210
Call the nerve back; dismiss the fear, the sadness.
Some day, perhaps, remembering even this
Will be a pleasure. We are going on
Through whatsoever chance and change, until
We come to Latium, where the fates point out
A quiet dwelling-place, and Troy recovered.
Endure, and keep yourself for better days."
He kept to himself the sorrow in the heart,
Wearing, for them, a mask of hopefulness.
They were ready for the feasting. Part lay bare   220
The flesh from the torn hides, part cut the meat
Impaling it, still quivering, on spits,
Setting the kettles, keeping the water boiling,

---

[19] Aeneas' most faithful companion.   [20] These perils are described in Book III.

And strong with food again, sprawling stretched out
On comfortable grass, they take their fill
Of bread and wine and venison, till hunger
Is gone, and the board cleared. And then they talk
For a long time, of where their comrades are,
Are, or may be, hopeful and doubtful both.
Could they believe them living? or would a cry   230
Fall on deaf ears forever? All those captains,
Brave Gyas, brave Cloanthus, Amycus,
Lycus, Orontes,—in his secret heart
Aeneas mourns them.
       Meanwhile, from the heaven
Jupiter watched the lands below, and the seas
With the white points of sails, and far-off people,
Turning his gaze toward Libya. And Venus
Came to him then, a little sadly, tears
Brimming in those bright eyes of hers. "Great father,"
She said, "Great ruler of the world   240
Of men and gods, great wielder of the lightning,
What has my poor Aeneas[21] done? what outrage
Could Trojans perpetrate, so that the world
Rejects them everywhere, and many a death
Inflicted on them over Italy?
There was a promise once, that as the years
Rolled onward, they would father Rome and rulers
Of Roman stock, to hold dominion over
All sea and land. That was a promise, father;
What changed it? Once that promise was my comfort;   250
Troy fell; I weighed one fate against another
And found some consolation. But disaster
Keeps on; the same ill-fortune follows after.
What end of it all, great king? One man, Antenor,
Escaped the Greeks, came through Illyrian waters
Safe to Liburnian regions, where Timavus[22]
Roars underground, comes up nine times, and reaches
The floodland near the seas. One man, Antenor,
Founded a city, Padua, a dwelling
For Trojan men, a resting-place from labor,   260
And shares their quietude. But we, your children,
To whom heaven's height is granted, we are betrayed,
We have lost our ships, we are kept from Italy,
Kept far away. One enemy—I tell you
This is a shameful thing! Do we deserve it?
Is this our rise to power?"
         He smiled, in answer,
The kind of smile that clears the air, and kissed her.

---

[21] Venus is Aeneas' mother; Anchises, his father, is a mortal.

[22] The river Timavus flows into the Adriatic Sea (east of Italy); Liburnia is part of the Adriatic coast.

"Fear not, my daughter; fate remains unmoved
For the Roman generations. You will witness
Lavinium's rise, her walls fulfill the promise;   270
You will bring to heaven lofty-souled Aeneas.
There has been no change in me whatever. Listen!
To ease this care, I will prophesy a little,
I will open the book of fate. Your son Aeneas
Will wage a mighty war in Italy,[23]
Beat down proud nations, give his people laws,
Found them a city, a matter of three years
From victory to settlement. His son,
The boy Ascanius, named Ilus once,
When Troy was standing, and now called Iulus,   280
Shall reign for thirty years, and great in power
Forsake Lavinium, transfer the kingdom
To Alba Longa, new-built capital.
Here, for three hundred years, the line of Hector
Shall govern, till a royal priestess bears
Twin sons to Mars, and Romulus, rejoicing
In the brown wolf-skin[24] of his foster-mother,
Takes up the tribe, and builds the martial walls
And calls the people, after himself, the Romans.
To these I set no bounds in space or time;   290
They shall rule forever. Even bitter Juno
Whose fear now harries earth and sea and heaven
Will change to better counsels, and will cherish
The race that wears the toga, Roman masters
Of all the world. It is decreed. The time
Will come, as holy years wheel on, when Troy
Will subjugate Mycenae, vanquish Phthia,
Be lord of Argos.[25] And from this great line
Will come a Trojan, Caesar, to establish
The limit of his empire at the ocean,   300
His glory at the stars, a man called Julius
Whose name recalls Iulus. Welcome waits
For him in heaven; all the spoils of Asia
Will weight him down, and prayer be made before him.
Then wars will cease, and a rough age grow gentler,
White Faith and Vesta,[26] Romulus and Remus,
Give law to nations. War's grim gates will close,
Tight-shut with bars of iron, and inside them
The wickedness of war sit bound and silent,
The red mouth straining and the hands held tight   310
In fastenings of bronze, a hundred hundred."
      With that, he sent down Mercury[27] from heaven

[23] The war is described in the second half of the poem, Books VII to XII.
[24] Romulus and his twin Remus were supposed to have been suckled by a she-wolf.
[25] Cities associated with the Trojans' Greek conquerors: Phthia with Achilles, Mycenae and Argos with Agamemnon, the Greek commander.
[26] Goddess of the hearth.   [27] Messenger of the gods.

That Carthage might be kindly, and her land
And new-built towers receive them with a welcome,
And their queen, Dido, knowing the will of fate,
Swing wide her doors. On the oarage of his wings
He flies through the wide sweep of air to Libya,
Where, at the will of the god, the folk make ready
In kindliness of heart, and their queen's purpose
Is gracious and gentle.

                 All night long Aeneas   320
Had pondered many a care, and with bright morning
Resolved to reconnoiter; the winds have brought him
To a new country: who lives in it, men
Or only beasts? The fields appear untended.
The fleet lies under a hollow cliff, surrounded
By spikes of shade, and groves arch overhead,
Ample concealment. Aeneas and Achates
Went forth together, armed, down the trail in the forest,
And there his mother met him, a girl, it seemed,
From Thrace or Sparta, trim as any huntress   330
Who rides her horses hard, or outspeeds rivers
In her swift going. A bow hung over her shoulder,
Her hair blew free, her knees were bare, her garments
Tucked at the waist and knotted. As she saw them,
"Ho there, young men," she cried, "have you seen my sister
Around here anywhere? She wears a quiver,
And a spotted lynx-hide; maybe you have heard her
Hunting the boar and shouting?"

                         But her son
Responded: "No; we have heard no sounds of hunting,
We have seen no one here. But tell me, maiden,   340
What name to call you by? In voice and feature
You are, I think, no mortal; a goddess, surely,—
Nymph, or Apollo's sister?[28] Whoever you are,
Be kind to us, lighten our trouble, tell us
Under what sky, along what coast of the world,
We wander, knowing neither land nor people,
Driven by gales and billows. Many a victim
We shall make ready for your altar." Venus
Answered: "I have no title to such honor.
The Tyrian girls all wear these crimson leggings   350
Like mine, and carry quivers. Tyrian folk
Live here; their city is Carthage; over the border
Lies Libya, warlike people. Our queen, Dido,
Came here from Tyre; she was fleeing from her brother,—
A long and complicated story; outrage,—
No matter, here it is, in brief. Her husband
Was Sychaeus, wealthiest of all Phoenicians,
At least in land, and Dido loved him dearly

[28] Diana, goddess of the hunt.

Since first her father gave her to him, virgin,
And then unlucky bride. She had a brother,   360
Pygmalion, king of Tyre, a monster, evil
In wickedness, and madness came between
Those men, the two of them. Pygmalion murdered
Sychaeus at the altar; he was crazy
And blind for gold and crafty; what did he care
About his sister's love? And he kept it quiet
For a long time, kept telling Dido something
To fool her with false comfort, but Sychaeus
Came to her in a dream, a ghost, unburied,
With the wounds in his breast, the story of the altar,   370
The pale lips blurting out the secret horror,
The crime in the dark of the household. *Flee,* he told her,
Forsake this land; and he told her where the treasure
Lay hidden in earth, uncounted gold and silver.
Dido was moved to flight, secured companions,
All those possessed by fear, all those whom hatred
Had made relentless; ships were standing ready,
As it so happened; they put the gold aboard,
And over the sea the greedy tyrant's treasure
Went sailing, with a woman for a captain.   380
They came here; you will see the walls arising
And the great citadel of the town called Carthage.
Here they bought ground; they used to call it Byrsa,
That being a word for bull's hide; they bought only
What a bull's hide could cover. And now tell me
Who you might be yourselves? what land do you come from,
Bound for what coast?"
                                    And he began his answer
With a long sigh: "O goddess, if I told you
All from the first beginning, if you had leisure
To listen to the record of our trouble,   390
It would take me all day long. From ancient Troy,
In case that name means anything, we come
Driven over many seas, and now a storm
Has whipped us on this coast. I am Aeneas,
A good, devoted man; I carry with me
My household gods, saved from the Greeks; I am known
In heaven; it is Italy I seek,
A homeland for me there, and a race descended
From lofty Jove. With a score of ships we started
Over the Phrygian ocean, following fate   400
And the way my mother pointed. Only seven
Are left us now, battered survivors, after
The rage of wind and wave. And here I wander
The wastes of Libya, unknown and needy,
Driven from Europe and Asia." And his mother
Broke in on his complaining:—"Whoever you are,
Some god must care for you, I think, to bring you

Here to the city of Carthage. Follow on,
Go to the royal palace. For, I tell you,
Your comrades have returned, your fleet is safe,   410
Brought to good haven by the turn of the winds,
Unless the augury my parents taught me
Was foolish nonsense. In the heaven yonder
You see twelve swans, rejoicing in long column,
Scattered, a little while ago, and driven
By the swooping eagle, over all the sky,
But now, it seems, they light on land, or watch
Those who came down before them; as they circle
In company, and make a cheerful sound
With whir of wing or song, so, let me tell you,   420
Your ships and men already enter harbor
Or near it under full sail. Keep on, go forward
Where the path leads."
                                And as she turned, her shoulders
Shone with a radiant light; her hair shed fragrance,
Her robes slipped to her feet, and the true goddess
Walked in divinity.[29] He knew his mother,
And his voice pursued her flight: "Cruel again!
Why mock your son so often with false phantoms?
Why may not hand be joined to hand, and words
Exchanged in truthfulness?" So, still reproachful,   430
He went on toward the city, with Achates,
But Venus cast dark air around their going,
A veil of mist, so that no man might see them
Or lay a hand on them, or halt them, asking
The reasons of their coming. She soared upward
To Paphos, happily home to temple and altars
Steaming with incense, redolent with garlands.
    And they went on, where the little pathway led them
To rising ground; below them lay the city,
Majestic buildings now, where once were hovels,   440
A wonder to Aeneas, gates and bustle
And well-paved streets, the busy Tyrians toiling
With stones for walls and citadel, or marking
Foundations for their homes, drainage and furrow,
All under ordered process. They dredge harbors,
Set cornerstones, quarry the rock, where someday
Their theater will tower. They are like bees
In early summer over the country flowers
When the sun is warm, and the young of the hive emerge,
And they pack the molten honey, bulge the cells   450
With the sweet nectar, add new loads, and harry
The drones away from the hive, and the work glows,
And the air is sweet with bergamot and clover.
"Happy the men whose walls already rise!"

---

[29] A goddess could be distinguished from a mortal by her gait and carriage.

Exclaims Aeneas, gazing on the city,
And enters there, still veiled in cloud—a marvel!—
And walks among the people, and no one sees him.
   There was a grove in the middle of the city,
Most happy in its shade; this was the place
Where first the Tyrians, tossed by storm and whirlwind,   460
Dug up the symbol royal Juno showed them,
The skull of a war-horse, a sign the race to come
Would be supreme in war and wealth, for ages,
And Dido here was building a great temple
In Juno's honor, rich in gifts, and blessed
With the presence of the goddess. Lintel and rafter
Were bronze above bronze stairways, and bronze portals
Swung on bronze hinges. Here Aeneas first
Dared hope for safety, find some reassurance
In hope of better days: a strange sight met him,   470
To take his fear away. Waiting the queen,
He stood there watching, under the great temple,
Letting his eyes survey the city's fortune,
The artist's workmanship, the craftsman's labor,
And there, with more than wonder, he sees the battles
Fought around Troy, and the wars whose fame had travelled
The whole world over; there is Agamemnon,
Priam, and Menelaus,[30] and Achilles,
A menace to them all. He is moved to tears.
"What place in all the world," he asks Achates,   480
"Is empty of our sorrow? There is Priam!
Look! even here there are rewards for praise,
There are tears for things, and what men suffer touches
The human heart. Dismiss your fear; this story
Will bring some safety to you." Sighing often,
He could not turn his gaze away; it was only
A picture on a wall, but the sight afforded
Food for the spirit's need. He saw the Greeks,
Hard-pressed, in flight, and Trojans coming after,
Or, on another panel, the scene reversed,   490
Achilles in pursuit, his own men fleeing;
He saw, and tears came into his eyes again,
The tents of Rhesus,[31] snowy-white, betrayed
In their first sleep by bloody Diomedes
With many a death, and the fiery horses driven
Into the camp, before they ever tasted
The grass of Troy, or drank from Xanthus' river.
Another scene showed Troilus, poor youngster,
Running away, his arms flung down; Achilles

---

[30] Priam was the patriarchal king of Troy, Menelaus was the cuckolded husband of Helen, brother of Agamemnon and co-commander of the Greek forces at Troy.

[31] Rhesus supported the Trojans against the Greeks. Troy could not fall, it was believed, if his horses tasted Troy's grass or drank from its river Xanthus. But before they could do either, Diomede and Ulysses carried the horses off.

Was much too good for him; he had fallen backward   500
Out of his car, but held the reins, and the horses
Dragged him along the ground, his hair and shoulders
Bounding in dust, and the spear making a scribble.
And there were Trojan women, all in mourning,
With streaming hair, on their way to Pallas' temple,
Bearing, as gift, a robe, but the stern goddess[32]
Kept her gaze on the ground. Three times Achilles
Had dragged the body of Hector around the walls,
And was selling it for money. What a groan
Came from Aeneas' heart, seeing that spoil,   510
That chariot, and helpless Priam reaching
His hands, unarmed, across the broken body!
And he saw himself there, too, fighting in battle
Against Greek leaders, he saw the Eastern columns,
And swarthy Memnon's[33] arms. Penthesilea,
The Amazon, blazes in fury, leading
Her crescent-shielded thousands, a golden buckle
Below her naked breast, a soldieress
Fighting with men.
                          And as he watched these marvels
In one long fascinated stare of wonder,   520
Dido, the queen, drew near; she came to the temple
With a great train, all majesty, all beauty,
As on Eurotas' riverside, or where
Mount Cynthus[34] towers high, Diana leads
Her bands of dancers, and the Oreads follow
In thousands, right and left, the taller goddess,
The quiver-bearing maiden, and Latona
Is filled with secret happiness, so Dido
Moved in her company, a queen, rejoicing,
Ordering on her kingdom's rising glory.   530
At Juno's portal, under the arch of the temple,
She took her throne, a giver of law and justice,
A fair partitioner of toil and duty,
And suddenly Aeneas, from the crowd,
Saw Trojan men approaching, brave Cloanthus,
Sergestus, Antheus, and all those others
Whom the black storm had driven here and yonder.
This he cannot believe, nor can Achates,
Torn between fear and joy. They burn with ardor
To seek their comrades' handclasp, but confusion   540
Still holds them in the cloud: what can have happened?
They watch from the cover of mist: men still were coming
From all the ships, chosen, it seemed, as pleaders

---

[32] Pallas (the Greek Athena or Roman Minerva) sided with the Greeks against the Trojans.
[33] Ethiopian king who sided with the Trojans.
[34] Birthplace of Diana, goddess of the hunt. In the passage following, *Oreads* are mountain nymphs, *the taller goddess* refers to Diana, *Latona* was another name for Leto, mother of Diana.

For graciousness before the temple, calling
Aloud: what fortune had been theirs, he wonders,
Where had they left the ships; why were they coming?
They were given audience; Ilioneus,
Senior to all, began: "O Queen, whom Jove
Has given the founding of a great new city,
Has given to bridle haughty tribes with justice,   550
We, pitiful Trojans, over every ocean
Driven by storm, make our appeal: keep from us
The terrible doom of fire; protect our vessels;
Have mercy on a decent race; consider
Our lot with closer interest. We have not come
To ravish Libyan homes, or carry plunder
Down to the shore. We lack the arrogance
Of conquerors; there is no aggression in us.
There is a place which Greeks have given a name,
The Land in the West; it is powerful in arms,   560
Rich in its soil; Oenotrians used to live there,
And now, the story goes, a younger people
Inhabit it, calling themselves Italians
After their leader's name.[35] We were going there
When, big with storm and cloud, Orion[36] rising
Drove us on hidden quicksands, and wild winds
Scattered us over the waves, by pathless rocks
And the swell of the surge. A few of us have drifted
Here to your shores. What kind of men are these,
What barbarous land permits such attitudes?   570
We have been denied the welcome of the beach,
Forbidden to set foot on land; they rouse
All kinds of war against us. You despise,
It may be, human brotherhood, and arms
Wielded by men. But there are gods, remember,
Who care for right and wrong. Our king Aeneas
May be alive; no man was ever more just,
More decent ever, or greater in war and arms.
If fate preserves him still, if he still breathes
The welcome air, above the world of shadows,   580
Fear not; to have treated us with kindly service
Need bring you no repentance. We have cities
In Sicily as well, and King Acestes
Is one of us, from Trojan blood. We ask you
To let us beach our battered fleet, make ready
Beams from the forest timber, mend our oarage,
Seek Italy and Latium, glad at knowing
Our king and comrades rescued. But if safety
Is hopeless for him now, and Libyan water
Has been his grave, and if his son Iulus   590
Is desperate, or lost, grant us permission

[35] Italus, a legendary ruler.   [36] The constellation was believed to presage storms.

At least to make for Sicily, whence we came here,
Where king Acestes has a dwelling for us."
The Trojans, as he ended, all were shouting,
And Dido, looking down, made a brief answer:
"I am sorry, Trojans; put aside your care,
Have no more fear. The newness of the kingdom
And our strict need compel me to such measures—
Sentries on every border, far and wide.
But who so ignorant as not to know   600
The nation of Aeneas, manly both
In deeds and people, and the city of Troy?
We are not as dull as that, we folk from Carthage;
The sun shines on us here. Whether you seek
The land in the west, the sometime fields of Saturn,[37]
Or the Sicilian realms and king Acestes,
I will help you to the limit; should you wish
To settle here and share this kingdom with me,
The city I found is yours; draw up your ships;
Trojan and Tyrian I treat alike.   610
Would, also, that your king were here, Aeneas,
Driven by that same wind. I will send good men
Along the coast to seek him, under orders
To scour all Libya; he may be wandering
Somewhere, in woods or town, surviving shipwreck."
    Aeneas and Achates both were eager
To break the cloud; the queen inspired their spirit
With her address. Achates asked Aeneas:—
"What do we do now, goddess-born? You see
They all are safe, our vessels and our comrades,   620
Only one missing, and we saw him drowning,
Ourselves, beneath the waves; all other things
Confirm what Venus told us." And as he finished,
The cloud around them broke, dissolved in air,
Illumining Aeneas, like a god,
Light radiant around his face and shoulders,
And Venus gave him all the bloom of youth,
Its glow, its liveliness, as the artist adds
Luster to ivory, or sets in gold
Silver or marble. No one saw him coming   630
Until he spoke:—"You seek me; here I am,
Trojan Aeneas, saved from the Libyan waves.
Worn out by all the perils of land and sea,
In need of everything, blown over the great world,
A remnant left by the Greeks, Dido, we lack
The means to thank our only pitier
For offer of a city and a home.
If there is justice anywhere, if goodness

[37] Italy, where Saturn dwelt after his dethronement by Jupiter and his new generation of gods. Saturn's reign is associated with an ancient "golden age" of simplicity.

Means anything to any power, if gods
At all regard good people, may they give 640
The great rewards you merit. Happy the age,
Happy the parents who have brought you forth!
While rivers run to sea, while shadows move
Over the mountains, while the stars burn on,
Always, your praise, your honor, and your name,
Whatever land I go to, will endure."[38]
His hand went out to greet his men, Serestus,
Gyas, Cloanthus, Ilioneus,
The others in their turn. And Dido marvelled
At his appearance, first, and all that trouble 650
He had borne up under; there was a moment's silence
Before she spoke: "What chance, what violence,
O goddess-born, has driven you through danger,
From grief to grief? Are you indeed that son
Whom Venus bore Anchises? I remember
When Teucer came to Sidon,[39] as an exile
Seeking new kingdoms, and my father helped him,
My father, Belus, conqueror of Cyprus.
From that time on I have known about your city,
Your name, and the Greek kings, and the fall of Troy. 660
Even their enemies would praise the Trojans,
Or claim descent from Teucer's line. I bid you
Enter my house. I, too, am fortune-driven
Through many sufferings; this land at last
Has brought me rest. Not ignorant of evil,
I know one thing, at least,—to help the wretched."
And so she led Aeneas to the palace,
Proclaiming sacrifice at all the temples
In honor of his welcome, and sent presents
To his comrades at the shore, a score of bullocks, 670
A hundred swine, a hundred ewes and lambs
In honor of the joyous day. The palace,
Within, is made most bright with pomp and splendor,
The halls prepared for feasting. Crimson covers
Are laid, with fine embroidery, and silver
Is heavy on the tables; gold, engraven,
Recalls ancestral prowess, a tale of heroes
From the race's first beginnings.
                                    And Aeneas,
Being a thoughtful father, speeds Achates
Back to the ships, with tidings for Iulus, 680
He is to join them; all the father's fondness
Is centered on the son. Orders are given

---

[38] Aeneas' words are ironic in the light of later events in the poem and in history.

[39] Teucer was a Greek exiled by his father; he is not to be confused with the Teucer who was the legendary ancestor of the Trojans (who are therefore sometimes called Teucrians). Sidon was a city near Tyre, Dido's former home.

To bring gifts with him, saved from the Trojan ruins,
A mantle stiff with figures worked in gold;
A veil with gold acanthus running through it,
Once worn by Helen, when she sailed from Sparta
Toward that forbidden marriage, a wondrous gift
Made by her mother Leda; and the sceptre
That Ilione, Priam's eldest daughter,
Had carried once; a necklace hung with pearls;   690
A crown of gold and jewels. Toward the ships
Achates sped the message.
                              Meanwhile Venus
Plotted new stratagems, that Cupid, changed
In form and feature, should appear instead
Of young Ascanius,[40] and by his gifts
Inspire the queen to passion, with his fire
Burning her very bones. She feared the house
Held dubious intentions; men of Tyre
Were always two-faced people, and Juno's anger
Vexed her by night. She spoke to her wingèd son:—   700
"O my one strength and source of power, my son,
Disdainful of Jove's thunderbolt, to you
I come in prayer for help. You know that Juno
Is hateful toward Aeneas, keeping him tossing
All over the seas in bitterness; you have often
Grieved with me for your brother. And now Dido
Holds him with flattering words; I do not trust
Juno's ideas of welcome; she will never
Pause at a point like this. Therefore I purpose
To take the queen by cunning, put around her   710
A wall of flame, so that no power can change her,
So that a blazing passion for Aeneas
Will bind her to us. Listen! I will tell you
How you can manage this. The royal boy,
My greatest care, has heard his father's summons
To come to the city, bringing presents, rescued
From the flames of Troy and the sea; and he is ready.
But I will make him drowsy, carry him off
In slumber over Cythera, or hide him
Deep on Idalium[41] in a secret bower   720
Before he learns the scheme or interrupts it.
You, for one night, no more, assume his features,
The boy's familiar guise, yourself a boy,
So that when Dido takes you to her bosom
During the royal feast, with the wine flowing,
And happiness abounding, you, receiving
The sweetness of her kiss, will overcome her

---

[40] Aeneas' son is sometimes called Ascanius, sometimes Iulus.
[41] Cythera was the island associated with Venus' birth; Idalium was a part of Cyprus associated with worship of her.

With secret fire and poison."
                    For his mother
Cupid put off his wings, and went rejoicing
With young Iulus' stride; the real Iulus   730
Venus had lulled in soft repose, and borne him
Warm in her bosom to Idalian groves,
Where the soft marjoram cradled him with blossom
Exhaling shadowy sweetness over his slumber.
And, with Achates leading, Cupid came
Obedient to his mother, bringing gifts.
The queen receives them, on a golden couch
Below the royal tapestries, where spreads
Of crimson wait Aeneas and his Trojans.
Servants bring water for their hands, and bread   740
In baskets, and fine napkins. At the fire
Are fifty serving-maids, to set the feast,
A hundred more, girls, and a hundred boys
To load the tables, and bring the goblets round,
As through the happy halls the Tyrians throng,
Admire the Trojan gifts, admire Iulus,
The young god with the glowing countenance,
The charming words, the robe, the saffron veil
Edged with acanthus. More than all the rest,
Disaster-bound, the unhappy queen takes fire,   750
And cannot have enough of looking, moved
Alike by boy and gifts. She watches him
Cling to his father's neck, or come to her
For fondling, and her eyes, her heart, receive him,
Alas, poor queen, not knowing what a god
Is plotting for her sorrow. He remembers
What Venus told him; she forgets a little
About Sychaeus; the heart unused to love
Stirs with a living passion.
When the first quiet settled over the tables,   760
And the boards were cleared, they set the great bowls down,
Crowning the wine with garlands. A great hum
Runs through the halls, the voices reach the rafters,
The burning lamps below the fretted gold,
The torches flaring, put the night to rout.
The queen commands the loving-cup of Belus,
Heavy with gems and gold, and fills it full,
And silence fills the halls before her prayer:—
"Jupiter, giver of laws for host and guest,
Grant this to be a happy day for all,   770
Both Tyrians and travellers from Troy,
And something for our children to remember!
May Bacchus,[42] giver of joy, attend, and Juno
Be kind, and all my Tyrians be friendly!"

[42] God of wine.

She poured libation on the table, touched
The gold rim with her lips, passed on the bowl
To Bitias, who dove deep, and other lords
Took up the challenge. And a minstrel played
A golden lyre, Iopas, taught by Atlas:[43]
Of the sun's labors and the wandering moon   780
He sang, whence came the race of beasts and man,
Whence rain and fire, the stars and constellations,
Why suns in winter hasten to the sea,
Or what delay draws out the dawdling nights.
The Tyrians roar, applauding, and the Trojans
Rejoice no less, and the poor queen prolongs
The night with conversation, drinking deep
Of her long love, and asking many questions
Of Priam, Hector; of the arms of Memnon;
How big Achilles was; and Diomedes,   790
What were his horses like? "Tell us, my guest,"
She pleads, "from the beginning, all the story,
The treachery of the Greeks, the wanderings,
The perils of the seven tiresome years."

BOOK II: THE FALL OF TROY

They all were silent, watching. From his couch
Aeneas spoke: "A terrible grief, O Queen,
You bid me live again, how Troy went down
Before the Greeks, her wealth, her pitiful kingdom,
Sorrowful things I saw myself, wherein
I had my share and more. Even Ulysses,[1]
Even his toughest soldiery might grieve
At such a story. And the hour is late
Already; night is sliding down the sky
And setting stars urge slumber. But if you long   10
To learn our downfall, to hear the final chapter
Of Troy, no matter how I shrink, remembering,
And turn away in grief, let me begin it.[2]

Broken in war, set back by fate, the leaders
Of the Greek host, as years went by, contrived,
With Pallas' help, a horse as big as a mountain.
They wove its sides with planks of fir, pretending
This was an offering for their safe return,
At least, so rumor had it. But inside

---

[43] The bard Iopas sings of astronomical science, which is associated with Atlas, the gigantic being who in mythology supports the heavens on his shoulders.

[1] The Latin name for Odysseus, the Greek hero.

[2] Typically, epic poems begin in the middle of the story, the earlier events being supplied in a flashback narrative like that of Aeneas in Books II and III.

They packed, in secret, into the hollow sides   20
The fittest warriors; the belly's cavern,
Huge as it was, was filled with men in armor.
There is an island, Tenedos, well-known,
Rich in the days of Priam; now it is only
A bay, and not too good an anchorage
For any ship to trust. They sailed there, hid
On the deserted shore. We thought they had gone,
Bound for Mycenae,[3] and Troy was very happy,
Shaking off grief, throwing the gates wide open.
It was a pleasure, for a change, to go   30
See the Greek camp, station and shore abandoned;
Why, this was where Achilles camped, his minions,
The Dolopes, were here; and the fleet just yonder,
And that was the plain where we used to meet in battle.
Some of us stared in wonder at the horse,
Astounded by its vastness, Minerva's gift,
Death from the virgin goddess, had we known it.
Thymoetes, whether in treachery, or because
The fates of Troy so ordered, was the first one
To urge us bring it in to the heart of the city,   40
But Capys, and some others, knowing better,
Suspicious of Greek plotting, said to throw it
Into the sea, to burn it up with fire,
To cut it open, see what there was inside it.
The wavering crowd could not make up its mind.

And, at that point, Laocoön came running,
With a great throng at his heels, down from the hilltop
As fast as ever he could, and before he reached us,
Cried in alarm: 'Are you crazy, wretched people?
Do you think they have gone, the foe? Do you think that any   50
Gifts of the Greeks lack treachery? Ulysses,—
What was his reputation? Let me tell you,
Either the Greeks are hiding in this monster,
Or it's some trick of war, a spy, or engine,
To come down on the city. Tricky business
Is hiding in it. Do not trust it, Trojans,
Do not believe this horse. Whatever it may be,
I fear the Greeks, even when bringing presents.'
With that, he hurled the great spear at the side
With all the strength he had. It fastened, trembling,   60
And the struck womb rang hollow, a moaning sound.
He had driven us, almost, to let the light in
With the point of the steel, to probe, to tear, but something
Got in his way, the gods, or fate, or counsel,
Ill-omened, in our hearts; or Troy would be standing
And Priam's lofty citadel unshaken.

---

[3] City in Greece ruled by Agamemnon, the Greek commander.

Meanwhile, some Trojan shepherds, pulling and hauling,
Had a young fellow, with his hands behind him,
Tied up, and they were dragging him to Priam.
He had let himself be taken so, on purpose,   70
To open Troy to the Greeks, a stranger, ready
For death or shifty cunning, a cool intriguer,
Let come what may. They crowd around to see him,
Take turns in making fun of him, that captive.
Listen, and learn Greek trickiness; learn all
Their crimes from one.
He stopped in the middle, frightened and defenceless,
Looked at the Trojan ranks,—'What land, what waters,
Can take me now?' he cried, 'There is nothing, nothing
Left for me any more, no place with the Greeks,   80
And here are the Trojans howling for my blood!'
Our mood was changed. We pitied him, poor fellow,
Sobbing his heart out. We bade him tell his story,
His lineage, his news: what can he count on,
The captive that he is? His fear had gone
As he began: 'O King, whatever happens,
I will tell the truth, tell all of it; to start with,
I own I am a Greek. Sinon is wretched,
Fortune has made him so, but she will never
Make him a liar. You may perhaps have heard   90
Rumors of Palamedes, son of Belus,[4]
A man of glorious fame. But the Greeks killed him,—
He was against the war, and so they killed him,
An innocent man, by perjury and lying
False witness. Now that he is dead they mourn him.
My father, his poor relative, had sent me
To soldier in his company; I was then
Scarcely beyond my boyhood. Palamedes
Held, for some time, some influence and standing
In royal councils, and we shared his glory,   100
But, and all men know this, Ulysses' hatred,
His cunning malice, pulled him down; thereafter
I lived in darkness, dragging out a lifetime
In sorrow for my innocent lord, and anger,
And in my anger I was very foolish,
I talked; I vowed, if I got home to Argos,
I would have vengeance: so I roused Ulysses
To hate me in his turn, and that began it,
Downfall and evil, Ulysses always trying
To frighten me with hint and accusation,   110
With rumors planted where the crowd would listen;
Oh yes, Ulysses knew what he was doing,

---

[4] Not to be confused with Dido's father Belus, mentioned in Book I.

He never stopped, until with Calchas[5] working
Hand in glove with him—why am I telling this,
And what's the use? I am stalling. All the Greeks,
You think, are all alike; what more do you want?
Inflict the punishment. That would be something
Ulysses would rejoice in, and some others
Pay handsome money for!'

But we were all on fire to hear him further.   120
Pelasgian[6] craft meant nothing to our folly.
Trembling and nervous, he resumed his lying:
'The Greeks were tired of the long war; they often
Wanted to sail from Troy for home. Oh, would
That they had only done it! But a storm
Would cut them off, or the wrong wind terrify them.
Especially, just after the horse was finished,
With the joined planks of maple, all the heaven
Roared loud with storm-clouds. In suspense and terror
We sent Eurypylus to ask Apollo   130
What could be done; the oracle was gloomy,
Foreboding: "Blood, O Greeks, and a slain virgin[7]
Appeased the winds when first you came here; blood
Must pay for your return, a life be given,
An Argive life." The word came to our ears
With terror in it, our blood ran cold in our veins,
For whom was fate preparing? who would be
The victim of Apollo? Then Ulysses
Dragged Calchas into our midst, with a great uproar,
Trying his best to make the prophet tell us   140
What the gods wanted. And there were many then
Who told me what was coming, or kept silent
Because they saw, and all too well, the scheme
Ulysses had in mind. For ten days Calchas
Said nothing at all, hid in his tent, refusing
To have a word of his pronounce the sentence,
And all the time Ulysses kept on shouting,
Till Calchas broke, and doomed me to the altar.
And all assented; what each man had feared
In his own case, he bore with great composure   150
When turned another way.
The terrible day was almost on me; fillets
Were ready for my temples, the salted meal
Prepared, the altars standing. But I fled,
I tore myself away from death, I admit it,

---

[5] As a Greek priest and prophet, Calchas' task was to discover and reveal the will of the gods.

[6] Here a synonym for "Greek."

[7] Iphigenia, daughter of Agamemnon; her life had been sacrificed to appease the gods and thus gain for the Greeks favorable winds for their expedition against Troy.

I hid all night in sedge and muddy water
At the edge of the lake, hoping, forever hoping,
They might set sail. And now I hope no longer
To see my home, my parents, or my children,
Poor things, whom they will kill because I fled them,   160
Whom they will murder for my sacrilege.
But oh, by the gods above, by any power
That values truth, by any uncorrupted
Remnant of faith in all the world, have pity,
Have pity on a soul that bears such sorrow,
More than I ever deserved.'
He had no need to ask us. Priam said,
Untie him, and we did so with a promise
To spare his life. Our king, with friendly words,
Addressed him, saying, 'Whoever you are, forget   170
The Greeks, from now on. You are ours; but tell me
Why they have built this monstrous horse? who made it,
Who thought of it? What is it, war-machine,
Religious offering?' And he, instructed
In every trick and artifice, made answer,
Lifting his hands, now free: 'Eternal fires,
Inviolable godhead, be my witness,
You altars, you accursèd swords, you fillets
Which I as victim wore, I had the right
To break those solemn bonds, I had the right   180
To hate those men, to bring whatever they hide
Into the light and air; I am bound no longer
To any country, any laws, but, Trojans,
Keep to the promise, if I tell the truth,
If I pay back with interest.
All the Greek hope, since first the war began,
Rested in Pallas, always. But Ulysses,
The crime-contriver, and the son of Tydeus[8]
Attacked Minerva's temple, stole her image
Out of the holy shrine, and slew the guards,   190
And laid their bloody hands upon the goddess,
And from that time the Danaan[9] hopes were broken,
Faltered and failed. It was no doubtful anger
Pallas revealed; she gave them signs and portents.
From her image in the camp the upraised eyes
Shot fire, and sweat ran salty down the limbs,
Thrice from the ground she seemed to flash and leap
With vibrant spear and clashing shield. The priest,
Calchas, made prophecy: they must take to flight
Over the sea, and Troy could not be taken   200
Without new omens; they must go to Argos,
Bring back the goddess again, whom they have taken
In curved ships over the sea. And if they have gone,

---

[8] His son was Diomede, one of the greatest of the Greek warriors.   [9] Greek.

They are bound for home, Mycenae, for new arms,
New gods, new soldiers; they will be here again
When least expected. Calchas' message warned them,
And so they built this image, to replace
The one they had stolen, a gigantic offering
For a tremendous sacrilege. It was Calchas,
Again, who bade them build a mass so mighty   210
It almost reached the stars, too big to enter
Through any gate, or be brought inside the walls.
For if your hands should damage it, destruction,
(May God avert it) would come upon the city,
But if your hands helped bring it home, then Asia
Would be invading Greece, and doom await
Our children's children.'
                We believed him, we
Whom neither Diomede nor great Achilles
Had taken, nor ten years, nor that armada,
A thousand ships of war. But Sinon did it   220
By perjury and guile.
                Then something else,
Much greater and more terrible, was forced
Upon us, troubling our unseeing spirits.
Laocoön, allotted priest of Neptune,
Was slaying a great bull beside the altars,
When suddenly, over the tranquil deep
From Tenedos,—I shudder even now,
Recalling it—there came a pair of serpents
With monstrous coils, breasting the sea, and aiming
Together for the shore. Their heads and shoulders   230
Rose over the waves, upright, with bloody crests,
The rest of them trailing along the water,
Looping in giant spirals; the foaming sea
Hissed under their motion. And they reached the land,
Their burning eyes suffused with blood and fire,
Their darting tongues licking the hissing mouths.
Pale at the sight, we fled. But they went on
Straight toward Laocoön, and first each serpent
Seized in its coils his two young sons, and fastened
The fangs in those poor bodies. And the priest   240
Struggled to help them, weapons in his hand.
They seized him, bound him with their mighty coils,
Twice round his waist, twice round his neck, they squeezed
With scaly pressure, and still towered above him.
Straining his hands to tear the knots apart,
His chaplets[10] stained with blood and the black poison,
He uttered horrible cries, not even human,
More like the bellowing of a bull when, wounded,
It flees the altar, shaking from the shoulder

---

[10] Garlands for the head.

The ill-aimed axe. And on the pair went gliding   250
To the highest shrine, the citadel of Pallas,
And vanished underneath the feet of the goddess
And the circle of her shield.
                                        The people trembled
Again; they said Laocoön deserved it,
Having, with spear, profaned the sacred image.
It must be brought to its place, they cried, the goddess
Must be appeased. We broke the walls, exposing
The city's battlements, and all were busy
Helping the work, with rollers underfoot
And ropes around the neck. It climbed our walls,   260
The deadly engine. Boys, unwedded girls
Sang alleluias round it, all rejoicing
To have a hand on the tow-rope. It came nearer,
Threatening, gliding, into the very city.
O motherland! O Ilium, home of gods,
O walls of Troy! Four times it stopped, four times
The sound of arms came from it, and we pressed on,
Unheedful, blind in madness, till we set it,
Ill-omened thing, on the citadel we worshipped.
And even when Cassandra[11] gave us warning,   270
We never believed her; so a god had ordered.
That day, our last, poor wretches, we were happy,
Garlanding the temples of the gods
All through the town.
                              And the sky turned, and darkness
Came from the ocean, the great shade covering earth
And heaven, and the trickery of the Greeks.
Sprawling along the walls, the Trojans slumbered,
Sleep holding their weary limbs, and the Greek armada,
From Tenedos, under the friendly silence
Of a still moon, came surely on. The flagship   280
Blazed at the masthead with a sudden signal,
And Sinon, guarded by the fates, the hostile
Will of the gods, swung loose the bolts; the Greeks
Came out of the wooden womb. The air received them,
The happy captains, Sthenelus, Ulysses,
Thessandrus, Acamas, Achilles' son
Called Neoptolemus, Thoas, Machaon,
Epeos, who designed the thing,—they all
Came sliding down the rope, and Menelaus
Was with them in the storming of a city   290
Buried in sleep and wine. The watch was murdered,
The open doors welcome the rush of comrades,
They marshal the determined ranks for battle.
        It was the time when the first sleep begins

---

[11] A daughter of the royal family of Troy; gifted with prophecy, she was nevertheless doomed always to have her true prophecies disbelieved.

For weary mortals, heaven's most welcome gift.
In sleep, before my eyes, I seemed to see
Hector, most sorrowful, black with bloody dust,
Torn, as he had been, by Achilles' car,
The thong-marks on his swollen feet. How changed
He was from that great Hector who came, once,   300
Triumphant in Achilles' spoil, from hurling
Fire at the Grecian ships. With ragged beard,
Hair matted with his blood, wearing the wounds
He earned around the walls of Troy, he stood there.
It seemed that I spoke first:—'O light of Troy,
Our surest hope, we have long been waiting for you,
What shores have kept you from us? Many deaths,
Much suffering, have visited our city,
And we are tired. Why do I see these wounds?
What shame has caused them?' Those were foolish questions;   310
He made no answer but a sigh or a groan,
And then: 'Alas, O goddess-born! Take flight,
Escape these flames! The enemy has the walls,
Troy topples from her lofty height; enough
Has been paid out to Priam and to country.
Could any hand have saved them, Hector's would have.
Troy trusts to you her household gods, commending
Her holy things to you; take them, companions
Of destiny; seek walls for them, and a city
To be established, a long sea-wandering over.'   320
From the inner shrine he carried Vesta's chaplets
In his own hands, and her undying fire.

    Meanwhile, the city is all confusion and sorrow;
My father Anchises' house, remote and sheltered
Among its trees, was not so far away
But I could hear the noises, always clearer,
The thickening din of war. Breaking from sleep,
I climb to the roof-top, listening and straining
The way a shepherd does on the top of a mountain
When fire goes over the corn, and the winds are roaring,   330
Or the rush of a mountain torrent drowns the fields
And the happy crops and the work of men and oxen
And even drags great trees over. And then I knew
The truth indeed; the craft of the Greeks was hidden
No longer from my sight. The house of a neighbor,
Deiphobus, went up in flames; next door,
Ucalegon was burning. Sigeum's[12] water
Gave back the glow. Men shouted, and the trumpets
Blared loud. I grab my arms, with little purpose,
There was no sense in it, but my heart was burning   340
To mass a band for war, rush to the hilltop

---

[12] A cape near Troy.

With comrades at my side. Anger and frenzy
Hurry me on. A decent death in battle
Is a helpful thought, sometimes.

    And here came Panthus, running from the weapons,
Priest of Apollo, and a son of Othrys,
With holy relics in his hands, and dragging
His little grandson, here came Panthus, running
In madness to my door. 'How goes it, Panthus?
What stronghold still is ours?' I had hardly spoken,   350
When he began, with a groan: 'It has come, this day
Will be our last, and we can not escape it.
Trojans we have been, Troy has been, and glory
Is ours no more. Fierce Jupiter has taken
Everything off to Argos, and Greeks lord it
In a town on fire. The horse, high in the city,
Pours out armed men, and Sinon, arrogant victor,
Lights up more fires. The gates are standing open,
And men are there by the thousands, ever as many
As came once from Mycenae; others block   360
The narrow streets, with weapons drawn; the blades
Flash in the dark; the point is set for murder.
A few of the guards are trying, striking blindly,
For all the good it does.'

    His words, or the gods' purpose, swept me on
Toward fire and arms, where the grim furies call,
And the clamor and confusion, reaching heaven.
Ripheus joined me, Epytus, mighty in arms,
Came to my side in the moonlight, Hypanis, Dymas,
And young Coroebus, Mygdon's son, poor youngster,   370
Mad with a hopeless passion for Cassandra,
He wanted to help Priam, but never heeded
The warnings of his loved one.
                    As they ranged
Themselves for battle, eager, I addressed them:
'O brave young hearts, it will do no good; no matter.
Even if your will is fixed, to follow a leader
Taking the final risk, you can't help seeing
The fortune of our state. The gods have gone,
They have left their shrines and altars, and the power
They once upheld is fallen. You are helping   380
A town already burnt. So let us die,
Rush into arms. One safety for the vanquished
Is to have hope of none.'
                    They were young, and angry.
Like wolves, marauders in black mist, whom hunger
Drives blindly on, whose whelps, abandoned, wait them
Dry-jawed, so we went on, through foes, through weapons,

To certain death; we made for the heart of the city,
Black night around us with its hollow shadow.
Who could explain that night's destruction, equal
Its agony with tears? The ancient city,   390
A power for many years, comes down, and corpses
Lie littering the streets and homes and altars.
Not only Trojans die. The old-time valor
Returns to the vanquished heart, and the Greek victors
Know what it is to fall. Everywhere sorrow,
Everywhere panic, everywhere the image
Of death, made manifold.

    Out of a crowd of Greeks comes one Androgeos,
Thinking us allies, hailing us as friendly:
'Why men, where have you been, you dawdling fellows?   400
Hurry along! Here is plunder for the taking,
Others are busy at it, and you just coming
From the high ships!' And then he knew he had blundered;
He had fallen in with foes, who gave no answer.
He stopped, stepped back, like a man who treads on a serpent
Unseen in the rough brush, and then in panic
Draws back as the purple neck swells out in anger.
Even so, Androgeos pulled away in terror.
We rush them, swarm all over them; they are frightened,
They do not know their ground, and fortune favors   410
Our first endeavor. Coroebus, a little crazy
With nerve and luck, cries out: 'Comrades, where fortune
First shows the way and sides with us, we follow.
Let us change our shields, put on the Grecian emblems!
All's fair in war: we lick them or we trick them,
And what's the odds?' He takes Androgeos' helmet,
Whose plume streams over his head, takes up the shield
With proud device, and fits the sword to his side.
And Ripheus does the same, and so does Dymas,
And all the others, happily being armed   420
With spoil, new-won. We join the Greeks, all going
Under no gods of ours, in the night's darkness
Wade into many a fight, and Greeks by the dozens
We send to hell. And some of them in panic
Speed to the ships; they know that shore, and trust it,
And some of them—these were the abject cowards—
Climb scrambling up the horse's sides, again
Take refuge in the womb.

    It is not for men to trust unwilling gods.
Cassandra was being dragged from Pallas' temple,   430
Her hair loosed to the wind, her eyes turned upward
To heaven for mercy; they had bound her hands.
Coroebus could not bear that sight; in madness

He threw himself upon them, and he died.
We followed, all of us, into the thick of it,
And were cut down, not only by Greeks; the rooftops,
Held by our friends, rained weapons: we were wearing
Greek crests and armor, and they did not know us.
And the Greeks came on, shouting with anger, burning
To foil that rescue; there was Menelaus,   440
And Agamemnon, and the savage Ajax,
And a whole army of them. Hurricanes
Rage the same way, when winds from different quarters
Clash in the sky, and the forest groans, and Neptune
Storms underneath the ocean. Those we routed
Once in the dark came back again from the byways
And alleys of the town; they mark our shields,
Our lying weapons, and our foreign voices.
Of course we are outnumbered. Peneleus
It was, who slew Coroebus, at the altar   450
Sacred to Pallas. Ripheus fell, a man
Most just of all the Trojans, most fair-minded.
The gods thought otherwise. Hypanis, Dymas,
Were slain by their own men, and Panthus' goodness
Was no protection, nor his priestly office.
I call to witness Troy, her fires, her ashes,
And the last agonies of all our people
That in that hour I ran from no encounter
With any Greek, and if the fates had been
For me to fall in battle, there I earned it.   460
The current swept me off, with two companions,
One, Iphitus, too slow with age, the other,
Pelias, limping from Ulysses' wound.
The noise kept calling us to Priam's palace.

    There might have been no fighting and no dying
Through all the city, such a battle raged
Here, from the ground to roof-top. At the threshold
Waves of assault were breaking, and the Greeks
Were climbing, rung by rung, along the ladders,
Using one hand, the right one up and forward   470
Over the battlements, the left one thrust
In the protecting shield. And over their heads
The Trojans pried up towers and planking, wrecking
The building; gilded beams, the spoils of their fathers,
Were ample weapons for the final moment.
Some had the doorways blocked, others, behind them,
Were ready with drawn swords. We had a moment
When help seemed possible; new reinforcement
Might yet relieve the palace.
There was a secret entrance there, a passage   480
All the way through the building, a postern gate,

Where, while the kingdom stood, Andromache[13]
Would go, alone, or bring the little boy,
Astyanax, to Hector's father and mother.
I climbed to the top of the roof, where the poor Trojans
Were hurling down their unavailing darts.
A tower stood on the very edge, a look-out
Over all Troy, the ships and camp of the Greeks.
This we attacked with steel, where the joints were weakest,
And pried it up, and shoved it over. It crashed,   490
A noisy ruin, over the hostile columns;
But more kept coming up; the shower of stones
And darts continued raining.
Before the entrance, at the very threshold
Stood Pyrrhus,[14] flashing proudly in bronze light,
Sleek as a serpent coming into the open,
Fed on rank herbs, wintering under the ground,
The old slough cast, the new skin shining, rolling
His slippery length, reaching his neck to the sun,
While the forked tongue darts from the mouth. Automedon   500
Was with him, Periphas, Achilles' driver,
A giant of a man, and the host from Scyros,[15]
All closing in on the palace, and hurling flames.
Among the foremost, Pyrrhus, swinging an axe,
Burst through, wrenched the bronze doors out of their hinges,
Smashed through the panelling, turned it into a window.
The long halls came to view, the inner chambers
Of Priam and the older kings; they see
Armed warriors at the threshold.
Within, it is all confusion, women wailing,   510
Pitiful noise, groaning, and blows; the din
Reaches the golden stars. The trembling mothers
Wander, not knowing where, or find a spot
To cling to; they would hold and kiss the doors.
Pyrrhus comes on, aggressive as his father;
No barrier holds him back; the gate is battered
As the ram[16] smashes at it; the doors come down.
Force finds a way; the Greeks pour in, they slaughter
The first one in their path; they fill the courtyard
With soldiery, wilder than any river   520
In flood over the banks and dikes and ploughland.
I saw them, Pyrrhus, going mad with murder,
And Atreus' twin sons,[17] and Hecuba
I saw, and all her daughters, and poor old Priam,
His blood polluting the altars he had hallowed.

---

[13] Wife of Hector and mother of Astyanax. Hector's parents are Priam and Hecuba, king and queen of Troy.
[14] Achilles' son, fierce like his war-loving father.   [15] Birthplace of Pyrrhus.
[16] The battering-ram.   [17] Agamemnon and Menelaus.

The fifty marriage-chambers,[18] the proud hope
Of an everlasting line, are violated,
The doors with the golden spoil are turned to splinters.
Whatever the fire has spared the Greeks take over.
    You would ask, perhaps, about the fate of Priam?   530
When he saw the city fall, and the doors of the palace
Ripped from the hinge, and the enemy pouring in,
Old as he was, he went and found his armor,
Unused so many years, and his old shoulders
Shook as he put it on. He took his sword,
A useless weapon, and, doomed to die, went rushing
Into the midst of the foe. There was an altar
In the open court-yard, shaded by a laurel
Whose shadow darkened the household gods, and here
Hecuba and her daughters had come thronging,   540
Like doves by a black storm driven. They were praying
Here at the altar, and clinging to the gods,
Whatever image was left. And the queen saw Priam
In the arms of his youth. 'O my unhappy husband,'
She cried, 'have you gone mad, to dress yourself
For battle, so? It is all no use; the time
Needs better help than yours; not even my Hector
Could help us now. Come to me, come to the altar;
It will protect us, or at least will let us
Die all together.' And she drew him to her.   550
    Just then through darts, through weapons, came Polites,
A son of Priam, fleeing deadly Pyrrhus,
Down the long colonnades and empty hallways,
Wounded, and Pyrrhus after him, vicious, eager
For the last spear-thrust, and he drives it home;
Polites falls, and his life goes out with his blood,
Father and mother watching. And then Priam,
In the very grip of death, cried out in anger:—
"If there is any righteousness in heaven,
To care about such wickedness, the gods   560
Will have the right reward and thanks to offer
A man like this, who has made a father witness
The murder of his son, the worst pollution!
You claim to be Achilles' son. You liar!
Achilles had some reverence, respected
A suppliant's right and trust; he gave me back
My Hector's lifeless body[19] for the tomb,
And let me go to my kingdom.' With the word
He flung a feeble spear, which dropped, deflected
From the rough bronze; it had hung there for a moment.   570

---

[18] The quarters of Priam's fifty sons and their wives; Priam also had fifty daughters.
[19] After killing Hector, Achilles agreed to return the corpse to Hector's father Priam. (See Homer's *Iliad*, Book XXIV.) Achilles himself has since been slain, struck in the heel (his one vulnerable spot) by an arrow from Paris' bow.

And Pyrrhus sneered: 'So, go and tell my father
The latest news: do not forget to mention,
Old messenger-boy, my villainous behavior,
And what a bastard Pyrrhus is. Now die!'
He dragged the old man, trembling, to the altar,
Slipping in his son's blood; he grabbed his hair
With the left hand, and the right drove home the sword
Deep in the side, to the hilt. And so fell Priam,
Who had seen Troy burn and her walls come down, once monarch,
Proud ruler over the peoples and lands of Asia.   580
He lies, a nameless body, on the shore,
Dismembered, huge, the head torn from the shoulders.
    Grim horror, then, came home to me. I saw
My father when I saw the king, the life
Going out with the cruel wound. I saw Creusa[20]
Forsaken, my abandoned home, Iulus,
My little son. I looked around. They all
Had gone, exhausted, flung down from the walls,
Or dead in the fire, and I was left alone.
    And I saw Helen, hiding, of all places,   590
At Vesta's shrine, and clinging there in silence,
But the bright flames lit the scene. That hated woman,
Fearing both Trojan anger and Greek vengeance,
A common fury to both lands, was crouching
Beside the altar. Anger flared up in me
For punishment and vengeance. Should she then,
I thought, come home to Sparta safe, uninjured
Walk through Mycenae,[21] a triumphant queen?
See husband, home, parents and children, tended
By Trojan slave-girls? This, with Priam fallen   600
And Troy burnt down, and the shore soaked in blood?
Never! No memorable name, I knew,
Was won by punishing women, yet, for me,
There might be praise for the just abolition
Of this unholiness, and satisfaction
In vengeance for the ashes of my people.
All this I may have said aloud, in frenzy,
As I rushed on, when to my sight there came
A vision of my lovely mother, radiant
In the dark night, a goddess manifest,   610
As tall and fair as when she walks in heaven.
She caught me by the hand and stopped me:[22]—'Son,
What sorrow rouses this relentless anger,
This violence? Do you care for me no longer?
Consider others first, your aged father,

---

[20] Aeneas' wife.
[21] The meaning is "Greece" (from the home city of Agamemnon, the Greek commander). Helen's actual home city was Sparta.
[22] Though she is Aeneas' mother, Venus as goddess of love naturally protects Helen, the most beautiful of all women.

Anchises; is your wife Creusa living?
Where is Iulus? Greeks are all around them,
Only my love between them, fire and sword.
It is not for you to blame the Spartan woman,
Daughter of Tyndareus, or even Paris.   620
The gods are the ones, the high gods are relentless;
It is they who bring this power down, who topple
Troy from the high foundation. Look! Your vision
Is mortal dull, I will take the cloud away,—
Fear not a mother's counsel. Where you see
Rock torn from rock, and smoke and dust in billows,
Neptune is working, plying the trident, prying
The walls from their foundations. And see Juno,
Fiercest of all, holding the Scaean gates,
Girt with the steel, and calling from the ships   630
Implacable companions. On the towers,—
Turn, and be certain—Pallas takes command
Gleaming with Gorgon and storm-cloud. Even Jove,
Our father, nerves the Greeks with fire and spirit,
And spurs the other gods against the Trojans.
Hasten the flight, my son; no other labor
Waits for accomplishment. I promise safety
Until you reach your father's house.' She had spoken
And vanished in the thickening night of shadows.
Dread shapes come into vision, mighty powers,   640
Great gods at war with Troy, which, so it seemed,
Was sinking as I watched, with the same feeling
As when on mountain-tops you see the loggers
Hacking an ash-tree down, and it always threatens
To topple, nodding a little, and the leaves
Trembling when no wind stirs, and dies of its wounds
With one long loud last groan, and dirt from the ridges
Heaves up as it goes down with roots in air.
Divinity my guide, I leave the roof-top,
I pass unharmed through enemies and blazing,   650
Weapons give place to me, and flames retire.

     At last I reached the house, I found my father,
The first one that I looked for. I meant to take him
To the safety of the hills, but he was stubborn,
Refusing longer life or barren exile,
Since Troy was dead. 'You have the strength,' he told me,
'You are young enough, take flight. For me, had heaven
Wanted to save my life, they would have spared
This home for me. We have seen enough destruction,
More than enough, survived a captured city.   660
Speak to me as a corpse laid out for burial,
A quick farewell, and go. Death I shall find
With my own hand; the enemy will pity,

Or look for spoil. The loss of burial[23]
Is nothing at all. I have been living too long
Hated by gods and useless, since the time
Jove blasted me[24] with lightning wind and fire.'
He would not move, however we wept, Creusa,
Ascanius, all the house, insistent, pleading
That he should not bring all to ruin with him.   670
He would not move, he would not listen. Again
I rush to arms, I pray for death; what else
Was left to me? 'Dear father, were you thinking
I could abandon you, and go? what son
Could bear a thought so monstrous? If the gods
Want nothing to be left of so great a city,
If you are bound, or pleased, to add us all
To the wreck of Troy, the way is open for it—
Pyrrhus will soon be here; from the blood of Priam
He comes; he slays the son before the father,   680
The sire at the altar-stone; O my dear mother,
Was it for this you saved me, brought me through
The fire and sword, to see our enemies
Here in the very house, and wife and son
And father murdered in each other's blood?
Bring me my arms; the last light calls the conquered.
Let me go back to the Greeks, renew the battle,
We shall not all of us die unavenged.'
      Sword at my side, I was on the point of going,
Working the left arm into the shield. Creusa   690
Clung to me on the threshold, held my feet,
And made me see my little son:—'Dear husband,
If you are bent on dying, take us with you,
But if you think there is any hope in fighting,
And you should know, stay and defend the house!
To whom are we abandoned, your father and son,
And I, once called your wife?' She filled the house
With moaning outcry. And then something happened,
A wonderful portent. Over Iulus' head,
Between our hands and faces, there appeared   700
A blaze of gentle light; a tongue of flame,
Harmless and innocent, was playing over
The softness of his hair, around his temples.
We were afraid, we did our best to quench it
With our own hands, or water, but my father
Raised joyous eyes to heaven, and prayed aloud:—
'Almighty Jupiter, if any prayer
Of ours has power to move you, look upon us,
Grant only this, if we have ever deserved it,

---

[23] Failure to receive proper burial was a grievous misfortune. See Book VI.
[24] The god took revenge because Anchises boasted of Venus' love for him.

Grant us a sign, and ratify the omen!'   710
He had hardly spoken, when thunder on the left
Resounded, and a shooting star from heaven
Drew a long trail of light across the shadows.
We saw it cross above the house, and vanish
In the woods of Ida,[25] a wake of gleaming light
Where it had sped, and a trail of sulphurous odor.
This was a victory: my father rose
In worship of the gods and the holy star,
Crying: 'I follow, son, wherever you lead;
There is no delay, not now; Gods of my fathers,   720
Preserve my house, my grandson; yours the omen,
And Troy is in your keeping. O my son,
I yield, I am ready to follow.' But the fire
Came louder over the walls, the flames rolled nearer
Their burning tide. 'Climb to my shoulders, father,
It will be no burden, so we are together,
Meeting a common danger or salvation.
Iulus, take my hand; Creusa, follow
A little way behind. Listen, you servants!
You will find, when you leave the city, an old temple   730
That once belonged to Ceres;[26] it has been tended
For many years with the worship of our fathers.
There's a little hill there, and a cypress tree;
And that's where we shall meet, one way or another.
And one thing more: you, father, are to carry
The holy objects and the gods of the household,
My hands are foul with battle and blood, I could not
Touch them without pollution.'
                                        I bent down
And over my neck and shoulders spread the cover
Of a tawny lion-skin, took up my burden;   740
Little Iulus held my hand, and trotted,
As best he could, beside me; Creusa followed.
We went on through the shadows. I had been
Brave, so I thought, before, in the rain of weapons
And the cloud of massing Greeks. But now I trembled
At every breath of air, shook at a whisper,
Fearful for both my burden and companion.
    I was near the gates, and thinking we had made it,
But there was a sound, the tramp of marching feet,
And many of them, it seemed; my father, peering   750
Through the thick gloom, cried out:—'Son, they are coming!
Flee, flee! I see their shields, their gleaming bronze.'
Something or other took my senses from me
In that confusion. I turned aside from the path,
I do not know what happened then. Creusa

---

[25] A mountain and mountain range near Troy.
[26] Goddess of the fields and harvest.

Was lost;[27] she had missed the road, or halted, weary,
For a brief rest. I do not know what happened,
She was not seen again; I had not looked back,
Nor even thought about her, till we came
To Ceres' hallowed home. The count was perfect,   760
Only one missing there, the wife and mother.
Whom did I not accuse, of gods and mortals,
Then in my frenzy? What worse thing had happened
In the city overthrown? I left Anchises,
My son, my household gods, to my companions,
In a hiding-place in the valley; and I went back
Into the city again, wearing my armor,
Ready, still one more time, for any danger.
I found the walls again, the gate's dark portals,
I followed my own footsteps back, but terror,   770
Terror and silence were all I found. I went
On to my house. She might, just might, have gone there.
Only the Greeks were there, and fire devouring
The very pinnacles. I tried Priam's palace;
In the empty courtyards Phoenix and Ulysses
Guarded the spoils piled up at Juno's altar.
They had Trojan treasure there, loot from the altars,
Great drinking-bowls of gold, and stolen garments,
And human beings. A line of boys and women
Stood trembling there.   780
I took the risk of crying through the shadows,
Over and over, 'Creusa!' I kept calling,
'Creusa!' and 'Creusa!' but no answer.
No sense, no limit, to my endless rushing
All through the town; and then at last I saw her,
Or thought I did, her shadow a little taller
Than I remembered. And she spoke to me
Beside myself with terror:—'O dear husband,
What good is all this frantic grief? The gods
Have willed it so, Creusa may not join you   790
Out of this city; Jupiter denies it.
Long exile lies ahead, and vast sea-reaches
The ships must furrow, till you come to land
Far in the West; rich fields are there, and a river
Flowing with gentle current; its name is Tiber.
And happy days await you there, a kingdom,
A royal wife. Banish the tears of sorrow
Over Creusa lost. I shall never see
The arrogant houses of the Myrmidons,[28]
Nor be a slave to any Grecian woman;   800

---

[27] The loss, literally, of Creusa (exactly what happens to her is not clear) may indicate
something about Aeneas' priorities, but it is providentially necessary that Aeneas be free to
marry Lavinia as part of the Trojans' later establishment of themselves in Italy.
[28] The Greek soldiers who had been led by Achilles.

I am a Dardan woman; I am the wife
Of Venus' son; it is Cybele[29] who keeps me
Here on these shores. And now farewell, and love
Our son.' I wept, there was more to say; she left me,
Vanishing into empty air. Three times
I reached out toward her, and three times her image
Fled like the breath of a wind or a dream on wings.
The night was over; I went back to my comrades.
    I was surprised to find so many more
Had joined us, ready for exile, pitiful people,   810
Mothers, and men, and children, streaming in
From everywhere, looking for me to lead them
Wherever I would. Over the hills of Ida
The morning-star was rising; in the town
The Danaans held the gates, and help was hopeless.
I gave it up, I lifted up my father,
Together we sought the hills.

BOOK III: THE WANDERINGS OF AENEAS

"After the gods' decision to overthrow
The Asian world, the innocent house of Priam,
And the proud city, built by Neptune, smoked
From the ruined ground, we were driven, different ways,
By heaven's auguries, seeking lands forsaken.
Below Antandros,[1] under Phrygian Ida,
We built a fleet, and gathered men, uncertain
Of either direction or settlement. The summer
Had scarce begun, when at my father's orders,
We spread our sails. I wept as I left the harbor,   10
The fields where Troy had been. I was borne, an exile
Over the deep, with son, companions, household,
And household gods.
                        Far off there lies a land,
Sacred to Mars; the Thracians[2] used to till it,
Whose king was fierce Lycurgus; they were friendly,
Of old, to Troy, when we were prosperous. Hither
I sailed, and on its curving shore established
A city site; Aeneadae, I called it.
This I began, not knowing fate was adverse.

---

[29] A goddess identified with Rhea, consort of Saturn during the reign of the older gods. It is possible that Creusa has not died but rather has been mysteriously inducted into the service of Cybele.
[1] A town near Troy.
[2] Inhabitants of Thrace, an area north of the Aegean Sea, northwest of the Hellespont strait (the modern Dardanelles).

I was offering my mother proper homage,   20
And other gods, to bless the new beginnings,
I had a white bull ready as a victim
To the king of the gods. There was a mound nearby,
Bristling with myrtle and with cornel-bushes.
I needed greenery to veil the altar,
But as I struggled with the leafy branches,
A fearful portent met my gaze. Black drops
Dripped from the ends of the roots, black blood was falling
On the torn ground, and a cold chill went through me.
I tried again; the shoot resisted; blood   30
Followed again. Troubled, I prayed to the Nymphs,
To the father of the fields, to bless the vision,
Remove the curse; and down on my knees I wrestled
Once more against the stubborn ground, and heard
A groan from under the hillock, and voice crying:
'Why mangle a poor wretch, Aeneas? Spare me,
Here in the tomb, and save your hands pollution.
You know me, I am Trojan-born, no stranger,
This is familiar blood. Alas! Take flight,
Leave this remorseless land; the curse of greed   40
Lies heavy on it. I am Polydorus,
Pierced by an iron harvest; out of my body
Rise javelins and lances.' I was speechless,
Stunned, in my terror.
        Priam, forever unfortunate, had sent
This Polydorus on a secret mission,
Once, to the king of Thrace, with gold for hiding
When the king despaired of the siege and the city's fortune.
And when Troy fell, and Fortune failed, the Thracian
Took Agamemnon's side, broke off his duty,   50
Slew Polydorus, took the gold. There is nothing
To which men are not driven by that hunger.
Once over my fear, I summoned all the leaders,
My father, too; I told them of the portent,
Asked for their counsel. All agreed, a land
So stained with violence and violation
Was not for us to dwell in. Southward ho!
For Polydorus we made restoration
With funeral rites anew; earth rose again
Above his outraged mound; dark fillets made   60
The altar sorrowful, and cypress boughs,
And the Trojan women loosed their hair in mourning.
We offered milk in foaming bowls, and blood
Warm from the victims, so to rest the spirit,
And cry aloud the voice of valediction.
        Then, when we trust the sea again, and the wind
Calls with a gentle whisper, we crowd the shores,

Launch ship again, leave port, the lands and cities
Fade out of sight once more.
                                   There is an island[3]
In the middle of the sea; the Nereids' mother[4]   70
And Neptune hold it sacred. It used to wander
By various coasts and shores, until Apollo,
In grateful memory, bound it fast, unmoving,
Unfearful of winds, between two other islands
Called Myconos and Gyaros. I sailed there;
Our band was weary, and the calmest harbor
Gave us safe haven. This was Apollo's city;
We worshipped it on landing. And their king,
Priest of Apollo also, came to meet us,
His temples bound with holy fillets, and laurel.   80
His name was Anius; he knew Anchises
As an old friend, and gave us joyful welcome.
      Apollo's temple was built of ancient rock,
And there I prayed: 'Grant us a home, Apollo,
Give walls to weary men, a race, a city
That will abide; preserve Troy's other fortress,
The remnant left by the Greeks and hard Achilles.
Whom do we follow? where are we bidden to go
To find our settlement? An omen, father!'
      I had scarcely spoken, when suddenly all things trembled,   90
The doors, and the laurel, and the whole mountain moved,
And the shrine was opened, and a rumbling sound
Was heard. We knelt, most humbly; and a voice
Came to our ears: 'The land which brought you forth,
Men of endurance, will receive you home.
Seek out your ancient mother. There your house
Will rule above all lands, your children's children,
For countless generations.' Apollo spoke,
And we were joyful and confused, together:
What walls were those, calling the wanderers home?   100
My father, pondering history, made answer:
'Hear, leaders; learn your hopes. There is a land
Called Crete, an island in the midst of the sea,
The cradle of our race; it has a mountain,
Ida, like ours, a hundred mighty cities,
Abounding wealth; if I recall correctly,
Teucer, our greatest father, came from there
To the Rhoetean[5] shores to found his kingdom.
Ilium was nothing then, the towers of Troy
Undreamed of; men lived in the lowly valleys.   110
And Cybele, the Great Mother, came from Crete
With her clashing cymbals, and her grove of Ida
Was named from that original; the silence

---

[3] Delos, an island in the Aegean, was the birthplace of Apollo.
[4] Doris; Nereids are sea-nymphs.   [5] Trojan.

Of her mysterious rites, the harnessed lions
Before her chariot wheels, all testify
To Cretan legend. Come, then, let us follow
Where the gods lead, and seek the Cretan kingdom.
It is not far; with Jupiter to favor,
Three days will see us there. With prayer, he made
Most solemn sacrifice, a bull to Neptune,   120
One to Apollo, to Winter a black heifer,
A white one for fair winds.

                    The story ran
That no one lived in Crete, Idomeneus[6]
Having left his father's kingdom, that the houses
Were empty now, dwellings vacated for us.
We sailed from Delos, flying over the water
Past Naxos, on whose heights the Bacchae revel,
Past green Donysa, snowy Paros,[7] skimming
The passages between the sea-sown islands.
No crew would yield to another; there is shouting,   130
And the cheer goes up, 'To Crete, and the land of our fathers!'
A stern wind follows, and we reach the land.
I am glad to be there; I lay out the walls
For the chosen city, name it Pergamea,[8]
And the people are happy. *Love your hearths,* I told them,
Build high the citadel. The ships were steadied
On the dry beach, the young were busy ploughing,
Or planning marriage, and I was giving laws,
Assigning homes. But the weather turned, the sky
Grew sick, and from the tainted heaven came   140
Pestilence and pollution, a deadly year
For people and harvest. Those who were not dying
Dragged weary bodies around; the Dog-Star[9] scorched
The fields to barrenness; grass withered, corn
Refused to ripen. 'Over the sea again!'
My father said, 'let us return to Delos,
Consult the oracle, implore Apollo
To show us kindliness; what end awaits
Our weary destiny, where does he bid us turn
For help in trouble?'   150
    Sleep held all creatures over the earth at rest;
In my own darkness visions came, the sacred
Images of the household gods I had carried
With me from Troy, out of the burning city.
I saw them plain, in the flood of light, where the moon

[6] Former king of Crete who fought against Troy. In fulfillment of a vow to kill the first living thing he saw after returning to Crete, he murdered his son. His people thereafter banished him, the gods having visited a plague on Crete as punishment.

[7] Naxos, Donysa, and Paros are islands in the south Aegean, passed during the southward voyage to Crete.

[8] Named for Pergamus, the citadel of Troy.

[9] Sirius, the brightest star in the sky, first visible in the hot days of late summer.

Streamed through the dormers. And they eased me, saying:
'Apollo would tell you this, if you went over
The sea again to Delos; from him we come
To you, with willing spirit. We came with you
From the burnt city, we have followed still   160
The swollen sea in the ships; in time to come
We shall raise your sons to heaven, and dominion
Shall crown their city. Prepare to build them walls,
Great homes for greatness; do not flee the labor,
The long, long toil of flight. Crete, says Apollo,
Is not the place. There is a land in the West,
Called by the Greeks, Hesperia:[10] anciency
And might in arms and wealth enrich its soil.
The Oenotrians lived there once; now, rumor has it,
A younger race has called it Italy   170
After the name of a leader, Italus.
Dardanus came from there, our ancestor,
As Iasius[11] was. There is our dwelling-place.
Be happy, then, waken, and tell Anchises
Our certain message: seek the land in the West.
Crete is forbidden country.'
        The vision shook me, and the voice of the gods;
(It was not a dream, exactly; I seemed to know them,
Their features, the veiled hair, the living presence.)
I woke in a sweat, held out my hands to heaven,   180
And poured the pure libation for the altar,
Then, gladly, to Anchises. He acknowledged
His own mistake, a natural confusion,
Our stock was double, of course; no need saying
We had more ancestors than one. 'Cassandra,'
Anchises said, 'alone, now I remember,
Foretold this fate; it seemed she was always talking
Of a land in the West, and Italian kingdoms, always.
But who would ever have thought that any Trojans
Would reach the shores in the West? Or, for that matter,   190
Who ever believed Cassandra? Let us yield
To the warning of Apollo, and at his bidding
Seek better fortunes.' So we obeyed him,
Leaving this place, where a few stayed, and sailing
The hollow keels over the mighty ocean.
        We were in deep water, and the land no longer
Was visible, sky and ocean everywhere.
A cloud, black-blue, loomed overhead, with night
And tempest in it, and the water roughened
In shadow; winds piled up the sea, the billows   200
Rose higher; we were scattered in the surges.
Clouds took away the daylight, and the night

[10] The western region of the world, associated with Hesperus, the evening star.
[11] Brother of Dardanus.

Was dark and wet in the sky, with lightning flashing.
We wandered, off our course, in the dark of ocean,
And our pilot, Palinurus, swore he could not
Tell day from night, nor the way among the waters.
For three lost days, three starless nights, we rode it,
Saw land on the fourth, mountains and smoke arising.
The sails came down, we bent to the oars; the sailors
Made the foam fly, sweeping the dark blue water.   210
I was saved from the waves; the Strophades received me,
(The word means Turning-point in the Greek language),[12]
Ionian islands where the dire Celaeno
And other Harpies[13] live, since Phineus' house
Was closed to them, and they feared their former tables.
No fiercer plague of the gods' anger ever
Rose out of hell, girls with the look of birds,
Their bellies fouled, incontinent, their hands
Like talons, and their faces pale with hunger.
We sailed into the harbor, happy to see   220
Good herds of cattle grazing over the grass
And goats, unshepherded. We cut them down
And made our prayer and offering to Jove,
Set trestles on the curving shore for feasting.
Down from the mountains with a fearful rush
And a sound of wings like metal came the Harpies,
To seize our banquet, smearing dirtiness
Over it all, with a hideous kind of screaming
And a stinking smell. We found a secret hollow
Enclosed by trees, under a ledge of rock,   230
Where shade played over; there we moved the tables
And lit the fire again; the noisy Harpies
Came out of somewhere, sky, or rock, and harried
The feast again, the filthy talons grabbing,
The taint all through the air. *Take arms,* I ordered,
We have to fight them. And my comrades, hiding
Their shields in the grass, lay with their swords beside them,
And when the birds swooped screaming, and Misenus
Sounded the trumpet-signal, they rose to charge them,
A curious kind of battle, men with sword-blades   240
Against the winged obscenities of ocean.
Their feathers felt no blow, their backs no wound,
They rose to the sky as rapidly as ever,
Leaving the souvenirs of their foul traces
Over the ruined feast. And one, Celaeno,
Perched on a lofty rock, squawked out a warning:—

[12] The Strophades are islands west of Greece, in the Ionian Sea. The Trojans have rounded the southwest corner of Greece; from this time until shortly after they leave Helenus and Andromache, their course will be northwest, along the shore and among the islands of Greece that face Sicily and southern Italy.

[13] Foul creatures sent originally by Jove to punish Phineus, king of Thrace, whence the Harpies have emigrated. Celaeno is their leader.

'Is it war you want, for slaughtered goats and bullocks,
Is it war you bring, you sons of liars, driving
The innocent Harpies from their father's kingdom?
Take notice, then, and let my words forever   250
Stick in your hearts; what Jove has told Apollo,
Apollo told me, and I, the greatest fury,
Shove down your throats; it is Italy you are after,
And the winds will help you, Italy and her harbors
You will reach, all right; but you will not wall the city
Till, for the wrong you have done us, deadly hunger
Will make you gnaw and crunch your very tables!'[14]
She flew back to the forest. My companions
Were chilled with sudden fear; their spirit wavered,
They call on me, to beg for peace, not now   260
With arms, but vows and praying, filthy birds
Or ill-foreboding goddesses, no matter.
Anchises prayed with outstretched hands, appeasing
The mighty gods with sacrifice:—'Be gracious,
Great gods, ward off the threats, spare the devoted!'
He bade us tear the cable from the shore,
Shake loose the sails. And a wind sprang up behind us,
Driving us northward; we passed many islands,
Zacynthus, wooded, Dulichium, and Same,
The cliffs of Neritus, Laertes' kingdom,   270
With a curse as we went by for Ithaca,
Land of Ulysses. Soon Leucate's headland
Came into view, a dreadful place for sailors,
Where Apollo had a shrine. We were very weary
As we drew near the little town; the anchor
Was thrown from the prow, the sterns pulled up on the beaches.

    This was unhoped-for land; we offered Jove
Our purifying rites, and had the altars
Burning with sacrifice. We thronged the shore
With games of Ilium. Naked, oiled for wrestling,   280
The young held bouts, glad that so many islands
Held by the Greeks were safely passed. A year
Went by, and icy winter roughened the waves
With gales from the north. A shield of hollow bronze,
Borne once by Abas,[15] I fastened to the door-posts,
And set a verse below it: *Aeneas won*
These arms from the Greek victors. I gave the order
To man the thwarts and leave this harbor; all
Obeyed, swept oars in rivalry. We left
Phaeacia's airy heights, coasting Epirus,   290
Drawn to Buthrotum, a Chaonian harbor.

[14] This prophecy will be fulfilled, in an unexpectedly casual way, in Book VII, when the
hungry Trojans eat the wheaten platters on which they have placed fruit.
[15] Not the Trojan mentioned in the storm-scene of Book I, but rather a Greek killed at
Troy. The present scene takes place at the site of the future naval battle of Actium, where in
31 B.C. Octavian defeated Mark Antony and Cleopatra; see the Introduction to Virgil.

And here we met strange news, that Helenus,
The son of Priam, was ruling Grecian cities,
Having won the wife of Pyrrhus and his crown,
And that Andromache once more had married
A lord of her own race. Amazed, I burn
With a strange longing to seek out that hero,
To learn his great adventures. It so happened,
Just as I left the landing, that was the day
Andromache, in a grove before the city,   300
By the waters of a river that resembled
The Simois at home, was offering homage,
Her annual mourning-gift to Hector's ashes,
Calling his ghost to the place which she had hallowed
With double altars, a green and empty tomb.
I found her weeping there, and she was startled
At the sight of me, and Trojan arms, a shock
Too great to bear: she was rigid for a moment,
And then lost consciousness, and a long time later
Managed to speak: 'Is it real, then, goddess-born?   310
What are you, living messenger or phantom,
Mortal or ghost? If the dear light has left you,
Tell me where Hector is.' I was moved, so deeply
I found it hard to answer to her tears
And through my own, but I did say a little:—
'I am alive; I seem to keep on living
Through all extremes of trouble; do not doubt me,
I am no apparition. And what has happened
To you, dear wife of Hector? Could any gain
Atone for such a loss? Has fortune tried   320
To even matters at all? Does Pyrrhus still
Presume on you as husband?' With lowered gaze
And quiet voice she answered:—'Happy the maiden
Slain at the foeman's tomb, at the foot of the walls;
Happy the daughter of Priam, who never knew
The drawing of the lots,[16] nor came to the bed
Of a conqueror, his captive. After the fire
I travelled different seas, endured the pride
Achilles filled his son with, bore him children
In bondage, till he tired of me and left me   330
For Leda's daughter and a Spartan marriage.
He passed me on to Helenus, fair enough,
Slave-woman to slave-man; but then Orestes,[17]
Inflamed with passion for his stolen bride,
And maddened by the Furies of his vengeance,
Caught Pyrrhus off-guard, and slew him at the altar
In his ancestral home. And Pyrrhus dying,

---

[16] For the division of the women among the conquerors.
[17] Pyrrhus married Hermione (daughter of Menelaus and Helen and thus Leda's grand-daughter, not her daughter), to whom Orestes had been betrothed.

Part of the kingdom came to Helenus,
Who named the fields Chaonian, the land
Chaonia, after a man from Troy,   340
And filled the heights, as best he could, with buildings
To look like those we knew. But what of yourself?
What winds, what fate, have brought you here, or was it
Some god? did you know you were on our coast? How is
The boy Ascanius, living still, whom Troy
Might have—does he ever think about his mother?
Does he want to be a hero, a manly spirit,
Such as his father was, and his uncle Hector?'
She was in tears again, when the son of Priam,
Helenus, with an escort, came from the city,   350
Happy to recognize us, bringing us in
With tears and greeting mingled. I went on,
Seeing a little Troy, low walls that copied
The old majestic ramparts, a tiny river
In a dry bed, trying to be the Xanthus,
I found the Scaean gates, to hold and cling to.
My Trojans, too, were fond of the friendly town,
Whose king received them in wide halls; libations
Were poured to the gods, and feasts set on gold dishes.
    Day after day went by, and the winds were calling   360
And the sails filling with a good south-wester.
I put my questions to the king and prophet:
'O son of Troy, the god's interpreter,
Familiar with the tripod and the laurel
Of great Apollo, versed in stars and omens,
Bird-song and flying wing, be gracious to me,
Tell me,—for heaven has prophesied a journey
Without mischance, and all the gods have sent me
The counsel of their oracles, to follow
Italy and a far-off country; one,   370
But one, Celaeno, prophesied misfortune,
Wrath and revolting hunger,—tell me, prophet,
What dangers first to avoid, what presence follow
To overcome disaster?'
                          Bullocks slain
With proper covenant, and the chaplets loosened,
He led me to the temple of Apollo,
The very gates, where the god's presence awed me,
And where he spoke, with eloquent inspiration:—
'O goddess-born, the journey over the sea
Holds a clear sanction for you, under Jove,   380
Who draws the lots and turns the wheel of Fate.
I will tell you some few things, not all, that safely
You may go through friendly waters, and in time
Come to Ausonian[18] harborage; the rest

_____
[18] Italian.

Helenus does not know, or, if he did,
Juno would stop his speaking. First of all,
Italy, which you think is near, too fondly
Ready to enter her nearest port, is distant,
Divided from you by a pathless journey
And longer lands between. The oar must bend   390
In the Sicilian ocean, and the ships
Sail on a farther coast, beyond the lakes
Of an infernal world, beyond the isles
Where dwells Aeaean Circe,[19] not till then
Can the built city rise on friendly ground.
Keep in the mind the sign I give you now:
One day, when you are anxious and alone
At the wave of a hidden river, you will find
Under the oaks on the shore, a sow, a white one,
Immense, with a new-born litter, thirty young   400
At the old one's udders; that will be the place,
The site of the city, the certain rest from labor.
And do not fear the eating of the tables,
The fates will find a way, Apollo answer.
Avoid this coast of Italy,[20] the lands
Just westward of our own; behind those walls
Dwell evil Greeks, Narycian Locri, soldiers
Of the Cretan king, Idomeneus; the plains
Are full of them; a Meliboean captain
Governs Petelia, a tiny town   410
Relying on her fortress! Philoctetes
Commands her walls. And furthermore, remember,
Even when the ships have crossed the sea and anchored,
When the altars stand on the shore, and the vows are paid,
Keep the hair veiled, and the robe of crimson drawn
Across the eyes, so that no hostile visage
May interfere, to gaze on the holy fire
Or spoil the sacred omens. This rite observe[21]
Through all the generations; keep it holy.
From that first landing, when the wind brings you down   420
To Sicily's coast, and narrow Pelorus widens
The waters of her strait, keep to the left,
Land on the left, and water on the left,
The long way round; the right is dangerous.
Avoid it. There's a story that this land

---

[19] A sorceress who, during Odysseus' wanderings as described in Homer's *Odyssey*, Book X, changed his men into swine. Aeaea is her home island.

[20] In the following lines, Helenus advises Aeneas to avoid the eastern coast of Italy (infested with people hostile to the Trojans) and to sail around Sicily rather than through the narrow passage (the modern straits of Messina) dividing Sicily from the Italian mainland. The straits are guarded on both sides, by a rock and whirlpool mythologized as, respectively, Scylla and Charybdis.

[21] As often in the poem, Virgil ascribes an ancient origin to Roman religious ritual of later times.

Once broke apart—(time brings so many changes)—
By some immense convulsion, though the lands
Had been one country once. But now between them
The sea comes in, and now the waters bound
Italian coast, Sicilian coast; the tide   430
Washes on severed shores, their fields, their cities.
Scylla keeps guard on the right; on the left Charybdis,
The unappeasable; from the deep gulf she sucks
The great waves down, three times; three times she belches
Them high up into the air, and sprays the stars.
Scylla is held in a cave, a den of darkness,
From where she thrusts her huge jaws out, and draws
Ships to her jagged rocks. She looks like a girl
Fair-breasted to the waist, from there, all monster,
Shapeless, with dolphins' tails, and a wolf's belly.   440
Better to go the long way round, make turning
Beyond Pachynus,[22] than to catch one glimpse
Of Scylla the misshapen, in her cavern,
And the rocks resounding with the dark-blue sea-hounds.
And one thing more than any, goddess-born,
I tell you over and over: pray to Juno,
Give Juno vows and gifts and overcome her
With everlasting worship. So you will come
Past Sicily and reach Italian beaches.
You will come to a town called Cumae,[23] haunted lakes,   450
And a forest called Avernus, where the leaves
Rustle and stir in the great woods, and there
You will find a priestess, in her wildness singing
Prophetic verses under the stones, and keeping
Symbols and signs on leaves. She files and stores them
In the depth of the cave; there they remain unmoving,
Keeping their order, but if a light wind stirs
At the turn of a hinge, and the door's draft disturbs them,
The priestess never cares to catch them fluttering
Around the halls of rock, put them in order,   460
Or give them rearrangement. Men who have come there
For guidance leave uncounselled, and they hate
The Sibyl's dwelling. Let no loss of time,
However comrades chide and chafe, however
The wind's voice calls the sail, postpone the visit
To this great priestess; plead with her to tell you
With her own lips the song of the oracles.
She will predict the wars to come, the nations
Of Italy, the toils to face, or flee from;
Meet her with reverence, and she, propitious,   470
Will grant a happy course. My voice can tell you

---

[22] The southeastern corner of Sicily, which is triangular.
[23] The meeting with the Sibyl of Cumae, in preparation for Aeneas' descent into the
Lower World, occurs in Book VI.

No more than this. Farewell; raise Troy to heaven.'
  After the friendly counsel, other gifts
Were sent to our ships, carved ivory, and gold,
And heavy silver, cauldrons from Dodona,
A triple breastplate linked with gold, a helmet
Shining with crested plume, the arms of Pyrrhus.
My father, too, has gifts; horses and guides
Are added, and sailing-men, and arms for my comrades.
Anchises bade the fleet prepare; the wind   480
Was rising, why delay? But Helenus
Spoke to Anchises, in compliment and honor:—
'Anchises, worthy of Venus' couch, and the blessing
Of other gods, twice saved from Trojan ruins,
Yonder behold Ausonia! Near, and far,
It lies, Apollo's offering; sail westward.
Farewell, made blest by a son's goodness. I
Am a nuisance with my talking.'
                              And his queen,
Sad at the final parting, was bringing gifts,
Robes woven with a golden thread, a Trojan   490
Scarf for Ascanius, all courteous honor
Given with these:—'Take them, my child; these are
The work of my own hands, memorials
Of Hector's wife Andromache, and her love.
Receive these farewell gifts; they are for one
Who brings my own son back to me; your hands,
Your face, your eyes, remind me of him so,—
He would be just your age.'
                              I, also, wept,
As I spoke my words of parting: 'Now farewell;
Your lot is finished, and your rest is won,   500
No ocean fields to plough, no fleeing fields
To follow, you have your Xanthus and your Troy,
Built by your hands, and blest by happier omens,
Far from the path of the Greeks. But we are called
From fate to fate; if ever I enter Tiber
And Tiber's neighboring lands, if ever I see
The walls vouchsafed my people, I pray these shores,
Italy and Epirus, shall be one,
The life of Troy restored, with friendly towns
And allied people. A common origin,   510
A common fall, was ours. Let us remember,
And our children keep the faith.'
    Over the sea we rode, the shortest run
To Italy, past the Ceraunian rocks.[24]
The sun went down; the hills were dark with shadow.

---

[24] After this point, the Trojan fleet changes its course; hereafter, until the storm that beaches it at Carthage, the fleet will sail southwest past the heel along the sole of the "boot" of southern Italy, then clockwise around Sicily.

The oars assigned, we drew in to the land
For a little welcome rest; sleep overcame us,
But it was not yet midnight when our pilot
Sprang from his blanket, studying the winds,
Alert and listening, noting the stars   520
Wheeling the silent heaven, the twin Oxen,
Arcturus and the rainy Kids. All calm,
He saw, and roused us; camp was broken; the sail
Spread to the rushing breeze, and as day reddened
And the stars faded, we saw a coast, low-lying,
And made out hills. 'Italy!', cried Achates,
'Italy!' all the happy sailors shouted.
Anchises wreathed a royal wine-bowl, stood
On the high stern, calling:—'Gods of earth and ocean
And wind and storm, help us along, propitious   530
With favoring breath!' And the breeze sprang up, and freshened;
We saw a harbor open, and a temple
Shone on Minerva's headland. The sails came down,
We headed toward the land. Like the curve of a bow
The port turned in from the Eastern waves; its cliffs
Foamed with the salty spray, and towering rocks
Came down to the sea, on both sides, double walls,
And the temple fled the shore. Here, our first omen,
I saw four horses grazing, white as snow,
And father Anchises cried:—'It is war you bring us,   540
Welcoming land, horses are armed for war,
It is war these herds portend. But there is hope
Of peace as well. Horses will bend to the yoke
And bear the bridle tamely.' Then we worshipped
The holy power of Pallas, first to hear us,
Kept our heads veiled before the solemn altar,
And following Helenus' injunction, offered
Our deepest prayer to Juno.
                                        And sailed on,
With some misgiving, past the homes of Greeks;
Saw, next, a bay, Tarentum, and a town   550
That rumor said was Hercules'; against it,
The towers of Caulon rose, and Scylaceum,[25]
Most dangerous to ships, and a temple of Juno.
Far off, Sicilian Etna[26] rose from the waves,
And we heard the loud sea roar, and the rocks resounding,
And voices broken on the coast; the shoals
Leaped at us, and the tide boiled sand. My father
Cried in alarm:—'This must be that Charybdis
Helenus warned us of. Rise to the oars,
O comrades, pull from the danger!' They responded   560
As they did, always, Palinurus swinging

[25] Tarentum, Caulon, and Scylaceum were cities lying along the sole of the "boot" of Italy.
[26] A volcano.

The prow to the waves on the left, and all our effort
Strained to the left, with oars and sail. One moment
We were in the clouds, the next in the gulf of Hell;
Three times the hollow rocks and reefs roared at us,
Three times we saw spray shower the very stars,
And the wind went down at sunset; we were weary,
Drifting, in ignorance, to the Cyclops[27] shores.

    There is a harbor, safe enough from wind,
But Etna thunders near it, crashing and roaring,   570
Throwing black clouds up to the sky, and smoking
With swirling pitchy color, and white-hot ashes,
With balls of flame puffed to the stars, and boulders,
The mountain's guts, belched out, or molten rock
Boiling below the ground, roaring above it.
The story goes that Enceladus, a giant,
Struck by a bolt of lightning, lies here buried
Beneath all Etna's weight, with the flames pouring
Through the broken furnace-flues; he shifts his body,
Every so often, to rest his weariness,   580
And then all Sicily seems to moan and tremble
And fill the sky with smoke. We spent the night here,
Hiding in woods, enduring monstrous portents,
Unable to learn the cause. There were no stars,
No light or fire in the sky; the dead of the night,
The thick of the cloud, obscured the moon.

                                 And day
Arrived, at last, and the shadows left the heaven,
And a man came out of the woods, a sorry figure,
In hunger's final stages, reaching toward us
His outstretched hands. We looked again. His beard   590
Unshorn, his rags pinned up with thorns, and dirty,
He was, beyond all doubt of it, a Greek,
And one of those who had been at Troy in the fighting.
He saw, far off, the Trojan dress and armor,
Stopped short, for a moment, almost started back
In panic, then, with a wild rush, came on,
Pleading and crying:—'By the stars I beg you,
By the gods above, the air we breathe, ah Trojans,
Take me away from here, carry me off
To any land whatever; that will be plenty.   600
I know I am one of the Greeks, I know I sailed
With them, I warred against the gods of Ilium,
I admit all that; drown me for evil-doing,
Cut me to pieces, scatter me over the waves.
Kill me. If I must die, it will be a pleasure
To perish at the hands of men.' He held
Our knees and clung there, grovelling before us.
We urged him tell his story, his race, his fortune.

[27] One-eyed giants.

My father gave him his hand, a pledge of safety,
And his fear died down a little.

                                'I come,' he said,   610
'From Ithaca, a companion of Ulysses;
My name is Achaemenides;[28] my father,
His name was Adamastus, was a poor man,
And that was why I came to Troy. My comrades
Left me behind here, in their terrible hurry,
To leave these cruel thresholds. The Cyclops live here
In a dark cave, a house of gore, and banquets
Soaking with blood. It is dark inside there, monstrous.
He hits the stars with his head—Dear gods, abolish
This creature from the world!—he is not easy   620
To look at; he is terrible to talk to.
His food is the flesh of men, his drink their blood.
I saw him once myself, with two of our men
In that huge fist of his; he lay on his back
In the midst of the cave, and smashed them on a rock,
And the whole place swam with blood; I watched him chew them
The limbs with black clots dripping, the muscles, warm,
Quivering as he bit them. But we got him!
Ulysses did not stand for this; he kept
His wits about him, never mind the danger.   630
The giant was gorged with food, and drunk, and lolling
With sagging neck, sprawling all over the cavern
Belching and drooling blood-clots, bits of flesh,
And wine all mixed together. And we stood
Around him, praying, and drew lots,—we had found a stake
And sharpened it at the end,—and so we bored
His big eye out; it glowered under his forehead
The size of a shield, or a sun. So we got vengeance
For the souls of our companions. But flee, I tell you,
Get out of here, poor wretches, cut the cables,   640
Forsake this shore. There are a hundred others
As big as he is, and just like him, keeping
Sheep in the caves of the rocks, a hundred others
Wander around this coast and these high mountains.
I have managed for three months, hiding in forests,
In the caves of beasts, on a rocky look-out, watching
The Cyclops, horribly frightened at their cries
And the tramp of their feet. I have lived on plants and berries,
Gnawed roots and bark. I saw this fleet come in,
And I did not care; whatever it was, I gladly   650
Gave myself up. At least, I have escaped them.
Whatever death you give is more than welcome.'
And as he finished, we saw that very giant,
The shepherd Polyphemus, looming huge

---

[28] One of Ulysses', or Odysseus', sailors. The story he summarizes here is told in Homer's
Odyssey, Book IX.

Over his tiny flock; he was trying to find
His way to the shore he knew, a shapeless monster,
Lumbering, clumping, blind in the dark, with a stumble,
And the step held up with trunk of a pine. No comfort
For him, except in the sheep. He reached the sand,
Wading into the sea, and scooped up water   660
To wash the ooze of blood from the socket's hollow,
Grinding his teeth against the pain, and roaring,
And striding into the water, but even so
The waves were hardly up to his sides. We fled
Taking on board our Greek; we cut the cable,
Strained every nerve at the oars. He heard, and struggled
Toward the splash of the wave, but of course he could not catch us,
And then he howled in a rage, and the sea was frightened,
Italy deeply shaken, and all Etna
Rumbled in echoing terror in her caverns.   670
Out of the woods and the thicket of the mountains
The Cyclops came, the others, toward the harbor,
Along the coast-line. We could see them standing
In impotent anger, the wild eye-ball glaring,
A grim assortment, brothers, tall as mountains
Where oak and cypress tower, in the groves
Of Jove or great Diana. In our speed
And terror, we sailed anywhere, forgetting
What Helenus had said: Scylla, Charybdis,
Were nothing to us then. But we remembered   680
In time, and a north wind came from strait Pelorus,
We passed Pantagia,[29] and the harbor-mouth
Set in the living-rock, Thapsus, low-lying,
The bay called Megara: all these were places
That Achaemenides knew well, recalling
The scenes of former wanderings with Ulysses.
    An island faces the Sicanian bay
Against Plemyrium, washed by waves; this island
Has an old name, Ortygia. The story
Tells of a river, Alpheus, come from Elis,[30]   690
By a secret channel undersea, to join
The Arethusan fountains, mingling here
With the Sicilian waters. Here we worshipped
The land's great gods; went on, to pass Helorus,
A rich and marshy land; and then Pachynus
Where the cliffs rose sharp and high; and Camerina,
With firm foundation; the Geloan plains,
And Gela, named for a river; then Acragas,

[29] The places named in the following lines are located on the east and south coasts of Sicily; Drepanum lies directly opposite Carthage, across a narrow part of the Mediterranean, and is thus approximately where the action of Book I begins.

[30] Part of Greece; thus the river Alpheus must flow under the Ionian and Mediterranean seas to join the fountain Arethusa. According to the myth, Alpheus was a river god in love with the nymph Arethusa.

A towering town, high-walled, and sometime famous
For its breed of horses; the city of palms, Selinus;   700
The shoals of Lilybaeum, where the rocks
Are a hidden danger; so at last we came
To Drepanum, a harbor and a shoreline
That I could not rejoice in, a survivor
Of all those storms of the sea. For here I lost
My comforter in all my care and trouble,
My father Anchises. All the storms and perils,
All of the weariness endured, seemed nothing
Compared with this disaster; and I had
No warning of it; neither Helenus,   710
Though he foretold much trouble, nor Celaeno,
That evil harpy, prophesied this sorrow.
There was nothing more to bear; the long roads ended
At that unhappy goal; and when I left there,
Some god or other brought me to your shores.'

And so he told the story, a lonely man
To eager listeners, destiny and voyage,
And made an end of it here, ceased, and was quiet.

BOOK IV: AENEAS AND DIDO

But the queen finds no rest. Deep in her veins
The wound is fed; she burns with hidden fire.
His manhood, and the glory of his race
Are an obsession with her, like his voice,
Gesture and countenance. On the next morning,
After a restless night, she sought her sister:
"I am troubled, Anna, doubtful, terrified,
Or am I dreaming? What new guest is this
Come to our shores? How well he talks, how brave
He seems in heart and action! I suppose   10
It must be true; he does come from the gods.
Fear proves a bastard spirit. He has been
So buffeted by fate. What endless wars
He told of! Sister, I must tell you something:
Were not my mind made up, once and for all,
Never again to marry, having been
So lost when Sychaeus left me for the grave,
Slain by my murderous brother at the altar,
Were I not sick forever of the torch[1]
And bridal bed, here is the only man   20
Who has moved my spirit, shaken my weak will.
I might have yielded to him. I recognize

[1] Carried in wedding processions; an emblem of marriage.

The marks of an old fire. But I pray, rather,
That earth engulf me, lightning strike me down
To the pale shades and everlasting night
Before I break the laws of decency.[2]
My love has gone with Sychaeus; let him keep it,
Keep it with him forever in the grave."
She ended with a burst of tears. "Dear sister,
Dearer than life," Anna replied, "why must you   30
Grieve all your youth away in loneliness,
Not know sweet children, or the joys of love?
Is that what dust demands, and buried shadows?
So be it. You have kept your resolution
From Tyre to Libya, proved it by denying
Iarbas and a thousand other suitors
From Africa's rich kingdoms. Think a little.
Whose lands are these you settle in? Getulians,
Invincible in war, the wild Numidians,
Unfriendly Syrtes, ring us round, and a desert   40
Barren with drought, and the Barcaean rangers.
Why should I mention Tyre, and wars arising
Out of Pygmalion's threats? And you, my sister,
Why should you fight against a pleasing passion?
I think the gods have willed it so, and Juno
Has helped to bring the Trojan ships to Carthage.
What a great city, sister, what a kingdom
This might become, rising on such a marriage!
Carthage and Troy together in arms, what glory
Might not be ours? Only invoke the blessing   50
Of the great gods, make sacrifice, be lavish
In welcome, keep them here while the fierce winter
Rages at sea, and cloud and sky are stormy,
And ships still wrecked and broken."
                                        So she fanned
The flame of the burning heart; the doubtful mind
Was given hope, and the sense of guilt was lessened.
And first of all they go to shrine and altar
Imploring peace; they sacrifice to Ceres,
Giver of law, to Bacchus, to Apollo,
And most of all to Juno, in whose keeping   60
The bonds of marriage rest. In all her beauty
Dido lifts up the goblet, pours libation
Between the horns of a white heifer, slowly,
Or, slowly, moves to the rich altars, noting
The proper gifts to mark the day, or studies
The sacrificial entrails for the omens.
Alas, poor blind interpreters! What woman
In love is helped by offerings or altars?
Soft fire consumes the marrow-bones, the silent

---

[2] Dido had sworn to remain faithful to her dead husband.

Wound grows, deep in the heart.   70
Unhappy Dido burns, and wanders, burning,
All up and down the city, the way a deer
With a hunter's careless arrow in her flank
Ranges the uplands, with the shaft still clinging
To the hurt side. She takes Aeneas with her
All through the town, displays the wealth of Sidon,
Buildings projected; she starts to speak, and falters,
And at the end of the day renews the banquet,
Is wild to hear the story, over and over,
Hangs on each word, until the late moon, sinking,   80
Sends them all home. The stars die out, but Dido
Lies brooding in the empty hall, alone,
Abandoned on a lonely couch. She hears him,
Sees him, or sees and hears him in Iulus,[3]
Fondles the boy, as if that ruse might fool her,
Deceived by his resemblance to his father.
The towers no longer rise, the youth are slack
In drill for arms, the cranes and derricks rusting,
Walls halt halfway to heaven.
                            And Juno saw it,
The queen held fast by this disease, this passion   90
Which made her good name meaningless. In anger
She rushed to Venus:—"Wonderful!—the trophies,
The praise, you and that boy of yours are winning!
Two gods outwit one woman—splendid, splendid!
What glory for Olympus! I know you fear me,
Fear Carthage, and suspect us. To what purpose?
What good does all this do? Is there no limit?
Would we not both be better off, to sanction
A bond of peace forever, a formal marriage?
You have your dearest wish; Dido is burning   100
With love, infected to her very marrow.
Let us—why not?—conspire to rule one people
On equal terms; let her serve a Trojan husband;
Let her yield her Tyrian people as her dowry."
    This, Venus knew, was spoken with a purpose,
A guileful one, to turn Italian empire
To Libyan shores: not without reservation
She spoke in answer: "Who would be so foolish
As to refuse such terms, preferring warfare,
If only fortune follows that proposal?   110
I do not know, I am more than a little troubled
What fate permits: will Jupiter allow it,
One city for the Tyrians and Trojans,
This covenant, this mixture? You can fathom
His mind, and ask him, being his wife. I follow
Wherever you lead." And royal Juno answered:

[3] The actual Iulus, not Cupid, who had been substituted for him in Book I.

"That I will tend to. Listen to me, and learn
How to achieve the urgent need. They plan,
Aeneas, and poor Dido, to go hunting
When sunlight floods the world to-morrow morning.   120
While the rush of the hunt is on, and the forest shaken
With beaters and their nets, I will pour down
Dark rain and hail, and make the whole sky rumble
With thunder and threat. The company will scatter,
Hidden or hiding in the night and shadow,
And Dido and the Trojan come for shelter
To the same cave. I will be there and join them
In lasting wedlock; she will be his own,
His bride, forever; this will be their marriage."
Venus assented,[4] smiling, not ungracious—   130
The trick was in the open.
        Dawn, rising, left the ocean, and the youth
Come forth from all the gates, prepared for hunting,
Nets, toils, wide spears, keen-scented coursing hounds.
And Dido keeps them waiting; her own charger
Stands bright in gold and crimson; the bit foams,
The impatient head is tossed. At last she comes,
With a great train attending, gold and crimson,
Quiver of gold, and combs of gold, and mantle
Crimson with golden buckle. A Trojan escort   140
Attends her, with Iulus, and Aeneas
Comes to her side, more lordly than Apollo
Bright along Delos' ridges in the springtime
With laurel in his hair and golden weapons
Shining across his shoulders. Equal radiance
Is all around Aeneas, equal splendor.
        They reach the mountain heights, the hiding-places
Where no trail runs; wild goats from the rocks are started,
Run down the ridges; elsewhere, in the open
Deer cross the dusty plain, away from the mountains.   150
The boy Ascanius, in the midst of the valley,
Is glad he has so good a horse, rides, dashing
Past one group or another: deer are cowards
And wild goats tame; he prays for some excitement,
A tawny lion coming down the mountain
Or a great boar with foaming mouth.
                                The heaven
Darkens, and thunder rolls, and rain and hail
Come down in torrents. The hunt is all for shelter,
Trojans and Tyrians and Ascanius dashing
Wherever they can; the streams pour down the mountains.   160
To the same cave go Dido and Aeneas,
Where Juno, as a bridesmaid, gives the signal,

[4] Having been told by Jove (in Book I) of the destined future of Trojans and Romans,
Venus is aware that Juno's plan will fail.

And mountain nymphs wail high their incantations,
First day of death, first cause of evil. Dido
Is unconcerned with fame, with reputation,
With how it seems to others. This is marriage
For her, not hole-and-corner guilt; she covers
Her folly with this name.
                                            Rumor goes flying
At once, through all the Libyan cities, Rumor
Than whom no other evil was ever swifter.   170
She thrives on motion and her own momentum;
Tiny at first in fear, she swells, colossal
In no time, walks on earth, but her head is hidden
Among the clouds. Her mother, Earth, was angry,
Once, at the gods, and out of spite produced her,
The Titans' youngest sister, swift of foot,
Deadly of wing, a huge and terrible monster,
With an eye below each feather in her body,
A tongue, a mouth, for every eye, and ears
Double that number; in the night she flies   180
Above the earth, below the sky, in shadow
Noisy and shrill; her eyes are never closed
In slumber; and by day she perches, watching
From tower or battlement, frightening great cities.
She heralds truth, and clings to lies and falsehood,
It is all the same to her. And now she was going
Happy about her business, filling people
With truth and lies: Aeneas, Trojan-born,
Has come, she says, and Dido, lovely woman,
Sees fit to mate with him, one way or another,   190
And now the couple wanton out the winter,
Heedless of ruling, prisoners of passion.
They were dirty stories, but the goddess gave them
To the common ear, then went to King Iarbas[5]
With words that fired the fuel of his anger.
      This king was Ammon's son, a child of rape
Begotten on a nymph from Garamantia;
He owned wide kingdoms, had a hundred altars
Blazing with fires to Jove, eternal outposts
In the gods' honor; the ground was fat with blood,   200
The temple portals blossoming with garlands.
He heard the bitter stories, and went crazy,
Before the presences of many altars
Beseeching and imploring:—"Jove Almighty,
To whom the Moorish race on colored couches
Pours festive wine, do you see these things, or are we
A pack of idiots, shaking at the lightning
We think you brandish, when it is really only
An aimless flash of light, and silly noises?

---

[5] A rejected African suitor of Dido, Iarbas is a son of Jove (identified here with Ammon).

Do you see these things? A woman, who used to wander   210
Around my lands, who bought a little city,
To whom we gave some ploughland and a contract,
Disdains me as a husband, takes Aeneas
To be her lord and master, in her kingdom,
And now that second Paris, with his lackeys,
Half-men, I call them, his chin tied up with ribbons,
With millinery on his perfumed tresses,
Takes over what he stole, and we keep bringing
Gifts to your temples, we, devout believers
Forsooth, in idle legend."
                          And Jove heard him   220
Making his prayer and clinging to the altars,
And turned his eyes to Carthage and the lovers
Forgetful of their better reputation.
He summoned Mercury:—"Go forth, my son,
Descend on wing and wind to Tyrian Carthage,
Speak to the Trojan leader, loitering there
Unheedful of the cities given by fate.
Take him my orders through the rapid winds:
It was not for this his lovely mother saved him
Twice[6] from Greek arms; she promised he would be   230
A ruler, in a country loud with war,
Pregnant with empire; he would sire a race
From Teucer's noble line; he would ordain
Law for the world. If no such glory moves him,
If his own fame and fortune count as nothing,
Does he, a father, grudge his son the towers
Of Rome to be? What is the fellow doing?
With what ambition wasting time in Libya?
Let him set sail. That's all; convey the message."
      Before he ended, Mercury made ready   240
To carry out the orders of his father;
He strapped the golden sandals on, the pinions
To bear him over sea and land, as swift
As the breath of the wind; he took the wand, which summons
Pale ghosts from Hell, or sends them there, denying
Or giving sleep, unsealing dead men's eyes,
Useful in flight through wind and stormy cloud,
And so came flying till he saw the summit
And towering sides of Atlas,[7] rugged giant
With heaven on his neck, whose head and shoulders   250
Are dark with fir, ringed with black cloud, and beaten
With wind and rain, and laden with the whiteness
Of falling snow, with rivers running over
His agèd chin, and the rough beard ice-stiffened.
Here first on level wing the god paused briefly,

[6] First in a combat with Diomede, then during the sack of Troy.
[7] The mountain in Africa, here personified as the giant.

Poised, plummeted to ocean, like a bird
That skims the water's surface, flying low
By shore and fishes' rocky breeding-ground.
So Mercury darted between earth and heaven
To Libya's sandy shore, cutting the wind   260
From the home of Maia's[8] father.
Soon as the winged sandals skim the rooftops,
He sees Aeneas founding towers, building
New homes for Tyrians; his sword is studded
With yellow jasper; he wears across his shoulders
A cloak of burning crimson, and golden threads
Run through it, the royal gift of the rich queen.
Mercury wastes no time:—"What are you doing,
Forgetful of your kingdom and your fortunes,
Building for Carthage? Woman-crazy fellow,   270
The ruler of the gods, the great compeller
Of heaven and earth, has sent me from Olympus
With no more word than this: what are you doing,
With what ambition wasting time in Libya?
If your own fame and fortune count as nothing,
Think of Ascanius at least, whose kingdom
In Italy, whose Roman land, are waiting
As promise justly due." He spoke, and vanished
Into thin air. Appalled, amazed, Aeneas
Is stricken dumb; his hair stands up in terror,   280
His voice sticks in his throat. He is more than eager
To flee that pleasant land, awed by the warning
Of the divine command. But how to do it?
How get around that passionate queen? What opening
Try first? His mind runs out in all directions,
Shifting and veering. Finally, he has it,
Or thinks he has: he calls his comrades to him,
The leaders, bids them quietly prepare
The fleet for voyage, meanwhile saying nothing
About the new activity; since Dido   290
Is unaware, has no idea that passion
As strong as theirs is on the verge of breaking,
He will see what he can do, find the right moment
To let her know, all in good time. Rejoicing,
The captains move to carry out the orders.
        Who can deceive a woman in love? The queen
Anticipates each move, is fearful even
While everything is safe, foresees this cunning,
And the same trouble-making goddess, Rumor,
Tells her the fleet is being armed, made ready   300
For voyaging. She rages through the city
Like a woman mad, or drunk, the way the Maenads

[8] Daughter of Atlas and mother of Mercury.

Go howling through the night-time on Cithaeron[9]
When Bacchus' cymbals summon with their clashing.
She waits no explanation from Aeneas;
She is the first to speak: "And so, betrayer,
You hoped to hide your wickedness, go sneaking
Out of my land without a word? Our love
Means nothing to you, our exchange of vows,
And even the death of Dido could not hold you.   310
The season is dead of winter, and you labor
Over the fleet; the northern gales are nothing—
You must be cruel, must you not? Why, even,
If ancient Troy remained, and you were seeking
Not unknown homes and lands, but Troy again,
Would you be venturing Troyward in this weather?
I am the one you flee from: true? I beg you
By my own tears, and your right hand—(I have nothing
Else left my wretchedness)—by the beginnings
Of marriage, wedlock, what we had, if ever   320
I served you well, if anything of mine
Was ever sweet to you, I beg you, pity
A falling house; if there is room for pleading
As late as this, I plead, put off that purpose.
You are the reason I am hated; Libyans,
Numidians, Tyrians, hate me; and my honor
Is lost, and the fame I had, that almost brought me
High as the stars, is gone. To whom, O guest—
I must not call you husband any longer—
To whom do you leave me? I am a dying woman;   330
Why do I linger on? Until Pygmalion,
My brother, brings destruction to this city?
Until the prince Iarbas leads me captive?
At least if there had been some hope of children
Before your flight, a little Aeneas playing
Around my courts, to bring you back, in feature
At least, I would seem less taken and deserted."
     There was nothing he could say. Jove bade him keep
Affection from his eyes, and grief in his heart
With never a sign. At last, he managed something:—   340
'Never, O Queen, will I deny you merit
Whatever you have strength to claim; I will not
Regret remembering Dido, while I have
Breath in my body, or consciousness of spirit.
I have a point or two to make. I did not,
Believe me, hope to hide my flight by cunning;
I did not, ever, claim to be a husband,
Made no such vows. If I had fate's permission

---

[9] A mountain where the Maenads (female worshipers of Bacchus) conducted their orgiastic rites.

To live my life my way, to settle my troubles
At my own will, I would be watching over   350
The city of Troy, and caring for my people,
Those whom the Greeks had spared, and Priam's palace
Would still be standing; for the vanquished people
I would have built the town again. But now
It is Italy I must seek, great Italy,
Apollo orders, and his oracles
Call me to Italy. There is my love,
There is my country. If the towers of Carthage,
The Libyan citadels, can please a woman
Who came from Tyre, why must you grudge the Trojans   360
Ausonian land? It is proper for us also
To seek a foreign kingdom. I am warned
Of this in dreams: when the earth is veiled in shadow
And the fiery stars are burning, I see my father,
Anchises, or his ghost, and I am frightened;
I am troubled for the wrong I do my son,
Cheating him out of his kingdom in the west,
And lands that fate assigns him. And a herald,
Jove's messenger—I call them both to witness—
Has brought me, through the rush of air, his orders;   370
I saw the god myself, in the full daylight,
Enter these walls, I heard the words he brought me.
Cease to inflame us both with your complainings;
I follow Italy not because I want to."
        Out of the corner of her eye she watched him
During the first of this, and her gaze was turning
Now here, now there; and then, in bitter silence,
She looked him up and down; then blazed out at him:—
"You treacherous liar! No goddess was your mother,
No Dardanus the founder of your tribe,   380
Son of the stony mountain-crags, begotten
On cruel rocks, with a tigress for a wet-nurse!
Why fool myself, why make pretense? what is there
To save myself for now? When I was weeping
Did he so much as sigh? Did he turn his eyes,
Ever so little, toward me? Did he break at all,
Or weep, or give his lover a word of pity?
What first, what next? Neither Jupiter nor Juno
Looks at these things with any sense of fairness.
Faith has no haven anywhere in the world.   390
He was an outcast on my shore, a beggar,
I took him in, and, like a fool, I gave him
Part of my kingdom; his fleet was lost, I found it,
His comrades dying, I brought them back to life.
I am maddened, burning, burning: now Apollo
The prophesying god, the oracles
Of Lycia, and Jove's herald, sent from heaven,
Come flying through the air with fearful orders,—

Fine business for the gods, the kind of trouble
That keeps them from their sleep. I do not hold you,   400
I do not argue, either. Go. And follow
Italy on the wind, and seek the kingdom
Across the water. But if any gods
Who care for decency have any power,
They will land you on the rocks; I hope for vengeance,
I hope to hear you calling the name of Dido
Over and over, in vain. Oh, I will follow
In blackest fire, and when cold death has taken
Spirit from body, I will be there to haunt you,
A shade, all over the world. I will have vengeance,   410
And hear about it; the news will be my comfort
In the deep world below." She broke it off,
Leaving the words unfinished; even light
Was unendurable; sick at heart, she turned
And left him, stammering, afraid, attempting
To make some kind of answer. And her servants
Support her to her room, that bower of marble,
A marriage-chamber once; here they attend her,
Help her lie down.
               And good Aeneas, longing
To ease her grief with comfort, to say something   420
To turn her pain and hurt away, sighs often,
His heart being moved by this great love, most deeply,
And still—the gods give orders, he obeys them;
He goes back to the fleet. And then the Trojans
Bend, really, to their work, launching the vessels
All down the shore. The tarred keel swims in the water,
The green wood comes from the forest, the poles are lopped
For oars, with leaves still on them. All are eager
For flight; all over the city you see them streaming,
Bustling about their business, a black line moving   430
The way ants do when they remember winter
And raid a hill of grain, to haul and store it
At home, across the plain, the column moving
In thin black line through grass, part of them shoving
Great seeds on little shoulders, and part bossing
The job, rebuking laggards, and all the pathway
Hot with the stream of work.
                   And Dido saw them
With who knows what emotion: there she stood
On the high citadel, and saw, below her,
The whole beach boiling, and the water littered   440
With one ship after another, and men yelling,
Excited over their work, and there was nothing
For her to do but sob or choke with anguish.
There is nothing to which the hearts of men and women
Cannot be driven by love. Break into tears,
Try prayers again, humble the pride, leave nothing

Untried, and die in vain:—"Anna, you see them
Coming from everywhere; they push and bustle
All up and down the shore: the sails are swelling,
The happy sailors garlanding the vessels.   450
If I could hope for grief like this, my sister,
I shall be able to bear it. But one service
Do for me first, dear Anna, out of pity.
You were the only one that traitor trusted,
Confided in; you know the way to reach him,
The proper time and place. Give him this message,
Our arrogant enemy: tell him I never
Swore with the Greeks at Aulis to abolish
The Trojan race, I never sent a fleet
To Pergamus, I never desecrated   460
The ashes or the spirit of Anchises:
Why does he, then, refuse to listen to me?
What is the hurry? Let him give his lover
The one last favor: only wait a little,
Only a little while, for better weather
And easy flight. He has betrayed the marriage,
I do not ask for that again; I do not
Ask him to give up Latium and his kingdom.
Mere time is all I am asking, a breathing-space,
A brief reprieve, until my luck has taught me   470
To reconcile defeat and sorrow. This
Is all I ask for, sister; pity and help me:
If he grants me this, I will pay it ten times over
After my death." And Anna, most unhappy,
Over and over, told her tears, her pleading;
No tears, no pleading, move him; no man can yield
When a god stops his ears. As northern winds
Sweep over Alpine mountains, in their fury
Fighting each other to uproot an oak-tree
Whose ancient strength endures against their roaring   480
And the trunk shudders and the leaves come down
Strewing the ground, but the old tree clings to the mountain,
Its roots as deep toward hell as its crest toward heaven,
And still holds on—even so, Aeneas, shaken
By storm-blasts of appeal, by voices calling
From every side, is tossed and torn, and steady.
His will stays motionless, and tears are vain.
     Then Dido prays for death at last; the fates
Are terrible, her luck is out, she is tired
Of gazing at the everlasting heaven.   490
The more to goad her will to die, she sees—
Oh terrible!—the holy water blacken,
Libations turn to blood, on ground and altar,
When she makes offerings. But she tells no one,
Not even her sister. From the marble shrine,
Memorial to her former lord, attended,

Always, by her, with honor, fleece and garland,
She hears his voice, his words, her husband calling
When darkness holds the world, and from the house-top
An owl sends out a long funereal wailing, 500
And she remembers warnings of old seers,
Fearful, foreboding. In her dreams Aeneas
Appears to hunt her down; or she is going
Alone in a lost country, wandering
Trying to find her Tyrians, mad as Pentheus,
Or frenzied as Orestes, when his mother
Is after him with whips of snakes, or firebrands,
While the Avengers menace at the threshold.[10]
    She was beaten, harboring madness, and resolved
On dying; alone, she plotted time and method; 510
Keeping the knowledge from her sorrowing sister,
She spoke with calm composure:—"I have found
A way (wish me good luck) to bring him to me
Or set me free from loving him forever.
Near Ocean[11] and the west there is a country,
The Ethiopian land, far-off, where Atlas
Turns on his shoulders the star-studded world;
I know a priestess there; she guards the temple
Of the daughters of the Evening Star; she feeds
The dragon there, and guards the sacred branches, 520
She sprinkles honey-dew, strews drowsy poppies,
And she knows charms to free the hearts of lovers
When she so wills it, or to trouble others;
She can reverse the wheeling of the planets,
Halt rivers in their flowing; she can summon
The ghosts of night-time; you will see earth shaking
Under her tread, and trees come down from mountains.
Dear sister mine, as heaven is my witness,
I hate to take these arts of magic on me!
Be secret, then; but in the inner courtyard, 530
Raise up a funeral-pyre, to hold the armor
Left hanging in the bower, by that hero,
That good devoted man, and all his raiment,
And add the bridal bed, my doom: the priestess
Said to do this, and it will be a pleasure
To see the end of all of it, every token
Of that unspeakable knave."
                And so, thought Anna,
Things are no worse than when Sychaeus perished.
She did not know the death these rites portended,
Had no suspicion, and carried out her orders. 540

---

[10] Pentheus was driven to madness by Bacchus for opposing worship of him. Orestes was pursued by the Furies ("Avengers") in revenge for the murder of his mother; see Aeschylus' *Oresteia.*

[11] The waters believed to surround the world.

  The pyre is raised in the court; it towers high
With pine and holm-oak, it is hung with garlands
And funeral wreaths, and on the couch she places
Aeneas' sword, his garments, and his image,
Knowing the outcome. Round about are altars,
Where, with her hair unbound, the priestess calls
On thrice a hundred gods, Erebus, Chaos,
Hecate, queen of Hell, triple Diana.
Water is sprinkled, from Avernus[12] fountain,
Or said to be, and herbs are sought, by moonlight   550
Mown with bronze sickles, and the stem-ends running
With a black milk, and the caul of a colt, new-born.
Dido, with holy meal and holy hands,
Stands at the altar, with one sandal loosened
And robes unfastened, calls the gods to witness,
Prays to the stars that know her doom, invoking,
Beyond them, any powers, if there are any,
Who care for lovers in unequal bondage.
  Night: and tired creatures over all the world
Were seeking slumber; the woods and the wild waters   560
Were quiet, and the silent stars were wheeling
Their course half over; every field was still;
The beasts of the field, the brightly colored birds,
Dwellers in lake and pool, in thorn and thicket,
Slept through the tranquil night, their sorrows over,
Their troubles soothed. But no such blessèd darkness
Closes the eyes of Dido; no repose
Comes to her anxious heart. Her pangs redouble,
Her love swells up, surging, a great tide rising   570
Of wrath and doubt and passion. "What do I do?
What now? Go back to my Numidian suitors,
Be scorned by those I scorned? Pursue the Trojans?
Obey their orders? They were grateful to me,
Once, I remember. But who would let them take me?
Suppose I went. They hate me now; they were always
Deceivers: is Laomedon[13] forgotten,
Whose blood runs through their veins? What then? Attend them,
Alone, be their companion, the loud-mouthed sailors?   580
Or with my own armada follow after,
Wear out my sea-worn Tyrians once more
With vengeance and adventure? Better die.
Die; you deserve to; end the hurt with the sword.
It is your fault, Anna; you were sorry for me,
Won over by my tears; you put this load
Of evil on me. It was not permitted,
It seems, for me to live apart from wedlock,
A blameless life. An animal does better.

---

[12]*Erebus . . . Avernus* were all associated with death or the Lower World.
[13]King of Troy before Priam; he was noted for deceitfulness.

I vowed Sychaeus faith. I have been faithless." 590
So, through the night, she tossed in restless torment.
    Meanwhile Aeneas, on the lofty stern,
All things prepared, sure of his going, slumbers
As Mercury comes down once more to warn him,
Familiar blond young god: "O son of Venus,
Is this a time for sleep? The wind blows fair,
And danger rises all around you. Dido,
Certain to die, however else uncertain,
Plots treachery, harbors evil. Seize the moment
While it can still be seized, and hurry, hurry! 600
The sea will swarm with ships, the fiery torches
Blaze, and the shore rankle with fire by morning.
Shove off, be gone! A shifty, fickle object
Is woman, always." He vanished into the night.
And, frightened by that sudden apparition,
Aeneas started from sleep, and urged his comrades:—
"Hurry, men, hurry; get to the sails and benches,
Get the ships under way. A god from heaven
Again has come to speed our flight, to sever
The mooring-ropes. O holy one, we follow, 610
Whoever you are, we are happy in obeying.
Be with us, be propitious; let the stars
Be right in heaven!" He drew his sword; the blade
Flashed, shining, at the hawser; and all the men
Were seized in the same restlessness and rushing.
They have left the shore, they have hidden the sea-water
With the hulls of the ships; the white foam flies, the oars
Dip down in dark-blue water.
                And Aurora[14]
Came from Tithonus' saffron couch to freshen
The world with rising light, and from her watch-tower 620
The queen saw day grow whiter, and the fleet
Go moving over the sea, keep pace together
To the even spread of the sail; she knew the harbors
Were empty of sailors now; she struck her breast
Three times, four times; she tore her golden hair,
Crying, "God help me, will he go, this stranger,
Treating our kingdom as a joke? Bring arms,
Bring arms, and hurry! follow from all the city,
Haul the ships off the ways, some of you! Others,
Get fire as fast as you can, give out the weapons, 630
Pull oars! What am I saying? O where am I?
I must be going mad. Unhappy Dido,
Is it only now your wickedness strikes home?
The time it should have was when you gave him power.
Well, here it is, look at it now, the honor,
The faith of the hero who, they tell me, carries

---

[14] Goddess of the dawn, mate of Tithonus.

With him his household gods, who bore on his shoulders
His agèd father! Could I not have seized him,
Torn him to pieces, scattered him over the waves?
What was the matter? Could I not have murdered   640
His comrades, and Iulus, and served the son
For a dainty at the table of his father?
But fight would have a doubtful fortune. It might have,
What then? I was going to die; whom did I fear?
I would have, should have, set his camp on fire,
Filled everything with flame, choked off the father,
The son, the accursèd race, and myself with them.
Great Sun, surveyor of all the works of earth,
Juno, to whom my sorrows are committed,
Hecate,[15] whom the cross-roads of the cities   650
Wail to by night, avenging Furies, hear me,
Grant me divine protection, take my prayer.
If he must come to harbor, then he must,
If Jove ordains it, however vile he is,
False, and unspeakable. If Jove ordains,
The goal is fixed. So be it. Take my prayer.[16]
Let him be driven by arms and war, an exile,
Let him be taken from his son Iulus,
Let him beg for aid, let him see his people dying
Unworthy deaths, let him accept surrender   660
On unfair terms, let him never enjoy the kingdom,
The hoped-for light, let him fall and die, untimely,
Let him lie unburied on the sand. Oh, hear me,
Hear the last prayer, poured out with my last blood!
And you, O Tyrians, hate, and hate forever
The Trojan stock. Offer my dust this homage.
No love, no peace, between these nations, ever!
Rise from my bones, O great unknown avenger,
Hunt them with fire and sword, the Dardan settlers,
Now, then, here, there, wherever strength is given.   670
Shore against shore, wave against wave, and war,
War after war, for all the generations."
    She spoke, and turned her purpose to accomplish
The quickest end to the life she hated. Briefly
She spoke to Barce, Sychaeus' nurse; her own
Was dust and ashes in her native country:—
"Dear nurse, bring me my sister, tell her to hurry,
Tell her to sprinkle her body with river water,
To bring the sacrificial beast and offerings,
And both of you cover your temples with holy fillets. 680
I have a vow to keep; I have made beginning

[15] A goddess associated with the Lower World, worshiped at crossways.
[16] Much of the curse that follows is fulfilled (though the poem does not describe the death of Aeneas).

Of rites to Stygian[17] Jove, to end my sorrows,
To burn the litter of that Trojan leader."
Barce, with an old woman's fuss and bustle,
Went hurrying out of sight; but Dido, trembling,
Wild with her project, the blood-shot eyeballs rolling,
Pale at the death to come, and hectic color
Burning the quivering cheeks, broke into the court,
Mounted the pyre in madness, drew the sword,
The Trojan gift, bestowed for no such purpose,   690
And she saw the Trojan garments, and the bed
She knew so well, and paused a little, weeping,
Weeping, and thinking, and flung herself down on it,
Uttering her last words:—
"Spoils that were sweet while gods and fate permitted,
Receive my spirit, set me free from suffering.
I have lived, I have run the course that fortune gave me,
And now my shade, a great one, will be going
Below the earth. I have built a noble city,
I have seen my walls, I have avenged a husband,   700
Punished a hostile brother. I have been
Happy, I might have been too happy, only
The Trojans made their landing." She broke off,
Pressed her face to the couch, cried:—"So, we shall die,
Die unavenged; but let us die. So, so,—
I am glad to meet the darkness. Let his eyes
Behold this fire across the sea, an omen
Of my death going with him."
                                    As she spoke,
Her handmaids saw her, fallen on the sword,
The foam of blood on the blade, and blood on the hands.   710
A scream rings through the house; Rumor goes reeling,
Rioting, through the shaken town; the palace
Is loud with lamentation, women sobbing,
Wailing and howling, and the vaults of heaven
Echo the outcry, as if Tyre or Carthage
Had fallen to invaders, and the fury
Of fire came rolling over homes and temples.
Anna, half lifeless, heard in panic terror,
Came rushing through them all, beating her bosom,
Clawing her face:—"Was it for this, my sister?   720
To trick me so? The funeral pyre, the altars,
Prepared this for me? I have, indeed, a grievance,
Being forsaken; you would not let your sister
Companion you in death? You might have called me
To the same fate; we might have both been taken,
One sword, one hour. I was the one who built it,

---

[17] Associated with Styx, a river in the Lower World. The "Stygian Jove" was Hades (also called Dis, Pluto, and Orcus).

This pyre, with my own hands; it was my voice
That called our fathers' gods, for what?—to fail you
When you were lying here. You have killed me, sister,
Not only yourself, you have killed us all, the people,   730
The town. Let me wash the wounds with water,
Let my lips catch what fluttering breath still lingers."
She climbed the lofty steps, and held her sister,
A dying woman, close; she used her robe
To try to stop the bleeding. And Dido tried
In vain to raise her heavy eyes, fell back,
And her wound made a gurgling hissing sound.
Three times she tried to lift herself; three times
Fell back; her rolling eyes went searching heaven
And the light hurt when she found it, and she moaned.   740
    At last all-powerful Juno, taking pity,
Sent Iris[18] from Olympus, in compassion
For the long racking agony, to free her
From the limbs' writhing and the struggle of spirit.
She had not earned this death, she had only sought it
Before her time, driven by sudden madness,
Therefore, the queen of Hades had not taken
The golden lock, consigning her to Orcus.[19]
So Iris, dewy on saffron wings, descending,
Trailing a thousand colors through the brightness   750
Comes down the sky, poises above her, saying,
"This lock I take as bidden, and from the body
Release the soul," and cuts the lock; and cold
Takes over, and the winds receive the spirit.

from BOOK V: THE FUNERAL GAMES FOR ANCHISES

The Trojans return to Sicily, where they solemnize the anniversary of Anchises' death through religious ritual and athletic contests. During the games some of the women, weary of travel and incited by Juno, try to burn the ships, but Jove sends a rainstorm that extinguishes the flames. Aeneas decides to leave the less hardy and zealous of the Trojans behind in Sicily, under the friendly ruler Acestes. The fleet then departs for Italy.

                            The masts are raised, and sail
Stretched from the halyards; right and left they bend
The canvas to fair winds: at the head of the fleet
Rides Palinurus, and the others follow,
As ordered, close behind him; dewy night
Has reached mid-heaven, while the sailors, sleeping,
Relax on the hard benches under the oars,   800
All calm, all quiet. And the god of Sleep
Parting the shadowy air, comes gently down,

[18] Goddess of the rainbow, Juno's messenger.
[19] The queen of Hades, or the Lower World, was Proserpina.

Looking for Palinurus, bringing him,
A guiltless man, ill-omened dreams. He settles
On the high stern, a god disguised as a man,
Speaking in Phorbas'[1] guise, "O Palinurus,
The fleet rides smoothly in the even weather,
The hour is given for rest. Lay down the head,
Rest the tired eyes from toil. I will take over
A little while." But Palinurus, barely   810
Lifting his eyes, made answer: "Trust the waves,
However quiet? trust a peaceful ocean?
Put faith in such a monster? Never! I
Have been too often fooled by the clear stars
To trust Aeneas to their faithless keeping."
And so he clung to the tiller, never loosed
His hand from the wood, his eyes from the fair heaven.
But lo, the god over his temples shook
A bough that dripped with dew from Lethe, steeped
With Stygian magic,[2] so the swimming eyes,   820
Against his effort, close, blink open, close
Again, and slumber takes the drowsy limbs.
Bending above him, leaning over, the god
Shoves him, still clinging to the tiller, calling
His comrades vainly, into the clear waves.
And the god is gone like a bird to the clear air,
And the fleet is going safely over its journey
As Neptune promised.[3] But the rocks were near,
The Siren-cliffs, most perilous of old,
White with the bones of many mariners,   830
Loud with their hoarse eternal warning sound.[4]
Aeneas starts from sleep, aware, somehow,
Of a lost pilot, and a vessel drifting,
Himself takes over guidance, with a sigh
And heartache for a friend's mishap, "Alas,
Too trustful in the calm of sea and sky,
O Palinurus, on an unknown shore,
You will be lying, naked."

---

[1] A friend of the helmsman Palinurus.

[2] Lethe, the river of forgetfulness, and Styx, the river of death, are part of the landscape of the Lower World, described in Book VI.

[3] In response to Venus' pleas, the ocean-god Neptune had promised her that the Trojan fleet should reach Italy in safety, but he had also stipulated that one sailor should be drowned.

[4] The Sirens, as described in Homer's *Odyssey*, Book XII, were females who enchanted sailors with their beautiful songs, luring them to destruction. Virgil associates this peril with certain actual rocks in the sea near modern Naples.

BOOK VI: THE LOWER WORLD

Mourning for Palinurus, he drives the fleet
To Cumae's[1] coast-line; the prows are turned, the anchors
Let down, the beach is covered by the vessels.
Young in their eagerness for the land in the west,
They flash ashore; some seek the seeds of flame
Hidden in veins of flint, and others spoil
The woods of tinder, and show where water runs.
Aeneas, in devotion, seeks the heights
Where stands Apollo's temple, and the cave
Where the dread Sibyl dwells, Apollo's priestess,   10
With the great mind and heart, inspired revealer
Of things to come. They enter Diana's grove,
Pass underneath the roof of gold.[2]
                                        The story
Has it that Daedalus fled from Minos' kingdom,
Trusting himself to wings he made, and travelled
A course unknown to man, to the cold north,
Descending on this very summit; here,
Earth-bound again, he built a mighty temple,
Paying Apollo homage, the dedication
Of the oarage of his wings. On the temple doors   20
He carved, in bronze, Androgeos' death, and the payment
Enforced on Cecrops' children, seven sons
For sacrifice each year: there stands the urn,
The lots are drawn—facing this, over the sea,
Rises the land of Crete: the scene portrays
Pasiphae in cruel love, the bull
She took to her by cunning, and their offspring,
The mongrel Minotaur, half man, half monster,
The proof of lust unspeakable; and the toil
Of the house is shown, the labyrinthine maze   30
Which no one could have solved, but Daedalus
Pitied a princess' love, loosened the tangle,
Gave her a skein to guide her way. His boy,
Icarus, might have been here, in the picture,
And almost was—his father had made the effort
Once, and once more, and dropped his hands; he could not

---

[1] A city, near the modern Naples, where Aeneas is to visit the Sybil named Deiphobe, mythical prophet and priestess of Apollo, in preparation for his visit to the Lower World.

[2] The temple and its environs were sacred to both Apollo and Diana, his sister. In her alter ego as Hecate, she was goddess of the Lower World and was sometimes associated with witchcraft.

Master his grief that much.[3] The story held them;
They would have studied it longer, but Achates[4]
Came from his mission; with him came the priestess,
Deiphobe, daughter of Glaucus,[5] who tends the temple   40
For Phoebus and Diana; she warned Aeneas:
"It is no such sights the time demands; far better
To offer sacrifice, seven chosen bullocks,
Seven chosen ewes, a herd without corruption."
They were prompt in their obedience, and the priestess
Summoned the Trojans to the lofty temple.
    The rock's vast side is hollowed into a cavern,
With a hundred mouths, a hundred open portals,
Whence voices rush, the answers of the Sibyl.
They had reached the threshold, and the virgin cried: 50
"It is time to seek the fates; the god is here,
The god is here, behold him." And as she spoke
Before the entrance, her countenance and color
Changed, and her hair tossed loose, and her heart was heaving,
Her bosom swollen with frenzy; she seemed taller,
Her voice not human at all, as the god's presence
Drew nearer, and took hold on her. "Aeneas,"
She cried, "Aeneas, are you praying?
Are you being swift in prayer? Until you are,
The house of the gods will not be moved, nor open   60
Its mighty portals." More than her speech, her silence
Made the Trojans cold with terror, and Aeneas
Prayed from the depth of his heart: "Phoebus Apollo,
Compassionate ever, slayer of Achilles
Through aim of Paris' arrow,[6] helper and guide
Over the seas, over the lands, the deserts,
The shoals and quicksands, now at last we have come
To Italy, we hold the lands which fled us:
Grant that thus far, no farther, a Trojan fortune

---

[3] Minos was king of Crete. His wife Pasiphae, in a bovine disguise fabricated by the crafts-man Daedalus, made love with a bull and then gave birth to the Minotaur, half bull and half human. Minos then forced Daedalus to construct a labyrinth to contain the Minotaur. After the Athenians killed Androgeos, the son of Minos, the king in revenge forced them (the "children" of Cecrops, an early king of Athens) to sacrifice to the Minotaur, each year, the lives of seven young men and seven young women, chosen by lots drawn from an urn. The Athenian hero Theseus went to Crete and succeeded in killing the monster that was devour-ing his compatriots. In this enterprise he was helped by Daedalus and the love-smitten Ari-adne, Minos' daughter, who gave Theseus a thread to guide him back out of the labyrinth. Imprisoned for his part in this feat, Daedalus with his son Icarus escaped from Crete on wings the father had constructed; Icarus, however, died when he flew too close to the sun, which melted the wax fastenings of his wings. Daedalus, after reaching Italy, built the temple and executed the carvings that Aeneas is examining, though Virgil represents the artist as having been incapable, in his grief, of representing his son's tragic story.
[4] Aeneas' most faithful friend.
[5] Glaucus was a sea-god gifted with prophetic powers.
[6] Apollo, patron of archers, helped Paris to slay Achilles by shooting him in the heel, the only part of his body not supernaturally protected.

Attend our wandering. And spare us now,   70
All of you, gods and goddesses, who hated
Troy in the past, and Trojan glory. I beg you,
Most holy prophetess, in whose foreknowing
The future stands revealed, grant that the Trojans—
I ask with fate's permission—rest in Latium
Their wandering storm-tossed gods. I will build a temple,
In honor of Apollo and Diana,
Out of eternal marble, and ordain
Festivals in their honor, and for the Sibyl
A great shrine in our kingdom, and I will place there   80
The lots and mystic oracles for my people
With chosen priests to tend them.[7] Only, priestess,
This once, I pray you, chant the sacred verses
With your own lips; do not trust them to the leaves,
The mockery of the rushing wind's disorder."[8]
    But the priestess, not yet subject to Apollo,
Went reeling through the cavern, wild, and storming
To throw the god, who presses, like a rider,
With bit and bridle and weight, tames her wild spirit,
Shapes her to his control. The doors fly open,   90
The hundred doors, of their own will, fly open,
And through the air the answer comes:—"O Trojans,
At last the dangers of the sea are over;
That course is run, but graver ones are waiting
On land. The sons of Dardanus will reach
The kingdom of Lavinia—be easy
On that account—the sons of Dardanus, also,
Will wish they had not come there. War, I see,
Terrible war, and the river Tiber foaming
With streams of blood. There will be another Xanthus,   100
Another Simois, and Greek encampment,
Even another Achilles, born in Latium,
Himself a goddess' son. And Juno further
Will always be there: you will beg for mercy,
Be poor, turn everywhere for help. A woman
Will be the cause once more of so much evil,
A foreign bride, receptive to the Trojans,
A foreign marriage.[9] Do not yield to evil,
Attack, attack, more boldly even than fortune
Seems to permit. An offering of safety,—   110

---

[7] The Sibylline books, venerated in Virgil's day, were supposed to contain prophetic oracles important to the guidance of Rome.

[8] See Helenus' instructions to Aeneas in III.455–63,466–67.

[9] In short, it will be the Trojan war all over again. Xanthus and Simois were rivers at Troy. The second Achilles will be the Italian hero Turnus (son of the nymph Venilia as Achilles had been the son of the nymph Thetis), who will become Aeneas' rival for the princess Lavinia. Thus, according to the prophecy, woman will again be at the root of the troubles, as with Helen and (it may be implied) Dido.

Incredible!—will come from a Greek city."[10]
　　So, through the amplifiers of her cavern,
The hollow vaults, the Sibyl cast her warnings,
Riddles confused with truth; and Apollo rode her,
Reining her rage, and shaking her, and spurring
The fierceness of her heart. The frenzy dwindled,
A little, and her lips were still. Aeneas
Began:—"For me, no form of trouble, maiden,
Is new, or unexpected; all of this
I have known long since, lived in imagination.   120
One thing I ask: this is the gate of the kingdom,
So it is said, where Pluto reigns, the gloomy
Marsh where the water of Acheron[11] runs over.
Teach me the way from here, open the portals
That I may go to my belovèd father,
Stand in his presence, talk with him. I brought him,
Once, on these shoulders, through a thousand weapons
And following fire, and foemen. He shared with me
The road, the sea, the menaces of heaven,
Things that an old man should not bear; he bore them,   130
Tired as he was. And he it was who told me
To come to you in humbleness. I beg you
Pity the son, the father. You have power,
Great priestess, over all; it is not for nothing
Hecate gave you this dominion over
Avernus' groves. If Orpheus could summon
Eurydice from the shadows with his music,
If Pollux could save his brother, coming, going,
Along this path,—why should I mention Theseus,
Why mention Hercules?[12] I, too, descended   140
From the line of Jupiter." He clasped the altar,
Making his prayer, and she made answer to him:
"Son of Anchises, born of godly lineage,
By night, by day, the portals of dark Dis
Stand open: it is easy, the descending
Down to Avernus.[13] But to climb again,

---

[10] Pallanteum, a city on the site of the future Rome; it had been founded by Evander, king of Arcadia (in Greece), who had emigrated to Italy.

[11] One of the rivers of the Lower World.

[12] The legendary musician Orpheus was allowed to lead his dead wife Eurydice out of the Lower World (though he lost her after all, being unable to obey the command not to look back as she followed him). Pollux, an immortal who was half-brother to the mortal Castor, wished to die with him but could not; Jupiter, however, agreed to let them exchange places daily, each living alternately in the heavens and in the world of the dead. Theseus and Pirithous had tried to abduct Proserpine, queen of the dead. (She is also called Proserpina and Persephone.) The most difficult of Hercules' famous "labors" was the theft of Cerberus, the three-headed dog guarding the Lower World. (See lines 415–21.)

[13] Dis, like Hades (Greek) and Orcus, is another name for the god Pluto, and also for his realm, the Lower World. Avernus in this passage also means the Lower World, named for a sulfurous volcanic lake near Cumae. See also line 136.

To trace the footsteps back to the air above,
There lies the task, the toil. A few, beloved
By Jupiter, descended from the gods,
A few, in whom exalting virtue burned,   150
Have been permitted. Around the central woods
The black Cocytus glides, a sullen river;
But if such love is in your heart, such longing
For double crossing of the Stygian lake,[14]
For double sight of Tartarus,[15] learn first
What must be done. In a dark tree there hides
A bough, all golden, leaf and pliant stem,
Sacred to Proserpine. This all the grove
Protects, and shadows cover it with darkness.
Until this bough, this bloom of light, is found,   160
No one receives his passport to the darkness
Whose queen requires this tribute. In succession,
After the bough is plucked, another grows,
Gold-green with the same metal. Raise the eyes,
Look up, reach up the hand, and it will follow
With ease, if fate is calling; otherwise,
No power, no steel, can loose it. Furthermore,
(Alas, you do not know this!), one of your men
Lies on the shore, unburied, a pollution
To all the fleet, while you have come for counsel   170
Here to our threshold.[16] Bury him with honor;
Black cattle slain in expiation for him
Must fall before you see the Stygian kingdoms,
The groves denied to living men."
                                                 Aeneas,
With sadness in his eyes, and downcast heart,
Turned from the cave, and at his side Achates
Accompanied his anxious meditations.
They talked together: who could be the comrade
Named by the priestess, lying there unburied?
And they found him on dry sand; it was Misenus,   180
Aeolus' son, none better with the trumpet
To make men burn for warfare. He had been·
Great Hector's man-at-arms; he was good in battle
With spear as well as horn, and after Hector
Had fallen to Achilles, he had followed
Aeneas, entering no meaner service.
Some foolishness came over him; he made
The ocean echo to the blare of his trumpet

---

[14] The four rivers of the Lower World (besides Lethe, the river of forgetfulness) were Styx, Acheron, Cocytus, and Phlegethon.

[15] The place in the Lower World where evil was punished. Aeneas actually sees only the walls of Tartarus, but it is described in lines 573–660. *Tartarus* can also mean the Lower World in general.

[16] An unburied corpse was offensive for religious reasons. See the meeting with Palinurus later in Book VI.

That day, and challenged the sea-gods to a contest
In martial music, and Triton, jealous, caught him,   190
However unbelievable the story,
And held him down between the rocks, and drowned him
Under the foaming waves.[17] His comrades mourned,
Aeneas most of all, and in their sorrow
They carry out, in haste, the Sibyl's orders,
Construct the funeral altar, high as heaven,
They go to an old wood, and the pine-trees fall
Where wild beasts have their dens, and holm-oak rings
To the stroke of the axe, and oak and ash are riven
By the splitting wedge, and rowan-trees come rolling   200
Down the steep mountain-side. Aeneas helps them,
And cheers them on; studies the endless forest,
Takes thought, and prays: "If only we might see it,
That golden bough, here in the depth of the forest,
Bright on some tree. She told the truth, our priestess,
Too much, too bitter truth, about Misenus."
No sooner had he spoken than twin doves
Came flying down before him, and alighted
On the green ground. He knew his mother's birds,
And made his prayer, rejoicing,—"Oh, be leaders,   210
Wherever the way, and guide me to the grove
Where the rich bough makes rich the shaded ground.
Help me, O goddess-mother!" And he paused,
Watching what sign they gave, what course they set.
The birds flew on a little, just ahead
Of the pursuing vision; when they came
To the jaws of dank Avernus, evil-smelling,
They rose aloft, then swooped down the bright air,
Perched on the double tree, where the off-color
Of gold was gleaming golden through the branches.   220
As mistletoe, in the cold winter, blossoms
With its strange foliage on an alien tree,
The yellow berry gilding the smooth branches,[18]
Such was the vision of the gold in leaf
On the dark holm-oak, so the foil was rustling,
Rattling, almost, the bract[19] in the soft wind
Stirring like metal. Aeneas broke it off
With eager grasp, and bore it to the Sibyl.
     Meanwhile, along the shore, the Trojans mourned,
Paying Misenus' dust the final honors.   230
A mighty pyre was raised, of pine and oak,

[17] Triton was a sea-deity, son of Neptune, and was often portrayed as blowing a conch-shell trumpet. The classical gods did not like to be challenged at their own specialties. Appropriately, the father of the trumpeter Misenus (line 181) is the namesake of the god of the winds, Aeolus.

[18] Mistletoe is a parasite with hardly visible roots, so that in winter it contrasts in appearance with the tree it grows on and seems to live a strange, self-sustaining life.

[19] A botanical term translating *brattea*, a thin metallic leaf.

The sides hung with dark leaves, and somber cypress
Along the front, and gleaming arms above.
Some made the water hot, and some made ready
Bronze caldrons, shimmering over fire, and others
Lave and anoint the body, and with weeping
Lay on the bier his limbs, and place above them
Familiar garments, crimson color; and some
Take up the heavy burden, a sad office,
And, as their fathers did, they kept their eyes   240
Averted, as they brought the torches nearer.
They burn gifts with him, bowls of oil, and viands,
And frankincense; and when the flame is quiet
And the ashes settle to earth, they wash the embers
With wine, and slake the thirsty dust. The bones
Are placed in a bronze urn by Corynaeus,
Who, with pure water, thrice around his comrades
Made lustral cleansing, shaking gentle dew
From the fruitful branch of olive; and they said
Hail and farewell! And over him Aeneas   250
Erects a mighty tomb, with the hero's arms,
His oar and trumpet, where the mountain rises
Memorial for ever, and named Misenus.[20]
    These rites performed, he hastened to the Sibyl.
There was a cavern, yawning wide and deep,
Jagged, below the darkness of the trees,
Beside the darkness of the lake. No bird
Could fly above it safely, with the vapor
Pouring from the black gulf (the Greeks have named it
Avernus, or A-Ornos, meaning *birdless*),[21]   260
And here the priestess for the slaughter set
Four bullocks, black ones, poured the holy wine
Between the horns, and plucked the topmost bristles
For the first offering to the sacred fire,
Calling on Hecate, a power in heaven,
A power in hell. Knives to the throat were driven,
The warm blood caught in bowls. Aeneas offered
A lamb, black-fleeced, to Night and her great sister,
A sterile heifer for the queen;[22] for Dis
An altar in the night, and on the flames   270
The weight of heavy bulls, the fat oil pouring
Over the burning entrails. And at dawn,
Under their feet, earth seemed to shake and rumble,
The ridges move, and bitches bay in darkness,
As the presence neared. The Sibyl cried a warning,
"Keep off, keep off, whatever is unholy,

---

[20]The promontory at the southwestern end of the Bay of Naples is still called Cape Miseno.
[21]Most authoritative manuscripts of *The Aeneid* omit this parenthetical statement.
[22]The sister of Night (Nox) was Earth (Tellus). The "queen" is Proserpine.

Depart from here!²³ Courage, Aeneas; enter
The path, unsheathe the sword. The time is ready
For the brave heart." She strode out boldly, leading
Into the open cavern, and he followed.   280
    Gods of the world of spirit, silent shadows,
Chaos and Phlegethon, areas of silence,
Wide realms of dark, may it be right and proper
To tell what I have heard, this revelation
Of matters buried deep in earth and darkness!
    Vague forms in lonely darkness, they were going
Through void and shadow, through the empty realm
Like people in a forest, when the moonlight
Shifts with a baleful glimmer, and shadow covers
The sky, and all the colors turn to blackness.   290
At the first threshold, on the jaws of Orcus,
Grief and avenging Cares have set their couches,
And pale Diseases dwell, and sad Old Age,
Fear, evil-counselling Hunger, wretched Need,
Forms terrible to see, and Death, and Toil,
And Death's own brother, Sleep, and evil Joys,
Fantasies of the mind, and deadly War,
The Furies' iron chambers, Discord, raving,
Her snaky hair entwined in bloody bands.
An elm-tree loomed there, shadowy and huge,   300
The aged boughs outspread, beneath whose leaves,
Men say, the false dreams cling, thousands on thousands.
And there are monsters in the dooryard, Centaurs,
Scyllas, of double shape, the beast of Lerna,
Hissing most horribly, Briareus,
The hundred-handed giant, a Chimaera
Whose armament is fire, Harpies, and Gorgons,
A triple-bodied giant.²⁴ In sudden panic
Aeneas drew his sword, the edge held forward,
Ready to rush and flail, however blindly,   310
Save that his wise companion warned him, saying
They had no substance, they were only phantoms
Flitting about, illusions without body.
    From here, the road turns off to Acheron,
River of Hell; here, thick with muddy whirling,
Cocytus boils with sand. Charon is here,

²³ At Roman religious ceremonies, the ritual dismissal of the uninitiated; here applied to
Aeneas' companions, who must now leave him. The approaching "presence" (line 275) is that
of the goddess Hecate, accompanied by her hounds.
²⁴ These lines are a catalogue of many of the most famous or fearsome monsters of ancient
fable. Centaurs were half man, half horse; Scylla was a six-headed monster (described in
III.432–44) who devoured sailors in the straits of Messina; the beast of Lerna was the Hydra,
a gigantic many-headed serpent; Briareus, as the text states, was a giant with a hundred
hands; the fire-breathing Chimaera was a combination of lion, goat, and serpent; the Harpies
were foul bird-women (described in III.213–57); the Gorgons (Medusa and her two sisters)
were snake-haired female monsters who literally petrified men who gazed on them; the triple-
bodied giant was named Geryon.

The guardian of these mingling waters, Charon,
Uncouth and filthy, on whose chin the hair
Is a tangled mat, whose eyes protrude, are burning,
Whose dirty cloak is knotted at the shoulder.   320
He poles a boat, tends to the sail, unaided,
Ferrying bodies in his rust-hued vessel.
Old, but a god's senility is awful
In its raw greenness. To the bank come thronging
Mothers and men, bodies of great-souled heroes,
Their life-time over, boys, unwedded maidens,
Young men whose fathers saw their pyres burning,
Thick as the forest leaves that fall in autumn
With early frost, thick as the birds to landfall
From over the seas, when the chill of the year compels them   330
To sunlight. There they stand, a host, imploring
To be taken over first. Their hands, in longing,
Reach out for the farther shore. But the gloomy boatman
Makes choice among them, taking some, and keeping
Others far back from the stream's edge. Aeneas,
Wondering, asks the Sibyl, "Why the crowding?
What are the spirits seeking? What distinction
Brings some across the livid stream, while others
Stay on the farther bank?" She answers, briefly:
"Son of Anchises, this is the awful river,   340
The Styx, by which the gods take oath; the boatman
Charon; those he takes with him are the buried,
Those he rejects, whose luck is out, the graveless.
It is not permitted him to take them over
The dreadful banks and hoarse-resounding waters
Till earth is cast upon their bones. They haunt
These shores a hundred restless years of waiting
Before they end postponement of the crossing."
Aeneas paused, in thoughtful mood, with pity
Over their lot's unevenness; and saw there,   350
Wanting the honor given the dead, and grieving,
Leucaspis, and Orontes, the Lycian captain,
Who had sailed from Troy across the stormy waters,
And drowned off Africa, with crew and vessel,
And there was Palinurus, once his pilot,
Who, not so long ago, had been swept over,
Watching the stars on the journey north from Carthage.
The murk was thick; Aeneas hardly knew him,
Sorrowful in that darkness, but made question:
"What god, O Palinurus, took you from us?   360
Who drowned you in the deep? Tell me. Apollo
Never before was false, and yet he told me
You would be safe across the seas, and come
Unharmed to Italy; what kind of promise
Was this, to fool me with?" But Palinurus

Gave him assurance:—"It was no god who drowned me,[25]
No falsehood on Apollo's part, my captain,
But as I clung to the tiller, holding fast
To keep the course, as I should do, I felt it
Wrenched from the ship, and I fell with it, headlong.   370
By those rough seas I swear, I had less fear
On my account than for the ship, with rudder
And helmsman overboard, to drift at the mercy
Of rising seas. Three nights I rode the waters,
Three nights of storm, and from the crest of a wave,
On the fourth morning, sighted Italy,
I was swimming to land, I had almost reached it, heavy
In soaking garments; my cramped fingers struggled
To grasp the top of the rock, when barbarous people,
Ignorant men, mistaking me for booty,[26]   380
Struck me with swords; waves hold me now, or winds
Roll me along the shore. By the light of heaven,
The lovely air, I beg you, by your father,
Your hope of young Iulus, bring me rescue
Out of these evils, my unconquered leader!
Cast over my body earth—you have the power—
Return to Velia's[27] harbor,—or there may be
Some other way—your mother is a goddess,
Else how would you be crossing this great river,
This Stygian swamp?—help a poor fellow, take me   390
Over the water with you, give a dead man
At least a place to rest in." But the Sibyl
Broke in upon him sternly:—"Palinurus,
Whence comes this mad desire? No man, unburied,
May see the Stygian waters, or Cocytus,
The Furies' dreadful river; no man may come
Unbidden to this bank. Give up the hope
That fate is changed by praying, but hear this,
A little comfort in your harsh misfortune:
Those neighboring people will make expiation,   400
Driven by signs from heaven, through their cities
And through their countryside; they will build a tomb,
Thereto bring offerings yearly, and the place
Shall take its name from you, Cape Palinurus."[28]
So he was comforted a little, finding
Some happiness in the promise.
                                    And they went on,
Nearing the river, and from the stream the boatman
Beheld them cross the silent forest, nearer,

[25] Palinurus is ignorant of the role of the god of Sleep in casting him overboard. Apollo's promise is not mentioned elsewhere in the poem.
[26] A man carrying valuable goods.   [27] A town near Cumae.
[28] As with Misenus and modern Cape Miseno (line 253), Palinurus' name is still given today to a promontory on the Italian coast (Point Palinuro).

Turning their footsteps toward the bank. He challenged:—
"Whoever you are, O man in armor, coming   410
In this direction, halt where you are, and tell me
The reason why you come. This is the region
Of shadows, and of Sleep and drowsy Night;
I am not allowed to carry living bodies
In the Stygian boat; and I must say I was sorry
I ever accepted Hercules and Theseus
And Pirithous, and rowed them over the lake,
Though they were sons of gods and great in courage.
One of them dared to drag the guard of Hell,
Enchained, from Pluto's throne, shaking in terror,   420
The others to snatch our queen from Pluto's chamber."
The Sibyl answered briefly: "No such cunning
Is plotted here; our weapons bring no danger.
Be undisturbed: the hell-hound in his cavern
May bark forever, to keep the bloodless shadows
Frightened away from trespass; Proserpine,
Untouched, in pureness guard her uncle's[29] threshold.
Trojan Aeneas, a man renowned for goodness,
Renowned for nerve in battle, is descending
To the lowest shades; he comes to find his father.   430
If such devotion has no meaning to you,
Look on this branch at least, and recognize it!"
And with the word she drew from under her mantle
The golden bough; his swollen wrath subsided.
No more was said; he saw the bough, and marvelled
At the holy gift, so long unseen; came sculling
The dark-blue boat to the shore, and drove the spirits,
Lining the thwarts, ashore, and cleared the gangway,
And took Aeneas aboard; as that big man
Stepped in, the leaky skiff groaned under the weight,   440
And the strained seams let in the muddy water,
But they made the crossing safely, seer and soldier,
To the far margin, colorless and shapeless,
Grey sedge and dark-brown ooze. They heard the baying
Of Cerberus, that great hound, in his cavern crouching,
Making the shore resound, as all three throats
Belled horribly; and serpents rose and bristled
Along the triple neck. The priestess threw him
A sop with honey and drugged meal; he opened
The ravenous throat, gulped, and subsided, filling   450
The den with his huge bulk. Aeneas, crossing,
Passed on beyond the bank of the dread river
Whence none return.
                              A wailing of thin voices
Came to their ears, the souls of infants crying,
Those whom the day of darkness took from the breast

---

[29] Proserpine's father, Jove, was Pluto's brother.

Before their share of living. And there were many
Whom some false sentence brought to death. Here Minos[30]
Judges them once again; a silent jury
Reviews the evidence. And there are others,
Guilty of nothing, but who hated living,   460
The suicides. How gladly, now, they would suffer
Poverty, hardship, in the world of light!
But this is not permitted; they are bound
Nine times around by the black unlovely river;
Styx holds them fast.
              They came to the Fields of Mourning,
So-called, where those whom cruel love had wasted
Hid in secluded pathways, under myrtle,
And even in death were anxious. Procris, Phaedra,
Eriphyle, displaying wounds her son
Had given her, Caeneus, Laodamia,   470
Caeneus, a young man once, and now again
A young man, after having been a woman.[31]
And here, new come from her own wound, was Dido,
Wandering in the wood. The Trojan hero,
Standing near by, saw her, or thought he saw her,
Dim in the shadows, like the slender crescent
Of moon when cloud drifts over. Weeping, he greets her:—
"Unhappy Dido, so they told me truly
That your own hand had brought you death. Was I—
Alas!—the cause? I swear by all the stars,   480
By the world above, by everything held sacred
Here under the earth, unwillingly, O queen,
I left your kingdom. But the gods' commands,
Driving me now through these forsaken places,
This utter night, compelled me on. I could not
Believe my loss would cause so great a sorrow.
Linger a moment, do not leave me; whither,
Whom, are you fleeing? I am permitted only
This last word with you."
              But the queen, unmoving
As flint or marble, turned away, her eyes   490
Fixed on the ground: the tears were vain, the words,
Meant to be soothing, foolish; she turned away,
His enemy forever, to the shadows
Where Sychaeus, her former husband, took her
With love for love, and sorrow for her sorrow.

---

[30] King of Crete, who had ordered the famous labyrinth built; he later was made judge of the dead.

[31] Some of these figures (all women) were evil, some admirable. Procris' jealousy of her husband led to his killing her by accident; Phaedra nursed a guilty, unrequited love for her stepson; Eriphyle, having been bribed, sent her husband to his death in war and was then, in return, killed by her son; Laodamia, on the other hand, was the faithful wife of the first man to die at Troy and gave up her life to be with him after his death. The sex-changed Caeneus had been seduced, as a maiden named Caenis, by Neptune.

And still Aeneas wept for her, being troubled
By the injustice of her doom; his pity
Followed her going.
                        They went on. They came
To the farthest fields, whose tenants are the warriors,
Illustrious throng. Here Tydeus came to meet him,   500
Parthenopaeus came, and pale Adrastus,[32]
A fighter's ghost, and many, many others,
Mourned in the world above, and doomed in battle,
Leaders of Troy, in long array; Aeneas
Sighed as he saw them: Medon; Polyboetes,
The priest of Ceres; Glaucus; and Idaeus
Still keeping arms and chariot;[33] three brothers,
Antenor's sons; Thersilochus; a host
To right and left of him, and when they see him,
One sight is not enough; they crowd around him,   510
Linger, and ask the reasons for his coming.
But Agamemnon's men, the Greek battalions,
Seeing him there, and his arms in shadow gleaming,
Tremble in panic, turn to flee for refuge,
As once they used to, toward their ships, but where
Are the ships now? They try to shout, in terror;
But only a thin and piping treble issues
To mock their mouths, wide-open.
                                One he knew
Was here, Deiphobus, a son of Priam,
With his whole body mangled, and his features   520
Cruelly slashed, and both hands cut, and ears
Torn from his temples, and his nostrils slit
By shameful wounds. Aeneas hardly knew him,
Shivering there, and doing his best to hide
His marks of punishment; unhailed, he hailed him:—
"Deiphobus, great warrior, son of Teucer,
Whose cruel punishment was this? Whose license
Abused you so? I heard, it seems, a story
Of that last night, how you had fallen, weary
With killing Greeks at last; I built a tomb,   530
Although no body lay there, in your honor,
Three times I cried, aloud, over your spirit,
Where now your name and arms keep guard. I could not,
Leaving my country, find my friend, to give him
Proper interment in the earth he came from."
And Priam's son replied:—"Nothing, dear comrade,
Was left undone; the dead man's shade was given
All ceremony due. It was my own fortune

---

[32] Three of the seven heroes who led a famous siege of the city of Thebes.
[33] Idaeus had been charioteer to Priam, king of Troy.

And a Spartan woman's[34] deadliness that sunk me
Under these evils; she it was who left me   540
These souvenirs. You know how falsely happy
We were on that last night; I need not tell you.
When that dread horse came leaping over our walls,
Pregnant with soldiery, she led the dancing,
A solemn rite, she called it, with Trojan women
Screaming their bacchanals;[35] she raised the torches
High on the citadel; she called the Greeks.
Then—I was worn with trouble, drugged in slumber,
Resting in our ill-omened bridal chamber,
With sleep as deep and sweet as death upon me—   550
Then she, that paragon of helpmates, deftly
Moved all the weapons from the house; my sword,
Even, she stole from underneath my pillow,
Opened the door, and called in Menelaus,
Hoping, no doubt, to please her loving husband,
To win forgetfulness of her old sinning.
It is quickly told: they broke into the chamber,
The two of them, and with them, as accomplice,
Ulysses came, the crime-contriving bastard.[36]
O gods, pay back the Greeks; grant the petition   560
If goodness asks for vengeance! But you, Aeneas,
A living man—what chance has brought you here?
Vagrant of ocean, god-inspired,—which are you?
What chance has worn you down, to come, in sadness,
To these confusing sunless dwelling-places?"
    While they were talking, Aurora's rosy car
Had halfway crossed the heaven; all their time
Might have been spent in converse, but the Sibyl
Hurried them forward:—"Night comes on, Aeneas;
We waste the hours with tears. We are at the cross-road,   570
Now; here we turn to the right, where the pathway leads
On to Elysium, under Pluto's ramparts.
Leftward is Tartarus, and retribution,
The terminal of the wicked, and their dungeon."
Deiphobus left them, saying, "O great priestess,
Do not be angry with me; I am going;
I shall not fail the roll-call of the shadows.
Pride of our race, go on; may better fortune
Attend you!" and, upon the word, he vanished.
    As he looked back, Aeneas saw, to his left,   580
Wide walls beneath a cliff, a triple rampart,

---

[34] Helen, who had left her husband Menelaus and run off to Troy with Paris; after Paris'
death she had become the wife of Deiphobus.

[35] Wild revels in honor of Bacchus, god of wine. Helen carried one of the torches customary in such revels but used it treacherously, as a signal to the Greeks.

[36] The insult is meant literally by Deiphobus, suggesting actual infidelity by Ulysses'
mother.

A river running fire, Phlegethon's torrent,
Rocks roaring in its course, a gate, tremendous,
Pillars of adamant, a tower of iron,
Too strong for men, too strong for even gods
To batter down in warfare, and behind them
A Fury, sentinel in bloody garments,
Always on watch, by day, by night. He heard
Sobbing and groaning there, the crack of the lash,
The clank of iron, the sound of dragging shackles.   590
The noise was terrible; Aeneas halted,
Asking, "What forms of crime are these, O maiden?
What harrying punishment, what horrible outcry?"
She answered:—"O great leader of the Trojans,
I have never crossed that threshold of the wicked;
No pure soul is permitted entrance thither,
But Hecate, by whose order I was given
Charge of Avernus' groves, my guide, my teacher,
Told me how gods exact the toll of vengeance.
The monarch here, merciless Rhadamanthus,[37]   600
Punishes guilt, and hears confession; he forces
Acknowledgment of crime; no man in the world,
No matter how cleverly he hides his evil,
No matter how much he smiles at his own slyness,
Can fend atonement off; the hour of death
Begins his sentence. Tisiphone, the Fury,
Leaps at the guilty with her scourge; her serpents
Are whips of menace as she calls her sisters.
Imagine the gates, on jarring hinge, rasp open,
You would see her in the doorway, a shape, a sentry,   610
Savage, implacable. Beyond, still fiercer,
The monstrous Hydra dwells; her fifty throats
Are black, and open wide, and Tartarus
Is black, and open wide, and it goes down
To darkness, sheer deep down, and twice the distance
That earth is from Olympus.[38] At the bottom
The Titans crawl, Earth's oldest breed, hurled under
By thunderbolts; here lie the giant twins,
Aloeus' sons, who laid their hands on heaven
And tried to pull down Jove; Salmoneus here   620
Atones for high presumption,—it was he
Who aped Jove's noise and fire, wheeling his horses
Triumphant through his city in Elis, cheering
And shaking the torch, and claiming divine homage,
The arrogant fool, to think his brass was lightning,
His horny-footed horses beat out thunder!
Jove showed him what real thunder was, what lightning
Spoke from immortal cloud, what whirlwind fury

---

[37] Brother of Minos and, like him, a judge in the Lower World.
[38] The dwelling-place of the gods.

Came sweeping from the heaven to overtake him.
Here Tityos, Earth's giant son, lies sprawling   630
Over nine acres, with a monstrous vulture
Gnawing, with crooked beak, vitals and liver
That grow as they are eaten; eternal anguish,
Eternal feast.[39] Over another hangs
A rock, about to fall; and there are tables
Set for a banquet, gold with royal splendor,
But if a hand goes out to touch the viands,
The Fury drives it back with fire and yelling.
Why name them all, Pirithous, the Lapiths,
Ixion?[40] The roll of crime would take forever.   640
Whoever, in his lifetime, hated his brother,
Or struck his father down; whoever cheated
A client, or was miserly—how many
Of these there seem to be!—whoever went
To treasonable war, or broke a promise
Made to his lord, whoever perished, slain
Over adultery, all these, walled in,
Wait here their punishment. Seek not to know
Too much about their doom. The stone is rolled,
The wheel keeps turning; Theseus forever   650
Sits in dejection; Phlegyas, accursed,
Cries through the halls forever: *Being warned,
Learn justice; reverence the gods!*[41] The man
Who sold his country is here in hell; the man
Who altered laws for money; and a father
Who knew his daughter's bed. All of them dared,
And more than dared, achieved, unspeakable
Ambitions. If I had a hundred tongues,
A hundred iron throats, I could not tell
The fullness of their crime and punishment."   660
And then she added:—"Come: resume the journey,
Fulfill the mission; let us hurry onward.
I see the walls the Cyclops[42] made, the portals
Under the archway, where, the orders tell us,
Our tribute must be set." They went together
Through the way's darkness, came to the doors, and halted,
And at the entrance Aeneas, having sprinkled
His body with fresh water, placed the bough

---

[39] The Titans, giant offspring of Heaven and Earth, fought alongside Saturn in his unsuccessful struggle against his son Jupiter. The sons of Aloeus, Otus and Ephialtes, were giants who tried to assault the gods by piling the mountains Ossa and Pelion on top of Olympus. Salmoneus imitated Jove's thunder, in a city sacred to Jove, by driving a brass chariot over a brass bridge. Tityos had sexually assaulted the goddess Latona, who was avenged by her children Apollo and Diana.

[40] Ixion, king of the Lapiths, had attempted a sexual assault on Juno; for Pirithous (son of Ixion), see lines 139–40 and note and lines 415–21.

[41] Theseus was punished, perhaps, for his attempt to abduct Proserpina. Phlegyas had burned Apollo's temple at Delphi.

[42] The laborers in the forge of Vulcan, the blacksmith god of fire.

Golden before the threshold. The will of the goddess
Had been performed, the proper task completed.   670
    They came to happy places, the joyful dwelling,
The lovely greenery of the groves of the blessèd.
Here ampler air invests the fields with light,
Rose-colored, with familiar stars and sun.
Some grapple on the grassy wrestling-ground
In exercise and sport, and some are dancing,
And others singing; in his trailing robe
Orpheus[43] strums the lyre; the seven clear notes
Accompany the dance, the song. And heroes
Are there, great-souled, born in the happier years,   680
Ilus, Assaracus; the city's founder,
Prince Dardanus.[44] Far off, Aeneas wonders,
Seeing the phantom arms, the chariots,
The spears fixed in the ground, the chargers browsing,
Unharnessed, over the plain. Whatever, living,
The men delighted in, whatever pleasure
Was theirs in horse and chariot, still holds them
Here under the world. To right and left, they banquet
In the green meadows, and a joyful chorus
Rises through groves of laurel, whence the river   690
Runs to the upper world.[45] The band of heroes
Dwell here, all those whose mortal wounds were suffered
In fighting for the fatherland; and poets,
The good, the pure, the worthy of Apollo;
Those who discovered truth and made life nobler;
Those who served others—all, with snowy fillets
Binding their temples, throng the lovely valley.
And these the Sibyl questioned, most of all
Musaeus,[46] for he towered above the center
Of that great throng:—"O happy souls, O poet,   700
Where does Anchises dwell? For him we come here.
For him we have traversed Erebus'[47] great rivers."
And he replied:—"It is all our home, the shady
Groves, and the streaming meadows, and the softness
Along the river-banks. No fixed abode
Is ours at all; but if it is your pleasure,
Cross over the ridge with me; I will guide you there
By easy going." And so Musaeus led them
And from the summit showed them fields, all shining,
And they went on over and down.   710
    Deep in a valley of green, father Anchises
Was watching, with deep earnestness, the spirits
Whose destiny was light, and counting them over,

[43] In myth, the prototype of poets and musicians. See note to lines 136–40.
[44] Three illustrious ancestors of the Trojans.
[45] The river is Eridanus, believed in fable to be the underground source of the river Po.
[46] Legendary poet, taught by Orpheus.
[47] The god of darkness; more generally, the Lower World itself.

All of his race to come, his dear descendants,
Their fates and fortunes and their works and ways,
And as he saw Aeneas coming toward him
Over the meadow, his hands reached out with yearning,
He was moved to tears, and called:—"At last, my son,—
Have you really come, at last? and the long road nothing
To a son who loves his father? Do I, truly,   720
See you, and hear your voice? I was thinking so,
I was hoping so, I was counting off the days,
And I was right about it. O my son!
What a long journey, over land and water,
Yours must have been! What buffeting of danger!
I feared, so much, the Libyan realm would hurt you."
And his son answered:—"It was your spirit, father,
Your sorrowful shade, so often met, that led me
To find these portals. The ships ride safe at anchor,
Safe in the Tuscan sea. Embrace me, father;   730
Let hand join hand in love; do not forsake me."
And as he spoke, the tears streamed down. Three times
He reached out toward him, and three times the image
Fled like the breath of the wind or a dream on wings.

    He saw, in a far valley, a separate grove
Where the woods stir and rustle, and a river,
The Lethe,[48] gliding past the peaceful places,
And tribes of people thronging, hovering over,
Innumerable as the bees in summer
Working the bright-hued flowers, and the shining   740
Of the white lilies, murmuring and humming.
Aeneas, filled with wonder, asks the reason
For what he does not know, who are the people
In such a host, and to what river coming?
Anchises answers:—"These are spirits, ready
Once more for life; they drink of Lethe's water
The soothing potion of forgetfulness.
I have longed, for long, to show them to you, name them,
Our children's children; Italy discovered,
So much the greater happiness, my son."   750
"But, O my father, is it thinkable
That souls would leave this blessedness, be willing
A second time to bear the sluggish body,
Trade Paradise for earth? Alas, poor wretches,
Why such a mad desire for light?" Anchises
Gives detailed answer: "First, my son, a spirit
Sustains all matter, heaven and earth and ocean,
The moon, the stars; mind quickens mass, and moves it.
Hence comes the race of man, of beast, of wingèd
Creatures of air, of the strange shapes which ocean   760
Bears down below his mottled marble surface.

[48] River of forgetfulness.

All these are blessed with energy from heaven;
The seed of life is a spark of fire, but the body
A clod of earth, a clog, a mortal burden.
Hence humans fear, desire, grieve, and are joyful,
And even when life is over, all the evil
Ingrained so long, the adulterated mixture,
The plagues and pestilences of the body
Remain, persist. So there must be a cleansing,
By penalty, by punishment, by fire,   770
By sweep of wind, by water's absolution,
Before the guilt is gone. Each of us suffers
His own peculiar ghost.[49] But the day comes
When we are sent through wide Elysium,
The Fields of the Blessed, a few of us, to linger
Until the turn of time, the wheel of ages,
Wears off the taint, and leaves the core of spirit
Pure sense, pure flame.[50] A thousand years pass over
And the god calls the countless host to Lethe
Where memory is annulled, and souls are willing   780
Once more to enter into mortal bodies."
        The discourse ended; the father drew his son
And his companion toward the hum, the center
Of the full host; they came to rising ground
Where all the long array was visible,
Anchises watching, noting, every comer.
"Glory to come, my son, illustrious spirits
Of Dardan lineage, Italian offspring,
Heirs of our name, begetters of our future!
These I will name for you and tell our fortunes:[51]   790
First, leaning on a headless spear, and standing
Nearest the light, that youth, the first to rise
To the world above, is Silvius; his name
Is Alban; in his veins Italian blood
Will run with Trojan; he will be the son
Of your late age; Lavinia will bear him,
A king and sire of kings; from him our race
Will rule in Alba Longa. Near him, Procas,
A glory to the Trojan race; and Capys,
And Numitor, and Silvius Aeneas,   800
Resembling you in name, in arms, in goodness,

---

[49] This notoriously elusive aphorism, typical of the difficulties in translating Virgil, probably means something like "Each endures his own penance and lives with his own purgatorial consciousness" (though other meanings have been suggested).

[50] Certain rare and noble spirits remain in Elysian bliss rather than being reincarnated. Anchises is one of these.

[51] In lines 791–808, Anchises describes the Trojan lineage in Italy up to the time of Romulus, legendary founder (in 753 B.C., several centuries after Aeneas) of Rome proper. Alba Longa, forerunner of Rome, was the city founded by Ascanius (as we are told in I.278–83). Silvius was third in the line to rule after Aeneas and Ascanius/Iulus. The persons listed in lines 798–800 were subsequent Alban kings (one of whom, Silvius Aeneas, was denied the throne for a long time). The aboriginal towns mentioned in lines 805–08 were near Rome.

If ever he wins the Alban kingdom over.
What fine young men they are! What strength, what prowess!
The civic oak already shades their foreheads.
These will found cities, Gabii, Fidenae,
Nomentum; they will crown the hills with towers
Above Collatia, Inuus fortress, Bola,
Cora, all names to be, thus far ungiven.
   "And there will be a son of Mars; his mother
Is Ilia, and his name is Romulus,   810
Assaracus' descendant. On his helmet
See, even now, twin plumes; his father's honor
Confers distinction on him for the world.
Under his auspices Rome, that glorious city,
Will bound her power by earth, her pride by heaven,
Happy in hero sons, one wall surrounding
Her seven hills, even as Cybele, riding
Through Phrygian cities, wears her crown of towers,
Rejoicing in her offspring, and embracing
A hundred children of the gods, her children,   820
Celestials, all of them, at home in heaven.[52]
Turn the eyes now this way; behold the Romans,
Your very own. These are Iulus' children,[53]
The race to come. One promise you have heard
Over and over: here is its fulfillment,
The son of a god, Augustus Caesar, founder
Of a new age of gold, in lands where Saturn
Ruled long ago;[54] he will extend his empire
Beyond the Indies, beyond the normal measure
Of years and constellations, where high Atlas   830
Turns on his shoulders the star-studded world.[55]
Maeotia[56] and the Caspian seas are trembling
As heaven's oracles predict his coming,
And all the seven mouths of Nile are troubled.
Not even Hercules, in all his travels,
Covered so much of the world, from Erymanthus
To Lerna; nor did Bacchus, driving his tigers
From Nysa's summit.[57] How can hesitation

[52] Cybele, a Phrygian (Trojan) deity considered the mother of the gods, was associated with the building and fortifying of cities.
[53] Iulus, Aeneas' son, was regarded as the progenitor of the Julian clan of Virgil's time, and thus of the line of Caesars.
[54] Augustus was "son of a god" because Julius Caesar, of whom Augustus was the adopted son, was deified at his death. Saturn, after being deposed by his son Jupiter, was supposed to have reigned in Italy during the mythical Age of Gold.
[55] The giant Atlas (sometimes identified with the north-African mountain) was imagined as supporting the heavens on his shoulders.
[56] Region north of the Black Sea.
[57] Erymanthus, a mountain range, and Lerna, a lake, were in Greece; among the Twelve Labors of Hercules were victories over monsters inhabiting these places. The mountain Nysa (located in India, according to one tradition) was the boyhood home of Bacchus, the god of wine, whose chariot was drawn by tigers.

Keep us from deeds to make our prowess greater?
What fear can block us from Ausonian[58] land?   840
    "And who is that one yonder, wearing the olive,
Holding the sacrifice? I recognize him,
That white-haired king of Rome, who comes from Cures,
A poor land, to a mighty empire, giver
Of law to the young town. His name is Numa.
Near him is Tullus; he will rouse to arms
A race grown sluggish, little used to triumph.
Beyond him Ancus, even now too boastful,
Too fond of popular favor.[59] And then the Tarquins,
And the avenger Brutus, proud of spirit,   850
Restorer of the balance. He shall be
First holder of the consular power; his children
Will stir up wars again, and he, for freedom
And her sweet sake, will call down judgment on them,
Unhappy, however future men may praise him,
In love of country and intense ambition.[60]
    "There are the Decii, and there the Drusi,
A little farther off, and stern Torquatus,
The man with the axe, and Camillus, the regainer
Of standards lost. And see those two, resplendent   860
In equal arms, harmonious friendly spirits
Now, in the shadow of night, but if they ever
Come to the world of light, alas, what warfare,
What battle-lines, what slaughter they will fashion,
Each for the other, one from Alpine ramparts
Descending, and the other ranged against him
With armies from the east, father and son
Through marriage, Pompey and Caesar.[61] O my children,
Cast out the thoughts of war, and do not murder
The flower of our country. O my son,   870
Whose line descends from heaven, let the sword
Fall from the hand, be leader in forbearing!
    "Yonder is one who, victor over Corinth,
Will ride in triumph home, famous for carnage
Inflicted on the Greeks; near him another,
Destroyer of old Argos and Mycenae

---

[58] Italian.

[59] The religious and civic lawgiver Numa Pompilius, the warlike Tullus, and Ancus (according to Virgil, a demagogue) were, respectively, the second, third, and fourth kings of Rome (Romulus having been the first).

[60] Brutus (not to be confused with the Brutus who assassinated Julius Caesar centuries later) expelled the last (seventh) of the Roman kings, Tarquinius Superbus, and founded the Roman republic in 509 B.C. He had his sons executed for attempting to restore the old monarchical line.

[61] The Decii, Torquatus, and Camillus were military or civic heroes of the fourth and third centuries B.C. The Drusi were ancestors of Livia, wife of Caesar Augustus. The civil war (49–45 B.C.) between the forces of Julius Caesar and those of his son-in-law Pompey, in Virgil's own lifetime, had been part of the chain of events culminating in the accession of Augustus.

Where Agamemnon ruled; he will strike down
A king descended from Achilles; Pydna
Shall be revenge for Pallas' ruined temple,
For Trojan ancestors. Who would pass over,   880
Without a word, Cossus, or noble Cato,
The Gracchi, or those thunderbolts of warfare,
The Scipios, Libya's ruin, or Fabricius
Mighty with little, or Serranus, ploughing
The humble furrow? My tale must hurry on:
I see the Fabii next, and their great Quintus
Who brought us back an empire by delaying.[62]
Others, no doubt, will better mould the bronze
To the semblance of soft breathing, draw, from marble,
The living countenance; and others plead   890
With greater eloquence, or learn to measure,
Better than we, the pathways of the heaven,
The risings of the stars; remember, Roman,
To rule the people under law, to establish
The way of peace, to battle down the haughty,
To spare the meek. Our fine arts, these, forever."[63]

    Anchises paused a moment, and they marvelled,
And he went on:—"See, how Marcellus[64] triumphs,
Glorious over all, with the great trophies
Won when he slew the captain of the Gauls,   900
Leader victorious over leading foeman.
When Rome is in great trouble and confusion
He will establish order, Gaul and Carthage
Go down before his sword, and triple trophies
Be given Romulus in dedication."

    There was a young man going with Marcellus,
Brilliant in shining armor, bright in beauty,
But sorrowful, with downcast eyes. Aeneas
Broke in, to ask his father: "Who is this youth[65]
Attendant on the hero? A son of his?   910
One of his children's children? How the crowd

---

[62] The "victor over Corinth" (line 873) was Mummius; the "another" of line 875 was probably Paullus (both second century B.C.). The latter, by defeating a Greek opponent, descended from Achilles, at the battle of Pydna, avenged Greek desecration of the Trojan temple of Pallas Athena during the Trojan War; see I.48–50, II.430–32. These two heroes, along with the other men named in lines 881–87, were among the greatest of the Roman military and political figures from the fifth through the second centuries B.C. The legacy of the episode with Dido is hinted at through the mention of the two Scipios and Quintus Fabius Maximus ("Cunctator," or "Delayer," famous for his drawn-out avoidance tactics), all three of whom won victories over Carthage in the Punic Wars (third and second centuries B.C.).

[63] In these memorable lines, one of the most famous passages in all of literature, the "Others" (line 888), with whose accomplishments Anchises is comparing those of the Romans, are primarily the Greeks. In oratory the Greeks were not in fact superior, but Anchises concedes even this area, so as to keep the distinction between the two peoples clean and emphatic.

[64] Roman general of the third century B.C.

[65] The Younger Marcellus—descendant of the Marcellus just described, nephew and son-in-law of Caesar Augustus, and presumed successor to him—died of malaria in 23 B.C. at the age of nineteen.

Murmurs and hums around him! what distinction,
What presence, in his person! But dark night
Hovers around his head with mournful shadow.
Who is he, father?" And Anchises answered:—
"Great sorrow for our people! O my son,
Ask not to know it. This one fate will only
Show to the world; he will not be permitted
Any long sojourn. Rome would be too mighty,
Too great in the gods' sight, were this gift hers.   920
What lamentation will the field of Mars[66]
Raise to the city! Tiber, gliding by
The new-built tomb, the funeral state, bear witness!
No youth from Trojan stock will ever raise
His ancestors so high in hope, no Roman
Be such a cause for pride. Alas for goodness,
Alas for old-time honor, and the arm
Invincible in war! Against him no one,
Whether on foot or foaming horse, would come
In battle and depart unscathed. Poor boy,   930
If you should break the cruel fates; if only—
You are to be Marcellus. Let me scatter
Lilies, or dark-red flowers, bringing honor
To my descendant's shade; let the gift be offered,
However vain the tribute."
      So through the whole wide realm they went together,
Anchises and his son; from fields of air
Learning and teaching of the fame and glory,
The wars to come, the toils to face, or flee from,
Latinus' city and the Latin peoples,   940
The love of what would be.
                              There are two portals,
Twin gates of Sleep, one made of horn, where easy
Release is given true shades, the other gleaming
White ivory, whereby the false dreams issue
To the upper air. Aeneas and the Sibyl
Part from Anchises at the second portal.[67]
He goes to the ships, again, rejoins his comrades,
Sails to Caieta's[68] harbor, and the vessels
Rest on their mooring-lines.

SUMMARY OF BOOKS VII–VIII

The Trojans continue their northward voyage along the western coast of Italy. They land and, while eating their meal off bread platters, suddenly realize that their acts fulfill the prophecy of

---

[66] The Campus Martius, site of Marcellus' tomb.

[67] Why Aeneas should emerge through the gate of falsehood is one of the most mystifying problems in the entire poem. Virgil may mean no more than that Aeneas ends his visit to the Lower World early in the night, since dreams dreamt at that time were considered deceiving. (The reliable dreams were those dreamt just before waking.) But the apparently deliberate effect of high-solemn mystery suggests some weightier meaning.

[68] A town about thirty-five miles up the coast from Cumae and the modern Naples.

*hunger and that they are at the destined place. On the following day they reach the river Tiber
and the city of King Latinus. He recognizes in Aeneas the realization of a prophecy that his
daughter Lavinia would marry a stranger. At Juno's instigation, the Italian hero Turnus,
a suitor of Lavinia who is jealous of Aeneas, stirs up opposition to the Trojans, and Aeneas prepares for war with him. Guided by a dream, Aeneas enlists the support of Evander,
whose city lies on the future site of Rome. Aeneas' mother Venus presents him with a shield,
made by the god Vulcan, on which important events in the future history of Rome have been
carved, a history that culminates in the victory of Augustus over Antony and Cleopatra at
Actium:*

from Book VIII: AENEAS AT THE SITE OF ROME

And the bright goddess through the clouds of heaven
Came bringing gifts, seeing her son alone
By the cold river in the quiet valley,
And spoke to him:—"Behold, the gifts made ready
By Vulcan's promised skill. Fear not, my son,
To face the wars with Turnus and the Latins!"
After the word, the embrace. She placed the armor,
All shining in his sight, against an oak-tree; 630
Rejoicing in the gift, the honor, he turned
His eyes to these, over and over again,
Could not be satisfied, took in his hands
The helmet with the terrible plumes and flame,
The fatal sword, the breastplate, made of bronze,
Fire-colored, huge, shining the way a cloud,
Dark-blue, turns crimson under the slanting sun,
The greaves of gold refined and smooth electrum,[1]
The spear, the final masterpiece, the shield.
    Hereon the great prophetic Lord of Fire 640
Had carved the story out, the stock to come,
The wars, each one in order, all the tale
Of Italy and Roman triumph.[2] Here
In Mars' green cave the she-wolf gives her udders
To the twin boys, turning half round to lick them,
And neither is afraid, and both are playing.[3]
Another scene presents the Circus-games,
When Romans took their Sabine brides, and war
Broke out between old Tatius and the sons
Of Romulus, and was ended, monarchs pledging 650

[1] Greaves were armor for the shins. Electrum was an alloy of gold and silver.
[2] The divinely made shield of Achilles in Homer's *Iliad*, Book XVIII, contains in pictures a
synopsis of the ways of human life, in fairly universal terms. Virgil's equivalent, for Aeneas, is
a vision of the glories of Roman history to come and of the Roman character.
[3] To make his usurped power secure, Amulius attempted to have his great-nephews, the
infant Romulus and his twin brother Remus, drowned in the Tiber, but they survived, being
suckled by a she-wolf in the cave of the Lupercal on the site of Rome. Romulus grew up to
found the city and establish its line of kings.

Peace at the altars over sacrifice.[4]
Mettus, the false, by the wild horses drawn
And quartered, sheds his life-blood over the brambles;[5]
Porsena, the besieger, rings the city
For Tarquin's sake, exile and tyrant; Romans
Rush on the steel for freedom; Clelia breaks
Her bonds to swim the river; and Horatius
Breaks down the bridge.[6] The guardian Manlius
Holds the high capitol and that crude palace
Fresh with the straw of Romulus; the goose   660
Flutters in silver through the colonnades
Shrieking alarm; the Gauls are near in darkness,
Golden their hair, their clothing, and their necks
Gleam white in collars of gold, and each one carries
Two Alpine javelins; they have long shields.
Near them, the Fire-god sets the priests with caps
Of wool, the miracle of the shields from heaven,
The Salii dancing, the Luperci naked,
And the chaste matrons riding through the city
In cushioned chariots.[7] Far off, he adds   670
The seats of Hell, the lofty gates of Pluto,
Penance for sin: Catiline, with the Furies
Making him cower; farther off, the good,
With Cato giving laws.[8] And all this scene
Bound with the likeness of the swelling ocean,
Blue water and whitecap, where the dolphins playing
Leap with a curve of silver. In the center

---

[4] The men of the newly founded city, having no women, seized them from Sabines who had come to watch the games in honor of Neptune being celebrated in the Circus, or amphitheater, of Rome. The seizing of the women caused war between the Romans and Sabines (ruled by Tatius), but it was halted through the intervention of the women, and the two peoples became allies.

[5] Mettus Fufetius was executed in the way described when, after having promised to fight for Rome during one of its early regional conflicts, he treacherously withdrew his troops from battle.

[6] After the Romans expelled their savage and tyrannical king Tarquinius Superbus, the Etrurian king Lars Porsena of Clusium attacked Rome in an attempt to restore Tarquinius to the throne. In the face of the enemy, Horatius held a bridge over the Tiber until it could be destroyed. This helped save the newborn (509 B.C.) Roman republic. Clelia was a young Roman woman who, having been taken hostage by Porsena, escaped by swimming the Tiber, was then returned to Porsena by the Romans, and finally was freed by Porsena, along with other prisoners, because he admired her courage.

[7] When Gauls from the Alps threatened the citadel of Rome in 390 B.C., the Roman consul Manlius was alerted to their night attack by the cackling of the sacred geese kept at the Capitol, where the early thatched hut of the founder Romulus was also preserved. Lines 666–70 describe religious celebrations of Roman victory and also acknowledge the Roman matrons, whose right to ride in luxury was earned by earlier contributions of their gold and jewels to the state.

[8] We see scenes of contrasted evil and good: Catiline, who in 63 B.C. plotted against the Roman government and is now punished in Hell by the Furies, and Cato the Younger (95–46 B.C.), the model of old-fashioned Roman virtue.

Actium,[9] the ships of bronze, Leucate[10] burning
Hot with the glow of war, and waves on fire
With molten gold. Augustus Caesar stands   680
High on the lofty stern; his temples flame
With double fire, and over his head there dawns
His father's star.[11] Agrippa[12] leads a column
With favoring wind and god, the naval garland
Wreathing his temples. Antony assembles
Egypt and all the East; Antony, victor
Over the lands of dawn and the Red Sea,
Marshals the foes of Rome, himself a Roman,
With—horror!—an Egyptian wife. The surge
Boils under keel, the oar-blades churn the waters,   690
The triple-pointed beaks drive through the billows,
You would think that mountains swam and battled mountains,
That islands were uprooted in their anger.
Fireballs and shafts of steel are slanting showers,
The fields of Neptune redden with the slaughter.
The queen drives on her warriors, unseeing
The double snakes of death;[13] rattle and cymbals
Compete with bugle and trumpet. Monstrous gods,
Of every form and fashion, one, Anubis,
Shaped like a dog, wield their outrageous weapons   700
In wrath at Venus, Neptune, and Minerva.
Mars, all in steel, storms through the fray; the Furies
Swoop from the sky; Discord exults; Bellona,[14]
With bloody scourge, comes lashing; and Apollo
From Actium bends his bow. Egypt and India,
Sabaeans and Arabians, flee in terror.
And the contagion takes the queen, who loosens
The sheets to slackness, courts the wind, in terror,
Pale at the menace of death. And the Nile comes
To meet her, a protecting god, his mantle   710
Spread wide, to bring a beaten woman home.
And Caesar enters Rome triumphant, bringing

---

[9] The climactic scene, at the center of the shield, shows the naval victory by the forces of Octavian (later Caesar Augustus) over the combined forces of Mark Antony, his rival for power, and Cleopatra, the Egyptian queen who had become Antony's consort. The great battle took place at Actium, off western Greece, in 31 B.C.; it ended decades of Roman civil war. Virgil presents this battle as a conflict between Roman virtue and Eastern luxury, decadence, and religious barbarism. Antony's and Cleopatra's fleets returned to Egypt, after she panicked, and a year later both he and she died defeated, leaving Octavian in sole power and bringing peace to Rome.

[10] A promontory near Actium that served as base for Octavian's fleet.

[11] A comet representing the spirit of the late Julius Caesar was supposed to have appeared in 43 B.C. in honor of Octavian, his adopted son; thereafter Octavian wore a star on his helmet.

[12] War minister and commander of Octavian's forces at Actium.

[13] The ill-omened double snakes are especially appropriate to Cleopatra because she afterward committed suicide by allowing herself to be bitten by asps.

[14] Goddess of war.

Immortal offerings, three times a hundred
New altars through the city. Streets are loud
With gladness, games, rejoicing; all the temples
Are filled with matrons praying at the altars,
Are heaped with solemn sacrifice. And Caesar,
Seated before Apollo's shining threshold,
Reviews the gifts, and hangs them on the portals.
In long array the conquered file, their garments,   720
Their speech, as various as their arms, the Nomads,
The naked Africans, Leleges, Carians,
Gelonians with quivers, the Morini,
Of mortals most remote, Euphrates moving
With humbler waves, the two-mouthed Rhine, Araxes,
Chafing beneath his bridge.[15]
                    All this Aeneas
Sees on his mother's gift, the shield of Vulcan,
And, without understanding, is proud and happy
As he lifts to his shoulder all that fortune,
The fame and glory of his children's children.   730

SUMMARY OF BOOKS IX–XII

Turnus' army has been laying siege to the Trojan camp in Aeneas' absence. Aeneas returns to the battlefield with new allies, including Evander's forces under the command of his young son Pallas. A general battle ensues. Evander's troops are nearly defeated when Pallas rallies them, but Pallas is then killed by Turnus, who savagely exults over the defeated youth and callously strips him of his armor. Aeneas is enraged and grief-stricken, all the more because he had been entrusted by Evander with the care of his dear son. Aeneas seeks Turnus in order to avenge Pallas' death, but Juno lures Turnus away from the battlefield. With great ceremony, Aeneas sends Pallas' body back to his father, and a twelve-day truce is declared.

An agreement is reached under which Aeneas and Turnus will settle the war through single combat. But the agreement is violated by the Latins and general fighting breaks out again:

from BOOK XII: THE FINAL COMBAT

And now his goddess-mother sent Aeneas
A change of purpose, to direct his column
More quickly toward the town, confuse the Latins   610
With sudden onslaught.[1] He was tracking Turnus
Here, there, all up and down the columns, watching,
Shifting his gaze, and so he saw that city
Immune from that fierce warfare, calm and peaceful.

---

[15] The list of names is primarily geographical symbolism honoring Caesar Augustus and Rome. The wandering Nomads (Numidians) were from Africa, the Leleges and Carians from Asia, the Gelonians and Morini from eastern and northern Europe. The Araxes is the river Aras, in Armenia.

[1] Aeneas decides to assault Latinus' city directly rather than engage the enemy troops on the field outside the city.

The vision of a greater fight comes to him:
He calls Sergestus, Mnestheus, brave Serestus,
And takes position on a mound; the Trojans
Come massing toward him, shield and spear held ready.
And as he stands above them, he gives the orders:—
"Let there be no delay: great Jove is with us.   620
Let no man go more slackly, though this venture
Is new and unexpected. That city yonder,
The cause of war, the kingdom of Latinus,
Unless they own our mastery, acknowledge
Defeat, declare obedience, I will topple,
Level its smoking roof-tops to the ground.
Or should I wait until it suits prince Turnus
To face the duel with me, and, once beaten,
Consent to fight again? This[2] is the head,
O citizens, this the evil crown of warfare.   630
Hurry, bring firebrands, win from fire the treaty!"
His words inflame their zeal, and, all together
They form a wedge; a great mass moves to the wall,
Ladders and sudden fire appear from nowhere;
The guards at the gate are butchered; steel is flying,
The sky is dark with arrows. Toward the city
Aeneas lifts his hand, rebukes Latinus,
Calling the gods to witness that his will
Was not for battle, it was forced upon him
By the Italians, double treaty-breakers,   640
His foes for now the second time.[3] The townsmen
Quarrel among themselves: "Open the town!",
Cry some, "Admit the Trojans!" and would drag
The king himself to the ramparts. Others hurry
With arms, man the defenses. When a shepherd
Trails bees to their hive in the cleft of a rock and fills it
With smarting smoke, there is fright and noise and fury
Within the waxen camp, and anger sharpened
With buzzing noises, and a black smell rises
With a blind sound, inside the rock, and rolling   650
Smoke lifts to empty air.
                         Now a new sorrow
Came to the weary Latins, shook the city
To its foundations, utterly. The queen
Had seen the Trojans coming and the walls
Under attack and fire along the gables
And no Rutulian column, nowhere Turnus
Coming to help. He had been killed, her hero,
She knew at last.[4] Her mind was gone; she cried

---

[2] This city.
[3] The Italians, or Latins, had first violated a treaty of alliance with the Trojans, including a
plan for Aeneas to marry Latinus' daughter Lavinia, then violated the single-combat treaty.
[4] Latinus' queen, Amata, had favored Turnus and bitterly opposed Aeneas as suitor for her
daughter Lavinia's hand. The Rutulians were Turnus' people.

Over and over:—"I am the guilty one,
I am the cause, the source of all these evils!"   660
And other wilder words. And then she tore
Her crimson robes, and slung a noose and fastened
The knot of an ugly death to the high rafter.
The women learned it first, and then Lavinia:
The wide hall rings with grief and lamentation;
Nails scratch at lovely faces, beautiful hair
Is torn from the head. And Rumor spreads the story
All up and down the town, and poor Latinus,
Rending his garments, comes and stares,—wife gone,
And city falling, an old man's hoary hair   670
Greyer with bloody dust.
                             And meanwhile Turnus
Out on the plain pursues the stragglers, slower
And slower now, and less and less exultant
In his triumphant car. From the city comes
A wind that bears a cry confused with terror,
Half heard, but known,—confusion, darkness, sorrow,
An uproar in the town. He checks the horses,
Pauses and listens. And his sister prompts him:[5]—
"This way, this way! The Trojans run, we follow
Where victory shows the path. Let others guard   680
The houses with their valor. The Italians
Fall in the fight before Aeneas. Let us
Send death to the Trojans, in our turn. You will not
Come off the worse, in numbers or in honor."
Turnus replies:—"O sister, I have known,
A long while since, that you were no Metiscus,
Since first you broke the treaty and joined the battle.
No use pretending you are not a goddess.
But who, from high Olympus, sent you down
To bear such labors? Was it to see your brother   690
In pitiful cruel death? What am I doing,
What chance will fortune grant me? I have seen
A man I loved more than the rest, Murranus,
A big man, slain by a big wound, go down.
Ufens is fallen, lucky or unlucky,
In that he never saw our shame; the Trojans
Have won his body and arms. Our homes are burning,
The one thing lacking up to now,—and shall I
Endure this, not refute the words of Drances
With this right hand?[6] Shall I turn my back upon them?   700

---

[5] Turnus' sister Juturna, seduced by Jupiter and granted immortality as a water-nymph in recompense, has disguised herself as Metiscus, her brother's charioteer, steering the chariot away from Aeneas in the hope of postponing Turnus' fated death.

[6] Drances, in an assembly of the Latins, had denounced Turnus and (unjustly) accused him of cowardice.

Is it so grim to die? Be kind, O shadows,[7]
Since the high gods have turned their favor from me.
A decent spirit, undisgraced, no coward,
I shall descend to you, never unworthy
Of all my ancient line."
                              He had hardly spoken
When a warrior, on foaming steed, came riding
Through all the enemy. His name was Saces,
And his face was badly wounded by an arrow.
He called the name of Turnus, and implored him:—
"We have no other hope; pity your people!   710
Aeneas is a lightning-bolt; he threatens
Italy's topmost towers; he will bring them down
In ruins; even now the brands[8] are flying
Along the roof-tops. They look to you, the Latins,
They look for you; and king Latinus mumbles
In doubt—who are his sons, who are his allies?[9]
The queen, who trusted you the most, has perished
By her own hand, has fled the light in terror.
Alone before the gates the brave Atinas
And Messapus hold the line. Around them, squadrons   720
Crowd close on either side, and the steel harvest
Bristles with pointed swords. And here is Turnus
Wheeling his car across a plain deserted."
    Bewildered by disaster's shifting image,
Turnus is silent, staring; shame and sadness
Boil up in that great heart, and grief and love
Driven by frenzy. He shakes off the shadows;
The light comes back to his mind. His eyes turn, blazing,
From the wheels of the car to the walls of that great city
Where the flame billowed upward, the roaring blast   730
Catching a tower, one he himself had fashioned
With jointed beams and rollers and high gangways.
"Fate is the winner now; keep out of my way,
My sister: now I follow god and fortune.
I am ready for Aeneas, ready to bear
Whatever is bitter in death. No longer, sister,
Shall I be shamed, and you behold me. Let me,
Before the final madness, be a madman!"
He bounded from the chariot, came rushing
Through spears, through enemies; his grieving sister   740
He left behind, forgotten. As a boulder
Torn from a mountain-top rolls headlong downward,
Impelled by wind, or washed by storm, or loosened

---

[7] The gods of the Lower World. They are contrasted with the "high gods," mentioned in the following line.
[8] Firebrands; flaming missiles.
[9] Latinus wonders whether the women among his people are to marry Trojans or Latins.

By time's erosion, and comes down the hillside
A mass possessed of evil, leaping and bounding,
And rolling with it men and trees and cattle,
So, through the broken columns, Turnus rushes
On to the city, where the blood goes deepest
Into the muddy ground, and the air whistles
With flying spears. He makes a sudden gesture,   750
Crying aloud:—"No more, no more, Rutulians!
Hold back your weapons, Latins! Whatever fortune
There may be here is mine. I am the one,
Not you, to make the treaty good, to settle
The issue with the sword. That will be better."
They all made way and gave him room.

                             Aeneas,
Hearing the name of Turnus, leaves the city,
Forsakes the lofty walls; he has no patience
With any more delay, breaks off all projects,
Exults, a terrible thunderer in armor,   760
As huge as Athos, or as huge as Eryx,
Or even father Apennine, that mountain
Roaring above the oaks, and lifting high
His crown of shimmering trees and snowy crest.[10]
Now all men turned their eyes, Rutulians, Trojans,
Italians, those who held the lofty ramparts,
Those battering at the wall below; their shoulders
Were eased of armor now. And king Latinus
Could hardly, in amazement, trust his senses
Seeing these two big men, born worlds apart,   770
Meeting to make decision with the sword.
The plain was cleared, and they came rushing forward,
Hurling, far off, their spears; the fight is on,
The bronze shields clang and ring. Earth gives a groan.
The swords strike hard and often; luck and courage
Are blent in one. And as on mighty Sila
Or on Taburnus' mountain,[11] when two bullocks
Charge into fight head-on, and trembling herdsmen
Fall back in fear, and the herd is dumb with terror,
And heifers, hardly lowing, stare and wonder   780
Which one will rule the woodland, which one the herd
Will follow meekly after, and all the time
They gore each other with savage horns, and shoulders
And necks and ribs run streams of blood, and bellowing
Fills all the woodland,—even so, Aeneas
And Daunus' son[12] clash shield on shield; the clamor
Fills heaven. And Jupiter holds the scales in balance

---

[10] Athos and Eryx were mountains in, respectively, northern Greece and Sicily. The Apennines were the mountains forming the geographical backbone of Italy.
[11] Sila was a mountain range and forest in southern Italy, Taburnus a mountain in central Italy.
[12] Turnus was the son of Daunus and the nymph Venilia.

With each man's destiny as weight and counter,
And one the heavier under the doom of death.
    Confident, Turnus, rising to the sword   790
Full height, is a flash of light; he strikes. The Trojans,
The Latins, cry aloud and come up standing.
But the sword is treacherous; it is broken off
With the blow half spent: the fire of Turnus finds
No help except in flight. Swift as the wind
He goes, and stares at a broken blade, a hand
Unarmed. The story is that in that hurry,
That rush of his, to arms, when the steeds were harnessed,
He took Metiscus' sword, not the one Daunus
Had left him.[13] For a while it served its purpose   800
While the Trojans ran away, but when it met
The armor Vulcan forged, the mortal blade
Split off, like brittle ice, with glittering splinters
Like ice on the yellow sand. So Turnus flies
Madly across the plain in devious circles:
The Trojans ring him round, and a swamp on one side,
High walls on the other.
                Aeneas, the pursuer,
Is none too swift: the arrow has left him hurt;[14]
His knees give way, but he keeps on, keeps coming
After the panting enemy, as a hound,   810
Running a stag to bay, at the edge of the water
Or hedged by crimson plumes,[15] darts in, and barks,
And snaps his jaws, closes and grips, is shaken
Off from the flanks again, and once more closes,
And a great noise goes up the air; the waters
Resound, and the whole sky thunders with the clamor.
Turnus has time, even in flight, for calling
Loud to Rutulians, each by name, demanding,
In terrible rage, the sword, the sword, the good one,
The one he knows. Let anybody bring it,   820
Aeneas threatens, and death and doom await him,
And the town will be a ruin. Wounded, still
He presses on. They go in five great circles,
Around and back: no game, with silly prizes,
Are they playing now; the life and blood of Turnus
Go to the winner.
        A wild olive-tree
Stood here, with bitter leaves, sacred to Faunus,[16]
Revered by rescued sailors, who used to offer

---

[13] Like Aeneas' armor, the sword Turnus inherited from Daunus had been made by the god Vulcan.

[14] Earlier in the day, Aeneas had been put temporarily out of action when he was wounded by an anonymous archer. His mother Venus had helped heal his wound.

[15] In hunting, barriers made of colorful feathers were used to scare game animals and keep them inside the hunting precincts.

[16] King Latinus' father, a rustic god.

Ex-votos[17] to the native gods, their garments
In token of gratitude. For this the Trojans   830
Cared nothing, lopped the branches off to clear
The run of the field. Aeneas' spear had fastened
Deep in the trunk where the force of the cast had brought it,
Stuck in the grip of the root. Aeneas, stooping,
Yanks at the shaft; he cannot equal Turnus
In speed of foot, but the javelin is wingèd.
And Turnus, in a terrible moment of panic,
Cries:—"Faunus, pity me, and Earth, most kindly,
If ever I was reverent, as Aeneas
And those he leads have not been, hold the steel,   840
Do not let go!" He prayed, and he was answered.
Aeneas tugged and wrestled, pulled and hauled,
But the wood held on. And, while he strained, Juturna
Rushed forward, once again Metiscus' double,
With the good sword for her brother. Then Venus, angry
Over such wanton interference, enters
And the root yields. The warriors, towering high,
Each one renewed in spirit, one with sword,
One with the spear, both breathing hard, are ready
For what Mars[18] has to send.
                                  And Juno, gazing   850
From a golden cloud to earth, watching the duel,
Heard the all-powerful king of high Olympus:—
"What will the end be now, O wife? What else
Remains? You know, and you admit you know it,
Aeneas is heaven-destined, the native hero
Become a god,[19] raised by the fates, exalted.
What are you planning? with what hope lingering on
In the cold clouds? Was it proper that a mortal
Should wound a god?[20] that the sword, once lost, be given
Turnus again?—Juturna, of course, is nothing   860
Without your help—was it proper that the beaten
Increase in violence? Stop it now, I tell you;
Listen to my entreaties: I would not have you
Devoured by grief in silence; I would not have you
Bring me, again, anxiety and sorrow,
However sweet the voice. The end has come.
To harry the Trojans over land and ocean,
To light up war unspeakable, to defile
A home with grief, to mingle bridal and sorrow,—
All this you were permitted. Go no farther!   870
That is an absolute order." And Juno, downcast

---

[17] Offerings made in fulfillment of a vow or in acknowledgment of a prayer answered.

[18] The god of war.

[19] In the future, Aeneas will be deified and regarded as their own hero by the natives of Italy.

[20] The "god" is Aeneas; the "mortal" is the anonymous bowsman who wounded Aeneas earlier.

In gaze, replied:—"Great Jove, I knew your pleasure:
And therefore, much against my will, left Turnus,
Left earth. Were it not so, you would not see me
Lonely upon my airy throne in heaven,
Enduring things both worthy and unworthy,
But I would be down there, by flame surrounded,
Fighting in the front ranks, and hauling Trojans
To battle with their enemies. Juturna,
I urged, I own, to help her wretched brother,   880
And I approved, I own, her greater daring
For his life's sake, but I did not approve,
And this I swear by Styx, that river whose name
Binds all the gods to truth, her taking weapons,
Aiming the bow.²¹ I give up now, I leave
These battles, though I hate to. I ask one favor
For Latium, for the greatness of your people,
And this no law of fate forbids: when, later,
And be it so, they join in peace, and settle
Their laws, their treaties, in a blessèd marriage,   890
Do not command the Latins, native-born,
To change their language, to be known as Trojans,
To alter speech or garb; let them be Latium,
Let Alban kings endure through all the ages,²²
Let Roman stock, strong in Italian valor,
Prevail: since Troy has fallen, let her name
Perish and be forgotten." Smiling on her,
The great creator answered:—"You are truly
True sister of Jove and child of Saturn, nursing
Such tides of anger in the heart!²³ Forget it!   900
Abate the rise of passion. The wish is granted.
I yield, and more than that,—I share your purpose.
Ausonians²⁴ shall keep their old tradition,
Their fathers' speech and ways; their name shall be
Even as now it is. Their sacred laws,
Their ritual, I shall add, and make all Latins
Men of a common tongue. A race shall rise
All-powerful, of mingled blood; you will see them
By virtue of devotion rise to glories
Not men nor gods have known, and no race ever   910
Will ·pay you equal honor."²⁵ And the goddess
Gave her assent, was happy, changed her purpose,

²¹ Juturna, in a different disguise, had been instrumental in the violation of the single-combat pact.
²² Latium was the region in west-central Italy where the action of the second half of the poem has been taking place. The royal line of Alba Longa, the city Iulus/Ascanius will found, was prophetically described by Anchises in VI.787–808.
²³ The Greek god Cronus, identified by the Romans with Saturn, was notoriously violent, fiercely devouring almost all his children.
²⁴ Italians.
²⁵ Juno was one of the three deities worshiped in the great Roman temple at the Capitol (the other two being Jupiter and Minerva).

Left heaven and quit the cloud.
                              This done, the father
Formed yet another purpose, that Juturna
Should leave her fighting brother. There are, men say,
Twin fiends, or triple, sisters named the Furies,
Daughters of Night, with snaky coils, and pinions[26]
Like those of wind. They are attendant spirits
Before the throne of Jove and whet the fears
Of sickly mortals, when the king of heaven   920
Contrives disease or dreadful death, or frightens
The guilty towns in war. Now he dispatches
One of the three to earth, to meet Juturna,
An omen visible; and so from heaven
She flew with whirlwind swiftness, like an arrow
Through cloud from bowstring, armed with gall or poison,
Loosed from a Parthian quiver,[27] cleaving shadows
Swifter than man may know, a shaft no power
Has power of healing over:—so Night's daughter
Came down to earth, and when she saw the Trojans   930
And Turnus' columns, she dwindled, all of a sudden,
To the shape of that small bird, which, in the night-time,
Shrills its late song, ill-omened, on the roof-tops
Or over tombs, insistent through the darkness.
And so the fiend, the little screech-owl, flying
At Turnus, over and over, shrilled in warning,
Beating the wings against the shield, and Turnus
Felt a strange torpor seize his limbs, and terror
Made his hair rise, and his voice could find no utterance.
    But when, far off, Juturna knew the Fury   940
By whir of those dread wings, she tore her tresses,
Clawed at her face, and beat her breast, all anguish
Over her brother:—"What can a sister do
To help you now, poor Turnus? What remains
For me to bear? I have borne so much already.
What skill of mine can make the daylight longer
In your dark hour? Can I face such a portent?[28]
Now, now, I leave the battle-line forever.
Foul birds, I fear enough; haunt me no further,
I know that beat of the wings, that deadly whirring;   950
I recognize, too well, Jove's arrogant orders,
His payment for my maidenhood. He gave me
Eternal life, but why? Why has he taken
The right of death away from me? I might have
Ended my anguish, surely, with my brother's,
Gone, at his side, among the fearful shadows,
But, no,—I am immortal. What is left me

---

[26] Wings.   [27] Parthia, in what is now Iran, was noted for skill in archery.
[28] Bad omen. The appearance here of one of the Furies, agents of retribution and punishing fate, gives the ending of the poem an effect like that of Greek tragedy.

Of any possible joy, without my brother?
What earth can open deep enough to take me,
A goddess, to the lowest shades?" The mantle,   960
Grey-colored, veiled her head, and the goddess, sighing,
Sank deep from sight to the greyness of the river.
    And on Aeneas presses: the flashing spear,
Brandished, is big as a tree; his anger cries:—
"Why put it off forever, Turnus, hang-dog?
We must fight with arms, not running. Take what shape
You will, gather your strength or craft; fly up
To the high stars, or bury yourself in earth!"
And Turnus shook his head and answered:—"Jove,
Being my enemy, scares me, and the gods,   970
Not your hot words, fierce fellow." And his vision,
Glancing about, beheld a mighty boulder,
A boundary-mark, in days of old, so huge
A dozen men in our degenerate era
Could hardly pry it loose from earth, but Turnus
Lifts it full height, hurls it full speed and, acting,
Seems not to recognize himself, in running,
Or moving, or lifting his hands, or letting the stone
Fly into space; he shakes at the knees, his blood
Runs chill in the veins, and the stone, through wide air going, 980
Falls short, falls spent. As in our dreams at night-time,
When sleep weighs down our eyes, we seem to be running,
Or trying to run, and cannot, and we falter,
Sick in our failure, and the tongue is thick
And the words we try to utter come to nothing,
No voice, no speech,—so Turnus finds the way
Blocked off, wherever he turns, however bravely.
All sorts of things go through his mind: he stares
At the Rutulians, at the town; he trembles,
Quails at the threat of the lance; he cannot see   990
Any way out, any way forward. Nothing.
The chariot is gone, and the charioteer,
Juturna or Metiscus, nowhere near him.
The spear, flung by Aeneas, comes with a whir
Louder than stone from any engine, louder
Than thunderbolt; like a black wind it flies,
Bringing destruction with it, through the shield-rim,
Its sevenfold strength, through armor, through the thigh.
Turnus is down, on hands and knees, huge Turnus
Struck to the earth. Groaning, the stunned Rutulians   1000
Rise to their feet, and the whole hill resounds,
The wooded heights give echo. A suppliant, beaten,
Humbled at last, his hands reach out, his voice
Is low in pleading:—"I have deserved it, surely,
And I do not beg off. Use the advantage.
But if a parent's grief has any power
To touch the spirit, I pray you, pity Daunus,

(I would Anchises), send him back my body.
You have won; I am beaten, and these hands go out
In supplication: everyone has seen it.   1010
No more. I have lost Lavinia. Let hatred
Proceed no further."
Fierce in his arms, with darting glance, Aeneas
Paused for a moment, and he might have weakened,
For the words had moved him, when, high on the shoulder,
He saw the belt of Pallas, slain by Turnus,
Saw Pallas on the ground, and Turnus wearing
That belt with the bright studs, of evil omen
Not only to Pallas now, a sad reminder,
A deadly provocation. Terrible   1020
In wrath, Aeneas cries:—"Clad in this treasure,
This trophy of a comrade, can you cherish
Hope that my hands would let you go? Now Pallas,
Pallas exacts his vengeance, and the blow
Is Pallas, making sacrifice!" He struck
Before he finished speaking: the blade went deep
And Turnus' limbs were cold in death; the spirit
Went with a moan indignant to the shadows.

Ovid
(43 B.C.–17 A.D.)

*Ovid and Virgil have been the two most influential Latin narrative poets—though
for very different reasons. Ovid was born into an old established family in the town
now called Sulmona, about a hundred miles east of Rome, in 43 B.C.—one year after
the assassination of Julius Caesar. He died in A.D. 17, during the reign of Tiberius,
Augustus' successor as emperor. Significantly, even symbolically, the twelve-year-old
Ovid was sent to Rome, to be educated for the law, at very nearly the same time
Augustus defeated Antony and Cleopatra in the battle of Actium. The victory brought
order and peace—if also efficient autocracy—to the Roman state for the first time in
generations. (See the Introduction to Virgil.) Virgil's values and sensibilities, shaped
and indeed scarred by the experience of civil war, were essentially conservative. Ovid
was a decade too young to have known that trauma; his formative years were not
shadowed by harrowing memories of iron, blood, and strife. Like a Parisian
boulevardier of the 1920's too young to have known the trenches, Ovid frequented a
somewhat younger set of artists less closely associated than Virgil's circle was with the
Augustan establishment.*

*After a few routine assignments in the Roman civil service and some travel in
Greece, Ovid abandoned the law to become a professional poet. Although the tradition that Ovid was a dissipated playboy probably has little truth, there is no doubt
that, as poet, Ovid was witty, skeptical, and almost subversively irreverent toward the*

austere official Augustan values. For example, his relatively early masterpiece, the Ars Amatoria, *or* Art of Love *(completed about 1 B.C.), a manual on how to conduct love affairs, is an amusingly amoral, worldly, though also psychologically sensitive treatment of men and women in love.*

Perhaps predictably, the poem got Ovid in serious trouble. In A.D. 8, though he was now the leading poet of Rome, he was summoned before Augustus, tried summarily, and banished to Tomis (in modern Romania), an outpost of the Roman empire, and indeed of civilization. One reason for Ovid's exile is known: his authorship of The Art of Love, *a work incompatible with Augustus' program for Roman piety. There was also a second reason, never explicitly identified by Ovid, that remains mysterious despite much detective work by scholars. Apparently it too was some personal or political offense against Augustus or his official code of values.*

This most urban and urbane of men now had to endure not just the absence of metropolitan society and amenities but also real danger from hostile border tribes. From Tomis the poet wrote a number of poignant works in verse, directly or indirectly pleading for permission to return to the city and to the people he knew and loved. But Augustus did not relent, nor, after his death, did Tiberius. Ovid was still in exile when he died. All this is ironic; whatever real or imaginary excesses Ovid may have been guilty of, they can hardly have rivaled the enormities that Roman historians have attributed to Tiberius, Nero, and their ages.

The Metamorphoses, *composed in the years immediately preceding his exile, belongs to Ovid's middle poetry, between the naughty early love poetry and the sad poetry of exile. The title signifies "miraculous transformations," though this theme sometimes has only perfunctory importance in the tales. Few poems of any age or language have shaped so much later literature. There are many reasons for this influence. For one thing, the poem is an almost exhaustive handbook of the best-known classical myths—it is thus a treasury of good stories and indeed a reference work. It is also a rhetorical tour de force, a model illustrating a great variety of poetic, linguistic, and stylistic tricks. (Ovid's training in the law and public speaking did not go to waste.) It is a wonderfully comic work—as, for example, in its portrait in Book X of Venus as a sexpot whose idea of roughing it is to hunt rabbits. Its characterizations of both gods and human beings are complex and sensitive. It is also, in places, a tragic work, especially if one defines tragedy so as to include painful conflicts within individual persons independent of historical, public, and other grand consequences.*

This interest in the idiosyncrasies, sometimes in the pathology, of feelings, especially of people in love, puts Ovid in somewhat the same relationship to Virgil that Euripides held to Aeschylus. Perhaps the nearest modern equivalent of the Metamorphoses *is Byron's* Don Juan *(1818–1823); defending his poem through a sneer at his brother Romantics' overintensity, Byron once wrote, "You have so many 'divine' poems; is it nothing to have written a human one?" Like* Don Juan, *the* Metamorphoses *is a seriocomic poem, simultaneously a spoof of the heroic tradition and a searching critique of it. In writing the poem, Ovid abandoned his usual poetic meter, the elegiac couplet, and chose instead the six-foot dactyllic line used in the* Iliad, *the* Odyssey, *and the* Aeneid. *The meter is one of many indications that Ovid meant his poem to be compared with Virgil's epic. Sometimes the relationship is that of mock-epic diminution: Virgil's grand vision of origins, which finds the seeds of history and empire in the past, becomes for Ovid an account of the origin of such things as flowers and trees—rather like modern nursery tales about how the tiger got his stripes; Aeneas' meeting with Venus-as-huntress in Book I of the* Aeneid *becomes in Ovid's Book X a facetious picture of the absurdity and discomfort of Venus in that unlikely role. Yet there is a saucy implication that Ovid can beat Virgil at his own game; if Virgil's epic could span a thousand years of legend and history, Ovid will outdo him by beginning, not with the fall of Troy, but with the aboriginal creation of the cosmos itself.*

Ovid repeatedly undermines Virgil's moralism. And yet, as with Byron, his technique of deflation is itself a kind of moral statement. In treating the gods and goddesses not religiously but as recognizable human beings, Ovid satirizes Virgil's religious piety and his implication that the universe, though mysterious, is just. The metamorphoses ordained by Ovid's deities often seem unjust, out of proportion to the offense and motivated by the wounded petty vanity of beings whose superiority to us humans consists merely in the lucky accidents of power and immortality.

From the late Middle Ages on, the Metamorphoses *has never lost its appeal, for readers and for authors both minor and great. A number of attempts have been made to rehabilitate Ovid's moral values, mainly by treating him allegorically. And the central idea of the work can be adapted to serious purposes, as Kafka demonstrates in our century in his novella* The Metamorphosis. *But the most typical attitude of later authors toward Ovid is not reverence but affection. His poetry is above all good entertainment, whether we define that term as diversion or as the deeper pleasure that comes from recognizing his wide range of sympathy and his understanding of human psychology.*

FURTHER READING *(prepared by F.S.N.):* Concise introductory material can be found in the pertinent sections of the *Latin Literature* volume, ed. E. J. Kenney and W. V. Clausen, 1982, of *The Cambridge History of Classical Literature;* and in Michael Grant, *Greek and Latin Authors, 800 B.C.–A.D. 1000,* 1980. In the influential book by Brooks Otis, *Ovid as an Epic Poet,* 1966, 2nd ed. 1970, a number of individual passages from Ovid are discussed, arranged according to topic. Ovid's life and literary art are treated by L. P. Wilkinson in *Ovid Recalled,* 1955, and in his shortened version *Ovid Surveyed,* 1962. Essays edited by J. W. Binns in *Ovid,* 1973, deal with a number of works by Ovid, and with the influence these works have had throughout the centuries. The *Metamorphoses* is treated in Charles P. Segal, *Landscape in Ovid's Metamorphoses: A Study in the Transformations of a Literary Symbol,* 1969, which is useful on symbol, unity, tradition, and the motif of moral order; and in Otto Steen Due, *Changing Forms: Studies in the Metamorphoses of Ovid,* 1974.

METAMORPHOSES

Translated by Rolfe Humphries

from BOOK I

My intention is to tell of bodies changed
To different forms; the gods, who made the changes,
Will help me—or I hope so—with a poem
That runs from the world's beginning to our own days.[1]

---

[1] The full fifteen-book poem ends with the transformations of Julius Caesar into a star and of Augustus, after his death (still in the future), into a god.

THE CREATION[2]

Before the ocean was, or earth, or heaven,
Nature was all alike, a shapelessness,
Chaos, so-called, all rude and lumpy matter,
Nothing but bulk, inert, in whose confusion
Discordant atoms warred: there was no sun
To light the universe; there was no moon   10
With slender silver crescents filling slowly;
No earth hung balanced in surrounding air;
No sea reached far along the fringe of shore.
Land, to be sure, there was, and air, and ocean,
But land on which no man could stand, and water
No man could swim in, air no man could breathe,
Air without light, substance forever changing,
Forever at war: within a single body
Heat fought with cold, wet fought with dry, the hard
Fought with the soft, things having weight contended   20
With weightless things.
                    Till God, or kindlier Nature,[3]
Settled all argument, and separated
Heaven from earth, water from land, our air
From the high stratosphere, a liberation;
So things evolved, and out of blind confusion
Found each its place, bound in eternal order.
The force of fire, that weightless element,
Leaped up and claimed the highest place in heaven;
Below it, air; and under them the earth
Sank with its grosser portions; and the water,   30
Lowest of all, held up, held in, the land.[4]

Whatever god it was, who out of chaos
Brought order to the universe, and gave it
Division, subdivision, he molded earth,
In the beginning, into a great globe,
Even on every side, and bade the waters
To spread and rise, under the rushing winds,
Surrounding earth; he added ponds and marshes,
He banked the river-channels, and the waters
Feed earth or run to sea, and that great flood   40
Washes on shores, not banks. He made the plains
Spread wide, the valleys settle, and the forest
Be dressed in leaves; he made the rocky mountains
Rise to full height, and as the vault of Heaven
Has two zones, left and right, and one between them

[2] The primordial transformation of chaos to order was itself a "metamorphosis." Compare the biblical account of creation in Genesis.
[3] The citing of two possible causes is a reflection of Ovid's wry religious skepticism.
[4] The four primal elements were believed to be fire, air, earth, and water.

Hotter than these, the Lord of all Creation
Marked on the earth the same design and pattern.
The torrid zone too hot for men to live in,
The north and south too cold, but in the middle
Varying climate, temperature and season.   50
Above all things the air, lighter than earth,
Lighter than water, heavier than fire,
Towers and spreads; there mist and cloud assemble,
And fearful thunder and lightning and cold winds,
But these, by the Creator's order, held
No general dominion; even as it is,
These brothers brawl and quarrel; though each one
Has his own quarter, still, they come near tearing
The universe apart. Eurus is monarch
Of the lands of dawn, the realms of Araby,   60
The Persian ridges under the rays of morning.
Zephyrus holds the west that glows at sunset,
Boreas, who makes men shiver, holds the north,
Warm Auster governs in the misty southland,
And over them all presides the weightless ether,[5]
Pure without taint of earth.
                              These boundaries given,
Behold, the stars, long hidden under darkness,
Broke through and shone, all over the spangled heaven,
Their home forever, and the gods lived there,
And shining fish were given the waves for dwelling   70
And beasts the earth, and birds the moving air.

But something else was needed, a finer being,
More capable of mind, a sage, a ruler,
So Man was born, it may be, in God's image,
Or Earth, perhaps, so newly separated
From the old fire of Heaven, still retained
Some seed of the celestial force which fashioned
Gods out of living clay and running water.
All other animals look downward; Man,
Alone, erect, can raise his face toward Heaven.   80

THE FOUR AGES

The Golden Age was first, a time that cherished
Of its own will, justice and right; no law,
No punishment, was called for; fearfulness
Was quite unknown, and the bronze tablets[6] held
No legal threatening; no suppliant throng
Studied a judge's face; there were no judges,

---

[5] The element of fire.
[6] The Roman laws were written and publicly displayed on such tablets.

There did not need to be. Trees had not yet
Been cut and hollowed, to visit other shores.
Men were content at home, and had no towns
With moats and walls around them; and no trumpets   90
Blared out alarums;[7] things like swords and helmets
Had not been heard of. No one needed soldiers.
People were unaggressive, and unanxious;
The years went by in peace. And Earth, untroubled,
Unharried by hoe or plowshare, brought forth all
That men had need for, and those men were happy,
Gathering berries from the mountain sides,
Cherries, or blackcaps, and the edible acorns.
Spring was forever, with a west wind blowing
Softly across the flowers no man had planted,   100
And Earth, unplowed, brought forth rich grain; the field,
Unfallowed, whitened with wheat, and there were rivers
Of milk, and rivers of honey, and golden nectar
Dripped from the dark-green oak-trees,
                              After Saturn[8]
Was driven to the shadowy land of death,
And the world was under Jove, the Age of Silver
Came in, lower than gold, better than bronze.
Jove made the springtime shorter, added winter,
Summer, and autumn, the seasons as we know them.
That was the first time when the burnt air glowed   110
White-hot, or icicles hung down in winter.
And men built houses for themselves; the caverns,
The woodland thickets, and the bark-bound shelters
No longer served; and the seeds of grain were planted
In the long furrows, and the oxen struggled
Groaning and laboring under the heavy yoke.

Then came the Age of Bronze, and dispositions
Took on aggressive instincts, quick to arm,
Yet not entirely evil. And last of all
The Iron Age succeeded, whose base vein   120
Let loose all evil: modesty and truth
And righteousness fled earth, and in their place
Came trickery and slyness, plotting, swindling,
Violence and the damned desire of having.
Men spread their sails to winds unknown to sailors,
The pines came down their mountain-sides, to revel
And leap in the deep waters, and the ground,
Free, once, to everyone, like air and sunshine,
Was stepped off by surveyors. The rich earth,
Good giver of all the bounty of the harvest,   130

---

[7]Calls to battle.
[8]Chief of the gods in the older generation of divinities. He reigned during the Golden Age, until he was deposed by Jove and his dynasty.

Was asked for more; they dug into her vitals,
Pried out the wealth a kinder lord had hidden
In Stygian[9] shadow, all that precious metal,
The root of evil. They found the guilt of iron,
And gold, more guilty still. And War came forth
That uses both to fight with; bloody hands
Brandished the clashing weapons. Men lived on plunder.
Guest was not safe from host, nor brother from brother,
A man would kill his wife, a wife her husband,
Stepmothers, dire and dreadful, stirred their brews   140
With poisonous aconite,[10] and sons would hustle
Fathers to death, and Piety lay vanquished,
And the maiden Justice, last of all immortals,
Fled from the bloody earth.
                                  Heaven was no safer.
Giants[11] attacked the very throne of Heaven,
Piled Pelion on Ossa, mountain on mountain
Up to the very stars. Jove struck them down
With thunderbolts, and the bulk of those huge bodies
Lay on the earth, and bled, and Mother Earth,
Made pregnant by that blood, brought forth new bodies,   150
And gave them, to recall her older offspring,
The forms of men. And this new stock was also
Contemptuous of gods, and murder-hungry
And violent. You would know they were sons of blood.

JOVE'S INTERVENTION

And Jove was witness from his lofty throne
Of all this evil, and groaned as he remembered
The wicked revels of Lycaon's table,
The latest guilt, a story still unknown
To the high gods. In awful indignation
He summoned them to council. No one dawdled.   160
Easily seen when the night skies are clear,
The Milky Way shines white. Along this road
The gods move toward the palace of the Thunderer,[12]
His royal halls, and, right and left, the dwellings
Of other gods are open, and guests come thronging.
The lesser gods live in a meaner section,
An area not reserved, as this one is,
For the illustrious Great Wheels of Heaven.
(Their Palatine Hill,[13] if I might call it so.)

---

[9] Pertaining to the underground world.
[10] A plant related to monkshood, often poisonous.
[11] The Giants were offspring of Earth and Heaven; Ossa and Pelion are mountains in Thessaly, a region of Greece.
[12] Jove.   [13] In the Rome of Ovid's time, the site of Caesar Augustus' dwelling.

They took their places in the marble chamber   170
Where high above them all their king was seated,
Holding his ivory sceptre, shaking out
Thrice, and again, his awful locks, the sign
That made the earth and stars and ocean tremble,
And then he spoke, in outrage: "I was troubled
Less for the sovereignty of all the world
In that old time when the snake-footed[14] giants
Laid each his hundred hands on captive Heaven.
Monstrous they were, and hostile, but their warfare
Sprung from one source, one body. Now, wherever   180
The sea-gods roar around the earth, a race
Must be destroyed, the race of men. I swear it!
I swear by all the Stygian rivers[15] gliding
Under the world, I have tried all other measures.
The knife must cut the cancer out, infection
Averted while it can be, from our numbers.
Those demigods, those rustic presences,
Nymphs, fauns, and satyrs, wood and mountain dwellers,
We have not yet honored with a place in Heaven,
But they should have some decent place to dwell in,   190
In peace and safety. Safety? Do you reckon
They will be safe, when I, who wield the thunder,
Who rule you all as subjects, am subjected
To the plottings of the barbarous Lycaon?"

They burned, they trembled. Who was this Lycaon,
Guilty of such rank infamy? They shuddered
In horror, with a fear of sudden ruin,
As the whole world did later, when assassins
Struck Julius Caesar down, and Prince Augustus[16]
Found satisfaction in the great devotion   200
That cried for vengeance, even as Jove took pleasure,
Then, in the gods' response. By word and gesture
He calmed them down, awed them again to silence,
And spoke once more:

THE STORY OF LYCAON

            "He has indeed been punished.
On that score have no worry. But what he did,
And how he paid, are things that I must tell you.
I had heard the age was desperately wicked,
I had heard, or so I hoped, a lie, a falsehood,

---

[14] The lower part of the Giants' body was serpentine.
[15] To swear by the river Styx was the most solemn and binding oath a god could take.
[16] A glance ahead to the very end of the poem, which celebrates the metamorphoses of these two Caesars.

So I came down, as man, from high Olympus,
Wandered about the world. It would take too long   210
To tell you how widespread was all that evil.
All I had heard was grievous understatement!
I had crossed Maenala, a country bristling
With dens of animals, and crossed Cyllene,
And cold Lycaeus'[17] pine woods. Then I came
At evening, with the shadows growing longer,
To an Arcadian palace, where the tyrant
Was anything but royal in his welcome.
I gave a sign that a god had come, and people
Began to worship, and Lycaon mocked them,   220
Laughed at their prayers, and said: 'Watch me find out
Whether this fellow is a god or mortal,
I can tell quickly, and no doubt about it.'
He planned, that night, to kill me while I slumbered;
That was his way to test the truth. Moreover,
And not content with that, he took a hostage,
One sent by the Molossians,[18] cut his throat,
Boiled pieces of his flesh, still warm with life,
Broiled others, and set them before me on the table.
That was enough. I struck, and the bolt of lightning   230
Blasted the household of that guilty monarch.
He fled in terror, reached the silent fields,
And howled, and tried to speak. No use at all!
Foam dripped from his mouth; bloodthirsty still, he turned
Against the sheep, delighting still in slaughter,
And his arms were legs, and his robes were shaggy hair,
Yet he is still Lycaon, the same grayness,
The same fierce face, the same red eyes, a picture
Of bestial savagery. One house has fallen,
But more than one deserves to. Fury reigns   240
Over all the fields of Earth. They are sworn to evil,
Believe it. Let them pay for it, and quickly!
So stands my purpose."
                          Part of them approved
With words and added fuel to his anger,
And part approved with silence, and yet all
Were grieving at the loss of humankind,
Were asking what the world would be, bereft
Of mortals: who would bring their altars incense?
Would earth be given the beasts, to spoil and ravage?
Jove told them not to worry; he would give them   250
Another race, unlike the first, created
Out of a miracle; he would see to it.

---

[17] Maenala, Cyllene, Lycaeus are mountains in Arcadia, a rustic region in Greece.
[18] Inhabitants of Molossus, a city in Crete.

He was about to hurl his thunderbolts
At the whole world, but halted, fearing Heaven
Would burn from fire so vast, and pole to pole
Break out in flame and smoke, and he remembered
The fates had said that some day land and ocean,
The vault of Heaven, the whole world's mighty fortress,
Besieged by fire, would perish. He put aside
The bolts made in Cyclopean[19] workshops; better,   260
He thought, to drown the world by flooding water.

THE FLOOD

So, in the cave of Aeolus,[20] he prisoned
The North-wind, and the West-wind, and such others
As ever banish cloud, and he turned loose
The South-wind, and the South-wind came out streaming
With dripping wings, and pitch-black darkness veiling
His terrible countenance. His beard is heavy
With rain-cloud, and his hoary locks a torrent,
Mists are his chaplet,[21] and his wings and garments
Run with the rain. His broad hands squeeze together   270
Low-hanging clouds, and crash and rumble follow
Before the cloudburst, and the rainbow, Iris,
Draws water from the teeming earth, and feeds it
Into the clouds again. The crops are ruined,
The farmers' prayers all wasted, all the labor
Of a long year comes to nothing.
                              And Jove's anger,
Unbounded by his own domain, was given
Help by his dark-blue brother. Neptune called
His rivers all, and told them, very briefly,
To loose their violence, open their houses,   280
Pour over embankments, let the river horses
Run wild as ever they would. And they obeyed him.
His trident[22] struck the shuddering earth; it opened
Way for the rush of waters. The leaping rivers
Flood over the great plains. Not only orchards
Are swept away, not only grain and cattle,
Not only men and houses, but altars, temples,
And shrines with holy fires. If any building
Stands firm, the waves keep rising over its roof-top,
Its towers are under water, and land and ocean   290
Are all alike, and everything is ocean,

---

[19] The Cyclops were workers under Vulcan, the blacksmith god of fire.
[20] God of the winds; with the following lines compare the storm at the beginning of Virgil's *Aeneid*, Book I.
[21] A garland for the head.   [22] The three-pronged spear wielded by the sea-god Neptune.

An ocean with no shore-line.
                       Some poor fellow
Seizes a hill-top; another, in a dinghy,
Rows where he used to plough, and one goes sailing
Over his fields of grain or over the chimney
Of what was once his cottage. Someone catches
Fish in the top of an elm-tree, or an anchor
Drags in green meadow-land, or the curved keel brushes
Grape-arbors under water. Ugly sea-cows
Float where the slender she-goats used to nibble   300
The tender grass, and the Nereids[23] come swimming
With curious wonder, looking, under water,
At houses, cities, parks, and groves. The dolphins
Invade the woods and brush against the oak-trees;
The wolf swims with the lamb; lion and tiger
Are borne along together; the wild boar
Finds all his strength is useless, and the deer
Cannot outspeed that torrent; wandering birds
Look long, in vain, for landing-place, and tumble,
Exhausted, into the sea. The deep's great license   310
Has buried all the hills, and new waves thunder
Against the mountain-tops. The flood has taken
All things, or nearly all, and those whom water,
By chance, has spared, starvation slowly conquers.

DEUCALION AND PYRRHA

Phocis,[24] a fertile land, while there was land,
Marked off Oetean from Boeotian fields.
It was ocean now, a plain of sudden waters.
There Mount Parnassus lifts its twin peaks skyward,
High, steep, cloud-piercing. And Deucalion came there
Rowing his wife. There was no other land,   320
The sea had drowned it all. And here they worshipped
First the Corycian[25] nymphs and native powers,
Then Themis, oracle and fate-revealer.
There was no better man than this Deucalion,
No one more fond of right; there was no woman
More scrupulously reverent than Pyrrha.
So, when Jove saw the world was one great ocean,
Only one woman left of all those thousands,
And only one man left of all those thousands,
Both innocent and worshipful, he parted   330
The clouds, turned loose the North-wind, swept them off,

[23] Sea-nymphs.
[24] A mountainous region separating Boeotia from Oeta, a mountain range on the border of Thessaly.
[25] Of Corycus, a sacred grotto. Themis, in the next line, was a goddess of justice who controlled the oracle of Delphi before it became associated with Apollo.

Showed earth to heaven again, and sky to land,
And the sea's anger dwindled, and King Neptune
Put down his trident, calmed the waves, and Triton,[26]
Summoned from far down under, with his shoulders
Barnacle-strewn, loomed up above the waters,
The blue-green sea-god, whose resounding horn
Is heard from shore to shore. Wet-bearded, Triton
Set lip to that great shell, as Neptune ordered,
Sounding retreat, and all the lands and waters   340
Heard and obeyed. The sea has shores; the rivers,
Still running high, have channels; the floods dwindle,
Hill-tops are seen again; the trees, long buried,
Rise with their leaves still muddy. The world returns.

Deucalion saw that world, all desolation,
All emptiness, all silence, and his tears
Rose as he spoke to Pyrrha: "O my wife,
The only woman, now, on all this earth,
My consort and my cousin and my partner
In these immediate dangers, look! Of all the lands   350
To East or West, we two, we two alone,
Are all the population. Ocean holds
Everything else; our foothold, our assurance,
Are small as they can be, the clouds still frightful.
Poor woman—well, we are not all alone—
Suppose you had been, how would you bear your fear?
Who would console your grief? My wife, believe me,
Had the sea taken you, I would have followed.
If only I had the power, I would restore
The nations as my father[27] did, bring clay   360
To life with breathing. As it is, we two
Are all the human race, so Heaven has willed it,
Samples of men, mere specimens."
                                           They wept,
And prayed together, and having wept and prayed,
Resolved to make petition to the goddess
To seek her aid through oracles. Together
They went to the river-water, the stream Cephisus,
Still far from clear, but flowing down its channel,
And they took river-water, sprinkled foreheads,
Sprinkled their garments, and they turned their steps   370
To the temple of the goddess, where the altars
Stood with the fires gone dead, and ugly moss
Stained pediment and column. At the stairs
They both fell prone, kissed the chill stone in prayer:
"If the gods' anger ever listens
To righteous prayers, O Themis, we implore you,

---

[26] A merman, son of Neptune.
[27] Prometheus, who made man from clay and also stole fire from heaven for human use.

Tell us by what device our wreck and ruin
May be repaired. Bring aid, most gentle goddess,
To sunken circumstance."
                And Themis heard them,
And gave this oracle: "Go from the temple,   380
Cover your heads, loosen your robes, and throw
Your mother's bones behind you!" Dumb, they stood
In blank amazement, a long silence, broken
By Pyrrha, finally: she would not do it!
With trembling lips she prays whatever pardon
Her disobedience might merit, but this outrage
She dare not risk, insult her mother's spirit
By throwing her bones around. In utter darkness
They voice the cryptic saying over and over,
What can it mean? They wonder. At last Deucalion   390
Finds the way out: "I might be wrong, but surely
The holy oracles would never counsel
A guilty act. The earth is our great mother,
And I suppose those bones the goddess mentions
Are the stones of earth; the order means to throw them,
The stones, behind us."
               She was still uncertain,
And he by no means sure, and both distrustful
Of that command from Heaven; but what damage,
What harm, would there be in trying? They descended,
Covered their heads, loosened their garments, threw   400
The stones behind them as the goddess ordered.
The stones—who would believe it, had we not
The unimpeachable witness of Tradition?—
Began to lose their hardness, to soften, slowly,
To take on form, to grow in size, a little,
Become less rough, to look like human beings,
Or anyway as much like human beings
As statues do, when the sculptor is only starting,
Images half blocked out. The earthy portion,
Damp with some moisture, turned to flesh, the solid   410
Was bone, the veins were as they always had been.
The stones the man had thrown turned into men,
The stones the woman threw turned into women,
Such being the will of God. Hence we derive
The hardness that we have, and our endurance
Gives proof of what we have come from.
                    Other forms
Of life came into being, generated
Out of the earth: the sun burnt off the dampness,
Heat made the slimy marshes swell; as seed
Swells in a mother's womb to shape and substance,   420
So new forms came to life. When the Nile river
Floods and recedes and the mud is warmed by sunshine,
Men, turning over the earth, find living things,

And some not living, but nearly so, imperfect,
On the verge of life, and often the same substance
Is part alive, part only clay. When moisture
Unites with heat, life is conceived; all things
Come from this union. Fire may fight with water,
But heat and moisture generate all things,
Their discord being productive. So when earth, 430
After that flood, still muddy, took the heat,
Felt the warm fire of sunlight, she conceived,
Brought forth, after their fashion, all the creatures,
Some old, some strange and monstrous.

*   *   *

BOOK X

THE STORY OF ORPHEUS AND EURYDICE

So Hymen[1] left there, clad in saffron robe,
Through the great reach of air, and took his way
To the Ciconian country, where the voice
Of Orpheus called him, all in vain. He came there,
True, but brought with him no auspicious words,
No joyful faces, lucky omens. The torch[2]
Sputtered and filled the eyes with smoke; when swung,
It would not blaze: bad as the omens were,
The end was worse, for as the bride went walking
Across the lawn, attended by her naiads,[3] 10
A serpent bit her ankle, and she was gone.
Orpheus mourned her to the upper world,
And then, lest he should leave the shades untried,
Dared to descend to Styx, passing the portal
Men call Taenarian.[4] Through the phantom dwellers,
The buried ghosts, he passed, came to the king
Of that sad realm, and to Persephone,
His consort, and he swept the strings,[5] and chanted:
"Gods of the world below the world, to whom
All of us mortals come, if I may speak 20
Without deceit, the simple truth is this:
I came here, not to see dark Tartarus,[6]

---

[1] Hymen, god of marriage, departs from Greece, where he has presided over a wedding described earlier, and arrives in Ciconia, a region of Thrace.
[2] Emblem of marriage.   [3] Water-nymphs.
[4] Taenarum was a cape in southern Greece believed to have an entrance to the world of the dead.
[5] Orpheus is the archetypal poet-musician.
[6] The place where evil is punished; it sometimes refers to the abode of the dead in general.

Nor yet to bind the triple-throated monster[7]
Medusa's offspring, rough with snakes. I came
For my wife's sake, whose growing years were taken
By a snake's venom. I wanted to be able
To bear this; I have tried to. Love has conquered.
This god is famous in the world above,
But here, I do not know. I think he may be
Or is it all a lie, that ancient story   30
Of an old ravishment,[8] and how he brought
The two of you together? By these places
All full of fear, by this immense confusion,
By this vast kingdom's silences, I beg you,
Weave over Eurydice's life, run through too soon.
To you we all, people and things, belong,
Sooner or later, to this single dwelling
All of us come, to our last home; you hold
Longest dominion over humankind.
She will come back again, to be your subject,   40
After the ripeness of her years; I am asking
A loan and not a gift. If fate denies us
This privilege for my wife, one thing is certain:
I do not want to go back either; triumph
In the death of two."
                                    And with his words, the music
Made the pale phantoms weep: Ixion's wheel
Was still, Tityos' vultures left the liver,
Tantalus tried no more to reach for the water,
And Belus' daughters rested from their urns,
And Sisyphus[9] climbed on his rock to listen.   50
That was the first time ever in all the world
The Furies[10] wept. Neither the king nor consort
Had harshness to refuse him, and they called her,
Eurydice. She was there, limping a little
From her late wound, with the new shades of Hell.
And Orpheus received her, but one term
Was set: he must not, till he passed Avernus,[11]
Turn back his gaze, or the gift would be in vain.

They climbed the upward path, through absolute silence,
Up the steep murk, clouded in pitchy darkness,   60
They were near the margin, near the upper land,

[7] The three-headed dog Cerberus, guardian of the world of the dead. Orpheus alludes to the binding and abduction of Cerberus by Hercules.

[8] Pluto, god of the dead, had stolen his bride, Persephone, or Proserpina, from her mother Ceres, goddess of the fields and harvest. Ovid had told the story in Book V.

[9] Ixion, Tityos, Tantalus, Belus' daughters, and Sisyphus were sinners being punished; Ixion was bound to a fiery wheel, Tityos' liver was eaten by vultures, Tantalus was placed up to the neck in water that he could not drink, Belus' daughters carried water in a vessel with holes in it, Sisyphus continually pushed a great stone uphill.

[10] The avengers of evil deeds.

[11] A lake, giving off noxious fumes, near the entrance to the underworld.

When he, afraid that she might falter, eager to see her,
Looked back in love, and she was gone, in a moment.
Was it he, or she, reaching out arms and trying
To hold or to be held, and clasping nothing
But empty air? Dying the second time,
She had no reproach to bring against her husband,
What was there to complain of? One thing, only:
He loved her. He could hardly hear her calling
Farewell! when she was gone.
                     The double death   70
Stunned Orpheus, like the man who turned to stone
At sight of Cerberus, or the couple of rock,
Olenos and Lethaea,[12] hearts so joined
One shared the other's guilt, and Ida's mountain,
Where rivers run, still holds them, both together.
In vain the prayers of Orpheus and his longing
To cross the river once more; the boatman Charon
Drove him away. For seven days he sat there
Beside the bank, in filthy garments, and tasting
No food whatever. Trouble, grief, and tears   80
Were all his sustenance. At last, complaining
The gods of Hell were cruel, he wandered on
To Rhodope and Haemus,[13] swept by the north winds,
Where, for three years, he lived without a woman
Either because marriage had meant misfortune
Or he had made a promise. But many women
Wanted this poet for their own, and many
Grieved over their rejection. His love was given
To young boys only, and he told the Thracians
That was the better way: *enjoy that springtime,*   90
Take those first flowers!
                   There was a hill, and on it
A wide-extending plain, all green, but lacking
The darker green of shade, and when the singer
Came there and ran his fingers over the strings,
The shade came there to listen. The oak-tree came,
And many poplars, and the gentle lindens,
The beech, the virgin laurel, and the hazel
Easily broken, the ash men use for spears,
The shining silver-fir, the ilex bending
Under its acorns, the friendly sycamore,   100
The changing-colored maple, and the willows
That love the river-waters, and the lotus
Favoring pools, and the green boxwood came,
Slim tamarisks, and myrtle, and viburnum
With dark-blue berries, and the pliant ivy,

---

[12] Lethaea had offended a deity (probably Venus) by boasting of her beauty; her husband
Olenos wished to assume her punishment, but both were turned to stone.
[13] Two mountains in Thrace.

The tendrilled grape, the elms, all dressed with vines,
The rowan-trees, the pitch-pines, and the arbute
With the red fruit, the palm, the victor's triumph,
The bare-trunked pine with spreading leafy crest,
Dear to the mother of the gods since Attis[14]   110
Put off his human form, took on that likeness,
And the cone-shaped cypress joined them, now a tree,
But once a boy, loved by the god Apollo
Master of lyre and bow-string, both together.

THE STORY OF CYPARISSUS

There was a deer, whom the Carthean[15] nymphs
Held sacred, a great stag, whose spreading antlers
Were his own shade-tree. Golden shone those horns,
And round his glossy neck a string of jewels
Fell to his shoulders, and a silver bubble,
Fastened with little straps, gleamed on his forehead,   120
With earrings, made of bronze, at either temple.
He had no fear at all, would enter houses,
Let even unfamiliar people pet him,
But most of all he was fond of Cyparissus,
The handsomest youth in Cea. Cyparissus
Would lead the animal to the green pastures,
Beside the running brooks, wreathe garlands for him
Of many-colored flowers, or ride him, bareback,
Guiding him gently with the crimson bridle.
One summer noon-day, when the heat of the sun   130
Held hot around the seashore, the deer was lying,
Tired, with his body on the grassy ground,
Under a tree's cool shadow, and Cyparissus
Shot him, by some ill luck, with pointed arrow,
And as he saw him dying from the wound,
Wanted to die himself. Apollo offered
Such consolation as he could, advised him
To keep his grief within some proper limit,
But he kept grieving still, and prayed the gods,
As a last boon, to let him grieve forever.   140
And his blood grew thin from that incessant weeping,
His limbs were green in color, and the hair
Over his snowy forehead, bristled, roughened
Like any bush, rose, tapering, toward Heaven.
Apollo spoke in sorrow: "I shall mourn you,
As you shall mourn for others, an attendant
On all who mourn their dead." And still the cypress

---

[14] Attis was metamorphosed into a pine tree; the pine was associated with the worship of Cybele ("mother of the gods").

[15] The city Carthea was located on the island of Cea (modern Keos) in the Aegean Sea.

Remains a tree of mourning.
                              Such was the grove
Orpheus had drawn to hear him, and the beasts
And birds made a circle all around him.   150
He tried the chords with his thumb, and found the tones
Different but harmonious, and began:
"From Jove, O Muse, my mother, for all things come
From Jove, inspire my song! I have often sung
His power before, his wars against the giants,
His thunderbolts, but now the occasion seeks
A gentler lyre, for I would sing of boys
Loved by the gods, and girls inflamed by love
To things forbidden, and earned punishment.

THE STORY OF GANYMEDE, A VERY BRIEF ONE

The king of the gods once loved a Trojan boy   160
Named Ganymede; for once, there was something found
That Jove would rather have been than what he was.
He made himself an eagle, the only bird
Able to bear his thunderbolts, went flying
On his false wings, and carried off the youngster
Who now, though much against the will of Juno,
Tends to the cups of Jove and serves his nectar.

THE STORY OF APOLLO AND HYACINTHUS

There was another boy, who might have had
A place in Heaven, at Apollo's order,
Had Fate seen fit to give him time, and still   170
He is, in his own fashion, an immortal.
Whenever spring drives winter out, and the Ram
Succeeds the wintry Fish, he springs to blossom
On the green turf. My father[16] loved him dearly,
This Hyacinthus, and left Delphi for him,
Outward from the world's center, on to Sparta,
The town that has no walls, and Eurotas River.
Quiver and lyre were nothing to him there,
No more than his own dignity; he carried
The nets for fellows hunting, and held the dogs   180
In leash for them, and with them roamed the trails
Of the rough mountain ridges. In their train
He fed the fire with long association.
It was noon one day: Apollo, Hyacinthus,
Stripped, rubbed themselves with oil, and tried their skill
At discus-throwing. Apollo sent the missile

[16] Apollo.

Far through the air, so far it pierced the clouds,
A long time coming down, and when it fell
Proved both his strength and skill, and Hyacinthus,
All eager for his turn, heedless of danger,   190
Went running to pick it up, before it settled
Fully to earth. It bounded once and struck him
Full in the face, and he grew deadly pale
As the pale god caught up the huddled body,
Trying to warm the dreadful chill that held it,
Trying to staunch the wound, to keep the spirit
With healing herbs, but all the arts were useless,
The wound was past all cure. So, in a garden,
If one breaks off a violet or poppy
Or lilies, bristling with their yellow stamens,   200
And they droop over, and cannot raise their heads,
But look on earth, so sank the dying features,
The neck, its strength all gone, lolled on the shoulder.
'Fallen before your time, O Hyacinthus,'
Apollo cried, 'I see your wound, my crime:
You are my sorrow, my reproach; my hand
Has been your murderer. But how am I
To blame? Where is my guilt, except in playing
With you, in loving you? I cannot die
For you, or with you either; the law of Fate   210
Keeps us apart: it shall not! You will be
With me forever, and my songs and music
Will tell of you, and you will be reborn
As a new flower whose markings will spell out
My cries of grief, and there will come a time
When a great hero's name will be the same[17]
As this flower's markings.' So Apollo spoke,
And it was truth he told, for on the ground
The blood was blood no longer; in its place
A flower grew, brighter than any crimson,   220
Like lilies with their silver changed to crimson.
That was not all; Apollo kept the promise
About the markings, and inscribed the flower
With his own grieving words: *Ai, Ai*
The petals say, Greek for *Alas!* In Sparta,
Even to this day, they hold their son in honor,
And when the day comes round, they celebrate
The rites for Hyacinthus, as did their fathers.

TWO INCIDENTS OF VENUS' ANGER

Amathus, a town of Cyprus, is rich in metals,
But never ask that town about her daughters,   230
Whose foreheads once bore horns, or the other ones,

---

[17] A pun on the Greek spelling (Aias) of Ajax, one of the heroes of the Trojan War.

Turned, later, into stone. The former had
An altar at their gates, sacred to Jove,
The god of host and guest: if any stranger
Had seen it, stained with blood, he would suppose
That sheep or calves were slain there, and how wrong
He would have been! That blood came from the murder,
Always, of innocent guests. Venus, offended,
Prepared to leave her Cyprian plains and cities,
And then reflected: 'But these lovely regions   240
Are not at fault, the cities are not guilty.
Let these Horned Girls, these wicked creatures, rather
Pay for their sins by exile or by death
Or by some punishment halfway between,
Let us say, a change of body.' As she wondered
What change, her eyes fell on the horns they carried:
Those they might keep. They were big women by nature,
Let them be bulls!
          "And even so, the others,
The foul Propoetides, would not acknowledge
Venus and her divinity, and her anger   250
Made whores of them, the first such women ever
To sell their bodies, and in shamelessness
They hardened, even their blood was hard, they could not
Blush any more; it was no transition, really,
From what they were to actual rock and stone.

THE STORY OF PYGMALION

One man, Pygmalion, who had seen these women
Leading their shameful lives, shocked at the vices
Nature has given the female disposition
Only too often, chose to live alone,
To have no woman in his bed. But meanwhile   260
He made, with marvelous art, an ivory statue,
As white as snow, and gave it greater beauty
Than any girl could have, and fell in love
With his own workmanship. The image seemed
That of a virgin, truly, almost living,
And willing, save that modesty prevented,
To take on movement. The best art, they say,
Is that which conceals art, and so Pygmalion
Marvels, and loves the body he has fashioned.
He would often move his hands to test and touch it,   270
Could this be flesh, or was it ivory only?
No, it could not be ivory. His kisses,
He fancies, she returns; he speaks to her,
Holds her, believes his fingers almost leave
An imprint on her limbs, and fears to bruise her.
He pays her compliments, and brings her presents

Such as girls love, smooth pebbles, winding shells,
Little pet birds, flowers with a thousand colors,
Lilies, and painted balls, and lumps of amber.
He decks her limbs with dresses, and her fingers   280
Wear rings which he puts on, and he brings a necklace,
And earrings, and a ribbon for her bosom,
And all of these become her, but she seems
Even more lovely naked, and he spreads
A crimson coverlet for her to lie on,
Takes her to bed, puts a soft pillow under
Her head, as if she felt it, calls her *Darling,*
My darling love!
           "And Venus' holiday
Came round, and all the people of the island
Were holding festival, and snow-white heifers,   290
Their horns all tipped with gold, stood at the altars,
Where incense burned, and, timidly, Pygmalion
Made offering, and prayed: 'If you can give
All things, O gods, I pray my wife may be—
(He almost said, *My ivory girl,* but dared not)—
One like my ivory girl.' And golden Venus
Was there, and understood the prayer's intention,
And showed her presence, with the bright flame leaping
Thrice on the altar, and Pygmalion came
Back where the maiden lay, and lay beside her,   300
And kissed her, and she seemed to glow, and kissed her,
And stroked her breast, and felt the ivory soften
Under his fingers, as wax grows soft in sunshine,
Made pliable by handling. And Pygmalion
Wonders, and doubts, is dubious and happy,
Plays lover again, and over and over touches
The body with his hand. It is a body!
The veins throb under the thumb. And oh, Pygmalion
Is lavish in his prayer and praise to Venus,
No words are good enough. The lips he kisses   310
Are real indeed, the ivory girl can feel them,
And blushes and responds, and the eyes open
At once on lover and heaven, and Venus blesses
The marriage she has made. The crescent moon
Fills to full orb, nine times, and wanes again,
And then a daughter is born, a girl named Paphos,
From whom the island later takes its name.

THE STORY OF CINYRAS AND MYRRHA

Her son was Cinyras; had he been childless,
He might have been a happier man. The story
Is terrible, I warn you. Fathers, daughters,   320
Had better skip this part, or, if you like my songs,

Distrust me here, and say it never happened,
Or, if you do believe it, take my word
That it was paid for. Nature, it may be,
Permits such things to happen. I would offer
Our land[18] congratulations, that it lies
So far away from such abominations.
Panchaia,[19] rich in cinnamon and balsam,
In frankincense and costmary, in flowers
Of every kind, has one more tree, remember,   330
Perhaps not worth its price, the myrrh. Now Myrrha,
Cinyras' daughter, Cupid claimed, had never
Been hurt by darts of his, nor had his torches
Kindled her fire; that was the work of the Furies,
Or one of them, with Stygian snake and firebrand.
Hating a father is a crime, but surely
Loving like this a greater crime than hatred.
Myrrha had many suitors: all the East
Had sent its ardent princes, eager rivals
For Myrrha's bed: make a selection, Myrrha,   340
Choose one of them, they are many, rule out only
One man of all the world!
                "Myrrha herself
Knew her own wickedness, and fought against it:
'What kind of thing is this that I am planning?
O gods, I pray you, keep me decent, keep me
Devoted, as I should be, to my parents,
Respectful of their rights! Keep off this sin,
This crime—or is it crime? Devotion cannot
Condemn such love as crime; the beasts, I notice,
Mate as they will, and no one calls a heifer   350
Disgraced to have her father on her back,
And no one thinks a filly should not welcome
Her sire as stallion; the ram goes in to ewes
He has begotten, and the birds are treaded
By cocks whose treading gave them life. How happy
They are, to be so free! But human culture
Has made malignant laws, laws against nature,
Envious, jealous laws. Yet there are people,
They say, where mothers wed their sons, and daughters
Sleep with their fathers, so that natural love   360
Is doubled. No such luck is mine; I might have
Been native to such countries; here I am,
Frustrated by geography! Why do I
Keep thinking of such matters? Foolish fancies!
Leave me alone! He is worthy to be loved,
Loved as a father. Were I not his daughter,

---

[18] The speaker is still Orpheus; his land is Thrace, which, however, had a reputation among Romans for sexual immorality.
[19] Legendary Eastern land, associated with luxury, spices, jewels.

I might have slept with Cinyras. He is mine
One way, not mine another; his very closeness
Keeps him far off. If I were foreign-born,
My power would be greater; I had better   370
Go from my home, my country, shun this passion,
This crime, that keeps me here, that keeps me watching
My Cinyras, touching him, and talking with him,
And kissing him, if nothing else is granted.
What else is there to look for? Virgin, wanton,
All names, all titles, vanish in confusion:
A mother's rival, and a father's mistress,
Sister of sons, and mother of your brothers!
Have you no fear of the sisters, the grim Furies
With the black snakes for hair, whose cruel torches   380
Threaten the eyes and faces of the guilty?
You have, so far, not sinned in body, Myrrha:
Try not to sin in mind; do not imagine
Embrace a natural law forbids. You want it,
I know, but fact forbids, and he is righteous,
Heedful of moral sanctions—and I wish
He had my kind of passion burning in him!'
All this she told herself, and Cinyras
Did not know what to do, so many suitors,
All worthy men, awaiting her decision.   390
He named them over to her, asked her questions,
Which one of them she would most prefer as husband.
She made no answer, only stared, and seemed
Confused in mind, and wept, and Cinyras
Thought this was natural for a girl, and, kindly,
Bade her not weep, and dried her cheeks, and kissed her.
That made her happy. So—*what kind of husband?*
'A man like you,' she said. He praised her answer
Not knowing what it really meant. 'Be such
A good girl always, dear!' he told her,   400
And Myrrha, like a good girl, kept her eyes
Downcast, too conscious of her guilt in goodness.

And midnight came,[20] with sleep to heal men's troubles,
To ease their bodies. Myrrha could not sleep,
Tossed all night long, unsatisfied, renewing
Her passionate wants, despaired, gave up, again
Wanted to try, knew shame, and knew desire,
Found no way out. As a great tree, deep wounded
By axe-blows, with the final stroke not given,
Wavers which way to fall, and every side   410
May be its dangerous earthward rush, so Myrrha,
Weakened by various wounds, uncertain, faltering,

---

[20] The passage and episode that follow are modeled, somewhat ironically, on Dido's situation as described by Virgil in the *Aeneid*, Book IV.

Leaned one way, then another, torn with conflict.
A love like hers, with neither rest nor limit,
Had no way out but death: death would be pleasant.
She rose, she swung a noose from the high rafter,
Crying, 'Farewell, dear Cinyras; understand
The reason for my death,' ghastly pale,
Fitting the noose around her neck.
                              "Some stir
Of action, or the murmur of her words,   420
Reached the old nurse who watched outside her doorway,
And she came flying, swung the door wide open,
Saw the grim preparations, screamed, and tore
Her garments, beat her breasts, and in a moment
Snatched loose the rope, and then found time for weeping,
For holding Myrrha in her arms, for asking
All kinds of questions. But Myrrha would not answer,
Would not look up, sullen, and grieving only
For her own slowness, and the nurse insisted,
Making a show of her gray hair, her skinny   430
Old useless breasts, begging her, by her cradle,
Her baby milk, to tell her all her trouble.
She turned away and groaned, but the old nurse
Was bound to find out more, and promised more
Than passive listening. 'Tell me, let me help you;
Old as I am, I have some wit. Is it madness?
I have a way to cure it by charms and simples.
Has some one put an evil spell upon you?
We can work it off with magic. Are the gods
Angry at you? Let sacrifice appease them!   440
What other reasons could there be? The fortunes
Of all your house go well; father and mother
Prosper in health.' Hearing the name of father,
Myrrha gave one long sigh, no clue to the nurse
Of the evil in her heart, but she suspected
Some love affair, and with persistent purpose
Kept up her questions, holding Myrrha close
With her old arms to her old breast. 'I know,'
She said, 'you are in love, and in this business,
Don't worry, I can more than help, and no one,   450
Not even your father, will ever know.' But Myrrha
Tore herself loose, and flung herself, face down,
Crying into her pillow. 'Go away,
Spare my unhappy shame!' But the nurse only
Urged and insisted. 'Go away, or stop it!
Stop asking why I grieve. It is a crime,
The thing you are trying to learn, a crime, I tell you!'
The poor old woman, horrified, held out
Her arms, all trembling with the weight of years,
The load of fear, and fell at her feet, imploring,   460
Coaxing and wheedling, sometimes even trying

To scare her into telling, making threats
To tell about the noose, about the try
At suicide, and giving reassurance
Of all her help, if only she can know
Who the man is. And Myrrha raised her head
To weep on the nurse's bosom, trying, often,
To get the truth out, failing, hiding her face
In the robes again, finally saying only:
'O mother, mother, happy in your husband!'   470
That was enough, and a cold horror crept
Through the old woman's limbs. She knew. She tried,
As best she could, to banish, if she might,
So mad a passion; Myrrha knew the warning
Was given in all truthfulness, but could not
Resign herself to living without having.
The one she loved. 'Live, then,' the other told her,
'You will have your—'(but she could not say it) *father.*

The time arrived when all the married women
Held festival for Ceres.[21] Robed in white,   480
They brought the first-fruits, wheaten ears as garlands,
And for nine nights to love a man or touch him
Was a forbidden thing. And the king's wife,
Queen Cenchreis, was one of them, most faithful
In those mysterious rites, and the king's bed
Was empty, and the nurse, losing no time,
Found him, a little drunk, and filled his ears
With a story of a girl who loved him truly,
Named—she made up a name, and praised her beauty.
Cinyras asked one question: how old was she?   490
'Just Myrrha's age.' 'Go get her!' So she went
Back home to Myrrha, crying out, 'My child,
Rejoice, we conquer!' In the heart of Myrrha
There was not all rejoicing, for her mind
Was filled with sad foreboding, but I could not
Say there was no rejoicing and be truthful.

It was the time when all things rest; in Heaven
The Driver of the Oxen[22] turned his team
To their downward course, the golden moon was gone,
The stars were in black cloud, and the night smouldered   500
Without the usual fires, as Myrrha came
On to her guilty deed. Three times she stumbled
At the edge of the threshold, and three times the owl
Wailed out his cry to warn her, but she came on,
Her shame diminished in the night's dark shadow.
Her left hand holds her nurse's hand, the other

[21] Goddess of the fields and harvest, and therefore also of fertility in general.
[22] The constellation Bootes; the time is midnight.

Gropes through the dark ahead, she comes to the door,
Opens the door, goes in, and her knees tremble,
Her face is pale and bloodless, and her spirit
Deserts her as she goes. Closer and closer   510
She nears her crime, and more and more she shudders,
Repents her boldness, wishes she might now
Turn back unknown, but the old woman leads her
Along, unwilling, to where the bedside towers,
Where Cinyras waits. 'Take her, she is your own,'
She says and is gone, leaving the two together,
Doomed and devoted. On the bed of incest
The father takes his daughter; words are spoken
To ease her virgin fears, to make the trembling
A little less. He might have called her *Daughter,*   520
Knowing how young she was; she might have answered
Dear father, so the names were right and proper
To suit the guilty deed.
                              "Filled with her father
She left the chamber, carrying in her womb
The seed of crime conceived, and she came back
The next night, and the next, till Cinyras,
After so many nights together, eager
To see the girl who loved him, called for lights
And so discovered his love, his crime, his daughter.
He could not speak, but drew the shining sword   530
Out of the sheath, and Myrrha fled, and darkness
And the blind night's favor kept death off. She wandered
Through the wide fields, beyond Arabian palm-trees,
Beyond Panchaia, till, with nine months gone,
In utter weariness she came to rest
In the Sabaean land.[23] Heavy of womb,
Not knowing what to pray for, torn between
Sickness of life and fear of death, she summoned
Her desperation in words of prayer: 'O gods,
If any gods will listen, I deserve   540
Punishment surely, I do not refuse it,
But lest, in living, I offend the living,
Offend the dead in death, drive me away
From either realm, change me somehow, refuse me
Both life and death!' There was a god to listen;
Her last petition had its gods to answer,
For even as she spoke, the earth closed over
Her legs, and slanting down between her toes
A root took hold, supporting the tall trunk,
The bones were stronger, and their central marrow   550
Suffered no change, but the blood was lymph or water,
Or watery sap, and the arms became long branches,
The fingers twigs, the skin rough bark. The tree

[23] Arabia.

Had bound the pregnant belly, held in tight
The swelling breasts, was on its way to cover
Shoulders and neck, and she could not bear the waiting,
Bent her face down to meet it, plunged her features
Into the bark, until her human senses
Had vanished with her human form, but still
She weeps, and the warm tear-drops trickle down,   560
Not without honor, for that distillation
Still keeps her name; men calling it myrrh,[24] no age
Will ever forget the word.
                     "Within the wood
The child, conceived in guilt, had grown toward life,
Sought its way out; the swollen bole dilated
Under the strain of the weight, and with no voice
To call Lucina:[25] like a woman in labor
The tree, contorted, cried and wept; the goddess
Stood near in pity, reached out helping hands,
Sang charms to aid the birth, and the tree cracked open,   570
The bark was split, the burden loosed, a baby
Gave his first cries, and naiads cradled him
On the soft leaves, and used his mother's tears
To wash him. Even Envy praised his beauty,
He looked so much like Cupid in a painting
All you would need to make them come out even
Would be to give a quiver to both, or neither.

THE STORY OF ADONIS

Time, in its stealthy gliding, cheats us all
Without our notice; nothing goes more swiftly
Than do the years. That little boy, whose sister   580
Became his mother, his grandfather's son,
Is now a youth, and now a man, more handsome
Than he had ever been, exciting even
The goddess Venus, and thereby avenging
His mother's passion. Cupid, it seems, was playing,
Quiver on shoulder, when he kissed his mother,
And one barb grazed her breast; she pushed him away,
But the wound was deeper than she knew; deceived,
Charmed by Adonis' beauty, she cared no more
For Cythera's shores nor Paphos' sea-ringed island,   590
Nor Cnidos, where fish teem, nor high Amathus,[26]
Rich in its precious ores. She stays away
Even from Heaven, Adonis is better than Heaven.
She is beside him always; she has always,
Before this time, preferred the shadowy places,

---

[24] A fragrant resin produced by the tree or shrub.   [25] Goddess of childbirth.
[26] Cythera, Paphos, Cnidos, and Amathus were Venus' usual earthly dwelling-places.

Preferred her ease, preferred to improve her beauty
By careful tending, but now, across the ridges,
Through woods, through rocky places thick with brambles,
She goes, more like Diana[27] than like Venus,
Bare-kneed and robes tucked up. She cheers the hounds,   600
Hunts animals, at least such timid creatures
As deer and rabbits; no wild boars for her,
No wolves, no bears, no lions. And she warns him
To fear them too, as if there might be good
In giving him warnings. 'Be bold against the timid,
The running creatures, but against the bold ones
Boldness is dangerous. Do not be reckless.
I share whatever risk you take; be careful!
Do not attack those animals which Nature
Has given weapons, lest your thirst for glory   610
May cost me dear. Beauty and youth and love
Make no impression on bristling boars and lions,
On animal eyes and minds. The force of lightning
Is in the wild boar's tusks, and tawny lions
Are worse than thunderbolts. I hate and fear them.'
He asks her why. She answers, 'I will tell you,
And you will wonder at the way old crime
Leads to monstrosities. I will tell you sometime,
Not now, for I am weary, all this hunting
Is not what I am used to. Here's a couch   620
Of grassy turf, and a canopy of poplar,
I would like to lie there with you. And she lay there,
Making a pillow for him of her breast,
And kisses for her story's punctuation.

VENUS TELLS ADONIS THE STORY OF ATALANTA

You may have heard (she said) about a girl
Who could outrun the swiftest men. The story
Is very true: she really could outrun them.
It would be hard to say, though, whether her speed
Or beauty earned more praise. She was very lovely.
She asked the oracle, one day, to give her   630
Advice on marriage. "You don't need a husband,"
The god replied, "Avoid that habit! Still,
I know you will not: you will keep your life,
And lose yourself." So Atalanta, frightened,
Lived in the shadowy woods, a single woman,
Harshly rejecting urgent throngs of suitors.
"No one gets me who cannot beat me running,
Race me!" she told them, "Wife and marriage-chamber

---

[27] The austere and "unfeminine" goddess of the hunt, mentioned to emphasize Venus'
new, uncharacteristic, and half-hearted attempt to live the outdoor life.

Go to the winner, but the slow ones get
The booby-prize of death. Those are my terms."   640
The terms were harsh, but beauty has such power
That those harsh terms were met by many suitors,
Foolhardy fellows. Watching the cruel race,
Hippomenes had some remarks to make:
"Is any woman worth it? These young men
Strike me as very silly." But when he saw her,
Her face, her body naked, with such beauty
As mine is, or as yours would be, Adonis,
If you were woman, he was struck with wonder,
Threw up his hands and cried: "I beg your pardon,   650
Young men, I judged you wrongly; I did not know
The value of the prize!" And he caught fire
From his own praising, hoped that no young runner
Would beat her, feared they might, was worried, jealous.
"Why don't I try?" he thought, "God helps the bold."
And, swifter than his thought, the girl sped by
On winged feet, swifter than Scythian arrow,
Yet not too swift for a young man's admiration,
And running made her lovelier: the breeze
Bore back the streaming pinions of her sandals,   660
Her hair was tossed back over ivory shoulders,
The colored ribbons fluttered at her knees,
And a light flush came over her girlish body
The way a crimson awning, over marble,
Tints it in pastel color. As he watched her,
She crossed the finish line, received the crown
Of victory, and the beaten suitors, groaning,
Were led away to death.
                                    'Hippomenes,
Undaunted, came from the crowd; he fixed his eyes
On Atalanta, and he made his challenge: 670
"This is too easy, beating all these turtles!
Race against me!" he said, "If you are beaten
It will be no disgrace. Megareus is my father,
Whose grandfather was Neptune, and that makes me
Great-grandson of the king of all the oceans.
Nor is my worth inferior to my race.
Beat me, and you will have something to boast of!"[28]
Listening, looking almost tenderly
At that young man, she wondered, in confusion,
Which would be better, to win or lose. "What god,"   680
She thought, "so hates the young and handsome
He wants to ruin this one, tempting him
To risk his precious life to marry me?
I do not think I am worth it. I am not moved
By his beauty (though I could be); I am moved

[28] Hippomenes' challenge parodies the epic hero's inflated challenge to armed combat.

Because he seems so young: he does not move me,
Only his age. What of his manly courage,
His nerve, his claim to proud descent, his love
For me, so great a love that death, he claims,
Is an advantage if he cannot have me?   690
Go while you may, O stranger, flee this marriage,
There is too much blood upon it. Any girl
Would marry you, and wisely. Why do I care,
Why worry for him, when I have slain so many?
Let him look out for himself, or let him die
Since the death of all those others has not warned him,
Since life is such a bore! Is he to die
Because he wants to live with me? Is death
To be the price of love? I shall be hated
In victory. It is not my fault. Poor fellow,   700
I wish you would forget it but, since you are crazy,
I wish at least you could run a little faster!
He looks like a girl, almost. I wish he had never
Laid eyes on me. He should have lived. If I
Were luckier, if the fates allowed me marriage,
He was the only one I would have taken
To bed with any pleasure." Atalanta
Was green in love, untutored—she did not know
What she was doing, and loved, and did not know it.

Meanwhile the people and her father, restless,   710
Were clamoring for the race. Hippomenes
Called me in supplication: "O, may Venus
Be near, I pray, assist my daring, favor
The love she gave me!" And a gentle breeze
Bore this soft prayer my way; it moved my heart,
I own, and there was little time to aid him.
There is a field the natives call Tamasus,
The richest part of Cyprus, which the ancients
Hallowed for me, and built my temples there,
And in a field there stands a golden tree,   720
Shining with golden leaves and branches rustling
With the soft click of gold, and golden apples
Are the fruit of that golden tree. I came from there
With three such apples in my hand, and no one
Saw me except Hippomenes, and I
Told him how he should use them.
                                   'The trumpets sounded
The start: the pair, each crouching low, shot forward,
Skimming the sand with flying feet, so lightly
They could run on waves and never wet their sandals,
They could run on fields of grain and never bend them.   730
He heard them cheering: "Go, Hippomenes,
Lean to the work, use all your strength: go, go,
You are sure to win!" I could not tell you whether

The cheering pleased him more, or Atalanta.
How many times, when she could have passed, she lingered,
Slowed down to see his face, and, most unwilling,
Sprinted ahead! And now his breathing labored,
Came in great sobbing gasps, and the finish line
Was a long way off, and he tossed one golden apple,
The first one, down. She looked at it with wonder,   740
Eager to have the shining fruit, she darted
Out of the course, and picked it up, still rolling,
The golden thing. He gained the lead again
As all the people roared applause. She passed him
Again, and once again lost ground to follow
The toss of the second apple, and once more
Caught up and sprinted past him. "O be near me,
Gift-bringing Goddess, help me now!" he cried,
And this time threw the last third apple farther,
Angling it off the course, way to one side.   750
She hesitated, only for a moment,
Whether to chase it, but I made her do it,
And made the fruit weigh more, so she was hindered
Both by the burden and her own delay.
To run my story quickly, as the race
Was run, the girl was beaten, and the winner
Led off his prize.
                    'Do you not think, Adonis,
He should have brought me incense, or at least
Given me thanks? He did not. I was angry:
Once slighted, I should not again be slighted.   760
I told myself I would make examples of them.
One day they were going by a temple, hidden
In the deep woods; in ancient times Echion
Had consecrated this to Cybele
In payment of a vow. Their trip was long,
And they were tired, or thought so, but I drove
Hippomenes half crazy with the passion
To take his wife. He saw, beside the temple,
A dimly-lighted cavern, roofed with rock,
A chapel it was, really, where the priesthood   770
Had placed for worship their old wooden idols.
He could not wait, here he took Atalanta,
And the gods turned their eyes away; Cybele,
The tower-crowned[29] Mother, had at first the impulse
To drown them, for their guilt, in the Stygian waters,
But that seemed much too easy. So their necks
Grew rough with tawny manes, their fingers, hooked,
Were claws, their arms were legs, their chests grew heavy,
Their tails swept over the sandy ground, and anger

---

[29]Cybele taught the arts of fortification; hence her crown of towers. The lovers are
profaning her shrine by their sexual act.

Blazed in their features, they conversed in growling,   780
Took to the woods to couple: they were lions,
Frightful to all but Cybele, whose bridle
And bit they champed in meekness. Do not hunt them,
Adonis: let all beasts alone, which offer
Breasts to the fight, not backs, or else your daring
Will be the ruin of us both.'

THE FATE OF ADONIS

                     "Her warning
Was given, and the goddess took her way,
Drawn by her swans through air. But the young hunter
Scorned all such warnings, and one day, it happened,
His hounds, hard on the trail, roused a wild boar,   790
And as he rushed from the wood, Adonis struck him
A glancing blow, and the boar turned, and shaking
The spear from the side, came charging at the hunter,
Who feared, and ran, and fell, and the tusk entered
Deep in the groin, and the youth lay there dying
On the yellow sand, and Venus, borne through air
In her light swan-guided chariot, still was far
From Cyprus when she heard his groans, and, turning
The white swans from their course, came back to him,
Saw, from high air, the body lying lifeless   800
In its own blood, and tore her hair and garments,
Beat her fair breasts with cruel hands, came down
Reproaching Fate. 'They shall not have it always
Their way,' she mourned, 'Adonis, for my sorrow,
Shall have a lasting monument: each year
Your death will be my sorrow,[30] but your blood
Shall be a flower. If Persephone
Could change to fragrant mint the girl called Mentha,[31]
Cinyras' son, my hero, surely also
Can be my flower.' Over the blood she sprinkled   810
Sweet-smelling nectar, and as bubbles rise
In rainy weather, so it stirred, and blossomed,
Before an hour, as crimson in its color
As pomegranates are, as briefly clinging
To life as did Adonis, for the winds
Which gave a name to the flower, anemone,
The wind-flower, shake the petals off, too early,
Doomed all too swift and soon."

[30] The reference is to an annual festival commemorating Adonis' death.
[31] A nymph favored by Persephone.

from BOOK XI

THE DEATH OF ORPHEUS

So with his singing Orpheus drew the trees,
The beasts, the stones, to follow, when, behold!
The mad Ciconian women,[1] fleeces flung
Across their maddened breasts, caught sight of him
From a near hill-top, as he joined his song
To the lyre's music. One of them, her tresses
Streaming in the light air, cried out: "Look there!
There is our despiser!" and she flung a spear
Straight at the singing mouth, but the leafy wand
Made only a mark and did no harm. Another   10
Let fly a stone, which, even as it flew,
Was conquered by the sweet harmonious music,
Fell at his feet, as if to ask for pardon.
But still the warfare raged, there was no limit,
Mad fury reigned, and even so, all weapons
Would have been softened by the singer's music,
But there was other orchestration: flutes
Shrilling, and trumpets braying loud, and drums,
Beating of breasts, and howling, so the lyre
Was overcome, and then at last the stones   20
Reddened with blood, the blood of the singer, heard
No more through all that outcry. All the birds
Innumerable, fled, and the charmed snakes,
The train of beasts, Orpheus' glory, followed.
The Maenads stole the show. Their bloody hands
Were turned against the poet; they came thronging
Like birds who see an owl wandering in daylight;
They bayed him down, as in the early morning
Hounds circle the doomed stag beside the game-pits.
They rushed him, threw the wands, wreathed with green leaves, 30
Not meant for such a purpose; some threw clods,
Some branches torn from the tree, and some threw stones,
And they found fitter weapons for their madness.
Not far away there was a team of oxen
Plowing the field, and near them farmers, digging
Reluctant earth, and sweating over their labor,
Who fled before the onrush of this army
Leaving behind them hoe and rake and mattock
And these the women grabbed, and slew the oxen
Who lowered horns at them in brief defiance   40
And were torn limb from limb, and then the women
Rushed back to murder Orpheus, who stretched out

---

[1] Maenads, female Thracian worshipers of Bacchus, the god of wine; they are enraged
because Orpheus has renounced women for boys, as is mentioned in Book X.

His hands in supplication, and whose voice,
For the first time, moved no one. They struck him down,
And through those lips to which the rocks had listened,
To which the hearts of savage beasts responded,
His spirit found its way to winds and air.

The birds wept for him, and the throng of beasts,
The flinty rocks, the trees which came so often
To hear his song, all mourned. The trees, it seemed,   50
Shook down their leaves, as if they might be women
Tearing their hair, and rivers, with their tears,
Were swollen, and their naiads and their dryads
Mourned in black robes. The poet's limbs lay scattered
Where they were flung in cruelty or madness,
But Hebrus River took the head and lyre
And as they floated down the gentle current
The lyre made mournful sounds, and the tongue murmured
In mournful harmony, and the banks echoed
The strains of mourning. On the sea, beyond   60
Their native stream, they came at last to Lesbos[2]
And grounded near the city of Methymna.
And here a serpent struck at the head, still dripping
With sea-spray, but Apollo came and stopped it,
Freezing the open jaws to stone, still gaping.
And Orpheus' ghost fled under the earth, and knew
The places he had known before, and, haunting
The fields of the blessed, found Eurydice
And took her in his arms, and now together
And side by side they wander, or Orpheus follows   70
Or goes ahead, and may, with perfect safety,
Look back for his Eurydice.
                        But Bacchus
Demanded punishment for so much evil.
Mourning his singer's loss, he bound those women,
All those who saw the murder, in a forest,
Twisted their feet to roots, and thrust them deep
Into unyielding earth. As a bird struggles
Caught in a fowler's snare, and flaps and flutters
And draws its bonds the tighter by its struggling,
Even so the Thracian women, gripped by the soil,   80
Fastened in desperate terror, writhed and struggled,
But the roots held. They looked to see their fingers,
Their toes, their nails, and saw the bark come creeping
Up the smooth legs; they tried to smite their thighs
With grieving hands, and struck on oak; their breasts
Were oak, and oak their shoulders, and their arms
You well might call long branches and be truthful.

---

[2] The island associated with lyric poets, especially with Sappho.

THE STORY OF MIDAS

And even this was not enough for Bacchus.
He left those fields, and with a worthier band
He sought the vineyards of his own Timolus[3]   90
And Pactolus, a river not yet gold
Nor envied for its precious sands. The throng
He always had surrounded him, the satyrs,
The Bacchanals; Silenus,[4] though, was missing.
The Phrygian rustics found him, staggering
Under the weight of years, and maybe also
From more than too much wine, bound him with wreaths
And led him to King Midas. Now this king
Together with the Athenian Eumolpus
Had learned the rites of Bacchic lore from Orpheus.   100
And therefore, since he recognized a comrade,
A brother in the lodge, he gave a party
For ten long days and nights, and then, rejoicing,
Came to the Lydian fields and gave Silenus
Back to his precious foster son. And Bacchus,
Happy and grateful, and meaning well, told Midas
To make his choice of anything he wanted.
And Midas, never too judicious, answered:
"Grant that whatever I touch may turn to gold!"
Bacchus agreed, gave him the ruinous gift,   110
Sorry the monarch had not chosen better.
So Midas went his cheerful way, rejoicing
In his own bad luck, and tried to test the promise
By touching this and that. It all was true,
He hardly dared believe it! From an oak-tree
He broke a green twig loose: the twig was golden.
He picked a stone up from the ground; the stone
Paled with light golden color; he touched a clod,
The clod became a nugget. Awns of grain
Were a golden harvest; if he picked an apple   120
It seemed a gift from the Hesperides.[5]
He placed his fingers on the lofty pillars
And saw them gleam and shine. He bathed his hands
In water, and the stream was golden rain
Like that which came to Danae.[6] His mind
Could scarcely grasp his hopes—all things were golden,
Or would be, at his will! A happy man,
He watched his servants set a table before him
With bread and meat. He touched the gift of Ceres
And found it stiff and hard; he tried to bite   130

---

[3] A mountain in Lydia, a country in Asia Minor; Sardis was its capital.
[4] The habitually drunk foster father of Bacchus.
[5] Islands at the western end of the world, noted for a garden of golden apples.
[6] Jupiter had come to Danae as a shower of golden rain.

The meat with hungry teeth, and where the teeth
Touched food they seemed to touch on golden ingots.
He mingled water with the wine of Bacchus;
It was molten gold that trickled through his jaws.

Midas, astonished at his new misfortune,
Rich man and poor man, tries to flee his riches
Hating the favor he had lately prayed for.
No food relieves his hunger; his throat is dry
With burning thirst; he is tortured, as he should be,
By the hateful gold. Lifting his hands to Heaven,   140
He cries: "Forgive me, father! I have sinned.
Have mercy upon me, save me from this loss
That looks so much like gain!" The gods are kind,
And Bacchus, since he owned his fault, forgave him,
Took back the gift. "You need not be forever
Smeared with that foolish color: go to the stream
That flows by Sardis, take your way upstream
Into the Lydian hills, until you find
The tumbling river's source. There duck your head
And body under the foaming white of the fountain,   150
And wash your sin away." The king obeyed him,
And the power of the golden touch imbued the water,
So that even now the fields grow hard and yellow
If that vein washes over them to flood
Their fields with the water of the touch of gold.

MIDAS NEVER LEARNS

Now Midas, hating wealth, haunted the forests,
The fields, and worshipped Pan,[7] who has his dwelling
In the mountain caves. But Midas still was stupid,
And once again his foolish wits were destined
To do their master damage. Where Timolus   160
Looks out to sea, towering high, one slope
Falling to Sardis and the other slanting
Toward little Hypaepa, Pan was singing tunes
Tossing them off to the soft nymphs, and warbling
A trill or two on the reeds joined with wax,
Remarking that the music of Apollo
Was poor beside his own, and offering challenge
To an unequal contest, with Timolus[8]
To be the umpire. So the ancient judge,
Seated on his own mountain, shook his ears   170
Loose from the trees. Around his dark-blue hair
An oaken chaplet twined; acorns hung down

[7] God of shepherds and of the woods.
[8] The god or personification of the mountain.

Around his hollow temples. He looked at Pan,
"The judge is ready," he said, and Pan made music
On the rustic reeds, and the barbaric song
Delighted Midas utterly—it so happened
Midas was listening. Then old Timolus
Turned to Apollo, and his forests followed
As he inclined his gaze. Apollo's hair,
Golden, was wreathed with laurel of Parnassus,[9]   180
His mantle, dipped in Tyrian crimson, swept
Along the ground. His lyre, inlaid with jewels,
With Indian ivory, his left hand held;
His right hand held the plectrum.[10] You could tell
The artist from his bearing. With his thumb
He plucked the strings, and charmed by that sweet music,
Timolus ordered Pan to lower his reeds,
Submissive to the lyre, and all approved
The judgment of the holy god of the mountain,
All except Midas, who began to argue,   190
Calling it most unfair. Such stupid ears,
Apollo thought, were surely less than human,
And so he made them longer, stuffed them full
Of gray and shaggy hair, and made their base
Unstable, giving them the power of motion.
The rest of him was human; this one feature
Alone was punished, and he wore the ears
Of the slow-going jackass. So, disfigured,
Ashamed, he tried to hide them with a turban,
But when he had his hair cut, then his barber   200
Saw, dared not tell, and wanted to, and could not
Keep matters to himself, no more than barbers
Today can do, and so he dug a hole
Deep in the ground, and went and whispered in it
What kind of ears King Midas had. He buried
The evidence of his voice, filled up the hole,
Sneaked silently away. But a thick growth
Of whispering reeds began to grow there; these,
At the year's end full-grown, betrayed the sower,
For when a light breeze stirred them, they would whisper   210
Midas has asses' ears! You can still hear them.

*   *   *

[9] Mountain in southern Greece, associated with Apollo and the Muses.
[10] A "pick," used to pluck the strings.

The New Testament

(First and Second Centuries A.D.*)*

The name given to the distinctively Christian part of the Bible, the New Testament, can also be rendered as New Covenant, a term that has the advantage of underlining the intimate relationship, of kinship and separation, between it and the Old Testament. The old covenant, sealed at Mount Sinai, was essentially a contract between God and the people of Israel. It was the culmination of a series of lesser covenants established between God and mankind, then between God and the Hebrew patriarchs. The contract spelled out the provisions by which God, on the occasion of the deliverance of the Hebrews from Egypt, revealed Himself to them and singled them out for special obligations and a special mission. Although the Exodus story, as told in the first six books of the Old Testament (the Hexateuch), has mythic content that links it to universal human religious insights, it nevertheless solemnizes a preeminently historical event, the establishment of the nation of Israel.

In later Old Testament times, written and popular traditions grew up stating that a divinely appointed Messiah would arise among the Jews to deliver them from their national tribulations and usher in a new era of triumph and glory. The Christians of the first century believed that this Messiah had in fact appeared, in the historical figure of Jesus of Nazareth. Through him God had established a new covenant, this time with a body of believers extending beyond the Jews. As the old covenant had been sealed with the ritual sprinkling of blood (Exodus 24:6–8), so had the new covenant, for this Messiah was—unexpectedly—a sacrificial victim. But he had risen from the dead as a pledge of an imminent second coming, or Parousia, that would vindicate God's newly adopted people. The doctrine of the Resurrection and the concomitant belief in the Parousia and final Judgment lay at the heart of Christian faith during the first century.

The canonical books of the New Testament, as finally defined several centuries after Jesus, number twenty-seven, all written in Greek: the four Gospels, of unknown authorship but named Matthew, Mark, Luke, and John; a history of the early Church written by the author of Luke and called Acts of the Apostles; twenty-one letters, or Epistles, the most important of which are by St. Paul; and a visionary, allegorical work of prophecy named Revelation, or the Apocalypse. The earliest of these books are the Pauline letters, which were written mainly over the sixth decade of the first century; the other books were written at various dates extending through the end of the first century into the early part of the second century. Most of the New Testament books are statements of doctrine and church discipline; the more biographical ones are Acts and the four Gospels that center on the life and teaching of Jesus.

Although the four Gospels contain substantially similar accounts of the trial, sufferings, and execution of Jesus (the Passion), and all present an empty tomb that points to his resurrection, their portrayals of the earlier phases of Jesus' life are significantly different from one another. John, on the one hand, has its own distinctive material. Matthew, Mark, and Luke (the "synoptic" Gospels), on the other hand, contain a common fund of different material, and many passages have almost identical wording. In fact, approximately 99 per cent of Mark, and much of its ordering of material, is paralleled (although sometimes recast) in Matthew and Luke. An enormous scholarly literature attempts to explain the significant overlap when these Gospels are "seen together" (the meaning of synoptic), and a consensus, called the

two-document hypothesis, has dominated the field of interpretation during this cen-
tury. The hypothesis proposes that Mark is the earliest Gospel (written around 65–70)
and that Matthew and Luke, although written independently of each other (between
about 80 and 95), are based partly on a direct knowledge of Mark. The shared but non-
Markan material in Matthew and Luke is derived from a now lost collection,
largely of sayings of Jesus, called Q (from German **Quelle,** *"source"). Some author-*
ities postulate that both Matthew and Luke also used other sources, called M and
L, respectively. The synoptic problem is of course important in itself, but it has
also intrigued scholars because it bears on the possibility of recovering facts about
the historical Jesus from the earliest accounts. This search for the "real" Jesus, inde-
pendent of later tendentious biases of the Gospel authors (the "evangelists"), was es-
pecially urgent in the nineteenth century. The goal no longer preoccupies biblical
scholars so insistently, however. They have attained some confidence concerning the
typical teaching and activity of Jesus from the earliest form of sayings and stories,
but they are doubtful that any of the evangelists, even the earliest, has provided an
account either of Jesus' acts or of the sequence of his acts that is free from substan-
tial interpretation.

That view may unsettle or puzzle readers accustomed to the goals of modern
biography and historiography. But to the earliest Christians it was the overwhelming
fact of the Messiah's death, resurrection, and imminent Parousia that was centrally
important, not the circumstantial details of his life. (It is significant that the word
*translated as "gospel"—*good news*—did not originally refer as it usually does now*
to the formal genre represented by Matthew, Mark, Luke, and John but rather to the
essential message *just outlined.) Moreover, the tradition of both Jewish and pagan*
historiography assumed that the truth about any event or person could best be re-
vealed by a respect for tradition and sources in the setting of the author's own creative
intuition. This combination operates even in the author of Luke and Acts, the New
Testament works governed most by the classical rules for writing history. The interest
among Christians in what Jesus had said and done during his life as a whole arose
only secondarily, and even then less from a modern need for historical accuracy in
itself than from a sense of Jesus as an enduring, living presence and a desire to
explore and authenticate the current doctrine and discipline of his living Church.
The earliest Christians did not feel that the circumstantial data were of value apart
from their significance.

It is important to recognize that each of the four Gospels has its own special
intention and effect. The readiest way to prove this true is to read a Gospel straight
through, an eye-opening experience for those readers whose acquaintance with the
New Testament comes entirely from exposure to brief and mixed excerpts such as are
found in prayer books and liturgies. The four Gospels contain basic stories about
Jesus' life and death that create an impression of coherence in the New Testament
(some apocryphal Gospels written later do not cohere with these accounts), but the
portraits differ unmistakably in their overtones: in Mark, Jesus is presented earthily,
almost naturalistically; in Luke, beautifully and heroically; in John, with a supernal
serenity; in Matthew, as compassionate but magisterial. More careful study reveals
also differences between the Gospels in their doctrinal emphases, their views of the
timing and nature of the coming apocalyptic Parousia, their definitions of ethical
and communal duties of Christians, and their notions of worship. Each Gospel ad-
dresses the needs of a different group of early Christians in its own place and set of
circumstances.

Matthew was probably written in Syria, as a manual of instruction for a well-established Christian community, containing both Jewish and Gentile converts, that was competing with Pharisaic Judaism after the destruction of the Jerusalem Temple in 70 A.D. The author is concerned to define the Church as the New Israel, replacing the old one by means of a way of righteousness surpassing the righteousness of the Pharisees (a difficult goal, because the Pharisees were the most fervently religious Jews within first-century Jewish society). Events of Jesus' life—especially healings, exorcisms, and other miraculous manifestations of messianic power—are integrated into a careful, fivefold structure framed at the outset by the infancy narrative establishing Jesus' descent through David from Abraham and at the end by the climactic Passion narrative. The gospel culminates five times in authoritative, didactic discourses. The first of these is the Sermon on the Mount (chapters 5–7), which outlines Christian ethics and its spiritual premises; the second (10) concerns missionary discipleship; the third (13) relates parables of God's kingdom; the fourth (18) is on the Church; and the fifth (24–25) is on the apocalyptic end of the world. Some interpreters see in this fivefold organization a deliberate parallel with the five books of the Torah or Mosaic Law.

In Mark, the fact that Jesus is the Messiah is a closely guarded secret, so much so that even the disciples are obtuse on the matter. Matthew, by contrast, is intent to show, beginning with the insistent opening genealogy and the story of the pagan wise men, not only that Jesus is the Messiah but that he was unmistakably that during his lifetime. Except in a few passages, the disciples, especially Peter, are clearly aware of this. There was thus no excuse, according to Matthew, for the perverse failure of the Jewish leaders to recognize Jesus as the Messiah, a failure that forfeits the claim by the Jews to be the special vehicle of God's providence. (Jesus first commissions the disciples to limit their preaching mission, as he has done, to the "lost sheep of the house of Israel"—10:5–6—but in the concluding words of the Gospel he dispatches them to "all nations.") Jesus is human but masterful, divinely sent, as the new star at his birth announced. Dozens of times Matthew quotes the Old Testament (sometimes drawing on the ancient Greek translation of it, the Septuagint) to show that Jesus is the fulfillment of the Old Testament promises.

Matthew's Gospel is a particularly Jewish one; it assumes an awareness, within Christianity and in its relations with its neighbors, of the Jewish scriptures, locutions, ideas, and heritage. These are the very air Matthew breathes. Jesus' disputes with the Pharisees, scribes, and Sadducees have a distinctively Jewish cast of thought, as in his verbal sparring over Old Testament texts (for example, 22:34–46) and in controversies over dietary and sabbatical rules. The position of Matthew's Jesus on such matters is generally that the expounders of the Law are either knowledgeable but hypocritical in their behavior, or ignorant ("the blind lead the blind"), or legalistic, intent on the letter of the Law at the expense of its spirit. A deep irony here, important for an understanding of Matthew, lies in the fact that a similar position was central in Pharisaism itself. The Pharisees believed that the Law had to be updated, adapted to the needs of the present, and supplemented by oral tradition if it was to retain its vitality. Matthew is thus leveling at the Pharisees (the dominant party in Judaism in Matthew's time) the kind of criticism that they leveled at ultra-conservative Jews and at rival groups within the ranks of the Pharisees. In short, the rancor expressed in Matthew toward the Pharisees is of the kind immemorially felt by religious groups toward others that are close enough in thought and proximity to be considered dangerous rivals.

This relationship—of friction between close kindred—must be kept in mind when one examines the ambivalence expressed in Matthew toward Jewry and Judaism. There is no mistaking the antagonism. Usually, however, Jesus does not repudiate the Law; when asked by a "lawyer" what the greatest commandment is, he dutifully cites Deuteronomy and Leviticus (Matthew 22:36–40), and in the Sermon on the Mount he emphatically endorses even the fine print: "Till heaven and earth pass, one jot or one tittle shall in no wise pass from the law, till all be fulfilled" (5:18). This seems to contradict other passages in Matthew where Jesus apparently sets aside at least the minutiae of the Law. Perhaps there is a contradiction, but not necessarily; much depends on the implications of the word fulfilled. *The frequent citations of Old Testament texts imply not that the Old Testament has been superseded or that a new chapter has merely been added to it. The new, Christian dispensation is not a repudiation of the Law so much as a living growth from it, and the new teaching no more negates its origins than the fruit of a tree negates the tree's earlier history of bud and leaf. It is no coincidence that central discourses and events such as the Sermon on the Mount, the Temptation, the Transfiguration, and the final commissioning of the disciples take place on "mountains" (hills, actually), for these settings all bear witness to their most solemn early archetype in the self-revelation of God at Mount Sinai. Matthew thus has a strong sense of iconography, of the symbolism of forms, settings, and stories from the Old Testament. Even the flight from Herod into Egypt and the later return to Palestine re-enact the migrations described in Genesis, Exodus, and Joshua. Matthew could not have felt or implied the force of such parallels if he thought of the Jewish past as simply annulled, a dead letter. It could be argued that what Matthew's Jesus attacks in the Jewish teachers and leaders is not their reverence for the law but virtually the opposite: their failure to recognize its living import. The apparent contrasts between new and old doctrine in the Sermon on the Mount can be seen as an actual intensifying of the old Law, an insistence that it be pushed to its ultimate implications.*

Although Matthew is a well-written and well-organized book, Luke is the most polished piece of literature among the Gospels. The author's stylistic versatility is impressive; he can write in an urbane classical manner (as in the preface to Theophilus—1:1–4) and also in the Old Testament manner, as in the following birth and infancy narratives, which also show a meticulous sense of structure in the elaborate parallelism of the stories of John the Baptist and of Jesus. The great anthems of the first two chapters, now deeply embedded in Christian liturgies, are filled with echoes of the Old Testament and strongly suggest the style of the Psalms. Even in our brief excerpt the warmth and joy characteristic of Luke shine through, and many of its key themes are sounded: the championing of the poor, the lowly, the outcasts; the call of the Gentiles; the importance of women; the workings of the Holy Ghost.

Uncertainty concerning the origins of the Gospels and their relationship to one another as documents should not be allowed to obscure the distinctive teaching and action that lie behind them. The literal ascription of the first five books of the Old Testament to Moses is untenable today, but it is equally difficult to ignore one's sense of their historical root in the experience and leadership of an unmistakably distinctive person. Similarly, it is difficult to imagine the Gospels as collections of loosely united traditions whose focus in Jesus is merely a pious convention. One senses a powerful dynamic, best understood as originating in Jesus' historical life and teaching, that has made the New Testament, especially in combination with the Old, the most influential book in human history.

FURTHER READING *(prepared by F.S.N.): Harper's Bible Dictionary,* general ed. Paul J. Achtemeier, 1985, is scholarly but accessible to general readers and contains articles of manageable length on such topics as "Jesus" and "Jerusalem." An excellent work of reference, containing general articles on the New Testament, introductions, exegesis, and expositions for individual books, is *The Interpreter's Bible,* ed. George A. Buttrick, 12 vols., 1952. Also very helpful is *The Interpreter's Dictionary of the Bible: An Illustrated Encyclopedia,* ed. George A. Buttrick, 4 vols., 1962, and its *Supplementary Volume,* ed. Keith Crim, 1976. For further useful articles, see John E. Steinmueller and Kathryn Sullivan, eds., *Catholic Biblical Encyclopedia: New Testament,* 1950. Werner Jaeger, *Early Christianity and Greek Paideia,* 1961, shows the influence of Greek civilization on Christianity; David Daube, *The New Testament and Rabbinic Judaism,* 1956, explores the relationship between Christianity and Judaism; and Howard Clark Kee, Franklin W. Young, and Karlfried Froehlich, *Understanding the New Testament,* 1957, 3rd ed. 1973, assembles excellent material on both the Hellenistic and the Jewish background to the Gospel narratives. Exegetical treatments of the individual books are given by A. E. Harvey, *The New English Bible: Companion to the New Testament,* 1970; and by Raymond E. Brown, Joseph A. Fitzmyer, and Roland E. Murphy, *The Jerome Biblical Commentary,* 1968. Early Christian beliefs, the expansion of the early Church, and its consolidation are discussed by James L. Price, *Interpreting the New Testament,* 1961. Anthony J. Tambasco, *In the Days of Jesus: The Jewish Background and Unique Teaching of Jesus,* 1983, is a short book capsulizing recent research on the Gospels and placing Jesus in the historical setting. Gerhard Lohfink, *Jesus and Community: The Social Dimension of Christian Faith,* trans. John P. Galvin, 1984, examines the life and mission of Jesus in the context of contemporary Judaism. David E. Aune, *Prophecy in Early Christianity and the Ancient Mediterranean World,* 1983, views the teaching of Jesus in the light of Jewish and Graeco-Roman prophetic traditions.

THE NEW TESTAMENT

King James Version (1611)

THE GOSPEL ACCORDING TO SAINT MATTHEW

The book of the generation of Jesus Christ, the son of David, the son of Abraham.[1]

Abraham begat Isaac; and Isaac begat Jacob; and Jacob begat Judah and his brethren; and Judah begat Pharez and Zerah of Tamar; and Pharez begat Hezron; and Hezron begat Ram; and Ram begat Amminadab; and Amminadab begat Nahshon; and Nahshon begat Salmon; and Salmon

---

[1] The introductory genealogy is intended to help affirm Jesus as the Messiah, the divinely sent hero who, Jewish tradition expected, would inaugurate a new era of glory and renewal. The list of names is only partly verifiable from the Old Testament. The Messiah, it was believed, would descend from the bloodline of David the king, and the descent from Abraham was important because he was the earliest patriarch of the Hebrews as God's people. The name Jesus means *saviour;* it is the Greek form of the Hebrew Yeshua, or Joshua, and thus the role of Jesus symbolically parallels that of the hero who, succeeding Moses, led the Israelites to triumph in the promised land. *Christ* is not a personal name but an epithet (meaning *Anointed One*) for the Messiah.

begat Boaz of Rachab; and Boaz begat Obed of Ruth; and Obed begat Jesse; and Jesse begat David the king.

And David the king begat Solomon of her that had been the wife of Uriah; and Solomon begat Rehoboam; and Rehoboam begat Abijah; and Abijah begat Asa; and Asa begat Jehoshaphat; and Jehoshaphat begat Jehoram; and Jehoram begat Uzziah; and Uzziah begat Jotham; and Jotham begat Ahaz; and Ahaz begat Hezekiah; and Hezekiah begat Manasseh; and Manasseh begat Amon; and Amon begat Josiah; and Josiah begat Jeconiah and his brethren, about the time they were carried away to Babylon.

And after they were brought to Babylon, Jeconiah begat Shealtiel; and Shealtiel begat Zerubbabel; and Zerubbabel begat Abiud; and Abiud begat Eliakim; and Eliakim begat Azor; and Azor begat Zadok; and Zadok begat Achim; and Achim begat Eliud; and Eliud begat Eleazar; and Eleazar begat Matthan; and Matthan begat Jacob; and Jacob begat Joseph the husband of Mary,[2] of whom was born Jesus, who is called Christ.

So all the generations from Abraham to David are fourteen generations; and from David until the carrying away into Babylon are fourteen generations; and from the carrying away into Babylon unto Christ are fourteen generations.[3] (1:1–17)

Now the birth of Jesus Christ was on this wise: When as his mother Mary was espoused to Joseph, before they came together, she was found with child of the Holy Ghost. Then Joseph her husband, being a just man, and not willing to make her a public example, was minded to put her away privily.[4] But while he thought on these things, behold, the angel of the Lord[5] appeared unto him in a dream, saying, "Joseph, thou son of David, fear not to take unto thee Mary thy wife: for that which is conceived in her is of the Holy Ghost. And she shall bring forth a son, and thou shalt call his name Jesus: for he shall save his people from their sins." Now all this was done, that it might be fulfilled which was spoken of the Lord by the prophet, saying,

> "Behold, a virgin shall be with child, and shall bring forth a son,
> And they shall call his name Emmanuel,"[6]

which being interpreted is, God with us. Then Joseph being raised from sleep did as the angel of the Lord had bidden him, and took unto him his

---

[2] The genealogy, apparently broken because Joseph is not Jesus' father, could be considered valid because Jewish law sanctioned the status of adopted sons as true ones.

[3] Matthew's tripartite genealogy, corresponding to three ages in Hebrew history, is typical of his concern with schematic structure in the gospel.

[4] Quietly, without making the matter a public issue as he was legally entitled to do.

[5] The dream, the angel, and the virgin birth are typical of the emphasis, especially strong in Matthew, on the miraculous and wondrously supernatural.

[6] Isaiah 7:14. This is the first of many Matthean quotations from the Old Testament to vindicate Jesus as the promised Messiah. Matthew quotes, as he often does, not from the Hebrew text but from the Septuagint, a Greek translation of the Old Testament used by non-Palestinian Jews ignorant of Hebrew. In the Septuagint the word here rendered as *virgin* can have that meaning; in the Hebrew text of Isaiah it means merely *young woman*. Matthew characteristically construes the Old Testament for his distinctive purposes, as foreshadowing the person and life of Jesus.

wife: and knew her not[7] till she had brought forth her firstborn son: and he called his name JESUS. (1:18–25)

Now when Jesus was born in Bethlehem of Judea in the days of Herod the king,[8] behold, there came wise men[9] from the east to Jerusalem, saying, "Where is he that is born King of the Jews? for we have seen his star in the east, and are come to worship him." When Herod the king had heard these things, he was troubled, and all Jerusalem with him. And when he had gathered all the chief priests and scribes[10] of the people together, he demanded of them where Christ should be born. And they said unto him, "In Bethlehem of Judea: for thus it is written by the prophet,

> 'And thou Bethlehem, in the land of Judah,
> Art not the least among the princes of Judah:
> For out of thee shall come a Governor,
> That shall rule my people Israel.'"

Then Herod, when he had privily called the wise men, enquired of them diligently what time the star appeared. And he sent them to Bethlehem, and said, "Go and search diligently for the young child; and when ye have found him, bring me word again, that I may come and worship him also." When they had heard the king, they departed; and, lo, the star, which they saw in the east, went before them, till it came and stood over where the young child was. When they saw the star, they rejoiced with exceeding great joy. And when they were come into the house, they saw the young child with Mary his mother, and fell down, and worshipped him: and when they had opened their treasures, they presented unto him gifts; gold, and frankincense, and myrrh. And being warned of God in a dream that they should not return to Herod, they departed into their own country another way. (2:1–12)

And when they were departed, behold, the angel of the Lord appeareth to Joseph in a dream, saying, "Arise, and take the young child and his mother, and flee into Egypt, and be thou there until I bring thee word: for Herod will seek the young child to destroy him." When he arose, he took the young child and his mother by night, and departed into Egypt: and was there until the death of Herod: that it might be fulfilled which was spoken of the Lord by the prophet, saying, "Out of Egypt have I called my son."[11] Then Herod, when he saw that he was mocked of the wise men, was exceeding wroth,[12] and sent forth, and slew all the children that were in Bethlehem, and in all the coasts thereof, from two years old and under,

---

[7] Did not have sexual intercourse with her.

[8] The ruler of Palestine, including Judea proper, the southern area of Palestine. He reigned under the authority of Caesar Augustus, because Palestine was part of the Roman empire. He was the father of the Herod who later examines Jesus at his trial. Bethlehem, a few miles south of Jerusalem, had been the home of David.

[9] Astrologers, not, as in later legend, kings. Celestial phenomena were regarded as portents of great events and the birth of august personages.

[10] Legal experts on and interpreters of Old Testament Jewish law.

[11] Hosea 11:1. In Hosea the reference is to God's deliverance of the Israelites out of captivity in Egypt.

[12] Angry.

according to the time which he had diligently enquired of the wise men. Then was fulfilled that which was spoken by Jeremiah the prophet, saying,

> "In Ramah was there a voice heard,
>   Lamentation, and weeping, and great mourning,
>   Rachel weeping for her children,
>   And would not be comforted,
>   Because they are not."[13]

But when Herod was dead, behold, an angel of the Lord appeareth in a dream to Joseph in Egypt, saying, "Arise, and take the young child and his mother, and go into the land of Israel: for they are dead which sought the young child's life." And he arose, and took the young child and his mother, and came into the land of Israel. But when he heard that Archelaus did reign in Judea in the room of his father Herod, he was afraid to go thither: notwithstanding, being warned of God in a dream, he turned aside into the parts of Galilee:[14] and he came and dwelt in a city called Nazareth: that it might be fulfilled which was spoken by the prophets, "He shall be called a Nazarene."[15] (2:13–23)

In those days[16] came John the Baptist,[17] preaching in the wilderness of Judea, and saying, "Repent ye: for the kingdom of heaven is at hand." For this is he that was spoken of by the prophet Isaiah, saying,

> "The voice of one crying in the wilderness,
>   Prepare ye the way of the Lord,
>   Make his paths straight."[18]

And the same John had his raiment of camel's hair, and a leathern girdle about his loins; and his meat was locusts and wild honey. Then went out to him Jerusalem, and all Judea, and all the region around about Jordan, and were baptized of him in Jordan, confessing their sins. But when he saw many of the Pharisees and Sadducees[19] come to his baptism, he said unto them, "O generation of vipers, who hath warned you to flee from the wrath to come? Bring forth therefore fruits meet for repentance: and think not to say within yourselves, 'We have Abraham to our father': for I say unto you,

---

[13] Jeremiah 31:15.   [14] The northern area of Palestine.

[15] Probably Matthew is creatively interpreting Isaiah 11:1. Strictly speaking, there is no mention of Nazareth in the Old Testament.

[16] A recurrent phrase that has no specific temporal reference. Here it marks the transition from the days of Jesus' infancy to those of his adulthood.

[17] John is a preacher in the tradition of Old Testament prophecy.   [18] Isaiah 40:3.

[19] Two prominent religious groups among Jews of the time, portrayed here as complacent, believing that as favorites of God and offspring of Abraham they have nothing to fear from any such divine judgment as John is proclaiming. The Sadducees were old-fashioned and aristocratic; they acknowledged as authoritative only the literal written Law of Moses and were especially concerned with the priesthood and sacrificial ritual. The Pharisees, although they too venerated the Torah, were more liberal in that they believed that the letter of the Law must be supplemented and applied with the help of tradition and orally transmitted authority. The Pharisees believed that the Scriptures, rightly interpreted, upheld the doctrine of the resurrection of the dead; the Sadducees denied this. (See 22:23–33.) After the sack of Jerusalem in 70 A.D. the Pharisees played a prominent role in preserving Jewish unity and integrity.

that God is able of these stones to raise up children unto Abraham. And now also the axe is laid unto the root of the trees: therefore every tree which bringeth not forth good fruit is hewn down, and cast into the fire. I indeed baptize you with water unto repentance: but he that cometh after me is mightier than I, whose shoes I am not worthy to bear: he shall baptize you with the Holy Ghost, and with fire: whose fan[20] is in his hand, and he will throughly purge his floor, and gather his wheat into the garner; but he will burn up the chaff with unquenchable fire." (3:1–12)

Then cometh Jesus from Galilee to Jordan unto John, to be baptized of him. But John forbade him, saying, "I have need to be baptized of thee, and comest thou to me?" And Jesus answering said unto him, "Suffer[21] it to be so now: for thus it becometh us to fulfil all righteousness." Then he suffered him. And Jesus, when he was baptized, went up straightway out of the water: and, lo, the heavens were opened unto him, and he saw the Spirit of God descending like a dove, and lighting upon him: and lo a voice from heaven, saying, "This is my beloved Son, in whom I am well pleased." (3:13–17)

Then was Jesus led up of the spirit into the wilderness to be tempted of the devil. And when he had fasted forty days and forty nights,[22] he was afterward ahungered. And when the tempter came to him, he said, "If thou be the Son of God, command that these stones be made bread." But he answered and said, "It is written, 'Man shall not live by bread alone, but by every word that proceedeth out of the mouth of God.'"[23] (4:1–4)

Then the devil taketh him up into the holy city, and setteth him on a pinnacle of the temple, and saith unto him, "If thou be the Son of God, cast thyself down: for it is written,

> 'He shall give his angels charge concerning thee:'
> And 'in their hands they shall bear thee up,
> Lest at any time thou dash thy foot against a stone.'"[24]

Jesus said unto him, "It is written again, 'Thou shalt not tempt the Lord thy God.'"[25] (4:5–7)

Again, the devil taketh him up into an exceeding high mountain, and sheweth him all the kingdoms of the world, and the glory of them; and saith unto him, "All these things will I give thee, if thou wilt fall down and worship me." Then saith Jesus unto him, "Get thee hence, Satan: for it is written, 'Thou shalt worship the Lord thy God, and him only shalt thou serve.'"[26] Then the devil leaveth him, and, behold, angels came and ministered unto him. (4:8–11)

Now when Jesus had heard that John was cast into prison,[27] he departed into Galilee; and leaving Nazareth, he came and dwelt in Capernaum,[28]

[20] Winnowing fan used to separate the grain from the chaff.   [21] Allow.
[22] The number forty is associated with several periods of preparation in the Old Testament, including the forty years the Israelites spent in the wilderness during the Exodus and the forty days and nights Moses spent on Mount Sinai.
[23] Deuteronomy 8:3; all three of Jesus' replies are from this book.   [24] Psalm 91:12.
[25] Deuteronomy 6:16.   [26] Deuteronomy 6:13.
[27] John's imprisonment is recounted later in 14:1–12.
[28] A town on the northern shore of the Sea of Galilee (actually a lake).

which is upon the sea coast, in the borders of Zebulun and Naphtali: that it might be fulfilled which was spoken by Isaiah the prophet, saying,

> "The land of Zebulun, and the land of Naphtali,
>   By the way of the sea, beyond Jordan,
>   Galilee of the Gentiles;
>   The people which sat in darkness
>   Saw great light;
>   And to them which sat in the region and shadow of death
>   Light is sprung up."[29]

From that time Jesus began to preach, and to say, "Repent: for the kingdom of heaven is at hand." (4:12–17)

And Jesus, walking by the sea of Galilee, saw two brethren, Simon called Peter, and Andrew his brother, casting a net into the sea: for they were fishers. And he saith unto them, "Follow me, and I will make you fishers of men." And they straightway left their nets, and followed him. And going on from thence, he saw other two brethren, James the son of Zebedee, and John his brother, in a ship with Zebedee their father, mending their nets; and he called them. And they immediately left the ship and their father, and followed him. (4:18–22)

And Jesus went about all Galilee, teaching in their synagogues, and preaching the gospel of the kingdom, and healing all manner of sickness and all manner of disease among the people. And his fame went throughout all Syria: and they brought unto him all sick people that were taken with divers diseases and torments, and those which were possessed with devils, and those which were lunatic, and those that had the palsy; and he healed them. And there followed him great multitudes of people from Galilee, and from Decapolis,[30] and from Jerusalem, and from Judea, and from beyond Jordan. (4:23–25)

And seeing the multitudes, he went up into a mountain: and when he was set, his disciples came unto him: and he opened his mouth, and taught them, saying,[31]

> "Blessed are the poor in spirit: for theirs is the kingdom of heaven.
> "Blessed are they that mourn: for they shall be comforted.
> "Blessed are the meek: for they shall inherit the earth.
> "Blessed are they which do hunger and thirst after righteousness: for they shall be filled.
> "Blessed are the merciful: for they shall obtain mercy.
> "Blessed are the pure in heart: for they shall see God.
> "Blessed are the peacemakers: for they shall be called the children of God.

[29] Isaiah 9:1–2.
[30] A region including ten Graeco-Roman towns east of the river Jordan.
[31] Here begins the Sermon on the Mount, which is often regarded as the quintessence of Christian ethical teaching. The discourse continues through Chapter 7. That it is given from a hill (or "mountain") underlines a basic theme in what follows: the relationship of the new teaching to the law of Moses, also delivered from a mountain (Sinai).

"Blessed are they which are persecuted for righteousness' sake: for theirs is the kingdom of heaven.

"Blessed are ye, when men shall revile you, and persecute you, and shall say all manner of evil against you falsely, for my sake. Rejoice, and be exceeding glad: for great is your reward in heaven: for so persecuted they the prophets which were before you. (5:1–12)

"Ye are the salt of the earth: but if the salt have lost his savor, wherewith shall it be salted? it is thenceforth good for nothing, but to be cast out, and to be trodden under foot of men. Ye are the light of the world. A city that is set on an hill cannot be hid. Neither do men light a candle, and put it under a bushel,[32] but on a candlestick; and it giveth light unto all that are in the house. Let your light so shine before men, that they may see your good works, and glorify your Father which is in heaven. (5:13–16)

"Think not that I am come to destroy the law, or the prophets: I am not come to destroy, but to fulfill. For verily I say unto you, Till heaven and earth pass, one jot or one tittle shall in no wise pass from the law, till all be fulfilled. Whosoever therefore shall break one of these least commandments, and shall teach men so, he shall be called the least in the kingdom of heaven: but whosoever shall do and teach them, the same shall be called great in the kingdom of heaven. For I say unto you, That except your righteousness shall exceed the righteousness of the scribes and Pharisees, ye shall in no case enter into the kingdom of heaven. (5:17–20)

"Ye have heard that it was said by them of old time, 'Thou shalt not kill'; and 'whosoever shall kill shall be in danger of the judgment':[33] but I say unto you, That whosoever is angry with his brother without a cause shall be in danger of the judgment: and whosoever shall say to his brother, 'Raca,'[34] shall be in danger of the council:[35] but whosoever shall say, 'Thou fool,' shall be in danger of hell fire. Therefore if thou bring thy gift to the altar, and there rememberest that thy brother hath ought against thee; leave there thy gift before the altar, and go thy way; first be reconciled to thy brother, and then come and offer thy gift. Agree with thine adversary quickly, whiles thou art in the way with him;[36] lest at any time the adversary deliver thee to the judge, and the judge deliver thee to the officer, and thou be cast into prison. Verily I say unto thee, Thou shalt by no means come out thence, till thou hast paid the uttermost farthing.[37] (5:21–26)

"Ye have heard that it was said by them of old time, 'Thou shalt not commit adultery': but I say unto you, That whosoever looketh on a woman to lust after her hath committed adultery with her already in his heart. And if thy right eye offend thee, pluck it out, and cast it from thee: for it is profitable for thee that one of thy members should perish, and not that thy whole body should be cast into hell. And if thy right hand offend thee, cut it off, and cast it from thee: for it is profitable for thee that one of thy

[32] A measuring-tub for meal.

[33] Prosecutable in court. Jesus goes on to say that even anger should be similarly prosecutable, like actual murder.

[34] Blockhead or idiot.   [35] The Sanhedrin, the highest Jewish law court.

[36] On the way to court.

[37] The last penny of the money owed for which one is being sued.

members should perish, and not that thy whole body should be cast into hell. It hath been said, 'Whosoever shall put away his wife, let him give her a writing of divorcement': but I say unto you, That whosoever shall put away his wife, saving for the cause of fornication, causeth her to commit adultery: and whosoever shall marry her that is divorced committeth adultery. (5:27–32)

"Again, ye have heard that it hath been said by them of old time, 'Thou shalt not forswear thyself, but shalt perform unto the Lord thine oaths': but I say unto you, Swear not at all; neither by heaven; for it is God's throne: nor by the earth; for it is his footstool: neither by Jerusalem; for it is the city of the great King. Neither shalt thou swear by thy head,[38] because thou canst not make one hair white or black. But let your communication be, 'Yea, yea'; 'Nay, nay': for whatsoever is more than these cometh of evil. (5:33–37)

"Ye have heard that it hath been said, 'An eye for an eye, and a tooth for a tooth': but I say unto you, That ye resist not evil: but whosoever shall smite thee on thy right cheek, turn to him the other also. And if any man will sue thee at the law, and take away thy coat, let him have thy cloak also. And whosoever shall compel thee to go a mile, go with him twain.[39] Give to him that asketh thee, and from him that would borrow of thee turn not thou away. (5:38–42)

"Ye have heard that it hath been said, 'Thou shalt love thy neighbor, and hate thine enemy.'[40] But I say unto you, Love your enemies, bless them that curse you, do good to them that hate you, and pray for them which despitefully use you, and persecute you; that ye may be the children of your Father which is in heaven: for he maketh his sun to rise on the evil and on the good, and sendeth rain on the just and on the unjust. For if ye love them which love you, what reward have ye? do not even the publicans[41] the same? And if ye salute your brethren only, what do ye more than others? do not even the publicans so? Be ye therefore perfect, even as your Father which is in heaven is perfect. (5:43–48)

"Take heed that ye do not your alms before men, to be seen of them: otherwise ye have no reward of your Father which is in heaven. Therefore when thou doest thine alms, do not sound a trumpet before thee, as the hypocrites do in the synagogues and in the streets, that they may have glory of men. Verily I say unto you, They have their reward. But when thou doest alms, let not thy left hand know what thy right hand doeth: that thine alms may be in secret: and thy Father which seeth in secret himself shall reward thee openly. (6:1–4)

"And when thou prayest, thou shalt not be as the hypocrites are: for they love to pray standing in the synagogues and in the corners of the streets, that they may be seen of men. Verily I say unto you, They have their reward. But thou, when thou prayest, enter into thy closet,[42] and

---

[38] By one's self.   [39] Two.

[40] The Old Testament enjoins love of one's neighbor but not explicitly hatred of enemies. That was, however, a popular inference from the former.

[41] Tax collectors, a generally despised group; elsewhere in the Gospels they are usually mentioned more sympathetically.

[42] Private room. Jesus is not condemning, however, congregational prayer in the temple or synagogue.

when thou hast shut thy door, pray to thy Father which is in secret; and thy Father which seeth in secret shall reward thee openly. But when ye pray, use not vain repetitions, as the heathen do: for they think that they shall be heard for their much speaking. Be not ye therefore like unto them: for your Father knoweth what things ye have need of, before ye ask him. After this manner therefore pray ye:

> Our Father which art in heaven,
> Hallowed be thy name.
> Thy kingdom come.
> Thy will be done
>   in earth as it is in heaven.
> Give us this day our daily bread.
> And forgive us our debts,
>   as we forgive our debtors.[43]
> And lead us not into temptation,
>   but deliver us from evil:[44]
> For thine is the kingdom, and the power, and the glory,
>   for ever. Amen.

For if ye forgive men their trespasses, your heavenly Father will also forgive you: but if ye forgive not men their trespasses, neither will your Father forgive your trespasses. (6:5–15)

"Moreover when ye fast, be not, as the hypocrites, of a sad countenance: for they disfigure their faces, that they may appear unto men to fast. Verily I say unto you, They have their reward. But thou, when thou fastest, anoint thine head, and wash thy face;[45] that thou appear not unto men to fast, but unto thy Father which is in secret: and thy Father, which seeth in secret, shall reward thee openly. (6:16–18)

"Lay not up for yourselves treasures upon earth, where moth and rust doth corrupt, and where thieves break through and steal: but lay up for yourselves treasures in heaven, where neither moth nor rust doth corrupt, and where thieves do not break through nor steal: for where your treasure is, there will your heart be also. The light of the body is the eye: if therefore thine eye be single,[46] thy whole body shall be full of light. But if thine eye be evil, thy whole body shall be full of darkness. If therefore the light that is in thee be darkness, how great is that darkness! (6:19–23)

"No man can serve two masters: for either he will hate the one, and love the other; or else he will hold to the one, and despise the other. Ye cannot serve God and mammon.[47] Therefore I say unto you, Take no thought for your life, what ye shall eat, or what ye shall drink; nor yet for your body, what ye shall put on. Is not the life more than meat, and the body than raiment? Behold the fowls of the air: for they sow not, neither do they reap, nor gather into barns; yet your heavenly Father feedeth them. Are ye

---

[43] The words *debts* and *debtors* can be rendered as, respectively, the wrongs we have committed and those that have been committed against us.

[44] In most of the earliest manuscripts, the Lord's Prayer ends here.

[45] Anointing and washing were part of preparing for a banquet.

[46] Healthy, as opposed to the "evil" (diseased) eye.

[47] Material possessions and money.

not much better than they? Which of you by taking thought can add one cubit[48] unto his stature? And why take ye thought for raiment? Consider the lilies of the field, how they grow; they toil not, neither do they spin: and yet I say unto you, That even Solomon in all his glory was not arrayed like one of these. Wherefore, if God so clothe the grass of the field, which today is, and tomorrow is cast into the oven,[49] shall he not much more clothe you, O ye of little faith? Therefore take no thought, saying, 'What shall we eat?' or, 'What shall we drink?' or, 'Wherewithal shall we be clothed?' (for after all these things do the Gentiles seek:) for your heavenly Father knoweth that ye have need of all these things. But seek ye first the kingdom of God, and his righteousness; and all these things shall be added unto you. Take therefore no thought for the morrow: for the morrow shall take thought for the things of itself. Sufficient unto the day is the evil thereof.[50] (6:24–34)

"Judge not, that ye be not judged. For with what judgment ye judge, ye shall be judged: and with what measure ye mete, it shall be measured to you again. And why beholdest thou the mote[51] that is in thy brother's eye, but considerest not the beam that is in thine own eye? Or how wilt thou say to thy brother, 'Let me pull out the mote out of thine eye'; and, behold, a beam is in thine own eye? Thou hypocrite, first cast out the beam out of thine own eye; and then shalt thou see clearly to cast out the mote out of thy brother's eye. (7:1–5)

"Give not that which is holy unto the dogs, neither cast ye your pearls before swine, lest they trample them under their feet, and turn again and rend you. (7:6)

"Ask, and it shall be given you; seek, and ye shall find; knock, and it shall be opened unto you: for every one that asketh receiveth; and he that seeketh findeth; and to him that knocketh it shall be opened. Or what man is there of you, whom if his son ask bread, will he give him a stone? Or if he ask a fish, will he give him a serpent? If ye then, being evil, know how to give good gifts unto your children, how much more shall your Father which is in heaven give good things to them that ask him? (7:7–11)

"Therefore all things whatsoever ye would that men should do to you, do ye even so to them: for this is the law and the prophets. (7:12)

"Enter ye in at the strait gate: for wide is the gate, and broad is the way, that leadeth to destruction, and many there be which go in thereat: because strait is the gate, and narrow is the way, which leadeth unto life, and few there be that find it. (7:13–14)

"Beware of false prophets,[52] which come to you in sheep's clothing, but inwardly they are ravening wolves. Ye shall know them by their fruits. Do men gather grapes of thorns, or figs of thistles? Even so every good tree bringeth forth good fruit; but a corrupt tree bringeth forth evil fruit. A good tree cannot bring forth evil fruit, neither can a corrupt tree bring

---

[48] About 20 inches.   [49] As fuel.

[50] Each day has anxieties enough of its own; one need not add to them worries about the future.

[51] A tiny speck of wood, as contrasted with a "beam," or large board.

[52] The caution against false prophets and that in the following passage against those who say "Lord, Lord" are less applicable to Jesus' own time than to the problems the early Church faced a half-century later (when Matthew was written).

forth good fruit. Every tree that bringeth not forth good fruit is hewn down, and cast into the fire. Wherefore by their fruits ye shall know them. (7:15–20)

"Not every one that saith unto me, 'Lord, Lord,' shall enter into the kingdom of heaven; but he that doeth the will of my Father which is in heaven. Many will say to me in that day, 'Lord, Lord, have we not prophesied in thy name? and in thy name have cast out devils? and in thy name done many wonderful works?' And then will I profess unto them, 'I never knew you: depart from me, ye that work iniquity.' (7:21–23)

"Therefore whosoever heareth these sayings of mine, and doeth them, I will liken him unto a wise man, which built his house upon a rock: and the rain descended, and the floods came, and the winds blew, and beat upon that house; and it fell not: for it was founded upon a rock. And every one that heareth these sayings of mine, and doeth them not, shall be likened unto a foolish man, which built his house upon the sand: and the rain descended, and the floods came, and the winds blew, and beat upon that house; and it fell: and great was the fall of it." (7:24–27)

And it came to pass, when Jesus had ended these sayings, the people were astonished at his doctrine: for he taught them as one having authority, and not as the scribes.[53] (7:28–29)

When he was come down from the mountain, great multitudes followed him. And, behold, there came a leper and worshipped him, saying, "Lord, if thou wilt, thou canst make me clean." And Jesus put forth his hand, and touched him, saying, "I will; be thou clean." And immediately his leprosy was cleansed. And Jesus saith unto him, "See thou tell no man; but go thy way, show thyself to the priest, and offer the gift that Moses commanded, for a testimony unto them."[54] (8:1–4)

And when Jesus was entered into Capernaum, there came unto him a centurion,[55] beseeching him, and saying, "Lord, my servant lieth at home sick of the palsy, grievously tormented." And Jesus saith unto him, "I will come and heal him." The centurion answered and said, "Lord, I am not worthy that thou shouldest come under my roof: but speak the word only, and my servant shall be healed. For I am a man under authority, having soldiers under me: and I say to this man, 'Go,' and he goeth; and to another, 'Come,' and he cometh; and to my servant, 'Do this,' and he doeth it." When Jesus heard it, he marvelled, and said to them that followed, "Verily I say unto you, I have not found so great faith, no, not in Israel. And I say unto you, That many shall come from the east and west, and shall sit down with Abraham, and Isaac, and Jacob, in the kingdom of heaven. But the children of the kingdom shall be cast out into outer darkness: there shall be weeping and gnashing of teeth." And Jesus said unto the centurion, "Go thy way; and as thou hast believed, so be it done unto thee." And his servant was healed in the selfsame hour. (8:5–13)

And when Jesus was come into Peter's house, he saw his wife's mother laid, and sick of a fever. And he touched her hand, and the fever left

---

[53] He did not teach with a cautious conformity to tradition, like the scribes, but rather like the prophets.

[54] Leviticus 14:2–9 describes the elaborate rite to be performed after the cure of leprosy.

[55] A military officer (here probably a Roman, certainly a Gentile) who commanded a hundred men.

her: and she arose, and ministered unto them. When the even was come, they brought unto him many that were possessed with devils: and he cast out the spirits with his word, and healed all that were sick: that it might be fulfilled which was spoken by Isaiah the prophet, saying, "Himself took our infirmities, and bare our sicknesses."[56] (8:14–17)

Now when Jesus saw great multitudes about him, he gave commandment to depart unto the other side.[57] And a certain scribe came, and said unto him, "Master, I will follow thee whithersoever thou goest." And Jesus saith unto him, "The foxes have holes, and the birds of the air have nests; but the Son of man[58] hath not where to lay his head." And another of his disciples said unto him, "Lord, suffer me first to go and bury my father." But Jesus said unto him, "Follow me; and let the dead bury their dead." (8:18–22)

And when he was entered into a ship, his disciples followed him. And, behold, there arose a great tempest in the sea, insomuch that the ship was covered with the waves: but he was asleep. And his disciples came to him, and awoke him, saying, "Lord, save us: we perish." And he saith unto them, "Why are ye fearful, O ye of little faith?" Then he arose, and rebuked the winds and the sea; and there was a great calm. But the men marvelled, saying, "What manner of man is this, that even the winds and the sea obey him!" (8:23–27)

And when he was come to the other side into the country of the Gergesenes, there met him two possessed with devils, coming out of the tombs, exceeding fierce, so that no man might pass by that way. And, behold, they cried out, saying, "What have we to do with thee, Jesus, thou Son of God? art thou come hither to torment us before the time?"[59] And there was a good way off from them an herd of many swine feeding. So the devils besought him, saying, "If thou cast us out, suffer us to go away into the herd of swine."[60] And he said unto them, "Go." And when they were come out, they went into the herd of swine: and, behold, the whole herd of swine ran violently down a steep place into the sea, and perished in the waters. And they that kept them fled, and went their ways into the city, and told every thing, and what was befallen to the possessed of the devils. And, behold, the whole city came out to meet Jesus: and when they saw him, they besought him that he would depart out of their coasts. (8:28–34).

And he entered into a ship, and passed over, and came into his own city.[61] And, behold, they brought to him a man sick of the palsy, lying on a bed: and Jesus seeing their faith said unto the sick of the palsy; "Son, be of good cheer; thy sins be forgiven thee." And, behold, certain of the scribes said within themselves, "This man blasphemeth."[62] And Jesus knowing their thoughts said, "Wherefore think ye evil in your hearts? For whether is

---

[56] Isaiah 53:4.   [57] The eastern side of the Sea of Galilee.

[58] *Son of man* can mean *individual human person*. It also came, by evolution from its first use in Daniel 7, to designate an apocalyptic figure expected to usher in the kingdom of God.

[59] Before God's final destruction of all evil.

[60] The devils ask that they be allowed one last display of their power. The herd of pigs (unclean animals to the Jews and fit to receive the devils) shows that this is Gentile country.

[61] Capernaum, Jesus' base during his ministry in Galilee.

[62] Because only God could forgive sins. Jesus' initial encouragement of the sick man ("be of good cheer") reflects the Jewish belief that God's forgiveness of sins was a prerequisite for recovery from illness.

easier, to say, 'Thy sins be forgiven thee'; or to say, 'Arise, and walk'? But that ye may know that the Son of man hath power on earth to forgive sins," (then saith he to the sick of the palsy,) "Arise, take up thy bed, and go unto thine house." And he arose, and departed to his house. But when the multitudes saw it, they marvelled, and glorified God, which had given such power unto men. (9:1–8)

And as Jesus passed forth from thence, he saw a man, named Matthew, sitting at the receipt of custom:[63] and he saith unto him, "Follow me." And he arose, and followed him. And it came to pass, as Jesus sat at meat in the house, behold, many publicans and sinners came and sat down with him and his disciples. And when the Pharisees saw it, they said unto his disciples, "Why eateth your Master with publicans and sinners?" But when Jesus heard that, he said unto them, "They that be whole need not a physician, but they that are sick. But go ye and learn what that meaneth, 'I will have mercy, and not sacrifice':[64] for I am not come to call the righteous, but sinners to repentance." (9:9–13)

Then came to him the disciples of John, saying, "Why do we and the Pharisees fast oft, but thy disciples fast not?" And Jesus said unto them, "Can the children of the bridechamber mourn, as long as the bridegroom is with them? but the days will come, when the bridegroom shall be taken from them, and then shall they fast. No man putteth a piece of new cloth unto an old garment, for that which is put in to fill it up taketh from the garment, and the rent is made worse. Neither do men put new wine into old bottles: else the bottles break, and the wine runneth out, and the bottles perish: but they put new wine into new bottles, and both are preserved."[65] (9:14–17)

While he spake these things unto them, behold, there came a certain ruler,[66] and worshipped him, saying, "My daughter is even now dead: but come and lay thy hand upon her, and she shall live." And Jesus arose, and followed him, and so did his disciples. (9:18–19)

And, behold, a woman, which was diseased with an issue of blood[67] twelve years, came behind him, and touched the hem of his garment: for she said within herself, "If I may but touch his garment, I shall be whole." But Jesus turned him about, and when he saw her, he said, "Daughter, be of good comfort; thy faith hath made thee whole." And the woman was made whole from that hour. And when Jesus came into the ruler's house, and saw the minstrels[68] and the people making a noise, he said unto them, "Give place: for the maid is not dead, but sleepeth." And they laughed him to scorn. But when the people were put forth, he went in, and took her by the hand, and the maid arose. And the fame hereof went abroad into all that land. (9:20–26)

---

[63] Customhouse; the disciple Matthew, a publican, would naturally be found there. He apparently goes on to invite Jesus to a dinner. Publicans were hated because they often used extortion in collecting the taxes.

[64] Hosea 6:6.

[65] The analogies from clothing and wine bottles (more exactly, wineskins) apparently serve to contrast the old Law with Jesus' teaching. But, significantly in Matthew, although Jesus' teaching is radically new, both the new and old wine, or doctrine, "are preserved."

[66] Identified in other Gospels as a synagogue official.   [67] Hemorrhage.

[68] The musicians and the other people are professional mourners.

And when Jesus departed thence, two blind men followed him, crying, and saying, "Thou son of David, have mercy on us." And when he was come into the house, the blind men came to him: and Jesus saith unto them, "Believe ye that I am able to do this?" They said unto him, "Yea, Lord." Then touched he their eyes, saying, "According to your faith be it unto you." And their eyes were opened; and Jesus straitly charged them, saying, "See that no man know it."[69] But they, when they were departed, spread abroad his fame in all that country. (9:27–31)

As they went out, behold, they brought to him a dumb man possessed with a devil. And when the devil was cast out, the dumb spake: and the multitudes marvelled, saying, "It was never so seen in Israel." But the Pharisees said, "He casteth out devils through the prince of the devils." (9:32–34)

And Jesus went about all the cities and villages, teaching in their synagogues, and preaching the gospel of the kingdom, and healing every sickness and every disease among the people. But when he saw the multitudes, he was moved with compassion on them, because they fainted, and were scattered abroad, as sheep having no shepherd. Then saith he unto his disciples, "The harvest truly is plenteous, but the laborers are few; pray ye therefore the Lord of the harvest, that he will send forth laborers into his harvest." (9:35–38)

And when he had called unto him his twelve disciples,[70] he gave them power against unclean spirits, to cast them out, and to heal all manner of sickness and all manner of disease. Now the names of the twelve apostles[71] are these; The first, Simon, who is called Peter, and Andrew his brother; James the son of Zebedee, and John his brother; Philip, and Bartholomew; Thomas, and Matthew the publican; James the son of Alpheus, and Lebbeus, whose surname was Thaddeus, Simon the Canaanite, and Judas Iscariot, who also betrayed him. These twelve Jesus sent forth, and commanded them, saying,

"Go not into the way of the Gentiles, and into any city of the Samaritans enter ye not:[72] but go rather to the lost sheep of the house of Israel. And as ye go, preach, saying, 'The kingdom of heaven is at hand.' Heal the sick, cleanse the lepers, raise the dead, cast out devils: freely ye have received, freely give. Provide neither gold, nor silver, nor brass in your purses, nor scrip[73] for your journey, neither two coats, neither shoes, nor yet staves: for the workman is worthy of his meat. And into whatsoever city or town ye shall enter, enquire who in it is worthy; and there abide till ye go thence. And when ye come into an house, salute it. And if the house be

---

[69] An allusion to the "Messianic secret"; according to some scholars, the early Church inserted in the Gospels such injunctions of secrecy (rare in Matthew) in order to explain the fact that Jesus was not recognized as Messiah until after his resurrection.

[70] The number twelve parallels the twelve sons of Jacob and tribes of the Jews.

[71] The word means those "sent out"; it is not used elsewhere in Matthew.

[72] The command not to proselytize the Gentiles is puzzling in light of the emphasis elsewhere in Matthew (see the conclusion, for example) on the Christian mission to them; perhaps the passage reflects the early Church's awareness that this mission belonged to a later stage. *Samaritans* were inhabitants of Samaria, in the mid-northern part of Palestine, south of Galilee and north of Judea; they shared much of the Jewish heritage but had a separate priesthood and did not recognize Jerusalem as the center of worship.

[73] Bag.

worthy, let your peace come upon it: but if it be not worthy, let your peace return to you. And whosoever shall not receive you, nor hear your words, when ye depart out of that house or city, shake off the dust of your feet. Verily I say unto you, It shall be more tolerable for the land of Sodom and Gomorrah[74] in the day of judgment, than for that city. (10:1–15)

"Behold, I send you forth as sheep in the midst of wolves: be ye therefore wise as serpents, and harmless as doves. But beware of men: for they will deliver you up to the councils,[75] and they will scourge you in their synagogues; and ye shall be brought before governors and kings for my sake, for a testimony against[76] them and the Gentiles. But when they deliver you up, take no thought how or what ye shall speak: for it shall be given you in that same hour what ye shall speak. For it is not ye that speak, but the Spirit of your Father which speaketh in you. And the brother shall deliver up the brother to death, and the father the child: and the children shall rise up against their parents, and cause them to be put to death. And ye shall be hated of all men for my name's sake: but he that endureth to the end shall be saved. But when they persecute you in this city, flee ye into another: for verily I say unto you, Ye shall not have gone over the cities of Israel, till the Son of man be come.[77] The disciple is not above his master, nor the servant above his lord. It is enough for the disciple that he be as his master, and the servant as his lord. If they have called the master of the house Beelzebub,[78] how much more shall they call them of his household? Fear them not therefore: for there is nothing covered, that shall not be revealed; and hid, that shall not be known. What I tell you in darkness, that speak ye in light: and what ye hear in the ear, that preach ye upon the housetops. And fear not them which kill the body, but are not able to kill the soul: but rather fear him[79] which is able to destroy both soul and body in hell. Are not two sparrows sold for a farthing? and one of them shall not fall on the ground without your Father. But the very hairs of your head are all numbered. Fear ye not therefore, ye are of more value than many sparrows. Whosoever therefore shall confess me before men, him will I confess also before my Father which is in heaven. But whosoever shall deny me before men, him will I also deny before my Father which is in heaven. (10:16–33)

"Think not that I am come to send peace on earth: I came not to send peace, but a sword. For I am come to set a man at variance against his father, and the daughter against her mother, and the daughter in law against her mother in law. And a man's foes shall be they of his own household. He that loveth father or mother more than me is not worthy of me: and he that loveth son or daughter more than me is not worthy of me. And he that taketh not his cross, and followeth after me, is not worthy of me. He that findeth his life shall lose it: and he that loseth his life for my sake shall find it. (10:34–39)

"He that receiveth you receiveth me, and he that receiveth me receiveth

---

[74] Sinful cities destroyed by God with brimstone and fire; see Genesis 19.   [75] Courts.
[76] To testify in the face of.
[77] A puzzling sentence; the apparent meaning, that the Last Judgment will come before the mission is extended to the Gentiles, can hardly be the meaning intended, because when this Gospel was written, half a century after Jesus, such an extension had occurred.
[78] Identified later (12:24) as "the prince of the devils."   [79] That is, fear God.

him that sent me. He that receiveth a prophet in the name of[80] a prophet shall receive a prophet's reward; and he that receiveth a righteous man in the name of a righteous man shall receive a righteous man's reward. And whosoever shall give to drink unto one of these little ones[81] a cup of cold water only in the name of a disciple, verily I say unto you, he shall in no wise lose his reward." (10:40–42)

And it came to pass, when Jesus had made an end of commanding his twelve disciples, he departed thence to teach and to preach in their cities.[82] Now when John had heard in the prison[83] the works of Christ, he sent two of his disciples, and said unto him, "Art thou he that should come, or do we look for another?" Jesus answered and said unto them, "Go and show John again those things which ye do hear and see: the blind receive their sight, and the lame walk, the lepers are cleansed, and the deaf hear, the dead are raised up, and the poor have the gospel preached to them. And blessed is he, whosoever shall not be offended in me."[84] (11:1–6)

And as they departed, Jesus began to say unto the multitudes concerning John, "What went ye out into the wilderness to see? A reed shaken with the wind?[85] But what went ye out for to see? A man clothed in soft raiment? behold, they that wear soft clothing are in kings' houses. But what went ye out for to see? A prophet? yea, I say unto you, and more than a prophet. For this is he, of whom it is written,

'Behold, I send my messenger before thy face,
Which shall prepare thy way before thee.'[86]

Verily I say unto you, Among them that are born of women there hath not risen a greater than John the Baptist: notwithstanding he that is least in the kingdom of heaven is greater than he.[87] And from the days of John the Baptist until now the kingdom of heaven suffereth violence, and the violent take it by force.[88] For all the prophets and the law prophesied until John. And if ye will receive it, this is Elijah[89] which was for to come. He that hath ears to hear, let him hear. (11:7–15)

"But whereunto shall I liken this generation? It is like unto children sitting in the markets, and calling unto their fellows, and saying, 'We have piped unto you, and ye have not danced; we have mourned unto you, and ye have not lamented.'[90] For John came neither eating nor drinking, and they say, 'He hath a devil.' The Son of man came eating and drinking, and they say, 'Behold a man gluttonous, and a winebibber, a friend of publicans and sinners.' But wisdom is justified of her children."[91] (11:16–19)

---

[80] "In the name of" can be translated as "because he is."   [81] Lowly disciples of Jesus.
[82] In towns nearby.   [83] For John's imprisonment, see 14:1–12.
[84] Shall not find me an obstacle to faith.
[85] Either a literal bed of reeds or (figuratively) a weak man.   [86] Malachi 3:1.
[87] Possibly because John lived before the new kingdom of heaven Jesus ushers in.
[88] The sentence is obscure; its meaning is conjectural.
[89] According to Jewish legend, the prophet Elijah, who had never died (2 Kings 2:11–12), would reappear just before the world ended.
[90] Jesus says that, like children at play who are out of tune with one another's moods, the Jews are dissatisfied with anything out of the ordinary—John the ascetic or the allegedly loose-living Jesus.
[91] The sentence is obscure; it may mean "Righteousness is vindicated by its results."

Then began he to upbraid the cities wherein most of his mighty works were done, because they repented not: "Woe unto thee, Chorazin! woe unto thee, Bethsaida! for if the mighty works, which were done in you, had been done in Tyre and Sidon, they would have repented long ago in sackcloth and ashes. But I say unto you, It shall be more tolerable for Tyre and Sidon at the day of judgment, than for you. And thou, Capernaum, which art exalted unto heaven, shalt be brought down to hell: for if the mighty works, which have been done in thee, had been done in Sodom, it would have remained until this day. But I say unto you, That it shall be more tolerable for the land of Sodom in the day of judgment, than for thee."[92] (11:20–24)

At that time Jesus answered and said, "I thank thee, O Father, Lord of heaven and earth, because thou hast hid these things from the wise and prudent, and hast revealed them unto babes. Even so, Father: for so it seemed good in thy sight. All things are delivered unto me of my Father: and no man knoweth the Son, but the Father; neither knoweth any man the Father, save the Son, and he to whomsoever the Son will reveal him." (11:25–27)

"Come unto me, all ye that labor and are heavy laden, and I will give you rest. Take my yoke upon you, and learn of me; for I am meek and lowly in heart: and ye shall find rest unto your souls. For my yoke is easy,[93] and my burden is light." (11:28–30)

At that time Jesus went on the sabbath day through the corn; and his disciples were ahungered, and began to pluck the ears of corn, and to eat. But when the Pharisees saw it, they said unto him, "Behold, thy disciples do that which is not lawful to do upon the sabbath day." But he said unto them, "Have ye not read what David did, when he was ahungered, and they that were with him; how he entered into the house of God, and did eat the showbread, which was not lawful for him to eat, neither for them which were with him, but only for the priests?[94] Or have ye not read in the law, how that on the sabbath days the priests in the temple profane the sabbath, and are blameless? But I say unto you, That in this place is one greater than the temple. But if ye had known what this meaneth, 'I will have mercy, and not sacrifice,'[95] ye would not have condemned the guiltless. For the Son of man is Lord even of the sabbath day." (12:1–8)

And when he was departed thence, he went into their synagogue: and, behold, there was a man which had his hand withered. And they asked him, saying, "Is it lawful to heal on the sabbath days?" that they might accuse him. And he said unto them, "What man shall there be among you, that shall have one sheep, and if it fall into a pit on the sabbath day, will he

[92] Chorazin, Bethsaida, and Capernaum (Jesus' city) have seen Jesus and his works but have been unresponsive; they are contrasted unfavorably with the Gentile cities Tyre and Sidon (seaports north of Palestine) and the notoriously wicked city of Sodom.

[93] The yoke of the Law construed spiritually is easy compared with a legalistically construed old Law.

[94] The disciples are accused of breaking sabbath rules about preparation of food. Jesus cites the enforced eating of the showbread (used in the Temple ritual; Leviticus 24:5–9), as told in 1 Samuel 21:1–6. He goes on to argue that the priests can without sin perform their Temple duties on the sabbath and that Jesus and his work are even more important than the Temple.

[95] Ritual sacrifice; Jesus is citing Hosea 6:6.

not lay hold on it, and lift it out? How much then is a man better than a sheep? Wherefore it is lawful to do well on the sabbath days." Then saith he to the man, "Stretch forth thine hand." And he stretched it forth; and it was restored whole, like as the other. (12:9–13)

Then the Pharisees went out, and held a council against him, how they might destroy him. But when Jesus knew it, he withdrew himself from thence: and great multitudes followed him, and he healed them all; and charged them that they should not make him known: that it might be fulfilled which was spoken by Isaiah the prophet, saying,

> "Behold my servant, whom I have chosen;
>   my beloved, in whom my soul is well pleased:
> I will put my spirit upon him,
>   and he shall show judgment to the Gentiles.
> He shall not strive, nor cry;
>   neither shall any man hear his voice in the streets.
> A bruised reed shall he not break,
>   and smoking flax shall he not quench,
> Till he send forth judgment unto victory.
> And in his name shall the Gentiles trust."[96] (12:14–21)

Then was brought unto him one possessed with a devil, blind, and dumb: and he healed him, insomuch that the blind and dumb both spake and saw. And all the people were amazed, and said, "Is not this the son of David?"[97] But when the Pharisees heard it, they said, "This fellow doth not cast out devils, but by Beelzebub the prince of the devils." And Jesus knew their thoughts, and said unto them, "Every kingdom divided against itself is brought to desolation; and every city or house divided against itself shall not stand: and if Satan cast out Satan, he is divided against himself; how shall then his kingdom stand? And if I by Beelzebub cast out devils, by whom do your children[98] cast them out? therefore they shall be your judges. But if I cast out devils by the Spirit of God, then the kingdom of God is come unto you. Or else how can one enter into a strong man's house, and spoil his goods,[99] except he first bind the strong man? and then he will spoil his house. He that is not with me is against me; and he that gathereth not with me scattereth abroad. Wherefore I say unto you, All manner of sin and blasphemy shall be forgiven unto men: but the blasphemy against the Holy Ghost shall not be forgiven unto men. And whosoever speaketh a word against the Son of man, it shall be forgiven him: but whosoever speaketh against the Holy Ghost, it shall not be forgiven him,[1] neither in this world, neither in the world to come. Either make the tree good, and his fruit good; or else make the tree corrupt, and his fruit corrupt: for the tree is known by his fruit. O generation of vipers, how can ye, being evil, speak good things? for out of the abundance of the heart the mouth speaketh. A

---

[96] Isaiah 42:1–4. The parallel is with the reticence just attributed to Jesus.
[97] The Messiah, who would be a descendant of David.   [98] Your own exorcists.
[99] The strong man is Satan; his "goods" are the persons demonically possessed by him.
[1] The nature of the unforgivable sin against the Holy Ghost is elusive; Jesus may mean there is no chance that people will repent (a prerequisite for God's forgiveness) who wilfully disregard the manifest signs of His works (as in the present casting out of devils).

good man out of the good treasure of the heart bringeth forth good things: and an evil man out of the evil treasure bringeth forth evil things. But I say unto you, That every idle word that men shall speak, they shall give account thereof in the day of judgment. For by thy words thou shalt be justified, and by thy words thou shalt be condemned." (12:22–37)

Then certain of the scribes and of the Pharisees answered, saying, "Master, we would see a sign[2] from thee." But he answered and said unto them, "An evil and adulterous[3] generation seeketh after a sign; and there shall no sign be given to it, but the sign of the prophet Jonah: for as Jonah was three days and three nights in the whale's belly; so shall the Son of man be three days and three nights in the heart of the earth.[4] The men of Nineveh[5] shall rise in judgment with this generation, and shall condemn it: because they repented at the preaching of Jonah; and, behold, a greater than Jonah is here. The queen of the south[6] shall rise up in the judgment with this generation, and shall condemn it: for she came from the uttermost parts of the earth to hear the wisdom of Solomon; and, behold, a greater than Solomon is here. (12:38–42)

"When the unclean spirit is gone out of a man, he walketh through dry places, seeking rest, and findeth none. Then he saith, 'I will return into my house from whence I came out'; and when he is come, he findeth it empty, swept, and garnished. Then goeth he, and taketh with himself seven other spirits more wicked than himself, and they enter in and dwell there: and the last state of that man is worse than the first.[7] Even so shall it be also unto this wicked generation." (12:43–45)

While he yet talked to the people, behold, his mother and his brethren stood without, desiring to speak with him.[8] Then one said unto him, "Behold, thy mother and thy brethren stand without, desiring to speak with thee." But he answered and said unto him that told him, "Who is my mother? and who are my brethren?" And he stretched forth his hand toward his disciples, and said, "Behold my mother and my brethren! For whosoever shall do the will of my Father which is in heaven, the same is my brother, and sister, and mother." (12:46–50)

The same day went Jesus out of the house, and sat by the sea side. And great multitudes were gathered together unto him, so that he went into a ship, and sat; and the whole multitude stood on the shore. And he spake many things unto them in parables, saying, "Behold, a sower went forth to sow; and when he sowed, some seeds fell by the way side, and the fowls came and devoured them up: some fell upon stony places, where they had not much earth: and forthwith they sprung up, because they had no deepness of earth: and when the sun was up, they were scorched; and because they had no root, they withered away. And some fell among

---

[2] That Jesus is the Messiah.   [3] Unfaithful to God.

[4] In the tomb, before rising from the dead. (This verse is a late addition to the text.)

[5] Though Gentiles, the inhabitants of Nineveh had repented in response to Jonah's preaching (Jonah 3:5).

[6] The Queen of Sheba, who had come from Arabia (1 Kings 10).

[7] Jesus is apparently describing an exorcism only temporarily successful because nothing good has replaced the cast-out evil. In applying this to his addressees, he may mean that although he has overcome evil, the relief will be only temporary for those who reject him.

[8] Some interpreters take the word here translated "brethren" to mean merely "relatives."

thorns; and the thorns sprung up, and choked them: but other fell into good ground, and brought forth fruit, some a hundredfold, some sixty-fold, some thirtyfold. Who hath ears to hear, let him hear." (13:1–9)

And the disciples came, and said unto him, "Why speakest thou unto them in parables?" He answered and said unto them, "Because it is given unto you to know the mysteries of the kingdom of heaven, but to them it is not given. For whosoever hath, to him shall be given, and he shall have more abundance: but whosoever hath not, from him shall be taken away even that he hath. Therefore speak I to them in parables: because they seeing see not; and hearing they hear not, neither do they understand. And in them is fulfilled the prophecy of Isaiah, which saith,

> 'By hearing ye shall hear, and shall not understand;
>   and seeing ye shall see, and shall not perceive:
> For this people's heart is waxed gross,
>   and their ears are dull of hearing,
>   and their eyes they have closed;
> Lest at any time they should see with their eyes,
>   and hear with their ears,
> And understand with their heart,
>   and should be converted, and I should heal them.'[9]

But blessed are your eyes, for they see: and your ears, for they hear. For verily I say unto you, That many prophets and righteous men have desired to see those things which ye see, and have not seen them; and to hear those things which ye hear, and have not heard them. Hear ye therefore the parable of the sower. When any one heareth the word of the kingdom, and understandeth it not, then cometh the wicked one, and catcheth away that which was sown in his heart. This is he which received seed by the way side. But he that received the seed into stony places, the same is he that heareth the word, and anon with joy receiveth it; yet hath he not root in himself, but dureth for a while: for when tribulation or persecution ariseth because of the word, by and by he is offended.[10] He also that received seed among the thorns is he that heareth the word; and the care of this world, and the deceitfulness of riches, choke the word, and he becometh unfruitful. But he that received seed into the good ground is he that heareth the word, and understandeth it; which also beareth fruit, and bringeth forth, some a hundredfold, some sixty, some thirty." (13:10–23)

Another parable put he forth unto them, saying, "The kingdom of heaven is likened unto a man which sowed good seed in his field: but while men slept, his enemy came and sowed tares[11] among the wheat, and went his way. But when the blade was sprung up, and brought forth fruit, then appeared the tares also. So the servants of the householder came and said unto him, 'Sir, didst not thou sow good seed in thy field? from whence then hath it tares?' He said unto them, 'An enemy hath done this.' The servants said unto them, 'Wilt thou then that we go and gather them up?' But he said,

---

[9] Isaiah 6:9–10.   [10] A modern translation might say "he lapses."
[11] Darnel, a weed resembling wheat and having poisonous seeds.

'Nay; lest while ye gather up the tares, ye root up also the wheat with them. Let both grow together until the harvest: and in the time of harvest I will say to the reapers, Gather ye together first the tares, and bind them in bundles to burn them: but gather the wheat into my barn.'" (13:24–30)

Another parable put he forth unto them, saying, "The kingdom of heaven is like to a grain of mustard seed, which a man took, and sowed in his field: which indeed is the least of all seeds: but when it is grown, it is the greatest among herbs, and becometh a tree, so that the birds of the air come and lodge in the branches thereof." (13:31–32)

Another parable spake he unto them; "The kingdom of heaven is like unto leaven, which a woman took, and hid in three measures of meal,[12] till the whole was leavened." All these things spake Jesus unto the multitude in parables; and without a parable spake he not unto them: that it might be fulfilled which was spoken by the prophet, saying,

"I will open my mouth in parables;
I will utter things which have been kept secret from the
foundation of the world."[13] (13:33–35)

Then Jesus sent the multitude away, and went into the house: and his disciples came unto him, saying, "Declare unto us the parable of the tares of the field." He answered and said unto them, "He that soweth the good seed is the Son of man; the field is the world; the good seed are the children of the kingdom; but the tares are the children of the wicked one; the enemy that sowed them is the devil; the harvest is the end of the world; and the reapers are the angels. As therefore the tares are gathered and burned in the fire; so shall it be in the end of this world. The Son of man shall send forth his angels, and they shall gather out of his kingdom all things that offend, and them which do iniquity; and shall cast them into a furnace of fire: there shall be wailing and gnashing of teeth. Then shall the righteous shine forth as the sun in the kingdom of their Father. Who hath ears to hear, let him hear. (13:36–43)

"Again, the kingdom of heaven is like unto treasure hid in a field; the which when a man hath found, he hideth, and for joy thereof goeth and selleth all that he hath, and buyeth that field. (13:44)

"Again, the kingdom of heaven is like unto a merchant man, seeking goodly pearls: who, when he had found one pearl of great price, went and sold all that he had, and bought it. (13:45–46)

"Again, the kingdom of heaven is like unto a net, that was cast into the sea, and gathered of every kind: which, when it was full, they drew to shore, and sat down, and gathered the good into vessels, but cast the bad away. So shall it be at the end of the world: the angels shall come forth, and sever the wicked from among the just, and shall cast them into the furnace of fire: there shall be wailing and gnashing of teeth." (13:47–50)

Jesus saith unto them, "Have ye understood all these things?" They say unto him, "Yea, Lord." Then said he unto them, "Therefore every scribe

---

[12] A large amount of dough.   [13] Psalm 78:2.

which is instructed unto the kingdom of heaven is like unto a man that is an householder, which bringeth forth out of his treasure things new and old."[14] (13:51–52)

And it came to pass, that when Jesus had finished these parables, he departed thence. And when he was come into his own country, he taught them in their synagogue, insomuch that they were astonished, and said, "Whence hath this man this wisdom, and these mighty works? Is not this the carpenter's son? is not his mother called Mary? and his brethren, James, and Joses, and Simon, and Judas? And his sisters, are they not all with us? Whence then hath this man all these things?" And they were offended in him. But Jesus said unto them, "A prophet is not without honor, save in his own country, and in his own house." And he did not many mighty works there because of their unbelief. (13:53–58)

At that time Herod the tetrarch[15] heard of the fame of Jesus, and said unto his servants, "This is John the Baptist; he is risen from the dead; and therefore mighty works do show forth themselves in him." For Herod had laid hold on John, and bound him, and put him in prison for Herodias' sake, his brother Philip's wife.[16] For John said unto him, "It is not lawful for thee to have her." And when he would have put him to death, he feared the multitude, because they counted him as a prophet. But when Herod's birthday was kept, the daughter of Herodias danced before them, and pleased Herod. Whereupon he promised with an oath to give her whatsoever she would ask. And she, being before instructed of her mother, said, "Give me here John Baptist's head in a charger."[17] And the king was sorry: nevertheless for the oath's sake, and them which sat with him at meat, he commanded it to be given her. And he sent, and beheaded John in the prison. And his head was brought in a charger, and given to the damsel: and she brought it to her mother. And his disciples came, and took up the body, and buried it, and went and told Jesus. (14:1–12)

When Jesus heard of it, he departed thence by ship into a desert place apart: and when the people had heard thereof, they followed him on foot out of the cities. And Jesus went forth, and saw a great multitude, and was moved with compassion toward them, and he healed their sick. And when it was evening, his disciples came to him, saying, "This is a desert place, and the time is now past; send the multitude away, that they may go into the villages, and buy themselves victuals." But Jesus said unto them, "They need not depart: give ye them to eat." And they say unto him, "We have here but five loaves, and two fishes." He said, "Bring them hither to me." And he commanded the multitude to sit down on the grass, and took the five loaves, and the two fishes, and looking up to heaven, he blessed, and brake, and gave the loaves to his disciples, and the disciples to the multitude. And they did all eat, and were filled: and they took up of the frag-

[14] The sentence probably means that a scribe, expert in the Old Testament law, who is also instructed in Jesus' new doctrine, can and should combine both.

[15] Herod Antipas, son of the Herod who sought the death of Jesus in chapter 2; he became tetrarch (prince) of Galilee after his father's death.

[16] According to the first-century Jewish historian Josephus, Herod had an adulterous relationship with Herodias. Her daughter, Josephus tells us, was named Salome.

[17] Platter.

ments that remained twelve baskets full. And they that had eaten were about five thousand men, beside women and children. (14:13–21)

And straightway Jesus constrained his disciples to get into a ship, and to go before him unto the other side, while he sent the multitudes away. And when he had sent the multitudes away, he went up into a mountain apart to pray: and when the evening was come, he was there alone. But the ship was now in the midst of the sea, tossed with waves: for the wind was contrary. And in the fourth watch[18] of the night Jesus went unto them, walking on the sea. And when the disciples saw him walking on the sea, they were troubled, saying, "It is a spirit"; and they cried out for fear. But straightway Jesus spake unto them, saying, "Be of good cheer; it is I; be not afraid." And Peter answered him and said, "Lord, if it be thou, bid me come unto thee on the water." And he said, "Come." And when Peter was come down out of the ship, he walked on the water, to go to Jesus. But when he saw the wind boisterous, he was afraid; and beginning to sink, he cried, saying, "Lord, save me." And immediately Jesus stretched forth his hand, and caught him, and said unto him, "O thou of little faith, wherefore didst thou doubt?" And when they were come into the ship, the wind ceased. Then they that were in the ship came and worshipped him, saying, "Of a truth thou art the Son of God." (14:22–33)

And when they were gone over, they came into the land of Gennesaret.[19] And when the men of that place had knowledge of him, they sent out into all that country round about, and brought unto him all that were diseased; and besought him that they might only touch the hem of his garment: and as many as touched were made perfectly whole. (14:34–36)

Then came to Jesus scribes and Pharisees, which were of Jerusalem, saying, "Why do thy disciples transgress the tradition of the elders? for they wash not their hands[20] when they eat bread." But he answered and said unto them, "Why do ye also transgress the commandment of God by your tradition? For God commanded, saying, 'Honor thy father and mother': and, 'He that curseth father or mother, let him die the death.' But ye say, 'Whosoever shall say to his father or his mother, "It is a gift, by whatsoever thou mightest be profited by me"; and honor not his father or his mother, he shall be free.'[21] "Thus have ye made the commandment of God of none effect by your tradition. Ye hypocrites, well did Isaiah prophesy of you, saying,

> 'This people draweth nigh unto me with their mouth,
> And honoreth me with their lips;
> But their heart is far from me.
> But in vain they do worship me,
> Teaching for doctrines the commandments of men.'"[22]

And he called the multitude, and said unto them, "Hear, and understand:

---

[18] About 3 A.M.   [19] Northwest of the Sea of Galilee.

[20] And thus violate religious ritual as ordained by tradition.

[21] By a legalism, a son could exempt himself from the duty to support his parents by uttering an oath reserving his goods to the Temple.

[22] Isaiah 29:13.

not that which goeth into the mouth defileth a man;[23] but that which cometh out of the mouth, this defileth a man." Then came his disciples, and said unto him, "Knowest thou that the Pharisees were offended, after they heard this saying?" But he answered and said, "Every plant, which my heavenly Father hath not planted, shall be rooted up. Let them alone: they be blind leaders of the blind. And if the blind lead the blind, both shall fall into the ditch." Then answered Peter and said unto him, "Declare unto us this parable." And Jesus said, "Are ye also yet without understanding? Do not ye yet understand, that whatsoever entereth in at the mouth goeth into the belly, and is cast out into the draught?[24] But those things which proceed out of the mouth come forth from the heart; and they defile the man. For out of the heart proceed evil thoughts, murders, adulteries, fornications, thefts, false witness, blasphemies: these are the things which defile a man: but to eat with unwashen hands defileth not a man." (15:1–20)

Then Jesus went thence, and departed into the coasts of Tyre and Sidon. And, behold, a woman of Canaan[25] came out of the same coasts, and cried unto him, saying, "Have mercy on me, O Lord, thou son of David; my daughter is grievously vexed with a devil." But he answered her not a word. And his disciples came and besought him, saying, "Send her away;[26] for she crieth after us." But he answered and said, "I am not sent but unto the lost sheep of the house of Israel." Then came she and worshipped him, saying, "Lord, help me." But he answered and said, "It is not meet to take the children's bread, and to cast it to dogs." And she said, "Truth, Lord: yet the dogs eat of the crumbs which fall from their masters' table." Then Jesus answered and said unto her, "O woman, great is thy faith: be it unto thee even as thou wilt." And her daughter was made whole from that very hour. (15:21–28)

And Jesus departed from thence, and came nigh unto the sea of Galilee; and went up into a mountain, and sat down there. And great multitudes came unto him, having with them those that were lame, blind, dumb, maimed, and many others, and cast them down at Jesus' feet; and he healed them: insomuch that the multitude wondered, when they saw the dumb to speak, the maimed to be whole, the lame to walk, and the blind to see: and they glorified the God of Israel. (15:29–31)

Then Jesus called his disciples unto him, and said, "I have compassion on the multitude, because they continue with me now three days, and have nothing to eat: and I will not send them away fasting, lest they faint in the way." And his disciples say unto him, "Whence should we have so much bread in the wilderness, as to fill so great a multitude?" And Jesus saith unto them, "How many loaves have ye?" And they said, "Seven, and a few little fishes." And he commanded the multitude to sit down on the ground. And he took the seven loaves and the fishes, and gave thanks, and brake them, and gave to his disciples, and the disciples to the multitude. And they did all eat, and were filled: and they took up of the broken meat that was

[23] Jesus apparently is questioning the prohibition of unclean foods (the issue of the observance of dietary laws was a vexed one in the early Church).

[24] Drain; privy.

[25] The woman is a Phoenician Gentile; in the Old Testament the name *Canaanite* refers to the original inhabitants of Palestine, who were considered sinful by the Jews.

[26] Give her what she wants and get rid of her.

left seven baskets full. And they that did eat were four thousand men, beside women and children.[27] (15:32–38)

And he sent away the multitude, and took ship, and came into the coasts of Magdala.[28] The Pharisees also with the Sadducees came, and tempting desired him that he would show them a sign from heaven. He answered and said unto them, "When it is evening, ye say, 'It will be fair weather: for the sky is red.' And in the morning, 'It will be foul weather today: for the sky is red and lowering.' O ye hypocrites, ye can discern the face of the sky; but can ye not discern the signs of the times? A wicked and adulterous generation seeketh after a sign; and there shall no sign be given unto it, but the sign of the prophet Jonah."[29] And he left them, and departed. (15:39–16:4)

And when his disciples were come to the other side, they had forgotten to take bread. Then Jesus said unto them, "Take heed and beware of the leaven of the Pharisees and of the Sadducees." And they reasoned among themselves, saying, "It is because we have taken no bread."[30] Which when Jesus perceived, he said unto them, "O ye of little faith, why reason ye among yourselves, because ye have brought no bread? Do ye not yet understand, neither remember the five loaves of the five thousand, and how many baskets ye took up? neither the seven loaves of the four thousand, and how many baskets ye took up? How is it that ye do not understand that I spake it not to you concerning bread, that ye should beware of the leaven of the Pharisees and of the Sadducees?" Then understood they how that he bade them not beware of the leaven of bread, but of the doctrine of the Pharisees and of the Sadducees. (16:5–12)

When Jesus came into the coasts of Caesarea Philippi,[31] he asked his disciples, saying, "Whom do men say that I the Son of man am?" And they said, "Some say that thou art John the Baptist: some, Elijah; and others, Jeremiah, or one of the prophets."[32] He saith unto them, "But whom say ye that I am?" And Simon Peter answered and said, "Thou art the Christ, the Son of the living God." And Jesus answered and said unto him, "Blessed art thou, Simon Bar-jona:[33] for flesh and blood hath not revealed it unto thee, but my Father which is in heaven. And I say also unto thee, That thou art Peter, and upon this rock I will build my church; and the gates of hell shall not prevail against it.[34] And I will give unto thee the keys of the kingdom of heaven: and whatsoever thou shalt bind on earth shall be bound in heaven:

[27] The near-repetition of the earlier episode (14:14–21, where the number of men is 5,000 rather than 4,000), which occurs also in Matthew's source in the Gospel of St. Mark, is a puzzle.

[28] On the west shore of the Sea of Galilee.   [29] See Matthew 12:38–40.

[30] The disciples think they are being charged with forgetfulness.

[31] A town about twenty miles north of the Sea of Galilee.

[32] The beliefs include the possibility that Jesus may be John reincarnate. For Elijah's significance as an apocalyptic precursor, see 11:14 and note. Jeremiah (seventh to sixth centuries B.C.) was one of the greatest of the Old Testament prophets.

[33] Son of Jonah.

[34] *Peter* is from the Greek word meaning *rock*. The phrase *gates of hell* is construed by modern translators as *power of death*. The present passage is one of the most interesting and controversial in the New Testament because of its implications about the nature and origin of the early Church and more particularly because some Roman Catholics believe it supports the primacy of papal authority.

and whatsoever thou shalt loose on earth shall be loosed in heaven." Then charged he his disciples that they should tell no man that he was Jesus the Christ. (16:13–20)

From that time forth began Jesus to show unto his disciples, how that he must go unto Jerusalem, and suffer many things of the elders and chief priests and scribes, and be killed, and be raised again the third day.[35] Then Peter took him, and began to rebuke him, saying, "Be it far from thee, Lord: this shall not be unto thee." But he turned, and said unto Peter, "Get thee behind me, Satan: thou art an offense[36] unto me: for thou savorest not the things that be of God, but those that be of men." Then said Jesus unto his disciples, "If any man will come after me, let him deny himself, and take up his cross, and follow me. For whosoever will save his life shall lose it: and whosoever will lose his life for my sake shall find it. For what is a man profited, if he shall gain the whole world, and lose his own soul? or what shall a man give in exchange for his soul? For the Son of man shall come in the glory of his Father with his angels; and then he shall reward every man according to his works. Verily I say unto you, There be some standing here, which shall not taste of death, till they see the Son of man coming in his kingdom."[37] (16:21–28)

And after six days Jesus taketh Peter, James, and John his brother, and bringeth them up into a high mountain[38] apart, and was transfigured before them: and his face did shine as the sun, and his raiment was white as the light. And, behold, there appeared unto them Moses and Elijah talking with him. Then answered Peter, and said unto Jesus, "Lord, it is good for us to be here: if thou wilt, let us make here three tabernacles;[39] one for thee, and one for Moses, and one for Elijah." While he yet spake, behold, a bright cloud overshadowed them: and behold a voice out of the cloud, which said, "This is my beloved Son, in whom I am well pleased; hear ye him." And when the disciples heard it, they fell on their face, and were sore afraid. And Jesus came and touched them, and said, "Arise, and be not afraid." And when they had lifted up their eyes, they saw no man, save Jesus only. (17:1–8)

And as they came down from the mountain, Jesus charged them, saying, "Tell the vision to no man, until the Son of man be risen again from the dead." And his disciples asked him, saying, "Why then say the scribes that Elijah must first come?" And Jesus answered and said unto them, "Elijah truly shall first come, and restore all things. But I say unto you, That Elijah is come already, and they knew him not, but have done unto him whatsoever they listed. Likewise shall also the Son of man suffer of them." Then

---

[35] The revelation that the Messiah must suffer rather than reign triumphantly on earth comes as a shock, as Peter's reaction indicates.

[36] An obstacle.

[37] This verse, like 10:23, is hard to construe. It seems to record an unfulfilled prophecy, and a gospel written a half century after Jesus would probably not have preserved so blatant a contradiction of fact. The reference here may be to something other than the triumphant return at the Last Judgment.

[38] The scene is symbolic, recalling the revelation by God on Mount Sinai, which is echoed in several details in the ensuing episode here (the Transfiguration). Moses and Elijah represent "the Law and the Prophets," in short, the total message of the Old Testament.

[39] Tents used as sanctuaries. The best-known tabernacle was that in which the Israelites carried the Ark of the Covenant during the Exodus.

the disciples understood that he spake unto them of John the Baptist.
(17:9–13)

And when they were come to the multitude, there came to him a certain
man, kneeling down to him, and saying, "Lord, have mercy on my son: for
he is lunatic, and sore vexed: for ofttimes he falleth into the fire, and oft
into the water. And I brought him to thy disciples, and they could not cure
him." Then Jesus answered and said, "O faithless and perverse generation,
how long shall I be with you? how long shall I suffer you? bring him hither
to me." And Jesus rebuked the devil; and he departed out of him: and the
child was cured from that very hour. Then came the disciples to Jesus
apart, and said, "Why could not we cast him out?" And Jesus said unto
them, "Because of your unbelief: for verily I say unto you, If ye have faith
as a grain of mustard seed, ye shall say unto this mountain, 'Remove hence
to yonder place'; and it shall remove; and nothing shall be impossible
unto you. Howbeit this kind goeth not out but by prayer and fasting."[40]
(17:14–21)

And while they abode in Galilee, Jesus said unto them, "The Son of man
shall be betrayed into the hands of men: and they shall kill him, and the
third day he shall be raised again." And they were exceeding sorry.
(17:22–23)

And when they were come to Capernaum, they that received tribute
money[41] came to Peter, and said, "Doth not your master pay tribute?" He
saith, "Yes." And when he was come into the house, Jesus prevented[42] him,
saying, "What thinkest thou, Simon? of whom do the kings of the earth
take custom or tribute? of their own children, or of strangers?" Peter saith
unto him, "Of strangers." Jesus saith unto him, "Then are the children
free.[43] Notwithstanding, lest we should offend them, go thou to the sea,
and cast an hook, and take up the fish that first cometh up; and when thou
hast opened his mouth, thou shalt find a piece of money: that take, and
give unto them for me and thee." (17:24–27)

At the same time came the disciples unto Jesus, saying, "Who is the
greatest in the kingdom of heaven?" And Jesus called a little child unto
him, and set him in the midst of them, and said, "Verily I say unto you,
Except ye be converted, and become as little children, ye shall not enter
into the kingdom of heaven. Whosoever therefore shall humble himself as
this little child, the same is greatest in the kingdom of heaven. And whoso
shall receive one such little child in my name receiveth me. But whoso shall
offend[44] one of these little ones which believe in me, it were better for him
that a millstone were hanged about his neck, and that he were drowned in
the depth of the sea. Woe unto the world because of offenses! for it must
needs be that offenses come; but woe to that man by whom the offense

---

[40] This sentence is omitted in some of the sources.

[41] A tax paid by Jews to defray the expenses of the Temple.

[42] Anticipated; spoke first to.

[43] Exempt. Supreme rulers (the Romans, for example) taxed aliens, not their own citizens;
by analogy, Jesus argues, Jews ought not to be legally bound to pay a tax to support their own
Temple. Here, however, it is implied, he goes on to pay the tax.

[44] Be a stumbling block. The term *little ones* here probably means simple, unsophisticated
believers, not children. Much of the present discourse is more relevant to the experience and
organization of the early Church than to the time of the Gospel story.

cometh! Wherefore if thy hand or thy foot offend thee, cut them off, and cast them from thee: it is better for thee to enter into life halt or maimed, rather than having two hands or two feet to be cast into everlasting fire. And if thine eye offend thee, pluck it out, and cast it from thee: it is better for thee to enter into life with one eye, rather than having two eyes to be cast into hell fire. (18:1–9)

"Take heed that ye despise not one of these little ones; for I say unto you, That in heaven their angels do always behold the face of my Father which is in heaven. For the Son of man is come to save that which was lost. How think ye? if a man have an hundred sheep, and one of them be gone astray, doth he not leave the ninety and nine, and goeth into the mountains, and seeketh that which is gone astray? And if so be that he find it, verily I say unto you, he rejoiceth more of that sheep, than of the ninety and nine which went not astray. Even so it is not the will of your Father which is in heaven, that one of these little ones should perish. (18:10–14)

"Moreover if thy brother shall trespass against thee, go and tell him his fault between thee and him alone: if he shall hear thee, thou hast gained thy brother. But if he will not hear thee, then take with thee one or two more, that in the mouth of two or three witnesses every word may be established. And if he shall neglect to hear them, tell it unto the church: but if he neglect to hear the church, let him be unto thee as a heathen man and a publican. Verily I say unto you, Whatsoever ye shall bind on earth shall be bound in heaven: and whatsoever ye shall loose on earth shall be loosed in heaven. Again I say unto you, That if two of you shall agree on earth as touching any thing that they shall ask, it shall be done for them of my Father which is in heaven. For where two or three are gathered together in my name, there am I in the midst of them." (18:15–20)

Then came Peter to him, and said, "Lord, how oft shall my brother sin against me, and I forgive him? till seven times?" Jesus saith unto him, "I say not unto thee, Until seven times: but, Until seventy times seven. Therefore is the kingdom of heaven likened unto a certain king, which would take account of his servants. And when he had begun to reckon, one was brought unto him, which owed him ten thousand talents.[45] But forasmuch as he had not to pay, his lord commanded him to be sold, and his wife, and children, and all that he had, and payment to be made. The servant therefore fell down, and worshipped him, saying, 'Lord, have patience with me, and I will pay thee all.' Then the lord of that servant was moved with compassion, and loosed him, and forgave him the debt. But the same servant went out, and found one of his fellowservants, which owed him a hundred pence: and he laid hands on him, and took him by the throat, saying, 'Pay me that thou owest.' And his fellowservant fell down at his feet, and besought him, saying, 'Have patience with me, and I will pay thee all.' And he would not: but went and cast him into prison, till he should pay the debt. So when his fellowservants saw what was done, they were very sorry, and came and told unto their lord all that was done. Then his lord, after that he had called him, said unto him, 'O thou wicked servant, I forgave thee all that debt, because thou desiredst me: shouldest not thou also have had

---

[45] A talent was a unit of weight and money. Ten thousand talents would be not just a large but an almost astronomical sum, in contrast to a hundred pence, a rather modest sum.

compassion on thy fellowservant, even as I had pity on thee?' And his lord was wroth, and delivered him to the tormentors,[46] till he should pay all that was due unto him. So likewise shall my heavenly Father do also unto you, if ye from your hearts forgive not every one his brother their trespasses." (18:21–35)

And it came to pass, that when Jesus had finished these sayings, he departed from Galilee,[47] and came into the coasts of Judea beyond Jordan; and great multitudes followed him; and he healed them there. (19:1–2)

The Pharisees also came unto him, tempting him, and saying unto him, "Is it lawful for a man to put away his wife for every cause?" And he answered and said unto them, "Have ye not read, that he which made them at the beginning made them male and female, and said, 'For this cause shall a man leave father and mother, and shall cleave to his wife: and they twain shall be one flesh?'[48] Wherefore they are no more twain, but one flesh. What therefore God hath joined together, let not man put asunder." They say unto him, "Why did Moses then command to give a writing of divorcement, and to put her away?"[49] He saith unto them, "Moses because of the hardness of your hearts suffered you to put away your wives: but from the beginning it was not so. And I say unto you, Whosoever shall put away his wife, except it be for fornication, and shall marry another, committeth adultery: and whoso marrieth her which is put away doth commit adultery." His disciples say unto him, "If the case of the man be so with his wife, it is not good to marry." But he said unto them, "All men cannot receive this saying,[50] save they to whom it is given. For there are some eunuchs, which were so born from their mother's womb: and there are some eunuchs, which were made eunuchs of men: and there be eunuchs, which have made themselves eunuchs for the kingdom of heaven's sake. He that is able to receive it, let him receive it." (19:3–12)

Then were there brought unto him little children, that he should put his hands on them, and pray: and the disciples rebuked them. But Jesus said, "Suffer little children, and forbid them not, to come unto me: for of such is the kingdom of heaven." And he laid his hands on them, and departed thence. (19:13–15)

And, behold, one came and said unto him, "Good Master, what good thing shall I do, that I may have eternal life?" And he said unto him, "Why callest thou me good? there is none good but one, that is, God: but if thou wilt enter into life, keep the commandments." He saith unto him, "Which?" Jesus said, "Thou shalt do no murder, Thou shalt not commit adultery, Thou shalt not steal, Thou shalt not bear false witness, Honor thy father and thy mother: and, Thou shalt love thy neighbor as thyself." The young

---

[46] The "lord" in the parable is best imagined as a kind of exotic oriental ruler; torture was not a feature of Palestinian culture in Jesus' time.

[47] Jesus begins his journey to Jerusalem, where he will spend the climactic last week of his life.

[48] Genesis 2:24.

[49] Deuteronomy (a book traditionally ascribed to Moses) 24:1–4. The interpretation of this passage was a controversial topic in Jesus' time.

[50] The reference is apparently to the disciples' stated inference that under such restrictions it is better not to marry, but the Greek text is ambiguous. In any event, Jesus' following statement that marriage should sometimes be renounced for the sake of holiness is radically opposed to Jewish doctrine about the duty to procreate.

man saith unto him, "All these things have I kept from my youth up: what lack I yet?" Jesus said unto him, "If thou wilt be perfect, go and sell that thou hast, and give to the poor, and thou shalt have treasure in heaven: and come and follow me." But when the young man heard that saying, he went away sorrowful: for he had great possessions. (19:16–22)

Then said Jesus unto his disciples, "Verily I say unto you, That a rich man shall hardly enter into the kingdom of heaven. And again I say unto you, It is easier for a camel to go through the eye of a needle, than for a rich man to enter into the kingdom of God." When his disciples heard it, they were exceedingly amazed,[51] saying, "Who then can be saved?" But Jesus beheld them, and said unto them, "With men this is impossible; but with God all things are possible."[52] (19:23–26)

Then answered Peter and said unto him, "Behold, we have forsaken all, and followed thee; what shall we have therefore?" And Jesus said unto them, "Verily I say unto you, That ye which have followed me, in the regeneration when the Son of man shall sit in the throne of his glory, ye also shall sit upon twelve thrones, judging the twelve tribes of Israel. And every one that hath forsaken houses, or brethren, or sisters, or father, or mother, or wife, or children, or lands, for my name's sake, shall receive a hundredfold, and shall inherit everlasting life. But many that are first shall be last; and the last shall be first. For the kingdom of heaven is like unto a man that is a householder, which went out early in the morning to hire laborers into his vineyard. And when he had agreed with the laborers for a penny a day, he sent them into his vineyard. And he went out about the third hour,[53] and saw others standing idle in the marketplace, and said unto them; 'Go ye also into the vineyard, and whatsoever is right I will give you.' And they went their way. Again he went out about the sixth and ninth hour, and did likewise. And about the eleventh hour he went out, and found others standing idle, and saith unto them, 'Why stand ye here all the day idle?' They say unto him, 'Because no man hath hired us.' He saith unto them, 'Go ye also into the vineyard; and whatsoever is right, that shall ye receive.' So when even was come, the lord of the vineyard saith unto his steward, 'Call the laborers, and give them their hire, beginning from the last unto the first.' And when they came that were hired about the eleventh hour, they received every man a penny. But when the first came, they supposed that they should have received more; and they likewise received every man a penny. And when they had received it, they murmured against the goodman of the house, saying, 'These last have wrought but one hour, and thou hast made them equal unto us, which have borne the burden and heat of the day.' But he answered one of them, and said, 'Friend, I do thee no wrong: didst not thou agree with me for a penny? Take that thine is, and go thy way: I will give unto this last, even as unto thee. Is it not lawful for me to do what I will with mine own? Is thine eye

---

[51] The amazement probably arises from the general belief that riches were a sign of a man's holiness.

[52] The meaning perhaps is that God can achieve the near-miracle involved in a man's renunciation of wealth.

[53] About 9 A.M. The hours are counted from daybreak.

evil,[54] because I am good?' So the last shall be first, and the first last: for many be called, but few chosen." (19:27–20:16)

And Jesus going up to Jerusalem took the twelve disciples apart in the way, and said unto them, "Behold, we go up to Jerusalem; and the Son of man shall be betrayed unto the chief priests and unto the scribes, and they shall condemn him to death, and shall deliver him to the Gentiles[55] to mock, and to scourge, and to crucify him: and the third day he shall rise again." (20:17–19)

Then came to him the mother of Zebedee's children[56] with her sons, worshipping him, and desiring a certain thing of him. And he said unto her, "What wilt thou?" She saith unto him, "Grant that these my two sons may sit, the one on thy right hand, and the other on the left, in thy kingdom." But Jesus answered and said, "Ye know not what ye ask. Are ye able to drink of the cup that I shall drink of, and to be baptized with the baptism that I am baptized with?" They say unto him, "We are able." And he saith unto them, "Ye shall drink indeed of my cup, and be baptized with the baptism that I am baptized with: but to sit on my right hand, and on my left, is not mine to give, but it shall be given to them for whom it is prepared of my Father." And when the ten heard it, they were moved with indignation against the two brethren. But Jesus called them unto him, and said, "Ye know that the princes of the Gentiles exercise dominion over them,[57] and they that are great exercise authority upon them. But it shall not be so among you: but whosoever will be great among you, let him be your minister; and whosoever will be chief among you, let him be your servant: even as the Son of man came not to be ministered unto, but to minister, and to give his life a ransom for many." (20:20–28)

And as they departed from Jericho,[58] a great multitude followed him. And, behold, two blind men sitting by the wayside, when they heard that Jesus passed by, cried out, saying, "Have mercy on us, O Lord, thou son of David." And the multitude rebuked them, because they should hold their peace: but they cried the more, saying, "Have mercy on us, O Lord, thou son of David." And Jesus stood still, and called them, and said, "What will ye that I shall do unto you?" They say unto him, "Lord, that our eyes may be opened." So Jesus had compassion on them, and touched their eyes: and immediately their eyes received sight, and they followed him. (20:29–34)

And when they drew nigh unto Jerusalem, and were come to Bethphage, unto the mount of Olives,[59] then sent Jesus two disciples, saying unto them, "Go into the village over against you, and straightway ye shall find an ass tied, and a colt with her: loose them, and bring them unto me. And if any man say ought unto you, ye shall say, 'The Lord hath need of

---

[54]"Are you envious?" This parable as a whole, apart from its implications about God's mercy, has been construed to apply to Jews versus Gentiles (who come to the truth late) and also to earlier versus later converted Christians.

[55]Romans.   [56]James and John, two of the twelve disciples.

[57]Over their subjects.

[58]A city near and northeast of Jerusalem, a little west of the river Jordan. The conquest of Jericho under Joshua (Joshua 6) marked the beginning of the Israelites' triumphant occupation of the promised land.

[59]Places on the route from Jericho to Jerusalem.

them'; and straightway he will send them." All this was done, that it might
be fulfilled which was spoken by the prophet, saying,

> "Tell ye the daughter of Sion,
> Behold, thy King cometh unto thee,
> Meek, and sitting upon an ass,
> And a colt the foal of an ass."[60]

And the disciples went, and did as Jesus commanded them, and brought
the ass, and the colt, and put on them their clothes, and they set him
thereon. And a very great multitude spread their garments in the way;
others cut down branches from the trees, and strewed them in the way.
And the multitudes that went before, and that followed, cried, saying, "Hosanna to the son of David: Blessed is he that cometh in the name of the
Lord;[61] Hosanna in the highest." And when he was come into Jerusalem,
all the city was moved, saying, "Who is this?" And the multitude said, "This
is Jesus the prophet of Nazareth of Galilee." (21:1–11)

And Jesus went into the temple of God, and cast out all them that sold
and bought in the temple,[62] and overthrew the tables of the moneychang-
ers, and the seats of them that sold doves, and said unto them, "It is written,
'My house shall be called the house of prayer'; but ye have made it a den of
thieves."[63] And the blind and the lame came to him in the temple; and he
healed them. And when the chief priests and scribes saw the wonderful
things that he did, and the children crying in the temple, and saying, "Hosanna to the son of David"; they were sore displeased, and said unto him,
"Hearest thou what these say?" And Jesus saith unto them, "Yea; have ye
never read,

> 'Out of the mouth of babes and sucklings
> Thou hast perfected praise'?"[64]

And he left them, and went out of the city into Bethany;[65] and he lodged
there. (21:12–17)

Now in the morning as he returned into the city, he hungered. And
when he saw a fig tree in the way, he came to it, and found nothing
thereon, but leaves only, and said unto it, "Let no fruit grow on thee
henceforward for ever." And presently the fig tree withered away. And
when the disciples saw it, they marvelled, saying, "How soon is the fig tree
withered away!" Jesus answered and said unto them, "Verily I say unto
you, If ye have faith, and doubt not, ye shall not only do this which is done
to the fig tree, but also if ye shall say unto this mountain, Be thou removed,
and be thou cast into the sea; it shall be done. And all things, whatsoever ye
shall ask in prayer, believing, ye shall receive." (21:18–22)

And when he was come into the temple, the chief priests and the elders
of the people came unto him as he was teaching, and said, "By what author-

---

[60] Zechariah 9:9.   [61] Psalm 118:26.   [62] In an outer court of the Temple.
[63] Isaiah 56:7; Jeremiah 7:11. Because such commercial activities could not have taken
place without the permission of the Temple priests, Jesus' attack is largely directed at them.
[64] Psalm 8:2.
[65] A village two miles from Jerusalem; there Jesus raised Lazarus from the dead (John 11).

ity doest thou these things? and who gave thee this authority?" And Jesus answered and said unto them, "I also will ask you one thing, which if ye tell me, I in like wise will tell you by what authority I do these things. The baptism of John, whence was it? from heaven, or of men?" And they reasoned with themselves, saying, "If we shall say, 'From heaven'; he will say unto us, 'Why did ye not then believe him?' But if we shall say, 'Of men'; we fear the people; for all hold John as a prophet." And they answered Jesus, and said, "We cannot tell." And he said unto them, "Neither tell I you by what authority I do these things.[66] (21:23–27)

"But what think ye? A certain man had two sons; and he came to the first, and said, 'Son, go work today in my vineyard.' He answered and said, 'I will not': but afterward he repented, and went. And he came to the second, and said likewise. And he answered and said, 'I go, sir': and went not. Whether of them twain did the will of his father?" They say unto him, "The first." Jesus saith unto them, "Verily I say unto you, That the publicans and the harlots go into the kingdom of God before you. For John came unto you in the way of righteousness, and ye believed him not: but the publicans and the harlots believed him: and ye, when ye had seen it, repented not afterward, that ye might believe him. (21:28–32)

"Hear another parable: There was a certain householder, which planted a vineyard, and hedged it round about, and digged a winepress in it, and built a tower, and let it out to husbandmen,[67] and went into a far country: and when the time of the fruit drew near, he sent his servants to the husbandmen, that they might receive the fruits of it. And the husbandmen took his servants, and beat one, and killed another, and stoned another. Again, he sent other servants more than the first: and they did unto them likewise. But last of all he sent unto them his son, saying, 'They will reverence my son.' But when the husbandmen saw the son, they said among themselves, 'This is the heir; come, let us kill him, and let us seize on his inheritance.' And they caught him, and cast him out of the vineyard, and slew him. When the lord therefore of the vineyard cometh, what will he do unto those husbandmen?" They say unto him, "He will miserably destroy those wicked men, and will let out his vineyard unto other husbandmen, which shall render him the fruits in their seasons." Jesus saith unto them, "Did ye never read in the scriptures,

> 'The stone which the builders rejected,
> The same is become the head of the corner:
> This is the Lord's doing,
> And it is marvellous in our eyes'?[68]

Therefore say I unto you, The kingdom of God shall be taken from you, and given to a nation bringing forth the fruits thereof. And whosoever

---

[66] As a mere interpreter of the Law, Jesus would need the approval of the Jewish authorities, but prophets have direct divine authority. The priests and elders have here confessed their incompetence to judge the basic question as to who are authentic prophets and who are not. Their incompetence, Jesus implies, makes it unnecessary for him to answer their question about authority.

[67] Farmers.   [68] Psalm 118:22–23.

shall fall on this stone shall be broken: but on whomsoever it shall fall, it will grind him to powder."[69] (21:33–44)

And when the chief priests and Pharisees had heard his parables, they perceived that he spake of them. But when they sought to lay hands on him, they feared the multitude, because they took him for a prophet. (21:45–46)

And Jesus answered and spake unto them again by parables, and said, "The kingdom of heaven is like unto a certain king, which made a marriage for his son, and sent forth his servants to call them that were bidden to the wedding: and they would not come. Again, he sent forth other servants, saying, 'Tell them which are bidden, Behold, I have prepared my dinner: my oxen and my fatlings are killed, and all things are ready: come unto the marriage.' But they made light of it, and went their ways, one to his farm, another to his merchandise: and the remnant took his servants, and entreated them spitefully, and slew them. But when the king heard thereof, he was wroth: and he sent forth his armies, and destroyed those murderers, and burned up their city.[70] Then saith he to his servants, 'The wedding is ready, but they which were bidden were not worthy. Go ye therefore into the highways, and as many as ye shall find, bid to the marriage.' So those servants went out into the highways, and gathered together all as many as they found, both bad and good: and the wedding was furnished with guests. And when the king came in to see the guests, he saw there a man which had not on a wedding garment: and he saith unto him, 'Friend, how camest thou in hither not having a wedding garment?'[71] And he was speechless. Then said the king to the servants, 'Bind him hand and foot, and take him away, and cast him into outer darkness; there shall be weeping and gnashing of teeth.' For many are called, but few are chosen." (22:1–14)

Then went the Pharisees, and took counsel how they might entangle him in his talk. And they sent out unto him their disciples with the Herodians,[72] saying, "Master, we know that thou art true, and teachest the way of God in truth, neither carest thou for any man: for thou regardest not the person of men. Tell us therefore, What thinkest thou? Is it lawful to give tribute unto Caesar, or not?" But Jesus perceived their wickedness, and said, "Why tempt ye me, ye hypocrites? Show me the tribute money." And they brought unto him a penny. And he saith unto them, "Whose is this image and superscription?" They say unto him, "Caesar's." Then saith he unto them, "Render therefore unto Caesar the things which are Caesar's; and unto God the things that are God's." When they had heard these words, they marvelled, and left him, and went their way. (22:15–22)

The same day came to him the Sadducees, which say that there is no

---

[69] This sentence is absent from some of the manuscripts and translations.

[70] Probably a reference to the Romans' sack of Jerusalem in 70 A.D.

[71] In failing to wear a proper wedding garment the guest is guilty of gross discourtesy. The allegorical significance of the guest is uncertain; perhaps he represents the "bad" who, along with the "good," accept the invitation—a suggestion that the early Church included both kinds.

[72] Followers of Herod and loyalists to Roman rule. The following question about paying taxes is intended to make Jesus liable to prosecution by the Romans if he answers no or else, by answering yes, make him acquiesce in the highly unpopular annual head tax. Jesus avoids the trap, partly by leaving open the question of what is rightfully due to Caesar.

resurrection,[73] and asked him, saying, "Master, Moses said, 'If a man die, having no children, his brother shall marry his wife, and raise up seed unto his brother.'[74] Now there were with us seven brethren: and the first, when he had married a wife, deceased, and, having no issue, left his wife unto his brother: likewise the second also, and the third, unto the seventh. And last of all the woman died also. Therefore in the resurrection whose wife shall she be of the seven? for they all had her." Jesus answered and said unto them, "Ye do err, not knowing the scriptures, nor the power of God. For in the resurrection they neither marry, nor are given in marriage, but are as the angels of God in heaven. But as touching the resurrection of the dead, have ye not read that which was spoken unto you by God, saying, 'I am the God of Abraham, and the God of Isaac, and the God of Jacob'?[75] God is not the God of the dead, but of the living." And when the multitude heard this, they were astonished at his doctrine. (22:23–33)

But when the Pharisees had heard that he had put the Sadducees to silence, they were gathered together. Then one of them, which was a lawyer, asked him a question, tempting him, and saying, "Master, which is the great commandment in the law?" Jesus said unto him,

"Thou shalt love the Lord thy God with all thy heart, and with all thy soul, and with all thy mind. This is the first and great commandment. And the second is like unto it, Thou shalt love thy neighbor as thyself.[76] On these two commandments hang all the law and the prophets." (22:34–40)

While the Pharisees were gathered together, Jesus asked them, saying, "What think ye of Christ?[77] whose son is he?" They say unto him, "The son of David." He saith unto them, "How then doth David in spirit[78] call him Lord, saying,

'The Lord said unto my Lord,
Sit thou on my right hand,
Till I make thine enemies thy footstool'?[79]

If David then call him Lord, how is he his son?" And no man was able to answer him a word, neither durst any man from that day forth ask him any more questions. (22:41–46)

Then spake Jesus to the multitude, and to his disciples, saying, "The scribes and the Pharisees sit in Moses' seat: all therefore whatsoever they bid you observe, that observe and do; but do not ye after their works: for they say, and do not. For they bind heavy burdens and grievous to be borne, and lay them on men's shoulders; but they themselves will not move them with one of their fingers. But all their works they do for to be seen of men: they make broad their phylacteries, and enlarge the borders of their

[73] Most Jews of Jesus' time had come to believe in the resurrection of the dead, although the belief had little if any support in the literal text of the Old Testament, which for the Sadducees, unlike the Pharisees, was the sole sanction for doctrine.

[74] Deuteronomy 25:5.   [75] Exodus 3:6.

[76] The two commandments are from Deuteronomy 6:5 and Leviticus 19:18.

[77] Of the Messiah. (*Christ* is not Jesus' personal name.)   [78] Inspired by God.

[79] Psalm 110:1. It was assumed that David was the author of the Psalms and also that the Messiah would be his descendant. The point of Jesus' quoting the passage is not to deny the latter belief but to turn the tables on the Pharisees by showing that despite their supposed expertise they do not know how to construe the passage.

garments,[80] and love the uppermost rooms at feasts, and the chief seats in the synagogues, and greetings in the markets, and to be called of men, Rabbi, Rabbi.[81] But be not ye called Rabbi: for one is your Master, even Christ; and all ye are brethren. And call no man your father upon the earth: for one is your Father, which is in heaven. Neither be ye called masters:[82] for one is your Master, even Christ. But he that is greatest among you shall be your servant. And whosoever shall exalt himself shall be abased; and he that shall humble himself shall be exalted. (23:1–12)

"But woe unto you, scribes and Pharisees, hypocrites! for ye shut up the kingdom of heaven against men: for ye neither go in yourselves, neither suffer ye them that are entering to go in.[83] (23:13)

"Woe unto you, scribes and Pharisees, hypocrites! for ye devour widows' houses, and for a pretense make long prayer: therefore ye shall receive the greater damnation. (23:14)

"Woe unto you, scribes and Pharisees, hypocrites! for ye compass sea and land to make one proselyte, and when he is made, ye make him two-fold more the child of hell than yourselves. (23:15)

"Woe unto you, ye blind guides, which say, 'Whosoever shall swear by the temple, it is nothing; but whosoever shall swear by the gold of the temple, he is a debtor'![84] Ye fools and blind: for whether is greater, the gold, or the temple that sanctifieth the gold? And, 'Whosoever shall swear by the altar, it is nothing; but whosoever sweareth by the gift that is upon it, he is guilty.' Ye fools and blind: for whether is greater, the gift, or the altar that sanctifieth the gift? Whoso therefore shall swear by the altar, sweareth by it, and by all things thereon. And whoso shall swear by the temple, sweareth by it, and by him that dwelleth therein. And he that shall swear by heaven, sweareth by the throne of God, and by him that sitteth thereon.[85] (23:16–22)

"Woe unto you, scribes and Pharisees, hypocrites! for ye pay tithe of mint and anise and cummin,[86] and have omitted the weightier matters of the law, judgment,[87] mercy, and faith: these ought ye to have done, and not to leave the other undone. Ye blind guides, which strain at[88] a gnat, and swallow a camel. (23:23–24)

"Woe unto you, scribes and Pharisees, hypocrites! for ye make clean the outside of the cup and of the platter, but within they are full of extortion and excess. Thou blind Pharisee, cleanse first that which is within the cup and platter, that the outside of them may be clean also. (23:25–26)

"Woe unto you, scribes and Pharisees, hypocrites! for ye are like unto

[80] Phylacteries (small boxes attached to the head and wrist and containing copies of important biblical texts) and tassels on the corners of the robe were worn by scriptural injunction.

[81] Aramaic for *Master*.   [82] Teachers.

[83] Jesus means that the Pharisees refuse to be saved and also prevent others from being saved. Here, and in much of what follows, is reflected the antagonism between Pharisees and Christians at the time this Gospel was written.

[84] Is bound or obligated.

[85] Jesus is attacking teaching that justifies the evasion of the obligation of oaths through legalistic technicalities.

[86] A tithe is a contribution of part of one's goods to the clergy. To pay tithes of substantial goods such as grain would make sense, but the Pharisees, Jesus charges, absurdly extend the principle to such insignificant things as herbs.

[87] Justice.   [88] Strain out of one's drink.

whited sepulchers, which indeed appear beautiful outward, but are within full of dead men's bones, and of all uncleanness. Even so ye also outwardly appear righteous unto men, but within ye are full of hypocrisy and iniquity. (23:27–28)

"Woe unto you, scribes and Pharisees, hypocrites! because ye build the tombs of the prophets, and garnish the sepulchers of the righteous, and say, 'If we had been in the days of our fathers, we would not have been partakers with them in the blood of the prophets.' Wherefore ye be witnesses unto yourselves, that ye are the children of them which killed the prophets. Fill ye up then the measure of your fathers.[89] Ye serpents, ye generation of vipers, how can ye escape the damnation of hell? (23:29–33)

"Wherefore, behold, I send unto you prophets, and wise men, and scribes: and some of them ye shall kill and crucify; and some of them shall ye scourge in your synagogues, and persecute them from city to city: that upon you may come all the righteous blood shed upon the earth, from the blood of righteous Abel unto the blood of Zechariah[90] son of Berechiah, whom ye slew between the temple and the altar. Verily I say unto you, All these things shall come upon this generation. (23:34–36)

"O Jerusalem, Jerusalem, thou that killest the prophets, and stonest them which are sent unto thee,[91] how often would I have gathered thy children together, even as a hen gathereth her chickens under her wings, and ye would not! Behold, your house is left unto you desolate.[92] For I say unto you, Ye shall not see me henceforth, till ye shall say, 'Blessed is he that cometh in the name of the Lord.'" (23:37–39)

And Jesus went out, and departed from the temple: and his disciples came to him for to show him the buildings of the temple.[93] And Jesus said unto them, "See ye not all these things? verily I say unto you, There shall not be left here one stone upon another, that shall not be thrown down." (24:1–2)

And as he sat upon the mount of Olives,[94] the disciples came unto him privately, saying, "Tell us, when shall these things be? and what shall be the sign of thy coming, and of the end of the world?" And Jesus answered and said unto them,

"Take heed that no man deceive you. For many shall come in my name, saying, 'I am Christ'; and shall deceive many. And ye shall hear of wars and rumors of wars: see that ye be not troubled: for all these things must come to pass, but the end is not yet. For nation shall rise against nation, and kingdom against kingdom: and there shall be famines, and pestilences, and earthquakes, in divers places. All these are the beginning of sorrows. (24:3–8)

---

[89] Finish the job (killing the prophets) of your fathers.

[90] In the Hebrew Bible, Abel was the first victim of murder, Zechariah the last.

[91] Jerusalem was not in fact the place where most of the prophets died. Although the Jews had shown hostility to some of them, the Old Testament does not record many murders of prophets by the Jews. The passage is probably meant to apply to Christian missionaries.

[92] Probably a reference to the destruction of Jerusalem and the Temple by the Romans in 70 A.D.

[93] Important renovations of the Temple had been made in recent years.

[94] This mount commanded a broad view of Jerusalem, with the Temple prominently in the foreground.

"Then shall they deliver you up to be afflicted, and shall kill you: and ye shall be hated of all nations for my name's sake. And then shall many be offended,[95] and shall betray one another, and shall hate one another. And many false prophets shall rise, and shall deceive many. And because iniquity shall abound, the love of many shall wax cold. But he that shall endure unto the end, the same shall be saved. And this gospel of the kingdom shall be preached in all the world for a witness unto all nations; and then shall the end come. (24:9–14)

"When ye therefore shall see the abomination of desolation,[96] spoken of by Daniel the prophet, stand in the holy place, (whoso readeth, let him understand:) then let them which be in Judea flee into the mountains: let him which is on the housetop not come down to take any thing out of his house: neither let him which is in the field return back to take his clothes. And woe unto them[97] that are with child, and to them that give suck in those days! But pray ye that your flight be not in the winter, neither on the sabbath day:[98] for then shall be great tribulation, such as was not since the beginning of the world to this time, no, nor ever shall be. And except those days should be shortened, there should no flesh be saved: but for the elect's sake those days shall be shortened. Then if any man shall say unto you, 'Lo, here is Christ,' or 'there'; believe it not. For there shall arise false Christs, and false prophets, and shall show great signs and wonders; insomuch that, if it were possible, they shall deceive the very elect. Behold, I have told you before.[99] Wherefore if they shall say unto you, 'Behold, he is in the desert'; go not forth: 'behold, he is in the secret chambers'; believe it not. For as the lightning cometh out of the east, and shineth even unto the west; so shall also the coming of the Son of man be. For wheresoever the carcass is, there will the eagles be gathered together. (24:15–28)

"Immediately after the tribulation of those days shall the sun be darkened, and the moon shall not give her light, and the stars shall fall from heaven, and the powers of the heavens shall be shaken: and then shall appear the sign of the Son of man in heaven: and then shall all the tribes of the earth mourn, and they shall see the Son of man coming in the clouds of heaven with power and great glory. And he shall send his angels with a great sound of a trumpet, and they shall gather together his elect from the four winds, from one end of heaven to the other. Now learn a parable of the fig tree; When his branch is yet tender, and putteth forth leaves, ye know that summer is nigh: so likewise ye, when ye shall see all these things, know that it is near, even at the doors. Verily I say unto you, This generation shall not pass, till all these things be fulfilled. Heaven and earth shall pass away, but my words shall not pass away. (24:29–35)

"But of that day and hour knoweth no man, no, not the angels of heaven, but my Father only. But as the days of Noah were, so shall also the coming of the Son of man be. For as in the days that were before the flood they were eating and drinking, marrying and giving in marriage, until the

---

[95] A modern translation would be *falter*.

[96] Daniel 9:27, 11:31, 12:11. The reference is to the installation of an image of a pagan god in the Temple. In this section, references to the invasion of Palestine and the destruction of Jerusalem are blended with a description of the end of the world.

[97] It will be hard for them; this is an expression of pity.

[98] When travel was forbidden.   [99] Beforehand.

day that Noah entered into the ark, and knew not until the flood came, and took them all away; so shall also the coming of the Son of man be. Then shall two be in the field; the one shall be taken, and the other left. Two women shall be grinding at the mill; the one shall be taken, and the other left. Watch therefore: for ye know not what hour your Lord doth come. (24:36–42)

"But know this, that if the goodman of the house had known in what watch the thief would come, he would have watched, and would not have suffered his house to be broken up. Therefore be ye also ready: for in such an hour as ye think not the Son of man cometh. Who then is a faithful and wise servant, whom his lord hath made ruler over his household, to give them meat in due season? Blessed is that servant, whom his lord when he cometh shall find so doing. Verily I say unto you, That he shall make him ruler over all his goods. But and if that evil servant shall say in his heart, 'My lord delayeth his coming'; and shall begin to smite his fellowservants, and to eat and drink with the drunken; the lord of that servant shall come in a day when he looketh not for him, and in an hour that he is not aware of, and shall cut him asunder, and appoint him his portion with the hypocrites: there shall be weeping and gnashing of teeth.[1] (24:43–51)

"Then shall the kingdom of heaven be likened unto ten virgins, which took their lamps, and went forth to meet the bridegroom.[2] And five of them were wise, and five were foolish. They that were foolish took their lamps, and took no oil with them: but the wise took oil in their vessels with their lamps. While the bridegroom tarried, they all slumbered and slept. And at midnight there was a cry made, 'Behold, the bridegroom cometh; go ye out to meet him.' Then all those virgins arose, and trimmed their lamps. And the foolish said unto the wise, 'Give us of your oil; for our lamps are gone out.' But the wise answered, saying, 'Not so; lest there be not enough for us and you: but go ye rather to them that sell, and buy for yourselves.' And while they went to buy, the bridegroom came; and they that were ready went in with him to the marriage:[3] and the door was shut. Afterward came also the other virgins, saying, 'Lord, Lord, open to us.' But he answered and said, 'Verily I say unto you, I know you not.' Watch therefore, for ye know neither the day nor the hour wherein the Son of man cometh. (25:1–13)

"For the kingdom of heaven is as a man traveling into a far country, who called his own servants, and delivered unto them his goods.[4] And unto one he gave five talents, to another two, and to another one; to every man according to his several ability; and straightway took his journey. Then he that had received the five talents[5] went and traded with the same, and made them other five talents. And likewise he that had received two, he also gained other two. But he that had received one went and digged in the earth, and hid his lord's money. After a long time the lord of those servants cometh, and reckoneth with them. And so he that had received five talents

---

[1] This parable may apply to good and bad stewardship by either Jewish or Christian leaders.

[2] Apparently to escort the bridegroom to the bride's house. Little is known of Jewish weddings of the time.

[3] The marriage feast. [4] Made them his commercial agents.

[5] A talent was a large sum, roughly equivalent to a bag of gold.

came and brought other five talents, saying, 'Lord, thou deliveredst unto me five talents: behold, I have gained beside them five talents more.' His lord said unto him, 'Well done, thou good and faithful servant: thou hast been faithful over a few things, I will make thee ruler over many things: enter thou into the joy of thy lord.' He also that had received two talents came and said, 'Lord, thou deliveredst unto me two talents: behold, I have gained two other talents beside them.' His lord said unto him, 'Well done, good and faithful servant; thou hast been faithful over a few things, I will make thee ruler over many things: enter thou into the joy of thy lord.' Then he which had received the one talent came and said, 'Lord, I knew thee that thou art a hard man, reaping where thou hast not sown, and gathering where thou hast not strewed:[6] and I was afraid, and went and hid thy talent in the earth: lo, there thou hast that is thine.' His lord answered and said unto him, 'Thou wicked and slothful servant, thou knewest that I reap where I sowed not, and gather where I have not strewed: thou oughtest therefore to have put my money to the exchangers,[7] and then at my coming I should have received mine own with usury.[8] Take therefore the talent from him, and give it unto him which hath ten talents. For unto every one that hath shall be given, and he shall have abundance: but from him that hath not shall be taken away even that which he hath. And cast ye the unprofitable servant into outer darkness: there shall be weeping and gnashing of teeth.' (25:14–30)

When the Son of man shall come in his glory, and all the holy angels with him, then shall he sit upon the throne of his glory: and before him shall be gathered all nations: and he shall separate them one from another, as a shepherd divideth his sheep from the goats: and he shall set the sheep on his right hand, but the goats on the left. (25:31–33)

"Then shall the King say unto them on his right hand, 'Come, ye blessed of my Father, inherit the kingdom prepared for you from the foundation of the world: for I was ahungered, and ye gave me meat: I was thirsty, and ye gave me drink: I was a stranger, and ye took me in: naked, and ye clothed me: I was sick, and ye visited me: I was in prison, and ye came unto me.' Then shall the righteous answer him, saying, 'Lord, when saw we thee ahungered, and fed thee? or thirsty, and gave thee drink? When saw we thee a stranger, and took thee in? or naked, and clothed thee? Or when saw we thee sick, or in prison, and came unto thee?' And the King shall answer and say unto them, 'Verily I say unto you, Inasmuch as ye have done it unto one of the least of these my brethren, ye have done it unto me.' (25:34–40)

"Then shall he say also unto them on the left hand, 'Depart from me, ye cursed, into everlasting fire, prepared for the devil and his angels: for I was ahungered, and ye gave me no meat: I was thirsty, and ye gave me no drink: I was a stranger, and ye took me not in: naked, and ye clothed me not: sick, and in prison, and ye visited me not.' Then shall they also answer him, saying, 'Lord, when saw we thee ahungered, or athirst, or a stranger, or naked, or sick, or in prison, and did not minister unto thee?' Then shall

---

[6] The "lord" is a tight-fisted man who is accustomed to making big profits on very small investments. The servant feared that he would take a loss on the money entrusted to him and have to make up at least part of the loss.

[7] Money changers, the equivalent of bankers.　　[8] Interest.

he answer them, saying, 'Verily I say unto you, Inasmuch as ye did it not to one of the least of these, ye did it not to me.' And these shall go away into everlasting punishment: but the righteous into life eternal." (25:41–46)

And it came to pass, when Jesus had finished all these sayings, he said unto his disciples, "Ye know that after two days is the feast of the passover,[9] and the Son of man is betrayed to be crucified." Then assembled together the chief priests, and the scribes, and the elders of the people, unto the palace of the high priest, who was called Caiaphas,[10] and consulted that they might take Jesus by subtilty, and kill him. But they said, "Not on the feast day, lest there be an uproar among the people." (26:1–5)

Now when Jesus was in Bethany, in the house of Simon the leper,[11] there came unto him a woman having an alabaster box of very precious ointment, and poured it on his head, as he sat at meat. But when his disciples saw it, they had indignation, saying, "To what purpose is this waste? for this ointment might have been sold for much, and given to the poor." When Jesus understood it, he said unto them, "Why trouble ye the woman? for she hath wrought a good work upon me. For ye have the poor always with you; but me ye have not always. For in that she hath poured this ointment on my body, she did it for my burial.[12] Verily I say unto you, Wheresoever this gospel shall be preached in the whole world, there shall also this, that this woman hath done, be told for a memorial of her." (26:6–13)

Then one of the twelve, called Judas Iscariot, went unto the chief priests, and said unto them, "What will ye give me, and I will deliver him unto you?" And they covenanted with him for thirty pieces of silver. And from that time he sought opportunity to betray him. (26:14–16)

Now the first day of the feast of unleavened bread the disciples came to Jesus, saying unto him, "Where wilt thou that we prepare for thee to eat the passover?"[13] And he said, "Go into the city to such a man, and say unto him, 'The Master saith, My time is at hand; I will keep the passover at thy house with my disciples.'" And the disciples did as Jesus had appointed them; and they made ready the passover. (26:17–19)

Now when the even was come, he sat down with the twelve. And as they did eat, he said, "Verily I say unto you, that one of you shall betray me." And they were exceeding sorrowful, and began every one of them to say unto him, "Lord, is it I?" And he answered and said, "He that dippeth his hand with me in the dish,[14] the same shall betray me. The Son of man goeth as it is written of him: but woe unto that man by whom the Son of man is betrayed! it had been good for that man if he had not been born." Then Judas, which betrayed him, answered and said, "Master, is it I?" He said unto him, "Thou hast said." (26:20–25)

---

[9] The Passover was the most sacred of the Jewish feasts, commemorating God's deliverance of the Israelites from slavery in Egypt. It is held in early spring, as is its Christian counterpart, Easter.

[10] He served as high priest from A.D. 18 to 36.

[11] Presumably a leper healed by Jesus.

[12] Anointing was customary before festive occasions. Corpses were also anointed for burial.

[13] Formerly eaten in the Temple area, the Passover feast was in Jesus' time eaten in private houses in Jerusalem.

[14] Ironically, to eat out of the same bowl would usually express fraternal amity.

And as they were eating, Jesus took bread, and blessed it, and brake it, and gave it to the disciples, and said, "Take, eat; this is my body."[15] And he took the cup, and gave thanks, and gave it to them, saying, "Drink ye all of it; for this is my blood of the new testament,[16] which is shed for many for the remission of sins. But I say unto you, I will not drink henceforth of this fruit of the vine, until that day when I drink it new with you in my Father's kingdom."[17] (26:26–29)

And when they had sung a hymn, they went out into the mount of Olives. Then saith Jesus unto them, "All ye shall be offended[18] because of me this night: for it is written, 'I will smite the shepherd, and the sheep of the flock shall be scattered abroad.'[19] But after I am risen again, I will go before you into Galilee." Peter answered and said unto him, "Though all men shall be offended because of thee, yet will I never be offended." Jesus said unto him, "Verily I say unto thee, That this night, before the cock crow, thou shalt deny me thrice." Peter said unto him, "Though I should die with thee, yet will I not deny thee." Likewise also said all the disciples. (26:30–35)

Then cometh Jesus with them unto a place called Gethsemane,[20] and saith unto the disciples, "Sit ye here, while I go and pray yonder." And he took with him Peter and the two sons of Zebedee, and began to be sorrowful and very heavy. Then saith he unto them, "My soul is exceeding sorrowful, even unto death: tarry ye here, and watch[21] with me." And he went a little farther, and fell on his face, and prayed, saying, "O my Father, if it be possible, let this cup pass from me: nevertheless not as I will, but as thou wilt." And he cometh unto the disciples, and findeth them asleep, and saith unto Peter, "What, could ye not watch with me one hour? Watch and pray, that ye enter not into temptation: the spirit indeed is willing, but the flesh is weak." He went away again the second time, and prayed, saying, "O my Father, if this cup may not pass away from me, except I drink it, thy will be done." And he came and found them asleep again: for their eyes were heavy. And he left them, and went away again, and prayed the third time, saying the same words. Then cometh he to his disciples, and saith unto them, "Sleep on now, and take your rest: behold, the hour is at hand, and the Son of man is betrayed into the hands of sinners. Rise, let us be going: behold, he is at hand that doth betray me." (26:36–46)

And while he yet spake, lo, Judas, one of the twelve, came, and with him a great multitude with swords and staves, from the chief priests and elders of the people. Now he that betrayed him gave them a sign, saying, "Whomsoever I shall kiss, that same is he: hold him fast." And forthwith he came to Jesus, and said, "Hail, master"; and kissed him. And Jesus said unto him, "Friend, wherefore art thou come?" Then came they, and laid hands on Jesus, and took him. And, behold, one of them which were with Jesus stretched out his hand, and drew his sword, and struck a servant of

[15] The main course at this Passover meal would have been the body of a sacrified lamb; Jesus thus implies that he too is a sacrificial victim.

[16] The new Covenant; the old Covenant, between God and the Israelites, had been ritually sealed by the sprinkling of blood; see Exodus 24:6–8.

[17] Jesus alludes to one of the images of the Messianic age: as a divine banquet.

[18] Lapse from your faith.   [19] Zechariah 13:7.   [20] The name means "oil press."

[21] Stay awake.

the high priest's, and smote off his ear. Then said Jesus unto him, "Put up again thy sword into his place: for all they that take the sword shall perish with the sword. Thinkest thou that I cannot now pray to my Father, and he shall presently give me more than twelve legions of angels? But how then shall the scriptures be fulfilled, that thus it must be?" In that same hour said Jesus to the multitudes, "Are ye come out as against a thief with swords and staves for to take me? I sat daily with you teaching in the temple, and ye laid no hold on me. But all this was done, that the scriptures of the prophets might be fulfilled." Then all the disciples forsook him, and fled. (26:47–56)

And they that had laid hold on Jesus led him away to Caiaphas the high priest, where the scribes and the elders were assembled. But Peter followed him afar off unto the high priest's palace, and went in, and sat with the servants, to see the end. Now the chief priests, and elders, and all the council,[22] sought false witness against Jesus, to put him to death; but found none: yea, though many false witnesses came, yet found they none. At the last came two false witnesses,[23] and said, "This fellow said, 'I am able to destroy the temple of God, and to build it in three days.'" And the high priest arose, and said unto him, "Answerest thou nothing? what is it which these witness against thee?" But Jesus held his peace. And the high priest answered and said unto him, "I adjure thee by the living God, that thou tell us whether thou be the Christ, the Son of God." Jesus saith unto him, "Thou hast said: nevertheless I say unto you, Hereafter shall ye see the Son of man sitting on the right hand of power, and coming in the clouds of heaven."[24] Then the high priest rent his clothes, saying, "He hath spoken blasphemy;[25] what further need have we of witnesses? behold, now ye have heard his blasphemy. What think ye?" They answered and said, "He is guilty of death." Then did they spit in his face, and buffeted him; and others smote him with the palms of their hands, saying, "Prophesy unto us, thou Christ, Who is he that smote thee?"[26] (26:57–68)

Now Peter sat without in the palace:[27] and a damsel came unto him, saying, "Thou also wast with Jesus of Galilee." But he denied before them all, saying, "I know not what thou sayest." And when he was gone out into the porch, another maid saw him, and said unto them that were there, "This fellow was also with Jesus of Nazareth." And again he denied with an oath, "I do not know the man." And after a while came unto him they that stood by, and said to Peter, "Surely thou also art one of them; for thy speech betrayeth thee." Then began he to curse and to swear, saying, "I know not the man." And immediately the cock crew. And Peter remembered the word of Jesus, which said unto him, "Before the cock crow, thou shalt deny me thrice." And he went out, and wept bitterly. (26:69–75)

[22] The Sanhedrin, the highest Jewish court.

[23] It was necessary for evidence to be valid that the same allegation be made independently by two witnesses.

[24] Daniel 7:13, Psalm 110:1.

[25] Blasphemy was a capital offense under Jewish law. Rending one's clothes was a ritual expression of sorrow over a serious breaking of the holy Law.

[26] That is, if Jesus is the Christ (Messiah), he should be able to identify even people he does not know.

[27] In an open-air inner courtyard.

When the morning was come, all the chief priests and elders of the people took counsel against Jesus to put him to death: and when they had bound him, they led him away, and delivered him to Pontius Pilate the governor.[28] (27:1–2)

Then Judas, which had betrayed him, when he saw that he was condemned,[29] repented himself, and brought again the thirty pieces of silver to the chief priests and elders, saying, "I have sinned in that I have betrayed the innocent blood." And they said, "What is that to us? see thou to that." And he cast down the pieces of silver in the temple, and departed, and went and hanged himself. And the chief priests took the silver pieces, and said, "It is not lawful for to put them into the treasury, because it is the price of blood." And they took counsel, and bought with them the potter's field, to bury strangers in. Wherefore that field was called, The field of blood, unto this day. Then was fulfilled that which was spoken by Jeremiah the prophet, saying,

> "And they took the thirty pieces of silver,
> The price of him that was valued,
> Whom they of the children of Israel did value;
> And gave them for the potter's field,
> As the Lord appointed me."[30] (27:3–10)

And Jesus stood before the governor: and the governor asked him, saying, "Art thou the King of the Jews?"[31] And Jesus said unto him, "Thou sayest." And when he was accused of the chief priests and elders, he answered nothing. Then said Pilate unto him, "Hearest thou not how many things they witness against thee?" And he answered him to never a word; insomuch that the governor marveled greatly. (27:11–14)

Now at that feast the governor was wont to release unto the people a prisoner, whom they would. And they had then a notable prisoner, called Barabbas. Therefore when they were gathered together, Pilate said unto them, "Whom will ye that I release unto you? Barabbas, or Jesus which is called Christ?" For he knew that for envy[32] they had delivered him. When he was set down on the judgment seat, his wife sent unto him, saying, "Have thou nothing to do with that just man: for I have suffered many things this day in a dream because of him." But the chief priests and elders persuaded the multitude that they should ask Barabbas, and destroy Jesus. The governor answered and said unto them, "Whether of the twain will ye that I release unto you?" They said, "Barabbas." Pilate saith unto them, "What shall I do then with Jesus which is called Christ?" They all say unto him, "Let him be crucified."[33] And the governor said, "Why, what evil hath he done?" But they cried out the more, saying, "Let him be crucified." When Pilate saw that he could prevail nothing, but that rather a tumult was

---

[28] Sentencing for a capital offense was reserved to the Roman authorities. Pilate, who was governor between the years 26 and 36, was often antagonistic to the Jews.

[29] That Jesus was condemned.   [30] Actually, not Jeremiah, but Zechariah 11:12–13.

[31] Pilate as Roman governor would not be interested in such religious charges as blasphemy; Jesus' enemies have apparently tried to depict him as a source of political danger. To judge from Pilate's later behavior, he does not take the charge very seriously.

[32] Malice.   [33] Crucifixion was the penalty imposed by the Romans for insurrection.

made, he took water, and washed his hands before the multitude, saying, "I am innocent of the blood of this just person: see ye to it." Then answered all the people, and said, "His blood be on us, and on our children."[34] Then released he Barabbas unto them: and when he had scourged Jesus, he delivered him to be crucified. (27:15–26)

Then the soldiers of the governor took Jesus into the common hall, and gathered unto him the whole band of soldiers. And they stripped him, and put on him a scarlet robe. And when they had platted a crown of thorns, they put it upon his head, and a reed in his right hand: and they bowed the knee before him, and mocked him, saying, "Hail, King of the Jews!" And they spit upon him, and took the reed, and smote him on the head. And after that they had mocked him, they took the robe off from him, and put his own raiment on him, and led him away to crucify him. And as they came out, they found a man of Cyrene, Simon by name: him they compelled to bear his cross. (27:27–32)

And when they were come unto a place called Golgotha, that is to say, a place of a skull, they gave him vinegar[35] to drink mingled with gall: and when he had tasted thereof, he would not drink. And they crucified him, and parted his garments, casting lots: that it might be fulfilled which was spoken by the prophet, "They parted my garments among them, and upon my vesture did they cast lots."[36] And sitting down they watched him there; and set up over his head his accusation written, *This is Jesus the King of the Jews.*" Then were there two thieves crucified with him, one on the right hand, and another on the left. (27:33–38)

And they that passed by reviled him, wagging their heads, and saying, "Thou that destroyest the temple, and buildest it in three days, save thyself. If thou be the Son of God, come down from the cross." Likewise also the chief priests mocking him, with the scribes and elders, said, "He saved others; himself he cannot save. If he be the King of Israel, let him now come down from the cross, and we will believe him. He trusted in God; let him deliver him now, if he will have him: for he said, 'I am the Son of God.'" The thieves also, which were crucified with him, cast the same in his teeth. (27:39–44)

Now from the sixth hour there was darkness over all the land unto the ninth hour.[37] And about the ninth hour Jesus cried with a loud voice, saying, "Eli, Eli, lama sabachthani?" that is to say, "My God, my God, why hast thou forsaken me?"[38] Some of them that stood there, when they heard that, said, "This man calleth for Elijah."[39] And straightway one of them ran, and took a sponge, and filled it with vinegar,[40] and put it on a reed, and gave him to drink. The rest said, "Let be, let us see whether Elijah will come to save him." (27:45–49)

Jesus, when he had cried again with a loud voice, yielded up the ghost. (27:50)

---

[34] Another allusion to the destruction of Jerusalem in 70 A.D.
[35] Probably cheap wine, intended as a narcotic.   [36] Psalm 22:18.
[37] From noon to mid-afternoon.   [38] Quoted from Psalm 22:1.
[39] The mistake probably arises from imperfect hearing of Jesus' utterance of "Eli" ("My God").
[40] Cheap wine.

And, behold, the veil of the temple was rent in twain from the top to the bottom; and the earth did quake, and the rocks rent; and the graves were opened; and many bodies of the saints which slept arose, and came out of the graves after his resurrection, and went into the holy city, and appeared unto many. Now when the centurion, and they that were with him, watching Jesus, saw the earthquake, and those things that were done, they feared greatly, saying, "Truly this was the Son of God." And many women were there beholding afar off, which followed Jesus from Galilee, ministering unto him: among which was Mary Magdalene,[41] and Mary the mother of James and Joses, and the mother of Zebedee's children. (27:51–56)

When the even was come, there came a rich man of Arimathea, named Joseph, who also himself was Jesus' disciple: he went to Pilate, and begged the body of Jesus. Then Pilate commanded the body to be delivered. And when Joseph had taken the body, he wrapped it in a clean linen cloth, and laid it in his own new tomb, which he had hewn out in the rock: and he rolled a great stone to the door of the sepulcher, and departed. And there was Mary Magdalene, and the other Mary, sitting over against the sepulcher. (27:57–61)

Now the next day, that followed the day of the preparation, the chief priests and Pharisees came together unto Pilate, saying, "Sir, we remember that that deceiver said, while he was yet alive, 'After three days I will rise again.' Command therefore that the sepulcher be made sure until the third day, lest his disciples come by night, and steal him away, and say unto the people, 'He is risen from the dead': so the last error shall be worse than the first." Pilate said unto them, "Ye have a watch:[42] go your way, make it as sure as ye can." So they went, and made the sepulcher sure, sealing the stone, and setting a watch. (27:62–66)

In the end of the sabbath, as it began to dawn toward the first day of the week, came Mary Magdalene and the other Mary to see the sepulcher. And, behold, there was a great earthquake: for the angel of the Lord descended from heaven, and came and rolled back the stone from the door, and sat upon it. His countenance was like lightning, and his raiment white as snow: and for fear of him the keepers did shake, and became as dead men. And the angel answered and said unto the women, "Fear not ye: for I know that ye seek Jesus, which was crucified. He is not here: for he is risen, as he said. Come, see the place where the Lord lay. And go quickly, and tell his disciples that he is risen from the dead; and, behold, he goeth before you into Galilee; there shall ye see him: lo, I have told you." And they departed quickly from the sepulcher with fear and great joy; and did run to bring his disciples word. And as they went to tell his disciples, behold, Jesus met them, saying, "All hail." And they came and held him by the feet, and worshipped him. Then said Jesus unto them, "Be not afraid: go tell my brethren that they go into Galilee, and there shall they see me." (28:1–10)

Now when they were going, behold, some of the watch came into the city, and showed unto the chief priests all the things that were done. And when they were assembled with the elders, and had taken counsel, they

[41] She is mentioned in the Gospel of Luke (8:2) as a woman out of whom Jesus cast seven devils.
[42] You may have a detachment to stand guard.

gave large money unto the soldiers, saying, "Say ye, 'His disciples came by night, and stole him away while we slept.' And if this come to the governor's ears, we will persuade him, and secure you."[43] So they took the money, and did as they were taught: and this saying is commonly reported among the Jews until this day. (28:11–15)

Then the eleven disciples went away into Galilee, into a mountain where Jesus had appointed them.[44] And when they saw him, they worshipped him: but some doubted. And Jesus came and spake unto them, saying, "All power is given unto me in heaven and in earth. Go ye therefore, and teach all nations,[45] baptizing them in the name of the Father, and of the Son, and of the Holy Ghost: teaching them to observe all things whatsoever I have commanded you: and, lo, I am with you alway, even unto the end of the world." Amen. (28:16–20)

from THE GOSPEL ACCORDING TO SAINT LUKE

Forasmuch as many have taken in hand to set forth in order a declaration of those things which are most surely believed among us, even as they delivered them unto us, which from the beginning were eyewitnesses, and ministers of the word; it seemed good to me also, having had perfect understanding of all things from the very first, to write unto thee in order, most excellent Theophilus,[1] that thou mightest know the certainty of those things, wherein thou hast been instructed. (1:1–4)

There was in the days of Herod, the king of Judea,[2] a certain priest named Zechariah, of the course of Abijah:[3] and his wife was of the daughters of Aaron, and her name was Elisabeth. And they were both righteous before God, walking in all the commandments and ordinances of the Lord blameless. And they had no child, because that Elisabeth was barren, and they both were now well stricken in years. And it came to pass, that while he executed the priest's office before God in the order of his course, according to the custom of the priest's office, his lot was to burn incense when he went into the temple of the Lord. And the whole multitude of the people were praying without at the time of incense. And there appeared unto him an angel of the Lord standing on the right side of the altar of incense. And when Zechariah saw him, he was troubled, and fear fell upon him. But the

---

[43] Protect you (from being punished for sleeping while on duty).

[44] Had said he would meet them. The "mountain" once more is the setting for a climactic event.

[45] The disciples' commission is now to the whole world, in contrast with their earlier-defined mission to the Jews only (10:5–6).

[1] An unidentified person, apparently of high rank. The name means "beloved by God." The stylistically elaborate opening, along with the address to a patron, indicates that Luke is attempting a highly polished work that follows classical literary and historiographical conventions. Luke's gospel is intended to have special relevance for the non-Jewish world. At the same time, the manner of the following narratives about the births and earliest years of John the Baptist and of Jesus are very much in the Old Testament style.

[2] For Herod, see Matthew 2:1 and note.

[3] *Course* means "division of the priesthood." The Jewish priesthood was descended from Moses' brother Aaron through his grandsons, of whom Abijah was one. The divisions took turns serving in the Temple, and within each division duties were assigned by drawing lots.

angel said unto him, "Fear not, Zechariah: for thy prayer is heard; and thy wife Elisabeth shall bear thee a son, and thou shalt call his name John. And thou shalt have joy and gladness; and many shall rejoice at his birth. For he shall drink neither wine nor strong drink; and he shall be filled with the Holy Ghost, even from his mother's womb. And many of the children of Israel shall he turn to the Lord their God. And he shall go before him in the spirit and power of Elijah,[4] to turn the hearts of the fathers to the children, and the disobedient to the wisdom of the just; to make ready a people prepared for the Lord." And Zechariah said unto the angel, "Whereby shall I know this? for I am an old man, and my wife well stricken in years." And the angel answering said unto him, "I am Gabriel, that stand in the presence of God; and am sent to speak unto thee, and to show thee these glad tidings. And, behold, thou shalt be dumb, and not able to speak, until the day that these things shall be performed, because thou believest not my words, which shall be fulfilled in their season." And the people waited for Zechariah, and marveled that he tarried so long in the temple. And when he came out, he could not speak unto them: and they perceived that he had seen a vision in the temple: for he beckoned unto them, and remained speechless. And it came to pass, that, as soon as the days of his ministration were accomplished, he departed to his own house. And after those days his wife Elisabeth conceived, and hid herself five months, saying, "Thus hath the Lord dealt with me in the days wherein he looked on me, to take away my reproach among men."[5] (1:5–25)

And in the sixth month the angel Gabriel was sent from God unto a city of Galilee,[6] named Nazareth, to a virgin espoused to a man whose name was Joseph, of the house of David; and the virgin's name was Mary. And the angel came in unto her, and said, "Hail, thou that art highly favored, the Lord is with thee: blessed art thou among women." And when she saw him, she was troubled at his saying, and cast in her mind what manner of salutation this should be. And the angel said unto her, "Fear not, Mary: for thou hast found favor with God. And, behold, thou shalt conceive in thy womb, and bring forth a son, and shalt call his name *Jesus*.[7] He shall be great, and shall be called the Son of the Highest: and the Lord God shall give unto him the throne of his father David: and he shall reign over the house of Jacob for ever; and of his kingdom there shall be no end."[8] Then said Mary unto the angel, "How shall this be, seeing I know not a man?" And the angel answered and said unto her, "The Holy Ghost shall come upon thee, and the power of the Highest shall overshadow thee: therefore also that holy thing which shall be born of thee shall be called the Son of God. And, behold, thy cousin[9] Elisabeth, she hath also conceived a son in her old age: and this is the sixth month with her, who was called barren. For with God nothing shall be impossible." And Mary said, "Behold the

---

[4] For Elijah's role as a precursor, see Malachi 4; for John the Baptist as Elijah, see Matthew 11:14 and note.

[5] Compare Genesis 30:23, where Rachel too refers to the "reproach" of being barren.

[6] The northern part of Palestine.

[7] For the significance of the name, see note to Matthew 1:1.

[8] On the Messiah and his descent from David, see note to Matthew 1:1.

[9] Kinswoman.

handmaid of the Lord; be it unto me according to thy word." And the angel departed from her. (1:26–38)

And Mary arose in those days, and went into the hill country[10] with haste, into a city of Judah; and entered into the house of Zechariah, and saluted Elisabeth. And it came to pass, that, when Elisabeth heard the salutation of Mary, the babe leaped in her womb; and Elisabeth was filled with the Holy Ghost: and she spake out with a loud voice, and said, "Blessed art thou among women, and blessed is the fruit of thy womb. And whence is this to me, that the mother of my Lord should come to me? For, lo, as soon as the voice of thy salutation sounded in mine ears, the babe leaped in my womb for joy. And blessed is she that believed: for there shall be a performance of those things which were told her from the Lord." (1:39–45)

And Mary said,

"My soul doth magnify the Lord,[11]
And my spirit hath rejoiced in God my Saviour.
For he hath regarded the low estate of his handmaiden:
For, behold, from henceforth all generations shall call me blessed.
For he that is mighty hath done to me great things;
And holy is his name.
And his mercy is on them that fear him
From generation to generation.
He hath shewed strength with his arm;
He hath scattered the proud in the imagination of their hearts.
He hath put down the mighty from their seats,
And exalted them of low degree.
He hath filled the hungry with good things;
And the rich he hath sent empty away.
He hath holpen his servant Israel,
In remembrance of his mercy;
As he spake to our fathers,
To Abraham, and to his seed for ever."

And Mary abode with her about three months, and returned to her own house. (1:46–56)

Now Elisabeth's full time came that she should be delivered; and she brought forth a son. And her neighbors and her cousins heard how the Lord had showed great mercy upon her; and they rejoiced with her. And it came to pass, that on the eighth day they came to circumcise the child; and they called him Zechariah, after the name of his father. And his mother answered and said, "Not so; but he shall be called John."[12] And they said unto her, "There is none of thy kindred that is called by this name." And they made signs to his father, how he would have him called. And he asked for a writing table, and wrote, saying, "His name is John." And they mar-

---

[10] The country near Jerusalem.
[11] The following anthem, the Magnificat, frequently echoes the Old Testament. Its sympathy with the humble and poor is entirely typical of Luke.
[12] The name means "The Lord has shown favor."

veled all.[13] And his mouth was opened immediately, and his tongue loosed, and he spake, and praised God. And fear came on all that dwelt round about them: and all these sayings were noised abroad throughout all the hill country of Judea. And all they that heard them laid them up in their hearts, saying, "What manner of child shall this be!" And the hand of the Lord was with him. (1:57–66)

And his father Zechariah was filled with the Holy Ghost, and prophesied, saying,

"Blessed be the Lord God of Israel;[14]
For he hath visited and redeemed his people,
And hath raised up a horn of salvation for us
In the house of his servant David;
As he spake by the mouth of his holy prophets,
Which have been since the world began:
That we should be saved from our enemies,
And from the hand of all that hate us;
To perform the mercy promised to our fathers,
And to remember his holy covenant;
The oath which he sware to our father Abraham,
That he would grant unto us, that we being delivered out of the hand
     of our enemies
Might serve him without fear,
In holiness and righteousness before him, all the days of our life.
And thou, child, shalt be called the prophet of the Highest:
For thou shalt go before the face of the Lord to prepare his ways;
To give knowledge of salvation unto his people
By the remission of their sins,
Through the tender mercy of our God;
Whereby the dayspring[15] from on high hath visited us,
To give light to them that sit in darkness and in the shadow of death,
To guide our feet into the way of peace."

And the child grew, and waxed strong in spirit, and was in the deserts till the day of his showing unto Israel. (1:67–80)

And it came to pass in those days, that there went out a decree from Caesar Augustus, that all the world should be taxed.[16] (And this taxing was first made when Cyrenius was governor of Syria.) And all went to be taxed, every one into his own city. And Joseph also went up from Galilee, out of the city of Nazareth, into Judea, unto the city of David, which is called Bethlehem;[17] (because he was of the house and lineage of David:) to be

---

[13] Because Zechariah is presumably deaf as well as dumb, his independent giving of the name evokes wonder.

[14] Like the Magnificat earlier, this song, the Benedictus, echoes the Old Testament frequently.

[15] The rising sun; an epithet for the Messiah.

[16] Such a census has been recorded, although it took place in 6–7 A.D.

[17] Bethlehem is about five miles south of Jerusalem and almost a hundred miles south of Nazareth.

taxed with Mary his espoused wife, being great with child. And so it was, that, while they were there, the days were accomplished that she should be delivered. And she brought forth her firstborn son, and wrapped him in swaddling clothes,[18] and laid him in a manger; because there was no room for them in the inn. (2:1–7)

And there were in the same country shepherds abiding in the field, keeping watch over their flock by night. And, lo, the angel of the Lord came upon them, and the glory of the Lord shone round about them: and they were sore afraid. And the angel said unto them, "Fear not: for, behold, I bring you good tidings of great joy, which shall be to all people. For unto you is born this day in the city of David a Saviour, which is Christ[19] the Lord. And this shall be a sign unto you; Ye shall find the babe wrapped in swaddling clothes, lying in a manger." And suddenly there was with the angel a multitude of the heavenly host praising God, and saying,

> "Glory to God in the highest,
> And on earth peace, good will toward men."

And it came to pass, as the angels were gone away from them into heaven, the shepherds said one to another, "Let us now go even unto Bethlehem, and see this thing which is come to pass, which the Lord hath made known unto us." And they came with haste, and found Mary, and Joseph, and the babe lying in a manger. And when they had seen it, they made known abroad the saying which was told them concerning this child. And all they that heard it wondered at those things which were told them by the shepherds. But Mary kept all these things, and pondered them in her heart. And the shepherds returned, glorifying and praising God for all the things that they had heard and seen, as it was told unto them. (2:8–20)

And when eight days were accomplished for the circumcising of the child, his name was called *Jesus,* which was so named of the angel before he was conceived in the womb. (2:21)

And when the days of her purification according to the law of Moses were accomplished, they brought him to Jerusalem, to present him to the Lord; (as it is written in the law of the Lord, "Every male that openeth the womb shall be called holy to the Lord";)[20] and to offer a sacrifice according to that which is said in the law of the Lord, "A pair of turtledoves, or two young pigeons."[21] And, behold, there was a man in Jerusalem, whose name was Simeon; and the same man was just and devout, waiting for the consolation of Israel: and the Holy Ghost was upon him. And it was revealed unto him by the Holy Ghost, that he should not see death, before he had seen the Lord's Christ. And he came by the Spirit into the temple: and when the parents brought in the child Jesus, to do for him after the custom of the law, then took he him up in his arms, and blessed God, and said,

---

[18] Bands of cloth, at the time used to ensure straight growth.

[19] Not a personal name but a title (literally, "the anointed one") designating the Messiah.

[20] Exodus 13:2,12.

[21] The ritual purification after conception and childbirth is described in Leviticus 12. The usual offering was a lamb, but the poor were allowed to substitute an extra turtledove or pigeon.

"Lord, now lettest thou thy servant depart in peace,
According to thy word:
For mine eyes have seen thy salvation,
Which thou hast prepared before the face of all people;
A light to lighten the Gentiles,
And the glory of thy people Israel."

And Joseph and his mother marveled at those things which were spoken of him. And Simeon blessed them, and said unto Mary his mother, "Behold, this child is set for the fall and rising again of many in Israel; and for a sign which shall be spoken against; (yea, a sword shall pierce through thy own soul also,) that the thoughts of many hearts may be revealed." (2:22–35)

And there was one Anna, a prophetess, the daughter of Phanuel, of the tribe of Asher; she was of a great age, and had lived with an husband seven years from her virginity; and she was a widow of about fourscore and four years, which departed not from the temple, but served God with fastings and prayers night and day. And she coming in that instant gave thanks likewise unto the Lord, and spake of him to all them that looked for redemption in Jerusalem. And when they had performed all things according to the law of the Lord, they returned into Galilee, to their own city Nazareth. And the child grew, and waxed strong in spirit, filled with wisdom: and the grace of God was upon him. (2:36–40)

Now his parents went to Jerusalem every year at the feast of the passover. And when he was twelve years old, they went up to Jerusalem after the custom of the feast. And when they had fulfilled the days, as they returned, the child Jesus tarried behind in Jerusalem; and Joseph and his mother knew not of it. But they, supposing him to have been in the company, went a day's journey; and they sought him among their kinsfolk and acquaintance. And when they found him not, they turned back again to Jerusalem, seeking him. And it came to pass, that after three days they found him in the temple, sitting in the midst of the doctors,[22] both hearing them, and asking them questions. And all that heard him were astonished at his understanding and answers. And when they saw him, they were amazed: and his mother said unto him, "Son, why hast thou thus dealt with us? behold, thy father and I have sought thee sorrowing." And he said unto them, "How is it that ye sought me? wist[23] ye not that I must be about my Father's business?" And they understood not the saying which he spake unto them. And he went down with them, and came to Nazareth, and was subject unto them: but his mother kept all these sayings in her heart. And Jesus increased in wisdom and stature, and in favor with God and man. (2:41–52)

[22] Teachers (of the Jewish Law).   [23] Knew.

The Middle Ages

✦✦✦✦✦✦✦✦✦✦

THE term *Middle Ages* as a description of the thousand-year period between the fifth and the fifteenth centuries—between the end of the Roman Empire and the Renaissance—is at once an oversimplification and a distortion of a long and complex period of European history. Coined by Renaissance and Enlightenment thinkers, the label *Middle Ages* (or its Latin form, the *Medieval* period) implies a mere transitional era, a long interruption in the continuity of Western history during which the classical culture of Greece and Rome, waiting to be revived in the Renaissance, lay dormant or dead.

From our perspective, we can see the Middle Ages in more positive terms, not as an interruption but as a fertile and dynamic period that produced a distinctive and permanently valuable culture of its own. It was more varied than a single, reductive label would imply. There is a certain unity in this long span of history that justifies our considering it as a single period, but within this unity is enormous diversity. Only the very early Middle Ages, from the sixth to the ninth centuries, were characterized by the cultural inertia often attributed to the whole period. The collapse of the Roman Empire left Europe for a time in chaos, with its economy, its social organization, and its culture brought almost to a halt. But even these "Dark Ages" were not without their rays of light, especially in areas where survivals of the Roman heritage or the Church preserved pockets of culture. In retrospect, we can see forces working during this fallow period that were to emerge later in a new and vital form of social organization. The new organization began to take shape in about the tenth century and led by the thirteenth century to a flowering of art and culture that anticipated and rivaled the Renaissance without forfeiting its own distinctively medieval character.

The formidable challenge to the early Middle Ages was to find a mode of social organization to replace the Roman Empire and to weave together the various threads of European culture: the remnants of Latin civilization, Christianity, and the northern, Germanic, "barbarian" tradition. The solution that gradually emerged over a period of several centuries lay in two institutions, the Roman Church and feudalism.

By the time of the Empire's final collapse, the Church had made great strides toward becoming a universal institution. Paul, the "Apostle of the Gentiles," was the chief architect in the conversion of Christianity from a parochial, nationalistic cult among dissident Jews to a universal religion. During the fourth century, Christianity gradually became the state religion of Rome; the emperor Theodosius at the end of the century formally proclaimed it as such, closed heathen temples, and forbade heathen sacrifices.

Within a few years, pagans were actively persecuted as the Christians had been persecuted earlier.

At the beginning of the fifth century, the centralizing forces in Christianity culminated in the claim by Pope Innocent I to jurisdiction over all Christendom. The centrally organized Church was to a large extent modeled on the Empire. As the Empire gradually wasted away, the Church emerged more and more clearly as its spiritual heir and as a universal source of authority. It also became, for a thousand years, the heir and the chief custodian of Latin culture. It preserved much of the classic Roman literature and over the centuries fostered a rich body of medieval Latin writing, largely ecclesiastical in nature. This work included philosophy such as that of St. Augustine, St. Anselm, and St. Thomas Aquinas; rhetoric, such as Geoffrey of Vinsauf's; chronicles and compilations of legendary history, such as the *Gesta Romanorum* and the Venerable Bede's *Ecclesiastical History of the English Nation;* a rich body of Latin religious poetry, especially hymns; and many other works.

The power of the medieval church was based upon two propositions, which it inculcated almost universally: that the visible scene of human life was a perpetual conflict between the Kingdom of God and the Kingdom of the Devil, and that salvation for the individual was available only through the offices of the Church. This world was seen as secondary to the world to come, a testing ground determining whether the individual would spend eternity in Heaven or Hell. Because participation in the sacraments of the Church was a requirement for salvation, the Church vitally affected the individual's fate through all eternity, a fate that at its worst was regarded with a fearful literalness.

The elaborate bureaucracy of the Roman Empire was reflected in the detailed hierarchy through which the Church performed its functions and which, in its meticulous emphasis upon rank and degree, expressed one of the deepest and most pervasive habits of medieval thought. The individual was linked to God through an elaborate chain of hierarchical relationships. Above the individual believer was the priest; above the priest were, in succession, bishop, archbishop, cardinal, and pope. The ranks rose, beyond the earthly Church, above the pope through the intricate orders of angels to God Himself. The pope was thus, in this minutely detailed scheme of things, the direct representative of God on earth, with absolute power to "bind and loose."

Quite apart from its religious function, the medieval Church was a vitally important social institution in the Middle Ages. In an era full of political disorder and conflict, it provided a slight check upon secular warfare, by asserting an authority that transcended political boundaries. It tempered social oppression by opening Church offices to commoners and upholding the doctrine of the equality of all men before God. It also helped unify and stabilize European culture by defining a broadly accepted system of values and beliefs.

The fixed hierarchy of the medieval Church was mirrored in feudalism, the secular social and economic system that gradually emerged to replace the fallen Empire. Feudalism originated in the human need to band together for mutual protection in a lawless and chaotic age. Inhabitants of a particular region placed themselves under the protection of the most powerful local lord and in return for his military protection pledged certain services. Like the Church, feudalism echoed certain aspects of the Roman Empire, notably the custom of clients gathering around wealthy patrons, but it also drew heavily upon the Germanic social organization, in which warriors gathered around a powerful chieftain, to whom they were bound by a complex system of obligations and rewards.

In its fully developed form, feudalism was, like the Church, a pyramidal structure encompassing all of society and organized by an intricate code of privileges and mutual commitments. The medieval king was the secular counterpart of the pope, subordinate to him only in matters of faith. The feudal system placed literal ownership of all the king's domain (except that controlled by the Church) in his hands. These lands, or "fiefs," were, in effect, leased and subleased down through hierarchical orders of nobility to the level of the individual manor, the basic social and economic unit of feudalism. Each nobleman became the "vassal" of his immediate superior and owed him, in return for the lands he was granted, money payments and, when demanded, military service. The exact terms of feudal obligations were never standardized across Europe. They depended on local custom, but they were quite precise and were ritualized in the ceremony of homage and investiture, in which the vassal knelt before his lord and, placing his hands between his lord's hands, vowed to fulfill the terms of his obligation. At the bottom of the feudal pyramid was the serf, bound to the land he worked and obliged to cultivate his lord's land as well, in a sort of peonage or sharecropper arrangement.

Feudal society thus consisted of only two classes, the people and the nobility, which included the orders of the Church as well as the secular feudal orders. There was no socially mobile middle class; such a class, outside the rigid ordering of rank, would have been incompatible with the idea of feudalism, and when it did begin to emerge late in the Middle Ages, it marked the beginning of the collapse of the whole system.

The first comparatively stable kingdom to be established after the fall of Rome was that of the Franks, founded by Clovis (465–511). Charlemagne (742–814), a descendant of Clovis, embarked upon a series of campaigns against the Saxons and Bavarians, the Moors of northeast Spain, and the Lombards in northern Italy, building an immense empire to rival that of the Caesars. He was crowned "Holy Roman Emperor" by Pope Leo III on Christmas Day, 800. Charlemagne's victories became the stuff of legend, and his deeds, along with those of his twelve "peers," were celebrated in a number of medieval works of which the *Song of Roland* is the most famous. The imperial court was also a great center of art and learning, the focal point of the "Carolingian renaissance." Charlemagne brought the learned monk Alcuin from England to found a palace school of theology and literature, imported architects from Italy to build a number of cathedrals, and encouraged the study of Latin literature as well as Germanic epics.

Another nucleus of culture in the early Middle Ages, the Benedictine monastic order, was founded in the late sixth century by St. Benedict of Nursia with the encouragement of the great medieval pope Gregory I (540–604), who launched a series of missions to Christianize the northern Germanic peoples. Within a century, the Benedictine monasteries had spread across Europe, succeeding the Roman schools as centers of learning. In these monasteries libraries were collected and copied, instruction was carried on, and medieval architecture was born, with many of the monks working as master masons in the construction of early cathedrals.

Charlemagne's empire was short-lived, crumbling under the impact of invasions from the north. The Vikings, seafaring warriors from Scandinavia, swept into England and northern France in the ninth century and established the kingdom of Normandy in 885. The result, however, was not a new age of barbarism. The Danish Vikings were gradually assimilated in England, where the reign of Alfred the Great of Wessex (871–899) accompanied a genuine revival of art and learning. The Vikings in Normandy were likewise assimilated with the Franks, and a similar revival of learning took place; when these Normans conquered England in 1066, they brought with them a culture superior to that of the Anglo-Saxons.

The eleventh and twelfth centuries were a time of explosive intellectual and cultural development. The Crusades, launched by Pope Urban II in 1095, were eventually a dismal failure as attempts to capture the Holy Lands from the "Saracens," but they had the unforeseen effect of bringing Europeans into contact with the riches of Muslim culture, literature, mathematics, and science. Industry and commerce began to revive across Europe, and a number of universities were founded: Oxford in 1167, Paris in 1170, Cambridge in 1209. Provence in southern France was a particularly fertile ground; a vigorous economic and cultural atmosphere brought the development of chivalry and a rich tradition of *troubadour* literature expressing chivalric values, a tradition paralleled in northern France by the poetry of the *trouvères*.

This rapid development culminated in the thirteenth century, the high point, in many ways, of medieval culture. Both the medieval papacy and the medieval monarchy reached the height of their power in the thirteenth century, the papacy under Innocent III, Gregory IX, and Nicholas III, the monarchy under such kings as Edward I of England, Louis IX of France, and Ferdinand III of Spain. The greatest of the Gothic cathedrals were built—Notre Dame de Paris, Mont-Saint-Michel, Rheims, Amiens, Chartres. The period also marked the golden age of Scholasticism, the philosophical project of reconciling the teachings of the Church with the logic of Aristotle, or faith with reason; St. Thomas Aquinas's *Summa Theologica*, the masterpiece of Scholasticism, was completed in 1273.

But already, at the peak of its triumph, the medieval system was beginning to show signs of its ultimate decline. The medieval monarchy received an ominous blow when the English barons forced King John to sign Magna Charta in 1215. The strains upon the medieval papacy surfaced in such conflicts as the prolonged struggles between the Guelphs (supporters of the Pope) and the Ghibellines (supporters of the Holy Roman Emperor) in the city-states of Italy. The rise in the thirteenth century of the guilds, organizations of skilled craftsmen, also heralded the rise of a middle class incompatible with the rigid categories of the feudal system and prophetic of its ultimate collapse.

These fragmenting tendencies gained momentum in the turbulent fourteenth century. The papacy was split, for most of the century, by the so-called Babylonian Captivity, 1305–1376, during which the papal see was removed to Avignon in France, and by the following Great Schism (1378–

1417), when there were two, and sometimes even three, rival popes. The chaos that followed the Black Death in mid-century further weakened the feudal system. The second half of the century was shaken by people's revolutions: the French Jacquerie in 1358 and the English Peasants' Revolt in 1381. These and other uprisings were put down, with great cruelty, but they foreshadowed the end of economic serfdom.

The greatest imaginative writers of medieval Europe emerged during its decline. The medieval world view is perhaps best expressed by such writers as Thomas Aquinas and John of Salisbury, but the masterpieces of medieval literature date from the fourteenth century: the *Divine Comedy,* the *Decameron,* the *Rhymes* of Petrarch, the *Canterbury Tales.* Paradoxically, none of these works is wholly medieval in spirit. The tension apparent in all of them between the passing medieval world and the emerging Renaissance world provides much of their energy.

That we can distinguish the "medieval" and the "modern" in such works, however tentatively, suggests that, despite the span and variety of the Middle Ages, there is a certain consistency in its world-view. At the risk of overgeneralizing, it is possible to point to three qualities pervasive enough to define the age: authoritarianism, comprehensiveness, and otherworldliness. The cathedral, often cited as the quintessential expression of the medieval spirit, illustrates all three tendencies. The system of communal engineering that made the building of cathedrals possible implies the subordination of individual creativity to collective authority. If one values the occasional evidences of individual personality, in the playful elaboration of a gargoyle carving, for instance, it is because such features are exceptions. Medieval literature, too, is often anonymous, and when we begin to hear, as in Petrarch, the sound of an individual voice, we know that a new element has entered the medieval literary world.

As for comprehensiveness, the cathedral was also a microcosm of an all-inclusive vision of life. Not only did it represent a synthesis of social values, art, and religion, but its art characteristically undertook to represent the whole Christian revelation, the divine plan from Creation to the Day of Judgment. The literary analogues were the compendiums, ambitious works that attempted a total view of human life, its individual parts placed in relation to a whole, as in Aquinas's *Summa Theologica* or Dante's *Divine Comedy.* And finally, the very shape of the cathedral, its great spires pointing away from the earth toward Heaven, suggests the pervasive otherworldliness of medieval life. This tendency made empirical science impossible but also, at its best, gave a hope and dignity to human life in an age when life was too often bleak and short. Medieval literature has its own distinctive form of earthiness, but it almost always provides a view of eternity too, whether in brief glimpses or in visionary panoramas.

The Middle Ages have a claim to the label the following age pre-empted; they were not merely a hiatus between the classic and modern worlds but in some ways themselves a renaissance, a rebirth after the collapse of Roman civilization. Much of the modern world has medieval origins: the modern state and the modern city, modern languages, and a large body of collective myth, including the idea of romantic love, are rooted in the Middle Ages. But the major medieval achievement was the welding together of the separate strands of Western culture—Hebrew, Greek, Roman, and Christian—into a single culture. This culture has been greatly amplified and modified by succeeding ages, but it still retains the general shape the Middle Ages gave it.

The literature of the Middle Ages is as varied as the time that produced it. Its characteristic forms are the epic, the romance, the allegory, the folktale, the lyric, and the drama.

The Germanic and Celtic tribes had a body of heroic legend as rich as that which Homer drew upon for the *Iliad* and the *Odyssey*. There is good reason to believe that this material was in oral circulation for centuries before Christian monks, in about the eighth century, began to write it down. The earliest of the folk epics is the English *Beowulf*, which may have been based upon the exploits of a sixth-century Scandinavian warrior but acquired a heavy overlay of folklore before an eighth-century English monk put it in written form. (The poem as we know it dates from a tenth-century manuscript.) Although *Beowulf*, like the *Iliad* and the *Aeneid*, celebrates the virtues of its culture's heroic past, these virtues are not precisely the same as those of Greece and Rome. The poem provides a fascinating glimpse into an ancient Germanic courtly culture held together by the complex, ritualized mutual obligations of the *comitatus* relationship, the bond between Germanic warriors and their lord. Magnanimity, loyalty, and the willingness to fight to the death to fulfill an obligation are the virtues celebrated, all against the background of a tragic belief in fate and eventual, inevitable defeat. This ethical system blends in *Beowulf* with other elements derived from Christianity and classical culture. Beowulf has a Christian gentleness; his monstrous antagonists are identified with Cain and the Devil himself, and in the end he, Christlike, lays down his life for his people. The *Beowulf* poet also apparently knew the *Aeneid*. Although he never alludes directly to Virgil's work, its influence is apparent in the poem's sophistication of organization and in the epic conception of Beowulf's character.

The other early medieval folk epics, in various ways, also depict the confrontation of pagan heroic ethics with the ethics of classical culture and Christianity. The *Elder,* or *Poetic, Edda,* composed in the ninth century but written down in the twelfth century, preserves the heroic legends of Iceland; the *Hildebrandslied* (ninth century) and *Nibelungenlied* (early thirteenth century) record German heroic tales; the Irish sagas of Cuchulain and Conchubar (eighth to tenth centuries) and the Welsh *Mabinogion* (eleventh century) preserve the heroic tales of the Celts. In France, the epic spirit was expressed in the *chansons de geste;* the greatest of these was the *Song of Roland* (twelfth century), which, like most of the *chansons de geste*, deals with legends of Charlemagne and his knights. The *Poem of My Cid* (twelfth century) presents a Spanish hero to rival Roland and Cuchulain. The Icelandic sagas, dealing with events in Iceland between about 930 and 1030 but written down several centuries later, represent a late survival of the epic impulse, perhaps because of the relative cultural isolation of Iceland.

In general, however, epic yielded some ground to romance in the eleventh and twelfth centuries. The term *romance* was originally applied to the Old French language as distinguished from the parent language, Latin or "Roman." In time, however, it came to refer to any work in the French language and ultimately to the most common form of French works, the tale of chivalric adventure. France remained pre-eminent in the romance form throughout the Middle Ages. Romances were fundamentally epics in which the center of interest had shifted from warfare to love, especially the elaborately ritualized cult of "courtly love," which first developed among the *troubadours* of Provence and the *trouvères* of northern France. Originally half-facetious, it transferred the homage the epic hero owed to his lord to the romance hero's lady, developing an elaborate code to govern the relation between the sexes. The idealization inherent in courtly love was probably, in part, a sublimation of youthful ungratified fervor; it arose in castles where numbers of young, unmarried knights surrounded their lords and the lords' remote, unattainable ladies. The revival of interest in Greek romances and in Ovid's *Art of Love* was also a factor, as was the growing cult of the Virgin Mary beginning in the second half of the tenth century.

The favorite subjects of medieval romance derived from the Matter of Britain (the Celtic sagas, especially those of King Arthur), the Matter of France (the Charlemagne legends), and the Matter of Rome the Great (Greek and Roman stories). Popular and widely circulated romances included those of Chrétien de Troyes, who wrote the first extant French romance, *Eric and Enid* (twelfth century) and a number of other Arthurian romances; Gottfried von Strassburg's *Tristan* (c. 1200); Wolfram von Eschenbach's *Parzival* (c. 1200); *Floris and Blanchefleur* (c. 1250); *Amis and Amiloun* (before 1300); and *Ipomedon* (fourteenth century). Among the most readable of these romances today are the twelve short *lais* of the twelfth-century Marie de France, sophisticated probings into the psychology of love within magical, "Breton" settings.

By the thirteenth century, the worldliness and sensuality of the romances had led the Church to regard them as detrimental to faith. Following its regular policy of assimilation and incorporation, however, the Church did not ban romances but rather encouraged the writing of a new kind, the "moral romance," which advanced Christian ideals while staying within the narrative conventions of the genre. The romances of the Holy Grail, the thirteenth-century French *Romance of the Rose,* and the fourteenth-century English *Sir Gawain and the Green Knight* all belong to this second phase. By the fifteenth century, the romance had become stale and formulaic, and after a period of rambling, inflated prose romances, uneasy blends of chivalric and moral elements, the genre was transformed and blended with new emphases in the Renaissance.

The *Romance of the Rose* also illustrates another major genre of medieval literature, the allegory. One of the most influential works of the Middle Ages, the *Romance of the Rose* is a dream-poem in which the poet visits the Garden of Delight, where he sees the Rose, which symbolizes his sweetheart. Major characters in the story are personified qualities: Idleness, Pleasure, Fair Welcome, Danger, Shame, and Evil Tongue. Primarily an allegory of courtly love, the poem is also a satire directed at a number of targets (including sexual infatuation, superstition, and the celibacy of the clergy) and a compendium of miscellaneous medieval lore. The work became immensely popular in France, England (where it was at least partly translated by Chaucer), and Italy (where it was translated into sonnet form, possibly by Dante). The use of a dream to introduce an allegorical narrative and of the dream-allegory structure to hold together a wide range of material was widely imitated for three hundred years. Chaucer's *Book of the Duchess, House of Fame,* and *Parliament of Fowls* are all dream allegories; even the *Canterbury Tales* exhibits some features of the genre, including the pilgrimage motif, the use of representative characters, and the inclusion of varied tales within a generally symbolic framework. The fourteenth-century *Confessio Amantis,* by Chaucer's contemporary John Gower, and *Piers Plowman,* by William Langland, both continue to use the form. Christine de Pizan's *Book of the City of Ladies* is a fascinating feminist dream-allegory, a refutation of the misogynistic *Romance of the Rose* which uses its own techniques to confound it. The supreme masterpiece of the genre is Dante's *Divine Comedy.* Allegory was also an important element in medieval drama. It survived vigorously into later ages, in such works as Edmund Spenser's *Faerie Queene* (1596) and John Bunyan's *Pilgrim's Progress* (1675). In fact, allegory has never died out.

Epic, romance, and allegory were all aristocratic narrative forms, written and read (or listened to) by the medieval aristocracy and gentry. There was also throughout the Middle Ages a flourishing body of popular oral narrative: folktales, beast fables, bawdy anecdotes called *fabliaux,* and folk ballads. These popular works were occasionally collected and written down; there are several collections of versified *fabliaux;* beast fables are the basis of several beast epics, the most famous of which is the French *Romance of Reynard* (twelfth century); and many popular ballads survive, though in versions dating from long after the Middle Ages. The importance of the oral folk tradition lies less in directly surviving texts than in the pervasive influence it exerted upon written literature—as sources, for example, of the stories in the *Decameron* and the *Canterbury Tales.*

Among medieval literary forms, the lyric is second in importance only to romance. There was a rich tradition of Latin lyric poetry that included Latin hymns; praises of rulers or patrons; nature songs; and "Goliardic" poetry (light occasional secular poetry, often satiric, written mainly by clerics in pretended praise of the fictional "Bishop Golias"). Vernacular poetry flowered earliest in twelfth-century Provence in southern France among the *troubadours.* The *troubadours* (or "finders" of treasure) were courtly singers who composed and sang elaborate, highly wrought poems, transmitting them orally to professional minstrels called *jongleurs,* who in turn spread them from place to place. Their major form was the *canzone,* an expression of idealized love written in a complex and rigid rhyme scheme, although they developed a number of other forms as well. The Provençal lyric influenced the *trouvères* of northern France and the *Minnesingers* of Germany. (*Trouvère* also means "finder," and *Minnesinger* means "singer of romantic love.") But its most vigorous influence was in Italy, which traveling troubadours visited in the early thirteenth century. There they inspired a school of imitators some of whom wrote in Provençal themselves, as a tribute to their mentors. Florence became the birthplace of the *dolce stil novo*—a "sweet new style" that combined the forms of the *troubadours* with a grave, philosophical content derived from Scholastic philosophy.

It is one of the more surprising facts about literary history that the very idea of drama had to be reinvented beginning in the tenth century. The plays of Plautus and Terence were read throughout the Middle Ages, and the tenth-century German nun Hroswitha of Gandersheim wrote several plays about saints' lives, imitating the form of Terence though not his ribald content. Medieval readers seem to have thought that the Roman plays were merely monologues or dialogues to be declaimed, not acted, and Hroswitha apparently had no notion of actual performance. There was a live tradition of popular entertainment—mimes, jugglers, and clowns, as well as a body of pagan fertility plays—but no conception of the sustained acting of a dramatic text.

Drama was reborn out of the liturgy of the Church, beginning in the tenth century with brief dramatized episodes (tropes) inserted into the Mass and then developed over several centuries into increasingly elaborate plays. The plays were separated from the Church in the thirteenth century and came to be performed outdoors at the spring Corpus Christi festivals. The major forms (which overlap considerably) were the mystery play, based upon scripture and performed at the festivals by "mysteries," or trade guilds; the miracle play, based upon a saint's life and staged on his or her feast day; and the morality play, a moral allegory dramatizing the spiritual life of the typical man. Secular forms included the folk play, which was independent of the religious drama and dramatized the deeds of a popular hero such as Robin Hood or St. George; the farce, a genre derived from popular and classical rather than religious models; and the secular interlude, a short play for performance between the parts of a banquet or other celebration.

Medieval drama, like most medieval art, was an international phenomenon, flourishing in England, France, Germany, Spain, and Italy. Although it produced few masterpieces—*Everyman* is one—it made possible the flowering of drama in the Renaissance, which built not only upon the rediscovered drama of Greece and Rome but upon native traditions as well.

Medieval literature, like the age that produced it, was rich and diverse. And, again like the age itself, it was not merely a prelude to what followed but, in many respects, the matrix of the future. Fiction, poetry, and drama since the Renaissance have drawn heavily upon the classical heritage, but the forms in which they developed were established in the Middle Ages.

FURTHER READING *(prepared by J. H.):* C. W. Previté-Orton's *Shorter Cambridge Medieval History,* 2 vols., 1952, is a standard history of the Middle Ages. See also Denys Hay, *The Medieval Centuries,* 1965; Friedrich Heer, *The Medieval World,* 1962; Johan Huizinga, *The Waning of the Middle Ages,* 1924; and R. W. Southern, *The Making of the Middle Ages,* 1953. An authoritative overview of medieval literature is J. A. Burrow's *Medieval Writers and Their Work,* 1982. *European Writers: The Middle Ages and the Renaissance,* ed. William T. H. Jackson and George Stade, 2 vols. (the second beginning with Petrarch), 1983, is a work of sound scholarship understandable by non-experts. E. R. Curtius's *European Literature and the Latin Middle Ages,* trans. Willard Trask, 1953, is challenging but rewarding. C. S. Lewis's *The Discarded Image,* 1964, is a very readable description of the popular world view that underlay medieval literature and culture. For aspects of medieval culture closely related to literature, see Henri Pirenne, *Mohammed and Charlemagne,* 1939; T. H. White, *The Book of Beasts,* 1956; Emile Male, *The Gothic Image,* trans. Dora Nussey, 1958; Erwin Panofsky, *Gothic Architecture and Scholasticism,* 1951; and David C. Fowler, *The Bible in Early English Literature,* 1976 (a broader treatment of cultural contexts than the title would suggest). Two readable and fairly concise books on medieval philosophy are John Marenbon, *Early Medieval Philosophy, 480–1150: An Introduction,* 1983; *and* Michael Haren, *Medieval Thought: The Western Intellectual Tradition from Antiquity to the Thirteenth Century,* 1985; both address the relationship between philosophy and religion. Especially interesting, on the subject the title announces, are the essays collected in *Women in the Middle Ages and the Renaissance: Literary and Historical Perspectives,* ed. Mary Beth Rose, 1986. On particular genres, see, for lyric poetry, Maurice Valency's *In Praise of Love,* 1958 (on Provençal and Italian poetry); James J. Wilhelm, *Medieval Song,* 1971; and Frederick Goldin, *Lyrics of the Troubadours and Trouvères,* 1973. On epic and romance, W. P. Ker's *Epic and Romance,* 1897, is, despite its date, still valuable. See also *Arthurian Literature in the Middle Ages,* ed. R. S. Loomis, 1959; and Eugene Vinaver, *The Rise of Romance,* 1971. Good on medieval drama are V. A. Kolve, *The Play Called Corpus Christi,* 1966; and Rosemary Woolf, *The English Mystery Plays,* 1972.

Beowulf
(Eighth Century?)

A recurring image in the great Old English epic Beowulf is a lonely island of light surrounded by vast and impenetrable darkness. The image is appropriate for the poem's own place in literary history. This earliest surviving example of the heroic poem in northern Europe rises up like a beacon across the intervening centuries. But it is shrouded in mysteries of the most basic kind. Scholars have succeeded in throwing some light upon these mysteries, both from the evidence of the poem itself and from such external sources as archeological discoveries. But much remains wrapped in darkness.

What is generally known about the poem can be quickly summed up. It is set in a half-historical, half-legendary past, perhaps in the sixth century A.D. (the historical King Hygelac was killed about 521) and among Germanic tribes in Scandinavia, in present-day Denmark and Sweden. The poem, most people agree, must have been composed between about 680 and 800, though minority views place it as late as the tenth century. It survives in a single manuscript, written in England about the year 1000. The poem was forgotten after its own day, and the manuscript lay buried, perhaps in a monastic library, until the sixteenth century, when it surfaced in the collection of an Elizabethan antiquarian. It eventually ended up in the British Museum, after being damaged in a fire in 1731. It was first printed in 1815.

So much for the external history of the poem (tentative as much of it is). For further light, we must look for the most part within the poem itself. The language and the versification of the poem need some explaining to modern readers. In the original Old English, Beowulf is written in alliterative verse. That is, instead of being built of poetic feet, each having the same number of syllables and the same pattern of accent, it has as its basic unit the line, which is divided into two half-lines separated by a caesura or short pause. Each half-line has two strong accents, with an indefinite number of syllables. The half-lines are tied together by alliteration; the same initial sound appears on at least one accented syllable in each of the half-lines. Kevin Crossley-Holland, in the excellent translation published here, has used a rather loose modern adaptation of this system. Take the first three lines for example:

> Lísten!
> The fáme   of Dánish kíngs
> in dáys gone bý,   the dáring féats
> wórked by those héroes   are wéll knówn to us.

Here the caesuras have been indicated with spaces, the accents have been marked, and the alliterating sounds underlined. The pattern is clear, although Crossley-Holland does not adhere to it strictly. The first line, for example, has neither a clear caesura nor alliterating words. Elsewhere in the translation, he sometimes omits the caesura or lets it fall somewhere other than between the second and third stresses. He also uses alliteration much more lightly than the original does. Nevertheless, the effect of the translation is very close to the original. It is a strongly oral poetry, meant to be chanted rhythmically rather than read silently.

The other most striking feature of the language, again carried over from the original Old English by the translator, is its heavy use of stock phrases such as *epithets. In the passage that introduces Grendel, for example, he is called within a few lines "the brutish demon," "the hellish fiend," "this gruesome creature," "notorious prowler of the borderland," "ranger of the moors," and "this cursed creature." Each of the major characters has a similar set of epithets, as do such things as the sea ("the whale's way," "the waves' domain," etc.).*

Formulaic language of this sort is a basic device of oral poets, to whom it serves as a means of fitting together traditional verbal elements into a new composition. Like the rhythmic alliterative verse, its use suggests that Beowulf *derives ultimately from oral verse. Some modern scholars have held that it was composed orally by an Old English* scop *or bard who was probably illiterate. The poem itself includes several references to such performances, not only the Creation song which maddens Grendel in lines 90–98, but even a song about Beowulf's exploits:*

> *And now and then one of Hrothgar's thanes*
> *who brimmed with poetry, and remembered lays,*
> *a man acquainted with ancient traditions*
> *of every kind, composed a new song*
> *in correct metre. Most skillfully that man*
> *began to sing of Beowulf's feat,*
> *to weave words together, and fluently*
> *to tell a fitting tale.*
>
> (lines 858–865)

It is perhaps not too fanciful to see in such an account a description of how Beowulf *itself came to be. In any case, the good reader of* Beowulf *will read it not as a modern poem designed mainly for the eye but as a "performance piece" intended primarily to be heard.*

Beowulf's *roots in orally transmitted, folk culture are also evident in its plot material, a curious mingling of circumstantial history and fairy-tale material. The poem is set in the historical past, and the poet places the central action against a background of historical events, sometimes presented rather elliptically and allusively, as in the story of the fight at Finnsburh (lines 1058ff.) or of the war between the Swedes and the Geats (lines 2902ff.). We can assume that the original readers (or hearers) of* Beowulf *would have had a good knowledge of this historical material and that a brief allusion would have called it to their minds. (We have tried to provide a substitute for this knowledge in the annotations to the historical passages.)*

The Beowulf *poet, though, keeps his history in the background; in the foreground is clearly fabulous material. Beowulf himself is part realistic Germanic warrior, part fairy-tale hero, with his supernatural strength and his ability to hold his breath under water for an entire day. Even his name betrays his folk-tale origins; he was originally part bear (bee-wolf means bear). And Grendel and his mother and the dragon have nothing to do with history at all.*

Why did the Beowulf *poet, obviously a sophisticated artist, choose to center his epic upon three fairy-tale monsters? Nineteenth-century scholars, eager for historical information about the early Middle Ages, tended to be impatient with the monsters and wish that the poet had gone into more detail about the history of the Germanic tribes. The great Victorian scholar W. P. Ker complained in 1904, for example, that the plot was "preposterous" and that, by concentrating in the main plot on the monsters and confining the historical allusions to the background, the poem put "the irrelevances in the centre and the serious things on the outer edges." Ker was an-*

swered in 1936 by the critic and novelist J. R. R. Tolkien, author of Lord of the Rings, *who argued that "the monsters are not an inexplicable blunder of taste; they are essential, fundamentally allied to the underlying ideas of the poem, which give it its lofty tone and high seriousness." For Tolkien, the monsters were symbolic of eternal forces of evil while remaining real monsters. The world of* Beowulf, *to him, is poised on the edge of the transition from pagan to Christian culture, and the monsters retain something of their pagan reality while anticipating also the allegorizing of the later Christian middle ages.*

However one interprets the monsters (and Tolkien's interpretation has not won universal agreement), it is clear that the sequence of monster-fights provides the structure of the poem. Tolkien, and others, have seen the poem as falling into two parts: the youthful Beowulf's adventure against Grendel and his mother and the aged king's struggle with the dragon. Some have even found in the two-part, balanced structure of the narrative an echo, on a larger scale, of the balanced structure of the divided single lines of alliterative verse. Certainly the poet uses pairings frequently. The royal ship-burial of Scyld Scefing which opens the poem is balanced by Beowulf's burial which ends it. Character is often developed by contrasted pairs: Beowulf as a good king is unlike Heremod the bad one, and the generous Queen Higd is not like the tyrannical Queen Thryth. Sometimes the contrast is ironic: the fortunate Queen Wealhtheow seems unlike the tragic Queen Hildeburh, but if we know the later history of the Danish court, they seem more alike than different.

There are, however, after all, three monsters, and other critics have considered triple patterns to be at least as important in Beowulf *as duple ones. In this poem of a little over three thousand lines, roughly a thousand lines are devoted to each of the three monsters, and it has been suggested that* Beowulf *was intended to be performed over three evenings, each devoted to a new monster. If the sequence of monsters is intended to suggest a progression, what is the point of the progression? There is an obvious contrast between Grendel and his mother, on the one hand, and the dragon on the other. Grendel and his mother are human, if horribly perverted, while the dragon seems to be evil itself. There is a similar progression from Grendel to his mother. The encounter with Grendel, dreadful as it is, at least takes place in a human habitation with other humans around; the fight with his mother takes place at the bottom of the fearful mere, in a psychologically suggestive setting that seems to move Beowulf closer to the heart of evil. On the other hand, the dragon does have some redeeming features; he has been wronged, as Grendel and his mother have not, and the poet treats him with some measure of respect.*

The monster-fights, important as they are, are not all of the poem, however. One of the most striking features of the poem is its use of inset narratives or "digressions." In a sense the poem begins with a digression—the story of Scyld Scefing—and at least seven more times the poet turns aside to tell a loosely related story, in the episodes of the later burning of Heorot (lines 81–85 and 769–773), Sigemund (lines 865–890), Heremod (lines 891–905 and 1694–1709), the fight at Finnsburh (lines 1058–1149), Thryth (lines 1915–1946), the Danish-Heathobard feud (lines 2006–2054), and the Geatish-Swedish wars (lines 2460–2480, etc.). But this list does not suggest the pervasiveness of the use of allusion and analogy in the poem, sometimes only in a phrase or in the use of the same formula in different situations. A continuing challenge in reading Beowulf *is exploring the relation of these inset stories to the main situation.*

Taken as a whole, the allusiveness in Beowulf *enriches the texture of the poem and gives it a curiously meditative, ruminative quality quite unlike the series of simple feats of strength it sometimes sounds like in summary. The three monster-fights are placed against a background of historical analogies and interwoven stories that some critics have seen as analogous to the complex, "interlaced" style of Old English art.*

Certain themes run through the complex interweaving of narratives in Beowulf, *and most of them center on the character of Beowulf himself as exemplar of a heroic code, first as a warrior and then as a king. The virtue that binds tribal society together is loyalty, both of a warrior to his king and of a king to his warriors. Wiglaf, in the dragon episode, is balanced as a good thane with the younger Beowulf, in one of the poem's many complex pairings, and the thanes who run away are implicitly compared with the loyal waiters by the lake in the episode with Grendel's mother. The emphasis upon heroic boasting and upon gift-giving may ring strange to modern ears. But pride and reward have different meanings in the world of* Beowulf. *In the last words of the poem, Beowulf is said to be, of all kings, the "most eager for fame," and the description seems to be wholly laudatory. The Germanic warrior's boasts and his jealousy over his reputation are regarded as virtues rather than vices, ways of reaffirming the values upon which the society depends. Rewards in* Beowulf *are similarly treated more as signs than for their material value. Hrothgar bestows great treasures upon Beowulf, but Beowulf surrenders them all to his king, Hygelac (receiving, to be sure, even greater ones). And the great treasure of the dragon is mostly buried with the hero. More than materialistic transactions, eagerness for reward and liberality in "ring-giving" are rituals confirming the heroic code.*

The Germanic heroic code in Beowulf *is, however, tempered with Christian values, although critics have been unable to agree upon their extent. Whoever put* Beowulf *in writing must have been a Christian, since at that time literacy was tied to a clerical vocation. Some critics have argued back from this fact and found* Beowulf *to be "profoundly Christian" or even an "allegory of salvation." The difficulty with such extreme positions is the absence of any specifically Christian references in the poem. The name "Christ" never appears, nor are there any references to the central doctrines of Christianity. Such biblical references as there are are to the Old Testament, perhaps the part of the Bible easiest to assimilate to Germanic tribal culture. A number of pious sentiments are expressed, but none is specifically Christian. Hrothgar, for example, after Beowulf kills Grendel, says, "Let us give thanks at once to God Almighty for this sight," and goes on to assign the victory not only to Beowulf but also to "the Almighty's power." Such statements are monotheistic but not explicitly Christian. The question of the exact relationship between the Germanic heroic ethic and Christianity in* Beowulf *may never be precisely answered. Tolkien thought that the author was a Christian, "a learned man writing of old times, who looking back on the heroism and sorrow [felt] in them something permanent and something symbolical." Kenneth Sisam, on the other hand, surveyed the debates about the Christianity in the poem and rather iconoclastically concluded that the* Beowulf *poet was less concerned about Christianity and paganism than his critics have been.*

The question of the Christianity of Beowulf *or the lack of it is, in other words, one of the many shadowy areas that remain in our understanding of the poem. But such uncertainties should not stand in the way of reading and responding to a magnificent poem that is worthy of the place it occupies at the threshold of modern European literature.*

FURTHER READING (*prepared by J. H.*): For students interested in looking at *Beowulf* in Old English, the standard edition is *Beowulf and the Fight at Finnsburg*, ed.

Friedrich Klaeber, 3rd ed., 1941. Somewhat less intimidating is *Beowulf: A Dual Language Edition,* ed. and trans. Howell D. Chickering, Jr., 2nd ed., 1982. Chickering prints a careful Anglo-Saxon text with a close, almost word-for-word modern English translation on facing pages. His hundred-page, section-by-section "Commentary" is an excellent starting point for the study of the poem. Among secondary works, Raymond W. Chambers' *Beowulf: An Introduction to the Study of the Poem,* 3rd ed., 1963, must be mentioned, although its voluminous presentation of background material is likely to tell the beginning reader more than he or she wants to know. Perhaps the best critical book on the poem is Arthur G. Brodeur's *The Art of Beowulf,* 1959. J. D. A. Ogilvy and Donald C. Baker's *Reading Beowulf: An Introduction to the Poem, Its Background, and Its Style,* 1983, provides the basic historical and critical background for a study of the poem. Fred C. Robinson, *Beowulf and the Appositive Style,* 1985, is a series of lectures on the style and structure of the poem which also argues for an interplay between Christian narrator and earlier, pagan subject. Among collections of important essays on *Beowulf* are *An Anthology of Beowulf Criticism,* ed. Lewis E. Nicholson, 1963, and *The Beowulf Poet,* ed. Donald K. Fry, 1968. Both include J. R. R. Tolkien's seminal "*Beowulf:* The Monsters and the Critics." *Beowulf* would seem to be the ultimate male poem, and one would not expect a study of its women to be very interesting. The reverse is proved by several recent studies, among them Alexandra Hennessey Olsen, "Women in *Beowulf*," in *Approaches to Teaching Beowulf,* ed. Jess B. Bessinger, Jr., and Robert F. Yeager, 1984; and Jane Chance, "Grendel's Mother as Epic Anti-Type of the Virgin and Queen," in *Woman as Hero in Old English Literature,* 1986. A recording of *Beowulf* read in Old English helps one get a feel for the oral quality of the poem; an excellent one is Jess B. Bessinger, Jr., *Beowulf, Caedmon's Hymn, and Other Old English Poems Read in Old English,* 1962. Readers of *Beowulf* may also be interested in John Gardner's modern novel based on the poem: *Grendel,* 1971.

BEOWULF

Translated by Kevin Crossley-Holland

Listen!
      The fame of Danish kings
in days gone by, the daring feats
worked by those heroes are well known to us.
  Scyld Scefing often deprived his enemies,
many tribes of men, of their mead-benches.[1]
He terrified his foes; yet he, as a boy,
had been found a waif; fate made amends for that.
He prospered under heaven, won praise and honour,
until the men of every neighbouring tribe,
across the whale's way, were obliged to obey him   10
and pay him tribute. He was a noble king!
Then a son was born to him, a child
in the court, sent by God to comfort
the Danes; for He had seen their dire distress,
that once they suffered hardship for a long while,

---

[1] The mead-bench—the high bench in a hall from which mead and gifts were distributed—was the symbol of the independence of a Germanic chieftain.

lacking a lord; and the Lord of Life,
King of Heaven, granted this boy glory;
Beow was renowned—the name of Scyld's son
became known throughout the Norse lands.
By his own mettle, likewise by generous gifts   20
while he still enjoys his father's protection,
a young man must ensure that in later years
his companions will support him, serve
their prince in battle; a man who wins renown
will always prosper among any people.

  Then Scyld departed at the destined hour,
that powerful man sought the Lord's protection.
His own close companions carried him
down to the sea, as he, lord of the Danes,
had asked while he could still speak.   30
That well-loved man had ruled his land for many years.
There in harbour stood the ring-prowed ship,[2]
the prince's vessel, icy, eager to sail;
and then they laid their dear lord,
the giver of rings,[3] deep within the ship
by the mast in majesty; many treasures
and adornments from far and wide were gathered there.
I have never heard of a ship equipped
more handsomely with weapons and war-gear,
swords and corslets; on his breast   40
lay countless treasures that were to travel far
with him into the waves' domain.
They gave him great ornaments, gifts
no less magnificent than those men had given him
who long before had sent him alone,
child as he was, across the stretch of the seas.
Then high above his head they placed
a golden banner and let the waves bear him,
bequeathed him to the sea; their hearts were grieving,
their minds mourning. Mighty men   50
beneath the heavens, rulers in the hall,
cannot say who received that cargo.

  When his royal father had travelled from the earth,
Beow of Denmark, a beloved king,
ruled long in the stronghold, famed
amongst men; in time Healfdene the brave
was born to him; who, so long as he lived,
grey-haired and redoubtable, ruled the noble Danes.
Beow's son Healfdene, leader of men,
was favoured by fortune with four children: 60
Heorogar and Hrothgar and Halga the good;
Yrse, the fourth, was Onela's queen,

---

[2] A ship with a high, scrolled prow, perhaps with carvings in a ring pattern.
[3] Generous dispenser of treasure (in the form of gold rings).

the beloved wife of that warlike Swedish king.
    Hrothgar won honour in war,
glory in battle, and so ensured
his followers' support—young men
whose number multiplied into a mighty troop.
And he resolved to build a hall,
a large and noble feasting-hall
of whose splendours men would always speak,   70
and there to distribute as gifts to old and young
all the things that God had given him—
but not men's lives or the public land.
Then I heard that tribes without number, even
to the ends of the earth, were given orders
to decorate the hall. And in due course
(before very long) this greatest of halls
was completed. Hrothgar, whose very word was counted
far and wide as a command, called it Heorot.[4]
He kept his promise, gave presents of rings   80
and treasure at the feasting. The hall towered high,
lofty and wide-gabled—fierce tongues of loathsome fire
had not yet attacked it, nor was the time yet near
when a mortal feud should flare between father-
and son-in-law, sparked off by deeds of deadly enmity.
    Then the brutish demon who lived in darkness
impatiently endured a time of frustration:
day after day he heard the din of merry-making
inside the hall, and the sound of the harp
and the bard's clear song. He who could tell   90
of the origin of men from far-off times lifted his voice,
sang that the Almighty made the earth,
this radiant plain encompassed by oceans;
and that God, all powerful, ordained
sun and moon to shine for mankind,
adorned all regions of the world
with trees and leaves; and sang that He gave life
to every kind of creature that walks about earth.
So those warrior Danes lived joyful lives,
in complete harmony, until the hellish fiend   100
began to perpetrate base crimes.
This gruesome creature was called Grendel,
notorious prowler of the borderland, ranger of the moors,
the fen and the fastness; this cursed creature
lived in a monster's lair for a time
after the Creator had condemned him
as one of the seed of Cain—the Everlasting Lord
avenged Abel's murder. Cain had
no satisfaction from that feud, but the Creator
sent him into exile, far from mankind,   110

[4]The name means "hart," an animal symbolic of kingship to the Anglo-Saxons.

because of his crime. He could no longer
approach the throne of grace, that precious place
in God's presence, nor did he feel God's love.
In him all evil-doers find their origin,
monsters and elves and spiteful spirits of the dead,
also the giants who grappled with God
for a long while; the Lord gave them their deserts.[5]
   Then, under cover of night, Grendel came
to Hrothgar's lofty hall to see how the Ring-Danes
were disposed after drinking ale all evening;   120
and he found there a band of brave warriors,
well-feasted, fast asleep, dead to worldly sorrow,
man's sad destiny. At once that hellish monster,
grim and greedy, brutally cruel,
started forward and seized thirty thanes
even as they slept; and then, gloating
over his plunder, he hurried from the hall,
made for his lair with all those slain warriors.
Then at dawn, as day first broke,
Grendel's power was at once revealed;   130
a great lament was lifted, after the feast
an anguished cry at that daylight discovery.
The famous prince, best of all men, sat apart in mourning;
when he saw Grendel's gruesome footprints,
that great man grieved for his retainers.
This enmity was utterly one-sided, too repulsive,
too long-lasting. Nor were the Danes allowed respite,
but the very next day Grendel committed
violent assault, murders more atrocious than before,
and he had no qualms about it. He was caught up in his crimes.   140
Then it was not difficult to find the man
who preferred a more distant resting-place,
a bed in the outbuildings, for the hatred
of the hall-warden was quite unmistakable.
He who had escaped the clutches of the fiend
kept further off, at a safe distance.
   Thus Grendel ruled, resisted justice,
one against all, until the best of halls
stood deserted. And so it remained:
for twelve long winters the lord of the Danes   150
was sorely afflicted with sorrows and cares;
then men were reminded in mournful songs
that the monster Grendel fought with Hrothgar
for a long time, fought with fierce hatred
committing crime and atrocity day after day
in continual strife. He had no wish for peace

---

[5] The story of a race of evil giants descended from Cain comes from early interpretations
of Genesis 6:4: "There were giants in the earth in those days, and also afterward, when the
sons of God had relations with the daughters of men, who bore children to them."

with any of the Danes, would not desist
from his deadly malice or pay *wergild*[6]—
No! None of the counsellors could hold out hope
of handsome compensation at that slayer's hands.   160
But the cruel monster constantly terrified
young and old, the dark death-shadow
lurked in ambush; he prowled the misty moors
at the dead of night; men do not know
where such hell-whisperers shrithe[7] in their wanderings.
Such were the many and outrageous injuries
that the fearful solitary, foe of all men,
endlessly inflicted; he occupied Heorot,
that hall adorned with treasures, on cloudless nights.
This caused the lord of the Danes deep,   170
heart-breaking grief. Strong men often sat
in consultation, trying in vain to devise
a good plan as to how best valiant men
could safeguard themselves against sudden attack.
At times they offered sacrifices to the idols
in their pagan tabernacles, and prayed aloud
to the soul-slayer[8] that he would assist them
in their dire distress. Such was the custom
and comfort of the heathen; they brooded in their hearts
on hellish things—for the Creator, Almighty God,   180
the judge of all actions, was neglected by them;
truly they did not know how to praise the Protector of Heaven,
the glorious Ruler. Woe to the man who,
in his wickedness, commits his soul to the fire's embrace;
he must expect neither comfort nor change.
He will be damned for ever. Joy shall be his
who, when he dies, may stand before the Lord,
seek peace in the embrace of our Father.

    Thus Healfdene's son endlessly brooded
over the afflictions of this time; that wise warrior
was altogether helpless, for the hardship upon them—   190
violent visitations, evil events in the night—
was too overwhelming, loathsome, and long-lasting.
    One of Hygelac's thanes, Beowulf by name,
renowned among the Geats[9] for his great bravery,
heard in his own country of Grendel's crimes;
he was the strongest man alive,
princely and powerful. He gave orders
that a good ship should be prepared, said he would sail

---

[6] "Man-gold," compensation, according to Germanic custom, for a murdered person, paid to his relatives.

[7] The translator's revival of an Anglo-Saxon word, *scrithan:* to slip along smoothly but menacingly, like a snake.

[8] A Germanic god, probably Woden, seen as a "soul-slayer" from a Christian perspective.

[9] The Germanic tribe called the Geats lived in southwestern Sweden. They flourished in the sixth century A.D.

over the sea to assist the famous leader,   200
the warrior king, since he needed hardy men.
Wise men admired his spirit of adventure.
Dear to them though he was, they encouraged
the warrior and consulted the omens.
Beowulf searched out the bravest of the Geats,
asked them to go with him; that seasoned sailor
led fourteen thanes to the ship at the shore.

   Days went by; the boat was on the water,
moored under the cliff. The warriors, all prepared,
stepped onto the prow—the water streams eddied,   210
stirred up sand; the men stowed
gleaming armour, noble war-gear
deep within the ship; then those warriors launched
the well-built boat and so began their journey.
Foaming at the prow and most like a sea-bird,
the boat sped over the waves, urged on by the wind;
until next day, at the expected time,
so far had the curved prow come
that the travellers sighted land,
shining cliffs, steep hills,   220
broad headlands. So did they cross the sea;
their journey was at its end. Then the Geats
disembarked, lost no time in tying up
the boat—their corslets clanked;
the warriors gave thanks to God
for their safe passage over the sea.

   Then, on the cliff-top, the Danish watchman
(whose duty it was to stand guard by the shore)
saw that the Geats carried flashing shields
and gleaming war-gear down the gangway,   230
and his mind was riddled with curiosity.
Then Hrothgar's thane leapt onto his horse
and, brandishing a spear, galloped
down to the shore; there, he asked at once:
"Warriors! Who are you, in your coats of mail,
who have steered your tall ship over the sea-lanes
to these shores? I've been a coastguard here
for many years, kept watch by the sea,
so that no enemy band should encroach
upon this Danish land and do us injury.   240
Never have warriors, carrying their shields,
come to this country in a more open manner.
Nor were you assured of my leaders' approval,
my kinsmen's consent. I've never set eyes
on a more noble man, a warrior in armour,
than one among your band; he's no mere retainer,
so ennobled by his weapons. May his looks never belie him,
and his lordly bearing. But now, before you step
one foot further on Danish land

like faithless spies, I must know   250
your lineage. Bold seafarers,
strangers from afar, mark my words
carefully: you would be best advised
quickly to tell me the cause of your coming."
   The man of highest standing, leader of that troop,
unlocked his hoard of words, answered him:
"We are all Geats, hearth-companions of Hygelac;
my father was famed far and wide,
a noble lord, Ecgtheow by name—
he endured many winters before he,   260
in great old age, went on his way; every wise man
in this world readily recalls him.
We have sailed across the sea to seek your lord,
Healfdene's son, protector of the people,
with most honourable intentions; give us your guidance!
We have come on an errand of importance
to the great Danish prince; nor, I imagine, will the cause
of our coming long remain secret. You will know
whether it is true—as we have heard tell—
that here among the Danes a certain evil-doer,   270
a fearful solitary, on dark nights commits deeds
of unspeakable malice—damage
and slaughter. In all good conscience
I can counsel Hrothgar, that wise and good man,
how he shall overcome the fiend,
and how his anguish shall be assuaged—
if indeed his fate ordains that these foul deeds
should ever end, and be avenged;
he will suffer endless hardship otherwise,
dire distress, as long as Heorot, best of dwellings,   280
stands unshaken in its lofty place."
   Still mounted, the coastguard,
a courageous thane, gave him this reply:
"The discriminating warrior—one whose mind is keen—
must perceive the difference between words and deeds.
But I see you are a company well disposed
towards the Danish prince. Proceed, and bring
your weapons and armour! I shall direct you.
And I will command my companions, moreover,
to guard your ship with honour   290
against any foe—your beached vessel,
caulked so recently—until the day that timbered craft
with its curved prow shall carry back
the beloved man across the sea currents
to the shores of the storm-loving Geats:
he who dares deeds with such audacity and valour
shall be granted safety in the squall of battle."
   Then they hurried on. The ship lay still;
securely anchored, the spacious vessel

rode on its hawser. The boar crest, brightly gleaming,   300
stood over their helmets: superbly tempered,
plated with glowing gold, it guarded the lives
of those grim warriors. The thanes made haste,
marched along together until they could discern
the glorious, timbered hall, adorned with gold;
they saw there the best-known building
under heaven. The ruler lived in it;
its brilliance carried across countless lands.
Then the fearless watchman pointed out the path
leading to Heorot, bright home of brave men,   310
so that they should not miss the way;
that bold warrior turned his horse, then said:
"I must leave you here. May the Almighty Father,
of His grace, guard you in your enterprise.
I will go back to the sea again,
and there stand watch against marauding bands."
    The road was paved; it showed those warriors
the way. Their corslets were gleaming,
the strong links of shining chain-mail
clinked together. When the sea-stained travellers   320
had reached the hall itself in their fearsome armour,
they placed their broad shields
(worked so skilfully) against Heorot's wall.
Then they sat on a bench; the brave men's
armour sang. The seafarers' gear
stood all together, a grey-tipped forest
of ash spears; that armed troop was well equipped
with weapons.
             Then Wulfgar, a proud warrior,
asked the Geats about their ancestry:
"Where have you come from with these gold-plated shields,   330
these grey coats of mail, these visored helmets,
and this pile of spears? I am Hrothgar's
messenger, his herald. I have never seen
so large a band of strangers of such bold bearing.
You must have come to Hrothgar's court
not as exiles, but from audacity and high ambition."
Then he who feared no man, the proud leader
of the Geats, stern-faced beneath his helmet,
gave him this reply: "We are Hygelac's
companions at the bench: my name is Beowulf.   340
I wish to explain to Healfdene's son,
the famous prince, your lord,
why we have come if he, in his goodness,
will give us leave to speak with him."
Wulfgar replied—a prince of the Vandals,
his mettle, his wisdom and prowess in battle
were widely recognized: "I will ask
the lord of the Danes, ruler of the Scyldings,

renowned prince and ring-giver,
just as you request, regarding your journey,   350
and bring back to you at once whatever answer
that gracious man thinks fit to give me."
   Then Wulfgar hurried to the place where Hrothgar sat,
grizzled and old, surrounded by his thanes;
the brave man moved forward until he stood
immediately before the Danish lord;
he well knew the customs of warriors.
Wulfgar addressed his friend and leader:
"Geatish men have travelled to this land,
come from far, across the stretch of the seas.   360
These warriors call their leader Beowulf;
they ask, my lord, that they should be allowed
to speak with you. Gracious Hrothgar,
do not give them *no* for answer.
They, in their armour, seem altogether worthy
of the highest esteem. I have no doubt of their leader's
might, he who has brought these brave men to Heorot."
Hrothgar, defender of the Danes, answered:
"I knew him when he was a boy;
his illustrious father was called Ecgtheow;   370
Hrethel the Geat gave him his only daughter
in marriage; now his son, with daring spirit,
has voyaged here to visit a loyal friend.
And moreover, I have heard seafarers say—
men who have carried rich gifts to the Geats
as a mark of my esteem—that in the grasp
of his hand that man renowned in battle
has the might of thirty men. I am convinced
that Holy God, of His great mercy,
has directed him to us West-Danes   380
and that he means to come to grips with Grendel.
I will reward this brave man with treasures.
Hurry! Tell them to come in and meet
our band of kinsmen; and make it clear, too,
that they are most welcome to the Danes!"
Then Wulfgar went to the hall door with Hrothgar's reply:
"My conquering lord, the leader of the East-Danes[10]
commands me to tell you that he knows your lineage
and that you, so bold in mind, are welcome
to these shores from over the rolling sea.   390
You may see Hrothgar in your armour,
under your helmets, just as you are;
but leave your shields out here, and your deadly ashen spears,
let them await the outcome of your words."

---

[10]The same as the "West-Danes" (l. 380). At various points in the poem, the Danes are called North-, South-, East-, and West-Danes, as well as Bright-Danes, Ring-Danes, and Spear-Danes. The variations are used for alliterative purposes.

Then noble Beowulf rose from the bench,
flanked by his fearless followers; some stayed behind
at the brave man's bidding, to stand guard over their armour.
Guided by Wulfgar, the rest hurried into Heorot
together; there went that hardy man, stern-faced
beneath his helmet, until he was standing under Heorot's roof.   400
Beowulf spoke—his corslet, cunningly linked
by the smith, was shining: "Greetings, Hrothgar!
I am Hygelac's kinsman and retainer. In my youth
I achieved many daring exploits. Word of Grendel's deeds
has come to me in my own country;
seafarers say that this hall Heorot,
best of all buildings, stands empty and useless
as soon as the evening light is hidden under the sky.
So, Lord Hrothgar, men known by my people
to be noble and wise advised me to visit you   410
because they knew of my great strength:
they saw me themselves when, stained by my enemies' blood,
I returned from the fight when I destroyed five,
a family of giants, and by night slew monsters
on the waves; I suffered great hardship,
avenged the affliction of the Storm-Geats and crushed
their fierce foes—they were asking for trouble.
And now, I shall crush the giant Grendel
in single combat. Lord of the mighty Danes,
guardian of the Scyldings, I ask one favour: 420
protector of warriors, lord beloved of your people,
now that I have sailed here from so far,
do not refuse my request—that I alone, with my band
of brave retainers, may cleanse Heorot.
I have also heard men say this monster
is so reckless he spurns the use of weapons.
Therefore (so that Hygelac, my lord,
may rest content over my conduct) I deny myself
the use of a sword and a broad yellow shield
in battle; but I shall grapple with this fiend   430
hand to hand; we shall fight for our lives,
foe against foe; and he whom death takes off
must resign himself to the judgement of God.
I know that Grendel, should he overcome me,
will without dread devour many Geats,
matchless warriors, in the battle-hall,
as he has often devoured Danes before. If death claims me
you will not have to cover my head,
for he already will have done so—
with a sheet of shining blood; he will carry off   440
the blood-stained corpse, meaning to savour it;
the solitary one will eat without sorrow
and stain his lair; no longer then
will you have to worry about burying my body.

But if battle should claim me, send this most excellent
coat of mail to Hygelac, this best of corslets
that protects my breast; it once belonged to Hrethel,
the work of Weland.[11] Fate goes ever as it must!"

 Hrothgar, protector of the Scyldings, replied:
"Beowulf, my friend! So you have come here,   450
because of past favours, to fight on our behalf!
Your father Ecgtheow, by striking a blow,
began the greatest of feuds. He slew Heatholaf of the Wylfings
with his own hand; after that, the Geats
dared not harbour him for fear of war.
So he sailed here, over the rolling waves,
to this land of the South-Danes, the honoured Scyldings;
I was young then, had just begun to reign
over the Danes in this glorious kingdom,
this treasure-stronghold of heroes; my elder brother, 460
Heorogar, Healfdene's son, had died
not long before; he was a better man than I!
I settled your father's feud by payment;
I sent ancient treasures to the Wylfings
over the water's back; and Ecgtheow swore oaths to me.
It fills me with anguish to admit to all the evil
that Grendel, goaded on by his hatred,
has wreaked in Heorot with his sudden attacks
and infliction of injuries; my hall-troop is depleted,
my band of warriors; fate has swept them 470
into Grendel's ghastly clutches. Yet God can easily
prevent this reckless ravager from committing such crimes.
After quaffing beer, brave warriors of mine
have often boasted over the ale-cup
that they would wait in Heorot
and fight against Grendel with their fearsome swords.
Then, the next morning, when day dawned,
men could see that this great mead-hall was stained
by blood, that the floor by the benches
was spattered with gore; I had fewer followers, 480
dear warriors, for death had taken them off.
But first, sit down at our feast, and in due course,
as your inclination takes you, tell how warriors
have achieved greatness."

     Then, in the feasting-hall,
a bench was cleared for the Geats all together,
and there those brave men went and sat,
delighting in their strength; a thane did his duty—
held between his hands the adorned ale-cup,
poured out gleaming liquor; now and then the poet sang,
raised his clear voice in Heorot; the warriors caroused, 490
no small company of Scyldings and Geats.

---

[11] The blacksmith of the Scandinavian gods.

Ecglaf's son, Unferth, who sat at the feet
of the lord of the Scyldings, unlocked his thoughts
with these unfriendly words—for the journey of Beowulf,
the brave seafarer, much displeased him
in that he was unwilling for any man
in this wide world to gain more glory than himself:
"Are you the Beowulf who competed with Breca,
vied with him at swimming in the open sea
when, swollen with vanity, you both braved   500
the waves, risked your lives on deep waters
because of a foolish boast? No one,
neither friend nor foe, could keep you
from your sad journey, when you swam out to sea,
clasped in your arms the water-streams,
passed over the sea-paths, swiftly moved your hands
and sped over the ocean. The sea heaved,
the winter flood; for seven nights
you both toiled in the water; but Breca outstayed you;
he was the stronger; and then, on the eighth morning,   510
the sea washed him up on the shores of the Heathoreams.
From there he sought his own country,
the land of the Brondings who loved him well;
he went to his fair stronghold where he had a hall
and followers and treasures. In truth, Beanstan's son
fulfilled his boast that he could swim better than you.
So I am sure you will pay a heavy price—
although you have survived countless battle storms,
savage sword-play—if you dare
ambush Grendel in the watches of the night."   520
Beowulf, the son of Ecgtheow, replied:
"Truly, Unferth my friend, all this beer
has made you talkative: you have told us much
about Breca and his exploits. But I maintain
I showed the greater stamina, endured
hardship without equal in the heaving water.
Some years ago when we were young men,
still in our youth, Breca and I made a boast,
a solemn vow, to venture our lives
on the open sea; and we kept our word.   530
When we swam through the water, we each held
a naked sword with which to ward off
whales; by no means could Breca
swim faster than I, pull away from me
through the press of the waves—
I had no wish to be separated from him.
So for five nights we stayed together in the sea,
until the tides tore us apart,
the foaming water, the freezing cold,
day darkening into night—until the north wind,   540
that savage warrior, rounded against us.

Rough were the waves; fishes in the sea
were roused to great anger. Then my coat of mail,
hard and hand-linked, guarded me against my enemies;
the woven war-garment, adorned with gold,
covered my breast. A cruel ravager
dragged me down to the sea-bed, a fierce monster
held me tightly in its grasp; but it was given to me
to bury my sword, my battle weapon,
in its breast; the mighty sea-beast   550
was slain by my blow in the storm of battle.
In this manner, and many times, loathsome monsters
harassed me fiercely; with my fine sword
I served them fittingly.
I did not allow those evil destroyers to enjoy
a feast, to eat me limb by limb
seated at a banquet on the sea-bottom;
but the next morning they lay in the sand
along the shore, wounded by sword strokes,
slain by battle-blades, and from that day on   560
they could not hinder seafarers from sailing
over deep waters. Light came from the east,
God's bright beacon; the swell subsided,
and I saw then great headlands,
cliffs swept by the wind. Fate will often spare
an undoomed man, if his courage is good.
As it was I slew nine sea-beasts
with my sword. I have never heard
of a fiercer fight by night under heaven's vault
nor of a man who endured more on the ocean streams.   570
But I escaped with my life from the enemies' clutches,
worn out by my venture. Then the swift current,
the surging water, carried me
to the land of the Lapps. I have not heard tell
that you have taken part in any such contests,
in the peril of sword-play. Neither you nor Breca
have yet dared such a deed with shining sword
in battle—I do not boast because of this—
though of course it is true you slew your own brothers,
your own close kinsmen. For that deed, however clever   580
you may be, you will suffer damnation in hell.
I tell you truly, son of Ecglaf,
that if you were in fact as unflinching
as you claim, the fearsome monster Grendel
would never have committed so many crimes
against your lord, nor created such havoc in Heorot;
but he has found he need not fear unduly
your people's enmity, fearsome assault
with swords by the victorious Scyldings.
So he spares none but takes his toll   590
of the Danish people, does as he will,

kills and destroys, expects no fight
from the Spear-Danes. But soon, quite soon,
I shall show him the strength, the spirit and skill
of the Geats. And thereafter, when day dawns,
when the radiant sun shines from the south
over the sons of men, he who so wishes
may enter the mead-hall without terror."
    Then the grizzled warrior, giver of gold,
was filled with joy; the lord of the Danes,   600
shepherd of his people, listened to Beowulf's
brave resolution and relied on his help.
The warriors laughed, there was a hum
of contentment. Wealhtheow came forward,
mindful of ceremonial—she was Hrothgar's queen;
adorned with gold, that proud woman
greeted the men in the hall, then offered the cup
to the Danish king first of all.
She begged him, beloved of his people,
to enjoy the feast; the king, famed   610
for victory, ate and drank in happiness.
Then the lady of the Helmings walked about the hall,
offering the precious, ornamented cup
to old and young alike, until at last
the queen, excellent in mind, adorned with rings,
moved with the mead-cup towards Beowulf.
She welcomed the Geatish prince and with wise words
thanked God that her wish was granted
that she might depend on some warrior for help
against such attacks. The courageous warrior   620
took the cup from Wealhtheow's hands
and, eager for battle, made a speech:
Beowulf, the son of Ecgtheow, said:
"When I put to sea, sailed
through the breakers with my band of men,
I resolved to fulfil the desire
of your people, or suffer the pangs of death,
caught fast in Grendel's clutches.
Here, in Heorot, I shall either work a deed
of great daring, or lay down my life."   630
Beowulf's brave boast delighted Wealhtheow:
adorned with gold, the noble Danish queen
went to sit beside her lord.
    Then again, as of old, fine words were spoken
in the hall, the company rejoiced,
a conquering people, until in due course
the son of Healfdene wanted to retire
and take his rest. He realized the monster
meant to attack Heorot after the blue hour,
when black night has settled over all—   640
when shadowy shapes come shrithing

dark beneath the clouds. All the company rose.
Then the heroes Hrothgar and Beowulf saluted
one another; Hrothgar wished him luck
and control of Heorot, and confessed:
"Never since I could lift hand and shield,
have I entrusted this glorious Danish hall
to any man as I do now to you.
Take and guard this greatest of halls.
Make known your strength, remember your might,   650
stand watch against your enemy. You shall have
all you desire if you survive this enterprise."
    Then Hrothgar, defender of the Danes,
withdrew from the hall with his band of warriors.
The warlike leader wanted to sleep with Wealhtheow,
his queen. It was said the mighty king
had appointed a hall-guard—a man who undertook
a dangerous duty for the Danish king,
elected to stand watch against the monster.   660
Truly, the leader of the Geats fervently trusted
in his own great strength and in God's grace.
Then he took off his helmet and his corslet
of iron, and gave them to his servant,
with his superb, adorned sword,
telling him to guard them carefully.
And then, before he went to his bed,
the brave Geat, Beowulf, made his boast:
"I count myself no less active in battle,
no less brave than Grendel himself: 670
thus, I will not send him to sleep with my sword,
so deprive him of life, though certainly I could.
Despite his fame for deadly deeds,
he is ignorant of these noble arts, that he might strike
at me, and hew my shield; but we, this night,
shall forego the use of weapons, if he dares fight
without them; and then may wise God,
the holy Lord, give glory in battle
to whichever of us He should think fitting."
Then the brave prince leaned back, put his head   680
on the pillow while, around him,
many a proud seafarer lay back on his bed.
Not one of them believed he would see
day dawn, or ever return to his family
and friends, and the place where he was born;
they well knew that in recent days
far too many Danish men had come to bloody ends
in that hall. But the Lord wove the webs of destiny,
gave the Geats success in their struggle,
help and support, in such a way   690
that all were enabled to overcome their enemy
through the strength of one man. We cannot doubt

that mighty God has always ruled
over mankind.
                    Then the night prowler
came shrithing through the shadows. All the Geats
guarding Heorot had fallen asleep—
all except one. Men well knew that the evil enemy
could not drag them down into the shadows
when it was against the Creator's wishes,
but Beowulf, watching grimly for his adversary Grendel,   700
awaited the ordeal with increasing anger.
Then, under night's shroud, Grendel walked down
from the moors; he shouldered God's anger.
The evil plunderer intended to ensnare
one of the race of men in the high hall.
He strode under the skies, until he stood
before the feasting-hall, in front of the gift-building
gleaming with gold. And this night was not the first
on which he had so honoured Hrothgar's home.
But never in his life did he find hall-wardens   710
more greatly to his detriment. Then the joyless warrior
journeyed to Heorot. The outer door, bolted
with iron bands, burst open at a touch from his hands:
with evil in his mind, and overriding anger,
Grendel swung open the hall's mouth itself. At once,
seething with fury, the fiend stepped onto
the tessellated floor; a horrible light,
like a lurid flame, flickered in his eyes.
He saw many men, a group of warriors,
a knot of kinsmen, sleeping in the hall.   720
His spirits leapt, his heart laughed;
the savage monster planned to sever,
before daybreak, the life of every warrior
from his body—he fully expected to eat
his fill at the feast. But after that night
fate decreed that he should no longer feed off
human flesh. Hygelac's kinsman,
the mighty man, watched the wicked ravager
to see how he would make his sudden attacks.
The monster was not disposed to delay;   730
but, for a start, he hungrily seized
a sleeping warrior, greedily wrenched him,
bit into his body, drank the blood
from his veins, devoured huge pieces;
until, in no time, he had swallowed the whole man,
even his feet and hands. Now Grendel stepped forward,
nearer and nearer, made to grasp the valiant Geat
stretched out on his bed—the fiend reached towards him
with his open hand; at once Beowulf perceived
his evil plan, sat up and stayed Grendel's outstretched arm.   740
Instantly that monster, hardened by crime,

realized that never had he met any man
in the regions of earth, in the whole world,
with so strong a grip. He was seized with terror.
But, for all that, he was unable to break away.
He was eager to escape to his lair, seek the company
of devils, but he was restrained as never before.
Then Hygelac's brave kinsman bore in mind
his boast: he rose from the bed and gripped
Grendel fiercely. The fiend tried to break free,   750
his fingers were bursting. Beowulf kept with him.
The evil giant was desperate to escape,
if indeed he could, and head for his lair
in the fens; he could feel his fingers cracking
in his adversary's grip; that was a bitter journey
that Grendel made to the ring-hall Heorot.
The great room boomed; all the proud warriors—
each and every Dane living in the stronghold—
were stricken with panic. The two hall-wardens   760
were enraged. The building rang with their blows.
It was a wonder the wine-hall withstood
two so fierce in battle, that the fair building
did not fall to earth; but it stood firm,
braced inside and out with hammered
iron bands. I have heard tell that there,
where they fought, many a mead-bench,
studded with gold, started from the floor.
Until that time, elders of the Scyldings
were of the opinion that no man could wreck   770
the great hall Heorot, adorned with horns,
nor by any means destroy it unless it were gutted
by greedy tongues of flame. Again and again
clang and clatter shattered the night's silence;
dread numbed the North-Danes, seized all
who heard the shrieking from the wall,
the enemy of God's grisly lay of terror,
his song of defeat, heard hell's captive
keening over his wound. Beowulf held him fast,
he who was the strongest of all men   780
ever to have seen the light of life on earth.
By no means did the defender of thanes
allow the murderous caller to escape with his life;
he reckoned that the rest of Grendel's days
were useless to anyone. Then, time and again,
Beowulf's band brandished their ancestral swords;
they longed to save the life, if they
so could, of their lord, the mighty leader.
When they did battle on Beowulf's behalf,
struck at the monster from every side,   790
eager for his end, those courageous warriors
were unaware that no war-sword,

not even the finest iron on earth,
could wound their evil enemy,
for he had woven a secret spell
against every kind of weapon, every battle blade.
Grendel's death, his departure from this world,
was destined to be wretched, his migrating spirit
was fated to travel far into the power of fiends.
Then he who for years had committed crimes   800
against mankind, murderous in mind,
and had warred with God, discovered
that the strength of his body could not save him,
that Hygelac's brave kinsman held his hand
in a vice-like grip; each was a mortal enemy
to the other. The horrible monster
suffered grievous pain; a gaping wound
opened on his shoulder; the sinews sprang apart,
the muscles were bursting. Glory in battle
was given to Beowulf; fatally wounded,   810
Grendel was obliged to make for the marshes,
head for his joyless lair. He was
well aware that his life's days were done,
come to an end. After that deadly encounter
the desire of every Dane was at last accomplished.
    In this way did the wise and fearless man
who had travelled from far cleanse Hrothgar's hall,
release it from affliction. He rejoiced in his night's work,
his glorious achievement. The leader of the Geats
made good his boast to the East-Danes;   820
he had removed the cause of their distress,
put an end to the sorrow every Dane had shared,
the bitter grief that they had been constrained
to suffer. When Beowulf, brave in battle,
placed hand, arm and shoulder—Grendel's
entire grasp—under Heorot's spacious roof,
that was evidence enough of victory.
    Then I have heard that next morning
many warriors gathered round the gift-hall;
leaders of men came from every region,   830
from remote parts, to look on the wonder,
the tracks of the monster. Grendel's death
seemed no grievous loss to any of the men
who set eyes on the spoor of the defeated one,
saw how he, weary in spirit, overcome in combat,
fated and put to flight, had made for the lake
of water-demons—leaving tracks of life-blood.
    There the water boiled because of the blood;
the fearful swirling waves reared up,
mingled with hot blood, battle gore;   840
fated, he hid himself, then joyless
laid aside his life, his heathen spirit,

in the fen lair; hell received him there.
    After this, the old retainers left the lake
and so did the company of young men too;
brave warriors rode back on their gleaming horses
from this joyful journey. Then Beowulf's exploit
was acclaimed; many a man asserted
time and again that there was no better
shield-bearer in the whole world, to north or south   850
between the two seas, under the sky's expanse,
no man more worthy of his own kingdom.
Yet they found no fault at all with their friendly lord,
gracious Hrothgar—he was a great king.
    At times the brave warriors spurred their bays,
horses renowned for their speed and stamina,
and raced each other where the track was suitable.
And now and then one of Hrothgar's thanes
who brimmed with poetry, and remembered lays,
a man acquainted with ancient traditions   860
of every kind, composed a new song
in correct metre. Most skilfully that man
began to sing of Beowulf's feat,
to weave words together, and fluently
to tell a fitting tale.
                      He recounted all he knew
of Sigemund, the son of Waels;[12] many a strange story
about his exploits, his endurance, and his journeys
to earth's ends; many an episode
unknown or half-known to the sons of men, songs
of feud and treachery. Only Fitela knew of these things,   870
had heard them from Sigemund who liked to talk
of this and that, for he and his nephew
had been companions in countless battles—
they slew many monsters with their swords.
After his death, no little fame attached to Sigemund's name,
that courageous man who had killed the dragon,
guardian of the hoard. Under the grey rock
the son of the prince braved that dangerous deed
alone; Fitela was not with him;
for all that, as fate had it, he impaled   880
the wondrous serpent, pinned it to the rock face
with his patterned sword; the dragon was slain.
Through his own bravery, that warrior ensured
that he could enjoy the treasure hoard
at will; the son of Waels loaded it all
onto a boat, stowed the shining treasure
into the ship; the serpent burned in its own flames.

---

[12] The singer is paying Beowulf a high compliment in comparing him to Sigemund, one of
the greatest Germanic heroes. Since Sigemund was renowned as a dragon-slayer (see ll. 875–
82), the lines may also foreshadow the end of the poem.

Because of all his exploits, Sigemund,
guardian of strong men, was the best known
warrior in the world—so greatly had he prospered—   890
after Heremod's prowess, strength and daring
had been brought to an end, when, battling with giants,
he fell into the power of fiends, and was at once
done to death.[13] He had long endured
surging sorrows, had become a source
of grief to his people, and to all his retainers.
And indeed, in those times now almost forgotten,
many wise men often mourned that great warrior,
for they had looked to him to remedy their miseries;
they thought that the prince's son would prosper   900
and attain his father's rank, would protect his people,
their heirlooms and their citadel, the heroes' kingdom,
land of the Scyldings. Beowulf, Hygelac's kinsman,
was much loved by all who knew him,
by his friends; but Heremod was stained by sin.
    Now and then the brave men raced their horses,
ate up the sandy tracks—and they were so absorbed
that the hours passed easily. Stout-hearted warriors
without number travelled to the high hall
to inspect that wonder; the king himself, too,   910
glorious Hrothgar, guardian of ring-hoards,
came from his quarters with a great company, escorted
his queen and her retinue of maidens into the mead-hall.
Hrothgar spoke—he approached Heorot,
stood on the steps, stared at the high roof
adorned with gold, and at Grendel's hand:
"Let us give thanks at once to God Almighty
for this sight. I have undergone many afflictions,
grievous outrages at Grendel's hands; but God,
Guardian of heaven, can work wonder upon wonder.   920
Until now, I had been resigned,
had no longer believed that my afflictions
would ever end: this finest of buildings
stood stained with battle blood,
a source of sorrow to my counsellors;
they all despaired of regaining this hall
for many years to come, of guarding it from foes,
from devils and demons. Yet now one warrior
alone, through the Almighty's power, has succeeded
where we failed for all our fine plans.   930
Indeed, if she is still alive,
that woman (whoever she was) who gave birth
to such a son, to be one of humankind,
may claim that the Creator was gracious to her

---

[13] Heremod was the Danish king before the legendary Scyld (l. 4). Through the rest of the
poem, he is the prototype of the bad king. (See, for example, ll. 1694ff.)

in her child-bearing. Now, Beowulf,
best of men, I will love you in my heart
like a son; keep to our new kinship
from this day on. You shall lack
no earthly riches I can offer you.
Most often I have honoured a man for less,   940
given treasure to a poorer warrior,
more sluggish in the fight. Through your deeds
you have ensured that your glorious name
will endure for ever. May the Almighty grant you
good fortune, as He has always done before!"
    Beowulf, the son of Ecgtheow, answered:
"We performed that dangerous deed
with good will; at peril we pitted ourselves
against the unknown. I wish so much
that you could have seen him for yourself,   950
that fiend in his trappings, in the throes of death.
I meant to throttle him on that bed of slaughter
as swiftly as possible, with savage grips,
to hear death rattle in his throat
because of my grasp, unless he should escape me.
But I could not detain him, the Lord
did not ordain it—I did not hold my deadly enemy
firm enough for that; the fiend jerked free
with immense power. Yet, so as to save
his life, he left behind his hand,   960
his arm and shoulder; but the wretched monster
has bought himself scant respite;
the evil marauder, tortured by his sins,
will not live the longer, but agony
embraces him in its deadly bonds,
squeezes life out of his lungs; and now this creature,
stained with crime, must await the day of judgement
and his just deserts from the glorious Creator."
    After this, the son of Ecglaf boasted less
about his prowess in battle—when all the warriors,   970
through Beowulf's might, had been enabled
to examine that hand, the fiend's fingers,
nailed up on the gables. Seen from in front,
each nail, each claw of that warlike,
heathen monster looked like steel—
a terrifying spike. Everyone said
that no weapon whatsoever, no proven sword
could possibly harm it, could damage
that battle-hardened, blood-stained hand.
    Then orders were quickly given for the inside of Heorot   980
to be decorated; many servants, both men and women,
bustled about that wine-hall, adorned that building
of retainers. Tapestries, worked in gold,
glittered on the walls, many a fine sight

for those who have eyes to see such things.
That beautiful building, braced within
by iron bands, was badly damaged;
the door's hinges were wrenched; when the monster,
damned by all his crimes, turned in flight,
despairing of his life, the hall roof only   990
remained untouched. Death is not easy
to escape, let him who will attempt it.
Man must go to the grave that awaits him—
fate has ordained this for all who have souls,
children of men, earth's inhabitants—
and his body, rigid on its clay bed,
will sleep there after the banquet.
                                        Then it was time
for Healfdene's son to proceed to the hall,
the king himself was eager to attend the feast.
I have never heard of a greater band of kinsmen   1000
gathered with such dignity around their ring-giver.
Then the glorious warriors sat on the benches,
rejoicing in the feast. Courteously
their kinsmen, Hrothgar and Hrothulf,
quaffed many a mead-cup, confident warriors
in the high hall. Heorot was packed
with feasters who were friends; the time was not yet come
when the Scyldings practised wrongful deeds.[14]
Then Hrothgar gave Beowulf Healfdene's sword,
and a battle banner, woven with gold,   1010
and a helmet and a corslet, as rewards for victory;
many men watched while the priceless, renowned sword
was presented to the hero. Beowulf emptied
the ale-cup in the hall; he had no cause
to be ashamed at those precious gifts.
There are few men, as far as I have heard,
who have given four such treasures, gleaming with gold,
to another on the mead-bench with equal generosity.
A jutting ridge, wound about with metal wires,
ran over the helmet's crown, protecting the skull,   1020
so that well-ground swords, proven in battle,
could not injure the well-shielded warrior
when he advanced against his foes.
Then the guardian of thanes ordered
that eight horses with gold-plated bridles
be led into the courtyard; onto one was strapped
a saddle, inlaid with jewels, skilfully made.
That was the war-seat of the great king,
Healfdene's son, whenever he wanted
to join in the sword-play. That famous man   1030

---

[14]This vague foreshadowing may refer to a story that after Hrothgar died Hrothulf
treacherously deposed and killed Hrothgar's son and successor Hrethric.

never lacked bravery at the front in battle,
when men about him were cut down like corn.
Then the king of the Danes, Ing's descendants,[15]
presented the horses and weapons to Beowulf,
bade him use them well and enjoy them.
Thus the renowned prince, the retainers' gold-warden,
rewarded those fierce sallies in full measure,
with horses and treasure, so that no man
would ever find reason to reproach him fairly.
Furthermore, the guardian of warriors gave   1040
a treasure, an heirloom at the mead-bench,
to each of those men who had crossed the sea
with Beowulf; and he ordered that gold
be paid for that warrior Grendel slew
so wickedly—as he would have slain many another,
had not foreseeing God and the warrior's courage
together forestalled him. The Creator ruled over
all humankind, even as He does today.
Wherefore a wise man will value forethought
and understanding. Whoever lives long   1050
on earth, endures the unrest of these times,
will be involved in much good and much evil.

   Then Hrothgar, leader in battle, was entertained
with music—harp and voice in harmony.
The strings were plucked, many a song rehearsed,
when it was the turn of Hrothgar's poet
to please men at the mead-bench, perform in the hall.
He sang of Finn's troop, victims of surprise attack,
and of how that Danish hero, Hnaef of the Scyldings,
was destined to die among the Frisian slain.[16]   1060

   Hildeburh, indeed, could hardly recommend
the honour of the Jutes; that innocent woman
lost her loved ones, son and brother,
in the shield-play; they fell, as fate ordained,
stricken by spears; and she was stricken with grief.
Not without cause did Hoc's daughter
mourn the shaft of fate, for in the light of morning
she saw that her kin lay slain under the sky,
the men who had been her endless pride
and joy. That encounter laid claim   1070
to all but a few of Finn's thanes,

[15] An older name for the Danes. Ing was a legendary Danish king.

[16] The story that the harpist tells is also the subject of a fragmentary Old English lay called *The Finnsburh Fragment.*.Finn, king of the Jutes (Frisians), married Hildeburh, daughter of the Danish king Hoc. During a visit from Hildeburh's brother Hnaef, who has succeeded to the Danish throne, to Finnsburh (Finn's stronghold), a quarrel breaks out between the Jutes and the Danes of Hnaef's party, and many are killed, including Hnaef and Finn's and Hildeburh's son. Hengest succeeds Hnaef as king of the Danes, and an uneasy truce is arranged which requires the Danes to live at peace with Finn, who has slain their king. After a winter of resentment and tension, violence breaks out again; Hengest and the Danes kill Finn and take Hildeburh back to Denmark.

and he was unable to finish that fight
with Hnaef's retainer, with Hengest in the hall,
unable to dislodge the miserable survivors;
indeed, terms for a truce were agreed:
that Finn should give up to them another hall,
with its high seat, in its entirety,
which the Danes should own in common with the Jutes;
and that at the treasure-giving the son of Folcwalda[17]
should honour the Danes day by day,   1080
should distribute rings and gold-adorned gifts
to Hengest's band and his own people in equal measure.
Both sides pledged themselves to this peaceful
settlement. Finn swore Hengest solemn oaths
that he would respect the sad survivors
as his counsellors ordained, and that no man there
must violate the covenant with word or deed,
or complain about it, although they
would be serving the slayer of their lord
(as fate had forced those lordless men to do);   1090
and he warned the Frisians that if, in provocation,
they should mention the murderous feud,
the sword's edge should settle things.
The funeral fire was prepared, glorious gold
was brought up from the hoard: the best of Scyldings,[18]
that race of warriors, lay ready on the pyre.
Blood-stained corslets, and images of boars
(cast in iron and covered in gold)
were plentiful on that pyre, and likewise the bodies
of many retainers, ravaged by wounds;   1100
renowned men fell in that slaughter.
Then Hildeburh asked that her own son
be committed to the flames at her brother's funeral,
that his body be consumed on Hnaef's pyre.
That grief-stricken woman keened over his corpse,
sang doleful dirges. The warriors' voices
soared towards heaven. And so did the smoke
from the great funeral fire that roared
before the barrow; heads sizzled,
wounds split open, blood burst out   1110
from battle scars. The ravenous flames
swallowed those men whole, made no distinction
between Frisians and Danes; the finest men departed.
Then those warriors,[19] their friends lost to them,
went to view their homes, revisit the stronghold
and survey the Frisian land. But Hengest
stayed with Finn, in utter dejection, all through
that blood-stained winter. And he dreamed
of his own country, but he was unable to steer

---

[17] Finn.   [18] Hnaef.   [19] The Jutish survivors.

his ship homeward, for the storm-beaten sea 1120
wrestled with the wind; winter sheathed the waves
in ice—until once again spring made its sign
(as still it does) among the houses of men:
clear days, warm weather, in accordance as always
with the law of the seasons. Then winter was over,
the face of the earth was fair; the exile
was anxious to leave that foreign people
and the Frisian land. And yet he brooded
more about vengeance than about a voyage,
and wondered whether he could bring about a clash 1130
so as to repay the sons of the Jutes.
Thus Hengest did not shrink from the duty of vengeance
after Hunlafing had placed the flashing sword,
finest of all weapons, on his lap;[20]
this sword's edges had scarred many Jutes.
And so it was that cruel death by the sword later
cut down the brave warrior Finn in his own hall,
after Guthlaf and Oslaf, arrived from a sea-journey,
had fiercely complained of that first attack,
condemned the Frisians on many scores: 1140
the Scyldings' restless spirits could no longer
be restrained. Then the hall ran red with the blood
of the enemy—Finn himself was slain,
the king with his troop, and Hildeburh was taken.
The Scylding warriors carried that king's
heirlooms down to their ship,
all the jewels and necklaces they discovered
at Finn's hall. They sailed over the sea-paths,
brought that noble lady back to Denmark
and her own people.

                  Thus was the lay sung, 1150
the song of the poet. The hall echoed with joy,
waves of noise broke out along the benches;
cup-bearers carried wine in glorious vessels.
Then Wealhtheow, wearing her golden collar, walked
to where Hrothgar and Hrothulf were sitting side by side,
uncle and nephew, still friends together, true to one another.
And the spokesman Unferth sat at the feet
of the Danish lord; all men admired
his spirit and audacity, although he had deceived
his own kinsmen in a feud. Then the lady of the Scyldings 1160
spoke these words: "Accept this cup, my loved lord,
treasure-giver; O gold-friend of men,
learn the meaning of joy again, and speak words
of gratitude to the Geats, for so one ought to do.

---

[20]Hunlafing means "son of Hunlaf." Hunlaf was apparently one of the Danes killed in Finnsburh and the brother of the Guthlaf and Oslaf mentioned in l. 1138. By placing his dead father's sword in Hengest's lap, Hunlafing is calling for vengeance.

And be generous to them too, mindful of gifts
which you have now amassed from far and wide.
I am told you intend to adopt this warrior,
take him for your son. This resplendent ring-hall,
Heorot, has been cleansed; give many rewards
while you may, but leave this land and the Danish people   1170
to your own descendants when the day comes
for you to die. I am convinced
that gracious Hrothulf will guard our children
justly, should he outlive you, lord of the Scyldings,
in this world; I believe he will repay our sons
most generously if he remembers all we did
for his benefit and enjoyment when he was a boy."
Then Wealhtheow walked to the bench where her sons,
Hrethric and Hrothmund, sat with the sons of thanes,
fledgling warriors; where also that brave man,   1180
Beowulf of the Geats, sat beside the brothers.
To him she carried the cup, and asked in gracious words
if he would care to drink; and to him she presented
twisted gold with courtly ceremonial—
two armlets, a corslet and many rings,
and the most handsome collar in the world.
I have never heard that any hero had a jewel
to equal that, not since Hama made off
for his fortress with the Brosings' necklace, that pendant
in its precious setting; he fled from the enmity   1190
of underhand Eormenric, he chose long-lasting gain.[21]
Hygelac the Geat, grandson of Swerting,
wore that necklace on his last raid
when he fought beneath his banner to defend his treasure,
his battle spoils; fate claimed him then,
when he, foolhardy, courted disaster,
a feud with the Frisians. On that occasion the famous prince
had carried the treasure, the priceless stones,
over the cup of the waves; he crumpled under his shield.
Then the king's body fell into the hands of Franks,   1200
his coat of mail and the collar also;
after that battle, weaker warriors picked at
and plundered the slain; many a Geat lay dead, guarding
that place of corpses.[22]

[21] The Brosings' necklace had been worn by the goddess Freya. Nothing is known of its
theft by Hama except what is given here. Eormenric was a famous king of the East Goths in
the fourth century. To "choose long-lasting gain" is to become a Christian and give up worldly
goods.

[22] The episode that is the subject of this digression is referred to three other times in the
poem: ll. 2340ff., 2492ff., and 2902ff. Hygelac, Beowulf's king, rashly led a raid on the
Frisians. He and his troop seized many Frisian treasures but on their way home by ship they
were attacked by Franks. Hygelac was killed. Beowulf killed Daeghrefn, the Frankish champion and standard-bearer, and escaped by swimming back to Geatland. There he was first
advisor to Heardred, Hygelac's young son and successor, and later king.

Applause echoed in the hall.
Wealhtheow spoke these words before the company:
"May you, Beowulf, beloved youth, enjoy
with all good fortune this necklace and corslet,
treasures of the people; may you always prosper;
win renown through courage, and be kind in your counsel
to these boys; for that, I will reward you further.   1210
You have ensured that men will always sing
your praises, even to the ends of the world,
as far as oceans still surround cliffs,
home of the winds. May you thrive, O prince,
all your life. I hope you will amass
a shining hoard of treasure. O happy Beowulf,
be gracious in your dealing with my sons.
Here, each warrior is true to the others,
gentle of mind, loyal to his lord;
the thanes are as one, the people all alert,   1220
the warriors have drunk well. They will do as I ask."
    Then Wealhtheow retired to her seat
beside her lord. That was the best of banquets,
men drank their fill of wine; they had not tasted
bitter destiny, the fate that had come and claimed
many of the heroes at the end of dark evenings,
when Hrothgar the warrior had withdrawn
to take his rest. Countless retainers
defended Heorot as they had often done before;
benches were pushed back; the floor was padded   1230
with beds and pillows. But one of the feasters
lying on his bed was doomed, and soon to die.
They set their bright battle-shields
at their heads. Placed on the bench
above each retainer, his crested helmet,
his linked corslet and sturdy spear-shaft
were plainly to be seen. It was their habit,
both at home and in the field,
to be prepared for battle always,
for any occasion their lord might need   1240
assistance; that was a loyal band of retainers.
    And so they slept. One man paid a heavy price
for his night's rest, as often happened
after Grendel first held the gold-hall
and worked his evil in it, until he met his doom,
death for his crimes. For afterwards it became clear,
and well known to the Scyldings, that some avenger
had survived the evil-doer, still lived after
that grievous, mortal combat.
                                Grendel's mother
was a monster of a woman; she mourned her fate—   1250
she who had to live in the terrible lake,

the cold water streams, after Cain slew
his own brother, his father's son,
with a sword; he was outlawed after that;
a branded man, he abandoned human joys,
wandered in the wilderness. Many spirits, sent
by fate, issued from his seed; one of them, Grendel,
that hateful outcast, was surprised in the hall
by a vigilant warrior spoiling for a fight.
Grendel gripped and grabbed him there,   1260
but the Geat remembered his vast strength,
that glorious gift given him of God,
and put his trust for support and assistance
in the grace of the Lord; thus he overcame
the envoy of hell, humbled his evil adversary.
So the joyless enemy of mankind journeyed
to the house of the dead. And then Grendel's mother,
mournful and ravenous, resolved to go
on a grievous journey to avenge her son's death.

    Thus she reached Heorot; Ring-Danes, snoring,   1270
were sprawled about the floor. The thanes suffered
a serious reverse as soon as Grendel's mother
entered the hall. The terror she caused,
compared to her son, equalled the terror
an Amazon inspires as opposed to a man,
when the ornamented sword, forged on the anvil,
the razor-sharp blade stained with blood,
shears through the boar-crested helmets of the enemy.
Then swords were snatched from benches, blades
drawn from scabbards, many a broad shield   1280
was held firmly in the hall; none could don helmet
or spacious corslet—that horror caught them by surprise.
The monster wanted to make off for the moors,
fly for her life, as soon as she was found out.
Firmly she grasped one of the thanes
and made for the fens as fast as she could.
That man whom she murdered even as he slept
was a brave shield-warrior, a well-known thane,
most beloved by Hrothgar of all his hall retainers
between the two seas. Beowulf was not there;   1290
the noble Geat had been allotted another lodging
after the giving of treasure earlier that evening.
Heorot was in uproar; she seized her son's
blood-crusted hand; anguish once again
had returned to the hall. What kind of bargain
was that, in which both sides forfeited
the lives of friends?
                  Then the old king,
the grizzled warrior, was convulsed with grief
when he heard of the death of his dearest retainer.

Immediately Beowulf, that man blessed with victory,   1300
was called to the chamber of the king. At dawn
the noble warrior and his friends, his followers,
hurried to the room where the wise man was waiting,
waiting and wondering whether the Almighty
would ever allow an end to their adversity.
Then Beowulf, brave in battle, crossed
the floor with his band—the timbers thundered—
and greeted the wise king, overlord of Ing's
descendants; he asked if the night had passed off
peacefully, since his summons was so urgent.   1310
  Hrothgar, guardian of the Scyldings, said:
"Do not speak of peace; grief once again
afflicts the Danish people. Yrmenlaf's
elder brother, Aeschere, is dead,
my closest counsellor and my comrade,
my shoulder-companion when we shielded
our heads in the fight, when soldiers clashed on foot,
slashed at boar-crests. Aeschere was all
that a noble man, a warrior should be.
The wandering, murderous monster slew him   1320
in Heorot; and I do not know where that ghoul,
drooling at her feast of flesh and blood,
made off afterwards. She has avenged her son
whom you savaged yesterday with vice-like holds
because he had impoverished and killed my people
for many long years. He fell in mortal combat,
forfeit of his life; and now another mighty
evil ravager has come to avenge her kinsman;
and many a thane, mournful in his mind
for his treasure-giver, may feel she has avenged   1330
that feud already, indeed more than amply;
now that hand lies still which once sustained you.
  I have heard my people say,
men of this country, counsellors in the hall,
that they have seen *two* such beings,
equally monstrous, rangers of the fell-country,
rulers of the moors; and these men assert
that so far as they can see one bears
a likeness to a woman; grotesque though he was,
the other who trod the paths of exile looked like a man,   1340
though greater in height and build than a goliath;
he was christened *Grendel* by my people
many years ago; men do not know if he
had a father, a fiend once begotten
by mysterious spirits. These two live
in a little-known country, wolf-slopes, windswept headlands,
perilous paths across the boggy moors, where a mountain stream
plunges under the mist-covered cliffs,

rushes through a fissure. It is not far from here,
if measured in miles, that the lake stands   1350
shadowed by trees stiff with hoar-frost.
A wood, firmly-rooted, frowns over the water.
There, night after night, a fearful wonder may be seen—
fire on the water; no man alive
is so wise as to know the nature of its depths.
Although the moor-stalker, the stag with strong horns,
when harried by hounds will make for the wood,
pursued from afar, he will succumb
to the hounds on the brink, rather than plunge in
and save his head. That is not a pleasant place.   1360
When the wind arouses the wrath of the storm,
whipped waves rear up black from the lake,
reach for the skies, until the air becomes misty,
the heavens weep. Now, once again, help may be had
from you alone. As yet, you have not seen the haunt,
the perilous place where you may meet this most evil monster
face to face. Do you dare set eyes on it?
If you return unscathed, I will reward you
for your audacity, as I did before,
with ancient treasures and twisted gold."   1370
    Beowulf, the son of Ecgtheow, answered:
"Do not grieve, wise Hrothgar! Better each man
should avenge his friend than deeply mourn.
The days on earth for every one of us
are numbered; he who may should win renown
before his death; that is a warrior's
best memorial when he has departed from this world.
Come, O guardian of the kingdom, let us lose
no time but track down Grendel's kinswoman.
I promise you that wherever she turns—   1380
to honeycomb caves, to mountain woods,
to the bottom of the lake—she shall find no refuge.
Shoulder your sorrows with patience
this day; this is what I expect of you."
    Then the old king leapt up, poured out his gratitude
to God Almighty for the Geat's words.
Hrothgar's horse, his stallion with plaited mane,
was saddled and bridled; the wise ruler
set out in full array; his troop of shield-bearers
fell into step. They followed the tracks   1390
along forest paths and over open hill-country
for mile after mile; the monster had made
for the dark moors directly, carrying the corpse
of the foremost thane of all those
who, with Hrothgar, had guarded the hall.
Then the man of noble lineage left Heorot far behind,
followed narrow tracks, string-thin paths
over steep, rocky slopes—remote parts

with beetling crags and many lakes
where water-demons lived. He went ahead   1400
with a handful of scouts to explore the place;
all at once he came upon a dismal wood,
mountain trees standing on the edge
of a grey precipice; the lake lay beneath,
blood-stained and turbulent. The Danish retainers
were utterly appalled when they came upon
the severed head of their comrade Aeschere
on the steep slope leading down to the lake;
all the thanes were deeply distressed.

    The water boiled with blood, with hot gore;   1410
the warriors gaped at it. At times the horn sang
an eager battle-song. The brave men all sat down;
then they saw many serpents in the water,
strange sea-dragons swimming in the lake,
and also water-demons, lying on cliff-ledges,
monsters and serpents of the same kind
as often, in the morning, molest ships
on the sail-road. They plunged to the lake bottom,
bitter and resentful, rather than listen
to the song of the horn. The leader of the Geats   1420
picked off one with his bow and arrow,
ended its life; the metal tip
stuck in its vitals; it swam more sluggishly
after that, as the life-blood ebbed from its body;
in no time this strange sea-dragon
bristled with barbed boar-spears, was subdued
and drawn up onto the cliff; men examined
that disgusting enemy.
                Beowulf donned
his coat of mail, did not fear for his own life.
His massive corslet, linked by hand   1430
and skilfully adorned, was to essay the lake—
it knew how to guard the body, the bone-chamber,
so that his foe's grasp, in its malicious fury,
could not crush his chest, squeeze out his life;
and his head was guarded by the gleaming helmet
which was to explore the churning waters,
stir their very depths; gold decorated it,
and it was hung with chain-mail, as the weapon smith
had wrought it long before, wondrously shaped it
and beset it with boar-images, so that   1440
afterwards no battle-blade could do it damage.
Not least amongst his mighty aids was Hrunting,
the long-hilted sword Unferth lent him in his need;
it was one of the finest of heirlooms; the iron blade
was engraved with deadly, twig-like patterning,
tempered with battle blood. It had not failed
any of those men who had held it in their hands,

risked themselves on hazardous exploits,
pitted themselves against foes. That was not
the first time it had to do a hard day's work.   1450
Truly, when Ecglaf's son, himself so strong,
lent that weapon to his better as a swordsman,
he had forgotten all those taunts he flung
when tipsy with wine; he dared not chance
his own arm under the breakers, dared not
risk his life; at the lake he lost
his renown for bravery. It was not so with Beowulf
once he had armed himself for battle.
    The Geat, son of Ecgtheow, spoke:
"Great son of Healfdene, gracious ruler,   1460
gold-friend of men, remember now—
for I am now ready to go—
what we agreed if I, fighting on your behalf,
should fail to return: that you would always
be like a father to me after I had gone.
Guard my followers, my dear friends,
if I die in battle; and, beloved Hrothgar,
send to Hygelac the treasures you gave me.
When the lord of the Geats, Hrethel's son,
sees those gifts of gold, he will know   1470
that I found a noble giver of rings
and enjoyed his favour for as long as I lived.
And, O Hrothgar, let renowned Unferth
have the ancient treasure, the razor sharp
ornamented sword; and I will make my name
with Hrunting, or death will destroy me."
    After these words the leader of the Geats
dived bravely from the bank, did not even
wait for an answer; the seething water
received the warrior. A full day elapsed   1480
before he could perceive the bottom of the lake.
    She who had guarded the lake's length and breadth
for fifty years, vindictive, fiercely ravenous for blood,
soon realized that one of the race of men
was looking down into the monsters' lair.
Then she grasped him, clutched the Geat
in her ghastly claws; and yet she did not
so much as scratch his skin; his coat of mail
protected him; she could not penetrate
the linked metal rings with her loathsome fingers.   1490
Then the sea-wolf dived to the bottom-most depths,
swept the prince to the place where she lived,
so that he, for all his courage, could not
wield a weapon; too many wondrous creatures
harassed him as he swam; many sea-serpents
with savage tusks tried to bore through his corslet,
the monsters molested him. Then the hero saw

that he had entered some loathsome hall
in which there was no water to impede him,
a vaulted chamber where the floodrush 1500
could not touch him. A light caught his eye,
a lurid flame flickering brightly.
   Then the brave man saw the sea-monster,
fearsome, infernal; he whirled his blade,
swung his arm with all his strength,
and the ring-hilted sword sang a greedy war-song
on the monster's head. Then that guest realized
that his gleaming blade could not bite into her flesh,
break open her bone-chamber; its edge failed Beowulf
when he needed it; yet it had endured 1510
many a combat, sheared often through the helmet,
split the corslet of a fated man; for the first time
that precious sword failed to live up to its name.
   Then, resolute, Hygelac's kinsman took his courage
in both hands, trusted in his own strength.
Angrily the warrior hurled Hrunting away,
the damascened sword with serpent patterns on its hilt;
tempered and steel-edged, it lay useless on the earth.
Beowulf trusted in his own strength,
the might of his hand. So must any man 1520
who hopes to gain long-lasting fame
in battle; he must risk his life, regardless.
Then the prince of the Geats seized the shoulder
of Grendel's mother—he did not mourn their feud;
when they grappled, that brave man in his fury
flung his mortal foe to the ground.
Quickly she came back at him, locked him
in clinches and clutched at him fearsomely.
Then the greatest of warriors stumbled and fell.
She dropped on her hall-guest, drew her dagger, 1530
broad and gleaming; she wanted to avenge her son,
her only offspring. The woven corslet
that covered his shoulders saved Beowulf's life,
denied access to both point and edge.
Then Ecgtheow's son, leader of the Geats,
would have died far under the wide earth
had not his corslet, his mighty chain-mail,
guarded him, and had not holy God
granted him victory; the wise Lord,
Ruler of the Heavens, settled the issue 1540
easily after the hero had scrambled to his feet.
   Then Beowulf saw among weapons an invincible sword
wrought by the giants, massive and double-edged,
the joy of many warriors; that sword was matchless,
well-tempered and adorned, forged in a finer age,
only it was so huge that no man but Beowulf
could hope to handle it in the quick of combat.

Ferocious in battle, the defender of the Scyldings
grasped the ringed hilt, swung the ornamented sword
despairing of his life—he struck such a savage blow   1550
that the sharp blade slashed through her neck,
smashed the vertebrae; it severed her head
from the fated body; she fell at his feet.
The sword was bloodstained; Beowulf rejoiced.

   A light gleamed; the chamber was illumined
as if the sky's bright candle were shining
from heaven. Hygelac's thane inspected
the vaulted room, then walked round the walls,
fierce and resolute, holding the weapon firmly
by the hilt. The sword was not too large   1560
for the hero's grasp, but he was eager to avenge
at once all Grendel's atrocities,
all the many visits the monster had inflicted
on the West-Danes—which began with the time
he slew Hrothgar's sleeping hearth-companions,
devoured fifteen of the Danish warriors
even as they slept, and carried off as many more,
a monstrous prize. But the resolute warrior
had already repaid him to such a degree
that he now saw Grendel lying on his death-bed,   1570
his life's-blood drained because of the wound
he had sustained in battle at Heorot. Then Grendel's corpse
received a savage blow at the hero's hands,
his body burst open: Beowulf lopped off his head.

   At once the wise men, anxiously gazing at
the lake with Hrothgar, saw that the water
had begun to chop and churn, that the waves
were stained with blood. The grey-haired Scyldings
discussed that bold man's fate, agreed
there was no hope of seeing that brave thane again—   1580
no chance that he would come, rejoicing in victory,
before their renowned king; it seemed certain
to all but a few that the sea-wolf had destroyed him.

   Then the ninth hour came. The noble Scyldings
left the headland; the gold-friend of men
returned to Heorot; the Geats, sick at heart,
sat down and stared at the lake.
Hopeless, they yet hoped to set eyes
on their dear lord.
                         Then the battle-sword
began to melt like a gory icicle   1590
because of the monster's blood. Indeed,
it was a miracle to see it thaw entirely,
as does ice when the Father (He who ordains
all times and seasons) breaks the bonds of frost,
unwinds the flood fetters; He is the true Lord.
The leader of the Geats took none of the treasures

away from the chamber—though he saw many there—
except the monster's head and the gold-adorned
sword-hilt; the blade itself had melted,
the patterned sword had burnt, so hot was that blood,   1600
so poisonous the monster who had died in the cave.
He who had survived the onslaught of his enemies
was soon on his way, swimming up through the water;
when the evil monster ended his days on earth,
left this transitory life, the troubled water
and all the lake's expanse was purged of its impurity.
    Then the fearless leader of the seafarers
swam to the shore, exulting in his plunder,
the heavy burdens he had brought with him.
The intrepid band of thanes hurried towards him,   1610
giving thanks to God, rejoicing
to see their lord safe and sound of limb.
The brave man was quickly relieved of his helmet
and corslet.   The angry water under the clouds,
the lake stained with battle-blood, at last became calm.
    Then they left the lake with songs on their lips,
retraced their steps along the winding paths
and narrow tracks; it was no easy matter
for those courageous men, bold as kings,
to carry the head away from the cliff   1620
overlooking the lake. With utmost difficulty
four of the thanes bore Grendel's head
to the gold-hall on a battle-pole;
thus the fourteen Geats, unbroken
in spirit and eager in battle, very soon
drew near to Heorot; with them, that bravest
of brave men crossed the plain towards the mead-hall.
Then the fearless leader of the thanes,
covered with glory, matchless in battle,
once more entered Heorot to greet Hrothgar.   1630
Grendel's head was carried by the hair
onto the floor where the warriors were drinking,
a ghastly thing paraded before the heroes and the queen.
Men stared at that wondrous spectacle.
    Beowulf, the son of Ecgtheow, said:
"So, son of Healfdene, lord of the Scyldings,
we proudly lay before you plunder from the lake;
this head you look at proves our success.
I barely escaped with my life from that combat
under the water, the risk was enormous;   1640
our encounter would have ended at once if God
had not guarded me. Mighty though it is,
Hrunting was no use at all in the battle;
but the Ruler of men—how often He guides
the friendless one—granted that I

should see a huge ancestral sword hanging,
shining, on the wall; I unsheathed it.
Then, at the time destiny decreed, I slew
the warden of the hall. And when the blood,
the boiling battle-blood burst from her body,   1650
that sword burnt, the damascened blade
was destroyed. I deprived my enemies
of that hilt; I repaid them as they deserved
for their outrages, murderous slaughter of the Danes.
I promise, then, O prince of the Scyldings,
that you can sleep in Heorot without anxiety,
rest with your retainers, with all the thanes
among your people—experienced warriors
and striplings together—without further fear
of death's shadow skulking near the hall."   1660
    Then the golden hilt, age-old work of giants,
was given to Hrothgar, the grizzled warrior,
the warlike lord; wrought by master-smiths,
it passed into the hands of the Danish prince
once the demons died; for that embittered fiend,
enemy of God, guilty of murder,
had abandoned this world—and so had his mother.
Thus the hilt was possessed by the best
of earthly kings between the two seas,
the best of those who bestowed gold on Norse men.   1670
    Hrothgar spoke, first examining the hilt,
the ancient heirloom. On it was engraved
the origins of strife in time immemorial,
when the tide of rising water drowned
the race of giants; their end was horrible;
they were opposed to the Eternal Lord,
and their reward was the downpour and the flood.
Also, on the sword-guards of pure gold,
it was recorded in runic letters, as is the custom,
for whom that sword, finest of blades,   1680
with twisted hilt and serpentine patterning
had first been made.
                        Then Healfdene's wise son
lifted his voice—everyone listened:
"This land's grizzled guardian, who promotes truth
and justice amongst his people, and forgets nothing
though the years pass, can say for certain that this man
is much favoured by fate! Beowulf my friend,
your name is echoed in every country
to earth's end. You wear your enormous might
with wisdom and with dignity. I shall keep   1690
my promise made when last we spoke. You will
beyond doubt be the shield of the Geats
for days without number, and a source
of strength to warriors.

            Heremod was hardly that
to Ecgwala's sons, the glorious Scyldings;
he grew to spread slaughter and destruction
rather than happiness amongst the Danish people.
In mad rage he murdered his table-companions,
his most loyal followers; it came about
that the great prince cut himself off   1700
from all earthly pleasures, though God had endowed him
with strength and power above all other men,
and had sustained him. For all that, his heart
was filled with savage blood-lust. He never gave
gifts to the Danes, to gain glory. He lived joyless,
agony racked him; he was long an affliction
to his people. Be warned, Beowulf,
learn the nature of nobility. I who tell you
this story am many winters old.
                 It is a miracle
how the mighty Lord in his generosity   1710
gives wisdom and land and high estate
to people on earth; all things are in His power.
At times he allows a noble man's mind to experience
happiness, grants he should rule over a pleasant,
prosperous country, a stronghold of men,
makes subject to him regions of earth,
a wide kingdom, until in his stupidity
there is no end to his ambition.
His life is unruffled—neither old age
nor illness afflict him, no unhappiness   1720
gnaws at his heart, in his land no hatred
flares up in mortal feuds, but all the world
bends to his will. He suffers no setbacks
until the seed of arrogance is sown and grows
within him, while still the watchman slumbers;
how deeply the soul's guardian sleeps
when a man is enmeshed in matters of this world;
the evil archer stands close with his drawn bow,
his bristling quiver. Then the poisoned shaft
pierces his mind under his helmet   1730
and he does not know how to resist
the devil's insidious, secret temptations.
What had long contented him now seems insufficient;
he becomes embittered, begins to hoard
his treasures, never parts with gold rings
in ceremonial splendour; he soon forgets
his destiny and disregards the honours
given him of God, the Ruler of Glory.
In time his transient body wizens and withers,
and dies as fate decrees; then another man   1740
succeeds to his throne who gives treasures and heirlooms
with great generosity; *he* is not obsessed with suspicions.

Arm yourself, dear Beowulf, best of men,
against such diseased thinking; always swallow pride;
remember, renowned warrior, what is more worthwhile—
gain everlasting. Today and tomorrow
you will be in your prime; but soon you will die,
in battle or in bed; either fire or water,
the fearsome elements, will embrace you,
or you will succumb to the sword's flashing edge,   1750
or to the arrow's flight, or to extreme old age;
then your eyes, once bright, will be clouded over;
all too soon, O warrior, death will destroy you.
   I have ruled the Ring-Danes under the skies
for fifty years, shielded them in war
from many tribes of men in this world,
from swords and from ash-spears, and the time had come
when I thought I had no enemies left on earth.
All was changed utterly, gladness
became grief, after Grendel,   1760
my deadly adversary, invaded Heorot.
His visitations caused me continual pain.
Thus I thank the Creator, the Eternal Lord,
that after our afflictions I have lived to see,
to see with my own eyes this blood-stained head.
Now, Beowulf, brave in battle,
go to your seat and enjoy the feast;
tomorrow we shall share many treasures."
   The Geat, full of joy, straightway went
to find his seat as Hrothgar had suggested.   1770
Then, once again, as so often before,
a great feast was prepared for the brave warriors
sitting in the hall.
                The shadows of night
settled over the retainers. The company arose;
the grey-haired man, the old Scylding,
wanted to retire. And the Geat, the shield-warrior,
was utterly exhausted, his bones ached for sleep.
At once the chamberlain—he who courteously
saw to all such needs as a thane,
a travelling warrior, had in those days—   1780
showed him, so limb-weary, to his lodging.
   Then Beowulf rested; the building soared,
spacious and adorned with gold; the guest
slept within until the black raven gaily
proclaimed sunrise. Bright light
chased away the shadows of night.
                  Then the warriors
hastened, the thanes were eager to return
to their own people; the brave seafarer
longed to see his ship, so far from that place.
Then the bold Geat ordered that Hrunting,   1790

that sword beyond price, be brought before Unferth;
he begged him to take it back and thanked him
for the loan of it; he spoke of it as an ally
in battle, and assured Unferth he did not
underrate it: what a brave man he was!
After this the warriors, wearing their chain-mail,
were eager to be off; their leader,
so dear to the Danes, walked to the daïs
where Hrothgar was sitting, and greeted him.
   Beowulf, the son of Ecgtheow, spoke: 1800
"Now we seafarers, who have sailed here from far,
beg to tell you we are eager
to return to Hygelac. We have been happy here,
hospitably entertained; you have treated us kindly.
If I can in any way win more of your affection,
O ruler of men, than I have done already,
I will come at once, eager for combat.
If news reaches me over the seas
that you are threatened by those around you
(just as before enemies endangered you)   1810
I will bring thousands of thanes,
all heroes, to help you. I know that Hygelac,
lord of the Geats, guardian of his people,
will advance me in word and deed
although he is young, so that I can back
these promises with spear shafts, and serve you
with all my strength where you need men.
Should Hrethric, Hrothgar's son, wish
to visit the court of the Geatish king,
he will be warmly welcomed. Strong men   1820
should seek fame in far-off lands."
   Hrothgar replied: "The wise Lord put these words
into your mind; I have never heard a warrior
speak more sagely while still so young.
You are very strong and very shrewd,
you speak with discerning. If your leader,
Hrethel's son, guardian of the people,
were to lose his life by illness or by iron,
by spear or grim swordplay, and if you survived him,
it seems to me that the Geats could not choose   1830
a better man for king, should you wish to rule
the land of your kinsmen. Beloved Beowulf,
the longer I know you, the more I like your spirit.
Because of your exploit, your act of friendship,
there will be an end to the gross outrages,
the old enmity between Geats and Danes;
they will learn to live in peace.
For as long as I rule this spacious land,
heirlooms will be exchanged; many men
will greet their friends with gifts, send them   1840

over the seas where gannets swoop and rise;
the ring-prowed ship will take tokens of esteem,
treasures across the waters. I know the Geats
are honourable to friend and foe alike,
always faithful to their ancient code."
    Then Healfdene's son, guardian of thanes,
gave him twelve treasures in the hall,
told him to go safely with those gifts
to his own dear kinsmen, and to come back soon.
That king, descendant of kings,   1850
leader of the Scyldings, kissed and embraced
the best of thanes; tears streamed down
the old man's face. The more that warrior thought,
wise and old, the more it seemed
improbable that they would meet again,
brave men in council. He so loved Beowulf
that he could not conceal his sense of loss;
but in his heart and in his head,
in his very blood, a deep love burned   1860
for that dear man.
                              Then Beowulf the warrior,
proudly adorned with gold, crossed the plain,
exulting in his treasure. The ship
rode at anchor, waiting for its owner.
Then, as they walked, they often praised
Hrothgar's generosity. He was an altogether
faultless king, until old age deprived him
of his strength, as it does most men.
    Then that troop of brave young retainers
came to the water's edge; they wore ring-mail,   1870
woven corslets. And the same watchman
who had seen them arrive saw them now returning.
He did not insult them, ask for explanations,
but galloped from the cliff-top to greet the guests;
he said that those warriors in gleaming armour,
so eager to embark, would be welcomed home.
Then the spacious ship, with its curved prow,
standing ready on the shore, was laden with armour,
with horses and treasure. The mast towered
over Hrothgar's precious heirlooms.   1880
    Beowulf gave a sword bound round with gold
to the ship's watchman—a man who thereafter
was honoured on the mead-bench that much the more
on account of this heirloom.
                              The ship surged forward,
butted the waves in deep waters;
it drew away from the shores of the Scyldings.
Then a sail, a great sea-garment, was fastened
with guys to the mast; the timbers groaned;
the boat was not blown off its course

by the stiff sea-breezes. The ship swept   1890
over the waves; foaming at the bows,
the boat with its well-wrought prow sped
over the waters, until at last the Geats
set eyes on the cliffs of their own country,
the familiar headlands; the vessel pressed forward,
pursued by the wind—it ran up onto dry land.
   The harbour guardian hurried down to the shore;
for many days he had scanned the horizon,
anxious to see those dear warriors once more.
He tethered the spacious sea-steed with ropes   1900
(it rode on its painter restlessly)
so that the rolling waves could not wrench it away.
Then Beowulf commanded that the peerless treasures,
the jewels and plated gold, be carried up from the shore.
He had not to go far to find the treasure-giver,
Hygelac son of Hrethel, for his house and the hall
for his companions stood quite close to the sea-wall.
That high hall was a handsome building;
it became the valiant king.
               Hygd, his queen,
Haereth's daughter, was very young; but she   1910
was discerning, and versed in courtly customs,
though she had lived a short time only
in that citadel; and she was not too thrifty,
not ungenerous with gifts of precious treasures
to the Geatish thanes.
             Queen Thryth[23] was proud
and perverse, pernicious to her people.
No hero but her husband, however bold,
dared by day so much as turn his head
in her direction—that was far too dangerous;
but, if he did, he could bargain on being cruelly   1920
bound with hand-plaited ropes; soon
after his seizure, the blade was brought into play,
the damascened sword to settle the issue,
to inflict death. It is not right for a queen,
compelling though her beauty, to behave like this,
for a peace-weaver to deprive a dear man of his life
because she fancies she has been insulted.
But Offa, Hemming's kinsman, put an end to that.
Ale-drinking men in the hall have said
that she was no longer perfidious to her people,   1930
and committed no crimes, once she had been given,
adorned with gold, to that young warrior

---

[23] The story of Queen Thryth is introduced so abruptly as a contrast to Queen Hygd and seems so marginally relevant that many scholars suspect that a transitional passage has been lost. The difficulties of the vocabulary make it uncertain even that her name is Thryth; it may be Modthryth. Offa was a famous fourth-century king of the Continental Angles. The other characters in the story are otherwise unknown.

of noble descent—once she had sailed,
at her father's command, to Offa's court
beyond the pale gold sea. After that,
reformed, she turned her life to good account;
renowned for virtue, she reigned with vision;
and she loved the lord of warriors in the high way
of love—he who was, as I have heard,
the best of all men, the mighty human race,   1940
between the two seas. Offa the brave
was widely esteemed both for his gifts
and his skill in battle; he ruled his land
wisely. He fathered Eomer, guardian
of thanes, who was Hemming's kinsman,
grandson of Garmund, a goliath in battle.

　　Then Beowulf and his warrior band walked
across the sand, tramped over
the wide foreshore; the world's candle shone,
the sun hastening from the south. The men hurried too   1950
when they were told that the guardian of thanes,
Ongentheow's slayer,[24] the excellent young king,
held court in the hall, distributing rings.
Hygelac was informed at once of Beowulf's arrival—
that the shield of warriors, his comrade in battle,
had come back alive to the fortified enclosure,
was heading for the hall unscathed after combat.
Space on the benches for Beowulf and his band
was hastily arranged, as Hygelac ordered.

　　The guardian of thanes formally greeted   1960
that loyal man; then they sat down—
the unfated hero opposite the king,
kinsman facing kinsman. Haereth's daughter
carried mead-cups round the hall,
spoke kindly to the warriors, handed the stoups
of wine to the thanes. Hygelac began
to ask his companion courteous questions
in the high hall; he was anxious to hear
all that had happened to the seafaring Geats:
"Beloved Beowulf, tell me what became of you   1970
after the day you so hurriedly decided
to do battle far from here over the salt waters,
to fight at Heorot. And were you able
to assuage the grief, the well-known sorrow
of glorious Hrothgar? Your undertaking
deeply troubled me; I despaired, dear Beowulf,
of your return. I pleaded with you
not on any account to provoke that monster,

---

[24] The story of the killing of Ongentheow, king of the Scylfings (Swedes), is told later in the poem (ll. 2914–2992). Actually Hygelac did not kill Ongentheow himself, but led the raid in which Ongentheow was killed.

but to let the South-Danes settle their feud
with Grendel themselves. God be praised   1980
that I am permitted to see you safe and home."
  Then Beowulf, the son of Ecgtheow, said:
"Half the world, lord Hygelac, has heard
of my encounter, my great combat
hand to hand with Grendel in that hall
where he had harrowed and long humiliated
the glorious Scyldings. I avenged it all;
none of Grendel's brood, however long
the last of that hateful race survives,   1990
steeped in crime, has any cause to boast about
that dawn combat.
                    First of all,
I went to the ring-hall to greet Hrothgar;
once Healfdene's great son knew of my intentions,
he assigned me a seat beside his own sons.
Then there was revelry; never in my life,
under heaven's vault, have I seen men
happier in the mead-hall. From time to time
the famous queen, the peace-weaver, walked across the floor,
exhorting the young warriors; often she gave   2000
some man a twisted ring before returning to her seat.
At times Hrothgar's daughter, whom I heard
men call Freawaru, carried the ale-horn
right round the hall in front of that brave company,
offered that vessel adorned with precious metals
to the thirsty warriors.
                    Young, and decorated
with gold ornaments, she is promised to Froda's noble son,
Ingeld of the Heathobards; that match was arranged
by the lord of the Scyldings, guardian of the kingdom;
he believes that it is an excellent plan   2010
to use her as a peace-weaver to bury old antagonisms,
mortal feuds. But the deadly spear rarely sleeps
for long after a prince lies dead in the dust,
however exceptional the bride may be!
  For Ingeld, leader of the Heathobards, and all
his retainers will later be displeased when he
and Freawaru walk on the floor—man and wife—
and when Danish warriors are being entertained.
For the guests will gleam with Heathobard heirlooms,
iron-hard, adorned with rings,   2020
precious possessions that had belonged
to their hosts' fathers for as long as they
could wield their weapons, until in the shield-play
they and their dear friends forfeited their lives.
Then, while men are drinking, an old
warrior will speak; a sword he has seen,
marvellously adorned, stirs his memory

of how Heathobards were slain by spears;
he seethes with fury; sad in his heart,
he begins to taunt a young Heathobard,   2030
incites him to action with these words:
    "Do you not recognize that sword, my friend,
the sword your father, fully armed, bore into battle
that last time, when he was slain by Danes,
killed by brave Scyldings who carried the field
when Withergyld fell and many warriors beside him?
See how the son of one of those
who slew him struts about the hall;
he sports the sword; he crows about that slaughter,
and carries that heirloom which is yours by right!"   2040
In this way, with acid words, he will endlessly
provoke him and rake up the past,
until the time will come when a Danish warrior,
Freawaru's thane, sleeps blood-stained,
slashed by the sword, punished by death
for the deeds of his father; and the Heathobard
will escape, well-acquainted with the country.
Then both sides will break the solemn oath
sworn by their leaders; and Ingeld will come
to hate the Scyldings, and his love for his wife   2050
will no longer be the same after such anguish and grief.
Thus I have little faith in friendship with Heathobards;
they will fail to keep their side of the promise,
friendship with the Danes.
                   I have digressed;
Grendel is my subject. Now you must hear,
O treasure-giver, what the outcome was
of that hand-to-hand encounter. When the jewel of heaven
had journeyed over the earth, the angry one,
the terrible night-prowler paid us a visit—
unscathed warriors watching over Heorot.   2060
A fight awaited Hondscio, a horrible end
for that fated man; he was the first to fall;
Grendel tore that famous young retainer to bits
between his teeth, and swallowed the whole body
of that dear man, that girded warrior.
And even then that murderer, mindful of evil,
his mouth caked with blood, was not content
to leave the gold-hall empty-handed
but, famed for his strength, he tackled me,
gripped me with his outstretched hand.   2070
A huge unearthly glove swung at his side,
firmly secured with subtle straps;
it had been made with great ingenuity,
with devils' craft and dragons' skins.
Innocent as I was, the demon monster
meant to shove me in it, and many another

innocent besides; that was beyond him
after I leapt up, filled with fury.
It would take too long to tell you how I repaid
that enemy of men for all his outrages;   2080
but there, my prince, I ennobled your people
with my deeds. Grendel escaped,
and lived a little longer; but he left
behind at Heorot his right hand; and, in utter
wretchedness, sank to the bottom of the lake.
 The sun rose; we sat down together
to feast, then the leader of the Scyldings
paid a good price for the bloody battle,
gave me many a gold-plated treasure.
There was talk and song; the grey-haired Scylding   2090
opened his immense hoard of memories;
now and then a happy warrior touched
the wooden harp, reciting some story,
mournful and true; at times the generous king
recalled in proper detail some strange incident;
and as the shadows lengthened, an aged thane,
cramped and rheumatic, raised his voice
time and again, lamenting his lost youth,
his prowess in battle; worn with winters,
his heart quickened to the call of the past.   2100
 In these ways we relaxed agreeably
throughout the long day until darkness closed in,
another night for men. Then, in her grief,
bent on vengeance, Grendel's mother
hastened to the hall where death had lain
in wait for her son—the battle-hatred
of the Geats. The horrible harridan avenged
her offspring, slew a warrior brazenly.
Aeschere, the wise old counsellor, lost
his life. And when morning came,   2110
the Danes were unable to cremate him,
to place the body of that dear man
on the funeral pyre; for Grendel's mother
had carried if off in her gruesome grasp,
taken it under the mountain lake.
Of all the grievous sorrows Hrothgar
long sustained, none was more terrible.
Then the king in his anger called upon your name
and entreated me to risk my life,
to accomplish deeds of utmost daring   2120
in the tumult of waves; he promised me rewards.
And so, as men now know all over the earth,
I found the grim guardian of the lake-bottom.
For a while we grappled; the water boiled
with blood; then in that battle-hall,
I lopped off Grendel's mother's head

with the mighty sword. I barely escaped
with my life; but I was not fated.
    And afterwards the guardian of thanes,
Healfdene's son, gave me many treasures.   2130
Thus the king observed excellent tradition:
in no wise did I feel unrewarded
for all my efforts, but Healfdene's son
offered me gifts of my own choosing;
gifts, O noble king, I wish now
to give to you in friendship. I still depend
entirely on your favours; I have few
close kinsmen but you, O Hygelac!"
    Then Beowulf caused to be brought in
a standard bearing the image of a boar,   2140
together with a helmet towering in battle,
a grey corslet, and a noble sword; he said:
"Hrothgar, the wise king, gave me
these trappings and purposely asked me
to tell you their history: he said that Heorogar,[25]
lord of the Scyldings, long owned them.
Yet he has not endowed his own brave son,
Heoroweard, with this armour, much as
he loves him. Make good use of everything!"
    I heard that four bays, apple-brown,   2150
were brought into the hall after the armour—
swift as the wind, identical. Beowulf gave them
as he gave the treasures. So should a kinsman do,
and never weave nets with underhand subtlety
to ensnare others, never have designs
on a close comrade's life. His nephew,
brave in battle, was loyal to Hygelac;
each man was mindful of the other's pleasure.
    I heard that he gave Hygd the collar,
the wondrous ornament with which Wealhtheow,   2160
daughter of the prince, had presented him,
and gave her three horses also, graceful creatures
with brightly-coloured saddles; Hygd
wore that collar, her breast was adorned.
    Thus Ecgtheow's son, feared in combat,
confirmed his courage with noble deeds;
he lived a life of honour, he never slew
companions at the feast; savagery was
alien to him, but he, so brave in battle,
made the best use of those ample talents   2170
with which God endowed him.
                    He had been despised
for a long while, for the Geats saw no spark
of bravery in him, nor did their king deem him

---

[25] Heorogar was Hrothgar's elder brother, who preceded him on the Danish throne.

worthy of much attention on the mead-bench;
people thought that he was a sluggard,
a feeble princeling. How fate changed,
changed completely for that glorious man!
   Then the guardian of thanes, the famous king,
ordered that Hrethel's[26] gold-adorned heirloom
be brought in; no sword was so treasured   2180
in all Geatland; he laid it in Beowulf's lap,
and gave him seven thousand hides of land,[27]
a hall and princely throne. Both men
had inherited land and possessions
in that country; but the more spacious kingdom
had fallen to Hygelac, who was of higher rank.

   In later days, after much turmoil,
things happened in this way: when Hygelac lay dead
and murderous battle-blades had beaten down
the shield of his son Heardred,   2190
and when the warlike Swedes, savage warriors,
had hunted him down amongst his glorious people,
attacked Hereric's nephew with hatred,
the great kingdom of the Geats passed
into Beowulf's hands.[28] He had ruled it well
for fifty winters—he was a wise king,
a grizzled guardian of the land—when, on dark nights,
a dragon began to terrify the Geats:
he lived on a cliff, kept watch over a hoard
in a high stone barrow; below, there was   2200
a secret path; a man strayed
into this barrow by chance, seized
some of the pagan treasures, stole drinking vessels.
At first the sleeping dragon was deceived
by the thief's skill, but afterwards he avenged
this theft of gleaming gold; people far and wide,
bands of retainers, became aware of his wrath.
   That man did not intrude upon the hoard
deliberately, he who robbed the dragon;
but it was some slave, a wanderer in distress   2210
escaping from men's anger who entered there,
seeking refuge. He stood guilty of some sin.
As soon as he peered in, the outsider
stiffened with horror. Unhappy as he was,
he stole the vessel, the precious cup.
There were countless heirlooms in that earth-cave,
the enormous legacy of a noble people,

---

[26] Hygelac's father.   [27] A hide was a unit of land measure, usually about 120 acres.
[28] Heardred succeeded his father Hygelac as king of the Geats. The story of the war with
the Swedes in which Heardred died is told more fully later (ll. 2366–2384).

ancient treasures which some man or other
had cautiously concealed there many years
before. Death laid claim to all that people   2220
in days long past, and then that retainer
who outlived the rest, a gold-guardian
mourning his friends, expected the same fate—
thought he would enjoy those assembled heirlooms
a little while only. A newly-built barrow
stood ready on a headland which overlooked
the sea, protected by the hazards of access.
To this barrow the protector of rings brought the heirlooms,
the plated gold, all that part of the precious treasure
worthy of hoarding; then he spoke a few words: 2230
"Hold now, O earth, since heroes could not,
these treasures owned by nobles! Indeed, strong men
first quarried them from you. Death in battle,
ghastly carnage, has claimed all my people—
men who once made merry in the hall
have laid down their lives; I have no one
to carry the sword, to polish the plated vessel,
this precious drinking-cup; all the retainers
have hurried elsewhere. The iron helmet
adorned with gold shall lose its ornaments;   2240
men who should polish battle-masks are sleeping;
the coat of mail, too, that once withstood
the bite of swords in battle, after shields were shattered,
decays like the warriors; the linked mail may no longer
range far and wide with the warrior,
stand side by side with heroes. Gone is the pleasure
of plucking the harp, no fierce hawk
swoops about the hall, nor does the swift stallion
strike sparks in the courtyard. Cruel death
has claimed hundreds of this human race."   2250
     Thus the last survivor mourned time passing,
and roamed about by day and night,
sad and aimless, until death's lightning
struck at his heart.   The aged dragon of darkness
discovered that glorious hoard unguarded,
he who sought out barrows, smooth-scaled
and evil, and flew by night, breathing
fire; the Geats feared him greatly.
He was destined to find the hoard
in that cave and, old in winters, guard   2260
the heathen gold; much good it did him!
     Thus the huge serpent who harassed men
guarded that great stronghold under the earth
for three hundred winters, until
a man enraged him; the wanderer carried
the inlaid vessel to his lord, and begged him

for a bond of peace. Then the hoard was raided
and plundered, and that unhappy man
was granted his prayer. His lord examined
the ancient work of smiths for the first time.   2270
   There was conflict once more after the dragon
awoke; intrepid, he slid swiftly
along by the rock, and found the footprints
of the intruder; that man had skilfully
picked his way right past the dragon's head.
Thus he who is undoomed will easily survive
anguish and exile provided he enjoys
the grace of God. The warden of the hoard
prowled up and down, anxious to find
the man who had pillaged it while he slept.   2280
Breathing fire and filled with fury,
he circled the outside of the earth mound
again and again; but there was no one
in that barren place; yet he exulted at the thought
of battle, bloody conflict; at times he wheeled back
into the barrow, hunting for the priceless heirloom.
He realized at once that one of the race of men
had discovered the gold, the glorious treasure.
Restlessly the dragon waited for darkness;
the guardian of the hoard was bursting with rage,   2290
he meant to avenge the vessel's theft
with fire.
                  Then daylight failed
as the dragon desired; he could no longer
confine himself to the cave but flew in a ball
of flame, burning for vengeance. The Geats
were filled with dread as he began his flight;
it swiftly ended in disaster for their lord.
   Then the dragon began to breathe forth fire,
to burn fine buildings; flame tongues flickered,
terrifying men; the loathsome winged creature   2300
meant to leave the whole place lifeless.
Everywhere the violence of the dragon, the venom
of that hostile one, was clearly to be seen—
how he had wrought havoc, hated and humiliated
the Geatish people. Then, before dawn he rushed back
to his hidden lair and the treasure hoard.
He had girdled the Geats with fire,
with ravening flames; he relied on his own strength,
and on the barrow and the cliff; his trust played him false.
   Then news of that terror was quickly brought   2310
to Beowulf, that flames enveloped
his own hall, best of buildings,
and the gift-throne of the Geats. That good man
was choked with intolerable grief.
Wise that he was, he imagined

he must have angered God, the Lord Eternal,
by ignoring some ancient law; he was seldom
dispirited, but now his heart was like lead.
    The fire dragon had destroyed the fortified hall,
the people's stronghold, and laid waste with flames   2320
the land by the sea. The warlike king,
prince of the Geats, planned to avenge this.
The protector of warriors, leader of men,
instructed the smith to forge a curious shield
made entirely of iron; he well knew
that a linden shield would not last long
against the flames. The eminent prince
was doomed to reach the end of his days on earth,
his life in this world. So too was the dragon,
though he had guarded the hoard for generations.   2330
    Then the giver of gold disdained
to track the dragon with a troop
of warlike men; he did not shrink
from single combat, nor did he set much store
by the fearless dragon's power, for had he not before
experienced danger, again and again
survived the storm of battle, beginning with that time
when, blessed with success, he cleansed
Hrothgar's hall, and crushed in battle
the monster and his vile mother?
                              That grim combat   2340
in which Hygelac was slain—Hrethel's son,
leader of the Geats, dear lord of his people,
struck down by swords in the bloodbath
in Frisia—was far from the least
of his encounters. Beowulf escaped
because of his skill and stamina at swimming;
he waded into the water, bearing no fewer
than thirty corslets, a deadweight on his arms.
But the Frankish warriors who shouldered
their shields against him had no cause to boast   2350
about that combat; a handful only
eluded that hero and returned home.
Then the son of Ecgtheow, saddened and alone,
rode with the white horses[29] to his own people.
Hygd offered him heirlooms there, and even
the kingdom, the ancestral throne itself; for she feared
that her son would be unable to defend it
from foreign invaders now that Hygelac was gone.
But the Geats, for all their anguish, failed
to prevail upon the prince—he declined   2360
absolutely to become Heardred's lord,
or to taste the pleasures of royal power.

---

[29] That is, the waves.

But he stood at his right hand,
ready with advice, always friendly,
and respectful, until the boy came of age
and could rule the Geats himself.
                                    Two exiles,[30]
Ohthere's sons, sailed to Heardred's court;
they had rebelled against the ruler of the Swedes,
a renowned man, the best of sea-kings,
gold-givers in Sweden. By receiving them,   2370
Heardred rationed the days of his life;
in return for his hospitality, Hygelac's son
was mortally wounded, slashed by swords.
Once Heardred lay lifeless in the dust,
Onela, son of Ongentheow, sailed home again;
he allowed Beowulf to inherit the throne
and rule the Geats; he was a noble king!
But Beowulf did not fail with help
after the death of the prince, although years passed;
he befriended unhappy Eadgils, Ohthere's son,   2380
and supplied him with weapons and warriors
beyond the wide seas. Eadgils afterwards
avenged Eanmund, he ravaged and savaged
the Swedes, and killed the king, Onela himself.

   Thus the son of Ecgtheow had survived
these feuds, these fearful battles, these acts
of single combat, up to that day
when he was destined to fight against the dragon.
Then in fury the leader of the Geats set out
with eleven to search for the winged serpent.   2390
By then Beowulf knew the cause of the feud,
bane of men; the famous cup
had come to him through the hands of its finder.
The unfortunate slave who first brought about
such strife made the thirteenth man
in that company—cowed and disconsolate,
he had to be their guide. Much against his will,
he conducted them to the entrance of the cave,
an earth-hall full of filigree work
and fine adornments close by the sea,   2400
the fretting waters. The vile guardian,
the serpent who had long lived under the earth,
watched over the gold, alert; he who hoped
to gain it bargained with his own life.

[30] The two exiles were Eanmund and Eadgils, sons of the Swedish king Ohthere, who had succeeded his father Ongentheow (see ll. 2914–2992). After Ohthere's death, his brother Onela usurped the throne. Eanmund and Eadgils fled to the Geatish court, where Heardred offered them protection. In retaliation, Onela attacked the Geats, killed both Eanmund and Heardred, and left Beowulf in charge of the conquered kingdom. Beowulf eventually helped the surviving son Eadgils overthrow Onela and regain the Swedish throne. (The poem tells this story so elliptically that many of the motivations and alliances remain obscure.)

Then the brave king sat on the headland,
the gold-friend of the Geats wished success
to his retainers. His mind was most mournful,
angry, eager for slaughter; fate hovered
over him, so soon to fall on that old man,
to seek out his hidden spirit, to split   2410
life and body; flesh was to confine
the soul of the king only a little longer.
Beowulf, the son of Ecgtheow, spoke:
"Often and often in my youth I plunged
into the battle maelstrom; how well I remember it.
I was seven winters old when the treasure guardian,
ruler of men, received me from my father.
King Hrethel took me into his ward, reared me,
fed me, gave me gold, mindful of our kinship;
for as long as he lived, he loved me no less   2420
than his own three sons, warriors with me
in the citadel, Herebeald, Haethcyn, and my dear Hygelac.
A death-bed for the firstborn was unrolled
most undeservedly by the action of his kinsman—
Haethcyn drew his horn-tipped bow
and killed his lord-to-be; he missed his mark,
his arrow was stained with his brother's blood.
That deed was a dark sin, sickening
to think of, not to be settled by payment of *wergild;*
yet Herebeald's death could not be requited.   2430
      Thus the old king, Hrethel, is agonized
to see his son, so young, swing
from the gallows.[31] He sings a dirge, a song
dark with sorrow, while his son hangs,
raven's carrion, and he cannot help him
in any way, wise and old as he is.
He wakes each dawn to the ache
of his son's death; he has no desire
for a second son, to be his heir
in the stronghold, now that his firstborn   2440
has finished his days and deeds on earth.
Grieving, he wanders through his son's dwelling,
sees the wine-hall now deserted, joyless,
home of the winds; the riders, the warriors,
sleep in their graves. No longer is the harp
plucked, no longer is there happiness in that place.
Then Hrethel takes to his bed, and intones
dirges for his dead son, Herebeald;
his house and his lands seem empty now,
and far too large. Thus the lord of the Geats   2450
endured in his heart the ebb and flow

---

[31] Since Haethcyn survives and inherits the throne, this hanging is apparently a ritual
hanging of the dead Herebeald, dictated by the fact that he did not die in battle.

of sorrow for his firstborn; but he could not
avenge that feud on the slayer—his own son;
although Hrethel had no love for Haethcyn,
he could no more readily requite death
with death. Such was his sorrow that he lost
all joy in life, chose the light of God;
he bequeathed to his sons, as a wealthy man does,
his citadel and land, when he left this life.
    Then there was strife, savage conflict 2460
between Swedes and Geats; after Hrethel's death
the feud we shared, the fierce hatred
flared up across the wide water.
The sons of Ongentheow, Onela and Ohthere,
were brave and battle-hungry; they had no wish
for peace over the sea but several times,
and wantonly, butchered the people of the Geats
on the slopes of Slaughter Hill. As is well known,
my kinsmen requited that hatred, those crimes;
but one of them paid with his own life— 2470
a bitter bargain; that fight was fatal
to Haethcyn, ruler of the Geats.
Then I heard that in the morning
one kinsman avenged another, repaid
Haethcyn's slayer with the battle-blade,
when Ongentheow attacked the Geat Eofor;
the helmet split, the old Swede fell,
pale in death; Eofor remembered
that feud well enough, his hand and sword
spared nothing in their death-swing. 2480
    I repaid Hygelac for his gifts of heirlooms
with my gleaming blade, repaid him in battle,
as was granted to me; he gave me land
and property, a happy home. He had
no need to hunt out and hire mercenaries—
inferior warriors from the Gepidae,
from the Spear-Danes or from tribes in Sweden;
but I was always at the head of his host,
alone in the van; and I shall still fight
for as long as I live and this sword lasts, 2490
that has often served me early and late
since I became the daring slayer
of Daeghrefn, champion of the Franks.
He was unable to bring adornments,
breast-decorations to the Frisian king,
but fell in the fight bearing the standard,
a brave warrior; it was my battle-grip,
not the sharp blade, that shattered his bones,
silenced his heartbeat. Now the shining edge,
hand and tempered sword, shall engage in battle 2500
for the treasure hoard. I fought many battles

when I was young; yet I will fight again,
the old guardian of my people, and achieve
a mighty exploit if the evil dragon dares
confront me, dares come out of the earth-cave!"
   Then he addressed each of the warriors,
the brave heroes, his dear companions,
a last time: "I would not wield a sword
against the dragon if I could grasp this hideous being
with my hands (and thus make good my boast),   2510
as once I grasped the monster Grendel;
but I anticipate blistering battle-fire,
venomous breath; therefore I have with me
my shield and corslet. I will not give an inch
to the guardian of the mound, but at that barrow
it will befall us both as fate ordains,
every man's master. My spirit is bold,
I will not boast further against the fierce flier.
Watch from the barrow, warriors in armour,
guarded by corslets, which of us will better   2520
weather his wounds after the combat.
This is not your undertaking, nor is it
possible for any man but me alone
to pit his strength against the gruesome one,
and perform great deeds. I will gain the gold
by daring, or else battle, dread destroyer
of life, will lay claim to your lord."
   Then the bold warrior, stern-faced beneath his helmet,
stood up with his shield; sure of his own strength,
he walked in his corslet towards the cliff;   2530
the way of the coward is not thus!
Then that man endowed with noble qualities,
he who had braved countless battles, weathered
the thunder when warrior troops clashed together,
saw a stone arch set in the cliff
through which a stream spurted; steam rose
from the boiling water; he could not stay long
in the hollow near the hoard for fear
of being scorched by the dragon's flames.
Then, such was his fury, the leader of the Geats   2540
threw out his chest and gave a great roar,
the brave man bellowed; his voice, renowned
in battle, hammered the grey rock's anvil.
The guardian of the hoard knew the voice for human;
violent hatred stirred within him. Now no time
remained to entreat for peace. At once
the monster's breath, burning battle vapour,
issued from the barrow; the earth itself snarled.
The lord of the Geats, standing under the cliff,
raised his shield against the fearsome stranger;   2550
then that sinuous creature spoiled

for the fight. The brave and warlike king
had already drawn his keen-edged sword,
(it was an ancient heirloom); a terror of each other
lurked in the hearts of the two antagonists.
While the winged creature coiled himself up,
the friend and lord of men stood unflinching
by his shield; Beowulf waited ready armed.
   Then, fiery and twisted, the dragon swiftly
shrithed towards its fate. The shield protected   2560
the life and body of the famous prince
for far less time than he had looked for.
It was the first occasion in all his life
that fate did not decree triumph for him
in battle. The lord of the Geats raised
his arm, and struck the mottled monster
with his vast ancestral sword; but the bright blade's
edge was blunted by the bone, bit
less keenly than the desperate king required.
The defender of the barrow bristled with anger   2570
at the blow, spouted murderous fire, so that flames
leapt through the air. The gold-friend of the Geats
did not boast of famous victories; his proven sword,
the blade bared in battle, had failed him
as it ought not to have done. That great Ecgtheow's
greater son had to journey on from this world
was no pleasant matter; much against his will,
he was obliged to make his dwelling
elsewhere—sooner or later every man must leave
this transitory life. It was not long   2580
before the fearsome ones closed again.
The guardian of the hoard was filled with fresh hope,
his breast was heaving; he who had ruled a nation
suffered agony, surrounded by flame.
And Beowulf's companions, sons of nobles—
so far from protecting him in a troop together,
unflinching in the fight—shrank back into the forest
scared for their own lives. One man alone
obeyed his conscience. The claims of kinship
can never be ignored by a right-minded man.   2590
   His name was Wiglaf, a noble warrior,
Weohstan's son, kinsman of Aelfhere,
a leader of the Swedes;[32] he saw that his lord,
helmeted, was tormented by the intense heat.
Then he recalled the honours Beowulf had bestowed
on him—the wealthy citadel of the Waegmundings,

---

[32] Wiglaf's father Weohstan seems to have been by blood both Swedish and Geatish. He fought and killed Eanmund on behalf of the Swedish king Onela; perhaps he moved to Geatland after Eadgils, the brother of the man he killed, ascended the Swedish throne. As a member of the Waegmunding family, Wiglaf is a kinsman of Beowulf.

the rights to land his father owned before him.
He could not hold back then; he grasped the round,
yellow shield; he drew his ancient sword,
reputed to be the legacy of Eanmund,   2600
Ohthere's son.
　　　　　　　　Weohstan had slain him
in a skirmish while Eanmund was a wanderer,
a friendless man, and then had carried off
to his own kinsmen the gleaming helmet,
the linked corslet, the ancient sword
forged by giants. It was Onela,
Eanmund's uncle, who gave him that armour,
ready for use; but Onela did not refer to the feud,
though Weohstan had slain his brother's son.
For many years Weohstan owned that war-gear,   2610
sword and corslet, until his son was old enough
to achieve great feats as he himself had done.
Then, when Weohstan journeyed on from the earth,
an old man, he left Wiglaf—who was
with the Geats—a great legacy of armour
of every kind.
　　　　　　　　This was the first time
the young warrior had weathered the battle storm,
standing at the shoulder of his lord.
His courage did not melt, nor did his kinsman's sword
fail him in the fight. The dragon found that out   2620
when they met in mortal combat.
　　Wiglaf spoke, constantly reminding
his companions of their duty—he was mournful.
"I think of that evening we emptied the mead-cup
in the feasting-hall, partook and pledged our lord,
who presented us with rings, that we would repay him
for his gifts of armour, helmets and hard swords,
if ever the need, need such as this, arose.
For this very reason he asked us
to join with him in this journey, deemed us   2630
worthy of renown, and gave me these treasures;
he looked on us as loyal warriors,
brave in battle; even so, our lord,
guardian of the Geats, intended to perform
this feat alone, because of all men
he had achieved the greatest exploits,
daring deeds. Now the day has come
when our lord needs support, the might
of strong men; let us hurry forward
and help our leader as long as fire remains,   2640
fearsome, searing flames. God knows
I would rather that fire embraced my body
beside the charred body of my gold-giver;
it seems wrong to me that we should shoulder

our shields, carry them home afterwards,
unless we can first kill the venomous foe,
guard the prince of the Geats. I know
in my heart his feats of old were such
that he should not now be the only Geat to suffer
and fall in combat; in common we shall share 2650
sword, helmet, corslet, the trappings of war."

   Then that man fought his way through the fumes,
went helmeted to help his lord. He shouted out:
"Brave Beowulf, may success attend you—
for in the days when you were young, you swore
that so long as you lived you would never allow
your fame to decay; now, O resolute king,
renowned for your exploits, you must guard your life
with all your skill. I shall assist you."

   At this the seething dragon attacked a second time; 2660
shimmering with fire the venomous visitor fell on his foes,
the men he loathed. With waves of flame, he burnt
the shield right up to its boss; Wiglaf's
corslet afforded him no protection whatsoever.
But the young warrior still fought bravely, sheltered
behind his kinsman's shield after his own
was consumed by flames. Still the battle-king
set his mind on deeds of glory; with prodigious strength
he struck a blow so violent that his sword stuck
in the dragon's skull. But Naegling snapped! 2670
Beowulf's old grey-hued sword
failed him in the fight. Fate did not ordain
that the iron edge should assist him
in that struggle; Beowulf's hand was too strong.
Indeed I have been told that he overtaxed
each and every weapon, hardened by blood, that he bore
into battle; his own great strength betrayed him.

   Then the dangerous dragon, scourge of the Geats,
was intent a third time upon attack; he rushed
at the renowned man when he saw an opening: 2680
fiery, battle-grim, he gripped the hero's neck
between his sharp teeth; Beowulf was bathed
in blood; it spurted out in streams.
Then, I have heard, the loyal thane
alongside the Geatish king displayed great courage,
strength and daring, as was his nature.
To assist his kinsman, that man in mail
aimed not for the head but lunged at the belly
of their vile enemy (in so doing his hand
was badly burnt); his sword, gleaming and adorned, 2690
sank in up to the hilt and at once the flames
began to abate. The king still had control then
over his senses; he drew the deadly knife,
keen-edged in battle, that he wore on his corslet;

then the lord of the Geats dispatched the dragon.
Thus they had killed their enemy—their courage
enabled them—the brave kinsmen together
had destroyed him. Such should a man,
a thane, be in time of necessity!
                            That was the last
of all the king's achievements, his last   2700
exploit in the world. Then the wound
the earth-dragon had inflicted with his teeth
began to burn and swell; very soon he
was suffering intolerable pain as the poison
boiled within him. Then the wise leader
tottered forward and slumped on a seat
by the barrow; he gazed at the work of giants,
saw how the ancient earthwork contained
stone arches supported by columns.
Then, with his own hands, the best of thanes   2710
refreshed the renowned prince with water,
washed his friend and lord, blood-stained
and battle-weary, and unfastened his helmet.
  Beowulf began to speak, he defied
his mortal injury; he was well aware
that his life's course, with all its delights,
had come to an end; his days on earth
were exhausted, death drew very close:
"It would have made me happy, at this time,
to pass on war-gear to my son, had I   2720
been granted an heir to succeed me,
sprung of my seed. I have ruled the Geats
for fifty winters; no king of any
neighbouring tribe has dared to attack me
with swords, or sought to cow and subdue me.
But in my own home I have awaited
my destiny, cared well for my dependants,
and I have not sought trouble, or sworn
any oaths unjustly. Because of all these things
I can rejoice, drained now by death-wounds;   2730
for the Ruler of Men will have no cause to blame me
after I have died on the count that I deprived
other kinsmen of their lives. Now hurry,
dear Wiglaf; rummage the hoard
under the grey rock, for the dragon sleeps,
riddled with wounds, robbed of his treasure.
Be as quick as you can so that I may see
the age-old golden treasure, and examine
all the priceless, shimmering stones; once I
have set eyes on such a store, it will be   2740
more easy for me to die, to abandon
the life and land that have so long been mine."

Then, I have been told, as soon as he heard
the words of his lord, wounded in battle,
Wiglaf hastened into the earth-cavern,
still wearing his corslet, his woven coat of mail.
After the fierce warrior, flushed with victory,
had walked past a daïs, he came upon
the hoard—a hillock of precious stones,
and gold treasure glowing on the ground;   2750
he saw wondrous wall-hangings; the lair
of the serpent, the aged twilight-flier;
and the stoups and vessels of a people
long dead, now lacking a polisher,
deprived of adornments. There were many old,
rusty helmets, and many an armlet
cunningly wrought. A treasure hoard,
gold in the ground, will survive its owner
easily, whosoever hides it!
And he saw also hanging high   2760
over the hoard a standard fashioned with gold strands,
a miracle of handiwork; a light shone from it,
by which he was able to distinguish the earth
and look at the adornments. There was no sign
of the serpent, the sword had savaged and slain him.
Then I heard that Wiglaf rifled the hoard
in the barrow, the antique work of giants—
he chose and carried off as many cups and salvers
as he could; and he also took the standard,
the incomparable banner; Beowulf's sword,   2770
iron-edged, had injured
the guardian of the hoard, he who had held it
through the ages and fought to defend it
with flames—terrifying, blistering,
ravening at midnight—until he was slain.
Wiglaf hurried on his errand, eager to return,
spurred on by the treasures; in his heart he was troubled
whether he would find the prince of the Geats,
so grievously wounded, still alive
in the place where he had left him.   2780
Then at last he came, carrying the treasures,
to the renowned king; his lord's life-blood
was ebbing; once more he splashed him
with water, until Beowulf revived a little,
began to frame his thoughts.
                      Gazing at the gold,
the warrior, the sorrowing king, said:
"With these words I thank
the King of Glory, the Eternal Lord,
the Ruler, for all the treasures here before me,
that in my lifetime I have been able   2790

to gain them for the Geats.
And now that I have bartered my old life
for this treasure hoard, you must serve
and inspire our people. I will not long be with you.
Command the battle-warriors, after the funeral fire,
to build a fine barrow overlooking the sea;
let it tower high on Whaleness
as a reminder to my people.
And let it be known as *Beowulf's barrow*
to all seafarers, to men who steer their ships   2800
from far over the swell and the saltspray."
    Then the prince, bold of mind, detached
his golden collar and gave it to Wiglaf,
the young spear-warrior, and also his helmet
adorned with gold, his ring and his corslet,
and enjoined him to use them well;
"You are the last survivor of our family,
the Waegmundings; fate has swept
all my kinsmen, those courageous warriors,
to their doom. I must follow them."   2810
    Those were the warrior's last words
before he succumbed to the raging flames
on the pyre; his soul migrated from his breast
to meet the judgement of righteous men.
    Then it was harrowing for the young hero
that he should have to see that beloved man
lying on the earth at his life's end,
wracked by pain. His slayer lay
there too, himself slain, the terrible
cave-dragon. That serpent, coiled evilly,   2820
could no longer guard the gold-hoard,
but blades of iron, beaten and tempered
by smiths, notched in battle, had taken him off;
his wings were clipped now, he lay
mortally wounded, motionless on the earth
at the mound's entrance. No more did he fly
through the night sky, or spread his wings,
proud of his possessions; but he lay prostrate
because of the power of Beowulf, their leader.
Truly, I have heard that no hero of the Geats,   2830
no fire-eater, however daring, could quell
the scorching blast of that venomous one
and lay his hands on the hoard in the lair,
should he find its sentinel waiting there,
watching over the barrow. Beowulf paid
the price of death for that mighty hoard;
both he and the dragon had travelled to the end
of this transitory life.
                              Not long after that
the lily-livered ones slunk out of the wood;

ten cowardly oath-breakers, who had lacked   2840
the courage to let fly with their spears
as their lord so needed, came forward together;
overcome with shame, they carried their shields
and weapons to where their leader lay;
they gazed at Wiglaf. That warrior, bone-weary,
knelt beside the shoulders of his lord; he tried
to rouse him with water; it was all in vain.
For all his efforts, his longing, he could not
detain the life of his leader on earth,
or alter anything the Ruler ordained.   2850
God in His wisdom governed the deeds
of all men, as He does now.
   Then the young warrior was not at a loss
for well-earned, angry words for those cowards.
Wiglaf, Weohstan's son, sick at heart,
eyed those faithless men and said:
"He who does not wish to disguise the truth
can indeed say that—when it was a question
not of words but war—our lord completely wasted
the treasures he gave you, the same war-gear   2860
you stand in over there, helmets and corslets
the prince presented often to his thanes on the ale-bench
in the feasting-hall, the very finest weapons
he could secure from far and wide.
The king of the Geats had no need to bother
with boasts about his battle-companions;
yet God, Giver of victories, granted
that he should avenge himself with his sword
single-handed, when all his courage was called for.
I could hardly begin to guard his life   2870
in the fight; but all the same I attempted
to help my kinsman beyond my power.
Each time I slashed at that deadly enemy,
he was a little weaker, the flames leaped
less fiercely from his jaws. Too few defenders
rallied round our prince when he was most pressed.
Now you and your dependants can no longer delight
in gifts of swords, or take pleasure in property,
a happy home; but, after thanes from far and wide
have heard of your flight, your shameful cowardice,   2880
each of your male kinsmen will be condemned
to become a wanderer, an exile deprived
of the land he owns. For every warrior
death is better than dark days of disgrace."
   Then Wiglaf ordered that Beowulf's great feat
be proclaimed in the stronghold, up along the cliff-edge,
where a troop of shield-warriors had waited all morning,
wondering sadly if their dear lord was dead,
or if he would return.

                        The man who galloped
to the headland gave them the news at once;   2890
he kept back nothing but called out:
"The lord of the Geats, he who gave joy
to all our people, lies rigid on his death-bed;
slaughtered by the dragon, he now sleeps;
and his deadly enemy, slashed by the knife,
sleeps beside him; he was quite unable
to wound the serpent with a sword. Wiglaf,
son of Weohstan, sits by Beowulf,
the quick and the dead—both brave men—
side by side; weary in his heart   2900
he watches over friend and foe alike.
    Now the Geats must make ready for a time
of war, for the Franks and the Frisians,
in far-off regions, will hear soon
of the king's death. Our feud with the Franks
grew worse when Hygelac sailed with his fleet
to the shores of Frisia. Frankish warriors
attacked him there, and outfought him,
bravely forced the king in his corslet
to give ground; he fell, surrounded   2910
by his retainers; that prince presented
not one ornament to his followers. Since then,
the king of the Franks has been no friend of ours.
    Nor would I in the least rely on peace
or honesty from the Swedish people; everyone
remembers how Ongentheow slew Haethcyn,
Hrethel's son, in battle near Ravenswood
when, rashly, the Geats first attacked the Swedes.
At once Ongentheow, Ohthere's father,
old but formidable, retaliated; he killed   2920
Haethcyn, and released his wife from captivity,
set free the mother of Onela and Ohthere,
an aged woman bereft of all her ornaments;
and then he pursued his mortal enemies
until, lordless, with utmost difficulty,
they reached and found refuge in Ravenswood.
Then Ongentheow, with a huge army, penned in
those warriors, exhausted by wounds,
who had escaped the sword; all night long
he shouted fearsome threats at those shivering thanes,   2930
swore that in the morning he and his men would let
their blood in streams with sharp-edged swords,
and string some up on gallows-trees
as sport for birds. Just as day dawned
those despairing men were afforded relief;
they heard the joyful song of Hygelac's
horn and trumpet as that hero came,
hurrying to their rescue with a band of retainers.

After that savage, running battle, the soil
was blood-stained, scuffled—a sign of how 2940
the Swedes and the Geats fomented their feud.
Then Ongentheow, old and heavy-hearted,
headed for his stronghold with his retainers,
that resolute man retreated; he realized
how spirit and skill combined in the person
of proud Hygelac; he had no confidence
about the outcome of an open fight with the seafarers,
the Geatish warriors, in defence of his hoard,
his wife and children; the old man thus withdrew
behind an earth-wall. Then the Swedes were pursued, 2950
Hygelac's banner was hoisted over that earth-work
after the Geats, sons of Hrethel, had stormed
the stronghold. Then grey-haired Ongentheow
was cornered by swords, the king of the Swedes
was constrained to face and suffer his fate
as Eofor willed it. Wulf, the son
of Wonred, slashed angrily at Ongentheow
with his sword, so that blood spurted
from the veins under his hair. The old Swede,
king of his people, was not afraid 2960
but as soon as he had regained his balance
repaid that murderous blow with interest.
Then Wonred's daring son could no longer
lift his hand against the aged warrior
but, with that stroke, Ongentheow had sheared
right through his helmet so that Wulf, blood-stained,
was thrown to the ground; he was not yet doomed to die
but later recovered from that grievous wound.
When Wulf collapsed, his brother Eofor,
Hygelac's brave thane, swung his broad sword, 2970
made by giants, shattered the massive helmet
above the raised shield; Ongentheow fell,
the guardian of the people was fatally wounded.
Then many warriors quickly rescued Wulf,
and bandaged his wounds, once they had won control
(as fate decreed) of that field of corpses.
Meanwhile Eofor stripped Ongentheow's body
of its iron corslet, wrenched the helmet
from his head, the mighty sword from his hands;
he carried the old man's armour to Hygelac. 2980
He received those battle adornments, honourably
promised to reward Eofor above other men;
he kept his word; the king of the Geats,
Hrethel's son, repaid Eofor and Wulf
for all they had accomplished with outstanding gifts
when he had returned home; he gave each of them
land and interlocked rings to the value
of a hundred thousand pence—no man on earth

had cause to blame the brothers for accepting
such wealth, they had earned it by sheer audacity.   2990
Then, as a pledge of friendship, Hygelac gave
Eofor his only daughter to grace his home.
  That is the history of hatred and feud
and deadly enmity; and because of it,
I expect the Swedes to attack us
as soon as they hear our lord is lifeless—
he who in earlier days defended a land
and its treasure against two monstrous enemies
after the death of its heroes, daring Scyldings,
he who protected the people, and achieved feats   3000
all but impossible.
                        Let us lose no time now
but go and gaze there upon our king
and carry him, who gave us rings,
to the funeral pyre. And let us not grudge gold
to melt with that bold man, for we have a mighty hoard,
a mint of precious metal, bought with pain;
and now, from this last exploit, a harvest
he paid for with his own life; these the fire
shall devour, the ravening flames embrace.
No thane shall wear or carry these treasures   3010
in his memory, no fair maiden shall hang
an ornament of interlinked rings at her throat,
but often and again, desolate, deprived of gold,
they must tread the paths of exile,
now that their lord has laid aside laughter,
festivity, happiness. Henceforth, fingers must grasp,
hands must hold, many a spear
chill with the cold of morning; no sound of the harp
shall rouse the warriors but, craving for carrion,
the dark raven shall have its say   3020
and tell the eagle how it fared at the feast
when, competing with the wolf, it laid bare the bones of corpses."
  Thus the brave messenger told of and foretold
harrowing times; and he was not far wrong.
Those events were fated. Every man in the troop
stood up, stained with tears, and set out
for Eagleness to see that strange spectacle.
There they found him lifeless on the sand,
the soft bed where he slept, who often before
had given them rings; that good man's days   3030
on earth were ended; the warrior-king,
lord of the Geats, had died a wondrous death.
But first they saw a strange creature
there, a loathsome serpent lying
nearby; the fire-dragon, fierce
and mottled, was scorched by its own flames.
It measured fifty paces from head to tail;

sometimes it had soared at night
through the cool air, then dived
to its dark lair; now it lay rigid in death, 3040
no longer to haunt caverns under the earth.
Goblets and vessels stood by·it,
salvers and valuable swords, eaten through
by rust, as if they had lain
for a thousand winters in the earth's embrace.
That mighty legacy, gold of men long dead,
lay under a curse; it was enchanted
so that no human might enter
the cavern save him to whom God,
the true Giver of Victories, Guardian of Men, 3050
granted permission to plunder the hoard—
whichever warrior seemed worthy to Him.
   Then it was clear that, whoever devised it,
the evil scheme of hiding the hoard under the rock
had come to nothing; the guardian had killed
a brave and famous man; that feud
was violently avenged. The day that a warrior,
renowned for his courage, will reach the end
(as fate ordains) of his life on earth,
that hour when a man may feast in the hall 3060
with his friends no longer, is always unpredictable.
It was thus with Beowulf when he tracked down
and attacked the barrow's guardian; he himself
was not aware how he would leave this world.
The glorious princes who first placed that gold there
had solemnly pronounced that until domesday
any man attempting to plunder the hoard
should be guilty of wickedness, confined,
tormented and tortured by the devil himself.
Never before had Beowulf been granted 3070
such a wealth of gold by the gracious Lord.
   Wiglaf, the son of Weohstan, said:
"Many thanes must often suffer
because of the will of one, as we do now.
We could not dissuade the king we loved,
or in any way restrain the lord of our land
from drawing his sword against the gold-warden,
from letting him lie where he had long lain
and remain in his lair until the world's end;
but he fulfilled his high destiny. The hoard, 3080
so grimly gained, is now easy of access;
our king was driven there by too harsh a fate.
I took the path under the earth-wall,
entered the hall and examined all
the treasures after the dragon deserted it;
I was hardly invited there. Hurriedly
I grasped as many treasures as I could,

a huge burden, and carried them here
to my king; he was still alive then,
conscious and aware of this world around him.   3090
He found words for his thronging thoughts,
born of sorrow, asked me to salute you,
said that as a monument to your lord's exploits
you should build a great and glorious barrow
over his pyre, for he of all men
was the most famous warrior on the wide earth
for as long as he lived, happy in his stronghold.
Now let us hurry once more together
and see the hoard of priceless stones,
that wonder under the wall; I will lead you   3100
so that you will come sufficiently close
to the rings, the solid gold. After we
get back, let us quickly build the bier,
and then let us carry our king,
the man we loved, to where he must
long remain in the Lord's protection."
　　　Then the brave warrior, Weohstan's son,
directed that orders be given to many men
(to all who owned houses, elders of the people)
to fetch wood from far to place beneath   3110
their prince on the funeral pyre:
　　　　　　　　　　　　　　　　"Now flames,
the blazing fire, must devour the lord of warriors
who often endured the iron-tipped arrow-shower,
when the dark cloud loosed by bow strings
broke above the shield-wall, quivering;
when the eager shaft, with its feather garb,
discharged its duty to the barb."
　　　I have heard that Weohstan's wise son
summoned from Beowulf's band his seven
best thanes, and went with those warriors   3120
into the evil grotto; the man leading
the way grasped a brand. Then those retainers
were not hesitant about rifling the hoard
as soon as they set eyes on any part of it,
lying unguarded, gradually rusting,
in that rock cavern; no man was conscience-stricken
about carrying out those priceless treasures
as quickly as he could. Also, they pushed the dragon,
the serpent over the precipice; they let the waves take him,
the dark waters embrace the warden of the hoard.   3130
Then the wagon was laden with twisted gold,
with treasures of every kind, and the king,
the old battle-warrior, was borne to Whaleness.
　　　Then, on the headland, the Geats prepared a mighty pyre
for Beowulf, hung round with helmets and shields
and shining mail, in accordance with his wishes;

and then the mourning warriors laid
their dear lord, the famous prince, upon it.
    And there on Whaleness, the heroes kindled
the most mighty of pyres; the dark wood-smoke 3140
soared over the fire, the roaring flames
mingled with weeping—the winds' tumult subsided—
until the body became ash, consumed even
to its core. The heart's cup overflowed;
they mourned their loss, the death of their lord.
And, likewise, a maiden of the Geats,
with her tresses swept up, intoned
a dirge for Beowulf time after time,
declared she lived in dread of days to come
dark with carnage and keening, terror of the enemy, 3150
humiliation and captivity.
                  Heaven swallowed the smoke.
    Then the Geats built a barrow on the headland—
it was high and broad, visible from far
to all seafarers; in ten days they built the beacon
for that courageous man; and they constructed
as noble an enclosure as wise men
could devise, to enshrine the ashes.
They buried rings and brooches in the barrow,
all those adornments that brave men
had brought out from the hoard after Beowulf died. 3160
They bequeathed the gleaming gold, treasure of men,
to the earth, and there it still remains
as useless to men as it was before.
    Then twelve brave warriors, sons of heroes,
rode round the barrow, sorrowing;
they mourned their king, chanted
an elegy, spoke about that great man:
they exalted his heroic life, lauded
his daring deeds; it is fitting for a man,
when his lord and friend must leave this life, 3170
to mouth words in his praise
and to cherish his memory.
Thus the Geats, his hearth-companions,
grieved over the death of their lord;
they said that of all kings on earth
he was the kindest, the most gentle,
the most just to his people, the most eager for fame.

The Song of Roland

(C. 1100 A.D.)

The name given to the Old French epics (written approximately between 1100 and 1500) is chansons de geste, or "songs of deeds." Those written during the first half of this period are heroic in spirit; thereafter they take on characteristics of the romance, assimilating love stories written in the spirit of "courtly love," a tradition that idealized women and turned the conventions of human love almost literally into a religion. The earlier chansons de geste, like the Roland, treat almost exclusively of men at war. The public matter of these poems is primarily the struggle of Christianity against the forces of evil as embodied in the Muslims, misrepresented as idolaters, partly out of ignorance and partly for propaganda purposes that sometimes were shaped by the Crusades against Islam waged in the eleventh, twelfth, and thirteenth centuries.

The central figures in most of the chansons de geste are Charlemagne (Charles the Great) and members of his court or dynasty. During his lifetime (742–814), the historical Charlemagne forged an empire extending from the Ebro river in Spain to the Elbe in middle Europe, spreading Christianity and centralizing rule. In 800 he was named by the Pope as Holy Roman Emperor, a title and office that, except for a break of a century or so soon after his death, continued to exist until 1806. A learned man himself, he patronized learning and the arts. The chansons de geste have, then, a basis in historical fact and are centered on a man who was a towering figure in the development of Western and Christian culture. In the interval between his lifetime and their composition, however, they took on overlays of poetic legend; in The Song of Roland, for example, Charlemagne is in intimate touch with the angels of God and is believed by the enemy to be two hundred years old.

The Roland is the earliest and best-known surviving specimen of chanson de geste. The poem was unknown until 1832, when the first of several manuscripts of the work was discovered. The best of these, located in the Bodleian Library at Oxford University, is a copy by an Anglo-Norman scribe of an earlier version. Scholarly interest in the poem has ever since been intense and widespread, and the Roland is now generally honored as the wellspring of French literature. Despite such interest and accolades, however, many basic facts about the poem remain mysteries, the subject of endless but inconclusive conjecture. The last line of the poem, ambiguous in almost every word, identifies the poet (or is it the scribe?) as a man named Turoldus, but nothing certain is known about him except that he was apparently a native of Normandy. The date of the poem is likewise uncertain, but the consensus, especially among those who regard the work as expressing the spirit of the First Crusade (1096–1108 in Palestine and Syria), points to a time near 1100. Moreover, opinion varies about the process of epic gestation that over the course of three centuries transformed the seed of historical fact into the existent poem. One theory is that the Roland is essentially a compilation of many separate folk compositions. A more recent, less romantic, hypothesis is that the poem is the work of a single masterful poet who drew on written works by traveling minstrels (jongleurs) who in turn drew on oral traditions kept alive along the pilgrimage routes between France and Spain. The controversy resembles closely the disputes about the identity of Homer, and as with Homer the case for a single great poet becomes stronger as readers and scholars come to recognize the distinctive artistry of Roland and the careful shaping that has been given the material.

The Song of Roland *is an epic, not in the loose sense implying mere grandeur of effect but in very technical ways. It includes many of the marks of the classical epic, including the hyperbolic praise of the past and the heroes of old, the appearance of prophetic dreams and omens, the intervention at key moments of supernatural beings, councils held in the camps of the opposing armies, catalogues of the armies on both sides, the divine commissioning of a half-reluctant hero—Charles—to do the will of Heaven (the last lines show a weary but acquiescent Charles accepting again God's charge to defend Christendom). If we accept the theory that the poem is meant to inspirit the warriors of the First Crusade, we can detect the strategy by which the epic poet defines the characteristic virtues of his people as they were evinced in the past so that these virtues can be extrapolated through the crisis of the present into a hoped-for glorious future. These features are all prominent in the Virgilian epic, with which the* Roland *poet was probably acquainted. Also heroic or epic in manner are the poet's relish in descriptions of fierce individual combats, the defiances and boasts that frame the duels, the stylized epithets ("Charles whose flowing beard is white"). One notes too the resemblance between Homer's willful Achilles and Roland (up to a point— Roland has no touch of Achilles' sulkiness).*

Like most epics, The Song of Roland *is also a portrait of the social structure and values of its age. The basis of its society is feudalism and its system of vassalage. Although some important aspects of feudalism persisted all through the Middle Ages and, more vestigially, into modern times in such systems as the British peerage, true feudalism, with its hierarchical yet also decentralized structure, flourished mainly through the eleventh century. The trend thereafter moved slowly toward concentration of power in the sovereign and in the centralized modern national state. The idea of an absolutist monarch ruling by divine right does not emerge until the sixteenth and seventeenth centuries. It is significant that in the* Roland *Charles, although clearly a revered instrument of God's will, must abide by the decisions of his counsellors and, in the trial of Ganelon, by the verdict of a jury of Ganelon's peers.*

The essence of feudalism is the system of reciprocal bonds between a chief and the vassals who serve him. At the pinnacle is a sovereign, such as Charles, to whom his knights owe service, particularly in war, and who in return is pledged to defend them. Each of these vassal knights has the same relationship to his immediate followers, and so on down the scale to the humblest of common men. Some vassals were maintained as part of their lord's household and were brought up together, forming in the process a bond of close comradeship. Other vassals might be granted lands, or "fiefs," by their liege-lord. Whatever the arrangement, the feudal code of chivalry stressed courage, loyalty, and honor, both inherently and in the eyes of others; Roland, for example, is resolved never to behave in such a way as to inspire mocking songs about him and his men. This intimate system of ties, one man to another, is important in understanding even the narrative method of The Song of Roland; *for example, one reason the poet dwells exclusively on the fights between prominent chiefs is that in the event of the leader's death his followers are entitled to quit the battle.*

The values governing the action of the Roland *are simply identified; they have to do almost exclusively with war and religion, which are intimately related to each other. (The union is epitomized with particular vividness in the archbishop Turpin, equally ready to perform priestly and martial service.) Success in battle is vital, not only for personal reasons but as a proof that God favors one's cause. The Christians are good. The Saracens are evil, although some of them may be attractive as persons and valiant as warriors. Philosophical subtleties are entirely absent from the poem, as are signs of inward conflict between inclination and duty. Even Ganelon, psychologically complex though he is, with no grudge against Charles, carries out his treacherous scheme without apparent misgivings. Complex ideas or sophistications of theology are foreign to the poem's ideological plainness of line. (In this respect the* Roland *is wholly unlike Virgil's* Aeneid.*) The poem's values are ultimately otherworldly and at the same time severely pragmatic.*

The narrative method and linguistic style are in keeping with this directness. Few poems ever written are so "unpoetical" if by "poetry" we mean embellishment, richness of language, and rhetorical dazzle. The poet, like Homer, almost completely effaces himself; we know from his occasional expressions of exultation, grief, or partisanship that he sides wholeheartedly with the Christians, but of the distinctive personal cast of his mind there are few signs. Atmospheric descriptions—of scenery, for example—are rare and brief. The vocabulary is simple and limited, the syntax forthright. Figurative language such as similes is almost entirely absent. The versification is similarly square-hewn, the typical unit of statement coinciding with the individual line. But it would be a serious mistake to think of the poet as an artless primitive. His ability to create suspense is extraordinary, enhanced rather than spoiled by occasional glances at the action to come, a strategy that can create an almost Sophoclean dramatic irony. He is also psychologically acute, although recognition of this quality depends entirely on the reader, because, like Homer, the poet prefers to reveal nuances of behavior and motive objectively, through speeches and deeds, without commentary. The very spareness of description enhances its power when it does occur, as in the account of the storm that afflicts France in sympathy with Roland's death (laisse CX), or the memorably ominous lines about the mountain pass at Roncevaux: "High are the hills, deep valleys shun the light; / The cliffs rise grey, the gorges hold dark fear" (laisse LXVI). The effect of the narrative method and style is of absolute, unwavering honesty. One might go farther and find in the poem sublimity, a quality archetypically evoked by grandeur of theme rendered with simplicity.

We should also credit the poet with a sense of structural unity. Some scholars have found the Baligant episode extraneous—an anticlimax after the high drama of Roland's death, a distracting break between that scene and the final punishment of Ganelon, or both. Implicit in some of these interpretations is the assumption that the poem is exclusively centered on Roland personally, that he is an otherwise admirable hero tragically flawed in his pride so that he refuses to sound his horn for help, his eyes opened only when it is too late. But other interpretations are possible. For example, we can see Roland not as flawed but as justified in his lack of "prudence," uniquely clear-sighted in recognizing that the only way to encounter the forces of evil is all-out warfare to the death, not shaky and specious temporizing. The episode of Charles' battle against Baligant, embodying as Baligant and his army do the worldwide forces of evil rather than the limited threat of Spanish paganism, might thus be seen as the vindication of Roland's uncompromising views and a symbolic apocalyptic vindication of Christianity in itself.

The basic narrative unit in The Song of Roland *is the verse paragraph, or laisse. Except in the* laisses similaires, *where the poet's repetitions serve to remove the action described from the flow of time and heighten its significance, each successive laisse moves the action at least slightly forward. Yet each is also a detached unit, making a new start and leading toward a focus of generalization or clarification in its last line. Thus the movement of the poem, from one laisse to another, has a fitful but compelling rhythm, like a series of short bursts of fire from a machine gun. The movement within each laisse has a similar staccato effect; each line is end-stopped and makes its own distinct statement in preparation for the final climax. Each line has ten syllables (not counting feminine endings), with a strong internal pause, or caesura, after the fourth (occasionally the sixth) syllable. Two stresses precede the caesura and two follow it. The ends of the lines throughout any one laisse are linked by assonance, the repetition of the same vowel sound. In the present translation by Patricia Terry, the caesura is indicated by a space in the middle of each line, and the climactic effect at the end of each laisse is suggested by assonance, which is sometimes also rhyme, in the last two lines. The following example, laisse CXXXVIII, is typical (in the Old French the caesuras are here represented by a space, as in the translation):*

> *Halt sont li pui   e tenebros e grant,*
> *Li val parfont   e les ewes coranz.*
> *Sonent cil graisle   e deriedre e devant,*
> *E tuit rachatent   encontre l'olifant.*
> *Li emperedre   chevalche iriedement,*
> *E li Françeis   coroços e dolent,*
> *Nen i at cel   n'i plort e se dement,*
> *E prient Deu   qu'il guarisset Rodlant*
> *Josqued il veignent   e'l champ comunement;*
> *Ensembl'od lui   i ferront veirement.*
> *De ço qui chalt?   car ne lor valt nient:*
> *Demorent trop,   n'i poedent estre a tens. AOI.*

> *High are the hills,   and shadowy and vast,*
> *Deep the defiles,   and swift the mountain streams.*
> *The trumpets sound   ahead and to the rear,*
> *Blaring replies   to Roland's Oliphant.*
> *In bitter wrath   the Emperor rides on,*
> *The men of France   in sorrow and in rage;*
> *Not one but grieves   and bitterly laments,*
> *Praying that God   will keep Count Roland safe*
> *Until they come   and join him in the field—*
> *How they will fight   when they are at his side!*
> *What does it matter   how loyally they strive?*
> *They'll be too late   whenever they arrive. AOI.*

FURTHER READING (*prepared by W.J.R.*): Anyone interested in exploring *The Song of Roland* in detail should consult Gerald S. Brault's *The Song of Roland: An Analytical Edition*, 1978. Brault's work, in two volumes, is a monumental work of scholarship. Volume I contains an introduction and a commentary; Volume II contains the Oxford text and a facing-page English translation. A general discussion of *Roland* is available in John Fox's *A Literary History of France: The Middle Ages*, 1974. Also very helpful is Joseph J. Duggan, "The *Chanson de Roland* and the *Chansons de Geste*," in *European Writers: Medieval and Renaissance*, Vol. I, ed. George Stade, 1984. Alain Renoir's "Roland's Lament: Its Meaning and Function in the *Chanson de Roland*," *Speculum*, 35 (1960), 572–83, examines Roland's lament upon seeing his massacred army and relates the passage's tone and meaning to the structure of the first part of the work. On the social ethic in *Roland*, see John Halverson's "Ganelon's Trial," *Speculum*, 42 (1967), 661–69. Halverson discusses the poem's foundation in the

Germanic feudal tradition and draws comparisons between *Roland* and *Beowulf* in order to illustrate the kinship-dominated social structure. Tony Hunt's "The Tragedy of Roland: An Aristotelian View," *Modern Language Review*, 74 (1979), 791–804, examines the poem's literary qualities and the reasons for its enduring appeal. John R. Allen's "Kinship in the *Chanson de Roland*," in *Jean Misrahi Memorial Volume: Studies in Medieval Literature,* ed. by Hans R. Runte and others, begins with a general discussion of the importance of blood ties in the poem and moves on to an investigation of a more complex type of kinship presented in *Roland*. The question of Roland's pride is considered in Jean Misrahi and William L. Hendrickson, "Roland and Oliver: Prowess and Wisdom, the Ideal of the Epic Hero," *Romance Philology*, 33 (1980), 357–72. The authors discuss what some have called Roland's "sinful" pride and make a defense of Roland's not calling for aid. Christian modifications of the Germanic ideal are also discussed.

from *THE SONG OF ROLAND*

Translated by Patricia Terry

I

The mighty Charles,[1] our emperor and king,
Seven long years has been at war in Spain;
That lofty land lies conquered to the sea.
No fortress now is standing in his way,
No walls, no towns remain for him to break,
Except for Saragossa, high on its hill,
Ruled by Marsile, who has no love for God;
He serves Apollo,[2] and to Mohammed prays—
But he will come, and soon, to evil days! AOI[3]

II

In Saragossa, the pagan king, Marsile,   10
Walks through an orchard whose trees give cooling shade.
The king reclines on a blue marble bench;
His host assembles, some twenty thousand men.
He speaks these words to all his dukes and counts:
"Now hear, my lords, what evils weigh us down!
For Charles has come, the ruler of sweet France,
To seize our lands, and bring us to our knees.
I have no army[4] to fight against his own;

[1] Charlemagne, or Charles the Great (742–814), who from 771 to 814 ruled the Franks (a tribe inhabiting, approximately, the lands of modern France and Germany). As a matter of historical fact, he did not become Emperor until 800, some 22 years later than the campaign (which lasted a few months, not seven years) upon which the poem seems to be based.

[2] According to the poet's distorted version of Islam, its three gods were Apollo, Mohammed, and Tervagant. In fact, the religion of Islam is emphatically monotheistic, worshipping Allah ("God") alone.

[3] These three letters, occurring usually at the end of sections ("laisses"), are one of the most puzzling mysteries about *Roland*. They may be some sort of exclamation.

[4] This statement is inconsistent with the later information that Marsile's army numbers 400,000.

No men of mine   will drive him to defeat—
Give me your counsel,   as you are true and wise,
Save me from death,   and from this bitter shame."
Mute are the pagans,   except for one alone:
Blancandrin speaks,   whose castle is Val-Fonde.

III

Among the pagans   Blancandrin was wise,
A trusted vassal,   a brave and loyal knight,
Clever enough   to think of good advice.
He tells the king,   "You need not be afraid.
Send word to Charles,   the arrogant, the proud,
That you in friendship   salute him as your lord,
Offer him gifts: bears and lions and dogs,
And seven hundred camels,   a thousand hawks,
Four hundred mule-loads   of silver and of gold,
And fifty carts   to form a wagon-train.
He'll have enough   to pay his hired men.
He has campaigned   so long here in this land,
He won't refuse   to go back home to Aix.[5]
Say you will meet him   in France, on Michael's Day,[6]
To be converted,   adopt the Christian law,
And do him homage   in friendship and good will.
If hostages are needed,   say you will send
Ten, even twenty,   to witness your good faith:
We'll have to yield   the sons our wives have borne—
The risk is death,   but I will send my own.
Better that they   should sacrifice their heads
Than that we lose   our honor and our pride,
And live as beggars   with all our rights denied!"   AOI

IV

Says Blancandrin,   "I swear by my right hand,
And by this beard   that ripples on my chest,
You'll see the French   disband their troops and go,
The Franks[7] will soon   be on their way to France.
And when each one   has found his home again,
Charles, in the chapel   that he has built in Aix,
Will give a feast   in honor of the saint,
On Michael's Day,   when we'll have sworn to come—
But of our coming   the French will see no sign.

[5] Aix-la-Chapelle, now also called Aachen, a city in the Rhineland, was the capital of Charlemagne's realm.

[6] September 29.

[7] "The 'Franks' (*Francs*) and 'French' (*Françeis*) are for the most part used as synonymous terms. Occasionally, however, the Franks of France are distinguished from the Franks from elsewhere in the Empire. It is stated that Charles prefers the men of France to all others (3031); in 3976–77 the bishops of France are mentioned separately from those of Bavaria and Germany. The boundaries of 'France' are also variable, sometimes including the whole of Charlemagne's empire (larger than life), sometimes more restricted."—Translator's note.

The king is proud,   and cruel is his heart;
He'll have the heads   of all our men cut off.
But better far   that they should lose their heads
Than that we lose   this shining land, fair Spain,
And be condemned   to hardship and disgrace."   60
The pagans say,   "That may well be the case!"

VI

Then King Marsile   declares the council closed.
He tells his men,   "Thus you shall go, my lords:
Hold in your hands   the olive branch of peace,   80
And speak for me   to Charlemagne the king;
In his God's name,   ask him to grant me grace.
Say that before   a single month has passed,
I'll bring to France   a thousand of my men,
There be converted,   adopt the Christian law,
Become his vassal   in loyalty and love.
For this he'll have   what hostages he will."
Says Blancandrin,   "Our wishes he'll fulfill."   AOI

VII

The ten white mules   are brought for them to ride;
Suatilie's king   had sent them to Marsile.   90
Their reins are gold,   their saddles silver-trimmed.
The envoys mount,   and as they ride away,
Each in his hand   holds high the olive branch.
They go to Charles,   who rules the Frankish land;
He will not see   the treachery they've planned.   AOI

VIII

The Emperor Charles   is jubilant and gay:
The lofty walls   of Cordres are torn down,
His catapults   have laid its towers low;
His knights rejoice,   for great is their reward—
Silver and gold,   and costly gear for war.   100
In all the city   no pagan now remains
Who isn't dead   or one of the true Faith.
In a great orchard,   Charlemagne sits in state.
With him are Roland,   and Oliver, his friend;
A duke called Samson,   and fiery Anseïs,
Geoffroy of Anjou,   flag-bearer for the king;
The two companions   Gerin and Gerier.
And with these barons   is no small group of men,
For fifteen thousand   came with them from sweet France.
The knights are seated   on carpets of white silk;   110
The older men,   or clever, pass the time
Playing backgammon,   or else they sit at chess;
The nimble youths   prefer to fence with swords.
Beneath a pine,   beside a briar-rose,

A throne is placed— it's made of purest gold.
There sits the king, the ruler of sweet France;
White is his beard, and silver streaks his hair,[8]
Handsome his form, his bearing very proud:
No stranger needs to have him pointed out.
The Saracens[9] dismount and come on foot   120
To greet the king, as friendly envoys would.

IX

Then Blancandrin begins to make his speech.
He says to Charles, "May God grant you His grace,
That glorious Lord to whom all men must pray!
We've come to you at King Marsile's command;
He's learned about the law that saves men's souls,
And of his wealth he wants to offer you
Lions and bears, and leash-trained hunting dogs,
And seven hundred camels, a thousand hawks,
Silver and gold four hundred mules will bear,   130
And fifty carts to form a wagon-train.
These will be loaded with silver coins and gold.
Enough for you to well reward your men.
You have campaigned so long here in this land,
It must be time to go back home to Aix;
My lord Marsile says he will follow you."
The Emperor Charles holds both hands up toward God;
He bows his head, and gives himself to thought. AOI

X

The Emperor Charles sits with his head bent low.
He was not known for answering in haste: 140
Always he liked to take his time to speak.
When he looked up, his face was stern and proud.
Thus he replies: "You've spoken well indeed.
But King Marsile has been no friend of mine;
Of what you say, although your words are fair,
How shall I know how much I can believe?"
"Take hostages," the Saracen replies,
"Ten or fifteen or twenty you shall have;
Though he risks death, I'll send a son of mine,
And there will be some even nobler men.   150
When, in your palace at Aix, you hold the feast
That celebrates Saint Michael of the Sea,[10]
My lord Marsile declares that he will come,

---

[8] Charles is depicted as old, although historically he was only thirty-six at the time of the
Spanish campaign.
[9] Arabs; Moslems.
[10] The reference is to Mont-Saint-Michel, the famous monastery on an island off the coast
of Brittany (northwest France).

And, in those baths[11]   which were God's gift to you,
He will be baptized,   adopt the Christian faith."
Then answers Charles,   "It still is not too late."   AOI

XI

Fair was the evening,   the sun set pure of cloud.
By Charles' command   the mules were led to stalls.
In the great orchard   he had a tent set up,
And there he lodged   the envoys of Marsile;   160
Twelve of his servants   attended to their needs.
There they remained   until it was bright day.
When, in the morning,   the emperor arose,
He heard a mass   and matins[12] first of all,
And then the king   sat down beneath a pine,
And called his barons: for what he must decide
The men of France   would always be his guide.   AOI

XIII

"Barons, my lords,"   says Charles the Emperor,   180
"This I have heard   from envoys of Marsile:
Of his great wealth   he'll send me a good part,
Lions and bears,   and leash-trained hunting dogs,
Seven hundred camels,   a thousand hawks,
Four hundred mule-loads   of fine Arabian gold,
And with these gifts,   some fifty heavy carts.
But he requests   that I return to France,
And says that when   I'm home again in Aix,
He'll come and yield   to holy Christian law,
He'll take the Faith,   and hold his lands from me;   190
But I don't know   the secrets of his heart."
"We must think twice,"   they say, "before we start!"   AOI

XIV

The king has brought   his discourse to an end.
And now Count Roland   has risen to his feet;
He speaks his mind   against the Saracens,
Saying to Charles,   "You can't believe Marsile!
It's seven years   since first we came to Spain;
For you I've conquered   Noples and Commibles,
I took Val-Terre   and all the land of Pine,
And Balaguer,   Tudela, Sedilie.   200
There King Marsile   displayed his treachery:
Of his vile pagans   he sent to you fifteen;
Each in his hand   held high the olive branch,
And when they spoke,   we heard this very speech.
You let your Franks   decide what should be done;
The plan they chose   was foolishness indeed:
You sent two counts   as envoys to the king,

---

[11] Aix is famous for its hot mineral springs.   [12] An early-morning prayer service.

Basant was one,   the other was Basile—
They left their heads   on a hill near Haltilies!
Finish the fight   the way it was begun: 210
To Saragossa   lead on your gathered host,
Though all your life   at war here you remain,
Avenge those men   so villainously slain!"   AOI

                                   XV

The Emperor Charles   has kept his head bowed down;
He strokes his beard,   arranges his moustache,
And to his nephew   says neither yes nor no.
The French are silent,   except for Ganelon;
He stands up straight   and comes before the king,
With wrathful pride   begins his argument,
Saying to Charles: "Believe no underling,   220
Not me, not Roland,   who speaks against your good!
When King Marsile   sends messengers to say
He'll place his hands in yours,   and be your man,
He'll do you homage   for all the lands of Spain,
And he'll observe   our holy Christian law—
Whoever urges you   to scorn this peace
Does not care, Sire,   what kind of death we die.
A man too proud   will recklessly advise;
Let's heed no fools,   and keep to what is wise!"   AOI

                                   XVI

When he had stopped,   Duke Naimon rose to speak;   230
In all the court   there was no better man.
He said to Charles,   "You've heard Count Ganelon;
I think the answer   that he has given you
Contains good sense,   if it be understood.
For King Marsile   there's no hope in this war:
All of his castles   have fallen to your hands,
Your catapults   have broken down his walls,
His towns are burned,   his men brought to defeat.
Now envoys ask   your mercy for the king—
If we refuse,   we're guilty of grave sin.   240
Since hostages will prove   he did not lie,
In this great war   there's no one left to fight."
The Frenchmen say,   "The duke is in the right!"

                                   XVII

"Barons, my lords,   which one of you shall go
To Saragossa,   to talk with King Marsile?"
Duke Naimon says,   "I'll do it, by your leave.
Yield to me now   the envoy's staff and glove."
Answers the king,   "The wisest of my men!
By this white beard,   by my moustache I swear
So far from me   I'll never let you go.   250
Sit down; if you are wanted,   I'll let you know!"

XVIII

"Barons, my lords,   what envoy can we send
To Saragossa,   held by the Saracen?"
Count Roland says,   "Let me talk to Marsile!"
"No, you shall not!"   Count Oliver replies,
"Your heart is fierce,   and you are quick to wrath—
If you are sent,   there's sure to be a fight.
By the king's leave,   I'll be the one to go."
Answers the king,   "Be quiet, both of you!
Not you nor he   will set foot in that town!   260
And by this beard   that you can see is white,
I'll tell you now   the twelve peers all must stay."
The French are silent;   they dare not disobey.

XIX

Turpin of Reims   has risen from his place.
He says to Charles,   "Leave all your Franks in peace.
For seven years   you've been here in this land
Where you have suffered   great hardships and fatigue.
Give, Sire, to me   the envoy's staff and glove,
And I will seek   the Spanish Saracen;
I would be glad   to know what he is like."   270
But much displeased   the emperor replies,
"I'll hear no more—   go to your place and sit.
Keep your advice   until I ask for it!"   AOI

XX

"My valiant knights,"   says Charles the Emperor,
"Choose for me now   the nobleman of France
Who is to take   my message to Marsile."
"I name," says Roland,   "Stepfather Ganelon."
The Franks reply,   "He'd do it very well;
We could not make   a wiser choice than this."
Count Ganelon   is furious indeed;   280
Casting aside   his cloak of marten furs,
He shows a tunic   made of the finest silk.
Steel-grey his eyes   and very proud his face,
His carriage noble,   his chest is large around;
He looks so handsome,   his peers all turn and stare.
He says, "You fool,   rash are your words, and wild.
Everyone knows   I'm stepfather to you,
Yet you name me   the envoy to Marsile!
If God should grant   that I come home again,
I won't forget—   and you'll face such a feud   290
That it will last   as long as you're alive!"
"I hear," says Roland,   "your foolishness and pride.
Everyone knows   I answer threats with scorn;
A man of wisdom   this embassy requires—
I'll take your place,   if the king so desires."   AOI

XXI

Ganelon says,   "You shall not take my place!
You're not my man,   nor am I your liege-lord.[13]
But Charles commands me   to serve him in this way:
In Saragossa   I'll talk to King Marsile.
But I will find   some little trick to play,   300
Fit to relieve   my fury at this wrong."
Roland replies   with laughter loud and long.   AOI

XXII

Count Ganelon,   when he hears Roland laugh,
Suffers such pain   he nearly splits with rage,
And he comes close   to falling in a faint.
He says to Roland,   "Now count me not your friend,
For you have swayed   this council to your will!
My rightful king,   you see me here at hand,
Ready to do   whatever you command.   AOI

XXIII

"To Saragossa   I know that I must go.   310
And from that journey   no man comes to his home.
Remember this: your sister is my wife;
She bore my son—   there is no fairer youth—
His name is Baldwin;   he'll make a valiant man.
To him I leave   my fiefdoms, all my lands.
Grant him your care;   I'll see him not again."
Then answers Charles,   "You have too soft a heart.[14]
You know my will;   it's time for you to start."   AOI

XXIV

Thus spoke the king,   "Come forward, Ganelon.
Take now from me   the envoy's staff and glove: 320
You've heard the Franks,   and they have chosen you."
Says Ganelon,   "Sire, this is Roland's work;
I'll have no love,   as long as I may live,
Either for him   or Oliver his friend.
All the twelve peers,   to whom he is so dear,
Sire, in your presence,   I challenge here and now!"
Then says the king,   "You yield too much to wrath.
Now you shall go,   since that is my command."
"I'll have the same   protection from Marsile
You gave Basant   and his brother Basile."   AOI   330

---

[13] Master to whom feudal loyalty is due.
[14] "Charles's irritated reply seems astonishing; one wonders if it does not conceal his embarrassed unwillingness to admit, once Ganelon has, to Charles's relief, been chosen, that the mission is indeed extremely dangerous."—Translator's note.

XXV

The Emperor Charles   holds out his right-hand glove,
But Ganelon,   who'd rather not be there,
Taking the gauntlet,[15]   lets it fall to the ground.
The Frenchmen say,   "Oh, God! What does this mean?
Surely this message   will bring us to our woe."
Says Ganelon,   "Your answer won't be slow."

XXVI

"Sire," says the count,   "now grant me leave to go;
Since go I must,   I care not for delay."
The king replies,   "In Jesu's name and mine!"
Then Charles' right hand   absolves the count from sin;   340
The staff and letter   are both given to him.

XXVII

Count Ganelon   returning to his tent,
Arrays himself   as if for waging war
With the best arms   his household can provide.
The spurs are gold   he fastens to his feet,
Murglais, his sword,   is hanging at his side,
And now he mounts   his war-horse Tachebrun,
The stirrup held   by his uncle Guinemer.
Then you could see   how many knights shed tears,
All of them saying,   "Alas! You go to die.   350
Long have you served   the great king at his court,
A noble vassal;   none fail to speak your praise.
The man who named you   the envoy to Marsile
Will not live long—   in spite of Charlemagne!
Roland was wrong   not to remember this:
Behind you stands   a mighty family."
And then they say,   "Let us go with you, lord."
The count replies,   "Almighty God forbid!
I'll die alone,   not sacrifice good knights.
But you must go,   my lords, back to sweet France   360
Where you will bring   my greetings to my wife,
To Pinabel,   my good friend and my peer,
And to my son,   Baldwin, whom you all know—
Give him your help,   and serve him as your lord."
Now toward Marsile   Ganelon sets his course. AOI

XXVIII

Ganelon rides   under tall olive trees;
Now he has met   the envoys from Marsile,
And Blancandrin   is riding at his side;
Both of them talk   with great diplomacy.
Says Blancandrin,   "I marvel at your king—   370

---

[15] A glove worn as part of a suit of armor. That it is dropped is an ill omen.

For he has conquered   the whole of Italy,
And then to England   he crossed the salty sea
So that the Saxons   would pay Saint Peter's fee.[16]
And what of Spain   will Charlemagne require?"
The count replies,   "That's hidden in his mind.
A greater king   no man will ever find."   AOI

XXIX

Says Blancandrin,   "The Franks are noble men;
But they do wrong,   those warlike dukes and counts
When by the counsel   they give to Charlemagne
They wear him out,   and others suffer too."   380
Ganelon says,   "Of this I could accuse
Only Count Roland—   who'll pay for it some day.
Not long ago,   when Charles sat at his ease,
His nephew came   dressed in his battle gear—
He'd gone for plunder   somewhere near Carcasonne.
In Roland's hand   an apple shone, bright red;
He told his uncle,   'Accept it, my fair lord!
I bring you here   the crowns of every king.'
But his great pride   will lead him on too far,
For every day   we see him risk his life.   390
If he were killed,   there'd be an end to strife."   AOI

XXX

Says Blancandrin,   "Evil is Roland's heart.
He'd have the world   surrender to his will,
Proclaim his right   to every land on earth!
But by whose help   can he attempt so much?"
"The Franks of France!   He so commands their love,
They'll never fail him,   they're with him to a man.
He gives them gifts   of silver and much gold,
War-horses, mules,   brocades and costly arms;
The king himself   won't cross him in the least: 400
By Roland's sword   he'll rule to the far East!"   AOI

XXXI

So Ganelon   and Blancandrin ride on
Until they've made   a solemn pact: they vow
That they will seek   to have Count Roland slain.
They go their way,   and then dismount at last
In Saragossa   where a tall yew tree stands.
Under a pine   a throne has been set up,
Draped in brocade   of Alexandrian silk.
There sits the king,   the ruler of all Spain;
Around him wait   his twenty thousand men.   410
Not one of them   lets fall a single word;

---

[16]Monetary tribute to Rome. These lines exaggerate the actual historical achievements of Charlemagne.

They're all intent   on what they hope to hear
From those two men   who even now appear.

XXXII

Now Blancandrin   has come before Marsile,
And by the fist   he holds Count Ganelon.
He speaks these words: "Hail, in Mohammed's name,
Apollo's too,   whose Law we all obey!
We have delivered   your message to King Charles;
When he had heard us,   he raised his hands on high
To praise his God,   but gave us no reply.   420
Now he has sent you   one of his noble lords,
A count of France,   a man of power and wealth.
From him you'll learn   if there is hope for peace."
Marsile replies,   "We'll hear him; let him speak."

XXXIII

Count Ganelon   has taken careful thought,
Now he begins   in well-considered words,
Subtly contrived—[17]   the count knows how to talk.
He tells Marsile: "May God grant you His grace,
That glorious Lord   to whom all men must pray!
Now by the will   of Charlemagne the King,   430
You must accept   the holy Christian law,
And half of Spain   he'll let you hold in fief.
Should you refuse   agreement to these terms,
You'll find yourself   a captive and in chains,
Taken by force   to answer Charles at Aix.
There you'll be judged,   and you will be condemned
To die a death   of infamy and shame."
At that Marsile   in fear and fury raised
A throwing spear—   its feathering was gold;
He would have struck,   but that his men took hold.   AOI   440

XXXIV

In the king's face   they see the color change;
He stands there raging,   shaking his javelin.
Ganelon's hand   reaches to grasp his sword,
Out of the scabbard   draws it two finger lengths;
He tells the blade: "Shining you are, and fair!
Long have we served,   we two, at King Charles' court!
The Emperor of France   shall never say
I died alone   here in this foreign land
Before their best   have bought you at your price."
The pagans say,   "We must not let them fight!"   450

---

[17] "Ganelon is not only an accomplished liar but an enthusiastic one (see his description of
the death of the Caliph, in laisse LIV). [In the speech that here follows] only the tone would
seem to misrepresent Charlemagne, except that Marsile will be allowed to keep only half of
Spain, in fief to Charles; the other half is to be ruled by Roland. Thus the latter is made, once
again, the focal point of the pagans' anger."—Translator's note.

XXXV

The Saracens   prevail upon Marsile
Until the king   will take his seat again.
Said the Caliph,[18]   "You don't do any good
When you are ready   to strike the Frenchman down.
Just let him speak,   and listen to him well."
Ganelon says,   "My lord, I'll suffer that.
But I won't stop,   for all the gold God made,
For all the treasure   that's gathered in this land,
Before I give him,   if he will grant me time,
The message Charles   confided to my care,   460
The words he sends   his mortal enemy."
Ganelon wore   a cloak of sable furs
Covered in folds   of Alexandrian silk.
He throws it down—   it's caught by Blancandrin—
But has no thought   of letting go his sword:
His right hand grasps   the handle made of gold.
The pagans say,   "Noble he is, and bold!" AOI

XXXVI

Count Ganelon   stands close beside the king,
And says to him,   "You have no cause for wrath
If Charlemagne   who rules the land of France   470
Says you must take   the holy Christian law:
One half of Spain   he'll let you hold in fief,
His nephew Roland   will rule the other part—
There you will have   a partner full of pride!
If you refuse   agreement to these terms,
In Saragossa   you soon will be besieged,
You'll find yourself   a prisoner in chains,
And straight away   you'll be led off to Aix.
And then no palfrey,   no war-horse will you have,
Nor yet a mule   to ride with dignity,   480
But you'll be thrown   onto some pack-beast's back,
And lose your head   at that long journey's end.
Here is the message   I've brought at Charles' command."
He puts the letter   into Marsile's right hand.

XXXVII

Now King Marsile,   his face gone white with rage,
Breaks the seal open   and throws the wax away,
Looks at the letter   and sees what it contains.
"Thus writes King Charles   who rules the land of France:
He won't forget   his anger and his grief
About Basant   and his brother Basile   490
Whose heads I took   on a hill near Haltilie.
If I would make amends,   there's just one way:
I'll have to send him   my uncle, the Caliph;

[18]Successor of Mohammed; here, the Ethiopian ruler.

If I refuse,   he'll have no love for me."
His son spoke up   and said to King Marsile,
"Wild empty words   we've had from Ganelon,
He's gone too far—   he well deserves to die.
Leave him to me,   and I'll do what is right."
Then Ganelon   prepared for the attack,
Brandished his sword,   the pine tree at his back.   500

XXXVIII

Into an orchard   the pagan king retired,
And with him went   the wisest of his men.
Blancandrin came   whose heavy beard was grey,
And Jurfaret,   Marsile's own son and heir,
And the Caliph,   his uncle and good friend.
Says Blancandrin,   "Summon the Frenchman here—
I have his word   that he will serve our cause."
Marsile replies,   "Then bring him to me now."
Blancandrin takes   the count by the right hand,
Walks through the orchard,   and leads him to Marsile.   510
They plot the treason   that cunning will conceal. AOI

XXXIX

Thus speaks the king: "My fair lord Ganelon,
I know I did   an ill-considered thing
When in my rage   I went to strike you down.
I pledge you now   by these fine sable furs—
The gold they're trimmed with   is worth five hundred pounds:
Tomorrow evening   I'll have made fair amends."
Says Ganelon,   "Your gift I won't refuse.
And if God please,   by this you shall not lose!" AOI

XLI

The pagan says,   "Truly, I am amazed
By Charlemagne   whose hair is grey with age—
I know he's lived   more than two hundred years.[19]
He's dragged his body   through so many far lands,   540
Taken such blows   from lances and from spears,
So many kings   reduced to beggary,
It must be time   for him to look for peace."
"That will not happen   while Roland is alive;[20]
There's no such vassal   under the high-domed sky;
And very brave   is Oliver his friend.

---

[19] An exaggeration typical of heroic poetry; the historical Charlemagne lived 72 years.
[20] "Here again Ganelon insists that only Roland is responsible for the pagans' misfortunes, and prepares the accomplishment of his own revenge, which depends on the separation of Roland and Charles. While the motive for this may be practical, as Marsile obviously could not hope to defeat the Emperor's entire army even with Ganelon's help, it seems that Ganelon really has no grudge against Charles in spite of the latter's obvious lack of enthusiasm for him. It should be remembered that Ganelon's wife is Charles's sister, and Roland's mother."
—Translator's note.

While the twelve peers   whom Charlemagne so loves
Serve as his vanguard   with twenty thousand knights,
The king is safe;   he fears no man alive." AOI

XLIII

"Fair Ganelon,"   then says the pagan king,
"You'll see no soldiers   better at war than mine,
And I can summon   four hundred thousand knights.
Can I not fight   King Charles and all his Franks?"
"If you should try it,"   Count Ganelon replies,
"I tell you this,   you'd massacre your men.
Forget that folly,   and hear what I advise:
To Charlemagne   send such a royal gift   570
As to amaze   and gratify the French.
Send twenty men   as hostages for you,
And then the king   will go home to sweet France.
Behind his army   the rear-guard will remain,
And with them Roland,   the nephew of the king,
And Oliver,   so gallant and so brave.
And there they die—   if you'll do as I say.
King Charles will see   the downfall of his pride;
He'll have no wish   to carry on the fight." AOI

XLIV

Answers Marsile,   "My fair lord Ganelon,   580
Tell me the way   Count Roland can be killed."
Ganelon says,   "Here is the plan I've made:
The king will cross   the mountain pass at Cize,[21]
With a strong guard   remaining far behind.
He'll leave his nephew,   Count Roland, in the rear,
Oliver too,   in whom he has such faith,
With them a host   of twenty thousand Franks.
Then of your pagans,   a hundred thousand men
Must be sent out   to launch the first attack.
You'll see the Frenchmen   wounded and overcome—   590
Not that I say   your men won't suffer too.
If you attack   a second time that way,
You can be sure   that Roland won't escape.
Once you have done   this brave and knightly deed,
All your life long   from warfare you'll be freed.

XLV

"With that same blow   that struck Count Roland down,
You would cut off   the Emperor's right arm;
His mighty host   you'd scatter and destroy,
Nor would he find   so great a force again.
All of his Empire   would be restored to peace."   600

---

[21] A valley in the northern Pyrenees, the mountains that divide France from Spain.

Marsile fell on his neck;   with joy he swore
That Ganelon   should loot his treasure-store.   AOI

XLVI

Then says Marsile,   "There's one thing more to do,
Since all good counsel   depends on perfect trust;
Give me your oath   that Roland is to die."
Ganelon says,   "That shall be as you wish."
He swore by relics[22]   he carried in his sword,
And so forever   turned from his rightful lord.   AOI

XLVII

A throne was there,   made all of ivory.
A book was brought   by King Marsile's command: 610
Laws of Mohammed   and Tervagant, his gods.
On this he swore,   the Spanish Saracen,
If he found Roland   was named to the rear-guard,
He would attack   with all his pagan knights,
And do his utmost   to see the Frenchman die.
"Amen to that!"   was Ganelon's reply.

LI

Then the king summons   his treasurer Malduit:
"Have they prepared   the tribute for King Charles?"
"The seven hundred camels,   by your command,
Have all been loaded   with silver and with gold,
And twenty men,   our noblest, set to go."   AOI

LII

King Marsile places   his arm around the count,
Saying to him,   "Valiant you are, and wise.
But as you keep   your God's most holy law,
I charge you never   to turn your heart from me!   650
Of all I own   I'll give you a good part:
Ten mules are loaded   with fine Arabian gold,
And every year   you'll have as much again.
Give Charles the keys   to this broad city's walls,
Tell him its treasures   will henceforth be his own,
And then name Roland   commander of the guard.
If I can find him   crossing some narrow pass,
There I'll attack   and fight him to the death."
Ganelon says,   "Then let us speed the day."
He mounts his horse,   and quickly rides away.   AOI   660

LIII

The Emperor Charles   has now retraced his steps
As far as Galne—   that was a captured town
Whose walls Count Roland   had leveled to the ground;

---

[22] Remains of the bodies or of the personal effects of the saints.

No one would live there   for the next hundred years.
He waits for news   of Ganelon's return,
And for the tribute   offered to him by Spain.
At dawn one morning,   just as the sky grows light,
Count Ganelon   comes back from his long ride.   AOI

LIV

The Emperor Charles   rose early on that day.
Now, having prayed   at matins and a mass,   670
He goes outside   and stands on the green grass.
Roland is with him,   the noble Oliver,
Naimon the Duke,   and many others too.
Ganelon comes,   treacherous and forsworn.
All of his cunning   he puts into his speech,
Saying to Charles,   "I greet you in God's name!
Here are the keys   to King Marsile's fair town;
From Saragossa,   treasures beyond all price,
And twenty nobles,   hostages—guard them well!
But King Marsile   has asked me to explain   680
Why you won't see   his uncle, the Caliph:
Before my eyes   a hundred thousand men
All armed in mail,   some with their helmets closed,
Swords at their belts,   the hilts inlaid with gold,
Sailed with that lord   out to the open sea.
They fled Marsile,   hating the Christian law
Which they refused   to honor and to keep.
They sailed away,   but had not gone four leagues
When they were caught   in such a frightful storm
They all were drowned.   So perished the Caliph.   690
Were he alive,   he'd be here with me now.
As for Marsile,   my lord, you can be sure
That well before   a single month has passed,
He'll follow you   when you return to France.
There he'll accept   the Faith that you uphold,
Both of his hands   he'll place between your own,
And do you homage   for all his lands in Spain."
Then said the king,   "For this may God be thanked!
You have done well,   and great shall be your prize."
Among the hosts,   a thousand trumpets sound;   700
The French break camp,   they load each mule and horse,
And toward sweet France   they gladly set their course.   AOI

LV

King Charles the Great   has conquered all of Spain,
Captured its forts,   its cities laid to waste;
His war, he says,   has now come to its end.
The emperor rides   once more toward his sweet France.
From Roland's spearhead   the flag of battle flies;
When, from a hilltop,   it waves against the sky,
The French make camp   throughout the countryside.

Pagans are riding   through valleys deep and dark,   710
Their coats of mail   are laced up to the chin,
Their helmets closed;   bright swords hang at their sides,
Shields at their necks,   a pennon on each lance;
Where trees grow thick   high on a hill they wait,
Four hundred thousand   watching for day's first light.
Alas! If only   the French could see that sight!   AOI

LVI

The day is over,   the night grows calm and still.
The Emperor Charles   goes to his bed and sleeps.
In dream he rides   through the great pass at Cize;
Clasped in his hands   he holds an ashwood spear: 720
Count Ganelon   wrenches it from his grasp,
With raging strength   shatters and breaks the wood,
And sends the splinters   flying against the sky.
King Charles sleeps on,   not opening his eyes.

LVIII

Darkness of night   gives way to shining dawn.
Throughout the host,   clarion trumpets sound.
Proud, on his horse,   the emperor appears.
"Barons, my lords,"   says Charlemagne the King,   740
"Narrow and dark   will be this mountain pass—
Who shall remain   to guard us from the rear?"
Ganelon says,   "Choose Roland, my stepson.
You have no baron   as valorous as he."
Fiercely the king   looks at the one who spoke,
And says to him: "Vile demon that you are!
You are insane,   possessed by deadly rage!
And in the vanguard—   who'll have the leader's place?"[23]
Ganelon says,   "Count Ogier the Dane.
None would do better,   and no one can complain."   750

LIX

Count Roland heard   what Ganelon proposed,
And then he answered   with knightly courtesy:
"Noble stepfather,   now I must hold you dear,
For you have named me   commander of this guard.
The King of France   won't lose by my neglect
War-horse or palfrey,   that I can promise you;
He shall not lose   a single riding-mule,
Saddle-horse, pack-horse—   none shall give up its life
Until our swords   take payment for that prize."
Ganelon says,   "I know you tell no lies."   AOI   760

---

[23] Charles asks who will assume Roland's usual position at the *head* of the army.

LX

When Roland heard   he'd stay with the rear-guard,
To his stepfather   he angrily replied:[24]
"Ignoble serf,   despicable foul wretch,
Do you suppose   I'll let the glove fall here
The way you dropped the staff[25]   at King Charles' feet?"   AOI

LXI

"My rightful lord,"   says Roland to the king,
"Give me the bow[26]   you're holding in your hand;
I promise you   that no man here will say
I let it fall,   like Ganelon that day
The envoy's staff   dropped out of his right hand."   770
The Emperor Charles   sits with his head bowed low,
Pulls his moustache,   and strokes his long white beard,
While in his eyes   unwilling tears appear.

LXII

At that Duke Naimon   stood up to speak his mind—[27]
The court could boast   no better man than he—
Saying to Charles,   "You have heard what's been said;
It's clear enough   that Roland is enraged.
He has been named   to go with the rear-guard;
You have no baron   who will dispute that now.
Give him the bow   that you yourself have bent;   780
Then choose good men   to fight at his command."
Charles puts the bow   in Roland's outstretched hand.

LXIII

The Emperor Charles   calls Roland to come forth.
"My noble nephew,   this is what I intend:
Half of my army   shall stay behind with you.
Accept their service,   and then you will be safe."
Count Roland answers,   "Never will I agree.
May God destroy me,   if I so shame my race!
Just twenty thousand   shall serve me, valiant Franks.
You'll cross the mountains,   safely in France arrive—   790
And fear no man   as long as I'm alive!"   AOI

LXIV

Roland has mounted   the horse he rides to war.
There comes to join him   his friend Count Oliver,
And Gerin comes,   the brave Count Gerier,
And Oton comes,   with him Count Bérengier,

---

[24] Roland's sudden shift from "knightly courtesy" (line 752) to anger may indicate that laisse LX is not authentic; possibly, as Joseph Bédier and the translator suggest, the shift shows that Roland's words in LIX are ironic.

[25] Ganelon had dropped a glove, not a staff (laisse XXV).   [26] An emblem of command.

[27] "Duke Naimon's advice is always followed, usually to disaster."—Translator's note.

And Astor comes,   and fiery Anseïs,
And old Gérard,   the Count of Roussillon,
The powerful and wealthy   Duke Gaïfier.
Says the Archbishop,   "My head on it, I'll go!"
"And I am with you,"   answers Count Gautier,   800
"I'm Roland's vassal—   my help is his by right."
Then they select   the twenty thousand knights.   AOI

                              LXV
Count Roland says   to Gautier de l'Hum:
"A thousand Franks,   men of our land, you'll take
To occupy   the hills and the ravines,
So that King Charles   may safely go his way."   AOI
Gautier answers,   "For you I'll do my best."
Leading away   a thousand Franks of France,
Gautier will guard   the mountains and ravines;
Whatever happens,   he won't come down again   810
Without a battle—   Almaris of Belferne
Gave them a fight;[28]   and seven hundred blades
Flashed from their scabbards   on that most evil day.

                              LXVI
High are the hills,   deep valleys shun the light;
The cliffs rise grey,   the gorges hold dark fear.
The French ride on   in misery and pain,
Their passing heard   some fifteen leagues around;
And when once more   they're back again in France,
In Gascony,   where Charlemagne is lord,
Then they remember   the lands they hold, their sons,   820
Their maiden daughters,   their fair and noble wives—
There is not one   who is not moved to weep
But of them all   none sorrows as does Charles,
For he has left   his nephew there in Spain;
And now his tears   the king cannot restrain.   AOI

                              LXVII
All the twelve peers   have stayed behind in Spain;
They guard the pass   with twenty thousand Franks,
Courageous men   who do not fear to die.
And now King Charles   is riding home again;
He drapes his cloak   to hide his grieving face.   830
Duke Naimon rides   next to the emperor;
He says to Charles,   "What weighs your spirits down?"
The king replies,   "Who asks me that does wrong.
I can't keep silent   the sorrow that I feel,
For Ganelon   will be the doom of France.
Last night an angel   sent me a warning dream:

---

[28]The poet anticipates the fighting to come.

I held a spear—   he broke it from my grasp,
That count who named   my nephew to the guard.
And I left Roland   among that pagan race—
God! If I lose him   no one can take his place." AOI   840

LXVIII

Charlemagne weeps;   he can't hold back his tears.
They grieve for him,   his hundred thousand Franks,
And for Count Roland   are suddenly afraid.
A traitor's lies   left him to die in Spain—
Rich gifts the pagan   bestowed on Ganelon:
Silver and gold,   brocades and silken cloaks,
Camels and lions,   fine horses, riding mules.
Now King Marsile   summons the lords of Spain,
His counts and viscounts,   his chieftains and his dukes,
His high emirs,[29]   and all their warrior sons: 850
Four hundred thousand   assemble in three days.
In Saragossa   the drums begin to sound;
They place Mohammed   high on the citadel—
No pagan fails   to worship him[30] and pray.
And then they ride   with all their might and main
Through Terre Certaine,[31]   through valleys, over hills,
Until they see   the battle-flags of France.
The twelve companions   are waiting with the guard;
When they are challenged,   the fighting will be hard.

LXIX

King Marsile's nephew   rides up before the host.   860
Laughing, he prods his mule   with a sharp goad,
And to his uncle   addresses this fair speech:
"For years, Lord King,   I've served you faithfully;
My only wages   were hardships, suffering,
And battles fought   and won on many fields.
I ask this boon: have Roland left to me![32]
I'll take his life   on my sharp-pointed spear,
And if Mohammed   protects me in the fight,
The land of Spain   once more shall be our own,
From the high passes   as far as Durestant![33]   870
Charles will be weary,   the Frenchmen will retreat;
In all your lifetime,   war will not touch your land."
King Marsile places   the gauntlet in his hand.[34] AOI

---

[29] Arab chieftains.   [30] In fact, the use of graven images is forbidden in Islam.
[31] Possibly the term refers to Cerdagne, a valley in Catalonia, a region bordering on France, possibly to the southern slope of the Pyrenees.
[32] Aelroth (we learn his name later, in XCIII) asks that he be the first to fight Roland.
[33] Where this is located is uncertain; the line apparently means "from the Pyrenees to the southern border."
[34] By placing the glove in his hand, Marsile grants his nephew's request.

*[Twelve pagan chieftains (including King Marsile's nephew Aelroth) vow to defeat Roland,
Oliver, and the other paladins (Charles' twelve peers). The pagans are identified as Falsaron,
Corsalis, Malprimis de Brigant, the emir (lord) of Balaguer, the emir of Moriane, Torgis of
Tortelose, Escrimiz of Valterne, Estorgant, Estramariz, Margariz of Seville, and Chernuble
de Munigre.]*

LXXIX

The pagans wear   Saracen coats of mail,
Most of them furnished   with triple-layered chains.
From Saragossa   come the good helms they lace;
They gird on swords   whose steel comes from Vienne;[35]
Their shields are strong;   Valencia made their spears;
Their battle flags   are crimson, blue and white.
All mules and palfreys   must now be left behind;   1000
Each mounts his war-horse;   in close-knit ranks they ride.
Fair is the day,   the sun shines bright and clear,
Weapons and armor   glitter with fiery light,
A thousand trumpets   command more splendor still.
That great shrill clamor   reaches the Frenchmen's camp.
Oliver says,   "Companion, it would seem
That we will have   some Saracens to fight."
Roland replies,   "God grant that you be right!
Here we will stand,   defending our great king.
This is the service   a vassal owes his lord: 1010
To suffer hardships,   endure great heat and cold,
And in a battle   to lose both hair and hide.
Now every Frank   prepare to strike great blows—
Let's hear no songs   that mock us to our shame![36]
Pagans are wrong,   the Christian cause is right.
A bad example   I'll be in no man's sight."   AOI

LXXX

Count Oliver   has climbed up on a hill.
From there he searches   the valley to his right,
And sees that host   of pagan Saracens.
Then he calls out   to Roland, his sworn friend: 1020
"Coming from Spain   I see the fiery glow
Of shining hauberks,[37]   the blazing steel of helms.
For our brave Franks   this means great toil and pain.
And that foul traitor,   false-hearted Ganelon,
Knew this—that's why   he named us to the guard."
Count Roland answers,   "Stop, Oliver, be still!
Of my stepfather   I'll let no man speak ill."

LXXXI

Count Oliver   has climbed up on a hill;
From there he sees   the Spanish lands below,

[35] A town on the Rhone river in France, noted for the manufacture of arms, as was Valencia in Spain.
[36] That is, let no mocking songs be written about us.   [37] Tunics of mail.

And Saracens   assembled in great force.   1030
Their helmets gleam   with gold and precious stones,
Their shields are shining,   their hauberks burnished gold,
Their long sharp spears   with battle flags unfurled.
He tries to see   how many men there are:
Even battalions   are more than he can count.
And in his heart   Oliver is dismayed;
Quick as he can,   he comes down from the height,
And tells the Franks   what they will have to fight.

LXXXIII

Oliver says,   "The pagan might is great—
It seems to me,   our Franks are very few!   1050
Roland, my friend,   it's time to sound your horn;
King Charles will hear,   and bring his army back."
Roland replies,   "You must think I've gone mad!
In all sweet France   I'd forfeit my good name!
No! I will strike   great blows with Durendal,
Crimson the blade   up to the hilt of gold.
To those foul pagans   I promise bitter woe—
They all are doomed   to die at Roncevaux!"   AOI

LXXXIV

"Roland, my friend,   let the Oliphant[38] sound!
King Charles will hear it,   his host will all turn back,   1060
His valiant barons   will help us in this fight."
Roland replies,   "Almighty God forbid
That I bring shame   upon my family,
And cause sweet France   to fall into disgrace!
I'll strike that horde   with my good Durendal;
My sword is ready,   girded here at my side,
And soon you'll see   its keen blade dripping blood.
The Saracens   will curse the evil day
They challenged us,   for we will make them pay."   AOI

LXXXV

"Roland, my friend,   I pray you, sound your horn!   1070
King Charlemagne,   crossing the mountain pass,
Won't fail, I swear it,   to bring back all his Franks."
"May God forbid!"   Count Roland answers then.
"No man on earth   shall have the right to say
That I for pagans   sounded the Oliphant!
I will not bring   my family to shame.
I'll fight this battle;   my Durendal shall strike
A thousand blows   and seven hundred more;
You'll see bright blood   flow from the blade's keen steel.
We have good men;   their prowess will prevail,   1080
And not one Spaniard   shall live to tell the tale."

[38] Horn made of ivory.

LXXXVI

Oliver says,   "Never would you be blamed;
I've seen the pagans,   the Saracens of Spain.
They fill the valleys,   cover the mountain peaks;
On every hill,   and every wide-spread plain,
Vast hosts assemble   from that alien race;
Our company   numbers but very few."
Roland replies,   "The better, then, we'll fight!
If it please God   and His angelic host,
I won't betray   the glory of sweet France!   1090
Better to die   than learn to live with shame—
Charles loves us more   as our keen swords win fame."

LXXXVII

Roland's a hero,   and Oliver is wise;
Both are so brave   men marvel at their deeds.
When they mount chargers,   take up their swords and shields,
Not death itself   could drive them from the field.
They are good men;   their words are fierce and proud.
With wrathful speed   the pagans ride to war.
Oliver says,   "Roland, you see them now.
They're very close,   the king too far away.   1100
You were too proud   to sound the Oliphant:
If Charles were with us,   we would not come to grief.
Look up above us,   close to the Gate of Spain:[39]
There stands the guard—   who would not pity them!
To fight this battle   means not to fight again."
Roland replies,   "Don't speak so foolishly!
Cursed be the heart   that cowers in the breast!
We'll hold our ground;   if they will meet us here,
Our foes will find us   ready with sword and spear."   AOI

LXXXIX

Archbishop Turpin   comes forward then to speak.
He spurs his horse   and gallops up a hill,
Summons the Franks,   and preaches in these words:
"My noble lords,   Charlemagne left us here,
And may our deaths   do honor to the king!
Now you must help   defend our holy Faith!
War is upon us—   I need not tell you that—   1130
Before your eyes   you see the Saracens.
Confess your sins,   ask God to pardon you;
I'll grant you absolution   to save your souls.
Your deaths would be   a holy martyrdom,
And you'll have places   in highest Paradise."
The French dismount;   they kneel upon the ground.

---

[39] The mountain pass.

Then the archbishop,   blessing them in God's name,
Told them, for penance,   to strike when battle came.[40]

XC

The kneeling Franks   have risen to their feet.
They are absolved,   and free from any sin;   1140
Archbishop Turpin   has signed them with the cross.
Now they have mounted   swift horses bred for war;
They bear the weapons   befitting them as knights.
Thus they await   the Saracen attack.
Count Roland calls   Oliver to his side:
"My lord companion,   the words you spoke were true;
This is the work   of faithless Ganelon—
He sold us all   for treasure, gold and coins.
Now may he suffer   the emperor's revenge!
As for the bargain   that King Marsile has made,   1150
Without good swords   he'll forfeit what he paid." AOI

XCI

At Roncevaux   Count Roland passes by,
Riding his charger,   swift-running Veillantif.
He's armed for battle,   splendid in shining mail.
As he parades,   he brandishes his lance,
Turning the point   straight up against the sky,
And from the spearhead   a banner flies, pure white,
With long gold fringes   that beat against his hands.
Fair to behold,   he laughs, serene and gay.
Now close behind him   comes Oliver, his friend,   1160
With all the Frenchmen   cheering their mighty lord.
Fiercely his eyes   confront the Saracens;
Humbly and gently   he gazes at the Franks,
Speaking to them   with gallant courtesy:
"Barons, my lords,   softly now, keep the pace!
Here come the pagans   looking for martyrdom.
We'll have such plunder   before the day is out,
As no French king   has ever won before!"
And at this moment   the armies join in war. AOI

XCII

Oliver says,   "I have no heart for words.   1170
You were too proud   to sound the Oliphant:
No help at all   you'll have from Charlemagne.
It's not his fault—   he doesn't know our plight,
Nor will the men   here with us be to blame.
But now, ride on,   to fight as you know how.

---

[40] The priest in confession administered absolution as God's agent, on condition that the sinner do penance; here fighting in battle is substituted for the usual forms of penance such as prayer, fasting, and almsgiving.

Barons, my lords,   in battle hold your ground!
And in God's name,   I charge you, be resolved
To strike great blows   for those you have to take.
Let's not forget   the war-cry of King Charles!"
He says these words,   and all the Franks cry out;   1180
No one who heard   that mighty shout, "Montjoie!"[41]
Would soon forget   the valor of these men.
And then, how fiercely,   God! they begin to ride,
Spurring their horses   to give their utmost speed,
They race to strike—   what else is there to do?
The Saracens stand firm;   they won't retreat.
Pagans and Christians,   behold! in battle meet.

XCIII

King Marsile's nephew,   Aelroth is his name,
First of the pagans,   rides out before the host,
Taunting our Franks   with loud malicious words: 1190
"Today, foul Frenchmen,   you'll break a lance with us;
You stand here now   abandoned and betrayed!
The king was mad   to leave you at the pass:
This day sweet France   will see its pride cast down.
The Emperor Charles   will lose his good right arm!"
Count Roland hears him,   God! with what pain and rage!
He spurs his horse   to run with all its might,
Levels his lance,   strikes Aelroth such a blow
His shield is shattered,   the hauberk split in two,
The pagan's bones   crack open in his chest,   1200
His broken spine   sticks out behind his back
So that the spear   drives out his very soul.
Under the thrust   the body starts to fall,
And Roland hurls him   a spear's length from his horse;
He falls down dead,   his neck broken in two.
But still Count Roland   gives him these parting words:
"Foul infidel,   King Charles is not a fool,
Nor was he ever   unfaithful to his trust.
Wisely he chose   that we should guard the pass;
Sweet France will lose   no glory here today.   1210
Strike on, you Franks!   First blood will win the fight!
Their cause is evil,   and we are in the right."   AOI

CX

Now fierce and grim   the battle rages on.
Oliver, Roland—   how valiantly they fight!
Turpin delivers   more than a thousand blows;
Among the peers   none dreams of holding back,
And all together,   the Franks, as one man, strike.

---

[41] Charles' battle cry. *Mont* means "hill" and *joie* means "joy." "Jenkins suggests also the pilgrims' cry of joy on seeing the end of their quest for Monte Gaudia or a similar hill near Jerusalem or Santiago, but no sure explanation exists." —Translator's note.

By hundreds, thousands,   the pagans fall and die;
There's no way out   except for those who flee:
Each one who stays   is living his last day.
But others die—   the best among the Franks—   1420
They'll never see   their families, their wives,
Or Charlemagne   who waits beyond the pass.
A fearful storm   that very day strikes France;
Through rushing winds   long peals of thunder roar,
And heavy rains,   enormous hailstones fall,
Great bolts of lightning   are striking everywhere.
Now the whole earth   is trembling dreadfully
From Saint Michel   all the way down to Seinz,
From Besançon   to Wissant on the sea;
There is no stronghold   without a shattered wall.   1430
At noontime shadows   darken the light of day;
The only brightness   comes when the black sky cracks,
And no man sees it   who isn't terrified.
Many declare,   "The world is at an end—
The Day of Wrath   has come upon us now!"
But they know nothing,   and they believe a lie.
The heavens grieve   that Roland is to die.

[*Laisses XCIV-CXXVI: Meeting the first assault force of the pagans, Charles' paladins kill
pagan chieftains in individual combat: Oliver kills Falsaron, Marsile's brother; Archbishop
Turpin kills Corsalis; Gerin kills Malprimis de Brigant; Gerier kills the emir of Balaguer;
Samson kills the emir of Moriane; Anseïs kills Torgis of Tortelose; Engelier kills Escrimiz of
Valterne; Oton kills Estorgant; Bérengier kills Estramariz; Roland kills Chernuble de
Munigre.*

    *After Marsile's reinforcements join the battle, however, it becomes more even, and Charles'
forces are gradually worn away by attrition. Most of the paladins are slain by pagans, though
at the cost of their own lives at the hands of Roland, Oliver, and Archbishop Turpin.*]

CXXVII

Count Roland says   to Oliver his friend:
"My lord companion,   I'm sure you will agree
That our archbishop   makes a most valiant knight—
There is none better   on earth beneath the sky;
With lance in hand,   or spear, how he can fight!"
The count replies,   "Then let's go to his side!"
When he has spoken,   the Franks attack once more.
Hard are the blows,   the slaughter pitiless;
Many a Christian   is brought to grievous pain.
Then to behold   Roland and Oliver   1680
Wielding their swords   to cut the pagans down!
Beside them Turpin   thrusts with his mighty spear.
We know what happened   according to the *Geste,*
Chronicles, records   bear witness to the fact:
Four thousand pagans   by those few Franks were slain.
Through four assaults   the Frenchmen hold their ground.
But with the fifth   their strength comes to an end.
That final charge   kills all the knights of France

Except for sixty   who by God's will survive—
They'll make the pagans   pay dearly for their lives!   AOI   1690

CXXVIII

Count Roland sees   the slaughter of the Franks.
He says these words   to Oliver his friend:
"Noble companion,   what do you counsel now?
So many Franks   lie dead upon the field—
Well could we weep   for that fair land, sweet France,
Which will not see   these valiant lords again.
Oh! Charles, my friend,   if only you were here!
Oliver, brother,   how can we call him back?
Is there no way   to tell the king our plight?"
Oliver answers,   "Not if we save our fame.   1700
Better to die   than learn to live with shame."   AOI

CXXIX

Then Roland says,   "I'll sound the Oliphant.
King Charles will hear it   on the high mountain pass;
I promise you,   the Franks will all turn back."
Oliver answers,   "Then you would bring disgrace
And such dishonor   on your whole family
The shame of it   would last them all their lives.
Three times I asked,   and you would not agree;
You still can do it,   but not with my consent.
To sound the horn   denies your valor now.   1710
And both your arms   are red with blood of foes!"
The count replies,   "I've struck some pretty blows."   AOI

CXXX

Then Roland says,   "This has become a war.
I'll blow my horn,   and Charlemagne will hear."
Oliver says,   "Then you'll disgrace your name.
Each time I asked you,   companion, you refused.
If Charles were with us,   we would not come to grief.
No one can say   our Franks have been to blame.
I promise you—   I swear it by my beard—
If I should live   to see my sister's face,   1720
You'll never lie   in Alda's[42] sweet embrace!"   AOI

CXXXI

Then says the count,   "You're angry at me. Why?"
Oliver answers,   "Roland, you are to blame.
There is no madness   in courage for good cause,
But men should listen   to reason, not blind pride.
You were too reckless,   and so these Franks have died.
Never again   will we serve Charlemagne.
Had you believed me,   my lord would be here now,

---

[42] Roland's fiancee.

We would have fought   and beat the Saracens,
Marsile would be   our prisoner, or dead.   1730
We are the victims   of your great prowess now!
We won't be there,   alas! to help King Charles,
A man whose peer   will not be seen on earth.
And you will die,   leaving sweet France to shame.
Brothers in arms   we've been until this day;
Now we have only   a last farewell to say."   AOI

CXXXII

Archbishop Turpin,   hearing their angry words,
Urges his horse   with spurs made of pure gold,
And riding up,   reproaches both of them:
"Roland, my lord,   and you, Lord Oliver,   1740
End your dispute,   I pray you, in God's name.
It's too late now   to blow the horn for help,
But just the same,   that's what you'd better do.
If the king comes   at least we'll be avenged—
Why should the Spaniards   go home safe to rejoice?
And then the Franks   will ride back to this place;
They'll find us dead,   our bodies hacked by swords
Put us in coffins   carried on horses' backs,
And they will weep   for pity and for grief.
We will be buried   with honor in a church,   1750
And not be eaten   by wolves and pigs and dogs."
Then Roland answers: "Your words are wise, my lord."

CXXXIII

Count Roland presses   the horn against his mouth;
He grasps it hard,   and sounds a mighty blast.
High are the hills,   that great voice reaches far—
They hear it echo   full thirty leagues around.
Charlemagne hears,   and so do all his men.
The Emperor says,   "Our Franks are in a fight!"
Count Ganelon   returns a swift reply:
"Except from you,   I'd take that for a lie!"   AOI   1760

CXXXIV

And now Count Roland,   in anguish and in pain,
With all his strength   sounds the great horn again.
Bright drops of blood   are springing from his mouth,
Veins in his forehead   are cracking with the strain.
That mighty voice   cries out a second time;
Charlemagne hears it,   high on the mountain pass,
Duke Naimon listens,   and so do all the Franks.
Then says the king,   "That is Count Roland's horn!
He'd never sound it,   except for an attack."
Ganelon says,   "What battle can there be?   1770
You have grown old,   your hair is streaked with white;
The words you speak   could well befit a child.

You ought to know   how great is Roland's pride—
The wonder is   God suffers it so long.
He captured Noples,   and not by your command,
And then flushed out   the Saracens inside;
He fought them all,   Roland, your loyal man,
And then took water   and washed the field of blood,
Hoping that you   would not detect the fight.
Just for a rabbit   he'll blow his horn all day!   1780
Now he is playing   some game to please his peers.
Who in the world   would dare make war on him!
Ride on, I tell you!   What are we waiting for?
We've far to go   to see our lands once more."   AOI

                              CXXXV
Count Roland's mouth   is crimson with his blood,
His temples broken   by the tremendous strain.
He sounds the horn   in anguish and in pain.
Charlemagne hears,   and so do all the Franks.
Then says the king,   "How long that horn resounds!"
Duke Naimon answers,   "Great valor swells the sound!   1790
Roland is fighting: he must have been betrayed—
And by that man   who tells you to hang back.
Take up your arms,   let your war-cry ring out!
Your household needs you,   now speed to its defense.
You've heard enough   how Roland's horn laments!"

                              CXXXVI
The Emperor Charles   orders his horns to sound.
The French dismount,   prepare themselves for war.
They put on hauberks,   helmets and golden swords;
Their shields are good,   heavy their spears and strong,
Their battle-flags   are crimson, blue and white.   1800
Riding their chargers,   the barons of the host
Spur on and gallop   back through the mountain pass.
Each to the other   pronounces this same vow:
"When we get there,   if Roland's still alive,
We'll fight beside him,   striking hard blows and straight."
What does it matter?   Their help will come too late.

                              CXXXVII
All afternoon   the sun shines bright and clear,
Armor and weapons   are gleaming in the light,
Hauberks and helmets   glitter as if on fire,
And all the shields,   brilliant with painted flowers,   1810
And all the spears   and gilded battle flags.
In bitter wrath   the Emperor rides on,
The men of France,   in sorrow and in rage.
There is not one   who can hold back his tears;
Because of Roland,   the Frenchmen are afraid.
King Charles commands   that Ganelon be seized;

Summoning forth   all of his household cooks,
He tells their chief,   Besgon, what should be done:
"Here is a felon   I'm leaving in your charge—
He has betrayed   the vassals of my house."   1820
The cook takes over;   a hundred kitchen boys,
The best and worst,   will guard Count Ganelon.
They pluck the hairs   from his moustache and beard,
Each with his fist   strikes him four mighty blows,
And then they beat him   with heavy sticks and clubs.
An iron collar   is put around his neck,
And then they chain him   as if he were a bear.
On a mule's back,   trussed up, he will remain.
They'll guard him well,   and wait for Charlemagne.   AOI

CXXXVIII

High are the hills,   and shadowy and vast,   1830
Deep the defiles,   and swift the mountain streams.
The trumpets sound   ahead and to the rear,
Blaring replies   to Roland's Oliphant.
In bitter wrath   the Emperor rides on,
The men of France   in sorrow and in rage;
Not one but grieves   and bitterly laments,
Praying that God   will keep Count Roland safe
Until they come   and join him in the field—
How they will fight   when they are at his side!
What does it matter   how loyally they strive?   1840
They'll be too late   whenever they arrive.   AOI

CXXXIX

Now Charlemagne   rides on in his great rage;
His beard, defiant,   outside his hauberk lies.
The lords of France   spur for the utmost speed,
There isn't one   but angrily laments
That they can't be   already on the field
Where Roland fights   against the Saracens.
I think his wound   won't let him long survive,
But God! the sixty   still fighting at his side—
No king or chieftain   has ever had their like.   AOI   1850

CXL

Count Roland sees   the mountains and the hills
Where all around him   the Franks are lying dead;
He weeps for them,   as a true knight would do.
"Barons, my lords,   may God forgive your sins,
And grant your souls   a place in Paradise,
On holy flowers   may you forever rest!
I've never seen   vassals better than you;
You followed me   so loyally and long,
For Charlemagne   we've won such mighty lands!
The king's own household,   alas! brings him to woe.   1860

And that fair country   where it is sweet to live
Today laid waste   and cruelly bereaved!
Barons of France,   because of me you die;
I can't protect you,   I cannot keep you safe:
Look now to God   who never failed a trust.
Oliver, brother,   I'll not break faith with you.
I'll die of grief,   if not by pagan spears.
My lord, companion,   there's still work for us here!"

CXLI

Roland has gone   back to the battlefield.
With Durendal   he strikes heroic blows: 1870
Faldrun de Pui   he cuts down first of all,
Then twenty-four   of the best pagan knights.
No man has ever   wanted revenge so much.
Just as the stag   runs to escape the hounds,
So do the pagans   before Count Roland flee.
Says the archbishop,   "Bravely you fight, and well!
Yours is the spirit   a chevalier must have,
If he bears arms   and has a horse to ride:
A man in battle   ought to be fierce and strong—
For one who isn't   I wouldn't give two cents.   1880
Instead of fighting   let him become a monk
And spend his days   praying for all our sins."
Roland replies,   "Strike on, and spare not one!"
With that the Franks   begin to fight once more.
Many a Christian   falls to the pagan swords.

CXLII

A man who knows   all captives will be slain
In such a battle   fights to the end of strength;
And so the Franks   like lions face their foes.
Behold Marsile: as a true knight would do,
He sits the horse   that he has named Gaignon,[43]   1890
Pricks with sharp spurs,   and rides against Bevon,
The lord of Beaune   and also of Dijon;
He breaks his shield,   the hauberk splits in two—
With that one blow   he fells the Frenchman dead.
Then Marsile kills   Ivoire and Ivon too,
And with them dies   Gérard of Roussillon.
Seeing that, Roland,   who isn't far away,
Says to the pagan,   "God smite you with His curse!
To you I owe   these good companions slain—
Nor shall we part   before that debt is paid!   1900
Now is the time   to teach you my sword's name."[44]
With that he charges   as a true knight would do;

---

[43] The name means "watchdog."
[44] "Thus it is apparent that the name 'Durendal' has significance, but nothing further can
be effectively said on the subject."—Translator's note.

The count's keen sword cuts off Marsile's right hand,
Then Jurfaleu surrenders his blond head—
He was a prince, the son of King Marsile.
The pagans cry, "Mohammed help us now!
Gods of our country, give us revenge on Charles,
For he has sent such felons here to fight
That death itself can't drive them from the field."
They tell each other, "Let's get away from here!"   1910
A hundred thousand run from the French attack;
Whoever calls, they won't be coming back.

CXLIII

What does it matter that King Marsile has fled?
They must still fight his uncle Marganice,[45]
The lord of Carthage, Alfrere, and Garmalie,
That land accursed called Ethiopia
Whose black men serve as Marganice commands.
They have big noses, their ears stick out too far;
Some fifty thousand have come to fight the Franks.
They gallop boldly, and in wild fury charge,   1920
Shouting the war-cry dear to the pagan hosts.
Then Roland says, "Here we'll win martyrdom.
Now I can see how little time is left;
But cursed be he who lets his life go cheap!
Strike them, my lords, strike with your shining swords!
Give them a battle whether you live or die,
That none may say we brought sweet France to shame.
When Charlemagne comes to this battlefield,
He'll see the hosts of slaughtered Saracens—
For each of us some fifteen pagans dead;   1930
Charles won't reproach us, he'll bless us all instead." AOI

CXLIV

When Roland sees this horde of infidels
Who all are darker than is the blackest ink,
With nothing white except their gleaming teeth,
He says aloud, "There isn't any doubt,
Today we'll die— I can believe it now.
Follow me, Frenchmen! We'll give them one more charge!"
Oliver says, "The devil take the last!"
The French attack; their blows fall hard and fast.

CXLV

And when the pagans see how few Franks are left,   1940
They take much pride and comfort from the fact,
Telling each other, "King Charles is in the wrong."
Then Marganice, astride a sorrel[46] horse,

---

[45] The Caliph mentioned in laisses XXXV and LIV.
[46] Light brown or orange-brown.

Pricks with gold spurs   and gallops from behind
To land his spear   deep in Oliver's back.
The gleaming hauberk   shatters and splits away,
The spear goes through   and opens up his chest.
Says Marganice,   "You've taken a hard blow!
Charlemagne left you   to wait here for your doom.
Let him not glory   in what he's done to Spain—   1950
Your death alone   avenges all our slain."

CXLVI

Oliver feels   how close he is to death.
He raises high   Halteclere's bright burnished blade,
Strikes Marganice,   and splits his tall gold helm,
Its jewels and flowers   fall shattered to the ground;
He cleaves his head   right down into the teeth,
Wrenching the sword,   he hurls the body down.
Then says the count,   "Be damned, you Saracen!
Whatever Charles   may have lost here today,
At least I'm sure   no wife or lady friend   1960
Will hear you boasting,   safe in your lands again,
Of how you captured   silver or gold from me:
Your triumphs here   will not be on parade."
He summons then   Count Roland to his aid. AOI

CXLVII

Oliver knows   he has a fatal wound.
He'll never have his fill   of vengeance now.
In the melee   he fights on valiantly,
He cuts through spears,   the pagans' studded shields,
And feet and fists   and saddle-trees and spines.
Whoever watched him   cut pagans limb from limb,   1970
Bodies piled up   around him on the ground,
Would know that once   he'd seen a noble lord.
The count remembers   the war-cry of King Charles,
And loud and clear   his voice rings out, "Montjoie!"
He calls to Roland,   summons his friend and peer,
"My lord, companion,   come fight beside me now!
We'll part in sorrow   before the sun goes down." AOI

CXLVIII

Roland is there;   he sees Oliver's face,
The skin is ashen,   so pallid it looks grey,
And from his wounds   bright blood is spurting out;   1980
Its heavy drops   flow down him to the ground.
"O God!" says Roland,   "I don't know what to do.
Was such great valor   destined to be cut down!
My noble friend,   you'll have no peer on earth.
Alas, sweet France!   You are bereft today
Of your good vassals,   laid waste and brought to shame;

The Emperor Charles   will sorely feel the lack."
With these words Roland   faints on his horse's back.   AOI

CXLIX

Here is Count Roland   unconscious on his horse;
Oliver, wounded   and very close to death,   1990
Has bled so much   that both his eyes are dimmed:
Now far or near   he can't see well enough
To give a name   to any man alive.
When he encounters   Count Roland in the field,
Oliver strikes him,   cleaving his golden helm
Brilliant with jewels—   the nose-piece cracks in two—
And yet the blade   does not touch face or head.
Roland's eyes open,   and looking at his friend,
Softly and gently   he asks him only this:
"My lord, companion,   it's Roland—did you know?   2000
I've always loved you;   did you intend that blow?
You gave no challenge   before you charged at me."
Oliver says,   "I recognize your voice,
But I can't see you—   God keep you in His sight!
I struck at you!   I pray you, pardon me."
Roland replies,   "I am not hurt at all;
I do forgive you,   here and in front of God."
When he had spoken,   each leaned down toward his friend.
So, with great love,   they parted in the end.

CL

Oliver suffers   the agonies of death;   2010
He feels his eyes   turn back into his head,
He cannot hear,   he cannot see at all.
Now he dismounts,   and kneeling on the ground,
Aloud he asks   forgiveness for his sins;
He clasps his hands,   and holds them toward the sky,
Praying that God   will grant him Paradise,
And give His blessing   to Charles and to sweet France,
And to Count Roland   above all other men.
Then his heart fails him,   his shining helmet bows.
All of his body   sinks down against the ground;   2020
The count is dead—   no longer did he stay.
Lord Roland weeps,   lamenting bitterly;
Many have grieved,   but no man more than he.

CLI

When Roland sees   that Oliver is dead,
Lying face downward   stretched out against the ground,
With tender words   he bids his friend farewell:
"Alas, companion!   Your valor ends in woe.
We were together   so many years and days;
You never wronged me,   and I kept faith with you.

Now you are dead,   I grieve to be alive."   2030
The marquis faints   just as he says these words,
Still on his horse,   whose name is Veillantif;
The fine gold stirrups   will keep him sitting straight,
So he won't fall   however he may sway.

CLII

Before Count Roland   recovers from his faint,
While he still sits   unconscious on his horse,
The battle brings   disaster to his men:
The Franks are dead—   he's lost them, every one
Save the archbishop   and Gautier de l'Hum[47]
Who from the mountains   has now returned at last.   2040
He fought a battle   with Spanish Saracens.
His men are dead;   their enemies have won.
Down toward the valleys,   he flees now, all alone,
Searching for Roland,   calling to him for help:
"Ah, noble count!   Where are you, valiant lord?
When you were with me,   I never was afraid.
It's Gautier—   I conquered Maelgut!
Droon is my uncle,   his aged head is grey.
You used to love me,   because you knew me brave.
My spear is broken,   my shield has been pierced through,   2050
My hauberk's links   scattered and snapped apart,
Deep in my body   a pagan lance has thrust;
I'm dying now,   but they have bought me dear."
Roland wakes up   to hear his final words;
Turning his horse,   toward Gautier he spurs.   AOI

CLIII

Count Roland, grieving   and filled with bitter rage,
Rides once again   through the thick of the fight.
Twenty Spaniards   he throws dead to the ground,
Gautier kills six,   Archbishop Turpin five.
The pagans say,   "These men are monstrous fierce!   2060
Take care, my lords,   don't let them get away.
If you aren't traitors,   we'll rush upon them now—
If you aren't cowards,   they won't escape alive!"
Then riding onward   with a great hue and cry,
They charge the Franks   once more from every side.   AOI

CLIV

There is Count Roland,   a noble warrior,
Gautier de l'Hum,   a worthy chevalier,
Archbishop Turpin,   a veteran and brave:
None would be willing   to fail the other two.
In the melee   they strike the pagans down.   2070
A thousand Spaniards   dismount to fight on foot,

---

[47] For Gautier, see LXIV-LXV.

While forty thousand   stay on their horses' backs—
And even so   they don't dare come too near.
They throw their lances,   hurl their keen-bladed spears,
All sorts of weapons   come flying at the Franks;
With the first blows,   Count Gautier is killed,
Turpin of Reims   soon finds his shield pierced through,
His helmet breaks—   he's wounded in the head—
His chain-mail hauberk   is cracked and splits apart,
Four pagan spears   strike deep into his flesh,   2080
His war-horse, dying,   carries him to the ground.
O God! What sorrow   to see Turpin go down!   AOI

CLV

Turpin of Reims,   finding himself unhorsed,
With four deep wounds   where spears thrust through his flesh,
Leaps up again,   great fighter that he is,
Looks for Count Roland,   and hastens to his side,
Saying just this: "I am not beaten yet!
No man of courage   gives up while he's alive."
He draws Almace   whose blade is burnished steel,
Strikes in the throng   a thousand blows and more.   2090
Soon Charles will say   that Turpin spared no foe:
They found four hundred   around him in the field,
Some of them wounded,   some of them thrust clean through,
And there were others   who parted with their heads.
So says the *Geste*,   and someone who was there:
Saint Giles[48] for whom   Our Lord works miracles
Left an account   in Laon's church in France;
Everyone knows this,   or nothing understands.

CLVI

Roland delivers   many a skillful blow,
But now his body   is fevered, drenched with sweat,   2100
His head is throbbing   under a dreadful pain,
His temples broken   from sounding his great horn.
Longing to know   if Charles is on his way,
Weakly, once more,   he blows the Oliphant.
King Charles stands still,   listening to that call;
"My lords," he says,   "now we have come to woe!
My nephew Roland   takes leave of us this day—
His horn's voice tells me   he won't be long alive.
Who wants to be there   had better speed his horse.
Let every trumpet   the host commands resound!"   2110
And sixty thousand   rang from the lofty peaks
Down through the valleys,   echoing loud and clear.
The pagans, listening,   think it no empty boast—
They say, "Here come   King Charles and all his host."   AOI

---

[48] The meaning apparently is that the saint, about whom there were numerous legends, was present in spirit. No account of the battle written by him is known.

CLVII

The pagans say,   "Now Charles is coming back.
Those trumpet calls   rally the men of France;
We'll have great losses   if the Emperor comes,
And if Count Roland   lives to make war again,
We may as well   surrender all of Spain."
About four hundred   assemble, helmeted,   2120
The best who fought   among the Saracens;
With all their might   these men attack anew,
And then Count Roland   has work enough to do. AOI

CLVIII

When Roland sees   the pagans closing in,
His heart grows stronger,   and prouder and more fierce.
He'll yield to none,   as long as he's alive.
Astride the horse   whose name is Veillantif,
He gallops toward them,   pricking with golden spurs;
Into the throng   he charges to attack.
Archbishop Turpin   is fighting at his side.   2130
The pagans say,   "Let's get away from here!
Those trumpet calls   mean that the Franks are near—
Their mighty king,   great Charles, will soon appear!"

CLIX

Count Roland's friendship   no coward ever knew,
Nor any man   false-hearted or too proud,
Nor any knight   who was not skilled at war.
To the archbishop   Roland addressed these words:
"I am on horseback,   my lord, and you're on foot;
For love of you,   here I shall take my stand—
We'll meet together   what good or evil comes,   2140
No mortal man   will make me leave your side.
We shall return   the Saracen attack.
What sword can equal   the blows of Durendal!
Turpin replies,   "Curse him whose arm grows slack!
We'll be avenged   when Charlemagne comes back."

CLX

The pagans say,   "Ours were unlucky stars!
Would that this evil day   had never dawned!
We've lost our peers,   our lords have all been slain,
The valiant Charles   is coming back again.
Now we can hear   the trumpets of his host,   2150
The mighty clamor   when the Franks shout 'Montjoie!'
And this Count Roland   is hideously fierce—
He can't be conquered   by men of flesh and blood.
Let's cast our lances   and then leave him alone."
The Saracens   throw many javelins,
Lances and darts,   and feathered throwing spears.

Count Roland's shield   is broken and pierced through,
His hauberk's mail   is cracked and split apart,
And still his body   has not been touched at all.
But Veillantif   has suffered thirty wounds;   2160
Beneath Count Roland   he falls dead to the ground.
Then all the pagans   yield to their fear and flee;
And Roland stands,   dismounted, on the field.   AOI

CLXI

The pagans flee,   furious and enraged,
Trying their best   to get away in Spain.
Count Roland lacks the means   to chase them now,
For he has lost   his war-horse Veillantif;
Against his will   he has to go on foot.
He went to give   Archbishop Turpin help,
Unlaced his helmet,   removed it from his head,   2170
And then took off   the hauberk of light mail;
The under-tunic   he cut into long strips
With which he stanched   the largest of his wounds.
Then lifting Turpin,   carried him in his arms
To soft green grass,   and gently laid him down.
In a low voice   Roland made this request:
"My noble lord,   I pray you, give me leave,
For our companions,   the men we held so dear,
Must not be left   abandoned now in death.
I want to go   and seek out every one,   2180
Carry them here,   and place them at your feet."
Said the archbishop,   "I grant it willingly.
The field belongs,   thank God, to you and me."

CLXII

Alone, Count Roland   walks through the battlefield,
Searching the valleys,   searching the mountain heights.
He found the bodies   of Ivon and Ivoire,
and then he found   the Gascon Engelier.
Gerin he found,   and Gerier his friend,
He found Aton   and then Count Bérengier,
Proud Anseïs he found,   and then Samson,   2190
Gérard the Old,   the Count of Roussillon.
He took these barons,   and carried every one
Back to the place   where the archbishop was,
And then he put them   in ranks at Turpin's knees.
Seeing them, Turpin   cannot restrain his tears;
Raising his hand,   he blesses all the dead.
And then he says,   "You've come to grief, my lords!
Now in His glory,   may God receive your souls,
Among bright flowers   set you in Paradise!
It's my turn now;   death keeps me in such pain,   2200
Never again   will I see Charlemagne."

CLXIII

Roland goes back   to search the field once more,
And his companion   he finds there, Oliver.
Lifting him in his arms,   he holds him close,
Brings him to Turpin   as quickly as he can,
Beside the others   places him on a shield;
Turpin absolves him,   signing him with the cross,
And then they yield   to pity and to grief.
Count Roland says,   "Brother in arms, fair friend,
You were the son   of Renier, the duke   2210
Who held the land   where Runers valley lies.
For breaking lances,   for shattering thick shields,
Bringing the proud   to terror and defeat,
For giving counsel,   defending what is right,
In all the world   there is no better knight."

CLXIV

When Roland sees   that all his peers are dead,
And Oliver   whom he so dearly loved,
He feels such sorrow   that he begins to weep;
Drained of all color,   his face turns ashen pale,
His grief is more   than any man could bear,
He falls down, fainting   whether he will or no.   2220
Says the archbishop,   "Baron, you've come to woe."

CLXV

When the archbishop   sees Roland on the ground,
He feels more sorrow   than he has ever known.
He reaches out   to grasp the Oliphant;
A swift stream waters   the plain at Roncevaux,
And there, for Roland,   he wants to fill the horn.
Taking short steps,   staggering, he sets out,
But in his weakness   he can't go very far—
He has no strength,   his wounds have bled too much;
He doesn't travel   even a hundred feet   2230
Before he falls—   his heart has given out.
Now death is trying   to put his soul to rout.

CLXVI

Meanwhile Count Roland   recovers from his faint,
He rises to his feet,   but with great pain.
He looks around him,   he searches up and down;
Beyond the place   where his companions lie,
Prone on the grass,   he sees the noble lord,
Archbishop Turpin,   God's delegate on earth.
Count Roland hears him   confessing he has sinned,
With his clasped hands   held upward toward the sky,   2240
Praying that God   will give him Paradise.
Turpin is dead   who fought for Charlemagne.
With mighty blows,   with wise and holy words,

Against the pagans   he championed the Faith.
May God in heaven   bless him and grant him grace.

CLXVII

Roland sees Turpin   lying there on the ground,
Entrails protruding   from his enormous wounds;
Above his forehead   his brains are bubbling out.
On Turpin's chest,   between his collarbones,
Roland has crossed   the beautiful white hands.   2250
Now he laments   as it is done in France:
"O nobly born,   illustrious chevalier,
To heaven's glory   I now commend your soul;
Our Lord will never   be served more willingly.
Since the Apostles,   there has been none like you
To keep the Law,   and bring men to the Faith.
From pain and sorrow   may your free soul arise;
May you find open   the gates of Paradise!"

CLXVIII

Now Roland knows   that death is very near.
His ears give way,   he feels his brain gush out.   2260
He prays that God   will summon all his peers;
Then, for himself,   he prays to Gabriel.[49]
Taking the horn,   to keep it from all shame,
With Durendal   clasped in his other hand,
He goes on, farther   than a good cross-bow shot,
West into Spain,   crossing a fallow field.
Up on a hilltop,   under two lofty trees,
Four marble blocks[50]   are standing on the grass.
But when he comes there,   Count Roland faints once more,
He falls down backward;   now he is at death's door.   2270

CLXIX

High are the hills   and very high the trees,
The four great blocks   of polished marble shine;
On the green grass   the count is lying still.
A Saracen   watches with steady eyes:
This man feigned death,   hiding among the slain;
His face and body   he had besmeared with blood.
Now he stands up   and dashes forward fast—
He's handsome, strong   and very valiant too,
But he won't live   to profit from his pride;
He falls on Roland,   seizing him and his arms   2280
And says these words: "Charles' nephew lost the fight!
When I go home,   his sword shall be my prize."
But as he pulls it,   Roland comes back to life.

---

[49] The great archangel; like Michael, he is a leader of the heavenly hosts.
[50] Possibly boundary stones.

CLXX

Count Roland feels   the pagan take his sword,
And opening his eyes,   he says just this:
"You look to me   like no one on our side!"
Raising the horn   he'd wanted to keep safe,
He strikes the helmet   shining with gold and jewels,
Shatters the steel,   smashes the skull and bones;
He puts both eyes   out of the pagan's head,   2290
And sends his body   crashing against the ground.
And then he asks him,   "How did you get so brave,
Dog, to attack me   with or without just cause?
Whoever heard this   would say you were insane!
But I have cracked   the Oliphant's broad bell;
Its gold and crystals   were shattered as it fell."

CLXXI

Count Roland feels   that he is going blind.
Now he stands upright,   using what strength remains;
All of the color   has vanished from his face.
In front of him   there is a dark grey stone.   2300
He strikes ten blows   in bitterness and grief;
The steel blade grates   but will not break or dent.
The count cries out,   "O Holy Mary, help!
O Durendal,   alas for your fair fame!
My life is over,   I'll care for you no more.
We've won such battles   together in the field,
So many lands   we've conquered, you and I,
For Charles to rule   whose beard is silver-grey.
No man must have you   who fights and runs away!
You have been long   in a good vassal's hands;   2310
You'll have no equal   in all of holy France."

CLXXIV

Count Roland feels   the very grip of death
Which from his head   is reaching for his heart.
He hurries then   to go beneath a pine;
In the green grass   he lies down on his face,
Placing beneath him   the sword and Oliphant;
He turns his head   to look toward pagan Spain.   2360
He does these things   in order to be sure
King Charles will say,   and with him all the Franks,
The noble count   conquered until he died.
He makes confession,   for all his sins laments,
Offers his glove   to God[51] in penitence.   AOI

CLXXVI

And now Count Roland,   lying beneath a pine,
Has turned his face   to look toward pagan Spain;

---

[51] A symbolic gesture of dependence, as by a feudal vassal to his chief.

And he begins   remembering these things:
The many lands   his valor won the king,
Sweet France, his home,   the men of his own line,
And Charlemagne   who raised him in his house—   2380
The memories   make him shed tears and sigh.
But not forgetting   how close he is to death,
He prays that God   forgive him all his sins:
"O my true Father,   O Thou who never lied,
Thou who delivered   Lazarus from the grave,
Who rescued Daniel[52]   out of the lions' den,
Keep now my soul   from every peril safe,
Forgive the sins   that I have done in life."
Roland, in homage,   offers his glove to God.
Saint Gabriel comes   and takes it from his hand.   2390
His head sinks down   to rest upon his arm;
Hands clasped in prayer,   the count has met his end.
God sends from heaven   the angel Cherubin,[53]
Holy Saint Michael   who saves us from the sea,
And with these two   the Angel Gabriel flies.
Count Roland's soul   they bring to Paradise.

CLXXVII

Roland is dead;   his soul rests now with God.
The Emperor Charles   rides into Roncevaux;
On every road,   on every mountain path,
On every ell,   on every foot of land,   2400
They find a body   of Frank or Saracen.
King Charles cries out,   "Fair nephew, where are you?
Where's the archbishop?   Where is Count Oliver?
Where is Count Gerin,   and Gerier his friend?
Oton—where is he, and noble Bérengier,
Ivoire and Ivon, those two I held so dear?
Tell me what happened   to Gascon Engelier,
Where are Duke Samson,   the valiant Anseïs,
And Old Gérard,   the Count of Roussillon?
Where are the peers,   the twelve who stayed behind?"   2410
What good is asking   when no one can reply?
"God!" says the king,   "Now have I cause to grieve,
For where was I   when fighting here began!"
He pulls his beard   in anguish and in pain;
The lords of France   are weeping bitter tears,
And twenty thousand   faint in their grief and fall.
Duke Naimon feels   great sorrow for them all.

---

[52] For these two famous biblical miracles—the resurrection of Lazarus by Jesus and the divine protection of Daniel when the Persian king Darius had him imprisoned in the lions' den—see John, chapters 11–12, and Daniel, chapter 6.

[53] Here the reference is to a particular angel, not to the order of angels the word usually signifies.

[*Laisses CLXXVIII–CLXXXVI: Leaving an honor guard to watch over Roland and the other slain heroes, Charles pursues the retreating Saracens. A divine miracle arrests the sun in the sky, allowing Charles' army to slay part of the enemy and to drive the rest to panic and death by drowning in the river Ebro.*]

CLXXXVII

To Saragossa   the pagan king has fled.   2570
There he dismounts   beneath an olive tree,
Gives up his sword,   his hauberk and his helm;
On the green grass   the king lies down in shame.
Marsile's right hand   was cut completely off,
And he is fainting   from loss of blood and pain.
In front of him,   his wife Queen Bramimonde,
Weeping for grief,   cries out a loud lament.
The queen has with her   some twenty thousand men,
All of them cursing   Charlemagne and sweet France.
Now they attack   Apollo in his crypt,   2580
Reviling him,   disfiguring his form:
"Why, evil god,   have you brought us to shame?
Why have you suffered   the downfall of our king?
For faithful service   you give a poor reward!"
Then they take off   his scepter[54] and his crown,
And to a column   they tie him by the hands;
They knock him down,   stamping him with their feet,
And with great clubs   they smash him into bits.
They take the ruby   away from Tervagant,
And then Mohammed   they thrust into a ditch   2590
Where he'll be trampled   and gnawed by dogs and pigs.

[*Laisses CLXXXVIII to CCLVII: On the following day, the great emir Baligant of "Babylon" (Cairo) arrives with his forces, too late for the battle but resolved to help Marsile and overcome Charles. He is told of the Saracens' defeat and of Roland's death.*

Charles, after camping overnight, returns to Roncevaux. He finds Roland's body and utters a lovingly elegiac lament for him. The dead are buried. Roland, Oliver, and the archbishop Turpin—who will be buried in France—receive special honors.

The army of Baligant suddenly appears; Charles and his forces prepare for war again. The poet recites an epic catalogue of Charles' armies, specifying what part of Europe each division comes from and who commands it. Charles prays for victory, he advances with his army, and they camp for the night.

The pagans too prepare for war. Baligant is described at some length, the poet expressing regret that so admirable a hero should not be a Christian. Baligant praises Charles. A catalogue, corresponding to that of the Franks, shows that Baligant's army comes from many parts of the world.

The battle is joined on a broad plain, Roland's horn sounding to hearten the Franks. Many men, on both sides, die in the fierce fighting. Duke Naimon, after felling Baligant's son, is seriously wounded by the emir's brother but is rescued by Charles. Informed of his son's death, Baligant grieves. He rallies the pagans; the Franks fall back.]

---

[54] That is, the idol's.

CCLVIII

The day goes by;   darkness begins to fall;   3560
Pagans and Franks   are fighting with their swords.
Two men of courage   command these mighty hosts.
They don't forget   to sound their battle-calls,
The great emir   shouting his "Précieuse!"
And Charlemagne,   his famous cry "Montjoie!"
Each recognizes   the other's strong clear voice,
And then they meet   upon the battlefield.
They charge head on;   each one lands with his spear
So great a blow   upon the other's shield
It cracks wide open   below the heavy boss;   3570
The hauberk panels   are cracked and split apart,
And yet the spearheads   don't penetrate the flesh.
The girths give way,   throwing the saddles off,
With them both kings   come crashing to the ground.
Then, in an instant,   both have regained their feet
And drawn their swords,   ready to fight it out.
No way to end   this combat will be found
Till one of them   lies dead upon the ground.   AOI

CCLIX

A mighty hero   is Charlemagne of France,
And Baligant   will meet him unafraid.   3580
With swords unsheathed,   they come together now,
Their heavy shields   receiving mighty blows
Which split the leathers,   the double wooden frames;
The nails fall out,   the bosses break apart.
Then nothing shelters   the hauberks from the blades,
And fiery sparks   come flashing from their helms.
This is a combat   which has to last as long
As neither man   admits that he is wrong.   AOI

CCLX

Says the emir,   "Charles, if you stop and think,
You will repent   of what you've done to me: 3590
You can't deny   that you have killed my son;
You do great wrong   when you invade my lands.
Become my vassal,   promise me fealty;
Come with me to the East   and serve me there."
King Charles replies,   "That would be vile disgrace.
I'll be no friend   to pagans, or make peace.
Receive the law   that is the gift of God,
Become a Christian,   and you shall know my love;
Serve Him, have faith   in that almighty King."
Says Baligant,   "Tediously you preach!"   3600
They draw their swords,   and there's an end to speech.

CCLXI

The great emir   is powerful and brave:
He strikes Charles' helmet   so terrible a blow

The burnished steel   is cracked and splits apart,
The sword blade cleaves   the emperor's thick hair
And slices off   a hand's breadth of his scalp,
Stripping the flesh   down to the naked bone.
Charlemagne staggers,   comes close to falling down,
But God won't have him   brought to defeat or slain:
Saint Gabriel   comes back to him once more,   3610
And says, "Great king,   what are you waiting for?"

CCLXII
Charlemagne hears   the angel's holy voice:
He's not afraid,   he knows he will not die.
His strength returns,   his mind is clear and calm.
And then he strikes   with the great sword of France;
The emir's helmet,   ablaze with jewels, cracks,
His head is broken   so that the brains spill out,
His face splits open   down to his long white beard:
He is stone dead   before he hits the ground.
Then Charles' "Montjoie!"   rings through the battlefield.   3620
Duke Naimon hears him   and hastens to his side
With Tencendur;[55]   the great king mounts his horse.
Now by God's will,   the pagans turn and flee;
The Frenchmen know   they've won their victory.

[*Laisses CCLXIII-CCLXIX: In Saragossa, the king Marsile dies in anguish when he hears of the Saracens' defeat. Charles' forces occupy the city, destroying its idols, baptizing many of the pagans, and putting resisters to death. Marsile's queen, Bramimonde, who is to be converted by gentler means, is forcibly led away with the army, which returns to France. On reaching the border, Charles has Roland, Oliver, and Archbishop Turpin honorably entombed. Back in his capital, Aix, Charles informs Roland's fiancee, Alda, of his death; rejecting Charles' compensatory offer of his own son and heir, she dies in grief.*]

CCLXX
The Emperor Charles   has come back home to Aix.
There Ganelon,   the traitor, bound with chains,
In the high town,   before the palace stands.
To a great stake   the serfs have bound him fast,
Both of his hands   are tied with deerskin thongs,
They beat him well   with heavy sticks and rods:
That way he's treated   in the most proper style,   3740
And he must wait   in torment for his trial.

CCLXXI
As it is written   in the old chronicles,
Charlemagne summoned   vassals from many lands;[56]
And in the chapel   at Aix they're gathered now.
The day is solemn,   the feast they celebrate
Is Saint Silvester's—[57]   so many people say.

---

[55] Charles' horse.
[56] Ganelon cannot be judged by Charlemagne himself; he must be tried by his peers.
[57] December 31.

The trial begins   with speeches on both sides,
And Ganelon,   who did a traitor's deed,
Is dragged before   the emperor to plead. AOI

CCLXXII

"Barons, my lords,"   says Charlemagne the king,   3750
"Give me your judgment   concerning Ganelon.
He was with me in Spain   among my host,
And there he robbed me   of twenty thousand Franks;
My nephew Roland   you'll never see again,
Nor Oliver,   so courteous and brave—
For gold and treasure   this man betrayed the peers."
"Sire," says the count,   "I won't conceal the truth:
Because of Roland   I lost both goods and gold.[58]
I wanted him   to suffer and to die;
But in that vengeance   there was no treachery."   3760
The Franks reply,   "We'll talk of this and see."

CCLXXIII

Before the king   behold Count Ganelon.
Stalwart he stands,   fair color in his face—
If he were loyal,   he'd look a noble lord.
He sees the French,   the judges who are there,
The thirty members   of his own family,
And then he speaks,   his great voice ringing out:
"Barons of France,   for God's sake hear me now!
My lords, I fought   beside the emperor,
And served him well   in loyalty and love.   3770
His nephew Roland,   hating me in his heart,
Had me condemned   to torment and sure death:
I was to bring   Charles' message to Marsile—
I had the wit   and wisdom to survive.
I faced Count Roland   and challenged him aloud,
And Oliver,   and all the other peers.
Charlemagne heard me,   so did these noble lords:
I am avenged,   but not by treachery."
The Franks reply,   "We'll go and judge your plea."

CCLXXIV

Ganelon sees   his great trial has begun.   3780
Thirty kinsmen   the count has with him there,
Among them one   looked up to by the rest
Called Pinabel—   his castle is Sorence.
This man can argue   so that his views prevail,
And he's a hero   not easy to defeat. AOI
Ganelon says,   "I place my trust in you—

---

[58] Ganelon may mean that Roland kept more than his proper share of the spoils of war in Spain. The basis of Ganelon's self-defense is that he opposed Roland openly, not in the secret manner that technically was necessary to the definition of treason.

Save me from death,   defend me in this trial!"
Says Pinabel,   "In no time you'll be free.
If any Frenchman   decides that you should hang,
The Emperor Charles   must have that judgment tried: 3790
My sword shall prove   these accusations lies."
Count Ganelon   with grateful thanks replies.

CCLXXV

Bavarians, Saxons,   have gone to judge the case,
Normans are with them,   Poitevins, men of France,
Germans are there,   and many Thiois too;
Those from Auvergne   show the most courtesy.
They speak more softly   because of Pinabel,
Telling each other,   "Let's bring this to an end,
Dismiss the trial,   and ask that Charles the King
For this one time   let Ganelon go free—   3800
He'll be his vassal   in loyalty and love.
Roland is dead;   you won't see him again.
No gold or treasure   will bring him back to life.
It would be madness   to fight for his sake now."
They all approve;   no one will disagree
But Geoffroy's[59] brother,   the chevalier Thierry.   AOI

CCLXXVI

And so the barons   return to Charlemagne,
Saying to him,   "Sire, we would ask for this:
Acquit your captive,   let Ganelon go free,
Henceforth to serve you   loyally and with love.   3810
Grant him his life,   for he is nobly born;
And no man's death   will bring Count Roland back,
Nor any gold—   there's nothing to be done."
Then says the king,   "You're traitors, every one!"   AOI

CCLXXVII

When King Charles sees   they all have failed his cause,
He bows his head   so none can see his face;
His words and looks   proclaim his bitter woe.
And then before him   he sees a chevalier,
Thierry, whose brother   is Geoffroy of Anjou.
Not very stalwart,   he's lean and spare of build,[60]   3820
His hair is black,   his face is rather dark;
He isn't tall,   nor could you call him short.
With courtesy   he tells the emperor:
"Fair sire and king,   do not give way to grief!
You know I've served you   a long time faithfully.

---

[59] Geoffroy of Anjou, Charles' flag bearer (see VIII) and one of his right-hand men.
[60] "The point is that Thierry will really need God's help if he is to prevail against Pinabel; thus the case will be better proved. And when he does win, the Franks immediately shout, 'A holy miracle!' (3931)."—Translator's note.

Now all my forebears   through me protest this trial:
However Roland   may have wronged Ganelon,
No one may harm   a man who serves the king.
Count Ganelon   is thus a traitor proved;
His oath to you   was broken and betrayed.   3830
And so I judge   that he should hang and die,
And that his body   be treated as befits
A criminal   who's guilty of a crime.
If he has kinsmen   who'd argue this with me,
I'll use this sword   girded here at my side
To give my judgment   a prompt and sure defense."[61]
The Franks reply,   "Your argument makes sense."

CCLXXVIII

Now Pinabel   stands up before the king;
He's tall and strong,   valiant and very swift:
The man he strikes   won't see another day.   3840
He says to Charles,   "Sire, you convoked this trial;
Pray, then, keep order—   let's not have so much noise.
And as for Thierry,   his judgment has been heard.
I say he's wrong—   now let him come and fight."
His right-hand glove   he offers to the king.[62]
The emperor says,   "I ask for hostages."[63]
His thirty kinsmen   will sponsor Pinabel.
Says Charlemagne,   "He's free then, in your place."
They will be guarded   till justice ends the case.   AOI

CCLXXIX

When Thierry sees   that Pinabel will fight,   3850
He gives his glove,   the right one, to the king,
And Charlemagne,   his hostage, sets him free.
Charles has four benches   arranged to mark the field;
Those who will fight   go out to take their seats.
All think the challenge   well given, rightly met;
Ogier explains   how they are to proceed.
Horses and arms   are sent for with all speed.

CCLXXX

The knights are ready   to meet for their ordeal.   AOI
They've made confession,   have been absolved and blessed,
They've heard a mass,   taken communion too;   3860
Great offerings   they've given to the church.
Now when the champions   appear before the king,
They both are wearing   sharp spurs upon their feet,

---

[61] Technically, Thierry is defending a minority verdict of the jury; Pinabel, his opponent, will defend the majority verdict just rendered. In trials by combat, it was believed, the victory or defeat of the combatants demonstrated God's own judgment.

[62] The offering of the glove symbolizes the surrender to Charles of the combatant's feudal estate if he should be killed.

[63] Hostages are kept to guarantee that the combatant will appear for the duel.

They've put on hauberks,   shining and light and strong,
Their burnished helmets   are closed around their heads,
They gird on swords   whose hilts are of pure gold,
Around their necks   they hang their quartered shields,
Their right hands grasp   the long sharp-pointed spears.
Now they have mounted   war-horses bred for speed.
Seeing them go,   a hundred thousand knights   3870
Remember Roland   and weep for Thierry—
For God knows what   the end of this will be!

CCLXXXI

In a broad meadow   below Aix la Chapelle,
The barons meet;   their battle has begun.
Both are courageous, both of them valiant lords,
And their war-horses   are spirited and swift.
They spur them hard,   and loosening the reins,
They charge each other   and strike with all their might.
Both shields are shattered—   they're broken into bits—
The hauberks break,   the girths are split apart,   3880
The saddles fall,   and with them both the knights.
A hundred thousand   are weeping at the sight.

CCLXXXII

Both chevaliers   have fallen to the ground.   AOI
Losing no time,   they're on their feet again.
Agile and swift   is Pinabel, and strong;
They face each other—   they have no horses now—
And raise their swords   whose hilts are made of gold
To strike and hew   each other's shining helms;
Those heavy blows   can cut right through the steel.
The French lament,   thinking their man must fail.   3890
"O God," says Charles,   "now let the right prevail!"

CCLXXXIII

Says Pinabel,   "Thierry, admit you've lost!
I'll be your vassal   in loyalty and love,
All I possess   shall be at your command—
But reconcile   the king and Ganelon."
Then Thierry answers,   "That's easy to decide!
I'll take no offer   unworthy of a knight!
Let God determine   which one of us is right!"   AOI

CCLXXXIV

And Thierry says,   "Pinabel, you are brave;
You're tall and strong,   your body is well built,   3900
That you are valiant   is known to all your peers.
This is a battle   you can afford to lose!
I'll make your peace   with Charlemagne the king,
But Ganelon   must get what he deserves—
No day will pass   without his death retold."

Says Pinabel,   "Almighty God forbid!
I stand here now   for all my family—
I won't surrender   to any man on earth!
Better to die   than live to merit blame."
So once again   they slash with their great swords,   3910
Striking the helmets   brilliant with gold and jewels—
Great fiery sparks   fly out against the sky.
Now neither champion   will to the other yield
Until a dead man   is lying on the field.   AOI

CCLXXXV

He's a strong fighter,   Pinabel of Sorence,
The blow he strikes   on Thierry's burnished helm
Sends out such sparks   the grass is set on fire.
Then he springs forward,   the point of his steel blade
Cutting right through   from Thierry's forehead down;
Along his face   the sword point slashes deep,   3920
And blood springs out   all over his right cheek;
Down to his waist   the hauberk links all tear—
Without God's help,   he'd have died then and there!   AOI

CCLXXXVI

When Thierry sees   he's wounded in the face,
His bright blood falling   over the meadow grass,
Pinabel's helmet   of burnished steel he strikes:
Down through the nose-piece   it cracks and splits in two,
His skull is broken   and spills the brains inside;
With one last flourish   Thierry has felled him dead—
With that great blow   he's master of the field.   3930
The Frenchmen shout,   "A holy miracle!
Justice demands   that Ganelon must die,
With all the kinsmen   who came and took his side."   AOI

CCLXXXIX

They all agree: Bavarians, Alemans,   3960
Poitevins, Bretons,   and men from Normandy,
And first of all   the Franks who come from France,
That Ganelon   should die most horribly.
And so they order   four war-horses[64] brought out
To which they tie   Ganelon's feet and hands.
These are proud chargers,   spirited, bred for speed:
Four servants urge them   the way they ought to go.
There where a river   across a meadow flows,
Count Ganelon   is utterly destroyed:
His ligaments   are twisted and stretched out,   3970
His every limb   is cracked and splits apart;
On the green grass   the bright blood runs in streams.

---

[64] The execution by quartering contradicts earlier statements that Ganelon was to be hanged.

So Ganelon   as a foul traitor died.
Let no man's treason   give comfort to his pride!

CCXC

The Emperor Charles,   his vengeance being done,
Summoned his bishops,   the ones who came from France,
Bavarians   and Alemans as well:
"A noble captive   is dwelling in this house;
She's heard such sermons   and edifying tales,
She trusts in God,   and wants to take the Faith.   3980
Baptize her now,   that God may have her soul."
The bishops answer,   "Let godmothers be found!"[65]

*   *   *

A great assembly   was gathered at the baths
To see the Queen of Spain   receive the Faith;
To Juliana   they now have changed her name.
She had true knowledge   when Christian she became.

CCXCI

The Emperor Charles,   once justice has been done,
And his great anger   is finally appeased,   3990
Has Bramimonde   baptized into the Faith.
The day is over,   and in the dark of night
The king lies sleeping   in his high vaulted room.
Saint Gabriel   is sent by God to say:
"Charlemagne, summon   your empire's mighty hosts!
You'll march in force   into the land of Bire;
You must relieve   King Vivien at Imphe[66]
Where pagans hold   his city under siege,
And Christian voices   are crying for your help."
The Emperor Charles   has no desire to go.
"God!" says the king,   "how weary is my life!"   4000
He pulls his beard,   the tears flow from his eyes.
Here ends the poem,   for Turoldus declines.[67]

---

[65] The following line, indicated here by the spaced asterisks, is defective in the manuscript. It apparently described the godmothers.

[66] "Nothing is known of Bire, Imphe, or Vivien except that they were all Christian." —Translator's note.

[67] "The ending of the poem, *Ci falt la geste que Turoldus declinet*, is very famous for being so enigmatic. *Que* may mean either 'which' or 'because' (Jenkins); *declinet* may mean 'to compose, sing, recite, or copy.' It may also mean to 'set,' as the sun sets, or to become infirm. While it is true that my version favors the idea of the poet's explaining why he does not continue his work with Charlemagne's new expedition, the reason for this disinclination is left as imprecise as possible. I hoped mainly to let the poem end with the same frustrating vagueness as does the original."—Translator's note.

Marie de France
(Twelfth Century)

*"The first woman novelist of our era": that is the contemporary novelist John Fowles'
description of Marie de France. The phrase is deliberately playful and paradoxical,
especially in calling the author of twelve very brief verse romances a "novelist." Yet it
is precise; Marie's gifts are those of a fiction writer rather than a poet. She excels in
storytelling: in shaping often simple, apparently naive stories so as to make them
powerfully evocative and anything but naive. Her characters are memorable, lightly
sketched and yet psychologically convincing, even when they are engaged in fabulous
actions. And she creates a highly distinctive fictional world, an imaginative "Brittany" that is simultaneously the world of fairy tales and a dream-like version of her
own courtly circle. Fowles' emphasis upon her femininity seems right, too. Marie
works on a small scale—Fowles calls her "a laborer on two inches of ivory"—but
within her miniature world she has a feminine eye for the nuances and often the
absurdities of human emotions. After eight centuries, we can still recognize Marie's
charming fictions as belonging to "our era."*

The historical Marie is a shadowy figure. She is thought to be the author of three
surviving works, the Lais, a collection of Fables, and a didactic, supernatural tale
called St. Patrick's Purgatory. All three date from the second half of the twelfth
century, and all three contain statements that they were written by someone named
"Marie." At the end of the Fables, she also gives her nationality: "I shall name
myself so that it will be remembered; / Marie is my name, I am of France." She also
tells us in a Prologue to the Lais that she wrote them for a "noble king." Scholars
have concluded that Marie must have been born in France but at some point went to
England and wrote for the English court, heavily French in the years following the
Norman Conquest. The noble king is probably Henry II, whose queen was Eleanor of
Aquitaine, a sophisticated patron of literature. It is even possible that Marie was
Henry II's half sister. Henry's father, Geoffrey Plantagenet, had an illegitimate
daughter named Marie, who became abbess of Shaftesbury about 1180, and some
scholars have identified her with the evidently well-educated, apparently highly
placed Frenchwoman who wrote under the name "Marie de France."

Whoever Marie was, her work is one of the finest literary expressions of the
Twelfth-Century Renaissance in European culture that marked the end of the so-
called "Dark Ages." The preoccupation with military prowess that marked earlier
medieval narrative gave way to an overwhelming interest in love as a literary subject,
as the new class of courtly aristocrats who clustered around the great courts of England and France sought to define and mythologize their class values. Ovid's Metamorphoses and especially his Art of Love and Remedy for Love were translated
and endlessly studied as a guide to the psychology of refined love. Classical stories
were translated and adapted to emphasize their romantic elements, as in the Romance of Aeneas and the Romance of Thebes. Legendary histories such as
William of Malmesbury's Deeds of the English Kings (about 1125) and Geoffrey
of Monmouth's History of the Kings of Britain (about 1135) introduced Arthurian material soon to be worked into romances. During Marie's lifetime, Chrétien
de Troyes, across the Channel, wrote the first account of the love of Lancelot and
Guinevere.

Marie's special interest, in the Lais, was the "matter of Britain," Celtic or
"Breton" stories. At the beginning of the first of the twelve Lais, "Guigemar," she

writes, *"The tales—and I know they're true— / from which the Bretons made their lais / I'll now recount for you briefly,"* and repeatedly through the collection, she refers to her "Breton" sources. Many of the stories do seem to be from Celtic folklore, but Marie perhaps reset even those from written French sources in a fairy-tale-like Wales or Brittany as a result of a literary vogue for Celtic material.

A certain amount of controversy centers around Marie's conception of a lai. Generally speaking, it is a short romance in rhyme which fuses supernatural elements, a fairy-tale "Celtic" setting, and a treatment of courtly love, originally performed by Breton minstrels to the accompaniment of a harp or a kind of lyre called a rote. Sometimes, Marie seems to use the term to refer to her sources, as in the prologue to "Guigemar"; at other times, she seems to use it to refer to her own work (although we are not sure that she gave her collection the title that the manuscript bears). Perhaps it is best to think of her poems as "literary lais," sophisticated adaptations of folk lais, probably intended to be read rather than chanted or sung.

Marie's twelve lais are enormously varied in length, form, and subject matter. But all of them center around the subject of love, like an elaborate set of variations on a single theme. The variations are so great that it is difficult to generalize about her view of love. It is remarkably open-minded; adulterous love is not ruled out, though generally she celebrates the possibilities for happiness within a loving marriage. She also celebrates sensuality, though she emphasizes the necessity for spiritual and emotional union as well. There is often tension in the lais between private ecstasy and public acknowledgement of love; love cannot survive the claustrophobia of secrecy and yet the world is often ranged against lovers who seek the endorsement of society. A recurring theme is what Marie calls desmesure, the passionate excess or loss of restraint characteristic of genuine love. This excess is one of the glories of love, but it carries within it the chief threat to continued love. Over and over in the stories, disaster ensues when one or the other of the lovers gives way to desmesure and oversteps the bounds of discretion and restraint.

The twelve stories in the Lais are so intricately interconnected by parallels, balances, and echoes that only a reading of the entire collection can convey the full range of Marie's variations on her theme. But Bisclavret and Yonec make a good pairing, partly because the first shows a false, disloyal love that is ultimately punished, while the other presents a genuine love that is ended by violence but is finally vindicated. Ironically, the false love is within marriage, the true one outside it. The two lais present a sharp contrast structurally as well. Bisclavret, like many of Marie's shorter lais, is centered around a single climactic scene, with the earlier part of the poem devoted to preparing for that scene. Yonec, on the other hand, covers a long span of time, with the emphasis upon the earlier scenes and the final scene only a sort of coda to the main action. Both illustrate Marie's fondness for organizing her work around a central symbolic creature or object that suggests the nature of the love and its moral problems. Marie takes the primitive figure of the werewolf in Bisclavret and turns it into an ironic and suggestive symbol of the central theme of the story, the conflict of bestiality and civilization in human nature. The bird-lover of Yonec is similarly suggestive as a representation of the story's themes of imprisonment and freedom, a symbol of love's power to enable us to liberate ourselves.

FURTHER READING (prepared by J. H.): The best introduction in English to the *Lais* is probably the present translators' *The Lais of Marie de France*, 1978. This volume contains a short appreciative foreword by John Fowles, a lengthy critical and historical introduction by the translators, translations of all the *lais*, and a short critical commentary on each. Marie's life, works, and milieu are well outlined in the Introduction to *The Fables of Marie de France*, trans. Mary Lou Martin, 1984. Paula Clifford's *Marie de France: Lais*, 1982, a volume in the Critical Guides to French Texts series, offers helpful critical analyses of the individual stories. Emanuel J. Mickel, Jr.'s *Marie de France*, 1974, in the Twayne's World Authors series, offers chapters on Marie's identity and intellectual background as well as on the nature of the *lai*, Marie's plots and sources, her concept of love, and the narrative structure of the *lais*. In the title novella of *The Ebony Tower*, 1974, the novelist John Fowles gives a modern treatment to some of Marie's themes, followed by a short "Personal Note" on Marie and a translation of "Eliduc"—all of which makes for a dazzling "metafictional" improvisation and a provocative interpretation of Marie. Glyn S. Burgess's *Marie de France*, 1977, is an annotated bibliography of scholarship up to its date. Readers interested in women's writing in general during the Middle Ages can find fifteen authors, including Marie de France, excerpted and succinctly discussed in *Medieval Women Writers*, ed. and with Introduction by Katharina M. Wilson, 1984; the section on Marie is by Joan M. Ferrante.

BISCLAVRET (THE WEREWOLF)

Translated by Robert Hanning and Joan Ferrante

Since I am undertaking to compose *lais*,
I don't want to forget Bisclavret;
In Breton, the *lai's* name is *Bisclavret*—
the Normans call it *Garwaf [The Werewolf]*.
In the old days, people used to say—
and it often actually happened—
that some men turned into werewolves
and lived in the woods.
A werewolf is a savage beast;
while his fury is on him   10
he eats men, does much harm,
goes deep in the forest to live.
But that's enough of this for now:
I want to tell you about the Bisclavret.

In Brittany there lived a nobleman
whom I've heard marvelously praised;
a fine, handsome knight
who behaved nobly.
He was close to his lord,
and loved by all his neighbors.   20
He had an estimable wife,
one of lovely appearance;
he loved her and she him,
but one thing was very vexing to her:
during the week he would be missing
for three whole days, and she didn't know
what happened to him or where he went.

Nor did any of his men know anything about it.
  One day he returned home
happy and delighted;   30
she asked him about it.
"My lord," she said, "and dear love,
I'd very much like to ask you one thing—
if I dared;
but I'm so afraid of your anger
that nothing frightens me more."
When he heard that, he embraced her,
drew her to him and kissed her.
"My lady," he said, "go ahead and ask!
There's nothing you could want to know,   40
that, if I knew the answer, I wouldn't tell you."
"By God," she replied, "now I'm cured!
My lord, on the days when you go away from me
I'm in such a state—
so sad at heart,
so afraid I'll lose you—
that if I don't get quick relief
I could die of this very soon.
Please, tell me where you go,
where you have been staying.   50
I think you must have a lover,
and if that's so, you're doing wrong."
"My dear," he said, "have mercy on me, for God's sake!
Harm will come to me if I tell you about this,
because I'd lose your love
and even my very self."
When the lady heard this
she didn't take it lightly;
she kept asking him,
coaxed and flattered him so much,   60
that he finally told her what happened to him—
he hid nothing from her.
"My dear, I become a werewolf:
I go off into the great forest,
in the thickest part of the woods,
and I live on the prey I hunt down."
When he had told her everything,
she asked further
whether he undressed or kept his clothes on [when he became a
          werewolf].
"Wife," he replied, "I go stark naked."   70
"Tell me, then, for God's sake, where your clothes are."
"That I won't tell you;
for if I were to lose them,
and then be discovered,
I'd stay a werewolf forever.

I'd be helpless
until I got them back.
That's why I don't want their hiding place to be known."
"My lord," the lady answered,
"I love you more than all the world;   80
you mustn't hide anything from me
or fear me in any way:
that doesn't seem like love to me.
What wrong have I done? For what sin of mine
do you mistrust me about anything?
Do the right thing and tell me!"
She harassed and bedeviled him so,
that he had no choice but to tell her.
"Lady," he said, "near the woods,
beside the road that I use to get there,   90
there's an old chapel
that has often done me good service;
under a bush there is a big stone,
hollowed out inside;
I hide my clothes right there
until I'm ready to come home."
   The lady heard this wonder
and turned scarlet from fear;
she was terrified of the whole adventure.
Over and over she considered   100
how she might get rid of him;
she never wanted to sleep with him again.
There was a knight of that region
who had loved her for a long time,
who begged for her love,
and dedicated himself to serving her.
She'd never loved him at all,
nor pledged her love to him,
but now she sent a messenger for him,
and told him her intention.   110
"My dear," she said, "cheer up!
I shall now grant you without delay
what you have suffered for;
you'll meet with no more refusals—
I offer you my love and my body;
make me your mistress!"
   He thanked her graciously
and accepted her promise,
and she bound him to her by an oath.
Then she told him   120
how her husband went away and what happened to him;
she also taught him the precise path
her husband took into the forest,
and then she sent the knight to get her husband's clothes.

So Bisclavret[1] was betrayed,
ruined by his own wife.
Since people knew he was often away from home
they all thought
this time he'd gone away forever.
They searched for him and made inquiries   130
but could never find him,
so they had to let matters stand.
The wife later married the other knight,
who had loved her for so long.
   A whole year passed
until one day the king went hunting;
he headed right for the forest
where Bisclavret was.
When the hounds were unleashed,
they ran across Bisclavret;   140
the hunters and the dogs
chased him all day,
until they were just about to take him
and tear him apart,
at which point he saw the king
and ran to him, pleading for mercy.
He took hold of the king's stirrup,
kissed his leg and his foot.
The king saw this and was terrified;
he called his companions.   150
"My lords," he said, "come quickly!
Look at this marvel—
this beast is humbling itself to me.
It has the mind of a man, and it's begging me for mercy!
Chase the dogs away,
and make sure no one strikes it.
This beast is rational—he has a mind.
Hurry up: let's get out of here.
I'll extend my peace to the creature;
indeed, I'll hunt no more today!"   160
Thereupon the king turned away.
Bisclavret followed him;
he stayed close to the king, and wouldn't go away;
he'd no intention of leaving him.
   The king led him to his castle;
he was delighted with this turn of events,
for he'd never seen anything like it.
He considered the beast a great wonder
and held him very dear.
He commanded all his followers,   170
for the sake of their love for him, to guard Bisclavret well,

---

[1] Until this point, "Bisclavret" is a common noun; hereafter it is used as the werewolf's name.

and under no circumstances to do him harm;
none of them should strike him;
rather, he should be well fed and watered.
They willingly guarded the creature;
every day he went to sleep
among the knights, near the king.
Everyone was fond of him;
he was so noble and well behaved
that he never wished to do anything wrong.   180
Regardless of where the king might go,
Bisclavret never wanted to be separated from him;
he always accompanied the king.
The king became very much aware that the creature loved him.
    Now listen to what happened next.
The king held a court;
to help him celebrate his feast
and to serve him as handsomely as possible,
he summoned all the barons
who held fiefs from him.   190
Among the knights who went,
and all dressed up in his best attire,
was the one who had married Bisclavret's wife.
He neither knew nor suspected
that he would find Bisclavret so close by.
As soon as he came to the palace
Bisclavret saw him,
ran toward him at full speed,
sank his teeth into him, and started to drag him down.
He would have done him great damage   200
if the king hadn't called him off,
and threatened him with a stick.
Twice that day he tried to bite the knight.
Everyone was extremely surprised,
since the beast had never acted that way
toward any other man he had seen.
All over the palace people said
that he wouldn't act that way without a reason:
that somehow or other, the knight had mistreated Bisclavret,
and now he wanted his revenge.   210
And so the matter rested
until the feast was over
and until the barons took their leave of the king
and started home.
The very first to leave,
to the best of my knowledge,
was the knight whom Bisclavret had attacked.
It's no wonder the creature hated him.
    Not long afterward,
as the story leads me to believe,   220
the king, who was so wise and noble,

went back to the forest
where he had found Bisclavret,
and the creature went with him.
That night, when he finished hunting,
he sought lodging out in the countryside.
The wife of Bisclavret heard about it,
dressed herself elegantly,
and went the next day to speak with the king,
bringing rich presents for him.   230
When Bisclavret saw her coming,
no one could hold him back;
he ran toward her in a rage.
Now listen to how well he avenged himself!
He tore the nose off her face.
What worse thing could he have done to her?
Now men closed in on him from all sides;
they were about to tear him apart,
when a wise man said to the king,
"My lord, listen to me!   240
This beast has stayed with you,
and there's not one of us
who hasn't watched him closely,
hasn't traveled with him often.
He's never touched anyone,
or shown any wickedness,
except to this woman.
By the faith that I owe you,
he has some grudge against her,
and against her husband as well.   250
This is the wife of the knight
whom you used to like so much,
and who's been missing for so long—
we don't know what became of him.
Why not put this woman to torture
and see if she'll tell you
why the beast hates her?
Make her tell what she knows!
We've seen many strange things
happen in Brittany!"   260
    The king took his advice;
he detained the knight.
At the same time he took the wife
and subjected her to torture;
out of fear and pain
she told all about her husband:
how she had betrayed him
and taken away his clothes;
the story he had told her
about what happened to him and where he went;   270

and how after she had taken his clothes
he'd never been seen in his land again.
She was quite certain
that this beast was Bisclavret.
The king demanded the clothes;
whether she wanted to or not
she sent home for them,
and had them brought to Bisclavret.
When they were put down in front of him
he didn't even seem to notice them;   280
the king's wise man—
the one who had advised him earlier—
said to him, "My lord, you're not doing it right.
This beast wouldn't, under any circumstances,
in order to get rid of his animal form,
put on his clothes in front of you;
you don't understand what this means:
he's just too ashamed to do it here.
Have him led to your chambers
and bring the clothes with him;   290
then we'll leave him alone for a while.
If he turns into a man, we'll know about it."
   The king himself led the way
and closed all the doors on him.
After a while he went back,
taking two barons with him;
all three entered the king's chamber.
On the king's royal bed
they found the knight asleep.
The king ran to embrace him.   300
He hugged and kissed him again and again.
As soon as he had the chance,
the king gave him back all his lands;
he gave him more than I can tell.
He banished his wife,
chased her out of the country.
She went into exile with the knight
with whom she had betrayed her lord.
She had several children
who were widely known   310
for their appearance:
several women of the family
were actually born without noses,
and lived out their lives noseless.

   The adventure that you have heard
really happened, no doubt about it.
The *lai* of Bisclavret was made
so it would be remembered forever.

YONEC

Translated by Robert Hanning and Joan Ferrante

Now that I've begun these *lais*
the effort will not stop me;
every adventure that I know
I shall relate in rhyme.
My intention and my desire
is to tell you next of Yonec,
how he was born and how his father
first came to his mother.
The man who fathered Yonec
was called Muldumarec.   10

There once lived in Brittany
a rich man, old and ancient.
At Caerwent, he was acknowledged
and accepted as lord of the land.
The city sits on the Duelas,
which at one time was open to boats.
The man was very far along in years
but because he possessed a large fortune
he took a wife in order to have children,
who would come after him and be his heirs.   20
The girl who was given to the rich man
came from a good family;
she was wise and gracious and very beautiful—
for her beauty he loved her very much.
Because she was beautiful and noble
he made every effort to guard her.
He locked her inside his tower
in a great paved chamber.
A sister of his,
who was also old and a widow, without her own lord,   30
he stationed with his lady
to guard her even more closely.
There were other women, I believe,
in another chamber by themselves,
but the lady never spoke to them
unless the old woman gave her permission.
So he kept her more than seven years—
they never had any children;
she never left that tower,
neither for family nor for friends.   40
When the lord came to sleep there
no chamberlain or porter
dared enter that room,
not even to carry a candle before the lord.

The lady lived in great sorrow,
with tears and sighs and weeping;
she lost her beauty,
as one does who cares nothing for it.
She would have preferred
death to take her quickly.   50

It was the beginning of April
when the birds begin their songs.
The lord arose in the morning
and made ready to go to the woods.
He had the old woman get up
and close the door behind him—
she followed his command.
The lord went off with his men.
The old woman carried a psalter
from which she intended to read the psalms.   60
The lady, awake and in tears,
saw the light of the sun.
She noticed that the old woman
had left the chamber.
She grieved and sighed
and wept and raged:
"I should never have been born!
My fate is very harsh.
I'm imprisoned in this tower
and I'll never leave it unless I die.   70
What is this jealous old man afraid of
that he keeps me so imprisoned?
He's mad, out of his senses;
always afraid of being deceived.
I can't even go to church
or hear God's service.
If I could speak to people
and enjoy myself with them
I'd be very gracious to my lord
even if I didn't want to be.   80
A curse on my family,
and on all the others
who gave me to this jealous man,
who married me to his body.
It's a rough rope that I pull and draw.
He'll never die—
when he should have been baptized
he was plunged instead in the river of hell;
his sinews are hard, his veins are hard,
filled with living blood.   90
I've often heard
that one could once find
adventures in this land

that brought relief to the unhappy.
Knights might find young girls
to their desire, noble and lovely;
and ladies find lovers
so handsome, courtly, brave, and valiant
that they could not be blamed,
and no one else would see them.   100
If that might be or ever was,
if that has ever happened to anyone,
God, who has power over everything,
grant me my wish in this."
When she'd finished her lament,
she saw, through a narrow window,
the shadow of a great bird.
She didn't know what it was.
It flew into the chamber;
its feet were banded; it looked like a hawk   110
of five or six moultings.
It alighted before the lady.
When it had been there awhile
and she'd stared hard at it,
it became a handsome and noble knight.
The lady was astonished;
her blood went cold, she trembled,
she was frightened—she covered her head.
The knight was very courteous,
he spoke first: 120
"Lady," he said, "don't be afraid.
The hawk is a noble bird,
although its secrets are unknown to you.
Be reassured
and accept me as your love.
That," he said, "is why I came here.
I have loved you for a long time,
I've desired you in my heart.
Never have I loved any woman but you
nor shall I ever love another,   130
yet I couldn't have come to you
or left my own land
had you not asked for me.
But now I can be your love."
The lady was reassured;
she uncovered her head and spoke.
She answered the knight,
saying she would take him as her lover
if he believed in God,
and if their love was really possible.   140
For he was of great beauty.
Never in her life
had she seen so handsome a knight—

nor would she ever.
"My lady," he said, "you are right.
I wouldn't want you to feel
guilt because of me,
or doubt or suspicion.
I do believe in the creator
who freed us from the grief   150
that Adam, our father, led us into
when he bit into the bitter apple.
He is, will be, and always was
the life and light of sinners.
If you don't believe me
send for your chaplain.
Say that you've suddenly been taken ill
and that you desire the service
that God established in this world
for the healing of sinners.   160
I shall take on your appearance
to receive the body of our lord God,
and I'll recite my whole credo for you.
You will never doubt my faith again."
She answered that she was satisfied.
He lay beside her on the bed
but he didn't try to touch her,
to embrace her or to kiss her.
Meanwhile, the old woman had returned.
She found the lady awake   170
and told her it was time to get up,
she would bring her clothes.
The lady said she was ill,
that the old woman should send for the chaplain
and bring him to her quickly—
she very much feared she was dying.
The old woman said, "Be patient,
my lord has gone to the woods.
No one may come in here but me."
The lady was very upset;   180
she pretended to faint.
When the other saw her, she was frightened;
she unlocked the door of the chamber
and sent for the priest.
He came as quickly as he could,
bringing the *corpus domini.*[1]
The knight received it,
drank the wine from the chalice.
Then the chaplain left
and the old woman closed the doors.   190
The lady lay beside her love—

---

[1] The "body of the Lord," bread for Communion.

there was never a more beautiful couple.
When they had laughed and played
and spoken intimately,
the knight took his leave
to return to his land.
She gently begged him
to come back often.
"Lady," he said, "whenever you please,
I will be here within the hour.   200
But you must make certain
that we're not discovered.
This old woman will betray us,
night and day she will spy on us.
She will perceive our love,
and tell her lord about it.
If that happens,
if we are betrayed,
I won't be able to escape.
I shall die."   210
With that the knight departed,
leaving his love in great joy.
In the morning she rose restored;
she was happy all week.
Her body had now become precious to her,
she completely recovered her beauty.
Now she would rather remain here
than look for pleasure elsewhere.
She wanted to see her love all the time
and enjoy herself with him.   220
As soon as her lord departed,
night or day, early or late,
she had him all to her pleasure.
God, let their joy endure!
Because of the great joy she felt,
because she could see her love so often,
her whole appearance changed.
But her lord was clever.
In his heart he sensed
that she was not what she had been.   230
He suspected his sister.
He questioned her one day,
saying he was astonished
that the lady now dressed with care.
He asked her what it meant.
The old woman said she didn't know—
no one could have spoken to her,
she had no lover or friend—
it was only that she was now more willing
to be alone than before.   240
His sister, too, had noticed the change.

Her lord answered:
"By my faith," he said, "I think that's so.
But you must do something for me.
In the morning, when I've gotten up
and you have shut the doors,
pretend you are going out
and leave her lying there alone.
Then hide yourself in a safe place,
watch her and find out   250
what it is, and where it comes from,
that gives her such great joy."
With that plan they separated.
Alas, how hard it is to protect yourself
from someone who wants to trap you,
to betray and deceive you!

Three days later, as I heard the story,
the lord pretended to go away.
He told his wife the story
that the king had sent for him by letter   260
but that he would return quickly.
He left the chamber and shut the door.
The old woman got up,
went behind a curtain;
from there she could hear and see
whatever she wanted to know.
The lady lay in bed but did not sleep,
she longed for her love.
He came without delay,
before any time had passed.   270
They gave each other great joy
with word and look
until it was time to rise—
he had to go.
But the old woman watched him,
saw how he came and went.
She was quite frightened
when she saw him first a man and then a bird.
When the lord returned—
he hadn't gone very far—   280
she told him and revealed
the truth about the knight
and the lord was troubled by it.
But he was quick to invent
a way to kill the knight.
He had great spikes of iron forged,
their tips sharpened—
no razor on earth could cut better.
When he had them all prepared
and pronged on all sides,   290

he set them in the window—
close together and firmly placed—
through which the knight passed
when he visited the lady.
God, he doesn't know what treachery
the villains are preparing.
The next day in the morning
the lord rose before dawn
and said he was going hunting.
The old woman saw him to the door   300
and then went back to bed
for day was not yet visible.
The lady awoke and waited
for the one she loved faithfully;
she said he might well come now
and be with her at leisure.
As soon as she asked,
he came without delay.
He flew into the window,
but the spikes were there.   310
One wounded him in his breast—
out rushed the red blood.
He knew he was fatally wounded;
he pulled himself free and entered the room.
He alighted on the bed, in front of the lady,
staining the bedclothes with blood.
She saw the blood and the wound
in anguish and horror.
He said, "My sweet love,
I lose my life for love of you.   320
I told you it would happen,
that your appearance would kill us."
When she heard that, she fainted;
for a short while she lay as if dead.
He comforted her gently,
said that grief would do no good,
but that she was pregnant with his child.
She would have a son, brave and strong,
who would comfort her;
she would call him Yonec.   330
He would avenge both of them
and kill their enemy.
But he could remain no longer
for his wound was bleeding badly.
He left in great sorrow.
She followed him with loud cries.
She leapt out a window—
it's a wonder that she wasn't killed,
for it was at least twenty feet high
where she made her leap,   340

naked beneath her gown.
She followed the traces of blood
that flowed from the knight
onto the road.
She followed that road and kept to it
until she came to a hill.
In the hill there was an opening,
red with his blood.
She couldn't see anything beyond it
but she was sure   350
that her love had gone in there.
She entered quickly.
She found no light
but she kept to the right road
until it emerged from the hill
into a beautiful meadow.
When she found the grass there wet with blood,
she was frightened.
She followed the traces through the meadow
and saw a city not far away.   360
The city was completely surrounded by walls.
There was no house, no hall or tower,
that didn't seem entirely of silver.
The buildings were very rich.
Going toward the town there were marshes,
forests, and enclosed fields.
On the other side, toward the castle,
a stream flowed all around,
where ships arrived—
there were more than three hundred sails.   370
The lower gate was open;
the lady entered the city,
still following the fresh blood
through the town to the castle.
No one spoke to her,
she met neither man nor woman.
When she came to the palace courtyard,
she found it covered with blood.
She entered a lovely chamber
where she found a knight sleeping.   380
She did not know him, so she went on
into another larger chamber.
There she found nothing but a bed
with a knight sleeping on it;
she kept going.
She entered the third chamber
and on that bed she found her love.
The feet of the bed were all of polished gold,
I couldn't guess the value of the bedclothes;
the candles and the chandeliers,   390

which were lit night and day,
were worth the gold of an entire city.
As soon as she saw him
she recognized the knight.
She approached, frightened,
and fell fainting over him.
He, who greatly loved her, embraced her,
lamenting his misfortune again and again.
When she recovered from her faint
he comforted her gently.   400
"Sweet friend, for God's sake, I beg you,
go away! Leave this place!
I shall die within the day,
there will be great sorrow here,
and if you are found
you will be hurt.
Among my people it will be well known
that they have lost me because of my love for you.
I am disturbed and troubled for you."
The lady answered: "Love,   410
I would rather die with you
than suffer with my lord.
If I go back to him he'll kill me."
The knight reassured her,
gave her a ring,
and explained to her
that, as long as she kept it,
her lord would not remember
anything that had happened—
he would imprison her no longer.   420
He gave her his sword
and then made her swear
no man would ever possess it,
that she'd keep it for their son.
When the son had grown and become
a brave and valiant knight,
she would go to a festival,
taking him and her lord with her.
They would come to an abbey.
There, beside a tomb,   430
they would hear the story of his death,
how he was wrongfully killed.
There she would give her son the sword.
The adventure would be recited to him,
how he was born and who his father was;
then they'd see what he would do.
When he'd told her and shown her everything,
he gave her a precious robe
and told her to put it on.
Then he sent her away.   440

She left carrying the ring
and the sword—they comforted her.
She had not gone half a mile
from the gate of the city
when she heard the bells ring
and the mourning begin in the castle,
and in her sorrow
she fainted four times.
When she recovered from the faints
she made her way to the hill.   450
She entered it, passed through it,
and returned to her country.
There with her lord
she lived many days and years.
He never accused her of that deed,
never insulted or abused her.
Her son was born and nourished,
protected and cherished.
They named him Yonec.
In all the kingdom you couldn't find   460
one so handsome, brave, or strong,
so generous, so munificent.
When he reached the proper age,
he was made a knight.
Hear now what happened
in that very year.
To the feast of St. Aaron,
celebrated in Caerleon
and in many other cities,
the lord had been summoned   470
to come with his friends,
according to the custom of the land,
and to bring his wife and his son,
all richly attired.
So it was; they went.
But they didn't know the way;
they had a boy with them
who guided them along the right road
until they came to a castle—
none more beautiful in all the world.   480
Inside, there was an abbey
of very religious people.
The boy who was guiding them to the festival
housed them there.
In the abbot's chamber
they were well served and honored.
Next day they went to hear Mass
before they departed,
but the abbot went to speak to them
to beg them to stay   490

so he could show them the dormitory,
the chapter house, and the refectory.
And since they were comfortable there,
the lord agreed to stay.
That day, after they had dined,
they went to the workshops.
On their way, they passed the chapter house,
where they found a huge tomb
covered with a cloth of embroidered silk,
a band of precious gold running from one side to the other.   500
At the head, the feet, and at the sides
burned twenty candles.
The chandeliers were pure gold,
the censers amethyst,
which through the day perfumed
that tomb, to its great honor.
They asked and inquired
of people from that land
whose tomb it was,
what man lay there.   510
The people began to weep
and, weeping, to recount
that it was the best knight,
the strongest, the most fierce,
the most handsome and the best loved,
that had ever lived.
"He was king of this land;
no one was ever so courtly.
At Caerwent he was discovered
and killed for the love of a lady.   520
Since then we have had no lord,
but have waited many days,
just as he told and commanded us,
for the son the lady bore him."
When the lady heard that news,
she called aloud to her son.
"Fair son," she said, "you hear
how God has led us to this spot.
Your father, whom this old man murdered,
lies here in this tomb.   530
Now I give and commend his sword to you.
I have kept it a long time for you."
Then she revealed, for all to hear,
that the man in the tomb was the father and this was his son,
and how he used to come to her,
how her lord had betrayed him—
she told the truth.
Then she fainted over the tomb
and, in her faint, she died.
She never spoke again.   540

When her son saw that she had died,
he cut off his stepfather's head.
Thus with his father's sword
he avenged his mother's sorrow.
When all this had happened,
when it became known through the city,
they took the lady with great honor
and placed her in the coffin.
Before they departed
they made Yonec their lord.   550

Long after, those who heard this adventure
composed a lay about it,
about the pain and the grief
that they suffered for love.

Dante Alighieri
(1265–1321)

The reputation of Dante Alighieri, already high in the time immediately following his death, is today such as to rank him with Homer and Shakespeare at the summit of world literature and his Divine Comedy *as perhaps the greatest single work of literary art. Dante's simple title was the* Commedia *(the epithet* Divina *was added on title pages beginning in the sixteenth century). The work was called a comedy because its style was a middle one beneath the high-serious tone of tragedy and because its movement was from sadness to joy. The* Comedy *is often described as the quintessence of the medieval world view, a codification of the values of the high Middle Ages in art, science, theology, and philosophy. This view has considerable truth. It is not without its ironies, however; Dante felt nostalgia for the past and entertained hopes for the future, but he considered his own age vicious, corrupt, and benighted. The circumstances of his life and its public backdrop bear out his judgment in many respects.*

Dante was born in 1265 in the independent, republican city-state of Florence, which in its commercial prosperity and its culture was beginning to rank with the leading cities of Europe. For decades before his birth an appallingly bloody feud had divided Florence into two factions: the Ghibellines, a feudal and military class allied with the Holy Roman Emperor, and the Guelfs, a middle-class party that tended to side with the Papacy in its struggle against the Empire. Dante's family were Guelfs. After an alternation of victories by one side over the other, the Guelfs triumphed decisively when Dante was a year old. But by the end of the century the Guelfs themselves had split into factions: the Blacks, who represented the nobility and were willing to tolerate papal political influence, and the Whites, who represented the commercial bourgeoisie and wanted political independence. Dante was a moderate White. After some military service, he held in his early thirties a succession of increasingly prominent political offices, becoming one of the chief magistrates of Florence in 1300, the year in which the events of the Divine Comedy *are imagined to take place. Fighting broke out in the streets. Dante's solution was to help banish the leaders of both factions, including his brother-in-law and also Guido Cavalcanti, one of his best friends and a fellow poet. But the Blacks conspired with Dante's detested Pope Boniface VIII, who wished to establish his power in Florence and the surrounding region of Tuscany, and with the help of a foreign army the Whites were ousted, while Dante was absent on a diplomatic mission to Rome. In 1302 he was unjustly accused of barratry (graft), tried in* absentia, *fined the large sum of 5,000 florins, and banished for two years. When he refused to pay the fine and thus admit guilt, the banishment was ruled perpetual, under penalty of being burned alive. Dante never saw his beloved—and henceforth also hated—Florence again, or his wife Gemma, whom he had married in his mid-twenties. The* Divine Comedy *refers often to this century-long saga of bloody and sleazy politics.*

For a time Dante nourished the hope that the Whites would regain control of Florence, but these hopes remained unfulfilled, and gradually Dante became a party of one, disillusioned with all the factions. He was thereafter dependent on a series of patrons who gave him asylum in various Italian cities, mainly in the north. Tradition has it that he spent some time in France and possibly in England, at Oxford. In 1308 his hopes for the regeneration, reordering, and pacification of Italy, including Florence, were rekindled by the election of a new, idealistic Holy Roman Emperor, Henry VII. Dante believed that most of the political evils of his country, and some of the spiritual ones too, sprang from a lack of guidance by an enlightened Emperor such as Rome had had in its best ancient days. But Henry's expedition to Italy failed, thwarted by party conflicts, the opposition of the Pope, and finally by Henry's death in 1313. Dante's hopes were once more disappointed. His very last years, however, were relatively serene; he had already circulated the first two parts of his Comedy, *the* Inferno *and* Purgatory, *the fame of which helped sustain him, and his children were again with him. His last patron, in Ravenna, was a nephew of the Francesca da Rimini whose story Dante had told so movingly in* Inferno *canto V. Dante died in 1321, not long after he completed the* Paradise *and with it the entire* Comedy.

As references in that work show, Dante's political vicissitudes are reflected in his art. Yet he lived another inner and creative life independent of public traumas. He seems to have had a happy childhood and a good education, probably under Dominican and Franciscan priests. He studied rhetoric under the philosopher-poet Brunetto Latini whom he honors in Inferno *XV. He was early influenced by French Provençal poetry and by the Italian vernacular poetry that had only recently begun to flourish. A protégé of Guido Cavalcanti, Dante developed a* dolce stil nuovo *("sweet new style"), rejecting elegant artifice for its own sake and emphasizing instead sincerity of feeling and substance in ideas. The central event of his earlier spiritual life is narrated in the* Vita Nuova *("New Life"), an amatory and spiritual autobiography with allegorical overtones, which he composed in Italian in 1292. It records, in a mixture of lyric verse and prose commentary, Dante's first love, inspired in him at the age of nine by the sight of Beatrice Portinari, a girl one year younger. He immediately conceived for her a lifelong, intensely idealistic passion that owes much to the medieval tradition of worship of woman, to which Dante adds a moral and philosophical dimension. Nine years later Dante and Beatrice greeted each other. There followed episodes of alienation and psychological distress (apparently idealized, for Dante seems not to have had much close contact with Beatrice). After she died in 1290, he turned to a compassionate lady who later became an emblem of the philosophical pursuits that occupied him after Beatrice's death. The composition of the* Vita Nuova, *when Dante was twenty-seven, marks the end of the third nine-year period, the number symbolism foreshadowing an even more elaborate dependence in the* Divine Comedy *on threes and nines. In all this it is difficult to separate fact from idealization, but perhaps such a symbol-making mind as Dante's would reject the distinction. The* Vita Nuova *ends with the mention of a wondrous vision and with the determination by Dante that he will write no more of Beatrice until he can write of her "what has not before been written of any woman." This decision is one seed of the* Divine Comedy, *in which Beatrice ("giver of blessings") reappears, the Florentine girl transfigured as the heavenly lady who, having helped rescue Dante from his dark night, conducts him through the spheres of the celestial paradise. She becomes both a symbol and vehicle of God's love and revelation.*

The study of philosophy and literature that Dante embarked on after the death of Beatrice was continued and deepened in later years until he had mastered most of the important ancient and medieval writers accessible in that time before the Renaissance revival of classical Greek. Indeed, he became one of the most learned men in Europe. He was indebted philosophically to Aristotle, by way of St. Thomas Aquinas. Poetically, he was immensely indebted to Virgil, whom he echoes again and again in the Comedy *and chooses to represent as his guide through Hell and most of Purgatory, the realms that can be largely understood by the human reason that (among other things) Virgil represents. Dante claimed to know the* Aeneid *by heart. His erudition led him to attempt several ambitious works. Much of what he had learned by 1305 or so he tried to put into a philosophically encyclopedic work called the* Convivio *("Banquet"), which was to contain fifteen treatises in alternating prose and verse, like the* Vita Nuova. *The* Convivio, *although abandoned by Dante in about 1308, is a landmark in its use of Italian prose instead of Latin for serious philosophical purposes, anticipating the choice of Italian for the* Comedy. *Conversely, Dante explored the general and practical principles involved in creating a worthy Italian language and literature in a Latin work of the same period,* De Vulgari Eloquentia *("Of Eloquence in the Vernacular Tongue"), which he also left incomplete. Somewhat later, at the time Dante's hero Henry VII was in Italy, he wrote the Latin* De Monarchia, *in which, picking up a theme treated in the* Convivio, *Dante argued the bold thesis that the rightful powers of emperor and pope, respectively temporal and spiritual, were both derived directly from God. The implication was that in a Christian state the two should be separate but equal authorities and should limit themselves to their own mutually exclusive spheres. This idea influences not just the thematic content of the* Divine Comedy *but its very rationale and symbolism; for example, at the end of the* Inferno, *at the bottom and center of Hell, the place of supreme dishonor in the jaws of Satan, the author of all evil, is shared by the spiritual traitor Judas and imperial traitors Brutus and Cassius.*

Dante wrote the Comedy *between 1308 and 1321, completing the* Inferno *by 1312 and the* Purgatory *by 1315. Literally, it is an account of a privileged journey taken by Dante the character (who should be distinguished from the Dante who writes the poem after the fact) into the world of the afterlife. On this level the* Comedy *is a theological work. The damned are those who, each in his or her own way, have definitively rebelled against God's law and defied or ignored His mercy; these include pagans, Jews, and Christians. The saved are those who, having repented and been forgiven by God, dwell with Him in the celestial paradise. Also among the saved are those who, having died at peace with God, are still spiritually imperfect and must refine away their potential for evil in Purgatory, which Dante locates on a mountain in the southern ocean. The Christian faith is a prerequisite for beatitude, although the righteous Jews of the Old Testament period are saved by their implicit faith in Christ to come; moreover, Jewish infants and baptized Christian infants are also among the saved. The virtuous pagans of antiquity and of more modern times cannot enter Heaven; instead they dwell in Limbo, the uppermost circle of Hell, where their only suffering is to live without hope of redemption. These righteous pagans include even Virgil. Dante shows, especially in the* Paradise, *that he is troubled by the lot of these blameless persons, and in fact in* Paradise XX *he opens a loophole, revealing that at least some good pagans can finally be saved. But this is only a loophole, a faint gleam of mysterious hope, and much pathos arises in the* Inferno *and* Purgatory *from the assumption that the magisterial and fatherlike Virgil is inexorably excluded from eternal bliss.*

Theologically, Purgatory is the most distinctively Catholic realm, reflecting one fundamental difference in belief between the Catholic and Protestant faiths. The basic Protestant position, as formulated two centuries later during the Reformation, is that man is saved by faith in God's mercy and grace; Catholics believe that man is saved by a combination of such faith and "works" (acts of goodness and remedial suffering). This latter view can make God seem a niggardly taskmaster, forgiving only grudgingly. But the Catholic view, if we can extrapolate from Dante's idea of the Redemption in Paradise VII, *is that God is like a generous creditor who might have forgiven a debt outright but instead asks that part be repaid so as to salvage the self-respect and elevate the dignity of the sinner-debtor. Dante's purgatorians thus suffer, in a discipline of compensation, but joyfully and willingly. Because they can rise to a higher slope of the mountain as soon as they feel ready and worthy, their own wills are the essential ministers of the purgatorial process.*

An awareness of such theological fundamentals is important for an understanding of the Comedy, *but the modern appeal of the work, even for believers, is not primarily theological but rather ethical and artistic. The* Comedy *is intended to be a picture of the world we live in; the journey into the afterlife is also the struggle in this life of every person who confronts evil, conquers it, and rises above it. Dante most obviously makes us aware of the temporal life by portraying known persons, great and commonplace, antique and modern, dead and living, and by commenting frequently on immediate, local issues, especially politics. In describing the three great realms and making clear his own emotional states, he draws vivid comparisons with the scenes and landscapes of recognizable life—the breaking of a gambler's lucky streak, the shipyards at Venice, a tailor's squint, fireflies on a summer evening, windmills seen through mist.*

Above all, Dante comments on earthly life through the descriptions of the punishments in Hell. These are not merely imposed from outside and after the fact; rather, they are symbols of the sins when they are truly understood and realized in imaginative fullness. Someone once said that the motto of the Inferno *might well be "They got what they wanted." Or, in Gerard Manley Hopkins' words, "The lost are like this, and their scourge [is] to be . . . their sweating selves." Thus the adulterous lovers Francesca and Paolo will be united forever, airborne on the winds of passion; the suicides who separated soul from body will remain so divided even after the Last Judgment, when other creatures have reassumed their flesh; the heretics who denied the immortality of the soul lie forever in sarcophagi, which will be sealed at the Judgment just as, in effect, they predicted; the popes who desecrated their office for money are all crammed, upside down and head to foot, into a single hole, in a parody of the apostolic succession and the laying on of hands by which the episcopal office is transmitted; the grafters continue their life of concealment and trickery.*

Moreover, the scheme of punishments in Hell reflects a theory of human nature and a rather complex scheme of ethics. (The divisions of Hell and of Purgatory are outlined by Virgil in Inferno XI *and* Purgatory XVII.*) The merely sensual sinners are the least guilty, and of them the sexual sinners least of all, possibly because sex retains some touch of the love that, properly understood, is God. The next most guilty are the violent. But the worst sinners are those who pervert the divine plan of creation by misusing the specifically human power of reason—that is, the fraudulent. But even fraud has gradations, and it is worst when it is treacherous. And the worst form of treachery is that shown to lords and benefactors. God as understood by Dante is associated with motion and energy, and it is therefore appropriate that the punishment for treacherous fraud is not the hell-fire of popular imagination but complete entropy in the form of a lake of ice. The Limbo and the circle of the heretics are conceived in the light of distinctively Christian beliefs, but the remainder of the* Inferno *is defined in terms of nearly universal human insights and values. Theologically, it may strike some people as arbitrary that in Dante salvation and damnation depend on the state of the human soul at the moment when, perhaps by sudden accident, death occurs, although in fact that notion is not uniquely Dantean or Christian. But from a moral rather than theological perspective, the idea suggests in the most powerful way possible that all actions in life are of incalculable consequence, each containing in itself the essence of utter good or utter evil. Perhaps it is Dante's sense of this urgency that makes him consign the contemptible trimmers, who were neither good nor evil, to the outer vestibule of Hell, lest their presence in Hell proper make "the wicked gain pride by comparison"* (Inferno III.42).

Probably no great work of literature has a structure so precisely articulated as the Divine Comedy. *It is governed, texturally and architecturally, by the numbers 3, 9, and 10. The entire* Comedy *has 100 cantos, the square of the perfect number 10. Each of the three great divisions has 33 cantos (the first of the 34 cantos in the* Inferno *serving as a prelude to the entire work). There are 9 (3 times 3) circles or spheres in each of the three realms, to which is added another region of a different order (the vestibule of Hell, the Garden of Eden, the empyrean Heaven), making a total of 10. The entire poem is written in tercets, three-line stanzas, and the Italian rhyme scheme is* terza rima *("third rhyme"), a system of interlocking rhymes in the pattern* aba bcb cdc, *each end rhyme thus sounding three times. The tercet is the normal syntactical unit of statement, producing along with the rhyme scheme an effect of powerful but deliberate forward movement. The symbolism of threes is an ever-present acknowledgment of the divine Trinity. Dante's mind, like others in the Middle Ages, could imagine a God who is both love and mathematical order.*

But the synthesizing imagination of Dante is best revealed not in such number symbolism but in the poem's total mode of understanding the structure of reality. Time is boldly conflated and twisted; sinners who have been in Hell for millennia coexist in an eternal now with those who have been dead for only a few years. The period of Dante's journey through Hell, from Good Friday to Easter Sunday, corresponds mythically to the time Jesus spent in the tomb. Cultures that were distinct on earth are homogenized in the hereafter, classical monsters and Christian demons reduced to a common denominator of allegorical and moral values. The boundaries between science, theology, philosophy, geography, history, and other branches of knowledge are virtually nonexistent; Dante hears lectures on politics and lunar astrophysics even in Paradise. Physical gravitation is closely identified with the spiritual operation of love, which is the motive power alike of the astronomical heavens and of every human act, good or bad. Evil and suffering, symbolized in Inferno XIV *by the tears of a gigantic Cretan statue weeping for the sorrows and sins of human history, move ever downward, channeled by Hell's four rivers to the motionless center of the universe; in the meantime, from the mountain of Purgatory on the other side of the globe the river of Lethe flows down to join the others in the same place, carrying with it the dead memories of the vices of the saved. Conversely, as the repentant move up the slopes of Purgatory, the burden of their evil propensities is quite literally lightened, so that like modern astronauts they feel the ascent easier and easier until, made perfect again in Eden, they rise to Heaven as naturally as flames fly upward.*

The ultimate goal of Dante the pilgrim and of the poem is the direct vision of God in the uncircumscribed empyrean heaven. In describing this experience, the last cantos of the Paradise *achieve a sublimity unsurpassed in literature. There Dante must realize for us what is utterly suprasensory and beyond speech without relinquishing the poetic tools of language and sense imagery that are the poet's only means of communication. His imagistic media, as throughout the* Paradise, *are mainly light, color, and nearly abstract patterns. His subject is not only the Deity but the relationship of Deity to the immensely variegated, differentiated world of things, places, and people so much of which the* Comedy *has revealed:*

> *In its depths I saw contained, bound with love*
> *in one volume, what is scattered*
> *on leaves throughout the world.* . . . *[Paradise XXXIII.85–87]*

The paradox, fundamental to any theistic vision, is that a God who is one and changeless created and sustains the teeming variety of our world.

It is impossible for translation to capture the exquisite sound effects of Dante's Italian, particularly the incantatory echoing of consonant and vowel sounds in lines such as Dei remi facemmo ali al folle volo *("we made wings of our oars for the mad flight"—*Inferno XXVI.125*). But in many other respects Dante's style and manner are unusually translatable. Although convoluted passages do occur, the hallmarks of Dante's usual style are directness and economy. He prefers verbs and nouns, using adjectives sparingly, and then more for utilitarian description than for atmosphere or ornament. (As an example, see Ulysses' famous speech in* Inferno XXVI.91–142.*) Exactly because he is describing what none of us has seen, he is compelled, as a good technical writer is, to furnish lucid visual descriptions and analogies. His method is eminently dramatic, realized in the overt gestures and speech of his characters. The characterizations are masterful; the most memorable—Francesca, Farinata, Brunetto Latini, Ulysses, Ugolino—are accomplished in a few dozen lines. Much of this can be captured by a literal translator who, renouncing the hopeless effort to compete with Dante's versification, lets this most literal of poets speak directly to us in language as nearly unclouded as his own.*

FURTHER READING *(prepared by W. J. R.):* A fine biography for the general reader is Monroe Stearns' *Dante: Poet of Love,* 1965, which is also a good introduction to *The Divine Comedy.* Michele Barbi, *Life of Dante,* 1933, trans. by Paul C. Ruggiers, 1954, is divided into sections on biography, the minor works, and *The Divine Comedy.* Carlo Golino's *Dante Alighieri,* 1979, which also provides both biographical information and criticism, has good discussions of works other than *The Divine Comedy.* Background material for the study of Dante's *Comedy,* a canto-by-canto summary, and critical analysis are combined in Aldo S. Bernardo and Anthony L. Pellegrini, *A Critical Study Guide to Dante's "Divine Comedy,"* 1968. The visual aids in this work are particularly useful. The notes and running commentary in Mark Musa's translation of *The Divine Comedy,* completed in 1984, are extremely helpful. Uberto Limentani's *Dante's Comedy: Introductory Readings of Selected Cantos,* 1985, provides an excellent model of how to read the poem as a whole. Joan M. Ferrante's *The Political Vision of the Divine Comedy,* 1984, is another excellent study, even broader in its critical scope than the title implies. A general appreciation of the *Comedy* is offered in Thomas Goddard Bergin's *Dante's "Divine Comedy,"* 1971, which is also good on the cosmology. George Holmes' *Dante,* 1980, in the Past Masters series, is a good introductory overview, of manageable length. For a historical introduction to the *Comedy,* see Erich Auerbach's *Dante, Poet of the Secular World,* 1929, trans. by Ralph Manheim, 1961. Auerbach's analysis of structure in the *Comedy* is also particularly readable and rewarding. *Dante: A Collection of Critical Essays,* ed. by J. Freccero, 1965, contains thirteen articles by Auerbach, Pirandello, and others. Selected cantos are interpreted in Mark Musa's *Advent at the Gates,* 1974. Musa's discussion of ambiguity in the characterization of Francesca is especially interesting. *From Time to Eternity,* ed. by Thomas Goddard Bergin, 1967, contains essays on Dante's Florence, religious theory of his time, and the genesis of the *Comedy.* Marianne Shapiro's *Woman, Earthly and Divine in the "Comedy" of Dante,* 1975, emphasizes the poet's relationship with Beatrice and offers a provocative discussion of Virgil's maternal and paternal aspects in the *Inferno.* Also valuable are David Nolan, ed., *Dante Commentaries: Eight Studies of "The Divine Comedy,"* 1977, and its companion volume, *Dante Soundings,* 1981.

THE DIVINE COMEDY

Translated, with interpolated summaries and bracketed glosses, by H. R. Huse.

INFERNO

A SAMPLE OF THE ORIGINAL VERSE

The opening tercets from Canto I will give readers an idea of the language and form of the original work.

Nel mezzo del cammin di nostra vita
  mi ritrovai per una selva oscura,
  chè la diritta via era smarrita.

Ah quanto a dir qual era è cosa dura
  esta selva selvaggia e aspra e forte
  che nel pensier rinnova la paura!

Tant'è amara che poco è più morte;
  ma per trattar del ben ch'io vi trovai,
  dirò dell'altre cose ch' i' v'ho scorte.

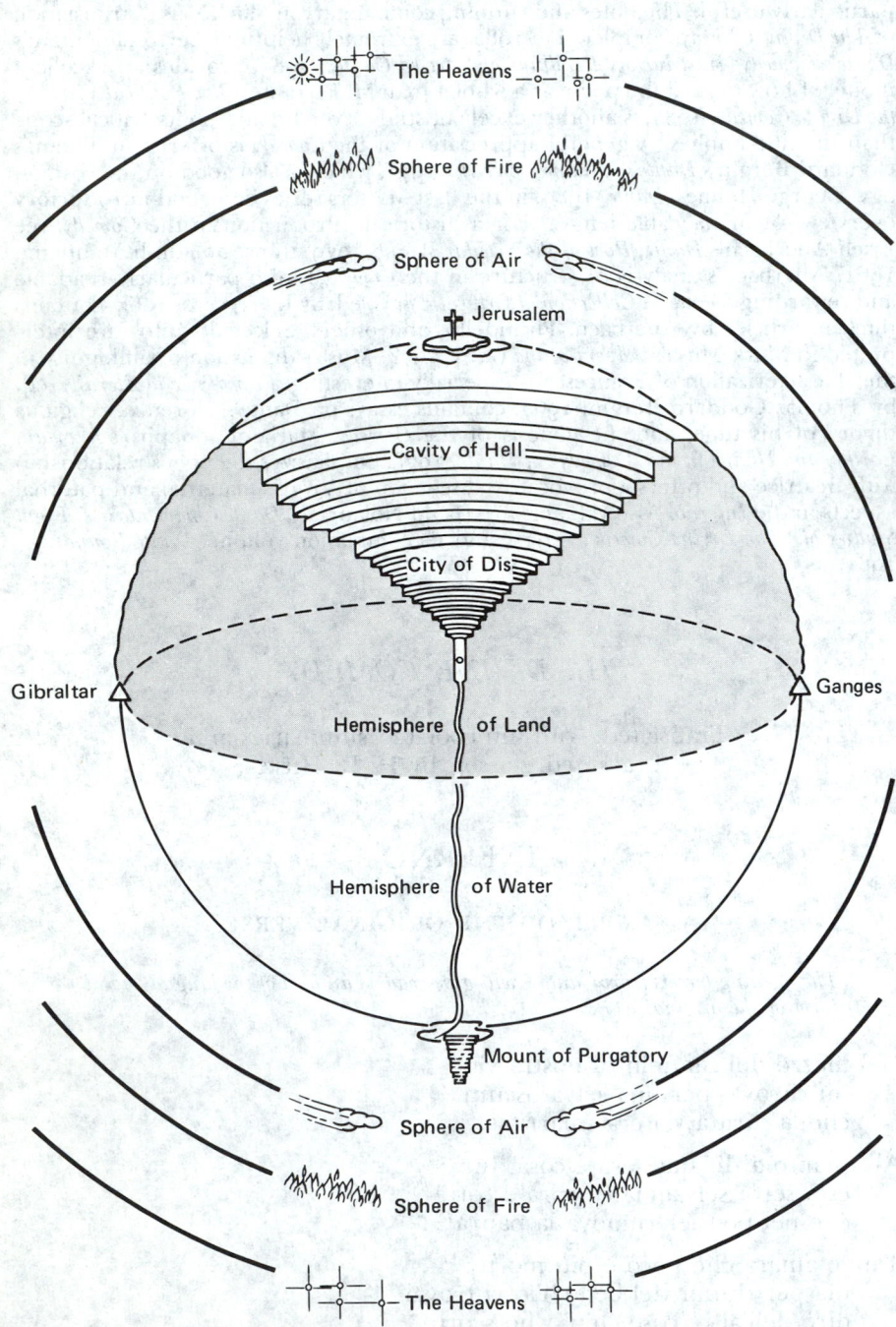

The Heavens

Sphere of Fire

Sphere of Air

Jerusalem

Cavity of Hell

City of Dis

Gibraltar

Ganges

Hemisphere of Land

Hemisphere of Water

Mount of Purgatory

Sphere of Air

Sphere of Fire

The Heavens

A diagram of the earth in the center of the universe.

Io non so ben ridir com'io v'entrai,
    tant'era pieno di sonno a quel punto
    che la verace via abbandonai. 12

Ma poi ch'i' fui al piè d'un colle giunto,
    là dove terminava quella valle
    che m'avea di paura il cor compunto,

guardai in alto, e vidi le sue spalle
    vestite già de' raggi del pianeta
    che mena dritto altrui per ogni calle.

Allor fu la paura un poco queta
    che nel lago del cor m'era durata
    la notte chi'i' passai con tanta pièta.

E come quei che con lena affannata
    uscito fuor del pelago alla riva
    si volge all'acqua perigliosa e guata, 24

così l'animo mio, ch'ancor fuggiva,
    si volse a retro a rimirar lo passo
    che non lasciò già mai persona viva.

OUTLINE OF THE INFERNO

Upper Hell, Incontinence

REGION	SINNERS	PUNISHMENTS
Vestibule	Trimmers, neutrals	Stung by insects, run after banners
Circle I	[Virtuous pagans, unbaptized infants]	Melancholy, desire without hope
Circle II	The lustful	Blown forever by storm winds
Circle III	The gluttons	Discomfort, all senses punished
Circle IV	The avaricious and the prodigal	Pushing rocks, useless labor
Circle V	The angry and the sullen	The angry thrashing about helplessly; the sullen submerged, emitting bubbles

Lower Hell, Malice (Violence and Fraud)

Circle VI	[Heretics]	In burning tombs
Circle VII	The violent	
Round 1	against neighbors, fellow men	Submerged in hot blood
Round 2	against self (suicides)	Enclosed in new bodies, as trees and bushes
Round 3	against God (blasphemers, sodomites, usurers)	On burning sand in rain of fire

OUTLINE OF THE INFERNO *(continued)*

Lower Hell (continued)

REGION	SINNERS	PUNISHMENTS
Circle VIII	Fraud against those who have no special trust	
Bolgia 1	Panders and seducers	Whipped by devils
Bolgia 2	Flatterers	Covered with filth
Bolgia 3	Simonists	Upside down in holes, feet on fire
Bolgia 4	Soothsayers	Heads twisted, turned backward
Bolgia 5	Barrators	Covered by boiling pitch
Bolgia 6	Hypocrites	Wearing leaden mantles
Bolgia 7	Thieves	In snake pit, transformations
Bolgia 8	Evil counselors	Concealed in flames
Bolgia 9	Sowers of discord	Wounds, mutilations
Bolgia 10	Falsifiers (alchemists, impersonators, counterfeiters, liars)	Diseases (leprosy, madness, dropsy, high fever)
Circle IX	Fraudulent against those who have special trust	
Caïna	Murderers of kindred	In ice to necks, heads bent forward
Antenora	Traitors to party or country	In ice to necks
Tolomea	Murderers of guests	In ice to necks, heads bent backward
Giudecca	Traitors to lords and benefactors	Completely submerged in ice

At the Center of the Earth (Universe)

Lucifer with Judas, Brutus, and Cassius in his three mouths, with three sets of wings sending forth a freezing blast of impotence, ignorance, and hatred.

NOTE: The souls in Circle I and Circle VI are outside of the classifications of Incontinence and Malice. They are guilty only from a Christian viewpoint, and Dante has to fit them as well as he can into the Aristotelian classification.

CANTO I

VIRGIL

The story begins on Thursday night, April 7, 1300. Dante, at the age of thirty-five, having completed half of man's traditional three-score years and ten, awakens to find himself in the forest of worldliness or sin. He cannot recall how he entered it: he had sunk, as men do, gradually and imperceptibly into sinful habits.

The night passes, and the sun (Divine Enlightenment or Righteous Choice) rises behind the Mount of Rectitude.

In the middle of the journey of our life
    I came to my senses in a dark forest,
      for I had lost the straight path.

Oh, how hard it is to tell
what a dense, wild, and tangled wood this was,
the thought of which renews my fear!

So terrible it is that death is hardly worse.
But to reveal the good that I found there,
I will speak first of other things.

I cannot tell how I entered it,
so heavy with slumber was I at the moment
when I abandoned the true way.   12

But when I had reached the foot of a hill,
there where the valley ended
which had filled my heart with fear,

I looked up, and saw its shoulders
clothed already with the rays of the planet
which leads men straight on every path.

Then the fear was somewhat quieted
which had lasted in the lake of my heart
during the night I had passed so piteously.

And as a seafarer, who has escaped from the storm
to the shore, turns with wearied breath
to the turbulent waters and gazes,   24

so I, still fleeing in my mind,
turned back to look at the pass
which no one before had ever left alive.

> *As Dante starts to climb the hill, a leopard, the symbol of luxury or lust, appears.
> It offers some opposition, but the early hour and the buoyant influence of Spring,
> the season when the universe was supposed to have been created, give him hope.
> Then a lion (Pride) assails him, rushing on with such fury that the very air
> around seems to tremble. And finally a she-wolf, the symbol of avarice or greed,
> the most widespread of vices. Dante (Mankind) feels that he could overcome the
> others, but at the sight of the wolf, he despairs.*[1]

After I had rested a little my weary body,
I took my way over the lonely slope
[climbing][2] so that the firm foot always was the lower.

And behold! almost at the beginning of the rise,
a leopard, light, and very nimble,
which was covered with a spotted hide!

It did not move from in front of me,
but instead so blocked my way
that several times I turned to go back.   36

---

[1] This is a traditional interpretation of the allegory of the three beasts. Other explanations
are possible—for example, that the leopard is Fraud, the lion Violence, and the wolf Incontinence. These three evils would correspond to the tripartite classification of sins in Dante's hell.

[2] The words within square brackets, here and later in *The Divine Comedy*, are explanations
inserted by the translator.

The time was the beginning of the morning,
    and the sun was rising with those stars
    that were with it when Divine Love

first set those beautiful things in motion,
    so that I found cause for good hope
    concerning the beast with the gaily spotted hide

in the hour of the day and in the sweet season;
    but even so I feared again
    at the sight of a lion that confronted me.

It appeared to be coming at me
    with head erect and with ravenous hunger,
    so that the air seemed afraid of it,   48

and a she-wolf came also, burdened
    in her leanness with all cravings,
    and which has indeed made many live in sorrow.

The sight of her brought such fear
    and such distress upon me
    that I lost hope of the ascent.

And as a gambler who gladly wins,
    but when the time comes for him to lose,
    weeps and is saddened in all his thoughts,

so I changed as the restless beast advanced
    against me, and little by little
    drove me down to where the sun is silent.   60

> *At this critical moment, Virgil (Reason, Philosophy), whose voice has long been
> unheard, appears. Dante forgets for a moment his despair, and bends reverently
> before his master. Then he mentions the wolf which has blocked his (and man-
> kind's) reform. Virgil explains the nature of the greed for which the wolf stands:
> it is an element in nearly all the crimes men commit. But a "hound," a redeemer
> (variously identified), possibly from between the towns of Feltro and Montefeltro,
> will ultimately come.*

While I was falling back to a lower place
    someone appeared before me whose voice
    from long silence seemed faint.

When I saw him in that desolation,
    "Have pity on me!" I cried to him,
    "whoever you are, whether a shade or a real man."

He answered, "Not a man now,
    a man once I was, and both my parents
    were Lombards, Mantuans by city.

I was born *sub Julio*[3] although late,
    and I lived in Rome under the good Augustus
    at the time of the false and lying gods.   72

I was a poet and sang of [Aeneas] that just son
    of Anchises who came from Troy
    after proud Ilion had been burned.

But why do you return to such misery?
    Why not climb the delightful mountain
    which is the beginning and the source of all joy?"

"Now are you that Virgil, that spring
    which pours forth so broad a stream of speech?"
    I answered him with bashful brow,

"Oh, honor and light of other poets,
    may the long study and great love help me
    which made me search through your volume!   84

You are my master and my author;
    you alone are the one from whom I took
    the style which has done me honor.

See the beast because of which I turned;
    save me from her, famous sage,
    for she makes my whole body tremble!"

"You must take another road," he answered
    after he had seen me weep,
    "if you want to escape from this wild place;

for the animal of which you complain
    lets no one pass along her way,
    but so hinders that she kills,   96

and she has a nature so vicious and perverse
    that she never satisfies her greedy desires,
    and after feeding is hungrier than before.

Many are the animals with which she mates,
    and there will be still more until the Hound comes
    that will make her die in pain.

He will not feed on earth or pelf,
    but on wisdom, love and virtue,
    and his nation will be between Feltro and Feltro.

He will be the savior of that humbled Italy
    for whom the virgin Camilla,
    Euryalus, Turnus, and Nisus[4] died of wounds.   108

---

[3] "Under Julius Caesar."
[4] Characters in the second half of Virgil's *Aeneid,* which describes war in Italy.

He will hunt her through every town
    until he has driven her back to Hell,
    whence Envy [of man's happiness] first released her.

> *Now Virgil proposes to lead Dante through Hell and Purgatory, and outlines the*
> *course of the journey. In Heaven, Beatrice (Revelation, Theology) will be the*
> *guide.*
>
> *In his humble submission to the mystery of Divine Justice, Virgil accuses himself*
> *of "rebellion" against God's law. There is a note of sadness in his words, con-*
> *demned as he is, for having lived before Christ, to an eternity of longing. Dante*
> *generously suggests his apology by a reference to the God the ancient poet did not*
> *and, of course, could not know.*

Therefore I think it best for you
    to follow me, and I will be your guide
    to take you through an eternal place [Hell]

where you will hear despairing cries
    and will see the tormented spirits
    each of whom proclaims the second death [damnation],

and you will see [in Purgatory] those who are contented
    in the fire, because they hope to come,
    whenever it may be, among the blessed,   120

to whom, then, if you wish to ascend,
    a guide worthier than I will take you:
    to her I will entrust you when I leave,

for that Emperor who reigns up there,
    because I was rebellious to His law,
    does not want me as a guide to His city.

Everywhere He reigns and there He rules;
    there is His seat and His high throne,
    O happy are those whom He chooses!"

And I to him, "Poet, I beg you
    by that God you did not know, in order
    that I may flee from this evil and worse,   132

take me where you have said,
    so that I may see St. Peter's gate
    and those you proclaim so sad."

Then he moved on, and I followed him.

CANTO II

BEATRICE

It is now the evening of Good Friday. The sun which had cheered Dante is going
down, and the animals on earth (all workers in God's universe) are returning
home from their labors of the day. In this dark moment, Dante's courage fails,

and he wonders about the advisability of the journey. It is true, he reflects, that both Aeneas and St. Paul, the "Chosen Vessel," visited the future world; but Aeneas' visit led to the founding of the Roman Empire, divinely ordained to be the seat of the papacy, and St. Paul brought from Heaven a confirmation of the true faith. Dante disclaims any such mission.

The day was departing, and the darkening air
    was taking the creatures that are on earth
    from their daily toil, and I alone

was preparing to endure the hardship
    both of the journey and of the pity
    which unerring memory will relate.

O Muses, O lofty genius, aid me now!
    O mind which inscribed what I saw,
    here your worth will be revealed.

I began, "Poet, you who guide me,
    consider my strength, whether it is great enough
    before you commit me to the arduous journey.   12

You say that [Aeneas] the father of Sylvius,
    still subject to corruption,
    went bodily to the eternal world;

but that the Adversary of all Evil [God]
    should be gracious to him, thinking of the result
    and of who and what he was,

does not seem unreasonable to a thoughtful man;
    for he was chosen in the Empyrean heaven
    to be father of glorious Rome

and of her empire, both of which
    were established for the holy place
    where the successors of St. Peter sit.   24

On this journey through which you honor him,
    he heard things which led to his victory
    and to the papal mantle.

Afterward the Chosen Vessel [St. Paul] went there
    to bring comfort to the faith
    which is the beginning of the way of salvation.

But why should I go? Who grants it?
    I am not Aeneas, nor am I Paul;
    for that neither I nor others believe me worthy.

Therefore, if I allow myself to go,
    I fear the journey may be folly: you are wise
    and understand better than I can speak."   36

And, as a person unwills what he wills,
    and with new thoughts changes purpose,
    holding back from what he has started,

so I became on that dark slope,
 for, by thinking, I delayed the undertaking
 that I had begun so quickly.

  Not deceived by this rationalizing, Virgil reproves Dante for being afraid. Then,
  to reassure him, he describes the occasion of his coming, a scene in the first circle
  of Hell where the souls of the virtuous pagans are "in suspense," longing for an
  understanding of God and of the mystery of life, with the realization that they can
  never attain it.

"If I have understood your words rightly,"
 answered that magnanimous shade,
 "your resolution is dulled by cowardice

which often distracts a man
 and turns him away from honorable deeds,
 as imperfect sight causes an animal to shy.   48

To free you from this fear, I will tell
 why I came and what I heard
 when I first took pity on you.

I was among those who are in suspense,
 and a lady [Beatrice] called to me
 so blessed and beautiful that I asked her to command.

Her eyes shone more than the stars,
 and with an angelic voice,
 softly and sweetly she spoke to me,

'O courteous Mantuan soul whose fame
 still lasts on the earth, and will last
 as long as the world,   60

my friend, but not the friend of Fortune,
 is so impeded on the deserted slope
 that in fear he has turned back,

and, from what I have heard in Heaven,
 I am afraid he is already so lost
 that I have come too late for his relief.

Now go to him, and with your eloquent speech
 and with all else needful for his escape
 help him, so that I may be consoled.

I am Beatrice, bidding you to go;
 I come from a place to which I would return;
 Love moved me and makes me speak.   72

When I am in the presence of my Lord
 I will praise you often to Him.'
 She was silent then and I began,

'O lady of virtue [Revelation] through whom alone
    the human race excels all creatures contained
    within the heaven of the smallest orbit [all on earth],

your command so pleases me that complying
    if already begun would seem slow;
    you need only to reveal your desire;

but tell me why you do not shrink
    from descending to this depth from the broad expanse
    to which you are eager to return.'   84

> *Beatrice explains how, although pitying Dante, she can feel no distress at the
> working of Divine Justice.*
>
> *The formal allegory of the scene in Heaven she then describes is as follows: Mary
> (Divine Mercy) sends Lucia (Illuminating Grace) to prepare the way for Beatrice
> (Revelation) whom Dante (Mankind) will perceive when Virgil (Reason) makes
> him ready to behold her.*

'Since you wish to know so much
    I will tell you briefly,' she answered,
    'why I do not fear to come here.

We should be afraid only of things
    which can harm, not of others,
    since they are not fearful.

Through God's grace I am formed in such a way
    that your misery does not touch me,
    nor does a flame of this burning hurt me.

There is a gentle lady in Heaven [Mary]
    whose pity is aroused by the distress of him
    to whom I send you, and who tempers harsh judgment.   96

She called upon Lucia and said in her request,
    "Your faithful one now has need of you,
    and I recommend him to you."

Lucia, the enemy of all cruelty,
    arose and came to where I was
    seated by the ancient Rachel.

She said, "Beatrice, true praise of God,
    why do you not help him who loved you so much
    that through you he arose above the common crowd?

Do you not hear the pity of his cries?
    Do you not see Death struggling with him
    on the river [of evil] not less terrible than the sea?"   108

On earth men were never so swift
    to seek gain and flee from harm
    as I was after these words were spoken

to come here from my blessed seat,
   trusting in your noble speech
   which honors you and those who have heard it.'

After she said this to me
   she turned away her shining eyes in tears,
   which made me still readier to go,

and to you I came as she desired.
   I freed you from the beast
   which had cut off the short way up the fair mount.   120

So what is it? Why, why do you hold back?
   Why keep such cowardice in your heart?
   Why are you not bold and free,

since three such holy ladies
   care for you in the court of Heaven,
   and my words promise you so much good?"

As little flowers, bent down and closed by the frost of night,
   stand up, all open on their stems,
   when the sun comes back to warm and brighten them,

so I revived my failing strength,
   and so much boldness rushed into my heart
   that I began like one set free,   132

"O compassionate lady who gave aid to me!
   O courteous shade who obeyed so quickly
   the true words she spoke to you!

You have disposed my heart
   with such desire for going by your account
   that I have regained my first intent.

Now go, for one wish is in both of us,
   you my leader [guide], my lord [superior], my master [teacher]!"
   Thus I spoke to him, and when he started

I followed on the deep and wild way.

CANTO III

THE ENTRANCE

In the faint light of the evening of Good Friday, the anniversary of the Crucifixion when, according to the Creed, Christ "entered into Hell," the two travelers move on to the gate over which appears a fearful inscription pointing out the woe within, the eternal pain, the people lost even to hope. Divine Justice (incomprehensible to reason alone) moved God in his three-fold attributes of Power, Wisdom, and Love to create Hell. It was made when only eternal things (the elements, the heavens, and the angels) existed, and it also will last and function eternally.

On reading these words Dante begins again to doubt, but, ashamed to confess his fear, he seeks delay or assurance by asking about their meaning which, incidentally, is painfully explicit. Virgil, undeceived, reproves Dante for his weakness.

Through me you go into the city of grief,
  Through me you go into the pain that is eternal,
  Through me you go among people lost.

Justice moved my exalted creator;
  The divine power made me,
  The supreme wisdom, and the primal love.

Before me all created things were eternal,
  And eternal i will last.
  Abandon every hope, you who enter here.

These words of a dark coloring
  I saw written above a gate; whereupon I said,
  "Master, their meaning is hard for me."   12

Then he spoke like one who understands:
  "Here you must give up all distrust,
  here all cowardice must end.

We have come to the place where I said
  that you would see the woeful people
  who have lost the good of the intellect.

And after he had taken me by the hand,
  with a cheerful look which comforted me,
  he drew me within the secret place [the eternal world].

On entering, Dante sees little because of the darkness, but hears sounds which he distinguishes gradually as cries, languages, words, accents, voices, and finally as the dull noise of blows. Virgil contemptuously refuses to waste words on the souls here. They are the trimmers, the mediocre, the poor in spirit, the neutrals, joined with the angels who refused to take sides in the revolt against God. They are in a kind of vestibule, outside of Hell proper. Their punishment is slight compared to those which come later, yet they are envious of every other lot.

There, sighs, lamentations, and deep wailings
  resounded through the starless air,
  so that at first I began to weep.   24

Diverse tongues, horrible languages,
  words of pain, accents of rage,
  voices loud and hoarse, and the sounds of blows

made a tumult which moved forever
  in that air unchanged by time,
  as sand eddies in a whirlwind.

And I said, my head girt with horror,
  "Master, what is it that I hear,
  and who are these people so overcome by pain?"

Then he to me, "This miserable fate
    afflicts the wretched souls of those
    who lived without infamy and without praise.   36

They are joined with that choir of wicked angels
    who were neither rebellious
    nor faithful to God, but for themselves.

The heavens, to remain beautiful, drove them out,
    nor would deep Hell receive them
    lest the wicked gain pride by comparison."

And I, "Master, what is so burdensome
    that it makes them lament loudly?"
    He answered, "Briefly I will tell you.

They have no hope of death,
    and their blind life is so debased
    that they are envious of every other lot.   48

The world does not grant them any fame;
    pity [of Heaven] and justice [of Hell] alike disdain them.
    Let us not speak of them, but look and pass on."

> *Some of these souls, neutral and perhaps sedentary in life, are condemned now to active partisanship. The poet recognizes one, but will not distinguish him with a name. Most commentators have identified him as Celestine V, a pope who, by his refusal to keep his office, allowed Dante's great enemy, Boniface VIII, to rise to power. There are less scandalous interpretations, however, notably as Pontius Pilate, who refused justice to Christ and who offers a better motivation for the extreme contempt shown here.*

And I, looking, saw a banner
    which, circling, moved so fast
    that it seemed to scorn all rest,

and behind it came such a throng of people
    that I never would have believed
    that death could have undone so many.

After I had recognized some of them,
    I saw and knew the shade of him
    who, through cowardice, made the great refusal.   60

At once I understood and was certain
    that this was the sect of the wicked
    displeasing both to God and to His enemies.

These wretches, who had never really lived,
    were naked and stung constantly
    by hornets and wasps that were there.

These made their faces stream with blood
    which, mixed with tears, was consumed
    by loathsome maggots at their feet.

When Dante asks about a crowd in the distance, Virgil tells him to wait and see. Taking this as a reproach, our poet remains silent for a long time.

As the travelers move on, Charon appears, the ancient boatman of the Styx, who prophesies Dante's ultimate salvation and whom Virgil appeases with a kind of conjuring formula.

When I began to look farther on
    I saw people on the shore of a great river;
    whereupon I said, "Master, now grant   72

that I should know who they are
    and what makes them so ready to pass over,
    as I discern through the faint light."

And he to me, "These things will be known to you
    when we stay our steps
    on the sad bank of the Acheron."

Then with eyes ashamed and lowered,
    fearing that my words might have offended him,
    I kept from speaking until we reached the stream.

And behold! coming toward us in a skiff
    an old man, white with ancient locks,
    shouting, "Woe to you, depraved spirits;   84

hope not ever to see Heaven.
    I come to take you to the other shore
    into eternal darkness, into heat and cold.

And you there, living soul,
    get away from these who are dead."
    But when he saw that I did not leave,

"By another way, at other ports," he said,
    "you will come ashore, not here;
    a lighter boat will carry you."

And my guide, "Charon, do not be disturbed;
    this is wished for where the power is
    to do what is wished; and ask no more."   96

Then were quieted the woolly cheeks
    of the boatman of the livid marsh
    who, around his eyes, had rings of flame.

The souls are impelled by a kind of instinct to seek their proper place, since sin leads inevitably to its own results, its own suffering.

We are not told how Dante crosses the river. There is a flash, an earthquake, and he falls unconscious. On awakening he is on the other bank.

But those weary and naked souls
    changed color and gnashed their teeth
    as soon as they heard the cruel words.

They cursed God and their parents,
    the human race, and the place, time, and seed
    of their begetting and of their birth.

Then, all together they withdrew,
    weeping loudly, to the accursed shore
    which awaits every man without fear of God.   108

Charon the demon, with eyes like glowing coals,
    beckoning to them, gathered them in,
    and hit with an oar any who delayed.

As in autumn the leaves fall
    one after the other, until the branch
    sees all its spoils upon the ground,

so, the evil seed of Adam
    fell to that shore, one by one, and at signals,
    as the falcon does at its recall.

Thus they go over the dark water,
    and before they have landed on the other shore,
    again on this side a new crowd assembles.   120

"My son," said the courteous master,
    "those who die in the wrath of God
    gather here from every country,

and they are ready to pass the river,
    for Divine Justice so spurs them
    that fear is changed into desire.

Along here no good spirit ever passes;
    therefore, if Charon complains of you,
    you can understand what his words imply."

When he had ended, the dark country
    trembled so that from fright
    my memory bathes me still with sweat.   132

The tearful land produced a blast
    which flashed a crimson light
    conquering all my senses;

and I fell, like one overcome by sleep.

CANTO IV

LIMBO

When Dante awakens from his swoon he is in Limbo, the first circle of Hell. He interprets Virgil's pallor as due to fear, but learns that it comes from pity for those in the ancient poet's own circle. Although Dante still refrains from questioning, Virgil is anxious to point out that the shades here committed no sin, but died unbaptized or lived before Christ. Their damnation is an article of faith, beyond man's understanding. Here there is no torment other than a sense of unfulfill-

ment, a feeling that expresses itself in melancholy, in suspense, in a vague
longing for knowledge of God and for a solution of the mystery of life without
hope of ever having either.

The deep sleep into which I fell was broken
    by heavy thunder, so that I started,
    like one awakened by force,

and having risen, I glanced around
    and looked intently with rested eyes
    to discover where I was.

In truth, I found myself on the brink
    of the dolorous valley of the abyss
    which resounds with the sound of countless cries.

It was so dark, deep, and cloudy
    that in looking toward the bottom
    I could discern nothing.   12

"Now, let us go into the blind world,"
    the poet began all pale,
    "I will be first and you second."

And I, noticing his color, said,
    "How shall I come if you are afraid,
    you who always comfort me in my doubt?"

And he to me, "The anguish
    of the people down there paints on my face
    the pity which you mistake for fear.

Let us go, for the long way impels us."
    Thus he moved on and made me enter
    the first circle which girds the abyss.   24

Here, so far as one could tell by listening,
    there was no lament, but only sighs
    which made the eternal air tremble.

They came from the sadness without torment
    felt by the great crowd
    of children and of women and of men.

My good master said to me, "You do not ask
    what spirits these are. Now,
    I want you to know before you go farther

that they did not sin, but having merit
    was not enough, for they lacked baptism,
    which is a portal of the faith you hold;   36

and if they lived before Christianity
    they did not worship God rightly;
    among such as these am I myself.

For such defects, not for other faults,
    are we lost, and afflicted only
    in that we live in longing without hope."

Great grief gripped my heart when I heard this,
    for I knew that people of much worth
    were in that Limbo in suspense.

> *Dante now risks a timid question. He wants to know about the "Harrowing of Hell," when Christ was supposed to have gone to Limbo to release the ancient Hebrews who had believed in His coming. After the explanation the poets move on to a special region reserved for the great men of the past. Virgil (as Reason) approves the recognition of Dante as the sixth in rank of the world's poets.*

"Tell me, Master, tell me, sir," I began,
    wishing to be assured of the faith
    that destroys every error,   48

"did any ever through his own merit
    or another's leave here to be blessed?"
    And he, understanding my veiled speech, answered,

"I was new in this condition
    when I saw a Powerful One [Christ]
    crowned with the sign of victory [the cross as an aureole].

He took from here our first parent,
    Abel his son, and Noah,
    obedient Moses, the lawgiver,

the patriarch Abraham, and David, the king,
    Israel [Jacob] with his father and his sons,
    and Rachel for whom he [Jacob] did so much,   60

and many others, and he made them blessed,
    and I wish you to know that before then
    no human souls were ever saved."

We did not stop because of his remarks,
    but kept passing through the forest—
    the forest, I mean, of crowded spirits.

Our way had not yet taken us far
    after my slumber when I saw a light
    which dispelled a hemisphere of darkness.

We were still distant from the glow
    but not too far for me to discern
    that notable people occupied that place.   72

"O you who honor every science and art," I said,
    "who are these whose great merit
    separates them from the others?"

And he answered, "The deserved fame
    which still honors them in your life
    gains favor in Heaven, and thus promotes them."

Meanwhile a voice was heard, saying,
    "Honor the greatest poet;
    his shade which had left is returning."

When this voice was silent
    I saw four great figures come to us,
    their faces neither sad nor gay.   84

My good master began to speak:
    "See that one with sword in hand,
    coming ahead of the others as their lord.

He is Homer, the sovereign poet;
    the other, following, is Horace, the satirist;
    Ovid is the third, and Lucan the last.

Since each shares with me the title 'poet'
    which the single voice pronounced,
    they do me honor, and in doing this do well."

Thus I saw assembled the school
    of that lord of the lofty song who soars
    above the others like an eagle.   96

After they had talked together a little
    they turned to me with signs of greeting,
    and my master smiled at that.

And still more honor they showed me
    by making me one of their group,
    so that I was the sixth among such sages.

> *The poets now come to the Castle of Wisdom or Fame, surrounded by the walls of the cardinal and speculative virtues and defended by a moat which may represent eloquence or desire for knowledge. They pass through the gates of the seven liberal arts. On a kind of enameled meadow within, the great spirits of the past appear: first the Trojans, Greeks, and legendary figures of early Rome; then philosophers, scientists, mathematicians, and doctors; and finally the Moorish scholar Averroës.*

Thus we continued toward the light,
    speaking of matters concerning which silence
    is as fitting now as speech was then,

and we arrived at the foot of a noble castle,
    seven times encircled by high walls,
    defended all around by a fair rivulet.   108

This we crossed as if on solid ground.
    Through seven gates I passed with these sages
    and we arrived on a meadow of fresh verdure.

There we saw people dignified and grave,
   of great authority in their semblance;
   they spoke seldom, and with soft voices.

Afterward we withdrew to one side
   to an open place, luminous and high,
   from which all could be seen.

There, standing on the green enamel,
   the great spirits were shown to me,
   to have seen whom I feel exalted.   120

I saw Electra[5] with many companions,
   among whom I recognized Hector and Aeneas,
   and Caesar clad in arms, with hawklike eyes.

I saw Camilla and Penthesilea
   on the other side, and I saw the Latian king,
   sitting with Lavinia, his daughter.

I saw that Brutus[6] who expelled the Tarquin,
   Lucretia, Julia, Marcia, and Cornelia;
   and alone, to one side, the Saladin.

When I had raised my eyes a little higher
   I saw the Master of the Knowing [Aristotle]
   sitting with his philosophic family.   132

All looked at him, all did him honor;
   there I saw Socrates and Plato
   who stood ahead of the others closest to him:

Democritus, who thought the world due to chance;
   Diogenes, Anaxagoras, and Thales,
   Empedocles, Heraclitus, and Zeno;

and I saw the good compiler of the qualities [of plants],
   Dioscorides, I mean; and Orpheus,
   Tully [Cicero], Linus, and Seneca, the moralist;

Euclid the geometer, and Ptolemy,
   Hippocrates, Avicenna, and Galen,
   and Averroës who made the great commentary [on Aristotle].   144

I cannot enumerate them all fully;
   my long theme so drives me on that many times
   my words fall short of the facts.

The sixfold company diminished to two [Virgil and Dante];
   by another way my wise guide took me,
   out of the quiet into the trembling air,

and I came to a place where no light shines.

[5] Not the daughter of Agamemnon and Clytemnestra but rather the mother of Dardanus, founder of Troy.

[6] This is not the assassin of Julius Caesar; that Brutus appears at the center of hell in Canto XXXIV. The Brutus referred to here founded the ancient Roman republic.

CANTO V

FRANCESCA DA RIMINI

Since Hell is like an inverted cone, the circumference of each succeeding circle diminishes.

The guardian of the second ring is Minos, the ancient judge of the dead, represented by Dante as having some of the characteristics of a medieval demon. Like Charon, Minos offers a slight opposition which is overcome by the conjuring formula.

Thus I descended from the first circle
    down to the second which encloses less space
    but so much more pain that it moves to tears.

There Minos stands, horrible and snarling,
    examining the offenses, judging,
    and sending down as he girds himself—

I mean that when an ill-born soul
    comes before him, it confesses wholly,
    and that discerner of sin,

seeing what place in Hell belongs to it,
    encircles himself with his tail as many times
    as the degrees he wants it to descend.   12

Always many stand in front of him;
    they come in turns to their judgment,
    confess and hear, and then are hurled below.

"O you who come to the painful refuge,"
    Minos said when he saw me,
    interrupting the work of his great office,

"consider how you entered and in whom you trust;
    do not let the breadth of the entrance deceive you."
    And my guide to him, "Why do you cry out?

Do not impede his fated going.
    It is wished for where the power is
    to do what is wished; so ask no more."   24

The poets hear and see the shades guilty of lust. A landslide caused by an earthquake at the time of the Crucifixion perhaps reminds the restless souls as they pass of the impossibility of their redemption. Dante pities more than blames these victims of the flesh and of the imagination. They pass like birds in autumn flight.

Now I begin to hear the sad notes of pain,
    now I have come to where
    loud cries beat upon my ears.

I have reached a place mute of all light
    which roars like the sea in a tempest
    when beaten by conflicting winds.

The infernal storm which never stops
    drives the spirits in its blast;
    whirling and beating, it torments them.

When they come in front of the landslide,
    they utter laments, moans, and shrieks;
    there they curse the Divine Power.   36

I learned that to such a torment
    carnal sinners are condemned
    who subject their reason to desire.

And, as starlings are borne by their wings
    in the cold season, in a broad and dense flock,
    so that blast carries the evil spirits.

Here, there, up, and down, it blows them;
    no hope ever comforts them
    of rest or even of less pain.

And as cranes go chanting their lays,
    making a long line of themselves in the air,
    so I saw coming, uttering laments,   48

shades born by that strife of winds.

> *Dante is eager to know who is punished here. No vulgar examples are cited but only glamorous figures of the ancient and medieval past whom love too completely mastered. Perhaps our poet suspects already that Francesca da Rimini and her lover are here. In any case he asks to speak to two who seem unusually light and is told to address them in the name of love, to which, in a nobler form, all his own life was a dedication. The real appeal, however, is in the sympathy expressed by the words, "O wearied souls!" Like doves borne on by desire, Francesca and Paolo leave their company, so responsive are they still to the slightest note of affection.*

I asked, "Master, who are these people
    whom the black air so punishes?"

"The first of those about whom
    you want to know," he said to me,
    "was an empress over many peoples,

by the vice of luxury so subdued
    that she made lust lawful in her decrees
    to take away the blame she had incurred.

She is Semiramis who, we read,
    succeeded Ninus, her spouse;
    she held the land that now the Sultan rules.   60

The other is she [Dido] who killed herself
    after breaking faith with the ashes of Sichaeus;
    next comes luxurious Cleopatra.

See Helen [of Troy] for whom
   so many bad years revolved, and the great Achilles
   whose last battle was with love.[7]

See Paris, Tristan,"—and he pointed out and named
   more than a thousand shades
   whom love had taken from our life.

After I had heard my teacher
   name the knights and ladies of olden times,
   pity overcame me, and I felt dismayed.   72

I began, "Poet, willingly would I speak
   with those two who go together
   and seem so light upon the wind."

And he to me, "Wait until they come closer,
   then entreat them by the love
   which impels them and they will come."

As soon as the wind brought them to us,
   I raised my voice, "O wearied souls,
   come speak to us if it is not forbidden."

As doves summoned by their desire,
   with wings raised and firm, sail through the air,
   borne on to their sweet nest by their will alone,   84

so those spirits moved from the band where Dido is,
   coming to us through the malignant air,
   so responsive were they to my affectionate cry.

> *Now Francesca speaks, and her first words are an implied prayer to God whose mysterious justice has condemned her beyond remission, an unselfish prayer for this living soul who has shown them pity. It is a prayer for the "peace" which romantic and illicit love can never know. In her heart's response to Dante's simple words, she treats him already as "gracious" and "benign" and exaggerates her own misdoing. Her story is a mere outline, told partly in terms of the maxims of courtly love. With ladylike reticence she does not name herself or Paolo, her brother-in-law and lover, or even the city where she was born. Death itself would not have been so tragic: one moment for repentance might have permitted her to be saved; it was the suddenness of her and Paolo's death that was so cruel. Caïna, at the bottom of Hell, where traitors to kindred are punished, awaits her husband who surprised and killed them.*

"O living creature, gracious and benign,
   going through the dark air
   visiting us who stained the earth with blood,

---

[7] Dante knew a medieval tradition according to which Achilles, as a result of love for a Trojan princess, was ambushed and killed.

if the King of the universe were friendly to us
   we would pray to Him for your peace,
     since you pity our perverse evil,

Whatever you are pleased to hear from us or say
   we will relate and listen to,
     while the wind, as now, is silent.   96

The city [Ravenna] where I was born
   lies on the shore where the Po descends
     with all its tributaries to find peace.

Love which flames quickly in noble hearts
   was kindled in this soul by the fair body
     taken from me; the manner [of that taking] still offends.

Love that exempts no one beloved from loving
   caught me so strongly with his charm
     that, as you see, it still does not leave me.

Love led us to one death together.
   Caïna waits for him who quenched our lives."
     These words were borne from them to us.   108

> *On hearing this delicate outline of the tragedy, Dante bows his head, perhaps
> recalling who the speaker is, and then naming Francesca, he asks, in words as
> respectful and delicate as her own, about the immediate cause and occasion of her
> sin. Although she dislikes to recall the intimate details, she speaks, unable to
> refuse an affectionate appeal. There was no premeditation in her sin. She and
> Paolo had been reading a love story without suspecting the effect it might have.
> One moment of weakness overcame them, a moment which ended their reading
> and their lives and which stands now in contrast to eternity.*

When I heard those afflicted souls
   I bent down my face, and held it low so long
     that the poet said, "Of what are you thinking?"

When I answered I began, "Alas!
   how many sweet thoughts, what desire
     led them to the woeful pass!"

Then I turned to them and said,
   "Francesca, your suffering
     makes me weep with sorrow and with pity,

But tell me, at the time of the sweet sighs,
   by what means and how love permitted you
     to know the dubious desires."   120

And she to me, "There is no greater pain
   than to recall a happy time in misery
     and this your teacher knows;

but if to learn the first root of our love
   you have such desire, I will answer
     like one who speaks and weeps.

One day for our delight we were reading
    about Lancelot, how love constrained him;
    alone we were and without any suspicion.

Several times that reading made our glances meet
    and changed the color of our faces;
    but one moment alone overcame us.   132

When we read how the fond smile [of Guinevere]
    was kissed by such a lover,
    he, who never will be separated from me,

kissed me, on my lips, all trembling.
    A Gallehaut [pander] was the book and he who wrote it.
    That day we read no farther."

While one spirit was saying this
    the other wept, so that from pity
    I fainted, as if I had been dying,

and I fell, as a dead body falls.

CANTO VI

THE GLUTTONS

On recovering my senses, which were stunned
    by pity for the two kinsfolk
    who overwhelmed me with sadness,

new torments and new tormented shades
    I see around me, wherever I move
    and wherever I turn to gaze.

The poets are now among the gluttons who are lying like pigs in a sty under a constant, unvarying rain. Although the punishments here are relatively mild, they are particularly distasteful to the luxury-loving. All the senses are afflicted: sight by the dismal setting, touch by the cold rain, smell and taste by the stench, and hearing by the loud barking of Cerberus, the three-headed dog, the bestial guardian of this circle. Cerberus is appeased, not by a honey cake, as in the Aeneid, but by dirt, to emphasize further the filthiness of gluttony.

I am in the third circle of the rain,
    eternal, accursed, cold, and heavy;
    its amount and kind never change.

Large hailstones, dirty water, and snow
    pour down through the dark air;
    the ground that receives them stinks.   12

Cerberus, the fierce and cruel beast,
    barks doglike with three throats
    over those submerged there.

His eyes are red, his beard greasy and black,
    his belly large, his paws armed with claws;
    grasping the spirits, he flays and tears them.

The rain makes them howl like dogs;
    they use one side to shelter the other;
    often they turn, the profane wretches.

When Cerberus, the monster, saw us,
    he opened his mouths and showed his teeth,
    trembling in all his limbs.   24

And my leader, opening his hands,
    took some earth and threw handfuls
    into the ravenous gullets.

As a barking dog, longing for food,
    grows quiet after he has seized it,
    since he thinks only of eating,

so did those filthy heads of the demon Cerberus
    who thunders over the shades,
    making them wish they were deaf.

*A soul nicknamed "Ciacco" (the pig) recognizes Dante but is himself unrecogniz-
able since the bestial vice of gluttony disfigures. To spare the feelings of this shade
Dante suggests that perhaps Ciacco's pain prevented the recognition.*

We passed over the spirits subdued
    by the heavy rain, placing our feet
    on their nothingness which appears as flesh.   36

They were all lying on the ground
    except one who sat up quickly
    as soon as he saw us pass in front of him.

"O you, led through this Hell,"
    he said to me, "recognize me if you can;
    you were made [born] before I was unmade [died]."

And I to him, "The anguish that you feel
    perhaps takes you from my memory
    so that I do not seem ever to have seen you,

but tell me who you are, placed here
    in such punishment that, if others
    are greater, none is so displeasing."   48

And he to me, "Your city [Florence] so full of envy
    that it can hold no more
    kept me in the bright life.

The citizens called me Ciacco;
    for the damning sin of gluttony,
    as you see, I lie helpless in the rain.

And I, sad spirit, am not alone,
    for all of these are in similar pain
    for a like sin,"—and he said no more.

I answered, "Ciacco, your distress weighs upon me
    so that it moves to tears;
    but tell me, if you can, the fate   60

of the citizens of the divided city;
    if any one of them is just, and tell me
    why such discord has assailed it."

Then he to me, "After long dispute
    they will come to blows, and the rustic party [the Whites]
    will drive out the other with much offense.

Afterward that faction will fall
    within three suns [years], and the other rise
    through one [Boniface VIII] who now is moving carefully.

For a long time it will hold high its head,
    keeping the other under heavy burdens,
    however much it may weep and be put to shame.   72

Two men are just, but are not listened to.
    Pride, envy, and avarice are the sparks
    which have enflamed all hearts."

Here he put an end to his sad words,
    and I said to him, "I wish to learn more,
    and beg you to grant me the gift of further speech.

Farinata and Tegghiaio, who were so worthy,
    Jacopo Rusticucci, Arrigo, and Mosca,
    and the others who set their minds to doing good,

tell me where they are, let me know about them,
    for a great desire urges me to find out
    if Heaven soothes or Hell embitters them."   84

And he, "They are among the blackest spirits;
    different sins weigh them to the bottom;
    if you go down so far, you will see them.

But when you are again in the sweet world,
    I beg you to recall me to the memory of others.
    More I will not say; this is all I answer."

He twisted his straight eyes asquint,
    looked at me a little, then bent his head,
    and fell to the level of the other blind ones.

My guide said to me, "No more will he awaken
    until the angelic trumpet sounds [on Judgment Day]
    when the hostile Power [hostile to sinners] will come.   96

Each then will find his sad tomb,
   will resume his flesh and form,
   and will hear what resounds to all eternity."

Thus we passed over the filthy mixture of the shades
   and of the rain, with slow steps,
   touching a little on the future life.

I asked, "Master, will these torments increase
   after the great judgment,
   or will they be less or equally painful?"

He answered, "Recall your science
   which maintains that the more perfect a thing is,
   the more bliss or pain it feels.   108

Although these accursed people
   never come to true perfection,
   they will be more complete after than before."

We bent our course along that way,
   saying much more than I relate,
   and came to a place for descending.

There we found Plutus, the great enemy.

CANTO VII

The Avaricious and the Prodigal
*Plutus, the ancient god of wealth and here the guardian of the circle of the
avaricious and the prodigal, is represented as an inflated monster. He speaks in
a high voice, like certain fat men, and his words are not clearly comprehensible.
A reference to the Power through which the archangel Michael defeated the
revolt of Satan easily deflates this weak, unhealthy, and puffy creature, who
collapses suddenly, without resistance.*

"Papè Satàn, Papè Satàn, aleppe,"[8]
   Plutus began with a clucking voice,
   and that noble sage [Virgil], who understood,

said to comfort me, "Do not fear,
   for whatever power he may have,
   he cannot prevent our descending this rock."

Then he turned to that inflated visage
   and said, "Keep still, accursed wolf;
   consume yourself inwardly with your rage.

Not without reason is our going to the depth.
   It is decreed on high where Michael
   took vengeance for the proud revolt."   12

---

[8] These words are not clearly understandable; perhaps a threat and a warning to Satan.
(Translator's note.)

As sails swelled by the wind
    fall entangled when the mast breaks,
    so the cruel monster fell to the ground.

The avaricious on one side and the prodigal on the other push great weights
around their respective semicircles. At the two points where they clash, like the
waves between Scylla and Charybdis, they exchange insults and turn, going to
the opposite point. Thus they work hard, like the avaricious on earth, but
uselessly, missing the spiritual pleasures which make this life and the next worth
while. All are alike, without distinction, and unrecognizable as individuals.

Thus we descended into the fourth cavity,
    taking in more of the dismal bank
    which holds all the evil of the universe.

Ah, Justice of God! Who can combine
    so many new pains and torments,
    and why does our sin so waste us?

As the waves above Charybdis break
    against each other as they meet,
    so in this place the souls must clash.   24

Here I saw more people than elsewhere
    on one side and the other, shouting loudly
    and pushing weights with their chests.

They bump against each other and then all turn,
    pushing back the load and crying,
    "Why do you hoard?" or "Why do you squander?"

Thus they go on each side
    of the dark circle to the opposite point,
    shouting their insulting refrains.

When they reach that place, they turn again
    through their half circles to the other clash.
    And I, my heart oppressed, said,   36

"Master, now tell me who these are
    and if all the tonsured ones
    on the left are of the clergy?"

And he to me, "In the first life
    all were so twisted mentally
    that they could not spend with moderation.

Quite clearly their voices bark this out
    when they come to the two points of the circle
    where contrary faults divide them.

Those whose heads are tonsured, as you see,
    were clerics and popes and cardinals
    in whom avarice shows its strength."   48

And I, "Master, among such as these
 I must surely recognize some
 who were defiled by these vices."

And he to me, "You conceive a vain thought;
 the undiscerning life which made them sordid
 now leaves them too obscure for recognition.

Throughout eternity they will clash;
 some will arise from the grave with fists closed,
 and the others [the prodigal] with their hair shorn.

Bad giving and bad keeping have taken from them
 the fair world and placed them in this strife
 which words of mine will not glorify.   60

> *Wealth, according to Dante, is in the hands of a special divinity, Fortune, who performs her functions as the angels guide and direct the various heavens. No reason or moral order is discernible in the distribution of wealth among individuals, families, and nations.*

Now, my son, you can see how wealth,
 committed to Fortune, and for which
 the human race struggles, mocks us.

All the gold that is under the moon
 or ever was, could not give rest
 to one of these weary souls."

"Master," I asked, "now tell me,
 who is this Fortune
 with the world's riches in her hands?"

And he to me, "Oh foolish creatures,
 how deep is the ignorance that blinds you!
 Now I want you to hear my judgment.   72

He [God] whose understanding transcends all
 made the heavens and gave them guides,
 so that each part shines on all the others,

distributing the light equally.
 Likewise, for mundane splendors,
 He ordained a general minister and guide

to transfer vain wealth in due time
 from people to people, and from one to another family,
 beyond the intervention of human intelligence.

Thus one people rules and another languishes,
 according to her judgment, which is hidden from us,
 like a snake in the grass.   84

Your knowledge is of no avail against her;
 she foresees, judges, and rules her province
 as the other gods [angels] do theirs.

Her activity has no truce;
    necessity makes her quick to act,
    so that changes [in fortune] come often.

She is the one so reviled
    even by those who should praise her
    but who, instead, give her ill repute.

Yet she is blessed and does not hear;
    happy with the other primal [angelic] creatures
    she rules her sphere and rejoices in her bliss.   96

> *It is now a little after midnight of Good Friday. In a swamp the poets see the
> bemired souls of the angry and the bubbles made by the sullen beneath the surface.
> The travelers make a long detour to the left, which indicates an approach to worse
> things.*

Now let us descend to greater misery;
    already each star that was rising when I started
    is falling, and staying too long is forbidden."

We crossed the circle to the inner bank
    along a stream which bubbled and flowed
    through a channel it had formed.

The water was darker than purplish-black;
    and, accompanying the murky waves,
    on a rough path, we reached the place below.

This dreary stream forms a marsh, the Styx,
    when it has reached the foot
    of the gray, malignant banks.   108

And I, who remained intent on looking,
    saw muddy people in that bog,
    naked, and with angry looks.

They struck each other not only with their hands,
    but with their heads, chests, and feet,
    and tore each other with their teeth, bit by bit.

My good master said, "Son, now see
    the souls of those whom anger overcame;
    I wish you to believe also

that under the water there are people sighing
    and making bubbles on the surface
    as your eyes tell you wherever you look.   120

Fixed in the slime they say, 'Sullen were we
    in the sweet air gladdened by the sun,
    keeping within us the fumes of spite;

now we are sullen in the black mire.'
    This hymn is gurgled in their throats,
    for they cannot speak in clear words."

Thus we covered a wide arc around the filthy slough
 between the dry bank and the swamp,
 with eyes turned to those swallowing the mire.

At last we came to the foot of a tower.

CANTO VIII

THE ANGRY AND THE SULLEN

*Continuing the account of the fifth circle, Dante anxiously inquires about the
meaning of certain signals. These are explained by the coming of a boat guided
by Phlegyas,*[9] *the guardian of this round.*

I say, continuing, that long before we reached
 the foot of the high tower
 our eyes were drawn to its top

by two little flames placed there;
 and another gave back a signal from so far
 that our eyes could hardly catch it.

Turning to the sea of all wisdom, I asked,
 "What does this mean? what does the other flame
 answer? and who are they who light it?"

And he to me, "Over the foul waters
 already you can see what is expected
 if the mist of the marsh does not hide it from you."   12

Never did a bowstring drive an arrow
 which sped so quickly through the air
 as a little boat I saw then

coming through the water toward us
 under the guidance of a single boatman
 who cried, "Now you are caught, fell spirit!"

"Phlegyas, Phlegyas, this time you cry out
 in vain," said my lord, "you will keep us
 only while crossing the slough."

As one who learns of a great trick
 played on him and who resents it,
 so Phlegyas became in his pent-up rage.   24

My guide stepped down into the boat,
 making me get in after him,
 and only then did it appear burdened.

As soon as my master and I had embarked,
 the ancient prow moved on,
 cleaving more of the water than it does with others.

---

[9] Enraged with Apollo for raping his daughter, Phlegyas set the god's temple on fire and
was killed by him.

Dante becomes angry at one of the shades, apparently incurring the very sin punished here, but is commended for it by Virgil. The episode is intended to show that righteous indignation is permissible. We cannot love gentleness and polite- ness intensely without disliking arrogance and incivility with equal intensity.

While we were going through the stagnant channel,
    a shade covered with mud rose up, saying [insolently],
    "Who are you, coming before your time?"

I answered, "If I come, I do not stay,
    but who are you, now so dirty?"
    And he, "You see I am one who weeps."   36

Then I to him, "With tears and grief
    stay here, damned spirit,
    for I recognize you for all your filth."

Then the shade stretched both hands toward the boat,
    but my wary master pushed him off, saying,
    "Get over there with the other dogs!"

And embracing me with both arms
    he kissed my face and said, "Indignant soul,
    may she be blessed who bore you!

In the world he was an arrogant person;
    no kindness adorned his memory,
    so his shade is furious here.   48

How many think themselves great kings
    who will lie like swine in the mire,
    leaving behind horrible censure."

And I, "Master, I would be glad
    to see him soused in this soup [muddy water]
    before we leave the pond."

He answered, "Before you see the shore
    you will be satisfied;
    it is proper that such a wish be granted."

In a little while I saw the muddy crowd
    wreak such havoc on him
    that I still praise and thank God for it.   60

All cried, "At Filippo Argenti!"
    and the raging Florentine spirit
    turned with his teeth upon himself.

Here we left him, and of him I say no more.
    A wailing now struck my ears,
    so that I looked ahead intently.

My good master said, "Now son,
    the City of Dis [Satan] draws near,
    with its grave citizens, its great garrison."

And I, "Master, already I discern its mosques
    clearly there within the valley,
    red, as if they had come out of fire."   72

He continued, "The eternal flames
    enkindling them make them glow
    as you see in this lower Hell."

We now arrived within the moats
    which surround the disconsolate city,
    the walls of which seemed of iron.

Not without making a wide circuit [to the left]
    did we come to where the boatman loudly cried,
    "Get out, here is the entrance!"

Above the gates more than a thousand [rebellious angels],
    rained down from Heaven, cried angrily,
    "Who is this one, without death,   84

going through the kingdom of the dead?"
    And my wise master signaled
    that he wished to speak with them secretly.

Then they held back their great anger
    and said, "You come alone and let him go
    who so boldly entered this kingdom.

Let him return by himself on the mad path;
    let him see if he can; for you will stay here,
    you who have led him through so dark a country."

> Threatened with the loss of Virgil (Reason), Dante begs not to be left alone. His
> guide tries to reassure him, but, as an intellectual rather than a suggestive force,
> he can do that only imperfectly. As Virgil leaves, Dante wonders whether the
> answer to a question about the success of the mission will be "yes," or "no." Virgil
> also is not sure, but, on returning, tries to comfort Dante by passing off his doubt
> and dismay as anger. He hopes, with the limited confidence reason gives, that an
> angel will bring divine aid.

Think, Reader, if I was frightened
    at the sound of the accursed words,
    for I did not believe I could ever return.   96

"O my dear guide, you who many times
    have made me safe and drawn me
    through deep peril confronting me,

do not leave me so undone," I said,
    "and if going farther is denied us,
    let us retrace our steps together rapidly."

Then that lord who had brought me there replied,
    "Do not fear, for no one can prevent our journey;
    by Such a One it has been granted.

Wait for me here, and with good hope
    comfort and feed your weary spirit,
    for I will not leave you in the lower world."   108

Thus my dear father went away
    and abandoned me, and I remained in doubt,
    for "yes" and "no" struggled within my mind.

I could not hear what he said to our adversaries,
    but he did not stay long with them
    before each of them raced back.

They closed the gates in the face
    of my lord, who remained outside
    and then came toward me with slow steps,

his eyes upon the ground and with a face
    shorn of all boldness. He asked, sighing,
    "Who has denied us the abode of woe?"   120

Then to me he said, "Although I may get angry,
    do not fear, for I will win the fight,
    whatever is contrived within.

This insolence of theirs is not new;
    they showed it once at a less secret gate
    which is now without a fastening.

Over it you saw the deadly inscription;[10]
    and already on this side of it,
    passing through the circles without escort,

someone descends who will open the city for us."

CANTO IX

THE CITY OF DIS

The hue that cowardice put on my face
    when I saw my guide come back
    made him repress more quickly his dismay.

He stopped, attentive, like a man listening;
    for sight could not go far
    through the dark air and thick mist.

"Still we must win the fight," he began,
    "if not . . . such help was offered us;
    oh, how I long for someone to come!"

I noticed how he covered up
    his first words with those that followed
    which expressed a different thought,   12

[10] The words written over hell's gate, III.1–9. Dante and Virgil are now about to enter the lower hell, where the sins of malice (violence and fraud) are punished.

and his remark made me afraid
  because I drew the words cut off
  into a meaning perhaps worse than he intended.

Dante asks indirectly if Virgil really knows the way.

"To this depth of the dismal hole
  does any ever descend from the first circle
  where hope cut off is the only punishment?"

This question I asked, and he answered,
  "It seldom happens that one of us
  makes the journey on which I am going.

It is true that I was down here once before,
  conjured by that cruel Erichtho [a sorceress],
  who brought shades back to their bodies.   24

Not for long had my flesh been without me
  when she made me go within those walls
  to bring out a spirit from Judas' circle.[11]

That is the lowest and darkest place, the one
  farthest removed from the heaven that encircles all.
  I know the road well; therefore be reassured.

This swamp exhaling the great stench
  surrounds the woeful city
  which we cannot enter now peacefully."

*Three Furies, handmaidens of Hecate, the ancient queen of Hell, symbols of
madness or remorseful terror, rise up, citing their error in letting Theseus enter
their region to rescue Persephone. Dante clings to Virgil with desperation. The
Furies then call upon the Gorgon (Medusa, Despair) to turn the intruder to
stone. Virgil warns his charge with great urgency not to look at her.*

*The allegorical meaning is perhaps as follows: the reforming Christian (Dante),
when confronted by remorseful terror (the Furies), may lose his reason (Virgil),
but as long as hope remains, he can appeal for divine aid. Only despair
(Medusa) cuts off irremediably the path to salvation.*

And more he said, but I do not recall it
  because my eyes drew all my thoughts
  to the glowing summit of the high tower   36

where suddenly three infernal Furies,
  with the shape and features of women,
  and stained with blood, stood upright.

They were girded with green hydras[12]
  and had serpents and horned snakes for hair
  with which their wild heads were bound.

[11] The very lowest and innermost circle of hell, described in Canto XXXIV.
[12] Monsters with several heads.

And he who knew well the handmaidens
    of the Queen of eternal lamentation
    said to me, "Behold! the fierce Erinyes [Furies].

The one on the left is Megaera;
    she on the right, weeping, is Alecto;
    Tisiphone is in the middle,"—and with that he was silent.   48

They were tearing their breasts with their nails,
    beating themselves with their hands, and shouting
    so loudly that in fear I drew close to my master.

"Let Medusa come, and we will change him to stone,"
    they all said, looking down,
    "badly did we avenge the assault of Theseus."

"Turn back and keep your eyes closed,
    for if the Gorgon [Medusa] shows herself
    and you see her, there will be no returning."

Thus my master spoke, and he himself
    turned me around, not trusting my hands,
    but with his also covered my eyes.   60

O you who have sound understanding,
    observe the meaning hidden
    beneath the veil of the strange verses.

And now over the turbid waters
    came a crash full of terror
    at which both the shores trembled,

a sound like that of a whirlwind
    made violent by conflicting currents
    which hits the forest without restraint,

shatters, beats down, and sweeps away the boughs.
    Behind a cloud of dust it moves on fiercely,
    and makes the beasts and shepherds flee.   72

My master freed my eyes and said,
    "Now direct your sight over that ancient foam
    to where the mist is thickest."

As frogs before their enemy the snake
    scatter through the water
    until each squats on the bottom,

so I saw more than a thousand ruined spirits
    fleeing before one [an angel] who,
    with dry feet, passed over the Styx.

From his face he fanned that gross air,
    moving his left hand in front of it,
    and only with that effort seemed weary.   84

I saw at once that he was sent from Heaven,
    and I turned to my master, who made a sign
    that I should keep quiet and bow to him.

How full of scorn he seemed to me!
    Coming to the gate, he opened it
    with a wand, for there was no resistance.

"O outcasts from Heaven, despised creatures!"
    he began, on the horrible threshold,
    "why do you harbor this insolence?

Why do you oppose that will
    whose purpose can never be hindered,
    and which has several times increased your pain?   96

Of what use is it to butt against fate?
    Your Cerberus [chained by Hercules] because of this
    still has a chin and throat without hair."[13]

Then he turned back over the filthy road
    and said no word to us, but seemed
    like one intent on other cares

than those of the people near him;
    and we moved on toward the city,
    safe, after the holy words.

> *On entering, Dante sees open tombs, hotter than iron in a blacksmith's forge.*
> *Each contains the leader of a heretical sect with his followers. Here, contrary to*
> *their custom, the travelers turn to the right, perhaps to indicate that heresy can be*
> *incurred honestly, although persistence in it is a sin of pride.*

We entered without any strife,
    and I, wanting to see what punishments
    such a fortress enclosed,   108

as soon as within glanced around
    and saw on every side a great plain
    full of grief and torment.

As at Arles where the Rhone spreads out
    or at Pola near [the bay of] Quarnero
    which encloses Italy and bathes her boundaries,

the tombs make the land uneven,
    so they did here, on all sides,
    except that these graves were more terrible;

for among the tombs flames spread
    by which they were so heated
    that no trade needs iron hotter.   120

---

[13] Theseus of Athens (line 54) tried to carry off Persephone (Hecate), queen of the underworld, but was himself held prisoner until he was rescued by Hercules, who in chaining the dog Cerberus tore the skin from its neck.

All their lids were open,
>and such harsh laments came from them
>as from the wretched and the suffering.

And I, "Master, who are the people
>buried within the tombs,
>making themselves heard by their painful sighs?"

And he to me, "Here are the archheretics[14]
>with their followers of every sect;
>and the tombs are laden much more than you think.

Like with like is buried,
>and the monuments are more and less hot."
>Then, after we had turned to the right,   132

we passed between the torments and the high battlements.

CANTO X

FARINATA DEGLI UBERTI

Now along a solitary path
>between the city wall and the torments,
>my master makes his way, and I behind him.

"O supreme genius, you who through the impious circles
>turn me [to the left or right] as you please," I began,
>"speak to me and satisfy my wishes.

The people lying in the sepulchres,
>might they be seen?—all the lids
>are raised and no one guards them."

And he to me, "All will be locked in
>when they return from Jehoshaphat [on Judgment Day]
>with the bodies they have left above.   12

>*Epicurus is with the heretics of Christian times since he, almost alone among*
>*ancient philosophers, denied the immortality of the soul.*

>*Still hesitant about asking questions, Dante represses his desire to see certain*
>*Florentines.*

On this side is the burial place
>of Epicurus and of all his followers
>who hold that the soul dies with the body.

---

[14] This circle of the heretics, like Limbo, is a special case, heresy being a mental or spiritual condition rather than one of the sins of behavior (Incontinence, Violence, Fraud) punished in the overall threefold scheme of Dante's hell. Moreover, heresy, like failure to be baptized, is a fault defined not by universal ethics but from a specifically Christian point of view.

But concerning the question you ask
   you will soon be satisfied,
   and also as to the wish you keep silent."[15]

And I, "Good guide, I hide my thought
   only to speak little; not long ago
   you disposed me to do that."

> *A deep voice sounds amid the silence of the graves. It is that of Farinata degli Uberti, a Ghibelline leader who, in 1260, won the bloody battle of Montaperti over the Florentine Guelfs, to which party Dante's family belonged. In recalling the bloodshed, Farinata has a moment of spontaneous repentance. Dante timidly draws closer to his guide who then directs him toward this proud, towering figure.*

"O Tuscan, you who through the city of fire
   go alive, speaking thus modestly,
   may it please you to remain in this place.   24

Your speech shows you a native
   of that noble fatherland
   to which, perhaps, I was too harmful."

Suddenly this sound came
   from one of the tombs, so that, startled,
   I drew closer to my guide.

He said to me, "Turn around! what are you doing?
   See Farinata, who has stood erect;
   from the waist upward, wholly, you can see him!"

I had already fixed my eyes on his,
   and he lifted up his chest and head,
   as if he had scorn for Hell,   36

and the bold and ready hands of my guide
   pushed me among the sepulchres to him,
   saying, "Let your words be well chosen."

> *Disappointed in not seeing someone of his own generation, Farinata asks about Dante's ancestors. On hearing the names of these former enemies, he tells angrily how he had scattered them. Now Dante's partisan spirit is aroused. He points out that his party has been able to return to Florence, whereas Farinata's has not learned the art of getting back. Dante's remark is an unexpected blow for the Ghibelline captain, who is unaware of all the events and who remains silent, trying to recover and to collect his thoughts.*

When I was at the foot of his tomb
   he looked at me a little; then, almost disdainfully,
   he asked, "Who were your ancestors?"

---

[15] Possibly a wish to see Farinata.

I, desirous to obey, did not hide them,
    but revealed them all,
    whereupon he raised his brows a little

and said, "Fiercely were they adverse
    to me and to my ancestors and to my party,
    so that twice I scattered them." 48

"If they were driven out, they came back from every side,"
    I answered him, "both the first and the second time,
    but yours did not learn well that art!"

*Now the shade of the father of Guido Cavalcanti, the latter a leading poet and
Dante's best friend, rises beside the great Ghibelline leader. He too is not interested in Dante. He assumes that our poet is allowed to visit Hell because of some
peculiar merit, and since he cannot conceive of greater nobility of mind than that
of his son, he wonders why Guido is not there also. Dante is perplexed, not
knowing that the shades are ignorant of immediate happenings on earth, and
replies ambiguously, implying lack of devotion on Guido's part to Virgil. The
important point, however, is the past tense of the verb he uses. Cavalcante assumes from it that his son is dead, and from the embarrassed tone of Dante's
remarks, suspects that Guido may have had a fate somewhat like his own. Dante's
delay in answering confirms his fear, and he falls back into his tomb.*

Now beside him there arose to sight
    a shade visible down to his chin;
    I believe he had risen on his knees.

He looked around me as if anxious
    to see if someone else were with me,
    but when this expectation was wholly spent,

weeping he said, "If through this blind prison
    you go because of the greatness of your mind,
    where is my son? why is he not with you?" 60

And I to him, "By myself I do not come;
    Virgil, waiting there, guides me,
    whom perhaps your Guido held in disdain."

His words and the manner of his punishment
    had already revealed his name to me;
    therefore my reply was so complete.

Rising suddenly he cried, "What did you say?
    he *held*? Does he not live still?
    Does not the sweet light strike his eyes?"

When he was aware of some delay
    before I answered, he fell back supine
    and showed himself no more. 72

*Meanwhile Farinata has been pondering over Dante's remark and, without tran-
sition, oblivious to the drama enacted at his feet, he returns the verbal blow by
predicting the poet's exile within four years. Relieved by this aggression, he asks*

*in a more kindly tone why the Florentines have persecuted his family, and he
points out proudly how, after the battle, when the Ghibelline leaders proposed
razing Florence to the ground, he alone defended and saved her. Now Dante's
partisan spirit is likewise softened, and in the conversation that follows he learns
that the shades remember the past and can predict the future, but, like farsighted
people, cannot see what is close at hand. This accounts for the misunderstanding
between him and Cavalcante, and he asks to have his error corrected.*

But that other magnanimous one, at whose instance
    I had stopped, did not change his expression,
    nor move his head, nor bend his body.

"And if," he said, continuing his first remark,
    "they have badly learned that art,
    it torments me more than this bed.

But not fifty times will be rekindled
    the face of her [Hecate, the moon] who rules here
    before you will know the hardness of that art!

And—so may you return sometime to the sweet world—
    tell me why the people are so fierce
    against my kindred in all their laws."   84

Then I to him, "The slaughter and havoc
    which dyed the [river] Arbia red
    cause such prayers to rise in our temple."

Sighing he shook his head and said,
    "In that I was not alone, nor certainly
    would I and the others have moved without cause,

but I was alone when all the rest
    agreed to wipe out Florence:
    I defended her openly before all."

"So may your descendants sometime have rest,"
    I replied, "please solve for me this puzzle
    which has now entangled my judgment.   96

It seems that you see, if I hear rightly,
    what the future brings,
    but for the present have a different vision."

"Like those with imperfect sight,
    we see things far from us," he said,
    "so much light the Supreme ruler still allows,

but when they come close, or exist, our minds
    do not perceive them, and, without news from others,
    we know nothing of your human state.

Therefore you can understand that our knowledge [gained from
      others]
    will be wholly dead after that moment [Judgment Day]
    when the gates of the future are closed."   108

Then, as if sorry for my fault,
    I said, "Now please tell that fallen one
    that his son is still joined with the living,

and if I was silent at his question,
    let him know it was because my thoughts
    were confused by the error you have corrected."

*Before moving on, Virgil declares emphatically that Beatrice will reveal to Dante
the course of his life. This is a mistake on Virgil's part: Cacciaguida, not Beatrice, makes the prophecy.*[16]

*(The treatment of the heretics is a comedy of errors which illustrates the fallibility
of human reason. The Epicureans, in their tombs, erred in thinking that the
grave ended all; Farinata is deceived in several ways; Cavalcante makes a series
of false assumptions; Dante likewise is bewildered. Finally Virgil [Reason itself]
is emphatically wrong.)*

Already my master was calling me back,
    so that I begged the spirit more hastily
    to tell me who was with him.

He said, "With more than a thousand I lie:
    here is the second Frederick [of Sicily]
    and the Cardinal [Ubaldino]; of the others I am silent."   120

Then he hid himself, and toward the ancient poet
    I turned my steps, meditating
    about the prophecy hostile to me.

My guide moved on and, as we were going,
    he said to me, "Why are you so bewildered?"
    and I satisfied his request.

"Let your mind retain what you have heard
    against you," that sage commanded me,
    "and now listen to this," and he raised his finger:

"When you face the sweet light
    of her [Beatrice] whose fair eyes see everything
    you will learn from her the journey of your life."   132

Then he turned his steps to the left;
    we went from the wall toward the center
    along a path which goes into a valley

which even up there stifled us with its stench.

---

[16] This occurs in *Paradise*, Canto XVII, where the exile of Dante, separated from the places
and people he cherished most, is poignantly outlined by Cacciaguida, Dante's great-great-
grandfather.

CANTO XI

The Classification of Sins

As the poets proceed toward the inner edge of the sixth circle, they observe a tomb inscribed with the name of Anastasius. There was confusion in Dante's time between a pope and a heretical Byzantine emperor of that name.

While waiting to become accustomed to the smell which rises from a river of hot blood below, Virgil explains the various divisions of Hell.

To explain why usurers are classed with blasphemers and sodomites as doing violence to God, Virgil points out that Nature, which offers man its bounty, derives from God; that man's art (industry) gives further value to the products of Nature and, in a sense, derives also from God; that man was intended to earn his living through the bounty of Nature and by the sweat of his brow, and that usurers violate this divine plan.

At the end of the canto we learn by the position of the stars that it is about three hours after midnight, Saturday, April 9, 1300.

On the edge of a high bank
    formed by a circle of broken rocks
    we stood above a more cruel pack;

and here because of the horrible stench
    which the deep abyss exhales
    we approached behind the cover of a great tomb

on which I saw an inscription saying,
    "I hold Anastasius, the pope,
    whom Photinus drew from the straight path."

"Our descent must be slow, so that our sense of smell
    may get used to the foul breath,
    and then we will not heed it."   12

Thus my master spoke, and I, "Please find compensation,
    so that time will not be wasted."
    And he, "That is what I have been thinking of.

My son," he then continued,
    "below us are three smaller circles
    like those you are leaving,

full of accursed spirits. In order
    that sight alone may suffice henceforth,
    observe how and why they are confined.

The malice which Heaven reproves
    causes injury and grief to others
    either by violence or by fraud,   24

but because fraud is peculiar to man
    it displeases God more; therefore
    the fraudulent are placed lower and have more pain.

The next circle [seventh] is for the violent,
    and, since force can be used
    against God, oneself, and one's fellow men—

I mean against them or their property—
    it is divided into three bands
    as you will clearly hear.

Death and painful wounds may be inflicted
    on one's fellows, and plunder, arson,
    and extortion on their property.   36

Thus the first round torments, in various groups,
    assassins, plunderers, and robbers,
    and all who strike maliciously.

A man may commit violence against himself
    and against his property; therefore, in the second round,
    all who deprive themselves of your world

or gamble and dissipate their wealth
    must unavailingly repent
    and weep instead of being happy.

Violence is committed against the Deity
    by cursing Him and denying Him in one's heart;
    and by scorning Nature and her bounty;   48

therefore the smallest band stamps with its seal
    both Sodom [the sodomites] and Cahors [the usurers]
    and those [the blasphemers] who speak disdaining God.

Fraud which hurts man's conscience
    can be used against those who trust
    and against those who have no special confidence.

In the latter case, only the love that Nature makes
    [the natural brotherhood of man] is violated;
    thus, in the following [eighth] circle are nested

hypocrisy, flattery, sorcery,
    falsifying, theft, and simony,
    panders, barrators, and similar filth.   60

The other fraud violates
    both the love Nature creates and that
    which implies a special trust.

Therefore, in the smallest circle
    at the center of the universe where Dis [Satan] holds forth
    whoever betrays is eternally consumed."

And I, "Master, your account proceeds clearly
    and makes plain the division
    of this abyss and those who are in it,

but tell me, the souls [above] in the slimy bog,
    those whom the wind blows, and those the rain beats,
    and those who meet with such sharp tongues,   72

why are they not inside the ruddy city
    if God is angry with them,
    and if not, why are they in such a plight?"

He answered, "Why does your mind
    go astray more than usual?
    or are you thinking of something else?

Do you not remember those words
    with which your *Ethics* [of Aristotle] treats
    the three dispositions Heaven does not admit—

incontinence, malice, and mad bestiality—
    and how incontinence offends God less
    and incurs less blame?   84

If you consider this teaching
    and recall who is being punished
    outside of the city,

you will see why they are separated
    from these and why, less angrily,
    Divine Justice torments them."

"O Sun, you who heal every troubled vision,
    I am so glad to hear you explain
    that to question pleases me no less than knowing;

but go back a little," I said,
    "to where you say that usury offends
    divine goodness, and solve the puzzle."   96

"Philosophy," he said,
    "states in more than one place
    that Nature takes her course

from the Divine Intellect and from Its operation,
    and if you note well your *Physics,*
    you will find after not many pages

that your activity follows the divine plan,
    as the pupil does his master, so that your art [industry]
    is, as it were, a grandchild of God.

From these two [Nature and Industry], if you recall
    the early part of Genesis,
    man should earn his living and prosper.   108

And because the usurer takes another way,
    he scorns Nature in itself and in its follower [Industry],
    since he places his hope in something else.

But follow me now, for I wish to go.
    The Fishes [Pisces] are quivering on the horizon
    and the Chariot [Big Dipper] lies wholly over Caurus [the north-
        west],

and the cliff we descend is far over there.

CANTO XII

THE VIOLENT

*Near a break in the cliff, a landslide caused by the revulsion of the earth at the
Crucifixion, is the Minotaur, a creature with a man's body and a bull's head, the
bestial guardian of the circle of the violent. To get around this monster, Virgil
puts him in a blind rage by mentioning the circumstances of his death, how his
half sister, Ariadne, had guided Theseus through the labyrinth to him.*

The place where we came to descend the bank
    was craggy and, because of what was there [the Minotaur],
    such that every eye would shun it.

As the landslide which, on this side of Trento,
    struck the Adige, either because of an earthquake
    or from being undermined—

for, from the top of the mountain
    to the plain, the cliff has so fallen
    that it provides a path for one above—

such was the descent into this ravine;
    and on the edge of the broken chasm,
    the infamy of Crete [the Minotaur], conceived   12

in the false [wooden] cow,[17] was stretched out.
    On seeing us the monster bit himself
    like one subdued by anger.

My sage cried to him, "Perhaps you think
    the Duke of Athens [Theseus] is here
    who killed you in the world.

Get away, beast, for this man does not come
    instructed by your sister,
    but journeys on to see your punishments."

As a bull that breaks loose at the moment
    when it receives a mortal blow
    and cannot go straight, but plunges here and there,   24

so I saw the Minotaur stagger,
    and my wary guide shouted, "Run to the pass;
    while he is raging it is well for you to go down."

[17] The Minotaur was born of Pasiphae, wife of Minos, king of Crete, after she hid herself
inside a wooden cow in order to have intercourse with a bull.

Thus we made our way over the loose rocks
    which often moved under my feet
    because of the unusual burden.

As I went on, thinking, my guide said,
    "Perhaps you are wondering about this landslide
    guarded by the bestial wrath I outwitted.

Now I want you to know that the other time
    I went down here into deep Hell
    this cliff had not yet been broken,   36

but, if I discern correctly, shortly before
    He [Christ] came to the first circle
    to remove the great prey from Dis [at the "harrowing"]

the loathsome pit trembled on all sides
    so that I thought the universe felt love
    because of which some [philosophers] believed

the world has many times reverted to chaos [a fusion
    of the elements]; and at that moment these old rocks
    here and elsewhere fell down.

But look below, for the river of blood
    is near, in which are boiled
    those who through violence harm others."   48

> *On the banks of the river are centaurs, creatures with horses' bodies, but whose*
> *heads (unlike that of the Minotaur) are human.*

O blind greed, wicked and foolish,
    which so spurs us in the brief life,
    and in the eternal condemns to such pain!

I saw a wide moat making a bend
    surrounding the level ground [of the circle]
    like the one my escort had mentioned,

and between the foot of the bank and the ditch
    centaurs, armed with arrows, were running, in single file,
    as they used to go hunting in our world.

Seeing us descend all stopped,
    and three came from the band,
    having armed themselves with bows and arrows.   60

One shouted from afar, "To what punishment
    are you coming? Tell us from there;
    if not, I'll draw the bow!"

My master answered, "We will reply
    to Chiron over there; unfortunately,
    you were always quick to act."

Then he touched me and said, "That is Nessus
 who died for the beautiful Dejanira
 and by himself took vengeance for himself.[18]

The one in the middle, looking at his breast,
 is the great Chiron, the teacher of Achilles,
 and the other is Pholus, who was so full of rage.　　　　72

Around the ditch they go by thousands
 shooting shades that rise from the blood
 farther than their sins allow."

As we drew near those rapid beasts
 Chiron took an arrow, and with the notch
 combed back the beard on his jaws,

and when he had uncovered his great mouth
 he said to his companions, "Did you notice
 that the one behind moves what he touches?

The feet of the dead do not do this."
 And my good guide, already close to the breast
 where the two natures were joined, answered,　　　　84

"He is indeed alive, and thus alone
 I must show him the dark valley.
 Necessity brings him here, not pleasure.

A lady [Beatrice] who came from singing hallelujah
 entrusted this mission to me;
 he is no robber nor am I a thief.

Therefore, by that power through which
 I move my feet over so rough a road,
 give us one of your band to be with us,

to show us where the ford is, and to carry
 this man on his back, for he is not a spirit
 that can go through the air."　　　　96

> *Chiron, turning to his better side, appoints Nessus as the leader. The party see
> first various Greek and Italian tyrants, sunk to their eyebrows in the blood; then
> assassins, among whom, shunned by the others, is the first Englishman men-
> tioned, Guy of Montfort who in a church at Viterbo killed Prince Henry. Henry's
> heart, it was said, was placed in a golden urn in Westminster Abbey.*

Chiron turned to his right
 and said to Nessus, "Go back and guide them,
 and if you meet another band, make it give way."

---

[18] While trying to abduct Dejanira, the centaur Nessus was killed by an arrow from her
husband Hercules. As he was dying, Nessus gave Dejanira a robe, stained with his blood, that
would supposedly preserve Hercules' love for her. But the robe killed Hercules, after which
she committed suicide.

We started with our trusted escort
    along the bank of the vermilion stream
    in which those boiled uttered loud cries.

I saw shades in it up to their eyebrows;
    and the great centaur said, "These are tyrants
    who engaged in bloodshed and in plunder.

Now they weep for their pitiless crimes.
    Here are Alexander and fierce Dionysius[19]
    who gave Italy years of woe,   108

and that head with such black hair
    is Azzolino; and the blond one,
    Opizzo da Este, who, in truth,

was killed by his stepson in the world above."
    Then I turned to the poet, who said,
    "Let him go first now and me second."

A little farther on the centaur stopped
    above a group who down to their throats
    appeared above the boiling stream.

Then he showed us a shade to one side, alone, saying,
    "That one, in God's bosom, pierced the heart
    that still is honored on the Thames."   120

Afterward I saw some who kept their heads
    and chests out of the stream,
    and of those I recognized many.

Thus, little by little, the blood grew shallow
    until it cooked only the feet,
    and there was our passage over the moat.

"As on this side you see the boiling river
    grow shallow," said the centaur,
    "so I wish you to believe

that on the other its bottom gets deeper
    until it reaches the place
    where tyrants must groan.   132

There Divine Justice torments
    that Attila who was a scourge on earth,
    and Pyrrhus and Sextus; and eternally it milks

the tears, which the boiling releases,
    from Rinieri da Corneto and Rinieri Pazzo
    who waged such warfare on the highways."

Then Nessus turned back and repassed the ford.

---

[19] Either Alexander the Great or another Alexander (of Pherae); Dionysius was tyrant of Syracuse (fourth century B.C.).

CANTO XIII

Pier delle Vigne

*The poets enter the wood of the Christian suicides. This wild forest represents the
world as it would be if all revolted against life. It is infested by the Harpies,
loathsome creatures, half human, half birds, which stand for the storm winds of
human passions.*

*In every way the suicides, now changed into trees or saplings, are frustrated.
They have used their power of movement to deprive themselves of what distinguished them from plants; but they have not found death. The Harpies they tried
to escape go with them, and the old agony is pent up in their new embodiments.*

Nessus had not yet reached the other side
   when we entered a wood
   that was marked by no path.

No green foliage was there, but of a dark color,
   no smooth branches, but knotty and twisted,
   no fruit, but poisonous thorns.

The wild beasts that shun cultivated places
   do not have such dense and tangled thickets
   [in the Maremma] between Cecina and Corneto.[20]

Here the ugly Harpies make their nests
   who with sad predictions of future harm
   drove the Trojans from the Strophades.[21]   12

They have wide wings and human necks and faces,
   feet with claws, and great feathered bellies;
   they utter laments on the strange trees.

My good master began to speak, saying,
   "Before you go any farther, know
   that you are in the second round and will be

until you come to the horrible sand.
   Therefore look closely and you will see
   what would seem incredible in my speech."

I heard moans on every side
   and saw no one to make them,
   so that I stopped, all bewildered.   24

I believe he believed that I believed
   that so many voices came from people
   hidden from us among the trees;

---

[20] Two towns, at the northern and southern edges of the Maremma, a swamp near Florence.
[21] Islands visited by Aeneas and the other Trojans in their wanderings after the fall of
Troy. This incident and one involving a bleeding shrub (referred to in line 48) occur in Virgil's
Aeneid, Book III.

therefore he said, "If you break
    a twig of one of these woody plants
    the thoughts you have will be corrected."

Then I stretched forth my hand
    and plucked a small branch from a great thorn tree,
    and its trunk cried, "Why do you break me?"

After it had grown dark with blood,
    it began again to lament, "Why do you tear me?
    have you no trace of pity?   36

We were men, and now are turned to wood;
    your hand should have been more merciful
    if we had been the souls of serpents."

As a green log, burning at one end,
    drips from the other and hisses
    with the steam that escapes,

so from the broken branch words and blood
    came out together; and I let the twig fall
    and stood like one afraid.

> The tree whose branch Dante has broken is that of Pier delle Vigne, a famous
> statesman, scholar, and poet at the court of Frederick II of Sicily. (In several
> curious, repetitious lines Dante imitates the style of the Frederician poets.) Fred-
> erick accused him of treason, had him blinded and led in derision on an ass from
> town to town. To escape this dishonor, Pier is said to have beaten his head against
> the walls of his prison. Dante presents him as innocent, as the model of a devoted
> public servant. He is proud of the office he once held and still loyal to the king
> who could do no wrong. It was Envy, he says, the harlot at every court, who
> caused his death. And he swears by his new body that he was never unfaithful.

"If he [Dante] could have believed, offended soul,"
    my master answered,
    "what he has seen only in my verse,   48

he would not have raised his hand against you,
    but the incredible thing made me prompt him
    to do what grieves me.

Now tell him who you were, so that
    to make amends, he may refresh your fame
    in the world above to which he is permitted to return."

Then the tree, "You so allure me with kind words
    that I cannot keep silent, and may you
    not be wearied if I grow sticky talking.

I am the one who held both keys [of consent and denial]
    to Frederick's heart, and who turned them,
    locking and unlocking so softly   60

that I kept almost everyone from his secrets.
    Such trust I bore to the glorious office
    that I lost sleep and strength.

The harlot [Envy] who never from Caesar's dwelling
    has turned aside her shameless eyes,
    the common bane and vice of courts,

inflamed all minds against me,
    and the inflamed so inflamed Augustus [Frederick]
    that my joyous honors changed to dismal sorrow.

My soul with disgust and scorn,
    hoping to escape disdain,
    made me unjust to my just self.   72

By the new roots of this tree, I swear to you
    that I never broke faith with my lord
    who was so worthy of honor.

And if either of you return to the world,
    comfort my memory which still lies crushed
    by the blow that Envy gave it."

Pier tells how the souls fall and become trees and bushes.

*After Judgment Day, the bodies the suicides could not endure for a few brief years
will hang on their branches forever. This is the final frustration.*

The poet waited a little and then said,
    "Since he is silent, do not lose the chance,
    but question him if you want to hear more."

And I answered, "*You* ask what you think
    will satisfy me, for I could not;
    such pity saddens me."   84

Then he began, "So may this man
    do freely for you what you ask,
    please tell us, imprisoned spirit,

how the soul becomes bound in these branches,
    and let us know if you can
    if any ever frees himself from them."

The tree blew loudly, and soon
    the wind changed into these sounds:
    "Briefly will you be answered.

When the fierce soul leaves the body
    from which it has torn itself,
    Minos sends it to the seventh depth.   96

It falls into the wood; no place is chosen for it,
    but where chance throws it
    it sprouts, like a grain of wheat.

It grows into a sapling and a wild tree;
    the Harpies, feeding then upon its leaves,
    give pain and to the pain an outlet.

Like the others we will come for our bodies,
    but not to be clothed again with them,
    for it is not right to get back what is rejected.

Here we will drag them, and
    in the sad wood our bodies will be hung
    on the branches of our injurious souls."   108

> *Two spirits rush by, chased by the hounds of ruin and crying for a second death
> they can never have. These are souls of reckless squanderers, destroyers of their
> estates and indirectly of themselves. One, Lano, in desperate circumstances, al-
> lowed himself to be killed in the battle of Toppo.*

We were still attentive to the tree,
    believing that it wished to say more,
    when a loud sound startled us

as it does the hunter who sees the boar and chase
    approach his post and who hears the beast
    and the crash of the branches.

And behold! two on the left,
    naked and scratched, fleeing so fast
    that they broke the brambles of the wood.

The one in the front cried, "Now come, now come, O Death!"
    and the other who saw himself outdistanced, called,
    "Lano, your legs were not so nimble   120

at the tournament of Toppo." And, perhaps
    because his breath had failed, he plunged
    into a bush, making a tangle of it and of himself.

Behind them the wood was full of black bitches,
    ravenous and running fast,
    like greyhounds just freed from the leash.

They fixed their teeth in the one who squatted
    and tore him to pieces,
    then carried off the suffering members.

My guide then took me by the hand
    and led me to the bush, which lamented vainly
    through its bleeding wounds.   132

"O Giacomo da Sant'Andrea," it cried,
    "what do you gain by making me a screen?
    what blame have I for your wicked life?"

My master had stopped beside it and asked,
    "Who were you, you who through so many breaks
    blow forth your woeful blood and words?"

The soul in the bush deplores the situation in Florence where martial virtue has been sacrificed for money-making (represented by John the Baptist whose image was stamped on Florentine coins); then he identifies himself briefly, not by a name but by an act: he desecrated his own home by making a gallows in it.

And the bush to us, "O souls coming
    to see the shameful ravage
    that has so separated my leaves from me,

gather them together at the foot of the poor plant.
    I was of the city which changed its first patron [Mars]
    for the Baptist, because of which   144

that god will always sadden it with his art,
    and if, at the bridge over the Arno
    there did not remain a trace of him [the ruins of a statue],

those citizens who rebuilt the city
    on the ashes left by Attila[22]
    would have done their work in vain.

I made a gibbet for myself of my own house."

CANTO XIV

THE VIOLENT AGAINST GOD

The round of the violent against God or Nature is characterized by sterility. On the hot sand the blasphemers are lying supine, the sodomites are running, the usurers sitting. Over all is falling a rain of fire which, here and elsewhere, symbolizes the direct wrath of God.

Because love for my native city moved me,
    I gathered the scattered leaves and gave them back
    to him whose voice was already faint.

Then we came to where the second round [the wood]
    is divided from the third [the plain]
    and where is seen a fearful kind of justice.

To make the new place manifest,
    I say that we reached a desert
    which repels every plant from its bed.

The doleful wood forms a garland around it,
    just as the dismal moat does to the wood.
    Here, at the very edge, we stopped.   12

The ground was of dry, thick sand,
    not different from that [of the Libyan desert]
    once trod by Cato's feet.[23]

---

[22] Attila the Hun, fifth-century invader of Europe, was supposed to have sacked Florence. See also XII.134.

[23] In 47 B.C., during the Roman civil war between Julius Caesar and Pompey, Cato led part of Pompey's army across Libya.

O how greatly the vengeance of God
    should be feared by everyone who reads
    what was apparent to my eyes!

I saw many groups of naked souls,
    all of whom wept miserably,
    but different positions were imposed on them.

Some were lying supine upon the ground,
    some were sitting, bent over,
    and others were running continually.   24

Those that kept moving were most numerous
    and those fewest who were lying in the torment,
    but their tongues were loosened by greater pain.

Over all the plain, falling slowly,
    dilated flakes of fire came down,
    like snow in Alps without a wind.

As Alexander in those hot parts
    of India saw flames fall on his host
    intact as far as to the ground,

and made his legions trample
    on the soil, since the fire
    could be extinguished better before it spread;   36

so fell the eternal heat
    by which the sand was kindled
    like tinder under flint, to double the pain.

Ever without rest was the dance
    of the miserable hands, now here, now there,
    brushing off the fresh burning.

> *Dante notices a shade still untamed, bold, indomitable, defying Jove and the
> thunderbolts which defeated the giants. Virgil has more contempt for this appar-
> ent superman than for anyone else in Hell. Flat on his back, feeling hour after
> hour eternally the power of the God he is defying, his attitude seems stupid rather
> than courageous, and is peculiarly disgusting to Reason.*

I began, "Master, you who have overcome everything
    except the fierce demons who rushed out against us
    at the entrance to the City,

who is that great shade not heeding the fire,
    lying scornful and contorted,
    whom the rain does not seem to ripen?"   48

And he, aware that I was asking my guide
    about him, shouted loudly,
    "As I was alive, so am I dead.

Though Jove exhaust his smith from whom,
    angrily, he took the sharp thunderbolt
    by which I was struck on my last day,

and though he weary the others [the Cyclops] one by one
    in Mongibello [Mt. Etna] at the black forge,
    crying, 'Help, help, good Vulcan!'—

as he did in the battle of Phlegra [against the giants]—
    and hit me with all his strength,
    he could not have the joy of vengeance."   60

Then my guide spoke with such feeling
    that I had never heard his voice so loud,
    "O Capaneus, since your pride

remains untamed you are punished more.
    No torture except your rage itself
    would be adequate for your fury."

Then he turned to me with a better look, saying,
    "This was one of the seven kings
    who besieged Thebes; he held and still seems

to hold God in contempt, and to fear Him little;
    but, as I told him, his blasphemy
    is a fitting ornament for his breast."   72

The travelers come to where the overflow from Phlegethon, the river of blood, crosses the plain. The water of this little stream is like the Bulicame, a hot spring near Viterbo, where special bathhouses were provided for prostitutes. Its sterile banks offer a passageway, since over the blood-stained water the fire is quenched, a confirmation or symbol of atonement, the appeasing of God's wrath by human suffering.

Now follow me and be careful
    not to put your feet on the burning sand,
    but always keep them close to the wood."

In silence we came to where, out of
    the forest, a little rivulet gushes,
    the redness of which still makes me shudder.

As from the Bulicame a stream flows
    which sinful women share among themselves,
    so this one flowed across the sand.

Its bottom and both its sides
    were made of stone and also the banks
    on which I perceived that our way led.   84

"Among all the things I have shown you
    since we entered the gate
    whose threshold is denied to none,

nothing has been seen by your eyes
   as notable as the present stream
   which quenches all the flames above it."

These words were spoken by my guide,
   and I asked him to grant the food
   for which he had given me an appetite.

> *With elaborate symbolism, Virgil now tells of man's fall from grace and the consequences. On Mount Ida, in Crete, the center of the ancient world and the supposed cradle of the human race, there is a statue which represents the history of mankind. Its back is turned toward the East, its face in the direction of the course of empire. Its head, representing the Golden Age of the Ancients or the period of the Garden of Eden, is of gold; other parts, according to the various ages, are of different metals. One foot is of iron (the Roman Empire), the other of clay (the Papacy), and the weight of the statue bears too heavily on the latter, the cause, in Dante's view, of much of the anarchy and disorder in the world. The whole statue except the head has been cracked by man's sin. From this fissure tears drip. They flow down to Hell, form the waters of the Acheron, the Styx, the Phlegethon, and ultimately the frozen Cocytus. Thus, by a kind of conservation of sorrow, the tears shed through cruelty are not lost, but flow down to punish those who cause them.*
>
> *Another river, the Lethe, descends to Hell from Purgatory carrying with it the last trace, that is, the very memory, of sin.*

"In the middle of the sea," he said then,
   "lies a waste land, called Crete,
   under whose kings the world once was chaste.   96

A mountain there, named Ida,
   was joyous with water and with leaves;
   now it is deserted, like a thing worn out.

Rhea chose it for the safe cradle
   of her son [Jupiter]; and to hide him better
   when he cried, she had a clamor made.[24]

On the mountain stands a great old man [a statue]
   with back turned toward Damietta [in the East]
   and looking toward Rome as in a mirror.

His head is formed of fine gold,
   his arms and breast are of pure silver;
   then he is of brass as far as to the fork.   108

From there down he is made of fine iron,
   except that the right foot is of baked clay,
   and he stands on that more than on the other.

Every part except the gold is broken
   by a fissure which drips tears
   and these, joining, cut through that bank,

---

[24] Rhea was the wife of Saturn, who devoured most of his sons. To save their son Jupiter, she had his protectors, the Curetes, make loud noises to drown out the infant's crying.

flow down to this pit, and form the Acheron,
   the Styx, and the Phlegethon;
   then, moving on through this narrow channel,

go down to where there can be no further descent.
   They form Cocytus; and since you will see
   how that lake is, I do not describe it."   120

And I to him, "If the present stream
   comes thus from our world,
   why does it appear only here?"

And he, "You know that the place is round,
   and, although you have come far
   always descending to the left,

you have not yet completed the circle;
   therefore, if something new appears,
   it should not cause marveling."

Then I asked, "Master, where are the Phlegethon
   and Lethe, for you are silent about one [Lethe]
   and say that this rain forms the other."   132

"In all your questions you please me,"
   he replied, "but the boiling red water
   ought to answer one [about the Phlegethon].

You will see Lethe outside of this pit
   where souls go to wash themselves
   when guilt, repented, is removed.

Now it is time to leave the wood;
   see that you come behind me;
   the banks, not burned, offer a way,

and over them all fire is extinguished."

CANTO XV

Brunetto Latini

*The banks of the rivulet are like the dikes built by the Flemings or those made
along the Brenta before the snow melts in the Chiarentana mountains. As the
poets pass, they are eyed intently by a band of sodomites. Dante recognizes one as
Brunetto Latini, a famous author and scholar, some of whose lectures Dante
evidently heard. Dante extends his hand with reverence and, using the polite
(voi) form of address, tells of his surprise at meeting him in this place.*

Now one of the hard banks offers us a way,
   and the vapor of the stream makes a shelter
   which protects the shores and water from the fire.

As the Flemings between Wissant and Bruges,
   fearing the flood which rushes toward them,
   make a bulwark to repel the sea,

and as the Paduans do along the Brenta
    to defend their cities and their castles,
    before Chiarentana feels the heat,

in such a manner those banks were formed,
    although their builder, whoever he was,
    made them not so high nor so thick.   12

Already we were so far from the wood
    that I could not have seen where it was
    if I had turned back

when we met a band of spirits
    coming along the banks, and each gazed at us
    as, at dusk, under a new moon,

men are wont to look at each other,
    sharpening their eyes at us
    as an old tailor does at his needle's eye.

Thus gazed at by such a group,
    I was recognized by one who grasped my skirt
    and cried, "What a marvel!"   24

And as he held out his arm toward me
    I fixed my glance on his baked aspect
    so that his burned face did not prevent

the recognition of him by my memory.
    Lowering my hand toward his face,
    I asked, "Are *you* here, *ser* Brunetto?"

> *Brunetto proposes to accompany Dante by walking along below him. He must
> keep moving: restlessness is common to the punishment of all sexual sinners.
> Dante shows the greatest affection for his old master, a feeling reciprocated by
> Brunetto, who prophesies Dante's quarrel with the Florentines. They, according
> to legend, represent a fusion of the descendants of a Roman colony and of the
> rough hill people from Fiesole. Dante wishes that Brunetto had not been banished
> in a double sense from human nature, and pays him the supreme tribute to a
> teacher: he taught, not the minutiae of scholarship and pedantry, but the impor-
> tant things, how man, through fame, can make himself eternal.*

And he, "O my son, may it not displease you
    if Brunetto Latini goes back with you a little,
    letting his company move on."

I said to him, "As much as I can I beg you to,
    and if you want me to sit down with you,
    I will do so, if he with whom I go permits."   36

"O son," he said, "whoever of this flock
    stops one instant, lies afterward a hundred years
    without brushing off the fire that strikes him;

therefore, go on; I will follow at your skirts
    and then I will rejoin my band
    which goes lamenting its eternal punishment."

I did not dare go down from the path
    to be with him, but I held my head low
    like one who walks with reverence.

He began, "What chance or destiny
    brings you here before your last day,
    and who is this one showing you the road?"   48

"Up there in the serene life," I answered,
    "I went astray in a valley,
    before my allotted time was spent.

Yesterday morning I turned my back on it;
    then, as I was falling into it again, this shade appeared
    who is taking me home by this road."

And he to me, "If you follow your star
    you cannot fail to reach a glorious port
    if I discerned rightly in the fair life.

And if I had not died so early,
    seeing the heavens so gracious to you,
    I would have cheered you in your work.   60

That ungrateful, malignant people who of old
    came down from Fiesole and still keep
    the roughness of the mountains and the rocks

will become your enemies because of your good deeds.
    And that is right, for among the bitter sorb trees
    it is not fitting that the sweet fig bear fruit.

Old report in the world calls them blind,
    an avaricious, envious, haughty people:
    see that you cleanse yourself from their ways.

Your fate reserves such honor
    that both parties will be hungry for you;
    but far from the goat will be the grass!   72

Let the beasts of Fiesole make fodder
    of themselves and not touch the plant
    if one grows on their dung heap

in whom the holy virtues are revived
    of those Romans who remained there
    when it was made the nest of such wickedness."

"If my request could be fully granted,"
    I answered him, "you would not yet
    be exiled from human nature;

for in my mind is fixed and my heart knows
    the dear and kindly image of you
    as a father when, from hour to hour,   84

you taught how man makes himself eternal;
  and while I am alive, it is fitting
  that my tongue show how grateful I am.

What you say about my life I write down
  and keep to be explained with another text
  by a lady [Beatrice] who can do this if I see her.

This much I would have plain to you—
  so may my conscience not chide me—
  I am prepared for Fortune as she wills.

Such warnings are not new to my ears;
  therefore, as they please, 'Let Fortune
  turn her wheel, and the churl his mattock.'"   96

My master turned to the right
  and looked at me, then said,
  "He listens well who notes what is told."

*Among the many famous and infamous men guilty of sodomy was Dante's bishop,
whom Boniface VIII, instead of punishing severely, merely transferred to another
see. Thus the two men whose duty was to teach Dante how to become eternal on
earth and in Heaven are together.*

Brunetto hurriedly commends his work, The Treasury, *to Dante and then
leaves, running fast, his loss of dignity showing the effect of one vice on an
otherwise venerable character.*

Nonetheless I continued talking
  to *ser* Brunetto, and I asked
  who were his most noted companions.

And he to me, "It is well to know of some;
  of the others it is more laudable to keep silent,
  for time would be short for so much speech.

Know briefly that all were clerks[25]
  and scholars and of great fame,
  by the same sin defiled on earth.   108

Priscian goes with that wretched crowd,
  and Francesco d'Accorso; moreover,
  if you had a hankering for such filth,

you might see him who by the Servant of the Servants
  was transferred from the Arno to the Bacchiglione,
  where he left his ill-strained muscles.

I would say more, but my going and my speech
  must not continue longer, since I see new smoke
  rising over there from the sand.

---

[25] Clerics.

People are coming with whom I must not be.
  Let my *Treasury*, in which I live
  be commended to you; more I do not ask."   120

Then he turned, and seemed like one of those
  who, at Verona, through the fields, run races
  for a green cloth; and of these he appeared to move

like the one who wins, and not like the one who loses.

CANTO XVI

THE WATERFALL

Already I had reached a place where the roar
  of the water falling into the next circle
  could be heard, like the hum of a beehive,

when three shades running together
  left a troop passing through the rain
  of the fiery torment.

They came toward us and each cried,
  "Stop, you who by your dress seem to us
  to come from our perverse city!"

Ah! what wounds I saw on their bodies,
  old and recent, burnt in by the flames!
  I still grieve whenever I recall it.   12

My teacher listened to their cries,
  then turned his face toward me and said,
  "Now wait, to these we must be courteous,

and if it were not for the fire
  which the nature of this place lets fall,
  I should say that haste befitted you more than them."

  Since the edge of the precipice is not far off, the shades propose to keep moving by
  circling around one spot.

As we stopped they began again their old lament,
  and when they had reached us
  all three made of themselves a circle,

as wrestlers, naked and oiled, are wont to do,
  watching for a hold and an advantage,
  before the tugs and blows begin.   24

Thus circling, all kept their eyes on me,
  so that their heads and necks,
  together with their feet, moved continually.

And one of them began, "If the misery of this sandy place
  and our scorched and burned faces
  cause scorn for us and for our prayers,

may our fame incline you to tell us
    who you are, you who move so securely
    your living feet through Hell.

The man in whose footsteps you see me tread,
    although he goes now bare and hairless,
    was of a higher rank than you might believe.   36

He was a grandson of the good Gualdrada;
    Guido Guerra was his name, and in his life
    he did much with counsel and with sword.

The other who treads the sand behind me
    is Tegghiaio Aldobrandi, whose voice
    should have been heeded in the world.

And I, placed on the cross with them,
    am Jacopo Rusticucci; and certainly my fierce wife
    troubles me more than anything else."

If I had been sheltered from the fire,
    I would have thrown myself down among them,
    and I believe my master would have permitted;   48

but since I would have been burned and cooked,
    fear overcame the good will
    which made me eager to embrace them.

Then I began, "Not contempt, but such grief
    as will not soon leave me,
    your condition caused in me

as soon as my lord spoke words
    through which I inferred
    that people like you were coming.

I am from your city; and always
    I have heard and told with affection
    of your honored deeds and names.   60

I leave the gall and go for the sweet fruit
    promised me by my truthful guide,
    but first I must descend to the center."

"So may your soul long guide your body,"
    he answered then,
    "and so may your fame shine after you,

tell us if courtesy and valor dwell
    in our city as they were wont
    or whether they have gone entirely,

for Guglielmo Borsiere who has suffered with us
    only a little while and is over there with his companions
    grieves us much with his remarks."   72

"New people and sudden gains, O Florence,
    have generated pride and excess in you
    so that already you are weeping!"

This I cried with my face raised, and the three
    who understood my words as a reply, glanced at each other
    as people do when the truth is spoken.

"If, at other times, it costs you so little
    to satisfy others," they all replied,
    "you are fortunate, speaking thus at will;

therefore, if you escape from this dark place
    and return to see the beautiful stars,
    when you can delight in saying 'I was there . . .'   84

see that you speak to others about us."
    Then they broke the wheel, and in their flight
    their nimble legs seemed wings.

An "amen" could not have been said
    so quickly as they disappeared;
    whereupon my master thought it best to go on.

I followed him, and we had not gone far
    before the waterfall was so near
    that we could hardly hear each other speak.

As the river which has its own channel at first
    from Monte Veso toward the east,
    on the left slope of the Apennines—   96

which is called Acquacheta up above
    before it flows to its lower bed,
    and at Forlì loses that name—

resounds there above San Benedetto dell'Alpe,
    because of falling in one single leap
    instead of being broken by a thousand,

so, down from a steep bank
    we found the colored water roaring so loudly
    that it soon would have hurt our ears.

A cord around Dante's waist probably stands for self-confidence, useful in com-
bating incontinence, but worse than useless in dealing with the fraud ahead. He
gives it to Virgil who throws it over the precipice as a signal. Dante waits anx-
iously to see what will happen.

I had a cord around my waist
    with which I had thought once
    to catch the leopard with the painted hide.   108

After I had loosened it from my body
    as my leader had ordered me,
    I handed it to him, coiled and knotted.

Then he turned to the right side,
    and threw it far from the bank
    down into that deep abyss.

"Surely," I said within myself, "something strange
    must respond to this new signal
    which my master so follows with his eyes."

Ah, how cautious we must be
    with those who see not only what we do
    but look also within our thoughts!   120

He said to me, "Soon what I am waiting for
    will come up, and what you are thinking about
    will be revealed to your eyes."

To the truth which appears to be a lie
    we should close our lips as long as we can,
    not to incur blamelessly a reproach;

but here I cannot keep silent and, Reader,
    by the notes of this Comedy, I swear to you—
    so may it not lack long favor—

that I saw, through that thick and dark air,
    a form marvelous to every steadfast heart
    come swimming up   132

as a swimmer rises after going down
    to loosen an anchor caught by a rock
    or something else hidden in the sea,

who stretches forth his arms and draws up his feet.

CANTO XVII

GERYON

The monster coming up is Geryon, a symbol of the fraud which is universal and more powerful than arms. His face has an honest look, but his body is reptilelike and covered with devious and intricate patterns, like oriental tapestries. He lies with his head on the bank as beavers were supposed to do when using their tails to throw their prey on the shore.

"Behold the beast with the pointed tail
    that can cross mountains and break through walls;
    behold the one that infects the whole world!"

Thus my guide began to speak to me
    and signaled to the beast to come ashore
    near the end of the stone banks we had walked on;

and that foul image of fraud came up
    and landed his head and breast,
    but did not put his tail upon the bank.

His face was that of an honest man,
   so kind an aspect it had outwardly,
   but all the rest was like a reptile.   12

He had two paws, hairy to the armpits;
   his back and breast and both sides
   were decorated with loops and circles;

never did Tartars nor Turks make cloth
   with more colors in groundwork and in pattern,
   nor did Arachne[26] ever put such webs on her loom.

As skiffs sometimes lie along the shore
   partly in the water and partly on land,
   and as up there among the gluttonous Germans

the beaver sits to carry on his war,
   so that worst of wild beasts lay
   on the edge which binds the sand with stone.   24

He darted his tail in the empty space,
   twisting up its venomous tip
   which was armed like that of a scorpion.

> The usurers (the remaining group of the violent against God) are crouching near the edge where it is easy to fall into the circle of fraud below. Dante treats them with the utmost contempt, as he does all mercenary souls. They are unrecognizable except by the coats of arms on their now empty purses.
>
> Virgil has warned Dante not to waste words on them: our poet does not speak at all. The usurers are still competing, quarreling, rivaling, and envying each other, without honor, courage, good manners, artistic or intellectual distinction.

My leader said, "We must now bend our course
   a little as far as to the wicked beast
   that is lying over there."

We descended to the right
   and took ten steps on the extreme edge
   in order to avoid the sand and the flames.

After we had reached the monster,
   I saw a little farther on some people on the sand
   sitting close to the empty space.   36

My master said, "So that you may take with you
   complete experience of this round,
   go and see their ways.

Let your talk with them be brief;
   until you return I will speak with this one
   so that he may lend us his strong shoulders."

---

[26] A skilled weaver who challenged the goddess Minerva to a competition; Minerva later changed her into a spider.

Thus I advanced along the extreme edge
    of the seventh circle all alone
    to where the sad souls were sitting.

Through their eyes their grief burst forth;
    on this side and that they used their hands,
    brushing off the fire and lifting themselves from the hot
        ground;   48

not otherwise are dogs busy in summer,
    now with their muzzles and now with their paws,
    when bitten by gadflies or fleas.

In looking at the faces of some
    on whom the painful fire was falling,
    I could recognize none, but I noticed

that from the necks of each a purse hung
    which had a certain color and design
    and on which it seemed that their eyes feasted.

As I came looking at them,
    on a yellow purse I saw in azure
    the head and the form of a lion.   60

Then continuing the course of my glances,
    I saw another, red as blood,
    showing a goose whiter than butter.

And one who had a white sack marked
    with an azure pregnant sow,
    said to me, "What are you doing in this hole?

Now go away and, since you are still alive,
    know that my neighbor Vitaliano
    will sit here on my left side.

With these Florentines I am a Paduan;
    many times they deafen my ears,
    shouting, 'Let the sovereign knight come   72

who will bring the pouch marked by three goats.'"
    Then he twisted his mouth and stuck out his tongue
    as an ox does to lick its nose.

And I, fearing that to stay longer
    might annoy my master, who had admonished me
    to be brief, turned my back on those wearied souls.

When Dante climbs on Geryon's back over the immense void, he is so frightened he cannot speak.

The transition from violence to deliberate, premeditated fraud is shown by the long and slow descent.

I found my leader already mounted
    on the back of the fierce animal.
    He said to me, "Now be strong and bold;

we descend here by such stairs.
    Mount in front, for I wish to be placed
    so that the tail cannot hurt you."   84

As one who has the chill of the quartan fever
    so close that his nails are already blue,
    and who shivers merely at the sight of shade,

so I became on hearing these words,
    but Virgil's admonition caused the shame
    which, in sight of his master, makes a servant strong.

I placed myself on those big shoulders.
    "See that you hold me," I wished to say,
    but my voice did not come out as I thought.

And he who at other times helped me
    in other fears, as soon as I had mounted,
    embraced and held me with his arms;   96

then said, "Geryon, move now;
    let the circles be large and the descent slow;
    think of the new burden that you have."

As a little ship moves from its berth,
    back, back, thus Geryon moved off,
    and when he felt his whole body clear,

he turned his tail to where his breast had been,
    and stretching it out, moved it like an eel,
    and with his paws drew in the air.

I do not believe there was greater fear when Phaëthon[27]
    let loose the reins [of the sun's chariot] so that the sky
    as still appears [by the Milky Way] was scorched,   108

nor when poor Icarus[28] [while flying] felt his loins unfeathered
    because of the melting of the wax,
    his father shouting to him, "The wrong way you're taking!"

than was mine when I saw myself in the air
    on every side and with every view hidden
    except that of the beast.

It went on swimming slowly, slowly,
    circled and descended, but I was aware of the movement
    only by the wind blowing in my face and from below.

---

[27] Son of Apollo, the charioteer of the sun. Entrusted with his father's chariot, Phaëthon lost control of it so that it burned the sky.

[28] Icarus, for whom his father Daedalus made wings cemented with wax, flew too near the sun and fell when it melted the wax.

Already I heard the torrent on the right
    roaring horribly beneath us,
    so that I stretched out my head to look down.   120

Then I was still more afraid,
    for I saw fires and heard laments,
    at which I crouched back, all trembling.

I noticed then the descending and the circling
    which I had not seen before
    by the torments drawing near on every side.

As a falcon that has long been on the wing
    without seeing a bird or lure, and that makes the falconer cry,
    "Alas, you are coming down!"

descends wearily, after many circles,
    to where it had swiftly started out,
    and lands far from its master, sullen and angry,   132

so Geryon set us down on the bottom,
    at the foot of the jagged rock;
    then freed of the weight of our bodies,

he darted off, like an arrow-notch from the string.

CANTO XVIII

PANDERS, SEDUCERS, AND FLATTERERS

*The matter-of-fact description of Malebolge contrasts with the deviousness of the
fraud it harbors. The term means "evil pouches" or "purses," perhaps with some
reference to the greed which motivates most fraud. Those who sinned through
violence are in the open. The fraudulent, appropriately, are hidden in dark
ditches. Over the moats are "scogli," rocky bridges, which come together at the
center like spokes of a wheel.*

There is a place in Hell called Malebolge,
    all of stone and of an iron color
    like the bank which surrounds it.

Right in the middle of the baleful space
    a well, rather wide and deep, opens up
    whose features I will describe in their place.

The belt that remains, then,
    between the well and the high, hard bank,
    had its bottom divided into ten valleys.

As the ground appears
    where several moats surround a castle
    as a protection for the walls,   12

such was the design these made.
    And, as from the thresholds of fortresses
    little bridges extend to the outer banks,

so from the bottom of the wall, rough spans
    crossed the ditches and the banks down to the well
    which brings them all together and cuts them off.

In this place, shaken from the back of Geryon,
    we found ourselves, and the poet started
    to the left, and I moved on behind him.

> *The souls in the first bolgia or ditch are guided by traffic regulations as was the crowd at the jubilee in Rome in 1300, the panders on the outside going to the right, the seducers on the inside to the left.*

> *We now meet the first devils. These, appropriately, wear the horns associated with adultery. We find also the first shade who is ashamed. When recognized, he tells how he sold his sister to the Marquis of Este. He confesses also for the other Bolognese panders, more numerous than the little children learning the dialect word for "yes" within the boundaries of their province.*

> *Here, as elsewhere, movement characterizes punishments for sins related to sexuality. Where the activity was natural, the agent of punishment is wind, a natural force; where unnatural, as on the plain, a supernatural fire is falling. Here, among the fraudulent, a devil plies the whip.*

On the right I saw new misery,
    new torments, and new tormentors
    with which the first ditch was filled.   24

The sinners along the bottom of the ditch were naked,
    coming on this side facing us, on the other
    moving with us, but with longer steps.

Thus the Romans because of the great throng
    in the year of the jubilee, chose a way
    to divide the traffic on the bridge,

so that on one side all had their faces
    toward the Castle [of Sant' Angelo], and went to St. Peter's,
    on the other side they advanced toward the Mount [Giordano].

On both sides of the dark rock
    I saw horned demons with great whips
    beating the shades fiercely from behind.   36

Ah, how they made them lift their legs
    at the first stroke! Indeed,
    none waited for the second or for the third.

While I was going on, my eyes fell on one;
    whereupon immediately I said,
    "I am not fasting for the sight of him!"[29]

Therefore I delayed advancing to look;
    and my dear leader stopped with me
    and consented that I go back a little.

[29] "I have seen this person before."

The whipped shade thought he could hide
    by lowering his face, but it availed him little,
    for I said, "You who cast your eyes on the ground,   48

if the features you wear are not false,
    are Venedico Caccianemico;
    but what brings you into such a pickle?"

And he to me, "Unwillingly I say it,
    but I am compelled by your clear speech
    which makes me recall the world.

I am the one who led Ghisolabella [his sister]
    to do the Marquis' [of Este's] will,
    however the vile tale may sound,

and I am not the only Bolognese weeping here;
    on the contrary the place is so full of them
    that as many tongues are not now being taught   60

to say 'sipa' between the Savena and the Reno;
    and if you want assurance of that,
    recall to your mind our avaricious hearts."

While he was speaking thus, a demon struck him
    with his whip, saying, "Away, pander!
    Here are no women to turn into cash!"

To see the seducers, who have been going to the left, the poets mount to the top of
the bridge. They observe Jason, a dignified figure, but whipped, like the others.
His principal crime, besides robbing the Colchians of the Golden Fleece and
deserting Medea, was the seduction of Hypsipyle. The latter, according to the
legend, had already shown her weakness by saving her father's life when the
disgusted women of Lemnos tried to kill off all the men.

I rejoined my escort; then,
    after a few steps, we came
    to where a rough bridge projects from the bank.

Quite easily we climbed it,
    and turning to the right over its ridge
    we moved away from that eternal bank.   72

When we reached the point below which the bridge opens
    to give passage for those whipped,
    my leader said, "Stop, and let your sight

fall on these other ill-born souls
    whose faces you have not yet seen,
    since they have been going with us."

From the old bridge we looked at the file
    coming toward us on the other side
    and whom the whip likewise drove on.

And my good master, without my asking, said,
    "Look at that great one coming,
    who, for his pain, sheds no tears;   84

what a regal bearing he still has!
    That is Jason who through courage and slyness
    deprived the Colchians of their ram [Golden Fleece].

He passed through the island of Lemnos
    after the bold and pitiless women
    had given up to death all their men.

There, with gifts and fine words,
    he deceived Hypsipyle, the young girl
    who first had deceived all the others.[30]

He abandoned her pregnant and forlorn.
    Such guilt condemns him to this punishment;
    and vengeance is taken also for Medea.   96

With him go all those who deceive in this way:
    let this knowledge suffice for the first vale
    and for those it holds in its grip."

> *The poets proceed to where they can see the flatterers in the second ditch. Dante
> chooses the elegant Thaïs as his ancient example, perhaps to emphasize the essen-
> tial filthiness of these sinners who, like dogs, lick the sores of those they exploit.
> The contrast is all the more striking because the charge against her seems trivial.
> Moreover, Dante had misread the incident in Cicero; the guilty one was Gnatho,
> not Thaïs. But the lesson is clear: even Thaïs could not make flattery clean.*

We had already come to where the narrow road
    crosses the second bank and makes of it
    an abutment for another arch.

Here we heard people moaning in the next ditch
    and puffing with their snouts
    and hitting themselves with their hands.

The banks were encrusted with a mold
    condensed from the vapor from below
    which offends both the eyes and nose.   108

The bottom was so deep it could be seen
    only by mounting to the summit of the arch
    where the bridge stands highest.

We reached that place, and down in the ditch
    I saw people plunged in excrement
    which seemed to have come from human privies.

---

[30] Hypsipyle spared her father and told the other women of Lemnos that he had been
killed along with the other males. For a version of the Jason-Medea story, see Euripides'
Medea.

And while I was searching down there with my eyes,
    I saw one with his head so smeared with filth
    that you could not tell if he were a layman or a clerk.

He bawled to me, "Why are you so eager
    to look at me more than at the other ugly ones?"
    And I to him, "Because, if I remember well,   120

I saw you once with dry hair;
    you are Alessio Interminei da Lucca;
    therefore, I eye you more than all the rest."

Then beating on his pate, he said,
    "The flatteries with which my tongue
    was never cloyed have put me down here."

After that my guide said to me,
    "See that you extend your gaze
    so that your eyes may reach the face

of that filthy and disheveled wench
    who is scratching herself with her dirty nails
    and now squats and now is standing on her feet.   132

Thaïs,[31] she is, the harlot
    who answered her paramour when he said,
    'Have I *great* favor with you?' 'No, *marvelous!*'

And with this let our sight be satisfied."

CANTO XIX

THE SIMONISTS

*Dante's objectivity ceases when we come to the simonists who by trafficking in
church offices and enriching themselves tend to destroy the Church itself. Their
fat feeds the fire which now punishes them.*

O Simon Magus![32] O rapacious followers,
    you who should be wedded to righteousness
    and instead prostitute the things of God

for gold and silver, now for you
    it is necessary that the trumpet sound,
    since you are in the third ditch.

Already we had mounted to that part
    of the following bridge
    which hangs over the middle of the moat.

[31] This is not the famous courtesan but a whore in a play by Terence, the Roman dramatist
(second century B.C.).

[32] Simon "the Magician," who, according to Acts of the Apostles 8, was rebuked by Peter
for attempting to buy the powers of the apostles that only God could give. The word *simony* is
derived from his name.

O Supreme Wisdom, how great is the art Thou showest
 in Heaven, on earth, and in the evil world,
 and how justly Thy power rewards!   12

I saw the livid stone covered with holes
 on the sides and on the bottom,
 all round, and of one breadth.

They appeared neither larger nor smaller
 than those in my beautiful San Giovanni
 made for the baptizers to stand in,

one of which, not many years ago, I broke
 to save a drowning child—and let this
 be my seal [on the truth] to undeceive all men.[33]

From the mouth of each a sinner's feet protruded
 and his legs up to the calf,
 and the rest remained within.   24

The soles of the feet of all were on fire,
 and their legs above the joints writhed so sharply
 that they would have broken withes or ropes.

As flames on oily things are wont
 to move only over the outer surface,
 so they did here from heel to toe.

"Who is that one, Master, who writhes so,
 twitching more than the others, his companions,
 and who feeds a ruddier flame?" I asked.

And he to me, "If you want me to carry you down there
 over the [inner] bank which slopes less steeply,
 you will learn from him about himself and his misdeeds."   36

And I, "Whatever you want is good for me;
 you are my lord, and you know that my will
 is like your own, and you know also what I keep silent."

Then we came to the fourth bank
 where we turned and descended on the left
 down into the narrow and pitted bottom.

My kind master still did not put me down,
 but carried me to the hole of the one
 who was so lamenting with his shanks.

The inverted shade, Pope Nicholas III, mistakes Dante for Boniface VIII (still living in 1300) who, after outraging the Church (the "Bride of Christ"), is to follow him here. Nicholas belonged to the Orsini family (orso, bear), and used his office to advance the cubs. In this mockery of the apostolic succession, Boni-

[33] Untrue rumors apparently had circulated about this incident, but what they were is not known.

face will be succeeded by Clement V, who, as the tool of Philip the Fair of France,
transferred the papacy to Avignon. A certain vulgarity characterizes the speech
of all mercenary sinners and the terms used to describe them.

"O, whoever you are, sad spirit,
    upside down, planted like a stake,"
    I began to say, "if you can, speak." 48

I stood like the friar confessing a treacherous assassin
    who, after being put in the hole [to be buried alive],
    calls the confessor back to delay his death,

and he shouted, "Are you already standing there,
    are you already there, O Boniface?—
    The writing [Book of Fate] lied to me by several years.

Are you so quickly sated with the wealth
    for which you were not afraid to seize the beautiful lady
    through guile and then to outrage her?"

I became like those who wonder
    if they are mocked, not understanding the words
    said to them, and who are unable to reply. 60

Then Virgil said, "Tell him quickly
    'I am not, I am not the one you think,'"
    and I answered as I had been bidden.

At that the spirit twisted both his feet,
    then sighing and with a tearful voice
    he said, "What do you ask of me?

If you want so much to learn who I am
    that you have come down the bank to hear,
    know that I was clothed with the great mantle,

and truly I was a son of the she-bear
    so covetous to advance the cubs
    that on earth I put wealth, and here myself, in a sack. 72

Below, under my head, the others[34]
    who preceded me in simony are compressed,
    squeezed into the fissures of the rock.

Down there I also will be pressed
    when he comes for whom I took you
    when I asked the sudden question.

But I have already been roasted
    and have stood thus upside down longer
    than he will stay planted with reddened feet,

for after him, out of the West, will come
    a shepherd without law, of uglier deed,
    fit to cover both him and me. 84

[34] That is, the other simoniacal popes, all of whom are thrust into the same hole.

He will be like the Jason[35] of whom we read in Maccabees,
    and as to Jason a king dealt gently,
    so will the ruler of France treat him."

*Dante addresses Nicholas with intense feeling, restrained only by reverence for
this sinner's past office. He mentions the Scarlet Woman, as the symbol of the
corrupt Church.*

*In this bolgia things are generally upside down. The clergy inverted their duties
and are now inverted themselves; Dante, a layman, hears a confession, like a
friar, and then preaches a sermon to an ex-pope.*

I do not know if I was now too bold,
    but I answered him in this strain:
    "Alas, now tell me, how much treasure

did our Lord ask of St. Peter
    before he put the keys in his hands?
    Surely he demanded only, 'Follow me!'

Nor did Peter and the others ask Matthias
    for gold or silver when he was chosen
    for the place the guilty soul [Judas] had lost.[36]   96

Therefore, stay there, for you are well punished,
    and keep securely the ill-got money
    which made you so bold against Charles [of Anjou].

And if I were still not prevented
    by reverence for the holy keys
    which you kept in the happy life,

I would use words still heavier;
    for your avarice afflicts the world,
    crushing the good and lifting up the bad.

The Evangelist [St. John] had shepherds like you in mind
    when she [the Scarlet Woman][37] that sitteth upon many waters
    was seen by him fornicating with kings,   108

she who was born with seven heads [virtues]
    and from ten horns [commandments] gained strength
    as long as virtue pleased the bridegroom [the papacy].

You have made a god of gold and silver,
    and how do you differ from the idolater,
    except that he worships one thing of gold, and you a hundred?

[35] In 2 Maccabees 4–5 (a book of the Roman Catholic Bible), the unworthy Jason obtains
from the king of Syria by bribery the office of Jewish high priest.

[36] In Acts 1, Matthias is chosen by prayer and the casting of lots as successor to Judas as one
of the twelve apostles.

[37] The details Dante gives are from Revelation 17; the passage refers to Rome.

*The papal claims to temporal power were based in part on the supposed gift of the
Western Empire to St. Sylvester by Constantine. The document confirming this
transfer was not recognized as a forgery until after Dante's time, but our poet
held that the emperor had no power to make such a gift nor the pope to receive it.*

*Virgil, as the representative of the Roman Empire in the political allegory, is so
delighted with Dante's sermon that he carries his pupil out of the ditch and to the
top of the next bridge.*

Ah, Constantine,[38] to how much ill gave birth
   not your conversion, but that dowry
   which the first rich father took from you!"

While I sang these notes to him,
   whether anger or conscience stung him,
   he kicked hard with both his feet.   120

I believe my leader was pleased,
   with such a contented look he listened
   to the true words I had expressed.

With both arms he took hold of me,
   and when he had me quite upon his breast,
   he remounted by the way we had come down,

nor did he tire of holding me tightly,
   but carried me to the top of the arch
   which crosses from the fourth to the fifth bank.

There, softly, he put down his burden—
   softly because of the rough and steep rocks
   which would have been a hard road even for goats.   132

From there another valley was disclosed.

CANTO XX

THE DIVINERS

*The sight of the soothsayers, diviners, and magicians, with their heads twisted
around and walking backward, makes Dante weep. He had previously shown
pity for the victims of our human defects, but now he is sorry for the punishment
itself. This is a kind of protest against the divine order, and he is severely rebuked
by Virgil. The scolding is most striking since Virgil had been considered a diviner, a master of magic art, and the sin punished here often tempted men of
learning like Dante himself.*

For new punishments I must make verses
   and provide matter for the twentieth canto
   of the first book, which is about the damned.

---

[38] Roman emperor from 306 to 337, a convert to Christianity who moved the capital of the
empire to Constantinople.

I was already placed where I could see
    into the uncovered depth
    which was bathed with tears of anguish,

and I saw people move silent and weeping
    through the circular valley, at the pace of those
    who chant litanies in this world.

When my eyes saw them more clearly
    each appeared to be twisted marvelously
    between the chin and the beginning of the chest,   12

for their faces were turned to the rear,
    and each was obliged to move backward,
    since seeing ahead was denied them.

Perhaps by the force of paralysis
    someone might be wholly twisted thus,
    but I have never seen the case nor believe it exists.

Reader, so may God let you profit
    by your reading, now think for yourself
    how I could keep my face dry

when I saw our [human] image, close at hand,
    so twisted that the tears from the eyes
    bathed the buttocks along the cleft.   24

Certainly I wept, leaning on a rock
    of the hard bridge, so that my escort said to me,
    "Are you, too, like the other fools?

Here pity lives when it is completely dead.
    Who is more impious than that one
    who feels sorrow for God's judgment?

> *Virgil now points out certain soothsayers of antiquity, characters chosen from various epic poems. The accounts of them are incorrect in some respects, perhaps to show once more the fallibility of men's minds. In discussing Manto, Virgil gives an account of the founding of Mantua different from one in the* Aeneid. *Moreover, in the* Purgatory, *Manto is mentioned as in a different circle. The digression interests even Dante only slightly.*

Lift up your head and see him [an augur] for whom
    the earth opened in the sight of the Thebans
    so that they cried, 'Where are you falling,

O Amphiaraus? why are you giving up the war?'
    and he did not stop rushing headlong
    down to Minos who seizes everyone;   36

observe how he has made a breast of his shoulders;
    because he wished to see too far ahead,
    he looks behind, and goes backward.

See Tiresias [a soothsayer] who changed his semblance
    when he became from man, a woman,
    transforming all his members,

and before he could regain his manly hair
    it was necessary for him to strike again
    the two entwined serpents with his wand.[39]

The one backing up to his belly
    is Aruns who, in the Luni mountains
    beneath which the Carrarese live and plow,   48

had a cave in the white marble for a dwelling
    from which no obstacle cut off
    a view of the sea or of the stars.

And she who covers her breasts
    which you do not see, with her loose tresses,
    and has on the other side all hairy skin,

was Manto, who sought through many lands
    before she settled where I was born
    and of her I would like for you to hear.

After her father had given up his life
    and Bacchus' city [Thebes] was enslaved
    she wandered a long time through the world.   60

In beautiful Italy, above the Tyrol,
    at the foot of the Alps which enclose Germany,
    lies a lake named Benaco.

A thousand brooks and more bathe the Apennino
    from Guarda to Val Canonica
    whose waters come to rest in this lake.

In the middle is a point where the pastors
    of Trento, Brescia, and Verona
    could give a blessing if they went that way.

Peschiera lies as a fair and powerful rampart
    to face the Brescians and the Bergamese
    where the shore is lowest.   72

There, all that the lap of Benaco
    cannot hold must overflow
    through green pastures and make a river.

When the water begins to flow,
    it is no longer called Benaco, but Mincio
    as far as Governo, where it falls into the Po.

---

[39] Tiresias had first been changed from a man into a woman when he struck two entwined serpents with his wand; years later he saw and struck them again, whereupon he was changed back into a man. Manto, mentioned later, was his daughter.

After a short course it finds a flat region
  over which it spreads and forms a marsh
  which in summer is wont to be noisome.

While passing there, the cruel virgin
  saw land in the middle of the fen
  uncultivated and devoid of inhabitants.   84

There, to shun all human intercourse,
  she, with her servants, stayed to practice her art,
  and lived, and left there her empty body.

Later the people scattered around
  gathered in that place which was strong
  because of the marsh on all sides.

They built the city on her bones
  and for her who first chose the place
  they called it Mantua, without other augury.

Once its people were more numerous
  before the madness of Casalodi [its ruler]
  was deceived by Pinamonte.   96

Therefore I warn you, that if you ever hear
  of another origin for my city,
  let no falsehood defraud the truth."

And I, "Master, your account is so certain
  and takes such hold on my belief
  that others would be like dead coals.

But tell me about the people passing by,
  whether you see any worthy of note,
  for to that alone my mind reverts."

> *The account of Eurypylus at the time of the Trojan wars differs also from its source in Virgil, a slip all the more striking since Dante implies that he knew the Aeneid by heart.*
>
> *Among the modern soothsayers is Michael Scott who lived at the court of Frederick II of Sicily. His legend survived in Scotland down to modern times. Other minor figures include Guido Bonatti, an astrologer of Forlì, Asdente, the cobbler of Parma, and various fortune-tellers and witches.*
>
> *In Italian folklore, the Man in the Moon is Cain. He is mentioned in indicating the time. It is about six o'clock on Saturday morning, April 9, 1300.*

Then he said, "That one who from his cheeks
  lets his beard fall on his dark shoulders
  was an augur [during the Trojan War] when Greece was so empty
    of males   108

that scarcely any remained for the cradles,
  and in Aulis, together with Calchas,
  he set the time for setting sail for Troy.

Eurypylus was his name, and my lofty tragedy
     sings of him in one place,
     as you know well, since you know it all.

The other, so slender in the flanks,
     was Michael Scott, who really knew
     the game of magic frauds.

See also Guido Bonatti, see Asdente
     who now wishes he had attended
     to his leather and his thread, but too late repents.   120

See the poor women who left the needle,
     the shuttle, and the spindle, and became fortunetellers;
     they wrought magic with herbs and images.

But come now, for Cain with his thorns
     is already on the confines of both hemispheres
     and below Seville is sinking in the sea,

and last night the moon was round;
     you must remember, since it was not unwelcome
     at times in the deep wood."

Thus he spoke as we moved on.

CANTO XXI

THE BARRATORS (GRAFTERS)

Thus we went from bridge to bridge, talking of things
     my Comedy does not care to mention,
     and reached the top of the next arch

where we stopped to see the ditch
     and to hear the other vain laments;
     and I found it marvelously dark.

As in the shipyards of the Venetians,
     in winter, the tenacious pitch boils
     to calk their damaged ships,

since the sailors cannot navigate, and instead
     some build new boats, some strengthen the ribs
     of one that has made many voyages;   12

some hammer at the prow and some at the stern;
     some make oars, and some twist ropes;
     some mend the jib and mainsail,

so, not by fire, but through divine art
     a dense tar boils down there
     which coats the banks on each side.

I saw the pitch, but did not see in it
     anything except the bubbles which rise,
     swell up, and then collapse.

While I was looking fixedly down there
    my guide drew me from where I was,
    saying, "Look! look!"   24

Then I turned like one suddenly dismayed,
    striving to see something
    from which he must escape

and who, to see, does not delay his start;
    and I noticed behind us a black devil
    coming at a run over the bridge.

Ah, how fierce he was in aspect,
    and how ferocious he seemed in act,
    with wings open, and light upon his feet!

His shoulders which were high and sharp
    were burdened by the haunches of a sinner
    the sinews of whose feet he clutched.   36

From our bridge he cried, "O Malebranche [devils],
    here is one of the elders[40] of Santa Zita [Lucca],
    put him under while I go back for more

to that city I have so well furnished with them.
    Everyone is a barrator there, except Bonturo;[41]
    there, for money, a 'no' becomes a 'yes.'"

Down he hurled him, and turned back
    over the rough bridge, and never was a mastiff
    in such haste to follow a thief.

The sinner plunged in, then rose doubled up,
    but the demons hiding under the bridge shouted,
    "Here there is no Holy Face [as at Lucca] to pray to!   48

Here you do not swim as in the Serchio!
    So, unless you want to feel our hooks,
    don't show yourself above the pitch!"

Then they struck him with more than a hundred prongs,
    saying, "Here you must dance under cover
    and pilfer secretly if you can!"

Not otherwise do cooks have their scullions
    dip the meat in the middle of the boiler
    with forks, so that it will not float.

> *Virgil holds a parley with the demons below the bridge. Then Dante rejoins his master, keeping as close to him (Reason) as he can, but using his eyes as well. The entire episode with the devils beginning here (a concession to the popular spirit of the Middle Ages) symbolizes incidentally Dante's narrow escape from Florence, where one of the false charges against him was barratry.*

[40] Public officials of Lucca, of which Zita was the patron saint.
[41] This is ironic; Bonturo was an especially notorious grafter.

My good master said, "So that it may not appear
    that you are here, crouch down
    behind a rock and remain hidden,   60

and whatever outrage is done to me
    do not be afraid, for I know about this business;
    once before I was in a like affray."

Then he went to the head of the bridge,
    and as he arrived on the sixth bank
    he needed a steadfast heart.

With that fury and that uproar
    with which dogs run out at a beggar
    who suddenly stops and begs from where he is,

those devils rushed out from under the bridge,
    turning against him all their hooks.
    But he cried, "Let none of you be headstrong.   72

Before your grapples touch me,
    let one of you come forward to hear me
    and then decide about hooking me."

All shouted, "Let Malacoda go"; whereupon one
    stepped forward while the others stood firm,
    and came to him saying, "What good will it do him?"

"Do you think, Malacoda,
    that you see me here," my master said,
    "safe from all your opposition,

without divine will and propitious fate?
    Let me go on, for it is willed in Heaven
    that I should show another this wild way."   84

Then Malacoda's pride collapsed so suddenly
    that he let his hook fall at his feet
    and said to the others, "Do not strike him."

And my guide called to me, "O you, crouching quietly
    behind the rocks of the bridge,
    you may come now securely."

I started out and went quickly to him,
    and all the devils pressed forward,
    so that I feared they might not keep their pact.

Thus I once saw foot soldiers afraid
    on leaving Caprona under safe conduct,
    when they saw themselves among so many enemies.   96

I drew close to my guide with my whole body,
    but did not take my eyes
    from the devils' looks, which were not good.

They lowered their hooks, one saying to another,
"Should I nick him on the rump?"
and being answered, "Yes, let him have it!"

But the demon who had held the parley
with my leader turned instantly,
and said, "Quiet, quiet, Scarmiglione!"

> *Malacoda proposes that a squad accompany the travelers to the next "unbroken" bridge. Since all the bridges over the next bolgia are broken, the devils understand that a trick is to be played on Virgil. To be more convincing in his fraud, Malacoda cites some statistics to show how much time has passed since the Crucifixion and the resultant earthquake. Dante, using his senses and intuition, would prefer to go on alone, but Virgil (Reason), taken in, tries to reassure him; and the grotesque company moves on.*

Then he said to us, "You cannot go farther
on this bridge, since the sixth arch
lies all broken on the bottom,   108

but if you still want to go ahead,
keep advancing along this bank;
nearby is another bridge that provides a way.

Yesterday, five hours later than this hour,
a thousand two hundred and sixty-six years[42]
were completed since the bridge here was broken.

I am sending some of my men over there
to see if any are airing themselves;
go with them, since they won't be harmful.

Step forward, Alichino and Calcabrina,"
he then began to say, "and Cagnazzo,
and you, Barbariccia, guide the squad.   120

Let Libicocco come and Draghignazzo,
Ciriatto with his tusks, and Graffiacane,
and Farfarello, and mad Rubicante.

Look around the boiling glue;
let these be safe as far as to the bridge
which *all unbroken* passes over the dens."

"Oh, Master, what is this I see?"
I exclaimed. "Ah, without escort, let us go alone
if you know the way; as for me, I ask for none.

If you are as wary as usual,
don't you see that they are gnashing their teeth,
and with their frowns threaten grief to us?"   132

[42] Christ died at the age of 33, and the present year is 1300, but Dante is presumably dating from Christ's conception, not his birth.

And he to me, "Do not be afraid,
    let them grind away as they like,
    because they do that for the wretches in the pitch."

The devils turned to the left on the bank,
    but first each pressed his tongue between his teeth,
    as a signal to their leader,

and he, for a trumpet, used his rump.[43]

CANTO XXII

CIAMPOLO OF NAVARRE

I have seen horsemen move camp
    and launch an attack, and hold their muster,
    and sometimes turn back to escape;

I have seen scouting parties in your land,
    O Aretines! and foragers start out,
    tournaments begin and races run,

sometimes at the sound of trumpets or of bells,
    with drums and with castle signals,
    and with familiar and strange devices,

but never yet did I see horse or footmen move
    to so strange a bugle call,
    or a ship at a sign on land or in the sky.   12

We went along with the ten demons;
    ah, fierce company! but "in church with saints,
    and in the tavern with the gluttons!"

I was attentive to the pitch
    to see what the bolgia contained
    and the people burning in it.

As dolphins make signs to sailors
    by the arching of their backs
    to prepare to save their ship,

so now and then, to relieve the pain,
    some of the sinners showed their backs
    and hid again as fast as lightning flashes;   24

and, as at the edge of the water of a ditch,
    frogs lie with just their muzzles out,
    hiding their feet and bodies,

so, on every side, the sinners lay;
    but when Barbariccia came near,
    they withdrew within the boiling.

[43] Farted.

I saw, and still my heart shudders at it,
 a soul waiting thus, just as it happens
 that one frog may remain when the others dart away,

and Graffiacane who was closest to him
 hooked his pitchy locks, and pulled him out
 so that he looked like an otter.   36

I already knew the names of all the demons
 so well did I note them when they were chosen,
 and as they called each other I noticed how.

"O Rubicante, see that you get your claws
 on him and skin him alive,"
 the accursed ones shouted all together,

and I, "Master, find out if you can
 who the unfortunate wretch is
 that has fallen into the hands of his enemies."

My guide went close to him and asked
 whence he came, and he replied,
 "I was born in the kingdom of Navarre. 48

My mother placed me as a servant to a lord,
 for she had borne me to a spendthrift,
 a destroyer of himself and of his property.

Then I was in the service of good King Thibault;
 there I began to commit barratry
 for which I give reckoning in this heat."

And Ciriatto from each side of whose mouth
 a tusk issued, as from a boar's,
 made him feel how one of them could rip.

The mouse had fallen among vicious cats;
 but Barbariccia took him in his arms
 and said, "Stand over there while I grip him." 60

And turning his face to my master,
 "Ask, if you want to hear more about him,"
 he said, "before the others mangle him."

My guide then said, "Now tell me, do you know
 any others under the pitch who are Italians?"
 And he answered, "A little while ago

I left one from a nearby island—
 (might I still be covered with him,
 for then I would fear neither claw nor hook!").

And Libicocco cried, "Too much have we endured,"
 and with his prong seized his arm
 and tearing it, carried off a sinew. 72

Draghignazzo also tried to lay hold
    of his legs, whereupon their corporal
    turned around with wicked looks.

When they were somewhat pacified
    my guide without delay addressed the sinner
    who was still looking at his wounds.

"Who is the one you say you left
    unluckily in order to come ashore?"
    and he replied, "It was Friar Gomita,

from Gallura, a vessel of every fraud
    who had his master's enemies in his hands
    and dealt with them so [gently] that all praise him.   84

Money he took, and let them off quietly
    as he says; and in other offices also
    he was not a little barrator, but a supreme one.

With him Don Michel Zanche of Logodoro
    keeps company, and their tongues
    are never tired of talking about Sardinia.

O me! see that one grinding his teeth;
    I would say more, but I am afraid
    he is getting ready to scratch my sticky coat!"

And their commander in chief, turning to Farfarello,
    who was rolling his eyes on the point of striking,
    said, "Get over there, vile bird!"   96

"If you wish to see or hear,"
    the frightened one [Ciampolo] then began,
    "some Tuscans or Lombards, I will have some come,

but let the Malebranche stand back a little
    so that their vengeance will not be feared,
    and I, sitting in this very place,

for one that I am, will make many come
    when I whistle, as it is our custom
    to do when any of us gets out."

Cagnazzo at these words raised his snout,
    shaking his head, and said, "Listen to the trick
    he has thought of to plunge down."   108

Then he [Ciampolo], who had a wealth of guile,
    answered, "I am too tricky indeed
    when I get greater sorrow for my friends!"

Alichino could hold back no longer
    and contrary to the others said,
    "If you plunge, I'll not gallop after you,

but will beat my wings above the pitch!
    Let the ridge be left and the bank made a screen
    to see if you can get the best of us."

O you who read will now hear new sport.
    All turned their eyes to the other side,
    and he first who had been most unwilling.   120

The Navarese chose well his time,
    steadied his feet upon the ground, and in an instant
    leaped, and from the marshal freed himself.

At that each was stung with guilt, and that one most
    who had been the cause of the mistake.
    He, swooping down, cried, "You're caught!"

but it availed little, for wings
    could not outstrip terror. The sinner went under,
    and his pursuer, flying, turned up his breast.

Not otherwise does the wild duck plunge
    when the falcon comes near
    which, defeated and angry, flies up again.   132

Calcabrina, furious at the trick,
    also went after him, eager for the sinner to escape
    so that he could start a quarrel.

And when the barrator had disappeared,
    he turned his claws on his companion
    and grappled with him above the ditch.

But Alichino was a full-grown hawk
    for clawing him back, and both fell
    into the middle of the boiling pond.

The heat at once broke their grip,
    but there was no way for them to rise,
    since their wings were so beglued.   144

Barbariccia, complaining with the rest,
    had four fly to the other bank
    with all their hooks, and quickly

on this side and that they went to their places
    and reached with their grapples to those stuck
    and already partly cooked within the crust;

and while they were embarrassed in this way we left them.

CANTO XXIII

THE HYPOCRITES

The devils' fight over the pitch has reminded Dante of a fable which tells how a frog offers to tow a mouse tied to himself over a stream, intending to pull the rodent under. A kite, seeing their struggle, swoops down and carries off both.

Silent, alone, and without company
    we went on, one in front of the other,
    as minor friars go along their way.

My thought was turned to Aesop's fable
    by the present quarrel, where he speaks
    of the frog and of the mouse;

for "mo" and "issa" [synonyms for "now"] are not more alike
    if one compares with close attention
    the beginning and the end of each case.

And, as one thought bursts from another,
    there arose from that one a second
    which caused my first fear to be doubled.   12

I reflected thus: "Those devils through us
    are mocked with such scorn and damage
    as, I believe, must enrage them.

If anger is added to ill will,
    they will rush after us more fiercely
    than a hound after the rabbit he snaps up."

Already I felt my hair stand on end from fear,
    and I looked back intently and said,
    "Master, if you do not quickly hide

yourself and me, I fear the Malebranche;
    we already have them right behind us,
    I so imagine it that I can feel them now."   24

And he, "If I were leaded glass [a mirror]
    I would not reflect your outer image
    more quickly than I do your inner feelings.

Just now your thoughts were coming among mine
    similar to them in force and in meaning,
    so that of them all I made one resolve.

If it happens that the right bank lies
    so that we can go into the next ditch,
    we will escape the dreaded chase."

He had not finished giving this counsel
    when I saw the demons not far away
    coming with wings extended to seize us.   36

My guide suddenly took hold of me and,
    as a mother who is awakened by a noise
    and sees close to her the burning flames,

who takes her son and flees, caring more for him
    than for herself, and who does not stop
    even long enough to put on any clothes,

so, down from the edge of the hard bank,
    lying on his back, my guide slid over the rock
    which walls one side of the ditch.

Water never ran so fast through a sluice
    to turn a millwheel, at the moment
    when it is closest to the paddles,   48

as my master went down over the bank,
    carrying me upon his breast,
    not as a companion, but as a son.

Scarcely had his feet touched the bottom
    when the devils reached the height above us,
    but there was nothing to fear,

for High Providence, which wished to put them
    as ministers of the fifth ditch,
    took from all of them the power to leave.

> *The hypocrites whom the travelers now see wear gowns brilliant outwardly but of lead, like those Frederick II was supposed to have had melted on the backs of offenders against the throne. Like all who affect a pose, they must carry the weight of it forever. They move slowly, watching their steps. A kind of whining reproach sounds in their affected reference to Dante's and Virgil's clothes and to their "running." Not willing to commit themselves, they qualify the slightest promise with a "perhaps."*

Down there we found a painted people
    who moved around the circle with slow steps,
    weeping, and, in countenance, wearied and overcome.   60

They wore capes with low hoods coming down
    in front of their eyes, cut in the style
    of those worn by the monks of Cluny,

outwardly gilded, so that they dazzled,
    but within of lead, and so heavy
    that [in comparison] those Frederick used were of straw.

O mantle eternally tiring! We turned once more
    to the left, moving with the sinners
    and listening to their sad lament;

but, because of their loads, those weary people
    came so slowly that at every step we took
    we found ourselves in new company.   72

Therefore I said to my guide, "Try to find someone
    who by name or deed might be recognized,
    and look around as we move on."

And one who understood the Tuscan speech
    shouted from behind us, "Stay your steps,
    you who are running so through the dark air;

perhaps you will hear from me what you ask for."
My guide turned around and said,
"Wait, and then come on at his pace."

I stopped and saw two showing by their looks
great eagerness to be with me,
but their burden and the narrow way delayed them.   84

When they came up, with sidelong glances
they looked at me, without saying a word,
then turned to each other and remarked,

"This man, by the movement of his throat, seems alive,
and if they are both dead, by what privilege
do they go divested of the heavy gown?"

Then they addressed me, "O Tuscan, you who have come
to the college of the sad hypocrites,
do not disdain to tell us who you are."

And I to them, "I was born and grew up
by the beautiful Arno river, in the great city,
and I am in the body I have always had.   96

But who are you whose distilled grief
drips down over your cheeks,
and what punishment glitters so on you?"

*The two shades had been chosen as arbiters in the party strife of Florence instead
of the usual one man. Far from being neutral, they favored the Guelfs. As a
result certain houses of Ghibelline leaders near the old Gardingo fortress were
destroyed and the site was made into a public square.*

*One shade, new to Virgil, naked, like Christ at the Crucifixion, is lying on the
ground. This is Caiaphas, the high priest who, with others of the council of the
Jews, favored sacrificing Christ.*

And one answered, "The orange-colored mantles
are of lead, so thick that their weight
would make any scales creak.

We are Jolly Friars, and Bolognese,
I Catalano, and he, Loderingo,
appointed together by your city

(as a single man usually is taken)
to preserve the peace, and what we did
can still be seen around the Gardingo.   108

I began, "O Brothers, your evil . . ."
but I said no more, for the sight of a shade on the ground,
crucified with three stakes, caught my eye.

When he saw me he writhed all his body,
breathing into his beard with sighs,
and Friar Catalano who noticed that

said to me, "The transfixed one at whom you are looking
    counseled the Pharisees that it was fitting
    to torture one man for the people.[44]

Now he is lying crosswise and naked on the road,
    as you see; and he must feel
    the weight of each one who passes.   120

In a similar way his father-in-law is tortured
    in this ditch, and the others of the Council
    which was a seed of evil for the Jews."

Then I saw Virgil marveling
    over the one stretched out so basely,
    like a cross, in the eternal exile.

*Virgil learns of the humiliating trick played on him by the devils of the fifth
bolgia. The hypocrites are more expert in perceiving this deception than Reason
itself. In his usual indirect manner, not committing himself, Catalano points out
that the Devil tells lies. Virgil, angry at the trick and disgusted with Catalano,
moves on contemptuously, without a word.*

Afterward he addressed to the friar these words,
    "Please tell us, if you can,
    whether there is a gap on the right side

by which we two can get out of here
    without constraining the black angels
    to come and extricate us from this bottom."   132

He answered, "Nearer than you expect
    is a bridge which begins at the outer circle
    and covers all the cruel valleys,

except that over this one it is broken.
    You will be able to climb up on its ruins
    which slope down the side and pile up on the bottom."

My guide stood a moment with his head lowered,
    then said, "Falsely did the one up there
    who hooks the sinners explain the matter."

And the friar added, "I once heard someone say at Bologna
    that the Devil has many vices, among which I heard
    that he is a liar and the father of lies."   144

Then with long steps my guide went on,
    a little disturbed in his looks by anger,
    and I also departed from the burdened ones,

following the imprints of the beloved feet.

---

[44] For the roles of Caiaphas and his father-in-law Annas in Jesus' passion, see John 11
and 18.

CANTO XXIV

Vanni Fucci

A dainty comparison takes us for a moment into the fresh air of late winter when the nights are beginning to get shorter and when the frost resembles for a while the snow.

The poets struggle laboriously to get out of the ditch of hypocrisy.

In that part of the young year
    when the sun warms his locks beneath Aquarius
    and the long nights are moving toward the south,

when the frost copies on the ground
    the image of her white sister
    although the point of her pen lasts but little,

the poor peasant whose fodder is getting low
    rises, looks out, and sees the fields all white;
    whereupon he strikes his thigh,

turns back and, lamenting, walks up and down
    like a wretch who does not know what to do.
    Later he looks out again and recovers hope   12

on seeing that the world, in a little while,
    has changed appearance; and he takes his crook
    and drives forth the lambs to feed.

Thus my master made me disheartened
    when I saw his face so troubled,
    and thus quickly to the sore the plaster came.

For, when we reached the ruins of the bridge
    my guide turned to me with that pleasant look
    which I saw first at the foot of the mountain.

He opened his arms, after having made a plan
    within his mind, and looking carefully
    at the rocks he took hold of me,   24

and like one who calculates while working,
    who always seems to provide ahead of time,
    on lifting me toward the top of one rock

he examined another crag, saying,
    "Afterward catch hold of that,
    but see first if it will bear your weight."

It was not a way for one clothed in a leaden cloak,
    for we, he a shade and I pushed,
    could hardly mount from jag to jag.

And were it not that on this side
    the slope was shorter than on the other,
    I do not know about him, but I would have been exhausted;   36

but, since Malebolge slopes wholly
    toward the edge of the lowest well,
    the position of each ditch demands

that one side be higher than the other.
    We came finally to the place
    where the last stone is broken off.

The breath had been so pumped from my lungs
    as I went up that at the top
    I could go no farther, and sat down at once.

"Now you must free yourself from sloth,"
    my master said, "for, sitting on down
    or lying under covers, no one comes to fame,   48

without which whoever consumes his life
    leaves such vestige of himself on earth
    as smoke in air or foam on water.

Therefore get up, overcome your panting
    with the spirit which wins every battle
    if it does not sink with its heavy body.

A longer stairs must be climbed;
    it is not enough to have left this one;
    if you understand, act so that it may profit you."

I then got up showing myself better furnished
    with breath than I was, and I said,
    "Go on, for I am strong and bold."   60

The travelers now come to the ditch of the thieves.

We made our way up over the bridge
    which was rocky, narrow, and difficult,
    and much steeper than the previous ones.

I kept talking in order not to appear faint;
    whereupon from the next ditch a voice issued
    unsuited for forming words.

I do not know what it said, although I was already
    on top of the arch that crosses there,
    but whoever spoke seemed moved to anger.

I had turned to look down, but my living eyes
    could not penetrate to the bottom
    through the darkness; therefore I said,   72

"Master, let us try to reach the next bank,
    for, just as I hear, but do not understand,
    so I look, and can distinguish nothing."

"No reply do I make except by an act,"
    he said, "for a modest request
    should be followed silently by the deed."

We went down the bridge to the place
    where it joins the eighth bank,
    and then the ditch was revealed to me.

I saw in it a terrible pack of serpents
    of such diverse appearance
    that the memory of it still chills my blood.   84

Let Libya with its sands boast no longer,
    for if it produced chelydri, jaculi, and phareae,
    and cencri with amphisbaena [fabulous snakes],

it has never shown so many plagues
    or such bad ones, together with all of Ethiopia
    and the land [Arabia] which lies above the Red Sea.

Amid this cruel and dismal swarm, I saw people running,
    naked and terrified, without hope of hiding place
    or of heliotrope [to make themselves invisible].

Their hands were tied behind them by serpents
    which stuck their heads and tails through their backs,
    and were knotted together in front.   96

And behold! at one that was near our bank
    a serpent sprang and transfixed him
    right where the neck meets the shoulders.

Neither I nor O was ever written so quickly
    as he took fire and burned and fell
    like a cinder to the ground.

Then when he was thus destroyed
    the ashes came together of themselves
    and took on instantly the previous form.

Thus it is maintained by great sages
    that the Phoenix[45] dies and then is reborn
    when the five-hundredth year approaches.   108

During its life it feeds on neither grain
    nor herb, but on incense and amomum,
    and nard and myrrh make up its shroud.

And like one [an epileptic] who falls not knowing how,
    through the force of a demon pulling him to the ground
    or through some obstruction that paralyzes him,

and who, when he gets up, looks around, all bewildered
    by the great anguish he has suffered,
    and while looking sighs,

such was the sinner after he arose.
    O Power of God, how severe it is
    in showering down such blows of vengeance!   120

---

[45] The mythical bird that was consumed in fire every 500 years and then arose to new life from the ashes of its dead self.

The stricken soul is Vanni Fucci, one of Dante's former political enemies, whom the poet had known, not as a thief, but only as hotheaded and violent. Vanni predicts obscurely and maliciously certain events which will lead to the defeat of the Florentine Whites.

My guide then asked the sinner who he was;
    whereupon he answered, "I rained down from
    Tuscany into this gullet a little while ago.

A bestial, not human life, I liked,
    mule [of irregular birth] that I was; I am Vanni Fucci,
    a beast, and Pistoia was a den worthy of me."

I said to my guide, "Tell him not to slip away
    and ask what sin thrusts him down here,
    for I saw him once a man of blood and rage."

And the soul, having heard, did not dissemble,
    but directed toward me his face
    and his attention with a look of dismal shame.   132

Then he said, "It grieves me more
    that you have caught me in this misery
    than when I was taken from the other world.

I cannot deny what you ask for;
    I have been put down this far for the theft
    of the fine ornaments of the sacristy,

for which another was falsely accused.
    But to keep you from enjoying this sight,
    if you ever get out of this dark place,

open your ears to my prophecy and hear:
    Pistoia first is thinned of Blacks,
    then Florence renews her masters and her ways;   144

Mars draws a fiery vapor [thunderbolt] from Val di Magra
    which is wrapped in turbid clouds,
    and in an impetuous and angry storm

a battle will be fought on the Piceno field;
    then the blast will pierce the mist
    so that every White will be wounded by it.

And I have told you this so that you may grieve."

CANTO XXV

The Metamorphosis of Thieves

At the end of his remarks the thief
    raised both hands, making the [obscene] sign of the fig,
    and shouting, "Take that, God, for at Thee I point them!"

From then on the serpents were my friends,
    for one coiled around his neck, as if saying,
    "I will not have you speak any more,"

and another encircled his arms and bound them,
    so clinching itself in front
    that he could not make a move with those members.

Ah, Pistoia, why do you not resolve to burn
    so that you will last no longer, since you surpass
    your own founders [followers of Catiline] in wickedness?   12

Through all the dark circles of Hell
    I saw no spirit so bold against God,
    not even him [Capaneus] who fell from the walls of Thebes.

The thief fled, saying nothing further.
    Then I saw a centaur, full of wrath, come calling,
    "Where is he? Where is the impious one?"

I do not believe Maremma has as many snakes
    as the centaur had on its back
    up to where our human form begins.

Upon his shoulders, behind his neck,
    a dragon was lying with open wings
    which set on fire all it met.   24

My master said, "That is Cacus [a fire-breathing monster]
    who, under the rocks of Mount Aventine,
    many times made a lake of blood.

He does not go on the same road as his brothers
        [the other centaurs]
    because of the theft he slyly made
    of the great herd [of cattle] kept near him,

which led to the end of his wicked life
    under the club of Hercules, who gave him
    perhaps a hundred blows, although hardly ten were felt."

While Virgil was saying this, the centaur ran off,
    and three spirits [Agnello, Buoso, and Puccio] came below us
    whom neither my master nor I had noticed   36

until they cried, "Who are you?"
    Whereupon our talking ceased,
    and we gave heed to them alone.

I did not recognize them, but it happened
    as sometimes occurs by chance
    that one needed to name the other,

saying, "Where can Cianfa [now a serpent] have remained?"
    In order to make my guide attentive,
    I held my finger against my mouth from chin to nose.

If you are slow, Reader, to believe
    what I am to relate, it will be no wonder,
    for I who saw it scarcely admit it to myself.   48

As I kept my eyes on them, a serpent [Cianfa]
    with six legs darted in front of one
    and fastened itself wholly to him.

With its middle feet it clasped his belly
    and with those in front seized his arms;
    then it set its fangs in both his cheeks.

It spread its hind feet over his thighs
    and thrust its tail between them
    drawing it up along his back.

Ivy never clung to a tree so tightly
    as the horrible beast
    entwined the other's members in its own;   60

then they grew together and exchanged their color
    as if they had been hot wax,
    nor did either one or the other appear as before.

Thus a dark hue moves ahead of a flame
    over a sheet of paper, as the whiteness
    dies away before it becomes black.

The other two [Buoso and Puccio] watched and shouted,
    "O me, Agnello, how you are changing!
    Behold! You are now neither two nor one."

The two heads had already fused into one,
    and the shapes of two faces appeared blended
    in the one in which the others had disappeared.   72

The two arms were formed of four strips;
    the thighs with the legs, the belly and the chest,
    became such members as were never seen.

All the former features were blotted out;
    the perverse image seemed two and none,
    and thus went away with slow steps.

As a lizard, under the great scourge
    of the dog days, passing from hedge to hedge,
    seems a flash as it crosses the path,

so appeared, making for the bellies
    of the remaining two, a small, fiery serpent,
    livid and black as a peppercorn,   84

and pierced that part in one of them
    where we first receive our nourishment;
    then fell, stretched out, in front of him.

The one transfixed [Buoso] looked at it, silently,
    and with feet motionless, yawned,
    as if sleep or a fever had come upon him.

He eyed the reptile, and the reptile him;
    from the wound of one and mouth of the other
    thick smoke issued and combined.

Let Lucan be silent now where he tells
    of poor Sabellus and of Nasidius [transformed by serpents],
    and wait to hear what is announced.   96

Let Ovid keep still concerning Cadmus and Arethusa,
    for if he changes one into a serpent in his verse
    and the other into a spring, I do not envy him,

since he never changed two natures
    face to face so that both forms
    were ready to exchange their substance.

The two responded to each other in such a way
    that the serpent made a fork of its tail,
    and the wounded shade drew its feet together.

The legs and the thighs united,
    so that in a little while there was no sign
    you could see of the joining.   108

The split tail took on the shape
    lost in the other; the skin of one became soft
    and that of the other hard.

I saw the arms withdraw through the armpits
    and the short legs of the reptile
    lengthen as much as the other's arms were shortened.

Then the hind feet, twisted together,
    became the member man hides,
    and the shade from his made two legs project.

As the smoke covered both with a new color
    it brought out hair on one
    and removed it from the other.   120

One got up and the other fell,
    neither, however, turning aside his gaze
    under which each had changed faces.

The one standing drew his snout toward his temples,
    and with the flesh left over
    ears were formed on the smooth cheeks.

What was not drawn back and remained
    in excess made a nose for the face
    and thickened the lips to a fit size.

The one on the ground stretched forth his nose,
    withdrew his ears within his head,
    as a snail does its horns,   132

and his tongue which had been undivided
    and apt for speech, split; and the forked tongue
    united; then the smoke stopped.

The soul that had become a brute
    fled hissing through the ditch,
    and after it the other, talking and sputtering.

Then he turned his new back to the reptile
    and said, "I want Buoso to run
    as I have, crawling over the way."

Thus I saw the seventh ballast change
    and interchange, and let the strangeness of it
    be my excuse if my pen has gone astray.   144

Although my eyes were somewhat confused
    and my mind bewildered, those shades
    could not slip away so secretly

that I did not recognize easily
    Puccio Sciancato, who was the only one
    of the three companions left unchanged.

The unidentified figure (originally the second snake) was Francesco de' Cavalcanti, killed by the people of Gaville. The town mourns because of the vengeance taken for him.

The other was he because of whom you, Gaville, weep.

CANTO XXVI

ULYSSES

The bitter tone of the beginning lines of an apostrophe to Florence ends quickly when Dante thinks of the misfortune certain to come to his city, a disaster wished for by neighboring towns, like Prato, not to mention enemies. Here, as elsewhere, the invective expresses deep concern, a kind of inverted love.

Rejoice, Florence, since you are so great
    that over land and over sea you beat your wings,
    and your name is famous in Hell!

Among the thieves I found five citizens of yours,
    such that shame comes over me;
    and you do not rise through them to great honor.

But if the truth is dreamed of near the morning,
    you will soon feel what Prato,
    not to mention others, craves for you.

And if that had already happened, it would not be
    too soon; so were it, since it has to be!
    for it will weigh heavier on me as I grow older.   12

> *The poets reach the summit of the bridge over the bolgia where evil counseling is*
> *punished. This sin, incurred mainly by those of superior intelligence, offered*
> *constant temptations to Dante, an exile dependent upon patronage.*
>
> *In the ditch below, lights appear, like fireflies at dusk on a summer evening. And*
> *just as Elisha saw Elijah rise up, enveloped in a cloud of flame, so here the fire*
> *concealed the spirits. Dante asks about a double flame, like that on the funeral*
> *pyre of Eteocles and Polynices, two brothers who had killed each other.*

We departed, and over the steps
    which stones had made for our descent,
    my guide remounted, and drew me up,

and continuing our solitary way
    over the stones and rocks of the bridge,
    feet did not advance without help from hands.

I grieved then, and now I grieve again
    when I direct my thought to what I saw,
    and I control my mind more than usual

so that virtue alone may guide it.
    Thus, if a kindly star or something better [Divine Grace]
    has given an advantage, it may not be harmful through abuse.   24

As a peasant who is resting on a slope
    in the season when the sun that lights the world
    keeps his face least hidden from us—

at the hour when gnats take the place of flies—
    sees fireflies down below in the valley,
    perhaps where he gathers grapes or plows;

so, with as many flames the eighth bolgia
    was all resplendent, as I noticed
    when I came to where I could see the bottom.

And, as he [Elisha] who avenged himself with the bears
    saw the chariot of Elijah depart
    when the horses rose erect to Heaven[46]—   36

for he could not follow so closely with his eyes
    that he could see anything except the flame itself,
    like a little cloud rising upward—

so each light moved through the ditch,
    none revealing what it hid,
    and yet each concealed a sinner.

[46] For the ascent of Elijah to Heaven and the story of Elisha's revenge on some children
who taunted him for his baldness (they were attacked by bears), see 2 Kings 2.

I was standing on the bridge leaning out to see,
    so that if I had not held to a rock,
    without being pushed I would have fallen,

and my guide, who saw me so attentive, said,
    "Within the fires are the spirits;
    each is wrapped in what is burning him."   48

"Master," I answered, "through hearing you
    I am more certain, but already I was aware
    that this was so, and wished to ask

who is in the fire which comes so divided at the top
    that it seems to rise from the pyre
    on which Eteocles was placed with his brother."

> *Ulysses and Diomed, in the double flame, are guilty on three counts: (1) the trick of the Trojan horse, which led to the destruction of Troy and the founding of Rome; (2) enticing Achilles to abandon Deidamia and to leave for the Trojan wars, and (3) the theft of the Palladium, a statue of Pallas on which the fate of Troy depended.*

He answered, "In that flame Ulysses and Diomed
    are tortured, and thus they go together
    in punishment as in their battles.

They groan within their flame for the ambush
    of the horse which was the portal
    through which came the noble ancestors of the Romans.[47]   60

Also they weep for the art on account of which
    Deidamia still grieves for Achilles,
    and they suffer too for the Palladium."

"If they can speak within those fires," I said,
    "Master, I beg you earnestly, and beg again
    (and may my prayer be worth a thousand),

that you do not deny our waiting
    until the horned flame comes here;
    you see how my desire bends me toward it!"

And he to me, "Your request is worthy
    of praise; therefore I grant it,
    but see that your tongue keeps silent.   72

Let me speak, for I have conceived
    what you want to know. Since they were Greeks,
    they might shy away from your words."

---

[47] The story of the Trojan horse is told in Virgil's *Aeneid*, Book II. The Greeks besieging Troy built a large wooden horse and concealed a band of troops inside it; the deluded Trojans brought it into their city, which was then destroyed by the Greeks. The exiled Trojans wandered to Italy, where their descendants founded Rome.

When Virgil, who had celebrated Ulysses in the Aeneid, *asks about his death, the latter, the representative of the spirit of adventure and of scientific discovery, answers with great dignity and relevance, pointing out how compelling was his desire for knowledge of the two worlds of things and of men. In the story Dante invents, instead of returning to Penelope and the comforts of home, Ulysses sails westward through the Mediterranean, then past Gibraltar, and out on the vast and terrifying Atlantic. His course, like that of Columbus almost two centuries after Dante, is west-southwest. Five months pass; the crew of old men see the constellations of the other hemisphere; then land (probably the island of Purgatory) appears. But a storm arises, and Ulysses ends his life in the glory of a last adventure.*

When the flame had come to where
    time and place seemed best to my guide,
    I heard him speak in these terms:

"O you two within one fire,
    if I merited thanks from you while I lived,
    if I deserved much or little

when in the world I wrote the lofty verses,[48]
    do not move, but let one of you tell
    where, lost, he went to die."   84

The greater horn of the ancient flame
    began to shake, murmuring like a fire
    struggling in the wind,

then moving the tip here and there,
    as if it were a tongue speaking,
    it formed words, and said:

"When I left Circe who detained me
    more than a year near Gaeta
    before Aeneas had named it thus,

neither fondness for my son, nor pity
    for an old father, nor the love for Penelope
    which should have made her happy,   96

could overcome in me the desire I had
    to gain experience of the world
    and of the vices and the worth of men.

I set out on the high, open sea,
    with only one ship, and with that little company
    by which I was not deserted.

Both coasts I saw as far as Spain,
    down to Morocco and the island of Sardinia,
    and the others that are bathed in that sea.

I and my companions were old and slow
    when we came to that narrow pass [Gibraltar]
    where Hercules set up his landmarks   108

[48] Dante had not read Homer's *Odyssey*. (Ulysses is the Latin name for Odysseus.)

so that men should not venture beyond.
> On the right I left Seville,
> and on the other side had already passed Ceuta.

'O brothers,' I said; 'you who
> through a thousand perils have come to the West,
> to the brief vigil of our senses

which is left, do not deny
> experience of the unpeopled world
> to be discovered by following the sun.

Consider what origin you had;
> you were not created to live like brutes,
> but to seek virtue and knowledge.'   120

With this little speech I made my companions
> so eager for the journey
> that scarcely then could I have held them back,

and, having turned our stern to the morning,
> we made wings of our oars for the mad flight,
> always gaining on the left.

The night already saw the stars
> of the other pole, and ours [the North Star] so low
> it did not rise from the ocean floor.

Five times the light upon the moon
> had shone and been extinguished
> since we started on the deep way,   132

when a mount appeared to us,
> dim in the distance, and which seemed
> higher than any I had ever seen.

We rejoiced; but soon our joy changed to sorrow,
> for, from the new land a whirlwind arose
> which struck the prow of our ship.

Three times it made it whirl with all the water;
> the fourth time it lifted high the stern
> and made the prow go down as pleased Another [God],

until at last the sea closed over us."

CANTO XXVII

GUIDO DA MONTEFELTRO

*A second flame roars like the brass statue of a bull in which prisoners were
burned alive. This instrument of torture was made for a tyrant of Agrigentum
and was tried out first on its inventor. The flame contains the soul of Guido da
Montefeltro, a famous Ghibelline leader referred to in the* Convivio *as "our most
noble Italian." Guido enquires about Romagna, and Dante outlines briefly the
conditions in that region, designating the various rulers by their armorial bearings.*

Already the flame was erect and quiet,
    having ended its speech, and was going from us
    with the leave of the dear Poet,

when another flame that came behind it
    made us turn our eyes to its tip
    because of a confused sound issuing from it.

As the Sicilian bull which roared first
    with the groans of the one who made it
    with his tools (and that was right)

bellowed with the voice of the tortured
    in such a way that, although it was of brass,
    it seemed transfixed with pain,   12

so, not having any opening or outlet
    from their source in the fire,
    the doleful words were transformed into its language.

After they had found their way
    up through the tip, giving it the vibration
    the tongue had imparted to them,

we heard it say, "O you to whom I direct my voice,
    and who were speaking Lombard just now,
    saying, 'Now go, further I do not urge you,'

although I have perhaps arrived somewhat late,
    do not be displeased to speak with me;
    you see it does not irk me, and I burn!   24

If you have just now fallen into this blind world
    from that sweet Latin land
    from which I bring all my sin,

tell me if the Romagnuols have peace or war,
    for I was from the mountains there
    between Urbino and the peak from which the Tiber comes."

I was still attentive and bent down
    when my leader nudged me, saying,
    "*You* speak, this is an Italian."

And I, having already prepared my reply,
    began without delay, "O soul,
    you who are hidden down there,   36

your Romagna is not and never was
    without strife in the hearts of its tyrants,
    but no open warfare did I leave there just now.

Ravenna stands as it has for many years,
    the eagle of Polenta brooding over it,
    and covering Cervia with its pinions.

The city [Forlì] which once bore the long siege,
    and made a bloody heap of the French,
    finds itself under the green claws [the Ordelaffi family].

The old and young mastiffs of Verrucchio [the Malatestas]
    who disposed badly of Mantagna [their prisoner],
    as usual, make an auger of their teeth.   48

The cities on the Lamone and the Santerno
    are ruled by the young lion in the white lair
        [Maghinardo da Susinana]
    who, from summer to winter, changes party.

And the city [Cesena] whose side the Savio bathes,
    as it lies between the mountain and the plain,
    lives [under party bosses] between tyranny and freedom.

Now I beg you to tell us who you are;
    do not be more reluctant than another has been;
    so may your name stay proudly in the world."

> *After a successful military career, Guido da Montefeltro withdrew from the world
> and joined the Franciscan order, hoping to make amends for the sins inseparable
> from military life and to prepare securely for the future world. His plan might
> have succeeded except for the pope, Boniface VIII, who asked him by what faith-
> less stratagem he might defeat his enemies, offering absolution in advance for the
> evil counsel. Obliged either to comply or to disobey his superior, Guido chose what
> seemed (to a soldier) the lesser evil, and told how the pope might, through treach-
> ery, secure Palestrina, the stronghold of his enemies.*

After the flame had roared a while in its manner,
    the sharp tip moved to and fro,
    and breathed forth this sound: 60

"If I believed that my reply were to anyone
    who would ever return to the world,
    this flame would remain quiet,

but since no one from this ditch
    has ever returned alive, if I hear the truth,
    I will answer without fear of infamy.

I was a man of arms, and then a Cordelier,
    believing, thus girt, to make amends;
    and certainly my intent would have been realized

except for the Great Priest (may ill befall him!)
    who put me back into my former sins;
    and how and why I want you to hear.   72

While I had the form of the flesh and bones
    my mother gave me, my deeds
    were not lionlike, but those of a fox.

The tricks and the secret ways,
    I knew them all, and so carried on their art
    that my fame spread to the ends of the earth.

When I saw that I had reached
    that point in life when everyone
    should lower sail and coil his ropes,

what first had pleased me became repugnant
    and, having repented and confessed, I gave myself to God,
    and alas! that should have availed.   84

The Prince of the new Pharisees [Boniface VIII],
    waging war close to the Lateran—
    and not with Saracens or with Jews,

for every enemy of his was a Christian,
    and none had been a renegade at Acre
    or a merchant in the Sultan's land—

considered neither his high office
    and sacred orders, nor in me that cord I wore
    which used to make those bound with it thinner.

But, as Constantine called upon Sylvester[49]
    in Soracte to cure him of his leprosy,
    so he called me, as his physician,   96

to cure the fever of his pride.
    He asked advice of me, and I kept silent,
    because his words seemed drunken,

and then he said, "Do not let your heart mistrust,
    right now I absolve you; let me know
    how to cast Palestrina to the ground.

I can open and close Heaven,
    as you know, since two are the keys
    that my predecessor [Celestine V] did not hold dear."[50]

The heavy arguments brought me to where
    silence seemed worse to me than complying,
    and I said, 'Father, since you wash away   108

the sin into which I now must fall,
    long promise with short fulfillment
    will make you triumph on your lofty seat.'

*At Guido's death, St. Francis came for him, but a "black Cherub" from the eighth
circle of Hell, the counterpart of those of the eighth heaven who likewise operate*

---

[49] For Constantine and Sylvester, see XIX.115–17, the translator's gloss, and the note.
Sylvester, according to legend, cured Constantine by baptizing him, in return for which Constantine yielded up the western part of the Roman empire.
[50] For Celestine V, see III.59–60 and translator's gloss.

through intelligence, objected, and pointed out the impossibility of absolution in advance.

Dante uses this extreme example to emphasize the point that salvation depends on the state of the soul at the moment of death. A similar contest, related in Purgatory, occurs in the case of Guido's son, but in almost exactly opposite circumstances.

When I was dead, Francis came for me,
 but one of the black Cherubim said to him,
 'Don't take him, don't wrong me.

He must come down among my minions
 because he gave the fraudulent advice,
 since when I have been lurking to grasp his hair.

For one who does not repent cannot be absolved,
 nor can *repenting* and *willing* go together
 because the contradiction does not allow it.'   120

Ah, wretched me, how I shuddered
 when he seized me, saying,
 'Perhaps you did not think I was a logician!'

To Minos he brought me, who twisted his tail
 eight times around his stiff back,
 and after he had bitten it in his rage, he said,

'This is one for the thievish fire.'
 Therefore I am lost here as you see,
 and while moving, clothed in fire, I grieve."

When he had finished speaking
 the sorrowing spirit went on
 twisting and shaking his sharp flame.   132

My guide and I passed over the bridge
 to the top of the next arch
 which crosses the ditch in which a fee is paid

by those who get a burden by dividing [sowing discord].

CANTO XXVIII

THE SOWERS OF DISCORD

If it were possible to bring together the wounded on the battlegrounds of southern Italy in the long series of wars from ancient times down to the Norman invasions and the wars of Charles of Anjou against Manfred, the scene would be similar to that of the ninth bolgia.

Who even in unrhymed words [prose]
 could ever fully tell in many narrations
 of the blood and of the wounds I now saw?

Every tongue certainly would fail
    because our language and our memories
    are insufficient to contain so much.

If all the soldiers were assembled
    who, on the stormy fields of Apulia,
    have groaned for their blood

shed by Trojans, and in the long [Punic] war
    which made so vast a spoil of rings
        [from fingers of dead Romans],
    as Livy writes, who does not err,   12

together with those who suffered painful wounds
    by opposing Robert Guiscard [the Norman conqueror]
    and others whose bones are still piled up

at Ceperano, where every Apulian [allied with Manfred]
    was a traitor, and at Tagliacozzo
    where old Alardo conquered without arms [by strategy],

and were one to show his limbs pierced,
    another his cut off, the view would not equal
    the awful sight of the ninth ditch.

Mahomet, the first shade recognized, had been considered as originally a Christian and as the deliberate cause of the separation of the world into two monotheistic faiths. Mahomet mentions prophetically and with malicious pleasure Fra Dolcino, the leader of a heretical sect who, besieged in 1306, was forced by hunger to surrender.

Indeed, a cask without a stave or endboard
    looks less mutilated than one I saw
    split from his chin down to where wind is broken.   24

His entrails hung between his legs,
    the vital parts appeared with the foul sack
    which makes excrement of what is swallowed.

While I was intently looking at him,
    he gazed at me, and with his hands opened his breast,
    saying, "Now see how I tear myself,

see how mangled Mahomet is!
    In front of me Ali [a son-in-law] goes weeping,
    his head split from chin to forelock;

and all the others you see here
    while alive were sowers of scandal and of schism
    and therefore are split like this.   36

A devil is here behind us who cuts us
    thus cruelly with the edge of his sword,
    reopening all the wounds

when we have gone around the doleful road,
    since they are healed
    before we come again before him.

But who are you, dallying on the bridge,
    perhaps to delay going to your punishment
    decreed upon your own confession?"

"Not yet has death come to him, nor does guilt
    bring him to torment," my master said,
    "but to give him complete experience,   48

I, who am dead, must take him
    down here from round to round, and this
    is as true as that I am speaking to you."

More than a hundred in the ditch,
    when they heard this, stopped to look at me,
    forgetting their pain in their marveling.

"Now tell Fra Dolcino, you who perhaps
    will soon see the sun again, that unless he wants
    to follow me he had better provide himself

with food, so that the snow
    will not bring victory to the Novarese,
    which otherwise would be hard for them to gain."   60

After he had lifted one foot to go
    Mahomet said these words to me,
    then placed it on the ground, moving on.

> *Pier da Medicina, another schismatic of whom little is known, adds the prophecy*
> *of the death of two citizens of Fano who will be called to a parley and treacher-*
> *ously thrown overboard. They will not need the usual protection from the squalls*
> *of Focara, since they will never reach that place. Then Curio is mentioned who*
> *from private motives urged Caesar to cross the Rubicon and begin the civil war.*
> *He wishes now he had never seen the town of Rimini near that river. Another*
> *sower of discord, Mosca, according to tradition advised the killing of an oppo-*
> *nent to settle a feud rather than a milder punishment, since that, he thought,*
> *would end the matter. Instead, the murder led to the first conflict between the*
> *Guelfs and Ghibellines in Florence. On seeing Mosca, Dante's Florentine spirit*
> *flares up, and he tells him of the banishment of his family, the Lamberti, from the*
> *city.*

Another who had his throat cut
    and his nose severed up to his eyebrows,
    and who had only a single ear,

having stopped to look with wonder,
    before the others cleared his windpipe
    which was all red outside, and said,

"O you whom sin does not condemn
    and whom I have seen in the Latin land,
    if too much resemblance does not deceive me,   72

recall to mind Pier da Medicina
    if ever you go back to see the sweet plain
    which from Vercelli slopes to Marcabò,

and make known to the two best men of Fano,
    to Messer Guido and to Angiolello,
    that, unless foresight here is vain,

they will be thrown from their ship
    and drowned near La Cattolica
    through the treachery of a base tyrant.

Between the islands of Cyprus and Majorca,
    Neptune has never seen so great a crime
    of pirates or of Argolic people [Greeks].   84

That traitor who sees with one eye only [Malatestino]
    and holds the city [Rimini] which someone here [Curio]
    would wish never to have seen,

will have them come for a parley with him,
    and will act so that to allay Focara's wind,
    they will need neither vow nor prayer."

And I to him, "Point out and tell me
    if you want me to take news of you above,
    who found the sight of that city bitter?"

Then he laid his hand on the jaw
    of one of his companions, and opened his mouth,
    saying, "This is he, and he does not speak.   96

While exiled, he quieted Caesar's fears,
    affirming that a man well prepared
    always loses by any delay."

Oh, how dismayed he seemed to me
    with his tongue cut in his throat,
    Curio, who before spoke so boldly!

And one who had both hands cut off,
    lifting the stumps in the dark air
    so that the blood dirtied his face,

cried, "Remember also Mosca
    who said, alas, 'A thing done has an end,'
    which was a seed of evil for the Tuscans."   108

And I added, "And death to your kindred,"
    whereupon he, heaping grief on grief,
    went off like one maddened by sorrow.

The last example is that of the Provençal poet Bertran de Born, who, Dante
believed, had fomented a quarrel between Henry, the "young English king," and
his father.

But I remained to look at the throng,
   and I saw a thing I would fear
   to tell about without more proof,

except that conscience reassures me,
   the good companion which emboldens man
   under the breastplate of conscious innocence.

I saw certainly, and I still seem to see
   a body without a head, going on
   like the others of the sad troop.   120

It held by the hair its severed head
   dangling from its hand like a lantern,
   which looked at us and said, "Woe is me!"

Of itself it made a lamp for itself,
   and they were two in one and one in two;
   how this can be He knows who so ordains.

When it was at the foot of the bridge,
   it lifted the head high with its arm
   to bring the words closer to me,

which were, "Now see my terrible penalty,
   you who, breathing, are visiting the dead;
   judge if any is as great as this.   132

And, that you may take news of me,
   know that I am Bertran de Born, the one
   who gave the young king the evil encouragement.

I made father and son rebellious to each other;
   Ahithophel did not do worse to Absalom
   and to David with his wicked plots.[51]

Because I separated persons thus joined,
   I now carry my brain, alas,
   detached from its source in this body.

Thus retribution is observed in me."

CANTO XXIX

THE FALSIFIERS

Fascinated by the sight of the horrible wounds, Dante keeps looking at them and incurs a reproach. He excuses himself (he is growing up in his relationship with his master) by mentioning that he believed that a relative was there, Geri del Bello, whose violent death had not been avenged. Dante pities Geri, perhaps for the latter's obvious adherence even here to the code of family vengeance.

---

[51] For Absalom's rebellion, incited by Ahithophel (or Achitophel), against his father King David, see 2 Samuel 14–18.

The time, as usual in Hell, is indicated by the position of the moon: it is now
shortly after noon on Saturday.

The great crowd and the diverse wounds
    had made my eyes so inebriated
    that they were eager to remain and weep.

But Virgil said, "What are you looking at?
    Why does your sight still rest down there
    on the sad, mutilated shades?

You have not done so at the other ditches.
    Consider, if you wish to count them,
    that the valley circles for twenty-two miles;

already the moon is under our feet;
    the time granted to us now is short,
    and there is much more to see."   12

"If you had taken note," I answered then,
    "of the cause that made me look,
    perhaps you would have granted me a longer stay."

Meanwhile my guide kept going on
    and I followed, making my reply
    and adding, "Within that hollow

on which I kept my eyes fixed so closely
    I believe a spirit of my own blood
    laments the sin that costs so much down here."

Then my master said, "From now on
    do not let your thoughts be distracted by him;
    attend to something else and let him stay there,   24

for I saw him at the foot of the little bridge
    pointing you out and threatening you with his finger,
    and I heard him called Geri del Bello.

You were then so completely occupied
    with him [Bertran de Born] who once held Altaforte
    that you did not look over there, and he departed."

"O my guide, his death by violence
    which has not yet been avenged," I said,
    "by [relatives] the partners of his shame,

made him indignant; therefore he went off
    without speaking to me, as I judge,
    and by that he has made me pity him the more."   36

The shades in the tenth bolgia are divided into four groups: falsifiers (1) of
metals (alchemists), punished by leprosy and paralysis; (2) of persons (impersona-
tors), punished by delirium or madness; (3) of coins (counterfeiters), afflicted
with dropsy; and (4) of words (liars), suffering from high fever. Dante treats
them with mild and amused contempt.

Thus we talked as far as to the point
    which would have shown the next ditch
    to the bottom if there had been more light.

Then, when we were above
    the last cloister of Malebolge, so that
    its lay brothers could be observed by us,

diverse laments kept striking me
    which had their arrows barbed with such pity
    that I covered my ears with my hands.

Such suffering as there would be if the sick
    in the hospitals of Valdichiana, Maremma, and Sardinia
    [malarious regions] between July and September   48

were all together in one ditch,
    was here; and such stench issued
    as comes from festered limbs.

We descended to the last bank of the long bridge,
    still keeping to the left,
    and then my sight was clearer

down toward the bottom, where the minister
    of the Supreme Lord, Infallible Justice,
    punishes the falsifiers registered here.

I do not believe there was greater sadness
    to see all the people of Aegina sick
    when the air was so full of pestilence   60

that the animals, even to the little worm,
    fell dead—and then the ancient people,
    as the poets hold as true,

were restored by the seed of ants[52]—
    than it was to see in the dark ditch
    the spirits languish in diverse heaps.

One lay upon the belly and one upon the shoulders
    of another, and one on all fours
    was crawling along the dismal path.

Step by step we went without speaking,
    observing and listening to the sick,
    who could not lift their bodies.   72

I saw two sitting, leaning on each other
    as stewpan is propped against stewpan to warm,
    spotted with scabs from head to foot,

---

[52] Juno inflicted on Aegina a plague that destroyed all living creatures except one man, Aeacus, at whose prayer Jupiter repopulated the island by changing ants into human beings. The story is told by Ovid.

and never have I seen a currycomb handled so quickly
    by a stable boy whose master was waiting for him
    or by one staying up against his will

as each of these plied the clawing of his nails
    on himself, because of the great rage
    of itching that had no other help;

and the nails scraped off the scabs
    as a knife does the scales from bream
    or some other fish that has them larger.   84

"O you who disarm yourself with your fingers,
    at times making pincers of them,"
    my guide began to say to one of them,

"tell us if any Latin is among those
    who are here; so may your nails
    suffice eternally for this work!"

"We are both Latins whom you see
    so disfigured here," one answered, weeping,
    "but who are you, asking about us?"

My guide replied, "I am one descending
    with this *live* man from ledge to ledge,
    and I intend to show Hell to him."   96

Then the mutual support broke,
    and each of them, trembling, turned to me,
    with others who had overheard the words.

My good master drew close to me, saying,
    "Ask them what you want to know."
    And I began to speak as he desired:

"So may your memory not fade
    from human minds in the first world,
    but may it live on for many suns,

tell me who you are, and of what people;
    let not your ugly and annoying punishment
    make you afraid to reveal yourselves to me."   108

> *Griffolino, a fraudulent alchemist, tells how he was burned by the presumptive*
> *father of the simple-minded Albero da Siena, who had taken seriously his remarks*
> *about flying. This prompts Dante to speak of the Sienese whose sometimes aristo-*
> *cratic folly was a standing joke in the bourgeois atmosphere of Florence. Dante is*
> *helped in his gibes by Capocchio, who mentions ironically the notorious spend-*
> *thrift Stricca and the "Spendthrifts' Club," a group of young Sienese who delib-*
> *erately ruined themselves by extravagance.*

"I was of Arezzo," one answered,
    "and Albero da Siena had me burned at the stake;
    but what I died for does not bring me here.

It is true that I told him, speaking in jest,
    that I could rise in the air in flight,
    and he who had the desire but little sense

wanted me to show him the art, and because
    I did not make him a Daedalus [a flyer], he had me burned
    by one who considered him as a son.

But to the last ditch of the ten,
    Minos, who cannot err, condemned me
    for the alchemy that I practiced in the world." 120

And I said to the poet, "Now was there ever
    a people as silly as the Sienese?
    Certainly the French are not so by far."

Thereupon the other leper who heard me
    answered my question and said, "Except Stricca
    who knew how to spend with moderation,

and Niccolò who first discovered
    the expensive use of the clove
    in the garden[53] where such seed takes root,

and except the company in which
    Caccia d'Ascian squandered vineyard and forest
    and the Abbagliato displayed his wit. 132

But that you may know who seconds your remarks
    against the Sienese, sharpen your eyes toward me,
    so that my face may give the right response.

Then you will see that I am the shade of Capocchio
    who falsified the metals by alchemy,
    and you must recall, if I see you correctly,

how good an ape of nature I became."

CANTO XXX

MASTER ADAM AND THE FALSE GREEK

Two terrible examples of insanity are cited at the beginning of this canto, the hallucination of Athamas and the hysterical grief of Hecuba. Two impersonators show a similar mania. One, Gianni Schicchi, had been engaged by Buoso Donati's son to impersonate his father and dictate a more favorable will. The commission was well performed except that the testator included himself in the legacy as the heir of the "queen of the herd," a valuable mare. The other example is that of Myrrha.

At the time when Juno because of Semele
    was angry at the Theban royal family,
    as she had shown already more than once,

[53] The "garden" is Siena.

Athamas was stricken with such madness
    that on seeing his wife coming
    burdened with two sons, one on either hand,

he shouted, "Let us spread the net, so that I
    may catch the lioness and cubs as they pass";
    then he stretched out his pitiless claws,

and seizing one, whose name was Learchus,
    whirled him around and dashed him on a rock;
    and she, with her other burden, drowned herself.[54]   12

And when Fortune had brought low
    the bold pride of the Trojans
    so that both king and kingdom were blotted out,

sad Hecuba, miserable and captive,[55]
    after she had seen her [daughter] Polyxena slain
    and, forlorn, recognized the body of [her son] Polydorus

on the shore of the sea, in her madness
    barked like a dog, so greatly
    had grief wrenched her mind.

But neither Theban nor Trojan Furies
    were ever seen anywhere so cruel
    in goading beasts, much less human bodies,   24

as those I saw in two spirits, pale and naked,
    who ran biting as a hungry boar does
    when just released from the sty.

One rushed on Capocchio and seized him
    by the neck, then dragging him,
    made his belly scrape on the hard bottom.

And the Aretine [Griffolino], who remained trembling,
    said to me, "That mad one is Gianni Schicchi,
    and he goes thus tearing others."

"Oh," I said to him, "so may the other
    not bite you, please tell us
    who it is before it gets away."   36

And he to me, "That is the ancient spirit
    of wicked Myrrha;[56] who was devoted to her father
    beyond the bounds of lawful love.

She came thus to sin with him,
    changing herself into another's form,
    just as the other who is running off

---

[54] Juno, angered at her consort Jupiter's love for Semele, a Theban princess who bore his son Bacchus, avenged herself on Semele's whole family. These included Semele's sister Ino, Ino's husband Athamas, and their children.

[55] Hecuba, queen of Troy, was carried off by the Greeks after they destroyed the city.

[56] The story of Myrrha's incestuous passion is told in Ovid's *Metamorphoses*, Book X.

undertook, to gain the mistress of the herd,
    to impersonate Buoso Donati,
    making a will and giving it a legal form."

After the two mad ones on whom
    I had kept my eyes had passed,
    I turned to look at the other ill-born shades.
        48

> *The counterfeiters are swollen with dropsy. One, a master of the art, had served
> the counts of Romena in one of the coolest, best watered of mountain regions, and
> the image of the place where he had worked increases the torture of his thirst.
> Amused at the size of Master Adam's belly, Dante asks about two shades on his
> boundaries. One, Sinon, suffering now from high fever, had pretended to be a
> fugitive from the Greeks, and had persuaded the Trojans to take in the wooden
> horse. The other liar is Potiphar's wife. Sinon objects to being called a "Greek
> from Troy," and we have a quarrel, the pot calling the kettle black. Sinon,
> considering each counterfeit coin as a separate indictment, charges Master Adam
> with the commission of more sins than any other demon. His opponent, in rebut-
> tal, mentions the infamous notoriety Sinon has gained through the works of
> Homer and Virgil. Dante is scolded for listening to the quarrel. He tries to reply,
> but is so ashamed that he cannot, and excuses himself by this embarrassment more
> effectively than if he had been able to speak.*

I saw one who would have looked like a lute
    if only he had had his legs cut off
    at the groin, where they join the body.

The heavy dropsy, disproportioning him thus
    with humors badly absorbed,
    left his head too small for his belly,

and made him hold his lips apart
    as the hectic does who, for thirst,
    has one turned up, the other down.

"O you who are without any punishment
    in this wretched world, and I don't know why,"
    he said to us, "see and take note
        60

of the misery of Master Adam!
    When alive I had enough of what I wanted,
    and now, alas! I long for a little drop of water.

The streams which from the green hills
    of Casentino flow down to the Arno,
    making their beds cool and soft,

always stand before my eyes and not in vain,
    for the vision of them dries me up
    more than the disease which wastes my features.

The rigid Justice which goads me
    takes advantage of the place where I sinned
    to put my sighs to quicker flight.
        72

There is Romena where I counterfeited
    the [Florentine] currency sealed with the Baptist's image,
    for which I left my body burned above.

But if I could see the miserable soul
    of Guido or of Alessandro or their brother [his employers]
    I would not trade the sight for Fonte Branda [a spring].

One is already in, if the mad shades
    that move around tell the truth,
    but of what avail is it, if my limbs are tied?

Yet, if I were still nimble enough
    to make an inch in a hundred years,
    I would already have started out   84

to find them among these disgusting people,
    although the ditch circles for eleven miles,
    and is not less than half a mile across.

Because of them I am in such a household;
    they induced me to stamp the florins
    which had indeed *three* carats of alloy!"

And I to him, "Who are the two wretches,
    steaming like wet hands in winter,
    lying close to your right frontier?"

"Here I found them on raining down in this ditch,"
    he answered, "since when they have not turned over,
    nor will they, I believe, in eternity.   96

One is the lying woman who accused Joseph;[57]
    the other is false Sinon, the Greek from Troy;
    because of their fever they emit such stench."

And one of them [Sinon] who perhaps
    took badly being named thus darkly,
    with his fist struck the vile belly

which sounded like a drum, and Master Adam
    struck him back in the face with his arm
    which did not seem less hard,

saying to him, "Although locomotion is impossible
    because of my heavy limbs,
    I have an arm free for such business!"   108

Whereupon the other answered, "When you went
    to the fire, you were not so quick,
    but you were still quicker when you made the coins."

---

[57] After Joseph, son of Jacob, was sold into Egypt, the wife of Potiphar, an officer of
Pharaoh, made sexual advances to Joseph. Rebuffed by him, she then accused him of making
the advances. See Genesis 39.

And he of the dropsy, "You tell the truth about this,
    but you were not so good a witness
    at Troy when the truth was asked of you."

"If I spoke falsely, you falsified the coins,"
    said Sinon, "and I am here for one fault,
    and you for more than any other demon."

"Remember, perjurer, the horse!" he of the swollen belly
    answered, "and let it be a plague to you
    that the whole world knows of it."   120

"And may the thirst that cracks your tongue
    be a curse to you," said the Greek, "and the foul water
    which makes a hedge before your eyes."

Then the counterfeiter, "Thus your mouth
    still opens to your harm, as usual,
    for, if I am thirsty and humor stuffs me up,

you have the burning and the headache,
    and to lick the mirror[58] of Narcissus
    you would not need a second invitation."

I was wholly intent on listening to them
    when my master said to me, "Now keep on gazing!
    a little more, and I will quarrel with you."   132

When I heard him speak to me with anger,
    I turned to him with such shame
    that the memory of it still haunts me.

As one who dreams of a misfortune
    and, while dreaming, hopes it is a dream,
    so that he longs for what is as if it were not,

so I became, not being able to speak
    although I wanted to excuse myself and did so,
    without knowing that I was doing it.

"Less shame washes away a greater fault,"
    said my master, "than yours has been;
    therefore, free yourself of all sadness   144

and take note that I am at your side
    if it happens again that chance catches you
    where people are in a similar wrangle,

for wishing to overhear it is a low desire."

[58] Water. Narcissus fell in love with his own reflected image.

CANTO XXXI

THE GIANTS

The same tongue first stung me
    so that it tinted both my cheeks,
    then offered me its cure.

Thus I hear that the lance of Achilles
    and of his father was wont first
    to wound and then to heal.

We turned our backs on the miserable ditch,
    going up without speaking
    over the bank which surrounds it.

Here it was less than night and less than day,
    so that my sight did not go far;
    but I heard a horn sound so loudly   12

that it would have made any thunder faint;
    and retracing the course the sound took
    I directed my eyes to one spot.

After the doleful rout,
    when Charlemagne lost his holy company,
    Roland did not blow so terribly.[59]

Only a short while did my eyes look toward the sound
    when I seemed to see many high towers,
    and I asked, "Master, tell me, what city is this?"

And he to me, "Since you are looking
    through the darkness from too far off
    your imagination leads you astray.   24

You will see when you arrive there
    how the senses are deceived by distance;
    therefore move a little faster."

Then he took me tenderly by the hand
    and said, "Before we go farther,
    to make the event seem less strange,

know that these are not towers, but giants,
    and they are in the well around the bank
    from the navel down, all of them."

As, when a mist has cleared somewhat,
    our eyes little by little make out
    what the vapor in the air had hidden,   36

---

[59] See *The Song of Roland.* When Charlemagne's army returned from Spain toward France, Roland commanded the elite rear guard. Set upon by the pagans and defeated, Roland refused to blow his great horn to call for help until it was too late.

so, piercing through the thick gloom
    on approaching closer and closer to the bank,
    my error fled, and my fear increased.

As, on the circle of its walls,
    Montereggione [a fortress] is crowned with towers,
    so, above the bank which surrounds the pit,

the horrible giants, whom Jove still threatens[60]
    when he thunders in the heavens,
    towered above us with half their bodies.

Already I saw the face, shoulders, and chest
    of one, and a large part of his belly,
    and both his arms down by his side.   48

Certainly when Nature gave up the art
    of producing these creatures she did well
    to deprive Mars of such agents;

and if she does not repent for elephants
    and whales, whoever looks closely
    will hold her more discreet and just,

for where the force of intellect [as in the giants]
    is added to ill will and strength,
    mankind can have no defense.

His face seemed to me as long and wide
    as the pine cone[61] at St. Peter's in Rome,
    and his other features were in proportion.   60

Thus the bank which was an apron
    from his middle down, showed so much of him
    that three Frieslanders [tall men] would have boasted

in vain to reach up to his hair.
    I saw, indeed, thirty great spans[62] of him
    down from [the neck] where a man buckles on his cloak.

> *Nimrod, the builder of the Tower of Babel, a "mighty hunter before the Lord," is
> with the giants who revolted against Jove. His words are meaningless. Virgil
> apostrophizes him for Dante's benefit. Then the travelers come to Antaeus, who
> was not present at the battle of the giants against the gods, and therefore is not
> bound like the others. Flattered by Virgil, who understands his fatuous character,
> Antaeus extends his hand and places the two poets on the bottom of the pit in the
> ninth and last circle.*

"Raphèl maỳ amèch zabì almì"
    the savage mouth for which sweeter
    hymns were unfitting began to say.

---

[60] Ovid's *Metamorphoses*, Book I, describes an attack on the gods by giants who piled mountains atop one another.
[61] A pine cone made of bronze, about ten feet high, is still visible in the Vatican.
[62] Hand spans.

And my guide to him, "Stupid soul,
   keep to your horn, and with it express yourself
   when anger or some other passion moves you.   72

Search around your neck and you will find the strap
   which holds it, O confused spirit;
   see it curving across your great chest."

Then he said to me, "He accuses himself.
   This is Nimrod, through whose evil thought
   a single tongue is not used in the world.[63]

Let us leave him and not speak in vain,
   for, as the language of others is to him,
   so is his to them, and is understood by none."

We kept on still to the left
   and at the distance of a crossbow shot
   we found another giant larger and fiercer.   84

Who the master was to bind him
   I cannot say, but his right arm
   at his back and the other in front

were bound by a chain, which held him tied
   from the neck down, so that over his exposed part
   it encircled him five times.

"This haughty creature wished to make trial
   of his power against supreme Jove,"
   said my master; "therefore, he has such a reward.

Ephialtes is his name; he fought in the great battle
   when the giants frightened the gods:
   the arms he used once, he never moves."   96

Then I to my guide, "If possible
   I should like for my eyes
   to gain experience of the immense Briareus."

Whereupon he answered, "You will see Antaeus
   nearby, who speaks and is unbound
   and who will put us in the lowest depth of guilt.

The one you wish to see is farther on
   and is bound and built like this one
   except that he looks more ferocious."

Never did an earthquake jar
   so violently a massive tower
   as Ephialtes suddenly shook himself.   108

Then I feared death more than ever,
   and fright alone would have caused it,
   if I had not seen the chains.

---

[63] For the story of the Tower of Babel and the consequent confusion of tongues in the world, see Genesis 11.

We went on then and came to Antaeus
    who protruded above the bank
    fully five ells,[64] not counting his head.

"O you who in the fateful valley
    which made Scipio an heir of glory,
    when Hannibal and his army turned back,[65]

you who once brought a thousand lions as prey—
    and, if you had fought in the great war,
    with your brothers, it seems that some believe   120

the sons of Earth [the giants] might have conquered—
    put us down, do not disdain to do so,
    to where cold locks up Cocytus.

Do not make us go to Tityus or to Typhon;
    this man can give what is longed for here;
    therefore bend over and do not scornfully refuse.

He can revive your fame in the world,
    for he lives and expects a long life, if Divine Grace
    does not call him to herself ahead of time."

Thus my master spoke, and Antaeus
    hurriedly held out the hand whose grip
    Hercules once felt, and took hold of my master.   132

When Virgil felt himself grasped,
    he said to me, "Come, let me take hold of you."
    Then, of himself and me he made one bundle.

As the Garisenda tower seems to fall
    if looked at under its leaning side
    when a cloud passes over it in the opposite direction,

so Antaeus appeared to me as I watched
    while he bent over; and he was such
    that I would have wished to go by another way.

But lightly in the depth which swallows
    Lucifer with Judas he placed us,
    nor did he delay long bent over   144

but rose like a mast set in a ship.

CANTO XXXII

The Traitors

*The tone of the Comedy now becomes harsh, scornful, vindictive. Dante again
calls upon the Muses, but this time on those who helped to build Thebes, "the
ancient home of crime."*

[64] An ell is about four or five feet.
[65] Scipio and Hannibal were, respectively, Roman and Carthaginian generals.

If I had rhymes rough and harsh enough
   to be fitting for the dismal hole
   on which all the other circles weigh,

I would press out the substance of my conception
   more fully; but since I do not have them,
   not without fear do I bring myself to speak.

For, to describe the bottom of the whole universe
   is not an enterprise to take up in jest,
   nor for a tongue that still cries "mamma" and "papa."

But may those ladies who helped Amphion
   to enclose Thebes aid my verse,
   so that words and facts will not differ.   12

O rabble, miscreated above all others,
   in this place to speak of which is hard,
   here [on earth] you would better have been sheep or goats!

When we were down in the dark well
   beyond the feet of the giant and much lower,
   and as I was still looking at the high wall,

I heard someone say, "Watch how you step!
   Move so you won't trample with your feet
   on the heads of the weary, miserable brothers."

Then I turned and saw a lake in front of me
   and under my feet which, frozen,
   had the appearance of glass and not of water.   24

The Danube in Austria never made in winter
   so thick a veil for its current,
   nor the Don up there under its cold skies,

as this did; for if Tambernicchi [a mountain]
   had fallen on it, or Pietrapana,
   it would not have given a creak even at the edge.

And as a frog lies croaking
   with just its muzzle out, in the season
   when the peasant woman thinks of gleaning,

so the shades were lying in the ice,
   livid up to where shame appears,
   their teeth chattering like storks' bills.   36

Each held his face down; their mouths
   gave evidence of the cold,
   and their eyes of their sad hearts.

Caïna, the first division of the ninth circle, contains traitors to kindred, among whom are the counts of Mangona, who killed each other in a quarrel over an inheritance. Other minor figures also are mentioned.

When I had looked around a little,
    I glanced at my feet and saw two so bound together
    that the hair on their heads was intermingled.

"Tell me, you who press your chests so close together,
    who you are," I asked, and they bent their necks,
    and after they had lifted their faces to me,

their eyes, which previously were wet only within,
    gushed through the lids, and the cold
    froze their tears and locked them up again.   48

A clamp never bound wood to wood so strongly.
    Then they, like two goats,
    butted each other, such anger overcame them.

And one who had lost both ears from the cold,
    with his face still downward, said,
    "Why do you look at us so much?

If you want to know who these two are,
    the valley from which the Bisenzio flows
    belonged to them and to their father, Albert.

They came from one body, and you might search
    through all Caïna[66] without finding a shade
    more worthy to be preserved in ice,   60

not him [Mordred] whose breast and shadow
    were laid open by a single blow from Arthur's hand,[67]
    not Focaccia; not this one who covers me

with his head, so that I cannot see beyond
    and whose name was Sassol Mascheroni,—
    if you are a Tuscan you know now who he was.

And, so that you will not put me to further speech,
    know that I was Camicion de' Pazzi, and am waiting
    for Carlino to make me [by comparison] seem innocent."

Afterward I saw a thousand faces made doglike
    by the cold; so that a shudder comes to me
    and always will at the sight of frozen pools.   72

> *Passing on to Antenora, the second division of the ninth circle, where traitors to party and country are kept, Dante accidentally kicks one shade who mentions Montaperti, the scene of a defeat of the Florentine Guelfs. Dante's suspicion is immediately aroused, and he tries by force to make the shade name himself. Another, however, treacherously gives him away as Bocca degli Abati who, at a*

[66] Named for Cain, who murdered his brother Abel (Genesis 4). All the treacherous sinners punished in this and the other three divisions of the ninth circle happen also to be involved in murder.

[67] Mordred was the evil nephew of King Arthur and a would-be usurper. Arthur killed him with a blow that penetrated his whole body.

critical moment in the battle, cut off the hand of the Florentine standardbearer,
an act which was thought to have caused the defeat. Dante's violence incurs no
reproach: the implication is that ordinary rules of conduct are inapplicable to the
completely depraved: one must keep away from them or act according to the code
they establish. This is the realistic Gresham's law of competitive behavior. Bocca
in turn mentions others, including Buoso da Duera, who had been bribed by
Charles of Anjou, and Ganelon, the traitor in the Song of Roland.

And while we were moving toward the center
    to which all weights are drawn
    and I was shivering in the eternal chill,

whether it was destiny or chance, I know not,
    but while walking among the heads
    my foot struck hard against the face of one.

Weeping it cried, "Why do you kick me?
    Unless you come to increase the vengeance
    for Montaperti, why do you molest me?"

And I, "Master, now wait for me here
    until this one relieves me of a doubt,
    then you can make me hurry as you wish."   84

My guide stood still, and I said to the shade
    who was still cursing loudly,
    "Who are you complaining thus of others?"

"Now who are you, going through Antenora[68]
    kicking others' cheeks," he answered,
    "harder than if you were alive?"

"I am alive," was my response,
    "and it may be dear to you, if you want fame,
    that I should include your name in my notes."

And he to me, "The contrary is what I want,
    get away from here; do not bother me,
    for you know badly how to flatter in this bottom."   96

Then I seized him by the scalp and said,
    "You will name yourself
    or not a hair will be left on your head."

And he to me, "Even if you tear it out
    and fall on my head a thousand times,
    I will not tell or show you who I am."

I had already twisted his hair in my hand
    and had pulled out more than one tuft,
    he howling with eyes cast down,

when another shouted, "What's the matter with you, Bocca?
    Isn't it enough to chatter with your jaws
    but you must bark?—What devil is after you?"   108

[68] Antenor was a Trojan who, according to medieval legend, betrayed his city to the
Greeks. He is treated favorably in Homer's *Iliad*.

"Now," I said, "I do not want you to speak,
    damned traitor, for to your shame
    I will carry off true news of you."

"Go," he answered, "and tell what you want,
    but if you get out of here, don't keep silent
    about him who has his tongue so ready.

He is weeping here for the money of the French.
    'I saw,' you can say, 'him of Duera,
    down there where sinners are put to cool.'

If any one asks about the others here,
    you have beside you the one of Beccheria
    whose throat was cut by Florence.   120

Gianni de' Soldanier, I believe,
    is farther on, with Ganelon, and Tebaldello
    who opened Faenza while it was sleeping."

We now see a bestial example of hatred. One shade is gnawing the head of another, as Tydeus, after being mortally wounded by Menalippus whom he in turn killed, called for the head of his enemy and chewed on it. Aghast at such a sight, Dante wonders what could motivate such hatred and offers to help in the vengeance by making the reason for it known in case there is just cause.

We had already departed from him
    when I saw two frozen in one hole,
    so that the head of one was a hood for the other,

and as bread is chewed from hunger,
    so the one on top set his teeth in the other
    where the brain joins the neck.

Not otherwise did Tydeus gnaw
    in his rage the temples of Menalippus
    than he did this one's skull and flesh.   132

"O you who show by such bestial signs
    hatred of him whom you are chewing,
    tell me why," I said, "on this condition

that if you rightfully complain of him,
    knowing who you are and his sin,
    I may repay you up in the world

if that [tongue] with which I speak is not dried up [by death]."

CANTO XXXIII

COUNT UGOLINO

Count Ugolino, a Pisan, had allied himself with the Florentine Guelfs and in 1285 was in control of his city. Perhaps he is among the traitors because of this change of party and because of the transfer of certain castles. In that year the

Ghibellines, led by the Archbishop Ruggieri, revolted. Ugolino was called treach-
erously to a parley, then imprisoned with two sons and two grandsons in what
was later known as the "Tower of Hunger." After some months the door of the
prison was nailed shut, and the five were left to die of starvation. The bodies, on
their removal, appeared mutilated, perhaps rat-bitten. Ugolino recognizes Dante
as a Florentine, therefore a Guelf, and explains why he is violating so terribly the
obligations of a neighbor.

The sinner raised his mouth from his fierce repast,
    wiping it on the hair of the head
    the back of which he had despoiled,

and then began, "You wish that I renew
    desperate grief, which wrings my heart,
    merely in thinking of it, before I speak.

But if my words can be seeds to bear infamy
    to the traitor I am gnawing,
    you will see me both speak and weep.

I do not know who you are, nor by what means
    you have come down here, but certainly
    you seem a Florentine when I hear you.   12

You must understand that I was Count Ugolino,
    and this is the Archbishop Ruggieri;
    now I will tell you why I am such a neighbor.

How, as the result of his evil thoughts,
    I was seized, trusting in him,
    and put to death, there is no need to tell,

but what you cannot have learned, that is,
    how cruel my death was, you will hear
    and know if he has offended me.

As in the Francesca episode, so here Dante reconstructs what could not be known,
that is, the lonely, unwitnessed death of the five in prison. In the tower (compared
to a "mew" in which falcons were kept while molting) several months had passed
when a symbolic and prophetic dream revealed to the prisoners their fate. In
describing it, Ugolino's fierce memory gets ahead of his words: the wolf becomes
"a father" and the whelps "sons," and he turns on Dante, reproaching the poet
for lack of feeling before he has told what happened.

A little loophole in the mew which
    because of me was called the 'Tower of Hunger'
    and in which others will be imprisoned   24

had shown through its opening several moons already
    when I had the evil dream
    which tore away the veil of the future.

This one seemed the lord and master of the hunt,
    chasing the wolf and whelps on the mountain
    which prevents the Pisans from seeing Lucca.

With lean, eager, and well-trained hounds [the mob],
    he had placed the Gualandi, Sismondi,
    and Lanfranchi [as leaders] in front of him.

After a short course, the father and the sons
    seemed to me weary, and I thought I saw
    their bodies torn by the sharp teeth.   36

When I had awakened before the dawn
    I heard my children who were with me
    weeping in their sleep and asking for bread.

You are cruel indeed not to grieve already
    in thinking of what my heart foreboded;
    and if you do not weep now, by what are you ever moved?

> *The drama passes in silence: almost nothing is said. On the first day Anselm, the smallest, showed concern for his father. On the second, Ugolino bit his hands from grief. That and the third day passed in complete silence. On the fourth, Gaddo weakened and died, and on the fifth and sixth, the others. On the seventh, Ugolino crawled over the bodies, and on the eighth, he succumbed, hunger having accomplished what grief could not do.*

> *The hatred of Ugolino is communicated to Dante who bursts out in an invective against Pisa.*

They were now awake, and the hour drew near
    when our food used to be brought to us,
    and each was afraid because of his dream;

and below I heard the door of the horrible tower
    nailed up; whereupon, without saying a word,
    I looked into the faces of my sons.   48

I did not weep, so stony did I become within.
    They cried, and my little Anselm said,
    'You look so [hard], father, what ails you?'

Still I shed no tears nor did I answer
    during all that day and the night after,
    until another sun came forth upon the world.

When a little light had entered
    the awful prison, and I saw
    on four faces my own aspect,

I bit both my hands from grief,
    and they, thinking I did it from hunger,
    suddenly got up and said,   60

'Father, it will be much less painful
    if you eat of us; you clothed us
    with this poor flesh; may you take it from us!'

I became quiet then not to make them more sad.
    That day and the next we all remained mute.
    Ah, hard earth, why did you not open!

After we had reached the fourth day,
    Gaddo fell stretched out at my feet, saying,
    'Father, why don't you help me?'

There he died; and as you see me ·
    I saw the three of them fall one by one
    between the fifth day and the sixth; then I began,   72

already blind, to crawl over each, and for two days
    I called them after they were dead.
    Then fasting did more than grief."[69]

When he had said this, with eyes awry,
    he seized again the wretched head with his teeth
    which gnawed upon the bone, like a dog's.

Ah, Pisa! shame of the people,
    of the beautiful land [Italy] where "si" ["yes"] is heard,
    since your neighbors are slow to punish you,

may the Capraia and Gorgona [islands] move
    and make a dam for the Arno at its mouth,[70]
    so that it may drown everyone in you;   84

for if Count Ugolino was reputed
    to have betrayed you of the castle,
    you should not have put his sons on such a cross.

Their young age made Uguccione
    and Brigata innocent, you modern Thebes![71]
    and the other two named by my song.

    The poets move on to Tolomea, the third division, where traitors to guests are
    punished. The heads of these sinners are thrown back, so that the tears, freezing
    in the cups of their eyes, cause a painful pressure.

We went farther on to where the frost
    roughly binds another people
    with faces thrown back, not turned down.

Weeping there prevents them from weeping:
    the tears which find a barrier in the eyes
    turn inward to increase the pain,   96

since they form a solid mass,
    and like visors of crystal fill
    the whole cavity beneath the eyebrows.

And, although, as in a callused spot,
    every feeling had gone from my face
    because of the intense cold,

[69] This line can mean that hunger could make him die as grief could not or else that
Ugolino was driven to cannibalism.
[70] Pisa is at the mouth of the river Arno.
[71] Thebes was considered the most wicked of the ancient cities.

already I seemed to notice a wind,
    so that I said, "Master, what causes this?
    Is not all vapor [atmospheric change] absent down here?"

And he to me, "Soon you will be
    where your eyes will see the cause
    of the blast and will give you the answer."   108

And one of the wretches in the cold crust
    shouted at us, "O souls so cruel
    that the last place is assigned to you,

take from my eyes the hard veils,
    so that I may relieve the pain a little
    that stuffs my heart before the tears freeze again."

> To induce this soul to speak, Dante makes a promise with false intent, that is, he commits fraud, as previously in this circle he had committed violence. Our poet is emphasizing again, in opposition to certain idealists, that golden rules and codes of honor presuppose a certain uniformity in the social group. To apply them without discrimination is merely to favor and give superior survival value to the fraudulent and dishonorable.
>
> The soul whom Dante has tricked had had guests murdered at a banquet, the signal for the execution being, "Bring on the fruit." He is now getting expensive dates for cheap figs, that is, being repaid with interest. His soul, apparently, has descended "quick" into Hell, and is replaced in his body by a demon.

And I to him, "If you want me to help you,
    tell me who you are, and if I do not relieve you,
    may I go to the bottom of the ice!"[72]

He answered then, "I am Friar Alberigo,
    he of the fruit of the evil garden,
    and am getting here dates for my figs."   120

"Oh," I said to him, "are you dead already?"
    And he to me, "How my body fares
    in the world above, I have no knowledge.

Such an advantage this Tolomea[73] has
    that often a soul falls into it
    before Atropos [a Fate] has thrust it forth.

And—so may you remove more willingly
    the frozen tears from my face—
    know that when a soul betrays as I did,

its body is taken from it by a demon
    who afterward controls the flesh
    until its allotted years have passed.   132

[72] Dante must in any event go beneath the ice, because that is the way out of hell; see the next canto.

[73] Probably named for Ptolemy, a soldier of Jericho who in 1 Maccabees 16 murders several of his relatives whom he invited to a banquet.

It falls into such a cistern as this,
    and perhaps the body of the shade
    wintering behind me appears on earth.

You must know him if you have just come down;
    He is Ser Branca d'Oria [a Genoese], and many years
    have passed since he was thus locked up."

"I believe that you are deceiving me,"
    I said to him, "for Branca d'Oria has not died,
    but eats and sleeps and puts on clothes."

"In the ditch of the Malebranche above,"
    he said, "where the tenacious pitch is boiling,
    Michel Zanche [his victim] had not yet arrived   144

when a devil took over his body
    and that of a close relative
    who did the treacherous act with him.

But reach out your hand, open my eyes";
    and I did not open them for him;
    and to be rude to him was fitting.

Ah, Genoese, men who are estranged
    from all good ways and full of all corruption,
    why are you not scattered from the earth,

for, with the worst spirit of Romagna [Alberigo],
    I found one of you whose soul
    for his deeds already bathes in Cocytus,   156

and in body seems still alive on earth!

CANTO XXXIV

SATAN

*To the first words of a Latin hymn to the cross, "The banners of the Lord come
forth, . . ." Dante adds the word* inferni, *applying them thus to Satan, the lord
of Hell. Dante is now in Giudecca where traitors to benefactors are completely
submerged in the ice.*

*Satan is represented as the counterpart of the Trinity, with heads of three colors,
yellow, black, and red, standing for impotence, ignorance, and hate, and corresponding to the divine power, wisdom, and love. His three pairs of wings send
forth a threefold blast which freezes Cocytus. In the mouths of Lucifer are Judas,
the traitor to Christ, and Brutus and Cassius, traitors to the Roman Empire. The
poets reach Satan at six o'clock on Saturday evening, having spent twenty-four
hours on the journey.*

"*Vexilla Regis prodeunt inferni*
    toward us, therefore, look ahead,"
    my master said, "and try to discern him."

As, when a thick mist covers the land
   or when night darkens our hemisphere,
   a windmill, turning, appears from afar,

so now I seemed to see such a structure;
   then because of the wind, I drew back
   behind my guide, for there was no other protection.

Already—and with fear I put it into verse—
   I was where the shades are covered in the ice
   and show through like bits of straw in glass.   12

Some were lying, some standing erect,
   some on their heads, others on their feet,
   still others like a bow bent face to toes.

When we had gone so far ahead
   that my master was pleased to show me
   the creature [Lucifer] that once had been so fair,

he stood from in front of me, and made me stop,
   saying, "Behold, Dis![74] Here is the place
   where you must arm yourself with courage."

How faint and frozen I then became,
   do not ask, Reader, for I do not write it down,
   since all words would be inadequate.   24

I did not die and did not stay alive:
   think now for yourself, if you have the wit,
   how I became, without life or death.

The emperor of the dolorous realm
   from mid-breast protruded from the ice,
   and I compare better in size

with the giants than they do with his arms.
   Consider how big the whole must be,
   proportioned as it is to such a part.

If he were once as handsome as he is ugly now,
   and still presumed to lift his hand against his Maker,
   all affliction must indeed come from him.   36

Oh, how great a marvel appeared to me
   when I saw three faces on his head!
   The one in front [hatred] was fiery red;

the two others which were joined to it
   over the middle of each shoulder
   were fused together at the top.

[74] Satan. (Dis, or Pluto, was the ancient god of the underworld.)

The right one [impotence] seemed between white and yellow;
　　the left [ignorance] was in color like those
　　who come from where the Nile rises.

Under each two great wings spread
　　of a size fitting to such a bird;
　　I have never seen such sails on the sea.　　　　　　　　　48

They had no feathers, and seemed
　　like those of a bat, and they flapped,
　　so that three blasts came from them.

Thence all Cocytus was frozen.
　　With six eyes he wept, and over his three chins
　　he let tears drip and bloody foam.

In each mouth he chewed a sinner with his teeth
　　in the manner of a hemp brake,[75]
　　so that he kept three in pain.

To the one in front the biting was nothing
　　compared to the scratching, for at times,
　　his back was stripped of skin.　　　　　　　　　　　　60

"The soul up there with the greatest punishment,"
　　said my master, "is Judas Iscariot. His head
　　is inside the mouth, and he kicks with his legs.

Of the other two whose heads are down,
　　the one hanging from the black face is Brutus;
　　see how he twists and says nothing.

The other who seems so heavy set is Cassius.[76]
　　But night is rising again now,
　　and it is time to leave, for we have seen all."

> At the center of the earth, also the center of gravity, the poets turn and begin
> climbing laboriously, the effort symbolizing the difficulty of getting rid of bad
> habits even when their ugliness is known. Lucifer now appears upside down, and
> the time changes to Saturday morning, since the travelers gain twelve hours in
> passing from Jerusalem time to that of Purgatory, directly opposite.
>
> Through the passage made by Lucifer as he fell, the poets reach the foot of
> Purgatory just before dawn on Easter Sunday.
>
> Each part of the Comedy ends with the word "stars," which stand for the goal of
> the journey, the objects farthest removed from Satan and the materialism of the
> earth, and whose beauty is most ethereal.

[75] A machine for crushing stalks of hemp.

[76] The place of Brutus and Cassius, the assassins of Julius Caesar, at the center of hell is a
surprise to modern readers accustomed to think of them as heroic opponents of tyranny. But
to Dante they were traitors to the Roman Empire (in the person of Caesar), the agency of
earthly rule that properly counterweighs spiritual authority (Christ through the papacy).

When my guide was ready, I embraced his neck,
    and he took advantage of the time and place
    so that when the wings were wide open   72

he caught hold of the shaggy sides
    and descended from tuft to tuft
    between the tangled hair and the frozen crust.

When we were at the place where the thigh
    revolves on the swelling of the haunches,
    my guide, with effort and with difficulty,

turned his head to where he had had his feet,
    and grappled the hair, like one mounting,
    so that I thought he was returning into Hell.

"Hold fast, for by such stairs,"
    my master said, panting like one weary,
    "we must depart from so much evil."   84

Then he came through the opening in a rock
    and put me on its edge, sitting,
    and climbed toward me with wary steps.

I raised my eyes and thought
    that I would find Lucifer as I had left him,
    but saw him holding up his legs,

and if I then became perplexed,
    let dull people imagine who do not see
    what the point was that I had passed.

"Get up on your feet," said my master,
    "the road is long and the path rough, and already
    the sun has returned to mid-tierce [at 7:30 A.M.]."   96

The place where we were
    was no palace hall, but a natural dungeon,
    dark and with an uneven floor.

"Before I uproot myself from the abyss, Master,"
    I said when I was standing,
    "speak to me a little to dispel my error.

Where is the ice? and how is Satan planted
    so upside down? and how in such a short time
    has the sun made its way from evening to morning?"

And he to me, "You still imagine you are
    on the other side of the center where I grasped the hair
    of the wicked monster that pierces the world.   108

You were over there as long as I descended;
    when I turned, you passed the point
    to which all weights are drawn.

Now you have arrived in the hemisphere
    opposite that which dry land covers
    and at whose summit [Jerusalem] was consumed

the man [Christ] who was born and lived without sin.
    You have your feet on a little circle
    which forms the other face of Giudecca.[77]

Here it is morning when it is evening there,
    and Satan who made a ladder for us
    with his hair is still as he was before.   120

On this side he fell from Heaven, and the earth here,
    through fear, made a veil for itself
    of the sea, and came to our hemisphere,

and perhaps the land [Purgatory] which shows on this side,
    to flee from him, rushed up
    and left this passageway empty."[78]

There is a place as remote
    from Beelzebub[79] as his tomb extends,
    not known by sight, but by the sound

of a little stream which descends in it
    along the hollow of a rock which it has eaten out
    with a slow and winding course."[80]   132

My guide and I started on that hidden way
    to return to the bright world,
    and, without caring for any rest,

we climbed, he first and I second,
    until I saw, through a round opening,
    the beautiful things that heaven bears,

and came forth to see again the stars.

---

[77] The innermost ring of the plain of ice; named for Judas.

[78] When Satan fell from heaven into the southern hemisphere, the land there recoiled from him into the northern hemisphere; also, the land within the earth rushed back from him to form the island of Purgatory in the southern ocean, leaving empty the cavern through which Virgil and Dante emerge from hell.

[79] Here, another name for Satan.

[80] The stream is the river Lethe, which from Eden atop the mountain of Purgatory flows down to the center of the earth to join the four rivers of hell, carrying with it the memory of the vices expiated in Purgatory. All evil, committed by the saved and the damned, thus comes to rest as dead weight, frozen and immobile, at the point of the universe farthest removed from God.

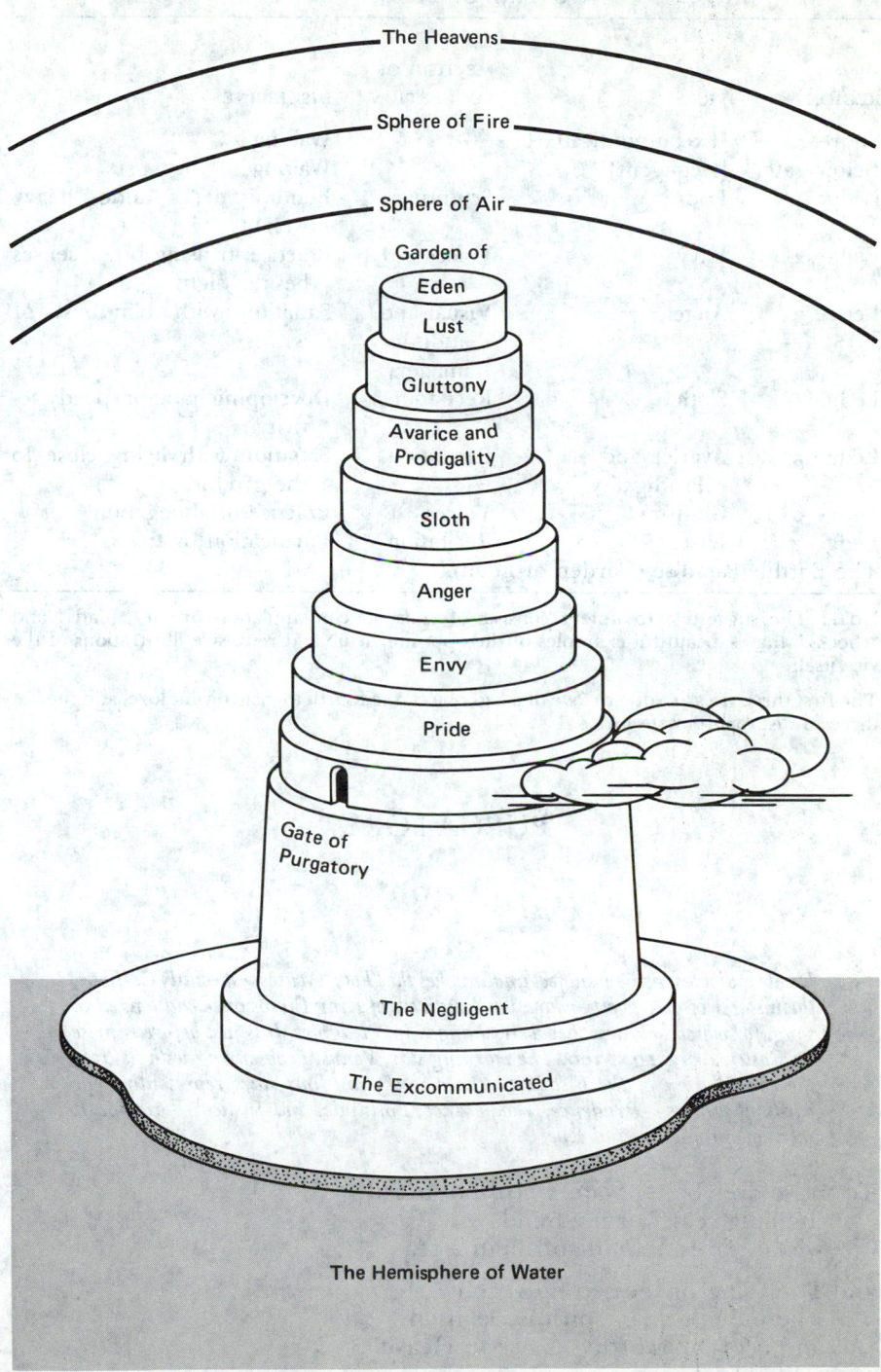

A diagram of Purgatory.

REGION	VICES	METHOD OF SUGGESTION	DISCIPLINES
Shore	[Excommunicated]		Waiting
Below gate	[Negligent]		Waiting
Ledge 1	Pride	Sculptures	Bending necks under heavy weights
Ledge 2	Envy	Voices	Practice in using other senses besides sight
Ledge 3	Anger	Visual and auditory imagery	Satiation with blindness of wrath
Ledge 4	Sloth	Recitation	Developing habit of speedy activity
Ledge 5	Avarice and Prodigality	Recitation	Satiation with living close to the ground
Ledge 6	Gluttony	Voices	Practice in abnegation
Ledge 7	Lust	Recitation	Purification by fire
The Earthly Paradise (Garden of Eden).			

NOTE: The suggestive treatment consists of constant contemplation of the "goads" and "checks," that is, beautiful examples of the opposite virtue and repulsive illustrations of the vice itself.

The first three vices are due to love of a bad object, the fourth to insufficient love, and the last three to disproportionate love.

PURGATORY

CANTO I

CATO

Dante indicates his new subject and invokes the "holy" Muses, especially Calliope, the inspirer of epic poetry whom the daughters of King Pieros once challenged in song, for which boldness they were changed into magpies. It is just before sunrise on Easter, April 10, 1300. The morning star, Venus, is obscuring with its light the constellation of the Fishes. In the new sky are four stars representing the cardinal virtues—Prudence, Temperance, Fortitude, and Justice[1]—previously seen only by Adam and Eve.

To move over better waters now hoists sail
    the little vessel of my mind
    which leaves behind so rough a sea;

and I will sing of the second realm
    where the human spirit is cleansed
    and becomes worthy to rise to Heaven.

[1] Also called the "natural virtues" or "moral virtues."

Here, O holy Muses, since I am yours,
>let dead poetry be revived
>and let Calliope arise a while,

accompanying my song with the music
>which struck the ears of the wretched magpies
>so that they despaired of pardon.   12

A sweet color of oriental sapphire
>which was forming in the clear sky,
>pure from the zenith to the horizon,

restored delight to my eyes
>as soon as I came out of the dead air
>that had afflicted both my eyes and lungs.

The beautiful planet which prompts to love
>made the whole east smile,
>veiling the Fishes that escorted her.

I turned to the right and set my mind
>on the other pole, and I noticed four stars
>never seen except by the first people.   24

The heavens seemed to rejoice in their light.
>O region of the north, widowed!
>since you are denied that view.

>*Cato, Dante's favorite hero of antiquity and the symbol of Free Will, appears, his*
>*face shining with the light of the four virtues. Rather than submit to Caesar, he*
>*had committed suicide, a Christian but not a pagan sin. For this devotion to*
>*freedom and for other merits he is made the guardian of Purgatory and will be*
>*saved on Judgment Day.*[2]

When I had withdrawn my eyes from them,
>turning for a moment to the north
>where the Great Bear [Dipper] had already disappeared,

I saw a solitary old man near me,
>in semblance worthy of so much reverence
>than no son owes more to his father.

The beard he wore was long
>and streaked with white, like his hair
>of which two tresses fell upon his breast.   36

The rays of the four holy lights
>so brightened his face that he appeared
>as if the sun were shining on him.

"Who are you who, moving up the dark stream,
>have fled from the eternal prison?"
>he asked, shaking his plumelike beard.

---

[2] There were two famous Romans named Cato. This one is Cato the Younger (95–46 B.C.).

"Who has guided you or given you a light
  to issue from the black night
  which darkens the infernal depth?

Are the laws of the abyss thus broken,
  or have decrees been changed in Heaven
  so that the damned may come to my cliffs?"   48

My guide then took hold of me,
  and with words and hands and gestures
  made reverent my knees and brow.

Then he answered, "By myself I do not come;
  a lady descended from Heaven, at whose prayers
  I helped this man with my companionship.

But, since it is your will that more
  of our present condition be explained,
  my will is not able to refuse you.

The man has not seen his last hour,
  but through his folly was so close to it
  that there was little time left.   60

I was sent to him, as I said,
  to rescue him, and there was no other way
  than this one on which I have started.

I have shown him all the wicked people
  and now propose to reveal those spirits
  who are purging themselves under your charge.

How I have brought him here would take long to tell;
  a Power from above has helped me
  to bring him to see and to hear you.

May it please you to welcome his coming;
  he is seeking freedom, which is precious,
  as one who gives up life for it knows.   72

You understand, since death for you was not bitter
  in Utica where you left the clothing of your flesh
  which, on the great day, will be so bright.

The eternal laws are not broken by us,
  for this man lives, and Minos does not condemn me.
  I am from the circle where the chaste eyes

of your Marcia still seem to supplicate,
  O holy breast! that you hold her for your own.
  For love of her, then, incline toward us;

let us go through your seven kingdoms;
  I will tell her of your grace
  if you deign to be mentioned down there."   84

Cato states plainly his indifference to the fate of his wife, Marcia: the felicity of
Heaven would be impaired if earthly relationships were not ended and if sorrow
could be felt for the damned. He directs Virgil to gird Dante with a reed (Humil-
ity) and to wash his face, so that he can appear properly before the guardians of
the ledges of Purgatory. The sun (Righteous Choice, Enlightenment) must be
their guide henceforth.

The two poets descend to the sea which Ulysses alone had sailed. There, the reed
which Virgil plucks for Dante replaces itself. Humility cannot be defeated: the
more it is crushed the more it grows.

"Marcia pleased my eyes so much
    while I was yonder," he said then,
    "that I granted all the favors she asked.

Now that she dwells beyond the evil stream
    she cannot move me because of the law
    which was made when I came from there.

But if a lady from Heaven sends and commands you,
    as you say, there is no need for coaxing;
    it is enough that you ask me for her sake.

Go then and see that you gird this man
    with a slender rush, and that you bathe his face,
    so that all stains are washed from it,   96

for it would not be fitting that eyes
    darkened by any mist should meet
    the first minister of those in Paradise.

This little island, around its very base,
    where the waves beat upon it,
    bears reeds upon the soft mud.

No other plant which brings forth leaves
    or grows hard could exist there,
    since it would not yield to the waves.

Afterward do not return along here;
    the sun which is rising now will show you
    the easiest way to climb the mount."   108

Then he disappeared, and I got up
    without speaking and drew close
    to my guide, my eyes fixed on him.

He began, "My son, follow my steps,
    let us turn back, for from here
    the plain slopes down to its low bounds."

The dawn was dispelling the morning hour
    which fled before it, so that from afar
    I recognized the trembling of the sea.

We went over the solitary plain
    like men returning to the road they have lost
    who, until they get there, seem to walk in vain.   120

When we reached the place where the dew
    contends with the sun and
    in shaded spots had dried but little,

my master softly placed both hands
    spread out on the wet grass,
    and I, aware of his purpose,

held toward him my tear-stained cheeks
    on which he wholly restored the color
    which the smoke of Hell had hidden.

We came then to the deserted shore
    whose waters had never been sailed
    by anyone who afterward was able to return.   132

There he girded me, as another [Cato] wished.
    O marvel! for, as he plucked the humble plant,
    it was suddenly reborn as it was

in the place from which he had torn it.

CANTO II. *As a beautiful day dawns, a boat arrives at the island (the counterpart of Charon's boat at the border of Hell), bearing souls of the saved. One of the new arrivals is the musician Casella, an old friend of Dante's. Casella performs for Dante a song Dante himself had written, a fact that shows the survival among the saved of personal attributes they had in their former lives on earth. Cato rebukes the company for this delay, and they hasten toward the mountain of Purgatory.*

CANTO III. *At the foot of the mountain, unable to begin their ascent as yet, though they are eager to do so, are persons who died in the state of excommunication from the Church. This ecclesiastical penalty is observed in Purgatory but limited in its effect: the souls in question must delay their cleansing on the mount for a period thirty times as long as they lived excommunicated.*

CANTO IV. *Dante and Virgil pass through a fissure in the rock and make the arduous climb to the lowermost slope of the mountain. Dante is startled to see the sun to the north rather than (as in the northern hemisphere) to the south. Virgil comforts the exhausted Dante by telling him that the ascent becomes progressively easier as they climb the mountain. (This is because the burden of inclination to sin is progressively lightened.) They come upon another group of souls debarred as yet from Purgatory proper; these are the persons who repented only at the last minute, and they must delay their purgation for a period as long as they remained unrepentant in life.*

CANTO V. *Continuing up and around the mountain (which they must ascend counter-clockwise), Dante and Virgil meet a group of late-repentant souls who were violently slain, including Jacopo del Cassero and a woman named Pia, who tells in a mere half-dozen lines a poignant story of death at her husband's hands. Here, as elsewhere in Purgatory, the souls are eager that the living pray for them, thus making their purgatorial process quicker and easier. Such mutual assistance and communication between the living and dead are part of the Dantean and Catholic understanding of the "communion of saints" mentioned in the Apostles' Creed.*

CANTO VI. *Virgil explains to Dante the nature of prayer—the fact, for example, that it does not deflect the divine will—but adds that a full explanation can come only from Christian revelation as embodied in Beatrice. At the mention of his beloved lady, Dante is excitedly eager to ascend. A cordial meeting between Virgil and Sordello, another man from Mantua, leads Dante to a sad comparison with the hatred and division that afflict the present cities of Italy, especially Florence.*

CANTO VII. *Virgil explains to Sordello, in a poignant passage, his own exclusion from salvation. Sordello explains to the two pilgrims that after sunset no one can ascend the mountain. He leads them to a peaceful valley where former monarchs who neglected the spiritual side of life must now delay their desired purgatorial discipline. In their fraternal amity, the rulers make a striking contrast with their former selves and many among the current generation of rulers.*

CANTO VIII. *Dante converses with some of the rulers, who, like other souls on the mountain, are astounded to learn that he still lives. The Valley, because it is outside Purgatory proper and therefore not immune to evil, is guarded by angels, who drive off an evil serpent that approaches. In the night sky are shining the three stars representing the "theological virtues" of faith, hope, and love. It is only during the day, however, when the four stars representing the moral virtues—prudence, justice, temperance, and fortitude—are above, that souls can ascend. This is a way of saying that the Purgatorial process leads essentially to natural rather than supernatural perfection.*

CANTO IX. *In sleep (his first since before the descent to Hell), Dante is borne upward by St. Lucia, to the outside of the gate of Purgatory proper. It is now morning, when ascent can take place. After ceremonially re-enacting the sacrament of Penance, or confession, Dante is admitted through the gate by the angel who guards it. On Dante's forehead the angel engraves seven P's standing for the seven capital sins (peccata). These will be erased, one by one, as Dante moves through the seven corresponding mountain ledges of Purgatory.*

CANTO X. *Being careful to observe the angel's command not to look back, Dante enters Purgatory proper and climbs upward with Virgil. They emerge on a terrace, some eighteen feet wide, its outer edge exposed dizzyingly to the sheer drop of the mountain wall. Here the vice of pride, which underlies all the others, is punished. The purgatorians must bend low under the weight of great stones they are carrying on their backs. On each terrace, "checks" and "goads" will appear, drawn from sacred and secular history. The checks are warnings about the vice punished; the goads are examples of the opposing virtue. On the terrace of pride, the goads consist of scenes, illustrating humility, carved on the inner wall.*

CANTO XI. *Dante must stoop down to converse with the proud souls. Thus, here as elsewhere in Purgatory, he participates in the discipline of suffering rather than simply observing it. Among the prideful is the painter Oderisi, who outlines the process by which new schools of painting and poetry (including Dante's own school) succeed one another. All will be superseded in turn, and therefore artists ought to feel no prideful sense of triumph. The same is true of military glory.*

CANTO XII. *On the ground the pilgrims walk upon are carved the checks: instances of proud behavior. The proud are thus brought low in contrast with the humble whose deeds are carved on the vertical inner wall. Before leaving the Terrace of Pride and climbing the stairs to the next terrace, Dante and Virgil meet an angel, who erases the first of the seven P's from Dante's brow, the incision of the other six P's thereby becoming shallower. The ascent will now become easier. A voice is heard quoting, from the gospel Beatitudes, the blessing on the poor in spirit. A corresponding angelic absolution and scriptural acclamation will recur on the other six terraces.*

CANTO XIII. *On the second terrace, of Envy, Dante meets souls whose eyelids are stitched shut, removing their perception of the beautiful and good things that they had once begrudged to others. They lean on one another in mutual dependency, and voices acclaim the virtue of generosity. Dante, in conversing with Sapia, one of the penitents, indicates that he too, after his death, will have to undergo this punishment, but only slightly compared with what he will have to suffer below, on the Terrace of Pride.*

CANTO XIV. *Another penitent, Guido del Duca, in response to Dante's apologetic reference to his birthplace on the Arno river, utters a scathing denunciation of the evil places the river passes through, notably Florence and Pisa. Voices sound in warning against the vice of envy.*

CANTO XV. *Guido had condemned humankind for fixing its attention on the things incompatible with partnership. Virgil explains to Dante the meaning of this cryptic statement: that, by being shared, material goods are diminished but spiritual goods are multiplied. The two reach the third terrace, of Wrath, where the souls are enveloped in smoke. In a vision that stuns him, Dante beholds instances of meekness.*

CANTO XVI. *As Virgil leads him, blinded, through the smoke, Dante hears the formerly wrathful souls singing harmoniously in praise of the Lamb of God. Dante meets Marco Lombardo, one of several purgatorians who condemn the degeneracy of the present world. In reply to Dante's question whether this degeneracy is due to stellar influence, or to the intrinsic degradation of life on earth, Marco indignantly rejects the determinism that those explanations would imply. He blames the evils of the times, rather, on the perversion of earthly rule caused by the Church's usurpation of temporal authority in addition to the spiritual authority that it rightfully exercises. Virgil and Dante approach the stair leading to the fourth terrace, of Sloth.*

CANTO XVII

THE RISE TO THE SLOTHFUL

Reader, if ever in the mountains a mist
    has caught you, through which your sight
    was like a mole's, through a membrane,

and if you remember how, when the thick vapors
    began to lighten, you could see faintly
    from within them the sphere of the sun,

it will be easy for you to imagine
    how I saw that planet which already
    was on the point of setting.

So, keeping step with my trusted master,
    I issued from the cloud into the sun's rays
    which were already dead on the shore below.   12

> *Among the checks on anger is the example of Procne who, to avenge a wrong done by her husband to her sister, made him eat, unsuspecting, the flesh of his own child. Later she was changed into a nightingale. Another example is that of the mother of Lavinia who committed suicide at the false report of the death of Turnus to whom her daughter had been betrothed. She feared that the victorious Aeneas would take Lavinia from her.*

O fantasy which at times steals us
    from ourselves, so that we are not aware
    if a thousand trumpets sound around us,

who creates you, since the senses give no impressions?
    A light formed in heaven moves you
    either by itself or by a will that directs it down.

A trace of the impiety of her [Procne]
    who changed into the bird that delights most
    to sing, appeared in my imagination,

and my mind was so intent
    within itself, that from without
    no impressions were received by it.   24

Then fell within my soaring fantasy
    one [Haman] crucified, scornful and fierce
    in looks even as he died.

Around him were the great Ahasuerus,
    Esther his wife, and the just Mordecai
    who was so honest in word and deed.[3]

And as this vision broke of itself,
    like a bubble as the water fails
    of which it is formed,

so there arose in my vision a maiden
    weeping loudly and saying, "O queen,
    why in your anger did you wish to be nothing?   36

You killed yourself for fear of losing Lavinia,
    yet you have lost her. I must mourn for you
    before mourning for another."

As sleep is broken when suddenly
    a light strikes the closed eyes,
    and being broken, wavers before it quite dies away,

so my imagining ended as soon as a light
    greater than any known here
    had struck my face.

I was turning to see where I was when a voice,
    banishing every other thought,
    said, "Here you mount."   48

It made my will so eager to see
    who was speaking that it could not rest
    until confronted with what it wanted.

---

[3] Ahasuerus was king of Persia. His minister Haman, angry with the upright Jew Mordecai, tried to annihilate the Jews, but Esther, wife of the king and cousin of Mordecai, caused Haman to be crucified (or hanged) instead. See Esther, chapters 3–7.

But as the sun burdens our sight
    and with its excess veils its form,
      so here my powers failed.

"This is a divine spirit, directing us
    on our way without our asking,
      and with his light he hides himself.

He acts as a man should; for whoever
    sees help needed and waits to be asked,
      may prompt an unkind refusal.   60

Now let our feet accept such an invitation;
    let us try to rise before dark,
      for afterward we cannot, until day returns."

Thus my master spoke, and with him
    I turned toward the stairway;
      and as soon as I was on the first step

I felt near my face the motion
    and the fanning of a wing, and heard the words,
      Beati pacifici[4] who are without sinful anger.

Already the last rays followed
    by the night were so high above us
      that stars appeared in several places.   72

"O my strength! why do you melt away?"
    I said to myself, for I felt [as the sun set]
      the power of my legs suspended.

We were at the top, where the stairs
    could not be climbed further,
      and were stranded, like a grounded ship.

I waited a while to see if I might hear
    some sound on the new ledge;
      then I turned to my master and said,

"My dear father, tell me what offense
    is purged on the round where we are;
      if our feet are stayed, do not end your words."   84

And he to me, "Love of good,
    when insufficient, is here restored;
      here the slackened oars are plied again.

But, in order to understand more clearly,
    direct your mind to me
      and you will gain good fruit for our tarrying."

[4] "Blessed are the peacemakers" (Matthew 5:9).

Virgil now classifies the various vices by relating them all to love (desire). Instinctive desires are primarily innocent, but acquired love may involve a bad object or be devoted to a legitimate one without moderation. A bad object implies injury to our fellow men, since all creatures are free from self-hatred or hatred of God. Proud men wish to dominate others; the envious wish for their decline; the angry are eager for vengeance. These vices are reformed on the first three ledges. Insufficient love for spiritual good (sloth) is punished on the fourth ledge. On the last three, disproportionate love for an object not bad in itself (avarice or prodigality, gluttony, and lust) is cured.

"Neither Creator nor creature, my son," he began,
  "was ever without love [desire] either instinctive
  or dependent upon the will [acquired], as you know.

The instinctive is always without error,
  but the other can err through a bad object
  or through too little or too much vigor.   96

While it is directed to primal [spiritual] good
  and is moderate in other things,
  it cannot be a cause of sinful pleasure.

But when it turns to evil or to legitimate pleasures
  with too much or too little care,
  the creature works against his Creator.

Hence you can understand that love
  must be the seed of every virtue in you
  and of every act that deserves punishment.

Now, since love can never turn
  from the welfare of its possessor,
  all things are free from self-hatred.   108

And because no one can be conceived
  as separate from the First [God] and existing by himself,
  every desire is cut off from hating Him.

It follows, if I distinguish rightly,
  that the evil we love is our neighbors',
  and this arises in three ways in our mortal clay.

Some [the proud] hoping to excel
  through their neighbors' decline
  long only to reduce their greatness.

Others [the envious] fear losing power,
  honor, and fame if another rises,
  and wish for the contrary.   120

Still others [the angry] feel so disgraced
  by injuries received that they long
  for vengeance and plan suffering for others.

This threefold love is wept for down below.
    Now I want you to hear about that love
    which seeks the good with wrong intensity.

Everyone conceives confusedly
    some ultimate [spiritual] good that will quiet
    all longing, and everyone desires it.

If insufficient love impels us
    toward it, this ledge,
    after due repentance, torments us.   132

There are other good things which do not make us happy;
    they do not give felicity, are not
    the essence and root of every good fruit.

Love which abandons itself too much to them
    is wept for above us in three rounds,
    but why it is described as threefold, I do not say,

so that you can discover it for yourself."

CANTO XVIII

MORAL RESPONSIBILITY—THE SLOTHFUL

*Dante is troubled by still another problem. He wants to understand better what
"love" is, to which all vices and virtues are related. He learns that natural,
instinctive desire is innocent. Love acquired through indulgence, however, may
be sinful and deserving of punishment, since man possesses innate ideas of right
and wrong, and a will which makes choice possible. But the question of moral
responsibility is too deep for Reason alone. Beatrice (Revelation) must give the
final answer.*

The eminent teacher had ended his explanation,
    and looked attentively in my face
    to see if I appeared content,

and I, tormented by a new thirst,
    outwardly kept silent, but inwardly said,
    "Perhaps too much questioning will bother him."

But that true father who knew
    of my timid, unexpressed wish
    gave me the boldness to ask.

Therefore I said, "Master, my sight is so quickened
    in your light that I discern clearly
    all that your explanations contain or describe;   12

so I beg you, dear father,
    to explain 'love' to me, to which you reduce
    every good action and its contrary."

"Direct toward me," he said, "the sharp eyes
    of your mind, and the errors of the blind
    who try to lead will be apparent to you.

The soul created ready to love
    is susceptible to everything that pleases
    as soon as it is awakened into activity.

Your perception of an object
    creates an impression in you
    which makes the soul turn toward it,   24

and if, so turned, it inclines in that direction,
    that inclination is love. It is a natural feeling
    reinforced in you through pleasure experienced.

Then as fire rises because of its form
    which makes it ascend
    to where it can remain in its element,

so the soul, captivated by a desire,
    a spiritual force, never rests
    until the thing loved makes it rejoice.

Now you know the truth
    hidden from those who maintain
    that every love is praiseworthy in itself,   36

because, although it may *appear* good,
    not every seal has worth
    even if impressed on good wax."

"Your words and my attentive mind," I answered,
    "have revealed to me what love is,
    but that has made me doubt still more

for, if love comes from without
    and the soul acts on no other basis,
    whether it goes straight or not, it has no merit."

And he to me, "Whatever reason can see in this
    I can tell you; expect to hear the rest
    only from Beatrice, since it requires faith.   48

Every substantial form [soul] distinct
    from body and united with it
    has in itself a specific virtue[5]

which is imperceptible except in operation
    and demonstrated only by its results,
    as life in plants is shown by their green leaves.

[5] The specific virtue (power) in the human soul is innate knowledge and a tendency to love.

Therefore, whence comes understanding
    of axiomatic truths, man does not know,
    nor his liking for the primal objects of desire

which is in you like the instinct in bees
    to make honey; and this first love
    does not admit of praise or blame.   60

Now, to make every desire conform,
    there is, innate in you, the virtue that counsels
    and which must defend the threshold of consent.

This is the source from which
    merit derives, according as good and bad loves
    are accepted or winnowed out.

Those who have gone deeply in philosophy
    have been aware of this innate liberty,
    and therefore have left ethics to the world.

Thus, supposing that every love
    by necessity is kindled in you,
    the power exists in you to resist it.   72

Beatrice understands this noble virtue as free will;
    therefore see that you have it in mind
    if she undertakes to speak to you about it."

> *The poets have spent the evening at the edge of the fourth ledge. Souls, formerly*
> *slothful, rush by, citing as the "goad" examples of haste and diligence and the*
> *opposite qualities as a "check."*

The moon, delayed almost to midnight,
    looked like a red-hot kettle,
    and made the stars seem fewer.

It proceeded against the sky's movement [backing up]
    on the path [the ecliptic] which the sun enflames
    when from Rome it is seen setting between Sardinia and Corsica,

and that noble soul [Virgil], on account of whom
    Pietola [his birthplace] is more famous than any other Mantuan
        city,
    had put down the burden of my loading.   84

So I, having received clear and plain answers
    to my questions, remained
    like one who lets his mind wander.

But this somnolence was dispelled suddenly
    by people who, behind our backs,
    had come around to where we were.

As [the rivers] Ismenus and Asopus once saw a tumult
    and a throng [the Bacchic orgies] at night along their banks
    whenever the Thebans had need of Bacchus,

so such a throng, judging by what I saw,
 bent its way around that ledge,
 driven on by good will and love.   96

That great crowd, because all in it
 were running, was soon upon us,
 and two in front, weeping, shouted,

"Mary *ran* in haste to the mountain,"[6]
 and "Caesar, to subdue Lerida,
 attacked Marseilles and then *rushed* to Spain."

"Quickly, quickly, let no time be lost
 through insufficient love," shouted the others,
 "so that our efforts to do good may renew grace."

"O people, you in whom keen fervor now
 makes up perhaps for negligence and delay
 shown previously in well-doing,   108

this man who lives (and certainly I do not lie)
 wishes to go up when the sun shines again;
 therefore, tell us where the nearest opening is."

These were the words of my guide,
 and one of those spirits said,
 "Come behind us, and you will find the pass.

We are so full of desire to move
 that we cannot stay; therefore pardon us
 if you take our punishment for rudeness.

I was the Abbot of San Zeno at Verona
 under the rule of the good Barbarossa
 of whom Milan still talks with sorrow.   120

And another already has a foot in the grave
 who will weep for having had power
 over that monastery,

because his son, deformed in body
 and worse in mind and a bastard,
 he has installed in place of its true pastor."

I do not know if he said more or was silent,
 so far had he already moved from us,
 but this I heard and gladly retained.

And Virgil, my help in every need,
 said, "Turn around, see two coming,
 giving sloth a curb [check]."   132

Behind the rest they were saying,
 "The people [sluggish Hebrews] for whom the sea opened
 were dead before Jordan [the Promised Land] saw its heirs," and,

---

[6] After learning that she would bear Jesus, Mary "arose in those days, and went into the hill country with haste" (Luke 1:39) to visit Elisabeth.

"Those that did not endure toil to the end
  with the son of Anchises [Aeneas]
  gave themselves up to a life without glory."

Then when those shades were so far from us
  that they could no longer be seen,
  a new thought came into my mind,

from which others, different, arose,
  and so much did I ramble from one to another
  that in my wandering I closed my eyes,   144

and transmuted thought into dreams.

CANTO XIX. *In the night Dante has another dream, this time of the Siren who represents the excessive indulgence in sensory pleasure. In accord with the scheme Virgil has outlined, the sensual vices will be cleansed on the next three terraces. Virgil, in the dream, strips the Siren, revealing the vileness that underlies her attractions. He and Dante climb to the fifth terrace, of the avaricious and prodigal. Penitents afflicted with these vices are lying face down, forced thus to confront their overattachment to the earth-bound senses. Dante now learns, from Pope Adrian V, that souls in Purgatory can skip terraces if they are free from the vices punished there. Dante kneels in reverence to the pope but is told by him not to do so; such earthly honors are no longer payable to individuals in the afterlife.*

CANTO XX. *Dante hears praises of generosity and poverty from one of the souls lying prone, who proves to be the progenitor of the line of French kings. (The contrary warnings against avarice are recited at night.) The many evils perpetrated by this royal house are denounced. Dante is frightened into haste by a sudden violent tremor, as of an earthquake, and from the whole mountain rises a loud cry in praise of God.*

CANTO XXI

STATIUS

The natural thirst which is never quenched
  except with the water [of truth] asked for,
  as a boon, by the woman of Samaria,[7]

tormented me, and haste goaded me
  over the encumbered road, behind my leader;
  and I was sorrowing for the just penance,

when, behold! as Luke tells how Christ,
  already risen from the grave, appeared
  to the two who were on the way,[8]

so a shade appeared to us as we were gazing
  at the crowd at our feet, having come from behind,
  nor were we aware of him until he spoke,   12

[7] In John 4:13–14, in a dialogue by a well, Jesus describes to the Samaritan woman "a well of water springing up into everlasting life" that will forever quench thirst.

[8] After his resurrection Jesus, remaining unrecognized for some time, joined two of his followers walking to the village of Emmaus; Luke 24.

saying, "Brothers, may God grant you peace!"
   We turned quickly, and Virgil,
   with a suitable gesture, returned his greeting

and began, "May the true court
   which keeps me in eternal exile
   take you into the council of the blessed!"

"What!" he [the newcomer] cried as we proceeded quickly,
   "If you are shades whom God does not allow above,
   who has brought you so far over the stairs?"

And my leader, "If you look at the marks
   traced by the angel and borne by this man,
   you will see that he must reign among the good.   24

But because she [the Fate] who spins
   day and night had not exhausted the thread
   prepared for everyone by Clotho,[9]

his soul [*anima*, fem.), the sister of yours and mine,
   could not come up alone,
   since it does not see as we do.

Therefore I was summoned from the wide throat of Hell
   to show him the way, and I will continue
   as far as my knowledge can take him.

But tell us if you can why the mountain
   trembled a little while ago, and why
   to its wet base all the souls seemed to shout?"   36

In asking this, he so threaded
   the needle's eye of my desire that
   with hope alone he made my thirst less burning.

> *The soul who has just joined them explains that on Purgatory meteorological changes and earthquakes from natural causes cannot happen. A trembling, however, occurs whenever a soul feels free to rise to Heaven, and a cry from all the ledges celebrates the happy event. As in Hell, a kind of determinism is at work here: the soul rises of its own accord when it is light enough to do so. Its "absolute" will to go up is conditioned previously by a compulsion, the need and desire to get rid of its vices.*

He began, "The holy rule of the mountain
   permits nothing that is disorderly
   or that is contrary to custom.

This place is free from variations;
   only what heaven takes into itself
   can cause change, nothing else,

---

[9] In the myth of the three Fates, Clotho prepares the thread of a person's life, Lachesis spins it out, and Atropos cuts it off.

so that no rain, hail, snow, dew, or frost
    falls higher than the stairs
    of the three short steps.   48

No heavy or light clouds appear, nor lightning,
    nor Thaumas' daughter [the rainbow]
    who often changes place on earth.

Dry vapor [lightning] does not rise above the top
    of the three steps of which I spoke
    where the vicar of St. Peter stands.

Perhaps below, the mountain quakes more or less
    from wind compressed in the earth
    (I know not how), but up here never.

It trembles here when a soul
    feels cleansed so that it may go up,
    and such a shout accompanies it.   60

Will alone gives proof of the purity
    which takes the soul by surprise, and helps it
    when it is free to change its cloister.

It wills indeed before, but this desire,
    conditioned by Divine Justice
    as formerly by sin, keeps it in its penance.

And I who have lain in this pain
    five hundred years and more, just now
    felt my will free for a better place.

Therefore you noticed the earthquake,
    and the devout spirits on the mountain gave praise
    to the Lord who, I pray, may soon send them up."   72

Thus he spoke to us, and since we enjoy drinking
    in proportion to our thirst,
    I cannot say how much good he did me.

My wise leader said, "Now I see the net
    which holds you here, and how it is broken,
    why the mountain quakes, and at what you rejoice.

Now please let me know who you were
    and let me learn from your words
    why you have lain here so long."

Statius, the newcomer, a pagan poet, the author of the Thebaid *and the unfinished* Achilleid *(whom Dante had confused with a Christian rhetorician of the
same name and who stands in the allegory for Reason illuminated by Christianity) identifies himself, and attributes his supposed conversion to certain works of
Virgil. Virgil signals to Dante not to reveal his identity, but the latter cannot
repress a smile, which Statius asks him to explain. Virgil finally relieves Dante's
embarrassment and allows him to speak freely. On learning who Virgil is, Statius
tries to embrace him, adding thus another affectionate tribute to the ancient poet
whom Dante must soon leave.*

"At the time when good Titus with the help
    of the Supreme King, avenged the wounds
    from which flowed the blood sold by Judas,[10]   84

I lived yonder," that spirit answered, "with the title
    [of poet] which lasts longest and honors most.
    I was famous but as yet did not have faith.

So sweet was the music of my verse that,
    although of Toulouse, Rome drew me to herself
    where I merited the myrtle crown.

People still mention my name, Statius.
    I sang of Thebes, and then of great Achilles,
    but I fell by the way with the second burden.

The sparks of the divine flame
    which has inspired more than a thousand
    kindled the fire that I felt in me—   96

I mean the *Aeneid* which was a mother to me
    and the nurse of my poetry;
    without it I would not have been worth a drachma,

and to have lived yonder when Virgil was alive,
    I would have agreed to do a year more
    than I owed before coming out of exile."

At these words, Virgil turned to me
    with a look that said, "Be quiet!"
    but the will cannot do all it wishes,

for laughter and tears are such close followers
    of the passion from which they spring
    that they obey least in those who are most sincere.   108

I merely smiled, making an involuntary sign,
    whereupon Statius was silent and looked
    in my eyes where the soul is most expressive,

and said, "So may you complete your task,
    why did your face just now
    reveal to me the flashing of a smile?"

Now I am caught on one side and the other;
    one bids me keep silent, the other asks
    that I speak; whereupon I sigh and am understood

by my master, who said to me,
    "Do not be afraid, but speak and tell him
    what he asks for so earnestly."   120

Then I, "Perhaps, ancient spirit,
    you are wondering at my smile,
    but I want you to marvel still more.

---

[10] The destruction of Jerusalem in 70 A.D. by the Romans under Titus was considered as a judgment on the Jews for the death of Jesus.

He who guides my eyes on high
　　is that Virgil from whom you gained
　　the power to sing of the gods and of men.

If you believe anything else caused my laughter
　　consider it as untrue and that the reason
　　was what you said about him."

Already he was bending to embrace my master's feet
　　when Virgil said, "Brother, do not do it,
　　for you are a shade and are looking at one."　　　　132

And he, on rising, "Now you can understand
　　the greatness of the love that warms me
　　for you when I forget our emptiness

and consider a shade as a solid thing."

CANTO XXII. *As the three men leave the fifth terrace, Virgil expresses surprise that so noble a soul as Statius should have been guilty of avarice but is informed by Statius that he was guilty rather of prodigality, which is punished in the same circle. Statius adds that he owes his freedom from avarice, and indeed his very salvation, to his having read Virgil, who, through his eclogue prophesying the birth of a wondrous child, led Statius to the Christian faith. Virgil is compared to a man who walks in darkness, carrying a lantern that lights the way for those who follow but not for himself. Virgil, in turn, describes the position, in Limbo, of himself and of other ancient poets and worthies. Entering the Terrace of Gluttony, the travelers see a great fruit tree, sprayed with water from a fall nearby. From the tree comes a voice citing examples of abstinence.*

CANTO XXIII. *Dante sees the formerly gluttonous purgatorians, now emaciated by the tantalizing prospect of the tree and of others like it around the ledge. Their penitential suffering brings them joy, however. Dante meets his old friend Forese Donati, who condemns the immoral dress of the Florentine women. Dante explains how he was delivered by Beatrice and Virgil from the worldliness in which he and Forese had formerly been immersed.*

CANTO XXIV. *Among the emaciated souls is Bonagiunta da Lucca, a poet from the old school superseded by that of Dante, with its* dolce stil nuovo, *"sweet new style." Dante explains its principle as stressing the truth in beautiful things rather than beautiful expression for its own sake. Bonagiunta approves this advance over the earlier poetic manner. From within another tree resembling the first one, a growth from the fatal tree in Eden, voices proclaim warnings against gluttony. Passing the angel of the circle, who emits a dazzling brightness and sweet odor, the three pilgrims leave the sixth terrace.*

CANTO XXV. *Dante is puzzled by the fact that bodily emaciation can be suffered by the souls they have just seen, although these souls have left their earthly bodies behind them. Virgil hints at an answer but must defer to Statius, who outlines to Dante the process of human embryology and God's inbreathing of the soul into the developing human being after it has passed the stages of lower plant and animal life. At death, this soul survives and renews its capacity for sense experience by projecting from itself an immaterial body. The travelers have now reached the seventh terrace, of the lustful; here fires burn around the terrace, forcing the three men to walk at its extreme outer edge. From within the flames are heard voices praising chastity.*

CANTO XXVI. *A group of purgatorians moving in the same direction as the pilgrims encounters another group, this one made up of former sodomites, moving in the other direction;*

both groups cry out warning examples of lust. All these sufferers remain within the flames, but Dante is able to talk with Guido Guinicelli, to whom he pays ardent tribute as the founder of his school of poetry. The troubador poet Arnaut Daniel, the foremost of the Provençal poets, is also honored and introduced. The implication is that poets, as singers of love, are especially prone to the vice of lust purged away on this terrace.

CANTO XXVII

THE DREAM OF LEAH
As this canto begins, the sun is setting in Purgatory and rising in Jerusalem; Spain (Ebro) is under the constellation of Libra, and it is noon in India.

The sun was darting its first beams
    on the place where its Maker shed his blood—
    the Ebro falling beneath the lofty scales,

and the waters of the Ganges made hot by noon—
    and [in Purgatory] day was departing
    when God's glad angel appeared.

Out of the flames he stood on the bank
    and sang, *"Beati mundo corde"*[11]
    in a voice much clearer than ours.

Then, "You cannot go farther, holy souls,
    unless the pain of fire is felt. Enter it
    and do not be deaf to the singing beyond."   12

This he said to us when we drew close,
    and when I heard his words I became
    like one who is laid in the grave.

I leaned over my clasped hands,
    looking at the fire and recalling vividly
    the burned human bodies I had seen.

The good escorts turned toward me
    and Virgil said, "My son,
    here there can be pain, but not death.

Remember! Remember!
    and if I guided you safely on Geryon,
    what will I do now, closer to God?   24

Be assured that if you stayed a thousand years
    in the midst of these flames
    they would not make you lose one hair;

and if perhaps you think that I deceive you,
    go toward them, and with your two hands
    and the hem of your dress gain assurance.

---

[11]"Blessed are the pure in heart" (Matthew 5:8).

Put aside, put aside all fear;
    turn this way, come, and enter securely."
    But I stood firm despite my conscience.

When he saw me remain still and stubborn,
    somewhat disturbed he said, "Now see, my son,
    this wall is between you and Beatrice!"   36

As Pyramus at the sound of Thisbe's name[12]
    opened his eyes and looked at her
    at the time when the mulberry became red,

so, my stubbornness softened, I turned
    to my wise leader, hearing the name
    which always springs up anew in my mind.

Then he shook his head and said, "What?
    do we want to stay on this side?" then smiled
    as to a child won over by an apple.

He stepped into the fire ahead of me,
    begging Statius to come behind
    who, for a long time, had divided us.   48

When I was in, I would have plunged
    into boiling glass to cool off,
    so extreme was the burning.

My sweet father, to comfort me,
    kept speaking of Beatrice,
    and adding, "I seem already to see her eyes."

A voice singing beyond guided us,
    and attentive only to it,
    we came to where the ascent began.

Venite, benedicti patris mei![13] sounded there
    within a light which so blinded me
    that I could not look at it.   60

"The sun is leaving," it added, "and evening
    comes; do not stop, but hasten
    while the west is still not dark."

The path rose straight within the rock
    so that the rays of the sun,
    already low, were broken in front of me.

The sages and I had mounted a few steps only
    when we noticed by my disappearing shadow
    that the sun was setting behind us.

---

[12] Pyramus and Thisbe had to confess their love through a chink in the wall between their houses. Later, Pyramus, thinking Thisbe dead, killed himself, his blood turning the fruit of the mulberry red.

[13] "Come ye blessed of my father," the words that welcome the saved into God's kingdom (Matthew 25:34).

And before the vast expanse
    of the horizon had become of one hue,
    and before Night held all its domain,   72

each of us made a bed of a step;
    for the nature of the mountain overcame,
    not our desire, but our strength to rise.

As goats, agile and wanton on the heights
    before they have eaten, become tame
    when ruminating, lying silent and quiet

in the shade while the sun is hot,
    watched over by the herdsman who leans
    on his staff, and while leaning guards them;

and as the shepherd who lodges in the open
    passes the night beside his flock,
    watching lest a wild beast scatter it,   84

so we were, all three of us,
    I like the goats and they like the shepherds,
    hemmed in on both sides by high walls.

There, little could be seen outside,
    but in that little the stars appeared
    clearer and larger than usual.

Thus, looking at them and musing,
    sleep came upon me, the sleep which often
    announces events before they occur.

*In a dream Dante sees Leah, who represents the innocent active life; Rachel, her
sister, stands for contemplation.*

At the hour, I believe, when Cytherea [Venus]
    always burning with the fire of love
    first shines from the east on the mount,   96

in a dream I seemed to see a lady,
    young and beautiful, going over a meadow
    gathering flowers and who while singing said,

"Let whoever asks for my name know
    that I am Leah, and I use my fair hands
    to make myself a garland.

I adorn myself to reflect a pleasant image;
    my sister Rachel never leaves her mirror,
    but sits before it all the day.

She likes to see her beautiful eyes
    as I to beautify myself with my hands;
    for her, seeing; for me, doing, satisfies."   108

And now amid the splendors before dawn
    which are the more welcome to pilgrims
    when, on returning, they spend the night nearer home,

on all sides the darkness fled
    and my sleep with it; and I got up
    seeing my great masters already risen.

> *After climbing to the top of the mountain, Virgil addresses Dante for the last time. The ancient poet has revealed all that Reason can disclose. Under his guidance Dante has freed himself not only of bad habits, but of the innate vices, the very potentiality for sin. He has attained a freedom from hereditary limitations and from environmental conditioning that no one on earth can ever have. The faith in the goodness of Nature, which later in the Renaissance deluded many, is appropriate for him. Free from the need for choice or thought or inner struggle, he can do as he pleases. To symbolize this freedom, this goal of man's reforming efforts, he is figuratively endowed with a crown and miter, the symbols of temporal and spiritual power.*

"That sweet fruit [happiness] for which,
    on so many branches, mortals search,
    today will satisfy your hunger."

These words Virgil addressed to me,
    and never were there gifts
    that caused such delight.   120

So greatly did desire rush upon desire
    to be above, that at every step
    I felt my wings grow for the flight.

When the stairway was wholly under us
    and we were on the top step,
    Virgil fixed his eyes on me and said,

"The temporal fire [of Purgatory] and the eternal [of Hell]
    you have seen, my son, and have come to a place
    where I, by myself, can discern nothing further.

I have brought you here with reason and with art;
    now take pleasure as your guide;
    you are free from the steep and narrow ways.   132

See the sun shining on your brow;
    see the grass, the flowers, and the shrubs
    which the earth here produces of itself.

Until the fair eyes [of Beatrice], now rejoicing, come—
    which in tears made me go to you—
    you can sit or walk among them.

Expect no further word or sign from me;
    free, upright, and whole is your will;
    it would be wrong not to do as it pleases.

Therefore, over yourself, I crown and miter you."

CANTO XXVIII

THE GARDEN OF EDEN

Eager now to look within and around
　　the dense and verdant forest which tempered
　　for our eyes the light of the new day,

without delay I left the mountain's edge,
　　and went slowly over the plain
　　on ground fragrant everywhere.

A sweet, unvarying breeze
　　touched my face as lightly
　　as a gentle wind

and made the leaves, quick to tremble,
　　bend in the direction
　　of the holy mountain's morning shadow,   12

not deflecting them, however, so far
　　that the birds there
　　must give up practicing their art;

but these, singing, full of joy, greeted the first hours
　　of the day from within the rustling leaves
　　which accompanied their song, just as,

in the pine grove on the shore of Chiassi
　　a sound swells from branch to branch
　　when Aeolus[14] lets the Sirocco blow.

Already my slow steps had taken me
　　so far within the ancient forest
　　that I could not see where I entered;   24

and behold! a stream prevented me
　　from going farther, which with little waves
　　bent leftward the grass growing on its banks.

The clearest waters on earth
　　would seem to have some mixture in them
　　compared with these which conceal nothing,

although they move darkly
　　under perpetual shade never pierced
　　by the rays of the sun or of the moon.

I held back my steps, but with my eyes
　　I glanced beyond the stream to see
　　the great variety of fresh May branches.   36

---

[14] God of the winds. The Sirocco is a hot Mediterranean wind.

And over there appeared, like something
    which, through the marveling it causes,
    turns every other thought aside,

a solitary lady who went along singing
    and choosing flowers from the flowers
    with which her path was painted.

"O fair lady, you who warm yourself
    in the rays of love (if I can believe your looks
    which are the witnesses of the heart),

may you be pleased to come forward
    toward this stream," I said to her,
    "so that I can understand what you sing.   48

You make me imagine where and how
    Proserpine[15] was at the time when her mother
    lost her, and when she lost the Spring."

As a lady when dancing turns
    with feet together and close to the ground,
    hardly moving one ahead of the other,

so she turned on the red and yellow flowers
    toward me, like a virgin,
    lowering her modest eyes.

And she fulfilled all my wishes,
    approaching so that the sweet sound
    of her voice came to me with its meaning.   60

As soon as she reached the place where the grass
    was bathed by the waves of the fair rivulet,
    she delighted me by lifting her eyes.

I do not believe that such light shone
    under the eyelids of Venus
    when she was wounded unintentionally by her son.[16]

She smiled, standing on the other bank,
    carrying in her hands flowers of many colors
    which the high land produces without seed.

The river kept us separated by three steps
    but Hellespont, where Xerxes passed—
    still a check on human pride—   72

---

[15] Proserpine was carried off in springtime by Pluto, god of the underworld, from the beautiful garden of Enna in Sicily.

[16] Venus was accidentally nicked by her son Cupid's arrow, which caused her to fall in love with Adonis.

was not more hated by Leander[17]
    for flowing between Sestos and Abydos
    than this stream by me for not opening.

"You are strangers here," she began,
    "and perhaps because I smile in this place
    chosen as the nest for human kind,

some wonder keeps you marveling;
    but the psalm *Delectasti*[18] gives light
    which can clear the mist from your minds.

And you in front who spoke to me,
    say if you wish to hear more, for I have come
    ready to satisfy all of your requests."   84

> *Matilda, the symbol of innocence and the guardian or presiding spirit of the Earthly Paradise, explains that the breeze is caused by the revolution of the heavens which communicate their movement to the sphere of air into which Purgatory projects. All plant life is represented in the Garden of Eden, and its reproductive power is dispersed over the earth by the moving air. Two streams, Lethe, which removes guilty memories, and Eunoè, which restores the recollection of all good deeds, are replenished by the will of God alone.*

> *Matilda adds, as a corollary, that the Ancients with their imperfect vision of the Christian truth mistook the Garden of Eden for the world in their "Golden Age." At this reference to their partial error, Virgil and Statius smile.*

"The water," I said, "and the sound of the forest
    combat in me a belief in something
    that denies the possibility of them."

Then she, "I will explain the cause
    of what makes you wonder
    and dispel the fog that has enveloped you.

The Supreme Good which follows only Its own pleasure
    made man good and for good, and gave this place
    to him as a pledge of eternal peace.

Through his fault he stayed here
    only a short time; through his fault he exchanged
    innocent laughter and play for tears and toil.   96

To prevent the vapors caused by the evaporation
    of land and water and which follow the heat
    as much as they can

---

[17] The Hellespont (modern Dardanelles) was a strait crossed by the Persian king Xerxes on his way to invade Greece. The strait also separated the lovers Leander of Abydos and Hero of Sestos.

[18] Psalm 92:4 ("For thou, Lord, hast made me glad through thy work").

from doing harm to man, this mountain rose
    so high toward Heaven, and is free
    from the gate upward from atmospheric change.

Now, since the air revolves
    with the primal revolution
    if its circling is not broken anywhere,

on this highest summit which projects
    in the air, such movement strikes
    and makes the dense wood give forth a sound;   108

and the smitten plants have such power
    that they impregnate the breeze with their virtues,
    and the air, revolving, scatters them,

and the land elsewhere, according as it is suited
    in itself and in its climate, conceives
    and produces from different virtues different growths.

Having heard this, it should not appear
    a marvel to you when some plant
    without apparent seed takes root.

And you must know that the sacred land
    where you are is full of every seed
    and has fruit not plucked in your world.   120

The water you see does not come from a spring
    restored by vapor condensed by cold,
    like rivers which rise and fall,

but comes from a stable and certain source,
    since it takes from the will of God
    what is poured forth in two streams.

On this side it descends with the power
    to take away memory of sin, and on the other
    it restores that of all good deeds.

Here it is called Lethe, over there
    Eunoè, and it is not effective
    unless drunk both here and there.   132

Its taste excels all other flavors.
    And, although your thirst may be quenched
    without my revealing more,

I will add as a favor a corollary;
    nor do I believe my remarks will be less dear
    if they go beyond my promise.

Those who in ancient times
    sang of the Golden Age and its happy state
    perhaps dreamed of this place on Parnassus.

Here the root of man's race was innocent,
     here is eternal Spring, and here is every fruit;
     this is the 'nectar' of which all sing."   144

I turned to my poets
     and saw that with smiles
     they had heard the last remark.

Then I turned my face to the fair lady.

CANTO XXIX. *Witnessing the landscape of Eden, Dante feels indignation at the sin that deprived humanity of so blissful a state. He sees approach a magnificent allegorical pageant, which Virgil is no longer capable of elucidating: seven candlesticks streaming colors (the gifts of the spirit); twenty-four elders (books of the Old Testament); four beasts (the Gospels); the Chariot of the Church, drawn by a griffon (Christ, with his two natures, human and divine); seven dancers (the three theological, or evangelical, virtues and the four cardinal, or moral, virtues); seven more elders (the remaining New Testament sources, namely Paul and the author of Acts; the four authors of other epistles; and the author of Revelation). The procession halts as a peal of thunder rings out.*

CANTO XXX

THE COMING OF BEATRICE (REVELATION)

The candlesticks are compared to the Septentrion, the constellation that contains the North Star. When they stop, all those in the procession turn expectantly toward the chariot of the Church which is to bring Beatrice (Revelation) to Dante (Mankind). At a call, angels hover over it, and within a rain of flowers that veil her, Beatrice appears, dressed in the colors of the three evangelical virtues. At this climactic moment, Latin phrases occur frequently, among them a line from the Aeneid (Manibus o date lilia plenis!), spoken by an angel as the last and supreme compliment to Virgil, who must now disappear, eclipsed. Dante feels the effect of Beatrice's presence as he had on earth, and in his distress turns to Virgil. But his former guide, denied the sight of Revelation, has already disappeared, and Dante is left alone before the overwhelming spectacle to accomplish the painful but necessary rites of contrition, confession, and satisfaction (penance).

When the Septentrion of the first heaven—
     which never knew rising or setting
     nor the veil of any mist except of sin

and which made everyone there aware
     of his duty, as the lower star does
     him who turns the helm to come to port—

had stopped, the true people who had come
     between it and the griffon[19]
     turned to the chariot as to their peace.

And one of them, as if sent from Heaven,
     cried three times in song *"Veni, sponsa, de Libano,"*[20]
     and all the others sang after him.   12

[19] A beast with an eagle's head and wings and a lion's body.
[20] "Come with me from Lebanon, my spouse" (Song of Solomon 4:8). Allegorically, the line represents Christ's greeting to the Church.

As the blessed, at the last trumpet call,
    will rise quickly from their graves,
    singing with regained voices "Hallelujah,"

so, above the divine vehicle
    a hundred [angels] rose *(ad vocem tanti senis)*[21]
    the ministers and messengers of eternal life.

All cried, *"Benedictus qui venis,"*[22]
    and scattering flowers above and around,
"Manibus o date lilia plenis!"[23]

I have often seen at the beginning of the day
    the eastern sky all rosy, the rest
    of the heavens beautifully clear,   24

and the sun's face appear veiled,
    so that, through the tempering of the vapors,
    the eyes could look steadily at it.

Thus, within a cloud of flowers,
    thrown by angelic hands, which rose
    and fell on and around the chariot,

underneath a white veil, crowned with olive,
    a lady appeared to me, under a green mantle,
    dressed in the color of living flame.

And my spirit which already had spent
    so long a time without the trembling
    from awe which her presence caused,   36

without seeing her more clearly,
    through a hidden influence which came from her,
    felt the great power of its old love.

As soon as on my eyes the great virtue fell
    which already had pierced me
    before I was out of childhood,[24]

I turned to the left with the expectation
    which a child has who runs to its mother
    when afraid or afflicted,

to say to Virgil, "Not a drop of blood
    unmoved is left in me;
    I recognize the signs of the old love!"[25]   48

[21] "At the voice of so great an elder."
[22] "Blessed are you who come" (cf. Matthew 21:9). This is a slight variation on the acclamation of Christ at his entrance into Jerusalem.
[23] "Oh, give lilies with full hands!"
[24] When Dante first saw the earthly Beatrice, he was less than nine years old. She died in 1290, when she was twenty-four, Dante twenty-five.
[25] This line is translated from Virgil's *Aeneid*, Book IV, where Dido tells her sister Anna that Aeneas has reawakened in her the symptoms of love after she thought she had banished it from her life.

But Virgil had left me without his company,
    Virgil, my beloved father, Virgil,
    to whom I gave myself up for my salvation;

nor could all that our ancient mother lost [Eden]
    keep my cheeks, cleaned with dew,
    from being darkened again by tears.

> *Now Beatrice speaks, not in her role as a tender friend, but severely, as a minister of the sacraments, calling Dante by his name (which appears here only), since the confession to follow must be personal and, in a manner, signed. Dante is paralyzed by this reception, but when the angels show sympathy for him, his awakened self-pity and his distress grow until he bursts into tears. Thus the first stage of the sacrament is accomplished.*

"Dante, although Virgil is leaving,
    do not weep yet, do not weep yet,
    for you must cry for another wound!"

As an admiral, at the prow or stern,
    looks at those who man the other ships,
    and heartens them to their work,   60

so—when I turned at the sound of my name,
    which is recorded here from necessity—
    at the left side of the chariot

I saw the lady who at first appeared
    veiled under the angelic shower
    directing her eyes at me from beyond the stream,

although the veil descending from her head,
    wreathed with Minerva's leaves [the olive],
    kept her from being completely manifest.

Queenlike, stern in her bearing,
    she continued, like one who speaks
    while holding back the sharpest words.   72

"Look at me! I am indeed, I am indeed Beatrice.
    How did you dare to approach the mount?
    Did you not know that here man is happy?"

My glances fell down to the clear stream;
    but seeing myself in it, I turned them
    to the grass, such shame burdened my face.

As a mother at times seems cruel
    to her son, so she appeared to me,
    since the taste of stern pity is bitter.

Then she was silent, and the angels sang
    at once, *"In te, Domine, speravi,"*[26]
    but did not go beyond *pedes meos.*[27]   84

---

[26] "In thee, O Lord, do I put my trust" (Psalm 31:1).

[27] "My feet." These words occur in verse 8 of the psalm; after this verse the tone changes from trust and assurance to despondency.

As snow on the living rafters [trees]
    of the back of Italy [the Apennines] congeals
    when blown and packed by Slavic winds,

then, melted, trickles down, if a breath comes
    from the land [Africa] without shadows,
    like fire melting a candle,

so was I without tears or sighs
    before those [angels] whose song is accompanied
    by the melodies of the eternal spheres;

but when I heard in their sweet notes
    their pity for me, more than if they had said,
    "Lady, why do you shame him so?"   96

the frost which had gripped my heart
    became breath and water, and with anguish
    through mouth and eyes came from my breast.

> *To prepare for the next stage, Beatrice tells how Dante, after her death, had*
> *devoted himself to the* donna pietosa *of the* Vita Nuova[28] *(profane philoso-*
> *phy), and to worldliness.*

She, still standing at the side
    of the chariot, then turned to address
    the angels who had shown pity for me.

"You watch in the eternal day,
    so that neither night nor sleep hides from you
    a step taken on the ways of the world;

therefore, my answer takes greater care
    that he, weeping over there, should understand,
    and that his sin and sorrow should be equal.   108

Not only by the operation of the great spheres
    which direct each seed to some end,
    according as the stars are conjoined,

but through the bounty of Divine Grace
    which has such high vapors for its rain
    that our sight cannot come close to them,

this man was such, potentially, in his young life
    that every good disposition
    might have come to marvelous fruition;

but the more vigor there is in the soil
    the more malignant and rank it becomes
    if uncultivated or sown with bad seed.   120

---

[28] The *New Life,* a quasi-allegorical work by Dante in which his spiritual autobiography is
traced in terms of his various loves. *Donna pietosa* means "compassionate lady."

For a while I sustained him with my countenance,
    and showing my youthful eyes to him,
    I led him with me in the right direction.

As soon as I was on the threshold
    of my second age, and changed life,
    he abandoned me, and gave himself to others.

When I had risen from flesh to spirit
    and beauty and virtue had increased in me,
    I was less dear to him and less esteemed,

and he turned his steps on an evil path,
    following false images of good
    which never fulfill their promise.   132

Nor did it avail me to invoke inspirations
    by which, in dreams and otherwise,
    I recalled him, so little did he care.

He fell so low that all means
    for his salvation would have been unavailing
    except to show him the lost people.

Therefore, I visited the portal of the dead,
    and to the one who brought him here,
    in sorrow I addressed my request.

The high decrees of God would be broken
    if Lethe were crossed and such a draught
    were tasted without any payment   144

of the penance that causes tears to flow."

CANTO XXXI

CONFESSION AND SATISFACTION
Beatrice now addresses Dante directly.

"O you beyond the sacred stream,"
    she continued without pausing,
    directing the point of her speech toward me

which even with the edge had seemed sharp,
    "say, say if this is true; to this accusation
    your confession must be joined."

My senses were so confused
    that my words began and were spent
    before released from their organs.

She waited a moment, then, "What are you thinking?"
    she questioned. "Answer me, for your sad memories
    are not yet impaired by the water [of Lethe]!"   12

Confusion and fear joined together
    sent forth such a "yes" from my mouth,
    that eyes were needed to hear it.

As a crossbow under too great a tension
    breaks both the string and the bow,
    so that the shaft hits its mark with less force,

so I burst under my heavy burden,
    pouring forth tears and sighs,
    and my voice died away on its passage.

Then she said, "In your desires for me [Revelation]
    which led you to love the good
    above which there is none to aspire to,   24

what chains or what hindering pitfalls
    did you find that you should lose
    the hope of going onward?

And what comforts or what advantages
    were displayed in the aspect of another good
    that you should seek it?"

After heaving a bitter sigh,
    scarcely had I voice for an answer,
    and my lips only with effort formed it.

Sobbing I said, "The present things,
    with their false pleasures, turned my steps away
    as soon as your face was hidden."   36

And she, "If you were silent or denied
    what you confess, your sin would not be concealed,
    known as it is by such a judge.

But when confession bursts
    from one's own mouth, the grindstone in our court
    turns back against the edge [of the sword of Justice].

Still to make you bear more shame
    for your error, and to make you stronger
    another time if you hear the sirens,

put aside your sowing of tears and listen,
    and you will hear how, when my flesh was buried,
    I should have led you in the opposite direction.   48

> *Beatrice refers again to the* pargoletta *(young girl). Then, by telling Dante to
> lift his "beard" instead of "chin," she points out indirectly that he is no child and
> should know better. Overcome by remorse, Dante falls in a faint, in this way
> giving "satisfaction," and accomplishing the last stage of the sacrament.*

Never did nature or art offer such delight
    as the fair members in which I was once enclosed
    and which are now in dust and scattered,

and if the supreme pleasure failed you
    at my death, what mortal thing
    should have drawn you with desire?

At the first shaft of fallacious things
    you should have lifted yourself up,
    following me, no longer [fallacious] like them.

No young girl or other vanity of such brief use
    should have weighed down your wings
    and exposed you to more blows.   60

A young bird takes two or three chances;
    but before the eyes of a full-grown one,
    the net is spread and the arrow shot in vain."

As children mute from shame stand listening,
    with their eyes on the ground,
    conscience-stricken and repentant,

so I stood; and she continued, "Since by hearing
    you suffer, lift up your beard,
    and you will have greater grief in looking."

With less effort a sturdy oak
    is uprooted by a wind of ours
    or by one from Iarbas' land [Libya]   72

than my chin was lifted at her command;
    and when by "beard" she meant my chin,
    I knew the venom of the argument.

Then when my face was raised,
    I saw the primal creatures [angels]
    resting from their scattering of flowers.

And my eyes, still insecure,
    saw Beatrice turned toward the beast
    which is one in two natures.

Under her veil and beyond the stream
    she seemed to surpass her former self
    more than she did others when on earth.   84

The thorn of repentance so pierced me then
    that of all things, those that had made me
    love them most now became most hateful to me.

Such remorse stung my heart
    that I fell, vanquished; and what became of me,
    she knows who caused this.

When my heart gave back a sense
    of outward things, I saw the lady [Matilda]
    above me, saying, "Hold to me, hold to me!"

She had drawn me into the river up to my throat,
  and pulling me behind her, moved on
  as lightly as a little boat over the water.   96

When I was near the sacred shore, *"Asperges me,"*[29]
  I heard so sweetly that I cannot keep the sound
  in mind, much less describe it.

The fair lady opened her arms,
  took my head, and held it down
  until I swallowed the water.

> *Matilda now takes Dante to the four nymphs (Prudence, Temperance, Fortitude,*
> *and Justice). These point out the deeper vision of the evangelical virtues (Faith,*
> *Hope, and Love) and bring Dante to the griffon (Christ), which he sees reflected*
> *in its twofold unity in the eyes of Revelation.*

Then she drew me forth, and led me, bathed,
  to the dance of the four nymphs,
  each of whom covered me with her arms.

"Here we are nymphs, and in Heaven stars.
  Before Beatrice came to the world
  we were ordained for her as handmaids.   108

We will lead you to her eyes; but the three
  over there who gaze more deeply
  will sharpen yours better for the light in them."

Thus they began to sing, and then took me
  with them to the breast of the griffon
  where Beatrice stood, turned toward us.

They said, "See that you do not spare your eyes;
  we have placed you before the jewels
  from which Love once shot his arrows."

A thousand desires hotter than flames
  bound my sight to the shining eyes
  which still were fixed upon the griffon.   120

As the sun in a mirror, not otherwise
  did the twofold creature shine in them,
  now with one, now with the other nature.

Think, Reader, if I marveled
  when I saw the object remain still
  and yet change in its image.

While full of joy and wonder, my soul
  tasted that [spiritual] food which,
  satisfying, gives hunger for itself;

---

[29]"Thou shalt sprinkle me" (King James Version "purge me") "with hyssop, and I shall be clean" (Psalm 51:7).

showing themselves of a higher order
    by their actions, the other three [Virtues] advanced,
    dancing to their angelic measure.   132

"Turn, Beatrice, turn your holy eyes,"
    was their song, "to your faithful one
    who, to see you, has taken so many steps!

Do us the favor of unveiling for him
    your smile, so that he may discern
    the second beauty which you conceal."

O splendor of the living, eternal light [of Beatrice]!
    who has become so pale in the shade of Parnassus,[30]
    or drunk so deeply at its well,

that he would not seem to have a clouded mind
    in trying to describe you as you appeared
    when the harmonious heavens alone veiled you,   144

and you disclosed yourself in the open air?

CANTO XXXII. *Dante is temporarily blinded by the sight of Beatrice. When he recovers, he and Statius follow as the procession moves to the tree of the knowledge of good and evil, which represents civic obedience and the authority of the Empire, or civil state. The griffon pays tribute to the tree, and, in a gesture symbolic of the ideal fraternal equality of ecclesiastical and civil authority, the pole of the chariot of the Church is bound to the tree. Dante is overcome by sleep; when he awakens, the pageant has disappeared, leaving him with Beatrice and the representatives of the seven virtues. He is granted a vision of the tragic perversions that will afflict the church and the state.*

CANTO XXXIII. *Beatrice hints at the coming of a political savior, but Dante fails to understand her. In consideration of his still-darkened mind, she promises to speak henceforth less enigmatically. Dante, with Statius, drinks from the fountain of Eunoè, which restores the memory of all good things as Lethe had obliterated the memory of evil ones. Now, in the full brightness of noonday, Dante is ready to leave Earth and ascend to the stars.*

---

[30]The mountain sacred to Apollo and the Muses.

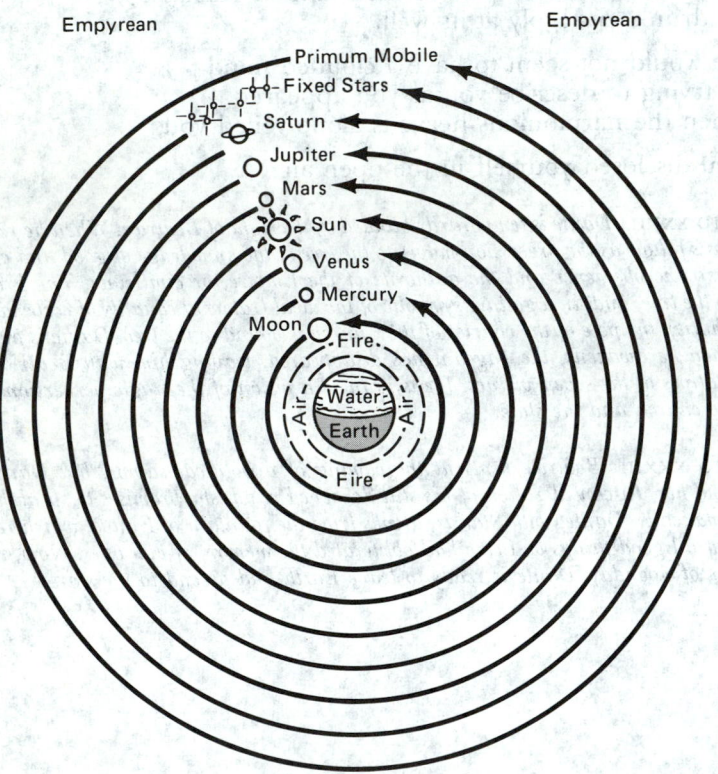

The Heavens.

Outline of Paradise

The Correspondences

PLANETS, HEAVENS	LIGHT	POSITION	PHYSICAL CHARACTERISTICS	WEAKNESS OR STRENGTH
1. Moon	Pearly		Changing phases, spots	Weakness in Faith
2. Mercury	Veiled, eclipsed by sun	Within shadow of earth	Smallness	Weakness in Hope
3. Venus	Color of flame		Double center of motion	Weakness in Love
4. Sun	White		Brightness	Strength in Prudence
5. Mars	Red	Beyond shadow of earth	Redness	Strength in Fortitude
6. Jupiter	Silvery		Temperate quality	Strength in Justice
7. Saturn	Crystal (cold)		Cold, ascetic	Strength in Temperance
8. Fixed Stars	Various	Along Golden Ladder	Variable	
9. Primum Mobile	Diaphanous		Diaphanous	
10. Empyrean				

The Correspondences

PLANETS, HEAVENS	SOULS REPRESENTED	SUBJECTS DISCUSSED	DENUNCIATIONS
1. Moon	Inconstant nuns	Vows	Ill-advised vows
2. Mercury	Lovers of earthly fame	Incarnation, atonement	Guelfs and Ghibellines
3. Venus	Sensual lovers	Heredity	Mercenary ecclesiastics
4. Sun	Theologians	God expounded in his creatures	Mendicant orders
5. Mars	Warriors of Faith	Decay of virility	Effeminacy of Florence
6. Jupiter	Just Rulers	Justice	Unjust rulers
7. Saturn	Monks	Predestination	Luxury and pomp of prelates

OUTLINE OF THE PARADISE *(continued)*

8. Fixed Stars	Apostles	Faith, Hope, Love	Unworthy popes
9. Primum Mobile		Angels	Popular preachers
10. Empyrean		[Beatific Vision]	Rejection of Henry VII

The Correspondences

PLANETS, HEAVENS	ANGELS	ANGELIC FUNCTION	HIERARCHIES	EARTHLY REPRESENTATIVES
1. Moon	Angels	Messengers to individuals		
2. Mercury	Archangels	Messengers to nations	Purifying	Deacons
3. Venus	Principalities	Guides of princes		
4. Sun	Powers	Subject to God		
5. Mars	Virtues	Divine motion	Illuminating	Priests
6. Jupiter	Dominations	Dominion		
7. Saturn	Thrones	Stability		
8. Fixed Stars	Cherubim	Knowledge	Perfecting	Bishops
9. Primum Mobile	Seraphim	Love		
10. Empyrean				

PARADISE

CANTO I

THE RISE UPWARD

After suggesting the majestic subject of the Paradiso, *that is, the splendor of the divine idea and its realization in Heaven, Dante invokes Apollo (God) and the Muses (his own talents), the "two peaks" of Parnassus. He hopes he may sing as Apollo did in the contest with Marsyas, who was flayed for his presumption in challenging the god.*

The glory of Him who moves all
    penetrates the universe, and is reflected
    in one place more, in another less.

I have been to the heaven which receives most of His light
    and seen things which one who descends
    has neither power nor knowledge to relate,

for, drawing near to its desire,
    our intellect is lost in such depths
    that memory cannot follow it.

Nevertheless, whatever my mind
    could treasure of the holy kingdom
    will now be the subject of my song.   12

O good Apollo, for the last task
    make me such a vessel of thy worth
    as the beloved laurel crown requires.

Until now one peak of Parnassus
    has been enough for me, but this time
    with both I must enter the arena which remains.

Enter my breast and breathe as thou didst
    when thou drewest Marsyas
    from the sheath of his body.

O divine Power, if Thou lendest Thyself to me,
    so that I may reveal even the shadow
    of the blessed realm imprinted on my mind,   24

Thou shalt see me come to Thy beloved tree [the laurel]
    and crown myself with those leaves
    of which Thou and my subject will make me worthy.

So rarely, Father, are they gathered
    for triumph of Caesar or of poet,—
    the fault and shame of human will—

that the Peneian leaf [the laurel] should bring joy
    to the Delphic deity [Apollo]
    when any is eager for it.

A great flame may follow a little spark;
    perhaps after me, with a better voice,
    prayers will be made to which Cyrrha [Apollo] may respond.   36

The various circles of the heavens, the celestial equator, the ecliptic, and the colure of the equinoxes, all of which cross the horizon, are most favorably related on March 21. It is now Wednesday noon, April 13, 1300, not far from this ideal moment, and the sun is still in Aries.

Dante rises swiftly from the Garden of Eden, passing through the sphere of fire which surrounds that of the air. By gazing at Beatrice he transcends his material self, his humanity.

The lamp of the world [the sun] rises for mortals
    by various paths, but on that
    which joins four circles with three crosses

it rises on its best course and is conjoined
    with its most propitious star, and tempers and seals
    the world's wax most perfectly.

Such a course had made morning there [in Eden]
    and evening here, and that hemisphere [at noon]
    was all aglow and ours dark

when I saw Beatrice turned to the left
    and gazing upon the sun:
    an eagle never looked at it so intently!   48

And, as a reflected ray
    is wont to rise upward,
    like a pilgrim wishing to return,

so her attitude, imaged in my mind,
    was copied by me, and I fixed my eyes
    on the sun, in a manner unknown here.

Much is possible to our faculties
    in the place [Eden] made for the human race
    not granted to us on earth.

I did not endure the sight long
    before I noticed a sparkling [the sphere of fire]
    like molten iron coming from a furnace.   60

Suddenly day seemed joined to day,
    as if He who had power to do so
    had adorned the heaven with another sun.

Beatrice remained with her eyes
    fixed on the eternal revolutions,
    and I turned mine, removed from above, on her.

While gazing at her, I became [transformed] like Glaucus[1]
    who tasted the herb which made him,
    in the sea, a companion of the gods.

"Transhumanizing" cannot be expressed in words;
    therefore, let the example suffice those
    for whom Grace reserves this experience.   72

If I were only that part of myself [the soul]
    created last, Thou alone, O Love, knowest,
    Thou that didst lift me with Thy light!

When the revolving [of the heavens] Thou makest eternal
    through desire made me attentive to it
    amid the harmony [of the spheres] Thou didst modulate,

so much of the sky seemed lit up
    by the flames of the sun that never rivers
    or rain ever made so large a lake.

---

[1] A fisherman transformed to a sea god by eating an herb.

The strangeness of the sound
    and the great light gave me a wish
    never before felt so keenly to know their cause;   84

whereupon she, who saw me as I see myself,
    to quiet my disturbed mind,
    spoke before I asked, and began,

"You become dull through false assumptions,
    so that you do not see
    what you would if you threw them off.

You are not on earth as you believe;
    a thunderbolt never fled down from its home
    as fast as you are going up to yours."

If I was freed of my first doubt
    by these brief words, spoken with a smile,
    I was caught more firmly in another,   96

and I said, "Already I was contented
    concerning one doubt; but now I wonder
    how I can rise through these light bodies."

Then, after a sigh of pity,
    she looked at me with that expression
    a mother has for a delirious child.

> *Beatrice explains that all things have certain characteristics or instincts which enable them to carry out the divine plan as, for example, that of fire to rise. Likewise men have an instinct that impels them to soar to Heaven, their true home, although this may be conditioned or diverted from its goal, just as fire in lightning sometimes descends. Since all hindrance has been removed, Dante's rise is no more marvelous than that water should flow down the side of a mountain.*

She began, "All things have order
    in them and this is the Form
    which makes the universe similar to God.

In it the exalted creatures see the imprint
    of the Eternal Power, the end
    for which the rule [order] was created.   108

To the order of which I speak
    all natures are obedient, by diverse lots,
    as more or less close to their source.

Thus they move to diverse ports
    over the great sea of being,
    and each with an instinct to lead it on.

This moves the fire upward toward the moon,
    this is the motive force in mortal hearts,
    this holds together and unites the earth.

Nor do the arrows of this bow
　　strike only creatures without intelligence,
　　but also those with understanding and love.　　　　　120

The Providence which ordains this
　　makes serene the heaven [the Empyrean] within which
　　turns the one [the Primum Mobile] that moves with greatest
　　　　speed.[2]

And now toward it, as to a goal decreed,
　　the power of that bow is carrying us
　　which aims its shots at a joyful mark.

It is true that, as the form, many times,
　　does not realize the intentions of the artisan
　　(since the material is slow to respond),

so the creatures thus impelled
　　sometimes deviate from their course,
　　since they have that power;　　　　　　　　　　　132

and as the fire in a cloud [lightning]
　　is seen to fall, so the creature's first impetus,
　　diverted by false pleasure, brings it to the ground.

If I judge correctly, you should not wonder more
　　at our rising than at the falling of a stream
　　from a high mountain to its base.

It would be a marvel if, unhindered,
　　you should remain seated down below,
　　as quietness would be in a living flame."

Then she turned her face again toward Heaven.

　　CANTO II. *Dante warns the reader of the immensity and profundity of the subject matter that is to follow. He and Beatrice reach the moon. Dante asks whether the dark patches on it are caused by their relatively low density. Beatrice demonstrates on scientific grounds that this explanation cannot be correct and then provides the true explanation: that the power of God, filtered through the guiding angelic intelligences, manifests itself more or less fully and brightly in the various parts of the material creation.*

CANTO III

PICCARDA AND THE EMPRESS CONSTANCE

In the lowest heaven, that of the moon, a slow-moving, changeable planet within the shadow of the earth, hardly more brilliant with divine light than a pearl, we find the inconstant nuns, their earthly images faintly visible. They serve as examples of the lowest degree of potential beatitude, and represent, perhaps, all weak and inconstant people. Among them are Piccarda, the sister of Dante's friend, Forese Donati, and the great Empress Constance, the two now equal in their rank.

[2] The empyrean heaven is the uncircumscribed abode of angels and the saved with God; the Primum Mobile (first mover) is the outermost shell of the material universe.

That sun which first had warmed my breast with love
    had unveiled, by proving and refuting,
    the fair face of truth to me

and, to confess myself corrected
    and assured, as was fitting,
    I raised my head to speak,

but a sight attracted
    my attention so closely
    that I forgot to make my confession.

As from transparent and polished glass
    or from clear and quiet water,
    not so deep that the bottom is lost to sight,   12

the outlines of our faces come back
    so faintly that a pearl on a white forehead
    appears as clearly to our eyes,

so I saw several faces ready to speak,
    which led me into the opposite error from that
    which kindled love between the man [Narcissus] and the
        spring:[3]

for, as I became aware of them,
    thinking that the countenances were mirrored,
    I turned to see whose they were

and perceived nothing. Then I looked ahead
    at the light of my sweet guide
    whose holy eyes glowed as she smiled.   24

"Do not marvel if I am amused," she said,
    "at your childish thought,
    since it still does not trust the truth

but turns you as usual toward delusions.
    What you saw are true substances [souls],
    relegated here through failure to keep their vows;

therefore, speak to them, and hear, and believe,
    since the light of the Truth which requites them
    does not let them turn from Itself."

I faced the shade which seemed
    most desirous of speaking, and began
    like one embarrassed by excessive desire,   36

"O well-created spirit, enjoying the rays
    of eternal life, the sweetness of which,
    untasted, can never be understood,

---

[3] Narcissus took his reflection in water for reality; Dante mistakes reality for reflection.

it would be gracious if you contented me
   with your name and your condition."
   Then she, ready and with smiling eyes,

"Our charity does not close the door
   on just wishes, any more than the Love
   which wants all Its court to resemble Itself.

In this world I was a virgin sister,
   and if your memory searches well
   my greater beauty will not hide me from you.   48

You will see that I am Piccarda,
   placed here with these others
   and blessed in the sphere that moves slowest.

Our feelings which are enflamed
   only by the pleasure of the Holy Spirit rejoice
   in being formed according to His plan.

This fate which seems so low
   is given us because we neglected our vows,
   left unfulfilled in some respect."

Then I to her, "In your countenances
   something divine is shining
   which makes you different from before;   60

therefore I was not quick to recall you,
   but what you say helps me now
   so that remembering is easier.

But tell me, while happy here,
   do you desire a higher place
   to see more or to make yourselves dearer?"

With those other spirits she smiled a little,
   then answered me so joyously
   that she seemed to burn in the first flame of love.

"My brother, a charity quiets our wills
   and makes us wish only for what we have,
   and we thirst for nothing else.   72

If we wanted to be higher
   our desires would be discordant
   with the will of Him who places us here,

which, as you will see, cannot happen
   in these spheres if loving is a necessity here
   and if you consider what love implies.

Rather it is essential in this blessed state
   to remain within the divine will
   so that ours can be one with it.

Thus wherever we may be from threshold to threshold
    throughout this kingdom pleases all the realm
    as it does the King who bends our wills to His.   84

And His will is our peace;
    it is that sea to which wholly moves
    what He and Nature create."

I understood then how everywhere in Heaven
    is Paradise, although the grace of the Supreme Good
    does not descend equally on all.

But, as it happens that one food satisfies
    while the craving for another remains,
    which we ask for as we refuse the first,

so by act and word I enquired
    if I might learn what the web [vow] was
    that she had not brought to completion.   96

"A perfect life and great merit place in a higher heaven
    a lady [St. Clare] under whose rule," she said,
    "in your world the veil and dress are worn

so that until death the wearers may wake and sleep
    with that Spouse who accepts every vow
    which love conforms to His pleasure.

To follow her, while a girl, I fled from the world
    and dressed myself in her gown,
    and pledged myself to the ways of her order.

> *Both Piccarda and Constance were taken by force from their convents and
> married against their will. Lethe, however, has effaced the memory of their
> submission.*

Afterward men more used to evil than to good
    tore me away from the sweet cloister;
    and God knows what my life then became;   108

and this other splendor which shows itself
    on my right, and which glows
    with all the light of our sphere

applies what I say to herself.
    She also was a sister, and likewise
    the shadow of the sacred veil was taken from her.

But after she had been led back to the world
    against her will and good custom,
    the veil was never loosened from her heart.

This is the light of the great Constance
    who from the second blast of Swabia [Henry VI]
    conceived the third and last power [Frederick II]."   120

Thus she spoke to me; then began to sing *Ave Maria*
    and while singing vanished
    like a heavy body in deep water.

My eyes followed her as far as they could,
    and, when they had lost her,
    turned to the goal of greater longing,

attentive to Beatrice alone
    who flashed so brightly that at first
    my eyes could not endure the light,

and this made me slower in my questioning.

CANTO IV. *Dante is puzzled by two things: since the inconstant nuns were forced into inconstancy, why should this diminish their heavenly glory? and does their appearance in the sphere of the moon indicate that Plato was correct in saying that human souls come from and return to the planets? Beatrice answers the first question by explaining that acquiescence cannot be fully exonerated even when it is forced. To his second question she replies that the souls of the saved all reside with God in the Empyrean heaven and are revealed to Dante in the lower heavens simply to manifest their spiritual conditions.*

CANTO V. *In reply to a question about vows, Beatrice explains that they must always be kept but that in some cases substitutions can be made for the thing vowed. Vows can never be altered where, as in monastic vows, no equivalent can be substituted. As for vows that are wrong in themselves, to keep them would simply magnify the original evil of making them. Dante and Beatrice now reach the heaven of Mercury, where they encounter spirits once tainted with ambition. One of these is the sixth-century Roman emperor and lawgiver Justinian.*

CANTO VI. *Justinian tells of his conversion to Christian orthodoxy and outlines the history of the Roman empire, the political entity that Dante would like to see restored to its proper authority. The former emperor champions the values of peace, law, and self-sacrifice and condemns factional divisions.*

CANTO VII

THE REDEMPTION

Justinian, in whom a double light of natural intelligence and illuminating grace shines, moves off with the other changeable, "mercurial," spirits.

Dante wonders how "just vengeance" could be "justly avenged," but, as he raises his head to ask, he is overcome by the awe he had felt on earth even for the mortal Bice (an affectionate shortening of the name Beatrice). She relieves his embarrassment by stating the question for him.

Osanna, sanctus Deus sabaoth,
    superillustrans claritate tua
    felices ignes horum malacoth![4]

---

[4]"Hosannah, holy God of Sabaoth, lighting from above with your brightness the blessed fires of these kingdoms."

Thus, revolving in his song,
    I saw this substance [Justinian] singing,
    in whom a double light shone.

Both it and others moved in their dance
    like rapid sparks veiling themselves
    from me by sudden distances.

I wondered, and said within myself,
    "O ask, ask her, ask my lady
    who quenches my thirst so sweetly!"   12

But that reverence which masters me completely,
    even for *Be* and *Ice*, again bowed down
    my head, as if I were drowsy.

Only a little while did Beatrice leave me thus,
    then she began to shine with such a smile
    as would make a man in fire happy:

"According to my infallible perception,
    how a just vengeance
    was justly punished has made you wonder;[5]

but I will quickly free your mind
    and do you listen, for my words
    will make you a gift of great doctrine.   24

In answer to Dante's question, Beatrice takes up the problem of the Redemption. The vengeance of the Cross was just if we consider the human element in Christ; it was unjust if we consider who assumed that human nature. The two aspects of Christ explain, therefore, how a just vengeance can justly be avenged. Dante now wonders why this particular method for man's redemption was chosen.

Man, created directly by God, was immortal, free, and godlike. The sin of Adam destroyed his dignity wholly, which could be regained only by adequate penance. But man was incapable of sufficient penance by himself, since his presumption was infinite, and his power to compensate for it limited. Only God could enable man to redeem himself. And by showing both justice and mercy, God was more generous than if He had pardoned outright, since His act included both manifestations of His goodness.

Beatrice also clears up another matter. The angels and man were created directly by God and are therefore immortal. Likewise the elements, but the various forms and combinations of these elements are the work of Nature or the stars, a second cause, and therefore undergo transformations and decay. Since man's body as well as his soul was created directly by God, we can assume the resurrection of the flesh.

By not enduring, for his own good, a curb
    on his will, the man never born [Adam],
    by damning himself, damned all his descendants,

---

[5] The reference is to a phrase used in Canto VI. The "just vengeance" is the punishment of man for original sin in the human person of the crucified Christ; "was justly punished" refers to the vengeance on the Jews in the form of the destruction of Jerusalem in 70 A.D.

so that the human race lay sick down below
    for many centuries, in great error,
    until it pleased the Word of God to descend,

when, by the act of His eternal love,
    He united with Himself
    the nature estranged from its Maker.

Now direct your sight to what is said:
    this [human] nature, united with its Maker,
    when created, was pure and good,   36

but, through its own act, it was banished
    from Paradise, since it turned
    from the way of truth and from its life.

The penalty, therefore, which the cross offered,
    if measured by the nature assumed,
    never struck anyone so justly,

and none ever did such great wrong
    if we consider the Person who suffered
    and by whom that nature was assumed.

Thus from one act different results ensue;
    for the same death which shook the earth
    and opened Heaven pleased God and the Jews.   48

It should not be hard to understand
    any longer that a just vengeance
    was avenged later by a just court.

But I see your mind bound from thought to thought
    in a knot, the loosening of which
    it waits for eagerly.

You say, 'I discern clearly what I hear,
    but why God should choose
    this means for our redemption is hidden from me.'

This decree, my brother, lies buried
    to the eyes of everyone whose mind
    has not matured in the flames of love.   60

Still, since this mark is gazed at much
    and little is discerned,
    I will tell why such a way was most worthy.

The Divine Goodness which spurns all envy,
    burning in Itself, so shines
    that It sends forth Its eternal beauty.

Whatever comes directly from It
    has no end, for when It has sealed,
    Its imprint cannot be removed.

What comes directly from It
    is wholly free, because not subject
    to the power of the new things [stars].   72

What is most conformed to It, therefore, pleases It most,
    for the holy ardor which shines on everything
    is brightest on what is most like Itself.

The human creature had all these advantages,
    and if one of them is lacking,
    he must fall from his nobility.

Only sin disqualifies him and makes him
    dissimilar to the Supreme Good,
    so that he is brightened little with Its light;

and he can never regain his dignity
    unless, with penance equal to his wicked pleasures,
    he makes up for the loss.   84

Your nature when it sinned wholly
    in its seed [Adam] was removed
    from this dignity as well as from Paradise.

Nor could man recover it,
    if you look closely, by any means
    except passing through one of these fords:

either God by his courtesy alone
    might have forgiven, or man by himself
    must have given satisfaction for his folly.

Look now into the abyss
    of the eternal counsel as far as you can,
    closely attentive to my speech.   96

Man with his limitations, afterward obedient,
    could never give satisfaction,
    through his inability to go down in humility

as far as he had risen in his presumption;
    and this is why man was prevented
    from compensating by himself.

Therefore it was necessary for God by His ways
    to restore man to perfect life,
    I mean by one way [mercy] or by both [justice and mercy].

But since a deed is more prized
    the more it displays of the goodness
    in the heart of the doer,   108

the Divine Goodness which puts Its stamp on the world
    was pleased to proceed by all His ways
    to lift you up, and, between the last night

and the first day, there has never been
　　or will be so exalted and magnificent an act,
　　either by one way or the other;

for, God was more generous to give Himself
　　to make man able to redeem himself
　　than if he had pardoned,

and all other ways would have been short
　　of justice unless the Son of God
　　humiliated Himself to become incarnate.   120

Now to fulfill well all your desires,
　　I go back to explain a certain point
　　so that you may see as I do.

You say, 'I see the water, I see the fire,
　　the air, and the earth, and all their mixtures
　　become corrupt and last only a short time.

And yet these things too were created,'
　　so that if what I said were true
　　they should be safe from corruption.

The angels, brother, and the perfect region
　　in which you are, can be considered created
　　as they are in their entire being,   132

but the elements you have named and the things
　　made of them have received their form
　　from a created power [a second cause].

The matter in them was created [directly],
　　the forming power likewise
　　in those stars which circle around them.

The rays and motion of the holy lights
　　draw from the potential elements [of matter]
　　the soul of every brute and of the plants.

But the Supreme Goodness breathes forth
　　your life directly, and enamors it of Itself,
　　so that ever after the soul desires It.   144

Hence you can infer from this
　　your resurrection, if you consider
　　how human flesh was made

when the first parents were formed."

CANTO VIII. *In the heaven of Venus, Dante and Beatrice encounter souls who in life were especially given to amorous pursuits but have converted their carnal impulses to heavenly love. Carlo Martello, who was king of Hungary and whom Dante knew, speaks with him. Dante asks him why it is that noble family lines sometimes produce base offspring. Carlo replies that all human capacities are fitted for some valuable function in the world and that these capacities are not inherited but instilled by the heavens. Society brings out the worst in people by assigning roles according to hereditary station that ought to be assigned according to inherent merit.*

CANTO IX. *In other conversations with souls in the heaven of Venus, Dante hears further denunciations of corruption, especially in Florence and the Papacy. He learns too that after reaching Heaven the saved feel no repentance for past sins, which are now seen to have been occasions for God's saving forgiveness. But we are given to understand that the degree of bliss enjoyed by the souls in these lower heavens is limited owing to the vices that stained them on earth.*

CANTO X. *Dante and Beatrice rise to the fourth heaven, of the Sun, where the theologians are manifested. The sun being now near the equinox, Dante points out to the reader that the degree of tilt of the earth's axis in relation to the ecliptic is divinely ordained for the best effect. The theologians, rejoicing in the doctrine of the Trinity, stand out in their brightness even against the sun. Dante raptly contemplates the idea of God, but his trance is broken by his awareness of the enhanced beauty of Beatrice's smile (which becomes more and more dazzling as they ascend). From a circling crown of twelve theologians who surround Dante, St. Thomas Aquinas, the greatest of medieval theologians, emerges to talk with him and introduce the other souls.*

CANTO XI. *St. Thomas, who belonged to the Dominican religious order, recites the history of and praises St. Francis of Assisi, founder of the other great medieval order, dwelling especially on Francis' marriage with poverty. Thomas deplores the degeneracy of the monks.*

CANTO XII. *A second circle surrounds the first one, circling it in an effect like that of twin rainbows. From this second circle St. Bonaventure, a Franciscan, emerges to reciprocate St. Thomas' gesture and praise St. Dominic, upholder of truth and orthodoxy and founder of the Dominicans. Bonaventure too deplores the deterioration of monastic orders.*

CANTO XIII. *Thomas Aquinas solves a problem of interpretation for Dante, namely how to reconcile the attribution of supreme wisdom to Solomon with the attribution of perfect knowledge to the new-created Adam and to Christ. After outlining the way in which God's creative power is manifested diversely in His creatures, Thomas distinguishes royal wisdom—the kind Solomon possessed—from wisdom and knowledge in general. Thomas warns Dante, through this example, of the dangers of facile inferences, a danger to which philosophy and theology are all too prone.*

CANTO XIV

THE GARMENT OF LIGHT—THE CROSS OF MARS

The sound waves coming from St. Thomas in the ring and from Beatrice in the center remind Dante of the ripples in a round vessel.

In answer to Dante's question as interpreted by Beatrice, Solomon explains that after Judgment Day the brightness of the souls will remain but will not dazzle their bodily eyes, which will have increased powers. The souls look forward to the time when, with their bodies, they will be more complete and therefore still happier.

From the center to the rim, and from the rim to the center,
    the water in a round vessel moves,
    according as it is struck from without or within.

What I say suddenly occurred
    to my mind when the glorious life
    of Thomas became silent,

because of the analogy with the speech
    of him and of Beatrice who, after him,
    was pleased to begin as follows:

"This man has a need which he does not express
    either in thought or with his voice
    to go to the root of another truth.   12

Tell him if the light which makes your substance
    flowerlike will remain eternally
    with you as it is now,

and if it remains tell how,
    when you are again made corporeal,
    your vision will not be harmed."

As, impelled and drawn by greater joy,
    those who dance in a round at times
    lift their voices and rejoice in their movements,

so, at the ready and devout prayer,
    the holy circles showed a new joy
    by their turning and wondrous melody.   24

Whoever laments because here we die
    to live up there, does not take account
    of the refreshment of the eternal rain [of light].

That One and Two and Three which always lives
    and always reigns in Three and Two and One,
    uncircumscribed and circumscribing all,

was sung of three times by each of those spirits
    with such melody that to hear it would be
    a just reward for every merit.

And I heard in the divinest light [that of Solomon]
    of the lesser circle, a modest voice,
    like that of the angel to Mary,   36

answer, "As long as the festival of Paradise
    exists, so long will our love
    radiate around us such a robe [of light].

Its brightness corresponds to our ardor,
    the ardor to our vision, and its intensity
    depends, apart from our merit, on a gift of grace.

When our glorious and holy flesh
    is reassumed, our persons
    through being entire will be more acceptable;

therefore whatever gratuitous light
    the Supreme Good gives us will be increased—
    a light which fits us to see Him;   48

so that our vision must increase,
　　　as well as the ardor lighted by it,
　　　and the resultant radiance.

Like a coal that produces flames
　　　but whose white incandescence shines through them
　　　so that it maintains its visibility,

this effulgence which already encircles us
　　　will be outshone by our flesh
　　　which all this time the earth has covered.

Nor can so much light fatigue us,
　　　for the organs of the body will be strong enough
　　　for all that can delight us."　　　　　　　　　　　　　　60

So ready were both choirs to say "amen"
　　　that they truly showed their desire
　　　for their dead bodies,

perhaps not only for themselves but for their mothers,
　　　fathers, and others who were dear
　　　before they became eternal flames.

*Now a third ring shines around the other two, composed of souls related to the
Holy Ghost, wise in the things of the spirit, to complete perhaps the symbolism of
the Trinity. Then Beatrice and Dante rise to the heaven of Mars. Here the
soldiers of holy crusades appear, ruddy with their love, on the white cross of their
Faith.*

And behold! a light of equal brightness
　　　shone around what was there
　　　like a horizon growing bright,

and, as in early evening, stars
　　　appear faintly in the sky,
　　　so that their sight seems real and not real,　　　　　　72

so I seemed to see new substances
　　　making a circle outside
　　　of the other two circumferences.

O true sparkling of the Holy Spirit,
　　　how suddenly glowing it became
　　　to my eyes which, overcome, endured it not!

But Beatrice showed herself so beautiful
　　　and smiling that her appearance must be left
　　　among the sights which overcame my mind.

Then my eyes gained strength to look up again,
　　　and I saw myself transported
　　　alone with my lady to more exalted salvation.　　　　84

I was well aware that I had risen higher
    because of the enkindled smile of the star
    which seemed to me ruddier than usual.

With all my heart, and in that speech [silent prayer]
    which is one in all, I made to God
    such an offering as befitted the new grace.

And the ardor of the sacrifice
    was not exhausted in my breast
    before I knew the offering had been accepted;

for, with such light and such ruddiness
    splendors appeared to me within two rays
    that I exclaimed, "O Helios! [Sun] who dost so adorn them!"   96

As, distinct with lesser and greater lights,
    the Milky Way shows white between the poles,
    making the wise wonder about it,

thus constellated, those rays formed
    in the depths of Mars the venerable emblem [the cross]
    which the joining of quadrants in a circle makes.

Here memory overcomes my mind,
    for that cross flashed forth Christ,
    so that I cannot find a comparison;

but whoever takes up his cross and follows Christ
    will excuse me for what I omit
    when he beholds Christ flashing in that glow.   108

From tip to tip and between the top and bottom
    lights moved shining brightly
    as they met and passed by.

Thus, on earth, particles long and short,
    straight and aslant, fast and slow,
    changing aspect, are seen moving

through a ray of sunlight which streaks
    the shade [in houses] which men provide,
    with intelligence and art, for their protection.

And as a viol and harp, tuned in harmony
    with many strings, make only a sweet tinkling sound
    to one unfamiliar with the music,   120

so from the lights I saw in the cross
    a melody sounded which carried me away
    without my understanding the hymn.

Well was I aware it was a song of lofty praise,
    since "Arise and conquer" came, as to one
    who hears but does not fully understand.

So enamored was I with the hymn
    that until then nothing had ever bound me
    with such sweet ties.

Perhaps these words seem too bold,
    slighting the delight of the beautiful eyes
    which give rest to all my longing,   132

but whoever knows that the living stamps of all beauty
    [the eyes of Beatrice] have more effect the higher they are,
    and that I had not yet turned to them,

can excuse me for what leads to my self-accusation
    and see that I speak the truth and that
    the holy delight, which becomes purer

as it rises, is not disparaged here.

    CANTO XV. *From the warriors appearing as lights on the cross in the heaven of Mars, one moves from it quickly and joyfully to accost Dante. He greets him with the joy Anchises, in the Sixth Book of Virgil's* Aeneid, *showed his son Aeneas when the latter visited Anchises in the realm of the dead. He identifies himself as Dante's great-great-grandfather, Cacciaguida, and describes the small town Florence was in earlier times. There he was born and lived before becoming a Crusader.*

    CANTO XVI. *Dante is overcome both by humility toward his ancestor and by pride in his lineage. Cacciaguida contrasts the small and still-uncorrupted Florence of his day with what it has since become, describing in detail the vicissitudes of the old families and mourning the afflictions of the city.*

    CANTO XVII. *On several occasions earlier in the* Comedy, *Dante had heard dire hints of calamity in his future. Cacciaguida, after explaining how his foreknowledge is consistent with free will, spells out plainly the sad future Dante has in store: his false indictment by Florence for the very acts of treachery that the city itself is guilty of; his impoverished and increasingly isolated exile; the hospitality that he will receive and be dependent on. But Cacciaguida bids Dante to have hopeful courage, to believe in his eventual vindication, and to publish his vision with unmitigated truthfulness.*

    CANTO XVIII. *Dante, after musing on what his ancestor has told him, is recalled to awareness by Beatrice's beauty. Cacciaguida identifies some of the warriors appearing on the cross, after which Dante and his guide ascend to the heaven of Jupiter, the keynote of which is justice. Here spirits arrange themselves so as to spell out an appropriate biblical verse; the last letter re-forms as the eagle symbolic of Roman law. The perversion of law and justice in the world, especially by the Papacy, is lamented.*

    CANTO XIX. *The souls that form the eagle are the just monarchs, who speak in unison. The heaven of justice seems the fitting place for Dante to explore his troubled doubts about the justice of excluding the righteous pagans from salvation. The kings answer by praising the justice of God, the Being who gives meaning to the very notion of justice, as beyond the comprehension and judgmental capacity of His creatures. They reaffirm that faith in Christ is necessary for salvation but then, intriguingly, declare that many heathens will be closer to God after the Last Judgment than some of those who are nominally Christians.*

CANTO XX

DIVINE GRACE

The eagle names the souls in the lights that form its eye. Among them are two pagans, Trajan and Ripheus. Dante wonders how these two could have been saved and learns that both had faith in Christ. Through the intercession of Gregory the Great, Trajan was allowed to return to earth from Limbus to be converted to Christianity and to die a second time. Ripheus, an inconspicuous character of the Aeneid, permitted somehow to believe in Christ to come, shows how Divine Grace is as unfathomable to our understanding as Divine Justice.

When the sun which lights the whole world
    disappears from our hemisphere
    so that the day on every side is spent,

the sky, before enkindled by it alone,
    suddenly makes itself apparent
    with many lights [stars] on which one splendor [the sun] shines,

and this change came to my mind
    when the ensign of the world and of its leaders
    became silent in its blessed beak,

since all those living lights,
    shining much more brightly, began songs
    which have fallen and disappeared from my memory.   12

O sweet Love, clothed in a smile,
    how ardent didst Thou appear in those pipes
    which had the breath alone of holy thoughts!

After the precious and shining gems
    with which I saw the sixth heaven jeweled
    imposed silence on their angelic chimes,

I seemed to hear the murmuring of a river
    descending clear from stone to stone,
    showing the abundance of its high source;

and, as at the neck of a lute
    the sound takes its form, and as the breath
    within a pipe at the holes,   24

so, without delay or waiting
    that murmuring of the eagle
    rose through its apparently hollow neck.

There it became voice and issued
    through its beak in the form of words,
    for which my heart that inscribed them waited.

"The part of me which sees," it began,
    "and which in mortal eagles endures the sun,
    now must be inspected closely,

for, of the lights with which I am formed,
    those that make my eye sparkle
    were supreme in all their ranks.   36

The one that shines in the middle as the pupil
    was [David] the singer of the Holy Spirit
    who bore the Ark [of the Covenant] from house to house.

Now he knows the merit of his song,
    insofar as a result of his own counsel,
    by the reward which is equally great.

Of the five which make a circle for an eyebrow,
    the one closest to my beak [Trajan]
    consoled the poor widow for her son.

Now he knows how dear it costs
    not to follow Christ by his experience
    with the sweet life and with its opposite.   48

And the one [King Hezekiah] who follows in the circumference
    of which I speak, upon the upper arch,
    delayed his death by his true penitence.

Now he knows that eternal decrees [plans]
    are not violated when a worthy prayer
    turns today into tomorrows down on earth [delays them].

The other [Constantine] with the laws and me [the eagle]
    became a Greek, and by giving [the Western Empire]
    to the shepherd [pope], with good intent, produced evil.

Now he knows how the wrong resulting
    from his good deed is not harmful to him
    although the world is destroyed by it.   60

And the one you see on the downward arc
    was William [II of Sicily], regretted by the land
    which weeps because of the living Charles and Frederick.

Now he knows how Heaven is enamored
    of righteous kings, and by his flashing
    he still is making that apparent.

Who down in the erring world
    would believe the Trojan, Ripheus, was the fifth
    of the holy lights in this circle?

Now he knows much about divine grace
    that the world cannot see, although even his sight
    does not penetrate to the bottom."   72

As a lark soaring in the air
    first sings and then is silent, content
    with the last sweetness which satisfies it,

so the image appeared to me
    under the imprint of the Eternal Pleasure
    by whose will everything becomes what it is,

and, although there in my doubt I was like glass
    [transparent] to the color that shows through it,
    this doubt did not endure to wait in silence,

but, from my tongue, "What things are these?"
    it urged with the force of its own weight;
    whereupon I saw a great revelry of flashing.   84

Then, soon, with a brighter eye,
    the blessed ensign answered me,
    not to keep me suspended in my wonder.

"I see that you believe these things
    because I say them, but do not see how,
    so that, although believed, they remain mysterious.

You do like those who apprehend a thing
    by name but cannot see its essence
    unless another discloses it.

Regnum coelorum[6] suffers violence [is moved]
    only from warm love and living hope
    which vanquish the divine will,   96

not as men overcome each other,
    but because it wishes to be overcome
    and, vanquished, it conquers with its own kindness.

The first and fifth life [souls] of the eyebrow [Trajan and Ripheus]
    make you marvel because you see
    the region of the angels embellished with them.

From their bodies they did not come, as you believe,
    as Gentiles,[7] but as Christians, with firm faith
    in the feet [of Christ] to be pierced or already pierced;

for one returned to his flesh from Hell
    whence there is no direct return to good will,
    and that was a reward for the living hope [of Gregory]—   108

for the living hope which put power
    into prayers made to God to resuscitate him,
    so that His will might be changed.

The glorious soul of whom I am speaking,
    having returned to the flesh for a while,
    believed in Him who could aid him,

and, believing, was so enkindled with flames
    of true love that, on his second death,
    he was worthy of coming to this festival.

[6]"The kingdom of the heavens."   [7]Pagans.

The other [Ripheus], through grace
    which is distilled from so deep a spring
    that no creature ever saw to the bottom,   120

put all his love below on uprightness;
    wherefore, from grace to grace,
    God opened his eyes to our future redemption,

and he believed in it and did not endure
    from then on the stench of paganism
    and reproached the perverse people for it.

Those three ladies [the Christian virtues] whom you saw
    at the right wheel [of the chariot] replaced baptism
    more than a thousand years before baptism.

O predestination! how remote your source is
    from the vision that does not see
    the First Cause entire!   132

And you, mortals, be careful
    about making judgments, for we who see God
    do not yet know all the elect;

and such a defect is sweet to us,
    for our good is so refined in this good
    that whatever God wishes we also want."

Thus, by that divine image,
    to clear up my short vision,
    a sweet medicine was given to me;

and, as a good lute player accompanies a singer
    with the vibration of the strings,
    and the song acquires a greater charm,   144

so, while it spoke, I recall
    that I saw the two blessed lights [Trajan and Ripheus]
    with the unison of blinking eyes

move their flames to the measure of the words.

CANTO XXI. *Beatrice and Dante rise to the heaven of Saturn, the realm of mystical contemplation. A replica of Jacob's ladder in Genesis extends down from above, and on it descend souls in light. Approached by one of them, the monk Peter Damiani, Dante inquires why Peter in particular has been singled out by God to address him. Peter replies that such individual particularities of Providence constitute a mystery even to the spirits in heaven. A former cardinal, Peter denounces the worldliness of high-ranking Church officials.*

CANTO XXII. *Dante has heard an outcry from the spirits, which, Beatrice explains to him, is a harbinger of divine vengeance. St. Benedict, the founder of Western monasticism, approaches Dante, who asks if he may see the saint in his full glory. Benedict replies that that will be accomplished in the Empyrean heaven beyond the realm of space and time. He too denounces the corruption of the monastic orders but holds out hope for their regeneration. The souls are swept up again out of sight, after which Dante and Beatrice rise to the heaven of the fixed stars. He gazes down at the heavens he has passed and at Earth, which appears tiny and insignificant.*

CANTO XXIII. *Dante experiences the stupendous vision of Christ amid the saved, a vision that stuns him into unconsciousness. When he comes to himself, however, his vision has been fortified by the sight, so that he is empowered to see the full beauty of Beatrice also, which is inexpressible in words. Christ having withdrawn in consideration of Dante's vulnerability, Dante gazes on the Virgin Mary and the Apostles. Mary is crowned by the angel Gabriel, and she too is lifted up beyond Dante's sight.*

CANTO XXIV. *As part of his preparation for the ultimate visions, Dante is examined, by St. Peter, on the nature and content of faith. As the foundation of faith, and of the existence of faith within him, Dante cites Scripture and the historical occurrence of miracles. He defines God first in terms of Aristotelian metaphysics and then in terms of the Trinity of which human-kind learns by divine revelation.*

CANTO XXV. *Having passed the examination in faith, Dante is examined on hope, by St. James the Apostle. Beatrice vouches for the presence of hope in Dante, as the very virtue that has brought him to the vision of the heavens. To James' direct queries about the nature of hope Dante replies in terms of Scriptural definition; the content of his hope he centers on the resurrection of the body and the immortality of the soul. Dante having passed this second test, St. John appears in the midst of impenetrable light. Dante is told that he cannot see John's body, since only Jesus and his mother Mary have been bodily assumed into Heaven.*

CANTO XXVI. *Blinded by the glory of John, Dante is examined by him on the third of the theological virtues: love. After testifying to the power of love instilled in him by Beatrice, he declares God to be the comprehensive object of all love. Dante identifies the love of good with the love of God, citing both Aristotle and Scripture. He declares that God is to be loved both in Himself and because of His goodness to humankind. His sight restored after passing the third test, Dante converses with Adam, who lovingly answers his questions about the Garden of Eden and the Fall.*

CANTO XXVII. *St. Peter angrily denounces the corruption of the Papacy, the office he was the first to hold, and the corrupt Pope Boniface VIII, charging Dante to relay this message of indignation to those on Earth. The spirits soar above, beyond sight. Dante again looks down toward Earth, seeing it lighted like a gibbous moon. He and Beatrice rise to the Primum Mobile (First Mover), the outermost of the spherical heavens and the realm from which every-thing spatial and temporal takes its origin. Beyond the Primum Mobile exists the unlocalized, timeless abode of God and the saved in eternity.*

CANTO XXVIII. *Dante now sees a vision of the adoration of God by the nine orders of angels. The vision consists of a single point of intense light, surrounded by nine revolving concentric circles, of which the innermost is both the brightest and the swiftest—that is to say, a model directly opposed to that of the nine physical heavens, of which the outermost is the most excellent. The unsearchable relationship of God to His creations can, then, be understood and represented through either of these opposite models.*

CANTO XXIX. *Beatrice explains to Dante that God created other beings not so as to en-hance Himself but so that joyful consciousness might exist outside of His own consciousness. She explains some metaphysical truths about Creation—for example, that the question what God did before Creation is meaningless, since time itself is meaningful only in connection with created reality. She narrates briefly the fall of the Satanic party and, among other truths about the angels, declares that each of these innumerable beings is wholly individualized.*

CANTO XXX. *The angelic spectacle fades away. Now, as Beatrice attains an indescriba-ble new intensity of beauty, she and Dante leave behind the world of time and space and enter the Empyrean heaven, where they will behold the eternal forms of the angels and of the human saved. A great flash of light strengthens Dante to see the vision of the blessed who are gazing on God Himself.*

CANTO XXXI

ST. BERNARD

In the form then of a white rose
    the holy company [the Church] which Christ with His blood
    made His spouse showed itself to me,

but the others [angels] who, flying, see and sing
    of the glory of Him who enamors them
    and of the goodness that has made them so numerous,

like a swarm of bees, at times lighting
    on a flower and then returning
    to where their toil is turned to sweetness,

descended into the great flower
    adorned with so many leaves, and then rose
    to where their love always dwells.   12

They all had faces of living flames,
    and golden wings, and the rest so white
    that no snow equals the whiteness.

When they sank into the flower
    from rank to rank, they bestowed
    the peace and ardor acquired as they flew,

nor did such a flying multitude
    between the flower and what was above
    obscure the vision of the splendor,

for divine light penetrates through the universe
    in proportion to its merit,
    so that there nothing can obscure it.   24

This secure and rejoicing realm,
    abounding in ancient and in new people,
    had eyes and love directed to one mark.

O Threefold Light which in a single star
    scintillating in their sight so satisfies them,
    look down here upon our storms!

If the barbarians coming from the regions [of the North]
    covered by Helice [the Great Dipper] circling
    with her son [Arcas, the Little Dipper] of whom she is fond,

were amazed on seeing Rome
    and her lofty monuments, when the Lateran [the papal palace]
    surpassed all mortal things,   36

I who had come from the human to the divine,
    from Time to Eternity, and from Florence
    to a people just and sane,

what amazement must I have felt!
    Certainly it and my joy made me content
    not to hear and to stand mute.

And as a pilgrim who gains fresh life
    in the temple of his vow as he looks
    and already hopes to report [at home] how it is,

so, through the living light,
    I cast my eyes over the ranks,
    now up, now down, and now around.   48

I saw faces persuasive of love adorned by the light
    of Another and by their own smiles,
    and with gestures graced by every dignity.

My sight had already taken in
    the general form of Paradise,
    but on no point had my eyes been fixed,

and I turned with rekindled desire
    to ask my lady about things
    that kept my mind in suspense.

> *Beatrice's role as Revelation is now ended, since Dante is in the actual presence
> of God, and she resumes her historical character as Beatrice Portinari, whom the
> poet addresses from now on with the familiar tu (for "you"). Her place is taken
> by St. Bernard, who was especially devoted to the Virgin Mary and who repre-
> sents Contemplation or perhaps Intuition.*

I expected one thing, and another responded;
    I thought I would see Beatrice, and instead
    I perceived an old man, clad like those in glory.   60

Benign joy was diffused
    over his eyes and face, his mien kindly,
    as is fitting in a tender father;

and, "Where is she?" I said suddenly;
    whereupon he, "To fulfill your desire
    Beatrice sent me from my place.

If you look at the third row
    of the highest tier you will see her again
    on the throne her merit allots to her."

Without speaking I lifted up my eyes
    and saw her, making herself a crown [a halo of light]
    and reflecting from herself the eternal rays.   72

From the region of the highest thunder
    no mortal eye is so distant
    although plunged deep into the sea

as my sight there from Beatrice,
    but that had no effect on me,
    for her image came down unblurred.

"O lady in whom my hope is strong,
    you who for my salvation endured
    to leave your footprints in Hell,

in all the things that I have seen
    I recognize the grace and the virtue
    of your power and goodness.   84

You have lifted me from slavery to freedom
    by all those ways, by all the means
    through which you had the power to do so.

Continue your generosity toward me,
    so that my soul that you redeemed
    may be freed from my body pleasing to you."

Thus I prayed, and she, so distant
    as it seemed, smiled, and looked at me;
    then turned to the Eternal Spring.

And the holy old man said, "In order
    that you may complete perfectly your journey
    for which purpose prayer and holy love sent me,   96

cast your eyes over this garden,
    for seeing it will prepare them
    for rising higher in the divine radiance.

And the Queen of Heaven for whom I burn
    wholly with love will grant us every grace,
    since I am her faithful Bernard."

As a pilgrim, perhaps from Croatia, who comes
    to see our Veronica [an image of Christ], and who,
    because of his long-felt hunger, is never satiated,

but says in his thoughts as long
    as it is shown, "My Lord, Jesus Christ, true God,
    now was Thy countenance really like this?"   108

so I was while gazing at the living love
    of him [Bernard] who in our world,
    through contemplation, enjoyed that peace.

"Son of Grace, if you keep your eyes
    only down here at this bottom," he began,
    "this joyous life will not be seen by you.

Look at the rows as far as the most remote
    until you see the Queen [Mary] sitting
    to whom this realm is loyal and devoted."

I lifted my eyes and, as in the morning
    the eastern part of the horizon
    outshines that where the sun goes down,   120

so, as if rising from a valley to a mountain,
    I saw with my eyes a part of the edge
    dominating with its light all the rim;

and, as on earth at sunrise, the pole of the chariot [of the sun]
    (which Phaëthon guided badly) is most enflamed
    and on either side the light decreases,

so that pacific oriflamme[8] [of Mary's] shone brighter
    in the middle, and on either side,
    gradually and equally decreased its light.

At that middle point, with wings spread,
    I saw more than a thousand rejoicing angels,
    each distinct in effulgence and in function.   132

I saw there smiling at their games
    and at their songs, a beauty which became a joy
    in the eyes of all the other saints.

And if I had such wealth in speech
    as in imagining, I would not dare
    to attempt the least of the delight she gave.

Bernard, when he saw my eyes
    fixed and intent on his warm love,
    turned his toward her with such affection

that he made mine more eager in their gazing.

CANTO XXXII

THE MYSTIC ROSE

*St. Bernard points out some of the souls that form the white rose. In the lower part
are the children, the little folk who "hastened to the true life."*

Intent on his delight, that contemplator [St. Bernard]
    freely assumed the office of teacher
    and began with these holy words:

"The wound that Mary healed and anointed
    the beautiful one [Eve] who is
    at her feet opened and enlarged.

In order, in the third row,
    Rachel sits beneath her
    with Beatrice, as you see.

[8] A gold-and-flame-colored pennant.

Sarah, Rebecca, Judith, and the great-grandmother [Ruth]
    of the singer [David] who, in sorrow
    for his sins, said '*Miserere mei*.'[9]   12

You can see them from rank to rank
    as with the name of each I go downward
    through the rose from petal to petal.

And from the seventh row on,
    as down to it, Hebrew women
    divide all the petals of the rose.[10]

According to the way their faith
    conceived of Christ they form the line
    by which the sacred stairway is divided.

On this side, where the flower is mature
    with all its leaves, are seated those
    who believed in Christ to come.   24

On the other, where the semicircles
    are broken by empty seats, are those
    who turned their faces to Christ already come.

And, just as on this side, the glorious seat
    of the Lady of Heaven and those below it
    make so great a division,

so, opposite her, does that of the great John
    who, always holy, endured martyrdom
    and the desert and then Hell for two years.[11]

And beneath him, Francis, Benedict, Augustine
    and others make a dividing line
    down to here from row to row.   36

Now marvel at the divine foresight, for both aspects
    of the Faith [the old Church and the new]
    will fill this garden equally;

and know that downward from the row
    which midway cleaves the two divisions,
    souls have a place through no merit of their own

but through that of others, under certain conditions;
    for all these are spirits released from the flesh
    [as children] before they could have a true choice.

Well can you see this by their faces
    and also by their childish voices
    if you look closely and listen to them.   48

---

[9] "Have mercy on me" (Psalm 51:1).

[10] The vertical line of Hebrew women seated below Mary forms a boundary between the two semicircles of the Jews and Christians. The amphitheater is also divided top and bottom, the children (Hebrew and Christian) in the bottom half.

[11] John the Baptist, martyred two years before Christ was crucified, spent the interval in Limbo awaiting the harrowing of hell by which Christ released the souls of the just.

The children enjoy varying felicity according to the grace they have received.

*Pre-Christian infants were saved through their parents' faith in Christ to come;
the others, in Christian times, through baptism.*

Now you wonder, and wondering, are silent;
    but I will undo the tight band
    by which your subtle thoughts are held.

Within the amplitude of this realm
    nothing can occur by chance
    any more than sadness, thirst, or hunger;

for whatever you see is established
    by eternal law, so that the ring
    fits the finger exactly.

Therefore, that those [little] people
    who hastened to the true life
    are more and less excellent is not *sine causa.*[12]   60

The King through whom this realm has rest
    in such love and in such delight
    that no desire ventures to have more,

creating all minds in His happy image
    endows with grace diversely, at His pleasure;
    and here let the fact suffice.

This is clearly and expressly noted for you
    in Holy Scripture in those twins [Jacob and Esau]
    who, within their mother, were stirred to wrath.

Therefore, according to the color
    of their hair, the light
    of grace must worthily crown them.[13]   72

Thus, without merit for their conduct
    they are placed in various ranks,
    differing only in primal keenness [of spiritual sight].

In the early centuries
    the parents' faith alone sufficed,
    with innocence, to receive salvation.

Then, after the first ages were completed,
    males were obliged through circumcision
    to gain power for their innocent wings;

but when the time of grace had come,
    without perfect baptism in Christ
    such innocence was held back there below.   84

[12] Latin, "without cause."
[13] God favored Jacob over his redheaded twin brother Esau from their time in the womb.
See Genesis 25.

Dante shifts his gaze to the upper part of the rose.

Look now on the face [of Mary]
 which bears most resemblance to Christ,
 for its brightness alone can prepare you for seeing Christ."

I saw such joy rain upon her
 borne in the holy minds [of the angels]
 created to fly over that height,

that nothing I had seen before
 had kept me suspended in such wonder
 or revealed to me such likeness to God.

And that love [Gabriel] which first descended
 on her singing *Ave Maria, gratia plena*,[14]
 spread his wings in front of her.   96

The blessed court on all sides
 sang responses to the divine song
 so that every face became brighter.

"O holy father, you who endure for my sake
 to be down here, leaving the sweet place
 where you sit by eternal lot,

who is that angel which, with such rapture,
 looks into the eyes of our Queen,
 so enamored that he seems aflame?"

Thus again I had recourse to the learning
 of him [St. Bernard] who grew beautiful through Mary
 as the morning star does through the sun.   108

And he said to me, "As much confidence and grace
 as there can be in an angel or in a soul
 are in him; and we want it so,

because he is the one who brought the palm [of victory over others]
 down to Mary when the Son of God
 was willing to take on the burden of our flesh.

But follow now with your eyes as I speak
 and note the great patricians
 of this most just and devout empire.

Those two [Eve and Rachel] who up there are happiest
 from being nearest to the Empress [Mary]
 are, as it were, two roots of this rose.   120

The one nearest her on the left
 is [Adam] the father whose bold tasting
 made the human race taste such bitterness.

[14] "Hail Mary, full of grace" ("thou that art highly favored" in the King James Version), the words of the angel Gabriel at the Annunciation; Luke 1:28.

On the right see the ancient father
    of Holy Church [St. Peter] to whom Christ
    entrusted the keys to this lovely flower;

and the one [John][15] who saw, before his death,
    the deplorable times of the fair Bride [the Church],
    won [by Christ] with the lance and with the nails,

sits beside him; and by the other
    that leader [Moses] rests under whom the fickle,
    ungrateful, and perverse people lived on manna.   132

Opposite Peter see Anna [the mother of Mary] so happy
    to gaze upon her daughter that she
    does not move her eyes while singing hosanna,

and opposite the greatest father of a family [Adam]
    Lucia sits, who sent your lady,[16] when your eyes
    were bent down for your destruction.

But because the time which keeps you in slumber
    is flying, here we will stop, like a tailor
    who makes the gown according to the cloth he has,

and we will direct our eyes to the First Love,
    so that looking toward Him you may penetrate
    as far as possible through His light.   144

But, lest in moving your wings
    you should go back while believing to advance,
    grace must be obtained by prayer—

grace from that one [Mary] who can help you;
    and may you follow me with your affection,
    so that your heart will not be discordant

from my words." And he began this holy prayer.

CANTO XXXIII

THE BEATIFIC VISION

*A prayer to the Blessed Virgin, later copied in great part by Chaucer, opens the
final canto.*

*The stages of the Beatific Vision are, in ascending order, a comprehension of the
world, a vision of the Trinity, and, as a final revelation, a view of the Incarnation.*

"Virgin mother, daughter of thy son,
    humble and exalted more than any creature,
    goal established by Eternal Counsel,

[15] The author of the Book of Revelation, or Apocalypse.   [16] See *Inferno*, II.97–108.

thou art the one by whom human nature
    was so ennobled that its Maker
    did not disdain to become its creature.

Within thy womb was rekindled the love
    through whose warmth this flower
    has blossomed in eternal peace.

Here thou art for us a noonday torch
    of charity, and down below, among mortals,
    a living fount of hope.   12

My lady, thou art so great and so triumphant
    that whoever wants and does not turn to thee
    would have his desire fly without wings.

Thy benignity succors not only those
    who ask, but many times
    freely anticipates the request.

In thee is mercy, in thee pity,
    in thee magnificence, in thee whatever goodness
    can be found in creatures is resumed.

Now, this man who from the deep well
    of the universe up to here
    has seen the spiritual lives, one after another,   24

begs thee of thy grace for strength,
    so that he may lift his eyes
    still higher toward the ultimate salvation.

And I who never for my own sight longed more
    than I do for his, offer thee all my prayers,
    and may they not be insufficient,

in order that thou, through thine, mayst dispel
    every cloud of his mortality, so that
    the Supreme Pleasure may reveal Itself to him.

I pray thee further, O Queen! thou who canst do
    what thou wilt, that thou keepest
    his affection sound after so great a vision.   36

May thy protection overcome his human impulses.
    Behold Beatrice with so many of the blessed
    clasping their hands to aid my prayer."

The eyes [of Mary] venerated and beloved
    by God, fixed on him who prayed, showed
    how gratefully devout prayers are heard.

Then they turned to the Eternal Light into which
    we must not think any mortal vision,
    however clear, can ever penetrate so deeply.

And I who drew near to the goal
    of all desires, ended, as I ought,
    within myself, the ardor of my longing.   48

Bernard signaled to me and smiled
    so that I might look up, but I
    already had made myself as he wished.

For my sight, growing pure, penetrated
    ever deeper into the rays
    of the Light which is true in Itself.

From then on my vision was greater
    than our speech which fails at such a sight,
    just as memory is overcome by the excess.

As one who in a dream sees clearly,
    and the feeling impressed remains afterward,
    although nothing else comes back to mind,   60

so am I; for my vision disappears
    almost wholly, and yet the sweetness
    caused by it is still distilled within my heart.

Thus, in sunlight, the snow melts away;
    thus the sayings of the Sibyl,[17] written
    on light leaves, were lost in the wind.

O Supreme Light that risest so high
    above mortal concepts, give back to my mind
    a little of what Thou didst appear,

and make my tongue strong,
    so that it may leave to future peoples
    at least a spark of Thy glory!   72

For, by returning to my memory
    and by sounding a little in these verses
    more of Thy victory will be conceived.

By the keenness of the living ray I endured
    I believe I would have been dazed
    if my eyes had turned away from it;

and I remember that I was bolder
    because of that to sustain the view
    until my sight *attained* the Infinite Worth.

O abundant grace through which I presumed
    to fix my eyes on the Eternal Light
    so long that I consumed my vision on it!   84

In its depths I saw contained, bound with love
    in one volume, what is scattered
    on leaves throughout the world—

[17] A prophetess (Virgil, *Aeneid*, Books III, VI) who inscribed her prophecies on the leaves of trees which were then scattered by the wind.

substances [things] and accidents [qualities] and their modes
    as if fused together in such a way
    that what I speak of is a single light.

The universal form [principle] of this unity
    I believe I saw, because more abundantly
    in saying this I feel that I rejoice.

One moment obscures more for me than twenty-five centuries
    have clouded since the adventure which made Neptune
    wonder at the shadow of the Argo [the first ship].[18]   96

Thus my mind with rapt attention
    gazed fixedly, motionless and attentive,
    continually enflamed by its very gazing.

In that light we become such
    that we can never consent
    to turn from it for another sight,

inasmuch as the good which is the object
    of the will is all in it, and outside of it
    whatever is perfect there is defective.

Now my speech, even for what I remember,
    will be shorter than that of an infant
    who still bathes his tongue at the breast.   108

Not that more than a single semblance
    was in the living light I gazed upon
    (for it is always as it was before),

but in my vision which gained strength
    as I looked the single appearance,
    through a change in me, was transformed.

Within the deep and clear subsistence
    of the great light three circles of three colors
    and of one dimension [the Trinity] appeared to me,

and one [the Son] seemed reflected from the other [the Father]
    as Iris by Iris,[19] and the third [the Holy Spirit]
    seemed fire emanating equally from both.   120

O how poor our speech is and how feeble
    for my conception! Compared to what I saw
    to say its power is "little" is to say too much.

O Eternal Light [Father], abiding in Thyself alone,
    Thou [Son] alone understanding Thyself, and Thou [Holy
        Spirit]
    understood only by Thee, Thou dost love and smile!

---

[18] The voyage of Jason and the Argonauts was considered to have taken place in the thirteenth century B.C. Dante means that the world has forgotten since then less than he has forgotten of the divine vision.

[19] Twin rainbows (Iris being the goddess of the rainbow).

The circle which appeared in Thee
 as a reflected light [the Son]
 when contemplated a while

seemed depicted with our image within itself
 and of its own [the Circle's] color,
 so that my eyes were wholly fixed on it.   132

Like the geometer who strives
 to square the circle and cannot find
 by thinking the principle he needs

I was at that new sight. I wanted to see
 how the [human] image was conformed
 to the [divine] circle and has a place in it,

but my own wings were not enough for that—
 except that my mind was illumined by a flash
 [of Grace] through which its wish was realized.

For the great imagination here power failed;
 but already my desire and will [in harmony]
 were turning like a wheel moved evenly   144

by the Love which turns the sun and the other stars.

Geoffrey Chaucer
(1340?–1400)

*One of the most versatile of English and of medieval poets, Chaucer was born in
1340 or a little later, the son of a London wine merchant. The comfortable middle-
class family had been rising socially, and young Geoffrey served as a page in the
household of the Countess of Ulster, where as an intimate of a noble family he was
well educated and early acclimated to aristocratic values and manners. In 1359 he
served on the Continent during one of the military campaigns of the Hundred Years'
War, waged in the fourteenth and fifteenth centuries for control of disputed territories in France. He was captured and then ransomed with the help of King Edward
III—an episode that marks the beginning of a series of favors, positions, and
preferments (interrupted by some tribulations in the 1380's) that Chaucer received
from English kings throughout his life. Besides serving again later in the army, he
filled several high posts in the country's service: customs supervisor, director of public
works, king's forester, and Member of Parliament. He undertook for the crown a
number of important diplomatic missions to France, the Low Countries, Spain, and
Italy. During his sojourns in Italy he was exposed to the work of the three fourteenth-
century Italian masters, Dante, Boccaccio, and Petrarch; their influence on his later*

work is strong. *Chaucer died in 1400, a year after the dethronement of Richard II by Henry IV, and was buried in what is now called the Poets' Corner of Westminster Abbey. That in a turbulent era he enjoyed the favor of three rulers says something about Chaucer as man and civil servant.*

Chaucer's lifelong close association with public affairs and men of high station helps explain his urbanity and his wide-ranging knowledge of the world. The often mordant portraits of moral delinquents and, conversely, of saintly types in The Canterbury Tales *testify that in his own way Chaucer is a social critic. But political matters do not play a large part in his works as they do in Dante's. Although he succeeded in portraying definitively the England of his time, Chaucer did so through the gifts he shares with the greatest storytellers: a sure and shrewd power of characterization, a keen eye for the quality of* things, *subtle and penetrating psychology, and an unfailing ear for good dialogue, which, like Shakespeare, he was able to accommodate naturally to a wide variety of verse forms, not to mention prose.*

Chaucer's narrative genius is in many ways best exemplified in Troilus and Criseyde *(1380s), one of his two supreme masterpieces. This poem of more than 8,000 lines, set during the Trojan War, allowed him to develop at book length a single story and to explore exhaustively the psychology of the characters, of whom the heroine Criseyde is the most complex. In* Troilus *Chaucer also develops one of his favorite themes: the nature of love as it reveals the conflicting values of this world and the next.*

The fullest range of Chaucer's powers emerges in his most popular work, The Canterbury Tales, *which he wrote in the late 1380s and early 1390s. The work is unfinished; the plan outlined in the General Prologue calls for four stories from each of thirty or so travelers, but we have only one tale apiece from twenty-four of them. Moreover, the work exists in ten fragments, the order of which has had to be reconstructed by scholarly detective work. Nevertheless, enough was completed and joined together to give the impression of a whole, although not a fully assembled or finally polished one.*

Like Boccaccio's Decameron *(which Chaucer apparently did not know),* The Canterbury Tales *is framed by an agreement among the principals to tell stories to one another. Chaucer's scheme, in which the characters are drawn from all vocations and social classes and the tales usually are emphatically appropriate to the tellers and their stations in life, allows him to achieve a variety at least as wide as Boccaccio's and at the same time to join the tales organically to the basic story of the pilgrimage. That Chaucer's framework is a* religious *pilgrimage is not insignificant; the pilgrims and the characters in their stories are revealed in the light both of the world with which so many of them are preoccupied and also of eternity. The variety of the pilgrims and of their moral conditions has a similar effect; the depravity of characters such as the Pardoner, the integrity of the Knight and sanctity of the Parson, the more ambiguous status of such figures as the fastidious Prioress and the worldly Monk imply, taken together, a moral concern almost as profound as Dante's, if less insistent.*

Chaucer is a distinctively English poet in many ways, but he also illustrates the characteristic internationalism of medieval culture and literature. Medieval authors were not expected to invent their own material, and Chaucer's tales, along with the frequent allusions and illustrations within them, are drawn mainly from non-English sources: French and Italian authors, classical legend and literature (notably Ovid), and the Bible (which Chaucer knew thoroughly). Chaucer reworks such materials in his own vein, infusing them with his distinctive qualities of drama, pathos, and wit. The media of the tales include an assortment of skillfully managed verse forms and genres. The Miller relates a fabliau, *a comically bawdy tale of ordinary or "low" life; the Wife of Bath relates a folktale; the Pardoner delivers a sermon and a morally pointed "exemplum"; the Nun's Priest's tale is a mock-heroic beast fable. The Canterbury Tales includes also specimens of romance, saint's legend, "tragedy" (defined simply as an account of the downfall of an eminent personage), and other narrative genres.*

Perhaps the most distinctive of Chaucer's gifts as storyteller is his ability to delineate characters and put them in realistic motion. They come most patently alive in the prologues to the individual tales and in the narrative links, but most of his people are realized three-dimensionally in the General Prologue as well. The pilgrims make up a human encyclopedia—comprehensive and universal but composed of unique individuals. Interpreting them can be problematical. The Wife of Bath, for example, projects to some readers an attractively earthy personality and to others a sinister moral obliquity. The Pardoner, unquestionably one of the most unsavory characters in world literature, raises questions too, most obviously about his motives in revealing his cynical duplicity so frankly to the company.

After the Normans conquered England in 1066, French became the language of polite society, while Latin continued to be the language of the learned. To a great extent this was still true in Chaucer's day. His decision to write in English at a time when the language was in a state of flux is a significant milestone in the development of English, like Dante's decision to write his Divine Comedy *in Italian. But English continued to change radically for a long time after Chaucer, and it was not until the late seventeenth century that the evolution so slowed that the average modern reader can understand the language of the time without elaborate glossing. Chaucer's language, "Middle English," is thus very different from the English of today. It is not so different, however, that modern readers should be discouraged from trying Chaucer in a good Middle English edition. The following is the beginning of the General Prologue:*

> *Whan that Aprille with his shoures soote*
> *The droghte of March hath perced to the rote,*
> *And bathed every veyne in swich licour*
> *Of which vertu engendred is the flour;*
> *Whan Zephirus eek with his swete breeth*
> *Inspired hath in every holt and heeth*
> *The tendre croppes, and the yonge sonne*
> *Hath in the Ram his halve cours yronne,*
> *And smale foweles maken melodye,*
> *That slepen al the nyght with open ye* 10
> *(So priketh hem nature in hir corages):*
> *Than longen folk to goon on pilgrymages,*
> *And palmers for to seken straunge strondes,*
> *To ferne halwes, kouthe in sondry londes;*
> *And specially from every shires ende*
> *Of Engelond to Caunterbury they wende,*
> *The holy blisful martir for to seke,*
> *That hem hath holpen whan that they were seke.*

FURTHER READING *(prepared by W. J. R.):* George Kane's *Chaucer,* 1984, in the Past Masters series, is a short general introduction to the poet's life and work, particularly interesting on the division between the poet and narrator. Two works by Derek Stanley Brewer provide vivid sketches of Chaucer and his England: Brewer's *Chaucer,* 1953, is intended for the new student of Chaucer; his *Chaucer and His World,* 1978, contains a generous selection of illustrations. Neither of these works offers critical material on Chaucer's poetry. D. W. Robertson, Jr., *A Preface to Chaucer,* 1962, is an important work in Chaucer scholarship, taking a deductive approach to Chaucer's work through an extensive analysis of background material. Robertson's work is noted for its many unconventional interpretations. Muriel Bowden's *A Reader's Guide to Geoffrey Chaucer,* 1964, takes a more centrist approach. This book offers a biographical sketch and a long section on *The Canterbury Tales* that discusses various influences on Chaucer's writing. Maurice Hussey and James Winny, *An Introduction to Chaucer,* 1965, contains material on Chaucer's England, the Church, science, and Chaucer's language. George Lyman Kittredge's *Chaucer and His Poetry,* 1915, reprinted in 1970, based on lectures delivered in 1914, remains fresh and instructive. Derek Albert Pearsall's *The Canterbury Tales,* 1985, includes a historical survey of the main critical issues raised by the work. David Aers, *Chaucer,* 1986, invites readers to examine the poet's work from modern perspectives. C. David Benson's *Chaucer's Drama of Style: Poetic Variety and Contrast in the "Canterbury Tales,"* 1986, discusses the topics mentioned in its title. One of the best essays on Chaucer's fabliaux can be found in Derek Brewer, *Chaucer: The Poet as Storyteller,* 1984, which also contains an essay on "The Nun's Priest's Tale" and another on Chaucer's place in European and English tradition. Critical perspectives from several centuries are represented in *Chaucer: "The Canterbury Tales": A Casebook,* ed. by J. J. Anderson, 1974. This volume includes Paul Ruggier's interesting "Irony in 'The Wife of Bath's Tale.'" Twenty-six essays, balanced between historical scholarship and literary criticism, are collected in *Chaucer: Modern Essays in Criticism,* ed. by Edward Wagenknecht, 1959. The emphasis is on *The Canterbury Tales,* including "The Pardoner's Tale" and "The Wife of Bath's Tale."

THE CANTERBURY TALES

Translated by Theodore Morrison

PROLOGUE

As soon as April pierces to the root
The drought of March, and bathes each bud and shoot
Through every vein of sap with gentle showers
From whose engendering liquor spring the flowers;
When zephyrs have breathed softly all about
Inspiring every wood and field to sprout,
And in the zodiac the youthful sun
His journey halfway through the Ram[1] has run;
When little birds are busy with their song
Who sleep with open eyes the whole night long
Life stirs their hearts and tingles in them so,

10

[1] The sun is in Aries (the Ram) during late March and early April.

Then off as pilgrims people long to go,
And palmers[2] to set out for distant strands
And foreign shrines renowned in many lands.
And specially in England people ride
To Canterbury[3] from every countryside
To visit there the blessed martyred saint
Who gave them strength when they were sick and faint.
    In Southwark at the Tabard[4] one spring day
It happened, as I stopped there on my way,   20
Myself a pilgrim with a heart devout
Ready for Canterbury to set out,
At night came all of twenty-nine assorted
Travelers, and to that same inn resorted,
Who by a turn of fortune chanced to fall
In fellowship together, and they were all
Pilgrims who had it in their minds to ride
Toward Canterbury. The stable doors were wide,
The rooms were large, and we enjoyed the best,
And shortly, when the sun had gone to rest,   30
I had so talked with each that presently
I was a member of their company
And promised to rise early the next day
To start, as I shall show, upon our way.
    But none the less, while I have time and space,
Before this tale has gone a further pace,
I should in reason tell you the condition
Of each of them, his rank and his position,
And also what array they all were in;
And so then, with a knight I will begin.   40
    A Knight was with us, and an excellent man,
Who from the earliest moment he began
To follow his career loved chivalry,
Truth, openhandedness, and courtesy.
He was a stout man in the king's campaigns
And in that cause had gripped his horse's reins
In Christian lands and pagan through the earth,
None farther, and always honored for his worth.
He was on hand at Alexandria's fall.[5]
He had often sat in precedence to all   50
The nations at the banquet board in Prussia.
He had fought in Lithuania and in Russia,
No Christian knight more often; he had been
In Moorish Africa at Benmarin,
At the siege of Algeciras in Granada,

[2] Zealous pilgrims who traveled to far-distant places.
[3] A city about sixty miles southeast of London. In Canterbury Cathedral was located the shrine of St. Thomas à Becket, murdered there in 1170.
[4] An inn in Southwark, a suburb of London on the south bank of the Thames.
[5] The places mentioned in the following lines were sites of battles, mostly fought against Mohammedans and other pagans.

And sailed in many a glorious armada
In the Mediterranean, and fought as well
At Ayas and Attalia when they fell
In Armenia and on Asia Minor's coast.
Of fifteen deadly battles he could boast, 60
And in Algeria, at Tremessen,
Fought for the faith and killed three separate men
In single combat. He had done good work
Joining against another pagan Turk
With the king of Palathia. And he was wise,
Despite his prowess, honored in men's eyes,
Meek as a girl and gentle in his ways.
He had never spoken ignobly all his days
To any man by even a rude inflection.
He was a knight in all things to perfection. 70
He rode a good horse, but his gear was plain,
For he had lately served on a campaign.
His tunic was still spattered by the rust
Left by his coat of mail, for he had just
Returned and set out on his pilgrimage.

His son was with him, a young Squire, in age
Some twenty years as near as I could guess.
His hair curled as if taken from a press.[6]
He was a lover and would become a knight.
In stature he was of a moderate height 80
But powerful and wonderfully quick.
He had been in Flanders, riding in the thick
Of forays in Artois and Picardy,
And bore up well for one so young as he,
Still hoping by his exploits in such places
To stand the better in his lady's graces.
He wore embroidered flowers, red and white,
And blazed like a spring meadow to the sight.
He sang or played his flute the livelong day.
He was as lusty as the month of May. 90
His coat was short, its sleeves were long and wide.
He sat his horse well, and knew how to ride,
And how to make a song and use his lance,
And he could write and draw well, too, and dance.
So hot his love that when the moon rose pale
He got no more sleep than a nightingale.
He was modest, and helped whomever he was able,
And carved as his father's squire at the table.

But one more servant had the Knight beside,
Choosing thus simply for the time to ride: 100
A Yeoman, in a coat and hood of green.
His peacock-feathered arrows, bright and keen,
He carried under his belt in tidy fashion.

---

[6]Curlers.

For well-kept gear he had a yeoman's passion.
No draggled feather might his arrows show,
And in his hand he held a mighty bow.
He kept his hair close-cropped, his face was brown.
He knew the lore of woodcraft up and down.
His arm was guarded from the bowstring's whip
By a bracer, gaily trimmed. He had at hip   110
A sword and buckler, and at his other side
A dagger whose fine mounting was his pride,
Sharp-pointed as a spear. His horn he bore
In a sling of green, and on his chest he wore
A silver image of St. Christopher,
His patron, since he was a forester.
   There was also a Nun, a Prioress,[7]
Whose smile was gentle and full of guilelessness.
"By St. Loy!"[8] was the worst oath she would say.
She sang mass well, in a becoming way,   120
Intoning through her nose the words divine,
And she was known as Madame Eglantine.
She spoke good French, as taught at Stratford-Bow,[9]
For the Parisian French she did not know.
She was schooled to eat so primly and so well
That from her lips no morsel ever fell.
She wet her fingers lightly in the dish
Of sauce, for courtesy was her first wish.
With every bite she did her skillful best
To see that no drop fell upon her breast.   130
She always wiped her upper lip so clean
That in her cup was never to be seen
A hint of grease when she had drunk her share.
She reached out for her meat with comely air.
She was a great delight, and always tried
To imitate court ways, and had her pride,
Both amiable and gracious in her dealings.
As for her charity and tender feelings,
She melted at whatever was piteous.
She would weep if she but came upon a mouse   140
Caught in a trap, if it were dead or bleeding.
Some little dogs that she took pleasure feeding
On roasted meat or milk or good wheat bread
She had, but how she wept to find one dead
Or yelping from a blow that made it smart,
And all was sympathy and loving heart.
Neat was her wimple[10] in its every plait,
Her nose well formed, her eyes as gray as slate.

---

[7] The head of a convent.
[8] A minor saint, popular with women at the royal court in Chaucer's day.
[9] A convent near London, where a dialect of French was spoken.
[10] A cloth worn around the face; part of a nun's habit.

Her mouth was very small and soft and red.
She had so wide a brow I think her head   150
Was nearly a span[11] broad, for certainly
She was not undergrown, as all could see.
She wore her cloak with dignity and charm,
And had her rosary about her arm,
The small beads coral and the larger green,
And from them hung a brooch of golden sheen,
On it a large A and a crown above;
Beneath, "All things are subject unto love."
    A Priest accompanied her toward Canterbury,
And an attendant Nun, her secretary.   160
    There was a Monk, and nowhere was his peer,
A hunter, and a roving overseer.[12]
He was a manly man, and fully able
To be an abbot. He kept a hunting stable,
And when he rode the neighborhood could hear
His bridle jingling in the wind as clear
And loud as if it were a chapel bell.
Wherever he was master of a cell
The principles of good St. Benedict,[13]
For being a little old and somewhat strict,   170
Were honored in the breach, as past their prime.
He lived by the fashion of a newer time.
He would have swapped that text for a plucked hen
Which says that hunters are not holy men,
Or a monk outside his discipline and rule
Is too much like a fish outside his pool;
That is to say, a monk outside his cloister.
But such a text he deemed not worth an oyster.
I told him his opinion made me glad.
Why should he study always and go mad,   180
Mewed[14] in his cell with only a book for neighbor?
Or why, as Augustine commanded, labor
And sweat his hands? How shall the world be served?
To Augustine be all such toil reserved!
And so he hunted, as was only right.
He had greyhounds as swift as birds in flight.
His taste was all for tracking down the hare,
And what his sport might cost he did not care.
His sleeves I noticed, where they met his hand,
Trimmed with gray fur, the finest in the land.   190
His hood was fastened with a curious pin
Made of wrought gold and clasped beneath his chin,

[11] A handspan.
[12] An "outrider," a person who supervised monastic property at some distance from the monastery.
[13] Sixth-century author of a famous rule, or code, laying down strict regulations for monastic life.
[14] Caged.

A love knot at the tip. His head might pass,
Bald as it was, for a lump of shining glass,
And his face was glistening as if anointed.
Fat as a lord he was, and well appointed.
His eyes were large, and rolled inside his head
As if they gleamed from a furnace of hot lead.
His boots were supple, his horse superbly kept.
He was a prelate to dream of while you slept.   200
He was not pale nor peaked like a ghost.
He relished a plump swan as his favorite roast.
He rode a palfrey brown as a ripe berry.

   A Friar was with us, a gay dog and a merry,
Who begged his district[15] with a jolly air.
No friar in all four orders[16] could compare
With him for gallantry; his tongue was wooing.
Many a girl was married by his doing,
And at his own cost it was often done.
He was a pillar, and a noble one,   210
To his whole order. In his neighborhood
Rich franklins[17] knew him well, who served good food,
And worthy women welcomed him to town;
For the license that his order handed down,
He said himself, conferred on him possession
Of more than a curate's[18] power of confession.
Sweetly the list of frailties he heard,
Assigning penance[19] with a pleasant word.
He was an easy man for absolution
Where he looked forward to a contribution,   220
For if to a poor order a man has given
It signifies that he has been well shriven,[20]
And if a sinner let his purse be dented
The Friar would stake his oath he had repented.
For many men become so hard of heart
They cannot weep, though conscience makes them smart.
Instead of tears and prayers, then, let the sinner
Supply the poor friars with the price of dinner.
For pretty women he had more than shrift.
His cape was stuffed with many a little gift,   230
As knives and pins and suchlike. He could sing
A merry note, and pluck a tender string,
And had no rival at all in balladry.
His neck was whiter than a fleur-de-lis,[21]
And yet he could have knocked a strong man down.
He knew the taverns well in every town.

[15] The friar is a "limiter," assigned a territory (limits) within which he can beg.
[16] The Franciscans, Dominicans, Carmelites, and Augustinians.
[17] Country gentlemen.   [18] Parish priest.
[19] After a sinner confesses to the priest, he is granted absolution (forgiveness of his sins), provided he does the assigned penance.
[20] Given shrift (absolution) in the sacrament of confession.   [21] Lily.

The barmaids and innkeepers pleased his mind
Better than beggars and lepers and their kind.
In his position it was unbecoming
Among the wretched lepers to go slumming.   240
It mocks all decency, it sews no stitch
To deal with such riffraff; but with the rich,
With sellers of victuals, that's another thing.
Wherever he saw some hope of profiting,
None so polite, so humble. He was good,
The champion beggar of his brotherhood.
Should a woman have no shoes against the snow,
So pleasant was his "*In principio*"[22]
He would have her widow's mite[23] before he went.
He took in far more than he paid in rent   250
For his right of begging within certain bounds.
None of his brethren trespassed on his grounds!
He loved as freely as a half-grown whelp.
On arbitration-days[24] he gave great help,
For his cloak was never shiny nor threadbare
Like a poor cloistered scholar's. He had an air
As if he were a doctor or a pope.
It took stout wool to make his semicope[25]
That plumped out like a bell for portliness.
He lisped a little in his rakishness   260
To make his English sweeter on his tongue,
And twanging his harp to end some song he'd sung
His eyes would twinkle in his head as bright
As the stars twinkle on a frosty night.
Hubert this gallant Friar was by name.
    Among the rest a Merchant also came.
He wore a forked beard and a beaver hat
From Flanders. High up in the saddle he sat,
In figured cloth, his boots clasped handsomely,
Delivering his opinions pompously,   270
Always on how his gains might be increased.
At all costs he desired the sea policed[26]
From Middleburg in Holland to Orwell.
He knew the exchange rates, and the time to sell
French currency, and there was never yet
A man who could have told he was in debt
So grave he seemed and hid so well his feelings
With all his shrewd engagements and close dealings.
You'd find no better man at any turn;
But what his name was I could never learn.   280

---

[22] Latin for "in the beginning," the opening words of St. John's gospel. The friar uses Latin
to show off.
[23] A tiny sum of money.
[24] "Love-days," when people settled their disputes, friars sometimes serving as judges.
[25] Jacket.   [26] That is, kept free of pirates.

There was an Oxford Student too, it chanced,
Already in his logic well advanced.
He rode a mount as skinny as a rake,
And he was hardly fat. For learning's sake
He let himself look hollow and sober enough.
He wore an outer coat of threadbare stuff,
For he had no benefice[27] for his enjoyment
And was too unworldly for some lay[28] employment.
He much preferred to have beside his bed
His twenty volumes bound in black or red   290
All packed with Aristotle from end to middle
Than a sumptuous wardrobe or a merry fiddle.
For though he knew what learning had to offer
There was little coin to jingle in his coffer.
Whatever he got by touching up a friend
On books and learning he would promptly spend
And busily pray for the soul of anybody
Who furnished him the wherewithal for study.
His scholarship was what he truly heeded.
He never spoke a word more than was needed,   300
And that was said with dignity and force,
And quick and brief. He was of grave discourse,
Giving new weight to virtue by his speech,
And gladly would he learn and gladly teach.
    There was a Lawyer, cunning and discreet,
Who had often been to St. Paul's porch to meet
His clients. He was a Sergeant of the Law,
A man deserving to be held in awe,
Or so he seemed, his manner was so wise.
He had often served as Justice of Assize[29]   310
By the king's appointment, with a broad commission,
For his knowledge and his eminent position.
He had many a handsome gift by way of fee.
There was no buyer of land as shrewd as he.
All ownership to him became fee simple.[30]
His titles were never faulty by a pimple.
None was so busy as he with case and cause,
And yet he seemed much busier than he was.
In all cases and decisions he was schooled
That were of record since King William[31] ruled.   320
No one could pick a loophole or a flaw
In any lease or contract he might draw.
Each statute on the books he knew by rote.
He traveled in a plain, silk-belted coat.
    A Franklin[32] traveled in his company.

---

[27] Position at a church.
[28] Secular. The student, or clerk, is preparing for a career in the Church.
[29] Lawcourt.   [30] Unqualified ownership.
[31] King William the Conqueror (ruled 1066–87).   [32] Country gentleman.

Whiter could never daisy petal be
Than was his beard. His ruddy face gave sign
He liked his morning sop of toast in wine.
He lived in comfort, as he would assure us,
For he was a true son of Epicurus[33]   330
Who held the opinion that the only measure
Of perfect happiness was simply pleasure.
Such hospitality did he provide,
He was St. Julian[34] to his countryside.
His bread and ale were always up to scratch.
He had a cellar[35] none on earth could match.
There was no lack of pasties in his house,
Both fish and flesh, and that so plenteous
That where he lived it snowed of meat and drink.
With every dish of which a man can think,   340
After the various seasons of the year,
He changed his diet for his better cheer.
He had coops of partridges as fat as cream,
He had a fishpond stocked with pike and bream.
Woe to his cook for an unready pot
Or a sauce that wasn't seasoned and spiced hot!
A table in his hall stood on display
Prepared and covered through the livelong day.
He presided at court sessions for his bounty
And sat in Parliament often for his county.   350
A well-wrought dagger and a purse of silk
Hung at his belt, as white as morning milk.
He had been a sheriff and county auditor.
On earth was no such rich proprietor!
   There were five Guildsmen, in the livery
Of one august and great fraternity,[36]
A Weaver, a Dyer, and a Carpenter,
A Tapestry-maker and a Haberdasher.
Their gear was furbished new and clean as glass.
The mountings of their knives were not of brass   360
But silver. Their pouches were well made and neat,
And each of them, it seemed, deserved a seat
On the platform at the Guildhall, for each one
Was likely timber to make an alderman.
They had goods enough, and money to be spent,
Also their wives would willingly consent
And would have been at fault if they had not.
For to be "Madamed" is a pleasant lot,
And to march in first at feasts for being well married,
And royally to have their mantles carried.   370

---

[33] Ancient Greek philosopher, often associated with love of pleasure, although this is an oversimplification of his teaching.
[34] Patron saint of hospitality.   [35] Wine cellar.
[36] Perhaps a religious lodge, since they all wear the same "livery," or uniform dress.

For the pilgrimage these Guildsmen brought their own
Cook to boil their chicken and marrow bone
With seasoning powder and capers and sharp spice.
In judging London ale his taste was nice.
He well knew how to roast and broil and fry,
To mix a stew, and bake a good meat pie,
Or capon creamed with almond, rice, and egg.
Pity he had an ulcer on his leg!
    A Skipper was with us, his home far in the west.
He came from the port of Dartmouth, as I guessed.   380
He sat his carthorse pretty much at sea
In a coarse smock that joggled on his knee.
From his neck a dagger on a string hung down
Under his arm. His face was burnished brown
By the summer sun. He was a true good fellow.
Many a time he had tapped a wine cask mellow
Sailing from Bordeaux while the owner slept.
Too nice a point of honor he never kept.
In a sea fight, if he got the upper hand,
Drowned prisoners floated home to every land.   390
But in navigation, whether reckoning tides,
Currents, or what might threaten him besides,
Harborage, pilotage, or the moon's demeanor,
None was his like from Hull to Cartagena.
He knew each harbor and the anchorage there
From Gotland to the Cape of Finisterre
And every creek in Brittany and Spain,
And he had called his ship the *Madeleine.*
    With us came also an astute Physician.
There was none like him for a disquisition   400
On the art of medicine or surgery,
For he was grounded in astrology.[37]
He kept his patient long in observation,
Choosing the proper hour for application
Of charms and images by intuition
Of magic, and the planets' best position.
For he was one who understood the laws
That rule the humors,[38] and could tell the cause
That brought on every human malady,
Whether of hot or cold, or moist or dry.   410
He was a perfect medico, for sure.
The cause once known, he would prescribe the cure,
For he had his druggists ready at a motion
To provide the sick man with some pill or potion—
A game of mutual aid, with each one winning.

---

[37] It was common for physicians in Chaucer's day to be guided by the position of the heavenly bodies.

[38] The relative proportion in a person of the four "humors" (blood, black bile, phlegm, yellow bile) was believed to influence character as well as health.

Their partnership was hardly just beginning!
He was well versed in his authorities,
Old Aesculapius, Dioscorides,
Rufus, and old Hippocrates, and Galen,
Haly, and Rhazes, and Serapion,   420
Averroës, Bernard, Johannes Damascenus,
Avicenna, Gilbert, Gaddesden, Constantinus.[39]
He urged a moderate fare on principle,
But rich in nourishment, digestible;
Of nothing in excess would he admit.
He gave but little heed to Holy Writ.
His clothes were lined with taffeta; their hue
Was all of blood red and of Persian blue,
Yet he was far from careless of expense.
He saved his fees from times of pestilence,   430
For gold is a cordial,[40] as physicians hold,
And so he had a special love for gold.
   A worthy woman there was from near the city
Of Bath, but somewhat deaf, and more's the pity.
For weaving she possessed so great a bent
She outdid the people of Ypres and of Ghent.[41]
No other woman dreamed of such a thing
As to precede her at the offering,[42]
Or if any did, she fell in such a wrath
She dried up all the charity in Bath.   440
She wore fine kerchiefs of old-fashioned air,
And on a Sunday morning, I could swear,
She had ten pounds of linen on her head.
Her stockings were of finest scarlet-red,
Laced tightly, and her shoes were soft and new.
Bold was her face, and fair, and red in hue.
She had been an excellent woman all her life.
Five men in turn had taken her to wife,
Omitting other youthful company—
But let that pass for now! Over the sea   450
She had traveled freely; many a distant stream
She crossed, and visited Jerusalem
Three times. She had been at Rome and at Boulogne,
At the shrine of Compostella, and at Cologne.
She had wandered by the way through many a scene.
Her teeth were set with little gaps between.[43]
Easily on her ambling horse she sat.
She was well wimpled, and she wore a hat
As wide in circuit as a shield or targe.[44]
A skirt swathed up her hips, and they were large.   460

[39] Famous ancient and medieval medical authorities.
[40] A medical stimulant. Gold was sometimes used as an ingredient.
[41] Centers of the weaving industry in Flanders.   [42] Offering at church.
[43] For a woman to be gap-toothed was considered a sign of being highly sexed.
[44] A type of shield.

Upon her feet she wore sharp-roweled spurs.
She was a good fellow; a ready tongue was hers.
All remedies of love she knew by name,
For she had all the tricks of that old game.
  There was a good man of the priest's vocation,
A poor town Parson of true consecration,
But he was rich in holy thought and work.
Learned he was, in the truest sense a clerk[45]
Who meant Christ's gospel faithfully to preach
And truly his parishioners to teach.   470
He was a kind man, fully of industry,
Many times tested by adversity
And always patient. If tithes[46] were in arrears,
He was loth to threaten any man with fears
Of excommunication;[47] past a doubt
He would rather spread his offering about
To his poor flock, or spend his property.
To him a little meant sufficiency.
Wide was his parish, with houses far asunder,
But he would not be kept by rain or thunder,   480
If any had suffered a sickness or a blow,
From visiting the farthest, high or low,
Plodding his way on foot, his staff in hand.
He was a model his flock could understand,
For first he did and afterward he taught.
That precept from the Gospel he had caught,
And he added as a metaphor thereto,
"If the gold rusts, what will the iron do?"
For if a priest is foul, in whom we trust,
No wonder a layman shows a little rust.   490
A priest should take to heart the shameful scene
Of shepherds filthy while the sheep are clean.
By his own purity a priest should give
The example to his sheep, how they should live.
He did not rent his benefice[48] for hire,
Leaving his flock to flounder in the mire,
And run to London, happiest of goals,
To sing paid masses in St. Paul's for souls,
Or as chaplain from some rich guild take his keep,
But dwelt at home and guarded well his sheep   500
So that no wolf should make his flock miscarry.
He was a shepherd, and not a mercenary.
And though himself a man of strict vocation
He was not harsh to weak souls in temptation,
Not overbearing nor haughty in his speech,

[45] A clergyman-scholar.
[46] One tenth of one's earnings, the sum due to the Church.
[47] Barring of a person from the church and sacraments—a serious penalty.
[48] Hire out his position as pastor of his church.

But wise and kind in all he tried to teach.
By good example and just words to turn
Sinners to heaven was his whole concern.
But should a man in truth prove obstinate,
Whoever he was, of rich or mean estate,   510
The Parson would give him a snub to meet the case.
I doubt there was a priest in any place
His better. He did not stand on dignity
Nor affect in conscience too much nicety,
But Christ's and his disciples' word he sought
To teach, and first he followed what he taught.
    There was a Plowman with him on the road,
His brother, who had forked up many a load
Of good manure. A hearty worker he,
Living in peace and perfect charity.   520
Whether his fortune made him smart or smile,
He loved God with his whole heart all the while
And his neighbor as himself. He would undertake,
For every luckless poor man, for the sake
Of Christ to thresh and ditch and dig by the hour
And with no wage, if it was in his power.
His tithes on goods and earnings he paid fair.
He wore a coarse, rough coat and rode a mare.
    There also were a Manciple,[49] a Miller,
A Reeve, a Summoner, and a Pardoner,[50]   530
And I—this makes our company complete.
    As tough a yokel as you care to meet
The Miller was. His big-beefed arms and thighs
Took many a ram put up as wrestling prize.
He was a thick, squat-shouldered lump of sins.
No door but he could heave it off its pins
Or break it running at it with his head.
His beard was broader than a shovel, and red
As a fat sow or fox. A wart stood clear
Atop his nose, and red as a pig's ear   540
A tuft of bristles on it. Black and wide
His nostrils were. He carried at his side
A sword and buckler. His mouth would open out
Like a great furnace, and he would sing and shout
His ballads and jokes of harlotries and crimes.
He could steal corn[51] and charge for it three times,
And yet was honest enough, as millers come,
For a miller, as they say, has a golden thumb.
In white coat and blue hood this lusty clown,
Blowing his bagpipes, brought us out of town.   550

---

[49] A steward.
[50] A reeve was an overseer for an estate; a summoner summoned to the ecclesiastical court
persons charged with offenses against the Church; a pardoner distributed or sold pardons for
sins in the name of the Pope.
[51] Grain.

The Manciple was of a lawyers' college,
And other buyers might have used his knowledge
How to be shrewd provisioners, for whether
He bought on cash or credit, altogether
He managed that the end should be the same:
He came out more than even with the game.
Now isn't it an instance of God's grace
How a man of little knowledge can keep pace
In wit with a whole school of learned men?
He had masters to the number of three times ten   560
Who knew each twist of equity and tort;
A dozen in that very Inn of Court
Were worthy to be steward of the estate
To any of England's lords, however great,
And keep him to his income well confined
And free from debt, unless he lost his mind,
Or let him scrimp, if he were mean in bounty;
They could have given help to a whole county
In any sort of case that might befall;
And yet this Manciple could cheat them all!   570
    The Reeve was a slender, fiery-tempered man.
He shaved as closely as a razor can.
His hair was cropped about his ears, and shorn
Above his forehead as a priest's is worn.
His legs were very long and very lean.
No calf on his lank spindles could be seen.
But he knew how to keep a barn or bin,
He could play the game with auditors and win.
He knew well how to judge by drought and rain
The harvest of his seed and of his grain.   580
His master's cattle, swine, and poultry flock,
Horses and sheep and dairy, all his stock,
Were altogether in this Reeve's control.
And by agreement, he had given the sole
Accounting since his lord reached twenty years.
No man could ever catch him in arrears.
There wasn't a bailiff, shepherd, or farmer working
But the Reeve knew all his tricks of cheating and shirking.
He would not let him draw an easy breath.
They feared him as they feared the very death.   590
He lived in a good house on an open space,
Well shaded by green trees, a pleasant place.
He was shrewder in acquisition than his lord.
With private riches he was amply stored.
He had learned a good trade young by work and will.
He was a carpenter of first-rate skill.
On a fine mount, a stallion, dappled gray,
Whose name was Scot, he rode along the way.
He wore a long blue coat hitched up and tied
As if it were a friar's, and at his side   600

A sword with rusty blade was hanging down.
He came from Norfolk, from nearby the town
That men call Bawdswell. As we rode the while,
The Reeve kept always hindmost in our file.
  A Summoner in our company had his place.
Red as the fiery cherubim his face.
He was pocked and pimpled, and his eyes were narrow.
He was lecherous and hot as a cock sparrow.
His brows were scabby and black, and thin his beard.
His was a face that little children feared. 610
Brimstone or litharge bought in any quarter,
Quicksilver, ceruse, borax, oil of tartar,[52]
No salve nor ointment that will cleanse or bite
Could cure him of his blotches, livid white,
Or the nobs and nubbins sitting on his cheeks.
He loved his garlic, his onions, and his leeks.
He loved to drink the strong wine down blood-red.
Then would he bellow as if he had lost his head,
And when he had drunk enough to parch his drouth,
Nothing but Latin issued from his mouth. 620
He had smattered up a few terms, two or three,
That he had gathered out of some decree—
No wonder; he heard law Latin all the day,
And everyone knows a parrot or a jay
Can cry out "Wat" or "Poll" as well as the pope;
But give him a strange term, he began to grope.
His little store of learning was paid out,
So *"Questio quod juris"*[53] he would shout.
He was a goodhearted bastard and a kind one.
If there were better, it was hard to find one. 630
He would let a good fellow, for a quart of wine,
The whole year round enjoy his concubine
Scot-free from summons, hearing, fine, or bail,
And on the sly he too could flush a quail.
If he liked a scoundrel, no matter for church law.
He would teach him that he need not stand in awe
If the archdeacon threatened with his curse—
That is, unless his soul was in his purse,
For in his purse he would be punished well.
"The purse," he said, "is the archdeacon's hell." 640
Of course I know he lied in what he said.
There is nothing a guilty man should so much dread
As the curse that damns his soul, when, without fail,
The church can save him, or send him off to jail.
He had the young men and girls in his control
Throughout the diocese; he knew the soul
Of youth, and heard their every last design.

---

[52] Remedies for skin diseases.
[53] Latin for "What law governs this case?"—a phrase picked up in courtrooms.

A garland big enough to be the sign
Above an alehouse balanced on his head,
And he made a shield of a great round loaf of bread.   650
   There was a Pardoner of Rouncivalle[54]
With him, of the blessed Mary's hospital,
But now come straight from Rome (or so said he).
Loudly he sang, "Come hither, love, to me,"
While the Summoner's counterbass trolled out profound—
No trumpet blew with half so vast a sound.
This Pardoner had hair as yellow as wax,
But it hung as smoothly as a hank of flax.
His locks trailed down in bunches from his head,
And he let the ends about his shoulders spread,   660
But in thin clusters, lying one by one.
Of hood, for rakishness, he would have none,
For in his wallet[55] he kept it safely stowed.
He traveled, as he thought, in the latest mode,
Disheveled. Save for his cap, his head was bare,
And in his eyes he glittered like a hare.
A Veronica[56] was stitched upon his cap,
His wallet lay before him in his lap
Brimful of pardons from the very seat
In Rome. He had a voice like a goat's bleat.   670
He was beardless and would never have a beard.
His cheek was always smooth as if just sheared.
I think he was a gelding or a mare;
But in his trade, from Berwick down to Ware,
No pardoner could beat him in the race,
For in his wallet he had a pillow case
Which he represented as Our Lady's veil;
He said he had a piece of the very sail
St. Peter, when he fished in Galilee
Before Christ caught him, used upon the sea.   680
He had a latten[57] cross embossed with stones
And in a glass he carried some pig's bones,
And with these holy relics, when he found
Some village parson grubbing his poor ground,
He would get more money in a single day
Than in two months would come the parson's way.
Thus with his flattery and his trumped-up stock
He made dupes of the parson and his flock.
But though his conscience was a little plastic
He was in church a noble ecclesiastic.   690
Well could he read the Scripture or saint's story,
But best of all he sang the offertory,[58]

---

[54] A hospital just outside London.   [55] Bag.
[56] An image of Christ's features supposed to have been made on the veil of St. Veronica
after she let him wipe his face on it before the Crucifixion.
[57] Made of a brasslike metal.   [58] Part of the Catholic Mass.

For he understood that when this song was sung,
Then he must preach, and sharpen up his tongue
To rake in cash, as well he knew the art,
And so he sang out gaily, with full heart.
  Now I have set down briefly, as it was,
Our rank, our dress, our number, and the cause
That made our sundry fellowship begin
In Southwark, at this hospitable inn   700
Known as the Tabard, not far from the Bell.[59]
But what we did that night I ought to tell,
And after that our journey, stage by stage,
And the whole story of our pilgrimage.
But first, in justice, do not look askance
I plead, nor lay it to my ignorance
If in this matter I should use plain speech
And tell you just the words and style of each
Reporting all their language faithfully.
For it must be known to you as well as me   710
That whoever tells a story after a man
Must follow him as closely as he can.
If he takes the tale in charge, he must be true
To every word, unless he would find new
Or else invent a thing or falsify.
Better some breadth of language than a lie!
He may not spare the truth to save his brother.
He might as well use one word as another.
In Holy Writ Christ spoke in a broad sense,
And surely his word is without offense.   720
Plato, if his are pages you can read,
Says let the word be cousin to the deed.
So I petition your indulgence for it
If I have cut the cloth just as men wore it,
Here in this tale, and shown its very weave.
My wits are none too sharp, you must believe.
  Our Host gave each of us a cheerful greeting
And promptly of our supper had us eating.
The victuals that he served us were his best.
The wine was potent, and we drank with zest.   730
Our Host cut such a figure, all in all,
He might have been a marshal in a hall.[60]
He was a big man, and his eyes bulged wide.
No sturdier citizen lived in all Cheapside,[61]
Lacking no trace of manhood, bold in speech,
Prudent, and well versed in what life can teach,
And with all this he was a jovial man.
And so when supper ended he began
To jolly us, when all our debts were clear.

---

[59] Another tavern.   [60] Managing official in a great medieval house.
[61] A commercial street in London.

"Welcome," he said. "I have not seen this year   740
So merry a company in this tavern as now,
And I would give you pleasure if I knew how.
And just this very minute a plan has crossed
My mind that might amuse you at no cost.
    "You go to Canterbury—may the Lord
Speed you, and may the martyred saint reward
Your journey! And to while the time away
You mean to talk and pass the time of day,
For you would be as cheerful all alone
As riding on your journey dumb as stone.   750
Therefore, if you'll abide by what I say,
Tomorrow, when you ride off on your way,
Now, by my father's soul, and he is dead,
If you don't enjoy yourselves, cut off my head!
Hold up your hands, if you accept my speech."
    Our counsel did not take us long to reach.
We bade him give his orders at his will.
"Well, sirs," he said, "then do not take it ill,
But hear me in good part, and for your sport,
Each one of you, to make our journey short,   760
Shall tell two stories, as we ride, I mean,
Toward Canterbury; and coming home again
Shall tell two other tales he may have heard
Of happenings that some time have occurred.
And the one of you whose stories please us most,
Here in this tavern, sitting by this post
Shall sup at our expense while we make merry
When we come riding home from Canterbury.
And to cheer you still the more, I too will ride
With you at my own cost, and be your guide.   770
And if anyone my judgment shall gainsay
He must pay for all we spend along the way.
If you agree, no need to stand and reason.
Tell me, and I'll be stirring in good season."
    This thing was granted, and we swore our pledge
To take his judgment on our pilgrimage,
His verdict on our tales, and his advice.
He was to plan a supper at a price
Agreed upon; and so we all assented
To this command, and we were well contented.   780
The wine was fetched; we drank, and went to rest.
    Next morning, when the dawn was in the east,
Up sprang our Host, who acted as our cock,
And gathered us together in a flock,
And off we rode, till presently our pace
Had brought us to St. Thomas' watering place.
And there our Host began to check his horse.
"Good sirs," he said, "you know your promise, of course.
Shall I remind you what it was about?

If evensong and matins don't fall out,[62]   790
We'll soon find who shall tell us the first tale.
But as I hope to drink my wine and ale,
Whoever won't accept what I decide
Pays everything we spend along the ride.
Draw lots, before we're farther from the Inn.
Whoever draws the shortest shall begin.
Sir Knight," said he, "my master, choose your straw.
Come here, my lady Prioress, and draw,
And you, Sir Scholar, don't look thoughtful, man!
Pitch in now, everyone!" So all began   800
To draw the lots, and as the luck would fall
The draw went to the Knight, which pleased us all.
And when this excellent man saw how it stood,
Ready to keep his promise, he said, "Good!
Since it appears that I must start the game,
Why then, the draw is welcome, in God's name.
Now let's ride on, and listen, what I say."
And with that word we rode forth on our way,
And he, with his courteous manner and good cheer,
Began to tell his tale, as you shall hear.   810

PROLOGUE TO THE MILLER'S TALE

When the Knight had finished,[1] no one, young or old,
In the whole company, but said he had told
A noble story, one that ought to be
Preserved and kept alive in memory,
Especially the gentlefolk, each one.
Our good Host laughed, and swore, "The game's begun,
The ball is rolling! This is going well.
Let's see who has another tale to tell.
Come, match the Knight's tale if you can, Sir Monk!"
      The Miller, who by this time was so drunk   10
He looked quite bloodless, and who hardly sat
His horse, he was never one to doff his hat
Or stand on courtesy for any man.
Like Pilate in the Church plays[2] he began
To bellow. "Arms and blood and bones," he swore,
"I know a yarn that will even up the score,
A noble one, I'll pay off the Knight's tale!"
      Our Host could see that he was drunk on ale.
"Robin," he said, "hold on a minute, brother.

---

[62] That is, if you feel this morning as you did last evening. Evensong and matins are evening and morning prayers.
[1] The Knight had led off the program of storytelling on the way to Canterbury; see the General Prologue, lines 745–810.
[2] The "mystery plays," based on the Bible, especially the Gospels.

Some better man shall come first with another.   20
Let's do this right. You tell yours by and by."
    "God's soul," the Miller told him, "that won't I!
Either I'll speak, or go on my own way."
    "The devil with you! Say what you have to say,"
Answered our Host. "You are a fool. Your head
Is overpowered."
                        "Now," the Miller said,
"Everyone listen! But first I will propound
That I am drunk, I know it by my sound.
If I can't get my words out, put the blame
On Southwark ale,[3] I ask you, in God's name!   30
For I'll tell a golden legend[4] and a life
Both of a carpenter and of his wife,
How a student put horns on the fellow's head."
    "Shut up and stop your racket," the Reeve said.[5]
"Forget your ignorant drunken bawdiness.
It is a sin and a great foolishness
To injure any man by defamation
And to give women such a reputation.
Tell us of other things; you'll find no lack."
    Promptly this drunken Miller answered back: 40
"Oswald, my brother, true as babes are suckled,
The man who has no wife, he is no cuckold.
I don't say for this reason that you are.
There are plenty of faithful wives, both near and far,
Always a thousand good for every bad,
And you know this yourself, unless you're mad.
I see you are angry with my tale, but why?
You have a wife; no less, by God, do I.
But I wouldn't, for the oxen in my plow,
Shoulder more than I need by thinking how   50
I may myself, for aught I know, be one.
I'll certainly believe that I am none.
A husband mustn't be curious, for his life,
About God's secrets or about his wife.
If she gives him plenty and he's in the clover,
No need to worry about what's left over."
    The Miller, to make the best of it I can,
Refused to hold his tongue for any man,
But told his tale like any low-born clown.
I am sorry that I have to set it down,   60
And all you people, for God's love, I pray,
Whose taste is higher, do not think I say
A word with evil purpose; I must rehearse

---

[3] Ale from the Host's inn, in the Southwark district of London, from which the pilgrimage had set out.
[4] A saint's life.
[5] The Reeve was a carpenter by trade; see the General Prologue, line 596.

Their stories one and all, both better and worse,
Or play false with my matter, that is clear.
Whoever, therefore, may not wish to hear,
Turn over the page and choose another tale;
For small and great, he'll find enough, no fail,
Of things from history, touching courtliness,
And virtue too, and also holiness.   70
If you choose wrong, don't lay it on my head.
You know the Miller couldn't be called well bred.
So with the Reeve, and many more as well,
And both of them had bawdy tales to tell.
Reflect a little, and don't hold me to blame.
There's no sense making earnest out of game.

THE MILLER'S TALE

There used to be a rich old oaf who made
His home at Oxford, a carpenter by trade,
And took in boarders. With him used to dwell
A student who had done his studies well,
But he was poor; for all that he had learned,
It was toward astrology his fancy turned.
He knew a number of figures and constructions
By which he could supply men with deductions
If they should ask him at a given hour
Whether to look for sunshine or for shower,   10
Or want to know whatever might befall,
Events of all sorts, I can't count them all.
    He was known as handy[1] Nicholas, this student.
Well versed in love, he knew how to be prudent,
Going about unnoticed, sly, and sure.
In looks no girl was ever more demure.
Lodged at this carpenter's, he lived alone;
He had a room there that he made his own,
Festooned with herbs, and he was sweet himself
As licorice or ginger. On a shelf   20
Above his bed's head, neatly stowed apart,
He kept the trappings that went with his art,
His astrolabe,[2] his books—among the rest,
Thick ones and thin ones, lay his *Almagest*[3]—
And the counters for his abacus as well.
Over his cupboard a red curtain fell
And up above a pretty zither lay

---

[1] "Chaucer's word is *hendë*, implying, I take it, both *ready to hand* and *ingratiating*. Nicholas was a Johnny-on-the-spot and also had a way with him."—Translator's note.
[2] An astronomical instrument, used to measure celestial altitudes.
[3] Handbook of the stars; from the treatise on astronomy by Ptolemy (2nd century A.D.).

On which at night so sweetly would he play
That with the music the whole room would ring.
"Angelus to the Virgin" he would sing   30
And then the song that's known as "The King's Note."[4]
Blessings were called down on his merry throat!
So this sweet scholar passed his time, his end
Being to eat and live upon his friend.
   This carpenter had newly wed a wife
And loved her better than he loved his life.
He was jealous, for she was eighteen in age;
He tried to keep her close as in a cage,
For she was wild and young, and old was he
And guessed that he might smack of cuckoldry.   40
His ignorant wits had never chanced to strike
On Cato's word, that man should wed his like;[5]
Men ought to wed where their conditions point,
For youth and age are often out of joint.
But now, since he had fallen in the snare,
He must, like other men, endure his care.
   Fair this young woman was, her body trim
As any mink, so graceful and so slim.
She wore a striped belt that was all of silk;
A piece-work apron, white as morning milk,   50
About her loins and down her lap she wore.
White was her smock, her collar both before
And on the back embroidered all about
In coal-black silk, inside as well as out.
And like her collar, her white-laundered bonnet
Had ribbons of the same embroidery on it.
Wide was her silken fillet,[6] worn up high,
And for a fact she had a willing eye.
She plucked each brow into a little bow,
And each one was as black as any sloe.[7]   60
She was a prettier sight to see by far
Than the blossoms of the early pear tree are,
And softer than the wool of an old wether.[8]
Down from her belt there hung a purse of leather
With silken tassels and with studs of brass.
No man so wise, wherever people pass,
Who could imagine in this world at all
A wench like her, the pretty little doll!
Far brighter was the dazzle of her hue
Than a coin struck in the Tower,[9] fresh and new.   70
As for her song, it twittered from her head
Sharp as a swallow perching on a shed.

   [4] That is, both sacred and secular music.
   [5] The *Distichs,* a book of Latin maxims used in schools, was attributed to Dionysius Cato
(4th century A.D.).
   [6] Headband.   [7] A small black fruit resembling a plum.   [8] Sheep.
   [9] The Tower of London, where coins were minted.

And she could skip and sport as a young ram
Or calf will gambol, following his dam.
Her mouth was sweet as honey-ale or mead
Or apples in the hay, stored up for need.
She was as skittish as an untrained colt,
Slim as a mast and straighter than a bolt.
On her simple collar she wore a big brooch-pin
Wide as a shield's boss underneath her chin. 80
High up along her legs she laced her shoes.
She was a pigsney,[10] she was a primrose
For any lord to tumble in his bed
Or a good yeoman honestly to wed.
　Now sir, and again sir, this is how it was:
A day came round when handy Nicholas,
While her husband was at Oseney,[11] well away,
Began to fool with this young wife, and play.
These students always have a wily head.
He caught her in between the legs, and said, 90
"Sweetheart, unless I have my will with you
I'll die for stifled love, by all that's true,"
And held her by the haunches, hard. "I vow
I'll die unless you love me here and now,
Sure as my soul," he said, "is God's to save."
　She shied just as a colt does in the trave,[12]
And turned her head hard from him, this young wife,
And said, "I will not kiss you, on my life.
Why, stop it now," she said, "stop, Nicholas,
Or I will cry out 'Help, help,' and 'Alas!' 100
Be good enough to take your hands away."
　"Mercy," this Nicholas began to pray,
And spoke so well and poured it on so fast
She promised she would be his love at last,
And swore by Thomas à Becket, saint of Kent,[13]
That she would serve him when she could invent
Or spy out some good opportunity.
"My husband is so full of jealousy
You must be watchful and take care," she said,
"Or well I know I'll be as good as dead. 110
You must go secretly about this business."
　"Don't give a thought to that," said Nicholas.
"A student has been wasting time at school
If he can't make a carpenter a fool."
And so they were agreed, these two, and swore
To watch their chance, as I have said before.
When Nicholas had spanked her haunches neatly

---

[10] Cuckoo-flower; a term of endearment.
[11] A town near Oxford, site of an abbey where the carpenter performed jobs.
[12] A frame used by blacksmiths to immobilize horses being shod.
[13] The saint whose shrine at Canterbury was the goal of Chaucer's pilgrims.

And done all I have spoken of, he sweetly
Gave her a kiss, and then he took his zither
And loudly played, and sang his music with her.   120
   Now in her Christian duty, one saint's day,
To the parish church this good wife made her way,
And as she went her forehead cast a glow
As bright as noon, for she had washed it so
It glistened when she finished with her work.
   Serving this church there was a parish clerk
Whose name was Absolom, a ruddy man
With goose-gray eyes and curls like a great fan
That shone like gold on his neatly parted head.
His tunic was light blue and his nose red,   130
And he had patterns that had been cut through
Like the windows of St. Paul's in either shoe.
He wore above his tunic, fresh and gay,
A surplice white as a blossom on a spray.
A merry devil, as true as God can save,
He knew how to let blood, trim hair, and shave,
Or write a deed of land in proper phrase,
And he could dance in twenty different ways
In the Oxford fashion, and sometimes he would sing
A loud falsetto to his fiddle string   140
Or his guitar. No tavern anywhere
But he had furnished entertainment there.
Yet his speech was delicate, and for his part
He was a little squeamish toward a fart.
   This Absolom, so jolly and so gay,
With a censer[14] went about on the saint's day
Censing the parish women one and all.
Many the doting look that he let fall,
And specially on this carpenter's young wife.
To look at her, he thought, was a good life,   150
She was so trim, so sweetly lecherous.
I dare say that if she had been a mouse
And he a cat, he would have made short work
Of catching her. This jolly parish clerk
Had such a heartful of love-hankerings
He would not take the women's offerings;
No, no, he said, it would not be polite.
   The moon, when darkness fell, shone full and bright,
And Absolom was ready for love's sake
With his guitar to be up and awake,   160
And toward the carpenter's, brisk and amorous,
He made his way until he reached the house
A little after the cocks began to crow.
Under a casement he sang sweet and low,
"Dear lady, by your will, be kind to me,"

---

[14] The vessel used in church to waft incense fumes.

And strummed on his guitar in harmony.
This lovelorn singing woke the carpenter
Who said to his wife, "What, Alison, don't you hear
Absolom singing under our bedroom wall?"
    "Yes, God knows, John," she answered, "I hear it all." 170
    What would you like? In this way things went on
Till jolly Absolom was woebegone
For wooing her, awake all night and day.
He combed his curls and made himself look gay.
He swore to be her slave and used all means
To court her with his gifts and go-betweens.
He sang and quavered like a nightingale.
He sent her sweet spiced wine and seasoned ale,
Cakes that were piping hot, mead sweet with honey,
And since she was town-bred, he proffered money. 180
For some are won by wealth, and some no less
By blows, and others yet by gentleness.
    Sometimes, to keep his talents in her gaze,
He acted Herod in the mystery plays
High on the stage. But what can help his case?
For she so loves this handy Nicholas
That Absolom is living in a bubble.
He has nothing but a laugh for all his trouble.
She leaves his earnestness for scorn to cool
And makes this Absolom her proper fool. 190
For this a true proverb, and no lie:
"It always happens that the nigh and sly
Will let the absent suffer." So 'tis said,
And Absolom may rage or lose his head
But just because he was farther from her sight
This nearby Nicholas got in his light.
    Now hold your chin up, handy Nicholas,
For Absolom may wail and sing "Alas!"
One Saturday when the carpenter had gone
To Oseney, Nicholas and Alison 200
Agreed that he should use his wit and guile
This simple jealous husband to beguile.
And if it happened that the game went right
She would sleep in his arms the livelong night,
For this was his desire and hers as well.
At once, with no more words, this Nicholas fell
To working out his plan. He would not tarry,
But quietly to his room began to carry
Both food and drink to last him out a day,
Or more than one, and told her what to say 210
If her husband asked her about Nicholas.
She must say she had no notion where he was;
She hadn't laid eyes on him all day long;
He must be sick, or something must be wrong;
No matter how her maid had called and cried

He wouldn't answer, whatever might betide.
  This was the plan, and Nicholas kept away,
Shut in his room, for that whole Saturday.
He ate and slept or did as he thought best
Till Sunday, when the sun was going to rest,   220
This carpenter began to wonder greatly
Where Nicholas was and what might ail him lately.
"Now, by St. Thomas, I begin to dread
All isn't right with Nicholas," he said.
"He hasn't, God forbid, died suddenly!
The world is ticklish these days, certainly.
Today I saw a corpse to church go past,
A man that I saw working Monday last!
Go up," he told his chore-boy, "call and shout,
Knock with a stone, find what it's all about   230
And let me know."
                        The boy went up and pounded
And yelled as if his wits had been confounded.
"What, how, what's doing, Master Nicholas?
How can you sleep all day?" But all his fuss
Was wasted, for he could not hear a word.
He noticed at the bottom of a board
A hole the cat used when she wished to creep
Into the room, and through it looked in deep
And finally of Nicholas caught sight.
This Nicholas sat gaping there upright   240
As though his wits were addled by the moon
When it was new. The boy went down, and soon
Had told his master how he had seen the man.
  The carpenter, when he heard this news, began
To cross himself. "Help us, St. Frideswide![15]
Little can we foresee what may betide!
The man's astronomy has turned his wit,
Or else he's in some agonizing fit.
I always knew that it would turn out so.
What God has hidden is not for men to know.   250
Aye, blessed is the ignorant man indeed,
Blessed is he that only knows his creed!
So fared another scholar of the sky,
For walking in the meadows once to spy
Upon the stars and what they might foretell,
Down in a clay-pit suddenly he fell!
He overlooked that! By St. Thomas, though,
I'm sorry for handy Nicholas. I'll go
And scold him roundly for his studying
If so I may, by Jesus, heaven's king!   260
Give me a staff, I'll pry up from the floor
While you, Robin, are heaving at the door.

---

[15] Eighth-century saint; she was the patron of Oxford, both city and university.

He'll quit his books, I think."
                          He took his stand
Outside the room. The boy had a strong hand
And by the hasp he heaved if off at once.
The door fell flat. With gaping countenance
This Nicholas sat studying the air
As still as stone. He was in black despair,
The carpenter believed, and hard about
The shoulders caught and shook him, and cried out   270
Rudely, "What, how! What is it? Look down at us!
Wake up, think of Christ's passion, Nicholas!
I'll sign you with the cross to keep away
These elves and things!" And he began to say,
Facing the quarters of the house, each side,
And on the threshold of the door outside,
The night-spell: "Jesu and St. Benedict[16]
From every wicked thing this house protect . . . ."
    Choosing his time, this handy Nicholas
Produced a dreadful sigh, and said, "Alas,   280
This world, must it be all destroyed straightway?"
    "What," asked the carpenter, "what's that you say?
Do as we do, we working men, and think
Of God."
            Nicholas answered, "Get me a drink,
And afterwards I'll tell you privately
Of something that concerns us, you and me.
I'll tell you only, you among all men."
    This carpenter went down and came again
With a draught of mighty ale, a generous quart.
As soon as each of them had drunk his part   290
Nicholas shut the door and made it fast
And sat down by the carpenter at last
And spoke to him. "My host," he said, "John dear,
You must swear by all that you hold sacred here
That not to any man will you betray
My confidence. What I'm about to say
Is Christ's own secret. If you tell a soul
You are undone, and this will be the toll:
If you betray me, you shall go stark mad."
    "Now Christ forbid it, by His holy blood,"   300
Answered this simple man. "I don't go blabbing.
If I say it myself, I have no taste for gabbing.
Speak up just as you like, I'll never tell,
Not wife nor child, by Him that harrowed hell."[17]
    "Now, John," said Nicholas, "this is no lie.
I have discovered through astrology

[16] Italian monk; founder, c. 529, of the first Western monastic order.
[17] The Harrowing of Hell was Jesus' descent into Hell (more exactly, into Limbo) after the Crucifixion, to liberate the souls of the pre-Christian just.

And studying the moon that shines so bright
That Monday next, a quarter through the night,
A rain will fall, and such a mad, wild spate
That Noah's flood was never half so great.   310
This world," he said, "in less time than an hour
Shall drown entirely in that hideous shower.
Yes, every man shall drown and lose his life."
   "Alas," the carpenter answered, "for my wife!
Alas, my Alison! And shall she drown?"
For grief at this he nearly tumbled down,
And said, "But is there nothing to be done?"
   "Why, happily there is, for anyone
Who will take advice," this handy Nicholas said.
"You mustn't expect to follow your own head.   320
For what said Solomon, whose words were true?
'Proceed by counsel, and you'll never rue.'[18]
If you will act on good advice, no fail,
I'll promise, and without a mast or sail,
To see that she's preserved, and you and I.
Haven't you heard how Noah was kept dry
When, warned by Christ beforehand, he discovered
That the whole earth with water should be covered?"
   "Yes," said the carpenter, "long, long ago."
   "And then again," said Nicholas, "don't you know   330
The grief they all had trying to embark
Till Noah could get his wife into the Ark?[19]
That was a time when Noah, I dare say,
Would gladly have given his best black wethers away
If she could have had a ship herself alone.
And therefore do you know what must be done?
This demands haste, and with a hasty thing
People can't stop for talk and tarrying.
   "Start out and get into the house right off
For each of us a tub or kneading-trough,[20]   340
Above all making sure that they are large,
In which we'll float away as in a barge.
And put in food enough to last a day.
Beyond won't matter; the flood will fall away
Early next morning. Take care not to spill
A word to your boy Robin, nor to Jill
Your maid. I cannot save her, don't ask why.
I will not tell God's secrets, no, not I.
Let it be enough, unless your wits are mad,
To have as good a grace as Noah had.   350
I'll save your wife for certain, never doubt it.

[18] Ecclesiasticus 32:19. This book of proverbs was canonical in the Roman Catholic Bible.
[19] "A stock comic scene in the mystery plays, of which the carpenter would have been an avid spectator."—Translator's note.
[20] A wooden tub for kneading dough.

Now go along, and make good time about it.
  "But when you have, for her and you and me,
Brought to the house these kneading-tubs, all three,
Then you must hang them under the roof, up high,
To keep our plans from any watchful eye.
When you have done exactly as I've said,
And put in snug our victuals and our bread,
Also an ax to cut the ropes apart
So when the rain comes we can make our start,   360
And when you've broken a hole high in the gable
Facing the garden plot, above the stable,
To give us a free passage out, each one,
Then, soon as the great fall of rain is done,
You'll swim as merrily, I undertake,
As the white duck paddles along behind her drake.
Then I shall call, 'How, Alison! How, John!
Be cheerful, for the flood will soon be gone.'
And 'Master Nicholas, what ho!' you'll say.
'Good morning, I see you clearly, for it's day.'   370
Then we shall lord it for the rest of life
Over the world, like Noah and his wife.
  "But one thing I must warn you of downright.
Use every care that on that selfsame night
When we have taken ship and climbed aboard,
No one of us must speak a single word,
Nor call, nor cry, but pray with all his heart.
It is God's will. You must hang far apart,
You and your wife, for there must be no sin
Between you, no more in a look than in   380
The very deed. Go now, the plans are drawn.
Go, set to work, and may God spur you on!
Tomorrow night when all men are asleep
Into our kneading-troughs we three shall creep
And sit there waiting, and abide God's grace.
Go along now, this isn't the time or place
For me to talk at length or sermonize.
The proverb says, 'Don't waste words on the wise.'
You are so wise there is no need to teach you.
Go, save our lives—that's all that I beseech you!"   390
  This simple carpenter went on his way.
Many a time he said, "Alack the day,"
And to his wife he laid the secret bare.
She knew it better than he; she was aware
What this quaint bargain was designed to buy.
She carried on as if about to die,
And said, "Alas, go get this business done.
Help us escape, or we are dead, each one.
I am your true, your faithful wedded wife.
Go, my dear husband, save us, limb and life!"   400
  Great things, in all truth, can the emotions be!

A man can perish through credulity
So deep the print imagination makes.
This simple carpenter, he quails and quakes.
He really sees, according to his notion,
Noah's flood come wallowing like an ocean
To drown his Alison, his pet, his dear.
He weeps and wails, and gone is his good cheer,
And wretchedly he sighs. But he goes off
And gets himself a tub, a kneading-trough,   410
Another tub, and has them on the sly
Sent home, and there in secret hangs them high
Beneath the roof. He made three ladders, these
With his own hands, and stowed in bread and cheese
And a jug of good ale, plenty for a day.
Before all this was done, he sent away
His chore-boy Robin and his wench likewise
To London on some trumped-up enterprise,
And so on Monday, when it drew toward night,
He shut the door without a candlelight   420
And saw that all was just as it should be,
And shortly they went clambering up, all three.
They sat there still, and let a moment pass.
   "Now then, 'Our Father,' mum!" said Nicholas,
And "Mum!" said John, and "Mum!" said Alison,
And piously this carpenter went on
Saying his prayers. He sat there still and straining,
Trying to make out whether he heard it raining.
   The dead of sleep, for very weariness,
Fell on this carpenter, as I should guess,   430
At about curfew time,[21] or little more.
His head was twisted, and that made him snore.
His spirit groaned in its uneasiness.
Down from his ladder slipped this Nicholas,
And Alison too, downward she softly sped
And without further word they went to bed
Where the carpenter himself slept other nights.
There were the revels, there were the delights!
And so this Alison and Nicholas lay
Busy about their solace and their play   440
Until the bell for lauds[22] began to ring
And in the chancel[23] friars began to sing.
   Now on this Monday, woebegone and glum
For love, this parish clerk, this Absolom
Was with some friends at Oseney, and while there
Inquired after John the carpenter.
A member of the cloister drew him away

---

[21] About 8 or 9 P.M.
[22] The earliest of the canonical hours, celebrated in monasteries around 3 or 4 A.M.
[23] The railed-in area of a church near the altar.

Out of the church, and told him, "I can't say.
I haven't seen him working hereabout
Since Saturday. The abbot sent him out 450
For timber, I suppose. He'll often go
And stay at the granary[24] a day or so.
Or else he's at his own house, possibly.
I can't for certain say where he may be."
     Absolom at once felt jolly and light,
And thought, "Time now to be awake all night,
For certainly I haven't seen him making
A stir about his door since day was breaking.
Don't call me a man if when I hear the cock
Begin to crow[25] I don't slip up and knock 460
On the low window by his bedroom wall.
To Alison at last I'll pour out all
My love-pangs, for at this point I can't miss,
Whatever happens, at the least a kiss.
Some comfort, by my word, will come my way.
I've felt my mouth itch the whole livelong day,
And that's a sign of kissing at the least.
I dreamed all night that I was at a feast.
So now I'll go and sleep an hour or two,
And then I'll wake and play the whole night through." 470
     When the first cockcrow through the dark had come
Up rose this jolly lover Absolom
And dressed up smartly. He was not remiss
About the least point. He chewed licorice
And cardamom to smell sweet, even before
He combed his hair. Beneath his tongue he bore
A sprig of Paris like a truelove knot.[26]
He strolled off to the carpenter's house, and got
Beneath the window. It came so near the ground
It reached his chest. Softly, with half a sound, 480
He coughed, "My honeycomb, sweet Alison,
What are you doing, my sweet cinnamon?
Awake, my sweetheart and my pretty bird,
Awake, and give me from your lips a word!
Little enough you care for all my woe,
How for your love I sweat wherever I go!
No wonder I sweat and faint and cannot eat
More than a girl; as a lamb does for the teat
I pine. Yes, truly, I so long for love
I mourn as if I were a turtledove." 490
     Said she, "You jack-fool, get away from here!
So help me God, I won't sing 'Kiss me, dear!'
I love another more than you. Get on,

---

[24] A barn, or perhaps farm, belonging to the abbey.
[25] The cock crowed around midnight and 3 A.M., and just before daybreak.
[26] A sprig of paris-herb, clover-shaped like a "truelove knot" and supposed to aid lovers.

For Christ's sake, Absolom, or I'll throw a stone.
The devil with you! Go and let me sleep."
   "Ah, that true love should ever have to reap
So evil a fortune," Absolom said. "A kiss,
At least, if it can be no more than this,
Give me, for love of Jesus and of me."
   "And will you go away for that?" said she.   500
   "Yes, truly, sweetheart," answered Absolom.
   "Get ready then," she said, "for here I come,"
And softly said to Nicholas, "Keep still,
And in a minute you can laugh your fill."
   This Absolom got down upon his knee
And said, "I am a lord of pure degree,[27]
For after this, I hope, comes more to savor.
Sweetheart, your grace, and pretty bird, your favor!"
   She undid the window quickly. "That will do,"
She said. "Be quick about it, and get through,   510
For fear the neighbors will look out and spy."
   Absolom wiped his mouth to make it dry.
The night was pitch dark, coal-black all about.
Her rear end through the window she thrust out.
He got no better or worse, did Absolom,
Than to kiss her with his mouth on the bare bum
Before he had caught on, a smacking kiss.
   He jumped back, thinking something was amiss.
A woman has no beard, he was well aware,
But what he felt was rough and had long hair.   520
   "Alas," he cried, "what have you made me do?"
   "Te-hee!" she said, and banged the window to.
   Absolom backed away a sorry pace.
   "You've bearded him!" said handy Nicholas.
"God's body, this is going fair and fit!"
   This luckless Absolom heard every bit,
And gnawed his mouth, so angry he became.
He said to himself, "I'll square you, all the same."
   But who now scrubs and rubs, who chafes his lips
With dust, with sand, with straw, with cloth and chips,   530
If not this Absolom? "The devil," says he,
"Welcome my soul if I wouldn't rather be
Revenged than have the whole town in a sack!
Alas," he cries, "if only I'd held back!"
His hot love had become all cold and ashen.
He didn't have a curse to spare for passion
From the moment when he kissed her on the ass.
That was the cure to make his sickness pass!
He cried as a child does after being whipped;
He railed at love. Then quietly he slipped   540
Across the street to a smith who was forging out

---

[27] In every way.

Parts that the farmers needed round about.
He was busy sharpening colter and plowshare[28]
When Absolom knocked as though without a care.
  "Undo the door, Jervice, and let me come."
  "What? Who are you?"
                          "It is I, Absolom."
  "Absolom, is it! By Christ's precious tree,[29]
Why are you up so early? Lord bless me,
What's ailing you? Some gay girl has the power
To bring you out, God knows, at such an hour!   550
Yes, by St. Neot,[30] you know well what I mean!"
  Absolom thought his jokes not worth a bean.
Without a word he let them all go by.
He had another kind of fish to fry
Than Jervice guessed. "Lend me this colter here
That's hot in the chimney, friend," he said. "Don't fear,
I'll bring it back right off when I am through.
I need it for a job I have to do."
  "Of course," said Jervice. "Why, if it were gold
Or coins in a sack, uncounted and untold,   560
As I'm a rightful smith, I wouldn't refuse it.
But, Christ's foot! how on earth do you mean to use it?"
  "Let that," said Absolom, "be as it may.
I'll let you know tomorrow or next day,"
And took the colter where the steel was cold
And slipped out with it safely in his hold
And softly over to the carpenter's wall.
He coughed and then he rapped the window, all
As he had done before.
                          "Who's knocking there?"
Said Alison. "It is a thief, I swear."   570
  "No, no," said he. "God knows, my sugarplum,
My bird, my darling, it's your Absolom.
I've brought a golden ring my mother gave me,
Fine and well cut, as I hope that God will save me.
It's yours, if you will let me have a kiss."
  Nicholas had got up to take a piss
And thought he would improve the whole affair.
This clerk, before he got away from there,
Should give *his* ass a smack; and hastily
He opened the window, and thrust out quietly,   580
Buttocks and haunches, all the way, his bum.
Up spoke this clerk, this jolly Absolom:
"Speak, for I don't know where you are, sweetheart."
  Nicholas promptly let fly with a fart
As loud as if a clap of thunder broke,

---

[28] The colter was the vertical cutting blade of the plowshare. It was customary for blacksmiths to begin work long before dawn.
[29] The Cross.   [30] Ninth-century saint.

So great he was nearly blinded by the stroke,
And ready with his hot iron to make a pass,
Absolom caught him fairly on the ass.
    Off flew the skin, a good handbreadth of fat
Lay bare, the iron so scorched him where he sat.   590
As for the pain, he thought that he would die,
And like a madman he began to cry,
"Help! Water! Water! Help, for God's own heart!"
    At this the carpenter came to with a start.
He heard a man cry "Water!" as if mad.
"It's coming now," was the first thought he had.
"It's Noah's flood, alas, God be our hope!"
He sat up with his ax and chopped the rope
And down at once the whole contraption fell.
He didn't take time out to buy or sell   600
Till he hit the floor and lay there in a swoon.
    Then up jumped Nicholas and Alison
And in the street began to cry, "Help, ho!"
The neighbors all came running, high and low,
And poured into the house to see the sight.
The man still lay there, passed out cold and white,
For in his tumble he had broken an arm.
But he himself brought on his greatest harm,
For when he spoke he was at once outdone
By handy Nicholas and Alison   610
Who told them one and all that he was mad.
So great a fear of Noah's flood he had,
By some delusion, that in his vanity[31]
He had bought himself these kneading-troughs, all three,
And hung them from the roof there, up above,
And he had pleaded with them, for God's love,
To sit there in the loft for company.
    The neighbors laughed at such a fantasy,
And round the loft began to pry and poke
And turned his whole disaster to a joke.   620
He found it was no use to say a word.
Whatever reason he offered, no one heard.
With oaths and curses people swore him down
Until he passed for mad in the whole town.
Wit, clerk, and student all stood by each other.
They said, "It's clear the man is crazy, brother."
Everyone had his laugh about this feud.
So Alison, the carpenter's wife, got screwed
For all the jealous watching he could try,
And Absolom, he kissed her nether eye,   630
And Nicholas got his bottom roasted well.
God save this troop! That's all I have to tell.

---

[31] Folly.

PROLOGUE TO THE WIFE OF BATH'S TALE

"Experience,[1] though all authority
Was lacking in the world, confers on me
The right to speak of marriage, and unfold
Its woes. For, lords, since I was twelve years old
—Thanks to eternal God in heaven alive—
I have married at church door no less than five
Husbands, provided that I can have been
So often wed,[2] and all were worthy men.
But I was told, indeed, and not long since,
That Christ went to a wedding only once   10
At Cana, in the land of Galilee.[3]
By this example he instructed me
To wed once only—that's what I have heard!
Again, consider now what a sharp word,
Beside a well, Jesus, both God and man,
Spoke in reproving the Samaritan:
'Thou hast had five husbands'—this for a certainty
He said to her—'and the man that now hath thee
Is not thy husband.' True, he spoke this way,
But what he meant is more than I can say   20
Except that I would ask why the fifth man
Was not a husband to the Samaritan?
To just how many could she be a wife?
I have never heard this number all my life
Determined up to now. For round and round
Scholars may gloze, interpret, and expound,
But plainly, this I know without a lie,
God told us to increase and multiply.[4]
That noble text I can well understand.
My husband—this too I have well in hand—   30
Should leave both father and mother and cleave to me.[5]
Number God never mentioned, bigamy,
No, nor even octogamy; why do men
Talk of it as a sin and scandal, then?
    "Think of that monarch, wise King Solomon.[6]
It strikes me that *he* had more wives than one!

---

[1] The Wife's appeal to experience is somewhat unorthodox, since written works were supposed to have stronger authority. She shows, however, that she can cite them too (though not always accurately).

[2] The Wife is not sure that all her marriages were valid.

[3] For the wedding at Cana, where Christ changed water to wine, see the gospel of John, 2:1–11. For Jesus' meeting with the sinful Samaritan woman, mentioned a few lines later, see John 4:3–30.

[4] God's command to Adam and Eve at the creation; Genesis 1:28.

[5] Adam's words about Eve, Genesis 2:24: "Therefore shall a man leave his father and his mother, and shall cleave unto his wife: and they shall be one flesh."

[6] The Old Testament king had 700 wives and 300 concubines.

To be refreshed, God willing, would please me
If I got it half as many times as he!
What a gift he had, a gift of God's own giving,
For all his wives! There isn't a man now living   40
Who has the like. By all that I make out
This king had many a merry first-night bout
With each, he was so thoroughly alive.
Blessed be God that I have married five,
And always, for the money in his chest
And for his nether purse, I picked the best.
In divers[7] schools ripe scholarship is made,
And various practice in all kinds of trade
Makes perfect workmen, as the world can see.
Five husbands have had turns at schooling me.   50
Welcome the sixth, whenever I am faced
With yet another. I don't mean to be chaste
At all costs. When a spouse of mine is gone,
Some other Christian man shall take me on,
For then, says the Apostle, I'll be free
To wed, in God's name, where it pleases me.
To marry is no sin, as we can learn
From him; better to marry than to burn,[8]
He says. Why should I care what obloquy
Men heap on Lamech and his bigamy?   60
Abraham was, by all that I can tell,
A holy man; so Jacob was as well,
And each of them took more than two as brides,
And many another holy man besides.
Where, may I ask, in any period,
Can you show in plain words that Almighty God
Forbade us marriage? Point it out to me!
Or where did he command virginity?
The Apostle, when he speaks of maidenhood,
Lays down no law. This I have understood   70
As well as you, milords, for it is plain.
Men may advise a woman to abstain
From marriage, but mere counsels aren't commands.
He left it to our judgment, where it stands.
Had God enjoined us all to maidenhood
Then marriage would have been condemned for good.
But truth is, if no seed were ever sown,
In what soil could virginity be grown?
Paul did not dare command a thing at best
On which his Master left us no behest.   80
    "But now the prize goes to virginity.
Seize it whoever can, and let us see

---

[7] Various.
[8] In 1 Corinthians 7:8–9, Paul recommends celibacy to the unmarried and widows, and then adds, "But if they cannot contain, let them marry: for it is better to marry than to burn."

What manner of man shall run best in the race!
But not all men receive this form of grace
Except where God bestows it by his will.
The Apostle was a maid, I know; but still,
Although he wished all men were such as he,
It was only *counsel* toward virginity.
To be a wife he gave me his permission,
And so it is no blot on my condition   90
Nor slander of bigamy upon my state
If when my husband dies I take a mate.
A man does virtuously, St. Paul has said,
To touch no woman—meaning in his bed.
For fire and fat are dangerous friends at best.
You know what this example should suggest.
Here is the nub: he held virginity
Superior to wedded frailty,
And frailty I call it unless man
And woman both are chaste for their whole span.   100
    "I am not jealous if maidenhood outweighs
My marriages; I grant it all the praise.
It pleases them, these virgins, flesh and soul
To be immaculate. I won't extol
My own condition. In a lord's household
You know that every vessel can't be gold.
Some are of wood, and serve their master still.
God calls us variously to do his will.
Each has his proper gift, of all who live,
Some this, some that, as it pleases God to give.   110
    "To be virgin is a high and perfect course,
And continence is holy. But the source
Of all perfection, Jesus, never bade
Each one of us to go sell all he had
And give it to the poor; he did not say
That all should follow him in this one way.
He spoke to those who would live perfectly,
And by your leave, lords, that is not for me!
The flower of my best years I find it suits
To spend on the acts of marriage and its fruits.   120
    "Tell me this also: why at our creation
Were organs given us for generation,
And for what profit were we creatures made?
Believe me, not for nothing! Ply his trade
Of twisting texts who will, and let him urge
That they were only given us to purge
Our urine; say without them we should fail
To tell a female rightly from a male
And that's their only object—say you so?
It won't work, as experience will show.   130
Without offense to scholars, I say this,
They were given us for both these purposes,

That we may both be cleansed, I mean, and eased
Through intercourse, where God is not displeased.
Why else in books is this opinion met,
That every man should pay his wife his debt?
Tell me with what a man should hope to pay
Unless he put his instrument in play?
They were supplied us, then, for our purgation,
But they were also meant for generation. 140
   "But none the less I do not mean to say
That all those who are furnished in this way
Are bound to go and practice intercourse.
The world would then grant chastity no force.
Christ was a maid, yet he was formed a man,
And many a saint, too, since the world began,
And yet they lived in perfect chastity.
I am not spiteful toward virginity.
Let virgins be white bread of pure wheat-seed.
Barley we wives are called, and yet I read 150
In Mark, and tell the tale in truth he can,
That Christ with barley bread cheered many a man.[9]
In the state that God assigned to each of us
I'll persevere. I'm not fastidious.
In wifehood I will use my instrument
As freely by my Maker it was lent.
If I hold back with it, God give me sorrow!
My husband shall enjoy it night and morrow
When it pleases him to come and pay his debt.
But a husband, and I've not been thwarted yet, 160
Shall always be my debtor and my slave.
From tribulation he shall never save
His flesh, not for as long as I'm his wife!
I have the power, during all my life,
Over his very body, and not he.
For so the Apostle has instructed me,[10]
Who bade men love their wives for better or worse.
It pleases me from end to end, that verse!"
   The Pardoner, before she could go on,
Jumped up and cried, "By God and by St. John, 170
Upon this topic you preach nobly, Dame!
I was about to wed, but now, for shame,
Why should my body pay a price so dear?
I'd rather not be married all this year!"
   "Hold on," she said. "I haven't yet begun.
You'll drink a keg of this before I'm done,
I promise you, and it won't taste like ale!

[9] The Wife alludes to the miracle in which Jesus fed 5,000 people with five barley loaves and two fishes.
[10] The Wife cites only the second half of the Apostle's (Paul's) statement (1 Corinthians 7:4): "The wife hath not power of her own body, but the husband: and likewise also the husband hath not power of his own body, but the wife."

And after I have told you my whole tale
Of marriage, with its fund of tribulation—
And I'm the expert of my generation,   180
For I myself, I mean, have been the whip—
You can decide then if you want a sip
Out of the barrel that I mean to broach.
Before you come too close in your approach,
Think twice. I have examples, more than ten!
'The man who won't be warned by other men,
To other men a warning he shall be.'
These are the words we find in Ptolemy.
You can read them right there in his *Almagest*."[11]
        "Now, Madame, if you're willing, I suggest,"   190
Answered the Pardoner, "as you began,
Continue with your tale, and spare no man.
Teach us your practice—we young men need a guide."
        "Gladly, if it will please you," she replied.
"But first I ask you, if I speak my mind,
That all this company may be well inclined,
And will not take offense at what I say.
I only mean it, after all, in play.
        "Now, sirs, I will get onward with my tale.
If ever I hope to drink good wine or ale,   200
I'm speaking truth: the husbands I have had,
Three of them have been good, and two were bad.
The three were kindly men, and rich, and old.
But they were hardly able to uphold
The statute which had made them fast to me.
You know well what I mean by this, I see!
So help me God, I can't help laughing yet
When I think of how at night I made them sweat,
And I thought nothing of it, on my word!
Their land and wealth they had by then conferred   210
On me, and so I safely could neglect
Tending their love or showing them respect.
So well they loved me that by God above
I hardly set a value on their love.
A woman who is wise is never done
Busily winning love when she has none,
But since I had them wholly in my hand
And they had given me their wealth and land,
Why task myself to spoil them or to please
Unless for my own profit and my ease?   220
I set them working so that many a night
They sang a dirge, so grievous was their plight!
They never got the bacon, well I know,

---

[11] The saying is not in the *Almagest*, although it was attributed to Ptolemy by a translator of the work. The same is true of the Wife's later citation of Ptolemy.

Offered as prize to couples at Dunmow[12]
Who live a year in peace, without repentance!
So well I ruled them, by my law and sentence,
They were glad to bring me fine things from the fair
And happy when I spoke with a mild air,
For God knows I could chide outrageously.
   "Now judge if I could do it properly!   230
You wives who understand and who are wise,
This is the way to throw dust in their eyes.
There isn't on the earth so bold a man
He can swear false or lie as a woman can.
I do not urge this course in every case,
Just when a prudent wife is caught off base;
Then she should swear the parrot's mad who tattled
Her indiscretions, and when she's once embattled
Should call her maid as witness, by collusion.
But listen, how I threw them in confusion: 240
   "'Sir dotard,[13] this is how you live?' I'd say.
'How can my neighbor's wife be dressed so gay?
She carries off the honors everywhere.
I sit at home. I've nothing fit to wear.
What were you doing at my neighbor's house?
Is she so handsome? Are you so amorous?
What do you whisper to our maid? God bless me,
Give up your jokes, old lecher. They depress me.
When I have a harmless friend myself, you balk
And scold me like a devil if I walk   250
For innocent amusement to his house.
You drink and come home reeling like a souse
And sit down on your bench, worse luck, and preach.
Taking a wife who's poor—this is the speech
That you regale me with—costs grievously,
And if she's rich and of good family,
It is a constant torment, you decide,
To suffer her ill humor and her pride.
And if she's fair, you scoundrel, you destroy her
By saying that every lecher will enjoy her;   260
For chastity at best has frail protections
If a woman is assailed from all directions.
   "'Some want us for our wealth, so you declare,
Some for our figure, some think we are fair,
Some want a woman who can dance or sing,
Some want kindness, and some philandering,
Some look for hands and arms well turned and small.
Thus, by your tale, the devil may take us all!

---

[12] A town in Essex, in southeastern England. Such a prize for peaceable couples was in fact given.
[13] A senile person.

Men cannot keep a castle or redoubt[14]
Longer, you tell me, than it can hold out.   270
Or if a woman's plain, you say that she
Is one who covets each man she may see,
For at him like a spaniel she will fly
Until she finds some man that she can buy.
Down to the lake goes never a goose so gray
But it will have a mate, I've heard you say.
It's hard to fasten—this too I've been told—
A thing that no man willingly will hold.
Wise men, you tell me as you go to bed,
And those who hope for heaven should never wed.   280
I hope wild lightning and a thunderstroke
Will break your wizened neck! You say that smoke
And falling timbers and a railing wife
Drive a man from his house. Lord bless my life!
What ails an old man, so to make him chide?
We cover our vices till the knot is tied,
We wives, you say, and then we trot them out.
Here's a fit proverb for a doddering lout!
An ox or ass, you say, a hound or horse,
These we examine as a matter of course.   290
Basins and also bowls, before we buy them,
Spoons, spools, and such utensils, first we try them,
And so with pots and clothes, beyond denial;
But of their wives men never make a trial
Until they are married. After that, you say,
Old fool, we put our vices on display.
   "'I am in a pique if you forget your duty
And fail, you tell me, to praise me for my beauty,
Or unless you are always doting on my face
And calling me "fair dame" in every place,   300
Or unless you give a feast on my birthday
To keep me in good spirits, fresh and gay,
Or unless all proper courtesies are paid
To my nurse and also to my chambermaid,
And my father's kin with all their family ties—
You say so, you old barrelful of lies!
   "'Yet just because he has a head of hair
Like shining gold, and squires me everywhere,
You have a false suspicion in your heart
Of Jenkin, our apprentice. For my part   310
I wouldn't have him if you died tomorrow!
But tell me this, or go and live in sorrow:
That chest of yours, why do you hide the keys
Away from me? It's my wealth, if you please,
As much as yours. Will you make a fool of me,

---

[14] A small fort or defensive hiding place.

The mistress of our house? You shall not be
Lord of my body and my wealth at once!
No, by St. James himself, you must renounce
One or the other, if it drives you mad!
Does it help to spy on me? You would be glad   320
To lock me up, I think, inside your chest.
"Enjoy yourself, and go where you think best,"
You ought to say; "I won't hear tales of malice.
I know you for a faithful wife, Dame Alice."
A woman loves no man who keeps close charge
Of where she goes. We want to be at large.
Blessed above all other men was he,
The wise astrologer, Don Ptolemy,
Who has this proverb in his *Almagest:*
"Of all wise men his wisdom is the best   330
Who does not care who has the world in hand."
Now by this proverb you should understand,
Since you have plenty, it isn't yours to care
Or fret how richly other people fare,
For by your leave, old dotard, you for one
Can have all you can take when day is done.
The man's a niggard to the point of scandal
Who will not lend his lamp to light a candle;
His lamp won't lose although the candle gain.
If you have enough, you ought not to complain.   340
"'You say, too, if we make ourselves look smart,
Put on expensive clothes and dress the part,
We lay our virtue open to disgrace.
And then you try to reinforce your case
By saying these words in the Apostle's name:
"In chaste apparel, with modesty and shame,
So shall you women clothe yourselves," said he,
"And not in rich coiffure or jewelry,
Pearls or the like, or gold, or costly wear."[15]
Now both your text and rubric, I declare,   350
I will not follow as I would a gnat!
"'You told me once that I was like a cat,
For singe her skin and she will stay at home,
But if her skin is smooth, the cat will roam.
No dawn but finds her on the neighbors calling
To show her skin, and go off caterwauling.
If I am looking smart, you mean to say,
I'm off to put my finery on display.
"'What do you gain, old fool, by setting spies?
Though you beg Argus[16] with his hundred eyes   360
To be my bodyguard, for all his skill
He'll keep me only by my own free will.

[15] See St. Paul's First Epistle to Timothy 2:9.
[16] In mythology, a hundred-eyed giant who served as a guard.

I know enough to blind him, as I live!
"'There are three things,[17] you also say, that give
Vexation to this world both south and north,
And you add that no one can endure the fourth.
Of these catastrophes a hateful wife—
You precious wretch, may Christ cut short your life!—
Is always reckoned, as you say, for one.
Is this your whole stock of comparison,   370
And why in all your parables of contempt
Can a luckless helpmate never be exempt?
You also liken woman's love to hell,
To barren land where water will not dwell.
I've heard you call it an unruly fire;
The more it burns, the hotter its desire
To burn up everything that burned will be.
You say that just as worms destroy a tree
A wife destroys her spouse, as they have found
Who get themselves in holy wedlock bound.'   380
    "By these devices, lords, as you perceive,
I got my three old husbands to believe
That in their cups they said things of this sort,
And all of it was false; but for support
Jenkin bore witness, and my niece did too.
These innocents, Lord, what I put them through!
God's precious pains! And they had no recourse,
For I could bite and whinny like a horse.
Though in the wrong, I kept them well annoyed,
Or oftentimes I would have been destroyed!   390
First to the mill is first to grind his grain.
I was always the first one to complain,
And so our peace was made; they gladly bid
For terms to settle things they never did!
    "For wenching I would scold them out of hand
When they were hardly well enough to stand.
But this would tickle a man; it would restore him
To think I had so great a fondness for him!
I'd vow when darkness came and out I stepped,
It was to see the girls with whom he slept.   400
Under this pretext I had plenty of mirth!
Such wit as this is given us at our birth.
Lies, tears, and needlework the Lord will give
In kindness to us women while we live.
And thus in one point I can take just pride:
In the end I showed myself the stronger side.
By sleight or strength I kept them in restraint,
And chiefly by continual complaint.
In bed they met their grief in fullest measure.

[17] Several of the examples of unpleasantness in the following lines are from Proverbs,
chapter 30.

There I would scold; I would not do their pleasure.   410
Bed was a place where I would not abide
If I felt my husband's arm across my side
Till he agreed to square accounts and pay,
And after that I'd let him have his way.
To every man, therefore, I tell this tale:
Win where you're able, all is up for sale.
No falcon by an empty hand is lured.
For victory their cravings I endured
And even feigned a show of appetite.
And yet in old meat I have no delight;   420
It made me always rail at them and chide them,
For though the pope himself sat down beside them
I would not give them peace at their own board.
No, on my honor, I paid them word for word.
Almighty God so help me, if right now
I had to make my last will, I can vow
For every word they said to me, we're quits.
For I so handled the contest by my wits
That they gave up, and took it for the best,
Or otherwise we should have had no rest.   430
Like a mad lion let my husband glare,
In the end he got the worst of the affair.
     "Then I would say, 'My dear, you ought to keep
In mind how gentle Wilkin looks, our sheep.
Come here, my husband, let me kiss your cheek!
You should be patient, too; you should be meek.
Of Job and of his patience when you prate
Your conscience ought to show a cleaner slate.
He should be patient who so well can preach.
If not, then it will fall on me to teach   440
The beauty of a peaceful wedded life.
For one of us must give in, man or wife,
And since men are more reasonable creatures
Than women are, it follows that *your* features
Ought to exhibit patience. Why do you groan?
You want my body yours, and yours alone?
Why, take it all! Welcome to every bit!
But curse you, Peter, unless you cherish it!
Were I inclined to peddle my *belle chose*,[18]
I could go about dressed freshly as a rose.   450
But I will keep it for your own sweet tooth.
It's your fault if we fight. By God, that's truth!'
     "This was the way I talked when I had need.
But now to my fourth husband I'll proceed.
     "This fourth I married was a roisterer.
He had a mistress, and my passions were,
Although I say it, strong; and altogether

---

[18] Literally, "beautiful thing" (French).

I was young and stubborn, pert in every feather.
If anyone took up his harp to play,
How I could dance! I sang as merry a lay 460
As any nightingale when of sweet wine
I had drunk my draft. Metellius,[19] the foul swine,
Who beat his spouse until he took her life
For drinking wine, had I only been his wife,
He'd never have frightened me away from drinking!
But after a drink, Venus gets in my thinking,
For just as true as cold engenders hail
A thirsty mouth goes with a thirsty tail.
Drinking destroys a woman's last defense
As lechers well know by experience. 470
  "But, Lord Christ, when it all comes back to me,
Remembering my youth and jollity,
It tickles me to the roots. It does me good
Down to this very day that while I could
I took my world, my time, and had my fling.
But age, alas, that poisons everything
Has robbed me of my beauty and my pith.
Well, let it go! Good-by! The devil with
What cannot last! There's only this to tell:
The flour is gone, I've only chaff to sell. 480
Yet I'll contrive to keep a merry cheek!
But now of my fourth husband I will speak.
  "My heart was, I can tell you, full of spite
That in another he should find delight.
I paid him for this debt; I made it good.
I furnished him a cross of the same wood,
By God and by St. Joce—in no foul fashion,
Not with my flesh; but I put on such passion
And rendered him so jealous, I'll engage
I made him fry in his own grease for rage! 490
On earth, God knows, I was his purgatory;
I only hope his soul is now in glory.
God knows it was a sad song that he sung
When the shoe pinched him; sorely was he wrung!
Only he knew, and God, the devious system
By which outrageously I used to twist him.
He died when I came home from Jerusalem.
He is buried near the chancel, under the beam
That holds the cross. His tomb is less ornate
Than the sepulcher where Darius[20] lies in state 500
And which the paintings of Appelles graced
With subtle work. It would have been a waste
To bury him lavishly. Farewell! God save

---

[19] The source of the story of Metellius is Valerius Maximus, one of Chaucer's favorite sources.
[20] According to legend, Darius, king of the ancient Persians, had a lavish tomb.

His soul and give him rest! He's in his grave.
    "And now of my fifth husband let me tell.
God never let his soul go down to hell
Though he of all five was my scourge and flail!
I feel it on my ribs, right down the scale,
And ever shall until my dying day.
And yet he was so full of life and gay   510
In bed, and could so melt me and cajole me
When on my back he had a mind to roll me,
What matter if on every bone he'd beaten me!
He'd have my love, so quickly he could sweeten me.
I loved him best, in fact; for as you see,
His love was a more arduous prize for me.
We women, if I'm not to tell a lie,
Are quaint in this regard. Put in our eye
A thing we cannot easily obtain,
All day we'll cry about it and complain.   520
Forbid a thing, we want it bitterly,
But urge it on us, then we turn and flee.
We are chary of what we hope that men will buy.
A throng at market makes the prices high;
Men set no value on cheap merchandise,
A truth all women know if they are wise.
    "My fifth, may God forgive his every sin,
I took for love, not money. He had been
An Oxford student once, but in our town
Was boarding with my good friend, Alison.   530
She knew each secret that I had to give
More than our parish priest did, as I live!
I told her my full mind, I shared it all.
For if my husband pissed against a wall
Or did a thing that might have cost his life,
To her, and to another neighbor's wife,
And to my niece, a girl whom I loved well,
His every thought I wouldn't blush to tell.
And often enough I told them, be it said.
God knows I made his face turn hot and red   540
For secrets he confided to his shame.
He knew he only had himself to blame.
    "And so it happened once that during Lent,
As I often did, to Alison's I went,
For I have loved my life long to be gay
And to walk out in April or in May
To hear the talk and seek a favorite haunt.
Jenkin the student, Alice, my confidante,
And I myself into the country went.
My husband was in London all that Lent.   550
I had the greater liberty to see
And to be seen by jolly company.
How could I tell beforehand in what place

Luck might be waiting with a stroke of grace?
And so I went to every merrymaking.
No pilgrimage was past my undertaking.
I was at festivals, and marriages,
Processions, preachings, and at miracle plays,[21]
And in my scarlet clothes I made a sight.
Upon that costume neither moth nor mite   560
Nor any worm with ravening hunger fell.
And why, you ask? It was kept in use too well.
    "Now for what happened. In the fields we walked,
The three of us, and gallantly we talked,
The student and I, until I told him he,
If I became a widow, should marry me.
For I can say, and not with empty pride,
I have never failed for marriage to provide
Or other things as well. Let mice be meek;
A mouse's heart I hold not worth a leek.   570
He has one hole to scurry to, just one,
And if that fails him, he is quite undone.
    "I let this student think he had bewitched me.
(My mother with this piece of guile enriched me!)
All night I dreamed of him—this too I said;
He was killing me as I lay flat in bed;
My very bed in fact was full of blood;
But still I hoped it would result in good,
For blood betokens gold, as I have heard.
It was a fiction, dream and every word,   580
But I was following my mother's lore
In all this matter, as in many more.
    "Sirs—let me see; what did I mean to say?
Aha! By God, I have it! When he lay,
My fourth, of whom I've spoken, on his bier,
I wept of course; I showed but little cheer,
As wives must do, since custom has its place,
And with my kerchief covered up my face.
But since I had provided for a mate,
I did not cry for long, I'll freely state.   590
And so to church my husband on the morrow
Was borne away by neighbors in their sorrow.
Jenkin, the student, was among the crowd,
And when I saw him walk, so help me God,
Behind the bier, I thought he had a pair
Of legs and feet so cleanly turned and fair
I put my heart completely in his hold.
He was in fact some twenty winters old
And I was forty, to confess the truth;
But all my life I've still had a colt's tooth.   600
My teeth were spaced apart;[22] that was the seal

---

[21] Plays based on the lives of the saints.   [22] A sign of lustiness.

St. Venus printed, and became me well.
So help me God, I was a lusty one,
Pretty and young and rich, and full of fun.
And truly, as my husbands have all said,
I was the best thing there could be in bed.
For I belong to Venus in my feelings,
Though I bring the heart of Mars to all my dealings.
From Venus come my lust and appetite,
From Mars I get my courage and my might,   610
Born under Taurus, while Mars stood therein.
Alas, alas, that ever love was sin!
I yielded to my every inclination
Through the predominance of my constellation;
This made me so I never could withhold
My chamber of Venus, if the truth be told,
From a good fellow; yet upon my face
Mars left his mark, and in another place.
For never, so may Christ grant me intercession,
Have I yet loved a fellow with discretion,   620
But always I have followed appetite,
Let him be long or short or dark or light.
I never cared, as long as he liked me,
What his rank was or how poor he might be.
    "What should I say, but when the month ran out,
This jolly student, always much about,
This Jenkin married me in solemn state.
To him I gave land, titles, the whole slate
Of goods that had been given me before;
But my repentance afterward was sore!   630
He wouldn't endure the pleasures I held dear.
By God, he gave me a lick once on the ear,
When from a book of his I tore a leaf,
So hard that from the blow my ear grew deaf.
I was stubborn as a lioness with young,
And by the truth I had a rattling tongue,
And I would visit, as I'd done before,
No matter what forbidding oath he swore.
Against this habit he would sit and preach me
Sermons enough, and he would try to teach me   640
Old Roman stories,[23] how for his whole life
The man Sulpicius Gallus left his wife
Only because he saw her look one day
Bareheaded down the street from his doorway.
    "Another Roman he told me of by name
Who, since his wife was at a summer's game
Without his knowledge, thereupon forsook
The woman. In his Bible he would look
And find that proverb of the Ecclesiast

---

[23] The following two stories are from Valerius Maximus.

Where he enjoins and makes the stricture fast 650
That men forbid their wives to rove about.
Then he would quote me this, you needn't doubt:
'Build a foundation over sands or shallows,
Or gallop a blind horse across the fallows,
Let a wife traipse to shrines that some saint hallows,
And you are fit to swing upon the gallows.'
Talk as he would, I didn't care two haws
For his proverbs or his venerable saws.
Set right by him I never meant to be.
I hate the man who tells my faults to me, 660
And more of us than I do, by your pleasure.
This made him mad with me beyond all measure.
Under his yoke in no case would I go.
  "Now, by St. Thomas, I will let you know
Why from that book of his I tore a leaf,
For which I got the blow that made me deaf.
  "He had a book, *Valerius,* he called it,
And Theophrastus, and he always hauled it
From where it lay to read both day and night
And laughed hard at it, such was his delight. 670
There was another scholar, too, at Rome
A cardinal, whose name was St. Jerome;
He wrote a book against Jovinian.
In the same book also were Tertullian,
Chrysippus, Trotula, Abbess Héloïse
Who lived near Paris; it contained all these,
Bound in a single volume, and many a one
Besides; the Parables of Solomon
And Ovid's *Art of Love.* On such vacation
As he could snatch from worldly occupation 680
He dredged this book for tales of wicked wives.[24]
He knew more stories of their wretched lives
Than are told about good women in the Bible.
No scholar ever lived who did not libel
Women, believe me; to speak well of wives
Is quite beyond them, unless it be in lives
Of holy saints; no woman else will do.
Who was it painted the lion,[25] tell me who?
By God, if women had only written stories
Like wits and scholars in their oratories,[26] 690
They would have pinned on men more wickedness
Than the whole breed of Adam can redress.
Venus's children clash with Mercury's;

[24] Jenkin's collection of anti-feminine literature is wide-ranging, including the Bible; ancient classical authors such as Theophrastus and Ovid; early Christian authors such as Tertullian and Jerome; and medieval writers such as the twelfth-century Héloïse (loved by Abelard).
[25] In a fable of Aesop, a lion who sees a picture of a man killing a lion says that if lions could paint, the roles in the picture might be reversed.
[26] Private chapels.

The two work evermore by contraries.
Knowledge and wisdom are of Mercury's giving,
Venus loves revelry and riotous living,
And with these clashing dispositions gifted
Each of them sinks when the other is uplifted.
Thus Mercury falls, God knows, in desolation
In the sign of Pisces, Venus's exaltation,   700
And Venus falls when Mercury is raised.
Thus by a scholar no woman can be praised.
The scholar, when he's old and cannot do
The work of Venus more than his old shoe,
Then sits he down, and in his dotage fond
Writes that no woman keeps her marriage bond!
    "But now for the story that I undertook—
To tell how I was beaten for a book.
    "Jenkin, one night, who never seemed to tire
Of reading in his book, sat by the fire   710
And first he read of Eve, whose wickedness
Delivered all mankind to wretchedness
For which in his own person Christ was slain
Who with his heart's blood bought us all again.
'By this,' he said, 'expressly you may find
That woman was the loss of all mankind.'
    "He read me next how Samson lost his hair.
Sleeping, his mistress clipped it off for fair;
Through this betrayal he lost both his eyes.[27]
He read me then—and I'm not telling lies—   720
How Deianeira, wife of Hercules,
Caused him to set himself on fire.[28] With these
He did not overlook the sad to-do
Of Socrates with *his* wives—he had two.
Xantippe emptied the pisspot on his head.
This good man sat as patient as if dead.
He wiped his scalp; he did not dare complain
Except to say 'With thunder must come rain.'
    "Pasiphaë,[29] who was the queen of Crete,
For wickedness he thought her story sweet.   730
Ugh! That's enough, it was a grisly thing,
About her lust and filthy hankering!
And Clytemnestra[30] in her lechery
Who took her husband's life feloniously,
He grew devout in reading of her treason.

[27] Judges, chapter 16. Samson confided to his beloved, Delilah, that his strength lay in his hair; she betrayed him by having it cut off while he was sleeping. Thus weakened, he was enslaved by the Philistines.
[28] In her jealousy she gave Hercules a poisoned robe, which caused him such agony that to escape the pain he had himself cremated.
[29] She fell in love with a bull and gave birth to a monster, half bull and half human.
[30] Wife of Agamemnon, commander of the Greeks against Troy. On his return from the war, she and her paramour killed him.

And then he told me also for what reason
Unhappy Amphiaraus lost his life.
My husband had the story of *his* wife,
Eriphyle, who for a clasp of gold
Went to his Grecian enemies and told   740
The secret of her husband's hiding place,
For which at Thebes he met an evil grace.[31]
Livia and Lucilia, he went through
Their tale as well; they killed their husbands, too.
One killed for love, the other killed for hate.
At evening Livia, when the hour was late,
Poisoned her husband, for she was his foe.
Lucilia doted on her husband so
That in her lust, hoping to make him think
Ever of her, she gave him a love-drink   750
Of such a sort he died before the morrow.[32]
And so at all turns husbands come to sorrow!
    "He told me then how one Latumius,
Complaining to a friend named Arrius,
Told him that in his garden grew a tree
On which his wives had hanged themselves, all three,
Merely for spite against their partnership.
'Brother,' said Arrius, 'let me have a slip
From this miraculous tree, for, begging pardon,
I want to go and plant it in my garden.'   760
    "Then about wives in recent times he read,
How some had murdered husbands lying abed
And all night long had let a paramour
Enjoy them with the corpse flat on the floor;
Or driven a nail into a husband's brain
While he was sleeping, and thus he had been slain;
And some had given them poison in their drink.
He told more harm than anyone can think,
And seasoned his wretched stories with proverbs
Outnumbering all the blades of grass and herbs   770
On earth. 'Better a dragon for a mate,
Better,' he said, 'on a lion's whims to wait
Than on a wife whose way it is to chide.
Better,' he said, 'high in the loft to bide
Than with a railing wife down in the house.
They always, they are so contrarious,
Hate what their husbands like,' so he would say.
'A woman,' he said, 'throws all her shame away
When she takes off her smock.' And on he'd go:
'A pretty woman, unless she's chaste also,   780

[31] In mythology, Amphiaraus was tricked by his wife (who had been bribed) into joining an
expedition against Thebes from which it was known that he would not return alive.
[32] In ancient Roman history there were two Livias, each of whom killed her husband.
Lucilia was married to the great Roman poet Lucretius (first century B.C.); the story of the love
potion is from St. Jerome.

Is like a gold ring stuck in a sow's nose.'
Who could imagine, who would half suppose
The gall my heart drank, raging at each drop?
    "And when I saw that he would never stop
Reading all night from his accursed book,
Suddenly, in the midst of it, I took
Three leaves and tore them out in a great pique,
And with my fist I caught him on the cheek
So hard he tumbled backward in the fire.
And up he jumped, he was as mad for ire   790
As a mad lion, and caught me on the head
With such a blow I fell down as if dead.
And seeing me on the floor, how still I lay,
He was aghast, and would have fled away,
Till I came to at length, and gave a cry.
'Have you killed me for my lands? Before I die,
False thief,' I said, 'I'll give you a last kiss!'
    "He came to me and knelt down close at this,
And said, 'So help me God, dear Alison,
I'll never strike you. For this thing I have done   800
You are to blame. Forgive me, I implore.'
So then I hit him on the cheek once more
And said, 'Thus far I am avenged, you thief.
I cannot speak. Now I shall die for grief.'
But finally, with much care and ado,
We reconciled our differences, we two.
He let me have the bridle in my hand
For management of both our house and land.
To curb his tongue he also undertook,
And on the spot I made him burn his book.   810
And when I had secured in full degree
By right of triumph the whole sovereignty,
And he had said, 'My dear, my own true wife,
Do as you will as long as you have life;
Preserve your honor and keep my estate,'
From that day on we had settled our debate.
I was as kind, God help me, day and dark
As any wife from India to Denmark,
And also true, and so he was to me.
I pray the Lord who sits in majesty   820
To bless his soul for Christ's own mercy dear.
And now I'll tell my tale, if you will hear."
    "Dame," laughed the Friar, "as I hope for bliss,
It was a long preamble to a tale, all this!"
    "God's arms!" the Summoner said, "it is a sin,
Good people, how friars are always butting in!
A fly and a friar will fall in every dish
And every question, whatever people wish.
What do you know, with your talk about 'preambling'?
Amble or trot or keep still or go scrambling,   830

You interrupt our pleasure."
"You think so,
Sir Summoner?" said the Friar. "Before I go,
I'll give the people here a chance or two
For a laugh at summoners, I promise you."
  "Curse on your face," the Summoner said, "curse me,
If I don't tell some stories, two or three,
On friars, before I get to Sittingborne,[33]
With which I'll twist your heart and make it mourn,
For you have lost your temper, I can see."
  "Be quiet," cried our Host, "immediately,"   840
And ordered, "Let the woman tell her tale.
You act like people who've got drunk on ale.
Do, Madame, tell us. That is the best measure."
  "All ready, sir," she answered "at your pleasure,
With the license of this worthy Friar here."
  "Madame, tell on," he said. "You have my ear."

THE WIFE OF BATH'S TALE

In the old days when King Arthur ruled the nation,
Whom Welshmen speak of with such veneration,
This realm we live in was a fairy land.
The fairy queen danced with her jolly band
On the green meadows where they held dominion.
This was, as I have read, the old opinion;
I speak of many hundred years ago.
But no one sees an elf now, as you know,
For in our time the charity and prayers
And all the begging of these holy friars   10
Who swarm through every nook and every stream
Thicker than motes of dust in a sunbeam,
Blessing our chambers, kitchens, halls, and bowers,
Our cities, towns, and castles, our high towers,
Our villages, our stables, barns, and dairies,
They keep us all from seeing any fairies,
For where you might have come upon an elf
There now you find the holy friar himself
Working his district on industrious legs
And saying his devotions while he begs.   20
Women are safe now under every tree.
No incubus[1] is there unless it's he,
And all they have to fear from him is shame.
  It chanced that Arthur had a knight who came
Lustily riding home one day from hawking,

---

[33] About forty miles from London.
[1] An evil spirit believed to have intercourse with women, in their sleep.

And in his path he saw a maiden walking
Before him, stark alone, right in his course.
This young knight took her maidenhead by force,
A crime at which the outcry was so keen
It would have cost his neck, but that the queen,   30
With other ladies, begged the king so long
That Arthur spared his life, for right or wrong,
And gave him to the queen, at her own will,
According to her choice, to save or kill.
   She thanked the king, and later told this knight,
Choosing her time, "You are still in such a plight
Your very life has no security.
I grant your life, if you can answer me
This question: what is the thing that most of all
Women desire? Think, or your neck will fall   40
Under the ax! If you cannot let me know
Immediately, I give you leave to go
A twelvemonth and a day, no more, in quest
Of such an answer as will meet the test.
But you must pledge your honor to return
And yield your body, whatever you may learn."
   The knight sighed; he was rueful beyond measure.
But what! He could not follow his own pleasure.
He chose at last upon his way to ride
And with such answer as God might provide   50
To come back when the year was at the close.
And so he takes his leave, and off he goes.
   He seeks out every house and every place
Where he has any hope, by luck or grace,
Of learning what thing women covet most.
But it seemed he could not light on any coast
Where on this point two people would agree,
For some said wealth and some said jollity,
Some said position, some said sport in bed
And often to be widowed, often wed.   60
Some said that to a woman's heart what mattered
Above all else was to be pleased and flattered.
That shaft, to tell the truth, was a close hit.
Men win us best by flattery, I admit,
And by attention. Some say our greatest ease
Is to be free and do just as we please,
And not to have our faults thrown in our eyes,
But always to be praised for being wise.
And true enough, there's not one of us all
Who will not kick if you rub us on a gall.   70
Whatever vices we may have within,
We won't be taxed with any fault or sin.
   Some say that women are delighted well
If it is thought that they will never tell
A secret they are trusted with, or scandal.

But that tale isn't worth an old rake handle!
We women, for a fact, can never hold
A secret. Will you hear a story told?
Then witness Midas! For it can be read
In Ovid that he had upon his head   80
Two ass's ears that he kept out of sight
Beneath his long hair with such skill and sleight
That no one else besides his wife could guess.
He loved her well, and trusted her no less.
He begged her not to make his blemish known,
But keep her knowledge to herself alone.
She swore that never, though to save her skin,
Would she be guilty of so mean a sin,
And yet it seemed to her she nearly died
Keeping a secret locked so long inside.   90
It swelled about her heart so hard and deep
She was afraid some word was bound to leap
Out of her mouth, and since there was no man
She dared to tell, down to a swamp she ran—
Her heart, until she got there, all agog—
And like a bittern booming in the bog
She put her mouth close to the watery ground:
"Water, do not betray me with your sound!
I speak to you, and you alone," she said.
"Two ass's ears grow on my husband's head!   100
And now my heart is whole, now it is out.
I'd burst if I held it longer, past all doubt."
Safely, you see, awhile you may confide
In us, but it will out; we cannot hide
A secret. Look in Ovid if you care
To learn what followed; the whole tale is there.[2]

   This knight, when he perceived he could not find
What women covet most, was low in mind;
But the day had come when homeward he must ride,
And as he crossed a wooded countryside   110
Some four and twenty ladies there by chance
He saw, all circling in a woodland dance,
And toward this dance he eagerly drew near
In hope of any counsel he might hear.
But the truth was, he had not reached the place
When dance and all, they vanished into space.
No living soul remained there to be seen
Save an old woman sitting on the green,
As ugly a witch as fancy could devise.
As he approached her she began to rise   120
And said, "Sir knight, here runs no thoroughfare.
What are you seeking with such anxious air?

---

[2] See Ovid, *Metamorphoses*, Book XI. In Ovid, however, it is Midas' barber, not his wife, who reveals the secret.

Tell me! The better may your fortune be.
We old folk know a lot of things," said she.
    "Good mother," said the knight, "my life's to pay,
That's all too certain, if I cannot say
What women covet most. If you could tell
That secret to me, I'd requite you well."
    "Give me your hand," she answered. "Swear me true
That whatsoever I next ask of you,   130
You'll do it if it lies within your might
And I'll enlighten you before the night."
    "Granted, upon my honor," he replied.
    "Then I dare boast, and with no empty pride,
Your life is safe," she told him. "Let me die
If the queen herself won't say the same as I.
Let's learn if the haughtiest of all who wear
A net or coverchief upon their hair
Will be so forward as to answer 'no'
To what I'll teach you. No more; let us go."   140
With that she whispered something in his ear,
And told him to be glad and have no fear.
    When they had reached the court, the knight declared
That he had kept his day, and was prepared
To give his answer, standing for his life.
Many the wise widow, many the wife,
Many the maid who rallied to the scene,
And at the head as justice sat the queen.
Then silence was enjoined; the knight was told
In open court to say what women hold   150
Precious above all else. He did not stand
Dumb like a beast, but spoke up at command
And plainly offered them his answering word
In manly voice, so that the whole court heard.
    "My liege and lady, most of all," said he,
"Women desire to have the sovereignty
And sit in rule and government above
Their husbands, and to have their way in love.
That is what most you want. Spare me or kill
As you may like; I stand here by your will."   160
    No widow, wife, or maid gave any token
Of contradicting what the knight had spoken.
He should not die; he should be spared instead;
He was worthy of his life, the whole court said.
    The old woman whom the knight met on the green
Sprang up at this. "My sovereign lady queen,
Before your court has risen, do me right!
It was I who taught this answer to the knight,
For which he pledged his honor in my hand,
Solemnly, that the first thing I demand,   170
He would do it, if it lay within his might.
Before the court I ask you, then, sir knight,

To take me," said the woman, "as your wife,
For well you know that I have saved your life.
Deny me, on your honor, if you can."
    "Alas," replied this miserable man,
"That was my promise, it must be confessed.
For the love of God, though, choose a new request!
Take all my wealth, and let my body be."
    "If that's your tune, then curse both you and me," 180
She said. "Though I am ugly, old, and poor,
I'll have, for all the metal and the ore
That under earth is hidden or lies above,
Nothing, except to be your wife and love."
    "My love? No, my damnation, if you can!
Alas," he said, "that any of my clan
Should be so miserably misallied!"
    All to no good; force overruled his pride,
And in the end he is constrained to wed,
And marries his old wife and goes to bed. 190
    Now some will charge me with an oversight
In failing to describe the day's delight,
The merriment, the food, the dress at least.
But I reply, there was no joy nor feast;
There was only sorrow and sharp misery.
He married her in private, secretly,
And all day after, such was his distress,
Hid like an owl from his wife's ugliness.
    Great was the woe this knight had in his head
When in due time they both were brought to bed. 200
He shuddered, tossed, and turned, and all the while
His old wife lay and waited with a smile.
"Is every knight so backward with a spouse?
Is it," she said, "a law in Arthur's house?
I am your love, your own, your wedded wife,
I am the woman who has saved your life.
I have never done you anything but right.
Why do you treat me this way the first night?
You must be mad, the way that you behave!
Tell me my fault, and as God's love can save, 210
I will amend it, truly, if I can."
    "Amend it?" answered this unhappy man.
"It can never be amended, truth to tell.
You are so loathsome and so old as well,
And your low birth besides is such a cross
It is no wonder that I turn and toss.
God take my woeful spirit from my breast!"
    "Is this," she said, "the cause of your unrest?"
    "No wonder!" said the knight. "It truly is."
    "Now sir," she said, "I could amend all this 220
Within three days, if it should please me to,
And if you deal with me as you should do.

"But since you speak of that nobility
That comes from ancient wealth and pedigree,
As if *that* constituted gentlemen,
I hold such arrogance not worth a hen!
The man whose virtue is pre-eminent,
In public and alone, always intent
On doing every generous act he can,
Take him—he is the greatest gentleman!   230
Christ wills that we should claim nobility
From him, not from old wealth or family.
Our elders left us all that they were worth
And through their wealth and blood we claim high birth,
But never, since it was beyond their giving,
Could they bequeath to us their virtuous living;
Although it first conferred on them the name
Of gentlemen, they could not leave that claim!
    "Dante the Florentine on this was wise:
'Frail is the branch on which man's virtues rise'—   240
Thus runs his rhyme—'God's goodness wills that we
Should claim from him alone nobility.'[3]
Thus from our elders we can only claim
Such temporal things as men may hurt and maim.
    "It is clear enough that true nobility
Is not bequeathed along with property,
For many a lord's son does a deed of shame
And yet, God knows, enjoys his noble name.
But though descended from a noble house
And elders who were wise and virtuous,   250
If he will not follow his elders, who are dead,
But leads, himself, a shameful life instead,
He is not noble, be he duke or earl.
It is the churlish deed that makes the churl.
And therefore, my dear husband, I conclude
That though my ancestors were rough and rude,
Yet may Almighty God confer on me
The grace to live, as I hope, virtuously.
Call me of noble blood when I begin
To live in virtue and to cast out sin.   260
    "As for my poverty, at which you grieve,
Almighty God in whom we all believe
In willful poverty chose to lead his life,
And surely every man and maid and wife
Can understand that Jesus, heaven's king,
Would never choose a low or vicious thing.
A poor and cheerful life is nobly led;
So Seneca and others have well said.
The man so poor he doesn't have a stitch,
If he thinks himself repaid, I count him rich.   270

---

[3] *Purgatory*, Canto VII.

He that is covetous, he is the poor man,
Pining to have the things he never can.
It is of cheerful mind, true poverty.
Juvenal[4] says about it happily:
'The poor man as he goes along his way
And passes thieves is free to sing and play.'
Poverty is a good we loathe, a great
Reliever of our busy worldly state,
A great amender also of our minds
As he that patiently will bear it finds.   280
And poverty, for all it seems distressed,
Is a possession no one will contest.
Poverty, too, by bringing a man low,
Helps him the better both God and self to know.
Poverty is a glass where we can see
Which are our true friends, as it seems to me.
So, sir, I do not wrong you on this score;
Reproach me with my poverty no more.
   "Now, sir, you tax me with my age; but, sir,
You gentlemen of breeding all aver   290
That men should not despise old age, but rather
Grant an old man respect, and call him 'father.'
   "If I am old and ugly, as you have said,
You have less fear of being cuckolded,
For ugliness and age, as all agree,
Are notable guardians of chastity.
But since I know in what you take delight,
I'll gratify your worldly appetite.
   "Choose now, which of two courses you will try:
To have me old and ugly till I die   300
But evermore your true and humble wife,
Never displeasing you in all my life,
Or will you have me rather young and fair
And take your chances on who may repair
Either to your house on account of me
Or to some other place, it well may be.
Now make your choice, whichever you prefer."
   The knight took thought, and sighed, and said to her
At last, "My love and lady, my dear wife,
In your wise government I put my life.   310
Choose for yourself which course will best agree
With pleasure and honor, both for you and me.
I do not care, choose either of the two;
I am content, whatever pleases you."
   "Then have I won from you the sovereignty,
Since I may choose and rule at will?" said she.
He answered, "That is best, I think, dear wife."
   "Kiss me," she said. "Now we are done with strife,

---

[4] Roman poet (about 60–140 A.D.). The reference is to his *Satires*, X.

For on my word, I will be both to you,
That is to say, fair, yes, and faithful too.   320
May I die mad unless I am as true
As ever wife was since the world was new.
Unless I am as lovely to be seen
By morning as an empress or a queen
Or any lady between east and west,
Do with my life or death as you think best.
Lift up the curtain, see what you may see."
    And when the knight saw what had come to be
And knew her as she was, so young, so fair,
His joy was such that it was past compare.   330
He took her in his arms and gave her kisses
A thousand times on end; he bathed in blisses.
And she obeyed him also in full measure
In everything that tended to his pleasure.
    And so they lived in full joy to the end.
And now to all us women may Christ send
Submissive husbands, full of youth in bed,
And grace to outlive all the men we wed.
And I pray Jesus to cut short the lives
Of those who won't be governed by their wives;   340
And old, ill-tempered niggards who hate expense,
God promptly bring them down with pestilence!

WORDS OF THE HOST TO THE PARDONER

"Now my fine friend," he said, "you Pardoner,
Be quick, tell us a tale of mirth or fun."[1]
    "By St. Ninian," he said, "it shall be done,
But at this tavern here, before my tale,
I'll just go in and have some bread and ale."
    The proper pilgrims in our company
Cried quickly, "Let him speak no ribaldry!
Tell us a moral tale, one to make clear
Some lesson to us, and we'll gladly hear."
    "Just as you wish," he said. "But I must think
Of something edifying while I drink."

PROLOGUE TO THE PARDONER'S TALE

"In churches," said the Pardoner, "when I preach,
I use, milords, a lofty style of speech
And ring it out as roundly as a bell,
Knowing by rote all that I have to tell.

---

[1] The Host, having heard a sad tale from the Physician, wants the Pardoner to tell a merrier one. The travelers are at a tavern.

My text is ever the same, and ever was:
Radix malorum est cupiditas.[2]
  "First I inform them whence I come; that done,
I then display my papal bulls,[3] each one.
I show my license first, my body's warrant,
Sealed by the bishop, for it would be abhorrent   10
If any man made bold, though priest or clerk,
To interrupt me in Christ's holy work.
And after that I give myself full scope.
Bulls in the name of cardinal and pope,
Of bishops and of patriarchs I show.
I say in Latin some few words or so
To spice my sermon; it flavors my appeal
And stirs my listeners to greater zeal.
Then I display my cases made of glass
Crammed to the top with rags and bones. They pass   20
For relics[4] with all the people in the place.
I have a shoulder bone in a metal case,
Part of a sheep owned by a holy Jew.
'Good men,' I say, 'heed what I'm telling you:
Just let this bone be dipped in any well
And if cow, calf, or sheep, or ox should swell
From eating a worm, or by a worm be stung,
Take water from this well and wash its tongue
And it is healed at once. And furthermore
Of scab and ulcers and of every sore   30
Shall every sheep be cured, and that straightway,
That drinks from the same well. Heed what I say:
If the good man who owns the beasts will go,
Fasting, each week, and drink before cockcrow
Out of this well, his cattle shall be brought
To multiply—that holy Jew so taught
Our elders—and his property increase.
  "'Moreover, sirs, this bone cures jealousies.
Though into a jealous madness a man fell,
Let him cook his soup in water from this well,   40
He'll never, though for truth he knew her sin,
Suspect his wife again, though she took in
A priest, or even two of them or three.
  "'Now here's a mitten that you all can see.
Whoever puts his hand in it shall gain,
When he sows his land, increasing crops of grain,
Be it wheat or oats, provided that he bring
His penny or so to make his offering.
  "'There is one word of warning I must say,
Good men and women. If any here today   50
Has done a sin so horrible to name

---

[2] "Greed is the root of all evil," adapted from 1 Timothy 6:10.   [3] Documents.
[4] That is, of saints or biblical personages.

He daren't be shriven[5] of it for the shame,
Or if any woman, young or old, is here
Who has cuckolded her husband, be it clear
They may not make an offering in that case
To these my relics; they have no power nor grace.
But any who is free of such dire blame,
Let him come up and offer in God's name
And I'll absolve him through the authority
That by the pope's bull has been granted me.'   60
   "By such hornswoggling I've won, year by year,
A hundred marks[6] since being a pardoner.
I stand in my pulpit like a true divine,
And when the people sit I preach my line
To ignorant souls, as you have heard before,
And tell skullduggeries by the hundred more.
Then I take care to stretch my neck well out
And over the people I nod and peer about
Just like a pigeon perching on a shed.
My hands fly and my tongue wags in my head   70
So busily that to watch me is a joy.
Avarice is the theme that I employ
In all my sermons, to make the people free
In giving pennies—especially to me.
My mind is fixed on what I stand to win
And not at all upon correcting sin.
I do not care, when they are in the grave,
If souls go berry-picking that I could save.
Truth is that evil purposes determine,
And many a time, the origin of a sermon: 80
Some to please people and by flattery
To gain advancement through hypocrisy,
Some for vainglory, some again for hate.
For when I daren't fight otherwise, I wait
And give him a tongue-lashing when I preach.
No man escapes or gets beyond the reach
Of my defaming tongue, supposing he
Has done a wrong to my brethren or to me.
For though I do not tell his proper name,
People will recognize him all the same.   90
By sign and circumstance I let them learn.
Thus I serve those who have done us an ill turn.
Thus I spit out my venom under hue
Of sanctity, and seem devout and true!
   "But to put my purpose briefly, I confess
I preach for nothing but for covetousness.
That's why my text is still and ever was
Radix malorum est cupiditas.

---

[5] Absolved of sins in the confessional.
[6] The equivalent today of a few thousand dollars.

For by this text I can denounce, indeed,
The very vice I practice, which is greed. 100
But though that sin is lodged in my own heart,
I am able to make other people part
From avarice, and sorely to repent,
Though that is not my principal intent.
  "Then I bring in examples, many a one,
And tell them many a tale of days long done.
Plain folk love tales that come down from of old.
Such things their minds can well report and hold.
Do you think that while I have the power to preach
And take in silver and gold for what I teach 110
I shall ever live in willful poverty?
No, no, that never was my thought, certainly.
I mean to preach and beg in sundry lands.
I won't do any labor with my hands,
Nor live by making baskets. I don't intend
To beg for nothing; that is not my end.
I won't ape the apostles; I must eat,
I must have money, wool, and cheese, and wheat,
Though I took it from the meanest wretch's tillage
Or from the poorest widow in a village, 120
Yes, though her children starved for want. In fine,
I mean to drink the liquor of the vine
And have a jolly wench in every town.
But, in conclusion, lords, I will get down
To business: you would have me tell a tale.
Now that I've had a drink of corny ale,
By God, I hope the thing I'm going to tell
Is one that you'll have reason to like well.
For though myself a very sinful man,
I can tell a moral tale, indeed I can, 130
One that I use to bring the profits in
While preaching. Now be still, and I'll begin."

THE PARDONER'S TALE

There was a company of young folk living
One time in Flanders, who were bent on giving
Their lives to follies and extravagances,
Brothels and taverns, where they held their dances
With lutes, harps, and guitars, diced at all hours,
And also ate and drank beyond their powers,
Through which they paid the devil sacrifice
In the devil's temple with their drink and dice,
Their abominable excess and dissipation.
They swore oaths that were worthy of damnation; 10
It was grisly to be listening when they swore.

The blessed body of our Lord they tore—
The Jews, it seemed to them, had failed to rend
His body enough—and each laughed at his friend
And fellow in sin. To encourage their pursuits
Came comely dancing girls, peddlers of fruits,
Singers with harps, bawds and confectioners
Who are the very devil's officers
To kindle and blow the fire of lechery
That is the follower of gluttony.   20
    Witness the Bible, if licentiousness
Does not reside in wine and drunkenness!
Recall how drunken Lot, unnaturally,
With his two daughters lay unwittingly,
So drunk he had no notion what he did.[1]
    Herod, the stories tell us, God forbid,
When full of liquor at his banquet board
Right at his very table gave the word
To kill the Baptist, John, though guiltless he.[2]
    Seneca[3] says a good word, certainly.   30
He says there is no difference he can find
Between a man who has gone out of his mind
And one who carries drinking to excess,
Only that madness outlasts drunkenness.
O gluttony, first cause of mankind's fall,[4]
Of our damnation the cursed original
Until Christ bought us with his blood again!
How dearly paid for by the race of men
Was this detestable iniquity!
This whole world was destroyed through gluttony.   40
    Adam our father and his wife also
From paradise to labor and to woe
Were driven for that selfsame vice, indeed.
As long as Adam fasted—so I read—
He was in heaven; but as soon as he
Devoured the fruit of that forbidden tree
Then he was driven out in sorrow and pain.
Of gluttony well ought we to complain!
Could a man know how many maladies
Follow indulgences and gluttonies   50
He would keep his diet under stricter measure
And sit at table with more temperate pleasure.
The throat is short and tender is the mouth,
And hence men toil east, west, and north, and south,
In earth, and air, and water—alas to think—
Fetching a glutton dainty meat and drink.

---

[1] See Genesis 19:30–36.
[2] See the versions of the story in the gospels of Matthew (chapter 14) and Mark (chapter 6).
[3] A Roman writer of the first century.
[4] Because Adam and Eve sinned by eating a forbidden fruit.

This is a theme, O Paul, that you well treat:
"Meat unto belly, and belly unto meat,
God shall destroy them both," as Paul has said.[5]
When a man drinks the white wine and the red—   60
This is a foul word, by my soul, to say,
And fouler is the deed in every way—
He makes his throat his privy through excess.
    The Apostle[6] says, weeping for piteousness,
"There are many of whom I told you—at a loss
I say it, weeping—enemies of Christ's cross,
Whose belly is their god; their end is death."
O cursed belly! Sack of stinking breath
In which corruption lodges, dung abounds!
At either end of you come forth foul sounds.   70
Great cost it is to fill you, and great pain!
These cooks, how they must grind and pound and strain
And transform substance into accident[7]
To please your cravings, though exorbitant!
From the hard bones they knock the marrow out.
They'll find a use for everything, past doubt,
That down the gullet sweet and soft will glide.
The spiceries of leaf and root provide
Sauces that are concocted for delight,
To give a man a second appetite.   80
But truly, he whom gluttonies entice
Is dead, while he continues in that vice.
    O drunken man, disfigured is your face,
Sour is your breath, foul are you to embrace!
You seem to mutter through your drunken nose
The sound of "Samson, Samson," yet God knows
That Samson[8] never indulged himself in wine.
Your tongue is lost, you fall like a stuck swine,
And all the self-respect that you possess
Is gone, for of man's judgment, drunkenness   90
Is the very sepulcher and annihilation.
A man whom drink has under domination
Can never keep a secret in his head.
Now steer away from both the white and red,
And most of all from that white wine keep wide
That comes from Lepe. They sell it in Cheapside
And Fish Street.[9] It's a Spanish wine, and sly
To creep in other wines[10] that grow nearby,
And such a vapor it has that with three drinks
It takes a man to Spain; although he thinks   100
He is home in Cheapside, he is far away

---

[5] See 1 Corinthians 6:13.   [6] St. Paul. See Philippians 3:18–19.
[7] Philosophical terms; "substance" is what a thing really is, "accident" is a nonessential quality or property of it.
[8] The Old Testament hero. His story is told in Judges, chapters 13–16.
[9] Main streets in London.   [10] Be mixed with other wines.

At Lepe. Then "Samson, Samson" will he say!
By God himself, who is omnipotent,
All the great exploits in the Old Testament
Were done in abstinence, I say, and prayer.
Look in the Bible, you may learn it there.
Attila,[11] conqueror of many a place,
Died in his sleep in shame and in disgrace
Bleeding out of his nose in drunkenness.
A captain ought to live in temperateness!   110
And more than this, I say, remember well
The injunction that was laid on Lemuel—
Not Samuel, but Lemuel, I say!
Read in the Bible; in the plainest way
Wine is forbidden to judges and to kings.[12]
This will suffice; no more upon these things.
    Now that I've shown what gluttony will do,
Now I will warn you against gambling, too;
Gambling, the very mother of low scheming,
Of lying and forswearing and blaspheming   120
Against Christ's name, of murder and waste as well
Alike of goods and time; and, truth to tell,
With honor and renown it cannot suit
To be held a common gambler by repute.
The higher a gambler stands in power and place,
The more his name is lowered in disgrace.
If a prince gambles, whatever his kingdom be,
In his whole government and policy
He is, in all the general estimation,
Considered so much less in reputation.   130
    Stilbon,[13] who was a wise ambassador,
From Lacedaemon once to Corinth bore
A mission of alliance. When he came
It happened that he found there at a game
Of hazard all the great ones of the land,
And so, as quickly as it could be planned,
He stole back, saying, "I will not lose my name
Nor have my reputation put to shame
Allying you with gamblers. You may send
Other wise emissaries to gain your end,   140
For by my honor, rather than ally
My countrymen to gamblers, I will die.
For you that are so gloriously renowned
Shall never with this gambling race be bound
By will of mine or treaty I prepare."

[11] Attila the Hun, fifth-century invader of Europe.
[12] In Proverbs, 31:4, Lemuel's mother admonishes him, "It is not for kings to drink wine." Not to be confused, the Pardoner insists, with Samuel, another Old Testament figure.
[13] This story and the following one about Demetrius are from a book by John of Salisbury, a learned English scholar of the twelfth century. Lacedaemon (Sparta) and Corinth were city-states of ancient Greece.

Thus did this wise philosopher declare.
　Remember also how the Parthians'[14] lord
Sent King Demetrius, as the books record,
A pair of golden dice, by this proclaiming
His scorn, because that king was known for gaming, 150
And the king of Parthia therefore held his crown
Devoid of glory, value, or renown.
Lords can discover other means of play
More suitable to while the time away.
　Now about oaths I'll say a word or two,
Great oaths and false oaths, as the old books do.
Great swearing is a thing abominable,
And false oaths yet more reprehensible.
Almighty God forbade swearing at all,
Matthew be witness; but specially I call 160
The holy Jeremiah on this head.
"Swear thine oaths truly, do not lie," he said.
"Swear under judgment, and in righteousness."[15]
But idle swearing is a great wickedness.
Consult and see, and he that understands
In the first table of the Lord's commands
Will find the second of his commandments this:
"Take not the Lord's name idly or amiss."
If a man's oaths and curses are extreme,
Vengeance shall find his house, both roof and beam. 170
"By the precious heart of God," and "By his nails"—
"My chance is seven, by Christ's blood at Hailes,[16]
Yours five and three." "Cheat me, and if you do,
By God's arms, with this knife I'll run you through!"—
Such fruit comes from the bones, that pair of bitches:
Oaths broken, treachery, murder. For the riches
Of Christ's love, give up curses, without fail,
Both great and small!—Now, sirs, I'll tell my tale.
　These three young roisterers of whom I tell
Long before prime[17] had rung from any bell 180
Were seated in a tavern at their drinking,
And as they sat, they heard a bell go clinking
Before a corpse being carried to his grave.
One of these roisterers, when he heard it, gave
An order to his boy: "Go out and try
To learn whose corpse is being carried by.
Get me his name, and get it right. Take heed."
　"Sir," said the boy, "there isn't any need.
I learned before you came here, by two hours.

---

[14] Parthia was an ancient region in what is now Iran.
[15] In the gospel of Matthew, 5:34 (part of the Sermon on the Mount), Christ says, "Swear not at all." See also Jeremiah 4:2.
[16] In the dice game of hazard, a player's "chance" was roughly the equivalent of his "point" in modern craps. Hailes was an English abbey supposed to possess a relic of Christ's blood.
[17] An early morning hour, between seven and nine.

He was, it happens, an old friend of yours,   190
And all at once, there on his bench upright
As he was sitting drunk, he was killed last night.
A sly thief, Death men call him, who deprives
All the people in this country of their lives,
Came with his spear and smiting his heart in two
Went on his business with no more ado.
A thousand have been slaughtered by his hand
During this plague. And, sir, before you stand
Within his presence, it should be necessary,
It seems to me, to know your adversary.   200
Be evermore prepared to meet this foe.
My mother taught me thus; that's all I know."
   "Now by St. Mary," said the innkeeper,
"This child speaks truth. Man, woman, laborer,
Servant, and child the thief has slain this year
In a big village a mile or more from here.
I think it is his place of habitation.
It would be wise to make some preparation
Before he brought a man into disgrace."
   "God's arms!" this roisterer said. "So that's the case!   210
Is it so dangerous with this thief to meet?
I'll look for him by every path and street,
I vow it, by God's holy bones! Hear me,
Fellows of mine, we are all one, we three.
Let each of us hold up his hand to the other
And each of us become his fellow's brother.
We'll slay this Death, who slaughters and betrays.
He shall be slain whose hand so many slays,
By the dignity of God, before tonight!"
   The three together set about to plight   220
Their oaths to live and die each for the other
Just as though each had been to each born brother.
And in their drunken frenzy up they get
And toward the village off at once they set
Which the innkeeper had spoken of before,
And many were the grisly oaths they swore.
They rent Christ's precious body limb from limb—
Death shall be dead, if they lay hands on him!
   When they had hardly gone the first half mile,
Just as they were about to cross a stile,   230
An old man, poor and humble, met them there.
The old man greeted them with a meek air
And said, "God bless you, lords, and be your guide."
   "What's this?" the proudest of the three replied.
"Old beggar, I hope you meet with evil grace!
Why are you all wrapped up except your face?
What are you doing alive so many a year?"
   The old man at these words began to peer
Into this gambler's face. "Because I can,

Though I should walk to India, find no man,"   240
He said, "in any village or any town,
Who for my age is willing to lay down
His youth. So I must keep my old age still
For as long a time as it may be God's will.
Nor will Death take my life from me, alas!
Thus like a restless prisoner I pass
And on the ground, which is my mother's gate,
I walk and with my staff both early and late
I knock and say, 'Dear mother, let me in!
See how I vanish, flesh, and blood, and skin!   250
Alas, when shall my bones be laid to rest?
I would exchange with you my clothing chest,
Mother, that in my chamber long has been
For an old haircloth rag to wrap me in.'
And yet she still refuses me that grace.
All white, therefore, and withered is my face.
   "But, sirs, you do yourselves no courtesy
To speak to an old man so churlishly
Unless he had wronged you either in word or deed.
As you yourselves in Holy Writ may read,   260
'Before an aged man whose head is hoar
Men ought to rise.'[18] I counsel you, therefore,
No harm nor wrong here to an old man do,
No more than you would have men do to you
In your old age, if you so long abide.
And God be with you, whether you walk or ride!
I must go yonder where I have to go."
   "No, you old beggar, by St. John, not so,"
Said another of these gamblers. "As for me,
By God, you won't get off so easily!   270
You spoke just now of that false traitor, Death,
Who in this land robs all our friends of breath.
Tell where he is, since you must be his spy,
Or you will suffer for it, so say I
By God and by the holy sacrament.
You are in league with him, false thief, and bent
On killing us young folk, that's clear to my mind."
   "If you are so impatient, sirs, to find
Death," he replied, "turn up this crooked way,
For in that grove I left him, truth to say,   280
Beneath a tree, and there he will abide.
No boast of yours will make him run and hide.
Do you see that oak tree? Just there you will find
This Death, and God, who bought again mankind,
Save and amend you!" So said this old man;
And promptly each of these three gamblers ran
Until he reached the tree, and there they found

---

[18] See Leviticus 19:32.

Florins of fine gold, minted bright and round,
Nearly eight bushels of them, as they thought.
And after Death no longer then they sought.   290
Each of them was so ravished at the sight,
So fair the florins glittered and so bright,
That down they sat beside the precious hoard.
The worst of them, he uttered the first word.
    "Brothers," he told them, "listen to what I say.
My head is sharp, for all I joke and play.
Fortune has given us this pile of treasure
To set us up in lives of ease and pleasure.
Lightly it comes, lightly we'll make it go.
God's precious dignity! Who was to know   300
We'd ever tumble on such luck today?
If we could only carry this gold away,
Home to my house, or either one of yours—
For well you know that all this gold is ours—
We'd touch the summit of felicity.
But still, by daylight that can hardly be.
People would call us thieves, too bold for stealth,
And they would have us hanged for our own wealth.
It must be done by night, that's our best plan,
As prudently and slyly as we can.   310
Hence my proposal is that we should all
Draw lots, and let's see where the lot will fall,
And the one of us who draws the shortest stick
Shall run back to the town, and make it quick,
And bring us bread and wine here on the sly,
And two of us will keep a watchful eye
Over this gold; and if he doesn't stay
Too long in town, we'll carry this gold away
By night, wherever we all agree it's best."
    One of them held the cut out in his fist   320
And had them draw to see where it would fall,
And the cut fell on the youngest of them all.
At once he set off on his way to town,
And the very moment after he was gone
The one who urged this plan said to the other:
"You know that by sworn oath you are my brother.
I'll tell you something you can profit by.
Our friend has gone, that's clear to any eye,
And here is gold, abundant as can be,
That we propose to share alike, we three.   330
But if I worked it out, as I could do,
So that it could be shared between us two,
Wouldn't that be a favor, a friendly one?"
    The other answered, "How that can be done,
I don't quite see. He knows we have the gold.
What shall we do, or what shall he be told?"
    "Will you keep the secret tucked inside your head?

And in a few words," the first scoundrel said,
"I'll tell you how to bring this end about."
  "Granted," the other told him. "Never doubt,   340
I won't betray you, that you can believe."
  "Now," said the first, "we are two, as you perceive,
And two of us must have more strength than one.
When he sits down, get up as if in fun
And wrestle with him. While you play this game
I'll run him through the ribs. You do the same
With your dagger there, and then this gold shall be
Divided, dear friend, between you and me.
Then all that we desire we can fulfill,
And both of us can roll the dice at will."   350
Thus in agreement these two scoundrels fell
To slay the third, as you have heard me tell.
  The youngest, who had started off to town,
Within his heart kept rolling up and down
The beauty of these florins, new and bright.
"O Lord," he thought, "were there some way I might
Have all this treasure to myself alone,
There isn't a man who dwells beneath God's throne
Could live a life as merry as mine should be!"
And so at last the fiend, our enemy,   360
Put in his head that he could gain his ends
If he bought poison to kill off his friends.
Finding his life in such a sinful state,
The devil was allowed to seal his fate.
For it was altogether his intent
To kill his friends, and never to repent.
So off he set, no longer would he tarry,
Into the town, to an apothecary,
And begged for poison; he wanted it because
He meant to kill his rats; besides, there was   370
A polecat living in his hedge, he said,
Who killed his capons; and when he went to bed
He wanted to take vengeance, if he might,
On vermin that devoured him by night.
  The apothecary answered, "You shall have
A drug that as I hope the Lord will save
My soul, no living thing in all creation,
Eating or drinking of this preparation
A dose no bigger than a grain of wheat,
But promptly with his death-stroke he shall meet.   380
Die, that he will, and in a briefer while
Than you can walk the distance of a mile,
This poison is so strong and virulent."
  Taking the poison, off the scoundrel went,
Holding it in a box, and next he ran
To the neighboring street, and borrowed from a man
Three generous flagons. He emptied out his drug

In two of them, and kept the other jug
For his own drink; he let no poison lurk
In that! And so all night he meant to work   390
Carrying off the gold. Such was his plan,
And when he had filled them, this accursed man
Retraced his path, still following his design,
Back to his friends with his three jugs of wine.
    But why dilate upon it any more?
For just as they had planned his death before,
Just so they killed him, and with no delay.
When it was finished, one spoke up to say:
"Now let's sit down and drink, and we can bury
His body later on. First we'll be merry,"   400
And as he said the words, he took the jug
That, as it happened, held the poisonous drug,
And drank, and gave his friend a drink as well,
And promptly they both died. But truth to tell,
In all that Avicenna[19] ever wrote
He never described in chapter, rule, or note
More marvelous signs of poisoning, I suppose,
Than appeared in these two wretches at the close.
Thus they both perished for their homicide,
And thus the traitorous poisoner also died.   410
    O sin accursed above all cursedness,
O treacherous murder, O foul wickedness,
O gambling, lustfulness, and gluttony,
Traducer of Christ's name by blasphemy
And monstrous oaths, through habit and through pride!
Alas, mankind! Ah, how may it betide
That you to your Creator, he that wrought you
And even with his precious heart's blood bought you,
So falsely and ungratefully can live?
    And now, good men, your sins may God forgive   420
And keep you specially from avarice!
My holy pardon will avail in this,
For it can heal each one of you that brings
His pennies, silver brooches, spoons, or rings.
Come, bow your head under this holy bull!
You wives, come offer up your cloth or wool!
I write your names here in my roll, just so.
Into the bliss of heaven you shall go!
I will absolve you here by my high power,
You that will offer, as clean as in the hour   430
When you were born. —Sirs, thus I preach. And now
Christ Jesus, our souls' healer, show you how
Within his pardon evermore to rest,
For that, I will not lie to you, is best.

---

[19] Arab philosopher, physician, and author of a medical textbook of the early eleventh
century.

But in my tale, sirs, I forgot one thing.
The relics and the pardons that I bring
Here in my pouch, no man in the whole land
Has finer, given me by the pope's own hand.
If any of you devoutly wants to offer
And have my absolution, come and proffer 440
Whatever you have to give. Kneel down right here,
Humbly, and take my pardon, full and clear,
Or have a new, fresh pardon if you like
At the end of every mile of road we strike,
As long as you keep offering ever newly
Good coins, not counterfeit, but minted truly.
Indeed it is an honor I confer
On each of you, an authentic pardoner
Going along to absolve you as you ride.
For in the country mishaps may betide— 450
One or another of you in due course
May break his neck by falling from his horse.
Think what security it gives you all
That in this company I chanced to fall
Who can absolve you each, both low and high,
When the soul, alas, shall from the body fly!
By my advice, our Host here shall begin,
For he's the man enveloped most by sin.
Come, offer first, Sir Host, and once that's done,
Then you shall kiss the relics, every one, 460
Yes, for a penny! Come, undo your purse!
    "No, no," said he. "Then I should have Christ's curse!
I'll do nothing of the sort, for love or riches!
You'd make me kiss a piece of your old britches
And for a saintly relic make it pass
Although it had the tincture of your ass.
By the cross St. Helen[20] found in the Holy Land,
I wish I had your balls here in my hand
For relics! Cut'em off, and I'll be bound
If I don't help you carry them around. 470
I'll have the things enshrined in a hog's turd!"
    The Pardoner did not answer; not a word,
He was so angry, could he find to say.
    "Now," said our Host, "I will not try to play
With you, nor any other angry man."
    Immediately the worthy Knight began,
When he saw that all the people laughed, "No more,
This has gone far enough. Now as before,
Sir Pardoner, be gay, look cheerfully,
And you, Sir Host, who are so dear to me, 480
Come, kiss the Pardoner, I beg of you,

---

[20] She was believed to have discovered the cross of Jesus about 200 years after the Crucifixion.

And Pardoner, draw near, and let us do
As we've been doing, let us laugh and play."
And so they kissed, and rode along their way.

THE KNIGHT'S INTERRUPTION
OF THE MONK'S TALE

"Stop!" cried the Knight.[1] "No more of this, good sir!
You have said plenty, and much more, for sure,
For only a little such lugubriousness
Is plenty for a lot of folk, I guess.
I say for me it is a great displeasure,
When men have wealth and comfort in good measure,
To hear how they have tumbled down the slope,
And the opposite is a solace and a hope,
As when a man begins in low estate
And climbs the ladder and grows fortunate,   10
And stands there firm in his prosperity.
That is a welcome thing, it seems to me,
And of such things it would be good to tell."
   "Well said," our Host declared. "By St. Paul's bell,
You speak the truth; this Monk's tongue is too loud.
He told how fortune covered with a cloud—
I don't know what-all; and of tragedy
You heard just now, and it's no remedy,
When things are over and done with, to complain.
Besides, as you have said, it is a pain   20
To hear of misery; it is distressing.
Sir Monk, no more, as you would have God's blessing.
This company is all one weary sigh.
Such talking isn't worth a butterfly,
For where's the amusement in it, or the game?
And so, Sir Monk, or Don Pierce by your name,
I beg you heartily, tell us something else.
Truly, but for the jingling of your bells
That from your bridle hang on every side,
By Heaven's King, who was born for us and died,   30
I should long since have tumbled down in sleep,
Although the mud had never been so deep,
And then you would have told your tale in vain;
For certainly, as these learned men explain,
When his audience have turned their backs away,
It doesn't matter what a man may say.
I know well I shall have the essence of it
If anything is told here for our profit.
A tale of hunting, sir, pray share with us."

---

[1] The Monk, whom the Knight interrupts, has been narrating a long series of "tragedies,"
tales about the fall of eminent personages.

"No," said the Monk, "I'll not be frivolous.   40
Let another tell a tale, as I have told."
    Then spoke our Host, with a rude voice and bold,
And said to the Nun's Priest, "Come over here,
You priest, come hither, you Sir John, draw near!
Tell us a thing to make our spirits glad.
Be cheerful, though the jade you ride is bad.
What if your horse is miserable and lean?
If he will carry you, don't care a bean!
Keep up a joyful heart, and look alive."
    "Yes, Host," he answered, "as I hope to thrive,   50
If I weren't merry, I know I'd be reproached."
And with no more ado his tale he broached,
And this is what he told us, every one,
This precious priest, this goodly man, Sir John.

THE NUN'S PRIEST'S TALE

Once a poor widow, aging year by year,
Lived in a tiny cottage that stood near
A clump of shade trees rising in a dale.
This widow, of whom I tell you in my tale,
Since the last day that she had been a wife
Had led a very patient, simple life.
She had but few possessions to content her.
By thrift and husbandry of what God sent her
She and two daughters found the means to dine.
She had no more than three well-fattened swine,   10
As many cows, and one sheep, Moll by name.
Her bower and hall were black from the hearth-flame
Where she had eaten many a slender meal.
No dainty morsel did her palate feel
And no sharp sauce was needed with her pottage.
Her table was in keeping with her cottage.
Excess had never given her disquiet.
Her only doctor was a moderate diet,
And exercise, and a heart that was contented.
If she did not dance, at least no gout prevented;   20
No apoplexy had destroyed her head.
She never drank wine, whether white or red.
She served brown bread and milk, loaves white or black,
Singed bacon, all this with no sense of lack,
And now and then an egg or two. In short,
She was a dairy woman of a sort.
    She had a yard, on the inside fenced about
With hedges, and an empty ditch without,
In which she kept a cock, called Chanticleer.
In all the realm of crowing he had no peer.   30

His voice was merrier than the merry sound
Of the church organ grumbling out its ground
Upon a saint's day. Stouter was this cock
In crowing than the loudest abbey clock.
Of astronomy instinctively aware,
He kept the sun's hours with celestial care,
For when through each fifteen degrees it moved,
He crowed so that it couldn't be improved.
His comb, like a crenelated[1] castle wall,
Red as fine coral, stood up proud and tall.   40
His bill was black; like polished jet it glowed,
And he was azure-legged and azure-toed.
As lilies were his nails, they were so white;
Like burnished gold his hue, it shone so bright.
This cock had in his princely sway and measure
Seven hens to satisfy his every pleasure,
Who were his sisters and his sweethearts true,
Each wonderfully like him in her hue,
Of whom the fairest-feathered throat to see
Was fair Dame Partlet. Courteous was she,   50
Discreet, and always acted debonairly.
She was sociable, and bore herself so fairly,
Since the very time that she was seven nights old,
The heart of Chanticleer was in her hold
As if she had him locked up, every limb.
He loved her so that all was well with him.
It was a joy, when up the sun would spring,
To hear them both together sweetly sing,
"My love has gone to the country, far away!"
For as I understand it, in that day   60
The animals and birds could sing and speak.
   Now as this cock, one morning at daybreak,
With each of the seven hens that he called spouse,
Sat on his perch inside the widow's house,
And next him fair Dame Partlet, in his throat
This Chanticleer produced a hideous note
And groaned like a man who is having a bad dream;
And Partlet, when she heard her husband scream,
Was all aghast, and said, "Soul of my passion,
What ails you that you groan in such a fashion?   70
You are always a sound sleeper. Fie, for shame!"
   And Chanticleer awoke and answered, "Dame,
Take no offense, I beg you, on this score.
I dreamt, by God, I was in a plight so sore
Just now, my heart still quivers from the fright.
Now God see that my dream turns out all right
And keep my flesh and body from foul seizure!
I dreamed I was strutting in our yard at leisure

---

[1] Having walls with notched openings at the top.

When there I saw, among the weeds and vines,
A beast, he was like a hound, and had designs 80
Upon my person, and would have killed me dead.
His coat was not quite yellow, not quite red,
And both his ears and tail were tipped with black
Unlike the fur along his sides and back.
He had a small snout and a fiery eye.
His look for fear still makes me almost die.
This is what made me groan, I have no doubt."
    "For shame! Fie on you, faint heart!" she burst out.
"Alas," she said, "by the great God above,
Now you have lost my heart and all my love! 90
I cannot love a coward, as I'm blest!
Whatever any woman may protest,
We all want, could it be so, for our part,
Husbands who are wise and stout of heart,
No blabber, and no niggard, and no fool,
Nor afraid of every weapon or sharp tool,
No braggart either, by the God above!
How dare you say, for shame, to your true love
That there is anything you ever feared?
Have you no man's heart, when you have a beard? 100
Alas, and can a nightmare set you screaming?
God knows there's only vanity in dreaming!
Dreams are produced by such unseemly capers
As overeating; they come from stomach vapors
When a man's humors[2] aren't behaving right
From some excess. This dream you had tonight,
It comes straight from the superfluity
Of your red choler, certain as can be,
That causes people terror in their dreams
Of darts and arrows, and fire in red streams, 110
And of red beasts, for fear that they will bite,
Of little dogs, or of being in a fight;
As in the humor of melancholy lies
The reason why so many a sleeper cries
For fear of a black bull or a black bear
Or that black devils have him by the hair.
Through other humors also I could go
That visit many a sleeping man with woe,
But I will finish as quickly as I can.
    "Cato, that has been thought so wise a man, 120
Didn't he tell us, 'Put no stock in dreams'?
Now, sir," she said, "when we fly down from our beams,
For God's sake, go and take a laxative!
On my salvation, as I hope to live,
I give you good advice, and no mere folly:

---

[2] The four substances in the body believed to determine personality types and states of health. Dame Partlet discusses two: choler (bile) and melancholy (black bile).

Purge both your choler and your melancholy!
You mustn't wait or let yourself bog down,
And since there is no druggist in this town
I shall myself prescribe for what disturbs
Your humors, and instruct you in the herbs   130
That will be good for you. For I shall find
Here in our yard herbs of the proper kind
For purging you both under and above.
Don't let this slip your mind, for God's own love!
Yours is a very choleric complexion.
When the sun is in the ascendant, my direction
Is to beware those humors that are hot.
Avoid excess of them; if you should not,
I'll bet a penny, as a true believer,
You'll die of ague, or a tertian fever.   140
A day or so, if you do as I am urging,
You shall have worm-digestives, before purging
With fumitory or with hellebore
Or other herbs that grow here by the score;
With caper-spurge, or with the goat-tree berry
Or the ground-ivy, found in our yard so merry.
Peck 'em up just as they grow, and eat 'em in!
Be cheerful, husband, by your father's kin!
Don't worry about a dream. I say no more."
    "Madame," he answered, "thanks for all your lore.   150
But still, to speak of Cato, though his name
For wisdom has enjoyed so great a fame,
And though he counseled us there was no need
To be afraid of dreams, by God, men read
Of many a man of more authority
Than this Don Cato could pretend to be
Who in old books declare the opposite,
And by experience they have settled it,
That dreams are omens and prefigurations
Both of good fortune and of tribulations   160
That life and its vicissitudes present.
This question leaves no room for argument.
The very upshot makes it plain, indeed.
    "One of the greatest authors that men read
Informs us that two fellow travelers went,
Once on a time, and with the best intent,
Upon a pilgrimage, and it fell out
They reached a town where there was such a rout
Of people, and so little lodging space,
They could not find even the smallest place   170
Where they could both put up. So, for that night,
These pilgrims had to do as best they might,
And since they must, they parted company.
Each of them went off to his hostelry
And took his lodging as his luck might fall.

Among plow oxen in a farmyard stall
One of them found a place, though it was rough.
His friend and fellow was lodged well enough
As his luck would have it, or his destiny
That governs all us creatures equally.   180
And so it happened, long before the day,
He had a dream as in his bed he lay.
He dreamed that his parted friend began to call
And said, 'Alas, for in an ox's stall
This night I shall be murdered where I lie.
Come to my aid, dear brother, or I die.
Come to me quickly, come in haste!' he said.
He started from his sleep, this man, for dread,
But when he had wakened, he rolled back once more
And on this dream of his he set no store.   190
As a vain thing he dismissed it, unconcerned.
Twice as he slept that night the dream returned,
And still another and third time his friend
Came in a dream and said, 'I have met my end!
Look on my wounds! They are bloody, deep, and wide.
Now rise up early in the morningtide
And at the west gate of the town,' said he,
'A wagon with a load of dung you'll see.
Have it arrested boldly. Do as bidden,
For underneath you'll find my body hidden.   200
My money caused my murder, truth to tell,'
And told him each detail of how he fell,
With piteous face, and with a bloodless hue.
And do not doubt it, he found the dream was true,
For on the morrow, as soon as it was day,
To the place where his friend had lodged he made his way,
And no sooner did he reach this ox's stall
Than for his fellow he began to call.
   "Promptly the stableman replied, and said,
'Your friend is gone, sir. He got out of bed   210
And left the town as soon as day began.'
   "At last suspicion overtook this man.
Remembering his dreams, he would not wait,
But quickly went and found at the west gate,
Being driven to manure a farmer's land
As it might seem, a dung cart close at hand
That answered the description every way,
As you yourself have heard the dead man say.
And he began to shout courageously
For law and vengeance on this felony.   220
'My friend was killed this very night! He lies
Flat in this load of dung, with staring eyes.
I call on those who should keep rule and head,
The magistrates and governors here,' he said.
'Alas! Here lies my fellow, done to death!'

"Why on this tale should I waste further breath?
The people sprang and flung the cart to ground
And in the middle of the dung they found
The dead man, while his murder was still new.
"O blessed God, thou art so just and true,   230
Murder, though secret, ever thou wilt betray!
Murder will out, we see it day by day.
Murder so loathsome and abominable
To God is, who is just and reasonable,
That he will never suffer it to be
Concealed, though it hide a year, or two, or three.
Murder will out; to this point it comes down.
"Promptly the magistrates who ruled that town
Have seized the driver, and put him to such pain,
And the stableman as well, that under strain   240
Of torture they were both led to confess
And hanged by the neck-bone for their wickedness.
"Here's proof enough that dreams are things to dread!
And in the same book I have also read,
In the very chapter that comes right after this—
I don't speak idly, by my hopes of bliss—
Two travelers who for some reason planned
To cross the ocean to a distant land
Found that the wind, by an opposing fate,
Blew contrary, and forced them both to wait   250
In a fair city by a harborside.
But one day the wind changed, toward eventide,
And blew just as it suited them instead.
Cheerfully these travelers went to bed
And planned to sail the first thing in the morning.
But to one of them befell a strange forewarning
And a great marvel. While asleep he lay,
He dreamed a curious dream along toward day.
He dreamed that a man appeared at his bedside
And told him not to sail, but wait and bide.   260
'Tomorrow,' he told the man, 'if you set sail,
You shall be drowned. I have told you my whole tale.'
He woke, and of this warning he had met
He told his friend, and begged him to forget
His voyage, and to wait that day and bide.
His friend, who was lying close at his bedside,
Began to laugh, and told him in derision,
'I am not so flabbergasted by a vision
As to put off my business for such cause.
I do not think your dream is worth two straws!   270
For dreams are but a vain absurdity.
Of apes and owls and many a mystery
People are always dreaming, in a maze
Of things that never were seen in all their days
And never shall be. But I see it's clear

You mean to waste your time by waiting here.
I'm sorry for that, God knows; and so good day.'
With this he took his leave and went his way.
But not the half his course had this man sailed—
I don't know why, nor what it was that failed— 280
When by an accident the hull was rent
And ship and man under the water went
In full view of the vessels alongside
That had put out with them on the same tide.
Now then, fair Partlet, whom I love so well,
From old examples such as these I tell
You may see that none should give too little heed
To dreams; for I say seriously, indeed,
That many a dream is too well worth our dread.
   "Yes, in St. Kenelm's life I have also read— 290
He was the son of Cynewulf, the king
Of Mercia—how this Kenelm dreamed a thing.
One day, as the time when he was killed drew near,
He saw his murder in a dream appear.
His nurse explained his dream in each detail,
And warned him to be wary without fail
Of treason; yet he was but seven years old,
And therefore any dream he could but hold
Of little weight, in heart he was so pure.
I'd give my shirt, by God, you may be sure, 300
If you had read his story through like me!
   "Moreover, Partlet, I tell you truthfully,
Macrobius[3] writes—and by his book we know
The African vision of great Scipio—
Confirming dreams, and holds that they may be
Forewarnings of events that men shall see.
Again, I beg, look well at what is meant
By the Book of Daniel in the Old Testament,
Whether *he* held that dreams are vanity!
Read also about Joseph. You shall see 310
That dreams, or some of them—I don't say all—
Warn us of things that afterward befall.
Think of the king of Egypt, Don Pharaoh;
Of his butler and his baker think also,
Whether they found that dreams have no result.[4]
Whoever will search through kingdoms and consult
Their histories reads many a wondrous thing
Of dreams. What about Croesus, Lydian king—
Didn't he dream he was sitting on a tree,
Which meant he would be hanged? Andromache, 320
The woman who was once great Hector's wife,

---

[3] A fifth-century author of a commentary on Cicero's *Dream of Scipio*.
[4] See Genesis, chapters 40–41. Joseph, imprisoned in Egypt, won his freedom by interpreting accurately the dreams of Pharaoh's butler and baker and later Pharaoh's own dreams.

On the day that Hector was to lose his life,
The very night before his blood was spilled
She dreamed of how her husband would be killed
If he went out to battle on that day.
She warned him; but he would not heed nor stay.
In spite of her he rode out on the plain,
And by Achilles he was promptly slain.
But all that story is too long to tell,
And it is nearly day. I must not dwell   330
Upon this matter. Briefly, in conclusion,
I say this dream will bring me to confusion
And mischief of some sort. And furthermore,
On laxatives, I say, I set no store,
For they are poisonous, I'm sure of it.
I do not trust them! I like them not one bit!
   "Now let's talk cheerfully, and forget all this.
My pretty Partlet, by my hope of bliss,
In one thing God has sent me ample grace
For when I see the beauty of your face,   340
You are so scarlet-red about the eye,
It is enough to make my terrors die.
For just as true as *In principio*
Mulier est hominis confusio—[5]
And Madame, what this Latin means is this:
'Woman is man's whole comfort and true bliss'—
When I feel you soft at night, and I beside you,
Although it's true, alas, I cannot ride you
Because our perch is built so narrowly,
I am then so full of pure felicity   350
That I defy whatever sort of dream!"
   And day being come, he flew down from the beam,
And with him his hens fluttered, one and all;
And with a "cluck, cluck" he began to call
His wives to where a kernel had been tossed.
He was a prince, his fears entirely lost.
The morning had not passed the hour of prime
When he treaded Partlet for the twentieth time.
Grim as a lion he strolled to and fro,
And strutted only on his either toe.   360
He would not deign to set foot on the ground.
"Cluck, cluck," he said, whenever he had found
A kernel, and his wives came running all.
Thus royal as a monarch in his hall
I leave to his delights this Chanticleer,
And presently the sequel you shall hear.
   After the month in which the world began,[6]
The month of March, when God created man,

---

[5] Literally, "In the beginning, woman is the ruin of man."
[6] According to tradition, the creation occurred at the beginning of spring.

Had passed, and when the season had run through
Since March began just thirty days and two, 370
It happened that Chanticleer, in all his pride,
While his seven hens were walking by his side,
Lifted his eyes, beholding the bright sun,
Which in the sign of Taurus had then run
Twenty and one degrees and somewhat more,
And knew by instinct, not by learned lore,
It was the hour of prime. He raised his head
And crowed with lordly voice. "The sun," he said,
"Forty and one degrees and more in height
Has climbed the sky. Partlet, my world's delight, 380
Hear all these birds, how happily they sing,
And see the pretty flowers, how they spring.
With solace and with joy my spirits dance!"
But suddenly he met a sore mischance,
For in the end joys ever turn to woes.
Quickly the joys of earth are gone, God knows,
And could a rhetorician's art indite it,
He would be on solid ground if he should write it,
In a chronicle, as true notoriously!
Now every wise man, listen well to me. 390
This story is as true, I undertake,
As the very book of Lancelot of the Lake
On which the women set so great a store.
Now to my matter I will turn once more.
  A sly iniquitous fox, with black-tipped ears,
Who had lived in the neighboring wood for some three years,
His fated fancy swollen to a height,
Had broken through the hedges that same night
Into the yard where in his pride sublime
Chanticleer with his seven wives passed the time. 400
Quietly in a bed of herbs he lay
Till it was past the middle of the day,
Waiting his hour on Chanticleer to fall
As gladly do these murderers, one and all,
Who lie in wait, concealed, to murder men.
O murderer, lurking traitorous in your den!
O new Iscariot, second Ganelon,
False hypocrite, Greek Sinon,[7] who brought on
The utter woe of Troy and all her sorrow!
O Chanticleer, accursed be that morrow 410
When to the yard you flew down from the beams!
That day, as you were well warned in your dreams,
Would threaten you with dire catastrophe.
But that which God foresees must come to be,

---

[7] Judas Iscariot betrayed Jesus; Ganelon is the traitor in *The Song of Roland;* Sinon, by means of the Trojan horse, betrayed the Trojans to the besieging Greeks (see Virgil's *Aeneid,* Book II).

As there are certain scholars who aver.
Bear witness, any true philosopher,
That in the schools there has been great altercation
Upon this question, and much disputation
By a hundred thousand scholars, man for man.
I cannot sift it down to the pure bran   420
As can the sacred Doctor, Augustine,
Or Boëthius, or Bishop Bradwardine,[8]
Whether God's high foreknowledge so enchains me
I needs must do a thing as it constrains me—
"Needs must"—that is, by plain necessity;
Or whether a free choice is granted me
To do it or not do it, either one,
Though God must know all things before they are done;
Or whether his foresight nowise can constrain
Except contingently, as some explain;   430
I will not labor such a high concern.
My tale is of a cock, as you shall learn,
Who took his wife's advice, to his own sorrow,
And walked out in the yard that fatal morrow.
Women have many times, as wise men hold,
Offered advice that left men in the cold.
A woman's counsel brought us first to woe
And out of Paradise made Adam go
Where he lived a merry life and one of ease.
But since I don't know whom I may displease   440
By giving women's words an ill report,
Pass over it; I only spoke in sport.
There are books about it you can read or skim in,
And you'll discover what they say of women.
I'm telling you the cock's words, and not mine.
Harm in no woman at all can I divine.
    Merrily bathing where the sand was dry
Lay Partlet, with her sisters all near by,
And Chanticleer, as regal as could be,
Sang merrily as the mermaid in the sea;   450
For the *Physiologus*[9] itself declares
That they know how to sing the merriest airs.
And so it happened that as he fixed his eye
Among the herbs upon a butterfly,
He caught sight of this fox who crouched there low.
He felt no impulse then to strut or crow,
But cried "cucock!" and gave a fearful start
Like a man who has been frightened to the heart.

---

[8] All three had discussed the notoriously difficult matter of reconciling God's foreknowledge with man's free will. Augustine (353–430), author of the *Confessions,* was one of the greatest Christian theologians; Boëthius (about 475–524) was a Roman who wrote *The Consolation of Philosophy,* one of the most influential works in the Middle Ages; Bradwardine was a theologian of Chaucer's own century.

[9] A book about animals, including legendary ones.

For instinctively, if he should chance to see
His opposite, a beast desires to flee,   460
Even the first time that it meets his eye.
    This Chanticleer, no sooner did he spy
The fox than promptly enough he would have fled.
But "Where are you going, kind sir?" the fox said.
"Are you afraid of me, who am your friend?
Truly, I'd be a devil from end to end
If I meant you any harm or villainy.
I have not come to invade your privacy.
In truth, the only reason that could bring
This visit of mine was just to hear you sing.   470
Beyond a doubt, you have as fine a voice
As any angel who makes heaven rejoice.
Also you have more feeling in your note
Than Boëthius,[10] or any tuneful throat.
Milord your father once—and may God bless
His soul—your noble mother too, no less,
Have been inside my house, to my great ease.
And verily, sir, I should be glad to please
You also. But for singing, I declare,
As I enjoy my eyes, that precious pair,   480
Save you, I never heard a man so sing
As your father did when night was on the wing.
Straight from the heart, in truth, came all his song,
And to make his voice more resonant and strong
He would strain until he shut his either eye,
So loud and lordly would he make his cry,
And stand up on his tiptoes therewithal
And stretch his neck till it grew long and small.
He had such excellent discretion, too,
That whether his singing, all the region through,   490
Or his wisdom, there was no one to surpass.
I read in that old book, *Don Burnel the Ass*,[11]
Among his verses once about a cock
Hit on the leg by a priest who threw a rock
When he was young and foolish; and for this
He caused the priest to lose his benefice.
But no comparison, in all truth, lies
Between your father, so prudent and so wise,
And this other cock, for all his subtlety.
Sing, sir! Show me, for holy charity,   500
Can you imitate your father, that wise man?"
    Blind to all treachery, Chanticleer began
To beat his wings, like one who cannot see
The traitor, ravished by his flattery.

---

[10] Boëthius, along with his other works, wrote a treatise on music.
[11] A twelfth-century poem by Nigel Wireker. The cock took his revenge by crowing late, thus causing the priest to oversleep on the day when he was to have been ordained.

Alas, you lords, about your court there slips
Many a flatterer with deceiving lips
Who can please you more abundantly, I fear,
Than he who speaks the plain truth to your ear.
Read in Ecclesiastes,[12] you will see
What flatterers are. Lords, heed their treachery!   510
    This Chanticleer stood tiptoe at full height.
He stretched his neck, he shut his eyelids tight,
And he began to crow a lordly note.
The fox, Don Russell, seized him by the throat
At once, and on his back bore Chanticleer
Off toward his den that in the grove stood near,
For no one yet had threatened to pursue.
    O destiny, that no man may eschew!
Alas, that he left his safe perch on the beams!
Alas, that Partlet took no stock in dreams!   520
And on a Friday happened this mischance!
    Venus, whose pleasures make the whole world dance,
Since Chanticleer was ever your true servant,
And of your rites will all his power observant
For pleasure rather than to multiply,
Would you on Friday[13] suffer him to die?
    Geoffrey,[14] dear master of the poet's art,
Who when your Richard perished by a dart
Made for your king an elegy so burning,
Why have I not your eloquence and learning   530
To chide, as you did, with a heart so filled,
Fridays? For on a Friday he was killed.
Then should I show you how I could complain
For Chanticleer in all his fright and pain!
    In truth, no lamentation ever rose,
No shriek of ladies when before its foes
Ilium fell, and Pyrrhus with drawn blade
Had seized King Priam by the beard and made
An end of him—the *Aeneid* tells the tale—[15]
Such as the hens made with their piteous wail   540
In their enclosure, seeing the dread sight
Of Chanticleer. But at the shrillest height
Shrieked Partlet. She shrieked louder than the wife
Of Hasdrubal, when her husband lost his life
And the Romans burned down Carthage; for her state

[12] The intended reference is apparently not to Ecclesiastes but to Ecclesiasticus (a book of the Roman Catholic Bible), 12:10ff, 27:26.

[13] Friday is Venus's day. (Compare the French for *Friday, vendredi.*)

[14] Geoffrey of Vinsauf, a twelfth-century author of a book on poetry. It includes as an example a poem, written in an elaborate style, about the death of King Richard the Lion-Hearted (Richard I).

[15] See Book II of Virgil's *Aeneid.* When the Greeks took Troy (Ilium), Pyrrhus, the son of Achilles, killed Priam, the Trojan king. The Nun's Priest goes on to compare the hens' lament over Chanticleer to the wailing when the Romans destroyed Carthage (second century B.C.) and when the emperor Nero supposedly burned Rome (A.D. 64).

Of torment and of frenzy was so great
She willfully chose the fire for her part,
Leaped in, and burned herself with steadfast heart.
    Unhappy hens, you shrieked as when for pity,
While the tyrant Nero put to flames the city   550
Of Rome, rang out the shriek of senators' wives
Because their husbands had all lost their lives;
This Nero put to death these innocent men.
But I will come back to my tale again.
    Now this good widow and her two daughters heard
These woeful hens shriek when the crime occurred,
And sprang outdoors as quickly as they could
And saw the fox, who was making for the wood
Bearing this Chanticleer across his back.
"Help, help!" they cried. They cried, "Alas! Alack!   560
The fox, the fox!" and after him they ran,
And armed with clubs came running many a man.
Ran Coll the dog, and led a yelping band;
Ran Malkyn, with a distaff[16] in her hand;
Ran cow and calf, and even the very hogs,
By the yelping and the barking of the dogs
And men's and women's shouts so terrified
They ran till it seemed their hearts would burst inside;
They squealed like fiends in the pit, with none to still them.
The ducks quacked as if men were going to kill them.   570
The geese for very fear flew over the trees.
Out of the beehive came the swarm of bees.
Ah! Bless my soul, the noise, by all that's true,
So hideous was that Jack Straw's[17] retinue
Made never a hubbub that was half so shrill
Over a Fleming they were going to kill
As the clamor made that day over the fox.
They brought brass trumpets, and trumpets made of box,
Of horn, of bone, on which they blew and squeaked,
And those who were not blowing whooped and shrieked.   580
It seemed as if the very heavens would fall!
    Now hear me, you good people, one and all!
Fortune, I say, will suddenly override
Her enemy in his very hope and pride!
This cock, as on the fox's back he lay,
Plucked up his courage to speak to him and say,
"God be my help, sir, but I'd tell them all,
That is, if I were you, 'Plague on you fall!
Go back, proud fools! Now that I've reached the wood,
I'll eat the cock at once, for all the good   590
Your noise can do. Here Chanticleer shall stay.'"
    "Fine!" said the fox. "I'll do just what you say."

---

[16] A long staff; part of a spinning wheel.
[17] In 1381, Jack Straw led into London a mob intent on killing foreigners.

But the cock, as he was speaking, suddenly
Out of his jaws lurched expeditiously,
And flew at once high up into a tree.
And when the fox saw that the cock was free,
"Alas," he said, "alas, O Chanticleer!
Inasmuch as I have given you cause for fear
By seizing you and bearing you away,
I have done you wrong, I am prepared to say.   600
But, sir, I did it with no ill intent.
Come down, and I shall tell you what I meant.
So help me God, it's truth I'll offer you!"
    "No, no," said he. "We're both fools, through and through.
But curse my blood and bones for the chief dunce
If you deceive me oftener than once!
You shall never again by flattery persuade me
To sing and wink my eyes, by him that made me.
For he that willfully winks when he should see,
God never bless him with prosperity!"   610
    "Ah," said the fox, "with mischief may God greet
The man ungoverned, rash, and indiscreet
Who babbles when to hold his tongue were needful!"
    Such is it to be reckless and unheedful
And trust in flattery. But you who hold
That this is a mere trifle I have told,
Concerning only a fox, or a cock and hen,
Think twice, and take the moral, my good men!
For truly, of whatever is written, all
Is written for our doctrine, says St. Paul.   620
Then take the fruit, and let the chaff lie still.
Now, gracious God, if it should be your will,
As my Lord teaches, make us all good men
And bring us to your holy bliss! Amen.

Christine de Pizan
(1364–1430?)

"Who was it painted the lion, tell me who?" asks the Wife of Bath in Chaucer's
Canterbury Tales. *The Wife is thinking of an Aesopian fable in which a lion looks
at a picture of a man killing a lion and remarks that if lions painted pictures, the
roles might be reversed. Her point is that if books were written by women instead of
elderly celibate clerics, the monotonous misogyny of medieval literature (of the sort
that Jenkin, her fifth husband, infuriatingly read aloud) might be reversed. "By
God," she goes on, "if women had only written stories / Like wits and scholars in their*

oratories, / They would have pinned on men more wickedness / Than the whole breed of Adam can redress."

It is a sentiment that Christine de Pizan, Chaucer's slightly younger contemporary, would have heartily endorsed. Only a few years after Chaucer wrote the Wife of Bath's Prologue, Christine was stung by her reading of a book by a dreary woman-hater named Mathéolus into breaking the long silence of medieval women and undertaking a sweeping universal history of women, defending her sex against the calumnies of the patriarchal tradition. The Book of the City of Ladies *is an extraordinary production. It is both quintessentially of its age—in its allegorizing, cataloguing, and universalizing tendencies—and startlingly fresh in its tough, realistic treatment of feminist issues. After five centuries, it still has much to teach us.*

Christine de Pizan was born in Venice. Both parents were from prominent Italian families. Her father was a noted physician and astrologer named Tommaso di Benvenuto da Pizzano (astrology was a respectable science in Christine's day, not very clearly differentiated from astronomy); her mother was a member of a well-known family named Mondino. When Christine was four, her family moved to Paris, where her father had accepted a position as court astrologer to King Charles V. Christine spent the rest of her life in France and thought of herself as a French writer.

Christine received some education from her father, against the wishes of her mother, apparently. When she was fifteen, she was married to a young man of her father's choosing, as was the custom. Her husband, about twenty-five years old, was Etienne de Castel, a young courtier who became secretary and notary to the king. The match was a happy one and produced three children. In 1390, however, after ten years of marriage, Castel suddenly died of a contagious disease. Pizzano had died three years before, after losing much of his fortune and suffering a long illness. The twenty-five-year-old widow was thus left with three children, a mother, and a niece to support. What money was left from her father's and husband's estates was tied up in litigation; it took fourteen years and large sums of money to settle her lawsuits.

Christine apparently resolved to earn her living by her pen. She launched into an intensive program of self-education, "like a child," she later wrote, "that one puts at first to studying his ABCs." She read ancient and then modern history, science, and finally poetry. During this period, in the early 1390s, she may also have worked in the book trade, as a manuscript copyist, according to a recent biographer. Throughout her life, she took an active interest in the physical format of her books, commissioning and overseeing their reproduction and illustration.

She had her first success as a writer around 1393, and by the end of the decade she was earning a dependable income from her work. She is thus often said to be the "first professional writer in Europe." Her writing falls into three periods. Between 1393 and 1400, she wrote mostly lyric poetry in the highly conventionalized forms popular at the time; these were eventually organized into three cycles of ballades. *By 1400, she had turned her attention to longer, narrative poems. Several of these were fashionable "love debates," which described various lovers' dilemmas that were to be presented to a "court of love" for settlement. Others were more serious.* The Long Road of Learning *(1403) is a utopian dream-vision in which Christine visits the Court of Reason to learn who should rule a better world.* The Mutation of Fortune *(also 1403) traces the role of Fortune through universal history. Also around 1400, Christine began to turn more frequently to prose; the output of her last period consists almost exclusively of long prose works. These include a commissioned biogra-*

phy of King Charles V (1404), The Book of the City of Ladies *(1405),* The Book of the Three Virtues *(1405), and a strange, semiautobiographical dream-vision called* Christine's Vision *(1405).*

France was in turmoil during Christine's later years. Charles VI was mentally unstable, and several powerful nobles competed for control of the kingdom. War with England also threatened. Faced with such dangers, Christine entered a convent, apparently around 1418, and turned her attention to government and advice to princes: The Book of the Body Politic *(1406–07),* Feats of Arms and of Chivalry *(1410), and* The Book of Peace *(1414). For her last work, she returned to poetry in* The Tale of Joan of Arc *to celebrate Joan's victory at Orléans in 1429. Joan's miraculous career seemed to vindicate not only Christine's faith in France but her faith in heroic women as well. Apparently, Christine died before Joan was captured by the English and burned at the stake in 1431.*

Christine de Pizan's masterpiece, among her voluminous writings, is The Book of the City of Ladies. *It perhaps had its origins in an interesting literary controversy she engaged in between 1399 and 1403 called the "Debate of* The Romance of the Rose." The Romance of the Rose *was an immensely long, immensely popular poem begun by Guillaume de Lorris around 1230 and completed by Jean de Meun in 1275–80. It tells the story of the attempt of Amant ("lover") to pick a beautiful Rose, guarded by various allegorical figures: Danger, Jealousy, and the like. Guillaume de Lorris' section is innocuous enough, but Jean de Meun's continuation is full of attacks on women. Christine had objected to Jean de Meun's slanders in* Cupid's Letter *(1399), but the debate really started in 1401, when one of the king's secretaries named Jean de Montreuil wrote an open letter to Christine praising Jean de Meun and rejecting her criticism. Christine replied, and before the debate ended more than twenty letters had been exchanged and several other people had entered the debate, including Jean Gerson, the chancellor of the University of Paris (on Christine's side) and Gontier Gol, another of the king's secretaries (on Jean de Montreuil's). The terms of the controversy were fairly complex, involving the literary merits of Jean de Meun's poem and its effect on public morality as well as its treatment of women, but it was the issue of misogyny that most interested Christine and that was to concern her two years later in* The Book of the City of Ladies.

The Book of the City of Ladies is cast in one of the Middle Ages' favorite forms: the dream-vision. After a short prologue, in which Christine broods about an attack on women she has just read, a strange light appears in her room. Shuddering, "as if wakened from sleep," she lifts her head to see three crowned ladies standing before her: Reason, Rectitude, and Justice. The rest of the book is devoted to the building of the City of Ladies under the instruction of these three ladies. Or perhaps the book is an anti-dream-vision. Christine says that she felt "as if wakened from sleep," not that she was wakened. (In dream-visions, falling asleep is ordinarily described as "waking" into a dream.) She may thus be distinguishing her work from The Romance of the Rose, *in which Amant does wake into his dream of the Rose, and suggesting that her book is truer than the* Romance. *The basic metaphor of the book—the building of a verbal, conceptual city—derives from St. Augustine's* City of God. *The City of Ladies is not meant to rival the City of God, of course, but the echo of Augustine's title and the personifications of virtue that preside over the building of the city are probably meant to place the whole enterprise within a Christian context. Christine echoes, too, the most famous dream-vision of the Middle Ages, the* Divine Comedy, *which she was among the first to introduce into France. The visionary experience, like Dante's, is presented as a response to confusion and dis-*

couragement, and the three feminine guides may owe something to the three ladies who watch over Dante's pilgrimage.

The most immediate source for The Book of the City of Ladies, *however, is* Boccaccio's Concerning Famous Women, *a compendium of sketches of famous women, both good and bad, starting with Eve and ending with Boccaccio's contemporary, Johanna of Naples, Queen of Sicily, but principally drawn from mythology and antiquity. Christine draws about three-fourths of her examples from Boccaccio. Her treatment of them, however, is completely different. For one thing, she treats only good women; for another, she goes out of her way to present pagan and Christian, ancient and contemporary women together, whereas Boccaccio kept them sharply separate.*

The third part of The Book of the City of Ladies, *presided over by Justice, is given over to a series of lives of female saints, climaxed by the life of Christine's own name-saint. It is given here as an example of a very widespread and popular medieval literary form.*

Christine, it hardly need be pointed out, is not a typical feminist in the modern sense. She never questions the medieval hierarchical social order; she merely wants women to hold an honored place within it. She also, as the climactic inclusion of the life of St. Christine demonstrates, remains firmly within a religious frame of reference. But she clearly is a feminist, if a medieval one. In her work, and preeminently in The Book of the City of Ladies, *we hear a voice otherwise largely silenced in medieval literature: the voice of a woman.*

FURTHER READING (*prepared by J. H.*): Much the fullest and best modern treatment in English of Christine de Pizan is Charity Cannon Willard's critical biography, *Christine de Pizan: Her Life and Works,* 1984. A more popularly written biography is Enid McLeod, *The Order of the Rose: The Life and Ideas of Christine de Pizan,* 1976. An excellent short critical overview is Earl Jeffrey Richards' introduction to his translation of *The Book of the City of Ladies,* 1982. A thoughtful treatment of Christine's feminism is F. Douglas Kelly, "Reflections on the Role of Christine de Pisan as a Feminist Writer," *Sub-Stances* 2 (1972), 63–71. A good collection of essays on the same topic is *Ideals for Women in the Works of Christine de Pizan,* ed. Diane Bornstein, 1981. Bibliographies include Edith Yenal, *Christine de Pisan: A Bibliography of Writings by Her and About Her,* 1982; and Angus J. Kennedy, *Christine de Pizan: A Bibliographical Guide,* 1984. For a survey of fifteen women authors of the Middle Ages, including excerpts from their works and succinct discussions of them, see *Medieval Women Writers,* ed. with Introduction by Katharina M. Wilson, 1984; the section on Christine de Pizan is by Charity Cannon Willard.

from *THE BOOK OF THE CITY OF LADIES*

Translated by Earl Jeffrey Richards

HERE BEGINS THE BOOK OF THE CITY OF LADIES, WHOSE FIRST CHAPTER TELLS WHY AND FOR WHAT PURPOSE THIS BOOK WAS WRITTEN.

One day as I was sitting alone in my study surrounded by books on all kinds of subjects, devoting myself to literary studies, my usual habit, my mind dwelt at length on the weighty opinions of various authors whom I had studied for a long time. I looked up from my book, having decided to leave such subtle questions in peace and to relax by reading some light poetry. With this in mind, I searched for some small book. By chance a strange volume came into my hands, not one of my own, but one which had been given to me along with some others. When I held it open and saw from its title page that it was by Mathéolus,[1] I smiled, for though I had never seen it before, I had often heard that like other books it discussed respect for women. I thought I would browse through it to amuse myself. I had not been reading for very long when my good mother called me to refresh myself with some supper, for it was evening. Intending to look at it the next day, I put it down. The next morning, again seated in my study as was my habit, I remembered wanting to examine this book by Mathéolus. I started to read it and went on for a little while. Because the subject seemed to me not very pleasant for people who do not enjoy lies, and of no use in developing virtue or manners, given its lack of integrity in diction and theme, and after browsing here and there and reading the end, I put it down in order to turn my attention to more elevated and useful study. But just the sight of this book, even though it was of no authority, made me wonder how it happened that so many different men—and learned men among them—have been and are so inclined to express both in speaking and in their treatises and writings so many wicked insults about women and their behavior. Not only one or two and not even just this Mathéolus (for this book had a bad name anyway and was intended as a satire) but, more generally, judging from the treatises of all philosophers and poets and from all the orators—it would take too long to mention their names—it seems that they all speak from one and the same mouth. They all concur in one conclusion: that the behavior of women is inclined to and full of every vice. Thinking deeply about these matters, I began to examine my character and conduct as a natural woman[2] and, similarly, I considered other women whose company I frequently kept, princesses, great ladies, women of the middle and lower classes, who had graciously told me of their most private and intimate thoughts, hoping that I could judge impartially and in good conscience whether the testimony of so many notable men could be true. To the best of my knowledge, no matter how long I confronted or dissected the problem, I could not see or realize how their claims could be true when compared to the natural behavior and character of women. Yet I still argued vehemently against women, saying that it would be impossible that so many famous men—such solemn scholars, possessed of such deep and great understanding, so clear-sighted in all things, as it seemed—could have spoken falsely on so many occasions that I could hardly find a book on morals where, even before I had read it in its entirety, I did not find several chapters or certain sections attacking women, no matter who the author was. This reason alone, in short, made me conclude that, although my intellect did not perceive my own great faults and, likewise, those of other

[1] The book is *The Book of the Lamentations of Mathéolus,* a long verse diatribe against women, written in Latin about 1300 and translated into French during Christine's lifetime.
[2] The phrase "natural woman" recalls *The Romance of the Rose,* in which the allegorical figure Nature argues that women are "naturally" unchaste.

women because of its simpleness and ignorance, it was however truly fitting that such was the case. And so I relied more on the judgment of others than on what I myself felt and knew. I was so transfixed in this line of thinking for such a long time that it seemed as if I were in a stupor. Like a gushing fountain, a series of authorities, whom I recalled one after another, came to mind, along with their opinions on this topic. And I finally decided that God formed a vile creature when He made woman, and I wondered how such a worthy artisan could have deigned to make such an abominable work which, from what they say, is the vessel as well as the refuge and abode of every evil and vice. As I was thinking this, a great unhappiness and sadness welled up in my heart, for I detested myself and the entire feminine sex, as though we were monstrosities in nature. And in my lament I spoke these words:

"Oh, God, how can this be? For unless I stray from my faith, I must never doubt that Your infinite wisdom and most perfect goodness ever created anything which was not good. Did You yourself not create woman in a very special way and since that time did You not give her all those inclinations which it pleased You for her to have? And how could it be that You could go wrong in anything? Yet look at all these accusations which have been judged, decided, and concluded against women. I do not know how to understand this repugnance. If it is so, fair Lord God, that in fact so many abominations abound in the female sex, for You Yourself say that the testimony of two or three witnesses lends credence, why shall I not doubt that this is true? Alas, God, why did You not let me be born in the world as a man, so that all my inclinations would be to serve You better, and so that I would not stray in anything and would be as perfect as a man is said to be? But since Your kindness has not been extended to me, then forgive my negligence in Your service, most fair Lord God, and may it not displease You, for the servant who receives fewer gifts from his lord is less obliged in his service." I spoke these words to God in my lament and a great deal more for a very long time in sad reflection, and in my folly I considered myself most unfortunate because God had made me inhabit a female body in this world.

Here Christine Describes How Three Ladies Appeared to Her and How the One Who Was in Front Spoke First and Comforted Her in Her Pain

So occupied with these painful thoughts, my head bowed in shame, my eyes filled with tears, leaning on the pommel of my chair's armrest, I suddenly saw a ray of light fall on my lap, as though it were the sun. I shuddered then, as if wakened from sleep, for I was sitting in a shadow where the sun could not have shone at that hour. And as I lifted my head to see where this light was coming from, I saw three crowned ladies standing before me, and the splendor of their bright faces shone on me and throughout the entire room. Now no one would ask whether I was surprised, for my doors were shut and they had still entered. Fearing that some phantom had come to tempt me and filled with great fright, I made the Sign of the Cross on my forehead.

Then she who was the first of the three smiled and began to speak,

"Dear daughter, do not be afraid, for we have not come here to harm or trouble you but to console you, for we have taken pity on your distress, and we have come to bring you out of the ignorance which so blinds your own intellect that you shun what you know for a certainty and believe what you do not know or see or recognize except by virtue of many strange opinions. You resemble the fool in the prank who was dressed in women's clothes while he slept; because those who were making fun of him repeatedly told him he was a woman, he believed their false testimony more readily than the certainty of his own identity. Fair daughter, have you lost all sense? Have you forgotten that when fine gold is tested in the furnace, it does not change or vary in strength but becomes purer the more it is hammered and handled in different ways? Do you not know that the best things are the most debated and the most discussed? If you wish to consider the question of the highest form of reality, which consists in ideas or celestial substances, consider whether the greatest philosophers who have lived and whom you support against your own sex have ever resolved whether ideas are false and contrary to the truth. Notice how these same philosophers contradict and criticize one another, just as you have seen in the *Metaphysics* where Aristotle takes their opinions to task and speaks similarly of Plato and other philosophers. And note, moreover, how even Saint Augustine and the Doctors of the Church have criticized Aristotle in certain passages, although he is known as the prince of philosophers in whom both natural and moral philosophy attained their highest level. It also seems that you think that all the words of the philosophers are articles of faith, that they could never be wrong. As far as the poets of whom you speak are concerned, do you not know that they spoke on many subjects in a fictional way and that often they mean the contrary of what their words openly say? One can interpret them according to the grammatical figure of *antiphrasis,* which means, as you know, that if you call something bad, in fact, it is good, and also vice versa. Thus I advise you to profit from their works and to interpret them in the manner in which they are intended in those passages where they attack women. Perhaps this man, who called himself Mathéolus in his own book, intended it in such a way, for there are many things which, if taken literally, would be pure heresy. As for the attack against the estate of marriage— which is a holy estate, worthy and ordained by God—made not only by Mathéolus but also by others and even by the *Romance of the Rose* where greater credibility is averred because of the authority of its author, it is evident and proven by experience that the contrary of the evil which they posit and claim to be found in this estate through the obligation and fault of women is true. For where has the husband ever been found who would allow his wife to have authority to abuse and insult him as a matter of course, as these authorities maintain? I believe that, regardless of what you might have read, you will never see such a husband with your own eyes, so badly colored are these lies. Thus, in conclusion, I tell you, dear friend, that simplemindedness has prompted you to hold such an opinion. Come back to yourself, recover your senses, and do not trouble yourself anymore over such absurdities. For you know that any evil spoken of women so generally only hurts those who say it, not women themselves."

Here Christine Tells How the Lady Who Had Said This Showed Her Who She Was and What Her Character and Function Were and Told Her How She Would Construct a City with the Help of These Same Three Ladies.

The famous lady spoke these words to me, in whose presence I do not know which one of my senses was more overwhelmed: my hearing from having listened to such worthy words or my sight from having seen her radiant beauty, her attire, her reverent comportment, and her most honored countenance. The same was true of the others, so that I did not know which one to look at, for the three ladies resembled each other so much that they could be told apart only with difficulty, except for the last one, for although she was of no less authority than the others, she had so fierce a visage that whoever, no matter how daring, looked in her eyes would be afraid to commit a crime, for it seemed that she threatened criminals unceasingly. Having stood up out of respect, I looked at them without saying a word, like someone too overwhelmed to utter a syllable. Reflecting on who these beings could be, I felt much admiration in my heart and, if I could have dared, I would have immediately asked their names and identities and what was the meaning of the different scepters which each one carried in her right hand, which were of fabulous richness, and why they had come here. But since I considered myself unworthy to address these questions to such high ladies as they appeared to me, I did not dare to, but continued to keep my gaze fixed on them, half-afraid and half-reassured by the words which I had heard, which had made me reject my first impression. But the most wise lady who had spoken to me and who knew in her mind what I was thinking, as one who has insight into everything, addressed my reflections, saying:

"Dear daughter, know that God's providence, which leaves nothing void or empty, has ordained that we, though celestial beings, remain and circulate among the people of the world here below, in order to bring order and maintain in balance those institutions we created according to the will of God in the fulfillment of various offices, that God whose daughters we three all are and from whom we were born. Thus it is my duty to straighten out men and women when they go astray and to put them back on the right path. And when they stray, if they have enough understanding to see me, I come to them quietly in spirit and preach to them, showing them their error and how they have failed, I assign them the causes, and then I teach them what to do and what to avoid. Since I serve to demonstrate clearly and to show both in thought and deed to each man and woman his or her own special qualities and faults, you see me holding this shiny mirror which I carry in my right hand in place of a scepter. I would thus have you know truly that no one can look into this mirror, no matter what kind of creature, without achieving clear self-knowledge. My mirror has such great dignity that not without reason is it surrounded by rich and precious gems, so that you see, thanks to this mirror, the essences, qualities, proportions, and measures of all things are known, nor can anything be done well without it. And because, similarly, you wish to know what are the offices of my other sisters whom you see here, each will reply in her own person about her name and character, and this way our testimony will be all the more certain to you. But now I myself will declare the reason for our coming. I must assure you, as we do nothing without good cause, that our appearance here is not at all in vain. For, although we are not common to many places and our knowledge does not come to all people, nevertheless you, for your great love of investigating the truth through long and continual study, for which you come here, solitary and separated from the world, you have deserved and deserve, our devoted friend, to be visited and consoled by us in your agitation and sadness, so that you might also see clearly, in the midst of the darkness of your thoughts, those things which taint and trouble your heart.

"There is another greater and even more special reason for our coming which you will learn from our speeches: in fact we have come to vanquish from the world the same error into which you had fallen, so that from now on, ladies and all valiant women may have a refuge and defense against the various assailants, those ladies who have been abandoned for so long, exposed like a field without a surrounding hedge, without finding a champion to afford them an adequate defense, notwithstanding those noble men who are required by order of law to protect them, who by negligence and apathy have allowed them to be mistreated. It is no wonder then that their jealous enemies, those outrageous villains who have assailed them with various weapons, have been victorious in a war in which women have had no defense. Where is there a city so strong which could not be taken immediately if no resistance were forthcoming, or the law case, no matter how unjust, which was not won through the obstinance of someone pleading without opposition? And the simple, noble ladies, following the example of suffering which God commands, have cheerfully suffered the great attacks which, both in the spoken and the written word, have been wrongfully and sinfully perpetrated against women by men who all the while appealed to God for the right to do so. Now it is time for their just cause to be taken from Pharaoh's hands, and for this reason, we three ladies whom you see here, moved by pity, have come to you to announce a particular edifice built like a city wall, strongly constructed and well founded, which has been predestined and established by our aid and counsel for you to build, where no one will reside except all ladies of fame and women worthy of praise, for the walls of the city will be closed to those women who lack virtue."

Here the Lady Explains to Christine the City Which She Has Been Commissioned to Build and How She Was Charged to Help Christine Build the Wall and Enclosure, and Then Gives Her Name.

"Thus, fair daughter, the prerogative among women has been bestowed on you to establish and build the City of Ladies. For the foundation and completion of this City you will draw fresh waters from us as from clear fountains, and we will bring you sufficient building stone, stronger and more durable than any marble with cement could be. Thus your City will be extremely beautiful, without equal, and of perpetual duration in the world.

"Have you not read that King Tros founded the great city of Troy with the aid of Apollo, Minerva, and Neptune, whom the people of that time considered gods, and also how Cadmus founded the city of Thebes with the admonition of the gods?[3] And yet over time these cities fell and have fallen into ruin. But I prophesy to you, as a true sybil, that this City, which you will found with our help, will never be destroyed, nor will it ever fall, but will remain prosperous forever, regardless of all its jealous enemies. Although it will be stormed by numerous assaults, it will never be taken or conquered.

"Long ago the Amazon kingdom was begun through the arrangement and enterprise of several ladies of great courage who despised servitude, just as history books have testified.[4] For a long time afterward they maintained it under the rule of several queens, very noble ladies whom they elected themselves, who governed them well and maintained their dominion with great strength. Yet, although they were strong and powerful and had conquered a large part of the entire Orient in the course of their rule and terrified all the neighboring lands (even the Greeks, who were then the flower of all countries in the world, feared them), nevertheless, after a time, the power of this kingdom declined, so that as with all earthly kingdoms, nothing but its name has survived to the present. But the edifice erected by you in this City which you must construct will be far stronger, and for its founding I was commissioned, in the course of our common deliberation, to supply you with durable and pure mortar to lay the sturdy foundations and to raise the lofty walls all around, high and thick, with mighty towers and strong bastions, surrounded by moats with firm blockhouses, just as is fitting for a city with a strong and lasting defense. Following our plan, you will set the foundations deep to last all the longer, and then you will raise the walls so high that they will not fear anyone. Daughter, now that I have told you the reason for our coming and so that you will more certainly believe my words, I want you to learn my name, by whose sound alone you will be able to learn and know that, if you wish to follow my commands, you have in me an administrator so that you may do your work flawlessly. I am called Lady Reason; you see that you are in good hands. For the time being then, I will say no more."

HERE CHRISTINE TELLS HOW THE SECOND LADY
TOLD HER NAME AND WHAT SHE SERVED AS AND HOW
SHE WOULD AID HER IN BUILDING THE CITY OF LADIES

When the lady above finished her speech, before I could resume, the second lady began as follows: "I am called Rectitude and reside more in Heaven than on Earth, but as the radiance and splendor of God and messenger of His goodness, I often visit the just and exhort them to do what is right, to give to each person what is his according to his capacity, to say and uphold the truth, to defend the rights of the poor and the innocent, not to hurt anyone through usurpation, to uphold the reputation of those unjustly accused. I am the shield and defense of the servants of God. I resist

---

[3] In connecting her City of Ladies with Thebes and Troy, Christine is following a commonplace of her time, which held that France was the natural heir to the culture of Greece and Rome. Legendary history held that the French kings were descended from Franco, the son of Hector of Troy.

[4] In Greek legend, the Amazons were a tribe of women who spent their time in hunting and warfare. In the Trojan War, they were supposed to have fought against the Greeks.

the power and might of evil-doers. I give rest to workers and reward those who act well. Through me, God reveals to His friends His secrets; I am their advocate in Heaven. This shining ruler which you see me carry in my right hand instead of a scepter is the straight ruler which separates right from wrong and shows the difference between good and evil: who follows it does not go astray. It is the rod of peace which reconciles the good and where they find support and which beats and strikes down evil. What should I tell you about this? All things are measured by this ruler, for its powers are infinite. It will serve you to measure the edifice of the City which you have been commissioned to build, and you will need it for constructing the façade, for erecting the high temples, for measuring the palaces, houses, and all public buildings, the streets and squares, and all things proper to help populate the City. I have come as your assistant, and this will be my duty. Do not be uneasy about the breadth and long circuit of the walls, for with God's help and our assistance you will build fair and sturdy mansions and inns without leaving anything vague; and you will people the City with no trouble."

Here Christine Tells How the Third Lady Told Her Who She Was and Her Function and How She Would Help Build the High Roofs of the Towers and Palaces and Would Bring to Her the Queen, Accompanied by Noble Ladies.

Afterward, the third lady spoke and said, "My friend Christine, I am Justice, the most singular daughter of God, and my nature proceeds purely from His person. My residence is found in Heaven, on Earth, or in Hell: in Heaven, for the glory of the saints and blessed souls; on Earth, for the apportionment to each man of the good or evil which he has deserved; in Hell, for the punishment of the evil. I do not bend anywhere, for I have not friend nor enemy nor changeable will; pity cannot persuade me nor cruelty move me. My duty is only to judge, to decide, and to dispense according to each man's just deserts. I sustain all things in their condition, nothing could be stable without me. I am in God and God is in me, and we are as one and the same. Who follows me cannot fail, and my way is sure. I teach men and women of sound mind who want to believe in me to chastise, know, and correct themselves, and to do to others what they wish to have done to themselves, to distribute wealth without favor, to speak the truth, to flee and hate lies, to reject all viciousness. This vessel of fine gold which you see me hold in my right hand, made like a generous measure, God, my Father, gave me, and it serves to measure out to each his rightful portion. It carries the sign of the fleur-de-lis of the Trinity,[5] and in all portions it measures true, nor can any man complain about my measure. Yet the men of the Earth have other measures which they claim depend upon and derive from mine, but they are mistaken. Often they measure in my shadow, and their measure is not always true but sometimes too much for some and too little for others. I could give a rather long account of the duties of my office, but,

---

[5] The fleur-de-lis, or lily, the symbol of France, also symbolized the Trinity, because of its three petals in one flower.

put briefly, I have a special place among the Virtues, for they are all based on me. And of the three noble ladies whom you see here, we are as one and the same, we could not exist without one another; and what the first disposes, the second orders and initiates, and then I, the third, finish and terminate it. Thus I have been appointed by the will of us three ladies to perfect and complete your City, and my job will be to construct the high roofs of the towers and of the lofty mansions and inns which will all be made of fine shining gold. Then I will populate the City for you with worthy ladies and the mighty Queen whom I will bring to you. Hers will be the honor and prerogative among all other women, as well as among the most excellent women. And in this condition I will turn the City over to you, completed with your help, fortified and closed off with strong gates which I will search for in Heaven, and then I will place the keys in your hands."

HERE CHRISTINE TELLS HOW SHE
SPOKE TO THE THREE LADIES

When the speeches of all three ladies were over—to which I had listened intently and which had completely taken away the unhappiness which I had felt before their coming—I threw myself at their feet, not just on my knees but completely prostrate because of their great excellence. Kissing the earth around their feet, adoring them as goddesses of glory, I began my prayer to them:

"Oh ladies of supreme dignity, radiance of the heavens and light of the earth, fountains of Paradise and joy of the blessed, where did such humility come from to Your Highnesses that you have deigned to come down from your pontifical seats and shining thrones to visit the troubled and dark tabernacle of this simple and ignorant student? Who could give fitting thanks for such a boon? With the rain and dew of your sweet words, you have penetrated and moistened the dryness of my mind, so that it now feels ready to germinate and send forth new branches capable of bearing fruits of profitable virtue and sweet savor. How will such grace be bestowed on me that I will receive the boon, as you have said, to build and construct in the world from now on a new city? I am not Saint Thomas the Apostle, who through divine grace built a rich palace in Heaven for the king of India,[6] and my feeble sense does not know the craft, or the measures, or the study, or the science, or the practice of construction. And if, thanks to learning, these things were within my ken, where would I find enough physical strength in my weak feminine body to realize such an enormous task? But nevertheless, my most respected ladies, although the awesomeness of this news seems strange to me, I know well that nothing is impossible for God. Nor do I doubt that anything undertaken with your counsel and help will not be completed well. Thus, with all my strength, I praise God and you, my ladies, who have so honored me by assigning me such a noble commission, which I most happily accept. Behold your handmaiden ready to serve. Command and I will obey, and may it be unto me according to your words."

---

[6]Thomas, one of the Twelve Apostles, was traditionally an apostle to Asia.

HERE CHRISTINE TELLS HOW, UNDER REASON'S
COMMAND AND ASSISTANCE, SHE BEGAN TO EXCAVATE
THE EARTH AND LAY THE FOUNDATION.

Then Lady Reason responded and said, "Get up, daughter! Without waiting any longer, let us go to the Field of Letters. There the City of Ladies will be founded on a flat and fertile plain, where all fruits and freshwater rivers are found and where the earth abounds in all good things. Take the pick of your understanding and dig and clear out a great ditch wherever you see the marks of my ruler, and I will help you carry away the earth on my own shoulders."

I immediately stood up to obey her commands and, thanks to these three ladies, I felt stronger and lighter than before. She went ahead, and I followed behind, and after we had arrived at this field I began to excavate and dig, following her marks with the pick of cross-examination. . . .

CHRISTINE ASKS REASON WHETHER GOD HAS EVER
WISHED TO ENNOBLE THE MIND OF WOMAN WITH THE
LOFTINESS OF THE SCIENCES; AND REASON'S ANSWER.

[I, Christine, spoke: "I would like to know whether it has ever pleased God, who has bestowed so many favors] on women, to honor the feminine sex with the privilege of the virtue of high understanding and great learning, and whether women ever have a clever enough mind for this. I wish very much to know this because men maintain that the mind of women can learn only a little."

She answered, "My daughter, since I told you before, you know quite well that the opposite of their opinion is true, and to show you this even more clearly, I will give you proof through examples. I tell you again—and don't doubt the contrary—if it were customary to send daughters to school like sons, and if they were then taught the natural sciences, they would learn as thoroughly and understand the subtleties of all the arts and sciences as well as sons. And by chance there happen to be such women, for, as I touched on before, just as women have more delicate bodies than men, weaker and less able to perform many tasks, so do they have minds that are freer and sharper whenever they apply themselves."

"My lady, what are you saying? With all due respect, could you dwell longer on this point, please. Certainly men would never admit this answer is true, unless it is explained more plainly, for they believe that one normally sees that men know more than women do."

She answered, "Do you know why women know less?"

"Not unless you tell me, my lady."

"Without the slightest doubt, it is because they are not involved in many different things, but stay at home, where it is enough for them to run the household, and there is nothing which so instructs a reasonable creature as the exercise and experience of many different things."

"My lady, since they have minds skilled in conceptualizing and learning, just like men, why don't women learn more?"

She replied, "Because, my daughter, the public does not require them to get involved in the affairs which men are commissioned to execute, just as I told you before. It is enough for women to perform the usual duties to

which they are ordained. As for judging from experience, since one sees
that women usually know less than men, that therefore their capacity for
understanding is less, look at men who farm the flatlands or who live in the
mountains. You will find that in many countries they seem completely savage because they are so simpleminded. All the same, there is no doubt that
Nature provided them with the qualities of body and mind found in the
wisest and most learned men. All of this stems from a failure to learn,
though, just as I told you, among men and women, some possess better
minds than others. Let me tell you about women who have possessed great
learning and profound understanding and treat the question of the similarity of women's minds to men's."

SHE BEGINS TO DISCUSS SEVERAL LADIES WHO WERE
ENLIGHTENED WITH GREAT LEARNING, AND FIRST
SPEAKS ABOUT THE NOBLE MAIDEN CORNIFICIA.

"Cornificia, the noble maiden, was sent to school by her parents along
with her brother Cornificius when they were both children, thanks to deception and trickery.[7] This little girl so devoted herself to study and with
such marvelous intelligence that she began to savor the sweet taste of
knowledge acquired through study. Nor was it easy to take her away from
this joy to which she more and more applied herself, neglecting all other
feminine activities. She occupied herself with this for such a long period of
time that she became a consummate poet, and she was not only extremely
brilliant and expert in the learnedness and craft of poetry but also seemed
to have been nourished with the very milk and teaching of perfect philosophy, for she wanted to hear and know about every branch of learning,
which she then mastered so thoroughly that she surpassed her brother,
who was also a very great poet, and excelled in every field of learning.
Knowledge was not enough for her unless she could put her mind to work
and her pen to paper in the compilation of several very famous books.
These works, as well as her poems, were much prized during the time of
Saint Gregory and he himself mentions them. The Italian, Boccaccio, who
was a great poet,[8] discusses this fact in his work and at the same time praises
this woman: 'O most great honor for a woman who abandoned all feminine activities and applied and devoted her mind to the study of the greatest scholars!' As further proof of what I am telling you, Boccaccio also talks
about the attitude of women who despise themselves and their own minds,
and who, as though they were born in the mountains totally ignorant of
virtue and honor, turn disconsolate and say that they are good and useful
only for embracing men and carrying and feeding children. God has given
them such beautiful minds to apply themselves, if they want to, in any of
the fields where glorious and excellent men are active, which are neither
more nor less accessible to them as compared to men if they wished to study
them, and they can thereby acquire a lasting name, whose possession is

---

[7] Cornificia, a first-century B.C. Roman aristocrat, was the sister of Cornificius, a Roman
general. Both were poets.

[8] The book referred to is Boccaccio's *Concerning Famous Women* (1360–74), which was translated into French about 1401. It is Christine's principal source for *The Book of the City of Ladies*.

fitting for most excellent men. My dear daughter, you can see how this author Boccaccio testifies to what I have told you and how he praises and approves learning in women." . . .

Here She Speaks of Sappho, That Most Subtle Woman, Poet, and Philosopher.

"The wise Sappho,[9] who was from the city of Mytilene, was no less learned. . . . This Sappho had a beautiful body and face and was agreeable and pleasant in appearance, conduct, and speech. But the charm of her profound understanding surpassed all the other charms with which she was endowed, for she was expert and learned in several arts and sciences, and she was not only well-educated in the works and writings composed by others but also discovered many new things herself and wrote many books and poems. Concerning her, Boccaccio has offered these fair words couched in the sweetness of poetic language: 'Sappho, possessed of sharp wit and burning desire for constant study in the midst of bestial and ignorant men, frequented the heights of Mount Parnassus, that is, of perfect study. Thanks to her fortunate boldness and daring, she kept company with the Muses, that is, the arts and sciences, without being turned away. She entered the forest of laurel trees filled with May boughs, greenery, and different colored flowers, soft fragrances and various aromatic spices, where Grammar, Logic, noble Rhetoric, Geometry, and Arithmetic live and take their leisure. She went on her way until she came to the deep grotto of Apollo, god of learning, and found the brook and conduit of the fountain of Castalia, and took up the plectrum and quill of the harp and played sweet melodies, with the nymphs all the while leading the dance, that is, following the rules of harmony and musical accord.' From what Boccaccio says about her, it should be inferred that the profundity of both her understanding and of her learned books can only be known and understood by men of great perception and learning, according to the testimony of the ancients. Her writings and poems have survived to this day, most remarkably constructed and composed, and they serve as illumination and models of consummate poetic craft and composition to those who have come afterward. She invented different genres of lyric and poetry, short narratives, tearful laments and strange lamentations about love and other emotions, and these were so well made and so well ordered that they were named 'Sapphic' after her. Horace recounts, concerning her poems, that when Plato, the great philosopher who was Aristotle's teacher, died, a book of Sappho's poems was found under his pillow.

"In brief this lady was so outstanding in learning that in the city where she resided a statue of bronze in her image was dedicated in her name and erected in a prominent place so that she would be honored by all and be remembered forever. This lady was placed and counted among the greatest and most famous poets, and, according to Boccaccio, the honors of the

---

[9] Sappho was a Greek poet of the seventh to sixth centuries B.C. Christine's semilegendary account of her is taken from Boccaccio. Christine could not have known Sappho's works directly, since by the fourteenth century, Sappho's ten volumes of collected works had long since been destroyed by clerical censors. A few of the poems were reconstructed, from scraps of papyrus and quotations by other authors, in the nineteenth century.

diadems and crowns of kings and the miters of bishops are not any greater, nor are the crowns of laurel and victor's palm.

"I could tell you a great deal about women of great learning. Leontium was a Greek woman and also such a great philosopher that she dared, for impartial and serious reasons, to correct and attack the philosopher Theophrastus,[10] who was quite famous in her time." . . .

AGAINST THOSE MEN WHO CLAIM IT IS NOT GOOD FOR WOMEN TO BE EDUCATED.

Following these remarks, I, Christine, spoke [to Lady Rectitude], "My lady, I realize that women have accomplished many good things and that even if evil women have done evil, it seems to me, nevertheless, that the benefits accrued and still accruing because of good women—particularly the wise and literary ones and those educated in the natural sciences whom I mentioned above—outweigh the evil. Therefore, I am amazed by the opinion of some men who claim that they do not want their daughters, wives, or kinswomen to be educated because their mores would be ruined as a result."

She responded, "Here you can clearly see that not all opinions of men are based on reason and that these men are wrong. For it must not be presumed that mores necessarily grow worse from knowing the moral sciences, which teach the virtues, indeed, there is not the slightest doubt that moral education amends and ennobles them. How could anyone think or believe that whoever follows good teaching or doctrine is the worse for it? Such an opinion cannot be expressed or maintained. I do not mean that it would be good for a man or a woman to study the art of divination or those fields of learning which are forbidden—for the holy Church did not remove them from common use without good reason—but it should not be believed that women are the worse for knowing what is good.

"Quintus Hortensius,[11] a great rhetorician and consumately skilled orator in Rome, did not share this opinion. He had a daughter, named Hortensia, whom he greatly loved for the subtlety of her wit. He had her learn letters and study the science of rhetoric, which she mastered so thoroughly that she resembled her father Hortensius not only in wit and lively memory but also in her excellent delivery and order of speech—in fact, he surpassed her in nothing. As for the subject discussed above, concerning the good which comes about through women, the benefits realized by this woman and her learning were, among others, exceptionally remarkable. That is, during the time when Rome was governed by three men, this Hortensia began to support the cause of women and to undertake what no man dared to undertake. There was a question whether certain taxes should be levied on women and on their jewelry during a needy period in Rome. This woman's eloquence was so compelling that she was listened to, no less readily than her father would have been, and she won her case.

[10] Theophrastus (third century B.C.) was a Greek Peripatetic philosopher and pupil of Aristotle. Leontium is known only in connection with this anecdote.

[11] Roman orator (114–50 B.C.). A leader of the aristocratic party, he was defeated (70 B.C.) by Cicero in the trial of Verres. His daughter Hortensia was as well educated and well known as Christine says she was.

"Similarly, to speak of more recent times, without searching for examples in ancient history, Giovanni Andrea, a solemn law professor in Bologna not quite sixty years ago, was not of the opinion that it was bad for women to be educated. He had a fair and good daughter, named Novella, who was educated in the law to such an advanced degree that when he was occupied by some task and not at leisure to present his lectures to his students, he would send Novella, his daughter, in his place to lecture to the students from his chair. And to prevent her beauty from distracting the concentration of her audience, she had a little curtain drawn in front of her. In this manner she could on occasion supplement and lighten her father's occupation. He loved her so much that, to commemorate her name, he wrote a book of remarkable lectures on the law which he entitled *Novella super Decretalium,* after his daughter's name.[12]

"Thus, not all men (and especially the wisest) share the opinion that it is bad for women to be educated. But it is very true that many foolish men have claimed this because it displeased them that women knew more than they did. Your father, who was a great scientist and philosopher, did not believe that women were worth less by knowing science; rather, as you know, he took great pleasure from seeing your inclination to learning. The feminine opinion of your mother, however, who wished to keep you busy with spinning and silly girlishness, following the common custom of women, was the major obstacle to your being more involved in the sciences. But just as the proverb already mentioned above says, 'No one can take away what Nature has given,' your mother could not hinder in you the feeling for the sciences which you, through natural inclination, had nevertheless gathered together in little droplets. I am sure that, on account of these things, you do not think you are worth less but rather that you consider it a great treasure for yourself; and you doubtless have reason to."

And I, Christine, replied to all of this, "Indeed, my lady, what you say is as true as the Lord's Prayer."

Here Christine Speaks to Rectitude, Who Argues Against Those Men Who Say That There Are Few Chaste Women, and She Tells of Susanna.

"From what I see, my lady, all good and virtuous things are found in women. Where does the opinion that there are so few chaste women come from? Were this so, then all their other virtues would be nothing, since chastity is the supreme virtue in women. But from what I have heard you say, the complete opposite of what those men claim seems to be the case."

She replied, "From what I have already actually told you and from what you know about this, the contrary is quite obvious to you, and I could tell you more about this and then some. How many valiant and chaste ladies does Holy Scripture mention who chose death rather than transgress against the chastity and purity of their bodies and thoughts, just like the beautiful and good Susanna, wife of Joachim, a rich man of great authority among the Jews?[13] Once when this valiant lady Susanna was alone relaxing

---

[12] Christine could have learned the story of Novella from her father, who was a colleague of Giovanni Andrea at the University of Bologna.

[13] The story of Susanna and the Elders is told in Daniel 13.

in her garden, two old men, false priests, entered the garden, approached her, and demanded that she sin with them. She refused them totally, whereupon, seeing their request denied, they threatened to denounce her to the authorities and to claim that they had discovered her with a young man. Hearing their threats and knowing that women in such a case were customarily stoned, she said, 'I am completely overwhelmed with anguish, for if I do not do what these men require of me, I risk the death of my body, and if I do it, I will sin before my Creator. However, it is far better for me, in my innocence, to die than to incur the wrath of my God because of sin.' So Susanna cried out, and the servants came out of the house, and, to put the matter briefly, with their disloyal testimony, these false priests managed to have Susanna condemned to death. Yet God who always provides for those dear to Him, opened the mouth of the prophet Daniel, who was a little child in his mother's arms and who, as Susanna was being led to her execution, with a great procession of people in tears following her, cried out that the innocent Susanna had been condemned because of a very grave mistake. So she was led back, and the false priests were thoroughly interrogated and found guilty by their own confessions. The innocent Susanna was freed and these men executed." . . .

REFUTING THOSE MEN WHO CLAIM WOMEN WANT TO BE RAPED, RECTITUDE GIVES SEVERAL EXAMPLES, AND FIRST OF ALL, LUCRETIA.[14]

Then I, Christine, spoke as follows, "My lady, I truly believe what you are saying, and I am certain that there are plenty of beautiful women who are virtuous and chaste and who know how to protect themselves well from the entrapments of deceitful men. I am therefore troubled and grieved when men argue that many women want to be raped and that it does not bother them at all to be raped by men even when they verbally protest. It would be hard to believe that such great villainy is actually pleasant for them."

She answered, "Rest assured, dear friend, chaste ladies who live honestly take absolutely no pleasure in being raped. Indeed, rape is the greatest possible sorrow for them. Many upright women have demonstrated that this is true with their own credible examples, just like Lucretia, the noblest Roman woman, supreme in chastity among Roman women, wife of a nobleman named Tarquin Collatinus. Now, when another man, Tarquin the Proud, son of King Tarquin, was greatly taken with love for this noble Lucretia, he did not dare to tell her because of the great chastity he saw in her, and, despairing of achieving his goal with presents or entreaties, he considered how he could have her through ruse. Claiming to be a close friend of her husband, he managed to gain entrance into her house whenever he wished, and once, knowing her husband was not at home, he went there and the noble lady received him with the honors due to someone whom she thought to be a close friend of her husband. However, Tarquin, who had something altogether different on his mind, succeeded in enter-

[14] The story of Lucretia and her rape by Tarquin the Proud is legendary history, set at the court of Tarquinius Superbus, traditionally the seventh and last king of Rome (sixth century B.C.).

ing Lucretia's bedroom and frightened her terribly. Put briefly, after trying
to coax her for a long time with promises, gifts, and favors, he saw that
entreaties were getting him nowhere. He drew his sword and threatened to
kill her if she made a sound and did not submit to his will. She answered
that he should go ahead and kill her, for she would rather die than consent.
Tarquin, realizing that nothing would help him, concocted a great malice,
saying that he would publicly declare that he had found her with one of his
sergeants. In brief, he so scared her with this threat (for she thought that
people would believe him) that finally she suffered his rape. Lucretia, however, could not patiently endure this great pain, so that when daylight came
she sent for her husband, her father, and her close relatives who were
among the most powerful people in Rome, and, weeping and sobbing,
confessed to them what had happened to her. Then, as her husband and
relatives, who saw that she was overwhelmed with grief, were comforting
her, she drew a knife from under her robe and said, 'This is how I absolve
myself of sin and show my innocence. Yet I cannot free myself from the
torment nor extricate myself from the pain. From now on no woman will
ever live shamed and disgraced by Lucretia's example.' Having said this,
she forcibly plunged the knife into her breast and collapsed dead before
her husband and friends. They rushed like madmen to attack Tarquin. All
Rome was moved to this cause, and they drove out the king and would have
killed his son if they had found him. Never again was there a king in Rome.
And because of this outrage perpetrated on Lucretia, so some claim, a law
was enacted whereby a man would be executed for raping a woman, a law
which is fitting, just, and holy." . . .

HERE [JUSTICE] SPEAKS OF SAINT CHRISTINE, VIRGIN.[15]

"If you want me to tell you about all the holy virgins who are in Heaven
because of their constancy during martyrdom, it would require a long history, including Saint Cecilia, Saint Agnes, Saint Agatha, and countless others. If you want more examples, you need only look at the *Speculum his-
toriale* of Vincent de Beauvais, and there you will find a great many.[16]
However, I will tell you about Saint Christine, both because she is your
patron and because she is a virgin of great dignity. Let me tell you at
greater length about her beautiful and pious life.

"The blessed Saint Christine, virgin, was from the city of Tyre and was
the daughter of Urban, master of the knights. Her father shut her up in a
tower because of her great beauty, and she had twelve maids with her. Her
father also had a very beautiful chapel with idols built near Christine's
chamber so that she could worship them. She, however, even as a twelve-
year-old child, had already been inspired by the faith of Jesus Christ and
did not pay any attention to the idols, so that her maids were astonished
and repeatedly urged her to sacrifice. Yet when she took the incense, as if

---

[15] There were two Saint Christines in the medieval church: Saint Christine of Tyre, whose
story Justice tells, and Saint Christine of Bolsena. The two became confused and came to share
the same legendary history. Saint Christine of Tyre probably never existed; Saint Christine of
Bolsena seems to have been a genuine martyr of the fourth century A.D. but was probably not
named Christine. Her history, as Justice tells it, is of course purely legendary.

[16] Vincent of Beauvais was a thirteenth-century French Dominican friar whose *Mirror of
History* was a compendium of knowledge, including many saints' lives.

to sacrifice to the idols, she knelt at a window facing east, looked up to Heaven, and offered her incense to the immortal God. She spent the greater part of the night at this window, watching the stars, and sighing, piously praying to God to help her against her enemies. The maids, clearly aware her heart was in Jesus Christ, would often kneel before her, their hands clasped together, begging her not to place her trust in a strange God but to worship her parents' gods, for if she were discovered they would all be killed. Christine would answer that the Devil was deceiving them by urging them to worship so many gods and that there was but one God. When her father at last realized that his daughter refused to worship his idols, he was terribly grieved and upbraided her a great deal. She replied that she would gladly worship the God of Heaven. He thought she meant Jupiter and he was overjoyed and wanted to kiss her, but she cried out, 'Do not touch my mouth, for I wish to offer a pure offering to the celestial God.' The father was even happy with this. She returned to her chamber and nailed the door shut, then she knelt down and offered a holy prayer to God, weeping all the while. And the angel of the Lord descended and comforted her and brought her white bread and meat which she ate, for she had not tasted food for three days. Once, afterward, when Christine saw from her window several poor Christians begging at the foot of her tower, seeing that she had nothing to give them, she searched for her father's idols which were made of gold and silver, and she smashed them all and gave the fragments to the poor. When her father learned of this, he beat her cruelly. She openly declared he was deceived to worship these false images and that there was but a single God in the Trinity and that her father should worship Him whom she confessed, and she refused to worship any other in order to escape death. Thereupon her enraged father had her tied up with chains and led from square to square to be beaten and then thrown into prison. He himself wanted to be the judge of this dispute, so on the following day he had her brought before him and threatened her with every conceivable torture if she would not worship his idols. After he realized that he could not convince her with entreaties or threats, he had her sprawled completely nude and beaten so much that twelve men wearied at the task. And the father kept asking her what she thought and he said to her, 'Daughter, natural affection wrings my heart terribly to torment you who are my own flesh, but the reverence I have for my gods forces me to do this because you scorn them.' And the holy virgin replied, 'Tyrant who should not be called my father but rather enemy of my happiness, you boldly torture the flesh which you engendered, for you can easily do this, but as for my soul created by my Father in Heaven, you have no power to touch it with the slightest temptation, for it is protected by my Savior, Jesus Christ.' The cruel father, all the more enraged, had a wheel brought in, which he had ordered built, and ordered her tied to it and a fire built below it, and then he had rivers of boiling oil poured over her body. The wheel turned and completely crushed her. But God, the Father of all mercies, took pity on His servant and dispatched His angel to wreck the torture machines and to extinguish the fire, delivering the virgin, healthy and whole, and killing more than a thousand treacherous spectators who had been watching her without pity and who blasphemed the name of God. And her father asked her, 'Tell me who taught you these evil practices!' She replied, 'Pitiless despot, have I not told you that my Father, Jesus Christ, taught me this long-suffering as well as every right thing in the faith of the Living God? Because of this, I scorn your tortures and will repel all the Devil's assaults with God's strength!' Beaten and confounded, he ordered her thrown into a horrible, dark prison. While she was there, contemplating the extraordinary mysteries of God, three angels came to her in great radiance and brought her food and comforted her. Urban did not know what to do with her but could not stop devising new tortures for her. Finally, fed up completely and wishing to be free of her, he had a great stone tied around her neck and had her thrown into the sea. But as she was being thrown in, the angels took her, and she walked on the water with them. Then, raising her eyes to heaven, Christine prayed to Jesus Christ, that it please Him for her to receive in this water the holy sacrament of baptism which she greatly desired to have; whereupon Jesus Christ descended in His own person with a large company of angels and baptized her and named her Christine, from His own name, and He crowned her and placed a shining star on her forehead and set her on dry land. That night Urban was tortured by the Devil and died. The blessed Christine, whom God wanted to receive through martyrdom (which she also desired), was led back to prison by these criminals. The new judge, named Dyon, knowing what had been done to her, summoned her to appear before him, and he lusted after her because of her beauty. When he saw that his alluring words were of no use, he had her tortured again. He ordered that a large cauldron be filled with oil and that a roaring fire be built beneath it; he had her thrown in, upside down, and four men used iron hooks to rotate her. And the holy virgin sang melodiously to God, mocking her torturers and threatening them with the pains of Hell. When this enraged criminal of a judge realized that nothing was of any avail, he ordered her to be hanged by her long golden hair in the square, in front of all. The women rushed up to her, and, wailing out of pity that such a young girl be so cruelly tortured, they cried out to the judge, saying, 'Cruel felon, crueler than a savage beast, how could a man's heart conceive such monstrous cruelty against such a beautiful and tender maiden?' And all the women tried to mob him. Then the judge, who was afraid, said to her, 'Christine, friend, do not let yourself be tortured anymore, but come with me and we will go worship the supreme God who has upheld you.' He meant Jupiter, who was considered the supreme god, but she understood him in a completely different way and so she replied, 'You have spoken well, so I consent.' He had her taken down and brought up to the temple, and a large crowd followed them. Then he led her before the idols, thinking she would worship them, and she knelt down, looked up at Heaven, and prayed to God. Thereupon she stood up and, turning toward the idol, said, 'I command you in the name of Jesus Christ, oh evil spirit residing in this idol, to come out.' Whereupon the Devil immediately came out and made a loud and frightening din which scared all the spectators, who fell to the ground in fear. When the judge stood up again, he said, 'Christine, you have moved our omnipotent god, and, out of pity for you, he came out to see his creature.' This remark angered her, and she reproached him harshly for being too blind to recognize divine virtue, so she prayed to God to overturn the idol and reduce it to dust, which was done. And more than three thousand men were converted through the words and signs of this virgin. The terrified judge exclaimed, "If the king finds out what this Christine has done against our god, he will utterly destroy me.' Thereupon, full of anguish, he went out of his mind and died. A third judge, named Julian, appeared, and he ordered Christine seized, boasting that he would make her worship the idols. In spite of all the force he could apply, he was unable physically to move her from the spot where she was standing, so he ordered a large fire built around her. She remained in the fire for three days, and from inside the flames were heard sweet melodies. Her tormentors were terrified by the amazing signs they saw. When the fire had burned out, she emerged fully healthy. The judge commanded that snakes be brought to him and had two asps (with their deadly poisonous bite) and two adders released upon her. But these snakes dropped down at her feet, their heads bowed, and did not harm her at all. Two horrible vipers were let loose, and they hung from her breasts and licked her. And Christine looked to Heaven and said, 'I give You thanks, Lord God, Jesus Christ, who have deigned to grant through Your holy virtues that these horrible serpents would come to know in me Your dignity.' The obstinate Julian, seeing these wonders, yelled at the snake-tender, 'Have you too been enchanted by Christine, so that you have no power to rouse the snakes against her?' Fearing the judge, he then tried to provoke the snakes into biting her, but they rushed at him and killed him. Since everyone was afraid of these serpents and no one dared approach, Christine commanded them in God's name to return to their cages without harming anyone, and they did so. She revived the dead man, who immediately threw himself at her feet and was converted. The judge, blinded by the Devil so that he was unable to perceive the divine mystery, said to Christine, 'You have sufficiently demonstrated your magic arts.' Infuriated, she replied, 'If your eyes would see the virtues of God, you would believe in them.' Then in his rage he ordered her breasts ripped off, whereupon milk rather than blood flowed out. And because she unceasingly pronounced the name of Jesus Christ, he had her tongue cut out, but then she spoke even better and more clearly than before of divine things and of the one blessed God, thanking Him for the bounties which He had given to her. She prayed that it please Him to receive her in His company and that the crown of her martyrdom be finally granted to her. Then a voice was heard from Heaven, saying, 'Christine, pure and radiant, the heavens are opened to you and the eternal kingdom waits, prepared for you, and the entire company of saints blesses God for your sake, for you have upheld the name of Your Christ from childhood on.' And she glorified God, turning her eyes to Heaven. The voice was heard saying, 'Come, Christine, my most beloved and elect daughter, receive the palm and everlasting crown and the reward for your life spent suffering to confess My name.' The treacherous Julian, who heard this voice, castigated the executioners and said they had not cut Christine's tongue short enough and ordered them to cut it so short that she could not speak to her Christ, whereupon they ripped out her tongue and cut it off at the root. She spat this cut-off piece of her tongue into the tyrant's face, putting out one of his eyes. She then said to him, speaking as clearly as ever, 'Tyrant, what does it profit you to have my tongue cut out so that it cannot bless God, when my soul will bless Him forever while yours languishes forever in eternal damnation? And because you did not heed my words, my tongue has blinded you, with good reason.' She ended her martyrdom then, having already seen Jesus Christ sitting on the right hand of His Father, when two arrows were shot at her, one in her side and the other in her heart. One of her relatives whom she had converted buried her body and wrote out her glorious legend."

O blessed Christine, worthy virgin favored of God, most elect and glorious martyr, in the holiness with which God has made you worthy, pray for me, a sinner, named with your name, and be my kind and merciful guardian. Behold my joy at being able to make use of your holy legend and to include it in my writings, which I have recorded here at such length out of reverence for you. May this be ever pleasing to you! Pray for all women, for whom your holy life may serve as an example for ending their lives well. Amen.

Everyman
(Late Fifteenth Century)

Everyman *was written in England by an anonymous clerical playwright in about* 1475. *There is a similar Dutch play of the same period named* Elckerlyc. Everyman *may be a translation of the Dutch play, or both may be derived independently from a Latin work named* Homulus. *Current scholarly opinion tends to conclude, however, that the English play is the original. Nothing is known of the author, and although the play was apparently produced with some frequency in the seventy-five years following its composition, no production records survive.*

Everyman *is the best example of the medieval "morality play," characterized by an allegorical plot that deals with some archetypal action in man's spiritual life and by characters who personify abstract ideas, such as Fellowship, Wealth, or Knowledge. Morality plays were only one genre in a rich body of drama that flourished in Europe from the tenth to the sixteenth century, fascinating both in its own right and as background to the flowering of an even richer and more varied drama in the Renaissance.*

By the time of the fall of Rome, classical drama had already declined to the level of crude entertainment, and the collapse of the Roman Empire ended dramatic performance altogether for more than five centuries. When drama began to re-emerge in the tenth century, it was again from religious roots. As classical drama had begun in the worship of Dionysus, so medieval drama was born in the Christian liturgy. The earliest bits of medieval drama were tropes, *brief exchanges of dialogue introduced into the chanted liturgy. These tropes were gradually elaborated until by the twelfth century practically all the narrative portions of the Bible had been dramatized in short, often crude, but vivid plays presented in the churches at Christmas and Easter. By the fourteenth century, these liturgical plays had attracted such large and unruly audiences that they were removed from the churches and presented in village streets, usually on Corpus Christi Day, in late May or early June. Production of the plays was taken over by the craft and trade guilds, although the clergy continued to play an active role, especially in writing the plays. By the end of the fourteenth century, every* town of any size in England had its own cycle of religious plays. Some idea of the numbers of plays involved is suggested by the four cycles that survive: the York cycle of forty-eight plays, the Wakefield cycle of thirty-two plays, the Chester cycle of twenty-five plays, and the Coventry cycle of forty-two plays. The subject matter was quite varied, ranging from authentic Biblical material to various folk accretions upon that material to saints' lives. (Scholars used to discriminate between mystery plays, based on the Bible, and miracle plays dealing with the lives of saints, but the distinction is so blurry in practice that they are now generally grouped together as liturgical plays.)

The morality play was the last of the medieval dramatic genres to emerge, in the middle of the fourteenth century, although there were many precedents for such didactic, allegorical works in nondramatic literature. The recurring subjects of morality plays are suggested by the titles of some of those that preceded Everyman: The Pride of Life, The Castle of Perseverance, and The Debate of the Body and the Soul.

Medieval plays were produced in several different ways. When they were still performed inside churches, they were staged on platforms distributed around the church, with a different platform, or mansion, for each locale. When they moved outside the churches, they were performed on large, two-decker pageant wagons. A curtained-off lower level was used as a dressing room, and a platform on the second level, reached by a ladder, was used as a stage. Sometimes the action spilled off the wagon-stage and into an open area in front of the wagon, the platea. These pageant wagons moved from one stopping place in the town to another on performance days, the actors performing their play at each stop. A spectator could station himself in one place and see the successive plays in the cycle performed in sequence.

By the time Everyman was performed, however, a somewhat different production method had been adopted for the longer morality plays. These were performed not as part of a cycle by members of a guild but independently by troupes of traveling players performing in town squares and on village greens. The original setting for Everyman was probably a stationary version of pageant-wagon staging: a two-story scaffold stage with an open space in front of it and probably two smaller sets, one on each side of the scaffold, for Goods and Good Deeds. This simple theater presented an elementary model of the medieval world view. God undoubtedly appeared on the "Heaven" of the top level, Death entered from the "Hell" of the covered lower level, and Everyman's main action was played on the "Earth" of the platea. In other respects as well, the theater and the conventions of staging allowed every element of the play to be translated into concrete, dramatic terms. The idea that earthly possessions weigh one down in the quest for salvation is vividly and amusingly presented by the immobilized Goods, unable to stir because of the chests and bags full of gold lying upon and around him. Similarly, the "scourge of penance" that Knowledge gives Everyman is no metaphor, but an actual whip.

The hasty reader of Everyman may dismiss it as crude and obvious, interesting only historically. It is true that the message of the play is presented with a crude directness and that its rhymed doggerel is naive, sometimes monotonous. But upon a closer reading, and especially after seeing a good performance, one's respect for the skill and artistry of the nameless playwright is likely to increase. The play presents a generalized, archetypal action, a sort of x-ray of human experience, but this generalizing tendency is everywhere in tension with a robust and earthy specificity. Everyman is not only all men, but a very particular man, economically but tellingly characterized. He is a fundamentally good-hearted but superficial sensualist who, at the existential moment when he must confront the reality of his impending death, *undergoes a radical and convincing psychological transformation. The secondary characters are handled with a similar economical skill and frequently with a mordant, ironic comic touch. Fellowship, Kindred and Cousin, Goods, and the rest are not mere walking abstractions but vivid embodiments of the qualities they represent. Fellowship, for example, within his short scene, is presented as hail-fellow-well-met, blustery, effusive, and full of reminiscences of drinking bouts, but quick to take his leave when he discovers that something more serious than a party is about to occur. The action, too, is poised on a delicate line between the general and the particular. The plot is often described as an archetypal journey through life, but it is actually not quite so general; it suggests the whole of life through focusing sharply upon its end. The story becomes not only a parable of all men's lives but a moving and personal study in one man's experience. Even the jogtrot language, at first distracting, comes to have a crude, direct power that is very moving.*

Paradoxically, Everyman, which seems so quintessentially of its age, has had a long and prominent history on the modern stage and has exercised a considerable influence upon modern drama. William Poel restaged the play in London in 1901 in the medieval manner; the revival attracted much favorable attention and was repeated a number of times during the following fifteen years. The great German director Max Reinhardt was inspired by Poel's production to present his own version, adapted by the poet and playwright Hugo von Hofmannsthal. Reinhardt's Jedermann *(German for* Everyman*) was first performed in 1911 in an elaborate production in an old Berlin circus building. In 1920, Reinhardt restaged his version of the play in front of the Salzburg Cathedral as part of the Salzburg Festival. The play was enormously successful and has been repeated every year since then to enormous festival crowds, except for a nine-year dark period between 1937 and 1946, when Hitler banned it as "Jewish." The Dutch version of the play has a similar annual production at the Holland Festival in the city of Delft.*

Everyman, *along with other pre-realistic plays, has had a strong influence upon the development of the post-realistic modern drama, especially as a model for dramatizing inner, psychological action. Its influence is especially clear in two modern plays that also deal with approaching death: Eugene Ionesco's* Exit the King *and Samuel Beckett's* Endgame.

FURTHER READING *(prepared by W.J.R.):* A discussion of medieval drama, by Joseph A. Dane, is included in *European Writers: Medieval and Renaissance,* Vol. I, ed. George Stade, 1984. A thorough background study of miracle, mystery, and morality plays is Hardin Craig's *English Religious Drama of the Middle Ages,* 1955. In A. P. Rossiter's *English Drama From Early Times to the Elizabethans,* 1950, morality plays are divided into two classes, those that view a man's life from cradle to grave and those that deal with a more specific situation. *The Castle of Perseverance* and *Everyman,* respectively, are discussed as representatives of these two classes, along with several other specimens. Glynne Wickham's *Shakespeare's Dramatic Heritage,* 1969, discusses the 1964 London production of *Everyman,* in which Everyman drifted onto stage wearing jeans and listening to music from *Bye-bye Birdie.* Wickham discusses the persistence of the play's appeal and its ability to survive when transposed to a new setting. The first chapter of W. Roy MacKenzie's *The English Moralities From the Point of View of Allegory,* 1966, discusses the nature of the morality play, specifically considering *Everyman* as its best representative. Two complementary essays on the play's structure, a somewhat neglected topic, are Lawrence V. Ryan's "Doctrine and Dramatic Structure in *Everyman,*" *Speculum,* 32 (1957), 722–35, and Thomas F. Van Laan's "*Everyman:* A Structural Analysis," *PMLA,* 78 (1963), 465–75. Ryan discusses the relationship between structure and doctrinal content, arguing that the play's moral lessons are a natural outgrowth of the action.

EVERYMAN

MESSENGER	KNOWLEDGE
GOD: *Adonai*[1]	CONFESSION
DEATH	BEAUTY
EVERYMAN	STRENGTH
FELLOWSHIP	DISCRETION
COUSIN	FIVE WITS
KINDRED	ANGEL
GOODS	DOCTOR
GOOD DEEDS	

Here beginneth a treatise how the High Father of Heaven sendeth Death to summon every creature to come and give account of their lives in this world, and is in manner of a moral play.

MESSENGER. I pray you all give your audience,
    And hear this matter with reverence,
    By figure[2] a moral play—
    The *Summoning of Everyman* called it is,
    That of our lives and ending shows   5
    How transitory we be all our day.
    This matter is wondrous precious,
    But the intent of it is more gracious,[3]
    And sweet to bear away.
    The story saith:—Man, in the beginning,   10
    Look well, and take good heed to the ending,
    Be you never so gay!
    Ye think sin in the beginning full sweet,
    Which in the end causeth the soul to weep,
    When the body lieth in clay.   15
    Here shall you see how Fellowship and Jollity,
    Both Strength, Pleasure, and Beauty,
    Will fade from thee as flower in May.
    For ye shall hear how our Heaven King
    Calleth Everyman to a general reckoning.   20
    Give audience, and hear what he doth say.   [*Exit.*]

[GOD *speaketh from above.*]

GOD. I perceive, here in my majesty,
    How that all creatures be to me unkind,
    Living without dread in worldly prosperity.
    Of ghostly sight[4] the people be so blind,   25
    Drowned in sin, they know me not for their God.
    In worldly riches is all their mind,

---

[1] Hebrew name for God.   [2] In form.   [3] Having to do with God's grace.
[4] Spiritual insight.

They fear not my rightwiseness,[5] the sharp rod;
My love that I showed when I for them died
They forget clean, and shedding of my blood red;   30
I hanged between two, it cannot be denied;
To get them life I suffered to be dead;
I healed their feet, with thorns hurt was my head.
I could do no more than I did, truly;
And now I see the people do clean forsake me.   35
They use the seven deadly sins damnable;
As pride, covetise, wrath, and lechery,
Now in the world be made commendable;
And thus they leave of angels the heavenly company.
Every man liveth so after his own pleasure,   40
And yet of their life they be nothing sure.
I see the more that I them forbear
The worse they be from year to year;
All that liveth appaireth[6] fast.
Therefore I will, in all the haste,   45
Have a reckoning of every man's person;
For, and[7] I leave the people thus alone
In their life and wicked tempests,
Verily they will become much worse than beasts;
For now one would by envy another up eat;   50
Charity they all do clean forget.
I hoped well that every man
In my glory should make his mansion,
And thereto I had them all elect;
But now I see, like traitors deject,[8]   55
They thank me not for the pleasure that I to them meant,
Nor yet for their being that I them have lent.
I proffered the people great multitude of mercy,
And few there be that asketh it heartily;
They be so cumbered with worldly riches,   60
That needs on them I must do justice,
On every man living, without fear.
Where art thou, Death, thou mighty messenger?

                        [*Enter* DEATH.]

DEATH. Almighty God, I am here at your will,
    Your commandment to fulfil.   65
GOD. Go thou to Everyman,
    And show him, in my name,
    A pilgrimage he must on him take,
    Which he in no wise[9] may escape;
    And that he bring with him a sure reckoning   70
    Without delay or any tarrying.

---

[5] Righteousness.   [6] Degenerates.   [7] If (frequently throughout the play).
[8] Abject.   [9] In no way (frequently throughout the play).

Death. Lord, I will in the world go run over all,
    And cruelly out search both great and small.   [God *withdraws*.]
    Every man will I beset that liveth beastly
    Out of God's laws, and dreadeth not folly.   75
    He that loveth riches I will strike with my dart,
    His sight to blind, and from heaven to depart,
    Except that alms be his good friend,
    In hell for to dwell, world without end.
    Lo, yonder I see Everyman walking;   80
    Full little he thinketh on my coming;
    His mind is on fleshly lusts and his treasure;
    And great pain it shall cause him to endure
    Before the Lord, Heaven King.
    Everyman, stand still! Whither art thou going   85
    Thus gaily? Hast thou thy Maker forgot?
Everyman. Why askest thou?
    Wouldst thou wete?[10]
Death. Yea, sir, I will show you;
    In great haste I am sent to thee   90
    From God out of his Majesty.
Everyman. What, sent to me?
Death. Yea, certainly.
    Though thou have forgot him here,
    He thinketh on thee in the heavenly sphere,   95
    As, ere we depart, thou shalt know.
Everyman. What desireth God of me?
Death. That shall I show thee;
    A reckoning he will needs have
    Without any longer respite.   100
Everyman. To give a reckoning longer leisure I crave;
    This blind matter troubleth my wit.
Death. On thee thou must take a long journey;
    Therefore thy book of count[11] with thee thou bring;
    For turn again thou can not by no way.   105
    And look thou be sure of thy reckoning,
    For before God thou shalt answer and show
    Thy many bad deeds, and good but a few,
    How thou hast spent thy life, and in what wise,
    Before the Chief Lord of paradise.   110
    Have ado[12] that we were in that way,
    For, wete thou well, thou shalt make none attorney.[13]
Everyman. Full unready I am such reckoning to give.
    I know thee not. What messenger art thou?
Death. I am Death, that no man dreadeth.   115
    For every man I 'rest, and no man spareth;

---

[10] Know.   [11] Accounts.   [12] Get ready.
[13] You cannot make anyone your representative.

For it is God's commandment
That all to me should be obedient.
EVERYMAN. O Death! thou comest when I had thee least in mind!
In thy power it lieth me to save,   120
Yet of my goods will I give thee, if thou will be kind;
Yea, a thousand pound shalt thou have,
If thou defer this matter till another day.
DEATH. Everyman, it may not be, by no way!
I set not by gold, silver, nor riches,   125
Nor by pope, emperor, king, duke, nor princes.
For, and I would receive gifts great,
All the world I might get;
But my custom is clean contrary.
I give thee no respite. Come hence, and not tarry.   130
EVERYMAN. Alas! shall I have no longer respite?
I may say Death giveth no warning.
To think on thee, it maketh my heart sick,
For all unready is my book of reckoning.
But twelve year and I might have abiding,   135
My counting-book I would make so clear,
That my reckoning I should not need to fear.
Wherefore, Death, I pray thee, for God's mercy,
Spare me till I be provided of remedy.
DEATH. Thee availeth not to cry, weep, and pray;   140
But haste thee lightly that thou were gone that journey,
And prove thy friends if thou can.
For wete thou well the tide abideth no man;
And in the world each living creature
For Adam's sin must die of nature.   145
EVERYMAN. Death, if I should this pilgrimage take,
And my reckoning surely make,
Show me, for saint charity,
Should I not come again shortly?
DEATH. No, Everyman; and thou be once there,   150
Thou mayst never more come here,
Trust me verily.
EVERYMAN. O gracious God, in the high seat celestial,
Have mercy on me in this most need!
Shall I have no company from this vale terrestrial   155
Of mine acquaintance that way me to lead?
DEATH. Yea, if any be so hardy,
That would go with thee and bear thee company.
Hie thee that thou were gone[14] to God's magnificence,
Thy reckoning to give before his presence.   160
What! weenest[15] thou thy life is given thee,
And thy worldly goods also?
EVERYMAN. I had weened so, verily.

---

[14] Hasten to be gone.   [15] Thinkest.

DEATH. Nay, nay; it was but lent thee;
    For, as soon as thou art gone,   165
    Another a while shall have it, and then go therefrom
    Even as thou hast done.
    Everyman, thou art mad! Thou hast thy wits[16] five,
    And here on earth will not amend thy life;
    For suddenly I do come.   170
EVERYMAN. O wretched caitiff![17] whither shall I flee,
    That I might 'scape endless sorrow?
    Now, gentle Death, spare me till tomorrow,
    That I may amend me
    With good advisement.   175
DEATH. Nay, thereto I will not consent,
    Nor no man will I respite,
    But to the heart suddenly I shall smite
    Without any advisement.
    And now out of thy sight I will me hie;   180
    See thou make thee ready shortly,
    For thou mayst say this is the day
    That no man living may 'scape away.   [*Exit* DEATH.]
EVERYMAN. Alas! I may well weep with sighs deep.
    Now have I no manner of company   185
    To help me in my journey and me to keep;
    And also my writing is full unready.
    How shall I do now for to excuse me?
    I would to God I had never been gete![18]
    To my soul a full great profit it had be;   190
    For now I fear pains huge and great.
    The time passeth; Lord, help, that all wrought.
    For though I mourn it availeth naught.
    The day passeth, and is almost a-go;[19]
    I wot[20] not well what for to do.   195
    To whom were I best my complaint to make?
    What if I to Fellowship thereof spake,
    And showed him of this sudden chance?
    For in him is all mine affiance,[21]
    We have in the world so many a day   200
    Been good friends in sport and play.
    I see him yonder, certainly;
    I trust that he will bear me company;
    Therefore to him will I speak to ease my sorrow.
    Well met, good Fellowship, and good morrow!   205

[FELLOWSHIP *speaketh*.]

FELLOWSHIP. Everyman, good morrow, by this day!
    Sir, why lookest thou so piteously?

---

[16] Senses.   [17] Knave.   [18] Born.   [19] Gone.   [20] Know.
[21] Trust.

If any thing be amiss, I pray thee me say,
  That I may help to remedy.
EVERYMAN. Yea, good Fellowship, yea,   210
  I am in great jeopardy.
FELLOWSHIP. My true friend, show to me your mind;
  I will not forsake thee to my life's end
  In the way of good company.
EVERYMAN. That was well spoken, and lovingly.   215
FELLOWSHIP. Sir, I must needs know your heaviness;
  I have pity to see you in any distress;
  If any have you wronged, ye shall revenged be,
  Though I on the ground be slain for thee,
  Though that I know before that I should die.   220
EVERYMAN. Verily, Fellowship, gramercy.[22]
FELLOWSHIP. Tush! by thy thanks I set not a straw!
  Show me your grief, and say no more.
EVERYMAN. If I my heart should to you break,
  And then you to turn your mind from me,   225
  And would not me comfort when you hear me speak,
  Then should I ten times sorrier be.
FELLOWSHIP. Sir, I say as I will do, indeed.
EVERYMAN. Then be you a good friend at need;
  I have found you true here before.   230
FELLOWSHIP. And so ye shall evermore;
  For, in faith, and thou go to hell,
  I will not forsake thee by the way!
EVERYMAN. Ye speak like a good friend. I believe you well;
  I shall deserve it, and I may.   235
FELLOWSHIP. I speak of no deserving, by this day!
  For he that will say and nothing do
  Is not worthy with good company to go;
  Therefore show me the grief of your mind,
  As to your friend most loving and kind.   240
EVERYMAN. I shall show you how it is:
  Commanded I am to go a journey,
  A long way, hard and dangerous,
  And give a strict count without delay
  Before the high judge, Adonai.   245
  Wherefore, I pray you, bear me company,
  As ye have promised, in this journey.
FELLOWSHIP. That is matter indeed! Promise is duty;
  But, and I should take such a voyage on me,
  I know it well, it should be to my pain.   250
  Also it maketh me afeared, certain.
  But let us take counsel here as well as we can,
  For your words would fright a strong man.
EVERYMAN. Why, ye said if I had need,

---

[22] Thank you.

Ye would me never forsake, quick nor dead,   255
   Though it were to hell, truly.
FELLOWSHIP. So I said, certainly,
   But such pleasures be set aside, the sooth[23] to say.
   And also, if we took such a journey,
   When should we come again?   260
EVERYMAN. Nay, never again till the day of doom.
FELLOWSHIP. In faith, then will not I come there!
   Who hath you these tidings brought?
EVERYMAN. Indeed, Death was with me here.
FELLOWSHIP. Now, by God that all hath bought,   265
   If Death were the messenger,
   For no man that is living today
   I will not go that loath journey—
   Nor for the father that begat me!
EVERYMAN. Ye promised otherwise, pardie.[24]   270
FELLOWSHIP. I wot well I said so, truly;
   And yet if thou wilt eat, and drink, and make good cheer,
   Or haunt to women the lusty company,
   I would not forsake you while the day is clear,
   Trust me verily!   275
EVERYMAN. Yea, thereto ye would be ready;
   To go to mirth, solace, and play,
   Your mind will sooner apply
   Than to bear me company in my long journey.
FELLOWSHIP. Now, in good faith, I will not that way.   280
   But and thou wilt murder, or any man kill,
   In that I will help thee with a good will!
EVERYMAN. O, that is a simple advice indeed!
   Gentle fellow, help me in my necessity;
   We have loved long, and now I need,   285
   And now, gentle Fellowship, remember me!
FELLOWSHIP. Whether ye have loved me or no,
   By Saint John, I will not with thee go.
EVERYMAN. Yet, I pray thee, take the labor, and do so much for me
   To bring me forward, for saint charity,   290
   And comfort me till I come without the town.
FELLOWSHIP. Nay, and thou would give me a new gown,
   I will not a foot with thee go;
   But, and thou had tarried, I would not have left thee so.
   And as now God speed thee in thy journey,   295
   For from thee I will depart as fast as I may.
EVERYMAN. Whither away, Fellowship? Will you forsake me?
FELLOWSHIP. Yea, by my fay,[25] to God I betake[26] thee.
EVERYMAN. Farewell, good Fellowship! For thee my heart is sore;
   Adieu for ever! I shall see thee no more.   300
FELLOWSHIP. In faith, Everyman, farewell now at the end!
   For you I will remember that parting is mourning.

[23] Truth.   [24] *Par dieu:* indeed. (Literally, "by God.")   [25] Faith.   [26] Commit.

[*Exit* FELLOWSHIP.]

EVERYMAN. Alack! shall we thus depart indeed
  (Ah, Lady, help!) without any more comfort?
  Lo, Fellowship forsaketh me in my most need.   305
  For help in this world whither shall I resort?
  Fellowship here before with me would merry make,
  And now little sorrow for me doth he take.
  It is said, "In prosperity men friends may find,
  Which in adversity be full unkind."   310
  Now whither for succor shall I flee,
  Sith that[27] Fellowship hath forsaken me?
  To my kinsmen I will, truly,
  Praying them to help me in my necessity;
  I believe that they will do so,   315
  For "kind will creep where it may not go."[28]
  I will go say,[29] for yonder I see them go.
  Where be ye now, my friends and kinsmen?

[*Enter* KINDRED *and* COUSIN.]

KINDRED. Here be we now, at your commandment.
  Cousin, I pray you show us your intent   320
  In any wise, and do not spare.
COUSIN. Yea, Everyman, and to us declare
  If ye be disposed to go any whither,
  For, wete you well, we will live and die together.
KINDRED. In wealth and woe we will with you hold,   325
  For over his kin a man may be bold.
EVERYMAN. Gramercy, my friends and kinsmen kind.
  Now shall I show you the grief of my mind.
  I was commanded by a messenger
  That is a high king's chief officer;   330
  He bade me go a pilgrimage, to my pain,
  And I know well I shall never come again;
  Also I must give a reckoning straight,
  For I have a great enemy that hath me in wait,[30]
  Which intendeth me for to hinder.   335
KINDRED. What account is that which ye must render?
  That would I know.
EVERYMAN. Of all my works I must show
  How I have lived, and my days spent;
  Also of ill deeds that I have used   340
  In my time, sith life was me lent;
  And of all virtues that I have refused.
  Therefore I pray you go thither with me,
  To help to make mine account, for saint charity.
COUSIN. What, to go thither? Is that the matter?   345

---

[27] Since.   [28] Walk.   [29] Try.   [30] Lies in wait for me.

    Nay, Everyman, I had liefer fast bread and water
    All this five year and more.
EVERYMAN. Alas, that ever I was bore!
    For now shall I never be merry
    If that you forsake me. 350
KINDRED. Ah, sir, what! Ye be a merry man!
    Take good heart to you, and make no moan.
    But one thing I warn you, by Saint Anne,
    As for me, ye shall go alone.
EVERYMAN. My Cousin, will you not with me go? 355
COUSIN. No, by our Lady! I have the cramp in my toe.
    Trust not to me; for, so God me speed,
    I will deceive you in your most need.
KINDRED. It availeth not us to tice.[31]
    Ye shall have my maid with all my heart; 360
    She loveth to go to feasts, there to be nice,[32]
    And to dance, and abroad to start;
    I will give her leave to help you in that journey,
    If that you and she may agree.
EVERYMAN. Now show me the very effect of your mind. 365
    Will you go with me, or abide behind?
KINDRED. Abide behind? Yea, that will I, and I may!
    Therefore farewell till another day.   [*Exit* KINDRED.]
EVERYMAN. How should I be merry or glad?
    For fair promises men to me make, 370
    But when I have most need, they me forsake.
    I am deceived; that maketh me sad.
COUSIN. Cousin Everyman, farewell now,
    For verily I will not go with you;
    Also of mine own life an unready reckoning 375
    I have to account; therefore I make tarrying.
    Now, God keep thee, for now I go.   [*Exit* COUSIN.]
EVERYMAN. Ah, Jesus! is all come hereto?
    Lo, fair words maketh fools fain;[33]
    They promise and nothing will do certain. 380
    My kinsmen promised me faithfully
    For to abide with me steadfastly,
    And now fast away do they flee.
    Even so Fellowship promised me.
    What friend were best me of to provide? 385
    I lose my time here longer to abide.
    Yet in my mind a thing there is:
    All my life I have loved riches;
    If that my Goods now help me might,
    He would make my heart full light. 390
    I will speak to him in this distress.
    Where art thou, my Goods and riches?

[31] Entice.   [32] Wanton.   [33] Glad.

GOODS [*from within*]. Who calleth me? Everyman? What, hast thou
    haste?
    I lie here in corners, trussed and piled so high,
    And in chests I am locked so fast,   395
    Also sacked in bags—thou mayst see with thine eye—
    I cannot stir; in packs low I lie.
    What would ye have? Lightly me say.
EVERYMAN. Come hither, Goods, in all the haste thou may.
    For of counsel I must desire thee.   400

[Enter GOODS.]

GOODS. Sir, and ye in the world have sorrow or adversity,
    That can I help you to remedy shortly.
EVERYMAN. It is another disease that grieveth me;
    In this world it is not, I tell thee so.
    I am sent for another way to go,   405
    To give a strict count general
    Before the highest Jupiter of all;
    And all my life I have had joy and pleasure in thee;
    Therefore I pray thee go with me,
    For, peradventure,[34] thou mayst before God Almighty   410
    My reckoning help to clean and purify;
    For it is said ever among,
    That "money maketh all right that is wrong."
GOODS. Nay, Everyman; I sing another song,
    I follow no man in such voyages;   415
    For, and I went with thee,
    Thou shouldst fare much the worse for me;
    For because on me thou did set thy mind,
    Thy reckoning I have made blotted and blind,
    That thine account thou cannot make truly;   420
    And that hast thou for the love of me.
EVERYMAN. That would grieve me full sore,
    When I should come to that fearful answer.
    Up, let us go thither together.
GOODS. Nay, not so! I am too brittle, I may not endure;   425
    I will follow no man one foot, be ye sure.
EVERYMAN. Alas! I have thee loved, and had great pleasure
    All my life-days on goods and treasure.
GOODS. That is to thy damnation, without lesing![35]
    For my love is contrary to the love everlasting.   430
    But if thou had me loved moderately during,
    As to the poor to give part of me,
    Then shouldst thou not in this dolor be,
    Nor in this great sorrow and care.
EVERYMAN. Lo, now was I deceived ere I was ware,   435
    And all I may wyte[36] my spending of time.
GOODS. What, weenest thou that I am thine?

---

[34] Perhaps.   [35] Lying.   [36] Blame upon.

EVERYMAN. I had weened so.
GOODS. Nay, Everyman, I say no;
　　As for a while I was lent thee,   440
　　A season thou hast had me in prosperity.
　　My condition is man's soul to kill;
　　If I save one, a thousand I do spill;[37]
　　Weenest thou that I will follow thee
　　From this world? Nay, verily.   445
EVERYMAN. I had weened otherwise.
GOODS. Therefore to thy soul Goods is a thief;
　　For when thou art dead, this is my guise—[38]
　　Another to deceive in the same wise
　　As I have done thee, and all to his soul's reprief.[39]   450
EVERYMAN. O false Goods, cursèd thou be!
　　Thou traitor to God, that hast deceived me
　　And caught me in thy snare.
GOODS. Marry! thou brought thyself in care,
　　Whereof I am right glad.   455
　　I must needs laugh, I cannot be sad.
EVERYMAN. Ah, Goods, thou hast had long my heartly love;
　　I gave thee that which should be the Lord's above.
　　But wilt thou not go with me indeed?
　　I pray thee truth to say.   460
GOODS. No, so God me speed!
　　Therefore farewell, and have good day.   [Exit GOODS.]
EVERYMAN. O, to whom shall I make my moan
　　For to go with me in that heavy journey?
　　First Fellowship said he would with me gone;   465
　　His words were very pleasant and gay,
　　But afterward he left me alone.
　　Then spake I to my kinsmen, all in despair,
　　And also they gave me words fair,
　　They lacked no fair speaking,   470
　　But all forsook me in the ending.
　　Then went I to my Goods, that I loved best,
　　In hope to have comfort, but there had I least;
　　For my Goods sharply did me tell
　　That he bringeth many into hell.   475
　　Then of myself I was ashamed,
　　And so I am worthy to be blamed;
　　Thus may I well myself hate.
　　Of whom shall I now counsel take?
　　I think that I shall never speed   480
　　Till that I go to my Good Deeds.
　　But alas! she is so weak
　　That she can neither go nor speak.
　　Yet will I venture on her now.
　　My Good Deeds, where be you?   485

[37] Ruin.   [38] Practice: trick.   [39] Reproof.

[GOOD DEEDS *speaks from the ground.*]

GOOD DEEDS. Here I lie, cold in the ground.
    Thy sins hath me sore bound,
    That I cannot stir.
EVERYMAN. O Good Deeds! I stand in fear;
    I must you pray of counsel,   490
    For help now should come right well.
GOOD DEEDS. Everyman, I have understanding
    That ye be summoned account to make
    Before Messias, of Jerusalem King;
    And you do by me,[40] that journey with you will I take.   495
EVERYMAN. Therefore I come to you my moan to make;
    I pray you that ye will go with me.
GOOD DEEDS. I would full fain, but I cannot stand, verily.
EVERYMAN. Why, is there anything on you fall?
GOOD DEEDS. Yea, sir, I may thank you of all;   500
    If ye had perfectly cheered[41] me,
    Your book of count full ready had be.
    Look, the books of your works and deeds eke;[42]
    Ah, see how they lie under the feet,
    To your soul's heaviness.   505
EVERYMAN. Our Lord Jesus help me!
    For one letter here I can not see.
GOOD DEEDS. There is a blind reckoning in time of distress!
EVERYMAN. Good Deeds, I pray you, help me in this need,
    Or else I am for ever damned indeed;   510
    Therefore help me to make my reckoning
    Before the Redeemer of all thing,
    That King is, and was, and ever shall.
GOOD DEEDS. Everyman, I am sorry of your fall,
    And fain would I help you, and I were able.   515
EVERYMAN. Good Deeds, your counsel I pray you give me.
GOOD DEEDS. That shall I do verily;
    Though that on my feet I may not go,
    I have a sister that shall with you also,
    Called Knowledge, which shall with you abide,   520
    To help you to make that dreadful reckoning.

[*Enter* KNOWLEDGE.]

KNOWLEDGE. Everyman, I will go with thee, and be thy guide
    In thy most need to go by thy side.
EVERYMAN. In good condition I am now in every thing,
    And am wholly content with this good thing;   525
    Thanked be God my Creator.
GOOD DEEDS. And when he hath brought thee there,
    Where thou shalt heal thee of thy smart,

---

[40] If you take my advice.   [41] Cherished.   [42] Also.

Then go you with your reckoning and your Good Deeds together
For to make you joyful at heart 530
Before the blesséd Trinity.
EVERYMAN. My Good Deeds, gramercy!
I am well content, certainly,
With your words sweet.
KNOWLEDGE. Now go we together lovingly 535
To Confession, that cleansing river.
EVERYMAN. For joy I weep; I would we were there!
But, I pray you, give my cognition
Where dwelleth that holy man, Confession.
KNOWLEDGE. In the house of salvation; 540
We shall find him in that place,
That shall us comfort, by God's grace.

[KNOWLEDGE *leads* EVERYMAN *to*
CONFESSION.]

Lo, this is Confession. Kneel down and ask mercy,
For he is in good conceit[43] with God almighty.
EVERYMAN [*kneeling*]. O glorious fountain, that all uncleanness doth
clarify, 545
Wash from me the spots of vice unclean,
That on me no sin may be seen.
I come, with Knowledge, for my redemption,
Redempt with hearty and full contrition;
For I am commanded a pilgrimage to take, 550
And great accounts before God to make.
Now, I pray you, Shrift,[44] mother of salvation.
Help my Good Deeds for my piteous exclamation.
CONFESSION. I know your sorrow well, Everyman.
Because with Knowledge ye come to me, 555
I will you comfort as well as I can,
And a precious jewel I will give thee,
Called penance, voider of adversity;
Therewith shall your body chastised be,
With abstinence, and perseverance in God's service. 560
Here shall you receive that scourge of me.

[*Gives* EVERYMAN *a scourge.*]

Which is penance strong, that ye must endure
To remember thy Savior was scourged for thee
With sharp scourges, and suffered it patiently;
So must thou ere thou 'scape that painful pilgrimage. 565
Knowledge, keep him in this voyage,
And by that time Good Deeds will be with thee.
But in any wise be seeker of mercy,
For your time draweth fast, and ye will saved be;
Ask God mercy, and He will grant truly; 570

[43]Esteem.   [44]The sacrament of confession.

When with the scourge of penance man doth him bind,
The oil of forgiveness then shall he find.   [*Exit* CONFESSION.]
EVERYMAN. Thanked be God for his gracious work!
  For now I will my penance begin;
  This hath rejoiced and lighted my heart,   575
  Though the knots be painful and hard within.
KNOWLEDGE. Everyman, look your penance that ye fulfil,
  What pain that ever it to you be,
  And Knowledge shall give you counsel at will
  How your account ye shall make clearly.   580

[EVERYMAN *kneels.*]

EVERYMAN. O eternal God! O heavenly figure!
  O way of rightwiseness! O goodly vision!
  Which descended down in a virgin pure
  Because he would Everyman redeem,
  Which Adam forfeited by his disobedience.   585
  O blesséd Godhead! elect and high divine,
  Forgive me my grievous offence;
  Here I cry thee mercy in this presence.
  O ghostly treasure! O ransomer and redeemer!
  Of all the world hope and conductor,   590
  Mirror of joy, and founder of mercy,
  Which illumineth heaven and earth thereby,
  Hear my clamorous complaint, though it late be.
  Receive my prayers; unworthy in this heavy life.
  Though I be a sinner most abominable,   595
  Yet let my name be written in Moses' table.
  O Mary! pray to the Maker of all thing,
  Me for to help at my ending,
  And save me from the power of my enemy,
  For Death assaileth me strongly.   600
  And, Lady, that I may by means of thy prayer
  Of your Son's glory to be partner,
  By the means of his passion I it crave;
  I beseech you, help my soul to save.   [*He rises.*]
  Knowledge, give me the scourge of penance.   605
  My flesh therewith shall give a quittance.
  I will now begin, if God give me grace.
KNOWLEDGE. Everyman, God give you time and space.
  Thus I bequeath you in the hands of our Savior,
  Now may you make your reckoning sure.   610
EVERYMAN. In the name of the Holy Trinity,
  My body sore punished shall be.   [*Scourges himself.*]
  Take this, body, for the sin of the flesh;
  Also thou delightest to go gay and fresh,
  And in the way of damnation thou did me bring;   615
  Therefore suffer now strokes of punishing.
  Now of penance I will wade the water clear,
  To save me from purgatory, that sharp fire.

[GOOD DEEDS *rises from floor.*]

GOOD DEEDS. I thank God, now I can walk and go,
    And am delivered of my sickness and woe.   620
    Therefore with Everyman I will go, and not spare;
    His good works I will help him to declare.
KNOWLEDGE. Now, Everyman, be merry and glad!
    Your Good Deeds cometh now, ye may not be sad;
    Now is your Good Deeds whole and sound,   625
    Going upright upon the ground.
EVERYMAN. My heart is light, and shall be evermore.
    Now will I smite faster than I did before.
GOOD DEEDS. Everyman, pilgrim, my special friend,
    Bléssed be thou without end.   630
    For thee is prepared the eternal glory.
    Ye have me made whole and sound,
    Therefore I will bide by thee in every stound.[45]
EVERYMAN. Welcome, my Good Deeds; now I hear thy voice,
    I weep for very sweetness of love.   635
KNOWLEDGE. Be no more sad, but ever rejoice;
    God seeth thy living in his throne above.
    Put on this garment to thy behoof,
    Which is wet with your tears,
    Or else before God you may it miss,   640
    When you to your journey's end come shall.
EVERYMAN. Gentle Knowledge, what do ye it call?
KNOWLEDGE. It is the garment of sorrow;
    From pain it will you borrow;
    Contrition it is   645
    That getteth forgiveness;
    It pleaseth God passing well.
GOOD DEEDS. Everyman, will you wear it for your heal?

[EVERYMAN *puts on garment of*
      contrition.]

EVERYMAN. Now bléssed be Jesu, Mary's Son,
    For now have I on true contrition.   650
    And let us go now without tarrying;
    Good Deeds, have we clear our reckoning?
GOOD DEEDS. Yea, indeed I have it here.
EVERYMAN. Then I trust we need not fear.
    Now, friends, let us not part in twain.   655
KNOWLEDGE. Nay, Everyman, that will we not, certain.
GOOD DEEDS. Yet must thou lead with thee
    Three persons of great might.
EVERYMAN. Who should they be?
GOOD DEEDS. Discretion and Strength they hight,[46]   660
    And thy Beauty may not abide behind.

---

[45] In every situation; always.   [46] Are called.

KNOWLEDGE. Also ye must call to mind
    Your Five Wits as for your counselors.
GOOD DEEDS. You must have them ready at all hours.
EVERYMAN. How shall I get them hither?   665
KNOWLEDGE. You must call them all together,
    And they will hear you incontinent.[47]
EVERYMAN. My friends, come hither and be present;
    Discretion, Strength, my Five Wits, and Beauty.

                    [*Enter* DISCRETION, STRENGTH,
                    FIVE WITS, *and* BEAUTY.]

BEAUTY. Here at your will we be all ready.   670
    What will ye that we should do?
GOOD DEEDS. That ye would with Everyman go,
    And help him in his pilgrimage.
    Advise you, will ye with him or not in that voyage?
STRENGTH. We will bring him all thither,   675
    To his help and comfort, ye may believe me.
DISCRETION. So will we go with him all together.
EVERYMAN. Almighty God, lovéd may thou be!
    I give thee laud that I have hither brought
    Strength, Discretion, Beauty, and Five Wits. Lack I naught;   680
    And my Good Deeds, with Knowledge clear,
    All be in company at my will here.
    I desire no more to my business.
STRENGTH. And I, Strength, will by you stand in distress,
    Though thou would in battle fight on the ground.   685
FIVE WITS. And though it were through the world round,
    We will not depart for sweet nor sour.
BEAUTY. No more will I, unto death's hour,
    Whatsoever thereof befall.
DISCRETION. Everyman, advise you first of all;   690
    Go with a good advisement and deliberation.
    We all give you virtuous monition
    That all shall be well.
EVERYMAN. My friends, hearken what I will tell:
    I pray God reward you in his heavenly sphere.   695
    Now hearken, all that be here,
    For I will make my testament
    Here before you all present:
    In alms half my goods I will give with my hands twain
    In the way of charity, with good intent,   700
    And the other half still shall remain;
    I it bequeath to be returned there it ought to be.
    This I do in despite of the fiend of hell,
    To go quite out of his peril
    Ever after and this day.   705

---

[47] At once.

KNOWLEDGE. Everyman, hearken what I say;
    Go to Priesthood, I you advise,
    And receive of him in any wise
    The holy sacrament and ointment together;
    Then shortly see ye turn again hither;   710
    We will all abide you here.
FIVE WITS. Yea, Everyman, hie you that ye ready were.
    There is no emperor, king, duke, nor baron,
    That of God hath commission
    As hath the least priest in the world being;   715
    For of the blesséd sacraments pure and benign
    He beareth the keys, and thereof hath the cure
    For man's redemption—it is ever sure—
    Which God for our soul's medicine
    Gave us out of his heart with great pain,   720
    Here in this transitory life, for thee and me.
    The blesséd sacraments seven there be:
    Baptism, confirmation, with priesthood good,
    And the sacrament of God's precious flesh and blood,
    Marriage, the holy extreme unction, and penance.   725
    These seven be good to have in remembrance,
    Gracious sacraments of high divinity.
EVERYMAN. Fain would I receive that holy body
    And meekly to my ghostly[48] father I will go.
FIVE WITS. Everyman, that is the best that ye can do.   730
    God will you to salvation bring,
    For priesthood exceedeth all other thing;
    To us Holy Scripture they do teach,
    And converteth man from sin, heaven to reach;
    God hath to them more power given,   735
    Than to any angel that is in heaven.
    With five words[49] he may consecrate
    God's body in flesh and blood to make,
    And handleth his Maker between his hands.
    The priest bindeth and unbindeth all bands,   740
    Both in earth and in heaven;
    Thou ministers all the sacraments seven;
    Though we kissed thy feet, thou wert worthy;
    Thou art the surgeon that cureth sin deadly:
    No remedy we find under God   745
    But all only priesthood.
    Everyman, God gave priests that dignity,
    And setteth them in his stead among us to be;
    Thus be they above angels, in degree.

              [*Exit* EVERYMAN.]

KNOWLEDGE. If priests be good, it is so, surely.   750

---

[48] Spiritual.   [49] The five words are *Hoc est enim corpus meum:* "For this is my body."

But when Jesus hanged on the cross with great smart,
There he gave out of his blesséd heart
The same sacrament in great torment.
He sold them not to us, that Lord omnipotent.
Therefore Saint Peter the Apostle doth say   755
That Jesus' curse hath all they
Which God their Savior do buy or sell,
Or they for any money do take or tell.
Sinful priests giveth the sinners example bad;
Their children sitteth by other men's fires, I have heard;   760
And some haunteth women's company
With unclean life, as lusts of lechery.
These be with sin made blind.
FIVE WITS. I trust to God no such may we find.
Therefore let us priesthood honor,   765
And follow their doctrine for our souls' succor.
We be their sheep, and they shepherds be
By whom we all be kept in surety.
Peace! for yonder I see Everyman come,
Which hath made true satisfaction.   770
GOOD DEEDS. Methinketh it is he indeed.

[Re-enter EVERYMAN.]

EVERYMAN. Now Jesu be your alder speed.[50]
I have received the sacrament for my redemption,
And then mine extreme unction.
Blesséd be all they that counseled me to take it!   775
And now, friends, let us go without longer respite.
I thank God that ye have tarried so long.
Now set each of you on this rod[51] your hand,
And shortly follow me.
I go before, there I would be. God be our guide.   780
STRENGTH. Everyman, we will not from you go,
Till ye have done this voyage long.
DISCRETION. I, Discretion, will bide by you also.
KNOWLEDGE. And though this pilgrimage be never so strong,
I will never part you fro.   785
Everyman, I will be as sure by thee
As ever I did by Judas Maccabee.[52]

[They go together to the grave.]

EVERYMAN. Alas! I am so faint I may not stand,
My limbs under me do fold.
Friends, let us not turn again to this land,   790
Not for all the world's gold;
For into this cave must I creep
And turn to earth, and there to sleep.
BEAUTY. What, into this grave? Alas!

---

[50] Jesus be the succor of all of you.   [51] Cross.   [52] Jewish patriot, second century B.C.

EVERYMAN. Yea, there shall you consume, more and less.   795
BEAUTY. And what, should I smother here?
EVERYMAN. Yea, by my faith, and never more appear.
   In this world live no more we shall,
   But in heaven before the highest Lord of all.
BEAUTY. I cross out all this; adieu, by Saint John!   800
   I take my cap in my lap and am gone.
EVERYMAN. What, Beauty, whither will ye?
BEAUTY. Peace! I am deaf. I look not behind me,
   Not and thou would give me all the gold in thy chest. [*Exit* BEAUTY.]
EVERYMAN. Alas, whereto may I trust?   805
   Beauty goeth fast away from me;
   She promised with me to live and die.
STRENGTH. Everyman, I will thee also forsake and deny.
   Thy game liketh me not at all.[53]
EVERYMAN. Why, then ye will forsake me all?   810
   Sweet Strength, tarry a little space.
STRENGTH. Nay, sir, by the rood[54] of grace,
   I will hie me from thee fast,
   Though thou weep till thy heart to-brast.[55]
EVERYMAN. Ye would ever bide by me, ye said.   815
STRENGTH. Yea, I have you far enough conveyed.
   Ye be old enough, I understand,
   Your pilgrimage to take on hand.
   I repent me that I hither came.
EVERYMAN. Strength, you to displease I am to blame;   820
   Yet promise is debt, this ye well wot.
STRENGTH. In faith, I care not!
   Thou are but a fool to complain.
   You spend your speech and waste your brain;
   Go, thrust thee into the ground.   [*Exit* STRENGTH.]   825
EVERYMAN. I had weened surer I should you have found.
   He that trusteth in his Strength
   She him deceiveth at the length.
   Both Strength and Beauty forsaketh me,
   Yet they promised me fair and lovingly.   830
DISCRETION. Everyman, I will after Strength be gone;
   As for me I will leave you alone.
EVERYMAN. Why, Discretion, will ye forsake me?
DISCRETION. Yea, in faith, I will go from thee;
   For when Strength goeth before   835
   I follow after evermore.
EVERYMAN. Yet, I pray thee, for the love of the Trinity,
   Look in my grave once piteously.
DISCRETION. Nay, so nigh will I not come.
   Farewell, every one!   [*Exit* DISCRETION.]   840
EVERYMAN. O all thing faileth, save God alone—
   Beauty, Strength, and Discretion;

[53] I do not like this game at all.   [54] Cross.   [55] Break into pieces.

For when Death bloweth his blast,
They all run from me full fast.

FIVE WITS. Everyman, my leave now of thee I take;   845
I will follow the other, for here I thee forsake.

EVERYMAN. Alas! then may I wail and weep,
For I took you for my best friend.

FIVE WITS. I will no longer thee keep;
Now farewell, and there an end.   [*Exit* FIVE WITS.]   850

EVERYMAN. O Jesu, help! All hath forsaken me!

GOOD DEEDS. Nay, Everyman; I will bide with thee,
I will not forsake thee indeed;
Thou shalt find me a good friend at need.

EVERYMAN. Gramercy, Good Deeds! Now may I true friends see.   855
They have forsaken me, every one;
I loved them better than my Good Deeds alone.
Knowledge, will ye forsake me also?

KNOWLEDGE. Yea, Everyman, when ye to death shall go;
But not yet, for no manner of danger.   860

EVERYMAN. Gramercy, Knowledge, with all my heart.

KNOWLEDGE. Nay, yet I will not from hence depart
Till I see where ye shall be come.

EVERYMAN. Methink, alas, that I must be gone
To make my reckoning and my debts pay,   865
For I see my time is nigh spent away.
Take example, all ye that this do hear or see,
How they that I loved best do forsake me,
Except my Good Deeds that bideth truly.

GOOD DEEDS. All earthly things is but vanity.   870
Beauty, Strength, and Discretion do man forsake,
Foolish friends and kinsmen, that fair spake,
All fleeth save Good Deeds, and that am I.

EVERYMAN. Have mercy on me, God most mighty;
And stand by me, thou Mother and Maid, holy Mary!   875

GOOD DEEDS. Fear not, I will speak for thee.

EVERYMAN. Here I cry God mercy!

GOOD DEEDS. Short our end, and 'minish our pain.
Let us go and never come again.

EVERYMAN. Into thy hands, Lord, my soul I commend.   880
Receive it, Lord, that it be not lost.
As thou me boughtest, so me defend,
And save me from the fiend's boast,
That I may appear with that blessèd host
That shall be saved at the day of doom.   885
In manus tuas—of might's most
For ever—*commendo spiritum meum.*[56]

> [EVERYMAN *and* GOOD DEEDS *de-
> scend into the grave.*]

---

[56]"Into thy hands I commend my spirit."

KNOWLEDGE. Now hath he suffered that we all shall endure;
    The Good Deeds shall make all sure.
    Now hath he made ending. 890
    Methinketh that I hear angels sing
    And make great joy and melody
    Where Everyman's soul received shall be.
ANGEL [*within*]. Come, excellent elect spouse to Jesu!
    Here above thou shalt go 895
    Because of thy singular virtue.
    Now the soul is taken the body fro,
    Thy reckoning is crystal clear.
    Now shalt thou into the heavenly sphere,
    Unto the which all ye shall come 900
    That liveth well before the day of doom.

> [*Exit* KNOWLEDGE. *Enter* DOC-
> TOR[57] *for Epilogue*.]

DOCTOR. This moral men may have in mind:
    Ye hearers, take it of worth, old and young,
    And forsake Pride, for he deceiveth you in the end,
    And remember Beauty, Five Wits, Strength, and Discretion, 905
    They all at the last do Everyman forsake,
    Save his Good Deeds there doth he take.
    But beware, and they be small
    Before God he hath no help at all.
    None excuse may be there for Everyman. 910
    Alas, how shall he do then?
    For, after death, amends may no man make,
    For then mercy and pity doth him forsake.
    If his reckoning be not clear when he doth come,
    God will say, "*Ite, maledicti, in ignem aeternum.*"[58] 915
    And he that hath his account whole and sound,
    High in heaven he shall be crowned.
    Unto which place God bring us all thither,
    That we may live body and soul together.
    Thereto help the Trinity! 920
    Amen, say ye, for saint charity.

THUS ENDETH THIS MORAL PLAY OF EVERYMAN.

---

[57] Theologian.   [58] "Go, cursed ones, into eternal fire."

The Renaissance

T HE word *Renaissance* means *rebirth*. The term purports to describe
a movement in European intellectual, cultural, and political history that first flourished in Italy, mainly from the mid-fourteenth
to the sixteenth centuries, and then in other parts of Europe during an
overlapping but generally later period that ended in the mid-seventeenth
century. The origin of the Renaissance, both the concept and the term, is of
considerable interest in exploring the question, much debated in the twentieth century, whether there was any genuine rebirth in the Renaissance
and whether the movement so labelled really had a distinctive existence.

To many people in the vanguard of Renaissance literature, art, and
thought, the age did in fact seem new. The first major spokesman for this
view was Petrarch (1304–1374), who believed that the thousand years separating his age from the fall of ancient Roman civilization had been a dark
night and that the first priority of his contemporaries should be to restore
ancient literature, for its own sake and in the interests of human virtue. His
followers, the humanists of Italy and later of northern Europe, extended
Petrarch's primarily literary emphasis to include important new directions
in the fine arts, religious studies, philosophy, mathematics, and political
theory. When the new heliocentric astronomy was developed (or rediscovered) by Copernicus (1473–1543), the new Protestant movement was
launched in 1517 by Luther (1483–1546), and maritime exploration in the
fifteenth and sixteenth centuries revealed the existence of the western
hemisphere, the age necessarily became aware that changes of awesome
momentousness, for better or worse, were in process. But for the most part
the consciousness by the age of its own novelty remained limited and was
primarily a matter of high culture. The term *rebirth* was popularized during
the Renaissance by the eminent art historian Giorgio Vasari in his *Lives of
the Most Eminent Italian Painters, Sculptors, and Architects* (1550), in which
Vasari acclaimed the new artists for having revived classical esthetic values
and recovered the faculty to see and depict nature.

The modern, much broader, concept of a Renaissance is largely the
creation not of the age itself but of retrospect. To eighteenth-century
Enlightenment thinkers the Renaissance was the age when medieval
"superstition," especially revealed religion, was overthrown. But it was not
until the nineteenth century that there emerged the model of the Renaissance familiar today, along with its mystique. The landmarks of this new
model were Jules Michelet's volume on the Renaissance in his *History of
France* (1855) and Jacob Burckhardt's *The Civilization of the Renaissance in
Italy* (1860), in combination with the work of Burckhardt's followers who
broadened his model of the early Italian Renaissance to include later peri-

ods, other parts of Europe, and fields such as economic life that Burck-hardt had not treated in depth. For these scholars and their intellectual heirs the Renaissance was not only or even primarily a revival of learning and the arts but a period with its own organic coherence, a sudden and radical break with the Middle Ages, and the point of departure for the modern world. In Michelet's phrase, it marked "the discovery of the world and of man." Above all, the Renaissance was an age of individual personali-ties, liberated from the political constraints of Holy Roman Emperor and pope, free to understand and express themselves for good or evil. The state, for Burckhardt, had become a "work of art," the product of events working through human personalities rather than something imposed by an external sanction such as tradition or the will of God. The age had a pagan vitality.

This view of the Renaissance has the obvious appeal of glamour, and it survives, as not only the popular model but also that of scholars, even when they feel they must reject or modify it as many of them have done. Medievalists especially have bridled. They insist that many of the suppos-edly new departures in the Renaissance—the revival of classical learning, the emergence of an urban culture that fostered the arts and a capitalist economy, exploration of distant lands, the development of the rationalist scientific mentality, the growth of a lay rather than clerical culture, and the rise of national states—were actually continuations of trends that be-gan centuries before Petrarch. It is also highly questionable, according to champions of the Middle Ages, that the most typical Renaissance trends were advances for humankind. For the most skeptical among them, the Renaissance was not a rebirth but the twilight of the great medieval era.

The conviction remains that the concept of a Renaissance (whether that is the right word or not) is useful and represents something real. But it can no longer be argued easily that the discontinuity with the Middle Ages was radical or that a single spirit dominated all of southern and western Europe for three centuries or that the Renaissance is simply an early stage of modernism. The tendency in Renaissance studies today is to examine dif-ferent places and stages of it closely, discriminating and qualifying consci-entiously in accord with concrete evidence rather than broad formulas, however exhilarating. In this brief essay there is not enough space to re-cord all the qualifications and exceptions that the complexity of the Renais-sance age and culture calls for. Almost all the generalizations that follow are challengeable. Even so, they may be helpful, especially because many of them originate in the Renaissance view of itself. Moreover, they provide an index to the history of sensibility. In the last century or so readers have developed the habit, when reading Renaissance literature, of isolating and responding selectively to those qualities in it that have the expansiveness of spirit which, accurately or not, has been understood as distinctively Renaissance.

We can begin with humanism, an aspect of the Renaissance that touches on virtually all the others. In a broad sense, the term *humanism* can be defined as any view of the world that places humankind at the center of things. It is as old as Greek antiquity but also quite modern, numbering among its adherents a wide variety of groups ranging from Marxists to existentialists (religious, atheistic, and agnostic) to educators who insist on the primacy of the liberal arts and humanities. In a more restricted though still rather elastic sense, humanism refers to a distinctive habit of thought that pervades Renaissance art and philosophy. Beginning roughly in the latter fourteenth century, with such men as Petrarch, it spread over the following centuries throughout Europe; in the north it reached its zenith of creative expression in the first decades of the sixteenth century in the great Dutch scholar, theologian, and satirist Desiderius Erasmus (1466?–1536) and in his English colleague Thomas More (1478–1535), the author of *Utopia*.

The humanists tended to think of themselves as a new breed, and they do represent at least a striking shift in emphasis. They accorded man a high degree of autonomy, an extreme form of which was expressed by the Italian humanist Pico della Mirandola (1463–1494) in his *Oration on the Dignity of Man*. In a famous passage from that work God addresses man: "I have given you, Adam, neither a predetermined place nor a particular aspect nor any special prerogatives in order that you may take and possess these through your own decision and choice. The limitations on the nature of other creatures are contained within my prescribed laws. You shall determine your own nature without constraint from any barrier, by means of the freedom to whose power I have entrusted you. . . . I have made you neither heavenly nor earthly, neither mortal nor immortal so that, like a free and sovereign artificer, you might mold and fashion yourself into that form you yourself shall have chosen." Asceticism was no longer necessarily the hallmark of sanctity, and pleasure became more respectable, whether celebrated riotously as in Rabelais or in the more spiritualized form it usually took for the northern humanists. (It must be stated, however, that the stereotype of Italian humanists as pagan rather than Christian is a misleading caricature.) The world and the life of the body were to be accepted and rejoiced in, regarded not as signs that man is alienated from his higher self but as avenues that, in parallel with the soul, humanity can use for its fulfillment. In "The Godly Feast," one of Erasmus's *Colloquies,* the host Eusebius urges his dinner guests: "But while we feast our minds plenteously, let us not neglect their partners." Asked who these partners are, he replies, "Our bodies; aren't they partners of our minds? For I prefer 'partners' to 'instruments' or 'dwellings' or 'tombs .'" The honorific status given in the Middle Ages to clerical authority and to the ideal of celibacy was considerably modified.

The vehicle for realizing the humanists' ideals was to be reason—more concretely, education of the most comprehensive kind: physical, moral, literary, philosophical. The ancient classics became major and indispensable tools of this education; without them the truly good life could not be envisioned in its wholeness. The humanists were therefore earnestly committed to the recovery and editing of ancient texts (which were not so much discovered as unearthed from churches and monasteries). The texts included both the secular and (especially for the northern humanists) the religious; Erasmus, most notably, did a landmark Greek edition of the New Testament. Moreover, this philological scholarship was not regarded as fastidious purism or as intellectual escapism; quite the contrary, for the humanists had as prime goals both the perfection of individual human character and the reform of public evils, in church and state. (More's *Utopia* is a clear case in point.) They were activist social scientists. In their educational systems, they wished to substitute for the medieval concern with elaborate formal logic an ideal of practical and moral wisdom instilled through a curriculum dominated by poetry, history, moral philosophy, and—in lieu of medieval theology—the Bible itself. Although they were in one way elitists, aiming to train a special educated cadre of reforming leaders, they were also egalitarian to the extent that they prized feudal nobility of birth less than a moral and intellectual nobility, the signs of which were rhetorical eloquence, refined diction, and urbane wit, all these combined with rectitude of conduct.

Humanist thought, elusive and ambiguous though it sometimes seems, was fundamentally concerned with wholeness, of the human personality and of world view. The clearest example is in their religious thought. Most of them were firm believers in Christianity (such occasional puzzles as Rabelais and Montaigne notwithstanding), which they did not regard as a system in rivalry with pagan antiquity. Nor did they regard antiquity as a mere allegorizing of Christian revelation (as often in Dante); the achievement of a genuinely historical point of view, by which the events and ideas of classical times could be understood as they really were in themselves, was another of their prime goals, akin to their passion for rejecting spurious literary texts and traditions. Rather, they saw Christianity and paganism as organic parts of total truth. In "The Godly Feast," Eusebius says, "whatever is devout and contributes to good morals should not be called profane. Sacred Scripture is of course the basic authority in everything; yet I sometimes run across ancient sayings or pagan writings—even the poets'—so purely and reverently and admirably expressed that I can't help believing their authors' hearts were moved by some divine power. And perhaps the spirit of Christ is more widespread than we understand, and the company of saints includes many not in our calendar. Speaking frankly among friends, I can't read [certain of Cicero's works] without sometimes kissing the book and blessing that pure heart, divinely inspired as it was. . . . So that I would much rather let all of Scotus [the medieval philosopher] and others of his sort perish than the books of a single Cicero or Plutarch." Some of the humanists went so far as to envisage a primal religious revelation of which all the world's creeds are reflections.

The complexity of the Renaissance age is well illustrated in the ambiguous relationship between humanism and the religious currents of the time, especially the Protestant Reformation, customarily dated from Luther's definitive rebellion against the Catholic Church in 1517. The papacy had been in dire trouble in the fourteenth and fifteenth centuries, sorely tried by its "Babylonian captivity" when the seat of the papacy was moved to Avignon in France, then weakened by a period of schism when there were rival popes, and after that by a period when a council laid claim to ecclesiastical authority. In the meantime, skeptical and heretical movements that had grown out of the late Middle Ages were flourishing, and powerful movements stressing mystical experience and simple piety were spreading rapidly among both clergy and laity. The last half of the fifteenth century and the first two decades of the sixteenth, immediately before Luther's revolt, saw a reinvigorated papacy at its height of cultural glory: the renowned Vatican Library was created, and Popes Julius II and Leo X, reigning from 1503 to 1521, patronized the work of great artists including Michelangelo and Raphael. But many of the popes of the time were concerned more with political and personal aggrandizement than with the spiritual welfare of the European church. Out of this background the Reformation emerged, claiming to reassert the values of authentic early Christianity, drawing for theological support on epistles by St. Paul and the writings of early church fathers like Augustine (and of course on the Gospels as the Reformers understood them), preaching that man was saved not by his own efforts ("works") but by faith. The Protestant opposition to indulgences (remissions of punishment in Purgatory) was therefore not merely a moral rebellion against the venal selling of them by Rome but a theological stance that rejected the whole idea of Purgatory, with its implication that man can satisfy divine justice in his own person rather than exclusively in Christ.

The Reformation is in different ways an expression of humanist ideals and a contradiction of them. The Protestant attempt to recover the ancient text and meaning of the Bible and to spread them widely, free of medieval theological overlays, is akin to and indeed part of the humanist movement, which conservative Catholic churchmen distrusted. Both Protestants and humanists agreed also in their contempt for medieval scholasticism in general, in pressing for institutional reform in the church, and in encouraging the active role of the laity in intellectual and religious life. Both put a high value on simple piety in contrast with elaborate formal liturgy and complicated systems of devotion such as the veneration of saints and their relics and the earning of indulgences. On the other hand, the two movements differed in some fundamental ways. The humanists were essentially optimistic about human nature, asserting the crucial role of free will. This emphasis contradicted the view, held by John Calvin (1509–1564) and the Protestant radicals who followed him, that humanity is weak in its fallen state ("totally depraved," to use the technical term) and therefore dependent on God's free gift of grace rather than its own spiritual exertions. Humanists tended not to be interested in sectarian dogma as such, except—as with Erasmus and More—to resist divisive innovations that threatened Church unity. Moreover, though the humanists scorned most things medieval, their essential internationalism, typified in the insistence by Erasmus and More that the Church remain unified, is closer to the medieval model than to the new localism and nationalism that evolved in parallel with the Protestant churches. And the advocacy of religious tolerance by humanists like Erasmus is antithetical to the intense sectarian partisanship expressed both in Protestantism and in the Catholic Counter-Reformation. (The latter is best exemplifed in the militant Society of Jesus, or Jesuits, founded on a military model in 1534 by the Spanish saint and former soldier Ignatius Loyola. In the literature of Protestant countries like England, the Jesuits generally appear not only as agents of "papist" religion but as unscrupulous, subversive machiavels working in the interest of foreign political powers. It is interesting, then, that Ignatius himself exhibited a kind of practical mysticism that owes something to the devotional trends, fostered by humanists, that had helped produce the Reformation.) Finally, the humanists' willingness to envisage the world in terms of classical models that might be compatible with Christianity but also existed independent of it did not square with the impulse in radical Protestantism to reject everything that was religiously neutral as pagan worldliness. The humanists were thus in a curious position after the Reformation, distrusted as sowers of heresy by many Catholics (despite his Catholicism, some of Erasmus's works were put on the *Index* of prohibited books) and rejected by many Protestants as faint-hearted, worldly temporizers, the lukewarm whom God, in the biblical phrase, would spew out of His mouth.

The role of the Renaissance and of humanism in the evolution of modern science is also ambivalent. The discovery of the world and the discovery of man that Michelet found in the Renaissance age are not necessarily parallel endeavors. It is true that the recovery of ancient authors made available to thinkers models of the cosmos not available in the Middle Ages, including the heliocentric astronomy with which Copernicus replaced the old Ptolemaic model, and some unknown works by ancient scientists like Archimedes were revived. Humanists encouraged the study of algebra and geometry, the latter overlapping with experiments by painters in visual perspective. Thus the way was prepared for the incomparable mathematical developments of the seventeenth century that provided the language of modern science. But the human-centeredness of the humanists, as is still true of some of their modern counterparts, sometimes took the form of an antagonism or at least indifference to science.

For modern science to develop, another radical change had also to occur: the medieval picture of the universe, with its beautiful model of correspondences between matter on one hand and theology and human psychology on the other, had to be replaced by a more objective view of nature as having its own autonomy independent of its roles of revealing God and reflecting man. The medieval correlation between the four humors in the human body and their corresponding psychological dispositions, and between the humors and the four elements in material nature; the systematic linking of the heavenly spheres with the hierarchical orders of angels; the notion that an apple falls from a tree because it loves the earth—such ideas had to go. (E. M. W. Tillyard argues in *The Elizabethan World Picture*, 1946, that assumptions like these continued to dominate much of Renaissance thought and art.) The trend in the Renaissance to study nature more objectively appears, for example, in the concern for accurate anatomy—systematically in the work of Vesalius (1514–1564) and esthetically in the proportions and musculature of painted or sculpted nudes. The dogmatic medieval reverence for Galen in medicine and for Aristotle in general was weakened.

The new empirical direction was, however, more an extrapolation of late medieval thought than a bold Renaissance innovation. Furthermore, although empiricism is fundamental to experimental method, it is probably less essential to pure science than the mental discipline of abstraction: one must learn, in accounting for the trajectory of the falling apple, to ignore certain quite objective facts about it—that it is a Winesap, is overripe, and has a worm in it—and concentrate exclusively on the abstract properties (mass, distance from other objects) it shares with all other gravitationally attracted bodies. It can be argued convincingly that this abstract habit of thinking is much closer than the humanists' practical wisdom to the medieval scholastic discipline.

In pure science, then, the Renaissance is probably best understood as a transition period. Technologically, however, there were some epochal advances. The most important by far was the invention in the late fifteenth century, by Johann Gutenberg (1400?–1468?) and others, of printing by movable type. In the last few decades of the century, several million books were printed, multiplying by an incalculable factor the impact of all the religious, intellectual, and literary trends in the later Renaissance. It is true that this invention too depended on earlier discoveries—in paper-making, for example—but the practical culmination of the technology of printing in the Renaissance itself marks one of the few unquestionable differences, not only from the Middle Ages but from all previous world history.

The new technology included also the navigational tools—again, drawing on pre-Renaissance and non-European cultures—that made possible the Renaissance age of geographical exploration. At the end of the fifteenth century Bartholomeu Dias and Vasco da Gama opened the route to India around the Cape of Good Hope and Columbus reached the New World; in the sixteenth century Magellan's crew and Francis Drake sailed around the globe. Such voyages had an enormous impact on the European imagination, influencing works like More's *Utopia* and Luiz Vaz de Camoëns' (1524–1580) Portuguese epic *The Lusiads,* which celebrates Vasco da Gama and vaunts his superiority to those mere Mediterranean sailors Odysseus and Aeneas. The new geographical discoveries also affected the politics and economics of Europe in important ways, accelerating the trends toward nationalism, middle-class power, economic capitalism, urbanization, and the shift of money and power from the Mediterranean to the countries on the Atlantic and the North Sea.

It is precisely in such sociological, political, and economic areas, however, that the nineteenth-century model of the Renaissance as a separate and distinct, organically whole age breaks down most seriously. It is beyond question that by the sixteenth century rulers such as Philip II in Spain and the Netherlands, Francis I in France, and Henry VIII in England had achieved unprecedented authority in their realms, built on their predecessors' consolidation of royal power, territory, and wealth in the fifteenth century. Because in many respects the feudal nobility was the greatest obstacle to royal authority, the monarchs' new power was wielded increasingly through complex bureaucracies staffed largely by a new kind of middle-class men distinguished less by birth than by talent or money. (Italy, with its city-states, was dominated by outside powers in the sixteenth century and was not unified as a nation until the nineteenth.) It is also true that these new national regimes, along with the Italian city-states, had begun to define themselves and their goals in increasingly secular and local terms, less dominated than in the past by the transnational authority of pope or Holy Roman Emperor or by the model of European Christendom as a unity. Populations boomed; banking flourished as money came to replace payment in kind and services; cities grew dramatically in size and importance, along with the intellectual and artistic activity that urban centers help foster. But the roots of all these movements go back, in some cases several centuries, into the medieval period. Moreover, the Renaissance is ridden by a great political-cultural paradox: while medieval internationalism was losing ground to the more local autonomy of city-state and national monarchy, in accordance with an ideal of patriotic citizenship that the humanists encouraged, the different parts of Europe were at the same time becoming more intellectually and culturally interdependent—a trend, greatly reinforced by the printing press, that also owes much to the humanists. A roughly similar paradox exists in the twentieth century: the breakup of the international colonial systems into scores of autonomous new states has coincided with the internationalist movement represented politically in the United Nations and with developments in technology and communication that have helped transform the world into a "global village."

Just as the humanists reacted contemptuously against things medieval in the name of a revived antiquity, so their classicizing counterparts in the visual arts often rejected medieval art, in theory at least. The Italians coined for it the pejorative term *Gothic* with a glance at the barbarians who overran ancient Rome. Today that term survives, but the accompanying value judgment has changed vastly. The Gothic style, alive from the twelfth to the fifteenth centuries (in some parts of Europe into the sixteenth), is now regarded as the expression of one of the great ages of world art. Much of its painting has disappeared, although a good deal is known about how it used two-dimensional media from tapestries, stained glass, and glorious color illuminations in manuscripts. Above all, its public architecture survives in the great European cathedrals, which embody an organic unity and a fusion with sculpture and other arts scarcely to be paralleled since the age of the Parthenon in ancient Greece.

The transition from Gothic to Renaissance art is problematical, like so many other aspects of the period when it happened. Compared with the Gothic, Renaissance art is more concerned with classical forms and subjects, with secular themes directed to a more secular clientele, with landscape and other aspects of nature, with the illusion of depth, with individual portraiture, and generally with greater representational realism. All these trends are also observable, however, in late medieval Gothic art as it developed from the Romanesque style that prevailed between the tenth and twelfth centuries. Further complications arise when one distinguishes between different parts of Europe, different stages of the Renaissance, and different art media. There remains nevertheless an immense difference between the Gothic and Renaissance periods in degree and also in consciousness, for the new trends were pursued with a programmatic deliberateness in the Renaissance that one does not find in the earlier era.

The most comprehensive of these trends was the revival of antiquity. Architectural models still existed, especially in Italy, and could be imitated directly. The spirituality implicit in the vertical-line composition and pointed arches of the Gothic cathedral yielded to the essentially horizontal classical emphasis. (Another way of looking at this shift is to see the cutting edge of architectural innovation as having shifted south to Italy, since the great Gothic cathedrals, with their mystically soaring vertical lines and spaces and their walls opened up with stained glass, had been an almost exclusively northern phenomenon.) The dome was revived by Filippo

Brunelleschi in his design for the Florence cathedral (1420), a landmark of the new style, and was used climactically by Michelangelo for St. Peter's in Rome. Classical columns, with their distinctive capitals marking the intersection of vertical with horizontal, took priority over the less clearly end-stopped Gothic pillars. In sculpture and painting, there were greater difficulties, since few antique models existed, especially in the early Renaissance before the discovery of statues such as the Apollo Belvedere. But artists in these media too did their enthusiastic best to classicize. Donatello (1386?–1466) pioneered in the revival of the free-standing nude and the equestrian statue. Painters, besides espousing the classical ideals of proportion and harmony, turned to ancient historical and mythological subjects—although the most frequent ones were still derived from the Bible and the lives of the saints.

The renewed interest in nature by Renaissance artists took many forms. The most obvious was an increased emphasis on landscape, though still almost always integrated with a human subject. The basic medieval world view had regarded the physical creation as sacramental and symbolic, and the Renaissance did not by any means discard that view; Renaissance pictures continued to be expressions of ideas, often retaining a system of symbols and icons inherited from the Middle Ages, as myriad Renaissance "emblem books" attest. At the same time, Renaissance art suggests also that, apart from its human or divine analogies, the world "out there" can be reproduced for what it is in itself. The picture frame became a window through which one glimpsed the living world. (According to Vasari, Leonardo da Vinci once played a practical joke on his father by creating a terrifying picture so lifelike that it was mistaken for reality.) Anatomy became a formal study for artists; drawing from nude models became commonplace, and the nude as a subject became ubiquitous. Color effects were perfected, especially by Titian and other Venetians. Portraits of individuals became an important genre, as exemplified in the masterfully realistic ones done by Hans Holbein the Younger (1497?–1543) of Erasmus, More, and Henry VIII. This individualism of subject reinforces the general motif of individualism ascribed to the Renaissance in the nineteenth-century model.

Even more to the point is the new individualistic role of the artist. The greatest medieval works of art, the cathedrals, had been collective, indeed communal achievements, a union of large vision with the painstaking efforts of hundreds of skilled artists and craftsmen who remained anonymous. Many of the best medieval artists are identified today only by the word *Master* linked to the name of his city or one of his masterpieces. But in the Renaissance, artists, often working for individual patrons whom they glorified as individuals, came to think of themselves also as unique men expressing their own unique visions and values. Some of them took to signing their canvases, a new practice, and even when they did not do so their works were figuratively signed by the unmistakable presence of their own personal styles. The medieval artist had been a maker and a servant of God; the Renaissance artist was a creator and, as such, God's rival.

Because it was essentially a literary movement, humanism naturally had its most direct impact on literature. Classical modes were revitalized—for example, the ode, the dialogue, and the pastoral, a form popular in Renaissance literary genres ranging from song to prose romance to drama. Besides serving as midwives of the revived classicism, some of the humanists created literary masterpieces themselves. They were at their best in the non-fictional or semi-fictional forms wherein inventiveness could be combined with the expression of ideas and opinions: letters, orations, dialogues, and treatises. Their admiration of Plato appears in the writings of Marsilio Ficino (1433–1499) and Pico della Mirandola, whose *Oration on the Dignity of Man* (1486) has already been mentioned. Dialogues included Erasmus's *Colloquies* (1519), More's *Utopia* (1516), and Baldassare Castiglione's *Book of the Courtier* (1514; published 1528), a vastly influential exposition of the ideal of the Renaissance gentleman. Erasmus's *Praise of Folly* (1509) is a many-sided ironic masterpiece which, like *Utopia,* shows the reformist side of humanism.

The most fundamental development in Renaissance literature was the growth of literary nationalism. All the important medieval vernacular languages of Europe had produced important literature, but it lived in the shadow of Latin, the international language, and the vernacular literatures themselves had typically reflected international rather than local traditions. In the Renaissance, political and personal allegiances to patrons, city-states, or national monarchies helped foster literary ambitions linked to the writers' own distinctive languages. Latin continued to thrive; among many other writers, More and Erasmus used it, in the works just mentioned, and into the seventeenth and eighteenth centuries it continued to be the normal vehicle for scientific discourse, including such monumental works as Isaac Newton's *Principia* (1687). It also remained the language of Roman Catholic liturgy and church government into the twentieth century. But the new Latin of the humanists was based on classical models such as Cicero's prose, and the concentration on such models helped to kill medieval Latin as a living language—a real loss, since in its spare directness medieval Latin had a beauty and functionality that the humanists did not properly appreciate. Their adulation for the classical tongues was also in some respects a roadblock to the development of the vernacular literatures; for example, humanism may have retarded for a time the development of Italian literature in the fifteenth century.

For the most part, though, the humanist impulse had the contrary effect: local patriotic feelings, reinforced by the humanist ideal of dedicated citizenship, inspired a desire to assert national identity while emulating in the national languages the achievements of antiquity. A notable example was the formation of the *Pléiade,* a group of sixteenth-century French writers that included Pierre de Ronsard (1524–1585), the greatest French poet of the Renaissance, and Joachim du Bellay (1522?–1560). Du Bellay, in his *Defense and Glorification of the French Language* (1549), produced the group's manifesto, calling for a French language and literature to rival that of Italy and antiquity in genres including tragedy, the ode, and the sonnet. The emergence of modern Italian vernacular literature had begun much earlier when Dante chose the Tuscan dialect for *The Divine Comedy,* supporting his program for Italian in a Latin treatise *On Eloquence in the Vernacular Tongue* (1304–1305), and later in the fourteenth century Petrarch and Boccaccio lent the weight of their prestige to Tuscan Italian. In Portugal, the achievements of Camoëns (1524–1580) in lyric and epic went a long way toward defining the Portuguese language. In the Protestant countries such as Germany, Holland, and England where the movement to translate the Bible into the vernacular could thrive, these translations were formative, especially Luther's German version (the New Testament in 1522, the Old Testament in 1534).

The most conscious and comprehensive assertions of Renaissance values appear in the long narrative works of the period, especially epics or works touched by the epic impulse. This is natural enough; the epic has always been a vehicle for communal ideas. If we did not know any of the great Renaissance epics and had to create a theoretical model for them on the basis of other tendencies of the time and clichés about it, we might arrive at something like this: a story of imposing events, written in a classical unrhymed verse, scornful of the outgrown medieval heritage, celebrating a modernist theme such as the recent achievements of the poet's own nation, and centered on a heroic but mentally elevated "Renaissance man" aglow with confidence and optimism. But, although virtually every Renaissance epic illustrates one or more of these motifs, what we most often find is a mixture, seemingly incongruous, of the modern, classical, and medieval, accompanied often by ambivalent value judgments. Some of these incongruities are attributable to the epic tradition itself, which since Virgil has tended to combine nationalist modernism with nostalgia, usually intimating a desire to keep alive what was best in the past and, on the other hand, a consciousness of having progressed beyond it.

Rabelais' *Gargantua and Pantagruel* (1532–1552), Cervantes' *Don Quixote* (1605, 1615), and Shakespeare's English history plays (1591–1599) are not epics in a strict formal sense, but they have the scale, comprehensiveness, and national flavor of epic. Rabelais' work is perhaps the showcase example of worldly Renaissance exuberance; yet it also recalls the medieval "goliardic," a student tradition of wining and wenching. The searching complexities of *Don Quixote* build from a direct confrontation between an idealism symbolized by the medieval romances and a contrasting pragmatism, and which set of values Cervantes endorses is not a question to answer simply. The *Quixote* is among other things an examination of the Spanish national character, but in the spirit of a sensitive critique rather than of panegyric. Of Shakespeare's ten English history plays, eight span the period from the end of the fourteenth century to the emergence in 1485 of the Tudor dynasty still reigning in Shakespeare's time, and these plays have been taken sometimes to constitute Shakespeare's epic. In it he celebrates the emergence of peace and order from a fragmented, dying medieval feudalism, but he also portrays the noble beauty of the chivalric code. None of these three authors, then, is simply heralding the glories of a new civilization unrooted in the medieval past.

When we turn to works more strictly describable as epics (almost all of them, interestingly, written in rhymed rather than in classical verse forms), we find the same mixture of allegiances. Perhaps the closest thing to our hypothetical national and modernist model is Camoëns' *Lusiad* (1572), a poem that intricately imitates Virgil's *Aeneid* and acclaims triumphantly the unprecedented Portuguese voyages around the Cape to the Far East for the glory of the nation and of Catholic Christianity. Here the sense of a vast new world in contrast to the constricted Mediterranean world of epic memory accords well enough with the nineteenth-century vision of an expansive

Renaissance spirit. Iberian interest in the new explorations is also reflected in several sixteenth-century Spanish epics by authors including Alonso de Ercilla y Zúñiga (1534–1594) and the great dramatist Lope de Vega (1562–1635).

The definitive Italian Renaissance epics are quite another matter. They consist of a series of poems written in Ferrara under the patronage of the Este family: the *Orlando in Love* (1483) of Matteo Boiardo, the *Orlando Driven Mad* (1516) of Ludovico Ariosto, and the *Jerusalem Delivered* (1575) of Torquato Tasso. (Boiardo and Ariosto built from an earlier work, *Morgante the Giant,* written about 1480 by Luigi Pulci.) All these authors belong unmistakably to the Renaissance; Ariosto especially, with his gaiety, sophistication, and sensuousness, and his theme of the impossible quest, expresses something quintessential to his time and place. But, like Pulci and Boiardo, he treats medieval matter and heroes derived from the traditions of King Arthur, Charlemagne, and Roland, although the hero of the great, austere *chanson de geste* is scarcely recognizable in this new Orlando ("Roland," in Italian). These poems are much closer to the magical atmosphere and free form of medieval romance than to the classical epic. Tasso's poem conforms more nearly to the ancient models, but it too has a medieval subject (the first Crusade) and owes much to the romance genre and atmosphere; moreover, the ideal it celebrates is a united Christian Europe that in the days of the Counter-Reformation had become no more than a wistful memory.

Edmund Spenser (1552?–1599), although a fervent Renaissance Protestant, wrote in this tradition of Italianate medievalism. In *The Faerie Queene* (published 1590–1595) he attempted a portrait of the ideal man based on a scheme of Aristotelian ethical virtues that medieval authors like Dante would probably have found congenial, and he chose for his vehicle a blend of romance, allegory, and archaic diction that also have strong medieval associations. On the other hand, Spenser's political allegory is modern and militantly Protestant, pitting Queen Elizabeth (Gloriana, the fairy queen) and her champions against evil popes and Catholic monarchs who serve as agents of the Satanic.

The culmination of Renaissance epic was achieved by Milton, who inherited many of Spenser's values but wrote an utterly different kind of poem. His *Paradise Lost*, influenced by *La Semaine* (*The Week,* 1578), an epic account of the creation by the French Protestant poet Guillaume du Bartas, treats the fall of humankind, a universal theme sanctioned by the divine truth of the Bible rather than the mere fictions of medieval legend or classic fable. In his close textural and structural use of Homer and Virgil, his anti-medievalism (reflected in a scornful passage abusing the monastic orders), his contemptuous rejection of rhyme as medieval barbarism, his deliberate disavowal of medieval romance as an epic mode ("fabled knights / In battles feigned")—in all these respects Milton adopts the humanist stance. Even more fundamentally, *Paradise Lost* is humanist in its relative freedom from sectarian factionalism (the passage about the monks notwithstanding) and in its ultimate theme: freedom, more specifically human free will. In rising above the doctrinaire polemics for his nation and theology that he reserved for his Puritan prose tracts, Milton may well have achieved in *Paradise Lost*, more than any other major Renaissance epic poet and at the very end of the Renaissance, the humanist goals that in so many ways define the age.

Renaissance values appear in the epics as broad, comprehensive visions, but equally characteristic is a new kind of literary intimacy and particularity akin to the vogue of portrait painting and the new self-expressive role of the artist. The best literary portraits are the characters in Shakespeare's plays; although they often owe something to earlier literary and dramatic traditions such as the morality play, scores of them are fully realized individuals. It may seem paradoxical, then, that Shakespeare reveals very little of himself. For the epitome of Renaissance self-revelation we can go to Montaigne (1533–1592), whose *Essays* (1580–1588) combine far-reaching speculation with the minutest factual details of his personal life and the quirks of his mind, all colored by his distinctive personality and voice.

But the principal medium for self-expression was the lyric. The prototype, once more, is Petrarch, whose lyrics focus so insistently on the poet himself. His Laura is clearly in the line of Dante's Beatrice, but, without denying that Beatrice is a real woman or that Laura is idealized, one senses that the latter is far more fully a unique individual. In the sonnet especially, Petrarch started a Renaissance fashion taken up by almost all the lyric poets of Europe, including Camoëns, Ronsard, Spenser, Sir Philip Sidney (1554–1586), Shakespeare, and Milton. It became the confessional love poem *par excellence*, but even when the subject was not inherently private or amatory (Shakespeare on time, Donne on religious experience), the viewpoint on these more universal matters was still usually subjective. This is not to say that the sonnets were reliably autobiographical; in fact, the genre became one of the most artificial, convention-ridden of forms, full of stylized sighing lovers, cruel but idealized mistresses (sometimes quite fictional), and other stock devices of the courtly love apparatus whose roots extend back beyond Petrarch into the Middle Ages. But even the most conventional of the sonnets reflect the vogue of self-expression, since the sonneteer had at least to assume the guise of a man revealing his intimate thoughts or feelings. "Fool," says Sidney's muse to him, "look in thy heart and write." (Ultimately the Petrarchan tradition of courtly praise fell by its own weight of artificiality; Donne in his lyrics scrutinizes the conventions ironically, and Shakespeare could satirize them as he does in his Sonnet 130: "My mistress' eyes are nothing like the sun; / Coral is far more red than her lips' red . . . .") Often, too, the sonneteers' self-consciousness took the form of commentary on their own work; poetry and the poets' ability to give immortality to their addressees were frequent themes, and beneath the overlays of this convention is an authentic new sense of the power of art that is characteristic of the Renaissance.

The heightened interest during the Renaissance in objectifying the world, portraying individuals, and exploring the complexities of human psychology as it is reflected in behavior—all these were favorable conditions for a resurgent interest in drama, which, especially in England and Spain, flourished as it had not done since Greek antiquity. The exact origins of this new dramatic impulse are hard to untangle from one another. The classical revival was unquestionably important: the plays of Terence, Plautus, and Seneca known to the Middle Ages were now approached less exclusively as rhetorical models and more as literary theater; the Greek dramatists were rediscovered along with some plays by Plautus that had disappeared; at schools and universities plays were studied avidly, and scholars began to write classically inspired dramas of their own, in both Latin and the vernacular. The printing press helped immeasurably; in the half-century or so after it came into use, the plays of all the great ancient dramatists—Aeschylus, Sophocles, Euripides, Aristophanes, Plautus, Terence, and Seneca—were published. The same period saw the publication of Aristotle's *Poetics,* and with it came a new consciousness of classical "rules" such as the preservation of the unities. Tragedians learned from Seneca how to write a long play that held together; comic playwrights learned the intricacies of tight plotting from Plautus and Terence. When the public theaters of London began to thrive in the 1580s and 1590s, the first important plays were written by men who, like Thomas Kyd (1557?–1595) and Christopher Marlowe (1564–1593), had learned their craft in the schools or universities.

Nevertheless, many of the greatest Renaissance plays are not in any obvious way classical. In both Spain and England, the most vital sources of the new drama were in native popular theatrical traditions which, in turn, had their ultimate roots in the medieval church. Shakespeare's friend and fellow playwright Ben Jonson (1572–1637), an aggressive advocate of classical form, felt himself to be in that role an enlightened exception among his formally footloose contemporaries. In Spain, the enormously prolific Lope de Vega (1562–1635) wrote a manifesto in 1609 rejecting classical rules; this anti-classical position was later modified by Calderón de la Barca (1600–1681), but he too in his more intellectual and theological vein was thoroughly Spanish in his religious preoccupations. Both Lope de Vega and Shakespeare blended the comic and the serious in a fashion closer to medievalism than to classicism. Even the staging of their plays, despite immense advances in professionalism and sophistication, recalls certain medieval features; for example, in the Elizabethan theater the areas below and above the main acting platform continued to be referred to as the "hell" and the "heaven," as in the three-level stage of the medieval period. (See the Introductions to *Everyman* and Shakespeare.)

The fact is that, although the Renaissance drama of England and Spain is unimaginable apart from either its medieval origins or the classical revival, it achieved expressive heights and explored human experience in ways not always clearly attributable to either strain. Religious themes continued to be immensely popular in Spain, but so were secular ones. In England these completely supplanted the overt devotional emphasis of the miracle, mystery, and morality plays. A Christian norm might be present, but, like the classicist goal of coherent unity, it was there organically and implicitly rather than texturally and explicitly. The history play perfected by Marlowe, Shakespeare, and Lope de Vega was an almost wholly new genre. Comedy owed something to medieval farce and to the stock characters of the Roman comedians (the "wily slave" transformed into the clowns and other clever "low" characters of playwrights such as Shakespeare), but in its highest reaches it became something new to the stage. In the Shakespearean comedies *Twelfth Night, As You Like It,* and *A Midsummer Night's Dream* (set, ludicrously, in ancient Athens but really in fairyland), laughter is combined with a warm and sympathetic insight into the romantic feelings of men and women, articulating a distinctive definition of love. Tragedy became both intimate and cosmic. The medieval notion of tragedy was simply the fall of a great personage from prosperous eminence (a strain vestigially recognizable in Shakespearean tragedies like *Macbeth*). The classical impulse in the Renaissance transformed this model radically—for example, Senecan models added a dimension of melodrama and a stoic sense of fatality, and from Aristotle came the notion of the hero's "tragic flaw." But no such formulas can define the great English tragedies of Marlowe, Shakespeare, or John Webster (1580?–1625). In Shakespeare's *Hamlet, King Lear, Othello,* and *Macbeth,* it is not only the hero's life and happiness but the entire vision of a morally ordered universe that is at stake, threatened by a demonic principle of evil that seems to have escaped human or divine control. Whether or not the principle of righteousness prevails in the end is a question that can be answered differently about different plays (opinion is notoriously divided about *King Lear*), but even when it does reassert itself, a terrible price has been paid in the suffering or destruction of precious, noble individuals. There is at the least a heartrending sense of human waste. But this sense is also mitigated by the very existence of human goodness, whether it triumphs or not. The integrity and love of Lear's daughter Cordelia are realities that in their nature cannot be denied or annulled, even by death. For dramatic visions so vast as these one must go back to Greek tragedy, and it might be argued that Shakespeare goes beyond the Greeks by combining with his cosmic themes a more intimate concern for the unique human person.

Italy, the original center of the humanist movement and the revival of antiquity, did not produce a great dramatic literature in the Renaissance, although some of its distinguished authors, including Ariosto and Tasso, produced notable plays, and there were occasional masterpieces such as Machiavelli's *Mandragola* (about 1518). Italy contributed influentially to post-Renaissance stagecraft, however; as in painting, it pioneered in the development of illusional perspective in stage settings, and it helped develop important architectural features like the proscenium arch. Such elements look past the Renaissance to the "picture-frame" stage that became the principal model for theater from the late seventeenth century until well into the twentieth. (Much of this new stagecraft reached other countries by way of Italian opera, a new art form developed around 1600 in rivalry with the integration of the arts in ancient Greek drama and crowned with immediate greatness in the works of Claudio Monteverdi—1567–1643.) The modern picture-frame stage, typically opening into someone's living room, is itself an emblem for the kind of realistically intimate drama often enacted on it, and the emblem represented by the physical theater is applicable to earlier dramatic traditions as well. The essentially public action of classical Greek drama took place before an unchanging background, the *skene* that typically represented a palace and concealed from the audience the merely domestic private scenes imagined to take place behind it. The medieval stage presented simultaneously to the audience three levels—heaven, earth, and hell—representing a constant awareness of the relationship between here and hereafter. The Renaissance stage of England and Spain was the vehicle for complete fluidity and variety, capable of representing, with the indispensable help of poetic language, any conceivable setting and of shifting from one to another instantaneously. The ceremonial and casual, the public and intimate, the lofty and low, the violent and serene, the realistic and romantic—all these manners and moods, in any combination, were at the service of the playwright and actors. It is therefore not surprising that Renaissance drama could encompass more of the world and of life than has been possible in the theater of any other age.

FURTHER READING *(prepared by W. J. R.):* One entry into the Renaissance is by way of Jacob Burckhardt's epoch-making and controversial study *The Civilization of the Renaissance in Italy,* first published in 1860 (discussed in the preceding Introduction), which emphasizes Renaissance individualism. More concise is J. H. Plumb's *The Italian Renaissance,* 1961, which in surveying the period refers often to Dante, Boccaccio, Petrarch, and Machiavelli. E. M. W. Tillyard's *The Elizabethan World Picture,* 1946, another historically influential study, identifies three models by which the cosmos was envisaged: as a chain, a set of correspondences, and a dance. Tillyard's *The English Renaissance: Fact or Fiction?,* 1952, identifies and discusses essential differences between Medieval and Renaissance thought in order to answer the question posed by the title; see also the excellent discussions in *The Renaissance: A Reconsideration of the Theories and Interpretations of the Age,* ed. Tinsley Helton, 1961. Two of the essays in this volume warrant special mention: Harry Levin's "English Literature of the Renaissance" and Paul Oskar Kristeller's "Changing Views of the Renaissance Since Jacob Burckhardt." The principles and attitudes reflected in Renaissance literature are treated in Douglas Bush's *Prefaces to Renaissance Literature,* 1965. Paul Oskar Kristeller's *Renaissance Thought and Its Sources,* ed. Michael Mooney, 1979, and Ernst Cassirer's *The Individual and the Cosmos in Renaissance Philosophy,* 1927, translated by Mario Domadi, 1963, are both careful and incisive; Kristeller begins with humanism and proceeds to study the classical forerunners of Renaissance thought, Renaissance attitudes toward the individual, and other topics; Cassirer's classic examines the Renaissance as a systematic unity. Surveys of literature and literary history include *The Continental Renaissance, 1500–1600,* by W. A. Coupe, A. J. Krailsheimer, J. A. Scott, and R. W. Truman, 1971, 1978; and A. C. Spearing, *Medieval to Renaissance in English Poetry,* 1985. (The reader can also consult the Further Reading list for Renaissance Lyric Poetry in the present volume.) Recently, progress toward understanding the Renaissance has been made through the study of a number of specific topics. One of the most important of these has been the role of women in the period, addressed in *Women in the Middle Ages and the Renaissance,* ed. Mary Beth Rose, 1986; *The Women's Sharp Revenge: Five Women's Pamphlets from the Renaissance,* ed. Simon Shepherd, 1985; and Angeline Goreau, *The Whole Duty of a Woman: Female Writers in Seventeenth-Century England,* 1985. Other works with large social implications include the collection of essays *Science and the Arts in the Renaissance,* ed. John W. Shirley and F. David Hoeniger, 1985; and J. R. Hale, *War and Society in Renaissance Europe, 1450–1620,* 1985. Derrick Henry, *The Listener's Guide to Medieval and Renaissance Music,* 1983, is largely a discography, but it serves also as a brief musical history of the periods. Complementing older studies of the humanist movement such as Douglas Bush, *The Renaissance and English Humanism,* 1939, and Myron P. Gilmore, *The World of Humanism, 1453–1517,* 1952, are such recent works as Charles Trinkaus, *The Scope of Renaissance Humanism,* 1983, and Benjamin G. Kohl, *Renaissance Humanism, 1300–1550: A Bibliography of Materials in English,* 1985.

Francis Petrarch
(1304–1374)

Possibly the greatest love poet in Western literature was Francis Petrarch, the four-teenth-century Italian classicist, humanist, and literary arbiter. Born in Arezzo in 1304, Petrarch was set to the study of law, first at Montpellier and then at Bologna. When his father died, the twenty-two-year-old Petrarch renounced law and moved to the lively city of Avignon, the seat of the papacy during its "Babylonian captivity" from 1309 to 1378. After briefly considering the Church, he entered instead the service of the wealthy and powerful Colonna family, the first of a series of patrons who made it possible for Petrarch to devote his life exclusively to literature. He has thus been called the first modern man of letters. By 1341 his reputation was so high that he received a laurel crown as poet laureate from the Roman Senate, an honor Petrarch always treasured as symbolizing not only his own achievement but his spirit-ual links with the great poets of classical Rome. For the rest of his life, Petrarch continued to be a celebrated public man, an intimate and counsellor of princes as well as an arbiter of literary taste. During his mature years, he moved from one residence to another, to Milan as guest of the Visconti, to Venice as guest of the Republic, and finally to Arqua, near Padua, where he spent the last four years of his life in a country retreat. He died in 1374, just before his seventieth birthday, his copy of Virgil open before him on his desk.

In his own day and his own estimation, Petrarch's major achievement was in his Latin works, which far outnumbered his Italian ones. In a letter to Boccaccio, written in his later years, he told of his decision, sometime in his thirties, to use Latin rather than Italian in his major literary work. He had, he said, already begun "a great work" in Italian but had given it up for fear that his words would be "mangled by the public." (Dante, who had visited Petrarch's family when Petrarch was seven, had completed The Divine Comedy *in Italian in 1321, about fifteen years before Petrarch decided in favor of Latin.) The most important of Petrarch's many Latin works are* Africa, *an unfinished epic poem about Scipio Africanus, the third-century* B.C. *conqueror of Hannibal; the* Secretum Meum *(My Secret), a spiritual autobi-ography in the form of three imaginary dialogues between Petrarch and St. Augus-tine; and his* Letters, *both in verse and prose, which Petrarch himself carefully edited and collected into a number of volumes. The humane and liberal spirit of Petrarch's classical studies was to be a major influence in the development of Renais-sance humanism throughout Europe.*

Later ages have known Petrarch less as a classicist, however, than as the author of the collection of poems in Italian which he called the Rerum vulgarium fragmenta *(Poetic Fragments in the Vernacular) and which is now generally known either as the* Canzoniere *(Lyric Poems) or simply the* Rhymes. *This collec-tion of poems was gradually built up through Petrarch's mature life. At least three times Petrarch arranged them in systematic collections, and he was still polishing and rearranging them when he died; the final version of the sequence contains 366 poems, intended to be read, like the Breviary, over the course of a year.*

The inspiration for the poems was Petrarch's crucial meeting, on April 6, 1327, with "Laura," in the church of St. Clare in Avignon. (Petrarch never revealed Laura's identity, but she is believed to have been Laurette de Noves, who had been married for two years when Petrarch met her and who had a number of children by the time of her death in 1348.) Petrarch adored her, hopelessly and from afar, until her death twenty-one years later and continued to cherish her memory in his poetry for another ten years, after which he professed to renounce earthly love and turn his thoughts only to God.

There is something faintly absurd to the modern reader about this protracted and self-conscious cultivation of a hopeless love (especially, perhaps, when one learns that Petrarch had two illegitimate children by different mothers during the time of his idealization of Laura). But there is more than a little of the conventional in Petrarch's adoration of Laura. By the time he wrote, there was already a long tradition of sequences of love poems addressed to an unattainable woman. Originating in the poems of the twelfth- and thirteenth-century troubadours of southern France, the tradition had found its most notable expression before Petrarch in Dante's La Vita Nuova *(The New Life), devoted to the transformation of the real Beatrice Portinari into "Beatrice," a symbol of Christian salvation (Latin* beata, *"blessed"). A friend of Petrarch, Giacomo Colonna, even suggested that Laura was not a real person but an invented symbol of the poetic "laurel." Petrarch replied with some vehemence that Laura was indeed real and that no one could counterfeit the "weariness and pallor" that his hopeless love had given him. But real passion for a real woman does not preclude making her also into a conventional poetic figure.*

What raised the Rhymes *above the level of its predecessors and made it one of the most widely read and imitated collections of poems in literary history was the wealth of classical learning in the poems, their scope and variety, their arrangement into a developing structure, and their sheer beauty. The classicism of the* Rhymes *is not obtrusive, but it is the more powerful for being so thoroughly assimilated. Virgil, Horace, Catullus, and especially Ovid are echoed throughout the* Rhymes. *One realizes with something of a shock, for example, that the poem "Upon the breeze she spread her golden hair" (XC), personal as it seems, is a close reworking of a passage from the* Aeneid. *Ovid is a pervasive presence in the* Rhymes, *not the Ovid of the* Art of Love *or the moralized, allegorical Ovid of the medieval interpreters, but the Ovid of the* Metamorphoses; *Ovid's Daphne, who, pursued by Apollo, was changed into a laurel tree, is one of the most important classical analogues for the Laura in Petrarch's sequence. The* Rhymes *are quite varied both in form and content. Sonnets predominate; 317 of the 366 poems in the collection are in this form. But there are also a number of* canzoni *(poems made up of five or six stanzas of equal length, followed by a shorter* envoy, *such as CXXVI and CXXIX), and several other forms appear. Most of the poems are about Laura, but a significant number have nothing to do with her, dealing instead with politics, moral problems, friendship, and other topics. The sequence begins and ends with a renunciation of the poet's passion for Laura. The poems between fall most obviously into two groups: Part One, consisting of 265 poems that deal with the living Laura, and Part Two, consisting of 99 poems devoted to the memory of the dead Laura. The poems are arranged in loose chronology, but more important than chronology is the range of moods of the speaker, a range that includes every emotion from spiritual ecstasy to agonized self-laceration and melancholy resignation, every mood associated with love, perhaps, except the joy of physical consummation.*

Laura comes to mean many things for Petrarch in the course of the poems; as Thomas G. Bergin has pointed out, they reveal at least four Lauras. One is the Laura of the poet's "laurel," his poetic ambitions which he pursues as Apollo pursued his Daphne. Another is Laura as a virtuous guide to Heaven, like Dante's Beatrice; this view of Laura comes to dominate the second part of the sequence, after Laura's death.

A third Laura represents beauty itself, especially as a fascinating temptation that draws the poet away from his proper pursuit of salvation; this Laura appears most explicitly in the sonnets of recantation: I and CCCLXV. And finally, Laura is, of course, merely a young woman with whom the poet fell in love on a spring day in 1327; many of the poems do not emphasize any metaphoric meanings for Laura but present her as a real human presence.

It is not Laura, however, but the poet who is the protagonist of the Rhymes. *His lady is described in loving detail, but always from outside, from the poet's point of view; Petrarch has no interest in the workings of Laura's mind or in her attitudes toward such subjects as, say, her husband or her children. The personality we remember after reading the poems is Petrarch's—nostalgic, melancholy, passionate and yet always curiously removed from life, an observer rather than a participant.*

The deeply personal and introspective quality of the Rhymes *and their brilliant technique established a vogue that endured for at least three centuries and left a permanent impression on Western poetry, especially love poetry. "Petrarchism" offered a way of portraying the loved one, as a fascinating combination of earthly and divine qualities; a characteristic stance for the lover; and a repertory of devices that could be endlessly imitated, sometimes well, sometimes clumsily and mechanically. These included a repertory of stock images—stormy seas, beautiful landscapes, marble tombs, battles—and a liberal use of antithesis (strong contrasts), oxymoron (contradictory terms), and hyperbole (exaggeration). (See Poem CXXXIV for examples of Petrarch's own use of such devices.) Exaggerated Petrarchan catalogues of the features of a stock, composite mistress had become so common by Shakespeare's time that he could parody them in his Sonnet 130:*

> *My mistress' eyes are nothing like the sun;*
> *Coral is far more red than her lips' red:*
> *If snow be white, why then her breasts are dun;*
> *If hairs be wires, black wires grow on her head.*

But pervasive as Petrarch's literary influence was, his influence upon attitudes toward love was probably even greater; even today, lovers who never heard of Petrarch tend to adopt Petrarchan attitudes. "The amatory attitudes of the Rhymes *have in fact been built into our culture," Thomas G. Bergin writes. "It is possible, of course, that some day there may be a revolution in human emotions, whether it be a new morality or a new erotic, but until that day comes we shall live by the code that Petrarch elaborated with such instinctive perception and such compelling sophistication." We may be somewhat more skeptical than Bergin about the desirability of some aspects of Petrarchan love, such as the radical split between the physical and the spiritual; the "revolution in human emotions" he mentions may now be taking place. But until it is completed, we must agree that lovers' meetings "will take place in the kingdom that Petrarch has explored for them."*

FURTHER READING *(prepared by W. J. R.):* Thomas G. Bergin's *Petrarch,* 1970, is an excellent introduction to the study of Petrarch. Bergin provides a concise survey of Petrarch's life and a clear and substantial commentary on the *Triumphs* and the *Rhymes.* Ernest Hatch Wilkins' *Life of Petrarch,* 1961, is a more detailed biography of the poet. Morris Bishop's *Petrarch and His World,* 1963, analyzes Petrarch and his times in great detail, but it is nonetheless suited for the new student of the poet. Nicholas Mann, *Petrarch,* 1984, in the Past Masters series, is a short book on

Petrarch's life and mind, emphasizing especially Petrarch's selfconsciousness and image of himself. Kenelm Foster, *Petrarch, Poet and Humanist*, 1984, is a comprehensive biographical and critical study, especially valuable on the relationship between the classical and religious sides of Petrarch. A Nobel Prize poet's thoughts on Petrarch are recorded in Salvatore Quasimodo's *The Poet and the Politician*, 1960, translated by Thomas G. Bergin, 1964. The second essay in this volume contains sections on both Petrarch's solitude and Dante's reputation. Stephen Minta's *Petrarch and Petrarchism: The English and French Traditions*, 1980, is an excellent anthology of poems by Petrarch and by English and French poets influenced by him. On the Renaissance humanists in general, see the Further Reading section of the Introduction to the Renaissance in the present book.

RHYMES

Translation and notes by Anthony Mortimer

I

All you that hear in scattered rhymes[1] the sound
of sighs on which I used to feed my heart
in my first youthful error when, in part,
I was another man, now left behind;

for the vain hopes, vain sorrows of my mind,   5
the tears and discourse of my varied art,
in any who have played a lover's part
pardon and pity too I hope to find.

But now I see too well how I became
a tale for common gossip everywhere,   10
so that I grow ashamed of what I am;

and of my raving still the fruit is shame
and penitence, and last the knowledge clear
that all the world loves is a passing dream.

III

It was that very day on which the sun
in awe of his creator dimmed the ray,[1]

---

[1] The poet regards his "scattered rhymes" as a collection of fragments (*Rerum vulgarium fragmenta*), but there is also the possibility that they are scattered through the world. The whole sonnet is, indeed, indicative of Petrarch's ambiguous attitude towards the *Canzoniere*: he deplores it as evidence of a "youthful error," but he still hopes to find readers. (Notes, unless otherwise indicated, are by the translator.)

[1] Petrarch first saw Laura at matins in the church of Saint Clare in Avignon on April 6, 1327. This was not the moveable feast of Good Friday, but, according to medieval calculations, the exact calendar anniversary of Christ's death.

when I was captured, with my guard astray,
for your fine eyes, my lady, bound me then.

It hardly seemed the time for me to plan   5
defence against Love's stroke; I went my way
secure, unwary; so upon that day
of general sorrow all my pains began.

Love found me with no armour for the fight,
my eyes an open highway to the heart,   10
eyes that are now a vent for tears to flow.

And yet he played no honourable part,
wounding me with his shaft in such a state;
he saw you armed and dared not lift the bow.

XC

Upon the breeze she spread her golden hair[1]
that in a thousand gentle knots was turned,
and the sweet light beyond all measure burned
in eyes where now that radiance is rare;

and in her face there seemed to come an air   5
of pity, true or false, that I discerned:
I had love's tinder in my breast unburned,
was it a wonder if it kindled there?

She moved not like a mortal, but as though
she bore an angel's form, her words had then   10
a sound that simple human voices lack;

a heavenly spirit, a living sun
was what I saw; now, if it is not so,
the wound's not healed because the bow grows slack.

CXXVI

Waters[1] fresh and sweet and clear
where the fair limbs reclined
of the one creature who to me seems woman;

---

[1] This sonnet is inspired by a description of Venus appearing to Aeneas in Virgil's *Aeneid*, Book I. (Editors' note.)
[1] The waters of the Sorgue in Vaucluse.

and gentle tree-trunk where,
with sighs I call to mind,   5
the leaning side once loved to find a column;
flowers and grass that often
the light gown hid from sight
with the angelic breast;[2]
airs breathing holy rest   10
where Love with those fair eyes opened my heart:
come, and together grant
a hearing to my last lament.

If it be destiny,
and heaven works for this,   15
that Love should close these weeping eyes of mine,
then may some kindness lay
the body in your midst
and the soul naked to its home return;
death shall become less stern   20
if such a hope I bear
into that fearful pass,
for the soul's weariness
could find no calmer haven anywhere,
nor could it ever leave   25
the troubled flesh in a more quiet grave.

A time may come again
when she perhaps will stray
to the old haunt, untamed, yet fair and meek,
and where she saw me then   30
upon that blessed day
will turn an eager and a happy look,
and there, O pity! seek
and find me turned to dust amid the stones:
at this may Love arise,   35
inspiring her with sighs
so sweet she forces heaven[3] and obtains
its mercy for my soul,
drying her eyes upon the lovely veil.

From the fair boughs there fell,   40
sweet in the memory,
upon her lap a rain of every flower,
and she sat there and still
was humble in such glory,

___

[2] Commentators have been unnecessarily puzzled here. The poet, in fact, recalls Laura in a number of different attitudes: bathing in the river, leaning against a tree, and sitting on the ground so that the gown which covers her breast also covers the grass and flowers.

[3] Bosco [a modern Italian critic] points out that heaven will be impressed not by Laura's sorrow or piety, but by the sweetness of her sighs and the elegance of her gestures. Even the intercession of the living for the dead is seen in aesthetic terms.

already covered by the loving shower;   45
upon the hem lay flowers,
and some the tresses crowned
which seemed that day to hold
both pearls and polished gold;
some rested on the waves, some on the ground;   50
some, sweetly turning through the air,
seemed in their drift to whisper: "Love reigns here."

How often I exclaimed,
seized by a sudden fear:
"For certain she was born in Paradise!"   55
Such deep oblivion came
from her celestial air,
the words, the gentle smiling, and the eyes,
so faintly did I seize
the image truth would show,   60
that I said sighing then:
"How came I here, or when?"
thinking myself in heaven, not here below.
And ever since I've loved this place
so much that elsewhere I can find no peace.   65

Song, had you beauty as you have desire,
intrepidly you could
go out among the crowd and leave this wood.

CXXIX

From thought to thought, from mountainside to mountain
Love leads me on, since every beaten trail
I feel as hostile to my peace of mind.
If some deserted heath has stream or fountain,
or if two hills should hide a shadowed vale,   5
the spirit sees its suffering decline,
and there, as Love designs,
now laughs and weeps, now fears and learns to trust;
the face that follows where the spirit leads
grows clear and overclouds,   10
and no condition ever seems to last:
so, at the sight, a man who knew that life
would say: "He burns, and stands in doubtful strife."

Among high mountains and wild woods I find
some kind of rest; but each frequented place   15
becomes an enemy that my eyes abhor.
At every step a new thought comes to mind
of my dear lady, often bringing gladness

out of the torment that I feel for her;
and hardly would I prefer   20
to change the sweet and bitter life I bear
when I reflect: "Perhaps Love keeps in view
a better time for you;
you hate yourself, but she may hold you dear."
And with this thought sighing I change again: 25
"Can it be ever true? but how? and when?"

Where a tall pine-tree or a hill gives shade
sometimes I stop, and on the nearest stone
my mind will draw her face. At last I find,
on coming to myself, my breast is bathed   30
with that emotion; then "alas," I groan,
"where are you now? what have you left behind?"
But while my wandering mind
can be kept steadfastly on that first thought
and I forget myself and gaze on her,   35
then I feel Love so near
the soul is sated with its own deceit:
I see her in so many things, so fair,
that if the illusion lasts I ask no more.

Often I've seen (who will believe me now?)   40
on the green grass or in transparent water
her living self, in beech-trees or the face
of a white cloud, and ever fashioned so
that Leda[1] would have surely said her daughter
fades like a star outshone by the sun's rays;   45
and the more wild the place
I come upon, the lonelier the shore,
the fairer does thought shadow forth[2] my love.
Then, when the truth removes
that sweet illusion, I sit as before,   50
cold and stone-dead upon the living stone,[3]
like one who thinks and weeps and writes alone.

To where the mountain shadows never lie,
towards the highest and best vantage-point,
a fierce desire often makes me start.   55
There I begin to measure with the eye
my sufferings, and tearfully give vent

[1] Leda, seduced by Zeus in the form of a swan, was the mother of Helen of Troy. (Editors' note.)
[2] The Italian word is *adombra*. More than "shadow forth" this suggests the conscious chiaroscuro of the painter, thus continuing the artist metaphor introduced in the previous stanza.
[3] The contrast is probably between the stone effigy on a tomb *(pietra morta)* and the natural stone *(pietra viva)* upon which the poet sits. Having transformed so many shapes into Laura's image, the poet now becomes an image himself. This reading is confirmed by the last line of the poem.

to the sad mists that thicken in my heart,
when both my gaze and thought
span all that lies between me and the fair   60
face that is still so near and far away;
then, whispering to myself, I say:
"What can you know? this moment over there
perhaps your absence makes her sigh for you;"
and in this thought the spirit breathes anew.   65

My song, beyond this alp,
where skies are happier and clear above,
you'll find me sitting by a stream that flows
where gentle aura blows
in from a fresh and fragrant laurel-grove: 70
there is my heart and she that stole it from me;
and here my image all that you can see.[4]

CXXXIV

I find no peace, and have no arms for war,
and fear and hope, and burn and yet I freeze,
and fly to heaven, lying on earth's floor,
and nothing hold, and all the world I seize.

My jailer opens not, nor locks the door,   5
nor binds me to her, nor will loose my ties;
Love kills me not, nor breaks the chains I wear,
nor wants me living, nor will grant me ease.

I have no tongue, and shout; eyeless, I see;
I long to perish, and I beg for aid;   10
I love another, and myself I hate.

Weeping I laugh, I feed on misery,
by death and life so equally dismayed:
for you, my lady, am I in this state.

CCLXV

Fierce heart and bitter, and most cruel will,
sweet, humble, and angelic to the sight,
if this first rigor last throughout the fight,
the honour of their trophies will be small;

---

[4]The envoi sends the poem to join the poet's heart which is with Laura beyond the Alps. For once I have attempted to translate the pun on Laura's name.

for when grass, leaf, and flower spring and fall,   5
when daylight comes, and in the dark of night,
always I weep. Indeed I have the right
on Love, my fate, my lady thus to call.

I live on hope alone, remembering
how I have seen a little moisture prove   10
to wear down marble and the solid stone:

there cannot be a heart so hard that weeping,
praying, and loving sometime will not move,
nor yet a will so cold it cannot burn.

CCXCII

The eyes I spoke of once in words that burn,
the arms and hands and feet and lovely face
that took me from myself for such a space
of time and marked me out from other men;

the waving hair of unmixed gold that shone,   5
the smile that flashed with the angelic rays
that used to make this earth a paradise,
are now a little dust, all feeling gone;

and yet I live, grief and disdain to me,
left where the light I cherished never shows,   10
in fragile bark on the tempestuous sea.

Here let my loving song come to a close,
the vein of my accustomed art is dry,
and this, my lyre, turned at last to tears.[1]

CCCLXV[1]

I keep lamenting over days gone by,
the time I spent loving a mortal thing,
with no attempt to soar, although my wing
might give no mean example in the sky.[2]

---

[1] See Job, 30:31, "My lyre is turned to mourning."

[1] The last sonnet, but not the last poem in the *Canzoniere*, which concludes with a canzone to the Virgin.

[2] The humility of the recantation is rendered more poignant by this lingering touch of human pride. Love for the "mortal thing" has been an obstacle to salvation, but there is also the explicit regret that it has prevented him from demonstrating his true worth in the eyes of the world.

You that my foul unworthy sins descry,   5
unseen and everlasting, heaven's King,
succour my soul, infirm and wandering,
and what is lacking let your grace supply;

so if I lived in tempest and in war,
I die in port and peace; however vain   10
the stay, at least the parting may be fair.

Now in the little life that still remains
and at my death may your quick hand be near:
in others, you well know, my hope is gone.

Giovanni Boccaccio
(1313–1375)

The great triumvirate of Italian literature in the fourteenth century consists of Dante, Petrarch, and Boccaccio. Boccaccio, the youngest, was born in 1313, the illegitimate son of a merchant-banker who had family roots in or near Florence. The legend, nurtured by Boccaccio, that he was born in Paris of an aristocratic mother is now regarded skeptically. He spent his childhood, not very happily, in Florence, moving with his businessman father to Naples when Boccaccio was about fourteen. His father gave him twelve years of education, first in commerce and then in church law, but Boccaccio wanted above all else to be a poet. His contact with the aristocracy of Naples, who had banking connections with his father's firm, gave Boccaccio the opportunity to develop as both writer and gentleman, since the Neapolitan court was highly cultivated and intellectual in tone. At the same time, his connection with commerce, in Naples and later in Florence, taught him about the life of middle-class people. It was in Naples too that Boccaccio is supposed to have met "Fiammetta," the object of his passionate love—the equivalent for Boccaccio of Dante's Beatrice and Petrarch's Laura. The identity of Fiammetta in real life is uncertain, and her very existence has been questioned. Real or fictitious, however, she was the occasion or focus for much of Boccaccio's early work. In this period, he wrote mainly in Italian rather than in the traditional learned language, Latin.

In 1340, Boccaccio reluctantly left Naples, where he had been very happy, and returned to Florence, where his literary art reached its full flower, culminating in The Decameron *(completed by 1353), or "Work of Ten Days." Boccaccio's earlier writing had been distinctly medieval in its concern with chivalric themes and its use of the genres of romance and allegory. Certain of his early works had revealed his gift of keen insight into human psychology, but nothing quite prepares us for* The Decameron, *with its brilliant dramatic and narrative styles and its rich variety of tones, from the wholly serious and tragic to the raucously farcical. Boccaccio had seen at first hand in Florence the ravages of the plague (the Black Death), and his vividly gruesome account of it at the beginning of* The Decameron *throws into relief the idyllic life led by the seven women and three men who tell the stories. The tone of their life in their country refuge is witty, refined, decorous, but relaxedly sensuous, in sharp contrast with the horrors they have escaped. The reader is aware, however, at some level of consciousness, of the terrible background. The most broadly comic parts of the work can be experienced as a reflex response to the plague, by characters and readers alike.*

The Decameron served as a model for Italian prose writers and had an enormous influence on later European literature. But Boccaccio wrote no later works in the same vein. In 1350, he met Petrarch (of whom he had already written a biography), and the two men enjoyed a close friendship for the rest of their lives. Petrarch influenced Boccaccio in some important ways, turning him toward the Latin tongue and various scholarly projects (for example, compendia of ancient myths, of famous men and women, and of place names in classical literature). Petrarch seems also to have been one cause, though not the only one, of an increasingly moral and religious tone in Boccaccio's later years. On the other hand, it was Petrarch who, when Boccaccio contemplated burning his earlier works, persuaded him not to do so. Having proved himself, in The Decameron, to be a humanist in the modern, popular sense, the older Boccaccio proved himself a humanist in the more technical sense that has to do with the revival of ancient classical learning and literature. He was instrumental, for example, in encouraging the translation of the epics of Homer. He also wrote, in Italian, a treatise on Dante and a commentary on the first half of Dante's Inferno. Despite the honor of public offices and of several ambassadorships, the last decades of Boccaccio's life were unsettled, often overshadowed by poverty. He died in 1375, a year later than Petrarch.

The much discussed question whether Boccaccio belongs to the Middle Ages or to the Renaissance is for some scholars a pseudoquestion, implying an overly simple view of the Middle Ages as piously ascetic and of the Renaissance as exclusively secular. Even if one allows for the distortions of stereotyping, however, it is difficult not to see in Boccaccio's work, or at least The Decameron, something distinctively modern. Much of his work looks backward to medieval chivalric values and beyond them to antiquity. But the worldly pragmatism of The Decameron, with its almost exclusive emphasis on human ingenuity and resourcefulness, is something genuinely new. Heaven and divine grace play almost no role in The Decameron. In the hundred tales, people are what the vicissitudes of life and their own characters make them, whether shrewd or gullible, high-minded or unscrupulous. Moreover, The Decameron also represents a transition to social realism; the ten storytellers have the manners of aristocrats, but many of the stories involve people of the lower and especially the middle classes. The essence of The Decameron is its variety—of subject matter, of tone, and of source (Boccaccio invented few, if any, of the tales in toto). The sense of a broad social and literary spectrum is one of the several parallels between Boccaccio and Chaucer, who was influenced by him.

Part of the worldliness of The Decameron is its notorious bawdiness, which is sometimes very explicit. Boccaccio's defensiveness on the matter shows that in his own time, and not only in later more prudish eras, some of the stories gave offense. Boccaccio tries to vindicate himself in his conclusion, advancing arguments that the reader may or may not find convincing. To them one may add the obvious: that the governing theme of The Decameron is love, and any comprehensive treatment of it must include the carnal as well as the psychological and spiritual. To many readers the main justification for the bawdiness will be the sparkling wit that characterizes many of the sexual episodes. It must be added too that the sexuality of The

Decameron *is intimately connected with its treatment of the sexes, particularly the very modern portrayal of women not as etherealized ideals but as realistic creatures of flesh and blood who are driven as much by desire as men are. The controversially patient Griselda is the exception that dramatizes the rule.*

FURTHER READING *(prepared by W. J. R.):* Thomas Bergin's *Boccaccio,* 1982, is a comprehensive introduction to the author's life and writings. Valuable as a general introduction is Judith Powers Serafini-Sauli, *Giovanni Boccaccio,* 1982. Vittore Branca's *Boccaccio: The Man and His Works,* translated by Richard Monges, 1976, provides a brief biographical sketch. Book II is devoted to *The Decameron,* with discussions of the medieval tradition in Boccaccio's work, his narrative art, and other topics. On style, see *An Anatomy of Boccaccio's Style,* ed. by Marga Cottino-Jones, 1968. Critical approaches in this volume range from linguistic to archetypal. The first essay offers an overview of Boccaccio criticism. Joan M. Ferrante's "Narrative Patterns in the *Decameron,*" *Romance Philology,* 31 (1978), 585–604, looks at the entire *Decameron,* seeking to clarify the meaning of narrative themes. "The Worlds of the *Decameron,*" Chapter Two in Yvonne Rodax's *The Real and the Ideal in the Novella of Italy, France and England,* 1968, discusses the achievement of vigorous reality in Boccaccio's tales, with a particular emphasis on medieval values. The first and third chapters in this work, on the novella and on *The Canterbury Tales,* are also of interest. Shirley S. Allen's "The Griselda Tale and the Portrayal of Women in the *Decameron,*" *Philological Quarterly,* 56 (1977), 1–13, considers previous interpretations of the tale of "patient Griselda" and argues that viewing the tale as an ironic plea for women's rights is in accord with the overall unity of *The Decameron.* Marga Cottino-Jones' "Comic Modalities in the *Decameron,*" in *Versions of Medieval Comedy,* ed. by Paul G. Ruggiers, 1977, investigates the varying comic tones and makes some general observations on the nature of Boccaccio's comedy. Cormac Cuilleanáin's "Man and Beast in the *Decameron,*" *Modern Language Review,* 75 (1980), 86–93, studies animal imagery and symbolism as it reveals Boccaccio's principal theme of man's existence in a social community. Demanding but exciting is Giuseppe Mazzotta, *The World at Play in Boccaccio's "Decameron,"* 1986, which relates the work in incisive ways to the culture of its time.

THE DECAMERON

Translated by Richard Aldington

THE FIRST DAY

Here begins the first day of the Decameron, *wherein, after the author has showed the reasons why certain persons gathered to tell tales, they treat of any subject pleasing to them, under the rule of Pampinea.*

Most gracious ladies, knowing that you are all by nature pitiful, I know that in your judgment this work will seem to have a painful and sad origin. For it brings to mind the unhappy recollection of that late dreadful plague,[1] so pernicious to all who saw or heard of it. But I would not have this frighten

---

[1] The "Black Death," probably bubonic plague, killed millions in Europe and Asia in the mid-fourteenth century.

you from reading further, as though you were to pass through nothing but sighs and tears in your reading. This dreary opening will be like climbing a steep mountain side to a most beautiful and delightful valley, which appears the more pleasant in proportion to the difficulty of the ascent. The end of happiness is pain, and in like manner misery ends in unexpected happiness.

This brief fatigue (I say brief, because it occupies only a few words) is quickly followed by pleasantness and delight, as I promised you above; which, if I had not promised, you would not expect perhaps from this opening. Indeed, if I could have taken you by any other way than this, which I know to be rough, I would gladly have done so; but since I cannot otherwise tell you how the tales you are about to read came to be told, I am forced by necessity to write in this manner.

In the year 1348 after the fruitful incarnation of the Son of God, that most beautiful of Italian cities, noble Florence, was attacked by deadly plague. It started in the East either through the influence of the heavenly bodies or because God's just anger with our wicked deeds sent it as a punishment to mortal men; and in a few years killed an innumerable quantity of people. Ceaselessly passing from place to place, it extended its miserable length over the West. Against this plague all human wisdom and foresight were vain. Orders had been given to cleanse the city of filth, the entry of any sick person was forbidden, much advice was given for keeping healthy; at the same time humble supplications were made to God by pious persons in processions and otherwise. And yet, in the beginning of the spring of the year mentioned, its horrible results began to appear, and in a miraculous manner. The symptoms were not the same as in the East, where a gush of blood from the nose was the plain sign of inevitable death; but it began both in men and women with certain swellings in the groin or under the armpit. They grew to the size of a small apple or an egg, more or less, and were vulgarly called tumors. In a short space of time these tumors spread from the two parts named all over the body. Soon after this the symptoms changed and black or purple spots appeared on the arms or thighs or any other part of the body, sometimes a few large ones, sometimes many little ones. These spots were a certain sign of death, just as the original tumor had been and still remained.

No doctor's advice, no medicine could overcome or alleviate this disease. An enormous number of ignorant men and women set up as doctors in addition to those who were trained. Either the disease was such that no treatment was possible or the doctors were so ignorant that they did not know what caused it, and consequently could not administer the proper remedy. In any case very few recovered; most people died within about three days of the appearance of the tumors described above, most of them without any fever or other symptoms.

The violence of this disease was such that the sick communicated it to the healthy who came near them, just as a fire catches anything dry or oily near it. And it even went further. To speak to or go near the sick brought infection and a common death to the living; and moreover, to touch the clothes or anything else the sick had touched or worn gave the disease to the person touching.

What I am about to tell now is a marvelous thing to hear; and if I and others had not seen it with our own eyes I would not dare to write it, however much I was willing to believe and whatever the good faith of the person from whom I heard it. So violent was the malignancy of this plague that it was communicated, not only from one man to another, but from the garments of a sick or dead man to animals of another species, which caught the disease in that way and very quickly died of it. One day among other occasions I saw with my own eyes (as I said just now) the rags left lying in the street of a poor man who had died of the plague; two pigs came along and, as their habit is, turned the clothes over with their snouts and then munched at them, with the result that they both fell dead almost at once on the rags, as if they had been poisoned.

From these and similar or greater occurrences, such fear and fanciful notions took possession of the living that almost all of them adopted the same cruel policy, which was entirely to avoid the sick and everything belonging to them. By so doing, each one thought he would secure his own safety.

Some thought that moderate living and the avoidance of all superfluity would preserve them from the epidemic. They formed small communities, living entirely separate from everybody else. They shut themselves up in houses where there were no sick, eating the finest food and drinking the best wine very temperately, avoiding all excess, allowing no news or discussion of death and sickness, and passing the time in music and suchlike pleasures. Others thought just the opposite. They thought the sure cure for the plague was to drink and be merry, to go about singing and amusing themselves, satisfying every appetite they could, laughing and jesting at what happened. They put their words into practice, spent day and night going from tavern to tavern, drinking immoderately, or went into other people's houses, doing only those things which pleased them. This they could easily do because everyone felt doomed and had abandoned his property, so that most houses became common property and any stranger who went in made use of them as if he had owned them. And with all this bestial behavior, they avoided the sick as much as possible.

In this suffering and misery of our city, the authority of human and divine laws almost disappeared, for, like other men, the ministers and the executors of the laws were all dead or sick or shut up with their families, so that no duties were carried out. Every man was therefore able to do as he pleased.

Many others adopted a course of life midway between the two just described. They did not restrict their victuals so much as the former, nor allow themselves to be drunken and dissolute like the latter, but satisfied their appetites moderately. They did not shut themselves up, but went about, carrying flowers or scented herbs or perfumes in their hands, in the belief that it was an excellent thing to comfort the brain with such odors; for the whole air was infected with the smell of dead bodies, of sick persons and medicines.

Others again held a still more cruel opinion, which they thought would keep them safe. They said that the only medicine against the plague-stricken was to go right away from them. Men and women, convinced of this and caring about nothing but themselves, abandoned their own city, their own houses, their dwellings, their relatives, their property, and went abroad or at least to the country round Florence, as if God's wrath in punishing men's wickedness with this plague would not follow them but strike only those who remained within the walls of the city, or as if they thought nobody in the city would remain alive and that its last hour had come.

Not everyone who adopted any of these various opinions died, nor did all escape. Some when they were still healthy had set the example of avoiding the sick, and, falling ill themselves, died untended.

One citizen avoided another, hardly any neighbor troubled about others, relatives never or hardly ever visited each other. Moreover, such terror was struck into the hearts of men and women by this calamity, that brother abandoned brother, and the uncle his nephew, and the sister her brother, and very often the wife her husband. What is even worse and nearly incredible is that fathers and mothers refused to see and tend their children, as if they had not been theirs.

Thus, a multitude of sick men and women were left without any care except from the charity of friends (but these were few), or the greed of servants, though not many of these could be had even for high wages. Moreover, most of them were coarse-minded men and women, who did little more than bring the sick what they asked for or watch over them when they were dying. And very often these servants lost their lives and their earnings. Since the sick were thus abandoned by neighbors, relatives and friends, while servants were scarce, a habit sprang up which had never been heard of before. Beautiful and noble women, when they fell sick, did not scruple to take a young or old manservant, whoever he might be, and with no sort of shame, expose every part of their bodies to these men as if they had been women, for they were compelled by the necessity of their sickness to do so. This, perhaps, was a cause of looser morals in those women who survived.

In this way many people died who might have been saved if they had been looked after. Owing to the lack of attendants for the sick and the violence of the plague, such a multitude of people in the city died day and night that it was stupefying to hear of, let alone to see. From sheer necessity, then, several ancient customs were quite altered among the survivors.

The custom had been (as we still see it today) that women relatives and neighbors should gather at the house of the deceased, and there lament with the family. At the same time the men would gather at the door with the male neighbors and other citizens. Then came the clergy, few or many according to the dead person's rank; the coffin was placed on the shoulders of his friends and carried with funeral pomp of lighted candles and dirges to the church which the deceased had chosen before dying. But as the fury of the plague increased, this custom wholly or nearly disappeared, and new customs arose. Thus, people died, not only without having a number of women near them, but without a single witness. Very few indeed were honored with the piteous laments and bitter tears of their relatives, who, on the contrary, spent their time in mirth, feasting and jesting. Even the women abandoned womanly pity and adopted this custom for their own safety. Few were they whose bodies were accompanied to church by more than ten or a dozen neighbors. Nor were these grave and honorable citizens but grave-diggers from the lowest of the people who got themselves called sextons, and performed the task for money. They took up the bier and hurried it off, not to the church chosen by the deceased but the church nearest, preceded by four or six of the clergy with few candles and often none at all. With the aid of the grave-diggers, the clergy huddled the bodies away in any grave they could find, without giving themselves the trouble of a long or solemn burial service.

The plight of the lower and most of the middle classes was even more pitiful to behold. Most of them remained in their houses, either through poverty or in hopes of safety, and fell sick by thousands. Since they received no care and attention, almost all of them died. Many ended their lives in the streets both at night and during the day; and many others who died in their houses were only known to be dead because the neighbors smelled their decaying bodies. Dead bodies filled every corner. Most of them were treated in the same manner by the survivors, who were more concerned to get rid of their rotting bodies than moved by charity towards the dead. With the aid of porters, if they could get them, they carried the bodies out of the houses and laid them at the doors, where every morning quantities of the dead might be seen. They then were laid on biers, or, as these were often lacking, on tables.

Often a single bier carried two or three bodies, and it happened frequently that a husband and wife, two or three brothers, or father and son were taken off on the same bier. It frequently happened that two priests, each carrying a cross, would go out followed by three or four biers carried by porters; and where the priests thought there was one person to bury, there would be six or eight, and often, even more. Nor were these dead honored by tears and lighted candles and mourners, for things had reached such a pass that people cared no more for dead men than we care for dead goats. Thus it plainly appeared that what the wise had not learned to endure with patience through the few calamities of ordinary life, became a matter of indifference even to the most ignorant people through the greatness of this misfortune.

Such was the multitude of corpses brought to the churches every day and almost every hour that there was not enough consecrated ground to give them burial, especially since they wanted to bury each person in the family grave, according to the old custom. Although the cemeteries were full they were forced to dig huge trenches, where they buried the bodies by hundreds. Here they stowed them away like bales in the hold of a ship and covered them with a little earth, until the whole trench was full.

Not to pry any further into all the details of the miseries which afflicted our city, I shall add that the surrounding country was spared nothing of what befell Florence. The villages on a smaller scale were like the city; in the fields and isolated farms the poor wretched peasants and their families were without doctors and any assistance, and perished in the highways, in their fields and houses, night and day, more like beasts than men. Just as the townsmen became dissolute and indifferent to their work and property, so the peasants, when they saw that death was upon them, entirely neglected the future fruits of their past labors both from the earth and from cattle, and thought only of enjoying what they had. Thus it happened that cows, asses, sheep, goats, pigs, fowls and even dogs, those faithful companions of man, left the farms and wandered at their will through the fields, where the wheat crops stood abandoned, unreaped and ungarnered. Many of these animals seemed endowed with reason, for, after they had pastured all day, they returned to the farms for the night of their own free will, without being driven.

Returning from the country to the city, it may be said that such was the cruelty of Heaven, and perhaps in part of men, that between March and July more than one hundred thousand persons died within the walls of Florence, what between the violence of the plague and the abandonment in which the sick were left by the cowardice of the healthy. And before the plague it was not thought that the whole city held so many people.

Oh, what great palaces, how many fair houses and noble dwellings, once filled with attendants and nobles and ladies, were emptied to the meanest servant! How many famous names and vast possessions and renowned estates were left without an heir! How many gallant men and fair ladies and handsome youths, whom Galen, Hippocrates and Aesculapius[2] themselves would have said were in perfect health, at noon dined with their relatives and friends, and at night supped with their ancestors in the next world!

But it fills me with sorrow to go over so many miseries. Therefore, since I want to pass over all I can leave out, I shall go on to say that when our city was in this condition and almost emptied of inhabitants, one Tuesday morning the venerable church of Santa Maria Novella had scarcely any congregation for divine service except (as I have heard from a person worthy of belief) seven young women in the mourning garments suitable to the times, who were all related by ties of blood, friendship or neighborship. None of them was older than twenty-eight or younger than eighteen; all were educated and of noble blood, fair to look upon, well-mannered and of graceful modesty.

I should tell you their real names if I had not a good reason for not doing so, which is that I would not have any of them blush in the future for the things they say and hearken to in the following pages. The laws are now strict again, whereas then, for the reasons already shown, they were very lax, not only for persons of their age but for those much older. Nor would I give an opportunity to the envious (always ready to sneer at every praiseworthy life) to attack the virtue of these modest ladies with vulgar speech. But so that you may understand without confusion what each one says, I intend to give them names wholly or partly suitable to the qualities of each.

The first and eldest I shall call Pampinea, the second Fiammetta, the third Filomena, the fourth Emilia, the fifth Lauretta, the sixth Neifile, and the last Elisa[3] (or "the virgin") for a very good reason. They met, not by arrangement, but by chance, in the same part of the church, and sat down

---

[2] The first two were ancient Greek physicians; Aesculapius was a Graeco-Roman god of medicine.

[3] Most of the names are derived from Greek and have something to do with love. The qualities or roles associated with the seven women are probably as follows: Pampinea (the eldest) is a leader and adviser; Fiammetta is loving and beloved; Filomena (related to "nightingale") is a lover of music; Emilia has pleasant manners; Lauretta (related to *laurel*) is learned; Neifile is young and naive; Elisa, who is also young, recalls *Elissa*, a name for Dido, the passionate Carthaginian queen in Virgil's *Aeneid*.

in a circle. After many sighs they ceased to pray and began to talk about the state of affairs and other things. After a short space of silence, Pampinea said:

"Dear ladies, you must often have heard, as I have, that to make a sensible use of one's reason harms nobody. It is natural for everybody to aid, preserve and defend his life as far as possible. And this is so far admitted that to save their own lives men often kill others who have done no harm. If this is permitted by the laws which are concerned with the general good, it must certainly be lawful for us to take any reasonable means for the preservation of our lives. When I think of what we have been doing this morning and still more on former days, when I remember what we have been saying, I perceive and you must perceive that each of us goes in fear of her life. I do not wonder at this, but, since each of us has a woman's judgment, I do wonder that we do not seek some remedy against what we dread.

"In my opinion we remain here for no other purpose than to witness how many bodies are buried, or listen whether the friars here (themselves reduced almost to nothing) sing their offices at the canonical hours,[4] or to display by our clothes the quantity and quality of our miseries to anyone who comes here. If we leave this church we see the bodies of the dead and the sick being carried about. Or we see those who had been exiled from the city by the authority of the laws for their crimes, deriding this authority because they know the guardians of the law are sick or dead, and running loose about the place. Or we see the dregs of the city battening on our blood and calling themselves sextons, riding about on horseback in every direction and insulting our calamities with vile songs. On every side we hear nothing but 'So-and-so is dead' or 'So-and-so is dying.' And if there were anyone left to weep we should hear nothing but piteous lamentations. I do not know if it is the same in your homes as in mine. But if I go home there is nobody left there but one of my maids, which fills me with such horror that the hair stands upon my head. Wherever I go or sit at home I seem to see the ghosts of the departed, not with the faces as I knew them but with dreadful looks which terrify me.

"I am ill at ease here and outside of here and at home; the more so since nobody who has the strength and ability to go away (as we have) now remains here, except ourselves. The few that remain (if there are any), according to what I see and hear, do anything which gives them pleasure or pleases their appetites, both by day and night, whether they are alone or in company, making no distinction between right and wrong. Not only laymen, but those cloistered in convents have broken their oaths and given themselves up to the delights of the flesh, and thus in trying to escape the plague by doing what they please, they have become lascivious and dissolute.

"If this is so (and we may plainly see it is) what are we doing here? What are we waiting for? What are we dreaming about? Are we less eager and active than other citizens in saving our lives? Are they less dear to us than to others? Or do we think that our lives are bound to our bodies with stronger

---

[4] Chant their prayers at the times of day specified by the Church.

chains than other people's, and so believe that we need fear nothing which might harm us? We were and are deceived. How stupid we should be to believe such a thing! We may see the plainest proofs from the number of young men and women who have died of this cruel plague.

"I do not know if you think as I do, but in my opinion if we, through carelessness, do not want to fall into this calamity when we can escape it, I think we should do well to leave this town, just as many others have done and are doing. Let us avoid the wicked examples of others like death itself, and go and live virtuously in our country houses, of which each of us possesses several. There let us take what happiness and pleasure we can, without ever breaking the rules of reason in any manner.

"There we shall hear the birds sing, we shall see the green hills and valleys, the wheat-fields rolling like a sea, and all kinds of trees. We shall see the open Heavens which, although now angered against man, do not withhold from us their eternal beauties that are so much fairer to look upon than the empty walls of our city. The air will be fresher there, we shall find a greater plenty of those things necessary to life at this time, and fewer troubles. Although the peasants are dying like the townsmen, still, since the houses and inhabitants are fewer, we shall see less of them and feel less misery. On the other hand I believe we are not abandoning anybody here. Indeed we can truthfully say that we are abandoned, since our relatives have either died or fled from death and have left us alone in this calamity as if we were nothing to them.

"If we do what I suggest, no blame can fall upon us; if we fail to do it, the result may be pain, trouble and perhaps death. Therefore I think that we should do well to take our servants and all things necessary, and go from one house to another, enjoying whatever merriment and pleasure these times allow. Let us live in this way (unless death comes upon us) until we see what end Heaven decrees to this plague. And remember that going away virtuously will not harm us so much as staying here in wickedness will harm others."

The other ladies listened to what Pampinea said, praised her advice, and in their eagerness to follow it began to discuss details, as if they were going to leave at once. But Filomena, who was a most prudent young woman, said:

"Ladies, although what Pampinea says is excellent advice, we must not rush off at once, as you seem to wish. Remember we are all women; and any girl can tell you how women behave together and conduct themselves without the direction of some man. We are fickle, wayward, suspicious, faint-hearted and cowardly. So if we have no guide but ourselves I greatly suspect that this company will very soon break up, without much honor to ourselves. Let us settle this matter before we start."

Elisa then broke in:

"Indeed men are a woman's head and we can rarely succeed in anything without their help; but how can we find any men? Each of us knows that most of her menfolk are dead, while the others are away, we know not where, flying with their companions from the end we wish to escape. To ask strangers would be unbecoming; for, if we mean to go away to save our lives we must take care that scandal and annoyance do not follow us where we are seeking rest and amusement."

While the ladies were thus arguing, three young men came into the church, the youngest of whom was not less than twenty-five. They were lovers whose love could not be quenched or even cooled by the horror of the times, the loss of relatives and friends, or even fear for themselves. The first was named Pamfilo, the second Filostrato, the third Dioneo.[5] They were pleasant, well-mannered men, and in this public calamity they sought the consolation of looking upon the ladies they loved. These ladies happened to be among our seven, while some of the others were related to one or other of the three men. They no sooner came into sight than the ladies saw them; whereupon Pampinea said with a smile:

"See how Fortune favors our plan at once by sending us these valiant and discreet young men, who will gladly act as our guides and servants if we do not refuse to accept them for such duties."

Neifile then became crimson, for she was one of the ladies beloved by one of the young men, and said:

"For God's sake, Pampinea, be careful what you are saying. I know quite well that nothing but good can be said of any of them and I am sure they could achieve greater things than this. I also think that their company would be fitting and pleasant, not only to us, but to ladies far more beautiful and charming than we are. But it is known to everyone that they are in love with some of us women here; and so, if we take them with us, I am afraid that blame and infamy will fall upon us, through no fault of ours or theirs."

Then said Filomena:

"What does that matter? If I live virtuously, my conscience never pricks me, whatever people may say. God and the truth will fight for me. If these men would come with us, then indeed, as Pampinea said, fortune would be favorable to our plan of going away."

The others not only refrained from censuring what she said, but agreed by common consent that the men should be spoken to, told their plan, and asked if they would accompany the ladies on their expedition. Without more ado, Pampinea, who was related to one of them, arose and went towards them where they stood looking at the ladies, saluted them cheerfully, told them the plan, and begged them in the name of all the ladies to accompany them out of pure and fraternal affection.

At first the young men thought this was a jest. But when they saw the lady was speaking seriously, they said they were willing to go. And in order to start without delay they at once gave the orders necessary for departure. Everything necessary was made ready, and word was sent on ahead to the place they were going. At dawn next morning, which was Wednesday, the ladies with some of their servants, and the young men with a man servant each, left the city and set out. They had not gone more than two miles when they came to the first place where they were to stay.

This estate was on slightly raised ground, at some distance from any main road, with many trees and plants, fair to look upon. At the top of the rise was a country mansion with a large inner courtyard. It had open colon-

---

[5] The name *Pamphilo* means "loving all"; *Filostrato* means "lover of strife" (perhaps the strife of being in love) and also "victim of love"; *Dioneo* is related to one of the names of Venus, goddess of sexual love.

nades, galleries and rooms, all beautiful in themselves and ornamented with gay paintings. Roundabout were lawns and marvelous gardens and wells of cool water. There were cellars of fine wines, more suitable to wine connoisseurs than to sober and virtuous ladies. The whole house had been cleaned, the beds were prepared in the rooms, and every corner was strewn with the flowers of the season and fresh rushes. All of which the company beheld with no little pleasure.

They all sat down to discuss plans, and Dioneo, who was a most amusing young man and full of witticisms, remarked:

"Ladies, your good sense, rather than our foresight, has brought us here. I do not know what you are thinking of doing with your troubles here, but I dropped mine inside the gates of the city when I left it with you a little time ago. Therefore, either you must make up your minds to laugh and sing and amuse yourselves with me (that is, to the extent your dignity allows), or you must let me go back to my troubles and stay in the afflicted city."

Pampinea, who had driven away her woes in the same way, cheerfully replied:

"Dioneo, you speak well, let us amuse ourselves, for that was the reason why we fled from our sorrows. But when things are not organized they cannot long continue. And, since I began the discussion which brought this fair company together and since I wish our happiness to continue, I think it necessary that one of us should be made chief, whom the others will honor and obey, and whose duty shall be to regulate our pleasures. Now, so that everyone—both man and woman—may experience the cares as well as the pleasures of ruling and no one feel any envy at not sharing them, I think the weight and honor should be given to each of us in turn for one day. The first shall be elected by all of us. At vespers[6] he or she shall choose the ruler for the next day, and so on. While their reigns last these rulers shall arrange where and how we are to spend our time."

These words pleased them all and they unanimously elected her for the first day. Filomena ran to a laurel bush, whose leaves she had always heard were most honorable in themselves and did great honor to anyone crowned with them, plucked off a few small branches and wove them into a fair garland of honor. When this was placed on the head of any one of them, it was a symbol of rule and authority over the rest so long as the party remained together.

Pampinea, thus elected queen, ordered silence. She then sent for the three servants of the young men and the four women servants the ladies had brought, and said:

"To set a first example to you all which may be bettered and thus allow our gathering to live pleasantly and orderly and without shame and to last as long as we desire, I appoint Dioneo's servant Parmeno as my steward, and hand over to him the care of the whole family and of everything connected with the dining hall. Pamfilo's servant Sirisco shall be our treasurer and buyer, and carry out Parmeno's instructions. Tindaro shall wait on Filostrato and Dioneo and Pamfilo in their rooms, when the other two servants are occupied with their new duties. Filomena's servant Licisca and

[6]One of the canonical hours; about 6 P.M.

my own servant Misia shall remain permanently in the kitchen and carefully prepare the food which Parmeno sends them. Lauretta's Chimera and Fiammetta's Stratilia shall take care of the ladies' rooms and see that the whole house is clean. Moreover we will and command that everyone who values our good grace shall bring back only cheerful news, wherever he may go or return from, and whatever he may hear or see."

Having given these orders, which were approved by everyone, she jumped gaily to her feet and said:

"Here are gardens and lawns and other delicious places, where each of us can wander and enjoy them at will. But let everyone be here at the hour of Tierce[7] so that we can eat together while it is still cool."

The company of gay young men and women, thus given the queen's permission, went off together slowly through the gardens, talking of pleasant matters, weaving garlands of different leaves, and singing love songs. After the time allotted by the queen had elapsed they returned to the house and found that Parmeno had carefully carried out the duties of his office. Entering a ground floor room decorated everywhere with broom[8] blossoms, they found tables covered with white cloths and set with glasses which shone like silver. They washed their hands and, at the queen's command, all sat down in the places allotted them by Parmeno. Delicately cooked food was brought, exquisite wines were at hand, and the three men servants waited at table. Everyone was delighted to see things so handsome and well arranged, and they ate merrily with much happy talk.

All the ladies and young men could dance and many of them could play and sing; so, when the tables were cleared, the queen called for musical instruments. At her command Dioneo took a lute and Fiammetta a viol, and began to play a dance tune. The queen sent the servants to their meal, and then with slow steps danced with the two young men and the other ladies. After that, they began to sing gay and charming songs.

In this way they amused themselves until the queen thought it was time for the siesta. So, at the queen's bidding, the three young men went off to their rooms (which were separated from the ladies') and found them filled with flowers as the dining hall had been. And similarly with the women. So they all undressed and went to sleep.

Not long after the hour of Nones,[9] the queen arose and made the other women and the young men also get up, saying that it was harmful to sleep too long during the daytime. Then they went out to a lawn of thick green grass entirely shaded from the sun. A soft breeze came to them there. The queen made them sit down in a circle on the grass, and said:

"As you see, the sun is high and the heat great, and nothing can be heard but the cicadas in the olive trees. To walk about at this hour would be foolish. Here it is cool and lovely, and, as you see, there are games of chess and draughts which everyone can amuse himself with, as he chooses. But, if my opinion is followed, we shall not play games, because in games the mind of one of the players must necessarily be distressed without any great pleasure to the other player or the onlookers. Let us rather spend this hot part of the day in telling tales, for thus one person can give pleasure to the whole company. When each of us has told a story, the sun will be going

---

[7] A canonical hour; 9 A.M.   [8] A shrub.   [9] A canonical hour; about 3 P.M.

down and the heat less, and we can then go walking anywhere we choose for our amusement. If this pleases you (for here I am ready to follow your pleasure) let us do it. If it does not please you, let everyone do as he likes until evening."

The women and men all favored the telling of stories.

"Then if it pleases you," said the queen, "on this first day I order that everyone shall tell his tale about any subject he likes."

She then turned to Pamfilo, who was seated on her right, and ordered him to begin with a tale. Hearing this command, Pamfilo at once began as follows, while all listened.[10]

THIRD DAY, TENTH TALE

Alibech becomes a hermit, and the monk Rustico teaches her how to put the devil in Hell. She is afterwards taken away and becomes the wife of Neerbale.

Dioneo had listened closely to the queen's story, and, when it was over and only he remained to tell a story, he did not wait to be commanded, but smilingly began as follows:

Most gracious ladies, perhaps you have never heard how the devil is put into hell; and so, without departing far from the theme[1] upon which you have all spoken today, I shall tell you about it. Perhaps when you have learned it, you also will be able to save your souls, and you may also discover that although love prefers to dwell in gay palaces and lovely rooms rather than in poor huts, yet he sometimes makes his power felt among thick woods and rugged mountains and desert caves. Whereby we may well perceive that all of us are subject to his power.

Now, to come to my story—in the city of Capsa[2] in Barbery there lived a very rich man who possessed among other children a pretty and charming daughter, named Alibech. She was not a Christian, but she heard many Christians in her native town crying up the Christian Faith and service to God, and one day she asked one of them how a person could most effectively serve God. The reply was that those best serve God who fly furthest from the things of this world, like the hermits who had departed to the solitudes of the Thebaid[3] Desert.

The girl was about fourteen and very simple minded. Urged by a mere childish enthusiasm and not by a well ordered desire, she secretly set out next morning quite alone, without saying a word to anyone, to find the Thebaid Desert. Her enthusiasm lasted several days and enabled her with great fatigue to reach those solitudes. In the distance she saw a little hut with a holy man standing at its entrance. He was amazed to see her there, and asked her what she was seeking. She replied that by God's inspiration she was seeking to serve Him, and begged the hermit to show her the right

---

[10] Here the series of a hundred tales, ten each day, begins. After the first day, when the choice of tales is unrestricted, each day has a prescribed theme.

[1] The stories told on the third day (ruled by Neifile) concern people who by cleverness gained or regained something desirable.

[2] A city in Tunisia; Barbery is in northern Africa.   [3] Near Thebes, in Egypt.

way to do so. But the holy man saw she was young and pretty, and feared that if he kept her with him he might be tempted of the devil. So he praised her good intentions, gave her some roots and wild apples to eat and some water to drink, and said:

"Daughter, not far from here dwells a holy man who is a far greater master of what you are seeking than I am; go to him."

And so he put her on the way. When she reached him, she was received with much the same words, and passing further on came to the cell of a young hermit named Rustico, to whom she made the same request as to the others. To test his spiritual strength, Rustico did not send her away, but took her into his cell. And when night came, he made her a bed of palm leaves and told her to sleep there.

Almost immediately after this, temptation began the struggle with his spiritual strength, and the hermit found that he had greatly over-estimated his powers of resistance. After a few assaults of the demon he shrugged his shoulders and surrendered. Putting aside holy thoughts and prayers and macerations,[4] he began to think of her beauty and youth, and then pondered how he should proceed with her so that she should not perceive that he obtained what he wanted from her like a dissolute man. First of all he sounded her by certain questions, and discovered that she had never lain with a man and appeared to be very simple minded. He then saw how he could bring her to his desire under pretext of serving God. He began by eloquently showing how the devil is the enemy of the Lord God, and then gave her to understand that the service most pleasing to God is to put the devil back into hell, to which the Lord God has condemned him. The girl asked how this was done, and Rustico replied:

"You shall soon know. Do what you see me do."

He then threw off the few clothes he had and remained stark naked, and the girl imitated him. He kneeled down as if to pray and made her kneel exactly opposite him. As he gazed at her beauty, Rustico's desire became so great that the resurrection of the flesh occurred. Alibech looked at it with amazement, and said:

"Rustico, what is that thing I see sticking out in front of you which I haven't got?"

"My daughter," said Rustico, "that is the devil I spoke of. Do you see? He gives me so much trouble at this moment that I can scarcely endure him."

Said the girl:

"Praised be God! I see I am better off than you are, since I haven't such a devil."

"You speak truly," said Rustico, "but instead of this devil you have something else which I haven't."

"What's that?" said Alibech.

"You've got hell," replied Rustico, "and I believe God sent you here for the salvation of my soul, because this devil gives me great trouble, and if you will take pity upon me and let me put him into hell, you will give me the greatest comfort and at the same time will serve God and please Him, since, as you say, you came here for that purpose."

---

[4] Starvation diets.

In all good faith the girl replied: "Father, since I have hell in me, let it be whenever you please."

Said Rustico: "Blessings upon you, my daughter. Let us put him in now so that he will afterwards depart from me."

So saying, he took the girl to one of their beds, and showed her how to lie so as to imprison the thing accursed of God. The girl had never before put any devil into her hell and at first felt a little pain, and exclaimed to Rustico:

"O father! This devil must certainly be wicked and the enemy of God, for even when he is put back into hell he hurts it."

"Daughter," said Rustico, "it will not always be so."

To prevent this from happening, Rustico put it into hell six times, before he got off the bed, and so purged the devil's pride that he was glad to rest a little. Thereafter he returned often and the obedient girl was always glad to take him in; and then the game began to give her pleasure, and she said to Rustico:

"I see that the good men of Capsa spoke the truth when they told me how sweet a thing is the service of God. I certainly do not remember that I ever did anything which gave me so much delight and pleasure as I get from putting the devil into hell. I think that everyone is a fool who does anything but serve God."

Thus it happened that she would often go to Rustico, and say:

"Father, I came here to serve God and not to remain in idleness. Let us put the devil in hell."

And once as they were doing it, she said:

"Rustico, I don't know why the devil ever goes out of hell. If he liked to remain there as much as hell likes to receive and hold him, he would never leave it."

The girl's frequent invitations to Rustico and their mutual pleasures in the service of God so took the stuffing out of his doublet[5] that he now felt chilly where another man would have been in a sweat. So he told the girl that the devil must not be chastened or put into hell except when pride made him lift his head. "And we," he said, "have so quelled his rage that he prays God to be left in peace." And in this way he silenced the girl for a time. But when she found that Rustico no longer asked her to put the devil in hell, she said one day:

"Rustico, your devil may be chastened and give you no more trouble, but my hell is not. You should therefore quench the raging of my hell with your devil, as I helped you to quell the pride of your devil with my hell."

Rustico, who lived on nothing but roots and water, made a poor response to this invitation. He told her that many devils would be needed to soothe her hell, but that he would do what he could. In this way he satisfied her hell a few times, but so seldom that it was like throwing a bean in a lion's mouth. And the girl, who thought they were not serving God as much as she wanted, kept murmuring.

Now, while there was this debate between the excess of desire in Alibech's hell and the lack of potency in Rustico's devil, a fire broke out in Capsa, and burned Alibech's father with all his children and servants. So

[5] Jacket.

Alibech became heir to all his property. A young man named Neerbale, who had spent all his money in riotous living, heard that she was still alive and set out to find her, which he succeeded in doing before the Court took over her father's property as that of a man who had died without heirs. To Rustico's great relief, but against her will, Neerbale brought her back to Capsa and married her, and together they inherited her large patrimony. But before Neerbale had lain with her, certain ladies one day asked her how she had served God in the desert. She replied that her service was to put the devil in hell, and that Neerbale had committed a great sin by taking her away from such service. The ladies asked:

"And how do you put the devil in hell?"

Partly in words and partly by gestures, the girl told them. At this they laughed so much that they are still laughing, and said:

"Be not cast down, my child, they know how to do that here, and Neerbale will serve the Lord God with you in that way."

As they told it up and down the city, it passed into a proverb that the service most pleasing to God is to put the devil into hell. And this proverb crossed the seas and remains until this day.

Therefore, young ladies, when you seek God's favor, learn to put the devil in hell, because this is most pleasing to God and to all parties concerned, and much good may come of it.

Dioneo's tale moved the chaste ladies to laughter hundreds of times, so apt and amusing did they find his words. When he had finished, the queen knew that the end of her reign had come, and therefore took the laurel wreath from her head and placed it upon Filostrato's, saying pleasantly:

"We shall soon find out if the wolf can guide the flock, as well as the flock has guided the wolves."

Filostrato laughingly replied:

"If my advice were followed, the wolves would have showed the flock how to put the devil in hell, as Rustico taught Alibech; and so they would not be called wolves, where you would not be the flock. However, since the rule now falls to me, I shall begin my reign."

Said Neifile:

"Filostrato, in trying to teach us, you might have learned wisdom, as Masetto da Lamporecchio learned it from the nuns,[6] and you might have regained your speech when your bones were rattling together from exhaustion!"

Filostrato, finding the ladies' sickles were as good as his shafts, ceased jesting, and occupied himself with the government of his kingdom. Calling the steward, he made enquiries into everything, and gave orders to ensure the well being and satisfaction of the band during his kingship. He then turned to the ladies and said:

"Amorous ladies, to my own misfortune—although I was quite aware of my disease—I have always been one of Love's subjects owing to the beauty of one of you. To be humble and obedient to her and to follow all her whims as closely as I could, was all of no avail to me, and I was soon abandoned for another. Thus I go from bad to worse, and believe I shall until I die. Tomorrow then it is my pleasure that we tell tales on a theme in

---

[6] A reference to another tale told earlier on the third day.

conformity with my own fate—that is, about those persons whose love ended unhappily. In the long run I expect a most unhappy end for myself, and the person who gave me the nickname of Filostrato, or the Victim of Love, knew what she was doing."

So saying, he rose to his feet, and gave them all leave to depart until supper time.

The garden was so delightful and so beautiful that they all chose to remain there, since no greater pleasure could be found elsewhere. The sun was now not so hot, and therefore some of them began to chase the deer and rabbits and other animals which had annoyed them scores of times by leaping in among them while they were seated. Dioneo and Fiammetta began to sing the song of Messer Guglielmo and the Lady of Vergiu. Filomena and Pamfilo played chess. Thus, with one thing and another, time passed so quickly that supper time arrived long before they expected. The tables were set round the fountain, and there they ate their evening meal with the utmost pleasure.

When they rose from table, Filostrato would not depart from the path followed by the preceding queens, and so ordered Lauretta to dance and sing a song. And she said:

"My lord, I do not know any songs of other persons, and I do not remember any of my own which are fitting for this merry band. But if you wish to have one of those I remember, I will gladly sing it."

"Nothing of yours could be anything but fair and pleasing," said the king, "so sing it just as it is."

Then to the accompaniment of the others, Lauretta sang as follows in a sweet but rather plaintive voice:

No helpless lady has such cause to weep as I, who vainly sigh, alas, for love.

He who moves the heavens and all the stars[7] made me for His delight so fair, so sweet, so gracious and so lovely that I might show to every lofty mind some trace of that high Beauty which ever dwells within His presence. But a weak man, who knew not Beauty, found me undelightful and scorned me.

Once there was one who held me dear, and in my early years took me into his arms and to his thoughts, being quite conquered by my eyes. And time, that flies so swiftly, he spent in serving me; and I in courtesy made him worthy of me. But now, alas, he is taken from me.

Then came a proud presumptuous man, who thought himself both noble and valorous, and made me his, but through false belief became most jealous of me. And then, alas, I came near to despair, for I saw that I, who came into the world to pleasure many, was possessed by one alone.

I curse my luckless fate that ever I said "yes" to man, and changed to a wife's garb. I was so gay in my old plain maiden's dress! Now in these finer clothes I lead so sad a life, reputed less than chaste. O hapless wedding feast! Would I had died before I knew the fate it held for me!

---

[7] The mover is God; the line is a close paraphrase of the last line of Dante's *Divine Comedy*.

O my first love, with whom I was so happy, who now in Heaven do stand before Him
    who created it, have pity on me. I cannot forget you for another. Let me feel that
    the flame wherewith you burned for me is not extinct, and pray that I may soon
    return to you.

Here ended Lauretta's song, which was noted carefully by them all, but interpreted differently. Some understood it in the Milanese sense—that it is better to be a good pig than a pretty girl.[8] Others were of a better, more sublime and truer understanding, but of this I shall not now speak.

After this the king had many torches brought and made them sing other songs as they sat on the grass and flowers, until the rising stars began to turn towards the west. Then, thinking it time for sleep, he said good night and sent each one to his room.

END OF THE THIRD DAY

FOURTH DAY, SECOND TALE

Frate Alberto persuades a lady that the Angel Gabriel is in love with her and thus manages to lie with her several times. From fear of her relatives he flies from her house and takes refuge in the house of a poor man, who next day takes him to the Piazza as a wild man of the woods. He is recognized, arrested, and imprisoned.

The tale told by Fiammetta many times drew tears from her companions' eyes, but when it was ended the king said with a stern face:

"I should value my life little in comparison with half the joy Ghismonda had with Guiscardo.[1] Nor should you marvel at this, since while I am alive I suffer a thousand deaths hourly, and yet not one particle of delight is granted me. But, putting aside my life and its fate, it is my will that Pampinea should continue with a tale in part similar to my own fate. If she continues as Fiammetta has begun, doubtless some drops of dew will fall upon my amorous fire, and I shall feel them."

Pampinea felt the wishes of the company more through her own affection than through the king's words, and, being more willing to amuse them than to please the king, she determined to tell an amusing tale without departing from the subject given, and so began:

They say commonly in proverbial style: A wicked man who is thought to be good can do evil and yet not have it believed. This gives me ample material to speak on the subject proposed, and at the same time to show the hypocrisy of the monks. Their gowns are long and wide, their faces artificially pale, their voices humble and pleading when they ask something, loud and rude when they denounce their own vices in others, and when they declare how they obtain salvation of themselves and others by their gift. Not as men who seek Paradise, like ourselves, but as if they were its

---

[8] That is, it is better to be an unhappy wife and alive than happily married and dead.

[1] Characters in the sad story with which Fiammetta had begun the fourth day's storytelling. The theme for the day, under Filostrato's rule, is love that ends unhappily.

owners and lords, they allot a more or less eminent place there to everyone
who dies, in accordance with the amount of money he leaves them; and
thereby they first deceive themselves—if they really believe it—and then
deceive those who put faith in their words. If I were permitted to do so, I
could soon show many simple minded persons what is hidden in their
ample gowns. Would to God that all their lies had the same fate as befell a
minor friar,[2] who was no paltry fellow, but was considered one of the best
casuists of Venice. It gives me the greatest pleasure to tell this tale, so that
perhaps I may divert your minds with laughter and amusement from the
pity you feel for Ghismonda's fate.

In Imola, most worthy ladies, there lived a man of wicked and corrupt
life, named Berto della Massa. His evil deeds were so well known to many
people of Imola that no one in Imola would believe him when he spoke
truth, let alone when he lied. Seeing, then, that his tricks were useless there,
he moved in despair to Venice, that welcomer of all wickedness, thinking
that in that town he might make a different use of his vices than he had
done before. As if conscience-stricken for his wicked deeds, he gave signs
of the greatest humility. He became not only the most Catholic of men, but
made himself a minor friar, and took the name of Friar Alberto da Imola.
In this guise he began to pretend to a severe life, praising penitence and
abstinence, and never eating flesh or drinking wine when he could not get
them good enough for him.

Never before had a thief, a ruffian, a forger, a murderer turned into a
great preacher without having abandoned those vices, even when he had
practiced them secretly. And after he had become a priest, whenever he
was celebrating Mass at the altar in the presence of a large congregation, he
always wept over the Saviour's Passion, for he was a man who could shed
tears whenever he pleased. In short, what with his sermons and his tears,
he so beguiled the Venetians that he was trustee and guardian of nearly
everyone's will, the keeper of many people's money, the confessor and
adviser of most men and women. Thus, from wolf he became shepherd,
and in those parts the fame of his sanctity was greater than San
Francesco's[3] ever was at Assisi.

Now, it happened that a silly stupid young woman, named Madonna
Lisetta da ca Quirino, the wife of a merchant who was away in Flanders
with the galleys, went with other women to confess to this holy friar. As she
knelt at his feet like the Venetian she was—and they are all fools—he asked
her half way through her confession if she had a lover. And she tartly
replied:

"Why, messer friar, have you no eyes in your head? Do you think my
beauties are no more than these other women's? I could have as many
lovers as I wanted. But my beauty is not to be yielded to the love of anybody. How many beauties do you see like mine, for I should be beautiful in
Paradise?"

And she went on to say so many things about her beauties that it was
tedious to listen to her. Friar Alberto at once saw her weakness, and, feeling

---

[2] A member of the Franciscan religious order (Order of Friars Minor).
[3] Saint Francis of Assisi (1182?–1226), of whose piety many stories were told. He is
eulogized in Dante's *Paradiso*, canto XI.

that she was ready made to his hand, he fell in love with her. But, reserving his flatteries for another time, he put on his saintly air and began to reprove her, and to say this was vain-glory and other things of the kind. So the lady told him he was a fool, and did not know how to distinguish one beauty from another. And Friar Alberto, not wanting to anger her too much, finished off the confession and let her go with the others.

A few days later he went with a trusted friend to Madonna Lisetta's house and took her aside into a room where they could not be seen. There he fell on his knees before her, and said:

"Madonna, I beseech you for God's sake to forgive me for what I said to you on Sunday when you spoke of your beauty, because I was so severely punished that night I have not been able to get up until today."

Then said Madonna Pot-stick: "And who punished you?"

"I will tell you," said Friar Alberto. "While I was praying that night, as I always do, I suddenly saw a bright light in my cell. Before I could turn to see what it was, I beheld a most beautiful young man with a large stick in his hand, who took me by the cowl, dragged me to my feet and beat me as if to break my bones. I asked him why he did this, and he replied: 'Because you presumed today to reprove the heavenly beauty of Madonna Lisetta whom I love more than anything except God himself.' And I asked: 'Who are you?' And he said he was the Angel Gabriel. 'O my lord,' said I, 'I beg you will pardon me.' And he said: 'I will pardon you on condition that you go to her as soon as you can and obtain her forgiveness. And if she does not forgive you I shall return here, and so deal with you that you will be miserable for the rest of your days.' What he afterwards said to me I dare not tell you until you have pardoned me."

Donna Windy-noddle, who was as sweet as salt, was enchanted at these words, and thought them all true.

"I told you, Friar Alberto," said she, "that mine were heavenly beauties. But, so help me God, I am sorry for you, and to spare you any further trouble I forgive you, if only you will tell me truly what the Angel then said."

"Madonna," replied Friar Alberto, "since you have pardoned me, I will tell you willingly. But, you must not repeat a word of what I tell you to anyone in the world, if you do not want to destroy your happiness, you who are the luckiest woman in the world.

"The Angel Gabriel told me to tell you that he loves you so much he would often have come to spend the night with you, but for his fear of terrifying you. He now sends you a message through me to say that he wants to come to you one night and to spend part of it with you. But he is an Angel, and if he came to you in the form of an Angel you could not touch him; and so he says that for your delight he will come in a man's shape and bids you tell him when you want him to come and in whose shape, and he will come. And so you ought to think yourself more blessed than any other woman living."

Madonna Silly then said she was very glad to have the Angel Gabriel in love with her, because she loved him and always put up a fourpenny candle to him wherever she saw him painted. Whenever he liked to come to her he would be welcome and he would find her alone in her room, on one condition, which was that he would not abandon her for the Virgin Mary whom he was said to be very fond of; and she was inclined to believe this since whenever she saw his picture he was kneeling before the Virgin.[4] In addition, she said that the Angel should come in any shape he pleased—she would not be afraid.

Then said Friar Alberto:

"Madonna, you speak wisely, and I will arrange with him as you say. But you can do me a great favor, which will cost you nothing. The favor is that you will allow him to come in my body. This will be a very great favor because he will take the soul from my body and put it in Heaven, and he will enter into me, and my soul will be in Paradise as long as he remains with you."

Then said Madonna Littlewit:

"I am content. I want you to have this consolation for the stripes[5] you received on my account."

Said Friar Alberto:

"Tonight leave the door of your house open, so that he can come in. Since he is coming in a human body, he can only enter by the door."

The lady replied that this should be done. Friar Alberto departed, and she remained in such a state of delight that her chemise did not touch her backside, and the time she had to wait for the Angel Gabriel seemed like a thousand years.

Friar Alberto thought it better to be a good horseman than an Angel that night, so he fortified himself with all sorts of good cheer, in order not to be unhorsed too easily. He obtained permission to be out that night, and went with his trusted friend to the house of a woman friend, which he had made his starting point more than once before when he was going to ride the mare. From there he went in disguise to the lady's house, and having transformed himself into an Angel with the fripperies[6] he had brought with him, he went upstairs into the lady's bedroom. When she saw something white come in, she kneeled down. The Angel gave her his benediction, raised her to her feet, and signed to her to get into bed. She did so immediately in her willingness to obey, and the Angel got into bed with his devotee.

Friar Alberto was a robust and handsome man and in excellent health. Donna Lisetta was fresh and pretty and found him a very different person from her husband to lie with. That night he flew many times with her without wings, which made her call herself blessed; and in addition he told her a great many things about heavenly glory. Just before dawn, he collected his trappings and returned to his friend, who had kept friendly company with the other woman so that she should not feel afraid by sleeping alone.

After the lady had dined, she went with a woman friend to see Friar Alberto, and gave him news of the Angel Gabriel, telling him how the Angel looked and what he had said about the glory of eternal life, to which she added all sorts of marvelous fables.

---

[4] The Annunciation, in which the angel Gabriel tells the Virgin Mary that she will be the mother of God, was a perennial subject of religious paintings.
[5] Blows.   [6] Gaudy costumes.

"Madonna," said Friar Alberto, "I know not how you were with him, all I know is that last night he came to me, and when I had delivered him your message, he suddenly took my soul to a place where there were more flowers and roses than ever I saw, one of the most delicious places that ever existed, where my soul remained until dawn this morning. But what happened to my body I do not know."

"Didn't I tell you?" said the lady. "Your body lay all night in my arms with the Angel Gabriel. And if you don't believe me, look under your left breast, where I gave the Angel such a kiss that the mark will remain for several days."

Then said Friar Alberto:

"I will do something today which I have not done for a very long time. I shall undress myself to see if what you say is true."

After a lot more chatter, the lady returned home. And Friar Alberto thereafter visited her many times in the guise of an Angel, without the slightest difficulty. But one day Madonna Lisetta was with one of her gossips,[7] and as they were discussing their beauties, she said like the empty-pated fool she was, in order to show off:

"If you knew who was in love with my beauty you would not speak of anyone else's."

The gossip was anxious to hear about it, and knowing Lisetta well, said:

"Madonna, you may be right, but as I do not know whom you mean I shall not change my opinion so easily."

The lady, who had very little sense, then said:

"Gossip, he does not want it talked about, but the person I mean is the Angel Gabriel, who loves me more than himself, so he says, because I am the most beautiful person in the world or the Maremma."[8]

The gossip felt like laughing outright, but restrained herself to keep the conversation going, and said:

"God's faith, Madonna, if you mean the Angel Gabriel and say so, it must be true, but I did not think the angels did such things."

"Gossip," said the lady, "you are wrong. By God's favor, he does it better than my husband, and he tells me they do it up above. But, because he thinks me more beautiful than anyone in Heaven, he has fallen in love with me, and often spends a night with me. So you see!"

As soon as the gossip had left Madonna Lisetta, it seemed like a thousand years to her before she had got into a company where she could laugh at all this. She went to a gathering of women, and told them the whole tale. These women told their husbands and other women, and they told others, and so in less than two days the story was all over Venice. Among others who heard it were the lady's cousins, and, without saying anything to her, they made up their minds to find this Angel and see whether he could fly. So they watched for him every night.

Some rumors of all this came to the ears of Friar Alberto, who went to the lady one night to scold her for it. He was scarcely undressed when her

---

[7] Intimate friends.

[8] A marshy region near Florence. The boast is ludicrous, since the Maremma is a mere local district.

cousins, who had seen him come in, were at the door. Friar Alberto heard them, and guessed what they were. He jumped up, and, having no other means of escape, opened a window overlooking the Grand Canal,[9] from which he threw himself into the water.

The water there was deep; he was a good swimmer, and so did himself no harm. He swam to the other side of the canal and immediately entered an open house there, begging the goodman[10] for the love of God to save his life, and told him all sorts of lies to explain why he was there naked at that hour of night.

The goodman, who was just setting off on his business, pitied Friar Alberto and put him into bed, telling him to stop there until he came back. He then locked the friar in, and went about his business.

When the lady's cousins entered her room, they found the Angel Gabriel had left his wings behind and flown away. They abused the lady indignantly, and, leaving her very disconsolate, returned home with the Angel's trappings.

Meanwhile, soon after dawn, the goodman was on the Rialto[11] and heard how the Angel Gabriel had gone to lie with Madonna Lisetta the night before, how he had been discovered by her relatives and had thrown himself into the canal, and nobody knew what had become of him. So he immediately realized that this was the man in his own house. He went home and after much discussion arranged that the Friar should pay him fifty ducats not to hand him over to the cousins; and this was done. Friar Alberto then wanted to leave, but the goodman said:

"There is only one way of doing this. There is a festival today where one man leads another dressed like a bear or a wild man of the woods or one thing or another, and then there is a hunt in the Piazza di San Marco,[12] and when that is over the festival ends. Then everyone goes off where he pleases with the person he has brought in disguise. Now, you may be spied out here, and so, if you like, I will lead you along in some disguise and can take you wherever you like. Otherwise I don't see how you can leave here without being recognized. The lady's relatives know you must be in some house in the neighborhood, and have posted guards everywhere to catch you."

Friar Alberto did not at all like the idea, but he was so much afraid of the lady's relatives that he agreed to it, and told the man where he wanted to go, and how he should be led along. The goodman smeared him all over with honey and then covered him with feathers, put a chain round his neck and a mask on his face. In one hand he gave him a large stick and in the other two great dogs which he had brought from the butcher; and then he sent someone to the Rialto who announced that everyone who wanted to see the Angel Gabriel should go to the Piazza di San Marco. That was true Venetian good faith!

Having done this, he took the Friar out, and, walking before him, led him along on a chain; and everybody came round saying: "What's this?

---

[9] The famous canals of Venice serve in lieu of streets.
[10] A title of respect for a man below the rank of gentry.
[11] The commercial center of Venice.
[12] The principal public square of Venice; St. Mark is the city's patron saint.

What's this?" And thus he took the Friar to the Piazza, where there was a great crowd of people, made up of those who had followed them and those who had come from the Rialto on hearing the announcement. He then led his wild man of the woods to a column in a conspicuous and elevated place, pretending that he was waiting for the hunt. The poor friar was greatly plagued by flies and gad-flies, because he was smeared all over with honey. And when the goodman saw that the Piazza was full of people, he pretended that he was going to unchain his wild man; but instead he took off Friar Alberto's mask, and shouted:

"Gentlemen, since the pig has not come to the hunt and since the hunt is off, I don't want you to have gathered here for nothing, and so I want you to see the Angel Gabriel who came down from Heaven to earth last night to console the ladies of Venice."

As soon as the mask was off, Friar Alberto was recognized by everybody, and there went up a great shout against him, everybody saying the most insulting things that ever were said to any scoundrel. And first one and then another threw all sorts of filth in his face. There he was kept a long time until the news reached the other friars of his convent. Six of them came down to the Piazza, threw a gown on his back and bound him, and then in the midst of a great tumult took him back to the monastery, where he was imprisoned. And it is believed that he soon died there after a life of misery.

Thus a man who was thought to be good and acted evilly without being suspected, tried to be the Angel Gabriel and was turned into a wild man of the woods; and, in the long run, was insulted as he deserved and came to weep in vain for the sins he had committed. Please God that this may happen to all like him.

FIFTH DAY, TENTH TALE

Pietro di Vinciolo goes out to sup. His wife brings a lover into the house; Pietro returns, and she hides the lover under a chicken coop. Pietro tells her how, while he was supping with Ercolano, a young man whom the wife had hidden was discovered. She blames Ercolano's wife, but an ass unhappily treads on the lover's finger as he is under the coop, and he gives a shriek; Pietro runs out, sees him, and perceives how his wife has tricked him; but in the end he pardons her fault.

The queen finished her tale, and they all praised God for having worthily rewarded Federigo; and then Dioneo began, without waiting to be ordered.[1]

I know not whether it be an accidental vice and the result of the corruption of men's manners, or whether it be a natural failing to laugh at bad things rather than at good deeds, especially when we are not directly concerned. Now since the task I undertook before and am about to carry out again, has no other object but to drive away melancholy from you and to raise mirth and merriment, I shall tell you this tale, enamored ladies, although its matter in part be less than chaste, because it may amuse you.

[1] The theme of the stories on the fifth day, under Fiammetta's rule, is love transformed from grief to happiness.

While you listen to it, do as you do when you enter a garden and, stretching out your delicate hands, pluck the roses and avoid the thorns. In so doing, leave the bad man in his misfortune with his woes, and laugh at the amorous tricks of the wife, and feel compassion for the misfortunes of others, where it is needed.

Not long ago in Perugia there was a rich man named Pietro di Vinciolo, who took a wife, more to deceive others and to avoid the general opinion of himself among the Perugians, than for any desire he had of her. And Fortune was so far conformable to his wish that the wife he took was a robust wench with lively red hair, who would rather have had two husbands than one, whereas she had chanced upon a man who would rather have had to do with another man than with her.

In process of time she found this out. And since she was fresh and pretty, and felt herself friskish and robust, she got angry and often exchanged sharp words with her husband; and they led a miserable life together. But, seeing that this exhausted her without improving her husband, she said to herself:

"This man leaves me in sorrow and goes off in his vice in wooden shoes through the dry, while I am trying to carry someone else in a ship through the rain.[2] I took him as my husband and gave him a good large dowry, knowing him to be a man, and thinking he wanted what men do and ought to want; and if I had not thought he was a man, I would never have taken him. He knew I was a woman; why did he marry me if he didn't like women? This is unendurable. If I had not wanted to live the life of the world, I should have become a nun. If I wait for delight and pleasure from him, I might perhaps wait in vain until I am an old woman, and then vainly regret my lost youth. He himself is an example to me, that I should find some consolation, and some pleasure as he does. In me this pleasure will be commendable, whereas in him it is blameworthy; for I only offend the laws, whereas he offends the laws and Nature too."

Having thought this over a good many times, the good woman, with an idea of carrying out her plan secretly, became familiar with an old woman, who yet seemed more like a pious old thing than a bawd, always going to church services with beads in her hand and never talking about anything but the lives of the Fathers or the stigmata of St. Francis,[3] so that almost everybody thought she was a saint. And when she thought it a fitting time, the wife told her everything she intended.

"My child," said the old woman, "God, who knows everything, knows that in this you will do well. And if you did it for no other reason, yet you and every other young woman should do it, in order not to waste the time of your youth, because to those who have any understanding there is no grief like having wasted time. What the devil good are we when we are old, except to watch the supper on the hearth? If anyone knows it and can bear witness to it, I can. Now I am an old woman I realize with bitter soul-prickings how I wasted my time. And although I did not lose it all (for I don't want you to think I was a simpleton), still I did not do what I could

---

[2] She means that sexually her husband goes against nature whereas she conforms to it.
[3] The Fathers were religious authorities in the ancient Christian church. St. Francis of Assisi was believed to have received in his own body the marks ("stigmata") of Christ's wounds.

have done. When I remember it, and see what I now am, and think how nobody would kindle up a spark of desire for me, God knows what grief I feel.

"The same thing does not happen to men. They are born fitted for a thousand things and not for this only, while the larger number of them are much better old than young. But women are only born to do it and make children, and so are esteemed. And if you haven't noticed anything else, you ought to have noticed this—that we are always ready for it, which does not happen with men. Moreover, one woman would tire out many men, whereas many men cannot tire one woman. Now, since we are born for this, I say once more you will be doing well to give your husband tit for tat, so that in your old age your mind will not have any reproach to bring against your flesh.

"Everyone gets from this world what he takes from it, especially women, who have far more necessity to make use of time while they have it than men, because, as you can see for yourself, when we get old, neither husband nor anyone else wants to see us, so we're chased in the kitchen to tell tales to the cat, and scour the pots and pans. Worse than that even, they make songs about us, saying: 'The best morsels for the girls, and quinsies[4] to the old women'; and they say lots of other similar things.

"To keep you no longer in talk, I say now that you could not have spoken to anyone in the world who can be more useful to you than me; for however haughty a man may be I am not afraid to say what is necessary to him, and however harsh or boorish, I can smooth him down and bring him to the point I want. Tell me the one you want, and leave the rest to me. But remember, my child, that I am poor, and that you will be remembered in all my church-goings and all the paternosters I say; and I shall pray God for the souls of all your departed dead."

Thus ended the old woman. And the young woman came to an agreement with the old one that, if she saw him, she was to bring her a young man who often passed through the district; and she described him in such a way that the old woman knew who he was. Then she gave her a piece of salt meat, and sent her away.

Not many days afterwards the old woman brought the young man described to her room, and soon afterwards another, according as the young woman wanted. And, although in fear of her husband, she did not miss the opportunity.

One evening her husband was going out to supper with a friend of his, named Ercolano, and so the girl arranged with the old woman to bring her a young man, who was one of the handsomest and pleasantest in Perugia. Which was quickly done. The young woman and the young man were just sitting down to supper, when they heard Pietro at the door, shouting to her to open it. When she heard it, the wife gave herself up for dead. Wanting to hide the young man if she could, and not having the cunning to get him out of the house or hide him elsewhere, she hid him under a chicken coop in a shed next to the room in which they were supping, and threw over it a piece of straw sacking she had emptied that day. After which, she quickly opened the door to her husband. When he came into the house, she said:

[4] Inflammations of the throat; the literal meaning in the Italian is "things to choke on."

"You've guzzled up that supper pretty quickly."

"We never even tasted it," said Pietro.

"How did that happen?" asked his wife.

"I'll tell you," said Pietro. "Ercolano and his wife and I were sitting down to table when we heard somebody sneeze near us, to which we paid no attention the first and second times. But the person sneezed a third, a fourth, a fifth and many other times, which greatly surprised us. Ercolano was already a little annoyed with his wife because she had kept him waiting a long time at the door, and said to her in a rage: 'What does this mean? Who is it sneezing like this?' He got up from the table, and went to the staircase near at hand, under which was a cupboard to store things away, as we see arranged in houses every day.

"It seemed to him that the sound of the sneezing came from this cupboard, so he opened a little door in it, and as soon as this was opened there suddenly came out the worst stink of sulphur imaginable, which he had noticed before and had complained of, whereupon his wife had said: 'I am whitening my veils in there with sulphur, and the pots too, which I sprinkled with sulphur so that they would get the fumes, and put them under the staircase, and the smell still comes from them.' And after Ercolano had opened the door and the fumes had cleared off a little, he looked inside and saw the person who had sneezed and was still sneezing owing to the sulphur fumes. And as he sneezed, the sulphur had got such a hold on his chest, that he was not far from never sneezing or doing anything else again.

"As soon as Ercolano saw him, he shouted: 'Now I see, wife, the man for whose sake you kept us waiting at the door so long without opening when we came. But may I never have anything please me again, if I don't make you pay for this!' The wife, hearing this and seeing that her fault was discovered, fled from the table without attempting any excuse; and I don't know where she went. Ercolano, not noticing that his wife had fled, told the sneezing man to come out; but he was beyond all power of moving, and did not stir for anything Ercolano said.

"Thereupon Ercolano took him by one of his feet and dragged him out, and ran for a knife to kill him. But, fearing the police on my own account, I jumped up and prevented him from killing the man or doing him any harm. My shouting and defending him aroused the neighbors who came in and took the almost swooning young man, and carried him somewhere—I don't know where—out of the house. So our supper was quite spoiled by all this, and I not only haven't guzzled it but never even tasted it, as I said."

At this tale the wife perceived that there were others who knew as much as she did, although some had bad luck She would have been glad to defend Ercolano's wife with words, but as blaming the faults of others seemed to her to make things easier for her own, she said:

"Here's fine doings! Here's a good and saintly woman! Here's the faith of a modest woman, who seemed to me so saintly that I would have confessed my sins to her. And, what's worse, she gives a mighty good example to the young, since she's getting old already. Cursed be the hour when she came into the world and the hour which allowed her to live, the wicked deceitful woman that she must be, the universal shame and scorn of all women on this earth! Curse her for leaving her chastity and the faith promised to her husband and the honor of the world, he that is such a good man and an honorable citizen and treated her so well, for another man, and not being ashamed to bring him to scorn and herself with him! So help me God, I'd have no pity on such women. They ought to be killed. They ought to be thrown into the fire and burned to ashes."

Then, recollecting that her lover was near at hand, hidden under the hen-coop, she began to urge Pietro to go to bed, as it was then bedtime. But Pietro was more anxious to have something to eat than to go to bed, and asked if there were not something for supper.

"Ah!" said the wife, "yes, indeed, there's supper! We're quite accustomed to have supper when you're not here! Yes, I'm Ercolano's wife, am I? Why don't you go to bed? Go to sleep this evening!"

Now, it happened that during the evening some of Pietro's workmen had brought certain things in from the country, and had stalled their asses without giving them any water to drink, in a little stable next to the shed. One of the asses was very thirsty indeed, and, managing to get his head out of the halter, walked out of the stable and went snuffing at everything, trying to find some water. And so he came up to the hen-coop where the young man was hidden.

He was on his hands and knees, and one of his fingers was outside the hen-coop. Now, as luck or ill luck would have it, the ass trod on his finger; whereupon, in his anguish, he uttered a yell. Pietro was astonished to hear it, and knew that someone must be in the house. He went out of the room and heard the young man moaning, for the ass had not yet taken its hoof off his finger and was still pressing heavily on it. Said Pietro: "Who's there?" He ran to the hen-coop, lifted it up, and saw the young man who, in addition to the pain he felt from the ass treading on his finger, was trembling with fear lest Pietro should do him an injury.

Pietro recognized him as a young man he had long been prowling after for his vicious pleasures, and asked him: "What are you doing here?" but the youth made no answer, and only begged him for the love of God to do him no harm.

"Get up," said Pietro, "I won't do you any harm; but tell me, how do you happen to be here, and why?"

The young man confessed everything. Pietro, no less joyous than his wife was distressed at the discovery, took him by the hand and led him into the room, where the wife was waiting in the greatest terror imaginable. Pietro made her sit down opposite and said:

"So you cursed so hard Ercolano's wife, and you said she ought to be burned and that she was the shame of you all—why didn't you say it of yourself? Or, if you didn't want to confess that, how could your conscience endure to say it of her, when you knew you had done the same thing as she had? Nothing, indeed, induced you to do it, except that all you women are alike, and you hope to hide your own sins under the failings of others. May fire come down from heaven and burn you all, vile generation that you are!"

The wife, seeing that at the first onslaught he had hurt her with nothing worse than words, and noticing that he was in high glee at holding such a handsome youth by the hand, plucked up heart and said:

"I am very sure that you would like fire to come from heaven and burn up all us women, since you are as fond of us as a dog is of sticks. But, God's

Cross! You won't see it happen. I should like to have a little discussion with you, to find out what you complain of. It is indeed well to compare me with Ercolano's wife, a hypocritical, snivelling old woman, who gets what she wants out of him, and he treats her as well as a wife can be treated, which doesn't happen to me. For, granted that I am well clad and shod, you know how I fare in other matters and how long it is since you lay with me. I'd go with rags on my back and broken shoes and be well treated by you in bed, rather than have all these things and be treated as you treat me. Understand plainly, Pietro, I'm a woman like other women, and I want what they want. So, if I go seeking for what I can't get from you, there's no need to abuse me. At least I do you so much honor that I don't go with boys and scrubby fellows."

Pietro saw that she could go on talking all night, and so, as he cared nothing about her, he said:

"That's enough, wife. I'll be content with that. Will you be so gracious as to get us some supper, for I rather fancy this boy has had no more supper than I have."

"No, indeed," said the wife, "he has had no supper; for when you arrived in an ill hour, we were just sitting down to table to sup."

"Go along then," said Pietro, "and get us some supper, and afterwards I will arrange this affair in such a way that you will have nothing to complain of."

Finding her husband so agreeable, the wife jumped up and re-laid the table, brought out the supper she had prepared, and supped merrily with her bad husband and the young man. What Pietro arranged after supper to satisfy all three of them has entirely gone out of my head. But I know that next morning the young man found himself in the piazza, not quite knowing whether the night before he had been with the wife or the husband. And so, dear ladies, I want to tell you: "He who does it to you, you do it to him." And if you can't, keep it in mind while you can, so that the ass may receive what he gets at home.

Dioneo's tale was now ended, and the ladies' laughter was restrained less from lack of amusement than from shame. The queen, seeing that the end of her reign was at hand, stood up and took off her garland, and gracefully placed it on Elisa's head, saying:

"Madonna, it is now for you to give orders."

Having received the honor, Elisa followed the adopted routine and first arranged with the steward for what was needed during the period of her rule; after which she said to the satisfaction of the company:

"We have already heard how many people by means of good sayings and prompt retorts and quick wits have been able to turn the teeth of others on themselves with a sharp nip or have averted threatened dangers. And since this is a good topic and may be useful, my will is that tomorrow, with God's help, we tell tales within these limits—that is, of such persons who have retorted a witticism directed at them, or with a quick retort or piece of shrewdness have escaped destruction, danger or contempt."

This was highly commended by them all. Whereupon the queen rose to her feet, and gave them all to do as they chose until supper time. The merry company arose as the queen arose, and according to custom, each of them gave himself up to what pleased him most. But when the cicadas ceased their song, everyone was called, and they all went to supper. After this had been festively served, they went to singing and music. Emilia danced at the queen's command, and then Dioneo was ordered to sing a song. He immediately began: "Old mother Hale, lift up your tail, and see the good news I bring you." Whereat all the ladies burst out laughing, especially the queen, who ordered him to abandon that song and start another.

"Madonna," said Dioneo, "if I had cymbals, I would sing: 'Up with your petties, Monna Lapa,' or 'Under the olive tree springs the grass,' or would you like me to sing: 'The waves of the ocean make me ill with their motion'? But then I haven't any cymbals, so see which of these others you would like. Do you like: 'Out you go to be chopped to shreds, like a melon down in the garden beds'?"

"No," said the queen, "sing something else."

"Well," said Dioneo, "shall I sing: 'Monna Simona, put it up in the cask, it isn't the month of October'?"

"No, no," said the queen laughing, "sing a nice song, if you like, but not that one."

"Don't get angry, madonna," said Dioneo. "Which do you like best? I know over a thousand. Would you like: 'If I don't tickle my little prickle,' or 'Gently, gently, husband dear,' or 'I'll buy a cock for a hundred dollars'?"

"Dioneo," said the queen rather angrily, although all the others were laughing, "cease joking, and sing a pleasant song. If you don't, you will discover how angry I can be."

At this Dioneo left his jests, and began to sing as follows:

Love, the fair light that issues from her eyes has made me slave to thee and her.

The splendor of her lovely eyes, passing through mine, moved me before your flame was kindled in my heart. However great your worth, I learned it through her beauteous face; imagining which, I found my self gathering every virtue and yielding them to her—another cause of sighs in me.

Now, dear my Lord, I have become one among your followers, and in obedience await your grace; but yet I know not if the high desire which you have set within my breast and my unshaken faith are wholly known to her, who so possesses all my mind that save from her I would not and I do not hope for peace.

Therefore I pray you, sweet my love, to show them to her, and make her feel a little of your flame, in grace to me who, as you see, am all consumed with love, and bit by bit worn down with pain. And then, when it is time, commend me to her, as you should, and gladly would I come with you to do it.

When Dioneo by his silence showed that his song was ended, the queen, after having highly praised it, had others sung. And when part of the night was spent and the queen felt that the heat of day was quenched in night's coolness, she ordered everyone to rest as he chose until the following day.

HERE ENDS THE FIFTH DAY

TENTH DAY, TENTH TALE

The Marquess of Saluzzo is urged by his subjects to take a wife and, to choose in his own way, takes the daughter of a peasant. He has two children by her and pretends to her that he has killed them. He then pretends that he is tired of her and that he has taken another wife and so brings their own daughter to the house as if she were his new wife, after driving her away in her shift. She endures it all patiently. He brings her back home, more beloved by him than ever, shows her their grown children, honors her and makes others honor her as Marchioness.

When the king[1] had ended his long tale, which, to judge by their looks, had greatly pleased everyone, Dioneo said, laughing:

"The good man who was waiting to bring down the ghost's stiff tail that night would not have given two cents for all the praise you give Messer Torello!"[2]

Then, knowing that he was the only one left to tell a tale, he began:

Gracious ladies, as far as I can see, today has been given up to Kings, Sultans and such like persons; so, not to wander away too far from you, I shall tell you about a Marquess, but not of his munificence. It will be about his silly brutality, although good came of it in the end. I do not advise anyone to imitate him, for it was a great pity that good did come to him.

A long time ago the eldest son of the Marquess of Saluzzo was a young man named Gualtieri. He was wifeless and childless, spent his time hunting and hawking, and never thought about marrying or having children, wherein he was probably very wise. This displeased his subjects, who several times begged him to take a wife, so that he might not die without an heir and leave them without a ruler, offering to find him a wife born of such a father and mother as would give him good hopes of her and content him. To which Gualtieri replied:

"My friends, you urge me to do something I was determined never to do, seeing how hard it is to find a woman of suitable character, and how many of the opposite sort there are, and how wretched is the life of a man who takes a wife unsuitable to him. It is foolishness of you to think you can judge a girl by the characters of her father and mother (from which you argue that you can find me one to please me), for I do not see how you can really know the fathers' or the mothers' secrets. And even if you did know them, daughters are often quite different from their fathers and mothers.

"But you want me to take these chains, and I am content to do so. If it turns out badly I want to have no one to complain of but myself, and so I shall choose for myself. And I tell you that if you do not honor the wife I choose as your lady you will find out to your cost how serious a thing it is to have compelled me by your entreaties to take a wife against my will."

They replied that they were content, if only he would take a wife.

For some time Gualtieri had been pleased by the character of a poor girl in a hamlet near his house. He thought her beautiful, and that he might live comfortably enough with her. So he decided that he would marry her

---

[1] Pamfilo, who rules over the tenth day. The theme of the day is liberal and munificent behavior.

[2] A reference to the immediately preceding story and to the first story of Day Seven.

without seeking any further, and, having sent for her father, who was a very poor man, he arranged to marry her. Having done this, Gualtieri called together all his friends from the surrounding country, and said:

"My friends, it has pleased you to desire that I should marry, and I am ready to do so, more to please you than from any desire I have of taking a wife. You know you promised me that you would honor anyone I chose as your lady. The time has now come for me to keep my promise to you and you to keep yours to me. I have found a girl after my heart quite near here; I intend to marry her and to bring her home in a few days. So take thought to make a handsome marriage feast and how you can honorably receive her, so that I may consider myself content with your promise as you may be with mine."

The good men cheerfully replied that they were glad of it, and that they would consider her their lady and honor her as their lady in all things. After which, they all set about preparing a great and handsome wedding feast, and so did Gualtieri. He prepared a great and fine banquet, and invited many friends and relatives and noblemen and others. Moreover, he had rich and beautiful dresses cut out and fitted on a girl, who seemed to him about the same build as the girl he proposed to marry. And he also purchased girdles and rings and a rich and beautiful crown, and everything necessary to a bride.

When the day appointed for the wedding arrived, Gualtieri about the middle of Terce³ mounted his horse, and so did those who had come to honor him. Everything being arranged, he said:

"Gentlemen, it is time to go for the bride."

Setting out with all his company he came to the hamlet and the house of the girl's father, where he found her drawing water in great haste, so that she could go with the other women to see Gualtieri's bride. And when Gualtieri saw her, he called her by her name, Griselda, and asked where her father was. She blushed and said:

"He is in the house, my lord."

Gualtieri dismounted, told everyone to wait for him, entered the poor little house where he found the girl's father (who was named Giannucole), and said to him:

"I have come to marry Griselda, but first I want to ask her a few things in your presence."

He then asked her whether, if he married her, she would try to please him, and never be angry at anything he said or did, and if she would be obedient, and several other things, to all of which she said "Yes." Gualtieri then took her by the hand and led her forth. In the presence of all his company he had her stripped naked, and then the clothes he had prepared were brought, and she was immediately dressed and shod, and he had a crown put on her hair, all unkempt as it was. Everyone marveled at this, and he said:

"Gentlemen, I intend to take this girl as my wife, if she will take me as her husband."

He then turned to her, as she stood blushing and irresolute, and said:

"Griselda, will you take me as your husband?"

³ 7:30 A.M.

"Yes, my lord," she replied.

"And I will take you as my wife," said he.

Then in the presence of them all he pledged his faith to her; and they set her on a palfrey and honorably conducted her to his house. The wedding feast was great and handsome, and the rejoicing no less than if he had married the daughter of the King of France.

The girl seemed to have changed her soul and manners with her clothes. As I said, she was beautiful of face and body, and she became so agreeable, so pleasant, so well-behaved that she seemed like the daughter of a nobleman, and not Giannucole's child and a cattle herder; which surprised everyone who had known her before. Moreover, she was so obedient and so ready to serve her husband that he felt himself to be the happiest and best matched man in the world. And she was so gracious and kindly to her husband's subjects that there was not one of them but loved her and gladly honored her, while all prayed for her good and her prosperity and advancement. Whereas they had said that Gualtieri had showed little wisdom in marrying her, they now said that he was the wisest and shrewdest man in the world, because no one else would have known the lofty virtue hidden under her poor clothes and village garb.

In short, before long she acted so well that not only in the marquisate but everywhere people were talking of her virtues and good actions; and whatever had been said against her husband for having married her was now turned to the opposite. She had not long been with Gualtieri when she became pregnant, and in due time gave birth to a daughter, at which Gualtieri rejoiced greatly.

Soon after this the idea came to him to test her patience with a long trial and intolerable things. He said unkind things to her, seemed to be angry, and said that his subjects were most discontented with her on account of her low birth, and especially when they saw that she bore children. He said they were very angry at the birth of a daughter and did nothing but murmur. When the lady heard these words, she did not change countenance or cheerfulness, but said to him:

"My lord, you may do with me what you think most to your honor and satisfaction. I shall be content, for I know that I am less than they and unworthy of the honor to which you have raised me by your courtesy."

Gualtieri liked this reply and saw that no pride had risen up in her from the honor done her by him and others.

Soon after, he informed his wife in general terms that his subjects could not endure the daughter she had borne. He then gave orders to one of his servants whom he sent to her. The man, with a dolorous visage, said:

"Madonna, if I am to avoid death I must do what my lord bids me. He tells me I am to take your daughter and . . ."

He said no more, but the lady, hearing these words and seeing the servant's face, and remembering what had been said to her, guessed that he had been ordered to kill the child. She went straight to the cradle, kissed and blessed the child, and although she felt great anguish in her heart, put the child in the servant's arms without changing her countenance, and said:

"Do what my lord and yours has ordered you to do. But do not leave her for the birds and animals to devour her body, unless you were ordered to do so."

The servant took the child and told Gualtieri what the lady had said. He marveled at her constancy, and sent the servant with the child to a relative at Bologna, begging her to bring her up and educate her carefully, but without ever saying whose daughter she was.

After this the lady again became pregnant, and in due time brought forth a male child, which delighted Gualtieri. But what he had already done was not enough for him. He pierced the lady with a worse wound, and one day said to her in pretended anger:

"Since you have borne this male child, I cannot live at peace with my subjects, who complain bitterly that a grandson of Giannucole must be their lord after me. If I am not to be driven out, I fear I must do now as I did before, and in the end abandon you and take another wife."

The lady listened to him patiently, and her only reply was:

"My lord, content yourself and do what is pleasing to you. Do not think about me, for nothing pleases me except as it pleases you."

Not many days afterwards Gualtieri sent for his son in the same way that he had sent for his daughter, and while pretending in the same way to kill the child, sent it to be brought up in Bologna, as he had sent the girl. And his wife said no more and looked no worse than she had done about the daughter. Gualtieri marveled at this and said to himself that no other woman could have done what she did; and if he had not seen that she loved her children while she had them, he would have thought she did it to get rid of them, whereas he saw it was from obedience to him.

His subjects thought he had killed his children, blamed him severely and thought him a cruel man, while they felt great pity for his wife. And when the women condoled with her on the death of her children, she never said anything except that it was not her wish but the wish of him who begot them.

Several years after his daughter's birth, Gualtieri thought the time had come for the last test of his wife's patience. He kept saying that he could no longer endure to have Griselda as his wife, that he knew he had acted childishly and wrongly when he married her, that he therefore meant to solicit the Pope for a dispensation to marry another woman and abandon Griselda; for all of which he was reproved by many good men. But his only reply was that it was fitting this should be done.

Hearing of these things, the lady felt she must expect to return to her father's house and perhaps watch cattle as she had done in the past, and see another woman take the man she loved; at which she grieved deeply. But she prepared herself to endure this with a firm countenance, as she had endured the other wrongs of Fortune.

Not long afterwards Gualtieri received forged letters from Rome, which he showed to his subjects, pretending that the Pope by these letters gave him a dispensation to take another wife and leave Griselda. So, calling her before him, he said to her in the presence of many of his subjects:

"Wife, the Pope has granted me a dispensation to leave you and to take another wife. Now, since my ancestors were great gentlemen and lords of this country while yours were always laborers, I intend that you shall no longer be my wife, but return to Giannucole's house with the dowry you brought me, while I shall bring home another wife I have found more suitable for me."

At these words the lady could only restrain her tears by a great effort, beyond that of women's nature, and replied:

"My lord, I always knew that my lowly rank was in no wise suitable to your nobility; and the rank I have had with you I always recognized as coming from God and you, and never looked upon it as given to me, but only lent. You are pleased to take it back, and it must and does please me to return it to you. Here is the ring with which you wedded me; take it. You tell me to take the dowry I brought you; to do this there is no need for you to pay anything nor shall I need a purse or a sumpter horse,[4] for I have not forgotten that I came to you naked. If you think it right that the body which has borne your children should be seen by everyone, I will go away naked. But in exchange for my virginity, which I brought here and cannot carry away, I beg you will at least be pleased to let me take away one shift[5] over and above my dowry."

Gualtieri, who was nearer to tears than anyone else present, managed to keep his countenance stern, and said:

"You shall have a shift."

Those who were present urged him to give her a dress, so that she who had been his wife for thirteen years should not be seen to leave his house so poorly and insultingly as it would be for her to leave it in a shift. But their entreaties were vain. So the lady, clad only in her shift, unshod and with nothing on her head, commended him to God, left his house, and returned to her father accompanied by the tears and lamentation of all who saw her.

Giannucole (who had never believed it was true that Gualtieri would keep his daughter as a wife and had always expected this event), had kept the clothes she had taken off on the morning when Gualtieri married her. So she took them and put them on, and devoted herself to drudgery in her father's house, enduring the assaults of hostile Fortune with a brave spirit.

After Gualtieri had done this, he told his subjects that he was to marry the daughter of one of the Counts of Panago. He therefore made great preparations for the wedding, and sent for Griselda to come to him; and when she came, he said:

"I am bringing home the lady I have just married, and I intend to do her honor at her arrival. You know there is not a woman in the house who can prepare the rooms and do many other things needed for such a feast. You know everything connected with the house better than anyone, so you must arrange everything that is to be done, and invite all the women you think fit and receive them as if you were mistress of the house. Then, when the marriage feast is over, you can return home."

These words were a dagger in Griselda's heart, for she had not been able to dispense with the love she felt for him as she had her good fortune, but she said:

"My lord, I am ready."

So, in her coarse peasant dress, she entered the house she had left a little before in her shift, and had the rooms cleaned and arranged, put out hangings and carpets in the halls, looked to the kitchen, and set her hand to everything as if she had been a scullery wench of the house. And she never paused until everything was ready and properly arranged.

---

[4] Pack horse.   [5] Loose undergarment; slip.

After this she invited all the ladies of the surrounding country in Gualtieri's name, and then awaited the feast. On the wedding day, dressed in her poor clothes, she received all the ladies with a cheerful visage and a womanly manner.

Gualtieri had had his children carefully brought up in Bologna by his relative, who was married into the family of the Counts of Panago. The daughter was now twelve years old, the most beautiful thing ever seen, and the boy was seven. He sent to her and asked her to come to Saluzzo with his son and daughter, to bring an honorable company with her, and to tell everyone that she was bringing the girl as his wife, and never to let anyone know that the girl was anything else. Her husband did what the Marquess asked, and set out. In a few days he reached Saluzzo about dinner time, with the girl and boy and his noble company; and all the peasants of the country were there to see Gualtieri's new wife.

The girl was received by the ladies and taken to the hall where the tables were spread, and Griselda went cheerfully to meet her, saying:

"Lady, you are welcome."

The ladies had begged Gualtieri, but in vain, to allow Griselda to stay in her room or to lend her one of her own dresses, so that she might not have to meet strangers in such a guise. They all sat down to table and began the meal. Every man looked at the girl and said that Gualtieri had made a good exchange, and Griselda above all praised her and her little brother.

Gualtieri now felt that he had tested his wife's patience as far as he desired. He saw that the strangeness of all this did not alter her and he was certain it was not the result of stupidity, for he knew her to be an intelligent woman. He thought it now time to take her from the bitterness which he felt she must be hiding behind a smiling face. So he called her to him, and in everyone's presence said to her smilingly:

"What do you think of my new wife?"

"My lord," replied Griselda, "I see nothing but good in her. If she is as virtuous as she is beautiful, as I well believe, I have no doubt that you will live with her the happiest lord in the world. But I beg you as earnestly as I can not to give her the wounds you gave the other woman who was your wife. I think she could hardly endure them, because she is younger and because she has been brought up delicately, whereas the other labored continually from her childhood."

Gualtieri saw that she really believed he was to marry the other, and yet spoke nothing but good of her. He made her sit down beside him, and said:

"Griselda, it is now time that you should reap the reward of your long patience, and that those who have thought me cruel and wicked and brutal should know that what I have done was directed towards a pre-determined end, which was to teach you to be a wife, then how to choose and keep a wife, and to procure me perpetual peace so long as I live with you. When I came and took you to wife, I greatly feared that this would not happen to me; and so, to test you, I have given you the trials and sufferings you know. I have never perceived that you thwarted my wishes by word or deed, and I think that in you I have the comfort I desire. I mean to give you back now what I deprived you of for a long time, and to heal the wounds I gave you with the greatest delight. Therefore, with a glad spirit, take her whom you think to be my wife and her brother as your children and mine. They are the children whom you and many others have long thought that I had cruelly murdered. And I am your husband, who loves you above all things, believing I can boast that no man exists who can so rejoice in his wife as I in you."

He then embraced and kissed her. She was weeping with happiness. They both arose and went to where their daughter was sitting, quite stupefied by what she had heard, and tenderly embraced her and her brother, thus undeceiving them and many of those present.

The ladies arose merrily from table and went with Griselda to her room. With better hopes they took off her old clothes and dressed her in one of her noble robes, and brought her back to the hall a lady, which she had looked even in her rags.

They rejoiced over their children, and everyone was glad at what had happened. The feasting and merrymaking were prolonged for several days, and Gualtieri was held to be a wise man, although they thought the testing of his wife harsh and intolerable. But above all they esteemed the virtue of Griselda.

The Count of Panago soon afterwards returned to Bologna. Gualtieri took Giannucole away from his labor and installed him as his father-in-law, so that he ended his days honorably and in great content. He afterwards married off his daughter to a nobleman of great wealth and distinction, and lived long and happily with Griselda, always honoring her as much as he could.

What more is to be said, save that divine souls are sometimes rained down from Heaven into poor houses, while in royal palaces are born those who are better fitted to herd swine than to rule over men? Who but Griselda could have endured with a face not only tearless but cheerful, the stern and unheard-of tests imposed on her by Gualtieri? It would perhaps not have been such a bad thing if he had chosen one of those women who, if she had been driven out of her home in a shift, would have let another man so shake her fur that a new dress would have come from it.

Dioneo's tale was over, and the ladies talked about it, taking first one part and then another, blaming some things and praising others. The king looked up at the sky and saw that the sun was already sinking towards the hour of Vespers,[6] and so, without rising, he spoke thus:

"Beautiful ladies, as I think you know, human wisdom does not wholly consist in remembering past things and knowing the present; but grave men esteem it the highest wisdom to be able to foresee the future from a knowledge of both.

"As you know, it will be a fortnight tomorrow since we left Florence to find some amusement to support our health and vitality, and to escape the melancholy, agony and woes which have continued in our city since the beginning of the plague. In my opinion we have virtuously performed this. We have told merry tales, which perhaps might incline to concupiscence; we have eaten and drunk well, played and sung music, all of which things incite weak minds to things less than virtuous; but so far as I have seen there has not been one word or one act on your part or on ours which could

---

[6] 6 P.M.

be blamed. I have noticed only continual virtue, concord and fraternal familiarity; which is certainly most pleasing to me in your honor and in mine. Now, through too long a habit something might arise which would turn to annoyance, and if we stay away too long an opportunity for scandal might occur; and moreover each of us has now for one day exercised the honor which now dwells in me. I therefore think, if you agree, that it would be well for us to return to the place from which we set out. And, if you consider the matter, our being together is already known round about, and so our company might be increased in such a way as to destroy our pleasure. If you approve my advice, I shall retain the crown until we leave, which I think should be tomorrow. If you decide otherwise, I am quite ready to crown someone for tomorrow."

The discussion between the ladies and young men was long, but at last the king's advice was adopted as wise and virtuous, and they determined to do as he had said. So, having called the steward, he discussed with him what should be done next morning, and then, standing up, gave the company their freedom until supper time.

The ladies and the rest arose, and as usual amused themselves in different ways. They came to supper merrily, and after that began to sing and dance and play music. After Lauretta had danced, the king ordered Fiammetta to sing a song, and she began pleasantly as follows:

If Love came to us without jealousy, no woman living—whoever she might be— would be so glad as I!

And if a woman should be pleased to find in her lover gay youth, the very pinnacle of virtue, eagerness and prowess, wisdom, manners, eloquent speech and perfect grace—I should be pleased, who love them all and see them in my hope.

But since I see that other ladies are as wise as I, I tremble with my fears and dread the worst—which is that others may desire the man I love; and so my wondrous fortune turns to woe and sighing, and all life seems ill.

If my lover were but as faithful as he is valiant, I should feel no jealousy. But now so many ladies seek for lovers that I think all men are faithless. This stabs my heart and makes me wish to die; I dread each woman who looks at him, and fear I may be robbed of him.

Therefore in God's name I beg all ladies not to work this wrong on me; for should any seek to do me harm by word or sign or flattery, either I shall turn fool at learning it or she shall weep her bitter foolishness!

When Fiammetta had ended her song, Dioneo, who was sitting beside her, said laughingly:

"Madonna, you would be very courteous to let all women know this, so that no one in ignorance may deprive you of a possession, whose loss would make you so angry!"

After this, they sang several other songs, and when it was nearly midnight, the king commanded that they should all go to bed.

Next morning they arose after the steward had already sent off all their baggage, and returned to Florence under the guidance of their prudent king. The three young men left the seven ladies in Santa Maria Novella, where they had met; and after taking leave of them went about their business. And the ladies returned home.

END OF THE TENTH AND LAST DAY

from CONCLUSION

Most noble ladies, for whose delight I have given myself over to this long task, I believe that with the aid of divine grace it is more through your pious prayers than any merit of mine that I have carried out what I promised to do at the beginning of this work. So now, after giving thanks, first to God and then to you, I shall rest my pen and weary hand. I know that these tales can expect no more immunity than any others, as I think I showed in the beginning of the Fourth Day;[1] and so before I rest, I mean to reply to certain objections which might be made by you or others.

Some of you may say that in writing these tales I have taken too much license, by making ladies sometimes say and often listen to matters which are not proper to be said or heard by virtuous ladies. This I deny, for there is nothing so unchaste but may be said chastely if modest words are used; and this I think I have done.

But suppose it to be true—and I shall not strive with you, for you are certain to win—I reply that I have many arguments ready. First, if there is any license in some of them, the nature of the stories demanded it; and if any understanding person looks at them with a reasonable eye he will see that they could not be related otherwise, unless I had altered them entirely. And if there are a few words rather freer than suits the prudes, who weigh words more than deeds and take more pains to appear than to be good, I say that I should no more be reproved for having written them than other men and women are reproved for daily saying "hole," "peg," "mortar," "pestle," "sausage," "Bologna sausage," and the like things.[2] My pen should be allowed no less power than is permitted the painter's brush; the painters are not censured for allowing Saint Michele to slay the serpent with a sword or lance and Saint Giorgio to kill the dragon as he pleases. They make Christ male and Eve female, and they fasten sometimes with one nail, sometimes with two, the feet of Him who died for the human race on the Cross.

In addition, anyone can see that these things were not told in church, where everything should be treated with reverent words and minds (although you will find plenty of license in the stories of the church); nor were they told in a school of philosophers, where virtue is as much required as anywhere else; nor among churchmen or other philosophers in any place;

---

[1] At the beginning of Day Four, Boccaccio had defended himself against detractors who had charged him, among other things, with too great a fondness for women. He replied that love for them was almost irresistibly natural.

[2] Words that can be used literally and innocently or with sexual meanings. Boccaccio goes on to cite paintings in which images that might be considered phallic can be used for pious purposes.

but they were told in gardens, in pleasure places, by young people who were old enough not to be led astray by stories, and at a time when everyone threw his cap over the mill and the most virtuous were not reproved for it.

But, such as they are, they may be amusing or harmful, like everything else, according to the persons who listen to them. Who does not know that wine is a most excellent thing, if we may believe Cinciglione and Scolaio,[3] while it is harmful to a man with a fever? Are we to say wine is wicked because it is bad for those who are feverish? Who does not know that fire is most useful and even necessary to mankind? And because it sometimes destroys houses, villages and towns, shall we say it is bad? Weapons defend the safety of those who wish to live in peace, but they also kill men, not through any wrong in them but through the wickedness of those who use them ill.

No corrupt mind ever understands words healthily. And just as such people do not enjoy virtuous words, so the well-disposed cannot be harmed by words which are somewhat less than virtuous, any more than mud can sully sunlight or earthy filth the beauty of the skies.

What books, what words, what letters are more holy, more worthy, more to be revered than those of the divine Scripture? Yet many people by perversely interpreting them have sent themselves and others to perdition. Everything in itself is good for something, and if wrongly used may be harmful in many ways; and I say the same of my tales. Whoever wants to turn them to bad counsel or bad ends will not be forbidden by the tales themselves, if by any chance they contain such things and are twisted and turned to produce them. Those who want utility and good fruits from them, will not find them denied; nor will the tales ever be thought anything but useful and virtuous if they are read at the times and to the persons for which they are intended. . . .

[3] Names used to represent drinkers.

Niccolò Machiavelli
(1469–1527)

Niccolò Machiavelli—historian, theorist of history and of politics, and dramatist—was born in 1469 in Florence, a city he loved passionately and served or wished to serve throughout his life. His family had long been prominent in the city, but his father was impoverished, and Niccolò did not receive the best of formal educations; he learned Latin but not Greek, and he was in certain respects self-taught. Nevertheless, after a youth of which we know little, he achieved in 1498 an important post in the Florentine government, and from that time until 1512 he held several key offices having to do with the internal, foreign, and military affairs of the city (Florence was then a republic, as it had been on and off for centuries). His military interests and assignments helped foster in him one of his key ideas: the desirability of a native soldiery as contrasted with venal, undependable mercenaries. He also was entrusted with a good many important diplomatic missions that took him to France, Switzerland, Austria, southern Germany, and several parts of Italy.

During his travels he gained firsthand experience of the turbulence and disunited vulnerability of Italy, experience that he was to draw on in his writings. He also learned much about the realities of contemporary intrigue and power politics during an era of notorious violence and corruption, in Italy and throughout much of Europe. (Compare Raphael Hythloday's mordant comments in Book One of More's Utopia.*) In 1502–1503 he observed at first hand the activities of Cesare Borgia, the unsavory political and military adventurer in whom Machiavelli, despite certain misgivings, found the boldness, acumen, and resourcefulness that he was to recommend in* The Prince. *Cesare's near-success in unifying central Italy provided in some respects a model for the larger unification of Italy that was one of Machiavelli's most cherished goals. The choice of such a model was to do Machiavelli's reputation no good when, later in the sixteenth century, gossip circulated about incestuous acts and murders by poison on the part of Cesare, his sister Lucrezia, and their father Pope Alexander VI.*

In 1512 the Medici family came to power in Florence, toppling the republic. Machiavelli was ousted from his posts and, suspected of disaffection as a member of the old government, was imprisoned and even tortured. Now in poverty, he retired to his modest patrimonial estate, where in 1513 he wrote The Prince *and much of the* Discourses on the First Decade of Titus Livius. *The former work, on which Machiavelli's popular fame rests, was intended on a personal level to win favor with and office from the Medici rulers; Machiavelli dedicated the book first to Giuliano de' Medici and then, after his death in 1516, to his nephew Lorenzo. On a higher level the book was meant to serve the cause of Italian independence and unity by instructing and inspiring the leader who might deliver the country from its abject condition. In or around 1518 Machiavelli wrote the comedy* Mandragola, *or* The Mandrake Root, *a masterpiece of world drama. In 1520 he wrote* On the Art of War, *a milestone in the theory of military tactics. In his last years Machiavelli was given a few minor diplomatic assignments by the Medici and also won their patronage for certain written works, including a history of Florence. In 1527 the forces of the Holy Roman Emperor, Charles V, sacked Rome, an event that helped drive the Medici from power in Florence. Although the republic was restored, Machiavelli was not in favor with the new regime either, and his hope to return to public office was disappointed. He died in the same year.*

Machiavelli's political writings, especially The Prince, *present a difficult challenge to interpreters; this much at least the author has in common with Thomas More, who two years later wrote the problematical* Utopia, *a book that seems to be the polar antithesis of* The Prince. *In the later sixteenth century Machiavelli came to be regarded as the epitome of coldblooded immorality; indeed, the "machiavel" became a stock character in Elizabethan drama, most notably in Christopher Marlowe's* Jew of Malta. *Marlowe's "Machiavelli" tells the audience, "I count religion but a childish toy, / And hold there is no sin but ignorance. . . . Might first made kings, and laws were then most sure / When . . . they were writ in blood." This myth about Machiavelli fed partly on itself, unbeholden to evidence from his writings, and it was reinforced in northern Europe by a stereotype of Italians as treacherous. What textual evidence there was came mainly from* The Prince; *the zealous republican Machiavelli of the* Discourses *seems a very different person. Certain passages in* The

Prince, *and perhaps even its general tenor, do seem to support the traditional and popular view, which is by no means dead today even among informed readers of Machiavelli. At the very least, however, we owe it to Machiavelli to read what he actually wrote and to consider in what sense, if any, he really taught the doctrine often ascribed to him that "the end justifies the means."*

But Machiavelli has many strong defenders. Besides appealing to the integrity of his private life and the evidence from works like the Discourses, *his partisans urge a reappraisal of* The Prince *itself. Some of them praise Machiavelli as a political realist; they consider him one of the first thinkers to treat politics as a science rather than as a branch of ethics. Others have read* The Prince *as sustained, straight-faced irony, a devastating indictment of tyranny that for satiric purposes advises exactly the evils it seeks to expose. Others take* The Prince *more nearly at its word but subordinate the details of Machiavelli's practical advice to his main purpose, stated stirringly in Chapter XXVI, of uniting and liberating his country. In their view, Machiavelli thus becomes a precursor of the patriots of the Risorgimento, the century-long movement to unify and free Italy that culminated in 1870. Other admirers turn the emphasis from political science to literary art, emphasizing Machiavelli's creative side and the indisputable fact of his preeminence as a master of Italian prose.*

In any case, there are many engrossing aspects of Machiavelli besides his morality. His prescriptions aside, his world view deserves attention in itself. In some ways he was a true Renaissance humanist, most clearly in his conviction that the classical past, which for Machiavelli meant primarily the Roman past, was directly relevant to the problems of modern times. This opinion is clearly not just sentimental nostalgia, for he finds in the ancients the same egocentric human nature he finds in his contemporaries. Yet out of selfishness and conflict, which for Machiavelli are givens in human nature and the state, the Romans created the greatest political entity the world has ever known. By the same token, since human nature does not change, he believes that the ancient glories can be revived, not by divine grace but by human skill and enterprise—within, admittedly, the limits of a fickle Fortune. The result is a unique and compelling vision, combining jaundiced caution with bracing self-assurance, unblinking realism with a peculiar brand of hope.

FURTHER READING *(prepared by W. J. R.):* Roberto Ridolfi's *The Life of Niccolò Machiavelli,* 1954, trans. by Cecil Grayson, 1963, is an excellent biography, as well as a comprehensive overview of Machiavelli's work. Ridolfi also provides an introductory account of the Italian Renaissance. The Past Masters series, which provides authoritative but fairly brief general introductions to great writers, includes Quentin Skinner's *Machiavelli,* 1981. Charles D. Tarlton's *Fortune's Circle,* 1970, uses Machiavelli's own writing to discover what it reveals about him. Works concentrating on the Italy of Machiavelli's time are numerous. Two suited for the general reader are J. H. Plumb's *The Italian Renaissance,* 1961, and J. R. Hale's *Machiavelli and Renaissance Italy,* 1960. Plumb's work is a concise survey of the period, with frequent references to Machiavelli, Dante, Petrarch, and other writers; Hale's work provides a clear account of Machiavelli's life and writings, with useful chronological tables and charts. E. Harris Harrison's "Machiavelli's *Prince* and More's *Utopia,*" in *Facets of the Renaissance,* ed. William H. Werkmeister, 1959, compares the two works in their cultural contexts, providing an excellent joint introduction to both writers. Machiavelli's literary art gets very good treatment in Peter Bondanella, *Machiavelli and the Art of Renaissance History,* 1974. Bondanella also has an essay on Machiavelli in *European Writers: Medieval and Renaissance,* Vol. 2, ed. George Stade, 1984. Silvia Ruffo-Fiore, *Niccolò Machiavelli,* 1982, attempts to draw together the political, historical, and literary aspects of Machiavelli. Proof that the image of him as an advocate of fraud and force is still alive is Mark Hulliung, *Citizen Machiavelli,* 1984. Sydney Anglo's *Machiavelli: A Dissection,* 1969, discusses each of Machiavelli's major works. For a sociological approach, see J. E. Siegel's "Violence and Order in Machiavelli," in *Violence and Aggression,* ed. Philip J. Wiener, 1974. Siegel examines Machiavelli's views on violence and attempts to reconcile Machiavelli's apparent brutality and his romantic idealism.

from *THE PRINCE*

Translated by Ninian Hill Thomson

CHAPTER I

OF THE VARIOUS KINDS OF PRINCEDOM, AND OF THE WAYS IN WHICH THEY ARE ACQUIRED

All the States and Governments by which men are or ever have been ruled, have been and are either Republics or Princedoms. Princedoms are either hereditary, in which the sovereignty is derived through an ancient line of ancestors, or they are new. New Princedoms are either wholly new, as that of Milan to Francesco Sforza;[1] or they are like limbs joined on to the hereditary possessions of the Prince who acquires them, as the Kingdom of Naples to the dominions of the King of Spain.[2] The States thus acquired have either been used to live under a Prince or have been free; and he who acquires them does so either by his own arms or by the arms of others, and either by good fortune or by merit.[3]

CHAPTER II

OF HEREDITARY PRINCEDOMS

Of Republics I shall not now speak, having elsewhere spoken of them at length.[4] Here I shall treat exclusively of Princedoms, and, filling in the outline above traced out, shall proceed to examine how such States are to be governed and maintained.

I say, then, that hereditary States, accustomed to the family of their Prince, are maintained with far less difficulty than new States, since all that

[1] Milan had formerly been ruled by the Duke Filippo Maria Visconti; after his death, his son-in-law Sforza (1401–1466) betrayed the succeeding republic and assumed control as Duke of Milan in 1450.

[2] In 1500, King Louis XII of France and Ferdinand "the Catholic," King of Spain, agreed to share the rule of the much-disputed Kingdom of Naples, but in 1503 it was seized by force by Ferdinand for Spain.

[3] *Merit* here translates the Italian *virtù.* A key word in Machiavelli, it can be variously interpreted as merit, ingenuity, human ability, worth, vigor, strength, and a number of related qualities. It rarely means "virtue."

[4] In the *Discourses on the First Decade of Titus Livius.* Livius, or Livy (59 B.C.–A.D. 17) wrote a history of ancient Rome from which Machiavelli believed much could be learned by the Italians of his own time. Livy's first ten books, or "decade," describe the early years of Rome, before it became an empire under the Caesars.

is required is that the Prince shall not depart from the usages of his ancestors, trusting for the rest to deal with events as they arise. So that if an
hereditary Prince be of average address,[5] he will always maintain himself in
his Princedom, unless deprived of it by some extraordinary and irresistible
force; and even if so deprived will recover it, should any, even the least,
mishap overtake the usurper. We have in Italy an example of this in the
Duke of Ferrara, who never could have withstood the attacks of the Venetians in 1484, nor those of Pope Julius[6] in 1510, had not his authority in
that State been consolidated by time. For since a Prince by birth has fewer
occasions and less need to give offense, he ought to be better loved, and will
naturally be popular with his subjects unless outrageous vices make him
odious. Moreover, the very antiquity and continuance of his rule will efface
the memories and causes which lead to innovation. For one change always
leaves a dovetail into which another will fit.

CHAPTER V

How Cities or Provinces Which
Before Their Acquisition Have
Lived Under Their Own
Laws Are To Be Governed

When a newly acquired State has been accustomed, as I have said, to live
under its own laws and in freedom, there are three methods whereby it
may be held. The first is to destroy it; the second, to go and reside there in
person; the third, to suffer it to live on under its own laws, subjecting it to
a tribute, and entrusting its government to a few of the inhabitants who will
keep the rest your friends. Such a Government, since it is the creature of
the new Prince, will see that it cannot stand without his protection and
support, and must therefore do all it can to maintain him; and a city accustomed to live in freedom, if it is to be preserved at all, is more easily controlled through its own citizens than in any other way.

We have examples of all these methods in the histories of the Spartans
and the Romans. The Spartans held Athens and Thebes[7] by creating oli-
garchies in these cities, yet lost them in the end. The Romans, to retain
Capua, Carthage, and Numantia,[8] destroyed them and never lost them. On
the other hand, when they thought to hold Greece as the Spartans had held
it, leaving it its freedom and allowing it to be governed by its own laws, they
failed, and had to destroy many cities of that Province before they could
secure it. For, in truth, there is no sure way of holding other than by destroying, and whoever becomes master of a City accustomed to live in freedom and does not destroy it, may reckon on being destroyed by it. For if it
should rebel, it can always screen itself under the name of liberty and its
ancient laws, which no length of time, nor any benefits conferred will ever
cause it to forget; and do what you will, and take what care you may, unless

---

[5] Adroitness or energy.
[6] For more on the warlike Julius II (reigned 1503–1513), see Chapters XVI and XXV.
[7] *Spartans . . . Thebes.* Athens fell to Sparta in 404 B.C. The Spartans seized Thebes in 382 B.C.
[8] *Romans . . . Numantia.* The Romans took Capua (in southwest Italy) in 211 B.C., Carthage
(in north Africa, near modern Tunis) in 146 B.C., and Numantia (in Spain) in 133 B.C.

the inhabitants be scattered and dispersed, this name, and the old order of things, will never cease to be remembered, but will at once be turned against you whenever misfortune overtakes you, as when Pisa rose against the Florentines after a hundred years of servitude.[9]

If, however, the newly acquired City or Province has been accustomed to live under a Prince, and his line is extinguished, it will be impossible for the citizens, used, on the one hand, to obey, and deprived, on the other, of their old ruler, to agree to choose a leader from among themselves; and as they know not how to live as freemen, and are therefore slow to take up arms, a stranger may readily gain them over and attach them to his cause. But in Republics there is a stronger vitality, a fiercer hatred, a keener thirst for revenge. The memory of their former freedom will not let them rest; so that the safest course is either to destroy them, or to go and live in them.

CHAPTER XV

Of the Qualities in Respect of Which Men, and Most of All Princes, Are Praised or Blamed

It now remains for us to consider what ought to be the conduct and bearing of a Prince in relation to his subjects and friends. And since I know that many have written on this subject, I fear it may be thought presumptuous in me to write of it also; the more so, because in my treatment of it I depart from the views that others have taken.

But since it is my object to write what shall be useful to whosoever understands it, it seems to me better to follow the real truth of things than an imaginary view of them. For many Republics and Princedoms have been imagined[10] that were never seen or known to exist in reality. And the manner in which we live, and that in which we ought to live, are things so wide asunder, that he who quits the one to betake himself to the other is more likely to destroy than to save himself; since any one who would act up to a perfect standard of goodness in everything, must be ruined among so many who are not good. It is essential, therefore, for a Prince who desires to maintain his position, to have learned how to be other than good, and to use or not to use his goodness as necessity requires.

Laying aside, therefore, all fanciful notions concerning a Prince, and considering those only that are true, I say that all men when they are spoken of, and Princes more than others from their being set so high, are characterized by some one of those qualities which attach either praise or blame. Thus one is accounted liberal,[11] another miserly (which word I use, rather than *avaricious,* to denote the man who is too sparing of what is his own, *avarice* being the disposition to take wrongfully what is another's); one is generous, another greedy; one cruel, another tenderhearted; one is faithless, another true to his word; one effeminate and cowardly, another

---

[9] Pisa, a city west of Florence where the Arno, the river of Florence, flows into the sea, was controlled by that city through most of the fifteenth century. When King Charles VIII of France swept through Italy in 1494, Pisa rebelled and was not subjugated by Florence again until 1509.

[10] For example, in Plato's *Republic.*   [11] Free-giving; generous.

high-spirited and courageous; one is courteous, another haughty; one impure, another chaste; one simple,[12] another crafty; one firm, another facile;[13] one grave, another frivolous; one devout, another unbelieving; and the like. Every one, I know, will admit that it would be most laudable for a Prince to be endowed with all of the above qualities that are reckoned good; but since it is impossible for him to possess or constantly practice them all, the conditions of human nature not allowing it, he must be discreet enough to know how to avoid the infamy of those vices that would deprive him of his government, and, if possible, be on his guard also against those which might not deprive him of it; though if he cannot wholly restrain himself, he may with less scruple indulge in the latter. He need never hesitate, however, to incur the reproach of those vices without which his authority can hardly be preserved; for if he well consider the whole matter, he will find that there may be a line of conduct having the appearance of virtue, to follow which would be his ruin, and that there may be another course having the appearance of vice, by following which his safety and well-being are secured.

CHAPTER XVI

OF LIBERALITY AND MISERLINESS

Beginning, then, with the first of the qualities above noticed, I say that it may be a good thing to be reputed liberal, but, nevertheless, that liberality without the reputation of it is hurtful; because, though it be worthily and rightly used, still if it be not known, you escape not the reproach of its opposite vice. Hence, to have credit for liberality with the world at large, you must neglect no circumstance of sumptuous display; the result being, that a Prince of a liberal disposition will consume his whole substance in things of this sort, and, after all, be obliged, if he would maintain his reputation for liberality, to burden his subjects with extraordinary taxes, and to resort to confiscations and all the other shifts[14] whereby money is raised. But in this way he becomes hateful to his subjects, and growing impoverished is held in little esteem by any. So that in the end, having by his liberality offended many and obliged few, he is worse off than when he began, and is exposed to all his original dangers. Recognizing this, and endeavoring to retrace his steps, he at once incurs the infamy of miserliness.

A Prince, therefore, since he cannot without injury to himself practice the virtue of liberality so that it may be known, will not, if he be wise, greatly concern himself though he be called miserly. Because in time he will come to be regarded as more and more liberal, when it is seen that through his parsimony his revenues are sufficient; that he is able to defend himself against any who make war on him; that he can engage in enterprises against others without burdening his subjects; and thus exercise liberality towards all from whom he does not take, whose number is infinite, while he is miserly in respect of those only to whom he does not give, whose number is few.

In our own days we have seen no Princes accomplish great results save

---

[12] Not double-dealing.   [13] Easygoing.   [14] Tricks; stratagems.

those who have been accounted miserly. All others have been ruined. Pope Julius II, after availing himself of his reputation for liberality to arrive at the Papacy, made no effort to preserve that reputation when making war on the King of France, but carried on all his numerous campaigns without levying from his subjects a single extraordinary tax, providing for the increased expenditure out of his long-continued savings. Had the present King of Spain been accounted liberal, he never could have engaged or succeeded in so many enterprises.

A Prince, therefore, if he is enabled thereby to forbear from plundering his subjects, to defend himself, to escape poverty and contempt, and the necessity of becoming rapacious, ought to care little though he incur the reproach of miserliness, for this is one of those vices which enable him to reign.

And should any object that Caesar by his liberality rose to power, and that many others have been advanced to the highest dignities from their having been liberal and so reputed, I reply, "Either you are already a Prince or you seek to become one; in the former case liberality is hurtful, in the latter it is very necessary that you be thought liberal; Caesar was one of those who sought the sovereignty of Rome; but if after obtaining it he had lived on without retrenching his expenditure, he must have ruined the Empire." And if it be further urged that many Princes reputed to have been most liberal have achieved great things with their armies, I answer that a Prince spends either what belongs to himself and his subjects, or what belongs to others; and that in the former case he ought to be sparing, but in the latter ought not to refrain from any kind of liberality. Because for a Prince who leads his armies in person and maintains them by plunder, pillage, and forced contributions, dealing as he does with the property of others this liberality is necessary, since otherwise he would not be followed by his soldiers. Of what does not belong to you or to your subjects you should, therefore, be a lavish giver, as were Cyrus, Caesar, and Alexander; for to be liberal with the property of others does not take from your reputation, but adds to it. What injures you is to give away what is your own. And there is no quality so self-destructive as liberality; for while you practice it you lose the means whereby it can be practiced, and become poor and despised, or else, to avoid poverty, you become rapacious and hated. For liberality leads to one or other of these two results, against which, beyond all others, a Prince should guard.

Wherefore it is wiser to put up with the name of being miserly, which breeds ignominy, but without hate, than to be obliged, from the desire to be reckoned liberal, to incur the reproach of rapacity, which breeds hate as well as ignominy.

CHAPTER XVII

Of Cruelty and Clemency, and Whether It Is Better To Be Loved or Feared

Passing to the other qualities above referred to, I say that every Prince should desire to be accounted merciful and not cruel. Nevertheless, he should be on his guard against the abuse of this quality of mercy. Cesare Borgia was reputed cruel, yet his cruelty restored Romagna, united it, and brought it to order and obedience; so that if we look at things in their true light, it will be seen that he was in reality far more merciful than the people of Florence, who, to avoid the imputation of cruelty, suffered Pistoja to be torn to pieces by factions.[15]

A Prince should therefore disregard the reproach of being thought cruel where it enables him to keep his subjects united and obedient. For he who quells disorder by a very few signal examples will in the end be more merciful than he who from too great leniency permits things to take their course and so to result in rapine and bloodshed; for these hurt the whole State, whereas the severities of the Prince injure individuals only.

And for a new Prince, of all others, it is impossible to escape a name for cruelty, since new States are full of dangers. Wherefore Virgil, by the mouth of Dido, excuses the harshness of her reign on the plea that it was new, saying:—

> "A fate unkind, and newness in my reign
> Compel me thus to guard a wide domain."[16]

Nevertheless, the new Prince should not be too ready of belief, nor too easily set in motion; nor should he himself be the first to raise alarms; but should so temper prudence with kindliness that too great confidence in others shall not throw him off his guard, nor groundless distrust render him insupportable.

And here comes in the question whether it is better to be loved rather than feared, or feared rather than loved. It might perhaps be answered that we should wish to be both; but since love and fear can hardly exist together, if we must choose between them, it is far safer to be feared than loved. For of men it may generally be affirmed that they are thankless, fickle, false, studious to avoid danger, greedy of gain, devoted to you while you are able to confer benefits upon them, and ready, as I said before, while danger is distant, to shed their blood, and sacrifice their property, their lives, and their children for you; but in the hour of need they turn against you. The Prince, therefore, who without otherwise securing himself builds wholly on their professions is undone. For the friendships which we buy with a price, and do not gain by greatness and nobility of character, though they be fairly earned are not made good,[17] but fail us when we have occasion to use them.

Moreover, men are less careful how they offend him who makes himself loved than him who makes himself feared. For love is held by the tie of obligation, which, because men are a sorry breed, is broken on every whisper of private interest; but fear is bound by the apprehension of punishment which never relaxes its grasp.

Nevertheless a Prince should inspire fear in such a fashion that if he do not win love he may escape hate. For a man may very well be feared and yet

---

[15] Pistoja was a city near Florence and under its control. Florence failed to assert its power and allowed a bloody civil war to continue.

[16] *Aeneid*, Book I.   [17] Made use of.

not hated, and this will be the case so long as he does not meddle with the property or with the women of his citizens and subjects. And if constrained to put any to death, he should do so only when there is manifest cause or reasonable justification. But, above all, he must abstain from the property of others. For men will sooner forget the death of their father than the loss of their patrimony. Moreover, pretexts for confiscation are never to seek,[18] and he who has once begun to live by rapine always finds reasons for taking what is not his; whereas reasons for shedding blood are fewer, and sooner exhausted.

But when a Prince is with his army, and has many soldiers under his command, he must needs disregard the reproach of cruelty, for without such a reputation in its Captain, no army can be held together or kept under any kind of control. Among other things remarkable in Hannibal[19] this has been noted, that having a very great army, made up of men of many different nations and brought to fight in a foreign country, no dissension ever arose among the soldiers themselves, nor any mutiny against their leader, either in his good or in his evil fortunes. This we can only ascribe to the transcendent cruelty, which, joined with numberless great qualities, rendered him at once venerable and terrible in the eyes of his soldiers; for without this reputation for cruelty these other virtues would not have produced the like results.

Unreflecting writers, indeed, while they praise his achievements, have condemned the chief cause of them; but that his other merits would not by themselves have been so efficacious we may see from the case of Scipio, one of the greatest Captains, not of his own time only but of all times of which we have record, whose armies rose against him in Spain from no other cause than his too great leniency in allowing them a freedom inconsistent with military strictness. With which weakness Fabius Maximus[20] taxed him in the Senate House, calling him the corrupter of the Roman soldiery. Again, when the Locrians[21] were shamefully outraged by one of his lieutenants, he neither avenged them, nor punished the insolence of his officer; and this from the natural easiness of his disposition. So that it was said in the Senate by one who sought to excuse him, that there were many who knew better how to refrain from doing wrong themselves than how to correct the wrong-doing of others. This temper, however, must in time have marred the name and fame even of Scipio, had he continued in it, and retained his command. But living as he did under the control of the Senate, this hurtful quality was not merely disguised, but came to be regarded as a glory.

Returning to the question of being loved or feared, I sum up by saying, that since his being loved depends upon his subjects, while his being feared depends upon himself, a wise Prince should build on what is his own, and not on what rests with others. Only, as I have said, he must do his utmost to escape hatred.

----

[18] Never lacking.

[19] Carthaginian general (247–182 B.C.), defeated by Scipio. One of Hannibal's most spectacular feats was to lead his invading army across the Alps from Spain to Italy.

[20] Fabius Cunctator ("The Delayer"), noted for his tactic of harassing Hannibal's army without meeting it head-on. He became dictator of Rome in 217 B.C.

[21] Scipio took Locri, in southern Italy, in 205 B.C.

CHAPTER XVIII

HOW PRINCES SHOULD KEEP FAITH

Every one understands how praiseworthy it is in a Prince to keep faith, and to live uprightly and not craftily. Nevertheless, we see from what has taken place in our own days that Princes who have set little store by their word, but have known how to overreach men by their cunning, have accomplished great things, and in the end got the better of those who trusted to honest dealing.

Be it known, then, that there are two ways of contending, one in accordance with the laws, the other by force; the first of which is proper to men, the second to beasts. But since the first method is often ineffectual, it becomes necessary to resort to the second. A Prince should, therefore, understand how to use well both the man and the beast. And this lesson has been covertly taught by the ancient writers, who relate how Achilles and many others of these old Princes were given over to be brought up and trained by Chiron the Centaur;[22] since the only meaning of their having for instructor one who was half man and half beast is, that it is necessary for a Prince to know how to use both natures, and that the one without the other has no stability.

But since a Prince should know how to use the beast's nature wisely, he ought of beasts to choose both the lion and the fox; for the lion cannot guard himself from the toils,[23] nor the fox from wolves. He must therefore be a fox to discern toils, and a lion to drive off wolves.

To rely wholly on the lion is unwise; and for this reason a prudent Prince neither can nor ought to keep his word when to keep it is hurtful to him and the causes which led him to pledge it are removed. If all men were good, this would not be good advice, but since they are dishonest and do not keep faith with you, you, in return, need not keep faith with them; and no Prince was ever at a loss for plausible reasons to cloak a breach of faith. Of this numberless recent instances could be given, and it might be shown how many solemn treaties and engagements have been rendered inoperative and idle through want of faith in Princes, and that he who has best known to play the fox has had the best success.

It is necessary, indeed, to put a good color[24] on this nature, and to be skillful in simulating and dissembling. But men are so simple, and governed so absolutely by their present needs, that he who wishes to deceive will never fail in finding willing dupes. One recent example I will not omit. Pope Alexander VI had no care or thought but how to deceive, and always found material to work on. No man ever had a more effective manner of asseverating, or made promises with more solemn protestations, or observed them less. And yet, because he understood this side of human nature, his frauds always succeeded.

It is not essential, then, that a Prince should have all the good qualities which I have enumerated above, but it is most essential that he should seem to have them; I will even venture to affirm that if he has and invariably practices them all, they are hurtful, whereas the appearance of having

---

[22] Centaurs were half man, half horse.   [23] Traps.   [24] Good appearance.

them is useful. Thus, it is well to seem merciful, faithful, humane, religious, and upright, and also to be so; but the mind should remain so balanced that were it needful not to be so, you should be able and know how to change to the contrary.

And you are to understand that a Prince, and most of all a new Prince, cannot observe all those rules of conduct in respect whereof men are accounted good, being often forced, in order to preserve his Princedom, to act in opposition to good faith, charity, humanity, and religion. He must therefore keep his mind ready to shift as the winds and tides of Fortune turn, and, as I have already said, he ought not to quit good courses if he can help it, but should know how to follow evil courses if he must.

A Prince should therefore be very careful that nothing ever escapes his lips which is not replete with the five qualities above named, so that to see and hear him, one would think him the embodiment of mercy, good faith, integrity, humanity, and religion. And there is no virtue which it is more necessary for him to seem to possess than this last; because men in general judge rather by the eye than by the hand, for every one can see but few can touch. Every one sees what you seem, but few know what you are, and these few dare not oppose themselves to the opinion of the many who have the majesty of the State to back them up.

Moreover, in the actions of all men, and most of all of Princes, where there is no tribunal to which we can appeal, we look to results. Wherefore if a Prince succeeds in establishing and maintaining his authority, the means will always be judged honorable and be approved by every one. For the vulgar are always taken by appearances and by results, and the world is made up of the vulgar, the few only finding room when the many have no longer ground to stand on.

A certain Prince[25] of our own days, whose name it is as well not to mention, is always preaching peace and good faith, although the mortal enemy of both; and both, had he practiced them as he preaches them, would, oftener than once, have lost him his kingdom and authority.

CHAPTER XXIII

That Flatterers Should Be Shunned

One error into which Princes, unless very prudent or very fortunate in their choice of friends, are apt to fall, is of so great importance that I must not pass it over. I mean in respect of flatterers. These abound in Courts, because men take such pleasure in their own concerns, and so deceive themselves with regard to them, that they can hardly escape this plague; while even in the effort to escape it there is risk of their incurring contempt.

For there is no way to guard against flattery but by letting it be seen that you take no offense in hearing the truth: but when every one is free to tell you the truth, respect falls short. Wherefore a prudent Prince should fol-

---

[25] King Ferdinand of Spain.

low a middle course, by choosing certain discreet men from among his subjects, and allowing them alone free leave to speak their minds on any matter on which he asks their opinion, and on none other. But he ought to ask their opinion on everything, and after hearing what they have to say, should reflect and judge for himself. And with these counsellors collectively, and with each of them separately, his bearing should be such, that each and all of them may know that the more freely they declare their thoughts the better they will be liked. Besides these, the Prince should hearken to no others, but should follow the course determined on, and afterwards adhere firmly to his resolves. Whoever acts otherwise is either undone by flatterers, or from continually vacillating as opinions vary, comes to be held in light esteem.

With reference to this matter, I shall cite a recent instance. Father Luke, who is attached to the Court of the present Emperor Maximilian, in speaking of his Majesty told me, that he seeks advice from none, yet never has his own way; and this from his following a course contrary to that above recommended. For being of a secret disposition, he never discloses his intentions to any, nor asks their opinion; and it is only when his plans are to be carried out that they begin to be discovered and known, and at the same time they begin to be thwarted by those he has about him, when he being facile[26] gives way. Hence it happens that what he does one day, he undoes the next; that his wishes and designs are never fully ascertained; and that it is impossible to build on his resolves.

A Prince, therefore, ought always to take counsel, but at such times and seasons only as he himself pleases, and not when it pleases others; nay, he should discourage every one from obtruding advice on matters on which it is not sought. But he should be free in asking advice, and afterwards, as regards the matters on which he has asked it, a patient hearer of the truth, and even displeased should he perceive that any one, from whatever motive, keeps it back.

But those who think that every Prince who has a name for prudence owes it to the wise counsellors he has around him, and not to any merit of his own, are certainly mistaken; since it is an unerring rule and of universal application that a Prince who is not wise himself cannot be well advised by others, unless by chance he surrender himself to be wholly governed by some one adviser who happens to be supremely prudent; in which case he may, indeed, be well advised; but not for long, since such an adviser will soon deprive him of his Government. If he listen to a multitude of advisers, the Prince who is not wise will never have consistent counsels, nor will he know of himself how to reconcile them. Each of his counsellors will study his own advantage, and the Prince will be unable to detect or correct them. Nor could it well be otherwise, for men will always grow rogues on your hands unless they find themselves under a necessity to be honest.

Hence it follows that good counsels, whencesoever they come, have their origin in the prudence of the Prince, and not the prudence of the Prince in wise counsels.

---

[26] Lacking in firmness.

CHAPTER XXV

What Fortune Can Effect in Human Affairs, and How She May Be Withstood

I am not ignorant that many have been and are of the opinion that human affairs are so governed by Fortune and by God, that men cannot alter them by any prudence of theirs, and indeed have no remedy against them; and for this reason have come to think that it is not worth while to labor much about anything, but that they must leave everything to be determined by chance.

Often when I turn the matter over, I am in part inclined to agree with this opinion, which has had the readier acceptance in our own times from the great changes in things which we have seen, and every day see happen contrary to all human expectation. Nevertheless, that our free will be not wholly set aside, I think it may be the case that Fortune is the mistress of one half our actions, and yet leaves the control of the other half, or a little less, to ourselves. And I would liken her to one of those wild torrents which, when angry, overflow the plains, sweep away trees and houses, and carry off soil from one bank to throw it down upon the other. Every one flees before them, and yields to their fury without the least power to resist. And yet, though this be their nature, it does not follow that in seasons of fair weather, men cannot, by constructing weirs and moles,[27] take such precautions as will cause them when again in flood to pass off by some artificial channel, or at least prevent their course from being so uncontrolled and destructive. And so it is with Fortune, who displays her might where there is no organized strength to resist her, and directs her onset where she knows that there is neither barrier nor embankment to confine her.

And if you look at Italy, which has been at once the seat of these changes and their cause, you will perceive that it is a field without embankment or barrier. For if, like Germany, France, and Spain, it had been guarded with sufficient skill, this inundation, if it ever came upon us, would never have wrought the violent changes which we have witnessed.

This I think enough to say generally touching resistance to Fortune. But confining myself more closely to the matter in hand, I note that one day we see a Prince prospering and the next day overthrown, without detecting any change in his nature or character. This, I believe, comes chiefly from a cause already dwelt upon, namely, that a Prince who rests wholly on Fortune is ruined when she changes. Moreover, I believe that he will prosper most whose mode of acting best adapts itself to the character of the times; and conversely that he will be unprosperous, with whose mode of acting the times do not accord. For we see that men in these matters which lead to the end that each has before him, namely, glory and wealth, proceed by different ways, one with caution, another with impetuosity, one with violence, another with subtlety, one with patience, another with its contrary; and that by one or other of these different courses each may succeed.

[27] Dams and breakwaters.

Again, of two who act cautiously, you shall find that one attains his end, the other not, and that two of different temperament, the one cautious, the other impetuous, are equally successful. All which happens from no other cause than that the character of the times accords or does not accord with their methods of acting. And hence it comes, as I have already said, that two operating differently arrive at the same result, and two operating similarly, the one succeeds and the other not. On this likewise depend the vicissitudes of Fortune. For if to one who conducts himself with caution and patience, time and circumstances are propitious, so that his method of acting is good, he goes on prospering; but if these change he is ruined, because he does not change his method of acting.

For no man is found so prudent as to know how to adapt himself to these changes, both because he cannot deviate from the course to which nature inclines him, and because, having always prospered while adhering to one path, he cannot be persuaded that it would be well for him to forsake it. And so when occasion requires the cautious man to act impetuously, he cannot do so and is undone: whereas, had he changed his nature with time and circumstances, his fortune would have been unchanged.

Pope Julius II proceeded with impetuosity in all his undertakings, and found time and circumstances in such harmony with his mode of acting that he always obtained a happy result. Witness his first expedition against Bologna, when Messer Giovanni Bentivogli[28] was yet living. The Venetians were not favorable to the enterprise; nor was the King of Spain. Negotiations respecting it with the King of France were still open. Nevertheless, the Pope with his wonted hardihood and impetuosity marched in person on the expedition, and by this movement brought the King of Spain and the Venetians to a check, the latter through fear, the former from his eagerness to recover the entire Kingdom of Naples; at the same time, he dragged after him the King of France, who, desiring to have the Pope for an ally in humbling the Venetians, on finding him already in motion saw that he could not refuse him his soldiers without openly offending him. By the impetuosity of his movements, therefore, Julius effected what no other Pontiff endowed with the highest human prudence could. For had he, as any other Pope would have done, put off his departure from Rome until terms had been settled and everything duly arranged, he never would have succeeded. For the King of France would have found a thousand pretexts to delay him, and the others would have menaced him with a thousand alarms. I shall not touch upon his other actions, which were all of a like character, and all of which had a happy issue,[29] since the shortness of his life did not allow him to experience reverses. But if times had overtaken him, rendering a cautious line of conduct necessary, his ruin must have ensued, since he never could have departed from those methods to which nature inclined him.

To be brief, I say that since Fortune changes and men stand fixed in their old ways, they are prosperous so long as there is congruity between them, and the reverse when there is not. Of this, however, I am well persuaded, that it is better to be impetuous than cautious. For Fortune is a woman who to be kept under must be beaten and roughly handled; and we

---

[28] Member of a family of Bologna, attacked by Julius in 1506. [29] Favorable outcome.

see that she suffers herself to be more readily mastered by those who so
treat her than by those who are more timid in their approaches. And always, like a woman, she favors the young, because they are less scrupulous
and fiercer, and command her with greater audacity.

CHAPTER XXVI

An Exhortation to Liberate
Italy from the Barbarians

Turning over in my mind all the matters which have above been considered, and debating with myself whether in Italy at the present hour the
times are such as might serve to confer honor on a new Prince, and
whether a fit opportunity now offers for a prudent and valiant leader to
bring about changes glorious for himself and beneficial to the whole Italian
people, it seems to me that so many conditions combine to further such an
enterprise, that I know of no time so favorable to it as the present. And if,
as I have said, it was necessary in order to display the valor of Moses that
the children of Israel should be slaves in Egypt, and to know the greatness
and courage of Cyrus that the Persians should be oppressed by the
Medes,[30] and to illustrate the excellence of Theseus[31] that the Athenians
should be scattered and divided, so at this hour, to prove the worth of some
Italian hero, it was required that Italy should be brought to her present
abject condition, to be more a slave than the Hebrew, more oppressed than
the Persian, more disunited than the Athenian, without a head, without
order, beaten, spoiled, torn in pieces, over-run and abandoned to destruction in every shape.

But though, heretofore, glimmerings may have been discerned in this
man or that, whence it might be conjectured that he was ordained by God
for her redemption, nevertheless it has afterwards been seen in the further
course of his actions that Fortune has disowned him; so that our country,
left almost without life, still waits to know who it is that is to heal her
bruises, to put an end to the devastation and plunder of Lombardy,[32] to the
exactions and imposts of Naples and Tuscany, and to stanch those wounds
of hers which long neglect has changed into running sores.

We see how she prays God to send some one to rescue her from these
barbarous cruelties and oppressions. We see too how ready and eager she is
to follow any standard were there only some one to raise it. But at present
we see no one except in your illustrious House[33] (pre-eminent by its virtues
and good fortune, and favored by God and by the Church whose headship
it now holds), who could undertake the part of a deliverer.

But for you this will not be too hard a task, if you keep before your eyes
the lives and actions of those whom I have named above. For although
these men were singular and extraordinary, after all they were but men,

---

[30] Inhabitants of Media, an ancient region in what is now northwestern Iran. Cyrus the
Great (sixth century B.C.) founded the Persian empire.

[31] A mythical king of Athens. The Athenians credited him with unifying the scattered
communities of Attica, the region near Athens.

[32] By the Swiss and then the French. Lombardy is in northern Italy, surrounding Milan.

[33] The Medici family.

not one of whom had so great an opportunity as now presents itself to you. For their undertakings were not more just than this, nor more easy, nor was God more their friend than yours. The justice of the cause is conspicuous; for that war is just which is necessary, and those arms are sacred from which we derive our only hope. Everywhere there is the strongest disposition to engage in this cause; and where the disposition is strong the difficulty cannot be great, provided you follow the methods observed by those whom I have set before you as models.

But further, we see here extraordinary and unexampled proofs of Divine favor. The sea has been divided; the cloud has attended you on your way; the rock has flowed with water; the manna has rained from heaven; everything has concurred to promote your greatness.[34] What remains to be done must be done by you; since in order not to deprive us of our free will and such share of glory as belongs to us, God will not do everything himself.

Nor is it to be marvelled at if none of those Italians I have named has been able to effect what we hope to see effected by your illustrious House; or that amid so many revolutions and so many warlike movements it should always appear as though the military virtues of Italy were spent; for this comes from her old system being defective, and from no one being found among us capable to strike out a new. Nothing confers such honor on the reformer of a State, as do the new laws and institutions which he devises; for these when they stand on a solid basis and have a greatness in their scope, make him admired and venerated. And in Italy material is not wanting for improvement in every form. If the head be weak the limbs are strong, and we see daily in single combats, or where few are engaged, how superior are the strength, dexterity, and intelligence of Italians. But when it comes to armies, they are nowhere, and this from no other reason than the defects of their leaders. For those who are skillful in arms will not obey, and every one thinks himself skillful, since hitherto we have had none among us so raised by merit or by fortune above his fellows that they should yield him the palm. And hence it happens that for the long period of twenty years, during which so many wars have taken place, whenever there has been an army purely Italian it has always been beaten. To this testify, first Taro, then Alessandria, Capua, Genoa, Vaila, Bologna, Mestri.[35]

If then your illustrious House should seek to follow the example of those great men who have delivered their country in past ages, it is before all things necessary, as the true foundation of every such attempt, to be provided with national troops, since you can have no braver, truer, or more faithful soldiers; and although every single man of them be good, collectively they will be better, seeing themselves commanded by their own Prince, and honored and esteemed by him. That you may be able, therefore, to defend yourself against the foreigner with Italian valor, the first step is to provide yourself with an army such as this.

And although the Swiss and the Spanish infantry are each esteemed

---

[34] The divided sea, the cloud, the water from the rock, and the manna were signs of divine favor when the Israelites escaped from bondage in Egypt; see Exodus 14, 13, 17, 16.

[35] *Taro . . . Mestri.* These defeats occurred between 1495 and 1513.

formidable, there are yet defects in both, by reason of which troops trained on a different system might not merely withstand them, but be certain of defeating them. For the Spaniards cannot resist cavalry, and the Swiss will give way before infantry if they find them as resolute as themselves at close quarters. Whence it has been seen, and may be seen again, that the Spaniards cannot sustain the onset of the French men-at-arms,[36] and that the Swiss are broken by the Spanish foot.[37] And although of this last we have no complete instance, we have yet an indication of it in the battle of Ravenna,[38] where the Spanish infantry confronted the German companies, who have the same discipline as the Swiss; on which occasion the Spaniards by their agility and with the aid of their bucklers[39] forced their way under the pikes, and stood ready to close with the Germans, who were no longer in a position to defend themselves; and had they not been charged by cavalry, they must have put the Germans to utter rout. Knowing, then, the defects of each of these kinds of troops, you can train your men on some different system, to withstand cavalry and not to fear infantry. To effect this, will not require the creation of any new forces, but simply a change in the discipline of the old. And these are matters in reforming which the new Prince acquires reputation and importance.

This opportunity then, for Italy at last to look on her deliverer, ought not to be allowed to pass away. With what love he would be received in all those Provinces which have suffered from the foreign inundation, with what thirst for vengeance, with what fixed fidelity, with what devotion, and what tears, no words of mine can declare. What gates would be closed against him? What people would refuse him obedience? What jealousy would stand in his way? What Italian but would yield him homage? This barbarian tyranny stinks in all nostrils.

Let your illustrious House therefore take upon itself this enterprise with all the courage and all the hopes with which a just cause is undertaken; so that under your standard this our country may be ennobled, and under your auspices be fulfilled the words of Petrarch:—

> Brief will be the strife
> When valor arms against barbaric rage;
> For the bold spirit of the bygone age
> Still warms Italian hearts with life.[40]

[36] Cavalry.   [37] Foot soldiers; infantry.   [38] In 1512.   [39] Shields.
[40] Canzone beginning "Italia mia"—an anti-German poem.

Thomas More
(*1478–1535*)

Renaissance humanism, of which Thomas More was one of the shining lights, encouraged religious tolerance. But this aspect of the movement could not coexist easily after the Protestant Reformation and the Catholic Counter-Reformation with the new sectarian antagonisms that embittered European religion in the latter sixteenth and seventeenth centuries. The tragedy of this factionalism gives a special poignancy to More's life and to his Utopia, written as it was in the last few years before the emergence of Luther.

More, the son of a lawyer, was born in 1478 in London, where he spent most of his life. He attended an excellent school there, St. Anthony's, and from about age twelve to fourteen he was maintained in the household of John Morton, the Lord Chancellor of England and Archbishop of Canterbury who is recalled admiringly by Raphael Hythloday in Book One of Utopia. At fourteen More entered Oxford, where his studies emphasized Latin and logic. Two years later he enrolled in one of London's Inns of Court, in accordance with his father's wishes that he become a lawyer. Although More had no great enthusiasm for that profession, his legal training was important in light of his later public service and the concomitant knowledge it fostered in him of all levels of society. In 1499 he met Desiderius Erasmus, with whom he was to have a lifelong friendship. (It was during a sojourn in More's house, in 1509, that Erasmus wrote his best-known work, The Praise of Folly, the Latin title of which, Moriae Encomium, puns affectionately on More's name.) There was an enduring ascetic strain in More (he continued throughout his life to wear a hair shirt that contrasted with his habitual cheerfulness), and for a while he considered becoming a Catholic priest. He also loved classical and theological learning, which always competed for his time with public and domestic duties. These preoccupations led him to spend about four years in a Carthusian monastery in London. He chose, however, a life in the world, and in 1505, soon after he left the monastery, he married Jane Colt. She died in 1511, leaving him with three young daughters and a son. He soon remarried a widow with two children. To these children and stepchildren were later added several other wards, who made up a school in More's household. An excellent humanist education, in religion, the classics, philosophy, and science, was imparted not only to the boys but also (which was noteworthy in More's time) to the girls. He once wrote, "The harvest will not be affected whether it be a man or woman who sows the seed. Both are reasonable beings, distinguished in this from the beasts; both therefore are suited equally for those studies by which reason is cultivated."

In 1509 Henry VIII succeeded Henry VII as King of England. The new monarch was welcomed hopefully by humanists as a potential social reformer, but they were soon disillusioned when Henry showed a penchant for military and political adventurism. At about the same time, More was himself embarking on a life of public service that, besides the office of Under-Sheriff of London, included diplomatic missions. During one such mission, to Flanders in 1515, to help settle a dispute about the wool trade, More took advantage of leisure occasioned by delays in the negotiations to write the second Book of Utopia. The first Book, which begins as a factual account of the stay in Flanders, was written in the following year, after More returned to England. (Some of More's writings were in English, but Utopia, designed mainly to be read by fellow humanists, statesmen, and intellectuals, was written in Latin.) At about this time More also wrote his History of Richard III, a landmark of English history-writing that was to shape Shakespeare's notorious (and unfair, according to some modern historians) portrait of Richard as an unscrupulous murderer.

More's own Hythloday, in Utopia, had advised that good men and philosophers should avoid the service of kings (advice that can be fruitfully contrasted with the role of adviser that Machiavelli adopts in The Prince, written only three years earlier). Nevertheless, More entered Henry's service, steadily winning the king's increasing *favor and attaining one high office after another: member of the King's Council in 1517, Under-Treasurer in 1521, knight in the same year, Speaker of the House of Commons in 1523, High Steward of Oxford in 1524 and of Cambridge in 1525, Chancellor of the duchy of Lancaster in 1525, and climactically, in 1529, Lord Chancellor, the highest post under the Crown. In 1526 More helped Hans Holbein the Younger attain the post of English court painter, and to Holbein we owe famous portraits of Henry, Erasmus, and More himself.*

These were also the first years of the Protestant Reformation, following on Luther's nailing of his theses to the church door at Wittenberg in 1517. More was a zealous propagandist against what he regarded as the new heresies. From the pope Henry VIII won for himself and subsequent British monarchs the title Defender of the Faith, by a piece of apologetics in which More had a hand—though, ironically in light of later events, More cautioned Henry against conceding to the pope in this tract more authority in England than was lawful. More's polemical writings reached a climax between 1529 and 1533. In the epitaph he composed for himself, More boasted of his severity to heretics, though it is also true that he once claimed to oppose "that vice of theirs and not their persons."

The final and most famous episode in More's life began in 1527. Henry, in love with Anne Boleyn (the mother of the future Queen Elizabeth I) and unhappy over the failure of his queen, Catherine of Aragon, to bear a male heir, expressed a desire that the pope, on tortuous grounds, approve a divorce. When the pope refused, Henry repudiated his authority and claimed for himself the headship of the Church in England. Asked in his role of Lord Chancellor to assent, More refused, believing that the pope's spiritual authority was essential to the Church unity More always cherished. He also refused to attend the coronation of Anne after Henry married her in 1533, an act of omission that was ominous for him. After being imprisoned in the Tower of London, where he lived contentedly, he was tried and beheaded for high treason in 1535, jesting whimsically with his captors on the way to his death. Exactly four centuries later, in 1935, he was canonized a saint of the Roman Catholic Church.

Another posthumous honor was rendered More in the twentieth century: the listing of his name on a monument in Moscow as a saint, so to speak, of Communism. That he should be enshrined, at virtually the same time, by the Church and also by the Soviets is an emblem of the enigmatic standing of More and particularly of his Utopia. More is one of several authors of the sixteenth century—Machiavelli, Erasmus, and Montaigne are also among them—whose works puzzle interpreters because they present internal problems of consistency in tone or viewpoint or because they seem anomalous in light of the author's life and other works.

The basic problem in interpreting Utopia is to explain it as a whole, without ignoring ideas and emphases that conflict with simplistic readings. One possibility is to see the work as a recreational, high-spirited intellectual game of the kind humanists liked to play, a teasing blend of realism and fancy to be savored more for its inventiveness than for a serious message. That a characteristic element of playfulness in More appears in Utopia is undeniable. But, although the humor in the book sometimes does seem an end in itself, as in the account of newborn artificially incubated chickens, the premarital inspection of prospective mates, and some of the etymologies, the humor can also sharpen the edge of the satire, as in the account of the showy Anemolian ambassadors. In any case, the social distress surveyed in Book One hardly seems the matter of comedy. It is possible that some of the humor is a protective packaging designed to preserve More from official reprisals.

Giving only light weight to evidence from More's other writings and to the central importance in the Utopian state of belief in God and in rewards and punishments after death, Marxists and other socialists focus on Raphael Hythloday's fervid attack on social and economic evils such as private property, commercial greed, and the selfishness of kings. In this reading, More's occasional polite objections to Hythloday's ideas are not to be taken very seriously.

Some Catholic interpreters, however, see Utopia not as a herald of a socialist future but as a defense of the medieval past, including the form of uncompetitive communal living practiced in monasteries. But it is one thing to celebrate ideals that even in the Middle Ages governed only small pockets of society and another thing to depict and apparently praise a whole state ruled by communist principles.

Another possibility is that More is using an a fortiori strategy: if the Utopians can achieve a society so just and attractive by using natural reason alone, it is shameful that Europeans blessed with the advantage of Christian revelation should live such evil and wretched lives in states so badly ruled. This view has some support in the text: the religion of the Utopians is in fact founded on such Christian premises as the immortality of the soul and the justice of divine providence, and the Utopians eagerly receive Christian teachings when they learn of them. But how then does one account for those Utopian practices—including euthanasia, a priesthood open to women and married men, and divorce on grounds of incompatibility—that do not so much fall short of the highest potential of Catholic Christianity as contravene Catholicism? Would More, who had his share of the humanist faith in reason, intimate that adherence to the doctrines and discipline of the Church was actually in defiance of reason?

Still another view holds that Utopia is not a scheme for a perfect commonwealth but rather a moral treatise, the details of Utopian sociology being merely ancillary to More's central purpose: to reform persons and not societies and particularly to root out the sin of pride that, in accordance with a Christian commonplace, underlies all other sins. To this reading at least two objections may be made: first, it seems unlikely that a general tract against personal pride should dwell so minutely and with such relish on social mechanics, and second, pride is attributed to a very specific social fact, the existence of private property—which brings us back to the socialist readings.

Most of the interpretations just outlined assume that in one way or another the values governing the Utopian commonwealth are desirable. But that is not a necessary assumption. It is perhaps unimportant that there are certain practical problems; for example, the small number of priests seems inadequate to their function as educators of the young. More cannot be expected to have worked out every detail. And the advantages of living in Utopia are heightened by contrast with the wretched conditions, especially of the poor, in More's time. It remains true, however, that there is a certain colorlessness, uniformity, and lack of passion in Utopian life. It is interesting that Book One, which focuses on the severely flawed Europe of More's day, contains a number of lively personal portraits, real and fictional. But Book Two, though in principle allowing for diversity among the Utopians (in their religious views, for example), presents few individual persons and none that are memorable.

This fact is important in connection with attempts in later literature to portray utopias and dystopias (evil polities). More was not, of course, the first writer who tried to envisage comprehensive human felicity; before him there were visions like Ovid's of the primitive Golden Age and hypothesized good societies like that of Plato's Republic, not to mention Christian images of heaven. More's Utopia differs, obviously, from the Christian heaven by being located on earth, from Plato's common-

wealth by the purported realism of Utopia and its democratic spirit and machinery, from primitivist images of the good life by its dependence not on simple, unsophisticated conditions of nature and mind but on an advanced rationality, expressed in an intricately structured social organization and in technology. It is this emphasis on structure, artifice, and mental discipline that tends to recur in later utopias and dystopias such as Francis Bacon's New Atlantis, *Book Four of Swift's* Gulliver's Travels, *Edward Bellamy's* Looking Backward, *several works by H. G. Wells, Aldous Huxley's* Brave New World, *George Orwell's* 1984, *and B. F. Skinner's* Walden Two. *The persistent theme of the relationship between social organization and mind in the utopian tradition has made it a continuing forum not only for confronting the desirable and undesirable possibilities of social structures but also for investigating the meaning of progress and the essential meaning of human nature. Such issues are implicit, apart from the values that inform any particular work, in the very notion of envisaging a thoroughly perfect or thoroughly evil society articulated in response to ideology.*

FURTHER READING *(prepared by W. J. R.):* Perhaps the best introduction to More for undergraduates and general readers is Anthony Kenny's short book *Thomas More,* 1983, in the Past Masters series, which surveys More's life, writings, and place in history. A full-scale biography, very well written and drawing on fresh material about More, is Richard Marius, *Thomas More: A Biography,* 1984. R. W. Chambers' *Thomas More,* 1935, despite its age, is still well worth reading. An excellent survey of More's intellectual development, through the phases of his life, is available in Alistair Fox, *Thomas More: History and Providence,* 1982. Penry Williams' *The Tudor Regime,* 1979, though not concerned directly with More, contains an excellent analysis of the process of Tudor government. An analysis of *Utopia* in the light of sixteenth-century social conditions and political philosophy can be found in Russell Ames' *Citizen Thomas More and His Utopia,* 1949. Richard Schoeck's *The Achievement of Thomas More,* 1976, is a fine introduction to More's other writings. Ligeia Gallagher's *More's "Utopia" and Its Critics,* 1964, contains the text of *Utopia,* a good introduction to it, and a collection of modern critical responses. Forty-seven articles are gathered in *Essential Articles for the Study of Thomas More,* ed. R. S. Sylvester, 1977, including Robert Bolt's preface to *A Man for All Seasons,* which could provide a useful starting point for the new reader of *Utopia.* The genesis of *Utopia* is intensively studied in J. H. Hexter's *More's "Utopia": The Biography of an Idea,* 1952. Part Two of this work contains a detailed analysis of *Utopia.* Walter R. Davis's "Thomas More's *Utopia* as Fiction," *Centennial Review,* 24 (1980), 249–68, treats Book I as exposition on the nature of fiction itself and Book II as a representative of such fiction. One of the most comprehensive readings of the work is George M. Logan, *The Meaning of More's "Utopia,"* 1983, which sees it as, in important ways, a critique of humanist theory. The basic notion of a utopia, along with several of its historical manifestations, provides the subject of the essays in *The Utopian Vision,* ed. E. D. S. Sullivan, 1983. Over the last three decades *The Complete Works of St. Thomas More,* in the Yale Edition, have been appearing in separate volumes, which include excellent critical apparatus.

UTOPIA

Translated by Peter K. Marshall

BOOK ONE

The most victorious King of England, Henry the Eighth, most accomplished in all the virtues of an outstanding prince, recently had a disagreement on certain matters of great importance with Charles, the most serene Prince of Castile. To settle and arrange this dispute, the King sent me as ambassador to Flanders,[1] together with that incomparable man Cuthbert Tunstall,[2] whom, to everyone's great joy, he recently made Master of the Rolls. But of this man's virtues I shall say nothing, not because I am afraid that a friend's evidence should be considered suspect, but because his goodness and learning are too great to be praised by me, and also too well known and famous everywhere to need my praise; unless, as the saying goes, I should wish to seem to be illuminating the sun with a lantern.

As had been arranged, all those excellent gentlemen met us at Bruges who had been entrusted with the affair by their prince. The chief and head of these was the Margrave of Bruges, a most distinguished gentleman. But their learned spokesman was George de Theimsecke, Provost of Kassel, a man eloquent by training and nature, greatly skilled in law and an unrivaled master in debating affairs both by his natural genius and by his constant experience in practical matters. We met once or twice, but could not sufficiently agree on certain points; so they said good-bye to us for a few days and left for Brussels to find out what their prince had in mind.[3] Meanwhile I set off to Antwerp; for so my affairs demanded.

While I was staying there, I had visits from several people but none was more welcome than Peter Giles,[4] a native of Antwerp. He is a man of great honesty and high position among his people, worthy of the highest. I cannot say which is greater, his learning or his excellence of character; for he is of the highest quality and deeply read in literature, with an open heart to everyone. Toward his friends he is so affectionate, loving, faithful, and sincere that you could scarcely find one or two people anywhere whom you would feel comparable to him in all respects of friendship. He has a rare modesty and no one could be less pretentious, no one could possess a wiser simplicity. Further, he is so graceful in talk and so harmlessly witty that by his sweet company and delightful conversation he greatly alleviated my

---

[1] The fictional tale that will be told by the fictional Raphael Hythloday is set in a context of historical fact. More was despatched in 1515 to serve as a negotiator in a commercial dispute, involving the wool trade, between England (then ruled by Henry VIII) and Flanders (approximately, modern Belgium), which was then ruled by Spain. The negotiations dragged on for six months, during which time More wrote the second Book of *Utopia*. Prince Charles (1500–1558) was later to become king of Spain and Holy Roman Emperor.

[2] A close friend of More; later Bishop of London.

[3] Charles spent a week in Brussels in July 1515.

[4] Peter Giles, a friend (like More) of the great Dutch humanist Desiderius Erasmus, was Chief Secretary of Antwerp.

longing for my own country and home, my wife and children, whom I was restless to see again as I had already been away from home for more than four months.

One day I had attended Mass in the Cathedral of Notre Dame, a most beautiful building, always crowded with people. When the service was finished, I was preparing to return to the place where I was staying, when I happened to see Peter Giles conversing with a stranger, a man approaching old age, with a sunburned face and a long beard, whose cloak was carelessly hanging from his shoulder. From his appearance and dress I judged him to be a sailor. When Peter saw me, he came up and greeted me. As I was about to reply, he drew me aside a little distance, and said, "Do you see this man?" at the same time pointing out the man with whom I had seen him talking. "I intended, " he said, "to bring him straight to you." "He would have been most welcome," I said, "for your sake." "No," said Peter, "for his own sake, if you knew him. For there is no one alive today who could tell you so much about unknown peoples and lands; and I know that you are most eager to hear about such things." "So," said I, "my guess was not far amiss. For at first glance, I felt that the man was a sailor." "And yet," said Peter, "you are very wrong. For he sailed certainly, not like Palinurus,[5] but like Ulysses, or rather, like Plato. Raphael Hythloday[6] over there (for this is his name) has a great knowledge of Latin and a profound one of Greek. He paid more attention to Greek than Latin because he had devoted himself entirely to philosophy, and on this subject he knew that nothing of any importance is extant in Latin except a few things of Seneca and Cicero. Well, he left to his brothers the inheritance he had at home (he is Portuguese), and from a desire to see the world joined himself to Amerigo Vespucci.[7] In the last three of those four voyages that everyone is reading about, he was Amerigo's constant companion, except that on the last voyage he did not return with him. For he, with the greatest difficulty, obtained permission from him to be among those twenty-three who at the end of the last voyage were left in the fort.[8] And so he was left behind, as a concession to his mind, which cared more for foreign travel than a grave; for he was constantly repeating the sayings: 'Who does not have an urn is covered by the sky,' and 'The road to heaven is the same length from all directions.' His attitude would have cost him dearly, if God had not been favorable to him.

"After Vespucci left, he visited many regions with five companions from the fort, and by good fortune at last came to Ceylon and from there to Calicut.[9] There he was lucky to find some Portuguese ships and at last, contrary to his expectations, he returned to his own country."

When Peter told me this, I thanked him for his kindness toward me for being so anxious that I should enjoy the talk of a man whose conversation

[5] Aeneas' pilot in Virgil's *Aeneid*, Book V; he fell asleep at the helm, went overboard, and drowned. By contrast, Ulysses (Homer's Odysseus) and Plato became wiser by traveling.

[6] The surname means "dispenser of nonsense."

[7] An Italian explorer in the service of Spain and Portugal who in 1507 published an account of four voyages, taken between 1497 and 1504, to the New World. The Americas are named for him.

[8] At Cape Frio, in Brazil; Vespucci describes leaving men there. During one voyage, he claimed, he encountered a people who (like the Utopians) owned property communally.

[9] The Portuguese discovered Ceylon in 1505. Calicut is in India.

he thought would be pleasant to me. Then I turned to Raphael. After an exchange of greetings and those pleasantries which people say on first meeting a stranger, we left that place and went to my house; and there in the garden we sat on a bench covered with green turf and began to talk together.

So he told us how he and his companions who had remained in the fort, after the departure of Vespucci, by kind approaches gradually won the favor of the natives of that land, and soon were able to move among them with no danger and with great ease, and how also they were regarded with great affection by a certain leader, whose country and name I have forgotten. By his generosity, he said, he and his five companions were given an abundance of supplies and money. For their journey (which was by boat on the water and by chariot on land) they were also given a very trusty guide to take them to other leaders whom they wished to see, and were supplied with the highest commendations. After traveling for many days, he said, he discovered towns and cities, and populous republics with excellent constitutions.

For under the Equator, and on both sides of it, for the distance taken in by the movement of the sun, there lie great deserts parched with constant heat. Everywhere the land is rough and harsh to the sight, terrible, untended, inhabited by wild beasts and serpents, or else men no less wild than the beasts nor less dangerous. But when you have traveled farther, gradually everything grows more gentle: the climate is less harsh, the land pleasantly green, the animals more mild. Eventually you meet peoples, cities, towns. In these there is constant commerce by land and sea, not merely among themselves and their neighbors, but also with far distant countries.

From there he had the opportunity to visit many lands far and wide, because he and his companions were readily welcomed on any ship that was being fitted out for any journey. He said that the ships they saw in the first regions had a flat keel; their sails were made from stitched reeds or osiers, in some places leather. But afterward they came across pointed keels and canvas sails, in short, everything like ours. Their sailors have a great knowledge of the sea and the sky.

But he said he won great favor by showing them how to use the magnet.[10] They had been previously quite ignorant of this, and consequently had been afraid to venture on the sea and did so only in the summer. But now, relying on the magnet, they are not worried by the winter, quite without fear but not without danger; for there is a great hazard that the very thing which they thought would bring them great good may, through their lack of prudence, be the cause of great ills.

He related what he saw in each place, but it would be too long for me to tell it all, and is not the purpose of this work. Perhaps I shall repeat it in another place, especially what it would be profitable to know; above all, those just and wise provisions which he observed among peoples continually living together in harmony. For we asked eagerly about these matters and he gladly discoursed on them. But we did not inquire about monsters, for there is nothing unusual about this subject. For everywhere you can

---

[10] The magnetic compass, invented in the East and first used by Europeans for navigation in the fifteenth century.

find Scyllas and greedy Celaenos and man-eating Laestrygonians,[11] and fearsome monsters of that kind; but people governed by healthy and wise laws cannot be found just anywhere.

But just as he observed many foolish practices among those new peoples, so he also told us of many institutions from which we might take suitable examples for correcting the errors of these cities, nations, peoples and kingdoms of ours. As I said, I shall relate these in another place. For the moment I want to repeat only what he said about the ways and institutions of the Utopians.[12] But first I will give the conversation which gradually led us to the mention of that republic.

Raphael had first with great wisdom touched upon the various mistakes both in our world and in that new one (and certainly they are very numerous in both places). Then he mentioned the wiser provisions that both we and they have. He so thoroughly understood the ways and practices of each people that it seemed that he had spent his whole life in whatever place he visited. In amazement at the man, Peter said, "My dear Raphael, I am surprised that you do not join yourself to some king. I am quite sure that you would be in great favor with any king, since by this learning and knowledge of places and men you could not merely give pleasure but also instruct by examples and aid by your advice. In this way you would look after your own interests admirably and also be able to help your family and friends greatly."

"As to my family and friends," he said, "I am not much worried, since I think that I have fulfilled my obligations toward them well enough. For other people do not part with their possessions unless they are old and sick, and even then with reluctance when they can no longer hold on to them; but I shared mine out to my family and friends not only when I was healthy and lively, but also when I was a young man. I think they ought to be content with this liberality of mine, and not demand and expect in addition that for their sakes I should give myself into servitude to kings."

"God forbid," said Peter. "My intention was that you should go not into servitude but into service of kings." "That," said he, "is only one syllable less than servitude." "But whatever name you give to it," said Peter, "my opinion is that this is the very road by which you could not only bring profit to others, both privately and publicly, but also make your own condition more prosperous."

"Should I make myself more prosperous," said Raphael, "by the road I find repulsive? And yet now I live just as I wish—a blessing which I suspect comes to very few men in high positions. But there are enough men of that kind who court the friendship of the powerful. So do not think it any great loss if they are going to do without me and one or two like me."

Then I said, "It is clear, Raphael, that you desire neither wealth nor power; and I for one respect and look up to a man of your mind no less than any of those who are in powerful positions. But you will be acting in a way worthy of your noble and philosophic spirit if you so dispose yourself,

---

[11] *Scyllas . . . Laestrygonians.* Scylla is a monster described in Homer's *Odyssey,* Book XII, who devours some of Odysseus' boatmen. Celaeno is one of Virgil's Harpies (*Aeneid,* Book III), birds with women's faces; the Laestrygonians, in the *Odyssey,* Book X, are gigantic cannibals.
[12] *Utopia* is from Greek, meaning "no place," with a pun on the Greek for "good place."

even though it may involve some private disadvantage, as to lend your ability and industry to public affairs. This you could most profitably do if you were a counselor to some great prince, and (as I am sure you would do) gave him advice both upright and honorable. For from a prince a river of all good or evil things flows upon the whole people as if from some perpetual fountain. But you have such perfect learning that even without much experience you could make yourself an indispensable counselor to any king, and such experience of affairs that you could do so without any learning."

"My dear More," said he, "you are twice wrong, first about me and secondly about the matter itself. For I do not have the ability you attribute to me, and even if I did, though I might disturb my own peace, I should not advance the state at all. For in the first place, practically all princes themselves take greater delight in spending their time on military pursuits than on the good arts of peace; and I neither have nor want skill in those matters. They are much more concerned how to get new kingdoms for themselves, by fair means or foul, than to administer well what they already have. Moreover, all the counselors of kings either are so wise as not to be in need of another's advice, or else think themselves so wise that they do not gladly welcome it. The only exception is when they flatter and agree to all the most ridiculous remarks of men whom, because of their great influence with the prince, they wish to win over by fawning. And certainly it is a natural failing for a man to be pleased with his own inventions. So a raven dotes on its chick and a monkey loves its young.

"But suppose that in that company of people who either are jealous of others' thoughts or prefer their own, a man should bring something forward which he has read of as done on other occasions, or has seen done in other parts. Those who hear it act exactly as if their whole reputation for wisdom were in danger, and as if after that they ought to be considered absolute fools if they cannot find some way to discredit others' discoveries. If all other means fail them, then they take refuge in saying, "These things pleased our forefathers. If only we could match their wisdom!" So with these words they are quite content, as if they had brought the discussion to a brilliant conclusion. As if it would involve terrible dangers if anyone were found wiser than his forefathers in any matter at all! Yet all their wisest decisions we are quite happy to let go; but if anywhere they might have made more prudent decisions, we eagerly fasten onto them, and hold on with our teeth. So I have come across these proud, stupid and bad-tempered judgments in many parts of the world, and in England too, once."

"Please tell me," said I. "Did you visit us?" "Yes," he said, "and I stayed there several months, not long after the western English rose in civil war against their king and were crushed with pitiful slaughter.[13] During that time I was much indebted to the Right Reverend Father John Morton,[14] Archbishop of Canterbury and Cardinal, and at that time Chancellor of England too. What I am about to say is well known to More, but believe me,

---

[13] In 1497, in the reign of Henry VII, 15,000 men of Cornwall, in southwest England, rebelled in protest against a tax designed to support a war against Scotland. The rebels marched on London but were defeated with much loss of life.

[14] As a boy, More had spent two years in Archbishop (later Cardinal) Morton's household. The high office of Lord Chancellor was attained by More himself, in 1529.

Peter, he was a man worthy of the highest respect not more for his authority than for his wisdom and goodness. He was of moderate height and
belied his advanced years. His face inspired reverence, not fear. In dealing
with people he was easy, yet serious and dignified. It was his pleasure on
occasions to speak harshly to those with requests to make of him, without
any malice, just to find out what readiness of mind and spirit each man
had. As long as a man kept away from impudence, he was delighted by
such readiness, as being congenial to his own nature, and he welcomed it as
a quality appropriate to a man of action. His conversation was polished and
to the point. He had great skill in law, an incomparable intellect and a
prodigious memory. He had these virtues in great abundance from birth,
but he advanced them still further by studying and practice.

"The King appeared to put great trust in his advice, and the state to rely
upon it heavily when I was there. For practically from his early youth he
was taken straight from school to court and was employed in important
matters all his life. Constantly tossed by the varying tides of fortune, he had
with many great dangers learned worldly wisdom. When it is won this way,
it does not easily leave.

"It happened one day that I was at his table, and a certain layman was
there, learned in your laws. On some pretext or other he began loudly to
sing the praises of that stern justice which was then being used in England
against thieves, who, he said, were strung up everywhere, sometimes
twenty on one gallows.[15] And so he said he was all the more puzzled, when
so few escaped punishment, what evil fate produced so many robbers all
over the country. Then, presuming to speak freely in front of the Cardinal,
I said, 'There is no reason why you should be surprised. For this punishment inflicted upon thieves is beyond the bounds of justice and not to the
public advantage. It is too severe for punishing robbery, but not sufficient
to restrain it. For simple theft[16] is not so great a crime as to deserve capital
punishment, nor is there any penalty strong enough to keep from theft
men who have no other means of gaining a livelihood. So in this matter not
only you, but a good part of this world also, seem to copy bad teachers, who
more readily beat their students than educate them. For harsh and terrible
punishments are inflicted upon thieves, when it would be much better to
see that they had a means to earn a living. In this way they would be freed
from the awful necessity of stealing and then being put to death.'

"'This has all been seen to well enough,' he said. 'There are manual
crafts and there is farming: from these a man may support his life, unless
by nature he prefers to be evil.' 'But you will not get out of it as easily as
this,' I said. 'In the first place, let us forget those who often come home
mutilated from foreign or civil wars, as recently happened among your
people in the Cornish war, and not so long ago in France.[17] These men give
their limbs to their country or their king; their disability does not allow
them to practice their former crafts, nor at such an age can they learn a

[15] In England capital punishment for theft was not outlawed until the early nineteenth
century.
[16] Theft is simple when it does not use violence.
[17] In 1492, under Henry VII, there had been a minor war in France.

new one. As I say, let us forget these, as wars come and go. Let us consider those cases that arise every day.

"'Now, there is a large number of noblemen who live in idleness like drones by the labors of others—in other words, they skin the tenants on their farms by increasing the rents. For that is the only thrift they know, though in other spheres they are so lavish as to beggar themselves. But as well as this, they take around an immense crowd of idle attendants, who have never learned any means of making a living. As soon as their master dies, or they themselves fall sick, they are thrown out straightaway. For masters are readier to support idlers than invalids, and often an heir cannot immediately afford the number of servants his dead father kept. Meanwhile they have the choice of violent hunger or violent robbery. For what are they to do? In wandering about, they wear out their clothes and health, and when they are unkempt with sickness and their clothes covered with patches, no gentleman deigns to receive them and no countryman dares. For they are well aware of the value of a man brought up softly in idleness and luxuries, who is used to sneering at the whole neighborhood with a braggart's look and despising everyone but himself, dressed up with his sword and shield. They know that he will be quite unsuited to be the faithful servant of a poor man, with a spade and a hoe, niggardly wages and scant food.'

"'No,' he said, 'this is the kind of man we ought especially to cultivate. For these are men of higher and nobler spirit than craftsmen or farmers, and in them lies the power and strength of the army whenever a battle must be fought.'

"'Of course,' I said, 'you might just as well say that we should cultivate thieves because of wars; for undoubtedly you will never be without wars as long as you have thieves. For neither are robbers fainthearted soldiers, nor are soldiers cowardly robbers; so nice an agreement is there between these two arts. But this is frequent among you, but not confined to you. For it belongs to practically all nations. Another more pestilential plague infests France as well; the whole country is filled and besieged with mercenary soldiers in peacetime too (if that can be called peace). They were brought in under the same belief through which you English thought that idle servants ought to be supported here: because, that is, the wise fools decided that the public safety depended upon the constant presence of a strong and firm garrison, especially of veterans. For they have no confidence in inexperienced men. The result is that they even have to seek out a war so as not to have unskilled soldiers, and wantonly to kill men so that (as Sallust[18] wittily puts it) their hands or spirits may not grow dull through lack of practice.

"'But how dangerous it is to keep beasts of this kind France has learned to her cost, and the same lesson is shown by the Romans, the Carthaginians, the Syrians and many other people. For their standing armies on various pretexts have overthrown their empires, and ravaged their country and cities. But how unnecessary this is can be seen from the example of the French: their soldiers, though trained to the fingertips, yet when matched

---

[18] Roman historian, first century B.C.

with your levies,[19] cannot often boast that they have come off superior—I say no more, so as not to seem to flatter you to your face. But neither those city craftsmen of yours nor the rough and uncouth farmers are believed to be very afraid of the idle attendants of the noblemen—except for those who do not happen to have a body to match their strength and boldness, or whose strength of spirit is broken by poverty. So there is no danger that these attendants might grow soft if they were trained in honest crafts for their livelihood and exercised in manly work; for as it is now, their strong and robust bodies (nobles choose to corrupt only picked men) grow feeble with idleness or soft with womanly tasks. Certainly, whatever is the truth of this matter, of one thing I am quite sure: that it is by no means to the interest of the state to keep, against the possibility of a war which you never have except when you wish, an immense crowd of the sort that destroys the peace—and we ought to have much more consideration for peace than war.

"'But this is not the only reason which drives men to steal. There is another one more peculiar to you English in my opinion.' 'What is that?' said the Cardinal. 'Your sheep,' I said, 'which are normally so gentle and need so little food. Now (so they say) they have begun to be so ravenous and wild that they even eat up men. They devastate and destroy fields, houses and towns. For in whatever parts of the kingdom fine and therefore more precious wool is produced, there the nobles and gentlemen, and also some holy abbots, are not content with the rents and annual profits that their predecessors used to get from their farms. They are not satisfied to live in luxury and idleness and be of no use to the state; they even harm it. They leave nothing for arable land, enclose everything for pasture,[20] destroy houses, tear down towns and leave only the church to house the sheep; and as if the forests and parks lost you too little ground, those good men turn all houses and cultivated land into a desert.

"'Thus, so that one glutton, the insatiable and terrible plague of the country, may join together fields and enclose several thousand acres, some tenants are ejected. Others are stripped of their own land by trickery or violence, or, wearied by their wrongs, are driven to sell. And so, however it happens, the wretched people leave, men, women, husbands, wives, orphans, widows, parents with small children, and with their large, but impoverished, band of servants (as farming needs many hands); they leave, I say, the home they knew so well, nor can they find anywhere to go. All their furniture, which would not bring a high price even if it could wait for a buyer, they sell for a pittance, since it must go out. This money they soon spend on their wanderings. What is there left for them then except to steal and hang (justly, of course), or else roam and beg? Although even then they are thrown into prison as vagrants, because they are traveling around with nothing to do. For no one will hire their services, even though they offer them eagerly. For those accustomed to farming have nothing to do

---

[19]Levies of unprofessional soldiers. They had helped defeat the French in several notable battles of the fourteenth and fifteenth centuries: Crecy (1346), Poitiers (1356), and Agincourt (1415). The victory at Agincourt, under the former "Prince Hal" of Shakespeare's *Henry the Fourth* plays, is a central episode in his *Henry the Fifth*.

[20]The "enclosure" movement, which converted crop fields into sheep pastures, was often attacked by social reformers in More's time.

where no crops are sown. One shepherd or attendant is enough to graze the land with cattle, although formerly many hands were needed to cultivate it so as to ensure a good harvest.

"'And this is the reason why in many places food is much dearer. The price of wool too has risen so high that it just cannot be bought by the poor, who usually make their cloth from it in England; and for that reason more people are driven from work to idleness. For after the institution of the enclosures, the rot destroyed a very large number of sheep. It was as if God punished the owners' greed by sending destruction to the sheep, although it would have been juster if it had fallen on their own heads. But even if the number of sheep increases enormously, yet the price does not come down. For although there cannot be said to be a monopoly on sheep, since more than one man is engaged in selling them, they are certainly in the control of a very small number. For they have almost all fallen into the hands of a few rich men who are under no necessity to sell before they want, and who do not want to until they may at their own price. Now there is the same reason why the other kinds of cattle are equally dear, or even more so, since there is no one left to look after their reproduction now that the houses have been pulled down and farming is neglected. Nor do those rich men rear the young of the larger cattle as they do of the sheep. Instead they buy them cheaply when they are lean, fatten them up on their pastures and sell them again at a great price. So in my opinion the entire evil effect of this affair has not yet been felt. For until now they have been raising the prices only in these places where they sell; but when eventually they remove them more quickly than they can be born, then the supply will gradually decrease in the places where they are bought too, and a great and troublesome shortage will follow there.

"'So now the wicked greed of a few has turned to a plague the very thing which made this island of yours seem so especially prosperous. For this dearness of food is the reason why everyone is dismissing as many servants as he can. Where are they going, I ask you, except to beg? Or on a course to which well-bred minds are more easily persuaded—to steal?

"'Now beside this wretched poverty and need we find wanton luxury. For among the servants of noblemen, and the craftsmen and even the countrymen too, among people of all ranks, are found many new styles in clothing and an excessive lavishness in food. Now places of ill repute, brothels, whorehouses and stews,[21] winehouses, alehouses, so many wicked games, dice, cards, the tables, tennis, bowls, quoits[22]—these all quickly exhaust their money and send their devotees straight off somewhere to steal.

"'Cast out these pernicious pests. Make a law that those who pulled them down should reconstruct the houses and country towns, or else give them up to people who are prepared to replace and rebuild them. Check the rich from buying everything up and put an end to their freedom in monopoly. Let fewer men be kept in idleness; bring back farming; reintroduce clothmaking to be an honorable business and a useful occupation for that idle mob, or for those whom until now poverty has made thieves, or those who are now vagrants or idle servants, both good material for future thieves. Certainly if you do not heal these ills, your boasts of justice exer-

---

[21] Brothels.   [22] A game resembling horseshoe-pitching.

cised in the punishment of theft are quite useless. This justice, in fact, is ostentatious rather than just or advantageous. When you allow people to be brought up in the worst possible way and their characters to be gradually corrupted from a tender age, and then punish them when they commit those crimes as men which they showed all signs of doing from their child-hood on—I ask you, what else are you doing than making men thieves and then punishing them?'

"While I was still saying this, the lawyer meanwhile had seriously got himself ready to speak and had decided to use that usual method of debaters[23] who repeat men's words with more care than they reply to them. In fact, they have a very high regard for memory. 'Yes,' he said, 'a good speech for a foreigner. You have been in a position to hear a little on these matters rather than gain any precise knowledge. I shall make this clear very quickly. First of all, I shall go over what you said in the same order. Then I shall demonstrate on what matters you have been misled by ignorance of our ways. Finally I shall destroy and refute all your reasoning. So, to begin with my first point, you seemed to me on four—' 'Hush,' said the Cardinal. 'To judge from your beginning, your reply is going to be lengthy. So for the moment we shall relieve you of the trouble of replying and keep it intact for you for your next meeting. If you or Raphael here has no other commitments, I should like that to take place tomorrow.

"'But meanwhile, Raphael, I should be very glad to hear from you why you think that theft ought not to be punished by death and what alternative penalty you suggest as being more to the public good. For not even you think that it ought to be tolerated. As things are now, men rush into theft despite the death penalty. Once you guarantee them their lives, what force or fear can restrain criminals? They would take the mitigation of the pen-alty as an inducement and invitation to crime.'

"'Reverend father,' I said, 'it seems to me outrageously unjust to take away a man's life for taking money. For in my opinion human life is worth more than all the possessions fortune can give. But if they say that this penalty is aimed against the violation of justice and breaking the laws rather than the theft, would we not be right in calling this extreme justice extreme injustice? For we must not approve of legal ordinances so severe that the slightest disobedience is immediately met with a drawn sword; nor of decrees so stoical[24] that all sins are considered equal, that it makes no difference whether you kill a man or steal money from him. If equity means anything, there is absolutely no similarity between these crimes. God has forbidden us to kill. Do we then kill so easily for the theft of a trifling sum? For if you interpret that commandment of God as forbidding killing except where human law declares a man ought to be killed, what is to prevent men from similarly deciding among themselves when it is permissi-ble to commit fornication, adultery and perjury? God has forbidden us to kill not merely others but ourselves too. Now, if human agreement on mutual slaughter, on fixed conditions, has such validity that it releases its followers from that divine commandment and with no example from God

---

[23] The lawyer's aborted rejoinder is in the medieval scholastic style of argument, which More is mocking.

[24] The ancient Stoics taught the doctrine outlined here.

allows them to kill people whom human sanction orders, are we not in this way giving only as much right to God's commandment as human law allows? And of course the result will be that in the same way men will decide in all matters how far it is convenient to observe God's commandments. The law of Moses, cruel and harsh though it was (for it was introduced against servants,[25] and stubborn ones at that), yet punished theft with a fine, not death. Let us not imagine that in the new law of kindness, by which He rules us as a father his children, God has granted us a greater license for cruelty against one another.

"'These are the reasons why I think it is not right. I am sure that everyone realizes how absurd it is and even dangerous for the state that a thief and murderer should be given the same punishment. For when a robber sees that no less a danger awaits a man condemned for theft than one convicted of homicide as well, by this single thought he is driven to murder the man he would otherwise merely have robbed. For if he is caught there is no more danger, and also there is greater safety in murder and a greater hope of concealing his crime if the witness is removed. So in trying to terrify thieves with excessive cruelty, we provoke them to kill good men.

"'To turn to the question of what punishment could be more suitable, in my opinion this is much easier to find than a worse one. For why should we doubt that the profitable way for punishing crime is the one approved of long ago by the Romans, men who had great experience in governing a state? For men found guilty of serious crimes were condemned to be sent to the stone quarries or mines, and kept in chains constantly.

"'Although in this connection nowhere have I seen a better institution than the one I noticed in my travels in Persia among the people called Polylerites.[26] These people are quite numerous and enjoy excellent institutions. They are free and governed by their own laws except that they pay an annual tribute to the King of Persia. They are far from the sea, practically shut in by mountains, and enjoy the fruits of a bountiful land. They do not visit others often, nor are they visited themselves. It is an ancient practice of their country not to try to extend their territory, and what they have is easily protected from all attack by the mountains and the tribute they pay to the powerful king. They are quite free from military service and lead a comfortable rather than a glorious life, prosperous rather than noble or distinguished. For I believe they are known to no one except their neighbors, even by name.

"'In this country those convicted of theft return what they stole to the owner, not to the king, as happens in other places. For they think that the king has as little right to the thing stolen as the thief himself. But if whatever is stolen cannot be recovered, the equivalent is paid from the thieves' property, which otherwise remains intact for their wives and children. The thieves themselves are condemned to hard labor. Unless the theft was a violent one, they are not shut up in prison, nor do they wear fetters, but they are free and unrestricted to do their work for the state. Those who

---

[25] Slaves; that is, the Jews of the Old Testament. The contrast is with the theological notion of Christian liberty, especially as developed in the Epistles of St. Paul.

[26] The name of this fictional people is from Greek, meaning "much nonsense"—a typical example of More's whimsical humor.

refuse to work or are halfhearted about it, they flog rather than imprison. Those who work hard suffer no violence and at night merely have a roll call and are shut up in their rooms. Apart from the constant work, there is nothing harsh about their lives. For their fare is not too severe, and as they are public servants, it comes out of public funds. Some variations occur: in some places the funds to support them come from charity. Although this way is not without risk, yet the people are so kindhearted that there is always plenty. In other parts some public revenues are marked out for that purpose. Elsewhere each man pays a tax for it. In several regions they do no public work, but any private citizen who needs laborers can hire their services in the marketplace for the day, at a fixed price which is slightly lower than what he would have paid for a free man. If such a servant is lazy he may be flogged.

"'So they are never without work, and besides paying for their keep, this system also brings something into the public treasury every day from each of them. They are one and all dressed in the same color clothing; their hair is not shaved but cut a little above their ears, and a small piece is taken from the tip of one ear. Each man may receive food and drink from his friends and clothing of the proper color. But to give money is a capital offense for the giver as well as the receiver. No less dangerous is it for a free man also to receive money from a convict for any reason whatever, and also for a slave (this is the name they give to the convicts) to touch weapons. Each district distinguishes its slaves by a special badge, which it is a capital offense to throw away—just as it is for them to be seen outside their own region, or to have any conversation with a slave of another district. It is no safer to plan to run away than it is actually to do so. To be an accomplice in such a plan means death for a slave and servitude for a free man. There are rewards decreed for an informer—for a free man money, for a slave freedom. Both classes of such informers are given pardon and impunity if they were involved in the plan, to prevent its being safer to go through with it than to repent.

"'I have shown you the law and arrangements dealing with this question. It is perfectly obvious how humane and advantageous it is. The anger of the law takes the form of destroying the vices but saving the men, who are so treated that they must be good and spend the rest of their lives repairing the damage they previously did.

"'So little fear is there of their falling back into their old ways, that travelers who have decided upon some journey think that the slaves are the safest of guides, and change them at each district. For if they want to commit robbery, they have everything against them: they have no weapons; money is merely an indication of crime; if they are caught, punishment is all ready for them; they have absolutely no hope of escaping anywhere. For how could a man conceal and hide his flight when his clothing is quite unlike everyone else's, except by escaping naked? Even if he did this, his ear would give him away. There is hardly any danger that they would enter a plot for conspiracy against the state. The only way for any district to entertain such hopes would be to win over the slaves of many other districts beforehand. But so far are they from being able to form a conspiracy, that they cannot even meet and talk together, or so much as exchange a greeting. Nor can it be imagined that they would fearlessly confide such a plan to their fellows, when they know that silence would be dangerous, but betrayal would be highly profitable. On the other hand, none is entirely without the hope that he may eventually recover his liberty by obedience and endurance and by showing that he is capable of leading a better life later. For every year several are freed as a reward for their patience.'

"After saying all this, I added that I saw no reason why this method should not be adopted in England too, with much greater profit than came from the justice the lawyer had so highly praised. At this the lawyer said, 'That plan could never be established in England without bringing the state into the greatest jeopardy.' While saying this, he shook his head, made a wry face and so fell silent. And all present gave their support to him.

"Then the Cardinal said, "It is not easy to guess whether the plan would work or not without making an experiment. But suppose that after pronouncing the death sentence the King ordered a stay of execution and tried this method out (after abolishing all rights of sanctuary[27]): if the plan worked out well, then it would be right to establish it permanently. If it did not, then those previously condemned could still be put to death. This would be no more against the interests of the state nor more unjust than if the execution were immediately carried out. Nor can any danger arise in the intervening period. I am quite sure that vagrants could well be treated in the same way. So far, in spite of all the legislation against them, we have achieved nothing.'

"After the Cardinal had finished, they all vied with one another to praise the suggestions that they had despised when they came from me—especially the point on vagrants, since this had been an addition of the Cardinal himself.

"Perhaps I ought not to repeat the absurd events that followed. Yet I will, as they were not bad and had some bearing on the subject.

"As it happened, there was standing nearby a parasite who wanted to seem to be playing the fool. But his imitation was quite lifelike. He tried for laughs with such feeble jokes that he was laughed at himself more often than his witticisms. Yet every now and then he brought out such a clever remark that it made us believe in the saying about dice: that eventually you are bound to throw two sixes. One of our company was saying that my suggestions had taken care of thieves and the Cardinal's of vagrants, and it now remained to give some public aid to people driven to poverty and rendered incapable of working for a living by sickness or age. The fool interrupted by saying, 'Allow me. I shall make good provision for this as well. For I should give anything to get rid of such people out of my sight. They have often made great nuisances of themselves by asking me for money with those whines and tears. But they have never been able to put them on successfully enough to get a penny out of me. For always one of two things happens: either I do not want to give, or else I just cannot, as I have nothing. And so they have now learned wisdom. For they do not waste their energy when they see me pass; they let me go by in silence. So they no longer have any hopes of getting anything from me, no more than if I were a priest. But I would pass a law to divide up all those beggars into the

---

[27] The right of a criminal to evade capture by taking refuge in a church.

Benedictine monasteries and make them lay brothers[28] and the women nuns.' The Cardinal smiled and applauded the joke, as the others genuinely did too.

"But a certain friar, who was a learned divine, was so amused by this witticism against priests and monks that he too began to joke, although normally he was a man of serious and grim appearance. 'No,' he said, 'you will not be rid of beggars so easily, if you do not also make some provision for us friars too.' 'And yet,' said the parasite, 'that is already taken care of. For the Cardinal made excellent provision for you when he decided that vagrants should be locked up and put to work. For you are the biggest vagrants of all.'[29]

"When everyone saw that the Cardinal did not disapprove, they began to take the joke up eagerly, all except the friar. For it was not surprising that after being made the object of such bitter wit, his anger flared up so hotly that he could not restrain himself from open abuse. He called the man a knave, a slanderer, a backbiter and a son of perdition. All the time he cited terrible threats from the Holy Scriptures. Now the jester began to play the jester in earnest and he was a master in his field. 'Do not be angry, good brother,' he said. 'It is written: "In your patience ye shall win your souls."'[30] Then the friar replied (for I shall repeat his actual words), 'I am not angry, you wretch, or at least I am not committing any sin. For the Psalmist says, "Stand in awe and sin not."'[31]

"Then the friar was gently warned by the Cardinal to control his feelings. 'My lord,' said the friar, 'I am only speaking out of good zeal, as I ought. For the saints had good zeal and so it is said: "For the zeal of thine house hath eaten me up,"[32] and in church we sing: "The mockers of Elisha, while he went up to the house of God, felt the zeal of the bald"[33]—just as perhaps he shall feel, that mocker, that ribald buffoon.' 'You are acting,' said the Cardinal, 'out of good feeling perhaps, but your action will probably be holier and certainly wiser if you do not get into a stupid quarrel with a foolish and stupid fellow.' 'No, my lord,' he said, 'I should not be acting more wisely. For Solomon himself, the wisest of men, says, "Answer a fool according to his folly,"[34] just as I am doing now, and I am showing him the pit into which he will fall if he does not take great care. For if the many mockers of Elisha, who was only one bald man, felt the zeal of the bald, how much more will it be felt by one mocker of many friars, among whom are many bald men?[35] And we also have a papal bull,[36] by which all who mock us are excommunicated.' When he saw that there was no end to this, the Cardinal dismissed the parasite with a nod, and gave the conversation a

---

[28] Unordained members of the monastic community, expected to perform lowly work.

[29] Friars, unlike monks, supported themselves by traveling around and begging.

[30] Luke 21:19.

[31] The quotation is from Psalms 4:4 (4:5 in the Vulgate [Catholic] version). The passage can also be translated "Be angry, and sin not."

[32] Psalms 69:9 (Vulgate 68:10).

[33] The Old Testament prophet Elisha, as related in 2 Kings 2:23-24, was taunted by children for his baldness. Elisha's punishing curse caused forty-two of the children to be destroyed by bears.

[34] Proverbs 26:5. This book was attributed to Solomon.

[35] The friars shaved their heads.   [36] A document sent out by the Pope.

convenient turn to another subject. Shortly after this, he rose from the table and dismissed us, to give his attention to the cases of his clients.

"My dear More, look what a long story I have burdened you with! I should have been quite ashamed to keep on for so long if you had not eagerly requested this of me and seemed so intent on the tale that you did not want a single detail left out. For although I did so rather briefly, I simply had to relate it to show up the judgment of those fellows. For when they had despised my words, they began to approve of them when the Cardinal immediately showed his favor. They so fawned upon him that they even flattered and seriously entertained his parasite's ideas, when, as a joke, his master did not reject them. From this you can judge what worth the courtiers would put upon me and my suggestions."

"My dear Raphael," I said, "you have given me great pleasure by the wisdom and charm of all you said. At times I thought I was in my own country and even somehow to become a child again, by the delightful remembrance of the Cardinal, in whose palace I was brought up as a child. When you praise his memory so, Raphael, you cannot imagine how much dearer you are made to me on this account, although you were very dear even before. But I still cannot change my opinion in any way. I am quite convinced that if you could school yourself to tolerate princes' courts, you could do a great deal of public good by your advice. So there is nothing more appropriate to your duty, that is the duty of a good man. Your Plato judges that states will become blessed only if philosophers become kings or kings philosophers.[37] How distant will such blessings be if philosophers do not even condescend to give their advice to kings?" "They are not so ungrateful," he said. "They would gladly do so. In fact, they have already done this in many published books, if only those in power were ready to listen to good advice. But Plato was clearly quite right: if kings do not become philosophers themselves, they will never approve of the advice of philosophers, since from childhood they have been infected and tainted with wrong beliefs. Plato himself found this out in the case of Dionysius.[38] If I were to put sound advice before some king and try to root out of him the pernicious seeds of evil, do you not think that I should be immediately thrown out or laughed to scorn?

"Now, suppose I were with the French King[39] and sitting on his council in secret consultation, in a circle of wise men, with the King himself as president. The question earnestly being discussed is: By what means and wiles can he hold on to Milan, and drag that fugitive Naples back? After that, how can he overthrow the Venetians and bring the whole of Italy into subjection? Then conquer Flanders, Brabant, the whole of Burgundy, and other countries as well which he has already invaded in his imagination? Here one advises that a treaty ought to be made with the Venetians, to last only as long as suits the King's convenience; their plan should be shared with them; even a part of the booty be deposited with them, which he can get back when matters are finished to his satisfaction. Another urges that the

---

[37] Plato, *Republic*, Book V.

[38] There was a plan for Plato to help educate Dionysius, the young ruler of Syracuse in Sicily; the effort failed and Plato was sorely mistreated.

[39] The ruses and strategems attributed to France in the following passage are founded on contemporary historical fact.

Germans should be hired, another that the Swiss ought to be won over
with money. Another thinks that the godhead of His Imperial Majesty[40]
ought to be appeased with a sacrifice of gold. Yet another advises that
peace should be made with the King of Aragon and that his own kingdom
of Navarre should be given up to him as a guarantee of peace. Another is
of the opinion that the King of Castile should be lured by some hope of
affinity[41] and some noble courtiers should be bribed to come over to their
party. The biggest stumbling block of all is the question of England. But
they agree that peace must be made and the alliance, always so feeble, should
be bound with the strongest ties, so that they can be called friends and
suspected as enemies. The Scots[42] should be kept ready as if on watch,
prepared for any opportunity, to be let loose immediately the English show
any signs of activity. Some noble exile also should be trained secretly (for
the treaties prevent this from happening openly) to maintain that the kingdom belongs to him so that the French King might have this weapon to
check the king he suspects. Here, I say, amid such weighty discussion, with
so many distinguished men vying to give their advice for war, suppose that
all on my own I should arise and advise a different course: that Italy should
be left alone and the French stay at home; that the kingdom of France is
practically too big to be conveniently administered by one man, so that the
King should not think of adding others. Then suppose I put before them
the decrees of the Achorians,[43] a people lying to the southeast of the island
of Utopia. They once waged a war to obtain another kingdom for their
king, which he claimed was his due inheritance because of some old affinity. When they finally won it, they saw that they had just as much trouble
holding on to it as they had endured in gaining it. And seeds of rebellion
were ever springing up within, or invasion from without. So they always
had to fight either for the people they had conquered or against them. They
never had an opportunity to dismiss their army and all the time their resources were being drained and their money going abroad. Their blood
was being spent on others' glory and peace was no safer. At home characters had become corrupted by war, people had tasted the joy of robbery,
boldness was strengthened by slaughter, the laws were held in contempt.
The King, divided between the cares of two realms, could not give his
proper attention to either. When they saw that there was no other end to
these ills, at last they devised a plot and very gently gave their king the
choice of retaining whichever kingdom he wanted. For they said he would
not be able to have both and they were too numerous to be governed by
half a king, since no one would willingly hire a muleteer to share with
another. So that good king was compelled to give his new kingdom to one
of his friends (who shortly after was thrown out) and be content with the
old. Suppose that besides this I showed that after so many nations had been
set in a turmoil for the French King's sake, when his coffers had been
drained and his people ruined, by some chance these preparations for war
would come to no purpose. I should tell him to look after the kingdom he

[40] The Holy Roman Emperor, at the time Maximilian of Austria.
[41] Alliance by marriage.
[42] Historically, Scotland has often opposed England and, backed by France, supported
rivals of the reigning English sovereigns.
[43] A fictional people; the name means "inhabitants of nowhere."

inherited, and embellish it as much as he could, and make it as flourishing as possible; to love his people and be loved by them; to live together with them and make his rule gentle; to say good-bye to other kingdoms, since the one that had fallen to his lot was enough and more than enough. If I were to say all this, my dear More, how do you think it would be received?" "Not readily, I am sure," said I.

"Let us go on then," he said. "Suppose that his counselors were debating with a king and devising means to pile up money for him. One advises that the value of money should be raised[44] when the king has to pay any out, and then lowered below its proper value when he has to take any, so that he may pay much money with little and receive much instead of little. Another advises him to feign a war and on that pretext to gather in much money; then, when it seems fit, to make peace with religious ceremonies to deceive the unfortunate people who suppose that he is a holy king with compassion for human blood. Another reminds him of certain ancient moth-eaten laws, outdated by long disuse. As no one remembers that they were passed, all have broken them. So the king ought to impose fines for their transgression. There could be no richer source, none more honorable, since it wears the mask of justice. Another advises him to forbid many things with heavy fines, especially such things as are against the interest of the people; then to give a dispensation for money to those whose interests are damaged by the decree. In this way he would gain favor with the people and profit in two ways: either from the fines imposed on those whose greed for gain has lured them into the snare, or else from the sale of immunities, which, of course, will be all the more expensive in proportion to the king's goodness. For it is only with the greatest reluctance that he allows any citizen to do anything against the interests of the people, and consequently only at a high price. Another recommends that he should bring the judges over to his side to give judgment for the king in every case; and that he should also summon them to the palace and invite them to discuss his affairs in his presence. In this way no case of his will be so manifestly unjust as not to allow one of them to find some crack in it for a false accusation—either because he likes to make objections, or because he hates agreeing with everyone, or else to win the king's favor. Thus while the judges differ and a perfectly clear case is disputed and the truth itself is questioned, the king is given a convenient opportunity to interpret the law to his own convenience. The others will support him either from shame or from fear. So afterward their sentence is delivered from the bench without any fear. For anyone pronouncing judgment for the king must have a good excuse; for it is enough for him to have equity on his side, or merely the words of a law, or the twisted meaning of a document, or—what outweighs all laws with conscientious judges—the king's indisputable prerogative. They all agree with that saying of Crassus:[45] 'No amount of money is enough for a king who has to keep an army.' They all agree too that a king can do no wrong, however much he may wish, since all men's possessions are his and the men

---

[44] That is, money should be declared to have a higher value than it actually has. Several of the fiscal expedients mentioned in the following passage were used in England under Henry VII.

[45] A rich Roman and financial opportunist of the first century B.C., partner in rule with Pompey and Julius Caesar.

themselves too; that a subject owns only as much as the king's kindness
allows him to keep; that it is greatly to the king's advantage that this should
be as little as possible, as he is safe only if his people do not run riot with
riches and freedom, since these are not so ready to bear harsh and unjust
commands; while on the other hand, need and poverty blunt their spirits,
make them more patient, beat them down and take away any brave hopes
of rebellion. Suppose that in my turn I should stand up and maintain that
all this advice is both dishonorable and disadvantageous for the king, since
his honor and safety rest upon the people's wealth more than his own. I
should show that they choose a king for themselves for their own sake, not
his,[46] so that by his toil and care they may live profitably and safe from
injury. So the king ought to concern himself with his people's well-being
rather than his own. It is just like the duty of a shepherd, who, insofar as he
is a shepherd, must tend his sheep rather than himself. The very facts show
how far wrong those people are who think that the people's poverty is a
guarantee of peace. For where could you find more quarrels than among
beggars? Who is more anxious for a change of government than a man who
is discontent with the present condition of his life? Or who is bolder in
stirring up revolution in the hope of gain from some source or other than
the man who now has nothing to lose? If a king were so despised or so
hated by his subjects that he could only keep them in their duty by outrageous measures, by plundering and appropriation, by reducing them to
poverty, it would surely be better for him to abdicate than to retain his
throne by measures by which he keeps the name of power but loses majesty. For it is not dignified for a king to exercise his power over beggars
instead of rich and prosperous citizens. This was realized by Fabricius,[47] a
man of lofty and sublime spirit, when he replied that he preferred to rule
the rich than be rich himself. And for one man to abound in pleasures and
delights, while the others are groaning and weeping around him—this is to
be the custodian not of a kingdom but of a prison. He is just like a bad
doctor who can cure a disease only by bringing on another; for a king who
can govern his subjects' lives only by taking away the comforts of life must
admit that he does not know how to rule free men. He should change
either his laziness or his pride. For it is mainly for these vices that his people
despise or hate him. Let him live harmlessly out of his own pocket, fit his
expenditure to his income, check ill-doing, by right training of his subjects
prevent abuses rather than let them grow and then punish them. Let him
not be quick to revive laws fallen into disuse, especially those which have
been out of use for a long time and never missed. Nor let him ever, under
the pretext of a fine, take anything which a judge would not allow a private
citizen to receive, because it is unjust and cunning. Suppose I suggest to
them the law of the Macarenses,[48] who also are not too far from Utopia. On
the day he ascends the throne, their king is bound, by an oath sanctioned
by great sacrifices, that he will never at one time have over a thousand
pounds of gold in his treasury or the equivalent weight of silver. They say
that this law was introduced by an excellent king, who had more care for

---

[46] This apparently modern view is actually medieval as well. The heyday of belief in the
absolute power of kings came later in the sixteenth and in the seventeenth centuries.

[47] A virtuous Roman, third century B.C.   [48] The name means "fortunate."

his country's well-being than his own wealth, as a bar to a king's piling up enough gold to create poverty among his people. For he realized that that amount would suffice, whether the king had to fight against rebels or the whole kingdom against an enemy's invasions. But it was not enough to incite him to invade other men's property. That was the main reason for passing the law. Another one was that he thought that provision was thereby made that there would be enough money in circulation for the citizens' daily trading. He also thought that since the king had to pay out whatever came into his treasury above the legal amount, he would not seek an occasion to do anyone an injustice. Such a king will be feared by the wicked and loved by the good. If then I were to put forward such suggestions to men violently inclined to the opposite, how deaf do you think they would be to my tale?"

"Very deaf indeed," I said. "Nor am I at all surprised, nor (to tell the truth) do I think that suggestions ought to be made or advice proffered which you are sure will never be taken. For how could so strange a tale do any good or work its way into their hearts, when the opposite belief is already firmly planted in their minds? This scholastic[49] philosophy is all right among friends in familiar conversation."

"That is precisely what I meant," he said, "when I said that there is no place for philosophy with kings." "No, there certainly is not," said I, "for this scholastic philosophy which thinks that everything is appropriate everywhere. But there is another philosophy of a more civil kind, which knows the stage it should act on, adapts itself accordingly in the play it has in hand and plays its part appropriately and with decorum. This is the one you should adopt. Otherwise, when a play of Plautus is being acted, and the servants are trifling among themselves, if you come on stage dressed like a philosopher and recite the passage from the *Octavia* where Seneca disputes with Nero, would it not have been better to act a dumb show than by reciting inappropriate lines to make it a tragicomedy?[50] For you would ruin and destroy the present play if you mixed in alien matter, even if the lines you brought were better. Whatever play is in hand, act it to the best of your ability, and do not wreck the whole of it because you remember another that is wittier.

"It is exactly the same in a state and the consultations of kings. If erroneous beliefs cannot be plucked out root and all, if you cannot heal long established evils to your satisfaction, you must not therefore desert the state and abandon the ship in a storm, because you cannot check the winds. Nor should you force upon people strange and unaccustomed discourses which you know will have no weight with them in their opposite beliefs. But you should try and strive obliquely to settle everything as best you may, and what you cannot turn to good, you should make as little evil as possible. For it is not possible for everything to be good unless all men are good, and I do not expect that that will come about for many years."

"The only result of this course," he said, "would be to make me as mad as

---

[49] Characteristic of the medieval universities.

[50] Plautus (c. 254–184 B.C.) and Seneca (4? B.C.–65 A.D.) were Roman playwrights, the former of low comedy, the latter of lofty tragedy.

the people whose insanity I am trying to cure. For if I want to speak the truth, this is what I must say. But whether it is appropriate for a philosopher to lie, I do not know. It certainly is not for me. Yet although my conversation might perhaps be unpleasant and annoying to them, I do not see why it ought to be outrageously strange. Suppose I were to say what Plato invents[51] in his *Republic* or what the Utopians do in theirs—although this might be better (as I am sure it is), yet it might seem out of place. For in our society every man has his private possessions, but there everything is held in common.

"Admittedly my discourse cannot please those who have decided to rush headlong by the opposite road, since it calls them back and points out the dangers. But otherwise what else did it contain which could not, or indeed ought not, to be said anywhere? For if we ought to omit everything, as being strange and inappropriate, which the corrupt ways of men have made appear odd, then we ought to cover up among Christians practically everything that Christ taught and so strongly forbade us to cover up that whatever He whispered in the ears of His disciples He ordered them to proclaim upon the housetops.[52] The greater part of His teaching is much further removed from men's ways than my speech was. But cunning preachers, following your advice, I suppose, because men were loath to adapt their ways to the rule of Christ, fitted His teaching to their ways like a lead rule,[53] so that at least they should join together somehow. I do not see what they have achieved by this, except that men may be evil with more safety. And I myself, I am sure, should achieve just as little in the councils of kings. For either I should be of a different opinion, which would be the same as having no opinion, or else I should be of the same and be a helper of their madness, as Micio says in Terence.[54] For I cannot see the point of that oblique way of yours, by which you think that if everything cannot be made good, I should strive at least to get it managed suitably and rendered as little evil as possible. For with a king there is no place for dissimulation or conniving. One must openly praise the vilest plans and put one's signature to the most disastrous decrees. He would be considered a spy and almost a traitor who gave faint praise to wicked decisions.

"Moreover, nothing happens in which you could be of any benefit, when you are put amid colleagues who would more easily corrupt even the best of men than be corrected themselves, by whose evil company either you will be depraved, or else, in your blameless and innocent state, you will act as a cloak to another's wickedness and folly. So far from possible is it to change anything for the better by that oblique path.

"For this reason Plato shows with a beautiful comparison why wise men rightly keep away from politics.[55] When they see the people swarm in the streets and get drenched with constant rain, and they cannot persuade them to move out of the rain and go to their houses, they know that they would achieve nothing by going out themselves, except to get wet with

---

[51] In *The Republic*, Book III, Socrates advocates a version of communism.
[52] See Matthew 10:27; Luke 12:3.
[53] Yardstick made of lead and thus easily bent out of a straight line.
[54] Roman comic dramatist, second century B.C.   [55] Plato, *Republic*, Book VI.

them, and so they keep themselves indoors. Since they cannot cure the folly of others, they are content if at least they are safe themselves.

"Although, my dear More, to speak the truth as it comes to mind, I think that wherever there are private possessions, where everything is measured by money, there a state can scarcely ever be justly and successfully managed—unless you think that is justice where all the best things come to the worst men, or that is success where everything is divided among a very few. Nor are they entirely prosperous, while the others are absolutely wretched.

"So I think over the wise and holy customs of the Utopians, who need so few laws for government so successful that virtue has its reward, and yet with equality of wealth all men have everything in abundance. Then I compare and contrast with their ways so many other nations, always making laws, but none of them all ever well enough governed, in which what each man gets he calls his own private possession. Their countless laws, passed every day, are not enough to help each man to obtain that which everyone calls his own, nor to protect it, nor to distinguish it from another's. This is clearly shown by those innumerable lawsuits which spring up all the time, but never come to an end. When I ponder on all this, I sympathize more with Plato and I am less surprised that he refused to pass any laws for men who refused those by which everyone shared all property equally.[56] For that wise man saw that the one and only path to public safety lay in equality of property. I do not think that this could ever come about where each man has his own possessions. For where each man by fixed titles appropriates as much as he can, a few share out all the wealth and leave poverty for the rest. It usually happens that the one class of men deserves the lot of the other. For the rich are greedy, wicked and useless, while the poor are modest and simple men, and by their daily labor contribute to the public good rather than their own.

"So I am convinced that things cannot be distributed in equity and justice, nor mortals' affairs be managed prosperously, unless private ownership is totally abolished. If it is left, the greatest and best part of mankind will always have the worrying and unavoidable burden of poverty and cares. I admit that this can be somewhat relieved, but maintain that it cannot be eradicated. But suppose that it were decreed that no one should have above a certain amount of land, and that each man could only have so much money. Suppose that laws were passed to prevent excessive power in the king and excessive arrogance in his people; that it were decided that offices should not be canvassed[57] or sold, and that no expense should be necessary for their tenure (otherwise an opportunity is given for repairing losses by trickery and plunder, and it is necessary to put rich men in charge of those posts which rather need the attention of the wise). By such laws, I say, just as desperately sick bodies can be supported by constant medication, so these evils too could be assuaged and lessened. But there is abso-

---

[56] Plato refused to make laws for the city of Megalopolis, in southwestern Greece, unless private ownership was given up. The incident is related in Diogenes Laertius' *Lives of the Eminent Philosophers.*

[57] Applied or campaigned for.

lutely no hope that they may be cured and restored to a good condition, as long as private property exists. While you attend to the cure of one part, you make the wound in the other parts more inflamed. So from the cure of the one grows the disease of the other, since nothing can be added to one without being taken from another."

"But," said I, "I am of the opposite opinion, that life can never be comfortable with community of possessions. For how could there be an abundant supply of things, when each man takes himself away from work? For considerations of his own profit do not urge him on, and confidence in another's industry makes him lazy. But when they are goaded by poverty and there is no law for a man to protect what he has gained, then must not constant murder and sedition vex the state? Above all, the authority of magistrates and their respect are abolished. I cannot even imagine what place there could be for such respect in men among whom there is no distinction." "I am not surprised," he said, "that you think this, when you have either no idea of what this would be like, or else a false one. But if you had been in Utopia with me and seen in person their habits and practices, as I did (for I lived there more than five years and would never have wanted to leave except to tell of that new world), then you would openly admit that this was the only place where you had seen a people properly governed."

"And yet," said Peter Giles, "you would have a hard time persuading me that a better governed people could be found in that new world than in this one known to us. For I think there are intellects just as good here and republics older than there, and long experience has discovered us many conveniences for life, not to mention certain chance discoveries of ours which no mind could ever have thought up."

"As far as concerns the oldness of republics," he said, "you could judge better if you had read the histories of that world. If they can be trusted, they had cities before we had men. Now, whatever up till now mind has discovered or chance found, could have come about in either place. But I am sure that although we excel them in brain, yet we are left far behind in enthusiasm and industry. For, as their annals show, before our arrival there, they had never heard anything of us (whom they call the Ultraequinoctials[58]), except that once over twelve hundred years ago a ship was carried by a storm to the island of Utopia and wrecked there. Some Romans and Egyptians were cast up on the shore and stayed there ever after.

"See what use their industry made of this one opportunity. Every art within the Roman empire which could be of any use, they learned from the shipwrecked strangers or discovered from the basis they offered. Such profit did they take from the single arrival of people from our world. But if any like chance brought anyone here from their world long ago, this has been quite blotted out, just as perhaps future generations will forget that I was once there. As they from one encounter immediately made their own all our happiest discoveries, so I think it would be a long time before we adopted any of their better ideas. This I think is the most important reason why their state is governed more wisely and is more prosperous, although we are in no way inferior to them in intellect or wealth."

[58] People from beyond the equator.

"So, my dear Raphael," I said, "I beg and beseech you to describe that island to us. Do not try to be brief, but unfold in due order their lands, rivers, cities, men, ways, institutes, laws—everything you think we wish to know. And you will think we wish to know everything of which we are so far ignorant." "There is nothing," he said, "I should be gladder to do, for I have it all ready. But it needs some leisure." "Let us go in then," I said, "to have lunch. Soon we shall take the time as we please." "Very well," said he. So we went in and had lunch.

After lunch we came back to the same place, and sat down on the same seat. The servants were told that no one should interrupt us, and Peter Giles and I urged Raphael to give us what he had promised. When he saw that we were anxious and eager to hear, he sat silent for a while, lost in thought, and then began in the following way.

BOOK TWO

CHAPTER ONE
ON THE COUNTRY AND ITS AGRICULTURE

The island of Utopia extends in the middle, where it is widest, for two hundred miles.[1] For a great part it is not much narrower, but gradually narrows at both ends. This makes a circumference of five hundred miles and gives the whole island the shape of a new moon, whose horns are separated by about eleven miles of sea. The water opens up to a large width inside, and as the winds are checked by land on all sides, it is like a big lake, placid and calm. It makes practically all the bay there one big harbor, which is very busy and sends ships in all directions. The entrance is made dangerous by shallows and rocks. In about the middle of the gap a single rock sticks up, but it is not dangerous, as it is visible. They have built a tower on this to house a garrison. The other rocks are hidden and treacherous. The channels are known only to the Utopians themselves, and so it is not often that a stranger makes his way into this bay except with a Utopian pilot. For even the inhabitants themselves hardly have a safe entrance, except by marking their passage by certain signs on the shore. By moving these to different places they could easily lure an enemy fleet to destruction, however numerous it might be. On the other side of the island there are also many harbors. But everywhere the landing is so well protected, either naturally or artificially, that a few defenders could ward off great hordes.

But, as they tell and as the appearance of the place shows, that land was once not surrounded by water. It was previously called Abraxa and received its present name from its conqueror, Utopus. It was he who brought his rough and rude people to that high point of culture and civilization whereby they now surpass practically all other men. As soon as he landed and conquered the place, he caused that part where it was joined to the mainland to be cut through and let the sea around the land. He put to work on that task not merely the original inhabitants, but so that they should not

---

[1] Utopia is approximately as big as England.

take this work as an insult, he also joined to them all his own soldiers. With the labor divided among so many men, the task was completed with unbelievable speed. The neighboring people, who at the beginning had laughed at this idle undertaking, were struck with admiration and fear at the success.

The island has fifty-four[2] cities, all of them large and magnificent. Their language, customs, institutions and laws are all the same. The layout of all the cities is the same, and, as far as the terrain allows, their appearance is the same everywhere. A distance of twenty-four miles separates the nearest cities, and none is so remote that a man cannot reach another in one day's journey.

From each city three experienced old men meet every year to discuss the common affairs of the island at Amaurote.[3] This is considered the chief city, as it lies in the center of the island and is convenient for the representatives from all parts. The territories are assigned to the cities in such a way that in no direction does any one of them have less than twenty miles and in some directions they have much more—that is, on the side where cities are separated by a greater distance. No city is anxious to extend its territory. For they think themselves farmers rather than masters of what they have.

In the country throughout their land they have well-arranged manors, well provided with farming equipment. The citizens take it in turns to live there. No country household has fewer than forty men and women, as well as two permanent slaves. In charge of all these are a man and wife of mature wisdom. Over each group of thirty households is put one phylarch.[4] From each household twenty return to the city every year after completing two years in the country. In their place are put twenty fresh men from the city, and they are trained by those who have spent a year in the country and are therefore more skilled in farming. They themselves will teach others the following year. This is done in case their inexperience should harm the crops if they were all equally new and ignorant of farming. This practice of renewing the farmers is rigidly observed so that no one should be compelled against his will to endure the harder life any longer. Nevertheless, many who by nature love farming are allowed to stay on there. The farmers till the land, feed the animals, gather wood and transport it to the city by land or sea, whichever is more convenient. They rear a very large number of chicks, by an amazing device. For the hens do not sit on the eggs. Instead they keep a great number of eggs warm with an even heat, and so hatch them. As soon as the chicks come out of the eggs, they follow the men and recognize them as if they were their mothers.

They keep very few horses, and only high-spirited ones. Their purpose is to exercise their young men in riding. For all the work of plowing and carrying is undertaken by oxen. They admit that oxen are inferior to horses in power, but think they excel them in endurance and are liable to

---

[2] Approximately the number of counties in England.

[3] The name means "dim" (like misty London, which Amaurote resembles in other ways as well).

[4] *Phylarch* means "ruler of a tribe."

fewer diseases. In addition to this, oxen need less expenditure of effort and money for their keep, and finally, when their working days are over, they can be used as food.

They use grain only for bread. For they drink wine, cider or perry,[5] or occasionally pure water, often also water in which they have boiled honey or licorice root, of which they have a large supply. When they have discovered (as they do very accurately) how much food is consumed by each city and the surrounding district, they yet plant a far greater crop and bring up far more cattle than their own needs require, and they share the surplus with their neighbors. They get from the city whatever supplies they need which are not kept in the country, and without any payment they get them from the city magistrates with no trouble at all. For each month several of them go to the city for a festival. When harvest time draws near, the farmers' phylarchs report to the city magistrates how many citizens should be sent to them. This crowd of harvesters, arriving on the appointed day, can finish practically the whole work on one fair day.

CHAPTER TWO
ON THE CITIES, AND ESPECIALLY AMAUROTE

Whoever knows one of their cities knows them all. As far as the nature of the ground allows they are absolutely identical. So I shall describe any one of them to you, as it does not much matter which. Which could be a better example than Amaurote? None deserves this more, as the others acknowledge it as head because of the presence of the Senate there, and none is better known to me, as I lived there for five years without a break.

Well now, Amaurote lies on a gentle slope of hill and is almost square in shape. Its side starts a little below the top of the hill and extends for two miles to the river Anyder.[6] Along the riverbank it is somewhat longer.

The Anyder rises eighty miles above Amaurote from a small spring; but it is increased by the addition of other rivers, two of which are quite sizable, and before it reaches the city itself it is half a mile wide. Soon it becomes even wider and flows on for another sixty miles before entering the ocean. In all this distance that lies between the city and the sea, and also several miles above the city, the water ebbs and flows with a swift tide for six hours at a time. When the sea rushes in for thirty miles, it fills the whole basin of the Anyder with its own water and pushes back the river. And it contaminates the water with brine a little farther than that too; but above this the water bit by bit becomes fresh and when it flows past the city it is pure. When the tide recedes, the river follows it, pure and untainted almost to its very mouth.

The city is joined to the other bank with a bridge made not out of piles and timber, but out of fine stone arches.[7] The bridge is in the part of the city farthest from the sea to allow ships to sail along all that side without any

---

[5] Pear cider.   [6] *Anyder* means "without water."   [7] Like London Bridge.

hindrance. They also have another small river, which is very calm and placid. It rises on the same hill the city is on and flows down right through the middle of it until it joins the Anyder. As the source of this stream lies a little outside the city, the Amaurotes have fenced it in and joined it to the city. This is done so that if ever they are attacked by an enemy, their water cannot be diverted or poisoned. The water is led off in brick channels in various directions to the lower parts of the city. If the ground prevents this anywhere, rainwater is collected in large tanks and is just as useful.

A high, thick wall surrounds the city, set with numerous towers and bastions. On three sides a moat surrounds the walls. This is dry, but deep and broad and entangled with briers. On the fourth side the river itself acts as a moat. The streets are well laid out for traffic and also to keep off the winds. The buildings are fine to see, as a long and unbroken row of them can be seen stretching along the whole street with their fronts facing you. These streets are twenty feet wide.[8] At the backs of the houses for the whole length of the streets lie wide gardens, closed in on all sides by the backs of streets. Every house has its own door to the street and also a back door to the garden. These doors are made of two leaves; they need only a slight push to open them, and close automatically. They let anyone enter and nothing is private anywhere. For they even change their houses by lot every ten years.

The gardens are very important to them. In them they have vines, fruits, herbs and flowers, all so neatly and carefully tended that I have never seen anything more prolific or more attractive. They are inspired to take this interest not merely because of the pleasure it gives, but by the rivalry between the streets for the excellence of their gardens. And certainly it would be hard to find anything in the whole city more profitable for the citizens or more pleasurable. It is for this reason that the founder seems to have paid more attention to the establishment of such gardens than to anything else.

For they say that the entire plan of the city right from the beginning was laid out by Utopus himself. But he left it to later generations to embellish and adorn it further, as he realized that this could hardly be done in a single life span. They keep records, written with great care and accuracy, covering the events of the 1,760 years from the conquest of the island. In these it is written that at first their houses were small, like cottages and huts, made out of any wood without discrimination; the walls were smeared with mud and the roofs rose to a ridge and were thatched. But now every house is remarkable for having three stories. The walls are faced with flint or plaster or brick, and are filled up with rubble. The roofs are flat and covered with an inexpensive substance so mixed that it cannot be harmed by fire and it is superior to lead for protection against the weather. They keep the wind out of the windows with glass, as it is quite plentiful there, or occasionally also with fine linen dipped in clear oil or amber. This dipping has two advantages, as by this means it lets in more light and less wind.

---

[8] By the standards of More's day, these streets would be grand boulevards.

CHAPTER THREE
ON THE MAGISTRATES

Every thirty households each year choose a magistrate for themselves, whom in the older language they call a syphogrant[9] and in the more modern a phylarch. Over ten syphogrants and their households there is an officer put in charge, previously called a tranibore, now a protophylarch.

The syphogrants are two hundred in number. They all swear to choose the man they think most suitable, and with a secret ballot elect a president, one of four previously nominated by the whole people. For one man is chosen from each quarter of the city to be put up for election before the Senate. The President holds his office for life, unless he is suspected of aiming at a dictatorship. They elect tranibores every year, but do not change them very often. All other offices are annual. The tranibores consult with the President every other day, occasionally more often if circumstances demand it. Their consultation is on matters of state and they quickly settle any disputes between private citizens, although these are very few. They always elect two syphogrants to sit with them in the Senate, a different pair each day. It is sanctioned that no legislation affecting the state should be passed unless it has been debated for three days previously in the Senate. To make plans on public affairs outside the Senate or the public elections is an offense punishable by death. The reason for this, they say, is to make it difficult for the President and tranibores to conspire together to oppress the people with a dictatorship and so change the constitution. And so matters considered of great importance are put before the syphogrants for their vote. These report on it to their households, consult among themselves and then report their decision to the Senate. Occasionally a matter is brought before the council of the whole island.

The Senate has the practice of debating nothing on the first day it is proposed to them, but it is put off for a full meeting of their body. This is to prevent someone from babbling the first thing that comes into his head, and then from a perverse and unnatural fear of seeming to have been shortsighted in the beginning, thinking up arguments to defend his plan rather than consulting the interests of the state, ready to damage the public good rather than his own reputation. Such a man ought to have seen to it right from the first that he spoke with more deliberation than haste.

CHAPTER FOUR
ON THE OCCUPATIONS OF THE UTOPIANS

All the men and women have one occupation in common—agriculture, in which everyone is skilled. They are all trained in this from childhood, partly by learning rules in school, and partly from being taken to the countryside near the city as if in play. As well as watching, they use the opportunity for exercise to gain some practical experience.

Besides agriculture (which, as I have said, is shared by all), each man is

[9] The meaning is uncertain, as also of *tranibore*.

taught one occupation as his own specialty. This is usually weaving of wool or flax, or the craft of a mason, a smith, an ironworker or a carpenter. Nor is there any other trade there that occupies any number of men worth mentioning. For throughout the island there is only one style of clothing, except that one sex is distinguished from another and unmarried from married people by their dress. This style is retained all through life. It is attractive, allows easy movement and is designed to be equally suitable for cold and hot weather. Each household makes its own clothes. But of those other crafts each person learns one or another, not merely men, but women too. But because of their comparative weakness, the women do lighter tasks. They usually work wool or flax. To the men are assigned the other, more laborious crafts. A person is generally trained to the craft of his father, as most men are naturally inclined that way. But if anyone's bent lies in a different direction, he is adopted into a household concerned with the craft he wants to practice. His father and the magistrates as well see to it that the new father he goes to is a worthy and honorable head of a family. If anyone learns one craft thoroughly and wishes to know another as well, he is likewise allowed. When he has a command of both, he practices which-ever he wishes, unless the state happens to need one more than the other.

It is the chief and almost the only task of the syphogrants to see that no one is idle, but that everyone diligently sets about his craft, but not like a beast, worn out by constant toil from early morning until late at night.[10] For even a slave is not as hard pressed as that. Nevertheless, this is the life of workmen practically everywhere except in Utopia. The Utopians divide night and day into twenty-four hours of equal length and assign only six to work: three before midday, after which they go to lunch; after lunch they have two hours in the afternoon for rest; after that they work for another three hours before dinner. Counting their first hour from midday, they go to bed around eight o'clock. Sleep claims eight hours. They are allowed to do as they please with the hours in between their work and sleep and meals. The purpose is not to allow them to waste this free time in wild living or idleness, but to enable them to apply their minds to whatever useful pursuit they wish in their free time. Most men devote their intervening hours to literature. For it is customary to hold public lectures every day before dawn. Only those are compelled to go who have been chosen by name to study literature. But a great number of men and women alike, from all classes, attend the lectures, their choice depending on their natural inclina-tion. If anyone would prefer to spend this time in the practice of his trade (as happens to many who are not inspired by the thought of learning) he is not prevented. In fact, he is even praised as being beneficial to the state.

After dinner they devote one hour to games, in the gardens during the summer, and in the winter in the common halls where they eat. There they practice music, or refresh themselves with conversation. They do not even know dice and such foolish and pernicious games. But they play two games not unlike chess: one is a battle of numbers in which one number makes booty of another; the second is a game where, in battle array, vices fight

---

[10] In More's time, the law dictated that laborers work from daybreak to dark between September and March, from about 5 A.M. to 7 or 8 P.M. in spring and summer.

with virtues. In this game a clever demonstration is given of the mutual discord of vices and their unity against virtues. It is also shown what vices oppose what virtues, with how much strength they openly assault, the wiles they use for oblique attack, the defenses virtues use to break the power of vices, the means they employ to foil their attempts and the ways in which either side gains victory.

But at this point, to avoid giving you a wrong impression, we must examine one aspect more closely. For as they spend only six hours in work, it might be that you think a shortage of supplies must follow. This is quite the reverse of the truth. In fact, this period of time is enough and more than enough to provide everything needed to support life or make it more comfortable. You will easily understand this if you remember how large a part of the population is idle in other countries. In the first place, there are all the women, a half of the total number; or if women are occupied in business anywhere, the men usually snore in their place. On top of this, there is a large and idle number of priests and religious, as they are called. Add to this all the rich men, especially the owners of estates, who are commonly called gentlemen, and the nobles. Add to these their servants, all that sewage of swashbuckling villains. Then count in the strong and healthy beggars, who use some sickness as a cloak for their laziness. You will certainly find that all these are far more numerous than the men whose labor provides all that human needs require. Of these latter, consider how few are engaged in necessary trades. For where we measure everything by money, many crafts are bound to be practiced which are quite useless and superfluous, merely the servants of luxury and vice. For if this large number now engaged in work were divided up to practice as few crafts as the convenient use of nature requires, then in the great abundance that would necessarily ensue, the prices would be too small to allow the craftsmen to earn a living. But take all those who now waste their time in idle occupations, and also all that mob enjoying the leisure of laziness and sloth, each one of whom consumes as much as two workmen who provide the goods; if they were all put to useful occupations, you can easily see how little time would amply suffice for supplying everything demanded by considerations of necessity or comfort, and of pleasure too if it is real and natural.

This is made clear by the state of affairs in Utopia. For there in the whole city and the surrounding neighborhood, scarcely five hundred persons of all the men and women strong and young enough to work are exempted.[11] Among these are the syphogrants, who are legally released from work; but they do not use this privilege, so that by their example they may more easily attract people to their occupations. The same immunity is enjoyed by those to whom the people, persuaded by the recommendation of the priests and secret election of the syphogrants, give a perpetual release to allow them to devote themselves to learning. If any one of these falls short of the hopes entertained of him, he is thrust back among the workers. Contrariwise, it often happens that a mechanic spends his leisure

---

[11] From figures given in Chapter Five, this works out to fewer than one person in a hundred.

time in such hard work on literature and makes such progress that he is taken from his trade and promoted to the class of scholars.

From this order are chosen ambassadors, priests, tranibores, and even the President himself, who is called in their old language Barzanes and in the newer one Ademus.[12] Since the remainder of the population is neither idle nor engaged in useless trades, it is easy to estimate how few hours produce so much good work. In addition to what I have said, there is also this advantage: they have to spend less time in the necessary crafts than other people. For in the first place, building or repairing houses requires the constant work of so many men everywhere simply because a spendthrift heir allows the house his father built gradually to crumble. So his successor must at great cost begin all over again what could have been safeguarded for so little. It also often happens that a man fastidiously turns his nose up at a house that cost another a great deal. So it is neglected and soon falls down. Then he builds another elsewhere at no less a price. But in Utopia, where everything is in good order and the state well established, it happens only very infrequently that a new site is chosen for building. They quickly repair present faults and also take precautionary measures against those that are likely to arise. So the buildings last for a long time with only a slight expenditure of labor, and workmen in that field occasionally have practically nothing to do—except that they are given timber to cut at home and stones to square and shape in the meanwhile, so that if any work does come it can rise more quickly.

Now see how few workmen they need for their clothing. When they are at work they are carelessly clothed in leather or skins, which will last seven years. When they go out of doors, they put a cloak on top to cover up their simple clothes. Throughout the whole island these cloaks are of the same natural color. So they need much less woolen cloth than is required in other countries and it also costs them much less. But linen is easier to produce and so is used more commonly. But in linen cloth only whiteness is observed, in woolen only cleanliness. No value is put upon a finer thread. Thus, while elsewhere four or five woolen cloaks of different colors are not enough for one man, and as many silk tunics, and for a more fastidious man not even ten are enough, in Utopia each man is content with one and it generally lasts him two years. For there is no reason why he should want more; if he obtained them, he would not be any better protected against the cold, nor would he seem one jot more attractive in his clothing.

So with everyone practicing useful crafts and fewer men needed for each, as there is a great abundance of supplies, occasionally they lead out a huge crowd to repair the public roads if any are worn away. Very often not even such work is required and so they make a public announcement of fewer working hours. For the magistrates do not exercise the citizens against their will in unnecessary work, since the institution of the republic has this one chief aim—that, as far as public necessity allows, all citizens should be given as much time as possible away from bodily service for the freedom and cultivation of the mind. For there, they think, lies happiness in life.

---

[12]*Barzanes* means "son of Zeus"; *Ademus* means "without people."

CHAPTER FIVE
ON THEIR LIVES TOGETHER

But now I must explain the interrelationships of the citizens, what mutual intercourse they have and what method there is for dividing everything up. Now, the city is composed of households and generally blood ties make up households. For when the women have matured, they are married and go to live in their husbands' homes. But male children and grandchildren remain in the household and obey the oldest of the parents, unless his mind is feeble from old age. Then the next in age takes his place.

Each city has six thousand such households, not counting the surrounding districts. To prevent the population from decreasing or expanding above the limit, no household is allowed to have fewer than ten or more than sixteen adults. No limit can be put upon the number of children. This number is easily maintained by transferring to smaller households those that are above the limit in larger ones. But if ever the number is exceeded for the whole city, they use the surplus to fill the gaps in their other cities. But if by any chance the numbers swell beyond the limit for the whole island, they choose citizens from any city and with their own laws set up a colony on the nearby mainland, wherever the inhabitants have too much land to cultivate. They take in any of the inhabitants of the country who wish to live with them. Thus joined with men who are willing, they easily merge into the same way of life and the same habits. That is advantageous for both peoples: for by their practices they bring it about that the land which appeared insufficient[13] and niggardly to the others is now more than enough for both. But those who refuse to live by their laws they drive out of the boundaries they mark out for themselves. If they resist, they go to war against them. For they think it the justest reason for war when any nation refuses to others the use and possession of that land which it does not use itself, but owns in idle emptiness, when the others by the law of nature ought to be nourished from it. It is said to have happened only twice ever, from a plague, that some of their cities are so reduced in numbers that they cannot be replenished from other parts of the island if each city is to keep its level. In that case citizens return from a colony to make up the numbers. For they prefer their colonies to die out rather than let any of the cities in the island decrease.

But to come back to the common lives of the citizens, as I said, the oldest member is head of each household. Wives serve their husbands, children their parents, and, in short, the younger serve the elder. Each city is divided into four equal parts. In the middle of each part is a marketplace for everything. There the produce of each household is brought and put in certain buildings. Each different kind of product is put separately into barns. From these each family head seeks what he and his family need, and he carries off whatever he seeks, without any money or exchange of any kind. For why should anything be refused him? There is more than enough of everything and there is no fear that anyone will ask for more than he needs. For why would he be likely to seek too much, when he knows for certain that his needs will always be met? A man is made greedy

---

[13] That is, not productive enough.

and grasping either by the fear of need (a fear common to all creatures) or else (in man alone) by pride, which thinks it glorious to surpass others in superfluous show. This kind of vice has no place at all in the ways of the Utopians.

Next to the markets I have mentioned are provision markets, where they bring vegetables, fruits and bread, as well as fish and the animals and birds that can be eaten. These markets are outside the city where the filth and muck can be washed away in the river. From there they bring the animals that have been killed and cleaned by the hands of their slaves. For they do not allow their own citizens to grow accustomed to the slaughter of animals, as they think that constant practice in this gradually destroys the kindness and gentle feeling of our souls. Nor do they allow anything filthy and impure to be brought into the city, whose corruption could pollute the air and carry in some disease.

Moreover, each street has certain large halls set at an equal distance apart, each one known by a separate name. The syphogrants live in these. Thirty households, fifteen from either side, are assigned to each hall and take their meals there. The caterers of each hall go into the market at a fixed hour and after telling the number of their charges, get the food.

But chief consideration is given to the sick, who are looked after in public hospitals. For they have four hospitals in the range of the city, a little outside the walls. These are so large that they could match as many small towns, and no number of patients, however great, would be cramped for lack of space. They also allow the isolation of patients who are suffering from a contagious disease. These hospitals are so well arranged, and so fully supplied with all things conducive to health, such tender and constant treatment is given, and the best doctors are so constantly in attendance, that while no one is sent there against his will, yet there is practically no one in the whole city who would not prefer to lie there when ill rather than at his own home. When the caterer for the sick has received the food in accordance with the doctor's prescription, then all the best remaining portions are divided equally among the halls, depending on the number in each. The only distinction is that some consideration is given to the President, the Bishop and the tranibores, and also to ambassadors and all foreigners—if there are any, as very rarely happens. These too, if there are any, are provided with certain houses properly equipped.

To these halls at the fixed hours of lunch and dinner come the whole syphograntia, summoned by the sound of a bronze trumpet, except for those who are sick in the hospitals or at home. Yet no one is prevented, after the halls have had enough, from taking food home from the market. For they know that no one does it for no reason. Although there is no rule forbidding eating at home, yet no one does this willingly, since it is not considered honorable, and in any case it is foolish to take the pains to prepare an inferior meal, when a rich and plentiful one is to be had at a nearby hall. In this hall, the slaves do all the tasks that are dirty or burdensome. But the job of cooking and preparing the food and making ready the whole meal is left to the women alone, each household taking its turn. Depending on their number, the people sit at three or more tables. The men are placed near the wall, the women nearer the door, so that if any sudden illness comes upon them (as occasionally happens in pregnancy) they may get up without disturbing the company and find their way to the nurses.

These nurses sit apart with the suckling children in a room set aside especially for that purpose. There is always a fire and clean water and also cradles, so that they can put the children down to rest and, when they wish, take off their swaddling clothes[14] in front of the fire and refresh them with play. Each mother is nurse to her own child, except where death or illness prevents this. When that happens, the wives of the syphogrants quickly find a nurse, and this is not difficult. For the women who can fulfill this function offer themselves to no task more willingly; since everyone praises this act of mercy and the child so brought up regards his nurse as his mother. In the nurses' room sit all the children under five years of age. All the other children of either sex who are below the age of marriage either serve at table or, if they are too young, stand nearby in absolute silence. Both classes of children eat what is offered to them by those at table, and they have no other set time for eating. The syphogrant and his wife sit in the middle of the first table, as this is the most distinguished place and from it can be seen the whole assembly, since the table runs across the highest part of the dining room. These are joined by two of the eldest present, as they sit four at a table. If there is a church located in that syphograntia, the priest and his wife sit with the syphogrant to preside. On each side sit the younger people and after them the older members, and so on throughout the whole hall. People of the same age sit together, but yet are mixed in with other age groups. They say that the reason for this practice is to allow the dignity and reverence of the old to check the young from unnecessary license in words and actions, since nothing can be done or said at table without being noticed by those nearby in one direction or another. The dishes are not served from the first place on, but first of all the older people, whose places are marked out in some special way, are given the choicest food; then the others are served impartially. If there are not enough tidbits[15] to distribute to the whole company, the older people share theirs at their discretion with those sitting near them. In this way respect for the elderly is preserved and at the same time all have the same advantages.

They begin every lunch and dinner with some reading suitable for forming the character. This is kept short to avoid boredom. Using this as a basis, the old men indulge in moral conversation, which nevertheless is not gloomy or lacking in wit. But they do not occupy the whole meal with lengthy dissertations. Rather, they gladly listen to the younger members also and even deliberately provoke them to speak so that they may discover the nature and mind of each, as these betray themselves in the freedom of the table. Their lunches are rather brief, their dinners more lavish. For lunch is succeeded by work, but dinner by sleep and rest for the night. This, they think, is more conducive to healthy digestion. No dinner passes without music, nor is the second course without its delights. They burn sweet-scented spices and scatter unguents and do everything to make the diners merrier. For they are readily inclined in this direction and think no kind of pleasure forbidden, as long as no inconvenience follows it.

---

[14] Wrappings for the bodies of infants. [15] Delicacies.

In this way, then, they live together in the city. But in the country, as they are more widely scattered, they all eat in their own homes. For no household lacks for food, as they are the source of supply for the city.

CHAPTER SIX
ON THE TRAVELS OF THE UTOPIANS[16]

But if any of the Utopians wish to see their friends who live in another city, or to visit the place itself, they easily obtain permission from their syphogrants and tranibores, unless some special need keeps them at home. So there is sent with such men a number of people with a letter from the President showing that they have permission to be away and also fixing the day of their return. They are given a wagon with a public servant to drive the oxen and look after them. But if they have no woman in their company, they send the wagon back as a burden and hindrance. For the whole journey they carry nothing with them, yet lack nothing; for everywhere they are at home. If they stay in any place longer than one day, each man practices his craft there and is treated with great kindness by the workers in his craft. If anyone wanders beyond his territory on his own authority, and is caught without written permission from the President, he is treated with much abuse and dragged back as a runaway and punished severely. If he dares to do it a second time, the penalty is slavery.

But if anyone has the urge to wander through the territory of his own city, he is allowed to do so after obtaining the permission of his father and the consent of his wife. But into whatever country district he arrives, he is given no food until he has completed the amount of work normally done there before midday, or dinnertime, as the case may be. With this provision, a man may go wherever he likes within the territory of his own city. For he will be no less useful to the city than if he were actually in it.

Now you see how little freedom they have for being idle. There is no pretext for laziness, no wine taverns, no alehouses, no brothels, no occasion for vice, no lurking places, no secret meetings. Thus, under the watchful eyes of all, they must perform their usual work or enjoy honorable leisure.

As the people have this practice, an abundant supply of all things must inevitably follow. As this is equally distributed among all, no one can be a pauper or a beggar. In the Senate of Amaurote (which, as I have said, three men from each city attend every year), as soon as it is decided what product is in plentiful supply anywhere, or what is not so plentiful elsewhere, then immediately the abundance of one place makes up the need of the other. And this they do free, receiving nothing in exchange for what they give. But if they have given anything from their supplies to a particular city without asking for anything in exchange, they receive whatever they themselves need from another city to which they have given nothing. So the whole island is just like one household.

But after they have made sufficient provision for themselves (and this they do not think achieved until they have provided for two years, in case

---

[16] Besides travel, this chapter outlines the Utopians' commerce; their moral, religious, and ethical philosophy; and their intellectual zeal.

the next year's crop should be unsatisfactory), then from the surplus they export to other countries a great abundance of grain, honey, wool, timber, scarlet and purple dye, sheepskins, wax, tallow, leather and also animals. They make a gift of a seventh part of all these commodities to the needy in that country. By this trade they import into their own country not merely what they need at home (for that is practically nothing except iron), but also a great abundance of silver and gold. By constantly following this practice, they now have a great surplus of those metals, more than one could believe. And so now they do not care whether they sell for ready cash or on credit, having by far the greatest amount owed to them. In making these loans, they give no credit to private individuals, but rather to whole cities, with the usual documents drawn up. When the day for repayment comes, the other city gathers in the debts of the private debtors and puts the amount into its treasury; it then enjoys the interest on that money until the Utopians ask for it back. For the most part they never ask for it. For they think it unjust to take away, from people who could use it, something for which they themselves have no use. But if circumstances demand that they should lend some part of that money to another country, then they ask for it back, or when they have to wage a war. For this single purpose they keep all the treasure they have at home, to protect them in extreme or sudden danger. They prefer to hire foreign soldiers for a huge wage, as they more willingly expose them to danger than their own citizens. For they realize that their very enemies can usually be bought by a huge sum of money, and either by treachery or civil strife be put in discord among themselves. For this reason they keep a treasury beyond value. Yet they keep it not as a treasury, but in a way I am really ashamed to relate, out of fear that my words will not be believed. My reticence is the more justified, as I realize that if I had not seen it in person, I could only with the greatest difficulty have been persuaded to believe the tale if told by another. For the less a thing fits the hearer's ways, the less credence is it always given. Yet a wise observer will perhaps be less surprised, since their other practices are so far removed from ours, if their use of silver and gold is suited to considerations of their ways rather than ours. For they do not use money, but save it for an eventuality which may or may not happen.

Meanwhile the gold and silver, of which money is made, no one of the Utopians values more than the nature of the things themselves deserves. In this respect, who does not see how vastly inferior they are to iron? Men could no more live without iron than without fire and water, though nature has given no use to gold and silver, which we might not easily go without, if man's folly had not put a price upon scarceness. Quite the reverse is truly the case: like a fond mother, nature has put all the best things in the open, like air, water and the earth itself, but has far removed empty and useless things. So if among the Utopians these metals were hidden away in some tower, the foolish cunning of people might suspect the President and Senate of tricking the people and getting some advantage themselves. Moreover, if they worked them into vessels and suchlike, if ever the occasion arose for melting them down again and paying them out as wages for the soldiers, they see, of course, that people would be very annoyed at being deprived of things they have come to enjoy as luxuries.

To remedy this, they have thought up a plan as harmonious with their

other practices as it is remote from ours (as we value gold so highly and
store it up so carefully). So only those who have observed it can readily
believe it. They eat and drink out of earthenware and glass vessels, most
elegant but yet cheap. But out of the gold and silver, not merely in common
halls, but in private houses too, they make chamberpots and all the most
humble utensils. In addition, from the same metals they fashion the chains
and thick fetters with which they confine their slaves. Finally, those in ill
repute for some crime have gold rings hanging from their ears, gold rings
on their fingers, gold necklaces and gold headbands. So they ensure in
every way that in their country gold and silver are in disgrace. So, although
other nations feel the removal of these metals as keenly as the removal of
their very entrails, yet no one in Utopia would think that he had lost one
penny if at any time circumstances demanded them all to be taken away.

They also gather pearls on the shore, and on certain rocks diamonds
and carbuncles. They do not go looking for them, but if they happen to
chance upon them they polish them up. With these they adorn their young
children. Although in early childhood they glory and delight in such ornaments, yet when they have grown a little older, without any warning from
their parents, they observe that only children use such trifles, and then they
put them aside in shame. This is exactly like our children, who, when they
grow up, throw away their nuts, brooches and dolls. These ways are so very
different from other nations', but how different are the mental attitudes
they produce, I never realized better than in the case of the ambassadors of
the Anemolians.[17]

These men came to Amaurote while I was there, and since they were
coming to discuss important matters, those three citizens from each city had
come before their arrival. All ambassadors from neighboring countries
were in the habit of coming in the plainest possible clothing, since they had
been there before and knew the character of the Utopians, and understood
that they paid no honor to sumptuous raiment, despised silk and even
rejected gold. But the Anemolians lived farther away and had had less
intercourse with them. Upon hearing that all Utopians used the same
rough kind of dress, they inferred that they just did not have what they
did not use. So, with more pride than wisdom, they decided to deck themselves like gods in the elegance of their equipment, and to dazzle the eyes of
the poor Utopians with the glitter of their finery. And so the three ambassadors made their entrance, with a hundred attendants, all in multicolored
clothing, mostly of silk. The ambassadors themselves, being nobles at
home, had gold clothes, huge necklaces and gold earrings, as well as gold
rings on their hands and chains hanging from their hats, which sparkled
with pearls and gems. In short, they were arrayed with all the things that in
Utopia were the punishment of slaves, or the shame of people in disgrace,
or the playthings of children. So it was worthwhile seeing how they
preened themselves when they compared their ornaments with the Utopians' clothes. (For the people had poured out into the streets.) On the other
hand, it was just as delightful to observe how wrong they had been in their
hopes and expectations, and how far they were from producing the impression they had imagined. For all the splendor of their equipment

---

[17] The name means "windy people."

seemed shameful to the eyes of all the Utopians, except a very few who had visited other countries for some worthy reason. They greeted the humblest members with reverence as if they were the masters, and considering the ambassadors themselves as slaves, because of their use of golden chains, passed them by with absolutely no mark of respect. You ought to have seen the children too! Those that had thrown away their gems and pearls, when they saw them on the ambassadors' hats, nudged their mothers and shouted to them, "Look, Mother! See that big booby still using his pearls and gems, just like a little boy!" But the mother, still taking it seriously, replied, "Hush, my son! He's one of the ambassadors' fools, I think." Others criticized those golden chains as being useless; for they were so thin that a slave could easily break them, yet so loose that he could shake them off whenever he wished to run away wherever he wanted, free and unfettered.

The ambassadors stayed there one or two days and observed that so much gold was thought so little of, and saw that it was despised there as much as it was honored in their own country. When they also learned that the chains and fetters of a single runaway slave took more gold and silver than all the trappings of the three of them, their feathers drooped and in shame they laid aside all that finery of which they had been so arrogantly proud. This came about especially after they had spoken more freely with the Utopians and learned their ways and opinions. For they are amazed that any man can be pleased with the feeble glow of a little gem or stone, when he can gaze at a star and the very sun itself; or that anyone is so crazy as to think himself more distinguished because of a thread of finer wool; for however fine a thread it may be, a sheep once wore it, and all the time it was nothing more than a sheep.

They are also amazed that gold, of its own nature so useless, is now everywhere so highly valued that man himself, through whom and for whose use it gained its worth, is valued much less than gold itself. This is so much so that some blockhead, with no more sense than a lump of wood and just as wicked as he is foolish, yet keeps many wise and good men in slavery, merely because he has a great pile of gold coins. If some chance or legal twist (which, no less than chance, exchanges high with low) transfers it from that master to the lowest wretch of all his household, soon he passes into the service of his servant, like an addition and tailpiece to his money. But much more are they amazed at and loathe the madness of men who pay practically divine honors to the rich, when they owe nothing to them, nor are they under any obligation to them, from no other consideration except their wealth; they do this even though they realize full well that they are so mean and greedy that, as long as the owners are alive, never will a penny come to them from such a huge pile of money.

They have formed these and similar opinions partly from their training, being brought up in a republic whose practices are very far removed from these kinds of stupidity, and partly from learning and literature. For although there are not many in each city who are exempt from other labors and are given over solely to learning (those, that is, in whom from childhood they have noticed an excellent character, an outstanding intellect and an inclination to good arts), yet all children are given a taste of literature; and a good part of the population, both men and women, throughout their lives spend those leisure hours we have mentioned in literature. They receive their learning in their own language. For it has a rich vocabulary, a pleasant sound and is an unsurpassed vehicle for expressing feelings. Practically the same language is current for a great area of that part of the world, except that it loses its purity outside Utopia in various ways.

Of all those philosophers whose names are so famous in the world known to us, not even a rumor had reached Utopia before our arrival. Yet in music and dialectic,[18] in arithmetic and geometry, their ancient philosophers made practically the same discoveries as ours. But although they match our ancients in almost everything, yet they are far behind the discoveries of our modern dialecticians.[19] For they have not discovered a single one of those rules which children learn everywhere in our world, about restrictions, amplifications and suppositions, all thought out with great acuteness in the handbooks on logic. Moreover, so far are they from finding "second intentions,"[20] that none of them could see Man Himself in the abstract,[21] as they call it, although (as you know) he is absolutely colossal and bigger than any giant, and although at that time we pointed to him with our fingers. But they are very learned in the course of the stars and the motions of the heavenly spheres. They have even skillfully devised instruments of various shapes in which they contain very precisely the movements and positions of the sun and moon and the other stars which appear on their horizon. But they do not even dream of the "friendships" and "dissensions" of the planets and all that fraud of divination from the stars.[22] They use certain signs seen long beforehand to forecast the rains, winds and other changes of the weather. But about the causes of all these things, and the tides and saltiness of the sea, and in general the origin and nature of the heavens and the earth, they partly put forward the same opinions as our old philosophers; partly also, as ours disagree among themselves, so they have different opinions from all of them, while they bring forward new explanations for things; nor yet do they agree everywhere among themselves.

In moral philosophy their discussions are the same as ours. They investigate the goods of the spirit and the body, and those of fortune; then whether the name "good" suits all these, or only those of the spirit. They discuss virtue and pleasure; but the first and foremost point of dispute is whether they think man's happiness lies in one thing or more. But on this point they seem to favor too much the side supporting pleasure, since by this they define the whole or the greatest part of human happiness. And what is more surprising, they seek support for so pleasure-loving an opinion from religion, despite its harsh, severe, sad and rigid nature. For they never discuss happiness without joining to rational philosophy some princi-

[18] Logic.

[19] The medieval scholastic thinkers, who were frequently ridiculed by Renaissance humanists for alleged over-subtlety.

[20] First intentions are the mind's direct apprehension of things; second intentions are notions derived from the mind's further reflection on the things.

[21] More refers to the great medieval debate between the "nominalists," who believed that such universals as "mankind" (as distinguished from individual men) were mere names, and the "realists," who believed that the universals were real.

[22] Astrology, ridiculed here, was still intellectually respectable in More's time.

ples taken from religion. Without these principles, they think that reason in itself is maimed and weak for the investigation of true happiness. Their principles are such as these: the soul is immortal and by the kindness of God born to happiness; for our virtues and good deeds, rewards are appointed after this life, and for our sins, punishments. Although these tenets belong to religion, yet they think that men are led to believe and accept them by reason. If they are abolished, they claim without any hesitation that no one is so stupid as not to feel that he ought to seek pleasure by right or wrong means. This merely would he watch, that a lesser pleasure should not stand in the way of a greater, or that he should not follow a pleasure which would be rewarded by pain. For they consider it sheer madness to pursue harsh and difficult virtue, and not merely to renounce a pleasant life but even willingly to endure pain, from which you might expect no profit. For what profit can there be if you gain nothing after death when you have passed the whole of this life unpleasantly, that is to say, miserably. But actually they do not think that happiness lies in all pleasure, but only in that which is good and honorable. For to this, as if to the highest good, our nature is drawn by virtue itself, to which alone those of the opposite belief attribute happiness. For they define virtue as "living in accordance with nature," since for that purpose were we created by God. Whoever obeys reason in desiring and avoiding anything is following the lead of nature. Moreover, reason primarily inflames men to the love and veneration of the divine majesty to whom we owe our existence and the possibility of attaining happiness. Secondly, it advises and urges us to lead a life with the least worry and the greatest joy, and also, in accordance with the kinship of nature, to offer ourselves as helpers to all others to attain that same end. For never has there been anyone so stern and severe a follower of virtue and hater of pleasure, a man to enjoin labors, vigils and penance upon you, who did not at the same time bid you exert all your efforts toward lightening the need and discomfort of others and who did not judge that in the name of humanity what is most deserving of praise is that a man should save and console another. For it is a most humane virtue, and none is more appropriate for a man than to lessen the misery of others, remove the anguish of their lives and restore them to joy, in other words, to pleasure. Why then should not nature urge a man to do the same for himself?

For there are two possibilities: either a life of joy, that is to say, pleasure, is evil, in which case you ought not to help anyone toward it, but rather deprive all men of it as far as you can, because of its harmful and deadly quality; or else, if you are not merely allowed but even commanded to win it for others as being something good, why can you not do this for yourself above all others? For it is only right to be as kind to yourself as to others. For when nature encourages you to be good to others, she does not then order you to be cruel and harsh to yourself. So, they say, the life of joy, that is, of pleasure, is prescribed to us by nature herself as the end of all our activities. They define virtue as living according to nature's prescription. But when nature encourages mankind to help one another to a happier life (and this she does with good reason; for no one is so far above the lot of the human race as to be nature's sole concern; for she looks after all men alike, whom she embraces with the common bond of similar appearance), you can be sure that she repeatedly exhorts you to see to it that you do not follow your own advantages to the extent of producing disadvantages for others.

Therefore they think that not only private agreements should be observed, but also public laws. For either a good president justly enacted them, or else the people as a whole, not being oppressed by a tyrant or ensnared by guile, sanctioned them by common agreement for sharing the advantages of life, that is to say, the material of pleasure. Provided that you do not violate these laws, it is a mark of wisdom to procure your own advantage, just as it is a mark of natural affection to procure that of the state as a whole. But to deprive another of his pleasure while you achieve your own—this is injustice. On the other hand, to deprive yourself of something to give it to others is a task of humanity and kindness; this never removes as much advantage as it restores. For it is compensated by the return of benefits, and also the very consciousness of having done a kindness, and the remembrance of the affection and good will of those to whom you have been kind, bring on pleasure to the mind much greater than the bodily pleasure would have been from which you abstained. Finally, as religion is easily able to persuade a mind which readily agrees, in the place of a brief and small pleasure God repays us with a great joy which will never die. Therefore in this way, after carefully examining and considering the matter, they think that all our actions, and among them the virtues themselves, look toward pleasure as their final state and happiness.

By "pleasure" they mean every motion and state of the body or mind in which, with nature's guidance, it is pleasant to be. To this they add, with good reason, the appetite of nature. For not merely the senses, but correct reason also follows whatever is pleasant by nature, provided that the way to it does not involve injustice, the loss of a greater pleasure, or hard work as an inevitable consequence. But what men contrary to nature imagine by idle agreement to be pleasant for them, as if it were in their power to change things just as they do their names—all these things the Utopians decree are of no use for the attainment of happiness. Instead, these practices even hinder it greatly, if it is only because when once they have settled in a man, they seize on all his mind with a false belief about pleasure and bring it about that there is no room anywhere for true and genuine delights. For there are many things which of their own nature contain no sweetness, and even on the whole a large share of bitterness; but by the perverse enticement of evil desires, they are not merely considered as the highest pleasures, but even counted among the chief reasons for life.

In this kind of spurious pleasure they include those people I mentioned before, who think themselves the better for wearing better clothes. On this point they are twice wrong. For they are just as mistaken in thinking their clothing better as they are in thinking this of themselves. For if you regard the use of a garment, why should finer wool be better than coarser? But yet those men, as if their superiority lay in their nature not their error, preen themselves and think that their value is increased in this way. And so, as if by right, they demand for their finer clothes a respect that they would not have dared hope for in cheaper attire, and if they are passed by and neglected they feel outraged.

But is it not part of the same ignorance to enjoy empty and useless honors? For what natural and true pleasure is brought by another's bared head or bent knees? Will this heal the pain in your own knees, or the frenzy in your own head? In this image of counterfeit pleasure, men enjoy sweet madness who flatter and applaud themselves in their belief in their nobility; for they happened to be born of ancestors whose wealth, above all in land, goes back many generations (for nobility is nothing else these days). They think themselves not in the slightest degree less noble even if their ancestors left them nothing of it at all, or if they themselves squandered what was left to them.

In this number they also include those who, as I said, are delighted with gems and precious stones, and who think that somehow they have become gods if they obtain an especially fine one, above all, one of the kind most highly valued by their own people at that particular time. For the same kinds of stones are not considered valuable by all people, nor at all times. But they buy them only if they are removed from their gold setting and displayed all alone. In fact, they will not buy them even under these circumstances unless the seller takes an oath and gives them a guarantee that the gem or stone is genuine; so careful are they that a counterfeit stone should not deceive their eyes into judging it real. But as far as sight is concerned, why should a fabricated stone give less pleasure when your eye cannot distinguish it from a real one? Each ought to have the same value for you as it does for a blind man. What of those people who guard excessive riches, not to get any advantage from the pile but merely to gaze at it? Do they get true pleasure, or are they not rather deceived by a false pleasure? Or what of those who, by an opposite failing, hide away gold that they will never use and perhaps not even see any more, and who, in their concern not to lose it, do in fact lose it? For what else is it when you return to the earth something that you have removed from your own use and perhaps that of all men too? And yet when you have hidden your treasure away, as if you were now free of all care, you jump for joy. Suppose someone stole it and you died ten years later in complete ignorance of the theft. During all those ten years of your life when the money was gone, what did it matter to you whether the money was stolen or still safe? You can be quite sure that in either way you got the same profit from it.

To these foolish pleasures they join those of gamblers (whose madness they know by hearsay, not experience) and hunters and hawkers. For, they say, what pleasure does it bring to throw the dice on the board, when you have done it so often that if there were any pleasure in it, you would have become bored with the constant experience? Or what pleasure can there be, rather than disgust, in hearing the barking and howling of dogs? Or what greater experience of pleasure is there when a dog chases a hare than when a dog chases a dog? For it is the same action in each case. For if running pleases you, there is running involved. But if you are held by the hope of slaughter and the expectation of seeing something torn to pieces before your eyes, it ought rather to move you to pity to see a little hare so weak, shy and harmless torn apart by a powerful, fierce and cruel dog. So the Utopians delegate this practice of hunting, as something unworthy of free men, to butchers (which trade, as I have said above, is carried on by slaves). For they think that hunting is the lowest part of that trade, while its other parts are both more useful and more honorable, since they produce much more advantage and kill animals merely out of necessity; while the hunter seeks nothing but pleasure from the slaughter and dismembering of a poor little animal. They think that this delight in seeing death arises in beasts too, either from an innate spirit of cruelty or else because the constant experience of so savage a pleasure turns into cruelty. Therefore they unambiguously decide that although the common crowd of men considers them pleasures, these and innumerable such-like practices have nothing to do with real pleasure, as there is nothing in them sweet by nature. For they are not moved from this opinion even though these practices stir the senses with delight and this appears to be the function of pleasure. The reason is not the inherent nature of the experience, but the corrupt habit of the men involved. From this fault they welcome the bitter for the sweet, just as pregnant women have a distorted sense of taste and think pitch and tallow sweeter than honey. Yet no man's judgment, corrupted by disease or habit, can change the nature of pleasure, any more than it can change that of anything else.

They make various divisions in the pleasures they call true. For they assign some to the mind and others to the body. To the mind they give intelligence and that joy which the contemplation of the truth produces. To this they add the sweet recollection of a life well led and the certain hope of future good. The pleasures of the body they divide into two categories. The first is that which affects the senses with a clear delight. This sometimes comes about by the renewal of those parts which our natural heat has dried up. For these are restored by food and drink. At other times it happens when those things are expelled of which our body has too great an abundance. This pleasure is produced when we empty our bowels, or have sexual intercourse, or else by rubbing or scratching relieve an itching in any part. But occasionally a pleasure arises that is not going to restore anything our limbs lack or remove anything they have in excess; yet it tickles, affects and attracts our sense with a clear feeling by some secret force—for example, the pleasure of music.

The second kind of bodily pleasure that they define is that which consists of a calm and balanced bodily condition; that is, each man's own bodily health interrupted by no ill. For if no pain assaults it, this state of health is delightful in itself, even if it is stirred by no external pleasure. For although it is less obvious and less clearly perceptible than the swelling desire of eating and drinking, yet nonetheless many men think this the greatest of pleasures. Almost all the Utopians claim that it is a great pleasure, the foundation and basis of all others; for even alone it can produce a calm and delightful state of life, but if it is removed there is no place left anywhere for any pleasure. For merely to be without pain they call insensibility, not pleasure, unless there is also present a state of health. The Utopians have long since rejected the opinion of those who thought that a stable and tranquil state of health (a question hotly debated among them) ought not to be considered a pleasure because its presence could not be felt except by some opposite emotion. But now they practically all agree on the opposite opinion that health must be considered a very special pleasure. For, they argue, since in sickness there is pain, the implacable enemy of pleasure, just as sickness is of health, why then should there not be pleasure in the placid state of good health? They do not think the question is affected if you say sickness *is* pain, or sickness *contains* pain. For the same effect is produced in either case. If health is a pleasure in itself, or if it necessarily produces pleasure (just as heat is produced by fire), then in either case a man who has constant good health must also have pleasure. Moreover, they say, when we eat, all that is happening is that health, which had begun to be impaired, is using food as an ally to fight against hunger. While health is gradually growing stronger, that very advance to its customary strength produces the pleasure, by which we are refreshed. So if health rejoices in the battle, will it not also be happy when it gains the victory? When it has at last successfully gained its former vigor (its only aim in the whole conflict), will it straightway become stupid, and not recognize and embrace its own goods? For they think the opinion that good health is not felt to be far from the truth. For, they argue, who when awake does not feel that he is healthy, except the man who is not? Who is afflicted by such stupor or lethargy as to say that health is not pleasant and delightful? But what is delight except pleasure under another name?

Therefore[23] they embrace chiefly the pleasures of the mind, thinking them the most important of all. They say that the most special part of them comes from the practice of the virtues and the realization of living a good life. Of the bodily pleasures they give first place to health. For they think that the joy of eating and drink, and whatever produces the same kind of delight, ought to be sought, but only for the sake of health. For such things are not pleasant in themselves, but only insofar as they oppose the stealthy attack of sickness. So just as the wise man avoids illness instead of hoping for medicine, and vanquishes pains instead of looking for consolations, so it will be better for him not to need this kind of pleasure instead of feeling its gratification. If anyone thinks himself blessed because of this kind of pleasure, then he must admit that he would be most fortunate if he spent his life in perpetual hunger, thirst, itching, eating, drinking, scratching and rubbing. Who does not see how disgusting and even how wretched such a life would be? Surely these are the lowest of all pleasures, just as they are the least pure. For they are never present unless joined to the opposite pains. For with the pleasure of eating is joined hunger, and by a very unequal law too. For the pain is more intense, as well as more enduring, since it is produced before the pleasure and is extinguished only when the pleasure dies too.

So they think that pleasures of this kind ought not to be highly valued, except insofar as they are necessary. But they do delight in these pleasures and gratefully recognize the kindness of fond mother nature, who uses the most alluring sweetness to entice her children to what must of necessity be done so often. For how miserable life would be if we had to drive away these daily illnesses of hunger and thirst with bitter drugs, like other sicknesses that attack us more rarely! But they gladly take care of their appearance, their strength and their suppleness as being the special delightful gifts of nature. They also pursue, as the delightful seasoning of life, those pleasures that come through the ears, eyes, and nostrils, which nature intended to be peculiar to man. For there is no other kind of animal that looks up to the beautiful appearance of the world, or is stirred by any sweetness of smell, except for choosing food, or is able to distinguish conso-

[23] That is, "to sum up."

nant or dissonant chords in music. But in all pleasures the Utopians have this reservation: that a lesser pleasure should not get in the way of a greater, and that a pleasure should not eventually produce pain. This they think necessarily ensues if it is not a worthy pleasure. But to despise physical beauty, to wear away one's strength, to turn nimbleness to sloth, to waste the body with fasting, to injure one's health and reject the other delights of nature (except if a man ignores his own advantage, while eagerly winning that of others or of the whole state, since in return for this toil he expects a greater pleasure from God), to punish oneself for the empty shadow of virtue, to no one's advantage, or to strive after greater fortitude for an adversity that may never come—all this they think is absolutely insane. It is the action of a mind at once cruel to itself and ungrateful to nature, all of whose kindness they reject, as if they scorned to owe her anything.

This is their opinion on virtue and pleasure. They think that human reason can find none truer, unless revealed religion inspires man with something more holy. Our time does not allow us to discuss whether they are right or wrong in this opinion, nor is it necessary to do so. For I have promised to tell you of their practices, not defend them.

But I am quite sure that whatever may be the status of their decisions, there is nowhere a more distinguished nation, nor a more prosperous republic. They are quick and nimble in body, with more strength than their height would suggest. Not that they are short. And although their soil is not fertile everywhere, nor their climate perfectly healthful, yet they so protect themselves against the weather by temperance in living, and make up the deficiencies of the soil by hard work so successfully, that nowhere in the world is there a greater production of grain and cattle, nowhere are men's bodies more lively and liable to fewer diseases. Of course, you can see them carefully attending to matters that farmers look after everywhere, so that by skill and hard work they can improve soil none too rich by nature. But you will also see the people pull up whole woods by the roots and transplant them elsewhere. In this they aim not to increase the production, but to make transportation easier, so that they can have timber nearer the sea, or the rivers, or the cities themselves. For it is less laborious to transport grain far over land than timber. The people are affable, witty, clever; they enjoy their leisure, but (when necessary) can endure physical labor well enough—although they do not go out of their way to look for it; they never tire of mental study.

When they heard from us about Greek literature and learning (for we did not think they would like much in Latin except the historians and poets), they were very anxious that we should explain and teach it all to them. So we began to lecture to them, at first more to show willingness than because we expected any profit would come of it. But when we had made some progress, their industry immediately made us realize that our efforts were not being wasted. For they began to imitate the Greek letters so easily, to pronounce the words so accurately, to commit things to memory so quickly and repeat them so exactly, that we were astounded, although most of them came from the company of the scholars, men of chosen intelligence and mature years, who were not merely fired with their own enthusiasm, but were also ordered by a decree of the Senate. So in less than three years there was nothing in Greek for them to learn. They were able to read the good authors without any stumbling (except where the text was faulty).[24]

In my opinion, they absorbed that literature all the more easily because, in a way, it was not alien to them. For I suspect that the Utopians have their origins in Greece, since their language, in other respects much like Persian, retains some traces of Greek in the names of their cities and magistrates. When I was planning my fourth voyage, I put on board ship a fair supply of books as cargo, since I had decided to stay a long while. Of these I gave to the Utopians several works of Plato and more of Aristotle; also Theophrastus' work *On Plants*, but, I am sorry to say, this was imperfect in many passages. For while we were sailing, I did not take enough care of this book and a monkey found it. In his play and frolicking he tore out several pages from different sections and ripped them up. Of the writers of grammar they have only Lascaris; for I did not bring Theodorus with me, nor any dictionary except Hesychius and Dioscorides. They are very fond of the works of Plutarch, and are also delighted with the wit and grace of Lucian. Of the poets they have Aristophanes, Homer and Euripides, as well as Sophocles in the small Aldine[25] edition; of the historians Thucydides and Herodotus, together with Herodian. On medicine, too, my companion Tricius Apinatus[26] had brought with him some minor works of Hippocrates, and Galen's *Microtechne*, which books they value very highly. For although they need medicine least of all people, yet nowhere is it more honored, since they count knowledge of medicine among the most beautiful and useful parts of philosophy. When by the help of this philosophy they search out the secrets of nature, they think that, besides gaining a wonderful pleasure from it, they also obtain the highest favor with its Author and Designer. They think that like other designers he has exposed the workings of this world to the sight of man (whom alone He created with ability to understand it), and therefore He is all the fonder of a careful and exact investigator and admirer of His work, than of a man who, like an animal without any mind, ignores so great and wonderful a sight, remaining dull and unmoved.

So from their reading the Utopians are amazingly clever at discovering devices to help make life more comfortable. But they owe two such pieces of knowledge to us, namely printing and papermaking. Yet their debt is not merely to us, but also to themselves to a large extent. For when we were showing them the printing of Aldus in paper books, and telling them about the material used in making paper and about the art of printing, just talking rather than explaining clearly (as none of us had precise knowledge of either process), yet they immediately worked it all out on their own with great skill. Although they previously wrote only on skin, bark or papyrus, now they immediately tried to make paper and print. At first they did not get very far, but by constantly experimenting they soon mastered both.

[24] To establish the best texts of the ancient classics was a prime endeavor of the humanists.

[25] The Aldine Press in Venice, founded in the late fifteenth century by Aldus Manutius, pioneered the printing of ancient Greek literature and was a center of Greek scholarship.

[26] An invented name (based on the names of two small towns in southern Italy), suggesting insignificance.

They made so much progress that, if they had the manuscripts of Greek books, they would not lack for printed copies. But as it is, they have only what I have told you about. But what they have, they have printed and multiplied into many thousand copies.

If anyone visits their country who is commended by some great intellectual gift or a knowledge of many lands from constant travel (which is why our landing pleased them so much), he is welcomed with open arms. For they are glad to hear what is done in every land. But only rarely do people go there for trade. For what would they bring? Only iron, or gold and silver, and then everyone would rather carry this away with him. As for their own exports, the Utopians think it better to transport them themselves rather than have others come to fetch them. In this way they can examine different people more carefully and not lose their experience and skill on the sea.

CHAPTER SEVEN
ON SLAVES[27]

For slaves they do not have men captured in war (unless they fought the war themselves), nor the children of slaves, nor anyone who could be bought as a slave in another country. Instead they have any of their own citizens who have been reduced to slavery for some offense, or the inhabitants of foreign cities who have been condemned to death for some crime they have committed. This latter class is by far the more common. For they take away many of these, sometimes for a small price, more often for nothing, just by asking for them. They keep this kind of slave not merely in constant labor, but also in chains. Their own people they treat more severely: they think they are the more hopeless and deserving of the harsher punishment, because after such an excellent training to virtue they still could not be restrained from crime.

There is another class of slaves, composed of poor overworked drudges from another country, who have deliberately chosen to be slaves in Utopia. These are decently treated, and handled with not much less kindness than Utopians, except that they have a little more work imposed on them as they are used to it. It does not often happen that one wishes to leave, but if he does, they do not hold him against his will, nor do they send him away empty-handed.

As I have said, they treat the sick with great kindness and leave nothing undone to restore their health, whether it is by drugs or by dieting. If anyone is suffering from an incurable disease, they console him by sitting with him, talking to him and supplying all the comforts they can. But if a disease is not merely beyond treatment, but also a constant source of pain and agony, the priests and magistrates remind him that he is not up to all the tasks of life, is troublesome to others and a burden to himself, and is now outliving his own death. Then they advise him not to resolve to feed that pestilence and sickness any longer, nor to hesitate to die, since life is a

---

[27] Besides slavery (more exactly, servitude), this chapter treats of euthanasia, marriage, penal law, and foreign relations.

torment to him. They bid him to take good hope and release himself from
that bitter life, as if from a prison or torture rack, or at least give his permission for others to remove him. They tell him that since he is going to put an
end not to pleasure but to punishment, he would be well advised to do it;
and since in that matter he is going to take the advice of priests, the interpreters of God, his action will also be pious and holy. Those who are persuaded by this either end their own lives by abstinence from food, or else
are released from it while they are asleep, without any sensation of death.
But they never remove anyone against his will, nor are they any the less
considerate to him. It is considered honorable to yield to persuasion and
die like this. But they think a man unworthy of burial or cremation who
commits suicide without having a reason approved of by the priests and
Senate. Instead, in great disgrace, he is flung unburied into some bog.

A woman does not marry before she is eighteen years old, and a man
not until he is four years older than that. If a man or woman is found guilty
of secret lust before marriage, the offender is severely punished and both
are forbidden to marry forever, unless the President pardons them and
forgives their offense. But also the head of the household and his wife in
whose home the shameful act was committed are held in great disgrace, on
the grounds that they were remiss in their duty. The reason for the severe
punishment of this crime is the realization that very few people would join
in married love, in which they saw they had to spend all their lives with one
person and endure all the consequent inconvenience, if they were not carefully restrained from random sexual relations.

Moreover, in choosing partners, they seriously and rigidly observe a
ritual that to us seemed quite absurd and ridiculous. A respectable and
honored matron shows the woman (whether she is a maiden or a widow) to
her suitor in complete nakedness. And in turn some trustworthy man
shows the suitor naked to the girl. When we were laughing at this custom as
being a silly one and were finding fault with it, the Utopians expressed
their surprise at the amazing stupidity of all other nations. For, they said, in
a matter involving a trifling sum of money, like buying a horse, other people are so careful that they refuse to buy the horse, however uncovered he
may be, if the saddle and harness are not taken off, in case there is a sore
hidden under those coverings. But in choosing a wife (a matter which will
bring pleasure or revulsion for the rest of one's life) they are so careless
that, while the rest of her body is concealed by clothes, they judge the whole
woman from a space of a few inches (for only her face is visible) and then
marry her—not without a great danger of a bad match if anything offends
their taste afterward. For not all men are wise enough to regard character
only, and in the marriages of such wise men bodily endowments make a
useful addition to the spiritual virtues. Naturally so foul a deformity can lie
concealed under those clothes that it can quite alienate the mind from one's
wife, when it is no longer possible he be bodily separated from her. If such
a deformity should happen to come about after marriage, then each man
must bear his lot. But there ought to be legal provision to prevent anyone
from being caught by such guile before marriage. The Utopians had to be
all the more cautious on this, as they are the only people in that world who
are content with one wife, and marriage is not often dissolved for them
except by death, unless the reason is adultery or some unendurable fault of

character. If either husband or wife is afflicted in this way, the Senate gives permission to him or her to find another partner. The other partner forever lives a single life, in disgrace. But they in no way tolerate a man to divorce his wife, if she is blameless, just because some physical misfortune strikes her. For they think it cruel to abandon anyone in his hour of greater need, and believe that it will also breed great distrust in old age, which both brings sickness and is a sickness itself. But it sometimes happens that the characters of husband and wife are quite irreconcilable, and they both discover others with whom they hope they can live more pleasantly. So they separate by mutual consent and contract new marriages. But this cannot be done without the permission of the Senate, which allows divorces only after its members and their wives have carefully examined the case. It is not easy even then, as they know that a ready hope of new marriage is most disadvantageous for strengthening the love of husband and wife.

Adulterers are punished with the severest slavery. If both offenders were married, the injured parties, if they wish, may gain a divorce and marry each other. Otherwise they may marry anyone they want. But if the injured party remains in love with so ill-deserving a partner, he is not forbidden to enjoy his right of marriage, as long as he is willing to follow the convicted partner in his hard labor. It sometimes happens that the repentance of the one and the constant kindness of the other move the President to compassion and gain them freedom once more. But if such a person falls back into his criminal ways, he is put to death.

For other crimes there is no fixed punishment regulated by any law, but the Senate judges the severity or mildness of the offense and decides upon an appropriate punishment. Husbands chastise their wives and parents their children, unless they have committed so terrible a crime that its public punishment is beneficial to morality. But usually the most serious crimes are punished with slavery. For they think this just as unpleasant for the criminals and more profitable for the state than if they hurried to execute the guilty and do away with them immediately. For their work brings more profit than their death, and by their example they can deter others from similar offenses for a longer time. But if in this treatment they rebel and fight against authority, then they are slaughtered like wild beasts that no prison or chain can confine. Yet if they are patient, not absolutely all hope is taken away. If after being subdued by long misfortune they clearly show enough repentance to demonstrate that their sin is more displeasing to them than their punishment, then sometimes by the President's prerogative, sometimes by the vote of the people, their slavery is mitigated or altogether remitted. To have tried to commit adultery is no less dangerous than to have succeeded. For in the case of every crime, they judge a fixed and clearly aimed attempt to be the equivalent of the deed itself. Nor do they think it ought to be in his favor that he did not go all the way, since it was not his doing that he failed.

They take great delight in fools. Although it is considered shameful to do them any harm, yet it is permissible to get pleasure from their foolishness. For they think that this is very good for the fools themselves. If anyone is so stern and severe that he cannot laugh at any word or action of theirs, to his safekeeping they refuse to entrust a fool. For they are afraid that a man who finds no use and no amusement in a fool (and this is a fool's only advantage) will not look after him with sufficient kindness.

To mock a man who is deformed or crippled is considered disgusting and disgraceful, not to the man mocked, but to the mocker. For he stupidly reproaches as a failing something that the man could not possibly avoid. They think a person lazy and slothful who does not look after his natural beauty; but with them it is a disgraceful arrogance to seek help from paint. For they know by experience how little husbands are attracted by their wives' beauty as compared with integrity and humility of character. For although some men are won by physical beauty alone, no one's affection is kept except by virtue and obedience.

They do not merely deter people from crimes by punishment; they also set up rewards to incite them to virtue. And so they put up statues in the marketplace to distinguished men and those who have been great benefactors to the state. This is done as a memorial to their benefactions, and also so that the glory of their ancestors may serve their descendants as a spur and incitement to virtue. Anyone who canvasses for an office is debarred from all promotion. They live together in love, as no magistrate is haughty or terrifying. They are called "fathers" and so do they act. Those who wish may pay them respect, as is only right, but this is not demanded of men against their will. Not even the President himself is distinguished by his clothing or by a crown. His only distinctive mark is a small sheaf of corn[28] which he carries, just as the Bishop's is a wax candle carried before him.

They have very few laws, as people so trained do not need many. The chief criticism they bring against other people is that an infinite number of books of laws and commentaries is not enough. The Utopians think it most unjust that any men should be bound by laws that are either too numerous to read or too obscure for anyone to understand. Moreover, they exclude absolutely all lawyers since these plead cases with cunning and slyly dispute the laws. For they think it useful that each man should plead his own case and repeat to the judge what he would have told his counsel. In this way there will be less doubt and the truth can be elicited more easily, since the speaker has not been taught any deceit by his lawyer, and the judge can shrewdly weigh up each point and help simpler minds against the false accusations of the cunning. It is hard for this procedure to be observed in other countries amid such a mass of tangled laws. But in Utopia every man has a good knowledge of law. For, as I have said, the laws are very few, and they think that the bluntest interpretation is the best. All laws, they say, are passed with the sole reason of reminding each man of his duty; therefore a more subtle interpretation reminds fewer people, as only few can follow it; whereas a more straightforward and simple meaning of the laws is open to everyone. Otherwise, as far as the common people are concerned (and they are the most numerous and most in need of being reminded), you might just as well pass no law at all as pass one and then interpret it in a sense that no one could possibly discover except by a very keen mind and much debate. For the blunt judgment of the common man could never discover

[28] Grain.

such an interpretation, nor does he have enough time, with his days spent in working for his living.

These virtues of the Utopians have incited their neighbors, who are free and under their own control (for the Utopians long ago freed many of them from tyranny), to take their magistrates from them, some every year, others for a period of five years. After they have completed their term of office, they escort them back with glory and honor, and take back fresh ones with them to their country. Now, these nations take an excellent and healthy care of their states. Since the safety or destruction of a state depends on the character of its magistrates, they could have made no wiser choice than men who are strangers in the land and could not be deflected from honesty by any bribe (since it would shortly be useless to them when they returned to their own country), nor influenced by favor or hatred toward anyone. If ever these two evils of bias and greed settle on the law courts, they immediately destroy all justice, the strongest sinew of the state. The Utopians call the people who fetch magistrates from them "allies," and the others to whom they have given aid they call "friends."

Other nations are in the habit of making treaties all the time, then breaking them and renewing them. But the Utopians make none at all. For what is the purpose of a treaty? they say. It is as if nature does not put enough love between man and man. If a man scorns nature, do you think he could care about words? They are led to this opinion particularly because in that part of the world the treaties and pacts of princes are not observed very faithfully. For in Europe, and especially those parts controlled by the faith and religion of Christ, the majesty of treaties is everywhere holy and unbreakable. This is partly because of the justice and goodness of the princes, partly because of the reverence and fear felt for the popes, who most religiously perform whatever they undertake and bid all other princes keep exactly to their promises, while those who seek to evade them they coerce with the severity of their pontifical censure. For they quite rightly think it most disgraceful if there is no faith in the treaties of men who are called by the special name of "faithful."[29]

But in that new world, as far separated from us by the equator as by their way of life and character, there is no confidence in treaties. The more numerous and sacred are the rites tying the knot, the more quickly is it undone. They easily find some verbal quibble, and occasionally formulate treaties deliberately in ambiguous language, so that they can never be bound by firm ties without having some loophole for wriggling out of the treaty and their good faith at the same time. If they found that this cunning, or rather this fraud and deceit, had played a part in an agreement between private individuals, they would look angry and shout "Sacrilege! They deserve the gallows!" while all the time they pride themselves on having given the same advice to their princes. This makes all justice seem either a lowly and humble virtue, far below princely eminence, or else capable of two divisions: The one befits the common people, going on foot and crawling along the ground, unable to leap over barriers, restricted with

---

[29] This heavily sarcastic passage is directed at, among other targets, the shifty diplomacy of Popes Alexander VI (reigned 1492–1503) and Julius II (reigned 1503–1513).

many fetters. The other is the virtue of princes, more august than the popular kind and much freer, which is allowed to do anything it wants.

As I said, I think that the reason why the Utopians make no treaties lies in the character of the princes there who keep their treaties so badly. Perhaps they would change their opinion if they lived here. However, they think that even if they are scrupulously observed, yet it was bad that the habit of making treaties started in the first place. This is the reason why nations think themselves born enemies and adversaries, just as if there were no natural bond uniting two peoples separated merely by a hill or a stream. Consequently such people think it right to plot the other's destruction if no treaties stand in the way. Even when they have entered upon a treaty they imagine that no friendship has been formed, rather that they still have freedom to plunder as far as the treaty has not been carefully worded and contains no sufficiently precise clause to ban this. But the Utopians are of the contrary opinion, that no one must be considered an enemy who has done no harm, that the fellowship of nature acts as a treaty, and that a better and more powerful bond exists between men from kindness than from treaties, that is to say, from the spirit rather than from words.

CHAPTER EIGHT

ON WARFARE

They absolutely detest war and battle as being quite beastly and employed by no kind of beast as constantly as man. Contrary to the custom of practically all nations, they think nothing as inglorious as the glory gained from war. The Utopians, both men and women, on fixed days give themselves to constant military training to keep themselves in practice for the time when war is necessary. Nevertheless, they do not deliberately look for war, except to protect their own territory, or to drive off an enemy who has invaded the land of their friends, or out of pity for a people oppressed by tyranny to free them with their own forces from the yoke and slavery of the tyrant, as they do out of compassion. Yet they give aid to their friends not always to allow them to defend themselves, but sometimes they help them pay back and avenge wrongs already done to them. But this they do only if they themselves are consulted while the matter is still fresh. If they approve of the cause and are satisfied that restitution has been demanded but not made, then they take the responsibility of waging war. They do not make this decision only when an enemy has come on a plundering expedition. Their response is much more violent when their friends' merchants in any country, either under cover of unjust laws or by the misrepresentation of good laws, suffer an unjust accusation under the name of justice. This was precisely the reason for the war that the Utopians waged a little before our time on behalf of the Nephelogetes against the Alaopolites.[30] For in the land of the Alaopolites some merchants of the Nephelogetes had suffered injustice, as the Utopians thought, under the guise of justice. To the power

---

[30] *Nephelogetes* means "born in the clouds"; *Alaopolites* means either "without a country" or "blind."

and malice of both sides were added the support and aid of neighboring countries too. The injustice, if such it was, was avenged by so savage a war, that of the most flourishing nations some were shattered and others were severely beaten, and these evils upon evils were finally ended by the slavery and surrender of the Alaopolites. As the Utopians were not fighting for themselves, by this surrender the Alaopolites came under the power of the Nephelogetes, although they were in no way to be compared to the Alaopolites at the height of their power.

So keenly do the Utopians avenge wrongs done to their friends even in money matters, although they are not so quick about their own. If they themselves are ever cheated and deprived of their goods, as long as there is no physical violence, their anger merely takes the form of abstaining from trade with that nation until satisfaction is given. This is not because they care less for their own citizens than for their allies, but yet they are more annoyed if their allies are cheated of money than if they themselves suffer this. For their friends' merchants lose their own private possessions and consequently suffer greatly by the loss. But their own citizens lose nothing except what belongs to the state and what was in great abundance and excess at home. Otherwise it would not have been sent abroad. Therefore no one feels the loss. So they think it excessively cruel to avenge a loss by the deaths of many men, when none of them feels any disadvantage from that loss in his life or way of living. But if any of their citizens are maimed in any country or killed, whether that is done by public or private plan, they investigate the matter through envoys. Unless the offenders are handed over, they cannot be restrained from declaring war immediately. If the offenders are handed over, they are punished with death or slavery.

If they gain a bloody victory, they are not merely sorry but even ashamed, considering it folly to have paid too great a price for merchandise, no matter how precious it is. They are very proud if they can conquer and overcome the enemy by guile and deceit. For this they arrange a public triumph and erect a trophy as if a great battle had been won. Then they boast that they have behaved manfully and courageously when they gain a victory in the way possible to no other animal than man, that is, by strength of mind. For bodily strength is the weapon of bears, lions, boars, wolves, dogs and the other beasts. Although most of them surpass us in strength and ferocity, they are all inferior to us in intelligence and reason.

The Utopians have only one aim in war—to gain that object which would have prevented them from going to war if they had previously won it. Or, if circumstances prevent this, they exact so terrible a penalty from their enemy that fear restrains others from attempting the same. These are the objectives they have, and these they aim at first of all. Yet they are more concerned with avoiding danger than winning praise and glory. So, as soon as they have declared war, they have many proclamations set up secretly all at one time in the most conspicuous parts of the enemy territory, signed with their public seal. In these they promise huge rewards if anyone kills the enemy leader. Then they announce smaller, but not inconsiderable, rewards for the head of each man whose name is contained in that same notice. These are the people they consider responsible, after their leader, for the hostile action against them. Whatever reward they announce for a killer is doubled if he brings any of the proscribed[31] to them alive. They also try to bring over the proscribed persons themselves to work against their former allies, by the same rewards with an additional promise of impunity.

Therefore their enemies soon come to suspect others, and are not faithful or trusting among themselves, but live in the greatest fear and danger. For it is well known that frequently a good part of the proscribed and, above all, the leader himself have been betrayed by those in whom they placed the greatest trust. So easily are men persuaded to any crime by gifts. The Utopians set no limit upon these gifts, but remembering the peril to which they are inciting others, they see to it that the greatness of the danger is compensated by the size of the recompense. Therefore they promise not merely great amounts of gold, but also estates with great returns to enjoy as their own forever in safe places among friends. They keep their promises most faithfully.

This way of bidding for and buying an enemy is held in bad repute by other nations, as being a cruel crime of a depraved mind. But the Utopians think it most praiseworthy and a mark of prudence, since they can rid themselves of great wars in this way without a single battle. They also consider it an act of mercy and compassion, since by the death of a few guilty persons they save the lives of many innocent who would have fallen in the fighting, on their own side and on their enemy's. They feel sorry for the common crowd of the enemy almost as much as their own, since they realize that they do not come to war of their own accord, but are driven to it by the madness of their leaders.

If no progress is made by these means, they sow and foster seeds of discord by bringing the leader's brother or one of the nobles to hope that he will win control of the country. If domestic factions fail, they stir up their enemy's neighbors and set them in conflict by digging up some old legal claim such as kings are never without. They promise support for the war and supply money plentifully, but their citizens sparingly. For they regard them as so precious and value them so highly that they would not willingly exchange any of their citizens for the enemy leader. But they pay out gold and silver lavishly, as this is the only purpose for which they keep them. For their lives would be no less comfortable even if they spent it all. In fact, besides their wealth in Utopia itself, they have unlimited treasure abroad, since, as I said before, very many nations are in their debt. So they hire soldiers from all lands and send them to the war, especially from the Zapoletes.[32] This nation is five hundred miles distant from Utopia toward the east, and it is rough, wild and savage. They prefer forests and craggy mountains, where they were brought up. They are a hard people, able to endure heat, cold and toil, unacquainted with luxuries, not concerned with agriculture. They pay little attention to their houses and clothing, devoting their energies merely to raising cattle. They live mainly by hunting and plunder. They are a nation born only for war, eagerly seeking any oppor-

---

[31] Outlawed by public proclamation.

[32] The name means "ready to sell"; More is thinking of the Swiss, many of whom served as mercenaries at the time.

tunity to wage war, and gladly embracing it once it is found. They go out in great numbers and for a low price offer their services to anyone needing soldiers. They know only this one art of life—that by which death is sought. They fight bitterly and faithfully for those under whom they are serving. But they do not bind themselves for any fixed length of time. They take sides on the condition that on the next day they will side even with the enemy if they offer a greater wage. On the next day after that they come back again if lured by a slightly higher sum. It is only rarely that there is a war in which a good number of them is not in each army. So it happens every day that men joined by ties of blood, who lived in great concord when hired on the same side, shortly after are separated to different sides and clash in war. With great ferocity, forgetting their birth and friendship, they plunge their swords into one another. No other reason incites them to this mutual slaughter than the trifling sum of money paid to them by opposing leaders. They are so careful about this money that if only one penny is added to their daily wage they are quite ready to change sides. So quickly have they drunk in avarice. Yet it is no use to them. For what they earn by their blood they immediately squander in luxury, and this luxury itself is not of a very high quality.

This nation fights for the Utopians against anyone, since they are hired at a price that cannot be matched anywhere else. For just as they seek good men to use, so the Utopians seek these worst of men to abuse. When necessity demands, they incite them with great promises and expose them to the greatest dangers, from which usually a great part never return to claim their rewards. To those that are left they faithfully pay what they promised so that they will be inspired to similar acts of daring. Nor do they care how many of these they send to their death, as they believe that they would earn the deepest thanks of the human race if they could cleanse the earth of all the filth of a people so foul and wicked.

After these, they use the forces of the people on whose behalf they are taking up arms, then auxiliary squadrons of their other friends. Last of all they join to them their own citizens. One of them, a man of proved bravery, they put in charge of the whole army. They also create two substitutes for him. If he is safe, they are both without any office; but if he is captured or killed, one of them succeeds to his position by a sort of inheritance. If it is rendered necessary by the many fortunes of war, the third man succeeds him to prevent the army being thrown into confusion because of the danger of its leader. A levy is held from each city out of those who volunteer. For no one is thrust out into military service against his will. They are convinced that if anyone is timid by nature, besides being no use in action, he will also make his companions afraid. But if any war presses close to their own country, provided that they are physically fit, they mix such cowards with men of better quality and put them on board ship, or else position them at intervals along the walls, from which they have nowhere to flee. So their fear is overcome by their sense of shame in front of their own people, the presence of the enemy and the impossibility of flight. And often extreme necessity turns into bravery.

Just as none of them is dragged to war against his will, so they do not prevent women who wish from accompanying their husbands on service. In fact, they encourage them and urge them on with praise. The women who go out are positioned each with her own husband together in line of battle. Also each man is surrounded by his children and relatives, so that those whom nature especially urges to supply help to one another may be of mutual assistance nearby. A husband who returns without his wife, or a wife without her husband, is held in the greatest disgrace, as is a son who returns after losing his father. So if the Utopians themselves come to be engaged in close fighting, as long as the enemy stand their ground, a long and bitter battle ensues, which is decided only by absolute destruction. As I have said, they try every means to avoid having to fight themselves, as long as they can wage war through the agency of mercenaries. But when they cannot help going into battle, they are fearless in handling what they wisely avoided as long as they could. They do not grow fierce at the first encounter, but rather by delaying they gradually gain their strength and become so resolute that they can more quickly be killed than repulsed. For that security of a livelihood that each has at home, and the absence of all anxious care for their families (a worry that breaks brave spirits everywhere), give them a nobility of spirit that disdains defeat. Their military training also gives them confidence. Finally, they are given courage by their right beliefs with which they have been filled from childhood by their training and the laws of the state. With this courage they do not hold life so cheap as to throw it away to no purpose, nor so outrageously dear as to cling to it greedily and shamefully when honor persuades them to lay it down.

When the battle is at its height and raging on all sides, a band of chosen young men sworn to one purpose makes for the enemy leader. They openly attack him, as well as creeping up on him stealthily. They aim at him from near and far, and assail him with a long, unbroken line, with fresh men constantly taking the place of those exhausted. If he does not flee, he rarely escapes death or being captured alive by his enemies. If the Utopians gain the victory themselves, they never follow it up with slaughter. For they prefer to capture those who flee rather than kill them. But they never give chase without leaving behind one line of troops in full array under their standards. They cling to this rule so firmly that, if they gain victory with their last line after being defeated in all other sections, they prefer to allow all the enemy to escape rather than throw their own ranks into confusion by giving chase. For they remember an experience that has been not infrequent with them: after the main body of their whole army had been defeated and crushed, the enemy were exultant at their victory and chased the fleeing troops in all different directions; a few of the Utopian reserves watching for their opportunities suddenly attacked the scattered and straggling enemy, who were careless from an unwarranted sense of security. So they changed the outcome of the whole battle, and by wresting so certain and undoubted a victory from their hands, though conquered they conquered the conquerors in turn.

It is not easy to say whether they are more cunning in setting ambushes or cautious in avoiding them. You would imagine they are getting ready to flee, when nothing is further from their minds. On the other hand, when they do plan flight, you would never suspect it was in their minds. For if they feel that they are being pressed too hard because of superior numbers or the unfavorable ground, then by night they shift camp in complete silence. Or they use some stratagem to deceive the enemy. Or else by day

they retreat so gradually, keeping such good order, that it is just as dangerous to attack them when they are retreating as when they are pressing
hard. They fortify their camps most carefully with a very deep and wide
ditch, and throw the earth so excavated on the inside. Nor do they use
slaves for this work. The task is done by the hands of the soldiers themselves and the whole army is engaged in the work, with the exception of
those who are on armed guard in front of the rampart for sudden attacks.
With so many helpers, they finish the large and extensive fortifications
more quickly than would ever be believed.

They use armor which is strong enough to take blows, yet is so suited to
any movement or gesture that they do not feel its weight even when swimming. For right at the beginning of their military training they get used to
swimming in full armor. For long-range weapons they have arrows, which
the infantry and cavalry can dispatch with great force as well as accuracy.
For short-range weapons they use not swords, but axes, which are deadly
with their sharp edge or sheer weight, according as the users slice or merely
strike. They are extremely clever at inventing engines of war. When they
have made them they are most careful to hide them in case their discovery,
before they are needed, might make them ridiculous rather than useful. In
manufacturing them, their chief aim is to make them easy to transport and
suitable for maneuvering.

When they have made a temporary truce with their enemies, they observe it so strictly that they do not break it even when provoked. They do
not devastate the enemy's land or burn his crops. In fact, they are careful
not even to trample them down with the feet of their soldiers or horses, as
far as possible, since they believe that the crops are growing for their own
use. They never harm an unarmed man, unless he is a spy. If a city surrenders to them they protect it. If they take one by storm, they do not plunder
it, but kill the men responsible for hindering the surrender and reduce the
other defenders to slavery. They leave untouched all the civilian population. If they discover that anyone advocated surrender, they give him a
share of the property of the condemned. They distribute the rest among
the auxiliary troops. For of the Utopians themselves no one takes any of the
booty.

But when a war is finished, they charge their expenses not to the friends
on whose behalf they incurred them, but to the vanquished. On this account they make them pay partly in money, which they put aside for similar
military purposes, and partly in land in the territory of the defeated country, to belong to the Utopians forever and provide them with a considerable revenue. They have revenues of this kind now in many countries. They
were obtained gradually for various reasons and have grown to over seven
hundred thousand ducats[33] a year. To these they send out some of their
citizens as financial agents, to live in great splendor in the foreign country
and play the part of millionaires. But yet there is plenty left to be paid into
the treasury, unless they prefer to lend it to the country producing it. They
often do this as long as the others have need of it. It hardly ever happens
that they ask for the whole amount back. They assign part of these landed
estates to the men who at the Utopians' request undergo the kind of danger

---

[33] Worth about 330,000 English pounds during More's time—a vast sum of money.

I described previously. If any king takes up arms against them and is ready to invade their territory, they immediately rush to oppose him in full strength outside their boundaries. For they do not like to make war on their own soil, nor is any necessity great enough to compel them to let foreign auxiliaries into their own island.

CHAPTER NINE
ON THE RELIGIONS OF THE UTOPIANS

They have different religions not merely in the island but even in single cities. Some worship the sun as a god, others the moon or any of the planets. Some look up to a man, not only as a god but as the highest god, if he was famed for virtue or glory long ago. But by far the largest section of the population, and the wisest too, adheres to none of these beliefs, but thinks that there is a certain single divinity, unknown, eternal, boundless, inexplicable, beyond the understanding of the human mind, diffused through the whole of this universe in virtue,[34] not bulk. They call him "the father." To this one divinity they attribute the beginnings, increases, advances, changes and ends of all things. They do not accord divine honors to anyone else.

Although all the others have different beliefs, yet they agree with them on this point: they believe that there is one Supreme Being who is responsible for the creation and protection of the universe. They all agree in calling him Mythra[35] in their native tongue, but they disagree in having different conceptions of him. Each man thinks that whatever he considers the Supreme Power is that selfsame person to whose divinity and majesty alone all nations assign the sum of all things. But they are gradually departing from that multiplicity of superstitions and coming together to that one religion which reason judges to surpass all others.[36] It is quite certain that the others would have disappeared long ago, except that when anyone planned to change his religion, whatever ill fortune occurred, he interpreted it in his terror not as a chance happening but as a sign from heaven, as if the power whose worship was being abandoned was punishing the wicked design against itself.

The Utopians heard from us the name of Christ, his teaching, his ways and his miracles, also the equally wonderful fortitude of the martyrs, whose blood willingly shed brought over so many countries to their beliefs in all parts of the world. You would not believe how readily they agreed to this, whether God was secretly inspiring them or our religion seemed closest to the belief most prevalent among them. Yet I believe they were also brought to this opinion because they heard that Christ favored communal living[37] among his followers and that this was still the practice in real Christian communities.[38] But whatever impelled them, many came over to our religion and were washed with the water of baptism.

There were four of us left, as two of our company had died, and unfor-

---

[34] Active power.   [35] The Persian god of light.

[36] That is, the religion ascribed a little earlier to the "wisest."

[37] On the communism of the early Christians, see Acts of the Apostles 2:44–45 and 4:32–35.

[38] Monasteries and convents.

tunately none of us was a priest.[39] The Utopians were initiated in the other points of Christianity, but still were without those sacraments which in our world only priests can supply. Yet they understand and make this their most earnest prayer. In fact, they even debate heatedly among themselves whether one of their own number could be chosen to receive the order of priesthood without the sending of a Christian bishop. And certainly it seemed as if they were going to choose one. But they had not yet chosen him when I left. Those who do not believe in Christianity nevertheless deter no one from it, nor attack a man instructed in it, except that one of our company was punished in my presence. He had been recently baptized, and much against our advice was discoursing in public on the worship of Christ with more enthusiasm than wisdom. So fervent did he grow that he not only extolled our beliefs above others, but absolutely condemned all others. He called the beliefs profane and their adherents impious and sacrilegious, deserving to be punished with everlasting fire. When he had been speaking like this for some time, they arrested him, then prosecuted and convicted him not for scorning a religion but for stirring up discord among the people. The penalty was exile. For it is one of their oldest established laws that no one should be penalized for his religious beliefs.

For right at the beginning King Utopus had heard that before his arrival the inhabitants fought constantly among themselves on religious issues, and he had observed that the reason for his conquest was that all the different sects were in strife and so fought singly for their country. So after his victory he first of all passed a law that everyone should be allowed to follow whatever religion he pleased; that a man might attempt to bring others over to his religion only to the extent of offering reasons calmly and soberly, without destroying others bitterly if he could not gain his end by persuasion; that he should not use any force and should refrain from abuse. If anyone goes beyond the limit in religious dispute, he is punished by exile or slavery.

Utopus introduced this law not merely to preserve peace, which he saw completely overthrown by constant strife and inextinguishable hatred, but also because he thought that such an enactment would further the cause of religion. He was never rash enough to give any definite view on religion, as if he was not sure whether God, desiring various and manifold worship, gave different inspiration to different people. But he thought it arrogant and foolish to demand by violence and threats that your views should be accepted by everyone. Even if one alone were true and all others idle, he easily foresaw that, provided the matter is handled with wisdom and moderation, the force of truth must eventually arise and stand out; but if there is armed strife and confusion, since the worst men are the most stubborn, the best and most holy religion would be overthrown by the empty superstitions, like crops among thorns and weeds. So he left the whole matter undecided and left each man the liberty to believe what he wished. But he issued severe and careful restrictions against anyone's so falling away from

---

[39] Of the seven Roman Catholic sacraments, two (Baptism and Matrimony) could be administered if necessary without a priest. Three (the Eucharist; Penance, or confession; and Extreme Unction, the rite for the dying) ordinarily required a priest. Two (Confirmation and Holy Orders, or the ordination of priests) required a bishop.

the dignity of human nature as to believe that the soul dies with the body or that the world revolves by chance without divine providence. And therefore they believe that after this life vice is punished and virtue rewarded. If anyone takes the contrary view, they do not even count him as a human being, since he has lowered the sublime nature of his soul to the cheapness of a beast's body. Much less do they consider him a citizen, as he would not have the slightest respect for laws and customs if fear did not compel him. For who can doubt that if a man has no fear outside the laws, no hope beyond the body, he will try to evade by stealth or overthrow by violence the public laws of his country, while gratifying his private desires. So if a man is of this opinion, he is given no share in public office, is entrusted with no magistracy and is put in charge of no public administration. Therefore he is despised on all sides as having a lazy and mean nature. Yet they inflict no actual punishment upon him, as they are convinced that no man is capable of believing anything he chooses. Nor do they force him by threats to conceal his mind. They do not tolerate deceit and lies, but hold them in the greatest detestation as being nearest to fraud. But they do prevent him from discussing his opinion, although this applies only to dispute before the common people. For they not merely allow but even encourage him to have private discussion with the priests and worthy citizens, being convinced that that madness will eventually yield to reason.

There are others of no inconsiderable number who are not so prohibited, as their beliefs are not entirely devoid of reason and they themselves are not evil men. These hold to a widely different error in believing that dumb animals too have eternal souls, although they are not to be compared to ours in dignity nor are they born to equal felicity. For they all believe as a sure and certain fact that man will enjoy such happiness, that while bewailing sickness, they lament no one's death, unless they see anyone being dragged from life in sadness and against his will. This they consider a very bad omen, as if the soul has given up all hope from a guilty conscience and is afraid to leave because of some hidden foreboding of imminent punishment. They also think that a man's arrival will not be welcome to God, if he does not run willingly when summoned, but has to be dragged protesting and unwilling. So those who witness this kind of death are appalled and conduct his funeral in sad silence. After praying for God's mercy on his soul and beseeching Him to pardon his weakness out of His kindness, they cover the corpse with earth.

On the other hand, whoever departs this life eagerly, full of good hope, is mourned by no one. They accompany his funeral with singing, commending his soul to God with great affection. At last they burn the body with reverence rather than grief, and set up a stone on the spot engraved with the dead man's titles. When they return home they recall his character and achievements, and no part of his life is told more often or more gladly than his happy death. This recollection of goodness they think is a most effective spur to virtue for the living and a most acceptable reverence for the dead. They believe that the dead are present at conversations about themselves, although they are invisible to dull mortal eyes. For it would not be appropriate to the lot of the blessed to be deprived of the freedom to journey where they wish, and it would be ungrateful to have thrown away all desire to see their friends, who were bound to them during life by mutual love and charity. They imagine that in good men, this love (like the other blessings) is increased rather than diminished after death. So they believe that the dead move among the living, as witnesses of their words and deeds. Therefore they go about their tasks with more confidence, relying upon these overseers. The belief in the presence of their ancestors also keeps them from secret dishonesty.

They completely discountenance and laugh at augury[40] and the other forms of divination springing from idle superstition, which are much in favor in other countries. But miracles, which arise by no natural agency, they respect as being the work and witness of the presence of God. They say that they have frequent miracles in their country, and on occasion, when important matters of state are in doubt, by public intercession and with absolute confidence they obtain and receive them.

They consider the contemplation and praise of nature an act of worship pleasing to God. But there are a good many people who, from their love of religion, ignore learning and are not concerned to acquire any knowledge, although they do not give themselves up to idleness. For they believe that future happiness after death is earned by work and kind actions to others. So some minister to the sick, others repair the roads, clean out ditches, mend bridges, dig up turf, sand or stones, fell trees and cut them up, transport wood, grain and other commodities to the cities in carts, and in both public and private life they act as servants and even more than slaves. For whatever task there is anywhere that is hard, difficult or filthy, which puts off others because of the toil, disgust or sheer impossibility, this they take entirely upon themselves with a willing and happy heart. They procure leisure for others, but spend their own lives in constant work and toil. However, they do not blame or rebuke the lives of others, nor praise their own. The lower they go in their servile work, the higher is the honor accorded to them by all.

Yet these people are divided into two sects. The first consists of those who do not marry and who keep away from sex, as well as from eating flesh, some of them from the meat of all living creatures. They absolutely renounce the pleasures of the present life as if they were harmful, and give all their attention to those of the next life by vigils and sweat, when in the meantime they are keen and energetic with the hope of soon winning the life to come. The other sect is just as desirous of work, but they prefer marriage. They do not despise the solace it brings, and believe that they owe a work to nature and children to their country. They avoid no pleasure, provided that it does not delay them in their work. They like the flesh of four-footed beasts, if only because they think that this food renders them stronger for any task. This sect the Utopians judge wiser, while they think the other sect more holy. They would laugh at them if they attempted a rational defense of their preference for celibacy over marriage and for the hard life over the easy. But since they claim they are led to it by religion, they look up to them and revere them. They have no more anxious concern than to avoid any forthright pronouncement on any religion. So this is what the people are like to whom in their own language they give the special name "bouthrescas," which may be translated as "religious."

---

[40]Supernatural foretelling of the future; divination.

They have priests who are very saintly and hence very few. For they do not have more than thirteen in each city, with an equal number of churches, except when they go to war. Then seven of them set out with the army and in the meanwhile their places are filled with others. But when they return, each takes up his old position. Those who are above the requisite number, until they duly succeed priests who die, are companions to the Bishop. He is the head of them all. They are chosen by the people, just like the other magistrates, by secret ballot to avoid party strife. When elected, they are consecrated by the college of priests. These are in charge of divine affairs, look after religious matters and act as moral censors. It is considered a great disgrace for anyone to be summoned or rebuked by them for loose living.

Their function is to exhort and admonish, but it is for the President and the other magistrates to check and punish the guilty. However, the priests are allowed to excommunicate anyone they find to be shamefully wicked. This is the greatest punishment they can suffer. For they are afflicted with severe disgrace and are tortured by an inward terror of religion, fearing that even their bodies will not be safe for long. If they do not quickly profess their repentance to the priests, they are arrested and punished by the Senate for impiety.

The priests instruct the boys and youths, and a concern for morals and virtue comes before that for learning. For they are very careful to instill immediately into the tender and obedient minds of the children good beliefs which are useful for preserving the republic. When these beliefs have settled in them as children, they follow them throughout life and prove extremely useful for maintaining the condition of the republic, which can be destroyed only by vices, and these are born from wicked beliefs.

Women also may be priests, but more rarely than men, and even then only aged widows are chosen. The male priests have as wives the most distinguished ladies in the country. For among the Utopians no magistrate is given greater honor, so much so that even if the priests commit a crime, they are not brought before a court. They are left merely to God and themselves. For they do not think it right to touch them with mortal hand, however criminal they may be, since they have so especially been consecrated to God, as a kind of offering. It is easier for them to observe this custom, as there are so few priests and such care is taken in choosing them. It does not easily happen that a man degenerates to corruption and vice, when he was advanced as the most virtuous of good men to a position of such dignity, with regard to his virtue alone. Even if this did happen (as human nature is so changeable), yet as they are so few and have no power except honor, there would be no great fear for the public safety from them. They have priests so few and far between to prevent the dignity of the order, held in such veneration by them now, from becoming debased by sharing their honor with many. This is all the more so since they think it difficult to find many people good enough for that dignity. To bear this office it is not enough to have average goodness.

Nor are they honored more among their own people than in foreign countries. The following tale will make this clear and also explain its origin. For when their forces are engaged in battle, the priests kneel down a short distance away, dressed in their sacred robes. They hold up their hands to heaven and pray above all for peace and secondly for victory for their country, but a bloody victory for neither side. When the Utopians are winning, they rush into the line of battle and stop them from showing cruelty to the vanquished foe. For an enemy merely to have seen them and addressed them in person is enough to save his life. To touch their flowing robes protects his other possessions from all outrage of war. Therefore with all nations they have acquired such veneration and so much true majesty that frequently they win no less safety from the enemy for their own men than they had brought to the enemy from their own citizens. For it is well known that on occasion, when their own troops have been pushed back and matters have looked hopeless, with the Utopians in flight and the enemy rushing in to kill and plunder, the slaughter has been stopped by the intervention of the priests, the troops of both sides separated and peace settled and arranged on equal terms. There has never been any race so fierce, cruel and barbarous as not to consider the priests' persons sacrosanct and untouchable.

For feast days they have the first and last days of each month and year, dividing the year into months. They measure the months by the course of the moon and the year by the sun. In their own language they call the first days Cynemerns and the last days Trapemerns.[41] These names mean "First Feast" and "Last Feast."

Their churches are wonderful to see. For they are not merely examples of excellent craftsmanship but, as was necessary because of the small number of churches, they can hold an immense number of people. But they are all fairly dark. They say this was done not from ignorance of how to build, but on the advice of the priests, as they think too much light scatters men's thoughts, while a darker, dim light gathers together the mind and increases devotion. Since religion is not the same for them all, and yet they all take the form, however varied and manifold they are, of coming by different ways to the goal of worship of the divine nature, therefore there is nothing seen or heard in their churches which would not fit them all alike. If any sect has its own special rite, each man performs it in his own home. The public rites they manage in such a way as to take nothing from the private.

Therefore no image of a god is seen in any church. So everyone is free to imagine God as he wishes according to his own religion. They have no special name for God except Mythra. By this name they all agree upon the single nature of a divine majesty, whatever it may be. Only those prayers are used which anyone could utter without offending his particular sect.

So on the days of the Last Feasts they come together to church in the evening, still fasting, to give thanks to God for the successful completion of the month or year of which it is the last day. The following day is the First Feast. They flock to the churches in the morning to pray for a happy and successful outcome of the year or month they are beginning with that feast day. But on the Last Feasts, before they go to church, at home the wives kneel before their husbands, and children before their parents, and confess that they have sinned by some actual deed or else by some carelessness in their duty. They then beg forgiveness for their mistake. So if any cloud

[41] The Greek derivations suggest the literal meanings, respectively, "dog-days" and "turning-days."

of discord has arisen at home, it is blown away by such atonement. So they take part in the services at church with a pure and peaceful mind. For it is an offense to be present with a troubled mind. For this reason, people do not go to the rites if they are aware of harboring anger or hatred against anyone, until they have become reconciled and purged their feelings, for fear of swift and great punishment.

When they come to church, the men sit on the right, and the women on their own on the left. They seat themselves so that the male members of each household sit in front of the head of the house and the females in front of his wife. In this way it is arranged that the gestures of every member in public are observed by those by whose authority and discipline they are controlled at home. They are also careful to see that a younger person is everywhere near an older, in case children put in the charge of other children should spend in childish frivolity the time in which they ought to be forming a religious fear toward God, a great and almost unique incitement to virtue.

They kill no animal in sacrifices, nor do they believe that the divine mercy delights in blood and slaughter. For He gave animals life that they might live. They burn incense and other sweet-smelling things. They also carry a large number of candles, not that they fail to realize that such things contribute no more to the divine nature than do men's prayers, but this harmless kind of worship pleases them. And by these scents and lights and the other ceremonies, men feel somehow that they are lifted up and rise to worship God with more fervent mind. In church the people wear white. The priest has many-colored robes, wonderful in workmanship and design, although the material is not very valuable. For they are not embroidered with gold or set with precious stones, but they are worked so cleverly and expertly from different feathers that no costly material could equal the value of the work. Moreover, in these birds' feathers and the definite arrangement they have in the priest's vestments, they say that there are contained certain mysteries. The priests zealously teach the interpretation of these feathers, and when it is known, people are reminded of God's goodness to them, the reverence they owe in turn to God, and their duties to one another.

When the priest first comes out of the vestry[42] in these vestments, they all immediately fall to the floor in reverence. There is such profound silence on all sides that the very scene inspires a kind of fear as if some divinity were present. They lie like this for a little while, and at a sign from the priest they stand up. Then they sing God's praises to the accompaniment of musical instruments, which are mainly of a form different from that seen in our world. Most of them far exceed ours in sweetness, but yet some of them are not even to be compared with ours. But in one matter they are clearly far ahead of us. All their music, whether it is played on instruments or performed by the human voice, so imitates and represents natural feelings that the sound is adapted to the subject. Whether it is a prayer or a tune of gladness, peace, trouble, sadness or anger, it so reproduces the feeling by the form of the melody that it affects the listeners' minds in an amazing way, sinks into them and inflames their spirits.

---

[42] The room where the priest puts on his vestments.

At the end the priest and people together recite solemn prayers in a fixed form of words. These are so composed that what they all say together, each man may apply privately to himself. In these everyone recognizes God as the author of creation and guidance of the world, and of all good things as well. He thanks God for so many benefits received, but specifically that by God's kindness he chanced to be born in that most blessed republic and that he was taught that religion which he hopes is truest. It is his prayer that God's goodness will bring it to his knowledge if he is in any way wrong in this, and if there is anything better than his country and religion and more acceptable to God. For he is ready to follow, he says, wherever God leads him. But if this form of republic is best and his religion most correct, then he prays God to grant him steadfastness and to lead all other men to that way of life and to the same belief about God, unless there is anything in this variety of religions that pleases God's inscrutable will. Finally he prays that he may have an easy death before being received to Him—how soon or late he does not dare to suggest. Although, if this does not offend His majesty, he would much rather die a difficult death and come to God than be kept from Him any longer in the most prosperous of lives. After this prayer they again fall to the floor. Shortly afterward they stand up and go to lunch. The remainder of the day they pass in games and military exercises.

I have described to you as truthfully as I could the form of the republic which I judge not merely the best, but the only one that can rightfully claim the name of republic. For elsewhere men talk of public good, but look after their private good. In Utopia, where nothing is private, they really do public business. In both places there is good reason for acting as they do. For elsewhere, everyone knows that however prosperous the republic may be, he will starve of hunger if he does not make some separate provision for himself. And so he is forced to believe that he ought to take account of himself rather than the people, that is, others. On the other hand, in Utopia, where all possessions are in common, everyone is certain that, provided that care is taken to keep the public barns full, everyone will have whatever he wants for his private use. For there is no unfair distribution of property, there are no paupers or beggars there, and though no one has anything, yet all are rich. What greater riches can there be than a life in happiness and peace, with all cares removed, without being worried about one's own food, or being harassed by one's wife's complaints and demands, or being afraid of poverty for one's son or anxious about a daughter's dowry? Instead they are assured of the livelihood and happiness of themselves and all their family, wife, sons, grandchildren, great-grandchildren, great-great-grandchildren and all the long list of descendants that nobles assume. Care is also taken of people who are incapable of the work they once did, just as much as for those still able.

At this point I should like someone to dare compare with this equity the justice of other nations. I'll be damned if I can find any trace of justice or equity among them. For what sort of justice is this when some noble or goldsmith[43] or moneylender or any one of those who do either nothing or

---

[43] Goldsmiths at the time often performed the functions of bankers.

else nothing very necessary to the republic achieves a glorious and splendid life either by idleness or unnecessary business? Meanwhile a laborer, carter, smith or farmer suffers heavy and constant toil that beasts could hardly endure, work so necessary that no republic could last without it for even one year. Yet they provide so poor a living for themselves and lead such a miserable life that the condition of beasts might seem far preferable. For the animals do not suffer such constant toil, and their food is not much worse and is pleasanter to them, nor do they meanwhile have any fear for the future. But men are incited for the present by barren and unprofitable work, and killed off by the recollection of an impoverished old age. For as they do not earn enough each day to keep them for that day, they certainly cannot have any surplus to put away for their old age each day.

Is this not an unjust and ungrateful republic which lavishes such riches upon the nobles, as they call them, and the goldsmiths and the others of that kind, who are idlers or mere flatterers and inventors of empty pleasures? Yet it makes no kindly provision for farmers, coal miners, laborers, carters and smiths, without whom there would be no republic at all. The republic abuses their labor when they are young and healthy, but when they are slow with age and sickness and utterly destitute, she forgets the sleepless nights they have spent and does not remember their many great benefits. Instead she shows her ingratitude by rewarding them with a wretched death. On top of this, from the daily wage of the poor, the rich wear something away every day, not merely by private fraud but even by public laws. So while it previously seemed unjust to give unkindness in return for good service to the state, the rich have twisted this and by passing laws made it justice.[44]

And so, when I examine and consider all the flourishing republics in the world today, believe me, nothing comes to mind except a conspiracy of the rich, who seek their own advantage under the name and title of the republic. They also devise and think up all sorts of ways and means to hold on to their ill-gotten gains with no fear of losing them, and then to hire the labor of all the poor at the lowest price and abuse them. When once the rich have decreed that these devices are to be observed in the public name (in other words, in the name of the poor too), they then become laws. But when vile men with their insatiable greed have shared among themselves what would have been enough for everybody, even so they are very far from the prosperity of the Utopian republic. Since all greed for money and also the use of it have been removed in Utopia, how great a burden of troubles has been cut back and how great a harvest of crimes has been torn up by the roots! For who does not realize that fraud, theft, plunder, quarrels, brawls, discord, sedition, murder, treachery, poisoning—all these are avenged by daily punishment, not checked; but if money is killed, they will die with it? Also fear, worry, care, toil and sleepless nights will also perish at the same moment as money. Yes, poverty itself, which alone seemed to lack money, would immediately decrease if money were absolutely abolished everywhere.

---

[44] In More's time, recent laws governing labor favored the employers' rather than the workers' interests.

To picture this more clearly, consider a barren and unfruitful year in which famine has taken away many thousand men. I firmly maintain that at the end of that shortage an examination of rich men's barns would reveal so much grain that, if it had been distributed among those killed by starvation, no one at all would have noticed the poor harvest. So easily could a living be made if that blessed thing money (a brilliant discovery to open up the way to a living) did not on its own shut off from us the path to a living. I am quite sure that the rich feel this too and are well aware how better a state it would be to lack nothing essential rather than abound in superfluities, to be taken from countless cares rather than be besieged by great wealth. Nor does it occur to me to doubt that the whole world could easily have been brought long ago to the laws of Utopia by the consideration of each man's advantage or by the authority of our Saviour Christ, who, with his great wisdom, could not fail to know what was best and, with his great kindness, could not fail to advise what he knew to be best. This would have been possible, if that single beast—the chief and parent of all plagues—pride did not fight against it.[45] Pride measures her prosperity not by her own advantages, but by others' disadvantages. She would not even wish to become a goddess if there were no wretches left over whom she could rule and exult, by comparison with whose wretchedness her own felicity might shine, whose need she might torture and inflame by displaying her own riches. This serpent of hell creeping over the breasts of men drags them back and stops them from seeking a better way of life.

Since she is too deeply fixed in the hearts of men to be easily plucked out, I am glad that the Utopians at least have achieved this form of republic, though I greatly wish all men had. The Utopians have followed those rules of life with which they laid such foundations for their republic as are most prosperous and also, as far as the human mind may conjecture, destined to last forever. For since they have cut out together with the other vices the roots of ambition and strife, there is no danger of internal discord, which alone has destroyed the well protected riches of many cities. With their concord safe at home and their institutions healthy, not even the jealousy of all the neighboring princes could shake or move that empire, although they have often tried in the past and always been driven back.

So Raphael finished his account. Many points occurred to me where the ways and laws of that people seemed regulated quite absurdly—for example, their method of waging war, their religious practices and other institutions of theirs too, but particularly the foundation stone of the whole government—I mean their communal life and living without any use for money, since by this one enactment are overthrown all nobility, magnificence, splendor and majesty, the true glory and ornaments, as popular opinion goes, of a republic. Yet I knew he was tired from his speech and I was not sure whether he could tolerate any contrary opinion, especially as I remembered he had censured others on that account, as if they were afraid

---

[45] It was a Christian commonplace that pride was the great sin comprehending or implying all the others.

of being thought unintelligent if they could not find something to criticize in others' discoveries. So I praised the Utopians' constitution and Raphael's speech, took him by the hand and led him indoors to dinner, saying that there would be another time for us to think more deeply on those matters and discuss them more fully with him. I hope this may happen someday. Meanwhile, although I cannot agree with everything he said, although he is otherwise beyond all doubt a most learned man with deep experience of human affairs, yet I readily admit that in the republic of Utopia there are very many things that I would pray might come to our cities rather than hope[46] they might ever be established.

[46] That is, expect.

Marguerite de Navarre
(1492–1549)

A very few periods in history have witnessed a wholesale reexamination and redefinition of fundamental values. The twentieth century, it seems certain, will be remembered as one of these periods. Another such period was the sixteenth century in Europe. Whether the spiritual life demanded immersion in the world or withdrawal from it; whether society was best served by the principle of authority or the principle of independence; what it meant to be a Christian; what the distinctive roles (if there were distinctive roles) of men and women should be; how the institution of marriage could best promote individual happiness and social order—these questions are woven deep into sixteenth-century literature. The writings of Marguerite de Navarre are a good case in point. They are particularly instructive in that Marguerite combined firm convictions and the temperament of a believer with a profound openmindedness.

The marvel is that Marguerite, sister of the king of France and queen of a neighboring country, had time in her life for any such spiritual and psychological concerns, occupied as she was almost constantly with some of the key public events of an especially momentous period of European history. She was born in 1492, the daughter of Charles d'Orléans, Count of Angoulême, and his wife Louise de Savoie (often identified with Oisille in The Heptameron*). The family was related to the reigning French royal house of Valois but lived on the outskirts of its favor and seemed unlikely to improve in fortunes. But the birth two years later of a son, François (Francis), kept dynastic hopes alive, and unexpected deaths among heirs to the throne made him king of France in 1515.*

Meanwhile Marguerite had received a thorough education, as a by-product of her mother's attention to the rearing of the royal heir. (The father had died in 1496.) As a girl Marguerite read widely in the family's excellent library of ancient and modern writers. A stimulating life in her mother's cultivated circle ended for six years when in 1509 Marguerite entered into an arranged marriage with Charles, Duke of Alençon, a soldier with none of the mental or other attractions calculated to win his bride's love. This period of eclipse ended when her brother acceded to the throne, as King Francis I, and called Marguerite to share with him in the splendors of the royal court. The king and his sister proceeded, virtually, to introduce the Italian Renaissance into France, inaugurating a brilliant new era of art, literature, and social elegance. Marguerite, far more than Francis' queen, and almost as much as he, was the central figure in this vibrant new society.

She also exercised considerable administrative and diplomatic authority, as an adviser to her brother and in implementing plans of military preparedness throughout the country. When, in 1524, Francis led his army into Italy against the Spanish Holy Roman Emperor, Charles V, Marguerite and her mother governed France in the king's absence. In the following year they had to cope with a major crisis when, the king having been taken prisoner abroad, France witnessed widespread insurrection by local governments, nobles, and merchants. By traveling to Spain to bargain for her brother's freedom, Marguerite was instrumental in ending the war.

She also had to nurse her ailing husband through part of this period; he died in 1525. Two years later Marguerite was married again, to Henri d'Albret, King of Navarre, a coastal kingdom at the west end of the Pyrenees Mountains separating France from Spain. This time Marguerite gave her heart with her hand, though for his part Henri felt much less bound by the canons of marital fidelity. (The couple were later to appear, in The Heptameron, *as Parlamente and Hircan.) For a time she continued to serve as a skilled diplomat on behalf of France. But increasingly her energies were occupied with the plight of her own new kingdom, largely under the control of Spain and, in its geographical position, symbolic of the new, ambiguous position she found herself in, as party to the complicated and not always edifying machinations of her husband, her brother, and the king of Spain. From that time on, until Francis died in 1547, Marguerite continued to act as a vitally important political agent for him, although the relationship was sometimes strained—notably by his high-handed treatment of her daughter Jeanne as an instrument, through marriage, of diplomatic policy. In her very last years Marguerite was able to spend a relatively (but only relatively) quiet life in Navarre. After two years of declining health, she died in 1549.*

All this might sound like enough for one person, but there was in fact much more to Marguerite's life. In addition to her political and diplomatic activity, she invested enormous, and effective, energies in what today we would call social work. She reformed monasteries and convents; she established hospitals. Her artistic and intellectual patronage was likewise very widespread—in commissioning new works and in gathering under her protection advocates of all sorts of new ideas, sometimes dangerous ones. She never allied herself with the Protestants who broke with the Catholic Church, but she was strongly caught up in several movements that, to conservatives, seemed tarred with the same brush—the evangelical and humanist reform movements of the time—and she associated with suspect people such as Calvin and Rabelais. Like Rabelais, she got into serious trouble with the Sorbonne, the militantly conservative university in Paris that represented everything in the old scholastic intellectual culture that was repellent to both the new reformers and the humanist sponsors of the New Learning. In 1533, the Sorbonne condemned as heretical Marguerite's then-recent devotional poem The Mirror of the Sinful Soul. *(It is ironic that, at exactly the same time, Thomas More, in many ways one of Marguerite's brothers in spirit, was adhering to the Roman church and thus digging his grave in Henry VIII's newly-Protestant England.)*

Thus far, a severely abridged account of Marguerite as a public figure has managed almost to avoid mentioning that she was an important writer. She is one of the very few authors to have distinguished themselves in all three of the major media of creative writing—prose fiction, in The Heptameron; *drama, such as her late allegorical play* The Comedy of Mont-de-Marsan *(1548); and verse, notably her near-epic* Prisons *(of about the same date), concerning the ascent of the soul through the successive prisons of mundane love, ambition, and learning. Her works reveal a mind of considerable versatility, subtlety, tolerance, and complexity—in short, fineness of grain. This last quality is particularly striking, in light of the widespread assumption that immersion in political and other public affairs coarsens the sensibilities and fosters reductionist, simpleminded views. (Plato's Socrates came close to believing as much—another irony, in light of Marguerite's deep devotion to Plato.) Her mind illustrates a quality missing even in some of the best minds: an ability to rise above, or surprisingly invert, some of its own firmest convictions, in the interests of a more comprehensive view of reality. Jules Gelernt, in a book about Marguerite, shows how this operates in, for example,* The Comedy of Mont-de-Marsan. *In the play, the Wise Woman, a character who speaks for Marguerite's own cherished beliefs in the humanist New Learning and enlightened piety, is ultimately overshadowed by another character, the Woman Ravished with Love of God, who exists on a plane of spiritual experience that transcends both learning and piety.*

In her last years Marguerite wrote (or so most scholars think) the work that became known, after its posthumous publication, as The Heptameron. *Only seventy-odd of the projected hundred stories were completed (or have survived). It is modeled, as the Prologue indicates, on Boccaccio's* Decameron, *and in some ways it clearly imitates that work—in the lush meadow setting, in the device of common flight from danger (a flood rather than the plague as in Boccaccio), in the conversational framework surrounding the ten tales told each day, in the recurrent themes (the wickedness of the friars, sexual plotting and trickery, and others), in the occasional bawdiness, and, not least, in the exploration of male-female relationships.*

The Heptameron *is, however, a very different kind of work, especially in its sustained concern with spiritual and ethical issues. Boccaccio's battle-of-the-sexes motif is much deepened and expanded, and the stakes are raised. (This may explain why Marguerite shapes her cast for a fair fight, with five men and five women instead of Boccaccio's three men and seven women.) The sexual sparring in Boccaccio is usually, by comparison, decorous and flirtatious, and feelings are seldom seriously ruffled. Marguerite's characters, however, often quarrel like undomesticated cats and dogs over the sex-related issues. The range of sensibilities and values is about as wide as it can possibly be. Among the women, Oisille is a model of otherworldliness; her male antithetical opposite is the brutally cynical Saffredent, who—for instance—sees rape as merely one method of seduction among others.*

This milieu and atmosphere would seem likelier to produce a shouting match (which, in fact, does occur at times) than to foster searching moral explorations and bring out psychological fine points, and yet these are what The Heptameron *is all about. One reason is that the author is willing to entertain, and apparently sometimes empathize with, viewpoints that go against the fundamental grain of her temperament. It is clear, for example, that a kind of lofty Platonism (or neoplatonism) is close to Marguerite's heart; Parlamente, her stand-in, delivers a memorable exposition of it at the end of Story Nineteen. It is also clear that the author, like other Renaissance humanists, connects Platonism with a Christian loftiness of vision, reflected—for example—by Simontaut's citation, in the same episode, of the First Epistle of John. But the spiritual "marriage" of the two lovers in Story Nineteen, with its subdued but lingering flavor of carnality, is likely to have disturbed some readers a little bit at least, and their misgivings are indeed expressed in the later post-mortem, not decorously but in terms of the roundest ridicule. As for the quotation from John, it too reappears, in a less reverent vein, after Story Thirty-Six. Among the males, Dagoucin is the most uncompromising spokesman for platonic love (in the modern as well as the classic sense), an attitude for which he has to pay dearly by way of the quite raw, mocking incredulity expressed by certain of his hearers. The author is entirely capable of seeing the comedy in Dagoucin, a man so serenely determined to create a hermetic seal around his uncontaminated love that he would never risk revealing it even to his lady, who thus, for practical purposes, might as well not exist.*

The fine grain of Marguerite's mind is reflected by the complexity of her vision, which in turn is reflected by the way in which different sets of values modify and interlock with one another. We get to appreciate this cumulatively, by reading various stories and noting more and more interconnections between matters that at first seem not to have much to do with one another. Take, for example, the very brief Story Fifty-Five, about a Spanish widow commissioned to carry out her late husband's dying bequest of the proceeds from the sale of a fine horse. The point of the story might seem a simple one: the widow's amusing cleverness in adhering to the letter of the testator's instructions while also preserving his wealth for herself and her children. The ensuing discussion, however, explicitly raises a number of controversial issues and suggests some others implicitly. One of them is the greed of the Franciscan friars, whom Marguerite also treats in certain of the stories as lustful sexual predators. (P. A. Chilton, in the Introduction to the translation used in this anthology, provides an especially illuminating discussion of this sexual aggression.) The witheringly unfavorable attitude toward the Franciscans was not, in fact, something new in literature; one finds it also in Boccaccio and Chaucer. But in The Heptameron *the friars are the focus for a whole complex of sociological, moral, and theological issues. For one thing, they stand for the old religious regime that the evangelical and humanist reformers found so benighted. They also stand for the monastic system, with its implicit hostility toward women and low valuation of marriage, which are central concerns in* The Heptameron *and were burning issues with the reformers and humanists, who fairly consistently attacked the enshrinement of the ideal of celibacy. As for deathbed bequests to the religious orders, the issue was not merely venal corruption in the Church but also the theological issue of belief in Purgatory, the concomitant belief in indulgences (remissions of punishment in Purgatory), and the notion that monetary gifts were one form of the "good works" that could earn indulgences. Behind that node of issues looms a still broader issue, the main theological battleground of the Reformation period: salvation by grace versus salvation by works. And even beyond that, at least for Marguerite, lies the problem of translating such theological concerns into a dynamic of love that can light up the heart with spiritual peace without ignoring the needs of a human society. Thus the feminist strands, for example, in Marguerite's work are part of a rich fabric of ideas and speculations. The intensity of the arguments that follow the stories is partly explained by the momentousness of such issues, far deeper-seated ones than those raised by, say, Boccaccio.*

The discussions following the stories also have a bearing on the artistry of The Heptameron. *Some of the stories—including the one about the horse—are elegantly crafted in themselves, but many of them are not. Some of them simply trail off or are otherwise knocked askew—Story Fifteen, for example, where we learn casually, in the last few sentences, that the protagonist ended by jilting the man for whose love she took so many pains and risked so much. The key here is to take the ensuing discussion (which addresses this final jilting, among other issues) not just as commentary but as integral to the tale. If the anecdote related had a rounded or climactic ending in itself, happy or unhappy, with the lady clearly triumphant or clearly foiled in her love, the ensuing discussion might well strike us as an extraneous intrusion on a story meant to be appreciated strictly as a self-contained artistic whole. As the story does end, however, it introduces a new psychological complexity, reminding us that life is usually less tidy than invented art and leading us directly into the discussion that, as often for Marguerite, is the climax of the narrative, not a mere appendage to it. The assertion made in the Prologue that the stories in* The Heptameron *are to be factual, not invented, may not always be literally true, but it is true at least in the sense that the barrier protecting the purity of literature from the unsettledness of life is often breached, in the interests of an urgent search, among many confusing options, for the most nearly comprehensive truth.*

A Note on the Text

The Heptameron *was first published some years after Marguerite's death, in printed editions significantly different from one another. Moreover, a large number of surviving manuscripts further complicate the problem of producing an authoritative text. The P. A. Chilton translation used in the present anthology prints certain manuscript variants in square brackets which, in the interests of smoother reading, have been removed in the pages that follow here. Readers interested in these textual discriminations should consult Chilton's volume in the Penguin Classics.*

FURTHER READING *(prepared by B. W.):* One of the most useful general introductions to Marguerite's life and the general tendencies of her mind and work can be found in the opening chapter of Jules Gelernt's *World of Many Loves: The Heptameron of Marguerite de Navarre,* 1966. Samuel Putnam's *Marguerite of Navarre,* 1935, is a clear, accurate account of both life and works. P. A. Chilton's introduction to his translation of the complete *Heptameron,* 1984, lays out the basic critical issues economically and thoughtfully and touches on textual complications and the merits of earlier translations. Brief, stimulating discussions of several facets of Marguerite's work are included in I. D. McFarlane, *A Literary History of France: Renaissance France 1470–1589,* 1974. C. J. Blaisdell, "Marguerite de Navarre and Her Circle," in *Female Scholars: A Tradition of Learned Women Before 1800,* 1980, places Marguerite in the tradition so identified. Three book-length studies in English of *The Heptameron* are Jules Gelernt's book already cited; Marcel Tetel, *Marguerite de Navarre's "Heptameron": Themes, Language, and Structure,* 1973; and Betty J. Davis, *The Storytellers in Marguerite de Navarre's "Heptameron,"* 1978. Gelernt explores the versions of love in the stories and Marguerite's neoplatonism, Tetel emphasizes figurative language and structure, and Davis looks at the characters in the frame-story and their interrelationships. Another good study of the framing is Glyn P. Norton, "Narrative Function in the *Heptameron* Frame-Story," in *La Nouvelle française à la Renaissance,* ed. Lionello Sozzi, 1981. On the relation to the Boccaccio model, see Donald Stone, "Boccaccio's *Decameron* and the *Heptameron,*" in his *From Tales to Truth: Essays on French Fiction in the Sixteenth Century,* 1973. Recent criticism has tended to concentrate on the feminist themes of the collection. Two good treatments of this subject are Paula Sommers, "Feminine Authority in the *Heptameron:* A Reading of Oysille," in *Modern Language Studies* 13 (1983), 52–59; and Robert W. Bernard, "Feminist Rhetoric for the Renaissance Woman in Marguerite de Navarre's *Heptameron,*" *Chimères* 15 (1982), 73–98.

THE HEPTAMERON

Translated by P. A. Chilton

The Heptameron is a series of tales told by ten persons of aristocratic birth who, owing to several misadventures, are marooned together at the abbey of Our Lady of Sarrance, in the Pyrenees mountains in southern France. All of them have been cut off, while returning from the mineral-spring town of Cauterets, by torrential floods. Although they are thrown together mostly by chance, they have known one another for some time.

The sage among the group is Oisille, a pious elderly widow interested in seeing the abbey for its own sake. The others take shelter there out of necessity and a desire to spend their time with friends and acquaintances.

The group includes a sub-group made up of two women named Parlamente and Longarine and three men named Hircan, Dagoucin, and Saffredent. Parlamente and her husband Hircan, along with young Longarine and her husband, had been traveling together, followed at a discreet distance by Dagoucin and Saffredent, two young devotees of Parlamente and Longarine. (Which man loves which woman is not explicitly stated.) The two married couples, while staying overnight as the unwitting guests of a bandit, became embroiled in a fight between their host and certain of his partners in crime. Dagoucin and Saffredent came to the rescue, but not before Longarine's husband was killed.

Two other young women, Nomerfide and Ennasuite, were driven to shelter while fleeing on horseback from a bear.

The two other men are Geburon, who narrowly escaped from a house where armed attackers had beset him, and Simontaut, who also narrowly escaped with his life, after rashly trying to ford the flood waters on horseback. Simontaut is secretly devoted to Parlamente. (There is also a hint that Parlamente's husband, Hircan, may be in love with an unidentified woman of the party.)

The travelers commission the building of a foot-bridge over a nearby river but find that the construction will take ten or twelve days. Anticipating boredom, they cast about for a way to pass the time. Oisille suggests scriptural readings and other pious exercises, but most of the travelers feel the need for more secular diversion also. Being informed by Parlamente that the French royal family have wanted a French equivalent of the hundred tales told in Boccaccio's *Decameron,* of which a translation from Italian has recently appeared, the travelers undertake to further the royal project by relating tales themselves, ten each day. Unlike those in Boccaccio, however, these tales are all to be based on actual fact. To tell their stories, the ten ladies and gentlemen assemble each afternoon in the lush grass and ample shade of a beautiful meadow adjoining the abbey.

(The work was completed only through the first seven days; it therefore never became a French Decameron but remained a "Heptameron" or "Work of Seven Days.") [*Editors' headnote.*]

"Since you speak so strongly in favor of women who get suspected wrongly, Longarine," said Hircan, "I choose you to tell us the eighth story, on condition that you don't make us all weep, like Madame Oisille did, with her excessive zeal for stories in praise of virtuous women."

Longarine broke into a hearty laugh, and said: "Since you want me to make you laugh, in my usual fashion, it won't be at the expense of women. Yet I *shall* tell you something to show how easy they are to deceive when they fill their heads with jealous thoughts, and pride themselves on their good sense for wanting to deceive their husbands."

STORY EIGHT

In the county of Alès[1] there was once a man by the name of Bornet, who had married a very decent and respectable woman. He held her honor and reputation very dear, as I am sure all husbands here hold the honor and reputation of *their* wives dear. He wanted her to be faithful to him, but was not so keen on having the rule applied to them both equally. He had become enamoured of his chambermaid, though the only benefit he got from transferring his affections in this way was the sort of pleasure one gets from varying one's diet. He had a neighbor called Sendras, who was of similar station and temperament to himself—he was a tailor and a drummer. These two were such close friends that, with the exception of the wife, there was nothing that they did not share between them. Naturally he told him that he had designs on the chambermaid.

Not only did his friend wholeheartedly approve of this, but did his best to help him, in the hope that he too might get a share in the spoils.

The chambermaid herself refused to have anything to do with him, although he was constantly pestering her, and in the end she went to tell her mistress about it. She told her that she could not stand being badgered by him any longer, and asked permission to go home to her parents. Now the good lady of the house, who was really very much in love with her husband, had often had occasion to suspect him, and was therefore rather pleased to be one up on him, and to be able to show him that she had found out what he was up to. So she said to her maid: "Be nice to him, dear, encourage him a little bit, and then make a date to go to bed with him in my dressing-room. Don't forget to tell me which night he's supposed to be coming, and make sure you don't tell anyone else."

The maid did exactly as her mistress had instructed. As for her master, he was so pleased with himself that he went off to tell his friend about his stroke of luck, whereupon the friend insisted on taking his share afterwards, since he had been in on the business from the beginning. When the appointed time came, off went the master, as had been agreed, to get into bed, as he thought, with his little chambermaid. But his wife, having abandoned her position of authority in order to serve in a more pleasurable one, had taken her maid's place in the bed. When he got in with her, she did not act like a wife, but like a bashful young girl, and he was not in the slightest suspicious. It would be impossible to say which of them enjoyed themselves more—the wife deceiving her husband, or the husband who thought he was deceiving his wife. He stayed in bed with her for some time, not as long as he might have wished (many years of marriage were beginning to tell on him), but as long as he could manage. Then he went out to rejoin his accomplice, and tell him what a good time he had had. The lustiest piece of goods he had ever come across, he declared. His friend, who was younger and more active than he was, said: "Remember what you promised?"

[1] A town in the Languedoc region of southern France. The theme of Stories 1–10, told on the first day, is dirty tricks played by women on men and vice versa.

"Hurry up, then," replied the master, "in case she gets up, or my wife wants her for something."

Off he went and climbed into bed with the supposed chambermaid his friend had just failed to recognize as his wife. *She* thought it was her husband again, and did not refuse anything he asked for (I say "asked," but "took" would be nearer the mark, because he did not dare open his mouth). He made a much longer business of it than the husband, to the surprise of the wife, who was not used to these long nights of pleasure. However, she did not complain, and looked forward to what she was planning to say to him in the morning, and the fun she would have teasing him. When dawn came, the man got up, and fondling her as he got out of bed, pulled off a ring she wore on her finger, a ring that her husband had given her at their marriage. Now the women in this part of the world are very superstitious about such things. They have great respect for women who hang on to their wedding rings till the day they die, and if a woman loses her ring, she is dishonored, and is looked upon as having given her faith to another man. But she did not mind him taking it, because she thought it would be sure evidence against her husband of the way she had hoodwinked him.

The husband was waiting outside for his friend, and asked him how he had got on. The man said he shared the husband's opinion, and added that he would have stayed longer, had he not been afraid of getting caught by the daylight. The pair of them then went off to get as much sleep as they could. When morning came, and they were getting dressed together, the husband noticed that his friend had on his finger a ring that was identical to the one he had given his wife on their wedding day. He asked him where he had got it, and when he was told it had come from the chambermaid the night before, he was aghast. He began banging his head against the wall, and shouted: "Oh my God! Have I gone and made myself a cuckold without my wife even knowing about it?"

His friend tried to calm him down. "Perhaps your wife had given the ring to the girl to look after before going to bed?" he suggested. The husband made no reply, but marched straight out and went back to his house.

There he found his wife looking unusually gay and attractive. Had she not saved her chambermaid from staining her conscience, and had she not put her husband to the ultimate test, without any more cost to herself than a night's sleep? Seeing her in such good spirits, the husband thought to himself: "She wouldn't be greeting me so cheerfully if she knew what I'd been up to."

As they chatted, he took hold of her hand and saw that the ring, which normally never left her finger, had disappeared. Horrified, he stammered: "What have you done with your ring?"

She was pleased that he was giving her the opportunity to say what she had to say.

"Oh! You're the most dreadful man I ever met! Who do you think you got it from? You think you got it from the chambermaid, don't you? You think you got it from that girl you're so much in love with, the girl who gets more out of you than I've ever had! The first time you got into bed you were so passionate that I thought you must be about as madly in love with her as it was possible for any man to be! But when you came back the *second* time, after getting up, you were an absolute devil! Completely uncontrolled you were, didn't know when to stop! You miserable man! You must have been blinded by desire to pay such tribute to my body—after all you've had me long enough without showing much appreciation for my figure. So it wasn't because that young girl is so pretty and so shapely that you were enjoying yourself so much. Oh no! You enjoyed it so much because you were seething with some depraved pent-up lust—in short the sin of concupiscence was raging within you, and your senses were dulled as a result. In fact you'd worked yourself up into such a state that I think any old nanny-goat would have done for you, pretty or otherwise! Well, my dear, it's time you mended your ways. It's high time you were content with me for what I am—your own wife and an honest woman, and it's high time that you found *that* just as satisfying as when you thought I was a poor little erring chambermaid. I did what I did in order to save you from your wicked ways, so that when you get old, we can live happily and peacefully together without anything on our consciences. Because if you go on in the way you have been, I'd rather leave you altogether than see you destroying your soul day by day, and at the same time destroying your physical health and squandering everything you have before my very eyes! But if you will acknowledge that you've been in the wrong, and make up your mind to live according to the ways of God and His commandments, then I'll overlook all your past misbehavior, even as I hope God will forgive me *my* ingratitude to Him, and failure to love Him as I ought."

If there was ever a man who was dumbfounded and despairing, it was this poor husband. There was his wife, looking so pretty, and yet so sensible and so chaste, and he had gone and left her for a girl who did not love him. What was worse, he had had the misfortune to have gone and made her do something wicked without her even realizing what was happening. He had gone and let another man share pleasures which, rightly, were his alone to enjoy. He had gone and given himself cuckold's horns and made himself look ridiculous for evermore. But he could see she was already angry enough about the chambermaid, and he did not dare tell her about the other dirty trick he had played. So he promised that he would leave his wicked ways behind him, asked her to forgive him and gave her the ring back. He told his friend not to breathe a word to anybody, but secrets of this sort nearly always end up being proclaimed from the roof-tops, and it was not long before the facts became public knowledge. The husband was branded as a cuckold without his wife having done a single thing to disgrace herself.

*　　*　　*

"Ladies, it strikes me that if all the men who offend their wives like that got a punishment like that, then Hircan and Saffredent ought to be feeling a bit nervous."

"Come now, Longarine," said Saffredent, "Hircan and I aren't the only married men here, you know."

"True," she replied, "but you're the only two who'd play a trick like that."

"And just when have you heard of us chasing our wives' maids?" he retorted.

"If the ladies in question were to tell us the facts," Longarine said, "then you'd soon find plenty of maids who'd been dismissed before their pay-day!"

"Really," intervened Geburon, "a fine one you are! You promise to make us all laugh, and you end up making these two gentlemen annoyed."

"It comes to the same thing," said Longarine. "As long as they don't get their swords out, their getting angry makes it all the more amusing."

"But the fact remains," said Hircan, "that if our wives were to listen to what this lady here has to say, she'd make trouble for every married couple here!"

"I know what I'm saying, and who I'm saying it to," Longarine replied. "Your wives are so good, and they love you so much, that even if you gave them horns like a stag's, they'd still convince themselves, and everybody else, that they were garlands of roses!"

Everyone found this remark highly amusing, even the people it was aimed at, and the subject was brought to a close. Dagoucin, however, who had not yet said a word, could not resist saying: "When a man already has everything he needs in order to be contented, it is very unreasonable of him to go off and seek satisfaction elsewhere. It has often struck me that when people are not satisfied with what they already have, and think they can find something better, then they only make themselves worse off. And they do not get any sympathy, because inconstancy is one thing that is universally condemned."

"But what about people who have not yet found their 'other half'?" asked Simontaut. "Would you still say it was inconstancy if they seek her wherever she may be found?"

"No man can know," replied Dagoucin, "where his other half is to be found, this other half with whom he may find a union so equal that between the parts there is no difference; which being so, a man must hold fast where Love constrains him and, whatever may befall him, he must remain steadfast in heart and will. For if she whom you love is your true likeness, if she is of the same will, then it will be your own self that you love, and not her alone."[2]

"Dagoucin, I think you're adopting a position that is completely wrong," said Hircan. "You make it sound as if we ought to love women without being loved in return."

"What I mean, Hircan, is this. If love is based on a woman's beauty, charm and favors, and if our aim is merely pleasure, ambition or profit, then such love can never last. For if the whole foundation on which our love is based should collapse, then love will fly from us and there will be no

---

[2] The allusion is to the fable related by Aristophanes in the *Symposium* of Plato, the ultimate ancient spokesman for the philosophy of idealism. According to the fable, each person is half of a primordial unified being, divided by the vindictive gods, and can find happiness only by being united with his or her separated soulmate.

love left in us. But I am utterly convinced that if a man loves with no other aim, no other desire, than to love truly, he will abandon his soul in death rather than allow his love to abandon his heart."

"Quite honestly, Dagoucin, I don't think you've ever really been in love," said Simontaut, "because if you had felt the fire of passion, as the rest of us have, you wouldn't have been doing what you've just been doing— describing Plato's republic,[3] which sounds all very fine in writing, but is hardly true to experience."

"If I have loved," he replied, "I love still, and shall love till the day I die. But my love is a perfect love, and I fear lest showing it openly should betray it. So greatly do I fear this, that I shrink to make it known to the lady whose love and friendship I cannot but desire to be equal to my own. I scarcely dare think my own thoughts, lest something should be revealed in my eyes, for the longer I conceal the fire of my love, the stronger grows the pleasure in knowing that it is indeed a perfect love."

"Ah, but all the same," said Geburon, "I don't think you'd be sorry if she did return your love!"

"I do not deny it. But even if I were loved as deeply as I myself love, my love could not possibly increase, just as it could not possibly decrease if I were loved less deeply than I love."

At this point, Parlamente, who was suspicious of these flights of fancy, said: "Watch your step, Dagoucin. I've seen plenty of men who've died rather than speak what's in their minds."

"Such men as those," he replied, "I would count happy indeed."

"Indeed," said Saffredent, "and worthy to be placed among the ranks of the Innocents—of whom the Church chants '*Non loquendo, sed moriendo confessi sunt*'![4] I've heard a lot of talk about these languishing lovers, but I've never seen a single one actually die. I've suffered enough from such torture, but I got over it in the end, and that's why I've always assumed that nobody else ever really dies from it either."

"Ah! Saffredent, the trouble is that you desire your love to be returned," Dagoucin replied, "and men of your opinions never die for love. But I know of many who *have* died, and died for no other cause than that they have loved, and loved perfectly."

*   *   *

"I choose Longarine," replied Simontaut. "I noticed a moment ago that she seemed to be talking to herself. I think she was rehearsing a piece for us. She's not in the habit of concealing the truth from anyone, man or woman, so it is she I choose to speak next."

"Since you regard me as such a truthful person," said Longarine, "I'll

---

[3] In another major dialogue, *The Republic*, Plato envisions the ideal society.
[4] From the Collect for the mass on the feast of the Holy Innocents: "not by speaking, but by dying have they confessed." This feast, celebrated on December 28, honors the infants slaughtered by Herod in his attempt to kill the newborn Jesus.

tell you a story, which, although it doesn't praise women as much as I'd like, does, as you will see, show that there are women who are just as courageous, just as intelligent and just as shrewd as men. If it is a little long, I ask you to bear with me."

STORY FIFTEEN

At the court of Francis I[1] there lived a certain gentleman, a gentleman whom I know well, but whose name I prefer not to tell you. He was poor. He did not have five hundred livres[2] a year to live on. But the King was very fond of him on account of his many excellent qualities, and he ended up marrying a woman rich enough to do justice to the highest lord of the land. As his wife was still only a young girl, the gentleman asked one of the greatest ladies of the court to take her into her household, which the lady in question gladly did. The gentleman himself was endowed with such good looks, such nobility, such charm and grace, that he was held in high esteem by the ladies at court, and in particular by one who happened at that time to be the object of the King's own affections. With this lady our handsome gentleman was passionately in love, though she was neither as beautiful nor as young as his own wife, of whom he took so little notice, that scarcely one night in a whole year did he sleep with her. What was even more insufferable to the girl was the fact that he never spoke to her or showed the least sign of affection. Moreover, although he drew on her wealth for his own pleasures, he gave her such a small share in it that she was not able to dress as she wished, or even as her station required. The lady in whose household she resided often complained to the husband about this state of affairs.

"Your wife is rich, beautiful and of good birth," she would say, "yet you treat her just as if she were the very opposite. So far she has put up with all this, being little more than a child, but I am afraid that when she grows up, and her mirror tells her how beautiful she really is, someone with little love for you will come along who will tell her the same thing. You have thought but little of her beauty, and I fear that in her resentment she will do things that she would never dare even to think about if she had been well treated by you."

But the gentleman's heart was set on other things, and remonstrate as she might, he merely laughed at her and carried on as before.

Two or three years passed by, and the young wife began to turn into one of the most beautiful women in all France. It was said that no other woman at court could match her. The more she realized that she deserved to be loved, the more she became upset at her husband's lack of consideration for her. So distressed did she become, in fact, that had it not been for the efforts her mistress made to console her, she would almost have despaired. She tried everything in her power to win him round. How could it

---

[1] One of the most famous kings of France (born 1494; reigned 1515–47). Marguerite de Navarre was his sister. Stories 11–20, told on the second day, do not have a prescribed subject.
[2] Pounds (money).

be possible, she asked herself, that he did not love her, when *she* loved *him* so dearly? In the end there seemed to her to be only one explanation—that his head had been turned by some fancy for another woman. She investigated this possibility with great shrewdness, until she eventually learned the truth. Every night he was occupied elsewhere. He had quite forgotten both his conscience and his duty to his wife.

Now that she knew for certain the kind of life her husband was leading, she sank into such a deep melancholy that she refused to wear anything but clothes of black and shunned all kinds of merrymaking. When her mistress noticed this, she did everything she could to draw her out of this gloomy frame of mind. But to no avail. The husband, although the situation was made abundantly clear to him, was more inclined to laugh at it than to do anything to remedy it.

Well now, as you know, Ladies, just as the heights of happiness may give way to tears, so the depths of misery may end in transports of joy. Thus it was that a certain noble lord of high estate, who was a close relative of the lady's mistress, and a frequent visitor, came to hear of the outlandish way the husband behaved towards her. He felt so sorry for her that he made an attempt to console her, and as he talked with her he was so struck by her goodness, her beauty and her modest demeanor, that he became rather more concerned to win her favor than to talk about her husband, except to show her what little cause she had to have any affection for the man. As for the lady herself, there she was, on the one hand abandoned by the very man who ought to have loved her, and on the other hand sought after and loved by a handsome prince, so it was hardly surprising that she felt overjoyed at having won his favor. Although she was concerned always to preserve her honor, nevertheless, starved as she was of love and consideration, she took the greatest delight in talking to him, and basking in his love and admiration. This tender friendship lasted for some time, but was eventually noticed by the King, who, being extremely fond of the lady's husband, was not prepared to let anybody cause him the least distress or disgrace. So he urged the prince to rid himself of his infatuation, and told him that if he did not, he was likely to incur royal displeasure. The prince was far more anxious to win the King's favor than he was to win all the favors of all the ladies in the world, so he promised that for the King's sake he would abandon his designs, and that he would go that very evening and take his leave of the lady.

True to his word, he went to the lady's house as soon as he was sure she had returned. As usual in the evening the husband was sitting at his window, so he saw the prince go into his wife's room, which was just beneath his own. But the prince, though he knew he had been seen, was not deterred. Once in her room, he told the fair lady, whose love was only beginning to blossom, that he was saying goodbye. The sole reason, he told her, was that he had been ordered to do so by the King himself. Till an hour after midnight the lady wailed and wept. Then by way of a parting speech she turned to him and said:

"Monseigneur, I give thanks to God that you no longer have the feelings you had before, for they must be weak indeed if you can pick them up and put them down again upon the orders of mere mortals! *I* asked permission neither from my mistress, nor from my husband, nor from myself, when I

fell in love with you. It was Love alone, with the help of your handsome
appearance and your charm, that had such authority over me that I recognized no other God and no other King. But since *your* heart is not so overflowing with love that all fear is banished from it, you cannot be a perfect
lover, and I have no desire to take one who is imperfect, and make him, as
once I was resolved to do, a lover loved with perfect love. So, Monseigneur,
since you are too craven[3] to deserve my true affection, I say farewell!'"

And the noble lord went off in tears. On his way out he noticed the
husband watching again at the window, so the next day he went to explain
to him why he had been to see his wife, and what the King had ordered him
to do. The gentleman was very gratified to hear all this, and thanked the
King. However, seeing his wife growing daily more beautiful, while he was
getting older and losing his good looks, he began to change his role. It was
his turn now to play the part he had imposed on his wife for so long, for he
spent more time with her than he had hitherto, and kept a constant watch
on her actions. But the more he followed her about, the more she kept out
of his way, since she had conceived a desire to pay him back for the sorrows
that his lack of love had brought her in the past. What is more, she was
beginning to learn the pleasures of love, and had no desire to be deprived
of them so soon. So she made advances to a young nobleman. He was a very
good-looking young man, very elegant, very nimble with his tongue, and
consequently much adored by all the ladies at court. She bemoaned her lot
to him, telling him how badly she was treated, and he was so moved by her
tale that he left no stone unturned in an attempt to comfort her. In order to
make up for the loss of her prince, she set about falling in love with this
young man with such passion that she eventually got over her earlier disappointment. She no longer had any other concern than to carry on her new
intrigue with as much finesse as possible. So careful was she, that her mistress, in whose presence she scrupulously avoided addressing the young
man, suspected nothing at all. But when she did want to talk to him, she
would go off to see some of the other ladies who resided at court, amongst
whom there happened to be one with whom her husband was affecting to
be in love.

One evening after supper, she slipped off in the dark on her own, and
went straight to the ladies' chamber, where she met the man she loved
more than life itself. She sat by his side, and, leaning over the table as if
they were reading a book together, they chatted intimately. The husband,
however, had set someone to watch her, and her whereabouts were soon
reported back to him. Being a cautious man he said nothing, but made his
way to the scene as fast as he could. He saw his wife sitting there reading as
soon as he went into the room, but pretending not to have noticed her, he
went straight over to the ladies on the other side. The poor wife, realizing
that her husband had discovered her with a man to whom she had never
spoken in his presence, was so unnerved that she completely lost her head.
Unable to move along the bench, she jumped over the top of the table, as if
her husband was after her with a naked sword, and went to find her mistress, who was just retiring for the night. Then she too undressed and
retired, but one of her women arrived with a message to say that her hus-

---

[3] Cowardly.

band was demanding her. She replied outright that she had no intention of going to him; he was so hard and cruel that she was afraid he might actually do her some harm. In the end, however, she did decide to go to him, for fear that worse might happen if she did not. The husband spoke not a word when she came in. But she, not so good at dissembling as he was, started to cry as soon as they were in bed. When he asked what was the matter with her, she replied that she was afraid he might be angry with her because he had found her reading a book with a gentleman. To this he answered that he had never forbidden her to speak to any man, and that he found nothing wrong with her talking to that one. What he did find suspicious was the way she had run off when she had seen her husband, as if she really was doing something reprehensible. And it was this alone, he said, which led him to think that she was in love with this particular gentleman. Consequently he was going to forbid her ever to speak to him again, either in private or in public. The first time he should catch her doing so, he warned her, he would kill her without pity or compassion. This she was ready to accept, resolving not to be so foolish a second time. But to forbid something is the surest way to make it even more ardently desired, and it was not very long before the poor young wife had forgotten her husband's threats, as well as the promises she herself had made. Indeed, that very evening, having gone back to sleep in another room with the other young ladies and their attendants, she sent word to her young gentleman that he was to come and see her during the night! But the husband, so racked by jealousy that he cannot sleep, gets up, dresses himself in a cloak, and calls a valet de chambre[4] to accompany him. This, so he had heard, was how his rival equipped himself for his nocturnal visits. Then off he goes to his wife's quarters, and knocks at the door. She gets up, puts on the furry shoes and wrap lying by her side, and, seeing that the three or four women she had with her were asleep, goes alone out of the room straight to the main door. Her husband was the last person she expected to find there.

"Who is it?" she called out.

A voice replied, giving the name of the young man she was in love with. But to make certain, she opened a grating in the door, saying:

"If you're who you say you are, let me feel your hand, and I shall recognize it."

As soon as she touched the hand, she knew it was her husband's. She slammed the grille shut, shouting, "Ah! Monsieur, it's *your* hand!"

He was beside himself with rage.

"Yes, it is indeed my hand!" he shouted. "And by this hand I shall keep my promise! Therefore do not fail to come when I command you!"

With these words he went back, and she, more dead than alive, returned to her room.

"Get up! Get up!" she shouted to her attendants. "You have slept too long! I thought I was going to outwit you, but instead it is I who have been outwitted!"

As she spoke she fell in a faint in the middle of the room. The poor women scrambled out of bed, astonished to hear their mistress talking like that, and then to see her collapse on the floor as if she were dead. There

---

[4] Personal valet; manservant.

was nothing to do but to run and find some means of reviving her. When she came round and could speak again, she said: "My dear friends, the woman you see before you is the most miserable creature in all the world!"

Then she told them what had befallen her, and begged them to give her their help, for she thought that she was already as good as dead. As they were trying to console her, one of her husband's valets de chambre came in with the order that she was to appear before him at once. She threw her arms round two of her women, screaming and crying, and beseeching them not to let her go, for she was sure she would be going to her death. But the valet de chambre assured her that she would be all right, and that he would answer for her safety with his own life. She saw there was no way out, and threw herself into the poor servant's arms, saying, "Since it must be so, bear this, my wretched body, unto death!"

In her despair she almost fainted, and the valet de chambre had to carry her bodily to his master. The poor lady fell at his feet, saying: "Monsieur, I beg you to have pity on me. I swear to you, by the faith I owe to almighty God, that I will tell you the whole truth."

"By God!" he replied, beside himself with rage, "tell me you certainly shall!"

He then ordered all his servants out of the room. Knowing that his wife had always been devout, he felt that she would not dare to perjure herself if she was made to swear by the true cross. So he had a cross sent for, a particularly fine specimen which he happened to have in his possession, and when they were alone again, he made her swear on it that she would tell the truth in reply to his questions. But having overcome her initial fears of death, she took courage, and while resolving not to conceal the truth before she died, she also resolved to say nothing which might cause the young gentleman she loved to suffer. So, having listened to her husband's questions, she replied thus.

"It is not my intention, Monsieur, to justify my love for the young gentleman who has roused your suspicions, or to make light of it. After the evidence you have had of it today you would not be able to believe me, nor is there any reason why you should. But I do wish to explain to you how this friendship came about in the first place. You know, Monsieur, that no wife ever loved her husband as dearly as I did. From the day I married you until my present age, my heart knew no love but my love for you. You know, too, that when I was still only a child, my parents were anxious for me to marry a man who was much richer than you, and of higher birth. But from the moment I met you, I could not agree to their plans for me. In opposition to their wishes, in spite of your lack of means and in spite of the way everyone criticized me for what I was doing, I insisted on having you and you alone. Nor can you be exactly ignorant of the way you have treated me since we were married, of the way you've failed to show me any love and respect! I've been so wretched, so miserable, that if it hadn't been for the lady who has looked after me, I would have sunk into the depths of despair. But then I grew up. Everybody—except you—considered me beautiful. I began to be so acutely aware of the wrong you had done me that instead of loving you as I did before, I began to hate you. Before I had longed to do your bidding, now my longing turned into a desire for revenge. This was the desperate state I was in when I was found by a certain

prince. And then, just as this honorable love was beginning to give me some
relief from all my sufferings, he left me too, because he preferred to obey
the dictates of the King rather than the dictates of Love. After he had left
me, I met this other man. There was no need for him to approach me. He
was handsome, refined, charming. He had manly qualities that made him
sought after by every woman with any discernment. It was because I sought
his love, not because he sought mine, that he came to love me with a love
that was pure and virtuous. Never once did he demand of me anything that
honor could not have granted. Although I had little enough reason to give
you my love and had every excuse to break my loyal vows, the love which I
have for God and for my honor have prevented me till now from doing
anything that I need to confess or be in any way ashamed of. I don't deny
that I went to talk to him as often as I could in a private room. I used to
pretend I was going there alone to say my prayers, because I trusted no
one, neither man nor woman, to assist me in this matter. I don't want to
deny, either, that when I was alone with him in that intimate room where
nobody could suspect us I often kissed him, and kissed him more gladly
than I do you. But may I answer to God, if anything more than that ever
passed between us, or if he ever demanded more, or if I ever had the
slightest desire that he should do so. It gave me joy just to see him. I could
have imagined nothing in the world more pleasurable. Now, Monsieur, do
you intend, after being the sole cause of all my misery, to take revenge on
me for the very kind of thing of which you yourself have been guilty for
years—with the difference that the example *you* set was completely devoid
of any scruple of honor or conscience? You know, and I know, that the
woman you love doesn't content herself with what lies within the commands of God and reason. However, although the law of men attaches
dishonor to women who fall in love with those who aren't their husbands,
the law of God does not exempt men who fall in love with women who
aren't their wives. Suppose that what each of us has done is weighed in the
balance. There are you, a mature man with experience of the ways of the
world, who ought to be able to tell right from wrong. There am I, young
and with no experience of the violence and the power of love. You have a
wife who wants to be with you, who admires you and loves you more than
life itself. And what have I got? A husband who keeps out of my way as
much as possible, who hates me and despises me more than if I were a
humble chambermaid. You are in love with a woman who's already getting
on in years, a shapeless creature far less beautiful than I, while my love is
for a gentleman who's younger than you, more handsome than you and
more worthy to be loved than you! Furthermore, this woman you're in love
with is the wife of one of the closest friends you have and at the same time
the mistress of your monarch, so that you violate the duty that you owe to
both of them, betraying not only the bond of friendship, but also the obligation of respect and esteem; whereas the young man whom I love is under
no bond, except the bond of love, the love that he bears for me. Well then,
judge without bias. Which of the two of us most deserves to be punished,
and which of us most deserves to be excused? Is it you, or is it I? Is it you,
the man considered experienced and wise, who not only shamefully
wrongs his wife, although she never gave him the least provocation, but
also wrongs his King, to whom he owes his loyalty? Or is it I, the young and

innocent girl, rejected and despised by you, who loves the finest and most honorable man in all France, and who loves him only because she despaired of ever being loved by you?"

The husband was overcome by these words, words so obviously full of truth, spoken from the lips of this beautiful woman, and spoken with such confident grace and bold assurance that it was evident she neither feared punishment nor considered she deserved it. So overcome was he that he did not know what to say, except that men's honor and women's honor were not the same thing. However, since she had sworn that there had been nothing sinful between her and the young man, it was not his intention to punish her further, provided that she did not see him again, and provided that both of them forgot all about the past. This she promised, and thus reconciled the two of them went to bed together.

The next day an elderly lady who attended the wife, and who had been extremely anxious for her mistress's life, came to her as she was rising, and asked: "And how are you, Madame?"

"My dear," replied the wife, laughing, "I have the best husband in all the world. He believed everything that I swore to him!"

For the next five or six days the husband kept her under such close observation that she was spied on night and day. But guard her as he might, he could not stop her meeting her young man in some dark and secret corner. In fact she kept the affair so well concealed that there was not a man or woman in the place who could have guessed the truth. However, some servant or other spread a rumor that he had found a young lady and gentleman in the stable underneath the room occupied by the wife's mistress, and the husband became so suspicious at this report that he finally made up his mind to have the young man murdered. He called together a large number of relatives and friends with the intention of having him killed, if they could catch him in some out-of-the-way place. But the foremost of the relatives happened to be a great friend of the young man himself, with the result that instead of helping to take the intended victim by surprise, he actually warned him of all the moves that were being made against him. In any case the young man was so well liked at court and always surrounded by so many people that he was not at all afraid of his enemy's superior forces, and was in fact never caught. Moreover, he managed to go to a church to meet the Princess, who was the mistress of the lady he loved, and who had learned nothing of what had passed between the couple, since neither had so much as spoken to the other in her presence. The young gentleman told her that the husband was suspicious of him and full of ill-will, and declared that although he himself was innocent he intended to go to distant parts to escape the rumors that were starting to spread. The noble Princess who had his lady in her charge was astonished to hear this. She swore that the husband was completely in the wrong to suspect his wife, whom she had always known to be a model of virtue and honor. However, because of the husband's high position, and in order to put an end to the malicious gossip, she advised the young man to absent himself for a good while, assuring him at the same time that she personally placed no credence in any of these wild suspicions. Both the young man and his lady were overjoyed that they were still well regarded and still favored by the Princess, who gave a final piece of advice—that the young man should speak to the husband before leaving, which he duly did.

It was in the gallery, near the King's own chamber, that he came across the husband. He approached him confidently, but with due respect for the man's rank, and said: "Monsieur, all my life it has been my wish to render you service, yet I learn that for my sole reward you sent people yesterday evening to seize and kill me. I would beg you to bear in mind, Monsieur, that although you may have more power and influence than I have, I am, like yourself, a gentleman, and I should be very disinclined to give up my life for nothing. I would also beg you to bear in mind that you have a virtuous wife, and that if any man dares to assert the contrary, then I shall tell him that he has uttered a wicked lie! As far as I myself am concerned, I do not think I have done anything that ought to give you cause to wish me harm. Therefore, I shall remain your servant, if it so please you, and if it does not, then I remain the servant of the King, and that is sufficient for me!"

In reply to these words the husband said that he had indeed been suspicious of him in the past, but that he considered him an honorable man whose friendship he preferred to his enmity. So saying, he embraced him like a bosom friend, and, hat in hand, bade him adieu. You can imagine what the people who only the night before had been commissioned to murder him said, when they saw him being given such tokens of friendship and respect! They all had something to say about it.

And so the young man set off. Since he was not so well endowed with riches as he was with good looks, his lady presented him with a ring which her husband had given her. It was worth three thousand écus,[5] and he pawned it for one thousand five hundred. Some time after he had left, the husband approached his wife's mistress, the Princess, and asked leave for his wife to go and stay for a while with one of his sisters in the country. The Princess thought this request rather curious, and insisted so strongly on being given a reason, that he was obliged to give her a partial, though not a complete, explanation. The young wife took leave of her mistress and the court without shedding a tear or showing any sign of regret. She then went off to the destination desired by her husband under the escort of a young gentleman who had been expressly instructed to keep a careful watch on her. In particular, he was to take care that she had no communication *en route* with the man who was the object of her husband's suspicions. She knew perfectly well what orders her escorts had been given, and every day took great delight in setting them on their guard and then teasing them for not being vigilant.

One day, as they were leaving the inn where they had spent the night, they came across a Franciscan friar on horseback. The lady rode along on her palfrey at his side, and chatted with him from midday till supper-time. When they were within a quarter of a league of their next lodging place, she said to him:

"Father, here are two écus for having been so kind to me this afternoon. I've wrapped them in a piece of paper, because I know you wouldn't dare

---

[5] Crowns (coin worth three francs).

to touch them with your bare hands![6] When you leave me will you please make off across the fields, taking care that the men don't see you. It's for your own good, and because of the debt I owe you."

The Franciscan, pleased with his two écus, galloped off at top speed across the fields. When he was quite a long way off, the lady started to shout out to her attendants.

"A fine lot of servants you are! You are conscientious guards, aren't you! That man you were supposed to watch out for, he's been talking to me all day, and you've not done a thing about it! To think that your master trusted you! Really, it's a good beating you deserve from him, not your wages!"

When the gentleman in charge of her heard this, he was so angry that he could think of nothing to say in reply. He dug in his spurs, called to two of his men, and riding for all he was worth, managed to catch up with the good friar, who saw them coming and did his best to get away. However, being better mounted than he was, they eventually caught the poor man. He had not the faintest idea what it was all about, and begged for mercy. To make his pleas more effective, he pulled his hood off and bared his head. They realized at once that it was not the man they were after, and that their mistress had made fools of them. When they got back, she teased them even more than before.

"So," she said, "this is the sort of people they entrust ladies to! They let them talk all day long, without finding out to whom, and then, believing anything they're told, they go and insult the servants of God!"

After teasing them all in this fashion, she went to the place to which her husband had ordered her to be taken, and there her two sisters-in-law and the husband of one of them held her in strict subjection. During this time her husband found out that his ring had been pawned for fifteen hundred écus and was extremely angry about it. In order to save his wife's honor and get his ring back, he told her through his sisters that she was to redeem it, and that he would pay the fifteen hundred écus himself. The wife could not have cared less about the ring itself, since the money was now in the hands of the young man, to whom she promptly wrote a letter explaining that it was her husband who had ordered her to redeem the ring. And in order that he should not think that she had done so because of any lessening of her goodwill, she sent him a diamond, which her mistress had given her, and which she prized above any of her rings. The young gentlemen willingly sent her the pawnbroker's bond, content to have had the fifteen hundred écus as well as the diamond, the assurance of his lady's favor— although, so long as the husband was alive, he was unable to address a single word to her except in writing. After the husband's death, assuming that she would be true to her word, he lost no time in seeking her hand in marriage, but he found that during his long absence, she had acquired another companion whom she now preferred. His sorrow was so great that

---

[6]The religious order founded by St. Francis of Assisi early in the thirteenth century had been dedicated to chastity, obedience, and especially poverty, but Marguerite and her contemporaries often portray the friars as mercenary and lecherous.

he thenceforth shunned all female company, preferring to court danger and risk his life in battle. Thus he ended his days, having won as much esteem as ever a young man could.

*   *   *

"Without being in any way lenient to our own sex, Ladies, the point of this example is to show all husbands that women of high spirit are more often dominated by anger and the desire for revenge than by the pleasures of love. The lady in the story was able to resist these emotions for a long time, but in the end was overcome by despair. No good woman should let this happen, because, whatever the circumstances, she should not look for an excuse to act badly. In fact the more excuses she is offered for doing wrong, the more she should prove her virtue by resisting and overcoming evil with good, rather than rendering evil for evil—especially as the wrong one intends to inflict on another person often rebounds on to oneself. Happy are they in whom God manifests the virtues of chastity, gentleness, patience and long-suffering!"

"It seems to me, Longarine," said Hircan, "that this lady you've told us about was moved more by resentment than by love, because if she'd loved the young gentleman as much as she pretended, she wouldn't have left him for another man. It follows that she could reasonably be said to be resentful, bitter, vindictive, stubborn and fickle!"

"It's easy for you to talk," said Ennasuite, "but you don't know how heart-rending it is to love without having your love returned."

"True," he replied, "because the moment a lady starts to be in the slightest way cold towards me, I forget all about love and all about her as well!"

"That may well be so," said Parlamente, "for you. All you care about is your own pleasure. But an honest woman shouldn't leave her husband in that fashion."

"However," said Simontaut, "the woman in the story completely forgot she was a woman for a while, for even a man could not have taken his revenge so well!"

"Because one woman is not virtuous," said Oisille, "one should not think that all others are like her."

"All the same," said Saffredent, "you *are* all women. You can cover yourselves up becomingly with all the finery you like, but the fact remains that anyone who looks carefully underneath all those skirts will find that you *are* all women!"

"If we listened to *you* all day," said Nomerfide, "we'd never stop arguing. But I'm waiting to hear another story, so I'll ask Longarine if she'll pick the next person to speak."

*   *   *

"I think," said Oisille, turning to Hircan, "that you are so fond of speaking ill of women, that you wouldn't have great difficulty in finding something good to say about men. So will you tell us the next story?"

"That's easy," he replied. "Not long ago I was told a tale that was very much to the credit of a certain gentleman. This was a man whose love, long-suffering and loyalty were so praiseworthy that I believe it my duty to prevent them sinking into oblivion."

STORY EIGHTEEN

My story is about a noble lord of excellent family. He was living in one of the important towns in the kingdom of France, and was studying at the schools there. His desire was to attain that knowledge which is the key to honor and virtue among men of worth. At the age of seventeen or eighteen he was so knowledgeable that one would have thought him a shining example, fit to instruct his fellow-students. However, he was also to become a pupil in the School of Love. Now Love is a subtle teacher, and to ensure that his lessons would be heard and taken to heart, he concealed himself behind the fair eyes and face of a certain lady. She was the most beautiful lady in all the land, and as chance would have it, was in the town at that time for some lawsuit. But before setting about the conquest of the heart of the noble young lord, Love first vanquished the heart of the lady herself, by bringing all his manly perfections before her eyes. For he was indeed so fair of face, so fair of speech, so fair in all his ways that there was not a man in all the land, whatever his station, who could surpass him. Those of you who know how quickly the fire of love spreads when it starts to smoulder in the heart and in the imagination will understand that once Love enters two such perfect subjects, he never stops until he has rendered them obedient to his commands, until indeed he has filled them both so full of his clear light that all their thoughts, all their desires and all their speech are nothing but the blazing forth of his flame. With the timidity of youth, the young lord pursued his desires with the utmost caution. But already the lady was conquered. There was no need of force. Yet Modesty, that persistent companion of ladies, prevented her for a while from showing her feelings. But in the end, the fortress of the heart where Honor dwells was destroyed, and the poor lady gave herself up to that which she had never wished to resist.

In order to test the long-suffering, constancy and love of her servant, she acceded to his demands on one exceedingly difficult condition. If he was able to keep this condition, then she would love him perfectly for evermore. If, however, he were to fail, then he would not possess her for as long as he should live. The condition was this. She would be happy to go to bed with him and to talk with him there. But they were both to keep their nightshirts on, and he was to demand nothing more than her discourse and chaste kisses! The young man, who felt that there was no joy in the world to be compared with that which she was promising him, agreed. Evening came, and the promise was kept. However much she encouraged him, however much he was tempted, he refused to break his word. Purgatory itself could not, he felt, be worse than what he went through that night. Yet so great was his love, so firm was his hope, that he was happy to wait in patience, for he was sure that the eternal love which it had cost him so much to win would in the end be his. So he left her bed without once asking of her anything that would have gone against his promise. But the lady was, I think, more astonished than pleased by his upright behavior, and began to think that either he did not love her as much as he had said, or that he had found her less attractive than he had expected. Completely disregarding his demonstration of honor, chastity, patience and fidelity, she decided to put the young man's love to another test before keeping her own promise. To this end, she asked him to approach one of the girls in her entourage, a girl who was extremely attractive and somewhat younger than herself. The idea was that he should make amorous overtures to this young girl, so that people would think it was because of her that he came to the house so often. The young lord, quite certain that his lady loved him as much as he loved her, carried out to the letter everything she ordered him to do. He forced himself for her sake to pursue her young companion, who, seeing what a handsome, gently spoken young man he was, believed his lies rather than the truth, and promptly fell in love with him, thinking he loved her. When the lady realized things had gone as far as this, she decided at last to permit the young man, who was still pressing her to fulfil her promise, to come to her room at one hour after midnight. She had, she told him, tried out his love and tested his obedience so thoroughly that it was only right that she should reward his long and patient wait. There can be no doubt about the joy which her loving and devoted servant experienced.

At the appointed hour he went to his lady's room. But she still wanted to test the strength of his love. So before he arrived, she took the young girl on one side, and said to her: "I know that there's a certain young gentleman who's in love with you, and I think you are no less passionately in love with him. Well, I feel so sorry for you both, that I've decided to give you the opportunity to talk on your own together for as long as you like."

The girl was so transported, that she could scarcely conceal the love she felt, and said that she could never refuse such a proposal. Following her mistress's advice, indeed her orders, she went to the appointed bedroom, undressed and lay down on the magnificent bed. The door was left half open, and all the candles lit, so that the girl and all her charms could be clearly seen. Then, pretending to go away, the lady herself hid near the bed in a spot where she could not be seen. It was not long before her poor devoted servant arrived, prompt at the appointed hour and fully expecting to find his beloved waiting for him as promised. In he crept, closed the door behind him, took off his gown and his fur-lined shoes, and went over to the bed, thinking to find there his heart's desire. No sooner did he stretch out his arms to embrace the recumbent figure he took to be his lady, than the poor girl, thinking he was all hers, flung her arms around his neck. The expression in her eyes and the passionate words she murmured would have been enough to put the holiest hermit off his paternosters![1] But prompted by his great love for his lady, the young man recognized both the voice and the face, and jumped out of the bed even faster than he

---

[1] "Our Fathers"; recitations of the Lord's Prayer.

had jumped in, when he realized that this was not the woman for whom he had suffered so long and so deeply!

Angry not only with the girl herself, but also with her mistress, he said: "I shall not be made other than I am either by your wild desires or by the wicked one who put you here! Seek to be an honest woman, for by no act of mine shall your good name be lost!"

Beside himself with rage, he marched out, and for a long time he did not come back to see his lady. However, Love, who never abandons hope, assured the young gentleman that the longer his constancy was tried and tested, the longer and pleasanter would be the enjoyment in the end. For her part, the lady, who had seen and heard everything, was surprised at the depth and constancy of his love, but it pleased her too, and she was anxious to see him again to ask his forgiveness for the pain she had inflicted in testing him. So at the earliest opportunity she addressed him in tones of such gracious tenderness that he not only forgot all his past torments, but even began to think of them with pleasure. For after all, it was through them that his constancy was honored at last, and through them that his lady was convinced of his love. From that hour on there were no more obstacles and no more trials, and from his lady he received all that his heart could desire.

*   *   *

"Now, Ladies, can you tell me of a woman as constant, as patient and as faithful in love as the man in this story? Anyone who's been through such temptations will find the temptations we are shown in pictures of St. Anthony[2] as nothing by comparison. Anyone who can remain patient and chaste when beautiful women offer not only their beauty and their love, but also time, place and opportunity, will surely be virtuous enough to resist every single devil in Hell!"

"It is a great shame," said Oisille, "that he did not address himself to a woman who had the same resources of virtue as he. We should then have had the most perfect example of pure and perfect love that has ever been heard of."

"Tell me," said Geburon, "which of the two trials do you think was the most difficult for the young man to bear?"

"I think the second," Parlamente said, "because disappointment and resentment are the strongest temptations of all."

Longarine, however, felt that the first trial was the hardest, "since he had to overcome Love as well as overcome himself, in order to keep his promise."

"It is easy for you to talk," said Simontaut, "but those of us who know the truth in such matters ought to say what they think. As far as I'm concerned, he acted like an idiot the first time, and like a madman the second. You see, I think that by keeping his promise he only made his lady suffer as much as, or more than, he himself suffered. The only reason she made him make such a promise in the first place was so that she could make herself

[2]Egyptian saint (251–356) and ascetic, the first monk. His sexual temptations during a sojourn in the desert were proverbial and were frequently portrayed by painters.

look more virtuous than she really was. She knew perfectly well that desperate love can't be held back by orders or oaths or by anything else in the whole world. But she wanted to make her vice look virtuous, and to make it appear that she could be won only by acts of virtue nothing less than heroic. The second time, he showed that he was mad to let the girl go, when she was so obviously in love with him and was certainly worth more than the woman he'd made his promise to. What is more, he had a good excuse, given the bitter disappointment he had just experienced."

Dagoucin objected to this, saying that his opinion was exactly the opposite, and that on the first occasion the young man had shown himself patient, constant and true to his word, while the second occasion showed that in his love he was perfect, true and faithful.

"And how do we know," said Saffredent, "that he wasn't one of those referred to in a certain chapter headed *De frigidis et maleficiatis*?[3] If Hircan had really wanted to sing this man's praises, he should have gone on to tell us how he acquitted himself once he got what he wanted. Then we could judge whether it was his virtue or his impotence that made him so well-behaved!"

"You may be quite sure," said Hircan, "that if he'd told me, I wouldn't have kept it back, any more than I have the rest of the story. But knowing him as well as I do, and knowing what his temperament is like, I shall always take the view that he acted the way he did because of the power of his love rather than because of frigidity or impotence."

"Well," Simontaut replied, "if he was the kind of man you say, then he ought to have broken his oath. After all, even if she had got annoyed at a little thing like that, it wouldn't have been too difficult to calm her down again!"

"But perhaps she didn't want him to do it just then?" said Ennasuite.

"So what? Wasn't he strong enough to force her," Saffredent said, "seeing that she led him on?"

"Holy Mary!" exclaimed Nomerfide. "That's a fine way to talk! Do you think that's the way to win the favor of a lady you believe to be chaste and virtuous?"

"In my opinion," said Saffredent, "when a man desires that sort of thing from a woman, the greatest honor he can do her is to take her by force. Because, however humble a girl may be, she will want you to beg and beseech over and over again. There are others who have to be given a lot of presents before you can win them round. Others are so stupid that they let themselves go at the slightest trick or guile, and with them it's merely a matter of finding the right method. But when you're faced with one that's too sensible and good to be tricked, and too well-behaved to be won round by presents and talk, is one not justified in trying every possible means of conquering her? Whenever you hear that a man's taken a woman by force, you can take it from me that the woman in question must have deprived him of all hope of success by other means. You shouldn't think the worse of a man who risks his life like that in order to give vent to his love."

[3] Latin: "On persons rendered frigid by magic spells," a papal document issued in the thirteenth century.

Geburon started to laugh. "I've often seen places besieged and taken by storm," he said, "because neither threats nor offers of money could persuade the defending forces to parley, for they say that once you engage in talks, you're already half defeated!"

"It would seem that all the love-affairs in the world are based on the kind of wicked passion that Simontaut and Saffredent have just been talking about!" said Ennasuite. "But there *are* people who have been in love, and loved long and constantly, without having those motives."

"If you know a story about somebody like that," said Hircan, "then I hand over to you for the next one."

"I do know such a story," she replied, "and shall be only too happy to tell it to you."

STORY NINETEEN

In the time of the Marquis of Mantua, who had married the sister of the Duke of Ferrara,[1] there was in the Duchess's household a lady-in-waiting by the name of Paulina. She was deeply beloved of a certain gentleman in the service of the Marquis. People marvelled at his attachment to Paulina, for, though poor, he was a man of valor, and one would have expected him, in view of his master's great liking for him, to have sought a match with a lady of means. But in his eyes Paulina was worth all the treasure in the world, and it was she alone whom he desired to marry and make his own. The Marchioness wanted to use her influence to bring about a better marriage for Paulina and did her best to deter her from marrying the gentleman who loved her so much, and often stopped them talking together. They would, she warned them, be the poorest and most miserable wretches in the whole of Italy if their marriage took place. But the gentleman could not be convinced by such arguments as these. For her part Paulina disguised her love as best she could—but dreamt about it none the less. Thus they continued in their love, living in the hope that one day their fortunes would improve.

During this time war broke out, and the gentleman was taken prisoner along with a Frenchman, who had left his love at home in France, just as he had left his in Italy. Finding that they were companions in the same misfortune, the two men began to tell one another their secrets. The Frenchman confessed that his heart too was captive, though he did not name its captor. He knew already that his comrade was in love with Paulina, for he too was in the service of the Marquis, and he urged him, as a friend concerned for his interests and well-being, to abandon this infatuation. The Italian gentleman of course swore that it was not within his power to do so. He said that if the Marchioness did not let him marry his beloved in recompense for his sufferings in captivity and all his other services, then he would become a Franciscan friar and serve no other master than God. His comrade could not believe this, for, apart from his devotion to Paulina, the Italian gentle-

[1] This marriage took place in 1490. Mantua and Ferrara are in northern Italy.

man did not seem to him to show the slightest sign of monastic piety. Nine months later the Frenchman was set free, and succeeded in obtaining the subsequent release of his comrade, who then immediately approached the Marquis and Marchioness and pursued the matter of his marriage to Paulina for all he was worth. But he had no success. They constantly reminded him that if he and Paulina were to marry they would have to live in poverty. Moreover, neither his family nor hers were in favor of the match, and they forbade him to speak to her in the hope that his infatuation would vanish if he was deprived of all means of meeting her. He realized that he had no alternative but to obey. So he asked the Marchioness if he might say farewell to Paulina, promising that he would never thereafter speak to her again. Permission was granted, and he immediately went to Paulina and began the following speech:

"I can see, Paulina, that both Heaven and earth are against us and desire not only that we should not marry, but that we should not even see one another and talk together. The orders of our master and our mistress are harsh indeed. Well might they boast that by uttering one word they have wounded two hearts, two hearts in two bodies that cannot now but languish unto death, and thus do our cruel master and our cruel mistress show that neither Love nor Pity ever entered their breasts. Their wish, I know, is that we should make rich marriages elsewhere, for they do not know that true riches are to be found in happiness alone. So badly have they treated me, so much grief have they caused me, it is impossible that I should any more do them service with a cheerful heart. If I had not mentioned marriage, I believe they are not so scrupulous that they would have prevented me meeting and talking with you. But I would sooner die than demean my love and, after having loved you with a love that is noble and good, seek to have that which I would defend against all others. Therefore, since to continue to be able to see you would be a penance too hard to bear, and since not to see you would fill my heart, which can never stay empty, with a despair that would bring me to a miserable end, I have resolved, and my resolve has long been firm, that I shall enter the religious life. It is not that I do not know well enough that all men can be saved, whatever their condition, but my wish is to have leisure to contemplate the divine Goodness, who will I hope take pity on my youthful faults and change my heart, that I may come to love spiritual things as I have loved those which are temporal. If God grants me this grace, it shall be my continual occupation to pray for you. And I beg you, in the name of this true and faithful love that is ours, to remember me in your devotions and to pray to Our Lord that He will give me as much constancy when I cease to see you as He gave me contentment when I was able to look upon you. My whole life I have lived in the hope that one day I would through marriage to you have that which honor and conscience allow, but now that I give up that hope, now that I can never expect that you will treat me as a wife treats a husband, I beseech you that you treat me as a brother, and permit me to kiss you."

Perceiving how deeply he was suffering, and yet how honorably even in the midst of such despair he contented himself with such a modest request, poor Paulina, who had always been severe, answered nothing, but threw her arms about his neck, weeping bitterly. So violent were her tears, that her voice, her faculty of speech and all her strength left her, and she fell into a faint in his arms. He, filled as he was with love and sorrow, was so overcome that he too fell in a faint. One of Paulina's companions, seeing them both collapse on the ground, called for help, and they were given medicaments which revived them.

When Paulina realized that she had revealed the strength of her feelings, she was overcome with shame, for she had always sought to disguise her love. But she was able to excuse herself on the grounds that she had been overwhelmed by compassion for the gentleman's plight. He, unable to bear the pain of uttering his final adieu, hastily left the scene, his face set, as he fought back the emotion that welled in his heart. No sooner had he returned home than he collapsed on his bed, a lifeless corpse. Throughout that night he lamented aloud, and his cries were so heart-rending that his servants thought he must have lost parents, friends and everything he had. The next day he commended himself to Our Lord, and shared out among his servants what little he possessed, taking only a small sum of money for himself. Then, forbidding anyone to follow him, he wended his way alone to the convent of the Observant Friars,[2] where, in the firm resolve never again to leave those walls, he requested the friar's habit.[3] The Superior, who had seen him in the past, thought at first that he must be dreaming or that it must be some sort of a joke. Indeed there could hardly have been a man in the whole land who was less endowed with the qualities and gifts required of a friar, for his gifts were the solid virtues of a gentleman of honor. But once the good father had heard the words he had to speak, once he had seen the tears pouring in torrents down his face, though he did not know their cause, he had compassion on him and took him in. It was not long afterwards that he acknowledged the gentleman's perseverance and granted him the habit, which the gentleman received with due devotion.

When the Marquis and Marchioness heard of this, they found it so strange that they could scarcely believe it. Paulina, desiring to show that she was not in any way subject to the dictates of love, covered up as best she was able the sorrow she felt at the gentleman's departure. So complete was her dissimulation that all those around her said that she had at last forgotten the feelings she had once had for her faithful and devoted servant. Five or six months passed by, and still she revealed nothing. One day during this time a monk visited her and showed her a song that had been composed by her faithful servant shortly after he had taken the habit. The tune was Italian and is quite well-known, but I have translated the words as closely as possible. They go like this:

> What will she say,
> My Lady, pray,
> What will she do, when her fair eyes
> See me thus dressed in monkish guise?

[2] A reformed branch of the Franciscan order.
[3] The robe worn as the uniform of the order.

Dear one, my own,
Sweet one alone,
Long speechless, wond'ring will she be,
Troubled and torn
Lady forlorn.
Strange will it seem, then presently
Her thoughts they will begin to dwell
On convent close and holy cell,
There to reside, eternally.
What will she say, etc.

What will they do,
Who from us two
Our love and joy did cause to go,
Seeing that love
Howe'er they strove
They yet more perfect caused to grow?
When they do look into our heart
They surely will repent their part
And bitter tears will surely flow.
What will she say, etc.

And if they say,
Oh come away!
And seek our souls so to divert,
Then you and I
Shall say, we'll die!
Far rather that than ever part,
For since we must their harshness bear,
We two do now the long robe wear
That we shall wear perpetually.
What will she say, etc.

And if again
With marriage then
They seek our souls to taunt and tempt,
While they relate
That pleasant state
And how we should be thus content,
Our soul, we'll say, is at God's side,
His holy spouse, His heavenly bride,
So shall it be, eternally.
What will she say, etc.

O love so great,
That through this gate
I have perforce for sorrow passed,
Ah! in this place
Grant me the grace

Without regret to pray and fast,
For this our love, our mutual love,
Shall rise so high, and dwell above
That God will be well pleased at last.
    What will she say, etc.

        Then put behind
        The joys that bind
In iron bonds so dire and fell!
        Quit worldly fame
        That leads in shame
Black souls through pride to depths of Hell!
Let us shun lust and vanity,
And take that love which in mercy
Lord Jesus gives, with Him to dwell.
    What will she say, etc.

        Come then away,
        Make no delay,
And with your best beloved go,
        Fear not, I pray,
        The habit gray,
Nor yet to flee this world below.
For with that love that's live and strong
From ashes must arise ere long
The phoenix true, enduringly.[4]
    What will she say, etc.

        Just as on earth
        Our love had birth,
Pure and perfect, noble, rare,
        It may appear,
        Hidden here
In cloistered cell, beyond compare.
For loyal love that's true and sure
And endlessly shall e'er endure
Must lead to heav'n, eventually.
    What will she say, etc.

She was sitting in a chapel as she read the song through, and when she had finished she wept bitterly, sprinkling the paper with the tears as they fell. Had it not been for her anxiety to avoid showing herself more moved than was becoming, she would even at that very moment have transported herself to some hermitage and shut herself away from all living creatures for evermore. But imbued as she was with the virtue of prudence, she was constrained to disguise her feelings for some little time longer. In her heart she was resolved to leave the world for ever, but in her outward appearance

---

[4] In myth, the phoenix was a single beautiful bird that was consumed in fire after living five hundred years in the desert but rose again to life from its own ashes.

it was the very opposite she showed, for when in company she wore an expression that revealed nothing of her true self. For five or six months more she kept her intentions secret, appearing to the world gayer and happier even than she had used to be.

Then, one day, she went with her mistress to the Observant convent to hear high mass. As the priest, deacon and subdeacon came out of the sacristy[5] and made their way to the high altar, she beheld her poor suitor, who had still not completed his one year of novitiate.[6] He was serving as acolyte[7] and walked with eyes bent to the ground, bearing in his hands the altar-cruets[8] covered in their white silk cloth. When she saw him attired thus in his vestments, his looks enhanced rather than diminished, she was so overcome with emotion that she made herself cough in order to cover up the color that had risen to her cheeks. Her poor servant could not fail to recognize the sound of her voice, a sound better known to him by far than the cloister bell. He dared not turn his head, yet as he passed by her, he could not prevent his eyes from turning in the direction that they had so long been accustomed to take. As he gazed sorrowfully upon her, he was so overwhelmed by the fire he believed almost extinct that in his desire to conceal it more than was in his power he fell to the ground at her feet. Fear lest the true cause be known led him to say that he had fallen over a broken pavingstone. But when Paulina realized that his change of habit could not change his heart, and that it was so long since he had entered the monastery that everyone would think she had forgotten him, she decided to carry out her long resolve. It was her desire that at the last their love should bring them together, that they should be alike in habit, condition and manner of life, just as at the beginning they had lived under the same roof, under the same master and under the same mistress. She had already more than four months previously made all the arrangements necessary for her entry into a convent, and one morning she asked the Marchioness for permission to go and hear mass at the convent of Saint Clare.[9] Permission was granted, although the Marchioness was ignorant of the true reason for the request. As Paulina went past the Franciscan house, she stopped and asked the Father Superior to send her devoted servant, who, she said, was a relative, to speak to her. They met in a quiet chapel, and she addressed him thus:

"If my honor had allowed me to dare to enter the cloister as soon as you did, I should not have waited till now. But I have waited patiently, and now that my waiting has thwarted those who prefer to think ill of others than to think well, I am resolved to adopt the same condition of life and the same robes as you have adopted. I do not ask what people will say. For if your chosen way has brought you joy, I shall have my part therein. If it has brought you suffering, I have no wish to be spared. Whatever path you tread to Paradise, I wish to follow in your steps. For I believe that He who alone is worthy to be called true and perfect Love has drawn us to His service through a love that is reasonable and good, a love that through His Holy Spirit He will turn wholly unto Himself. And I beg you that we may

---

[5] The deacon and subdeacon were the priest's assistants in celebrating mass. The sacristy was the room where the priest's vestments and the sacred vessels were stored.
[6] The trial period before becoming a full member of the order.   [7] Altar-boy.
[8] The vessels containing the wine, water, and oil used by the priest in the mass.
[9] St. Clare (1193–1253) founded the order of Franciscan nuns known as the Poor Clares.

put away the flesh of the old Adam that perisheth, and accept and put on that of Jesus Christ our Spouse."

Paulina's devoted servant, now a servant of God, was so filled with joy when he heard her express this sacred wish that, weeping tears of happiness, he strove to strengthen her resolve. Since he could have nothing of her but the enjoyment of the words she spoke, he held his lot happy indeed, for henceforth he would always be able to hear her, and her words would be such that both he and she would profit by them, living as they would in one love, one heart and one spirit, drawn and guided by the goodness of God. And he prayed that God would hold them in His hand, for in His hands no man can perish. As he spoke, he shed tears of love and joy. Then he bent to kiss her hand, but Paulina lowered her face to his, and in true charity they exchanged the holy kiss of love. Her soul thus filled with happiness, Paulina departed and went to the sister convent of Saint Clare, where after being received she took the veil.

Later she had the news conveyed to the Marchioness, who was so surprised she could not believe it, and went the very next day to try to make her change her mind. But Paulina's reply was firm. The Marchioness might have the power to remove her fleshly husband, the one in the world whom she had loved above all others, but that being so, she should now be satisfied and not seek to separate her from Him who was immortal and invisible, for neither the Marchioness nor any creature on earth had such power. Seeing that Paulina was resolute, the Marchioness kissed her, and filled with sorrow and regret, went on her way. From that time on Paulina and her servant lived devout and holy lives in their Observant houses. So devout and so holy were they, one cannot doubt that He whose law has its end in charity would tell them at their lives' end, even as He told Mary Magdalen, that their sins were forgiven, for they had loved much,[10] and that He would transport them in peace to the place whose recompenses surpass all human merits.

*   *   *

"Now you can't deny, Ladies, that the man's love was clearly the stronger. But it was so well repaid, that I only wish that everybody who fell in love had the same recompense."

"If that were the case," said Hircan, "there'd be more self-declared fools around than ever!"

"Do you call it folly if one loves with an honorable love in one's youth, and then converts this love entirely unto God?" asked Oisille.

"If melancholy and despair deserve praise," he replied laughing, "then Paulina and her devoted servant certainly deserve praise!"

"Yet God has many ways of drawing us to Him," said Geburon, "ways whose beginnings may seem bad, but whose end is good."

"Furthermore," said Parlamente, "I hold the view that no man will ever perfectly love God, unless he has perfectly loved some creature in this world."

"What do you mean by perfectly loved?" said Saffredent. "Is a perfect

[10]See Luke 7:47. Mary Magdalen was often interpreted to be a reformed harlot.

lover for you one of those paralytic individuals who adore their ladies from afar and never dare to bring their desires out into the open?"

"Those whom I call perfect lovers," replied Parlamente, "are those who seek in what they love some perfection, whether it be beauty, goodness or grace, those whose constant goal is virtue and whose hearts are so lofty and so pure that they would die rather than make their goal that which is low and condemned by honor and conscience. For the soul, which was created solely that it might return to its Sovereign Good, ceaselessly desires to achieve this end while it is still within the body. But the senses, by means of which the soul is able to have intelligence of its Sovereign Good, are dim and carnal because of the sins of our forefather Adam and consequently can reveal to the soul only those things which are visible and have some nearer approximation to perfection. The soul runs after these things, vainly thinking that in some external beauty, in some visible grace and in the moral virtues it will find the sovereign beauty, the sovereign grace and the sovereign virtue. But once the soul has searched out these things and tried and tested them, once it has failed to find in them Him whom it loves, it passes beyond. In the same way children, when they are small, like dolls and all manner of little things that are attractive to the eye and think that the pebbles they collect will make them rich; but then, as they grow up, the dolls they love are living people and the things they collect are the necessities of human life. Then, when they learn through experience that in earthly and transitory things there is neither perfection nor felicity, they desire to seek the source and maker of these things. Yet, if God does not open the eyes of faith, they will be in danger of leaving ignorance behind only to become infidel philosophers. For only faith can reveal and make the soul receive that Good which carnal and animal man cannot understand."

"Do you not see," said Longarine, "that uncultivated ground is desirable, although it bears nothing but useless trees and grasses, because it offers the hope that one day, when it is sown, it will bring forth good fruit? In the same way, if the heart of man feels no love for visible things, it will never attain the love of God when His word is sown therein. For the earth of his heart is sterile, cold and damned."

"So that's why most of your doctors of theology aren't spiritual doctors!" said Saffredent. "It's because all they'll ever like is good wine and ugly, sluttish chambermaids. They never try out what it's like to love ladies who are more refined!"

"If I could speak Latin properly," said Simontaut, "I'd quote St John to you. He says 'he who loves not his brother whom he has seen, how can he love God whom he cannot see?'[11] For it is through things visible that one is drawn to the love of things invisible."

"But who is the man who is so perfect?" asked Ennasuite. "*Quis est ille, et laudabimus eum?*"[12]

To this Dagoucin replied: "There *are* men," he said, "who love so deeply and so perfectly that they would rather die than feel any desire that was contrary to the honor and conscience of their ladies, and yet they would not wish their ladies or anyone else to be aware of their feelings."

[11] First Epistle of John 4:20.   [12] Latin: "Who is he, and we will praise him?"

"Men like that," said Saffredent, "are chameleons—they live on nothing but air! The fact is that there's no such thing as a man who doesn't want to declare his love and know it's returned. What is more, if it *isn't* returned, I don't think there was ever a love fever that wasn't cured instantaneously. I've seen miracles enough to prove it!"

*   *   *

"But [said Parlamente] I don't think that these days there is a single man alive who is genuinely good with regard to ladies, and who can be trusted with a lady's honor and conscience. Women who believe it is otherwise, and accordingly act in complete confidence, end up by being deceived! They enter into such liaisons by way of God, and often get out of them by way of the Devil. I know many women who, under the guise of talking about God, embarked on a liaison which they later wanted to break but couldn't, because they were caught up in their own cloak of respectability. You see, vicious love disintegrates of its own accord, and is unable to survive in a heart that is pure. But 'virtuous' love has such subtle bonds that one gets caught before one notices them."

"From what you say," said Ennasuite, "no woman would ever want to be in love with a man. But your law is so harsh that it cannot endure."

"I know," said Parlamente, "but in spite of that, I still think it desirable that every woman should be content with her own husband, as I am with mine!"

Ennasuite felt that these words were aimed at her and colored: "I don't think you should assume the rest of us are any different at heart from yourself," she said, "unless you regard yourself as more perfect than we are."

"Well," said Parlamente, "so as not to get into an argument, let's see who Hircan will pick to speak next."

"I choose Ennasuite," he said, "to make up for what my wife has said."

"Well, since it's my turn," said Ennasuite, "I shall spare neither men nor women, in order to make everything equal. And seeing that you can't bring yourselves to admit that men can be good and virtuous, I'll take up the thread of the last story, and tell you one that is very similar."

STORY THIRTY-SIX

It is about a man who was president of the Parlement of Grenoble[1]— a man whose name I can't reveal, although I can tell you he wasn't a

---

[1]The Court of Justice of Grenoble, a city in southeastern France. The President, in this story, is modeled on a certain Geoffroy Carles, a north-Italian, who died in 1516. (His method of disposing of his wife was somewhat different, however, from what the story relates.) The theme of Stories 31–40, told on the fourth day, is the virtuous patience of wives in cementing their marriages and the prudence of men in preserving the honor of their houses.

Frenchman. He was married to a very beautiful woman, and they lived a happy and harmonious life together. However, the President was getting on in years, and the wife began an affair with a young clerk who was called Nicolas. Every morning, when her husband went off to the Palais de Justice,[2] Nicolas would go to her bedroom to take his place. This was noticed by one of the President's servants, a man who had been in his household for thirty years, and who, being loyal to his master, could not do otherwise than tell him. The President was a prudent man, and was not prepared to believe the story without further evidence. He said that the servant was merely trying to sow discord between his wife and himself. If it was true, he said, then he ought to be able to show him the living proof. If he could not do so, then he would conclude that the man had been lying in order to destroy the love which he and his wife had for one another. The servant assured him that he should see with his own eyes what he had described.

One morning, as soon as the President had left for the courts and Nicolas had gone into the bedroom, the servant sent one of his fellow-servants to tell the master to come, while he stayed by the door to make sure Nicolas did not leave. When the President saw the servant give him the signal, he pretended he was feeling unwell, left the court, and hurried back home, where he found his other faithful old servant by the bedroom door assuring him that Nicolas was inside and that he had indeed only just gone in.

"Do not move from here," said the President. "As you know, there is no way in or out except through the small private room to which I alone have the key."

In went the President and found his wife and Nicolas in bed together. Nicolas, who had nothing on but his shirt, threw himself at the President's feet, begging forgiveness, while the wife started to weep.

"Your misdemeanor is a serious one, as you well know," said the President to his wife. "However, I do not wish to see my household dishonored or the daughters I have had by you disadvantaged. Therefore, I order you to cry no more and to listen to what I mean to do. And you, Nicolas, hide in my private room and make no noise."

Then he opened the door, called his old servant, and said:

"Did you not tell me that you would show me Nicolas and my wife in bed together? I came here on the strength of your word and might have killed my poor wife. I have found nothing to bear out what you have told me. I have looked all over the room and there is no one here, as I now desire to demonstrate to you."

So saying, he made the servant look under the beds and everywhere else in the room. When he found nothing, the old man was amazed, and said to his master: "The Devil must have carried him off! I saw him come in, and he didn't come out through the door—yet I can see that he is not here!"

Then his master replied: "You are a miserable servant to try to sow discord between my wife and myself. Therefore I give you leave to depart. For the services that you have rendered I shall pay what I owe you and more. But leave quickly and take care not to be found in this town when twenty-four hours have passed!"

The President gave him five or six years' wages in advance, and know-

[2] The law-court building.

ing how loyal he was, said that he hoped to reward him further. So the servant went off in tears, and the President brought Nicolas out of his hiding-place. After telling his wife and her lover what he thought of their wicked behavior, he forbade them to give any hint of it to anyone. He then instructed his wife to dress more elegantly than usual and to take part in all the social gatherings, dances and festivities. He ordered Nicolas too to make merry more than before, but added that the moment he whispered in his ear the words "Leave this place!", he should take care to be out of town within three hours. So saying, he returned to the Palais de Justice without the slightest hint that anything had happened.

For the next fortnight he set about entertaining his friends and neighbors—something he had not at all been in the habit of doing. After the banquets which he gave, there were musicians with drums for the ladies to dance to. On one occasion he noticed that his wife wasn't dancing, and told Nicolas to be her partner. Nicolas, thinking the President had forgotten what had happened, danced with her quite gaily. But after the dance was over, the President, on the pretext of giving him some instructions about domestic duties, whispered into Nicolas's ear: "Leave this place and never return!"

Now Nicolas was sorry indeed to leave his lady, but none the less glad to escape with his life. The President impressed upon all his relatives, friends and neighbors how much he loved his wife. Then, one fine day in the month of May, he went into his garden and picked some herbs for a salad. After eating it, his wife did not live more than twenty-four hours, and the grief that the President showed was so great that nobody suspected that he was the agent of her death. And so he avenged himself on his enemy and saved the honor of his house.

*   *   *

"It is not my wish, Ladies, to praise the President's conscience, but rather to portray a woman's laxity, and the great patience and prudence of a man. And do not take offense, Ladies, I beg you, because the truth sometimes speaks just as much against you as against men. Both men and women have their share of vice as well as of virtue."

"If all those women who've had affairs with their domestics," said Parlamente, "were obliged to eat salads like that one, then I know a few who wouldn't be quite so fond of their gardens as they are, but would pull up all their herbs to avoid the ones that restore the honor of families by taking the lives of wanton mothers!"

Hircan, who guessed full well why she said this, replied angrily, "A woman of honor ought never to accuse another of doing things she herself would never do!"

"Knowing something is not the same as making foolish accusations," said Parlamente. "The fact remains that this poor woman paid a penalty which not a few deserve. And I think that the husband, considering that he was intent on revenge, conducted himself with remarkable prudence and good sense."

"And also with great malice," said Longarine, "as well as vindictiveness that was both protracted and cruel—which shows that he had neither God nor conscience in mind."

"And what would you have wanted him to do, then," asked Hircan, "to avenge himself for the worst outrage a woman can perpetrate against a man?"

"I would rather," she said, "that he had killed her out of anger, for the learned doctors say that such a sin is remissible,[3] because the first movements of the soul are not within man's powers. So if he had acted out of anger he might have received forgiveness."

"Yes," said Geburon, "but his daughters and his descendants would have borne the stigma for ever."

"He shouldn't have killed her," said Longarine, "for once rage had subsided, she could have lived with him as an honorable woman and the whole thing would have been forgotten."

"Do you really think," said Saffredent, "that he had really calmed down, just because he had managed to conceal his anger? I think that the day he made the salad he was just as angry as at first, because there are people whose first movements never subside till their passion is put into effect. And I'm glad to say the theologians regard this kind of sin as readily pardonable. I share their view on this."

"One needs to watch one's words with people as dangerous as you," said Parlamente, "but what I said was meant to apply to cases where the passion is so great that it suddenly overwhelms the senses, and does so to such an extent that reason cannot operate."

"Taking that point further," said Saffredent, "I would argue that a man who is deeply in love does not commit a sin, or only commits a venial sin, whatever he does. Because I'm certain that if he is in the grip of perfect love, he will not hear the voice of reason, either in his heart or in his understanding. And, if we're truthful about it, there's not one among us who's not experienced this wild passion, which, I believe, is readily pardonable. What is more, I believe that God is not even angered by sin of this kind, since it is one step in the ascend to perfect love of Him, to which one cannot ascend without passing up the ladder of worldly love. For St John says: 'How shall you love God, whom you see not, unless you love him whom you see?'"[4]

"There is not a single text in Holy Scripture, however beautiful," Oisille said, "that you would not turn to your own ends. But take care lest, like the spider, you turn wholesome meat into poison. Be you assured that it is indeed dangerous to draw on Scripture out of place and without necessity."

"Do you call telling the truth 'out of place' and 'without necessity'?" said Saffredent. "Do you mean to say, then, that when we're talking to you unbelieving ladies and call God to our aid, do you mean that we're taking His name in vain? But if there's any sin in *that*, it's you who should take the blame—because it's *your* unbelief that obliges us to look for all the oaths we

---

[3] Forgivable. The "doctors" are theologians.
[4] First Epistle of John 4:20. Compare the quotation of this text in the discussion following Story Nineteen.

can possibly think of. And even then we can't kindle the fire of charity in your icy hearts!"

"That just shows," said Longarine, "that you're all liars—for the truth is so mighty that we could do no other than believe you, were truth in the words you spoke. But the danger is that the daughters of Eve are too ready to believe this serpent."

"I can see, Parlamente, that women are invincible," replied Saffredent. "So I shall keep quiet, to see who Ennasuite will choose to speak next."

*   *   *

"You make me laugh when you mention conscience," said Simontaut. "Conscience is something I would rather a woman never troubled herself about."

"It would serve you right," said Nomerfide, "to have a wife like the one who, after her husband's death, turned out to be more concerned about his cash than his conscience."

"Then will you tell us the story," asked Saffredent, "if I invite you to be the next speaker?"

"I hadn't intended to tell such a short story," replied Nomerfide, "but since it is to the point, I will do so."

STORY FIFTY-FIVE

In the town of Saragossa[1] there was a rich merchant. Seeing that his death was near, and that he could not take his wealth with him—wealth which perhaps he had not acquired altogether honestly—he thought that he might make some amends for his sins by making some little donation or other to God. As if God grants his grace in return for money! Anyway, he made arrangements regarding his house, and gave instructions that a fine Spanish horse of his should be sold, and the proceeds distributed to the poor mendicants.[2] It was his wife whom he requested to carry out these instructions as soon as possible after his death. No sooner was the burial over and the first few tears shed, than the wife, who to say the least was no more stupid than Spanish women in general, approached her servant, who had also heard her husband's wishes.

"I think I've lost enough," said she, "in losing my husband whom I loved so dearly, without losing his property as well. Not that I want to disobey his instructions. In fact, I want to carry out his wishes even better than he

[1] A city in northeastern Spain. Stories 51–60, told on the sixth day, concern deceptions motivated by greed, hatred, and vengeance.
[2] Beggars soliciting alms.

intended. You see, the poor man was so taken in by those greedy priests. He thought he would make a sacrifice to God after his death by giving away a sum of money, not a single écu[3] of which he would have given away during his lifetime, however great the need, as you know. So I've made up my mind that we shall do what he instructed us to do after his death— indeed we shall do better, and do what he *would* have done himself, had he lived a fortnight longer. Only not a soul must hear of it!"

The servant gave his word, and she went on: "You will go and sell his horse, and when they ask you how much you want, you will say one ducat.[4] But I also have an excellent cat that I want to sell, and you will sell it at the same time, for ninety-nine ducats. Together the horse and the cat will fetch a hundred ducats, which is what my husband wanted for the horse alone."

So the servant promptly went off to do as his mistress requested. As he was leading the horse across the square, carrying the cat in his arms, he was approached by a certain nobleman who had seen the horse before and was interested in acquiring it. Having asked the price, the nobleman received the answer: "One ducat!"

"I should be obliged if you would be serious," said the man.

"I assure you, Monsieur, that the price is one ducat. You have to buy the cat with it, of course. I can't let the cat go for less than ninety-nine ducats!"

The nobleman thought this was a fair enough bargain. On the spot he paid one ducat for the horse, and ninety-nine for the cat, as requested, and led his purchases away. The servant took the money back to his mistress, who was extremely pleased, and lost no time in giving away the proceeds from the sale of the horse to the poor mendicants. As for the rest, that went to provide for the wants of herself and her children.

*   *   *

"Well, what do you think of her? Wasn't she wiser than her husband, and wasn't she just as much concerned about his conscience as she was about doing well for her family?"

"I think she loved her husband," said Parlamente, "but realized that most men's minds wander when they're on their deathbeds, and knowing what his real intention was, she wanted to interpret his wishes for the benefit of their children, and I think it was very wise of her to do so."

"What!" exclaimed Geburon. "Do you not think it a grave error to fail to execute the last will and testament of deceased friends?"

"Indeed I do!" replied Parlamente. "Provided the testator is sound of mind and not deranged."

"Do you call it deranged," replied Geburon, "to give away one's goods to the Church and to the poor mendicants?"

"I do not call it deranged," she replied, "if a man distributes to the poor that which God has placed within his power. But to give away as alms what belongs to other people—I do not think that shows great wisdom. It's all too common to see the world's greatest usurers putting up ornate and impressive chapels, in the hope of appeasing God for hundreds of thousands of ducats' worth of sheer robbery by spending ten thousand ducats on a building! As if God didn't know how to count!"

---

[3] A coin worth three francs.   [4] A gold coin.

"Indeed, I am frequently astonished," said Oisille, "that they presume to be able to appease God by means of the very things, which, when He came to earth, He condemned—things such as fine buildings, gilded ornaments, decorations and paintings. But, if they had rightly understood what God has said of human offerings in a certain passage—that 'the sacrifice of God is a troubled spirit: a broken and contrite heart, O God, shalt thou not despise'—and again, in another passage, what Saint Paul has said—that 'ye are the temple of the living God, in which He will dwell'—if they had rightly heard these words, I say, they would have taken pains to adorn their conscience while they were yet alive.[5] They would not have waited till a time when man can do neither good nor evil. Nor would they have done what is even worse and placed upon those who remain the burden of dispensing their alms to those upon whom, during their lifetime, they did not even deign to look. But He who reads men's hearts will not be deceived, and He will judge them not only according to their works, but according to the faith and charity that they have shown towards Him."

"Why is it, then," said Geburon, "that the Franciscans and Mendicants[6] talk of nothing else when a man's dying but of how we ought to make bequests to their monasteries, with the assurance that they will send us to Paradise whether we want or not?"

"What, Geburon!" broke in Hircan. "Have you forgotten your story about the Franciscans, that you're asking how men like that can possibly lie? I'll tell you, as far as I'm concerned, there's no one on this earth tells lies like they do. It may be that those who speak for the good of their community as a whole aren't to be criticized; but there are some who forget their vow of poverty in order to satisfy their own greed."

[5] The biblical quotations are from Psalms 51:17 and 2 Corinthians 6:16.
[6] Religious orders of begging friars.

François Rabelais
(*1494?–1553*)

Of François Rabelais, the great French historian Jules Michelet wrote that no man had ever better captured the spirit of his age. Rabelais, he said, was a man "who contained the genius of his century and overflowed it at every moment." This would seem to be a strange judgment to make of the author of a book as seemingly fantastic and unreal as Gargantua and Pantagruel. *The rambling and obscene adventures of two folklore giants seem at first glance to be little more than a string of sexual and excremental jokes. But what Michelet saw in* Gargantua and Pantagruel *were the explosive energies and conflicts of a world in transition between two ages.*

The century Michelet had in mind, the sixteenth (Rabelais lived from about 1494 to 1553), rivaled our own in terms of rapidity and violence of change. Within Rabelais' lifetime, Europeans discovered the New World and sailed around the globe, the glory of the Italian Renaissance spread to northern Europe, and printing presses began to disseminate the New Learning that followed the rediscovery of classical civilization. In France, King Francis I was locked in a struggle with the Spanish Holy Roman Emperor, Charles V, for control of Europe. The Catholic Church was under attack by reformers from without—Luther, Zwingli, and Calvin all flourished during Rabelais' lifetime—and from within—the great Dutch humanist and reformer Erasmus was Rabelais' contemporary and intellectual father. The Church stiffened in response to these challenges, and, in France, the Faculty of Theology at the Sorbonne university used the stake freely to enforce orthodoxy and repress dissent.

Rabelais threaded his way through these tumultuous times, frequently in danger because of his beliefs and his satiric writing. Born in Chinon, in the province of Touraine, the son of a prominent lawyer, he was by the age of twenty-seven a priest and a monk in a Franciscan monastery and an avid student of Greek. After the Sorbonne forbade the study of Greek in France and Rabelais' books were confiscated, he moved to a more liberal Benedictine monastery and resumed his studies. In 1527 or 1528, he left the monastery and took up the study of medicine, first in Paris and then at Montpellier, where he became a bachelor of medicine in 1530 and a doctor in 1537.

In 1532, Rabelais was in Lyons, editing Greek medical texts for a printer and serving as a doctor in a hospital. In the summer of that year, he read an anonymous book published in Lyons: The Great and Inestimable Chronicles of the Great and Enormous Giant Gargantua, a crudely comic tale of a family of giants created by Merlin to serve King Arthur. The name and character of Gargantua were not original with the anonymous author; they had been a part of French folklore for centuries. The great success of the book and a visit to his familial home, which was then suffering from a severe drought, inspired Rabelais to write a sequel to the anonymous best seller. Pantagruel appeared in the autumn of 1532 and was an enormous success. Like Gargantua, Pantagruel originated in folk tradition, as a demon who poured salt down the throats of drunkards. He had appeared in a French mystery play half a century before, and by Rabelais' day the demon's name had become a proverbial term for a parching thirst. Pantagruel, like the anonymous Gargantua which inspired it, was a collection of traditional tales, but Rabelais made them his own through his exuberant style and satiric wit.

The following summer, Rabelais met his greatest patron, Jean Du Bellay, the Bishop of Paris who was later to become archbishop and cardinal. He accompanied Du Bellay to Rome in 1534, where Rabelais unsuccessfully sought papal absolution for having left the monastic life without permission. Upon his return, he published his own version of the anonymous Gargantua, as a sort of prologue to Pantagruel. It appears that Rabelais wanted not only to capitalize upon his success with Pantagruel, but also to write a similar work which would exploit more fully and more pointedly the satiric possibilities of the material. Gargantua is consequently much more satiric and outspoken than the earlier Pantagruel.

Pantagruel incurred the disapproval of the Sorbonne as an obscene book, and increasing religious persecution drove Rabelais into hiding for a time. In 1535, however, he accompanied Du Bellay on a second trip to Rome, and this time he was successful in obtaining absolution for having left the monastery. He was permitted to return to a Benedictine monastery, if he wished, and to practice medicine. Officially at least, Rabelais remained in good standing with the Church for the rest of his life.

Rabelais traveled to Italy once again in 1539, this time with Jean Du Bellay's older brother Guillaume, seigneur de Langey, remaining there until 1541. A new, definitive edition of Gargantua and Pantagruel *was published in that year. In this edition, Rabelais tempered his satire considerably; the term* theologians *was changed to* sophists *throughout. Nevertheless, in 1543, the Sorbonne officially condemned the book, forbidding its sale or possession. Despite this action, Rabelais obtained the King's permission in 1545 to publish a* Third Book, *which appeared in 1546. This book continued the adventures of Pantagruel and Panurge but was addressed to a more learned audience. Almost wholly lacking in narrative, it deals primarily with Panurge's desire to marry. After a series of thirteen consultations, his advisors conclude that if Panurge marries, he will almost certainly be cuckolded, beaten, and robbed by his wife. Despite the King's sanction and the comparative mildness of Rabelais' satire, soon after its publication the Sorbonne condemned the* Third Book *as well.*

Rabelais went again to Rome in 1548. Opposition to Gargantua and Pantagruel *intensified during his absence, but in 1550 Rabelais obtained the King's permission not only to republish the first three books, "revised and corrected," but also to bring out sequels. The* Fourth Book *therefore appeared in 1552. This volume told the fantastic tale of Pantagruel's and his friends' quest for the oracle of the Divine Bottle. The Sorbonne banned the book almost immediately, a year before Rabelais died in mid-1553. A* Fifth Book *of* Gargantua and Pantagruel *appeared posthumously in 1564. This book is almost certainly not entirely authentic, though it probably incorporates sketches and uncompleted fragments of a concluding book. It is notable mainly for completing the story of the voyage of Pantagruel and his friends; they finally reach the Divine Bottle, receive its oracle ("Drink!"), and set out for home again.*

Gargantua and Pantagruel *is easy to read but hard to describe or interpret. We look in vain for traditional elements of plot, character, and theme. The plot is rambling, episodic, and at times incoherent, and the major as well as the minor characters are little more than monstrous caricatures. Nor is it easy to identify the book's theme. It has traditionally been read as a satire, but the satirical element seems sporadic. There is some satire on medieval ways of teaching, the Sorbonnists, and scholastic modes of discourse. But it is hard to account for the overall impact of the flood of energetic obscenity merely in terms of satire.*

Nor is the book only an entertaining story about giants. There have been such giant stories throughout literary history—for example, the stories of the Cyclops in the Odyssey *and of Goliath in the Old Testament; the folktale of "Jack and the Beanstalk"; and the story of the Brobdingnagians in the second book of Swift's* Gulliver's Travels. *But none of these is much like the giants in* Gargantua and Pantagruel. *Giants in literature tend to be either monstrous ogres, as in "Jack and the Beanstalk," or kindly big people whose stature echoes their magnanimity, as in* Gulliver's Travels. *The giants in* Gargantua and Pantagruel *seem to be great babies, whose size parallels their gigantic appetites—for food, wine, sex, and every other gratification. Nor does Rabelais seem to take the fact that they are giants very seriously. Swift gets a great deal of fun out of calculating his giants' precise size and exploring the implications of such size. Rabelais is wildly inconsistent in his treatment of his giants' relationship to normal-sized people and objects. Through much of the book, he presents them as ordinary people.*

Gargantua and Pantagruel *is not pornography, either, despite the liberal references to copulation. Grangousier and Gargamelle may "play the two-backed beast, rubbing and grinding their respective bacons together," but the effect is hardly erotic. The sexual act, like Panurge's "tailrasping bumswinks," is invariably presented as grotesque and absurd, parallel to other bodily functions such as eating, drinking, defecating, urinating, and vomiting.*

The meaning of Rabelais' comedy, modern critics have concluded, does not lie in either satire, folk-fantasies of gigantism, or pornography, but in its "carnivalesque" character. Rabelais' comedy is derived from the rich, bawdy comedy of the medieval carnivals and feast days, in which traditional authority was overturned, at least for the day, the king becoming a fool and the fool a king. Such comedy was full of extravagance, of oaths and curses, of distorted physical dimensions and appetites, and of fantastic combats, couplings, feastings, and drinkings. Its meaning was the celebration of the body and of experience in opposition to rigid forms of social authority; its effect was release and renewal.

Rabelais expresses this carnival spirit through an overwhelming exuberance of language. One critic has spoken of his ivresse lexicographique, *his "lexicographical drunkenness." His style is strongly oral—the book begins, "Hail, O most valiant and illustrious drinkers! Your health, my precious pox-ridden comrades"—and it explodes in truly gigantic lists, bravura speeches, threats, imprecations, curses, invented languages, mock-heroic descriptions, and other extravagances of verbal invention, indulged almost for their own sake.*

This sprawling and ebullient narrative is held together by the central metaphor of drinking. Gargantua comes tumbling out of Gargamelle's womb crying, "Drink, drink, drink!" and the entire book ends with the Oracle of the Divine Bottle: "Drink!" The thirst which began in a topical allusion to the great drought of 1532 becomes, as the book progresses, a thirst for experience and for life itself.

But "Drink!" is not the only counsel of the book. As modern critics such as Donald M. Frame have pointed out, two main voices dominate Gargantua and Pantagruel. *One is the voice of Rabelais' mock persona, Alcofribas Nasier, and that of the wily Panurge. This is the voice we ordinarily call "Rabelaisian"—lusty, obscene, jolly, and sometimes cruel. There is something infantile about this voice, something the English writer John Cowper Powys described as "becoming like a little child literally, in the sense of becoming like an ordinary, harmless, healthy, sense-absorbed, indecently shameless babe or suckling." This is the voice that opens the book, loudly hailing the readers as "most valiant and illustrious drinkers!" and proceeding to delight in unrestrained accounts of gratifications of all sorts. (We might add that there is profound misogyny in this voice, too, a quality that appears strongly in Panurge's cruel revenge upon the "Parisienne of high degree.")*

But there is another voice in the book, too, a restrained, stoic, tranquil voice of moderation identified in the later books with Pantagruel but also characteristic of Gargantua, once he becomes educated. It is heard, for example, in the description of how Ponocrates organized Gargantua's education and, at its most serious, in Gargantua's long letter to Pantagruel in Paris. This letter expresses quite directly and without a trace of the "Panurgian" voice the high conception of education and of human possibilities that underlies this extraordinary book.

FURTHER READING (*prepared by W. J. R.*): Jean Plattard's *The Life of François Rabelais*, 1931, trans. by Louis P. Roche, 1968, contains a detailed account of the writer's phases of development and gives much attention to his writing. Marcel Tetel's *Rabelais*, 1967, examines his artistry, explaining why Rabelais' reputation remains high in spite of the topicality of many of his ideas. A comprehensive, im-

mensely valuable scholarly study of Rabelais' work is Michael Andrew Screech's
Rabelais, 1979. Mikhail Bakhtin's *Rabelais and His World,* 1965, translated from Russian by Helene Iswolsky, 1968, discusses Rabelais' roots in popular culture; the
significance of this influential study is treated by Krystyna Pomorska and Michael
Holquist in the prefatory material of a 1984 edition. Thomas M. Greene, *Rabelais: A
Study in Comic Courage,* 1970, in the Landmarks in Literature series, is an introductory study that discusses Rabelais' works in their intellectual context and delineates
his main themes. Abraham C. Keller's *The Telling of Tales in Rabelais,* 1963, concentrates on his narrative art, with interesting observations on the integration of
didacticism and entertainment. Rabelais' method is also discussed in Barbara C.
Bowen's *The Age of Bluff: Paradox and Ambiguity in Rabelais and Montaigne,* 1972.
Defining "bluff" as a deliberate intention to disconcert the reader and to provoke
thought, Bowen discusses Rabelais' use of paradox, enigma, antithesis, and other
devices. Marcel Tetel's "The Function and Meaning of the Mock Epic Framework
in Rabelais," *Neophilologus,* 59 (1975), 157–164, argues that the mock epic served
Rabelais as the most expedient vehicle for several of his literary purposes. Tetel
discusses *Gargantua and Pantagruel* in relation to the heroic epic, the quest epic,
and the Bildungsroman. Chapter Two of Harcourt Brown's *Science and the Human
Comedy,* 1976, examines why Rabelais has always been of great interest to medical
people. Many of the episodes included in the present anthology are on a 1982
Caedmon recording of excerpts, *The Histories of Gargantua and Pantagruel,* read by
James Mason using J. M. Cohen's translation.

GARGANTUA AND PANTAGRUEL

Translated by Jacques LeClercq

TO MY READERS

Dear friends and readers who may scan these tomes,
Lay by all sense of prejudiced objection,
My pages bring no virus or infection
Across the thresholds of your virtuous homes.
True they can teach you only scant perfection
Save laughter's joys—though I confess I find
No theme more welcome to my heart and mind,
As I observe your melancholy fears,
Your gib-cat airs, your saturnine dejection. . . .
Better to write of laughter than of tears,
For laughter is the essence of mankind.

LIVE HAPPY!

from THE FIRST BOOK

*The Very Horrendous Life of the Great Gargantua, Father of Pantagruel, Set
Down of Yore by Monsieur Alcofribas,[1] Abstractor of Quintessence, A Book
Filled with Pantagruelism.[2]*

---

[1] Alcofribas (Nasier) is an anagram of *François Rabelais.* The first two books of *Gargantua
and Pantagruel* were published under this pseudonym.
[2] The name Rabelais gave to the half-serious philosophy expressed in his books.

THE AUTHOR'S PROLOGUE

Hail, O most valiant and illustrious drinkers! Your health, my precious pox-ridden comrades! To you alone, I dedicate my writings. Suffer me, therefore, to draw your attention to a dialogue of Plato's called *The Banquet*.

In this work, Alcibiades, praising his master Socrates (undoubtedly the prince of philosophers), happens, among other things, to liken him to sileni.

Sileni, in the days of yore, were very small boxes such as you may see nowadays at your apothecary's. They were named for Silenus, foster father to Bacchus. The outside of these boxes bore gay, fantastically painted figures of harpies, satyrs, bridled geese, hares with gigantic horns, saddled ducks, winged goats in flight, harts in harness and many other droll fancies. They were pleasurably devised to inspire just the sort of laughter Silenus, Bacchus' master, inspired.

But inside these sileni, people kept priceless drugs such as balsam of Mecca, ambergris from the sperm whale, amomum from the cardamon, musk from the deer and civet from the civet's arsehole—not to mention various sorts of precious stones, used for medical purposes, and other invaluable possessions.

Well, Alcibiades likened Socrates to these boxes, because, judging by his exterior, you would not have given an onion skin for him. He was ill-shaped, ridiculous in carriage, with a nose like a knife, the gaze of a bull and the face of a fool. His ways stamped him a simpleton, his clothes a bumpkin. Poor in fortune, unlucky when it came to women, hopelessly unfit for all office in the republic, forever laughing, forever drinking neck to neck with his friends, forever hiding his divine knowledge under a mask of mockery. . . .

Yet had you opened this box, you would have found in it all sorts of priceless, celestial drugs: immortal understanding, wondrous virtue, indomitable courage, unparalleled sobriety, unfailing serenity, perfect assurance and a heroic contempt for whatever moves humanity to watch, to bustle, to toil, to sail ships overseas and to engage in warfare.

Alcibiades? Socrates? The sileni? Why all this introductory flourish? Let me explain to you only, O my beloved disciples, and to such other idlers and idiots as read my works. Having noted the flippant titles of certain books of my invention—*Gargantua, Pantagruel, Drownbottle, The Dignity of Codpieces and Trouserflies, Of Peas and Bacon, with Tables and Sauce Material, etc.*—you jump to the conclusion that these tomes are filled with mere jests, vulgarities and buffoonery. Alas! you leap at the outward and visible sign; you swallow that title in a spirit of levity and derision without pausing to make further inquiry. How unseemly to consider so frivolously the works of humankind! Is it you who profess that clothes do not make the man nor robes the monk? Do I quote you when I declare that a fellow most monasterially apparelled may turn out to be a downright infidel whereas another, draped in a Spanish cloak, may possess every virtue on earth except Castilian pride and daring? Well then, you see why you should look beyond my title, open my book and seriously weigh its subject matter. The spice secreted within the box is more precious, far, than its exterior promised. In other words, the topics treated are not so foolish as the title suggested at first hand.

Again, supposing you find enough tomfoolery to live up to the title, must you tarry there, as Ulysses tarried at the song of the sirens?[3] Certainly not. Instead, you should lend a loftier sense to what you first believed written in the exuberance of humor. . . .

III

HOW GARGANTUA WAS BORNE
ELEVEN MONTHS IN HIS
MOTHER'S WOMB

In his day, Grangousier or Greatgullet was a rollicking blade and a superlative toper.[4] With him it was always bottoms-up and no heel taps, for he drank deep as any man on the face of the earth. And he was ever ready to eat salted meat, which serves to rouse the thirst. Thus he was ordinarily well provided with hams from Mainz in Westphalia and Bayonne in Gascony; with oxtongues and chitterlings[5] in season; with salted beef and mustard; with sausages galore—not from Bologna, for he feared the Italian poisoner as a curer of bacon, but from Bigorre, Longaulnay, Brenne and Rouergue, all places nearer home.

Having attained manhood, appropriately enough he married Gargamelle—the name means gullet, also—daughter to the King of the Parpaillos or Butterflies, a jolly hoyden with a pleasing mug. Together the pair often played the two-backed beast, rubbing and grinding their respective bacons together so blithesomely and to such good purpose that she was soon big with a fair son, whom she bore for eleven months.

Does this sound strange? Perhaps. But a woman *can* bear offspring in her belly as long or even longer, especially when that offspring is a masterpiece of nature, destined to accomplish mighty exploits in his due time. Homer, himself, cites the child with which Neptune swelled the nymph Tyro: it was born a whole year after the conception. As Aulus Gellius comments, in Book III of the *Attic Nights,* such gestation was merely in keeping with the Sea God's majesty and assured the child its perfect form. By the same token, Jupiter miraculously protracted the duration of the night he bedded with Alcmena to forty-eight full hours. A shorter period could never have sufficed for the forging of Hercules, who purged the world of its monsters and tyrants. . . .

VI

THE STRANGE AND
WONDERFUL MANNER OF
GARGANTUA'S BIRTH

. . . Gargamelle began to feel slightly upset in her lower parts. Grangousier immediately rose from the grass and proceeded to comfort her most feel-

---

[3]In Book XII of Homer's *Odyssey*. The Sirens lured ships onto their rocks with their songs; Odysseus stopped his men's ears with wax and had them tie him to the mast so that he could listen without danger.

[4]Drinker.   [5]The small intestines of pigs.

ingly. She must now be in travail, he suspected. So he told her to lie down on the grass under the willows and expect shortly to see a pair of new feet next to her own. She must therefore pluck up her courage at the prospect of the babe's arrival; though the pain was somewhat grievous, it would be brief. More, her joy when it was over would banish even the memory of what she had suffered.

"I can prove it to you," he said, "for God, that is our Saviour, says in the *Gospel According to St. John* (Chapter XVI): 'A woman in travail hath sorrow because her hour is come; but as soon as she is delivered of the child, she remembereth no more the anguish.'"

"Ha!" Gargamelle broke in. "You speak nobly. I derive greater pleasure and profit in hearing such thoughts from the Gospel than in listening to the *Life of St. Margaret* or to other like cant prescribed for women in childbearing."[6]

"Courage, girl," Grangousier continued, "all you need is the courage of a sheep! Dispatch this boy and we shall be busy soon making another!"

"Ha," she countered, "it's easy for you men to dismiss it so lightly! Ah, well! by the help of God, I shall strive my utmost, since such is your wish, Grangousier. But would to God it had been cut off you!"

"What?" asked Grangousier.

"Ha," she said, "what an innocent you are! You heard what I said."

"Do you mean my member?" he cried. "'Sblood![7] if you wish it, I'll have a knife brought me."

"Oh, never! God forbid! God forgive me, I didn't speak it from my heart, so don't take any notice of what I said. But I shall be having plenty of work to-day, unless God come to my aid, and all because of your member, that you might have pleasure."

"Courage, courage!" he urged. "The worst is over. Once the plow is out of the mire, sit tight and let the four front oxen do the pulling. For my part, I'm off to swill up a few more draughts of wine. Meantime, should any harm befall you, I shall be near by. Halloo through your hands and I shall rush to your side!"

A few moments later she began to groan, lament and cry out. Suddenly crowds of midwives came rushing up from all directions. Feeling and groping her below, they found certain loose shreds of skin, of a rather unsavory odor, which they took to be the child. It was, on the contrary, her fundament which had escaped with the mollification of her right intestine (you call it the bumgut) because she had eaten too much tripe, as I explained above.

Thereupon, a grimy old baggage of the company, who had come from Brisepaille near St. Genou threescore years before, and was reputed to be a great she-physician, administered an astringent. So horrible was this restrictive medicine that it obstructed and contracted the sphincters of Gargamelle's vents and flues, until you could barely have pried them open with your teeth. A truly revolting thought, this, but one suggested by the story of the Devil at St. Martin's Mass noting down the chatter of two

---

[6] The *Life of St. Margaret,* patron saint of childbearing, was often read to women during labor.

[7] A distortion of "God's blood!," a common oath.

trollops and with his teeth stretching the parchment he wrote on, in a vain effort to keep up with them.[8]

As a result of Gargamelle's discomfort, the cotyledons of the placenta of her matrix were enlarged. The child, leaping through the breech and entering the hollow vein, ascended through her diaphragm to a point above her shoulders. Here the vein divides into two; the child accordingly worked his way in a sinistral direction, to issue, finally, through the left ear.

No sooner born, he did not, like other babes, cry: "Whaay! Whaay!" but in a full, loud voice bawled: "Drink, drink, drink!" as though inviting the company to fall to. What is more, he shouted so lustily that he was heard throughout the regions of Beuxe (pronounced "booze") and Bibarois (which in sound evokes bibbers and is how the Gascons pronounce "Vivarais").

Now I suspect that you do not thoroughly believe this strange nativity. If you do not, I care but little, though an honest and sensible man always believes what he is told and what he finds written. Does not Solomon say in *Proverbs* (XIII, 15): "*Innocens credit omni verbo,* the innocent believeth every word," and does not St. Paul (*I Corinthians*, 13) declare: "*Charitas omnia credit,* Charity believeth all."

Why should you not believe what I tell you? Because, you reply, there is no evidence. And I reply in turn that for this very reason you should believe with perfect faith. For the gentlemen of the Sorbonne say that faith is the argument of non-evident truths.

Is anything I have related beyond our law or faith, contrary to our reason, or opposed to Divine Scriptures? For my part, I find nothing in the Holy Bible that stands against it. And if such had been the will of God, would you affirm that He could not accomplish it? Ha, I pray you, do not ambiguembrangle your minds with such vain conceits. I tell you that nothing is impossible to God and, if He but pleased, women would henceforth give birth to their children through the left ear.

Was not Bacchus engendered out of the very thigh of Jupiter? Was not Roquetaillade or Cleftrock ushered into the world through his mother's heel? Did not Croquemouche or Craunchfly first see the light out of his nurse's slipper? Was not Minerva progenerated out of the brain and through the ear of Jupiter? Was not the bark of a myrrh tree brought to bed of Adonis? And did not an eggshell, laid and hatched by Leda, extravasate Castor and Pollux into being?[9]

You would be infinitely more surprised and stunned were I presently to expose to you the entire chapter in which Pliny deals with fantastic and unnatural births, yet I am not nearly so accomplished a liar as he was. Read his *Natural History,* Book VII, Chapter III, yourselves, and do not plague me further with the subject.

---

[8] The episode referred to here appears in the mystery play of the *Life of St. Martin.* The devil at St. Martin's Mass is so frustrated by being unable to keep up with the gossip of two young women or to keep his parchment unrolled to write it down that he strikes his head against a pillar.

[9] The stories of the miraculous births of Bacchus, Minerva, Adonis, and Castor and Pollux appear in classical mythology; those of Roquetaillade and Croquemouche are whimsical inventions by Rabelais.

VII

HOW GARGANTUA CAME BY
HIS NAME AND HOW HE
SWILLED DOWN THE WINE

That excellent man Grangousier was drinking and making merry with the others, when he heard a horrible tumult. It was his son emerging into the light of this world, bellowing, "Drink, drink, drink!"

At once Grangousier exclaimed: *"Que grand tu as le gousier"* or "What a great gullet you have!" Hearing this, the company declared that the child should indeed be named *"grand tu as"*: Gargantua or Greatgullet. Were these not the first sounds the father had uttered after the child's birth? And was this not an ancient Hebrew custom well worth following? Grangousier assented; Gargamelle was delighted with the idea.

Next, to quiet the babe, they made him drink till his throat almost burst. Then, carrying him to the font, they baptized him, as is the custom among all good Christians.

Shortly after, they appointed seventeen thousand nine hundred and thirteen cows from Pontille and Bréhémont to furnish him with milk in ordinary,[10] for, considering his enormous needs, it was impossible to find a satisfactory nurse in all the country. Nevertheless, certain learned doctors, disciples of Duns Scotus,[11] have affirmed that his own mother suckled him. She could, they say, draw from her breasts two thousand one hundred and three hogsheads and eighteen pints at one time. This seems scarcely probable. Indeed, this point has been condemned by the Sorbonne as mammarily scandalous and reeking with heresy.

Gargantua was thus looked after until he was twenty-two months old. Then, on the advice of the physicians, they began to carry him, and Jean Denyau built a special ox-drawn cart for him. They drove him about in it here, there and everywhere with the greatest pleasure; and a fine sight he was, too, with a great, open face and almost eighteen chins! He cried very little but he beshitted himself at all times. For he was wondrously phlegmatic of bum, as much by natural complexion as from an accidental predisposition, due to exaggerated quaffing of the juices of Septembral mash.[12] Yet he never touched a drop without good reason; for whenever he happened to be out of sorts, vexed, angry or melancholy, if he stamped, wept or shouted, they brought him a drink. This invariably restored his native good humor and at once made him as quiet and happy as before.

One of his governesses told me on oath what a rooted habit this tippling had become. Indeed, the mere clinking of pints and flagons sent him off into the ecstasy of one who tastes the joys of Paradise. Accordingly, in view of this divine character, they used to delight him every morning by making music on glasses with knives, on bottles with their stoppers, and on pots

[10] For everyday use.

[11] British or Irish scholastic philosopher (d. 1308). He was a favorite satirical target of Rabelais; the fact that our modern word *dunce* comes from his name suggests his low reputation in the Renaissance.

[12] New autumn wine.

with their lids. At this he would turn gay, thrill with joy, wag his head and rock from side to side, monochording with his fingers and barytoning through his tail.

XI

OF GARGANTUA'S ADOLESCENCE

From three to five years of age, Gargantua was, by his father's orders, brought up and instructed in all proper discipline. He spent his time like other small children; namely, in drinking, eating and sleeping; in eating, sleeping and drinking; in sleeping, drinking and eating. . . .

Do you know what else he did, my brave lads? May the drunkard's pip rot your guts if the little lecher wasn't forever groping his nurses upside-down, arsey-turvy, *hirdie-girdie, giddy-up, whoah, Hinny!*—and if he wasn't beginning to bring his codpiece into play and turn it to account. Every morning his governesses prinked and dizened it with lovely nosegays and fine silken tassels. Their favorite pastime was to feel and finger his organ, to knead and mold it lovingly as pharmacists handle ointment and salve to make a large, solidified cylindrical suppository. Then they would burst out laughing for joy at the sport as, under their skilled hands, it would prick up its ears.

One called it her darling faucet, another her corking pin, a third her coral branch, a fourth her bungpeg, a fifth her stopgap. Others named it variously their ramrod, their spikebit, their swagdangle, their trunnion, their private hardware because it must be hard where they stocked it, their lever, their borer, their little ruddy sausage, their nutty little booby prize.

"It belongs to me!" one cried.

"No, it's mine!" another protested.

"What about me?" piped up a third. "Shall I have no share in it? By my faith, I'll cut it off then."

"Ha!" said the other. "You would hurt him, Madame, if you cut it off. Do you propose to cut a child's penial utensil? He'd be Master Bobtail, then!"

And so that he might play like other little children they made him a fine whirligig with the wings from a windmill in the Mirebelais region of the Poitou.

XIV

HOW GARGANTUA WAS TAUGHT
LATIN BY A THEOLOGIAN
AND SOPHIST

The excellent Grangousier was rapt with admiration as he listened to his son talking. Truly this lad was marvellously gifted! What a vast intelligence, what cogent understanding! Turning to the governesses:

"Philip, King of Macedon," he declared, "recognized the sound judgment of Alexander, his son, when he saw how skillfully the lad managed his horse. This beast Bucephalus was so fierce and unruly that it threw all its riders. It cracked one man's neck, smashed another's legs, brained a third, and crushed the jawbone of a fourth. No one, then, dared mount it. Alexander happened to be in the hippodrome watching them breaking in and training the horses; he noticed at once that the beast's frenzy came from fright at its own shadow. He therefore made short shrift of vaulting upon its back and heading it towards the sun. There, its shadow falling behind it, he easily mastered it. Philip, by this token, realized the divine insight rooted in his son's intelligence and had him most carefully reared by Aristotle, then the most renowned philosopher in Greece.

"For my part, the brief conversation I have just had with Gargantua in your presence suffices to convince me that his mind is illumined by the divine spark. How else, pray, could he have proved so acute, so subtle, so profound and withal so serene? Give the boy proper schooling, say I, and he will attain a supreme degree of wisdom! Accordingly, I intend to trust him to some scholar who will instruct him to his capacity. What is more, I shall spare no cost."

The name of Master Tubal Holofernes, a great sophist and Doctor of Theology, was proposed to Grangousier.[13] Subsequently this savant taught Gargantua his A B C so thoroughly that he could say it by heart backwards. This took five years and three months. A succession of standard texts followed; the *Facet* (a treatise of puerile moral precepts), the *Ars Grammatica* of Actius Donatus, the fourth-century grammarian; the *Theodolet* (in which Theodulus, Bishop of Syria in the fifth century, exposed in Latin the falsity of mythology and the truth of Holy Scripture) and the *Alanus in Parabolis* (a series of moral quatrains by Alanus of Lille, a thirteenth-century worthy). It took Gargantua thirteen years, six months and two weeks to master these authorities.

It is only fair to add, however, that Gargantua, in the process, learned to write in Gothic characters. (Printing had not yet been invented and the young student had to write out his own texts.)

He had, therefore, to carry in front of him a tremendous writing apparatus that weighed more than seven hundred thousand pounds. The pencase was as large and as tall as the great columns of the Church of St. Martin of Ainay in Lyons; the inkhorn was suspended to it by great iron chains wide enough to hold five cubic yards of merchandise.

Another book, *De Modis Significandi*—a work of speculative grammar by Thomas Aquinas, or Albert of Saxony or probably Duns Scotus—was Gargantua's next reading, together with comments by Hurtebize or Windjammer, by Fasquin or Roadheaver, by Tropditeux or Toomanysuch, by Gualehault or Galahad, by Jean Le Veau or John Calf, by Billonio or Lickspittle, by Brelinguandus or Timeserver, and by a rabble of others. This took more than eighteen years and eleven months, but Gargantua knew the texts so well that at examinations he could recite them by heart backwards. And he could prove to his mother on his fingers' ends that *de modis significandi non erat scientia*, grammar was no science.

---

[13]Tubal Holofernes' names are both biblical; see Genesis 4:22 and the book of Judith. Master Holofernes' instruction of Gargantua parodies the medieval method of teaching, including reading to the pupil, rote drill, endless repetition, and a very slow pace. The books named were standard medieval textbooks, currently being discredited by the New Learning.

Next he read the *Compost* or *Popular Calendar,* and had spent sixteen years and two months at it, when suddenly, in 1420, his tutor died of the pox.

Holofernes' successor was another wheezy old pedant named Master Jobelin Bridé or Jolter Clotpoll, who read him the *Liber Derivationum* or *Latin Vocabulary* of Hugutio of Pisa, thirteenth-century Bishop of Ferrara . . . the *Grecism* by Everard de Béthune, a philological lexicon illustrating the Latin words derived from the Greek . . . *De Octo Partibus Orationis* or *Of the Eight Parts of Speech* . . . the *Quid Est?* or *What is it?* a school manual in the form of questions and answers . . . the *Supplementum,* a collection of commentaries . . . the *Mammotreptus,* a monkish or monkeyish commentary on the Psalter and the Saints . . . the *Libellus de Moribus in Mensa Servandis* or *Essay on Manners in Serving at Table,* a rhymed treatise on youthful propriety and morals by Sulpizio de Veroli . . . Seneca's *De Quatuor Virtutibus Cardinalibus* or *Of the Four Cardinal Virtues,* a moral work by Martin de Braga, Bishop of Mondonedo in the sixth century . . . the *Specchio della vera Penitenza* or *Mirror of True Penitence* by Jacobo Passaventi, the Florentine monk of the sixteenth century—with its inevitable commentary! . . . a book of sermons, *Dormi Secure* or *Sleep in Peace,* a collection designed to save the preacher the pains of composing his sermons . . . and finally, other stuff of the same ilk, feather, kidney and broth. . . .

Indeed, Gargantua grew as even as any down ever smoothed, as full of matter as any goose liver ever crammed!

XV

HOW GARGANTUA WAS PUT
UNDER OTHER PROFESSORS

At last his father realized that though Gargantua was studying most industriously and spending all his time at it, he was profiting not at all. Worse, this training had actually made the lad over into a fool, a dunce, a booby and a nincompoop.

One day Grangousier happened to complain of it to Don Philippe des Marais, Viceroy of Papeligosse, a kingdom of Cockaigne.[14] That monarch assured Grangousier that Gargantua would be better off learning nothing than studying books of the sort with pedagogues of that school. Their knowledge, said Don Philippe, was but rubbish, their wisdom flapdoodle; they succeeded merely in bastardizing noble spirits and corrupting the flower of youth.

"Upon my word, I'll prove it!" Don Philippe declared. "Take any lad of to-day with but two years' schooling. If he is not superior to your son in judgment, speech, bearing and personality, then I'm the greatest loggerhead and shallowpate from here to Brenne."

This challenge pleased Grangousier mightily; he at once gave orders that a match of wits take place.

---

[14] An imaginary country of idleness and luxury.

That evening, at supper, Don Philippe brought in a young page of his named Eudemon, which means "the fortunate." The lad hailed from Villegongis near St. Genou in Touraine. He was so neat, so spruce, so handsome and his hair was so beautifully combed that he looked more like an angel than like a man.[15]

Don Philippe turned to Grangousier:

"Do you see this lad? He's not twelve years old. Let us prove, if you will, the difference between the pedantic balderdash of yesterday's wiseacres and the intelligence of our modern boys."

Grangousier was agreeable to such a test and bade the page begin the debate. Whereupon Eudemon, asking leave of the Viceroy, his master, to do so, rose, hat in hand. His face was open and frank, his lips red, his glance confident. Looking at Gargantua with youthful modesty, he proceeded to praise and commend the boy—first for his virtues and good manners, next for his knowledge, thirdly for his nobility, fourthly for his bodily excellences and, in the fifth place, exhorted him most gracefully to reverence his father in all respects, because his father was so careful to have him well brought up. Finally, Eudemon prayed Gargantua to admit him among the least of his bondsmen. He added that the only boon he craved from Heaven, at present, was to serve Gargantua in some agreeable manner. Eudemon accompanied the whole speech with gestures so appropriate, his delivery was so distinct, his voice rang so eloquent, his idiom was so elegant and he couched his phrases in such perfect Latin that he seemed rather a Tiberius Gracchus, a Cicero or an Aemilius Lepidus of old,[16] than a youth of our own day.

Gargantua's only reaction was to burst into tears. He bawled like a sick cow, hung his head and hid his face in his cap, until there was about as much possibility of drawing a word from him as a salvo of farts from the rump of a dead donkey.

This so incensed his father that Grangousier vowed to slay Master Jobelin Clotpoll, but Don Philippe remonstrated with him and, by fair persuasions, soothed his ire. Grangousier thereupon ordered them to pay the pedagogue off and to get him as properly fuddled up as your finest scholar of the Sorbonne. This accomplished, let him go to the devil!

"There is this consolation!" cried Grangousier. "To-day at least, he will not cost his host much if by chance he dies in his cups like an Englishman."

When Master Jobelin Clotpoll had gone away, Grangousier asked Don Philippe's advice about a tutor for Gargantua. They finally decided to appoint Ponocrates, Eudemon's teacher, to the position; auspiciously enough, in Greek the name means "vigorous." And soon, the three were to go to Paris in order to find out what studies young men were at this period pursuing in France.

---

[15] Eudemon represents the new education, in contrast to Gargantua's old-fashioned education. He speaks in Ciceronian Latin and, in his speech, follows an orderly mode of developing a thesis.

[16] The Roman orator Cicero (106–43 B.C.) praised both Tiberius Gracchus and Aemilius Lepidus for their skill in oratory.

XVI

How Gargantua Went to
Paris Upon an Enormous
Mare Which Destroyed
the Oxflies of the Beauce

In the same season, Fayolles, fourth king of Numidia, sent Grangousier a mare from Africa. It was the hugest and most enormous mare ever seen, the strangest monster in the world; for Africa, as the saying goes, may always be relied upon to produce something wonderfully new. The beast was as big as six elephants; like Julius Caesar's charger, her feet were cloven into human toes; her ears hung down like those of the goats of Languedoc; and a little horn grew out of one buttock. Save for a few dapple-gray spots as overlay, her coat was the color of burnt sorrel, which shows that she partook of the four elements, earth, water, air and fire. Above all, she had a horrible tail. It was more or less as tall as the tower of St. Mars near Langeais; and just as square, with tufts of hair as tightly spun and woven as the beards on ears of corn.

Do you marvel at this? You have greater cause to marvel at the tails of the rams of Scythia, which weighed more than thirty pounds each, or—if Jean Thenaud speaks truthfully in his *Voyage from Angoulême to Cairo*—at those of the Syrian sheep which are so long and heavy that, to hold them up, the natives have to hitch a small cart to the beast's rump. Ha! my lusty country wenchthumpers, you've no such tails as these!

The mare Fayolles sent Grangousier was brought overseas in three Genoese carracks and a brigantine; she landed at Les Sables d'Olonne in Talmondais.

When Grangousier laid eyes upon her:

"Ah!" he exclaimed. "Here is just what my son needs to bear him to Paris! So now, in God's name, all will go well: Gargantua shall be a great scholar one of these days! Were it not for dumb brutes we should all be scholars!"

Next day, having drunk liberally, as you may imagine, Gargantua set out on his journey, accompanied by his tutor Ponocrates, the young page Eudemon and his train. And, because the weather was serene and temperate, Grangousier had a pair of dun-colored boots made for him. According to Babin and the Chinon cobblers, these are technically known as buskins.

So they travelled along the highway very merrily, living on the fat of the land and making the best of cheer, until a little beyond Orléans they came to a huge forest, about thirty-five leagues long and seventeen wide. Alas! the woods were aswarm with oxflies and hornets of all varieties, so the wretched mares, asses and horses suffered a veritable massacre. But, by means of a trick they never suspected, Gargantua's mare handsomely avenged all the outrages visited upon her kind. For suddenly, when in the heart of the forest the wasps attacked her, she swished her tail and, sweeping all about her, not only felled the stingers but uprooted all the trees. Up and down, right and left, lengthwise and athwart, here and there, over and under, before her and aback, this way and that, she mowed down the woods like so much grass. And this region, which she thus turned into fallow land, has never known tree or wasp since.

Gargantua, delighted by the spectacle, forbore to boast, merely commenting to his followers:

"*Je trouve beau ce!* I find this pleasant!"

Whence this pleasant land has been known as Beauce ever since.

However, when it came to breakfasting, they had to content themselves with their yawns; in memory of which the gentlemen of the Beauce, proverbially poor, still subsist on a diet of yawns and gaping, and find it very nourishing. Indeed, they spit all the better for it.

At last they reached Paris, where Gargantua rested two or three days, making merry with his followers and inquiring about what scholars were then in the city and what wines people drank.

XVII

Of the Treat Gargantua
Gave the Parisians on
His Arrival and How He
Carried Off the Great
Bells of Notre Dame

After a few days' rest, Gargantua went sightseeing. He attracted the attention of all the townsmen because Parisians are such fools, dolts and gulls that a mountebank, a hawker of relics and indulgences,[17] a mule with a bell on its neck or a fiddler on a street corner, collects a greater mob than the most distinguished and authoritative preacher.

They thronged so thick about him that he said in a loud clear voice:

"Upon my word, I think these boobies want me to pay my welcome here and give the Bishop an offertory.[18] Quite right, too! I'll treat them! They'll get their drink! I recognize my obligations and liquidate I shall!—but only *par ris,* for sport!"

Then, smiling, he unfastened his noble codpiece and lugging out his great pleasure-rod, he so fiercely bepissed them that he drowned two hundred and sixty thousand four hundred and eighteen, exclusive of women and children.

By sheer fleetness of foot, a certain number escaped this mighty pissflood, and reaching the top of the Montagne Ste. Geneviève, beyond the University, sweating, coughing, hawking and out of breath, they began to swear and curse, some in anger, others in jest:

—"God's plague and a pox take it! I'll deny God, if . . ."

—"'Sblood!"

—"Christ, look ye, it's *Mère de . . . merde . . .* shit . . . Mother of God!"

—"*Pocapedion!* God's head!" roared a Gascon.

—"*Das dich Gots leyden Schend!*" bellowed a German trooper. "Christ's passion roil you!"

—"*Pote de Christo!*" an Italian voice rang out. "Christ's power!"

—"*Ventre St. Quenet!* . . . By the bellies of all the apostles . . . God's virtue . . . by St. Fiacre of the land of Brie!"

---

[17] Memorials of saints and papers remitting temporal punishments for sins.
[18] Fee paid to bishops after their ordination.

They called upon the renowned saint who cured miraculously such ailments as hemorrhoids and chancres, and who was patron to gardeners and husbandmen; one, doubtless a Scots Guard, invoked St. Andrew; and St. Theobald of Vico, the patron of shoemakers, was duly implored to intercede.

—*"Pasques Dieu!* God's passover!" said one, using an oath consecrated by King Louis XI.

—*"Bonjour Dieu!* God's light!" said another, after the manner of Charles VII.

—*"Le Diable m'emporte!* Devil take me!" said a third, quoting Louis XII.

—*"Foy de Gentilhomme!* My faith as a gentleman!" said a fourth, like Francis I.

—*"Par St. Andouille* . . . by St. Chitterling . . . by St. Godegran stoned to death with apple dumplings . . . by St. Foutin, the fornicators' friend! . . . by St. Vitus and his jig! . . . *Carimari, Carimara, hocus, pocus!* . . . by St. Mamica, the virgin martyr, by our lusty mammical duty to all virgins. . . ."

But, whatever protector each invoked, one and all cried:

"Nous sommes baignés par ris, we are drenched *par ris,* for sport."

Accordingly, the city which Strabo (Book IV) calls Leucetia—the name, signifying "whiteness" in Greek, pays a pretty tribute to the thighs of the local ladies—was, ever after Gargantua's exploit, named *par ris* or Paris.

And, since at this new christening every single townsman present swore by all the saints in his parish, the Parisians, who are made up of all nations and all varieties of men, will quite naturally swear at, to or by anything. Indeed they are not a little presumptuous and conceited, whence Joaninus de Barranco in his *Liber de Copiositate Reverentiarum* or *Of the Abundance of Venerable Things* opines that the word *Parisian* comes from the Greek *Parrhesieus,* a bold talker.

His account liquidated, Gargantua considered the great bells in the Towers of Notre Dame and made them ring out most harmoniously. The music suggested to him that they might sound very sweet tinkling on his mare's neck when he sent her back to his father laden with Brie cheese and fresh herring. So he promptly picked up the bells of the Cathedral and carried them home. . . .

XXI

GARGANTUA'S EDUCATION AND SOCIAL LIFE UNDER THE DIRECTION OF HIS PRECEPTORS AT THE SORBONNE

The . . . bells put back in place, the citizens of Paris, in acknowledgment of Gargantua's civility, offered to feed and maintain his mare as long as he wished. Gargantua accepted this courtesy, so the Parisians sent the beast to graze in the Forest of Bière or Fontainebleau. (I do not believe she is still there.)

This accomplished, Gargantua resolved with all his heart to study under the direction of Ponocrates. But the latter, wishing to learn how the lad's former teachers had wasted so much time making a crackbrained, addle-pated dunce of him, decided he should do exactly as he had in the past.

Gargantua therefore arranged his schedule so as to awake usually be-tween eight and nine o'clock, rain or shine, dark or daylight, simply be-cause his preceptors had decided this on the strength of the Psalmist's saw: *"Vanum est vobis ante lucem surgere,* it is vain for you to rise up betimes."

Then he wriggled and writhed, wallowing in his bed and tossing about like a parched pea, the better to stimulate his vital spirits. Next, he would dress, according to the season, but he was always happy to don a long, hanging gown of heavy wool lined with fox. Next, he combed out his hair with the comb of Jacques Almain, the Sorbonne theologian, known in Eng-lish as John Handy—a comb consisting of four fingers and a thumb—for his mentors maintained that to brush one's hair, wash one's face and make oneself clean were, in this world, a pure waste of time.

Next Gargantua dunged, piddled, vomited, belched, broke wind, yawned, spat, coughed, hiccoughed, sneezed and snotted himself as majes-tically and bountifully as an archdeacon. Next he proceeded to breakfast in order to fortify himself against the morning mist and cold. His menu con-sisted of splendid fried tripe, choice meats grilled on charcoal, rich hams, succulent roast venison and numerous soups and brews, with toast, cheese, parsley and chopped meat floating on the surface.

Ponocrates objected that he should not eat so soon after rising without having taken any exercise. To which he replied:

"Exercise? Good God, didn't I tumble and jounce in bed six or seven times before I got up? Surely, that is exercise enough? Pope Alexander VI did this on the advice of his Jew physician, Bonnet de Lates, and lived till the day of his death in spite of his enemies. My first masters taught me this habit, for breakfast, they said, gave man a good mind. So they started the day by drinking. It suits me perfectly and I manage to dine the better for it. Master Tubal Holofernes, who was graduated Licentiate in Paris at the head of his class, used to tell me that to hasten was not enough, one must set out betimes. By the same token, the total health of mankind does not con-sist in drinking down and lapping up, *glub, glub, glub,* like so many ducks, but rather in falling to, early in the morning. *Unde versus;* so runs the rune:

> *Lever matin n'est point bonheur*
> *Boire matin est le meilleur.*
>
> *To rise betimes is not enough,*
> *To drink at morning, that's the stuff!"*

After an abundant breakfast, Gargantua repaired to church, with, in his train, a varlet bearing a basket. The latter contained a huge breviary swad-dled in velvet and weighing about twelve hundred and six pounds includ-ing the filth of thumbmarks, dogeared corners, golden clasps and nonpa-reil parchment. Twenty-six, if not thirty, masses ensued for the benefit of Gargantua and his chaplain. Under his tall hood, this chaplain looked for all the world like a peewit . . . and had very thoroughly antidoted his breath against possible poisons with much syrup of the vine! Chaplain and pupil babbled the mumbo jumbo of the litany, thumbing their rosaries so carefully that not one single bead fell to the ground.

As he left the church, they brought him an oxcart laden with a huge heap of paternosters, chaplets and relics from St. Claude in the Jura, each bigger than a hatblock.[19] Gargantua and his chaplain then strolled in the cloisters, galleries or garden, saying more aves than sixteen hermits.

After, Gargantua would study for a short half-hour, his eyes glued to his book but his mind, to quote Terence's *Eunuch*,[20] wool-gathering in the kitchen. Then he proceeded to make water, filling a large urinal to capacity, after which he sat down at table, and, being naturally phlegmatic, began his meal with a few dozen hams, smoked tongues of beef, caviar, sausages and other like forerunners of wine.

Then four servants in turn shovelled mustard into his mouth by the spadeful, thus preparing him to drain a horrific draught of white wine to relieve his kidneys. Then the meal proper began with viands to his liking, according to the season; Gargantua ceasing to eat only when his belly had reached bursting point.

When it came to drinking, he acknowledged neither end nor rule; for, he said, there were no limits and boundaries to swilling until the tosspot felt the cork soles of his shoes swell up a half-foot from the ground.

XXIII

How Ponocrates Gave Gargantua Such Instruction That Not an Hour of the Day Was Wasted

When Ponocrates saw Gargantua's vicious mode of life, he determined to bring him up otherwise. But for the first few days he bore with him, for he realized that nature cannot endure sudden and violent changes.

To begin his work the better, Ponocrates requested a learned physician of the times, Master Theodore—the name means "God-given"—to examine Gargantua thoroughly with a view to steering him on the right course. The scholar purged Gargantua canonically with Anticyrian hellebore, an herb indicated for cerebral disorders and insanity, thus cleansing his brain of its unnatural, perverse condition. Ponocrates, by the same aperient means, made the lad forget all he had learned under his former teachers, just as Timotheus of old treated pupils who had already studied under other musicians. Timotheus, incidentally, used to charge this class of students double!

For Gargantua's further edification, Ponocrates made him mingle among learned men whose company fired him with a desire to emulate them, to study more profitably and to make his mark. Next, Ponocrates so arranged the lad's schedule that not a moment of the day was wasted; all his time was spent in the pursuit of learning and honest knowledge.

By this new dispensation, Gargantua awoke at about four in the morning. While the servants massaged him, he would listen to some page of

---

[19] St. Claude was famous for rosaries.
[20] A comedy by the Roman dramatist Terence (c. 185–c. 159 B.C.).

Holy Scripture, read aloud in clear tones and pronounced with fitting respect for the text. A young page, a native of Basché, near Chinon, was appointed reader, as his name, Anagnostes, shows. According to the purpose and argument of this lesson, Gargantua frequently turned to worship, adore, pray and reverence Almighty God, Whose majesty and wondrous wisdom were made manifest in the reading.

Next, he would repair to secret places to make excretion of his natural digestions; here his tutor repeated what had been read, expounding its more obscure and difficult features. Returning to the house, they would study the heavens. Was it the same sky they had observed the night before? Into what signs was the sun entering that day? and the moon?

After this astronomical survey, Gargantua was dressed, combed, curled, trimmed and perfumed, and, while this was being done, he heard the lessons of the day before. Then, having recited them by heart, he would argue certain practical, human and utilitarian cases based upon the principles enunciated. This part of the program sometimes took two or three hours, though usually he had exhausted it by the time he was fully clad.

Then, for three good hours, he was read or lectured to, after which they went to the Tennis Court at the Grande Bracque in the Place de l'Estrapade or to the playing fields.

On the way, they discussed various aspects of the subject previously treated. Then they would play tennis, handball and three-cornered catch, exercising their bodies as vigorously as they had exercised their minds before.

All their play was free for they left off when they pleased, which was usually when they had sweated a good bit or were otherwise tired. They were thoroughly wiped and rubbed down, after which they changed their shirts and walked quietly home to see if dinner were ready. As they waited, they would go over certain points they had retained of the lectures.

Meanwhile My Lord Appetite put in an appearance and they sat down most opportunely to table.

At the beginning of the meal, they listened to the reading of some agreeable chronicle of chivalry in ancient times, until Gargantua gave the signal for wine to be served. Then, if they wished, the reading went on or they could talk merrily together. Often they discussed the virtues, property, efficacy and nature of what was served at table: bread, wine, water, salt, meat, fish, fruit, herbs, roots and their preparation. Thus Gargantua soon knew all the relevant passages in Pliny's *Natural History* . . . in the grammarian Athenaeus' *Deipnosophistes* or *The Banquet of the Sages*, which treats of flowers, fruits and their various uses . . . in Dioscorides' famous medical treatise, the bible of apothecaries . . . in the *Vocabularium* by Julius Pollux, a grammarian and sophist of Marcus Aurelius' day, who wrote of hunting and fishing . . . in Galen's numerous dissertations upon alimentation . . . in the works of Porphyrius, the third-century Greek author of a *Treatise upon Abstinence from Meat* . . . in Oppian's two poems, *Cynegetica* which deals with venery and *Halieutica* with angling . . . in *Of Healthy Diet* by Polybius of Cos, disciple and son-in-law of Hippocrates . . . in Heliodorus of Emesa, Syrian Bishop of Tricca and a celebrated novelist of the fourth century . . . in Aristotle's essays on natural history . . . in the Greek works upon animals by Claudius Aelianus, a Roman contemporary of Heliogobalus

. . . and in various other tomes. . . . Often for surer authority as they argued, they would have the book in question brought to the table. Gargantua so thoroughly and cogently learned and assimilated all he heard that no physician of his times knew one-half so much as he.

They discussed the lessons they had learned that morning and topped their meal off with quiddany, a sort of quince marmalade and an excellent digestive. After which Gargantua picked his teeth with a fragment of mastic,[21] washed his hands and daubed his eyes with cool clear water, and, instead of saying grace, sang the glory of God in noble hymns, composed in praise of divine bounty and munificence.

Presently cards were brought them and they played, not for the sake of the pastime itself but to learn a thousand new tricks and inventions all based on arithmetic.

Thus Gargantua developed a keen enthusiasm for mathematics, spending his leisure after dinner and supper every evening as pleasantly as once he had, dicing and gaming. As a result, he knew so much about its theory and practice that Cuthbert Tunstal, Bishop of Durham and secretary to King Henry VIII, a voluminous writer on the subject, confessed that, beside Gargantua, he knew no more about arithmetic than he did about Old High Gothic. Nor was it arithmetic alone our hero learned, but also such sister sciences as geometry, astronomy and music.

Now the digestion of foods is a most important matter. There is the first stage which occurs in the stomach, where the viands are changed into chyle; the second, in the liver, where the chyle is transformed into blood; the third, in the habit of the body, where the blood is finally converted into the substance of each part. So, whilst Gargantua awaited the first stage of digestion, they made a thousand delightful instruments, drew geometrical figures and even applied the principles of astronomy.

After, they amused themselves singing a five-part score or improvising on a theme chosen at random. As for musical instruments, Gargantua learned to play the lute, the spinet, the harp, the nine-holed transverse or German flute, the viol and the sackbut or trombone.

Having spent an hour thus and completed his digestion, he discharged his natural excrements and then settled down again to work three hours or more at his principal study. Either he revised the morning reading, or proceeded in the text at hand or practised penmanship in the most carefully formed characters of modern Roman and ancient Gothic script.

Next, they went out with a young gentleman of Touraine, the esquire Gymnastes, who instructed Gargantua in the art of horsemanship. Having changed his clothes, he proceeded to mount a fiery Italian charger, a Flemish dray horse, a Spanish jennet, an Arab thoroughbred and a hackney. These he would put vigorously through their paces, letting them "career" or gallop a short distance at full speed, making them leap high in the air, jump ditches, clear stiles, and turn short in a ring both to the right and to the left. Next he wielded but did not break his lance, for it is arrant stupidity to boast: "I have broken ten lances in a tilt or fight." A wretched carpenter can do the same. On the contrary, the whole glory of such combat lies in besting ten enemies with one and the same lance. So with a strong, stiff,

---

[21] An aromatic resin from a tree.

steel-tipped lance, Gargantua would force the outer door of some house, pierce an adversary's armor, beat down a tree, pick up a ring, carry off a cuirassier saddle, a hauberk or a gauntlet. And he performed these feats armed cap-à-pie.[22]

In the technique of parading his horse with prances and flourishes to a fanfare of trumpets—the ceremonial of knights as they enter the lists—he had no equal. As for the divers terms of the equine vocabulary from *giddy-up* and *cluck* to *whoa* and *grrr,* no horseman could hold a candle to him. Indeed Cesare Fieschi, the celebrated jockey of Ferrara, was a mere monkey in comparison.

He learned, too, to leap hastily and with singular dexterity from one horse to another without setting foot to the ground (the nags were circus horses or, to be technical, "desultories"). Further, lance in hand, he could leap on horseback from either side without stirrups and rule the beast at will without a bridle, for such accomplishments are highly useful in military engagements.

Another day he would practice wielding the battle-axe, which he managed so skillfully, in the nimblest thrusts, the most powerful lunges and the vast encircling sweeps of the art, that he passed knight-at-arms in the field and at all tests. Sometimes unarmed, sometimes carrying a buckler or a rolled cape of mail over his arm or a small shield over his wrist, Gargantua brandished the pike, plied the double-edged, two-handed sword, the bastard claymore used by archers, the Spanish rapier, the dagger and the poniard.

He hunted, too: stag, roebuck, bear, fallow deer, wild boar, hare, partridge, pheasant and otter . . . he played at ball, ever ready with well-aimed foot or powerful fist to send the great sphere whizzing through the air . . . he learned to wrestle and to run. . . . As for jumping, he did not go in for the various forms of running jumps, such as the three-steps-and-a-leap, the hop-step-and-jump or the German high-jump. As Gymnastes pointed out, these were quite useless in warfare. Instead, he practiced the standing jumps. Starting from scratch, he could in one leap top a hedge, clear a ditch, mount six paces upon a wall and thus reach a window-ledge one lance's height from the ground.

Gargantua could swim in the deepest water, breaststroke, back and sidestroke, using his whole body or his feet alone. He could cross the breadth of the Seine or the Loire at Montsoreau, dragging his cloak along in his teeth and holding a book high and dry over the waters—thus renewing the exploit with which Plutarch credits Julius Caesar during the Alexandrian War. Then, using one hand only, he could, with a single great pull, climb into a boat, whence a moment later he would dive headlong into the water again, sound its utmost depths, touch bottom, explore the hollows of rocks and plunge into any pits and abysses he fancied. He would turn the boat about, managing it perfectly, bringing it swiftly or slowly upstream or down and arresting its course at a milldam. He could guide it with one hand while he plied hard about him with a great oar; he could run up a sail, hoist himself up a mast by the shrouds, dance along the yards, operate the compass, tackle the bowlines to sail close to the wind and steer the helm.

---

[22] From head to foot.

His water sports done, he would dash full speed up a mountain, then down quite as fast. He climbed trees like a cat, hopping from one to the next like a squirrel and pulling down great boughs—like the celebrated Milo of Crotona who, Pausanias tells us, met his death devoured by wolves, his hands caught in the cleft of an oak he had sought to split. With two well-steeled daggers and a pair of well-tried mason's punches, he could scurry up the side of a house like a rat, then leap down again, from roof to ground, so expertly that he landed without hurt. Gargantua also cast the dart, threw the iron bar, put the stone, tossed the boar-spear, hurled the javelin, shied the halberd. He drew the bow to breaking point; he could shoulder a harquebuss—a great siege piece weighing fifty pounds—and fire it off like a crossbow. He could set a huge cannon on its carriage, hit buttmarks and other targets for horizontal shooting, or, point-blank, bring down papgays (stuffed figures of parrots on poles), clay pigeons and other vertical marks, facing them on a level or upwards, or downwards or sidewise. Like the ancient Parthians, he could even hit them as he retreated.

They would tie a cable to a high tower and let it dangle to the ground. Gargantua hoisted himself up with both hands, then slipped down again as evenly, surely and plumb as a man running along a flat meadow. Or they would set a great pole across two trees for Gargantua to hang from by his hands. He moved along the pole from tree to tree so swiftly, without setting foot on *terra firma,* that a man, running on the ground below, could not have caught him. To expand his chest and exercise his lungs, he would roar like all the devils in hell. Once indeed, I heard him call Eudemon across all Paris, from the Porte St. Victor, the gate by the University, all the way to Montmartre, a village on a hill two miles beyond the walls of the city. Stentor, who cried louder than forty men, displayed no such vocal power, even at the siege of Troy.

To develop his sinews, they made him two great pigs of lead, each weighing eight hundred and five tons. These pigs (called salmons in France because the metal is shaped like this fish) Gargantua named *alteres,* an ancient Greek term for the weights used to give jumpers their initial spring— our modern dumb-bells. Taking one in each hand, Gargantua then performed an inimitable feat. He would raise them high above his head and, never turning a hair, stock-still as a statue, hold them aloft for three-quarters of an hour. He played at Barriers or Tug-of-War with the stoutest champions. When his turn came he took root so firmly as to defy the sturdiest to budge him. Nor was it thus alone he emulated Milo of Crotona. Like the ancient athlete, he could hold a pomegranate so fast in his hand that none could wrest it from him, yet so adroitly that he did not crush it.

Having spent his time in such manly sports, he had himself washed, rubbed down and given a change of clothes. Then he returned home at a leisurely pace, passing through some meadow or grassy space to examine the trees and plants. These he would compare with what the authorities wrote of them in their books: among the Ancients, Theophrastus, the successor of Aristotle and teacher of Menander . . . or Palladius, whose poem *De re rustica* was translated by Pietro Marini . . . or Dioscorides Pedanius, the Greek physician of the first century . . . or Pliny or Nicander or Aemilius Macer, the Roman, or Galen himself. . . . Gargantua and his companions picked specimens by the handful and took them home to a young page named Rhizotome or Rootcutter, who watched over them and the various small mattocks, pickaxes, hooks, hoes, pruning-knives, shears and other botanical instruments.

At home, whilst the servants prepared dinner, our young men repeated certain passages of what had been read. Then they sat down to table. Here I would have you note that their dinner was simple and frugal; they ate no more than necessary to quiet the baying of the belly. Supper, on the contrary, was a large and copious meal; they ate what they needed for their sustenance and nourishment. Such indeed is the true system prescribed by the art of sound, self-respecting physicians though a rabble of dunderhead quacks, wrangling eternally in the claptrap routine of the Arab nostrum shop of Avicenna, recommend the exact opposite. During supper, they continued the lesson given at dinner as long as they saw fit; the rest of the meal was spent in earnest and profitable discussion.

Having said grace, they applied their voices to sing tunefully or they played upon harmonious instruments. Or they amused themselves with such minor pastimes as cards, dice cups and dice afforded. Sometimes they tarried here enjoying themselves and making merry until bedtime; they would visit learned men or such as had travelled in foreign lands. Well into the night, before retiring, they would go to the most exposed spot in the house, whence they examined the face of the sky, noting the comets, if any were visible, and the various figures, positions, aspects, oppositions and conjunctions of the heavenly bodies.

According to the Pythagorean system, Gargantua would, with his tutor, recapitulate briefly all that he had read, seen, learned, done and assimilated in the course of the day.

Then they prayed to God the Creator, doing Him worship and confirming their faith in Him, glorifying Him for His immense goodness, vouchsafing thanks for all the mighty past and imploring His divine clemency for all the future.

And so they retired to rest.

XXIV

How Gargantua Spent His Time in Rainy Weather

In intemperate or rainy weather, things went on much the same as usual before dinner except that Gargantua had a fine bright fire lighted to correct the inclemency of the air. But after dinner, instead of gymnastics, they stayed indoors and, by way of apotherapy or exercise amused themselves by bundling hay, splitting logs, sawing wood and threshing sheaves in the barn. Then they studied the arts of painting and sculpture. Or they revived the ancient Roman game of *Tali*, dicing as the Italian humanist Nicolaus Leonicus Thomaeus wrote of it in his dialogue *Sannutus, Of the Game of Dice*, and as our good friend Janus Lascaris, librarian to our sovereign king, plays at the game. In their sport, they reviewed such passages of ancient authors as mention or quote some metaphor drawn from this play.

In much the same way, they might go to watch workmen forging metals or casting pieces of ordnance. Or they might visit the lapidaries, goldsmiths

and cutters of precious stones in their ateliers, the alchemists in their labo-
ratories, the coiners at the mint, the tapestry-workers, velvet-workers and
weavers at their looms, the watchmakers, looking-glass framers, printers,
lutemakers, dyers and other such artisans in their workshops. Wherever
they went, they would distribute gratuities, invariably investigating and
learning the various inventions and industry of the trade.

Or they might attend public lectures, official convocations, oratorical
performances, speeches, pleadings by eloquent attorneys and sermons by
evangelical preachers—that is, such priests as wished to restore Christianity
to the primitive tradition of the Gospel. Gargantua also frequented fencing
halls and tested his skill at all weapons against the masters, proving to them
by experience that he knew as much as they and, indeed, even more.

Instead of herborizing, they would inspect the shops of druggists, herb-
alists and apothecaries, studiously examining the sundry fruits, roots,
leaves, gums, seeds and exotic unguents and learning how they could be
diluted or adulterated. He viewed jugglers, mountebanks and medicast-
ers—who sold Venice treacle, a cure for all ills—carefully observing their
tricks and gestures, their agile capers and smooth oratory. His favorites
were those from Chauny in Picardy who are born jabberers and the
readiest expounders of mealy-mouthed flimflam concerning their ability to
weave ropes of sand, extract sunbeams from cucumbers and milk a he-goat
into a sieve.

Returning home to supper, they would eat more sparingly than on fine
days. Their meats would, by the same token, be more desiccative and extenuating so as to counteract the humidity communicated to their bodies by
the necessary contiguity of the atmosphere and to nullify what harm might
arise from lack of their customary exercise.

Such was Gargantua's program and so he continued from day to day,
benefiting as you would expect a young man of his age and intelligence to
benefit under such a system faithfully applied. To be sure, the whole thing
may have seemed incredibly difficult to him at the outset, but it soon
proved so light, so easy and so pleasant as to appear more like a king's
pastime than the study of a schoolboy.

However, Ponocrates was careful to supply relaxation from this violent
bodily and mental tension. Once a month, on some very bright serene day,
they would clear out of town early in the morning, bound for the near-by
villages of Gentilly, Boulogne, Montrouge, Pont-de-Charenton, Vanves or
St. Cloud. There they spent the whole day enjoying themselves to their
heart's content, sporting and merrymaking, drinking toast for proffered
toast, playing, singing, dancing, tumbling about or loafing in some fair
meadow, turning sparrows out of their nests, bagging quail and fishing for
frogs and crayfish.

But though this holiday was free of books and reading, it was not spent
unprofitably. Lying in the green meadow, they usually recited certain delightful lines from Virgil's *Georgics,* from Hesiod's *Works and Days* or from
Politian's *Husbandry.* Or they broached some savory epigram in Latin, then
turned it into a French roundelay or ballade.

In their feasting, they would sometimes separate the twin elements,
isolating the wine and the water in their drink by pouring the latter into a
cup of ivy-wood, as Cato teaches in his *De re rustica,* and Pliny elsewhere.

Then they would wash the wine in a basin full of water and draw it out with a funnel, as pure as ever. And they pumped the water with a syphon from one glass to another, manufacturing several sorts of automatic or self-operating devices.

LII

How Gargantua Had the Abbey of Thélème Built for the Monk[23]

There remained only the monk to provide for. Gargantua offered him the Abbey of Seuilly: he refused. What about the Benedictine abbeys of Bourgueil or St. Florent, among the richest in France: he might have either or both? Again, the offer met with a flat refusal: Friar John of the Funnels answered peremptorily that he did not seek the charge or government of monks.

"For," he explained, "how shall I govern others when I cannot possibly govern myself?" There was a pause. "But—" he hesitated. "But if you believe I have given and can give you good service, let me found an abbey after my own heart."

The notion delighted Gargantua: he forthwith offered his estate of Thélème, by the Loire, two leagues away from Port Huault. Thélème in Greek means free will, an auspicious name for Friar John's abbey. Here indeed he could institute a religious order contrary to all others.

"First," said Gargantua, "you must not build a wall around it, for all other abbeys are solidly enclosed."

"Quite so," agreed the monk, "for where there are *mures,* walls, before, and *mures,* walls, behind, we have *murmures,* murmurs of envy and plotting."

Now in certain monasteries it is a rule that if any women enter (I mean honest and chaste ones) the ground they tread upon must be swept over. Therefore it was decreed that if a monk or nun should by any chance enter Thélème, every place that religious passed through should be thoroughly disinfected.

Similarly because all monasteries and convents on earth are compassed, limited and regulated by hours, at Thélème no clock or dial of any sort should be tolerated. On the contrary, their time here would be governed by what occasions and opportunities might arise. As Gargantua sagaciously commented:

"I can conceive of no greater waste of time than to count the hours. What good comes of it? To order your life by the toll of a bell instead of by reason or common sense is the veriest piece of asininity imaginable."

By the same token, they established the qualifications for entrance into

---

[23] "The monk" is Friar John, a major character in the episode of the Picrocholine War, here omitted, and in later books of *Gargantua and Pantagruel*. The Picrocholine War, an absurdly inflated contest begun with a dispute with some cake-peddlers, parodies a quarrel in Rabelais' own Chinon country over navigation rights on the River Loire. In this episode, Rabelais reveals his hatred of war, his discrimination between just and unjust wars, and his humane attitudes on the treatment of defeated enemies.

their order. Was it not true that at present women took the veil only if they were wall-eyed, lame, hunchbacked, ill-favored, misshapen, half-witted, unreasonable or somewhat damaged? That only such men entered monasteries as were cankered, ill-bred idiots or plain nuisances?

("Incidentally," said Friar John, "if the woman is neither fair nor good, of what use is the cloth?"

"Let the clot hump her," Gargantua replied.

"I said 'cloth' not 'clot.' "

"Well, what's the answer?"

"To cover her face or her arse with!")

Accordingly, they decided to admit into the new order only such women as were beautiful, shapely, pleasing of form and nature, and such men as were handsome, athletic and personable.

Again, because men entered the convents of this world only by guile and stealth, it was decreed that no women would be in Thélème unless men were there also, and vice-versa.

Moreover, since both men in monasteries and women in convents were forced after their year of noviciate to stay there perpetually, Gargantua and Friar John decided that the Thélèmites, men or women, might come and go whenever they saw fit.

Further, since the religious usually made the triple vow of chastity, poverty and obedience, at Thélème all had full leave to marry honestly, to enjoy wealth and to live in perfect freedom.

As for the age of initiation, they stipulated that women were admissible between the ages of ten and fifteen, men between twelve and eighteen.

LIII

How the Abbey of Thélème
was Built and Endowed

To build and furnish the abbey, Gargantua paid in cash twenty-seven hundred thousand eight hundred and thirty-one crowns in current coin of the realm, fresh from the mint, with a sheep on the obverse and the king's head on the reverse. He undertook to pay yearly, until the project was completed, sixteen hundred and sixty-nine thousand crowns, with the sun on the obverse, and as many again with the seven stars, the whole to be levied upon custom receipts.

For the foundation and maintenance of Thélème, he settled in perpetuity twenty-three hundred and sixty-nine thousand, five hundred and fourteen nobles (a coin stamped by the English kings with the rose of York), free of all tax, burden or fealty, payable yearly at the abbey gate. These privileges were all corroborated by letters patent.

The building was hexagonal; in each corner rose a great, circular tower, each identical, sixty yards in diameter. To the north, the river Loire flowed past the first tower which was named *Arctice* or Northern. East of it rose *Calaer* which means "situated in the balmy air"; then, successively, *Anatole* or Eastern; *Mesembrine* or Southern; *Hesperia* or Occidental; and the last, *Cryere* or Glacial. The distance between each tower was three hundred and twelve yards. The building was throughout six stories high, counting the underground cellar for one. The ground floor was vaulted like a basket handle; the others, covered with Flanders mistletoe,[24] jutting out like brackets and pendants. The roof, of finest slate, was lined with lead and bore little figures of mannikins and animals well assorted and gilt. The gutters jutted out from the walls between the casement arches; they were painted diagonally gold and blue down to the ground, where they ended in pipes which carried the water into the river below.

This building was a hundred times more magnificent than Bonnivet, Chambord or Chantilly.[25] There were nine thousand three hundred and thirty-two suites, each with a salon, a study, a dressing room, an oratory and an exit into a great hall. In the wing between each tower was a winding stairway. The steps, grouped in units of twelve between each landing, were of porphyry, of Numidian stone, of serpentine marble; they were twenty-two feet long and three fingers thick. At each landing, two spendid round antique archways admitted the light and led to an open loggia of the same dimensions. The stairway, rising to the roof, ended in a pavilion; on either side lay a great hall which in turn led to the apartments.

The wing between the towers called *Arctice* and *Cryere* contained rich libraries of Greek, Latin, Hebrew, French, Italian and Spanish volumes, grouped in their respective sections. In the center rose a marvellous winding ramp conceived in such ample proportions that six soldiers with their lances at rest could ride up it abreast to the top of the palace. Its entry, outside the house, was an archway six fathoms wide.

Between *Anatole* and *Mesembrine* were spacious galleries with murals representing heroic feats of olden times, scenes from history and pictures of the earth. Here again were a stairway and gate as described upon the river side. On this gate, couched in great antique letters, ran the following legend.

LIV

INSCRIPTION ENGRAVED ON
THE MAIN GATE AT THÉLÈME

Here enter not, smug hypocrites or holy loons,
Bigots, sham-Abrahams, impostors of the cloth,
Mealy-mouthed humbugs, holier-than-thou baboons,
Lip-service lubbers, smell-feast picaroons.
Else had we to admit the Goth and Ostrogoth,
Precursors of the ape and others of that broth.
Hence, sneaks and mischief-makers, colporteurs of lies,
Be off to other parts to sell your merchandise.

    Being foul you would befoul
    Man, woman, beast or fowl.   10
    The vileness of your ways

---

[24] A kind of plaster.   [25] Three of the most magnificent castles in France.

　　　　Would sully my sweet lays,
　　　　Owls—And your own black cowl,
　　　　Being foul, you would befoul.

Here enter not, defenders of dishonest pleas,
Clerks, barristers, attorneys who make freemen slaves,
Canon Law pettifoggers, censors, Pharisees,
Judges, assessors, arbitrators, referees
Who blithely doom good people to untimely graves,
The gibbet is your destination, legal knaves!   20
Be off: indict the rope if you should find it short,
Here there is no abuse; we do not need your court.

　　　　　Tangle, wrangle, brangle
　　　　　We loathe, from any angle.
　　　　　Our aim is joy and sport,
　　　　　Time's swift, youth's fleet, life's short.
　　　　　You, go and disentangle
　　　　　Tangle, wrangle, brangle!

Here enter not, curmudgeon, loan shark, muckworm, hunks,
Bloodsucking usurer, extortioner, pennystint, . . .   30
Hence, lawsuit-chasing crimps, greedy as starving punks
Tracking a patron; lickgolds, hiding cash in trunks,
Harpyclaws, crunchfists, jaundiced zealots of the mint,
Your crackling, sallow palms are itching. Skin a flint!
Heap up your hoard, O scrub-faced curs, heap up afresh,
And as you grudge and gripe and screw, God rot your flesh!

　　　　　Those grim and grisly faces
　　　　　Bear all the ravaged traces
　　　　　Of hidebound avarice;
　　　　　We cannot stomach this.   40
　　　　　Banish from all blithe places
　　　　　Those grim and grisly faces.

Here enter not, you churls, sour boors, invidious fools,
Old, jealous brabblers, scolds, neither by night nor day,
Nor grumblers, soreheads, sulkers, badgers bred in schools
Of hate; nor ghosts of malaperts; nor firebrands' ghouls
From Rhineland, Greece or Rome, fiercer than wolves at bay;
Nor you, riddled with pox, your face a Milky Way
Of scars not stars; nor you, clapstricken to the bone:
Enjoy your shameless crusts and blemishes alone.   50

　　　　　Honor, praise and pleasure
　　　　　Are here in goodly measure:
　　　　　Health reigns supreme because
　　　　　We follow Nature's laws.

Ours is a triple treasure:
Honor, praise and pleasure.

But enter here thrice welcome, men of goodly parts,
Gallants and noble gentlemen, thrice welcome be!
Here you will find an abbey after your own hearts,
Where living is esteemed the highest of the arts.   60
Come in your tens and hundreds, come in thousands, we
Shall clasp you to our bosoms in fond amity:
Come wise, come proud, come gay, come courteous, come mellow,
Come true sophisticate, come worldling, come, good fellow!

Comrades, companions, friends,
Assemble from the ends
Of earth in this fair place
Where all is mirth and grace.
Felicity here blends
Comrades, companions, friends.   70

Here enter, all ye loyal scholars who expound
Novel interpretations of the Holy Writ.
Here is a fort and refuge; from this favored ground
You may confound the error that is elsewhere found,
You may found a profound new faith instead of it,
Sweeping away false teachings, bit by fallacious bit.
Come unto us and make your cogent meanings heard:
Destroy the foes of God and of his Holy Word.

The Holy Word of God
Shall never be downtrod   80
Here in this holy place,
If all deem reason grace,
And use for staff and rod
The Holy Word of God.

Here enter, ladies fair of eminent degree,
Come soon with starry eyes, lips smiling, comely face,
Flowers of loveliness, angels of harmony,
Resplendent, proud yet of the rarest modesty,
Sprightly of flesh, lithe-waisted and compact of grace,
Here is your home. A gallant lord designed this place   90
For you, that beauty, charm and virtue might find room
Deliciously to breathe, exquisitely to bloom.

Who makes a priceless gift
Wins pardon without shrift.
Donor, recipient
Alike find rich content.
To him your voices lift
Who makes a priceless gift.

LV

How the Monks and Nuns
Lived at Thélème

In the middle of the lower court stood a magnificent alabaster fountain, surmounted by the Three Graces holding cornucopias and spouting water through their breasts, mouths, ears, eyes and other orifices. The buildings above this court stood upon great pillars of chalcedony and porphyry, forming classical arches about lengthy wide galleries adorned with paintings and trophies of various animals: the horns of bucks, unicorns and hippopotami, elephants' tusks and sundry other curiosities.

The ladies' quarters ran from *Arctice* all the way to the *Mesembrine* Gate; the rest of the abbey was reserved for men. In front of this part, between the outer two towers, lay the recreational facilities: the tilting yard, the riding school, the theater and the natatorium[26] which included wonderful swimming pools on three different levels, with every sort of equipment and myrtle water aplenty.

Near the river was the fine pleasure garden, with, in the middle, a maze. Tennis courts and football fields spread out between the next two towers. Close to *Cryere,* an orchard offered a mass of fruit trees laid out in quincunxes, with, at its end, a sizy park abounding in venison.

The space between the third pair of towers was reserved for the shooting ranges: here were targets and butts for harquebuss, long bow and crossbow. The servants' quarters, one story high, were situated outside *Hesperia*. Beyond was the falconry, managed by expert falconers and hawk trainers and annually supplied by the Cretans, Venetians and Sarmatian Poles with all manner of birds. There were priceless eagles for hunting hares, foxes and cranes. There were gerfalcons, goshawks, sakers for hunting wild geese, herons and bitterns. There were falcons, lanners, sparhawks and merlins for hunting larks and partridges. Other birds there were, too, in great quantities, so well trained that when they flew afield for their own sport they never failed to catch every bird they encountered. . . . The venery with its hounds and beagles stood a little further along towards the park.

All the halls, apartments and chambers were richly hung with tapestries varying with the season; the floors were covered with green cloth, the beds all embroidered. Each rear chamber boasted a pierglass set in a heavy gold frame adorned with pearls. Near the exits of the ladies' halls were the perfumers and hairdressers who ministered to the gentlemen before the latter visited the ladies. These attendants furnished the ladies' rooms with rose water, orange-flower water and angelica,[27] supplying a precious small atomizer to give forth the most exquisite aromatic perfumes.

---

[26] Swimming area.   [27] An aromatic herb.

LVI

HOW THE MONKS AND NUNS OF
THÉLÈME WERE APPARELLED

When first the abbey was founded, the ladies dressed according to their taste and pleasure. Subsequently of their own free will they modified their costume as follows.

They wore hose, of scarlet or kermes-red, reaching some three inches above the knee, the edge being exquisitely embroidered or slashed. Their garters, which matched their bracelets, came both a whit over and under the knee. Their shoes, pumps and slippers were of red, violet or crimson velvet and jagged as a lobster's claws.

Over their slips, they put on a tight tunic of pure silk camlet, and over that a taffeta farthingale or petticoat, red, white, beige, gray or of any other color. Above this farthingale went a skirt of silver taffeta, with fine gold embroidery and delicate cross-stitch work. According to the temperature, the season or the ladies' whim, these skirts might be satin, damask or velvet and, in color, orange, green, cendré, blue, canary yellow, scarlet, crimson or white, or of cloth-of-gold, cloth-of-silver, or any other choice material variously embroidered, stitched, brocaded or spangled according to the occasion for which they were worn.

Their gowns, or over-garments, were also governed by timely considerations. They might be cloth-of-gold with silver embossing or red satin with gold brocade or taffeta, white, blue, black or tawny. Or they might be silk rep, silk camlet, velvet, cloth-of-silver, cloth-of-gold or satin variously figured with gold and silver thread.

In summer, instead of these gowns, they wore lovely light smocks made of the same material, or capes, Moorish-fashion, with hoods to protect and shade their faces from the sun. These Moresco capes were of violet velvet, having raised gold stitching over silver purl or gold piping and cording, with small Indian pearls at their ends. And ever a gay colored plume, the color of their sleeves, bravely garnished with gold! In winter, their gowns were of taffeta in all the colors mentioned above, but lined with lynx, weasel, Calabrian marten, sable and other rare fur. Their beads, rings, chains and necklaces were of precious stones: carbuncles, rubies, balas rubies, diamonds, sapphires, emeralds, turquoises, garnets, agates, beryls and priceless pearls.

Their headgear also varied with the season. In winter, it was in the French fashion with a cap over the temples covered by a velvet hood with hanging veil. In spring it was in the Spanish, with laces and veils. In summer it was in the Tuscan, the hair elaborately entwined with gold chains and jewels. On Sundays and holidays, however, they followed the French mode which is more seemly and modest.

The men, too, dressed according to their personal taste. Their hose were of light wool or serge cloth, white, black, scarlet or kermes-red. Their velvet breeches were of the same hue or almost; they were embroidered or slashed to their taste. The doublet was of cloth-of-gold, cloth-of-silver, velvet, satin or damask, embroidered, panelled or slashed on one model, the points silk to match and the ornaments of fine enamelled gold.

Their cloaks and jerkins were of cloth-of-gold, cloth-of-silver, gold tissue or velvet, purfled or brocaded at pleasure; their over-garments were every whit as costly as the ladies'. Their girdles were silk, matching their doublets. Each wore on his side a handsome sword with gilt hilt and pommel; the scabbard velvet, matching his breeches, and the ferrule a wondrous example of the goldsmith's art. So too the dagger. Their caps were of black velvet, trimmed with jewels and rings and buttons of gold, with a white plume set in jauntily and parted by many rows of spangles from which hung splendent emeralds and various other stones.

Such was the sympathy between the gallants and their ladies that they matched one another's costumes every day. And in order to be sure of it, certain gentlemen were appointed to report every morning to the youths what garments their ladies planned to wear on that occasion. All here was done for the pleasure of the fair.

Handsome though the clothes were and rich the accoutrements, lads or girls wasted no time in dressing. The wardrobe masters had everything ready before their gentlemen arose and the maids were so nimble that in a trice their mistresses were apparelled from head to toe.

To facilitate matters, over a distance of half-a-league, a row of light, well-appointed cottages housed the goldsmiths, lapidaries, embroiderers, tailors, gold drawers, velvet weavers, tapestry makers and upholsterers. Here each worked at his trade, and all for the jolly friars and comely nuns of the new abbey. They received materials and stuffs from My Lord Nausiclete, famous for his ships, as the name indicates. Each year brought them seven vessels from the Pearl and Cannibal Islands or Antilles, laden with ingots of gold, raw silk, pearls and precious stones.

If pearls through age tended to lose their luster, the jewellers, following the method of Avicenna, fed them to the roosters, and they regained their native sparkle.

LVII

How Those of Thélème Were
Governed in Their Manner
of Living

Their whole life was ordered not by law, statute or rule, but according to their free will and pleasure. They arose when they pleased. They ate, drank, worked and slept when the spirit moved them. No one awoke them, forced food or drink upon them or *made* them do anything else. Gargantua's plan called for perfect liberty. The only rule of the house was:

DO AS THOU WILT

because men that are free, of gentle birth, well-bred and at home in civilized company possess a natural instinct that inclines them to virtue and saves them from vice. This instinct they name their honor. Sometimes they may be depressed or enslaved by subjection or constraint; for we all long for forbidden fruit and covet what is denied us. But they usually apply the fine forces that tend to virtue in such a way as to shake off the yoke of servitude.

The Thélèmites, thanks to their liberty, knew the virtues of emulation. All wished to do what they saw pleased one of their number. Let some lad or maid say "Let us drink" and all of them drank, "Let us play" and all of them played, "Let us frolic in the fields" and all of them frolicked. When falconry or hawking were in order, the ladies sat high upon their saddles on fine nags, a sparhawk, lanner or merlin on one daintily gloved wrist, while the men bore other kinds of hawks.

They were so well-bred that none, man or woman, but could read, write, sing, play several instruments, speak five or six languages and readily compose verse and prose in any of them. Never had earth known knights so proud, so gallant, so adroit on horseback and on foot, so athletic, so lively, so well-trained in arms as these. Never were ladies seen so dainty, so comely, so winsome, so deft at handwork and needlework, so skillful in feminine arts, so frank and so free as these.

Thus when the time came for a man to leave the abbey (either at his parents' request or for some other reason) he took with him one of the ladies—the particular one who had chosen him for her knight—and they were married. And though they had lived in devotion and friendship at Thélème, their marriage relations proved even more tender and agreeable. Indeed to the end of their lives they loved one another as they had on the day of their wedding. . . .

from THE SECOND BOOK

Pantagruel, King of the Dipsodes,[1] *Restored to His True Nature, Together with His Deeds and Horrendous Feats. Set Down by the Late Monsieur Alcofribas, Abstractor of Quintessence.*

II

OF THE NATIVITY OF THE MOST REDOUBTABLE PANTAGRUEL

At the age of four hundred fourscore and forty-four years, Gargantua begat his son Pantagruel upon his wife named Badebec, daughter to the king of the dimly-seen Amaurotes in Utopia.[2] She died in the throes of childbirth. Alas! Pantagruel was so extraordinarily large and heavy that he could not possibly come to light without suffocating his mother.

If you would fully understand how he came to be christened Panta-gruel, you must remember that a terrible drought raged that year through-

---

[1] *Dipsodes* means "Thirsty Ones." The Dipsodes appear in a later section of *Pantagruel*, here omitted.

[2] *Amaurote*, which means "dimly seen" (hence "imaginary"), is the principal city in Thomas More's *Utopia* (1516).

out the land of Africa. For thirty-six months, three weeks, four days, thirteen hours and even longer, there was no drop of rain. And the sun blazed so fiercely that the whole earth was parched.

Even in the days of Elijah,[3] the soil was no drier, for now no tree on earth bore leaf or flower. The grass had no verdure; rivers and springs ran dry; the luckless fishes, abandoned by their element, crawled on solid earth, crying and screaming most horribly. Birds fell from the air for want of moisture; wolves, foxes, harts, wild boars, fallow deer, hares, rabbits, weasels, martens, badgers and other beasts were found dead in the fields, their mouths agape.

As for the men, their state was very piteous. You should have seen them with their tongues dangling like a hound's after a run of six hours. Not a few threw themselves into the wells. Others lay under a cow's belly to enjoy the shade—these it is whom Homer calls *Alibantes*, the desiccated.[4] The whole country was at a standstill. The strenuous efforts of mortals against the vehemence of this drought was a horrible spectacle. It was hard enough, God knows, to save the holy water in the churches from being wasted; but My Lords the Cardinals and our Holy Father laid down such strict rules that no man dared take more than a lick of it. In the churches, scores of parched, unhappy wretches followed the priest who distributed it, their jaws yawning for one tiny driblet. Like the rich man in *Luke*, who cried for Lazarus to dip his fingers in water,[5] they were tormented by a flame, and would not suffer the slightest drop to be wasted. Ah! thrice happy that year the man who had a cool, well-plenished wine cellar underground!

In discussing the question: "Why is sea water salty?" the philosopher Aristotle, after Empedocles,[6] supplies the following reason. When Phoebus[7] gave the reins of his luminous chariot to Phaëton, his son, the latter, unskilled in the art of driving, was incapable of following the ecliptic lines between the two tropics of the sun's sphere. Accordingly, he strayed from the appointed path and came so close to earth that he dried up all the countries under his course. He also burnished that great portion of heaven which philosophers call *Via Lactea* or the Milky Way, and good drinkers St. James' Way, since it is the starry line that guides pilgrims to Santiago de Compostella.[8] (On the other hand, poets declare that it is here Juno's milk dropped while she was suckling Hercules.)[9]

Earth at that time was so excessively heated that it broke into an enormous sweat which ran over the sea, making the latter salty, since all sweat is salt. If you do not admit this last statement, then taste of your own sweat. Or savor the perspiration of your pox-stricken friends when they are put in sweatboxes for treatment.[10] It is all one to me.

Practically the same thing happened the year I am speaking of. On a

[3] During Elijah's time, there was a three-year drought. See I Kings 17.

[4] Plutarch (46?–c. 120 A.D.) discusses the word *alibantes* ("dried up"). It does not appear in Homer, though this passage is in Plutarch's commentary on Homer in the *Symposiaca*.

[5] The rich man in Hell asked Lazarus in Heaven for a drop of water (Luke 16:24).

[6] Fifth-century B.C. Greek philosopher. In his *Meteorologica*, Aristotle cites Empedocles' explanation but refutes it.

[7] God of the sun.

[8] Shrine in northwest Spain, built over the supposed tomb of the apostle St. James.

[9] Juno was wife of Jupiter and queen of the gods.

[10] A common method for treating syphilis at the time.

certain Friday, all the people were intent upon their devotions. A noble procession was in progress with plenty of litanies and fine preachings. Supplications arose toward Almighty God beseeching Him to cast His eye of mercy upon them in their affliction. Suddenly they clearly saw some great drops of water stand out upon the ground, exactly as from a person sweating copiously.

The wretched populace began to rejoice as though here were a great blessing. Some declared that, since the air lacked all moisture, earth was supplying the deficiency. Other scientists asseverated that it was a shower of the Antipodes, as described by Seneca in *Quaestiones Naturales,* Book IV, where he treats of the Nile's source, attributing its floods to distant rains washed underground into the river. But they were thoroughly deceived. For, the procession done, when each sought to gather up this dew and drink it up by the bowlful, they found it was only pickle, far saltier than the saltiest water of the sea.

Another great mishap befell Gargantua that week. A dungchafing lout, bearing two great bags of salt and a hambone in his gamepouch, walked into poor Gargantua's mouth as the giant lay snoring. The clod spilled a quantity of salt in Gargantua's throat. Gargantua, crazy with thirst he could not slake, angrily snapped his mouth shut. He gnashed his teeth fiercely; they ground like millstones. Later the rascal told me he was so terrified you could have stopped up his nose with a bale of hay. He fell flat on his face like a dead man, dropping the two saltbags that had tormented Gargantua. They were at once swallowed up and entombed.

My rogue vowed vengeance. Thrusting his hand in his gamepouch, he drew out a great hambone, highly salted, still covered with hair, and twenty-eight inches long. Ragefully he rammed it down Gargantua's throat. The giant, drier than ever, felt the pig's hair tickling his belly and, willy-nilly, spewed up all he had. Eighteen tumbrils could not have drawn away the rich nauseous yield. My dungchafer, hidden in the cavity of one of his teeth, was forced to take French leave[11] in such pitiful condition that all who saw him were horrified. Gargantua, looking down, noticed this jackpudding whirling about in a great puddle.

"Here is some worm that sought to sting me in the belly," he mused, happy to have expelled him from his body.

Because he was born that very day, his father called him Pantagruel or All-Athirst, a name derived from the Greek *panta* meaning all, and the Hagarene or Saracen *gruel* meaning athirst.[12] Gargantua inferred thereby that at his son's birth the entire universe was wholly parched. Prophetically, too, he realized that some day Pantagruel would become Supreme Lord of the Thirsty, a fact indicated even more surely by a further portent.

For while his mother Badebec was bringing him forth and the midwives stood by ready to receive him, there first issued from her belly seventy-eight salt-vendors, each leading a salt-laden mule by the halter. They were followed by nine dromedaries, bearing hams and smoked oxtongues; seven

---

[11] Hasty departure without permission.

[12] A facetious etymology. Pantagruel was a demon in medieval French plays, who made everyone he met thirsty. The Saracen language is Moorish, called "Hagarene" because the Moors were said to be descended from the biblical Hagar.

camels bearing chitterlings; twenty-five cartloads of leeks, garlic, onions and chives. This terrified some midwives, but others said:

"Here is good provision! As it is, we drink but lazily, instead of vigorously. This must be a good omen, since these victuals are spurs to bibbing wine!"

As they were tattling away, out pops Pantagruel, hairy as a bear! At which, prophetically, one of them exclaimed:

"God help us, he is born hair and all, straight from the arse of Satan in flight. He will do terrible wonders. If he lives, he will grow to a lusty age!"

Of Pantagruel's race are those who drink so heavily in the evening that they must rise at night to drink again, quenching the coals of fire and blistering thirst in their throats. This form of thirst is called Pantagruel, in memory of the giant.

V

The Noble Pantagruel's Adolescence

Pantagruel grew and developed visibly from day to day, which naturally delighted his father. While he was still a tiny mite, his father had a crossbow made for him to shoot at small birds. It is still preserved in the great tower at Bourges; they call it the crossbow of Chantelle, because it was made in the famous arsenal there.[13]

Desiring the lad to study during his formative years, Gargantua sent him to Poitiers, where he profited greatly. It was here he noticed how heavy time hung on the students' hands, pitied them for it, and determined to remedy the situation. So one fine day he picked up a great stone off a ledge of rocks called Passelourdin and, though it was two thousand yards square and fourteen feet thick, easily set it on four pillars in the middle of a field. Thus, when the university students wanted something to do, they could spend their time climbing on top of it, banquet there abundantly upon flagons of wine, hams and pasties, and carve their names upon it with a knife.

To-day, this stone is known as La Pierre Levée, the Lifted Stone. In memory of Pantagruel's feat, no student can register at the University of Poitiers without first drinking in the mystic fountain of Croûtelle, going to Passelourdin and scaling the Lifted Stone.[14] . . .

VI

How Pantagruel Met a Limousin Who Spoke Spurious French

One evening after supper—I cannot say exactly when—Pantagruel was strolling with some friends near the north gate of Orléans, by the road to Paris. Here he met a neat young student walking down the road. After they had bowed to one another, Pantagruel asked:

---

[13] The "crossbow of Chantelle" was a large siege engine at the castle of Chantelle.
[14] There was such a stone formation in Poitiers. It is now broken in two.

"Well, friend, where are you coming from at this time of day?"

The scholar replied:

"From the alme, inclyte and celebrate academy which is vocitated Lucetia."

"What on earth does he mean?" Pantagruel asked one of his men.

"He means: 'From Paris!'"

"So you come from Paris, eh?" Pantagruel resumed. "And how do you gentlemen students spend your time in Paris?"

The scholar replied:

"We transfretate the Sequana at the dilucul and crepuscul; we deambulate by the compites and quadrives of the metropolis; we despume the Latin verbocination and, like verisimilary amorabonds, we captate the benevolence of the omnijugal, omniform and omnigeneous muliebrine sex. At certain diecules, we invisitate upon the lupanars and, amid a venerean ecstasis, we inculcate our virilia into the most antipodean recesses of the pudenda of these supremely amicable meretricules. Then we proceed to pabulate in the mercantile taberna of the *Fir Cone,* the *Castle,* the *Magdalen* and the *Mule,* upon rare vervicina spatula perforaminated with petrosil. If by misfortune, there be rarity or penury of numismatical in our marsupia, or if we be exhausted of ferrugine metal, to pay, we demit our codexes and we oppignerate our vestments while we prestolate the Tabellaries who are to come from our patriotic Lares and Penates."

"What the devil is this jargon?" cried Pantagruel. "By God, I think you must be some sort of heretic."

(There was no interpreter here to tell Pantagruel that what the fellow meant was this: "We cross the Seine at dawn and dusk; we walk through the thoroughfares and crossroads of the city; we rake up Latin to speak and, as true lusty fellows, we win the favors of women. Occasionally we go to brothels and, hot with love, push our cods into the depths of these friendly little harlots' cunnies. Then, in the taverns of the *Fir Cone,* the *Castle,* the *Magdalen* and the *Mule,* we eat shoulders of mutton garnished with parsley; should we have little money in our purses or be out of cash, we settle the bill by pledging our books and pawning our clothes while awaiting remittances from home.")

So then, Pantagruel having taxed the Limousin student with heresy:

"Nay, my Lord," he replied, "for libentissimally as soon as it illucesces a minutule fragment of the day, I demigrate to some one of those so well architected ecclesiastical abodes. There, irrorigating myself with sweet lustral water, I rattle off little slices of some missic precation of our sacrificula. Submurmurating my horary precules, I elave and absterge my anima of its nocturnal inquinations; I revere the Olympicoles; I latrially venerate the supernal astripotent; I dilige and redame my proxims; I observe the Decalogical precepts and, according to the facultatule of my vires, I do not discede from them one unguicule. However it is veriform that since Mammona does not supergurgitate anything in my loculas, I am somewhat rare and tardigrade in supererogating the eleemosynaries to these indigents who hostially queritate their stipend."

(Poor Pantagruel! He could not know the fellow meant: "For when day breaks I withdraw to a well-built church, and there, sprinkling myself with holy water, I mumble a few words of the mass. While saying my prayers, I wash and cleanse my soul of the pollution of the night; I worship the high gods; I adore the master of the spheres; I love and cherish my neighbors; I follow the Ten Commandments and, within the measure of my power, I do not deviate a nail's breadth from these teachings. It is certain that because the Goddess of Wealth puts nothing in my purse, I very rarely give alms to the beggars who seek money from door to door.")

So, hearing the Limousin's mad flow of words:

"Midden and dung!" Pantagruel roared. "What does this lunatic mean? I think he is forging some diabolic tongue and laying a spell of witchcraft upon us."

To which one of his followers replied:

"Doubtless, My Lord, this rascal is trying to imitate the language of the Parisians. But all he is doing is to flay the Latin tongue, under the impression that he is using the noble style of Pindar. He fancies himself no end of an orator in French because he disdains our usual mode of speech."

"Is that true?" Pantagruel asked the scholar.

"Ah, My Lord!" the scholar replied, "my genius is not natively adept to what this flagitious nebulon manifests, as he excoriates the cuticle of our vernacular Gallic. On the contrary, I applicate my scruples viceversally and with the auxiliary of both sails and oars—*veles et rames*—I effortize to locupletate it with Latinicome redundance."

(All of which simply meant: "My genius is not naturally apt to grasp what this worthless vagabond says as he accuses me of flaying the skin of our French vernacular. On the contrary, I devote all my attention and make every possible effort to endow it with a Latin richness.")

"By God," Pantagruel growled, "I'll teach you how to speak. But come here, first, and tell me where you hail from?"

"The primeval origin of my aves and ataves," said the scholar, "was indigenous to the Lemovican regions where requiesces the cadaver of the hagiotate St. Martial."

(Which being interpreted meant: "My ancestors were born in the Limousin where St. Martial is buried.")

"I understand you perfectly," Pantagruel roared. "It all boils itself down to the fact that you're a Limousin trying to play the Parisian. Come here, my lad, and I'll curry your hair for you."

Seizing him by the throat:

"You're a flayer of Latin, eh? By St. John, I'll make you flay the fox—or vomit, ay, since you don't understand French. Unless I flay you alive!"

The wretched Limousin at once changed his tune.

"Eh but lawd gen'leman! Ho, Sint Martiaw, ho, cum to me help! Ooh, ho, leave me but be, and do ye not tech me!"

To which Pantagruel answered:

"Now you are speaking naturally."

So he let him go, for the unhappy Limousin had completely befouled his breeches, which were cut like a codfish tail, with a slash and not full-bottomed. At which Pantagruel cried:

"By St. Alipentin, what a civet, what a stew! The devil take this turnip-fed bumpkin. Phew! he whiffs to high heaven!"

And Pantagruel fled. But the scholar was thoroughly impressed by Pantagruel's throat-squeezing influence. He declared ever after that Pantagruel held him by the gullet. And he repented throughout his life, until some years later he died the death of Roland—from thirst![15] Thus the law of divine vengeance vindicated the instructions of Favorinus, the philosopher, in Aulus Gellius' *Attic Nights* where we are warned to speak the common idiom and where Octavius Augustus urges us to steer clear of unusual words even as mariners avoid reefs at sea.

VIII

How Pantagruel in Paris
Received a Letter From
His Father Gargantua

As you may suppose, Pantagruel studied very hard and profited much by his study, for his intelligence was naturally active and his memory as full as twelve casks of olives. While in Paris, he received the following letter from his father:

> *My beloved son,*
>
> *Among the gifts, graces and prerogatives with which our sovereign Creator, God Almighty, blessed and enriched humanity from the beginning, there is one that I deem supreme. By its means, though we be mortal, we can yet achieve a sort of immortality; through it, we may, in the course of our transitory lives, yet perpetuate our name and race.*
>
> *To be sure, what we gain by a progeny born of lawful wedlock cannot make up for what we lost through the sin of our first parents. Adam and Eve disobeyed the commandments of the Lord their God: mortality was their punishment. By death the magnificent mold in which Man was fashioned vanished into the dust of oblivion.*
>
> *However, thanks to seminal propagation, what a man loses his children revive and, where they fail, their children prevail. So it has gone, and so it shall be, from generation to generation, until the Day of Judgment, when Christ shall restore to God the Father His kingdom pacified, secured and cleansed of all sin. Then all generation and corruption shall cease, for the elements will have completed their continuous transmutations. The peace humanity has craved so anxiously will have been attained; all things will have been reduced to their appointed end and period.*
>
> *I therefore have reason to give thanks to God, my Saviour, for having granted me the joy of beholding my old age blossom anew in your youth. When, by His pleasure, which rules and orders everything, my soul must abandon this human habitation, I shall not believe I am dying utterly, but rather passing from one place to another. For in you my visible image will continue to live on earth; by you, I shall go on frequenting honorable men and true friends, as I was wont to do.*
>
> *My associations have not been without sin, I confess. We all transgress and must continually beseech God to forgive us our trespasses. But they have been without reproach in the eyes of men.*
>
> *That is why if, beside my bodily image, my soul did not likewise shine in you, you would not be accounted worthy of guarding the precious immortality of my name. In that case, the least part of me (my body) would endure. Scant satisfaction, that, when*

---

[15] In the *Song of Roland*, Roland, grieving over his fallen knights, dies craving a drink of water. The Archbishop dies trying to get the water for him.

*the best part (my soul, which should keep my name blessed among men) had degener-
ated and been bastardized. I say this not through any doubt as to your virtue, which I
have already often tested, but to encourage you to go on doing ever better and
profiting by your constant improvement.*

*My purpose is not so much to keep you absolutely on your present virtuous course
as to make you rejoice that you have kept and are keeping on it. I seek to quicken your
heart with resolutions for the future. To help you make and carry these out, remember
that I have spared nothing. I have helped you as though my sole treasure on earth
were once in my lifetime to see you well-bred and accomplished in honesty and valor
as well as in knowledge and civility. Ay, I have longed to leave you after my death as
a mirror of your father's personality. The reflection may not prove perfect in practice,
but certainly I could not more studiously wish for its perfection.*

*My late father Grangousier, of blessed memory, made every effort that I might
achieve mental, moral and technical excellence. The fruit of my studies and labors
matched, indeed surpassed, his dearest wish. But you can realize that conditions were
not as favorable to learning as they are to-day. Nor had I such gifted teachers as you.
We were still in the dark ages; we still walked in the shadow of the dark clouds of
ignorance; we suffered the calamitous consequences of the destruction of good literature by the Goths.*[16] *Now, by God's grace, light and dignity have been restored to
letters, and I have lived to see it. Indeed, I have watched such a revolution in
learning that I, not erroneously reputed in my manhood the leading scholar of the
century, would find it difficult to enter the bottom class in a grammar school.*

*I tell you all this not through boastfulness, though in writing to you I might be
proud with impunity. Does not Marcus Tullius*[17] *authorize it in his book* OF OLD
AGE, *and Plutarch in* HOW A MAN MAY PRAISE HIMSELF WITHOUT ENVY? *Both
authors recognize that such pride is useful in fostering the spirit of emulation. No—I
do it simply to give you a proof of my love and affection.*

*To-day, the old sciences are revived, knowledge is systematized, discipline
reëstablished. The learned languages are restored: Greek, without which a man would
be ashamed to consider himself educated; Hebrew, Chaldean and Latin. Printing is
now in use, an art so accurate and elegant that it betrays the divine inspiration of its
discovery, which I have lived to witness. Alas! Conversely, I was not spared the
horror of such diabolic works as gunpowder and artillery.*

*To-day, the world is full of learned men, brilliant teachers and vast libraries: I
do not believe that the ages of Plato, Cicero or Papinian*[18] *afforded such facilities for
culture. From now on, it is unthinkable to come before the public or move in polite
circles without having worshipped at Minerva's*[19] *shrine. Why, the robbers, hang-
men, adventurers and jockeys of to-day are infinitely better educated than the doctors
and preachers of my time. More, even women and girls aspire to the glory, the
heavenly manna of learning. Thus, at my advanced age, I have been forced to take
up Greek. Not that I had despised it, like Cato; I never had the opportunity to learn
it. Now I delight in reading Plutarch's* MORALS, *Plato's noble* DIALOGUES, *the*
MONUMENTS *of Pausanias and the* ANTIQUITIES *of Athenaeus, as I await the hour
when it shall please God, my Creator, to call me back to His bosom.*

*That is why, my dear son, I urge you to spend your youth making the most of your
studies and developing your moral sense. You are in Paris, which abounds in noble
men upon whom to pattern yourself; you have Epistemon, an admirable tutor, who*

---

[16]*Goths* meant any barbarians.   [17]Cicero (106–43 B.C.).
[18]A learned Roman jurist of the third century A.D.   [19]Goddess of wisdom.

can inspire you by direct oral teaching. But I demand more of you. I insist you learn languages perfectly! Greek first, as old Quintilian prescribes; then Latin; then Hebrew for the sake of the Holy Scripture; then Chaldee and Arabic, too. Model your Greek style on Plato, your Latin on Cicero. Let no history slip your memory; cultivate cosmography, for you will find its texts helpful.

As for the liberal arts of geometry, arithmetic and music, I gave you a taste of them when you were a little lad of five or six. Proceed further in them yourself, learning as much as you can. Be sure to master all the rules of astronomy; but dismiss astrology and the divinatory art of Lullius as but vanity and imposture.[20] *Of civil law, I would have you know the texts of the Code by heart, then compare them with philosophy.*

A knowledge of nature is indispensable; devote yourself to this study with unflagging curiosity. Let there be no sea, river or fountain but you know the fish that dwell in it. Be familiar with all the shrubs, bushes and trees in forest or orchard, all the plants, herbs and flowers that grow on the ground, all the birds of the air, all the metals in the bowels of earth, all the precious stones in the orient and the south. In a word, be well informed in everything that concerns the physical world we live in.

Then carefully consult the works of Greek, Arabian and Latin physicians, without slighting the Jewish doctors, Talmudists and Cabbalists.[21] *By frequent exercises in dissection, acquire a perfect knowledge of that other world, which is man.*

Devote a few hours a day to the study of Holy Writ. Take up the New Testament and the Epistles in Greek; then, the Old Testament in Hebrew. Strive to make your mind an inexhaustible storehouse of knowledge. For you are growing to manhood now: soon you will have to give up your studious repose to lead a life of action. You will have to learn to bear arms, to achieve knighthood, so as to defend my house and help our allies frustrate the attacks of evildoers.

Further, I wish you soon to test what profit you have gained from your education. This you can best do by public discussion and debate on all subjects against all comers, and by frequenting learned men both in Paris and elsewhere.

But remember this. As Solomon says, wisdom entereth not into a malicious soul, and science without conscience spells but destruction of the spirit. Therefore serve, love and fear God, on Him pin all your thoughts and hopes; by faith built of charity, cling to Him so closely that never a sin come between you. Hold the abuses of the world in just suspicion. Set not your heart upon vanity, for this life is a transitory thing, but the Word of God endureth forever. Be serviceable to your neighbor, love him as you do yourself. Honor your teachers. Shun the company of all men you would not wish to resemble; receive not in vain the favors God has bestowed upon you.

When you realize that you have acquired all the knowledge Paris has to offer, come back so I may see you and give you my blessing before I die.

My son, the peace and grace of Our Lord be with you. Amen.

Your father,

Gargantua

From Utopia, the seventeenth day of September.

Having read this letter, Pantagruel, greatly encouraged, strove more ardently than ever to profit in his work. Had you seen him studying vigor-

---

[20] *Lullius* was Raymond Lully, thirteenth-century astrologer and philosopher.
[21] The Talmudists and Cabbalists wrote commentaries on Jewish law as well as on Scriptures.

ously, practically and tirelessly, you would have compared his spirit moving among his books to flames blazing through a bonfire of dry branches.

IX

How Pantagruel Met
Panurge Whom He Loved
All His Life

One day Pantagruel was walking in the country towards the Abbey of St. Antoine, conversing and philosophizing with his servants and some students. Suddenly he met a man of fine stature and handsome mien, but severely wounded in several places, and so tattered that he must have been fighting a pack of mastiffs. His clothes were as ragged as a Norman apple-picker's.

Seeing him from afar:

"Do you see that fellow coming from the Charenton bridge?" Pantagruel asked his companions. "Upon my word, he is poor only in fortune; his face bespeaks a rich and noble family. Doubtless the misadventures that invariably beset too-curious people have reduced him to his present misery."

When the fellow drew close, Pantagruel addressed him.

"Stop, friend, I beg you, and answer a few questions," he said. "I assure you you'll have no cause to regret it. The calamity that has befallen you moves me to pity; I am eager to help you however I can. Tell us, friend: who are you? Where are you going? What do you wish? And what is your name?"

The fellow answered:

"Juncker, Gott geb euch glück unnd hail. Zuvor, Lieber Juncker, ich las euch wissen das da ir mich von fragt, ist ein arm unnd erbarmglich ding, unnd wer vil darvon zu sagen, welches euch verdruslich zu hoeren, unnd mir zu erzelen wer, viewol die Poeten unnd Orators vorzeiten haben gesagt in iren Sprüchen unnd Sentenzen, das die Gedechtnus des Ellends unnd Armuot vorlangs erlitten ist ain grosser Lust."

(He spoke in German, saying: "Young gentleman, God prosper you and bring you joy. But first, my dear young gentleman, I must inform you that what you seek to know is a wretched and pitiful thing. It would make an endless story. And it would prove no pleasanter for you to hear than for me to tell, though the poets and orators of ancient times have stated in maxim and adage that the remembrance of sorrows endured is a great joy.")

"My friend," said Pantagruel, "I cannot understand this gibberish. If you expect us to understand, then speak another tongue."

The stranger replied:

"Al barildim gotfano dech min brin alabo dordin falbroth ringuam albaras. Nin porth zadikim almucathin milko prin al elmim enthoth dal heben ensouim: kuthim al dum alkatim nim broth dechoth porth min michais im endoth, pruch dal maisoulum hol moth dansrilrim lupaldas im voldemoth. Nin hur diavosth mnarbotim dal gousch

palfrapin duch im scoth pruch galeth dal Chinon *min foulchrich al conin butathen doth dal prim."*

(The words sounded vaguely like Arab, but it was a fantastic jargon he spoke. His hearers could make out only a single place-name: Chinon.)

"Can you make head or tail of it?" Pantagruel appealed to the others.

"I think it is the language of the Antipodes," Epistemon ventured. "But it's such a jawbreaker not even the devil himself would dare twist his tongue to it."

"My friend," said Pantagruel, "the walls may understand you, if they have ears to hear. But not one man jack among us can follow a syllable."

The stranger sighed. Then:

"Signor mio: voi videte par exempio che la cornamusa non suona mai s'ella non ha il ventre pieno," he went on. *"Cosi io parimente non vi saperei contare le mie fortune, se prima il tribulato ventre non a la solita refettione, alquale é adviso che le mani et li denti abbui perso il loro ordine naturale et del tuto annichillati."*

(A person conversant in Italian would have gathered: "My Lord, you know, for example, that no bagpipe ever makes a sound without a full belly. By the same token, I couldn't possibly tell you my adventures unless my tormented stomach first received its usual refreshment. To my paunch, it appears as though my hands and teeth had lost their natural functions and were utterly annihilated.")

"We're no better off than before," Epistemon grumbled.

The stranger continued:

"Lord geft tholb be sua virtiuss be Intelligence ass yi Body schal biss be naturall relvtht, tholb suld of me pety have, for Natur hass ulss equaly maide; bot Fortune sum exaltit hess, and oyis deprevit. Non ye less viois mou virtius deprevit and virtius men descrevis; for anen ye lad end, iss non good."

(This was Scots English. Its purport: "My Lord, if your generosity of spirit is as lofty as your body is by nature, you will have pity on me. For Nature hath created us equal, but Fortune hath exalted some, and others she hath brought low. Nevertheless, though virtue be often beggarly and the upright scorned, yet till the hour of death, no man may boast that he is good.")

"Floored again," cried Pantagruel. Panurge immediately resumed:

"Jona andie, guaussa goussy etan behar da erremedio, beharde, versela ysser lan da. Anbates, otoyyes nausu, eyn essassu gourr ay proposian ordine den. Non yssena bayta fascheria egabe, genherassy badia sadassu noura assia. Aran Rondovan gualde eydassu nay dessuna. Estou oussyc eguinan soury hin, er darstura eguy harm, Genicoa plasar vadu."

(A bastard Basque, this. Most Gascon lackeys could have told Pantagruel it meant: "Great Lord, all things have their remedy: if unapparent, then we must sweat to find it. I implore you therefore to let me know clearly if my suggestion is in order. If you see no inconvenience, then give me my fill. Once you have done that, ask me what you will: I shall not fail you. Please God, I speak the truth from the depths of my heart.")

"Are you there, Genoica?" mocked Eudemon. "My God!!!"[22]

"By St. Ninnyhammer," cried Carpalim, Gargantua's valet. "May your bum burst if I didn't almost get the drift of it."

"Prug frest strinst," the stranger continued, *"sorgdmand strochdt drhds pag brleland* Gravot, Chavigny, La Pomardière, *rusth pkallhdracg* La Devinière près Nays, Seuilly. *Halmuch monach drupp delmeupplistrincq drlnd dodelb up drent loch minc stzrinquald* de vins *der Cordelis hur jocst-stzampenards."*

Again, in this mad balderdash, all they made out was the placenames Gravot, Chavigny, La Pomardière, La Devinière, Nays, Seuilly and the word "wines."

"Do you speak Christian, my friend," Epistemon asked, "or Gipsy language, Welsh or Czech?"

"No," said another, "that's Lantern Language, spoken in the Isles of Nowhere."

The stranger changed his tack:

"Herre, ie en spreeke anders gheen taele, dan kersten taele; my dunct nochtans, al en seg icu met een woordt, mynen noot verklaert ghenonch wat ie begeere; gheeft my uyt bermherticheyt yet waer vn ic ghevoct magh zunch."

(Translated from the Dutch this meant: "Sir, I speak no tongue that is not Christian. Yet I should think that, without my saying a word, my rags betray clearly enough what it is I wish. In human charity, give me something to revive me!")

"It's all of one piece," Pantagruel grumbled. "And about as clear as mud."

"Seignor, de tanto hablar yo soy cansado. Por que suplico a Vostra Reverentia que mire a los preceptos evangeliques, para que ellos movant vostra Reverentia a lo que as de conscientia, y, si ellos non bastarent para mover Vostra Reverentia a piedad, suplico que mire a la piedad natural, la qual yo creo que la movra, como es de razon, y con esto non digo mas."

(The Spanish means: "My Lord, I am tired from so much speaking. So I beg your Reverence to consider the precepts of the Gospel, so that they may move your Reverence to fulfill the demands of conscience. If they do not suffice to move your Reverence to pity, then I implore you to consider natural compassion, which I think must reasonably do so. On this head, I shall say no more.")

"By God, I've no doubt you can speak a score of languages fluently," said Pantagruel. "But tell us what you want in some language we can understand."

---

[22] *Genoica* means "from God."

"Myn Herre," the stranger said, *"endog jeg med ingen tunge talede, lygesom boeen, ocg uskielig creatuer; myne kledebon och myne legoms magerhed uudviser allyguevel klarlig huvad tyng meg meest behoff girered, som aer sandeligh mad och drycke: hwarfor forbarme teg omsyder ofvermeg, oc befael at gyffue meg nogeth, aff huglket jeg kand styremyne groeendes maghe, lygeruüss son mand Cerbero en soppe forsetthr: Soa shal tue loeffve lenge och lyksaligth."*

(Translating the Danish: "Sir, even if like a babe or beast I spoke no language whatever, my clothing and my emaciated body should plainly show what I need: food and drink. Have pity on me then and order them to give me something to master my baying belly, even as sops are tossed to Cerberus.[23] Do this and you will live long and happy."

"I think," Epistemon said, "that is how the Goths spoke. Were God willing we would all speak thus—through our tailpieces!"

"Adoni, scolom techa," the stranger cried. *"Im ischar harob hal hebdeca bemeherah thithen li kikar lehem, chancathub: Laah al Adonai cho nen ral."*

(In Hebrew: "Sir, the peace of God be upon you. If you wish to do good to your servitor, give me a loaf of bread at once, for it is written: 'He that hath pity upon the poor lendeth to the Lord.'")

"Ha!" cried Epistemon. "This time I understand. That's Hebrew, well turned and rhetorically pronounced."

The wag resumed:

"Despota tinyn panagathe, doiti sy mi uc artodotis? Horas gar limo analiscomenon eme athlios. Ce en to metaxy eme uc eleis udamos, zetis de par emu ha u chre, ce homos philologi pamdes homologusi tote logus te ce rhemeta peritta hyrparchin, opote pragma afto pasi delon esti. Entha gar anancei monon logi isin, hina pragmata, hon peri amphibitumen, me prosphoros epithenete."

(In Greek: "Excellent master, why do you give me no bread? You see me miserable and perishing of hunger, yet instead of coming to my aid, you ask me irrelevant questions. Nevertheless, all intelligent people agree unanimously that discourse and words are superfluous when the facts are patent to all. The only words needful here are those you should speak to give me what we are arguing about.")

"Good Lord! That's Greek!" cried Carpalim. "I've heard it spoken before. How do you know it? Have you ever lived in Greece?"

The stranger, for only answer, said:

"Agonou dont oussoys von denaguez algarou, nou den farou zamist vous mariston ulbrou, fousquez vous brol, tam bredaguez moupreton den goul houst, daguez daguez nou croupys fost bardounnoflist nou grou. Agou paston tol nalprissys hourtou los ecbatonous prou dhouquys brol panygou den bascrou noudous caguons goulfren goul oust troppassou."

---

[23] The dog that guarded the entrance to Hades in classical mythology.

"I believe I understand him," said Pantagruel. "Either that language is my native Utopian or it is much like it in sound."

But as he sought to address him, the stranger interrupted:

"Jam toties vos per Sacra perque Deos Deasque omnis obtestatus sum ut, si qua vos pietas permovet, egestatem meam solaremini, nec hilum proficio clamans et ejulans. Sinite, quaeso, sinite, viri impii, Quo me fata vocant abire, nec ultra vanis vestris interpellationibus obtundatis, memores veteris illius adagii, quo Venter famelicus auriculis carere dicitur."

(Which Latin meant: "Already, by all I hold sacred, by the gods and goddesses above, I have repeatedly implored you to allay my suffering, if pity can move you. But I have gained nothing by my prayers and supplications. Leave me, therefore, I pray you, O impious men; let me go whither destiny calls. Cease wearying me with your vain questions and remember the ancient adage: 'The empty belly hath no ears to hear.'")

"By God, friend, can't you speak French?" Pantagruel demanded.

"Why of course, I can speak French very well," the stranger answered. "It is my natural language, praise God, my mother-tongue, for I was born and brought up in Touraine, the garden of France."

"Then tell us what is your name," Pantagruel urged, "and explain where you have come from. By my faith, I've already taken such a liking to you that if you incline to my wishes, you shall never budge out of my company. God's truth, you and I shall make a pair of friends to match Aeneas and Achates."[24]

"My Lord, my true and proper Christian name is Panurge. I have just returned from Turkey whither I was taken prisoner after the disaster at Mytilene.[25] I shall be only too pleased to tell you of my adventures, which are more wonderful than those of Ulysses. But you are pleased to attach me to your person; I heartily accept the offer and swear never to leave you, should you go to all the devils in hell. I shall therefore have more leisure at another time to give an account of myself. For the moment, I most urgently need to feed. My teeth are sharp, my belly empty, my throat dry and my appetite a devouring flame. All is ready if you will but give the word. To see me fall to, would be a feast for the eyes. For God's sake, order me some food."

Pantagruel bade them take him home and provide him with victuals aplenty. Panurge ate abundantly that evening, went to bed with the chickens, and slept until the morrow at dinner time. Thus the interval from bed to board was but three steps and a jump.

XVI

OF THE CHARACTER AND
CONDITION OF PANURGE

Panurge was then about thirty-five years old and as fine to gild as a dagger of lead. Of medium height, neither too tall nor too short, he had an aqui-

---

[24] Companion and friend of Aeneas in Virgil's *Aeneid*.

[25] The French besieged the Greek island of Mytilene in 1502 but were defeated by the Turks. The name Panurge comes from the Greek *panourgos*, "apt at everything, a knave."

line nose, shaped like the handle of a razor. He cut a very gallant figure though he was a trifle lewd by nature, and subject to a disease at that time called impecunitis, an incomparable malady.

Yet when he needed money, he knew thirty-three methods of acquiring it, the most ordinary and honorable of which was filching. He was a quarrelsome fellow, a sharper, a toper, a roisterer and a profligate, if ever there was one in the city of Paris. In every other respect, he was the best fellow in the world.

He was constantly plotting against the sergeants and the watch. Sometimes he assembled three or four sportsmen, plied them with drink until they were boozy as Knights Templars, then took them up the hill to Ste. Geneviève or near the Collège de Navarre. Placing his sword on the pavement and his ear to his sword, he waited till he heard the blade shake—an infallible sign that the watch was not far off. Then he and his companions took a dung cart and rolled it down hill. Ere it was halfway down, they had fled in the opposite direction, for in less than two days Panurge knew every street and alley in Paris as well as his postprandial grace: *Deus det nobis pacem suam*, God grant us His peace.

Another time he laid down a train of gunpowder where the watch was due to pass. Just as the troop debouched,[26] he set fire to it, vastly delighted in observing how gracefully they took to their heels, in mortal terror that St. Anthony's fire had caught them by the legs.

The luckless Masters of Arts and theologians he persecuted more than any other class of men. When he met one, he never failed to do him some harm, either slipping a turd into his hood or pinning little foxtails or hares' ears to his back.

One day when all the theologians had been summoned to the Sorbonne to examine the articles of the faith, he made a tart of garlic, asafoetida, galbanum, castoreum and steaming excrement, which he steeped and tempered in the corrupt manner of chancres and pockbiles. Very early in the morning he so theologically greased and anointed the lattices and grates of the trellised gallery of the Hall of Records that not even the devil himself had dared stay there. The worthy pedagogues puked in public as abundantly as though they had flayed the fox. Ten or twelve died of the plague, fourteen contracted leprosy, eight came down with pestiferous ulcers, and more than twenty-eight caught the pox. But Panurge was jubilant.

Usually he carried a whip under his gown with which he mercilessly belabored such pages as he met bearing wine for their masters, in order to speed them on their way.

In his coat he had more than twenty-six little pockets and pouches which were always full. One held a pair of loaded dice and a small knife like a glover's awl to cut purses with. Another, verjuice[27] to throw in the eyes of those who annoyed him. A third, burrs, penned with gosling or capon feathers, to stick on to the robes and bonnets of honest people. He often gave married men a fine pair of horns which they bore through the city sometimes all their lives long. To the back of the women's hoods, he liked to affix various knickknacks shaped like the sexual organ of man.

---

[26] Marched out.

[27] An acid juice made from crab apples or unripe grapes, used in cooking.

Another pocket held a lot of little packages filled with fleas and lice which he recruited from the tramps at St. Innocent's graveyard and cast with small sticks or quills down the backs of the smartest gentlewomen he could find. He did this even in church, for he never sat up in the choir, preferring to stand in the nave among the women during mass, vespers or sermon. Another pocket held a large supply of bent nails with which he would couple men and women together where they sat. This was particularly amusing when the victims wore gowns of costly sarsenet taffeta, because they ripped them to shreds as they sought to separate. Still another pocket held a squib with tinder, flints, matches, vesuvians, sulphur and other combustibles. Another, two or three burning-glasses with which he tortured and disconcerted men and women at church. For he said there was only an antistrophe between *femme folle à la messe* and *molle à la fesse* or working a cunning stunt and a stunning cunt. Another pouch held needles, threads and pins for all manner of minor deviltries.

Once at the door of the Great Hall in the Palais de Justice, Panurge saw a Cordelier father[28] getting ready to say mass before the proceedings of the day. Immediately he ran up to help the holy man don his vestments and, in the process, managed to sew his alb[29] to his robe and shirt. Then, as the magistrates arrived for mass, Panurge withdrew. Mass done, as he reached the formula *Ite, missa est,* the wretched friar tried to take off his alb. But, at the same time, off came the robe and shirt solidly sewn to it. Our Cordelier, thus stripped to the shoulders, revealed his dangledingus to all the world—and it was no small crosier, as you may imagine. The harder he tugged, the more he exposed himself. So much so indeed, that one of the counselors cried:

"What is the matter? Is this good friar making an offering of his tail for us to kiss? No, by heaven, let St. Anthony's fire kiss it for us!"

From then on, an ordinance forbade the poor good fathers to disrobe before the world, the vestry-room being indicated as the only fit place for this. They were especially warned against doing so in the presence of women, lest it tempt the latter to sin through longing. When people wondered why the fathers were genitally so well-equipped, Panurge solved the problem.

"What makes the ears of asses so long?" he asked, and answering his own question: "Their dams put no caps on their ears. Alliacus, Chancellor of the University and Chaplain to Charles VI, proves this in his *Suppositiones.* Similarly, what makes the whangletools of our holy fathers hang so low? Well, they never wear dark breeches, so their lusty organs, dangling down at liberty like a horse given head, knock against their knees like women's beads. Why are they correspondingly large? Because, with all this waggling to and fro, the humors of the body sink down into these parts. Do not the legists point out that continual agitation and continual motion are the cause of attraction?"

Another of Panurge's pouches held stone-alum, an itching-powder which he poured down the backs of those he considered the proudest and most stately ladies. Some would at once strip off their clothes then and

[28] Franciscan friar (so called from the knotted cord worn around the waist).
[29] White linen robe worn by a priest.

there before the public . . . others danced like cats on hot coals or a drumstick on a tabor . . . others again rushed madly into the street and he at their heels. . . . Those inclined to disrobe, he assisted by sheltering them under his cape, as any courteous and gallant gentleman would have done.

In another pocket he had a small leather bottle full of old oil. If he saw a man or woman in a handsome costume, he would grease and stain it in the most conspicuous places. His technique here was an art. Pretending to admire the material, he would finger it.

"Rare cloth, this, sir," or "Fine satin, upon my word!" or "Oh, what lovely taffeta, Madame!" he would exclaim. "God give you all your noble heart desires. You have a new suit, My Lord! And you a new dress, My Lady. Well, you know the saying: New clothes, new friends. God give you joy in them!"

As he spoke, his hands passed lightly over the shoulders and a long ugly smear remained

> So indelible a spot
> Stamped on body, soul and fame
> That the devil could not blot
> Out its testament of shame.

As he took his leave of the ladies, he would say:

"Madame, take care not to fall. You've a huge filthy hole out of sight in front of you, there!"

In another pocket he kept euphorbium,[30] very finely pulverized and spread over a dainty handkerchief he had stolen from a pretty salesgirl in the Galleries of the Sainte-Chapelle, hard by the law courts and frequented by the gallants of the day. (He filched it while removing from between her breasts a louse he had dropped there.)

When he happened to be in gentle company, he would steer the conversation on to the subject of lace and lingerie. Then, thrusting his hands into some lady's bosom:

"Glorious work, this. Is it Flanders or Hainault?"

Then, drawing his handkerchief:

"Just look at this kerchief, Madame. Would you say it was Frontignan or Fontarabia?"

Shaking it hard under her nose, he would make her sneeze for hours at a time. Then he would fart like a dray horse.

"Tut, tut," the lady would say. "Are you whiffling, Panurge?"

"No, Madame," he would reply gallantly, "I am merely tuning my tail to the plain song you make with your nose."

Panurge was never without pincers, a picklock, a pelican, a jimmy, a crook or other tools against which no chest or door could avail. Finally, in another pocket he kept a whole battery of small goblets which he worked with amazing skill, for his fingers were nimble and adroit as those of Minerva or Arachne.[31] He had indeed once been an itinerant quack, barking

---

[30] An acrid medicinal powder.

[31] Minerva and Arachne, in Greek mythology, were both renowned for their skill in weaving. When Arachne defeated Minerva in a weaving contest, she was turned into a spider.

antidotes for poison. When he presented a sum of money and asked for change, the changer had to be spry as Argus[32] to catch Panurge spiriting away five, six or seven coins at a time, visibly, openly, manifestly, without lesion or hurt, whilst all the changer noticed was a slight draught.

XXI

HOW PANURGE FELL IN LOVE
WITH A PARISIENNE OF
HIGH DEGREE

As a result of his debate with the English scholar, Panurge had acquired quite a reputation in Paris. The activity of his codpiece was proportionally greater, and, to that effect, he had it pinked and slashed with ornate embroidery, after the Roman fashion. His praises became a topic of general conversation. There was even a song written to celebrate his exploits; the little children sang it as they went to fetch mustard. Best of all, he was made welcome in the most elegant circles. But it went to his head; he actually had the presumption to beleaguer one of the great ladies of the city.

Scorning the rigmarole of prefaces and preliminaries dear to such languishing, dreamy lovers as never touch meat in Lent, Panurge popped the question outright.

"Madame," he told this lofty lady, "it would prove beneficent to the commonwealth, pleasurable to your person, honorable to your progeny and necessary to me that I cover you for the propagation of my race. You may take my word for this, Madame; experience will prove it to you conclusively."

The lady, indignant, thrust him a thousand leagues away.

"You crazy knave, how dare you talk like that? Who do you think I am? Get out of here at once and never let me lay eyes upon you again. For two pins, I'd have your arms and legs sawed off!"

"Madame," he protested, "I would not care two pins if my arms and legs were sawed off, providing you and I had first fought a merry bout of spermary-snuggery. For," he showed her his long codpiece, "here is Master Johnny Inigo, a master instrumentalist who begs to fiddle and thrum, sweep the *viola d'amore*, play the manichord, tweedle the gittern, strike the lyre, beat the drum, wind the horn and grind the organ until you feel his music throbbing in the marrow of your bones. A wily gallant, Master Johnny: he will not fail to find all the cranks, winches, wedges, pullies, nippers, clutches, teeth, springs and rigging stored in your delicate cockpit. You'll be needing no scouring or brushing up after *him*."

"Go to, scoundrel, and away! One more word out of you and I'll shout for help; I'll have my servants beat you to death."

"No, Madame," Panurge protested. "You are not as cruel as you pretend. You cannot be or else your face is a living lie. Let earth soar upward into the firmament, let high heaven sink into the bottomless pit, let the

---

[32] In Greek mythology, a giant with a hundred eyes, set to guard the heifer Io.

whole concert of nature be annihilated ere your beauty and grace secrete one drop of gall or malice. They say that is is virtually impossible for man:

> To find in women beauty unallied
> With arrogance or cruelty or pride

but that holds only for vulgar beauties. Your own is so priceless, so unique, so heavenly that I vow Nature has bestowed it on you as a paragon to prove what she can do when she cares to muster all her power and science. Everything in you is honey, sugar, celestial manna. To you Paris should have awarded the golden apple, not to Venus or Juno or Minerva.[33] For Juno possessed no such nobility, Minerva no such wisdom, Venus no such comeliness.

"O ye heavenly gods and goddesses! how happy the man whom you allow to kiss and fondle you, to cosset, nuzzle and cockle you, to thrust his prolific engine of pleasure into the pod of your quivering quim. By God, I am that man, I plainly feel it. Already she loves me her bellyful I swear; ay, Panurge is predestined to it by the nixies and fairies. Let us lose no time: come, slap-dash, helter-skelter, holus-bolus, to horse and fair riding, tantivy, hoicks!"

Whereupon he sought to embrace her; but she moved towards the window as if to call for help, so Panurge made off hastily. Yet ere retreating:

"Madame," he said, "wait for me here; I'll call your friends, don't bother!"

And he withdrew, unfeased and no less cheerful despite the rebuff.

Next day, as she arrived at church, Panurge stood waiting at the door, offered her holy water, bowed deep as she passed, then kneeled familiarly beside her:

"Madame," he declared, "you must know how madly in love with you I am. Why, I can neither piddle nor cack for love of you! I don't know how *you* feel, but, Madame, suppose I took ill from it, wouldn't you be responsible?"

"Go away, I don't care anything about it. Leave me alone to my prayers."

"One moment!" Panurge begged. "Please equivocate on '*à Beaumont le Viconte?*' or on 'Runt and Codger are fellow-muckers!' "

"I don't know what you mean!"

"Quite easy! '*A beau con le vit monte*,' 'Cunt and Rodger are mellow fuckers!' Now, pray to God that He grant whatever your noble heart desires. And oh, Madame, I beg you: give me those beads a moment."

"Here you are, stop bothering me."

She was about to take off her rosary—it was of cestrin wood with gold ornamentation—when Panurge promptly drew one of his knives and neatly cut it. Before carrying it off to pawn:

"Would you like my knife?" he asked.

---

[33] The shepherd Paris awarded a golden apple to Venus for her beauty, over Juno and Minerva, indirectly causing the Trojan War.

"No, certainly not!"

"It's yours to grind or sheathe, Madame, body and soul, bag and baggage, tripe and guts."

But the lady was worried over the loss of her beads, so many implements to help her keep her countenance in church:

"This chattering scoundrel must be some eccentric foreigner," she mused. "He will never return my rosary. What will my dear husband say? He'll be furious! But I'll tell him a sneak thief cut it off me at church. He must believe me: I've still the end fastened on my girdle."

After dinner, Panurge went to call on her with, in his sleeve, a purse full of tokens specially struck for use in the law courts.

"Which of us is the better lover, Madame, you or I?"

"For my part I cannot hate you," she said magnanimously. "God commands us to love our neighbors."

"Aren't you in love with me?"

"I've told you repeatedly not to talk to me like that!" she insisted. "If you mention it again, I'll show you I'm not to be trifled with. Go away, I tell you. But give me back my rosary; my husband might ask me for it."

"Give you back your rosary? No, by heaven, I shall do nothing of the sort. But I'll tell you what I *will* do: I'll gladly give you another. Would you like one in beautifully enamelled gold with beads shaped like great pendulous knockers? Or like loveknots or ingots, heavy in the hand? Or ebony or broad zircons or square-cut garnets with mountings of rare turquoises, or costly topazes or priceless sapphires or precious rubies set with glittering diamonds of twenty-eight facets? No, no, that is a trumpery gift. I know of a marvellous rosary: it's made of exquisite emeralds with a mounting of speckled gray amber; at the buckle there's a Persian pearl fat as an orange . . . and the bauble costs but a paltry five-and-twenty thousand ducats. I will make you a present of it; I've heaps of cash!"

He made his tokens ring as though they were genuine, authentic golden crowns with the shining sun of France stamped upon them.

"Do you fancy a piece of violet or crimson velure, dyed in grain, or a piece of scarlet or brocaded satin? Is it your pleasure to accept chains, brooches, tiaras or rings? You have but to say the word: fifty thousand is a trifle!"

His offer made her mouth water. Yet she stood her ground.

"No, thank you, I want nothing to do with you."

"By God, I certainly want to do something with *you!* What I want will cost you nothing; you'll be out nothing when you've given it. Look, Madame," and he showed her his long codpiece. "Here is Master Johnny Scramblecunney who craves lodging."

He was about to strike root there, when she started to cry out, though none too loud. The mask of courtesy fell from Panurge's face.

"So you won't let me have a little harmless fun, eh? Not even a morsel for me, eh? A bucket of turds to you! you don't deserve the honor or pleasure of it. But by God! I'll make the dogs ride you!"

With which he beat a hasty retreat in dread of blows. (He was by nature fearful of them.)

XXII

How Panurge Played a
None Too Pleasant Trick
on the Parisienne of
High Degree

Next day was Corpus Christi, a feast on which the ladies of Paris put on their stateliest apparel. Panurge's charmer was decked out in a rich gown of crimson velvet, with a skirt of costly white velure.

The day before, Panurge scoured the town for a bitch in heat. Having found one, he tied his belt around her neck and took her home. All that day and through the night, he fed her abundantly; in the morning he killed her, plucked out that part the Greek geomancians know, cut it as fine as he could, tucked it away in one of his innumerable pockets and went to the church. He was sure his lady would soon arrive to take part in the procession always held on that day.

When she entered, Panurge bowed courteously, offered her some holy water and, shortly after she had finished her petty devotions, sat down on the bench beside her. As she looked up, he passed her a paper on which he had written the following rondeau:

> Sweet lady, once, once only I expressed
> My admiration; you denied my quest,
> You drove me irremediably away
> Although I never harmed you (welladay!)
> In act or word or libel or the rest. . . .
> Granted my wooing stirred no answering zest,
> You could have been more honest, and confessed:
> "I do not wish it, friend. Leave me, I pray!"
>   Sweet lady, once,
> Once more and never again I shall protest
> Ere love's flame utterly consume my breast,
> One boon alone I languish for: to lay
> My peacock, shoveller, cockerel, popinjay
> Deep in the shelter of your downy nest.
>   Sweet lady, once!

While she was unfolding the paper to see what was inside, Panurge deftly sprinkled his drug all over her, spilling it impartially in the folds of her sleeves and skirt.

"Madame," he said before taking his leave, "a lover's life is not always a bed of roses. In my case I can only hope the anguished nights, the sorrows and tribulation I undergo for love of you will be deducted from my trials in purgatory. At least pray God He give me patience to bear my affliction."

Panurge had scarcely spoken when all the dogs in the church, attracted by the odor of the drug, scurried over to the lady. Big and little, large and small, one and all came up, sniffed, raised their legs, cocked their members and let fly on her dress. It was the most horrible sight imaginable.

Panurge pretended to chase them off, then bowed and retired to watch the sport from the vantage point of a chapel. Those wretched curs were squirting all over her clothes. One huge greyhound placed a paw on her shoulder to aim at her head . . . other dogs pumped in her sleeves . . . still others drenched her backside, while the puppies piddled in her shoes. . . . The women close to her sought to keep the beasts off, but with scant success. Meanwhile, holding his sides, Panurge, between guffaws of laughter, told certain lords who were next to him:

"I think that lady's in heat. Or some wolfhound covered her recently."

Seeing the dogs crowded as thick about her as about a bitch in heat, he ran off to fetch Pantagruel. On the way, he stopped to kick every dog he met, crying:

"To church with you! To your genuflexions! Follow the odor of sanctity! Be off and join your fellows at the urinarian baptism! Forward, by all the devils, be off, devil take you!"

"Master," he said breathlessly to Pantagruel, "please come and see all the dogs of the country gathered about the loveliest lady in town, and every one of them agog to scrounge her!"

Pantagruel, delighted at the novelty of it, accompanied Panurge back to church and enjoyed the fun immensely. By the time the procession began, matters had reached a crisis. There were more than six hundred thousand and fourteen dogs thronging about her and finding one thousand and one means of harassing her. Whichever way she turned, the newcomers followed the scent, dogged her heels and flooded whatever spot her dress touched. The only course left her was to go home. As she fled through the streets, every one stopped to watch the dogs leaping high as her neck, turning her elegant toilette into a very toilet, as she ran on, helpless and steaming. It was impossible to give them the slip, the trail was too pungent. So they followed her to her residence.

While she hid in her room and her chambermaids burst into laughter behind politely raised aprons, all the dogs within a radius of a half-league came rushing up and showered so hard against the gate as to form a stream in which ducks might very well have swum. To-day this same current, now called the creek of Bièvre, flows through the grounds of the Abbey of St. Victor and past the Gobelin dye-works. Materials steeped in its waters turn a rare scarlet thanks to some special virtue of these pissdogs, as our learned Master Doribus recently pointed out in a brilliant sermon. God help us; a mill could have ground corn there, though not so much as the famous Bazacle in Toulouse on the Garonne.

Michel de Montaigne

(1533–1592)

"I have no more made my book than my book has made me," Michel de Montaigne wrote, *"'tis a book consubstantial with the author, of a peculiar design, a member of my life, and whose business is not designed for others, as that of all other books is."* The book is his Essays, and perhaps no other work has ever coincided so precisely with the personality of its author, who was an extraordinarily complex, attractive, and in some ways baffling man.

Montaigne was born in 1533, the son of Pierre Eyquem, a wealthy merchant and mayor of Bordeaux. (Montaigne later discarded the name Eyquem and took instead the name of the family estate, the château de Montaigne in Périgord, in southwestern France.) Montaigne's father was deeply impressed with Renaissance ideas, and he attempted to give his son an experimental education that would fit him for the spirit of the new age. He sent his son to be nursed by a peasant woman in a village on his estate, so that the young Montaigne would develop a love and respect for common people. A Latin tutor came from Germany to oversee his first attempts at speech, to keep him from hearing French until he had mastered Latin, and thus to make Latin his native tongue.

When he was six, Montaigne was sent to school at the famous Collège de Guienne in Bordeaux, where he studied under a number of learned men destined to become key figures in Renaissance thought. After he had completed his course at Bordeaux, he went on to the study of law, probably at Toulouse, home of one of the famous law schools of France. When he was twenty-one, he became a member of a court and, three years later, a member of the Parlement of Bordeaux, where he was one of sixty magistrates whose duty it was to enforce the king's law. In his function as magistrate, Montaigne was an observer of, and sometimes a participant in, the religious conflicts between Catholics and Protestant Huguenots and in the brutal suppression of Huguenot "heretics." Here he seems to have developed the strong distaste for cruelty and brutal punishments that appears frequently in the Essays. The other notable influence upon Montaigne during these years was an intense friendship with another young member of the Parlement, Étienne de la Boétie, which lasted six years and ended only with the early death of La Boétie. La Boétie was a Humanist and a fine scholar who translated Xenophon and Plutarch and wrote poetry in both Latin and French.

In 1570, Montaigne resigned from the Parlement of Bordeaux and retired to his estate, *"to the bosom of the learned Virgins"* (the Muses), as he put it. For the rest of his life, his chief employment was the writing of his Essays, though there were many interruptions and temporary returns to active life: a year and a half of traveling in 1580–81, two terms as Mayor of Bordeaux (during which the Plague killed almost a third of the population of that city), and a period of exile from his château during the height of the Plague and the Wars of Religion. The first two volumes of his Essays were published in 1580; in 1586–88, he thoroughly revised and expanded the earlier volumes and wrote a third one. Even after the publication of the edition of 1588, he continued to revise and expand the Essays through marginal annotations during the last four years of his life. He died of a severe inflammation of the throat on September 13, 1592.

Montaigne's Essays represent a new genre in Western literature. The nine-

1945

teenth-century English critic Edmund Gosse wrote, "It is not often that we can date with any approach to accuracy the arrival of a new class of literature into the world. But it was in the month of March 1571 that the essay was invented." This exaggeration neglects the long process by which Montaigne developed his characteristic form, but it does suggest the originality of his achievement. Montaigne began his work as a modest set of quotations from his readings, annotated with his own comments; a reminder of these origins remains in the many Latin quotations which punctuate the Essays *in their final form. As he continued to write, however, his own comments began to outweigh the quotations and develop their own loose, rambling, almost free-associational structure. Frequently, the title of an essay serves only as the jumping-off place for a series of meditations that have little or no connection with the presumed subject. The style is easy and informal, though it can rise when appropriate to great eloquence; Montaigne's literary voice is distinctively witty, self-deprecating, and charming. Often long passages consist merely of a series of amusing and ingenious anecdotes, illustrations, and quotations spiraling around the subject. The nineteenth-century French critic Sainte-Beuve described Montaigne's style as "a continual epigram or a metaphor always renewing itself."*

Montaigne's ideas have been the subject of almost continuous controversy since the Essays *were first published. Some readers, noting that he regards human reason as powerless and the world as essentially unknowable, have concluded that his work implies indifference and resignation to ignorance. Others have found the essential spirit of modern science in his skeptical, inquiring spirit and his unwillingness to take anything merely on authority. His religious views are also variously interpreted. Few of his contemporaries found anything unorthodox in the* Essays, *but the Church later found their skeptical spirit questionable and in 1676 placed them on the* Index. *Some close students of Montaigne have found him profoundly Christian, while Ralph Waldo Emerson called his essay on Montaigne "The Skeptic," and Sainte-Beuve believed that he worked deliberately to undermine the teachings of Christianity. Equally controversial, across the centuries, has been the meaning of Montaigne's preoccupation with himself. In the seventeenth century, the French scientist and philosopher Pascal spoke of Montaigne's work as "the foolish project of painting himself." Others have seen this self-preoccupation as inspired both by the classical injunction to "Know Thyself" and the Renaissance emphasis upon the importance of the individual mind, while modern readers have found in Montaigne a vivid anticipation of twentieth-century literature's intense interest in the inner world of the individual self.*

The disagreements regarding Montaigne's work probably arise from attempts to impose a unity and consistency upon them that they do not have. Critics now usually divide his thought into three stages of development. In the first stage, he was deeply influenced by the philosophy of Seneca and by the personal model of Cato of Utica. During this period he held "Stoic" ideas of indifference to death, suffering, and misfortune. A second, "Skeptical" stage is marked by his writing of the long and important Apology for Raymond Sebond *(too long to reprint here). Sebond, a Spanish professor of medicine at Toulouse, had written a Latin work called* Liber Creaturarum, *or* Natural Theology, *which Montaigne had translated into French for his father. Sebond's aim was to prove that the major tenets of Christianity could be arrived at by natural reason and reference to the natural world. In the course of writing his essay on Sebond, Montaigne came close to defending the precisely opposite view: the inability of the human mind to know anything with certainty. This skeptical view had such a hold upon Montaigne that in about 1576 he had a*

*medal struck which depicted an evenly balanced scale above the personal motto,
"Que Scay-je?" or "What do I know?" The third and last stage is often called the
"Epicurean" stage; Montaigne's emphasis now shifts to the achievement of happiness
through the exercise of the human faculties, physical as well as intellectual.*

*This tripartite scheme seems accurate as far as it goes, but even it may imply more
consistency and order in Montaigne's work than actually exists. The real core of
Montaigne's work is not a consistent set of ideas, but the continual presence of the
man himself. He is constantly shifting and changing but is always vividly present at
center stage. It is through Montaigne's constant attention to the details of his own life
that he captures not only the quality of his own personality but also the rich variety
and delight of life itself. The twentieth-century novelist and critic Virginia Woolf
summed up this vitality in her essay on Montaigne: "It is life that emerges more and
more clearly as these essays reach not their end, but their suspension in full career. It
is life that becomes more and more absorbing as death draws near, one's self, one's
soul, every part of existence: that one wears silk stockings summer and winter; puts
water in one's wine; has one's hair cut after dinner; must have glass to drink from;
has never worn spectacles; has a loud voice; carries a switch in one's hands; bites
one's tongue; fidgets with one's feet; is apt to scratch one's ears; likes meat to be high;
rubs one's teeth with a napkin (thank God, they are good!); must have curtains to
one's bed; and, what is rather curious, began by liking radishes, then disliked them,
and now likes them again. No fact is too little to let it slip through one's fingers."*

*Montaigne's spirit, as well as some of his recurring ideas and his characteristic
style, are well illustrated in the two essays reprinted here. Montaigne's love of
simplicity and "naturalness" is expressed vividly in the quaint but pointed essay "Of
Cannibals." Montaigne, like most of his European contemporaries, was fascinated by
reports of the New World; he had seen natives of Brazil at the court celebrations in
Rouen in 1560 (celebrating the coming of age of Charles IX) and, as he tells us, had
some Brazilian artifacts in his home. He delights in the curious details of cannibal
life but, characteristically, lets his mind spiral around the implications of a comparison between the lives of these "noble savages" and his own life. "We may then call
these people barbarous, in respect to the rules of reason," he writes, "but not in respect
to ourselves, who in all sorts of barbarity exceed them." (This essay has an extrinsic
interest in that Shakespeare adapted a passage from it, in John Florio's Elizabethan
translation, and incorporated it into* The Tempest.*)*

*In the essay "Of Repentance," Montaigne comes close to what his contemporaries
would have called heresy as he examines from a skeptical and ironic point of view an
important religious conception. The Church enjoins penitence and contrition, a hatred of one's old life and a turning to a new life in Christ, but Montaigne builds his
essay around an explanation of the blunt statement "I very rarely repent." A person
may regret an action, he says, or give up "impetuous, prompt, and sudden" sins, but
as for changing one's fundamental nature, being "reborn," that, Montaigne says, "is
very hard for me to imagine or form." Montaigne's critics have taken this view as an
attempt to justify his own self-indulgence and self-satisfaction, but Montaigne's conclusions are quite different. By denying the possibility of a sudden transformation of
one's nature through divine intervention, Montaigne puts the responsibility for virtue completely upon the everyday struggles of the individual, alone with his own
conscience. "The virtue of the soul," he writes, "does not consist in flying high, but in
walking orderly," and his ideal is not the grandeur of an Alexander but the modesty
of a Socrates, who wanted not to conquer the world but to "carry on human life
conformably with its natural condition."*

FURTHER READING *(prepared by W. J. R.):* A good starting point is the essay on Montaigne by Donald M. Frame, an eminent Montaigne scholar, in *European Writers: Medieval and Renaissance*, Vol. 2, ed. George Stade, 1984. Frame's *Montaigne, A Biography*, 1965, a lengthy but readable portrait, follows the writer's life closely but does not consider his writing at length. Marcel Tetel's *Montaigne*, 1974, is a general introduction; another good one is Peter Burke's *Montaigne*, 1981, a medium-length study in the Past Masters series. Reflections on Montaigne by two creative writers provide a good introduction to the *Essays:* Ralph Waldo Emerson's "Montaigne, or The Skeptic," in *Representative Men*, 1850, is interesting on Montaigne's skepticism; Virginia Woolf's "Montaigne," in *The Common Reader*, 1925, considers autobiography and self-knowledge. Phillip P. Hallie's *The Scar of Montaigne: An Essay in Personal Philosophy*, 1966, provides a good introductory essay on Montaigne's historical background. Hallie also examines doubt in French Renaissance thought in connection with the evolution of Montaigne's personal philosophy. Jean Starobinski, *Montaigne in Motion*, beautifully translated by Arthur Goldhammer, 1985, is a major study, approaching Montaigne topically and emphasizing his awareness of the contrast between illusion and reality. Margaret M. McGowan's *Montaigne's Deceits: The Art of Persuasion in the "Essais,"* 1974, examines Montaigne's art of dissimulating in order to persuade his readers indirectly. McGowan examines his concern with surviving in his age and his interest in the difficulties of communicating. Several types of imagery and their contribution to Montaigne's persuasiveness are studied in Carol Clark's *The Web of Metaphor*, 1978. Montaigne's language is discussed in depth in Richard L. Regosin's *The Matter of My Book: Montaigne's "Essais" as the Book of the Self*, 1977. Regosin studies closely the phenomenon of objectified man as both the subject and object of discourse, considering Montaigne's own awareness of this situation and the way it shaped his style.

ESSAYS

Translated by Charles Cotton

OF CANNIBALS

When King Pyrrhus invaded Italy, having viewed and considered the order of the army the Romans sent out to meet him: "I know not," said he, "what kind of barbarians," (for so the Greeks called all other nations) "these may be; but the disposition of this army, that I see, has nothing of barbarism in it."[1] As much said the Greeks of that which Flaminius brought into their country;[2] and Philip, beholding from an eminence the order and distribution of the Roman camp formed in his kingdom by Publius Sulpicius Galba, spake to the same effect.[3] By which it appears how cautious men ought to be of taking things upon trust from vulgar opinion, and that we are to judge by the eye of reason, and not from common report.

I long had a man in my house that lived ten or twelve years in the New

[1] Pyrrhus (318–272 B.C.) was King of Epirus. This story is told in Plutarch's *Life of Pyrrhus*.
[2] T. Quintius Flaminius (230–144 B.C.) was a Roman general. See Plutarch's *Life of Flaminius* for this story.
[3] The reference is to Philip V, King of Macedon (221–179 B.C.). This story is told by the Roman historian Livy.

World, discovered in these latter days, and in that part of it where Villegaignon landed, which he called Antarctic France.[4] This discovery of so vast a country seems to be of very great consideration. I cannot be sure, that hereafter there may not be another, so many wiser men than we having been deceived in this. I am afraid our eyes are bigger than our bellies, and that we have more curiosity than capacity; for we grasp at all, but catch nothing but wind.

Plato brings in Solon, telling a story that he had heard from the priests of Sais in Egypt, that of old, and before the Deluge, there was a great island called Atlantis, situate directly at the mouth of the Straits of Gibraltar, which contained more countries than both Africa and Asia put together; and that the kings of that country, who not only possessed that isle, but extended their dominion so far into the continent that they had a country of Africa as far as Egypt, and extending in Europe to Tuscany, attempted to encroach even upon Asia, and to subjugate all the nations that border upon the Mediterranean Sea, as far as the Black Sea; and to that effect overran all Spain, the Gauls, and Italy, so far as to penetrate into Greece, where the Athenians stopped them: but that sometime after, both the Athenians, and they and their island, were swallowed by the Flood.[5]

It is very likely that this extreme irruption and inundation of water made wonderful changes and alterations in the habitations of the earth, as 'tis said that the sea then divided Sicily from Italy—

> "Haec loca, vi quondam, et vasta convulsa ruina,
> Dissiluisse ferunt, quum protenus utraque tellus
> Una foret."[6]

—Cyprus from Syria, the isle of Negropont from the continent of Boeotia, and elsewhere united lands that were separate before, by filling up the channel between them with sand and mud:

> "Sterilisque diu palus, aptaque remis,
> Vicinas urbes alit, et grave sentit aratrum."[7]

But there is no great appearance that this isle was this New World so lately discovered: for that almost touched upon Spain, and it were an incredible effect of an inundation, to have tumbled back so prodigious a mass, above twelve hundred leagues: besides that our modern navigators have already almost discovered it to be no island, but *terra firma*,[8] and continent with the East Indies on the one side, and with the lands under the two poles on the other side; or, if it be separate from them, it is by so narrow a strait and channel, that it none the more deserves the name of an island for that.

It should seem, that in this great body, there are two sorts of motions,

---

[4] The French explorer Villegaignon explored Brazil (Antarctic France) in 1557.

[5] The story of Atlantis appears in Plato's *Timaeus*.

[6] "These lands, they say, once with violence and vast desolation convulsed and burst asunder, which until then were one" (Virgil, *Aeneid*).

[7] "That which was once a sterile marsh and bore vessels on its bosom now feeds neighboring cities and admits the plow" (Horace).

[8] Dry land.

the one natural, and the other febrific,[9] as there are in ours. When I consider the impression that our river of Dordoigne has made in my time, on the right bank of its descent, and that in twenty years it has gained so much, and undermined the foundations of so many houses, I perceive it to be an extraordinary agitation: for had it always followed this course, or were hereafter to do it, the aspect of the world would be totally changed. But rivers alter their course, sometimes beating against the one side, and sometimes the other, and sometimes quietly keeping the channel. I do not speak of sudden inundations, the causes of which everybody understands. In Medoc,[10] by the seashore, the Sieur d'Arsac, my brother, sees an estate he had there, buried under the sands which the sea vomits before it: where the tops of some houses are yet to be seen, and where his rents and domains are converted into pitiful barren pasturage. The inhabitants of this place affirm, that of late years the sea has driven so vehemently upon them, that they have lost above four leagues of land. These sands are her harbingers: and we now see great heaps of moving sand, that march half a league before her, and occupy the land.

The other testimony from antiquity, to which some would apply this discovery of the New World, is in Aristotle; at least, if that little book of unheard-of miracles be his.[11] He there tells us, that certain Carthaginians, having crossed the Atlantic Sea without the Straits of Gibraltar, and sailed a very long time, discovered at last a great and fruitful island, all covered over with wood, and watered with several broad and deep rivers; far remote from all *terra-firma*, and that they, and others after them, allured by the goodness and fertility of the soil, went thither with their wives and children, and began to plant a colony. But the senate of Carthage perceiving their people by little and little to diminish, issued out an express prohibition, that none, upon pain of death, should transport themselves thither; and also drove out these new inhabitants; fearing, 'tis said, lest in process of time they should so multiply as to supplant themselves and ruin their state. But this relation of Aristotle no more agrees with our new-found lands than the other.

This man that I had was a plain ignorant fellow,[12] and therefore the more likely to tell truth: for your better bred sort of men are much more curious in their observation, 'tis true, and discover a great deal more, but then they gloss upon it, and to give the greater weight to what they deliver and allure your belief, they cannot forbear a little to alter the story; they never represent things to you simply as they are, but rather as they appeared to them, or as they would have them appear to you, and to gain the reputation of men of judgment, and the better to induce your faith, are willing to help out the business with something more than is really true, of their own invention. Now, in this case, we should either have a man of irreproachable veracity, or so simple that he has not wherewithal to contrive, and to give a color of truth to false relations, and who can have

9 Feverish.

10 Home of Montaigne's brother, Medoc is a district in southwestern France, northwest of Bordeaux.

11 The book referred to is the apocryphal *Of Unheard-Of Wonders*, which contains an account of Atlantis.

12 That is, the traveler referred to at the beginning of the essay.

no ends in forging an untruth. Such a one was mine; and besides, he has at divers times brought to me several seamen and merchants who at the same time went the same voyage. I shall therefore content myself with his information, without inquiring what the cosmographers say to the business. We should have topographers to trace out to us the particular places where they have been; but for having had this advantage over us, to have seen the Holy Land, they would have the privilege, forsooth, to tell us stories of all the other parts of the world besides. I would have every one write what he knows, and as much as he knows, but no more; and that not in this only, but in all other subjects; for such a person may have some particular knowledge and experience of the nature of such a river, or such a fountain, who, as to other things, knows no more than what everybody does, and yet to keep a clutter with this little pittance of his, will undertake to write the whole body of physics: a vice from which great inconveniences derive their original.

Now, to return to my subject, I find that there is nothing barbarous and savage in this nation, by anything that I can gather, excepting, that every one gives the title of barbarism to everything that is not in use in his own country. As, indeed, we have no other level of truth and reason, than the example and idea of the opinions and customs of the place wherein we live: there is always the perfect religion, there the perfect government, there the most exact and accomplished usage of all things. They are savages at the same rate that we say fruit are wild, which nature produces of herself and by her own ordinary progress; whereas in truth, we ought rather to call those wild, whose natures we have changed by our artifice, and diverted from the common order. In those, the genuine, most useful and natural virtues and properties are vigorous and sprightly, which we have helped to degenerate in these, by accommodating them to the pleasure of our own corrupted palate. And yet for all this our taste confesses a flavor and delicacy, excellent even to emulation of the best of ours, in several fruits wherein those countries abound without art or culture. Neither is it reasonable that art should gain the pre-eminence of our great and powerful mother nature. We have so surcharged her with the additional ornaments and graces we have added to the beauty and riches of her own works by our inventions, that we have almost smothered her; yet in other places, where she shines in her own purity and proper luster, she marvelously baffles and disgraces all our vain and frivolous attempts.

> "Et veniunt hederae sponte sua melius;
> Surgit et in solis formosior arbutus antris;
> Et volucres nulla dulcius arte canunt."[13]

Our utmost endeavors cannot arrive at so much as to imitate the nest of the least of birds, its contexture, beauty, and convenience: not so much as the web of a poor spider.

All things, says Plato, are produced either by nature, by fortune, or by

---

[13] "The ivy grows best spontaneously, the arbutus best in shady caves, and the wild notes of birds are sweeter than art can teach" (Propertius).

art; the greatest and most beautiful by the one or the other of the former, the least and the most imperfect by the last.[14]

These nations then seem to me to be so far barbarous, as having received but very little form and fashion from art and human invention, and consequently to be not much remote from their original simplicity. The laws of nature, however, govern them still, not as yet much vitiated with any mixture of ours: but 'tis in such purity, that I am sometimes troubled we were not sooner acquainted with these people, and that they were not discovered in those better times, when there were men much more able to judge of them than we are. I am sorry that Lycurgus and Plato had no knowledge of them:[15] for to my apprehension, what we now see in those nations, does not only surpass all the pictures with which the poets have adorned the golden age, and all their inventions in feigning a happy state of man, but, moreover, the fancy and even the wish and desire of philosophy itself; so native and so pure a simplicity, as we by experience see to be in them, could never enter into their imagination, nor could they ever believe that human society could have been maintained with so little artifice and human patchwork. I should tell Plato, that it is a nation wherein there is no manner of traffic, no knowledge of letters, no science of numbers, no name of magistrate or political superiority; no use of service, riches or poverty, no contracts, no successions, no dividends, no properties, no employments, but those of leisure, no respect of kindred, but common, no clothing, no agriculture, no metal, no use of corn or wine; the very words that signify lying, treachery, dissimulation, avarice, envy, detraction, pardon, never heard of. How much would he find his imaginary republic short of his perfection?[16] *"Viri a diis recentes."*[17]

"Hos natura modos primum dedit."[18]

As to the rest, they live in a country very pleasant and temperate, so that, as my witnesses inform me, 'tis rare to hear of a sick person, and they moreover assure me, that they never saw any of the natives, either paralytic, blear-eyed, toothless, or crooked with age. The situation of their country is along the seashore, enclosed on the other side toward the land, with great and high mountains, having about a hundred leagues in breadth between. They have great store of fish and flesh, that have no resemblance to those of ours: which they eat without any other cookery, than plain boiling, roasting and broiling. The first that rode a horse thither, though in several other voyages he had contracted an acquaintance and familiarity with them, put them into so terrible a fright, with his centaur[19] appearance, that they killed him with their arrows before they could come to discover who he was. Their buildings are very long, and of capacity to hold two or

---

[14] Montaigne is paraphrasing a passage in Plato's *Laws*.

[15] Lycurgus was a Spartan lawgiver. Like Plato, he wrote of ideal societies, and, Montaigne suggests, both would have profited from knowing the culture of the New World cannibals.

[16] The two sentences preceding are the famous passage adapted by Shakespeare in *The Tempest*, II.i.147.

[17] "Men fresh from the gods" (Seneca).

[18] "These were the manners first taught by nature" (Virgil).

[19] A creature half horse and half man.

three hundred people, made of the barks of tall trees, reared with one end upon the ground, and leaning to and supporting one another, at the top, like some of our barns, of which the coverings hang down to the very ground, and serves for the side walls. They have wood so hard, that they cut with it, and make their swords of it, and their grills of it to broil their meat. Their beds are of cotton, hung swinging from the roof, like our seaman's hammocks, every man his own, for the wives lie apart from their husbands. They rise with the sun, and so soon as they are up, eat for all day, for they have no more meals but that: they do not then drink, as Suidas[20] reports of some other people of the East that never drank at their meals; but drink very often all day after, and sometimes to a rousing pitch. Their drink is made of a certain root, and is of the color of our claret, and they never drink it but lukewarm. It will not keep above two or three days; it has a somewhat sharp, brisk taste, is nothing heady, but very comfortable to the stomach; laxative to strangers, but a very pleasant beverage to such as are accustomed to it. They make use, instead of bread, of a certain white compound, like coriander comfits;[21] I have tasted of it; the taste is sweet and a little flat. The whole day is spent in dancing. Their young men go a-hunting after wild beasts with bows and arrows; one part of their women are employed in preparing their drink the while, which is their chief employment. One of their old men, in the morning before they fall to eating, preaches to the whole family, walking from the one end of the house to the other, and several times repeating the same sentence, till he has finished the round, for their houses are at least a hundred yards long. Valor toward their enemies and love toward their wives, are the two heads of his discourse, never failing in the close, to put them in mind, that 'tis their wives who provide them their drink warm and well seasoned. The fashion of their beds, ropes, swords, and of the wooden bracelets they tie about their wrists, when they go to fight, and of the great canes, bored hollow at one end, by the sound of which they keep the cadence of their dances, are to be seen in several places, and among others, at my house. They shave all over, and much more neatly than we, without other razor than one of wood or stone. They believe in the immortality of the soul, and that those who have merited well of the gods, are lodged in that part of heaven where the sun rises, and the accursed in the west.

They have I know not what kind of priests and prophets, who very rarely present themselves to the people, having their abode in the mountains. At their arrival, there is a great feast, and solemn assembly of many villages: each house, as I have described, makes a village, and they are about a French league distant from one another. This prophet declaims to them in public, exhorting them to virtue and their duty: but all their ethics are comprised in these two articles, resolution in war, and affection to their wives. He also prophesies to them events to come, and the issues they are to expect from their enterprises, and prompts them to or diverts them from war: but let him look to't; for if he fail in his divination, and anything happen otherwise than he has foretold, he is cut into a thousand pieces, if he be caught, and condemned for a false prophet: for that reason, if any of them has been mistaken, he is no more heard of.

---

[20] A tenth-century Greek lexicographer.   [21] Cakes flavored with the herb coriander.

Divination is a gift of God, and therefore to abuse it, ought to be a punishable imposture. Among the Scythians, where their diviners failed in the promised effect, they were laid, bound hand and foot, upon carts loaded with furze and bavins, and drawn by oxen, on which they were burned to death.[22] Such as only meddle with things subject to the conduct of human capacity, are excusable in doing the best they can: but those other fellows that come to delude us with assurances of an extraordinary faculty, beyond our understanding, ought they not to be punished, when they do not make good the effect of their promise, and for the temerity of their imposture?

They have continual war with the nations that live further within the mainland, beyond their mountains, to which they go naked, and without other arms than their bows and wooden swords, fashioned at one end like the heads of our javelins. The obstinacy of their battles is wonderful, and they never end without great effusion of blood: for as to running away, they know not what it is. Every one for a trophy brings home the head of an enemy he has killed, which he fixes over the door of his house. After having a long time treated their prisoners very well, and given them all the regales they can think of, he to whom the prisoner belongs, invites a great assembly of his friends. They being come, he ties a rope to one of the arms of the prisoner, of which, at a distance, out of his reach, he holds the one end himself, and gives to the friend he loves best the other arm to hold after the same manner; which being done, they two, in the presence of all the assembly, despatch him with their swords. After that they roast him, eat him among them, and send some chops to their absent friends. They do not do this, as some think, for nourishment, as the Scythians anciently did, but as a representation of an extreme revenge; as will appear by this: that having observed the Portuguese, who were in league with their enemies, to inflict another sort of death upon any of them they took prisoners, which was to set them up to the girdle in the earth, to shoot at the remaining part till it was stuck full of arrows, and then to hang them, they thought those people of the other world (as being men who had sown the knowledge of a great many vices among their neighbors, and who were much greater masters in all sorts of mischief than they) did not exercise this sort of revenge without a meaning, and that it must needs be more painful than theirs, they began to leave their old way, and to follow this. I am not sorry that we should here take notice of the barbarous horror of so cruel an action, but that, seeing so clearly into their faults, we should be so blind to our own. I conceive there is more barbarity in eating a man alive, than when he is dead; in tearing a body limb from limb by racks and torments, that is yet in perfect sense; in roasting it by degrees;[23] in causing it to be bitten and worried by dogs and swine (as we have not only read, but lately seen, not among inveterate and mortal enemies, but among neighbors and fellow-citizens, and, which is worse, under color of piety and religion), than to roast and eat him after he is dead.

---

[22] The Scythians were the inhabitants of a region in southeastern Europe and Asia, legendary for their barbarity. "Furze and bavins" are dry heather and straw. This story appears in the work of the Greek historian Herodotus.

[23] These were accepted modes of execution in Montaigne's day.

Chrysippus and Zeno,[24] the two heads of the Stoic sect, were of opinion that there was no hurt in making use of our dead carcasses, in what way soever for our necessity, and in feeding upon them too; as our own ancestors, who being besieged by Caesar in the city of Alexia, resolved to sustain the famine of the siege with the bodies of their old men, women, and other persons who were incapable of bearing arms.[25]

> "Vascones, ut fama est, alimentis talibus usi
> Produxere animas."[26]

And the physicians make no bones of employing it to all sorts of use, either to apply it outwardly; or to give it inwardly for the health of the patient. But there never was any opinion so irregular, as to excuse treachery, disloyalty, tyranny, and cruelty, which are our familiar vices. We may then call these people barbarous, in respect to the rules of reason: but not in respect to ourselves, who in all sorts of barbarity exceed them. Their wars are throughout noble and generous, and carry as much excuse and fair pretense, as that human malady is capable of; having with them no other foundation than the sole jealousy of valor. Their disputes are not for the conquest of new lands, for these they already possess are so fruitful by nature, as to supply them without labor or concern, with all things necessary, in such abundance that they have no need to enlarge their borders. And they are moreover, happy in this, that they only covet so much as their natural necessities require: all beyond that, is superfluous to them: men of the same age call one another generally brothers, those who are younger, children; and the old men are fathers to all. These leave to their heirs in common the full possession of goods, without any manner of division, or other title than what nature bestows upon her creatures, in bringing them into the world. If their neighbors pass over the mountains to assault them, and obtain a victory, all the victors gain by it is glory only, and the advantage of having proved themselves the better in valor and virtue: for they never meddle with the goods of the conquered, but presently return into their own country, where they have no want of anything necessary, nor of this greatest of all goods, to know happily how to enjoy their condition and to be content. And those in turn do the same; they demand of their prisoners no other ransom, than acknowledgment that they are overcome: but there is not one found in an age, who will not rather choose to die than make such a confession, or either by word or look, recede from the entire grandeur of an invincible courage. There is not a man among them who had not rather be killed and eaten, than so much as to open his mouth to entreat he may not. They use them with all liberality and freedom, to the end their lives may be so much the dearer to them; but frequently entertain them with menaces of their approaching death, of the torments they are to suffer, of the preparations making in order to it, of the mangling their limbs, and of the feast that is to be made, where their carcass is to be the

---

[24] Chrysippus (291–208 B.C.) and Zeno (d. 264 B.C.) were, as noted, Stoic philosophers.
[25] This story of cannibalism appears in Caesar's *Gallic Wars*.
[26] "It is said that the Gascons with such meat appeased their hunger" (Juvenal).

only dish. All which they do, to no other end, but only to extort some gentle or submissive word from them, or to frighten them so as to make them run away, to obtain this advantage that they were terrified, and that their constancy was shaken; and indeed, if rightly taken, it is in this point only that a true victory consists.

> "Victoria nulla est,
> Quam quae confessos animo quoque subjugat hostes."[27]

The Hungarians, a very warlike people, never pretend further than to reduce the enemy to their discretion; for having forced this confession from them, they let them go without injury or ransom, excepting, at the most, to make them engage their word never to bear arms against them again. We have sufficient advantages over our enemies that are borrowed and not truly our own; it is the quality of a porter, and no effect of virtue, to have stronger arms and legs; it is a dead and corporeal quality to set in array; 'tis a turn of fortune to make our enemy stumble, or to dazzle him with the light of the sun; 'tis a trick of science and art, and that may happen in a mean base fellow, to be a good fencer. The estimate and value of a man consist in the heart and in the will: there his true honor lies. Valor is stability, not of legs and arms, but of the courage and the soul; it does not lie in the goodness of our horse or our arms: but in our own. He that falls obstinate in his courage—*"Si succiderit, de genu pugnat"*[28]—he who, for any danger of imminent death, abates nothing of his assurance; who, dying, yet darts at his enemy a fierce and disdainful look, is overcome not by us, but by fortune; he is killed, not conquered; the most valiant are sometimes the most unfortunate. There are defeats more triumphant than victories. Never could those four sister victories, the fairest the sun ever beheld, of Salamis, Plataea, Mycale, and Sicily, venture to oppose all their united glories, to the single glory of the discomfiture of King Leonidas and his men, at the pass of Thermopylae.[29] Whoever ran with a more glorious desire and greater ambition, to the winning, than Captain Iscolas to the certain loss of a battle?[30] Who could have found out a more subtle invention to secure his safety, than he did to assure his destruction? He was set to defend a certain pass of Peloponnesus against the Arcadians, which, considering the nature of the place and the inequality of forces, finding it utterly impossible for him to do, and seeing that all who were presented to the enemy, must certainly be left upon the place; and on the other side, reputing it unworthy of his own virtue and magnanimity and of the Lacedaemonian name to fail in any part of his duty, he chose a mean between these two extremes after this manner; the youngest and most active of his men, he preserved for the service and defense of their country, and sent

---

[27] "No victory is complete which the conquered do not admit to be so" (Claudius).
[28] "If his legs fail him, he fights on his knees" (Seneca).
[29] Salamis, Plataea, Mycale, and Sicily were the sites of notable victories of the Greeks over the Persians and Carthaginians in the fifth century B.C. At Thermopylae, a narrow mountain pass in eastern Greece, a small band of Spartans held off the Persian army in 480 B.C.
[30] This story is told by the Greek historian Diodorus Siculus (first century B.C.).

them back; and with the rest, whose loss would be of less consideration, he resolved to make good the pass, and with the death of them, to make the enemy buy their entry as dear as possibly he could; as it fell out, for being presently environed on all sides by the Arcadians, after having made a great slaughter of the enemy, he and his were all cut in pieces. Is there any trophy dedicated to the conquerors, which was not much more due to these who were overcome? The part that true conquering is to play, lies in the encounter, not in the coming off; and the honor of valor consists in fighting, not in subduing.

But to return to my story: these prisoners are so far from discovering the least weakness, for all the terrors that can be represented to them that, on the contrary, during the two or three months they are kept, they always appear with a cheerful countenance; importune their masters to make haste to bring them to the test, defy, rail at them, and reproach them with cowardice, and the number of battles they have lost against those of their country. I have a song made by one of these prisoners, wherein he bids them "come all, and dine upon him, and welcome, for they shall withal eat their own fathers and grandfathers, whose flesh has served to feed and nourish him. These muscles," says he, "this flesh and these veins, are your own: poor silly souls as you are, you little think that the substance of your ancestors' limbs is here yet; notice what you eat, and you will find in it the taste of your own flesh:" in which song there is to be observed an invention that nothing relishes of the barbarian. Those that paint these people dying after this manner, represent the prisoner spitting in the faces of his executioners and making wry mouths at them. And 'tis most certain, that to the very last gasp, they never cease to brave and defy them both in word and gesture. In plain truth, these men are very savage in comparison of us; of necessity, they must either be absolutely so or else we are savages; for there is a vast difference between their manners and ours.

The men there have several wives, and so much the greater number, by how much they have the greater reputation for valor. And it is one very remarkable feature in their marriages, that the same jealousy our wives have to hinder and divert us from the friendship and familiarity of other women, those employ to promote their husbands' desires, and to procure them many spouses; for being above all things solicitous of their husbands' honor, 'tis their chiefest care to seek out, and to bring in the most companions they can, forasmuch as it is a testimony of the husband's virtue. Most of our ladies will cry out, that 'tis monstrous; whereas in truth, it is not so; but a truly matrimonial virtue, and of the highest form. In the Bible, Sarah, with Leah and Rachel, the two wives of Jacob, gave the most beautiful of their handmaids to their husbands; Livia preferred the passions of Augustus to her own interest; and the wife of King Deiotarus, Stratonice, did not only give up a fair young maid that served her to her husband's embraces, but moreover carefully brought up the children he had by her, and assisted them in the succession to their father's crown.[31]

---

[31] The story of Sarah and her maid Hagar appears in Genesis, chapter 16, that of Leah and Rachel in Genesis, chapter 30. The story of Livia is in Suetonius' *Life of Augustus* and that of Stratonice in Plutarch's *Bravery of Women*.

And that it may not be supposed, that all this is done by a simple and servile obligation to their common practice, or by any authoritative impression of their ancient custom, without judgment or reasoning and from having a soul so stupid, that it cannot contrive what else to do, I must here give you some touches of their sufficiency in point of understanding. Besides what I repeated to you before, which was one of their songs of war, I have another, a love-song, that begins thus: "Stay, adder, stay, that by thy pattern my sister may draw the fashion and work of a rich ribbon, that I may present to my beloved, by which means thy beauty and the excellent order of thy scales shall forever be preferred before all other serpents." Wherein the first couplet, "Stay, adder," etc., makes the burden of the song. Now I have conversed enough with poetry to judge thus much: that not only, there is nothing of barbarous in this invention, but, moreover, that it is perfectly Anacreontic.[32] To which may be added, that their language is soft, of a pleasing accent, and something bordering upon the Greek terminations.

Three of these people, not foreseeing how dear their knowledge of the corruptions of this part of the world will one day cost their happiness and repose, and that the effect of this commerce will be their ruin, as I presuppose it is in a very fair way (miserable men to suffer themselves to be deluded with desire of novelty and to have left the serenity of their own heaven, to come so far to gaze at ours!) were at Rouen at the time that the late King Charles IX was there.[33] The king himself talked to them a good while, and they were made to see our fashions, our pomp, and the form of a great city. After which, some one asked their opinion, and would know of them, what of all the things they had seen, they found most to be admired? To which they made answer, three things, of which I have forgotten the third, and am troubled at it, but two I yet remember. They said, that in the first place they thought it very strange, that so many tall men wearing beards, strong, and well armed, who were about the king ('tis like they meant the Swiss of his guard) should submit to obey a child, and that they did not rather choose out one among themselves to command. Secondly (they have a way of speaking in their language, to call men the half of one another), that they had observed, that there were among us men full and crammed with all manner of commodities, while, in the meantime, their halves were begging at their doors, lean, and half-starved with hunger and poverty; and they thought it strange that these necessitous halves were able to suffer so great an inequality and injustice, and that they did not take the others by the throats, or set fire to their houses.

I talked to one of them a great while together, but I had so ill an interpreter, and one who was so perplexed by his own ignorance to apprehend my meaning, that I could get nothing out of him of any moment. Asking him, what advantage he reaped from the superiority he had among his own people (for he was a captain, and our mariners called him king), he told me: to march at the head of them to war. Demanding of him further, how

---

[32] Like the poetry of Anacreon (c. 563–c. 478 B.C.), a Greek poet known for his love poems.
[33] King Charles IX of France died in 1574.

many men he had to follow him? he showed me a space of ground, to signify as many as could march in such a compass, which might be four or five thousand men; and putting the question to him, whether or no his authority expired with the war? he told me this remained: that when he went to visit the villages of his dependence, they plained[34] him paths through the thick of their woods, by which he might pass at his ease. All this does not sound very ill, and the last was not at all amiss, for they wear no breeches.

OF REPENTANCE

Others form man; I only report him: and represent a particular one, ill fashioned enough, and whom, if I had to model him anew, I should certainly make something else than what he is: but that's past recalling. Now, though the features of my picture alter and change, 'tis not, however, unlike: the world eternally turns round; all things therein are incessantly moving, the earth, the rocks of Caucasus, and the pyramids of Egypt, both by the public motion and their own. Even constancy itself is no other but a slower and more languishing motion. I cannot fix my object; 'tis always tottering and reeling by a natural giddiness: I take it as it is at the instant I consider it; I do not paint its being, I paint its passage; not a passing from one age to another, or, as the people say, from seven to seven years, but from day to day, from minute to minute. I must accommodate my history to the hour: I may presently change, not only by fortune, but also by intention. 'Tis a counterpart of various and changeable accidents, and of irresolute imaginations, and, as it falls out, sometimes contrary: whether it be that I am then another self, or that I take subjects by other circumstances and considerations: so it is, that I may peradventure contradict myself, but, as Demades said, I never contradict the truth.[1] Could my soul once take footing, I would not essay but resolve: but it is always learning and making trial.

I propose a life ordinary and without luster: 'tis all one; all moral philosophy may as well be applied to a common and private life, as to one of richer composition: every man carries the entire form of human condition. Authors communicate themselves to the people by some especial and extrinsic mark; I, the first of any, by my universal being; as Michel de Montaigne, not as a grammarian, a poet, or a lawyer. If the world find fault that I speak too much of myself, I find fault that they do not so much as think of themselves. But is it reason, that being so particular in my way of living, I should pretend to recommend myself to the public knowledge? And is it also reason that I should produce to the world, where art and handling have so much credit and authority, crude and simple effects of nature, and of a weak nature to boot? Is it not to build a wall without stone or brick, or

---

[34] Cleared.
[1] Demades (d. 318 B.C.) was an Athenian orator. A version of this remark appears in Plutarch's *Life of Demosthenes*.

some such thing, to write books without learning and without art? The fancies of music are carried on by art; mine by chance. I have this, at least, according to discipline, that never any man treated of a subject he better understood and knew, than I what I have undertaken, and that in this I am the most understanding man alive: secondly, that never any man penetrated farther into his matter, nor better and more distinctly sifted the parts and sequences of it, nor ever more exactly and fully arrived at the end he proposed to himself. To perfect it, I need bring nothing but fidelity to the work; and that is there, and the most pure and sincere that is anywhere to be found. I speak truth, not so much as I would, but as much as I dare; and I dare a little the more, as I grow older; for, methinks, custom allows to age more liberty of prating, and more indiscretion of talking of a man's self. That cannot fall out here, which I often see elsewhere, that the work and the artificer contradict one another: "Can a man of such sober conversation have written so foolish a book?" Or "Do so learned writings proceed from a man of so weak conversation?" He who talks at a very ordinary rate, and writes rare matter, 'tis to say that his capacity is borrowed and not his own. A learned man is not learned in all things: but a sufficient man is sufficient throughout, even to ignorance itself; here my book and I go hand in hand together. Elsewhere men may commend or censure the work, without reference to the workman; here they cannot: who touches the one, touches the other. He who shall judge of it without knowing him, will more wrong himself than me; he who does know him, gives me all the satisfaction I desire. I shall be happy beyond my desert, if I can obtain only thus much from the public approbation, as to make men of understanding perceive that I was capable of profiting by knowledge, had I had it; and that I deserved to have been assisted by a better memory.

Be pleased here to excuse what I often repeat, that I very rarely repent, and that my conscience is satisfied with itself, not as the conscience of an angel, or that of a horse, but as the conscience of a man, always adding this clause, not one of ceremony, but a true and real submission, that I speak inquiring and doubting, purely and simply referring myself to the common and accepted beliefs for the resolution. I do not teach, I only relate.

There is no vice that is absolutely a vice which does not offend, and that a sound judgment does not accuse; for there is in it so manifest a deformity and inconvenience, that, peradventure, they are in the right who say that it is chiefly begotten by stupidity and ignorance: so hard is it to imagine that a man can know without abhorring it. Malice sucks up the greatest part of its own venom, and poisons itself. Vice leaves repentance in the soul, like an ulcer in the flesh, which is always scratching and lacerating itself; for reason effaces all other grief and sorrows, but it begets that of repentance, which is so much the more grievous, by reason it springs within, as the cold and heat of fevers are more sharp than those that only strike upon the outward skin. I hold for vices (but every one according to its proportion), not only those which reason and nature condemn, but those also which the opinion of men, though false and erroneous, have made such, if authorized by law and custom.

There is likewise no virtue which does not rejoice a well-descended nature; there is a kind of, I know not what, congratulation in well doing that gives us an inward satisfaction, and a generous boldness that accompanies a good conscience: a soul daringly vicious may, peradventure, arm itself with security, but it cannot supply itself with this complacency and satisfaction. 'Tis no little satisfaction to feel a man's self preserved from the contagion of so depraved an age, and to say to himself: "Whoever could penetrate into my soul would not there find me guilty either of the affliction or ruin of any one, or of revenge or envy, or any offense against the public laws, or of innovation or disturbance, or failure of my word; and though the license of the time permits and teaches every one so to do, yet have I not plundered any Frenchman's goods, or taken his money, and have lived upon what is my own, in war as well as in peace; neither have I set any man to work without paying him his hire." These testimonies of a good conscience please, and this natural rejoicing is very beneficial to us, and the only reward that we can never fail of.

To ground the recompense of virtuous actions upon the approbation of others is too uncertain and unsafe a foundation, especially in so corrupt and ignorant an age as this, wherein the good opinion of the vulgar is injurious: upon whom do you rely to show you what is recommendable? God defend me from being an honest man, according to the descriptions of honor I daily see every one make of himself. *"Quæ fuerant vitia, mores sunt."*[2] Some of my friends have at times schooled and scolded me with great sincerity and plainness, either of their own voluntary motion, or by me entreated to it as to an office, which to a well-composed soul surpasses not only in utility, but in kindness all other offices of friendship: I have always received them with the most open arms, both of courtesy and acknowledgment; but, to say the truth, I have often found so much false measure, both in their reproaches and praises, that I had not done much amiss, rather to have done ill, than to have done well according to their notions. We, who live private lives, not exposed to any other view than our own, ought chiefly to have settled a pattern within ourselves by which to try our actions; and according to that, sometimes to encourage and sometimes to correct ourselves. I have my laws and my judicature to judge of myself and apply myself more to these than to any other rules: I do, indeed, restrain my actions according to others; but extend them not by any other rule than my own. You yourself only know if you are cowardly and cruel, loyal and devout: others see you not, and only guess at you by uncertain conjectures, and do not so much see your nature as your art; rely not therefore upon their opinions, but stick to your own: *"Tuo tibi judicio est utendum . . . Virtutis et vitiorum grave ipsius conscientiæ pondus est: qua sublata, jacent omnia."*[3]

But the saying that repentance immediately follows the sin seems not to have respect to sin in its high estate, which is lodged in us as in its own proper habitation. One may disown and retract the vices that surprise us, and to which we are hurried by passions; but those which by a long habit are rooted in a strong and vigorous will are not subject to contradiction.

---

[2] "What before were vices are now right manners" (Seneca).

[3] "You might employ your own judgment upon yourself. Great is the weight of your own conscience in the discovery of your own virtues and vices. If that is taken away, all is lost" (Cicero).

Repentance is no other but a recanting of the will and an opposition to our fancies, which lead us which way they please. It makes this person disown his former virtue and continency:

> "Quæ mens est hodie, cur eadem non puero fuit?
> Vel cur his animis incolumes non redeunt genæ?"[4]

'Tis an exact life that maintains itself in due order in private. Every one may juggle his part, and represent an honest man upon the stage: but within, and in his own bosom, where all may do as they list, where all is concealed, to be regular—there's the point. The next degree is to be so in his house, and in his ordinary actions, for which we are accountable to none, and where there is no study nor artifice. And therefore Bias, setting forth the excellent state of a private family, says: "of which the master is the same within, by his own virtue and temper, that he is abroad, for fear of the laws and report of men."[5] And it was a worthy saying of Julius Drusus, to the masons who offered him, for three thousand crowns, to put his house in such a posture that his neighbors should no longer have the same inspection into it as before; "I will give you," said he, "six thousand to make it so that everybody may see into every room."[6] 'Tis honorably recorded of Agesilaus, that he used in his journeys always to take up his lodgings in temples, to the end that the people and the gods themselves might pry into his most private actions.[7] Such a one has been a miracle to the world, in whom neither his wife nor servant has ever seen anything so much as remarkable; few men have been admired by their own domestics; no one was ever a prophet, not merely in his own house, but in his own country, says the experience of histories: 'tis the same in things of naught, and in this low example the image of a greater is to be seen. In my country of Gascony, they look upon it as a drollery to see me in print; the further off I am read from my own home, the better I am esteemed. I am fain to purchase printers in Guienne; elsewhere they purchase me. Upon this it is that they lay their foundation who conceal themselves present and living, to obtain a name when they are absent and dead. I had rather have a great deal less in hand, and do not expose myself to the world upon any other account than my present share; when I leave it I quit the rest. See this functionary whom the people escort in state, with wonder and applause, to his very door; he puts off the pageant with his robe, and falls so much the lower by how much he was higher exalted: in himself within, all is tumult and degraded. And though all should be regular there, it will require a vivid and well-chosen judgment to perceive it in these low and private actions; to which may be added, that order is a dull, somber virtue. To enter a breach, conduct an embassy, govern a people, are actions of renown: to reprehend, laugh, sell, pay, love, hate, and gently and justly converse with a man's own family, and with himself; not to relax, not to give a man's self the lie is more

---

[4] "Why was I not of the same mind when I was a boy that I am now? Or why do not the ruddy cheeks of my youth return to help me now?" (Horace).

[5] Bias of Priene (c. 570 B.C.) was one of the "Seven Sages."

[6] "Julius Drusus" is an error for Marcus Livius, a second-century B.C. Roman tribune. Montaigne is citing Plutarch, *On Managing Affairs of State*.

[7] Agesilaus (c. 440–360 B.C.) was king of Sparta.

rare and hard, and less remarkable. By which means, retired lives, whatever is said to the contrary, undergo duties of as great or greater difficulty than the others do; and private men, says Aristotle, serve virtue more painfully and highly, than those in authority do:[8] we prepare ourselves for eminent occasions, more out of glory than conscience. The shortest way to arrive at glory, would be to do that for conscience which we do for glory: and the virtue of Alexander appears to me of much less vigor in his great theater, than that of Socrates in his mean and obscure employment.[9] I can easily conceive Socrates in the place of Alexander, but Alexander in that of Socrates, I cannot. Who shall ask the one what he can do, he will answer, "Subdue the world:" and who shall put the same question to the other, he will say, "Carry on human life conformably with its natural condition:" a much more general, weighty, and legitimate science than the other.

The virtue of the soul does not consist in flying high, but in walking orderly; its grandeur does not exercise itself in grandeur, but in mediocrity. As they who judge and try us within, make no great account of the luster of our public actions, and see they are only streaks and rays of clear water springing from a slimy and muddy bottom: so, likewise, they who judge of us by this gallant outward appearance, in like manner conclude of our internal constitution; and cannot couple common faculties, and like their own, with the other faculties that astonish them, and are so far out of their sight. Therefore it is, that we give such savage forms to demons: and who does not give Tamerlane great eyebrows, wide nostrils, a dreadful visage, and a prodigious stature, according to the imagination he has conceived by the report of his name?[10] Had any one formerly brought me to Erasmus,[11] I should hardly have believed but that all was adage and apothegm he spoke to his man or his hostess. We much more aptly imagine an artisan upon his close-stool, or upon his wife, than a great president venerable by his port and sufficiency: we fancy that they, from their high tribunals, will not abase themselves so much as to live. As vicious souls are often incited by some foreign impulse to do well, so are virtuous souls to do ill; they are therefore to be judged by their settled state, when they are at home, whenever that may be; and, at all events, when they are nearer repose, and in their native station.

Natural inclinations are much assisted and fortified by education: but they seldom alter and overcome their institution: a thousand natures of my time have escaped toward virtue or vice, through a quite contrary discipline;

> "Sic ubi desuetæ silvis in carcere clausæ
> Mansuevere feræ, et vultus posuere minaces,
> Atque hominem didicere pati, si torrida parvus

---

[8] *Nicomachean Ethics* X.7.

[9] Alexander the Great (356–323 B.C.) was king of Macedonia; he conquered the Greek city-states and the Persian Empire.

[10] Tamerlane, or Tamburlaine (1336?–1405), was the Mongol conqueror of most of southern and western Asia.

[11] Erasmus (1466?–1536) was the famous Dutch Humanist, scholar, and satirist.

Venit in ora cruor, redeunt rabiesque furorque,
Admonitæque tument gustato sanguine fauces;
Fervet, et a trepido vix abstinet ira magistro;"[12]

these original qualities are not to be rooted out; they may be covered and concealed. The Latin tongue is as it were natural to me; I understand it better than French; but I have not been used to speak it, nor hardly to write it these forty years. Yet, upon extreme and sudden emotions which I have fallen into twice or thrice in my life, and once, seeing my father in perfect health fall upon me in a swoon, I have always uttered my first outcries and ejaculations in Latin; nature starting up, and forcibly expressing itself, in spite of so long a discontinuation; and this example is said of many others.

They who in my time have attempted to correct the manners of the world by new opinions, reform seeming vices, but the essential vices they leave as they were, if indeed, they do not augment them; and augmentation is, therein, to be feared; we defer all other well doing upon the account of these external reformations, of less cost and greater show, and thereby expiate cheaply, for the other natural consubstantial and intestine vices.[13] Look a little into our experience: there is no man, if he listen to himself, who does not in himself discover a particular and governing form of his own, that jostles his education, and wrestles with the tempest of passions that are contrary to it. For my part, I seldom find myself agitated with surprises; I always find myself in my place, as heavy and unwieldy bodies do; if I am not at home, I am always near at hand; my dissipations do not transport me very far, there is nothing strange nor extreme in the case; and yet I have sound and vigorous turns.

The true condemnation, and which touches the common practice of men, is, that their very retirement itself is full of filth and corruption; the idea of their reformation composed; their repentance sick and faulty, very nearly as much as their sin. Some, either from having been linked to vice by a natural propension, or long practice, cannot see its deformity. Others (of which constitution I am) do indeed feel the weight of vice, but they counterbalance it with pleasure, or some other occasion; and suffer, and lend themselves to it, for a certain price, but viciously and basely. Yet there might, haply, be imagined so vast a disproportion of measure, where with justice the pleasure might excuse the sin, as we say of utility; not only if accidental, and out of sin, as in thefts, but the very exercise of sin, as in the enjoyment of women, where the temptation is violent, and 'tis said, sometimes not to be overcome.

Being the other day at Armaignac, on the estate of a kinsman of mine, I there saw a country fellow who was by every one nicknamed the thief. He thus related the story of his life; that being born a beggar, and finding that he should not be able, so as to be clear of indigence, to get his living by the sweat of his brow, he resolved to turn thief, and by means of his strength of

---

[12] "So savage beasts, when shut up in cages and grown unaccustomed to the woods, become tame and lay aside their fierce looks and submit to the rule of man; if again they taste blood, their rage and fury return, their jaws thirst for blood, and they scarcely forbear to assail their trembling masters" (Lucan).

[13] "Consubstantial" means "of the same substance"; "intestine" means "internal." "Natural consubstantial and intestine vices" are those which are basic and deep-seated.

body, had exercised this trade all the time of his youth in great security; for he ever made his harvest and vintage in other men's grounds, but a great way off, and in so great quantities, that it was not to be imagined one man could have carried away so much in one night upon his shoulders; and, moreover, was careful equally to divide and distribute the mischief he did, that the loss was of less importance to every particular man. He is now grown old, and rich for a man of his condition, thanks to his trade, which he openly confesses to every one. And to make his peace with God, he says, that he is daily ready by good offices to make satisfaction to the successors of those he has robbed, and if he do not finish (for to do it all at once he is not able) he will then leave it in charge to his heirs to perform the rest, proportionably to the wrong he himself only knows he has done to each. By this description, true or false, this man looks upon theft as a dishonest action, and hates it, but less than poverty, and simply repents; but to the extent he has thus recompensed, he repents not. This is not that habit which incorporates us into vice, and conforms even our understanding itself to it; nor is it that impetuous whirlwind that by gusts troubles and blinds our souls and for the time precipitates us, judgment and all, into the power of vice.

I customarily do what I do thoroughly and make but one step on't; I have rarely any movement that hides itself and steals away from my reason, and that does not proceed in the matter by the consent of all my faculties, without division or intestine sedition; my judgment is to have all the blame or all the praise; and the blame it once has, it has always; for almost from my infancy it has ever been one; the same inclination, the same turn, the same force; and as to universal opinions, I fixed myself from my childhood in the place where I resolved to stick. There are some sins that are impetuous, prompt, and sudden; let us set them aside; but in these other sins so often repeated, deliberated, and contrived, whether sins of complexion or sins of profession and vocation, I cannot conceive that they should have so long been settled in the same resolution, unless the reason and conscience of him who has them, be constant to have them; and the repentance he boasts to be inspired with on a sudden, is very hard for me to imagine or form. I follow not the opinion of the Pythagorean sect, "that men take up a new soul when they repair to the images of the gods to receive their oracles," unless he mean that it must needs be extrinsic, new, and lent for the time; our own showing so little sign of purification and cleanness, fit for such an office.[14]

They act quite contrary to the stoical precepts, who do indeed, command us to correct the imperfections and vices we know ourselves guilty of, but forbid us therefore to disturb the repose of our souls; these make us believe that they have great grief and remorse within; but of amendment, correction, or interruption, they make nothing appear.[15] It cannot be a cure if the malady be not wholly discharged; if repentance were laid upon the scale of the balance, it would weigh down sin. I find no quality so easy to

[14] Pythagoras, the Greek philosopher, mathematician, and religious reformer (c. 582– c. 500 B.C.), taught the transmigration of souls.

[15] Stoicism was a Greek school of philosophy founded about 315 B.C. It taught, among other things, self-control and self-reformation, subduing passion and indulgence in order to attain inner freedom.

counterfeit as devotion, if men do not conform their manners and life to the profession; its essence is abstruse and occult; the appearances easy and ostentatious.

For my own part, I may desire in general to be other than I am; I may condemn and dislike my whole form, and beg of Almighty God for an entire reformation, and that He will please to pardon my natural infirmity: but I ought not to call this repentance, methinks, no more, than the being dissatisfied that I am not an angel or Cato.[16] My actions are regular, and conformable with what I am, and to my condition; I can do no better; and repentance does not properly touch things that are not in our power; sorrow does. I imagine an infinite number of natures more elevated and regular than mine; and yet I do not for all that improve my faculties, no more than my arm or will grow more strong and vigorous for conceiving those of another to be so. If to conceive and wish a nobler way of acting than that we have, should produce a repentance of our own, we must then repent us of our most innocent actions, forasmuch as we may well suppose that in a more excellent nature they would have been carried on with greater dignity and perfection; and we would that ours were so. When I reflect upon the deportments of my youth, with that of my old age, I find that I have commonly behaved myself with equal order in both, according to what I understand: this is all that my resistance can do. I do not flatter myself; in the same circumstances I should do the same things. It is not a patch, but rather an universal tincture, with which I am stained. I know no repentance, superficial, half-way and ceremonious; it must sting me all over before I can call it so, and must prick my bowels as deeply and universally as God sees into me.

As to business, many excellent opportunities have escaped me for want of good management; and yet my deliberations were sound enough, according to the occurrences presented to me: 'tis their way to choose always the easiest and safest course. I find that, in my former resolves, I have proceeded with discretion, according to my own rule, and according to the state of the subject proposed, and should do the same a thousand years hence in like occasions; I do not consider what it is now, but what it was then, when I deliberated on it: the force of all counsel consists in the time; occasions and things eternally shift and change. I have in my life committed some important errors, not for want of good understanding, but for want of good luck. There are secret, and not to be foreseen, parts in matters we have in hand, especially in the nature of men; mute conditions, that make no show, unknown sometimes even to the possessors themselves, that spring and start up by incidental occasions; if my prudence could not penetrate into nor foresee them, I blame it not: 'tis commissioned no further than its own limits; if the event be too hard for me, and take the side I have refused, there is no remedy; I do not blame myself, I accuse my fortune, and not my work; this cannot be called repentance.

Phocion,[17] having given the Athenians an advice that was not followed,

---

[16] Marcus Porcius Cato (95–46 B.C.)—Cato the Younger—was a Roman statesman known for his Stoical convictions and his incorruptible honesty.

[17] Phocion (402–317 B.C.) was an Athenian statesman and general. This story appears in Plutarch.

and the affair nevertheless succeeding contrary to his opinion, some one said to him; "Well, Phocion, art thou content that matters go so well?" "I am very well content," replied he, "that this has happened so well, but I do not repent that I counseled the other." When any of my friends address themselves to me for advice, I give it candidly and clearly, without sticking, as almost all other men do, at the hazard of the thing's falling out contrary to my opinion, and that I may be reproached for my counsel; I am very indifferent as to that, for the fault will be theirs for having consulted me, and I could not refuse them that office.

I, for my own part, can rarely blame any one but myself for my oversights and misfortunes, for indeed I seldom solicit the advice of another, if not by honor of ceremony, or excepting where I stand in need of information, special science, or as to matter of fact. But in things wherein I stand in need of nothing but judgment, other men's reasons may serve to fortify my own, but have little power to dissuade me; I hear them all with civility and patience: but to my recollection, I never made use of any but my own. With me, they are but flies and atoms, that confound and distract my will; I lay no great stress upon my opinions; but I lay as little upon those of others, and fortune rewards me accordingly: if I receive but little advice, I also give but little. I am seldom consulted, and still more seldom believed, and know no concern, either public or private, that has been mended or bettered by my advice. Even they whom fortune had in some sort tied to my direction, have more willingly suffered themselves to be governed by any other counsels than mine. And as a man who am as jealous of my repose as of my authority, I am better pleased that it should be so; in leaving me there, they humor what I profess, which is to settle and wholly contain myself within myself. I take a pleasure in being uninterested in other men's affairs, and disengaged from being their warranty, and responsible for what they do.

In all affairs that are past, be it how it will, I have very little regret; for this imagination puts me out of my pain, that they were so to fall out; they are in the great revolution of the world, and in the chain of stoical causes: your fancy cannot, by wish and imagination, move one tittle, but that the great current of things will not reverse both the past and the future.

As to the rest, I abominate that incidental repentance which old age brings along with it. He, who said of old, that he was obliged to his age for having weaned him from pleasure,[18] was of another opinion than I am; I can never think myself beholden to impotency, for any good it can do to me; *"Nec tam aversa unquam videbitur ab opere suo providentia, ut debilitas inter optima inventa sit."*[19] Our appetites are rare in old age; a profound satiety seizes us after the act; in this I see nothing of conscience; chagrin and weakness imprint in us a drowsy and rheumatic virtue. We must not suffer ourselves to be so wholly carried away by natural alterations, as to suffer our judgments to be imposed upon by them. Youth and pleasure have not formerly so far prevailed with me, that I did not well enough discern the face of vice in pleasure; neither does the distaste that years have brought

---

[18] This remark was attributed to Sophocles by Cicero.
[19] "Nor can Providence ever be seen so averse to her own work that debility should be ranked among the best things" (Quintilian).

me, so far prevail with me now, that I cannot discern pleasure in vice. Now that I am no more in my flourishing age, I judge as well of these things as if I were. I, who narrowly and strictly examine it, find my reason the very same it was in my most licentious age, except, perhaps, that 'tis weaker and more decayed by being grown older; and I find that the pleasure it refuses me upon the account of my bodily health, it would no more refuse now, in consideration of the health of my soul, than at any time heretofore. I do not repute it the more valiant for not being able to combat; my temptations are so broken and mortified, that they are not worth its opposition; holding but out my hands, I repel them. Should one present the old concupiscence before it, I fear it would have less power to resist it than heretofore; I do not discern that in itself it judges anything otherwise now, than it formerly did, nor that it has acquired any new light: wherefore, if there be convalescence, 'tis an enchanted one. Miserable kind of remedy, to owe one's health to one's disease! 'Tis not that our misfortune should perform this office, but the good fortune of our judgment. I am not to be made to do anything by persecutions and afflictions, but to curse them: that is for people who cannot be roused but by a whip. My reason is much more free in prosperity, and much more distracted, and put to't to digest pains than pleasures: I see best in a clear sky; health admonishes me more cheerfully, and to better purpose, than sickness. I did all that in me lay to reform and regulate myself from pleasures, at a time when I had health and vigor to enjoy them; I should be ashamed and envious, that the misery and misfortune of my old age should have credit over my good, healthful, sprightly, and vigorous years; and that men should estimate me, not by what I have been, but by what I have ceased to be.

In my opinion, 'tis the happy living, and not (as Antisthenes said) the happy dying, in which human felicity consists. I have not made it my business to make a monstrous addition of a philosopher's tail to the head and body of a libertine; nor would I have this wretched remainder give the lie to the pleasant, sound, and long part of my life: I would present myself uniformly throughout. Were I to live my life over again, I should live it just as I have lived it; I neither complain of the past, nor do I fear the future; and if I am not much deceived, I am the same within that I am without. 'Tis one main obligation I have to my fortune, that the succession of my bodily estate has been carried on according to the natural seasons; I have seen the grass, the blossom, and the fruit; and now see the withering; happily, however, because naturally. I bear the infirmities I have the better, because they came not till I had reason to expect them, and because also they make me with greater pleasure remember that long felicity of my past life. My wisdom may have been just the same in both ages; but it was more active, and of better grace while young and sprightly, than now it is when broken, peevish and uneasy. I repudiate, then, these casual and painful reformations. God must touch our hearts; our consciences must amend of themselves, by the aid of our reason, and not by the decay of our appetites; pleasure is, in itself, neither pale nor discolored, to be discerned by dim and decayed eyes.

We ought to love temperance for itself, and because God has commanded that and chastity; but that which we are reduced to by catarrhs, and for which I am indebted to the stone,[20] is neither chastity nor temperance; a man cannot boast that he despises and resists pleasure, if he cannot see it, if he knows not what it is, and cannot discern its graces, its force, and most alluring beauties; I know both the one and the other, and may therefore the better say it. But, methinks, our souls, in old age, are subject to more troublesome maladies and imperfections than in youth; I said the same when young and when I was reproached with the want of a beard; and I say so now that my gray hairs give me some authority. We call the difficulty of our humors and the disrelish of present things wisdom; but, in truth, we do not so much forsake vices as we change them, and, in my opinion, for worse. Besides a foolish and feeble pride, an impertinent prating, froward and insociable humors, superstition, and a ridiculous desire of riches when we have lost the use of them, I find there more envy, injustice and malice. Age imprints more wrinkles in the mind than it does on the face; and souls are never, or very rarely seen, that in growing old do not smell sour and musty. Man moves all together, both toward his perfection and decay. In observing the wisdom of Socrates, and many circumstances of his condemnation, I should dare to believe, that he in some sort himself purposely, by collusion, contributed to it, seeing that, at the age of seventy years, he might fear to suffer the lofty motions of his mind to be cramped, and his wonted luster obscured. What strange metamorphoses do I see age every day make in many of my acquaintance! 'Tis a potent malady, and that naturally and imperceptibly steals into us; a vast provision of study and great precaution are required to evade the imperfections it loads us with, or at least, to weaken their progress. I find that, notwithstanding all my entrenchments, it gets foot by foot upon me; I make the best resistance I can, but I do not know to what at last it will reduce me. But fall out what will. I am content the world may know, when I am fallen, from what I fell.

[20] The *stone* is the chronic kidney stones from which Montaigne suffered.

Miguel de Cervantes Saavedra
(*1547–1616*)

Don Quixote is one of the greatest works of art in Western literature, but in a sense it is surprising that it should have been a work of art at all. It began its life as a humble parody of contemporary popular literature, written by an elderly failed playwright in a more or less desperate attempt to make money, possibly even as he lay in prison for shortages in his accounts as a petty government official. Cervantes may have conceived of the total work in all its complexity and grandeur from the very beginning, but it seems more likely that even he was surprised at the way the work developed, from an unpretentious extended joke to an almost mythic narrative. Grow-

ing from roots deep in the popular culture of his time, it reached the loftiest heights of man's questionings of human nature.

Miguel de Cervantes Saavedra was born in 1547, the fourth of seven children of an impoverished physician. During Miguel's childhood the family moved from one village to another to flee from creditors. By 1564, when he was sixteen, the family had settled in Seville, where Miguel was enrolled in a Jesuit school; he seems later to have studied for a time at the University of Salamanca. Any hopes he may have had for an academic career, however, were blasted when he got involved, at the age of twenty-one, in a duel within the precincts of the royal palace in Madrid. The royal court sentenced him to lose his right hand and be exiled for ten years; Cervantes fled to Italy to escape the execution of the sentence.

He was not to return to Spain for twelve years, and those years were filled with hardships and adventures more spectacular than any in the romances he was to parody in Don Quixote. *After a brief period of service in Rome in the retinue of the cardinal-elect Giulio Acquaviva, he enlisted in the Spanish forces of the Holy League opposing Turkish control of the Mediterranean. His first engagement was the famous Battle of Lepanto. Cervantes was on board a ship called the* Marquesa *when the battle began, sick with a fever and confined to his bunk. Despite his condition, he immediately asked to be placed in the most dangerous position and fought gallantly throughout the battle. In the action, he received two shots in the chest and his left hand was shattered; he was never to recover full use of it. Cervantes received an increase in pay for his bravery and a letter of commendation from his commander, Don John of Austria, brother of King Philip II. After his convalescence, he spent four more years in the army, campaigning in Sardinia, Naples, and South Italy.*

Finally, in 1575, Cervantes set sail for Spain again in the company of his brother Rodrigo, who had joined the colors at the same time as Cervantes. Off the coast of southern France, the ship was attacked by pirates and captured, and everyone on board was carried off to Algiers to be sold as slaves. Cervantes remained in slavery for five years, conducting himself with the utmost gallantry. Four times he attempted to organize a general rising among the 24,000 Christian slaves in Algiers. All these attempts failed, and each time Cervantes took full responsibility, in spite of the potential penalty of death by torture. The Dey of Algiers, Hassan Pacha, each time pardoned him, however, since he privately admired Cervantes' courage. Rodrigo was ransomed comparatively early by his family back in Spain, but Cervantes' ransom price was much higher because of the letter of commendation to the Spanish king his captors found in his possession. He was not ransomed until 1580, half of the money coming from his hard-pressed family and the other half from sympathetic Spanish residents of Algiers.

Cervantes was thirty-three when he finally returned to Spain. He was crippled and without a job; his family was deeply in debt. Don John was by now dead, and since his memory was hated by the king, Cervantes could not use his commendation to get preferment. He spent the next twenty-five years trying desperately to earn a meager living. He wrote a number of plays, none notably successful. During his theatrical days he fell in love with an actress, Ana Franca de Rojas. They had a child, Isabel, whom Cervantes was left to rear when Ana deserted him. In 1584, at the age of thirty-seven, he married a nineteen-year-old girl, Catalina de Palacios y Salazar Vozmediano; he then had to support a household consisting of his wife, Isabel, his mother, his two sisters, and his widowed mother-in-law. He finally succeeded in getting a government post as a traveling agent charged with requisitioning supplies for the Invincible Armada, the massive fleet that Philip was preparing to launch against England in 1588. As a "commissary," he not only had to face angry mobs of villagers who resented the army's appropriation of their goods, but had to deal also with a government bureaucracy that at one point was two years behind with his salary. Cervantes was twice imprisoned for shortages in his accounts, owing to a combination of his superiors' own chaotic records, an untimely bank failure, and doubtless his own inadequacies as a bookkeeper. There is a tradition, based on an ambiguous passage in the Prologue to Book I of Don Quixote *(the story was "just what might be begotten in a prison, where every discomfort is lodged and every dismal noise has its dwelling"), that he began his great novel in the prison at Seville in 1597.*

However this may be, soon after his release Cervantes was hard at work on Don Quixote, *which was first published in 1605, the year in which his contemporary Shakespeare produced* King Lear. *Cervantes' book was an immediate bestseller; it went through a number of printings the first year and was very promptly translated into French, Italian, and other European languages. Its success brought Cervantes little except the satisfaction of fame; he received no royalties beyond the small initial sum paid him by the publisher.*

From the time the first part was published, Cervantes had planned a continuation, but it did not appear for ten years. In 1614, he had written fifty-nine chapters of the sequel when he learned that a pirated continuation had been published by one Alonso Fernandez de Avellaneda. Furious, he rushed through the ending of Part II, incorporating in the part he had already finished an attack upon the "false Quixote." Part II was also successful, but again it did little to relieve the author's chronic poverty. Aged and ill, he spent the last two years of his life finishing Persiles and Sigismunda, *an episodic romance he had begun in 1609. (It was published posthumously.) In the dedication to this work, written on his deathbed to his patron the Conde de Lemos, he wrote the famous lines, adapted from an old ballad, "With one foot in the stirrup, and in the anguish of death, My Lord, I write to thee." He died on April 23, 1616; ten days later in England, Shakespeare died, also on April 23 (since the English calendar was still unreformed).*

Don Quixote *is a long novel, one of the longest ever written, but it is not a word too long. An abridgment can only suggest the cumulative effect of the book's movement from primitive burlesque to the mysteriously moving climax. At the heart of the novel are the mad knight himself, his commonsensical squire Sancho, and their gradually unfolding relationship. Quixote and Sancho are inseparable, bound together like spirit and flesh as are their fictional descendants Sherlock Holmes and Dr. Watson, Stephen Dedalus and Leopold Bloom in Joyce's* Ulysses, *and Didi and Gogo in Beckett's* Waiting for Godot. *The division is not absolute: Quixote has his earthy side, and it is Sancho who clings to a dream of being governor of an island. It is not Sancho, finally, who represents the claims of unimaginative reality, but the barber and the curate, guardians of flesh and spirit in the everyday world in their respective roles as bleeder and spiritual advisor. Similarly, it is not Don Quixote himself who represents dreams kicked loose from all contact with the earth, but the romances with which he has addled himself. Quixote and Sancho are not allegorical figures but real human beings, each torn between dream and reality. The novel traces their profound, moving, and richly comic negotiation with each other. This negotiation consists of the gradual "Sanchification" of Quixote and the "Quixotification" of Sancho; the Knight moves from a world of pure delusion to a vision of real life ennobled by idealism, while Sancho begins to see the substantial world through the eyes of his master, as touched by the dream. By the end of the novel, all hope of his island gone, Sancho still longs for the quest: "Up with you this instant, out of your bed! . . . Who knows but we may find Lady Dulcinea behind a hedge, disenchanted and as fresh as a daisy!"*

As, for his protagonists, Cervantes draws upon the most fundamental of human relationships, so for his plot he turns to the most basic of narratives, the journey. The key to all the great quest stories is the goal of the quest. Odysseus, on his journey home, is in quest of Ithaca and Penelope, the world of ordinary life after the heroic but distorted world of military action. Dante, in his dream journey through the afterlife, seeks to leave the Dark Wood of worldly confusion and find the security of God's holy order. Quixote's quest remains in the Dark Wood on this earth: the dusty and sterile landscape of La Mancha, the emblem of a modern world from which it seems all glory has fled. His quest, literally for chivalric adventure, is more fundamentally for the spark of imagination that redeems ordinary life. And ultimately he finds this spark, not in absurd romances but within himself.

FURTHER READING *(prepared by W. J. R.):* Melveena McKendrick's biography *Cervantes,* 1980, is a good introduction for the general reader. Manuel Duran's *Cervantes,* 1974, a somewhat more succinct biography, contains a good introductory chapter on Spanish culture in Cervantes' time and includes a long discussion of *Don Quixote.* An excellent evaluation of Cervantes as a critical theorist can be found in E. C. Riley's *Cervantes' Theory of the Novel,* 1962, which places Cervantes' ideas in the literary context of his time and discusses such topics as structural unity, verisimilitude, and the function of history. Riley's later, more comprehensive study, *Don Quixote,* 1986, is an excellent historical and critical analysis of the work. Diverse critical approaches are represented in *Cervantes: A Collection of Critical Essays,* ed. Lowry Nelson, Jr., 1969. This volume includes Erich Auerbach's "The Enchanted Dulcinea" and Thomas Mann's "Voyage with Don Quixote." The essays on *Don Quixote* gathered in the Norton Critical Edition, ed. Joseph R. Jones and Kenneth Douglas, 1981, are also well selected. Ruth El Saffar's *Distance and Control in "Don Quixote,"* 1975, explores a wide variety of narrative techniques employed by Cervantes, concentrating on the dynamics of role-switching by the characters. John C. Weiger's *The Individuated Self,* 1979, distinguishes "individuation" from individualism in an examination of personal freedom in *Don Quixote* and is interesting on the emergence of self-knowledge in the novel. John J. Allen's *Don Quixote: Hero or Fool?: A Study in Narrative Techniques,* 1969, discusses stylistic devices, levels of fiction, and the relationship between author, reader, and character. The subject of chivalry is the starting point for a provocative study in Howard Mancing's *The Chivalric World of Don Quixote: Style, Structure, and Narrative Technique,* 1982.

DON QUIXOTE

Translated by Walter Starkie

from PART I

CHAPTER I

Which tells of the quality and manner of life of the famous gentleman Don Quixote of La Mancha

At a village of La Mancha, whose name I do not wish to remember,[1] there lived a little while ago one of those gentlemen who are wont to keep a lance in the rack, an old buckler, a lean horse, and a swift greyhound. His stew had more beef than mutton in it and most nights he ate a hodgepodge, pickled and cold. Lentil soup on Fridays, "tripe and trouble" on Saturdays,[2] and an occasional pigeon as an extra delicacy on Sundays consumed three quarters of his income. The remainder was spent on a jerkin of fine puce, velvet breeches, and slippers of the same stuff for holidays, and a suit of good, honest homespun for weekdays. His family consisted of a house-keeper about forty, a niece not yet twenty, and a lad who served him both in the field and at home and could saddle the horse or use the pruning knife. Our gentleman was about fifty years of age, of a sturdy constitution, but wizened and gaunt-featured, an early riser and a devotee of the chase. They say that his surname was Quixada or Quesada (for on this point the authors who have written on this subject differ), but we may reasonably conjecture that his name was Quixana. This, however, has very little to do with our story; enough that in its telling we swerve not a jot from the truth. You must know that the above-mentioned gentleman in his leisure moments (which was most of the year) gave himself up with so much delight and gusto to reading books of chivalry that he almost entirely neglected the exercise of the chase and even the management of his domestic affairs. Indeed his craze for this kind of literature became so extravagant that he sold many acres of arable land to purchase books of knight-errantry, and he carried off to his house as many as he could possibly find. Above all, he preferred those written by the famous Feliciano de Silva[3] because of the clarity of his writing and his intricate style, which made him value those books more than pearls, especially when he read of those courtships and letters of challenge that knights sent to ladies, often containing expressions such as: "The reason for your unreasonable treatment of my reason so enfeebles my reason that I have reason to complain of your beauty." And again: "The high heavens, which with your divinity divinely fortify you with stars, make you the deserver of the desert that is deserved by your greatness." These and similar rhapsodies bewildered the poor gentleman's understanding, for he racked his brain day and night to unbowel their meaning, which not even Aristotle himself could have done if he had been raised from the dead for that very purpose. He was not quite convinced of the number of wounds that Don Belianís gave and received in battle, for he considered that however skillful the surgeons that cured him may have been, the worthy knight's face and body must have been bedizened with scars and scabs. Nevertheless he praised the author for concluding his book with the promise of endless adventure, and many times he felt inclined to take up his pen and finish it off himself, as it is there promised. He doubt-

---

[1] Cervantes was purposely vague in describing Don Quixote's birthplace. An old Spanish ballad begins "At a village in La Mancha." (Notes are adapted and expanded from those of the translator.)

[2] Spaniards ate meagerly on Saturdays, in commemoration of a victory over the Moors in 1212.

[3] A sixteenth-century writer of romances, famous for *Don Florisel de Niquea* (1532), from which the following quotation is taken.

less would have done so, and successfully too, had he not been diverted by other plans and purposes of greater moment. He often debated with the curate of the village—a man of learning, a graduate of Sigüenza—on the relative merits of Palmerin of England and Amadis of Gaul. But Master Nicholas, the village barber, affirmed that no one could be compared with the Knight of the Sun and that if, indeed, any could be matched with him, it was Don Galaor, the brother of Amadis of Gaul, for he had a nature adapted to every whim of fortune; he was not so namby-pamby and whimpering a knight as his brother, and as for valor, he was in every respect his equal.

In short, he so immersed himself in those romances that he spent whole days and nights over his books; and thus with little sleeping and much reading, his brains dried up to such a degree that he lost the use of his reason. His imagination became filled with a host of fancies he had read in his books—enchantments, quarrels, battles, challenges, wounds, courtships, loves, tortures, and many other absurdities. So true did all this phantasmagoria from books appear to him that in his mind he accounted no history in the world more authentic. He would say that the Cid Ruiz Díaz was a very gallant knight, but not to be compared with the Knight of the Burning Sword, who with a single thwart blow cleft asunder a brace of hulking, blustering giants. He was better pleased with Bernardo del Carpio, because at Roncesvalles he had slain Roland the Enchanted by availing himself of the stratagem Hercules had employed on Antaeus, the son of the Earth, whom he squeezed to death in his arms. He praised the giant Morgante, for he alone was courteous and well bred among that monstrous brood puffed up with arrogance and insolence. Above all, he admired Rinaldo of Montalbán,[4] especially when he saw him sallying out of his castle to plunder everyone who came his way, and when beyond the seas he made off with the idol of Mohammed which, as history says, was of solid gold. But he would have parted with his housekeeper and his niece into the bargain for the pleasure of rib roasting the traitor Galalón.[5]

At last, having lost his wits completely, he stumbled upon the oddest fancy that ever entered a madman's brain. He believed that it was necessary, both for his own honor and for service of the state, that he should become a knight-errant, roaming through the world with his horse and armor in quest of adventures and practicing all that had been performed by the knights-errant of whom he had read. He would follow their life, redressing all manner of wrongs and exposing himself to continual dangers, and at last, after concluding his enterprises, he would win everlasting honor and renown. The poor gentleman fancied himself already crowned emperor of Trebizond for the valor of his arm. And thus excited by these agreeable delusions, he hastened to put his plans into operation.

The first thing he did was to refurbish some rusty armor that had belonged to his great grandfather and had lain moldering in a corner. He

[4] One of Charlemagne's knights and the hero of Boiardo's romance *Orlando Innamorato (Roland in Love)*. Palmerin of England, Amadis of Gaul, The Knight of the Sun, The Cid Ruiz Diaz, The Knight of the Burning Sword, Bernardo del Carpio, and Morgante are all characters in actual romances.

[5] Galalón, or Ganelon of Mayence, was another of Charlemagne's knights who betrayed him at Rouncevalles. See *The Song of Roland*.

cleaned it and repaired it as best he could, but he found one great defect: instead of a complete helmet there was just the simple morion.[6] This want he ingeniously remedied by making a kind of visor out of pasteboard, and when it was fitted to the morion, it looked like an entire helmet. It is true that in order to test its strength and see if it was swordproof, he drew his sword and gave it two strokes, the first of which instantly destroyed the result of a week's labor. It troubled him to see with what ease he had broken the helmet in pieces, so to protect it from such an accident, he remade it and fenced the inside with a few bars of iron in such a manner that he felt assured of its strength, and without caring to make a second trial, he held it to be a most excellent helmet. Then he went to see his steed, and although it had more cracks in its hoof than there are quarters in a Spanish real[7] and more faults than Gonella's jade, which was all skin and bone,[8] he thought that neither the Bucephalus of Alexander nor the Cid's Babieca could be compared with it.[9] He spent four days deliberating over what name he would give the horse, for (as he said to himself) it was not right that the horse of so famous a knight should remain without a name. So he endeavored to find one that would express what the animal had been before he had been the mount of a knight-errant, and what he now was. It was indeed reasonable that when the master changed his state, the horse should change his name too and assume one pompous and high-sounding, as suited the new order he was about to profess. So after having devised, erased, and blotted out many other names, he finally decided to call the horse Rozinante—a name, in his opinion, lofty, sonorous, and significant, for it explained that he had been only an ordinary hack before he had been raised to his present status of first of all the hacks in the world.[10]

Now that he had given his horse a name so much to his satisfaction, he resolved to choose one for himself, and after seriously considering the matter for eight whole days, he finally determined to call himself Don Quixote. For that reason the authors who have related this most true story have deduced that his name must undoubtedly have been Quixada and not Quesada, as others would have it. Then, remembering that the valiant Amadis had not been content to call himself simply Amadis, but added thereto the name of his kingdom and native country to render it more illustrious, calling himself Amadis of Gaul, so he, like a good knight, also added the name of his province and called himself Don Quixote of La Mancha. In this way he openly proclaimed his lineage and country, and at the same time he honored it by taking its name.

Now that his armor was scoured, his morion made into a helmet, his horse and himself newly named, he felt that nothing was wanting but a lady of whom to be enamored, for a knight-errant who was loveless was a tree without leaves and fruit, a body without soul. "If," said he, "for my sins or through my good fortune I encounter some giant—a usual occurrence to

[6] Headpiece of a helmet, without the visor.

[7] A *real* was a silver coin. There were eight *cuartos*, or "cracks," in a *real*.

[8] Pedro Gonella was the clown of the Duke of Ferrara in the fifteenth century; his horse, all skin and bones, was the theme of many of his jokes.

[9] Bucephalus was Alexander the Great's horse, Babieca that of Ruy Diaz, hero of the twelfth-century Spanish epic *The Cid*.

[10] *Rozin*, or *rocin*, means an ordinary horse; *ante*, before.

knights-errant—and bowling him over at the first onset or cleaving him in twain, I finally vanquish and force him to surrender, would not it be better to have some lady to whom I may send him as a trophy? Then, when he comes into her presence, he may kneel before her and humbly say: 'Madam, I am the giant Caraculiambro, Lord of the Island of Malindrania, whom the never-adequately-praised Don Quixote of La Mancha has overcome in single combat. He has commanded me to present myself before you so that your highness may dispose of me as you wish.'" How glad was our knight when he had made these discourses to himself, but chiefly when he had found one whom he might call his lady! It happened that in a neighboring village there lived a good-looking country lass with whom he had been in love, although it is understood that she never knew or was aware of it. She was called Aldonza Lorenzo, and it was to her that he thought fit to entrust the sovereignty of his heart. He sought a name for her that would not vary too much from her own and yet would approach that of a princess or a lady of quality. At last he resolved to call her Dulcinea of El Toboso (she was a native of that town), a name in his opinion musical, uncommon, and expressive, like the others he had devised.

CHAPTER II

Which deals with our imaginative hero's first sally from his home

Once these preparations were made he was anxious to put his designs into operation without delay, for he was spurred on by the conviction that the world needed his immediate presence; so many were the grievances he intended to rectify, the wrongs he resolved to set right, the harms he meant to redress, the abuses he would reform, and the debts he would discharge. And so, without acquainting a living soul with his intentions, and wholly unobserved, one morning before daybreak (it was one of the hottest in the month of July), he armed himself cap-a-pie, mounted Rozinante, placed his ill-constructed helmet on his head, braced on his buckler, grasped his lance, and through the door of his back yard sallied forth into the open country, mightily pleased to note the ease with which he had begun his worthy enterprise. But scarcely had he issued forth when he was suddenly struck by so terrible a thought that he almost gave up his whole undertaking, for he just then remembered that he had not yet been dubbed a knight, and therefore, in accordance with the laws of chivalry, he neither could nor ought to enter the lists against any knight. Moreover, even if he had been dubbed, he should, as a novice, have worn white armor without any device on his shield until he had won it by force of arms. These thoughts made him stagger in his purpose; but as his madness prevailed over every reason, he determined to have himself knighted by the first person he should meet, like many others of whom he had read in the books that distracted him. As to white armor, he intended at the first opportunity to scour his own so that it would be whiter than ermine. In this way he calmed himself and continued his journey, letting his horse choose the way, believing that in this consisted the true spirit of adventure.

As our brand-new adventurer proceeded, he kept conversing with himself in this manner: "Who doubts but that in future ages, when the true story of my famous deeds is brought to light, the wise man who writes it will describe my first sally in the morning as follows: 'Scarcely had the rubicund Apollo spread over the face of the vast and spacious earth the golden tresses of his beautiful hair, and scarcely had the little painted birds with their tuneful tongues saluted in sweet and melodious harmony the coming of rosy Aurora, who, leaving the soft couch of her jealous husband, revealed herself to mortals through the gates and balconies of the Manchegan horizon, when the famous knight Don Quixote of La Mancha, quitting his downy bed of ease, mounted his renowned steed, Rozinante, and began to ride over the ancient and memorable plain of Montiel.' "[11] (And indeed he was doing so.) Continuing his discourse, he added: "O happy era, O happy age, wherein my famous deeds shall be revealed to the world, deeds worthy to be engraved in bronze, sculptured in marble, and painted in pictures for future record! O thou wise enchanter, whosoever thou mayest be, whose duty it will be to chronicle this strange history, do not, I beseech thee, forget my good horse, Rozinante, the everlasting companion of my wanderings." Then, as if really enamored, he cried: "O Dulcinea, my princess! Sovereign of this captive heart! Grievous wrong hast thou done me by dismissing me and by cruelly forbidding me by decree to appear in thy beauteous presence. I pray thee, sweet lady, to remember this poor, enslaved heart, which for love of thee suffers so many pangs."

To such words he added a sequence of other foolish notions all in the manner of those that his books had taught him, imitating their language as nearly as he could. And all the while he rode slowly on while the sun rose with such intense heat that it would have been enough to dissolve his brains, if he had had any left. He traveled almost the whole of that day without meeting any adventure worthy of note, wherefore he was much troubled, for he was eager to encounter someone upon whom he could try the strength of his doughty arm. Some authors say his first adventure was that of the Pass of Lápice; others hold it was that of the windmills; but according to my investigations and according to what is written in the annals of La Mancha, he traveled all that day, and at dusk both he and his horse were tired and nearly dead with hunger. He looked around him on every side to see whether he could discover any castle or shepherd's hut where he might rest and find nourishment. He then saw, not far from the road, an inn, which was as welcome to him as a star leading him not to the portals but to the very palace itself of his redemption. So he hastened on and reached it before dark.

Now there chanced to be standing at the door two young wenches who belonged to the category of women of the town, as they say. They were on their way to Seville in the company of certain carriers who halted for the night in that inn. As all our adventurer saw, thought, or imagined seemed to happen in accordance with what he had read in his books of chivalry, no sooner did he see the inn than it assumed in his eyes the semblance of a castle with four turrets, the pinnacles of which were of glittering silver, including drawbridge, deep moat, and all the appurtenances with which such castles are depicted. And so he drew near to the inn (which he thought

[11] Memorable because it was the scene of a famous battle in 1369.

was a castle), and at a short distance from it, he halted Rozinante, expecting that some dwarf would mount the battlements to announce by trumpet blast the arrival of a knight-errant at the castle. But when he saw that they tarried, and as Rozinante was pawing the ground impatiently in eagerness to reach the stable, he approached the inn door and there saw the two young doxies, who appeared to him to be two beautiful damsels or graceful ladies enjoying the fresh air at the castle gate. It happened also at this very moment that a swineherd, as he gathered his hogs (I ask no pardon,[12] for so they are called) from the stubblefield, blew a horn that assembled them, and instantly Don Quixote imagined it was what he expected, namely, that some dwarf was giving notice of his arrival. Therefore, with extraordinary satisfaction he went up to the inn and the ladies. But when they saw a man armed in that manner draw near with lance and buckler, they started to take to their heels, full of fear. Don Quixote, perceiving their alarm, raised his pasteboard visor, and displaying his withered and dusty countenance, accosted them gently and gravely: "I beseech your ladyships, do not flee, nor fear the least offense. The order of chivalry that I profess does not permit me to do injury to anyone, and least of all to such noble maidens as your presences denote you to be."

The wenches kept gazing earnestly, endeavoring to catch a glimpse of his face, which its ill-fashioned visor concealed; but when they heard themselves called maidens, a thing so out of the way of their profession, they could not restrain their laughter, which was so boisterous that Don Quixote exclaimed in anger: "Remember that modesty is becoming in beautiful ladies, whereas laughter without cause denotes much folly. However," added he, "I do not say this to offend you or to incur your displeasure, for my one desire is to do you honor and service." The strange language of the knight was not understood by the ladies, and this, added to his uncouth appearance, increased their laughter and his annoyance, and he would have proceeded further but for the timely appearance of the innkeeper, a man who by reason of his extreme corpulence was of very peaceable disposition. As soon as he saw that uncomely figure all armed, in accouterments so ill-sorted as were the bridle, lance, buckler, and corselet, he felt inclined to join the damsels in their mirth. But out of fear of such a medley of warlike gear, he resolved to be civil, and so he said: "Sir knight, if you are seeking a lodging, you will find all in abundance here, with the exception of a bed, for there are none in this inn." Don Quixote, observing the humility of the governor of the fortress (for such the landlord and the inn appeared to him), answered: "Anything, sir castellan, suffices me:

> My ornaments are arms,
> My pastime is in war."

The host thought he called him a castellan because he took him to be one of the Simple-Simon Castilians,[13] whereas he was an Andalusian, one

---

[12] Spanish peasants still beg one's pardon when mentioning pigs, a custom picked up from the neighboring Moslems, who abhor pork.

[13] *Castellano* means both "castellan" (a governor of a castle) and "Castilian" (a native of Castile).

of those from the Sanlúcar shore, no less a thief than Cacus[14] and not less mischievous than a truant scholar or court page. And so he made the following reply: "If so, your worship's beds must be hard rocks and your sleep an everlasting watching;[15] wherefore you may boldly dismount and I can assure you that you can hardly miss being kept awake all year long in this house, much less one single night." Saying this, he went and held Don Quixote's stirrup, who forthwith dismounted, though with much difficulty, for he had not broken his fast all that day. He then told the host to take great care of his horse, saying that he was one of the finest pieces of horse-flesh that ever ate bread. The innkeeper looked him over but thought him not so good by half as his master had said. After stabling him, he returned to receive his guest's orders and found the damsels (who had now become reconciled to him) disarming him, but though they were able to take off the back- and breast-plates, they did not know how to undo his gorget[16] or remove his counterfeit helmet, which he had tied on with green ribbons in such a way that they could not be untied. It was necessary to cut them because the knots were so intricate, but he would not allow this to be done, and so remained all that night with his helmet on, and was the strangest and pleasantest sight imaginable.

And while he was being disarmed by those lights-o'-love whom he imagined to be ladies of quality of that castle, he said to them with great charm:

> "There never was on earth a knight
> So waited on by ladies fair
> As once was he, Don Quixote hight,
> When first he left his village dear:
> Damsels to serve him ran with speed
> And princesses to dress his steed.[17]

"Rozinante, ladies, is the name of my horse, and Don Quixote of La Mancha my own. I never intended to discover myself until deeds performed in your service should have proclaimed me, but the need of adapting to my present purpose the old ballad of Sir Lancelot has made my right name known to you prematurely. But the day will come when your ladyships shall command and I obey, and the valor of my arm make plain my desire to serve you."

The girls, unaccustomed to such flourishes of rhetoric, made no reply but asked whether he would eat anything. "Fain would I break my fast," answered Don Quixote, "for I think that a little food would be of great service to me." That day happened to be a Friday and there was nothing in the inn but some pieces of fish, called in Castile pollack, in Andalusia codfish, in some parts ling, and in others troutlets, or Poor Jack. They asked him if he would eat some troutlets, for they had no other fish to offer him. "Provided there are many little trout," answered Don Quixote, "they will supply the place of one salmon trout, for it is the same to me whether I receive eight single reals or one piece of eight. Moreover, those troutlets

---

[14] Cacus, in Roman mythology, stole some of Hercules' cattle.
[15] The innkeeper quotes the same ballad Quixote quotes above.   [16] Throatpiece.
[17] Quixote is quoting, and altering, a ballad about Sir Lancelot, as he acknowledges below.

may turn out to be like unto veal, which is better than beef, and kid, which is superior to goat. Be that as it may, let it come in quickly, for the toil and weight of arms cannot be sustained without the good government of the guts." As the air was cool, they placed the table at the door of the inn, and the landlord brought a portion of ill-soaked and worse-cooked codfish and a piece of bread as black and moldy as the knight's arms. It was a laughable sight to see him eat, for as he had his helmet and his visor up, he could not feed himself, and so one of the ladies performed that service for him. But it would have been impossible for him to drink had not the innkeeper bored a cane, and placing one end in his mouth, poured in the wine at the other end. All this he endured patiently rather than cut the ribbons of his helmet.

While he was at his meal, a hog-gelder happened to sound his reed flageolet four or five times as he came near the inn. This was a still more convincing proof to Don Quixote that he was in a famous castle where they were entertaining him with music, that the codfish was salmon trout, the bread of the purest white, the whores ladies, and the innkeeper the governor of the fortress. All this made him applaud his own resolution and his enterprising sally. There was only one thing that vexed him: he regretted that he was not dubbed a knight, for he thought that he could not lawfully undertake any adventure until he had received the order of knighthood.

CHAPTER III

Which relates the pleasant method by which Don Quixote had himself dubbed knight

As he was tormented by that thought, he made short work of his meager, pothouse supper. Then he called for his host, shut himself up with him in the stable, and fell upon his knees, saying: "I will never rise from this place, valorous knight, until your courtesy grants me the boon I seek, one that will redound to your glory and to the advantage of the human race." The innkeeper, seeing his guest at his feet and hearing such words, stared at him in bewilderment, without knowing what to do or say. He tried to make him get up, but in vain, for the latter would not consent to do so until the boon he demanded was granted. "I expected no less from your magnificence," answered Don Quixote, "and so I say unto you that the boon I have demanded and that you, out of your liberality, have granted unto me is that tomorrow morning you will dub me knight. This night I shall watch over my arms in the chapel of your castle,[18] and tomorrow, as I have said, you will fulfill my earnest desires so that I may sally forth through the four parts of the world in quest of adventures on behalf of the distressed, as is the duty of knighthood and knights-errant who, like myself, are devoted to such achievements."

The host, who was, as we said before, a bit of a wag and already had some doubts about his guest's sanity, now found all his suspicions confirmed, but he resolved to humor him so that he might have sport that

[18] In chivalric romances, the "vigil" (watching over one's arms overnight) was an important part of the ceremony of knighthood.

night. He told the knight that his wishes were very reasonable, for such pursuits were natural to knights so illustrious as he seemed and his gallant bearing showed him to be. He added that he himself in the days of his youth had devoted himself to the same honorable profession and had wandered over various parts of the world in search of adventures; and, moreover, he had not failed to visit the curing grounds of Málaga, the Isles of Riarán, the Precinct of Seville, the Quicksilver Square of Segovia, the Olive field of Valencia, the Circle of Granada, the Strand of Sanlúcar, the Colt Fountain of Córdoba, the Taverns of Toledo, and divers other haunts where he had proved the nimbleness of his feet and the lightness of his fingers, committing wrongs in plenty, accosting many widows, deflowering sundry maidens, tricking some minors, and finally making himself known and famous to all the tribunals and courts over the length and breadth of Spain.[19] At last he had retired to this castle, where he lived on his own and on other men's revenues, entertaining therein knights-errant of every quality, solely for the great affection he bore them, and that they might share their goods with him in return for his benevolence. He further told him that in his castle there was no chapel where he could watch over his arms, for he had knocked it down to build it anew. However, in case of necessity, he might watch over the arms wherever he pleased, and therefore, he might watch that night in the castle courtyard. Then, the following morning, with God's help, the required ceremonies would be carried out in such a way that he would be dubbed a knight so effectively that nowhere in the world could one more perfect be found. He asked if Don Quixote had brought any money. "Not a farthing," answered the knight, "for I have never read in the stories of knights-errant that they ever carried money with them."

"You are mistaken," answered the landlord, "for although the stories are silent on this matter, seeing that the authors did not think it necessary to specify such obvious requirements as money and clean shirts, yet there is no reason to believe that the knights had none. On the contrary, it was an established fact that all knights-errant (whose deeds fill many a volume) carried their purses well lined against accidents, and moreover, they carried, in addition to shirts, a small chest of ointments to heal their wounds, for in the plains and deserts where they fought and were wounded, there was no one to cure them unless they were lucky enough to have some wise enchanter for friend who straightaway would send through the air in a cloud some damsel or dwarf with a vial of water possessed of such power that upon tasting a single drop of it, they would instantly find their wounds as perfectly cured as if they had never received any. But when the knights had no such friend, they always insisted that their squires should be provided with money and such necessities as lint and ointments; and when they had no squires (which was very seldom), they themselves carried those things on the crupper of their horse in saddlebags so small that they were scarcely visible, for except in such a case, the custom of carrying saddlebags was not allowed among knights-errant. I must, therefore, advise you," he continued, "nay, I might even command you, seeing that you are shortly to become my godson in chivalry, never from this day forward to travel with-

---

[19] The places the innkeeper names were all associated with robbers and thieves.

out money or without the aforesaid necessities, and you will see how serviceable you will find them when least you expect it."

Don Quixote promised to follow his injunctions carefully, and an order was given for him to watch over his armor in a large yard adjoining the inn. When the knight had collected all his arms together, he laid them on a stone trough that was close by the side of a wall. Then embracing his buckler and grasping his lance, he began with stately air to pace up and down in front of the trough, and as he began his parade, night began to close in.

The landlord, meanwhile, told all who were in the inn of the madness of his guest, the arms vigil, and the knighthood dubbing that was to come. They were astonished at such a strange kind of madness and flocked to observe him from a distance. They saw that sometimes he paced to and fro and at other times he leaned on his lance and gazed fixedly at his arms for a considerable time. It was now night, but the moon shone so clearly that she might have almost vied with the luminary that lent her splendor, and thus every action of our new knight could be seen by the spectators.

Just at this moment one of the carriers in the inn took it into his head to water his team of mules, to do which would necessitate removing Don Quixote's arms from the trough. But the knight, as he saw him approach, cried out in a loud voice: "O thou, whosoever thou art, rash knight that dost prepare to lay hands upon the arms of the most valiant knight-errant who ever girded sword, take heed and touch them not if thou wouldst not leave thy life in guerdon[20] for thy temerity." The carrier paid no heed to this warning (it would have been better for him if he had), but seizing hold of the armor by the straps, he threw it a good way from him. No sooner did Don Quixote perceive this than, raising his eyes to heaven and fixing his thoughts (as it seemed) upon his lady, Dulcinea, he said: "Assist me, O lady, in this first affront that is offered to thy vassal's heart. Let not thy favor and protection fail me in this first encounter." Uttering these and similar words, he let slip his buckler, and raising the lance in both hands, he gave the carrier such a hefty blow on the pate that he felled him to the ground in so grievous a plight that if he had followed it with a second, there would have been no need of a surgeon to cure him. This done, he put back his arms and began to pace to and fro as peacefully as before.

Soon after, another carrier, not knowing what had happened (for the first still lay unconscious), came out with the same intention of watering his mules and began to take away the arms that were encumbering the trough, when Don Quixote, not saying a word or imploring assistance from a soul, once more dropped his buckler, lifted up his lance, and without breaking it to pieces, opened the second muleteer's head in four places. All the people in the inn rushed out when they heard the noise, and the landlord among them. As soon as Don Quixote saw them, he braced on his buckler and laid his hands upon his sword, saying: "O lady of beauty, strength and vigor of my enfeebled heart! Now is the time for thee to turn the eyes of thy greatness upon this thy captive knight, who stands awaiting so great an adventure." These words, it seemed to him, filled him with such courage that if all the muleteers in the world had attacked him he would not have retreated one step. The wounded men's companions, seeing them in such an

---

[20] Recompense.

evil plight, began from afar to rain a shower of stones upon Don Quixote, who defended himself as best he could with his buckler, but he did not dare to leave the trough for fear of leaving his arms unprotected. The landlord shouted at them to let him alone, for he had told them the man was mad, and as such, he would be acquitted even if he killed every one of them. Don Quixote shouted still louder, called them caitiffs and traitors, and the lord of the castle a cowardly, baseborn knight for allowing knights-errant to be treated in such a manner. "I would make thee understand," cried he, "what a traitorous scoundrel thou art had I but been dubbed a knight. But as for you, ye vile and base rabble, I care not a fig for you; fire on, advance, draw near, and hurt me as much as you dare. Soon ye shall receive the reward for your folly and presumption." Such was the undaunted boldness with which he uttered these words that his attackers were struck with terror. And so, partly through fear and partly through the persuasive words of the landlord, they ceased to fling stones at him, and he allowed them to carry off their wounded, after which he returned to the guard of his arms with as much calm gravity as before.

The landlord did not relish the mad pranks of his guest, so he determined to make an end of them and give him his accursed order of chivalry before any further misfortune occurred. And so, going up to him, he excused himself for the insolent way those low fellows had treated him, without his knowledge or consent, adding that they had been well chastised for their rashness. He repeated what he had said before: that there was no chapel in that castle, nor was one necessary for what remained to be done; that the chief point of the knighting ceremony consisted in the accolade and the tap on the shoulders, according to the ceremonial of the order,[21] and that might be administered in the middle of a field; that he had performed the duty of watching over his armor, for he had watched more than four hours, whereas only two were required. All this Don Quixote believed and said that he was then ready to obey him, but yet begged him to conclude with all the brevity possible, for if he should be attacked again when he was armed a knight, he was determined not to leave one person alive in the castle, except those whom, out of respect for the governor of the fortress and at his request, he would spare. The governor, being warned and alarmed at possible consequences, brought out forthwith a book in which he kept his account of the straw and barley supplied to the carriers, and with a stump of candle, which a boy held lighted in his hands, and accompanied by the two above-mentioned damsels, he went over to Don Quixote and ordered him to kneel. He then read in his manual as if he had been repeating some pious oration. In the midst of the prayer he raised his hand and gave him a good blow on the neck, and after that gave a royal thwack on the shoulders, all the time mumbling between his teeth as if praying. After this he commanded one of the ladies to gird on his sword, which she did with much discretion and aplomb, plenty of which was needed to prevent them all from bursting with laughter at every stage of the ceremonies; but the prowess they had beheld in the new knight made them restrain their laughter. As she girded on his sword, the good lady said: "God make

---

[21] The "accolade" (a ceremonial embrace) and a ceremonial tap on the shoulders with a sword were part of the ceremony conferring knighthood.

you fortunate, knight, and give you success in your contests." Don Quixote demanded then how she was called that he might henceforward know to whom he was beholden for the favor received, for he was resolved to give her a share of the honor that his valor should merit. And she answered with great humility that she was called La Tolosa and was a cobbler's daughter from Toledo, who lived near Sancho Bienaya Square, and that she would always serve him and consider him her lord wherever she happened to be. Don Quixote replied, requesting her for his sake to call herself henceforth Lady Tolosa, which she promised to do. Then the other lady buckled on his spur and he addressed her in very nearly the same terms as the lady of the sword. He asked her name, and she said she was called La Molinera and was daughter of an honest miller of Antequera. He begged her to take a title and call herself Lady Molinera, at the same time making new offers of service.

Don Quixote could not rest until he found himself mounted on horseback and sallying forth in quest of adventures, and after saddling Rozinante, he mounted, but not before he had embraced his host and said so many extravagant words in thanking him for having dubbed him knight that it is impossible to tell them. The landlord, that he might speed the parting guest, answered him in no less rhetorical flourishes but in briefer words, and without asking him to pay for his lodging, he let him go with a godspeed.

CHAPTER IV

What happened to our knight when he sallied from the inn

It was about daybreak when Don Quixote sallied forth from the inn, so happy, so lively, and so excited at finding himself knighted that his very horse girths were ready to burst for joy. But calling to mind the advice of his host concerning the necessary accouterments for his travels, especially the money and the clean shirts, he resolved to return home to provide himself with them and with a squire. He had in view a certain laboring man of the neighborhood who was poor and had children but was otherwise very well fitted for the office of squire to a knight. With this thought in mind he turned Rozinante toward his village, and the horse, knowing full well the way to his stable, began to trot so briskly that his hoofs seemed hardly to strike the ground. The knight had not traveled far when he thought he heard the faint cries of someone in distress from a thicket on his right hand. No sooner had he heard them than he said: "I render thanks to heaven for such a favor. Already I have an opportunity of performing the duty of my profession and of reaping the harvest of my good ambition. Those cries must surely come from some distressed man or woman who needs my protection." Then turning his reins, he guided Rozinante toward the place from which he thought the cries came. A short distance within the wood he saw a mare tied to an oak and to another a youth of about fifteen years of age naked from the waist up. It was he who was crying out, and not without reason, for a lusty countryman was flogging him with a leather strap, and every blow he accompanied with a word of warning and advice, saying, "Keep your mouth shut and your eyes skinned." The boy answered: "I'll never do it again, master. By God's passion, I won't do it again and I promise in future to be more careful of your flock."

When Don Quixote saw what was happening, he said in an angry voice: "Discourteous knight, it is a caitiff's deed to attack one who cannot defend himself. Get up on your horse and take your lance" (for the farmer, too, had a lance leaning against the oak tree to which the mare was tied) "I will show you that you have been acting a coward's part." The countryman, at the sight of the strange apparition in armor brandishing a lance over him, gave himself up for lost and so replied submissively: "Sir knight, this youth I am chastising is a servant of mine, whom I employ to look after a flock of sheep in the neighborhood, but he is so careless that every day he loses one, and when I punish him for his negligence or rascality, he says I do it because I am a skinflint and will not pay him his wages. Upon my life and soul, he lies."

"Have you the impudence to lie in my presence, vile serf?" said Don Quixote. "By the sun that shines on us I will pierce you through and through with this lance of mine. Pay him instantly and none of your denials. If not, by almighty God who rules us all, I will annihilate you this very moment. Untie him at once."

The countryman lowered his head and without a word untied his servant. Don Quixote then asked the boy how much his master owed him. He replied nine months' wages at seven reals a month. Don Quixote, having calculated the sum, found that it came to sixty-three reals and told the farmer to pay up the money unless he wished to die. The farmer, who was shaking with fear, then answered that on the word of one in a tight corner and also upon his oath (yet he had sworn nothing), he did not owe so much, for they must deduct three pairs of shoes that he had given the boy and a real for two bloodlettings that he had when he was sick.

"That is all very well," answered Don Quixote, "but let the shoes and the bloodletting stand for the blows that you have given him for no fault of his own; if he wore out the leather of the shoes you gave him, you wore out his skin, and if the barber drew blood from him when he was sick,[22] you drew blood from him when he was in good health; so in this matter he owes you nothing."

"The trouble is, sir knight," said the countryman, "that I have no money on me. If Andrés comes home with me, I'll pay him ready money down."

"I go home with him?" said the boy. "Not on your life, sir! I would not think of doing such a thing; the moment he gets me alone he'll flay me like a Saint Bartholomew."[23]

"He will not do so," answered Don Quixote. "I have only to command and he will respect me and do my behest. So I shall let him go free and guarantee payment to you, provided he swears by the order of knighthood that he has received."

---

[22] Barbers also functioned as surgeons.
[23] Saint Bartholomew, one of the twelve apostles and martyrs, was said to have been flayed to death.

"Take heed, sir, of what you are saying," said the boy. "My master is no knight; he has not received any order of knighthood. He is Juan Haldudo the wealthy, a native of Quintanar."

"That matters little," answered Don Quixote; "there may be Haldudos who are knights, especially as every man is the son of his own works."

"That's true," said Andrés, "but what kind of works is my master the son of? Isn't he denying me the wages of my sweat and toil?"

"I'm not denying them, brother Andrés," answered the countryman. "Do, please, come with me and I swear by all the orders of knighthood there are in the world to pay you, as I said before, every real down and even perfumed into the bargain."

"I'll spare you the perfume," said Don Quixote. "Give them to him in good, honest reals and I shall be satisfied; but see to it that you carry out your oath. If not, I swear by the same oath to return and chastise you, and I am sure to find you, even if you hide away from me more successfully than a lizard. And if you want to know who it is who gives you this command, learn that I am the valiant Don Quixote of La Mancha, the undoer of wrongs and injuries. So, God be with you, and do not forget what you have promised and sworn, on pain of the penalty I have stated." With these words he spurred Rozinante and in a moment he was far away.

The countryman gazed after him, and when he saw that he had gone through the wood and was out of sight, he turned to his servant, Andrés, saying: "Come here, my boy; I want to pay you what I owe you in accordance with the commands of that undoer of wrongs."

"So you will, I swear," said Andrés; "and you had better obey the orders of that good knight—may he live a thousand years. He is such a courageous man and such a fair judge that by Saint Roch, if you don't pay me, he'll be back and he'll do what he threatened."

"And I'll swear I will too," answered the countryman, "and to show you my goodwill, I'll double the debt so that I can double the pay." Catching the boy by the arm, he tied him again to the oak and gave him such a drubbing that he left him for dead. "Now, master Andrés," said he, "call out to that undoer of wrongs and you'll find that he won't undo this one. Indeed I don't think I'm finished with you yet, for I've a mind to flay you alive as you feared a moment ago." At last he untied him and gave him leave to go off and fetch his judge to carry out the threatened sentence. As for Andrés, he went off sorely fretful, swearing that he would seek out the valiant Don Quixote of La Mancha and tell him all that happened, and he would make his tormentor pay sevenfold. However, he departed in tears, while his master stayed behind laughing.

Such was the manner in which the valiant Don Quixote undid that wrong.

Meanwhile the knight was quite pleased with himself, for he believed that he had begun his feats of arms in a most successful and dignified manner, and he went on riding toward his village, saying to himself in a low voice: "Well mayest thou call thyself the happiest of all women on earth, O Dulcinea of El Toboso, peerless among beauties, for it was thy fortune to have subject to thy will so valiant and celebrated a knight as is and shall be Don Quixote of La Mancha, who, as all the world knows, received only yesterday the order of knighthood and today has undone the greatest wrong that ever ignorance designed or cruelty committed. Today from the hand of that pitiless foe he seized the lash with which he so unjustly scourged that tender child."

Just then he came to a road that branched into four directions, and forthwith he was reminded of the crossroads where knights-errant would halt to consider which road they should follow. To imitate their example, he paused for a moment's meditation, and then he slackened the reins, leaving Rozinante to choose the way. The horse followed his original intention, which was to make straight in the direction of his stable.

When Don Quixote had ridden about two miles, he saw a big company of people who, as it appeared later, were traders of Toledo on their way to buy silk in Murcia. There were six of them and they carried sunshades. They were accompanied by four servants on horseback and three muleteers on foot. No sooner had Don Quixote perceived them than he fancied a new adventure was at hand. So, imitating as closely as possible the exploits he had read about in his books, he resolved now to perform one that was admirably molded to the present circumstances. So, with a lofty bearing he fixed himself firmly in his stirrups, grasped his lance, covered himself with his buckler, and stood in the middle of the road waiting for those knights-errant to approach (for such he supposed them to be). As soon as they came within earshot, Don Quixote, raising his voice, cried out in an arrogant tone: "Let all the world stand still if all the world does not confess that there is not in all the world a fairer damsel than the Empress of La Mancha, the peerless Dulcinea of El Toboso."

At the sound of those words the traders pulled up and gazed in amazement at the grotesque being who uttered them. Both the tone and the appearance of the horseman gave clear proof of his insanity, but they wished to consider in more leisurely fashion the meaning of this confession that he insisted upon. So one of them, who was a trifle waggish in humor and had plenty of wit, addressed him as follows: "Sir knight, we do not know this lady you speak of. Show her to us, and if she is as beautiful as you say, we shall willingly and universally acknowledge the truth of your claim."

"If I were to show her to you," answered Don Quixote, "what merit would there be in acknowledging a truth so manifest to all? The important point is that you should believe, confess, affirm, swear, and defend it without setting eyes on her. If you do not, I challenge you to try battle with me, ye presumptuous and overweening band. Come on now, one by one as the traditions of chivalry declare, or else all together according to the foul custom of your breed. Here I stand waiting for you, trusting in the justice of my cause."

"Sir knight," answered the trader, "I beseech you in the name of all the princes here present not to force us to burden our consciences by confessing something we have never seen or heard, especially when it is so prejudicial to the empresses and queens of Alcarria and Extremadura.[24] Please show us some picture of that lady, even if it is no bigger than a grain of wheat, for a thread will enable us to judge the whole skein and we shall be satisfied and you yourself happy and content. I believe that we already are so much on your side that even if your lady's picture shows that one eye

---

[24] Both backward, primitive regions.

squints and the other drips vermilion and sulphur, yet in spite of all, to gratify you, we shall say all that you please in her favor."

"Drip indeed, you infamous scoundrels!" cried Don Quixote in a towering rage. "Nothing of the kind drips from her eyes, but only ambergris and civet in cotton wool. She is not squint-eyed nor hunchbacked, but straighter than a Guadarrama spindle. But you shall pay the penalty for the great blasphemy you have uttered against so peerless a beauty as my lady." With those words he attacked the man who had spoken to him, so fiercely with couched lance that if good fortune had not caused Rozinante to stumble and fall midway, the merchant would have paid dearly for his rashness. Rozinante fell and his master rolled a good distance over the ground. Although he tried to rise, he could not, for he was so impeded by the lance, the buckler, the spurs, the helmet, and the weight of the ancient armor. However, as he was struggling to arise, he kept on crying: "Flee not, cowardly rabble! Wait, slavish herd! It is not my fault, but the fault of my horse, that I am stretched here."

One of the muleteers of the company, who indeed was not very good-natured, when he heard the poor fallen knight say such arrogant words, could not resist the temptation to give him the answer on his ribs. So he went up to him, took the lance, broke it into pieces, and with one of them he so belabored our poor Don Quixote that in spite of his armor he thrashed him like a measure of wheat. His masters shouted to him not to beat him so much and to leave off; but the fellow was angry and would not stop the game until he had spent what remained of his rage. Then, running to get the rest of the pieces of the lance, he splintered them all on the wretched knight, who, in the midst of all this tempest of blows that rained on him, did not for a moment close his mouth, but bellowed out threats to heaven and earth and those villainous cutthroats (for so they appeared to him). At last the muleteer became wearied and the traders pursued their journey, carrying with them plenty of matter for conversation at the expense of the poor drubbed knight. And when he was alone, he tried to see if he could get up, but if he could not do so when he was hale and hearty, how could he do it when he was bruised and battered? And yet he counted himself lucky, for he thought that his misfortune was peculiar to knights-errant and he attributed the whole accident to the fault of his horse. But so bruised was his whole body that it was impossible for him to get up.

CHAPTER V

In which is continued the account of our knight's mishap

Seeing that he couldn't stir, he resolved to have recourse to his usual remedy, which was to think of some incident from one of his books. His madness made him remember that of the Marquess of Mantua and Baldwin, whom Carloto left wounded on the mountainside[25]—a story familiar to children, not unknown to youths, celebrated and even believed by old men, yet for

---

[25] Carloto, son of Charlemagne, was the hero of a well-known ballad, which Quixote quotes below.

all that, no more authentic than the miracles of Mohammed. Now this story, so he thought, exactly fitted his present circumstances, so with great display of affliction he began to roll about on the ground and to repeat in a faint voice the words that the wounded knight in the wood was supposed to have said:

> "Where art thou, lady of my heart,
> That for my woe thou dost not grieve?
> Alas, thou do know'st not my distress,
> Or thou art false and pitiless."

In this manner he repeated the ballad until he came to those verses that say: "O noble Marquess of Mantua, my uncle and liege lord." By chance there happened to pass by at that very moment a peasant of his own village, a neighbor, who was returning from bringing a load of wheat to the mill. And he, seeing a man lying stretched out on the ground, came over and asked him who he was and what was the cause of his sorrowful lamentation. Don Quixote, firmly believing that the man was the Marquess of Mantua, his uncle, would not answer but continued reciting his ballad, which told of his misfortunes and of the loves of the Emperor's son with his wife, just as the book relates it. The peasant was amazed to hear those extravagant words. Then taking off his visor, which had been broken to pieces in the drubbing, he wiped the dust off his face. No sooner had he done so than he recognized him and said: "Master Quixana" (for that must have been how people called him when he had his wits and had not been transformed from a staid gentleman into a knight-errant) "who left you in such a state?" But he kept on reciting his ballad and made no answer to what he was asked. The good man then, as best as he could, took off his breast- and back-plate to see if he was wounded, but he saw no blood or scar upon him. He managed to lift him up from the ground and with the greatest difficulty hoisted him on to his ass, thinking that beast an easier mount. Then he gathered together all his arms, not omitting even the splinters of the lance, tied them into a bundle, and laid them upon Rozinante's back. Then taking the horse by the bridle and the ass by the halter, he set off toward his village, meditating all the while on the foolish words that Don Quixote kept saying. And Don Quixote on his part was no less pensive, for he was so beaten and bruised that he could hardly hold himself onto the ass, and from time to time he uttered such melancholy sighs that seemed to pierce the skies that the peasant felt again moved to ask him what was the cause of his sorrow. But it must have been the Devil himself who supplied him with stories so similiar to his circumstances, for at that instant, forgetting Baldwin, he remembered the Moor Abindarráez whom the governor of Antequera, Rodrigo de Narváez, took prisoner to his castle.[26] So when the peasant asked him again how he was, he answered word for word as the captive Abindarráez answered Rodrigo de Narváez, just as he had read in Montemayor's *Diana*, where the story is told. And he applied it so artfully

---

[26] There were a number of romance tales about the love of the captive Moor Abindarráez for the beautiful Jarifa. One version of the story is in Jorge de Montemayor's romance *Diana* (1561), which Quixote mentions.

to his own case that the peasant wished he were in Hell rather than to have to listen to such a hodgepodge of foolishness. This convinced him that his neighbor was mad, so he made haste to reach the village and thereby escape being further plagued by Don Quixote's long discourse. The latter ended by saying: "I would have you know, Master Rodrigo de Narváez, that the beauteous Jarifa I have mentioned is now the fair Dulcinea of El Toboso, for whom I have done, still do, and shall do the most famous deeds of chivalry that ever have been, are, or ever shall be seen in the world." To this the peasant answered: "Take heed, sir, that I am neither Don Rodrigo de Narváez nor the Marquess of Mantua, but Pedro Alonso, your neighbor, and you are neither Baldwin nor Abindarráez, but the honorable gentleman Master Quixana."

"I know who I am," answered Don Quixote, "and I know that I can be not only those I have mentioned but also the Twelve Peers of France and even the Nine Worthies, for my exploits will surpass all they have ever jointly or separately achieved."[27]

With this and sundry topics of conversation they reached the village at sunset, but the peasant waited until it was dark so that no one would see the belabored knight so sorrily mounted. When he thought the time had come, he entered the village and went to Don Quixote's house, which he found in an uproar. The curate and the village barber, great friends of Don Quixote, happened to be there and the housekeeper was addressing them in a loud voice: "What do you think, Master Licentiate Pedro Pérez" (that was the curate's name) "of my master's misfortune? For the past six days neither he, nor his horse, nor his buckler, nor his lance, nor his armor has appeared. Woe is me! I'm now beginning to understand, and I'm as sure of it as I am of death that those accursed books of chivalry that he continually reads have turned his brain topsy-turvy. Now that I think of it I remember hearing him say to himself many a time that he wished to become a knight-errant and go through the world in search of adventures. The Devil and Barabbas[28] take such books, for they have ruined the finest mind in all La Mancha!" The niece said the same and a little more: "You must know, Master Nicholas" (this was the name of the barber) "that it was a frequent occurrence for my uncle to read these soulless books of misadventures for days and nights on end. At the end of that time he would cast the book from his hands, clutch his sword, and begin to slash the walls. Then, when he was grown very weary, he would say that he had killed four giants as big as towers and that the sweat that dripped off him after his great exertions, he would say, was blood from the wounds he had received in battle. Then he would drink a great jugful of water and become calm and peaceable, saying that the water was a most precious liquor that his friend the great enchanter Esquife had given him. I, however, blame myself for all, for not having warned you of my uncle's extravagant behavior. You might have cured him before things reached such a state, and you would have burned

---

[27] The Twelve Peers were Charlemagne's chief knights, all equal in rank. The Nine Worthies, in medieval lore, were nine famous men, three Jewish, three pagan, and three Christian, subjects of a number of tales and chronicles.
[28] The robber whom Pilate pardoned instead of Christ; see, for example, Matthew 27: 15–26.

all those excommunicated books (he has many, mind you), for they all deserve to be burned as heretics."

"I agree with that," said the curate, "and I hold that tomorrow must not pass without a public inquiry being made into them. They should be condemned to the fire to prevent them from tempting those who read them to do what my poor master must have done."

All this Don Quixote and the peasant heard. The latter finally understood the infirmity of his neighbor and began to shout: "Open your doors, all of you, to Sir Baldwin and the Marquess of Mantua, who is grievously wounded, and to the Moor Abindarráez, who is led captive by the valiant Rodrigo de Narváez, governor of Antequera."

Hearing these cries, they all rushed out and straightaway recognized their friend. They ran to embrace him, but he had not yet dismounted from the ass, for he was not able to do so. He said: "Stand back, all of you. I have been sorely wounded through the fault of my horse; carry me to my bed and, if possible, call the wise Urganda to examine and cure my wounds."

"A thousand curses," said the housekeeper then. "My heart told me clearly on which foot my master limped. Come on upstairs, sir; we'll know how to look after you here without that Urganda woman. Curses, aye, a hundred curses on those books of chivalry that have driven you to this!"

They carried him to his bed and searched his body for wounds, but could find none. He said he was all bruised after a great fall he had with his horse, Rozinante, when he was fighting ten giants, the fiercest and most overweening in the world.

"Aha!" said the curate. "So there are giants too in the dance. By the sign of the Cross I swear I'll burn the lot of them before tomorrow night."

They questioned Don Quixote a thousand times, but he would give no answer. He only asked them to give him food and allow him to sleep, for rest was what he needed most. . . .

[In a chapter omitted here, the curate and the barber examine the contents of Don Quixote's library and burn all the books on knight-errantry. They examine the title pages and comment critically on the absurd contents.]

CHAPTER VII

Of the second sally of our good knight Don Quixote of La Mancha

. . . . That same night the housekeeper burned all the books she could find in the courtyard and in the house, and some that perished in the flames deserved to be preserved forever in the archives, but fate and the laziness of the inquisitor did not allow it, and thus in their case the saying was fulfilled that the saint sometimes pays for the sinner. One of the remedies that the curate and the barber then prescribed for their friend's infirmity was to wall up the room where the books had been stored so that when he rose he should not find them, for once the cause had been removed, the effect might cease. And they agreed to tell him that an enchanter had whisked books, room, and all away. The plan was carried out with great speed.

Two days later Don Quixote got up, and the first thing he did was to go and see his books, and as he could not find the room in which he had left them, he went up and down and all over the house looking for it. He came to the place where the door used to be and felt the wall with his hands, staring around him on all sides without saying a word. At last he asked the housekeeper where was the study in which he kept his books. The housekeeper, who knew exactly what she had to answer, said: "What manner of study is your worship looking for? There are no studies or books in this house now, for the Devil in person took all away."

"It was not the Devil," said the niece, "but an enchanter who arrived on a cloud one night after you went away from here. He got down off the serpent on which he was riding and went into the room. I don't know what he did in there, but soon after he went flying out through the roof, leaving the house full of smoke. When we looked to see what he had done, we could see no books or room, but we remember very well, myself and the housekeeper, that when the wicked old man was about to depart, he said in a loud voice that owing to the secret enmity he bore against the owner of those books and of the room, he had done damage that would soon be clear. He also said that he was called Muñatón the wizard."

"Frestón was the name he wished to say," answered Don Quixote.

"I don't know," said the housekeeper, "whether he was called Frestón or Fritón; I only know that his name ended in *-tón.*"

"That is true," said Don Quixote. "He is a wise enchanter, a great enemy of mine, and looks upon me with a malicious eye, for he knows by his skill and wisdom that in the course of time I shall fight in single combat with a knight whom he favors, and I shall win, in spite of all his machinations; so, he tries to do me all the hurt he can. But I affirm that he will never prevail over what has been ordained by Heaven."

"Who has any doubts on that score?" said the niece. "But, dear uncle, what have you to do with such quarrels? Is it not better to stay peacefully at home instead of roaming the world in search of better bread than is made of wheat, not to mention that many who go for wool come home shorn?"

"My dear niece," answered Don Quixote, "how far you are off the mark! Before they ever shear me, I'll have plucked and lopped off the beards of all who think they can touch the tip of a single hair of mine."

The two would not make any further reply, for they saw that his anger was rising. As a matter of fact, he remained a fortnight peacefully at home without showing any signs of wanting to repeat his former vagaries. During those days he held many pleasant arguments with his two old friends the curate and the barber. He would maintain that what the world needed most of all was plenty of knights-errant and that he himself would revive knight-errantry. The curate sometimes contradicted him; at other times he would give in to him, for had he not adopted this procedure, he could never have dealt with him.

During this interval Don Quixote made overtures to a certain laboring man, a neighbor of his and an honest fellow (if such a term can be applied to one who is poor), but with very little wit in his pate. In effect, he said so much to him and made so many promises that the poor wight resolved to set out with him and serve him as squire. Among other things Don Quixote told him that he should be most willing to go with him because some time or another he might meet with an adventure that would earn for him, in the twinkling of an eye, some island, and he would find himself governor of it. With those and other promises, Sancho Panza (for that was the fellow's name) left his wife and children and engaged himself as squire to his neighbor. Don Quixote then set about raising money, and by selling one thing, pawning another, and throwing away the lot for a mere song, he gathered a respectable sum. He furnished himself likewise with a buckler borrowed from a friend, repaired his broken helmet as best he could, and informed his squire, Sancho, of the day and hour when he intended to sally forth so that the latter might supply himself with all that was needed. He charged him particularly to carry saddlebags. Sancho said he would do so and added that he was thinking of bringing an ass with him, for he had a good one and he was not used to travel on foot. At the mention of the ass Don Quixote hesitated a little, racking his brains to remember any case of a knight-errant who was attended by a squire mounted on ass-back, but he could not remember any such case. Nevertheless, he resolved to let him take his ass, for he intended to present him with a more dignified mount when he got the opportunity, by unhorsing the first discourteous knight he came across. He also provided himself with shirts and other necessities, thus following the advice the innkeeper had given him.

After all these preparations had been made, Don Quixote, without saying farewell to his housekeeper and niece, Panza to his wife and children, set out one night from the village without being seen. They traveled so far that night that at daybreak they were sure that no one would find them, even if they were pursued.

Sancho Panza rode along on his ass like a patriarch, with his saddlebags and wineskin, full of a huge longing to see himself governor of the island his master had promised to him. Don Quixote happened to take the same road as on his first journey, that is, across the Plain of Montiel, which he now traveled with less discomfort than the last time, for as it was early in the morning, the rays of the sun did not beat down directly upon them, but slantwise, and so did not trouble them. Presently Sancho Panza said to his master: "Mind, your worship, sir knight-errant, you don't let slip from your memory the island you've promised me; I'll be able to rule it well, no matter how big it is."

To which Don Quixote replied: "I would have you know, my friend Sancho, that knights-errant of long ago were accustomed to make their squires governors of the islands or kingdoms they won, and I have resolved not to neglect so praiseworthy a custom. Nay, I wish to surpass them in it, for they sometimes, perhaps even on the majority of occasions, waited till their squires were grown old, and then when they were cloyed with service after enduring bad days and worse nights, they conferred upon them some title, such as count or at least marquess, of some valley of more or less account. But if you live and I live, I may, before six days have passed, even conquer a kingdom with a string of dependencies, which would fall in exactly with my plan of crowning you king of one of them. Do not, however, think this strange, for knights-errant of my kind meet with such extraordinary and unexpected chances that I might easily give you still more than I am promising."

"And so," answered Sancho Panza, "by that token, if I became king by one of those miracles you mention, at least my chuck[29] Juana Gutiérrez would become queen and my children princes."

"Who doubts it?" answered Don Quixote.

"I doubt it," replied Sancho Panza, "for I truly believe that even if God were to rain kingdoms down upon earth, none would sit well on the head of Mari Gutiérrez.[30] Believe me, sir, she's not worth two farthings as queen; countess would suit her better, and even then, God help her."

"Leave all in God's hands, Sancho," answered Don Quixote. "He will do what is best for her, but do not humble yourself so far as to be satisfied with anything less than the title of lord-lieutenant."

"I'll not indeed, sir," replied Sancho, "for a famous master like yourself will know what is fit for me and what I can carry."

CHAPTER VIII

Of the valiant Don Quixote's success in the terrifying and never-before-imagined adventure of the windmills, with other events worthy of happy remembrance

Just then they came in sight of thirty or forty windmills that rise from that plain, and no sooner did Don Quixote see them than he said to his squire: "Fortune is guiding our affairs better than we ourselves could have wished. Do you see over yonder, friend Sancho, thirty or forty hulking giants? I intend to do battle with them and slay them. With their spoils we shall begin to be rich, for this is a righteous war and the removal of so foul a brood from off the face of the earth is a service God will bless."

"What giants?" asked Sancho Panza.

"Those you see over there," replied his master, "with their long arms; some of them have them well-nigh two leagues in length."

"Take care, sir," cried Sancho. "Those over there are not giants but windmills, and those things that seem to be arms are their sails, which when they are whirled around by the wind turn the millstone."

"It is clear," replied Don Quixote, "that you are not experienced in adventures. Those are giants, and if you are afraid, turn aside and pray whilst I enter into fierce and unequal battle with them."

Uttering these words, he clapped spurs to Rozinante, his steed, without heeding the cries of his squire, Sancho, who warned him that he was not going to attack giants but windmills. But so convinced was he that they were giants that he neither heard his squire's shouts nor did he notice what they were, though he was very near them. Instead, he rushed on, shouting in a loud voice: "Fly not, cowards and vile caitiffs; one knight alone attacks you!" At that moment a slight breeze arose and the great sails began to move. When Don Quixote saw this, he shouted again: "Although you flourish more arms than the giant Briareus, you shall pay for it!"[31]

Saying this and commending himself most devoutly to his lady, Dulcinea, whom he begged to help him in this peril, he covered himself

[29] A term of endearment. Juana is Sancho's wife.

[30] Gutiérrez is Juana's (or Mari's) maiden name; elsewhere she is called Juana Panza.

[31] Briareus was a hundred-armed, fifty-headed giant in Greek mythology. He helped Zeus to overthrow the Titans.

with his buckler, couched his lance, charged at Rozinante's full gallop, and rammed the first mill in his way. He ran his lance into the sail, but the wind twisted it with such violence that it shivered the lance in pieces and dragged both rider and horse after it, rolling them over and over on the ground, sorely damaged.

Sancho Panza rushed up to his assistance as fast as his ass could gallop, and when he reached the knight, he found that he was unable to move, such was the blow that Rozinante had given him in the fall.

"God help us!" cried Sancho. "Did I not tell you, sir, to mind what you were doing, for those were only windmills? Nobody could have mistaken them unless he had windmills in his brain."

"Hold your peace, good Sancho," replied Don Quixote. "The affairs of war are, above all others, subject to continual change. Moreover, I am convinced, and that is the truth, that the magician Frestón, the one who robbed me of my study and books, has changed those giants into windmills to deprive me of the glory of victory; such is the enmity he bears against me. But in the end his evil arts will be of little avail against my doughty sword."

"God settle it in His own way," cried Sancho as he helped his master to rise and remount Rozinante, who was well-nigh disjointed by his fall.

They conversed about the recent adventure as they followed the road toward the Pass of Lápice, for there, Don Quixote said, they could not fail to find many and various adventures, seeing that it was a much frequented spot. Nevertheless he was very downcast at the loss of his lance, and in mentioning it to his squire, he said: "I remember having read of a Spanish knight called Diego Pérez de Vargas, who, when he broke his sword in a battle, tore off a huge branch from an oak and with it did such deeds of prowess that day and pounded so many Moors that he earned the surname of Machuca,[32] and so he and his descendants were called from that day onwards Vargas y Machuca. I mention this because I intend to tear from the first oak tree we meet such a branch, with which I am resolved to perform such deeds that you will consider yourself fortunate to witness, exploits that men will scarcely credit."

"God's will be done," said Sancho. "I'll believe all your worship says; but straighten yourself a bit in the saddle, for you seem to be leaning over on one side, which must be from the bruises you received in your fall."

"That is true," replied Don Quixote, "and if I do not complain, it is because knights-errant must never complain of any wound, even though their guts are protruding from them."

"If that be so, I've no more to say," answered Sancho, "but God knows I'd be glad to hear you complain when anything hurts you. As for myself, I'll never fail to complain at the smallest twinge, unless this business of not complaining applies also to squires."

Don Quixote could not help laughing at the simplicity of his squire and told him that he might complain whenever he pleased and to his heart's content, for he had never read anything to the contrary in the order of chivalry. Sancho then bade his master consider that it was now time to eat, but the latter told him to eat whenever he fancied. As for himself, he had

---

[32] The verb *machucar* means "to pound." The story of Diego Pérez de Vargas, a sort of Spanish Hercules, is told in another old ballad.

no appetite at the moment. Sancho no sooner had obtained leave than he settled himself as comfortably as he could upon his ass, and taking out of his saddlebags some of the contents, he jogged behind his master, munching deliberately; and every now and then he would take a stiff pull at the wineskin with such gusto that the ruddiest tapster in Málaga would have envied him. While he rode on, swilling away in that manner, he did not remember any promise his master might have made to him, and so far from thinking it a labor, he thought it a life of ease to go roaming in quest of adventures, no matter how perilous they might be.

They spent that night under some trees, and from one of them Don Quixote tore a withered branch that might, at a pinch, serve him as a lance, and he fixed to it the iron head of the one he had broken. All that night he did not sleep, for he kept thinking of his lady, Dulcinea. In this way he imitated what he had read in his books, where knights spent many sleepless nights in forests and wastes, reveling in memories of their fair ladies. Not so Sancho Panza, whose belly was full of something more substantial than chicory water. He made one long sleep of it, and if his master had not roused him, not even the rays of the sun beating on his face nor the joyful warbling of the hosts of birds would have awakened him. When he got up he tested the wineskin once more and found it somewhat flabbier than the night before. This saddened him, for he thought that they were not in the way to remedy that loss as soon as would satisfy him. Don Quixote would not break his fast, for as we have said before, he was resolved to nurture himself on savory remembrances. . . .

[In the following chapters, Don Quixote attacks two monks and some muleteers who he thinks are necromancers carrying off a princess; he encounters a beautiful maiden, Marcella, who is as independent and idealistic as Quixote himself; he is beaten by herdsmen who object to Rozinante's amorous attentions to their mares; and he becomes embroiled in a dispute in an inn when he mistakenly thinks a servant girl is a beautiful princess who has fallen in love with him. This incident ends with Sancho being tossed in a blanket.]

CHAPTER XVIII

In which an account is given of the conversation that took place between Sancho Panza and his master, Don Quixote, with other adventures worth recording

. . . . Suddenly Don Quixote saw a large, dense cloud of dust rolling toward them. Turning to Sancho, he said: "This is the day, Sancho, on which shall be clearly seen the good that fate has in store for us; this is the day, I say, on which I shall show the might of my arm and on which I intend to do deeds that shall be written in the books of fame for succeeding ages. Do you see that dust cloud, Sancho? Know then that it is churned up by a mighty army composed of sundry and innumerable people who are marching this way."

"If so, there must be two armies," said Sancho, "for here on this side there is as great a cloud of dust."

Don Quixote turned around to look at it, and seeing it was so, he rejoiced, for he fancied that there were indeed two armies coming to fight each other in the midst of that spacious plain. For his imagination at all hours of the day and night was full of battles, enchantments, adventures, follies, loves, and challenges as are related in the books of chivalry, and all his words, thoughts, and actions were turned to such things. As for the clouds of dust he had seen, they were raised by two large flocks of ewes and rams that were being driven along the same road from opposite directions, which, because of the dust, could not be seen until they came near.

So earnest was Don Quixote in calling them armies that Sancho came to believe it and asked: "Well, what are we to do?"

"What?" said Don Quixote. "Why, favor and help the distressed and needy. You must know, Sancho, that the army marching toward us in front is led by the mighty emperor Alifanfarón, lord of the great island of Trapobana;[33] the other, which is marching at our back, is the army of his foe, the king of the Garamantans, Pentapolín of the Naked Arm, for he always goes into battle with his right arm bare."

"Why do these two gentlemen hate each other so much?" asked Sancho.

"They are enemies," replied Don Quixote, "because Alifanfarón is a furious pagan and is in love with the daughter of Pentapolín, a beautiful, graceful lady and a Christian. Her father refuses to give her to the pagan king unless he abandon first the false religion of Mohammed and turn Christian."

"By my beard," said Sancho, "Pentapolín does right, and I'll help as best I can."

"Then you will do your duty," said Don Quixote, "for it is not necessary to be dubbed a knight to engage in battles such as these."

"I understand," replied Sancho, "but where shall we tie this ass that we may be sure of finding him after the scuffle is over? I think it was never customary to go into battle mounted on such a beast."

"That is true," said Don Quixote. "What you must do is to leave the ass to his own devices. Let him take his chance whether he get lost or not, for after winning this battle we shall have so many horses that even Rozinante runs the risk of being exchanged for another. Now listen to me carefully while I give you an account of the principal knights in the two approaching armies. Let us withdraw to that hillock over there to get a better view of the two armies."

They did so, and standing on the top of the hill, they could have discerned the two flocks that Don Quixote had converted into armies had their eyes not been blinded by the clouds of dust. But seeing in his imagination what did not exist, he began to say in a loud voice: "The knight you see yonder with the yellow armor, who bears on his shield a crowned lion couchant at a damsel's feet, is the valiant Laurcalco, lord of the Silver Bridge. The other with armor flowered with gold, who bears on his shield three crowns argent on an azure field, is the fearsome Micocolembo, grand duke of Quirotia. The other, with gigantic limbs, who marches on his right, is the undaunted Brandabarbarán of Boliche, lord of the Three Arabias. He is wearing a serpent's skin and bears a gate as a shield, which, fame says, was one of those belonging to the temple that Samson pulled down when

---

[33] Most of the high-sounding names in this passage are imaginary. Trapobana, or Taprobana, is the ancient name given the island of Ceylon.

by his death he took revenge on his enemies.[34] Now turn your eyes to this other side, and there you will see, in front of this other army, the victorious and never vanquished Timonel of Carcajona, prince of New Biscay, who comes clad in armor quartered azure, vert, argent, and or. He bears on his shield a cat or on a field gules with a scroll inscribed *Miau,* which is the beginning of his mistress' name—according to report—the peerless Miaulina, daughter of Alfeñiquén, duke of Algarbe. The other, who weighs down and oppresses the back of that powerful and spirited charger, with armor as white as snow and a white shield without a device, is a novice knight of the French nation called Pierre Papin, lord of the baronies of Utrique. The other pricking with iron heel the flanks of that nimble zebra and carrying for arms the azure cups is the doughty duke of Nerbia, Espartafilardo of the Wood, who bears on his shield the device of an asparagus plant, with a motto in Castilian which says: *My fortune trails.*"

So he went on, naming many imaginary knights in each squadron as his fancy dictated and giving extemporaneously to each his armor, colors, devices, and mottoes, for he was completely carried away by his strangely deluded imagination. He continued without a pause: "That squadron in the front is composed of men of various nations: Here are they who drink of the sweet waters of the famous Xanthus; mountaineers who tread the Massilian fields; those who sift the pure and fine gold of Arabia; dwellers on the celebrated cool shores of clear Thermodon; those who drain in various ways the golden Pactolus; the Numidians, unreliable in their promises; Persians, famous for their bows and arrows; Parthians; Medes, who fight as they flee; Arabs, with their movable houses; Scythians as cruel as they are fair; Ethiopians with pierced lips; and countless other nations, whose faces I recognize and behold, although their names I do not recollect. In that other squadron come drinkers of the crystal waters of the olive-bearing Betis; men who burnish and polish their faces with the liquor of the ever-rich and golden Tagus; men who enjoy the health-giving waters of the divine Genil; dwellers in the Tartessian plain with their abundant pastures; men who enjoy the Elysian fields of Jérez; men of La Mancha rich and crowned with golden corn; men clad in iron, survivors of the ancient Gothic race; bathers in the Pisuerga, famous for its mild current; men who graze their flock on the broad pastures of the winding Guadiana, famous for its hidden current;[35] men who shiver with the cold of the wooded Pyrenees and among the white snows of the lofty Apennines; as many as all Europe contains and encloses."

By God! How many provinces did he name! How many nations did he enumerate, giving to each, with wonderful speed, its peculiar attributes, so absorbed and wrapped up was he in all that he had read in his lying books! Sancho Panza hung on his words without uttering one. Now and then he turned his head to see whether he could perceive the knights and giants his master named. Seeing none, he said at last: "Master, I'll commend to the Devil any man, giant, or knight of all those you mentioned who is actually here. At least I do not see them. Perhaps all may be enchantment like last night's specters."

---

[34] See Judges 16.
[35] The Guadiana river runs underground through part of La Mancha.

"Why do you say that?" said Don Quixote. "Do you not hear the neighing of the horses, the blaring of the trumpets, and the rattle of the drums?"

"I hear nothing," answered Sancho, "but the bleating of sheep and lambs." And so it was, for now the two flocks were close at hand.

"The fear you are in," said Don Quixote, "allows you neither to see nor to hear correctly, for one of the effects of fear is to disturb the senses and make things seem different from what they are. If you are so afraid, stand to one side and leave me alone, for I alone am sufficient to give the victory to the side that I shall assist." With these words he clapped spurs to Rozinante, and with lance couched, rode down the hillside like a thunderbolt.

Sancho shouted at him: "Come back, master, come back! I swear to God that those you are going to charge are only sheep and lambs. Come back! Woe to the father who begat me! What madness is this? Look! There is neither giant, nor knight, nor cats, nor arms, nor shield quartered or entire, nor azures true or bedeviled. Sinner that I am, what are you doing?"

Don Quixote, however, did not turn back, but charged on, shouting as he went: "Ho! You knights who fight under the banners of the valiant emperor Pentapolín of the Naked Arm! Follow me, all of you, and you will see how easily I will take vengeance for him on his enemy, Alifanfarón of Trapobana."

With these words he dashed into the midst of the flock of sheep and began to spear them with as much courage and fury as if he were fighting his mortal enemies. The shepherds and herdsmen who came with the flock shouted to him to stop, but seeing that words were of no avail, they unloosed their slings and began to salute his ears with stones as big as one's fist. Don Quixote took no notice of their stones but galloped to and fro, crying out: "Where are you, proud Alifanfarón? Where are you? Come to me, for I am but one knight and wish to try my strength with you, man to man, and take away your life for the wrong you do to the valiant Pentapolín." At that instant a smooth pebble hit him in the side and buried two ribs in his entrails. Finding himself in such a bad way, he thought for certain that he was killed or sorely wounded, and remembering his balsam, he took out his cruse[36] and raised it to his mouth to drink. But before he could swallow what he wanted, another pebble struck him full on the hand, broke the cruse to pieces, carried away with it three or four teeth and grinders out of his mouth, and badly crushed two fingers of his hand. And such was the force of those two blows that the poor knight fell off his horse onto the ground. The shepherds ran up to him, and believing that they had killed him, they collected their flocks in great haste, carried away their dead sheep, which were more than seven, and departed without further inquiry.

All this time Sancho stood on the hillock watching his master's mad escapade and tearing his beard and cursing the unlucky hour and moment when he first met him. But seeing him lying on the ground and the shepherds out of sight, he came down the hill, went up to his master, and found him in a very bad way, although not quite unconscious. So he said to him: "Did I not tell you, sir, to come back, for those you went to attack were not armies, but flocks of sheep?"

---

[36] An earthen pot. "Balsam" is any soothing medicine.

"That rascal of an enchanter, my enemy, can counterfeit and make men vanish. Know, Sancho, that it is a very easy matter for such men to make us see what they please, and this malignant persecutor of mine, envious of the glory that I was to reap in this battle, has changed the squadrons of enemy into flocks of sheep. Now, for my sake, Sancho, do one thing to undeceive yourself and see the truth of what I am telling you. Get up on your ass and follow them softly, and you will see that when they have gone a little distance away, they will return to their original shapes, and ceasing to be sheep, will become grown-up, mature men as when I described them to you at first. But do not go now, for I need your assistance. Come and see how many of my teeth are missing, for I do not think I have a single one left in my mouth."

Sancho went so close that he almost thrust his eyes into his mouth, and it was precisely at the fatal moment when the balsam that had been fretting in Don Quixote's stomach came up to the surface; and with the same violence that a bullet is fired out of a gun, all that he had in his stomach discharged itself upon the beard of the compassionate squire.

"Holy Mary!" cried Sancho. "What has happened to me? The poor sinner must be at death's door, for he's puking blood at the mouth." But reflecting a little, he was soon convinced by the color, smell, and taste that it was not blood, but the balsam that he had seen him drink; and so great was the loathing he felt that his own stomach turned, and he emptied its full cargo upon his master, and both were in a precious pickle. Sancho rushed to his ass to take something out of his saddlebags to clean himself and his master, and when he did not find them, he was on the verge of losing his mind. He cursed himself again and vowed in his heart to leave his master and return to his home, although he would lose his wages for service and his hopes of becoming governor of the promised island.

Don Quixote had now risen, and keeping his left hand to his mouth lest the rest of his teeth fall out, with the other he took hold of Rozinante's bridle (who had not stirred from his master's side, such was his well-bred loyalty) and went over to his squire, who stood leaning against his ass with his cheek upon his hand, looking like the picture of a man lost in thought.

The knight, seeing him in that mood and so full of melancholy, said to him: "Learn, Sancho, that one man is not more than another unless he achieves more than another. All those storms that fall upon us are signs that soon the weather will be fair and that things will go smoothly, for it is not possible for evil or good to last forever. Hence we may infer that as our misfortunes have lasted so long, good fortunes must be near. So, you must not vex yourself about my mischances, for you have no share in them."

"How not?" replied Sancho. "I suppose him they tossed in a blanket yesterday was not my father's son? And the saddlebags that are missing today with all my chattels is someone else's misfortune?"

"What, are the saddlebags missing, Sancho?" asked Don Quixote.

"Yes, they are missing," answered Sancho.

"In that case, we have nothing to eat today," said Don Quixote.

"Very true," said Sancho, "if these fields are barren of the herbs that your worship says he knows all about and with which unfortunate knights-errant like yourself generally supply their wants."

"Nevertheless," answered Don Quixote, "at the present moment I would rather have a quarter-loaf of bread or a cottage loaf and a couple of heads of salted pilchards than all the herbs that Dioscorides describes, though his book be illustrated by Doctor Laguna.[37] But, good Sancho, get up on your ass and follow me, for God, who provides for all, will not desert us, especially being engaged, as we are, in His service. He does not abandon the gnats of the air, nor the worms of the earth, nor the tadpoles of the water, and He is so merciful that He maketh His sun shine on the good and the evil and He causeth the rain to fall upon the just and the unjust."

"Your worship," said Sancho, "were fitter to be a preacher than a knight-errant."

"Knights-errant, Sancho," said Don Quixote, "knew, and ought to know, somewhat of all things, for there have been knights-errant in past ages who were as ready to make a sermon or a speech on the king's highway as though they had taken their degrees at the University of Paris; whence it may be inferred that the lance never blunted the pen, nor the pen the lance."

"Well, may it turn out as you say," answered Sancho. "But let us be gone and endeavor to get a lodging tonight; and I pray to God we may find a place where there are no blankets, blanketeers, specters, or enchanted Moors; and if there are, may the Devil keep the lot of them."

"Ask that of God, my son," said Don Quixote, "and lead me where you please, for on this occasion I will leave the choice of lodging to you. But give me your hand and feel with your finger how many teeth and grinders I have lost on this right side of my upper jaw, for there I feel the pain."

Sancho put in his finger, and feeling about, asked: "How many grinders did your worship have before on this side?"

"Four," answered Don Quixote, "besides the wisdom tooth, all of them whole and sound."

"Mind well, master, what you say," answered Sancho.

"I say four, if not five," said Don Quixote, "for in all my life I have never had a tooth or grinder pulled from my mouth, nor has any fallen out or been destroyed by decay."

"Well then, on this lower side," said Sancho, "you have only two grinders and a half, but on the upper, not even half a one, for it is as smooth as the palm of my hand."

"Woe is me," cried Don Quixote, hearing these sad tidings from his squire. "I would rather they lopped off an arm, provided it were not my sword arm; for you must know, Sancho, that a mouth without grinders is like a mill without grindstone, and a tooth is far more to be prized than a diamond. But all this must be suffered by those who profess the stern order of chivalry. Mount, friend, and lead the way, for I will follow you at what pace you please. . . ."

[*In the succeeding sections, Don Quixote attacks a funeral party, mistakes a cloth mill for a supernatural danger, and deprives a barber of his basin, which he takes to be the "golden helmet of Mambrino," referred to in Ariosto's* Orlando Furioso.]

---

[37] Andrés de Laguna, a famous sixteenth-century physician, translated the work of Dioscorides, a first-century A.D. Greek physician and pharmacologist.

CHAPTER XXII

Of the liberty Don Quixote gave to a number of unfortunates who were being borne, much against their will, where they had no wish to go

Cide Hamete Benengeli, the Arabian and Manchegan author,[38] relates in this most grave, high-sounding, precise, pleasant, and imaginative history that after the conversation between the famous Don Quixote of La Mancha and Sancho Panza, his squire, which is reported at the end of the twenty-first chapter, Don Quixote raised his eyes and saw coming, along the road he was taking, about a dozen men on foot strung together like beads on a great iron chain. The chain was fastened around their necks and they were handcuffed. With them were two men on horseback, and two others followed on foot. The horsemen had firelocks, and those on foot pikes and swords.

As soon as Sancho Panza saw them he said: "Here's a chain of galley slaves, men forced by the king, going to serve in the galleys."

"How! Men forced?" answered Don Quixote. "Is it possible that the king forces anybody?"

"I don't say that," answered Sancho, "but they are people condemned for their offenses to serve the king in the galleys."

"Then it is a fact," replied Don Quixote, "however you put it, that these men are being taken to their destination by force and not by their own free will."

"That is so," said Sancho.

"Then," said his master, "here is the opportunity for me to carry out my duty: to redress grievances and give help to the poor and the afflicted."

"I beg you, sir," said Sancho, "to consider that justice, which is the king himself, does no violence to these men, but only punishes those who have committed crime."

By this time the chain gang came up, and Don Quixote in very courteous words asked those in charge to be good enough to inform him why they conducted people away in that manner. One of the guardians on horseback replied that they were slaves condemned by His Majesty to the galleys and that there was no more to be said, nor ought Don Quixote to desire any further information.

"Nevertheless," answered Don Quixote, "I would like to hear from each one of them individually the cause of his disgrace." To this the guardian on horseback answered: "Though we have here the register of the crimes of all these unlucky fellows, this is no time to produce and read them. Draw near, sir, and ask it from themselves. No doubt they'll tell you their tales, for men of their sort take delight in boasting of their rascalities."

With this leave, which Don Quixote would have taken for himself if they had not given it, he went up to the gang and asked the first man for what

---

[38] Cide Hamete Benengeli is the imaginary author Cervantes has earlier introduced as the writer of an old manuscript, in Arabic, containing the history of Don Quixote. This device allows the narrator to step in and out of the story, commenting on the presentation as well as on the content of the narrative.

crimes he found himself in such straits. The man answered that it was for being in love.

"For that and no more?" cried Don Quixote. "If men are sent to the galleys for being in love, I should have been pulling an oar there long ago."

"My love was not of the kind your worship imagines," replied the galley slave. "Mine was that I loved too much a basket of fine linen, which I embraced so lovingly that if the law had not taken it from me by violence, I should not of my own free will have forsaken it even to this present day. I was caught in the act, so there was no need for torture. The case was a short one. They gave my shoulders a hundred lashes and in addition three years' hard labor in the *gurapas,* and that's an end of it."

"What are *gurapas?*" said Don Quixote.

"*Gurapas* are galleys," answered the convict, who was a young man of about twenty-four, born, as he said, at Piedrahita.

Don Quixote put the same question to the second, who returned no answer, for he seemed too downcast and melancholy to speak. But the first one spoke for him and said: "Sir, this gentleman goes for being a canary bird—I mean a musician or singer."

"Is it possible," said Don Quixote, "that musicians and singers are sent to galleys?"

"I should say so, sir," replied the galley slave. "There's nothing worse than to sing under torture."

"Well," said Don Quixote, "I, on the contrary, have heard it said: 'Who sings in grief, procures relief.'"

"Down here it's the exact opposite," said the slave, "for he who sings once, weeps the rest of his life."

"I do not understand it," said Don Quixote. One of the guards then said to him: "You know, sir, among these unsanctified folk 'to sing under torture' means to confess on the rack. They put this poor sinner to the torture, and he confessed his crime of being a rustler, which means that he was a cattle thief; and because he confessed, he was condemned to the galleys for six years, with the addition of two hundred lashes that he carries on his shoulders. He's always sad and pensive, for the other thieves bully, abuse, and despise him because he confessed and hadn't the courage to say a couple of *nos.* For as they say, 'A *nay* has as many letters as a *yea,*' and it is good luck for a criminal when there are no witnesses and proofs and his fate depends on his own tongue. In my opinion there's much truth in that."

"I think so also," said Don Quixote, and he passed on to where the third slave stood, and put to him the same question as to the others. The man replied quickly and coolly, saying: "I'm off to their ladyship the galleys because I wanted ten ducats."

"I will give you twenty with all my heart to free you from that misfortune," said Don Quixote.

"That," replied the slave, "would be like one who has money in the middle of the sea and yet is perishing of hunger because he has nowhere to buy what he needs. I say this because, if I'd had the twenty ducats your worship offers me at the right time, I would have greased the lawyer's palm with them and so sharpened my advocate's wit that I would now be strolling about in the marketplace at Toledo instead of being trailed along here like a greyhound. But God is great; patience is enough."

Don Quixote passed on to the fourth, who was a man of venerable appearance, with a white beard reaching below his chest. No sooner was he asked the reason for his being there than he began to weep and would not answer a word; but the fifth convict lent him a tongue and said: "This honest gentleman is off for four years to the galleys after having appeared in the usual procession dressed in full pomp and mounted."[39]

"That means, I suppose," said Sancho, "carried to shame in view of the whole people."

"You have said it," answered the galley slave, "and the offense for which they gave him this punishment was for having been an ear broker, and a body broker too. What I mean to say is that this gentleman goes for pimping and for fancying himself as a bit of a wizard."

"If it had been merely for pimping," said Don Quixote, "he certainly did not deserve to go rowing in the galleys, but rather to command them and be their captain. For the profession of pimp is no ordinary office, but one requiring wisdom and most necessary in any well-governed state. None but wellborn persons should practice it. In fact, it should have its overseers and inspectors, as there are of other offices, limited to a certain appointed number, like exchange brokers.[40] If this were done, many evils would be prevented, which now take place because this profession is practiced only by foolish and ignorant persons such as silly women, page boys, and mountebanks of few years' standing and less experience, who, in moments of difficulty, when the utmost skill is needed, allow the tidbit to freeze between their fingers and their mouth and scarcely know which is their right hand. I should like to go on and give reasons why it is right to make special choice of those who have to fill such an important office in the state, but this is not the place to do it. Some day I will tell my views to those who may provide a remedy; at present I only wish to say that the sorrow I felt at seeing your gray hairs and venerable countenance in so much distress for pimping has entirely vanished when I learn that you are a wizard; though I know well that there are no sorceries in the world that can affect and force the will, as some simple people imagine. Our will is free and no herb nor charm can compel it. What such gullible wenches and lying rascals do is to mix some potion or poison that drives men crazy, claiming that it has the power to rouse love; whereas I maintain that it is impossible to force a man's will."

"That is true, sir," said the worthy old man; "and indeed I was not guilty of witchcraft; as for being a pimp, I couldn't deny it, but I never thought there was any harm in it, for all my intention was that the whole world should enjoy themselves and live together in peace and quiet without quarrels or troubles. But my good intentions could not save me from going to a place from which I have no hope of return, laden as I am with years and so worried with a bladder trouble that does not give me a moment's rest." He now began to weep as before, and Sancho felt so sorry for him that he drew from his purse a four-real piece and gave it to him as alms.

[39] Those condemned for witchcraft or wizardry were dealt with by the Holy Office. They were mounted on mules with face to the tail and led in procession through the streets accompanied by a noisy crowd. They wore a *coroza* or paper miter, carried a lighted candle, and were flogged through the streets.

[40] Don Quixote's ironic praise of pimps echoes a stock joke in sixteenth-century Spanish literature.

Don Quixote passed on and asked another what his offense was. He answered with much more pleasantness than the former: "I am here because I played a little too much of a game with two cousins of mine and with two other sisters who were not mine. In short, I carried the game so far with them all that the result of it was the increasing of my kindred so intricately that no devil could make it out. It was all proved against me; I hadn't a friend, and I hadn't a groat; my neck was in the utmost danger; they gave me six years in the galleys; I concurred: it's fair punishment for my guilt; I'm young; if only my life lasts, all will turn out for the best. If you, sir, have anything about you to relieve us poor devils, God will repay you in Heaven and we will have care on earth to ask God in our daily prayers to give you as long and prosperous a life and health as your kind presence deserves."

This convict was dressed in a student's habit, and one of the guards told Don Quixote that he was a great talker and a fine Latin scholar.

Behind all these came a man about thirty years of age, of very comely looks, except that he had a slight squint. He was differently tied from the rest, for he wore a chain to his leg so long that it wound around his whole body. He had, besides, around his neck two iron rings, one of which was fastened to the chain, and the other, called a keep friend or friend's foot, had two irons that came down from it to his waist, at the ends of which were fixed two manacles. These held his hands locked with a great padlock so that he could neither put his hands to his mouth nor bend down his head to his hands.

Don Quixote asked why this man was loaded with more fetters than the rest. The guard answered that it was because he had committed more crimes than all the rest put together and that he was such a desperate rascal that, though they carried him fettered in that way, they were not sure of him but feared that he might give them the slip.

"What crimes did he commit," said Don Quixote, "that have deserved no greater penalty than being sent to the galleys?"

"He is going for ten years," said the guard, "which is the same as civil death. I need only tell you that this man is the famous Ginés de Pasamonte, alias Ginesillo de Parapilla."

"Master commissary," said the galley slave, "don't go so fast and don't let us start defining names and surnames. Ginés is my name, not Ginesillo, and Pasamonte is my family name, not Parapilla as you say. Let every man first look to himself and he'll do a good deal."

"Keep a civil tongue, mister out-and-out robber," answered the commissary. "Otherwise we'll shut you up, whether you like it or not."

"I know," answered the galley slave, "that man goes as God pleases; but one day someone will know whether my name is Ginesillo de Parapilla or not."

"Don't they call you that, you lying trickster?"

"They do," answered Ginés, "but I'll make them stop calling me by that name or I'll shear them where I don't care to mention in company. And now, sir, if you have something to give us, hand it out and good-bye, for you tire us with your inquiries about other men's lives. If you want to know mine, I am Ginés de Pasamonte, whose life has been written by these very fingers of mine."

"He speaks the truth," said the commissary. "He himself has written his own history—as good a one as you could wish, and he pawned the book in jail for two hundred reals."

"Aye, and I intend to redeem it," said Ginés, "even if it stood at two hundred ducats."

"Is it good?" said Don Quixote.

"It is so good," answered Ginés, "that it means trouble for *Lazarillo de Tormes*[41] and for all that has been written or ever shall be written in that style. I assure you it deals with truths and truths so attractive and entertaining that no fiction could compare with them."

"What is the title of the book?" asked Don Quixote.

"*The Life of Ginés de Pasamonte*," answered Ginés himself.

"Is it finished yet?" asked Don Quixote.

"How can it be finished," answered Ginés, "when my life isn't finished yet? What is written tells everything from my birth down to this last time I was packed off to the galleys."

"Then you have been there before?" said Don Quixote.

"To serve God and the king," answered Ginés; "on the last occasion I was there for four years, and I know already the taste of hard tack and the lash. I'm not too sorry to return there, for I'll have an opportunity to finish my book. I've still many things to say, and in the galleys of Spain there's more than enough leisure, though I don't need much for what I have to write because I know it by heart."

"You seem to be a clever fellow," said Don Quixote.

"Aye. And an unlucky one," replied Ginés, "for bad luck always pursues genius."

"It pursues knaves," interrupted the commissary.

"I've already told you, sir commissary," answered Pasamonte, "not to go so fast. The lords of the land didn't give you that rod to mistreat us but to guide us and take us where His Majesty has ordered. If not, by Heaven— But enough! Perhaps one day the dirty work that was done in the inn may come out in the wash; in the meantime mum's the word, and let every man live well and speak better. Now let us move on, for we've had too much of this diversion."

The commissary raised his rod to strike Pasamonte in answer to his threats, but Don Quixote intervened, asking him not to ill-treat the convict since it was only fair that one who had his hands so tied should be somewhat free with his tongue. Then, turning toward the gang, he said: "I have gathered from all you have said, dearest brethren, that although they punish you for your faults, yet the pains you suffer do not please you, and that you go to them with ill will and against your inclination. I realize, moreover, that perhaps it was the lack of courage of one fellow on the rack, the want of money of another, the want of friends of a third, and finally the biased sentence of the judge that have been the cause of your not receiving the justice to which you were entitled. Now all this prompts and even compels me to perform on your behalf the task for which I was sent into the world, and for which I became a knight-errant, and to which end I vowed to succor the needy and help those who are oppressed by the powerful. But as it is prudent not to do by evil means what can be done by fair, I wish to

[41] An anonymous "rogue novel" published in 1554.

entreat these gentlemen, your guardians and the commissary, to be kind enough to loose you and let you go in peace, for there will be plenty of men to serve the king on worthier occasions; it seems to me a harsh thing to make slaves of those whom God and nature made free. What is more, gentlemen of the guard," added Don Quixote, "these unfortunate creatures have done nothing against you yourselves. Let each man be answerable for his own sins; there is a God in Heaven who does not fail to punish the wicked nor to reward the good. It is not right that honest men should be executioners of others when they have nothing to do with the case. I ask this boon of you in a peaceable and quiet manner, and if you grant it, I shall give you my thanks. If, on the other hand, you will not grant it willingly, then shall this lance and sword of mine, wielded by my invincible arm, force you to do my bidding."

"This is a pleasant jest," answered the commissary. "You have ended your ranting with a fine joke. Do you want us to hand over to you those the king has imprisoned, as if we had the authority to let them go or you to order us to do it? Go your way, good sir, and a pleasant journey. Settle the basin straight on your pate, and don't go looking for a cat with three legs."[42]

"You are a cat, a rat, and a knave," answered Don Quixote. Without another word he ran at him so fiercely that, not giving him time to defend himself, he struck him to the ground badly wounded by his lance. It was lucky for the knight that this was the one who carried the firelock. The guards were astounded at this unexpected event. But they recovered themselves, and the horsemen drew their swords, the footmen clutched their pikes, and all of them threw themselves upon Don Quixote, who quietly waited for their attack. No doubt he would have been in great danger if the slaves, seeing a chance of liberty, had not broken the chain by which they were tied together. The confusion was such that the guards, first trying to prevent the galley slaves from getting loose, then defending themselves against Don Quixote, who attacked them, did nothing to any purpose. Sancho, for his part, helped to release Ginés de Pasamonte, who was the first that leaped free and unfettered upon the plain. The latter then set upon the fallen commissary and relieved him of his sword and firelock, with which, aiming first at one and then at another, although he never fired it, he cleared the plain of guards, for they all fled no less from Pasamonte's firelock than from the showers of stones that the liberated slaves flung at them.

Sancho was much worried by all that had happened, for he had a shrewd suspicion that the guards who had fled would report the matter to the Holy Brotherhood,[43] who would raise the alarm and sally out in pursuit of the criminals, and he said so to his master, begging him to leave that place at once and hide themselves in the neighboring sierra.

"That is all very well," answered Don Quixote, "but I know what we should do now." Then he called all the galley slaves, who were now running hither and thither in a riotous mood and had stripped the commissary to the skin, and when they had gathered around him in a circle, he addressed

---

[42] A proverbial expression that means "Don't go looking for the impossible."
[43] A tribunal organized to punish highway robbers.

them as follows: "It is the duty of well-bred people to be grateful for benefits received, and ingratitude is one of the most hateful sins in the eyes of
God. I say this, sirs, because you know what favor you have received from
me, and the only return I wish and demand is that you all go from here,
laden with the chains from which I have just freed your necks, to the city of
El Toboso. There you are to present yourselves before Lady Dulcinea of El
Toboso and tell her that her Knight of the Rueful Figure sent you there to
commend his service to her. You are to tell her, point by point, the details
of this famous adventure, and when you have done this, you may then go
whichever way you please and good luck be with you."

Ginés de Pasamonte answered for all the rest, saying: "That which you
demand, sir, is impossible to perform, because we must not travel the roads
together, but go alone and separate so that we may not be found by the
men of the Holy Brotherhood, who will be sure to come out to search for
us. What you can do, and ought to do, is to change this service and duty to
the Lady Dulcinea of El Toboso into a certain number of Ave Marias and
credos that we shall say for your worship's intention. And this we may do by
night or by day, resting or on the run, at peace or at work; but if you think
that we are now going to return to the fleshpots of Egypt—to our chains, I
mean—and start off on the road to El Toboso, you might as well imagine
that it's already nighttime, whereas it is not yet ten o'clock in the morning.
To expect this from us is like expecting pears off an elm tree."

"I vow then," said Don Quixote in a rage, "sir whoreson, Don Ginesillo
de Parapilla, or whatever you call yourself, that you will go alone, with your
tail between your legs and the whole length of chain on your back."

Pasamonte, who was a truculent fellow (he now understood that Don
Quixote was not very sane, seeing the foolish thing he had done by setting
them free), would not stand being abused in this manner; so he winked at
his companions, and they from a distance began to rain a shower of stones
on Don Quixote, whose buckler gave him scant cover; and poor Rozinante
paid no more attention to the spur than if his flanks were made of bronze.
Sancho took cover behind his ass and thus sheltered himself against the
squall of stones that burst about them. Don Quixote was less able to shield
himself against the countless stones that hit him with such force that at last
they stretched him on the ground. Scarcely had he fallen when the student
Ginés jumped upon him, and taking the basin from his head, gave him
three or four blows with it on the shoulders and then struck it repeatedly
on the ground, almost breaking it into pieces. They then stripped him of a
tunic he wore over his armor, and they would have seized his hose too had
they not been hindered by his greaves.[44] They took Sancho's cloak, leaving
him in his underclothes, and after dividing among themselves the rest of
the spoils, each went his own way, with more thought of escaping the Holy
Brotherhood than of dragging their chains to Lady Dulcinea of El Toboso.

All that remained were the ass, Rozinante, Sancho, and Don Quixote.
The ass pensively hanging his head, shaking his ears every now and then as
if he thought the storm of stones was not yet over; Rozinante prostrate
lying beside his master on the ground; Sancho in his underclothes,

---

[44] Armor for the lower legs.

trembling at the thought of the Holy Brotherhood; and Don Quixote, in the dumps at finding himself so ill-treated by those for whom he had done so much.

[Don Quixote decides to do penance in the wilderness of the Sierra Morena as other knights-errant do who have been absent too long from their mistresses. He sends Sancho to deliver a letter to Dulcinea. Quixote then meets a young man, Cardenio (whom Quixote calls the "Knight of the Wood"), who has lost his love to a false friend, Ferdinand. Meanwhile Sancho meets the curate and the barber, and they persuade him to join in a strategem to get Don Quixote to return to his village. They and Cardenio meet Dorothea, a woman deceived and abandoned by Cardenio's betrayer Ferdinand; she agrees to help them deceive the knight by playing the role of a princess, "Micomicona." They return to Quixote, and charmed by "Micomicona," he agrees to help her regain her "kingdom." The party stops at an inn on the way back to the village—the same inn where Sancho was tossed in a blanket. Here the curate reads them a manuscript called A Tale of Ill-Advised Curiosity, *in which a husband comes to grief through testing his wife's fidelity. The story raises some of the same questions of reality and illusion explored in the novel itself. At the inn, Cardenio is reunited with his Lucinda, and Ferdinand claims Dorothea as his true wife. A returned captive of the Turks arrives at the inn and tells the party of his experiences and his escape (experiences reminiscent of Cervantes' own). Other guests arrive, including a judge with a beautiful young daughter who is pursued by a lovesick boy posing as a muleteer. After the ugly servant woman Maritornes plays a cruel trick on Quixote, the curate and the barber place him in a barred oxcart to take him back to his village. On the journey, Sancho manages to free his master from the cart. Quixote meets a goatherd and offers to rescue his lover from a nunnery; the goatherd, however, becomes angry and beats Quixote.]*

CHAPTER LII

Of the quarrel that Don Quixote had with the goatherd, with the rare adventure of the disciplinants, which he successfully achieved with the sweat of his brow

. . . . It so happened that year that the clouds had denied the earth their moisture; so, throughout the valleys of that region, processions, public prayers, and penances were ordered to beseech Heaven to open the flood gates of its mercy and send them rain. It was for this purpose, therefore, that the people of a neighboring village were coming in procession to a holy shrine that stood on a hill at the edge of the valley. Don Quixote, as soon as he saw the strange attire of the disciplinants, did not pause to recall the many occasions on which he had seen a similar sight before but immediately imagined that it was some kind of adventure that was reserved for him alone as knight-errant. He was all the more confirmed in his opinion by mistaking an image that they carried all swathed in mourning for some noble lady whom those ruffians and unmannerly churls were carrying away against her will. No sooner did this thought flash through his mind than he rushed over to Rozinante, who was grazing nearby, and taking off the bridle and buckler that hung from the pommel of the saddle, he bridled him in an instant. Then, asking Sancho for his sword, he mounted Rozinante, and bracing his buckler, he cried in a loud voice to all those present: "Now, valiant company, ye shall see how necessary it is that there be in the world knights who profess the order of knight-errantry; now, I say, shall ye see, in the restoration of that captive lady to liberty, whether knights-errant ought to be valued!"

Saying this, he clapped his heels to Rozinante (for spurs he had none), and at a half gallop (for nowhere in all this truthful history can one read that Rozinante ever went at full speed) he advanced to encounter the disciplinants, though the curate and the barber tried to stop him. But all their efforts were in vain, nor could he be stopped by the screams of Sancho, who shouted: "Master, where are you going? What devils in your heart are driving you on to attack our Catholic faith? Mind, sir! Bad 'cess to it! That is a procession of disciplinants and the lady they're carrying on the bier is the most blessed image of the Immaculate Virgin. Take heed, sir what you're doing; this time I can assure you that it's not what you think."

Sancho wasted his breath, for his master was so set upon encountering the sheeted ones and upon freeing the lady in black that he heard not a word, and even if he had, he would not have turned back though the king himself had commanded him. When he reached the procession, he stopped Rozinante, who already wanted to rest a little, and in a hoarse, angry voice he cried out: "You there, who cover up your faces probably because you are evil, halt and pay heed to my words!"

The first to halt were those who were carrying the image. Then, one of the four priests who chanted the litanies, noticing the strange appearance of Don Quixote, the leanness of Rozinante, and other ludicrous details, answered him, saying: "Brother, if you have anything to say, say it quickly, for these brethren are scourging their flesh, and we cannot, nor is it right that we should, stop to listen to anything that may not be said in two words."

"I will say it in one," replied Don Quixote. "You must instantly free that beauteous lady whose tears and sad appearance show clearly that you are bearing her away against her will and that you have done her some grievous wrong. But I, who came into the world to redress such injuries, will not allow you to move one single step forward till you have restored to her the liberty she desires and deserves."

From these words all who heard them concluded that Don Quixote must be some madman, and they began to laugh heartily. But their laughter only served to add gunpowder to the knight's fury, for without another word he drew his sword and attacked the litter. One of those who carried it, leaving the burden to his comrades, stepped forward to encounter Don Quixote, brandishing a forked pole on which they propped the litter while resting, and with it he parried the heavy stroke that the knight aimed at him. The force of the stroke snapped the pole in two, but with the remaining stump that was left in his hand he dealt the knight such a thwack on the shoulder of his sword-arm that his buckler was unable to shield him against the rustic onslaught, and down came poor Don Quixote to the ground in a bad way. Sancho, who came panting after him, seeing him fall, called out to his assailant not to strike him again, for he was a poor enchanted knight who had done nobody any harm all his life. The peasant stopped, not, however, on account of Sancho's appeal, but because he saw that Don Quixote stirred neither hand nor foot. And, believing that he had killed him, he hastily tucked up his habit to his girdle and set off, racing like a deer across the country.

By that time everyone in Don Quixote's company had reached where he lay, but when the men in the procession saw them running in their direction and with them troopers of the Holy Brotherhood with their crossbows, they feared some trouble. So, they clustered in a circle about the image: the penitents lifted their hoods and grasped their lashes; the priests brandished their tapers, and all waited for the attack with the firm resolve to defend themselves, and if they could, to take the offensive against their aggressors. But Fortune arranged matters better than they expected, for Sancho did nothing but cast himself upon the body of his master, making over him the most sorrowful and drollest lament in the world, for he truly believed that Don Quixote was dead. Our curate was recognized by one of the priests in the procession, and this calmed the apprehension of both sides. Our curate in a few words told the second curate of Don Quixote's condition; then, he and the whole crowd of disciplinants went to see whether or not the poor knight was dead, and heard Sancho Panza proclaim with tears in his eyes: "O flower of chivalry, one single blow of a cudgel has finished the course of your well-spent years! O glory of your race, honor and credit to all La Mancha, and even to the whole world, which, now that you are gone, will be overrun with evildoers, who will no longer fear punishment for their iniquities! O liberal above all the Alexanders, since for a mere eight months' service you have given me the best island that the sea surrounds! O humble to the haughty and arrogant to the humble! Resister of perils, sufferer of affronts, lover without cause, imitator of the good, scourge of the wicked, enemy of the base! In a word, knight-errant, which is the highest thing anyone could say!"

At the cries and groans of Sancho, Don Quixote revived, and the first words he said were: "He who lives absent from thee, sweet Dulcinea, endures far greater sufferings than these. Help me, friend Sancho, to lift myself into the enchanted cart, for I am no longer in a condition to press the saddle of Rozinante; this shoulder of mine is broken to pieces."

"That I'll do with all my heart, dear master," replied Sancho, "and let us go back to our village in the company of these gentlemen, and there we will make schemes for another sally that may be more profitable to us."

"You speak well, Sancho," answered the knight. "It is prudent for us to wait until the evil influence of the stars that now reigns passes away."

The canon, the curate, and the barber approved this resolution, and after they had enjoyed Sancho Panza's fooleries to the full, they placed Don Quixote on the cart as before. The procession resumed its former order and went on its way. The goatherd took his leave of them all, and as the troopers refused to go any further, the curate paid them what he owed them. The canon then begged the curate to let him know what might happen to Don Quixote (whether he recovered from his madness or remained in it), and with this he took his leave. Thus they all parted and went their several ways.

The party now consisted only of the curate, the barber, Don Quixote, Sancho, and good Rozinante, who bore all the ups and downs as patiently as his master. The wagoner yoked his oxen, and having laid Don Quixote on a bundle of hay, plodded his way at his usual calm, deliberate pace, following the directions of the curate; and at the end of six days they reached Don Quixote's village. They made their entrance at noon, and as it happened to be Sunday, all the people were in the marketplace when the wagon passed through. Everyone rushed to see who was in it, and when they recognized their townsman, they were amazed. A boy ran off at full speed to give the news to his housekeeper and his niece that their master and uncle was coming home lean and yellow, stretched out on a bundle of hay in an oxcart. It was a pathetic thing to hear the cries of the two ladies, the blows they gave themselves, the execrations they uttered afresh against the books of chivalry, all of which were repeated when they saw Don Quixote enter the door of his house.

As soon as she received news of Don Quixote's arrival, Sancho Panza's wife ran there, and as soon as she saw Sancho, her first inquiry was whether the ass had come home in good condition. Sancho replied that he was in better health than his master.

"Thanks be to God," said she, "for this great favor. Now tell me, husband, what good have you got from your squireship? What petticoat have you brought for me? What dainty shoes for your children?"

"I've brought you nothing of the kind, dear wife," said Sancho, "But I've other things of more consequence."

"I'm glad to hear so," answered the wife. "Show me those things of more consequence. I'm dying to see them to gladden my heart, for I've been mournful and down in the mouth all those ages you've been away."

"I'll show them to you at home, wife," said Sancho. "For the present, hold your soul in patience. Please God we may sally out another time in search of adventures and you'll soon see me count or governor of an island, and not one of those around here, but the finest that can be found."

"May the Lord be pleased to grant it, husband, for we're in sore need of it. Tell me now; what's all this about islands? I don't catch your meaning."

"Honey is not for an ass's mouth," answered Sancho. "You'll see in good time, wife, aye, and you'll be all agape at hearing yourself called ladyship by all your vassals."

"What are you prating about ladyships, islands, and vassals?" cried Juana Panza, for that was the name of Sancho's wife, not because they were relatives, but because in La Mancha it is customary for wives to take their husbands' last name.

"Don't fret yourself, Juana, and be in such a hurry to know everything at once; it's enough for you to know that I'm telling the truth, so mum's the word; but I can tell you one thing by the way, namely, that there's nothing in this world so pleasant as for an honest man to be squire to a knight-errant on the prowl for adventures. It's true that most of those we encountered were not as comfortable as a body would wish, for out of a hundred adventures, ninety-nine usually turned out cross and crooked. I know by experience, for from some I came off blanketed and from others bruised and battered, but when all's said and done, it's a fine thing to be gadding about spying for chances, crossing mountains, exploring woods, climbing rocks, visiting castles, lodging in inns at our own sweet will, with devil a maravedi to pay."

While this conversation was passing between Sancho Panza and Juana

Panza, his wife, Don Quixote's housekeeper and niece received the knight, undressed him, and put him into his old bed. He looked at them with squinting eyes, for he could not make out where he was. The curate told the niece to take very good care of her uncle and to be very watchful lest he should make another sally, telling her the trouble it had cost to get him home. The two women began their lamentations once more, again execrating the books of chivalry and imploring Heaven to plunge the authors of so many lies and absurdities into the bottomless abyss. In fact, they were at their wits' end, for they were afraid they might lose their master and uncle the moment he felt a little better. And events turned out as they feared.

But though the author of this history has eagerly and diligently inquired after Don Quixote's exploits on his third sally, he has not been able to discover any account of them, at least from any authentic documents. Only tradition has preserved in the memory of La Mancha that the third time Don Quixote left his home he went to Saragossa, where he took part in some famous jousts in that city, and that he had adventures there worthy of his valor and of his sound intelligence. Nor would our author have been able to discover any details of his death, nor would he even have heard of it, if Fortune had not thrown in his path an aged physician who had in his possession a leaden box that he said he had discovered among the ruined foundations of an ancient hermitage that was being rebuilt. In this box he had found certain parchments written in the Gothic script, but in Castilian verse, which contained many of his exploits and emphasized the beauty of Dulcinea of El Toboso, the shape of Rozinante, the fidelity of Sancho Panza, and the burial of Don Quixote himself, with various epitaphs and eulogies on his life and character. Such as could be deciphered and interpreted the trustworthy author of this original and matchless history has set down here, and he asks no recompense from his readers for the immense pains it has cost him to ransack all the archives of La Mancha to drag it into light. All he asks is that they should give it as much credit as sensible men are wont to give to the books of chivalry, which are held in such high esteem in the world. With this he will reckon himself well paid and satisfied, and he will be encouraged to go in search of other histories, perhaps less truthful than this one, but at least as inventive and entertaining. . . .

from PART II

CHAPTER I

What passed between the curate, the barber, and Don Quixote regarding the knight's infirmity

Cide Hamete Benengeli in the second part of this history concerning Don Quixote's third sally relates that the curate and the barber remained nearly a month without seeing him, in order not to revive past events and bring them back to his memory. But this did not prevent them from visiting his niece and his housekeeper, whom they charged to be careful to treat him

well and give him to eat such food as was comforting and good for heart
and brain, for they had every reason to believe that all his misfortunes
proceeded from that quarter. The two women declared that they were
doing so and that they would continue to lavish care and affection on their
master, for they had noticed that he gave signs at times of being in his right
mind. This news gave the curate and the barber great satisfaction, for it
seemed to prove that they had done right in bringing him back enchanted
in the ox wagon, as has been related in the last chapter of the first part of
this great and accurate history. So, they resolved to visit him and test his
recovery, though they thought that was scarcely possible, and they agreed
not to touch in any way on knight-errantry, so as not to run the risk of
ripping open wounds that were still so tender.

They paid him a visit at last and found him sitting up in his bed, dressed
in a green-baize jacket and a red Toledo cap and so lean and shriveled that
he looked as if he had been turned into a mummy. He welcomed them
cordially and to their questions about his health he replied intelligently in
very well-chosen words. In the course of conversation they discoursed on
so-called affairs of state and systems of government, correcting this abuse
and condemning that, reforming one practice and abolishing another, each
one of the three setting himself up as a new lawgiver, a modern Lycurgus,
or a brand-new Solon.[1] And to such a degree did they remodel the state
that they might as well have cast it into a furnace and forged a new one.
And Don Quixote spoke with such good sense on all the subjects they
treated that the two examiners believed, without shadow of doubt, that he
was quite recovered and in full possession of his wits. The niece and the
housekeeper were present at the conversation and could not find adequate
words to thank God when they saw that their master was so clear in his
mind. The curate, however, changed his original plan, which was not to
touch on the subject of chivalry, and resolved to test Don Quixote's recovery thoroughly to see whether it was genuine or not; so, changing from one
subject to another, he came at last to talk of some news that had come from
the capital. Among other things he said that they had it for certain that the
Turk was descending with a powerful fleet, but no one knew what his
designs were or where the mighty storm would burst. And owing to this
fear, which almost every year rouses men to arms, all Christendom was on
the alert, and His Majesty had made provision for the defense of the coast
of Naples, Sicily, and island of Malta.

"His Majesty has acted like a most prudent warrior," replied Don Quixote, "in fortifying his realms in time, so that the enemy may not find him
unprepared; but if he would take my advice, I would counsel him to take
one precaution of which His Majesty is not aware at the present moment."

No sooner did the curate hear this than he said to himself: "God protect
you, my poor Don Quixote, for it looks to me as if you are tumbling
from the pinnacle of your madness into the deep abyss of your simplemindedness."

But the barber, who already had the same suspicions as the curate,
asked Don Quixote what kind of measures he thought they should adopt,

---

[1] The legendary Lycurgus (seventh century B.C.) reformed the Spartan constitution; Solon
reformed the Athenian government in 594 B.C.

for perhaps they might be added to the long list of unpractical projects usually offered to princes.

"Mine, Mr. Scrapebeard," said Don Quixote, "are not unpractical but highly practical."

"No harm meant," replied the barber, "but experience has shown that all or most of the projects presented to His Majesty are either impossible, absurd, or damaging to the king and the country."

"But mine," rejoined Don Quixote, "is neither impossible nor ridiculous, but the easiest, the justest, the readiest, and the simplest that could enter the mind of any thinking man."

"Your worship is slow in telling us about it, Don Quixote," said the curate.

"I do not wish to tell it now," said Don Quixote, "and have it reach by tomorrow morning the ears of the lords of the Council, and for someone else to get the thanks and the reward for my pains."

"As for me," said the barber, "I give my word here and before God that I'll not repeat what you say to king, or rook, or earthly man,[2] an oath I learned from the ballad of the priest, who in the prologue warns the king against the thief who had robbed him of a hundred doubloons and his ambling mule."

"I do not know the story," said Don Quixote, "but I know that the oath is a good one, because I believe that the barber is an honest man."

"Even if he were not," said the curate, "I will go bail for him and vouch that he'll speak as much as a dumb man, under pain of any penalty imposed by the court."

"And who will go bail for your reverence?" said Don Quixote.

"My profession," replied the curate, "which is to keep secrets."

"Bless my heart!" exclaimed Don Quixote. "What else has His Majesty to do but to order by public crier all the knights-errant who are wandering about Spain to assemble at the capital on a certain day, and even if no more than half a dozen came, might there not be one among them who alone would be strong enough to annihilate the whole army of the Turk? Let your worships give me your attention and follow me. Is it, mark you, an unheard-of exploit for a single knight-errant to cut to bits an army of two hundred thousand men as if all together had but one throat or were made of almond paste? Now tell me, how many histories are there full of such marvels? If there were living today—to my misfortune, though I shall not say to anyone else's—the famous Don Belianís or any one of those of the innumerable offspring of Amadis of Gaul![3] If any of them were living today and were to face the Turk, I would not be in the latter's shoes. But God will take care of his people and will provide someone who, if not as resolute as the knights-errant of old, will at least not be behind them in spirit. God understands me, and I say no more."

"Alas!" cried the niece, at this point. "Strike me dead if my master doesn't want to turn knight-errant again."

To which Don Quixote replied: "A knight-errant I shall die, and let the

---

[2] A metaphor from chess; kings and rooks are chess pieces.

[3] Heroes of Fernández' *Don Belianio of Greece* (1547) and the anonymous Spanish romance *Amadis of Gaul* (thirteenth or fourteenth century).

Turk make his descent or ascent whenever he will and with whatever power he can. I say once more that God understands, and I say no more."

At this the barber chimed in: "Allow me, your worships, to tell you a short tale about something that took place at Seville, for as it fits this situation like a glove, I'm dying to tell it."

Don Quixote and the curate gave him leave, and the others pricked up their ears; so, the barber began as follows: "In the madhouse at Seville was a certain man whose relations had put him there because he had lost his wits. He had graduated in common law at Osuna, but even if it had been at Salamanca, many think he would have been just as mad. This graduate, at the end of some years of confinement, convinced himself that he was sane and in his right mind, and in this frame of mind he wrote to the archbishop, imploring him earnestly and in convincing terms to order his release from the misery in which he lived, for his relatives kept him there in order to enjoy his share of the estate, and in spite of the clearest evidence, they wished to have him stay mad till his death. The archbishop, impressed by his many sensible and well-reasoned letters, ordered one of his chaplains to ascertain from the governor of the madhouse whether what the licentiate wrote was true. He asked him to speak to the madman, and if he seemed to be in his senses, to set him at liberty. The chaplain did so, and the governor informed him that the man was still mad, and that though he often talked like a person of great intelligence, in the end he would break out into wild tirades as crazy and exaggerated as his previous talk had been sensible, as he would find out by speaking to him. The chaplain wished to do so, and when he visited the madman, he talked with him for an hour and more, and in all that time he never said a queer or crazy word but spoke so sensibly that the chaplain was obliged to believe him sane. Among other things that the madman said was that the governor had an edge against him because he did not want to lose the bribes his relations paid him for declaring that he was still mad, though with lucid intervals. The greatest obstacle he had to deal with in his misfortunes, he said, was his great wealth, for in order to enjoy it his enemies misjudged him and cast doubts upon the mercy that Our Lord had done him by turning him from a beast into a man. In short, he spoke so convincingly as to throw suspicion on the governor and to make his relatives appear covetous and inhuman and himself so sane that the chaplain resolved to take him away with him, so that the archbishop might see him and verify the truth for himself. In all good faith, then, the worthy chaplain begged the governor to give orders for the licentiate to be given back the clothes in which he had arrived. But the governor once more bade him mind what he was doing, for the licentiate undoubtedly was still mad. However, the governor's warning could not prevail upon the chaplain to leave the madman behind; so, seeing that the archbishop had given the order, the governor obeyed, and the madman was given back his clothes, which were new and decent. When he found himself stripped of his lunatic's dress and clothed in the garb of sanity, he begged the chaplain out of charity to allow him to bid farewell to his mad companions. The chaplain told him he would like to accompany him and see the inmates who were lodged there. So they went upstairs, accompanied by some other people who were present, and the madman went up to a cage in which was a raging maniac who happened to be calm and quiet at the time, and said to him: 'My brother, see if you have any commands for me. I am going home, for God in His infinite mercy and goodness has been pleased to restore me to my senses, though I don't deserve it. Now I am sane and in my right mind, for to God's power nothing is impossible. Put great hope and trust in Him; since He has restored me to my former state, He will restore you too, if you have faith in Him. I will send you some dainties to eat, and be sure you eat them, for I must tell you that I am convinced, as one who has gone through it, that all our madness proceeds from our having our bellies empty and our brains full of wind. Take heart! Have courage! For despondency in our misfortunes weakens our health and hastens death.'

"Another madman in another cage opposite the raging lunatic's overheard all that the graduate said, and rising from an old mat on which he was lying stark naked, he asked in a loud voice who this man was who was going away cured and sane. The graduate replied: 'It is I, brother, who am going. I have no need to stay here any longer, for which I give infinite thanks to Heaven, which has done me this great favor.'

"'Mind what you say, graduate, and don't let the Devil deceive you,' answered the madman. 'Rest your feet and stay snugly and quietly at home, and you'll spare yourself the return journey.'

"'I know that I am well,' rejoined the graduate, 'and shall not have to go the rounds again.'

"'You well?' cried the madman. 'Good! We shall see. God be with you, but I vow to Jupiter, whose majesty I represent on earth, that for the sin that Seville is committing today in releasing you from this house and treating you as a sane man, I shall inflict such punishment on her as shall be remembered for centuries and centuries to come, amen. Do you not know, you mean little graduate, that I have the power to do so? For let me tell you, I am Jupiter the thunderer and hold in my hands the flaming thunderbolts with which I can and do threaten to destroy the world. But with one punishment alone I mean to chastise this ignorant city. For three whole years I will not rain on it and on all the surrounding districts, and the time is to be reckoned from the instant I utter this threat. You free, you sane, you in your right senses? And I mad and sick and in chains? I would as soon think of raining as hang myself.'

"The madman's loud burst of oratory attracted the attention of the bystanders, but our graduate, turning to our chaplain and seizing him by the hands, cried: 'Don't be concerned, my dear sir; take no notice of what this lunatic says, for if he is Jupiter and will not rain, I am Neptune, the father and god of the waters, and I will rain as often as I please and whenever it is necessary.'

"To which the chaplain replied: 'All the same, Lord Neptune, it would not be right to annoy Lord Jupiter. Your worship may remain at home, and we will come back for you another day when we have more time.'

"The governor and the bystanders burst out laughing, and the chaplain was half ashamed at their jeering. The graduate was stripped and clapped in his cage, and that is the end of my story."

"So that, Master Barber, is the story," said Don Quixote, "that suited our situation so well that you had to tell it? O Master Scrapebeard! How blind is he who cannot see through a sieve! Is it possible that your worship does not know that comparisons between wit and wit, valor and valor, beauty and beauty, birth and birth, are always hateful and cause resentment? I, Master Barber, am not Neptune, the god of the waters, and I am not setting myself up as a wise man when I am not. I only strive to convince the world of its errors in not reviving that most fortunate age in which the order of chivalry flourished. But our depraved age does not deserve to enjoy so great a blessing as did those in which knights-errant undertook and burdened their shoulders with the defense of kingdoms, the protection of damsels, the relief of children and orphans, the chastisement of the proud, and the rewarding of the humble. Most of our knights nowadays prefer to nestle in the damasks, brocades, and other rich silks they wear than in armored coats of mail. There are now no knights who sleep in the fields, exposed to the rigor of the heavens in full armor from head to foot. There is no one now who snatches a nap, as they say, resting on his lance and with his feet on the stirrups as knights-errant did of old. There is no one now to sally forth from this wood and enter that mountain, and from there to go to a wasted and deserted shore of the sea, most often stormy and tempestuous, and to find there on the beach a little boat without oars, sail, mast, or tackle, and with undaunted heart to fling himself in and entrust himself to the implacable waves of the deep sea, which at one moment toss him up to the sky, and at another engulf him in the abyss. Then, exposing his chest to the irresistible tempest, he finds himself, when he least expects it, more than nine thousand miles from the place where he embarked; and leaping on to a remote and unknown shore, he undergoes experiences worthy to be inscribed not on parchment, but on brass. Today sloth triumphs over industry, idleness over labor, vice over virtue, arrogance over bravery, and theory over the practice of arms, which only lived and flourished in the Golden Age and among knights-errant. If I am not right, tell me, who was more virtuous and valiant than the renowned Amadis of Gaul? Who was wiser than Palmerin of England? Who more pleasant and dexterous than Tirante the White? Who more gallant than Lisuarte of Greece? Who a greater slasher or more slashed than Don Belianís? Who more undaunted than Perión of Gaul, or more eager to face peril than Felixmarte of Hyrcania? Or more sincere than Esplandian? Who more impetuous than Cirongilio of Thrace? Who more fearless than Rodamante? Who more prudent than King Sobrino? Who bolder than Rinaldo? Who more invincible than Orlando? And who more high-spirited and courteous than Ruggiero, from whom are descended today the dukes of Ferrara, according to Turpin's cosmography?[4] All these knights and many more I could mention, Master Priest, were knights-errant, the light and glory of chivalry. These, and such as these, I should wish to take part in my project, and if they did, His Majesty would find himself well served at great saving of expense, and the Turk would be left tearing his beard. Therefore I wish to remain at home, since the chaplain is not taking me out, and if Jupiter, as the barber has said, will not rain, here am I who will rain whenever I please. This I say so that Master Basin may see that I understand him."

---

[4] The heroes mentioned are all characters in Spanish romances or in romances by Ariosto and Boiardo. Turpin's cosmography is a fictitious work.

"Really, Don Quixote," said the barber, "that wasn't why I told you the tale. I meant well by it, so help me God, and your worship shouldn't take offense."

"I know best whether I took offense or not," replied Don Quixote.

The curate then remarked: "Although I've hardly said a word up to now, I should like to relieve myself of a scruple that is gnawing and scraping at my conscience upon hearing Don Quixote's last remarks."

"The curate has license for other more solemn matters," answered Don Quixote, "so he can declare his scruple, for it is unpleasant to go about with scruples on one's conscience."

"Well, with your leave," replied the curate, "I shall reveal my scruple. It is that I am unable to convince myself in any way, Don Quixote, that all this crew of knights-errant your worship has mentioned have really and truly been people of flesh and blood living in this world. On the contrary, I think that it is all fiction, fable, and lies, dreams told by men awake, or rather half asleep."

"That is another mistake," replied Don Quixote, "into which many have fallen who do not believe that such knights have ever existed. Often with different people and at different times I have tried to expose this almost universal error to the light of truth. On some occasions I have not succeeded in my purpose; on others I have, supporting my argument with evidence so infallible that I might say I have seen Amadis of Gaul with my own eyes. He was a man tall of stature and fair of face, with a well-trimmed black beard, and his looks were half mild and half severe. He was short of speech, slow to anger, and quickly appeased. Now in the same manner in which I have portrayed Amadis, I could, I believe, paint and describe all the knights-errant who wander in the histories, for I have absolute faith that they were exactly as the histories tell us, and my knowledge of their deeds and their characters makes it possible for me by sound philosophy to make out their features, their complexions, and their statures."

"How big then, my dear Don Quixote," inquired the barber, "would the giant Morgante have been in your worship's opinion?"

"As to the existence of giants," replied Don Quixote, "there are various opinions. But Holy Scripture, which cannot depart from the truth by so much as an inch, proves that they existed by telling us the story of that great Philistine, Goliath, who was seven cubits and a half tall, which is a prodigious height.[5] There have been also found in the island of Sicily shinbones and shoulder blades of a size that shows that their owners were giants and as tall as great towers; geometry proves this beyond a doubt. Nevertheless, I am unable to say with certainty what was the size of Morgante, although I imagine he could not have been so very tall, and I am inclined to this opinion by discovering in the history where special emphasis is laid upon his deeds that he often slept under a roof, and since he found houses to contain him, it is clear that his size was not excessive."

"That is true," said the curate, who, delighted to hear him talk such

---

[5] The story of Goliath is told in I Samuel 17, where his height is given as six and a half cubits, about nine feet nine inches. The giant Morgante appears in a sixteenth-century romance by Pulci.

nonsense, then asked him what he felt about the features of Rinaldo of Montalban and of Orlando and the other Peers of France, for they all were knights-errant.

"Of Rinaldo," replied Don Quixote, "I make bold to say that he was broad in face, red-complexioned, with rolling and rather prominent eyes, very thin-skinned and choleric, friendly to robbers and to vagabonds. About Roland, or Rotolando, or Orlando—for histories give him all these names—I am positively convinced that he was of middle stature, broad-shouldered, rather bowlegged, dark-complexioned, and red-bearded, with a hairy body and a threatening appearance, abrupt in speech, but very polite and well bred."

"If Orlando was no more of a gentleman than your worship has made out," said the curate, "it was no wonder that the lady Angélica the Fair rejected him for the gaiety, the dash, and the charm of the downy-cheeked Moorling to whom she gave herself. She showed good sense in falling in love with Medoro's gentleness rather than with the roughness of Orlando."[6]

"That Angélica, sir priest," answered Don Quixote, "was a giddy, wanton damsel, and a trifle flighty, and she left the world as full of her indiscretions as of her famous beauty. She scorned a thousand lords—a thousand valiant and a thousand wise lords—and contented herself with a smooth-faced little chit of a page with no other fortune than the reputation he gained by his loyalty to his friend. The great singer of her beauty, the celebrated Ariosto, did not dare, or perhaps did not care, to relate what happened to this lady after her base surrender—for no doubt her conduct was not too chaste—and left her with these lines:

'And how she won the scepter of Cathay,
Another bard will sing to a mellower lay.'

"This, no doubt, was a kind of prophecy, for poets are also called *vates*, which means diviners. This truth can be plainly seen, for since then a famous Andalusian poet has wept and sung about her tears, and another celebrated and unique Castilian poet has sung her beauty."[7]

"Tell me, Don Quixote," interposed the barber, "has there been no poet who has made some satire on this lady Angélica, among all those who have praised her?"

"I truly believe," replied Don Quixote, "that if Sacripante or Orlando had been poets, they would have given the damsel a trouncing, for it is right and natural for poets who have been scorned or not accepted by their ladies, either fictitious or modeled on those they have chosen as mistresses of their thoughts, to revenge themselves in satires and lampoons, a vengeance assuredly unworthy of generous hearts. But up to now there has come to my notice no defamatory verse against the lady Angélica, who turned the whole world topsy-turvy."

---

[6] Quixote and the curate are referring to the Italian comic romance *Orlando Furioso (Roland Driven Mad)*, 1532, by Ludovico Ariosto. Quixote misquotes a couplet from this work below.

[7] The Andalusian poet is Luis Barahona de Soto, and the Castilian is Lope de Vega, both of whom wrote poems about the romance heroine Angélica.

"A miracle," exclaimed the curate.

But at this point they heard the housekeeper and the niece, who had withdrawn from their conversation, making an outcry in the yard, and they all ran out to see what the noise was about.

CHAPTER II

Which deals with the notable quarrel between Sancho Panza and Don Quixote's niece and housekeeper, with other amusing incidents

The story tells that the noise Don Quixote, the curate, and the barber heard were the niece and the housekeeper screaming indignantly at Sancho Panza, who was struggling to get in and see Don Quixote, while they were holding the door against him.

"What does that feckless gadabout want in this house? Off with you to your own haunts, brother, for it's you and none other who deludes my master and leads him gallivanting over hill and dale."

To which Sancho replied: "Housekeeper of Satan! I'm the one who is deluded and led gallivanting over hill and dale, and not your master; it is he who led me on a jaunt all over the world, and you are wide off the mark. It was he who tricked me away from home, with his colloguing, promising me an island, and I'm still waiting for it."

"May those foul islands choke you," replied the niece, "damn you, Sancho. And what are those isles of yours? Are they something to eat, you glutton and gormandizer?"

"They are not anything to eat," answered Sancho, "but to govern and rule, and better than any four cities and richer than four judgeships at court."

"You shan't come in here, all the same," said the housekeeper, "you bag of mischief, you sack of villainies! Go and govern your house, till your plot, and rid your empty pate of isles and islands."

The curate and the barber were greatly amused to hear this conversation of the three, but Don Quixote was afraid Sancho would blurt out a whole heap of mischievous nonsense and touch upon points that might not be wholly to his credit. So, he called to him and bade the two women to hold their tongues and let him enter. Sancho went in, and the curate and the barber took their leave of the knight. They despaired of his cure, for they saw how fixed he was in his crazy notions and how deeply absorbed by his accursed nonsensical knight-errantry. And so the curate said to the barber: "You will see, my friend; when we least expect it, our knight will be off bush-ranging."

"I've no doubt of that," replied the barber, "but I'm less surprised at the knight's madness than at the squire's foolishness in believing the story of the isle, for I'm sure that all the disappointments imaginable will not drive it out of his head."

"May God help them," said the curate, "and let us keep our eyes open and see what comes of this crazy alliance of knight and squire. Both of them seem to be cast in the same mold, and the master's eccentricities would not be worth a farthing without the squire's foolishness."

"That's true," said the barber, "and I should be very glad to know what the two of them are talking about this moment."

"I dare wager," replied the curate, "that the niece or the housekeeper will tell us by and by, for they are not the kind to refrain from listening."

In the meantime Don Quixote had shut himself in his room with Sancho, and when they were alone, he said: "I am deeply grieved, Sancho, that you have said and still say that it was I took you from your cottage, when you know that I myself did not stay at home. We set out together, together we lived, together we wandered. One and the same fortune, one and the same destiny has fallen upon us both; if they tossed you in a blanket once, they have beaten me a hundred times, and this is the one advantage I have over you."

"That is quite right," answered Sancho, "for as your worship says, disasters belong rather to knights-errant than to their squires."

"You are mistaken, Sancho," said Don Quixote. "Remember the saying: *quando caput dolet*, etc."[8]

"I understand no language but my own," replied Sancho.

"I mean," said Don Quixote, "that when the head aches, all the limbs feel pain; and so, as I am your lord and master, I am your head, and you are a part of me because you are my servant; and for that reason the evil that touches me, or shall touch me, should hurt you, and yours should hurt me."

"So it should be," said Sancho, "but when they tossed me, the limb, in the blanket, my head was outside the wall, watching me fly through the air and not feeling any pain. But since the limbs have to suffer the head's pain, the head should also be made to suffer for the limbs."

"Do you mean to suggest, Sancho," replied Don Quixote, "that I felt no pain when they were tossing you? If that is what you say, you are wrong. You should not even think such a thing, for I felt more pain then in my spirit than you did in your body. But let us put that aside for the present, for there will be a time when we can consider the matter and come to a proper conclusion. Now tell me, Sancho, my friend, what do they say about me in the village? What opinion of me have the common people and the gentry and the knights? What do they say of my valor, of my deeds, and of my courtesy? How do they speak of the enterprise I have undertaken to revive and restore to the world the forgotten order of chivalry? In short, Sancho, I want you to tell me all that has come to your ears. You must answer me without exaggerating praise or mitigating blame. For it is the duty of loyal vassals to speak the truth to their lords without exaggerating it through flattery or lessening it through vain deference. And I would have you know, Sancho, that if the naked truth reached the ears of princes without the trappings of flattery, these times would be different, and other ages would more fitly be reputed iron than ours, which I reckon to be of gold. Take this warning, Sancho, and discreetly and faithfully give me the true answer to the questions I have asked you."

"I'll do so with all my heart, sir," replied Sancho, "on condition that your worship does not get angry at what I say, for you want me to tell

---

[8] *Quando caput dolet, caetera membra dolent* is the complete proverb. Quixote translates it below: "When the head aches, all the limbs feel pain."

you the naked truth and not to dress it in any clothes, except those I found it in."

"On no account shall I be angry," answered Don Quixote. "You can speak freely, Sancho, without beating about the bush."

"Then the first thing I'll say is that the common people take your worship for a mighty great madman, and they think I'm no less of a simpleton. The gentry say that you're not content with being a country gentleman and that you have turned yourself into a don and thrust yourself into knighthood with no more than a few miserable vinestocks and two acres of land, with a tatter behind and another in front to bless your name. The knights say they don't relish seeing the petty gentry setting themselves up against them, especially those squireens who black their shoes and darn their black stockings with green silk."

"That," said Don Quixote, "has nothing to do with me, for I am always well dressed and never patched. Ragged I may be, but ragged more from the wear and tear of my armor than from time."

"As to your worship's valor, courtesy, and exploits," continued Sancho, "there are different opinions. Some say, 'mad but droll'; others, 'valiant but unfortunate'; others, 'courteous but saucy'; and so they go sticking their noses into this and that until they don't leave a whole bone either in your body or in mine."

"Observe, Sancho," said Don Quixote, "that whenever virtue is found in an eminent degree, it is persecuted. Few or none of the famous heroes of old have escaped being slandered by malicious tongues. Julius Caesar, a most high-spirited, most prudent, and most valiant captain, was branded as ambitious and not too clean either in his garments or in his morals. Alexander, whose exploits achieved for him the name of Great, was said to have been somewhat of a drunkard. And Hercules, the hero of the many labors, according to gossips was lascivious and effeminate. Don Galaor, the brother of Amadis of Gaul, is rumored to have been over-lecherous and his brother to have been a sniveler. So, Sancho, seeing that there is so much slander against good men, what they say about me may pass if it is no more than what you have told me."

"Ah, but there's the rub, body of my father!" replied Sancho.

"Is there anything more then?" asked Don Quixote.

"Faith an' we still have to skin the tail,' said Sancho. "Why, up to now it has been tarts and fancy bread, but if your worship wants to know all about the calumnies they fling at you, I'll bring you here presently one who will tell you the lot of them without missing an atom, for last night Bartolomé Carrasco's son arrived from studying at Salamanca, where he was made a bachelor. And when I went up to welcome him, he told me that the history of your worship is already told in a book by the name of *The Ingenious Gentleman Don Quixote of La Mancha*. And he says that they also mention me in it by my own very name of Sancho Panza, and Lady Dulcinea of El Toboso, too, and many a thing that happened to us in private, which made me cross myself in amazement to think how the history writer could have got wind of what he wrote."

"You may be sure, Sancho," said Don Quixote, "that the author of our history is some wise enchanter, for nothing can be hidden from them."

"But if the author of this history was a wise enchanter," replied Sancho, "how comes it about that according to the bachelor Sansón Carrasco—for that's the man's name—the author of our history is called Cide Hamete Berengena?"

"That is a Moor's name," rejoined Don Quixote.

"So it may be," answered Sancho, "for I have heard that Moors for the most part are very fond of eggplants."[9]

"You must be mistaken, Sancho," said Don Quixote, "in the name of this Cide, which in Arabic means lord."

"Very likely," replied Sancho, "but if you would like to have me bring the bachelor here, I'll go for him like a shot."

"You will do me a great favor, my friend," said Don Quixote. "What you have told me makes me anxious, and I shall not eat a mouthful that will do me good until I am informed of everything."

"Then I'll go to fetch him," answered Sancho.

So, leaving his master, he went off to find the bachelor, with whom he returned in a short while. And between these three a most entertaining conversation took place.

CHAPTER III

Of the ridiculous conversation that passed between Don Quixote, Sancho Panza, and the bachelor Sansón Carrasco

Don Quixote remained very pensive, waiting for the bachelor Sansón Carrasco, from whom he expected to hear how he had been put into a book, as Sancho had told him. He could not convince himself that such a history could exist, for the blood of the enemies he had slain was hardly dry on the blade of his sword, yet they were already saying that his high deeds of chivalry were in print. Nevertheless, he imagined that some sage, either friend or enemy, by his magic art had given them to the press; if a friend, to magnify and exalt them above the most renowned feats of any knight-errant; if an enemy, to annihilate them and place them below the meanest ever written of some base squire, although, he said to himself, the deeds of squires were never written of. If, however, it were true that such history was in existence, seeing that it was about a knight-errant, it must of necessity be grandiloquent, lofty, distinguished, and true. This thought consoled him somewhat, but he was worried to think that its author was a Moor, as the name Cide suggested, for he could expect no truth from the Moors, since they are all impostors, forgers, and schemers. He also dreaded that his love affairs might be treated indelicately, which might lead to the disparagement and prejudice of Lady Dulcinea of El Toboso's good name. For he was anxious that it should be made quite clear that he had always been faithful to her and had always shown her respect, turning a blind eye to all queens, empresses, and damsels of every degree for her sake. And so, Sancho, when he returned with Carrasco, found him rapt and absorbed in

---

[9] The "Arabic manuscript" is supposed to have been found at Toledo, where the inhabitants were jokingly called *berengeneros* (the eggplanters).

these and countless other fancies, but the knight received the new guest with courtesy.

The bachelor, though his name was Sansón, was no giant in stature, but was a very great wag. He was of sallow complexion, very sharp witted, about twenty-four years of age, with a round face, a flat nose, and a large mouth—all signs of a mischievous disposition and of one who is fond of joking and making fun, as he showed straightaway, for no sooner did he see Don Quixote than he dropped to his knees before him, saying: "Let your mightiness give me your hands to kiss, Sir Don Quixote of La Mancha. By the habit of St. Peter[10] that I wear—though I've taken no more than the first four orders—your worship is one of the most famous knights-errant there has ever been or ever shall be in all the rotundity of the earth. Blessings on Cide Hamete Benengeli, who has written the history of your doughty deeds, and double blessings on the connoisseur who took the trouble to have it translated from Arabic into our Castilian vulgar tongue for the universal entertainment of mankind."

Don Quixote made him rise and said: "So it is true that there is a history of me and that it was a Moor and a wise man who wrote it."

"So true is it," said Sansón, "that I believe there are today in print more than twelve thousand volumes of the said history. For proof you have only to ask Portugal, Barcelona, and Valencia, where they have been printed, and it is rumored that it is being printed at Antwerp, and I am convinced that there is not a country or language in the world in which it will not be translated."[11]

"One of the things," said Don Quixote in reply, "which shall give the greatest pleasure to a virtuous and eminent man is to see himself in his lifetime printed and in the press, and with a good name on people's tongues, a good name, I repeat, for were it the contrary, no death could be so bad."

"If it is a question of a good reputation and a good name," said the bachelor, "your worship singly carries off the palm from all knights-errant, for the Moor in his language and the Christian in his have taken great pains to portray for us, quite realistically, your worship's gallantry, your great courage in facing perils, your patience in adversity and in sufferings, whether because of misfortunes or because of wounds, and the chastity and continence in the platonic loves of your worship and my lady, Doña Dulcinea of El Toboso."

"Never," butted in Sancho at this point, "have I heard Lady Dulcinea called doña, but plain Lady Dulcinea of El Toboso. So, history has gone astray."

"That's not an important objection," replied Carrasco.

"No, surely," replied Don Quixote, "but tell me, Master Bachelor, which of my deeds are most highly praised in this history?"

"About that point," answered the bachelor, "opinions vary as tastes vary. Some favor the adventure of the windmills, which seemed to your

[10] The ecclesiastical dress worn by university students.
[11] Ten editions had already been published of the first part of *Don Quixote* by 1612–13, when Cervantes is thought to have written this chapter.

worship to be Briareuses and giants; others, the adventure of the fulling mills.[12] One is all for the description of the two armies, which afterward turned out to be two flocks of sheep; another praises the one of the corpse they were carrying to Segovia for burial. This one declares that the best of all is the freeing of the galley slaves, that one says that none equals that of the Benedictine giants and the combat with the valiant Biscayan."

"Tell me, Master Bachelor," cried Sancho, "does the adventure with the Yanguesans come in, when our good Rozinante had the notion of looking for mushrooms at the bottom of the sea?"[13]

"The sage left nothing in the inkhorn," answered Sansón. "He tells everything and touches on every point, even the capers that the worthy Sancho cut on the blanket."

"I cut no capers on the blanket," answered Sancho, "but in the air I did, and more than I would have liked."

"In my opinion," said Don Quixote, "there is no human history in the world which has not its ups and downs, especially those that deal with knight-errantry. They can never be full of lucky incidents alone."

"For all that," replied the bachelor, "some who have read your history say that they would have been glad if the author had omitted some of the countless drubbings that were given Don Quixote in his various encounters."

"Ah! There's where the truth of the story comes in," rejoined Sancho.

"Yet, they might in all fairness have kept quiet about them," said Don Quixote, "for there is no point in writing about actions that do not change or affect the truth of the story, if they tend to diminish the stature of the hero. Aeneas, I am sure, was not as pious as Virgil made him out to be, nor Ulysses as prudent as he is described in Homer."[14]

"That is true," replied Sansón, "but it is one thing to write as a poet, and another as a historian. The poet can tell or sing of things, not as they were, but as they ought to have been; the historian must relate them not as they should have been, but as they were, without adding to or subtracting from the truth."

"Well, if this Moor is out for truth," said Sancho, "then my beatings will be found there as well as my master's, for they never took measure of his worship's shoulders without measuring my whole body. But there's no wonder in that, for that same master of mine says that the limbs must take their fair share of the head's pain."

"You're a cunning rogue, Sancho," answered Don Quixote, "I swear your memory never fails you when you want to remember something."

"Even if I wanted to forget the cudgelings I got," said Sancho, "devil a bit would the bruises let me, for they're still as plain as paint on my ribs."

"Be quiet, Sancho," said Don Quixote, "and don't interrupt the bachelor, who, I hope, will now tell me what they say of me in this history he has referred to."

---

[12] Cloth mills. (The episode is omitted in this selection.)

[13] The adventures of the funeral party, the Benedictine "giants," the valiant Biscayan, and the Yanguesans are all omitted here.

[14] The references are to Virgil's *Aeneid* and Homer's *Odyssey*. Ulysses is Odysseus.

"And of me," said Sancho, "for I'm told that I am one of the principal presonages in it."

"*Personage*, not *presonages*, Sancho, my friend," said Sansón.

"So, here we have another word corrector!" rejoined Sancho. "If it goes on like this, we'll never come to the end of it in this life."

"May I be blowed, Sancho," replied the bachelor, "if you're not the second person in the history! Why, there are some who prefer to hear you talk than the best parts in the whole book, though, to be sure, there are others who say you were much too credulous in taking as Gospel truth that island Don Quixote has promised you."

"The sun is still shining on the thatch,"[15] said Don Quixote, "and in the meantime, as Sancho is growing older and riper in experience, wit, and years, he will become fitter and more able for the post of governor than he is at present."

"By God, sir," said Sancho, "any island I can't govern at my age, I'll never govern, even if I live to be as old as Methuselah.[16] The worst of it is that this isle of yours keeps itself hidden away the Lord knows where, and not that I haven't brains enough to govern it."

"Commend it to God, Sancho," said Don Quixote, "and all will be well, perhaps better than you think, for not a leaf stirs on a tree without God's will."

"That is true," said Sansón, "for if God is willing, Sancho will not lack a thousand isles, much less one."

"I have seen governors about here," said Sancho, "who, in my opinion, don't come up to the sole of my shoe. Yet, for all that they're called lordship and served on silver."

"Those are not governors of isles," answered Sansón, "but of other governments that are easier handled. Governors of isles must at least be grammarians."

"I'll deal with the *gram*," said Sancho, "but as to the *marians*, I'll let them be, for I don't understand them. But leaving this matter of a governorship in God's hands—may He put me where I can serve Him best—let me say, Master Bachelor, that I'm mighty glad the author of this history has spoken of me in such a way that the things told of me don't give offense, for as I'm a good squire, if he'd said any derogatory things about me, not becoming the old Christian I am, our quarrel would reach the ears of the deaf."

"That would be to work miracles," said Sansón.

"Miracles or no miracles," said Sancho, "let everyone mind how he speaks or writes about persons, and not jot down helter-skelter the first thing that comes into his noddle."

"One of the blemishes they find in this history," said the bachelor, "is that the author has inserted in it a novel called 'The Tale of Ill-Advised Curiosity'—not that it is bad or badly told, but that it is out of place and has nothing to do with the history of his worship, Don Quixote."[17]

---

[15] A proverbial expression, meaning "the day is not over yet" or "there is still time."

[16] 969 years, according to Genesis 5:25.

[17] This episode is omitted in this selection. Here and below, Cervantes is citing actual criticisms of Part I.

"I'll bet," rejoined Sancho, "that the son of a dog has made a pretty kettle of fish of everything."

"Now I am sure," said Don Quixote, "that the author of my story is no sage but some ignorant prater who set himself blindly and aimlessly to write it down and let it turn out anyhow, like Orbaneja, the painter of Ubeda, who, when they asked him what he was painting, used to answer: 'Whatever it turns out.' Sometimes he would paint a cock in such a way and so little like one that it was necessary to write beside it in Gothic characters: 'This is a cock.' And so it must be with my history, which will need a commentary to be understood."

"No," replied Sansón, "for it's so plain that there is nothing in it to cause any difficulty. Children finger it, young people read it, grown men know it by heart, and old men praise it. It is so thumbed and read and so familiar to all kinds of people that no sooner do they catch sight of a lean hack than they cry out: 'There goes Rozinante.' Those who are most given to reading it are pages, for there's no lord's antechamber in which you will not find a *Don Quixote*. When one lays it down, another picks it up; some grab at it, others beg for it. This story, in fact, is the most delightful and least harmful entertainment ever seen to this day, for nowhere in it can one detect even the shadow of an indelicate expression or an uncatholic thought."

"To write in any other way," said Don Quixote, "would be to write not truths but lies, and historians who resort to lying ought to be burned like coiners of false money. But I do not know what induced the author to make use of novels and irrelevant tales when he had so much to write of in mine. No doubt he felt bound by the proverb: 'With straw or with hay, what odds we say!' For really if he had confined himself to my thoughts, my sighs, my tears, my righteous desires, and my enterprises, he could have compiled a volume greater than all the works of El Tostado, or at least as big.[18] So, my conclusion is, Master Bachelor, that one needs good judgment and ripe understanding to write histories or books of any sort whatsoever. To be witty and write humorously requires great genius. The most cunning part in a comedy is the clown's, for a man who wants to be taken for a simpleton must never be one. History is like a sacred text, for it has to be truthful, and where the truth is, there is God. But in spite of this, there are some who write books and toss them off into the world as though they were pancakes."

"There is no book so bad," said the bachelor, "that there is not something good in it."[19]

"No doubt of that," replied Don Quixote, "but it often happens that authors who have deservedly reaped and won great fame by their books have lost it all, or at least lessened it, when they have given them to the press."

"The reason of that is," answered Sansón, "that printed books are viewed at leisure, and so their faults are easily noticed, and the greater the fame of their authors, the more closely they are examined. Celebrated men

[18] Alonso de Madrigal, bishop of Ávila, who wrote under the pen name "El Tostado," was so prolific a writer of devotional works that there was a proverb, "He writes more than El Tostado."

[19] Carrasco is quoting the Roman naturalist Pliny the Elder.

of genius, great poets, and famous historians are always, or as a rule, envied by those who make it their pleasure and special pastime to judge the writings of others, without having published anything of their own."

"That is no wonder," said Don Quixote, "for there are many theologians who are no good in the pulpit, but excellent at recognizing the faults or excesses of those who preach."

"All that is so, Don Quixote," said Carrasco, "but I would be happy if those censors would be more merciful and less scrupulous and if they refrained from pitilessly stressing the specks on the bright sun of the work they are crabbing. For if *aliquando bonus dormitat Homerus*,[20] let them reflect how long he stayed awake to give us the light of his work with the least possible shadow. And it is possible that what seem to be faults to them are moles, which at times heighten the beauty of the face that has them. And so, I say that he who prints a book runs a very great risk, for it is absolutely impossible to write one that will satisfy and please every reader."

"The one that treats of me," said Don Quixote, "must have pleased but few."

"Rather the opposite, for as there are an infinite number of fools in the world, an infinite number of people have enjoyed that history. But there are some who have found fault and assailed the author's memory for forgetting who it was who robbed Sancho of his ass, for it is not then stated and it is only from the context that we infer that it was stolen. Yet, a little later on we find Sancho riding on this same ass, and we are never told how he turned up again. They also say that he forgot to put down what Sancho did with the hundred crowns he found in the leather bag in the Sierra Morena, for they were never mentioned again. Many people want to know what he did with them and how did he spend them, for it is one of the major omissions in the work."

"I'm not prepared now, Master Sansón," replied Sancho, "to go into details or accounts, for I feel faint in the stomach and if I don't cure it with a few swigs of the old stuff, it will put me on St. Lucy's thorn.[21] I have a drop at home, and my old woman is waiting for me. When I've had my dinner, I'll come back and answer all your worship's questions, and all the world's whether it's about my losing the ass or spending the hundred crowns."

Then, without waiting for an answer or saying another word, he went home.

Don Quixote begged and prayed the bachelor to stay and take potluck with him. He accepted the invitation and stayed for the meal, and a pair of pigeons were added to the usual fare. Knight-errantry was discussed at table, and Carrasco was careful to humor the knight. When the meal was over, they took their siesta until Sancho returned. . . .

[In the following chapters, Sancho supplies Sansón Carrasco with certain details of his and Quixote's adventures and reassures his wife Teresa that his quest with Quixote will result in his being governor of an island. Quixote's niece Antonia tries to dissuade him from further adventures, but he resolves to embark on a "third sally." He and Sancho ride out, bound first for

---

[20] "Worthy Homer sometimes nods." (Horace, *Art of Poetry*, line 359.)
[21] Make me weak with hunger (proverbial).

Toboso, to see Dulcinea. There Sancho tricks Quixote by telling him that Dulcinea has been changed by enchantment into a country wench; he introduces him to three such wenches. Quixote, discouraged, rides on with Sancho; they encounter a band of strolling players. The actors have just performed a morality play called The Parliament of Death *and are costumed as Death, an angel, and a knight. The Fool of the company frightens Rozinante and Sancho's ass Dapple, who throw their riders, but Quixote yields to Sancho's advice not to do battle with these false Kings, Princes, and Emperors.]*

CHAPTER XII

Of the strange adventure that befell the gallant Don Quixote with the brave Knight of the Mirrors

Don Quixote and his squire spent the night following their encounter with Death beneath some tall and shady trees, and the former, at Sancho's persuasion, partook of the food from the store carried by Dapple. While they were at supper, Sancho said to his master: "Sir, what a fool I should have been if I had chosen for my reward the spoils of the first adventure accomplished by your worship, instead of the foals of the three mares![22] Well, well, a sparrow in the hand is better than a vulture on the wing."

"Nevertheless, Sancho," replied Don Quixote, "if you had let me attack as I wished, the Empress' gold crown and Cupid's painted wings would have fallen to you as spoils, for I would have seized them by force and put them into your hands."

"The scepters and crowns of stage emperors," answered Sancho Panza, "are never made of real gold, but only of brass or tinfoil."

"That is true," said Don Quixote, "the ornaments of the drama should not be real, but only make-believe and fiction like the drama itself. Indeed, Sancho, I want you to turn a kindly eye upon the play and in consequence upon those who represent and compose it, for they are all productive of much good to the state, placing before us at every step a mirror in which we may see vividly portrayed the action of human life. Nothing, in fact, more truly portrays us as we are and as we would be than the play and the players. Now tell me, have you never seen a play acted in which kings, emperors, pontiffs, knights, ladies, and divers other characters are introduced? One plays the bully, another the rogue; this one the merchant, that the soldier; one the wise fool, another the foolish lover. When the play is over and they have divested themselves of the dresses they wore in it, the actors are all again upon the same level."

"Yes, I've seen it," answered Sancho.

"Well, then," said Don Quixote, "the same happens in the comedy and life of this world, where some play emperors, others popes, and in short, all the parts that can be brought into a play; but when it is over, that is to say, when life ends, death strips them all of the robes that distinguished one from the other, and all are equal in the grave."

"A brave comparison!" said Sancho. "Though not so new, for I've heard it many a time, as well as that one about the game of chess: so long as the game lasts, each piece has its special office, and when the game is finished,

---

[22] The reward Quixote has promised Sancho for news of Dulcinea.

they are all mixed, shuffled, and jumbled together and stored away in the bag, which is much like ending life in the grave."

"Each day, Sancho," said Don Quixote, "you are becoming less doltish and more wise."

"Yes, master, for some of your wisdom must stick to me," said Sancho, "just as land that is of itself barren and dry will eventually, by dint of dunging and tilling, come to yield a goodly crop. What I mean to say is that your worship's talk has been the dung that has fallen upon the barren soil of my poor wit and that the time during which I have served you and enjoyed your company has been the tillage. With the help of this I hope to yield fruit that are like blessings and such that will not slide away from the paths of good breeding that you have made in my shallow understanding."

Don Quixote laughed at Sancho's affected style of speech and perceived that what he said about his improvement was true, for from time to time he spoke in a way that astonished him; though on most occasions when Sancho tried to talk in argument and in a lofty style, his speech would end by toppling down from the peak of his simplicity into the abyss of his ignorance. And where he showed his culture and his memory best was in his use of proverbs, no matter whether they came pat to the subject or not, as must have been seen already and noted in the course of this history.

In such a conversation they spent a great part of the night, but Sancho felt a wish to let down the hatches of his eyes, as he used to say when he wanted to sleep. So, having unharnessed Dapple, he left him free to crop the abundant pasture. He did not take the saddle off Rozinante, as his master's express orders were that as long as they were in the field or not sleeping under a roof, Rozinante was not to be unsaddled; it was, by the way, an ancient custom, established and observed by knights-errant, to take off the bridle and hang it on the saddlebow; but to remove the saddle from the horse—never on your life! Sancho observed this rule and gave him the same liberty he had given Dapple, whose friendship for Rozinante was so unequaled and so close that a tradition handed down from father to son says that the author of this true history wrote some chapters on the subject that, in order to preserve the propriety and decorum due to so heroic a history, he did not include. At times, however, he forgets this resolve and describes how, as soon as the two beasts were together, they would scratch one another, and how, when they were tired or satisfied, Rozinante would lay his neck across Dapple's more than half a yard beyond, and the pair would stand in that position, gazing thoughtfully at the ground, for three days, or at least, as long as they were left alone and hunger did not compel them to look for food.

It is said that the author left on record a comparison between their friendship and that of Nisus and Euryalus, and of Pylades and Orestes, and if this is true, it can be understood how steadfast must the friendship of these two animals have been to the wonder of the world and to the shame of humankind, who fail so lamentably to preserve friendship for one another.[23] Because of this it has been said:

---

[23] Nisus and Euryalus were two friends who accompanied Aeneas to Italy, in Virgil's *Aeneid*. Pylades, son of the king of Phocis, accompanied Orestes back to Argos to avenge his father Agamemnon's death; see Aeschylus' *The Libation Bearers,* in the *Oresteia*.

   Friend to friend no more draws near,
   And the jouster's cane has become a spear.[24]

And that other song that goes:

   Says friend to friend: "Here's mud in your eye!"

  But let no one imagine that the author went off the tracks when he compared the friendship of these animals to that of men, for men have received many lessons from dumb beasts and learned many things of value, as for example: from storks the enema, from dogs vomiting and gratitude, from cranes watchfulness, from ants thrift, from elephants chastity, and loyalty from the horse.

  At last, Sancho fell asleep at the foot of a cork tree, and Don Quixote dozed under a robust oak. But a short time had elapsed when a noise he heard behind awoke the latter, and standing up, he gazed in the direction the noise came from, and spied two men on horseback, one of whom, letting himself slip from the saddle, said to the other: "Dismount, friend, and take the bridles off the horses, for this spot seems to me both rich in grass for them and in silence and solitude for my love-sick thoughts."

  Saying this, he stretched himself upon the ground, and as he flung himself down, the armor he wore clattered—a manifest proof by which Don Quixote knew him to be a knight-errant—and going over to Sancho, who was fast asleep, he pulled him by the arm, and after rousing him with no small difficulty, he said to him in a low voice: "Brother Sancho, we have an adventure."

  "God send us a good one," said Sancho, "and where, master, may Mistress Adventure be?"

  "Where, Sancho?" answered Don Quixote. "Turn your eyes and there you will see stretched a knight-errant, who, I believe, is not too happy, for I saw him fling himself off his horse and throw himself on the ground with signs of dejection, and as he fell, his armor clattered."

  "But how does your worship make out that this is an adventure?" said Sancho.

  "I do not insist," answered Don Quixote, "that this is a full adventure, but it is the beginning of one, for this is the way adventures begin. But listen, for he seems to be tuning a viol or lute, and by the way he is spitting and clearing his throat, he must be preparing to sing something."

  "Faith and so he is," answered Sancho. "He must be a lovesick knight."

  "There is no knight-errant who is not," said Don Quixote. "Let us listen to him, for if he sings, by that thread we shall gain a clue to his thoughts, for the tongue speaks out of the abundance of the heart."

  Sancho was about to reply to his master, but the voice of the Knight of the Wood, which was neither very bad nor very good, prevented him, and the two, listening attentively, heard the following sonnet:[25]

---

[24] A line from a popular ballad.
[25] Cervantes is parodying conventional love poetry of his time.

> O cruel one, bestow on me
> Some token of your sovereign sway,
> Which I may follow earnestly,
> And never from its precepts stray.
> If you would have me fade away
> In silence, then account me dead,
> But if you'd hear my ancient lay,
> Then Love himself my cause shall plead.
> My soul to contraries inured
> Is made of wax and adamant,
> And well prepared for Cupid's law.
> Whether soft or hard my heart is yours,
> To grave it leave to you I'll grant,
> And to your will I'll bow with awe.

With a sigh that seemed to spring from the depths of his heart, the Knight of the Wood ended his song, and after a short pause he exclaimed in a sad and sorrowful voice: "O most beautiful and ungrateful woman in all the world! Is it possible, most serene Casildea of Vandalia, for thee to allow thy captive knight to be consumed and to perish in perpetual wandering and in harsh and unkind labors? Is it not enough that I have compelled all the knights of Navarra, of León, of Tartessus, Castile, and all the knights of La Mancha as well, to acknowledge thee to be the most beautiful lady in the world?"

"Not so," cried Don Quixote at this, "for I am of La Mancha, and I have acknowledged no such thing, nor could I, nor ought I, acknowledge anything so prejudicial to the beauty of my mistress. This knight, as you can see, Sancho, is raving. But let us listen; perhaps he will give himself away still more."

"That he will surely," answered Sancho, "for he seems the kind who'll go on mourning and groaning for a month on end."

This was not so, however, for the Knight of the Wood, overhearing voices nearby, proceeded no further with his lamentations, but sprang to his feet and called out in a loud but courteous voice: "Who goes there? Who are you? Are you by any chance one of the band of the happy or of the afflicted?"

"Of the afflicted," answered Don Quixote.

"Then come to me," replied the Knight of the Wood, "and you will come to the very fountainhead of sorrow and affliction."

Don Quixote, when he heard such gentle and courteous words, went over to him, and Sancho likewise. The melancholy knight then took Don Quixote by the arm and said: "Sit down here, sir knight. Now that I know that I have found you in this place, where solitude and the night dews, the natural couch and proper dwelling of knights-errant, keep you company, I need no further proof that you belong to their number."

To which Don Quixote answered: "I am a knight, and of the order you mention; and although sorrows, misfortunes, and disasters keep their abode in my soul, they have not scored away my compassion for the misfortunes of others. From what you were singing a moment ago I gathered that yours are amorous woes—I mean, of the love you have for that ungrateful beauty whom you named in your lament."

While this conversation was proceeding, they were seated side by side upon the hard sward, in peace and good company, not in the manner of men who at break of day would have to break one another's heads.

"Are you, sir knight, perchance, in love?" inquired the Knight of the Wood.

"To my woe, I am," answered Don Quixote, "though the sorrows arising from well-placed affections should be accounted blessings rather than calamities."

"That is true," replied he of the Wood, "provided disdain does not unbalance our reason and understanding, for if exaggerated, it resembles vengeance."

"I was never disdained by my lady," said Don Quixote.

"No, surely not," said Sancho, who stood close by, "my lady is as meek as a yearling ewe and softer than butter."

"Is this your squire?" asked he of the Wood.

"Yes, he is," said Don Quixote.

"This is the first time I have ever seen a squire," said he of the Wood, "who dared to speak while his master was speaking. Anyhow, there is mine over there, who is as tall as his father, and it cannot be proved that he has ever opened his lips when I was speaking."

"By my faith," said Sancho, "I have spoken and am fit to speak before one as great, and even—But let it be, it'll be worse to stir it about."

The squire of the Wood then took Sancho by the arm, saying: "Let us two go where we can talk squirelike together, and leave these gentlemen, our masters, to butt at each other, telling the story of their loves. I wager the day will find them at it without having settled anything."

"With all my heart," said Sancho, "and I'll tell your worship who I am so that you may judge whether I deserve to be counted among the number of most talkative squires."

The two squires then withdrew to one side, and a dialogue passed between them as droll as that of their masters was serious.

CHAPTER XIII

In which the adventure of the Knight of the Wood is continued, with the wise, novel, and agreeable conversation between the two squires

The knights and squires were separated, the latter telling the stories of their lives, the former of their loves; but the history tells first of the conversation between the servants, and then follows with that between their masters. And so, it relates that he of the Wood, when they had drawn a little aside, said to Sancho: "It's a wearisome life we lead, sir, those of us who are squires to knights-errant. We certainly eat our bread in the sweat of our brows, which is one of the curses God laid on our first parents."[26]

"It may be said, too," added Sancho, "that we eat it in the chill of our

[26] See Genesis 3:1.

bodies, for who suffers the heat and the cold worse than the wretched squires of knight-errantry? It wouldn't be so bad if we had something to eat, for sorrows are lighter when there's bread to eat, but there are times when we go a day or two without breaking our fast, unless it be on the wind that blows."

"All that can be put up with," said he of the Wood, "when we have hopes of a reward, for unless he serves an especially unlucky knight-errant, a squire is sure after a little time to find himself at least rewarded with a handsome government of some island or a tidy countship."

"I have told my master already," said Sancho, "that I'll be content with the government of some island, and he's so noble and generous that he has promised it to me many a time."

"As for me," said he of the Wood, "I'll be content with a canonry[27] for my services, and my master has already assigned me one."

"Your master," said Sancho, "must then be a knight in the ecclesiastical line and can grant such favors to his good squire, but mine is only a layman, though I do remember some wise, but in my opinion, intriguing folks who tried to persuade him to have himself made archbishop. He, however, would be nothing but an emperor, and I was trembling all the time lest he should become bitten with the fancy of going into the Church, for I didn't consider myself suitable to hold offices in it. In fact, I may as well tell you that, though I look like a man, I'm just a beast as far as the Church is concerned."

"Ah! That's where you are wrong," said he of the Wood. "Those insular governorships are not all plain sailing. Some are twisted, some poor, some dreary, and in short, the loftiest and best regulated brings with it a heavy load of worry and trouble, which the unlucky wight to whose lot it has fallen bears upon his shoulders. Far better would it be for us who profess this plague-stricken service to return to our homes and there spend our days in more pleasant occupations, such as hunting and fishing, for where in the world would you find a squire so poor as not to have a hack, a couple of greyhounds, and a fishing rod with which to while away the time in his own village?"

"I'm not short of any of these things," said Sancho. "It's true I've no hack, but I've an ass that is worth twice as much as my master's horse. God send me a bad Easter, and may it be the next one, if I would swap him, even if I got four bushels of barley to boot. You'll laugh at the value I'm putting on my Dapple, for dapple is the color of my ass. As for greyhounds, I'm in no want, for there are plenty of them in my home town, and surely the finest sport of all is where it's at other people's expense."

"Truly and earnestly, sir squire," said he of the Wood, "I've made up my mind to give up the drunken frolics of these knights of ours and go back to my village and bring up my children, for I've three like three oriental pearls."

"I've two," said Sancho, "fit to be presented to the Pope in person, especially a girl whom I'm rearing to be a countess, please God, though against her mother's wishes."

---

[27] A minor ecclesiastical appointment.

"And how old is this lady who is being brought up to be a countess?" inquired he of the Wood.

"Fifteen years, more or less," replied Sancho, "but she's as tall as a lance and as fresh as an April morning and as strong as a porter."

"Those qualities," said he of the Wood, "make her fit to be not only a countess but a nymph of the greenwood. Ah, the frisky whore! What spunk the jade must have!"

To this Sancho replied somewhat sulkily: "She's no whore, nor was her mother, nor will either of them be, please God, so long as I'm alive. And do keep a civiller tongue on you. Considering that you've been reared among knights-errant, who are the last word in courtesy, I don't think your language is becoming."

"Oh, how little you understand the language of compliments, sir squire," answered he of the Wood. "Do you mean to tell me that you don't know that when a horseman lands a good lance thrust at a bull in the square, or when anyone does anything very well, the people are accustomed to say: 'How well the whoreson rogue has done it!' and what seems to be insulting in the phrase is high praise? Come, sir, let you disown the sons or daughters whose actions don't earn their parents such compliments."

"Yes, I do disown them," answered Sancho, "and in the same way you may heap the whole of whoredom straightaway on me, my wife, and my children, for all they do and say is over and above deserving of like praise. And that I may see them again, I pray God deliver me from mortal sin, which is the same as delivering me from this dangerous squire business into which I've fallen for the second time, baited and bribed by a purse with a hundred ducats in it that I found one day in the heart of the Sierra Morena.[28] And I tell you the Devil is always putting before my eyes, here, there, and everywhere, a bag full of doubloons, which I'm forever turning over with my hand and hugging it and carrying it home with me to make investments and settle rents and live like a prince. So long as I think of this, I don't care a fig for all the toils I endure with this fool of a master of mine, whom I know to be more of a madman than a knight."

"Hence the common saying that 'covetousness bursts the bag,'" said he of the Wood; "but if you mean to talk of such men, let me tell you that there is no greater in the world than my master, for he is one of those of whom it is said: 'Care for his neighbor kills the ass,' for he makes a madman of himself in order that another knight may recover the wits he has lost,[29] and he goes about looking for what, were he to find it, may, for all I know, hit him in the snout."

"Is he by any chance in love?" asked Sancho.

"He is," said he of the Wood, "with a certain Casildea of Vandalia, the rawest[30] and most hard-boiled lady in the world, but it is not on the score of rawness that he limps, for he has other greater plans rumbling in his belly; you'll hear him speak of them before long."

---

[28] Sancho is referring to an incident in Part I, omitted here.

[29] In the incident in the Sierra Morena, Don Quixote has tried to imitate such romance heroes as Ariosto's Orlando by going mad with love.

[30] The Spanish puns here on *crudo,* which means both "raw" and "cruel."

"No matter how smooth the road, there's sure to be some rut or hollow in it," said Sancho. "In other houses they cook beans, but in mine it is by the potful;[31] madness has always more followers and hangers-on than wisdom; but if the common saying is true, that 'to have a friend in grief gives some relief,' I may draw consolation from you, for your master is as crazy as mine."

"Crazy but valiant," answered he of the Wood, "and more roguish than crazy or valiant."

"Mine is not like that," replied Sancho. "I mean, he has nothing of the rogue in him. On the contrary, he has a soul as simple as a pitcher; he could do no harm to anyone, but good to all, nor has he any malice in him; why, a child would convince him it is night at noonday, and it is on account of this simplicity that I love him as I love the cockles of my heart, and I can't invent a way of leaving him, no matter what piece of foolishness he does."

"Nevertheless, brother and sir," said he of the Wood, "if the blind lead the blind, both are in danger of falling into the ditch. It is better for us to retire quickly and get back to our dens, for those who seek adventures don't always find good ones."

Sancho kept spitting from time to time, and as the charitable Squire of the Wood noticed that his spittle was gluey and somewhat dry, he said: "It seems to me that all this talk of ours has made our tongues stick to our palates, but I have a loosener, hanging from the saddlebow of my horse, which is quite good." And getting up, he came back a moment later with a large skin of wine and a pasty half a yard long, which is no exaggeration, for it was composed of a domestic rabbit so big that Sancho, as he held it, took it to be a goat, not to say a kid, and gazing at it, he said: "Is this what you carry along with you, sir?"

"What were you thinking then?" said the other. "Am I perchance some homespun, water-drinking squire? I carry better food supplies on my horse's crupper than a general does when he is on the march."

Sancho fell to, without any need of pressing. In the dark he gobbled lumps as large as knots on a tether, observing as he ate: "You are indeed a trusty and a loyal squire, round and sound, grand and gorgeous, as is proved by this feast, which, if it has not come here by magic, seems like it at least; and not like me, poor devil, who am only carrying in my saddlebags a scrap of cheese so hard that you could brain a giant with it, and to keep it company, a few dozen carob pods and as many filberts and walnuts. Thanks to the poverty of my master and the idea he has and the rule he follows that knights-errant must not feed on anything except dried fruits and the herbs of the field."

"By my faith," replied he of the Wood, "my stomach is not made for thistles or wild pears from the woods. Let our masters keep to their opinions and laws of chivalry, and eat what is prescribed. As for me, I carry my meat baskets and this wineskin slung from my saddlebow, whether they like it or not, and I'm so devoted to her, aye, and so arrantly fond of her, that hardly a minute passes without my giving her a thousand kisses and hugs."

Saying this, he put the skin into Sancho's hands, who, raising it up,

---

[31] Sancho means his bad luck comes in quantity. This paragraph is a good example of Sancho's "proverbial" style; he quotes four proverbs.

pressed it to his mouth and remained gazing at the stars for a quarter of an hour. When he had finished his drink, he let his head fall on one side, and heaving a deep sigh, he exclaimed: "Whoreson rogue, what a tip-top liquor it is!"

"There you are," said he of the Wood when he heard Sancho's exclamation. "See how you have praised my wine by calling it 'whoreson.'"

"Well," said Sancho, "I confess that I'm aware it's no dishonor to call somebody whoreson when we mean to praise him. Now tell me, sir, by the life you love best, is this Ciudad Real wine?"

"O peerless wine taster!" said he of the Wood, "From there and from nowhere else has it come, and it is a few years old, too."

"Trust me in that," said Sancho. "I knew I'd make a successful guess as to where it came from. Would you believe me, sir, when I tell you that I've such a great natural instinct in testing wines that no sooner do I smell one of them than I tell its country, its kind, its flavor and age, the changes it will undergo, and every detail concerning the wine. But you needn't wonder, for I've had in my family, on my father's side, the two finest wine tasters La Mancha has known for many a long year, and to prove what I'm saying, I'll tell you what happened to them. They were both given wine from a cask to try, and they were asked their opinion about its condition, quality, goodness or badness. One of them tested it with the tip of his tongue, the other did no more than hold it to his nose. The first said that the wine tasted of iron; the second that it had a flavor of cordovan leather. The owner declared that the cask was clean, and that the wine had no blending that could have imparted a taste of iron or leather. Notwithstanding this, the two famous wine tasters stuck to their point. Time went by, the wine was sold, and when the cask was cleaned, a small key was found in it hanging to a cordovan thong. Consider now whether one who comes of such a stock is able to give an opinion in such matters."

"Since that is so," said he of the Wood, "let us give up going in search of adventures; and since we have loaves, don't let us go looking for tarts, but return to our cots, for there God will find us if it be His will."

"I'll serve my master till he gets to Saragossa," said Sancho, "then maybe we'll come to an understanding."

Finally, the two worthy squires talked so much and drank so much that they had need of sleep to tie up their tongues and allay their thirst, for to quench it was impossible. And so the pair of them, clinging to the now nearly empty wineskin and with half-chewed morsels in their mouths, fell fast asleep; and there we will leave them for the present to relate what took place between the Knight of the Wood and him of the Rueful Figure.

CHAPTER XIV

In which the adventure of the Knight of the Wood is continued

Among the many speeches that passed between Don Quixote and the Knight of the Wood, our history tells us that the latter said to Don Quixote: "In a word, sir knight, I wish you to know that my destiny, or rather my choice, led me to become enamored of a certain lady, the peerless Casildea of Vandalia. I call her peerless, because she has no peer in bodily stature, rank, or beauty. This Lady Casildea repaid my honorable desires by forcing me, as his stepmother did Hercules,[32] to engage in many perilous exploits, promising me at the end of each that, with the end of the next, I should obtain the object of all my hopes. But my labors have gone increasing link by link until they are past counting, nor do I know which is to be the one that will finally announce the accomplishment of my honorable wishes. On one occasion she ordered me to go and challenge that famous giantess of Seville known as the Giralda,[33] who is as valiant and strong as if made of brass, and though never stirring from one spot, is the most changeable and volatile woman in the world. I came, I saw, I conquered, and I made her keep still and on one point, for none but north winds blew for more than a week. On another occasion she made me go and weigh the mighty Bulls of Guisando,[34] an enterprise that should have been recommended to porters rather than to knights. Another time she commanded me to fling myself into the pit of Cabra,[35] an unheard-of peril, and bring her back a detailed account of what is hidden in its abyss. I stopped the motion of the Giralda; I weighed the Bulls of Guisando; I descended into the pit and drew to the light of day the secrets of its abyss; yet my hopes are as dead as dead can be, and her orders and disdains as much alive as ever. And now her last command is for me to go through all provinces of Spain and compel all the knights-errant wandering about to confess that she is the most beautiful woman alive today and that I am the most valiant and the most enamored knight on earth. In accordance with her demand I have already traveled over the greater part of Spain and have vanquished many knights who have had the presumption to gainsay me. But my greatest pride and boast is that I have conquered in single combat that so famous knight Don Quixote of La Mancha, and made him confess that my Casildea is more beautiful than his Dulcinea. By this victory alone I consider that I have conquered all the knights in the world, for the said Don Quixote has vanquished them all, and since I have vanquished him, his glory, his fame, and his honor are forthwith transferred to my person, and his innumerable exploits are now set down to my account and have become mine."

Don Quixote was astounded to hear such words from the Knight of the Wood, and he was a thousand times on the point of telling him he lied and had the *you lie!* on the tip of his tongue, but he restrained himself as best he could in order to make him confess the lie out of his own mouth. So, he said to him calmly: "I say nothing about your worship, sir knight, having vanquished most of the knights of Spain, and even of the world, but I doubt that you have conquered Don Quixote of La Mancha. Perhaps it may have been some other knight who resembled him, though, indeed, there are few like him."

"How! Not vanquished him?" said he of the Wood. "By Heaven above

---

[32] Hercules' "stepmother" was Hera, since he was the son of Zeus by the mortal Alcmena. Hera imposed the labors of Hercules.

[33] The Giralda is actually a fourteen-foot brass statue of Faith on the top of the great tower of the Cathedral of Seville.

[34] The Bulls of Guisando are four rough granite figures of animals in the district of Ávila.

[35] The pit of Cabra in the district of Córdoba is traditionally supposed to be the shaft of an ancient mine.

us, I fought Don Quixote and vanquished him and overcame him. He is a man of tall stature, gaunt features, lanky shriveled limbs; his hair is turning gray, his nose is aquiline and a little hooked, and his moustaches are long, black, and drooping. He goes into battle under the name of the Knight of the Rueful Figure, and he has for squire a peasant called Sancho Panza. He presses the back and curbs the reins of a famous horse called Rozinante, and finally, he has for mistress of his will a certain Dulcinea of El Toboso, once upon a time known as Aldonza Lorenzo, just as mine, whose name is Casildea and who comes from Andalusia, I call Casildea of Vandalia. If all these tokens do not suffice to vindicate the truth of my words, here is my sword, which will compel incredulity itself to give credence to it."

"Softly, sir knight," said Don Quixote, "and listen to what I am about to say. You must know that this Don Quixote you speak about is the greatest friend I have in the world; in fact, I may say that I regard him as I would my very self, and by the precise tokens you have given of him I am sure that he must be the same whom you vanquished. On the other hand, I see with my eyes and feel with my hands that it is impossible for him to be the same, unless, perhaps, that particular enemy of his, who is an enchanter, may have taken his shape in order to allow himself to be vanquished so as to cheat him of the fame that his noble exploits as a knight have won him throughout the world. To confirm this I must tell you that only two days ago these said enchanters, his enemies, changed the shape and person of the fair Dulcinea of El Toboso into a vulgar and mean village lass,[36] and in the same manner they must have transformed Don Quixote. If all this does not suffice to convince you of the truth of my words, here stands Don Quixote himself: he will maintain it by arms, on foot or on horseback or in any way you wish."

With these words he stood up and grabbed his sword, waiting for the decision of the Knight of the Wood, who in a voice equally calm replied: "A good prayer needs no sureties. He who managed to vanquish you once when transformed, Señor Don Quixote, may well hope to conquer you in your person. But since it is not right for knights to perform their deeds in the dark like highwaymen and bullies, let us wait till daylight, that the sun may look down on our achievements. And it must be a condition of our battle that the vanquished shall remain entirely at the mercy of the conqueror, provided that what is imposed shall be becoming a knight."

"I am more than satisfied with these conditions," answered Don Quixote.

And so saying, they went to seek their squires, whom they found snoring in the same posture as when sleep first waylaid them. They roused them and ordered them to prepare the steeds, for at sunrise the two knights would engage in bloody single combat. When Sancho heard the news, he was thunderstruck, fearing for the safety of his master, because of the tales that he had heard the Squire of the Wood tell of his knight's powers. Without saying a word, however, the two squires went off in search of their beasts, for the three horses and the dapple had smelled each other and were by this time all together.

On the way, he of the Wood said to Sancho: "You must know, brother, that fighting men from Andalusia are accustomed, when they are seconds

---

[36] An episode omitted here, in which Sancho plays a thoughtless trick on Quixote.

in any combat, not to stand idle with their hands folded while their champions are engaged. I'm saying this to remind you that while our masters are fighting, we, too, must have a fight and knock one another to splinters."

"That custom, sir squire," replied Sancho, "may be current among the bullies and fighting men you mention, but never in any circumstances among the squires of knights-errant. At least I have never heard my master speak of such a custom, and he knows all the rules of knight-errantry by heart. But even if it is an express rule that squires should fight while their masters are fighting, I don't intend to follow it, but to pay the penalty that might be imposed on peacefully minded squires like myself, for I'm sure it will not be more than a couple of pounds of wax.[37] I would prefer to pay that, for I know it will cost me less than the plasters I'll need to heal my head, which I already reckon to be smashed in two pieces. Furthermore, I cannot fight, for I've no sword and never in my life carried one."

"I know a good remedy for that," said he of the Wood. "I've here two linen bags of the same size; you take one and I'll take the other, and we'll have a bout of bag-blows on equal terms."

"If that's the way it goes," answered Sancho, "I'm game, for such a fight will beat the dust off us rather than hurt us."

"That mustn't happen," replied the other, "for we'll put in the bags, to keep the wind from blowing them away, half a dozen fine smooth stones, all of the same weight. In this way we'll be able to pound one another without doing much damage."

"Body of my father," said Sancho, "what a nice kind of sable skins and pads of cotton wool he's putting into the bags to save breaking our heads and mashing our bones to powder! But even if they were filled with pads of raw silk, I tell you, my dear sir, there's to be no fighting for me. Let our masters fight and take their medicine, but let us eat, drink, and be merry, for Time is anxious enough to snatch away our lives from us without our going out in search of appetizers to finish them off before they reach their season and drop off the tree for very ripeness."

"Still," said he of the Wood, "we must fight, if only for half an hour."

"Not on your life," replied Sancho; "I'm not going to be so churlish or ungrateful as to pick any quarrel, no matter how trifling, with one whom I have eaten and drunk with; besides, who the devil could manage to fight in cold blood, without anger or annoyance?"

"I'll provide a remedy for that," said he of the Wood. "Before we start fighting I'll walk nicely and gently up to your worship and give you three or four buffets that will land you at my feet. By this means I'll rouse your choler though it be sleeping sounder than a dormouse."

"I've a trick against yours that's just as good," replied Sancho. "I'll take up a stout cudgel, and before your worship gets near enough to raise my choler, I'll send yours to sleep with such sound whacks that it will not awake unless it be in the next world, where all know that I am not the kind of man to let my face be messed about by anyone. Let each man watch out for his own arrow, though, mind you, the better way would be for everyone to let his choler sleep in peace, for no one knows the heart of his neighbor, and

---

[37] Fines payable in wax were imposed for trifling offenses; the wax was used to make church candles.

many a man comes for wool and goes back shorn; and God always blessed the peacemakers and cursed the peace-breakers; for if a baited cat who's shut in turns into a lion, God knows what I, who am a man, shall turn into. So, from now on I warn you, Mister Squire, that I'll put down to your account all the harm and damage that may come of our quarrel."

"I agree," said he of the Wood; "God will send the dawn and all will be as right as rain."

And now a thousand kinds of little painted birds began to warble in the trees, and with their blithe and jocund notes they seemed to welcome and salute the fresh Aurora, who already was showing her beautiful countenance through the gates and balconies of the East, shaking from her tresses countless liquid pearls. The plants, bathing in that fragrant moisture, seemed likewise to shed a spray of tiny white gems, the willow trees distilled sweet manna, the fountains laughed, the brooks murmured, and the meadows clad themselves in all their glory at her coming. But hardly had the light of the day allowed things to be seen and distinguished, when the first object that Sancho Panza caught sight of was the Squire of the Wood's nose, which was so big that it almost overshadowed his whole body. It is said, indeed, that it was of huge size, hooked in the middle, all covered with warts, and of a mulberry color like an eggplant, and that it hung down two fingers' length below his mouth. The size, the color, the warts, and the hook of the aforesaid nose made its owner's face so hideous that Sancho, as he gazed at it, began to shudder hand and foot like a child in a fit of epilepsy, and he resolved in his heart to let himself be given two hundred buffets rather than to allow his choler to provoke him into attacking that monster.

Don Quixote looked at his adversary and found that he already had his helmet on, with the visor down, so that he could not see his face, but he noticed that he was a muscular man, though not very tall in stature. Over his armor he wore a surcoat or cassock of a cloth that seemed to be of the finest gold, all bedizened with many little moons of glittering mirrors, which gave him a most gallant and showy appearance. Above his helmet fluttered a great cluster of green, yellow, and white plumes, and his lance, which was leaning against a tree, was very long and thick and had a steel point more than a palm in length.

Don Quixote noticed everything, and from what he saw he inferred that the said knight must be very powerful; but for all that he did not fear as Sancho did, but with noble courage he addressed the Knight of the Mirrors, saying: "If your great longing to fight, sir knight, has not exhausted your courtesy, I would beg you earnestly to raise your visor a little that I may see if the gallantry of your countenance corresponds with that of your accouterment."

"Whether you are vanquished or victor in this enterprise, sir knight," answered he of the Mirrors, "you will have more than enough time and opportunity to see me. If I do not now satisfy your request, it is because, in my opinion, I should wrong the beauteous Casildea of Vandalia by wasting time in raising my visor before forcing you to confess what you know I demand."

"Well," said Don Quixote, "while we are mounting our steeds you can surely tell me if I am the Don Quixote whom you said you vanquished."

"To that we answer," said he of the Mirrors, "that you are as like the knight whom I vanquished as one egg is like another, but as you say that enchanters persecute you, I dare not say whether you are the aforesaid or not."

"That is enough," said Don Quixote, "to convince me of your deception; however, to relieve you of your misapprehensions, let our horses be brought, and in less time than you would take in raising your visor, if God, my lady, and my arm prevail, I shall see your face, and you shall see that I am not the vanquished Don Quixote you consider me to be."

Therefore, cutting short further words, they mounted their horses, and Don Quixote turned Rozinante's reins in order to take up the requisite ground for charging back upon his rival, while he of the Mirrors did the same; but Don Quixote had hardly gone twenty paces when he heard himself called by the Knight of the Mirrors, who said, when each had returned halfway: "Remember, sir knight, that the condition of our battle is that the vanquished, as I said before, shall be at the disposal of the victor."

"I know it already," answered Don Quixote, "but there is a proviso that what is commanded and imposed upon the vanquished must not transgress the bounds of chivalry."

"That is understood," replied he of the Mirrors.

Just at this moment the amazing nose of the squire presented itself to Don Quixote's view, and he was no less astonished to see it than Sancho had been, so much so that he took him for some monster or else for a human being of some new species that is rarely seen on the face of the earth. Sancho, seeing his master go off to take his ground, did not want to remain alone with the nosy individual, for he was afraid that one flick of that nose on his own would end the battle as far as he was concerned and leave him stretched on the ground either because of the blow or because of fright; so, he ran after his master, holding on to one of Rozinante's stirrups, and when he thought it was time to turn about, he said: "I beg your worship, master, before you turn to charge, to help me climb up on that cork tree, from where I may witness your gallant encounter with this knight at better ease and comfort than from the ground."

"I am rather of the opinion, Sancho," said Don Quixote, "that you would even mount a scaffold to see the bulls without danger."

"To tell you the truth," replied Sancho, "the fearsome nose of that squire has me all in a dither and full of terror, so that I dare not stay near him."

"It is, indeed, such a one," said Don Quixote, "that were I not what I am, it would strike fear in me, too. So, come, I will help you to climb up where you will."

While Don Quixote stopped to let Sancho climb into the cork tree, he of the Mirrors took as much ground as he considered necessary, and thinking that Don Quixote had done likewise, without waiting for any sound of trumpet or other signal to direct them, he wheeled his horse, which was no swifter or better-looking than Rozinante, and at his top speed, which was no more than an easy trot, advanced to meet his foe, but noticing that he was busy hoisting Sancho up into the tree, he drew reins and halted midway, for which his steed was profoundly grateful, for it was unable to move. Don Quixote, imagining that his rival was careering down on top of him, drove his spurs vigorously into the lean flanks of Rozinante and made him dash along in such a way that, as the history relates, this was the one occasion when he was seen to make an attempt to gallop, for on all others he did no more than plain easy trotting; and with this unheard-of fury he charged at him of the Mirrors, who was digging the spurs into his horse up to the buttons, without being able to make him stir an inch from the spot where he had halted in his career. At this critical moment did Don Quixote bear down upon his adversary, who was in difficulties with his horse and embarrassed with his lance, for he could neither manage it nor was there time to put it into the rest. Don Quixote, however, paid scant heed to such embarrassments, but in perfect safety and without taking any risk crashed into him of the Mirrors with such force that in spite of himself, he threw him to the ground over the horse's rump and so great was the fall that he lay apparently dead, not stirring hand or foot. No sooner did Sancho see him fall than he slid down the cork tree and ran at top speed to where his master was, who, after dismounting from Rozinante, stood over the Knight of the Mirrors. Unlacing his helmet to see if he was dead and to give him air if haply he were alive, he saw— Who can say what he saw without arousing the wonder, astonishment, and awe of all who hear it? He saw, the history says, the very face, the very figure, the very aspect, the very physiognomy, the very effigy, the very image of the bachelor Sansón Carrasco. As soon as he saw him, he cried out in a loud voice: "Come, Sancho, and behold what you have to see but not to believe; make haste, my son, and learn what wizards and enchanters are able to accomplish."

Sancho came up, and when he saw the face of the bachelor Carrasco, he began to cross himself a thousand times and bless himself as many more. All this time the prostrate knight showed no signs of life, and Sancho said to Don Quixote: "In my opinion, master, you should stick your sword into the mouth of this one who looks like the bachelor Carrasco, and perhaps in him you will kill one of your enemies, the enchanters."

"That is good advice," said Don Quixote, "for the fewer enemies, the better."

Then, drawing his sword, he was about to put into operation Sancho's advice, when the Squire of the Mirrors came up, now minus the nose that had made him so hideous, and cried out in a loud voice: "Mind what you are doing, Señor Don Quixote, for that man lying at your feet is your friend the bachelor Sansón Carrasco, and I am his squire."

"And what about the nose?" said Sancho, seeing him without his former hideous appendage.

"I have it here in my pocket," said the latter, and sticking his hand into his right pocket, he drew out a clownish nose of varnished pasteboard of the kind we have already described.

Sancho, then, after peering at him more and more closely, exclaimed in a loud voice of amazement: "Holy Mary, protect us! Isn't it Tomé Cecial, my neighbor and comrade?"

"Who else would I be?" replied the unnosed squire. "Tomé Cecial I am, comrade and friend, Sancho Panza, and I'll tell you presently of the means, the vagaries, the schemings, that brought me here; but in the meantime, beg and beseech your master not to touch, maltreat, wound, or kill the

Knight of the Mirrors, whom he has lying at his feet, for without doubt he is the bold and ill-advised bachelor Sansón Carrasco, our compatriot."

At this moment he of the Mirrors came to his senses, and Don Quixote no sooner saw it than he held the naked point of his sword to his face, saying: "You are a dead man, knight, unless you confess that the peerless Dulcinea of El Toboso surpasses your Casildea of Vandalia in beauty; besides, you have to promise that if you survive this combat and fall, you will go to the city of El Toboso and present yourself before her on my behalf, letting her do with you what she pleases. And if she leaves you to your own devices, you must return and look for me (the trail of my deeds will guide you in my direction) and tell me all that has taken place between her and you. These are conditions that do not depart from the terms of knight-errantry."

"I confess," said the fallen knight, "that the torn and dirty shoe of Lady Dulcinea of El Toboso is better than the ill-combed though clean beard of Calsildea, and I promise to go and return from her presence to yours and give you a complete and detailed account of what you ask me."

"You have also to confess and believe," added Don Quixote, "that the knight you vanquished was not, nor could be, Don Quixote of La Mancha, but somebody else who resembles him, just as I confess and believe that you, though you appear to be the bachelor Sansón Carrasco, are not he, but another like him, and that my enemies have conjured you up before me in his shape that I may restrain and moderate my impetuous wrath and make humane use of my glorious victory."

"I confess, judge, and consider everything to be as you confess, judge, and consider it," answered the crippled knight. "Let me rise, I pray you, if the shock of my fall will allow it, for I am indeed in a very bad way."

Don Quixote helped him to rise, with his squire Tomé Cecial, off whom Sancho never for an instant took his eyes and whom he questioned incessantly, proving thereby to his own satisfaction that the latter was truly the Tomé Cecial he said he was. But Sancho was so impressed by what his master had said about the enchanters having changed the figure of the Knight of the Mirrors into that of the bachelor Sansón Carrasco that he was unable to believe the truth of what he saw with his own eyes. In the end, both master and man remained under their delusion; and so he of the Mirrors and his squire, feeling down in the dumps and out of tune with the world, took their departure from Don Quixote and Sancho, intending to look for some place where the knight's ribs might be plastered and strapped.

Don Quixote and Sancho continued to make their way toward Saragossa, and the history leaves them at this point in order to give an account of who were the Knight of the Mirrors and his nosy squire.

CHAPTER XV

In which is told who the Knight of the Mirrors and his squire were

Don Quixote rode onward in great spirits. He was extremely pleased, elated, and vainglorious at having won a victory over such a valiant knight as he imagined him of the Mirrors to be, and from his knightly word he expected to learn whether his lady still continued to be enchanted, for the said vanquished knight was bound, on pain of ceasing to be one, to return and give him a report of what took place between himself and her. But if Don Quixote was thinking of one thing, he of the Mirrors was certainly thinking of another. In fact, the latter had no other thought at the moment than to find some place where he might get poulticed, as we have said before.

The history then says that when the bachelor Sansón Carrasco counseled Don Quixote to resume his relinquished knight-errantry, he did so in consequence of a conference he had previously held with the curate and the barber upon the measures to be taken to induce Don Quixote to stay at home in peace and quiet, without exciting himself over his accursed adventures. At that conclave it was decided by the unanimous vote of all, and at the special instance of Carrasco, that Don Quixote should be allowed to set out, as it was impossible to restrain him, that Sansón should sally forth as a knight-errant, join battle with him, for which a pretext could readily be found, and vanquish him—an easy matter they thought—and that it should be agreed and regulated that the one conquered should remain at the mercy of his conqueror. And once Don Quixote was vanquished, the knight-bachelor would order him to go back to his village and home and not leave it for two years or until some other command was imposed upon him, all of which conditions Don Quixote would carry out without fail rather than break the laws of chivalry. During the period of his seclusion, he might possibly forget his foolish notions, or else an opportunity might be found of discovering a sure remedy for his madness.

Carrasco undertook the task, and Tomé Cecial, Sancho's comrade and neighbor, a merry, scatterbrained fellow, offered his services as squire. Sansón armed himself as has been described, and Tomé Cecial, to avoid being recognized by his comrade when they met, fitted on over his natural nose the false one already mentioned. And so they followed the same road as Don Quixote and very nearly reached him in time to be present at the adventure of the cart of Death, and at last they met in the wood, where everything that the wise reader has read took place. And if it had not been for the extraordinary fancies of Don Quixote, who took it into his head that the bachelor was not the bachelor, Master Bachelor would be forever incapacitated from taking his degree as licentiate, because he did not find nests where he expected to find birds. Tomé Cecial, seeing how badly their plans had turned out and what a wretched end their expedition had come to, said to the bachelor: "For sure, Master Sansón Carrasco, we've met with our deserts. It's easy to plan and start an enterprise, but most times it's hard to get out of it safe and sound. Don Quixote is mad, and we are sane, but he comes off safe and in high spirits, while you, master, are left drubbed and downcast. Tell us, now, who is the greater madman, he who is so because he can't help it, or he who is so of his own free will?"

To which Sansón replied: "The difference between these two madmen is that he who is so perforce will be one forever, but he who is so of his own accord can leave off being one whenever he likes."

"That being so," said Tomé Cecial, "I was mad of my own accord when

I agreed to become your squire, and of my own accord, I wish to leave off being one and go back home."

"You may please yourself," replied Sansón, "but to imagine that I am going home before I have given Don Quixote a beating is an absurdity, and it is not my wish to make him recover his wits that will drive me to hunt him now, but a lust for revenge, for the aching of my ribs will not let me form a more charitable resolve."

The two conversed in such a manner until they reached a town where by good fortune they found a bone-setter who cured the hapless Sansón. Then, Tomé Cecial went home, leaving the bachelor behind nursing his revenge. Our history will return to him at the proper time, but now it must frolic along with Don Quixote.

CHAPTER XVI

Of what happened when Don Quixote met a wise gentleman of La Mancha

Don Quixote continued his journey full of the joy, satisfaction, and high spirits we have described, fancying himself, owing to his late victory, the most valiant knight-errant in the world. All the adventures that might happen to him from that day on he reckoned as already successfully accomplished; he despised enchanters and enchantments; he gave no thought to the innumerable beatings he had received in the course of his knight-errantry, nor to the stoning that had knocked out half his teeth, nor to the ingratitude of the galley slaves, nor to the bold insolence of the Yanguesans who had belabored him with their staves. Finally he said to himself that if he could only discover a method of disenchanting his Lady Dulcinea, he would not envy the highest good fortune that the most fortunate knight-errant of past ages ever achieved or could achieve.

He was riding along entirely absorbed in these fancies when Sancho said to him: "Isn't it strange, master, that I've still before my eyes that monstrous and hugeous nose of my comrade Tomé Cecial?"

"Can it be, Sancho, that you really believe that the Knight of the Mirrors was the bachelor Sansón Carrasco, and his squire, Tomé Cecial, your comrade?"

"I don't know what I'm to say to that," answered Sancho. "I only know that the details he gave me about my house, my wife, and my children, no one but himself could have given me; and as for his face, once he had removed the nose, it was the very face of Tomé Cecial, for I've often seen him in my village—there was but a wall between my house and his—and the tone of his voice was just the same."

"Let us be reasonable, Sancho," replied Don Quixote. "Now tell me, how it can be argued that the bachelor Sansón Carrasco would come as a knight-errant, armed with arms offensive and defensive, to do battle with me? Have I, perchance, ever been his enemy? Have I ever given him cause to have a grudge against me? Am I his rival, or does he make profession of arms that he should envy the fame I have earned in them?"

"But what shall we say, master," replied Sancho, "about that knight, whoever he was, being the very image of the bachelor Carrasco, and his squire the dead spit of my comrade Tomé Cecial? And if that is enchantment, as your worship says, was there no other form in the world for them to take the likeness of?"

"It is all," said Don Quixote, "an artifice and trick of the malignant magicians who persecute me and who, guessing that I was to be victorious in the conflict, settled that the vanquished knight should display the face of my friend the bachelor in order that my affection for him might intervene to halt my sharp blade and restrain my mighty arm and moderate the righteous indignation of my heart, so that he who sought to rob me of my life by trickery should save his own. And in proof, you know already, Sancho, through experience, which cannot lie or deceive, how easy it is for enchanters to change some countenances into others, making the beautiful ugly and the ugly beautiful, for not two days ago you saw with your own eyes the beauty and elegance of the peerless Dulcinea in all its perfection and natural grace, while I saw her in the ugly and mean form of a coarse country wench, with cataracts in her eyes and a stinking breath from her mouth. Seeing that the perverse enchanter caused such a wicked transformation, it is no wonder that he effected that of Sansón Carrasco and of your comrade in order to snatch away my victory. Nevertheless, I console myself, because when all is said and done, I have been victorious over my enemy, no matter what shape he took."

"God knows the truth of it all," answered Sancho. Knowing as he did that the transformation of Dulcinea had been a device and trick of his own, he was not at all pleased by his master's wild fancies; but he did not like to reply, for fear of saying anything that would reveal his trickery.

While they were conversing, they were overtaken by a man who was riding on the same road behind them, mounted on a very handsome gray mare and dressed in an overcoat of fine green cloth slashed with tawny velvet and a hunting cap of the same to match. His mare's trappings were rustic and for riding with short stirrups, and were also of purple and green. He wore a Moorish scimitar hanging from a broad baldric[38] of green and gold, and his leggings were of the same make. His spurs were not gilt but covered with green lacquer and so glossy and burnished that, because they matched the rest of his apparel, they looked better than if they had been made of pure gold. When the stranger overtook them, he greeted them courteously and would have pressed on ahead, had not Don Quixote accosted him, saying: "Gallant sir, if your worship is taking the same road as ourselves and if haste is not your object, I should be grateful if we could ride together."

"Indeed," replied the man on the mare, "I should not have passed on ahead of you if I had not been afraid that your horse would be disturbed by my mare's company."

"You may, sir," answered Sancho, "in all safety rein in your mare, for our horse is the most modest and well behaved in the world. He has never misconducted himself on such an occasion as this, and the only time he didn't behave, my master and I paid for it seven times over. Your worship, I repeat, may pull up, if you wish; why, if they served your mare to him

---

[38] Shoulder strap.

between two courses, our horse wouldn't even look her in the face, I assure you."

The traveler drew rein and gazed with amazement at the figure and face of Don Quixote, who was riding without his helmet, which Sancho carried like a wallet on the pommel of Dapple's saddle. And the more the man in green stared at Don Quixote, the more did Don Quixote stare at the man in green, who seemed to him a man of substance. He appeared to be about fifty years of age; his gray hairs were few, his face aquiline, his expression between cheerful and grave—in short, his dress and general appearance stamped him as a man of fine endowments. What the man in green thought of Don Quixote was that he had never seen a man of that kind or physiognomy; he was amazed at his long scrawny neck, his tall body, his gaunt sallow face, his armor, his gestures and his carriage, a figure and image not seen in those parts for many a year.

Don Quixote observed how attentively the traveler was staring at him and assumed that his astonishment was due to his curiosity. So, being courteous and eager to oblige everybody, he anticipated the latter's questions and said to him: "I should not wonder if your worship were surprised at my appearance, which is both strange and out of the ordinary. But you will cease to do so when I tell you, as I do now, that I am a knight

'Of those, as people say, who ride
In quest of valiant enterprise.'

I have left my native country; I have pledged my estate; I have forsaken my comfort and delivered myself into the arms of Fortune to lead where she will. I have sought to revive the now extinct order of knight-errantry, and for many a day, stumbling here, falling there, flung down in one place and rising up in another, I have been accomplishing a great part of my design, succoring widows, protecting maidens, and relieving wives, orphans, and young children, the proper and natural office of knights-errant; and so, by my many valiant and Christian deeds I have been found worthy to appear in print in almost all, or at least most, of the nations of the earth. Thirty thousand volumes of my history have been printed, and it is on the way to be printed thirty thousand times more, if Heaven does not prevent it. In fact, to sum up all in a few words, or in one word, I must tell you that I am Don Quixote of La Mancha, otherwise called the Knight of the Rueful Figure. And though to praise oneself is degrading, I am compelled at times to sound my own, though naturally only when there is no one present to sound them. So, gentle sir, neither this horse, nor this lance, nor this shield, nor this squire, nor all these arms together, nor the sallowness of my face, nor my lanky limbs, should henceforth astonish you, now that I have informed you who I am and what profession I follow."

After saying this Don Quixote remained silent, and the man in green delayed so long in answering that he seemed unable to find words, but after a while he said: "You rightly guessed my thoughts, sir knight, when you noted my amazement, but you have not managed to dispel the wonder the sight of you causes in me. Though you say that it should be removed once I know who you are, it has not done so. On the contrary, now that I know, I am all the more perplexed and astounded. What! Is it possible that there are knights-errant in the world today and that histories are printed about real knight-errantries? I cannot persuade myself that there is anyone on earth today who favors widows, protects maidens, honors wives, and succors orphans, and I would not have believed it had I not seen it in your worship with my own eyes. Blessed be Heaven for that history of your noble and authentic chivalries, which your worship says is in print, for it will cast into oblivion the innumerable books of counterfeit knights-errant with which the world is filled, that do such harm to good morals and such damage and discredit to genuine history."

"There is much to be said," answered Don Quixote, "on this point of whether the stories of knights-errant are fictions or not."

"But is there anyone who doubts their falsity?" asked the man in green.

"I doubt it," replied Don Quixote, "but there let the matter rest. If our journey lasts, I hope, with God's help, to convince your worship that you have done wrong in going along with the stream of those who declare that they are not true."

From this last remark of Don Quixote the traveler began to suspect that he must be some crazy fellow, but he waited for further evidence to confirm his suspicions. But before they could broach any other subject, Don Quixote begged him to say who he was, since he had told him already something about his way of life.

To which the man in green replied: "I, Knight of the Rueful Figure, am a gentleman and native of a village where, please God, we shall go to dine today. I am more than moderately rich, and my name is Don Diego de Miranda. I spend my life with my wife, my children, and my friends. My pursuits are hunting and fishing, but I keep neither hawk nor hounds, but only a quiet pointer and a saucy ferret or two. I have about six dozen books, some in Spanish and some in Latin, some historical and some devotional, but books of chivalry have never even crossed my threshold. I read profane books more than devotional, provided they give me honest entertainment, delight me by their language, and startle and keep me in suspense by their plots, though there are very few of this kind in Spain. Sometimes I dine with my neighbors and friends, and very often they are my guests. My table is clean, well appointed, and never stinted. I take no pleasure in scandal and allow none in my presence; I do not pry into my neighbors' lives, nor do I spy on other men's actions. I hear Mass every day; I share my goods with the poor, without boasting of my good works, lest hypocrisy and vainglory worm themselves into my heart, for they are foes that subtly waylay even the wariest. I try to make peace between those I know to be at loggerheads. I am devoted to Our Lady and always put my trust in the infinite mercy of Our Lord."

Sancho listened most attentively to the account of the gentleman's life and occupation, and he said to himself that it was a good and holy life and that the man who led it must be able to work miracles. So, flinging himself off Dapple and hastily seizing the gentleman's right stirrup, devoutly and almost in tears he kissed his feet again and again.

At this the gentleman exclaimed: "What are you doing, brother? Why these kisses?"

"Let me kiss you," answered Sancho, "for I do believe your worship's the first saint I've seen riding with short stirrups in all the days of my life."

"I am no saint," replied the gentleman, "but a great sinner. But you, brother, must be good; your simplicity proves it."

Sancho regained his saddle, after having succeeded in extracting a laugh out of his melancholy master and causing fresh amazement in Don Diego. Don Quixote then asked the gentleman how many children he had and said that the ancient philosophers, who were devoid of the true knowledge of God, held that the highest good lay in the gifts bestowed by Nature and Fortune, and in the number of friends and good children.

"I, Don Quixote," rejoined the gentleman, "have one son, and if he did not exist, perhaps I might count myself more fortunate than I do at present, not because he is wicked, but because he is not as good as I would wish. He is eighteen years old; he has been for six years in Salamanca studying Latin and Greek, and when I wished him to proceed to the study of other sciences, I found him so steeped in the one of Poetry—if it can be called a science—that there was no way of getting him to take cheerfully to Law, which I would like him to study, or to the queen of all the sciences, Theology. I wish him to be a credit to his family, for we live in an age when our princes highly reward virtuous and deserving learning, for learning without virtue is like pearls on a dunghill. All his day he spends in discussing whether Homer expressed himself well or ill in such and such verse of the *Iliad*; whether Martial was indecent or not in some epigram; whether such and such verses of Virgil are to be understood in this way or in that. In short, all his conversation concerns the books of those poets, and those of Horace, Persius, Juvenal, and Tibullus, for he has no high opinion of modern writers in Spanish. Yet, in spite of his dislike for poetry in the vernacular, his thoughts are now absorbed in making a gloss on four verses they have sent him from Salamanca, which, I believe, refer to some literary competition."

To all this Don Quixote replied: "Children, sir, are part of their parents' bowels, and so we must love them, whether they are good or bad, as we love the souls that give us life. It is the duty of their parents to guide them from infancy along the paths of virtue, good breeding, and Christian behavior, so that, grown up, they may be the staff of their parents' old age and the glory of their posterity. But when it comes to forcing them to study this or that science, I consider it unwise, although there may be no harm in persuading them; and seeing that they are in no need of studying to earn their daily bread, as the student is lucky enough to be endowed by Heaven with parents who spare him that, my advice is that they should be permitted to pursue the branch of learning to which they are most inclined. And although that of Poetry is less useful than it is pleasurable, it is certainly not one of those that dishonor their votary. Poetry, my dear sir, I would compare to a tender, young, and ravishingly beautiful maiden, whom many other maidens, namely, all the other sciences, strive to enrich, to polish, and to adorn. And she has to exact service from all, and all of them can only become exalted through her. But this maiden refuses to be manhandled, or dragged through the streets, or exposed to the public at the market corners or in the antechambers of palaces, for she is fashioned of an alchemy of such power that anyone who knows how to treat her will transmute her into purest gold of inestimable price. He who possesses her must keep her within bounds, not letting her descend to base lampoons or impious sonnets; she must not be displayed for sale, unless in heroic poems, in mournful tragedies, or in merry and artificial comedies. She must not suffer herself to be handled by buffoons, nor by the vulgar mob, who are incapable of recognizing or valuing the treasures she enshrines. Do not imagine, sir, that by vulgar I mean only the common and humble people, for everyone who is ignorant, be he a prince or a lord, can and should be included in the category of the vulgar; so anyone with the qualifications I have mentioned who takes up and treats Poetry will become famous and his name will be held in esteem among all the civilized nations of the world. As to what you say, sir, of your son not appreciating the poetry in our Spanish tongue, I am convinced that he is wrong there, and the reason in this: the great Homer did not write in Latin because he was a Greek, nor Virgil in Greek because he was a Latin. In short, all the ancient poets wrote in the tongues they sucked with their mother's milk, and they did not go out in quest of strange ones to express the greatness of their conceptions; and this being so, it is only reasonable that the fashion should extend to all nations, and the German poet should not be undervalued because he writes in his language, nor the Castilian, nor even the Biscayan, who writes in his. But your son, sir, as I believe, does not dislike the poetry in the vulgar tongue, but only the poets who are merely vernacular and know no other tongues or other sciences to adorn, jog, and stimulate their natural inspiration. And yet, even in this we may be mistaken, for according to true belief, the poet is born—that is to say, the natural poet sallies forth from his mother's womb a poet, and with that impulse that Heaven has given him, without further study or art, he composes things that prove the truth of the saying: *est Deus in nobis,*[39] etc. Let me also say that the natural poet who makes use of art will improve himself and be much greater than the poet who relies only on his knowledge of the art. The reason is clear, for art is not better than nature, but merely perfects her. So, nature combined with art and art with nature will produce a most perfect poet. To conclude my speech, noble sir, your worship should allow your son to go where his star calls him, for if he is as good a student as he should be and if he has successfully mounted the first step of learning, which is that of the languages, he will ascend of his own accord to the summit of humane letters, which so well become a gentleman of leisure, and adorn, honor, and exalt him as miters do bishops or robes learned doctors of law. But your worship should chide your son if he writes lampoons to the prejudice of the characters of others, and punish him and tear them up; but if he writes satires after the manner of Horace, reproving vice in general terms and as elegantly as the Roman did, praise him, for a poet may lawfully castigate envy and upbraid the envious in his verses and flagellate other vices, too, provided he does not single out any particular person, though there are poets who run the risk of banishment to the Isles of Pontus for the sake of uttering one malicious jibe.[40] If the poet, however, is chaste in his morals, he will be chaste also in his verses. The pen is the tongue of the soul, and the thoughts begotten there will

---

[39] The complete quotation is "There is a god in us; he stirs and lo! we feel his fire." (Ovid, *Festivals,* VI.5.)

[40] Ovid was banished thus by the Emperor Augustus, presumably for writing *The Art of Love.*

burgeon in whatever he writes. And when kings and princes behold the miraculous science of Poetry in subjects who are wise, virtuous, and grave, they honor, esteem, and reward them, and even crown them with the leaves of the tree that lightning never strikes, as a warning that no one should attack men whose temples are honored and adorned by such crowns."[41]

The man in green was lost in amazement at Don Quixote's reasoning, so much so that he began to alter the opinion he had formed of the knight's craziness. But in the middle of the conversation, which was not much to his taste, Sancho had strayed from the road to beg a little milk from some shepherds who were milking their ewes close by; and just as the gentleman was about to renew the conversation, highly delighted with Don Quixote's wisdom and good sense, the latter, lifting his head, saw a cart decorated with the king's colors coming along the road by which they were traveling. Imagining that this must be some new adventure, he shouted to Sancho to come and bring him his helmet. Sancho, hearing himself called, left the shepherds, and spurring on Dapple, hastened toward his master, to whom befell a stupendous and fearful adventure.

CHAPTER XVII

In which is set forth the highest point that Don Quixote's unheard-of courage ever reached, with the happily terminated adventure of the lions

Our history relates that when Don Quixote called Sancho to bring him his helmet, the latter was buying some curds from the shepherds, and being flustered by his master's pressing call, he did not know what to do with them nor how to carry them. So, in order not to lose them, as he had already paid for them, he thought it best to pour them into his master's helmet, and using this clever shift, he turned back to see what his master needed. Don Quixote cried out to him: "Give me that helmet, my friend, for either I know precious little of adventures, or what I see yonder is one that should, and does, require me to arm myself."

The man in green heard this and gazed around in all directions without seeing anything but a cart coming toward them with two or three small flags, which made him think that it was carrying the king's treasure, and so he told Don Quixote. But the knight did not believe it, for he always firmly imagined that everything that befell him must be adventures and still more adventures. So, he replied: "Forewarned is forearmed. Nothing is lost by taking precautions, for I know by experience that I have enemies visible and invisible, and I never know when or where, nor in what moment, nor in what shape they may attack me."

And turning to Sancho, he asked him for his helmet, and as the squire had no time to take out the curds, he had to give it to him as it was. Don Quixote took it, and without noticing what was in it, he clapped it on his head hastily, and as the curds were pressed and squeezed, the whey began

---

[41] This refers to the laurel tree.

to pour down over Don Quixote's face and beard, which gave him such a start that he exclaimed to Sancho: "What's this, Sancho? I think my head is softening, or my brains are melting, or else I am sweating from head to foot. But if I am sweating, it is certainly not from fear, though I am truly sure the adventure I have to face is a terrible one. Give me something to wipe myself with, for this copious sweat is blinding my eyes."

Sancho held his tongue and handed him a cloth, thanking God that his master had not found out the truth.

Don Quixote wiped himself and took off the helmet to see what it was that made his head feel cool, and seeing the white mess inside the helmet, he put it up to his nose, and sniffing he said: "By my Lady Dulcinea of El Toboso, these are curds you have put here, you treacherous, impudent, ill-favored squire!"

To which with calm composure Sancho replied: "If they are curds, master, give them to me, and I'll eat them; but let the Devil eat them, for it must be he who put them there! How could you ever imagine that I would have the impudence to soil your worship's helmet? Indeed, you must already know the culprit! In faith, master, from the understanding which God has given me, I am convinced that I, too, must have enchanters who persecute me as a creature and limb of your worship, and they must have put that nasty mess there in order to rouse your patience to anger and make you drub my ribs as you are wont to do. But this time they have missed their mark, for I put my trust in my master's good sense; he must have considered that I have no curds or milk, or anything of the kind, and if I had, it is in my belly I would put them and not in the helmet."

"That may be," replied Don Quixote.

The gentleman had observed all with amazement, especially when Don Quixote, after wiping clean his head, face, beard, and helmet, put it on again, stood up in his stirrups, and feeling for his sword and grasping his lance, cried: "Now, come what may, I stand ready to face Satan himself in battle."

At this moment the cart with the flags approached. In it was nobody but the carter, who rode one of the mules, and a man who was seated in front. Don Quixote stood in front of it and said: "Whither are you going, brothers? What cart is this? What have you got in it? What flags are those?"

To this the carter replied: "The cart is mine, but in it is a fine pair of caged lions that the general is sending from Oran as a present to His Majesty, and the flags are of the king, our master, which signify that what is inside the cart is his property."

"Are the lions big?" asked Don Quixote.

"So big," said the man at the door of the cart, "that none bigger, or even as big, have ever crossed from Africa into Spain. I am the keeper and I've carried many, but never a pair like these. They are male and female; the male is in the front cage, and the female in the one behind. They are now very hungry, for they've eaten nothing today; so it would be best for your worship to stand aside, for we must make haste to reach the place where we may give them their feed."

To this Don Quixote answered, smiling slightly: "Lion cubs to me? To me lion cubs? At such a time, too? Then, by God, those gentlemen who send them here will soon see whether I am the man to be frightened by lions. Dismount, my good man, and since you are the keeper, open the cages and drive out these beasts. In the midst of this open field I will let them know who Don Quixote of La Mancha is, in spite of the enchanters who have sent them to me."

"Goodness gracious!" muttered the gentleman in green at this. "Our good knight is giving me proof of his nature. The curds, no doubt, have softened his skull and mellowed his brains."

At this point Sancho came up to him and exclaimed: "Sir, for God's sake, try and stop my master fighting with these lions; if he fights them, they'll tear us all to pieces."

"Is your master so crazy," the gentleman replied, "that you actually fear and believe he will really fight those furious beasts?"

"He's not crazy," replied Sancho, "but foolhardy."

"I'll make him stop," said the gentleman. And going up to Don Quixote, who was pressing the keeper to open the cages, he said: "Sir knight, knights-errant should engage in enterprises that hold out some prospect of success, but not in those that are entirely devoid of it, for valor that verges on temerity has more of madness about it than bravery. Moreover, these lions have not come against you, nor do they dream of doing so. They are going to be presented to His Majesty, and it is not right to detain them or hinder their journey."

"Get you gone, my dear sir," answered Don Quixote, "and look to your tame partridge and your spry ferret, and let every man look to his own duty; this is mine, and I know whether these gentlemen, the lions, are coming against me or not." Then turning to the keeper, he said sharply: "I swear, sir rascal, that if you don't open the cage at once, I'll stitch you to the cart with this lance."

The carter saw the armed phantom's grim determination and said to him: "Please, sir, for charity's sake, let me unhitch the mules and place myself in safety along with them before the lions are unleashed, for if they kill my beasts, I'm ruined for life, seeing that all I possess is this cart and the mules."

"O man of little faith!" replied Don Quixote. "Get down and unyoke, and do what you will; soon you will see that your toils were in vain and that you might have spared yourself the trouble."

The carter got down and in haste unyoked, and the keeper called out in a loud voice: "Bear witness, all who are here, how against my will and under compulsion I open the cages and let loose the lions. And I protest to this gentleman that all the harm and mischief these beasts shall do will be put to his account, together with my wages and dues as well. You, sir, take cover before I open; as for myself, I am sure they will do me no harm."

Once more the gentleman in green entreated the knight not to commit such an act of madness, for to engage in such freakish folly was to tempt Providence, but Don Quixote answered that he knew what he was up to. The gentleman warned him once more to mind what he was doing, for he was surely mistaken.

"Well, sir," replied Don Quixote, "if your worship does not wish to witness what you believe is about to be a tragedy, clap spurs to your gray mare and retire to safety."

Hearing this, Sancho besought his master with tears in his eyes to give up such an enterprise, compared with which the adventure of the wind-mills and the fearsome one of the fulling mills and, in fact, all the deeds his master had attempted in the whole course of his life were nothing but cakes and fancy bread. "Look sir," said he, "here there is no enchantment nor anything of the kind, for through the chinks and bars of the cage I have seen the claw of a live lion, and I'm sure that a lion with such a claw must be bigger than a mountain."

"Fear, at any rate," answered Don Quixote, "will make it seem bigger to you than half the earth. Retire, Sancho, and leave me. If I die here, you know our old compact. You will go straight to Dulcinea; I say no more."

Other words he added to those declarations that took away all hope that he would give up his insane purpose. The man in green would have re-sisted him, but not being so well armed, he thought it would be imprudent to fight with a madman, for he now was convinced that the knight was stark, staring mad. Don Quixote then went on pressing the keeper and repeating his threats, which gave the gentleman a chance to spur his mare, Sancho to prod Dapple, and the carter his mules—all trying to get away from the cart as far as possible before the lions erupted from their cages. Sancho wept for his master's death, for this time he truly believed he would perish at the claws of the lions, He cursed his luck and the unlucky hour when he took it into his head to return to his service. Nevertheless, in spite of all his tears and groans, he took good care to flog up Dapple so as to drive him farther away from the cart. Then, when the keeper saw that those who had fled were far enough away, he again entreated and warned Don Quixote as he had done before, but the knight replied that he heard him but would listen to no more warnings or entreaties and bade him make haste. While the keeper was opening the first cage, Don Quixote was con-sidering whether it would be better to do battle on foot or on horseback, and in the end he decided to fight on foot, for he was afraid Rozinante would take fright at the lions. He, therefore, sprang off his horse, flung his lance aside, and braced his buckler on his arm. Then, unsheathing his sword with marvelous valor and undaunted heart, he advanced at a lei-surely pace and posted himself in front of the cart, commending his soul to God and then to his lady, Dulcinea.

We now must observe that when the author of our true history came to this point, he exclaimed: "O brave and incomparably courageous Don Quixote of La Mancha! Mirror wherein all the valiant may behold them-selves! You second Don Manuel of León,[42] who was the honor and glory of Spanish knights! With what words shall I describe this most fearful exploit, or how make it credible to future ages? What praises can be unfitting and unmeet for you, though hyperbole be piled on hyperbole? You on foot, you alone, you bold and undaunted with only a simple sword and no trenchant Toledo blades of the little dog make,[43] with a shield of not very bright and shining steel, you stand watchful and ready for the two fiercest lions ever bred in African forests! Let your deeds themselves, valiant Manchegan, extol you; here I leave them in all their glamor, for I lack words to glorify them."

[42] A famous knight of the time of Ferdinand and Isabella.
[43] A little dog was the trademark of Julián del Rey, a famous armorer of Toledo.

Here the author broke off his apostrophe and proceeded to take up the thread of his history, saying:

The keeper, seeing that Don Quixote had taken up his position and that it was impossible to avoid letting loose the male lion without falling under the rage of the wrathful and undaunted knight, opened wide the doors of the first cage, containing, as we have said, the male lion. The beast was now seen to be of extraordinary size and of grim and awful aspect. The first thing he did was to turn around in the cage in which he lay and to extend his claws and stretch himself out to his full length. Then, he opened his mouth and yawned very leisurely, and with about two palms' lengths of tongue, which he put out, he licked the dust from his eyes and washed his face. When this was done, he put his head out of the cage and gazed all around with eyes like blazing coals, a sight that would have struck terror in temerity itself. Don Quixote alone stood looking at him intently, longing for him to leap out of the cart and come to close grips with him, when he hoped to hack him to pieces. Up to such a point did his unheard-of madness raise him. The noble lion, however, more courteous than arrogant, took scant notice of such childish bravado, and after looking around about him, as we have said, he turned his back and showed Don Quixote his hind parts, after which coolly and calmly he flung himself down in the cage. Seeing this, Don Quixote ordered the keeper to prod him and tease him to make him come out.

"I will not do so," replied the keeper, "for if I excite him, the first he will tear to pieces will be myself. Be content, sir, with what you have done, which leaves no more to be said on the score of courage, and don't try to tempt Fortune a second time. The lion has the door open; he's free to come out or not; since he hasn't come out up to now, he won't come out all day. Your worship's sturdy heart has been already shown to the world; no gallant champion, to my way of thinking, is bound to do more than to challenge his enemy and wait for him in the field. If his rival doesn't come, to him sticks the disgrace, and the man who waits his ground carries off the crown of victory."

"That is true," replied Don Quixote; "so, shut the door, my friend, and give me a sworn statement of what you have seen me do here, in the best form you can; to wit, that you did open for the lion, that I waited for him, that he did not come out, that still I waited for him, that still he did not come out, and that he lay down again. I am not bound to do more. Away with enchantments and God protect right, truth, and true chivalry! Shut the door, friend, while I signal to the fugitive and absent to return that they may learn of this exploit from your lips."

The keeper did so, and Don Quixote, sticking on the point of his lance the cloth with which he had wiped the shower of curds off his face, began to signal to those who were still continuing to flee, though looking around at every step, urged on by the gentleman in green. Sancho, happening to notice the signal of the white cloth, exclaimed: "May I be blowed if my master has not conquered the wild beasts, for he's calling us!"

They all stopped, and seeing that it was Don Quixote who was making the signals, losing some of their fear, they approached little by little until they clearly heard the voice of Don Quixote calling to them. At length they reached the cart, and as they came up, Don Quixote said to the carter:

"Yoke your mules once more, my friend, and continue your journey, and you, Sancho, give him two gold crowns for himself and for the keeper as a compensation for the delay they have had through me."

"I'll give them with a heart and a half," said Sancho; "but what has happened to the lions? Are they alive or dead?"

Then the keeper gave a detailed account of the encounter, praising to the skies the power and valor of Don Quixote, at whose sight the cowed lion dared not to come out of his cage, though he had held the door open a good while, and that it was only because he had told the knight that it was tempting Providence to excite the lion and force him to come out, as he wanted him to do, that the knight had, against his will, allowed him to close the door.

"What do you think of this, Sancho?" said Don Quixote. "Are any enchantments able to prevail against true valor? The enchanters may be able to rob me of good luck, but of courage they cannot."

Sancho gave them the gold crowns, the carter yoked up, the keeper kissed Don Quixote's hands for the guerdon received and promised him to give an account of the brave exploit to the king himself as soon as he saw him at court.

"Then," said Don Quixote, "if His Majesty should happen to ask who performed it, you must say that it was the Knight of the Lions, for it is my wish that from this day on there may be changed, altered, and transformed the name that till now I have borne of the Knight of the Rueful Figure. In this I follow the ancient custom of knights-errant, who changed their names when they pleased or when it suited them."

The cart went on its way and Don Quixote, Sancho, and the gentleman in the green coat continued theirs.

All this while Don Diego de Miranda had not opened his mouth, so carefully was he watching and noting every word and action of Don Quixote, who appeared to him to be at once a sane man turned mad and a madman who had glimmers of sanity. The first part of this history had not yet come to his notice, for if he had read it, he would have ceased to wonder at the knight's deeds, since he would have ascertained the nature of his madness. But as he did not know it, he sometimes took him for sane, sometimes for mad. For what Don Quixote said was consistent, elegant, and well expressed, but what he did was eccentric, rash, and absurd. "What could be madder," he reflected, "than to put on a helmet full of curds and believe that enchanters had melted one's brains? And what could be rasher and more absurd than to insist on fighting with lions?"

Don Quixote interrupted his soliloquy by saying: "No doubt, Don Diego de Miranda, your worship regards me as both foolish and mad. And it would be no wonder if you did, for my actions can have no other interpretation. Nevertheless, I wish your worship to note that I am not so mad or foolish as I must have appeared to you. It is a fine sight to see a gallant knight under the eyes of his king give effective lance thrusts at a brave bull in the midst of a great square; it is a fine sight to see a knight, all armed in burnished armor, pace the lists in merry jousts before the ladies; and it is a fine sight to see all those knights who in military exercises or the like entertain, cheer, and if one may say so, honor the courts of their princes. But finer than all these is to see a knight-errant roaming through deserts and solitudes, by crossroads and forests and mountains, in quest of perilous adventures, in order to bring them to a happy and fortunate conclusion only for the sake of glory and lasting renown. It is a finer sight, I say, to see a knight-errant succoring a widow in some lonely waste than a courtier knight dallying with a maiden in the cities. All knights have their particular offices; let the courtier serve the ladies, lend pomp and circumstance to the royal court by his gay liveries, support poor knights at his beautiful table, arrange jousts, maintain tourneys, and show himself generous, liberal and lavish, and a good Christian above everything, for in this way he will fulfill his precise obligations. But let the knight-errant explore the corners of the world, penetrate the most intricate labyrinths, encounter at every step the impossible, brave the scorching rays of the sun in midsummer on high and unpeopled deserts, and in winter the grim inclemency of the winds and frosts; let no lions daunt him, nor hobgoblins scare him, nor dragons terrify him, for to seek them, attack them, and conquer them all are his principal duties. And as the lot has fallen on me to be of the number of knights-errant, I cannot then fail to attempt everything that seems to me to fall within the bounds of my duty. So, it was strictly my right to attack these lions whom I attacked just now, although I knew it to be rash temerity, for I know well what valor is, namely, a virtue that is situated between the two vicious extremes, which are cowardice and rashness. But it is far better for the brave man to mount to the height of rashness than to sink into the depths of cowardice, for just as it is easier for the generous than for the miser to be prodigal, so it is easier for the daring than for the cowardly to become truly valiant. And in the matter of encountering adventures, let your worship, Don Diego, believe me that it is better to lose the game by a card too much than by one too little, for 'this knight is rash and foolhardy' sounds better in the hearer's ears than 'such a knight is timid and cowardly.'"

"Let me admit, Don Quixote," replied Don Diego, "that all that your worship has said and done is adjusted by the balance of reason itself, and I believe that if the laws and ordinances of knight-errantry had been lost, they would be found in your worship's heart, as in their right repository and archive. . . .

[Quixote and Sancho remain four days at the home of the "Knight of the Green Coat," Don Diego de Miranda; Quixote converses with Don Lorenzo, his host's son. Riding on, they attend a village wedding. The bride, Quiteria, is marrying the wealthy Comacho rather than her real lover, the impoverished Basilio. At the wedding, Basilio appears, stabs himself, and as a dying wish, asks to be married to Quiteria, who can then marry Comacho within a few minutes as a widow. She consents, but after the ceremony Basilio jumps up, unhurt, and claims the bride. A riot almost breaks out, but Quixote defends the newlyweds. He spends three days with them and lectures Basilio on marriage.]

CHAPTER XXII

In which is given an account of the great adventure of the cave of Montesinos, in the heart of La Mancha, which our gallant Don Quixote brought to a happy conclusion

. . . . "Remember, O wise Basilio," added Don Quixote, "that a certain sage, I know not who, held that there was not more than one good woman in all the world, and he advised everyone to think and believe that this one good woman was his own wife, and so he would live happy. I myself am not married, nor, so far, has it even come into my mind to be so; nevertheless, I would dare to give advice to anyone who might ask it, as to the mode in which he should seek a wife to marry. The first thing I would advise him is to pay more attention to reputation than to fortune, for the good woman does not win a good name solely by being good, but by appearing so, for looseness and public frivolity do greater injury to a woman's honor than secret misdeeds. If you bring a good woman to your house, it will be an easy matter to keep her good, and even improve her in that goodness. But if you bring home a bad one, you will find it a hard task to mend her ways, for it is not easy to pass from one extreme to another. I do not say it is impossible, but I consider it difficult."

Sancho, who had been listening to all this, said to himself: "Whenever I say a word that has a bit of marrow and substance about it, this master of mine straightaway says that I ought to take a pulpit in my hand and roam the world preaching fine sermons; but I say of him that when he starts stringing sentences and giving counsels, not only might he take a pulpit in his hand, but two on each finger, and go into the marketplaces with the cry, 'Who'll buy my wares?' on his lips. Devil take him for a knight-errant, what a number of things he knows! I used to think to myself that the only things he knew had to do with chivalry, but there's not a thing he doesn't peck at nor dip his spoon into."

Sancho kept mumbling to himself so loud that his master overheard him and asked: "What are you muttering about, Sancho?"

"I'm not saying or murmuring anything," said Sancho, "only saying to myself that I wish I had heard what your worship has just said before I got married. Perhaps I'd say now: 'The ox that's loose licks himself well!'"

"Is Teresa[44] so bad then, Sancho?" said Don Quixote.

"She's not too bad," replied Sancho, "but she's not very good; at least, she's not as good as I would like her to be."

"You do wrong, Sancho," said Don Quixote, "to speak ill of your wife, for she is the mother of your children."

"We don't owe each other a thing," answered Sancho, "for she speaks ill of me when she's got the whim, especially when she's jealous; then Satan himself couldn't stomach her."

They remained three days with the newlyweds by whom they were treated and served as royalty. Don Quixote asked the nimble licentiate to get them a guide to conduct them to the cave of Montesinos, of which so many wonderful things were related in those parts, for he had a great wish to explore it and to see with his own eyes if the wonders reported were true. The licentiate replied that he would get him a cousin of his own, a famous scholar, one much given to reading books of chivalry, who would be very glad to guide him to the mouth of the cave and would show him the lagoons of Ruidera, which were also famous all over La Mancha, and even all over Spain. He also said that Don Quixote would enjoy his kinsman's

---

[44] In Part I, Sancho's wife's name is given as Juana (or Mari) Gutiérrez; in Part II, Cervantes calls her Teresa Cascajo, apparently by mistake.

company, who was well versed in writing books and in dedicating them to princes.

The cousin arrived later on, with a she-ass in foal, whose packsaddle was covered with a many-colored rug or sackcloth. Sancho saddled Rozinante, harnessed Dapple, and stocked his saddlebags, to which we should add those of the cousin, which likewise were well supplied. And so, commending themselves to God and taking leave of all, they set out on the road leading to the famous cave of Montesinos.[45]

On the way Don Quixote asked the cousin of what kind were his pursuits, his profession, and studies. To which he replied that his profession was that of a humanist, and his pursuits and studies were to write books for publication, all of great profit and no less entertainment to the state; that one of them was entitled *The Book of Liveries,* in which he described seven hundred and three devices, with their colors, mottoes, and ciphers, from which the gentlemen at court could select and use whichever they pleased on the occasion of festivals and revels, without having to beg them from anybody or rack their brains, as they say, to invent them to suit their wishes and purposes.

"For," he said, "I give appropriate devices to the jealous, the scorned, the forgotten, and the absent, which fit them like a glove. I have another book as well, which I mean to call *Metamorphoses,* or *The Spanish Ovid,* a new and most original work in which, while parodying Ovid, I describe the Giralda of Seville, the Angel of the Magdalen, the Gutter of Vecinguerra at Córdoba, and the Bulls of Guisando, the Sierra Morena, the fountains of Leganitos and Lavapiés in Madrid, not forgetting that of the Piojo, that of the Golden Gutter, and that of the Priora; and all these with such allegories, metaphors, and transformations that they will entertain, astonish, and instruct at the same time.[46] I also have another book that I call the *Supplement to Polydore Virgil,*[47] which deals with the invention of things. It is a work of deep learning and research, because I clarify and verify in most elegant style the subjects of great importance that Polydore omitted. He forgot to tell us who was the first man who ever had catarrh and who was the first to use ointments to cure himself of the French pox.[48] All this I explain with the utmost precision on the testimony of twenty-five authorities. So your worship may judge whether I have not worked well, and whether this book will not be indispensable to the whole world."

Sancho, who had been listening carefully to the cousin's narrative, said to him: "Tell me, sir, and best of luck with the printing of your books, but

[45] There is an actual cave of Montesinos in La Mancha. It is very deep and is said to end in the feudal castle of Rochefrías.

[46] The Giralda of Seville and the Angel of the Magdalen were statues on the tops of churches in Seville and Salamanca. The Gutter of Vecinguerra was a sewer in Córdoba. The Bulls of Guisando (referred to, like the Giralda of Seville, earlier) were rough stone statues in Ávila, reportedly marking the site of one of Caesar's victories. The Sierra Morena is a range of mountains. The other wonders are fountains in Madrid. The cousin wants to imitate the Roman poet Ovid (43 B.C.–A.D. 18), whose *Metamorphoses* are a collection of mythological stories of transformations.

[47] Polydore Virgil (c. 1470–1550) was an Italian historian who wrote a book named *On the Invention of Things.* The cousin's projects parody those of the Renaissance Humanists.

[48] A reference to the use of mercury ointments to cure syphilis.

can you inform me—of course you can, as you know everything—who was the first man who scratched his head? I'm of the opinion that it must have been our father Adam."

"Yes, it must have been," answered the cousin, "for there is no doubt Adam had a head and hair; and that being so, and as he was the first man in the world, he must sometimes have scratched himself."

"So I believe," answered Sancho; "tell me now, who was the first tumbler in the world?"

"Frankly, brother," replied the cousin, "I am not able to solve that at present, until I have gone further in my studies. I shall look into the matter when I get back to my books, and I'll answer you when we meet again, for this must not be the last time."

"Look here, sir," answered Sancho, "don't go to any trouble about it, for I've hit upon the answer to my question. The first tumbler in the world, let me tell you, was Lucifer, for when they threw or pitched him out of Heaven, he went tumbling into the pit of hell."

"You are right, my friend," said the cousin.

"That question and answer," said Don Quixote, "are not yours, Sancho. You have heard them from someone else."

"Whist, sir," answered Sancho, "for if I start questioning and answering, I shan't be done till tomorrow morning. Yes, for if it's just a matter of asking idiotic questions and giving silly replies, I needn't go begging help from the neighbors."

"You have said more than you know, Sancho," said Don Quixote, "for there are some people who tire themselves out learning and proving things that, once learned and proved, don't matter a straw as far as the mind or memory is concerned."

That day was spent in such pleasant discussions, and at night they put up in a little village that the cousin told Don Quixote was no more than six miles from the cave of Montesinos. He added that if he was determined to enter it, he would need to provide himself with ropes so that he might be tied up and lowered into its depths.

Don Quixote said that even if it reached to the abyss, he was determined to see where it ended. So, they bought about a hundred fathoms of rope, and next day at two o'clock in the afternoon they arrived at the cave. Its mouth is wide and spacious, but full of thorns and wild fig bushes and brambles and briars, so thick and intertwined that they completely close it up.

When they caught sight of it, the cousin, Sancho, and Don Quixote dismounted, and the first two straightaway tied up the latter very firmly with the ropes, and while they were binding him and winding them around him, Sancho said: "Mind what you're doing, master; don't bury yourself alive, or put yourself where you'll be like a flask lowered down into a well to cool. Surely it's no affair of yours to be exploring this place, which must be worse than an underground dungeon."

"Tie me up and hold your peace," replied Don Quixote. "Such an enterprise as this has been reserved for me."

The guide then said: "I pray you, Señor Don Quixote, to note and examine with a hundred eyes all that is inside the cave. Perhaps there may be things that I may include in one of my books."

"The drum is in hands that will know well how to beat it," said Sancho.

When Don Quixote's binding was complete, which went over his doublet but not over his armor, he said: "It was remiss of us not to have provided ourselves of a little bell to be tied on the rope close to me. By the sound you would know that I was still descending and was alive. However, since that is impossible, let God's hand guide me."

Saying this, he fell upon his knees, and in a low voice he offered up a prayer to Heaven, beseeching God to help him and give him success in his new perilous adventure. Then, in a loud voice he cried: "O mistress of my actions and movements, most illustrious and peerless Dulcinea of El Toboso, if it is possible for the prayers and the supplications of thy venturesome lover to reach thy ears, by thy incomparable beauty I beseech thee to listen to them, for they do but beg thee not to refuse me thy favor and protection at this moment when I need them so urgently. I am about to plunge, to engulf, and to sink myself in the abyss that yawns at my feet, only to make the world recognize that if thou dost favor me, there is no impossible feat that I may not accomplish."

With those words he approached the cavern, and finding that it was not possible to let himself down or make an entrance unless by force of arm or by cutting a passage, he drew his sword and began to cut away the brambles at the mouth of the cave. At the noise he made, a great number of crows and jackdaws fluttered out so thickly and with such a rush that they knocked Don Quixote down, and if he had been as superstitious as he was a good Catholic, he would have taken it for an evil omen and would have refused to bury himself in such a place. At last, he rose to his feet, and seeing that no more crows came out, or night birds such as bats, which had flown out at the same time as the crows, he let the cousin and Sancho give him rope, and he began to lower himself into the depths of the dreaded cave. As he entered it, Sancho gave him his blessing and made a thousand signs of the Cross over him, saying: "May God and the Rock of France and the Trinity of Gaeta[49] guide you, O flower, cream, and skimming of knights-errant! There you go, you bully of the world, heart of steel, and of arm of bronze. Once more, may God guide you and bring you back safe and sound to the light of this world of ours you are leaving to bury yourself in darkness."

The cousin likewise offered up similar prayers and supplications.

Don Quixote, as he descended, called out for more and more rope, and they gave it to him little by little. When his shouts, which sounded from the cave as through a funnel, could not be heard, they had already uncoiled the hundred fathoms of rope. They were of the opinion that they should pull up Don Quixote, for they had no more rope to give him. They waited, however, for about half an hour and then began to gather in the rope with great ease and without any weight, a sign that made them believe that Don Quixote had remained inside. Sancho, when he realized this, wept bitterly and pulled away in great haste in order to learn the worst. But when they came to about eighty fathoms, they felt a weight, which cheered them up

---

[49] The Rock of France is a statue of the Virgin discovered in the fifteenth century, on the road between Salamanca and Cuidad Rodrigo. The chapel of the Holy Trinity of Gaeta was north of Naples.

considerably. At last, at ten fathoms they saw Don Quixote clearly, and Sancho shouted to him, saying: "Welcome back, master, we fancied you were staying down there to found a family."

Don Quixote answered not a word, and when they had pulled him all the way up, they saw that his eyes were shut and that he appeared to be fast asleep.

They laid him on the ground and untied him, but still he did not awake. Then, they turned him over this way and that, and so shook him and rolled him about that at last he came to himself and stretched himself as if he had just awakened from a deep sleep. Looking around him from one side to another like one who had great fear on him, he cried: "God forgive you, friends; you have snatched me from the most delightful vision that any human being has ever beheld. Now indeed I know that all the pleasant things of this life pass away like a shadow and a dream, or wither like the flowers of the field.[50] O hapless Montesinos! O sorely wounded Durandarte! O unlucky Belerma! O tearful Guadiana, and ye luckless daughters of Ruidera, who show by your waters the tears your eyes did shed!"[51]

The cousin and Sancho listened with great attention to the words of Don Quixote, who uttered them as though they were torn from his very bowels. They besought him to explain what he meant and to tell them what he had seen in the hell below.

"Hell do you call it?" said Don Quixote. "Do not call it thus, for it does not deserve such a name, as you will see presently."

He then begged them to give him something to eat, for he was very hungry. They spread the cousin's saddlecloth on the grass, visited their saddlebags, and seated together in good brotherly fellowship, they lunched and supped at the same time.

Then, when the saddlecloth was removed, Don Quixote said: "Let no one stir. Now, my sons, give me all your attention."

CHAPTER XXIII

Of the wonderful things that the consummate Don Quixote said he had seen in the deep cave of Montesinos, whose impossibility and immensity have caused this adventure to be considered apocryphal

It was then about four o'clock in the afternoon when the sun veiled itself behind clouds and shone with subdued light, so that Don Quixote was enabled to relate without heat and discomfort what he had seen in the cave of Montesinos to his two illustrious auditors. He began as follows: "About twelve or fourteen fathoms down in the depth of this dungeon, on the right hand, there is a recess big enough to contain a large cart with its mules. A tiny ray of light enters through some chinks or crevices that are open to the earth's surface. This recess I saw when I was weary and downcast at finding myself dangling in the air by the rope and traveling down through that

---

[50] The idea and the language are biblical. See, for example, Psalm 102:11: "My days are like an evening shadow; I wither away like grass." For the idea that "life is a dream," see Calderón's play of that title.

[51] These are all characters in chivalric romances.

dark region below without any clear idea of where I was going; so, I determined to enter it and rest for a moment. I shouted to you not to let out more rope until I should ask for it, but you must not have heard me. I then gathered in the rope you were letting down, and after making a coil of it, I sat down upon it, meditating all the while on what I ought to do in order to lower myself to the bottom of the cavern, seeing that I had no one to hold me up. While I was thus perplexed, suddenly and without warning a deep sleep fell upon me, and without knowing the why or the wherefore, I awoke and found myself in the midst of the most delightful meadow that Nature could create or the most vivid imagination visualize. I opened my eyes, I rubbed them, and I found that I was not asleep but wide awake. Nevertheless, I felt my head and my heart to make sure that I myself was there and not some vain specter, but the touch, the feeling, the discourse I held with myself, proved to me that I was the same then as I am here at this moment. Then I saw before me a sumptuous royal palace or castle, with walls that seemed to be made of clear, transparent crystal, and through two great doors that opened I saw a venerable old man come toward me, clad in a long cloak of purple-colored serge that trailed on the ground. He wore over his shoulders and breast a scholar's green-satin hood, and his head was covered with a black Milanese cap, and his snow-white beard fell below his waist. He carried no arms at all, only a rosary of beads that were bigger than fair-sized walnuts—indeed, each tenth bead was like a moderate-sized ostrich egg. His bearing, his gait, his gravity, and his imposing presence, each thing by itself and all of them together, held me spellbound with admiration. He came up to me, and the first thing he did was to embrace me closely. Then he said: 'For many an age, valiant knight Don Quixote of La Mancha, we who inhabit these enchanted solitudes have waited to see you, that you may announce to the world what lies buried in the deep cavern that you have entered, called the cave of Montesinos, an exploit reserved for your invincible heart and spirit. Come with me, illustrious sir, for I wish to show you the wonders that this transparent palace contains, whereof I am the governor and perpetual chief warden, for I am Montesinos himself, after whom the cave is named.'

"No sooner had he said that he was Montesinos than I asked him if the story told in the world above was true, that he had cut the heart of his great friend Durandarte out of his breast with a little dagger and carried it to Lady Belerma, in accordance with Durandarte's instructions at the point of death.[52] He replied that the story was correct in all particulars save in the matter of the dagger, for it was not a dagger, nor little, but a burnished poniard sharper than an awl."

"That same poniard," said Sancho, "must be one of those made by Ramón de Hoces, the Sevillian."[53]

"I do not know," said Don Quixote, "but it could not have been made by that poniard maker, for Ramón de Hoces lived yesterday, whereas the affair of Roncesvalles, where this misfortune took place, was many years

<hr />

[52] This story is told in the chivalric "Ballads of Montesinos." Through this whole section, the story of the heart is told with an absurd literalness.

[53] Unidentified. Presumably a contemporary knife-maker.

ago. But this matter is not of importance; it does not disturb or alter the truth of the story."

"You are right," said the cousin. "Pray proceed, Señor Don Quixote, for I am listening to you with the greatest pleasure in the world."

"And I am no less pleased to tell the story," said Don Quixote. "Well, to continue, the venerable Montesinos led me into the palace of crystal, where in a lower hall, all made of alabaster and extremely cool, there stood an elaborately carved marble tomb, on top of which I saw a knight stretched out full length, not of bronze or marble, but of actual flesh and bone. He had his right hand (which to my eyes appeared somewhat hairy and sinewy, a sign that its owner was of great muscular strength) placed over his heart, but before I could question Montesinos, he, seeing me gaze in amazement at the tomb, said: 'This is my friend Durandarte, flower and mirror of the true lovers and valiant knights of his time. He is kept enchanted here, as I am myself and many other men and women, by that Gallic enchanter Merlin,[54] who, they say, was the Devil's son; but, in my opinion, he is no Devil's son, for he knows, as the saying goes, a deal more than the Devil. How or why he enchanted us, no one knows, but time will reveal the reason at no distant date. What amazes me is that I know as surely as that it is now day that Durandarte ended his life in my arms and that after his death I extracted his heart with my own hands; indeed, it must have weighed a couple of pounds, for according to scientists, he who has a large heart is endowed with greater valor than he who has a small one. Now since the knight did really die, how comes it that he moans and complains from time to time as if he were alive?'

"As he said these words that wretched Durandarte cried aloud:

> " 'O my cousin Montesinos!
>   Heed, I pray, my last request:
>   When thou seest me lying dead
>   And my soul from my corpse has fled,
>   With thy poniard or thy dagger
>   Pluck the heart from out my breast,
>   And hie thee with it to Belerma.' "[55]

"On hearing these words the venerable Montesinos sank upon his knees before the hapless knight, and with tears in his eyes, he exclaimed: 'Long since, Sir Durandarte, my dearest cousin, have I done what you bade me on the rueful day when I lost you. I took out your heart as best I could, without leaving the slightest piece of it in your breast; I wiped it with a lace handkerchief; I went off with it by the road to France, after having first laid you in the bosom of the earth with tears so plentiful that they sufficed to wash and cleanse my hands of the blood that stained them when I groped in your bowels. Then, O cousin of my soul, as further proof, at the first place I reached after leaving Roncesvalles, I sprinkled a few pinches of salt on your heart that it might not smell badly and that I might bring it, if

---

[54] The wizard in the Arthurian legends. He was Welsh, not "Gallic," though he was claimed by the Bretons.
[55] Cervantes is quoting, and combining, two actual ballads.

not fresh, at least pickled, into the presence of Lady Belerma, whom, along with you and me, and Guadiana, your squire, and the duenna Ruidera and her seven daughters and two nieces, and other friends, Merlin the Wizard keeps here enchanted these many years. And though five hundred years have passed, not one of us has died. Ruidera and her daughters and nieces alone are missing, for Merlin, pitying them for the tears they had shed, changed them into so many lagoons, which now in the world of the living and in the province of La Mancha the people call the lagoons of Ruidera.[56] The seven daughters belong to the kings of Spain and the two nieces to the knights of a very holy order, called the Order of St. John.[57] Guadiana, your squire, who also was bewailing your fate, was changed into a river of his own name, but when he reached the surface of the earth and saw the sun of another Heaven, so great was his sorrow at finding that he was leaving you that he plunged into the bowels of the earth.[58] Nevertheless, as he cannot avoid following his natural course, from time to time he comes forth and shows himself to the sun and the world. The lagoons I have mentioned supply him with their waters, and with their help and the help of many others he enters Portugal in all his pomp and glory. But wherever he goes he shows his sadness and melancholy and takes no pride in breeding choice and tasty fish, but only coarse and tasteless kinds, very different from those of the golden Tagus.[59] All this, my cousin, I have told you many times before, but since you make me no answer, I am afraid you do not believe me, or do not hear me, which greatly distresses me, as God knows. Now I have news to give you, which, while it may not alleviate your sorrows, will by no means increase them. Learn that you have here before you (open your eyes and you will see him) that great knight about whom the magician Merlin has prophesied so many things; that Don Quixote of La Mancha, I say, who once again and to better purpose than in the past has revived in the present the already forgotten order of knight-errantry. By his aid and favor we may be disenchanted, for great deeds are reserved for great men.'

" 'And if this does not take place,' replied the hapless Durandarte in a swooning voice; 'if this may not be, then, O cousin, I say: patience and shuffle the cards.'[60] And turning over on his side, he relapsed into his former silence without speaking another word.

"And now a great outcry and lamentations arose, accompanied by deep groans and pitiful sobbings. I turned around and saw through the walls of crystal in another hall a procession of two lines of fair damsels all clad in mourning, with white turbans of Turkish fashion on their heads. Behind, in the rear of the procession, walked a lady, for so her dignity proclaimed her to be, also clothed in black, with a white veil so long and ample that it kissed the ground. Her turban was twice as large as the largest of any of the others; she had eyebrows that met, and her nose was rather flat; her mouth was large, but her lips were red; her teeth, which at times she showed, were few and not well set, though as white as peeled almonds. She carried in her

---

[56] The "lagoons of Ruidera" were a series of lakes in the vicinity of the ancient Moslem castle of Ruidera.

[57] Two of the lakes (the "nieces") were in the domain of the Order of St. John.

[58] The fact that the Guadiana river in La Mancha flows underground for some distance has already been mentioned in Part I.

[59] A river in central Spain.   [60] A proverb among card players.

hands a fine handkerchief, and in it, as well as I could make out, a mummi-fied heart, for it was all dried up and pickled. Montesinos said that all those in the procession were servants of Durandarte and Belerma, who were enchanted there with their master and mistress, and that the last one, she who bore the heart wrapped up in the handkerchief, was the Lady Belerma, who with her damsels, four days a week, walked in that proces-sion and sang, or rather wept, her sorrowful dirges over the body and wretched heart of his cousin. He added that if she appeared to me some-what ugly, or at least, not as beautiful as fame reported, it was because of the bad nights and the worse days she spent in that enchantment, as I could see by the great dark circles around her eyes and her sickly complexion. 'And,' said he, 'her sallowness and the rings around her eyes do not come from the periodical ailment common to women, for it is many months, and even years, since it has appeared at her gates, but from the grief her own heart suffers for that object that she continually holds in her hands; it brings back to her memory the misfortune of her luckless lover. If it were not for this, scarcely would the great Dulcinea of El Toboso, so renowned in all these parts, and even in all the world, equal her in beauty, charm, and wit.'

"'Go slow, Don Montesinos,' said I. 'Tell your story rightly, for you are aware that all comparisons are odious, and there is no reason to compare one person with another. The peerless Dulcinea of El Toboso is what she is, and Doña Belerma is what she is and has been, and there let the matter rest.'

"To which he answered: 'Forgive me, Don Quixote, for I confess that I was wrong in saying that Lady Dulcinea could scarcely equal Lady Belerma, for it was enough for me to learn, I know not by what indications, that you are her knight, to make me bite my tongue rather than compare her to anything but Heaven itself.' After this satisfaction that the great Mon-tesinos gave me, my heart recovered from the shock it had received at hearing my lady compared to Belerma."

"And yet I'm amazed," cried Sancho, "that your worship did not jump upon the old fellow and kick every bone in his body and tear out his beard, without leaving a hair in it."

"No, Sancho, my friend," said Don Quixote, "it would not have been right for me to do so, for we are all bound to show respect to the aged, even though they be not knights, but especially to those who are and who be-come enchanted. I am certain that I owed him nothing in the matter of the many questions and answers that passed between us."

At this point the cousin remarked: "I cannot understand, Don Quixote, how in so short a space of time as you were down below you were able to see so many things and to say and answer so much."

"How long is it since I went down?" asked Don Quixote.

"A little more than an hour," replied Sancho.

"That cannot be," answered Don Quixote, "for night came when I was down there, and then morning, and again a night and a morning three times, so that, by my reckoning, I have been three days in these remote regions hidden from the upper world."

"My master must be right," said Sancho, "for since everything that has happened to him is by enchantment, perhaps what seems an hour to us would seem three days and nights down there."

"That must be so," said Don Quixote.

"Did you, dear sir, eat anything all that time?" asked the cousin.

"I have not broken my fast," answered Don Quixote, "nor did I feel hunger, even in my imagination."

"Do the enchanted eat?" inquired the cousin.

"They do not eat," answered Don Quixote, "nor do they void excrement, but it is thought that their nails, hair, and beard grow."

"And do the enchanted ones sleep, master?" asked Sancho.

"Certainly not," replied Don Quixote, "at any rate, during the three days I spent with them no one closed an eye; neither did I."

"This is a point," said Sancho, "where the proverb comes pat: 'Tell me the company you keep and I'll tell you what you are.' You, master, kept company with enchanted fellows who were fasting and watching. What wonder, then, that you neither ate nor slept while you were with them? But forgive me, master, if I tell you that of all you've said up to the present, God seize me—I was just going to say the devil—if I believe a single word."

"What!" cried the cousin. "Could Don Quixote tell a lie? Why, even if he wished to do so, this was no time for him to invent such a load of lies."

"I don't believe my master tells lies," answered Sancho.

"If not, what do you believe?" asked Don Quixote.

"I believe," said Sancho, "that this fellow Merlin, or these enchanters who bewitched the whole crew your worship says you saw and talked to down below, has piled your imagination with all that hodgepodge you have been telling and with everything else that you still have to tell."

"That might be, Sancho," replied Don Quixote, "but as a matter of fact, it is not so, for all that I have told you I saw with my own eyes and touched with my own hands. Now, what will you say when I tell you that among the countless marvelous things Montesinos showed me, he pointed out three peasant girls who were capering and frisking like she-goats over those delightful fields, and no sooner had I caught sight of them than I recognized one as the peerless Dulcinea of El Toboso and the other two as the same country wenches that were with her and to whom we spoke on the road from El Toboso? I asked Montesinos if he knew them. He answered that he did not, but that he thought they must be some enchanted ladies of quality, for it was but a few days since they had made their appearance in those meadows. He added that I should not be surprised at that, because many ladies of past and present times were enchanted there in various strange shapes, and among them he recognized Queen Guinevere and her duenna, Quintañona, who poured out the wine for Lancelot 'When from Brittany he came.' "[61]

As soon as Sancho Panza heard his master say this, he thought he would lose his wits, or else die with laughter, for since he knew the truth about the pretended enchanting of Dulcinea and had been himself the enchanter and the concocter of all the evidence, he made up his mind, beyond all

[61] From the ballad on Lancelot that Don Quixote quoted in the first adventure in the inn in Part I.

shadow of a doubt, that his master was out of his wits and mad as a March hare. So, he said to him: "It was a bitter day, dear master, when you went below to the other world, and it was an unlucky moment when you met Señor Montesinos, who has so transmogrified you for us. Up here, master, you were in your full senses, just as God has given you, uttering your maxims and giving counsels at every turn, and not as you are now, blabbing the greatest balderdash that ever was known."

"I know you, Sancho," replied Don Quixote, "so, I pay no heed to your words."

"No more do I to yours," said Sancho, "even though you beat me or kill me for those I've spoken or mean to speak if you don't correct and mend your own. But tell me, now that we're at peace, what made you recognize the lady our mistress? If you did speak to her, what did you say, and what did she say in reply?"

"I recognized her," said Don Quixote, "because she wore the same clothes as when you showed her to me. I spoke to her, but she did not answer a word, but only turned her back on me and fled, and she ran at such a pace that an arrow would not have overtaken her. I wanted to follow her and would have done so if Montesinos had not advised me not to weary myself in doing so, for it would be vain, especially as the hour was approaching when it would be necessary for me to leave the cave. He told me, moreover, that in time he would tell me how he, Belerma, Durandarte, and all who were there were to be disenchanted. What pained me most of all was that while Montesinos was speaking to me, one of the two attendants of the hapless Dulcinea came up to me without my having seen her coming, and with tears in her eyes, she said to me in a low agitated voice: 'My Lady Dulcinea of El Toboso kisses your worship's hand and beseeches you to let her know how you are; because she is in great need, she also entreats your worship as earnestly as she can to be so good as to lend her, upon this new dimity petticoat I have here, half a dozen reals, or as many as you have, which she promises to repay in a very short time.' Such a message amazed me; so, turning to Montesinos, I said: 'Is it possible, Señor Montesinos, that persons of quality who are enchanted can suffer need?' He replied: 'Believe me, Don Quixote of La Mancha, what is called want is the fashion all over the world; it extends throughout, touches everyone, and doesn't even spare the enchanted. And since Lady Dulcinea of El Toboso sends to borrow the six reals, and the security is apparently good, there is nothing to do but to give them to her, for she must no doubt be in sore straits.'

"'I will not take a pledge for her,' I replied, 'nor can I yet give her what she asks, for all I have is four reals,' which I gave her (they were those that you, Sancho, gave me the other day to hand as alms to the poor I met on the road), and I said: 'Tell your mistress, my dear friend, that I am distressed to hear of her troubles and that I wish I were a Fúcar[62] to relieve them; I would have her know that I cannot be, and ought not to be, in good health, seeing that I lack her pleasant company and witty conversation. So, I beseech her as earnestly as I can to allow herself to be seen and greeted by

---

[62]"Fúcar" is the Spanish form of "Fugger," the name of a famous family of Bavarian bankers and financiers in the Middle Ages.

this her captive and foot-weary cavalier. You must tell her also that when she least expects it, she will hear that I have made a vow, like the one that the Marquess of Mantua made to avenge his nephew Baldwin when he found him dying on the mountainside, which was not to eat bread off a tablecloth, with some other trifles he added, until he had avenged him.[63] And I will do the same: not to rest, and to wander over the seven regions of the earth more diligently than the Infante Don Pedro of Portugal,[64] until I have freed her from her enchantment.'

"'All that and more, your worship should do for my lady,' said the damsel in answer, and taking the four reals, instead of making me a curtsy she cut a caper that lifted her two yards up into the air."

"Holy God!" shouted Sancho at this point. "Is it possible that such things can happen in the world and that enchanters and enchantments can have the power to change the good sense of my master into such crazy folly? O master, master, for God's sake, mind yourself, consider your honor and give no credit to this empty balderdash that has destroyed your senses."

"You talk this way, Sancho, because you love me," said Don Quixote, "and because you are inexperienced in the affairs of the world. Everything that presents points of difficulty appears to you impossible. But after time has passed I shall tell you about some of the things I saw below that will make you believe what I have related, for its truth admits no reply or question."

CHAPTER XXIV

In which a thousand trifles are recounted, as nonsensical as they are necessary to the true understanding of this great history

The translator of this great history from the original written by its first author, Cide Hamete Benengeli, says that when he came to the adventure of the cave of Montesinos, he found written in the margin, in the hand of Hamete, these words: "I am unable to understand or to persuade myself that all that is written in the previous chapter literally happened to the valiant Don Quixote. The reason is that all the adventures until now have been feasible and probable, but this one of the cave I can find no way of accepting it as true, seeing that it exceeds all reasonable bounds. Nevertheless, I cannot possibly believe that Don Quixote, who was the most truthful gentleman and the noblest knight of the times, could tell a lie; why, he could not lie, even if they riddled him with arrows. On the other hand, when I consider the minute and detailed manner in which he has spoken, I find it still more impossible to believe that he could have fashioned such a tissue of absurdities in so short time.

"So, if this adventure seems apocryphal, it is not I who am to blame, for I write it down without vouching its truth or falsity. You, cautious reader, as you are wise, must judge for yourself, for I cannot, and should not, do

---

[63] The story of Carloto and Baldwin has already been told in Part I.

[64] A celebrated traveler. His account of his travels in the East was published in 1554.

more. One thing, however, is certain, that finally he retracted it on his deathbed and confessed that he had invented it, since he believed that it fitted in well with the adventures he had read of in his histories." . . .

[In a long section which follows, Don Quixote and Sancho, among other adventures, are entertained in the home of a duke and duchess who have read the First Part of their history and who play an elaborate series of practical jokes on them. The duke pretends to make Sancho the governor of an island, where he surprises everyone by the wisdom of his decisions. Meanwhile at the castle, Quixote is the victim of a series of jests, but he maintains his dignity; both he and Sancho grow in stature as the duke and duchess appear progressively more foolish. Leaving the palace, Quixote and Sancho encounter a group setting up a pastoral Arcadia, who treat them kindly. They then meet a Robin Hood-like highwayman, Roque Guinart, who befriends them. They go to Barcelona, where they are the guests of Don Antonio Moreno, who plays tricks on Quixote even more cruel than those in the castle of the duke and duchess.]

CHAPTER LXIV

Of the adventure that gave Don Quixote more sorrow than any that had ever befallen him

. . . . One morning when Don Quixote was riding out for an airing on the strand, armed cap-a-pie—for, as he often said, "my ornaments are arms, my rest the battle fray," and he was never a moment without them— he spied a knight riding toward him, armed like himself from head to foot, with a shining moon painted on his shield, who, when he came within hearing, called out to him: "Illustrious knight and never-enough-renowned Don Quixote of La Mancha, I am the Knight of the White Moon, whose unheard-of exploits perchance may have reached your ears. I come to enter into combat with you and to compel you by sword to own and confess that my mistress, whoever she may be, is incomparably more beautiful than your Dulcinea of El Toboso. If you will fairly confess this truth, you will spare your own life and me the trouble of taking it. If you are resolved to fight and if victory be mine, my terms require that you relinquish arms and the quest of adventures and retire to your home for the space of one year, where you shall live quietly and peaceably, without laying hand to your sword, for thus you will improve your temporal and spiritual welfare. But should you vanquish me, my head shall be at your mercy, my arms and my steed shall be yours, and the fame of my deeds shall be added to yours. Consider what is best for you and give me your answer without delay, for this day must decide the issue of this affair."

Don Quixote was surprised, not to say dumbfounded, as much by the arrogance of the Knight of the White Moon's challenge, as at the subject of it; so, with solemn gravity and composure he replied: "Knight of the White Moon, whose exploits have not yet come to my ears, I will make you swear that you have never set eyes upon the illustrious Dulcinea, for if you had done so, I am confident that you would never have made this claim, since the sight of her perfections must have convinced you that there never was, or ever can be, beauty comparable to hers. And so, without calling you a liar, I declare that you are mistaken and accept your challenge upon the spot, this very day. Furthermore, I accept all your conditions, with the exception of the transfer of your exploits, for they are unknown to me; I must remain contented with my own, such as they are. Choose, then, your ground and I shall do the same, and may St. Peter bless him whom God favors."

Meanwhile the viceroy, who had been informed of the arrival of the Knight of the White Moon and of the conversation that he was holding with Don Quixote, hastened to the scene of action accompanied by Don Antonio and others, firmly convinced that this must be some new jest invented by Don Antonio Moreno or by some other gentleman of the city. They arrived just as Don Quixote was wheeling Rozinante about to take his ground, and perceiving that they were on the point of attacking one another, the viceroy intervened and asked what was the reason for such a sudden encounter. The Knight of the White Moon replied that it was a question of preeminence in beauty, and then he briefly told what he had said to Don Quixote concerning the conditions of the duel. The viceroy then went up to Don Antonio and asked him in a whisper if he knew who the Knight of the White Moon was, or whether it was some trick they wished to play upon Don Quixote. Don Antonio answered that he did not know who he was, or whether the challenge was in earnest or not. The viceroy was troubled by that answer and wondered whether he ought or ought not to let the battle continue. At length, by dint of persuading himself that it was some jest, he withdrew, saying: "Gentlemen, if there be no other remedy than confession or death, and if Don Quixote is stubborn in his resolve, and you, Knight of the White Moon, are obstinate likewise, then in God's name go to it."

The Knight of the White Moon in courteous and well-chosen words thanked the viceroy for what he had done, and Don Quixote did likewise. And after recommending himself to Heaven and to his Dulcinea, he retired to take a longer compass of the ground, for he saw his opponent do the same; then, without any flourish of trumpets or any other martial instrument to give the signal for the outset, they both turned their horses around at the same instant. But he of the White Moon, who was mounted on the fleeter steed, met Don Quixote two-thirds down the course and hurtled into him with such a fierce onslaught that, without touching him with his lance, which he seemed purposely to hold aloof, he brought both horse and rider to the ground. He then sprang upon him and said as he clapped his lance to his opponent's visor: "Knight, you are vanquished and a dead man if you don't confess in accordance with the conditions of our challenge."

Don Quixote, who was bruised and stunned, without lifting his visor and as though speaking from the tomb, said in a faint low voice: "Dulcinea of El Toboso is the most beautiful woman in the world, and I am the most unfortunate knight on earth, and it isn't just that my weakness should discredit this truth. Go on, knight, press on with your lance and take away my life, since you have robbed me of my honor."

"That I shall certainly never do," said he of the White Moon. "Long may the fame of Lady Dulcinea of El Toboso's beauty live and flourish! All I demand is that the great Don Quixote should retire to his village for one year, or for a period to be fixed by me, in accordance with the agreement drawn up before this battle."

The viceroy, Don Antonio, and many others witnessed all that passed, and they heard Don Quixote promise that he would fulfill all the terms of their engagement like a genuine and punctilious knight, provided nothing was required to the prejudice of Lady Dulcinea. When this declaration was made, he of the White Moon turned about his horse, and after bowing to the viceroy, he rode at a half gallop into the city.

The viceroy commanded Don Antonio to go after him and to ascertain by all possible means who he was. Then, they raised Don Quixote from the ground, and uncovering his face, they found him pale and bathed in sweat. Rozinante was in such a plight that he was unable to stir for some time. As for Sancho, he was so sorrowful and cast down that he knew not what to say or do; he fancied that all had taken place in dreams and that the whole business was the result of enchantment. He saw his master overthrown and bound to lay aside his arms for a whole year. He imagined that his master's glory had been finally eclipsed and his own hopes from the latter's recent promises vanished like smoke in the wind. He was afraid that Rozinante might be crippled forever and his master's bones be permanently knocked out of joint, though it would be no small blessing if his madness were knocked out of him. In the end they carried the knight into the city on a hand-chair that the viceroy had sent for. The viceroy himself returned, eager to ascertain who was this Knight of the White Moon who had left Don Quixote in such a piteous state.

CHAPTER LXV

Which reveals who the Knight of the White Moon was, with the liberation of Don Gregorio and other incidents

Don Antonio Moreno rode after the Knight of the White Moon, and a great number of boys also followed, pestering him until he took refuge in an inn inside the city. Don Antonio entered there, too, as he was eager to make his acquaintance. A squire came forward to receive him and take off his armor, and he shut himself up in a lower room, where he was followed by Don Antonio, who was on tenterhooks to know who he was. Then, when the Knight of the White Moon found that the gentleman would not leave him, he said: "I know very well, sir, what you have come here for: to find out who I am. As it happens, there is no reason for me to conceal myself; so, while my servant is taking off my armor, I shall tell you the whole truth of my story, without omitting a single detail. You must know sir, that I am called the bachelor Sansón Carrasco; I come from the same town as Don Quixote of La Mancha, whose madness and folly have been the cause of deep sorrow to his friends and neighbors. I myself felt particular sympathy for his sad case, and as I believed his recovery to depend upon his remaining quietly at home, I earnestly endeavored to accomplish that end. And so, about three months ago I sallied forth myself as a knight-errant, calling myself the Knight of the Mirrors and intending to fight and vanquish him without doing him any harm and to impose as the condition of our combat that the vanquished should be at the mercy of the conqueror. Feeling certain of my success, I expected to send him home for twelve months, hoping that during that time he might be restored to health. But Fortune willed otherwise, for it was he who vanquished me; he unhorsed me, and my scheme was of no avail. He continued his journey, and I returned home vanquished, ashamed, and injured by my fall. Nevertheless, I did not abandon my scheme, as you have seen this day, and as he is so punctilious and so particular in observing the laws of knight-errantry, he is sure to perform his promise. This, sir, is my whole story, and I beseech you not to reveal me to Don Quixote, in order that my good intentions may produce their fruit and that the worthy gentleman may recover his sense, for when he is freed from the follies of chivalry, he is a man of excellent understanding."

"O sir!" replied Don Antonio. "May God forgive you for the wrong you have done in robbing the world of the most diverting madman who was ever seen. Is it not plain, sir, that his cure can never benefit mankind half as much as the pleasure he affords by his eccentricities? But I feel sure, sir, that all your art will not cure such deep-rooted madness; were it not uncharitable, I would express the hope that he may never recover, for by his cure we would lose not only the knight's good company, but also the drollery of his squire, Sancho Panza, which is enough to transform melancholy itself into mirth. All the same, I shall hold my peace and not breathe a word to him, to see whether I am right in suspecting that all Mister Carrasco's efforts will have no effect."

The bachelor answered that the business in any case was far advanced and that he was confident there would be a favorable result. And so, after Don Antonio had offered to follow the latter's instructions, the bachelor took his leave that same day. He had his armor tied on a mule; he mounted the charger on which he had done battle and left the city for home, meeting no adventure on the way worthy of mention in this true history.

Don Antonio told the viceroy everything that Carrasco had said. The viceroy was not too pleased by it, for Don Quixote's retirement would mean a loss to all those who were entertained by the tales of his mad adventures.

For six days Don Quixote was confined to his bed, dejected, melancholy, thoughtful, out of humor, and full of bleak reflections on his luckless overthrow. Sancho strove hard to comfort him, saying: "Raise your head, master, cheer up and thank your stars that you've come off without even a broken rib. Remember, sir, that 'They that give must take'; and that 'Where there are hooks there aren't always flitches.' Come now, sir, a fig for the doctor! You've no need of him. Let us be off for home, and give up this gallivanting up and down in search of adventures in lands and places, God knows where. And when you come to think of it, I'm the one who's the greater loser by this, though it's your worship who is in a worse pickle. Though with my government I gave up all desire of being a governor again, I've never lost the hankering to be a count. But I may as well say good-bye to all that if your worship gives up trying to be a king and resigns your profession of chivalry! So all my hopes end in smoke."

"Be quiet, Sancho. Do you not see that my seclusion and retirement need only last a year? After that I shall return to my honored calling, and I am bound to win a kingdom, and some countship or other for you."

"God grant you may," said Sancho, "and let sin be deaf, for I've always heard that good hopes are better than poor holdings. . . ."

[On the journey home, Quixote considers becoming a pastoral shepherd; he and Sancho meet several people from their past adventures, including the duke and duchess, who play one last trick on them. Sancho continues the self-flagellation the duke claimed was necessary to free Dulcinea from her enchantment, though he whips trees instead of himself whenever possible. Without realizing it, they arrive at their village.]

CHAPTER LXXIII

Of the omens that Don Quixote met at the entrance to his village, with other incidents that embellish and accredit this great history

As they entered the village, Cide Hamete informs us, Don Quixote noticed two boys pummeling one another on the threshing floor, and heard one say to the other: "Don't fash[65] yourself, Periquillo, for you'll never see her in all the days of your life."

Don Quixote, overhearing this, said to Sancho: "Did you catch what the boy said, 'You'll never see her in all the days of your life?'"

"Well," rejoined Sancho, "what does it matter what the boy said?"

"What?" retorted his master. "Don't you realize that such words, when applied to my affairs, clearly portend that I shall never see my Dulcinea?"

Sancho was about to answer again, but was hindered from so doing by a great hue and cry of hounds and huntsmen in full pursuit of a hare, which was so hard pressed that she came and squatted for shelter just between Dapple's feet. Immediately Sancho laid hold of her and presented her to Don Quixote, but the knight kept muttering to himself: "*Malum signum! Malum signum!*[66] A hare runs away, hounds pursue her, and Dulcinea does not appear."

"You are a strange man, sir," said Sancho. "Let us suppose that poor bunny here is Mistress Dulcinea, the greyhounds that followed her are the wicked enchanters who transmogrified her into a country lass; she races away, I catch her and hand her safe and sound to your worship, and you hold her in your arms and pet her: what harm is there in this, and what bad omen is this?"

By this time the two boys who had been fighting came up to see the hare, and when Sancho inquired why they had been fighting, he was answered by the boy who had uttered the ominous words, that he had snatched from his playmate a cage full of crickets, which he would not give back to him again. Sancho pulled a threepenny piece out of his pocket and gave it to the boy for his cage; and giving it to Don Quixote, he said: "There you are, sir; all the tokens of bad luck have been brought to nothing, and though I am a blockhead, I'm convinced all these things have no more to do with our affairs than the clouds of yesteryear. And if I remember right, I've heard the curate of our village say that no decent self-respecting Christian should give ear to such foolishness; and I've heard you yourself, master, say not many days ago that all those Christians who troubled their heads with fortune-telling rubbish were no better than nincompoops. So, without more ado let us make straight for our homes."

---

[65] Worry.   [66] "A bad sign."

By now the huntsmen had come up and asked for their hare, which Don Quixote delivered up to them. They passed on, and just as they were entering the town, they perceived the curate and the bachelor Sansón Carrasco at their devotions in a small field. We must add that Sancho had thrown over Dapple and the bundle of arms, as a cover, the buckram robe painted with flames of fire that they had put on him in the duke's castle on the night when Altisidora rose from the dead.[67] He had also fitted the miter on Dapple's head, and this ornament transformed him as strangely as ever an ass was transformed in all the world. The curate and the bachelor recognized them at once and hastened toward them with open arms. Don Quixote dismounted and embraced them affectionately. Meanwhile the boys, who are as sharp-eyed as lynxes and miss no detail, sighted the ass's miter and rushed up to look at it, saying: "Have a look, boys! Here is Sancho's ass gaudier than Mingo, and Don Quixote's hack leaner than ever."[68]

Surrounded by the boys of the town and attended by the curate and the bachelor, they moved toward the house of Don Quixote, where they found the housekeeper and his niece, who had heard of their arrival, waiting for them on the doorstep. News had also reached Teresa, the wife of Sancho Panza, and she came running half-naked and with her hair all tousled, leading by the hand her daughter, Sanchica. But when she found that her husband was not quite dressed up to her notions of what a governor should wear, she said: "What's all this, husband? You look as if you'd plodded all the way on shanks' mare! You look more misgoverned than governor, I'm thinking."

"Whisht, Teresa!" said Sancho. "Many a time there's a hook but devil a flitch on it.[69] First of all, let us go home, and then I'll tell you wonders. I've money, and after all, that is what counts, and I made it by my own labors without harming a soul."

"Bring home the money, my dear," said Teresa, "no matter how or where you've earned it; after all there's nothing new in that."

Sanchica then hugged her father and asked what he had brought her, for she longed for his return as the flowers do for the dew in May. So, she caught hold of her father's waistband with one hand and pulled Dapple after her by the halter with the other, and her mother took Sancho by the arm on the other side, and away they all went to his cottage, leaving Don Quixote in his own house under the care of his niece and housekeeper with the curate and the bachelor to keep him company.

Don Quixote drew the last two aside, and without observing time or season, he gave them a short account of his defeat and the obligation he lay under of remaining in his village for a year, which, like a true knight-errant, he was determined to observe most faithfully. He added that he intended to become a shepherd and spend that year in the solitude of the fields and woods, giving rein to his amorous thoughts and practising the virtues of the pastoral life. Furthermore, he begged them, if more impor-

[67] The story of this practical joke in the duke's castle is omitted here.
[68] A reference to a popular fifteenth-century poem named *Mingo Revulgo*, in which Mingo is dressed in a blue smock and red doublet.
[69] A proverb: "Sometimes there's a hook, but no bacon on it."

tant duties were not a hindrance, to become his companions, and he assured them that he would furnish them with sufficient sheep and cattle to
enable them to belong to such a profession. He let them know that the
principal part of the business was already done, for he had planned names
that would fit them exactly. The curate asked him what they were, and Don
Quixote replied that he was to call himself the shepherd Quixotiz, the bachelor the shepherd Carrascón, the curate the shepherd Curiambro, and
Sancho Panza the shepherd Panzino. They were all astonished at Don
Quixote's new strain of madness, but considering that this might be a
means of preventing him from wandering from home and hoping at the
same time that within the year he might be cured of his mad knight-
errantry, they applauded his pastoral folly as a wise idea and offered to
become his companions in carrying it out.

"Better still," said Sansón Carrasco, "as all the world is now aware that I
am a very celebrated poet, I shall compose pastoral or courtly verses at
every turn, or such as may best assist our cause, so that we may entertain
ourselves in the lonely wastes where we may have to wander. But what is
most important, gentlemen, is for each one of us to choose the name of the
shepherdess he intends to celebrate in his verses, and not to have a single
tree, no matter how tough its bark, on which her name is not inscribed and
cut on it, as is the custom of love-sick shepherds."

"That is quite right," answered Don Quixote, "though for myself I have
no need to seek for the name of any imaginary shepherdess, for I have the
peerless Dulcinea of El Toboso, glory of these banks, ornament of these
meadows, the prop of beauty, the cream of grace, and in short, the cyno-
sure of all praise, however exaggerated it may be."

"That is true," said the curate, "but we must look around for indulgent
shepherdesses who are easy to manage, and we may have to trim their
angles if they don't square with us."

"And if they should fail," added Sansón Carrasco, "we'll give them the
names in print that are known to all the world: Phyllidas, Amaryllises,
Dianas, Fleridas, Galateas, and Belisardas;[70] since they're for sale in the
markets, we can easily buy them and keep them for our own. If my lady—
my shepherdess, I should say—by chance be called Ana, I'll celebrate her
under the name of Anarda; if Francisca, I'll call her Francenia; and if
Lucía, Lucinda: that is all it will come to. And if Sancho Panza is to enter
our confraternity, he can celebrate his wife, Teresa Panza, under the name
Teresaina."

Don Quixote smiled at the application of the name and the curate extolled his chaste and honorable resolution, repeating his offer to bear him
company for as long as he could spare from compulsory duties. With this
they took leave of him, advising him to take care of his health and to adopt
a healthy diet.

As luck would have it, the housekeeper and the niece heard the conversation between the three on the subject of the pastoral life, and no sooner
had the priest and the bachelor gone than they both burst into Don Quixote's room, and the niece cried: "Mercy on us, uncle! What does this mean?
We thought that you had come to stay at home and live here like a quiet,

---

[70] Common names in pastoral poetry.

honest gentleman, and here you are longing to wander off into fresh labyrinths, becoming a 'gentle shepherd, come and go.' In truth, uncle, the straw is too old to make pipes of."

"Heaven help us, sir!" added the housekeeper. "How will your worship be able to stand the summer's heat, the winter's frost, and the howling of the wolves in the open country? Pray, sir, you mustn't think of it; it's a business for strong men who are born and bred to it from the days when they were babes in arms. And if it comes to worst, better to be a knight-errant than a shepherd. Mark my words, master, and heed my counsel; I'm not full of food and drink, but fasting, and I'm no chicken, but fifty years of age, and I say to you: Stay at home, look after your property, go to confession often, do good to the poor, and let me take the blame if you go wrong."

"My dear girls, do cease your prating," Don Quixote answered. "I know best what I have to do; only help me to my bed, for I do not feel very well. Remember that whether I be a knight-errant or an errant shepherd, you will always find me ready to provide for you, and you may rely on my good faith."

And his affectionate daughters—for so the niece and the housekeeper undoubtedly were—undressed him, put him to bed, where they brought him something to eat, and made him as comfortable as possible.

CHAPTER LXXIV

Of how Don Quixote fell ill, of the will he made, and of his death

As all human things, especially the lives of men, are not eternal, and even their beginnings are but steps to their end, and as Don Quixote was under no special dispensation of Heaven, he was snatched away by death when he least expected it. Whether his sickness was caused by his melancholic reflections on his defeat, or whether it was so preordained by Providence, he was stricken down by a violent fever that confined him to his bed for six days. All that time his good friends, the priest, the bachelor, and the barber, often visited him, and his trusty squire, Sancho Panza, never left his bed-side. They were convinced that his sickness was due to his sorrow at having been defeated and his disappointment in the matter of Dulcinea's disenchantment; and so, they tried in every way to cheer him up. The bachelor begged him to pluck up his spirits and get up from his bed so that they might begin their pastoral life, adding that he had already written an eclogue that would put Sannazaro's[71] nose out of joint, and that he had bought with his own money from a shepherd of Quintanar two pedigreed dogs to watch the flock, one called Barcino and the other Butrón. But this had no effect, for Don Quixote continued to mope as before. A physician was sent for, who, after feeling his pulse, took a rather gloomy view of the case and told him that he should provide for his soul's health, for that of his body was in dangerous condition. Don Quixote received the news calmly and serenely, but his niece, his housekeeper, and his squire began to weep as

---

[71] Jacapo Sannazaro (1456–1533) was famous for his pastoral novel *Arcadia*.

bitterly as if he had been laid out already. The physician was of the opinion that melancholy and mortification had brought him to death's door. Don Quixote then asked them to leave him for a little while, as he wished to sleep. They retired, and he slept at a stretch, as they say, for more than six hours, and the housekeeper and the niece were afraid that he might not waken from it. At length he did awaken and cried out in a loud voice: "Blessed be the Almighty for this great benefit He has granted me! Infinite are His mercies, and undiminished even by the sins of men."

The niece, who was listening very attentively to these words of her uncle, found more sense in them than there was in his usual talk, at least since he had fallen ill, and she questioned him: "What do you mean, uncle? Has anything strange taken place? What mercies and what sins of men are you talking about?"

"Mercies," answered Don Quixote, "that God has just this moment granted to me in spite of all my sins. My judgment is now clear and unfettered, and that dark cloud of ignorance has disappeared, which the continual reading of those detestable books of knight-errantry had cast over my understanding. Now I see their folly and fraud, and my sole regret is that the discovery comes too late to allow me to amend my ways by reading others that would enlighten my soul. I find, dear niece, that my end approaches, but I would have it remembered that though in my life I was reputed a madman, yet in my death this opinion was not confirmed. Therefore, my dear child, call my good friends, the priest, the bachelor Sansón Carrasco, and Master Nicholas, the barber, for I wish to make my confession and my will."

There was no need for the niece to go to the trouble, for presently all three arrived at the house, and Don Quixote no sooner saw them than he said: "My dear friends, welcome the happy news! I am no longer Don Quixote of La Mancha, but Alonso Quixano, the man whom the world formerly called the Good, owing to his virtuous life. I am now the sworn enemy of Amadis of Gaul and his innumerable brood; I now abhor all profane stories of knight-errantry, for I know only too well, through Heaven's mercy and through my own personal experience, the great danger of reading them."

When his three friends heard him talk thus, they concluded that he was stricken with some new madness. Sansón then said to him: "What does all this mean, Don Quixote? Now that we have just received news that Lady Dulcinea is disenchanted, and now that we are just about to become shepherds and spend our days singing and living like princes, you talk about turning yourself into a hermit. No more foolish tales, I beg you, and come back to your senses."

"Those foolish tales," replied Don Quixote, "that up to now have been my bane may with Heaven's help turn to my advantage at my death. Dear friends, I feel that I am rapidly sinking; therefore, let us put aside all jesting. I want a priest to hear my confession, and a notary to draw up my will. At such a moment a man must not deceive his soul; therefore, I beg you to send for the notary while the priest hears my confession."

Don Quixote's words amazed his hearers, but though they were at first skeptical about the return of his sanity, they were forced to take him at his word. One of the symptoms that made them fear he was near the point of death was the suddenness with which he had recovered his intellect, for after what he had already said, he conversed with such good sense and displayed such true Christian resignation that they believed his wits had been restored at last. The curate, therefore, told the company to leave the room, and he confessed Don Quixote. In the meantime the bachelor hastened to fetch the notary, and presently he returned with him and with Sancho Panza. The latter (who had already heard from the bachelor the news of his master's plight), finding the niece and the housekeeper in tears, began to make wry faces and finally burst out crying. After the priest had heard the sick man's confession, he came out saying: "There is no doubt that Alonso Quixano is at the point of death, and there is also no doubt that he is in his entire right mind; so, we should go in and enable him to make his will."

These sad tidings burst open the floodgates of the housekeeper's, the niece's, and the good squire's swollen eyes; their tears flowed fast and furious, and a thousand sighs rose from their breasts, for, indeed, as it has been noted, the sick gentleman, whether as Alonso Quixano the Good or as Don Quixote of La Mancha, had always been so good-natured and so agreeable that he was beloved not only by his family, but by all who knew him.

The notary, with the rest of the company, then went into the sick man's chamber, and Don Quixote stated the preamble to the will, commending his soul to Heaven and including the customary Christian declarations. When he came to the legacies he said:

"Item, I give and bequeath to Sancho Panza, whom in my madness I made my squire, whatever money he has of mine in his possession; and whereas there are accounts and reckonings to be settled between us for what he has received and disbursed, my will and pleasure is that he should not be required to furnish any account of such sums, and whatever may remain due to me, which must be but little, be enjoyed by him as my free gift, and may he prosper with it. And as when I was mad, he was through my means made governor of an island, I would now, in my right senses, give him the government of a kingdom, were it in my power, for his honesty and his faithfulness deserve it.

"And now, my friend," said he, turning to Sancho, "forgive me for making you appear as mad as I was myself, and for drawing you into my errors and persuading you that there have been and still are knights-errant in the world."

"Woe is me!" cried Sancho all in tears. "Don't die on me; but take my advice and live on for many a year; the maddest trick a man can play in his life is to yield up the ghost without more ado, and without being knocked on the head or stabbed through the belly to mope away and die of the doldrums. Shame on you, master; don't let the grass grow under your feet. Up with you this instant, out of your bed, and let us put on our shepherd's clothing and off with us to the fields as we had resolved a while back. Who knows but we may find Lady Dulcinea behind a hedge, disenchanted and as fresh as a daisy. If it's your defeat that is tearing your heart, lay the blame on me and say that it was my fault in not tightening Rozinante's girths enough, and that was why you were unhorsed. You must remember, too, sir, from your books on knight-errantry how common it was for knights to jostle one another out of the saddle, and he who's lying low today may be crowning his victory tomorrow."

"Just so," said Sansón; "there is good sense in what honest Sancho says."

"Go softly, I pray you, gentlemen," replied Don Quixote; "one should never look for birds of this year in the nests of yesteryear. I was mad, but I am now in my senses; I was once Don Quixote of La Mancha, but I am now, as I said before, Alonso Quixano the Good, and I hope that my repentance and my sincere words may restore me to the same esteem as you had for me before. So now proceed, Mr. Notary.

"Item, I declare and appoint Antonia Quixano, my niece, here present, sole heiress of all my estate, both real and personal, after all my just debts and legacies have been paid and deducted out of my goods and chattels; and the first charges on the estate shall be salaries due to my housekeeper, together with twenty ducats over and above her salary wages, which I leave and bequeath her to buy a gown.

"Item, I appoint the curate and the bachelor Sansón Carrasco, here present, to be the executors of this my last will and testament.

"Item, it is my will that if my niece Antonia Quixano should wish to marry, it will be with none but a person who, upon strict investigation, shall be found never to have read a book of knight-errantry in his life; but if it should be ascertained that he is acquainted with such books and she still insists on marrying him, she is then to lose all rights to my bequest, which my executors may then distribute in charity as they think fit.

"Item, I entreat the said executors that if at any time they happen to meet with the author of a certain book entitled *The Second Part of the Exploits of Don Quixote of La Mancha*, they will in my name most heartily beg his pardon for my having been unwittingly the cause of his writing such an amount of folly and triviality as he has done. Indeed, as I depart from this life my conscience troubles me that ever I was the cause of his publishing such a book."

After finishing the will, he swooned away and stretched his body to its full length in the bed. The company were alarmed and ran to his assistance; but these fainting attacks were repeated with great frequency during the three days that he lived after he had made his will. The household was in grief and confusion; and yet, after all, the niece continued to eat her meals, the housekeeper drowned her sorrows in wine, and Sancho Panza puffed himself up with satisfaction, for the thought of a legacy possesses a magic power to remove, or at least to soothe, the pangs that the heir should otherwise feel for the death of his friend.

At length Don Quixote's last day came, after he had received all the sacraments and expressed his abhorrence of books of knight-errantry. The notary, who was present, said that he had never read of any knight who ever died in his bed so peacefully and like a good Christian as Don Quixote. And so, amid the tears and lamentations of his friends, who knelt by his bedside, he gave up the ghost, that is to say, he died. And when the priest saw that he had passed away, he bade the notary give him a certificate stating that Alonso Quixano the Good, commonly known as Don Quixote of La Mancha, had died a natural death. This he desired lest any other author, except Cide Hamete Benengeli, take the opportunity of raising him from the dead and presume to write endless histories of his pretended adventures.

Such was the death of that imaginative gentleman Don Quixote of La Mancha, whose native place Cide Hamete did not wish to ascertain, with the intention that all the towns and villages in La Mancha should vie with one another for the honor of having given him birth, as the seven cities of Greece did for Homer. We shall omit the lamentations of Sancho and those of the niece and the housekeeper, as well as the epitaphs that were composed for his tomb, and we shall only quote the following, which the bachelor Sansón Carrasco inscribed on it:

> Here lies the noble fearless knight,
> Whose valor rose to such a height;
> When Death at last did strike him down,
> His was the victory and renown.
> He reck'd the world of little prize,
> And was a bugbear in men's eyes;
> But had the fortune in his age
> To live a fool and die a sage.[72]

And said the most prudent Cide Hamete to his pen: "Here you shall rest, hanging from this rack by this copper wire, my quill. Whether you are well cut or badly pointed here you shall live long ages, unless presumptuous and unworthy historians take you down to profane you. But before they touch you, warn them in as strong terms as you are able:

> Beware, beware, all petty knaves,
> I may be touched by none:
> This enterprise, my worthy king,
> Is kept for me alone.[73]

For me alone Don Quixote was born, and I for him. He knew how to act, and I knew how to write. We two alone are as one, despite that fictitious and Tordesillescan scribe who has dared, and may dare again with his coarse and ill-trimmed ostrich quill, to write the exploits of my valorous knight.[74] This is no burden for his shoulders, no subject for his frost-bound muse; and should you by chance get to know him, do warn him to let Don Quixote's weary and moldering bones rest in the grave, and not seek, against all canons of death, to carry him off to Old Castile, compelling him to leave the tomb where he really and truly lies stretched out full length, powerless to make a third expedition[75] and new sally. Surely his two, which have met with approval and have delighted all the people who knew about them, both here and abroad, are enough to make a mockery of all the innumerable sallies undertaken by all the countless knights-errant.

[72] Samuel Putnam points out that these lines are "a doggerel imitation of the epitaphs composed by village poets."

[73] A quotation from an old ballad.

[74] Another attack on the "false Quixote," whose author was reputedly from Tordesillas.

[75] This should be "fourth expedition." Don Quixote had three expeditions, one alone and two with Sancho.

Thus you will comply with your Christian profession by offering good advice to one who wishes you ill, and I shall be proud to be the first author who ever enjoyed witnessing the full effect of his writing. For my sole aim has been to arouse men's scorn for the false and absurd stories of knighterrantry, whose prestige has been shaken by this tale of my true Don Quixote, and which will, without any doubt, soon crumble in ruin. Vale."[76]

[76] Farewell.

William Shakespeare
(1564–1616)

Shakespeare's plays and poems, taken together, have a quality of impersonality, or suprapersonality, transcending the limitations and biases that one normally finds in a single author. If we try to understand Shakespeare through his works, he is everything and everyone. Each of his plays is its own place, with a distinctive mood, method, and thematic emphasis; collectively, they define a mind and a sensibility that seem nearly as inclusive as the world itself. It is appropriate, then, if also tantalizing, that we know so little about the inner workings of the mind of Shakespeare as an individual and artist. Nineteenth-century critical tradition tended to find autobiographical revelations in the plays and some of the poems (especially the Sonnets), *and modern psychoanalytic criticism finds in them revelations of Shakespeare's unconscious mind, but all the hard facts we have about him are impersonal or external: records of law and vital statistics, annals of the Elizabethan and Jacobean stage, and references to him by contemporary authors and playgoers.*

Shakespeare was born in the town of Stratford, in the geographical heart of England, in April, 1564. His father was a tradesman and prominent member of the town government, his mother a descendant of a very old family. Although he did not go to a university, he got a good education at the Stratford grammar school, especially in the Latin classics. (Ovid seems to have been one of his favorite authors.) In 1582 he married Anne Hathaway, by whom he had two daughters and a son who died in boyhood. How and where Shakespeare spent his early twenties is obscure; by 1590 or so, however, he was active in the London theater. During the next decade he became highly popular as a playwright and poet (among his nondramatic works are Venus and Adonis, The Rape of Lucrece, *and the famous* Sonnets), *apparently making a good living and also acquiring influential friends. In 1596, almost certainly through Shakespeare's efforts, his family was granted a coat of arms. By 1612 or so, when he stopped writing, he had composed more than three dozen plays. He died on April 23, 1616—very nearly on the same day Cervantes died.*

Shakespeare wrote his plays for performance; he had little or no interest in having them printed and published. A reading audience for plays did exist, however, and many of Shakespeare's were in fact published during his lifetime—some in good versions, others in very poor ones. In 1623, seven years after Shakespeare died, the "First Folio," a comprehensive collection of almost all his plays, was issued under the supervision of two members of Shakespeare's old company. The Folio contains, among other tributes, a famous one by the eminent contemporary poet and playwright Ben Jonson. Not a man to bestow praise lightly, Jonson rated Shakespeare above all his contemporary dramatists. His true peers, according to Jonson, were Aeschylus, Sophocles, and Euripides; in comedy, Jonson asserted, Shakespeare was peerless. This tribute has proved to be an accurate prophecy of Shakespeare's reputation in later ages.

Beginning with the First Folio, it has been customary to divide Shakespeare's plays into three categories: tragedies, comedies, and histories. But these labels are inadequate; Shakespeare's plays are typically blends of different tones and genres. Certain of the histories (Richard the Second, for example) can accurately be called tragedies. The comedies are of several different kinds; the early Comedy of Errors *and* Taming of the Shrew *are mainly farcical;* A Midsummer Night's Dream *combines farce with lyrical fantasy; the "romantic" comedies of Shakespeare's middle period (including* As You Like It *and* Twelfth Night*) are warmly exuberant works that place fairly realistic characters in never-never-land settings; the "dark" comedies like* Measure for Measure *include some disturbing, uncomic elements; the late* Winter's Tale *and* Tempest *treat serious themes but with a disregard for realism that has earned for them the name romances. Some of the tragedies mingle comic episodes with their prevalent high seriousness (as in* Romeo and Juliet *and* Macbeth*), and several are based on history, especially that of ancient Rome (*Julius Caesar, Antony and Cleopatra, Coriolanus*).*

To enumerate briefly the qualities that make Shakespeare great is impossible, since the individual plays and poems are so different from one another. Every age from Shakespeare's time to the present has found something different in him to admire. All ages, however, have recognized his supreme skill in inventing sharply etched characters; it frequently happens that long after one has forgotten the exact story of a play one remembers its people with absolute vividness. It is true, paradoxically, that many of Shakespeare's characters represent universal types; Romeo's name has become a synonym for the fervent young lover, and the adjective Falstaffian *has entered the common vocabulary of English as an epithet for robust, expansive heartiness. But none of Shakespeare's characters is merely a type. Scores of them are fully realized persons, absolutely individualized new creations even when they are adapted from earlier sources. (Few of Shakespeare's stories were wholly invented by him.) More than anything else, it is his power to create such characters that has prompted extravagant praise of Shakespeare's "godlike" genius. Some critics, in fact, have speculated about the characters, even those Shakespeare wholly invented, almost as though they had a real existence outside of the plays. Such excesses, odd as they may seem, are understandable, for the characters do seem to speak and act as of their own volition, with the combination of inevitability and unpredictability that one finds in living human beings.*

The power to create characters and tell compelling stories underlies one traditional view of Shakespeare: that his plays are children of "nature" rather than of "art." That view of him no longer has much currency. Both in their total conception and in their craftsmanship, most Shakespearean plays are both powerful and skillfully controlled. He is expert in managing plot-lines and is particularly fond of double-plotting. King Lear *is an excellent example. The Gloucester plot is in intricate parallel and contrast with the story of the king's education in suffering, with the result that the theme has a breadth and universality it might not otherwise have.*

Perhaps the ultimate reason for Shakespeare's power is simply his mastery of language as an expressive and poetic medium. The many pages given to Shakespeare in dictionaries of quotations attest the beauty and memorability of his words. But such excerpting, which removes Shakespeare's lines from their dramatic context, also does him a disservice, suggesting as it does that he was a gnomic philosopher at large. The well known lines from Hamlet *"To thine own self be true, / And it must follow, as the night the day, / Thou canst not then be false to any man" have been quoted countless times without an awareness that in the play they illustrate a pompous old man's self-importance. The true measure of Shakespeare's language is its effectiveness in the play where it occurs; much of Shakespeare's artistry lies in his skill in giving different characters different poetic imaginations and voices. Moreover, the quality of a play's language—plain or ornate, ceremonial or colloquial, quiet or declamatory, direct or fraught with images and figures of speech—is intimately wedded to the governing themes and distinctive atmospheres. Whether the plays generated their linguistic texture or the other way around is a difficult question. Whatever the answer, it remains true that language—prose or verse—is the principal shaping force of Shakespearean drama.*

No one play can represent adequately Shakespeare's many facets, but for many people, especially in the twentieth century, King Lear *is his most powerful, disturbing, and sublime work. Its setting is a virtually prehistoric darkness (despite the medieval tone of the scene in which Edgar challenges Edmund)—an apt background for the play's ferocity, its pain, and its questionings of providence. The play is so disturbing that for a long time after it was created it was performed with a rewritten ending in which Cordelia survives to marry Edgar. In our own time, the play has come into its own, perhaps because it explores so unflinchingly the existential question of man's difficult search for meaning in a moral and natural world where agony and injustice seem to reign. The play's moral vision is very complex and has stirred controversy, especially over Shakespeare's implied answer to the problem of evil—if, indeed, he does suggest an answer. In theme and atmosphere—for example, the inscrutable mystery with which the cosmos seems to be governed—*Lear *invites comparison with ancient Greek tragedy. (The play refers continually to "the gods" rather than "God.") The parallel with Sophocles is especially compelling. In its theme of poetic justice, its story of filial and sibling relationships, its atmosphere of suffering, its tentative gropings toward positive affirmation, its imagery (of blindness, for example),* King Lear *has striking affinities with the Oedipus plays and with* Antigone.

NOTE ON SHAKESPEARE'S STAGE

The public theaters of Shakespeare's day were modeled architecturally on inn-yards, where, a generation or so earlier, plays had commonly been presented by itinerant troupes of actors. The theaters were large three-story structures, round, square, or multisided in shape, surrounding an open-air arena. Three sides of the theater consisted of galleries, facing inward toward the arena. From the fourth side, a large platform stage, about five feet high, perhaps forty feet deep and twenty-five feet wide, projected into the arena; around it stood those spectators ("groundlings") who paid the lowest price of admission. At the back of this stage were two doors and a curtained alcove used for "discovery" scenes. There was some sort of acting space on the second level, as well, perhaps another curtained alcove and perhaps a projecting balcony,

A reconstruction of the Fortune Theater by Walter H. Godfrey. (From Shakespeare's Theatre by Ashley H. Thorndike.)

supported by posts rising from the main stage. There may have been a third level as well, occasionally used by actors but intended primarily for musicians. To avoid harassment by the Puritanically-minded London government, the theaters were built outside the city limits, especially on the south bank of the Thames. A theater could accommodate about two thousand people, drawn from every social level from the laboring class through the titled aristocracy.

As in ancient Greek drama, spectacle was important on Shakespeare's stage. Costumes were elaborate, and the style of acting was emphatic and declamatory. All the actors were male; the female roles were played by boys. There was little or no scenery, and action flowed continuously without scene or act divisions. Because the plays were performed in the afternoon, under the sky, settings like the storm in King Lear or night scenes had to be evoked by the play's language; the imagination of the audience thus played a crucial part, as in modern radio drama.

Shakespeare's theater was literally what a modern director and critic has called "the empty space," to be filled by the playwright's, the actors', and the audience's imaginations. The Greek skene building and orchestra were well suited for plays that took place "before the palace" and dramatized the public lives of scapegoat-kings. The neutral, fluid space of the Elizabethan stage was ideally suited to drama calling for the free movement of the imagination. The line between illusion and reality, nebulous in any kind of theater, was especially so in Shakespeare's, and his plays are full of scenes that question what is "real," as in King Lear, Act IV, scene vi, in which the blind Gloucester thinks he is on the top of a cliff. Edgar knows that Gloucester is "really" in a flat field, while we see that the field is as imaginary as the cliff and that the characters are really on a wooden stage.

FURTHER READING *(prepared by W. J. R.):* S. Schoenbaum's *William Shakespeare: A Compact Documentary Life,* 1977, a revision of an earlier biography, discusses the major stages of Shakespeare's life and the contemporary theatrical world. For a handsome biography, full of color photographs, see Anthony Burgess' *Shakespeare,* 1970. A stimulating introductory overview, treating Shakespeare topically and discussing the metaphysics of *King Lear,* is Germaine Greer's *Shakespeare,* 1986. *King Lear* is treated in Volume 2 of *Shakespearean Criticism: Excerpts . . . from the First Published Appraisals to Current Evaluations,* ed. Laurie Lanzen Harris and Mark W. Scott, 1985, a book appropriate for introductory-level students. Eight authorities on Shakespeare discuss *King Lear,* from a variety of perspectives, in *On King Lear,* ed. Lawrence Danson, 1982, a collection of very readable essays. Other good introductions to Shakespearean criticism are *The New Century Shakespeare Handbook,* ed. Sandra Clark, 1974, and Stanley Wells' *Shakespeare: The Writer and His Work,* 1978. Clark's work contains a brief biographical sketch, notes on productions of Shakespeare's work in his own time, and numerous photographs of modern productions. Wells discusses Shakespeare's England and his theater and provides an overview of Shakespearean criticism. On Shakespeare's great tragedies, A. C. Bradley's *Shakespearean Tragedy,* 1904, is still valuable and readable. This work, which greatly influenced interpretations of the tragedies, studies *Hamlet, Othello, King Lear,* and *Macbeth.* An overview of criticism is provided in *Shakespeare and His Critics,* ed. F. E. Halliday, 1947, revised 1957, which contains commentary on all the first folio plays and the minor poems. Two fine works on staging and related topics are Cécile de Banke's *Shakespearean Stage Production, Then and Now,* 1953, and S. Schoenbaum's *Shakespeare: The Globe and the World,* 1979. Banke's work is a detailed study of staging, acting, costuming, and other aspects of production relevant for the modern amateur producer of Shakespeare. Schoenbaum's work is filled with color photographs, drawings, and diagrams; modern productions of Shakespeare, including film adaptations, are also treated. Very valuable on the stage history and staging of *King Lear* is Gamini Salgado, *King Lear: Text and Performance,* 1985. The crucial role of the performers is discussed in connection with *King Lear* and other tragedies in Michael Goldman, *Acting and Action in Shakespearean Tragedy,* 1985. *Lear* is examined along with Shakespeare's other tragedies in Paul A. Jorgensen, *William Shakespeare: The Tragedies,* 1985. John Russell Brown, *Discovering Shakespeare: A New Guide to the Plays,* 1981, invites new readers to consider the plays as performance rather than through traditional methods of literary analysis.

KING LEAR

Footnotes by Oscar James Campbell

DRAMATIS PERSONAE

LEAR, *king of Britain.*
KING OF FRANCE.
DUKE OF BURGUNDY.
DUKE OF CORNWALL.
DUKE OF ALBANY.
EARL OF KENT.
EARL OF GLOUCESTER.
EDGAR, *son to Gloucester.*
EDMUND, *bastard son to Gloucester.*
CURAN, *a courtier.*
OLD MAN, *tenant to Gloucester.*
DOCTOR.
FOOL.

OSWALD, *steward to Goneril.*
A CAPTAIN *employed by Edmund.*
GENTLEMAN *attendant on Cordelia.*
A HERALD.
SERVANTS *to Cornwall.*
GONERIL,
REGAN,　*daughters to Lear.*
CORDELIA,
KNIGHTS *of Lear's train,* CAPTAINS,
　MESSENGERS, SOLDIERS, *and*
　ATTENDANTS.

SCENE: *Britain.*

ACT I

SCENE I
KING LEAR'S *palace*

[*Enter* KENT, GLOUCESTER, *and* EDMUND.]

KENT. I thought the king had more affected[1] the Duke of Albany[2] than Cornwall.

GLOU. It did always seem so to us: but now, in the division of the kingdom, it appears not which of the dukes he values most; for equalities are so weighed,[3] that curiosity in neither can make choice of either's moiety.[4]

KENT. Is not this your son, my lord?

GLOU. His breeding, sir, hath been at my charge:[5] I have so often blushed to acknowledge him, that now I am brazed[6] to it.

KENT. I cannot conceive[7] you.　10

GLOU. Sir, this young fellow's mother could: whereupon she grew round-wombed, and had, indeed, sir, a son for her cradle ere she had a husband for her bed. Do you smell a fault?

KENT. I cannot wish the fault undone, the issue of it being so proper.[8]

---

[1] Favored.　[2] An old name for Scotland.
[3] **equalities . . . weighed,** shares are so (evenly) balanced.
[4] **curiosity . . . moiety,** careful examination cannot decide which portion (moiety) is to be preferred.
[5] Expense.　[6] Hardened.　[7] Understand.　[8] Handsome.

GLOU. But I have, sir, a son by order of law,[9] some year[10] elder than
this, who yet is no dearer in my account: though this knave came
something[11] saucily into the world before he was sent for, yet was
his mother fair; there was good sport at his making, and the
whoreson[12] must be acknowledged. Do you know this noble gentle-
man, Edmund?   20

EDM. No, my lord.

GLOU. My lord of Kent: remember him hereafter as my honourable
friend.

EDM. My services to your lordship.

KENT. I must love you, and sue to know you better.

EDM. Sir, I shall study deserving.[13]

GLOU. He hath been out[14] nine years, and away he shall again. The
king is coming.

[*Sennet.*[15] *Enter* KING LEAR, CORN-
WALL, ALBANY, GONERIL, REGAN,
CORDELIA, *and* ATTENDANTS.]

LEAR. Attend the lords of France and Burgundy, Gloucester.

GLOU. I shall, my liege.   30

[*Exeunt* GLOUCESTER *and* ED-
MUND.]

LEAR. Meantime we shall express our darker[16] purpose.
Give me the map there. Know that we have divided
In three our kingdom: and 'tis our fast intent[17]
To shake all cares and business from our age;
Conferring them on younger strengths, while we
Unburthen'd crawl toward death. Our son of Cornwall,
And you, our no less loving son of Albany,
We have this hour a constant[18] will to publish[19]
Our daughters' several dowers, that future strife
May be prevented[20] now. The princes, France[21] and Bur-
gundy,[22]   40
Great rivals in our youngest daughter's love,
Long in our court have made their amorous sojourn,
And here are to be answer'd. Tell me, my daughters,—
Since now we will divest us, both of rule,
Interest of[23] territory, cares of state,—
Which of you shall we say doth love us most?
That we our largest bounty may extend
Where nature doth with merit challenge.[24] Goneril,
Our eldest-born, speak first.

---

[9]**by . . . law,** legally.   [10]About a year.   [11]Somewhat.
[12]Lit., son of a whore, hence bastard.   [13]To deserve your favor.
[14]Out of England, abroad.   [15]A series of notes sounded on a trumpet.
[16]More secret.   [17]Firm purpose.   [18]Firm.   [19]Make known.   [20]Forestalled.
[21]King of France.   [22]Duke of Burgundy.   [23]Claim to.
[24]**Where . . . challenge,** where your merit and my natural affection lay equal claim (to my
generosity).

GON. Sir, I love you more than words can wield the matter;[25]   50
    Dearer than eye-sight, space,[26] and liberty;[27]
    Beyond what can be valued, rich or rare;
    No less than life, with grace,[28] health, beauty, honour;
    As much as child e'er loved, or father found;[29]
    A love that makes breath poor, and speech unable;
    Beyond all manner of so much[30] I love you.
COR. [*Aside*] What shall Cordelia do? Love, and be silent.
LEAR. Of all these bounds, even from this line to this,
    With shadowy forests and with champains rich'd,[31]
    With plenteous rivers and wide-skirted meads,   60
    We make thee lady: to thine and Albany's issue
    Be this perpetual. What says our second daughter,
    Our dearest Regan, wife to Cornwall? Speak.
REG. Sir, I am made
    Of the self-same metal that my sister is,
    And prize me at her worth.[32] In my true heart
    I find she names my very deed of love;[33]
    Only she comes too short: that[34] I profess
    Myself an enemy to all other joys,
    Which the most precious square of sense possesses;[35]   70
    And find I am alone felicitate[36]
    In your dear highness' love.[37]
COR.   [*Aside*] Then poor Cordelia!
    And yet not so; since, I am sure, my love's
    More richer than my tongue.[38]
LEAR. To thee and thine hereditary ever
    Remain this ample third of our fair kingdom;
    No less in space, validity,[39] and pleasure,
    Than that conferr'd on Goneril. Now, our joy,
    Although the last, not least; to whose young love
    The vines of France and milk[40] of Burgundy   80
    Strive to be interess'd;[41] what can you say to draw
    A third more opulent than your sisters? Speak.
COR. Nothing, my lord.
LEAR. Nothing!
COR. Nothing.
LEAR. Nothing will come of nothing: speak again.
COR. Unhappy that I am, I cannot heave
    My heart into my mouth. I love your majesty
    According to my bond;[42] nor more nor less.

[25] **wield the matter,** serve to express the fact. [26] Freedom from imprisonment.
[27] Liberty of action. [28] Favor. [29] **found,** i.e., in a child's love.
[30] **all . . . much,** every sort of similar comparison. [31] Enriched with fertile fields.
[32] **And . . . worth,** and estimate my value to be the same as hers.
[33] **very . . . love,** my love as it actually is. [34] In that.
[35] **Which . . . possesses,** which the most delicate test of feeling takes for joys.
[36] Made happy. [37] Love of your dear highness.
[38] **More . . . tongue,** i.e., greater than I can express in words. [39] Value.
[40] Pastures. [41] **to be interess'd,** to have a right in.
[42] Obligation (as a daughter).

LEAR. How, how, Cordelia! mend your speech a little,   90
  Lest it may mar your fortunes.
COR.   Good my lord,
  You have begot me, bred me, loved me: I
  Return those duties back as are right fit,[43]
  Obey you, love you, and most honour you.
  Why have my sisters husbands, if they say
  They love you all?[44] Haply, when I shall wed,
  That lord whose hand must take my plight[45] shall carry
  Half my love with him, half my care and duty:
  Sure, I shall never marry like my sisters,
  To love my father all.   100
LEAR. But goes thy heart with this?
COR.   Ay, good my lord.
LEAR. So young, and so untender?
COR. So young, my lord, and true.
LEAR. Let it be so; thy truth, then, be thy dower.
  For, by the sacred radiance of the sun,
  The mysteries[46] of Hecate,[47] and the night;
  By all the operation[48] of the orbs[49]
  From whom we do exist, and cease to be;
  Here I disclaim all my paternal care,
  Propinquity and property[50] of blood,   110
  And as a stranger to my heart and me
  Hold thee, from this, for ever. The barbarous Scythian,[51]
  Or he that makes his generation messes[52]
  To gorge his appetite, shall to my bosom
  Be as well neighbour'd, pitied, and relieved,
  As thou my sometime daughter.
KENT.   Good my liege,—
LEAR. Peace, Kent!
  Come not between the dragon[53] and his wrath.[54]
  I loved her most, and thought to set my rest[55]
  On her kind nursery.[56] Hence, and avoid[57] my sight!   120
  So be my grave my peace, as here I give
  Her father's heart from her! Call France; who stirs?
  Call Burgundy. Cornwall and Albany,
  With my two daughters' dowers digest[58] this third:
  Let pride, which she calls plainness,[59] marry her.
  I do invest you jointly with my power,
  Pre-eminence, and all the large effects[60]

---

[43] **as . . . fit,** which are most fitting (for a daughter).
[44] **They . . . all,** i.e., give you all their love. [45] Pledge. [46] Secret religious rites.
[47] Goddess of the lower world, of witchcraft and of magic. [48] Influence.
[49] Stars. [50] Identity.
[51] Inhabitant of Southern Russia, since classical times regarded as complete barbarians.
[52] **makes . . . messes,** makes food of his children. [53] i.e., his crest.
[54] Object of his wrath. [55] **set my rest,** rely entirely. [56] Nursing. [57] Leave.
[58] Assimilate, combine. [59] Frankness. [60] Lavish manifestations.

That troop with[61] majesty. Ourself, by monthly course,
With reservation of an hundred knights,
By you to be sustain'd, shall our abode   130
Make with you by due turns. Only we still retain
The name, and all the additions[62] to a king;
The sway, revenue, execution of the rest,[63]
Belovèd sons, be yours: which to confirm,
This coronet part betwixt you.

                                                  [Giving the crown.]

KENT.   Royal Lear,
Whom I have ever honour'd as my king,
Loved as my father, as my master follow'd,
As my great patron thought on in my prayers,—
LEAR. The bow is bent and drawn, make from the shaft.[64]
KENT. Let it fall[65] rather, though the fork[66] invade   130
The region of my heart: be Kent unmannerly,   140
When Lear is mad. What wilt thou do, old man?
Think'st thou that duty shall have dread to speak,
When power to flattery bows? To plainness honour's bound,
When majesty stoops to folly. Reverse thy doom;[67]
And, in thy best consideration, check
This hideous rashness: answer my life my judgement,[68]
Thy youngest daughter does not love thee least;
Nor are those empty-hearted whose low sound
Reverbs[69] no hollowness.
LEAR.   Kent, on thy life, no more.   150
KENT. My life I never held but as a pawn
To wage[70] against thy enemies; nor fear to lose it,
Thy safety being the motive.
LEAR.   Out of my sight!
KENT. See better, Lear; and let me still remain
The true blank[71] of thine eye.
LEAR. Now, by Apollo,—
KENT.   Now, by Apollo, king,
Thou swear'st thy gods in vain.
LEAR.   O, vassal! miscreant![72]

                                      [Laying his hand on his sword.]

ALB. ⎫
CORN. ⎬ Dear sir, forbear.
     ⎭
KENT. Do;
Kill thy physician, and the fee bestow   160
Upon thy foul disease. Revoke thy doom;

---

[61] March in company with.   [62] Titles.   [63] The rest of my royal prerogatives.
[64] **make . . . shaft,** avoid the arrow (of my anger).   [65] Fly.   [66] Arrowhead.
[67] Judgment (pronounced against Cordelia).
[68] **answer . . . judgement,** I'll stake my life on the correctness of my opinion.
[69] Reverberates with.   [70] Stake.   [71] White center of a target.
[72] Vile wretch.

Or, whilst I can vent clamour from my throat,
I'll tell thee thou dost evil.

LEAR.   Hear me, recreant![73]
On thine allegiance, hear me!
Since thou hast sought to make us break our vow,
Which we durst never yet, and with strain'd[74] pride
To come between our sentence and our power,
Which nor our nature nor our place can bear,
Our potency[75] made good,[76] take thy reward.
Five days we do allot thee, for provision[77]   170
To shield thee from diseases[78] of the world;
And on the sixth to turn thy hated back
Upon our kingdom: if, on the tenth day following,
Thy banish'd trunk be found in our dominions,
The moment is thy death. Away! by Jupiter,
This shall not be revoked.

KENT. Fare thee well, king: sith[79] thus thou wilt appear,
Freedom lives hence, and banishment is here.
[*To* CORDELIA] The gods to their dear shelter take thee, maid,
That justly think'st, and hast most rightly said!   180
[*To* REGAN *and* GONERIL] And your large speeches may your
    deeds approve,[80]
That good effects may spring from words of love.
Thus Kent, O princes, bids you all adieu;
He'll shape his old course[81] in a country new.
                            [*Exit.*]

                            [*Flourish. Re-enter* GLOUCESTER,
                            with FRANCE, BURGUNDY, *and*
                            ATTENDANTS.]

GLOU. Here's France and Burgundy, my noble lord.
LEAR. My lord of Burgundy,
    We first address towards you, who with this king
    Hath rivall'd for our daughter: what, in the least,
    Will you require in present dower with her,
    Or cease your quest of love?
BUR.   Most royal majesty,   190
    I crave no more than what your highness offer'd,
    Nor will you tender less.
LEAR.   Right noble Burgundy,
    When she was dear to us, we did hold her so;
    But now her price is fall'n. Sir, there she stands:
    If aught within that little seeming substance,[82]
    Or all of it, with our displeasure pieced,
    And nothing more, may fitly like[83] your grace,
    She's there, and she is yours.

---

[73] Breaker of your oath (of allegiance to me).   [74] Excessive.   [75] Authority
[76] Effective.   [77] To provide means.   [78] Distresses, pains.   [79] Since.   [80] Justify
[81] Conduct.
[82] **that . . . substance,** that little person who only seems to be genuine.   [83] Please.

BUR.   I know no answer.

LEAR. Will you, with those infirmities[84] she owes,[85]
    Unfriended, new-adopted to our hate,   200
    Dower'd with our curse, and stranger'd with our oath,
    Take her, or leave her?

BUR.   Pardon me, royal sir;
    Election makes not up on such conditions.[86]

LEAR. Then leave her, sir; for, by the power that made me,
    I tell you all her wealth. [*To* FRANCE] For[87] you, great king,
    I would not from your love make such a stray,
    To match you where I hate; therefore beseech you
    To avert your liking[88] a more worthier way
    Than on a wretch whom nature is ashamed
    Almost to acknowledge hers.

FRANCE.   This is most strange,   210
    That she, that even but now was your best object,[89]
    The argument[90] of your praise, balm of your age,
    Most best, most dearest, should in this trice[91] of time
    Commit a thing so monstrous, to[92] dismantle
    So many folds of favour. Sure, her offence
    Must be of such unnatural degree,
    That monsters[93] it, or your fore-vouch'd affection
    Fall'n into taint:[94] which to believe of her,
    Must be a faith that reason without miracle
    Could never plant in me.

COR.   I yet beseech your majesty,—   220
    If for[95] I want that glib and oily art,
    To speak and purpose not;[96] since what I well intend,
    I'll do 't before I speak,—that you make known
    It is no vicious blot,[97] murder, or foulness,[98]
    No unchaste action, or dishonour'd step,
    That hath deprived me of your grace and favour;
    But even for want of that for which[99] I am richer,
    A still-soliciting[1] eye, and such a tongue
    As I am glad I have not, though not to have it
    Hath lost me in your liking.[2]

LEAR.   Better thou   230
    Hadst not been born than not to have pleased me better.

FRANCE. Is it but this,—a tardiness in nature[3]
    Which often leaves the history unspoke
    That it intends to do? My lord of Burgundy,

---

[84] Defects.   [85] Owns.
[86] **Election . . . conditions,** i.e., choice of wife is not made under such conditions.
[87] As for.   [88] **avert your liking,** turn your affection.
[89] **your best object,** the main object of your love.   [90] Topic.   [91] Instant.
[92] As to.   [93] Makes monstrous.   [94] Decay.   [95] Because.
[96] **purpose not,** not to mean what one says.   [97] Stain made by a vice.
[98] Lack of chastity.   [99] For lack of which.   [1] Ever-begging.
[2] **lost . . . liking,** made me lose your affection.
[3] **tardiness in nature,** natural reticence.

> What say you to the lady? Love's not love
> When it is mingled with regards that stand
> Aloof from the entire point.[4] Will you have her?
> She is herself a dowry.
>
> BUR.   Royal Lear,
> Give but that portion which yourself proposed,
> And here I take Cordelia by the hand,   240
> Duchess of Burgundy.
>
> LEAR. Nothing: I have sworn; I am firm.
>
> BUR. I am sorry, then, you have so lost a father
> That you must lose a husband.
>
> COR.   Peace be with Burgundy!
> Since that respects[5] of fortune are his love,
> I shall not be his wife.
>
> FRANCE. Fairest Cordelia, that art most rich, being poor;
> Most choice, forsaken; and most loved, despised!
> Thee and thy virtues here I seize upon:
> Be it lawful I take up what's cast away.   250
> Gods, gods! 'tis strange that from their cold'st neglect
> My love should kindle to inflamed[6] respect.
> Thy dowerless daughter, king, thrown to my chance,
> Is queen of us, of ours, and our fair France:
> Not all the dukes of waterish[7] Burgundy
> Can buy this unprized[8] precious maid of me.
> Bid them farewell, Cordelia, though unkind:
> Thou losest here, a better where to find.
>
> LEAR. Thou hast her, France: let her be thine; for we
> Have no such daughter, nor shall ever see   260
> That face of hers again. Therefore be gone
> Without our grace,[9] our love, our benison.[10]
> Come, noble Burgundy.

> [*Flourish. Exeunt all but* FRANCE,
> GONERIL, REGAN, *and* CORDELIA.]

> FRANCE. Bid farewell to your sisters.
>
> COR. The jewels of our father, with wash'd eyes
> Cordelia leaves you: I know you what you are;
> And like a sister am most loath to call
> Your faults as they are named.[11] Use well our father:
> To your professèd[12] bosoms I commit him:
> But yet, alas, stood I within his grace,   270
> I would prefer[13] him to a better place.
> So, farewell to you both.
>
> REG. Prescribe not us our duties.

---

[4] **regards . . . point,** considerations that have nothing to do with the essence of the matter.
[5] Considerations.   [6] Heightened.   [7] Marshy.   [8] Unappreciated.   [9] Favor.
[10] Blessing.   [11] **as . . . named,** by their proper names.
[12] Full of professions (of love).   [13] Recommend.

GON.   Let your study
    Be to content your lord, who hath received you
    At fortune's alms. You have obedience scanted,[14]
    And well are worth the want that you have wanted.[15]
COR. Time shall unfold what plaited[16] cunning hides:
    Who cover faults, at last shame them derides.
    Well may you prosper!
FRANCE.   Come, my fair Cordelia.
                      [*Exeunt* FRANCE *and* CORDELIA.]
GON. Sister, it is not a little I have to say of what most nearly   280
    appertains to us both. I think our father will hence to-night.
REG. That's most certain, and with you; next month with us.
GON. You see how full of changes his age is; the observation we have
    made of it hath not been little: he always loved our sister most; and
    with what poor judgement he hath now cast her off appears too
    grossly.[17]
REG. 'Tis the infirmity of his age: yet he hath ever but slenderly
    known himself.
GON. The best and soundest of his time[18] hath been but rash;[19] then
    must we look to receive from his age, not alone the imperfections   290
    of long-engraffed condition,[20] but therewithal[21] the unruly way-
    wardness that infirm and choleric years bring with them.
REG. Such unconstant starts[22] are we like[23] to have from him as this
    of Kent's banishment.
GON. There is further compliment[24] of leave-taking between France
    and him. Pray you, let's hit[25] together: if our father carry author-
    ity with such dispositions as he bears, this last surrender of his will
    but offend[26] us.
REG. We shall further think on't.
GON. We must do something, and i' the heat.[27]   [*Exeunt.*]   300

SCENE II
The EARL OF GLOUCESTER'S *castle*

[*Enter* EDMUND, *with a letter.*]
EDM. Thou, nature, art my goddess; to thy law
    My services are bound. Wherefore should I
    Stand in the plague of custom,[1] and permit

---

[14] **At . . . alms,** i.e., when Fortune was giving alms, i.e., petty gifts; **scanted,** grudged.
   [15] **And . . . wanted,** and well deserved that lack of affection (from your husband) in which you have been lacking.
   [16] Folded.   [17] Obviously.   [18] **The . . . time,** the best and soundest time of his life.
   [19] Headlong, hasty.
   [20] **long-engraffed condition,** temperament that has long been deeply embedded in his nature.
   [21] With it.   [22] **unconstant starts,** freakish sudden impulses.   [23] Likely.
   [24] Ceremony.   [25] Agree.   [26] Injure.   [27] **i' the heat,** i.e., while the iron is hot.
   [1] **Stand . . . custom,** occupy a position in which I suffer from disabilities dictated by mere custom.

The curiosity of nations[2] to deprive me,[3]
For that I am some twelve or fourteen moonshines
Lag of[4] a brother? Why bastard? wherefore base?
When my dimensions are as well compact,[5]
My mind as generous,[6] and my shape as true,[7]
As honest[8] madam's issue? Why brand they us
With base? with baseness? bastardy? base, base?   10
Who, in the lusty stealth of nature, take
More composition[9] and fierce quality
Than doth, within a dull, stale, tired bed,
Go to the creating a whole tribe of fops,
Got 'tween asleep and wake? Well, then,
Legitimate Edgar, I must have your land:
Our father's love is to the bastard Edmund
As to the legitimate: fine word,—legitimate!
Well, my legitimate, if this letter speed,[10]
And my invention[11] thrive, Edmund the base   20
Shall top the legitimate. I grow; I prosper:
Now, gods, stand up for bastards!

                        [*Enter* GLOUCESTER.]

GLOU. Kent banish'd thus! and France in choler parted![12]
    And the king gone to-night! subscribed his power![13]
    Confined to exhibition![14] All this done
    Upon the gad![15] Edmund, how now! what news?
EDM. So please your lordship, none.

                        [*Putting up the letter.*]

GLOU. Why so earnestly seek you to put up that letter?
EDM. I know no news, my lord.
GLOU. What paper were you reading?   30
EDM. Nothing, my lord.
GLOU. No? What needed, then, that terrible dispatch of it[16] into your
    pocket? the quality[17] of nothing hath not such need to hide itself.
    Let's see: come, if it be nothing, I shall not need spectacles.
EDM. I beseech you, sir, pardon me:[18] it is a letter from my brother,
    that I have not all o'er-read; and for so much as I have perused, I
    find it not fit for your o'er-looking.
GLOU. Give me the letter, sir.
EDM. I shall offend, either to detain[19] or give it. The contents, as in
    part I understand them, are to blame.[20]   40
GLOU. Let's see, let's see.

---

[2] **curiosity of nations,** nice distinction of universal law.
[3] **deprive me,** i.e., of my just inheritance.   [4] Behind.
[5] **dimensions . . . compact,** structure of my body is as well built.   [6] Noble.
[7] Regular.   [8] Chaste.   [9] A stronger constitution.   [10] Succeed.   [11] Scheme.
[12] Departed.   [13] **subscribed his power,** his power signed away.
[14] An allowance.   [15] Spur (of the moment).
[16] **terrible . . . it,** frantic haste to put it.   [17] Nature.
[18] Excuse my not sharing it with you. [19] Withhold.   [20] Blameworthy.

EDM. I hope, for my brother's justification, he wrote this but as an essay[21] or taste of my virtue.

GLOU. [*Reads*] "This policy and reverence[22] of age makes the world bitter to the best of our times;[23] keeps our fortunes from us till our oldness cannot relish them. I begin to find an idle and fond bondage[24] in the oppression of aged tyranny; who sways, not as it hath power, but as it is suffered.[25] Come to me, that of this I may speak more. If our father would sleep till I waked him, you should enjoy half his revenue for ever, and live the beloved of your brother,   50

"EDGAR."

Hum—conspiracy!—"Sleep till I waked him,—you should enjoy half his revenue,"—My son Edgar! Had he a hand to write this? a heart and brain to breed it in?—When came this to you? who brought it?

EDM. It was not brought me, my lord; there's the cunning of it; I found it thrown in at the casement of my closet.[26]

GLOU. You know the character[27] to be your brother's?

EDM. If the matter[28] were good, my lord, I durst swear it were his; but, in respect of[29] that, I would fain think it were not.   60

GLOU. It is his.

EDM. It is his hand, my lord; but I hope his heart is not in the contents.

GLOU. Hath he never heretofore sounded you in this business?

EDM. Never, my lord: but I have heard him oft maintain it to be fit, that, sons at perfect age,[30] and fathers declining,[31] the father should be as ward to the son, and the son manage his revenue.

GLOU. O villain, villain! His very opinion in the letter! Abhorred villain! Unnatural, detested, brutish villain! worse than brutish! Go, sirrah, seek him; I'll apprehend him: abominable villain! Where   70
is he?

EDM. I do not well know, my lord. If it shall please you to suspend your indignation against my brother till you can derive from him better testimony of his intent, you shall run a certain course; where,[32] if you violently proceed against him, mistaking his purpose, it would make a great gap in your own honour, and shake in pieces the heart of his obedience. I dare pawn down my life for him, that he hath wrote this to feel my affection[33] to your honour, and to no further pretence of danger.[34]

GLOU. Think you so?   80

EDM. If your honour judge it meet, I will place you where you shall hear us confer of this, and by an auricular assurance have your

---

[21] Trial.   [22] **policy and reverence,** established convention of revering the old.

[23] **best of our times,** best part of our life.

[24] **idle . . . bondage,** a useless and foolish servitude.

[25] **who . . . suffered,** which prevails not by virtue of its power, but as a result of our submission.

[26] Private room.   [27] Handwriting.   [28] Subject matter.   [29] Regard to.

[30] Full maturity.   [31] Growing old.   [32] Whereas.

[33] **feel my affection,** test my feeling.   [34] **pretence of danger,** dangerous intention.

satisfaction; and that without any further delay than this very evening.

GLOU. He cannot be such a monster—

EDM. Nor is not, sure.

GLOU. To his father, that so tenderly and entirely loves him. Heaven
and earth! Edmund, seek him out; wind me into him,[35] I pray
you: frame the business after your own wisdom. I would unstate
myself,[36] to be in a due resolution.[37]   90

EDM. I will seek him, sir, presently;[38] convey[39] the business as I shall
find means, and acquaint you withal.

GLOU. These late eclipses in the sun and moon portend no good to
us: though the wisdom of nature[40] can reason it thus and thus, yet
nature finds itself scourged by the sequent effects:[41] love cools,
friendship falls off, brothers divide: in cities, mutinies;[42] in countries, discord; in palaces, treason; and the bond cracked 'twixt son
and father. This villain of mine comes under the prediction;
there's son against father: the king falls from bias[43] of nature;
there's father against child. We have seen the best of our time: 100
machinations, hollowness, treachery, and all ruinous disorders,
follow us disquietly to our graves. Find out this villain, Edmund; it
shall lose thee nothing; do it carefully. And the noble and true-
hearted Kent banished! his offence, honesty! 'Tis strange.

                                     [*Exit.*]

EDM. This is the excellent foppery[44] of the world, that, when we are
sick in fortune,—often the surfeit[45] of our own behaviour,—we
make guilty of our disasters the sun, the moon, and the stars: as if
we were villains by necessity; fools by heavenly compulsion;
knaves, thieves, and treachers,[46] by spherical predominance;[47]
drunkards, liars, and adulterers, by an enforced obedience of   110
planetary influence; and all that we are evil in, by a divine
thrusting on: an admirable evasion of whoremaster man, to lay his
goatish[48] disposition to the charge of a star! My father compounded with[49] my mother under the dragon's tail; and my nativity
was under Ursa major; so that it follows, I am rough and lecherous. Tut, I should have been that I am,[50] had the maidenliest star
in the firmament twinkled on my bastardizing. Edgar—

                              [*Enter* EDGAR.]

and pat[51] he comes like the catastrophe of the old comedy: my

---

[35] **wind . . . him,** worm your way into his confidence for my sake.
[36] **unstate myself,** surrender the privileges of my rank.
[37] **due resolution,** proper certainty.   [38] At once.   [39] Manage secretly.
[40] **wisdom of nature,** scientific theory.   [41] **sequent effects,** results which follow.
[42] Tumults.   [43] The curve of a bowling ball, hence "tendency."   [44] Foolishness.
[45] Overeating, indigestion.   [46] Traitors.
[47] **spherical predominance,** because of the controlling influence of some planet.
[48] Licentious.   [49] Came to terms with.   [50] **that I am,** what I am.
[51] Opportunely.

cue is villanous melancholy, with a sigh like Tom o' Bedlam.[52] O,
these eclipses do portend these divisions! fa, sol, la, mi.   120

EDG. How now, brother Edmund! what serious contemplation are
you in?

EDM. I am thinking, brother, of a prediction I read this other day,
what should follow these eclipses.

EDG. Do you busy yourself about that?

EDM. I promise you, the effects he writes of succeed[53] unhappily; as
of unnaturalness between the child and the parent; death,
dearth,[54] dissolutions of ancient amities; divisions in state, menaces and maledictions against king and nobles; needless diffi-
dences,[55] banishment of friends, dissipation of cohorts,[56] nuptial   130
breaches, and I know not what.

EDG. How long have you been a sectary astronomical?[57]

EDM. Come, come; when saw you my father last?

EDG. Why, the night gone by.

EDM. Spake you with him?

EDG. Ay, two hours together.

EDM. Parted you in good terms? Found you no displeasure in him by
word or countenance?

EDG. None at all.

EDM. Bethink yourself wherein you may have offended him: and at   140
my entreaty forbear[58] his presence till some little time hath qualified[59] the heat of his displeasure; which at this instant so rageth in
him, that with the mischief of your person[60] it would scarcely allay.

EDG. Some villain hath done me wrong.

EDM. That's my fear. I pray you, have a continent[61] forbearance till
the speed of his rage goes slower; and, as I say, retire with me to
my lodging, from whence I will fitly[62] bring you to hear my lord
speak: pray ye, go; there's my key: if you do stir abroad, go armed.

EDG. Armed, brother!

EDM. Brother, I advise you to the best; go armed: I am no honest   150
man if there be any good meaning towards you: I have told you
what I have seen and heard; but faintly, nothing like the image
and horror[63] of it: pray you, away.

EDG. Shall I hear from you anon?[64]

EDM. I do serve you in this business.

[*Exit* EDGAR.]

A credulous father! and a brother noble,
Whose nature is so far from doing harms,
That he suspects none; on whose foolish honesty

---

[52] Common name of lunatics of Bethlehem Hospital (Bedlam), an insane asylum, who were
sent out to beg.

[53] Follow.   [54] Famine.   [55] Suspicions.

[56] **dissipation of cohorts,** breaking up of military organizations.

[57] **sectary astronomical,** believer in astrology.   [58] Avoid.   [59] Lessened.

[60] **mischief . . . person,** harm to your body.   [61] Restrained.

[62] Opportunely.   [63] **image and horror,** the horrible truth.   [64] Shortly.

My practices[65] ride easy! I see the business.
Let me, if not by birth, have lands by wit: 160
All with me's meet that I can fashion fit.[66]   [*Exit.*]

SCENE III
The DUKE OF ALBANY'S *palace*

[*Enter* GONERIL, *and* OSWALD, *her steward.*]
GON. Did my father strike my gentleman for chiding of his fool?
OSW. Yes, madam.
GON. By day and night he wrongs me; every hour
    He flashes into one gross crime or other,
    That sets us all at odds: I'll not endure it:
    His knights grow riotous, and himself upbraids us
    On every trifle. When he returns from hunting,
    I will not speak with him; say I am sick:
    If you come slack of former services,
    You shall do well; the fault of it I'll answer.   10
OSW. He's coming, madam; I hear him.
                      [*Horns within.*]
GON. Put on what weary negligence you please,
    You and your fellows; I'ld have it come to question:[1]
    If he dislike it, let him to our sister,
    Whose mind and mine, I know, in that are one,
    Not to be over-ruled. Idle[2] old man,
    That still would manage those authorities
    That he hath given away! Now, by my life,
    Old fools are babes again; and must be used[3]
    With checks as[4] flatteries,—when they are seen abused.[5]   20
    Remember what I tell you.
OSW.   Well, madam.
GON. And let his knights have colder looks among you;
    What grows of it, no matter; advise your fellows so:[6]
    I would breed from hence occasions,[7] and I shall
    That I may speak: I'll write straight to my sister,
    To hold my very course. Prepare for dinner.   [*Exeunt.*]

SCENE IV
A hall in the same

[*Enter* KENT, *disguised.*]
KENT. If but as well I other accents borrow,
    That can my speech defuse,[1] my good intent

---

[65] Plots.   [66] **fashion fit,** make fitting by fraudulent management.
[1] **to question,** i.e., to a showdown.   [2] Foolish.   [3] Managed.
[4] Rebukes as well as.   [5] Deceived.
[6] **advise . . . so,** tell your servants to act the same way.   [7] Opportunities.
[1] Disguise.

May carry through itself to that full issue
For which I razed my likeness.[2] Now, banish'd Kent,
If thou canst serve[3] where thou dost stand condemn'd,
So may it come, thy master, whom thou lovest,
Shall find thee full of labours.

> [*Horns within. Enter* LEAR, KNIGHTS,
> *and* ATTENDANTS.]

LEAR. Let me not stay a jot for dinner; go get it ready. [*Exit an*
   ATTENDANT.] How now! what art thou?

KENT. A man, sir.   10

LEAR. What dost thou profess?[4] what wouldst thou with us?

KENT. I do profess to be no less than I seem; to serve him truly that
   will put me in trust; to love him that is honest; to converse[5] with
   him that is wise, and says little; to fear judgement; to fight when I
   cannot choose;[6] and to eat no fish.[7]

LEAR. What art thou?

KENT. A very honest-hearted fellow, and as poor as the king.

LEAR. If thou be as poor for a subject as he is for a king, thou art poor
   enough. What wouldst thou?

KENT. Service.   20

LEAR. Who wouldst thou serve?

KENT. You.

LEAR. Dost thou know me, fellow?

KENT. No, sir; but you have that in your countenance[8] which I would
   fain call master.

LEAR. What's that?

KENT. Authority.

LEAR. What services canst thou do?

KENT. I can keep honest counsel,[9] ride, run, mar a curious[10] tale in
   telling it, and deliver a plain message bluntly: that which ordinary   30
   men are fit for, I am qualified in; and the best of me is diligence.

LEAR. How old art thou?

KENT. Not so young, sir, to love a woman for singing, nor so old to
   dote on her for any thing: I have years on my back forty-eight.

LEAR. Follow me; thou shalt serve me: if I like thee no worse after
   dinner, I will not part from thee yet. Dinner, ho, dinner! Where's
   my knave?[11] my fool? Go you, and call my fool hither.

> [*Exit an* ATTENDANT.]

> [*Enter* OSWALD.]

You, you, sirrah, where's my daughter?

OSW. So please you,—   [*Exit.*]

LEAR. What says the fellow there? Call the clotpoll[12] back. [*Exit a*   40
   KNIGHT.] Where's my fool, ho? I think the world's asleep.

---

[2] **razed my likeness,** erased any likeness to myself.   [3] Act as a servant.
[4] **What . . . profess?** What is your profession?   [5] Associate.   [6] i.e., help it.
[7] **eat no fish,** i.e., a Protestant and not disloyal like the fish-eating Catholics.
[8] Bearing.   [9] Keep an honorable secret.   [10] Elaborate.   [11] Boy.
[12] Blockhead.

[*Re-enter* KNIGHT.]

How now! where's that mongrel?

KNIGHT. He says, my lord, your daughter is not well.

LEAR. Why came not the slave back to me when I called him?

KNIGHT. Sir, he answered me in the roundest[13] manner, he would not.

LEAR. He would not!

KNIGHT. My lord, I know not what the matter is; but, to my judgement, your highness is not entertained[14] with that ceremonious affection[15] as you were wont; there's a great abatement of kind-   50
ness appears as well in the general dependants[16] as in the duke himself also and your daughter.

LEAR. Ha! sayest thou so?

KNIGHT. I beseech you, pardon me, my lord, if I be mistaken; for my duty cannot be silent when I think your highness wronged.

LEAR. Thou but rememberest[17] me of mine own conception:[18] I have perceived a most faint[19] neglect of late; which I have rather blamed as mine own jealous curiosity[20] than as a very pretence[21] and purpose of unkindness: I will look further into 't. But where's my fool? I have not seen him this two days.   60

KNIGHT. Since my young lady's going into France, sir, the fool hath much pined away.

LEAR. No more of that; I have noted it well. Go you, and tell my daughter I would speak with her. [*Exit* KNIGHT.] Go you, call hither my fool.   [*Exit an* ATTENDANT.]

[*Re-enter* OSWALD.]

O, you sir, you, come you hither, sir: who am I, sir?

OSW. My lady's father.

LEAR. "My lady's father!" My lord's knave: you whoreson dog! you slave! you cur!

OSW. I am none of these, my lord; I beseech your pardon.   70

LEAR. Do you bandy[22] looks with me, you rascal?   [*Striking him.*]

OSW. I'll not be struck, my lord.

KENT. Nor tripped neither, you base football player.
                                            [*Tripping up his heels.*]

LEAR. I thank thee, fellow; thou servest me, and I'll love thee.

KENT. Come, sir, arise, away! I'll teach you differences:[23] away, away! If you will measure your lubber's[24] length again, tarry: but away! go to; have you wisdom? so.
                                            [*Pushes* OSWALD *out.*]

LEAR. Now, my friendly knave, I thank thee: there's earnest of[25] thy service.
                                            [*Giving* KENT *money.*]

---

[13] Plainest.   [14] Treated.   [15] The affection which shows itself in formal respect.
[16] The house-servants.   [17] Remind.   [18] Idea.   [19] Half-hearted.
[20] **jealous curiosity,** overscrupulous watchfulness (for slights).
[21] **very pretence,** deliberate intention.   [22] Strike a ball back and forth (as in tennis).
[23] Proper distinctions in rank.   [24] Awkward lout's.   [25] Advance payment for.

[*Enter* FOOL.]

FOOL. Let me hire him too: here's my coxcomb.   80
[*Offering* KENT *his cap.*]

LEAR. How now, my pretty knave! how dost thou?

FOOL. Sirrah, you were best[26] take my coxcomb.[27]

KENT. Why, fool?

FOOL. Why, for taking one's part that's out of favour: nay, an[28] thou
canst not smile as the wind sits, thou'lt catch cold shortly: there,
take my coxcomb: why, this fellow has banished two on 's[29] daughters, and did the third a blessing against his will; if thou follow
him, thou must needs wear my coxcomb. How now, nuncle![30]
Would I had two coxcombs and two daughters!

LEAR. Why, my boy?   90

FOOL. If I gave them all my living, I'ld keep my coxcombs myself.
There's mine; beg another of thy daughters.

LEAR. Take heed, sirrah; the whip.

FOOL. Truth's a dog must to kennel; he must be whipped out, when
Lady the brach[31] may stand by the fire and stink.

LEAR. A pestilent gall[32] to me!

FOOL. Sirrah, I'll teach thee a speech.

LEAR. Do.

FOOL. Mark it, nuncle:
Have more than thou showest,   100
Speak less than thou knowest,
Lend less than thou owest,[33]
Ride more than thou goest,[34]
Learn more than thou trowest,[35]
Set[36] less than thou throwest;[37]
Leave thy drink and thy whore,
And keep in-a-door,[38]
And thou shalt have more
Than two tens to a score.

KENT. This is nothing, fool.   110

FOOL. Then 'tis like the breath of an unfee'd lawyer; you gave me
nothing for 't. Can you make no use of nothing, nuncle?

LEAR. Why, no, boy; nothing can be made out of nothing.

FOOL. [*To* KENT] Prithee, tell him, so much the rent of his land comes
to: he will not believe a fool.

LEAR. A bitter fool!

FOOL. Dost thou know the difference, my boy, between a bitter fool
and a sweet fool?

LEAR. No, lad; teach me.

---

[26] Had better.
[27] The hood crested with red like a cock's comb, worn by the professional fool.
[28] If.   [29] Of his.   [30] Contraction for "mine uncle."   [31] Bitch, personifying flattery.
[32] **pestilent gall,** annoying irritation.   [33] Ownest.   [34] Walkest.   [35] Knowest.
[36] Stake.   [37] Have a chance to throw, i.e., don't bet your all.
[38] Indoors, i.e., at home.

FOOL. That lord[39] that counsell'd thee   120
    To give away thy land,
  Come place him here by me,
    Do thou for him stand:[40]
  The sweet and bitter fool
    Will presently[41] appear;
  The one in motley here,
    The other found out there.

LEAR. Dost thou call me fool, boy?

FOOL. All thy other titles thou hast given away; that thou wast born
  with.   130

KENT. This is not altogether fool, my lord.

FOOL. No, faith, lords and great men will not let me; if I had a
  monopoly[42] out,[43] they would have part on't:[44] and ladies too,
  they will not let me have all fool to myself; they'll be snatching.
  Give me an egg, nuncle, and I'll give thee two crowns.

LEAR. What two crowns shall they be?

FOOL. Why, after I have cut the egg i' the middle, and eat up the
  meat, the two crowns of the egg. When thou clovest thy crown i'
  the middle, and gavest away both parts, thou borest thy ass on thy
  back o'er the dirt: thou hadst little wit in thy bald crown, when   140
  thou gavest thy golden one away. If I speak like myself[45] in this,
  let him be whipped that first finds it so.
    [*Singing*] Fools had ne'er less wit in a year;
      For wise men are grown foppish,[46]
    They know not how their wits to wear,
      Their manners are so apish.

LEAR. When were you wont to be so full of songs, sirrah?

FOOL. I have used it,[47] nuncle, ever since thou madest thy daughters
  thy mother: for when thou gavest them the rod, and put'st down
  thine own breeches,   150
    [*Singing*] Then they for sudden joy did weep,
      And I for sorrow sung,
    That such a king should play bo-peep,[48]
      And go the fools among.
  Prithee, nuncle, keep a schoolmaster that can teach thy fool to lie:
  I would fain learn to lie.

LEAR. An you lie, sirrah, we'll have you whipped.

FOOL. I marvel what kin thou and thy daughters are: they'll have me
  whipped for speaking true, thou'lt have me whipped for lying;
  and sometimes I am whipped for holding my peace. I had rather   160

---

[39] Perhaps a reference to the Lord Skalligi in the old *King Lear* who suggests the love test.
Nobody in this play gives Lear this stupid advice.
    [40] Impersonate him.   [41] Immediately.
    [42] A royal patent granting a monopoly on something.   [43] Granted me.
    [44] **they . . . on't,** the lords who helped him get the monopoly would demand a share in it.
    [45] **like myself,** i.e., outspokenly.
    [46] **Fools . . . foppish,** there is nothing left for fools to do, now that wise men have become
fools (**foppish,** foolish).
    [47] **I . . . it,** it has been my custom.
    [48] **play bo-peep,** be so childish as to play "Hide and Go Seek."

be any kind o' thing than a fool: and yet I would not be thee,
nuncle; thou hast pared thy wit o' both sides, and left nothing i' the
middle: here comes one o' the parings.

[*Enter* GONERIL.]

LEAR. How now, daughter! what makes that frontlet[49] on? Methinks
    you are too much of late i' the frown.
FOOL. Thou wast a pretty fellow when thou hadst no need to care for
    her frowning; now thou art an O[50] without a figure; I am better
    than thou art now; I am a fool, thou art nothing. [*To* GON.] Yes,
    forsooth, I will hold my tongue; so your face bids me, though you
    say nothing. Mum, mum,   170
          He that keeps nor crust nor crum,
          Weary of all, shall want some.
    [*Pointing to* LEAR] That's a shealed peas-cod.[51]
GON. Not only, sir, this your all-licensed fool,
    But other of your insolent retinue
    Do hourly carp[52] and quarrel; breaking forth
    In rank and not-to-be-endurèd riots. Sir,
    I had thought, by making this well known unto you,
    To have found a safe redress; but now grow fearful,
    By what yourself too late have spoke and done,   180
    That you protect this course, and put it on[53]
    By your allowance;[54] which if you should, the fault
    Would not 'scape censure, nor the redresses[55] sleep,
    Which, in the tender of a wholesome weal,[56]
    Might in their working do you that offence,
    Which else were shame, that then necessity
    Will call discreet proceeding.[57]
FOOL. For, you know, nuncle,
    The hedge-sparrow fed the cuckoo[58] so long,
    That it had it head bit off by it[59] young.
    So, out went the candle, and we were left darkling.[60]   190
LEAR. Are you our daughter?
GON. Come, sir,
    I would you would make use of that good wisdom,
    Whereof I know you are fraught;[61] and put away
    These dispositions, that of late transform you
    From what you rightly are.
FOOL. May not an ass know when the cart draws the horse? Whoop,
    Jug! I love thee.[62]

---

[49] Band worn on the forehead, here = frown.   [50] Cipher.   [51] Shelled pea pod.
[52] Find fault.   [53] Encourage it.   [54] With your approval.   [55] Acts of redress.
[56] **in the tender . . . weal,** in our care to make the commonwealth sound.
[57] **which . . . proceeding,** which would be shameful but which the demands (of the situation) would force one to call prudent action (discreet procedure).
[58] The cuckoo lays its eggs in other birds' nests.   [59] **it . . . it,** its . . . its.
[60] In the dark.   [61] Stored.
[62] **Whoop, Jug! . . . thee,** the tag of some song. The fool takes refuge in nonsense whenever he suspects that one of his sallies has been too impertinent.

LEAR. Doth any here know me? This is not Lear: 200
Doth Lear walk thus? speak thus? Where are his eyes?
Either his notion[63] weakens, his discernings
Are lethargied[64]—Ha! waking?[65] 'tis not so.
Who is it that can tell me who I am?

FOOL. Lear's shadow.

LEAR. I would learn that; for, by the marks of sovereignty, knowledge, and reason, I should be false persuaded I had daughters.

FOOL. Which[66] they will make an obedient father.

LEAR. Your name, fair gentlewoman?

GON. This admiration,[67] sir, is much o' the savour   210
Of other your new pranks. I do beseech you
To understand my purposes aright:
As you are old and reverend, you should be wise.
Here do you keep a hundred knights and squires;
Men so disorder'd, so debosh'd[68] and bold,
That this our court, infected with their manners,
Shows like a riotous inn: epicurism[69] and lust
Make it more like a tavern or a brothel
Than a graced[70] palace. The shame itself doth speak
For instant remedy: be then desired   220
By her, that else will take the thing she begs,
A little to disquantity[71] your train;
And the remainder, that shall still depend,[72]
To be such men as may besort[73] your age,
And know themselves and you.

LEAR.   Darkness and devils!
Saddle my horses; call my train together.
Degenerate bastard! I'll not trouble thee:
Yet have I left a daughter.

GON. You strike my people; and your disorder'd rabble
Make servants of their betters.   230

[*Enter* ALBANY.]

LEAR. Woe, that too late repents,— [*To* ALB.] O, sir, are you come?
Is it your will? Speak, sir. Prepare my horses.
Ingratitude, thou marble-hearted fiend,
More hideous when thou show'st thee in a child
Than the sea-monster![74]

ALB.   Pray, sir, be patient.[75]

LEAR. [*To* GON.] Detested kite! thou liest:
My train are men of choice and rarest parts,[76]
That all particulars of duty know,

[63] Understanding.   [64] Paralyzed.   [65] Am I awake?   [66] Whom.
[67] Pretended astonishment.   [68] Debauched.   [69] Unrestrained indulgence.
[70] Honored.   [71] Reduce the numbers of.   [72] Remain as your dependents.
[73] Befit.
[74] (1) Perhaps the hippopotamus, which had a reputation for ingratitude, or (2) any sea
monster of classical mythology.
[75] Exercise self-control.   [76] Accomplishments.

And in the most exact regard support
The worships of their name.[77] O most small fault,　　　　　　240
How ugly didst thou in Cordelia show!
That, like an engine, wrench'd my frame of nature[78]
From the fix'd place; drew from my heart all love,
And added to the gall. O Lear, Lear, Lear!
Beat at this gate, that let thy folly in,
　　　　　　　　　　　　[Striking his head.]
And thy dear judgement out! Go, go, my people.

ALB. My lord, I am guiltless, as I am ignorant
　　Of what hath moved you.

LEAR.　　　　　　　　　　　It may be so, my lord.
　　Hear, nature, hear; dear goddess, hear!
　　Suspend thy purpose, if thou didst intend　　　　　　250
　　To make this creature fruitful!
　　Into her womb convey sterility!
　　Dry up in her the organs of increase;[79]
　　And from her derogate[80] body never spring
　　A babe to honour her! If she must teem,[81]
　　Create her[82] child of spleen;[83] that it may live,
　　And be a thwart[84] disnatured[85] torment to her!
　　Let it stamp wrinkles in her brow of youth;
　　With cadent[86] tears fret[87] channels in her cheeks;
　　Turn all her mother's pains and benefits　　　　　　260
　　To laughter and contempt; that she may feel
　　How sharper than a serpent's tooth it is
　　To have a thankless child! Away, away!
　　　　　　　　　　　　　　[Exit.]

ALB. Now, gods that we adore, whereof comes this?

GON. Never afflict yourself to know the cause;
　　But let his disposition[88] have that scope
　　That dotage gives it.

　　　　　　　　　　[Re-enter LEAR.*]*

LEAR. What, fifty of my followers at a clap!
　　Within a fortnight!

ALB.　　　　　　　　　What's the matter, sir?

LEAR. I'll tell thee: *[To* GON.*]* Life and death! I am ashamed　　270
　　That thou hast power to shame my manhood thus;
　　That these hot tears, which break from me perforce,
　　Should make thee worth them. Blasts and fogs[89] upon thee!
　　The untented[90] woundings of a father's curse
　　Pierce every sense about thee! Old fond[91] eyes,

---

[77]**And . . . name,** and in the smallest details uphold the honorable names they bear.
　　[78]**like . . . nature,** like a powerful piece of mechanism, dislodged the whole structure of my nature.
　　[79]Child-bearing.　　[80]Deteriorated, blighted.　　[81]Be fruitful.　　[82]For her.
[83]Malice.　　[84]Perverse.　　[85]Unnatural.　　[86]Falling.　　[87]Wear.　　[88]Mood.
[89]Fogs and mists were supposed to be laden with the seeds of pestilence.
[90]Too deep to be cleansed with a tent (a piece of lint).　　[91]Foolish.

Beweep this cause again, I'll pluck ye out,
And cast you, with the waters that you lose,
To temper[92] clay. Yea, is it come to this?
Let it be so: yet have I left a daughter,
Who, I am sure, is kind and comfortable:[93]   280
When she shall hear this of thee, with her nails
She'll flay thy wolvish visage. Thou shalt find
That I'll resume the shape which thou dost think
I have cast off for ever: thou shalt, I warrant thee.

> [*Exeunt* LEAR, KENT, *and* ATTEND-
> ANTS.]

GON. Do you mark that, my lord?
ALB. I cannot be so partial, Goneril,
　　To the great love I bear you,—
GON. Pray you, content.[94] What, Oswald, ho!
　　[*To the* FOOL] You, sir, more knave than fool, after your
　　　　master.
FOOL. Nuncle Lear, nuncle Lear, tarry and take the fool with thee.   290
　　　　A fox, when one has caught her,
　　　　And such a daughter,
　　　　Should sure to the slaughter,
　　　　If my cap would buy a halter:
　　　　So the fool follows after.   [*Exit.*]
GON. This man hath had good counsel:—a hundred knights!
　　'Tis politic[95] and safe to let him keep
　　At point[96] a hundred knights: yes, that, on every dream,
　　Each buzz,[97] each fancy, each complaint, dislike,
　　He may enguard his dotage with their powers,   300
　　And hold our lives in mercy.[98] Oswald, I say!
ALB. Well, you may fear too far.
GON.   Safer than trust too far:
　　Let me still[99] take away the harms I fear,
　　Not fear still to be taken:[1] I know his heart.
　　What he hath utter'd I have writ my sister:
　　If she sustain him and his hundred knights,
　　When I have show'd the unfitness,—

> [*Re-enter* OSWALD.]

　　　　　　　　　　　　　　How now, Oswald!
　　What, have you writ that letter to my sister?
OSW. Yes, madam.
GON. Take you some company, and away to horse: 310
　　Inform her full of my particular fear;
　　And thereto add such reasons of your own
　　As may compact it more.[2] Get you gone;

---

[92] Soften.　　[93] Bringing comfort.　　[94] Be satisfied.　　[95] Prudent.
[96] Completely equipped.　　[97] Rumor.　　[98] At his mercy.　　[99] Always.
　[1] **Let . . . taken,** let me always remove what I fear will harm me, rather than always live in fear of being attacked by some harm.
　[2] **compact it more,** give it more substance, i.e., make the argument more convincing.

And hasten your return. [*Exit* OSWALD.] No, no, my lord,
This milky gentleness and course[3] of yours
Though I condemn not, yet, under pardon,
You are much more attask'd[4] for want of wisdom
Than praised for harmful mildness.

ALB. How far your eyes may pierce I cannot tell:
Striving to better, oft we mar what's well.   320

GON. Nay, then—

ALB. Well, well; the event.[5]   [*Exeunt.*]

SCENE V
Court before the same

[*Enter* LEAR, KENT, *and* FOOL.]

LEAR. Go you before to Gloucester with these letters. Acquaint my
daughter no further with any thing you know than comes from
her demand out of the letter. If your diligence be not speedy, I
shall be there afore you.

KENT. I will not sleep, my lord, till I have delivered your letter.
                    [*Exit.*]

FOOL. If a man's brains were in 's heels, were't not in danger of
kibes?[1]

LEAR. Ay, boy.

FOOL. Then, I prithee, be merry; thy wit shall ne'er go slip-shod.[2]

LEAR. Ha, ha, ha!   10

FOOL. Shalt see thy other daughter will use thee kindly;[3] for though
she's as like this as a crab's[4] like an apple, yet I can tell what I
can tell.

LEAR. Why, what canst thou tell, my boy?

FOOL. She will taste as like this as a crab does to a crab. Thou canst tell
why one's nose stands i' the middle on 's face?

LEAR. No.

FOOL. Why, to keep one's eyes of either side's nose; that what a man
cannot smell out, he may spy into.

LEAR. I did her wrong—   20

FOOL. Canst tell how an oyster makes his shell?

LEAR. No.

FOOL. Nor I neither; but I can tell why a snail has a house.

LEAR. Why?

FOOL. Why, to put his head in; not to give it away to his daughters,
and leave his horns without a case.

LEAR. I will forget my nature. So kind a father! Be my horses ready?

FOOL. Thy asses are gone about 'em. The reason why the seven stars[5]
are no more than seven is a pretty reason.

---

[3]**milky . . . course,** mild gentleness of this course.   [4]To be blamed.
[5]**the event,** i.e., let's see what will be the outcome.   [1]Chilblains.
[2]In slippers (and so in danger of chilblains).
[3](1) according to her nature, (2) with kindness.   [4]Crab-apple's.   [5]Pleiades.

LEAR. Because they are not eight?   30
FOOL. Yes, indeed: thou wouldst make a good fool.
LEAR. To take 't again perforce![6] Monster ingratitude!
FOOL. If thou wert my fool, nuncle, I'ld have thee beaten for being
    old before thy time.
LEAR. How's that?
FOOL. Thou shouldst not have been old till thou hadst been wise.
LEAR. O, let me not be mad, not mad, sweet heaven!
    Keep me in temper:[7] I would not be mad!

                        [*Enter* GENTLEMAN.]

How now! are the horses ready?
GENT. Ready, my lord.
LEAR. Come, boy.   40
FOOL. She that's a maid now, and laughs at my departure,
    Shall not be a maid long, unless things be cut shorter.

                              [*Exeunt.*]

ACT II

SCENE I
The EARL OF GLOUCESTER'S *castle*

[*Enter* EDMUND, *and* CURAN *meets him.*]
EDM. Save thee, Curan.
CUR. And you, sir. I have been with your father, and given him notice
    that the Duke of Cornwall and Regan his duchess will be here with
    him this night.
EDM. How comes that?
CUR. Nay, I know not. You have heard of the news abroad; I mean
    the whispered ones, for they are yet but ear-kissing arguments?[1]
EDM. Not I: pray you, what are they?
CUR. Have you heard of no likely wars toward, 'twixt the Dukes of
    Cornwall and Albany?   10
EDM. Not a word.
CUR. You may do, then, in time. Fare you well, sir.   [*Exit.*]
EDM. The duke be here to-night? The better![2] best!
    This weaves itself perforce into my business.
    My father hath set guard to take my brother;
    And I have one thing, of a queasy question,[3]
    Which I must act: briefness and fortune, work!
    Brother, a word; descend:[4] brother I say!

                       [*Enter* EDGAR.]

---

[6] **To . . . perforce,** I will recover my kingdom by force.
[7] Natural emotional equilibrium, i.e., sane.
[1] **ear-kissing arguments,** whispered remarks.   [2] So much the better!
[3] **of . . . question,** of a ticklish nature.
[4] Edgar is in the balcony which represents Edmund's room.

My father watches: O sir, fly this place;
Intelligence is given where you are hid;   20
You have now the good advantage of the night:
Have you not spoken 'gainst the Duke of Cornwall?
He's coming hither; now, i' the night, i' the haste,
And Regan with him: have you nothing said
Upon his party 'gainst the Duke of Albany?
Advise yourself.
EDG.   I am sure on 't, not a word.
EDM. I hear my father coming: pardon me;
In cunning[5] I must draw my sword upon you:
Draw; seem to defend yourself; now quit you[6] well.
Yield: come before my father. Light, ho, here!   30
Fly, brother. Torches, torches! So, farewell.
                              [*Exit* EDGAR.]
Some blood drawn on me would beget opinion[7] [*Wounds
    his arm.*]
Of my more fierce endeavour: I have seen drunkards[8]
Do more than this in sport. Father, father!
Stop, stop! No help?

                    [*Enter* GLOUCESTER, *and* SER-
                    VANTS *with torches.*]

GLOU. Now, Edmund, where's the villain?
EDM. Here stood he in the dark, his sharp sword out,
    Mumbling of wicked charms, conjuring the moon
    To stand auspicious mistress,—
GLOU.   But where is he?
EDM. Look, sir, I bleed.
GLOU.   Where is the villain, Edmund?   40
EDM. Fled this way, sir. When by no means he could—
GLOU. Pursue him, ho! Go after. [*Exeunt some* SERVANTS.] By no
    means what?
EDM. Persuade me to the murder of your lordship;
    But that[9] I told him, the revenging gods
    'Gainst parricides did all their thunders bend;[10]
    Spoke, with how manifold and strong a bond
    The child was bound to the father; sir, in fine,
    Seeing how loathly opposite[11] I stood
    To his unnatural purpose, in fell motion,[12]
    With his preparèd[13] sword, he charges home   50
    My unprovided[14] body, lanced mine arm:
    But when he saw my best alarum'd spirits,[15]
    Bold in the quarrel's right, roused to the encounter,

---

[5] As a pretense.   [6] Acquit yourself.   [7] Give the impression.
[8] An Elizabethan gallant, when a little drunk, sometimes cut his arm to mix his blood with wine, to be drunk to his mistress's health.
[9] When.   [10] Aim.   [11] Loathingly opposed.   [12] Fierce thrust.   [13] Drawn.
[14] Undefended.   [15] **my . . . spirits,** my best energies aroused (as by a call to arms).

Or whether gasted[16] by the noise I made,
Full suddenly he fled.

GLOU.   Let him fly far:
Not in this land shall he remain uncaught;
And found—dispatch.[17] The noble duke my master,
My worthy arch and patron,[18] comes to-night:
By his authority I will proclaim it,
That he which finds him shall deserve our thanks,   60
Bringing the murderous coward to the stake;
He that conceals him, death.

EDM. When I dissuaded him from his intent,
And found him pight[19] to do it, with curst[20] speech
I threaten'd to discover him:[21] he replied,
"Thou unpossessing bastard! dost thou think,
If I would stand against thee, would the reposal
Of any trust, virtue, or worth in thee
Make thy words faith'd?[22] No: what I should deny,—
As this I would; ay, though thou didst produce   70
My very character,[23]—I'ld turn it all
To thy suggestion, plot, and damnèd practice:[24]
And thou must make a dullard of the world,
If they not thought the profits of my death
Were very pregnant and potential[25] spurs
To make thee seek it."

GLOU.   Strong and fasten'd[26] villain!
Would he deny his letter? I never got[27] him.

                         [*Tucket*[28] *within.*]
Hark, the duke's trumpets! I know not why he comes.
All ports[29] I'll bar;[30] the villain shall not 'scape;
The duke must grant me that: besides, his picture   80
I will send far and near, that all the kingdom
May have due note of him; and of my land,
Loyal and natural boy, I'll work the means
To make thee capable.[31]

                    [*Enter* CORNWALL, REGAN, *and*
                         ATTENDANTS.]

CORN. How now, my noble friend! since I came hither,
Which I can call but now, I have heard strange news.
REG. If it be true, all vengeance comes too short
Which can pursue the offender. How dost, my lord?
GLOU. O, madam! my old heart is crack'd, is crack'd!
REG. What, did my father's godson seek your life?   90
He whom my father named? your Edgar?
GLOU. O, lady, lady, shame would have it hid!

---

[16]Terrified.   [17]Finish him off.   [18]**arch and patron,** chief patron.
[19]Determined.   [20]Angry.   [21]Reveal his plan.   [22]Believed.   [23]Handwriting.
[24]Plotting.   [25]**pregnant and potential,** cogent and powerful.   [26]Confirmed.
[27]Begot.   [28]A flourish on the trumpet, a fanfare.   [29]Sea-ports.   [30]Guard.
[31]i.e., of inheriting, i.e., he promises to legitimize him.

Reg. Was he not companion with the riotous knights
    That tend upon my father?
Glou. I know not, madam: 'tis too bad, too bad.
Edm. Yes, madam, he was of that consort.[32]
Reg. No marvel, then, though[33] he were ill affected:[34]
    'Tis they have put him on[35] the old man's death,
    To have the expense[36] and waste of his revenues.
    I have this present evening from my sister
    Been well inform'd of them; and with such cautions,   100
    That if they come to sojourn at my house,
    I'll not be there.
Corn.   Nor I, assure thee,[37] Regan.
    Edmund, I hear that you have shown your father
    A child-like office.[38]
Edm.   'Twas my duty, sir.
Glou. He did bewray[39] his practice;[40] and received
    This hurt you see, striving to apprehend him.
Corn. Is he pursued?
Glou.   Ay, my good lord.
Corn. If he be taken, he shall never more
    Be fear'd of doing harm: make your own purpose,[41]   110
    How in my strength you please.[42] For you, Edmund,
    Whose virtue and obedience doth this instant
    So much commend itself, you shall be ours:
    Natures of such deep trust we shall much need;
    You we first seize on.
Edm.   I shall serve you, sir,
    Truly, however else.
Glou.   For him I thank your grace.
Corn. You know not why we came to visit you,—
Reg. Thus out of season, threading[43] dark-eyed night:
    Occasions, noble Gloucester, of some poise,[44]
    Wherein we must have use of your advice: 120
    Our father he hath writ, so hath our sister,
    Of difference,[45] which[46] I least thought it fit
    To answer from[47] our home; the several messengers
    From hence attend dispatch.[48] Our good old friend,
    Lay comforts to your bosom; and bestow
    Your needful counsel to our business,
    Which craves the instant use.[49]
Glou.   I serve you, madam:
    Your graces are right welcome.   [*Exeunt.*]

---

[32] Company.   [33] If.   [34] **ill affected,** evilly disposed.
[35] **put him on,** incited him to.   [36] Expenditure.   [37] Be assured.
[38] **child-like office,** filial service.   [39] Disclose.   [40] Plot.   [41] Plans.
[42] **How . . . please,** using my authority however you please.   [43] Passing through.
[44] Weight.   [45] Quarrels.   [46] i.e., letters.   [47] Away from.
[48] **attend dispatch,** wait to be sent.
[49] **the instant use,** to be carried out instantly.

SCENE II
Before GLOUCESTER'S *castle*

[*Enter* KENT *and* OSWALD, *severally*.]

Osw. Good dawning to thee, friend: art of this house?

KENT. Ay.

Osw. Where may we set our horses?

KENT. I' the mire.

Osw. Prithee, if thou lovest me, tell me.

KENT. I love thee not.

Osw. Why, then, I care not for thee.

KENT. If I had thee in Lipsbury pinfold,[1] I would make thee care
    for me.

Osw. Why dost thou use me thus? I know thee not.   10

KENT. Fellow, I know thee.

Osw. What dost thou know me for?

KENT. A knave; a rascal; an eater of broken meats; a base, proud,
    shallow, beggarly, three-suited,[2] hundred-pound, filthy, worsted-
    stocking knave; a lily-livered,[3] action-taking knave,[4] a whoreson,
    glass-gazing,[5] super-serviceable,[6] finical[7] rogue; one-trunk-inher-
    iting[8] slave; one that wouldst be a bawd, in way of good service,
    and art nothing but the composition[9] of a knave, beggar, coward,
    pandar, and the son and heir of a mongrel bitch: one whom I will
    beat into clamorous whining, if thou deniest the least syllable of   20
    thy addition.[10]

Osw. Why, what a monstrous fellow art thou, thus to rail on one that
    is neither known of thee nor knows thee!

KENT. What a brazen-faced varlet art thou, to deny thou knowest me!
    Is it two days ago since I tripped up thy heels, and beat thee before
    the king? Draw, you rogue: for, though it be night, yet the moon
    shines; I'll make a sop o' the moonshine of you:[11] draw, you
    whoreson cullionly barber-monger,[12] draw. [*Drawing his sword.*]

Osw. Away! I have nothing to do with thee.

KENT. Draw, you rascal: you come with letters against the king; and   30
    take Vanity the puppet's part[13] against the royalty of her father:
    draw, you rogue, or I'll so carbonado[14] your shanks: draw, you
    rascal; come your ways.[15]

Osw. Help, ho! murder! help!

---

[1] **Lipsbury pinfold,** pinfold is a pound for stray animals. Regarding Lipsbury pinfold, says
Nares: "The enclosure adjacent to my teeth, in my jaws," so, in my clutches.

[2] Alludes to the three suits a year regularly allowed to a man-servant.

[3] A white liver was devoid of blood, i.e., of courage.

[4] A man who settles his quarrels by going to the law.   [5] Vain.

[6] One who serves in ways other than honorable, e.g., as a bawd.   [7] Fussy.

[8] **one . . . inheriting,** whose possessions would fill only one trunk.   [9] Mixture.

[10] Descriptive titles.

[11] **make . . . of you,** steep you in moonshine, i.e., steep you in your own blood even if we
fight by the uncertain light of the moon.

[12] **cullionly . . . monger,** rascally haunter of barber shops (where he was beautified).

[13] **Vanity . . . part,** Lady Vanity was a character in the morality-like puppet plays.

[14] Slash.   [15] Come on then.

KENT. Strike, you slave; stand, rogue, stand; you neat[16] slave, strike.
                                                    [*Beating him.*]
Osw. Help, ho! murder! murder!

                              [*Enter* EDMUND, *with his rapier
                              drawn,* CORNWALL, REGAN, GLOU-
                              CESTER, *and* SERVANTS.]

EDM. How now! What's the matter?
KENT. With you, goodman boy, an you please: come, I'll flesh[17] ye:
    come on, young master.
GLOU. Weapons! arms! What's the matter here?   40
CORN. Keep peace, upon your lives;
    He dies that strikes again. What is the matter?[18]
REG. The messengers from our sister and the king.
CORN. What is your difference?[19] Speak.
Osw. I am scarce in breath, my lord.
KENT. No marvel, you have so bestirred your valour. You cowardly
    rascal, nature disclaims[20] in thee: a tailor made thee.[21]
CORN. Thou art a strange fellow: a tailor make a man?
KENT. Ay, a tailor, sir: a stone-cutter or a painter could not have
    made him so ill, though he had been but two hours at the trade.   50
CORN. Speak yet, how grew your quarrel?
Osw. This ancient ruffian, sir, whose life I have spared at suit of his
    gray beard,—
KENT. Thou whoreson zed![22] thou unnecessary[23] letter! My lord, if
    you will give me leave, I will tread this unbolted[24] villain into mor-
    tar, and daub the walls of a jakes[25] with him. Spare my gray beard,
    you wagtail?[26]
CORN. Peace, sirrah!
    You beastly knave, know you no reverence?
KENT. Yes, sir; but anger hath a privilege.   60
CORN. Why art thou angry?
KENT. That such a slave as this should wear a sword,
    Who wears no honesty.[27] Such smiling rogues as these,
    Like rats, oft bite the holy cords[28] a-twain
    Which are too intrinse[29] t' unloose; smooth[30] every passion
    That in the natures of their lords rebel;
    Bring oil to fire, snow to their colder moods;
    Renege,[31] affirm, and turn their halcyon beaks[32]
    With every gale and vary[33] of their masters,
    Knowing nought, like dogs, but following.   70

[16] Foppish.   [17] Feed with flesh for the first time, i.e., initiate you.
[18] Cause of the quarrel.   [19] Dispute.   [20] Disowns.
[21] **a . . . thee,** i.e., you are nothing but clothes.   [22] i.e., the letter "z."
[23] **unnecessary,** because "s" can express its sound.   [24] Unsifted, coarse.
[25] Privy.   [26] A ridiculously active bird.   [27] Sense of honor.
[28] **holy cords,** sacred family bonds.   [29] Intricately tied.
[30] Flatter (into uncontrolled expression).   [31] Deny.
[32] **halcyon beaks,** it was believed that if a halcyon (kingfisher) were hung by the neck, he
would turn his beak into the wind.
[33] **gale and vary,** varying gale.

A plague upon your epileptic[34] visage!
Smile you my speeches, as I were a fool?[35]
Goose, if I had you upon Sarum plain,[36]
I'ld drive ye cackling home to Camelot.[37]

CORN. What, art thou mad, old fellow?
GLOU. How fell you out? say that.
KENT. No contraries hold more antipathy
Than I and such a knave.
CORN. Why dost thou call him knave? What's his offence?
KENT. His countenance likes me not.[38]   80
CORN. No more, perchance, does mine, nor his, nor hers.
KENT. Sir, 'tis my occupation to be plain:[39]
I have seen better faces in my time
Than stands on any shoulder that I see
Before me at this instant.
CORN.   This is some fellow,
Who, having been praised for bluntness, doth affect
A saucy roughness, and constrains the garb[40]
Quite from[41] his nature: he cannot flatter, he,
An honest mind and plain, he must speak truth!
An they will take it, so;[42] if not, he's plain.[43]   90
These kind of knaves I know, which in this plainness
Harbour more craft and more corrupter ends
Than twenty silly ducking observants[44]
That stretch their duties nicely.[45]
KENT. Sir, in good sooth, in sincere verity,[46]
Under the allowance of your great aspect,[47]
Whose influence, like the wreath of radiant fire
On flickering Phoebus' front,[48]—
CORN.   What mean'st by this?
KENT. To go out of my dialect, which you discommend so much. I
know, sir, I am no flatterer: he that beguiled you in a plain accent   100
was a plain knave; which for my part I will not be, though I should
win your displeasure to entreat me to 't.
CORN. What was the offence you gave him?
OSW. I never gave him any:
It pleased the king his master very late
To strike at me, upon his misconstruction;[49]
When he, conjunct,[50] and flattering his displeasure,
Tripp'd me behind; being down, insulted, rail'd,

---

[34] Distorted by a (frightened) smile.   [35] Professional jester.
[36] **Sarum plain,** Salisbury plain where geese were bred.
[37] The site of King Arthur's Court.   [38] **His . . . not,** I do not like his face.
[39] Plain-spoken.   [40] **constrains the garb,** forces himself to assume a bearing.
[41] **Quite from,** completely foreign to.   [42] Well and good.   [43] Frank.
[44] **ducking observants,** obsequious (continually bowing) courtiers.   [45] Punctiliously.
[46] Kent parodies the speech of "ducking observants."   [47] An astrological term.
[48] Forehead.   [49] Misapprehending [me].   [50] Joined with him (Lear).

And put upon him such a deal of man,[51]
That worthied him,[52] got praises of the king   110
For him attempting who was self-subdued;[53]
And, in the fleshment[54] of this dread exploit,
Drew on me here again.

KENT.   None of these rogues and cowards
But Ajax is their fool.[55]

CORN.   Fetch forth the stocks!
You stubborn ancient knave, you reverend braggart,
We'll teach you—

KENT.   Sir, I am too old to learn:
Call not your stocks for me: I serve the king;
On whose employment I was sent to you:
You shall do small respect, show too bold malice
Against the grace and person of my master,   120
Stocking his messenger.

CORN. Fetch forth the stocks! As I have life and honour,
There shall he sit till noon.

REG. Till noon! till night, my lord; and all night too.

KENT. Why, madam, if I were your father's dog,
You should not[56] use me so.

REG.   Sir, being his knave, I will.

CORN. This is a fellow of the self-same colour[57]
Our sister speaks of. Come, bring away[58] the stocks!
                          [*Stocks brought out.*]

GLOU. Let me beseech your grace not to do so:
His fault is much, and the good king his master   130
Will check[59] him for 't: your purposed low correction
Is such as basest and contemnèd'st wretches
For pilferings and most common trespasses
Are punish'd with: the king must take it ill,
That he, so slightly valued in his messenger,
Should have him thus restrain'd.

CORN.   I'll answer[60] that.

REG. My sister may receive it much more worse,
To have her gentleman abused, assaulted,
For following her affairs. Put in his legs.
                          [KENT *is put in the stocks.*]
Come, my good lord, away.   140
                          [*Exeunt all but* GLOUCESTER *and*
                          KENT.]

---

[51] **deal of man,** lot of manhood, i.e., he swaggered.
[52] As made him appear worthy.
[53] **For . . . self-subdued,** for assailing one who makes no self-defense.
[54] Ferocious excitement.
[55] **Ajax . . . fool,** the cowardly swashbuckler Ajax is vastly inferior to them (in braggart talk).
[56] Surely would not.   [57] Sort.   [58] Along.   [59] Reprove.
[60] Be responsible for.

GLOU. I am sorry for thee, friend; 'tis the duke's pleasure,
  Whose disposition, all the world well knows,
  Will not be rubb'd[61] nor stopp'd: I'll entreat for thee.
KENT. Pray, do not, sir: I have watched[62] and travell'd hard;
  Some time I shall sleep out, the rest I'll whistle.
  A good man's[63] fortune may grow out at heels:
  Give you[64] good morrow!
GLOU. The duke's to blame in this; 'twill be ill taken.   [*Exit.*]
KENT. Good king, that must approve the common saw,[65]
  Thou out of heaven's benediction comest   150
  To the warm sun!
  Approach, thou beacon to this under globe,
  That by thy comfortable[66] beams I may
  Peruse this letter! Nothing almost sees miracles
  But misery: I know 'tis from Cordelia,
  Who hath most fortunately been inform'd
  Of my obscurèd course;[67] [*Reads*] "And shall find time
  From this enormous state,[68] seeking to give
  Losses their remedies." All weary and o'erwatch'd,[69]
  Take vantage,[70] heavy eyes, not to behold   160
  This shameful lodging.
  Fortune, good night: smile once more; turn thy wheel![71]
                                                                        [*Sleeps.*]

                        SCENE III
                         A wood

[*Enter* EDGAR.]
EDG. I heard myself proclaim'd;
  And by the happy[1] hollow of a tree
  Escaped the hunt. No port is free; no place,
  That guard, and most unusual vigilance,
  Does not attend my taking.[2] Whiles I may 'scape,
  I will preserve myself: and am bethought[3]
  To take the basest and most poorest shape
  That ever penury, in contempt of man,
  Brought near to beast: my face I'll grime with filth;
  Blanket my loins; elf[4] all my hair in knots;   10
  And with presented nakedness out-face[5]
  The winds and persecutions of the sky.

---

[61] Obstructed; a "rub" in bowling was anything that deflected the course of the ball.
[62] Stayed awake.   [63] Even a good man's.   [64] God give you.
[65] Proverb, i.e., "To run out of God's blessing [of shade] into the sun" is "to go from bad to worse."
[66] Comforting.   [67] **obscured course,** career in disguise.
[68] The present abnormal political situation.   [69] Exhausted from lack of sleep.
[70] Advantage (of feeling sleepy).   [71] i.e., Fortune's wheel.   [1] Helpful.
[2] **attend my taking,** wait to arrest me.   [3] It occurs to me.
[4] Tangle; tangled hair was thought to be the work of mischievous elves.   [5] Defy.

The country gives me proof and precedent
Of Bedlam beggars,[6] who, with roaring voices,
Strike in their numb'd and mortified[7] bare arms
Pins, wooden pricks,[8] nails, sprigs of rosemary;
And with this horrible object,[9] from low[10] farms,
Poor pelting[11] villages, sheep-cotes, and mills,
Sometime with lunatic bans,[12] sometime with prayers,
Enforce their charity. Poor Turlygod![13] poor Tom!
That's something yet:[14] Edgar I nothing am.   [*Exit.*]   20

SCENE IV
Before GLOUCESTER'S *castle*—KENT *in the stocks*

[*Enter* LEAR, FOOL, *and* GENTLEMAN.]
LEAR. 'Tis strange that they should so depart from home,
And not send back my messenger.
GENT.   As I learn'd,
The night before there was no purpose in them
Of this remove.[1]
KENT.   Hail to thee, noble master!
LEAR. Ha!
Makest thou this shame thy pastime?
KENT.   No, my lord.
FOOL. Ha, ha! he wears cruel[2] garters. Horses are tied by the heads,
dogs and bears by the neck, monkeys by the loins,[3] and men by the
legs: when a man's over-lusty at legs, then he wears wooden
nether-stocks.[4]   10
LEAR. What's he that hath so much thy place[5] mistook
To set thee here?
KENT.   It is both he and she;
Your son and daughter.
LEAR. No.
KENT. Yes.
LEAR. No, I say.
KENT. I say, yea.
LEAR. No, no, they would not.
KENT. Yes, they have.
LEAR. By Jupiter, I swear, no.   20
KENT. By Juno, I swear, ay.
LEAR.   They durst not do 't;
They could not, would not do 't; 'tis worse than murder,

---

[6] Inhabitants of Bedlam (Bethelem Hospital), an insane asylum, were sent out on the roads
to beg.
[7] Insensible.   [8] Skewers.   [9] Spectacle.   [10] Humble.   [11] Paltry.   [12] Curses.
[13] A name beggars applied to themselves; its meaning is unknown.
[14] **That's . . . yet,** i.e., in that character I have a future.   [1] Change of residence.
[2] Pun on crewel = worsted.
[3] **monkeys . . . loins,** the chain of pet-monkeys was so affixed.
[4] Stockings.   [5] Position (as my messenger).

To do upon respect[6] such violent outrage:
Resolve me,[7] with all modest[8] haste, which way
Thou mightst deserve, or they impose, this usage,
Coming from us.

KENT.   My lord, when at their home
I did commend your highness' letters to them,
Ere I was risen from the place that show'd
My duty kneeling, came there a reeking post,[9]
Stew'd in his haste, half breathless, panting forth   30
From Goneril his mistress salutations;
Deliver'd letters, spite of intermission,[10]
Which presently[11] they read: on[12] whose contents,
They summon'd up their meiny,[13] straight took horse;
Commanded me to follow, and attend
The leisure of their answer; gave me cold looks:
And meeting here the other messenger,
Whose welcome, I perceived, had poison'd mine,—
Being the very fellow that of late
Display'd so saucily[14] against your highness,—   40
Having more man[15] than wit about me, drew:
He raised the house with loud and coward cries.
Your son and daughter found this trespass worth
The shame which here it suffers.

FOOL. Winter's not gone yet, if the wild-geese fly that way.
      Fathers that wear rags
          Do make their children blind;
      But fathers that bear bags[16]
          Shall see their children kind.
      Fortune, that arrant whore,   50
      Ne'er turns the key[17] to the poor.

But, for all this, thou shalt have as many dolours[18] for thy daughters as thou canst tell[19] in a year.

LEAR. O, how this mother[20] swells up toward my heart!
      Hysterica passio, down, thou climbing sorrow,
      Thy element's[21] below! Where is this daughter?

KENT. With the earl, sir, here within.

LEAR.   Follow me not,
      Stay here.   [*Exit.*]

GENT. Made you no more offence but what you speak of?

KENT. None.   60
      How chance the king comes with so small a train?

---

[6] **upon respect,** contrary to the respect due me as their father and their King.
[7] Explain to me.   [8] Moderate.   [9] Messenger stinking from sweat.
[10] In spite of interrupting me.   [11] Immediately.   [12] As a result of.
[13] Household servants.   [14] **Display'd so saucily,** behaved so impudently.
[15] Manhood.   [16] **bear bags,** i.e., are rich.   [17] **turns the key,** i.e., opens the door.
[18] Grief, with a pun on "dollars."   [19] Count.
[20] Hysteria, supposed to be caused by wind rising from the stomach to cloud the brain
and cause dizziness.
[21] Proper sphere is.

FOOL. An thou hadst been set i' the stocks for that question, thou
hadst well deserved it.[22]

KENT. Why, fool?

FOOL. We'll set thee to school to an ant, to teach thee there's no la-
bouring i' the winter. All that follow their noses are led by their
eyes but blind men; and there's not a nose among twenty but can
smell him that's stinking. Let go thy hold when a great wheel runs
down a hill, lest it break thy neck with following it; but the great
one that goes up the hill, let him draw thee after. When a wise man   70
gives thee better counsel give me mine again: I would have none
but knaves follow it, since a fool gives it.[23]

    That sir[24] which serves and seeks for gain,
        And follows but for form,
    Will pack[25] when it begins to rain,
        And leave thee in the storm.
    But I will tarry; the fool will stay,
        And let the wise man fly:
    The knave turns fool that runs away;
        The fool no knave,[26] perdy.[27]   80

KENT. Where learned you this, fool?

FOOL. Not i' the stocks, fool.

                    [*Re-enter* LEAR, *with* GLOUCESTER.]

LEAR. Deny[28] to speak with me? They are sick? they are weary?
    They have travell'd all the night? Mere fetches;[29]
    The images[30] of revolt[31] and flying off.
    Fetch me a better answer.

GLOU.   My dear lord,
    You know the fiery quality of the duke;
    How unremoveable and fix'd he is
    In his own course.

LEAR. Vengeance! plague! death! confusion!   90
    Fiery? what quality? Why, Gloucester, Gloucester,
    I'ld speak with the Duke of Cornwall and his wife.

GLOU. Well, my good lord, I have inform'd them so.

LEAR. Inform'd them! Dost thou understand me, man?

GLOU. Ay, my good lord.

LEAR. The king would speak with Cornwall; the dear father
    Would with his daughter speak, commands her service:
    Are they inform'd of this? My breath and blood!
    Fiery? the fiery duke? Tell the hot duke that—
    No, but not yet: may be he is not well: 100

---

[22] **deserved it,** i.e., for asking a silly question.

[23] The fool in stringing together these wise sayings describing Lear's situation is showing
Kent how much wiser the Fool is than he.

[24] Great man.   [25] Run away.

[26] **The . . . no knave,** the fool that runs away from his master is a knave, but the fool who,
like him, remains faithful is no knave.

[27] "Par dieu," literally: "by God," but is a mild oath about = "forsooth."   [28] Refuse.

[29] Pretexts.   [30] Exact likenesses, i.e., clearest signs.   [31] Gross departure from duty.

Infirmity doth still neglect all office[32]
Whereto our health is bound; we are not ourselves
When nature, being oppress'd, commands the mind
To suffer with the body: I'll forbear;
And am fall'n out with my more headier[33] will,
To take[34] the indisposed and sickly fit
For the sound man. Death on my state![35] wherefore
                          [*Looking on* KENT.]
Should he sit here? This act persuades me
That this remotion[36] of the duke and her
Is practice[37] only. Give me my servant forth.   110
Go tell the duke and 's wife I'ld speak with them,
Now, presently:[38] bid them come forth and hear me,
Or at their chamber-door I'll beat the drum
Till it cry sleep to death.[39]
GLOU. I would have all well betwixt you.
                        [*Exit.*]
LEAR. O me, my heart, my rising heart! but, down!
FOOL. Cry to it, nuncle, as the cockney[40] did to the eels when she put
    'em i' the paste alive; she knapped[41] 'em o' the coxcombs[42] with a
    stick, and cried "Down, wantons, down." 'Twas her brother that, in
    pure kindness to his horse, buttered his hay.   120

                    [*Enter* CORNWALL, REGAN, GLOU-
                    CESTER, *and* SERVANTS.]

LEAR. Good morrow to you both.
CORN.   Hail to your grace![43]
                    [KENT *is set at liberty.*]
REG. I am glad to see your highness.
LEAR. Regan, I think you are; I know what reason
    I have to think so: if thou shouldst not be glad,
    I would divorce me from thy mother's tomb,
    Sepulchring[44] an adultress. [*To* KENT] O, are you free?
    Some other time for that. Belovèd Regan,
    Thy sister's naught:[45] O Regan, she hath tied
    Sharp-tooth'd unkindness, like a vulture, here:
                  [*Points to his heart.*]
    I can scarce speak to thee; thou'lt not believe   130
    With how depraved a quality[46]—O Regan!
REG. I pray you, sir, take patience:[47] I have hope
    You less know how to value her desert
    Than she to scant her duty.
LEAR.   Say, how is that?
REG. I cannot think my sister in the least
    Would fail her obligation: if, sir, perchance

---

[32]Duty.   [33]Impulsive.   [34]For taking.   [35]Royal power.   [36]Removal.
[37]Trickery.   [38]At once.   [39]**cry . . . death,** murder sleep.
[40]Cook, perhaps a London cook who knows nothing about eels.   [41]Rapped.
[42]Jocular for heads.   [43]i.e., Majesty.   [44]i.e., as containing.   [45]Wicked.
[46]Character.   [47]**take patience,** be calm.

She have restrain'd the riots of your followers,
'Tis on such ground, and to such wholesome end,
As clears her from all blame.
LEAR. My curses on her!
REG.   O, sir, you are old;   140
Nature in you stands on the very verge
Of her confine:[48] you should be ruled and led
By some discretion, that discerns your state[49]
Better than you yourself. Therefore, I pray you,
That to our sister you do make return;
Say you have wrong'd her, sir.
LEAR.   Ask her forgiveness?
Do you but mark how this becomes the house:[50]
"Dear daughter, I confess that I am old;
                    [*Kneeling.*]
Age is unnecessary:[51] on my knees I beg
That you'll vouchsafe me raiment, bed, and food."   150
REG. Good sir, no more; these are unsightly tricks:
Return you to my sister.
LEAR.   [*Rising*] Never, Regan:
She hath abated me of half my train;[52]
Look'd black upon me; struck me with her tongue,
Most serpent-like, upon the very heart:
All the stored vengeances of heaven fall
On her ingrateful top! Strike her young bones,[53]
You taking[54] airs, with lameness!
CORN.   Fie, sir, fie!
LEAR. You nimble lightnings, dart your blinding flames
Into her scornful eyes! Infect her beauty,   160
You fen-suck'd fogs, drawn by the powerful sun,
To fall[55] and blast her pride!
REG. O the blest gods! so will you wish on me,
When the rash mood is on.
LEAR. No, Regan, thou shalt never have my curse:
Thy tender-hefted[56] nature shall not give
Thee o'er to harshness: her eyes are fierce; but thine
Do comfort and not burn. 'Tis not in thee
To grudge my pleasures, to cut off my train,
To bandy hasty words, to scant my sizes,[57]   170
And in conclusion to oppose the bolt
Against my coming in: thou better know'st
The offices[58] of nature, bond of childhood,[59]
Effects of courtesy,[60] dues of gratitude;

---

[48] Assigned boundary.   [49] i.e., mental state.
[50] **becomes the house,** is a fitting family relationship.
[51] **Age is unnecessary,** old people are of no use.
[52] **abated . . . train,** reduced my retinue by half.   [53] i.e., Goneril's youthful figure.
[54] Infecting.   [55] Fall upon.   [56] Swayed by tender feelings.   [57] Allowances.
[58] Duties.   [59] **bond of childhood,** the duties of a child to its parents.
[60] **effects of courtesy,** courteous action.

Thy half o' the kingdom hast thou not forgot,
Wherein I thee endow'd.

REG.   Good sir, to the purpose.[61]

LEAR. Who put my man i' the stocks?

                         [*Tucket within.*]

CORN.   What trumpet's that?

REG. I know 't, my sister's: this approves her letter,
That she would soon be here.

                    [*Enter* OSWALD.]

                    Is your lady come?

LEAR. This is a slave, whose easy-borrow'd[62] pride   180
Dwells in the fickle grace of her he follows.
Out, varlet,[63] from my sight!

CORN.   What means your grace?

LEAR. Who stock'd my servant? Regan, I have good hope
Thou didst not know on 't. Who comes here? O heavens,

                    [*Enter* GONERIL.]

If you do love old men, if your sweet sway
Allow[64] obedience, if yourselves are old,
Make it your cause; send down, and take my part!
[*To* GON.] Art not ashamed to look upon this beard?
O Regan, wilt thou take her by the hand?

GON. Why not by the hand, sir? How have I offended?   190
All's not offence that indiscretion finds
And dotage terms so.

LEAR.   O sides, you are too tough;
Will you yet hold? How came my man i' the stocks?

CORN. I set him there, sir: but his own disorders
Deserved much less advancement.[65]

LEAR.   You! did you?

REG. I pray you, father, being weak, seem so.
If, till the expiration of your month,
You will return and sojourn with my sister,
Dismissing half your train, come then to me:
I am now from home, and out of that provision   200
Which shall be needful for your entertainment.[66]

LEAR. Return to her, and fifty men dismiss'd?
No, rather I abjure all roofs, and choose
To wage[67] against the enmity o' the air;
To be a comrade with the wolf and owl,—
Necessity's sharp pinch! Return with her?
Why, the hot-blooded France, that dowerless took
Our youngest born, I could as well be brought
To knee[68] his throne, and, squire-like,[69] pension beg
To keep base life afoot. Return with her?   210

---

[61] Talk sense.   [62] Easily assumed.   [63] Scoundrel.   [64] Approve.   [65] Honor.
[66] Maintenance.   [67] Wage war with.   [68] Kneel before.   [69] As if I were a servant.

Persuade me rather to be slave and sumpter[70]
To this detested groom.[71]   [*Pointing at* OSWALD.]
GON.   At your choice, sir.
LEAR. I prithee, daughter, do not make me mad:
  I will not trouble thee, my child; farewell:
  We'll no more meet, no more see one another:
  But yet thou art my flesh, my blood, my daughter;
  Or rather a disease that's in my flesh,
  Which I must needs call mine: thou art a boil,
  A plague-sore, an embossèd[72] carbuncle,
  In my corrupted blood. But I'll not chide thee;   220
  Let shame come when it will, I do not call it:
  I do not bid the thunder-bearer shoot,
  Nor tell tales of thee to high-judging Jove:
  Mend when thou canst; be better at thy leisure:
  I can be patient; I can stay with Regan,
  I and my hundred knights.
REG.   Not altogether so:
  I look'd not for you yet, nor am provided
  For your fit welcome. Give ear, sir, to my sister;
  For those that mingle reason with your passion[73]
  Must be content to think you old, and so—   230
  But she knows what she does.
LEAR.   Is this well spoken?
REG. I dare avouch[74] it, sir: what, fifty followers?
  Is it not well? What should you need of more?
  Yea, or so many, sith that both charge[75] and danger
  Speak 'gainst so great a number? How, in one house,
  Should many people, under two commands,
  Hold amity? 'Tis hard; almost impossible.
GON. Why might not you, my lord, receive attendance
  From those that she calls servants or from mine?
REG. Why not, my lord? If then they chanced to slack[76] you,   240
  We could control them. If you will come to me,—
  For now I spy a danger,—I entreat you
  To bring but five and twenty: to no more
  Will I give place or notice.[77]
LEAR. I gave you all—
REG.   And in good time you gave it.
LEAR. Made you my guardians, my depositaries;[78]
  But kept a reservation to be follow'd
  With such a number. What, must I come to you
  With five and twenty, Regan? said you so?
REG. And speak 't again, my lord; no more with me.   250
LEAR. Those wicked creatures yet do look well-favour'd,[79]
  When others are more wicked; not being the worst

---

[70]Packhorse, drudge.   [71]Menial.   [72]Swollen.
[73]**mingle . . . passion,** consider your violence in the light of reason.   [74]Affirm.
[75]Expense.   [76]Neglect.   [77]Recognition.   [78]Trustees.   [79]Handsome.

Stands in some rank of praise. [*To* Gon.] I'll go with thee:
Thy fifty yet doth double five-and-twenty,
And thou art twice her love.

Gon.   Hear me, my lord:
What need you five and twenty, ten, or five,
To follow in a house where twice so many
Have a command to tend you?

Reg.   What need one?

Lear. O, reason[80] not the need: our basest beggars
Are in the poorest thing superfluous:[81]   260
Allow not nature more than nature needs,
Man's life is cheap as beast's: thou art a lady;
If only to go warm were gorgeous,
Why, nature needs not what thou gorgeous wear'st,
Which scarcely keeps thee warm. But, for true need,—
You heavens, give me that patience,[82] patience I need!
You see me here, you gods, a poor old man,
As full of grief as age; wretched in both!
If it be you that stir these daughters' hearts
Against their father, fool me not so much   270
To bear it tamely;[83] touch me with noble anger,
And let not women's weapons, water-drops,
Stain my man's cheeks! No, you unnatural hags,
I will have such revenges on you both,
That all the world shall—I will do such things,—
What they are, yet I know not; but they shall be
The terrors of the earth.[84] You think I'll weep;
No, I'll not weep:
I have full cause of weeping; but this heart
Shall break into a hundred thousand flaws,[85]   280
Or ere I'll weep. O fool, I shall go mad!

                              [*Exeunt* Lear, Gloucester,
                              Kent, *and* Fool. *Storm and
                              tempest.*]

Corn. Let us withdraw; 'twill be a storm.
Reg. This house is little: the old man and his people
        Cannot be well bestow'd.[86]
Gon. 'Tis his own blame;[87] hath put himself from rest,
        And must needs taste[88] his folly.
Reg. For his particular,[89] I'll receive him gladly,
        But not one follower.
Gon.   So am I purposed.
        Where is my lord of Gloucester?

---

[80] Discuss.
[81] **Are . . . superfluous,** have in their most meagre possessions more than the barest necessities.
[82] Endurance.
[83] **fool . . . tamely,** do not make me so much of a weakling as to endure it tamely.
[84] **The . . . earth,** deeds to terrify the whole world.   [85] Fragments.   [86] Lodged.
[87] Fault.   [88] i.e., digest.   [89] As for him alone.

CORN. Follow'd the old man forth: he is return'd. 290

[*Re-enter* GLOUCESTER.]

GLOU. The king is in high rage.
CORN.   Whither is he going?
GLOU. He calls to horse; but will I know not whither.
CORN. 'Tis best to give him way; he leads himself.
GON. My lord, entreat him by no means to stay.
GLOU. Alack, the night comes on, and the bleak winds
    Do sorely ruffle;[90] for many miles about
    There's scarce a bush.
REG.   O, sir, to wilful men,
    The injuries that they themselves procure
    Must be their schoolmasters. Shut up your doors:
    He is attended with a desperate train; 300
    And what they may incense[91] him to, being apt[92]
    To have his ear abused,[93] wisdom bids fear.
CORN. Shut up your doors, my lord; 'tis a wild night:
    My Regan counsels well: come out o' the storm. [*Exeunt.*]

ACT III

SCENE I
A heath

[*Storm still. Enter* KENT *and a* GENTLEMAN, *meeting.*]
KENT. Who's there, besides foul weather?
GENT. One minded like the weather, most unquietly.
KENT. I know you. Where's the king?
GENT. Contending with the fretful element;
    Bids the wind blow the earth into the sea,
    Or swell the curlèd waters 'bove the main,[1]
    That things[2] might change or cease; tears his white hair,
    Which the impetuous blasts, with eyeless[3] rage,
    Catch in their fury, and make nothing of;[4]
    Strives in his little world of man[5] to outscorn 10
    The to-and-fro-conflicting wind and rain.
    This night, wherein the cub-drawn[6] bear would couch,[7]
    The lion and the belly-pinchèd wolf
    Keep their fur dry, unbonneted[8] he runs,
    And bids what will take all.[9]
KENT.   But who is with him?
GENT. None but the fool; who labours to out-jest
    His heart-struck injuries.

[90] Bluster.   [91] Incite.   [92] Ready.   [93] Deceived.   [1] Mainland.   [2] World.
[3] **eyeless,** hence undirected, indiscriminate.
[4] **make nothing of,** show no respect for.
[5] **little . . . man,** man was regarded as a universe (macrocosm) in miniature (microcosm).
[6] Sucked dry by her cubs.   [7] Lie protected from the storm.   [8] Without a hat.
[9] **take all,** the cry of a gambler when he stakes his last penny; so a gesture of desperation.

KENT.   Sir, I do know you;
        And dare, upon the warrant of my note,[10]
        Commend a dear thing[11] to you. There is division,
        Although as yet the face of it be cover'd   20
        With mutual cunning, 'twixt Albany and Cornwall;
        Who have—as who have not, that their great stars
        Throned and set high?—servants, who seem no less,[12]
        Which are to France the spies and speculations[13]
        Intelligent of our state;[14] what hath been seen,
        Either in snuffs[15] and packings[16] of the dukes,
        Or the hard rein which both of them have borne
        Against the old kind king; or something deeper,
        Whereof perchance these are but furnishings;[17]
        But, true it is, from France there comes a power[18]   30
        Into this scatter'd[19] kingdom; who already,
        Wise in our negligence, have secret feet[20]
        In some of our best ports, and are at point[21]
        To show their open banner. Now to you:
        If on my credit[22] you dare build so far
        To[23] make your speed to Dover, you shall find
        Some that will thank you, making just[24] report
        Of how unnatural and bemadding sorrow
        The king hath cause to plain.[25]
        I am a gentleman of blood and breeding;   40
        And, from some knowledge and assurance, offer
        This office[26] to you.
GENT. I will talk further with you.
KENT.   No, do not.
        For confirmation that I am much more
        Than my out-wall,[27] open this purse, and take
        What it contains. If you shall see Cordelia,—
        As fear not but you shall,—show her this ring;
        And she will tell you who your fellow[28] is
        That yet you do not know. Fie on this storm!
        I will go seek the king.   50
GENT. Give me your hand: have you no more to say?
KENT. Few words, but, to effect,[29] more than all yet;
        That, when we have found the king,—in which your pain
        That way,[30] I'll this,—he that first lights on him
        Holla the other.   [*Exeunt severally.*]

---

[10] Knowledge (of the situation).
[11] **Commend . . . thing,** entrust a momentous matter.
[12] **no less,** not more nor less than servants.   [13] Observers.
[14] **Intelligent . . . state,** giving information about our political situation.
[15] Resentments.   [16] Plots.   [17] Deceptive shows.   [18] Armed force.   [19] Divided.
[20] Infantry.   [21] **at point,** all ready.   [22] **my credit,** your trust in me.   [23] As to.
[24] **making just,** if you make accurate.   [25] Complain.   [26] Duty.
[27] Exterior, i.e., the garb of a serving man.   [28] Companion.
[29] **to effect,** in their importance.
[30] **your . . . way,** i.e., your efforts to find him lie in that direction.

SCENE II
Another part of the heath—storm still

[*Enter* LEAR *and* FOOL.]

LEAR. Blow, winds, and crack your cheeks! rage! blow!
    You cataracts and hurricanoes,[1] spout
    Till you have drench'd our steeples, drown'd the cocks![2]
    You sulphurous and thought-executing[3] fires,
    Vaunt-couriers[4] to oak-cleaving thunderbolts,
    Singe my white head! And thou, all-shaking thunder,
    Smite flat the thick rotundity o' the world!
    Crack nature's moulds,[5] all germens[6] spill[7] at once,
    That make ingrateful man!

FOOL. O nuncle, court holy-water[8] in a dry house is better than this   10
    rain-water out o' door. Good nuncle, in, and ask thy daughters'
    blessing: here's a night pities neither wise man nor fool.

LEAR. Rumble thy bellyful! Spit, fire! spout, rain!
    Nor rain, wind, thunder, fire, are my daughters:
    I tax[9] not you, you elements, with unkindness;
    I never gave you kingdom, call'd you children,
    You owe me no subscription:[10] then let fall
    Your horrible pleasure; here I stand, your slave,
    A poor, infirm, weak, and despised old man:
    But yet I call you servile ministers,[11]   20
    That have with two pernicious daughters join'd
    Your high engender'd[12] battles[13] 'gainst a head
    So old and white as this. O! O! 'tis foul!

FOOL. He that has a house to put 's head in has a good head-piece.
    The cod-piece[14] that will house
        Before the head has any,
    The head and he shall louse;[15]
        So beggars marry many.
    The man that makes his toe
        What he his heart should make[16]   30
    Shall of a corn cry woe,
        And turn his sleep to wake.
    For there was never yet fair woman but she made mouths in a
    glass.[17]

LEAR. No, I will be the pattern of all patience;
    I will say nothing.

[*Enter* KENT.]

---

[1] Water-spouts.   [2] Weathercocks.   [3] Having the speed of thought.
[4] Forerunners.   [5] i.e., molds in which nature fashions men.   [6] Seeds.
[7] Destroy.   [8] **court holy-water,** i.e., flattery.   [9] Reproach.   [10] Obedience.
[11] Agents.   [12] Engendered on high.   [13] Battalions.
[14] An appendage worn on the front of men's trousers.
[15] **The cod-piece . . . louse,** the man who begets children before he has a house will live a lousy existence.
[16] **The . . . make,** the man who puts his heart where his toe should be.
[17] **made . . . glass,** grimaced before a looking-glass.

KENT. Who's there?

FOOL. Marry, here's grace[18] and a cod-piece; that's a wise man and a
   fool.

KENT. Alas, sir, are you here? things that love night   40
   Love not such nights as these; the wrathful skies
   Gallow[19] the very wanderers of the dark,
   And make them keep their caves: since I was man,
   Such sheets of fire, such bursts of horrid thunder,
   Such groans of roaring wind and rain, I never
   Remember to have heard: man's nature cannot carry[20]
   The affliction[21] nor the fear.

LEAR.   Let the great gods,
   That keep this dreadful pother[22] o'er our heads,
   Find out their enemies now. Tremble, thou wretch,
   That hast within thee undivulgèd crimes,   50
   Unwhipp'd of justice: hide thee, thou bloody hand;
   Thou perjured, and thou simular man of[23] virtue
   That art incestuous: caitiff,[24] to pieces shake,
   That under covert and convenient seeming[25]
   Hast practised on[26] man's life: close pent-up guilts,
   Rive your concealing continents,[27] and cry
   These dreadful summoners[28] grace.[29] I am a man
   More sinn'd against than sinning.

KENT.   Alack, bare-headed!
   Gracious my lord, hard by here is a hovel;
   Some friendship will it lend[30] you 'gainst the tempest: 60
   Repose you there; while I to this hard[31] house—
   More harder than the stones whereof 'tis raised;
   Which even but now, demanding after[32] you,
   Denied[33] me to come in—return, and force
   Their scanted courtesy.

LEAR.   My wits begin to turn.
   Come on, my boy: how dost, my boy? art cold?
   I am cold myself. Where is this straw, my fellow?
   The art[34] of our necessities is strange,
   That can make vile things precious. Come, your hovel.
   Poor fool and knave, I have one part in my heart   70
   That's sorry yet for thee.

FOOL. [*Singing*] He that has and a little tiny wit,—
      With hey, ho, the wind and the rain,—
   Must make content with his fortunes fit,
      For the rain it raineth every day.

LEAR. True, my good boy. Come, bring us to this hovel.
                                              [*Exeunt* LEAR *and* KENT.]

---

[18] An honorable gentleman.   [19] Terrify.   [20] Bear.   [21] The bodily pain.
[22] Uproar.   [23] **simular man of,** pretender to.   [24] Despicable creature.
[25] Hypocrisy.   [26] Plotted against.
[27] **Rive . . . continents,** rip open your coverings.   [28] Police of an ecclesiastical court.
[29] **cry . . . grace,** beg for mercy.   [30] Afford.   [31] Cruel.   [32] Asking for.
[33] Forbade.   [34] A reference to alchemy.

FOOL. This is a brave[35] night to cool a courtezan.
　　　I'll speak a prophecy ere I go:
　　　When priests are more in word than matter;[36]
　　　When brewers mar their malt with water;　　　　　　　　　　　80
　　　When nobles are their tailors' tutors;
　　　No heretics burn'd, but wenches' suitors;
　　　When every case in law is right;
　　　No squire in debt, nor no poor knight;
　　　When slanders do not live in tongues;
　　　Nor cutpurses come not to throngs;
　　　When usurers tell[37] their gold i' the field;
　　　And bawds and whores do churches build;
　　　Then shall the realm of Albion[38]
　　　Come to great confusion:[39]　　　　　　　　　　　　　　90
　　　Then comes the time, who lives to see 't,
　　　That going[40] shall be used with feet.
This prophecy Merlin[41] shall make; for I live before his time.
　　　　　　　　　　　　　　　　　　　　　　　[*Exit.*]

SCENE III
GLOUCESTER'S *castle*

[*Enter* GLOUCESTER *and* EDMUND.]

GLOU. Alack, alack, Edmund, I like not this unnatural dealing. When
　　I desired their leave that I might pity him, they took from me the
　　use of mine own house; charged me, on pain of their perpetual
　　displeasure, neither to speak of him, entreat for him, nor any way
　　sustain[1] him.

EDM. Most savage and unnatural!

GLOU. Go to; say you nothing. There's a division betwixt the dukes;
　　and a worse matter than that: I have received a letter this night; 'tis
　　dangerous to be spoken; I have locked the letter in my closet:
　　these injuries the king now bears will be revenged home;[2] there's　　　10
　　part of a power[3] already footed:[4] we must incline to the king.[5] I
　　will seek him, and privily[6] relieve him: go you and maintain talk
　　with the duke, that my charity be not of him perceived: if he ask
　　for me, I am ill, and gone to bed. Though I die for it, as no less is
　　threatened me, the king my old master must be relieved. There is
　　some strange thing toward,[7] Edmund; pray you, be careful.　[*Exit.*]

EDM. This courtesy, forbid thee,[8] shall the duke
　　　Instantly know; and of that letter too:
　　　This seems a fair deserving,[9] and must draw me
　　　That which my father loses; no less than all:　　　　　　　20
　　　The younger rises when the old doth fall.　　　　[*Exit.*]

---

[35] Fine.　　[36] **more . . . matter,** better in their talk than in deeds.　　[37] Count.
[38] Britain.　　[39] Ruin.　　[40] Walking.
[41] Magician and prophet of King Arthur's Court.　　[1] Relieve.　　[2] Fully.　　[3] Army.
[4] Landed.　　[5] **incline to the King,** take the King's part.　　[6] Secretly.
[7] In preparation.　　[8] Forbidden to thee.
[9] **This . . . deserving,** this will seem a meritorious action.

SCENE IV
The heath—before a hovel

[*Enter* LEAR, KENT, *and* FOOL.]

KENT. Here is the place, my lord; good my lord, enter:
 The tyranny of the open night's[1] too rough
 For nature to endure.   [*Storm still.*]

LEAR.   Let me alone.

KENT. Good my lord, enter here.

LEAR.   Wilt break my heart?

KENT. I had rather break mine own. Good my lord, enter.

LEAR. Thou think'st 'tis much that this contentious storm
 Invades us to the skin: so 'tis to thee;
 But where the greater malady is fix'd,
 The lesser is scarce felt. Thou 'ldst shun a bear;
 But if thy flight lay toward the raging sea,   10
 Thou 'ldst meet the bear i' the mouth.[2] When the mind's free,[3]
 The body's delicate:[4] the tempest in my mind
 Doth from my senses take all feeling else
 Save what beats there. Filial ingratitude!
 Is it not as[5] this mouth should tear this hand
 For lifting food to 't? But I will punish home:
 No, I will weep no more. In such a night
 To shut me out! Pour on; I will endure.
 In such a night as this! O Regan, Goneril!
 Your old kind father, whose frank[6] heart gave all,—   20
 O, that way madness lies; let me shun that;
 No more of that.

KENT.   Good my lord, enter here.

LEAR. Prithee, go in thyself; seek thine own ease:
 This tempest will not give me leave to ponder
 On things would hurt me more. But I'll go in.
 [*To the* FOOL] In, boy; go first. You houseless poverty,—
 Nay, get thee in. I'll pray, and then I'll sleep.
                          [FOOL *goes in.*]
 Poor naked wretches, wheresoe'er you are,
 That bide[7] the pelting of this pitiless storm,
 How shall your houseless heads and unfed sides,   30
 Your loop'd and window'd[8] raggedness, defend you
 From seasons such as these? O, I have ta'en
 Too little care of this! Take physic, pomp;
 Expose thyself to feel what wretches feel,
 That thou mayst shake the superflux[9] to them,
 And show the heavens more just.

EDG. [*Within*] Fathom[10] and half, fathom and half! Poor Tom!

---

[1] **open night,** night in the open.   [2] **i' the mouth,** face to face.   [3] i.e., from trouble.
[4] Sensitive.   [5] As if.   [6] Generous.   [7] Endure.
[8] **loop'd and window'd,** the two words are synonymous, meaning "full of holes."
[9] Superfluity (i.e., what pomp does not need).
[10] **Fathom, etc.,** Tom pretends to be a sailor, taking soundings in a storm at sea.

[*The* FOOL *runs out from the hovel.*]

FOOL. Come not in here, nuncle, here's a spirit. Help me, help me!

KENT. Give me thy hand. Who's there?

FOOL. A spirit, a spirit: he says his name's poor Tom. 40

KENT. What art thou that dost grumble there i' the straw? Come forth.

[*Enter* EDGAR *disguised as a madman.*]

EDG. Away! the foul fiend follows me!
    Through the sharp hawthorn blows the cold wind.
    Hum! go to thy cold bed, and warm thee.

LEAR. Hast thou given all to thy two daughters?
    And art thou come to this?

EDG. Who gives any thing to poor Tom? whom the foul fiend hath led through fire and through flame, through ford and whirlpool, o'er bog and quagmire; that hath laid knives under his pillow,[11] and halters in his pew;[12] set ratsbane by his porridge; made him proud of heart, to ride on a bay trotting-horse over four-inched bridges, to course[13] his own shadow for a traitor. Bless thy five wits! Tom's a-cold,—O, do de, do de, do de. Bless thee from whirlwinds, star-blasting, and taking![14] Do poor Tom some charity, whom the foul fiend vexes: there could I have him[15] now,— and there,—and there again, and there. 50

[*Storm still.*]

LEAR. What, have his daughters brought him to this pass?
    Couldst thou save nothing? Didst thou give them all?

FOOL. Nay, he reserved a blanket, else we had been all shamed. 60

LEAR. Now, all the plagues that in the pendulous[16] air
    Hang faded o'er men's faults light on thy daughters!

KENT. He hath no daughters, sir.

LEAR. Death, traitor! nothing could have subdued[17] nature[18]
    To such a lowness but his unkind daughters.
    Is it the fashion, that discarded fathers
    Should have thus little mercy on their flesh?[19]
    Judicious punishment! 'twas this flesh begot
    Those pelican daughters.[20]

EDG. Pillicock[21] sat on Pillicock-hill: 70
    Halloo, halloo, loo, loo!

FOOL. This cold night will turn us all to fools and madmen.

EDG. Take heed o' the foul fiend: obey thy parents; keep thy word justly; swear not; commit[22] not with man's sworn spouse; set not thy sweet heart on proud array. Tom's a-cold.

---

[11] **knives . . . pillow,** i.e., tempted him to commit suicide.
[12] A gallery of a house, not a church pew.   [13] Chase.   [14] Infection.
[15] **there . . . him,** i.e., he snatches at vermin.   [16] Overhanging.   [17] Reduced.
[18] i.e., man's nature.
[19] **mercy . . . flesh,** Edgar has stuck thorns or skewers into his flesh.
[20] **pelican daughters,** it was believed that young pelicans fed on their mother's blood.
[21] Suggested by *pelican;* it meant darling.   [22] i.e., commit adultery.

LEAR. What hast thou been?

EDG. A serving-man, proud in heart and mind; that curled my hair; wore gloves in my cap;[23] served the lust of my mistress' heart, and did the act of darkness with her; swore as many oaths as I spake words, and broke them in the sweet face of heaven: one that slept   80
in the contriving of lust, and waked to do it: wine loved I deeply, dice dearly; and in woman out-paramoured[24] the Turk:[25] false of heart, light of ear,[26] bloody of hand; hog in sloth, fox in stealth, wolf in greediness, dog in madness, lion in prey. Let not the creaking of shoes nor the rustling of silks betray thy poor heart to woman: keep thy foot out of brothels, thy hand out of plackets,[27] thy pen from lenders' books, and defy the foul fiend.
Still through the hawthorn blows the cold wind:
Says suum, mun, ha, no, nonny.
　　Dolphin[28] my boy, my boy, sessa![29] let him trot by.   90
　　　　　　　　　　　　[Storm still.]

LEAR. Why, thou wert better in thy grave than to answer[30] with thy uncovered body this extremity of the skies.[31] Is man no more than this? Consider him well. Thou owest the worm no silk, the beast no hide, the sheep no wool, the cat[32] no perfume. Ha! here's three on's are sophisticated! Thou art the thing itself: unaccommodated man[33] is no more but such a poor, bare, forked animal as thou art. Off, off, you lendings![34] come, unbutton here.
　　　　　　　　　　　　[Tearing off his clothes.]

FOOL. Prithee, nuncle, be contented; 'tis a naughty[35] night to swim in. Now a little fire in a wild field were like an old lecher's heart; a small spark, all the rest on 's body cold. Look, here comes a walk-   100
ing fire.

　　　　　　　　　　[Enter GLOUCESTER, with a torch.]

EDG. This is the foul fiend Flibbertigibbet: he begins at curfew, and walks till the first cock; he gives the web and the pin,[36] squints the eye, and makes the hare-lip; mildews the white[37] wheat, and hurts the poor creature of earth.
　　Saint Withold[38] footed[39] thrice the 'old;[40]
　　He met the night-mare,[41] and her nine-fold;[42]
　　　　Bid her alight,
　　　　And her troth plight,[43]
　　And, aroint[44] thee, witch, aroint thee!   110

---

[23] **gloves . . . cap,** a gallant often wore his lady's glove in his hat.
[24] Had more mistresses than.　　[25] The Sultan.
[26] **light of ear,** foolishly credulous of evil gossip.　　[27] Slits in petticoats.
[28] **Dolphin, my boy,** reference to a ballad ridiculing the French Dauphin.
[29] Hurry, go it.　　[30] Oppose.　　[31] **extremity . . . skies,** violence of the storm.
[32] Civet cat.
[33] **unaccommodated man,** man unprovided with clothes and other furnishings of civilization.
[34] Lent by art to the natural man.　　[35] Very wicked.
[36] **web and the pin,** old term for "cataract."　　[37] i.e., ripening.　　[38] i.e., St. Vitalis.
[39] Walked across.　　[40] Wold, an upland plain.　　[41] A demon.　　[42] Nine offspring.
[43] Pledge her faith (to do no harm).　　[44] Begone.

KENT. How fares your grace?[45]

LEAR. What's he?

KENT. Who's there? What is 't you seek?

GLOU. What are you there? Your names?

EDG. Poor Tom; that eats the swimming frog, the toad, the tadpole,
the wall-newt and the water;[46] that in the fury of his heart, when
the foul fiend rages, eats cow-dung for sallets;[47] swallows the old
rat and the ditch-dog; drinks the green mantle[48] of the standing[49]
pool; who is whipped from tithing to tithing,[50] and stock-punished,[51]
and imprisoned; who hath had three suits to his back, six shirts to   120
his body, horse to ride, and weapon to wear;

> But mice and rats, and such small deer,[52]
> Have been Tom's food for seven long year.

Beware my follower.[53] Peace, Smulkin; peace, thou fiend!

GLOU. What, hath your grace no better company?

EDG. The prince of darkness is a gentleman:
Modo he's call'd, and Mahu.

GLOU. Our flesh and blood is grown so vile, my lord,
That it doth hate what gets[54] it.

EDG. Poor Tom's a-cold.   130

GLOU. Go in with me: my duty cannot suffer[55]
To obey in all your daughters' hard commands:
Though their injunction be to bar my doors,
And let this tyrannous night take hold upon you,
Yet have I ventured to come seek you out,
And bring you where both fire and food is ready.

LEAR. First let me talk with this philosopher.[56]
What is the cause of thunder?

KENT. Good my lord, take his offer; go into the house.

LEAR. I'll talk a word with this same learned Theban.[57]   140
What is your study?[58]

EDG. How to prevent[59] the fiend, and to kill vermin.

LEAR. Let me ask you one word in private.

KENT. Importune him once more to go, my lord;
His wits begin to unsettle.

GLOU. Canst thou blame him?   [*Storm still.*]
His daughters seek his death; ah, that good Kent!
He said it would be thus, poor banish'd man!
Thou say'st the king grows mad; I'll tell thee, friend,
I am almost mad myself: I had a son,   150
Now outlaw'd from my blood; he sought my life,
But lately, very late: I loved him, friend:
No father his son dearer: truth to tell thee,
The grief hath crazed my wits. What a night's this!
I do beseech your grace,—

---

[45] Majesty.   [46] **wall . . . water,** the wall-lizard and the water-lizard.   [47] Salads.
[48] Scum.   [49] Stagnant.   [50] **tithing to tithing,** parish to parish.
[51] Put in the stocks.   [52] Animal.   [53] Attendant fiend.   [54] Begets.
[55] Permit me.   [56] Scientist.   [57] i.e., Greek philosopher.   [58] Specialty.
[59] Forestall.

LEAR.   O, cry you mercy,[60] sir.
       Noble philosopher, your company.
EDG. Tom's a-cold.
GLOU. In, fellow, there, into the hovel: keep thee warm.
LEAR. Come, let's in all.
KENT.   This way, my lord.
LEAR.   With him;
       I will keep still[61] with my philosopher.   160
KENT. Good my lord, soothe[62] him; let him take the fellow.
GLOU. Take him you on.
KENT. Sirrah, come on; go along with us.
LEAR. Come, good Athenian.
GLOU. No words, no words: hush.
EDG. Child[63] Rowland[64] to the dark tower came,
       His word was still,—Fie, foh, and fum,
       I smell the blood of a British man.   [*Exeunt.*]

SCENE V
GLOUCESTER'S *castle*

[*Enter* CORNWALL *and* EDMUND.]
CORN. I will have my revenge ere I depart his house.
EDM. How, my lord, I may be censured,[1] that nature thus gives way to
       loyalty, something fears me[2] to think of.
CORN. I now perceive, it was not altogether your brother's evil dispo-
       sition made him seek his death; but a provoking merit,[3] set a-work
       by a reproveable badness in himself.[4]
EDM. How malicious is my fortune, that I must repent to be just![5]
       This is the letter he spoke of, which approves[6] him an intelligent
       party[7] to the advantages of France.[8] O heavens! that this treason
       were not, or not I the detector!   10
CORN. Go with me to the duchess.
EDM. If the matter of this paper be certain, you have mighty business
       in hand.
CORN. True or false, it hath made thee earl of Gloucester. Seek out
       where thy father is, that he may be ready for our apprehension.[9]
EDM. [*Aside*] If I find him comforting[10] the king, it will stuff his suspi-
       cion more fully.—I will persevere in my course of loyalty, though
       the conflict be sore between that and my blood.[11]
CORN. I will lay trust upon thee; and thou shalt find a dearer father
       in my love.   [*Exeunt.*]   20

---

[60]**cry you mercy,** beg your pardon (for not paying attention).   [61]Always.
[62]Humor.   [63]A candidate for knighthood.
[64]Charlemagne's nephew and legendary hero. The line is probably a snatch from a lost
ballad.
[1]Judged.   [2]**something fears me,** I am somewhat frightened.
[3]**provoking merit,** i.e., the fact that your father deserved to die also incited him.
[4]i.e., Gloucester.   [5]Righteous.   [6]Proves.   [7]**intelligent party,** a spy.
[8]King of France.   [9]Arrest.   [10]Giving aid and comfort.   [11]Natural instincts.

SCENE VI
A chamber in a farmhouse adjoining the castle

[*Enter* GLOUCESTER, LEAR, KENT, FOOL, *and* EDGAR.]

GLOU. Here is better than the open air; take it thankfully. I will piece
out the comfort with what addition I can: I will not be long from
you.

KENT. All the power of his wits have given way to his impatience: the
gods reward your kindness!   [*Exit* GLOUCESTER.]

EDG. Fraretetto[1] calls me; and tells me Nero is an angler in the lake of
darkness. Pray, innocent,[2] and beware the foul fiend.

FOOL. Prithee, nuncle, tell me whether a madman be a gentleman or
a yeoman?[3]

LEAR. A king, a king!   10

FOOL. No, he's a yeoman that has a gentleman to his son; for he's a
mad yeoman that sees his son a gentleman before him.[4]

LEAR. To have a thousand with red burning spits
    Come hissing in upon 'em,—

EDG. The foul fiend bites my back.

FOOL. He's mad that trusts in the tameness of a wolf, a horse's health,
a boy's love, or a whore's oath.

LEAR. It shall be done; I will arraign them straight.
    [*To* EDGAR] Come, sit thou here, most learned justicer;[5]
    [*To the* FOOL] Thou, sapient sir, sit here. Now, you she foxes!   20

EDG. Look, where he stands and glares!
    Wantest thou eyes at trial,[6] madam?
    Come o'er the bourn,[7] Bessy, to me,—[8]

FOOL. Her boat hath a leak,
    And she must not speak
Why she dares not come over to thee.

EDG. The foul fiend haunts poor Tom in the voice of a nightingale.
Hopdance[9] cries in Tom's belly for two white[10] herring. Croak
not,[11] black angel; I have no food for thee.

KENT. How do you, sir? Stand you not so amazed:[12]   30
    Will you lie down and rest upon the cushions?

LEAR. I'll see their trial first. Bring in the evidence.[13]
    [*To* EDGAR] Thou robed man of justice, take thy place;
    [*To the* FOOL] And thou, his yoke-fellow of equity,
Bench[14] by his side: [*To* KENT] you are o' the commission,[15]
Sit you too.

EDG. Let us deal justly.
    Sleepest or wakest thou, jolly shepherd?

---

[1] The name of a fiend.   [2] Simpleton.
[3] A small landed proprietor, in rank lower than a gentleman.
[4] **before him,** before he is one.   [5] Judge.
[6] **Wantest . . . trial?** Don't you see you have a spectator at your trial, i.e., the fiend?
[7] Brook.   [8] **Come . . . me,** first line of an old ballad.   [9] A fiend.   [10] Fresh.
[11] **Croak not,** addressed to his rumbling belly.   [12] In a daze.   [13] Witnesses.
[14] Sit on the judge's bench.   [15] A commissioned Justice of the Peace.

Thy sheep be in the corn;[16]
And for one blast[17] of thy minikin[18] mouth,   40
Thy sheep shall take no harm.
Purr! the cat is gray.

LEAR. Arraign her first; 'tis Goneril. I here take my oath before this
honourable assembly, she kicked the poor king her father.

FOOL. Come hither, mistress. Is your name Goneril?

LEAR. She cannot deny it.

FOOL. Cry you mercy, I took you for a joint-stool.[19]

LEAR. And here's another, whose warp'd[20] looks proclaim
What store[21] her heart is made on. Stop her there!
Arms, arms, sword, fire! Corruption in the place![22]   50
False justicer, why hast thou let her 'scape?

EDG. Bless thy five wits!

KENT. O pity! Sir, where is the patience now,
That you so oft have boasted to retain?

EDG. [*Aside*] My tears begin to take his part so much,
They'll mar my counterfeiting.

LEAR. The little dogs and all,
Tray, Blanch, and Sweet-heart, see, they bark at me.

EDG. Tom will throw his head at them.
Avaunt, you curs!   60
Be thy mouth or black or white,
Tooth that poisons if it bite;
Mastiff, greyhound, mongrel grim,
Hound or spaniel, brach or lym,[23]
Or bobtail tike[24] or trundle-tail,[25]
Tom will make them weep and wail:
For, with throwing thus my head,
Dogs leap the hatch,[26] and all are fled.
Do de, de, de. Sessa![27] Come, march to wakes and fairs and mar-
ket-towns. Poor Tom, thy horn is dry.[28]   70

LEAR. Then let them anatomize[29] Regan; see what breeds about her
heart. Is there any cause in nature that makes these hard hearts?
[*To* EDGAR] You, sir, I entertain[30] for one of my hundred; only I
do not like the fashion of your garments: you will say they are
Persian[31] attire; but let them be changed.

KENT. Now, good my lord, lie here and rest awhile.

LEAR. Make no noise, make no noise; draw the curtains:[32] so, so, so.
We'll go to supper i' the morning. So, so, so.[33]

FOOL. And I'll go to bed at noon.

[*Re-enter* GLOUCESTER.]

---

[16] Wheat field.   [17] The time it takes to blow one blast.   [18] Pretty little.
[19] Stool made by a joiner.   [20] Distorted.   [21] Stuff.
[22] **Corruption . . . place,** bribery in the court.   [23] **brach or lym,** bitch or bloodhound.
[24] Cur.   [25] Drooping-tail.   [26] Lower half of a divided [Dutch] door.
[27] about = "Let's go!"   [28] **horn is dry,** a beggar's appeal for drink; horn was a bottle.
[29] Dissect.   [30] Engage.   [31] Gorgeous.   [32] i.e., imaginary bed curtains.
[33] **So . . . so,** an indication that Lear goes through the motions of drawing curtains.

GLOU. Come hither, friend: where is the king my master? 80
KENT. Here, sir; but trouble him not, his wits are gone.
GLOU. Good friend, I prithee, take him in thy arms;
    I have o'erheard a plot of death upon[34] him:
    There is a litter ready; lay him in 't,
    And drive towards Dover, friend, where thou shalt meet
    Both welcome and protection. Take up thy master:
    If thou shouldst dally[35] half an hour, his life,
    With thine, and all that offer to defend him,
    Stand in assurèd loss:[36] take up, take up;
    And follow me, that will to some provision[37] 90
    Give thee quick conduct.
KENT.   Oppressèd nature sleeps;
    This rest might yet have balm'd thy broken sinews,[38]
    Which, if convenience will not allow,
    Stand in hard cure.[39] [*To the* FOOL] Come, help to bear thy
        master;
    Thou must not stay behind.
GLOU.   Come, come, away.
                      [*Exeunt all but* EDGAR.]
EDG. When we our betters see bearing our woes,
    We scarcely think our miseries our foes.
    Who alone suffers suffers most i' the mind,
    Leaving free[40] things and happy shows[41] behind:
    But then the mind much sufferance[42] doth o'erskip,[43] 100
    When grief hath mates, and bearing[44] fellowship.
    How light and portable[45] my pain seems now,
    When that which makes me bend makes the king bow,
    He childed as I father'd![46] Tom, away!
    Mark the high noises;[47] and thyself bewray,[48]
    When false opinion, whose wrong thought defiles thee,
    In thy just proof,[49] repeals[50] and reconciles thee.
    What[51] will hap more to-night, safe 'scape the king!
    Lurk, lurk.[52]   [*Exit.*]

SCENE VII
GLOUCESTER'S castle

[*Enter* CORNWALL, REGAN, GONERIL, EDMUND, *and* SERVANTS.]
CORN. Post speedily to my lord your husband; show him this letter:
    the army of France is landed. Seek out the villain Gloucester.

---

[34] Against.   [35] Delay.   [36] **Stand . . . loss,** are sure to be lost.   [37] i.e., for safety.
[38] **balm'd . . . sinews,** healed your racked nerves.
[39] **Stand . . . cure,** are hard to cure.   [40] Carefree.
[41] **happy shows,** appearances of happiness.   [42] Suffering.   [43] Escape.
[44] i.e., of sorrow.   [45] Endurable.
[46] **childed . . . father'd,** having children like my father (in cruelty).
[47] **high noises,** sounds of discord among the high and mighty.
[48] You reveal yourself, i.e., put off your disguise.
[49] **In . . . proof,** on proof that you are guiltless.   [50] Restores (i.e., to favor).
[51] Whatever.   [52] Hide.

[*Exeunt some of the* SERVANTS.]

REG. Hang him instantly.

GON. Pluck out his eyes.

CORN. Leave him to my displeasure. Edmund, keep you our sister
company: the revenges we are bound to take upon your traitorous
father are not fit for your beholding. Advise the duke, where you
are going, to a most festinate preparation:[1] we are bound to the
like.[2] Our posts[3] shall be swift and intelligent[4] betwixt us. Farewell,
dear sister: farewell, my lord of Gloucester.[5]   10

[*Enter* OSWALD.]

How now! where's the king?

OSW. My lord of Gloucester[6] hath convey'd him hence:
    Some five or six and thirty of his knights,
    Hot questrists[7] after him, met him at gate;
    Who, with some other of the lords dependants,
    Are gone with him towards Dover; where they boast
    To have well-armèd friends.

CORN.   Get horses for your mistress.

GON. Farewell, sweet lord, and sister.

CORN. Edmund, farewell.

[*Exeunt* GONERIL, EDMUND, *and*
Oswald.]

        Go seek the traitor Gloucester,
    Pinion[8] him like a thief, bring him before us.   20

[*Exeunt other* SERVANTS.]

    Though well we may not pass[9] upon his life
    Without the form of justice, yet our power
    Shall do a courtesy[10] to our wrath, which men
    May blame, but not control. Who's there? the traitor?

[*Enter* GLOUCESTER, *brought in by
two or three.*]

REG. Ingrateful fox! 'tis he.

CORN. Bind fast his corky[11] arms.

GLOU. What mean your graces? Good my friends, consider
    You are my guests: do me no foul play, friends.

CORN. Bind him, I say.

[SERVANTS *bind him.*]

REG.   Hard, hard. O filthy traitor!

GLOU. Unmerciful lady as you are, I'm none.   30

CORN. To this chair bind him. Villain, thou shalt find—

[REGAN *plucks his beard.*]

GLOU. By the kind gods, 'tis most ignobly done

---

[1] **to . . . preparation,** to make a most hasty preparation (for war).
[2] **bound to the like,** getting ready for the like preparation.   [3] Messengers.
[4] Carry information.
[5] i.e., Edmund, who has been given the title as a reward for his treachery.
[6] The old Earl.   [7] Searchers.   [8] i.e., bind his elbows together.   [9] Pass judgment.
[10] Act in accordance with.   [11] Withered.

    To pluck me by the beard.
REG. So white, and such a traitor!
GLOU.   Naughty[12] lady,
    These hairs, which thou dost ravish from my chin,
    Will quicken,[13] and accuse thee: I am your host:
    With robbers' hands my hospitable favours[14]
    You should not ruffle[15] thus. What will you do?
CORN. Come, sir, what letters had you late from France?
REG. Be simple[16] answerer, for we know the truth.   40
CORN. And what confederacy have you with the traitors
    Late footed[17] in the kingdom?
REG. To whose hands have you sent the lunatic king?
    Speak.
GLOU.   I have a letter guessingly set down,
    Which came from one that's of a neutral heart,
    And not from one opposed.
CORN.   Cunning.
REG.   And false.
CORN. Where hast thou sent the king?
GLOU. To Dover.
REG. Wherefore to Dover? Wast thou not charged at peril[18]—
CORN. Wherefore to Dover? Let him first answer that.   50
GLOU. I am tied to the stake, and I must stand the course.[19]
REG. Wherefore to Dover, sir?
GLOU. Because I would not see thy cruel nails
    Pluck out his poor old eyes; nor thy fierce sister
    In his anointed[20] flesh stick boarish fangs.
    The sea, with such a storm as his bare head
    In hell-black night endured, would have buoy'd up,[21]
    And quench'd the stelled fires:[22]
    Yet, poor old heart, he holp[23] the heavens to rain.
    If wolves had at thy gate howl'd[24] that stern time,   60
    Thou shouldst have said "Good porter, turn the key,"
    All cruels else subscribed:[25] but I shall see
    The wingèd vengeance overtake such children.
CORN. See 't shalt thou never. Fellows, hold the chair.
    Upon these eyes of thine I'll set my foot.
GLOU. He that will think to live till he be old,
    Give me some help! O cruel! O you gods!
REG. One side will mock another;[26] the other too.
CORN. If you see vengeance,—

---

[12] Wicked.   [13] Come to life.   [14] **hospitable favours,** the features of your host.
[15] Treat with violence.   [16] Straightforward.   [17] Landed.
[18] Under peril (of death).   [19] Attack (of the dogs in bear-baiting).
[20] i.e., with the consecrated oil at his coronation.   [21] Heaved aloft.
[22] **stelled fires,** the fires of the stars.   [23] Helped.   [24] i.e., for shelter.
[25] **All . . . subscribed,** all other cruel creatures except you gave way (to their need for shelter).
[26] **One . . . another,** i.e., one good eye will mock the other blind one.

FIRST SERV.   Hold your hand, my lord:
    I have served you ever since I was a child;   70
    But better service have I never done you
    Than now to bid you hold.
REG.   Hold now, you dog!
FIRST SERV. If you did wear a beard upon your chin,
    I'd shake it on this quarrel.[27] What do you mean?
CORN. My villain![28]   [*They draw and fight.*]
FIRST SERV. Nay, then, come on, and take the chance of anger.
REG. Give me thy sword. A peasant stand up thus!
                [*Takes a sword, and runs at him
                behind.*]
FIRST SERV. O, I am slain! My lord, you have one eye left
    To see some mischief[29] on him. O!
                [*Dies.*]
CORN. Lest it see more, prevent[30] it. Out, vile jelly!   80
    Where is thy lustre now?
GLOU. All dark and comfortless. Where's my son Edmund?
    Edmund, enkindle all the sparks of nature,
    To quit[31] this horrid act.
REG.   Out, treacherous villain!
    Thou call'st on him that hates thee: it was he
    That made the overture[32] of thy treasons to us;
    Who is too good to pity thee.
GLOU. O my follies! then Edgar was abused.[33]
    Kind gods, forgive me that,[34] and prosper him!
REG. Go thrust him out at gates, and let him smell   90
    His way to Dover. [*Exit one with* GLOUCESTER.] How is 't, my
    lord? how look you?
CORN. I have received a hurt: follow me, lady.
    Turn out that eyeless villain; throw this slave
    Upon the dunghill. Regan, I bleed apace:[35]
    Untimely[36] comes this hurt: give me your arm.
                [*Exit* CORNWALL, *led by* REGAN.]
SEC. SERV. I'll never care what wickedness I do,
    If this man come to good.
THIRD SERV.   If she live long,
    And in the end meet the old course of death,
    Women will all turn monsters.[37]
SEC. SERV. Let's follow the old earl, and get the Bedlam[38]   100
    To lead him where he would: his roguish madness
    Allows itself to any thing.[39]

---

[27] This cause (over which I quarrel with you).   [28] Bondman, serf.   [29] Harm.
[30] Forestall.   [31] Repay, revenge.   [32] Disclosure.   [33] Deceived (by Edmund).
[34] i.e., my treatment of Edgar.   [35] Fast.   [36] Inopportunely.
[37] **Women . . . monsters,** because they will know there is no divine justice.
[38] Lunatic, i.e., Edgar.
[39] **Allows . . . thing,** permits him to do anything with impunity.

THIRD SERV. Go thou: I'll fetch some flax and whites of eggs
    To apply to his bleeding face. Now, heaven help him!

                                      [Exeunt severally.]

ACT IV

SCENE I
The heath

[Enter EDGAR.*]*

EDG. Yet better thus, and known to be contemn'd,[1]
    Than still contemn'd and flatter'd. To be worst,
    The lowest and most dejected thing of fortune,
    Stands still in esperance,[2] lives not in fear:
    The lamentable change is from the best;
    The worst returns to laughter.[3] Welcome, then,
    Thou unsubstantial air that I embrace!
    The wretch that thou hast blown unto the worst
    Owes nothing to thy blasts. But who comes here?

                     [Enter GLOUCESTER, *led by an*
                     OLD MAN.*]*

    My father, poorly led?[4] World, world, O world!   10
    But that thy strange mutations[5] make us hate thee,
    Life would not yield to age.
OLD MAN. O, my good lord, I have been your tenant, and your fa-
    ther's tenant, these fourscore years.
GLOU. Away, get thee away; good friend, be gone:
    Thy comforts can do me no good at all;
    Thee they may hurt.
OLD MAN. Alack, sir, you cannot see your way.
GLOU. I have no way,[6] and therefore want no eyes;
    I stumbled when I saw: full oft 'tis seen,   20
    Our means secure us,[7] and our mere defects
    Prove our commodities.[8] O dear son Edgar,
    The food[9] of thy abusèd[10] father's wrath!
    Might I but live to see thee in my touch,
    I'ld say I had eyes again!
OLD MAN.   How now! Who's there?
EDG. *[Aside]* O gods! Who is 't can say "I am at the worst"?
    I am worse then e'er I was.
OLD MAN.   'Tis poor mad Tom.

---

[1] Despised.   [2] Hope.   [3] **returns to laughter,** changes to happiness.
[4] **poorly led,** led by one poor old man, instead of his former attendants.
[5] Changes (of fortune).   [6] **I . . . way,** no course in life is left me.
[7] **Our . . . secure us,** prosperity makes us careless and overconfident.
[8] **our mere . . . commodities,** our very deprivations prove to be benefits.
[9] i.e., object.   [10] Deceived.

EDG. [*Aside*] And worse I may be yet: the worst is not
    So long as we can say "This is the worst."
OLD MAN. Fellow, where goest?
GLOU.   Is it a beggar-man?   30
OLD MAN. Madman and beggar too.
GLOU. He has some reason, else he could not beg.
    I' the last night's storm I such a fellow saw;
    Which made me think a man a worm: my son
    Came then into my mind; and yet my mind
    Was then scarce friends with him: I have heard more since.
    As flies to wanton[11] boys, are we to the gods,
    They kill us for their sport.
EDG.   [*Aside*] How should this be?
    Bad is the trade that must play fool to sorrow,
    Angering[12] itself and others.—Bless thee, master!   40
GLOU. Is that the naked fellow?
OLD MAN.   Ay, my lord.
GLOU. Then, prithee, get thee gone: if, for my sake,
    Thou wilt o'ertake us, hence a mile or twain,
    I' the way toward Dover, do it for ancient love;
    And bring some covering for this naked soul,
    Who I'll entreat to lead me.
OLD MAN.   Alack, sir, he is mad.
GLOU. 'Tis the times' plague,[13] when madmen lead the blind.
    Do as I bid thee, or rather do thy pleasure;[14]
    Above the rest,[15] be gone.
OLD MAN. I'll bring him the best 'parel that I have,   50
    Come on 't what will.   [*Exit.*]
GLOU. Sirrah, naked fellow,—
EDG. Poor Tom's a-cold. [*Aside*] I cannot daub it[16] further.
GLOU. Come hither, fellow.
EDG. [*Aside*] And yet I must.—Bless thy sweet eyes, they bleed.
GLOU. Knowst thou the way to Dover?
EDG. Both stile and gate, horse-way and foot-path. Poor Tom hath
    been scared out of his good wits: bless thee, good man's son, from
    the foul fiend! five fiends have been in poor Tom at once; of lust,
    as Obidicut; Hobbididance, prince of dumbness; Mahu, of steal-   60
    ing; Modo, of murder; Flibbertigibbet, of mopping and mowing,[17]
    who since[18] possesses chambermaids and waiting-women. So, bless
    thee, master!
GLOU. Here, take this purse, thou whom the heavens' plagues
    Have humbled to all strokes:[19] that I am wretched
    Makes thee the happier: heavens, deal so still![20]
    Let the superfluous and lust-dieted man,[21]

---

[11] Playful.   [12] Distressing.   [13] **times' plague,** world's calamity.
[14] **thy pleasure,** what you wish.   [15] **above the rest,** above all.   [16] **daub it,** dissemble.
[17] **mopping and mowing,** grimacing and making faces.   [18] i.e., since a long time ago.
[19] **Have . . . strokes,** have humbled you so that you accept every sort of adversity.
[20] **deal so still,** i.e., continue to treat men overconfident in their prosperity as you have me.
[21] **superfluous . . . man,** the man who has all that he needs, all that he lusts after.

That slaves your ordinance,[22] that will not see
Because he doth not feel, feel your power quickly;
So distribution[23] should undo[24] excess,   70
And each man have enough. Dost thou know Dover?
EDG. Ay, master.
GLOU. There is a cliff, whose high and bending head
Looks fearfully[25] in the confinèd[26] deep.[27]
Bring me but to the very brim of it,
And I'll repair the misery thou dost bear
With something rich about me: from that place
I shall no leading need.
EDG.   Give me thy arm:
Poor Tom shall lead thee.   [*Exeunt.*]

SCENE II
Before the DUKE OF ALBANY'S *palace*

[*Enter* GONERIL *and* EDMUND.]
GON. Welcome, my lord: I marvel our mild husband
Not met us on the way.

                              [*Enter* OSWALD.]

                              Now, where's your master?
OSW. Madam, within; but never man so changed.
I told him of the army that was landed;
He smiled at it: I told him you were coming;
His answer was "The worse:" of Gloucester's treachery,
And of the loyal service of his son,
When I inform'd him, then he call'd me sot,[1]
And told me I had turn'd the wrong side out:[2]
What most he should dislike seems pleasant to him;   10
What like, offensive.
GON. [*To* EDM.]   Then shall you go no further.
It is the cowish[3] terror of his spirit,
That dares not undertake:[4] he'll not feel wrongs
Which tie him to an answer. Our wishes on the way[5]
May prove effects.[6] Back, Edmund, to my brother;
Hasten his musters and conduct his powers:[7]
I must change[8] arms[9] at home, and give the distaff
Into my husband's hands. This trusty servant
Shall pass between us: ere long you are like to hear,

---

[22] **slaves your ordinance,** that makes heaven's will subservient to his own.
[23] Distributive justice.   [24] Correct.
[25] In a way to arouse terror in anyone who looks over it down to the sea.
[26] Shut in.   [27] **confined deep,** i.e., the Straits of Dover.   [1] Fool.
[2] **turn'd . . . out,** completely misinterpreted the situation.   [3] Cowardly.
[4] Take the initiative.   [5] **on the way,** expressed on our way here.
[6] **prove effects,** come to pass.   [7] Forces.   [8] Exchange.
[9] Emblems of our professions.

If you dare venture in your own behalf,   20
A mistress's command. Wear this; spare speech;
                    [*Giving a favor.*]
Decline your head: this kiss, if it durst speak,
Would stretch thy spirits up into the air:
Conceive,[10] and fare thee well.
EDM. Yours in the ranks of death.
GON.   My most dear Gloucester!
                    [*Exit* EDMUND.]
O, the difference of man and man!
To thee a woman's services are due:
My fool[11] usurps[12] my body.
OSW.   Madam, here comes my lord.
                    [*Exit.*]

                    [*Enter* ALBANY.]

GON. I have been worth the whistle.[13]
ALB.   O Goneril!
You are not worth the dust which the rude wind   30
Blows in your face. I fear your disposition:[14]
That nature, which contemns its origin,
Cannot be border'd certain in itself;[15]
She that herself will sliver and disbranch[16]
From her material sap,[17] perforce must wither
And come to deadly use.[18]
GON. No more; the text is foolish.
ALB. Wisdom and goodness to the vile seem vile:
Filths savour but themselves.[19] What have you done?
Tigers, not daughters, what have you perform'd?   40
A father, and a gracious[20] agèd man,
Whose reverence even the head-lugg'd[21] bear would lick,
Most barbarous, most degenerate! have you madded.[22]
Could my good brother suffer you to do it?
A man, a prince, by him so benefited!
If that the heavens do not their visible[23] spirits
Send quickly down to tame these vile offences,
It will come,[24]
Humanity must perforce prey on itself,
Like monsters of the deep.
GON.   Milk-liver'd[25] man!   50

[10] Understand.   [11] i.e., fool of a husband.   [12] Possesses without right.
[13] **the whistle,** whistling for.   [14] Temperament.
[15] **Cannot . . . itself,** can have no sure restraints in its own nature.
[16] **sliver and disbranch,** both mean "break off."
[17] **material sap,** its nourishing substance (i.e., the sap of the tree).
[18] **deadly use,** i.e., to destruction.
[19] **Filths . . . themselves,** everything tastes filthy to the filthy.   [20] Kindly.
[21] Pulled along by the head, showing he is surly.   [22] Driven insane.
[23] In visible form.   [24] **It will come,** this will be the result.
[25] White-livered, cowardly.

That bear'st a cheek for blows, a head for wrongs:
Who hast not in thy brows an eye discerning[26]
Thine honour[27] from thy suffering; that not know'st
Fools[28] do those villains pity who are punish'd
Ere they have done their mischief. Where's thy drum?
France[29] spreads his banners in our noiseless[30] land,
With plumèd helm thy state[31] begins to threat;
Whiles thou, a moral[32] fool, sit'st still, and criest
"Alack, why does he so?"

ALB.   See thyself, devil!
Proper[33] deformity seems not in the fiend   60
So horrid as in woman.

GON.   O vain[34] fool!

ALB. Thou changèd[35] and self-cover'd[36] thing, for shame,
Be-monster not thy feature.[37] Were 't my fitness[38]
To let these hands obey my blood,[39]
They art apt[40] enough to dislocate and tear
Thy flesh and bones: howe'er[41] thou art a fiend,
A woman's shape doth shield thee.

GON. Marry, your manhood now[42]—

                    [*Enter a* MESSENGER.]

ALB. What news?

MESS. O, my good lord, the Duke of Cornwall's dead;   70
That slain by his servant, going to put out
The other eye of Gloucester.

ALB.   Gloucester's eyes!

MESS. A servant that he bred, thrill'd with remorse,[43]
Opposed against the act, bending[44] his sword
To[45] his great master; who, thereat enraged,
Flew on him, and amongst them fell'd[46] him dead;
But not without that harmful stroke, which since
Hath pluck'd him after.[47]

ALB.   This shows you are above,
You justicers, that these our nether crimes
So speedily can venge! But, O poor Gloucester!   80
Lost he his other eye?

MESS.   Both, both, my lord.
This letter, madam, craves a speedy answer;
'Tis from your sister.

---

[26] Able to distinguish.   [27] **Thine honour,** things you can endure with honor.
[28] i.e., only fools.   [29] The King of France.
[30] Quiet, i.e., unprepared for warlike resistance.   [31] Realm.   [32] Moralizing.
[33] Suitable to a fiend.   [34] Silly, futile.   [35] Transformed.
[36] i.e., covering your real fiend's nature with a woman's form.
[37] **Be-monster . . . feature,** don't allow your whole appearance to be changed to that of a
monster.
[38] **were't my fitness,** if it were proper for me.   [39] Passion.   [40] Ready.
[41] However much.   [42] **your . . . now,** what a fine specimen of manhood you are now!
[43] Pity.   [44] Directing.   [45] Against.   [46] They felled.
[47] **pluck'd him after,** i.e., pulled Cornwall down after him.

GON. [*Aside*] One way I like this well;
     But being widow, and my Gloucester with her,
     May all the building in my fancy pluck
     Upon my hateful[48] life: another way,
     The news is not so tart.[49]—I'll read, and answer.
                                        [*Exit.*]
ALB. Where was his son when they did take his eyes?
MESS. Come with my lady hither.
ALB.   He is not here.   90
MESS. No, my good lord; I met him back[50] again.
ALB. Knows he the wickedness?
MESS. Ay, my good lord; 'twas he inform'd against him;
     And quit the house on purpose, that their punishment
     Might have the freer course.
ALB.   Gloucester, I live
     To thank thee for the love thou show'dst the king,
     And to revenge thine eyes. Come hither, friend:
     Tell me what more thou know'st.   [*Exeunt.*]

SCENE III
The French camp near Dover

[*Enter* KENT *and a* GENTLEMAN.]
KENT. Why the King of France is so suddenly gone back know you
     the reason?
GENT. Something he left imperfect in the state, which since his com-
     ing forth is thought of; which imports[1] to the kingdom so much
     fear and danger that his personal return was most required and
     necessary.
KENT. Who hath he left behind him general?
GENT. The Marshal of France, Monsieur La Far.
KENT. Did your letters pierce the queen to any demonstration of
     grief?   10
GENT. Ay, sir; she took them, read them in my presence;
     And now and then an ample tear trill'd[2] down
     Her delicate cheek; it seem'd she was a queen
     Over her passion;[3] who, most rebel-like,
     Sought to be king o'er her.
KENT.   O, then it moved her.
GENT. Not to a rage:[4] patience and sorrow strove
     Who should express her goodliest.[5] You have seen
     Sunshine and rain at once: her smiles and tears
     Were like a better way:[6] those happy smilets,[7]

---

[48] **May . . . hateful,** may pull down all my castles in the air (her plan to marry Edmund) and
make my life a hated ruin.
[49] Painful.   [50] On his way back.   [1] Portends.   [2] Trickled.   [3] Emotion, i.e., grief.
[4] Outburst (of grief).
[5] **express her goodliest,** give her the most beautiful expression.
[6] **like . . . way,** like mingled sunshine and rain, only more beautiful.   [7] Little smiles.

That play'd on her ripe lip, seem'd not to know   20
What guests were in her eyes; which[8] parted thence,
As pearls from diamonds dropp'd. In brief,
Sorrow would be a rarity most beloved,
If all could so become it.[9]

KENT.   Made she no verbal question?[10]

GENT. 'Faith, once or twice she heaved the name of "father"
Pantingly forth, as if it press'd her heart;
Cried "Sisters! sisters! Shame of ladies! sisters!
Kent! father! sisters! What, i' the storm? i' the night?
Let pity not be believed!"[11] There she shook
The holy water from her heavenly eyes,   30
And clamour moisten'd:[12] then away she started
To deal with grief alone.

KENT.   It is the stars,
The stars above us, govern our conditions;[13]
Else one self[14] mate and mate could not beget
Such different issues. You spoke not with her since?

GENT. No.

KENT. Was this before the king return'd?

GENT.   No, since.

KENT. Well, sir, the poor distressèd Lear's i' the town;
Who sometime,[15] in his better tune,[16] remembers
What we are come about, and by no means   40
Will yield[17] to see his daughter.

GENT.   Why, good sir?

KENT. A sovereign[18] shame so elbows[19] him: his own unkindness,
That stripp'd her from his benediction,[20] turn'd her
To foreign casualties,[21] gave her dear rights
To his dog-hearted daughters, these things sting
His mind so venomously, that burning shame
Detains him from Cordelia.

GENT.   Alack, poor gentleman!

KENT. Of Albany's and Cornwall's powers[22] you heard not?

GENT. 'Tis so, they are afoot.

KENT. Well, sir, I'll bring you to our master Lear,   50
And leave you to attend him: some dear[23] cause
Will in concealment wrap me up awhile;
When I am known aright, you shall not grieve
Lending me[24] this acquaintance. I pray you, go
Along with me.   [*Exeunt.*]

---

[8] i.e., the tears.   [9] **all . . . become it,** it were so becoming to all (as to her).
[10] **Made . . . question?** Did she say nothing? (**question,** speech).   [11] Believed in.
[12] **clamour moisten'd,** moistened her cries of grief (by weeping).   [13] Temperaments.
[14] **one self,** one and the same.   [15] Sometimes.   [16] **better tune,** more lucid intervals.
[17] Assent.   [18] Overmastering.   [19] Stands at his elbow.   [20] Parting blessing.
[21] **foreign casualties,** hazards in a foreign land.   [22] Troops.   [23] Important.
[24] **Lending me,** for having granted me.

SCENE IV
The same—a tent

[*Enter, with drum and colours,* CORDELIA, DOCTOR, *and* SOLDIERS.]

COR. Alack, 'tis he: why, he was met even now
    As mad as the vex'd sea; singing aloud;
    Crown'd with rank fumiter and furrow-weeds,[1]
    With bur-docks, hemlock, nettles, cuckoo-flowers,[2]
    Darnel, and all the idle[3] weeds that grow
    In our sustaining corn.[4] A century[5] send forth;
    Search every acre in the high-grown field,
    And bring him to our eye. [*Exit an* OFFICER.] What can man's
      wisdom[6]
    In the restoring his bereavèd sense?
    He that helps him take all my outward worth.[7]   10
DOCT. There is means, madam:
    Our foster-nurse of nature[8] is repose,
    The which he lacks; that to provoke[9] in him,
    Are many simples operative,[10] whose power
    Will close the eye of anguish.
COR.   All blest secrets,[11]
    All you unpublish'd virtues[12] of the earth,
    Spring with my tears! be aidant and remediate[13]
    In the good man's distress! Seek, seek for him;
    Lest his ungovern'd rage[14] dissolve the life
    That wants the means[15] to lead it.

[*Enter a* MESSENGER.]

MESS.   News, madam;   20
    The British powers are marching hitherward.
COR. 'Tis known before; our preparation stands
    In expectation of[16] them. O dear father,
    It is thy business that I go about;
    Therefore great France
    My mourning and important[17] tears hath pitied.
    No blown[18] ambition doth our arms incite,
    But love, dear love, and our aged father's right:
    Soon may I hear and see him!   [*Exeunt.*]

---

[1] **rank . . . furrow-weeds,** luxuriant fumitory (earth-smoke) and weeds growing in furrows of a plowed field.
[2] Flowers blooming when the cuckoo is abroad, i.e., in April and May—perhaps cowslips.
[3] Useless.   [4] **sustaining corn,** wheat that gives sustenance.
[5] Detail of a hundred men.   [6] **What . . . wisdom,** what can science do.   [7] Property.
[8] **Our foster . . . of,** the nurse that fosters our nature.   [9] Induce.
[10] **simples operative,** effective medicinal herbs.   [11] Private remedies.
[12] **unpublish'd virtues,** secret efficacious medicinal plants.
[13] **be . . . remediate,** be helpful and remedial.   [14] Delirium.
[15] **the means,** i.e., his reason.   [16] **In . . . of,** ready to meet.   [17] Importunate.
[18] Swollen.

SCENE V
GLOUCESTER'S *castle*

[*Enter* REGAN *and* OSWALD.]

REG. But are my brother's powers set forth?

OSW.   Ay, madam.

REG. Himself in person there?

OSW.   Madam, with much ado:[1]
    Your sister is the better soldier.

REG. Lord Edmund spake not with your lord at home?

OSW. No, madam.

REG. What might import[2] my sister's letter to him?

OSW. I know not, lady.

REG. 'Faith, he is posted[3] hence on serious matter.[4]
    It was great ignorance,[5] Gloucester's eyes being out,
    To let him live: where he arrives he moves   10
    All hearts against us: Edmund, I think, is gone,
    In pity of his misery, to dispatch
    His nighted life; moreover, to descry
    The strength o' the enemy.

OSW. I must needs after him, madam, with my letter.

REG. Our troops set forth to-morrow: stay with us;
    The ways are dangerous.

OSW.   I may not, madam:
    My lady charged my duty in this business.

REG. Why should she write to Edmund? Might not you
    Transport her purposes by word? Belike,[6]   20
    Something—I know not what: I'll love thee much,
    Let me unseal the letter.

OSW.   Madam, I had rather—

REG. I know your lady does not love her husband;
    I am sure of that: and at her late being here
    She gave strange oeillades[7] and most speaking looks
    To noble Edmund. I know you are of her bosom.[8]

OSW. I, madam?

REG. I speak in understanding; you are, I know 't:
    Therefore I do advise you, take this note:
    My lord is dead; Edmund and I have talk'd;[9]   30
    And more convenient[10] is he for my hand
    Than for your lady's: you may gather more.[11]
    If you do find him, pray you, give him this;
    And when your mistress hears thus much[12] from you,
    I pray, desire her call her wisdom to her.
    So, fare you well.

---

[1] **with much ado,** as a result of much effort.   [2] Mean.   [3] **is posted,** has ridden fast.
[4] Business.   [5] Stupidity.   [6] Probably.   [7] Amorous glances.
[8] **of her bosom,** in her confidence.
[9] **have talk'd,** have come to an understanding (about marrying).   [10] Suitable.
[11] **gather more,** i.e., make further inferences.
[12] **thus much,** as much as I have told you.

If you do chance to hear of that blind traitor,
Preferment[13] falls on him that cuts him off.
Osw. Would I could meet him, madam! I should show
What party I do follow.
Reg.   Fare thee well.   [*Exeunt.*]   40

SCENE VI
Fields near Dover

[*Enter* Gloucester, *and* Edgar *dressed like a peasant.*]
Glou. When shall we come to the top of that same hill?
Edg. You do climb up it now: look, how we labour.
Glou. Methinks the ground is even.
Edg.   Horrible steep.
Hark, do you hear the sea?
Glou.   No, truly.
Edg. Why, then, your other senses grow imperfect
By your eyes' anguish.
Glou.   So may it be, indeed:
Methinks thy voice is alter'd; and thou speak'st
In better phrase and matter than thou didst.
Edg. You're much deceived: in nothing am I changed
But in my garments.
Glou.   Methinks you're better spoken.[1]   10
Edg. Come on, sir; here's the place: stand still. How fearful
And dizzy 'tis, to cast one's eyes so low!
The crows and choughs[2] that wing the midway air
Show scarce so gross[3] as beetles: half way down
Hangs one that gathers samphire,[4] dreadful trade!
Methinks he seems no bigger than his head:
The fishermen, that walk upon the beach,
Appear like mice; and yond tall anchoring bark,
Diminish'd to her cock;[5] her cock, a buoy
Almost too small for sight: the murmuring surge,   20
That on the unnumber'd[6] idle[7] pebbles chafes,
Cannot be heard so high. I'll look no more;
Lest my brain turn, and the deficient sight[8]
Topple[9] down headlong.
Glou.   Set me where you stand.
Edg. Give me your hand: you are now within a foot
Of the extreme verge: for all beneath the moon
Would I not leap upright.[10]
Glou.   Let go my hand.

---

[13] Advancement.   [1] i.e., you speak with more propriety.
[2] Crow-like birds, something like grackles.   [3] Large.
[4] An aromatic herb, gathered from the face of cliffs by men lowered by a rope.
[5] Cock-boat, tender.   [6] Innumerable.   [7] Useless, barren.
[8] **the . . . sight,** my sight failing.   [9] Cause me to topple.   [10] i.e., even straight up.

Here, friend, 's another purse; in it a jewel
Well worth a poor man's taking: fairies[11] and gods
Prosper it with thee! Go thou farther off;   30
Bid me farewell, and let me hear thee going.

EDG. Now fare you well, good sir.

GLOU.   With all my heart.

EDG. Why I do trifle thus with his despair
Is done to cure it.

GLOU. [*Kneeling*]   O you mighty gods!
This world I do renounce, and in your sights,
Shake patiently my great affliction off:
If I could bear it longer, and not fall
To quarrel with[12] your great opposeless[13] wills,
My snuff[14] and loathèd part of nature should
Burn itself out. If Edgar live, O, bless him!   40
Now, fellow, fare thee well.   [*He falls forward.*]

EDG.   Gone, sir; farewell.
And yet I know not how conceit[15] may rob
The treasury of life,[16] when life itself
Yields to the theft:[17] had he been where he thought,
By this, had thought been past. Alive or dead?
Ho, you sir! friend! Hear you, sir! speak!
Thus might he pass[18] indeed: yet he revives.
What are you, sir?

GLOU.   Away, and let me die.

EDG. Hadst thou been aught but gossamer,[19] feathers, air,
So many fathom down precipitating,   50
Thou 'dst shiver'd like an egg: but thou dost breathe;
Hast heavy substance; bleed'st not; speak'st; art sound.
Ten masts at each[20] make not the altitude
Which thou hast perpendicularly fell:
Thy life's a miracle. Speak yet again.

GLOU. But have I fall'n, or no?

EDG. From the dread summit of this chalky bourn.[21]
Look up a-height;[22] the shrill-gorged[23] lark so far
Cannot be seen or heard: do but look up.

GLOU. Alack, I have no eyes.   60
Is wretchedness deprived that benefit,
To end itself by death? 'Twas yet some comfort,
When misery could beguile[24] the tyrant's rage,
And frustrate his proud will.

EDG.   Give me your arm:
Up: so. How is 't? Feel you your legs? You stand.

GLOU. Too well, too well.

EDG.   This is above all strangeness.

---

[11] fairies, because they were supposed to make it increase miraculously.
[12] Rebel against.   [13] Irresistible.   [14] Burnt and smoking wick.   [15] Imagination.
[16] Life's treasury.   [17] **Yields . . . theft,** i.e., death's theft of the treasury of life.
[18] Die.   [19] Floating cobweb.   [20] **at each,** end to end.   [21] Boundary.
[22] On high.   [23] Shrill-throated.   [24] Cheat.

Upon the crown o' the cliff, what thing was that
Which parted from you?

GLOU.   A poor unfortunate beggar.

EDG. As I stood here below, methought his eyes
Were two full moons; he had a thousand noses,   70
Horns whelk'd[25] and waved like the enridgèd sea:
It was some fiend; therefore, thou happy father,
Think that the clearest[26] gods, who make them honours
Of men's impossibilities,[27] have preserved thee.

GLOU. I do remember now: henceforth I'll bear
Affliction till it do cry out itself
"Enough, enough," and die. That thing you speak of,
I took it for a man; often 'twould say
"The fiend, the fiend:" he led me to that place.

EDG. Bear free[28] and patient thoughts. But who comes here?   80

> [*Enter* LEAR, *fantastically dressed
> with wild flowers.*]

The safer[29] sense will ne'er accommodate[30]
His master thus.

LEAR. No, they cannot touch[31] me for coining;[32]
I am the king himself.

EDG. O thou side-piercing sight!

LEAR. Nature's above art in that respect. There's your press-money.[33]
That fellow handles his bow like a crow-keeper:[34] draw me a clothier's yard.[35] Look, look, a mouse! Peace, peace; this piece of toasted
cheese will do 't. There's my gauntlet; I'll prove[36] it on a giant.
Bring up the brown bills.[37] O, well flown, bird![38] i' the clout,[39] i'   90
the clout: hewgh![40] Give the word.[41]

EDG. Sweet marjoram.

LEAR. Pass.

GLOU. I know that voice.

LEAR. Ha! Goneril, with a white beard! They flattered me like a dog;
and told me I had white hairs in my beard ere the black ones were
there. To say "ay" and "no" to every thing that I said!—"Ay" and
"no" too was no good divinity. When the rain came to wet me once,
and the wind to make me chatter; when the thunder would not
peace[42] at my bidding; there I found 'em, there I smelt 'em out.   100
Go to, they are not men o' their words: they told me I was every
thing; 'tis a lie, I am not ague-proof.

GLOU. The trick[43] of that voice I do well remember:
Is 't not the king?

---

[25] Twisted.   [26] Most glorious.   [27] **men's impossibilities,** things impossible to men.
[28] i.e., from grief.   [29] Saner.   [30] Equip.   [31] Arrest.
[32] Making counterfeit money.   [33] Money to a recruit pressed into military service.
[34] A boy stationed to scare away crows.
[35] **clothier's yard,** arrow a cloth-yard in length.   [36] Defend it by combat.
[37] Halberds, painted brown to prevent rust.   [38] i.e., arrow.   [39] Bulls-eye.
[40] Imitation of the whizzing of the arrow.   [41] Password.   [42] Hold its peace.
[43] Peculiarity.

LEAR.   Ay, every inch a king:
When I do stare, see how the subject quakes.
I pardon that man's life. What was thy cause?
Adultery?
Thou shalt not die: die for adultery! No:
The wren goes to 't, and the small gilded fly
Does lecher in my sight.   110
Let copulation thrive; for Gloucester's bastard son
Was kinder to his father than my daughters
Got 'tween the lawful sheets.
To 't, luxury,[44] pell-mell! for I lack soldiers.
Behold yond simpering dame,
Whose face between her forks presages snow;[45]
That minces virtue,[46] and does shake the head
To hear of pleasure's name;
The fitchew,[47] nor the soilèd[48] horse, goes to 't
With a more riotous appetite.   120
Down from the waist they are Centaurs,[49]
Though women all above:
But[50] to the girdle do the gods inherit,[51]
Beneath is all the fiends';
There's hell, there's darkness, there's the sulphurous pit,
Burning, scalding, stench, consumption; fie, fie, fie! pah, pah!
Give me an ounce of civet,[52] good apothecary, to sweeten my
imagination: there's money for thee.
GLOU. O, let me kiss that hand!
LEAR. Let me wipe it first; it smells of mortality.   130
GLOU. O ruin'd piece[53] of nature! This great world
Shall so wear out to nought.[54] Dost thou know me?
LEAR. I remember thine eyes well enough. Dost thou squiny[55] at me?
No, do thy worst, blind Cupid;[56] I'll not love. Read thou this chal-
lenge; mark but the penning of it.
GLOU. Were all the letters suns, I could not see one.
EDG. I would not take[57] this from report; it is,
And my heart breaks at it.
LEAR. Read.
GLOU. What, with the case[58] of eyes?   140
LEAR. O, ho, are you there with me?[59] No eyes in your head, nor no
money in your purse? Your eyes are in a heavy case,[60] your purse
in a light: yet you see how this world goes.
GLOU. I see it feelingly.

---

[44] Lust.   [45] i.e., chastity.
[46] **minces virtue,** makes a show of virtue by her mincing (affected) bearing.
[47] Skunk, a supposedly oversexed animal.   [48] Fed full with spring grass.
[49] Lustful fabulous monsters, half man, half horse.   [50] Only.   [51] Rule.
[52] Perfume.   [53] Masterpiece.   [54] **Shall . . . nought,** shall likewise come to nothing.
[55] Squint.   [56] **blind Cupid,** the sign usually hung over a brothel.
[57] Accept, believe.   [58] Sockets.
[59] **are . . . me?** i.e., Is that what you are telling me?
[60] **heavy case,** bad condition, with a pun on case-socket.

LEAR. What, art mad? A man may see how this world goes with no
    eyes. Look with thine ears: see how yond justice rails upon yond
    simple[61] thief. Hark, in thine ear: change places; and, handy-
    dandy,[62] which is the justice, which is the thief? Thou hast seen a
    farmer's dog bark at a beggar?
GLOU. Ay, sir.   150
LEAR. And the creature run from the cur? There thou mightst be-
    hold the great image[63] of authority: a dog's obeyed in office.
        Thou rascal beadle, hold thy bloody hand!
        Why dost thou lash that whore? Strip thine own back;
        Thou hotly lust'st to use her in that kind[64]
        For which thou whipp'st her. The usurer hangs the cozener.[65]
        Through tatter'd clothes small vices do appear;
        Robes and furr'd gowns hide all. Plate sin with gold,[66]
        And the strong lance of justice hurtless breaks;
        Arm it in rags, a pigmy's straw does pierce it.   160
        None does offend, none I say, none; I'll able[67] 'em:
        Take that[68] of me, my friend, who have the power
        To seal the accuser's lips. Get thee glass eyes;[69]
        And, like a scurvy politician,[70] seem
        To see the things thou dost not. Now, now, now, now:
        Pull off my boots: harder, harder: so.
EDG. O, matter and impertinency[71] mix'd!
        Reason in madness!
LEAR. If thou wilt weep my fortunes, take my eyes.
        I know thee well enough; thy name is Gloucester: 170
        Thou must be patient; we came crying hither:
        Thou know'st, the first time that we smell the air,
        We wawl and cry. I will preach to thee: mark.
GLOU. Alack, alack the day!
LEAR. When we are born, we cry that we are come
        To this great stage of fools: this's a good block;[72]
        It were a delicate stratagem, to shoe
        A troop of horse with felt: I'll put 't in proof;[73]
        And when I have stol'n upon these sons-in-law,
        Then, kill, kill, kill, kill, kill, kill!   180

                            [*Enter a* GENTLEMAN, *with* ATTEN-
                            DANTS.]

GENT. O, here he is: lay hand upon him. Sir,
        Your most dear daughter—
LEAR. No rescue? What, a prisoner? I am even

---

[61] Mere.
[62] **handy-dandy,** "Which hand will you have?" (a formula in a well-known child's game).
[63] Figure.   [64] Way.   [65] Cheater, sharper.
[66] **Plate . . . with gold,** clothe sin in golden armor-plates.   [67] Authorize.
[68] i.e., an imaginary pardon.   [69] Spectacles.   [70] **scurvy politician,** vile trickster.
[71] **matter and impertinency,** sense and incoherence.   [72] Hat.
[73] **put 't in proof,** make a trial of it.

The natural fool of fortune.[74] Use me well;
You shall have ransom. Let me have surgeons;
I am cut to the brains.
GENT.   You shall have any thing.
LEAR. No seconds? all myself?
Why, this would make a man a man of salt,[75]
To use his eyes for garden water-pots,
Ay, and laying autumn's dust.
GENT.   Good sir,—   190
LEAR. I will die bravely,[76] like a bridegroom. What!
I will be jovial: come, come; I am a king,
My masters, know you that.
GENT. You are a royal one, and we obey you.
LEAR. Then there's life in 't. Nay, if you get it, you shall get it with
running. Sa, sa, sa, sa.[77]   [*Exit running;* ATTENDANTS *follow.*]
GENT. A sight most pitiful in the meanest wretch,
Past speaking of in a king! Thou hast one daughter,
Who redeems nature from the general[78] curse
Which twain have brought her to.   200
EDG. Hail, gentle[79] sir.
GENT.   Sir, speed you: what's your will?
EDG. Do you hear aught, sir, of a battle toward?[80]
GENT. Most sure and vulgar:[81] every one hears that,
Which[82] can distinguish sound.
EDG.   But, by your favour,
How near's the other army?
GENT. Near and on speedy foot; the main descry[83]
Stands on the hourly thought.[84]
EDG.   I thank you, sir: that's all.
GENT. Though that the queen on special cause is here,
Her army is moved on.
EDG.   I thank you, sir.
                              [*Exit* GENTLEMAN.]
GLOU. You ever-gentle gods, take my breath from me;   210
Let not my worser spirit[85] tempt me again
To die before you please!
EDG.   Well pray you, father.
GLOU. Now, good sir, what are you?
EDG. A most poor man, made tame to fortune's blows;
Who, by the art of known and feeling[86] sorrows,
Am pregnant to[87] good pity. Give me your hand,
I'll lead you to some biding.[88]

---

[74] **The . . . fortune,** man reduced by fortune to the condition of a fool.
[75] Of salt tears.   [76] In fine clothes.
[77] **Sa . . . sa,** a hunter's cry to urge on the dogs.   [78] Universal.   [79] Noble.
[80] At hand.   [81] i.e., known to everyone.   [82] Who.
[83] **the main descry,** the view of the main body of troops.
[84] **Stands . . . thought,** is expected any time.   [85] Worse side of my nature.
[86] Heartfelt.   [87] **pregnant to,** able to conceive.   [88] Abiding place.

Glou.   Hearty thanks:
  The bounty[89] and the benison[90] of heaven
  To boot,[91] and boot![92]

                        [*Enter* Oswald.]

Osw.   A proclaim'd prize! Most happy!
  That eyeless head of thine was first framed flesh   220
  To raise my fortunes. Thou old unhappy traitor,
  Briefly thyself remember:[93] the sword is out
  That must destroy thee.
Glou.   Now let thy friendly hand
  Put strength enough to 't.
                        [Edgar *interposes.*]
Osw.   Wherefore, bold peasant,
  Darest thou support a publish'd[94] traitor? Hence;
  Lest that the infection of his fortune take
  Like hold on thee. Let go his arm.
Edg. Chill[95] not let go, zir, without vurther 'casion.
Osw. Let go, slave, or thou diest!
Edg. Good gentleman, go your gait, and let poor volk pass. An   230
  chud[96] ha' bin zwaggered out of my life, 'twould not ha' bin zo
  long as 'tis by a vortnight. Nay, come not near th' old man;
  keep out, che vor ye,[97] or ise[98] try whether your costard[99] or
  my ballow[1] be the harder: chill be plain with you.
Osw. Out, dunghill!
Edg. Chill pick your teeth, zir: come; no matter vor your foins.[2]
                        [*They fight, and* Edgar *knocks
                            him down.*]
Osw. Slave, thou hast slain me: villain, take my purse:
  If ever thou wilt thrive, bury my body;
  And give the letters which thou find'st about me
  To Edmund earl of Gloucester; seek him out   240
  Upon the British party:[3] O, untimely death!
                        [*Dies.*]
Edg. I know thee well: a serviceable villain;
  As duteous[4] to the vices of thy mistress
  As badness would desire.
Glou.   What, is he dead?
Edg. Sit you down, father; rest you.
  Let's see these pockets: the letters that he speaks of
  May be my friends. He's dead; I am only sorry
  He had no other death's-man.[5] Let us see:
  Leave,[6] gentle wax; and, manners, blame us not:

---

[89]Favor.   [90]Blessing.   [91]**To boot,** besides.
[92]**and boot,** and may it be your reward.   [93]**thyself remember,** repent your past sins.
[94]Publicly proclaimed.   [95]I will. The following passage is in stage rustic dialect.
[96]If I could.   [97]**che vor ye,** I warn you.   [98]I will.   [99]Apple, slang for head.
[1]Cudgel.   [2]Sword thrusts.   [3]**British party,** side of the British.   [4]Compliant.
[5]Executioner.   [6]Allow me.

To know our enemies' minds, we'ld rip their hearts;   250
Their papers, is more lawful.
[*Reads*] "Let our reciprocal vows be remembered. You have many
opportunities to cut him off: if your will want not, time and place
will be fruitfully[7] offered. There is nothing done, if he return the
conqueror: then am I the prisoner, and his bed my gaol; from the
loathed warmth whereof deliver me, and supply the place for your
labour.
       "Your—wife, so I would say—
          Affectionate servant,[8]
              GONERIL."   260
O undistinguish'd space[9] of woman's will![10]
A plot upon her virtuous husband's life;
And the exchange my brother! Here, in the sands,
Thee I'll rake up,[11] the post[12] unsanctified
Of murderous lechers: and in the mature time[13]
With this ungracious[14] paper strike the sight
Of the death-practised duke:[15] for him 'tis well
That of thy death and business I can tell.
GLOU. The king is mad: how stiff is my vile sense,[16]
That I stand up, and have ingenious feeling[17]   270
Of my huge sorrows! Better I were distract:[18]
So should my thoughts be sever'd from my griefs,
And woes by wrong imaginations lose
The knowledge of themselves.
EDG.   Give me your hand:
                         [*Drum afar off.*]
Far off, methinks, I hear the beaten drum:
Come, father, I'll bestow you with a friend.   [*Exeunt.*]

SCENE VII

A tent in the French camp—LEAR *on a bed asleep, soft
music playing;* GENTLEMAN, *and others attending*

[*Enter* CORDELIA, KENT, *and* DOCTOR.]
COR. O thou good Kent, how shall I live and work,
To match thy goodness? My life will be too short,
And every measure[1] fail me.
KENT. To be acknowledged, madam, is o'erpaid.
All my reports go with the modest truth;[2]
Nor more nor clipp'd,[3] but so.
COR.   Be better suited:[4]

---

[7] Amply.   [8] **servant,** lover.   [9] **undistinguish'd space,** limitless range.   [10] Lust.
[11] Bury hastily.   [12] Messenger.   [13] **in . . . time,** when the time is ripe.   [14] Wicked.
[15] **death . . . duke,** duke whose death is plotted.
[16] **stiff . . . sense,** strong is my sanity.   [17] **ingenious feeling,** keen consciousness.
[18] Insane.   [1] i.e., measuring out (of benefits).
[2] **modest truth,** moderate statement of the facts.   [3] Abridged.   [4] Clothed.

These weeds[5] are memories[6] of those worser hours:
I prithee, put them off.
KENT.   Pardon me, dear madam;
Yet to be known shortens my made intent:[7]
My boon I make it,[8] that you know me not   10
Till time and I think meet.
COR. Then be 't so, my good lord. [*To the* DOCTOR] How does the king?
DOCT. Madam, sleeps still.
COR. O you kind gods,
Cure this great breach in his abusèd nature!
The untuned and jarring senses, O, wind up[9]
Of this child-changèd[10] father!
DOCT.   So please your Majesty
That we may wake the king: he hath slept long.
COR. Be govern'd by your knowledge, and proceed
I' the sway of your own will. Is he array'd?   20
GENT. Ay, madam; in the heaviness of his sleep
We put fresh garments on him.
DOCT. Be by, good madam, when we do awake him;
I doubt not of his temperance.[11]
COR.   Very well.
DOCT. Please you, draw near. Louder the music there!
COR. O my dear father! Restoration hang
Thy medicine on my lips; and let this kiss
Repair those violent harms that my two sisters
Have in thy reverence made![12]
KENT.   Kind and dear princess!
COR. Had you not been their father, these white flakes   30
Had challenged pity of them. Was this a face
To be opposed against the warring winds?
To stand against the deep dread-bolted[13] thunder?
In the most terrible and nimble stroke
Of quick, cross[14] lightning? to watch—poor perdu![15]—
With this thin helm?[16] Mine enemy's dog,
Though he had bit me, should have stood that night
Against my fire; and wast thou fain,[17] poor father,
To hovel thee with swine, and rogues[18] forlorn,
In short and musty straw? Alack, alack!   40
'Tis wonder that thy life and wits at once
Had not concluded all.[19] He wakes; speak to him.
DOCT. Madam, do you; 'tis fittest.

---

[5] Garments.   [6] Reminders.
[7] **shortens . . . intent,** makes me fall short of my prearranged plan.
[8] **My . . . it,** I ask it as a favor to me.
[9] i.e., tighten the strings (as of a musical instrument) of his untuned senses.
[10] Whose nature has become childish.   [11] Self-control, i.e., sanity.
[12] **in thy . . . made,** done to you to whom they owe reverence.
[13] With its dreadful bolts.   [14] Zigzag.
[15] A soldier on an isolated post of great danger.   [16] i.e., hair.   [17] Glad.
[18] Tramps.   [19] Altogether come to an end.

COR. How does my royal lord? How fares your majesty?
LEAR. You do me wrong to take me out o' the grave:
　　　Thou art a soul in bliss; but I am bound
　　　Upon a wheel of fire, that[20] mine own tears
　　　Do scald like molten lead.
COR.　　　　　　　　　　　　Sir, do you know me?
LEAR. You are a spirit, I know: when did you die?
COR. Still, still, far wide![21]　　　　　　　　　　　　　　50
DOCT. He's scarce awake: let him alone awhile.
LEAR. Where have I been? Where am I? Fair daylight?
　　　I am mightily abused.[22] I should e'en die with pity,
　　　To see another thus. I know not what to say.
　　　I will not swear these are my hands: let's see;
　　　I feel this pin prick. Would I were assured
　　　Of my condition![23]
COR.　　　　　　　　　　O, look upon me, sir,
　　　And hold your hands in benediction o'er me:
　　　No, sir, you must not kneel.
LEAR.　　　　　　　　　　　　Pray, do not mock me:
　　　I am a very foolish fond[24] old man,　　　　　　　　　60
　　　Fourscore and upward, not an hour more nor less;
　　　And, to deal plainly,
　　　I fear I am not in my perfect mind.
　　　Methinks I should know you, and know this man;
　　　Yet I am doubtful: for I am mainly[25] ignorant
　　　What place this is; and all the skill[26] I have
　　　Remembers not these garments; nor I know not
　　　Where I did lodge last night. Do not laugh at me;
　　　For, as I am a man, I think this lady
　　　To be my child Cordelia.
COR.　　　　　　　　　　And so I am, I am.　　　　　　　70
LEAR. Be your tears wet? yes, 'faith. I pray, weep not:
　　　If you have poison for me, I will drink it.
　　　I know you do not love me; for your sisters
　　　Have, as I do remember, done me wrong:
　　　You have some cause, they have not.
COR.　　　　　　　　　　　　　　No cause, no cause.
LEAR. Am I in France?
KENT.　　　　　　　In your own kingdom, sir.
LEAR. Do not abuse[27] me.
DOCT. Be comforted, good madam: the great rage,[28]
　　　You see, is kill'd in him: and yet it is danger
　　　To make him even o'er the time[29] he has lost.　　　　80
　　　Desire him to go in; trouble him no more
　　　Till further settling.[30]

---

[20] So that.　　[21] i.e., of the mark.　　[22] Deluded.　　[23] Situation.　　[24] Doting.
[25] Completely.　　[26] Intelligence.　　[27] Deceive.　　[28] Delirium.
[29] **even o'er the time,** fill the interval by recalling what happened.
[30] **Till . . . settling,** until he becomes calmer.

COR. Will 't please your highness walk?[31]
LEAR.   You must bear with me:
    Pray you now, forget and forgive: I am old and foolish.
                                    [*Exeunt all but* KENT *and* GEN-
                                            TLEMAN.]
GENT. Holds it true, sir, that the Duke of Cornwall was so slain?
KENT. Most certain, sir.
GENT. Who is conductor of his people?
KENT. As 'tis said, the bastard son of Gloucester.
GENT. They say Edgar, his banished son, is with the Earl of Kent in
    Germany.   90
KENT. Report is changeable. 'Tis time to look about; the powers[32] of
    the kingdom approach apace.
GENT. The arbitrement[33] is like to be bloody.
    Fare you well, sir.   [*Exit.*]
KENT. My point and period[34] will be throughly wrought,[35]
    Or well or ill, as this day's battle's fought.   [*Exit.*]

ACT V

SCENE I
The British camp, near Dover

[*Enter, with drum and colours,* EDMUND, REGAN, GENTLEMEN, *and* SOLDIERS.]
EDM. Know of the duke if his last purpose hold,
    Or whether since he is advised[1] by aught
    To change the course: he's full of alteration
    And self-reproving: bring his constant pleasure.[2]
                                    [*To a* GENTLEMAN, *who goes out.*]
REG. Our sister's man is certainly miscarried.[3]
EDM. 'Tis to be doubted, madam.
REG.   Now, sweet lord,
    You know the goodness I intend upon you:
    Tell me—but truly—but then speak the truth,
    Do you not love my sister?
EDM.   In honour'd love.
REG. But have you never found my brother's way   10
    To the forfended[4] place?
EDM.   That thought abuses[5] you.
REG. I am doubtful[6] that you have been conjunct[7]
    And bosom'd[8] with her, as far as we call hers.[9]
EDM. No, by mine honour, madam.
REG. I never shall endure her: dear my lord,
    Be not familiar with her.

[31] i.e., come with me.   [32] Armed forces.   [33] Forcing of the decision.
[34] **My point and period,** the final attainment of my ends.   [35] Worked out.
[1] Induced.   [2] **constant pleasure,** settled decision.   [3] Come to grief.   [4] Forbidden.
[5] Dishonors.   [6] **am doubtful,** suspect.   [7] Joined.   [8] Intimate.
[9] **as . . . hers,** i.e., in all that she has.

EDM.   Fear me not:[10]
       She and the duke her husband!

                              [*Enter, with drum and colours,* AL-
                              BANY, GONERIL, *and* SOLDIERS.]

GON. [*Aside*] I had rather lose the battle than that sister
       Should loosen him and me.
ALB. Our very loving sister, well be-met.[11]   20
       Sir, this I hear; the king is come to his daughter,
       With others whom the rigour of our state[12]
       Forced to cry out.[13] Where I could not be honest,[14]
       I never yet was valiant: for[15] this business,
       It toucheth us, as France[16] invades our land,
       Not bolds[17] the king, with others, whom, I fear,
       Most just and heavy causes[18] make oppose.[19]
EDM. Sir, you speak nobly.
REG.   Why is this reason'd?[20]
GON. Combine together 'gainst the enemy;
       For these domestic and particular[21] broils   30
       Are not the question here.
ALB.   Let's then determine
       With the ancient of war[22] on our proceedings.
EDM. I shall attend you presently at your tent.
REG. Sister, you'll go with us?
GON. No.
REG. 'Tis most convenient;[23] pray you, go with us.
GON. [*Aside*] O, ho, I know the riddle.[24]—I will go.

                              [*As they are going out, enter* EDGAR
                              disguised.]

EDG. If e'er your grace had speech with man so poor,
       Hear me one word.
ALB.   I'll overtake you. Speak.

                              [*Exeunt all but* ALBANY *and* EDGAR.]

EDG. Before you fight the battle, ope this letter.   40
       If you have victory, let the trumpet sound
       For him that brought it: wretched though I seem,
       I can produce a champion that will prove
       What is avouchèd there. If you miscarry,[25]
       Your business of the world hath so an end,
       And machination[26] ceases. Fortune love you!
ALB. Stay till I have read the letter.
EDG.   I was forbid it.

---

[10] **Fear me not,** don't worry about me.   [11] Met.   [12] Administration.   [13] Protest.
[14] Honorable.   [15] As for.   [16] The King of France.   [17] Emboldens.
[18] **heavy causes,** weighty reasons.   [19] **make oppose,** force to oppose us.
[20] **Why . . . reason'd,** Why do you search for reasons [for an action]?
[21] Family and personal.   [22] **ancient of war,** veteran soldiers.   [23] Fitting.
[24] Hidden reason (i.e., you want to be alone with Edmund).   [25] i.e., are killed.
[26] Intrigue (against you).

When time shall serve, let but the herald cry,
And I'll appear again.
ALB. Why, fare thee well: I will o'erlook[27] thy paper. [*Exit* EDGAR.]   50

[*Re-enter* EDMUND.]

EDM. The enemy's in view; draw up your powers.
Here is the guess of their true strength and forces
By diligent discovery;[28] but your haste[29]
Is now urged on you.
ALB.   We will greet the time.[30]   [*Exit.*]
EDM. To both these sisters have I sworn my love;
Each jealous[31] of the other, as the stung
Are of the adder. Which of them shall I take?
Both? one? or neither? Neither can be enjoy'd,
If both remain alive: to take the widow
Exasperates, makes mad her sister Goneril;   60
And hardly shall I carry out my side,[32]
Her husband being alive. Now then we'll use
His countenance[33] for the battle; which being done,
Let her who would be rid of him devise
His speedy taking off. As for the mercy
Which he intends to Lear and to Cordelia,
The battle done, and they within our power,
Shall never see his pardon; for my state
Stands on me to defend, not to debate.[34]   [*Exit.*]

SCENE II
A field between the two camps

[*Alarum*[1] *within. Enter, with drum and colours,* LEAR, CORDELIA, *and* SOL-
DIERS, *over the stage; and exeunt.*]

[*Enter* EDGAR *and* GLOUCESTER.]

EDG. Here, father, take the shadow of this tree
For your good host; pray that the right may thrive:
If ever I return to you again,
I'll bring you comfort.
GLOU.   Grace[2] go with you, sir!
[*Exit* EDGAR.]

[*Alarum and retreat within. Re-
enter* EDGAR.]

EDG. Away, old man; give me thy hand; away!

---

[27] Glance at.   [28] Scouting.   [29] **your haste,** prompt action on your part.
[30] **greet the time,** meet the situation.   [31] Suspiciously afraid.   [32] Plans.
[33] Authority.
[34] **my state . . . debate,** my situation requires defense by arms, not debate (as to the justification of my actions).
[1] A call to arms.   [2] The protection of the gods.

   King Lear hath lost, he and his daughter ta'en:
   Give me thy hand; come on.
GLOU. No farther, sir; a man may rot even here.
EDG. What, in ill thoughts again? Men must endure
   Their going hence, even as their coming hither: 10
   Ripeness[3] is all: come on.
GLOU.   And that's true too.   *[Exeunt.]*

SCENE III
The British camp near Dover

[Enter, in conquest, with drum and colours, EDMUND; LEAR *and* CORDELIA,
prisoners; CAPTAIN, SOLDIERS, &c.]
EDM. Some officers take them away: good guard,
   Until their greater pleasures[1] first be known
   That are to censure[2] them.
COR.   We are not the first
   Who, with best meaning, have incurr'd the worst.
   For thee, oppressèd king, am I cast down;
   Myself could else out-frown false fortune's frown.
   Shall we not see these daughters and these sisters?
LEAR. No, no, no, no! Come, let's away to prison:
   We two alone will sing like birds i' the cage:
   When thou dost ask me blessing, I'll kneel down,   10
   And ask of thee forgiveness: so we'll live,
   And pray, and sing, and tell old tales, and laugh
   At gilded butterflies,[3] and hear poor rogues[4]
   Talk of court news; and we'll talk with them too,
   Who loses and who wins; who's in, who's out;
   And take upon 's the mystery of things,[5]
   As if we were God's spies: and we'll wear out,[6]
   In a wall'd prison, packs[7] and sects of great ones,
   That ebb and flow by the moon.
EDM.   Take them away.
LEAR. Upon such sacrifices, my Cordelia,   20
   The gods themselves throw incense. Have I caught thee?
   He that parts us shall bring a brand from heaven,
   And fire us hence like foxes.[8] Wipe thine eyes;
   The good-years[9] shall devour them, flesh and fell,[10]
   Ere they shall make us weep: we'll see 'em starve first.
   Come.   *[Exeunt* LEAR *and* CORDELIA,
         guarded.]

---

[3] Readiness (for death).
[1] **their greater pleasures,** the wishes of those of higher rank.   [2] Pass judgment upon.
[3] i.e., dandified courtiers.   [4] Wretches.
[5] **take . . . things,** assume that we can explain the mysteries of human life.
[6] i.e., forget.   [7] Parties.
[8] **fire . . . foxes,** foxes can be driven from their holes by smoke and fire.
[9] Evils, perhaps "pestilence."   [10] Skin.

EDM.   Come hither, captain; hark.
             Take thou this note[11] [*giving a paper*]; go follow them to prison:
             One step I have advanced thee; if thou dost
             As this instructs thee, thou dost make thy way
             To noble fortunes: know thou this, that men   30
             Are as the time is:[12] to be tender-minded
             Does not become a sword: thy great employment
             Will not bear question;[13] either say thou'lt do 't,
             Or thrive by other means.[14]
CAPT.   I'll do' t, my lord.
EDM. About it; and write happy[15] when thou hast done.
             Mark, I say, instantly; and carry it[16] so
             As I have set it down.
CAPT. I cannot draw a cart, nor eat dried oats;
             If it be man's work, I'll do it.   [*Exit.*]

                           [*Flourish. Enter* ALBANY, GON-
                           ERIL, REGAN, *another* CAPTAIN,
                           and SOLDIERS.]

ALB. Sir, you have shown to-day your valiant strain.[17]   40
             And fortune led you well: you have the captives
             That were the opposites of[18] this day's strife:
             We do require them of you, so to use them
             As we shall find their merits and our safety
             May equally determine.
EDM.   Sir, I thought it fit
             To send the old and miserable king
             To some retention and appointed guard;[19]
             Whose age has charms in it, whose title more,
             To pluck the common bosom[20] on his side,
             And turn our impress'd lances[21] in our eyes   50
             Which[22] do command them. With him I sent the queen;
             My reason all the same; and they are ready
             To-morrow, or at further space, to appear
             Where you shall hold your session. At this time
             We sweat and bleed: the friend hath lost his friend;
             And the best quarrels,[23] in the heat, are cursed
             By those that feel their sharpness:
             The question of Cordelia and her father
             Requires a fitter place.[24]
ALB.   Sir, by your patience,[25]

---

[11] i.e., an order for the execution of Lear and Cordelia.
[12] **as . . . is,** as the situation demands.   [13] Permit discussion.
[14] **other means,** i.e., than my favor.
[15] **write happy,** write yourself down as fortunate.   [16] Carry it out.   [17] Stock.
[18] **the opposites of,** our opponents in.
[19] **some retention . . . guard,** to the custody of some guards appointed for the purpose.
[20] **pluck . . . bosom,** enlist the sympathies of the common soldiers.
[21] **impress'd lances,** drafted troops.   [22] Who.   [23] Causes.
[24] i.e., than the battlefield.   [25] i.e., if you will pardon my plain talk.

I hold you but a subject of this war,   60
Not as a brother.

REG.   That's as we list to grace him.[26]
Methinks our pleasure[27] might have been demanded,
Ere you had spoke so far. He led our powers;
Bore the commission of my place and person;[28]
The which immediacy[29] may well stand up,
And call itself your brother.

GON.   Not so hot:
In his own grace[30] he doth exalt himself,
More than in your addition.[31]

REG.   In my rights,
By me invested, he compeers[32] the best.

GON. That were the most,[33] if he should husband you.   70

REG. Jesters do oft prove prophets.

GON.   Holla, holla!
That eye that told you so look'd but a-squint.[34]

REG. Lady, I am not well; else I should answer
From a full-flowing stomach.[35] General,
Take thou my soldiers, prisoners, patrimony;
Dispose of them, of me; the walls are thine:[36]
Witness the world, that I create thee here
My lord and master.

GON.   Mean you to enjoy him?

ALB. The let-alone lies not in your good will.[37]

EDM. Nor in thine, lord.

ALB.   Half-blooded[38] fellow, yes.   80

REG. [*To* EDMUND] Let the drum strike, and prove[39] my title thine.

ALB. Stay yet; hear reason. Edmund, I arrest thee
On capital treason; and, in thine attaint,[40]
This gilded serpent [*pointing to* GONERIL.]. For your claim,[41]
    fair sister,
I bar it in the interest of my wife;
'Tis she is sub-contracted[42] to this lord,
And I, her husband, contradict your bans.
If you will marry, make your loves to me,
My lady is bespoke.

---

[26] **That's . . . him,** that depends on how far I wish to honor him.
[27] Wishes in the matter.
[28] **Bore . . . person,** exercised the authority of my rank and person.
[29] **The which immediacy,** and this fact of immediate representation [of me].
[30] His personal deserts.   [31] **your addition,** the title you gave him.   [32] Equals.
[33] **the most,** most fully realized.
[34] **That eye . . . asquint,** a reference to the proverb, "Love being jealous, makes a good eye look asquint."
[35] Anger.   [36] **the walls are thine,** i.e., you have taken my outer defenses by storm.
[37] **let-alone . . . will,** the prohibition does not depend on what you wish.   [38] Bastard.
[39] i.e., by combat.   [40] **in . . . attaint,** i.e., as a sharer in your corruption.
[41] i.e., to Edmund.
[42] i.e., has made a contract depending on the abrogation of a previous one.

GON.   An interlude!⁴³
ALB. Thou art arm'd, Gloucester: let the trumpet sound: 90
    If none appear to prove upon thy head
    Thy heinous, manifest, and many treasons,
    There is my pledge [*throwing down a glove*]; I'll prove it on thy
       heart,
    Ere I taste bread, thou art in nothing⁴⁴ less
    Than I have here proclaim'd thee.
REG.   Sick, O, sick!
GON. [*Aside*] If not, I'll ne'er trust medicine.
EDM. There's my exchange [*throwing down a glove*]: what⁴⁵ in the world
      he is
    That names me traitor, villain-like he lies:
    Call by thy trumpet: he that dares approach,
    On him, on you, who not? I will maintain   100
    My truth and honour firmly.
ALB. A herald, ho!
EDM.   A herald, ho, a herald!
ALB. Trust to thy single virtue;⁴⁶ for thy soldiers,
    All levied in my name, have in my name
    Took their discharge.
REG.   My sickness grows upon me.
ALB. She is not well; convey her to my tent.   [*Exit* REGAN, *led.*]

[Enter a HERALD.]

    Come hither, herald,—Let the trumpet sound,—
    And read out this.
CAPT. Sound, trumpet!⁴⁷ [*A trumpet sounds.*]
HER. [*Reads*] "If any man of quality or degree⁴⁸ within the lists of the   110
    army will maintain upon Edmund, supposed Earl of Gloucester,
    that he is a manifold traitor, let him appear by the third sound of
    the trumpet: he is bold in his defence."
EDM. Sound!   [*First trumpet.*]
HER. Again!   [*Second trumpet.*]
HER. Again!   [*Third trumpet.*]
                        [*Trumpet answers within.*]

                [Enter EDGAR, *at the third sound,*
                armed, with a trumpet before him.]

ALB. Ask him his purposes, why he appears
    Upon this call o' the trumpet.
HER.   What are you?
    Your name, your quality? and why you answer
    This present summons?
EDG.   Know, my name is lost;   120
    By treason's tooth bare-gnawn and canker-bit:⁴⁹

---

⁴³ Comedy (a reference to Albany's elaborate irony).   ⁴⁴ No respect.
⁴⁵ Whoever and whatever.   ⁴⁶ Valor.   ⁴⁷ Trumpeter.
⁴⁸ **quality or degree,** rank or high social position.   ⁴⁹ Eaten away by a canker-worm.

Yet am I noble as the adversary
I come to cope.[50]

ALB.   Which is that adversary?

EDG. What's he that speaks for Edmund Earl of Gloucester?

EDM. Himself: what say'st thou to him?

EDG.   Draw thy sword,
That, if my speech offend a noble heart,
Thy arm[51] may do thee justice: here is mine.
Behold, it is the privilege of mine honours,[52]
My oath,[53] and my profession: I protest,
Maugre[54] thy strength, youth, place, and eminence,   130
Despite thy victor sword and fire-new[55] fortune,
Thy valour and thy heart,[56] thou art a traitor;
False to thy gods, thy brother, and thy father;
Conspirant[57] 'gainst this high-illustrious prince;
And, from the extremest upward[58] of thy head
To the descent[59] and dust below thy foot,
A most toad-spotted[60] traitor. Say thou "No,"
This sword, this arm, and my best spirits, are bent
To prove upon thy heart, whereto I speak,
Thou liest.   140

EDM. In wisdom[61] I should ask thy name;
But, since thy outside looks so fair and warlike,
And that thy tongue some say of breeding[62] breathes,
What safe and nicely[63] I might well delay
By rule of knighthood, I disdain and spurn:
Back do I toss these treasons[64] to thy head;
With the hell-hated[65] lie o'erwhelm thy heart;
Which, for[66] they yet glance by and scarcely bruise,
This sword of mine shall give them instant way,
Where they shall rest for ever. Trumpets, speak!   150

                    [*Alarums. They fight.* EDMUND *falls.*]

ALB. Save him, save him!

GON.   This is mere practice,[67] Gloucester:
By the law of arms thou wast not bound to answer[68]
An unknown opposite;[69] thou art not vanquish'd,
But cozen'd[70] and beguiled.

ALB.   Shut your mouth, dame,
Or with this paper[71] shall I stop it. Hold, sir;

---

[50] Cope with.   [51] Weapon.   [52] **mine honours,** my rank, i.e., as knight.
[53] i.e., which I swore when dubbed knight, i.e., to protect the honor of knighthood from such evils as treason.
[54] In spite of.   [55] Brand-new.   [56] Courage.   [57] Conspirator.   [58] Top.
[59] Lowest part [of you].   [60] Marked with poisonous spots.
[61] **In wisdom,** i.e., a knight was not obliged to accept the challenge of an unknown opponent.
[62] **say of breeding,** accent of a gentleman.
[63] **safe and nicely,** safely and punctiliously.   [64] Accusations of treason.
[65] Hateful as hell.   [66] Because.   [67] **mere practice,** out-and-out foul play.
[68] Accept the challenge of.   [69] Opponent.   [70] Cheated.
[71] i.e., her love letter which Edgar has found on Oswald's body.

Thou worse than any name, read thine own evil:
No tearing, lady; I perceive you know it.

[*Gives the letter to* EDMUND.]

GON. Say, if I do, the laws are mine, not thine:[72]
Who can arraign me for 't?

ALB.   Most monstrous! oh!
Know'st thou this paper?

GON.   Ask me not what I know.   [*Exit.*]   160

ALB. Go after her: she's desperate; govern[73] her.

EDM. What you have charged me with, that have I done;
And more, much more; the time will bring it out:
'Tis past, and so am I. But what art thou
That hast this fortune[74] on me? If thou'rt noble,
I do forgive thee.

EDG.   Let's exchange charity.
I am no less in blood than thou art, Edmund;
If more, the more thou hast wrong'd me.
My name is Edgar, and thy father's son.
The gods are just, and of our pleasant vices   170
Make instruments to plague us:
The dark and vicious place where thee he got[75]
Cost him his eyes.

EDM.   Thou hast spoken right, 'tis true;
The wheel[76] is come full circle; I am here.

ALB. Methought thy very gait[77] did prophesy
A royal nobleness: I must embrace thee:
Let sorrow split my heart, if ever I
Did hate thee or thy father!

EDG.   Worthy[78] prince, I know't.

ALB. Where have you hid yourself?
How have you known the miseries of your father?   180

EDG. By nursing them, my lord. List a brief tale;
And when 'tis told, O, that my heart would burst!
The bloody proclamation to escape,[79]
That follow'd me so near,—O, our lives' sweetness!
That we the pain of death would hourly die
Rather than die at once![80]—taught me to shift
Into a madman's rags; to assume a semblance
That very dogs disdain'd: and in this habit
Met I my father with his bleeding rings,
Their precious stones new lost; became his guide,   190
Led him, begg'd for him, saved him from despair;
Never,—O fault![81]—reveal'd myself unto him,
Until some half-hour past, when I was arm'd:

---

[72] **the laws . . . thine,** I, as ruler, make the laws, not you.   [73] Restrain.
[74] Success.   [75] Begot.   [76] i.e., of Fortune.   [77] Bearing.   [78] Honorable.
[79] **The . . . escape,** in order to escape from the proclamation for my arrest.
[80] **That . . . once,** that we prefer to suffer the pain of death hour by hour than to die at
once.
[81] Mistake.

Not sure, though hoping, of this good success,
I ask'd his blessing, and from first to last
Told him my pilgrimage: but his flaw'd[82] heart,
Alack, too weak the conflict to support!
'Twixt two extremes of passion, joy and grief,
Burst smilingly.

EDM.　　　　　　　　This speech of yours hath moved me,
And shall perchance do good: but speak you on;　　　　　　200
You look as you had something more to say.

ALB. If there be more, more woeful, hold it in;
For I am almost ready to dissolve,[83]
Hearing of this.

EDG.　　　　　　　　This would have seem'd a period[84]
To such as love not sorrow; but another,
To amplify too much, would make much more,
And top extremity.[85]
Whilst I was big in clamour[86] came there in a man,
Who, having seen me in my worst estate,[87]
Shunn'd my abhorr'd society; but then, finding　　　　　　210
Who 'twas that so endured, with his strong arms
He fasten'd on my neck, and bellow'd out
As he'ld burst heaven; threw him on my father;
Told the most piteous tale of Lear and him
That ever ear received: which in recounting
His grief grew puissant,[88] and the strings of life[89]
Began to crack: twice then the trumpets sounded,
And there I left him tranced.[90]

ALB.　　　　　　　　　　　　　But who was this?

EDG. Kent, sir, the banish'd Kent; who in disguise
Follow'd his enemy king, and did him service　　　　　　220
Improper for[91] a slave.

　　　　　　　　　　[*Enter a* GENTLEMAN, *with a
　　　　　　　　　　bloody knife.*]

GENT. Help, help, O, help!

EDG.　　　　　　　　What kind of help?

ALB.　　　　　　　　　　　　Speak, man.

EDG. What means that bloody knife?

GENT.　　　　　　　　　　　'Tis hot, it smokes;
It came even from the heart of—O, she's dead!

ALB. Who dead? speak, man.

GENT. Your lady, sir, your lady: and her sister
By her is poisoned; she hath confess'd it.

EDM. I was contracted to them both: all three
Now marry in an instant.

---

[82] Cracked.　　[83] i.e., in tears.　　[84] End (of sorrow).
[85] **top extremity,** exceed the extreme limit.　　[86] **big in clamour,** loud in lament.
[87] Condition.　　[88] Overpowering.　　[89] **strings of life,** heart-strings.　　[90] In a swoon.
[91] Even for.

EDG.   Here comes Kent.

ALB. Produce their bodies, be they alive or dead: 230
    This judgement of the heavens, that makes us tremble,
    Touches us not with pity.   [*Exit* GENTLEMAN.]

                          [*Enter* KENT.]

                      O, is this he?
    The time will not allow the compliment[92]
    Which very manners urges.

KENT.   I am come
    To bid my king and master aye[93] good night:
    Is he not here?

ALB.   Great thing of[94] us forgot!
    Speak, Edmund, where's the king? and where's Cordelia?
    See'st thou this object, Kent?

                          [*The bodies of* GONERIL *and* RE-
                          GAN *are brought in.*]

KENT. Alack, why thus?

EDM.   Yet Edmund was beloved:
    The one the other poison'd for my sake,   240
    And after slew herself.

ALB. Even so. Cover their faces.

EDM. I pant for life: some good I mean to do,
    Despite of mine own nature. Quickly send,
    Be brief in it, to the castle; for my writ
    Is on the life of Lear and on Cordelia:
    Nay, send in time.

ALB.   Run, run, O, run!

EDG. To who, my lord? Who hath the office? send
    Thy token of reprieve.

EDM. Well thought on: take my sword,   250
    Give it the captain.

ALB.   Haste thee, for thy life.   [*Exit* EDGAR.]

EDM. He hath commission from thy wife and me
    To hang Cordelia in the prison, and
    To lay the blame upon her own despair,
    That she fordid[95] herself.

ALB. The gods defend her! Bear him hence awhile.

                          [EDMUND *is borne off.*]

                          [*Re-enter* LEAR, *with* CORDELIA
                          dead in his arms; EDGAR, CAP-
                          TAIN, *and others following.*]

LEAR. Howl, howl, howl, howl! O, you are men of stones:
    Had I your tongues and eyes, I'ld use them so
    That heaven's vault should crack. She's gone for ever!

[92] Ceremony.   [93] Forever.   [94] By.   [95] Destroyed.

I know when one is dead, and when one lives;   260
She's dead as earth. Lend me a looking-glass;
If that her breath will mist or stain the stone,[96]
Why, then she lives.

KENT.   Is this the promised end?[97]

EDG. Or image[98] of that horror?

ALB.   Fall, and cease![99]

LEAR. This feather stirs; she lives! if it be so,
It is a chance which does redeem[1] all sorrows
That ever I have felt.

KENT. [*Kneeling*] O my good master!

LEAR. Prithee, away.

EDG.   'Tis noble Kent, your friend.

LEAR. A plague upon you, murderers, traitors all!
I might have saved her; now she's gone for ever!   270
Cordelia, Cordelia! stay a little. Ha!
What is 't thou say'st? Her voice was ever soft,
Gentle, and low, an excellent thing in woman.
I kill'd the slave that was a-hanging thee.

CAPT. 'Tis true, my lords, he did.

LEAR.   Did I not, fellow?
I have seen the day, with my good biting falchion[2]
I would have made them skip: I am old now,
And these same crosses[3] spoil me. Who are you?
Mine eyes are not o' the best: I'll tell you straight.[4]

KENT. If fortune brag of two she loved and hated,   280
One of them we behold.[5]

LEAR. This is a dull sight. Are you not Kent?

KENT.   The same,
Your servant Kent. Where is your servant Caius?

LEAR. He's a good fellow, I can tell you that;
He'll strike, and quickly too: he's dead and rotten.

KENT. No, my good lord; I am the very man,—

LEAR. I'll see that[6] straight.

KENT. That, from your first of difference and decay,[7]
Have follow'd your sad steps.

LEAR.   You are welcome hither.

KENT. Nor no man else:[8] all's cheerless, dark, and deadly.   290
Your eldest daughters have fordone[9] themselves,
And desperately[10] are dead.

LEAR.   Ay, so I think.

---

[96] Crystal mirror.   [97] i.e., of the world, the Last Judgment.   [98] Exact likeness.
[99] **Fall, and cease,** i.e., let Doomsday come and all things cease to be.   [1] Repay.
[2] A curved, broad-bladed sword.   [3] Troubles.   [4] Straightway.
[5] **One . . . behold,** certainly no more than two men in all human history have experienced such violent ups and downs of Fortune as Lear.
[6] **see that,** see to that.
[7] **from . . . decay,** from the beginning of the decline and decay of your fortunes.
[8] **Nor . . . else,** not I nor any one else.   [9] Killed.   [10] In despair.

ALB. He knows not what he says: and vain it is
    That we present us to him.
EDG.   Very bootless.

                    [*Enter a* CAPTAIN.]

CAP. Edmund is dead, my lord.
ALB.   That's but a trifle here.
    You lords and noble friends, know our intent.
    What comfort to this great decay[11] may come
    Shall be applied: for us, we will resign
    During the life of this old majesty,
    To him our absolute power:[12] [*To* EDGAR *and* KENT] you, to
        your rights;   300
    With boot,[13] and such addition as your honours
    Have more than merited. All friends shall taste
    The wages of their virtue, and all foes
    The cup of their deservings. O, see, see!
LEAR. And my poor fool[14] is hang'd! No, no, no life!
    Why should a dog, a horse, a rat, have life,
    And thou no breath at all? Thou'lt come no more,
    Never, never, never, never, never!
    Pray you, undo this button: thank you, sir.
    Do you see this? Look on her, look, her lips,   310
    Look there, look there!   [*Dies.*]
EDG.   He faints! My lord, my lord!
KENT. Break, heart; I prithee, break!
EDG.   Look up, my lord.
KENT. Vex not his ghost:[15] O, let him pass! he hates him much
    That would upon the rack of this tough world
    Stretch him out longer.
EDG.   He is gone, indeed.
KENT. The wonder is, he hath endured so long:
    He but usurp'd his life.[16]
ALB. Bear them from hence. Our present business
    Is general woe. [*To* KENT *and* EDGAR] Friends of my soul, you
        twain
    Rule in this realm, and the gored state sustain.   320
KENT. I have a journey, sir, shortly to go;
    My master calls me,[17] I must not say no.
ALB. The weight of this sad time we must obey;
    Speak what we feel, not what we ought to say.
    The oldest[18] hath borne most: we that are young
    Shall never see so much, nor live so long.[19]
                    [*Exeunt, with a dead march.*]

[11] **great decay,** great man fallen into decay.
[12] **our absolute power,** the sovereign power I now exercise.
[13] Something given in the bargain.
[14] i.e., Cordelia; "fool" was used as a term of endearment.
[15] Departing spirit.   [16] **usurp'd his life,** i.e., lived longer than the usual term of life.
[17] i.e., to follow him through Death.   [18] i.e., Lear and Gloucester.
[19] **Shall . . . long,** i.e., even if we shall live as long as Lear has, we should never experience
so much misery.

John Milton
(1608–1674)

John Milton was one of the world's greatest and most influential poets, the author of the definitive English epic, the last towering figure of the European Renaissance, and a prominent partisan, on the Puritan and Republican side, in the momentous English Civil War, fought in the seventeenth century over issues of church and civil government. The issues of his day in certain ways mark the beginning of the modern political era.

Milton was born in London in 1608; his father, disinherited for converting from Roman Catholicism to Protestantism, was a successful businessman (and a gifted musician) who found it proper, the family having risen in the world, to give his son John the best of humanist educations, through private tutors and at St. Paul's School. The precocious evidence John gave of intellectual and poetic ability made the church, rather than a more worldly profession, seem his natural calling, and, although Milton later in his life chose not to be ordained, he remained grateful that his education had not been narrow and merely pragmatic. In 1625 he entered Cambridge University; there, after problems with his first tutor, he achieved distinction, though he chafed at what he considered the university's intellectual conservatism. At Cambridge he earned the nickname "The Lady" because of his delicate good looks, his religious seriousness, and the ascetic tendencies that (as his later life would reveal) coexisted with a passionate and even sensuous side of his character. In 1629 he wrote his first great poem in English (he composed in Latin and Italian also), the Ode on the Morning of Christ's Nativity, *which anticipates* Paradise Lost *by its references to the overcoming of the heathen gods at the coming of Christ. After taking his B.A. in 1629 and his M.A. in 1632, he retired to his father's estate, where he studied intensively, preparing himself, as he felt, for some great enterprise in literature or public life. Before the age of thirty, when this period of retirement ended, Milton had also written* L'Allegro *and* Il Penseroso *(twin poems praising, respectively, the cheerful and contemplative characters), the brief masque* Arcades, *the longer masque* Comus *(a platonic celebration of the triumph of virtue and chastity over evil and sensuality), and* Lycidas, *a pastoral elegy that some critics consider the greatest lyric poem in English. Written to commemorate the premature death of an acquaintance,* Lycidas *dramatizes Milton's concern over the mystery and injustice of death, the possible unfulfillment of his own hopes in life, and the assurance of spiritual victory through submission to divine Providence—all this in the context of an almost unbelievably rich pattern of classical allusion and creative imitation.*

In 1638 Milton left England to spend fifteen months on the Continent, mainly in Florence, Rome, and Naples. During this "grand tour," he met a number of eminent men of learning and culture, including Hugo Grotius, the Dutch expositor of international law, and Galileo, who at the time was in trouble with the Church because of his speculations in astronomy. Milton was for the most part gratified by his reception, which gave him increased confidence in his powers. It is both characteristic and prophetic that, as Milton later put it, he "openly defended . . . the reformed religion in the very metropolis of popery" despite plots said to have been hatched against him by the Jesuits. He aborted a trip to Sicily and Greece when he learned of the outbreak of civil disturbances in England, and some months later he was back there. Around the time of his return, King Charles I was forced to convene a hostile Parliament; over the next two decades, during which many battles were fought between the

Royalists/Episcopalians and their Republican/Puritan antagonists, the Presbyterian party first rose to power, being succeeded later by an even more radical party of Independents; Charles I was beheaded in 1649; a republic (the "Commonwealth") was declared; Oliver Cromwell was named Lord Protector (dictator, virtually) between 1653 and his death in 1658; his ineffectual son Richard succeeded him but abdicated; and finally, to Milton's dismay, the monarchy was restored in 1660 in the person of the heretofore exiled Charles II.

After returning from his Italian tour, Milton pondered an ambitious literary work, particularly a drama on an English or scriptural subject, and it is possible that he did begin a play on his favorite topic, the fall of man, which he later chose for his epic. But his sense of commitment to the cause of religious and civil freedom as he understood it made him put aside his ambitious literary plans for the greater part of two decades, during which he composed many treatises and pamphlets directed against his personal and political enemies and those of the revolutionary government. His first efforts dealt with the evils of the episcopal system (rule by bishops) in the Church of England, an issue that Milton conceived to be part of the larger issue of general human freedom. An ill-considered marriage, which for a time was broken off, prompted a series of tracts boldly arguing for the legality of divorce on grounds of incompatibility, a position that in its alleged libertinism alienated not only the Royalists but the Presbyterians as well. In 1644, in opposition to a Parliamentary censorship law, he wrote Areopagitica, *a classic rationale for freedom of the press and individual responsibility that, curiously, uses arguments against an artificially sheltered, untested virtue that seem at least to be similar to those Satan and Eve use in Book IX of* Paradise Lost *to justify eating the fruit of the Tree of Knowledge of Good and Evil. He also wrote on education, history, and theology. In 1649, the year Charles was beheaded, he wrote* The Tenure of Kings and Magistrates, *a tract that earned him the favor of the regicide regime by arguing that a king's tenure and very life were subject to the will of the people. Milton was made Latin Secretary in the government, a post that involved foreign correspondence and official defenses of the regime against its opponents at home and abroad. But his eyesight, which for some time had been failing, deteriorated until total blindness came in 1652, after which time he was gradually relieved of official duties and was able (especially after 1654) to turn his energies again to literature. Milton was sustained in part by his belief that loss of literal vision was compensated by a strengthened inner light and vision—a hope that was later expressed movingly in the hymn to light that opens Book III of* Paradise Lost. *In the latter 1650s he began his epic* Paradise Lost, *which he completed by 1665; it was published in 1667, in a ten-book version that he later altered to twelve. Meanwhile, the restoration of the Royalists brought Milton's life into peril, though for reasons not entirely clear he was released, after being arrested, with just a fine. Thereafter, despite reduced financial circumstances and some friction with his relatives, he lived a fairly regular and outwardly uneventful life, composing verse (the inspiration for which is said to have come mainly in the winter during the hours before dawn), singing and playing music, walking in his garden, meditating and being read to, receiving admiring visitors. In 1671 were published the "short epic"* Paradise Regained *(a sequel to* Paradise Lost *that centers on Christ's resistance to Satan's temptations in the wilderness as narrated, for example, in the fourth chapter of Matthew's gospel) and the drama* Samson Agonistes. *The latter, based on the story of Samson in Judges 13–16, has irresistible autobiographical relevance as the story of a blinded hero, living his last days in captivity, who undergoes a spiritual renewal and finally triumphs over his wicked captors.* Samson

Agonistes *has been praised as the nearest English equivalent of ancient Greek drama and as a work on the same level of greatness as* Paradise Lost. *Thus Milton's stature as a poet is attested in all three traditional poetic modes: lyric (his sonnets must be mentioned along with works already named), epic, and drama. After a final pamphlet in 1673 warning against resurgent "popery" under Charles II, Milton died, in 1674, of gout.*

In Paradise Lost *Milton aimed at grandeur, comprehensiveness, and universal relevance. This is most clearly true in the choice of subject itself, for to Christians no theme could be more awesome than that of the fall of man, which "Brought death into the world, and all our woe" (I.3) and the counterpoised Redemption that is outlined theologically in Book III and historically in Book XII. It was a theme, Milton tells us, that he was "long choosing and beginning late" (IX.26). The question to what extent the poem transcends the interests of Christian theology has been much debated. Milton's approach can be cited on both sides: on one hand, he is careful to integrate into his poem the whole fabric of pagan antiquity, thus achieving something like mythic universality; on the other hand, he takes pains to distinguish the distorted versions of truth expressed by the pagans from the literal and naked truth of biblical revelation on which his epic is based. The pagan gods, for example, are the true devils in disguise. Aiming at universality, Milton subordinates in* Paradise Lost *the notes of political and religious partisanship he sounds in his tracts. His political opposition to the restored monarchy appears chiefly by innuendo, and although there is in the poem some peculiarly Miltonic theology (his apparently unorthodox view of the Trinity, for example), and some direct sectarian invective, his treatment of the Son's redeeming self-sacrifice is essentially in the mainstream of Christian tradition.*

Whatever limitations Milton's theology, idiosyncratic or more broadly Christian, may imply for the persuasiveness of his answers, it is hardly questionable that he defines compellingly the ultimate issues explored in all theodicies (attempts to "justify God's ways")—questions of cosmic justice, the origin of physical suffering and of moral evil, and the relationship of these to human free will. Indeed, the motif of liberty is at the heart of Paradise Lost *and is perhaps the most vital link between the values of the poem and those Milton cherished in his personal and public life. Moreover, his treatment of liberty is complex. His belief that man stands or falls essentially on his own, without either the compulsion or the effective help of earthly authority, is part both of radical Protestantism and of modern libertarianism. Yet it is also true that the Son's obedient submission to the Father is for Milton the prototype of all true liberty.* Paradise Lost *thus raises some questions about the relationship between absolute human autonomy and acquiescence in the cosmic order that assert themselves in any age, under any system.*

Milton's claim to have raised the subject matter of epic to a new level of grandeur and truth is itself part of the epic tradition. In this claim he is following the precedent of Virgil, who (to apply a phrase of Milton's) also tried to be "doctrinal and exemplary to a nation" by implicitly substituting for Homeric objectivity and concern with war a set of values that, while still communal, are more inward, ethical, philosophical. Like Virgil, Milton tells a story whose historical, and not merely mythical, dimension is important to him. The matter is of the greatest possible public import. Yet Milton, while insisting on the literal existence of hell, heaven, and the earthly paradise, gives them also an extended spiritual dimension. Hell is a state of mind, one that Satan creates for himself and carries with him everywhere he goes. Paradise is lost by Adam and Eve, but Book XII assures them that, through faith in and imitation of the redeeming Son of God, they can achieve "A Paradise within thee, happier far"

(XII.587) than the one they forfeited. In a passage where he both acknowledges and repudiates his epic ancestry, Milton substitutes for "Wars, hitherto the only argument / Heroic deemed" the "better fortitude / Of patience and heroic martyrdom" (IX.28– 32). It is enormously significant that in Paradise Regained *he balances against the "disobedience" (*Paradise Lost, *I.1) of the fallen Adam not the climax of Jesus' public life in the Passion and Resurrection but the most private incident in his career, the obedience to his Father manifested in the Temptation in the Wilderness.*

Much of the power of Paradise Lost *comes from qualities that might seem alien to the opinionated Milton: a kind of evenhandedness or at least intellectual and imaginative empathy that he extends to ideas and characters opposed to what he is championing. Easily the best example is Satan, one of the supreme triumphs of literary characterization. Shelley and other interpreters in the Romantic tradition went so far as to consider him the real hero of the poem. That was surely not Milton's intent, yet it remains true that Satan is given dramatic autonomy. He is treated with grandeur, in, for example, Books I and II, and sometimes with touches of pathos as in the soliloquy that opens Book IV. (Ironically, as it has seemed to some readers, the Milton who in life defended rebellion against monarchy identifies the insubordinate Satan in the epic poem as the origin of evil.) Belial, whom Milton calls "lewd," "gross," and one who could "make the worse appear / The better reason" (I.490– 491; II.113–114), is endowed with breathtaking imagination and made to utter a noble encomium on the human mind, "this intellectual being, / Those thoughts that wander through eternity" (II.147–148). And, as mentioned earlier, Satan and Eve sound somewhat like* Areopagitica. *Such anomalies can suggest a failure by Milton to control the tone of the poem or else, as William Blake's* Marriage of Heaven and Hell *charges, a lapse in self-knowledge by Milton. Against which it might be argued that in true epics heroes and heroism have worthy, however evil, adversaries. If the temptations and errors of Satan and mankind had no plausibility and seductive power, their fall would seem not tragic but fatuous.*

Paradise Lost *is a consummate work of art, in architecture and surface. The sublime hymn to light in Book III, for example, serves structurally to emphasize the emergence of Satan, and the poem, from the sulphurous horror of hell and darkness to the ambrosial brightness of heaven. These same transitional lines also mark the elaborate parallelism between the council-scenes of Books II and III, including the antithetical offers by Satan and the Son of God respectively to destroy man and to save him. Figures of speech are powerful; the modulation of the metaphysical praise of light into Milton's mourning for his personal blindness is capped by a sublime metaphor in which the outward-radiating natural sun that fertilizes the world and dispels darkness becomes the emblem of a fertilizing spiritual sun that shines toward a center:*

> *So much the rather thou celestial Light*
> *Shine inward, and the mind through all her powers*
> *Irradiate, there plant eyes, all mist from thence*
> *Purge and disperse, that I may see and tell*
> *Of things invisible to mortal sight. (III.51–55)*

The grand style in Paradise Lost, *the style generally called "Miltonic," is the high ceremonial one that Milton recognized as appropriate to epic. Vowel sounds are often sonorous ("To bellow through the vast and boundless deep"—I.177). Half- repetitions (the "Miltonic turn") have an effect that can be both epigrammatic and swelling ("Thus high uplifted beyond hope, aspires / Beyond thus high"—II.7–8). Exotic, evocative proper names are heaped on one another (IV. 268–83). Long-extended similes are used as in Homer and Virgil (I.302–13, 768–92), often with even greater psychological suggestiveness. Sentences are prolonged through whole "verse paragraphs," the sense drawn out inexorably from one line to the next— sustaining elevation of tone or creating suspense or introducing bold imaginative surprises that one is not allowed to linger over as climaxes.*

In fact, however, the poem has many voices. The speeches in the infernal council in Book II are not just magniloquent; they are specifically modeled on parliamentary oratory. Moreover, even this section is varied within itself, the headlong Moloch sounding not at all like the subtle, intellectually speculative Belial. Satan's soliloquy in Book IV is in itself a mixture of tones, from subdued remorse to anguish to desperate recklessness. Adam and Eve can address each other like royal consorts in their unfallen state but with colloquial acrimony at the end of Book IX after their fall. Milton abandoned the dramatic genre for the epic, but he retained the variety of speech one finds in the best dramas.

Although Shakespeare may have been rated as highly, Milton's influence on English literature in the 150 years following his death in 1674 was much greater, indeed incalculable. To imitate Shakespeare, who created in his plays and poems a score of different worlds, is nearly equivalent to imitating the whole variety of human experience. But Milton's work, despite its wide variety of genre and tone, has a kind of finished architectural coherence that, blending with the events of his life and his forcefully expressed ideas, has the effect of a single massive literary and personal presence. He dominated the eighteenth-century imagination as Newton dominated its science, partly because of his grandeur of manner, partly because of the fascination of his theological argument, partly because he synthesized while he transformed a vast body of ancient and Renaissance culture. The English Romantic poets, especially Blake, Wordsworth, Shelley, and Keats, all took Milton, in one way or another, as a touchstone for their most considered statements about human values and the place of humanity in the cosmic order.

FURTHER READING (*prepared by W. J. R.*): William Riley Parker's *Milton: A Biography*, 2 vols., 1968, is the definitive modern biography; as an introduction, Douglas Bush's *John Milton: A Sketch of His Life and Writings*, 1964, is recommended. Also very good, especially for new readers of Milton, is A. N. Wilson, *The Life of John Milton*, 1983. The subject identified in his book's title is treated topically in James Thorpe, *John Milton: The Inner Life*, 1983. An admirable introduction to *Paradise Lost*, discussing the poem as psychology, doctrine, drama, and from several other perspectives, is G. K. Hunter, *Paradise Lost*, 1980. Arnold Stein's *Answerable Style: Essays on "Paradise Lost,"* 1953, is an excellent study of the poem. C. S. Lewis's *A Preface to "Paradise Lost,"* 1942, rev. 1960, discusses the poem's ideas and style in a lively, rigorous fashion, in the contexts of classical and Christian tradition. An excellent introduction is David M. Miller's *John Milton: Poetry*, 1978, which includes a biographical introduction and discussions of *Paradise Lost*, *Paradise Regained*, and *Samson Agonistes*, in a manner suitable for general readers. Northrop Frye's *The Return of Eden*, 1965, contains excellent essays, including Frye's celebrated analysis of foreground and background action in *Paradise Lost*. Douglas Bush's *"Paradise Lost" in Our Time*, 1945, discusses the negative reaction to Milton's epic in the twentieth century, Milton's religion and ethics, methods of characterization, and other topics. Helen Gardner's *A Reading of "Paradise Lost,"* 1965, contains a helpful discussion of the modern meaning of *Paradise Lost*; an appendix contains Gardner's earlier (1948) and important essay on Satan and his appeal as a heroic figure. Joan Webber's *Milton and His Epic Tradition,* 1979, surveys early epics beginning with Homer and relates this tradition to *Paradise Lost* and *Paradise Regained.* *New Essays on "Paradise Lost,"* ed. Thomas Kranidas, 1971, contains good essays on the theme of Book III, innocence and experience in *Paradise Lost,* the Fall, and other topics. Don Cameron Allen's *The Harmonious Vision,* 1954, deals with nearly all of Milton's poetry in an attempt to define the overall unity of Milton's thought. Diane Kelsey McColley, *Milton's Eve,* 1983, asserts Eve's positive role in the scheme of *Paradise Lost,* taking issue with the idea that the portrayal of her is antifeminist. Stevie Davies, *Images of Kingship in "Paradise Lost,"* 1983, evaluates the poem's figures in light of the ruler-subject relationship. Milton's theology, especially in connection with the problem of evil, is addressed in Dennis Richard Danielson, *Milton's Good God: A Study in Literary Theodicy,* 1982.

PARADISE LOST

Selected Notes by James Holly Hanford

THE VERSE: The measure is English heroic verse without rime, as that of Homer in Greek, and of Virgil in Latin; rime being no necessary adjunct or true ornament of poem or good verse, in longer works especially, but the invention of a barbarous age, to set off wretched matter and lame metre; graced indeed since by the use of some famous modern poets, carried away by custom, but much to their own vexation, hindrance, and constraint to express many things otherwise, and for the most part worse than else they would have expressed them. Not without cause, therefore, some both Italian and Spanish poets of prime note have rejected rime both in longer and shorter works, as have also, long since, our best English tragedies, as a thing of itself, to all judicious ears, trivial and of no true musical delight; which consists only in apt numbers, fit quantity of syllables, and the sense variously drawn out from one verse into another, not in the jingling sound of like endings, a fault avoided by the learned ancients both in poetry and all good oratory. This neglect then of rime so little is to be taken for a defect, though it may seem so perhaps to vulgar readers, that it rather is to be esteemed an example set, the first in English, of ancient liberty recovered to heroic poem from the troublesome and modern bondage of riming.

from BOOK I

THE ARGUMENT

This first book proposes first in brief the whole subject, Man's disobedience, and the loss thereupon of Paradise wherein he was placed: then touches the prime cause of his fall, the Serpent, or rather Satan in the Serpent; who revolting from God, and drawing to his side many legions of angels, was by the command of God driven out of Heaven with all his crew into the great Deep. Which action passed over, the poem hastes into the midst of things, presenting Satan with his angels now fallen into Hell, described here, not in the center (for Heaven and Earth

may be supposed as yet not made, certainly not yet accursed) but in a place of
utter darkness, fitliest called Chaos. Here Satan with his angels lying on the
burning lake, thunderstruck and astonished, after a certain space recovers, as
from confusion, calls up him who next in order and dignity lay by him; they
confer of their miserable fall. Satan awakens all his legions, who lay till then in
the same manner confounded; they rise: their numbers, array of battle, their chief
leaders named, according to the idols known afterwards in Canaan and the
countries adjoining. To these Satan directs his speech, comforts them with hope
yet of regaining Heaven, but tells them lastly of a new world and new kind of
creature to be created, according to an ancient prophecy or report in Heaven; for
that angels were long before this visible creation, was the opinion of many ancient
Fathers. To find out the truth of this prophecy, and what to determine thereon, he
refers to a full council. What his associates thence attempt. Pandemonium the
palace of Satan rises, suddenly built out of the Deep; the infernal peers there sit
in council.

Of Man's first disobedience, and the fruit*
Of that forbidden tree, whose mortal taste
Brought death into the world, and all our woe,
With loss of Eden, till one greater Man
Restore us, and regain the blissful seat,
Sing Heavenly Muse, that on the secret top
Of Oreb, or of Sinai, didst inspire
That shepherd, who first taught the chosen seed,
In the beginning how the Heavens and Earth
Rose out of Chaos; or if Sion hill   10
Delight thee more, and Siloa's brook that flowed
Fast by the oracle of God, I thence
Invoke thy aid to my adventurous song,
That with no middle flight intends to soar
Above the Aonian mount, while it pursues
Things unattempted yet in prose or rhyme.
And chiefly thou O Spirit, that dost prefer
Before all temples the upright heart and pure,
Instruct me, for thou knowest; thou from the first
Wast present, and with mighty wings outspread   20

*All footnotes are by Hanford unless otherwise stated. Some notes are abridged. The
Arguments are by Milton.

1 ff. Milton follows the conventional epic procedure in his opening. For the various
elements or steps in this procedure, cf. *Iliad* i. 1 ff., *Aeneid* i. 1 ff.

2. mortal, deadly.

6. Heavenly Muse. The Christian poets adopted the classical muse of Astronomy, whose
name (Urania, the Heavenly) qualified her for the new office, as the patroness of their divine
inspiration. Milton identifies her with the Holy Spirit of Scripture and so turns his invocation
into a prayer.

7. of Oreb or of Sinai. Cf. Exod. 19:20 and Deut. 4:10. Milton carefully follows Scripture
even in its apparent contradiction.

8. That shepherd, Moses.

10. Sion hill, Mount Zion, one of the hills on which the city of Jerusalem is built.

11. Siloa's brook, "the waters of Shiloah that go softly" (Isa. 8:6).

12. Fast by the oracle of God, i.e., close to the Temple of Jerusalem.

15. Above the Aonian mount. Milton means that his theme is loftier than any that the
Pagan poets could sing. The **Aonian mount** is Helicon, sacred to the muses.

Dove-like sat'st brooding on the vast Abyss
And madest it pregnant: what in me is dark
Illumine, what is low raise and support;
That to the height of this great argument
I may assert Eternal Providence,
And justify the ways of God to men.
   Say first, for Heaven hides nothing from thy view,
Nor the deep tract of Hell, say first what cause
Moved our grand parents in that happy state,
Favored of Heaven so highly, to fall off   30
From their Creator, and transgress his will
For one restraint, lords of the world besides?
Who first seduced them to that foul revolt?
The infernal Serpent; he it was, whose guile,
Stirred up with envy and revenge, deceived
The Mother of Mankind; what time his pride
Had cast him out from Heaven, with all his host
Of rebel angels, by whose aid aspiring
To set himself in glory above his peers,
He trusted to have equalled the Most High,   40
If he opposed; and with ambitious aim
Against the throne and monarchy of God,
Raised impious war in Heaven and battle proud
With vain attempt. Him the Almighty Power
Hurled headlong flaming from the ethereal sky
With hideous ruin and combustion down
To bottomless perdition, there to dwell
In adamantine chains and penal fire,
Who durst defy the Omnipotent to arms.
   Nine times the space that measures day and night   50
To mortal men, he with his horrid crew
Lay vanquished, rolling in the fiery gulf
Confounded though immortal. But his doom
Reserved him to more wrath; for now the thought
Both of lost happiness and lasting pain
Torments him; round he throws his baleful eyes,
That witnessed huge affliction and dismay
Mixed with obdurate pride and steadfast hate.
At once as far as angel's ken he views
The dismal situation waste and wild: 60

   21. Gen. 1:1, 2. The Hebrew word translated in the Authorized Version "moved" can also
be rendered "brooded." The Holy Spirit takes the form of a dove in Luke 3:22.
   24. argument, subject.   **25. assert,** maintain the cause of.
   26. justify, make apparent the justice of. The real issue in Milton's mind is whether an
intelligent and righteous will rules man's destiny, or a blind or capricious or malicious one.
The justification hinges on (1) the affirmation of man's freedom and responsibility, and (2)
the scheme of salvation through Christ which is set forth in the poem as a whole.
   29. our grand parents, i.e., our original ancestors, Adam and Eve.
   32. for, because of. **53. Confounded,** defeated and ruined.
   57. witnessed, bore witness to, expressed.
   59. angel's ken, an angel's range of vision.

A dungeon horrible, on all sides round
As one great furnace flamed, yet from those flames
No light, but rather darkness visible
Served only to discover sights of woe,
Regions of sorrow, doleful shades, where peace
And rest can never dwell, hope never comes
That comes to all; but torture without end
Still urges, and a fiery deluge, fed
With ever-burning sulphur unconsumed:
Such place Eternal Justice had prepared　　　　　　　　70
For those rebellious, here their prison ordained
In utter darkness, and their portion set
As far removed from God and light of Heaven
As from the center thrice to the utmost pole.
Oh how unlike the place from whence they fell!
There the companions of his fall, o'erwhelmed
With floods and whirlwinds of tempestuous fire,
He soon discerns, and weltering by his side
One next himself in power, and next in crime,
Long after known in Palestine, and named　　　　　　80
Beëlzebub. To whom the Arch-Enemy,
And thence in Heaven called Satan, with bold words
Breaking the horrid silence thus began.
　　"If thou beest he; but Oh how fallen! how changed
From him, who in the happy realms of light
Clothed with transcendent brightness didst outshine
Myriads, though bright: if he whom mutual league,
United thoughts and counsels, equal hope
And hazard in the glorious enterprise,
Joined with me once, now misery hath joined　　　　90
In equal ruin: into what pit thou seest
From what height fallen, so much the stronger proved
He with his thunder, and till then who knew
The force of those dire arms? Yet not for those,
Nor what the potent victor in his rage
Can else inflict, do I repent or change,
Though changed in outward luster, that fixed mind
And high disdain, from sense of injured merit,

63. darkness visible, darkness not quite absolute. The words perhaps express also the idea of the darkness having a positive quality.
　　64. discover, reveal.
　　66. Cf. Dante, *Inferno,* iii: "All hope abandon, ye who enter here."
　　68. urges, afflicts.
　　72. utter, outer—as in Scripture. But there is also a suggestion of the modern sense.
　　74. from the center thrice to the utmost pole. The center is the center of the earth; the **utmost pole** is the pole of the outermost sphere of the visible heavens. The distance from hell to the empyrean (the supreme heaven) is ordinarily felt by Milton to be much greater than this exact calculation makes it.
　　81. Beëlzebub. Cf. Matt. 12:24. **Arch-Enemy.** Satan in Hebrew means "adversary."
　　84 ff. If thou beest he, etc. The sentence is not completed. The entire speech is made disjointed to indicate Satan's emotional stress.

That with the Mightiest raised me to contend,
And to the fierce contention brought along   100
Innumerable force of spirits armed
That durst dislike his reign, and, me preferring,
His utmost power with adverse power opposed
In dubious battle on the plains of Heaven,
And shook his throne. What though the field be lost?
All is not lost; the unconquerable will,
And study of revenge, immortal hate,
And courage never to submit or yield:
And what is else not to be overcome?
That glory never shall his wrath or might   110
Extort from me. To bow and sue for grace
With suppliant knee, and deify his power
Who from the terror of this arm so late
Doubted his empire, that were low indeed,
That were an ignominy and shame beneath
This downfall; since by fate the strength of gods
And this empyreal substance cannot fail,
Since through experience of this great event,
In arms not worse, in foresight much advanced,
We may with more successful hope resolve   120
To wage by force or guile eternal war,
Irreconcilable to our grand foe,
Who now triumphs, and in the excess of joy
Sole reigning holds the tyranny of Heaven."
    So spake the apostate Angel, though in pain,
Vaunting aloud, but racked with deep despair;
And him thus answered soon his bold compeer.
    "O Prince, O Chief of many thronèd Powers,
That led the embattled Seraphim to war
Under thy conduct, and in dreadful deeds   130
Fearless, endangered Heaven's perpetual King,
And put to proof his high supremacy,
Whether upheld by strength, or chance, or fate;
Too well I see and rue the dire event,
That with sad overthrow and foul defeat
Hath lost us Heaven, and all this mighty host
In horrible destruction laid thus low,
As far as gods and heavenly essences
Can perish: for the mind and spirit remains
Invincible, and vigor soon returns,   140

---

110. That glory, i.e., the glory of subduing Satan's will.   **114. Doubted,** feared for.
    116 ff. since by fate, etc. Satan denies that he was created by and is therefore subordinate to God. His egotism makes him a polytheist or more specifically a Manichee.
    120. successful hope, hope of success.
    128–29. throned Powers, Seraphim. The angelic orders in Dante and the Catholic theologians are, from lowest to highest, as follows: Angels, Archangels, Principalities, Powers, Virtues, Dominions, Thrones, Cherubim, Seraphim. Milton uses many of these names interchangeably.

Though all our glory extinct, and happy state
Here swallowed up in endless misery.
But what if he our conqueror (whom I now
Of force believe almighty, since no less
Than such could have o'erpowered such force as ours)
Have left us this our spirit and strength entire,
Strongly to suffer and support our pains,
That we may so suffice his vengeful ire,
Or do him mightier service as his thralls
By right of war, whate'er his business be,   150
Here in the heart of Hell to work in fire,
Or do his errands in the gloomy deep;
What can it then avail, though yet we feel
Strength undiminished, or eternal being
To undergo eternal punishment?"
  Whereto with speedy words the Arch-Fiend replied.
"Fallen Cherub, to be weak is miserable,
Doing or suffering: but of this be sure,
To do aught good never will be our task,
But ever to do ill our sole delight,   160
As being the contrary to his high will
Whom we resist. If then his providence
Out of our evil seek to bring forth good,
Our labor must be to pervert that end,
And out of good still to find means of evil;
Which oft-times may succeed, so as perhaps
Shall grieve him, if I fail not, and disturb
His inmost counsels from their destined aim.
But see the angry victor hath recalled
His ministers of vengeance and pursuit   170
Back to the gates of Heaven; the sulphurous hail
Shot after us in storm, o'erblown hath laid
The fiery surge, that from the precipice
Of Heaven received us falling, and the thunder,
Winged with red lightning and impetuous rage,
Perhaps hath spent his shafts, and ceases now
To bellow through the vast and boundless deep.
Let us not slip the occasion, whether scorn,
Or satiate fury yield it from our foe.
Seest thou yon dreary plain, forlorn and wild,   180
The seat of desolation, void of light,
Save what the glimmering of these livid flames
Casts pale and dreadful? Thither let us tend
From off the tossing of these fiery waves,
There rest, if any rest can harbor there,
And re-assembling our afflicted powers,
Consult how we may henceforth most offend

---

148. **suffice,** satisfy.   167. **if I fail not,** unless I mistake.
178. **Let us not slip,** Let us not let slip.   186. **afflicted powers,** routed forces.

Our enemy, our own loss how repair,
How overcome this dire calamity,
What reinforcement we may gain from hope;   190
If not, what resolution from despair."
    Thus Satan talking to his nearest mate
With head uplift above the wave, and eyes
That sparkling blazed; his other parts besides,
Prone on the flood, extended long and large,
Lay floating many a rood, in bulk as huge
As whom the fables name of monstrous size,
Titanian or Earth-born, that warred on Jove,
Briareos or Typhon, whom the den
By ancient Tarsus held, or that sea-beast   200
Leviathan, which God of all his works
Created hugest that swim the ocean stream:
Him haply slumbering on the Norway foam,
The pilot of some small night-foundered skiff,
Deeming some island, oft, as seamen tell,
With fixèd anchor in his scaly rind,
Moors by his side under the lee, while night
Invests the sea, and wishèd morn delays:
So stretched out huge in length the Arch-Fiend lay
Chained on the burning lake; nor ever thence   210
Had risen or heaved his head, but that the will
And high permission of all-ruling Heaven
Left him at large to his own dark designs,
That with reiterated crimes he might
Heap on himself damnation, while he sought
Evil to others, and enraged might see
How all his malice served but to bring forth
Infinite goodness, grace and mercy shown
On Man by him seduced, but on himself
Treble confusion, wrath and vengeance poured.   220
    Forthwith upright he rears from off the pool
His mighty stature; on each hand the flames
Driven backward slope their pointing spires, and rolled
In billows, leave in the midst a horrid vale.
Then with expanded wings he steers his flight
Aloft, incumbent on the dusky air
That felt unusual weight, till on dry land
He lights, if it were land that ever burned

    197. as whom, as those whom.
    198. Titanian, or Earth-born. The Titans and Giants in classical mythology were sons of
Heaven (Uranus) and Earth (Ge).
    199. Briareos or Typhon. The former was a Titan, the latter a Giant.
    201. Leviathan. Cf. Psalms 104:26, and Job 41. The monster was often associated with the
whale or the crocodile. Milton does not specifically identify it with either, although he suggests
characteristics of both.
    203 ff. This is an old traveller's story, the most familiar version being in the *Arabian Nights*.
night-foundered, i.e., lost in the darkness as completely as a sunken ship is lost in the ocean.
    208. invests, covers as with a garment.   **226. incumbent,** leaning on.

With solid, as the lake with liquid fire,
And such appeared in hue; as when the force   230
Of subterranean wind transports a hill
Torn from Pelorus, or the shattered side
Of thundering Ætna, whose combustible
And fuellèd entrails thence conceiving fire,
Sublimed with mineral fury, aid the winds,
And leave a singèd bottom all involved
With stench and smoke: such resting found the sole
Of unblest feet. Him followed his next mate,
Both glorying to have scaped the Stygian flood
As gods, and by their own recovered strength,   240
Not by the sufferance of supernal power.
   "Is this the region, this the soil, the clime,"
Said then the lost Archangel, "this the seat
That we must change for Heaven, this mournful gloom
For that celestial light? Be it so, since he
Who now is sovran can dispose and bid
What shall be right. Farthest from him is best,
Whom reason hath equalled, force hath made supreme
Above his equals. Farewell happy fields
Where joy for ever dwells: Hail horrors, hail   250
Infernal world, and thou profoundest Hell
Receive thy new possessor: one who brings
A mind not to be changed by place or time.
The mind is its own place, and in itself
Can make a Heaven of Hell, a Hell of Heaven.
What matter where, if I be still the same,
And what I should be, all but less than he
Whom thunder hath made greater? Here at least
We shall be free; the Almighty hath not built
Here for his envy, will not drive us hence: 260
Here we may reign secure, and in my choice
To reign is worth ambition, though in Hell:
Better to reign in Hell than serve in Heaven.
But wherefore let we then our faithful friends,
The associates and co-partners of our loss,

---

232. **Pelorus,** Cape Faro in Sicily, near Mt. Aetna.
   235. **sublimed,** sublimated, converted to gaseous form, but also with the original sense of lifted up; **the winds,** i.e., the winds or gases within the earth which were supposed to be the cause of earthquakes.
   236. **involved,** wrapped in.   244. **change for,** take in exchange for.
   246. **sovran,** sovereign, supreme in power.
   254–55. The supremacy of the mind is one of Milton's favorite ideas. The corollary of this utterance of Satan's is to be found in IV, 20–23.
   257–58. **all but less than,** etc. Usually interpreted as "all but equal to" or "less only than," but other or additional meanings are possible. "What I should be" is, in Satan's mind, God's equal. He would rather be anything but inferior and, since the mind is its own place, he *can* be equal in everything but power. The confusion of grammar is no greater than the confusion of frustrated human emotion.

Lie thus astonished on the oblivious pool,
And call them not to share with us their part
In this unhappy mansion; or once more
With rallied arms to try what may be yet
Regained in Heaven, or what more lost in Hell?"   270
  So Satan spake, and him Beëlzebub
Thus answered. "Leader of those armies bright,
Which but the Omnipotent none could have foiled,
If once they hear that voice, their liveliest pledge
Of hope in fears and dangers, heard so oft
In worst extremes, and on the perilous edge
Of battle when it raged, in all assaults
Their surest signal, they will soon resume
New courage and revive, though now they lie
Grovelling and prostrate on yon lake of fire,   280
As we erewhile, astounded and amazed;
No wonder, fallen such a pernicious height!"
  He scarce had ceased when the superior Fiend
Was moving toward the shore; his ponderous shield,
Ethereal temper, massy, large, and round,
Behind him cast; the broad circumference
Hung on his shoulders like the moon, whose orb
Through optic glass the Tuscan artist views
At evening from the top of Fesolë,
Or in Valdarno, to descry new lands,   290
Rivers or mountains in her spotty globe.
His spear, to equal which the tallest pine
Hewn on Norwegian hills, to be the mast
Of some great ammiral, were but a wand,
He walked with, to support uneasy steps
Over the burning marle, not like those steps
On Heaven's azure; and the torrid clime
Smote on him sore besides, vaulted with fire.
Nathless he so endured, till on the beach
Of that inflamëd sea, he stood and called   300
His legions, angel forms, who lay entranced,
Thick as autumnal leaves that strew the brooks

---

266. oblivious, causing forgetfulness. Milton is thinking of the classical Lethe.

276. edge. Latin *acies,* edge, means also battle line.

288. the Tuscan artist, Galileo, whom Milton had visited during his stay in Italy.

289. Fesolë, Fiesole, a small town located on a hill just outside Florence.

290. Valdarno, the valley of the Arno, in which Florence is located. Galileo's last residence was at Arcetri, west of the main part of the city. He was blind or almost so when Milton visited him and lamented that he could no longer look at the universe which his discoveries had made more wonderful.

294. ammiral, admiral, flagship.   **296. marle,** soil.

299. Nathless, nevertheless.

302 ff. Note the series of brilliant Homeric similes used to emphasize the numbers of the fallen angels. They are compared (1) when lying on the lake, to fallen leaves and floating sea-weed; (2) when flying, to a cloud of locusts; (3) when alighted, to a huge invading army.

In Vallombrosa, where the Etrurian shades
High over-arched embower; or scattered sedge
Afloat, when with fierce winds Orion armed
Hath vexed the Red-Sea coast, whose waves o'erthrew
Busiris and his Memphian chivalry
While with perfidious hatred they pursued
The sojourners of Goshen, who beheld
From the safe shore their floating carcasses   310
And broken chariot wheels; so thick bestrewn
Abject and lost lay these, covering the flood,
Under amazement of their hideous change.
He called so loud, that all the hollow deep
Of Hell resounded. "Princes, Potentates,
Warriors, the flower of Heaven, once yours, now lost,
If such astonishment as this can seize
Eternal spirits; or have ye chosen this place
After the toil of battle to repose
Your wearied virtue, for the ease you find   320
To slumber here, as in the vales of Heaven?
Or in this abject posture have ye sworn
To adore the conqueror, who now beholds
Cherub and Seraph rolling in the flood
With scattered arms and ensigns, till anon
His swift pursuers from Heaven gates discern
The advantage, and descending tread us down
Thus drooping, or with linkèd thunderbolts
Transfix us to the bottom of this gulf.
Awake, arise, or be for ever fallen!"   330
   They heard and were abashed, and up they sprung
Upon the wing, as when men wont to watch
On duty, sleeping found by whom they dread,
Rouse and bestir themselves ere well awake.
Nor did they not perceive the evil plight
In which they were, or the fierce pains not feel;
Yet to their general's voice they soon obeyed
Innumerable. As when the potent rod
Of Amram's son in Egypt's evil day
Waved round the coast, up called a pitchy cloud   340

---

303. Vallombrosa, a district about eighteen miles from Florence, containing a famous monastery which Milton is said to have visited. The name is Italian for "shady valley."
   305. Orion, a constellation proverbially associated with storms.
   307 ff. Cf. Exod. 14. **Busiris** was an ancient Egyptian king, whom Milton for some reason identifies with the Pharaoh whose hosts were drowned in the Red Sea. **Memphian** is here equivalent to Egyptian, Memphis being the ancient capital of Egypt. **The sojourners of Goshen** are of course the Israelites.
   312. Abject, cast down (Latin *abjectus*).   **320. virtue,** valor, strength (Latin *virtus*).
   328. linkèd thunderbolts. The thunderbolts are compared to linked cannon balls.
   335. Nor did they not, i.e., they did.
   338 ff. As when the potent rod, etc. Cf. Exod. 10:12–15. Moses was Amram's son.
   340. pitchy, dark as pitch.

Of locusts, warping on the eastern wind,
That o'er the realm of impious Pharaoh hung
Like night, and darkened all the land of Nile:
So numberless were those bad angels seen
Hovering on wing under the cope of Hell
'Twixt upper, nether, and surrounding fires;
Till, as a signal given, the uplifted spear
Of their great Sultan waving to direct
Their course, in even balance down they light
On the firm brimstone, and fill all the plain;   350
A multitude, like which the populous North
Poured never from her frozen loins, to pass
Rhene or the Danaw, when her barbarous sons
Came like a deluge on the South, and spread
Beneath Gibraltar to the Libyan sands.
Forthwith from every squadron and each band
The heads and leaders thither haste where stood
Their great commander; godlike shapes and forms
Excelling human, Princely Dignities,
And Powers that erst in Heaven sat on thrones;   360
Though of their names in heavenly records now
Be no memorial, blotted out and rased
By their rebellion from the Books of Life.
Nor had they yet among the sons of Eve
Got them new names, till wandering o'er the Earth,
Through God's high sufferance for the trial of Man,
By falsities and lies the greatest part
Of mankind they corrupted to forsake
God their Creator, and the invisible
Glory of him that made them to transform   370
Oft to the image of a brute, adorned
With gay religions full of pomp and gold,
And devils to adore for deities:
Then were they known to men by various names,
And various idols through the heathen world.

*   *   *

341. **warping,** working slowly forward with a bending or swerving motion. The term is primarily nautical.

345. **cope,** vault or canopy.

351. **A multitude,** etc. Milton concentrates in a simile the history of the barbarian invasions of the Roman Empire. Successive inroads were made by the Goths, the Vandals, and the Huns.

353. **Rhene,** the Rhine (from Latin *Rhenus*). **Danaw,** the Danube (from German *Donau*).

355. **Beneath Gibraltar,** i.e., south of Gibraltar. The Vandals crossed from Spain into North Africa.

364 ff. **Nor had they yet,** etc. The idea that the fallen angels become the pagan divinities goes back to early Patristic sources. The identification furnishes Milton with abundant biblical and mythological data regarding the inhabitants of hell.

Meanwhile the wingèd heralds by command
Of sovran power, with awful ceremony
And trumpet's sound, throughout the host proclaim
A solemn council forthwith to be held
At Pandemonium, the high capitol
Of Satan and his peers; their summons called
From every band and squarèd regiment
By place or choice the worthiest; they anon
With hundreds and with thousands trooping came   760
Attended. All access was thronged, the gates
And porches wide, but chief the spacious hall
(Though like a covered field, where champions bold
Wont ride in armed, and at the Soldan's chair
Defied the best of Paynim chivalry
To mortal combat or career with lance)
Thick swarmed, both on the ground and in the air,
Brushed with the hiss of rustling wings. As bees
In spring time, when the sun with Taurus rides,
Pour forth their populous youth about the hive   770
In clusters; they among fresh dews and flowers
Fly to and fro, or on the smoothèd plank,
The suburb of their straw-built citadel,
New rubbed with balm, expatiate and confer
Their state affairs. So thick the airy crowd
Swarmed and were straitened; till the signal given,
Behold a wonder! they but now who seemed
In bigness to surpass Earth's giant sons,
Now less than smallest dwarfs, in narrow room
Throng numberless, like that Pygmean race   780
Beyond the Indian mount, or fairy elves,
Whose midnight revels, by a forest side
Or fountain, some belated peasant sees,
Or dreams he sees, while overhead the Moon
Sits arbitress, and nearer to the Earth
Wheels her pale course; they on their mirth and dance
Intent, with jocund music charm his ear;
At once with joy and fear his heart rebounds.
Thus incorporeal spirits to smallest forms
Reduced their shapes immense, and were at large,   790

753. **awful,** awe-inspiring.

756. **Pandemonium,** the abode of all the demons. The name, which is a Miltonic coinage, may have been suggested by *Pantheon,* the abode of all the gods.

757 ff. **their summons,** etc. The council is in reality a sort of military Parliament.

763–66. The allusion is to the single combats between Pagans and Crusaders described in the Italian romances of chivalry. **Soldan** is a variant of Sultan.

769. **when the Sun with Taurus rides,** i.e., when the sun is in the zodiacal sign of the Bull (between April 19 and May 20).

774. **expatiate and confer,** walk abroad and discuss.   776. **straitened,** crowded.

780 ff. The **Indian mount** is probably Imaus in the Himalayas.

781 ff. Milton is here drawing on the traditions of English fairy poetry.

785. **arbitress,** spectator.   790. **were at large,** had ample room.

Though without number still, amidst the hall
Of that infernal court. But far within,
And in their own dimensions like themselves,
The great Seraphic Lords and Cherubim
In close recess and secret conclave sat,
A thousand demi-gods on golden seats,
Frequent and full. After short silence then
And summons read, the great consult began.

from BOOK II

THE ARGUMENT

The consultation begun, Satan debates whether another battle is to be hazarded
for the recovery of Heaven: some advise it, others dissuade. A third proposal is
preferred, mentioned before by Satan, to search the truth of that prophecy or
tradition in Heaven concerning another world, and another kind of creature,
equal, or not much inferior, to themselves, about this time to be created. Their
doubt who shall be sent on this difficult search; Satan, their chief, undertakes
alone the voyage; is honoured and applauded. The council thus ended, the rest
betake them several ways and to several employments, as their inclinations lead
them, to entertain the time till Satan return. He passes on his journey to Hell
gates, finds them shut, and who sat there to guard them; by whom at length they
are opened, and discover to him the great gulf between Hell and Heaven; with
what difficulty he passes through, directed by Chaos, the Power of that place, to
the sight of this new world which he sought.

High on a throne of royal state, which far
Outshone the wealth of Ormus and of Ind,
Or where the gorgeous East with richest hand
Showers on her kings barbaric pearl and gold,
Satan exalted sat, by merit raised
To that bad eminence; and from despair
Thus high uplifted beyond hope, aspires
Beyond thus high, insatiate to pursue
Vain war with Heaven, and by success untaught,
His proud imaginations thus displayed.   10
   "Powers and Dominions, Deities of Heaven,
For since no deep within her gulf can hold
Immortal vigor, though oppressed and fallen,
I give not Heaven for lost. From this descent
Celestial Virtues rising, will appear

---

793. like themselves, i.e., in their own shapes.   **795. recess,** retirement.
797. frequent, crowded.
   2. Ormus, a city on the Persian Gulf, famous as a market for precious stones. It is often
mentioned by Renaissance travelers. **Ind,** India.
   4. barbaric pearl and gold. The sprinkling of powdered pearls and gold dust on a monarch at his coronation was an Oriental custom.
   9. success, i.e., ill-success, the outcome of his former attempt.

More glorious and more dread than from no fall,
And trust themselves to fear no second fate.
Me though just right, and the fixed laws of Heaven
Did first create your leader, next, free choice,
With what besides, in counsel or in fight, 20
Hath been achieved of merit, yet this loss
Thus far at least recovered, hath much more
Established in a safe unenvied throne
Yielded with full consent. The happier state
In Heaven, which follows dignity, might draw
Envy from each inferior; but who here
Will envy whom the highest place exposes
Foremost to stand against the Thunderer's aim
Your bulwark, and condemns to greatest share
Of endless pain? Where there is then no good 30
For which to strive, no strife can grow up there
From faction; for none sure will claim in Hell
Precedence, none whose portion is so small
Of present pain, that with ambitious mind
Will covet more. With this advantage then
To union, and firm faith, and firm accord,
More than can be in Heaven, we now return
To claim our just inheritance of old,
Surer to prosper than prosperity
Could have assured us; and by what best way, 40
Whether of open war or covert guile,
We now debate; who can advise, may speak."
 He ceased, and next him Moloch, sceptred king,
Stood up, the strongest and the fiercest spirit
That fought in Heaven; now fiercer by despair.
His trust was with the Eternal to be deemed
Equal in strength, and rather than be less
Cared not to be at all; with that care lost
Went all his fear: of God, or Hell, or worse
He recked not, and these words thereafter spake. 50
 "My sentence is for open war. Of wiles,
More unexpert, I boast not; them let those
Contrive who need, or when they need, not now.
For while they sit contriving, shall the rest,
Millions that stand in arms, and longing wait
The signal to ascend, sit lingering here
Heaven's fugitives, and for their dwelling-place
Accept this dark opprobrious den of shame,

17. trust themselves, etc., i.e., their experience has given them such confidence that they will not fear to fall again.
24 ff. Satan, like Belial (112 ff.), knows how to "make the worse appear the better reason."
50. thereafter spake, spoke accordingly.
51. sentence, judgment, opinion (Latin *sententia*). Moloch is the type of blunt warrior who knows no other method of winning an object than to fight for it. Milton must have known such among the leaders of the Commonwealth.

The prison of his tyranny who reigns
By our delay? No, let us rather choose,   60
Armed with Hell flames and fury, all at once
O'er Heaven's high towers to force resistless way,
Turning our tortures into horrid arms
Against the Torturer; when to meet the noise
Of his almighty engine he shall hear
Infernal thunder, and for lightning see
Black fire and horror shot with equal rage
Among his angels, and his throne itself
Mixed with Tartarean sulphur and strange fire,
His own invented torments. But perhaps   70
The way seems difficult and steep to scale
With upright wing against a higher foe.
Let such bethink them, if the sleepy drench
Of that forgetful lake benumb not still,
That in our proper motion we ascend
Up to our native seat; descent and fall
To us is adverse. Who but felt of late
When the fierce foe hung on our broken rear
Insulting, and pursued us through the deep,
With what compulsion and laborious flight   80
We sunk thus low? The ascent is easy then;
The event is feared; should we again provoke
Our stronger, some worse way his wrath may find
To our destruction; if there be in Hell
Fear to be worse destroyed; what can be worse
Than to dwell here, driven out from bliss, condemned
In this abhorrèd deep to utter woe;
Where pain of unextinguishable fire
Must exercise us without hope of end
The vassals of his anger, when the scourge   90
Inexorably, and the torturing hour
Calls us to penance? More destroyed than thus
We should be quite abolished and expire.
What fear we then? what doubt we to incense
His utmost ire? which to the height enraged,
Will either quite consume us, and reduce
To nothing this essential, happier far
Than miserable to have eternal being;

    63. tortures, i.e., the flames which torture.
    65. engine, instrument—referring to the thunderbolt.
    69. Tartarean, infernal (from Tartarus, a classical name for hell).
    73. such, i.e., those who reason thus. **sleepy drench,** sleep-producing drink. The word
drench suggests contempt.
    74. forgetful, causing forgetfulness. Cf. I, 266 and note.
    75–77. The natural (**proper**) motion of Spirits, as of fire, is upward. For them to fall is
therefore unnatural (**adverse**).
    79. Insulting. The original Latin meaning (*insultans,* leaping upon) is implied.
    82. event, outcome.   **89. exercise,** torment.
    94. what doubt we, i.e., why do we hesitate.   **97. essential,** essence, spiritual being.

Or if our substance be indeed divine,
And cannot cease to be, we are at worst   100
On this side nothing; and by proof we feel
Our power sufficient to disturb his Heaven,
And with perpetual inroads to alarm,
Though inaccessible, his fatal throne;
Which if not victory is yet revenge."
He ended frowning, and his look denounced
Desperate revenge, and battle dangerous
To less than gods. On the other side up rose
Belial, in act more graceful and humane;
A fairer person lost not Heaven; he seemed   110
For dignity composed and high exploit;
But all was false and hollow; though his tongue
Dropped manna, and could make the worse appear
The better reason, to perplex and dash
Maturest counsels: for his thoughts were low;
To vice industrious, but to nobler deeds
Timorous and slothful: yet he pleased the ear,
And with persuasive accent thus began.
    "I should be much for open war, O Peers,
As not behind in hate, if what was urged   120
Main reason to persuade immediate war,
Did not dissuade me most, and seem to cast
Ominous conjecture on the whole success:
When he who most excels in fact of arms,
In what he counsels and in what excels
Mistrustful, grounds his courage on despair
And utter dissolution, as the scope
Of all his aim, after some dire revenge.
First, what revenge? The towers of Heaven are filled
With arméd watch, that render all access   130
Impregnable; oft on the bordering deep
Encamp their legions, or with óbscure wing
Scout far and wide into the realm of Night,
Scorning surprise. Or could we break our way
By force, and at our heels all Hell should rise
With blackest insurrection, to confound
Heaven's purest light, yet our great enemy
All incorruptible would on his throne
Sit unpolluted, and the ethereal mould

---

104. fatal, upheld by fate. Admitting that the throne is so upheld, Moloch is forced to grant its inaccessibility.
   106. denounced, proclaimed.   **109. act,** bearing.
   113. manna. Cf. Exod. 16:31: "the taste of it was like wafers made with honey."
   119 ff. Cf. with the abrupt beginning of Moloch's speech the insinuating oratory of Belial. Like a skilled debater, he turns his opponent's own argument against him.
   124. fact of arms, feat of arms (Latin *factum*, deed).
   136. blackest insurrection. Cf. 65–70. Belial answers Moloch point by point.
   139. mould, substance.

Incapable of stain would soon expel   140
Her mischief, and purge off the baser fire,
Victorious. Thus repulsed, our final hope
Is flat despair; we must exasperate
The almighty victor to spend all his rage,
And that must end us, that must be our cure,
To be no more; sad cure; for who would lose,
Though full of pain, this intellectual being,
Those thoughts that wander through eternity,
To perish rather, swallowed up and lost
In the wide womb of uncreated Night,   150
Devoid of sense and motion? And who knows,
Let this be good, whether our angry foe
Can give it, or will ever? How he can
Is doubtful; that he never will is sure.
Will he, so wise, let loose at once his ire,
Belike through impotence, or unaware,
To give his enemies their wish, and end
Them in his anger, whom his anger saves
To punish endless? 'Wherefore cease we then?'
Say they who counsel war; 'we are decreed,   160
Reserved, and destined to eternal woe;
Whatever doing, what can we suffer more,
What can we suffer worse?' Is this then worst,
Thus sitting, thus consulting, thus in arms?
What when we fled amain, pursued and struck
With Heaven's afflicting thunder, and besought
The Deep to shelter us? this Hell then seemed
A refuge from those wounds. Or when we lay
Chained on the burning lake? that sure was worse.
What if the breath that kindled those grim fires   170
Awaked should blow them into sevenfold rage
And plunge us in the flames? or from above
Should intermitted vengeance arm again
His red right hand to plague us? What if all
Her stores were opened, and this firmament
Of Hell should spout her cataracts of fire,
Impendent horrors, threatening hideous fall
One day upon our heads; while we perhaps
Designing or exhorting glorious war,
Caught in a fiery tempest shall be hurled   180
Each on his rock transfixed, the sport and prey
Of racking whirlwinds, or for ever sunk
Under yon boiling ocean, wrapped in chains;

141. **Her mischief,** i.e., the damage or pollution caused by hell-fire.
152. **Let this be good,** i.e., granting that this (annihilation) is desirable.
156. **Belike,** no doubt. As frequently in Shakespeare, the word implies irony. **impotence,**
lack of self-control.
165. **What when,** i.e., how was it when. **amain,** with all haste, precipitately.
177. **Impendent,** overhanging.   182. **racking,** twisting, torturing.

There to converse with everlasting groans,
Unrespited, unpitied, unreprieved,
Ages of hopeless end; this would be worse.
War therefore, open or concealed, alike
My voice dissuades; for what can force or guile
With him, or who deceive his mind, whose eye
Views all things at one view? He from Heaven's height   190
All these our motions vain, sees and derides;
Not more almighty to resist our might
Than wise to frustrate all our plots and wiles.
Shall we then live thus vile, the race of Heaven
Thus trampled, thus expelled to suffer here
Chains and these torments? Better these than worse,
By my advice; since fate inevitable
Subdues us, and omnipotent decree,
The victor's will. To suffer, as to do,
Our strength is equal, nor the law unjust   200
That so ordains: this was at first resolved,
If we were wise, against so great a foe
Contending, and so doubtful what might fall.
I laugh when those who at the spear are bold
And venturous, if that fail them, shrink and fear
What yet they know must follow, to endure
Exile, or ignominy, or bonds, or pain,
The sentence of their conqueror: this is now
Our doom; which if we can sustain and bear,
Our súpreme foe in time may much remit   210
His anger, and perhaps, thus far removed,
Not mind us not offending, satisfied
With what is punished; whence these raging fires
Will slacken, if his breath stir not their flames.
Our purer essence then will overcome
Their noxious vapor, or inured not feel,
Or changed at length, and to the place conformed
In temper and in nature, will receive
Familiar the fierce heat, and void of pain;
This horror will grow mild, this darkness light,   220
Besides what hope the never-ending flight
Of future days may bring, what chance, what change
Worth waiting, since our present lot appears
For happy though but ill, for ill not worst,
If we procure not to ourselves more woe."

185. Note how the repetition of the prefix intensifies the effect of utter hopelessness.
186. **of hopeless end,** without hope of end.   191. **motions,** proposals, plots.
213. **With what is punished,** i.e., with the punishment already inflicted.
219. **Familiar the fierce heat,** etc., i.e., the fierce heat, by becoming familiar, will be no longer painful. The considerations which move Belial are in complete accordance with his character and philosophy.
224. **For happy,** etc., i.e., viewed as a happy situation the present one is bad, but it is not so bad as it might be.

    Thus Belial with words clothed in reason's garb,
Counselled ignoble ease, and peaceful sloth,
Not peace; and after him thus Mammon spake.
    "Either to disenthrone the King of Heaven
We war, if war be best, or to regain   230
Our own right lost. Him to unthrone we then
May hope, when everlasting Fate shall yield
To fickle Chance, and Chaos judge the strife:
The former, vain to hope, argues as vain
The latter; for what place can be for us
Within Heaven's bound, unless Heaven's Lord supreme
We overpower? Suppose he should relent
And publish grace to all, on promise made
Of new subjection; with what eyes could we
Stand in his presence humble, and receive   240
Strict laws imposed, to celebrate his throne
With warbled hymns, and to his Godhead sing
Forced halleluiahs; while he lordly sits
Our envied Sovran, and his altar breathes
Ambrosial odors and ambrosial flowers,
Our servile offerings. This must be our task
In Heaven, this our delight; how wearisome
Eternity so spent in worship paid
To whom we hate. Let us not then pursue,
By force impossible, by leave obtained   250
Unacceptable, though in Heaven, our state
Of splendid vassalage, but rather seek
Our own good from ourselves, and from our own
Live to ourselves, though in this vast recess,
Free, and to none accountable, preferring
Hard liberty before the easy yoke
Of servile pomp. Our greatness will appear
Then most conspicuous, when great things of small,
Useful of hurtful, prosperous of adverse
We can create, and in what place soe'er   260
Thrive under evil, and work ease out of pain
Through labor and endurance. This deep world
Of darkness do we dread? How oft amidst
Thick clouds and dark doth Heaven's all-ruling Sire
Choose to reside, his glory unobscured,
And with the majesty of darkness round
Covers his throne; from whence deep thunders roar,
Mustering their rage, and Heaven resembles Hell!
As he our darkness, cannot we his light
Imitate when we please? This desert soil   270
Wants not her hidden luster, gems and gold;
Nor want we skill or art, from whence to raise

---

234. argues, proves.   **249. pursue,** seek to regain.
271. Wants not, is not without.

Magnificence; and what can Heaven show more?
Our torments also may in length of time
Become our elements, these piercing fires
As soft as now severe, our temper changed
Into their temper; which must needs remove
The sensible of pain. All things invite
To peaceful counsels, and the settled state
Of order, how in safety best we may   280
Compose our present evils, with regard
Of what we are and where, dismissing quite
All thoughts of war: ye have what I advise."
    He scarce had finished, when such murmur filled
The assembly, as when hollow rocks retain
The sound of blustering winds, which all night long
Had roused the sea, now with hoarse cadence lull
Seafaring men o'erwatched, whose bark by chance
Or pinnace anchors in a craggy bay
After the tempest: such applause was heard   290
As Mammon ended, and his sentence pleased,
Advising peace; for such another field
They dreaded worse than Hell: so much the fear
Of thunder and the sword of Michaël
Wrought still within them; and no less desire
To found this nether empire, which might rise
By policy and long process of time,
In emulation opposite to Heaven.
Which when Beëlzebub perceived, than whom,
Satan except, none higher sat, with grave   300
Aspéct he rose, and in his rising seemed
A pillar of state; deep on his front engraven
Deliberation sat and public care;
And princely counsel in his face yet shone,
Majestic though in ruin: sage he stood,
With Atlantean shoulders fit to bear
The weight of mightiest monarchies; his look
Drew audience and attention still as night
Or summer's noontide air, while thus he spake.
    "Thrones and imperial Powers, Offspring of Heaven,   310

---

278. sensible, sense. The use of an adjective for a noun is a Latinism which Milton frequently adopts.
    281. Compose, adjust.
    290 ff. such applause, etc. Mammon's proposal is an improvement on Belial's in that it supplies an activity consistent with the abandonment of a futile renewal of the attempt on Heaven. But the desire for revenge expressed by Moloch and felt by all the demons remains to be satisfied.
    299. Beëlzebub. Cf. I, 79–81 and note. In the Old Testament the name is applied to the sun-god of the Philistines.
    302. front, forehead.
    306. Atlantean shoulders, shoulders like those of Atlas, who in Greek mythology supported the heavens.

Ethereal Virtues; or these titles now
Must we renounce, and changing style, be called
Princes of Hell? for so the popular vote
Inclines, here to continue, and build up here
A growing empire; doubtless; while we dream,
And know not that the King of Heaven hath doomed
This place our dungeon, not our safe retreat
Beyond his potent arm, to live exempt
From Heaven's high jurisdiction, in new league
Banded against his throne, but to remain   320
In strictest bondage, though thus far removed,
Under the inevitable curb, reserved
His captive multitude. For he, be sure,
In height or depth, still first and last will reign
Sole king, and of his kingdom lose no part
By our revolt, but over Hell extend
His empire, and with iron scepter rule
Us here, as with his golden those in Heaven.
What sit we then projecting peace and war?
War hath determined us, and foiled with loss   330
Irreparable; terms of peace yet none
Vouchsafed or sought; for what peace will be given
To us enslaved, but custody severe,
And stripes, and arbitrary punishment
Inflicted? and what peace can we return,
But to our power hostility and hate,
Untamed reluctance, and revenge though slow,
Yet ever plotting how the conqueror least
May reap his conquest, and may least rejoice
In doing what we must in suffering feel?   340
Nor will occasion want, nor shall we need
With dangerous expedition to invade
Heaven, whose high walls fear no assault or siege
Or ambush from the Deep. What if we find
Some easier enterprise? There is a place
(If ancient and prophetic fame in Heaven
Err not), another world, the happy seat
Of some new race called Man, about this time
To be created like to us, though less
In power and excellence, but favored more   350
Of him who rules above; so was his will
Pronounced among the gods, and by an oath,
That shook Heaven's whole circumference, confirmed.

---

313. the popular vote, i.e., the state of opinion indicated by the applause given Mammon.
315. doubtless. The word is used sarcastically.
330. determined us, ended us or perhaps determined our future.
336. to our power, up to the limits of our power.
337. Untamed reluctance, untamable resistance.   **346. fame,** rumor.

Thither let us bend all our thoughts, to learn
What creatures there inhabit, of what mould
Or substance, how endued, and what their power,
And where their weakness, how attempted best,
By force or subtlety. Though Heaven be shut,
And Heaven's high Arbitrator sit secure
In his own strength, this place may lie exposed,   360
The utmost border of his kingdom, left
To their defence who hold it; here perhaps
Some advantageous act may be achieved
By sudden onset, either with Hell fire
To waste his whole creation, or possess
All as our own, and drive as we were driven,
The puny habitants; or if not drive,
Seduce them to our party, that their God
May prove their foe, and with repenting hand
Abolish his own works. This would surpass   370
Common revenge, and interrupt his joy
In our confusion, and our joy upraise
In his disturbance; when his darling sons
Hurled headlong to partake with us, shall curse
Their frail original, and faded bliss,
Faded so soon. Advise if this be worth
Attempting, or to sit in darkness here
Hatching vain empires." Thus Beëlzebub
Pleaded his devilish counsel, first devised
By Satan, and in part proposed; for whence,   380
But from the author of all ill, could spring
So deep a malice, to confound the race
Of Mankind in one root, and Earth with Hell
To mingle and involve, done all to spite
The great Creator? But their spite still serves
His glory to augment. The bold design
Pleased highly those infernal States, and joy
Sparkled in all their eyes; with full assent
They vote: whereat his speech he thus renews.
    "Well have ye judged, well ended long debate,   390
Synod of gods, and like to what ye are,
Great things resolved; which from the lowest deep
Will once more lift us up, in spite of Fate,

---

354. Thither let us, etc. Beëlzebub's proposal does not exclude Mammon's, which had itself appropriated Belial's; but it goes beyond both in supplying a rational project of revenge. The whole movement of the discussion has been constructively forward toward the formation of a policy satisfactory to all, and Beëlzebub, who is Satan's mouthpiece, has been simply waiting the opportune moment to introduce Satan's own scheme. His intelligence is far more comprehensive than that of the preceding speakers. It is easy to believe that Milton had been present at deliberations of the Council of State, and that he had noted with care the play of mind in them.
    356. endued, equipped.   **375. original,** originator, i.e., Adam.
    380. in part proposed, i.e., in an earlier speech, I, 645 ff.
    382. confound, destroy completely.   **387. States,** princes or representatives.

Nearer our ancient seat; perhaps in view
Of those bright confines, whence with neighboring arms
And opportune excursion we may chance
Re-enter Heaven; or else in some mild zone
Dwell not unvisited of Heaven's fair light
Secure, and at the brightening orient beam
Purge off this gloom; the soft delicious air,   400
To heal the scar of these corrosive fires
Shall breathe her balm. But first whom shall we send
In search of this new world? whom shall we find
Sufficient? who shall tempt with wandering feet
The dark unbottomed infinite Abyss
And through the palpable obscure find out
His uncouth way, or spread his airy flight
Upborne with indefatigable wings
Over the vast abrupt, ere he arrive
The happy isle; what strength, what art can then   410
Suffice, or what evasion bear him safe
Through the strict senteries and stations thick
Of angels watching round? Here he had need
All circumspection, and we now no less
Choice in our suffrage; for on whom we send,
The weight of all and our last hope relies."
    This said, he sat; and expectation held
His look suspense, awaiting who appeared
To second, or oppose, or undertake
The perilous attempt; but all sat mute,   420
Pondering the danger with deep thoughts; and each
In other's countenance read his own dismay
Astonished; none among the choice and prime
Of those Heaven-warring champions could be found
So hardy as to proffer or accept
Alone the dreadful voyage; till at last
Satan, whom now transcendent glory raised
Above his fellows, with monarchal pride
Conscious of highest worth, unmoved thus spake.
    "O Progeny of Heaven, empyreal Thrones,   430
With reason hath deep silence and demur
Seized us, though undismayed. Long is the way
And hard, that out of Hell leads up to light;
Our prison strong, this huge convex of fire,
Outrageous to devour, immures us round
Ninefold, and gates of burning adamant
Barred over us prohibit all egress.

----

404. tempt, attempt, try.   **406. palpable obscure,** tangible darkness.
407. uncouth, unknown, strange.
409. the vast abrupt, the region of Chaos, which is a gulf or breach (Lat. *abruptum*), an
emptiness.
412. stations, outposts, guards.   **415. Choice in our suffrage,** care in our selection.
418. suspense, suspended.   **431. demur,** hesitation.

These passed, if any pass, the void profound
Of unessential Night receives him next
Wide gaping, and with utter loss of being   440
Threatens him, plunged in that abortive gulf.
If thence he scape into whatever world,
Or unknown region, what remains him less
Than unknown dangers and as hard escape.
But I should ill become this throne, O Peers,
And this imperial sovranty, adorned
With splendor, armed with power, if aught proposed
And judged of public moment, in the shape
Of difficulty or danger, could deter
Me from attempting. Wherefore do I assume   450
These royalties, and not refuse to reign,
Refusing to accept as great a share
Of hazard as of honor, due alike
To him who reigns, and so much to him due
Of hazard more, as he above the rest
High honored sits? Go therefore mighty Powers,
Terror of Heaven, though fallen; intend at home,
While here shall be our home, what best may ease
The present misery, and render Hell
More tolerable; if there be cure or charm   460
To respite or deceive, or slack the pain
Of this ill mansion; intermit no watch
Against a wakeful foe, while I abroad
Through all the coasts of dark destruction seek
Deliverance for us all: this enterprise
None shall partake with me." Thus saying rose
The Monarch, and prevented all reply;
Prudent, lest from his resolution raised
Others among the chief might offer now
(Certain to be refused) what erst they feared;   470
And so refused might in opinion stand
His rivals, winning cheap the high repute
Which he through hazard huge must earn. But they
Dreaded not more the adventure than his voice
Forbidding; and at once with him they rose;
Their rising all at once was as the sound
Of thunder heard remote. Towards him they bend
With awful reverence prone; and as a god

---

439. unessential, having no real being. Night and Chaos are thought of by Milton as merely negative, not really created.

441. abortive, prematurely brought forth and therefore unformed.

445 ff. But I should ill, etc. Satan's offer is parallel to that of Christ in III, 217 ff.

450. Me. Note the emphasis given by the meter.   **457. intend,** plan, consider.

461. deceive, beguile.

467. prevented, anticipated (a good example of the transition from the older, literal meaning of the word to the modern).

468. from his resolution raised, encouraged by his bravery.

477–79. This deification of Satan is a precedent for the idolatries of men.

Extol him equal to the Highest in Heaven.
Nor failed they to express how much they praised,   480
That for the general safety he despised
His own: for neither do the spirits damned
Lose all their virtue; lest bad men should boast
Their specious deeds on Earth, which glory excites,
Or close ambition varnished o'er with zeal.
   Thus they their doubtful consultations dark
Ended rejoicing in their matchless chief:
As when from mountain tops the dusky clouds
Ascending, while the North wind sleeps, o'erspread
Heaven's cheerful face, the louring element   490
Scowls o'er the darkened landscape snow or shower;
If chance the radiant sun with farewell sweet
Extend his evening beam, the fields revive,
The birds their notes renew, and bleating herds
Attest their joy, that hill and valley rings.
O shame to men! Devil with devil damned
Firm concord holds, men only disagree
Of creatures rational, though under hope
Of heavenly grace; and God proclaiming peace,
Yet live in hatred, enmity, and strife   500
Among themselves, and levy cruel wars,
Wasting the Earth, each other to destroy:
As if (which might induce us to accord)
Man had not hellish foes enow besides,
That day and night for his destruction wait!

*   *   *

from BOOK III

THE ARGUMENT

*God, sitting on his throne, sees Satan flying towards this World, then newly
created; shows him to the Son, who sat at his right hand; foretells the success of
Satan in perverting mankind; clears his own justice and wisdom from all imputation, having created Man free and able enough to have withstood his tempter;
yet declares his purpose of grace towards him, in regard he fell not of his own
malice, as did Satan, but by him seduced. The Son of God renders praises to his*

    483. virtue, merit—but not moral goodness, for that, Milton would hold, is inconsistent
with disobedience to God.
    484. specious deeds, deeds which, though having all the appearance of being public-
spirited and self-sacrificing, are really the fruit of personal ambition masquerading as zeal for
the common good. Under Milton's theory the demons can furnish a precedent for all that is
great and magnanimous in men except the one essential of a righteous will. He never forgets
that Satan and the rest are angels fallen.
    490. element, sky.   **492. If chance,** if it chances that.

Father for the manifestation of his gracious purpose towards Man; but God again declares that grace cannot be extended towards Man without the satisfaction of Divine Justice: Man hath offended the majesty of God by aspiring to Godhead, and therefore, with all his progeny, devoted to death, must die, unless some one can be found sufficient to answer for his offence, and undergo his punishment. The Son of God freely offers himself a ransom for Man: the Father accepts him, ordains his incarnation, pronounces his exaltation above all names in Heaven and Earth; commands all the angels to adore him: they obey, and hymning to their harps in full choir, celebrate the Father and the Son. Meanwhile Satan alights upon the bare convex of this World's outermost orb; where wandering he first finds a place since called the Limbo of Vanity; what persons and things fly up thither; thence comes to the gate of Heaven, described ascending by stairs, and the waters above the firmament that flow about it. His passage thence to the orb of the sun: he finds there Uriel, the regent of that orb, but first changes himself into the shape of a meaner angel, and pretending a zealous desire to behold the new creation, and Man whom God had placed here, inquires of him the place of his habitation, and is directed; alights first on Mount Niphates.

Hail holy Light, offspring of Heaven first-born,
Or of the Eternal coeternal beam
May I express thee unblamed? since God is light,
And never but in unapproachëd light,
Dwelt from eternity, dwelt then in thee,
Bright effluence of bright essence increate.
Or hear'st thou rather pure ethereal stream,
Whose fountain who shall tell? Before the sun,
Before the Heavens thou wert, and at the voice
Of God, as with a mantle didst invest   10
The rising world of waters dark and deep,
Won from the void and formless infinite.
Thee I revisit now with bolder wing,
Escaped the Stygian pool, though long detained
In that obscure sojourn, while in my flight
Through utter and through middle darkness borne
With other notes than to the Orphean lyre
I sung of Chaos and eternal Night,
Taught by the heavenly Muse to venture down
The dark descent, and up to re-ascend,   20
Though hard and rare: thee I revisit safe,
And feel thy sovran vital lamp; but thou
Revisit'st not these eyes, that roll in vain
To find thy piercing ray, and find no dawn;

2–3. May I, without blame, call thee coeternal with God?

6. Light is God's essence and as such is uncreated; but it is also what flows from him (effluence) and was the first created thing.

7–8. **Or hear'st.** Milton now says that the relation of the effluence to the essence is a mystery.

16. **utter,** outer, i.e., Hell.

17. **Orphean lyre.** There was an Orphic hymn to night. Milton means that his poem is of higher inspiration, being based on Scripture.

So thick a drop serene hath quenched their orbs,
Or dim suffusion veiled. Yet not the more
Cease I to wander where the Muses haunt
Clear spring, or shady grove, or sunny hill,
Smit with the love of sacred song; but chief
Thee Sion, and the flowery brooks beneath   30
That wash thy hallowed feet, and warbling flow,
Nightly I visit; nor sometimes forget
Those other two equalled with me in fate,
So were I equalled with them in renown,
Blind Thamyris and blind Mæonides,
And Tiresias and Phineus prophets old:
Then feed on thoughts, that voluntary move
Harmonious numbers; as the wakeful bird
Sings darkling, and in shadiest covert hid
Tunes her nocturnal note. Thus with the year   40
Seasons return; but not to me returns
Day, or the sweet approach of even or morn,
Or sight of vernal bloom, or summer's rose,
Or flocks, or herds, or human face divine;
But cloud instead, and ever-during dark
Surrounds me, from the cheerful ways of men
Cut off, and for the book of knowledge fair
Presented with a universal blank
Of Nature's works to me expunged and razed,
And wisdom at one entrance quite shut out.   50
So much the rather thou celestial Light
Shine inward, and the mind through all her powers
Irradiate, there plant eyes, all mist from thence
Purge and disperse, that I may see and tell
Of things invisible to mortal sight.
    Now had the Almighty Father from above,
From the pure Empyrean where he sits
High throned above all height, bent down his eye,
His own works and their works at once to view.
About him all the sanctities of Heaven   60
Stood thick as stars, and from his sight received
Beatitude past utterance; on his right
The radiant image of his glory sat,
His only Son; on Earth he first beheld
Our two first parents, yet the only two
Of mankind, in the happy garden placed,
Reaping immortal fruits of joy and love,
Uninterrupted joy, unrivalled love

---

25. **drop serene,** a translation of the medical term *gutta serena,* used of blindness in which
the eye is not clouded. The "clear drop" is a humor which blocks the optic nerve.
26. **dim suffusion,** cataract.
29. **sacred song,** poetry, which is divine as coming from the muses.
30. To visit the brooks by Sion is to read Scripture.   35. **Mæonides,** Homer.

In blissful solitude. He then surveyed
Hell and the gulf between, and Satan there   70
Coasting the wall of Heaven on this side Night
In the dun air sublime, and ready now
To stoop with wearied wings and willing feet
On the bare outside of this World, that seemed
Firm land imbosomed without firmament,
Uncertain which, in ocean or in air.
Him God beholding from his prospect high,
Wherein past, present, future he beholds,
Thus to his only Son foreseeing spake.
　"Only begotten Son, seest thou what rage   80
Transports our Adversary, whom no bounds
Prescribed, no bars of Hell, nor all the chains
Heaped on him there, nor yet the main Abyss
Wide interrupt can hold; so bent he seems
On desperate revenge, that shall redound
Upon his own rebellious head. And now
Through all restraint broke loose he wings his way
Not far off Heaven, in the precincts of light,
Directly towards the new-created World,
And Man there placed, with purpose to assay   90
If him by force he can destroy, or worse,
By some false guile pervert; and shall pervert;
For Man will hearken to his glozing lies,
And easily transgress the sole command,
Sole pledge of his obedience; so will fall
He and his faithless progeny. Whose fault?
Whose but his own? Ingrate, he had of me
All he could have; I made him just and right,
Sufficient to have stood, though free to fall.
Such I created all the Ethereal Powers   100
And spirits, both them who stood and them who failed;
Freely they stood who stood, and fell who fell.
Not free, what proof could they have given sincere
Of true allegiance, constant faith, or love,
Where only what they needs must do, appeared,
Not what they would? what praise could they receive?
What pleasure I from such obedience paid,
When will and reason (reason also is choice)

　72. sublime, elevated.
　74–76. Satan is ready to light on the *primum mobile*, the outer shell of the created universe, not on the earth itself. The substance of this shell is indeterminate. The "firmament" is the visible sky, which separates the waters above from the waters beneath the earth. The shell is "without," i.e., outside of this firmament, or perhaps rather not composed of it, as the other spheres must be. The "waters above" constitute the crystalline sphere, inside the *primum mobile*, but also make a sea on top of it. Milton is not only adjusting the biblical account of creation to the Ptolemaic idea of the spheres but making the conception philosophic as well. The *primum mobile* is a link between God and his universe.
　76. Uncertain which, it being uncertain whether the shell hung in water or in air. Milton suggests that the business about the firmament and the waters is obscure, as indeed it is.

Useless and vain, of freedom both despoiled,
Made passive both, had served necessity,   110
Not me. They therefore as to right belonged,
So were created, nor can justly accuse
Their Maker, or their making, or their fate,
As if predestination overruled
Their will, disposed by absolute decree
Or high foreknowledge; they themselves decreed
Their own revolt, not I. If I foreknew,
Foreknowledge had no influence on their fault,
Which had no less proved certain unforeknown.
So without least impulse or shadow of fate,   120
Or aught by me immutably foreseen,
They trespass, authors to themselves in all,
Both what they judge and what they choose; for so
I formed them free, and free they must remain,
Till they enthrall themselves: I else must change
Their nature, and revoke the high decree
Unchangeable, eternal, which ordained
Their freedom; they themselves ordained their fall.
The first sort by their own suggestion fell,
Self-tempted, self-depraved; Man falls, deceived   130
By the other first; Man therefore shall find grace,
The other none. In mercy and justice both,
Through Heaven and Earth, so shall my glory excel,
But mercy first and last shall brightest shine."
   Thus while God spake, ambrosial fragrance filled
All Heaven, and in the blessed spirits elect
Sense of new joy ineffable diffused.
Beyond compare the Son of God was seen
Most glorious; in him all his Father shone
Substantially expressed; and in his face   140
Divine compassion visibly appeared,
Love without end, and without measure grace,
Which uttering thus he to his Father spake.
   "O Father, gracious was that word which closed
Thy sovran sentence, that Man should find grace;
For which both Heaven and Earth shall high extol
Thy praises with the innumerable sound
Of hymns and sacred songs, wherewith thy throne
Encompassed shall resound thee ever blest.
For should Man finally be lost, should Man   150
Thy creature late so loved, thy youngest son
Fall circumvented thus by fraud, though joined
With his own folly? that be from thee far,
That far be from thee, Father, who art judge

---

114 ff. Predestination, in Milton's theology, was a conditional decree of God, not an absolute one, as in strict Calvinism. Milton is not the first or the last thinker to maintain the paradox that God foresees but not immutably.

Of all things made, and judgest only right.
Or shall the Adversary thus obtain
His end, and frustrate thine, shall he fulfil
His malice, and thy goodness bring to nought,
Or proud return though to his heavier doom,
Yet with revenge accomplished, and to Hell   160
Draw after him the whole race of mankind,
By him corrupted? or wilt thou thyself
Abolish thy creation, and unmake,
For him, what for thy glory thou hast made?
So should thy goodness and thy greatness both
Be questioned and blasphemed without defence."
   To whom the great Creator thus replied.
"O Son, in whom my soul hath chief delight,
Son of my bosom, Son who art alone
My word, my wisdom, and effectual might,   170
All hast thou spoken as my thoughts are, all
As my eternal purpose hath decreed:
Man shall not quite be lost, but saved who will,
Yet not of will in him, but grace in me
Freely vouchsafed; once more I will renew
His lapsëd powers, though forfeit and enthralled
By sin to foul exorbitant desires;
Upheld by me, yet once more he shall stand
On even ground against his mortal foe,
By me upheld, that he may know how frail   180
His fallen condition is, and to me owe
All his deliverance, and to none but me.
Some I have chosen of peculiar grace
Elect above the rest; so is my will.
The rest shall hear me call, and oft be warned
Their sinful state, and to appease betimes
The incensëd Deity, while offered grace
Invites; for I will clear their senses dark,
What may suffice, and soften stony hearts
To pray, repent, and bring obedience due.   190
To prayer, repentance, and obedience due,
Though but endeavored with sincere intent,
Mine ear shall not be slow, mine eye not shut.
And I will place within them as a guide
My umpire Conscience, whom if they will hear,
Light after light well used they shall attain,
And to the end persisting, safe arrive.

   175–76. Man's free will, like Satan's, has lapsed with his disobedience. Because his sin came
from an outside suggestion his power to choose good is renewed by an act of Grace, as Satan's
is not.
   184. Elect. In Calvinistic thought the elect include all who are to be saved, in contrast to the
"reprobate," who are predestined before their birth to be damned; with Milton, on the other
hand, the elect are only a special group of saints to whom goodness and salvation come easily.
The rest of mankind are prone to sin but capable of repentance.

This my long sufferance and my day of grace
They who neglect and scorn shall never taste;
But hard be hardened, blind be blinded more,   200
That they may stumble on, and deeper fall;
And none but such from mercy I exclude.
But yet all is not done; Man disobeying,
Disloyal breaks his fealty, and sins
Against the high supremacy of Heaven,
Affecting Godhead, and so losing all,
To expiate his treason hath nought left,
But to destruction sacred and devote,
He with his whole posterity must die;
Die he or justice must; unless for him   210
Some other able, and as willing, pay
The rigid satisfaction, death for death.
Say Heavenly Powers, where shall we find such love?
Which of ye will be mortal to redeem
Man's mortal crime, and just the unjust to save?
Dwells in all Heaven charity so dear?"
    He asked, but all the heavenly choir stood mute,
And silence was in Heaven; on Man's behalf
Patron or intercessor none appeared,
Much less that durst upon his own head draw   220
The deadly forfeiture, and ransom set.
And now without redemption all mankind
Must have been lost, adjudged to Death and Hell
By doom severe, had not the Son of God,
In whom the fulness dwells of love divine,
His dearest mediation thus renewed.
    "Father, thy word is passed, Man shall find grace;
And shall grace not find means, that finds her way,
The speediest of thy wingèd messengers,
To visit all thy creatures, and to all   230
Comes unprevented, unimplored, unsought?
Happy for Man, so coming; he her aid
Can never seek, once dead in sins and lost;
Atonement for himself or offering meet,
Indebted and undone, hath none to bring.
Behold me then, me for him, life for life
I offer; on me let thine anger fall;
Account me Man; I for his sake will leave
Thy bosom, and this glory next to thee
Freely put off, and for him lastly die   240
Well pleased; on me let Death wreak all his rage;
Under his gloomy power I shall not long

    203 ff. God's immutable decree cannot be evaded. If justice is to be satisfied there must be
death for sin. The solution is the sacrifice of Christ, who, like Adam, is the representative of
mankind.
    236 ff. Christ's highly dramatic offer, with its reception, is in studied contrast to Satan's in
Book II, 430 ff.

Lie vanquished; thou hast given me to possess
Life in myself for ever; by thee I live;
Though now to Death I yield, and am his due
All that of me can die, yet that debt paid,
Thou wilt not leave me in the loathsome grave
His prey, nor suffer my unspotted soul
For ever with corruption there to dwell;
But I shall rise victorious, and subdue   250
My vanquisher, spoiled of his vaunted spoil;
Death his death's wound shall then receive, and stoop
Inglorious, of his mortal sting disarmed.
I through the ample air in triumph high
Shall lead Hell captive maugre Hell, and show
The powers of darkness bound. Thou at the sight
Pleased, out of Heaven shalt look down and smile,
While by thee raised I ruin all my foes,
Death last, and with his carcass glut the grave:
Then with the multitude of my redeemed,   260
Shall enter Heaven long absent, and return,
Father, to see thy face, wherein no cloud
Of anger shall remain, but peace assured
And reconcilement; wrath shall be no more
Thenceforth, but in thy presence joy entire."
   His words here ended, but his meek aspéct
Silent yet spake, and breathed immortal love
To mortal men, above which only shone
Filial obedience. As a sacrifice
Glad to be offered, he attends the will   270
Of his great Father. Admiration seized
All Heaven, what this might mean, and whither tend
Wondering; but soon the Almighty thus replied.
   "O thou in Heaven and Earth the only peace
Found out for mankind under wrath, O thou
My sole complacence! well thou know'st how dear
To me are all my works, nor Man the least
Though last created, that for him I spare
Thee from my bosom and right hand, to save,
By losing thee a while, the whole race lost!   280
Thou therefore whom thou only canst redeem,
Their nature also to thy nature join;
And be thyself Man among men on Earth,
Made flesh, when time shall be, of virgin seed,
By wondrous birth; be thou in Adam's room
The head of all mankind, though Adam's son.
As in him perish all men, so in thee
As from a second root shall be restored,
As many as are restored; without thee, none.
His crime makes guilty all his sons; thy merit   290
Imputed shall absolve them who renounce
Their own both righteous and unrighteous deeds,

And live in thee transplanted, and from thee
Receive new life. So Man, as is most just,
Shall satisfy for Man, be judged and die,
And dying rise, and rising with him raise
His brethren, ransomed with his own dear life.
So heavenly love shall outdo hellish hate,
Giving to death, and dying to redeem,
So dearly to redeem what hellish hate   300
So easily destroyed, and still destroys
In those who, when they may, accept not grace. . . ."

*   *   *

from BOOK IV

THE ARGUMENT

Satan, now in prospect of Eden, and nigh the place where he must now attempt the bold enterprise which he undertook alone against God and Man, falls into many doubts with himself, and many passions, fear, envy, and despair; but at length confirms himself in evil, journeys on to Paradise, whose outward prospect and situation is described, overleaps the bounds, sits in the shape of a cormorant on the Tree of Life, as highest in the Garden, to look about him. The Garden described; Satan's first sight of Adam and Eve; his wonder at their excellent form and happy state, but with resolution to work their fall; overhears their discourse; thence gathers that the Tree of Knowledge was forbidden them to eat of under penalty of death, and thereon intends to found his temptation by seducing them to transgress; then leaves them a while, to know further of their state by some other means. Meanwhile Uriel, descending on a sunbeam, warns Gabriel, who had in charge the gate of Paradise, that some evil spirit had escaped the Deep, and passed at noon by his sphere, in the shape of a good angel, down to Paradise; discovered after by his furious gestures in the mount. Gabriel promises to find him ere morning. Night coming on, Adam and Eve discourse of going to their rest: their bower described; their evening worship. Gabriel, drawing forth his bands of night-watch to walk the round of Paradise, appoints two strong angels to Adam's bower, lest the evil spirit should be there doing some harm to Adam or Eve sleeping; there they find him at the ear of Eve, tempting her in a dream, and bring him, though unwilling, to Gabriel; by whom questioned, he scornfully answers, prepares resistance, but hindered by a sign from Heaven, flies out of Paradise.

O for that warning voice, which he who saw
The Apocalypse heard cry in Heaven aloud,
Then when the Dragon, put to second rout,
Came furious down to be revenged on men,
"Woe to the inhabitants on Earth!" that now,
While time was, our first parents had been warned

---

1 ff. This opening passage is based on the vision of St. John recorded in Rev. 12.

The coming of their secret foe, and scaped,
Haply so scaped, his mortal snare; for now
Satan, now first inflamed with rage, came down,
The tempter ere the accuser of mankind,   10
To wreak on innocent frail Man his loss
Of that first battle, and his flight to Hell.
Yet not rejoicing in his speed, though bold,
Far off and fearless, nor with cause to boast,
Begins his dire attempt, which nigh the birth
Now rolling, boils in his tumultuous breast,
And like a devilish engine back recoils
Upon himself; horror and doubt distract
His troubled thoughts, and from the bottom stir
The Hell within him, for within him Hell   20
He brings, and round about him, nor from Hell
One step no more than from himself can fly
By change of place. Now conscience wakes despair
That slumbered, wakes the bitter memory
Of what he was, what is, and what must be
Worse; of worse deeds worse sufferings must ensue.
Sometimes towards Eden which now in his view
Lay pleasant, his grievèd look he fixes sad,
Sometimes towards Heaven and the full-blazing sun,
Which now sat high in his meridian tower.   30
Then much revolving, thus in sighs began.
    "O thou that with surpassing glory crowned,
Look'st from thy sole dominion like the god
Of this new world; at whose sight all the stars
Hide their diminished heads; to thee I call,
But with no friendly voice, and add thy name
O Sun, to tell thee how I hate thy beams
That bring to my remembrance from what state
I fell, how glorious once above thy sphere;
Till pride and worse ambition threw me down   40
Warring in Heaven against Heaven's matchless King.
Ah wherefore! He deserved no such return
From me, whom he created what I was
In that bright eminence, and with his good
Upbraided none; nor was his service hard.
What could be less than to afford him praise,
The easiest recompense, and pay him thanks,

---

10. The tempter ere the accuser. In St. John's vision, Satan, routed from heaven for the second time, comes down to earth as "the accuser of our brethren" (Rev. 12:10). But, as Milton points out, he first came to earth in the role of tempter. The word "devil" is a corruption of the Greek *diabolos*, meaning literally "slanderer" or "accuser."

11. wreak, avenge.   **27.** The literal meaning of **Eden** is "delight."

31. much revolving, pondering many things.

41. Cf. I, 116, 117 and note. The uncompromising egotism of Satan's public utterances now gives way to a secret admission of God's supremacy.

How due! Yet all his good proved ill in me,
And wrought but malice; lifted up so high
I 'sdeined subjection, and thought one step higher　　　　50
Would set me highest, and in a moment quit
The debt immense of endless gratitude,
So burdensome still paying, still to owe;
Forgetful what from him I still received,
And understood not that a grateful mind
By owing owes not, but still pays, at once
Indebted and discharged; what burden then?
Oh had his powerful destiny ordained
Me some inferior angel, I had stood
Then happy; no unbounded hope had raised　　　　60
Ambition. Yet why not? some other Power
As great might have aspired, and me though mean
Drawn to his part; but other Powers as great
Fell not, but stand unshaken, from within
Or from without, to all temptations armed.
Hadst thou the same free will and power to stand?
Thou hadst. Whom hast thou then or what to accuse,
But Heaven's free love dealt equally to all?
Be then his love accurst, since love or hate,
To me alike it deals eternal woe.　　　　70
Nay cursed be thou; since against his thy will
Chose freely what it now so justly rues.
Me miserable! which way shall I fly
Infinite wrath and infinite despair?
Which way I fly is Hell; myself am Hell;
And in the lowest deep a lower deep
Still threatening to devour me opens wide,
To which the Hell I suffer seems a Heaven.
O then at last relent: is there no place
Left for repentance, none for pardon left?　　　　80
None left but by submission; and that word
Disdain forbids me, and my dread of shame
Among the spirits beneath, whom I seduced
With other promises and other vaunts
Than to submit, boasting I could subdue
The Omnipotent. Ay me, they little know
How dearly I abide that boast so vain,
Under what torments inwardly I groan;
While they adore me on the throne of Hell,
With diadem and scepter high advanced　　　　90
The lower still I fall, only supreme
In misery; such joy ambition finds.

---

　　50. 'sdeined, disdained.　　**51. quit,** requite, pay.
　　52–57. Satan means that gratitude is in itself payment, whereas payment alone does not
release from a debt of gratitude.
　　87. abide, suffer for.　　**90. advanced,** elevated. **Me** (89) is the word modified.

But say I could repent, and could obtain
By act of grace my former state; how soon
Would height recall high thoughts, how soon unsay
What feigned submission swore: ease would recant
Vows made in pain, as violent and void.
For never can true reconcilement grow
Where wounds of deadly hate have pierced so deep;
Which would but lead me to a worse relapse   100
And heavier fall: so should I purchase dear
Short intermission bought with double smart.
This knows my Punisher; therefore as far
From granting he, as I from begging peace.
All hope excluded thus, behold instead
Of us, outcast, exiled, his new delight,
Mankind created, and for him this World.
So farewell hope, and with hope farewell fear,
Farewell remorse! All good to me is lost;
Evil be thou my good; by thee at least   110
Divided empire with Heaven's King I hold
By thee, and more than half perhaps will reign;
As Man ere long, and this new World shall know."
    Thus while he spake, each passion dimmed his face
Thrice changed with pale, ire, envy, and despair,
Which marred his borrowed visage, and betrayed
Him counterfeit, if any eye beheld.
For heavenly minds from such distempers foul
Are ever clear. Whereof he soon aware,
Each perturbation smoothed with outward calm,   120
Artificer of fraud; and was the first
That practised falsehood under saintly show,
Deep malice to conceal, couched with revenge.
Yet not enough had practised to deceive
Uriel once warned; whose eye pursued him down
The way he went, and on the Assyrian mount
Saw him disfigured, more than could befall
Spirit of happy sort. His gestures fierce
He marked and mad demeanor, then alone,
As he supposed, all unobserved, unseen.   130
    So on he fares, and to the border comes
Of Eden, where delicious Paradise,
Now nearer, crowns with her enclosure green,
As with a rural mound the champaign head
Of a steep wilderness, whose hairy sides
With thicket overgrown, grotesque and wild,

115. Thrice changed with pale, i.e., each of the passions (**ire, envy, and despair**) dims the natural luster of his countenance. **Pale** is of course used as a noun.
    123. couched with, lying hidden with.   **126. the Assyrian mount,** Niphates.
    132 ff. Eden is apparently thought of as embracing the greater part of the Tigris and Euphrates region. Paradise is a garden in the east of Eden.
    134. champaign head, level summit.

Access denied; and overhead up grew
Insuperable height of loftiest shade,
Cedar, and pine, and fir, and branching palm,
A sylvan scene, and as the ranks ascend   140
Shade above shade, a woody theater
Of stateliest view. Yet higher than their tops
The verdurous wall of Paradise up sprung;
Which to our general sire gave prospect large
Into his nether empire neighboring round.
And higher than that wall a circling row
Of goodliest trees loaden with fairest fruit,
Blossoms and fruits at once of golden hue
Appeared, with gay enamelled colors mixed;
On which the sun more glad impressed his beams   150
Than in fair evening cloud, or humid bow,
When God hath showered the earth; so lovely seemed
That landscape. And of pure now purer air
Meets his approach, and to the heart inspires
Vernal delight and joy, able to drive
All sadness but despair; now gentle gales
Fanning their odoriferous wings dispense
Native perfumes, and whisper whence they stole
Those balmy spoils. As when to them who sail
Beyond the Cape of Hope, and now are past   160
Mozambic, off at sea north-east winds blow
Sabæan odors from the spicy shore
Of Araby the Blest, with such delay
Well pleased they slack their course, and many a league
Cheered with the grateful smell old Ocean smiles.
So entertained those odorous sweets the Fiend
Who came their bane, though with them better pleased
Than Asmodëus with the fishy fume,
That drove him, though enamored, from the spouse
Of Tobit's son, and with a vengeance sent   170
From Media post to Egypt, there fast bound.
    Now to the ascent of that steep savage hill
Satan had journeyed on, pensive and slow;
But further way found none, so thick entwined,
As one continued brake, the undergrowth
Of shrubs and tangling bushes had perplexed
All path of man or beast that passed that way.
One gate there only was, and that looked east
On the other side; which when the Arch-Felon saw,
Due entrance he disdained, and in contempt,   180

145. **nether empire,** i.e., the outlying territories of Eden.
149. **enamelled,** bright and variegated.
167 ff. The allusion is to an episode related in the apocryphal Book of Tobit, 8. Tobit's son
is married to a maiden of Media, who is beloved by the evil spirit Asmodeus; to get rid of this
spirit he is instructed by the angel Raphael to burn the heart and liver of a fish. The odor
drives Asmodeus into Egypt, where the angel binds him.
172. **savage,** woody.   176. **perplexed,** made difficult.

At one slight bound high overleaped all bound
Of hill or highest wall, and sheer within
Lights on his feet. As when a prowling wolf,
Whom hunger drives to seek new haunt for prey,
Watching where shepherds pen their flocks at eve
In hurdled cotes amid the field secure,
Leaps o'er the fence with ease into the fold;
Or as a thief bent to unhoard the cash
Of some rich burgher, whose substantial doors,
Cross-barred and bolted fast, fear no assault,   190
In at the window climbs, or o'er the tiles:
So clomb this first grand thief into God's fold;
So since into his Church lewd hirelings climb.
Thence up he flew, and on the Tree of Life,
The middle tree and highest there that grew,
Sat like a cormorant; yet not true life
Thereby regained, but sat devising death
To them who lived; nor on the virtue thought
Of that life-giving plant, but only used
For prospect, what well used had been the pledge   200
Of immortality. So little knows
Any, but God alone, to value right
The good before him, but perverts best things
To worst abuse, or to their meanest use.
    Beneath him with new wonder now he views
To all delight of human sense exposed
In narrow room Nature's whole wealth, yea more,
A Heaven on Earth, for blissful Paradise
Of God the garden was, by him in the east
Of Eden planted; Eden stretched her line   210
From Auran eastward to the royal towers
Of great Seleucia, built by Grecian kings,
Or where the sons of Eden long before
Dwelt in Telassar. In this pleasant soil
His far more pleasant garden God ordained;
Out of the fertile ground he caused to grow
All trees of noblest kind for sight, smell, taste;
And all amid them stood the Tree of Life,
High-eminent, blooming ambrosial fruit
Of vegetable gold; and next to life   220
Our death the Tree of Knowledge grew fast by,
Knowledge of good bought dear by knowing ill.
Southward through Eden went a river large,

---

181. bound . . . bound. Note the play on words.   **194. Tree of Life.** Cf. Gen. 2:9.
196. like a cormorant, i.e., in the shape of a ravenous bird of prey.
211. Auran, a district of Syria, about fifty miles south of Damascus.
212. Seleucia, a city on the Tigris, about twenty miles southeast of modern Bagdad.
214. Telassar, an ancient site in Mesopotamia.   **219. blooming,** bearing.
223 ff. Southward . . . no account. Cf. Gen. 2:10. In IX, 71–73 Milton identifies this river
with the Tigris.

Nor changed his course, but through the shaggy hill
Passed underneath ingulfed, for God had thrown
That mountain as his garden mould, high raised
Upon the rapid current, which through veins
Of porous earth with kindly thirst up drawn,
Rose a fresh fountain, and with many a rill
Watered the garden; thence united fell   230
Down the steep glade, and met the nether flood,
Which from his darksome passage now appears,
And now divided into four main streams,
Runs diverse, wandering many a famous realm
And country whereof here needs no account;
But rather to tell how, if art could tell,
How from that sapphire fount the crispèd brooks,
Rolling on orient pearl and sands of gold,
With mazy error under pendent shades
Ran nectar, visiting each plant, and fed   240
Flowers worthy of Paradise, which not nice art
In beds and curious knots, but Nature boon
Poured forth profuse on hill and dale and plain,
Both where the morning sun first warmly smote
The open field, and where the unpierced shade
Imbrowned the noon-tide bowers. Thus was this place,
A happy rural seat of various view;
Groves whose rich trees wept odorous gums and balm,
Others whose fruit burnished with golden rind
Hung amiable, Hesperian fables true,   250
If true, here only, and of delicious taste.
Betwixt them lawns, or level downs, and flocks
Grazing the tender herb, were interposed,
Or palmy hillock, or the flowery lap
Of some irriguous valley spread her store,
Flowers of all hue, and without thorn the rose.
Another side, umbrageous grots and caves
Of cool recess, o'er which the mantling vine
Lays forth her purple grape, and gently creeps
Luxuriant; meanwhile murmuring waters fall   260
Down the slope hills, dispersed, or in a lake,
That to the fringèd bank with myrtle crowned
Her crystal mirror holds, unite their streams.
The birds their choir apply; airs, vernal airs,

---

233. **four main streams.** Cf. Gen. 2:10–14.   238. **orient,** lustrous.
239. **error,** wandering (the literal meaning of Latin *error*).
241–42. The natural profusion of Paradise is contrasted with the artificial arrangement of an Italian garden. **nice,** fastidious. **boon,** bounteous. This passage played a part in supporting later preference for the so-called English garden and for the love of natural scenery generally.
247. **various view,** varied aspect.
250–51. Milton means that here, if anywhere, was to be found such fruit as classical myth attributed to the Garden of the Hesperides. **amiable,** lovely.
255. **irriguous,** well-watered.

Breathing the smell of field and grove, attune
The trembling leaves, while universal Pan,
Knit with the Graces and the Hours in dance,
Led on the eternal Spring. Not that fair field
Of Enna, where Proserpine gathering flowers
Herself a fairer flower by gloomy Dis   270
Was gathered, which cost Ceres all that pain
To seek her through the world; nor that sweet grove
Of Daphne by Orontes, and the inspired
Castalian spring, might with this Paradise
Of Eden strive; nor that Nyseian isle,
Girt with the river Triton, where old Cham
Whom Gentiles Ammon call and Lybian Jove,
Hid Amalthea and her florid son
Young Bacchus from his stepdame Rhea's eye;
Nor where Abassin kings their issue guard,   280
Mount Amara, though this by some supposed
True Paradise, under the Ethiop line
By Nilus' head, enclosed with shining rock,
A whole day's journey high, but wide remote
From this Assyrian garden, where the Fiend
Saw undelighted all delight, all kind
Of living creatures new to sight and strange.
Two of far nobler shape erect and tall,
God-like erect, with native honor clad
In naked majesty seemed lords of all,   290
And worthy seemed, for in their looks divine
The image of their glorious Maker shone,
Truth, wisdom, sanctitude severe and pure,
Severe but in true filial freedom placed;
Whence true authority in men; though both

266 ff. Classical writers often made "the dance of the Hours" symbolic of the orderly succession of the seasons.

269 ff. Enna, etc. Proserpine (Greek Persephone), the daughter of Ceres, goddess of agriculture (Greek Demeter), was abducted by Dis, god of the underworld, from her garden in Enna (in Sicily). After a long search, Ceres found her daughter in the underworld and arranged that she should spend part of her time there and part on the earth. The myth obviously describes the alternation of the seasons. (Editors' note.)

273. Daphne, a town situated on the river **Orontes,** about five miles from Antioch. It contained a grove and fountain sacred to Apollo, the fountain being named after the more famous **Castalian spring** at Delphi.

275. that Nyseian isle, the island of Nysa, situated in the midst of the river **Triton** in northern Africa. The identification of Jupiter Ammon with Noah's son Ham (**Cham**) is an interesting Miltonic touch.

281. Mount Amara, a high hill on the Abyssinian plateau, the place of seclusion where, according to tradition, the Abyssinian princes were sent to be educated.

282. Ethiop line, the equator.

289. God-like erect. Milton makes man's upright stature a symbol of his superiority to the brutes and of his instinctive aspiration.

295 ff. Throughout the poem Milton carefully distinguishes between the relative endowments and obligations of man and woman. The sexes are not equal, he insists, and authority quite properly belongs to the male. But the position which he accords woman, when considered in the light of theological tradition, is exceedingly high.

Not equal, as their sex not equal seemed;
For contemplation he and valor formed,
For softness she and sweet attractive grace;
He for God only, she for God in him.
His fair large front and eye sublime declared   300
Absolute rule; and hyacinthine locks
Round from his parted forelock manly hung
Clustering, but not beneath his shoulders broad:
She as a veil down to the slender waist
Her unadornëd golden tresses wore
Dishevelled, but in wanton ringlets waved
As the vine curls her tendrils, which implied
Subjection, but required with gentle sway,
And by her yielded, by him best received,
Yielded with coy submission, modest pride,   310
And sweet reluctant amorous delay.
Nor those mysterious parts were then concealed;
Then was not guilty shame; dishonest shame
Of Nature's works, honor dishonorable,
Sin-bred, how have ye troubled all mankind
With shows instead, mere shows of seeming pure,
And banished from man's life his happiest life,
Simplicity and spotless innocence.
So passed they naked on, nor shunned the sight
Of God or angel, for they thought no ill;   320
So hand in hand they passed, the loveliest pair
That ever since in love's embraces met:
Adam the goodliest man of men since born
His sons, the fairest of her daughters Eve.
Under a tuft of shade that on a green
Stood whispering soft, by a fresh fountain side
They sat them down; and after no more toil
Of their sweet gardening labor than sufficed
To recommend cool Zephyr, and made ease
More easy, wholesome thirst and appetite   330
More grateful, to their supper-fruits they fell,
Nectarine fruits which the compliant boughs
Yielded them, sidelong as they sat recline
On the soft downy bank damasked with flowers.
The savory pulp they chew, and in the rind
Still as they thirsted scoop the brimming stream;
Nor gentle purpose, nor endearing smiles
Wanted, nor youthful dalliance, as beseems
Fair couple linked in happy nuptial league,

---

300. front, brow.   **301. hyacinthine,** i.e., dark in color.
306. wanton, loose, unbound.   **313. dishonest,** unchaste.
323. the goodliest man of men since born, etc. The idiom is obviously illogical, but it has ample precedent in Elizabethan English as well as in Greek and Latin.
333. recline, i.e., reclining.
334. damasked, ornamented with a variegated pattern.   **337. purpose,** conversation.

Alone as they. About them frisking played   340
All beasts of the earth, since wild, and of all chase
In wood or wilderness, forest or den;
Sporting the lion ramped, and in his paw
Dandled the kid; bears, tigers, ounces, pards,
Gambolled before them; the unwieldy elephant
To make them mirth used all his might, and wreathed
His lithe proboscis; close the serpent sly
Insinuating, wove with Gordian twine
His braided train, and of his fatal guile
Gave proof unheeded; others on the grass   350
Couched, and now filled with pasture gazing sat,
Or bedward ruminating; for the sun
Declined was hasting now with prone career
To the Ocean Isles, and in the ascending scale
Of Heaven the stars that usher evening rose:
When Satan still in gaze, as first he stood,
Scarce thus at length failed speech recovered sad.
　　"Oh Hell! what do mine eyes with grief behold!
Into our room of bliss thus high advanced
Creatures of other mould, earth-born perhaps,   360
Not spirits, yet to heavenly spirits bright
Little inferior; whom my thoughts pursue
With wonder, and could love, so lively shines
In them divine resemblance, and such grace
The hand that formed them on their shape hath poured.
Ah gentle pair, ye little think how nigh
Your change approaches, when all these delights
Will vanish and deliver ye to woe,
More woe, the more your taste is now of joy;
Happy, but for so happy ill secured   370
Long to continue, and this high seat your Heaven
Ill fenced for Heaven to keep out such a foe
As now is entered; yet no purposed foe
To you whom I could pity thus forlorn
Though I unpitied. League with you I seek,
And mutual amity so strait, so close,
That I with you must dwell, or you with me
Henceforth; my dwelling haply may not please
Like this fair Paradise, your sense, yet such
Accept your Maker's work; he gave it me,   380
Which I as freely give; Hell shall unfold,
To entertain you two, her widest gates,
And send forth all her kings; there will be room,

343. ramped, reared on his hind legs.
348. Gordian twine, intricate tangle. The reference is to the famous Gordian knot, which no one could untie but which Alexander the Great finally cut with his sword.
352. ruminating, chewing the cud.
354. the Ocean Isles, i.e., the extreme west. Milton may here have in mind the Azores, but the figure is used by classical writers without definite geographical reference.

Not like these narrow limits, to receive
Your numerous offspring; if no better place,
Thank him who puts me loath to this revenge
On you who wrong me not, for him who wronged.
And should I at your harmless innocence
Melt, as I do, yet public reason just,
Honor and empire with revenge enlarged,   390
By conquering this new World, compels me now
To do what else though damned I should abhor."
    So spake the Fiend, and with necessity,
The tyrant's plea, excused his devilish deeds.
Then from his lofty stand on that high tree
Down he alights among the sportful herd
Of those four-footed kinds, himself now one,
Now other, as their shape served best his end
Nearer to view his prey, and unespied
To mark what of their state he more might learn   400
By word or action marked. About them round
A lion now he stalks with fiery glare;
Then as a tiger, who by chance hath spied
In some purlieu two gentle fawns at play,
Straight couches close, then rising changes oft
His couchant watch, as one who chose his ground
Whence rushing he might surest seize them both
Griped in each paw; when Adam first of men
To first of women Eve thus moving speech,
Turned him all ear to hear new utterance flow.   410
    "Sole partner and sole part of all these joys,
Dearer thyself than all, needs must the Power
That made us, and for us this ample World,
Be infinitely good, and of his good
As liberal and free as infinite,
That raised us from the dust and placed us here
In all this happiness, who at his hand
Have nothing merited, nor can perform
Aught whereof he hath need, he who requires
From us no other service than to keep   420
This one, this easy charge, of all the trees
In Paradise that bear delicious fruit
So various, not to taste that only Tree
Of Knowledge, planted by the Tree of Life,
So near grows death to life, whate'er death is,
Some dreadful thing no doubt; for well thou know'st
God hath pronounced it death to taste that Tree;
The only sign of our obedience left

    389. By excusing his crime on the ground of political expediency, Satan once more demon-
strates his proficiency in Machiavellian statecraft. That he can feel human pity is a survival of
the divine endowment which he has perverted.
    411. Note the double play on words: **partner . . . part; sole . . . sole.** The first *sole* is used
in the ordinary sense of "only," the second in the sense of "unrivaled," or "chief."

Among so many signs of power and rule
Conferred upon us, and dominion given   430
Over all other creatures that possess
Earth, air, and sea. Then let us not think hard
One easy prohibition, who enjoy
Free leave so large to all things else, and choice
Unlimited of manifold delights;
But let us ever praise him, and extol
His bounty, following our delightful task
To prune these growing plants, and tend these flowers,
Which were it toilsome, yet with thee were sweet."
    To whom thus Eve replied. "O thou for whom   440
And from whom I was formed flesh of thy flesh,
And without whom am to no end, my guide
And head, what thou hast said is just and right.
For we to him indeed all praises owe,
And daily thanks, I chiefly who enjoy
So far the happier lot, enjoying thee
Pre-eminent by so much odds, while thou
Like consort to thyself canst nowhere find.
That day I oft remember, when from sleep
I first awaked, and found myself reposed   450
Under a shade on flowers, much wondering where
And what I was, whence thither brought, and how.
Not distant far from thence a murmuring sound
Of waters issued from a cave and spread
Into a liquid plain, then stood unmoved
Pure as the expanse of Heaven; I thither went
With unexperienced thought, and laid me down
On the green bank, to look into the clear
Smooth lake, that to me seemed another sky.
As I bent down to look, just opposite   460
A shape within the watery gleam appeared
Bending to look on me: I started back,
It started back, but pleased I soon returned,
Pleased it returned as soon with answering looks
Of sympathy and love; there I had fixed
Mine eyes till now, and pined with vain desire,
Had not a voice thus warned me. 'What thou seest,
What there thou seest, fair creature, is thyself,
With thee it came and goes; but follow me,
And I will bring thee where no shadow stays   470
Thy coming, and thy soft embraces, he
Whose image thou art, him thou shalt enjoy
Inseparably thine; to him shalt bear
Multitudes like thyself, and thence be called
Mother of human race.' What could I do
But follow straight, invisibly thus led?

470. stays, awaits.

Till I espied thee, fair indeed and tall,
Under a platane; yet methought less fair,
Less winning soft, less amiably mild,
Than that smooth watery image; back I turned,   480
Thou following cried'st aloud, 'Return fair Eve,
Whom fliest thou? whom thou fliest, of him thou art,
His flesh, his bone; to give thee being I lent
Out of my side to thee, nearest my heart,
Substantial life, to have thee by my side
Henceforth an individual solace dear.
Part of my soul I seek thee, and thee claim
My other half.' With that thy gentle hand
Seized mine, I yielded, and from that time see
How beauty is excelled by manly grace   490
And wisdom, which alone is truly fair."
  So spake our general mother, and with eyes
Of conjugal attraction unreproved,
And meek surrender, half embracing leaned
On our first father; half her swelling breast
Naked met his under the flowing gold
Of her loose tresses hid. He in delight
Both of her beauty and submissive charms
Smiled with superior love, as Jupiter
On Juno smiles, when he impregns the clouds   500
That shed May flowers; and pressed her matron lip
With kisses pure. Aside the Devil turned
For envy, yet with jealous leer malign
Eyed them askance, and to himself thus plained.
  "Sight hateful, sight tormenting! thus these two
Imparadised in one another's arms,
The happier Eden, shall enjoy their fill
Of bliss on bliss, while I to Hell am thrust,
Where neither joy nor love, but fierce desire,
Among our other torments not the least,   510
Still unfulfilled with pain of longing pines;
Yet let me not forget what I have gained
From their own mouths. All is not theirs, it seems;
One fatal tree there stands, of Knowledge called,
Forbidden them to taste. Knowledge forbidden?
Suspicious, reasonless. Why should their Lord
Envy them that? can it be sin to know,
Can it be death? and do they only stand
By ignorance, is that their happy state,
The proof of their obedience and their faith?   520

479. less amiably mild, i.e., less fitted to inspire love.   **486. individual,** inseparable.
493. unreproved, unreprovable.
500. impregns, impregnates. Hera typifies the lower air or haze which surrounds the
earth, Zeus the upper air (aether). The mingling of the two produces the spring with its
flowers.
504. plained, complained, murmured.

O fair foundation laid whereon to build
Their ruin! Hence I will excite their minds
With more desire to know, and to reject
Envious commands, invented with design
To keep them low whom knowledge might exalt
Equal with gods. Aspiring to be such,
They taste and die; what likelier can ensue?
But first with narrow search I must walk round
This garden, and no corner leave unspied;
A chance but chance may lead where I may meet   530
Some wandering spirit of Heaven, by fountain side,
Or in thick shade retired, from him to draw
What further would be learned. Live while ye may,
Yet happy pair; enjoy, till I return,
Short pleasures, for long woes are to succeed."
  So saying, his proud step he scornful turned,
But with sly circumspection, and began
Through wood, through waste, o'er hill, o'er dale, his roam.

*   *   *

  Now came still Evening on, and Twilight gray
Had in her sober livery all things clad;
Silence accompanied, for beast and bird,   600
They to their grassy couch, these to their nests
Were slunk, all but the wakeful nightingale;
She all night long her amorous descant sung;
Silence was pleased. Now glowed the firmament
With living sapphires; Hesperus that led
The starry host, rode brightest, till the Moon
Rising in clouded majesty, at length
Apparent queen unveiled her peerless light,
And o'er the dark her silver mantle threw.
When Adam thus to Eve. "Fair consort, the hour   610
Of night, and all things now retired to rest
Mind us of like repose, since God hath set
Labor and rest, as day and night to men
Successive, and the timely dew of sleep
Now falling with soft slumberous weight inclines
Our eye-lids; other creatures all day long
Rove idle, unemployed, and less need rest;
Man hath his daily work of body or mind
Appointed, which declares his dignity,

---

521 ff. Satan's own experience has taught him the allurement of godlike power, and the outcome of any attempt to gain it. He therefore has little difficulty in determining the most effective temptation. Cf. IX, 705 ff.

530. A chance but, there is a chance that.

603. descant, a song, or rather a soprano part.   **605. Hesperus,** the evening star.

608. Apparent, manifest.

And the regard of Heaven on all his ways;   620
While other animals unactive range,
And of their doings God takes no account.
To-morrow ere fresh morning streak the east
With first approach of light, we must be risen,
And at our pleasant labor, to reform
Yon flowery arbors, yonder alleys green,
Our walks at noon, with branches overgrown,
That mock our scant manuring, and require
More hands than ours to lop their wanton growth.
Those blossoms also, and those dropping gums,   630
That lie bestrown unsightly and unsmooth,
Ask riddance, if we mean to tread with ease;
Meanwhile, as Nature wills, night bids us rest."
    To whom thus Eve with perfect beauty adorned.
"My author and disposer, what thou bidd'st
Unargued I obey; so God ordains.
God is thy law, thou mine; to know no more
Is woman's happiest knowledge and her praise.
With thee conversing I forget all time,
All seasons and their change, all please alike.   640
Sweet is the breath of Morn, her rising sweet,
With charm of earliest birds; pleasant the Sun
When first on this delightful land he spreads
His orient beams, on herb, tree, fruit, and flower,
Glistering with dew; fragrant the fertile Earth
After soft showers; and sweet the coming on
Of grateful Evening mild, then silent Night
With this her solemn bird and this fair Moon,
And these the gems of Heaven, her starry train:
But neither breath of Morn when she ascends   650
With charm of earliest birds, nor rising Sun
On this delightful land, nor herb, fruit, flower,
Glistering with dew, nor fragrance after showers,
Nor grateful Evening mild, nor silent Night,
With this her solemn bird, nor walk by moon,
Or glittering star-light, without thee is sweet.
But wherefore all night long shine these? for whom
This glorious sight, when sleep hath shut all eyes?"
    To whom our general ancestor replied.
"Daughter of God and Man, accomplished Eve,   660
Those have their course to finish, round the Earth

628. manuring, cultivating.

640. All seasons, i.e., all times of the day. Spring is the only season of the year that Eve has
yet experienced.

642. charm, song.

650 ff. Note how the imagery of the preceding nine lines is repeated with subtle variations
in phrasing. Milton frequently makes effective use of repetition, but nowhere else does he
work it into so elaborate a pattern. He is adorning or sophisticating a Homeric device, as he
does in his use of similes, and in his structural adaptation of the epic throwback.

By morrow evening, and from land to land
In order, though to nations yet unborn,
Ministering light prepared, they set and rise;
Lest total Darkness should by night regain
Her old possession, and extinguish life
In nature and all things; which these soft fires
Not only enlighten, but with kindly heat
Of various influence foment and warm,
Temper or nourish, or in part shed down   670
Their stellar virtue on all kinds that grow
On Earth, made hereby apter to receive
Perfection from the sun's more potent ray.
These then, though unbeheld in deep of night,
Shine not in vain, nor think, though men were none,
That Heaven would want spectators, God want praise;
Millions of spiritual creatures walk the Earth
Unseen, both when we wake, and when we sleep.
All these with ceaseless praise his works behold
Both day and night. How often from the steep   680
Of echoing hill or thicket have we heard
Celestial voices to the midnight air,
Sole, or responsive each to other's note,
Singing their great Creator; oft in bands
While they keep watch, or nightly rounding walk,
With heavenly touch of instrumental sounds
In full harmonic number joined, their songs
Divide the night, and lift our thoughts to Heaven."
   Thus talking, hand in hand alone they passed
On to their blissful bower; it was a place   690
Chosen by the sovran Planter, when he framed
All things to Man's delightful use; the roof
Of thickest covert was inwoven shade,
Laurel and myrtle, and what higher grew
Of firm and fragrant leaf; on either side
Acanthus, and each odorous bushy shrub
Fenced up the verdant wall; each beauteous flower,
Iris all hues, roses, and jessamine
Reared high their flourished heads between, and wrought
Mosaic; underfoot the violet,   700
Crocus, and hyacinth with rich inlay
Broidered the ground, more colored than with stone
Of costliest emblem. Other creature here,
Beast, bird, insect, or worm durst enter none;
Such was their awe of Man. In shadier bower
More sacred and sequestered, though but feigned,

---

665. total Darkness, i.e., the darkness of Chaos.

667 ff. The doctrine of stellar influence, which formed the basis of astrology, was still widely current in the seventeenth century. Milton seems to take its validity for granted.

688. Divide the night, i.e., into watches.

703. emblem, embossed or inlaid ornamentation.

Pan or Sylvanus never slept, nor Nymph
Nor Faunus haunted. Here in close recess
With flowers, garlands, and sweet-smelling herbs
Espousëd Eve decked first her nuptial bed,   710
And heavenly choirs the hymenæan sung,
What day the genial angel to our sire
Brought her in naked beauty more adorned,
More lovely than Pandora, whom the gods
Endowed with all their gifts, and O too like
In sad event, when to the unwiser son
Of Japhet brought by Hermes, she ensnared
Mankind with her fair looks, to be avenged
On him who had stole Jove's authentic fire.
      Thus at their shady lodge arrived, both stood,   720
Both turned, and under open sky adored
The God that made both sky, air, Earth, and Heaven,
Which they beheld, the moon's resplendent globe
And starry pole: "Thou also mad'st the night,
Maker Omnipotent, and thou the day,
Which we in our appointed work employed
Have finished happy in our mutual help
And mutual love, the crown of all our bliss
Ordained by thee, and this delicious place
For us too large, where thy abundance wants   730
Partakers, and uncropped falls to the ground.
But thou hast promised from us two a race
To fill the Earth, who shall with us extol
Thy goodness infinite, both when we wake,
And when we seek, as now, thy gift of sleep."
      This said unanimous, and other rites
Observing none, but adoration pure
Which God likes best, into their inmost bower
Handed they went; and eased the putting off
These troublesome disguises which we wear,   740
Straight side by side were laid, nor turned, I ween,
Adam from his fair spouse, nor Eve the rites
Mysterious of connubial love refused;
Whatever hypocrites austerely talk

707. Pan, Sylvanus, and **Faunus** were classical deities of the fields and woods. The qualifying **though but feigned** phrase, used with reference to their haunts, implies a judgment on much of the subject matter of pagan poetry. Milton frequently asserts the superior truth of his own materials. Cf. 250, 251, and note.
    712. genial, nuptial, instrumental to marriage.
    714 ff. The allusion is to a myth related by Hesiod. To be avenged on Prometheus, who had stolen fire from heaven for the use of mortals, Jove sent to earth **Pandora** ("the all-gifted"), on whom each of the gods had bestowed some fatal charm. Hermes conducted her to Epimetheus, the **unwiser son of Japhet,** who married her, despite the warning of his brother. Thereupon all the ills which she had brought from heaven were released to afflict humanity.
    719. authentic, original.   **739. Handed,** hand in hand.
    744 ff. Whatever hypocrites, etc. Throughout this passage, Milton is quite obviously taking issue with the advocates of monasticism and celibacy.

Of purity and place and innocence,
Defaming as impure what God declares
Pure, and commands to some, leaves free to all.
Our Maker bids increase; who bids abstain
But our destroyer, foe to God and Man?
Hail wedded Love, mysterious law, true source   750
Of human offspring, sole propriety
In Paradise of all things common else.
By thee adulterous lust was driven from men
Among the bestial herds to range; by thee,
Founded in reason, loyal, just, and pure,
Relations dear, and all the charities
Of father, son, and brother first were known.
Far be it, that I should write thee sin or blame,
Or think thee unbefitting holiest place,
Perpetual fountain of domestic sweets,   760
Whose bed is undefiled and chaste pronounced,
Present or past, as saints and patriarchs used.
Here Love his golden shafts employs, here lights
His constant lamp, and waves his purple wings,
Reigns here and revels; not in the bought smile
Of harlots, loveless, joyless, unendeared,
Casual fruition; nor in court-amours,
Mixed dance, or wanton mask, or midnight ball,
Or serenate, which the starved lover sings
To his proud fair, best quitted with disdain.   770
These lulled by nightingales, embracing slept,
And on their naked limbs the flowery roof
Showered roses, which the morn repaired. Sleep on
Blest pair; and O yet happiest if ye seek
No happier state, and know to know no more.

*   *   *

BOOK V: THE ARGUMENT

Morning approached, Eve relates to Adam her troublesome dream; he likes it not,
yet comforts her; they come forth to their day labors; their morning hymn at the
door of their bower. God, to render Man inexcusable, sends Raphael to admonish
him of his obedience, of his free estate, of his enemy near at hand—who he is, and
why his enemy, and whatever else may avail Adam to know. Raphael comes down

751. sole propriety, sole property. Their love for each other is the one thing in Paradise
which Adam and Eve have as their exclusive possession.
756. charities, affections.
767. nor in court-amours, etc. Milton may be thinking specifically of the court of Charles
II; but he is also thinking of the general chivalric tradition, the artificial conventions of which
he believes to be irreconcilable with the ideal domestic relationship.
769. serenate, serenade. **starved,** i.e., suffering from cold.
775. know to know no more, i.e., are wise enough not to seek further knowledge.

to Paradise; his appearance described; his coming discerned by Adam afar off, sitting at the door of his bower; he goes out to meet him, brings him to his lodge, entertains him with the choicest fruits of Paradise got together by Eve; their discourse at table. Raphael performs his message, minds Adam of his state and of his enemy; relates, at Adam's request, who that enemy is, and how he came to be so, beginning from his first revolt in Heaven, and the occasion thereof; how he drew his legions after him to the parts of the North, and there incited them to rebel with him, persuading all but only Abdiel, a Seraph, who in argument dissuades and opposes him, then forsakes him.

BOOK VI: THE ARGUMENT

Raphael continues to relate how Michael and Gabriel were sent forth to battle against Satan and his angels. The first fight described; Satan and his Powers retire under night. He calls a council; invents devilish engines, which, in the second day's fight, put Michael and his angels to some disorder; but they at length, pulling up mountains, overwhelmed both the force and machines of Satan. Yet, the tumult not so ending, God, on the third day, sends Messiah his Son, for whom he had reserved the glory of that victory. He, in the power of his Father, coming to the place, and causing all his legions to stand still on either side, with his chariot and thunder driving into the midst of his enemies, pursues them, unable to resist, towards the wall of Heaven; which opening, they leap down with horror and confusion into the place of punishment prepared for them in the deep. Messiah returns with triumph to his Father.

BOOK VII: THE ARGUMENT

Raphael, at the request of Adam, relates how and wherefore this World was first created: that God, after the expelling of Satan and his angels out of Heaven, declared his pleasure to create another World, and other creatures to dwell therein; sends his Son with glory, and attendance of angels, to perform the work of creation in six days: the angels celebrate with hymns the performance thereof, and his reascension into Heaven.

BOOK VIII: THE ARGUMENT

Adam inquires concerning celestial motions; is doubtfully answered, and exhorted to search rather things more worthy of knowledge. Adam assents, and still desirous to detain Raphael, relates to him what he remembered since his own creation: his placing in Paradise, his talk with God concerning solitude and fit society, his first meeting and nuptials with Eve. His discourse with the angel thereupon; who, after admonitions repeated, departs.

BOOK IX

THE ARGUMENT

Satan, having compassed the Earth, with meditated guile returns as a mist by night into Paradise; enters into the serpent sleeping. Adam and Eve in the morning go forth to their labors, which Eve proposes to divide in several places, each laboring apart: Adam consents not, alleging the danger, lest that enemy, of whom they were forewarned, should attempt her found alone. Eve, loth to be thought not circumspect or firm enough, urges her going apart, the rather desirous to make trial of her strength; Adam at last yields. The Serpent finds her alone: his subtle approach, first gazing, then speaking, with much flattery extolling Eve above all other creatures. Eve, wondering to hear the Serpent speak, asks how he attained to human speech and such understanding, not till now; the Serpent answers, that by tasting of a certain tree in the garden he attained both to speech and reason, till then void of both. Eve requires him to bring her to that tree, and finds it to be the Tree of Knowledge forbidden. The Serpent, now grown bolder, with many wiles and arguments induces her at length to eat; she, pleased with the taste, deliberates a while whether to impart thereof to Adam or not; at last brings him of the fruit; relates what persuaded her to eat thereof. Adam, at first amazed, but perceiving her lost, resolves through vehemence of love to perish with her, and, extenuating the trespass, eats also of the fruit. The effects thereof in them both; they seek to cover their nakedness; then fall to variance and accusation of one another.

No more of talk where God or angel guest
With Man, as with his friend, familiar used
To sit indulgent, and with him partake
Rural repast, permitting him the while
Venial discourse unblamed. I now must change
Those notes to tragic; foul distrust and breach
Disloyal on the part of man, revolt
And disobedience; on the part of Heaven
Now alienated, distance and distaste,
Anger and just rebuke, and judgment given,   10
That brought into this World a world of woe,
Sin and her shadow Death, and Misery
Death's harbinger. Sad task, yet argument
Not less but more heroic than the wrath
Of stern Achilles on his foe pursued
Thrice fugitive about Troy wall; or rage
Of Turnus for Lavinia disespoused;
Or Neptune's ire or Juno's, that so long
Perplexed the Greek and Cytherea's son;
If answerable style I can obtain   20

1 ff. The long conversation between Raphael and Adam, forming the substance of Books V–VIII, has introduced the antecedent action and illuminated more fully the existing situation. Now before entering upon the climax of his narrative, Milton pauses for a brief meditative interlude. The personal allusions in the opening lines of this book are of exceptional interest.

6–12. Cf. I, 3. The theme announced at the beginning of the poem is repeated in expanded form.

13 ff. Having restated his theme, Milton here asserts its superiority to the themes of the three great classical epics: (1) the *Iliad*, which deals with **the wrath of stern Achilles;** (2) the *Odyssey*, which relates the outcome of **Neptune's ire** against the Greek Odysseus; (3) the *Aeneid*, the first part of which is motivated by the hostility of **Juno** toward Aeneas (**Cytherea's son**), and the second part by the anger of **Turnus** at the loss of **Lavinia.**

20. answerable style, i.e., a style commensurate with the dignity of the theme.

Of my celestial patroness, who deigns
Her nightly visitation unimplored,
And dictates to me slumbering, or inspires
Easy my unpremeditated verse;
Since first this subject for heroic song
Pleased me long choosing and beginning late;
Not sedulous by nature to indite
Wars, hitherto the only argument
Heroic deemed, chief mastery to dissect
With long and tedious havoc fabled knights   30
In battles feigned; the better fortitude
Of patience and heroic martyrdom
Unsung; or to describe races and games,
Or tilting furniture, imblazoned shields,
Impresses quaint, caparisons and steeds,
Bases and tinsel trappings, gorgeous knights
At joust and tournament; then marshalled feast
Served up in hall with sewers and seneshals,
The skill of artifice or office mean,
Not that which justly gives heroic name   40
To person or to poem. Me of these
Nor skilled nor studious, higher argument
Remains, sufficient of itself to raise
That name, unless an age too late, or cold
Climate, or years damp my intended wing
Depressed, and much they may, if all be mine,
Not hers who brings it nightly to my ear.
    The sun was sunk, and after him the star
Of Hesperus, whose office is to bring
Twilight upon the Earth, short arbiter   50
'Twixt day and night, and now from end to end
Night's hemisphere had veiled the horizon round;
When Satan who late fled before the threats
Of Gabriel out of Eden, now improved
In meditated fraud and malice, bent

21–23. Cf. III, 29–40. The implication is that with Milton composition was a spontaneous process, based on a passive reception of impressions and ideas.

25 ff. From the Cambridge MS. it is evident that the subject of *Paradise Lost* (together with various other subjects drawn from biblical and British history) was in Milton's mind by 1640 or soon after. The actual composition of the epic could not have been begun much before 1658.

33. races and games. Milton is thinking of the detailed accounts in *Iliad* xxiii, and *Aeneid* v.

34. tilting furniture, etc., i.e., the trappings of chivalry.

35. impresses, devices on shields.

36. bases, kilt-like garments worn by knights on horseback.

41–43. Me . . . remains. To me, who am, etc., there remains.

44–45. an age too late, i.e., too late a period in the world's history. The notion of universal retrogression was fairly common in the seventeenth century. Though Milton had argued against the theory, he here shows that he is not unaffected by fear that it may be true. **or cold Climate.** The idea that a northern climate is unfavorable to works of the mind goes back to Aristotle.

On Man's destruction, maugre what might hap
Of heavier on himself, fearless returned.
By night he fled, and at midnight returned
From compassing the Earth, cautious of day,
Since Uriel, regent of the sun, descried   60
His entrance, and ·forewarned the Cherubim
That kept their watch; thence full of anguish driven,
The space of seven continued nights he rode
With darkness, thrice the equinoctial line
He circled, four times crossed the car of Night
From pole to pole, traversing each colure;
On the eighth returned, and on the coast averse
From entrance or cherubic watch, by stealth
Found unsuspected way. There was a place,
Now not, though sin, not time, first wrought the change,   70
Where Tigris at the foot of Paradise
Into a gulf shot under ground, till part
Rose up a fountain by the Tree of Life;
In with the river sunk, and with it rose
Satan involved in rising mist, then sought
Where to lie hid; sea he had searched and land
From Eden over Pontus, and the pool
Mæotis, up beyond the river Ob;
Downward as far antarctic; and in length
West from Orontes to the ocean barred   80
At Darien, thence to the land where flows
Ganges and Indus. Thus the orb he roamed
With narrow search, and with inspection deep
Considered every creature, which of all
Most opportune might serve his wiles, and found
The serpent subtlest beast of all the field.
Him after long debate, irresolute
Of thoughts revolved, his final sentence chose
Fit vessel, fittest imp of fraud, in whom
To enter, and his dark suggestions hide   90
From sharpest sight; for in the wily snake,
Whatever sleights none would suspicious mark,
As from his wit and native subtlety
Proceeding, which in other beasts observed,

56. maugre, in spite of.

66. traversing each colure. The colures are two great circles intersecting at the poles, one passing through the equinoxes, the other (at right angles to it) through the solstices. Satan follows each of these lines from south to north and back, keeping always within the earth's shadow.

69 ff. Cf. IV, 223–30. Satan makes his entrance from the north side. Satan's wanderings, first described astronomically, are here described geographically. Northward he had gone over the Black Sea (**Pontus**) and the Sea of Azof (**the pool Mæotis**), beyond the Siberian river **Ob** to the pole; thence southward to the Antarctic. Westward he had gone along the Syrian river **Orontes,** over the Mediterranean and Atlantic to the Isthmus of Panama (**Darien**), and from there across the Pacific to India (the land of **Ganges and Indus**).

82. orb, the world.   **88. sentence,** decision.   **89. imp,** offspring.

Doubt might beget of diabolic power
Active within beyond the sense of brute.
Thus he resolved, but first from inward grief
His bursting passion into plaints thus poured.
  "O Earth, how like to Heaven, if not preferred
More justly, seat worthier of Gods, as built   100
With second thoughts, reforming what was old!
For what God after better worse would build?
Terrestrial Heaven, danced round by other Heavens
That shine, yet bear their bright officious lamps,
Light above light, for thee alone, as seems,
In thee concentring all their precious beams
Of sacred influence. As God in Heaven
Is center, yet extends to all, so thou
Centring receivest from all those orbs; in thee,
Not in themselves, all their known virtue appears   110
Productive in herb, plant, and nobler birth
Of creatures animate with gradual life
Of growth, sense, reason, all summed up in Man.
With what delight could I have walked thee round,
If I could joy in aught, sweet interchange
Of hill and valley, rivers, woods, and plains,
Now land, now sea, and shores with forest crowned,
Rocks, dens, and caves; but I in none of these
Find place or refuge; and the more I see
Pleasures about me, so much more I feel   120
Torment within me, as from the hateful siege
Of contraries; all good to me becomes
Bane, and in Heaven much worse would be my state.
But neither here seek I, no nor in Heaven
To dwell, unless by mastering Heaven's Supreme;
Nor hope to be myself less miserable
By what I seek, but others to make such
As I, though thereby worse to me redound:
For only in destroying I find ease
To my relentless thoughts; and him destroyed,   130
Or won to what may work his utter loss,
For whom all this was made, all this will soon
Follow, as to him linked in weal or woe;
In woe then, that destruction wide may range.
To me shall be the glory sole among
The infernal Powers, in one day to have marred
What he Almighty styled, six nights and days
Continued making, and who knows how long
Before had been contriving, though perhaps

---

  99 ff. "O Earth," etc. Cf. Satan's soliloquy on first gaining sight of Eden, IV, 32 ff. As then, he is torn by passion, but now there is less of remorse, more of bitterness and despair.
  103. danced round by other Heavens. Milton frequently compares the motion of the heavenly bodies to a dance.

Not longer than since I in one night freed   140
From servitude inglorious well nigh half
The angelic name, and thinner left the throng
Of his adorers. He to be avenged,
And to repair his numbers thus impaired,
Whether such virtue spent of old now failed
More angels to create, if they at least
Are his created, or to spite us more,
Determined to advance into our room
A creature formed of earth, and him endow,
Exalted from so base original,   150
With heavenly spoils, our spoils. What he decreed
He effected; Man he made, and for him built
Magnificent this World, and Earth his seat,
Him lord pronounced, and, O indignity!
Subjected to his service angel wings,
And flaming ministers to watch and tend
Their earthy charge. Of these the vigilance
I dread, and to elude, thus wrapped in mist
Of midnight vapor glide obscure, and pry
In every bush and brake, where hap may find   160
The serpent sleeping, in whose mazy folds
To hide me, and the dark intent I bring.
O foul descent! that I who erst contended
With Gods to sit the highest, am now constrained
Into a beast, and, mixed with bestial slime,
This essence to incarnate and imbrute,
That to the height of deity aspired;
But what will not ambition and revenge
Descend to? Who aspires must down as low
As high he soared, obnoxious first or last   170
To basest things. Revenge, at first though sweet,
Bitter ere long back on itself recoils;
Let it; I reck not, so it light well aimed,
Since higher I fall short, on him who next
Provokes my envy, this new favorite
Of Heaven, this man of clay, son of despite,
Whom us the more to spite his Maker raised
From dust: spite then with spite is best repaid."
    So saying, through each thicket dank or dry,
Like a black mist low creeping, he held on   180
His midnight search, where soonest he might find
The serpent. Him fast sleeping soon he found
In labyrinth of many a round self-rolled,
His head the midst, well stored with subtle wiles;

---

142. name, race, stock.
163 ff. Satan's imbruting himself within the serpent is the final step in his progressive degeneration. His own words explain the symbolism.
170. obnoxious, liable, subject.

Not yet in horrid shade or dismal den,
Nor nocent yet, but on the grassy herb
Fearless unfeared he slept. In at his mouth
The Devil entered, and his brutal sense,
In heart or head, possessing soon inspired
With act intelligential, but his sleep   190
Disturbed not, waiting close the approach of morn.
    Now whenas sacred light began to dawn
In Eden on the humid flowers, that breathed
Their morning incense, when all things that breathe,
From the Earth's great altar send up silent praise
To the Creator, and his nostrils fill
With grateful smell, forth came the human pair
And joined their vocal worship to the choir
Of creatures wanting voice; that done, partake
The season, prime for sweetest scents and airs;   200
Then commune how that day they best may ply
Their growing work; for much their work outgrew
The hands' dispatch of two gardening so wide.
And Eve first to her husband thus began.
    "Adam, well may we labor still to dress
This garden, still to tend plant, herb, and flower,
Our pleasant task enjoined, but till more hands
Aid us, the work under our labor grows,
Luxurious by restraint; what we by day
Lop overgrown, or prune, or prop, or bind,   210
One night or two with wanton growth derides
Tending to wild. Thou therefore now advise
Or hear what to my mind first thoughts present:
Let us divide our labors, thou where choice
Leads thee, or where most needs, whether to wind
The woodbine round this arbor, or direct
The clasping ivy where to climb, while I
In yonder spring of roses intermixed
With myrtle, find what to redress till noon.
For while so near each other thus all day   220
Our task we choose, what wonder if so near
Looks intervene and smiles, or object new
Casual discourse draw on, which intermits
Our day's work, brought to little, though begun
Early, and the hour of supper comes unearned."
    To whom mild answer Adam thus returned.
"Sole Eve, associate sole, to me beyond
Compare above all living creatures dear,
Well hast thou motioned, well thy thoughts employed
How we might best fulfil the work which here   230

199–200. partake The season, i.e., share the beauties of the morning. As in IV, 640, **season** refers to the time of day.
    218. spring, clump, thicket.   **229. motioned,** proposed.

God hath assigned us, nor of me shalt pass
Unpraised; for nothing lovelier can be found
In woman, than to study household good,
And good works in her husband to promote.
Yet not so strictly hath our Lord imposed
Labor, as to debar us when we need
Refreshment, whether food, or talk between,
Food of the mind, or this sweet intercourse
Of looks and smiles, for smiles from reason flow,
To brute denied, and are of love the food,   240
Love not the lowest end of human life.
For not to irksome toil, but to delight
He made us, and delight to reason joined.
These paths and bowers doubt not but our joint hands
Will keep from wilderness with ease, as wide
As we need walk, till younger hands ere long
Assist us. But if much converse perhaps
Thee satiate, to short absence I could yield;
For solitude sometimes is best society,
And short retirement urges sweet return.   250
But other doubt possesses me, lest harm
Befall thee severed from me; for thou know'st
What hath been warned us, what malicious foe
Envying our happiness, and of his own
Despairing, seeks to work us woe and shame
By sly assault; and somewhere nigh at hand
Watches, no doubt, with greedy hope to find
His wish and best advantage, us asunder,
Hopeless to circumvent us joined, where each
To other speedy aid might lend at need;   260
Whether his first design be to withdraw
Our feälty from God, or to disturb
Conjugal love, than which perhaps no bliss
Enjoyed by us excites his envy more;
Or this, or worse, leave not the faithful side
That gave thee being, still shades thee and protects.
The wife, where danger or dishonor lurks,
Safest and seemliest by her husband stays,
Who guards her, or with her the worst endures."
    To whom the virgin majesty of Eve,   270
As one who loves, and some unkindness meets,
With sweet austere composure thus replied.
    "Offspring of Heaven and Earth, and all Earth's lord,
That such an enemy we have, who seeks
Our ruin, both by thee informed I learn,
And from the parting angel overheard

---

245. wilderness, wildness (i.e., too luxuriant growth of vegetation).
265. Or this, or worse, i.e., whether his design (261) be this or worse.
276. from the parting angel, i.e., from Raphael as he was parting from Adam.

As in a shady nook I stood behind,
Just then returned at shut of evening flowers.
But that thou shouldst my firmness therefore doubt
To God or thee, because we have a foe   280
May tempt it, I expected not to hear.
His violence thou fear'st not, being such,
As we, not capable of death or pain,
Can either not receive, or can repel.
His fraud is then thy fear, which plain infers
Thy equal fear that my firm faith and love
Can by his fraud be shaken or seduced;
Thoughts, which how found they harbor in thy breast,
Adam, misthought of her to thee so dear?"
   To whom with healing words Adam replied.   290
"Daughter of God and Man, immortal Eve,
For such thou art, from sin and blame entire;
Not diffident of thee do I dissuade
Thy absence from my sight, but to avoid
The attempt itself, intended by our foe.
For he who tempts, though in vain, at least asperses
The tempted with dishonor foul, supposed
Not incorruptible of faith, not proof
Against temptation. Thou thyself with scorn
And anger wouldst resent the offered wrong,   300
Though ineffectual found. Misdeem not then,
If such affront I labor to avert
From thee alone, which on us both at once
The enemy, though bold, will hardly dare,
Or daring, first on me the assault shall light.
Nor thou his malice and false guile contemn;
Subtle he needs must be, who could seduce
Angels, nor think superfluous others' aid.
I from the influence of thy looks receive
Access in every virtue, in thy sight   310
More wise, more watchful, stronger, if need were
Of outward strength; while shame, thou looking on,
Shame to be overcome or overreached,
Would utmost vigor raise, and raised unite.
Why shouldst not thou like sense within thee feel
When I am present, and thy trial choose
With me, best witness of thy virtue tried."
So spake domestic Adam in his care
And matrimonial love; but Eve, who thought
Less attributed to her faith sincere,   320
Thus her reply with accent sweet renewed.
   "If this be our condition, thus to dwell
In narrow circuit straitened by a foe,

---

292. entire, untouched.   **310. access,** growth, increase.
318. domestic, devoted to home life and its duties.   **320. less,** too little.

Subtle or violent, we not endued
Single with like defence, wherever met,
How are we happy, still in fear of harm?
But harm precedes not sin: only our foe
Tempting affronts us with his foul esteem
Of our integrity; his foul esteem
Sticks no dishonor on our front, but turns   330
Foul on himself; then wherefore shunned or feared
By us? who rather double honor gain
From his surmise proved false, find peace within,
Favor from Heaven, our witness, from the event.
And what is faith, love, virtue, unassayed
Alone, without exterior help sustained?
Let us not then suspect our happy state
Left so imperfect by the Maker wise,
As not secure to single or combined.
Frail is our happiness, if this be so,   340
And Eden were no Eden thus exposed."
     To whom thus Adam fervently replied.
"O Woman, best are all things as the will
Of God ordained them; his creating hand
Nothing imperfect or deficient left
Of all that he created, much less Man,
Or aught that might his happy state secure,
Secure from outward force: within himself
The danger lies, yet lies within his power;
Against his will he can receive no harm.   350
But God left free the will, for what obeys
Reason is free, and Reason he made right,
But bid her well be ware, and still erect,
Lest by some fair appearing good surprised
She dictate false, and misinform the will
To do what God expressly hath forbid.
Not then mistrust, but tender love enjoins,
That I should mind thee oft, and mind thou me.
Firm we subsist, yet possible to swerve,
Since Reason not impossibly may meet   360
Some specious object by the foe suborned,
And fall into deception unaware,
Not keeping strictest watch, as she was warned.

328. affronts. The literal meaning "strikes on the forehead" is implied (Latin *ad + frons*).
Note how the image is expanded in the two lines following.
   335. And what is faith, love, virtue, etc., i.e., what value have these qualities unless they
have been tested and found able to stand by their own merits. Milton here puts in the mouth
of Eve an argument which he himself used in *Areopagitica*. Cf. the famous passage: "I cannot
praise a fugitive and cloistered virtue," etc.
   339. to single or combined, i.e., to us singly or together.
   341. no Eden, no place of delight. Cf. note on IV, 27, 28.
   348 ff. within himself . . . no harm. The principle of human responsibility is fundamental
to Milton's whole philosophy.
   353. still erect, ever alert.

Seek not temptation then, which to avoid
Were better, and most likely if from me
Thou sever not; trial will come unsought.
Wouldst thou approve thy constancy, approve
First thy obedience; the other who can know,
Not seeing thee attempted, who attest?
But if thou think trial unsought may find   370
Us both securer than thus warned thou seem'st,
Go; for thy stay, not free, absents thee more;
Go in thy native innocence, rely
On what thou hast of virtue, summon all,
For God towards thee hath done his part, do thine."
    So spake the patriarch of mankind, but Eve
Persisted; yet submiss, though last, replied.
    "With thy permission then, and thus forewarned,
Chiefly by what thy own last reasoning words
Touched only, that our trial, when least sought,   380
May find us both perhaps far less prepared,
The willinger I go, nor much expect
A foe so proud will first the weaker seek;
So bent, the more shall shame him his repulse."
    Thus saying, from her husband's hand her hand
Soft she withdrew, and like a wood-nymph light,
Oread or Dryad, or of Delia's train,
Betook her to the groves, but Delia's self
In gait surpassed and goddess-like deport,
Though not as she with bow and quiver armed,   390
But with such gardening tools as art yet rude,
Guiltless of fire had formed, or angels brought.
To Pales, or Pomona, thus adorned,
Likest she seemed, Pomona when she fled
Vertumnus, or to Ceres in her prime,
Yet virgin of Proserpina from Jove.
Her long with ardent look his eye pursued
Delighted, but desiring more her stay.
Oft he to her his charge of quick return
Repeated, she to him as oft engaged   400
To be returned by noon amid the bower,
And all things in best order to invite
Noontide repast, or afternoon's repose.
O much deceived, much failing, hapless Eve,
Of thy presumed return! event perverse!

---

367. approve, give proof of, confirm.   **371. securer,** i.e., "less prepared" (381).
    387. Oread or Dryad, a nymph of the mountains or of the trees. **Delia,** the goddess Diana,
born on the island of Delos.
    392. Guiltless of fire. The uses of fire are not discovered until after the fall.
    393 ff. Pales was a Roman goddess of flocks, **Pomona** of fruits, **Ceres** of agriculture;
Vertumnus was god of the changing seasons.
    396. Yet virgin of, not yet the mother of.
    402. And all things in best order, i.e., to have all things in best order.

Thou never from that hour in Paradise
Found'st either sweet repast or sound repose;
Such ambush, hid among sweet flowers and shades,
Waited with hellish rancor imminent
To intercept thy way, or send thee back   410
Despoiled of innocence, of faith, of bliss.
    For now, and since first break of dawn the Fiend,
Mere serpent in appearance, forth was come,
And on his quest, where likeliest he might find
The only two of mankind, but in them
The whole included race, his purposed prey.
In bower and field he sought, where any tuft
Of grove or garden-plot more pleasant lay,
Their tendance or plantation for delight,
By fountain or by shady rivulet.   420
He sought them both, but wished his hap might find
Eve separate; he wished, but not with hope
Of what so seldom chanced; when to his wish,
Beyond his hope, Eve separate he spies,
Veiled in a cloud of fragrance, where she stood,
Half spied, so thick the roses bushing round
About her glowed, oft stooping to support
Each flower of slender stalk, whose head though gay
Carnation, purple, azure, or specked with gold,
Hung drooping unsustained; them she upstays   430
Gently with myrtle band, mindless the while
Herself, though fairest unsupported flower,
From her best prop so far, and storm so nigh.
Nearer he drew, and many a walk traversed
Of stateliest covert, cedar, pine, or palm,
Then voluble and bold, now hid, now seen
Among thick-woven arborets and flowers
Imbordered on each bank, the hand of Eve:
Spot more delicious than those gardens feigned
Or of revived Adonis, or renowned   440
Alcinous, host of old Laertes' son,
Or that, not mystic, where the sapient king
Held dalliance with his fair Egyptian spouse.
Much he the place admired, the person more.
As one who long in populous city pent,

432. **Herself . . . flower.** The metaphor is repeated from IV, 270.
436. **voluble,** rolling (Latin *volubilis*).   437. **arborets,** small trees, shrubs.
438. **hand,** handiwork.
439 ff. The gardens of Alcinous, the Phaeacian ruler who entertained Odysseus (**old Laertes' son**), are described in *Odyssey* vii. The garden of Solomon (**the sapient king**) is mentioned in Scripture; hence, from Milton's point of view, it is not **feigned** or **mystic** (i.e., mythical) like the others. Cf. Song of Sol. 7:2, and I Kings 3:1.
440, 442. **Or . . . or,** either . . . or.
445 ff. The attitude toward nature revealed in this simile anticipates Wordsworth's. Note especially the idea that natural objects, lovely in themselves, are enhanced in meaning by their human associations. Milton's treatment is ordinarily more impersonal.

Where houses thick and sewers annoy the air,
Forth issuing on a summer's morn to breathe
Among the pleasant villages and farms
Adjoined, from each thing met conceives delight,
The smell of grain, or tedded grass, or kine,   450
Or dairy, each rural sight, each rural sound;
If chance with nymph-like step fair virgin pass,
What pleasing seemed, for her now pleases more,
She most, and in her look sums all delight.
Such pleasure took the Serpent to behold
This flowery plat, the sweet recess of Eve
Thus early, thus alone; her heavenly form
Angelic, but more soft and feminine,
Her graceful innocence, her every air
Of gesture or least action overawed   460
His malice, and with rapine sweet bereaved
His fierceness of the fierce intent it brought.
That space the Evil One abstracted stood
From his own evil, and for the time remained
Stupidly good, of enmity disarmed,
Of guile, of hate, of envy, of revenge;
But the hot hell that always in him burns,
Though in mid Heaven, soon ended his delight,
And tortures him now more, the more he sees
Of pleasure not for him ordained; then soon   470
Fierce hate he recollects, and all his thoughts
Of mischief, gratulating, thus excites.
   "Thoughts, whither have ye led me, with what sweet
Compulsion thus transported to forget
What hither brought us, hate, not love, nor hope
Of Paradise for Hell, hope here to taste
Of pleasure, but all pleasure to destroy,
Save what is in destroying; other joy
To me is lost. Then let me not let pass
Occasion which now smiles, behold alone   480
The woman, opportune to all attempts,
Her husband, for I view far round, not nigh,
Whose higher intellectual more I shun,
And strength, of courage haughty, and of limb
Heroic built, though of terrestrial mould,
Foe not informidable, exempt from wound,
I not; so much hath Hell debased, and pain
Enfeebled me, to what I was in Heaven.
She fair, divinely fair, fit love for Gods,
Not terrible, though terror be in love   490

446. **annoy,** pollute, render noisome.
450. **tedded grass,** grass just mown and spread out for drying.
465. **Stupidly good,** i.e., stupefied into goodness.
485. **of terrestrial mould,** of earthly substance.

And beauty, not approached by stronger hate,
Hate stronger, under shew of love well feigned,
The way which to her ruin now I tend."
    So spake the Enemy of mankind, enclosed
In serpent, inmate bad, and toward Eve
Addressed his way, not with indented wave,
Prone on the ground as since, but on his rear,
Circular base of rising folds, that towered
Fold above fold a surging maze; his head
Crested aloft, and carbuncle his eyes;   500
With burnished neck of verdant gold, erect
Amidst his circling spires, that on the grass
Floated redundant. Pleasing was his shape,
And lovely, never since of serpent kind
Lovelier; not those that in Illyria changed
Hermione and Cadmus, or the god
In Epidaurus; nor to which transformed
Ammonian Jove, or Capitoline was seen,
He with Olympias, this with her who bore
Scipio the height of Rome. With tract oblique   510
At first, as one who sought access, but feared
To interrupt, sidelong he works his way.
As when a ship by skilful steersman wrought
Nigh river's mouth or foreland, where the wind
Veers oft, as oft so steers, and shifts her sail;
So varied he, and of his tortuous train
Curled many a wanton wreath in sight of Eve,
To lure her eye; she busied heard the sound
Of rustling leaves, but minded not, as used
To such disport before her through the field,   520
From every beast, more duteous at her call,
Than at Circean call the herd disguised.
He bolder now, uncalled before her stood,
But as in gaze admiring. Oft he bowed
His turret crest, and sleek enamelled neck,
Fawning, and licked the ground whereon she trod.
His gentle dumb expression turned at length

500. **carbuncle,** i.e., deep red, suggesting passion.   502. **spires,** coils.
505. **changed,** took the place of.
506. **Hermione** and her husband **Cadmus,** king of Thebes, were changed into serpents at their own request, in order to escape the miseries of human life. The god of medicine, Aesculapius, took the form of a serpent when going from **Epidaurus** to Rome for the purpose of staying a pestilence.
507. **nor to which transformed,** etc., i.e., nor those serpents into which Jove was seen transformed. According to a myth told by Plutarch, Jupiter Ammon (**Ammonian Jove**) was the father of Alexander the Great, having been observed in the shape of a serpent with **Olympias,** Alexander's mother. A similar myth portrayed Jupiter Capitolinus as the father of Scipio Africanus.
517. **wanton,** playful.
522. **Circean call.** The allusion is to the well-known myth of Circe, an enchantress who changed men into beasts and kept them in complete subjection to her will.

The eye of Eve to mark his play; he glad
Of her attention gained, with serpent tongue
Organic, or impulse of vocal air,   530
His fraudulent temptation thus began:
    "Wonder not, sovran mistress, if perhaps
Thou canst, who art sole wonder, much less arm
Thy looks, the heaven of mildness, with disdain,
Displeased that I approach thee thus, and gaze
Insatiate, I thus single, nor have feared
Thy awful brow, more awful thus retired.
Fairest resemblance of thy Maker fair,
Thee all things living gaze on, all things thine
By gift, and thy celestial beauty adore,   540
With ravishment beheld, there best beheld
Where universally admired; but here
In this enclosure wild, these beasts among,
Beholders rude, and shallow to discern
Half what in thee is fair, one man except,
Who sees thee? (and what is one?) who shouldst be seen
A Goddess among Gods, adored and served
By angels numberless, thy daily train."
    So glozed the Tempter, and his proem tuned;
Into the heart of Eve his words made way,   550
Though at the voice much marvelling; at length
Not unamazed she thus in answer spake.
    "What may this mean? Language of man pronounced
By tongue of brute, and human sense expressed?
The first at least of these I thought denied
To beasts, whom God on their creation-day
Created mute to all articulate sound;
The latter I demur, for in their looks
Much reason, and in their actions, oft appears.
Thee, Serpent, subtlest beast of all the field   560
I knew, but not with human voice endued;
Redouble then this miracle, and say,
How cam'st thou speakable of mute, and how
To me so friendly grown above the rest
Of brutal kind, that daily are in sight?
Say, for such wonder claims attention due."
    To whom the guileful Tempter thus replied.
"Empress of this fair World, resplendent Eve,
Easy to me it is to tell thee all
What thou command'st, and right thou shouldst be obeyed.   570

    529. with serpent tongue, etc. Satan either uses the serpent's vocal organs directly or
causes his words seemingly to come from them.
    544. shallow, i.e., too shallow.
    549. glozed, smoothed over his real motive with flattery.
    558. demur, remain in doubt about.
    563. How cam'st thou speakable of mute, i.e., how did you, being mute, become capable of
speech.

I was at first as other beasts that graze
The trodden herb, of abject thoughts and low,
As was my food, nor aught but food discerned
Or sex, and apprehended nothing high:
Till on a day roving the field, I chanced
A goodly tree far distant to behold
Loaden with fruit of fairest colors mixed,
Ruddy and gold. I nearer drew to gaze;
When from the boughs a savory odor blown,
Grateful to appetite, more pleased my sense   580
Than smell of sweetest fennel or the teats
Of ewe or goat dropping with milk at even,
Unsucked of lamb or kid, that tend their play.
To satisfy the sharp desire I had
Of tasting those fair apples, I resolved
Not to defer; hunger and thirst at once,
Powerful persuaders, quickened at the scent
Of that alluring fruit, urged me so keen.
About the mossy trunk I wound me soon,
For high from ground the branches would require   590
Thy utmost reach or Adam's: round the tree
All other beasts that saw, with like desire
Longing and envying stood, but could not reach.
Amid the tree now got, where plenty hung
Tempting so nigh, to pluck and eat my fill
I spared not, for such pleasure till that hour
At feed or fountain never had I found.
Sated at length, ere long I might perceive
Strange alteration in me, to degree
Of reason in my inward powers, and speech   600
Wanted not long, though to this shape retained.
Thenceforth to speculations high or deep
I turned my thoughts, and with capacious mind
Considered all things visible in Heaven,
Or Earth, or middle, all things fair and good;
But all that fair and good in thy divine
Semblance, and in thy beauty's heavenly ray
United I beheld; no fair to thine
Equivalent or second, which compelled
Me thus, though importune perhaps, to come   610
And gaze, and worship thee of right declared
Sovran of creatures, universal Dame."
   So talked the spirited sly Snake; and Eve
Yet more amazed unwary thus replied.
   "Serpent, thy overpraising leaves in doubt

---

581. According to popular belief, serpents were especially fond of fennel and were in the habit of sucking milk from sheep and goats.
605. middle, i.e., the air.   **612. universal Dame,** mistress of the universe.
613. spirited, i.e., inspired by Satan.

The virtue of that fruit, in thee first proved.
But say, where grows the tree, from hence how far?
For many are the trees of God that grow
In Paradise, and various, yet unknown
To us; in such abundance lies our choice,   620
As leaves a greater store of fruit untouched,
Still hanging incorruptible, till men
Grow up to their provision, and more hands
Help to disburden Nature of her birth."
     To whom the wily Adder, blithe and glad.
"Empress, the way is ready, and not long;
Beyond a row of myrtles, on a flat,
Fast by a fountain, one small thicket past
Of blowing myrrh and balm; if thou accept
My conduct, I can bring thee thither soon."   630
     "Lead then," said Eve. He leading swiftly rolled
In tangles, and made intricate seem straight,
To mischief swift. Hope elevates, and joy
Brightens his crest, as when a wandering fire,
Compact of unctuous vapor, which the night
Condenses, and the cold environs round,
Kindled through agitation to a flame,
Which oft, they say, some evil spirit attends,
Hovering and blazing with delusive light,
Misleads the amazed night-wanderer from his way   640
To bogs and mires, and oft through pond or pool,
There swallowed up and lost, from succor far.
So glistered the dire Snake, and into fraud
Led Eve our credulous mother, to the tree
Of prohibition, root of all our woe;
Which when she saw, thus to her guide she spake.
     "Serpent, we might have spared our coming hither,
Fruitless to me, though fruit be here to excess,
The credit of whose virtue rest with thee,
Wondrous indeed, if cause of such effects.   650
But of this tree we may not taste nor touch;
God so commanded, and left that command
Sole daughter of his voice; the rest, we live
Law to ourselves, our reason is our law."
     To whom the Tempter guilefully replied.
"Indeed? Hath God then said that of the fruit
Of all these garden trees ye shall not eat,
Yet lords declared of all in Earth or air?"

     622. incorruptible, incapable of decay.
     624. birth, i.e., the products to which she has given birth.
     629. blowing, blossoming.
     634 ff. This description of the ignis fatuus combines a semiscientific explanation with a popular superstition. Whether Milton actually believed the phenomenon the work of an evil spirit he does not say.
     643. fraud, offense, harm.   **653. the rest,** as for the rest.

To whom thus Eve yet sinless. "Of the fruit
Of each tree in the garden we may eat,   660
But of the fruit of this fair tree amidst
The garden, God hath said, 'Ye shall not eat
Thereof, nor shall ye touch it, lest ye die.'"
　　She scarce had said, though brief, when now more bold
The Tempter, but with show of zeal and love
To Man, and indignation at his wrong,
New part puts on, and as to passion moved,
Fluctuates disturbed, yet comely and in act
Raised, as of some great matter to begin.
As when of old some orator renowned   670
In Athens or free Rome, where eloquence
Flourished, since mute, to some great cause addressed,
Stood in himself collected, while each part,
Motion, each act won audience ere the tongue,
Sometimes in height began, as no delay
Of preface brooking through his zeal of right.
So standing, moving, or to height upgrown,
The Tempter all impassioned thus began.
　　"O sacred, wise, and wisdom-giving Plant,
Mother of science, now I feel thy power   680
Within me clear, not only to discern
Things in their causes, but to trace the ways
Of highest agents, deemed however wise.
Queen of this Universe, do not believe
Those rigid threats of death; ye shall not die:
How should ye? by the fruit? it gives you life
To knowledge; by the threatener? look on me,
Me who have touched and tasted, yet both live,
And life more perfect have attained than fate
Meant me, by venturing higher than my lot.   690
Shall that be shut to Man, which to the beast
Is open? or will God incense his ire
For such a petty trespass, and not praise
Rather your dauntless virtue, whom the pain
Of death denounced, whatever thing death be,
Deterred not from achieving what might lead
To happier life, knowledge of good and evil;
Of good, how just? of evil, if what is evil
Be real, why not known, since easier shunned?
God therefore cannot hurt ye, and be just;   700
Not just, not God; not feared then, nor obeyed:

661–63. Milton here follows very closely the phraseology of Gen. 3:1–3.
　　668. Fluctuates. The word is used literally. Milton means that the serpent moves his body
to and fro, in order to give visible expression to his assumed emotion.
　　679 ff. "O sacred, wise . . ." The serpent's speech is a masterpiece of persuasion, uniting
intense emotional fervor with closely packed and seemingly irrefutable arguments. Milton
does not wish to make Eve too easy a victim.
　　680. science, knowledge (Latin *scientia*).　　　**687. To,** in addition to.

Your fear itself of death removes the fear.
Why then was this forbid? Why but to awe,
Why but to keep ye low and ignorant,
His worshippers; he knows that in the day
Ye eat thereof, your eyes that seem so clear,
Yet are but dim, shall perfectly be then
Opened and cleared, and ye shall be as Gods,
Knowing both good and evil as they know.
That ye should be as Gods, since I as Man,   710
Internal Man, is but proportion meet,
I of brute human, ye of human Gods.
So ye shall die perhaps, by putting off
Human, to put on Gods, death to be wished,
Though threatened, which no worse than this can bring.
And what are Gods, that Man may not become
As they, participating godlike food?
The Gods are first, and that advantage use
On our belief, that all from them proceeds;
I question it, for this fair Earth I see,   720
Warmed by the sun, producing every kind,
Them nothing. If they all things, who enclosed
Knowledge of good and evil in this tree,
That whoso eats thereof, forthwith attains
Wisdom without their leave? and wherein lies
The offence, that Man should thus attain to know?
What can your knowledge hurt him, or this tree
Impart against his will, if all be his?
Or is it envy, and can envy dwell
In heavenly breasts? These, these and many more   730
Causes import your need of this fair fruit.
Goddess humane, reach then, and freely taste!"
  He ended, and his words replete with guile
Into her heart too easy entrance won.
Fixed on the fruit she gazed, which to behold
Might tempt alone, and in her ears the sound
Yet rung of his persuasive words, impregned
With reason, to her seeming, and with truth;
Meanwhile the hour of noon drew on, and waked
An eager appetite, raised by the smell   740
So savory of that fruit, which with desire,
Inclinable now grown to touch or taste,
Solicited her longing eye; yet first
Pausing a while, thus to herself she mused.
  "Great are thy virtues, doubtless, best of fruits,
Though kept from Man, and worthy to be admired,
Whose taste, too long forborne, at first assay

---

732. humane, gracious, gentle in demeanor.   **737. impregned,** impregnated.
739–43. Physical appetite is an important factor in Eve's decision, but she does not admit it
to herself.

Gave elocution to the mute, and taught
The tongue not made for speech to speak thy praise.
Thy praise he also who forbids thy use   750
Conceals not from us, naming thee the Tree
Of Knowledge, knowledge both of good and evil;
Forbids us then to taste, but his forbidding
Commends thee more, while it infers the good
By thee communicated, and our want;
For good unknown sure is not had, or had
And yet unknown, is as not had at all.
In plain then, what forbids he but to know,
Forbids us good, forbids us to be wise?
Such prohibitions bind not. But if Death   760
Bind us with after-bands, what profits then
Our inward freedom? In the day we eat
Of this fair fruit, our doom is, we shall die.
How dies the Serpent? He hath eaten and lives,
And knows, and speaks, and reasons, and discerns,
Irrational till then. For us alone
Was death invented? or to us denied
This intellectual food, for beasts reserved?
For beasts it seems; yet that one beast which first
Hath tasted, envies not, but brings with joy   770
That good befallen him, author unsuspect,
Friendly to man, far from deceit or guile.
What fear I then, rather what know to fear
Under this ignorance of good and evil,
Of God or death, of law or penalty?
Here grows the cure of all, this fruit divine,
Fair to the eye, inviting to the taste,
Of virtue to make wise; what hinders then
To reach, and feed at once both body and mind?"
    So saying, her rash hand in evil hour   780
Forth reaching to the fruit, she plucked, she eat.
Earth felt the wound, and Nature from her seat
Sighing through all her works gave signs of woe,
That all was lost. Back to the thicket slunk
The guilty Serpent, and well might, for Eve
Intent now only on her taste, nought else
Regarded; such delight till then, as seemed,
In fruit she never tasted, whether true
Or fancied so, through expectation high
Of knowledge, nor was Godhead from her thought.   790

758. **In plain,** frankly (i.e., in plain terms).
771. **author unsuspect,** informant not to be suspected.
778. **Of virtue,** i.e., having the power.
781. **eat.** Milton regularly uses this form of the preterite. Since the pronunciation corresponds to the spelling, lines 781 and 782 form a rhymed couplet, giving effective emphasis to a crucial point in the action.

Greedily she ingorged without restraint,
And knew not eating death. Satiate at length,
And heightened as with wine, jocund and boon,
Thus to herself she pleasingly began.
  "O sovran, virtuous, precious of all trees
In Paradise, of operation blest
To sapience, hitherto obscured, infamed,
And thy fair fruit let hang, as to no end
Created; but henceforth my early care,
Not without song, each morning, and due praise,   800
Shall tend thee, and the fertile burden ease
Of thy full branches offered free to all;
Till dieted by thee I grow mature
In knowledge, as the Gods who all things know;
Though others envy what they cannot give;
For had the gift been theirs, it had not here
Thus grown. Experience, next to thee I owe,
Best guide; not following thee, I had remained
In ignorance, thou open'st Wisdom's way,
And givest access, though secret she retire.   810
And I perhaps am secret; Heaven is high,
High and remote to see from thence distinct
Each thing on Earth; and other care perhaps
May have diverted from continual watch
Our great Forbidder, safe with all his spies
About him. But to Adam in what sort
Shall I appear? Shall I to him make known
As yet my change, and give him to partake
Full happiness with me, or rather not,
But keep the odds of knowledge in my power   820
Without copartner? so to add what wants
In female sex, the more to draw his love,
And render me more equal, and perhaps,
A thing not undesirable, sometime
Superior; for inferior who is free?
This may be well. But what if God have seen
And death ensue? then I shall be no more,
And Adam wedded to another Eve,

791. **Greedily she ingorged without restraint.** In terms of human ethics as opposed to theology, Milton interprets the sin of Adam and Eve as a sin of excess, a violation of temperance. Eve's initial greed is therefore a symbol of all the other forms of excess in which she and Adam afterwards indulge.

792. **knew not eating,** i.e., knew not that she was eating.   793. **boon,** gay.

795. **virtuous, precious of all trees,** i.e., most virtuous, most precious, etc. The idiom is classical.

796–97. **of operation blest To sapience,** i.e., so blest as to have the power of conferring wisdom.

797. **infamed,** not known.   815. **safe,** not likely to do harm.

817 ff. **Shall I to him,** etc. The first fruits of Eve's sin are selfishness and jealousy—the negation of her original qualities.

Shall live with her enjoying, I extinct;
A death to think. Confirmed then I resolve   830
Adam shall share with me in bliss or woe.
So dear I love him, that with him all deaths
I could endure, without him live no life."
   So saying, from the tree her step she turned,
But first low reverence done, as to the power
That dwelt within, whose presence had infused
Into the plant sciential sap, derived
From nectar, drink of Gods. Adam the while
Waiting desirous her return, had wove
Of choicest flowers a garland to adorn   840
Her tresses, and her rural labors crown,
As reapers oft are wont their harvest queen.
Great joy he promised to his thoughts, and new
Solace in her return, so long delayed;
Yet oft his heart, divine of something ill,
Misgave him; he the faltering measure felt;
And forth to meet her went, the way she took
That morn when first they parted. By the Tree
Of Knowledge he must pass; there he her met,
Scarce from the tree returning; in her hand   850
A bough of fairest fruit that downy smiled,
New gathered, and ambrosial smell diffused.
To him she hasted; in her face excuse
Came prologue, and apology to prompt,
Which with bland words at will she thus addressed.
   "Hast thou not wondered, Adam, at my stay?
Thee I have missed, and thought it long, deprived
Thy presence, agony of love till now
Not felt, nor shall be twice, for never more
Mean I to try what rash untried I sought,   860
The pain of absence from thy sight. But strange
Hath been the cause, and wonderful to hear:
This tree is not as we are told, a tree
Of danger tasted, nor to evil unknown
Opening the way, but of divine effect
To open eyes, and make them Gods who taste;
And hath been tasted such. The Serpent wise,
Or not restrained as we, or not obeying,
Hath eaten of the fruit, and is become

835–36. Eve's perverted conception of God quickly manifests itself in idolatry.
837. sciential, capable of bestowing knowledge.
838–44. Adam the while . . . delayed. The situation closely parallels that in *Iliad* xxii, where Andromache is described making preparations for Hector's return, not knowing that he is already slain.
845. divine of, foreboding.
846. faltering measure, i.e., the uneven beating of his heart.
853–54. in her face . . . prompt. Milton means that the appearance of Eve's face served as a fitting introduction to her verbal apology. The stage imagery is perhaps intended to suggest her insincerity; she approaches Adam in an assumed character.

Not dead as we are threatened, but thenceforth   870
Endued with human voice and human sense,
Reasoning to admiration, and with me
Persuasively hath so prevailed, that I
Have also tasted, and have also found
The effects to correspond, opener mine eyes,
Dim erst, dilated spirits, ampler heart,
And growing up to Godhead; which for thee
Chiefly I sought, without thee can despise.
For bliss, as thou hast part, to me is bliss;
Tedious, unshared with thee, and odious soon.   880
Thou therefore also taste, that equal lot
May join us, equal joy, as equal love;
Lest thou not tasting, different degree
Disjoin us, and I then too late renounce
Deity for thee, when fate will not permit."
    Thus Eve with countenance blithe her story told;
But in her cheek distemper flushing glowed.
On the other side, Adam, soon as he heard
The fatal trespass done by Eve, amazed,
Astonied stood and blank, while horror chill   890
Ran through his veins, and all his joints relaxed;
From his slack hand the garland wreathed for Eve
Down dropped, and all the faded roses shed.
Speechless he stood and pale, till thus at length
First to himself he inward silence broke.
    "O fairest of creation, last and best
Of all God's works, creature in whom excelled
Whatever can to sight or thought be formed,
Holy, divine, good, amiable, or sweet!
How art thou lost, how on a sudden lost,   900
Defaced, deflowered, and now to death devote!
Rather how hast thou yielded to transgress
The strict forbiddance, how to violate
The sacred fruit forbidden! Some cursèd fraud
Of enemy hath beguiled thee, yet unknown,
And me with thee hath ruined, for with thee
Certain my resolution is to die;
How can I live without thee, how forgo
Thy sweet converse and love so dearly joined,
To live again in these wild woods forlorn?   910
Should God create another Eve, and I
Another rib afford, yet loss of thee
Would never from my heart; no, no! I feel
The link of nature draw me: flesh of flesh,

---

872. **to admiration,** in a way to be admired.

877–78. **which for . . . Chiefly I sought.** Eve ends her plea with an open falsehood.
Cf. 816–25.

901. **devote,** doomed, accursed.   914 ff. **flesh of flesh,** etc. Cf. Gen. 2:23.

Bone of my bone thou art, and from thy state
Mine never shall be parted, bliss or woe."
  So having said, as one from sad dismay
Recomforted, and after thoughts disturbed
Submitting to what seemed remediless,
Thus in calm mood his words to Eve he turned.   920
  "Bold deed thou hast presumed, adventurous Eve,
And peril great provoked, who thus hast dared,
Had it been only coveting to eye
That sacred fruit, sacred to abstinence,
Much more to taste it under ban to touch.
But past who can recall, or done undo?
Not God Omnipotent, nor Fate. Yet so
Perhaps thou shalt not die; perhaps the fact
Is not so heinous now, foretasted fruit,
Profaned first by the Serpent, by him first   930
Made common and unhallowed ere our taste,
Nor yet on him found deadly; he yet lives,
Lives, as thou saidst, and gains to live as Man
Higher degree of life, inducement strong
To us, as likely tasting to attain
Proportional ascent, which cannot be
But to be Gods, or angels, demi-gods.
Nor can I think that God, Creator wise,
Though threatening, will in earnest so destroy
Us his prime creatures, dignified so high,   940
Set over all his works, which in our fall,
For us created, needs with us must fail,
Dependent made; so God shall uncreate,
Be frustrate, do, undo, and labor lose,
Not well conceived of God, who though his power
Creation could repeat, yet would be loth
Us to abolish, lest the Adversary
Triumph and say: 'Fickle their state whom God
Most favors, who can please him long? Me first
He ruined, now mankind; whom will he next?'   950
Matter of scorn not to be given the Foe;
However, I with thee have fixed my lot,
Certain to undergo like doom: if death
Consort with thee, death is to me as life;
So forcible within my heart I feel
The bond of nature draw me to my own,
My own in thee, for what thou art is mine;
Our state cannot be severed; we are one,
One flesh; to lose thee were to lose myself."

---

    928. fact, deed (Latin *factum*).
    932. he yet lives, etc. Having determined his course on nonrational grounds, Adam proceeds to rationalize just as Eve had done.
    953. Certain, resolved.

So Adam, and thus Eve to him replied.   960
"O glorious trial of exceeding love,
Illustrious evidence, example high!
Engaging me to emulate, but short
Of thy perfection, how shall I attain,
Adam, from whose dear side I boast me sprung,
And gladly of our union hear thee speak,
One heart, one soul in both; whereof good proof
This day affords, declaring thee resolved,
Rather than death or aught than death more dread
Shall separate us, linked in love so dear,   970
To undergo with me one guilt, one crime,
If any be, of tasting this fair fruit,
Whose virtue (for of good still good proceeds,
Direct, or by occasion) hath presented
This happy trial of thy love, which else
So eminently never had been known.
Were it I thought death menaced would ensue
This my attempt, I would sustain alone
The worst, and not persuade thee, rather die
Deserted, than oblige thee with a fact   980
Pernicious to thy peace, chiefly assured
Remarkably so late of thy so true,
So faithful love unequalled; but I feel
Far otherwise the event, not death, but life
Augmented, opened eyes, new hopes, new joys,
Taste so divine, that what of sweet before
Hath touched my sense, flat seems to this and harsh.
On my experience, Adam, freely taste,
And fear of death deliver to the winds."
    So saying, she embraced him, and for joy   990
Tenderly wept, much won that he his love
Had so ennobled, as of choice to incur
Divine displeasure for her sake, or death.
In recompense (for such compliance bad
Such recompense best merits) from the bough
She gave him of that fair enticing fruit
With liberal hand; he scrupled not to eat
Against his better knowledge, not deceived,
But fondly overcome with female charm.
Earth trembled from her entrails, as again   1000
In pangs, and Nature gave a second groan;
Sky loured, and muttering thunder, some sad drops

977–83. Were it I thought . . . unequalled. Cf. 826–33. **oblige,** render liable to punishment.
    1000 ff. Earth trembled, etc. The idea that the fall was marked by convulsions of the earth and other signs of nature's grief is a literary and theological tradition. While it has no direct scriptural authority, it may have been suggested by the analogous portents accompanying the crucifixion of Christ (Matt. 27:51).

Wept at completing of the mortal sin
Original; while Adam took no thought,
Eating his fill, nor Eve to iterate
Her former trespass feared, the more to soothe
Him with her loved society, that now
As with new wine intoxicated both
They swim in mirth, and fancy that they feel
Divinity within them breeding wings   1010
Wherewith to scorn the Earth. But that false fruit
Far other operation first displayed,
Carnal desire inflaming: he on Eve
Began to cast lascivious eyes, she him
As wantonly repaid; in lust they burn,
Till Adam thus 'gan Eve to dalliance move.
    "Eve, now I see thou art exact of taste,
And elegant, of sapience no small part,
Since to each meaning savor we apply,
And palate call judicious; I the praise   1020
Yield thee, so well this day thou hast purveyed.
Much pleasure we have lost, while we abstained
From this delightful fruit, nor known till now
True relish, tasting; if such pleasure be
In things to us forbidden, it might be wished
For this one tree had been forbidden ten.
But come; so well refreshed, now let us play,
As meet is, after such delicious fare;
For never did thy beauty since the day
I saw thee first and wedded thee, adorned   1030
With all perfections, so inflame my sense
With ardor to enjoy thee, fairer now
Than ever, bounty of this virtuous tree."
    So said he, and forbore not glance or toy
Of amorous intent, well understood
Of Eve, whose eye darted contagious fire.
Her hand he seized, and to a shady bank,
Thick overhead with verdant roof embowered,
He led her nothing loth; flowers were the couch,
Pansies, and violets, and asphodel,   1040
And hyacinth, Earth's freshest softest lap.
There they their fill of love and love's disport
Took largely, of their mutual guilt the seal,
The solace of their sin, till dewy sleep
Oppressed them, wearied with their amorous play.
    Soon as the force of that fallacious fruit,

1003–4. the mortal sin Original. This is Milton's only use in the poem of the theological term "original sin."

1019. The word **savor** is derived from Latin *sapere*, which means both "to taste" and "to be wise." Milton represents Adam as playing on this double meaning in explaining why Eve's *taste* can properly be called **judicious.**

1034. toy, caress.

That with exhilarating vapor bland
About their spirits had played, and inmost powers
Made err, was now exhaled, and grosser sleep,
Bred of unkindly fumes, with conscious dreams   1050
Encumbered, now had left them, up they rose
As from unrest, and each the other viewing,
Soon found their eyes how opened, and their minds
How darkened; innocence, that as a veil
Had shadowed them from knowing ill, was gone,
Just confidence, and native righteousness,
And honor from about them, naked left
To guilty Shame. He covered, but his robe
Uncovered more. So rose the Danite strong,
Herculean Samson, from the harlot-lap   1060
Of Philistean Delilah, and waked
Shorn of his strength, they destitute and bare
Of all their virtue. Silent, and in face
Confounded, long they sat, as strucken mute,
Till Adam, though not less than Eve abashed,
At length gave utterance to these words constrained.
    "O Eve, in evil hour thou didst give ear
To that false worm, of whomsoever taught
To counterfeit Man's voice, true in our fall,
False in our promised rising; since our eyes   1070
Opened we find indeed, and find we know
Both good and evil, good lost and evil got,
Bad fruit of knowledge, if this be to know,
Which leaves us naked thus, of honor void,
Of innocence, of faith, of purity,
Our wonted ornaments now soiled and stained,
And in our faces evident the signs
Of foul concupiscence; whence evil store,
Even shame, the last of evils; of the first
Be sure then. How shall I behold the face   1080
Henceforth of God or angel, erst with joy
And rapture so oft beheld? those heavenly shapes
Will dazzle now this earthly, with their blaze
Insufferably bright. Oh might I here
In solitude live savage, in some glade
Obscured, where highest woods impenetrable
To star or sunlight, spread their umbrage broad
And brown as evening! Cover me ye pines,
Ye cedars, with innumerable boughs
Hide me, where I may never see them more.   1090
But let us now, as in bad plight, devise

1050. **unkindly,** contrary to nature.
1058. **He covered,** etc. i.e., shame covered them with his robe, but in so doing revealed to them their nakedness.
1059. **So rose the Danite strong,** etc. Cf. Judg. 16:4–20.   **1068. worm,** serpent.
1079. **the last of evils,** i.e., the greatest (Latin *extremus*). **the first,** i.e., the lesser.

What best may for the present serve to hide
The parts of each from other that seem most
To shame obnoxious, and unseemliest seen,
Some tree whose broad smooth leaves together sewed,
And girded on our loins, may cover round
Those middle parts, that this new comer, Shame,
There sit not, and reproach us as unclean."
   So counselled he, and both together went
Into the thickest wood; there soon they chose   1100
The fig-tree, not that kind for fruit renowned,
But such as at this day to Indians known
In Malabar or Decan spreads her arms
Branching so broad and long, that in the ground
The bended twigs take root, and daughters grow
About the mother tree, a pillared shade
High overarched, and echoing walks between;
There oft the Indian herdsman shunning heat
Shelters in cool, and tends his pasturing herds
At loop-holes cut through thickest shade. Those leaves   1110
They gathered, broad as Amazonian targe,
And with what skill they had, together sewed,
To gird their waist, vain covering if to hide
Their guilt and dreaded shame; Oh how unlike
To that first naked glory. Such of late
Columbus found the American so girt
With feathered cincture, naked else and wild
Among the trees on isles and woody shores.
Thus fenced, and as they thought, their shame in part
Covered, but not at rest or ease of mind,   1120
They sat them down to weep, nor only tears
Rained at their eyes, but high winds worse within
Began to rise, high passions, anger, hate,
Mistrust, suspicion, discord, and shook sore
Their inward state of mind, calm region once
And full of peace, now tossed and turbulent;
For Understanding ruled not, and the Will
Heard not her lore, both in subjection now
To sensual Appetite, who from beneath
Usurping over sovran Reason claimed   1130
Superior sway. From thus distempered breast,
Adam, estranged in look and altered style,
Speech intermitted thus to Eve renewed.
   "Would thou hadst hearkened to my words, and stayed
With me, as I besought thee, when that strange

1094. obnoxious. Cf. note on 170.
1103. Malabar refers to the western coast of Hindustan, especially the southern part.
Decan, or **Deccan,** is a name applied to the entire peninsula.
1111. Amazonian targe, shield of the Amazons.
1127 ff. For Understanding . . . sway. The tripartite division of the soul, which underlies
this passage, is Platonic. Cf. 351–56.

Desire of wandering this unhappy morn,
I know not whence possessed thee; we had then
Remained still happy, not as now, despoiled
Of all our good, shamed, naked, miserable.
Let none henceforth seek needless cause to approve   1140
The faith they owe; when earnestly they seek
Such proof, conclude, they then begin to fail."
   To whom soon moved with touch of blame thus Eve.
"What words have passed thy lips, Adam severe!
Imputest thou that to my default, or will
Of wandering, as thou call'st it, which who knows
But might as ill have happened thou being by,
Or to thyself perhaps? Hadst thou been there,
Or here the attempt, thou couldst not have discerned
Fraud in the Serpent, speaking as he spake;   1150
No ground of enmity between us known,
Why he should mean me ill, or seek to harm.
Was I to have never parted from thy side?
As good have grown there still a lifeless rib.
Being as I am, why didst not thou the head
Command me absolutely not to go,
Going into such danger as thou saidst?
Too facile then, thou didst not much gainsay,
Nay didst permit, approve, and fair dismiss.
Hadst thou been firm and fixed in thy dissent,   1160
Neither had I transgressed, nor thou with me."
   To whom then first incensed Adam replied.
"Is this the love, is this the recompense
Of mine to thee, ingrateful Eve, expressed
Immutable when thou wert lost, not I,
Who might have lived and joyed immortal bliss,
Yet willingly chose rather death with thee?
And am I now upbraided, as the cause
Of thy transgressing? not enough severe,
It seems, in thy restraint. What could I more?   1170
I warned thee, I admonished thee, foretold
The danger, and the lurking enemy
That lay in wait; beyond this had been force,
And force upon free will hath here no place.
But confidence then bore thee on, secure
Either to meet no danger or to find

1141. owe, possess.

1163 ff. Adam's statement is a fascinating mixture of right and wrong judgment, self-knowledge, and self-deception. In Milton's theory he is the superior being, but his reasoning is flawed by passion: "Understanding ruled not." Lines 1166–67 are certainly not a fair representation of the facts, being inconsistent with what he said in lines 908–10, above: "How can I live without thee?" On the other hand, he has come to the point of partly recognizing his own weakness: "And perhaps I also erred." How detached Milton himself is in all this it is really very difficult to say.

1164. expressed, demonstrated.

Matter of glorious trial; and perhaps
I also erred in overmuch admiring
What seemed in thee so perfect, that I thought
No evil durst attempt thee, but I rue   1180
That error now, which is become my crime,
And thou the accuser. Thus it shall befall
Him who to worth in women overtrusting
Lets her will rule; restraint she will not brook,
And left to herself, if evil thence ensue,
She first his weak indulgence will accuse."
Thus they in mutual accusation spent
The fruitless hours, but neither self-condemning,
And of their vain contest appeared no end.

from BOOK X

THE ARGUMENT

*Man's transgression known, the guardian angels forsake Paradise, and return
up to Heaven to approve their vigilance, and are approved; God declaring that
the entrance of Satan could not be by them prevented. He sends his Son to judge
the transgressors; who descends, and gives sentence accordingly; then in pity
clothes them both, and reascends. Sin and Death, sitting till then at the gates of
Hell, by wondrous sympathy feeling the success of Satan in this new world, and
the sin by Man there committed, resolve to sit no longer confined in Hell, but to
follow Satan, their sire, up to the place of Man. To make the way easier from
Hell to this world to and fro, they pave a broad highway or bridge over Chaos,
according to the track that Satan first made; then, preparing for Earth, they meet
him, proud of his success, returning to Hell; their mutual gratulation. Satan
arrives at Pandemonium; in full assembly relates, with boasting, his success
against Man; instead of applause is entertained with a general hiss by all his
audience, transformed, with himself also, suddenly into serpents, according to his
doom given in Paradise; then, deluded with a show of the Forbidden Tree springing up before them, they greedily reaching to take of the fruit chew dust and bitter
ashes. The proceedings of Sin and Death; God foretells the final victory of his
Son over them, and the renewing of all things; but for the present commands his
angels to make several alterations in the heavens and elements. Adam, more and
more perceiving his fallen condition, heavily bewails, rejects the condolement of
Eve; she persists, and at length appeases him: then, to evade the curse likely to
fall on their offspring, proposes to Adam violent ways, which he approves not,
but, conceiving better hope, puts her in mind of the late promise made them, that
her seed should be revenged on the Serpent, and exhorts her with him to seek
peace of the offended Deity by repentance and supplication.*

                                 Thus began
Outrage from lifeless things; but Discord first,
Daughter of Sin, among the irrational,
Death introduced through fierce antipathy.
Beast now with beast 'gan war, and fowl with fowl,   710
And fish with fish; to graze the herb all leaving,
Devoured each other; nor stood much in awe
Of Man, but fled him, or with countenance grim

Glared on him passing. These were from without
The growing miseries, which Adam saw
Already in part, though hid in gloomiest shade,
To sorrow abandoned, but worse felt within,
And in a troubled sea of passion tossed,
Thus to disburden sought with sad complaint.
   "O miserable of happy! is this the end   720
Of this new glorious World, and me so late
The glory of that glory, who now, become
Accurst of blessed, hide me from the face
Of God, whom to behold was then my height
Of happiness. Yet well, if here would end
The misery; I deserved it, and would bear
My own deservings; but this will not serve:
All that I eat or drink, or shall beget,
Is propagated curse. O voice once heard
Delightfully, 'Increase and multiply,'   730
Now death to hear! for what can I increase
Or multiply, but curses on my head?
Who of all ages to succeed, but feeling
The evil on him brought by me, will curse
My head: 'Ill fare our Ancestor impure,
For this we may thank Adam'; but his thanks
Shall be the execration; so besides
Mine own that bide upon me, all from me
Shall with a fierce reflux on me redound,
On me as on their natural center light   740
Heavy, though in their place. O fleeting joys
Of Paradise, dear bought with lasting woes!
Did I request thee, Maker, from my clay
To mould me Man, did I solicit thee
From darkness to promote me, or here place
In this delicious garden? As my will
Concurred not to my being, it were but right
And equal to reduce me to my dust,
Desirous to resign and render back
All I received, unable to perform   750
Thy terms too hard, by which I was to hold
The good I sought not. To the loss of that,
Sufficient penalty, why hast thou added
The sense of endless woes? inexplicable
Thy justice seems; yet to say truth, too late
I thus contest; then should have been refused
Those terms whatever, when they were proposed.
Thou didst accept them; wilt thou enjoy the good,
Then cavil the conditions? And though God
Made thee without thy leave, what if thy son   760
Prove disobedient, and reproved, retort,
'Wherefore didst thou beget me? I sought it not.'
Wouldst thou admit for his contempt of thee

That proud excuse? yet him not thy election,
But natural necessity begot.
God made thee of choice his own, and of his own
To serve him, thy reward was of his grace,
Thy punishment then justly is at his will.
Be it so, for I submit, his doom is fair,
That dust I am, and shall to dust return.   770
O welcome hour whenever! Why delays
His hand to execute what his decree
Fixed on this day? Why do I overlive,
Why am I mocked with death, and lengthened out
To deathless pain? How gladly would I meet
Mortality my sentence, and be earth
Insensible, how glad would lay me down
As in my mother's lap! There I should rest
And sleep secure; his dreadful voice no more
Would thunder in my ears, no fear of worse   780
To me and to my offspring would torment me
With cruel expectation. Yet one doubt
Pursues me still, lest all I cannot die,
Lest that pure breath of life, the spirit of Man
Which God inspired, cannot together perish
With this corporeal clod; then in the grave
Or in some other dismal place, who knows
But I shall die a living death? O thought
Horrid, if true! Yet why? It was but breath
Of life that sinned; what dies but what had life   790
And sin? the body properly hath neither.
All of me then shall die: let this appease
The doubt, since human reach no further knows.
For though the Lord of all be infinite,
Is his wrath also? Be it, Man is not so,
But mortal doomed. How can he exercise
Wrath without end on Man whom death must end?
Can he make deathless death? That were to make
Strange contradiction, which to God himself
Impossible is held, as argument   800
Of weakness, not of power. Will he draw out,
For anger's sake, finite to infinite
In punished Man, to satisfy his rigor
Satisfied never? That were to extend
His sentence beyond dust and Nature's law,
By which all causes else according still
To the reception of their matter act,
Not to the extent of their own sphere. But say
That death be not one stroke, as I supposed,
Bereaving sense, but endless misery   810

805–8. In all other matters where causes produce effects, the effect is in accordance with
the nature and properties of the thing being acted on. (Editors' note.)

From this day onward, which I feel begun
Both in me and without me, and so last
To perpetuity: Ay me, that fear
Comes thundering back with dreadful revolution
On my defenceless head; both Death and I
Am found eternal, and incorporate both,
Nor I on my part single, in me all
Posterity stands cursed. Fair patrimony
That I must leave ye, sons; oh were I able
To waste it all myself, and leave ye none!   820
So disinherited how would ye bless
Me now your curse! Ah, why should all mankind
For one man's fault thus guiltless be condemned,
If guiltless? But from me what can proceed
But all corrupt, both mind and will depraved,
Not to do only, but to will the same
With me? How can they then acquitted stand
In sight of God? Him after all disputes
Forced I absolve; all my evasions vain
And reasonings, though through mazes, lead me still   830
But to my own conviction: first and last
On me, me only, as the source and spring
Of all corruption, all the blame lights due;
So might the wrath. Fond wish! couldst thou support
That burden heavier than the Earth to bear,
Than all the World much heavier, though divided
With that bad woman? Thus what thou desirest
And what thou fearst, alike destroys all hope
Of refuge, and concludes thee miserable
Beyond all past example and future,   840
To Satan only like, both crime and doom.
O Conscience, into what abyss of fears
And horrors hast thou driven me; out of which
I find no way, from deep to deeper plunged!"
    Thus Adam to himself lamented loud
Through the still night, not now, as ere Man fell,
Wholesome and cool and mild, but with black air
Accompanied, with damps and dreadful gloom,
Which to his evil conscience represented
All things with double terror. On the ground   850
Outstretched he lay, on the cold ground, and oft
Cursed his creation, Death as oft accused
Of tardy execution, since denounced
The day of his offence. "Why comes not Death,"
Said he, "with one thrice-acceptable stroke
To end me? Shall Truth fail to keep her word,
Justice divine not hasten to be just?
But Death comes not at call, Justice divine
Mends not her slowest pace for prayers or cries.
O woods, O fountains, hillocks, dales, and bowers,   860

With other echo late I taught your shades
To answer, and resound far other song."
Whom thus afflicted when sad Eve beheld,
Desolate where she sat, approaching nigh,
Soft words to his fierce passion she assayed;
But her with stern regard he thus repelled.
  "Out of my sight, thou serpent, that name best
Befits thee with him leagued, thyself as false
And hateful; nothing wants, but that thy shape,
Like his, and color serpentine, may show   870
Thy inward fraud, to warn all creatures from thee
Henceforth; lest that too heavenly form, pretended
To hellish falsehood, snare them. But for thee
I had persisted happy, had not thy pride
And wandering vanity, when least was safe,
Rejected my forewarning, and disdained
Not to be trusted, longing to be seen
Though by the Devil himself, him overweening
To overreach, but with the Serpent meeting
Fooled and beguiled, by him thou, I by thee,   880
To trust thee from my side, imagined wise,
Constant, mature, proof against all assaults,
And understood not all was but a show
Rather than solid virtue, all but a rib
Crooked by nature, bent, as now appears,
More to the part sinister from me drawn;
Well if thrown out, as supernumerary
To my just number found. Oh why did God,
Creator wise, that peopled highest Heaven
With spirits masculine, create at last   890
This novelty on Earth, this fair defect
Of Nature, and not fill the World at once
With men as angels without feminine,
Or find some other way to generate
Mankind? This mischief had not then befallen,
And more that shall befall, innumerable
Disturbances on Earth through female snares,
And strait conjunction with this sex. For either
He never shall find out fit mate, but such
As some misfortune brings him, or mistake,   900
Or whom he wishes most shall seldom gain,
Through her perverseness, but shall see her gained
By a far worse, or if she love, withheld
By parents, or his happiest choice too late
Shall meet, already linked and wedlock-bound
To a fell adversary, his hate or shame;
Which infinite calamity shall cause
To human life, and household peace confound."
  He added not, and from her turned, but Eve
Not so repulsed, with tears that ceased not flowing,   910

And tresses all disordered, at his feet
Fell humble, and embracing them, besought
His peace, and thus proceeded in her plaint:
    "Forsake me not thus, Adam, witness Heaven
What love sincere and reverence in my heart
I bear thee, and unweeting have offended,
Unhappily deceived; thy suppliant
I beg, and clasp thy knees; bereave me not,
Whereon I live, thy gentle looks, thy aid,
Thy counsel in this uttermost distress,   920
My only strength and stay. Forlorn of thee,
Whither shall I betake me, where subsist?
While yet we live, scarce one short hour perhaps,
Between us two let there be peace, both joining,
As joined in injuries, one enmity
Against a foe by doom express assigned us,
That cruel Serpent. On me exercise not
Thy hatred for this misery befallen,
On me already lost, me than thyself
More miserable. Both have sinned, but thou   930
Against God only, I against God and thee,
And to the place of judgment will return,
There with my cries importune Heaven, that all
The sentence from thy head removed may light
On me, sole cause to thee of all this woe,
Me, me only, just object of his ire."
    She ended weeping, and her lowly plight,
Immovable till peace obtained from fault
Acknowledged and deplored, in Adam wrought
Commiseration; soon his heart relented   940
Towards her, his life so late and sole delight,
Now at his feet submissive in distress,
Creature so fair his reconcilement seeking,
His counsel whom she had displeased, his aid;
As one disarmed, his anger all he lost,
And thus with peaceful words upraised her soon:
    "Unwary, and too desirous, as before,
So now, of what thou knowst not, who desirest
The punishment all on thyself; alas,
Bear thine own first, ill able to sustain   950
His full wrath whose thou feel'st as yet least part,
And my displeasure bear'st so ill. If prayers
Could alter high decrees, I to that place
Would speed before thee, and be louder heard,
That on my head all might be visited,
Thy frailty and infirmer sex forgiven,
To me committed and by me exposed.
But rise, let us no more contend, nor blame
Each other, blamed enough elsewhere, but strive
In offices of love, how we may lighten   960

Each other's burden in our share of woe;
Since this day's death denounced, if aught I see,
Will prove no sudden, but a slow-paced evil,
A long day's dying to augment our pain,
And to our seed (O hapless seed!) derived."
  To whom thus Eve, recovering heart, replied.
"Adam, by sad experiment I know
How little weight my words with thee can find,
Found so erroneous, thence by just event
Found so unfortunate; nevertheless,   970
Restored by thee, vile as I am, to place
Of new acceptance, hopeful to regain
Thy love, the sole contentment of my heart
Living or dying, from thee I will not hide
What thoughts in my unquiet breast are risen,
Tending to some relief of our extremes,
Or end, though sharp and sad, yet tolerable,
As in our evils, and of easier choice.
If care of our descent perplex us most,
Which must be born to certain woe, devoured   980
By Death at last, (and miserable it is
To be to others cause of misery,
Our own begotten, and of our loins to bring
Into this cursèd World a woeful race,
That after wretched life must be at last
Food for so foul a monster), in thy power
It lies, yet ere conception, to prevent
The race unblest, to being yet unbegot.
Childless thou art, childless remain; so Death
Shall be deceived his glut, and with us two   990
Be forced to satisfy his ravenous maw.
But if thou judge it hard and difficult,
Conversing, looking, loving, to abstain
From love's due rites, nuptial embraces sweet,
And with desire to languish without hope,
Before the present object languishing
With like desire, which would be misery
And torment less than none of what we dread,
Then both our selves and seed at once to free
From what we fear for both, let us make short,   1000
Let us seek Death, or he not found, supply
With our own hands his office on ourselves;
Why stand we longer shivering under fears
That show no end but death, and have the power,
Of many ways to die the shortest choosing,
Destruction with destruction to destroy."
  She ended here, or vehement despair
Broke off the rest; so much of death her thoughts
Had entertained as dyed her cheeks with pale.
But Adam with such counsel nothing swayed,   1010

To better hopes his more attentive mind
Laboring had raised, and thus to Eve replied.
    "Eve, thy contempt of life and pleasure seems
To argue in thee something more sublime
And excellent than what thy mind contemns;
But self-destruction therefore sought, refutes
That excellence thought in thee, and implies,
Not thy contempt, but anguish and regret
For loss of life and pleasure overloved.
Or if thou covet death, as utmost end   1020
Of misery, so thinking to evade
The penalty pronounced, doubt not but God
Hath wiselier armed his vengeful ire than so
To be forestalled; much more I fear lest death
So snatched will not exempt us from the pain
We are by doom to pay; rather such acts
Of contumacy will provoke the Highest
To make death in us live. Then let us seek
Some safer resolution, which methinks
I have in view, calling to mind with heed   1030
Part of our sentence, that thy seed shall bruise
The Serpent's head; piteous amends, unless
Be meant, whom I conjecture, our grand foe
Satan, who in the serpent hath contrived
Against us this deceit. To crush his head
Would be revenge indeed; which will be lost
By death brought on ourselves, or childless days
Resolved, as thou proposest; so our foe
Shall scape his punishment ordained, and we
Instead shall double ours upon our heads.   1040
No more be mentioned then of violence
Against ourselves, and wilful barrenness,
That cuts us off from hope, and savors only
Rancor and pride, impatience and despite,
Reluctance against God and his just yoke
Laid on our necks. Remember with what mild
And gracious temper he both heard and judged,
Without wrath or reviling; we expected
Immediate dissolution, which we thought
Was meant by death that day, when lo, to thee   1050
Pains only in child-bearing were foretold,
And bringing forth, soon recompensed with joy,
Fruit of thy womb; on me the curse aslope
Glanced on the ground: with labor I must earn
My bread; what harm? Idleness had been worse;
My labor will sustain me; and lest cold

    1015. what thy mind contemns, the life and pleasure your mind shows contempt for.
(Editors' note.)

Or heat should injure us, his timely care
Hath unbesought provided, and his hands
Clothed us unworthy, pitying while he judged;
How much more, if we pray him, will his ear   1060
Be open, and his heart to pity incline,
And teach us further by what means to shun
The inclement seasons, rain, ice, hail, and snow,
Which now the sky with various face begins
To show us in this mountain, while the winds
Blow moist and keen, shattering the graceful locks
Of these fair spreading trees; which bids us seek
Some better shroud, some better warmth to cherish
Our limbs benumbed, ere this diurnal star
Leave cold the night, how we his gathered beams   1070
Reflected, may with matter sere foment,
Or by collision of two bodies grind
The air attrite to fire, as late the clouds
Justling or pushed with winds rude in their shock
Tine the slant lightning, whose thwart flame driven down
Kindles the gummy bark of fir or pine,
And sends a comfortable heat from far,
Which might supply the sun. Such fire to use,
And what may else be remedy or cure
To evils which our own misdeeds have wrought,   1080
He will instruct us praying, and of grace
Beseeching him, so as we need not fear
To pass commodiously this life, sustained
By him with many comforts, till we end
In dust, our final rest and native home.
What better can we do, than to the place
Repairing where he judged us, prostrate fall
Before him reverent, and there confess
Humbly our faults, and pardon beg, with tears
Watering the ground, and with our sighs the air   1090
Frequenting, sent from hearts contrite, in sign
Of sorrow unfeigned, and humiliation meek.
Undoubtedly he will relent and turn
From his displeasure; in whose look serene,
When angry most he seemed and most severe,
What else but favor, grace, and mercy shone?"
   So spake our father penitent, nor Eve
Felt less remorse. They forthwith to the place
Repairing where he judged them, prostrate fell
Before him reverent, and both confessed   1100

1070–78. Various means of inventing or producing fire.
1071. **matter sere,** dry materials. **foment,** increase the heat of.
1073. **attrite,** rubbed together.   1075. **Tine,** kindle. **thwart,** slanting.
1078. **supply the sun,** replace the heat of the sun. (Editors' notes.)

Humbly their faults, and pardon begged, with tears
Watering the ground, and with their sighs the air
Frequenting, sent from hearts contrite, in sign
Of sorrow unfeigned, and humiliation meek.

BOOK XI: THE ARGUMENT

The Son of God presents to his Father the prayers of our first parents now
repenting, and intercedes for them. God accepts them, but declares that they must
no longer abide in Paradise; sends Michael with a band of Cherubim to
dispossess them, but first to reveal to Adam future things; Michael's coming
down. Adam shows to Eve certain ominous signs; he discerns Michael's ap-
proach; goes out to meet him; the Angel denounces their departure. Eve's lamen-
tation. Adam pleads, but submits; the Angel leads him up to a high hill; sets
before him in vision what shall happen till the Flood.

from BOOK XII

THE ARGUMENT

The Angel Michael continues from the Flood to relate what shall succeed; then,
in the mention of Abraham, comes by degrees to explain, who that Seed of the
Woman shall be which was promised Adam and Eve in the Fall; his incarnation,
death, resurrection, and ascension; the state of the Church till his second coming.
Adam greatly satisfied and recomforted by these relations and promises descends
the hill with Michael; wakens Eve, who all this while had slept, but with gentle
dreams composed to quietness of mind and submission. Michael in either hand
leads them out of Paradise, the fiery sword waving behind them, and the Cheru-
bim taking their stations to guard the place.

Here Adam interposed. "O sent from Heaven,   270
Enlightener of my darkness, gracious things
Thou hast revealed, those chiefly which concern
Just Abraham and his seed. Now first I find
Mine eyes true opening, and my heart much eased,
Erewhile perplexed with thoughts what would become
Of me and all mankind; but now I see
His day, in whom all nations shall be blest,
Favor unmerited by me, who sought
Forbidden knowledge by forbidden means.
This yet I apprehend not, why to those   280
Among whom God will deign to dwell on Earth
So many and so various laws are given;
So many laws argue so many sins
Among them; how can God with such reside?"
    To whom thus Michael. "Doubt not but that sin
Will reign among them, as of thee begot;

And therefore was law given them to evince
Their natural pravity, by stirring up
Sin against law to fight; that when they see
Law can discover sin, but not remove,   290
Save by those shadowy expiations weak,
The blood of bulls and goats, they may conclude
Some blood more precious must be paid for Man,
Just for unjust, that in such righteousness
To them by faith imputed, they may find
Justification towards God, and peace
Of conscience, which the law by ceremonies
Cannot appease, nor man the moral part
Perform, and not performing cannot live.
So law appears imperfect, and but given   300
With purpose to resign them in full time
Up to a better covenant, disciplined
From shadowy types to truth, from flesh to spirit,
From imposition of strict laws, to free
Acceptance of large grace, from servile fear
To filial, works of law to works of faith.
And therefore shall not Moses, though of God
Highly beloved, being but the minister
Of law, his people into Canaan lead;
But Joshua whom the Gentiles Jesus call,   310
His name and office bearing, who shall quell
The adversary Serpent, and bring back
Through the world's wilderness long-wandered Man
Safe to eternal Paradise of rest.
Meanwhile they in their earthly Canaan placed
Long time shall dwell and prosper, but when sins
National interrupt their public peace,
Provoking God to raise them enemies,
From whom as oft he saves them penitent
By judges first, then under kings; of whom   320
The second, both for piety renowned
And puissant deeds, a promise shall receive
Irrevocable, that his regal throne
For ever shall endure; the like shall sing
All prophecy: that of the royal stock
Of David (so I name this king) shall rise
A Son, the Woman's Seed to thee foretold,
Foretold to Abraham, as in whom shall trust

---

287. evince, to demonstrate. In Milton's theology the Mosaic law was given "for the hardness of men's hearts." It was abrogated by the new testament of love in Christ, the "better covenant" of line 302.

303. shadowy types. Christian interpretation found allegorical illustrations of the truth everywhere in Old Testament history. Thus the burnt offerings are a symbol of the true sacrifice of a contrite heart; Moses is a mediator and foreshadows the office of the Redeemer; Joshua, leading his people into the promised land, is again Christ making possible salvation for the elect.

All nations, and to kings foretold, of kings
The last, for of his reign shall be no end.   330
But first a long succession must ensue,
And his next son for wealth and wisdom famed,
The clouded ark of God till then in tents
Wandering, shall in a glorious temple enshrine.
Such follow him, as shall be registered
Part good, part bad, of bad the longer scroll,
Whose foul idolatries and other faults
Heaped to the popular sum, will so incense
God, as to leave them, and expose their land,
Their city, his temple, and his holy ark   340
With all his sacred things, a scorn and prey
To that proud city, whose high walls thou saw'st
Left in confusion, Babylon thence called.
There in captivity he lets them dwell
The space of seventy years, then brings them back,
Remembering mercy, and his covenant sworn
To David, stablished as the days of Heaven.
Returned from Babylon by leave of kings
Their lords, whom God disposed, the house of God
They first re-edify, and for a while   350
In mean estate live moderate, till grown
In wealth and multitude, factious they grow;
But first among the priests dissension springs,
Men who attend the altar, and should most
Endeavor peace; their strife pollution brings
Upon the temple itself; at last they seize
The scepter and regard not David's sons,
Then lose it to a stranger, that the true
Anointed King Messiah might be born
Barred of his right; yet at his birth a star   360
Unseen before in Heaven proclaims him come,
And guides the eastern sages, who inquire
His place, to offer incense, myrrh, and gold;
His place of birth a solemn angel tells
To simple shepherds, keeping watch by night;
They gladly thither haste, and by a choir
Of squadroned angels hear his carol sung.
A Virgin is his mother, but his Sire
The Power of the Most High; he shall ascend
The throne hereditary, and bound his reign   370
With Earth's wide bounds, his glory with the Heavens."
    He ceased, discerning Adam with such joy
Surcharged, as had like grief been dewed in tears,
Without the vent of words, which these he breathed.
    "O prophet of glad tidings, finisher

332. his next son. Solomon. See I Kings 6–7 and II Chron. 3–4.
373. had, would have.

Of utmost hope! now clear I understand
What oft my steadiest thoughts have searched in vain,
Why our great Expectation should be called
The Seed of Woman: Virgin Mother, hail,
High in the love of Heaven, yet from my loins　　　　　　380
Thou shalt proceed, and from thy womb the Son
Of God Most High; so God with Man unites.
Needs must the Serpent now his capital bruise
Expect with mortal pain: say where and when
Their fight, what stroke shall bruise the Victor's heel."
　　To whom thus Michael. "Dream not of their fight
As of a duel, or the local wounds
Of head or heel: not therefore joins the Son
Manhood to Godhead, with more strength to foil
Thy enemy; nor so is overcome　　　　　　　　　　　390
Satan, whose fall from Heaven, a deadlier bruise,
Disabled not to give thee thy death's wound;
Which he, who comes thy Savior, shall recure,
Not by destroying Satan, but his works
In thee and in thy seed. Nor can this be,
But by fulfilling that which thou didst want,
Obedience to the law of God, imposed
On penalty of death, and suffering death,
The penalty to thy transgression due,
And due to theirs which out of thine will grow:　　　　400
So only can high justice rest appaid.
The law of God exact he shall fulfil
Both by obedience and by love, though love
Alone fulfil the law; thy punishment
He shall endure by coming in the flesh
To a reproachful life and cursèd death,
Proclaiming life to all who shall believe
In his redemption, and that his obedience
Imputed becomes theirs by faith, his merits
To save them, not their own, though legal works.　　　410
For this he shall live hated, be blasphemed,
Seized on by force, judged, and to death condemned
A shameful and accursed, nailed to the cross
By his own nation, slain for bringing life;
But to the cross he nails thy enemies,
The law that is against thee, and the sins
Of all mankind, with him there crucified,
Never to hurt them more who rightly trust
In this his satisfaction; so he dies,
But soon revives, Death over him no power　　　　　420
Shall long usurp; ere the third dawning light
Return, the stars of morn shall see him rise

---

383. capital, of the head, but with the idea also of "chief."

Out of his grave, fresh as the dawning light,
Thy ransom paid, which Man from Death redeems,
His death for Man, as many as offered life
Neglect not, and the benefit embrace
By faith not void of works. This godlike act
Annuls thy doom, the death thou shouldst have died,
In sin for ever lost from life; this act
Shall bruise the head of Satan, crush his strength   430
Defeating Sin and Death, his two main arms,
And fix far deeper in his head their stings
Than temporal death shall bruise the Victor's heel,
Or theirs whom he redeems, a death like sleep,
A gentle wafting to immortal life.
Nor after resurrection shall he stay
Longer on Earth than certain times to appear
To his disciples, men who in his life
Still followed him; to them shall leave in charge
To teach all nations what of him they learned   440
And his salvation, them who shall believe
Baptizing in the profluent stream, the sign
Of washing them from guilt of sin to life
Pure, and in mind prepared, if so befall,
For death, like that which the Redeemer died.
All nations they shall teach; for from that day
Not only to the sons of Abraham's loins
Salvation shall be preached, but to the sons
Of Abraham's faith wherever through the world;
So in his seed all nations shall be blest.   450
Then to the Heaven of Heavens he shall ascend
With victory, triumphing through the air
Over his foes and thine; there shall surprise
The Serpent, Prince of air, and drag in chains
Through all his realm, and there confounded leave;
Then enter into glory, and resume
His seat at God's right hand, exalted high
Above all names in Heaven; and thence shall come,
When this world's dissolution shall be ripe,
With glory and power to judge both quick and dead,   460
To judge the unfaithful dead, but to reward
His faithful, and receive them into bliss,
Whether in Heaven or Earth, for then the Earth
Shall all be Paradise, far happier place
Than this of Eden, and far happier days."
  So spake the Archangel Michael, then paused,
As at the world's great period; and our Sire
Replete with joy and wonder thus replied.
  "O goodness infinite, goodness immense!
That all this good of evil shall produce,   470
And evil turn to good; more wonderful

Than that which by creation first brought forth
Light out of darkness! full of doubt I stand,
Whether I should repent me now of sin
By me done and occasioned, or rejoice
Much more, that much more good thereof shall spring,
To God more glory, more good will to men
From God, and over wrath grace shall abound.
But say, if our Deliverer up to Heaven
Must reascend, what will betide the few   480
His faithful, left among the unfaithful herd,
The enemies of truth; who then shall guide
His people, who defend? will they not deal
Worse with his followers than with him they dealt?"
   "Be sure they will," said the Angel; "but from Heaven
He to his own a Comforter will send,
The promise of the Father, who shall dwell
His Spirit within them, and the law of faith
Working through love, upon their hearts shall write,
To guide them in all truth, and also arm   490
With spiritual armor, able to resist
Satan's assaults, and quench his fiery darts,
What man can do against them, not afraid,
Though to the death, against such cruelties
With inward consolations recompensed,
And oft supported so as shall amaze
Their proudest persecutors. For the Spirit
Poured first on his Apostles, whom he sends
To evangelize the nations, then on all
Baptized, shall them with wondrous gifts endue   500
To speak all tongues, and do all miracles,
As did their Lord before them. Thus they win
Great numbers of each nation to receive
With joy the tidings brought from Heaven: at length
Their ministry performed, and race well run,
Their doctrine and their story written left,
They die; but in their room, as they forewarn,
Wolves shall succeed for teachers, grievous wolves,
Who all the sacred mysteries of Heaven
To their own vile advantages shall turn   510
Of lucre and ambition, and the truth

473 ff. The paradox which makes the Fall of Man at once the greatest of human calamities and the occasion of man's highest experience of good is a commonplace of Christian thinking.

508 ff. Wolves shall succeed for teachers. In this review of the perversion of the Church Milton touches on every essential point in the attack of Protestant against Catholic, of Puritan against Anglican. The clergy have substituted "man-made tradition" for the "plain truth of Scripture"; they have sought rank and title instead of imitating the simplicity of the early church; they have invoked secular power for the suppression of dissent; they have taught that authority and not inner conviction should rule the individual in matters of belief, and that salvation may be obtained by ritualistic observance rather than by repentance. Milton had been saying these things more or less all his life.

With superstitions and traditions taint,
Left only in those written records pure,
Though not but by the Spirit understood.
Then shall they seek to avail themselves of names,
Places and titles, and with these to join
Secular power, though feigning still to act
By spiritual, to themselves appropriating
The Spirit of God, promised alike and given
To all believers; and from that pretence,   520
Spiritual laws by carnal power shall force
On every conscience; laws which none shall find
Left them enrolled, or what the Spirit within
Shall on the heart engrave. What will they then
But force the Spirit of Grace itself, and bind
His consort Liberty; what but unbuild
His living temples, built by faith to stand,
Their own faith, not another's: for on earth
Who against faith and conscience can be heard
Infallible? yet many will presume: 530
Whence heavy persecution shall arise
On all who in the worship persevere
Of Spirit and Truth; the rest, far greater part,
Will deem in outward rites and specious forms
Religion satisfied; Truth shall retire
Bestuck with slanderous darts, and works of faith
Rarely be found. So shall the world go on,
To good malignant, to bad men benign,
Under her own weight groaning till the day
Appear of respiration to the just,   540
And vengeance to the wicked, at return
Of Him so lately promised to thy aid,
The Woman's Seed, obscurely then foretold,
Now amplier known thy Savior and thy Lord,
Last in the clouds from Heaven to be revealed
In glory of the Father, to dissolve
Satan with his perverted world, then raise
From the conflagrant mass, purged and refined,
New Heavens, new Earth, ages of endless date
Founded in righteousness and peace and love,   550
To bring forth fruits joy and eternal bliss."
    He ended; and thus Adam last replied.
"How soon hath thy prediction, Seer blest,
Measured this transient world, the race of time,
Till time stand fixed: beyond is all abyss,
Eternity, whose end no eye can reach.
Greatly instructed I shall hence depart,
Greatly in peace of thought, and have my fill
Of knowledge, what this vessel can contain;
Beyond which was my folly to aspire.   560
Henceforth I learn, that to obey is best,

And love with fear the only God, to walk
As in his presence, ever to observe
His providence, and on him sole depend,
Merciful over all his works, with good
Still overcoming evil, and by small
Accomplishing great things, by things deemed weak
Subverting worldly strong, and worldly wise
By simply meek; that suffering for truth's sake
Is fortitude to highest victory,   570
And to the faithful death the gate of life;
Taught this by his example whom I now
Acknowledge my Redeemer ever blest."
  To whom thus also the Angel last replied.
"This having learned, thou hast attained the sum
Of wisdom; hope no higher, though all the stars
Thou knew'st by name, and all the ethereal powers,
All secrets of the deep, all Nature's works,
Or works of God in heaven, air, earth, or sea,
And all the riches of this world enjoy'dst,   580
And all the rule, one empire; only add
Deeds to thy knowledge answerable, add faith,
Add virtue, patience, temperance, add love,
By name to come called charity, the soul
Of all the rest: then wilt thou not be loth
To leave this Paradise, but shalt possess
A Paradise within thee, happier far.
Let us descend now therefore from this top
Of speculation; for the hour precise
Exacts our parting hence; and see the guards,   590
By me encamped on yonder hill, expect
Their motion, at whose front a flaming sword,
In signal of remove, waves fiercely round;
We may no longer stay: go, waken Eve;
Her also I with gentle dreams have calmed
Portending good, and all her spirits composed
To meek submission: thou at season fit
Let her with thee partake what thou hast heard,
Chiefly what may concern her faith to know,
The great deliverance by her seed to come   600
(For by the Woman's Seed) on all mankind.
That ye may live, which will be many days,
Both in one faith unanimous though sad,
With cause for evils past, yet much more cheered
With meditation on the happy end."
  He ended, and they both descend the hill;
Descended, Adam to the bower where Eve
Lay sleeping ran before, but found her waked;
And thus with words not sad she him received.
  "Whence thou return'st, and whither went'st, I know;   610

591–92. expect Their motion, await the moment of moving.

For God is also in sleep, and dreams advise,
Which he hath sent propitious, some great good
Presaging, since with sorrow and heart's distress
Wearied I fell asleep. But now lead on;
In me is no delay; with thee to go,
Is to stay here; without thee here to stay,
Is to go hence unwilling; thou to me
Art all things under Heaven, all places thou,
Who for my wilful crime art banished hence.
This further consolation yet secure   620
I carry hence; though all by me is lost,
Such favor I unworthy am vouchsafed,
By me the Promised Seed shall all restore."
   So spake our mother Eve, and Adam heard
Well pleased, but answered not; for now too nigh
The Archangel stood, and from the other hill
To their fixed station, all in bright array
The Cherubim descended; on the ground
Gliding meteorous, as evening mist
Risen from a river o'er the marish glides,   630
And gathers ground fast at the laborer's heel
Homeward returning. High in front advanced,
The brandished sword of God before them blazed
Fierce as a comet; which with torrid heat,
And vapor as the Libyan air adust,
Began to parch that temperate clime; whereat
In either hand the hastening angel caught
Our lingering parents, and to the eastern gate
Led them direct, and down the cliff as fast
To the subjected plain; then disappeared.   640
They looking back, all the eastern side beheld
Of Paradise, so late their happy seat,
Waved over by that flaming brand, the gate
With dreadful faces thronged and fiery arms.
Some natural tears they dropped, but wiped them soon;
The world was all before them, where to choose
Their place of rest, and Providence their guide.
They hand in hand with wandering steps and slow,
Through Eden took their solitary way.

614 ff. Eve's words suggest those of Ruth, "Whither thou goest I will go," but also Andromache's to Hector in the *Iliad*.

Renaissance Lyric Poetry
(c.1500–c.1660)

One traditional model in the study of literature suggests that we can assign to epic the expression of national and broadly religious values, to drama the expression of social values, and to lyric poetry the expression of individual values and states of feeling. The Renaissance was an era of great achievement in all three of these literary modes. The lyric poetry of the era has a special significance; even if we regard skeptically the nineteenth-century exaggeration that the Renaissance was a sudden explosion of individualism, that view has a certain amount of truth. Just as painters of the period began to sign their names to their canvases, thus staking a claim to some kind of achievement or style different from those of other painters, so poets also cultivated voices that were uniquely their own. The following section of this anthology presents a concert, so to speak, of such voices. Seven of them are Spanish: Garcilaso de la Vega (c.1501–1536), Santa Teresa de Jesús, or St. Teresa of Jesus (1515–1582), Fray Luis de León (c.1527–1591), San Juan de la Cruz, or St. John of the Cross (1542–1591), Luis de Góngora (1561–1627), Bartolomé Leonardo de Argensola (1562–1631), and Lope de Vega (1562–1635). Two are French: Joachim Du Bellay (1522–1560) and Pierre de Ronsard (1524–1585). Seven are English: Edmund Spenser (1552–1599), Michael Drayton (1563–1631), William Shakespeare (1564–1616), Thomas Campion (1567–1620), John Donne (1572–1631), Robert Herrick (1591–1674), and John Milton (1608–1674). A number of facts are worth noting incidentally in connection with this roster: that some of the poets are even better known for their work in the larger genres, for example Lope de Vega and Shakespeare in drama, Spenser and Milton in epic; that the Spanish poetry has an especially strong religious coloring (except for Garcilaso, all seven Spanish poets were priests or belonged to other religious orders, and two are canonized saints); and that, as the dates indicate, the distinctively Renaissance lyric impulse flourished later in England than on the continent.

If the poems included here had been recently discovered, without the poets' names, it would be no harder to determine who wrote them than it is for music enthusiasts today to identify established singers or composers; in both cases, distinctive rhythms, ways of handling melody and theme, and other stylistic traits would permit firm identification. (The two included poems by Campion, incidentally, are literally song lyrics, the music for which has survived.) It is also true, however, that artists of any given era tend to share certain habits of style, attitude, and preference in subject matter. In the Renaissance lyric these habits, most easily identifiable in the poetry of love and religion, are essentially a blending of classical with late-medieval Christian elements.

The main model for this blending was the lyric poetry of the fourteenth-century Italian humanist Francis Petrarch, whose presence loomed over almost all the significant lyric poets of the following two or three centuries. In his time Petrarch had been the foremost apostle of the revival of the ancient classical spirit, tone, and forms. He was involved, for example, in rediscovering the passionate but formally elegant love poetry of Catullus, perhaps the most powerful expression in ancient poetry of both the bliss and agony of love. But behind Petrarch lay several other, more recent European traditions: the courtly love tradition of the troubadors of southern France, which made a kind of religion of the worship of an unattainable beloved; the Divine Comedy and Vita Nuova ("New Life") of Dante, whose sensuously beautiful Bea-

trice was an emblem of God's revealed truth; and a number of other Christian influences including medieval "Mariolatry," a quasi-worship of the Virgin Mary often expressed in terms of sensuous art and lyrical language. All these strands, along with others, went into the poetic creation of Petrarch's beloved Laura, celebrated in the sonnet form that became a hallmark of the poet and in other lyric forms he developed from classical precedents. Laura was the occasion for the poet's highest happiness and sorest suffering, and in her very name femininity blended with the associations of the laurel wreath that, in classic antiquity, had symbolized the loftiest achievements in the sphere of poetry. Petrarch, far more even than Dante, set the example for the Renaissance thought-pattern by which religious experience could be described in terms of sexual love and love described in terms of religion.

The result, in Petrarch and his countless followers, was a poetry that fused with one another the supernal fervor of Christianity, the secular discipline of classical form, and overtones of ancient philosophy. Plato's works, with their combination of lyricism and otherworldliness, exerted an especially strong influence as they became better known in the centuries after Petrarch, reinforcing the blend of sensuousness and idealism in the "religion" of love. Significantly, this "religion" was developed almost exclusively from a male point of view. To the poets, most of them men, women were the desired but alien Other and were treated with profound ambivalence. On the one hand, they were regarded with something of the old distrust (the more primitive inheritance from the Middle Ages), so that misplaced devotion to them was a bar to salvation, but they could also be regarded as avenues to the highest reaches of spiritual experience, not to mention other varieties of ecstasy. Such a state of mind has an obvious seductive appeal, a form of having one's cake and eating it too. It is, just as obviously, a fragile construction singularly open to the jeers of the skeptical and irreverent. The Petrarchan tradition ultimately was to undergo this kind of undercutting and ironic subversion, most notably at the hands of John Donne.

In the Renaissance, every country of western Europe had to come to terms with this Italian influence and the Italian cast given in the Renaissance to classical models. The result, commonly, was another immensely powerful cultural ambivalence. The Italian models had obvious attractions, not to mention the fact that Rome, a still-flourishing modern city, was a present reminder of classical glories. On the other hand, the Italian states and city-states were perennial pawns or enemies in the wars of expansion conducted by France and Spain, which were flexing their muscles as newly-centralized modern nations. In the countries of northern Europe where the Protestant Reformation made headway, most obviously in England, Italian religion and culture were also suspect for other reasons. And on top of that, the generally recognized cultural superiority of Italy engendered in other parts of Europe a kind of militant inferiority complex that imitated Italian achievements while sometimes chafing under the awareness of an allegiance or debt to Italy. Ronsard, Du Bellay, and the other five members of the sixteenth-century French group called the Pléiade wanted to create a new, consciously French literature that could compete with Italian excellence but also by-pass Italy for more direct use of ancient literary models. In some countries and authors, this ambivalence produced a powerful tension; for example, Edmund Spenser in England (with his medievally flavored epic The Faerie Queene*) and Lope de Vega in Spain (with his old-Spanish type of ballads) were both in many ways modernists (which in the Renaissance meant being classicists) but were reluctant to join any modernist movement that would jeopardize the more popular medieval heritage, which was dear to them as a repository of their respective national traditions.*

Thus the Petrarchan and classicizing craze that became epidemic in Europe was accompanied by a self-consciousness that could be very intense. Even the simplest, most straightforward repetitions of ancient themes—for example, adaptations by Garcilaso de la Vega, Ronsard, and Herrick of the carpe diem *("seize the day") theme traceable to such ancient poems as Catullus' "Come, Lesbia, let us live and love"—could be construed as cultural gestures of international import. Edmund Spenser's "Epithalamion," perhaps the most heartfelt and beautiful wedding poem ever written, a personal statement if there ever was one, could also be seen, with its repeated appeals to mythology and its recollections of Catullus' wedding poems, as part of a general European classicizing program. To invoke the religious theme of the Good Shepherd familiar in the Old and New Testaments was a half-automatic temptation to imitate the pastoral genre of ancient pagan literature.*

The more direct indebtedness to Petrarch was even more self-conscious, whether it was being followed meekly or subverted. Shakespeare's Sonnet 18, "Shall I compare thee to a summer's day?", works without restlessness within the Petrarchan gallery of images and similes, but his Sonnet 130, "My mistress' eyes are nothing like the sun," is a direct repudiation of Petrarchism, and the self-loathing in Sonnet 129, "The expense of spirit in a waste of shame," is conveyed partly through the Petrarchan images, now reviled, of heaven and hunted game animals. The sonneteering cliché that lovers are sustained by sighs and tears is evoked by John Donne in "Love's Diet" with a literalism that amusingly calls the whole convention into question while also, in a wry way, affirming its validity: the speaker, tired of being in love, tries to cure the obesity of his (personified) love by calorie-counting, as it were, as he indulges in sighs and tears. Luis de Góngora, writing at the time when the Spanish Renaissance is beginning to yield to the Baroque era, does similarly jarring things with the Petrarchan and sonneteering conventions. His poem "A Rose" mourns not so much the flower's brevity of life and beauty as its being born at all. "The Spring" compares the mistress' beauty to the sun not as life-giving but as killing. "Allegory of the Brevity of Things Human" (if we take the speaker to be a human being) reverses the usual similitudes by asking flowers to take a lesson from the brevity of human life. More cheerfully, "The Rosemary Spray" has flowers turning not to ashes and dust but to honey.

To some modern readers, of course, the wonder is not that poets should eventually have come to look askance at such apparently artificial conventions but rather that they should have survived in any form, heartfelt or ironic, for three hundred years. One reason is their hallowed pedigree, and another is that they were not wholly conventional; for example, the medieval view (expressed by Dante and many others) that the celestial spheres of the sun and planets literally dispensed love and other heavenly favors was still significantly alive. In any case, to the extent that we recognize and accept those many Petrarchan clichés that have survived and been infinitely repeated in modern popular music (my sweetheart is an angel) and other equally shopworn clichés of emotion (I'm laughing, but I'm crying inside, etc.), we ought to be careful about casting stones. Or, if those examples seem too lightweight, we might ponder the recurrence in the more solemn black spirituals and folk songs of certain interchangeable phrases and images ("The river of Jordan [death and deliverance] is muddy and cold, / It chills the body but not the soul"). It would be rash indeed to regard these perennial formulas as emotional posing.

It might seem that by the time one has enumerated all the traditions governing the Renaissance lyric—survivals of medieval attitudes such as the contemptus mundi *(disdain of the world), biblical and other Christian influences, classical models of form and of attitude, neoplatonism, and the rest—all traces of original expression will have been explained away. What such enumeration cannot explain is the peculiar energy of Renaissance poetry at its best—its freshness, fragrance, and intensity. To say that these qualities are the product of the spiritual challenge of a rapidly changing world, full of new perils and opportunities, political and cultural, may sound romantic, but it also may well be true. The greatest era of Spanish literature, for example, undoubtedly coincides closely with the era of Spain's greatest influence on the world's stage. Nor would it be at all accurate to regard Spain as an enclave sealed off from the energy and ferment of the Reformation. The Counter-Reformation launched in and from Spain was not merely an attempt to contain the Protestant movement; it was also a genuine deepening of spiritual experience, and it involved some risks. The three greatest religious poets of sixteenth-century Spain—St. Teresa of Jesus, Fray Luis de León, and St. John of the Cross—were all members of religious orders, but they were also innovators who, in their own day, were challenged by the Inquisition or imprisoned or both. Teresa and John collaborated in vitally important conventual and monastic reform movements, and in John's poetry and other writings are expressed some of the most powerful mystical religious experiences of which we have a record.*

One especially interesting thing about Spanish Renaissance poetry is the way in which it daringly unites different traditions, modes of poetry, and modes of feeling. Lope de Vega (another cleric, though an unlikely one in light of his amorous and other adventures), in his sonnet "The Good Shepherd," St. John of the Cross, in "A Shepherd, Young and Mournful, Grieves Alone," and Luis de León, in "The Life of the Blessed," all combine the settings of ancient pastoral with the biblical Good Shepherd motif. In his "Ode to Francisco Salinas," Fray Luis yokes together Christian otherworldliness, neoplatonism, Ptolemaic cosmology, and Pythagorean philosophy, while in certain other poems his impulse to withdraw from the fevered world owes something to the let's-get-away-from-the-city theme in the ancient Latin poems of Horace. But the most daring conjunctions are those of eroticism and mysticism, as achieved by St. John of the Cross in certain of his poems, where he sometimes also inverts surprisingly the sexual role of the speaker. In his pastoral poem noted earlier, he also inverts the role of the Saviour and humankind, so that the Saviour is the lovesick shepherd. This strategy of daring and surprise in religious poetry is by no means unique; it has its roots in the eroticism of the Song of Songs in the Old Testament, and it reappears later in the love-songs sung by Christ and the soul in the church music of J. S. Bach (not to mention other centrist Protestant hymns such as "The Church's One Foundation"). But St. John carries the strategy much farther than in most realizations of the "bride of Christ" tradition. In this respect, the closest analogues to St. John's poems are those of Donne, who has long been notorious for converting sex into religion and vice versa.

The most lasting formal legacy of Petrarch was the sonnet—a fourteen-line poem broken by rhyme scheme and strategy into an eight-line octave and a six-line sestet. (In England, the Shakespearean form, three quatrains and a couplet, was often used instead.) Considered simply as a verse form, the sonnet has its attractions and advantages, and poets have demonstrated its enormous versatility. (It has never gone out of style in English poetry except during the century or so after Milton.) That it should have become popular is not surprising, but that it became so nearly universal an obsession during the Renaissance is one of the mysteries of literary history. It is possible, though unlikely, that the sonnet form provides a basic, if unconscious, satisfaction, as the AABA song form apparently does. The sonnet's expressiveness was well demonstrated by Milton in "On the Late Massacre in Piedmont," where all the lines end with a howling, angry wail in o and a sounds and the poem's compression is important to its effect. It is not clear, however, why this effect would not be equally powerful in other short lyric forms.

We get a clue to the secret of the sonnet's fascination from Shakespeare's play Romeo and Juliet, *where the protagonists fall in love at first sight, in the course of speaking a perfect sonnet in dialogue. In the first quatrain, Romeo flirts his way (to the accompanying Petrarchan obbligato of religious imagery) to kissing Juliet's hand:*

> If I profane with my unworthiest hand
> This holy shrine, the gentle fine is this,
> My lips, two blushing pilgrims, ready stand
> To smooth that rough touch with a tender kiss.

She proffers some maidenly resistance, telling him that handshakes should be enough, and introducing a pun on palm *and* palmer *(religious pilgrim):*

> Good pilgrim, you do wrong your hand too much,
> Which mannerly devotion shows in this:
> For saints have hands that pilgrims' hands do touch,
> And palm to palm is holy palmer's kiss.

Seizing on this last hint, Romeo presses his advantage:

> ROM. Have not saints lips, and holy palmers too?
> JUL. Ay, pilgrim, lips that they must use in pray'r.
> ROM. O then, dear saint, let lips do what hands do,
> They pray—grant thou, lest faith turn to despair.
> JUL. Saints do not move, though grant for prayers' sake.
> ROM. Then move not while my prayer's effect I take.

He is now ready to kiss her, on the lips, and does so twice as they speak a few more lines. "You kiss by th' book," says the bemused Juliet, in one of Shakespeare's best lines. Both she and Romeo understand sonnet form, including the climactic effect of the end couplet.

Like the limerick, the sonnet is a way of saying things "by the book," of living within certain arbitrarily hard-and-fast rules, and if this is true, it perhaps explains why certain quite expressive variations on sonnet form, invented by Spenser, John Keats, and certain other poets, have not taken hold. Poets rely on formal expectations that are themselves part of the poem's effect. Drayton's sonnet "Since There's No Help," another poem about handshakes and kisses, is of the Shakespearean type, divided 4-4-4-2, and the movement of supposedly cooling love between the parting kiss that opens the first quatrain and the handshake that opens the second one is inseparable from the sonnet form itself. The ultimate specimen of the game aspect of the genre is Lope de Vega's "Sonnet All of a Sudden," which is totally devoid of substantive content, an example of poetic form concerned entirely with itself. Even when the sonnet is used to comment on serious events of great moment, as in Milton's massacre poem, formal expectations play a part, in this case (Petrarchan, 8–6) because the poet's rage pushes him past the paltry barrier that is supposed to neatly separate the octave and sestet. Even that effect, however, of disdain for mere calcu-

*lated art, was presumably calculated, the poem's ferocious anger and high-minded-
ness notwithstanding. If so, we are reminded that our present-day distinction between
sincerity and artifice is something the Renaissance poets probably would not have
appreciated or perhaps even understood.*

FURTHER READING *(prepared by B.W.)*: Extensive bilingual collections of Spanish-
language poetry, for those who wish to sample it more extensively, include John A.
Crow, ed., *An Anthology of Spanish Poetry from the Beginnings to the Present Day,* 1979;
Angel Flores, ed., *An Anthology of Spanish Poetry from Garcilaso to García Lorca in
English Translation,* 1961; and Eleanor L. Turnbull and Pedro Salinas, eds., *Ten
Centuries of Spanish Poetry,* 1955. Stephen Minta's *Petrarch and Petrarchism: The English and French Traditions,* 1980, is a collection of poems by Petrarch and by French
and English poets whom he influenced. *The Continental Renaissance: 1500–1600,*
1978, by W. A. Coupe, A. J. Krailsheimer, J. A. Scott, and R. W. Truman, is a
helpful and well-written general survey of the period and includes discussions of
individual French and Spanish poets (and of poets of other nationalities as well). An
analogous survey of French Renaissance literature appears in I. D. McFarlane, *A
Literary History of France: Renaissance France 1470–1589,* 1974. Surveys and other
general treatments of English Renaissance lyrics include J. W. Lever, *The Elizabethan
Love Sonnet,* 1956; Douglas Peterson, *The English Lyric from Wyatt to Donne: A History
of the Plain and Eloquent Styles,* 1967; Hallett Smith, *Elizabethan Poetry: A Study in
Convention, Meaning, and Expression,* 1952; and Rosemond Tuve, *Elizabethan and
Metaphysical Imagery: Renaissance Poetic and Twentieth Century Critics,* 1947. On individual authors, see the following books, all either overviews or studies described by
their titles: Helmut Hatzfeld, *Santa Teresa de Ávila,* 1969; A. W. Satterthwaite, *Spenser, Ronsard, and Du Bellay: A Renaissance Comparison,* 1960; K. R. W. Jones, *Pierre de
Ronsard,* 1970; Manuel Durán, *Luis de León,* 1971; Gerald Brenan, *St. John of the
Cross,* with translations by Lynda Nicholson, 1973; A. Kent Hieatt, *Short Time's Endless Monument: The Symbolism of Numbers in Edmund Spenser's Epithalamion,* 1960;
Francis C. Hayes, *Lope de Vega,* 1968; Angel Flores, *Lope de Vega: Monster of Nature,*
1969; John Carey, *John Donne: Life, Mind, and Art,* 1981; Arnold Stein, *John Donne's
Lyrics: The Eloquence of Action,* 1962; and James Winny, *A Preface to Donne,* 1970. The
introduction, notes, and apparatus in *The Complete English Poems of John Donne,* ed.
C. A. Patrides, 1985, are very helpful and useful.

Garcilaso de la Vega
(C.1501–1536)

YOUR FACE IS WRITTEN IN MY SOUL . . . [1]

> Your face is written in my soul, and when
> I want to write about you, you alone
> Become the writer, I but read the line;
> I watch you where you still watch me, within.

[1] Spanish title: *Escrito está en mi alma vuestro gesto;* translated by Edwin Morgan.

This state I am and always will be in.   5
For though my soul imprints a half-design
Of what I see in you, the good unknown
Is taken on a trusting regimen.

What was I born for if not to adore you?
My ills have shaped you to the bent they give.   10
I love you by a daily act of soul.

All that I have I must confess I owe you.
For you I came to life, for you I live,
For you I'd die, and do die, after all.

WHILE THERE IS STILL THE COLOR OF A ROSE . . . [1]

While there is still the color of a rose
And of a lily in your countenance,
And you with such an ardent candid glance
Can fire the heart, and check the flames it shows;

And while that golden hair of yours that flows   5
Into a knot can leap into a dance
As the wind blows with livelier dalliance
Upon the fairest proud white neck it knows:

Gather together from your happy spring
Fruits that are sweet, before time ravages   10
With angry snow the beauty of your head.

The rose will wither as the cold wind rages,
And age come gently to change everything,
Lest our desire should change old age instead.

Santa Teresa de Jesús
(*1515–1582*)

IF, LORD, THY LOVE FOR ME IS STRONG[1]

If, Lord, Thy love for me is strong
As this which binds me unto Thee,
What holds me from Thee, Lord, so long,
What holds Thee, Lord, so long from me?

[1] *En tanto que de rosa y azucena;* translated by Edwin Morgan.
[1] Spanish title: *Si el amor que me tenéis;* translated by Arthur Symons.

O soul, what then desirest thou?   5
—Lord, I would see Thee, who thus choose Thee.
What fears can yet assail thee now?
—All that I fear is but to lose Thee.

Love's whole possession I entreat,
Lord, make my soul Thine own abode,   10
And I will build a nest so sweet
It may not be too poor for God.

O soul in God hidden from sin,
What more desires for thee remain,
Save but to love, and love again,   15
And, all on flame with love within,
Love on, and turn to love again?

LET NOTHING DISTURB THEE[1]

Let nothing disturb thee,
Nothing affright thee;
All things are passing;
God never changeth;
Patient endurance   5
Attaineth to all things;
Who God possesseth
In nothing is wanting;
Alone God sufficeth.

[1] *Nada te turbe;* translated by Henry Wadsworth Longfellow. This poem is also known as "St. Teresa's Bookmark." It was found, after her death, inscribed on the bookmark she used in her breviary (the book of prescribed prayers and readings used by members of religious orders).

Joachim Du Bellay
(1522–1560)

REGRETS, XXXI[1]

How happy is the man who has traveled the ways
Of Jason or Ulysses,[2] and then returned
To his home again, wise, and having learned
To live among his own the rest of his days.

When will I see again the wisps which rise   5
From the chimneys of my town, what spring or fall
Will I see the little garden behind my wall—
Greater than any province in my eyes?

More pleasant is my family's humble home
Than any gaudy palace front in Rome,   10
More than their marble does that slate roof please.

I'd rather have my Loire and hilltop town
Than the Latin Tiber and Mount Palatine,
And rather than salty air, the sweet Anjou breeze.[3]

FROM A WINNOWER OF WHEAT TO THE WINDS[1]

To you, light airy flock,
Who, on the wing, pass
Over this world of ours
And softly sweep the grass,
And make the treetops shake,   5
With soft, rustling murmurs,

I offer these violets,
These daisies, these lilies,
And some roses, too,
Scarlet roses, all these   10
Newly blossomed florets,
And carnations, for you.

---

[1] French title: *Les Regrets, XXXI, Heureux, qui, comme Ulysse;* translated by David Sanders.
[2] Two great travelers and adventurers from Greek myth: Jason captained the Argonauts in their voyage to capture the Golden Fleece, Odysseus sailed all over the Mediterranean in his ten-years' voyage home from the Trojan war.
[3] The Loire is a river flowing through the old province of Anjou, in western France. The Tiber is the river of Rome, the Palatine one of the city's seven hills.
[1] *D'un Vanneur de blé aux vents;* translated by David Sanders.

So fan this tract of land
With your sweet breath,
Fan this farm, while I   15
Separate the chaff
From the wheat I fan
In the heat of the day.

Pierre de Ronsard
(1524–1585)

TO CASSANDRE[1]

I'm sending you this fresh bouquet of flowers
Which, if my fingers hadn't picked them tonight,
Would all be withered up and shriveled tight,
And have dropped their petals in a few short hours.

There is in this a lesson meant for you: 5
The delicate flower your beauty has become
Will also wither up and drop in time
And someday, like these flowers, perish too.

Time goes on, my dearest, time goes on.
Alas! not time, it's we who have to go,   10
And we who'll lie beneath the family stone.

And the love of which we've both been talking so
Will mean just nothing when our lives are through;
So love me, while your beauty is still new.

ON THE DEATH OF MARIE[1]

Just as the rose on the branch one sees in May,
In youthful beauty budding, in first flower,
Turns the sky jealous of its deep color
When the Dawn's tears bathe it at break of day

---

[1] French title: *Je vous envoie un bouquet, que ma main;* translated by David Sanders.
[1] *Sonnet sur la mort de Marie;* translated by David Sanders.

(Grace held in its leaf and Love that lies   5
Inside anoint the gardens and trees with scents),
But beaten by rain or by the sun's intense
Heat, leaf by open leaf, it dies;

So in your young and first unfolding bloom
While the earth and sky honored your beauty's powers,   10
The Fates killed you, and laid you in an ashen bed.

Accept these tears I offer at your tomb,
This vase of milk, this basket full of flowers,
And let your body be roses, alive and dead.

TO HÉLÈNE[1]

When you are old and sitting by the fire,
Spinning your threads of yarn by candlelight,
Singing my songs, you'll say to yourself one night,
"Ronsard praised me when I was his desire."

You'll have no maid who hears you tell this story   5
Though already half-asleep from working hard,
Who won't wake up at the sound of the name Ronsard,
Blessing your name with songs of lasting glory.

By then I'll be a ghost, long since dead,
Buried in the shade of the myrtle overhead,   10
And you'll be an old crone crouching at the fire

Regretting my lost love and your cold scorning.
Live now, if you believe me, don't wait till morning;
Come out and cut the roses from your brier.

SONNET TO AN UNNAMED PERSON[1]

I give these eggs to you. The egg is a sphere
Resembling heaven, which holds within its girth
The water of oceans, the fire, the air and earth,[2]
And contains without confining all that's here.

The egg's membrane is like the air; the raw   5
Egg white, the sea from which all things spring;
The yolk, a fire igniting everything;
The shell, the fertile earth which can bear them all.

[1] *Sonnets pour Hélène: Quand vous serez bien vieille;* translated by David Sanders.
[1] *Les Amours diverses, XLVIII: Je vous donne des oeufs;* translated by David Sanders.
[2] This line names the four elements of which all things were believed to be constituted.

Both heaven and eggs are covered with white. It's this,
My gift to you in a shell: the universe.   10
The present is perfection—if you care.

As perfect as it is, it cannot equal
The perfection of you, to which nothing can compare,
And of which the gods alone are entitled to tell.

Fray Luis de León
(C. 1527–1591)

ODE TO FRANCISCO SALINAS[1]

The air grows calm and clear
And clothes itself in beauty and strange light,
Salinas, when the extreme
Art of your music strikes
Out from that skilled and tempering hand I admire.   5

It is a heavenly sound
That makes my dull, all-too-forgetful soul
Find its senses and rouse
Its lost recollections of those
First days in its primordial glorious home.   10

Yes, it goes back, it remembers;
In thoughts, and fate, it grows a better thing;
For gold, it loses fervor:
Let that brittle glint
Trap the adoring slavelike mob, not this   15

Soul that crosses space,
Climbs till it has reached the highest sphere,[2]
And hears a music there
That's made for other ears,
Unfading notes and the first notes to speak.[3]   20

---

[1] Spanish title: *Oda a Francisco Salinas;* translated by Edwin Morgan. Salinas (1530–90),
who was blind, was a distinguished musician and music theorist on the faculty of the University of Salamanca.

[2] The Primum Mobile, or first mover, the outermost shell of the universe in the Ptolemaic
system.

[3] The "music of the spheres" was produced, according to ancient Pythagorean philosophy,
by the ordered movements of the heavens. This philosophy also posited the existence of
numerical correspondences between the heavens and the soul.

It sees the master player
With that great cosmic cithern[4] in his arms
Pluck out sure and clear
The sacred chord that guards
This everlasting temple from all harm.[5]   25

And since it is itself
Composed of many chords, it quickly gives
Its answer in an echo,
And both together mix
Their vying sounds in sweetest harmony.   30

Now through a sea of sweetness
The soul goes voyaging on, until at last
It plunges drowned so deep there
That neither eye nor heart
Takes notice of what happens above or apart.   35

O blessed loss of sense!
O life-enhancing death! O sweet forgetting!
If I could enjoy your rest
Without regaining, ever,
This consciousness so earthbound and so wretched!   40

To this blessing I call you,
Glory of Apollo's holy choir,[6] friends
I love more dearly than all the
Things that are treasured well,
For what is all the rest but a lament?   45

O play, still play, Salinas,
Still sound the sound of music in my ear;
Let this unblind the feelings
Till the divine good appears
And every other thing stays sunk in sleep.   50

THE LIFE OF THE BLESSED[1]

Region of life and light!
Land of the good whose earthly toils are o'er!
Nor frost nor heat may blight
Thy vernal beauty, fertile shore,
Yielding thy blessed fruits for evermore!   5

---

[4] A guitar-like instrument of the sixteenth century.
[5] The harmony of chords is also based on numerical ratios.
[6] Fellow-poets (Apollo being the god of poets).
[1] *Morada del cielo;* translated by William Cullen Bryant.

There, without crook or sling,
Walks the Good Shepherd; blossoms white and red
   Round his meek temples cling;
   And, to sweet pastures led,
His own loved flock beneath his eye is fed.   10

   He guides, and near him they
Follow delighted; for he makes them go
   Where dwells eternal May,
   And heavenly roses blow,
Deathless, and gathered but again to grow.   15

   He leads them to the height
Named of the infinite and long-sought Good,
   And fountains of delight;
   And where his feet have stood,
Springs up, along the way, their tender food.   20

   And when, in the mid skies,
The climbing sun has reached his highest bound,
   Reposing as he lies,
   With all his flock around,
He witches the still air with numerous[2] sound.   25

   From his sweet lute flow forth
Immortal harmonies, of power to still
   All passions born of earth,
   And draw the ardent will
Its destiny of goodness to fulfil.   30

   Might but a little part,
A wandering breath, of that high melody
   Descend into my heart,
   And change it till it be
Transformed and swallowed up, O love! in thee: 35

   Ah! then my soul should know,
Beloved! where thou liest at noon of day;
   And from this place of woe
   Released, should take its way
To mingle with thy flock, and never stray.   40

[2] Musical; metrical.

AT THE ASCENSION[1]

Good Shepherd, have You skipped away, to leave
Your flock in this deep, hidden vale,
Their lonely legacy to grieve
Their stay, while You, beyond the blue sky's trail,
Attain assuring immortality.   5

They are now reft of joy who once were filled
From the fond kindness of Your breast;
Where can the leaderless, who willed
To follow, turn? the hungry, lest
They lose their way, seek out Your company?   10

What vision in this world can satisfy
Those who have gazed upon Your face?
Less beauty but disturbs the eye;
The music in this world is dull, lacks grace,
For those who heard Your words' sweet harmony.   15

Who is there now to calm the white-foamed lake?
Who now to still the roaring gales?
Now that a cloud has lowered to take
And cover You, how can we set our sails
For port? What north star pilots destiny?   20

Why do you run so fast, O cloud, as though
You envied us brief happiness?
Why hoard the sun, only to show
How rich you are?—miser without largesse,
Scorning our blindness and our poverty!   25

THE ASSUMPTION OF THE VIRGIN[1]

Lady! thine upward flight
The opening heavens receive with joyous song;
Blest, who thy garments bright
May seize, amid the throng,
And to the sacred mount float peacefully along.   5

---

[1] *En la Ascensión;* translated by James Edward Tobin. According to Luke 24:52–53, after
the Ascension of Jesus into heaven his disciples "returned to Jerusalem with great joy, and
were continually in the temple, praising and blessing God."
[1] *A la Asunción de Nuestra Señora;* translated by Henry Wadsworth Longfellow. Roman Catholics believe that the Virgin Mary was bodily assumed into heaven at her death.

Bright angels are around thee,
They that have served thee from thy birth are here:
   Their hands with stars have crowned thee;
   Thou,—peerless Queen of air,
As sandals to thy feet the silver moon dost wear.   10

   Celestial dove! so meek
And mild and fair! oh, let thy peaceful eye
   This thorny valley seek,
   Where such sweet blossoms lie,
But where the sons of Eve in pain and sorrow sigh.   15

   For if the imprisoned soul
Could catch the brightness of that heavenly way,
   'Twould own its sweet control
   And gently pass away,
Drawn by the magnet power to an eternal day.   20

San Juan de la Cruz
(1542–1591)

ONE DISMAL NIGHT . . . [1]

   One dismal night
With the ardors of love aflame
   O venture bright!
Unobserved I slipped away
While my dwelling still unstirring lay.   5

   In disguise of night
By the secret stair's security
   O venture bright!
Into the dark and stealthily
While my dwelling still unstirring lay.   10

   In the secrecy
Of the glorious night, unseen my face
Nor able any part to see
Having no light to guide my way
Save the one within my heart ablaze.   15

[1] Spanish title: *En una noche obscura;* translated by Kate Flores. The poem is probably, to some extent, literal description, of the author's escape from a Toledo prison, in which he had been confined by fellow-friars opposed to his attempts at monastic reform. Juan (St. John of the Cross) also wrote a prose commentary expanding on the mystical significance of the poem, as he did with certain others including "O Living Flame of Love."

This more luminously
Led me than the radiance of noon
Thence to where in waiting for me
One to me well known
Kept a place where no one had been drawn.   20

O that night that guided me
O night lovelier than the dawn
O that night of ecstasy
When Beloved and Lover joined,
Into Lover the Beloved transformed!   25

On my flowering breast,
Kept for Him alone away,
Him I caressed
And He drowsed and stayed
And all my senses languished there.   30

The turreted breeze
In stroking His hair
With fingers serene
My throat touched near
And all my senses languished there.   35

Lingering and forgetting
Face in the Lover reposing fair
All lapsed and I surrendered
Surrendering my care
Amidst the lilies remembering no more.   40

O LIVING FLAME OF LOVE . . . [1]

O living flame of love,
   How tender is your wound,
Your burning at the center of my soul!
   You are no longer shy—
   Please finish, know me at the source;   5
Break the hymen of our sweet intercourse!

O easy cautery![2]
   Oh wound that is really gift!
Oh gentle hand! Oh delicate touch of a knife
   That brings eternal life   10
   And pays all petty debts!
Killing, you turn my death into flaming life!

[1] *¡Oh llama de amor viva!;* translated by Stephen Stepanchev. See the note to "One Dismal
Night."
[2] Medical treatment with a hot iron or needle.

O lamps of living fire,
In whose renewing splendors
The deep and smoking caverns of the senses,   15
Which once were black and blind,
Provide amazing delights,
Give heat and light to their awaking lover!

How tender, mild, and blessed
Is your image in my breast,   20
Where, secretly, you live alone, a king;
And with your soft breathing,
The bliss and glory of the Dove,
How delicately you induce my love!

I ENTERED WHERE I DID NOT KNOW . . . [1]

I entered where I did not know,
And there remained unknowing,
All reason now transcended.

I did not know the door
But when I found the way,   5
Unknowing where I was,
I learned unheard of things,
But what I heard I cannot say,
For I remained unknowing,
All reason now transcended.   10

My knowledge was fulfilled
With piety and peace.
In deepest solitude
I found the narrow way:
A secret giving such release   15
That I was left there stammering,
All reason now transcended.

I was so fully drunk,
So dazed and far away,
My senses were released   20
From feelings of my own.
My mind had found a surer way:
A knowledge of unknowing,
All reason now transcended.

And he who does arrive,   25
Collapses as in sleep;
For all he knew before

[1] *Entréme donde no supe;* translated by Willis Barnstone.

Now seems of little worth,
And so his knowledge grows so deep
That he remains unknowing,   30
All reason now transcended.

The higher he ascends,
The darker is the wood;
It is the shadowy cloud
That clarified the night,   35
And so the one who understood
Remains at last unknowing,
All reason now transcended.

This knowledge by unknowing
Is such a soaring force   40
That scholars argue long
But never leave the ground.
Their reason always fails the source:
To understand unknowing,
All reason now transcended.   45

This knowledge is supreme
And meets a blazing height,
Though formal reason tries,
It crumbles in the dark.
For one who would control the night,   50
By knowledge of unknowing
He will have all transcended.

This is my final word,
The highest learning lead
To an ecstatic feeling   55
Of the most holy Being;
And from his mercy comes his deed:
To make one stay unknowing,
All reason now transcended.

A SHEPHERD, YOUNG AND MOURNFUL, GRIEVES ALONE . . . [1]

A shepherd, young and mournful, grieves alone,
Alien his pleasure, absent his content;
The shadow-memory of his shepherdess
Strikes at his heart as though love were a stone.

---

[1] *Un pastorcico solo está penado;* translated by James Edward Tobin.

Physical pain does not evoke lament,   5
Such suffering is not what brings the hurt;
Although his heart is battered by the blow,
He weeps to realize neglect is meant.

In realizing thus that he is not
The center of his shepherdess's life   10
He sadly finds his heart is wounded more;
Alien to joy, he hears love taunt: Forgot.

The shepherd cries: Why does she stand apart?
Ah, woe to him who holds her distantly,
Keeps her in willing absence from my side,   15
Shutting her eyes to how love tears my heart.

He stretched his lovely, loving arms out wide,
Climbing a tree in time to hold them so;
His heart still deeply wounded by her love,
He clung there, waiting her, until he died.   20

I KNOW FULL WELL THE WATER'S
FLOWING POWER . . . [1]

I know full well the water's flowing power,
Though it be dark.

A secret font, an everlasting force—
I know exactly where it has its source,
Though it be dark.   5

And yet I do not know; for therein lies
The origin from which origins rise,
Though it be dark.

I know that nothing can be quite so fair
And that earth drinks from it as well as air,   10
Though it be dark.

I know its depth cannot be sounded, know
That none can cross against the eddies' flow,
Though it be dark.

[1] *Que bien sé yo la fonte que mana y corre;* translated by James Edward Tobin. As with "One Dismal Night," this devotional and theological poem may have had a circumstantial origin, in the darkness of Juan's imprisonment in Toledo. The poem's images develop the idea of the divine Trinity.

Nothing can dim its ever-brilliant gleam,   15
From which all other light and wisdom stream,
Though it be dark.

I know its many branches stretch and wind
To reach all heights and depths and all mankind,
Though it be dark.   20

I know how well this nourished current laves
Each bank, how very powerful its waves,
Though it be dark.

Both source and swirling stream are one, I sense—
Their unity permits no precedence—   25
Though it be dark.

Its deathless strength, its hidden riverhead,
Are in grace-giving eucharistic Bread,
Though it be dark.

And all mankind is called and asked to share   30
The nourishment of hidden mystery there,
Though it be dark.

Desiring and desired, this mystery
Within the Bread of life I clearly see,
Though it be dark.   35

Edmund Spenser
(*1552–1599*)

EPITHALAMION[1]

Ye learnèd sisters,[2] which have oftentimes
Been to me aiding, others to adorn,
Whom ye thought worthy of your graceful rhymes,
That even the greatest did not greatly scorn
To hear their names sung in your simple lays,[3]   5

---

[1]*Epithalamion*, or *epithalamium*, is the generic name (derived from Greek) for a wedding song. Spenser was married on June 11, 1594, to Elizabeth Boyle.
[2]The Muses, the goddesses of inspiration.
[3]Poems. Spenser's longest and greatest work, *The Faerie Queene*, was written to honor Queen Elizabeth I.

But joyèd in their praise;
And when ye list[4] your own mishaps to mourn,
Which death, or love, or fortune's wreck did raise,
Your string could soon to sadder tenor turn,
And teach the woods and waters to lament   10
Your doleful dreariment:
Now lay those sorrowful complaints aside;
And, having all your heads with garlands crowned,
Help me mine own love's praises to resound;
Nor let the same of any be envide: 15
So Orpheus did for his own bride![5]
So I unto myself alone will sing;
The woods shall to me answer, and my echo ring.

Early, before the world's light-giving lamp
His golden beam upon the hills doth spread,   20
Having dispersed the night's uncheerful damp,
Do ye awake; and, with fresh lusty-hed,[6]
Go to the bower of my belovèd love,
My truest turtle dove;
Bid her awake; for Hymen[7] is awake,   25
And long since ready forth his mask to move,[8]
With his bright Tead[9] that flames with many a flake,
And many a bachelor to wait on him,
In their fresh garments trim.
Bid her awake therefore, and soon her dight,[10]   30
For lo! the wishèd day is come at last,
That shall, for all the pains and sorrows past,
Pay to her usury of long delight:
And, whilst she doth her dight,
Do ye to her of joy and solace sing,   35
That all the woods may answer, and your echo ring.

Bring with you all the Nymphs that you can hear,
Both of the rivers and the forests green,
And of the sea that neighbors to her near,[11]
All with gay garlands goodly well beseen.   40
And let them also with them bring in hand
Another gay garland,
For my fair love, of lilies and of roses,
Bound truelove wise with a blue silk riband;
And let them make great store of bridal posies,   45

---

[4] It pleases you.
[5] Orpheus, the mythical poet and musician, loved his wife Eurydice so strongly that he undertook to rescue her from the realm of the dead.
[6] Zestful pleasure.   [7] The god of weddings.
[8] To lead the festive wedding procession.   [9] Torch.   [10] Array; adorn.
[11] The bride's residence was near the ocean. The Nymphs were minor nature-goddesses: they included naiads (of rivers), dryads (of trees), nereids (of ocean).

And let them eke[12] bring store of other flowers,
To deck the bridal bowers.
And let the ground whereas her foot shall tread,
For fear the stones her tender foot should wrong,
Be strewed with fragrant flowers all along,   50
And diapered like the discolored mead;[13]
Which done, do at her chamber door await,
For she will waken straight;[14]
The whiles do ye this song unto her sing,
The woods shall to you answer, and your echo ring.   55

Ye Nymphs of Mulla,[15] which with careful heed
The silver scaly trouts do tend full well,
And greedy pikes which use therein to feed
(Those trouts and pikes all others do excel);
And ye likewise, which keep the rushy lake,   60
Where none do fishes take;
Bind up the locks the which hang scattered light,
And in his waters, which your mirror make,
Behold your faces as the crystal bright,
That when you come whereas my love doth lie,   65
No blemish she may spy.
And eke, ye lightfoot maids, which keep the deer,
That on the hoary mountain used to tower;[16]
And the wild wolves, which seek them to devour,
With your steel darts do chase from coming near;   70
Be also present here,
To help to deck her, and to help to sing,
That all the woods may answer, and your echo ring.

Wake, now, my love, awake! for it is time;
The rosy morn long since left Tithon's bed,[17]   75
All ready to her silver coach to climb;
And Phoebus[18] 'gins to show his glorious head.
Hark, how the cheerful birds do chant their lays[19]
And carol of love's praise.
The merry lark her matins[20] sings aloft;   80
The thrush replies; the mavis descant[21] plays;
The ouzel shrills; the ruddock warbles soft;
So goodly all agree, with sweet consent,
To this day's merriment.
Ah! my dear love, why do ye sleep thus long,   85
When meeter[22] were that ye should now awake,

---

[12] Also.   [13] *diapered*: decorated. *discolored mead*: many-colored meadow.
[14] Straightway; immediately.
[15] A river valley in Ireland, where the wedding is taking place.
[16] To dwell in a high place.
[17] Tithonus was the mate of Eos, or Aurora, goddess of the dawn.
[18] Apollo, god of the sun.   [19] Songs.   [20] Morning prayers.   [21] Treble part.
[22] More fitting.

To await the coming of your joyous mate,
And hearken to the birds' love-learnèd song,
The dewy leaves among!
For they of joy and pleasance to you sing,   90
That all the woods them answer, and their echo ring.

My love is now awake out of her dreams,
And her fair eyes, like stars that dimmèd were
With darksome cloud, now show their goodly beams
More bright than Hesperus[23] his head doth rear.   95
Come now, ye damsels, daughters of delight,
Help quickly her to dight:
But first come, ye fair hours, which were begot
In Jove's sweet paradise of Day and Night;[24]
Which do the seasons of the year allot,   100
And all that ever in this world is fair,
Do make and still repair:
And ye three handmaids of the Cyprian queen,[25]
The which do still adorn her beauty's pride,
Help to adorn my beautifulest bride;   105
And as ye her array, still throw between
Some graces to be seen,
And, as ye use to Venus, to her sing,
The whiles the woods shall answer, and your echo ring.

Now is my love all ready forth to come: 110
Let all the virgins therefore well await:
And ye fresh boys, that tend upon her groom,
Prepare yourselves; for he is coming straight;
Set all your things in seemly good array,
Fit for so joyful day: 115
The joyfulest day that ever sun did see.
Fair Sun! show forth thy favorable ray,
And let thy life-full heat not fervent be,
For fear of burning her sunshiny face,
Her beauty to disgrace.   120
O fairest Phoebus! father of the Muse![26]
If ever I did honor thee aright,
Or sing the thing that might thy mind delight,
Do not thy servant's simple boon[27] refuse;
But let this day, let this one day, be mine;   125
Let all the rest be thine.

[23] Venus as evening star.
[24] The Hours were goddesses of order and the seasons. In Renaissance poetry Jove, king of the gods, was a near-synonym for God.
[25] The three Graces were minor goddesses personifying charm, brilliance, and freshness. They were attendants on Aphrodite/Venus, the goddess of love, who was worshiped especially in Cyprus.
[26] Phoebus Apollo was god both of the sun and of poetry.   [27] Requested favor.

Then I thy sovereign praises loud will sing,
That all the woods shall answer, and their echo ring.

Hark! how the Minstrels 'gin to shrill aloud
Their merry music that resounds from far. 130
The pipe, the tabor, and the trembling croud,
That well agree withouten breach or jar.[28]
But, most of all, the Damsels do delight
When they their timbrels[29] smite,
And thereunto do dance and carol sweet, 135
That all the senses they do ravish quite;
The whiles the boys run up and down the street,
Crying aloud with strong confusèd noise,
As if it were one voice,
Hymen, iö Hymen, Hymen, they do shout;[30] 140
That even to the heavens their shouting shrill
Doth reach, and all the firmament doth fill;
To which the people standing all about,
As in approvance, do thereto applaud,
And loud advance her laud;[31] 145
And evermore they Hymen, Hymen sing,
That all the woods them answer, and their echo ring.

Lo! where she comes along with portly pace,
Like Phoebe,[32] from her chamber of the East,
Arising forth to run her mighty race, 150
Clad all in white, that seems a virgin best.
So well it her beseems, that ye would ween
Some angel she had been.
Her long loose yellow locks like golden wire,
Sprinkled with pearl, and pearling flowers atween, 155
Do like a golden mantle her attire;
And, being crownèd with a garland green,
Seem like some maiden queen.
Her modest eyes, abashèd to behold
So many gazers as on her do stare, 160
Upon the lowly ground affixèd are;
Nor dare lift up her countenance too bold,
But blush to hear her praises sung so loud,
So far from being proud.
Nathless do ye still loud her praises sing, 165
That all the woods may answer, and your echo ring.

Tell me, ye merchants' daughters, did ye see
So fair a creature in your town before:
So sweet, so lovely, and so mild as she,

---

[28] *tabor:* drum. *croud:* fiddle. *jar:* dissonance. [29] Tambourines.
[30] The traditional exclamation of joy in classical wedding poetry, such as Catullus' Poem 62.
[31] Praise. [32] Goddess of the moon; sister of Phoebus Apollo.

Adorned with beauty's grace and virtue's store?   170
Her goodly eyes like sapphires shining bright,
Her forehead ivory white,
Her cheeks like apples which the sun hath ruddied,
Her lips like cherries charming men to bite,
Her breast like to a bowl of cream uncrudded,[33]   175
Her paps[34] like lilies budded,
Her snowy neck like to a marble tower;
And all her body like a palace fair,
Ascending up, with many a stately stair,
To honor's seat and chastity's sweet bower.   180
Why stand ye still, ye virgins, in amaze,
Upon her so to gaze,
Whiles ye forget your former lay to sing,
To which the woods did answer, and your echo ring?

But if ye saw that which no eyes can see,   185
The inward beauty of her lively spright,[35]
Garnished with heavenly gifts of high degree,
Much more then would ye wonder at that sight,
And stand astonished like to those which read
Medusa's mazeful head.[36]   190
There dwells sweet love, and constant chastity,
Unspotted faith, and comely womanhood,
Regard of honor, and mild modesty;
There virtue reigns as queen in royal throne,
And giveth laws alone,   195
The which the base affections[37] do obey,
And yield their services unto her will;
Nor thought of thing uncomely ever may
Thereto approach to tempt her mind to ill.
Had ye once seen these her celestial treasures,   200
And unrevealèd pleasures,
Then would ye wonder, and her praises sing,
That all the woods should answer, and your echo ring.

Open the temple gates unto my love,
Open them wide that she may enter in,   205
And all the posts adorn as doth behove,
And all the pillars deck with garlands trim,
For to receive this Saint with honor due,
That cometh in to you.
With trembling steps, and humble reverence,   210
She cometh in, before the Almighty's view;
Of her ye virgins learn obedience,

---

[33] Uncurdled.   [34] Nipples.   [35] Spirit.
[36] *read:* saw. Medusa was a monster, with snakes for hair, who turned to stone anyone who
gazed on her.
[37] Lower passions and feelings.

When so ye come into those holy places,
To humble your proud faces:
Bring her up to the high altar, that she may   215
The sacred ceremonies there partake,
The which do endless matrimony make;
And let the roaring organs loudly play
The praises of the Lord in lively notes;
The whiles, with hollow throats,   220
The Choristers the joyous Anthem sing,
That all the woods may answer, and their echo ring.

Behold, whiles she before the altar stands,
Hearing the holy priest that to her speaks,
And blesseth her with his two happy hands,   225
How the red roses flush up in her cheeks,
And the pure snow, with goodly vermill stain
Like crimson dyed in grain:[38]
That even the Angels, which continually
About the sacred altar do remain,   230
Forget their service and about her fly,
Oft peeping in her face, that seems more fair,
The more they on it stare.
But her sad[39] eyes, still fastened on the ground,
Are governèd with goodly modesty,   235
That suffers not one look to glance awry,
Which may let in a little thought unsound.
Why blush ye, love, to give to me your hand,
The pledge of all our band?[40]
Sing, ye sweet Angels, Alleluja sing,   240
That all the woods may answer, and your echo ring.

Now all is done: bring home the bride again;
Bring home the triumph of our victory:
Bring home with you the glory of her gain;
With joyance bring her and with jollity.   245
Never had man more joyful day than this,
Whom heaven would heap with bliss.
Make feast therefore now all this live-long day;
This day for ever to me holy is.
Pour out the wine without restraint or stay,   250
Pour not by cups, but by the belly full,
Pour out to all that will,
And sprinkle all the posts and walls with wine,
That they may sweat, and drunken be withal.
Crown ye God Bacchus[41] with a coronal,   255
And Hymen also crown with wreaths of vine;
And let the Graces dance unto the rest,
For they can do it best:

---

[38] *vermill:* vermilion. *grain:* fast dye.   [39] Serious.   [40] Union.   [41] God of wine.

The whiles the maidens do their carol sing,
To which the woods shall answer, and their echo ring.   260

Ring ye the bells, ye young men of the town,
And leave your wonted[42] labors for this day:
This day is holy; do ye write it down,
That ye for ever it remember may.
This day the sun is in his chiefest height,   265
With Barnaby the bright,[43]
From whence declining daily by degrees,
He somewhat loseth of his heat and light,
When once the Crab[44] behind his back he sees.
But for this time it ill ordainèd was,   270
To choose the longest day in all the year,
And shortest night, when longest fitter were:
Yet never day so long, but late would pass.
Ring ye the bells, to make it wear away,
And bonfires make all day;   275
And dance about them, and about them sing,
That all the woods may answer, and your echo ring.

Ah! when will this long weary day have end,
And lend me leave to come unto my love?
How slowly do the hours their numbers spend?   280
How slowly does sad Time his feathers move?
Haste thee, O fairest Planet,[45] to thy home,
Within the Western foam:
Thy tirèd steeds long since have need of rest.
Long though it be, at last I see it gloom,   285
And the bright evening-star with golden crest
Appear out of the East.
Fair child of beauty! glorious lamp of love!
That all the host of heaven in ranks dost lead,
And guidest lovers through the night's sad dread,   290
How cheerfully thou lookest from above,
And seems to laugh atween thy twinkling light,
As joying in the sight
Of these glad many, which for joy do sing,
That all the woods them answer, and their echo ring!   295

Now, cease, ye damsels, your delights fore-past;[46]
Enough is it that all the day was yours:
Now day is done, and night is nighing fast,
Now bring the bride into the bridal bowers.
The night is come, now soon her disarray,   300

---

[42] Usual.

[43] June 11, the feast of St. Barnabas, was the longest day of the year before the Gregorian calendar was adopted, which omitted the dates of ten consecutive days. Since then, June 21 has been the longest day.

[44] The constellation Cancer, which the sun enters at the summer solstice.

[45] The sun.   [46] Gone by.

And in her bed her lay;
Lay her in lilies and in violets,
And silken curtains over her display,
And odored sheets, and Arras[47] coverlets.
Behold how goodly my fair love does lie,   305
In proud humility!
Like unto Maia, when as Jove her took
In Tempe, lying on the flowery grass,
'Twixt sleep and wake, after she weary was,
With bathing in the Acidalian brook.[48]   310
Now it is night, ye damsels may be gone,
And leave my love alone,
And leave likewise your former lay to sing:
The woods no more shall answer, nor your echo ring.

Now welcome, night! thou night so long expected,   315
That long day's labor dost at last defray,
And all my cares, which cruel Love collected,
Hast summed in one, and cancellèd for aye:
Spread thy broad wing over my love and me,
That no man may us see;   320
And in thy sable mantle us enwrap,
From fear of peril and foul horror free.
Let no false treason seek us to entrap,
Nor any dread disquiet once annoy
The safety of our joy;   325
But let the night be calm, and quietsome,
Without tempestuous storms or sad affray:
Like as when Jove with fair Alcmena lay,
When he begot the great Tirynthian groom:[49]
Or like as when he with thyself[50] did lie   330
And begot Majesty.
And let the maids and young men cease to sing;
Nor let the woods them answer, nor their echo ring.

Let no lamenting cries, nor doleful tears,
Be heard all night within, nor yet without: 335
Nor let false whispers, breeding hidden fears,
Break gentle sleep with misconceivèd doubt.
Let no deluding dreams, nor dreadful sights,
Make sudden sad affrights;
Nor let house-fires, nor lightning's helpless[51] harms,   340
Nor let the Puck,[52] nor other evil sprites,
Nor let mischievous witches with their charms,

[47] A city in France where tapestries were made.
[48] Maia was the mother of the god Hermes, or Mercury. Tempe was a valley near Mt. Olympus, the home of the gods in northern Greece. The Acidalian brook was sacred to Aphrodite.
[49] Hercules, son of Alcmena, born at Tiryns; the greatest of the Greek heroes.
[50] Night.   [51] For which there is no help.   [52] A mischievous fairy.

Nor let hobgoblins, names whose sense we see not,
Fray[53] us with things that be not:
Let not the screech-owl nor the stork be heard,   345
Nor the night raven, that still deadly yells;
Nor damnèd ghosts, called up with mighty spells,
Nor grizzly vultures, make us once afraid:
Nor let the unpleasant choir of frogs still croaking
Make us to wish their choking.   350
Let none of these their dreary accents sing;
Nor let the woods them answer, nor their echo ring.

But let still Silence true night-watches keep,
That sacred Peace may in assurance reign,
And timely Sleep, when it is time to sleep,   355
May pour his limbs forth on your[54] pleasant plain;
The whiles an hundred little wingèd loves,
Like divers-feathered doves,
Shall fly and flutter round about your bed,
And in the secret dark, that none reproves,   360
Their pretty stealths shall work, and snares shall spread
To filch away sweet snatches of delight,
Concealed through covert night.
Ye sons of Venus,[55] play your sports at will!
For greedy pleasure, careless of your toys,[56]   365
Thinks more upon her paradise of joys,
Than what ye do, albeit good or ill.
All night therefore attend your merry play,
For it will soon be day:
Now none doth hinder you, that say or sing;   370
Nor will the woods now answer, nor your echo ring.

Who is the same, which at my window peeps?
Or whose is that fair face that shines so bright?
Is it not Cynthia,[57] she that never sleeps,
But walks about high heaven all the night?   375
O! fairest goddess, do thou not envy
My love with me to spy:
For thou likewise didst love, though now unthought,
And for a fleece of wool, which privily[58]
The Latmian shepherd once unto thee brought,   380
His pleasures with thee wrought.
Therefore to us be favorable now;
And since of women's labors thou hast charge,
And generation goodly dost enlarge,
Incline thy will to effect our wishful vow,   385

[53] Frighten.   [54] Night's.   [55] Cupids (the "loves" of line 357).
[56] Trivial amusements.
[57] Another name for the goddess of the moon. Proverbially chaste, she nevertheless fell in
love with Endymion, a shepherd of Mt. Latmos, to whom she came in his sleep.
[58] Secretly.

And the chaste womb inform with timely seed,
That may our comfort breed:
Till which we cease our hopeful hap[59] to sing;
Nor let the woods us answer, nor our echo ring.

And thou, great Juno![60] which with awful might   390
The laws of wedlock still dost patronize,
And the religion of the faith first plight[61]
With sacred rites hast taught to solemnize;
And eke for comfort often callèd art
Of women in their smart;[62]   395
Eternally bind thou this lovely band,
And all thy blessings unto us impart.
And thou, glad Genius![63] in whose gentle hand
The bridal bower and genial bed remain,
Without blemish or stain: 400
And the sweet pleasures of their love's delight
With secret aid dost succor and supply,
Till they bring forth the fruitful progeny;
Send us the timely fruit of this same night.
And thou, fair Hebe![64] and thou, Hymen free!   405
Grant that it may so be.
Till which we cease your further praise to sing;
Nor any woods shall answer, nor your echo ring.

And ye high heavens, the temple of the gods,
In which a thousand torches flaming bright   410
Do burn, that to us wretched earthly clods
In dreadful darkness lend desirèd light;
And all ye powers which in the same remain,
More than we men can feign,[65]
Pour out your blessing on us plenteously,   415
And happy influence upon us rain,
That we may raise a large posterity,
Which from the earth, which they may long possess
With lasting happiness,
Up to your haughty[66] palaces may mount;   420
And, for the guerdon[67] of their glorious merit,
May heavenly tabernacles there inherit,
Of blessèd Saints for to increase the count.
So let us rest, sweet love, in hope of this,
And cease till then our timely joys to sing: 425
The woods no more us answer, nor our echo ring!

---

[59] Good fortune.   [60] Queen of the gods; goddess of matrimony.
[61] *religion:* tie. *plight:* pledged.   [62] Pains of childbirth.
[63] Spirit of fertility; compare *genial* in the following line.   [64] Goddess of youth.
[65] Imagine.   [66] Lofty.   [67] Reward.

Song! made in lieu of many ornaments,
With which my love should duly have been decked,
Which cutting off through hasty accidents,[68]
Ye would not stay your due time to expect,   430
But promised both to recompense;
Be unto her a goodly ornament,
And for short time[69] *an endless monument.*

Luis de Góngora
(*1561–1627*)

A ROSE[1]

Blown[2] in the morning, thou shalt fade ere noon,
What boots[3] a life which in such haste forsakes thee?
Thou'rt wondrous frolic, being to die so soon,
And passing proud a little colour makes thee.
If thee thy brittle beauty so deceives,   5
Know then the thing that swells thee is thy bane;[4]
For the same beauty doth, in bloody leaves,
The sentence of thy early death contain.
Some clown's[5] coarse lungs will poison thy sweet flower,
If by the careless plough thou shalt be torn;   10
And many Herods lie in wait each hour
To murder thee as soon as thou art born[6]—
Nay, force thy bud to blow—their tyrant breath
Anticipating life, to hasten death!

A NIGHTINGALE[1]

With such variety and dainty skill
Yon nightingale divides[2] her mournful song,
As if ten thousand of them through one bill

---

[68] Accidents caused by haste. The wedding poem is a gift in lieu of "ornaments" (presents) which have not yet arrived.
[69] *for short time:* of this one brief (wedding) day.
[1] Spanish title: *Vana rosa;* translated by Sir Richard Fanshawe (1608–66).
[2] Blossomed.   [3] Profits.   [4] Ruin.   [5] Peasant's; boor's.
[6] King Herod ordered a wholesale massacre of infants with the intent of killing the new-born Jesus; Matthew 2:1–16.
[1] *Con diferencia tal, con gracia tanta;* translated by Sir Richard Fanshawe.
[2] A musical term, meaning to sing a rapid melody in harmony.

Did sing in parts the story of their wrong.[3]
Nay, she accuses with such vehemence   5
Her ravisher, I think she would incline
The conscious grove thereof to have a sense
And print it on the leaves of that tall pine.
Yet happy she, who may her pain declare
In moving notes, and wandering through the woods   10
With uncut wings, but change divert her care!
But let Him melt away in silent floods,
Whom his Medusa turned into a stone,[4]
That he might neither change, nor make his moan.

THE SPRING[1]

Those whiter lilies which the early morn
Seems to have newly woven of sleaved[2] silk,
To which (on banks of wealthy Tagus[3] borne)
Gold was their cradle, liquid pearl their milk:
These blushing roses, with whose virgin leaves   5
The wanton wind to sport himself presumes,
Whilst from their rifled wardrobe he receives
For his wings purple, for his breath perfumes:
But those, and these,[4] my Celia's pretty foot
Trod up. But if she should her face display,   10
And fragrant breast, they'd dry down to the root,
(As with the blasting of the midday's ray)
And this soft wind which both perfumes and cools
Pass like the unregarded breath of Fools.

SOAR HIGH, MY LOVE[1]

Soar high, my Love, check not thy gallant flight
With thought of that ill-fated youth, to whom
(Fallen like a star from his presumptuous height)
The grey sea was a diaphanous tomb.[2]
Thy downy wings stretch to the gentle wind,   5
Avoiding the dead sea of cold despair,

---

[3] In the Greek myth, Philomela was raped by her brother-in-law Tereus, who cut out her tongue to prevent her revealing the fact. She was later transformed into a nightingale.
[4] Medusa, one of the Gorgons, turned those who gazed on her to stone.
[1] *Los blancos lilios que de ciento en ciento;* translated by Sir Richard Fanshawe.
[2] Made from finely separated threads.
[3] A river flowing through Spain and Portugal.   [4] Both the lilies and the roses.
[1] *No enfrene tu gallardo pensamiento;* translated by Sir Richard Fanshawe.
[2] Daedalus, the legendary master-craftsman, made wings for himself and his son Icarus, but Icarus flew too near the sun, which melted the wax fastenings. He then fell to his death in the sea.

And raised above the clouds, a passage find,
To the most flaming region of the air.
With active circles crown that golden sphere,
'Gainst which the Royal Bird[3] refines his sight,   10
Showing what kind he is by looking there,
And melt thy wings yet at the noblest light.
Since to the Ocean and her pearly shore,
My glorious ruin now adds one title more.

LIFE'S GREATEST MISERY. ADDRESSED TO A FRIEND ON HIS MARRIAGE[1]

To dine on meats high-spiced, and find your flask
    Has leak'd, and not a drop your thirst to tame;
To reach your posting-house[2] dead-tired, and ask
    For mules, and find one trotting brute dead-lame;
    To try new boots, with luck not quite the same,   5
One with great pain you fit, and one you tear;
    To play Primero,[3] and,—to win your game
Wanting the King,—to find the Knave is there;
To ply with gifts a thankless lady fair;
    To owe to bankers punctual as the day;   10
To ride uncloak'd, unfenced, through spungy air;[4]
    To feed bad grooms who steal your corn and hay:
Count all the griefs you've known since life began;
The worst remains—to be a married man.

ALLEGORY OF THE BREVITY OF THINGS HUMAN[1]

Learn, flowers, from me, what parts we play
From dawn to dusk. Last noon the boast
And marvel of the fields, today
I am not even my own ghost.

The fresh aurora was my cot,   5
The night my coffin and my shroud;
I perished with no light, save what
The moon could lend me from a cloud.
And thus, all flowers must die—of whom
Not one of you can cheat the doom.   10

---

[3] The eagle, proverbially keen-sighted and able to gaze at the sun.
[1] *Comer salchicas y hallar sin gota;* translated by Edward Churton.
[2] Station for changing mounts.   [3] A sixteenth- and seventeenth-century card game.
[4] *unfenced:* unprotected. *spungy:* damp.
[1] *Alegoría de la brevedad de las cosas humanas;* translated by Roy Campbell. The speaker can be thought of as the poet or as a flower, the morning glory.

Learn, flowers, from me, what parts we play
From dawn to dusk. Last noon the boast
And marvel of the fields, today
I am not even my own ghost.

What most consoles me from my fleetness   15
Is the carnation fresh with dew,
Since that which gave me one day's sweetness
To her conceded scarcely two:
Ephemerids[2] in briefness vie
My scarlet and her crimson die.   20

Learn, flowers, from me, what parts we play
From dawn to dusk. Last noon the boast
And marvel of the fields, today
I am not even my own ghost.

The jasmine, fairest of the flowers,   25
Is least in size as in longevity.
She forms a star, yet lives less hours
Than it has rays. Her soul is brevity.
If amber could a flower be grown
It would be she, and she alone!   30

Learn, flowers, from me, what parts we play
From dawn to dusk. Last noon the boast
And marvel of the fields, today
I am not even my own ghost.

The gillyflower, though plain and coarse,   35
Enjoys on earth a longer stay.
And sees more suns complete their course
—As many as there shine in May.
Yet better far a marvel die
Than live a gillyflower, say I!   40

Learn, flowers, from me, what parts we play
From dawn to dusk. Last noon the boast
And marvel of the fields, today
I am not even my own ghost.

To no flower blooming in our sphere did   45
The daystar[3] grant a longer pardon
Than to the Sunflower, golden-bearded
Methusaleh[4] of every garden.
Eying him through as many days
As he shoots petals forth like rays.   50

---

[2] Short-lived creatures.   [3] The sun.
[4] A biblical figure who lived 969 years; Genesis 5:27.

Yet learn from me, what parts we play
From dawn to dusk. Last noon the boast
And marvel of the fields, today
I am not even my own ghost.

THE ROSEMARY SPRAY[1]

The flowers upon the rosemary spray,
  Young Maid, may school thy sorrow;
The blue-eyed flower, that blooms to-day,
  To honey turns to-morrow.

A tumult stirs thy tender breast,   5
  With jealous pain true-hearted,
That he, whom thy first love hath bless'd
  From thee hath coldly parted.

Ungracious boy, who slights thy love,
  And overbold, disdaining   10
To ask forgiveness, and remove
  The cause of thy complaining.

Hope, come and drive those tears away!
  For lovers' jealous sorrow,
Like dewy blue-eyed flower on spray,   15
  To honey turns to-morrow.

By thine own joy thou wast undone:
  A bliss thou could'st not measure,
Like star at dawn too near the sun,
  Eclipsed thee by its pleasure.   20

Walk forth with eyes serene and fair;
  The pearls that deck the morning,
Are wasted in the day's fierce glare;
  With calmness tame his scorning.

Disperse those clouds that but dismay;   25
  Distrust that jealous sorrow:
The blue-eyed flower, that blooms to-day,
  To honey turns to-morrow.

[1] *Las flores del romero;* translated by Edward Churton.

Bartolome Leonardo de Argensola
(1562–1631)

I MUST CONFESS, DON JUAN[1]

I must confess, Don Juan, on due inspection,
That dame Elvira's[2] charming red and white,
Though fair they seem, are only hers by right,
In that her money purchased their perfection;
But thou must grant as well, on calm reflection,   5
That her sweet lie hath such a luster bright,
As fairly puts to shame the paler light,
And honest beauty of a true complexion!
And yet no wonder I distracted go
With such deceit, when 'tis within our ken[3]   10
That nature blinds us with the self-same spell;
For that blue heaven above that charms us so,
Is neither heaven nor blue! Sad pity then
That so much beauty is not truth as well.

MARY MAGDALENE[1]

Blessed, yet sinful one, and broken-hearted!
The crowds are pointing at the thing forlorn,
In wonder and in scorn!
Thou weepest days of innocence departed;
Thou weepest, and thy tears have power to move   5
The Lord to pity and love.

The greatest of thy follies is forgiven,
Even for the least of all the tears that shine
On that pale cheek of thine.
Thou didst kneel down to Him who came from heaven,   10
Evil and ignorant, and thou shalt rise
Holy, and pure, and wise.

It is not much that to the fragrant blossom
The ragged brier should change; the bitter fir
Distill Arabian myrrh;   15

---

[1] Spanish title: *Yo os quiero confesar, Don Juan;* translated by James Young Gibson.
[2] Wife of the legendary lover and seducer Don Juan.   [3] Range of observation.
[1] *A Santa María Magdalena;* translated by William Cullen Bryant. Mary Magdalene was
traditionally identified with the repentant harlot (Luke 7:36–50) who washes Jesus' feet with
her tears and wipes them with her hair. An onlooker is scandalized, but Jesus says of her, "Her
sins, which are many, are forgiven, for she loved much."

Nor that, upon the wintry desert's bosom,
The harvest should rise plenteous, and the swain
Bear home the abundant grain.

But come and see the bleak and barren mountains
Thick to their tops with roses; come and see   20
Leaves on the dry, dead tree:
The perished plant, set out by living fountains,
Grows fruitful, and its beauteous branches rise
For ever towards the skies.

Lope de Vega
(1562–1635)

THE GOOD SHEPHERD[1]

Shepherd! who with thine amorous, sylvan song
Hast broken the slumber that encompassed me,
Who mad'st Thy crook from the accursèd tree
On which Thy powerful arms were stretched so long!
    Lead me to mercy's ever-flowing fountains;   5
For Thou my shepherd, guard, and guide shalt be;
I will obey Thy voice, and wait to see
Thy feet all beautiful upon the mountains.
    Hear, Shepherd, Thou who for Thy flock art dying,
Oh, wash away these scarlet sins, for Thou   10
Rejoicest at the contrite sinner's vow!
    Oh, wait! to Thee my weary soul is crying,
Wait for me: Yet why ask it, when I see,
With feet nailed to the cross, Thou'rt waiting still for me!

TOMORROW[1]

Lord, what am I, that with unceasing care
Thou did'st seek after me, that Thou did'st wait
Wet with unhealthy dews before my gate,
And pass the gloomy nights of winter there?

---

[1] Spanish title: *Rimas sacras, Soneto XIV: Pastor, que con tus silbos amorosos;* translated by Henry Wadsworth Longfellow.
[1] *Rimas sacras, Soneto XVIII: ¿Qué tengo yo, que mi amistad procuras?;* translated by Henry Wadsworth Longfellow.

Oh, strange delusion, that I did not greet 5
Thy blest approach, and oh, to heaven how lost
If my ingratitude's unkindly frost
Has chilled the bleeding wounds upon Thy feet.
    How oft my guardian angel gently cried,
"Soul from thy casement look, and thou shalt see 10
How He persists to knock and wait for thee!"
    And oh, how often to that Voice of sorrow,
"Tomorrow we will open," I replied,
And when the morrow came I answered still "Tomorrow."

AT DAWN THE VIRGIN IS BORN . . . [1]

At dawn the Virgin is born
And with her the sun,
Banishing the night
Of our griefs.
The bright dawn 5
Tramples down the night;
Heaven's smile
Tells of her peace
And time stands still
To gaze upon her 10
Banishing the night
Of our griefs.

That she may be
Mistress of heaven, this holy
Child lifts up 15
Her light, which is the dawn;
And the light sings while she weeps
Divine pearls,
Banishing the night
Of our griefs. 20

That pure light
From the sun proceeds,
For all beauty which is
His to give he gives her:
The dawn, whose promise is 25
That he follows after,
Banishing the night
Of our griefs.

[1] *Nace el Alba María;* translated by W. S. Merwin.

ICE AND FIRES CONTEND WITH MY CHILD . . . [1]

Ice and fires
Contend with my child;
Only love
Would suffer such torment.

The fire of love   5
And the cold of time
Rob my sweet love
Of his peace.
So that I say
When I find him smiling: 10
Only love
Would suffer such torment.

Whatever breast freeze
Or soul blaze
It will be seen that love   15
Alone could have wrought it.
Child contented
With ice and fire,
Only love
Would suffer such torment.   20

WHERE ARE YOU GOING, MAIDEN . . . ?[1]

Where are you going, maiden,
Alone on the mountain?[2]
But who bears the sun
Does not fear the night.

Where are you going, Mary,   5
Divine bride,
Glorious mother
Of him who made us?
What would you do if the day
Should sink in the west   10
And night overtake you
On the mountain?

---

[1] *A mi niño combaten fuegos y hielos;* translated by W. S. Merwin.
[1] *¿Dónde vais, zagala?;* translated by W. S. Merwin.
[2] "And Mary arose in those days, and went into the hill country with haste" (Luke 1:39).
The reference is to Mary's journey, after the Annunciation, to her cousin Elisabeth, herself
then pregnant with John the Baptist.

But who bears the sun
Does not fear the night.

The sight of the stars   15
Troubles me,
But your eyes
Are brighter than they.
Now with the stars
The dark night comes,   20
And the light of your beauty
Is hidden away,
But who bears the sun
Does not fear the night.

A LITTLE CAROL OF THE VIRGIN[1]

Angels walking under the palm trees,
holy angels,
let my child sleep,
hold back the branches.

Palms of Bethlehem,   5
tossing in angry wind,
rustling so loud:
for his sake quieten, sway gently—
let my child sleep,
hold back the branches.   10

The holy child
is tired
of crying for his rest
on earth;
he craves a little respite   15
from his pathetic plaint.
Let my child sleep,
hold back the branches.

All about him
the bitter frost;   20
see, I have nothing
with which to shelter him.
Blessed angels,
flying past,
let my child sleep,   25
hold back the branches.

---

[1] *Cantarcillo de la Virgen;* translated by Denise Levertov.

A SONNET ALL OF A SUDDEN[1]

Violante has commanded me to write
A sonnet. Oh! what trouble I am in!
Though here go three lines, eager to begin,
A sonnet's lines must number fourteen, quite!

I never thought that I should find a rhyme,   5
And look! the second quatrain[2] is begun:
But nothing in the quatrains would I shun
If I reach the first tercet[3] in good time.

I enter the first tercet in effect,
And I came in on the right foot, it seems,   10
Because the end of this verse is in sight.

Already in the second, I suspect
That I am finishing just thirteen lines:
Count them! If there are fourteen, it is right.

Michael Drayton
(1563–1631)

HOW MANY PALTRY, FOOLISH, PAINTED THINGS

How many paltry, foolish, painted things,
That now in coaches trouble ev'ry street,
Shall be forgotten, whom no poet sings,
Ere they be well wrapped in their winding sheet![1]
Where I to thee eternity shall give,   5
When nothing else remaineth of these days,
And queens hereafter shall be glad to live
Upon the alms of thy superfluous praise;
Virgins and matrons reading these my rhymes
Shall be so much delighted with thy story   10
That they shall grieve they lived not in these times,
To have seen thee, their sex's only[2] glory.
So shalt thou fly above the vulgar throng,
Still to survive in my immortal song.

---

[1] *Soneto de repente,* from the play *La niña de plata;* translated by Doreen Bell.
[2] Unit of four lines.   [3] Unit of three lines.   [1] Shroud.
[2] Preeminent (but perhaps with the modern meaning also).

SINCE THERE'S NO HELP

Since there's no help, come let us kiss and part;
Nay, I have done, you get no more of me,
And I am glad, yea glad with all my heart
That thus so cleanly I myself can free;
Shake hands forever, cancel all our vows,   5
And when we meet at any time again,
Be it not seen in either of our brows
That we one jot of former love retain.
Now at the last gasp of love's latest breath,
When, his pulse failing, passion speechless lies,   10
When faith is kneeling by his bed of death,
And innocence is closing up his eyes,
Now if thou wouldst, when all have given him over,
From death to life thou mightst him yet recover.

William Shakespeare
(1564–1616)

SONNET 18

Shall I compare thee to a summer's day?
Thou art more lovely and more temperate.
Rough winds do shake the darling buds of May,
And summer's lease hath all too short a date.
Sometime too hot the eye of heaven shines,   5
And often is his gold complexion dimmed.
And every fair from fair[1] sometime declines,
By chance or nature's changing course untrimmed.[2]
But thy eternal summer shall not fade,
Nor lose possession of that fair thou owest,[3]   10
Nor shall Death brag thou wander'st in his shade
When in eternal lines to time thou grow'st.
So long as men can breathe, or eyes can see,
So long lives this, and this gives life to thee.

---

[1]*fair from fair:* beauty from beauty.   [2]Deprived of adornment.   [3]Possess; own.

SONNET 30

When to the sessions of sweet silent thought
I summon up remembrance of things past,
I sigh the lack of many a thing I sought,
And with old woes new wail my dear time's waste.
Then can I drown an eye, unused to flow,   5
For precious friends hid in death's dateless[1] night,
And weep afresh love's long since canceled woe,
And moan the expense of many a vanished sight.
Then can I grieve at grievances foregone,
And heavily from woe to woe tell o'er[2]   10
The sad account of forebemoanèd moan,
Which I new-pay as if not paid before.
But if the while I think on thee, dear friend,
All losses are restored and sorrows end.

SONNET 64

When I have seen by Time's fell[1] hand defaced
The rich-proud cost of outworn buried age;
When sometime[2] lofty towers I see down-razed,
And brass eternal slave to mortal rage;
When I have seen the hungry ocean gain   5
Advantage on the kingdom of the shore,
And the firm soil win of the watery main,
Increasing store[3] with loss, and loss with store;
When I have seen such interchange of state,
Or state itself confounded to decay;   10
Ruin hath taught me thus to ruminate,
That Time will come and take my love away.
This thought is as a death, which cannot choose
But weep to have that which it fears to lose.

SONNET 73

That time of year thou mayst in me behold
When yellow leaves, or none, or few, do hang
Upon those boughs which shake against the cold,
Bare ruined choirs where late the sweet birds sang.
In me thou see'st the twilight of such day   5
As after sunset fadeth in the west,
Which by and by black night doth take away,

---

[1]Eternal.   [2]Total up.   [1]Cruel; evil.   [2]Formerly.   [3]Plenty; supply.

Death's second self, that seals up all in rest.
In me thou see'st the glowing of such fire,
That on the ashes of his youth doth lie   10
As the deathbed whereon it must expire,
Consumed with that which it was nourished by.
This thou perceivest, which makes thy love more strong,
To love that well which thou must leave ere long.

SONNET 116

Let me not to the marriage of true minds
Admit impediments. Love is not love
Which alters when it alteration finds,
Or bends with the remover to remove:
O, no! it is an ever-fixed mark,   5
That looks on tempests and is never shaken;
It is the star to every wandering bark,[1]
Whose worth's unknown, although his height be taken.[2]
Love's not Time's fool, though rosy lips and cheeks
Within his bending sickle's compass come;   10
Love alters not with his brief hours and weeks,
But bears it out even to the edge of doom.
If this be error, and upon me proved,
I never writ, nor no man ever loved.

SONNET 129

The expense[1] of spirit in a waste of shame
Is lust in action; and till action, lust
Is perjured, murderous, bloody, full of blame,
Savage, extreme, rude, cruel, not to trust;
Enjoyed no sooner but despisèd straight;[2]   5
Past reason hunted, and no sooner had,
Past reason hated, as a swallowed bait,
On purpose laid to make the taker mad.
Mad in pursuit, and in possession so;
Had, having, and in quest to have, extreme;   10
A bliss in proof; and proved,[3] a very woe;
Before, a joy proposed; behind, a dream.
All this the world well knows, yet none knows well
To shun the Heaven that leads men to this Hell.

---

[1] Sailing ship.   [2] *his height be taken:* its celestial altitude be measurable.
[1] Spending.   [2] Straightway; immediately.
[3] *in proof:* while being tried or experienced. *proved:* after being experienced.

SONNET 130

My mistress' eyes are nothing like the sun;
Coral is far more red than her lips' red;
If snow be white, why then her breasts are dun;[1]
If hairs be wires, black wires grow on her head.
I have seen roses damasked, red and white,   5
But no such roses see I in her cheeks;
And in some perfumes is there more delight
Than in the breath that from my mistress reeks.
I love to hear her speak, yet well I know
That music hath a far more pleasing sound;   10
I grant I never saw a goddess go;[2]
My mistress, when she walks, treads on the ground:
And yet, by heaven, I think my love as rare
As any she belied with false compare.

SONNET 138

When my love swears that she is made of truth,
I do believe her, though I know she lies,
That she might think me some untutor'd youth,
Unlearned in the world's false subtleties.
Thus vainly thinking that she thinks me young,   5
Although she knows my days are past the best,
Simply I credit her false-speaking tongue:
On both sides thus is simple truth supprest.
But wherefore says she not she is unjust?[1]
And wherefore say not I that I am old?   10
O, love's best habit is in seeming trust,
And age in love loves not to have years told:[2]
Therefore I lie with her, and she with me,
And in our faults by lies we flatter'd be.

---

[1] Lightless, dull brown.
[2] Walk. Gait and carriage were distinctive marks of a goddess.   [1] Unfaithful.
[2] Counted.

Thomas Campion
(1567–1620)

I CARE NOT FOR THESE LADIES

I care not for these ladies
That must be wooed and prayed,
Give me kind Amaryllis,
The wanton country maid;
Nature art disdaineth,   5
Her beauty is her own;
   Her when we court and kiss,
   She cries forsooth let go,
   But when we come where comfort is,
   She never will say no.   10

If I love Amaryllis
She gives me fruit and flowers,
But if we love these ladies
We must give golden showers.[1]
Give them gold that sell love;   15
Give me the nut-brown lass
   Who when we court and kiss
   She cries forsooth let go,
   But when we come where comfort is,
   She never will say no.   20

These ladies must have pillows
And beds by strangers wrought;
Give me a bower of willows,
Of moss and leaves unbought,
And fresh Amaryllis   25
With milk and honey fed,
   Who when we court and kiss
   She cries forsooth let go,
   But when we come where comfort is,
   She never will say no.   30

FOLLOW YOUR SAINT

Follow your saint, follow with accents sweet;
Haste you, sad notes, fall at her flying feet.
There, wrapped in cloud of sorrow, pity move,
And tell the ravisher of my soul I perish for her love.

---

[1] In Greek myth, Zeus made love to Danaë in the guise of a shower of gold.

But if she scorns my never-ceasing pain,   5
Then burst with sighing in her sight and ne'er return again.

All that I sung still[1] to her praise did tend,
Still she was first, still she my songs did end.
Yet she my love and music both doth fly,
The music that her echo is and beauty's sympathy.   10
Then let my notes pursue her scornful flight:
It shall suffice that they were breathed and died for her delight.

John Donne
(1572–1631)

THE GOOD-MORROW

I wonder by my troth, what thou and I
Did, till we lov'd? were we not wean'd till then?
But suck'd on country pleasures,[1] childishly?
Or snorted we in the seven sleepers' den?[2]
'Twas so; but this,[3] all pleasures fancies be.   5
If ever any beauty I did see,
Which I desir'd, and got, 'twas but a dream of thee.

And now good-morrow to our waking souls,
Which watch not one another out of fear;
For love all love of other sights controls,   10
And makes one little room[4] an everywhere.
Let sea-discoverers to new worlds have gone,
Let maps to other, worlds on worlds have shown,
Let us possess one world, each hath one, and is one.[5]

My face in thine eye, thine in mine appears,   15
And true plain hearts do in the faces rest;
Where can we find two better hemispheres[6]
Without sharp North, without declining West?
What ever dies, was not mixt equally;[7]
If our two loves be one, or thou and I   20
Love so alike that none do slacken, none can die.

---

[1] Always; constantly.   [1] Rural pleasures, but also a sexual pun.
[2] The seven sleepers were seven Christian youths of Ephesus who were said to have taken refuge in a cave during the persecution of the Emperor Decius and slept for two centuries.
[3] Compared to this love.   [4] Their bedroom.
[5] That is, each has the world of the other, and each is a world to the other.
[6] Donne may have been thinking of "cordiform" maps which depicted each hemisphere as a heart.
[7] An axiom in alchemy. *Equally* here means "uniformly."

SONG

Go, and catch a falling star,
   Get with child a mandrake root,[1]
Tell me, where all past years are,
   Or who cleft the Devil's foot,[2]
Teach me to hear Mermaids singing,   5
   Or to keep off envy's stinging,
          And find
          What wind
Serves to advance an honest mind.

If thou be'st born to strange sights,   10
   Things invisible to see,
Ride ten thousand days and nights,
   Till age snow white hairs on thee,
Thou, when thou return'st, wilt tell me
All strange wonders that befell thee,   15
          And swear
          No where
Lives a woman true, and fair.

If thou find'st one, let me know,
   Such a Pilgrimage were sweet;   20
Yet do not, I would not go,
   Though at next door we might meet,
Though she were true, when you met her,
And last, till you write your letter,
          Yet she   25
          Will be
False, ere I come, to two, or three.

THE CANONIZATION

For God's sake hold your tongue, and let me love;
   Or chide my palsy, or my gout,
My five grey hairs, or ruin'd fortune flout;
   With wealth your state, your mind with arts improve,
      Take you a course,[1] get you a place,[2]   5
      Observe his Honour, or his Grace,[3]
Or the King's real, or his stamped face[4]

---

[1] The forked root of the mandrake looks like the lower half of a human body.
[2] The devil is said to be recognizable by his cloven hoof.
[1] That is, a course of action leading to worldly success.   [2] A job.
[3] 1) A judge or a nobleman, 2) the qualities of honor and grace.
[4] Stamped on a coin.

Contemplate; what you will, approve,[5]
So you will let me love.

Alas, alas, who's injur'd by my love?   10
    What merchant's ships have my sighs drown'd?
Who says my tears have overflow'd his ground?
    When did my colds a forward spring remove?
        When did the heats which my veins fill
        Add one more to the plaguy bill?[6]   15
Soldiers find wars, and lawyers find out still
    Litigious men, which quarrels move,[7]
    Though she and I do love.

Call us what you will, we are made such by love;
    Call her one, me another fly,[8]   20
We're tapers too, and at our own cost die,[9]
    And we in us find the Eagle and the Dove.[10]
        The Phoenix riddle[11] hath more wit
        By us; we two being one, are it.
So to one neutral thing both sexes fit,   25
    We die and rise the same,[12] and prove
    Mysterious by this love.

We can die by it, if not live by love,
    And if unfit for tombs and hearse[13]
Our legend be, it will be fit for verse;   30
    And if no piece of Chronicle we prove,[14]
        We'll build in sonnets pretty rooms;[15]
        As well a well-wrought urn becomes
The greatest ashes, as half-acre tombs,
    And by these hymns, all shall approve   35
    Us canonized for Love:

And thus invoke us; You whom reverend love
    Made one another's hermitage;
You, to whom love was peace, that now is rage;

---

[5] Try out, test.   [6] The list of deaths from the plague.   [7] Who start quarrels.
    [8] The taper-fly, which was attracted to flame and burned itself in it, was said to be hermaphroditic and resurrectable.
    [9] Sexual intercourse was thought to shorten life. Therefore lovers are like candles, which get shorter as they burn. *Die* is a slang term for having sexual intercourse.
    [10] Symbols, in medieval literature, of righteousness and mercy.
    [11] The Phoenix bird, which was resurrected from its own ashes, was also said to be hermaphroditic.
    [12] In sexual intercourse, we become sexless (*neutral*), because one sex cancels out the other. But after intercourse, we mysteriously are two different sexes again. *Die* and *rise* also have sexual meanings.
    [13] Funereal poems were pinned to hearses.
    [14] If we are not recorded in history, or if we do not beget children as described in I Chronicles 1–9.
    [15] Mausoleum rooms and stanzas (in Italian).

Who did the whole world's soul contract, and drove   40
    Into the glasses of your eyes[16]
    (So made such mirrors, and such spies,
  That they did all to you epitomize,)
    Countries, Towns, Courts: beg from above
    A pattern of your love![17]   45

THE FUNERAL

Whoever comes to shroud me, do not harm
    Nor question much
That subtle wreath of hair, which crowns my arm;[1]
The mystery, the sign you must not touch,
    For 'tis my outward Soul,   5
Viceroy to that, which then to heaven being gone,
    Will leave this to control,
And keep these limbs, her Provinces, from dissolution.

For if the sinewy thread my brain lets fall
    Through every part,[2]   10
Can tie those parts, and make me one of all;
These hairs which upward grew, and strength and art
    Have from a better brain,
Can better do 't;[3] except[4] she meant that I
    By this should know my pain,   15
As prisoners then are manacled, when they're condemn'd to die.

Whate'er she meant by it, bury it with me,
    For since I am
Love's martyr, it might breed idolatry,
If into others' hands these Reliques came;   20
    As 'twas humility
To afford to it all that a Soul can do,[5]
    So, 'tis some bravery,
That since you would save none of me, I bury some of you.

---

[16] That is, drove the whole world into each other's eyes by gazing at each other.
[17] Ask the god of love for a pattern of your love.
[1] Such bracelets found on corpses are described by several medieval writers, including Giraldus Cambrensis.
[2] The nervous system which makes him one being.
[3] That is, tie the parts of the body together.   [4] Unless.
[5] It was submission to give to it all that a soul can do.

THE FLEA

Mark but this flea, and mark in this,
How little that which thou deny'st me is;
It suck'd me first, and now sucks thee,
And in this flea, our two bloods mingled be;[1]
Thou know'st that this cannot be said   5
A sin, nor shame, nor loss of maidenhead,
    Yet this enjoys before it woo,
    And pamper'd swells with one blood made of two,
    And this, alas, is more than we would do.

Oh stay, three lives in one flea spare,   10
Where we almost, yea more than married are.
This flea is you and I, and this
Our marriage bed, and marriage temple is;
Though parents grudge, and you, we're met,
And cloistered in these living walls of jet.   15
    Though use make you apt to kill me,
    Let not to that, self murder added be,
    And sacrilege,[2] three sins in killing three.

Cruel and sudden, hast thou since
Purpled thy nail, in blood of innocence?   20
Wherein could this flea guilty be,
Except in that drop which it suck'd from thee?
Yet thou triumph'st, and say'st that thou
Find'st not thyself, nor me the weaker now;
    'Tis true, then learn how false, fears be;   25
    Just so much honour, when thou yield'st to me,
    Will waste, as this flea's death took life from thee.

A VALEDICTION: FORBIDDING MOURNING[1]

    As virtuous men pass mildly away,
      And whisper to their souls, to go,
    Whilst some of their sad friends do say,
      The breath goes now, and some say, no:

    So let us melt, and make no noise,   5
      No tear-floods, nor sigh-tempests move,

[1] The three united in the flea—the flea himself, the lover, and the mistress—thus echo the Trinity, an idea that recurs throughout the poem.
[2] Sacrilege because the flea is a "marriage temple."
[1] Donne wrote this poem to his wife when he went to the Continent with Sir Robert Drury in 1611.

'Twere profanation of our joys
    To tell the laity our love.

Moving of th' earth brings harms and fears,
    Men reckon what it did and meant,   10
But trepidation of the spheres,[2]
    Though greater far, is innocent.

Dull sublunary[3] lovers' love
    (Whose soul is sense[4]) cannot admit
Absence, because it doth remove   15
    Those things which elemented[5] it.

But we by a love, so much refin'd,
    That ourselves know not what it is,
Inter-assurèd of the mind,
    Care less eyes, lips, and hands to miss.   20

Our two souls therefore, which are one,
    Though I must go, endure not yet[6]
A breach, but an expansion,
    Like gold to aery thinness beat.

If they be two, they are two so   25
    As stiff twin compasses[7] are two,
Thy soul the fixed foot, makes no show
    To move, but doth, if th' other do.

And though it in the centre sit,
    Yet when the other far doth roam,   30
It leans, and hearkens after it,
    And grows erect, as that comes home.

Such wilt thou be to me, who must
    Like th' other foot, obliquely[8] run;
Thy firmness makes my circle just,   35
    And makes me end, where I begun.

---

[2] *Trepidation* was the term used for the trembling of the outermost sphere (the *primum mobile*) in the Ptolemaic universe; this gave movement to the other spheres. The word also means "fear" of heavenly disturbances.

[3] Beneath the moon; earthly.   [4] Dependent upon sensual gratification.

[5] Created or composed.   [6] Nevertheless do not allow.

[7] That is, the two legs of a compass.

[8] Not in a straight line. The lover travels in a circle, and then, when the compass is closed, returns to his starting place.

LOVE'S DIET

To what a cumbersome unwieldiness
And burdenous corpulence my love had grown,
    But that I did, to make it less,
    And keep it in proportion,
Give it a diet, made it feed upon   5
That which love worst endures, *discretion*.

Above one sigh a day I allow'd him not,
Of which my fortune, and my faults had part;
    And if sometimes by stealth he got
    A she sigh from my mistress' heart,   10
And thought to feast on that, I let him see
'Twas neither very sound, nor meant to me.[1]

If he wrung from me a tear, I brined[2] it so
With scorn or shame, that him it nourish'd not;
    If he suck'd hers, I let him know   15
    'Twas not a tear, which he had got,
His drink was counterfeit, as was his meat;
For, eyes which roll towards all, weep not, but sweat.

Whatever he would dictate, I writ that,
But burnt my letters; when she writ to me,   20
    And that that favour made him fat,
    I said, if any title be
Convey'd by this, Ah, what doth it avail,
To be the fortieth name in an entail?[3]

Thus I reclaim'd my buzzard[4] love, to fly   25
At what, and when, and how, and where I choose;
    Now negligent of sport I lie,
    And now as other falconers use,
I spring[5] a mistress, swear, write, sigh and weep:
And the game kill'd, or lost, go talk, and sleep.   30

---

[1] This is a difficult line. It probably means either, "The *she sigh* was neither a true ("very") sound, nor meant *for* me," or "The *she sigh* was to me neither a true sound nor sincerely intended."

[2] Salted.

[3] An *entail* is a paper documenting a line of descent of ownership or inheritance. The lover doubts that he will win the mistress, since he is so far down on the list.

[4] That is, rapacious but slow.   [5] Rouse from hiding, as in hunting with falcons.

ELEGY XIX
TO HIS MISTRESS GOING TO BED

Come, Madam, come, all rest my powers defy,
Until I labour, I in labour lie.[1]
The foe oft-times having the foe in sight,
Is tired with standing though he never fight.[2]
Off with that girdle, like heaven's Zone glistering,   5
But a far fairer world encompassing.
Unpin that spangled breastplate which you wear,
That th' eyes of busy fools may be stopt there.
Unlace yourself, for that harmonious chime
Tells me from you, that now it is bed time.   10
Off with that happy busk,[3] which I envy,
That still can be, and still can stand so nigh.
Your gown going off, such beauteous state reveals,
As when from flowry meads th' hill's shadow steals.
Off with that wiry Coronet and show   15
The hairy Diadem which on you doth grow:
Now off with those shoes, and then safely tread
In this love's hallow'd temple, this soft bed.
In such white robes, heaven's Angels used to be
Receiv'd by men; thou Angel bring'st with thee   20
A heaven like Mahomet's Paradise;[4] and though
Ill spirits walk in white, we easily know,
By this these Angels from an evil sprite,
Those set our hairs, but these our flesh upright.
   Licence my roving hands, and let them go,   25
Before, behind, between, above, below.
O my America! my new-found-land,
My kingdom, safeliest when with one man mann'd,
My Mine of precious stones, My Empery,
How blest am I in this discovering thee!   30
To enter in these bonds, is to be free;
Then where my hand is set, my seal[5] shall be.
   Full nakedness! All joys are due to thee,
As souls unbodied, bodies uncloth'd must be,
To taste whole joys. Gems which you women use   35
Are like Atlanta's balls,[6] cast in men's views,
That when a fool's eye lighteth on a Gem,
His earthly soul may covet theirs, not them.
Like pictures, or like books' gay coverings made

---

[1] Until I get to work at sexual intercourse, I lie in agony waiting.
[2] Note sexual double meanings.   [3] Corset.
[4] The paradise of Islam was supposed to be full of fleshly pleasure.
[5] Both "impression" and "sign of ownership."
[6] Atalanta (usually so spelled) lost a race to Hippomenes because she paused three times to pick up three golden apples which Venus had given him and which he threw in her path.

For lay-men, are all women thus array'd;   40
Themselves are mystic books, which only we
(Whom their imputed grace will dignify)
Must see reveal'd. Then since that I may know,[7]
As liberally,[8] as to a Midwife, show
Thyself: cast all, yea, this white linen hence,   45
There is no penance due to innocence.
    To teach thee, I am naked first; why then
What needst thou have more covering than a man.

HOLY SONNETS

X

Death be not proud, though some have called thee
Mighty and dreadful, for, thou art not so,
For, those, whom thou think'st, thou dost overthrow,
Die not, poor death, nor yet canst thou kill me.
From rest and sleep, which but thy pictures be,   5
Much pleasure, then from thee, much more must flow,
And soonest our best men with thee do go,
Rest of their bones, and soul's delivery.
Thou art slave to Fate, Chance, kings, and desperate men,
And dost with poison, war, and sickness dwell,   10
And poppy, or charms can make us sleep as well,
And better than thy stroke; why swell'st thou then?
One short sleep past, we wake eternally,
And death shall be no more; death, thou shalt die.

XIV

Batter my heart, three-person'd God; for, you
As yet but knock, breathe, shine, and seek to mend;
That I may rise, and stand, o'erthrow me, and bend
Your force, to break, blow, burn and make me new.
I, like an usurp'd town, to another due,   5
Labour to admit you, but Oh, to no end,
Reason your viceroy in me, me should defend,
But is captiv'd, and proves weak or untrue.
Yet dearly I love you, and would be loved fain,
But am betroth'd unto your enemy: 10
Divorce me, untie, or break that knot again,
Take me to you, imprison me, for I
Except you enthral me, never shall be free,
Nor ever chaste, except you ravish me.

---

[7] Both "have knowledge" and "have intercourse."   [8] Both "freely" and "lewdly."

A HYMN TO GOD THE FATHER

I

Wilt Thou forgive that sin where I begun,[1]
  Which is my sin, though it were done before?[2]
Wilt Thou forgive that sin, through which I run,
  And do run still: though still I do deplore?
    When Thou hast done, Thou hast not done,   5
      For I have more.

II

Wilt Thou forgive that sin by which I have won
  Others to sin? and, made my sin their door?
Wilt Thou forgive that sin which I did shun
  A year, or two: but wallowed in, a score?   10
    When Thou hast done, Thou hast not done,
      For I have more.

III

I have a sin of fear, that when I have spun
  My last thread, I shall perish on the shore;[3]
Swear by Thyself, that at my death Thy son   15
  Shall shine as He shines now, and heretofore;
    And, having done that, Thou hast done,
      I fear no more.

Robert Herrick
(*1591–1674*)

TO THE VIRGINS, TO MAKE MUCH OF TIME

Gather ye rosebuds while ye may,
  Old time is still[1] a-flying,
And this same flower that smiles today
  Tomorrow will be dying.

The glorious lamp of heaven, the sun,   5
  The higher he's a-getting,

---

[1] Original sin.   [2] Note the pun on Donne's name, here and below.
[3] As opposed to going to heaven.   [1] Always.

The sooner will his race be run,
    And nearer he's to setting.

That age is best which is the first,
    When youth and blood are warmer;   10
But being spent, the worse, and worst
    Times still succeed the former.

Then be not coy,[2] but use your time,
    And while ye may, go marry;
For having lost but once your prime,   15
    You may for ever tarry.

TO DAFFODILS

Fair daffodils, we weep to see
    You haste away so soon;
As yet the early-rising sun
    Has not attained his noon.
        Stay, stay,   5
Until the hasting day
        Has run
But to the even-song;[1]
And, having prayed together, we
    Will go with you along.   10

We have short time to stay as you,
    We have as short a spring,
As quick a growth to meet decay
    As you, or any thing.
        We die   15
As your hours do, and dry
        Away,
Like to the summer's rain,
Or as the pearls of morning's dew,
    Ne'er to be found again.   20

---

[2] Unwilling; retiring.   [1] Evensong is the Church of England evening prayer service.

John Milton
(*1608–1674*)

ON THE LATE MASSACRE IN PIEDMONT[1]

Avenge, O Lord, thy slaughtered saints, whose bones
Lie scattered on the Alpine mountains cold;
Even them who kept thy truth so pure of old,
When all our fathers worshipped stocks and stones,
Forget not: in thy book record their groans   5
Who were thy sheep, and in their ancient fold
Slain by the bloody Piedmontese, that rolled
Mother with infant down the rocks. Their moans
The vales redoubled to the hills, and they
To heaven. Their martyred blood and ashes sow   10
O'er all the Italian fields, where still doth sway
The triple tyrant;[2] that from these may grow
A hundredfold, who, having learnt thy way,
Early may fly the Babylonian woe.[3]

WHEN I CONSIDER HOW MY LIGHT IS SPENT[1]

When I consider how my light is spent
Ere half my days, in this dark world and wide,
And that one talent which is death to hide,
Lodged with me useless, though my soul more bent
To serve therewith my Maker, and present   5
My true account, lest he returning chide,
"Doth God exact day-labour, light denied?"
I fondly ask;[2] but Patience, to prevent
That murmur, soon replies, "God doth not need
Either man's work or his own gifts; who best   10
Bear his mild yoke, they serve him best. His state
Is kingly. Thousands at his bidding speed
And post o'er land and ocean without rest:
They also serve who only stand and wait."

[1] In April 1655, the Waldenses, an early-Protestant sect dwelling in the Piedmont (Alpine foothills) of northern Italy, were victims of a religious massacre by soldiers under the Duke of Savoy.
[2] The Pope, with his three-crowned tiara.
[3] The biblical book of Revelation (chapters 17, 18) portrayed ancient Rome as the Whore of Babylon; militant Protestants often applied the figure to the contemporary Church of Rome.
[1] Milton, whose eyesight had deteriorated over several years, became totally blind in the early 1650s. *Spent* means gone or exhausted.
[2] Lines 3–8 refer to the parable of the talents in Matthew 25:14–30, which compares God to a rich man who demands that his servants invest, at a profit, the talents (sums of money) he allots to them. The master punishes harshly the servant who failed to multiply his capital.

Chronology

✦❦✧❦✦❦✧

Political and Social Events	Intellectual and Cultural Events

B.C.

13th *c.* Hebrew Exodus from Egypt into Canaan

1193–1184 Trojan War

ca. 1100 Dorians migrate into Peloponnesus

953 Dedication of Temple at Jerusalem

10th *c.* Oral traditions of Jews attain first written form (the J strand); oral epics in circulation among the Greeks

931 Jews split into the Northern Kingdom of Israel and the Southern Kingdom of Judah

826 Founding of Carthage

776 First Olympic games in Greece

753 Traditional date of founding of Rome by Romulus and Remus

750–500 Era of Greek colonization

6th *c.* Rise of free statuary and Doric and Ionic temple architecture

597 Babylonian captivity of the Jews

6th *c.* Ascendancy of the Persian empire

586 The piper Sakadas wins the pipe contest at the Greek Pythian games with a piece representing Apollo's fight with a dragon

538 The Persians under Cyrus capture Babylon and free the Jews

585 Thales makes the first prediction of a solar eclipse

534 Thespis' dramatic performances in Athens

509 Traditional date of the founding of the Roman Republic

490 Athenians defeat Persians at the Battle of Marathon

480 The Greek fleet defeats the Persians at the Battle of Salamis

461–429 The Periclean Age in Athens

432 The Parthenon completed

429 The Acropolis completed

431–404 Peloponnesian War and the fall of Athens

399 The death of Socrates

336–323 Conquests of Alexander

334 Foundation of the Library at Alexandria

264–146 Punic Wars

146 Roman conquest of Greece

ca. 150 Frieze from the Altar of Zeus at Pergamon

Homer (8th *c.*)

Sappho (7th–6th *c.*)

Old Testament (10th–2nd *c.*)

Aeschylus (*ca.* 525–456)

Sophocles (496–406)

Euripides (*ca.* 480–406)

Aristophanes (*ca.* 450–*ca.* 386)

Plato (*ca.* 427–*ca.* 348)

Aristotle (384–322)

60 First Triumvirate (Pompey, Julius
   Caesar, Crassus)
58–50 Caesar's Gallic Wars
44 Assassination of Caesar
43 Second Triumvirate (Antony,
   Octavian, Lepidus)
27–A.D. 14 Augustus Caesar Emperor of Rome
ca. 4 Birth of Christ

A.D.
ca. 29 Crucifixion of Christ
64 Burning of Rome and first Christian persecutions
70 Titus, son of Emperor Vespasian,   70 Colosseum begun at Rome
   suppresses a Jewish revolt, de-
   stroys the Temple at Jerusalem,
   and massacres and exiles Jews
   (the *Diaspora,* or Scattering)

                                         81 Arch of Titus completed at Rome
84 Roman conquest of Britain
                                         118–126 Construction of the Pan-
                                            theon at Rome
132 Jews rebel again, recapture Je-
   rusalem, and set up a state of Israel
135 Jewish revolt crushed; the Final
   Diaspora   211–217 Construction of Roman
250 Decius, Emperor of Rome,   Baths of Caracalla
   makes emperor-worship compul-
   sory and orders persecution of
   Christians
286 Emperor Diocletian divides the
   Empire into Eastern and Western
   Empires
323–337 Constantine Emperor in
   the East. He moves the capital to
   Constantinople and allows Christianity in the Empire
351 Emperor Julian attempts to reintroduce paganism in place of
   Christianity
395 Emperor Theodosius makes
   Christianity the official religion of
   Rome

Catullus
(*ca.* 84–*ca.* 54)

Virgil (70–19)

Ovid (43 B.C.–A.D. 17)

New Testament (1st and 2nd c.)

401 Pope Innocent I claims universal jurisdiction over the Roman Church

413 St. Augustine, *The City of God*
ca. 450 Establishment of the seven liberal arts as regular course of study

476 The end of the Roman Empire

❧ THE MIDDLE AGES

527–565 Construction of the Hagia Sophia, Constantinople

622–624 Beginning of Mohammedan Era and Holy War

622 Hegira of Mohammed

711 Conquest of Spain by Arabs

ca. 750 Arabic science brought to Europe

768–814 Charlemagne Ruler of Franks and Holy Roman Emperor

9th *c.* Feudal system develops among the Franks and spreads across Europe

9th *c.* Music cultivated in monasteries; development of "sequences" (elaborated passages) in liturgical music

856–875 Vikings overrun England

ca. 925 The *Quem Quaeritis* trope, earliest surviving example of the staged sections of the Mass which were to form the basis of medieval drama

ca. 1025 Guido of Arezzo's earliest writings on the theory of music

1066 Norman conquest of England

ca. 1080 The Bayeux Tapestry

1086 The Domesday Book compiled in England

1094 Construction begins on St. Mark's Cathedral, Venice

1095–1291 Period of the Crusades

1145 Chartres Cathedral begun

ca. 1150 Troubadours flourish in Provence; rise of universities in Europe; flourishing of Scholasticism

1163 Cornerstone laid for Notre Dame in Paris

Beowulf (8th century?)

Song of Roland (ca. 1100)

Marie de France
(12th century)

Political and Social Events	Intellectual and Cultural Events
	1167 Oxford University founded
	1170 Beginning of the University of Paris
	ca. 1200 Trouvères flourish in northern France, Minnesingers in Germany
	1209 Cambridge University founded
	1213–1380 Construction of the Alhambra
1233 Inquisition established in Spain	
	ca. 1240 The motet becomes the most important form of polyphonic composition
	ca. 1250 Period of the *ars antiqua* polyphonic style in music
	1270 St. Thomas Aquinas, *Summa Theologica*
1271 Beginning of Marco Polo's travels	
	1300–1370 Period of *ars nova* in France, the "new art" of musical composition
1309–1378 The "Babylonian Captivity": papal see removed to Avignon, France	1305 Giotto, the Arena chapel frescoes
	1308 Duccio begins painting the Siena panels
	1327 Petrarch meets Laura
1337–1453 The Hundred Years' War between France and England	
1348 Outbreak of Black Death in Europe	
	1360 Guillaume Machaut, Mass of Notre Dame
	1376 Wycliffe's translation of the Bible
1431 Joan of Arc burned as a witch	1426 Jan and Hubert Van Eyck begin the Ghent Altarpiece
	1436 Guillaume Dufay, *Nuper rosarum flores*
	ca. 1450 Ascendancy of humanism in Italy
1453 Fall of Constantinople to Ottoman Turks ends the Byzantine Empire and marks the end of the Middle Ages	

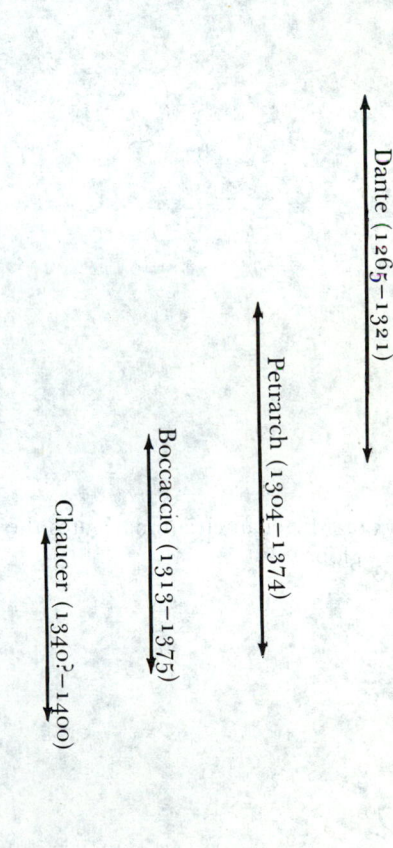

Dante (1265–1321)

Petrarch (1304–1374)

Boccaccio (1313–1375)

Chaucer (1340?–1400)

Christine de Pizan
(1364–1430?)

✤ THE RENAISSANCE

Political and Social Events	Intellectual and Cultural Events
	1454 Printing by movable type perfected by Gutenberg
1455–1485 English Wars of the Roses	
	1478 Lorenzo de' Medici patronizes arts in Florence; Sandro Botticelli, *La Primavera*
	1487 Giovanni Bellini, San Giobbe Altarpiece
1492 Columbus reaches America	
	1495 Hieronymus Bosch, *Temptation of St. Anthony;* Leonardo da Vinci, *The Last Supper*
	1501 Publication of Josquin des Prez's first book of Masses
	1503 Leonardo da Vinci, the *Mona Lisa*
	1504 Michelangelo Buonarotti, *David*
	1506 St. Peter's begun in Rome
	1508 Michelangelo begins Sistine Chapel ceiling
	1511 Desiderius Erasmus' *Praise of Folly*
	1516 Raphael, the *Sistine Madonna;* Lodovico Ariosto, *Orlando Furioso*
	1517 Martin Luther nails his ninety-five theses to a church door in Wittenberg to begin the German Reformation
1522 Magellan circumnavigates the globe	
	1525 Titian, *Deposition*
	1533 First Italian madrigals
	1540 Society of Jesus (the Jesuits) founded
	1547 Benvenuto Cellini, *Perseus*
	1554 Giovanni Palestrina, first book of Masses
	1555 Pieter Breughel the Elder, *The Wedding Dance*
1572 Saint Bartholomew's Day massacre: French Protestants massacred	
	1575–1625 The school of "English virginalist" composers, including William Byrd, Thomas Morley, and Orlando Gibbons
1588 England defeats the invading Spanish Armada	

● *Everyman* (late 15th *c.*)

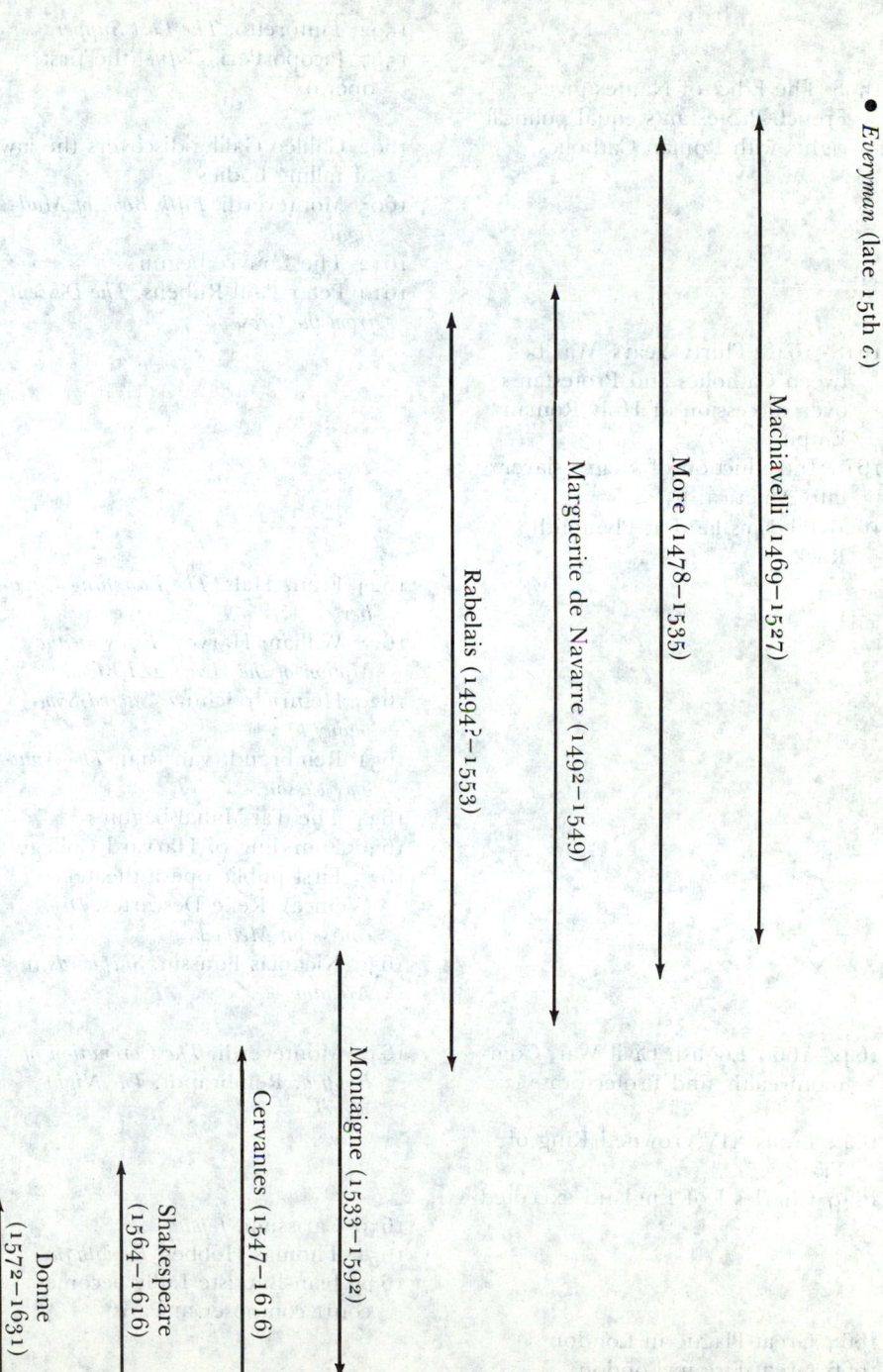

Machiavelli (1469–1527)

More (1478–1535)

Marguerite de Navarre (1492–1549)

Rabelais (1494?–1553)

Montaigne (1533–1592)

Cervantes (1547–1616)

Shakespeare (1564–1616)

Donne (1572–1631)

Political and Social Events	Intellectual and Cultural Events
	1592 Tintoretto, *The Last Supper*
	1597 Jacopo Peri, *Dafne* (the first opera)
1598 The Edict of Nantes gives French Protestants equal political rights with Roman Catholics	
	1602 Galileo Galilei discovers the law of falling bodies
	1605 Monteverdi, *Fifth Book of Madrigals*
	1612 The Louvre begun
	1614 Peter Paul Rubens, *The Descent from the Cross*
1618–1648 Thirty Years' War between Catholics and Protestants over succession of Holy Roman Empire	
1619 Introduction of Negro slavery into America	
1620 Pilgrims land at Plymouth Rock	
	1624 Franz Hals, *The Laughing Cavalier*
	1628 William Harvey, *Essay on the Motion of the Heart and Blood*
	1629 Heinrich Schütz, *Sacred Symphony I*
	1631 Rembrandt van Rijn, *The Anatomy Lesson*
	1634 The Taj Mahal begun
	1636 Founding of Harvard College
	1637 First public opera theater (Venice); René Descartes, *Discourse on Method*
	1639 Nicholas Poussin, *Shepherds in Arcadia*
1642–1660 English Civil War, Commonwealth, and Protectorate	1642 Monteverdi, *The Coronation of Poppea;* Rembrandt, *The Night Watch*
1643 Louis XIV crowned King of France	
1649 Charles I of England executed	
	1650 Carissimi, *Jephta*
	1651 Thomas Hobbes, *Leviathan*
	1653 Jean-Baptiste Lully becomes court composer at Paris
1665 Great Plague in London	
1666 Great Fire in London	

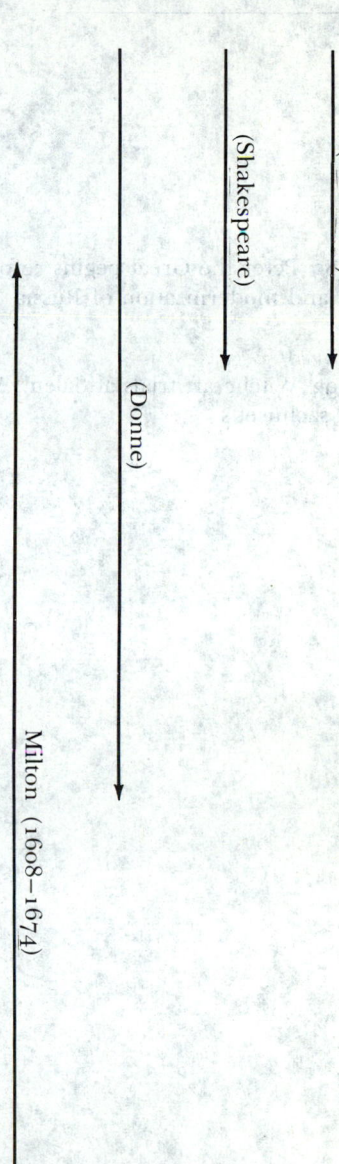

(Cervantes)

(Shakespeare)

(Donne)

Milton (1608–1674)

Political and Social Events	*Intellectual and Cultural Events*
	1667 Giovanni Lorenzo Bernini, colonnade of St. Peter's
	1670 Blaise Pascal, *Pensées*
	1675 Sir Christopher Wren begins St. Paul's Cathedral
	1687 Isaac Newton, *Principia Mathematica*
1689 Peter the Great begins reform and modernization of Russia	1689 Henry Purcell, *Dido and Aeneas*
	1690 John Locke, *An Essay Concerning Human Understanding*
1692 Witchcraft trials at Salem, Massachusetts	

(Milton) ↓

Index

Note: First lines of short poems and titles of books of the Bible are in roman type. Titles of long works are in italics. Titles of short works are in italics in the general alphabetical listing but in roman type when listed as sub-entries under their authors' names.